TROUBLESHOOTING, MAINTAINING & REPAIRING PCS

FIFTH EDITION

ABOUT THE AUTHOR

Stephen J. Bigelow is the founder and president of Dynamic Learning Systems, a technical writing, research, and small publishing company specializing in electronic and PC service topics. Bigelow is the author of 15 feature-length books for TAB/McGraw-Hill, and over 100 major articles for mainstream electronics magazines such as *Popular Electronics*, *Electronics NOW*, *Circuit Cellar INK*, and *Electronic Service & Technology*. Bigelow is a contributing editor at *CNET* (the "PC Mechanic" column and feature articles) and a regular contributor with *SmartComputing*. Bigelow is also the editor and publisher of *The PC Toolbox*™, a premier PC service newsletter for computer enthusiasts and technicians. He is an electrical engineer with a BS EE from Central New England College in Worcester, MA. You may contact him at **www.dlspubs.com**.

TROUBLESHOOTING, MAINTAINING & REPAIRING PCS

FIFTH EDITION

STEPHEN J. BIGELOW

Osborne/**McGraw-Hill**

New York   Chicago   San Francisco
Lisbon   London   Madrid   Mexico City
Milan   New Delhi   San Juan
Seoul   Singapore   Sydney   Toronto

Osborne/**McGraw-Hill**
2600 Tenth Street
Berkeley, California 94710
U.S.A.

To arrange bulk purchase discounts for sales promotions, premiums, or fund-raisers, please contact Osborne/**McGraw-Hill** at the above address. For information on translations or book distributors outside the U.S.A., please see the International Contact Information page immediately following the index of this book.

Troubleshooting, Maintaining & Repairing PCs, Fifth Edition

234567890 DOC DOC 0198765432

Book p/n 0-07-213270-1 and CD p/n 0-07-213271-X
parts of
ISBN 0-07-213272-8

Publisher
  Brandon A. Nordin

Vice President & Associate Publisher
  Scott Rogers

Acquisitions Editor
  Michael Sprague

Project Editor
  Janet Walden

Acquisitions Coordinator
  Paulina Pobocha

Copy Editors
  William McManus, Jan Jue, Carl Wikander,
  Sally Engelfried, Claire Splan, Judith Brown

Proofreaders
  Pat Mannion, John Schindel, Stefany Otis,
  Steve Anderson

Indexer
   David Heiret

Computer Designer
  Carie Abrew, Melinda Moore Lytle

Illustrator
  Jackie Sieben, Richard Coda

Series Design
  Michelle Galicia

Cover Design
  Will Voss

This book was composed with Corel VENTURA™ Publisher.

Pentium 4 image courtesy of Intel Corporation.

CONTENTS AT A GLANCE

The following appendixes are on the accompanying CD:

CONTENTS

The following appendixes are on the accompanying CD:

Appendix B   **PC99 System Compliance Standards**

Appendix C   **PC Standards**

Appendix D   **Index of Filename Extensions**

Appendix E   **Standard ASCII Chart (0 to 127)**

Appendix F   **Windows 9x/Me Shortcut Keys**

Appendix G   **PC-related Related FAQs and Newsgroups**

Appendix H   **Preparing for A+**

Appendix I   **The DLS Technician's Certificate 4**

CST CERTIFICATION

The Computer Service Technician (CST) certification program was initiated in 1998 by the ETA-I. It has since gained popularity as the standard computer certification program for electronics technicians. The CST certification examination consists of 50 questions. The test covers nine basic areas related to personal computer maintenance, repair, upgrading and troubleshooting. The areas of competencies tested include

- Microprocessor architecture and operational characteristics
- Video display systems
- Memory
- Bus architectures
- Hard drive installation and troubleshooting
- Printers
- I/O hardware characteristics
- Networking—basic features of LAN's, network protocols
- Network operating systems

Certified ETA-I examiners at various locations in the United States, Canada, and other countries administer the CST examinations. The fee for the exam, as well as recertification after four years, is $50.00. Information regarding ETA-I certifications, local test sites, exam results, and re-certification may be obtained from the Electronics Technicians Association—International headquarters by calling one of the following numbers: 800-288-3824 or 765-653-4301. Or you can visit the ETA-I Web site at **www.eta-sda.com**.

DISCLAIMER AND CAUTIONS

It is *important* that you read and understand the following information. Please read it carefully!

Personal Risk and Limits of Liability

The repair of personal computers and their peripherals involves some amount of personal risk. Use extreme caution when working with AC and high-voltage power sources. Every reasonable effort has been made to identify and reduce areas of personal risk. You are instructed to read this book carefully *before* attempting the procedures discussed. If you are uncomfortable following the procedures that are outlined in this book, *do not attempt them*—refer your service to qualified service personnel.

Neither the author, the publisher, nor anyone directly or indirectly connected with the publication of this book and accompanying computer software shall make any warranty either expressed or implied, with regard to this material, including, but not limited to, the implied warranties of quality, merchantability, and fitness for any particular purpose.

Further, neither the author, publisher, nor anyone directly or indirectly connected with the publication of this book and computer software shall be liable for errors or omissions contained herein, or for incidental or consequential damages, injuries, or financial or material losses resulting from the use, or inability to use, the material and software contained herein. This material and software is provided as-is, *and the reader bears all responsibilities and risks connected with its use.*

Virus Warning

Although the software included with this book was thoroughly checked for viruses before publication, you are *strongly* advised to inspect *all* new software, including the software on this book's companion CD, for the presence of computer viruses *before* executing the software. Antivirus software can be obtained through commercial and shareware sources. Neither the author, publisher, nor anyone directly or indirectly connected with this book assume any liability whatsoever for incidental or consequential damages, financial loss, or material loss, resulting from the occurrence of computer viruses on your system or network. You use this software at your own risk.

Vendor Warning

The products, materials, equipment, manufacturers, service providers, and distributors listed and presented in this book are shown for reference purposes only. Their mention and use in this book shall not be construed as an endorsement of any individual or organization, nor the quality of their products or services, nor their performance or business integrity. The author, publisher, and anyone directly or indirectly associated with the production of this book expressly disclaim all liability whatsoever for any financial or material losses or incidental or consequential damages that might occur from contacting or doing business with any such organization or individual.

INTRODUCTION: A BOOK FOR CHANGING TIMES

It used to be that when a PC failed, it wound up sitting on a test bench surrounded by a battalion of test equipment. An experienced technician would be hovering over the PC, logic probe or test leads in-hand. They relied on their knowledge of electronics and microprocessor operations to track the problem to a faulty chip or passive component that could then be replaced with relatively simple soldering tools. There were few add-ons or peripherals to worry about, and only a few megabytes of memory or so to work with. Compatibility problems and proprietary interfaces often plagued the few expansion devices that did exist.

Well, times certainly *have* changed. Today's PC is largely a collection of very inexpensive subassemblies, most of which are now manufactured in the Pacific Rim and assembled in high volumes at factories around the world. The diverse array of peripherals that are now available (including tape drives, CD-RWs, video accelerators, DVD-ROMs, pointing devices, and so on) enjoy a remarkable level of hardware compatibility using well-established interface schemes (such as AGP, SCSI, UDMA/100, USB, PCI, and FireWire). The labor cost involved in a component-level repair today is usually more expensive than the cost of a replacement assembly. There is little doubt that the day of component-level PC repair is over.

However, PCs still fail, and they fail in ways that continue to exhaust even the most patient mind. When you realize that there are now well over 100 million PCs in operation (and growing at an astonishing rate each year), you can see that *effective* troubleshooting requires *more* than simply an arbitrary swapping of boards and drives. Now, more than ever, efficient and cost-effective troubleshooting requires an understanding of PC hardware and operating systems, along with a keen knowledge of symptoms and diagnostics. Setting up, optimizing, and upgrading a PC are three other important areas that demand the attention of today's technician.

IN THIS EDITION

This book is intended for the modern computer enthusiast, working technician, or PC student. It is *not* designed to explain computer theory—there are already plenty of theory books out there. Instead, this book is designed to be a hands-on desktop (or workbench) reference for PC repair, maintenance, and upgrading. This book concentrates on the symptoms and problem areas that occur in every area of the modern PC, as well as proper *diagnosis* of problems. Online resources are included for almost every chapter making the book ideal for classroom or home study. Previous editions have been extremely popular, but this fifth edition has been completely revised to keep pace with the improvements in PC technology, and updated software versions have been added to the companion CD.

This book is meant to be a lifeline and a resource to help you repair your PC, keep it running, and get the most out of it. You'll find almost 2,000 PC problems fully detailed and explained. There are references to hundreds more POST and diagnostic codes to help you identify even the most obscure problems. But the support you'll find here goes far beyond these book pages. You'll find an entire CD-ROM full of over 120 *power-tools*—shareware and freeware diagnostics and utilities designed to help you identify even the peskiest PC problems. This is one of the only PC hardware books to bundle so many Windows 9x/Me diagnostic software products with the text.

SUBSCRIBE TO THE PC TOOLBOX

Many readers also complain that PC books suffer from a limited "life-span." All too often, a book is dated as soon as it gets on bookstore shelves. You can avoid this kind of technical obsolescence by subscribing to our #1 newsletter, *The PC Toolbox*™, to stay informed of the latest hands-on service articles, optimization techniques, and find the answers to your PC questions. Even if you don't fix computers for a living, a subscription can save you hundreds of dollars in shop costs. You can learn more about *The PC Toolbox*™ and enter your subscription at **www.dlspubs.com**.

TEST YOUR KNOWLEDGE

Worried about keeping yourself employable? Go for the Dynamic Learning Systems Technician's Certificate 4. As the purchaser of this book, you can take the DLS Technician's Certificate Exam included in Appendix I (on the accompanying CD). Those readers that pass will receive a high-quality certificate showing your mastery of the material in this book. But the certificate is not just for framing—readers who successfully complete the examination are much better prepared to tackle the industry-recognized A+ examination, and even to move on to acquire CST certification through the ETA (Electronic Technician's Association).

I'M INTERESTED IN YOUR SUCCESS

I've taken a lot of time and effort to see that this edition is the most comprehensive and understandable book on PC/peripheral repair available. If you have any questions or comments about the book, please don't hesitate to contact me through Dynamic Learning Systems at **www.dlspubs.com**.

—Stephen J. Bigelow

SYMPTOMS AT A GLANCE

AN INSIDE LOOK AT
A CONTEMPORARY PC

In order to upgrade or troubleshoot a PC effectively, a technician must be familiar with the general mechanical and physical aspects of the PC. They must be able to disassemble the unit quickly (without causing damage to the case or internal assemblies in the process), and then accurately identify each subassembly, expansion board, and connector. Once a diagnosis and repair has been completed, the technician must be able to reassemble the PC and its enclosures (again without damaging assemblies or enclosures). Remember that there's no such thing as an *unimportant* part—every device serves a vital purpose, and can have an impact on the overall performance and reliability of your system. This chapter is designed to provide you with a "guided tour" of a typical PC, point out the various operating subassemblies, and offer a series of assembly guidelines.

The Contemporary PC

A PC doesn't just appear—it is carefully crafted into being by combining a series of key component devices and assemblies. Before you start troubleshooting a PC, it is important that you recognize each major device on sight, and understand its role in the system. If you're new to personal computers, this part of the chapter will give you a thorough introduction to the devices that you'll find. Once you're comfortable tearing off a cover and poking around inside of the system, you can focus on upgrade and troubleshooting procedures.

ENCLOSURES

The *enclosure* (also called the *case* or *chassis*) is the most obvious and least glamorous element of a PC. Yet, the enclosure serves some very important functions. First, the enclosure forms the mechanical foundation of every PC. Every other subassembly is bolted securely to this chassis. Second, the chassis is electrically grounded through the power supply. Grounding prevents the buildup or discharge of static electricity from damaging other subassemblies. Whenever you work inside of a PC, be sure to use a properly grounded antistatic wrist strap to prevent electrostatic discharge from your body from accidentally damaging circuitry inside the system. If you do not have an antistatic wrist strap handy, you can discharge yourself on the PC's metal chassis as long as the power supply is plugged in. However, since you are *strongly* urged to protect yourself by unplugging the power supply AC, do *not* rely on the chassis to discharge you. Grounding also prevents a serious shock or fire hazard if AC should come in contact with the metal case. There are three general classifications of case: baby, desktop, and tower.

Baby Cases

The *baby case* lives up to its name. It is a small desktop case that fits an absolute minimum of items. You're usually limited to two drives, because the 130–175W power supply is typically located right behind the drives, and there's no room left for an internally mounted hard drive. You are also limited to using a small motherboard—typically with a minimum of features or ports. Finally, the small case and motherboard will usually limit the number of expansion slots available. A baby desktop case really limits your upgrade and expandability options. The only real benefit of a baby case is when you only need a minimum system (in other words, a network terminal), and desk space is at a premium.

Desktop Cases

Desktop cases come in a variety of shapes and sizes, but generally offer a lot more versatility and upgrade potential than baby cases. With regular desktop cases, you can usually count on two external drive bays, and two internal drive bays—great for a floppy drive, CD or DVD drive, and one or two hard drives. If you find a desktop case with three external drive bays, you can even add a second CD drive or a tape drive. The other advantages to regular desktop cases is that they have the physical space to support larger power supplies (usually 200–250W+), they fit larger motherboards, and they support more expansion cards. A desktop case will support a low to moderate number of upgrades with few headaches.

Tower Cases

The *tower case* is typically a large vertically mounted case, which is designed to hold the maximum number of drives. There are often four or more external drive bays, and at least four internal drive bays. The extra space also allows the largest power supplies (300W+), which are vital to support an array of different drives. Tower cases can hold the very largest of motherboards (though in practice the motherboards are rarely larger than those found in a regular desktop). Tower cases also provide the best air ventilation, and can sport two or more fans and air filters. The other advantage of good airflow is that high-end CPUs (even multiprocessor motherboards) can be cooled most effectively. In spite of their larger size, tower cases are rarely more expensive than desktop enclosures. Towers can also be placed on the floor (off of your desk or other work area). Tower cases are often available in minitower, midtower, and full-tower styles, so you can usually pick the tower size that meets your particular needs and esthetic preference. Figure 1-1 illustrates a typical generic midtower case.

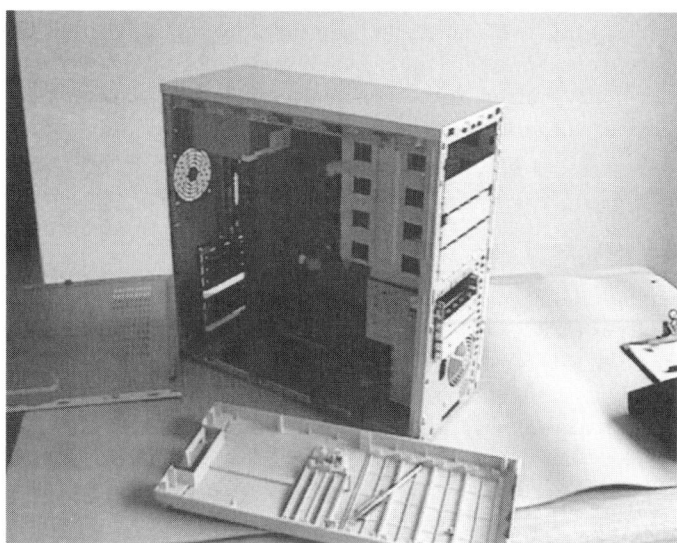

FIGURE 1-1   A generic midtower case

Enclosure Issues

Most technicians do not concern themselves with PC enclosures, because they don't "break" and are almost never upgraded, and thus last the life of the PC. However, other upgrades (such as new motherboards or advanced processors) may necessitate the selection of another enclosure. For example, the AMD Athlon processor is known to be rather particular about the case it is in—so much so that compatible cases are listed at the AMD Web site: **www1.amd.com/athlon/config**. As another example, Intel calls for a minimum of 250W (power supply) and support for an ATX 2.01 case when working with the Pentium III processor. Take a moment to understand some important enclosure issues.

The Importance of Drive Bays   One of the most important aspects of a case is the number of drive bays it provides. There are two types of drive bays: external and internal. *External* drive bays are open to the outside of the case. Floppy drives, CD-ROM/CD-R/CD-RW drives, DVD-ROM/DVD-RAM drives, and tape drives all require external drive bays. *Internal* drive bays are mounting frames located inside of the case. Typically, only hard drives use internal drive bays. As a minimum, your case should have two external drive bays (for a floppy drive and CD or DVD drive) and one internal drive bay (for the hard drive). If additional drive bays are available, you'll have room for future expansion.

Fitting Power Supplies and Motherboards   You also need to remember that your case will have to hold a power supply and motherboard—these things actually have to *mount* to the case, so be sure that your enclosure provides ample space and mounting points for a clean fit. There's nothing more frustrating than receiving a replacement motherboard and finding out that it won't fit in the case (or the mounting holes don't line up). Fortunately, cases are often offered with built-in power supplies, so that's one less headache to deal with. If you are upgrading to a new (typically larger) case, it may also help you to get a matched case and power supply. The new supply should offer more power capacity than your original supply, and you will probably have an easier time getting rid of or reusing the old case if it has a working power supply with it.

Mechanical Specifications   Given the problems matching motherboards, cases, and power supplies, the computer industry has responded by developing a series of physical specifications (called *form factors*) for the construction of motherboards, cases, and power supplies. The idea is that power supplies, motherboards, and cases all built to a certain specification will fit correctly without the problems of mixing and matching. The three most popular specifications are AT (and baby AT), ATX, and NLX. See "Standardized Form Factors" at the end of this chapter for more information.

POWER SUPPLIES

You should next familiarize yourself with the *power supply,* as shown in Figure 1-2. Whether you're replacing a failed supply, upgrading to a larger supply, or building a new system from scratch, do yourself a favor and *don't* skimp on the power supply. Buy plenty of power capacity, and go with a reputable manufacturer—marginal supplies will cause no end of trouble with erratic system operation and premature failures. Power is measured in *watts* (W). Each device in the computer demands power, so enough power must be available from the supply to run the motherboard, the drives, and all of the expansion boards in your system. Don't be afraid to "buy power"—it's OK to have too much—problems occur when there isn't enough. If you go with a desktop case, plan on a 200–250W supply. For tower cases (with lots of drives), go with a 300–350W unit (servers or systems packed with devices may need a 400W supply).

If you really want to apply some numbers when estimating the size for a power supply, you can use the 150+12 rule. This is a baseline of 150W for the motherboard and CPU, and then 12W for every drive and expansion board you plan to add. If you want a system with a floppy drive, hard drive, CD-ROM, modem board, and video board, figure on about (150+12+12+12+12+12) 210W. If you buy a 220W to 250W supply, you'll have plenty of power, though your upgrade options may be a bit limited.

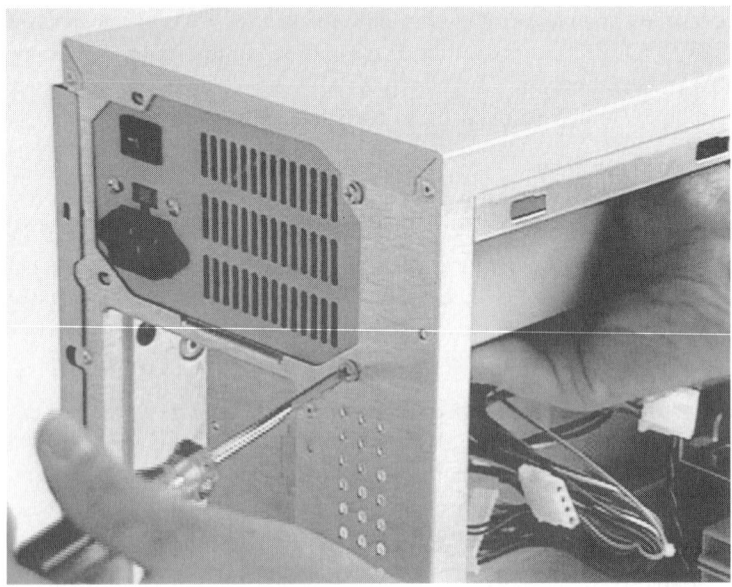

FIGURE 1-2   A typical PC power supply unit

Power Connectors

When you look at the power supply, you'll notice two different sets of cables. One set of cables plugs into the motherboard. The other set of cables provides power to each drive. There must be enough drive power cables to run each drive in your system. Otherwise, you'll need Y cables to split power. In practice, these Y cables should be avoided, so the more drive power cables, the better off you'll be. As a rule, the more wattage offered by the power supply, the more drive cables that will be available.

There are two well-accepted sets of cables to power the motherboard: the baby AT configuration, shown in Figure 1-3, and the ATX configuration, shown in Figure 1-4. The classic baby AT configuration uses two 6-pin Molex connectors (usually marked P8 and P9), which are inserted adjacent to each other. The rule here is "black wires together." A baby AT power supply provides four voltage levels (+5V, −5V, +12V, and −12V) along with a "Power Good" signal. The ATX power supply uses a slightly different 20-pin single-connector scheme, which includes a +3.3V supply along with the other conventional voltages. It is important to stress that baby AT power supply connectors will *not* mate with an ATX motherboard (and vice versa).

An auxiliary power connector (6-pin, P4 connector) is included with some newer ATX power supplies, but not many motherboards support or use this connector. When the connector is unsupported or unused, just leave it detached.

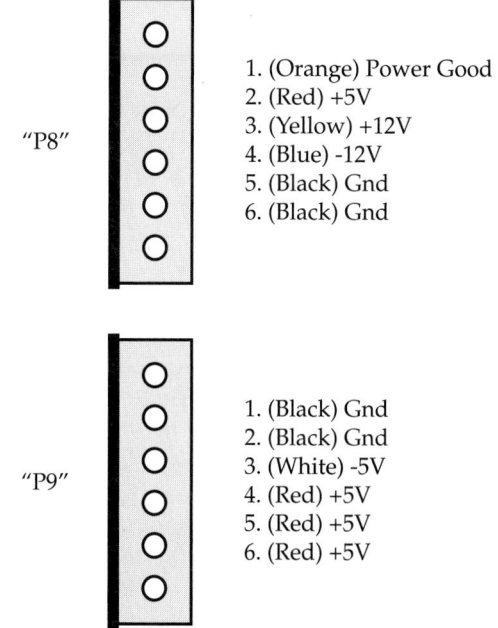

"P8"

1. (Orange) Power Good
2. (Red) +5V
3. (Yellow) +12V
4. (Blue) -12V
5. (Black) Gnd
6. (Black) Gnd

"P9"

1. (Black) Gnd
2. (Black) Gnd
3. (White) -5V
4. (Red) +5V
5. (Red) +5V
6. (Red) +5V

FIGURE 1-3   Baby AT-style power connectors

1. +3.3V	11. +3.3V
2. +3.3V	12. -12V
3. Gnd	13. Gnd
4. +5V	14. PW_ON
5. Gnd	15. Gnd
6. +5V	16. Gnd
7. Gnd	17. Gnd
8. PWRGD	18. -5V
(Power Good)	19. +5V
9. +5V SB	
(Standby for RTC)	

FIGURE 1-4   ATX-style power connectors

Mounting Points

Of course, you actually have to mount that power supply into the case. This can get a little bit tricky with older baby AT systems, because nobody tells the case makers and the power supply makers to put their screw holes in the same places. You should make sure that the power supply will mount properly in the case. If you can find a case with a suitable power supply already mounted, that might take some of the guesswork out of your assembly. Also remember that you'll need to turn the supply on and off—this means the case has to have a hole for the power switch, as well as the AC line cord and fuse opening. Remember that ATX- and NLX-style cases and power supplies should be easier to match. Today, there are relatively few mechanical compatibility problems between power supplies and cases, but keep those mounting issues in mind.

Most ATX-style power supply units do *not* use an on/off switch. Instead, the ATX standard uses "soft power" signals from the case power button to the motherboard. Don't get rattled if you don't see an on/off switch on your ATX supply.

Choosing a Supply

Power supplies are some of the most overlooked parts of a PC—probably because you never see them in operation the way you do with video boards or hard drives. Also, once a supply is operating, there is really no reason to replace it. The only two reasons to replace a power supply are to exchange a defective unit, or to support the power demands of more devices added during a PC upgrade. The supply needs to provide adequate power to the computer, needs to fit in the physical space available, needs to mount properly and securely, and should have an ample number of drive power cables available without having to resort to Y cables. Once again, buy reputable! While all power supplies perform the same basic jobs, they are *not* all created equal—go with a manufacturer that uses top-quality parts in a well-designed and reliable supply that is backed with a strong warranty and friendly return policy. The best PC components in the world cannot make up for a poor power supply.

Power supply assemblies are generally regarded as extremely safe, because it is virtually impossible to come into contact with exposed high-energy circuitry. Still, exercise caution and common sense whenever working with a running power supply.

MOTHERBOARDS AND RELATED PARTS

The *motherboard* is absolutely the heart and soul of every computer. Motherboards and the components on them (CPUs, chipsets, RAM, BIOS, and integrated controllers) largely define the capabilities and limitations of any given system. This part of the chapter covers the major elements of a motherboard, and shows you the important points to consider. Table 1-1 lists the specifications for the example motherboard shown in Figure 1-5. You can see the specifications at **english.aopen.com.tw/products/mb/ak72.htm**.

Form Factor Support

The dimensions and mounting points for the motherboard are typically defined by the *form factor,* and this is often the first specification you see when evaluating the new motherboard. Your choices are generally; baby AT, ATX, or NLX (though ATX is by far the most common and popular form factor). The dimensions for a typical ATX motherboard are illustrated in Figure 1-6. The form factor is certainly not the most exciting motherboard issue when compared to processors and chipsets, but you need to understand it right up front—all the processing power in the world won't do you much good if the motherboard doesn't fit in the case.

Expansion Slot Support

Motherboards alone rarely offer all of the features that you need for your computer. Fortunately, you can easily add other devices to the motherboard by plugging them into *expansion slots* (or *bus slots*). There are five different architectures that you should be familiar with: ISA, PCI, AGP, USB, and AMR. You should be familiar with each of these five bus types because virtually all new motherboards offer some (or all) of these busses, and the capabilities of your new system will largely be defined by the busses that are available on your particular motherboard. For example, you can't use an AGP video card on a motherboard that only has PCI slots. These bus types are defined next.

FIGURE 1-5   An AMD Athlon-compatible motherboard

TABLE 1-1 **BASIC SPECIFICATIONS FOR AN AOPEN AK72 ATHLON MOTHERBOARD**

CHARACTERISTIC	DESCRIPTION
CPU	AMD Athlon (K7) CPU; CPU clock ratio from 5.0 to 10.5
Chipset	VIA Apollo KX133 (VT8371/VT82C686A)
Busses	1 ISA slot, 5 PCI slots, 1 AGP slot, and 1 AMR slot; support 1X/2X/4X AGP mode
Main memory	Up to 1.5GB SDRAM (PC100 or PC133)
DIMM types	8/16/32/64/128/256/512MB
Sound	Analog Devices AD1881 AC'97 CODEC onboard
BIOS	Award Plug and Play 2MB Flash ROM BIOS
Onboard I/O	2 serial ports (UART 16C550 support) 1 parallel port (SPP/EPP/ECP support) 2 channel EIDE (Mode 4 and bus master Ultra-DMA 33/66 support) 1 floppy drive connector (1.2/1.44/2.88MB) 2 Universal Serial Bus (USB) ports 2 USB connectors (with cable) 1 PS/2 mouse port 1 PS/2 keyboard port Game/MIDI port Speaker-Out, Line-In, and Mic-In connectors
Connectors	CD audio, modem audio, IrDA, Wake On Modem, Wake On LAN, CPU fan, chassis fan
Battery	3V lithium battery
Form factor	244mm x 305mm, ATX form factor

ISA This is the classic *Industry Standard Architecture* (ISA) 16-bit, 8.3MHz expansion bus. Although it offers limited data throughput and resources when compared to other busses, you'll still find numerous 16-bit cards like modems, SCSI adapters, and sound cards. Your motherboard may have two to four ISA slots onboard—though some of the newest Pentium III/Athlon motherboards eliminate

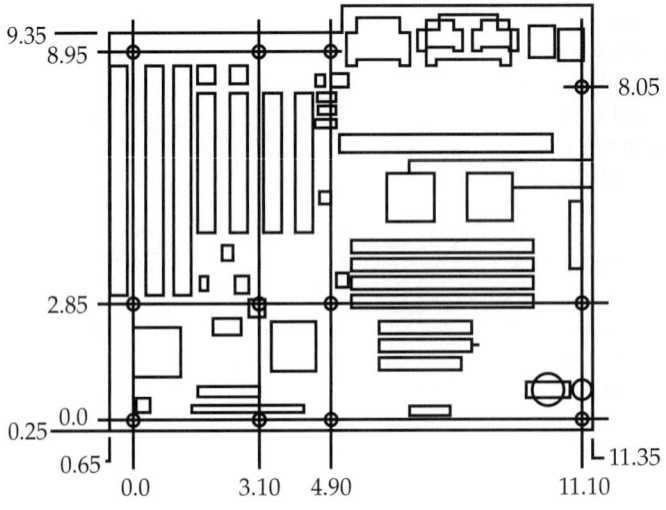

FIGURE 1-6 ATX motherboard dimensions

the ISA bus completely. If you *must* use older ISA cards carried over from an existing system, make sure that your motherboard offers ISA slots. Otherwise, it's a good idea to avoid the use of ISA devices in favor of PCI and AGP devices.

PCI   The *Peripheral Component Interconnect* (PCI) bus originally evolved as a 32/64-bit answer to the aged *Video Local Bus* (VLB). Whereas the VLB is generally geared toward video systems, the PCI bus is designed to support general-purpose devices (though network cards, modems, and drive controllers are some of the most common). PCI is clearly a better-performing bus with superior data throughput. Its fixed 30MHz/33MHz clock speed makes PCI much more stable than VLB, and its bus mastering features make it ideal for high-performance devices. A modern motherboard may sport between four and six PCI slots.

AGP   Video continues to be a bottleneck for cutting-edge graphics applications that push video resolution, color depth, and image complexity to the limit (especially for video and real-time 3-D images). The *Accelerated Graphics Port* (AGP) is a high-performance port using a superset of PCI architecture designed to handle huge volumes of video data. Where the 32-bit PCI bus implementation can handle 133MB/s, the 32-bit implementation of an AGP can handle 533MB/s—future implementations of AGP are expected to handle 1GB/s of video data and higher. This opens up whole new possibilities for games and visualization software. However, you will require AGP support in the motherboard's PCI chipset, as well as the BIOS and operating system. Microsoft now fully supports AGP in Windows 98. The AGP also accesses main system RAM for storing graphics textures, so video RAM is not so critical. But it is still a good idea to select replacement AGP cards (or any video card) with as much onboard video memory as possible.

USB   Expanding a PC has always been a hassle—setting jumpers and DIP switches often leads to hardware conflicts that cause system crashes and lockups. Plug-and-play (PnP) technology has helped ease the burden of installations and upgrades to some extent, but adding new devices remains troublesome. The *Universal Serial Bus* (USB) is a relatively new architecture that allows you to add devices "outside of the PC" simply by daisy-chaining devices together without worrying about resource allocation. The devices can also be installed and removed while the system is running (called *hot insertion and removal*). USB is slanted primarily toward external devices such as monitors, joysticks, keyboards, and so on. Many modern motherboards will offer one or two USB ports.

AMR   The relatively new *Audio/Modem Riser* (AMR) specification defines a hardware-scaleable OEM (original equipment manufacturer) motherboard riser board and interface that supports both audio and modem features. This allows the development and use of specialized low-cost sound/modem "combo cards" that can be used in this slot. While numerous motherboards include an AMR slot, few AMR devices are available at this time. Consequently, you may need to use a separate modem card and sound card. If your motherboard already offers a built-in sound device, you can stick with a PCI modem card.

CPU Support

The *central processing unit* (called a *processor* or *CPU*) is the main processing component on your motherboard (see Figure 1-7). All program instructions and data are eventually processed through the CPU. The faster and more powerful a CPU is, the more performance your computer will offer. Keep in mind that a CPU also has to operate in conjunction with other elements of the motherboard, so a newer CPU installed into an older motherboard may not offer the same performance as a new CPU installed into a state-of-the-art motherboard. When selecting a CPU for upgrade or replacement, always verify that your motherboard will support it. In virtually all cases, the motherboard (or system) documentation will list the

CPUs that are compatible with the motherboard. For example, the Intel PD440FX motherboard will support a Pentium II CPU operating at 233MHz or 266MHz, but the AOpen AK72 motherboard (shown earlier in Figure 1-5) supports AMD Athlon processors from 500MHz to 1000MHz. Improved CPUs are one of the most popular upgrades for a motherboard, so choose a motherboard to accommodate the CPUs that may be added in the future. Otherwise, you'll find yourself having to replace the entire motherboard outright.

It's a good idea to keep potential future upgrades in mind. When selecting a motherboard for upgrade or replacement, go for the *fastest* motherboard that you can afford. Later, it's a simple matter to upgrade to a faster processor once their price falls.

Heat Sinks and Fans   Modern CPUs also run hot—*very* hot. If you don't want to ruin your CPU investment, you'll need to think about ways to keep the CPU cool. As a rule, use a heat sink/CPU fan that mounts directly to the CPU itself. The heat sink is basically a metal radiator that carries heat away from the CPU. The fan—built right into the heat sink—forces air through the heat sink, which makes the cooling process much more efficient (you can see the cooling unit in Figure 1-7). You can typically buy a heat sink/fan when buying the CPU.

Select a "boxed" processor that is certain to include an appropriate heat sink/fan assembly. An "unboxed" or OEM processor version will offer an identical processor, but is not always certain to include the heat sink/fan.

Main Memory (RAM) Support

All computers need memory to hold program data and instructions while the CPU is executing them, so *random access memory* (RAM) is needed on the motherboard. Older motherboards usually incorporated 1 or 2MB of RAM on the motherboard, then allowed you to add more memory in the form of Single Inline Memory Module (SIMMs). Today, all motherboards use memory modules exclusively—Dual Inline Memory Modules (DIMMs) or Rambus Inline Memory Modules (RIMMs)—which makes it much easier to

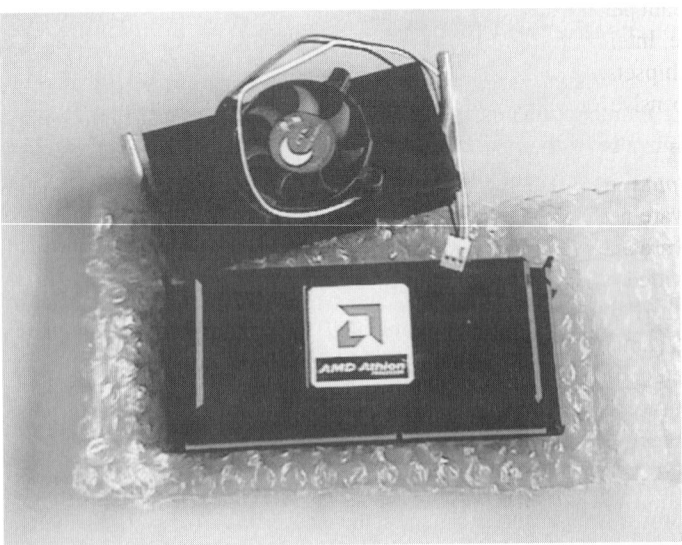

FIGURE 1-7   An 800MHz AMD Athlon processor

replace defective memory without having to replace the entire motherboard. You generally choose some preinstalled amount of RAM when you select your motherboard, or purchase the RAM separately and install it yourself. Many types of RAM are available for the PC, but you should be familiar with the three most popular types, described next.

SDRAM   *Synchronous DRAM* is a type of enhanced memory that allows data to be transferred at any point in the system's clock cycle rather than just at certain points. This makes for dramatically faster overall memory performance. SDRAM can also "burst" large amounts of data to and from memory. All the newest chipsets support SDRAM. SDRAM was introduced for 66MHz motherboards (often referred to as PC66 SDRAM). A variation of SDRAM is PC100 SDRAM. With newer motherboards using a bus speed of 100MHz, the RAM timing becomes far more critical. PC100 RAM is basically SDRAM that has been certified to run properly on 100MHz motherboards. If you do *not* select PC100 RAM, make sure that your SDRAM is suitable for operation at 100MHz. PC133 SDRAM is available for motherboards using a bus speed of 133MHz. You can often use 100MHz SDRAM on a 133MHz motherboard, but you'll need to slow the motherboard's bus speed to 100MHz—this will result in a terrible loss of performance for the system. You should also be able to use PC133 RAM on 100MHz systems, but the expense of PC133 RAM makes this a bit of a waste. SDRAM is available in DIMM form.

DDR SDRAM   Double data rate (DDR) SDRAM is a relatively recent enhancement to SDRAM technology that can transfer data on two edges of the system's clock rather than on just one edge. This makes it possible to increase (ideally double) the effective performance of RAM. In actual practice, DDR SDRAM does not double memory performance over ordinary SDRAM, but it does offer a real improvement. DDR SDRAM is available in DIMM form.

RDRAM   *Rambus DRAM* (or just plain *Rambus*) has dramatically grown in popularity over the last few years, and is supported in most new PCs (namely PCs using the Intel 800 series of chipsets). Rambus (**www.rambus.com**) uses dedicated data channels to transfer data using speeds of up to 800MHz, and this is often dubbed PC800 RAM. PCs fitted for Rambus operation can often achieve 2-byte transfers at 800MHz, giving the system a memory throughput of up to 1.6GB/sec. In actual practice, Rambus has not enjoyed the significant performance improvements that the technology had promised, but improvements are still being made. Intel originally did not plan on offering PC133 SDRAM support in its 800 family (810, 820, 840) of chipsets, but it was added to provide backward-compatibility with widely available and comparatively inexpensive SDRAM. RDRAM is available in RIMM form, which is a bit bigger than DIMM.

BIOS Support

The *basic input/output system* (BIOS) is a form of permanent memory that holds the instructions that your motherboard hardware needs to communicate with the operating system. In short, BIOS "drives" your motherboard hardware and supports features like PnP, power conservation, and specialized busses like USB. BIOS is provided *with* the motherboard, so you don't have to select it separately, but you may choose to upgrade the BIOS later on.

Normally, BIOS should only be upgraded when there is a clear problem with the BIOS that prevents an important feature or function from working, or a BIOS upgrade would expand the capabilities of your hardware. For example, suppose you're using a motherboard video system, and you decide to upgrade the video system by adding a new video board—you'd need to disable the motherboard video system. Some poorly designed motherboards may be unable to fully disable their onboard video because of a flaw in the BIOS, and an upgrade might fix the problem. As another example, some older motherboards needed a BIOS upgrade to support the AMD K6 and K6-2, or the Cyrix MII. It would not be a surprise to see a few motherboards require a BIOS upgrade to support newer third-party CPUs, such as the AMD K6-III or the Cyrix MIII.

Chipset Support

In the early days of PCs, motherboards were built with hundreds of discrete logic chips (just take a look at any original IBM PC/AT). It didn't take long for designers to realize that the major PC functions could be condensed onto application-specific chips. This philosophy not only reduced the total number of chips needed to build a motherboard, but also allowed performance to improve, and reduced the power demands and costs for a motherboard. Eventually, chip design evolved to the point where *all* the major features needed for a motherboard could be provided with just a couple of related (and very complex) chips. These related chips became known as *chipsets*. Modern motherboard capabilities are largely defined by their chipset. In fact, most chipsets are specific to certain CPU families. When replacing a motherboard, be sure to select one with a chipset that supports the important features that you need (such as USB ports, advanced processors, and so on).

Motherboard Ports and Controllers

As you've seen already, motherboards rarely provide every possible feature or device needed to make a working computer—there are countless other devices that could (and should) be added to the system. Most external devices are attached to the motherboard through ports. Figure 1-8 illustrates some of the ports available for external devices.

- **Serial ports**   Get a motherboard with two serial ports. One serial port is usually for a serial mouse, and another serial port is typically for an external modem. If your motherboard does not offer serial ports, you can add serial ports by installing a multi-I/O card into an available expansion slot.

- **Parallel ports**   If you plan to use a printer, at least one parallel port will be a necessity. Virtually all motherboards provide one parallel port. If your motherboard does not offer a parallel port, you can add one by installing a multi-I/O card into an available expansion slot.

- **Keyboard port**   This is really a no-brainer—there has to be a connector on the motherboard to accept the input from a keyboard. The keyboard port may be soldered directly to the motherboard itself, or there may be a cable header from the motherboard to a keyboard connector at the case. Modern motherboards include a built-in PS/2 keyboard port.

- **Mouse port**   Although you can easily install a serial mouse on an existing serial port, you may choose to get a motherboard with a built-in PS/2 mouse port. This frees up the second serial port for other uses (such as a serial printer). Keep in mind that some motherboards will require a small adapter cable to connect a PS/2 header on the motherboard to a PS/2 connector in the case.

- **USB port(s)**   While a USB port is not required, it is standard equipment on most new motherboards (**www.usb.org**). When used in conjunction with Windows 98, the USB port offers a fast and convenient means of connecting several USB devices without even having to turn off the PC. You can even use USB keyboards and mice. USB supports a port speed of 12Mbits/s (1.5MBs—up to ten times faster than serial or parallel port speed). It can connect up to 127 devices, provide up to 0.5 amps to external devices, and handle the *hot swapping* of devices (connecting and disconnecting devices with power on).

- **IEEE 1394 (a.k.a. FireWire)**   While USB will be the accepted standard for lower-speed peripherals (such as keyboards, mice, game controllers, speakers, scanners, or printers), high-end digital audio/video peripherals require a high-speed port. FireWire meets this requirement with throughput speeds reaching 400Mbits/s (50MB/s) at this time, and is scheduled to reach 800Mbps (100MB/s) soon. FireWire uses a *tiered star* topology and supports peer-to-peer connections without hubs, allowing up to 63 same-speed devices to be connected to the same bus, and up to 1,023 buses to be interconnected. FireWire is also designed to be hot-swappable. Many companies involved in the development of FireWire are doing so in conjunction with a computer case standard named Device Bay. The combination of high-speed FireWire, hot-swapping, and Device Bay technologies will allow high-speed peripherals to be inserted and removed at any time (and even moved from computer to computer). Motherboards supporting FireWire are just now being introduced, but you can learn more about FireWire at **www.dtvgroup.com/DigVideo/FireWire/Adaptec/1394main.html**.

Controllers are generally used to connect devices inside of the PC. Many of today's motherboards incorporate video and drive controllers (a few also provide a sound feature). This adds convenience to the motherboard because it saves two expansion slots (one for the video controller, and one for the drive controller). If you choose to upgrade the motherboard's video or drive controller later, you can always disable the motherboard's controllers and install the replacement controllers in the form of expansion boards. The following are common motherboard controllers:

- **Floppy drive controllers (FDCs)**   You will find a 34-pin IDC header (or *ribbon cable connector*) on the motherboard for your floppy drives (usually labeled FDD). The floppy drive port will support two floppy drives (A and B) and can be disabled through a jumper on the motherboard. If you install a drive controller expansion board later, you need to disable the floppy drive port.

- **Hard drive controllers (HDCs)**   You will probably find two 40-pin IDC headers (or *ribbon cable connectors*) on the motherboard for your hard drives (usually labeled "primary HDD" and "secondary HDD"). The primary hard drive port should support two Ultra-DMA/100 hard drives (C and D). The secondary hard drive port should also support two Ultra-DMA/100 drives, but may be limited to slightly older devices such as Ultra-DMA/66 or Ultra-DMA/33. If you install a drive controller expansion board later, you will need to disable these hard drive ports.

- **Video controllers**   Your motherboard will probably offer a 15-pin high-density SVGA connector and 2 or 4MB of video RAM. This allows you to connect your monitor directly to the motherboard. The constant pressure to lower overall system costs has produced increased video integration. Intel 810 and 810E chipsets include built-in AGP graphics support. ALi and VIA offer chipsets that are tightly integrated with onboard AGP graphic engines from well-known video component manufacturers (ALi Aladdin TNT2 and VIA Apollo MVP4, PM601). If you need higher resolutions, color depths, more video memory, or better overall video performance, you can always disable the motherboard video system and install a video controller expansion board later on.

FIGURE 1-8   A typical selection of motherboard I/O ports

If maximum system performance and upgradeability are important, you should avoid motherboards with onboard video and select a motherboard containing a separate AGP slot. Current high-performance standards call for motherboard support for AGP 4X and video cards with at least 32MB of DDR memory.

VIDEO SYSTEMS

All computers need a video system to display the text, graphics, and multimedia images associated with everyday computing. This is even more important for demanding video applications such as 3-D rendering and visualization. A video system generally consists of two elements—the video controller and the monitor. This part of the chapter explains the issues involved with a typical video system, and shows you some important considerations in part selection.

Video Controllers

Next to your motherboard, the video controller (see Figure 1-9) is a vitally important device. Indirectly, the video controller defines the "visualization capabilities" of your PC. With the intense interest in multimedia, video, and computer graphics, video systems are evolving at an incredible rate. The advantage of a motherboard-based video controller is convenience—you save money, and need only plug a monitor into the motherboard's video connector. However, motherboard video controllers are limited in terms of memory and sophistication, and they cannot be upgraded without replacing the motherboard or installing a stand-alone video board. If you do not have a video controller already available on your motherboard (or wish to install a more powerful video system), you will have to install a stand-alone video board into a motherboard expansion slot. If your motherboard provides an AGP slot, an AGP video board will certainly offer superior performance.

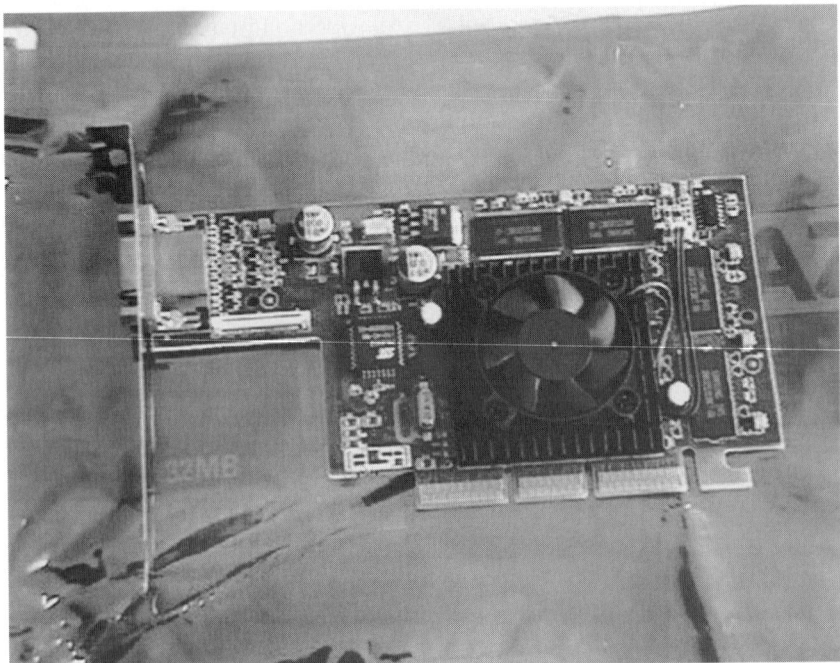

FIGURE 1-9   A high-performance AGP video card

Resolutions and Color Depth   Video boards are rated in terms of their resolution and color depth. The *resolution* is the number of pixels, which can be displayed on a monitor. Resolution is usually rated in terms of width×height (for example, 640×480). *Color depth* is the number of colors that can be displayed at a given resolution. Most current video boards can support resolutions up to 1280×1024 at color depths from 16 colors to 16 million colors. As a rule, Windows 95/98 work fine with 800×600 resolution at 65k colors (high-color mode), but if you're considering the use of a DVD drive for MPEG-2 video, you should go for a video board that will support a minimum of 800×600 resolution in true color (16M color) mode.

Table 1-2 illustrates the capabilities of a typical high-end video board. For each standard resolution, you can see the various color depths that the board can handle. Note that color depths are often expressed as bits per pixel (or bits/pixel). Below each bits/pixel entry is the amount of video memory available. Note that more video memory allows higher resolutions and color depths. The relationship of bits to colors is as follows: 8 bits yields 265 colors, 16 bits supports 65 thousand colors (called *high color* mode), 24 bits provides 16 million colors (called *true color* mode), and 32 bits supplies an astounding 4 billion colors.

Video Memory   As you probably noticed in Table 1-2, video memory holds the data that composes your image. Higher resolutions and color depths require more video memory. The actual formula for memory is

```
total pixels x bits/pixel
```

Suppose you have an 800×600 image at 16 bits/pixel (65 thousand colors). That's (800×600) 480,000 pixels. You would need (480,000×16) 7,680,000 bits (960,000 bytes or 960KB) of video memory to show one complete image on the screen. As a rule, select a video board with at *least* 8MB of video memory—preferably 16MB. If you're planning on a high-end 3-D video board, plan on 16–32MB of video RAM.

Video BIOS and Drivers   All video boards running above 640×480×16 require the use of *video drivers* to support higher resolutions and color depths. While protected-mode drivers for Windows 98 or Me can easily support a wide range of enhanced video modes, this presents some unique problems for older DOS applications (especially games). When you select a video board, make sure that the video BIOS supports VESA 2.0 extensions or later. This eliminates the need for DOS VESA drivers. If you're using an older video board without VESA support in BIOS, try the Universal VESA display driver available from SciTech Software, Inc. at **www.scitechsoft.com**. Some game manufacturers also distribute the Universal VESA driver in their technical support Web site.

Given the importance of drivers, don't even think of buying a video board unless it comes with the very latest video drivers for Windows 98/Me. Older Windows 3.1 video drivers will *not* work well with

TABLE 1-2   VIDEO RESOLUTION AND COLOR DEPTH

RESOLUTION	BITS/PIXEL (2MB)	BITS/PIXEL (4MB)	BITS/PIXEL (8MB)
640×480	8, 16, 24, 32	8, 16, 24, 32	8, 16, 24, 32
800×600	8, 16, 24, 32	8, 16, 24, 32	8, 16, 24, 32
1024×768	8, 16	8, 16, 24, 32	8, 16, 24, 32
1152×864	8, 16	8, 16, 24, 32	8, 16, 24, 32
1280×1024	8	8, 16, 24	8, 16, 24, 32
1600×1200	8	8, 16	8, 16, 24

Windows 98/Me. Another issue to consider is driver age. Video drivers are some of the most frequently updated items, and you can usually find a video driver update on the video card manufacturer's technical support Web site. If you're installing a used video board that's a few years old, be sure to check for the latest drivers first.

Monitors

The video controller drives your monitor, which actually displays the video image. In a sense, the monitor is your "window" into the PC. Choose a monitor with care—a poor-quality monitor can ruin the finest video image. In most cases, a 15- to 17-inch SVGA monitor with a dot spacing (or *pitch*) of 0.28 or less (preferably 0.26 or less) should produce a fine-looking image. If your customer works with computers extensively, you should recommend spending the extra money for a 20- or 21-inch monitor. Larger monitors support higher resolutions, and allow you to "zoom" documents and drawings with far more clarity than you could achieve with a smaller monitor. You should also recommend monitors that are *non-interlaced*. Interlaced monitors tend to show more flicker, and cause more eye fatigue. You will notice that the monitor's signal cable has a 15-pin high-density connector on the end, which will fit perfectly with the connector on your video board. You can actually use any compatible monitor to test the video output of a system. The information contained at the Hitachi Web site can take some of the mystery out of all of those monitor specifications: **www.hitachidisplays.com/how_monitors/index.htm**.

SOUND SYSTEMS

Originally driven by the needs of game developers, sound boards evolved as a replacement for the obnoxious beeping and tweeting of a PC speaker. Over the last 15 years, sound has become a prominent feature of virtually all new systems. Today, good-quality sound boards provide efficient sound-file play-back, extremely precise sound synthesis, and orchestral-quality music. Whether you plan to play audio CDs, use the newest games, watch your favorite DVD movie, or make multimedia presentations, you will almost certainly need a good-quality sound device in your computer. Many traditional sound cards use an ISA slot because of its low cost and simplicity. This has generally worked well because of the relatively low bandwidth demanded by sound systems. However, in the interests of creating complete plug-and-play systems, select a newer sound card using a PCI slot, if possible.

If your motherboard already incorporates an onboard sound device, you will *not* need a separate sound board.

Sound Issues

Unless you're a real audiophile, you probably won't be able to detect a significant sound difference between good-quality sound cards, so feel free to compare prices. Still, there are some issues to consider while you're recommending sound hardware for upgrades, replacements, or new builds.

Drive Interfaces   Many sound boards (typically older sound boards) come with a CD-ROM drive port already incorporated. If you plan to attach a CD-ROM to the sound board, make sure that the port is compatible with your CD-ROM drive. Older sound boards provided several proprietary CD-ROM ports (such as Sony, Panasonic, and Mitsumi), but that has largely been abandoned by major sound cards in favor of a standard ATAPI IDE port (the same interface used for hard drives). Today, drive interfaces are a rare commodity on sound devices, and you're often better off to avoid sound cards with drive interfaces entirely.

MIDI/Game Port You'll also probably notice a 15-pin connector on the sound board. This is the MIDI port—if you have a MIDI instrument, you can connect it to the sound board and compose your own music. If you're "musically challenged," you can switch the MIDI port to serve as a standard joystick port. You can enable or disable the game port through a jumper on the sound board. If you already have another game port (or multi-I/O card) in the system, you can leave the port disabled.

MIDI Memory High-end sound boards (such as the Sound Blaster AWE32) often provide SIMM slots for additional memory. This is MIDI memory and is used when composing MIDI music, or taking sound samples. If you're not going to be composing music, don't bother buying extra memory for the sound board.

CD Audio Connector When selecting a sound board, look for the CD audio connector. It's a small, 4-pin connector usually located at the top of the sound board, roughly in the middle. You'll run a thin, 4-wire cable between the CD drive's audio output and the sound board—this is how you get your favorite CD to play through your sound board's speakers. Today's high-end sound boards may have two or three audio connectors to support audio from CD-ROM/CD-RW and DVD-ROM drives in the same system. A connector is also sometimes supplied for a voice modem's input/output. If there is no CD audio connector, you'll have to run a patch cable from the CD-ROM drive's headphone output to the sound card's line input, and then adjust the sound board's mixer to set the correct CD audio level.

Speakers You'll also need to connect some powered speakers for the sound board. Do your customer a favor and recommend a few extra dollars for some decent powered speakers capable of a wide frequency range. Inexpensive speakers can sound "tinny," and can ruin the output of even the best sound board. If you have a choice, avoid battery-powered speakers (unless you can afford a regular stream of new batteries). Other multimedia (such as DVD movies) will also benefit from good-quality speakers. Try to avoid the speakers that are incorporated into monitors. While they are a convenience, their sound quality is often poor.

DRIVE SYSTEMS

PCs use a wide range of drives that you should be familiar with. Drives serve two vital purposes. First, drives provide permanent storage for your programs and files (including the operating system). Second, drives allow for the convenient and economical distribution or exchange of programs and files. In most cases, you're going to use a minimum of three drives: a floppy drive, a hard drive, and a CD drive (which could be a CD-ROM, CD-R, CD-RW, or even a DVD drive), such as shown in Figure 1-10. However, there are other drives that you should also be familiar with. This part of the chapter explores the various drives that you will commonly encounter, and cover the essential points that you should be aware of.

IDE Drive Controllers

It is quite common for a motherboard to provide two IDE-type (40-pin) drive controller ports and one floppy controller (34-pin) port. If so, you do not need to use a separate drive controller card. If your motherboard does not offer an onboard drive controller, you *will* need to add one in an available expansion slot (though that is rare today). As a *minimum,* the drive controller should support up to two Ultra-DMA/66 (preferably two Ultra-DMA/100) hard drives on a *primary* controller port (C and D), and up to two more UDMA/EIDE/IDE devices on a *secondary* controller port (E and F). The controller should also support at least one floppy drive (usually the A drive). If a motherboard has PCI bus slots, you should certainly recommend a PCI drive controller for best performance.

FIGURE 1-10   A typical PC sporting a CD-RW, DVD-ROM, and floppy drive

If you're going to use Ultra-DMA/66 or Ultra-DMA/100 drives, but your motherboard does not support the corresponding Ultra-DMA drive interface, you may choose to disable the motherboard's controller and install an appropriate Ultra-DMA controller card. You can use the existing controller, but the performance of your drives will be limited to that controller.

SCSI Controllers

Now is a good time to bring up the subject of *Small Computer System Interface* (SCSI) controllers. SCSI is a "bus-type" system that allows numerous different devices to all share a common signal bus cable. SCSI hard drives, SCSI CD-ROM drives, SCSI tape drives, SCSI scanners, SCSI Zip or Jaz drives, and numerous other SCSI devices can all coexist and share a single SCSI cable. In fact, most drives can be obtained with a SCSI interface rather than an IDE-type (40-pin) interface. While many motherboards support the UDMA interface, few support a native SCSI interface. If you plan on supporting SCSI devices in your new PC, you'll almost certainly need to add a SCSI controller board to the system.

If a motherboard provides PCI bus slots, be sure to recommend a PCI SCSI controller for optimum performance. Keep in mind that installing a SCSI controller will demand system resources (namely an IRQ and some amount of I/O space, as well as space for the SCSI BIOS). Another major issue with SCSI is *termination*—both ends of a signal cable must be properly terminated, or none of the SCSI devices may function properly. Termination is certainly not difficult, but can be tricky to master, and termination oversights are one of the most frequent causes of SCSI installation and upgrade problems.

SCSI and UDMA/EIDE   Contrary to popular belief, SCSI and UDMA/EIDE interfaces can coexist just fine. It is certainly possible to have Ultra-DMA hard drives and a SCSI scanner and CD-ROM, or an ATAPI CD-ROM with two SCSI hard drives, or Ultra-DMA and SCSI hard drives, and so on. The trick is that your system will try to boot from UDMA/EIDE drives *first*. In other words, if you have an Ultra-DMA hard drive and a SCSI hard drive in the same system, the Ultra-DMA drive will traditionally be the boot device. However, late-model SCSI controllers are starting to offer an option that will override the UDMA/EIDE boot device and allow a SCSI drive to boot the system even if there is another drive present (this is a feature of the latest SCSI BIOS versions).

SCSI vs. UDMA/EIDE   Even though UDMA/EIDE and SCSI devices will work together (as long as there are no hardware conflicts between the SCSI and non-SCSI controllers), the question remains as to which is better. The line between SCSI and Ultra-DMA has grown a bit murky over the last few years. It used to be that if you needed very large drives and top performance, you stuck with SCSI. Today, SCSI and IDE-type devices share remarkably similar performance characteristics. Today, SCSI drives are typically smaller than the available Ultra-DMA models (which are exceeding 60GB), and the largest SCSI drives are generally quite expensive. Both are fine interfaces, but you need to make your choice based on the advantages and disadvantages of each interface.

SCSI only requires one controller to handle up to seven SCSI devices (like hard drives, tape drives, scanners, and so on). All of those drives can be connected to the same SCSI signal bus. As a result, the hardware and cabling requirements are simpler. When you deal with SCSI, you also need to deal with drivers—you need an ASPI driver for the SCSI controller, and all other SCSI devices in your system (except for hard drives, which are handled by the SCSI BIOS). This can be a problem if you install protected-mode drivers for Windows 98/Me, and then need to use the devices under DOS. On the other hand, installing real-mode drivers for DOS can interfere with Windows 98/Me operation. Finally, not all SCSI devices are equally compatible with every SCSI controller. For example, if you replace your SCSI controller with a different make and model, you'll need to install a whole new set of drivers—and probably even have to reformat your SCSI hard drives.

By comparison, Ultra-DMA offers its own set of challenges. Most UDMA/EIDE controllers provide one fast Ultra-DMA channel, and one slower channel—both channels can only support two devices. You usually put the fast devices (your hard drives) on the Ultra-DMA channel, and put the slower devices (such as your CD drives) on the secondary channel. This complicates the installation and cabling a bit, and you may run into trouble mixing slow and fast devices (such as CD-ROM drives and hard drives) on the same channel. However, Ultra-DMA devices are readily available, and can be as much as several hundred dollars cheaper than their SCSI counterparts. UDMA/EIDE is also supported directly in BIOS, so you don't need drivers to run the drive controller (though you still need ATAPI drivers for some devices like CD-ROM drives). This makes UDMA/EIDE equally robust under DOS and Windows 98/Me.

In short, Ultra-DMA is the choice when price is your top concern, and you won't need to expand your system very much. SCSI is the way to go when you need the very best multitasking performance and capacity, and you plan to add a large number of devices to the system (such as building your own Windows 2000 server).

SCSI BIOS and Drivers   SCSI BIOS is required in order to operate SCSI hard drives. If you have SCSI hard drives in your system, you'll need to have the SCSI BIOS enabled. Keep in mind that the SCSI BIOS will occupy space in the upper memory area (UMA) along with the motherboard BIOS, video BIOS, and any other BIOS in the system. If you need a SCSI controller for such things as a scanner, and there are no SCSI hard drives, you can almost always disable the SCSI BIOS.

Drivers are another important SCSI issue. The SCSI controller, and all other SCSI devices (except for hard drives), uses drivers. You'll need real-mode drivers to operate the SCSI system under DOS, and protected-mode drivers to run your SCSI devices under Windows 98/Me. Drivers are always provided with the respective SCSI device, but always make it a point to keep your SCSI drivers updated. The latest SCSI drivers are typically available for download from each particular SCSI manufacturer.

Floppy Drives

Floppy drives are the classical "removable media," and floppy disks remain a simple and convenient means of distributing simple software, or moving files, between PCs. Your drive controller will support at least one floppy drive, but may handle up to two (A and B drives). You will need a 34-pin ribbon cable to attach your floppy drive(s) to the drive controller. Today, all you really need is one 3.5-inch floppy drive—though you can get dual drives (a 3.5- and 5.25-inch drive in the same drive assembly).

Floppy Cables and Jumpers   Take a look at the floppy drive cable. You'll notice that there is a single 34-pin connector at one end, and two 34-pin connectors at the other. The end with the single connector attaches to the drive controller, the "middle" connector attaches to drive B, and the endmost connector attaches to drive A. The cable should not exceed about 2 feet (around 60 cm) in length. If the system supports only one floppy drive, the cable may not offer any middle connector.

If you look closely, you'll also notice that the floppy drive probably has several jumpers. These jumpers serve several purposes, but as a general rule, you should *not* move them. Most floppy drives are jumpered as drive B—that's OK—the little twist you see near the drive end of your floppy cable converts the endmost drive back to A.

Hard Drives

The *hard drive* is really the center of your mass-storage strategy. The media is not removable, but hard drives provide huge amounts of very fast storage. An Ultra-DMA drive controller will typically support up to two fast UDMA drives, and up to two UDMA/EIDE devices, so expect to find at least one Ultra-DMA hard drive (20GB or larger) on the (primary) UDMA channel. If you use an ATAPI IDE CD drive, you can place it on the secondary channel. Drive prices drop so fast that you can get very large drives for a reasonable price.

Hard Drive Cable   Take a look at the hard drive cable. You'll notice that there is one 40-pin connector at one end, and two 40-pin connectors at the other. The end with the single connector plugs into the drive controller, and the other connectors plug into the drives. Unlike floppy drive cables, the hard drive cable has no effect on drive letter assignments. The Ultra-DMA/66 and Ultra-DMA/100 cable is a 40-pin/80-conductor cable, but it is almost identical in appearance to the regular 40-pin/40-conductor IDE cable—be sure to use the correct cable for UDMA/66 or UDMA/100 drives.

It is critical that *all* the components for supporting UDMA/66 or UDMA/100 are in place before you enable it on the drive. If you place an UDMA/66- or UDMA/100-enabled drive in a system that does not fully support it, you will easily find yourself with lost or corrupt data. For example, without the proper cable, the signal will deteriorate as it passes through the cable at such high speeds. Also, there are BIOS versions in many systems that do not support UDMA/66 or UDMA/100. For example, these BIOS versions will detect that the drive supports Ultra-DMA/66 and instruct the drive to operate in Ultra-DMA/66 mode. The result could be corrupted data.

Drive Jumpers   UDMA/EIDE hard drives use jumpers to define their relationship. Drives can be set as the primary drive ("master") or the secondary drive ("slave"). A primary and secondary drive can be installed on each of the two drive channels, so the controller can support up to four drives. The first drive installed on the first (UDMA) channel should be jumpered as the primary drive (this will be C). The second drive installed on the first (UDMA) channel should be jumpered as the secondary drive (this will be D). The first drive installed on the second (UDMA or EIDE) channel should be jumpered as the primary drive (this will be E), and the second drive installed on the second (UDMA or EIDE) channel should be jumpered as the secondary drive (this will be F). As a rule, do *not* use the "cable select" (or CS) jumper option if one is available.

SCSI devices are identified in a slightly different manner using eight ID numbers (0 to 7). The SCSI controller is typically assigned ID7, and the first two SCSI hard drives are usually given ID0 (the boot drive) and ID1. Other SCSI devices use the remaining SCSI IDs. All SCSI IDs are selected through the use of jumpers.

The preceding example drive letters assume a single partition on each drive (such as FAT32). Multiple partitions will alter the actual drive letter assignments. This Microsoft article explains the procedure used by DOS/Windows to assign drive letters: **support.microsoft.com/support/ kb/articles/Q51/9/78.asp**.

Drive Parameters   When installing a hard drive, you need to configure drive parameters in the system's CMOS Setup. Parameters usually include: cylinders, sectors/track, heads, landing zone, and write precompensation. You'll need to locate those parameters in the drive's documentation, and be sure to record them for future reference. If your BIOS and drives support *autodetection* (as virtually all do today), you may be able to get away with autodetecting the hard drive rather than entering specific parameters. Modern motherboards and BIOS versions make installing a hard drive extremely easy—enable LBA (Logical Block Addressing) and Auto-Detect in BIOS after you attach the drive. You should see the hard drive identified and entered in the BIOS automatically. The numbers entered for Cylinders, Heads, and Sectors (if any) may not match the actual numbers for the drive (because LBA uses a mathematical formula to determine these numbers instead). Still, the size of the hard drive (in MB or GB) entered automatically by the BIOS should be correct. The auto detection routine of the BIOS may display a list of optional results after examining your hard drive. You are then able to select between Normal, Large, and LBA modes for actually recording your drive parameters in your BIOS. LBA is almost always the best option.

If you're transferring a hard drive containing information from one system to another, you must enter the hard drive information in the new system *exactly* as it was in the original system. Be sure to make a record of the original drive parameters before removing it.

CD-ROM Drives

Virtually all major software applications are now distributed on CD (and many are even partially run from the CD). As a consequence, CD-ROM drives have emerged as an absolute necessity in the modern computer. The typical CD-ROM drive is an inexpensive and reliable device that requires almost no maintenance. More recently, CD-ROM drives have become "bootable," though you need a suitable drive, BIOS, and bootable CD media to make use of this feature. Plan on at least one CD-ROM drive for your new system, or select a fast model to replace a failed or aging drive.

Many current systems are using CD-RW drives rather than ordinary CD-ROM drives. CD-RW drives provide the rewritability of CD-RW technology, the writability of a CD-R, and the fast disc reading of a CD-ROM drive.

CD-ROM drives are rated in terms of seek time and transfer speed. *Seek time*—the time required to locate desired information—can be as much as 100 or 200 milliseconds (ms). *Transfer speed*—the rate at which data is transferred from the drive to the interface—is a multiple of the original floppy drive transfer speed of 150KB/sec. For example, a 2X CD transfers data at 300KB/s, a 4X CD transfers data at 600KB/s, and so on. Today, you can get 24X and 36X drives at very reasonable prices—48X to 56X versions are readily available. With the recent emergence of CD-R, CD-RW, and DVD technology, it is unlikely that ordinary CD-ROM drives will become much faster.

CD-ROM Interfaces   Older CD-ROM drives used any one of several proprietary interfaces (such as Mitsumi, Panasonic, and so forth). That worked fine with "multimedia kits," where the drive's controller was integrated into the sound board (or other proprietary card). If you didn't have a controller handy, though, you were stuck. Today, all major CD-type drives offer an ATAPI IDE interface, which is exactly the same interface as your hard drive. You can then install the CD-ROM with any IDE/EIDE/UDMA drive controller. If you have a secondary channel on your drive controller, an ATAPI IDE CD-ROM drive is a perfect fit. As a rule, never install a hard drive and CD-ROM drive together on the same channel.

CD Audio   If you want to play CD audio through your sound board, you will need to connect the audio output of your CD-ROM drive to your sound board or motherboard (if you have built-in sound support) through a thin, 4-wire audio cable. Some sound boards offer two or three input connectors to support systems with both CD-ROM/CD-RW and DVD-ROM/DVD-RAM drives. Verify that the CD-ROM drive comes with a suitable connector for CD audio.

CD-RW Drives

The decreasing costs of CD-ROM and CD-R technology, a delay in DVD recordable drive introduction, and the need to re-record a CD led to the development of CD-RW (rewriteable) drives. These drives can accomplish all the tasks of a standard CD-ROM and CD-R drive, yet you can record and erase files from a CD-RW disc with the same ease as a floppy disk. In addition, they can use both CD-R and CD-RW media for recording. The expanding number of newer CD-ROM drives with MultiRead capability also improves the likelihood of other systems being able to read a CD-R or a CD-RW disk created on a CD-RW drive.

You should only consider purchasing MultiRead-capable CD-ROM or CD-RW drives.

Modern CD-RW drives offer a wide variety of possibilities to meet the file management needs of the average computer owner. You can make copies of entire music and data CDs (or only copy individual files or songs). You can make your own custom CDs by recording a preselected group of files, or by creating an image file on your hard drive before using your CD-RW to record it. You can even tackle unattended backups of over 450MB per disc. CD-R discs created with a modern CD-RW drive can be read by just about every present-day system, which allows you to send large files through the mail on a single disc.

A major disadvantage of earlier CD-RW drives was their lack of support for drag-and-drop file copying—to copy even a single file, you had to launch the application for controlling the CD-RW drive. Modern CD-RW drives can format an entire CD-RW disk through the UDF file system. You can then leave the CD-RW disk in the drive and use it just like a big floppy drive. Any of the methods you would normally use to manipulate files on or between your floppy and hard drive can now be used with your CD-RW drive and disc. This includes drag and drop, copy and paste, right-click context menu commands, and menu bar commands.

UDF-formatted CD-RW discs can be read only by systems that have a UDF Reader utility installed. Roxio offers a free reader at its Web site (**www.roxio.com**).

CD-RW Characteristics   The two major considerations in selecting a CD-RW drive are the *interface* connection and the drive *speed*. You can choose between an ATAPI IDE or SCSI CD-RW drive. SCSI is considered a better data-transfer method (and might prevent buffer underrun problems), but you'll need to include SCSI support (such as by installing a SCSI controller). SCSI drives are also more expensive than IDE. IDE-type drives (for example, IDE, EIDE, or UDMA) are more popular and widely used. Almost all motherboards include two UDMA/EIDE channels supporting up to four IDE-type devices. In terms of speed, you'll see three numbers used to characterize a CD-RW drive: *record×rewrite×read* (for example, 4×2×16 or 4×6×32). For example, a modern 10×4×32 CD-RW drive offers 10X writing speed, 4X rewriting speed, and 32X reading speed (like an ordinary CD-ROM).

DVD Drives

Today, the CD-ROM technology is showing its age, and a single CD no longer provides enough storage for the increasing demands of data-intensive applications and multimedia. A new generation of high-density optical storage called DVD-ROM is now appearing on many new systems. The acronym DVD stands for several different things. In the early phase of DVD development, it stood for *digital video disc.* Later on, it stood for *digital versatile disc* (because it could hold programs and data as well as video and sound). But regardless of what you call it, DVD technology promises to supply up to 17GB of removable optical storage on your desktop PC. In addition, the DVD drive is fully backward-compatible with CD audio, CD-ROM, CD-I, and other popular CD formats, so the DVD can actually replace your existing CD-ROM drive.

DVD Interfaces and Jumpers   DVD drives are now available with either SCSI or ATAPI IDE interfaces, so no proprietary interface card is required. This simplifies installation and replacement quite a bit. The ATAPI IDE version can easily coexist as a secondary (or "slave" drive) with your existing hard drive on the same controller channel (unlike older CD-ROM drives, which could interfere with high-performance data transfers). You can also install the DVD drive on a secondary controller channel. Jumpers on the drive allow you to define the DVD drive as a "master," "slave," or "cable select." As a rule, avoid the use of cable select (CS). As a SCSI drive, you can place the DVD drive almost anywhere in the SCSI chain. The most critical aspect of SCSI installations is to terminate the SCSI chain properly, and jumper the DVD drive with an unused SCSI ID number (usually between ID2 and ID6).

The DVD drive does not require a stand-alone MPEG-2 decoder board for basic drive operation (such as reading files from a DVD disc), but the decoder is usually recommended for the reliable playback of DVD-video and Dolby audio.

CD-Audio   If you want to play audio from the DVD drive through your sound board, you will need to connect the audio output of your DVD-ROM drive to your sound board through a thin, 4-wire audio cable. Make sure that the DVD-ROM drive comes with a suitable connector for CD audio. Remember, unless you buy a DVD-ROM and MPEG-2 decoder board together as a multimedia kit, you may have to buy the CD audio cable separately.

Even though a sound board is not included in a DVD kit, the CD audio cable is typically included in a DVD kit. If you already have a CD-ROM or other drive feeding CD audio to the sound card, you may wish to connect the DVD drive's audio signal there instead, or select a sound card that offers more than one CD audio connection.

MPEG-2 Decoder Board   One of the major advances with DVD technology is the development of high-quality video and audio playback—however, the immense volume of data required would demand several DVD discs worth of storage. To provide full-length feature movies on a single 4GB disc, the video and audio data must be highly *compressed* using the MPEG-2 standard. When the presentation is played, the DVD passes audio and video data to a PCI MPEG-2 decoder board for processing. The use of hardware decoding removes a large processing burden from the system CPU. The MPEG-2 board then passes video data directly to the monitor, and audio directly to the sound board's "line input" (a pass-through is provided so that signals from your existing video board are routed through the MPEG-2 board).

Keep in mind that a decoder board is not an interface for the DVD drive, but rather a supplemental part of the complete DVD package. The decoder is not used when running programs or accessing other data from a DVD disc. With the processing power of today's computers, hardware decoder boards are often omitted in favor of "SoftDVD Player" software. Decoder software may work adequately on some systems, but hardware decoding offloads a great deal of processing from the CPU, and may provide more reliable playback—especially on somewhat older PCs.

Other Drives

Of course, there are many other possible drives that you may choose to complement the particular needs of your system. These drives are *not* required to make a working computer, but they can enhance the versatility of your new system. You can spend the money for other drives during your initial construction, or wait and add the drives as upgrades later. Perhaps the most recognized manufacturer of "removable media" drives is Iomega (**www.iomega.com**). The Zip and Ditto drives are very popular with computer users.

Iomega Zip   The Zip drive has become perhaps the single most popular semistandard drive in production today. Zip drives offer relatively fast seek times at 29ms, and can sustain data rates of 300KB/s across the parallel port (an external Zip drive), or 1MB/s via SCSI or IDE interfaces (an internal Zip drive). Each cartridge (which resembles an ordinary floppy disk) can hold up to 100MB, which is large enough to hold huge illustrations, CAD layouts, and even small multimedia presentations. A 250MB version of the Zip drive is now available. When used with a SCSI interface and a properly configured Adaptec SCSI controller, you may even boot from the Zip drive. Zip drives are available in both internal and external versions.

Iomega Ditto   Tape backups are typically time-consuming and troublesome, so Iomega has gone to great lengths to develop a tape drive that can be set up and used as quickly and easily as possible. The result is its Ditto drive. There are several versions of the Ditto, providing 420MB, 800MB, and 2GB backups, respectively. According to Iomega, the external Ditto can be installed in just five minutes, and the Ditto software makes backup operations almost intuitive (it will even accomplish backups in the background while you work on other things). There are two factors to keep in mind when considering a Ditto drive. First, the Ditto 2GB drive *requires* a high-performance floppy drive interface to function properly. If you're using an ordinary 500KB/s floppy interface, you will need to install the Ditto Dash accelerator card. Second, the 2GB tape is a *proprietary* tape manufactured exclusively for Iomega. The Ditto 2GB tape cartridge uses a slightly wider tape (.315 inch) than the QIC-80 and QIC-40 minicartridges (note that the uncompressed capacity for Ditto 2GB tapes is only 1GB). The 2GB tape drive can read and write to the 2GB cartridge, but cannot format this cartridge, so all Ditto 2GB tapes are preformatted.

MODEMS

The Internet has become an icon of the global information age. You can access information, make purchases, read articles, solve technical problems, or even chat and exchange mail with anyone else online. If you've ever considered going online (or already have online accounts), you're going to need a modem to access the Internet, and other online resources like America Online or FTP sites. Rapid advances in modem technology have resulted in dramatic increases in connection speeds, while competition has lowered the cost of modems. Intense competition between online service providers has also lowered the costs of going online. Chances are that you'll be installing or upgrading numerous modems (see Figure 1-11) for your customers.

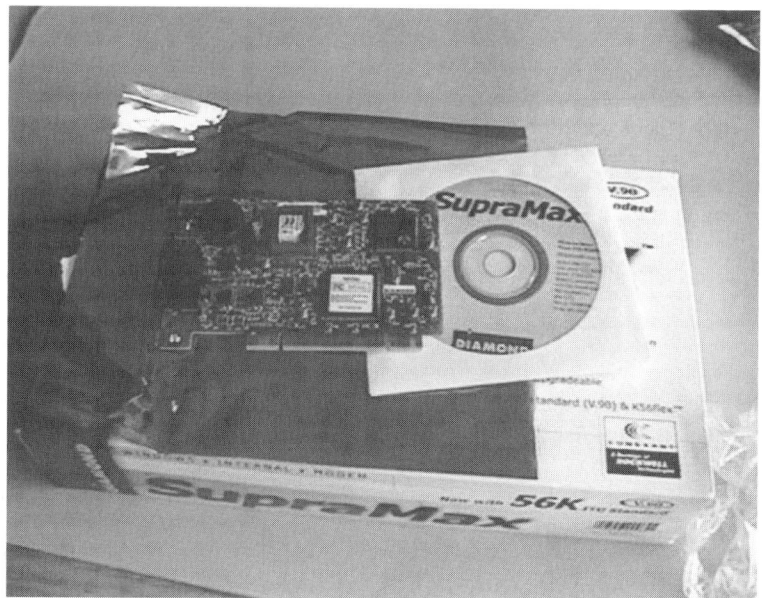

FIGURE 1-11   A typical analog 56Kbps modem

Internal vs. External

You have the choice between internal and external modems. From a practical standpoint, both offer equivalent performance. The trade-off comes in considering your installation issues. *Internal* modems do not require a separate power supply, and do not take up space outside of the PC, but they do use their own built-in COM port (and IRQ). This means you may need to disable or reconfigure any corresponding COM port already in the system to avoid potential hardware conflicts. By comparison, *external* modems do need an separate power source and take up a bit of space, but you can connect it directly to any open COM port in the system—this simplifies installation a bit. Also, the external modem is mobile, and you can take it from system to system if necessary.

Modem Speed

The rule with modems is "the faster the better," but "faster" does not always *guarantee* top-speed commu-nication. *Both* ends of the communication link must be capable of the same top speed, or the link will be limited by the speed of the *slowest* modem. For example, if you buy a 56Kbps modem and call an *Internet Service Provider* (ISP) with only a 33.6Kbps modem, the top speed you'll get is only 33.6Kbps. Other factors such as poor telephone connections and incorrect drivers may also serve to hamper your communication performance. Opt for 56Kbps, V.90-standard modems if your ISP will support such speeds. If you really need the highest possible speeds on your desktop, contact your local telephone or cable company to check out the costs involved with advanced technologies such as cable modem or DSL service.

Check with your local cable provider or telephone company before selecting a cable modem or DSL modem. You must verify that the respective service is available in your area, evaluate the pricing plan(s), and set up an account. If you do opt for an advanced modem, the cable company or tele-phone company may even provide the appropriate modem for you as part of your service, so you might be able to save the cost of a device.

One other note—try to avoid the use of WinModems if at all possible. WinModem-type products compensate for highly simplified (though cheap) hardware by making heavy use of Windows 98/Me resources. While this may not be a problem for high-powered Windows 98/Me platforms, older systems may be bogged down by the demands of a WinModem. A WinModem will also not function under DOS.

Modem Drivers and Software

Modems demand drivers and communication software to function. The new modem will come with drivers on disk, but you should also check the modem manufacturer's Web site to see if there are any updates or patches available (especially if you have trouble getting the modem to work). You're also going to need communication software to run your modem. HyperTerminal—which comes with Windows 95/98/Me—is a good utility for simple BBS-type connections, but a full-featured software package such as SmartCom for Windows can offer better control and performance. Finally, you'll need online access software, such as an Internet Winsock, Web browser, e-mail program, and FTP utility (you may choose to use Internet Explorer as well as the mail and other features that typically accompany Windows 95/98/Me).

INPUT DEVICES

Of course, you also need to get commands and selections to the PC. This is accomplished through the use of *input devices*. As a minimum, you'll need a mouse and keyboard for your new system. If you play any sort of flight simulator or other interactive game, you should also plan on a joystick.

Mouse

Select a good-quality pointing device. It can be a mouse or a trackball (depending on your personal taste). You generally have the choice between a *serial* mouse, *PS/2* mouse, and *USB* mouse. There is also a *bus* mouse, but that has fallen into disuse. Serial and PS/2 mice are basically the same thing—the port connectors are just a bit different. A bus mouse uses an expansion card as a dedicated mouse controller. A USB mouse simply connects to a USB port on the PC, or USB hub. There are no real advantages of any one type of mouse. The bus mouse frees up a serial port at the expense of a bus slot. The bus mouse controller card also demands an interrupt (or IRQ) for proper operation, so that is one less IRQ that you will have available when adding other devices to the system. System resources are an important issue to keep in mind when choosing a mouse.

Two-Button or Three-Button   The choice of two-button and three-button mice is really a matter of personal preference. Most programs only recognize two buttons (left-click or right-click). A middle button is generally used only by specialized programs (like CAD software)—otherwise, it is ignored. Unless your customer has a specific use for that third mouse button, recommend that they save a few dollars and go with a two-button unit.

Mouse Drivers   All mice will require a mouse driver. If you use DOS applications, you'll need a real-mode mouse driver loaded in CONFIG.SYS or AUTOEXEC.BAT. If you use Windows, you'll use a protected-mode mouse driver. The drivers will accompany your mouse on floppy disk. Once you install the mouse drivers, you shouldn't need to mess with them again, but if you change the mouse later, you'll need to remove the old mouse drivers before installing the new ones.

Routine Maintenance   A mouse requires periodic routine maintenance to clean out the dust, debris, and hair that accumulates around the mouse ball and rollers. This typically involves removing the mouse ball, and then cleaning it and the rollers. In actual practice, the process takes no longer than five minutes. Cleaning is indicated when the mouse cursor starts to "skip" or "stall" while moving the mouse.

Keyboard

Obviously, every computer needs a keyboard. There are about as many different sizes, shapes, and features for a keyboard as there are for a mouse. But there are some key points to consider. First, make sure that the keyboard connector is compatible with the keyboard connector on the motherboard. Today, most keyboards use the small PS/2-type barrel connector, and a growing number use a USB port.

Comfort and Ergonomics   Try the keyboard if you can, and make sure that the keys *feel* comfortable. You may also care to try an "ergonomic" keyboard, which is typically a bit easier on the hands and wrists. This may seem like a trivial matter now, but better ergonomics now can prevent persistent wrist pain and fatigue later.

QWERTY vs. Dvorak   You generally have two keyboard styles to choose from; QWERTY and Dvorak. The QWERTY style is the conventional typewriter key layout. This has been the standard typewriter layout for 125 years, so you will have no trouble finding QWERTY keyboards. Dvorak keyboards use a more efficient placement of keys, which results in less finger and hand movement—this reduces hand strain (and makes typing a bit faster). Dvorak keyboards are harder to find, but it is possible to convert your QWERTY keyboard to Dvorak under Windows 95.

Joystick

Joysticks are not required for a PC, but if your customer plans to do any serious flight simulation or other interactive 3-D gaming, a good-quality joystick will be an absolute necessity. By themselves, joysticks are fairly simple devices—really little more than a couple of potentiometers, a few buttons, and a couple of springs. But when used for PC games, the joystick adds a level of control that is simply impossible to achieve with any other input device.

Game Ports   All joysticks require a 15-pin game port to function. Most sound boards and I/O boards incorporate a game port already, so obtaining a game port is not a problem. However, only one game port can be active in the system at any given time. If you have more than one game port in the PC, it is vital that you remember to disable all but one. Otherwise, you'll find that your joystick behaves erratically, and that you have little (if any) control.

Joystick Drivers and Calibration   In the DOS world, joystick drivers were not required—each individual application was required to service the joystick. Under Windows 95/98/Me, joystick drivers allow a single, uniform joystick environment that any Windows game can use. Regardless of whether you use DOS or Windows, you still have to calibrate the joystick periodically, because of the way in which the game port reads the analog signals from the joystick.

Routine Maintenance   In general, joysticks require no routine maintenance. Still, you'll find that the exposed pivot of a joystick is a magnet for dust and debris. You should make it a point to occasionally blow out any accumulations of dust or dirt. If the joystick experiences "dead areas" (where moving the stick causes no change in the program), it could be that the X or Y potentiometers are wearing out, and you should consider replacing the joystick.

Disassembly/Reassembly Notes

All to often, the *mechanics* of PC repair—taking the system apart and putting it back together again—are overlooked or treated as an afterthought. As you saw in the first part of this chapter, PC assemblies are not terribly complicated, but a careless or rushed approach to the repair can do more harm than good. Lost parts and collateral damage to the system are certain ways to loose a customer (and perhaps open yourself to legal recourse). This section outlines a set of considerations that can help ensure a speedy, top-quality repair effort.

THE VALUE OF DATA

It is a fact of modern computing that the *data* contained on a customer's hard drive(s) is usually more valuable than the PC hardware itself. If your customer is an entrepreneur or corporate client, you can expect that the system contains valuable accounting, technical, reference, design, or operations information that is vital to their business. As a consequence, you should make it a priority to protect yourself from any potential liability issues connected with your customer's data. Even if the drives are *causing* the problem, a customer may hold you responsible if you are unable to restore or recover their precious information. Start a consistent regimen of written and oral precautions. Such precautions should include (but are not limited to):

- Always advise your customers to *back up* their systems regularly. Before the customer brings in their system, advise them to perform a complete backup of their drives *if possible*.

- Always advise your customers to *check* (or verify) their backups—a backup is useless if it can't be restored.

- When a customer delivers a system for repair, be sure that they sign a *work order*. Work orders should expressly give you authority and permission to work on the customer's system, outline such things as your hourly rate, labor minimums for evaluation and service, and show all applicable disclaimers. Your work order should include a strong disclaimer expressly relieving you of any and all liability for the contents of any magnetic media (for example, hard drives) in the system. If you attempt data recovery, the disclaimer should also disclaim any warranty or guarantee of results—that way, you're not liable if you are *unable* to recover vital files. Since liability issues vary from state to state and country to country, a local attorney can advise you on specific wording.

OPENING THE SYSTEM

Most desktop and tower systems use a metal chassis covered by a painted metal cover or shroud that is secured with a series of screws. There are often nine screws—two on either side of the enclosure, and five at the rear of the chassis. While this pattern covers many of the desktop PCs in service, you are likely to encounter a number of variations. You may find that the screws are bolted in from the bottom rather than from the sides. There may also be more or fewer screws in the rear of the chassis. Only on very rare occasions will you find screws used to secure the enclosure at its front—the molded plastic housing found on most desktop PCs does not accommodate screws without spoiling the finished look.

Tower cases are a bit different. The metal shroud also uses about nine screws—all secured from the rear. The bottom and front edges of the enclosure are typically bent inward to interlock with the chassis when seated properly. This approach allows the entire enclosure to fit securely along the whole chassis while using only a minimum of screws. Enclosures that do not interlock, however, may require screws along the bottom and front edges. As a general rule, PC enclosure manufacturers tend to minimize the use of visible screws in order to enhance a "seamless" appearance—this is why most screws are relegated to the back of the chassis.

There are three factors to keep in mind when removing screws and other mounting hardware. First, be extremely careful not to mark or gouge the painted metal enclosure. Customers are rightfully possessive of their PC investment, and putting a scratch or dent in an enclosure is tantamount to dinging their new car (a careless reputation is very bad for business). Be equally careful of the enclosure after removing and setting it aside. Second, store the screws in a safe, organized place. The old "egg carton" trick may seem cliché, but it really does work. Of course, you are free to use plastic bags or organizer boxes as well—the idea here is to keep screws and other hardware *off* the work surface (unless you enjoy picking them up off the floor). Third, take note of each screw as you remove it, and keep groups of screws separated. This allows you to put the right screws back into the corresponding locations. Since most enclosures use screws of equal size and length, this is rarely an issue at this phase of disassembly. But as you dismantle other subassemblies for upgrade or repair, keeping track of hardware becomes an important concern.

Use care when sliding the enclosure off the chassis. Metal inserts or reinforcements welded to the cover can easily catch on ribbon cables or other wiring. This can result in damage to the cable, and damage to whatever the cable is attached to. The rule here is simple: force nothing! If you encounter any resistance at all, stop and search for the obstruction carefully—it's faster to clear an obstruction than to replace a damaged cable.

CLOSING THE SYSTEM

After your repair or upgrade is complete, you need to close the system. Before sliding the enclosure back into place, however, make it a point to check the PC carefully. Make sure that every subassembly is installed and secured into place with the proper screws and hardware—leftover parts are *unacceptable*. A little care in organizing and sorting hardware during disassembly really pays off here. Remember to reattach power and signal cables as required. Each cable must be installed properly and completely (in its correct orientation). Take time to route each signal cable with care, and avoid jamming them into the system haphazardly. Careless cable runs stand a good chance of being caught and damaged by the enclosure during reassembly, or the next time the system needs to be disassembled. Properly routed cables also reduce the chance of signal problems (such as noise or crosstalk) that can result in unstable long-term operation. Also check the installation of any auxiliary cables, such as CD-ROM sound cables, the speaker cable, and the keylock cable.

Once the system components are reassembled securely, you can apply power to the PC and run final diagnostics to test the system. When the system checks properly, you can slide the enclosure into place (being careful not to damage any cables or wiring) and secure the enclosure with its full complement of screws.

TIPS FOR WORKING INSIDE A DESKTOP OR TOWER PC

Whether you're troubleshooting, upgrading, or building your own PC from scratch, there's no doubt that you'll get plenty of hands-on time inside desktop and tower PCs. Unfortunately, many potential problems can be overlooked (or even caused) while working inside a PC. The following tips should help you make the most of your PC experience, and minimize the chances of collateral problems:

■ *Be extremely careful of any sharp edges along the metal cover, or inside the metal chassis itself.* Case manufacturers often save costs by omitting such production steps as burr removal and dulling sharp edges.

■ *Make sure that the chassis assembly is tight.* All chassis are *not* created equal—some stand solid as a house, while others can seem to sway freely. Take note of the chassis condition, and tighten the chassis if necessary.

■ *Watch your vents and fans for good air flow.* Make sure that the fan blades, grills, and any intake and exhaust filters are kept clean. Check to see that all fans are working.

■ *Watch for dust and debris.* When you're examining the enclosure, check for accumulations of dust or other debris. Dust is generally a thermal insulator and electrical conductor, and can easily block the flow of air inside a chassis, so it is important to avoid accumulations of dust and debris wherever possible.

■ *Choose new chassis with care.* Replacing a chassis (or building a new PC from scratch) is an exciting but time-consuming effort, so plan for adequate expansion in terms of drive bays, expansion slot openings, power supply capacity, and drive power cables.

■ *Go with standardized cases, power supplies, and motherboards.* New PC systems have largely abandoned the use of AT-style cases (baby AT or full AT) in favor of ATX or NLX versions. As you'll see in the following sections, standard dimensioning ensures that cases, motherboards, and power supplies will *all* fit together.

■ *Keep drives mounted snugly.* All PC drives (whether in an internal or external drive bay) should be mounted with at least four screws. Fewer screws can allow the drive to vibrate, and this can shorten the drive's working life. Make sure that all four screws are in place and secure, but do not over-tighten the screws. Over-tightening can actually warp a drive's internal frame and cause premature failures as well.

■ *Be careful when mounting the motherboard.* Under no circumstances should you ever flex a motherboard, or install it in such a way that it is uneven. Ensure that no metal edges or standoffs touch the motherboard, and that the motherboard is not sitting flush against any part of the PC chassis.

■ *Check your cables closely.* There are myriad cables inside a PC. Make it a point to check the installation and routing of each cable. Each end of a cable should be installed evenly and completely. Cables should be run (where possible) to minimize any interruptions to air flow.

■ *Check your expansion boards.* Whenever you're working inside a PC, make sure that any expansion boards inside the system are inserted evenly and completely into their bus slots. Often, exchanging external cables can accidentally wiggle a card loose—resulting in possible system problems. Also verify that each expansion board is secured with a screw in the PC chassis.

■ *Check your memory devices.* While you're in the system, take a look at the memory devices. Make sure that each SIMM or DIMM module is clipped securely into place (especially if you're replacing or upgrading memory). If your motherboard uses COAST (cache-on-a-stick) modules for cache RAM, also verify that the COAST module is installed properly.

■ *Check the CPU heat sink/fan.* Chances are that your CPU is fitted with a heat sink/fan assembly. Check to see that the heat sink is attached securely to the CPU, and verify that the fan portion of the assembly is working once the system is powered up. The CPU itself should also be mounted securely into place.

Standardized Form Factors

Selecting traditional PC chassis has always been somewhat of a "hit or miss" proposition. You'd choose cases, power supplies, and motherboards, and *hope* that everything would fit properly. All too often, screw holes wouldn't line up, and you'd be forced to return assemblies, or "kluge" the assemblies together—aligning as many screw holes as possible, and ignoring, clipping, or removing standoffs outright. Over the last few years, the PC industry has come together to develop a set of standard dimensions for key PC components (cases, motherboards, and power supplies). The three current standards are known as LPX, ATX, and NLX. This part of the chapter looks at these standards in more detail, and you can learn more at **www.formfactors.org**.

 The use of new form factors does not have any bearing on the capabilities or performance of any new PC—only the dimensions of the motherboard, case, and power supply are affected.

LPX FORM FACTOR

The Low-Profile Extended (or LPX) form factor proved to be the PC industry's first major step beyond AT- and baby AT–style motherboards. Developed jointly by Intel and Western Digital some years ago, the LPX specification covers the physical layout, power requirements, and electrical issues for such motherboards. A standard LPX motherboard has the same *maximum* dimensions as a baby AT board—no more than 8.5 inches wide by 13 inches long (see Figure 1-12). It also shares the same baby AT mounting hole arrangements.

The LPX approach does not support expansion cards on the motherboard. Instead, it uses a riser card inserted into a single board slot, and any cards added into the system attach to the riser card. LPX power connectors are the same as the original IBM AT power connectors: two 6-pin connectors attached to the motherboard (usually labeled P8 and P9). The LPX format also provides a strict series of I/O ports arranged from left to right across the back of a board:

- A VGA monitor connector
- A parallel port
- Two serial ports
- A PS/2-style mouse port
- A PS/2-style keyboard port

 Later variations in LPX design may alter the placement of external connectors, substitute two USB interfaces in place of serial connectors, and perhaps even add local area network (LAN) and sound connectors.

In addition, an LPX motherboard typically provides two IDE drive controllers, a floppy disk controller, and 72-pin SIMM sockets. The LPX riser card slot conforms to the older EISA standard (both physically and electronically), but LPX is generally compatible with newer high-performance expansion architectures, such as PCI. As a result, it's not uncommon to find LPX riser cards offering ISA and PCI slots for expansion devices.

LPX was embraced widely by popular name-brand PC makers, such as AST, Compaq, Digital, Dell, Gateway, Hewlett-Packard, IBM, NCR, NEC, Packard-Bell, and Zenith, and LPX-type motherboards have been produced up to the introduction of Pentium II processors. The main problem with LPX was its

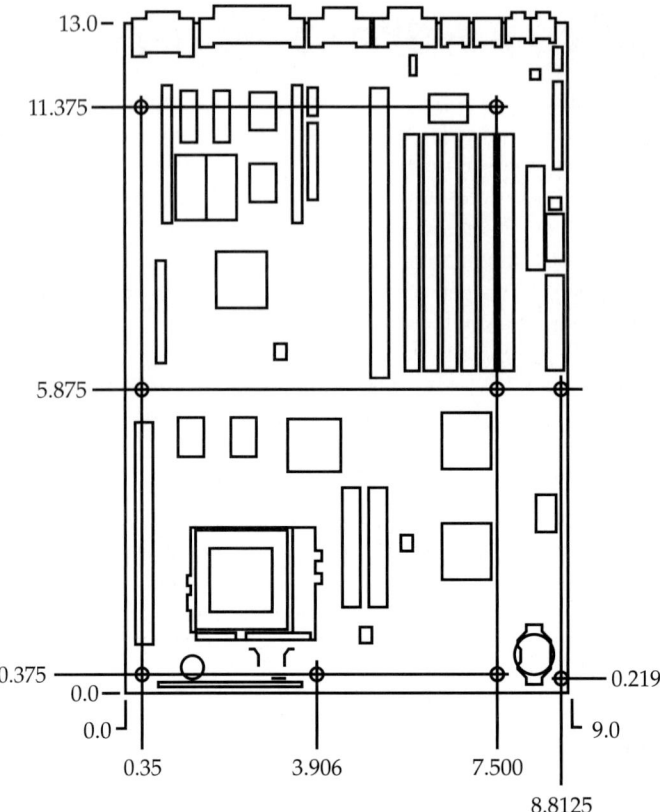

FIGURE 1-12   Image of an LPX motherboard

proprietary use of riser cards. Riser cards need to meet the LPX physical and electrical connector standard—but *that's* the extent of LPX standardization. Otherwise, every computer manufacturer was free to choose its own riser card layout (such as the number of slots, the type of slots [ISA or PCI], the distance of the slots from the top of the LPX connector, and the size of the riser card). Table 1-3 illustrates the known compatibility issues with major LPX system manufacturers.

As a consequence of this weak standardization, riser cards were rarely interchangeable among various cases (often even for the same manufacturer), and this made it extremely difficult to replace and upgrade LPX motherboards. Eventually, the PC industry abandoned LPX in favor of the more uniform ATX and NLX form factors.

ATX FORM FACTOR

The version 2.03 ATX form factor (see Figure 1-13) represents the most popular and well-established effort to standardize the major assemblies of a PC. In addition to the use of well-established mounting holes, the ATX approach makes several key improvements to the layout of a system. The CPU is relocated to a position on the motherboard that will not interfere with the use of full-length expansion boards (a common complaint of baby/full AT motherboard users). Since full-length cards can now be used in *all* the

TABLE 1-3   COMMON NONSTANDARD LPX ISSUES

BRAND/MODEL	NONSTANDARD FEATURE(S)
AST Advantage (before Socket 5)	LPX physical connector
AST Bravo LC, Bravo LC CX, Bravo MS-L, Bravo MS-T	LPX physical connector
Compaq DeskPro (All)	LPX physical connector
DEC Celebris and Venturis 4xx and 5xx, DECpc LPV+	LPX physical connector
DEC Starion 200/300	Riser w/ 5 ISA slots; connector may be ISA
DEC Starion 200i/300i * (Trio 32)	Riser w/ ISA, PCI, shared; connector may be standard
DEC Starion 400/500 (C&T 63400)	Riser w/ 2 ISA, PCI, shared; connector appears nonstandard
DEC Starion 400i thru 900i * (Trio 32)	Riser w/ 3 ISA, PCI, shared; connector may be standard
DEC Starion 910 thru 920 * (Trio 32)	Riser w/ 8-bit, 2 ISA, PCI, shared; connector may be standard
DEC Starion 930 to 942 and 2001 (64-bit)	Riser w/ 8-bit, 2 ISA, PCI, shared; connector may be standard
Dell Optiplex 4xx/L	Board mounting uses two screws, oblong holes; wires that connect board to front panel of case
Gateway 2000 486 low-profile (ISA & PCI)	LPX physical connector
IBM PC350	LPX physical connector
NCR 3000 series	LPX physical connector, motherboard mounting holes, power supply connector
Packard-Bell PB600 motherboard	Non-Intel board; connector order is VGA, keyboard, mouse (e.g. Axcel 461CDT), serial, parallel
Packard-Bell 386s and 486s	Connectors sometimes in different order on rear of case; some LPX riser cards have an ISA bus connector, but the card slots are placed closer to the rear of the computer case

slots, it won't be necessary to shuffle expansion cards around to avoid interfering with the CPU. The CPU itself can also be upgraded without having to remove expansion cards. SIMM and DIMM connectors are also located away from drive bays and expansion slots for easier access. The use of rear I/O ports (see Figure 1-14) and front panel connections have been standardized on the ATX motherboard, which simplifies case design and reduces the wiring on the motherboard. Integrated drive controller connections are now located closer to the drive bays to reduce drive cable lengths and reduce clutter. The ATX power supply provides power (including a native 3.3 volts) through a single 20-pin cable rather than through the two 6-pin cables used in traditional baby/full AT systems. Finally, the ATX case design is configured to be cooled by a single fan located in the ATX power supply. This not only simplifies the case and reduces power demands, but it makes the system quieter.

ATX Motherboard Dimensions

A full-size ATX board is 12 inches wide by 9.6 inches deep (305mm×244mm). The Mini-ATX board is 11.2 inches by 8.2 inches (284mm×208mm). The microATX form factor is the newest iteration of ATX, and allows for motherboards down to 9.6 inches by 9.6 inches (244mm×244mm). Designers have attempted to use as many mounting holes as possible from older baby/full AT–style motherboards to allow existing chassis to use ATX motherboards with a minimum of modification (though it's certainly preferable to use an ATX case with ATX motherboards).

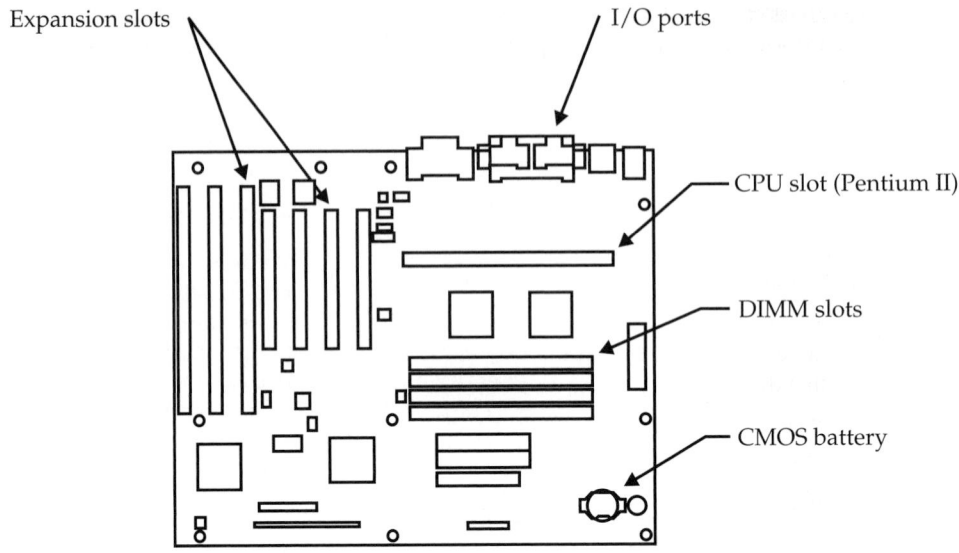

FIGURE 1-13   Layout of an ATX motherboard

 When using a microATX motherboard, it may be necessary to use a small form factor power supply (SFX Power Supply) if the system is to be built into a low-profile chassis.

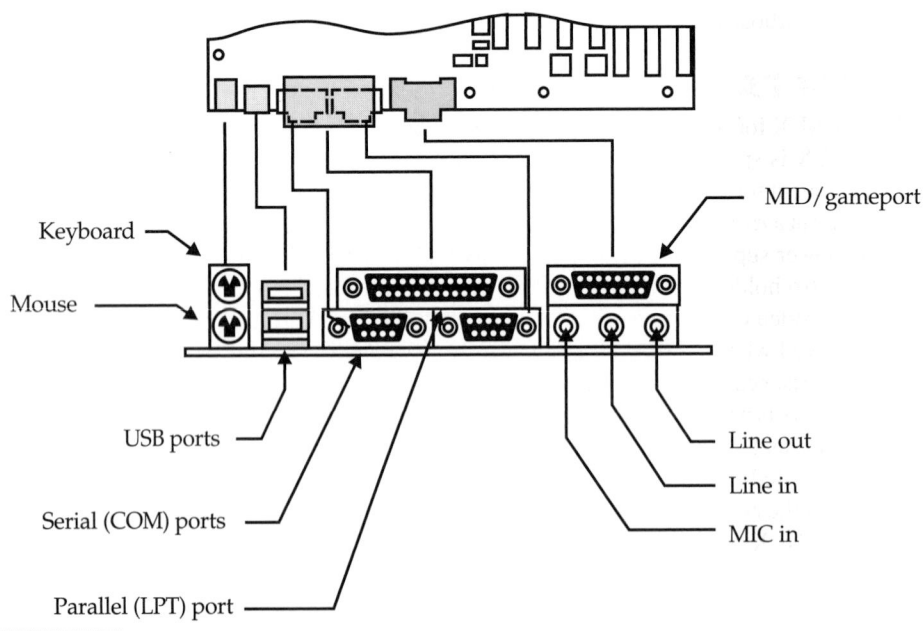

FIGURE 1-14   Layout of an ATX I/O port panel

ATX Motherboard Connectors

Aside from the board size and placement of mounting holes, an ATX motherboard is also characterized by the general placement of various connectors. The following list outlines the major connectors:

- Expansion slots (PCI/ISA) are located at the left rear of the motherboard.
- The power input connector is placed along the right edge of the board (near CPU).
- Drive signal connectors are located along the front edge of the board near the drive bays.
- Front panel I/O connectors (power switch and LED) are located along the front edge of the board—usually to the right of the expansion slots.
- Back panel I/O connectors (COM ports, parallel port, USB port, and so on) are all located on a single panel to the right rear of the motherboard. There is no single accepted layout for ATX connections, so you may find that different ATX motherboards offer unique I/O port layouts.
- Memory module connectors are located between the CPU and expansion slots, or between the CPU and drive signal connectors (usually visible on inspection).
- The CPU is usually located on the right side of the motherboard in front of the back panel I/O connectors.

ATX Power Supply and Case

An ATX power supply is about 6.1 inches long, 5.7 inches wide, and 3.5 inches deep—roughly equivalent to a PS/2 power supply footprint. The supply must generate the four traditional PC voltage levels (+5V, −5V, +12V, −12V), as well as a 3.3V level to better support low-voltage logic being used in modern PCs. Power is provided to the motherboard through a single 20-pin connector. A single exhaust fan assembly located in the supply must be capable of maintaining a minimum airflow of 23CFM (cubic feet/minute).

The only distinguishing characteristic of an ATX case is the rear opening corresponding to the motherboard's back panel I/O connector plate. You may need to obtain an I/O shield that matches the layout of your specific motherboard's I/O ports.

NLX FORM FACTOR

The version 1.2 NLX form factor (see Figure 1-15) is one of the newest dimensioning specifications for modern PCs. NLX is specifically designed to accommodate low-profile PC systems, while providing superior management for heat control, and easy maintainability. The key to the NLX configuration is not the motherboard, but a *riser board* (similar in nature to the LPX form factor). The vertical riser board connects directly to the power supply (not the motherboard), and holds all of the expansion boards horizontally. The riser board also holds the drive cable connectors (the floppy connectors and hard drive connectors) that previously resided on the motherboard. This means that the NLX motherboard has no cables to be attached or removed when servicing the NLX system. An NLX motherboard can simply be undocked from the system's riser card, and another one can be installed in a matter of moments. A wide area for back panel I/O connectors is provided on the rear of the NLX motherboard, which allows for a large variety of high-end ports such as TV, sound, game ports, and so on. NLX motherboards were also some of the first to support the Accelerated Graphics Port (AGP) for better graphics performance on PCs. The CPU is placed toward the front of the NLX motherboard (close to the fan) to ensure better system cooling. You can get a better view of the NLX riser, motherboard, and back panel in Figure 1-16.

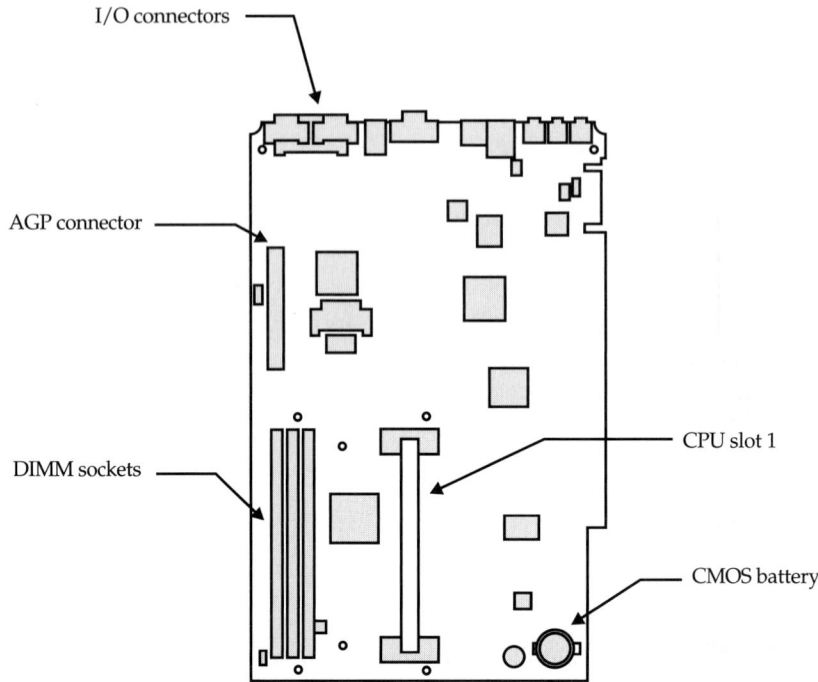

FIGURE 1-15   Layout of an NLX motherboard

NLX Motherboard Sizes

NLX motherboards are not as straightforward as ATX units. The NLX specification defines motherboards of 9.0 inches by 13.6 inches (maximum) and 8.0 inches 10.0 inches (minimum)—this means an NLX motherboard might run *anywhere* between these two sizes, and an NLX case must be able to support all possible sizes, though the typical NLX motherboard dimensions will be as follows (in inches):

- 8.0×10.0
- 9.0×10.0
- 8.0×11.2
- 9.0×11.2
- 8.0×13.6
- 9.0×13.6

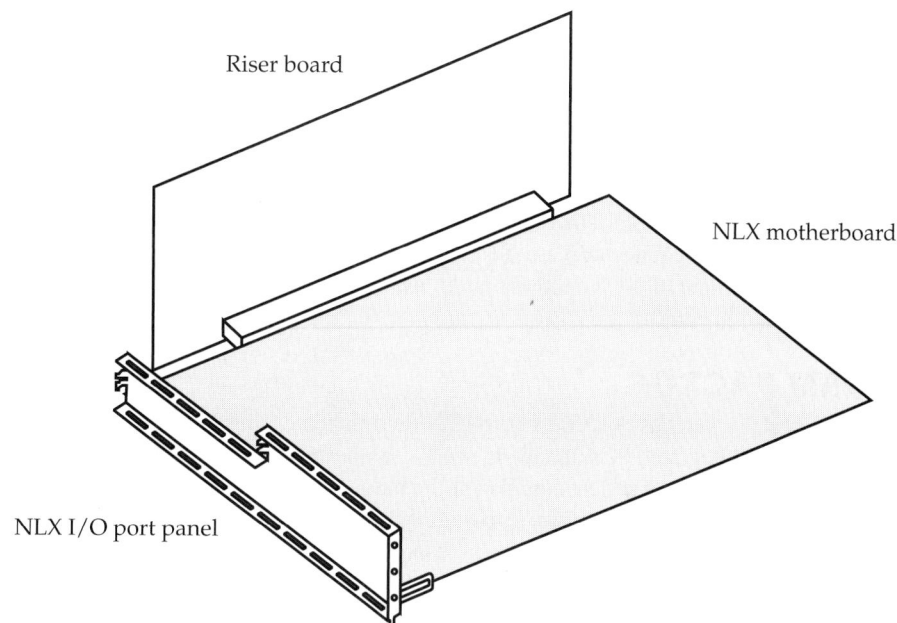

FIGURE 1-16   View of an NLX riser, motherboard, and I/O panel

NLX Motherboard Connectors

Perhaps the most noticeable difference between an NLX motherboard and other motherboards is the apparent lack of expansion board connectors and drive port connectors, which have been implemented on the riser card. You'll also note the presence of a 340-pin card edge connector that interfaces to the riser card. The following list outlines the disposition of important connections:

■ Expansion slots (PCI/ISA) are located on the riser card in a horizontal orientation.

■ The power input connector is attached to the riser card.

■ Drive signal connectors are attached to the riser card.

■ Back panel I/O connectors (COM ports, parallel port, USB port, and so on) are all located on a single panel to the right rear of the motherboard. This back panel occupies the entire rear of the motherboard.

■ Memory module connectors are typically located somewhere between the CPU and expansion slots, or behind the CPU toward the rear of the motherboard.

■ The CPU is usually located on the left front of the motherboard in direct proximity to an NLX case intake fan.

■ The AGP connector is located along the left side of the motherboard several inches from the left rear corner of the motherboard.

NLX Power Supply and Case

An NLX power supply uses the same dimensions as an ATX power supply (about 6.1 inches long, 5.7 inches wide, and 3.5 inches deep). The supply must generate the four traditional PC voltage levels (+5V, −5V, +12V, −12V), as well as a 3.3V level to better support low-voltage logic being used in modern PCs. Power is provided to the riser card through a single 20-pin connector. A single exhaust fan assembly located in the supply must be capable of maintaining a minimum airflow of 23CFM.

The only distinguishing characteristic of an NLX case is the long rear opening corresponding to the motherboard's back panel I/O connector plate. There may also be hinged access or other provision to ease the installation or replacement of NLX motherboards. An additional inlet fan is located in the front left part of the chassis to aid in cooling the CPU.

WTX FORM FACTOR

Most recent form factors, such as ATX or microATX (and the emerging FlexATX), have focused on smaller and more highly integrated PCs. In fact, FlexATX motherboards are only a little over half the size of ATX motherboards. This trend reflects the rise of the burgeoning lower-end, sub-$1,000 PC market. Still, as PC technology continues to increase in power and performance, PCs are emerging as powerful players in the high-end professional market for high-performance workstations and network servers. Most of the current form factors are simply too small for high-end multiprocessor systems using numerous hard drives and a large amount of RAM. To address the needs of this high-end market, Intel introduced the new WTX form factor in 1998 (the *W* stands for workstation). The WTX form factor is intended to standardize the current proliferation of different large PC-based workstation and server designs.

Maximum WTX motherboard size is a whopping 14 inches by 16.75 inches—over twice the maximum size of a regular ATX board. Since the goal of the WTX form factor is to support both current and future high-end motherboard and CPU technologies (as well as other features in demand by workstation and server users), the form factor is geared specifically toward flexibility of design. For example, exact mounting hole locations are not prescribed for the case. Rather, the motherboard is designed to mount to a metal plate that comes with it, and the plate is installed into the case. Since the WTX form factor is still emerging, we won't discuss it any further.

Further Study

AGP Implementers' Forum   www.agpforum.org/
Amtrade Products   www.amtrade.com
Enlight   www.enlightcorp.com.tw
Fong Kai Industrial   www.fkusa.com
Form factor information   www.formfactors.org/
Intel AGP Web site   developer.intel.com/technology/agp/
Intel chipsets   developer.intel.com/design/chipsets/
Intel motherboards   developer.intel.com/design/motherbd/
InWin Development   www.in-win.com
Iomega   www.iomega.com
ProCase   www.procase.com.tw/68.htm

AN INSIDE LOOK AT MONITORS

The ability to display images and information has evolved right along with CPUs, memory, hard drive space, and all of the other computer attributes that we associate with PC performance. Although the essential principles of a "monitor" have remained virtually unchanged, the small, drab monochrome displays of years past have long since been replaced by flicker-free, high-resolution monitors capable of producing photo-realistic color images (Figure 2-1). Today's monitor is more than just an output device—it has become our window into the complex virtual world created by computers. This chapter shows you what is inside the typical color monitor, and provides some guidelines for monitor disassembly and reassembly.

Monitor Assembly

As you can see from Figure 2-2, a typical computer monitor is not terribly complicated. Compared to notebook computers and low-profile desktop systems, the monitor assembly is spacious. This is not an accident—monitors require substantial amounts of energy for operation. Much of this energy is dissipated as heat. Extra space prevents a buildup of heat from damaging the monitor's circuitry, and heat is allowed to escape through ventilation slots in the enclosure. Another reason for ample enclosure space is to ensure ample high-voltage insulation. Some monitors generate up to 30kV during normal operation (sometimes

FIGURE 2-1   A modern PC monitor (CTX International, Inc.)

more for very large monitors), and normal plastic-wire insulation is hardly sufficient to ensure safety. High-voltage insulation and plenty of unobstructed space keep high-voltage from arcing to other circuits. The typical monitor can be broken down into five sections: the enclosure, the CRT, a CRT drive board (or video drive board), a raster drive board, and a power supply.

ENCLOSURE

Monitor enclosures are built as two pieces. The front enclosure (*1* in Figure 2-2) is used to mount the CRT and degaussing coil. This is bolted to a frame (*2*), which forms the base of the monitor. Once other circuit boards are attached to the frame, the rear enclosure (*3*) forms a shroud over almost all of the monitor. In most cases, the rear enclosure can be freed by removing four screws (*4*). A few monitor enclosures are held together by plastic latches in addition to screws. If the rear enclosure does not slide away easily, suspect the presence of snap-in latches, or extra screws installed into the frame from the bottom.

CRT

Although color monitors rely on extra video circuitry to process color signals, it is the design and construction of the CRT itself (*CRT* in Figure 2-2) that really makes color monitors possible. The basic principles of a color CRT (Figure 2-3) are very similar to a monochrome monitor—electrons "boil" off the cathode and are accelerated toward the phosphor-coated front face by a high positive potential. Color CRTs use three cathodes and video control grids—one for each of the three primary colors. Control (brightness), screen, and focus grids serve the same purpose as they do in monochrome CRTs. The *control grid* regulates the overall brightness of the electron beams, the *screen grid* begins accelerating the electron beams toward the front screen, and the *focus grid* narrows the beams. Once the electron beams are focused, vertical and horizontal deflection coils (or deflection yokes) apply magnetic force to direct the beams around the screen.

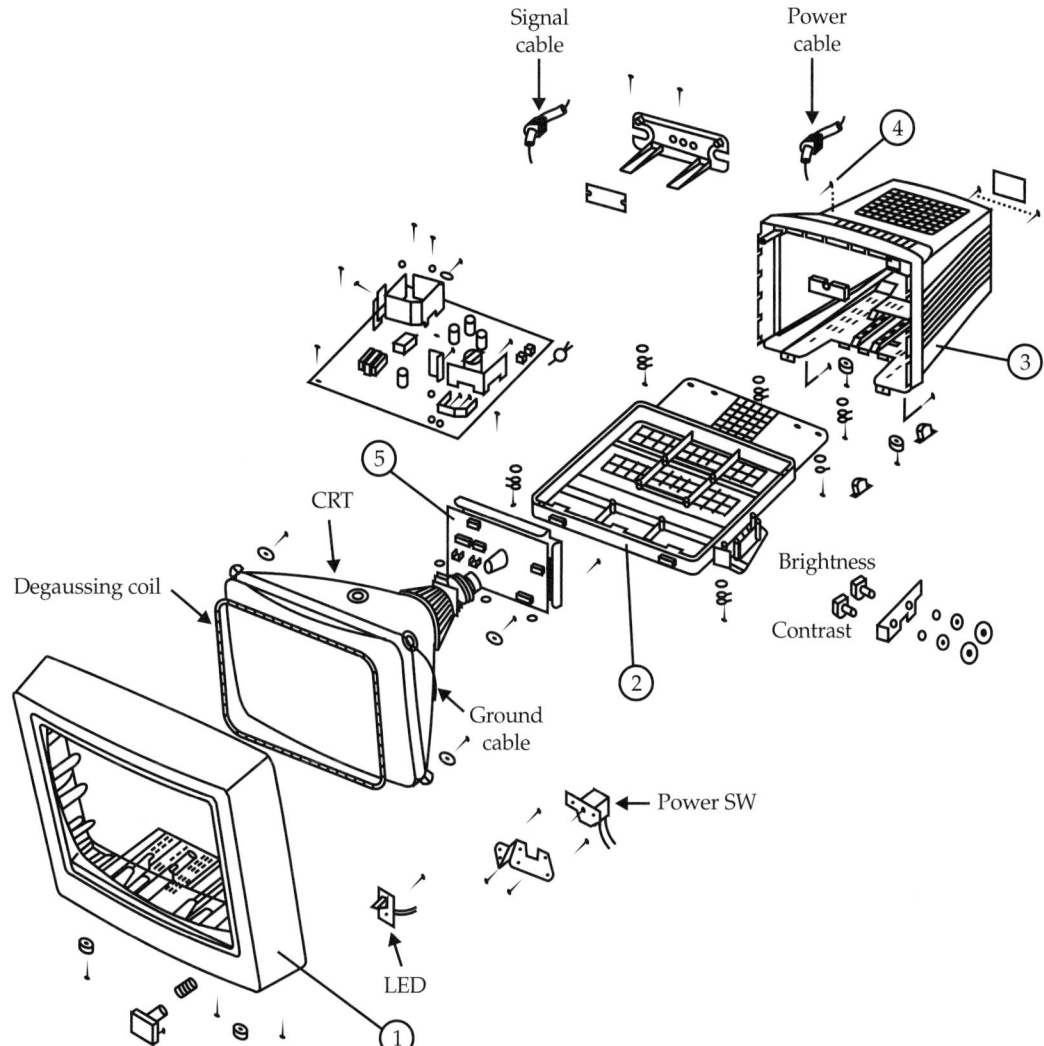

Signal cable

Power cable

Degaussing coil

CRT

Ground cable

Brightness

Contrast

Power SW

LED

FIGURE 2-2   Exploded diagram of a Tandy VGM220 monitor (Tandy Corp.)

You will notice a *shadow mask* added to the color CRT. A shadow mask is a thin plate of metal that contains thousands of microscopic perforations (one perforation for each screen pixel). The mask is placed in close proximity to the phosphor face. Many more recent monitor designs abandon a shadow mask in favor of layered grids called *aperture grilles*. There is also a substantial difference in the screen phosphors. Whereas a monochrome CRT uses a homogeneous layer of phosphor across the entire face, a color CRT uses phosphor *triads,* as shown in Figure 2-4 (note that the distance between the shadow mask/aperture grille and phosphor screen is shown greatly exaggerated). Red, green, and blue phosphor dots are arranged in sets such that the red, green, and blue electron beams will strike the corresponding

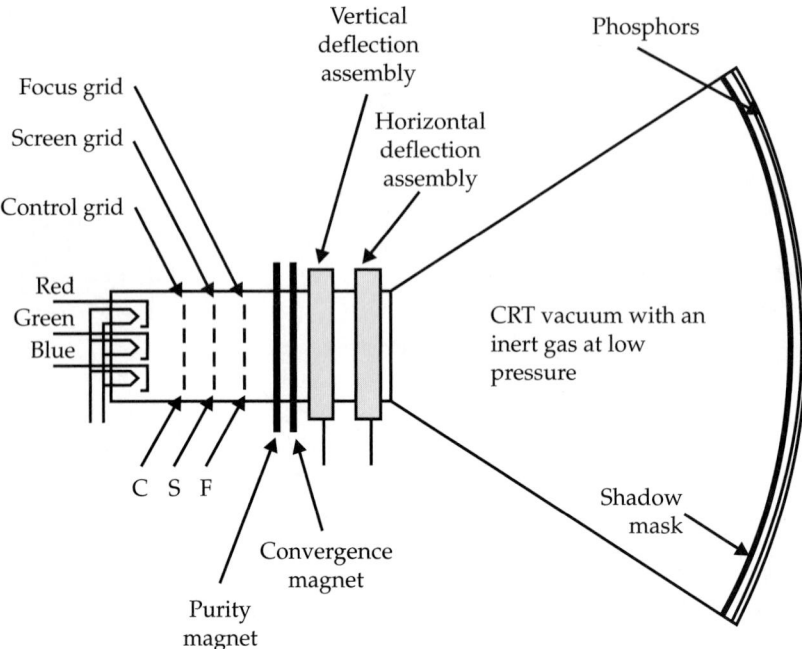

FIGURE 2-3 Diagram of a typical color CRT assembly

phosphor. In actual operation, the color dots are so close together that each triad appears as a single point (or pixel). A *degaussing coil* (shown in Figure 2-2) mounted in front of the CRT works to keep the shadow mask demagnetized.

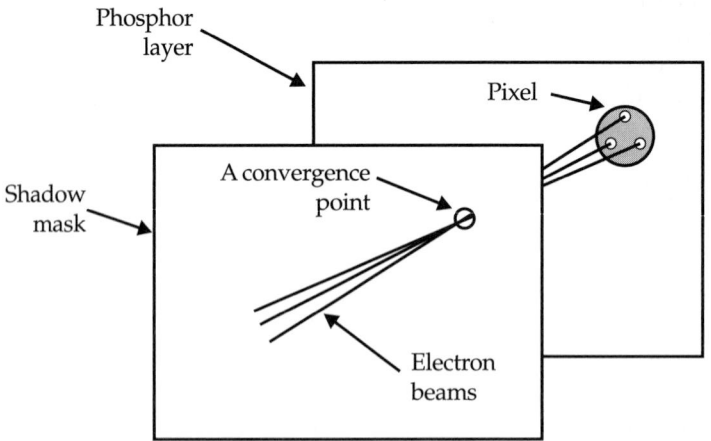

*Sizes and distances are NOT shown to scale

FIGURE 2-4 The relationship of a shadow mask and color phosphors

Color CRTs must also be more precise in how the three electron beams are directed around the screen. Since there are now three phosphors instead of just one, it is critical that each electron beam strike only its corresponding phosphor color, not adjoining phosphors. This is known as *color purity*. A *purity magnet* added to the CRT yoke helps to adjust fine beam positioning. By using a shadow mask, the electron beams are allowed to reach the phosphors only where there are holes in the mask. Also remember that each of the three electron beams must converge at each hole in the shadow mask. A *convergence magnet* added to the CRT yoke adjusts beam convergence in the display center (known as *static convergence*), while a convergence coil driven by the raster circuitry optimizes beam convergence at the edges of the display (known as *dynamic convergence*). It is this delicate balance of purity and convergence adjustments—as well as the presence of a shadow mask—that give today's color monitors such rich, precise color.

CRT DRIVE BOARD

The CRT drive board (5 in Figure 2-2) attaches directly to the CRT pins through a circular connector. Control (brightness), screen, and focus grid voltages are applied to the CRT through this board. The CRT drive board also contains the red, green, and blue video amplifiers and drivers. Since more CRT drive circuitry is needed for a color monitor than for a monochrome monitor, the CRT drive board for a color monitor is usually much larger than that for a monochrome monitor. Once the monitor is unplugged and discharged, make sure that this board is attached evenly and securely to the CRT. It is the CRT drive circuit that regulates the strength of each electron beam by adjusting signal strength on the corresponding video control grid in the CRT. The CRT drive circuit must convert a small video signal (usually no more than 0.7 volts) into a signal large enough to drive the CRT (typically around 50 volts). For color monitors with three analog video lines, three separate video drive circuits are required.

Problems can strike the CRT drive circuits in a number of ways, but there are clues to help you identify the source of the problem. If the display disappears but the raster remains (*raster* is that dim haze you see by turning up the monitor's brightness), the video signal may have failed at the video adapter board in your PC. If there is suddenly not enough (or far too much) red, green, or blue in the displayed image, the corresponding DAC (digital-to-analog converter) on the video adapter may have failed, or the corresponding CRT drive circuit in the monitor may have broken down. Try a monitor that you know is working properly. If the correct image appears, you know the video adapter is producing the desired output, and the original monitor is probably defective. If no display appears on the good monitor, suspect the video adapter board in your PC. If the screen is black, suffers from fixed brightness (with or without video input), or looses focus, one or more grids in the CRT may have shorted and failed.

RASTER DRIVE BOARD

The main raster board contains the vertical raster, horizontal raster, and high-voltage circuits that actually drive the CRT and direct the electron beam(s) around the screen. Depending on the design of your particular monitor, the raster board may contain part or all of the power supply circuit as well, along with some microcontroller-driven circuitry to operate on-screen monitor adjustments. Just about all monitors mount the raster board directly to the frame horizontally below the CRT neck. This assembly can be difficult to remove, because it is obstructed by the CRT neck and yoke, as well as the interconnecting wiring that connects to the power supply, front panel controls, and flyback transformer.

The vertical drive circuit is used to operate the vertical deflection yoke. This is accomplished with a *vertical sweep oscillator,* which is little more than a free-running oscillator set to run at 60, 70, 75, or 85 Hz (perhaps more, depending on the design of the particular monitor). When the oscillator is triggered, it produces a sawtooth wave. The start of the sawtooth wave corresponds to the top of the screen, while the end of the sawtooth wave corresponds to the bottom of the screen. When the sawtooth cycle is complete, there is a blank period for blanking and retrace. One vertical sweep will be accomplished in less than 1/60th of a second.

Trouble with the vertical drive circuit usually strikes the vertical output driver circuit. If part of the driver fails, either the upper or lower half of the image disappears. If the entire driver fails, the screen image compresses to a straight horizontal line in the center of the screen (there would be no vertical deflection—only horizontal deflection). Another problem is vertical oversweep, which elongates the picture to the extent where it "wraps back" on itself in the lower portion of the screen. The area where the vertical image oversweeps will appear with a whitish haze and is typically the fault of the vertical oscillator circuit.

The horizontal drive circuit is the second part of the color monitor's raster circuit, and it is designed to operate the horizontal deflection yoke. This is accomplished with a *horizontal oscillator*, which is little more than a free-running oscillator set to run at a frequency between 15 kHz and 95 kHz. For example, a classic CGA monitor will typically use a horizontal sweep frequency of about 15.75 kHz, but a current high-resolution (1600×1200) monitor may run as high as 93.7 kHz. Table 2-1 illustrates the typical relationships between resolution and vertical/horizontal drive frequencies. The actual oscillator may be based on a transistor, but is usually designed around an integrated circuit, which is more stable at the higher frequencies that are needed. When a horizontal synchronization trigger pulse is received from the video adapter board, the oscillator is forced to fire. When the oscillator is triggered, it produces a square wave. The start of the square wave corresponds to the left side of the screen. When the cycle is complete, there is a blank period for blanking and retrace. At an operating frequency of 31.5 kHz, one horizontal sweep will be accomplished in about 31.7μS.

Trouble with the horizontal drive circuit usually strikes the horizontal output drive circuit since that is the circuit that sustains the greatest stress in the monitor. If the drive circuit fails, the entire image disappears, because high-voltage generation will also be affected. Unfortunately, a fault in the horizontal oscillator will also result in an image loss, because high-voltage generation depends on a satisfactory

TABLE 2-1	RELATIONSHIP BETWEEN VERTICAL AND HORIZONTAL DRIVE FREQUENCIES	
RESOLUTION	**HORIZONTAL FREQUENCY**	**VERTICAL FREQUENCY**
640×400	31.5 kHz	70 Hz
640×480	31.5 kHz	60 Hz
640×480	37.5 kHz	75 Hz
640×480	43.3 kHz	85 Hz
800×600	46.9 kHz	75 Hz
800×600	53.7 kHz	85 Hz
1024×768	60.0 kHz	75 Hz
1024×768	68.6 kHz	85 Hz
1152×870	68.7 kHz	75 Hz
1280×1024	80.0 kHz	75 Hz
1280×1024	91.1 kHz	85 Hz
1600×1200	93.7 kHz	75 Hz
1600×1200	106.3 kHz	85 Hz
1800×1350	120.4 kHz	85 Hz
1800×1440	120.6 kHz	80 Hz

horizontal pulse. If the horizontal oscillator or amplifier fails, high-voltage fails as well, and the image becomes too faint to see. This makes troubleshooting horizontal problems a bit more difficult than troubleshooting vertical problems.

The high-voltage system is actually part of the horizontal drive circuit. A monitor's power supply generates relatively low voltages (usually not much higher than 140 volts). This means that the high positive potential needed to excite the CRT's anode is *not* developed in the power supply. Instead, the 15kV to 30kV or more needed to power a CRT anode is generated from the horizontal output. The amplified, high-frequency pulse signal generated by the horizontal driver circuit is provided to the primary winding of a device known as the *flyback transformer* (or FBT). It is the FBT that produces the high voltage. The principle is similar to the ignition system used in automobiles.

POWER SUPPLY

The power supply is typically a hand-sized assembly that converts AC into several DC voltage levels (usually +135, +20, +12, +6.3, and +87 volts DC) that will be needed by other monitor circuits. The AC itself may be filtered and fused by a separate small assembly near the monitor's base. If there is no stand-alone power supply board in your particular monitor, the supply is probably incorporated into the raster board. As you saw earlier, the only voltage that is *not* produced in the power supply is the high-voltage source. A stand-alone power supply is typically mounted vertically to the frame. The metal frame not only provides a rigid mounting platform, but it serves as a chassis common, and helps to contain radio-frequency (RF) signals generated by the monitor.

Working with On-Screen Controls

PC monitors have traditionally been analog devices that include manually adjusted controls to configure proper operation. However, as monitor sizes, viewing areas, refresh rates, and screen resolutions continue to increase, users demand more control over the image's appearance. The use of microcontrollers in large modern monitors allows many display adjustments to be made through the front control panel, which otherwise would require a tedious and time-consuming internal alignment. Such changes can then be easily saved in the monitor's internal memory. Since adjustments can be set for major resolutions independently, the monitor can "remember" your optimum display configuration for your most frequently used display modes—there is almost no tinkering with the monitor each time you change a screen mode. On-screen controls are listed through a series of icons that indicate the general action of each control.

BASIC CONTROLS

The basic on-screen controls may seem overwhelming at first glance—that's understandable, because most PC users never get to use more than brightness and contrast knobs. Still, the basic controls are designed to help you set the overall image position and quality for your current display mode. Figure 2-5 illustrates some of the most popular icons for basic on-screen monitor adjustments.

Some of these adjustments can cause severe image distortion if set improperly. Before making any adjustments (beyond contrast and brightness), be sure to note the starting level of each adjustment, or find the "factory default" button, which can restore default levels automatically.

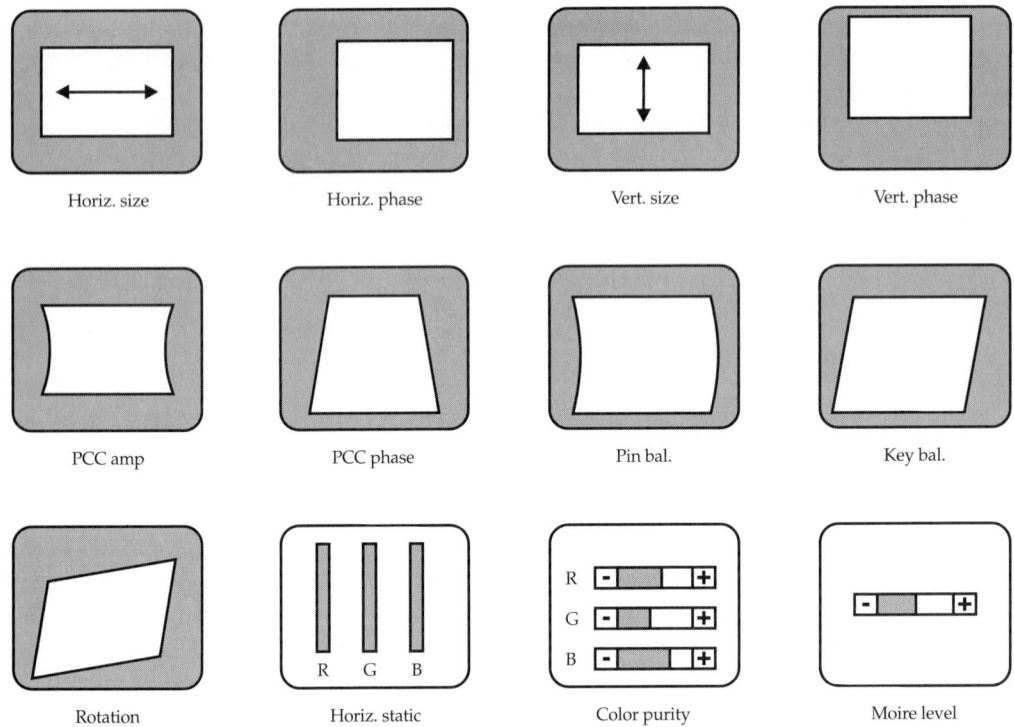

FIGURE 2-5   Basic on-screen monitor adjustment icons

■ **Horizontal Size**   Also called *H-size*, this makes the image fatter or thinner. If the image is too wide (where one or both ends are "lost" beyond the edges of the display area), you can use the H-size control to pull the image inside the display area.

■ **Horizontal Phase**   Also called *H-phase* or *H-posi*, this control lets you position the image left or right in the display area. For example, if the image is too far to the right, use H-phase to shift the image to the left. You may use H-phase and H-size alternately to size the image properly.

■ **Vertical Size**   Also called *V-size*, this makes the image taller or shorter. If the image is too tall (where one or both ends are "lost" beyond the top and bottom of the display area), you can use the V-size control to pull the image inside the display area.

■ **Vertical Phase**   Also called *V-phase* or *V-posi*, this control lets you position the image higher or lower in the display area. For example, if the image is too low, use V-phase to shift the image upward. You may use V-phase and V-size alternately to size the image properly.

■ **PCC Amp**   Also known as the *pincushion adjustment*, this control lets you straighten the left and right sides of the image. If the PCC control is set too low, the image will bow outward. If the PCC control is set too high, the image will draw inward. Ideally, the sides of the image should be straight.

■ **PCC Phase**   Also known as the *trapezoidal adjustment,* this control lets you make the image perfectly rectangular. If the adjustment is set too low, the top of the image may be narrower than the bottom. If the adjustment is set too high, the top of the image may be wider than the bottom.

■ **Pin Balance**   Also known as the *curvature adjustment,* this control also lets you straighten the image. If the control is too high, the image may curve to the left. If the image is too low, the image may curve to the right. Note that this is not a pincushion (PCC amp) adjustment, because the left and right sides of the image are being affected in the same direction.

■ **Key Balance**   Also referred to as a *slant control* or *tilt adjustment,* this control also lets you straighten the image. If the control is set too high, the top of the image may be pulled right, and the bottom of the image may be pulled left. If the control is set too low, the top of the image may be pulled left, and the bottom of the image may be pulled right.

■ **Rotation**   Also referred to as the *twist adjustment,* this control affects the rotation of the entire image in the display. Ideally, the image should appear straight in the display—the two bottom corners of the image should be exactly the same distance from the desk.

■ **Horizontal Static**   This is an adjustment of color alignment. Use this control to adjust the alignment of the red, green, and blue electron beams.

■ **Color Purity**   You may also see this called *color balance.* Ideally, white should be a "pure" white—containing the exact same amounts of red, green, and blue. However, age may affect CRT color guns and video driver levels, so you can tweak the RGB settings to restore color purity.

■ **Moire Level**   *Moire* is a form of distortion that occurs when certain conditions of resolution, dot pitch, screen size, and image coloring are met. The moire pattern usually appears as wavy or elliptical patterns in the display. Use this control to adjust the amount of moire distortion that may appear in an image.

ADVANCED CONTROLS

The advanced on-screen image adjustments are often quite similar to the basic adjustments, but advanced adjustments allow more precise and subtle corrections—especially in the corners of an image, which are the most difficult to set correctly. Figure 2-6 highlights the advanced controls that you'll encounter most frequently.

■ **Vertical Linearity**   This is also called *V-lin.* Linearity is the geometric "correctness" of the display. For example, in an image of small colored boxes that are the same size throughout, each box should "appear" to be the same size. If not, linearity might be a problem. This control adjusts linearity in the vertical direction.

■ **Vertical Linearity Balance**   Also called *V-lin balance,* this control effectively centers the linearity of the display's vertical axis. For example, it may be necessary to shift the linearity balance when changing linearity, to avoid making uniform linearity changes across the entire display.

■ **Center PCC**   Also called *center pincushion,* this is a precision adjustment that allows you to tweak the pincushion adjustment near the vertical center of the image, instead of across the entire left and right sides of the image. This adjustment should be used only when there is limited pincushioning around the middle of the image.

- **Corner PCC**   Also called *corner pincusion,* this is a precision adjustment that allows you to tweak the pincushion adjustment near the corners of the image, instead of across the entire left and right sides of the image. This adjustment should be used only when there is limited pincushioning around the edges of the image.

- **Center Balance**   This feature (similar to pin balance) adjusts the curvature of the left and right sides of the display near the vertical center of the image, instead of across the entire image. Use this adjustment to correct minor curvature in the center of the image.

- **Corner Balance**   This feature (similar to pin balance) adjusts the curvature of the left and right sides of the display at the corners of the image, instead of across the entire image. Use this adjustment to correct minor curvature at the corners of the image.

- **Clamp Pulse Position**   This feature is not needed with RGB inputs, such as those provided by your 15-pin video cable, but may be needed when using Sync-on-Green signals through a BNC connector. Clamp pulse controls allow you to eliminate the excessive green or white background that can occur when using Sync-on-Green or external sync signals at the monitor.

- **Purity**   This feature allows you to adjust the color purity, or color uniformity, of the display. Do not adjust this level unless absolutely necessary. This is sometimes referred to as the monitor's *color temperature* setting.

- **Power Management**   This option can be used to disable the power management (a.k.a. "Energy Star") features of your monitor. When disabled, the monitor will not power-down after a given period of system inactivity.

- **Degaussing**   This feature allows you to manually degauss the monitor if you notice unusual screen discoloration. Use this feature with extreme caution, and only on an as-needed basis.

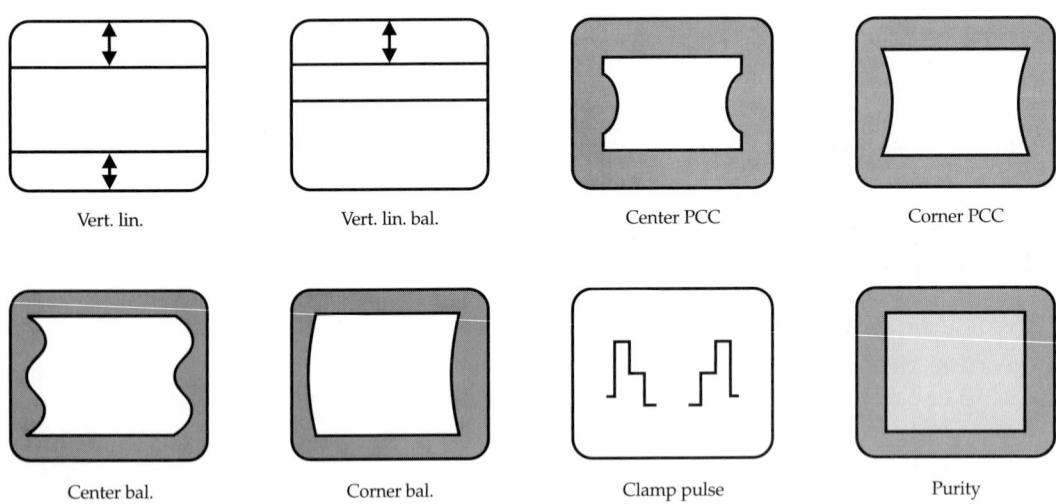

| Vert. lin. | Vert. lin. bal. | Center PCC | Corner PCC |
| Center bal. | Corner bal. | Clamp pulse | Purity |

FIGURE 2-6   Advanced on-screen monitor adjustments

Notes on Monitor Disassembly and Reassembly

The process of monitor disassembly is remarkably straightforward. In most cases, only the rear enclosure must be removed to expose the entire inner workings of the monitor. The rear enclosure itself typically is held in place with only four screws (there may be additional screws inserted at the bottom). On some occasions, you may also encounter a number of plastic latches, but this is rare. After removing the rear enclosure, you will see the bell and neck of the CRT, the CRT drive board, the raster board, and the power supply (if a separate supply is used).

The computer monitor operates with exposed voltages that are potentially lethal! This makes monitors unusually dangerous in the hands of novice or inexperienced troubleshooters. Make sure that the monitor is *unplugged* and allowed several minutes to discharge before reaching into the assembly. Do not operate the monitor without its X-ray and RF shields in place (if applicable). It is also advisable to work with a second person nearby.

You should take note of any metal shrouds or coverings that are included with the monitor assembly. Metal shielding serves two very important purposes. First, the oscillators and amplifiers in a monitor produce RF signals that have the potential to interfere with radio and TV reception. The presence of metal shields or screens helps to attenuate any such interference, so make it a point to always replace shields securely before testing or operating the monitor. Second, large CRTs (larger than 17 inches) use *very* high voltages (30kV or more) at the CRT anode. With such high potentials, X-radiation becomes a serious concern. CRTs with lower anode voltages can usually contain X-rays with lead in the CRT glass. Metal shields are added to the larger CRTs as supplemental shielding to stop X-rays from escaping the monitor enclosure. When X-ray shielding is removed, it is vital that it be replaced *before* the monitor is tested and returned to service. X-ray shields will usually be clearly marked when you remove the monitor's rear cover.

DISCHARGING THE CRT

Before removing any wiring or boards from the monitor, it is important to be sure that the CRT is fully discharged. Even though unplugging the monitor will prevent AC and high-voltage electrocution, there may still be enough high-voltage charge stored in the CRT to provide a fair kick to the careless. Make sure the monitor is turned off and allow several minutes for the AC supply to discharge. Use a regular-blade screwdriver with a heavy-duty alligator clip attached between the screwdriver shaft and the metal chassis. *Gently* insert the screwdriver blade under the high-voltage anode cap, as shown in Figure 2-7. You will probably hear a mild crackle as the CRT is grounded. *Do not rotate the screwdriver or force it in the CRT.* Remember that the CRT is still a glass assembly, and excessive force can damage it easily. Once the crackling noise stops, remove the screwdriver and unplug the monitor's AC cord. The assembly should now be safe to work on.

REMOVING SUBASSEMBLIES

Removing boards is often a simple matter. The CRT drive board is simply plugged into the CRT through a circular connector. Rock the video board back and forth gently to pull it away from the CRT. The raster board is typically mounted to the frame with several screws. After the screws are removed, the raster

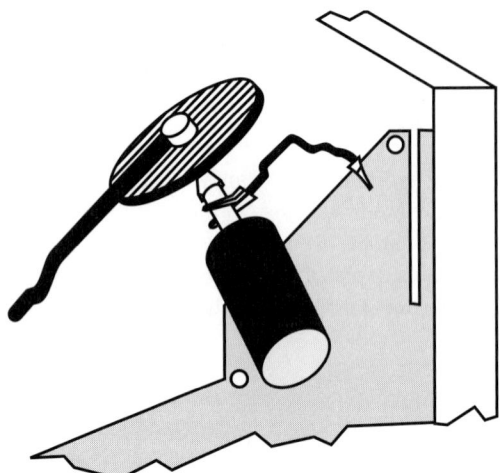

FIGURE 2-7   Discharging an unpowered CRT before servicing

board should be free. When removing any board, be sure to make a careful note of each connector's location and orientation. A CRT is held in place with a metal bracket bolted to the front enclosure. Unfortunately, replacing the CRT usually means removing the video and raster boards along with the frame. If you must place the monitor (or front enclosure alone) face down onto a work surface, be sure to use a layer of soft towels or foam to prevent scratches to the front enclosure or CRT.

REPLACING SUBASSEMBLIES

The most important rule to remember when exchanging a board or CRT is to use an *exact* replacement part. Monitors are precisely timed, high-energy systems, so "close" doesn't count. An improper replacement assembly may cause the monitor to malfunction, or it may work only for a limited amount of time. When reassembling a monitor, be extremely careful of the wiring interconnecting each board and the CRT. Be sure that all wiring and connectors are installed properly and completely. Loose connectors can cause erratic or intermittent operation. Pay close attention to wire paths—do not allow wiring to be pinched under boards or against the metal chassis. Finally, make it a point to reinstall any RF or X-ray shielding that may have been removed during the repair.

Remember that a monitor may need to be realigned after completing a repair. In many cases, this is as simple as using the monitor's on-screen controls to tweak the image.

TIPS FOR WORKING WITH A MONITOR

Of all the PC peripherals, monitors are perhaps the most potentially dangerous in careless hands. The following tips will help you protect yourself from injury, and get the most working life from your monitor investment:

- For best monitor images, always keep the 15-pin video cable secured to the video adapter board. Also avoid using monitor cable extensions, which can cause image ghosting.

■ The viewable area of a computer monitor is typically 1 inch less than the rated diagonal screen area. For example, a monitor with a 20.9-inch CRT size generally offers a viewing area of about 20 inches.

■ Use simple ammonia-based cleaner to clean the monitor case, but never spray cleaner onto the monitor, only onto the cleaning cloth.

■ CRT coatings (such as antiglare coatings) can be extremely sensitive to chemicals, so never use any sort of cleaner other than demineralized water to clean the CRT. Remember to wet the cleaning cloth, not the CRT.

■ Monitors use convection for cooling. Be sure to keep all of the vent openings on the monitor case unobstructed and free of dust and debris. Vacuum out any accumulations of dust within the monitor.

■ When working on a monitor, always use a soft pillow or plush towel to cushion the CRT and avoid scratches.

■ Monitors can contain potentially dangerous voltages. Be sure to keep the monitor turned off and unplugged before working inside it. Discharge the CRT's high-voltage anode before performing any service.

■ Do not use metal tools when working inside a monitor, especially when attempting to make alignments.

■ When reassembling a monitor, be extremely careful to avoid damaging wiring and connectors.

■ Monitors (especially large monitors) are extremely sensitive to the influences of magnetic fields. Be sure to keep any motorized or magnetic devices well clear of the monitor. Even unshielded multimedia speakers can adversely affect the monitor.

■ Monitors are particularly heavy devices, so be very careful when lifting a monitor. Lift from the knees, not from the back. Hold the CRT face toward your chest.

Further Study

Anatek Corporation   www.anatekcorp.com
CTX   www.ctxintl.com/
Electronix Corporation   www.electronix.com/
Monitor Testing Software   www.csf.org.uk/csf/download/main.htm
NEC   www.nec.com
Sony   www.ita.sel.sony.com/support/displays/
Viewsonic   www.viewsonic.com/desk/desk.htm

3

AN INSIDE LOOK AT OPERATING SYSTEMS AND THE BOOT PROCESS

As a technician, it is vital for you to understand the relationship between PC hardware and software. In the early days of computers, hardware was typically the center of attention. Since early software was written for a specific computer (such as a DEC PDP system or IBM VAX), and early computers were very limited in their storage and processing capacity, software often arrived as an afterthought. (We still see software development lagging behind hardware advances to this day.) With the introduction of personal computers in the mid-1970s, designers realized that a wide selection of software would be needed to make PCs

52

attractive. Instead of writing software specifically for particular machines, a uniform operating environment would be needed to manage system resources and launch applications. In this way, applications would be *portable* between systems whose hardware resources would otherwise be incompatible. This uniform applications environment became known as the *operating system* (OS). When IBM designed the early PC, it chose to license a simple command-line–based operating system from a fledgling company called Microsoft—and the rest is history.

Although this book is dedicated to dealing with PC hardware (since it is the hardware that "breaks"), you should realize that the operating system has a profound effect on PC resources and how those resources are allocated to individual software applications. This is especially true of the more sophisticated operating systems such as Windows 98/Me/NT/2000, Linux, and OS/2. Every good technician is sensitive to the fact that problems with an OS (or its configuration) will result in problems with PC performance. This chapter explains the relationship between PC hardware and software, highlights some of the major features found in typical operating systems, and walks you through a typical PC boot process.

The PC Hierarchy

Before we dig into the OS itself, you should understand the complex (and often frustrating) relationship between computer hardware and software. This relationship is often expressed as a *hierarchy,* as shown in Figure 3-1. Each layer in the hierarchy serves a very specific function in PC operation. This hierarchy has four levels: the hardware, the BIOS, the OS, and the application(s).

HARDWARE

As you might expect, hardware forms the core of a PC hierarchy—without the hardware, the computer doesn't exist. The hardware includes all the circuits, drives, expansion boards, power supplies, peripheral devices, and their interconnecting wiring or cables. This extends not only to the PC itself, but also to monitors,

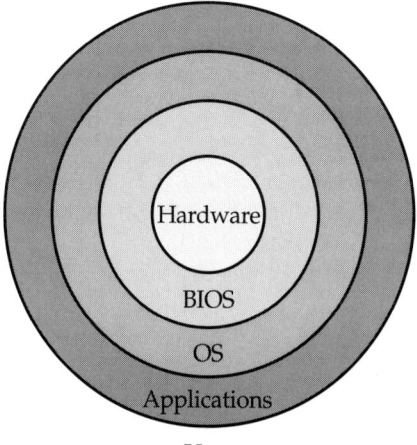

User

FIGURE 3-1   A standard PC hierarchy

keyboards, pointing devices, printers, and so on. By sending digital information to various ports or addresses in memory, it is possible to manipulate almost anything attached to the system CPU. Any physical aspect of the PC is regarded as hardware. (Chapter 1 provides a thorough review of PC hardware.)

Unfortunately, controlling PC hardware is a difficult process that requires an intimate knowledge of a PC's electronic architecture. How is it that Microsoft can sell an OS that works on an i386-based AT, as well as on a new Pentium 4 system? Since each PC manufacturer designs its circuitry (especially motherboard circuitry) differently, it is virtually impossible to create a universal OS without some sort of interface between the one standard OS and the myriad variations of hardware in the marketplace. This interface is accomplished by the *Basic Input/Output System* (BIOS).

BIOS

Simply stated, a BIOS is a set of small programs (or *system services*) that are designed to operate each major PC subsystem (video, disk, keyboard, and so on). Each of these system services is invoked by a set of standard calls (originally developed by IBM) that are made as needed through the OS. When the OS requests a standard BIOS service, the particular BIOS program performs the appropriate function that has been tailored to the particular hardware. Thus, each motherboard design requires its own BIOS. Using this methodology, BIOS acts as a glue that allows diverse (and older) hardware to operate with a single uniform OS. In addition to system services, the BIOS executes a power-on self-test (POST) program each time the PC is initialized. POST checks the major subsystems before attempting to load an OS.

In practice, most BIOS code is written by a limited number of companies, such as Award or AMI. Motherboard manufacturers then license the generic BIOS code and tweak the BIOS for each particular motherboard design.

Since BIOS is specific to each motherboard design, BIOS resides on the motherboard in the form of a read-only memory (ROM) chip, although newer systems employ electrically rewritable (or *flash*) ROMs that allow the BIOS to be updated without having to replace the BIOS ROM chip. You may see BIOS referred to as *firmware* rather then software, because the BIOS instructions are permanently recorded on a chip. As you might imagine, the efficiency and elegance of BIOS code would have a profound impact on the overall operation of a PC; better BIOS routines will result in superior system performance, while clumsy, inefficient BIOS routines can easily bog down a system. *Bugs* (software errors) in BIOS can have very serious consequences for the system (including lost files and system lockups).

OPERATING SYSTEM

The operating system serves two very important functions in the modern PC. First, an OS interacts with (and provides an extension to) the BIOS. This extension provides applications with a rich selection of high-level file handling and disk control functions. It is this large number of disk-related functions that added the term "disk" to "operating system" to give us *disk operating system,* or *DOS.* You can see how Windows 98 reports disk capacity in Figure 3-2. When an application needs to perform disk access or file handling, the OS layer performs most of the work. By providing access to a library of frequently used functions through the OS, application programs can be written without the need to incorporate the code for such complex functions into each application itself. In actual operation, the OS and BIOS work closely together to give an application easy access to system resources.

Second, an OS forms an environment (or *shell*) through which applications can be executed, and provides a user interface allowing you and your customers to interact with the PC. MS-DOS uses a

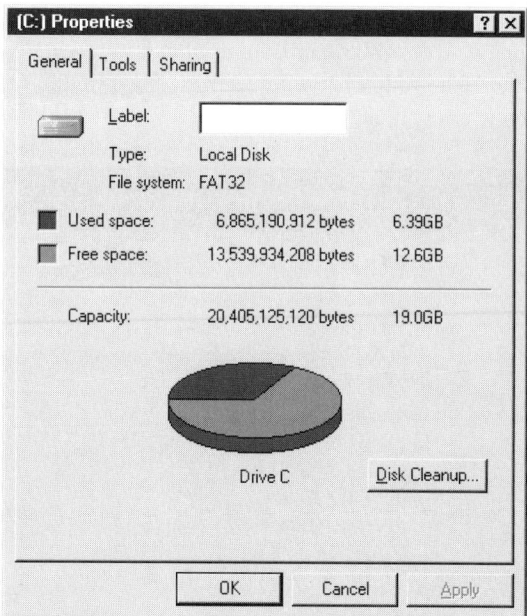

FIGURE 3-2   Locating disk information through a Windows dialog box

keyboard-driven, command-line interface signified by the command-line prompt (such as C:>_), which is now almost universally recognized. By contrast, the Windows family of operating systems provides a graphical user interface (GUI) that relies on symbols, icons, and dialog boxes that are selected with a mouse or other pointing device.

APPLICATIONS

Ultimately, the aim of any computer is to execute applications (such as games, word processors, spread-sheets, and so on). An OS loads and allows the user to launch the desired application(s). As the application requires system resources during run time, it makes an appropriate call to the OS or BIOS, which in turn accesses the needed function and returns any needed information to the calling application. The actual dynamics of such an exchange are more complex than described here, but this description should give you the general idea. Now that you have an overview of the typical PC hierarchy and understand how each layer interacts with one another, it is time to take a closer look at the OS layer itself.

Understanding Popular OS Features

Many different operating systems are written for today's computers. The range and sophistication of operating systems span the entire spectrum of features and complexity—some are large, complex, commercial giants (such as Windows 98/Me, Windows 2000, and Windows NT), while others are small, freely distributed packages (like FreeBSD). Other operating systems are tailored for such features as real-time operation, true or high-performance multitasking, or networking. New, specialized operating systems are regularly being introduced to support particular systems, such as process control, manufacturing, or other mission-critical needs. Table 3-1 offers a partial listing of today's available operating systems. As a technician, you should understand the important features of today's operating systems, and why one OS might be selected over another. The following sections offer some highlights of the major commercial operating systems offered by Microsoft and IBM.

TABLE 3-1   PARTIAL LIST OF CONTEMPORARY OPERATING SYSTEMS

OPERATING SYSTEM	FURTHER STUDY
98Lite	www.98lite.net/
A/UX	jagubox.gsfc.nasa.gov/aux/
BeOS 5	www.be.com/products/freebeos/
CP/M	www.herne.com/cpm.htm
CTOS	www.dogstar.com/Sirius/Menu/TechLibrary.NewsletterExcerpts.html
DR-DOS v6.0	support.novell.com/Ftp/Updates/dsktop/drdos60/Date0.html
EROS	www.cis.upenn.edu/~eros/
Freedows OS	www.freedows.org/
GEOS	users.bergen.org/~edwdig/geos/
GNU	www.delorie.com/gnu/
GNU Hurd	www.gnu.ai.mit.edu/software/hurd/hurd.html
HP/UX	eigen.ee.ualberta.ca/
JOS (Java OS)	www.jos.org/
Linux, Caldera	www.caldera.com/
Linux, Debian	www.debian.org/
Linux, Mandrake	www.linux-mandrake.com/en/
Linux, Real-Time	www.rtlinux.org/
Linux, Red Hat	www.redhat.com/
Linux, SuSE	www.suse.com/
Linux, ZipSlack	www.slackware.com/zipslack/
Mach	www.cs.cmu.edu/afs/cs.cmu.edu/project/mach/public/www/mach.html
MacMinix	www.pliner.com/macminix/
MacOS	www.apple.com/macos/
MacOS X Server	www.apple.com/macosx/server/
Novell NetWare	www.novell.com/
OS/2	www-4.ibm.com/software/os/warp/
PC-DOS v7.0 (2000)	www-4.ibm.com/software/os/dos/index.html
PertOS	www.trumpet.com/products.html
Plan9	www.fywss.com/plan9/
QNX	get.qnx.com/
ReactOS	www.reactos.com/
UNIX, BSD	www.bsd.org/
UNIX, FreeBSD	www.freebsd.org/
UNIX, KDE	www.kde.org/
UNIX, Minix	www.disi.unige.it/person/DoderoG/minix/minix.htm
UNIX, NetBSD	www.netbsd.org/
UNIX, OpenBSD	www.openbsd.org/
UNIX, SCO	www.sco.com/

TABLE 3-1   PARTIAL LIST OF CONTEMPORARY OPERATING SYSTEMS (*CONTINUED*)

OPERATING SYSTEM	FURTHER STUDY
UNIX, Solaris	www.sun.com/solaris/
UNIX, Tru64	www.tru64unix.compaq.com/
UNIX, XFree86	www.xfree86.org/
V2 OS	www.v2.nl/v2_os/
VMS (OpenVMS)	www.levitte.org/~ava/index.htmlx
Windows 95, 98, Me	www.microsoft.com/windows/default.asp
Windows CE	www.microsoft.com/windows/default.asp
Windows NT/2000	www.microsoft.com/windows/default.asp
Windows XP	www.microsoft.com/windows/default.asp
Wine	www.winehq.com/
X Window System	www.rahul.net/kenton/xsites.html

MS-DOS 6.22

MS-DOS 6.22 is the last stand-alone command-line OS designed by Microsoft for the PC, and is generally considered to be one of the most versatile and reliable DOS-type OSs ever released by Microsoft. It has numerous safety features and enhancements designed to provide the safest possible computing environment of any MS-DOS version. And the most notable features of MS-DOS 6.22. Table 3-2 highlights the system requirements for MS-DOS 6.22 and other popular operating systems. And the most notable features of MS-DOS 6.22 are outlined in the following list.

> Today, stand-alone real-mode operating systems such as MS-DOS and PC-DOS are considered obsolete. It is increasingly difficult to locate information on these operating systems (even technical support resources are gradually disappearing). When faced with DOS, you may consider upgrading the system to a version of Windows or Linux.

TABLE 3-2   COMPARISON OF SYSTEM REQUIREMENTS FOR MAJOR OPERATING SYSTEMS

FEATURE	DOS	WINDOWS 95	WINDOWS 98	WINDOWS NT	WINDOWS 2000	WINDOWS ME
PC platform	Any	486/25 MHz	486/66 MHz	486/25 MHz, Alpha, MIPS R4X00, PowerPC	Pentium 166 MHz	Pentium 150 MHz
RAM	1MB	8MB	16MB	16–32MB	64MB	32MB
Install drive	1.44MB (disks)	CD-ROM	CD-ROM	CD-ROM	CD-ROM	CD-ROM
HDD space	6MB	40–50MB	250MB	110MB	250MB	480–645MB
Display	Mono text	VGA	VGA	VGA	VGA	VGA
Mouse	Optional	Required	Required	Required	Required	Required

■ **Anti-Virus**   This utility can identify and remove more than 1000 different computer viruses. MS-DOS 6.22 includes a version of Anti-Virus for both DOS and Windows 3.1x.

■ **Backup**   Backup is a utility for backing up your hard disk drive. MS-DOS 6.22 includes a version of Backup for both DOS and Windows 3.1x.

■ **Defrag**   MS-DOS 6.22 includes a later version of Defrag that reorganizes files on your hard disk to minimize the time it takes your computer to access them.

■ **DriveSpace and DoubleGuard**   DriveSpace integrates disk compression into the OS and supports both hard disks and floppy disks. DriveSpace includes DoubleGuard safety checking, which protects data by verifying data integrity before writing to the disk.

■ **Interactive start**   The interactive start feature gives you the ability to bypass startup commands when you turn on your computer, by pressing F8. This allows you to choose which CONFIG.SYS and AUTOEXEC.BAT commands MS-DOS should carry out.

■ **Interlink**   This feature enables you to easily transfer files between computers. With Interlink and a cable, you can access information on another computer without using floppy disks to copy data from one computer to another.

■ **MultiConfig**   MultiConfig allows you to define more than one configuration in your CONFIG.SYS file. If your CONFIG.SYS file defines multiple configurations, MS-DOS displays a menu that enables you to choose the configuration you want to use each time you boot the computer.

■ **ScanDisk**   MS-DOS 6.22 includes a more current version of ScanDisk (limited to FAT16) that detects, diagnoses, and repairs disk errors on uncompressed drives and DriveSpace-compressed drives. ScanDisk can repair file system errors (such as cross-linked files and lost clusters) and physical disk errors.

■ **SmartDrive**   The SmartDrive program included with MS-DOS 6.22 speeds up your computer by using a disk cache that stores information being read from your hard disk or CD-ROM drive. SmartDrive can also be set to cache information being written to your hard disk.

■ **Undelete**   This feature allows you to recover deleted files. MS-DOS 6.22 includes a version of Undelete for both DOS and Windows 3.1x.

PC-DOS 7.0

PC-DOS is IBM's answer to MS-DOS. Early versions of PC-DOS were actually licensed to IBM from Microsoft, but the two giants eventually parted company, and IBM continued the development of PC-DOS under its own banner. Today, PC-DOS 7.0 is roughly equivalent in features and performance to MS-DOS 6.22, including disk compression, antivirus software, and limited networking features. However, PC-DOS is not as widely distributed. System requirements are about the same, but PC-DOS 7.0 includes PCMCIA support, a DOS file update feature (to keep files synchronized between PCs), and a high-level programming language called REXX. The more important features of PC-DOS 7.0 are listed here:

■ **Anti-virus**   PC-DOS 7.0 includes IBM Anti-Virus, which checks for more than 2100 viruses.

■ **File update**   A new PC DOS file update feature automatically synchronizes files between your desktop and notebook PCs so that they're always up to date.

■ **Improved utilities**   There are numerous enhancements to DOS and Windows utilities, including Central Point's Backup utility, Phoenix Technology's PCMCIA support utility, and the RAMBoost Memory Optimizer.

- **REXX**   PC-DOS 7.0 includes a new integrated REXX high-level programming language.
- **Stacker**   Stacker 4.0 disk compression delivers an excellent mix of compression and performance.

WINDOWS 95

Microsoft released Windows 95 in August 1995 as the major upgrade to Windows 3.1x. Windows 95 was designed to offer superior performance while taking advantage of emerging PC hardware and PC platform technologies such as plug-and-play, power conservation, PCI bus architecture, and so on. Windows 95 runs most Windows 3.1x and DOS programs, but also supports improved features like a built-in uninstaller, dial-up networking, multitasking, and long file names. Though aging and no longer available preinstalled on new computers, Windows 95 is still the OS used on a large number of personal computers. Its most popular features include the following:

- **Active right mouse button**   Use the right mouse button to accomplish many common tasks quickly and easily. Click almost anything in Windows 95 with your right mouse button to see a context-sensitive menu of options.
- **Dial-up networking**   This feature allows easy access to online resources (like the Internet) and supports communication between connected PCs.
- **Long file names**   Windows 95 supports long file names (up to 250 characters) to make your files and folders easier to organize and find. File names can now have sensible titles.
- **Multitasking**   Windows 95 offers improved multitasking capabilities that truly allow the system to handle multiple tasks simultaneously without system interruptions.
- **Plug-and-play**   This feature allows you to insert the card for a hardware device into your computer, and Windows automatically recognizes and sets up the hardware for you.
- **Shortcuts**   You can create links for easy access to important files, folders, drives, programs, or Web sites.
- **Taskbar**   The Taskbar acts as a home base from which you can start programs (with the Start button) and keep track of what programs have been launched. You can use the Taskbar to switch between programs, as needed, for convenient multitasking.
- **Windows Explorer**   The traditional File Manager of earlier Windows versions has been replaced by Windows Explorer for browsing through and managing your files, drives, and network connections.

OS/2 WARP 4.X

OS/2 Warp has long been IBM's premier OS. Originally codeveloped with Microsoft, OS/2 development continued in-house after IBM and Microsoft ceased their cooperative ventures. OS/2 is a GUI-based operating system capable of running most Windows and DOS software, as well as native OS/2 applications in a true multitasking environment. OS/2 Warp 4.x focuses on network operations and connectivity—including built-in Internet applications—and offers an advantage over competing operating systems with its use of voice input controls. In spite of these advantages, OS/2 is noted for a surprising lack of hardware support. For example, it can be surprisingly difficult to find suitable OS/2 drivers for devices such as CD-ROM drives and sound boards. Today, OS/2 is rarely used and is generally considered to be obsolete. The following are its more noteworthy features:

- **Connectivity**   OS/2 is particularly noted for its strong network connectivity.

- **Reliability**   A true multitasking environment is well suited to critical applications, and OS/2 is relatively crash-proof when compared to Windows 95 and NT.

- **Software compatibility**   OS/2 runs DOS and most Windows 3.1x applications, along with native OS/2 and Java applications. OS/2 also supports features like TrueType, OpenGL, OpenDOC, Open32, and plug-and-play.

- **Speech recognition**   OS/2 includes VoiceType for OS/2 Warp speech recognition software.

- **Systems management**   OS/2 offers powerful system management features, including DMI (Desktop Management Interface) support.

WINDOWS CE

Windows CE is designed to serve as an operating system for a broad range of communications, entertainment, and mobile-computing devices. It also enables new types of non-PC business and consumer devices that can communicate with each other, share information with Windows-based PCs, and connect to the Internet (for example, wallet PCs, digital information pagers, cellular smart phones, DVD players, and Internet Web phones). The first handheld PC products based on Windows CE began shipping in November 1996. It is important to note that Windows CE is released strictly as an OEM product and cannot be purchased through retail channels. Its major features are listed here:

- **Communication with Windows-based PCs**   Windows CE can seamlessly synchronize, communicate, and exchange information with Windows-based PCs.

- **Companion applications**   The Windows CE operating system supports Windows CE–based companion applications that share or synchronize information with their counterparts for Windows.

- **Internet Explorer**   Windows CE includes a version of Internet Explorer that offers built-in Web access for many types of communications, entertainment, and mobile-computing devices.

- **Windows development environment**   The Windows CE development environment supports a comprehensive and expandable subset of Win32 APIs, and uses familiar off-the-shelf development tools, with the goal of ensuring a strong aftermarket for Windows CE applications.

WINDOWS NT (WORKSTATION)

Windows NT represents Microsoft's emphasis on business communication and networking. While the look and feel of Windows NT may seem quite similar to Windows 95, NT incorporates a powerful suite of networking and Internet-related features backed up by detailed security, cryptography, and system policies configurations. Windows NT also abandons DOS-mode support. Windows NT undoubtedly represents one of the most complex and versatile operating systems now in service for business and networking environments. It is surpassed only by the more recent Windows 2000 family of operating systems. The primary features of Windows NT are listed here:

- **Client support for NDS**   Windows NT Workstation includes an improved version of Client Services for NetWare that supports Novell NetWare Directory Services (NDS). This enables users to log on to Novell NetWare 4.x servers running DNS to access files and print resources.

- **Client support for PPTP**   Point-to-Point Tunneling Protocol provides a secure path to use public data networks (such as the Internet) to create virtual private networks. PPTP allows you to safely transmit confidential communications over the Internet.

- **Cryptography APIs**   Windows NT includes a set of encryption APIs that allows developers to easily create applications that work securely over nonsecure networks (such as the Internet).

■ **Dial-up networking**   Improved dial-up networking provides the ability to easily and automatically dial up on demand.

■ **Dial-up networking multilink channel aggregation**   Dial-up networking now provides channel aggregation that enables users to combine all available dial-up lines to achieve higher transfer speeds. For example, you can combine two or more PPP ISDN B channels to achieve speeds of up to 128 Kbps.

■ **Distributed Component Object Model (DCOM)**   Windows NT provides the infrastructure that allows DCOM applications (also known as *Network OLE*) to communicate across networks without needing to redevelop applications.

■ **Hardware profiles**   Windows NT hardware profiles allow you to have different computer settings depending on the environment in which a computer is being used, and they make it easier to use computers in different configurations (such as docked and undocked laptop configurations).

■ **Internet Explorer**   Windows NT Workstation comes with Internet Explorer, which gives you full support to explore the Internet.

■ **Management and control**   Windows NT includes remote management and troubleshooting tools, and allows administrators to implement policies and standards for systemwide desktop configurations.

■ **Multimedia APIs**   Windows NT supports the multimedia APIs found in Windows 95: DirectDraw, DirectInput, DirectPlay, and DirectSound. Supporting these APIs allows developers to create games and other applications for both platforms simultaneously.

■ **Peer Web Services (PWS)**   PWS enables easy publication of personal Web pages, and lets systems share that Web information over Intranets. It's also ideal for developing, testing, and staging Web applications and content.

■ **Setup Manager**   This Windows NT utility assists administrators in creating installation scripts and reduces the time and effort of deploying Windows NT.

■ **System policies and user profiles**   System policies are used to provide a standardized, controlled desktop environment for users. User profiles contain all user-definable settings and can be stored on a Windows NT Server so that users can receive the same desktop regardless of their location.

■ **Task Manager**   An integrated tool for managing applications and tasks, Task Manager maintains detailed information on each application and process running on the desktop. It also provides an effective way to terminate applications and processes that are not responding.

■ **Telephony APIs**   Telephony API (TAPI) integrates telephones and PCs. Using the TAPI interface, communications applications can ask for access to a modem or telephone device, allowing them to be shared.

■ **Windows messaging client**   This is a universal e-mail inbox that you can use with many different e-mail systems. It includes full Messaging API (MAPI) 1.0 support. You can send, receive, organize, and store e-mail and file system objects.

■ **Windows NT Explorer**   This is the Windows NT tool for browsing and managing files, drive, and network connections. It displays your computer's contents as a hierarchy, or tree, allowing you to see the contents of each drive, folder, and network connection.

■ **WINS and DNS integration**   Windows NT takes advantage of the integration between Windows Internet Name Service and Domain Name System to provide a form of dynamic DNS that makes it easier to connect to network resources.

WINDOWS 98

With the many new hardware standards and features being developed for the PC, Windows 95 became increasingly hard-pressed to make the fullest use of system resources. Windows 98 builds on Windows 95 by adding a rich suite of refinements and improvements to a full 32-bit OS. New wizards, utilities, and resources work proactively to keep systems running more smoothly. Performance is faster for many common tasks such as application loading, system startup, and shutdown. Full integration with the Internet's World Wide Web aids online work and system versatility. After numerous delays, Windows 98 was finally released in June 1998, and an upgrade containing a year's worth of learning and improvements named "Windows 98 Second Edition" (or "Windows 98 SE") was released in September 1999. Microsoft has since released the Millennium Edition (called Windows Me), intended to focus on a broad spectrum of home users, but Windows 98/SE continues to be a popular and versatile OS for home and small office users. The most notable features and improvements of Windows 98/SE are outlined here:

- **Backup utility**   A new backup applet supports SCSI tape devices and makes backing up your data easier and more versatile.

- **Broadcast architecture**   With a TV tuner board installed, Windows 98 allows a PC to receive and display television and other data distributed over the broadcast networks, including enhanced television programs (which combine standard television with HTML information related to the programs).

- **Dial-up networking improvements**   The dial-up networking included with Windows 98 has been updated to support features like dial-up scripting and support for multilink channel aggregation, which enables users to combine all available dial-up lines to achieve higher transfer speeds.

- **Disk Defragmenter Optimization wizard**   This new wizard uses the process of disk defragmentation to increase the speed with which your most frequently used applications run.

- **Display configuration enhancements**   Display setting enhancements provide support for dynamically changing screen resolution and color depth. Adapter refresh rates can also be set with most newer display driver chipsets.

- **Distributed Component Object Model (DCOM)**   Windows 98 (and Windows NT 4.0) provides the infrastructure that allows DCOM applications (the technology formally known as *Network OLE*) to communicate across networks without needing to redevelop applications.

- **Dr. Watson**   Windows 98 includes an enhanced version of the Dr. Watson utility. When a software fault occurs (such as a general protection fault or system hang), Dr. Watson intercepts it and indicates what software failed (and why). Dr. Watson also collects detailed information about the state of your system at the time the fault occurred. A Log file is created and can be used by a technician to troubleshoot the problem. Dr. Watson does not run by default; it must be started manually or from a shortcut placed in the Startup folder.

- **Faster shutdown**   The time it takes to shut down the system has been dramatically reduced in Windows 98.

- **FAT32**   This improved version of the FAT file system allows disks over 2GB to be formatted as a single drive. FAT32 also uses smaller clusters than FAT drives, resulting in a more efficient use of space on large disks.

- **Infrared Data Association (IrDA) 3.0 support**   Windows 98 supports IrDA for wireless connectivity, which means users can easily connect to peripheral devices or other PCs without using connecting cables. Infrared-equipped laptop or desktop computers have the capability of networking, transferring files, and printing wirelessly with other IrDA-compatible infrared devices.

- **Intel MMX processor support** Windows 98 provides support for software that uses the Pentium Multimedia Extensions (MMX and SSE) for fast audio and video support on future generations of the Pentium processor.

- **Internet connection sharing (for Windows 98 SE)** This feature enables you to configure your home computer network to share a single connection to the Internet.

- **Multiple display support** This feature allows you to use multiple monitors and/or multiple graphics adapters on a single PC.

- **NetWare Directory Services (NDS) support** Windows 98 includes Client Services for NetWare that support Novell NDS. This enables Windows 98 users to log on to Novell NetWare 4.x servers running NDS to access files and print resources.

- **New hardware support** Windows 98 provides support for an array of innovations that have occurred in computer hardware over the last few years. Some of the major hardware standards supported by Windows 98 include Universal Serial Bus (USB), IEEE 1394, Accelerated Graphics Port (AGP), Advanced Configuration and Power Interface (ACPI), and Digital Video Disc (DVD).

- **PCMCIA enhancements** There have been several enhancements to Windows 98 for PCMCIA support, including support for PC Card32 (CardBus) to implement high-bandwidth applications such as video capture and 100 Mbps networking. There is also support for PC Cards that operate at 3.3 volts, and for multifunction PC Cards (such as LAN and modem, or SCSI and sound) to operate on a single physical PC Card.

- **PPTP support** The Point-to-Point Tunneling Protocol provides a way to use public data networks (such as the Internet) to create virtual private networks connecting client PCs with servers. PPTP offers protocol encapsulation to support multiple protocols via TCP/IP connections and data encryption for privacy, making it safer to send information over nonsecure networks.

- **Power management improvements** Windows 98 includes support for the Advanced Configuration and Power Interface (ACPI), and support for the Advanced Power Management (APM) 1.2 extensions, including: disk spindown, PCMCIA modem power down, and resume on ring.

- **Remote Access Server** Windows 98 includes all the components necessary to enable your desktop to act as a dial-up server. This allows dial-up clients to remotely connect to a Windows 98 machine for local resource access.

- **System Configuration utility** This utility allows for the fine-tuning of the Windows 98 startup and shutdown. Individual items in AUTOEXEC.BAT, CONFIG.SYS, SYSTEM.INI, WIN.INI, and the Startup folder can be enabled or disabled to troubleshoot conflicts or problems. It replaces and vastly improves on Windows 95 Sysedit.

- **System File Checker** This utility provides an easy way to verify that the Windows 98 system files (*.dll, *.com, *.vxd, *.drv, *.ocx, *.inf, *.hlp, and so on) have not been modified or corrupted. This utility also provides an easy mechanism for restoring the original versions of system files that have changed.

- **System Information tool** This utility provides extensive information on the system hardware and software environment. Many of the new troubleshooting, repair, and report utilities are available from the System Information utility through the Tools menu.

- **System Troubleshooter** This utility automates the routine troubleshooting steps used by support personnel and users when diagnosing issues with the Windows configuration. The troubleshooters are designed to address specific areas and devices. You can find the troubleshooters listed under the Help utility.

- **Windows 98 Report tool**   Available under Tools in the System Information utility, this program allows you to submit a problem report to Microsoft. It automatically includes the information about your system that the Microsoft technicians need to have to examine the problem.

- **Windows Media Player**   Windows 98 supports a new media-streaming architecture called ActiveMovie that delivers high-quality video playback of popular media types, including MPEG audio, WAV audio, MPEG video, AVI video, and Apple QuickTime video. The Media Player supports many popular audio, video, and combined media file formats. Updated Media Players are available for download from Microsoft.

- **Windows System Update**   This feature helps you ensure that you're using the latest drivers and file systems available. The new Web-based service scans your system to determine what hardware and software you have installed, and then compares that information to a back-end database to determine whether newer drivers or system files are available. If there are newer drivers or system files, the service can automatically install the drivers.

WINDOWS 2000

Released in early 2000, Windows 2000 is the successor to Windows NT and is intended for high-end business workstations and servers. Windows 2000 is a true 32-bit operating system (no DOS support) and also contains code to support 64-bit operations. Windows 2000 is divided into four versions targeted for different workplace requirements. Windows 2000 Professional is intended for desktop or workstation use and replaces Windows NT Workstation in the Microsoft product line. Windows 2000 Server Standard Edition supercedes NT Server and is intended for use in general-purpose network server environments, such as found in small- to medium-sized businesses. Windows 2000 Advanced Server is intended for use in mission-critical environments of any medium- to large-sized business, including Internet Service Providers (ISPs). These last two versions replace Windows NT Server and Windows NT Server Enterprise Edition. A third (even more powerful) server version named Windows 2000 Datacenter Server was released in mid-2000.

The publicized goal of Microsoft is eventually to integrate the personal (Windows 98/Me) and business (Windows 2000) versions of Windows into a single product line (code-named "XP"), with every version using the same basic OS files. Windows 98, including Second Edition and any other improvements, may be the last Windows OS able to run 16-bit and DOS programs.

Windows 2000 Professional includes all the features of Windows NT Workstation with numerous additions and improvements. The added features are meant to combine the ease of use of Windows 98 with the stability, speed, and security of Windows NT. Many of the improvements are listed here:

- **64-bit ready**   Microsoft has enabled the Windows 2000 code base to be 64-bit ready and is working toward delivering a full-featured 64-bit OS in the future (this will be fully compatible with existing 32-bit applications). The goal is to take full advantage of Intel's 64-bit "Itanium" processor when it is released.

- **Active Directory**   This is the integral directory service within Windows 2000. This service improves manageability, enables security, and extends the compatibility between Windows 2000 and other operating systems.

- **Group Policy**   Group Policy allows an administrator to define and control the state of computers and/or users in an organization. The effect of Group Policy may be adjusted using memberships in security groups.

■ **Hardware wizard**   This wizard gives you a single, simple interface for dealing with many hardware issues. The options include the ability to add, configure, remove, troubleshoot and upgrade the peripherals that you use.

■ **Index Server**   This utility runs in the background and creates an index of the contents of the local hard drive or files on a network (if connected). It includes the ability to select what directories and file properties to index. Index Server can operate locally or across a network to improve speed and accuracy, and search results can be ranked according to relevance.

■ **Intellimirror desktop management**   This feature allows users to work at any station on a network and maintain their personal desktop settings, application data, and documents. Intellimirror gives administrators the ability to automatically distribute software (including remote OS installation). Administrators can also remotely control desktop configuration and maintenance.

■ **Internet Explorer 5.x**   The latest Microsoft browser is fully integrated in the Windows 2000 Professional edition.

■ **Network Connections wizard**   A Network Connections folder in My Computer replaces the Network Settings item in the NT 4.0 Control Panel. Clicking on the Make New Connection icon opens Windows 2000's Network Connection wizard. The wizard guides you through fewer steps than were required in NT 4.0 to create a new connection. When used with Windows 2000 Server's Active Directory, the OS also adds a series of new management functions designed to simplify running a network.

■ **Open/Save/Save As dialog boxes**   Windows 2000 provides an Outlook-like directory tree displayed to the left of the Open or Save dialog box, allowing for quick and easy navigation to different folders on the hard drive.

■ **Personalized Start menu**   Windows 2000 tracks programs and files launched from Start | Programs. After the first six sessions, it alters the Programs menu to show just the most used items. The other entries are collapsed and available by clicking on the double arrows displayed. Windows 2000 continues to monitor file use and make adjustments to the Start menu.

■ **Plug-and-play**   Windows 2000 is compatible with current plug-and-play standards, including support for the latest busses (such as USB, IEEE 1394 or "FireWire," and AGP) and other devices, such as DVD players, scanners, and digital cameras.

■ **SMP support**   Symmetric Multiprocessing allows for multiple processors in the different versions of Windows 2000. The Professional and Standard Server editions support two processors, while the most advanced server edition can support up to eight processors.

■ **Windows 2000 Explorer**   The Explorer in Windows 2000 includes all the individual customizable features of Windows 98 Explorer. Added improvements include enabling Thumbnail View on all files instead of on a folder-by-folder basis, customized Windows Explorer toolbars, and Folder Options in Control Panel with a new streamlined Folder Options dialog box.

■ **Windows Installer**   This utility allows for easier program installation and reduces problems caused by replacing shared DLL files with different versions during the install process. Windows Installer allows applications to examine existing DLL files in order to keep common files already installed. It also allows for adding program components at a later time and can be used to repair damaged applications. Windows Installer needs cooperative applications, so software publishers must write programs with MSI scripts that take advantage of Installer features.

WINDOWS ME

Microsoft sought to solidify its hold on the home user PC market with its introduction of Windows Millennium Edition (Me) in September 2000. While benchmarking tests show no real performance advantages with Windows Me over Windows 98/SE, the update package does offer a wide range of enhancements, primarily focused on entertainment, multimedia, and home networking.

Major enhancements over Windows 98/SE include multimedia features such as an automated video editor with high-powered compression and simple import from video cameras, a wizard to automate scanner and still-image camera captures, and a media jukebox/recorder. New system-protection features include a wizard that restores an unstable system to an earlier, functional state, and new easy setup features simplify home networking and broadband access. In addition, support for the Universal Plug-and-Play specification will let Windows communicate with devices such as refrigerators and wearable computers (not that there are immediate applications for such features).

Two important changes are the removal of the standard Windows 9x option to restart or boot to the MS-DOS command prompt (though DOS applications are still usable in DOS windows), and an overhaul of Windows Internet services that improves performance. Windows Me uses the same desktop interface as Windows 2000 Professional, along with the new TCP/IP stack that connects to the Internet, but the new stack causes incompatibilities with some widely used Internet software. The help system has vastly improved troubleshooters and more informative error messages—the whole system is intended to be friendlier to experts and novices alike.

The System Restore feature backs up crucial system files when the computer is idle, making a snapshot of the system state every ten hours of computing time. Additional snapshots can be created at any time by running the System Restore wizard. If the system stops working, and if you can at least reboot (even if only in Safe mode), you can run the wizard and choose from among the earlier saved system states to restore. The current state of your documents and e-mail won't be overwritten, but the damaged system files will be overwritten with working copies. The System Restore component springs into action whenever you delete any potentially important files from the Windows or Program Files folder. For example, if you delete data from the Program Files folder, Windows will work in the background to restore the damage.

The System File Protection feature (based on the similar Windows File Protection in Windows 2000) silently prevents applications from overwriting crucial DLL files with older or nonstandard versions, and should drastically reduce the chance that a newly installed application will stop other programs from working. Users can also switch on the new AutoUpdate feature that downloads newer versions of system files in the background and then prompts you to restore them.

Multimedia

Windows Movie Maker records video from an attached camera or imports existing files, and then splits the video into clips for editing that uses technology borrowed from high-end video-editing software. Existing videos can be imported from all standard formats (except RealMedia), but can be output only in Windows Media Format, not AVI or MPEG.

The Windows Image Acquisition (WIA) feature uses a wizard interface for previewing, creating, and managing images from scanners and digital still cameras. Basic features can be used with any plug-and-play scanner, but with a WIA-compatible camera, you can preview and manage pictures without downloading them. More than 60 WIA-enabled camera models (including most released in recent months) are now on the market. The wizard runs automatically when a WIA-enabled camera is plugged into a USB port or a button is pressed on a plug-and-play scanner.

The new Windows Media Player 7 works with most standard audio and video formats, with the exception of RealMedia, and includes a Web radio tuner, a jukebox, and a file-transfer utility that copies and compresses existing files or streaming media to portable MP3 players and Windows CE devices. The interface is less convoluted than most third-party media players, but Microsoft wastes a lot of screen space in an attempt to make the Media Player look cool, and the program is more crash-prone than anything else in Windows Me.

Networking

A home networking wizard walks you through the process of setting up and customizing file, printer, and Internet sharing on a Windows Me machine connected to any peer-to-peer network. The wizard optionally creates a disk that can be used to install the Windows Me network software on other computers that you want to include on the same network, even if the other computers are running Windows 95 or 98. A new Folder Options applet in the Control Panel provides a direct route to file association and other customization features. To protect against reckless use, crucial system files cannot be viewed in Windows Explorer unless you mark a checkbox in the applet.

If you have ever installed a home network, virtual private network, or broadband software under Windows 95 or 98, you probably bumped into an error message telling you that you could use only six instances of TCP/IP. This meant that Windows 9x could connect to the Internet through no more than six networking components, and that no Internet connections were available for the new software you wanted to install. The new TCP/IP software built into Windows Me removes this limitation, and you can install as many networking features as you want without being forced to remove existing ones.

Internet Explorer 5.5 and Outlook Express 5.5 come with Windows Me, but the only notable enhancement over earlier versions is a new print preview feature in IE. NetMeeting 3.1 is also a part of the package, but its home-networking features are already available in downloadable versions.

Upgrade Recommendations

So, as a technician, should you suggest that your clients upgrade to Windows Me? While Windows Me adds a lot of tools that home users may love, the stability of Windows Me is still being addressed, and benchmark tests suggest that Windows Me is just slightly *slower* than Windows 98/SE. As a rule, wait until Windows Me has undergone some more development (and wait for one or two service packs to become available) before jumping into an upgrade from Windows 98/SE.

A Closer Look at MS-DOS

The operating system provides I/O resources to application programs, as well as an environment that can be used to execute programs or interact with the OS. To accomplish these two tasks, MS-DOS uses three files: IO.SYS, MSDOS.SYS, and COMMAND.COM. Note that the myriad other files shipped with MS-DOS technically are not part of the OS itself, but rather are a library of utilities intended to help you optimize and maintain the system. The following sections examine each of the three core MS-DOS files in more detail. Keep in mind that loading and running an OS properly relies on adequate processing, memory, and disk system resources.

 While any study of DOS files may seem obsolete today, serious system problems may require you to boot to DOS from a floppy disk or bootable CD. As a technician, you should have a brief knowledge of DOS so that you can make the most of real-mode (DOS) troubleshooting.

IO.SYS

The IO.SYS file provides many of the low-level routines (or *drivers*) that interact with BIOS. Some versions of IO.SYS are customized by original equipment manufacturers (OEMs) to supplement the particular BIOS for their system. However, OS customization is extremely rare today because it leads to system incompatibilities. In addition to low-level drivers, IO.SYS contains a system initialization routine. The entire contents of the file (except for the system initialization routine) are kept in low memory throughout system operation. IO.SYS is a file assigned with a hidden-file attribute, so you will not see the file when searching a bootable disk with an ordinary DIR command. Although Microsoft uses the file name IO.SYS, other OS makers may use a different name. For example, the corresponding file name in IBM's PC-DOS is IBMBIO.COM.

In order for a disk (floppy or hard disk) to be bootable under MS-DOS 3.x or 4.x, IO.SYS must be the first file in the disk directory, and it must occupy at least the first available cluster on the disk (usually cluster 2). This is the disk's OS volume boot sector (VBS). Of course, subsequent clusters containing IO.SYS can be placed anywhere in the disk just like any other ordinary file. MS-DOS 5.x and later versions eliminate this requirement and allow IO.SYS to be placed in any root directory location anywhere on the disk. When disk access begins during the boot process, the bootable drive's boot sector is read, which loads IO.SYS into memory and gives it control of the system. Once IO.SYS is running, the boot process can continue (as you'll learn later in this chapter). If this file is missing or corrupt, you will see some type of boot failure message, or the system may lock up.

MSDOS.SYS

This is the core of MS-DOS versions up through 6.22. The MSDOS.SYS file is listed second in the boot disk's directory, and is the second file to be loaded during the boot process. It contains the routines that handle OS disk and file access. Like IO.SYS, the MSDOS.SYS file is loaded into low memory where it resides throughout the system's operation. If the file is missing or corrupt, you will see some kind of boot failure message, or the system may lock up.

IO.SYS AND MSDOS.SYS VARIATIONS UNDER WINDOWS

With the introduction of Windows 95 (and continued with Windows 98/Me), the classical DOS files have been redesigned to streamline the boot process. Windows places all the functions found in IO.SYS and MSDOS.SYS into a single hidden file called IO.SYS (this file may be renamed WINBOOT.SYS if you start the PC with a previous OS). Most of the options formerly set with entries in the CONFIG.SYS file are now incorporated into the Windows IO.SYS file. The settings that are selected with IO.SYS can be superseded by entries in a CONFIG.SYS file, but the defaults used with IO.SYS are listed here:

dos=high	DOS components are automatically loaded into high memory.
himem.sys	The real-mode memory manager is loaded.
ifshlp.sys	The file system enhancement utility is loaded.
setver.exe	The MS-DOS version utility is loaded.
files=60	File handle buffers are allocated.
Lastdrive=z	This specifies the last drive letter available for assignment.
Buffers=30	File buffers are allocated.
stacks=9,256	Stack frames are created.
shell=command.com	This sets the desired command processor.
fcbs=4	This sets the maximum number of file control blocks.

Few of the default settings in IO.SYS are really needed by Windows, but they are included to provide a level of backward compatibility with preexisting system configurations.

The MSDOS.SYS file has also been dramatically altered under Windows. Whereas older versions of MS-DOS relied on MSDOS.SYS for disk and file code, all of that functionality has been worked into IO.SYS. MSDOS.SYS under Windows. It is now little more than a text INI file that is used to configure the boot properties of Windows and list important paths to key Windows files (including the registry).

ADJUSTING MSDOS.SYS UNDER MS-DOS 7.X

Windows essentially eliminates the function of the MSDOS.SYS file by including a text file that is used to tailor the startup process. Normally, there is little need to access the MSDOS.SYS text file, but you may be faced with the need to adjust the Windows boot process. This part of the chapter takes you inside the MSDOS.SYS file for MS-DOS 7.x (Windows 9x/Me) and illustrates the various options you can use to enhance the Windows 9x/Me platform.

One issue to remember is that some programs expect the MSDOS.SYS file to be at least 1024 bytes in length. If it is not that length, those programs may not work correctly. For example, if an antivirus program detects that the MSDOS.SYS file is less than 1024 bytes in length, the program may assume that the MSDOS.SYS file is infected with a virus. However, the version of the MSDOS.SYS file on your system may not be 1024 bytes or longer. If you use the SYS command to transfer system files from your Windows startup disk (or other boot disk) to the hard drive, the MSDOS.SYS file that is copied to the hard disk is less than 1024 bytes in length. You can edit the MSDOS.SYS file by typing the following command line:

```
C:\>attrib -s -h -r c:\msdos.sys edit c:\msdos.sys
```

Examine the MSDOS.SYS file shown in Figure 3-3 and make the following changes, if necessary:

1. Replace <Windows> with the name of the folder containing Windows (for example, C:\WINDOWS).

2. If you are using disk compression software (such as DriveSpace), change the letter in the HostWinBootDrv= line to the letter of the host drive.

3. Add the lines with all Xs to make the MSDOS.SYS file at least 1024 bytes in length.

4. Save the edited file and then exit EDIT.COM.

5. Reset the attributes of the MSDOS.SYS file by using a command line such as this:

```
C:\>attrib +s +h +r c:\msdos.sys
```

and then restart your computer.

There are two main sections to the MSDOS.SYS file: the [Paths] section defines the directory paths to major Windows file areas, and the [Options] section enables you to configure many of the available attributes used to boot a Windows 9x/Me system. The variables for these two sections are listed in Table 3-3.

```
[Paths]
WinDir=<Windows>
WinBootDir=<Windows>
HostWinBootDrv=C
[Options]
BootGUI=1
;
;Some programs on this system expect the MSDOS.SYS file to be at least
;1024 bytes in length; hence, the following lines create an MSDOS.SYS
;file that is greater than 1024 bytes in length. These lines are not
;needed for Windows to boot or run.
;xxxxxxxxxxxxxxxxxxxxxxxxxxxxxxxxxxxxxxxxxxxxxxxxxxxxxxxxxxxxxxxxa
;xxxxxxxxxxxxxxxxxxxxxxxxxxxxxxxxxxxxxxxxxxxxxxxxxxxxxxxxxxxxxxxxb
;xxxxxxxxxxxxxxxxxxxxxxxxxxxxxxxxxxxxxxxxxxxxxxxxxxxxxxxxxxxxxxxxc
;xxxxxxxxxxxxxxxxxxxxxxxxxxxxxxxxxxxxxxxxxxxxxxxxxxxxxxxxxxxxxxxxd
;xxxxxxxxxxxxxxxxxxxxxxxxxxxxxxxxxxxxxxxxxxxxxxxxxxxxxxxxxxxxxxxxe
;xxxxxxxxxxxxxxxxxxxxxxxxxxxxxxxxxxxxxxxxxxxxxxxxxxxxxxxxxxxxxxxxf
;xxxxxxxxxxxxxxxxxxxxxxxxxxxxxxxxxxxxxxxxxxxxxxxxxxxxxxxxxxxxxxxxg
;xxxxxxxxxxxxxxxxxxxxxxxxxxxxxxxxxxxxxxxxxxxxxxxxxxxxxxxxxxxxxxxxh
;xxxxxxxxxxxxxxxxxxxxxxxxxxxxxxxxxxxxxxxxxxxxxxxxxxxxxxxxxxxxxxxxi
;xxxxxxxxxxxxxxxxxxxxxxxxxxxxxxxxxxxxxxxxxxxxxxxxxxxxxxxxxxxxxxxxj
;xxxxxxxxxxxxxxxxxxxxxxxxxxxxxxxxxxxxxxxxxxxxxxxxxxxxxxxxxxxxxxxxk
;xxxxxxxxxxxxxxxxxxxxxxxxxxxxxxxxxxxxxxxxxxxxxxxxxxxxxxxxxxxxxxxxl
;xxxxxxxxxxxxxxxxxxxxxxxxxxxxxxxxxxxxxxxxxxxxxxxxxxxxxxxxxxxxxxxxm
;xxxxxxxxxxxxxxxxxxxxxxxxxxxxxxxxxxxxxxxxxxxxxxxxxxxxxxxxxxxxxxxxn
;xxxxxxxxxxxxxxxxxxxxxxxxxxxxxxxxxxxxxxxxxxxxxxxxxxxxxxxxxxxxxxxxo
;xxxxxxxxxxxxxxxxxxxxxxxxxxxxxxxxxxxxxxxxxxxxxxxxxxxxxxxxxxxxxxxxp
;xxxxxxxxxxxxxxxxxxxxxxxxxxxxxxxxxxxxxxxxxxxxxxxxxxxxxxxxxxxxxxxxq
;xxxxxxxxxxxxxxxxxxxxxxxxxxxxxxxxxxxxxxxxxxxxxxxxxxxxxxxxxxxxxxxxr
;xxxxxxxxxxxxxxxxxxxxxxxxxxxxxxxxxxxxxxxxxxxxxxxxxxxxxxxxxxxxxxxxs
```

FIGURE 3-3   An example of the MSDOS.SYS text file under Windows

If Windows 95 is installed in its own directory, the earlier version of MS-DOS is preserved on the hard disk. If you set BootMulti=1 in MSDOS.SYS, you can start the earlier version of MS-DOS by pressing F4 when starting Windows 95. Windows 98 offers the same feature.

COMMAND.COM

The COMMAND.COM file serves as the MS-DOS shell and command processor. This is the program that you are interacting with at the command-line prompt. COMMAND.COM is the third file loaded when a PC boots, and it is stored in low memory along with IO.SYS and MSDOS.SYS. The number of commands that you have available depends on the version of MS-DOS in use. MS-DOS uses two types of commands in normal operation: resident and transient.

TABLE 3-3   THE VARIABLES USED IN THE MSDOS.SYS FILE

[Paths]

WinDir=	Indicates the location of the Windows 9x directory specified during setup.
WinBootDir=	Indicates the location of the necessary startup files. The default is the directory specified during the setup process (C:\WINDOWS).
HostWinBootDrv=c	Indicates the location of the boot drive root directory.

[Options]

BootMulti=	Enables dual-boot capabilities. The default is 0. Setting this value to 1 enables the user to start MS-DOS by pressing F4, or by pressing F8 to use the Windows Startup menu.
BootGUI=	Enables automatic graphical startup into Windows 9x. The default is 1.
BootMenu=	Enables automatic display of the Windows 9x Startup menu (the user must press F8 in Windows 95, or press and hold the CTRL key in Windows 98 to see the menu). The default is 0. Setting this value to 1 eliminates the need to press F8 to see the menu.
BootKeys=	Enables the startup option keys (F5, F6, and F8). The default is 1.
BootWin=	Enables Windows 9x as the default OS. Setting this value to 0 disables Windows 9x as the default (useful only with MS-DOS version 5 or 6.x on the computer). The default is 1.
BootDelay=n	Sets the initial startup delay to n seconds (default is 2). A BootKeys=0 entry disables the delay. The only purpose of the delay is to give the user sufficient time to press F8 after the "Starting Windows" message appears.
BootFailSafe=	Enables Safe mode for system startup. The default is 0.
BootMenuDefault=#	Sets the default menu item on the Windows Startup menu; the default is 3 for a computer with no networking components, and 4 for a networked computer.
BootMenuDelay=#	Sets the number of seconds to display the Windows Startup menu before running the default menu item. The default is 30 seconds.
Logo=	Enables display of the Windows 9x logo. The default is 1. Setting this value to 0 also avoids hooking a variety of interrupts that can create incompatibilities with certain memory managers from other vendors.
BootWarn=	Enables the Safe mode startup warning. The default is 1.
DblSpace=	Enables automatic loading of DBLSPACE.BIN. The default is 1.
DrvSpace=	Enables automatic loading of DRVSPACE.BIN. The default is 1.
DoubleBuffer=	Enables loading of a double-buffering driver for a SCSI controller. The default is 0. Setting this value to 1 enables double-buffering (if required by the SCSI controller).
LoadTop=	Enables the loading of COMMAND.COM or DRVSPACE.BIN at the top of 640KB memory. The default is 1. Set this value to 0 with Novell NetWare or any software that makes assumptions about what is used in specific memory areas.
Network=	Enables "Safe Mode with Networking" as a menu option. The default is 1 for computers with networking installed. This value should be 0 if network software components are not installed.

Resident commands (also called *internal commands*) are procedures that are coded directly into COMMAND.COM. As a result, resident commands execute almost immediately when called from the command line. CLS and DIR are two typical resident commands. *Transient commands* (also called *external commands*) represent a broader and more powerful group of commands. However, transient commands are not loaded with COMMAND.COM. Instead, the commands are available as small COM or EXE utility files in the DOS directory (such as DEBUG and EMM386). Transient commands must be loaded from the disk and executed each time they are needed. By pulling out complex commands as separate utilities, the size of COMMAND.COM can be kept relatively small.

RECOGNIZING AND DEALING WITH OS PROBLEMS

Since the operating system is an integral part of the PC, any problems with using or upgrading the OS can adversely affect system operation. Software does not fail like hardware—once software is loaded and running, it will not eventually break down from heat or physical stress. Unfortunately, software is hardly perfect. Upgrading from one OS to another can upset the system's operation, and *bugs* in the OS can result in an unforeseen operation that might totally destroy a system's reliability.

Virtually all versions of operating systems have bugs in them, especially in early releases. In most cases, such bugs are found in the transient commands that are run from the command line rather than in the three core files (IO.SYS, MSDOS.SYS, and COMMAND.COM). Even the latest stand-alone version of MD-DOS (6.22) has endured several incarnations since its initial release as 6.0. As a technician, you should be sensitive to the version of DOS (and Windows) being used by your customer. Whenever the customer complains of trouble using a DOS utility (such as BACKUP or EMM386) or of difficulties using particular software under DOS, one of your first steps should be to ensure that the version in use is appropriate. If it has been updated, you should try the new release. Remember that a software fault can manifest itself as a hardware problem—that is, the hardware may malfunction or refuse to respond. Check with the OS maker to find its newest releases and fixes. Microsoft maintains an extensive Web site for the support of its operating systems. Check in regularly to find error reports and upgrades. If your customer is using Windows 98, check the Windows Help file for a troubleshooter that deals with the error or the device that is causing the problem.

Another concern for technicians is dealing with old versions of an OS. Remember that part of the task of an OS is to manage system resources (disk space, memory, and so on). New OS versions such as MS-DOS 5.0 and later do a much better job of disk and memory management than MS-DOS 4.x and earlier. Should you recommend an upgrade to your customer? As a general rule, any MS-DOS version older than 5.0 is worth upgrading to MS-DOS 6.22, especially if your customer is planning to keep or upgrade the PC. If the MS-DOS version is 5.0 or later, the only good reason to upgrade would be to take advantage of advanced utilities such as MemMaker or DoubleSpace, which have been refined and included with MS-DOS 6.22. If the PC hardware will support an upgrade to Windows 95 or Windows 98, it should also be considered as a potential OS upgrade.

The Boot Process

Computer initialization is a *process,* not an event. From the moment power is applied until the system sits idle at the command-line prompt or graphical desktop, the PC boot process is a sequence of predictable steps that verifies the system and prepares it for operation. By understanding each step in system initialization, you can develop a real appreciation for the way that hardware and software relate to one another. You also stand a much better chance of identifying and resolving problems when a system fails to boot properly. This part of the chapter provides a step-by-step review of a typical PC boot process.

APPLYING POWER

PC initialization starts when you turn on the system. When all output voltages from the power supply are valid, the supply generates a Power Good (PG) logic signal. It can take between 100ms and 500ms for the supply to generate a PG signal. When the motherboard timer chip receives the PG signal, the timer stops forcing a Reset signal to the CPU. At this point, the CPU starts processing.

THE BOOTSTRAP

The very first operation performed by a CPU is to fetch an instruction from address FFFF:0000h. Since this address is almost at the end of available ROM space, the instruction is almost always a jump command (JMP) followed by the actual BIOS ROM starting address. By making all CPUs start at the same point, the BIOS ROM can then send program control anywhere in the particular ROM (and each ROM *is* usually different). This initial search of address FFFF:0000h and the subsequent redirection of the CPU is traditionally referred to as the *bootstrap,* because the PC "pulls itself up by its bootstraps," or gets itself going. Today, we have shortened the term to *boot* and have broadened its meaning to include the entire initialization process.

CORE TESTS

The core tests are part of the overall power-on self-test (POST) sequence, which is the most important use of a system BIOS during initialization. As you might expect, allowing the system to initialize and run with flaws in the motherboard, memory, or drive systems can have catastrophic consequences for files in memory or on disk. To ensure system integrity, a set of hardware-specific self-test routines checks the major motherboard components and identifies the presence of any other specialized BIOS chips in the system (drive controller BIOS, video BIOS, SCSI BIOS, and so on).

BIOS starts with a test of the motherboard hardware, such as the CPU, math coprocessor, timer chips, direct memory access (DMA) controllers, and interrupt (IRQ) controllers. If an error is detected in this early phase of testing, a series of beeps (or *beep codes*) are produced. By knowing the BIOS manufacturer and the beep code, you can determine the nature of the problem. Chapter 18 deals with beep and error codes in more detail. Beep codes are used because the video system has not been initialized.

Next, BIOS looks for the presence of a video ROM from memory location C000:0000h through C780:000h. In just about all systems, the search will reveal a video BIOS ROM on a video adapter board plugged into an available expansion slot. If a video BIOS is found, its contents are evaluated with a checksum test. If the test is successful, control is transferred to the video BIOS, which loads and initializes the video adapter. When initialization is complete, you see a cursor on the screen, and control returns to the system BIOS. When no external video adapter BIOS is located, the system BIOS provides an initialization routine for the motherboard's video adapter, and a cursor also appears. Once the video system initializes, you are likely to see a bit of text on the display identifying the system or video BIOS ROM maker and revision level. If the checksum test fails, you will see an error message such as "C000 ROM Error" or "Video ROM Error." Initialization will usually halt right there.

Now that the video system is ready, system BIOS will scan memory from C800:0000h through DF80:0000h in 2KB increments to search for any other ROMs that might be on other adapter cards in the system. If other ROMs are found, their contents are tested and run. As each supplemental ROM is executed, it will show manufacturer and revision ID information. In some cases, a supplemental (or *adapter*) ROM may alter an existing BIOS ROM routine. For example, an Ultra DMA/100 drive controller board with its own on-board ROM will replace the motherboard's older drive routines. When a ROM fails the checksum test, you will see an error message such as "XXXX ROM Error." The XXXX indicates the segment address where the faulty ROM was detected. When a faulty ROM is detected, system initialization will usually halt.

POST

BIOS then checks the memory location at 0000:0472h. This address contains a flag that determines whether the initialization is a cold start (power first applied) or a warm start (reset button or CTRL-ALT-DEL key combination). A value of 1234h at this address indicates a warm start, in which case the POST routine is skipped. If any other value is found at that location, a cold start is assumed, and the full POST routine will be executed.

The full POST checks many of the other higher-level functions on the motherboard, memory, keyboard, video adapter, floppy drive, math coprocessor, printer port, serial port, hard drive, and other subsystems. Dozens of tests are performed by the POST. When an error is encountered, the single-byte POST code is written to I/O port 80h, where it may be read by a POST code reader. In other cases, you may see an error message on the display (and system initialization will halt). Keep in mind that POST codes and their meanings will vary slightly between BIOS manufacturers. If the POST completes successfully, the system will respond with a single beep from the speaker. Chapter 18 covers I/O port POST codes.

FINDING THE OS

The system now needs to load an operating system (usually DOS or Windows 9x). The first step here is to have the BIOS search for a DOS VBS on the A: drive. If there is no disk in the drive, you will see the drive light illuminate briefly, and then BIOS will search the next drive in the boot order (usually drive C:). If there is a disk in drive A:, BIOS will load sector 1 (head 0 cylinder 0) from the disk's DOS VBS into memory starting at 0000:7C00h. There are a number of potential problems when attempting to load the VBS. Otherwise, the first program in the directory (IO.SYS) will begin to load, followed by MSDOS.SYS.

- If the first byte of the DOS VBS is less than 06h (or if the first byte is greater than or equal to 06h, and the next nine words of the sector contain the same data pattern), you will see an error message similar to "Diskette boot record error."

- If IO.SYS and MSDOS.SYS are not the first two files in the directory (or some other problem is encountered in loading), you'll see an error such as "Non-system disk or disk error."

- If the boot sector on the floppy disk is corrupt and cannot be read (DOS 3.3 or earlier), you'll probably get a "Disk boot failure" message.

If the OS cannot be loaded from any floppy drive, the system will search the first fixed drive (hard drive). Hard drives are a bit more involved than floppy drives. BIOS loads sector 1 (head 0 cylinder 0) from the hard drive's master partition boot sector (called the *master boot sector,* or *MBS*) into memory starting at 0000:7C00h, and the last two bytes of the sector are checked. If the final two bytes of the master partition boot sector are not 55h and AAh, respectively, the boot sector is invalid; you will see an error message similar to "No boot device available," and system initialization will halt. Other systems may depict the error differently or attempt to load ROM BASIC. If the BIOS attempts to load ROM BASIC, and there is no such feature in the BIOS, you'll see a "ROM BASIC error" message.

Otherwise, the disk will search for and identify any extended partitions (up to 24 total partitions). Once any extended partitions have been identified, the drive's original boot sector will search for a boot indicator byte marking a partition as active and bootable. If none of the partitions is marked as bootable (or if more than one partition is marked as bootable), a disk error message will be displayed, such as "Invalid partition table." Some older BIOS versions may attempt to load ROM BASIC, but will generate an error message in most cases anyway.

When an active bootable partition is found in the master partition boot sector, the DOS VBS from the bootable partition is loaded into memory and tested. If the DOS VBS cannot be read, you will see an error message similar to "Error loading operating system." When the DOS VBS *does* load, the last two bytes are tested for a signature of 55h and AAh, respectively. If these signature bytes are missing, you will see an error message such as "Missing operating system." Under either error condition, system initialization will halt.

After the signature bytes are identified, the DOS VBS (now in memory) is executed as if it were a program. This "program" checks the root directory to ensure that IO.SYS and MSDOS.SYS (or IBMBIO.COM and IBMDOS.COM) are available. In older MS-DOS versions, IO.SYS and MSDOS.SYS have to be the first two directory entries. If the DOS VBS was created with MS-DOS 3.3 or earlier, and the two startup files are not the first two files in the directory (or there is an error in loading the files), the system will produce an error code such as "Non-System disk or disk error." If the boot sector is corrupt, you may see a message like "Disk boot failure."

LOADING THE OS

If no problems are detected in the disk's DOS VBS, IO.SYS (or IBMBIO.COM) is loaded and executed. If Windows 98/Me is on the system, IO.SYS may be renamed WINBOOT.SYS, which will be executed instead. IO.SYS contains extensions to BIOS that start low-level device drivers for such things as the keyboard, printer, and block devices. Remember that IO.SYS also contains initialization code that is only needed during system startup. A copy of this initialization code is placed at the top of conventional memory, which takes over initialization. The next step is to load MSDOS.SYS (or IBMDOS.COM), which is loaded such that it overlaps the part of IO.SYS containing the initialization code. MSDOS.SYS (the MS-DOS kernel) is then executed to initialize base device drivers, detect system status, reset the disk system, initialize devices such as the printer and serial port, and set up system default parameters. The MS-DOS essentials are now loaded, and control returns to the IO.SYS/WINBOOT.SYS initialization code in memory.

Remember that for Windows 9x/Me systems, IO.SYS (or WINBOOT.SYS) combines the functions of IO.SYS and MSDOS.SYS.

ESTABLISHING THE ENVIRONMENT

If a CONFIG.SYS file is present, it is opened and read by IO.SYS/WINBOOT.SYS. The DEVICE statements are processed first in the order they appear, and then INSTALL statements are processed in the order they appear. A SHELL statement is handled next. If no SHELL statement is present, the COMMAND.COM processor is loaded. When COMMAND.COM is loaded, it overwrites the initialization code left over from IO.SYS (which is now no longer needed). Under Windows 9x/Me, COMMAND.COM is loaded only if an AUTOEXEC.BAT file is present to process the AUTOEXEC.BAT statements. Finally, all other statements in CONFIG.SYS are processed, and WINBOOT.SYS also looks for the SYSTEM.DAT registry file.

When an AUTOEXEC.BAT file is present, COMMAND.COM (which now has control of the system) will load and execute the batch file. After batch file processing is complete, the familiar DOS prompt will appear. If no AUTOEXEC.BAT file is in the root directory, COMMAND.COM will request the current DATE and TIME, and then show the DOS prompt. You may now launch applications or use any available OS commands. AUTOEXEC.BAT may also call a shell (such as Windows 3.1x) or start an application. Under Windows 9x/Me, IO.SYS/WINBOOT.SYS automatically loads HIMEM.SYS, IFSHLP.SYS, and SETVER.EXE, and then loads the WIN.COM kernel to officially start Windows.

Creating a DOS Boot Disk

The most persistent problem with PC troubleshooting is that booting a system successfully can be difficult, especially if there are hard drive problems. Thus, it is particularly important to have a bootable floppy disk on hand. There are two means of creating a boot disk: automatically through an existing Windows 9x/Me platform, or manually through a DOS 6.22 platform. In either case, you need access to a running PC with an OS similar to the version you plan to install on the new PC (or that is already installed on the suspect PC).

WINDOWS 9X/ME

Windows 95 and Windows 98 come with an automatic Startup Disk maker. If you have access to a Windows 9x system, use the following procedure to create a DOS 7.x startup disk:

1. Label a blank diskette and insert it into your floppy drive.

2. Click on Start | Settings | Control Panel.

3. Double-click on the Add/Remove Programs icon.

4. Select the Startup Disk tab.

5. Click on Create Disk.

6. The utility will remind you to insert a diskette, and then prepare the disk automatically. When the preparation is complete, test the disk.

The preparation process takes several minutes, and the Windows 95 creation process will copy the following files to your disk: ATTRIB, CHKDSK, COMMAND, DEBUG, DRVSPACE.BIN, EDIT, FDISK, FORMAT, REGEDIT, SCANDISK, SYS, and UNINSTAL. All of these files are DOS 7.x–based files, so you can run them from the A: prompt. Other versions of Windows will copy different suites of files to the disk.

The startup disk made with the Windows 98 Startup Disk utility is much more powerful and useful. The major difference between the disk made by Windows 95 and the one made by Windows 98 is that the Windows 98 disk includes the generic drivers for your CD-ROM. If you want a Windows 95 startup disk with CD-ROM support, you have to create CONFIG.SYS and AUTOEXEC.BAT files and add the real-mode (DOS) drivers yourself. In addition, Windows 98 compresses a lot of utilities into a CAB file, EBD.CAB. Windows 98 creates a Ramdrive in memory and then expands the files in EBD.CAB to the Ramdrive. Without the compressed file, there would not be enough room on a single floppy disk to contain all the startup files, drivers, and utilities.

The early Windows 95 FDISK utility reportedly has a bug that can cause problems when creating more than one partition on the same drive. Later releases of Windows 95 (such as OSR 2) claim to have corrected this issue, but if you encounter problems with FDISK, use the version with Windows 98/Me.

DOS 6.22

If you don't have access to a system with Windows 9x/Me already, you need to make a boot disk manually, using DOS 6.22 utilities. Create a bootable diskette by using the SYS feature, as shown here:

```
C:\DOS\> SYS A:    <Enter>
```

or use the FORMAT command to make a bootable diskette, like this:

```
C:\DOS\> FORMAT A: /S    <Enter>
```

Once the disk is bootable, copy the following DOS utilities (usually from the DOS directory): FDISK, FORMAT, SYS, MEM, DEFRAG, SCANDISK, EDIT, HIMEM, EMM386, and EDIT. You may not need all of these utilities, but it can be handy to have them accessible in case you need to check a disk or memory.

Windows 9x/Me Maintenance Tips

Although troubleshooting individual devices and subsystems is covered in their respective chapters, it is useful to note some general setup and maintenance issues with Windows 9x/Me here. A careful installation followed by a routine maintenance schedule will prevent a lot of problems for you and your customers.

Under Windows 9x, for example, the SETUP.TXT file in the \Win9x folder on your Windows 9x CD contains an extensive list of setup error messages, problems, and resolutions. Most problems occur when upgrading an existing system that has numerous peripherals and programs already installed. This increases the chances for conflicts, setup errors, and failures. Upgrading or installing a new operating system over an old one also increases the chances for an error. If you have trouble installing Windows as an upgrade, you may need to consider installing the full version from scratch.

The SETUP.TXT file also contains directions on how to prepare the computer system for Windows 9x installation. The idea is to *simplify* the system hardware and software as much as possible before installing Windows 9x. The best way to avoid setup errors and achieve a good installation is to start with a freshly formatted hard drive on a system with as few peripherals attached as possible. This is generally referred to as a *clean* install. You can follow this policy even with the "Upgrade" version of Windows 98/SE (simply run Setup on the freshly formatted hard drive and insert your Windows 95 CD when the Setup program requests proof of ownership for a pervious version of Windows).

Once Windows 9x/Me is installed and operating smoothly, it's a good idea to set up a regular schedule for the maintenance programs included with Windows. The basic maintenance programs included with Windows 9x/Me are ScanDisk and Disk Defragmenter (a.k.a. Defrag). Running these programs on a regular basis can prevent some file system problems, and warn you far enough in advance of more serious problems to give you time to catch and fix the trouble before permanent data loss occurs.

ScanDisk can be run in Standard or Thorough mode. Standard mode checks files and folders for errors. Thorough mode adds an extensive check of the hard disk surface to the file and folder check, so Thorough testing requires a great deal more time than Standard testing. This should be scheduled at a time when the computer is not in use (any activity on the drive being scanned will cause ScanDisk to restart the file and folder check). After ten restarts, ScanDisk stops and a dialog box asks if you want to continue, so it is best to run a Thorough test when nothing will cause restarts.

 You might need the Windows Plus pack or another utility to schedule running programs under Windows 95.

Windows 98/Me includes a third general maintenance utility named Disk Cleanup, which finds and removes useless files that accumulate over time, such as TMP temp files, Internet Cache files, and other unnecessary program files. Windows 98/Me allows you to schedule these and other programs to run at any time you set. You can use Maintenance wizard or Scheduled Tasks to establish a suite of regular maintenance times and help keep the computer systems under your supervision running smoothly. Preventive maintenance is a good way to establish a reputation of reliability.

Further Study

IBM   www-4.ibm.com/software/os/warp/

Linux Online   www.linux.org/

Linux Resources   www.linuxrx.com/

Microsoft Support   support.microsoft.com/support/

Microsoft Troubleshooters   support.microsoft.com/support/tshoot/

Novell   www.novell.com

V Communications (System Commander)   www.v-com.com

Windows Home Page   www.microsoft.com/windows/default.asp

Yahoo (Operating Systems)   dir.yahoo.com/computers_and_internet/software/operating_systems/

4

ARRANGING THE PRESERVICE CHECKOUT

As a professional PC technician, you must understand one basic rule of business: time is money. Whether you're the boss or work for someone else, the ability to identify and isolate a PC or peripheral fault quickly and decisively is a critical element to your success. It requires a keen eye, some common sense, and a bit of intuition. It also requires an understanding of the troubleshooting process and a reliable plan of action, because even though the number of PC configurations and setups is virtually unlimited, the methodology used to approach each repair is always about the same. This chapter illustrates the concepts of basic troubleshooting and shows you how to apply a suite of cause-and-effect relationships that will help you narrow down the problem before you even take a screwdriver to the enclosure. By applying a consistent technique, you can shave precious time from every repair.

The Universal Troubleshooting Process

Regardless of how complex your particular computer or peripheral device may be, a dependable trouble-shooting procedure can be broken down into four basic steps, as illustrated in Figure 4-1: define your symptoms, identify and isolate the potential source (or location) of your problem, repair or replace the suspected subassembly, and retest the unit thoroughly to be sure that you have solved the problem. If you have not solved the problem, start again from step 1. This procedure isn't limited to troubleshooting PC equipment, but rather is a universal procedure that you can apply to *any* sort of troubleshooting.

DEFINE YOUR SYMPTOMS

When a PC breaks down, the cause may be as simple as a loose wire or connector, or as complicated as a chip or subassembly failure. Before you open your toolbox, you must have a firm understanding of all the symptoms. Think about the symptoms carefully and consider questions such as these:

■ Is the disk, CD, or tape inserted properly?

■ Is the power or activity LED lit?

■ Does this problem occur only when the computer is tapped or moved?

By recognizing and understanding your PC's symptoms, tracing a problem to the appropriate assembly or component may be much easier. Take the time to write down as many symptoms as you can. This note taking may seem tedious now, but once you have begun your repair, a written record of symptoms and circumstances will help to keep you focused on the task at hand. This list will also help to jog your

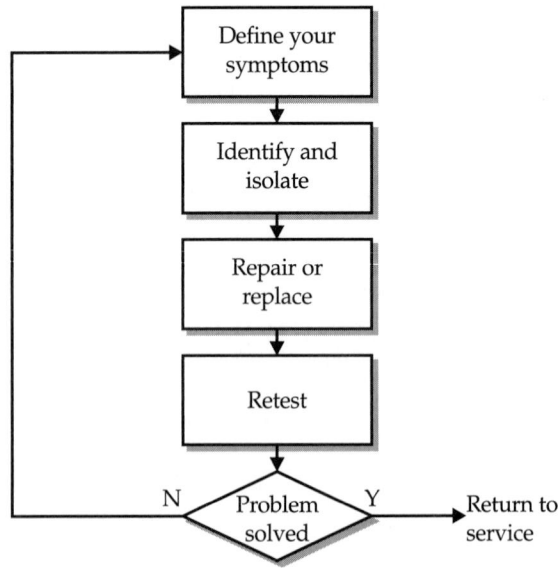

FIGURE 4-1   The universal troubleshooting process

memory if you must explain the symptoms to someone else at a later date. As a professional trouble-shooter, you must often log problems or otherwise document your activities anyway.

IDENTIFY AND ISOLATE

Before you try to isolate a problem within a piece of computer hardware, you must first be sure that the equipment itself is causing the problem. In many circumstances, this will be fairly obvious, but you may encounter situations in which the cause appears ambiguous (for example, there is no power, no DOS prompt, and so on). Always remember that a PC operates because of an intimate mingling of hardware and software. A faulty or improperly configured piece of software can cause confusing system errors. Chapter 3 touched on just a few of the problems that operating systems can encounter.

When you're confident that the failure lies in your system's hardware, you can begin to identify possible problem areas. Since this book is designed to deal with subassembly troubleshooting, start your diagnostics there. The troubleshooting procedures throughout this book will guide you through the major sections of today's popular PC components and peripherals, and aid you in deciding which subassembly may be at fault. When you have identified a potential problem area, you can begin the actual repair process and swap the suspect subassembly.

REPAIR OR REPLACE

Since computers and their peripherals are designed as collections of subassemblies, it is almost always easier to replace a subassembly outright than to attempt to troubleshoot the subassembly to its component level. Even if you had the necessary time, documentation, and test equipment to isolate a defective component, many complex parts are proprietary, so it is highly unlikely that you would be able to obtain replacement components without a significant hassle. The labor and frustration factor involved in such an endeavor is often more expensive than replacing the entire subassembly to begin with. On the other hand, manufacturers and their distributors often stock a selection of subassemblies and supplies. Keep in mind that you may need to know the manufacturer's part number for the subassembly in order to obtain a new one.

During a repair, you may reach a roadblock that requires you to leave your equipment for a day or two, or maybe longer. This generally happens after an order has been placed for new parts, and you are waiting for those parts to come in. Make it a point to reassemble your system as much as possible before leaving it. Gather any loose parts in plastic bags, seal them shut, and mark them clearly. If you are working with electronic circuitry, make sure to use good-quality antistatic boxes or bags for storage. Partial reassembly (combined with careful notes) will help you remember how the unit goes together later on.

Another problem with the fast technological progress we enjoy is that parts rarely stay on the shelf long. That high-performance video card you bought last year is no longer available, is it? How about that 10x CD-ROM drive you put in some time back? Today there's something newer and faster in its place. When a PC fails and you need to replace a broken device, chances are that you'll need to upgrade simply because you cannot obtain an identical replacement device. From this standpoint, upgrading is often a proxy of troubleshooting and repair.

RETEST

When a repair is finally complete, the system must be reassembled carefully before testing it. All guards, housings, cables, and shields must be replaced before final testing. If symptoms persist, you will have to reevaluate the symptoms and narrow the problem to another part of the equipment. If normal operation is restored (or greatly improved), test the computer's various functions. When you can verify that your symptoms have stopped during actual operation, the equipment may be returned to service. As a general rule, it is wise to let the system run for at least 24 hours to ensure that the replacement subassembly will not fail prematurely. This is known as letting the system *burn-in*. Burn-in can usually be accomplished by leaving the system idle (and retesting various functions periodically). However, you can use various benchmark and burn-in software utilities to stress various parts of the system before returning it to service. PassMark BurnIn Test 2.2 (Figure 4-2) is one such burn-in utility (**www.passmark.com/**).

Don't be discouraged if the equipment still malfunctions. Perhaps you missed a jumper setting. Maybe software settings and device drivers must be updated to accommodate the replacement subassembly. If you get stuck, simply walk away, clear your head, and start again by defining your current symptoms. Never continue with a repair if you are tired or frustrated—tomorrow is another day, and even the most experienced troubleshooters get overwhelmed from time to time. You should also realize that there may be more than one bad assembly to deal with. Remember that a PC is just a collection of assemblies, and each assembly is a collection of parts. Normally, everything works together, but when one assembly fails, it may cause one or more interconnected assemblies to fail as well.

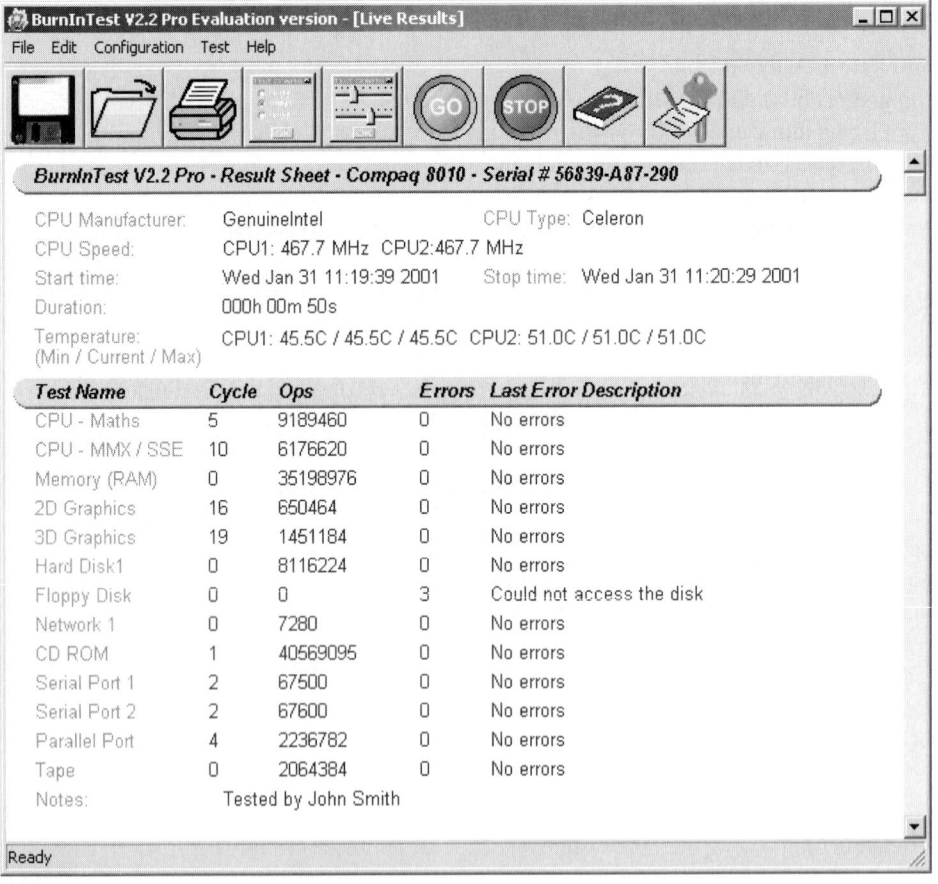

FIGURE 4-2   Typical PassMark BurnIn 2.2 test results

DOCUMENT YOUR WORK

Documentation is another important practice that is frequently overlooked. When you perform a successful repair, you should take some time to record your findings and solutions on paper. This is a habit that takes time and discipline to develop, but it's well worth the trouble. You can refer to your notes for future repairs, possibly saving hours of trial and error. Notes can also be an invaluable asset to other technicians faced with problems that you have already learned how to resolve.

THE SPARE PARTS DILEMMA

Once a problem is isolated, technicians face another problem: the availability of spare parts. Novice technicians often ask what kinds and quantity of spare parts they should keep on hand. The best answer to give here is, simply, none at all. The reason for this somewhat drastic answer is best explained by the two realities of modern PC service: parts are always changing, and inventory costs money.

Parts Are Always Changing

After more than 20 years, the PC is in its eighth generation, with processors such as the AMD Athlon and Pentium 4. As a result, a new generation matures every 24 to 36 months (although the newer generations have been arriving in 18 to 24 months). Even standardized products such as CD-ROM/R/RW and DVD drives have proliferated in different speeds and versions (for example, CD-ROM drives can be found at speeds as high as 50x). Once production stops for a drive or board, stock rarely remains for very long. Thus, even if you know what the problem is, the chances of locating an exact replacement part are often quite slim if the part is over two years old. Note the word "exact"—this is the magic word in PC repair, and is the reason why so many repairs involve an upgrade. For example, why replace a failed EGA board with another EGA board when you can install a state-of-the-art video card (which is typically fully compatible) for the same price or less? Choosing the right parts to stock is like hitting a moving target, so don't bother.

Inventory Costs Money

Financial considerations also play a big role in choosing parts. For computer enthusiasts or novice technicians just tinkering in their spare time, the expense and space demands required for inventory are simply out of the question. For more serious repair businesses, the expense of inventory can burden the bottom line. And what happens if you don't actually use a part? After a while, you're stuck with an "antique." The economics of inventory are further complicated by razor-thin profit margins and the proliferation of sub-$1000 PCs that are often not worth putting additional money into.

A Better Strategy

Unless you're in the business of selling replacement parts and upgrade components, don't waste your money and space stocking parts that are going to be obsolete in less than 24 months. Rather than worry about stocking parts yourself, work to cultivate new vendors and develop your contacts with computer parts stores and superstores that specialize in PC parts and subassemblies. Let them stock the parts for you. Since parts stores generally have an inside line with distributors and manufacturers, parts that they do not stock can often be ordered for you. Even many reputable mail-order firms can provide parts in under 48 hours with today's delivery services.

Benchmarking the PC

We all know that today's personal computers are capable of astounding performance (if you doubt that, consider any popular 3D game like Quake III or Unreal). However, it is often important to *quantify* the performance of a system. Just saying that a PC is "faster" than another system is simply not enough. Technicians often must apply a number to that performance, against which to measure the impact of improvements offered by an upgrade or to objectively compare the performance of various systems. *Benchmarks* are used to test and report the performance of a PC by running a set of well-defined tasks on the system. A benchmark program has several different uses in the PC industry depending on what your needs are:

- **System comparisons** Benchmarks are often used to compare a system to one or more competing machines (or to compare a newer system to older machines). Just flip through any issue of *PC Magazine* or *PC World* and you'll see a flurry of PC ads all quoting numerical performance numbers backed up by benchmarks. You may also run a benchmark to establish the overall performance of a new system before making a purchase decision.

- **Upgrade improvements** Benchmarks are frequently used to gauge the value of an upgrade. By running the benchmark before and after the upgrade process, you can get a numerical assessment of just how much that new CPU, RAM, drive, or motherboard may have improved (or hindered) system performance. For example, if a system scores a benchmark of 1,000 before a video card upgrade, and then scores a 1,250 after the video card upgrade, you know the upgrade improved performance by 25 percent.

- **Diagnostics** Benchmarks sometimes have a role in system diagnostics. Systems that are performing poorly can be benchmarked as key components are checked or reconfigured. This helps the technician isolate and correct performance problems far more reliably than using just simple visual observations.

AVOIDING BENCHMARK PROBLEMS

One of the most serious problems encountered with benchmarks is the integrity of their numbers. You've probably heard that "statistics can lie," and the same thing is true of benchmarks. You must apply benchmarks objectively and consistently for them to be useful. In order for benchmarks to provide you with reliable results, you must take certain precautions:

- *Note the complete system configuration.* When you run a benchmark and achieve a result, be sure to note the entire system configuration (CPU, RAM, cache, OS version, and so on). A benchmark may yield vastly different numbers on different configurations of the same system.

- *Run the same benchmark on every system.* Benchmarks are still software, and the way in which benchmark code is written can impact the way it produces results on a given computer. Often, two different versions of the same benchmark will yield two different results. When you use benchmarks for comparisons between systems, be sure to use the same program and version number.

- *Minimize hardware differences between hardware platforms.* A computer is an assembly of many interdependent subassemblies (motherboard, drive controllers, drives, CPU, and so on), but when a benchmark is run to compare a difference between systems, that difference can be masked by other elements in the system. For example, suppose you're using a benchmark to test the hard drive data transfer on two systems. Different hard drives and drive controllers will yield different results (that's expected). However, even if you're using identical drives and controllers, other differences between the systems (such as BIOS versions, TSRs, OS versions, or motherboard chipsets) can also produce different results.

■ *Run benchmarks under the same load.* The results generated by a benchmark do not guarantee that same level of performance under real-world applications. This was one of the flaws of early computer benchmarking—small, tightly written benchmark code resulted in artificially high performance, but the system still performed poorly when real applications were used. Use benchmarks that use (or simulate) actual programs, or otherwise simulate your true workload.

OBTAINING BENCHMARKS

Benchmarks have been around since the earliest computers, and there are now a vast array of benchmark products to measure all aspects of the PC, as well as more specialized issues such as networking, real-time systems, and UNIX (or other operating system) platforms. Table 4-1 highlights a cross-section of common computer benchmarks for your reference (including a URL where you can download the complete benchmark program). The benchmarks denoted with an asterisk are described in more detail following Table 4-1. Today, Ziff Davis (**www.zdnet.com/etestinglabs/filters/benchmarks/**) publishes a suite of freeware benchmark utilities that have become standard tools for end users and technicians alike.

TABLE 4-1   INDEX OF MODERN PC BENCHMARKS

BENCHMARK	DESCRIPTION	AVAILABILITY
3D-Bench	PC 3D graphics benchmark	www.sysopt.com/3dbench.html www.sysopt.com/cbench.html
3D WinBench 2000 (1.1)*	PC 3D graphics benchmark	www.zdnet.com/etestinglabs/stories/ benchmarks/0,8829,2326154,00.html
Audio WinBench 99 (1.0.1)*	PC audio subsystem performance benchmark	www.zdnet.com/etestinglabs/stories/ benchmarks/0,8829,2326212,00.html
BatteryMark (4.0)*	Mobile PC battery benchmark	www.zdnet.com/etestinglabs/stories/ benchmarks/0,8829,2326219,00.html
Business Winstone 2001 (1.0.1)*	Windows 98/Me/2000 application performance benchmark	www.zdnet.com/etestinglabs/stories/ benchmarks/0,8829,2326103,00.html
CD WinBench 99 (1.1.1)*	CD/DVD drive performance benchmark	www.zdnet.com/etestinglabs/stories/ benchmarks/0,8829,2326197,00.html
Content Creation Winstone	Windows 98/Me/2000 performance with content applications benchmark	www.zdnet.com/etestinglabs/stories/ benchmarks/0,8829,2384408,00.html
CPUMark99 (1.1)	CPU/cache/RAM performance benchmark	www8.zdnet.com/pcmag/pclabs/ bench/cpumark99.html
i-Bench (2.0)*	Web client performance benchmark	http://i-bench.zdnet.com/ibench/ i-bench.htm
JMark 1.01	Java applications performance benchmark	www8.zdnet.com/pcmag/pclabs/ bench/benchjm.htm
NetBench (7.0.1)*	File server performance benchmark	www.zdnet.com/etestinglabs/stories/ benchmarks/0,8829,2326318,00.html
Oracle Applications Standard Benchmark	Oracle applications benchmark performance benchmark	www.oracle.com/apps_benchmark/
ServerBench 4.1	PC network server benchmark	www.zdnet.com/etestinglabs/stories/ benchmarks/0,8829,2349035,00.html

TABLE 4-1   INDEX OF MODERN PC BENCHMARKS (*CONTINUED*)

BENCHMARK	DESCRIPTION	AVAILABILITY
SPEC (Standard Performance Evaluation Corporation)	General-purpose benchmarks	www.specbench.org/
SYSmark2000 (BAPCo)	General system performance benchmark	www.bapco.com/ www.bapco.com/ sysmark2000primer.htm
SYSmarkJ (BAPCo)	Java applications benchmark	www.bapco.com/ www.bapco.com/SYSmarkJ.html
TPC (Transaction Processing Council)	POS transaction processing benchmark	www.tpc.org/
WebBench (4.0.1)*	Web server performance benchmark	www.zdnet.com/etestinglabs/stories/ benchmarks/0,8829,2326243,00.html
Webmark2001 (BAPCo)	Internet performance benchmark	www.bapco.com/ www.bapco.com/SYSmarkJ.html
WinBench 99 (1.2)	General system benchmark	www.zdnet.com/etestinglabs/stories/ benchmarks/0,8829,2326114,00.html
WinTune (1.0.43)*	General Windows system benchmark	wintune.winmag.com/

3D WinBench 2000

3D WinBench 2000 (version 1.1) measures the performance of a computer's 3D subsystem, which includes the Direct3D software, the monitor, the graphics adapter, the graphics driver, and the bus used to carry information between the graphics adapter and the processor subsystem (the AGP bus). You can use 3D WinBench 2000 to test hardware graphics adapters, drivers, and the value of such enhancing technologies as MMX. 3D WinBench 2000 runs only on Microsoft Windows 98, Windows 98 SE, Windows 2000, and Windows Me. It won't work under Windows NT 4.0 because NT doesn't support hardware acceleration of the Windows Direct3D interface that 3D WinBench 2000 uses. 3D WinBench 2000 uses the DirectX 7.0 interface, which means you can see the benefits and performance of features such as hardware transformation and lighting effects. Version 1.1 also includes a new processor test suite and new quality tests for the latest innovations in 3D rendering.

Audio WinBench 99

The Audio WinBench 99 benchmark takes you deep into the heart of your PC's audio system by offering objective and subjective tests to measure CPU usage, hardware voices, 3D positioning, and more. Audio WinBench 99 measures the performance of a PC's audio subsystem, which includes the sound card and its driver, the processor, the DirectSound and DirectSound 3D software, and the speakers. Audio WinBench 99 runs on Microsoft Windows 98, Windows 98 SE, Windows NT, Windows 2000, and Windows Me. You'll need DirectX 6 (which includes DirectSound and DirectSound3D) to run all the Audio WinBench 99 tests. Version 1.0.1 is now available, which includes several minor updates.

BatteryMark 4.0

BatteryMark 4.0 measures the battery life on notebook computers running Windows 95, Windows 98, Windows ME, Windows NT 4.0, or Windows 2000. BatteryMark exercises several different 32-bit software workload engines to simulate processor, disk, and graphics tasks. BatteryMark mixes these workloads together and adds periodic breaks in the work that reflect the way users pause while working. The latest major release of BatteryMark (4.0.1) fixes a memory problem in version 3.0 that only showed up on faster processors (400 MHz processors and faster).

The BatteryMark 4.0 License Agreement no longer requires you to use the ZDigit II device if you wish to publish your BatteryMark 4.0 scores. If your Windows 98, Windows ME, or Windows 2000 noteook computer correctly supports the Advanced Configuration and Power Interface (ACPI), Battery-Mark can keep the screen on during its tests without external intervention. Even without ACPI, you may be able to configure your BIOS to keep the screen on during testing.

Business Winstone 2001

Business Winstone 2001 is a system-level, application-based benchmark that measures a system's overall performance when running today's top-selling Windows-based 32-bit applications on Windows 98/SE, Windows NT 4.0 (SP6 or later), Windows 2000, or Windows Me. Business Winstone doesn't simply mimic various PC applications, it actually runs real applications through a series of scripted activities, and uses the time a PC takes to complete those activities to produce its performance scores. (The CD-ROM that contains Business Winstone also includes all the files and application portions the benchmark needs to run.)

Ziff Davis has released version 1.0.1 of Business Winstone 2001, which contains numerous bug fixes. The executable update converts an installed version 1.0 of Business Winstone 2001 into the new 1.0.1 version. To install the update, you must have already installed a complete version 1.0 of Business Winstone 2001 (including Business Winstone support files) on your system.

This benchmark generally replaces the aging Winstone 99.

CD WinBench 99

CD WinBench 99 measures the performance of a PC's CD-ROM or DVD-ROM drive subsystem (which includes the CD/DVD drive, controller, and driver, and the system processor). This benchmark isn't available as a download, so you have to run it from the CD WinBench 99 CD-ROM while it's spinning in your system's CD drive. Version 1.1.1 of CD WinBench 99 includes numerous minor updates. Keep in mind that this benchmark will not test music CDs or DVD movies.

i-Bench 2.0

i-Bench 2.0 is a comprehensive, cross-platform benchmark that tests the performance and capability of Web clients as they use the latest Web technologies and features. A *Web client* is any combination of hardware and software that you can use to retrieve content from a Web site. The benchmark provides a series of tests that measure both how well the client handles features and the degree to which network access speed affects performance. You can also use the i-Bench CD-ROM to test Web performance over a LAN.

NetBench 7.0.1

NetBench 7.0.1 is a portable benchmark program that measures how well a file server handles file I/O requests from 32-bit Windows clients while those clients pepper the server with requests for network file operations. NetBench reports file throughput and client response time measurements. Version 7.0 of NetBench provides for greater disk coverage and more disk-testing flexibility. To run NetBench, you need a file server PC (called the controller) running Windows NT or Windows 2000 to start and monitor the tests, as well as clients that are running either Windows 95/98 or Windows NT/2000. To run NetBench, you'll need to download both the client and the controller files.

WebBench 4.0.1

WebBench 4.0 lets you measure Web server software performance by running different Web server packages on the same server hardware or by running a given Web server package on different hardware platforms. Version 4.0.1 of WebBench allows for more connections and other facilities that put more stress on bigger servers—more accurately modeling real-world server workloads. WebBench standard test suites produce two overall scores for the server: requests per second, and throughput (measured in bytes per second). WebBench provides both static standard test suites and dynamic standard test suites (which execute applications that actually run on the server). In addition, you can easily create your own test suites. No matter which test suites you use, your PC clients must be running either Windows 95/98 or Windows NT/2000, and the controller must be running Windows NT or Windows 2000.

To run WebBench, you need to download the client files, the controller files, and the workload tree for your server operating system. The workload trees that come with the workload downloads contain everything you need to run both the e-commerce and regular WebBench 4.0.1 test suites. Note that WebBench no longer supports the OS/2 Warp server platform.

WinTune 1.0.43

WinTune for Windows 98/Me/NT/2000 is an established benchmark entry from CMP, the publishers of *Windows Magazine*. WinTune is an overall benchmark to measure Windows platform performance. It has a fast user interface that allows the program to load much faster than the earlier versions, and will now support testing of the latest Pentium III/4 systems. WinTune tests video systems on the fastest new computers at full-screen resolution. In addition, you can use WinTune to test the system while it's online (if your system uses IE 3.02 or later). Of course, you may download and install an offline version for individual system testing.

Viruses and Computer Service

Few developments in the personal computer field have caused more concern and alarm than the computer virus. Although viruses do not physically damage computer hardware, they can irrevocably destroy vital data, disable your PC (or shut down a network), and propagate to other systems through networks, disk swapping, and online services. Even though virus infiltration is generally regarded as rare, a good PC technician will always protect themselves (and their customers) by checking the system for viruses before and after using their diagnostic disks on the PC. A careful process of virus isolation can detect viruses on the customer's system before any hardware-level work is done. Virus isolation tactics also prevent your diagnostic disks from becoming infected and subsequently transferring the virus to other systems (for which you might be legally liable). This part of the chapter outlines a virus screening procedure for PCs.

COMPUTER VIRUSES EXPLAINED

There have been many attempts to define a computer virus, and most definitions have a great deal of technical merit. For the purposes of this book, however, we can consider a *virus* to be some length of computer code (a program or program fragment) that performs one or more, often destructive, functions and replicates itself wherever possible to other disks and systems. Since viruses generally want to escape detection, they may also hide by copying themselves as hidden, system, or read-only files. However, this only prevents casual detection. More elaborate viruses affect the boot sector code on floppy and hard disks, or attach themselves to other executable programs. Each time the infected program is executed, the virus has a chance to wreak havoc. Still other viruses infect the partition table. Most viruses exhibit a code sequence that can be detected. Many virus scanners work by checking the contents of memory and disk files for such virus *signatures.* As viruses become more complex, however, they are using encryption techniques to escape detection. Encryption changes the virus signature each time the virus replicates itself, and for a well-designed virus, this can make detection extremely difficult.

Just as a biological virus is an unwanted (and sometimes deadly) organism in a body, "viral" code in software can lead to a slow, agonizing death for your customer's data. In actual practice, few viruses *immediately* crash a system (with notable exceptions, such as the much-publicized Michelangelo virus). Most viruses make only small changes each time they are executed, creating a pattern of chronic problems. This slow manifestation gives viruses a chance to replicate and infect backups and floppy disks, which are frequently swapped, thereby infecting other systems.

Frequent system backups are an effective protection against computer viruses because you can restore files damaged by viruses. Even if the backup is infected, the infected files can often be cleaned once they are restored from the backup.

The Tell-Tale Signs

Viruses are especially dangerous since you are rarely made aware of their presence until it is too late and the damage is already done. However, there are a number of behaviors that might suggest the presence of a virus in your system. Once again, remember that one of the best protections against viruses (or other drive failures) is to maintain regular backups of your data. None of these symptoms alone guarantees the presence of a virus (there *are* other reasons why such symptoms can occur), but when symptoms do surface, it is always worth running an antivirus checker just to be safe. The following symptoms are typical of virus activity:

■ *The hard drive is running out of disk space for no apparent reason.* Some viruses multiply by attaching copies of themselves to EXE and COM files, often multiple times. This increases the file size of infected files (sometimes dramatically) and consumes more disk space. If left unchecked, files can grow until the disk runs short of space. However, disk space can also be gobbled up by many CAD, graphics, and multimedia applications, such as video capture systems. Be aware of what kind of applications are on the disk.

■ *You notice that various EXE and COM programs have increased in size for no reason.* This is a classic indicator of a virus at work. In actual practice, few rational people make it a habit to keep track of file sizes, but dates can be a giveaway. For example, if most of the files in a subdirectory are dated six months ago when a software package was first installed, but the main EXE file is dated yesterday, it's time to run that virus checker.

■ *You notice substantial hard drive activity but were not expecting it.* It is hardly unusual to see the drive indicator LED register activity when programs are loaded and run. In disk-intensive systems such as Windows Me or 2000, you should expect to see extensive drive activity due to swap file operation. However, you should not expect to see regular or substantial disk activity when the system is idle. If the drive runs for no apparent reason—especially under DOS—run the virus checker.

■ *System performance has slowed down noticeably.* This symptom is usually coupled with low drive space, and may very well be the result of a filled and fragmented disk, such as those found in systems that deal with CAD and multimedia applications. Run the virus checker first. If no virus is detected, try eliminating any unneeded files and defragment the drive completely.

■ *Files have been lost or corrupted for no apparent reason, or there are an unusual number of access problems.* Under ordinary circumstances, files should not be lost or corrupted on a hard drive. Even though bad sectors will crop up on extremely rare occasions, you should expect the drive to run properly. Virus infiltration can interrupt the flow of data to and from the drives and result in file errors. Such errors may occur randomly, or they may be quite consistent. You may see error messages such as "Error in .EXE file." Regular errors may even simulate a drive failure. Try running a virus checker before running a diagnostic like ScanDisk. Inadequate power problems can also have an effect on drive reliability.

■ *The system locks up frequently or without explanation.* Faulty applications and corrupted files can freeze a system. Memory and motherboard problems can also result in system lockups. While viruses rarely manifest themselves in this fashion, it is possible that random or consistent system lockups may suggest a virus (or virus damage to key files).

■ *There are unexplained problems with system memory or memory allocation.* Although there may be one or more memory defects, it is quite common for viruses to exist in memory where other files can be infected. In some cases, this can affect the amount of free memory available to other applications. You may see error messages such as "Program too big to fit in memory." If you are having trouble with free memory or memory allocation, run a virus checker that performs a thorough memory check. If the system checks clear of viruses, you can run diagnostics to check the memory.

ANTIVIRUS SOFTWARE

In the race between good and evil, evil usually has the head start. As a result, antivirus detection and elimination packages are constantly trying to keep up with new viruses and their variations (in addition to dealing with the tens of thousands of viruses that have already been identified). This leads to an important conclusion about antivirus software: they all quickly become obsolete. Even though first-class shareware and commercial packages can be quite comprehensive, they must all be updated frequently. Some of the most notable antivirus products are found in Symantec's Norton AntiVirus (NAV), and VirusScan from Network Associates. If you use DOS 6.0 or later, you already own Microsoft AntiVirus (MSAV).

Another important factor in antivirus programs is their inability to successfully remove all viruses from executable (EXE) files. Files with a .COM extension are simply reflections of memory, but EXE files contain header information that is easily damaged by a virus (and are subsequently unrecoverable). It is always worth trying to eliminate the virus—if the EXE header is damaged, you've lost nothing in the attempt, and you can reload the damaged EXE file from a backup or its original distribution disks if necessary. Remember that there is no better protection against viruses and other hardware faults than keeping regular backups. It is better to restore an infected backup and clean it than to forego backups entirely.

Sterilizing Your Shop

Sterilization starts by assuming that *all* machines coming in for service are infected with a virus. You should assume the possibility of an infection even if the complaint is something innocent (for example, the keyboard is "acting up"). This part of the chapter shows you how to create antivirus work disks that will be used to boot and check the systems brought in for service. Guard your master antivirus disks by placing them somewhere away from the shop. That way they won't be infected accidentally. *Immediately write-protect your work disks!* Also, be ready to discard your work disks frequently. Replacing a 15-cent work disk is much cheaper than having to scan and clean every disk in your shop. If the antivirus software, DOS, and the DISKCOPY program can all fit, you should use double-density disks rather than high-density disks. Double-density disks can be used in high-density drives (but not vice versa).

Routine, preservice virus scanning makes good sense. It will save time by detecting virus-related problems right away. You won't waste time disassembling cabinets and troubleshooting hardware. Also, eliminating viruses is much easier than reformatting or replacing the hard drive (a devastating choice if your customer has no current backup). Reformatting a hard drive on a system with a virus may *not* solve the problem and result in a callback. On the other hand, *not* wiping out your customer's entire drive is a sure way to make a friend. Finally, preservice virus checking is quick—the computer is on the bench anyway. Sticking in a disk and turning on the computer is all the labor required.

The following procedure assumes that your floppy disk is A:, your main hard drive is C:, and your CD-ROM (if installed) is D:. If your particular system is configured differently, please substitute the correct drive letters.

1. Start at the DOS command line. You should exit Windows 95/98 to the DOS prompt before proceeding.

2. Ensure your system is virus-free. Run a current virus checker that checks for the most important types of viruses, including memory-resident viruses. Once the system is clean, you can proceed.

3. Format ten floppy disks as bootable (system) disks. If your disks are totally blank, use the FORMAT command, as shown here:

```
C:\DOS\> format a:          <Enter>
```

Next, make the disks bootable by transferring system files. Use the SYS command to make the disks bootable, as shown here:

```
C:\DOS\> sys a:             <Enter>
```

If you purchase your disks preformatted, simply use the SYS command.

4. Test a disk. Reboot your computer and see that the system will boot successfully to the A: DOS prompt. If so, you have created simple boot disks (you need only test one disk), but there are other steps required to complete a virus-checking disk.

5. Copy the virus checker to your first bootable floppy disk. Virus checkers are typically self-conained, single-file tools, such as Norton's NAV.EXE, Microsoft's MSAV.EXE, or the shareware tool FPROT.EXE. Copy the necessary DOS executable file(s) to your disk.

6. Create an AUTOEXEC.BAT file that will start the virus checker. Ideally, you want the virus checker to start automatically, so create a simple AUTOEXEC.BAT file that will start the virus checker. For example, MSAV.EXE could use a command line such as this:

```
a:\msav.exe
```

You might also add command-line arguments to streamline the virus checker even further. Save the AUTOEXEC.BAT file to your floppy disk.

7. Test the disk again. Reboot the system with your master antivirus floppy disk. The system should boot clean—with no drivers or TSRs loaded that might confuse the virus checker—and the antivirus program should load. Depending on exactly which virus checker and command-line options you choose, the checker may run through a complete scan automatically, or you may have to start testing manually from the program's menu.

8.   Duplicate the original disk to the other work disks. Use the DOS DISKCOPY command to duplicate your original virus-checking disk to the other nine disks you have prepared. You may have to
swap back and forth between the source (original) and target (new) disks several times. When the
new disk is done, DISKCOPY will ask if you want to repeat the procedure.

9.   Mark the disks carefully. You have just created a batch of antivirus work disks. They should be
immediately write-protected and kept together as a set.

Step 8 instructs you to create nine copies of the virus-checking software. Even though the disks are
exclusively for your use, and you will use only one disk at a time, this kind of multiple duplication may
violate the license agreement for your antivirus software. Be sure your license allows multiple copies
of the software before proceeding.

Using the Virus Work Disks   Whenever a PC comes in for service, use one of your antivirus work
disks to boot and check the system first, before trying a boot disk or diagnostic disk. Professionals always
create antivirus disks in batches because the disks are disposable. That is, if a virus is detected and
cleaned, the disk that detected the infection should be destroyed, and you should boot the system with a
new work disk to locate any other instances of the same virus, or any different viruses. This may seem rad-
ical, but it is cheap insurance against cross-contamination of the disk. Once a system is booted with a work
disk and checks clean, you can put that work disk away and boot the system again with a diagnostic or boot
disk as required. It is also advisable to check the PC for viruses again once the repair is complete.

Problems with Antivirus Tools   The protocol previously outlined should help to protect you (and
your customer) from virus attacks. Still, there are two situations in which trouble can occur. First, viruses
are proliferating with the aid of powerful new programming languages and vast avenues of distribution
such as the Internet. You need to update your virus work disks regularly with the very latest antivirus software and signature updates. Too often, technicians buy an antivirus package and continue to use it for
years. The software certainly remains adept at detecting the viruses it was designed for, but does not take
into account the many new strains that crop up regularly. As a result, older virus checkers may allow
newer viruses to pass undetected.

Second, technicians tend to get cheap with their floppy disks. If a work disk detects and eliminates a
virus, it should be considered contaminated, and you should throw it away. Start again with a fresh work
disk. Continue checking and eradicating viruses until the system checks clean. The 15 cents or so that the
disk is worth is not worth the risk of contracting the virus.

You can usually find a selection of free or trial antivirus software at **freebyte.com/antivirus/#scanners**.

Quick-Start Bench Testing

Of the many problems that can plague the PC, perhaps the most troubling problems occur during startup,
when the computer fails to start at all or does not start completely. Startup problems make it almost impossible to use diagnostics or other utilities that we depend on to help isolate problems. With the advent of
graphics-oriented operating systems such as Windows 98/Me, there are even more difficulties that can
develop. This part of the chapter offers you a series of possible quick-start explanations for full and partial
system failures.

THE SYSTEM DOESN'T START AT ALL

These types of problems are easy to spot—you push the power button, and nothing happens. The solution to these kinds of problems is usually quite straightforward, but the following symptoms will show you some of the wrinkles that may occur. Start with the following checklist:

- Check for AC from your wall outlet
- Reattach or replace the AC line cord
- Reattach the power cables at the motherboard
- Replace the power supply
- Replace the motherboard
- Replace the CPU

SYMPTOM 4-1   **There is no power light, and you cannot hear any cooling fan**
Chances are that there is insufficient power to the computer. Use a voltmeter and confirm that there is adequate AC voltage at the wall outlet. Check the AC cord next to make sure it isn't loose or disconnected. See that the power switch is turned on and connected properly. Check the power supply fuse(s). The main fuse may have opened. Replace any failed fuse. If the trouble continues, try another power supply, and then replace the motherboard if necessary. In many cases, a poor-quality power supply will allow voltage transients to pass through and damage the motherboard (preventing any system activity). This rarely damages the CPU or RAM.

SYMPTOM 4-2   **There is no power light, but you hear the cooling fan running**
This usually means that there is some level of AC power reaching the system. Use a voltmeter and confirm that there is adequate AC voltage at the wall outlet. Unusually low AC voltages (such as during brownout conditions) can cause the power supply to malfunction. Verify that the power supply cables are attached properly and securely to the motherboard. Use a voltmeter to verify that each output from the power supply is correct (Table 4-2 illustrates the proper voltage levels at each wire color). If any output is very low or absent (especially the +5 volt output), replace the power supply. Finally, use a voltmeter and verify that the Power Good (or PwrOK) signal is +5 volts. If this signal is below 1.0 volts, it may inhibit the CPU from running by forcing a continuous Reset condition. Since the Power Good signal is generated by the power supply, try replacing the power supply. Otherwise, try another CPU.

SYMPTOM 4-3   **The power light is on, but there is no apparent system activity**
Check the power supply voltages. Use a voltmeter to verify that each output from the power supply is correct. Table 4-2 lists the proper voltage for each wire color. If any output is very low or absent (especially the +5 volt output), replace the power supply. Use a voltmeter and verify that the Power Good signal is +5 volts. If this signal is below 1.0 volts, it may inhibit the CPU from running, by forcing a continuous Reset condition. Since the Power Good signal is generated by the power supply, try replacing the power supply.

Check that the CPU is cool, that the heat-sink/fan assembly is fitted on correctly, and that the CPU itself is inserted properly and completely into its socket. Check the CPU socket. If the CPU is seated in a ZIF (Zero Insertion Force) socket, make sure that the socket's tension lever is closed and locked into place. For Pentium II/III/4 processors, verify that the retention mechanism is secure. Next, check the expansion boards to make sure that they all are seated properly. Any boards that are not secured properly, or that are inserted unevenly, can short bus signals and prevent the PC from starting. Check the motherboard for shorts. Inspect the motherboard at every metal standoff and see that no metal traces are being

TABLE 4-2   STANDARD POWER CONNECTOR PINOUTS

ATX POWER CONNECTOR

Color	Voltage	Pin	Color	Voltage	Pin
Orange	+3.3 Vdc	1	Brown	3.3V Sense	11
Orange	+3.3 Vdc	2	Blue	-12 Vdc	12
Black	Ground	3	Black	Ground	13
Red	+5 Vdc	4	Green	PS-ON	14
Black	Ground	5	Black	Ground	15
Red	+5 Vdc	6	Black	Ground	16
Black	Ground	7	Black	Ground	17
Gray	PwrOK	8	White	-5 Vdc	18
Purple	+5V standby	9	Red	+5 Vdc	19
Yellow	+12 Vdc	10	Red	+5 Vdc	20

BABY AT POWER CONNECTORS

Color	Voltage	Pin	Color	Voltage	Pin
Orange	PwrOK	1 (P8)	Black	Ground	1 (P9)
Red	+5 Vdc	2 (P8)	Black	Ground	2 (P9)
Yellow	+12 Vdc	3 (P8)	White	-5 Vdc	3 (P9)
Blue	-12 Vdc	4 (P8)	Red	+5 Vdc	4 (P9)
Black	Ground	5 (P8)	Red	+5 Vdc	5 (P9)
Black	Ground	6 (P8)	Red	+5 Vdc	6 (P9)

shorted against a standoff or screw. You may want to free the motherboard and see if the system starts. If it does, use nonconductive spacers (such as a small piece of manila folder) to insulate the motherboard from each metal standoff. If the system still fails to start (and all voltages from the power supply are correct), replace the motherboard.

THE SYSTEM STARTS BUT WON'T INITIALIZE

Now things start to get a bit more complicated. Power is clearly reaching the system, and the POST process is starting, but a serious problem somewhere very early in the system initialization process is preventing the system from finishing the POST or loading the operating system. In many cases, you'll find this to be a motherboard fault, or an assembly problem (for example, an expansion card is not properly seated in its expansion slot). Start with the following checklist:

■ Reattach the power cables at the motherboard

■ Reattach the power cables to all drives

■ Reinstall all expansion cards

■ Check and reinstall all signal cabling

■ Check for POST errors using a POST reader card (if available)

■ Check the CMOS Setup

■ Replace the motherboard

SYMPTOM 4-4   **The power light is on, but you hear two or more beeps**   There is no video. Check the video board first. Video problems can easily halt the initialization process. Turn off and unplug the PC, and then make sure that your video board is inserted completely into its expansion slot. Consider the beep code itself—a catastrophic fault has been detected in the power-on self-test (POST) before the video system could be initialized. BIOS makers use different numbers and patterns of beeps to indicate failures. You can determine the exact failure by finding the BIOS maker (usually marked on the motherboard BIOS chip), and then finding the error message in Chapter 18. In the vast majority of cases, the fault will be traced to the CPU, RAM, motherboard circuitry, video controller, or drive controller.

SYMPTOM 4-5   **The power light is on, but the system hangs during initialization**
Video may be active, but there may be no text in the display. The POST has detected a fault and is unable to continue with the initialization process. BIOS makers mark the completion of each POST step by writing single-byte hexadecimal completion codes to port 80h. Turn off and unplug the PC, and then insert a POST board to read the completion codes. Reboot the computer and find the last code to be written before the initialization stops—that is the likely point of failure. You can determine the meaning of that POST code by finding the BIOS maker (usually displayed in the initial moments of power-up) and then locating the corresponding error message in Chapter 18. Note that without a POST board available, identifying the problem will be extremely difficult.

SYMPTOM 4-6   **You see a message indicating a CMOS Setup problem**   The system parameters entered into CMOS RAM do not match the hardware configuration found during the POST, and the boot process will not continue. Enter your CMOS Setup routine. If you are working on an older system (early i386 and i286 systems), you will probably need to boot the PC from a setup disk. If no setup disk is available, you may be able to find a suitable routine at one of the sites at **oak.oakand.edu:/SimTel/msdos/at** or **ftp.uu.net:/systems/msdos/simtel/at**.

Review each entry in the CMOS Setup—especially things like drive parameters and installed memory—and make sure that the CMOS entries accurately reflect the actual hardware installed on your system. If not, correct the error(s), save your changes, and reboot the system. In most current PCs, you can opt to load BIOS Default values. Finally, test the CMOS battery. See if CMOS RAM will hold its contents by turning off the PC, waiting several minutes, and then rebooting the PC. If setup problems persist and you find that the values you entered have been lost, change the CMOS backup battery.

SYMPTOM 4-7   **You see no drive light activity**   The boot drive cannot be located. The most frequent cause of drive problems is power connections. Inspect the 4-pin power cable and see that it is attached properly and completely to the drive. Check the power supply voltages next. Use a voltmeter and verify that the +5 and +12 voltage levels (especially +12 volts) are correct at the 4-pin connector. If either voltage is low or absent, replace the power supply. Locate the wide ribbon cable that connects to the drive and make sure it is attached correctly and completely at the drive and controller ends. Look for any scrapes or nicks along the cable that might cause problems. Start the CMOS Setup. If you are working on an older system (early i386 and i286 systems), you will probably need to boot the PC from a setup disk. If there is no setup disk available, you may be able to find a suitable routine at **oak.oakland.edu:/SimTel/msdos/at** or **ftp.uu.net:/systems/msdos/simtel/at**.

Review the drive parameters entered in the CMOS Setup and make sure that the CMOS entries accurately reflect the actual boot drive installed on your system. If they do not, correct the error(s), save your changes, and reboot the system. Also make sure that the drive controller board is installed properly and completely in its expansion slot, and see that any jumpers are set correctly.

Try booting the system from your boot floppy. If the system successfully boots to the A: prompt, your problem is limited to the hard drive system. Now try switching to the C: drive. If the drive responds (and you can access its information), there may be a problem with the boot sector. Try a package like Norton Utilities to try to fix the boot sector. If you can't access the hard drive, try a diagnostic to check the drive controller and drive. Check for boot sector viruses. A boot sector virus can render the hard drive unbootable. If you haven't checked for viruses yet, use your antivirus work disk now, and focus on boot sector problems. If you cannot determine the problem at this point, try replacing the drive with a known-good working drive. Remember that you will have to change the CMOS Setup parameters to accommodate the new drive. If all else fails, try a new drive controller board or motherboard.

SYMPTOM 4-8 **The drive light remains on continuously** The boot drive cannot be located. This typically happens if the signal cable is inserted backward at one end. In most cases, this type of problem happens after replacing a drive or upgrading a controller. Make sure the cable is inserted in the correct orientation at both the drive and controller ends. If you cannot determine the problem at this point, try replacing the drive with a known-good working drive. Remember that you will have to change the CMOS Setup parameters to accommodate the new drive. If all else fails, try a new drive controller board or motherboard.

SYMPTOM 4-9 **You see normal system activity, but there is no video** Make sure the monitor is plugged in and turned on. This type of oversight is really more common than you might think. Make sure that the monitor works (you may want to try the monitor on a known-good system). If the monitor fails on a known-good system, replace the monitor. Next, trace the monitor cable to its connection at the video board, and verify that the connector is inserted securely. Check the video board. It is possible that the video board has failed. If the problem persists, replace the video board.

THE SYSTEM STARTS BUT CRASHES/REBOOTS INTERMITTENTLY

These are undoubtedly some of the most perplexing and frustrating problems that any technician can face. It's not that the solutions are particularly difficult, but there are so many possible causes that positively identifying the culprit can be difficult. Spontaneous crashes or reboots can be triggered by a wide range of problems, including resource conflicts, power anomalies, hardware faults, software conflicts, and outdated or buggy drivers (as well as many other causes).

Isolating the Trouble

Given the many possible causes of crashes and reboots, the first step in dealing with such problems is to determine whether the trouble is related to hardware or software. This can save you countless hours of trial and error, because if the trouble is hardware-based, you can focus on the devices in your system and how they're configured, and if the trouble is software-based, you can focus on isolating and updating the offending software. The following tips can help you locate common problems.

■ *Viruses can impair stability.* It's best to start with a virus checker. Viruses can damage files that are necessary for the proper functioning of the PC. While the probability of a virus problem is rare, it's a quick and easy check. Damaged files should be replaced from a backup or from original installation CDs. Then, run the system and see if stability returns. If the system checks clean, you can move on to the next point.

■ *Conflicts can impair stability.* Start by checking your Windows Device Manager (Figure 4-3). Each device classification should appear without markings such as yellow exclamation marks or red Xs. If Device Manager does not report any troubles, go to the next check. If one or more devices are marked with a problem, you should resolve that problem and see if the system stabilizes. In most cases, device problems can be resolved by reconfiguring the offending device, reinstalling it, or upgrading the device driver(s). (See Chapter 12 for more-detailed information on device conflict troubleshooting.)

■ *Buggy/damaged applications can impair stability.* Not all software works smoothly on every system, or coexists well with other software. If you find that the system is less stable when certain programs are running, try shutting down those applications. Also shut down unneeded applications that may be running in the background. If the system crashes or reboots regardless of what is running, go to the next step. If you identify a suspect piece of software, try uninstalling and reinstalling it, or check for upgrades/patches from the software maker.

■ *Damaged/conflicting utilities can impair stability.* Start Windows in the Safe Mode. This is a diagnostic mode that loads Windows with a minimum of drivers and device support. Run the system this way for a bit and see if stability returns. If the system still crashes or reboots, go to the next step. If stability improves, chances are that software is causing the trouble. Restart the system normally, and systematically disable applications from the Startup folder and System Tray. See if you can find a tool or utility that is causing the problem. For example, if you remove the Speaker icon from the System Tray and the system stabilizes, chances are that the problem was caused by (or is related to) that software. It is not uncommon for unique tools loaded in the System Tray or at startup (for example, a photo printer utility) to cause stability problems. This process of isolation takes some patience and persistence, but it's often necessary.

■ *Buggy/outdated/conflicting drivers can impair stability.* Older or buggy device drivers may compromise system stability. Check for updated device drivers for each key device on the system. Update DirectX drivers, video drivers, sound drivers, printer drivers, modem drivers, USB device drivers, and so on. Update one driver at a time and see if the system stabilizes. If the system continues to crash/reboot, chances are that you're faced with a hardware problem.

■ *AC problems can impair stability.* Now it's time to look at the hardware devices in your system. Try your PC on another AC outlet, preferably one that's free of high-load devices like air conditioners, coffeemakers, fans, motors, and other power-hungry electrical equipment. Install a new surge/spike suppressor (even an inexpensive UPS) on the AC outlet and see if the system stabilizes. If it does not, go to the next step.

■ *Device installation problems can impair stability.* Make sure that all expansion boards and signal cables are seated properly. Any boards that are not secured properly, or that are inserted unevenly, can short bus signals and cause spurious reboots. Inspect the motherboard at every metal standoff and make sure that no metal traces are being shorted against a standoff or screw. You may want to free the motherboard and see if the crashes or reboots go away. If so, use nonconductive spacers (such as a small piece of manila folder) to insulate the motherboard from each metal standoff. If no traces are touching but stability returns when one or more screws are removed, the motherboard may be suffering a hairline stress fracture and may need to be replaced. Also make sure that all SIMMs/DIMMs/RIMMs are seated properly in their holders and locked into place. You may try removing each module, cleaning the contacts, and reinstalling the module. If problems persist, go to the next step.

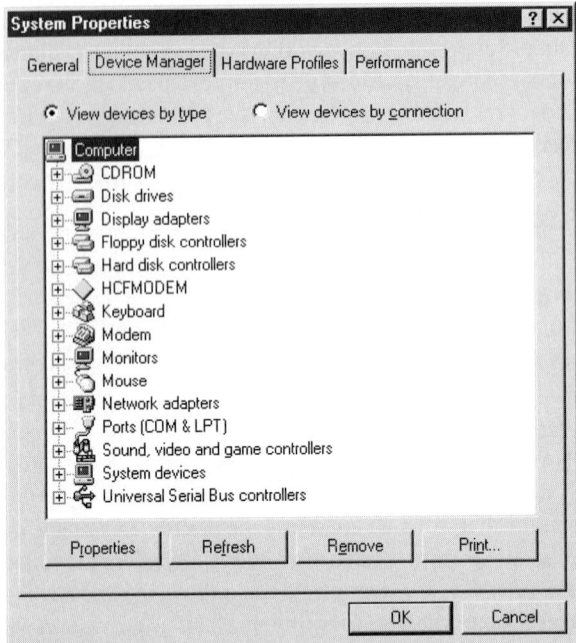

FIGURE 4-3   Checking Device Manager for device problems

■ *Power supply problems can impair stability.* Double-check the power supply connections to the motherboard and drives. Use a voltmeter to verify that each output from the power supply is correct as outlined in Table 4-2. If any output is low (especially the +5 volt output), replace the power supply. Even if the supply outputs seem okay, you may wish to try another power supply anyway, just to eliminate the possibility of internal supply problems. If another power supply does not stabilize the system, go to the last step.

■ *CPU heating can impair stability.* With all power off, check to see that the CPU is cool, that the heat-sink/fan assembly is fitted on correctly, and that the CPU itself is inserted properly and completely into its socket. If the CPU overheats, it will stall, taking the entire system with it. If the CPU is seated in a ZIF socket, make sure that the socket's tension lever is closed and locked into place. For Pentium II/III/4 processors, verify that the retention mechanism is secure.

Divide and Conquer

If you've come this far and the system is still unstable, chances are that there's an issue with one or more system devices that has escaped your detection. Now we're down to "hack and slash" troubleshooting. Remove one device at a time from the system and see if the system stabilizes. Start with unnecessary devices, such as Zip drives, and work your way to secondary hard drives, CD drives, optional cards (such as SCSI cards, sound cards, video capture cards, modems, and so on). Restart the system after removing each device and see if stability returns. If so, the last device you removed is probably the culprit. Once you've identified the troublesome item, you can try reinstalling it from scratch using the very latest drivers and applet software downloaded from the manufacturer's Web site. If the problem returns after reinstallation, you can try reconfiguring it (if possible). For example, if the system doesn't like your DVD-ROM drive as a slave device on a secondary controller channel, you can try making it the master device instead (and resetting the current master device as a slave device).

AFTER AN UPGRADE

Upgrades are prime places for system startup problems. In most cases, a new device is installed improperly, is incompatible with your current platform, or is conflicting with another device in the system. Fortunately, problems occurring after an upgrade are relatively simple to correct because you already know the change(s) performed on the system. There are three typical symptoms that you may encounter.

SYMPTOM 4-10 **The system fails to boot, freezes during boot, or freezes during operation for no apparent reason** This is the classic sign of a hardware conflict. A PC is designed with a limited number of resources (memory, I/O addresses, interrupt [IRQ] lines, DMA channels, and so on). For the PC to function properly, each device added to the system must use its own unique resources. For example, no two devices can use the same IRQ, DMA, or I/O resources. When such an overlap of resources occurs, the PC can easily malfunction and freeze. Unfortunately, it is virtually impossible to predict when the malfunction will occur, so a conflict can manifest itself early (any time during the boot process), or later on (after DOS is loaded) while an application is running.

Resolving a conflict is not difficult, but it requires patience and attention to detail. Examine the upgrade and its adapter board and check the IRQ, DMA, and I/O address settings of other boards in the system. Make sure that the upgrade hardware is set to use resources that are not in use by other devices already in the system. For example, some motherboards offer built-in video controller circuits. Before another video adapter can be added to the system, the motherboard video adapter must be disabled—usually with a single motherboard jumper, or through the CMOS Setup. Some sophisticated adapter boards (especially high-end video adapters and video capture boards) require the use of extra memory space. If memory exclusions are needed, be sure that the appropriate entries are made in the CONFIG.SYS and AUTOEXEC.BAT files. If memory exclusions are not followed, multiple devices may attempt to use the same memory space, which will result in a conflict. (See Chapter 12 for more-detailed information on device conflict troubleshooting.)

SYMPTOM 4-11 **The system fails to recognize the newly installed device** Even if the hardware is installed in a system correctly, the PC may not recognize the upgrade device(s) without the proper software loaded. A great example of this is the CD-ROM drive in real mode (DOS). It is a simple matter to install the drive (and a controller card if necessary), but the PC will not even recognize the drive unless the low-level CD-ROM device driver is added to CONFIG.SYS, and the MS-DOS CD-ROM extension (MSCDEX) is included in AUTOEXEC.BAT. If the PC is running in a stable fashion but does not recognize the expansion hardware, make sure that you have loaded all required software correctly. If you're having trouble with a device under Windows, recheck the device's installation procedure and see if any software needed to be loaded before the actual installation of the hardware. For example, some high-end USB devices may need software before attaching the device for the first time.

If you are mixing and matching existing subassemblies from new and old systems, make sure that each device is fully compatible with the PC. Incompatibilities between vintages and manufacturers can lead to operational problems. For example, adding a 3.5-inch floppy drive to an i286 AT system can result in problems because the older BIOS cannot format 3.5-inch high-density (1.44MB) floppy disks. A DOS utility (such as DRIVER.SYS) is needed to correct this deficiency.

It is also possible that the upgrade device may simply be defective or installed incorrectly. Open the system and double-check your installation. Pay particular attention to any cables, connectors, or drive jumpers. When you confirm that the hardware and software installations are correct, suspect a hardware defect. Try the upgrade in another system if possible. If the problem persists when you attempt the upgrade on another PC, one or more elements of the upgrade hardware are probably defective. Return the upgrade hardware to the vendor for a prompt refund or replacement. If the upgrade works on another system, the original system may be incompatible with the upgrade, or you may have a hardware conflict in the original system that is preventing the new hardware from being detected.

SYMPTOM 4-12   **One or more applications fail to function as expected after an upgrade**   This is not uncommon among video adapter and sound board (multimedia) upgrades. Often, applications are configured to work with various sets of hardware. When that hardware is altered, the particular application(s) may no longer run properly (this is especially true under Windows 98/Me). The best way to address this problem is to check and change the hardware configuration for each affected application. Most DOS applications come with an EXE setup utility. Under Windows 98/Me, you can access system configuration settings through the System icon under the Control Panel (a.k.a. Device Manager).

In other cases, the drivers that were installed with the new device may have broken the link to important program relations. For example, you may have trouble playing DVD movies after installing a new video card, because the new video drivers that "took over" from the existing DVD drivers may not be compatible with the DVD drive. Reinstalling the affected device (the DVD drivers or playback software) may reestablish that "link" and restore normal operation.

WINDOWS 98/ME BOOT SYMPTOMS

After the POST finishes checking hardware, BIOS looks for a master boot record and tries to initiate loading the operating system, which is some version of Windows in virtually all cases today. Even when the hardware checks out properly, there are many different problems that can plague a complicated operating system such as Windows and prevent it from loading. For our purposes, the most common issues to consider are software interference (such as old drive overlay software) and damaged Windows components (such as a damaged kernel file or other DLL). The symptoms described next are typical of Windows startup problems. If problems persist, removing and reinstalling Windows will often correct the trouble.

SYMPTOM 4-13   **The Windows 98/Me boot drive is no longer bootable after restoring data with the DOS Backup utility**   This happens frequently when a replacement drive is installed and you attempt to restore the Windows 98/Me backup data. Unfortunately, the DOS version of Backup is not configured to restore system files. Start Backup and restore your root directory with System Files, Hidden Files, and Read Only Files checked. Next, boot the system from an MS-DOS 6.x upgrade setup disk 1, or a Windows 98/Me startup disk, and then use the SYS command to make the hard drive bootable, as shown here:

```
A:\> sys c:              <Enter>
```

You should then be able to restore the remainder of your files. When backing up a Windows 98/Me system, your best approach is to use a current Windows Backup program. Once the new drive is installed, partitioned, and formatted, install a new copy of Windows 98/Me, start the Windows Backup program, and then restore the remaining files to the drive.

SYMPTOM 4-14   **Windows 98/Me will not boot, and ScanDisk reports bad clusters that it cannot repair**   This is a problem encountered with Western Digital hard drives. If your WD drive fails in this way, you can recover the drive, but you will lose all information on it. Back up as much information from the drive as possible before proceeding:

1.   Download the Western Digital service files WDATIDE.EXE and WD_CLEAR.EXE from WD at **www.wdc.com/**. You can also get these files from AOL by typing the keyword WDC.

2.   Copy these files to a clean boot floppy disk.

3.   Boot to DOS from a clean disk (no CONFIG.SYS or AUTOEXEC.BAT files) and run WD_CLEAR.EXE. This utility clears all data on the media (and destroys all data).

4.   Run the WDATIDE.EXE utility to perform a comprehensive surface scan.

5.   Repartition and reformat the drive, and then restore your data.

SYMPTOM 4-15   **You see a "Bad or missing <filename>" error on startup**   A file used by Windows 98/Me during startup has probably become corrupt. Locate the file mentioned in the error message. If you can find the file, erase it and try reinstalling it from the original Windows 98/Me installation CD.

SYMPTOM 4-16   **Windows 98/Me reports damaged or missing files, or a "VxD error"**   During startup, Windows 98/Me depends on several key files being available. If a key file is damaged or missing, Windows will not function properly (if it loads at all). You can use System File Checker to verify the integrity of your operating system files, to restore them if they are corrupted, and to extract compressed files (such as drivers) from your installation disks. You can have System File Checker back up the existing files before restoring the original files. You can start System File Checker by clicking Start, highlighting Programs, pointing to Accessories, selecting System Tools, and then clicking System Information. In System Information, click Tools, and then click System File Checker. Otherwise, you may need to reinstall Windows from scratch.

SYMPTOM 4-17   **After installing Windows 98/Me, you can't boot from a different drive**   The Windows setup program checks all hard disks to find just one that contains the 80h designator in the DriveNumber field of a boot sector. Windows 98/Me will typically force the first drive to be bootable, and prevent other drives from booting. However, there are two ways to correct the problem after Windows is installed:

■   Use the version of FDISK included with Windows 95/98 to set the primary active partition.

■   Use a disk editor utility to change a disk's DriveNumber field so that you can boot from that hard disk.

SYMPTOM 4-18   **Windows 98/Me registry files are missing**   There are two registry files: USER.DAT and SYSTEM.DAT. They are also backed up automatically as USER.DA0 and SYSTEM.DA0. If a DAT file is missing, Windows will automatically load the corresponding DA0 file. If both the DAT and DA0 registry files are missing or corrupt, Windows will start in the Safe Mode, offering to restore the registry. However, this cannot be accomplished without a backup. Either restore the registry files from a tape or disk backup, or run Windows setup to create a new registry. Unfortunately, restoring an old registry or creating a new registry from scratch will reload programs and re-add hardware to restore the system to its original state, which is a long and difficult procedure. Use RegEdit to back up your registry files, or use the following DOS procedure to back up the registry files to a floppy disk:

```
attrib -r -s -h system.da?
attrib -r -s -h user.da?
copy system.da? A:\
copy user.da? A:\
attrib +r +s +h system.da?
attrib +r +s +h user.da?
```

SYMPTOM 4-19   **During the Windows 98/Me boot, you get an "Invalid System Disk" error**   This often happens during the first reboot during Windows setup, or when you boot from the startup disk. When you a see a message such as "Invalid system disk. Replace the disk, and then press any key," there may be several possible problems. First, your disk may be infected with a boot-sector virus. Run your antivirus work disk and check closely for boot sector viruses. Windows setup may also fail if there is antivirus software running as a TSR, or your BIOS has enabled boot sector protection. Make sure that any boot sector protection is turned off before installing Windows 98/Me. Check for disk overlay software (Windows 98/Me may not detect older versions of overlay software such as Disk Manager, EZ-Drive, or DrivePro), and overwrite the master boot record (MBR). See the documentation that accompanies your particular management software for recovering the MBR. To reinstall the Windows 98/Me system files, follow these steps:

1.   Boot the system using the Windows 98/Me emergency boot disk.

2.   At the DOS command prompt, type the following lines:

```
c:
cd\windows\command
attrib c:\msdos.sys -h -s -r
ren c:\msdos.sys c:\msdos.xxx
a:
sys c:
del c:\msdos.sys
ren c:\msdos.xxx c:\msdos.sys
attrib c:\msdos.sys +r +s +h
```

3.   Remove the emergency boot disk and reboot the system.

SYMPTOM 4-20   **Windows 9x/Me will not install on a compressed drive**   You are probably using an old version of the compression software that Windows does not recognize. Although Windows 9x/Me should be compatible with all versions of SuperStor, it does require version 2.0 or later of Stacker. Make sure your compression software is recent, and that enough free space exists on the host drive to support Windows 9x/Me installation. If you have a PlusPack for Windows, you should be able to install DriveSpace 3 for best Windows support.

SYMPTOM 4-21   **Windows Me won't mount a compressed volume**   Information contained on a DriveSpace-compressed volume is not available after you upgrade to Windows Me; the compressed volume appears in My Computer as a drive labeled "Host for Drive *X*:" (where *X* is the drive letter assigned to the compressed volume). Windows Me does not support fixed-disk compressed volumes, and will not start with the compressed volume mounted. To have the compressed volume mount after every reboot:

1. Right-click Start and then click Explore.

2. In the right Windows Explorer pane, double-click the Programs folder.

3. In the right Windows Explorer pane, double-click the Startup folder.

4. In the right Windows Explorer pane, right-click an empty area, point to New, and then click Shortcut.

5. In the Command Line box, type **drvspace /mount x:**, where *x* is the drive letter of the host drive.

6. Click Next, and then click Finish.

SYMPTOM 4-22   **You receive a kernel error when starting Windows 98/Me**   When you start Windows, you see an error such as "Error Loading Kernel. You must reinstall Windows." Windows quits after you receive this message. This error can occur if the KERNEL32.DLL file is missing or damaged. You need to extract a new copy of the KERNEL32.DLL file from your original Windows CD:

1. Restart your computer. When you see the "Starting Windows" message, press the F8 key and choose Command Prompt Only from the Startup menu. If you're using Windows Me, start your computer with the Windows Me startup disk.

2. Type the following commands (press ENTER after each line):

   ```
   cd\windows\system
   ren kernel32.dll kernel32.xxx
   ```

3. Extract a new copy of the KERNEL32.DLL file from your original Windows CD to the Windows\System folder. If you need help extracting a file, see article Q129605 in the Microsoft Knowledge Base.

4. Restart your computer.

SYMPTOM 4-23   **A drive indicates that it is in "MS-DOS compatibility mode"**
For some reason, Windows is using a real-mode (DOS) driver instead of a protected-mode (32-bit) driver. Make sure that any software related to the hard drive (especially hard disk drivers) is using the protected-mode version. Windows 98/Me should install equivalent protected-mode software, but you may need to contact the drive manufacturer and obtain the latest Windows drivers. If you are using Disk Manager, make sure that you're using version 6.0 or later. You can get the latest patch (DMPATCH.EXE) from the Ontrack Web site at **www.ontrack.com/**. Finally, check your motherboard BIOS. Windows may use DOS compatibility mode on large EIDE hard disks (hard disks with more than 1024 cylinders) in some computers. This may occur because of an invalid drive geometry translation in the system ROM BIOS that prevents the protected-mode IDE device driver from being loaded. Contact your system manufacturer for information about obtaining an updated BIOS.

SYMPTOM 4-24   **Disabling protected-mode disk driver(s), hides the partition table when FDISK is used**   As with Symptom 4-23, there are problems preventing 32-bit operation of your hard drive(s). Do not use the "Disable all 32-bit protected-mode disk drivers" option. Instead, upgrade your motherboard BIOS to a later version.

SYMPTOM 4-25   **You cannot achieve 32-bit disk access under Windows 98/Me**
If the Windows 98/Me system refuses to allow 32-bit disk access, there may be a conflict between the motherboard CMOS Setup entries and the BIOS on your EIDE controller. For example, if both BIOS have settings for Logical Block Addressing (LBA), make sure only one entry is in use.

SYMPTOM 4-26   **Windows 98/Me does not recognize a new device**   In some cases, Windows is unable to recognize a new device. When this happens, check to see if a hardware conflict exists between the device and other devices in the system (conflicts are represented in Device Manager with small yellow exclamation marks). Also make sure that any necessary drivers have been installed properly. If problems continue, remove the new device through your Device Manager, and reinstall it through the Add New Hardware wizard (or perform a full reboot and allow Windows to redetect the device at start time).

SYMPTOM 4-27   **Windows 98/Me malfunctions when installed over Disk Manager**
Current versions of Disk Manager should typically be compatible with Windows 98/Me, but there are some points to keep in mind. Check your Disk Manager version first. If you are using Disk Manager, make sure that you're using version 6.0 or later. You can get the latest patch (DMPATCH.EXE) from the Ontrack Web site at **www.ontrack.com/**. Check the slave drive with Disk Manager. Although the Windows 98/Me file system is supposed to work properly with a slave drive only using Disk Manager, problems can occur in some circumstances:

- When an obsolete Windows 3.1*x* virtual driver replaces the Windows protected-mode driver (such as WDCDRV.386), which can happen after several OS upgrades
- When the cylinder count in CMOS for the slave drive is greater than 1024 cylinders
- When the motherboard CMOS settings for the slave drive are set to autodetect

SYMPTOM 4-28   **You have problems using a manufacturer-specific hard disk driver (such as Western Digital's FastTrack driver WDCDRV.386) for 32-bit access under Windows 9x/Me**   Generally speaking, Windows has 32-bit protected-mode drivers for a wide variety of EIDE devices—in practice, you should not need a manufacturer-specific driver. If Windows has not removed all references to the driver from SYSTEM.INI, you should edit the file and remove those references manually, and then reboot the system. Be sure to make a backup copy of SYSTEM.INI before editing it.

TIPS FOR SLOW WINDOWS STARTUPS

Windows 98/Me is a complex operating system, and loading the many components and drivers that are required to make it run takes time. It takes even longer when you've installed additional software and applets that must load at start time. However, there are some circumstances that can make Windows really drag. If your Windows 98/Me system seems to be taking an unusually long time to start, follow the tips provided next to help streamline your platform.

Shut Down Unneeded Programs   The first thing to do is examine what programs you're launching at startup, and decide whether you really need them. Remember that programs can be launched from the Startup folder (under the Start menu), from the RUN= and LOAD= lines of your WIN.INI file, or from entries in the registry. Under Windows 95, you'd have to check each of these locations manually, but Windows 98/Me has a convenient one-stop location to tweak them all (Figure 4-4). Just click Start, select Run, and then type **MSCONFIG**. Under the Startup tab, you'll see all the programs you are launching. By clearing the check box next to any item, you'll prevent it from running at startup.

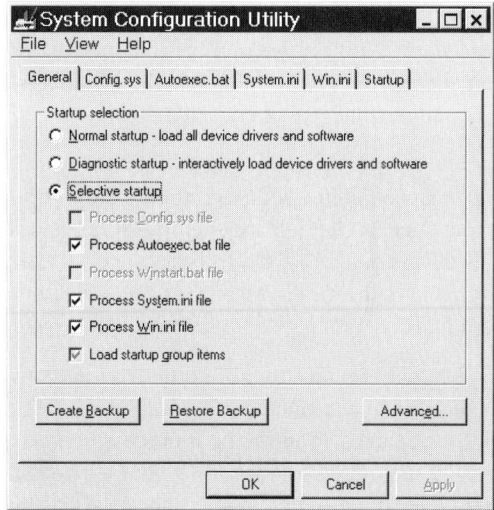

FIGURE 4-4   The MSCONFIG utility

Disable Real-Time Virus Scanning   Many of today's antivirus utilities offer real-time scanning for viruses. Unfortunately, since the scanner loads at startup, it can seriously impact performance, because it must scan every program file as it is being loaded into memory. If you're willing to accept a bit less virus protection, you can accelerate your boot times by turning off real-time scanning; instead, schedule a task to run a standard virus scan at least once a day. Not only will this shorten boot times, but it will make your system faster during any disk access.

Don't Check the Floppy Drive   Among its many other startup checks, Windows 98/Me checks whether you've added or changed floppy drives each time the system starts up. Chances are that you'll never reconfigure your floppy, so tell Windows to stop checking it. Click Start, highlight Settings, select Control Panel, and then double-click the System icon. Click the Performance tab, click the File System button, and then select the Floppy Disk tab. Clear the check box marked "Search for new floppy disk drives each time your computer starts." Apply your changes and try rebooting the computer.

Check Your Network Settings   Network settings are often a cause of slow boot times. One common problem occurs when a network card has the TCP/IP protocol loaded and is set to obtain an IP address from a DHCP server, but no server is available. The PC will wait up to a minute for an answer from the server before it continues booting. Click Start, highlight Settings, select the Control Panel, and double-click the Network icon. (Don't make changes if you're on a company network that is supported by a network administrator. Check with the administrator first.)

If you're not using TCP/IP on your local network (only for ISP dial-up), then just remove the binding between the network card and the TCP/IP protocol. You'll see this in the Network dialog box as a line that reads "TCP/IP -> (network card name)," as shown in Figure 4-5. Select that item and click Remove. If you are using TCP/IP on your local network, you either need to have a DHCP server running on the network or use manually assigned IP addresses. For most small networks of Windows 98/Me systems, manually assigned addresses work fine. Give each PC on the network a unique IP number in a sequence such as 10.0.0.1, 10.0.0.2, 10.0.0.3, and so on. You set this number in the Network dialog box. Select the entry "TCP/IP -> (network card name)" and click Properties. On the IP Address tab, choose "Specify an IP address" and enter the unique IP number that you've chosen for this system. For the subnet mask, try using **255.0.0.0** for all systems.

Tweak Your CMOS Setup Check your CMOS Setup routine for options that can speed your system's boot time. Enabling options such as Quick Boot or Quick POST and shortening drive initialization delays can shave a few seconds off the system's POST process. You'll also get a faster boot sequence if the system can boot directly from the C: drive rather than first checking for a floppy, LS-120, or CD drive (this also prevents viruses from infecting your system via a boot floppy).

Examine the Boot Log You may be faced with a problematic hardware component or software driver. These can be a bit difficult to diagnose, but the BOOTLOG.TXT feature can help. This allows you to generate a boot log that indicates each step in the boot process. You'll need to access the Windows startup menu, which will give you the option to generate a boot log. After the BIOS has completed its POST, hold down the CTRL key. The boot menu should appear (if the Windows 98/Me logo appears instead, you probably didn't press the CTRL key soon enough).

From the boot menu, select a "logged startup." Once Windows has finished booting up, the file BOOTLOG.TXT will be in the root of your C: drive, and you can view this file with Notepad. On a normal system, it's unusual to have any step in the boot process take more than a second or two. Large delays (10 or 20 seconds) usually indicate some sort of problem with a driver or its associated hardware.

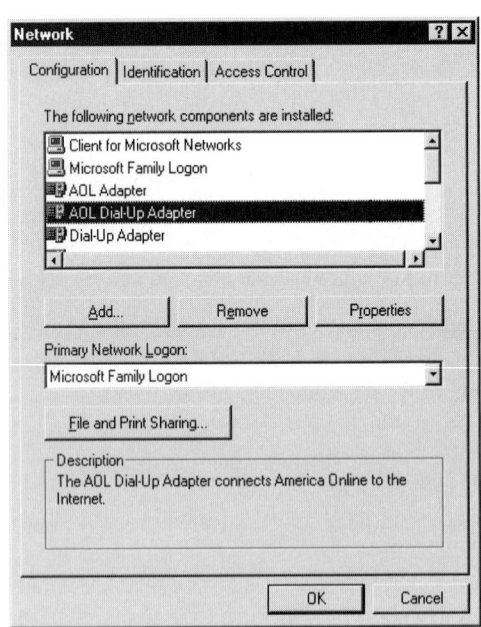

FIGURE 4-5   Checking Windows 98 network bindings

TIPS FOR WINDOWS STARTUP PROBLEMS

It's bad enough when Windows takes a long time to load, but when Windows fails to start at all, it may be difficult (or impossible) to use diagnostics and Windows tools to identify and correct the problem. This part of the chapter outlines a suite of tips that can help you track down and correct serious startup faults.

Try the Safe Mode   One of your first options is to try starting Windows 98/Me in the Safe Mode. For Windows 98, hold down the CTRL key right after the BIOS finishes its POST (but before Windows starts to load). You should get a Startup menu of options to select from. Choose Safe Mode and allow Windows to boot. If the boot is successful, right-click My Computer and select Properties, and then click the Device Manager tab. If any hardware is malfunctioning, the Manager tab will show it with a yellow exclamation point. (You can also use Device Manager to disable hardware manually and see if that lets you boot normally.) If you cannot boot Windows to the Safe Mode, chances are that a serious hardware problem exists in the system.

Try a Clean Boot Under Windows Me   You can use a clean boot technique to disable common startup programs, settings, and drivers under Windows Me:

1.   Click Start, click Run, type **MSCONFIG** in the Open box, and then click OK.
2.   On the General tab, click Selective Startup.
3.   Click to clear all of the check boxes under Selective Startup.
4.   On the Startup tab, click to select the *StateMgr check box.
5.   Click OK, and click Yes when you're prompted to restart your computer.
6.   After the computer restarts, click Start, click Run, type **MSCONFIG**, and then click OK again. Review the General tab and ensure that the check boxes you cleared are still cleared. If you see a disabled or gray check box, your computer is not truly clean-booted.

   Now you can isolate the problem. If the trouble does not reoccur after a clean boot, select one item at a time under Selective Startup, and then restart the computer to see if the additional entry reproduces the original issue. If so, that is the cause of the trouble. When you're done troubleshooting, you may return to a normal boot process:

1.   Click Start, click Run, type **MSCONFIG** in the Open box, and then click OK.
2.   On the General tab, click Normal Startup.
3.   Click OK, and click Yes when you're prompted to restart your computer.

Check for Disk Errors   If you cannot start Windows due to a disk error, it may be that the drive's power or signal cable has become loose. Check the cables and see that the drive is receiving adequate power. Try booting from a floppy disk. If you can reach a DOS prompt from a boot disk, the system hard drive may be defective.

Use the Automatic Skip Driver Agent   If your system crashes or hangs during the startup process, Windows 98/Me tries to avoid crashing again by skipping the operation that it "thinks" caused the problem. This is the Automatic Skip Driver (ASD) agent at work. However, the ASD may cause other problems (such as disabling some of your hardware) when a driver is skipped. To see if Windows is skipping any boot-up operations on your system, select Start, choose Run, and type **ASD**. If everything is okay, you'll receive a dialog box that says "There are no current ASD critical operation failures on this machine." If your system has had boot problems, they will be listed in this dialog box. You can put a check next to any or all of the skipped drivers to have Windows 98 retry them the next time you boot. After you boot the system again, run ASD and see if the function was disabled again; if so, you may have a problem with that hardware (or your BIOS).

Check for Missing Files   If you see the message "A file needed by Windows is missing" during a boot cycle, it's often due to a poor uninstallation of an application. This can sometimes occur when you uninstall and then immediately reinstall an application without rebooting first. Take a look at the name of the missing file to see whether it yields any clue as to which application might be causing the problem, and if it does, then try to uninstall, reboot, and reinstall that application. If the offending file relates to an application that you no longer need, you can use RegEdit to find and delete the registry keys that refer to the file (be sure that you have good backups before trying this). As a last resort, you may need to reinstall Windows to fix this problem cleanly.

Windows Protection Errors   In some cases, Windows may refuse to boot, returning the message "Windows Protection Error. You need to restart your computer." At this point, you're stuck unless you boot from a floppy disk. One cause in Windows 95 is a problem between SmartDrive and a large number of installed device drivers. If you see something about "initializing IOS" in the error message, try booting from a floppy, find the file SMARTDRV.EXE (usually in the Windows directory), and rename it **SMARTDRV.BAD**. Now try booting the system from the hard drive again.

There is also a known problem in Windows 95 that affects AMD K6 processors that run at 350 MHz or higher speeds, and this will sometimes give a Windows Protection Error message. (You can refer to Microsoft's document Q192841 for more-detailed information and a patch file.) Other solutions to Windows Protection Errors can be identified in Microsoft's document Q149962.

Other Startup Problems   You can refer to the Microsoft Web site and Knowledge Base to learn about numerous other startup problems:

Q132571	Cannot Start Windows or Programs in Windows
Q267079	Norton AntiVirus 2000 Real Mode Virus Scanner May Not Work in Windows Me
Q272381	System Configuration Utility Error Occurs at Startup
Q273738	How to Troubleshoot Windows Millennium Edition Startup Problems
Q273746	How to Troubleshoot Windows Me Shutdown Problems
Q143053	Mouse Systems Driver May Cause Windows Protection Error
Q186351	Norton AntiVirus 4.0 May Cause Windows Protection Error
Q186844	"Windows Protection Error" with EZ-SCSI 4.0 and Easy-CD Pro 95
Q175930	Illegal Operations or Access Violations When Starting Windows
Q141898	Windows 95/98 Boots Directly to "Shut Down" Screen
Q187524	MS-DOS Based Program Starts When You Start Your Computer

Further Study

IBM setup routines   oak.oakland.edu:/SimTel/msdos/at or ftp.uu.net:/systems/msdos/simtel/at
Innoculan AntiVirus   www.networldwide.com/products/cheyenne.htm
McAfee Anti-Virus   www.mcafee.com/
Microsoft   www.microsoft.com
Norton AntiVirus   www.symantec.com
Ontrack Software   www.ontrack.com/
PassMark BurnIn 2.2   www.passmark.com/
Ziff Davis   www.zdnet.com/etestinglabs/filters/benchmarks/

5

BACKUP GUIDE

Few events are as frightening or disturbing as losing your valuable data. It really doesn't make much difference how it happens—virus damage, drive failure, sabotage, user error, an improper software installation, or old age are all equally effective at disabling your computer and rendering your data inaccessible. There are countless preventative maintenance tools and data recovery tactics available, but regardless of manufacturers' claims, all of those recovery techniques have limitations—especially when the drive fails outright. The only certain means of protecting your valuable data is to back up your system. This chapter covers some important backup considerations, offers some guidelines for preparing backups, and explains the major limitations and pitfalls of backup strategies.

Backup Considerations

Although it is not terribly expensive or difficult to start a backup regimen, it is hardly a trivial concern. Whether protecting your system against data loss or archiving unused applications and data, proper backups depend on understanding the needs of the particular system being backed up. One of the most common misconceptions about backups is that they are used solely for the purposes of protecting data. True, the threat of data loss is a major factor in any backup strategy, but there are other advantages of backups as well.

For example, backups are often used to archive older or unused files. Let's face it, even the largest hard drive will eventually run short of space. Older applications and work files can be off-loaded through a backup, then erased from the hard drive—thus freeing valuable drive space. Backups also play an important role in periodic drive maintenance. As magnetic media ages, the sector and track IDs decay slowly. In extreme cases, this identification data may become irretrievable and result in the loss of an application or its data. By maintaining timely backups, a drive can be low-level formatted (using a formatting program designed for the particular drive) to rewrite sector and track ID information, then reloaded from a most recent backup. The "refreshed" drive may then continue providing years of trouble-free service. Effective backups also demand a variety of other considerations:

- *Consider the backup frequency.* How often should a backup be performed? This is one of the most perplexing questions surrounding tape backups—and the answer is always different depending on who you talk to. The most common yardstick is need. If you can't afford to lose what you've got, back it up. While this guideline may be effective for individual PC owners, it is not quite so simple to evaluate the backup needs of business and professional users. In such cases, need should be based on the value of data contained in the PC and how often it changes. For example, a graphic design or desktop publishing firm may need to back up every week or two. On the other hand, a busy order-entry system would probably be best served making daily backups.

- *Consider the most effective type of backup.* Traditionally, there are three types of backup: total, selective, and modified. The *total* backup is just as the name implies—all files and directories on the specified drive are saved to the backup device. Total backups provide the best protection of data, and files can be restored selectively. (But total backups take the longest to complete.) *Selective* backups allow you to back up only desired files or directories. This is particularly handy for archival purposes, or if the majority of new data on the system is limited to a number of known directories. Selective backups also take less time than total backups (depending on the number of files selected). *Modified* backups (also known as *differential* backups) copy only the files that were changed since the last backup. This is the fastest but least flexible type of backup. It is often a combination of these strategies that provides the best level of data protection.

- *Consider the hardware and media requirements.* There are many means of producing backups. Floppy disks, removable media disks such as the Iomega Zip drive, tape drives (in all their variations), and optical disks such as CD-Rs or CD-RWs are just a few of the available options. Some years ago, floppy disks were often used for backups. Today, however, it would take thousands of disks to perform a total backup of one contemporary hard drive. Floppy disks are still used for small groups of files (for example, DTP files, graphics, and data files) that are considered "work-in-progress," but they are hardly useful for serious backup work. At the other end of the range, *magneto-optical* (MO) devices provide tremendous storage capacity, but their price and sophistication are often best suited for busy networks and high-end workstations. For the individual PC or a small network, tape drives or CD-R/-RW drives generally provide the best cost/performance trade-off. A single low-end tape drive can back up 2GB on one tape—more expensive drives can hold over 8GB. In most installations, a tape drive will provide more than adequate backup capability.

■ *Get the media preformatted.* If you've ever had to format a box of floppy disks, you know what a cumbersome, time-consuming process it can be. Tapes are even more difficult to deal with. A typical mini-cartridge can take up to one hour to format. While this may not be a problem for individual users who back up infrequently, business users may have trouble committing hours of PC time to tape formatting. Use factory-formatted media wherever possible. Even though preformatted media may cost a bit more, the savings in time are often well worth it.

■ *Consider where to store the backups.* Since backups can serve a number of practical purposes, it is important to plan where the backups will be kept and who will have access to them. Again, individuals who use their PC for casual applications can probably keep their backup tape in a desk drawer or filing cabinet without a second thought. For businesses and busy professional systems, the problem becomes a bit more complicated. One of the key reasons for backups is disaster recovery, so the backup should be protected from disaster. Often, this means securing backups in a fireproof safe or fireproof file cabinet in another room away from the original system—sometimes away from the site of business entirely. Another reason for this concern is security—you would not want confidential files falling into the wrong hands. In many companies, backup, restoration, and security are assigned to authorized individuals.

■ *Consider compression.* Data compression is an excellent means of expanding the storage capacity of a tape. For example, compression may allow a 4GB tape to hold up to 8GB of data. If your backup software provides the capability of tape compression, use it. There may be a small penalty in reading or writing speed, but the extra capacity is usually worth it.

■ *Consider manual vs. automatic backups.* If you run your system for regular, prolonged periods, automatic backups can be configured with a scheduler feature of most backup software (or the Task Manager feature of Windows 98/Me). This makes it possible to save desired files at regular times while remaining virtually transparent to the user. Businesses with extensive computer time can usually take advantage of automatic backups. Individuals who use PCs inconsistently are probably best served with manual backups. Keep in mind that tape drives require routine cleaning, so automatic backups should also include periods of downtime for regular scheduled cleanings.

TAPE ROTATION TACTICS

Tape cartridges are the most common medium for backup systems. Although the number of backups you perform per week or per month will depend entirely on the amount of activity on your system or network, the tapes themselves limit backup integrity. By using more than one tape as part of your backup regimen, you will not find yourself writing over a current backup (potentially disastrous if the backup process is interrupted). Tape rotation is a tactic that helps to ensure that data is protected and integral at all times.

Two Tapes

This is generally considered to be the most rudimentary strategy—ideal for individual or infrequent PC users. There are usually two variations with a two-tape strategy. The most common implementation is simply to make full backups—alternating the tapes each time. For example, tape A is reformatted and used for a backup on March 1, tape B is reformatted and used on April 1, then tape A is reformatted and reused for a complete backup on May 1, and so on. This approach guarantees that you are never overwriting a "current" backup. An alternative strategy is to create a total backup on tape A, then make modified backups on tape B as needed.

Three Tapes

The three-tape cycle is frequently used for small offices or home offices where there are a limited number of files changing from day to day. The process is easy to understand if you look at it over a one-week period. On Monday, make a complete backup on tape A. Tuesday through Friday, make modified (a.k.a. "incremental") backups on tape B (each modified backup should have its own tape volume). The next week, make a total backup on tape C, and store tape A in a secure location off-site. Erase or reformat tape B, and then use it for modified backups throughout the week. On Monday of the subsequent week, store tape C off-site, and return tape A to be erased or reformatted for a new complete backup. Thus tapes A and C are alternated each week for complete system backups, while tape B remains on-site for daily modified backups.

If you're not using the system enough to justify daily maintenance, try a weekly approach. Use tape A for a total backup on the first of the month, and then use tape B for modified backups once a week during the month (or whenever important new files must be protected). The first of the next month, perform a total backup on tape C and store tape A in a secure location off-site. Erase tape B and reuse it for modified backups throughout the month. On the first of the third month, move tape C off site, erase tape A and perform a complete backup, and then erase tape B and use it for modified backups. This way, tapes A and C are alternated the first of every month rather than the first of every week.

Six Tapes

The six-tape rotation is intended for businesses and busy offices where important files are changed and updated daily. Start the week by erasing or reformatting tapes A and F, then creating total backups on both tapes. Store tape F in a secure location off-site. Use tapes B, C, D, and E to perform modified (incremental) backups on Tuesday through Friday. On the subsequent Monday, tapes A and F would be erased and backed up once again. Each day through the week, the tape designated for that particular day would be erased and saved with a modified backup.

Ten Tapes

When you need to maintain weekly and monthly off-site archives of ongoing work, you can use a ten-tape rotation cycle (which is really just an adjustment to the six-tape cycle). By adding four more tapes to the six-tape cycle, you can create a total backup the first of every week, and then store those weekly backups off-site. For example, on the first Monday of the month, a total backup is made on tapes A and F (just as in the six-tape rotation), and tape F is stored off-site. On Tuesday through Friday, tapes B, C, D, and E hold modified backups of each day. Tape F becomes the archive of week 1. The next week, total backups are made on tapes A and G, while tapes B, C, D, and E provide modified backups. Tape G would be the archive for week 2. The third week, tapes A and H would be the total backups, and tape H would archive the third week. Tapes A and I would hold total backups on the fourth week, so tape I would archive the fourth week. Finally, tape J would be used as a total backup on the last day of the month. While this process is overkill for many businesses, it may come in handy for businesses that require long-term archives of their work (for example, government contractors).

BACKUP LIMITATIONS

While backups are usually considered to be a cost-effective form of data archiving and a reliable means of data protection, backups are hardly perfect. There is a whole array of limitations that can adversely effect your backup efforts (or those of your customer). This part of the chapter is designed to illustrate the pitfalls to look out for when planning and executing backups:

- *Irregular or inconsistent backups.* This is probably the single most troublesome problem when implementing a backup strategy. To be effective, backups must be performed regularly. All too often, users make some initial backups on schedule, but fail to follow through with subsequent backups. Before long, the backups that *were* made fall so far out of date that they become useless. When trouble occurs, the investment in equipment and media just does not pay off. Make it a point to implement regular backups and follow through with them consistently.

- *Poorly labeled and stored backups.* This problem is typical of large tape rotations. Often, tapes and other backup media are left strewn around an office or department with little or no idea what is on them. Effective backup strategies demand that each tape be marked and identified clearly so that no one will accidentally discard or overwrite it. Groups of tapes should always be kept together in a drawer or on a shelf the same way you would organize volumes of books. It's hard enough to keep regular backups without having to search for the tapes and guess which ones to use. Make it a point to keep tapes (and all magnetic media) away from telephones, monitors, power supplies, excessive heat, extreme cold, and all forms of moisture.

- *Inadequate disaster preparation.* Here's another real impediment to successful backups. Too often, businesses invest serious money in backup equipment—only to leave the tapes sitting on top of the backed-up system. If you rely on backups to store your vital files, those tapes should be stored in a location that is reasonably safe from disasters (for example, fire, flood, theft, or sabotage). Often, a fireproof safe or file cabinet will perform quite well. The same concern is true for off-site storage.

- *Inadequate testing and maintenance.* Some businesses are so preoccupied with performing a backup that they do not check to confirm that the backup is any good. When trouble strikes, they are horrified to find that the backup lacks vital files, is unreadable, or does not restore properly—leaving the backup virtually useless. After a backup is made, it should be tested using a "compare" or "verify" function of the backup software to check the tape contents against the disk files. Although this takes a bit longer, it need not be done each time a backup is made. When errors are indicated, it usually means that the drive is failing or has not been routinely cleaned as required. Try cleaning the backup drive as recommended by the manufacturer, and perform the backup again. Every so often, it may be worth testing your backup capability with a "backup drill."

- *Inadequate attention to the media.* Like floppy disks, tapes are magnetic media. Unfortunately, magnetic media does not last forever. One of the big problems with frequent backups is that users mistake backup or compare errors for a problem with the drive or backup software, when it is actually the tape that has worn out. As a general rule, plan on replacing your tapes at least once a year. If you are performing frequent backups, plan on replacing your tapes even more frequently. Tape life is also dependent on tape quality. High-quality tapes last longer than low-quality tapes. It is often more prudent to spend a bit more for a reliable, good-quality tape, than to save a little money on a low-cost tape—only to find that the tape wears out much sooner or loses data.

Using Microsoft Backup

There are numerous backup utilities available today, but Microsoft includes a version of Backup with each copy of Windows 9x/Me. Backup is generally regarded as a basic end-user utility, but there are some important issues to remember when installing and using Backup. This part of the chapter outlines the essentials for using Backup and covers many of the most common Backup problems.

BACKUP GUIDELINES

When using Backup, it's important that you remember the following points—otherwise, you may encounter problems setting up or using Backup for Windows 9x/Me.

■ *Tape drive support.* The Backup program supports the following QIC-40, QIC-80, and QIC-3010 tape backup units made by the following companies (and connected to the primary floppy disk controller): Colorado Memory Systems (CMS), Conner, Iomega, and Wangtek (in "hardware phantom mode" or "Drive B sharing mode"). Backup also supports CMS QIC-40, QIC-80, and QIC-3010 tape drives connected to a parallel port. However, the following drives are not compatible with Backup:

  ■ Drives connected to a secondary floppy disk controller (or to a floppy accelerator card)

  ■ Archive drives

  ■ Irwin AccuTrak tapes (and other Irwin drives)

  ■ Mountain drives

  ■ QIC Wide tapes (Backup supports QIC Wide drives using QIC 80 tapes)

  ■ QIC 3020 drives

  ■ SCSI tape drives

  ■ Summit drives

  ■ Proprietary tape drive controllers of any type

  ■ Travan drives

 Some floppy controller–driven tape backup units may require firmware (BIOS) revisions to work properly with the Backup program.

■ *FC-20 tape controller support.* Backup does not support proprietary controller cards for tape drives. Similar unsupported controllers include FC-10 and FC-15 controllers, and controllers from Iomega.

■ *Using other backup sets.* Backup can restore data from backup sets created by third-party DOS-based or Windows 3.1–based tape backup programs. However, the third-party tape backup program must conform to the QIC standard for implementing compression. Unfortunately, Backup cannot restore data sets created by earlier versions of Backup.

■ *Backup types.* Backup supports full and incremental backup sets, but does not support differential backups. To enable incremental backup, click Options on Backup's Settings menu, and then click the Incremental option button on the Backup tab.

■ *Restoring without Windows.* Backup requires Windows. If you're reinstalling Windows for any reason, you need at least a minimum install (including Backup). Then you can use the Backup utility to restore your backup set.

■ *Registry errors when restoring files.* When restoring just one or two files from a backup set, you may receive a message such as "There may have been an error restoring the registry. Your computer may not work properly" even though you chose not to restore the registry. This message appears when you restore files from the "Full System Backup Set" collection, which is intended to be used only to perform a full system backup or restore. The Full System Backup Set collection contains the files necessary to restore your Windows configuration to its original state. Keep this backup set in a safe place in case your hard disk partition or the Windows folder is damaged, and create separate backup sets for backing up other data.

■ *Tape drive detection.* Tape drive detection is performed by Microsoft Backup when it loads. Backup does not rely on the operating system for information about tape drive units attached to the system, so it is not necessary for your tape drive to be listed in Device Manager.

INSTALLING BACKUP

Although the Backup utility is included with Windows 9x/Me, it is not installed by default when Windows is installed. Instead, you'll need to install Backup manually from the Windows installation CD. Follow these steps to install Backup:

1. Open your Control Panel, and then double-click the Add/Remove Programs icon.

2. On the Windows Setup tab, click Disk Tools (or System Tools), and then click Details.

3. Click the Backup check box to select it, and then click OK.

4. Click OK again. The installation will proceed automatically.

BACKUP AND RESTORE

Using Microsoft Backup is not a terribly complicated process, but there are a few guidelines that might make the procedure a bit easier. Use the following steps when creating a backup set:

1. Click Start, highlight Programs, select Accessories, highlight System Tools, and then click Backup.

2. Click the Backup tab.

3. Create a backup set. (A *backup set* is an index of the files you plan to back up.) The first time you run Backup, a Full System Backup Set is created. This set includes every file on your hard disk.

4. To create a smaller set of selected files, use the Select Files To Backup dialog box. Each drive, folder, and file has a check box next to it. If a check appears in a given box, that file, folder, or the contents of the selected drive will be backed up. If a check appears in a check box with a dark background, some items in the folder or drive (but not everything) will be backed up.

5. Click Next Step.

6. In the "Select a destination for the backup" window, click the desired destination for your backup. If you have a supported tape backup drive that is detected by Backup, it appears at the bottom of the "Select a destination for the backup" window. If you do not have a tape drive (or your tape drive is not detected), you can select a floppy disk drive or a location on your hard disk.

 You can also back up your files to a network drive by mapping a drive letter to the network destination where you want to back up your files. If you have mapped a drive letter to a network drive, Backup shows it in the "Select a destination for the backup" window.

7. Click Start Backup and allow the process to proceed. If you have created a new backup set, you are prompted to name the new set. Backup will inform you when the operation is finished.

You can use the following steps to restore your backup set:

1. Click Start, highlight Programs, select Accessories, highlight System Tools, and then click Backup.

2. Click the Restore tab.

3. In the Restore From window, select the drive or folder where the backup is stored.
   In the Backup Set window, select the backup set that you need to restore, and then click Next Step.

4. Click the check boxes by the files you want to restore (a check will appear in the check box), or clear the check boxes for any files you do not want to restore.

5. Click Start Restore and allow the process to proceed. Backup will inform you when the operation is finished.

RESTORING EARLIER BACKUP SETS

It is important to remember that the Backup utility included with a given version of Windows cannot restore files that were saved with an earlier version of Backup (for example, the versions of Backup included with DOS versions 5.0 and 6.x). To restore files saved with earlier versions of Backup, you must use the RESTORE.EXE or MSBACKUP.EXE utilities located on the Windows CD. Before using RESTORE.EXE or MSBACKUP.EXE, you should refer to the LFNBK.TXT file in the \admin\apptools\lfnback folder on your Windows CD.

To restore files saved with the Backup program included with DOS 5.0, use the RESTORE.EXE program located in the \other\oldmsdos folder on your Windows 95 CD. To run this program, copy it to a folder on your hard drive, and then run it from a command prompt (making sure to use the appropriate syntax). For detailed information about the RESTORE.EXE program, type the following line:

```
restore /?
```

If you receive the error message "Incorrect DOS version" when you try to use RESTORE.EXE, type the following line to modify the version table:

```
setver restore.exe 6.22
```

After you type this line, restart your computer and try to run RESTORE.EXE again.

To restore files created with the backup program included with DOS 6.x, use the MSBACKUP.EXE utility located in the \other\oldmsdos\msbackup folder on your Windows 95 CD. To run this program, copy all the files from the folder on that CD to a folder on your hard drive. Double-click the MSBACKUP.EXE file in Windows Explorer to start it. For detailed information about the MSBACKUP.EXE program, start the program and click Restore on the Help menu.

RESTORING WINDOWS 98 FROM A BACKUP

The Windows 98/SE System Recovery wizard restores the data on your computer by installing Windows 98 with a custom MSBATCH.INF file. This installation of Windows 98 allows the protected-mode Microsoft Backup program to restore a previously created full system backup. To use the System Recovery wizard to restore your Windows 98 installation, you must have a Windows 98 Startup disk, a CD-ROM drive supported by the Windows 98 Startup disk, the Windows installation CD, a backup device connected to your computer, and a full system backup created with Backup. Use the following steps to restore Windows 98 on your computer:

Use these steps to restore data only to the same hardware on which it was backed up. If your computer hardware has changed since the backup was made, you can use these steps to restore your data, but you will need to reinstall all of your Windows-based software after the process is complete.

1. Insert your Windows 98 Startup disk into the floppy disk drive, and then start your computer.

2. On the Windows 98 Startup menu, choose Start Computer With CD-ROM Support.

3. At the command prompt, type the following line (then press ENTER):

    ```
    <cdrom>: cd tools\sysrec pcrestor
    ```

    where <cdrom> is the drive letter of your CD-ROM drive.

4. After Windows 98 Setup starts, remove the Windows 98 Startup disk from the floppy disk drive.

5. In the System Recovery wizard, click Next.

6. Type your name and company name, and then click Next.

7. In the System Recovery wizard, click Finish. The Backup Welcome screen appears.

8. In the Backup dialog box, click Restore Backed Up Files, and then click OK.

9. In the Restore wizard, use the following options when you are prompted:

    ■ **Restore From**   Select the location where your backup is stored.

    ■ **Select Backup Sets**   Select the most recent full system backup.

    ■ **What To Restore**   Click to select the check box next to each local drive.

    ■ **Where To Restore**   Click Original Locations.

    ■ **How To Restore**   Click "Always replace the file on my computer."

10. Click Start to start the restore process.

Using Backup Exec

Another popular backup application is Seagate's Backup Exec utility. With Backup Exec, you can create and test emergency recovery floppy disks that allow you to recover files without having to first reinstall the operating system or backup software—this is a powerful advantage when it becomes necessary to recover your system from a catastrophic loss. Backup Exec also supports many QIC and SCSI backup devices. This part of the chapter is intended to highlight some features of Backup Exec and to identify some potential problems that you should keep in mind.

CREATING EMERGENCY RECOVERY DISKS

Backup Exec's Emergency Restore feature enables you to rebuild the operating system and the latest "Selected Files" backup without having to reinstall the operating system or the backup software. Your entire local drive can be restored using the Emergency Recovery (ER) disks and a backup of your drive. The first time Backup Exec launches, you are prompted to create ER disks. The ER disks enable you to restore your files even if Windows will not start. If you do not create ER disks the first time Backup Exec launches, you may do so later by choosing Emergency Diskettes from the Tools menu. You may use the following procedure to create ER disks:

You cannot use the File option for Emergency Recovery. Instead, you must use a backup device when creating your ER disks. If you installed a new backup device since you created your ER disks, you must create new ER disks to accompany your new backup device.

1. With Backup Exec running, select Emergency Diskettes from the Tools menu.

2. If you have more than one backup device, your backup devices appear on the Tools menu under Emergency Diskettes. Select the device you want to use to store your local drive and registry files. You may need to select the correct DOS ASPI drivers at this time (for SCSI backup drives).

3. Follow the on-screen instructions.

4. A message appears when the ER disks are complete.

The Emergency Recovery feature of Backup Exec will not restore a dual boot system (for example, Windows 98 and NT). Also, Emergency Recovery will not restore data to a compressed hard drive. If you have used a disk compression program to increase the capacity of your hard drive, you may not be able to restore your data—Emergency Recovery may run out of space on the hard drive before your data is fully recovered.

TESTING EMERGENCY RECOVERY DISKS

After you create your Emergency Recovery (ER) disks, it is highly recommended that you test them. This is particularly important if your backup device requires a DOS driver:

1. Insert ER Disk #1 into the floppy drive.

2. Restart your computer. The README.ER file appears. After reading the text, press ALT-F, and then press X to exit the editor.

3. Insert ER Disk #2.

4. To start the Recovery process, type **restore** and press ENTER.

5. Insert your media containing the backup sets you want to recover, and then press ENTER.

6. If prompted, select the specific backup set to recover. (The backup set is selected automatically if your media contains only one backup set.)

7. If your backup set is password protected, you are prompted to enter your password. Type your password and press ENTER.

8. Ensure that all of your selections are correct before continuing. If so, then you have verified that "Emergency Recovery" will be able to read data from the media in case of an actual emergency.

9. If you see any error messages during this process, there is a problem communicating with the backup device. Most likely the problem is a missing DOS driver that is required for your backup device (or incorrect command-line parameters for the driver).

USING EMERGENCY RECOVERY

The Emergency Recovery (ER) process enables you to recover from hard disk failure and should be used in emergency situations only. Before using Emergency Recovery, decide if another recovery method can be implemented instead. For example, if the problem appears to be a Windows 9x system problem (such as a corrupt registry), try to recover as suggested by the operating system instructions. Otherwise, you should go ahead and use your ER disks:

1. Insert ER Disk #1 into the floppy drive.

2. Turn on your computer.

3. If necessary, you may prepare your hard disk using FDISK, FORMAT, and SYS, all located on ER Disk #1.

If you alter your drives by using FDISK (or another partition utility), you must reboot with ER Disk #1 *before* using the FORMAT and SYS utilities (or continuing with Emergency Recovery).

4. Insert ER Disk #2. At the command prompt, type **restore**.

5. If prompted, select your specific backup device. The backup device is selected automatically if only one device is connected to your computer.

6. Insert the media containing your backup sets to be recovered, and then press ENTER.

7. If prompted, select the most recent All Selected Files (Full) backup set to recover. The backup set is selected automatically if your media contains only one backup set.

8. If the backup set is password protected, you are prompted to enter the password. Type your password and press ENTER.

9. Select the drive volume where you want to recover your data.

10. Ensure that all of your selections are correct before proceeding, and then press ENTER.

The Emergency Recovery process now begins restoring the Windows 9x file system on your selected drive. If your selected backup set spans two or more media, you are prompted to insert the next medium in the sequence after all the current files are recovered. When the recovery is complete, a summary of the recovery process appears. This summary includes the number of files selected and the number actually recovered. If these numbers are different, refer to the RESTORE.RPT file for a listing of what files could not be recovered. Press ENTER to close the summary and return to DOS.

If you want to recover other backup sets or drive volumes, run the RESTORE.EXE utility again. When you're finished restoring files, remove the ER disk from the floppy drive and restart your computer. It may be necessary to reboot your computer more than once if any hardware has changed in your system since your backup was made.

CONFLICTS FROM OTHER BACKUP PROGRAMS

Although Backup Exec is generally regarded as a stable and reliable utility, there are drivers from other backup programs (or Windows 3.1 applications) that may conflict with Backup Exec. To troubleshoot problems with Backup Exec, it may be necessary to disable suspect driver files in order to try clearing the problem. Note the following driver files that are known to cause problems:

device=cmswtape.386	;Colorado Backup for Windows
device=cmsdtape.386	;Colorado Backup for DOS
device=vfintd.386	;Backup Exec, Conner, Iomega, and Norton Backup
device=cpbvxd.386	;Central Point Backup
device=symevnt.386	;Symantec Norton Utilities
device=adw30.386	;After Dark Screen Savers
device=awdos.386	;PC Anywhere for DOS
device=vpcaw.386	;PC Anywhere for Windows
device=fastback.386	;Fastback Backup
device=irw286.drv	;Irwin EZtape Backup
device=novabkp.386	;Novastor Backup
device=virwt.386	;Irwin EZtape Backup

You can use the following steps to disable suspect drivers:

1. Make a copy of your SYSTEM.INI file (found in your Windows folder), and name the copy SYSTEMBKUP.INI. (This provides a copy of your original file.)

2. Click Start and then click Run.

3. Type **system.ini** and click OK. The SYSTEM.INI file will open in Notepad.

4. In the [386Enh] section of your SYSTEM.INI file, type a semicolon (;) at the beginning of the driver file line(s) that you need to disable.

5. Save the modified SYSTEM.INI file and restart your computer.

If the problem persists, use the following steps to disable other potential problem programs:

1. Make a copy of your WIN.INI file (found in your Windows folder), and name the copy WINBKUP.INI. (This provides a copy of your original file.)

2. Click Start and then click Run.

3. Type **win.ini** and click OK. The WIN.INI file will open in Notepad.

4. Type a semicolon (;) at the beginning of the "load=" and "run=" lines of any files that need to be disabled, and then save the updated file.

5. Restart your computer and run Backup Exec.

If you're using a SCSI backup device, try disabling any real-mode drivers loading in CONFIG.SYS:

1. Click Start and then click Run.

2. Type **sysedit.exe** and click OK.

3. Click on the CONFIG.SYS window.

4. Type **rem** at the beginning of each line that contains a real-mode driver. For example:

```
rem device=c:\aspi\aspi4dos.sys
```

5. Save the CONFIG.SYS file.

6. Restart your computer and run Backup Exec.

Backup Troubleshooting

Microsoft Backup offers most Windows 9x/Me users a simple and convenient tool for backing up their important files or day-to-day work. While Backup is compatible with a wide range of drives, it is certainly not foolproof. When you encounter problems with Backup, check the following tips before diving into the troubleshooting issues next.

TAPE DRIVE NOT DETECTED

When you cannot get Backup to recognize a specific tape drive, verify that the drive is compatible with Backup. Windows Backup should support the following tape backup units: QIC 40, QIC 80, and QIC 3010 tape drives that are connected to the primary floppy disk controller generally *are* compatible with Backup. Typical drives include those made by Colorado Memory Systems (CMS), Conner, Iomega, and Wangtek (only in "hardware phantom mode" or "Drive B sharing mode"). Also, Colorado Memory Systems (CMS) QIC 40, QIC 80, and QIC 3010 tape drives connected to a parallel port generally *are* compatible with Backup. However, there is a long list of devices that are *not* compatible with Backup, and these fall into a few broad categories:

■ Any drives connected to a secondary floppy disk controller (or to a floppy accelerator card)

■ Archive drives, Irwin (including AccuTrak) tapes/drives, Mountain drives, QIC Wide tapes (Backup supports QIC Wide drives using QIC 80 tapes), QIC 3020 drives, SCSI tape drives, Summit drives, and Travan drives

■ Any type of tape drive controller

Some floppy controller–driven tape backup units may require firmware revisions in order to work properly with the Windows Backup utility.

PROBLEMS RESTORING FILES

File restoration problems are often the result of drive maintenance and system (or OS) configuration issues. Use the following tips to help troubleshoot file problems:

■ Clean the read/write heads.

■ Set your computer to a slower speed (for example, disable the "turbo" mode).

■ Try to restore the files in Safe Mode. If the tape backup drive requires a protected-mode driver, it will not work in Safe Mode. For example, Colorado Trakker drives do not work in Safe Mode because the VCOMM driver doesn't load.

■ Try to restore the files on a different computer.

■ Verify that there is enough swap file space on your hard drive.

NETWORK BACKUP/RESTORE PROBLEMS

This problem is usually related to the network or network configuration rather than to the Backup utility. If you can't back up or restore files through a network, try a different network protocol, or try to copy a large file across the network with the XCOPY command. You may also need to disconnect the PC from its network and backup/restore files locally.

TAPE CANNOT BE FORMATTED

Formatting is a critical process when preparing or refurbishing tapes for backup operations. Formatting problems are usually the result of defective tapes, incompatible formats, or OS driver conflicts:

■ See that you're using a compatible tape format. For example, you cannot format a 3010 tape in a QIC-80 drive, and you cannot format a QIC-80 Wide tape in a QIC-80 drive.

■ The tape may be bad or worn out. Try to format a different tape. Do not try to format bulk-erased tapes.

■ Try to format the tape in Windows Safe Mode. If the tape backup drive requires a protected-mode driver, it will not work in Safe Mode. For example, Colorado Trakker drives do not work in Safe Mode because the VCOMM driver doesn't load.

■ There may be a video DMA conflict (typically encountered on older PCs). Minimize the progress indicator. If formatting still fails, change the video resolution to 640×480×16 colors. If problems persist, try formatting the tape in a full-screen DOS command prompt session. (If this works, use Device Manager to look for a DMA conflict between the video card and the floppy drive controller.)

THE TAPE DESPOOLS

If your tapes frequently despool, the end-of-tape (EOT) sensor in your tape drive may be dirty or damaged. This prevents the drive from accurately determining when the end of the tape has been reached. Many drive manufacturers recommend cleaning the end-of-tape sensor after every eight hours of drive operation, when excessive dust or other debris accumulates on the sensor, or when a tape used in the drive becomes despooled. For specific cleaning information, refer to the documentation that came with your drive.

TAPE COMPARISON FAILS

Tapes should always be verified (or compared) after a backup is performed. Failed comparisons almost always mean that the tape itself has failed. Try a known-good or good-quality tape.

CANNOT ACCESS TAPE DRIVE

You may find that Backup stops responding. If Backup is unable to access the tape drive and appears to stop responding, there may be a resource conflict between IDE devices in your computer. For example, your SyQuest removable drive may be configured to use the same resources as your tape drive. Use the Device Manager to check for hardware conflicts in the system.

COLORADO TRAKKER TAPE BACKUP ISSUES

If you're experiencing random Backup problems with a Colorado Trakker tape drive on a parallel port, make sure the parallel port is not configured in the computer's CMOS Setup as an ECP or EPP port. If it is, reconfigure the port to a "standard" (or bidirectional) parallel port.

IOMEGA QIC-80 TAPE BACKUP ISSUES

Iomega suggests that these drives require new drivers from Iomega (**www.iomega.com**). You may also need to verify that the following line exists in the CONFIG.SYS file:

```
buffers=30
```

MISCELLANEOUS SUGGESTIONS

There are numerous other problems that may not be covered by the preceding points. If you continue to have problems with Backup, try some of these tips:

■ Clean the tape drive carefully (especially the read/write heads).

■ Verify that all of the power connections and signal cables are securely and properly attached.

■ Verify that any jumpers on the drive (and drive controller) are set in a compatible mode for your system.

■ If you have an internal tape drive, position it as far as possible from the hard disk. If you have an external tape drive, position it as far as possible from the monitor.

BACKUP SYMPTOMS

When you cannot isolate problems with the tips and guidelines provided earlier, you can refer to specific symptoms for advice and solutions. This part of the chapter examines many common issues that are known to occur with Backup under Windows.

SYMPTOM 5-1   **You encounter errors with Backup under Windows 9x/Me**   When you use Backup to create a full system backup under Windows 9x/Me or a backup that includes the \Windows folder, the status box may indicate that errors occurred during the backup process. When you click Report to view the backup report, you may see error messages such as:

```
Error: C:\WINDOWS\Cookies\index.dat - busy
Error: C:\WINDOWS\History\index.dat - busy
Error: C:\WINDOWS\Temporary Internet Files\index.dat - busy
```

This problem can occur because the INDEX.DAT files that are in each of these locations are open if Internet Explorer is running. Since IE is part of the Windows 98/Me *graphical user interface* (GUI), these files are always open and therefore cannot be backed up. This behavior occurs in Windows 95 if you're running IE when you run Backup (or if IE 4.0 or 4.01 is installed on the system, and you have enabled the Windows Desktop Update component). Remember that the INDEX.DAT files are re-created each time IE starts, so it is not necessary to back up these files. All other files that you selected are successfully backed up.

SYMPTOM 5-2   **Backup has trouble spanning multiple disks when backing up to a removable media drive under Windows**   When you're using Backup to store files to a removable disk (other than floppy disks), Backup doesn't prompt you to insert a second disk. If the entire backup doesn't fit on one disk, you'll receive an error such as "Errors occurred during this operation—do you want to view them now?" The incomplete backup volume on the first disk is damaged and cannot be restored.

This is a limitation of the Backup utility. While Backup does support the use of removable disk drives (for example, Bernoulli and SyQuest drives), it does not support performing backups that span multiple disks. Backup can span multiple disks only on floppy disk drives connected to the primary floppy drive controller. When you're using Backup to store files to a removable disk, perform only backups that fit on one disk. Large backups that require more than one disk should be broken up into smaller backups—each of which fits on one disk.

SYMPTOM 5-3   **Backup cannot restore a file from multiple disks**   When you try to use the Backup utility in Windows 98/Me to restore a backup set created in Microsoft Windows 95 that spans multiple disks, a new folder may be created, but the file in the backup set may not be restored. This trouble occurs when your backup set contains a file that spans multiple disks. Windows 98/Me cannot restore a Windows 95 backup set that consists of a single file that spans two or more disks. To work around this problem, use the Backup utility in Windows 95 to restore your file. To correct this problem for the future, do not use the Backup tool in Windows 95 to back up a single file that spans multiple disks. Alternatively, back up more than one file from your Windows 95–based computer, and verify that the additional file is on the first disk—in its entirety.

SYMPTOM 5-4   **Backup performance appears poor under Windows**   Performing a backup operation through Backup may take (significantly) longer than you expect. This poor backup performance might also be accompanied by diminished hard drive performance while you perform other tasks in Windows. There are several important factors that can affect backup performance. First, check your available memory. A lack of available memory is typically caused by having too many programs open at the same time, or by not having enough physical RAM installed in the computer. Close all running programs before starting the backup process. If that does not improve performance, remove all programs from the Startup folder and from the "load=" and "run=" lines of your WIN.INI file. If performance remains poor after restarting Windows, try adding more RAM to the system.

Also check for DOS Compatibility Mode. Double-click the System icon in Control Panel, and then click the Performance tab. If the Performance tab in System properties shows that one or more of the hard drives are operating in DOS Compatibility Mode, resolve this problem as soon as possible to improve performance in Backup. Check the hard drive performance next. Even if your hard drives are not stuck in DOS Compatibility Mode, Backup performance may be affected by overall drive performance. If you're using an IDE-type hard drive, its performance may be affected by another device on the same controller channel (for example, tape drives and CD-ROMs). Move the slower device(s) to a separate IDE controller channel.

Update any compression software. When using "disk compression" on an older (slower) computer, hard drive performance may suffer. If you're using third-party disk compression software that employs real-mode drivers to access your compressed drives, you may be able to improve performance by replacing the real-mode driver with a protected-mode driver. Also check and correct any file fragmentation. Badly fragmented hard disks can affect the performance of Backup (as well as the performance of many other tasks under Windows). Click the Start button, highlight Programs, point to Accessories, point to System Tools, and then click Disk Defragmenter. Run "Defrag" to reorganize the files on your hard drive(s).

Finally, check the tape for defects. Backup can detect and avoid unusable sectors on a tape, but the process that it uses for this type of checking can be time-consuming. If you suspect that performance problems in Backup are caused by unusable sectors on a tape, try using a new tape, or use a tape that you know does not contain bad sectors.

SYMPTOM 5-5 **Backup files demand more space than originally expected** When you create a backup by using the Backup utility included with Windows Me, the number of files and amount of space used by the backup are larger than estimated by MSBACKUP.EXE. In other cases, you receive messages stating that files cannot be restored when you restore a backup that includes the _Restore folder. This problem occurs when the System Restore feature is enabled during backup. If System Restore is enabled during a backup, System Restore saves the temporary backup files. If you back up the _Restore folder, the files that System Restore saves from the temporary backup files are also backed up. To prevent temporary backup files from being saved by System Restore (and decrease the backup size), do not back up the _Restore folder. Click the plus sign (+) next to drive C in Backup, and then clear the check box next to the _Restore folder.

SYMPTOM 5-6 **You cannot restore a Travan tape backup after upgrading to Windows Me** Your internal Travan tape drive is typically configured as the primary device on the UDMA 33 controller. After you upgrade your system to Windows Me, when you attempt to restore a backup from your Travan drive (firmware revision 2.08) using the Hewlett-Packard Colorado Backup II program (version 6.0), your computer may hang up. To work around this issue, configure the Travan drive as a slave device on the UDMA 33 controller.

SYMPTOM 5-7   **The HP Colorado Backup utility doesn't detect your tape drive under Windows 98**   When you try to use the HP Colorado Backup for Windows 95 software under Windows 98, the Colorado Backup software does not detect your tape drive—even though your tape drive is listed in Device Manager. This might happen if Backup is currently installed (or has been installed in the past). Backup makes subtle changes to the registry. You'll need to remove unneeded files and correct the changes to the registry. To utilize Colorado Backup software instead of Backup, uninstall Microsoft Backup first, and then reinstall Colorado Backup from scratch:

Be sure to make a complete backup of your registry files (as well as the REGEDIT utility) to your emergency boot floppy disk. If you make a mistake editing the registry, you can install the original files from your boot floppy.

1. Click Start, highlight Settings, and then click Control Panel.

2. Double-click Add/Remove Programs, and then click the Windows Setup tab.

3. Click on System Tools (not the check box), and then click Details.

4. Click the Backup check box to clear it, click OK, click OK again, and then click Yes to restart your computer.

5. Delete or rename the following files (if they exist):
    - PNPWPROP.DLL in \Windows\System
    - PNPWRENU.DLL in \Windows\System
    - PNPWFDC.INF in \Windows\Inf
    - PNPWIDE.INF in \Windows\Inf
    - PNPWPPT.INF in \Windows\Inf
    - PNPWTAPE.INF in \Windows\Inf
    - PNPWTAPE.CAT in \Windows

6. Use the Registry Editor (REGEDIT) to delete the following registry keys (if they exist):
    ```
    HKEY_LOCAL_MACHINE\System\CurrentControlSet\Services\Class\Tape
    HKEY_LOCAL_MACHINE\System\CurrentControlSet\Services\Class\TapeController
    HKEY_LOCAL_MACHINE\System\CurrentControlSet\Services\Class\TapeDetection
    ```

7. Restart your computer.

8. Now check Device Manager to verify that the Windows 98 tape icons and drivers no longer exist. Remove them if they are present.

9. Reinstall the Colorado Backup software, and test it to determine if the problem is resolved. (Your tape drive should be detected properly.)

Microsoft Backup is not installed by default in Windows 98. If Backup is installed in Windows 95 before you install Windows 98, Backup is upgraded to the Windows 98 version automatically.

SYMPTOM 5-8   **When starting Backup under Windows 98, you receive a driver installation error**   The error may appear similar to "Driver already installed Ref 00-02-00-00-0000." After Backup starts, you may receive another error message such as "No device found." Chances are that the backup devices in your computer will not work correctly, and running the Add New Hardware wizard will probably not correctly detect your backup device(s). In most cases, the problem is caused when Seagate Direct Tape Access (version 2.0 or 3.0) is installed on your computer. Uninstall the Seagate Direct Tape Access (version 2.0 or 3.0) software, or uninstall Microsoft Backup for Windows 98. To uninstall Backup:

1. Click Start, highlight Settings, click Control Panel, and then double-click Add/Remove Programs.

2. Click the Windows Setup tab, click on System Tools (not the check box), click Details, click the Backup check box to clear it, and then click OK.

3. Follow the instructions on the screen to finish uninstalling Backup.

SYMPTOM 5-9   **You cannot change the destination folder in Backup under Windows 98**
When you select a destination folder under Where To Back Up in Microsoft Backup and then change your backup options by clicking Options under How To Back Up, the destination folder may be changed to the default folder instead of the folder you specified. This can occur if you click the Browse button to locate the destination folder, and you change the Backup options after you specify the destination folder. To resolve this problem, manually type the path to the destination folder, or change the Backup options before you specify the destination folder.

SYMPTOM 5-10   **You encounter an error while writing backup data**   When you attempt to back up data using the Backup utility under Windows 98/SE, you may receive an error message such as:

```
An error occurred while writing the backup data. The end of the media was
approached unexpectedly. (08-22-07-01-0000)
```

This issue can occur if you compress a floppy disk (or other removable media) using DriveSpace, then try to back up more data than you have available free space on the compressed disk/media. When this happens, Backup does not prompt you to insert another blank disk or media as expected. This issue can also occur when you try to span multiple CD-RW discs. The version of Backup included with Windows 98/SE does not support CD-RW disc spanning. If compression is the problem, do not use DriveSpace if you want to back up data onto more than one blank disc or removable media. If you wish to span multiple CD-RW discs, upgrade to the full version of the Seagate backup software.

SYMPTOM 5-11   **Backup cannot perform unattended backups that have been scheduled**   When you set Task Scheduler to start an unattended backup job using Backup under Windows 98, the backup job doesn't complete if it's left unattended. This occurs even if you have configured Backup to perform an unattended backup and then added this task to Task Scheduler. Task Scheduler only starts Backup—not the backup job itself. The version of Backup that is included with Windows 98 does not support starting a backup job automatically, so you must be present to begin the backup job. To resolve this problem permanently, upgrade to a backup program that supports completely unattended backup jobs.

SYMPTOM 5-12   **Backup doesn't see removable media drives as backup devices**
When you click the Where To Back Up box in Backup under Windows 98 to view your backup devices, removable media devices (such as floppy drives, Zip drives, Jaz drives, and so on) do not appear on the list. Unfortunately, a removable media drive is not recognized as a backup device (such as a tape drive), but instead is recognized as a regular drive with a drive letter (such as a hard disk). If you want to back up to removable media, click File in the Where To Back Up box when you make a backup.

If your PC only has a removable media drive for backup use, you receive a message stating there are no backup devices when you start Backup for the first time. When you're prompted to use Add New Hardware to find a backup device (or to continue without looking for a backup device), click No.

SYMPTOM 5-13   **You cannot restore from multiple tapes if one or more tapes is damaged**   For example, when you try to use Backup for Windows 98 to restore files from a backup that spans multiple tapes, you may receive an error message that says the backup media is damaged. If you then click OK or Cancel, the restore process stops, and you are not prompted to insert the next tape. This trouble occurs when one of the backup tapes is damaged. To circumvent this problem, manually restore the files on each tape:

1.   Click Start, highlight Programs, point to Accessories, point to System Tools, and then click Backup.

2.   Insert one of the tapes from your backup set into the tape drive, and then click Refresh on the Restore tab. Note that you cannot restore damaged files from the tape.

3.   When you receive a message that says your backup spans multiple tapes, click No.

4.   From the list of files on that tape, highlight the files you want to restore, and then click Start. Repeat this process with each tape in the set until you restore all the files you want, and then quit Backup.

SYMPTOM 5-14   **Windows 98 runs poorly when backing up a large number of files**   When you're backing up a very large number of files to a tape drive (or other large-capacity device), or you're comparing an existing backup to the original files on the hard drive, Windows 98 may appear to run slowly. This problem typically occurs if you back up a large number of files (for example, 2000 to 3000+ files) while the backup software is configured to perform a comparison. A comparison will check the files on the tape versus the original files on the hard drive. This problem may also occur when you're comparing a set of files that had been backed up previously. For example, this problem is known to occur with the Onstream 30GB digital drive.

This problem is caused by a fault in the Windows 98 protected-mode disk cache (VCACHE.VXD). The error occurs when the maximum value used to track the age of blocks in the cache has been exceeded. If this occurs while the protected-mode disk cache tries to free the oldest blocks to make room for new data, it takes a long time for the operation to finish. Windows will run slowly (and continues to do so until the computer is restarted). You can download and install an updated version of VCACHE.VXD (version 4.10.2183, dated 4/7/99).

SYMPTOM 5-15   **You see a Windows 98 error message such as "You have restored a good registry"**   When you start your computer, you may receive the following error message: "You have restored a good registry. Windows found an error in your system files and restored a recent backup of the files to fix the problem." When you restart your computer, you may receive the error message again. This problem can occur if the Registry backup file you're trying to restore is damaged (or if the "damage" flag in the current Registry file is not being reset by the Registry Checker utility). To fix this problem, run the Registry Checker tool using the **/fix** and **/opt** switches:

1.   Start your computer to the Safe Mode command prompt.

2.   At the DOS prompt, type **scanreg /fix** and press ENTER. The **/fix** switch causes the Registry Checker tool to repair any damaged portions of the registry.

3.   Press ENTER after the Registry Checker tool finishes repairing the registry.

4.   At the DOS prompt, type **scanreg /opt** and press ENTER. The **/opt** switch causes the Registry Checker tool to optimize the registry by removing unused space.

5.   Restart your computer.

6.   If the problem persists, try restoring a different registry backup file using the **/restore** switch.

SYMPTOM 5-16   **You encounter "Out of Memory" errors when running SCANREG.EXE under Windows 98**   When you run Registry Checker (SCANREG.EXE) with the **/fix** or **/restore** switch, you may receive an "Out of Memory" error message. You may also receive this error message when SCANREG.EXE creates a backup copy of the registry (during Windows startup). This error may occur with less than 340KB of free conventional memory. When you try to launch SCANREG.EXE with the **/fix** or **/restore** switch, more than 340KB of free conventional memory may be required—depending on the size of the Registry. Increase the free conventional memory to more than 340KB. The easiest way to do this is to reboot the computer to the Safe Mode command prompt; then run SCANREG.EXE with the appropriate switches.

SYMPTOM 5-17   **When backing up to tape under Windows 98, you get a media error** When you use Backup to read a backup tape, you may receive an error such as:

```
The media is not supported by this product - please insert another media.
```

Using a different tape generates the same error message. The error message may occur with any operation that attempts to read the tape. The error occurs if the tape drive fails to support the Quick File Access (QFA) format—also known as *media partitioning.* Backup requires that the tape drive support QFA. The QFA format allows tapes to be divided into a large data partition and a small directory partition. The directory partition holds information about each of the backup sets on the tape and can also be used to store the exact block address of each file on the tape. This feature allows for fast file retrieval with the tape drive.

SYMPTOM 5-18   **The tape backup drive is not detected**   While Microsoft Backup (or simply "Backup") is a handy tool, it has rather limited compatibility with tape drives. If Backup reports that it cannot detect your drive, you should make sure that your tape drive is compatible. You can check the Help file in your version of Backup for a more current listing of compatible drives.

SYMPTOM 5-19   **You encounter problems restoring files with Backup**   No backup has value unless it can be restored, and PC users often forget to test their backup. The only thing worse than losing your work, is discovering that your backup is inaccessible. If Backup reports trouble restoring your files, there are some steps you can take to address the problem:

■   *Clean the drive.* If the drive's read/write heads are dirty, it will not be able to read the tape reliably and errors will result. This should not damage the tape or its contents, but will make restoring difficult until the heads are cleaned. Refer to the drive's particular cleaning instructions and clean the heads. (This is good routine maintenance anyway.)

■   *Use a slower tape speed.* Some parallel ports become sensitive when the PC is operating in its "turbo" mode. Often, the tape drive is forced to work much harder—pulling the tape back and forth across the heads (an undesirable behavior called *shoeshining*). If your backup or restoration process appears to be taking an unusually long time, try disabling the PC's turbo mode, or reconfiguring the parallel port to "compatibility" mode. This does not seem to be an issue with floppy interface tape drives.

■ *Try the Windows Safe Mode.* Some drivers may interfere with the proper restoration of tape files. Try restarting Windows in the Safe Mode and then restoring files. Note that if the tape drive requires a protected-mode driver (such as Colorado Trakker's VCOMM file), the tape drive will not work in the Safe Mode.

■ *Check your drive space.* Make sure there is enough space on your hard drive. File restoration under Windows involves the use of a swap file. Since the swap file size can change dynamically under Windows, the swap file can grow to be quite large (depending on the number of files involved). If there is very limited drive space, free some space and try again.

SYMPTOM 5-20   **You find that there are problems formatting your tapes**   As with any magnetic media, you must format a tape before using it to store files. Today, many common tapes are available already formatted, but if the drive does not recognize the format (or you have trouble formatting the tape yourself), here are some things to consider:

■ *Check your tape standard.* Remember that you cannot format a 3010 tape in a QIC-80 drive, and you cannot format a QIC-80 Wide tape in a QIC-80 drive. Make sure you are using the right tape in the drive.

■ *Try a different tape.* If you have trouble formatting or working with a particular tape (but similar tapes behave correctly), it may be worn out or otherwise defective. Throw the tape away; it is not worth trying to reuse.

Do *not* attempt to reuse the tape by degaussing it (a.k.a. "bulk erasing"). This will not restore a worn tape or repair damage to it. If data is subsequently written to bad blocks, it may render your backup unusable.

■ *Try the Windows Safe Mode.* Some drivers may interfere with the proper operation of the drive. Start Windows in the Safe Mode, and then try formatting the tape. Note that if the tape drive requires a protected-mode driver, the tape drive will not work in the Safe Mode.

■ *Check for hardware conflicts.* This is typical of floppy interface tape drive installations. There may be a conflict between the video board and floppy drive controller. Start the format operation and minimize the progress indicator. If problems persist, change the video mode to 640×480×16. If problems continue, try formatting in a full-screen DOS session. Use the Device Manager to look for conflicts between the video board and floppy drive controller.

SYMPTOM 5-21   **You find that tape comparisons fail**   After a backup has been completed, Backup (and most other tape backup utilities) allows you to perform a comparison that checks the tape contents against your original files. This is how you know the data is good. When you encounter errors in comparison, it also means you will probably have trouble restoring from the tape later on. Comparison errors almost always mean that data was lost writing to the tape, or that the tape itself is defective (for example, a bad block is encountered). First, clean the tape drive read/write heads, and then check the comparison again. If the problem persists, try creating another backup now that the heads have been cleaned. If the problem still continues, the tape itself is probably worn out (or is otherwise defective) and should be replaced.

SYMPTOM 5-22   **There is a serious error in the memory manager**   When Backup attempts to perform a backup, restore, or compare operation, you may receive an important error message that typically reads as follows:

```
Microsoft Backup has encountered a serious error in the Memory Manager.
Quit and restart Backup, and then try again.
```

This error message contains the word "serious" because the potential causes for this problem all demand your careful consideration:

- *Suspect incompatible device drivers.* If you have just recently installed a new application or updated any of your system drivers, you may be faced with an incompatible device driver or memory-resident program being loaded through your AUTOEXEC.BAT, CONFIG.SYS, SYSTEM.INI, or WIN.INI file. Try starting Windows 9x in the Safe Mode. If the problem disappears, locate and correct the conflicting driver(s)—usually the last change you made to the system before the problem occurred.

- *Check your Windows swap file.* This error may also be caused if the swap file is damaged. Check the swap file's condition by opening the Control Panel, selecting the System icon, selecting the Performance page, and clicking on Virtual Memory. Click on "Let me specify my own virtual memory settings," and then select the Disable Virtual Memory box. Select OK and restart the computer. Next, go into the virtual memory dialog box again, select "Let Windows manage my virtual memory settings," and then click OK. This should re-create your swap file and set it to automatic control under Windows.

You cannot select the Disable Virtual Memory box on a PC with only 8MB of RAM. If your computer has only 8MB of RAM, restart your computer to the command prompt, delete any SWP file in the Windows folder, and then restart your computer and create a new swap file.

- *Suspect your tape or drive.* The particular tape drive may be malfunctioning or incompatible with Backup. (The backup tape itself may also be damaged or improper for the drive.)

- *Reinstall Backup.* One or more files under Microsoft Backup may be corrupt. To ensure that your installation is correct, open your Control Panel, select the Add/Remove Programs icon, click the Windows Setup page, select Disk Tools, and then click Details. Find the entry for Backup, clear its check box, and then click OK. Restart the PC if necessary. This removes Backup from your PC. Next, go to the Backup check box again, reselect it, and then click OK. This will reinstall the Backup application.

SYMPTOM 5-23   **Errors are reported after the backup is complete**   When you try to back up files or folders that are located on a password-protected network share under Windows 98, you may receive an error message such as "Backup complete—error reported." If you view the backup log, you may see errors such as:

```
Error: \\<share> - access denied
Error: \\<share> - could not be accessed
```

where <share> is the name of the network share. This trouble occurs because Backup does not prompt you for a password to access password-protected network shares. Connect to the network share, and enter your password before you try to back up files or folders from this share.

SYMPTOM 5-24   **Backup hesitates when providing a network list**   When you are using Backup under Windows 98 and you select a network location to back up by double-clicking the Networks icon and then double-clicking the Microsoft Network icon, the list of computers on the network may take a long time to appear. This occurs because Backup compiles a list of all the computers on your net-work—not just your workgroup. There isn't much you can do about this issue.

BACKUP EXEC SYMPTOMS

Backup Exec software will generally run well and allow you an added measure of protection when recovering from a system failure. However, when troubles occur with the software, you can often refer to the following symptoms for more specific corrective action.

SYMPTOM 5-25   **The system locks up immediately after Backup Exec is installed**
In most cases, there may be conflicts between Backup Exec and other applications. You can try disabling possible conflicting programs:

1.   Press CTRL-ALT-DEL to display the Close Program dialog box. (The only application that must be running is the Explorer.)

2.   Close other applications by highlighting the desired application and clicking the End Task button.

3.   If all applications have been disabled and Backup Exec is still not responding, rename (using the .OLD extension) any Backup Exec drivers not being used.

SYMPTOM 5-26   **Backup Exec locks up when displaying a selection**   Files in your Recycle Bin may be conflicting with other files on your hard drive. Delete the files in your Recycle Bin before using Backup Exec. Click the right mouse button on the Recycle Bin located on the desktop, and then select Empty Recycle Bin.

SYMPTOM 5-27   **The tape controller is not responding during backup, compare, or restore**   If you have an internal QIC backup device that is attached to the floppy disk controller, use the Device Manager to verify that there are no extra backup device entries. If there are, you should delete additional backup device entries:

1.   Right-click the My Computer icon and select Properties.

2.   Click the Device Manager tab.

3.   Locate the Tape Drive Controller section. If you find an entry in this section that has an X on the icon, remove it by selecting the item and clicking the Remove button.

4.   Restart Windows 9x.

If the problem continues and you are using a high-speed controller (a.k.a. accelerator card), make sure that the settings on the card match those reported by the Device Manager.

SYMPTOM 5-28   **There is a DMA conflict during backup or compare**   You may need to reduce the data transfer speed used in your system:

1.   Go to Device Manager and double-click the "backup device" item.

2.   Select the "backup device" and click Properties.

3. Select the Settings tab and disable "high speed burst mode," "concurrent video update," and "concurrent hard disk access" settings.

4. Reduce the transfer rate to its lowest setting (500 Kbps).

If you still have a DMA conflict problem, use the lowest resolution setting available on your video card—if this corrects the problem, contact your video card or computer manufacturer for available driver updates for Windows 9x.

SYMPTOM 5-29   **You receive an error such as "media not formatted or unreadable"**
You may need to disable the high-speed burst transfer option under your system properties:

1. Right-click the My Computer icon and select Properties.

2. Click the Device Manager tab in your System Properties dialog box.

3. Click the plus (+) sign next to your "backup device type" to expand the entries, and then double-click your backup device.

4. Click the Settings tab in the Properties dialog box.

5. Uncheck the "High speed burst transfers" option and click OK.

6. Restart your computer.

Further Study

@Backup   www.atbackup.com/
Micro Solutions   www.micro-solutions.com
Microsoft (Backup)   www.microsoft.com
PowerQuest   www.powerquest.com
Seagate   www.seagate.com
Symantec   www.symantec.com

6

BATTERIES

Of all the elements in a PC, few are as overlooked and ignored as the battery. Batteries play an important role in all PCs by maintaining the system's configuration data while main AC power is turned off (just imagine how inconvenient it would be to reenter the *entire* system setup in CMOS before being able to use the system each time). For portable systems such as notebook and sub-notebook PCs, battery packs also provide main power for the entire system. This chapter outlines the technologies and operating characteristics of today's battery families, and illustrates a selection of battery-related problems that can plague a PC.

A Battery Primer

The battery is perhaps the most common and dependable source of power ever developed. It is an electro-chemical device that uses two dissimilar metals (called *electrodes*) that are immersed or encapsulated in a chemical catalyst (or *electrolyte*). The chemical reaction that takes place in a battery causes a voltage differential to be developed across its electrodes. When a battery is attached to a circuit, the battery provides current. The more current required by a load, the faster a chemical reaction will occur. As the chemical reaction continues, electrodes are consumed. As a result of this chemical consumption, the voltage differential will gradually drop, and the battery will eventually wear out. It is important to realize that a *battery* and a *cell* are not necessarily the same. A *cell* is the basic element of a battery, but a *battery* may be made up of several individual cells.

For some batteries, the chemical reaction is irreversible. When the battery is dead, it must be discarded (in an environmentally responsible manner). These are known as non-rechargeable (or *primary*) batteries. Most PCs use small primary-type batteries to sustain the contents of CMOS RAM. However, some types of batteries can be recharged. By applying current to the battery from an external source (for example, a battery charger), the expended chemical reaction can be almost entirely reversed. Such rechargeable batteries are referred to as *secondary* batteries. Rechargeable batteries are used to supply main power for all mobile computers.

BATTERY RATINGS

Batteries carry two important ratings: cell voltage and ampere-hours (Ah). *Cell voltage* refers to the cell's working voltage. Most everyday cells operate around +1.5 Vdc, but can range from +1.2 to +3.0 Vdc (or more) depending on the particular battery chemistry being used. The *ampere-hour* rating is a bit more involved, but it reflects the energy storage capacity of a battery. A high Ah rating suggests a high-capacity battery, and a low rating, a low capacity.

As an example, suppose your battery is rated for 2.0 Ah. Ideally, you should be able to draw 2 amps from the battery for one hour before it is exhausted. However, you should also be able to draw 1 amp for 2 hours, 0.5 amp for 4 hours, 0.1 amp for 20 hours, and so on. Keep in mind that the ampere-hour relationship is not always precisely linear. Higher current loads may shorten battery life to less than that expected by the ampere-hour rating, while small loads may allow slightly more battery life than expected. Regardless of the ampere-hour rating, all batteries have an upper current limit—attempting to draw excess current can destroy the battery (causing it to rupture and leak caustic chemicals). Physically large batteries can usually supply more current (and last longer) than smaller batteries. Another way to express a battery's energy capacity is in watt-hours per kilogram (Wh/kg) or watt-hours per pound (Wh/lb). For example, a 1 kg battery rated at 60 Wh could provide 60W of power for 1 hour, 30W of power for 2 hours, 10W of power for 6 hours, and so on.

CHARGING

In its simplest sense, *charging* is the replacement of electrical energy to batteries whose stored chemical energy has been discharged. By applying an electrical current to a discharged battery over a given period, it is possible to cause a chemical recombination at the battery's electrodes, which will restore most of the battery's spent potential. Essentially, you must back-feed the battery at a known, controlled rate.

Recharging only works for secondary cells such as nickel-cadmium (NiCd), nickel metal-hydride (NiMH), or lithium-ion (Li-ion) batteries. Attempting to recharge a primary battery will quickly destroy it.

Before you dive into an overview of charging circuits and troubleshooting, you must understand the concept of C. The term *C* designates the normal current capacity of a battery (in amperes). In most circumstances, the value of C is the same as the ampere-hour current level. For example, a battery rated for 1300 mAh (1.30 Ah) would be considered to have a C value of 1.30 amps. A battery rated for 700 mAh (0.70 Ah) would have a C of 0.70 amps. Charging rates are based upon fractions or multiples of C.

To charge a battery, you must apply a reverse voltage that will cause the appropriate amount of charging current to flow back into the battery. Traditionally, a battery should be charged at a rate of 0.1C. For batteries with a C of 500 mA (0.5A), 0.1C would be 50 mA (0.05A). At 0.1C, the battery could be left connected in the charger indefinitely without damage. Low-current charge rates such as 0.1C are sometimes referred to as a *slow charge* or *trickle charge*. Slow charging produces the least physical or thermal stress within a battery and ensures the maximum possible number of charge/discharge cycles.

Many current secondary batteries can be charged well above the 0.1C rate. The *quick charge* approach uses current levels of 0.3C (three times the rate of a slow charge) to recharge the battery in four to six hours. For a battery with a C of 600 mA (0.60A), the 0.1C charging rate would be 60 mA (0.06A), but the quick charge rate would be 180 mA (0.18A). However, the quick charging process runs the risk of *overcharging* a battery. Once a battery is fully recharged, additional current at or above the quick charge rate causes temperature and pressure buildups within the cell(s). In extreme cases, a severely overcharged battery may rupture and be destroyed. When quick charging, the 0.3C charging rate should be used only long enough to restore the bulk of a battery's energy. The rate should be reduced to 0.1C (or less) for continuous operation (a.k.a. trickle charging).

New NiCd and NiMH battery designs allow for an even faster charge of one hour. The *one-hour charge* uses a rate of 1.5C, which is 1.5 times the amount of current that the battery is intended to provide. A battery with a C of 1400 mA (1.40A) would use a one-hour charge rate of 2100 mA (2.10A). Remember that only specially designed secondary cells can be safely charged in one hour or less. With one-hour charging, current control and timing become critical issues. The battery charging current *must* be reduced as soon as the battery approaches its full charge, or catastrophic battery failure will almost certainly result. Rapid charging causes substantial temperature and pressure increases that eventually take their toll on a battery's working life. You should expect the working life of any battery to be curtailed when it is regularly operated in a one-hour charge mode.

The *constant-current charger* is designed to automatically compensate for changes in battery terminal voltage in order to maintain charging current at a constant level. Constant-current charging is very efficient, but it is not adjustable. If the charger were set to deliver substantial charging currents, the battery pack could charge quickly, but overcharging could eventually damage the pack. The charger could be set to a lower level for safe charging (perhaps 0.1C), but the low charging rate means very long charge times for a battery pack (ten hours or more). Such limitations make constant-current chargers poorly suited for use in mobile computers. Instead, constant-current chargers are typically used in stand-alone battery pack charging units.

A more effective approach for portable computers is a *variable-current* (constant-voltage) scheme. When a battery is deeply discharged and its terminal voltage is low, there will be a substantial difference between the power supply source and battery voltage level. This difference results in a sizable current flow to the battery. Charging usually starts out around the 0.5C to 0.3C rate for fast charge operation. As the battery takes on a charge, its terminal voltage increases. Higher battery voltage reduces the difference between the supply and battery—current flow into the battery decreases. When the battery pack reaches full charge, there is almost no voltage difference between the charger and battery, so only a small amount of current trickles into the battery. Current flow may reach levels as low as 0.05C.

STORING BATTERIES

At some point, you'll probably need to store unused batteries for some time. Remember that the chemical process that makes batteries work will always continue regardless of whether the battery is installed—this means your battery will eventually go dead even if you don't use it. You can extend your battery's shelf life by reducing its temperature. Typically, this means storing your batteries in the refrigerator (in a vapor-proof container to prevent drying the battery's electrolyte due to the low humidity). The cold will slow the chemical reaction and keep the battery "fresh" much longer. Just remember to remove the battery from the refrigerator and to allow it to stabilize at room temperature for at least 24 hours before using it.

CMOS Backup Batteries

When IBM released its PC/AT in the early 1980s, one of the many design changes over the older PC/XT was the elimination of DIP switches used to set the system configuration. Instead of discrete physical switches, PC designers chose to set system parameters using bit sequences stored in small areas of low-power static RAM. Since it would be necessary to maintain the contents of this RAM even when system power is off, designers choose to use RAM chips based on *Complementary Metal Oxide Semiconductor* (CMOS) fabrication. This extremely low-power memory became known as CMOS RAM. CMOS RAM can be maintained for years using only a single small battery or battery pack incorporated onto the motherboard (Figure 6-1) called a *CMOS backup battery.* All motherboards require a CMOS backup battery.

Do not confuse CMOS batteries with standby batteries. Mobile computers such as IBM's ThinkPad series often employ additional batteries to serve as a standby power source. These *standby batteries* are rechargeable battery packs frequently used to supplement the main battery in mobile computers. Traditionally, you'd need to shut down a laptop and replace a main battery pack, then reboot the system in order to

FIGURE 6-1 A Rayovac Computer Clock battery (Courtesy of Rayovac Corp.)

keep working. If the main battery pack were to fail, you'd lose any work in progress (and perhaps corrupt important files). With a standby power source, the system can automatically enter a "suspend" mode where almost no power is used, but files and data can be kept active in memory. You can then replace the main battery and leave the suspend mode to keep working without the time and trouble to reboot and reload your applications. If the main battery should fail, the standby batteries can keep your work intact for up to several days until you can exchange the main battery pack, or find an AC outlet for a battery eliminator.

LITHIUM BATTERIES

Lithium/manganese-dioxide (Li/MnO_2 or simply "lithium") batteries are commonly employed as CMOS backup batteries. Lithium batteries use a layer of lithium as the anode, a specially formulated manganese-dioxide alloy as the cathode, and a conductive organic electrolyte. Depending on the overall size and shape of the cell, a lithium battery can supply +3.0 Vdc at up to 330 Wh/kg of energy density. Lithium cells also offer a five-year shelf life with almost no loss of power. While their energy density is quite high, lithium cells offer only low ampere-hour ratings between 70 mAh (0.70 Ah) and 1300 mAh (1.30 Ah). Limited Ah ratings allow lithium cells to maintain an almost constant output voltage over a long working life.

The classical type of lithium battery is the *coin cell*. The typical coin cell is designed in two halves with a lithium anode at the top and a manganese-dioxide cathode layer on the bottom. Both halves are separated by a thin membrane containing a conductive electrolyte. The finished electrochemical assembly is then packaged into a small metal can. The lid forms the negative electrode, while the side walls and bottom of the coin form the positive electrode. The lid is physically isolated from the rest of the metal can by a thin insulating grommet—thus, the coin cell is not sealed. A grommet keeps moisture and contaminants out, yet will allow any pressure buildup to escape the battery.

BACKUP BATTERY REPLACEMENT

Battery life has a limit. Eventually, all backup batteries will discharge to the point where they can no longer sustain the system. When the battery finally does fail, CMOS information is lost. The next time you attempt to turn the PC on, the system will generate an error code or message indicating that the system configuration does not match the CMOS Setup information. The loss of a CMOS Setup suddenly leaves a system disabled until new (and correct) CMOS information is entered. This presents a serious problem for most PC users, since few users bother to back up or record their CMOS Setup. As you might imagine, it then becomes an exercise in frustration to load the setup routine and reconstruct the system setup from scratch.

Fortunately, there are two things you can do to avoid this problem. First, make it a point to routinely replace the backup battery every two years (no more than three years). If you change the backup battery for a customer, note the battery part number and replacement date on a sticker, and then place the sticker inside the PC enclosure (you might also note the next replacement date on your customer's bill). Second, back up the system CMOS entries *before* replacing the battery. You can note the entries on paper (using the form included in the appendix of this book) and tape the page inside the enclosure, or you can use a shareware utility to back up CMOS contents as a disk file. CMOS backup as a disk file is quick and easy, and the file can be restored in a matter of seconds. A backup utility is especially handy when there is no SETUP disk available for the system being worked on. Make it a point to keep the backup current as system parameters change. (Otherwise, you would be restoring information that is no longer valid.)

The actual process of backup battery replacement is simply a matter of removing the old battery and inserting a new one. Since the battery is often located prominently on the motherboard, it is possible to replace a backup battery with system power applied (this lets the system maintain its CMOS settings). However, working inside a "hot" system is against the safety protocols that we have established for this book, so be sure to record the CMOS settings on floppy disk or paper first; then power-down and unplug the PC before opening it. Replace the battery, and then restart the PC and reload the CMOS settings from disk or paper. Replacing the backup battery in a notebook or sub-notebook PC is sometimes easier since the battery is usually accessible from a small panel on the bottom enclosure (you do not have to disassemble the notebook enclosures to replace the battery). Even with easy access, you should make it a point to remove power before replacing the battery.

If you act quickly when replacing the CMOS backup battery, there may be enough of a latent charge in CMOS RAM that the contents will remain intact for several minutes after the old battery is removed. However, each motherboard is designed differently, and there is no guarantee how long CMOS RAM contents may remain intact once the battery is removed. Always be prepared to restore CMOS settings from scratch *before* removing the CMOS backup battery.

BACKUP BATTERY TROUBLESHOOTING

Lithium CMOS backup batteries are typically rugged and reliable devices whose greatest threat is simply old age. Since lithium cells are the primary type, they cannot be recharged, so they must be replaced periodically. Under most circumstances, only a few symptoms account for the majority of backup battery problems. In a few cases, you may find a motherboard that employs a nickel-cadmium (rechargeable) battery to maintain the CMOS RAM. In that case, the backup battery is recharged whenever the system is running. The problem with NiCd backup batteries is that NiCd has a very short "shelf life," so you must run the system periodically to keep the backup battery charged—otherwise, you may lose your CMOS data just letting the system sit idle.

Checking the CMOS Backup Battery

It is usually a simple matter to check the CMOS backup battery. Power-down the system and expose the motherboard. Locate the CMOS backup battery, and find the two battery terminals leading from the battery to the motherboard. Measure the voltage between those two terminals—you should read between 2.5 and 3.7 Vdc. If the backup battery voltage is correct, there may be a software program or motherboard failure. If the backup battery reads low, replace the battery. If the battery discharges again quickly, there is a problem on the motherboard that is shorting the CMOS backup battery.

Do not remove the CMOS backup battery from the motherboard in order to check it—this will clear your CMOS configuration and make it difficult for the system to boot until the CMOS settings are restored. Check the battery level "in circuit," but be sure to keep the PC power *off*.

Symptoms

The following symptoms outline some of the more common problems that you may encounter when working with typical CMOS RAM backup batteries:

SYMPTOM 6-1   **You see an error such as "System hardware does not match CMOS configuration"**   For some reason(s), the BIOS has identified different hardware than that listed in the CMOS Setup, or the CMOS RAM contents have been lost. Start by checking your CMOS RAM contents through the CMOS Setup routine. Make sure that the CMOS Setup is configured properly (configuration errors can happen frequently when new drives or RAM is added to the system). Remember to save your changes to CMOS RAM before exiting the Setup routine. If the CMOS RAM contents won't hold, check the battery connector to see that the battery is secure. A loose or corroded battery connector may effectively "disconnect" the battery—even if the battery is working perfectly. If the CMOS RAM contents still won't hold, you should replace the CMOS backup battery outright. When replacing the battery, be sure to install the new battery in the proper orientation and to verify that it is secure in its connector.

This error often happens when RAM is added to the system—even though there is no entry for installed RAM anywhere in the CMOS Setup. Try to "exit saving changes" though you may not have actually changed any settings.

SYMPTOM 6-2   **You notice corrosion from the CMOS battery on the battery holder and motherboard**   This frequently occurs with older motherboards (i386 and i486 vintage motherboards) that have been stored for prolonged periods. The battery has ruptured and electrolyte has leaked onto the holder, or onto the motherboard itself. Battery chemicals are very caustic to metals, and chances are that any traces or solder connections that have come in contact with the battery leakage have been ruined. Unfortunately, this also means that the motherboard has been ruined and must be replaced.

If you're planning to remove and store a motherboard for any period, take a PRINT SCREEN of all CMOS Setup pages before removing the motherboard, and then store the old motherboard with the battery *removed.* You may place the battery in a small, heavy-gauge plastic bag at the bottom of the motherboard's antistatic box. When resurrecting the motherboard later, you can replace the battery and restore the CMOS settings from your printed record.

SYMPTOM 6-3   **The system configuration is lost intermittently**   A lithium battery generally produces a very stable output voltage until the very end of its operating life. When the battery finally dies, it tends to be a permanent event. When a system loses its setup configuration without warning, but seems to hold the configuration once it is restored, a loose or intermittent connection is suggested. Turn the PC off and unplug it. Check the battery and make sure it is inserted correctly and completely in its holder. A coin cell should fit snugly. If the cell is loose, gently tighten the holder's prongs to hold the cell more securely. Make sure to remove any corrosion or debris that may be interfering with the contacts. High-quality electrical contact cleaner on a moistened swab is particularly effective at cleaning contacts. When the battery is attached by a short cable, see that the cable is not broken or frayed, and make sure it is inserted properly into its receptacle. If problems persist, replace the CMOS backup battery.

SYMPTOM 6-4   **The backup battery is going dead frequently**   This is a rare and perplexing problem that is often difficult to detect because it may only manifest itself several times a year. Ideally, a lithium coin cell should last for several years (perhaps three years or more). A lithium or alkaline battery pack can last five years or more. When a system loses its setup more than once a year due to battery failures, it is very likely that an error in the motherboard design is draining the backup batteries faster than normal. Unfortunately, the only way to *really* be sure is to replace the motherboard with a different or updated version. Before suggesting this option to your customer, you may wish to contact technical support for the original motherboard manufacturer and find out if similar cases have been reported. If so, find if there is a fix or correction that will rectify the problem (it may be necessary to return the motherboard to the manufacturer for corrective action).

SYMPTOM 6-5   **You see a "161" error or message indicating that the system battery is dead**   Depending on the particular system you are working with, there may also be a message indicating that the CMOS Setup does not match the system configuration. In either case, the backup battery has probably failed and should be replaced. Remember to turn off the system before replacing the battery. Once the backup battery is replaced, restart the system. You will likely receive a message that the CMOS

Setup does not match the system configuration. Restore the configuration from paper notes or a file backup. The system should now function normally.

Mobile Batteries

Besides providing power to back up the system's configuration, notebook and sub-notebook computers rely on batteries for main power when operating away from AC. Such power is typically provided from one or more battery packs installed from the bottom or side of the computer. The requirements for battery packs are ever more stringent—packs have to provide as much power for as long as today's technology will allow, yet be as light and small as possible. Further, today's battery packs must be quickly rechargeable and offer a long working life through hundreds of recharging cycles. The three battery technologies best suited to these requirements are nickel-cadmium, nickel metal-hydride, and lithium-ion.

NICKEL-CADMIUM

The nickel-cadmium (NiCd) battery is one of the most cost-effective power sources in mass production today. Large NiCd battery packs have been widely used in mobile computers (primarily laptops and notebooks) as a main power source. Since NiCd cells can be manufactured in almost limitless shapes and sizes, they are ideal for systems requiring unusual battery configurations. Although NiCd batteries initially cost more than primary batteries, they can be recharged often—usually recovering their initial cost many times over.

Nickel-cadmium batteries are secondary (rechargeable) devices using an anode of nickel hydroxide and a cathode consisting of a specially formulated cadmium compound. The electrolyte is made of potassium hydroxide. NiCd cells can supply up to +1.2 Vdc each with ampere-hour ratings from 500 mAh (0.50 Ah) to 2300 mAh (2.30 Ah). Energy densities in NiCd cells can approach 50 Wh/kg (23 Wh/lb). Respectable ampere-hour ratings allow NiCd cells to supply sizable amounts of current, but their inherently low energy density means that NiCds must be recharged fairly often.

The NiCd *memory effect* is a unique phenomenon that is not entirely understood. In operation, a NiCd battery can develop a "memory" that serves to limit either the capacity or terminal voltage of a cell. As you might expect, either limit can result in problems with the battery. *Voltage memory* is generally caused by prolonged charging over weeks and months. High ambient temperatures and high charging currents can accelerate this condition. In effect, the battery is charged for so long, or at such a high rate or temperature, that the efficiency of the electrochemical reaction is impaired. As a result, the battery suffers from low terminal voltage.

The *memory capacity* problem is probably more widely recognized and is usually expressed as the loss of a NiCd's ability to deliver its full power capacity. The generally accepted cause of capacity problems is the result of frequent partial battery discharge, followed by a full recharge. Over several such cycles, the battery "learns" that only a portion of its capacity is used. This renders the battery unable to deliver a full discharge when needed. Although the chemical reason for memory capacity is not fully understood, it is believed to be caused by oxidation reactions that temporarily coat the electrodes with non-reactive chemical compounds. There are several application errors that can cause issues resembling the "memory effect":

■ **Cutoff voltage too high**   Since NiCds have a flat voltage versus discharge characteristic, using voltage sensing to determine when the battery is nearly empty can be tricky. An improper setting coupled with a slight voltage depression can cause many battery-measuring devices to call a battery "dead" even when nearly the full capacity remains usable.

■ **Operating temperature too high**   NiCds suffer under high-temperature conditions. Excessive heating will reduce both the charge that will be accepted by the cells when charging and the voltage across the battery when charged.

■ **Voltage depression due to overcharge**   NiCds can drop 0.1–0.15 V/cell if exposed to a long-term overcharge (a period of months). Such overcharge conditions are not uncommon with inexpensive consumer electronics—especially if you're in the habit of leaving the unit in a simple charger. As a precaution, do not leave any NiCd-powered gear on a charger longer than the recommended time unless the charger is specifically designed for long-term "trickle charge" operation.

■ **Operating temperature too low**   Do not operate NiCd batteries below 0°C.

■ **Discharge rates are too high**   NiCd batteries are generally not designed for extremely fast discharge rates (above 5C). If they're not, the battery will essentially behave as if it has short-circuited. Reduce the load on the battery, or install a "fast discharge" battery pack.

■ **The battery may be worn out**   NiCd batteries do not last forever. Over time, one or more cells may wear out or fail, and this can lower the terminal voltage of the entire battery. Old or worn batteries should be replaced.

Fortunately, the memory effect appears to be only a temporary condition that can usually be cleared by forcing the battery through several *full* discharge/recharge cycles. If you are in the habit of using your notebook or laptop PC until you receive low-battery warnings, you will probably not have to worry about NiCd memory problems. It is interesting to note that the newer lithium-ion (Li-ion) batteries do not seem to suffer from memory problems.

NiCd cells also have a very limited charged life when sitting idle. While alkaline and lithium cells can hold close to their original charge for years, NiCds will lose approximately 25 percent to 35 percent of their remaining charge each month. After several months of inactivity, a NiCd battery pack will need to be recharged before use. As a general rule, you should fully recharge any new or rarely used NiCd battery or battery pack prior to use. Today, NiCd batteries have largely been phased out of mobile computer use in favor of more robust NiMH and Li-ion batteries.

NICKEL METAL-HYDRIDE

Nickel metal-hydride (NiMH) batteries are a somewhat newer type of rechargeable battery designed to offer substantially greater energy density than NiCd cells for mobile computer applications. Since their introduction in 1990, NiMH cells have already undergone some substantial improvements and cost reductions that have made NiMH the dominant type of battery for mobile computers.

NiMH batteries are remarkably similar in construction and operating principles to NiCds. A positive electrode of nickel-hydroxide remains the same as that used in NiCds, but the negative electrode replaces cadmium with a metal-hydroxide alloy. When combined with a uniquely formulated electrolyte, NiMH cells are rated to provide at least 40 percent more capacity than similarly sized NiCd cells. NiMH batteries can provide +1.2 Vdc with discharge ratings from 800 mAh (0.80 Ah) to more than 2400 mAh (2.40 Ah) at continuous discharge currents of 9A or more. Energy densities can exceed 80 Wh/kg (38.1 Wh/lb). This means a NiMH battery can power a laptop and support additional features (for example, a larger active-matrix color display) for longer times. NiMH batteries also seem to suffer the "memory effects" that plague NiCd batteries, but certainly not to the same extent. Keep in mind that NiMH has a fairly short shelf life (often a matter of days)—so you'll need to keep your NiMH batteries fully charged before traveling.

LITHIUM-ION AND ZINC-AIR

Lithium-ion (Li-ion) batteries are a relatively recent development, but they are now readily available for the current generation of mobile computers. The formulation of the Li-ion battery allows 20–30 percent more running time than a similarly sized NiMH battery (at about 115 Wh/kg) and retains a charge for a long time while on the shelf. Li-ion batteries are also free of the memory effects found in NiCd and NiMH batteries and will last through well over 800 recharge cycles. Li-ion batteries represent the newest generation of "smart" batteries, because status information on the battery's remaining charge can be communicated to the host system for an accurate determination of running time.

Zinc-air batteries are another recent development in mobile battery design, and the batteries now appearing in the field offer almost twice the energy density of Li-ion batteries (at a whopping 220 Wh/kg). In actual practice, however, zinc-air batteries have proven extremely large and heavy. They are also quite expensive. These factors have kept zinc-air batteries out of most small mobile systems. Still, the high energy potential of zinc-air will keep development active. Over the next few years, Li-ion and zinc-air batteries should continue to be the major power sources for mobile systems.

IDENTIFYING NICD AND NIMH BATTERIES

Although it is often difficult to distinguish between a NiCd and NiMH battery pack at first glance, there are some tips that might help you tell the difference. NiCd battery packs typically use three metal contacts (a slightly longer "negative" contact bridges contacts in the laptop and indicates the presence of the battery to the system). By comparison, NiMH battery packs are newer and "smarter" than NiCd packs, so the NiMH packs will typically include a type and temperature sensing contact located near the positive terminal of the battery pack. The firmware of some laptops will not begin charging the battery pack if the battery temperature is over 104°F (or if the temperature rises above 140°F while charging).

If the battery pack is unmarked, you may be able to identify the technology of the battery pack based on the pack's output voltage. NiCd packs will be a multiple of 1.2V, lead-acid packs will be a multiple of 2.0V, and alkaline packs will be a multiple of 1.5V. For example, if you measure 3.6 Vdc across a battery pack, you can guess that it is probably a NiCd pack.

IDENTIFYING A RESERVE BATTERY

Many current laptop designs employ a *reserve battery,* which powers the system for a few minutes—allowing the main battery to be replaced without having to shut down the system or connect to AC power. In most cases, the internal reserve battery is a pack of four half-length AA-size, 270 mAh, NiCd batteries in an inline stack. When fully charged, this pack can power the system for about eight minutes before being fully discharged. In operation, the reserve battery is permitted to support the computer for two to three minutes at the most before forcing a system shutdown.

RECHARGEABLE BATTERY GUIDELINES

Rechargeable batteries are reliable and robust devices, but there are a number of guidelines that need to be observed to get the most from them:

■ *Plan on charging the battery before use.* For safety reasons, rechargeable batteries are typically shipped in a discharged state. You will need to prepare (or *condition*) your battery pack (according to manufacturer's instructions) prior to placing the battery pack into use.

■ *Cycle the battery pack as recommended.* Rechargeable batteries generally need to be *cycled* (fully charged and discharged) as many as five times before they will perform at full load capacity.

■ *New batteries may fool a status indicator.* A new battery may cause the battery status indicator on your computer to indicate a dead or low battery condition. If this happens, try letting the battery charge in the system overnight so that the PC's charging circuit might synchronize with the battery pack. If you have trouble using battery packs with a certain make and model of mobile PC, the system's BIOS may be at fault (check with the system maker for a BIOS upgrade).

■ *Store the battery carefully.* When the battery pack is not in use, remove it from the system and store it in a cool, dry place.

■ *Never short-circuit the battery terminals.* Although some battery packs are protected by internal self-resetting fuses, short circuits can still cause considerable damage to the battery. Use extreme care when packing spare batteries with other equipment during transit or storage.

■ *Handle the battery pack carefully.* Do not drop, hit, or abuse the battery pack in any way. Not only might this damage the battery's internal cells, but a break in the casing may also release electrolyte or expose cell contents—this material is corrosive and can damage circuitry in the PC.

■ *Check for excessive heat.* It is perfectly normal for a battery pack to become warm to the touch when charging or discharging. However, if the battery pack gets extremely warm (that is, over 50°C or 122°F), there may be a problem with the charging circuit. If you're using a stand-alone battery charger, do not leave the battery connected to the charger—this can overcharge the battery and shorten its life.

■ *Keep an eye on your running time.* Running time depends on the power demands of your system components and the way in which the computer is used. Changing screen types and adding accessories will often shorten actual run times. After 300 to 500 recharges, a shortened run time may indicate that the battery needs to be replaced.

Battery Charging and Replacement Tips

For best results with rechargeable batteries, use the following guidelines:

■ Remember that AC adapters are generally designed for specific laptops in order to handle the specific power requirements of the laptop and its add-on devices (for example, a Dell Token Ring Advanced Port Replicator). This means you typically cannot mix and match AC adapters. Be sure to use only the AC adapter intended for your laptop model.

■ Each time the computer is connected to AC power (or a battery is installed in a computer that is connected to AC power), the computer checks the battery's charge. The AC adapter then charges the battery (if needed) and the reserve battery, and then maintains the battery's charge.

■ For lithium-ion battery packs with built-in charge indicators, you can check the battery's charge by pressing the Battery Test button. For a fully charged battery pack, all the indicators should light up. Otherwise, the number of indicators lit will correspond to the amount of battery power remaining. For example, if there are five LEDs, each LED would represent 20 percent of the battery's capacity. If one of the battery cells is shorted, you'll probably see a blinking indicator for that cell (the battery pack should be replaced).

■ Do not attempt to replace the main battery while running on battery power without first placing the computer in battery-swap (reserve battery) or "suspend-to-disk" mode. Otherwise, a loss of data will probably result.

- Today, an AC adapter requires about 1.25–1.5 hours to charge a battery if the computer is off. The battery charges in 2.75–3 hours if the computer is on.

- For maximum battery performance, charge the battery only at normal room temperature.

- The battery starts charging immediately. The corresponding battery indicator lights while the battery is being charged and turns off when the cycle is complete.

- If a battery indicator blinks while the AC adapter is connected to the computer, the battery may be defective or installed improperly. Check the documentation for your particular laptop, and verify that you're seeing the correct charging indicator.

Conserving Mobile Battery Power

Battery life is affected by the current drawn by a computer—higher current demands result in shorter battery life, and lower demands result in longer battery life. A large portion of battery troubleshooting is to ensure that your system setup is adequate. The following steps should help you to optimize battery life (Table 6-1 illustrates typical settings for power conservation):

- Take advantage of special power modes like suspend or hibernation. These modes use very little power and should be selected when you'll be away from the running laptop for any period of time.

- Remove or disable any unnecessary devices in the laptop. For example, you may not need that PCMCIA modem card or sound card during that flight cross-country, so remove the card. If you can *disable* unneeded devices (that is, shut down power to the built-in infrared communication unit), that will also save substantial power.

- Use the lowest screen brightness that you are comfortable with by adjusting the display's brightness and contrast control(s).

- LCD backlights gobble up substantial amounts of power, so set a short timeout interval for the backlight (one or two minutes is often a good selection).

- A setting with light characters and images on a dark background generally consumes less power than dark characters or images on a light background. Try setting your screen mode to a "light on dark" configuration. If you're using Windows 98/Me, select a dark color scheme.

- The hard disk drive is another major power user—not only by spinning, but during spinup as well. Select a moderate timeout interval for the hard drive (not so long that it spins forever, and not so short that it is constantly starting). Otherwise, you will waste more power constantly spinning up the drive than you save by turning it off. Also, constant starting and stopping can reduce the life expectancy of the drive.

- RAM consumes much less power than hard drives, so try setting up a disk cache or RAM disk to reduce the number of disk accesses. This allows the hard drive to shut down fairly quickly and not require access for a relatively long time.

- Microprocessor speed can be a serious drain on battery power. If your laptop computer allows you to select processor speed, use the slowest speed possible for all but the most demanding applications. Most word processors and conventional DOS utility software runs just fine with slower processor speeds.

- Most mobile batteries have trouble retaining their full charge capacity when left unused for prolonged times. For example, IBM tests suggest that after a one-year shelf life at room temperature, a Li-ion battery retained 95 percent of its original capacity (about 90 percent for NiMH). If you purchase several batteries for a mobile computer, be sure to alternate the use of each battery.

- Avoid playing CDs or DVDs while the PC is on battery power.

TABLE 6-1   RECOMMENDED POWER-SAVING SETTINGS

FOR THIS FEATURE...	CONFIGURE THE SYSTEM TO...
Power button mode	Standby/Resume
PM Control	Battery
Power Savings	Maximum Battery Life
Sleep Timeout	2 Minutes
Standby Timeout	10 Minutes
Hard Disk Timeout	2 Minutes
Video Timeout	4 Minutes
Audio Timeout	2 Minutes
Battery Low Standby	Enabled
Auto Dim With Battery Only	On
Cooling control	Silence

MOBILE BATTERY TROUBLESHOOTING

When discussing batteries as main power sources, not only are the batteries or battery pack involved, but a whole host of other circuitry is included as well (such as battery charging, battery protection, and power management circuits). As a result, you should understand that problems running or charging the battery may be originating *outside* of the battery compartment itself. Since batteries power notebook and sub-notebook systems, trouble may be on the motherboard (where most charging and power management functions are located).

Recognizing Rechargeable Battery Failures

Rechargeable batteries can and do fail. The process of discharge and recharge generates physical stress in the battery that will eventually wear it out. As a rule of thumb, a NiCd battery will last from about three to five years (through 500 to 1500 complete charge cycles). NiMH and lithium-ion batteries will generally last somewhat longer. However, proper charging in a cool environment can extend battery life much further (up to as many as 10,000 complete charge cycles have been reported). Over the life of a rechargeable battery, microscopic "whiskers" of conductive compounds develop between the electrodes. Ultimately, these deposits work to short-circuit the battery from inside. Although "zapping" techniques have been developed using brief surges of current to remove these deposits, such techniques are very risky since the battery stands a good chance of exploding. Another failure mode is the premature loss of liquid electrolyte during high-current or high-temperature charging. Improperly designed "quick-charge" chargers can drive a battery so hard that electrolyte starts to corrode the battery's pressure-relief vent. If the vent is damaged or frozen in the open position, electrolyte will continue to evaporate and the battery will fail.

Check the Battery Pack

When the battery refuses to take or hold a charge, it will often be necessary for you to verify the integrity of your mobile battery. The following steps outline the procedure:

1. Power-down the laptop or notebook computer, and remove the battery pack according to the instructions for your particular system.

2. Once the battery pack is removed, measure the voltage between battery terminals. If there are more than two terminals (as in Figure 6-2 for an IBM ThinkPad battery), be sure to measure across the proper two terminals. For the example of Figure 6-2, you would measure across pins 1 and 4. If you read 0 Vdc, the battery pack is defective and should be replaced.

Pin 1	Positive (+) voltage output
Pin 2	Send terminal
Pin 3	Thermal feedback signal
Pin 4	Ground (–)
Pin 5	Select terminal

FIGURE 6-2   Battery terminals for an IBM ThinkPad battery pack

The remaining pins on the battery pack are used for thermal sensors and other communication between the mobile PC and the battery.

3. If the voltage across the battery terminals is less than the optimum value (usually less than +11.0 Vdc), the battery pack has been discharged through self-discharge (being left on the shelf) or use in the PC. Recharge the battery pack. If the voltage is still less than what the fully charged voltage should be after recharging, replace the battery pack.

4. If the voltage is more than +11.0 Vdc, measure the resistance between the thermal sensor and ground terminals (pins 3 and 4 in Figure 6-2). The resistance should be about 4 to 30 kOhms. If the resistance is not correct, the thermal sensor has failed. This can make it impossible to charge the battery properly, so replace the battery pack.

5. If the resistance is correct, the battery charging circuit has probably failed.

Recalibrate the Battery

Today's "smart" lithium-ion batteries are designed to communicate with your laptop system and provide the system with vital information about the amount of charge that remains in the battery pack—this feature allows you to monitor the amount of charge (or running time) left on your battery. To provide the proper information to your laptop, a battery must be *calibrated* so that it "knows" the difference between a full charge and an empty charge.

When your laptop goes into a standby mode prematurely and without warning (for example, while you're typing or watching a DVD video), it's possible that the battery has "forgotten" the difference between a full and empty charge. When this occurs, the battery may need to be *recalibrated*. The following steps outline a general procedure, but check with your laptop maker for more specific details:

1. Power-up your notebook.

2. Start the laptop's CMOS Setup routine.

3. Check the Advanced or Power Management menus and locate a "Battery Calibrate" or "Recalibrate" feature (some laptops refer to this function as "Recalibrate Gas Gauge").

4. Press ENTER. A screen opens prompting you to start the recalibration program.

5. Press ENTER to start discharging the battery. A message appears indicating the amount of time the discharge process will take.

6.   When the battery has been fully discharged, the notebook will turn itself off.

7.   You can now fully charge the battery, and the laptop's battery meter should display an accurate status of your battery's charge level.

> If you're connected to AC power, you'll be prompted to disconnect the AC power adapter (after you have disconnected the AC power, the discharge process should start automatically).

Symptoms

The following symptoms highlight a wide range of problems that you may encounter while working with rechargeable batteries:

SYMPTOM 6-6   **You cannot deep discharge the main battery on your laptop**   Often, early laptop systems needed to *deep discharge* the main battery when battery life became shorter—this feature was designed to help correct the "memory" problem encountered with NiCd and some NiMH batteries. Some laptops (such as the Dell Latitude LX or Latitude M) provide a deep discharge feature. Try the following procedure:

1.   Reboot your system and enter the CMOS Setup. Select Power Management Control from the main menu.

2.   Check for a submenu in Power Management Control, and then select the Deep Discharge option and enable it.

3.   Save your changes and reboot the system again. When the system reboots, it will be in deep discharge mode—this means that it is using battery power as quickly as possible. Now allow the system to run on battery power until it powers-off.

4.   Recharge the battery fully, and then repeat the process (you may need to repeat this process as many as three times). If your battery will still not hold a charge (or has a weak charge), you may need to replace the battery pack.

Use extreme caution when employing this tactic. Some batteries may not tolerate this deep discharge process very well, and battery damage may result. Check with the laptop maker to see if deep discharging is permitted (or if an alternative deep discharge process is recommended).

SYMPTOM 6-7   **The battery pack does not charge**   In this type of situation, the computer may run fine from the AC-powered supply, and the system may very well run from its onboard battery when the AC-powered supply is removed. However, the battery pack does not appear to charge when the AC supply is connected and running. Without a charge, the battery will eventually go dead. Remember that some computers (especially older laptops) may not recharge their battery packs while the system is on—the computer may have to be turned off with the AC supply connected in order for the battery pack to charge. Refer to the user manual for your particular system to review the correct charging protocol.

Your clue to the charging situation comes from the computer's battery status indicator. Most notebook/laptop systems incorporate a multicolor LED or an LCD status bar to show battery information. For example, the LED may be red when the small-computer is operating from its internal battery. Yellow may appear when the AC-powered supply is connected to indicate the battery is charging. The LED may turn green when the battery is fully charged. If the battery status indicator fails to show a charging color when the AC-powered supply is being used, that is often a good sign of trouble. Table 6-2 lists the status indicators for an IBM ThinkPad (check the user manual for your particular computer).

TABLE 6-2   STATUS INDICATORS FOR AN IBM THINKPAD COMPUTER

MODE	COLOR	MEANING
Charging	Green	Battery fully charged
	Orange	Battery charging
	Blinking orange	Battery needs charging
Conservation	Green	Computer is in suspend mode
	Blinking green	Computer is entering suspend mode or hibernation mode, or resuming normal operation
Status	Green	Power on

Check the battery pack with all computer power off. Make sure that the battery pack is inserted properly and completely into its compartment. Also check any cabling and connectors that attach the battery pack to the charging circuit. Loose or corroded connectors, as well as faulty cable wiring, can prevent energy from the AC-powered supply from reaching the battery. Reseat any loose connectors and reattach any loose wiring that you may find.

After you are confident of your connections, you should trace charging voltage from the AC-powered supply to the battery terminals. If charging voltage does not reach the battery, the battery can never charge. Set your multimeter to measure DC voltage (probably in the 10 to 20 Vdc range), and measure the voltage across your battery pack. You should read some voltage below the pack's rated voltage because the battery pack is somewhat discharged. Now, connect the computer's AC-powered supply, and measure voltage across your battery pack again. If charging voltage is available to the battery, your voltage reading should climb above the battery pack's rated voltage. If charging still does not seem to take place, try replacing the battery pack, which may be worn out or damaged. If charging voltage is not available to your battery pack, the charging circuit is probably faulty. Replace the charging circuit. Since the charging circuit is typically located on the motherboard, it may be necessary to replace the entire motherboard assembly.

SYMPTOM 6-8   **The system does not run on battery power, but runs properly from main (AC) power**   This symptom usually suggests that your computer runs fine whenever the AC-powered supply is being used, but the system will not run from battery power alone. The system may or may not initialize, depending on the extent of the problem. Before you disassemble the computer or attempt any sort of repair, make sure that you have a fully charged battery pack in the system. Remove the battery pack and measure the voltage across its terminals. You should read approximately the battery voltage marked on the pack. A measurably lower voltage may indicate that the battery is not fully charged. Try a different battery pack, or try to let the battery pack recharge. The charging process may take several hours on older systems, but newer small-computer battery systems can charge in an hour or so.

When you have a fully charged battery, check to be sure that it is inserted completely and connected properly. Inspect any wiring and connectors that attach the battery pack to its load circuit. Faulty wiring, corroded connections, or loose connectors can cut off the battery pack entirely. At this point, it is safe to assume that battery power is not reaching the laptop circuit(s). In this event, the battery charging/protection circuit may be defective and should be replaced. If the circuit is incorporated into the motherboard, the motherboard should be replaced.

SYMPTOM 6-9   **Your laptop no longer has a Standby option on the Shutdown menu**
You notice that the plug icon always appears in the system tray while using battery power (rather than the battery icon). In virtually all cases, you'll need to reinstall the laptop's *Advanced Power Management* (APM) feature. Here is the process for Windows 98:

1.   Shut down all running applications.

2.   Click Start, highlight Settings, select Control Panel, and then double-click the System icon.

3.   Click the Device Manager tab, and then click the View Devices By Type radio button.

4.   Click the plus (+) next to "System Devices," select Advanced Power Management, select Remove, and then click OK. Restart the system when prompted to do so.

5.   Once the system has rebooted, click Start, highlight Settings, select Control Panel, and then double-click the Add New Hardware icon.

6.   Click Next to search for new hardware. Click Next again to search for any new plug-and-play devices. The system may find new hardware (and list the items). If Advanced Power Management Support is not listed, select Yes for Windows to search for your new hardware, and then click Next to begin the search.

7.   Once device detection is finished, select Details—it should find Advanced Power Management Support.

8.   Select Finish to begin the installation. The system will prompt you to insert your Windows 98 CD. After the necessary files are installed, you'll be promoted to reboot the system.

9.   Once the system has rebooted, the system will find the APM Battery Slot.

After the system finishes booting, click Start, select Shut Down, and you should see Standby as one of the Shutdown options. Switch from AC power to battery power, and the plug icon should change to a battery icon.

SYMPTOM 6-10   **The system suffers from a short battery life**   Today's mobile computers are designed to squeeze up to six hours of operation (or more) from every charge. Most systems get at least two hours from a charge. Short battery life can present a perplexing problem—especially if you do a great deal of computing on the road. All other computer functions are assumed to be normal.

Begin your investigation by inspecting the battery pack itself. Check for any damaged batteries. Make sure the battery pack is inserted properly into the computer, and see that its connections and wiring are clean and intact. Try replacing the battery pack. Keep in mind that rechargeable batteries do not last forever. Typical NiCd packs are usually good for about 800 cycles, NiMH packs are often suitable for 500 cycles, and Li-ion packs are usually rated for 1200 cycles. Fast-charge battery packs are subject to the greatest abuse and can suffer the shortest life spans. It is possible that one or more cells in the battery pack may have failed. The battery pack may also have developed a "memory" problem. Try several cycles of completely discharging and recharging the pack. If the problem remains, replace the battery pack.

The computer's configuration itself can largely determine the amount of running time that is available from each charge. The CPU, the display (and its backlight), the hard drive, and floppy drive/CD-ROM drive access consume substantial amounts of power. Many mobile computers are designed to shut down each major power consumer after some preset period of disuse. For example, an LCD screen may shut off if there is no keyboard activity after two minutes, or the hard drive may stop spinning after three minutes if there is no hard drive access, and so on. Even reducing CPU clock speed during periods of inactivity will reduce power consumption. The amount of time required before shutdown can usually be adjusted through setup routines in the computer or through the operating system. See the "Conserving Mobile Battery Power" section earlier.

SYMPTOM 6-11   **The battery pack becomes extremely hot during charging**   As you learned earlier in the chapter, current must be applied to a battery from an external source in order to restore battery charge. When a battery receives significant charging current (during or after the charging process), its temperature will begin to rise. Temperature rise continues as long as current is applied. If high charging current continues unabated, battery temperature may climb high enough to actually damage the cells. Even under the best circumstances, prolonged high-temperature conditions can shorten the working life of a battery pack. Today's high-current charging circuits must be carefully controlled to ensure a full, rapid battery charge and to prevent excessive temperature rise and damage.

Battery packs or compartments are fitted with a *thermistor* (a temperature-sensitive resistor). When the battery pack is fully charged, the thermistor responds to the subsequent temperature increase and signals charging circuitry to reduce or stop its charging current. In this way, temperature is used to detect when full charge has been reached. It is normal for most battery packs to become a bit warm during the charging process—especially packs that use fast-charge currents. However, the cell(s) should not give off an obnoxious odor or become too hot to touch. Hot batteries are likely to be damaged. In many cases, the thermistor (or thermistor's signal conditioning circuitry) has failed and is no longer shutting down charge current. Try another battery pack. If the new pack also becomes very hot, the fault is in the charging circuit, which should be replaced. If the new pack remains cooler, the fault is probably in the original battery pack.

SYMPTOM 6-12   **After several days of disuse, your laptop may not power up properly** This may happen regardless of whether you use the AC adapter or battery. You find that the battery shows a full charge. The system may have failed to detect (or have misdetected) the available power. With the system powered off, unplug the AC adapter from the back of the computer, and remove the battery from the case so that both power sources are removed. Then replace the battery and AC adapter cord before turning the unit on—your laptop should power up normally.

SYMPTOM 6-13   **Your laptop locks up if you hot- or warm-swap a CD-ROM module with a battery**   This lockup is caused from system detection problems. If a CD-ROM drive is detected by Windows at boot time, and then at some point that drive is removed, the operating system is not made aware of this (and will attempt to poll the device when My Computer is opened). At this point, the operating system will continue to wait for a response from the device until it times out. This can take anywhere from four to six minutes—during which the system appears to be locked up. Swapping the CD-ROM is currently not supported by Windows 95 CD-ROM drivers. Later versions of the OS may need a driver update or OS patch to correct the trouble.

SYMPTOM 6-14   **A "battery problem" indicator comes on and will not go out**   This is a known problem on systems like the Gateway Solo 2300/9100 and is almost always caused by a problem with the BIOS. Generally, a BIOS upgrade will correct the problem and allow the computer to communicate properly with the "smart" battery. Once the BIOS is upgraded, be sure to charge the battery to 100 percent. If the battery indicator light still turns red, it should only last four to five seconds, and then return to orange (charging) or green (charged fully).

SYMPTOM 6-15   **The computer quits without producing a low-battery warning**

Computers are rarely subtle with regard to low-power warnings. Once a battery pack falls below a certain voltage threshold, the computer initiates a series of unmistakable audible (and sometimes visual) cues that tell you there are only minutes of power remaining. Such a warning affords you a last-minute opportunity to save your work and switch over to AC power if possible. If you choose to ignore a low-power warning, the system will soon reach a minimum working level and crash.

Mobile computers measure their battery voltage levels constantly. A custom chip on the motherboard is typically given the task of watching over battery voltage. When voltage falls below a preset level, the detector chip produces a logic alarm signal. The alarm, in turn, drives an interrupt to the CPU, or passes the signal to a power management chip, which then deals with the CPU or system controller. Once the alarm condition reaches the CPU, the computer typically initiates a series of tones, flashes a "power" LED, or sometimes both (see Table 6-2).

Most PCs produce at least one beep during initialization in order to test the internal speaker. If you do not hear this beep, the speaker or its driving circuit may be damaged. Try replacing the speaker; then try replacing the motherboard. When a beep is heard during initialization, there is probably a fault in the computer's battery detection or power management circuits. Try cleaning the battery contacts first, and then try replacing the laptop's motherboard.

SYMPTOM 6-16   **Your battery indicator displays a 0 percent charge, even though the battery has been fully charged**   After attempting to charge a laptop's battery, the battery may display a status of 0 percent (and may not accept a charge). This typically occurs only after the battery has been left completely discharged for an extended time, or after a fully charged battery has been left completely out of a computer for several months or more. This issue is often avoided by regularly charging the battery. For example, seat or reseat the battery and AC adapter as necessary, and (with the computer plugged into the adapter) allow the battery to charge up to approximately 100 percent. Here are some tips to resolve the issue:

■ Verify that the latest version of the computer's BIOS is installed on the system.

■ Reseat the battery and AC adapter to ensure a good connection.

■ If your laptop uses battery monitoring/conditioning software, be sure to install the latest version (which can typically be downloaded directly from the laptop manufacturer).

■ If the battery still shows 0 percent (or does not accept a charge), the battery may be defective and need to be replaced.

Recycling

Most types of batteries use metals and electrolyte chemicals that are harmful to the environment. As a consequence, many states and provinces have enacted legislation that prohibits the dumping or discarding of batteries (especially lead-acid, NiCd, and alkaline). NiMH and lithium batteries are somewhat less toxic, but often can also be recycled. To support a cleaner environment, many vendors who sell PC batteries are accepting returns of the old defective batteries to be recycled. For example, 1-800-Batteries (a major battery vendor) accepts returns (at 408-879-1930). Before purchasing new batteries, verify that the vendor will accept your spent batteries—if not, contact your local town recycling center to see if they will take exhausted batteries.

If the alarming number of old PCs being dumped into landfills has you worried, IBM is now offering a PC recycling program. For the relatively low cost of $29.99 (including UPS shipping), you can send your old PC to Envirocycle, where they will recycle any manufacturer's system in an "environmentally friendly" manner, or refurbish the system and arrange for its donation to Gifts in Kind International. You can learn more about IBM's recycling offer at **www.ibm.com/news/2000/11/142.phtml**.

Further Study

Direct Power   www.dpp.com/index.html
Duracell   www.duracell.com/
Energizer   www.energizer.com/
Fedco   www.fedcoelectronics.com/home.tmpl
Rayovac   www.rayovac.com/
Tadiran   www.tadiranbat.com/
Varta   www.varta.com/index.html

7

BIOS

Although every personal computer uses the same essential subassemblies, each subassembly is designed a bit differently. This is especially true of the processing components (that is, chipsets and controllers) contained on a motherboard. This is understandable given the tremendous speed at which PC components and technology are advancing. Unfortunately, such dramatic variations in hardware make it difficult to use a single standard operating system. Instead of tailoring an operating system (and applications) to specific computers, a *Basic Input/Output System* (BIOS) is added on ROM chips to provide an interface between the raw PC hardware and the standardized operating system. BIOS gives an OS access to a standard set of functions. As a result, every system uses a slightly different BIOS, but each BIOS contains the same set of functions that an OS can interface to. This chapter explains the internal workings of a typical BIOS, illustrates some means of identifying BIOS versions, and shows you the many features a modern BIOS must support.

Of course, BIOS is not limited solely to the motherboard. (Although most BIOS versions carry enough routines to support video and drive controller operations in addition to other motherboard features.) But what happens when a new video card is developed that the system BIOS does not know how to work with, or an advanced drive controller board becomes available? A common practice in computer design is to include a BIOS ROM chip for major subsystems such as video and drive control. One of the early steps of system initialization is to check for the presence of other valid BIOS ROMs located in upper memory (between 640KB and 1024KB). These are usually referred to as expansion, option, or adapter BIOS. When another BIOS is located, it is also checksum-tested and used by the PC. In general, a PC may be fitted with up to six or more BIOS ROMs such as:

- System (motherboard) BIOS
- Video adapter firmware (BIOS)
- Drive controller firmware (BIOS)
- Network adapter board BIOS
- Modem card firmware (BIOS)
- SCSI adapter BIOS

Typical Motherboard BIOS

The typical BIOS ROM occupies 128KB of space in the system's *upper memory area* (UMA) from E0000h to FFFFFh (within the PC's first megabyte of memory). Contrary to popular belief, BIOS is not a single program, but an arsenal of individual routines—most quite small. In general, BIOS contains three sections, as shown in Figure 7-1: the *power-on self-test* (POST), the CMOS Setup routine, and the system services routines. The particular section of BIOS code that is executed depends on the computer's state and its activities at any given moment.

POWER-ON SELF-TEST (POST)

Although many novice technicians are aware that POST checks the system, few are aware that POST actually manages the entire system startup. The power-on self-test handles virtually all of the initialization activities for a PC. POST performs a low-level diagnostic and reliability test of the main processing components—including ROM programs and system RAM. It tests the CPU, initializes the motherboard's chipset, checks the 128 bytes (or more) of CMOS for system configuration data, and sets up an index of

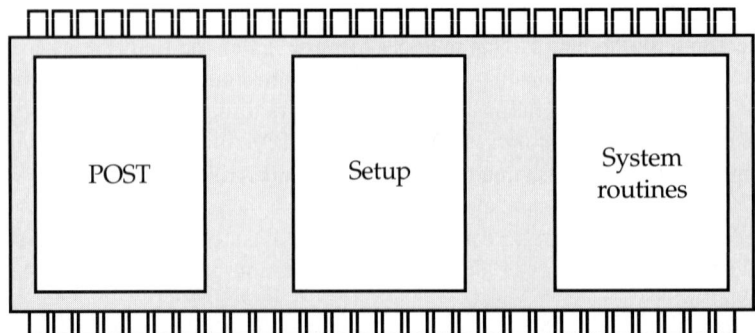

FIGURE 7-1   Main functions of a typical motherboard BIOS

interrupt vectors for the CPU from 0000h to 02FFh. POST then sets up a BIOS Stack Area from 0300h to 03FFh, loads the *BIOS Data Area* (BDA) in low memory 0400h to 04FFh, detects any optional equipment (adapter BIOS ROMs) in the system, and proceeds to boot the operating system from an available disk.

CMOS SETUP ROUTINE

The hardware configuration for any given computer is maintained in a small amount of very low-power CMOS RAM, and a CMOS Setup routine is required for you to access the system's configuration. Older i286 and i386 systems provided the CMOS Setup routine as a separate utility included with the system on a floppy disk. In most cases, the setup disk was promptly misplaced or discarded. Starting with late-model i386 and later systems, the CMOS Setup routine has been integrated into the motherboard BIOS itself. At boot time, the POST gathers information about the system's hardware and compares it with the settings in CMOS RAM. If the information matches, the hardware is deemed to be operational and the boot process may continue. Otherwise, the boot process halts and a "system setup" error appears. The actual CMOS Setup program can vary tremendously between system manufacturers and motherboards, so there is no one standard for what settings can be controlled, or where those entries are located.

Many Compaq systems place the setup routine on a *diagnostic partition* on the hard drive. If the drive fails (or is repartitioned), the diagnostic partition may be lost—it may be impossible to adjust the system's configuration until the diagnostic partition is restored.

SYSTEM SERVICE ROUTINES

The system services (also referred to as *BIOS services*) are a set of individual functions that form the layer between hardware and the operating system. It is this versatility that allows a single operating system to work with such a proliferation of motherboard designs, bus architectures, processor types, and chipsets. Services are called through the use of interrupts. An *interrupt* essentially causes the CPU to stop whatever it was working on and send program control to another address in memory that usually starts a subroutine designed specifically to deal with the particular interrupt. When the interrupt handling routine is complete, the CPU's original state is restored, and control is returned to where the PC left off before the interrupt occurred. There is a wide range of interrupts that can attract the attention of a CPU, and interrupts can be produced from three major sources: the CPU itself, a hardware condition, and a software condition.

Interrupts produced by the CPU itself (known as *processor interrupts*) are often the result of an unusual, unexpected, or erroneous program result. For example, if a program tries to divide a number by zero, the CPU will generate INT 00h, which causes a "Divide by zero" error message. There are five processor interrupts (00h to 04h).

The *hardware interrupts* are generated when a device needs the CPU's attention to perform a certain task. Hardware interrupts are invoked by asserting a logic level on a physical *interrupt request* (IRQ) line. The CPU suspends its activities and executes the interrupt handling routine. When the interrupt handler is finished, the CPU resumes normal operation. For example, each time a keyboard key is pressed, the keyboard buffer asserts a logic line corresponding to INT 09h (IRQ 1). This invokes a keyboard handling routine. PC/AT-compatible systems typically provide 16 hardware interrupts (IRQ 0 to IRQ 15) that correspond to INT 08h to 0Fh and 70h to 77h, respectively.

Software interrupts are generated when a hardware device must be checked or manipulated by the PC. The "print screen" function is a prime example of a software interrupt. When the PRINTSCREEN button is pressed on the keyboard, an INT 05h is generated. The interrupt routine dumps the contents of its video character buffer to the printer port.

BIOS Features

PC technology is constantly advancing in CPUs, chipsets, memory, video, drives, and so on. As the hardware continues to advance, the BIOS must also advance to keep pace with the resources emerging on today's systems. As a result, it is important for you to recognize the key features that are included in a modern BIOS. You do not need to understand the details of each feature right now, but you should at least recognize a "current" BIOS by reviewing its feature set. Table 7-1 lists the feature set for a current version of MR BIOS. While many of the items listed in a BIOS feature set may seem a bit incidental, the core features of a modern BIOS can be broken down into a number of major areas:

- **CPU support**   BIOS should support a rich range of CPUs, preferably from various CPU makers like Intel, AMD, and Cyrix. Look for Pentium, Pentium MMX, Pentium Pro, Pentium II, Pentium III, Pentium 4, AMD Athlon, and AMD Duron support (though one BIOS will certainly not support all these CPU families).

- **Chipset support**   The BIOS should support the latest chipset families (such as Intel's 840 or 850 chipset). Chipset support is critical because it is the chipset that allows motherboard designers to implement other features like power management, USB, and advanced memory architectures such as DDR-SDRAM.

- **Memory support**   The BIOS should be able to autosize and support the most modern forms of memory (for example, SDRAM, DDR-SDRAM, and Rambus). Memory error checking (such as "parity" and "ECC") should also be supported. Modern BIOS can support up to 4GB of RAM (far more for servers), though the system's motherboard may not handle that much.

TABLE 7-1   SPECIFICATION LIST FOR A RECENT VERSION OF MR BIOS

Built-In Setup	
Menu driven	
Dynamic screen generation	
Hardware summary	
Intelligent defaults	
Password Security	
Three modes	SETUP Only
	Power-up/SETUP
	Boot-up/SETUP
Hardware switch master override	
Boot Sequence	
Boot any drive: A–F	
Screen prompt or autosearch boot	
Programmable boot-delay (0–30 sec)	
Memory testing: full test or quick scan	
Fixed Disk	
Enhanced IDE support	LBA and CHS translations
	EDPT table support
	IBM/Microsoft INT 13 extensions
	Eight disks max—each to 137GB

TABLE 7-1   SPECIFICATION LIST FOR A RECENT VERSION OF MR BIOS (*CONTINUED*)

Fixed Disk

	Name any disk C:
	Boot SCSI (ahead of IDE)
FAST-ATA support	ATA mode 4/5 (to 20MB/S)
	Built-in IDE drivers (AD12, CMD, OPTI, and more)
Raid-0 disk striping	Interleave 2-8 IDE drives for very fast data throughput
Data transfer modes: 32-bit, block, polling, and standard	
Autoconfigure IDE drives	
Greater than 1024 cylinder support	
Two user-programmable drive types	
47 "scroll-through-table" selections	
Built-in low-level format utility	

Floppy

Five floppy support: 360KB, 720KB, 1.2MB, 1.44MB, and 2.88MB	
Four floppy/tape drives max	
Secondary controller setup	
Configurable slow/fast step-rate	
Enhanced floppy support	
Rename any floppy drive as A	

PCI and Bridge Support

Auto resource (IRQ) steering	

Plug-and-Play Card Support

Auto resource steering	
Windows 95 and 98 compatible	

ATAPI and Removable IDE

CD-ROM recognition	
SyQuest and other ejectable media	

I/O Ports

Dynamic port mapping in SETUP	
Four serial, four parallel ports supported	
Enhanced parallel support (IEEE 1284)	-SPP, Bidirectional, EPP, and ECP modes
Automatic combo-chip support	
USB support	

Power Management

APM for Windows and DOS	
VESA DPMS video management	
SMI and STPCLK, all x86s	

Video

Automatic detection (no jumpers needed)	
Dual monitor management	
Mono-VGA compatibility	

Clock

Set time: AM/PM or 24-hour	
Set date: U.S. or international	

TABLE 7-1   SPECIFICATION LIST FOR A RECENT VERSION OF MR BIOS (*CONTINUED*)

Keyboard and Mouse

XT, AT, PS/2 83-102 key supported

XT/AT autoswitch compatibility

Selectable boot-up Num Lock state

Programmable typematic rates

Automatic PS/2 mouse recognition

Cache

586 write-back support

Autodetection and autosizing

Full SRAM/TagRAM cache testing

Enable/disable cache via SETUP utility

486: Internal and external set independently

On-the-fly hot-key cache control

Cacheable/non-cache regions

Memory

Support up to 4GB

View memory map in SETUP

Autoscan: 256KB to 16MB DRAMs

Ten-level memory testing

Shadow RAM

E000,F000 (System ROMs): 64KB granularity

C000-DFFF (Video, Adapters): 16KB
granularity

Each block: read/write or write protect

SETUP: View present ROMs and vacancies

User Programmable

DMA

Chipset setup

Memory timing and refresh

AT-bus clock

Turbo and cache

Gate A20 control

Configuration Flexibility

No video

No floppy drive

No fixed disk

No keyboard

Automatic

PCI configuration

Memory wait-state configuration

AT bus speed settings

Cache wait-states

Autodetection of Cyrix CPU cache

XT/AT/PS2 keyboard selection

■ **Power management support**   The BIOS should fully comply with the *Advanced Configuration and Power Interface* (ACPI) specification (revision 1.0 or later), and support APM BIOS specifications through version 1.2 or later. Power management is vitally important for mobile systems and is widely used in desktop/tower systems to reduce energy waste. The BIOS should also support DPMS (*Display Power Management System*) for monitors and other display devices.

■ **Drive support**   The BIOS must support 32-bit disk transfers and large Ultra-ATA hard drives (over 1024 cylinders) with very fast data transfer modes like Ultra-DMA/33, Ultra-DMA/66, and Ultra-DMA/100. It is increasingly common for BIOS support to also involve removable media devices such as Zip or SyQuest drives. In some cases, the BIOS may even include support for basic RAID functions such as RAID 1 (striping).

■ **PC 99 support**   The BIOS should comply with the current Microsoft PC 99 BIOS requirements (or later).

■ **I^{2}O support**   The BIOS may support I^{2}O (Intelligent I/O), which allows the dynamic assignment of ports and resources for I/O devices in the PC. This is more commonly found in server platforms.

■ **Boot versatility support**   The BIOS should be able to boot from a number of different drives, and include the BIOS Boot Specification for *Initial Program Load* (IPL) devices. This currently supports booting from up to four IDE-type drives (including CD-ROM drives), SCSI drives, and network cards. Support for removable media drives (for example, Iomega Zip or SyQuest drives) is an advantage.

■ **Plug-and-play support**   The BIOS must detect and configure PnP devices during POST. The BIOS also communicates with Windows 95/98 to determine system resources, and to support IRQ Steering for PCI bus devices. Support of Microsoft's AML permits compatibility with PnP capability in future Windows operating systems (such as Windows 2000).

■ **Parallel port support**   The BIOS should support a full range of parallel port modes including *Standard Parallel Port* (SPP or "compatibility" mode), bidirectional mode, *Enhanced Capabilities Port* (ECP), and *Enhanced Parallel Port* (EPP)—collectively part of the IEEE 1284 standard.

■ **PCI and AGP support**   The BIOS must support Intel's *Peripheral Component Interconnect* (PCI) bus specification (version 2.1 or later), including PCI-to-PCI and PCI-to-ISA bridging. The BIOS must also support the Accelerated Graphics Port (AGP) version 2.0 or later.

■ **USB support**   The BIOS should support both Universal and Open HCI standards. It should maintain full core compatibility and provide legacy support for USB hardware and multilayered USB hubs. You may also find support for USB 2.0 (high-speed USB) in the very newest BIOS versions.

■ **Antivirus protection**   The BIOS should offer the option of virus protection. At a minimum, the BIOS should prevent changes to the master boot record (often a classic sign of virus activity).

Whether you're trying to learn the capabilities of your current BIOS or planning a BIOS upgrade, you can learn a lot about a BIOS and its features by studying the BIOS ID codes. This part of the chapter explains several means of identifying popular BIOS versions and will help you to understand the information encoded in the BIOS ID string.

AMI BIOS

American Megatrends (AMI) has been a major player in the development of leading BIOS versions for the PC and has been very popular with Pacific Rim motherboard makers. (Though popularity with domestic U.S. motherboard makers is growing.) The AMI BIOS code appears in the lower portion of the POST display—usually during the memory count. The code's format will indicate the relative age of the BIOS. The following format indicates an older AMI BIOS made between 1986 and 1990:

```
DINT-1123-040990-K8
```

This older BIOS code uses an **AAAA-BBBB-DDMMYY-Kx** format where:

■ **AAAA** *BIOS type*. This includes chipset identification codes.

■ **BBBB** *AMI customer reference number*. This code identifies the motherboard manufacturer that AMI tailored the BIOS for (see Table 7-2 to reference the motherboard maker).

■ **DDMMYY** *BIOS release date*. This is in day/month/year format.

■ **Kx** *Keyboard BIOS*. This indicates the revision level of the keyboard BIOS code.

A more recent AMI BIOS (released after 1990) normally appears as shown next:

```
51-0102-zz5123-00111111-101094-AMIS123-P
```

This recent BIOS code uses an **A#-BBBB-CCCCCC-DDDDDDDD-EEEEEE-FFFFFFFF-G** format where:

■ **A** *CPU type*. This code identifies the CPU vintage, where 0 = 8086 (or 8088), 2 = 80286, 3 = 80386, 4 = 80486, 5 = Pentium, and so on.

■ **#** *BIOS size*. This code tells the size of the BIOS chip, where 0 = 64KB, and 1 = 128KB.

■ **BBBB** *BIOS version number*. This is the main version number that you would use to identify the BIOS currently on the system.

■ **CCCCCC** *AMI customer reference number*. This code identifies the motherboard manufacturer that AMI tailored the BIOS for. (See Table 7-2 to reference the motherboard maker.)

■ **DDDDDDDD** *AMIBCP settings*. This is a set of eight logical "flags" that define several key operating parameters of the BIOS (0 = no, 1 = yes):

  1 Halt on error during POST

  2 Initialize CMOS RAM at every boot

  3 Keyboard controller output pin 23, 24 blocked

  4 Mouse support in BIOS and keyboard controller

  5 Wait for in case of POST error

  6 Display floppy error during POST

  7 Display video error during POST

  8 Display keyboard error during POST

■ **EEEEEE** *BIOS release date*. This is in day/month/year format.

■ **FFFFFFFF** *BIOS type*. This includes chipset identification codes.

■ **G** *Keyboard BIOS*. This indicates the revision level of the keyboard BIOS code.

In this version, the BIOS identification number for this BIOS identification string would be zz5123. If the first of the **bold** numbers is

- **1, 2, 8**, or a **letter**, you have a non-AMI Taiwanese-manufactured motherboard
- **3, 4**, or **5**, you have a true AMI motherboard
- **50** or **6**, you have a non-AMI U.S.-made motherboard
- **9**, you have an evaluation BIOS for a Taiwanese manufacturer

The second set of numbers (BBBB or 1123 in this case) would immediately identify the BIOS as a Non-AMI foreign-made motherboard. The complete code identifies Magtron Technology Co., Ltd. (from Table 7-2) as the consumer of this BIOS version released on 09/04/90. The second set of numbers (5123) would indicate that the motherboard is a true AMI motherboard (not listed in Table 7-2).

AMI provides a utility called AMIMBID that is designed to help technicians identify the manufacturer of a motherboard using AMI BIOS. You can obtain the utility from **www.ami.com/support/ mbid.html**.

TABLE 7-2   AMI CUSTOMER IDENTIFICATION CODES

NON-U.S. MOTHERBOARD MANUFACTURERS		NON-U.S. MOTHERBOARD MANUFACTURERS	
Code	Customer	Code	Customer
1101	Sunlogix, Inc.	1133	Seritech Enterprise Co., Ltd.
1102	Soyo Technology Co., Ltd.	1135	Acer Inc.
1105	Autocomputer Co., Ltd.	1136	Sun's Electronics Co., Ltd.
1106	Dynasty Computer Inc.	1138	Win-Win Electronic Co., Ltd.
1107	DataExpert Corp.	1140	Angine Ltd. Taiwan Branch (H.K.)
1108	Chaplet Systems Inc.		
1109	Fair Friend Ent. Co., Ltd.	1141	Nuseed Technology Inc.
1111	Paoku P&C Co., Ltd.	1142	Firich Enterprises Co., Ltd.
1112	Aquarius Systems Inc.	1143	Crete Systems Inc.
1113	Micro Leader Enterprises Corp.	1144	Vista Technology Co., Ltd.
1114	Iwill Corp.	1146	Taste Corp.
1115	Senor Science Co., Ltd.	1147	Integrated Technology Express, Inc.
1116	Chicony Electronics Co., Ltd.		
1117	A-Trend Technology Co., Ltd.	1150	Achitec Corp. Ltd.
1120	Unicorn Computer Corp.	1151	Accos Enterprise Co., Ltd.
1121	First International Computer, Inc.	1152	Top-Thunder Technology Co., Ltd.
1122	Microstar Computer Corp.		
1123	Magtron Technology Co., Ltd.	1154	San Li Technology Co., Ltd.
1124	Tekram Technology Co., Ltd.	1156	Technica House Inc.
1126	Chuntex Elex., Co., Ltd.	1158	Hi-Com Industrial Co., Ltd.
1128	Chaintech Computer Co., Ltd.	1159	Twinhead International Corp.
1130	Pai Jung Electronic Ind. Co., Ltd.	1161	Monterey International Corp.
1131	Elitegroup Computer Co., Ltd.	1163	Softek Systems Co., Ltd.
1132	Dkine Enterprise Co., Ltd.	1165	Mercury Computer Corp.

TABLE 7-2   AMI CUSTOMER IDENTIFICATION CODES (CONTINUED)

NON-U.S. MOTHERBOARD MANUFACTURERS		NON-U.S. MOTHERBOARD MANUFACTURERS	
Code	Customer	Code	Customer
1169	Micro-Star International Co., Ltd.	1297	DD&TT Enterprise Inc.
1170	Taiwan Igel Co., Ltd.	1301	Taken Corp.
1171	Shing Yunn Electronics Enterprise Corp.	1304	Dual Enterprises Corp.
		1309	Protronic Enterprises Corp.
1176	Sigma Computer Corp.	1317	New Comm
1178	Clevo Co.		Technology Co., Ltd.
1188	Quanta Computer Inc.	1318	Unitron Inc.
1195	GNS Technologies Inc.	1343	Holco Enterprise Co., Ltd.
1196	Universal Scientific	1346	Snobol Industrial Corp.
	Industrial Co.	1351	Singdak Electronic Co., Ltd.
1197	Golden Way Electronic Corp.	1353	J. Bond Computer
1199	GigaByte Co., Ltd.		Systems Corp.
1201	New Tech International Co., Ltd.	1354	Protech Systems Co., Ltd.
1203	Sunrex Technology Corp.	1367	Coxswain Technology Co. Ltd.
1204	Bestek Computer Co., Ltd.	1371	ADI Corp.
1209	Puretek Industrial Co., Ltd.	1373	Silicon Integrated Systems Corp.
1210	Rise Computer Inc.	1379	Win Technologies Co., Ltd.
1211	Diamond Flower	1391	Aten International Co., Ltd.
	Electronic Co., Ltd.	1392	Acc Taiwan Inc.
1214	Rever Computer Inc.	1393	Plato Technology Co., Ltd.
1218	Elite Computer Co., Ltd.	1396	Tatung Co.
1223	Biostar Microtech	1398	Spring Circle Computer Inc.
	International Corp.	1404	Alptech Logic Products Inc.
1225	Yunglin Technology Corp.	1421	Well Join Industry Co., Ltd.
1234	Leadman Electronic Co., Ltd.	1422	Labway Computer Co., Ltd.
1241	Mustek Corp.	1437	Hsing Tech Enterprise Co., Ltd.
1242	Amptek Technology Co., Ltd.	1440	Great Electronics Corp.
1244	Flytech Technology Co., Ltd.	1451	Ecel Systems Corp.
1246	Cosmotech Computer Corp.	1452	United Hitech Corp.
1247	Abit Computer Corp.	1453	Kai Mei Electronic Corp.
1256	Lucky Star Technology Co., Ltd.	1461	Hedonic Computer Co., Ltd.
1258	Four Star Computer Co., Ltd.	1462	Arche Technologies Inc.
1259	GVC Corp.	1470	Flexus Computer Technology
1262	Arima Computer Corp.	1472	Datacom Technology Co., Ltd.
1266	Modula Tech. Co., Ltd.	1484	Mitac International Corp.
1271	Tidal Technologies Inc.	1490	Great Tek Corp.
1273	UFO Computer Co., Ltd.	1491	President Technology Inc.
1274	Full Yes Industrial Corp.	1493	Artdex Computer Corp.
1276	Jet Way Information Co., Ltd.	1494	Pro Team Computer Corp.
1277	Tarng Bow Co., Ltd.	1500	Netcon Co., Ltd.
1281	EFA Corp.	1503	Up Right Tech Co., Ltd.
1283	Advance Creative	1514	Wuu Lin Electronics Co., Ltd.
	Computer Corp.	1519	Epox Computer Co., Ltd.
1284	Lung Hwa Electronics Co., Ltd.	1526	Eagle Computer
1291	Taiwan Mycomp Co., Ltd.		Technology Co., Ltd.
1292	AsusTek Computer Inc.	1531	Force System Inc.

TABLE 7-2   AMI CUSTOMER IDENTIFICATION CODES (*CONTINUED*)

NON-U.S. MOTHERBOARD MANUFACTURERS		NON-U.S. MOTHERBOARD MANUFACTURERS	
Code	Customer	Code	Customer
1540	BCM Computers Co., Ltd.	1774	Acer Sertek Inc.
1546	Golden Horse Computer Co., Ltd.	1776	Joss Technology, Ltd.
1549	CT Continental Corp.	1780	Acrosser Technology Co., Ltd.
1564	Random Technology Inc.	1783	Efar Microsystems, Inc.
1576	Jetta Computer Co., Ltd.	1788	Systex Corp.
1585	Gleem Industries Co., Ltd.	1792	U-Board Computerize Ltd.
1588	Boser Technology Co., Ltd.	1794	CMT-Taiwan, Inc.
1593	Advantech Co., Ltd.	1796	J&J Technology Co., Ltd.
1608	Consolidated Marketing Corp.	1801	Palit Microsystems Inc.
1612	Datavan International Corp.	1806	Interplanetary Information Co., Ltd.
1617	Honotron Corp.	1807	Expert Electronic Corp.
1618	Union Genius Computer Co., Ltd.	1810	Elechands International Co., Ltd.
1621	New Paradise Enterprise Co., Ltd.	1815	Powertech Electronic Co., Ltd.
1622	R.P.T. Intergroups International Ltd.	1820	Ovis Enterprises Co., Ltd.
1628	Digital Equipment International Ltd.	1823	Inlog Micro Systems Co., Ltd.
		1826	Tercomputer Technologies Corp.
1630	Iston Computer Corp.	1827	Anpro Inc.
1647	Lantic Inc.	1828	Axiom Technology Co., Ltd.
1652	ASE Technologies Inc.	1840	New Union H.K. Ltd.
1655	Kingston Technology Inc.	1845	PC Direct Technology Co., Ltd.
1656	Storage System Inc.	1846	Garnet International Corp.
1658	Macrotek International Corp.	1847	Brain Power Co.
1666	Cast Technology Inc.	1850	HTR Asia Pacific Inc.
1671	Cordial Far East Corp.	1853	Veridata Electronics Inc.
1672	Lapro Corp.	1856	Smart D&M Technology Co., Ltd.
1675	Advanced Scientific Corp.	1867	LTH Rong Electronic Enterprise Co.
1685	High Ability Computer Co., Ltd.	1868	Soyo Technology Co., Ltd. (H.K. office)
1691	Gain Technology Co., Ltd.	1879	Aeontech International Co., Ltd.
1707	Chaining Computer & Communication Co.	1881	Manufacturing Technology Resources
1708	E-San Electronic Co., Ltd.	1888	Seal International Corp.
1719	Taiwan Turbo Technology Co., Ltd.	1889	Rock Technology Co., Ltd.
1720	Fantas Technology Co., Ltd.	1906	Freedom Data Technology Co., Ltd.
1723	NTK Computer Inc.	1914	Aquarius Systems Inc.
1727	Tripod Technology Corp.	1917	Source of Computer Co., Ltd.
1737	Ay Ruey International Co., Ltd.	1918	Lanner Electronics Inc.
1739	Jetpro Infotech Co., Ltd.	1920	Ipex ITG International Ltd.
1743	Mitac Inc.	1924	Join Inc.
1762	Ansoon Technology Co.	1926	Kou Sheng Computer Co., Ltd.
1770	Acer Inc.	1927	Seahill Technology Co., Ltd.
1771	Toyen Computer Co., Ltd.	1928	Nexcom International Co., Ltd.
		1929	CAM Enterprise Inc.

TABLE 7-2   AMI CUSTOMER IDENTIFICATION CODES (*CONTINUED*)

NON-U.S. MOTHERBOARD MANUFACTURERS

Code	Column
1931	Aaeon Technology Co., Ltd.
1932	Kuei Hao Industrial Co., Ltd.
1933	ASMT Corp.
1934	Silver Bally Inc.
1935	Prodisti Co., Ltd.
1936	Codegen Technology Co., Ltd.
1937	Orientech Electronics Corp.
1938	Project Information Company Ltd.
1939	Arbor Technology Corp.
1940	Suntop Computer Systems Corp.
1941	Funtech Entertainment Corp.
1942	Sunflower Systems Inc.
1943	Needs System Development Co., Ltd.
1945	Norm Advanced Technology Corp.
1947	Ten Yun Co., Ltd.
1948	Beneon Co., Ltd.
1949	National Advantages Computer Inc.
1950	MITS Technology Co.
1951	Macromate Corp.
1953	Orlycon Enterprise Co., Ltd.
1954	Chung Yu Electronics Co., Ltd.
1955	Yamashita Systems Corp.
1957	High Large Corp.
1958	Young Micro Systems
1959	Fastfame Computer Co., Ltd.
1960	Acqutek Corp.
1961	Deson Trade Inc.
1962	Astra Communication Corp.
1963	Dimensions Electronics Co., Ltd.
1964	Micron Design Technology, Ltd.
1965	Cantta Enterprises Co., Ltd.
1968	Khi Way Enterprise Co., Ltd.
1969	Gemlight Computer Ltd.

NON-U.S. MOTHERBOARD MANUFACTURERS

Code	Column
1970	Mat Technologies, Ltd.
1971	Norm Advanced Technology Corp.
1973	Fugu Tech Enterprise Co., Ltd.
1974	Green Taiwan Computer Co., Ltd.
1975	Supertone Electronic Co., Ltd.
1977	AT&T Taiwan Telecommunications Co.
1978	Winco Electronic Co., Ltd.
1980	Teryang Systems Co., Ltd.
1981	Nexcom International Co., Ltd.
1982	China Semiconductor Corp.
1985	Top Union Electronics Corp.
1986	DMP Electronics Co., Ltd.
1988	Concierge Co., Ltd.
1989	Atherton Technology Co., Ltd.
1990	Expen Tech Electronics Co., Ltd.
1994	Japan Cere'Bro Computers Inc.
1996	Ikon Technologies Corp.
1998	Chang Tseng Corp.

U.S. MOTHERBOARD MANUFACTURERS

Code	Column
6105	Dolch Computer Systems
6132	Technology Power Enterprises
6156	Genoa
6259	Young Micro
6285	Tyan
6326	Crystal
6328	Alaris
6386	Pacific Information, Inc.
6389	Supermicro
6423	APC
8003	QDI
8045	VTech/PCPartner
428003	Quantum Designs (H.K.) Ltd.
428054	Pine

AWARDS BIOS

Award is another popular BIOS maker with many years of BIOS development experience behind them. As with most other BIOS versions, the Award BIOS code appears in the lower portion of the POST display—usually during the memory count—and can be used to reveal the supported chipset and motherboard manufacturer. The typical Award BIOS ID format is

Award uses the first five characters (that is, 2A59I) to indicate the chipset used on the motherboard. The 2A59I entry indicates the Intel Triton TX chipset, and you can find many more chipset codes in Table 7-3. The sixth and seventh characters are used to represent the motherboard manufacturer. For example, the Z1 code indicates a Tomato motherboard made by Zida. Table 7-4 provides a comprehensive listing of manufacturers.

TABLE 7-3   CHIPSET SUPPORT CODES FOR AWARD BIOS

BIOS CODE STRING	CORRESPONDING CHIPSET
213V1	SARC RC2018
21480	HiNT SC9204 (Sierra), HMC82C206
214D1	HiNT SC9204 (Sierra), HMC82C206
214I8	SiS 85C471
214I9	SiS 85C471E
214L2	VIA VT82C486A
214L6	VIA Venus VT82C486A, VT82C495, and VT82C496G
214W3	VD 88C898
214X2	UMC 491 Chipset
215UM	OPTi 82C546 and 82C597
21917	ALD Chipset
219V0	SARC RC2016
2A431	Cyrix MediaGx Cx5510 Chipset
2A432	Cyrix GXi Cx5520 Chipset
2A433	Cyrix GXm Cx5520 Chipset
2A434	Cyrix GXm Cx5530 Chipset
2A496	Intel Saturn Chipset
2A498	Intel Saturn II Chipset
2A499	Intel Aries Chipset
2A4H2	Contaq 82C596-9 Chipset
2A4IB	SiS 496/497 Chipset
2A4J6	Winbond W83C491(SL82C491 "Symphony Wagner")
2A4KA	ALi (unknown)
2A4KC	ALi 1439/45/31 Chipsets
2A4KD	ALi 1487/1489 Chipsets
2A4L4	VIA 486A/482/505 Chipsets
2A4L6	VIA 496/406/505 Chipsets
2A4O3	EFAR EC802GL and EC100G Chipsets
2A4UK	OPTi 802G-822 Chipsets
2A4X5	UMC 8881E/8886B Chipsets
2A4Z0	(unknown)
2A597	Intel Mercury Chipset
2A59A	Intel Natoma (Neptune) Chipset
2A59B	Intel Mercury Chipset
2A59C	Intel Triton FX chipset (Socket 7 based motherboard)
2A59F	Intel Triton II HX chipset (a.k.a. 430HX PCIset—Socket 7–based motherboard)
2A59G	Intel Triton VX chipset (Socket 7–based motherboard)
2A59H	Intel Triton VX chipset (Socket 7–based motherboard) with an "illegal" BIOS

TABLE 7-3   CHIPSET SUPPORT CODES FOR AWARD BIOS (*CONTINUED*)

BIOS CODE STRING	CORRESPONDING CHIPSET
2A59I	Intel Triton TX chipset (Socket 7–based motherboard)
2A5C7	VIA VT82C570 Chipset
2A5G7	VLSI VL82C594 Chipset
2A5GB	VLSI Lynx VL82C541/VL82C543 Chipset
2A5IA	SiS 501/02/03 Chipsets
2A5IC	SiS 5501/02/03 Chipsets
2A5ID	SiS 5511/12/13 Chipsets
2A5IE	SiS 5101-5103 Chipsets
2A5IF	SiS 5596/5597 Chipsets
2A5IH	SiS 5571 Chipset
2A5II	SiS 5582/5597/5598 Chipsets
2A5IJ	SiS 5120 Mobile Chipset
2A5IK	SiS 5591 Chipset
2A5IM	SiS 530 Chipset
2A5KB	Ali 1449/61/51 Chipsets
2A5KE	ALI 1511 Chipset
2A5KF	ALI 1521/23 Chipsets
2A5KI	ALI IV+ M1531/M1543 Chipset (a.k.a. Super TX chipset)
2A5KK	Ali Aladdin V Chipset
2A5L5	VIA (unknown)
2A5L7	VIA VT82C570 Chipset
2A5L9	VIA VT82C570M Chipset
2A5LA	VIA Apollo VP1 (VT82C580VP) Chipset—sometimes relabeled as VXPro chipset
2A5LC	VIA Apollo VP2 Chipset—sometimes relabeled as AMD640 chipset
2A5LD	VIA VPX Chipset—sometimes relabeled as VXPro+ chipset
2A5LE	VIA Apollo (M)VP3 Chipset
2A5LH	VIA Apollo VP4 Chipset
2A5R5	Forex FRX58C613/601A Chipsets
2A5R6	Forex FRX58C613A/602B/601B
2A5T6	ACC Micro 2278/2188 (Auctor) Chipset
2A5UI	OPTi 82C822/596/597 or OPTi 596/546/82 Chipsets
2A5UL	OPTi 82C822/571/572 Chipsets
2A5UM	OPTi 82C822/546/547 Chipsets
2A5UN	OPTi Viper-M 82C556/557/558 or OPTi Viper 82C556/557/558 Chipsets
2A5UP	OPTi Viper Max
2A5X7	UMC 82C890 Chipset
2A5X8	UMC UM8886BF/UM8891BF/UM8892BF Chipsets
2A5XA	UMC 890C Chipset
2A69H	Intel 440FX Chipset (Pentium II/Pentium Pro-based chipset)
2A69J	Intel 440LX/EX Chipset (Pentium II-based chipset)
2A69K	Intel 440BX/ZX Chipset (Pentium II/III-based chipset)
2A69L	Intel "Camino" 820 Chipset
2A69M	Intel "Whitney" 810 Chipset
2A69N	Intel Banister Mobile ChipSet with C&T 69000 Video

TABLE 7-3   CHIPSET SUPPORT CODES FOR AWARD BIOS (CONTINUED)

BIOS CODE STRING	CORRESPONDING CHIPSET
2A6IL	SiS 5600 Chipset
2A6IN	SiS 620 Chipset
2A6KL	ALi 1621/1543C Chipsets
2A6KO	ALi M1631/M1535D
2A6LF	VIA Apollo Pro (691/596) Chipsets
2A6LG	VIA Apollo Pro Plus (692/596) Chipsets
2A6LI	VIA MVP4 VIA 601(Trident on-chip video)/686A (on-chip modem, on-chip sound)
2A6LJ	VIA 694X/596B and VIA 694X/686A (on-chip modem and on-chip sound)
2A9KG	ALi M6117/M1521/M1523 Chipsets
2AG9H	Intel Neptune ISA Chipset
2B496	Intel Saturn I EISA Chipset
2B597	Intel Mercury EISA Chipset
2B59A	Intel Neptune EISA Chipset
2B59F	Intel 430HX EISA Chipset
2B69D	Intel Orion EISA Chipset
2C470	HYF82481 Chipset
2C4D2	HiNT SC8006 (Sierra), HMC82C206
2C4I7	SiS 461 Chipset
2C4I8	SiS 85C471B Chipset
2C4I9	SiS 85C471B/E/G Chipsets
2C4J6	Winbond W83C491(SL82C491 "Symphony Wagner")
2C4K9	ALi 14296 Chipset
2C4KC	ALi 1439/45/31 Chipsets
2C4L2	VIA 82C486A Chipset
2C4L6	VIA VT496G Chipset
2C4L8	VIA VT425MV Chipset
2C4O3	EFAR EC802G-B Chipset
2C4S0	AMD Elan 470
2C4T7	ACC Micro 2048 (Auctor)
2C4UK	OPTi 82C895/82C602
2C4X2	UMC UM82C491/82C493 Chipsets
2C4X6	UMC UM498F/496F
3A6LF	VIA Apollo Pro (691/596) Chipset with Award BIOS v4.60PGA
6A69L	Intel "Camino" i820 Chipset with Award BIOS v6.00
6A69M	Intel i810(E) Chipset with Award BIOS v6.00
6A69R	Intel "Solano" i815(E) Chipset with Award BIOS v6.00
6A6LJ	VIA 694X/686A (Apollo Pro 133A) Chipset with Award BIOS v6.00
6A6LK	VIA VT8371 (KX-133) Chipset with Award BIOS v6.00
6A6LM	VIA VT8363 (KT-133) Chipset with Award BIOS v6.00
6A6S2	AMD 751 Chipset with Award BIOS v6.00
JA6LM	VIA VT8363 (KT-133) chipset (only used on Matsonic motherboards)

TABLE 7-4   MANUFACTURER CODES FOR AWARD BIOS

BIOS CODE STRING	CORRESPONDING MANUFACTURER
00	Unknown—it may be necessary to contact Unicore (a subsidiary of Award Software) for more information.
A0	Asus
A1	Abit
A2	Atrend
A3	Bcom (ASI)
A7	AVT (formerly Concord)
A8	Adcom
AB	AOpen
AD	Amaquest
AK	Advantech
AM	Achme
AT	ASK Technology
AX	Achitec
B0	Biostar
B1	BEK-Tronic Technology
B2	Boser
B3	BCM
C0	Matsonic
C1	Clevo
C2	Chicony
C3	Chaintech
C5	Chaplet
C9	Computrend
CF	Flagpoint
CS	Gainward or CSS Labs
D0	DataExpert
D1	DTK
D2	Digital
D3	Digicom
D4	DFI (Diamond Flower)
D7	Daewoo
DE	Dual Tech
DI	Domex (DTC)
DJ	Darter
DL	Delta Electronics
E1	Elitegroup (ECS)
E3	EFA
E4	ESPCo
E6	Elonex
E7	Expen Tech
EC	ENPC

TABLE 7-4   MANUFACTURER CODES FOR AWARD BIOS (*CONTINUED*)

BIOS CODE STRING	CORRESPONDING MANUFACTURER
F0	FIC (FICA)
F1	Flytech Group
F2	Free Tech
F3	Full Yes
F5	Fugutech
F8	Formosa Industrial Computing
F9	Fordlian
FG	Fastfame Technology Co., Ltd.
FI	FIC (FICA)
G0	GigaByte
G1	(unknown)
G3	Gemlight
G5	GVC
G9	Global Circuit Technology
GA	Giantec
GE	Zaapa
H0	Hsing-Tech (PCChips)
H2	Shuttle (HolCo)
HH	HighTech Information System
I3	Iwill
I4	Inventa
I5	Informtech
I9	ICP
IA	Infinity
IC	Inventec
IE	Itri
J1	Jetway (a.k.a. Jetboard or Acorp)
J2	Jamicon
J3	J-Bond
J4	Jetta
J6	Joss
K0	Kapok
K1	Kamei
KF	Kinpo
L1	Lucky Star
L7	Lanner Electronics, Inc.
L9	Lucky Tiger
LB	LeadTek
M0	Matra
M2	Mycomp (TMC) and Megastar
M3	Mitac
M4	Micro-Star
M8	Mustek
M9	Micro Leader Enterprises (MLE)
MH	Macrotek

TABLE 7-4   MANUFACTURER CODES FOR AWARD BIOS (CONTINUED)

BIOS CODE STRING	CORRESPONDING MANUFACTURER
N0	Nexcom
N5	NEC
NM	New Media Communication (NMC)
NX	Nexar
O0	Ocean (Octek)
P1	PCChips
P4	Asus
P6	Pro-Tech
P8	Azza
P9	Powertech
PA	Epox and 2TheMax
PC	Pine
PF	President
PN	Procomp
PS	Palmax
PX	Pionix
Q0	Quanta
Q1	QDI
RA	RioWorks Solutions Inc.
R0	Mtech (Rise)
R2	Rectron
R3	Datavan International Corp.
S2	Soyo
S3	Smart D&M Technology
S5	Shuttle (HolCo)
S9	Spring Circle
SA	Seanix
SC	Sukjung (Auhua Electronics)
SE	Newtech or SMT or Professional Technologies
SH	SYE (Shining Yuan Enterprises)
SJ	Sowah
SL	Winco
SM	San-Li, Hope Vision, and Superpower
SN	Soltek
SR	(unknown)
SW	S&D (Some A-Corp and Zaapa motherboards use this code.)
T0	Twinhead
T1	Taemung, Fentech, or Trang Bow
T4	Taken
T5	Tyan
T6	Trigem
TB	Taeil

TABLE 7-4   MANUFACTURER CODES FOR AWARD BIOS (*CONTINUED*)

BIOS CODE STRING	CORRESPONDING MANUFACTURER
TG	Tekram
TJ	Totem
TL	Transcend Information Inc.
TP	Commate, Ozzo
U0	U-Board
U1	USI (Universal Scientific Industrial)
U2	AIR (UHC)
U4	Unicorn
U5	Unico
U6	Unitron
U9	Warp Speed
V3	Vtech (PC Partner)
V5	Vision Top Technology
V6	Vobis
V7	YKM (Dayton Micro)
W0	Wintec (Edom)
W1	Well Join
W5	Winco
W7	Win Lan
XA	ADLink Technology
X3	A-Corp
X5	Arima
Y2	Yamashita
Z1	Zida (Tomato motherboards)
Z2	(unknown)
Z3	ShenZhen Zeling Industrial

MICROID RESEARCH BIOS (MR BIOS)

The MR BIOS identification string is located at the top-right corner of the Summary screen (and all or most of the Setup screens). The code directly relates to a specific motherboard model and manufacturer, as shown in Table 7-5. For example, a code of ACER309 means the MR BIOS was designed for an Acer/ALI M1209 motherboard using a Cyrix 486SLC processor.

TABLE 7-5   IDENTIFICATION STRINGS FOR MR BIOS

CODE	MOTHERBOARD
ACER300	Acer/ALI M1209
ACER301	Acer/ALI M1209
ACER304	Acer/ALI M1209
ACER305	Acer/ALI M1209
ACER306	Acer/ALI M1209
ACER307	Acer/ALI M1209
ACER308	Acer/ALI M1209—Cyrix 486SLC

TABLE 7-5   IDENTIFICATION STRINGS FOR MR BIOS (*CONTINUED*)

CODE	MOTHERBOARD
ACER309	Acer/ALI M1209—Cyrix 486SLC
ACER30C	Acer/ALI M1209—Cyrix 486SLC
ACER30D	Acer/ALI M1209—Cyrix 486SLC
ACER30E	Acer/ALI M1209—Cyrix 486SLC
ACER30F	Acer/ALI M1209—Cyrix 486SLC
ACER310	Acer/ALI M1217
ACER311	Acer/ALI M1217
ACER314	Acer/ALI M1217
ACER315	Acer/ALI M1217
ACER316	Acer/ALI M1217
ACER317	Acer/ALI M1217
ACER318	Acer/ALI M1217—Cyrix 486SLC
ACER319	Acer/ALI M1217—Cyrix 486SLC
ACER31C	Acer/ALI M1217—Cyrix 486SLC
ACER31D	Acer/ALI M1217—Cyrix 486SLC
ACER31E	Acer/ALI M1217—Cyrix 486SLC
ACER31F	Acer/ALI M1217—Cyrix 486SLC
C&T_300	Chips & Technologies CS8230
C&T_304	Chips & Technologies CS8230
C&T_305	Chips & Technologies CS8230
C&T_308	Chips & Technologies CS8230
C&T_309	Chips & Technologies CS8230
CNTQ400	Contaq 82C591/82C592 WriteBack
CNTQ404	Contaq 82C591/82C592 WriteBack
CNTQ405	Contaq 82C591/82C592 WriteBack
CNTQ406	Contaq 82C591/82C592 WriteBack
CNTQ407	Contaq 82C591/82C592 WriteBack
CNTQ410	Contaq 82C596 WriteBack
CNTQ411	Contaq 82C596 WriteBack
CNTQ412	Contaq 82C596 WriteBack
EFAR400	Efar Microsystems 82EC495 WriteBack
EFAR401	Efar Microsystems 82EC495 WriteBack—82C711 Combo I/O
EFAR402	Efar Microsystems 82EC495 WriteBack—PC87310 Super I/O
EFAR404	Efar Microsystems 82EC495 WriteBack
EFAR405	Efar Microsystems 82EC495 WriteBack
EFAR406	Efar Microsystems 82EC495 WriteBack
EFAR407	Efar Microsystems 82EC495 WriteBack
EFAR408	Efar Microsystems 82EC495 WriteBack—82C711 Combo I/O
EFAR409	Efar Microsystems 82EC495 WriteBack—82C711 Combo I/O
EFAR40A	Efar Microsystems 82EC495 WriteBack—82C711 Combo I/O
EFAR40B	Efar Microsystems 82EC495 WriteBack—82C711 Combo I/O
EFAR40C	Efar Microsystems 82EC495 WriteBack—PC87310 Super I/O
EFAR40D	Efar Microsystems 82EC495 WriteBack—PC87310 Super I/O
EFAR40E	Efar Microsystems 82EC495 WriteBack—PC87310 Super I/O
EFAR40F	Efar Microsystems 82EC495 WriteBack—PC87310 Super I/O

TABLE 7-5   IDENTIFICATION STRINGS FOR MR BIOS (*CONTINUED*)

CODE	MOTHERBOARD
EFAR410	Efar Microsystems 82EC798 WriteBack
EFAR411	Efar Microsystems 82EC798 WriteBack—82C711 Combo I/O
EFAR412	Efar Microsystems 82EC798 WriteBack—PC87310 Super I/O
EFAR414	Efar Microsystems 82EC798 WriteBack
EFAR415	Efar Microsystems 82EC798 WriteBack
EFAR416	Efar Microsystems 82EC798 WriteBack
EFAR417	Efar Microsystems 82EC798 WriteBack
EFAR418	Efar Microsystems 82EC798 WriteBack—82C711 Combo I/O
EFAR419	Efar Microsystems 82EC798 WriteBack—82C711 Combo I/O
EFAR41A	Efar Microsystems 82EC798 WriteBack—82C711 Combo I/O
EFAR41B	Efar Microsystems 82EC798 WriteBack—82C711 Combo I/O
EFAR41C	Efar Microsystems 82EC798 WriteBack—PC87310 Super I/O
EFAR41D	Efar Microsystems 82EC798 WriteBack—PC87310 Super I/O
EFAR41E	Efar Microsystems 82EC798 WriteBack—PC87310 Super I/O
EFAR41F	Efar Microsystems 82EC798 WriteBack—PC87310 Super I/O
EFAR41G	Efar Microsystems 82EC798 WriteBack—Cyrix 486DLC
EFAR41H	Efar Microsystems 82EC798 WriteBack—Cyrix 486DLC—82C711 Combo I/O
EFAR41J	Efar Microsystems 82EC798 WriteBack—Cyrix 486DLC—PC87310 Super I/O
EFAR41K	Efar Microsystems 82EC798 WriteBack—Cyrix 486DLC
EFAR41L	Efar Microsystems 82EC798 WriteBack—Cyrix 486DLC
EFAR41M	Efar Microsystems 82EC798 WriteBack—Cyrix 486DLC
EFAR41N	Efar Microsystems 82EC798 WriteBack—Cyrix 486DLC
EFAR41P	Efar Microsystems 82EC798 WriteBack—Cyrix 486DLC—82C711 Combo I/O
EFAR41Q	Efar Microsystems 82EC798 WriteBack—Cyrix 486DLC—82C711 Combo I/O
EFAR41R	Efar Microsystems 82EC798 WriteBack—Cyrix 486DLC—82C711 Combo I/O
EFAR41S	Efar Microsystems 82EC798 WriteBack—Cyrix 486DLC—82C711 Combo I/O
EFAR41T	Efar Microsystems 82EC798 WriteBack—Cyrix 486DLC—PC87310 Super I/O
EFAR41U	Efar Microsystems 82EC798 WriteBack—Cyrix 486DLC—PC87310 Super I/O
EFAR41V	Efar Microsystems 82EC798 WriteBack—Cyrix 486DLC—PC87310 Super I/O
EFAR41W	Efar Microsystems 82EC798 WriteBack—Cyrix 486DLC—PC87310 Super I/O
EFAR41X	Efar Microsystems 82EC798 WriteBack—Cyrix 486DLC
ELIT320	Elite Microelectronics Eagle Rev. A1
ELIT324	Elite Microelectronics Eagle Rev. A1
ELIT325	Elite Microelectronics Eagle Rev. A1
ELIT420	Elite Microelectronics Eagle Rev. A1
ELIT424	Elite Microelectronics Eagle Rev. A1
ELIT425	Elite Microelectronics Eagle Rev. A1
ELIT426	Elite Microelectronics Eagle Rev. A1
ELIT427	Elite Microelectronics Eagle Rev. A1
ETEQ301	Eteq Microsystems 82C491/82C493 Bobcat Rev. A
ETEQ303	Eteq Microsystems 82C491/82C492 Cougar Rev. B, C
ETEQ304	Eteq Microsystems 82C491/82C492 Cougar Rev. B, C
ETEQ305	Eteq Microsystems 82C491/82C492 Cougar Rev. B, C
ETEQ311	Eteq Microsystems 82C491/82C493 Bobcat Rev. A
ETEQ314	Eteq Microsystems 82C491/82C493 Bobcat Rev. A

TABLE 7-5   IDENTIFICATION STRINGS FOR MR BIOS (*CONTINUED*)

CODE	MOTHERBOARD
ETEQ315	Eteq Microsystems 82C491/82C493 Bobcat Rev. A
ETEQ321	Eteq Microsystems 82C4901/82C4902 Bengal WriteBack
ETEQ324	Eteq Microsystems 82C4901/82C4902 Bengal WriteBack
ETEQ325	Eteq Microsystems 82C4901/82C4902 Bengal WriteBack
ETEQ401	Eteq Microsystems 82C491/82C493 Bobcat Rev. A
ETEQ403	Eteq Microsystems 82C491/82C492 Cougar Rev. B, C
ETEQ404	Eteq Microsystems 82C491/82C492 Cougar Rev. B, C
ETEQ405	Eteq Microsystems 82C491/82C492 Cougar Rev. B, C
ETEQ421	Eteq Microsystems 82C4901/82C4902 Bengal WriteBack
ETEQ428	Eteq Microsystems 82C4901/82C4902 Bengal WriteBack
ETEQ429	Eteq Microsystems 82C4901/82C4902 Bengal WriteBack
FORX300	Forex 36C300/200 [36C300/46C402] WriteThru
FORX303	Forex 36C300/200 [36C300/46C402] WriteThru
FORX320	Forex 36C311 Single Chip 386SX with Cache
FORX323	Forex 36C311 Single Chip 386SX with Cache
FORX410	Forex 46C411/402 WriteThru
FORX413	Forex 46C411/402 WriteThru
FORX418	Forex 46C411/402 WriteThru
FORX419	Forex 46C411/402 WriteThru
FORX420	Forex 46C521 WriteBack or Forex 46C421A/422 WriteBack
FORX421	Forex 46C521 WriteBack or Forex 46C421A/422 WriteBack
FORX422	Forex 46C521 WriteBack or Forex 46C421A/422 WriteBack
FORX423	Forex 46C521 WriteBack or Forex 46C421A/422 WriteBack
FORX424	Forex 46C521 WriteBack or Forex 46C421A/422 WriteBack
FORX425	Forex 46C521 WriteBack or Forex 46C421A/422 WriteBack
FORX426	Forex 46C521 WriteBack or Forex 46C421A/422 WriteBack
FORX427	Forex 46C521 WriteBack or Forex 46C421A/422 WriteBack
FORX428	Forex 46C521 WriteBack or Forex 46C421A/422 WriteBack
FORX429	Forex 46C521 WriteBack or Forex 46C421A/422 WriteBack
FTDI400	FTDI 82C3480 WriteBack/WriteThru
FTDI401	FTDI 82C3480 WriteBack/WriteThru with 82C711 Combo I/O
FTDI402	FTDI 82C3480 WriteBack/WriteThru with PC87310 Super I/O
FTDI408	FTDI 82C3480 WriteBack/WriteThru
FTDI409	FTDI 82C3480 WriteBack/WriteThru with 82C711 Combo I/O
FTDI40A	FTDI 82C3480 WriteBack/WriteThru with PC87310 Super I/O
HDK_200	EverTech 286 Hedaka
HDK_210	EverTech 286 Hedaka—built-in EMS
HKT_301	Hong Kong Technology HK3000 (Phoenix 8242 Keyboard Controller)
HKT_302	Hong Kong Technology HK3000 (MR BIOS 8042 Keyboard Controller)
HT12200	Headland Technologies HT12/HT12+
HT12201	Headland Technologies HT12/HT12+
HT12202	Headland Technologies HT12/HT12+
HT12210	Headland Technologies HT12/HT12+ with built-in EMS
HT12211	Headland Technologies HT12/HT12+ with built-in EMS
HT22300	Headland Technologies HT22/HT18C

TABLE 7-5   IDENTIFICATION STRINGS FOR MR BIOS (*CONTINUED*)

CODE	MOTHERBOARD
HT22302	Headland Technologies HT22/HT18C
HT22303	Headland Technologies HT22/HT18C
HT2230A	Headland Technologies HT22/HT18C with 82C711 Combo I/O
HT2230B	Headland Technologies HT22/HT18C with PC87310 Super I/O
HT2230C	Headland Technologies HT22/HT18C with 82C711 Combo I/O
HT2230D	Headland Technologies HT22/HT18C with PC87310 Super I/O
HT2230E	Headland Technologies HT22/HT18C with 82C711 Combo I/O
HT2230F	Headland Technologies HT22/HT18C with PC87310 Super I/O
HT32300	Headland Technologies HT320 Shasta
HT32302	Headland Technologies HT320 Shasta
HT32303	Headland Technologies HT320 Shasta
HT3230A	Headland Technologies HT320 Shasta with 82C711 Combo I/O
HT3230B	Headland Technologies HT320 Shasta with PC87310 Super I/O
HT3230C	Headland Technologies HT320 Shasta with 82C711 Combo I/O
HT3230D	Headland Technologies HT320 Shasta with PC87310 Super I/O
HT3230E	Headland Technologies HT320 Shasta with 82C711 Combo I/O
HT3230F	Headland Technologies HT320 Shasta with PC87310 Super I/O
HT34400	Headland Technologies HT340 Shasta
HT34408	Headland Technologies HT340 Shasta
HT34409	Headland Technologies HT340 Shasta
HT3440A	Headland Technologies HT340 Shasta with 82C711 Combo I/O
HT3440B	Headland Technologies HT340 Shasta with PC87310 Super I/O
HT3440C	Headland Technologies HT340 Shasta with 82C711 Combo I/O
HT3440D	Headland Technologies HT340 Shasta with PC87310 Super I/O
HT3440E	Headland Technologies HT340 Shasta with 82C711 Combo I/O
HT3440F	Headland Technologies HT340 Shasta with PC87310 Super I/O
MOSL400	Mosel MS400 Single Chip
MOSL403	Mosel MS400 Single Chip
MOSL404	Mosel MS400 Single Chip
MOSL410	Mosel MS400 Single Chip with 82C711 Combo I/O
MOSL413	Mosel MS400 Single Chip with 82C711 Combo I/O
MOSL415	Mosel MS400 Single Chip with 82C711 Combo I/O
MXIC300	Micronix MX83C305/306 (with built-in 8KB cache)
MXIC302	Micronix MX83C305/306 (with built-in 8KB cache)
MXIC303	Micronix MX83C305/306 (with built-in 8KB cache)
MXIC304	Micronix MX83C305/306 (with built-in 8KB cache)
MXIC305	Micronix MX83C305/306 (with built-in 8KB cache)
MXIC308	Micronix MX83C305/306 (with built-in 8KB cache)
MXIC30A	Micronix MX83C305/306 (with built-in 8KB cache)
MXIC30B	Micronix MX83C305/306 (with built-in 8KB cache)
MXIC30C	Micronix MX83C305/306 (with built-in 8KB cache)
MXIC30D	Micronix MX83C305/306 (with built-in 8KB cache)
OPTI306	OPTi 82C381 WriteThru
OPTI308	OPTi 82C381 WriteThru
OPTI309	OPTi 82C381 WriteThru

TABLE 7-5   IDENTIFICATION STRINGS FOR MR BIOS (*CONTINUED*)

CODE	MOTHERBOARD
OPTI315	OPTi 82C281 SxPW Single-Chip Posted-Write
OPTI316	OPTi 82C281 SxPW Single-Chip Posted-Write
OPTI317	OPTi 82C283 SxPI Single-Chip
OPTI318	OPTi 82C283 SxPI Single-Chip
OPTI319	OPTi 82C281 SxPW Single-Chip Posted-Write with 82C711 Combo I/O
OPTI31A	OPTi 82C281 SxPW Single-Chip Posted-Write with PC87310 Super I/O
OPTI31B	OPTi 82C283 SxPI Single-Chip with 82C711 Combo I/O
OPTI31C	OPTi 82C283 SxPI Single-Chip with PC87310 Super I/O
OPTI31D	OPTi 82C283 SxPI Single-Chip
OPTI31E	OPTi 82C283 SxPI Single-Chip
OPTI31F	OPTi 82C283 SxPI Single-Chip with 82C711 Combo I/O
OPTI31G	OPTi 82C283 SxPI Single-Chip with 82C711 Combo I/O
OPTI31H	OPTi 82C283 SxPI Single-Chip with PC87310 Super I/O
OPTI31J	OPTi 82C283 SxPI Single-Chip with PC87310 Super I/O
OPTI31K	OPTi 82C281 SxPW Single-Chip Posted-Write
OPTI31L	OPTi 82C281 SxPW Single-Chip Posted-Write
OPTI31M	OPTi 82C281 SxPW Single-Chip Posted-Write with 82C711 Combo I/O
OPTI31N	OPTi 82C281 SxPW Single-Chip Posted-Write with 82C711 Combo I/O
OPTI31P	OPTi 82C281 SxPW Single-Chip Posted-Write with PC87310 Super I/O
OPTI31Q	OPTi 82C281 SxPW Single-Chip Posted-Write with PC87310 Super I/O
OPTI324	OPTi 82C391 WriteBack Rev. A & Rev. B
OPTI32B	OPTi 82C391 WriteBack Rev. A & Rev. B with 82C711 Combo I/O
OPTI32C	OPTi 82C391 WriteBack Rev. A & Rev. B with PC87310 Super I/O
OPTI32E	OPTi 82C391 WriteBack Rev. A & Rev. B
OPTI32F	OPTi 82C391 WriteBack Rev. A & Rev. B
OPTI32G	OPTi 82C391 WriteBack Rev. A & Rev. B
OPTI32H	OPTi 82C391 WriteBack Rev. A & Rev. B
OPTI32J	OPTi 82C391 WriteBack Rev. A & Rev. B with 82C711 Combo I/O
OPTI32K	OPTi 82C391 WriteBack Rev. A & Rev. B with 82C711 Combo I/O
OPTI32L	OPTi 82C391 WriteBack Rev. A & Rev. B with 82C711 Combo I/O
OPTI32M	OPTi 82C391 WriteBack Rev. A & Rev. B with 82C711 Combo I/O
OPTI32P	OPTi 82C391 WriteBack Rev. A & Rev. B with PC87310 Super I/O
OPTI32Q	OPTi 82C391 WriteBack Rev. A & Rev. B with PC87310 Super I/O
OPTI32R	OPTi 82C391 WriteBack Rev. A & Rev. B with PC87310 Super I/O
OPTI32S	OPTi 82C391 WriteBack Rev. A & Rev. B with PC87310 Super I/O
OPTI330	OPTi 82C496/497 DxPI Rev. A & Rev. B
OPTI331	OPTi 82C496/497 DxPI Rev. A & Rev. B with 82C711 Combo I/O
OPTI332	OPTi 82C496/497 DxPI Rev. A & Rev. B with PC87310 Super I/O
OPTI334	OPTi 82C496/497 DxPI Rev. A & Rev. B
OPTI335	OPTi 82C496/497 DxPI Rev. A & Rev. B
OPTI336	OPTi 82C496/497 DxPI Rev. A & Rev. B
OPTI337	OPTi 82C496/497 DxPI Rev. A & Rev. B
OPTI338	OPTi 82C496/497 DxPI Rev. A & Rev. B with 82C711 Combo I/O
OPTI339	OPTi 82C496/497 DxPI Rev. A & Rev. B with 82C711 Combo I/O
OPTI33A	OPTi 82C496/497 DxPI Rev. A & Rev. B with 82C711 Combo I/O

TABLE 7-5   IDENTIFICATION STRINGS FOR MR BIOS (*CONTINUED*)

CODE	MOTHERBOARD
OPTI33B	OPTi 82C496/497 DxPI Rev. A & Rev. B with 82C711 Combo I/O
OPTI33C	OPTi 82C496/497 DxPI Rev. A & Rev. B with PC87310 Super I/O
OPTI33D	OPTi 82C496/497 DxPI Rev. A & Rev. B with PC87310 Super I/O
OPTI33E	OPTi 82C496/497 DxPI Rev. A & Rev. B with PC87310 Super I/O
OPTI33F	OPTi 82C496/497 DxPI Rev. A & Rev. B with PC87310 Super I/O
OPTI340	OPTi 82C291 SxWB Single-Chip WriteBack
OPTI341	OPTi 82C291 SxWB Single-Chip WriteBack with 82C711 Combo I/O
OPTI342	OPTi 82C291 SxWB Single-Chip WriteBack with PC87310 Super I/O
OPTI344	OPTi 82C291 SxWB Single-Chip WriteBack
OPTI345	OPTi 82C291 SxWB Single-Chip WriteBack
OPTI346	OPTi 82C291 SxWB Single-Chip WriteBack
OPTI347	OPTi 82C291 SxWB Single-Chip WriteBack
OPTI348	OPTi 82C291 SxWB Single-Chip WriteBack with 82C711 Combo I/O
OPTI349	OPTi 82C291 SxWB Single-Chip WriteBack with 82C711 Combo I/O
OPTI34A	OPTi 82C291 SxWB Single-Chip WriteBack with 82C711 Combo I/O
OPTI34B	OPTi 82C291 SxWB Single-Chip WriteBack with 82C711 Combo I/O
OPTI34C	OPTi 82C291 SxWB Single-Chip WriteBack with PC87310 Super I/O
OPTI34D	OPTi 82C291 SxWB Single-Chip WriteBack with PC87310 Super I/O
OPTI34E	OPTi 82C291 SxWB Single-Chip WriteBack with PC87310 Super I/O
OPTI34F	OPTi 82C291 SxWB Single-Chip WriteBack with PC87310 Super I/O
OPTI406	OPTi 82C481 WriteThru
OPTI408	OPTi 82C481 WriteThru
OPTI409	OPTi 82C481 WriteThru
OPTI424	OPTi 82C491 WriteBack (original)
OPTI428	OPTi 82C491 WriteBack Rev. A & Rev. B
OPTI42B	OPTi 82C491 WriteBack Rev. A & Rev. B with 82C711 Combo I/O
OPTI42C	OPTi 82C491 WriteBack Rev. A & Rev. B with PC87310 Super I/O
OPTI42E	OPTi 82C491 WriteBack Rev. A & Rev. B
OPTI42F	OPTi 82C491 WriteBack Rev. A & Rev. B
OPTI42G	OPTi 82C491 WriteBack Rev. A & Rev. B
OPTI42H	OPTi 82C491 WriteBack Rev. A & Rev. B
OPTI42J	OPTi 82C491 WriteBack Rev. A & Rev. B with 82C711 Combo I/O
OPTI42K	OPTi 82C491 WriteBack Rev. A & Rev. B with 82C711 Combo I/O
OPTI42L	OPTi 82C491 WriteBack Rev. A & Rev. B with 82C711 Combo I/O
OPTI42M	OPTi 82C491 WriteBack Rev. A & Rev. B with 82C711 Combo I/O
OPTI42P	OPTi 82C491 WriteBack Rev. A & Rev. B with PC87310 Super I/O
OPTI42Q	OPTi 82C491 WriteBack Rev. A & Rev. B with PC87310 Super I/O
OPTI42R	OPTi 82C491 WriteBack Rev. A & Rev. B with PC87310 Super I/O
OPTI42S	OPTi 82C491 WriteBack Rev. A & Rev. B with PC87310 Super I/O
OPTI430	OPTi 82C496/497 DxPI Rev. A & Rev. B
OPTI431	OPTi 82C496/497 DxPI Rev. A & Rev. B with 82C711 Combo I/O
OPTI432	OPTi 82C496/497 DxPI Rev. A & Rev. B with PC87310 Super I/O
OPTI434	OPTi 82C496/497 DxPI Rev. A & Rev. B
OPTI435	OPTi 82C496/497 DxPI Rev. A & Rev. B
OPTI436	OPTi 82C496/497 DxPI Rev. A & Rev. B

TABLE 7-5   IDENTIFICATION STRINGS FOR MR BIOS (*CONTINUED*)

CODE	MOTHERBOARD
OPTI437	OPTi 82C496/497 DxPI Rev. A & Rev. B
OPTI438	OPTi 82C496/497 DxPI Rev. A & Rev. B with 82C711 Combo I/O
OPTI439	OPTi 82C496/497 DxPI Rev. A & Rev. B with 82C711 Combo I/O
OPTI43A	OPTi 82C496/497 DxPI Rev. A & Rev. B with 82C711 Combo I/O
OPTI43B	OPTi 82C496/497 DxPI Rev. A & Rev. B with 82C711 Combo I/O
OPTI43C	OPTi 82C496/497 DxPI Rev. A & Rev. B with PC87310 Super I/O
OPTI43D	OPTi 82C496/497 DxPI Rev. A & Rev. B with PC87310 Super I/O
OPTI43E	OPTi 82C496/497 DxPI Rev. A & Rev. B with PC87310 Super I/O
OPTI43F	OPTi 82C496/497 DxPI Rev. A & Rev. B with PC87310 Super I/O
OPTI450	OPTi 82C498 DxWB WriteBack
OPTI451	OPTi 82C498 DxWB WriteBack with 82C711 Combo I/O
OPTI452	OPTi 82C498 DxWB WriteBack with PC87310 Super I/O
OPTI454	OPTi 82C498 DxWB WriteBack
OPTI455	OPTi 82C498 DxWB WriteBack
OPTI456	OPTi 82C498 DxWB WriteBack
OPTI457	OPTi 82C498 DxWB WriteBack
OPTI458	OPTi 82C498 DxWB WriteBack with 82C711 Combo I/O
OPTI459	OPTi 82C498 DxWB WriteBack with 82C711 Combo I/O
OPTI45A	OPTi 82C498 DxWB WriteBack with 82C711 Combo I/O
OPTI45B	OPTi 82C498 DxWB WriteBack with 82C711 Combo I/O
OPTI45C	OPTi 82C498 DxWB WriteBack with PC87310 Super I/O
OPTI45D	OPTi 82C498 DxWB WriteBack with PC87310 Super I/O
OPTI45E	OPTi 82C498 DxWB WriteBack with PC87310 Super I/O
OPTI45F	OPTi 82C498 DxWB WriteBack with PC87310 Super I/O
OPTI470	OPTi 82C495SxLC
OPTI471	OPTi 82C495SxLC with 82C711 Combo I/O
OPTI472	OPTi 82C495SxLC with PC87310 Super I/O
OPTI474	OPTi 82C495SxLC
OPTI475	OPTi 82C495SxLC
OPTI476	OPTi 82C495SxLC
OPTI477	OPTi 82C495SxLC
OPTI478	OPTi 82C495SxLC with 82C711 Combo I/O
OPTI479	OPTi 82C495SxLC with 82C711 Combo I/O
OPTI47A	OPTi 82C495SxLC with 82C711 Combo I/O
OPTI47B	OPTi 82C495SxLC with 82C711 Combo I/O
OPTI47C	OPTi 82C495SxLC with PC87310 Super I/O
OPTI47D	OPTi 82C495SxLC with PC87310 Super I/O
OPTI47E	OPTi 82C495SxLC with PC87310 Super I/O
OPTI47F	OPTi 82C495SxLC with PC87310 Super I/O
OPTI47G	OPTi 82C495SxLC
OPTI47H	OPTi 82C495SxLC with 82C711 Combo I/O
OPTI47J	OPTi 82C495SxLC with PC87310 Super I/O
OPTI47K	OPTi 82C495SxLC
OPTI47L	OPTi 82C495SxLC
OPTI47M	OPTi 82C495SxLC

TABLE 7-5   IDENTIFICATION STRINGS FOR MR BIOS (*CONTINUED*)

CODE	MOTHERBOARD
OPTI47N	OPTi 82C495SxLC
OPTI47P	OPTi 82C495SxLC with 82C711 Combo I/O
OPTI47Q	OPTi 82C495SxLC with 82C711 Combo I/O
OPTI47R	OPTi 82C495SxLC with 82C711 Combo I/O
OPTI47S	OPTi 82C495SxLC with 82C711 Combo I/O
OPTI47T	OPTi 82C495SxLC with PC87310 Super I/O
OPTI47U	OPTi 82C495SxLC with PC87310 Super I/O
OPTI47V	OPTi 82C495SxLC with PC87310 Super I/O
OPTI47W	OPTi 82C495SxLC with PC87310 Super I/O
OPTI480	OPTi 82C499 DxSC Single Chip
OPTI481	OPTi 82C499 DxSC Single Chip with 82C711 Combo I/O
OPTI482	OPTi 82C499 DxSC Single Chip with PC87310 Super I/O
OPTI484	OPTi 82C499 DxSC Single Chip
OPTI485	OPTi 82C499 DxSC Single Chip
OPTI486	OPTi 82C499 DxSC Single Chip
OPTI487	OPTi 82C499 DxSC Single Chip
OPTI488	OPTi 82C499 DxSC Single Chip with 82C711 Combo I/O
OPTI489	OPTi 82C499 DxSC Single Chip with 82C711 Combo I/O
OPTI48A	OPTi 82C499 DxSC Single Chip with 82C711 Combo I/O
OPTI48B	OPTi 82C499 DxSC Single Chip with 82C711 Combo I/O
OPTI48C	OPTi 82C499 DxSC Single Chip with PC87310 Super I/O
OPTI48D	OPTi 82C499 DxSC Single Chip with PC87310 Super I/O
OPTI48E	OPTi 82C499 DxSC Single Chip with PC87310 Super I/O
OPTI48F	OPTi 82C499 DxSC Single Chip with PC87310 Super I/O
OPTI48G	OPTi 82C499 DxSC Single Chip
OPTI48H	OPTi 82C499 DxSC Single Chip with 82C711 Combo I/O
OPTI48J	OPTi 82C499 DxSC Single Chip with PC87310 Super I/O
OPTI48K	OPTi 82C499 DxSC Single Chip
OPTI48L	OPTi 82C499 DxSC Single Chip
OPTI48M	OPTi 82C499 DxSC Single Chip
OPTI48N	OPTi 82C499 DxSC Single Chip
OPTI48P	OPTi 82C499 DxSC Single Chip with 82C711 Combo I/O
OPTI48Q	OPTi 82C499 DxSC Single Chip with 82C711 Combo I/O
OPTI48R	OPTi 82C499 DxSC Single Chip with 82C711 Combo I/O
OPTI48S	OPTi 82C499 DxSC Single Chip with 82C711 Combo I/O
OPTI48T	OPTi 82C499 DxSC Single Chip with PC87310 Super I/O
OPTI48U	OPTi 82C499 DxSC Single Chip with PC87310 Super I/O
OPTI48V	OPTi 82C499 DxSC Single Chip with PC87310 Super I/O
OPTI48W	OPTi 82C499 DxSC Single Chip with PC87310 Super I/O
OPTI48Z	OPTi 82C499 DxSC Single Chip with PC87311/312 Super I/O
OPTI490	OPTi 82C495 SLC
OPTI491	OPTi 82C495 SLC with 82C711 Combo I/O
OPTI492	OPTi 82C495 SLC with PC87310 Super I/O
OPTI493	OPTi 82C495 SLC
OPTI494	OPTi 82C495 SLC with 82C711 Combo I/O

TABLE 7-5 IDENTIFICATION STRINGS FOR MR BIOS (*CONTINUED*)

CODE	MOTHERBOARD
OPTI495	OPTi 82C495 SLC with PC87310 Super I/O
OPTI496	OPTi 82C495 SLC
OPTI497	OPTi 82C495 SLC with 82C711 Combo I/O
OPTI498	OPTi 82C495 SLC with PC87310 Super I/O
OPTI499	OPTi 82C495 SLC
OPTI49A	OPTi 82C495 SLC with 82C711 Combo I/O
OPTI49B	OPTi 82C495 SLC with PC87310 Super I/O
OPTI4A0	OPTi 82C801 SCWB2 Single Chip WriteBack
OPTI4A1	OPTi 82C801 SCWB2 Single Chip WriteBack with 82C711 Combo I/O
OPTI4A2	OPTi 82C801 SCWB2 Single Chip WriteBack with PC87310 Super I/O
OPTI4A3	OPTi 82C801 SCWB2 Single Chip WriteBack with PC87311 Super I/O
OPTI500	OPTi 586 VHP Pentium Chipset
PKDM301	Chips & Technologies CS82310 PEAKset DM Rev-0
PKDM304	Chips & Technologies CS82310 PEAKset DM Rev-0
PKDM305	Chips & Technologies CS82310 PEAKset DM Rev-0
PKDM311	Chips & Technologies CS82310 PEAKset DM Rev-0—82C711 Combo I/O
PKDM314	Chips & Technologies CS82310 PEAKset DM Rev-0—82C711 Combo I/O
PKDM315	Chips & Technologies CS82310 PEAKset DM Rev-0—82C711 Combo I/O
PKDM321	Chips & Technologies CS82310 PEAKset DM Rev-B1
PKDM322	Chips & Technologies CS82310 PEAKset DM Rev-B1
PKDM323	Chips & Technologies CS82310 PEAKset DM Rev-B1
PKDM324	Chips & Technologies CS82310 PEAKset DM Rev-B1
PKDM325	Chips & Technologies CS82310 PEAKset DM Rev-B1
PKDM331	Chips & Technologies CS82310 PEAKset DM Rev-B1—82C711 Combo I/O
PKDM332	Chips & Technologies CS82310 PEAKset DM Rev-B1—82C711 Combo I/O
PKDM333	Chips & Technologies CS82310 PEAKset DM Rev-B1—82C711 Combo I/O
PKDM334	Chips & Technologies CS82310 PEAKset DM Rev-B1—82C711 Combo I/O
PKDM335	Chips & Technologies CS82310 PEAKset DM Rev-B1—82C711 Combo I/O
PKDM420	Chips & Technologies CS82310 PEAKset DM Rev-B1
PKDM421	Chips & Technologies CS82310 PEAKset DM Rev-B1
PKDM424	Chips & Technologies CS82310 PEAKset DM Rev-B1
PKDM425	Chips & Technologies CS82310 PEAKset DM Rev-B1
PKDM428	Chips & Technologies CS82310 PEAKset DM Rev-B1
PKDM429	Chips & Technologies CS82310 PEAKset DM Rev-B1
PKDM430	Chips & Technologies CS82310 PEAKset DM Rev-B1—82C711 Combo I/O
PKDM431	Chips & Technologies CS82310 PEAKset DM Rev-B1—82C711 Combo I/O
PKDM434	Chips & Technologies CS82310 PEAKset DM Rev-B1—82C711 Combo I/O
PKDM435	Chips & Technologies CS82310 PEAKset DM Rev-B1—82C711 Combo I/O
PKDM438	Chips & Technologies CS82310 PEAKset DM Rev-B1—82C711 Combo I/O
PKDM439	Chips & Technologies CS82310 PEAKset DM Rev-B1—82C711 Combo I/O
SARC302	SARC RC2016A Rev. A3 (standard)
SARC306	SARC RC2016A Rev. A3 with built-in EMS
SARC30A	SARC RC2016A Rev. A3 Cyrix
SARC30E	SARC RC2016A Rev. A3 Cyrix, with built-in EMS
SCAT300	Chips & Technologies 82C236 SCATsx

TABLE 7-5   IDENTIFICATION STRINGS FOR MR BIOS (*CONTINUED*)

CODE	MOTHERBOARD
SCAT304	Chips & Technologies 82C236 SCATsx
SCAT305	Chips & Technologies 82C236 SCATsx
SIS_303	SiS 85C310/320/330 Rabbit Rev. A, B & C
SIS_306	SiS 85C310/320/330 Rabbit Rev. A, B & C
SIS_307	SiS 85C310/320/330 Rabbit Rev. A, B & C
SIS_308	SiS 85C310/320/330 Rabbit Rev. A, B & C
SIS_309	SiS 85C310/320/330 Rabbit Rev. A, B & C
SIS_400	SiS 85C460 & 85C461V Single-Chip
SIS_404	SiS 85C460 & 85C461V Single-Chip
SIS_405	SiS 85C460 & 85C461V Single-Chip
SLGC301	SysLogic 386 non-cache
SLGC302	SysLogic 386 with cache
SLGC304	SysLogic 386 non-cache
SLGC305	SysLogic 386 non-cache
SLGC306	SysLogic 386 with cache
SLGC307	SysLogic 386 with cache
SLGC401	SysLogic 486 no external cache
SLGC404	SysLogic 486 no external cache
SLGC405	SysLogic 486 no external cache
STD_202	Generic 286 (TTL/Discrete Logic)
STD_203	Generic 286 (TTL/Discrete Logic)
STD_286	Generic 286 (TTL/Discrete Logic)
STD_302	Generic 386 (TTL/Discrete Logic)
STD_303	Generic 386 (TTL/Discrete Logic)
STD_386	Generic 386 (TTL/Discrete Logic)
STD_408	Generic 486 (TTL/Discrete Logic)
STD_409	Generic 486 (TTL/Discrete Logic)
STD_486	Generic 486 (TTL/Discrete Logic)
SYML401	Symphony Labs SL82C46x Haydn Rev. 1.1
SYML402	Symphony Labs SL82C46x Haydn Rev. 1.1 with 82C711 Combo I/O
SYML403	Symphony Labs SL82C46x Haydn Rev. 1.1 with PC87310 Super I/O
SYML404	Symphony Labs SL82C46x Haydn Rev. 1.1
SYML405	Symphony Labs SL82C46x Haydn Rev. 1.1
SYML406	Symphony Labs SL82C46x Haydn Rev. 1.1 with 82C711 Combo I/O
SYML407	Symphony Labs SL82C46x Haydn Rev. 1.1 with 82C711 Combo I/O
SYML408	Symphony Labs SL82C46x Haydn Rev. 1.1 with PC87310 Super I/O
SYML409	Symphony Labs SL82C46x Haydn Rev. 1.1 with PC87310 Super I/O
SYML411	Symphony Labs SL82C46x Haydn Rev. 1.2
SYML412	Symphony Labs SL82C46x Haydn Rev. 1.2 with 82C711 Combo I/O
SYML413	Symphony Labs SL82C46x Haydn Rev. 1.2 with PC87310 Super I/O
SYML414	Symphony Labs SL82C46x Haydn Rev. 1.2
SYML415	Symphony Labs SL82C46x Haydn Rev. 1.2
SYML416	Symphony Labs SL82C46x Haydn Rev. 1.2 with 82C711 Combo I/O

TABLE 7-5   IDENTIFICATION STRINGS FOR MR BIOS (*CONTINUED*)

CODE	MOTHERBOARD
SYML417	Symphony Labs SL82C46x Haydn Rev. 1.2 with 82C711 Combo I/O
SYML418	Symphony Labs SL82C46x Haydn Rev. 1.2 with PC87310 Super I/O
SYML419	Symphony Labs SL82C46x Haydn Rev. 1.2 with PC87310 Super I/O
TACT300	Texas Instruments TACT83000 Tiger non-cache
TACT302	Texas Instruments TACT83000 Tiger with Intel 82385 cache
TACT303	Texas Instruments TACT83000 Tiger with Austek cache
TACT30A	Texas Instruments TACT83000 Tiger non-cache
TACT30B	Texas Instruments TACT83000 Tiger non-cache
TACT30C	Texas Instruments TACT83000 Tiger with Austek cache
TACT30D	Texas Instruments TACT83000 Tiger with Austek cache
TACT30E	Texas Instruments TACT83000 Tiger with Intel 82385 cache
TACT30F	Texas Instruments TACT83000 Tiger with Intel 82385 cache
TACT400	Texas Instruments TACT83000 Tiger no external cache
TACT40A	Texas Instruments TACT83000 Tiger no external cache
TACT40B	Texas Instruments TACT83000 Tiger no external cache
UMC_301	UMC 82C48x WriteBack Rev. 0
UMC_302	UMC 82C48x WriteBack Rev. A & Rev. B
UMC_304	UMC 82C48x WriteBack Rev. A & Rev. B
UMC_310	UMC 82C330 Twinstar
UMC_314	UMC 82C330 Twinstar
UMC_315	UMC 82C330 Twinstar
UMC_401	UMC 82C48x WriteBack Rev. 0
UMC_402	UMC 82C48x WriteBack Rev. A & Rev. B
UMC_403	UMC 82C48x WriteBack Rev. A & Rev. B
UMC_404	UMC 82C48x WriteBack Rev. A & Rev. B
UMC_405	UMC 82C48x WriteBack Rev. A & Rev. B
UMC_406	UMC 82C48x WriteBack Rev. A & Rev. B
UMC_407	UMC 82C48x WriteBack Rev. A & Rev. B
UMC_40A	UMC 82C48x WriteBack Rev. B
UMC_40B	UMC 82C48x WriteBack Rev. B
UMC_40C	UMC 82C48x WriteBack Rev. B
UMC_40D	UMC 82C48x WriteBack Rev. B
UMC_40E	UMC 82C48x WriteBack Rev. B
UMC_40F	UMC 82C48x WriteBack Rev. B
UMC_40G	UMC 82C48x WriteBack Rev. A & Rev. B
UMC_410	UMC 82C491 Single-Chip
VLSI301	VLSI Technology 386 Topcat—Intel 82340 non-cache
VLSI302	VLSI Technology 386 Topcat—Intel 82340 non-cache with 82C106 IPC
VLSI312	VLSI Technology 386 Topcat—Intel 82340 with 82385 cache and 82C106 IPC
VLSI401	VLSI Technology 386 Topcat—Intel 82340
VLSI402	VLSI Technology 386 Topcat—Intel 82340 with 82C106 IPC
VLSI404	VLSI Technology 386 Topcat—Intel 82340 with 82C106 IPC

IDENTIFYING YOUR BIOS CHIP

There may also be times when it becomes necessary to identify the flash BIOS chip itself in order to replace the chip or more closely identify the motherboard. The most obvious sign of a BIOS chip is the presence of a sticker carrying the name of a known BIOS maker such as AMI, Award, Phoenix, MR BIOS, and so on. When you gently peal back the sticker, you can determine the characteristics of your flash BIOS chip from the part number. Table 7-6 identifies many of the most popular flash chips.

TABLE 7-6   IDENTIFYING BIOS CHIPS BY PHYSICAL PART NUMBER

PART NUMBER	IDENTIFICATION
27Cxxx	With window—EPROM—read-only, requires programmer to write and UV to erase
28Cxxx	EEPROM—not flash memory
28EE011	SST 5-volt flash ROM
28F001BX-B	Intel 12-volt flash ROM
28F001BX-T	Intel 12-volt flash ROM
28F010	Fujitsu 12-volt flash ROM (or ISSI 12-volt flash ROM)
28F010	Intel 12-volt flash ROM
29EE010	SST 5-volt flash ROM
29LVxxx	3-volt Flash memory (rare)
A28F010	Intel 12-volt flash ROM
Am28F010	AMD 12-volt flash ROM
Am28F010A	AMD 12-volt flash ROM
Am29F010	AMD 5-volt flash ROM
AT28C010	Atmel 5-volt flash ROM
AT28MC010	Atmel 5-volt flash ROM
AT29C010	Atmel 5-volt flash ROM
AT29LC010	Atmel 5-volt flash ROM
AT29MC010	Atmel 5-volt flash ROM
CAT28F010	Catalyst 12-volt flash ROM
CAT28F010I	Catalyst 12-volt flash ROM
CAT28F010V5	Catalyst 5-volt flash ROM
CAT28F010V5I	Catalyst 5-volt flash ROM
DQ28C010	SEEQ 5-volt flash ROM
DQ47F010	SEEQ 12-volt flash ROM
DQ48F010	SEEQ 12-volt flash ROM
DQM28C010A	SEEQ 5-volt flash ROM
DYM28C010	SEEQ 5-volt flash ROM
HN28F101	Hitachi 12-volt flash ROM
HN29C010	Hitachi 12-volt flash ROM
HN29C010B	Hitachi 12-volt flash ROM
HN58C1000	Hitachi 5-volt flash ROM
HN58C1001	Hitachi 12-volt flash ROM
HN58V1001	Hitachi 12-volt flash ROM
KM29C010	Samsung 5-volt flash ROM
M28F010	SGS-Thomson 12-volt flash ROM
M28F1001	SGS-Thomson 12-volt flash ROM
M5M28F101FP	Mitsubishi 12-volt flash ROM

TABLE 7-6	IDENTIFYING BIOS CHIPS BY PHYSICAL PART NUMBER (*CONTINUED*)
PART NUMBER	**IDENTIFICATION**
M5M28F101P	Mitsubishi 12-volt flash ROM
M5M28F101RV	Mitsubishi 12-volt flash ROM
M5M28F101VP	Mitsubishi 12-volt flash ROM
MSM28F101	OKI 12-volt flash ROM
MX28F1000	MXIC 12-volt flash ROM
PH29EE010	SST ROM Chip—Flashable
TMS28F010	Texas Instruments 12-volt flash ROM
TMS29F010	Texas Instruments 5-volt flash ROM
W27F010	Winbond 12-volt flash ROM
W29EE011	Winbond 5-volt flash ROM
X28C010	XICOR 5-volt flash ROM
X28C010I	XICOR 5-volt flash ROM
XM28C010	XICOR 5-volt flash ROM
XM28C010I	XICOR 5-volt flash ROM

Anything without a quartz window that doesn't have a "28" or "29" as the preceding digits of the part number is most likely a standard ROM chip that cannot be reprogrammed.

BIOS and Boot Sequences

The next step in understanding the BIOS is to recognize how it *boots*—the series of steps that takes a PC from power-on to the point where it's loading an operating system. While every BIOS follows a similar pattern of steps, each BIOS is written a bit differently and may have more or fewer steps than comparable BIOS versions. This part of the chapter looks at the boot sequences for several popular BIOS versions.

AMERICAN MEGATRENDS

American Megatrends (AMI) is renowned for their BIOS, PC diagnostics, and motherboards. AMI BIOS performs a fairly comprehensive suite of 24 steps in order to check and initialize the PC. The general AMI BIOS POST procedure follows:

1. *Disable the NMI.* BIOS disables the nonmaskable interrupt line to the CPU. A failure here suggests a problem with the CMOS RAM chip or its associated circuitry.

2. *Power-on delay.* The system resets the soft and hard reset bits. A fault here indicates a problem with the keyboard controller chip or system clock generator chip.

3. *Initialize chipsets.* BIOS initializes any particular motherboard chipsets (such as the Intel or VIA chipsets) that may be present in the system. A problem here may be caused by the BIOS, the clock generator chip, or the chipset itself.

4. *Reset determination.* The system reads the reset bits in the keyboard controller to determine whether a hard or soft reset (cold or warm boot) is required. A failure here may be caused by the BIOS or keyboard controller chip.

5. *BIOS ROM checksum.* The system performs a checksum test of ROM contents and adds a factory preset value that should make the total equal to 00h. If this total does not equal 00h, the BIOS ROM is defective.

6. *Keyboard test.* A command is sent to the 8042 (keyboard controller), which performs a test and sets a buffer space for commands. After the buffer is defined, the BIOS sends a command byte, writes data to the buffer, checks the high order bits (pin 23) of the internal keyboard controller, and issues a *No Operation* (NOP) command. A fault here is likely caused by the keyboard controller chip.

7. *CMOS shutdown check.* BIOS tests the shutdown byte in CMOS RAM, calculates the CMOS checksum, and updates the CMOS diagnostic byte. The system then initializes a small CMOS area in conventional memory and updates the date and time. A problem here is likely in the RTC/CMOS chip, or in the CMOS backup battery.

8. *Controller disable.* BIOS now disables the DMA and IRQ controller chips before proceeding. A fault at this point suggests trouble in the respective controller.

9. *Disable video.* BIOS disables the video controller chip. If this procedure fails, the trouble is probably in the video adapter board.

10. *Detect memory.* The system proceeds to check the amount of memory available. BIOS measures system memory in 64KB blocks. A problem here may be in the memory chip(s).

11. *PIT test.* BIOS tests the *programmable interrupt timer* (PIT), vital for memory refresh. A problem with the PIT test may reflect a fault in the PIT IC or in the RTC chip.

12. *Check memory refresh.* BIOS now uses the PIT to try refreshing memory. A failure indicates a problem with the PIT chip.

13. *Check low address lines.* The system checks the first 16 address lines controlling the first 64KB of RAM. A problem with this test typically means a fault in an address line.

14. *Check low 64KB RAM.* The system now checks the first 64KB of system RAM. This is vital since this area must hold information that is critical for system initialization. A problem here is usually the result of a bad RAM chip.

15. *Initialize support chips.* BIOS proceeds to initialize the *programmable interrupt timer* (PIT), the *programmable interrupt controller* (PIC), and the *Direct Memory Access* (DMA) chips. A fault here would be located in one of those locations.

16. *Load INT vector table.* BIOS loads the system's interrupt vector table into the first 2KB of system RAM.

17. *Check the keyboard controller (KBC).* BIOS reads the keyboard controller buffer at I/O port 60h. A problem here indicates a fault in the keyboard controller chip.

18. *Video tests.* The system checks for the type of video adapter in use, then tests and initializes the video memory and adapter. A problem with this test typically indicates a fault with the video memory or adapter, respectively. After a successful video test, the video system will be operational.

19. *Load the BDA.* The system now loads the *BIOS data area* (BDA) into conventional memory.

20. *Test memory.* BIOS checks all memory below 1MB. A problem here is typically the fault of one or more RAM modules, the keyboard controller chip, or a bad data line.

21. *Check DMA registers.* BIOS performs a register-level check of the DMA controller(s) using binary test patterns. A problem here is often due to a failure of the DMA chip(s).

22. *Check the keyboard.* The system performs a final check of the keyboard interface. An error at this point is usually the fault of the keyboard.

23. *Perform high-level tests.* This step involves a whole suite of tests that check such high-level devices as the floppy and hard disks, serial adapters, parallel adapters, mouse adapter, and so on. The number and complexity of these tests vary with the BIOS version. When an error occurs, a corresponding text message will be displayed. If the system hardware does not match the setup shown in the CMOS Setup, a corresponding error code will be displayed.

24. *Load the OS.* At this point, BIOS triggers INT 19h, which is the routine that loads an operating system. An error here generally results in an error message such as "Non-system disk."

AWARD SOFTWARE

Award is another popular and well-established BIOS maker whose products can be found in a wide range of PCs spanning almost every generation. The procedure outlined next is generally found with Award BIOS v4.2 and later.

1. *Test the CPU.* The BIOS checks the error flags in the CPU, then performs a register test by writing and reading bit patterns. Failure here is normally due to the CPU or clock chip.

2. *Initialize support chips.* Video is disabled along with parity/DMA and NMI; then the PIT/PIC and DMA chips are initialized. Failure at this point is normally due to the PIT or DMA chips.

3. *Initialize the keyboard.* The keyboard and *keyboard controller* (KBC) are initialized. Problems here are due to keyboard connection faults, or a failure of the KBC chip.

4. *ROM BIOS test.* A checksum is performed on the ROM BIOS. Failure here is normally due to the ROM BIOS chip that would normally be reprogrammed or replaced.

5. *CMOS RAM test.* A test of the CMOS chip is performed (which should also detect a bad battery). Trouble here is due to either the CMOS chip or the CMOS backup battery.

6. *Memory test.* The first 356KB of memory is tested with any diagnostic routines in the chipsets. A fault at this point is normally due to defective memory chips, SIMMs, or DIMMs.

7. *Cache initialization.* Any cache external to the main chipset is activated. Failure to control the cache here is normally caused by a fault in the cache controller or cache chips.

8. *Initialize the vector table.* Interrupt vectors are initialized, and the interrupt table is installed into low memory. Failure here is normally caused by the BIOS or a fault in low memory.

9. *CMOS RAM checksum.* The CMOS RAM is checksum tested (BIOS defaults are loaded if the CMOS RAM checksum is invalid). When trouble occurs here, it may be necessary to replace the CMOS RAM chip.

10. *Keyboard initialization.* The keyboard is initialized, and the Num Lock is set On. Check the keyboard or *keyboard controller* (KBC) if you have problems here.

11. *Video circuit test.* The video adapter circuit is tested and initialized.

12. *Video memory test.* Memory is tested on "Mono" and "CGA" adapters (if installed). Check the adapter card if trouble occurs here.

13. *DMA controller test.* The DMA controllers and page registers are tested. Check the DMA chips when problems occur here.

14. *PIC tests.* The 8259 PIC chips are tested.

15. *EISA mode test.* A checksum is performed on the extended data area of CMOS where EISA information is stored. If the test passes, the EISA adapter is initialized.

16. *Enable EISA slots.* Slots 0–15 (for EISA adapters) are enabled if the test passes.

17. *Check memory size.* Memory addresses above 265KB are written to in 64KB blocks, and any addresses found are initialized. If a bit is bad, the entire block containing it (and those above it) will not be seen. Replace any defective memory chips, SIMMs, or DIMMs.

18. *Memory test.* A read/write test is performed on memory over 256KB. A failure would be due to a bad bit in RAM, and the defective memory chip, SIMM, or DIMM should be replaced.

19. *Check EISA memory.* This checks memory on any adapters initialized previously. If there are problems here, check the memory chips/devices on those adapters.

20. *Mouse initialization.* This checks for a mouse and installs the appropriate interrupt vectors if one is found. Check the mouse adapter if there is a problem.

21. *Cache initialization.* The cache controller is initialized (if present).

22. *Shadow RAM setup.* Any shadow RAM that is present (according to the CMOS Setup) is enabled.

23. *Floppy test.* Test and initialize the floppy controller and drive.

24. *Hard drive test.* Test and initialize the hard disk controller and drive. If there is trouble here, there may be an improper setup, a bad controller, or a defective hard drive.

25. *Serial/parallel port test.* Any serial and parallel ports found at the proper addresses are initialized.

26. *Initialize math coprocessor.* The MCP is initialized if found.

27. *Boot speed.* This sets the default speed at which the computer boots.

28. *POST loop.* A reboot occurs if the "loop pin" is set. (This is used only for manufacturing purposes.)

29. *Security.* The system will ask for the password (if one has been configured). If this does not happen, check the CMOS data or the CMOS RAM chip. For example, a CMOS password may have been cleared if the CMOS backup battery was removed.

30. *Write to CMOS RAM.* The BIOS tries to write the CMOS values from setup to CMOS RAM. Failure here is normally due to an invalid CMOS configuration.

31. *Initialize adapter ROM(s).* Any adapter ROMs between C800h and EFFFh are initialized. The ROM will do an internal test before giving back control to the system ROM. Failure here is normally due to the adapter ROM or the attached hardware that should be replaced.

32. *Set up the time.* This sets the CMOS time to the value located at 40h of the *BIOS Data Area* (BDA).

33. *Boot the system.* Control is given to the INT 19 boot loader.

PHOENIX TECHNOLOGIES

Phoenix Technologies is one of the premier BIOS manufacturers for IBM-compatible PCs, known for their extensive POST and versatility with OEMs. A typical Phoenix BIOS performs essentially the same steps as an AMI BIOS, but there are several variations, as shown next:

1. *Check the CPU.* The registers and control lines of the CPU are checked. Any problems will usually be the result of a faulty CPU or clock chip.

2. *Test CMOS RAM.* The CMOS chip is tested. A fault is usually due to a failure of the RTC/CMOS chip.

3.   *BIOS ROM checksum.* A checksum is performed on the BIOS ROM. If the calculated checksum does not match the factory-set value, an error is generated. A checksum problem is typically the result of a faulty BIOS ROM. Try replacing the BIOS ROM.

4.   *Test chipset(s).* The system checks any chipsets (such as the Intel or VIA chipsets) for proper operation with the BIOS. A problem here is typically due to a fault in the chipset. Replace the motherboard.

5.   *Test PIT.* The *programmable interrupt timer* (PIT) is tested to ensure that all interrupt requests are handled properly. A problem here indicates that the PIT chip is defective.

6.   *Test DMA.* The *Direct Memory Access* (DMA) controller is tested next. A fault at this point is typically caused by the CPU, the DMA chip, or an address line problem.

7.   *Test base 64KB memory.* BIOS checks the lowest 64KB of system RAM. A problem here is due to a fault in memory, or an address line problem.

8.   *Check serial and parallel ports.* The system checks the presence of serial and parallel port hardware, and I/O data areas are assigned for any devices found.

9.   *Test PIC.* The *programmable interrupt controller* (PIC) is tested to see that proper interrupt levels can be generated. A problem here is typically due to a fault in the PIC chip.

10.   *Check keyboard controller (KBC).* The keyboard controller chip is tested for proper operation. When a problem occurs, the keyboard controller is likely defective.

11.   *Verify CMOS data.* Data within the CMOS is checked for validity. If the extended area returns a failure, CMOS data has probably been set up incorrectly. However, continuous failures typically represent a faulty RTC/CMOS chip.

12.   *Verify video system.* Video RAM is tested; then the video controller is located, tested, and initialized. A fault is usually the result of a defective video controller. If the controller is located on an expansion board, try replacing the video board.

13.   *Test RTC.* The *real-time clock* (RTC) is tested next, and each frequency output is verified. A problem here is usually due to a fault in the RTC, PIT, or system crystal.

14.   *Test CPU in protected mode.* The CPU is switched to protected mode and returned to POST at the point indicated in CMOS RAM offset 0Fh. When this step fails, the CPU, keyboard controller chip, CMOS chip, or address line(s) may be at fault.

15.   *Verify PIC 2.* Counter #2 is tested on the PIC chip. If this test fails, the PIC chip is likely defective.

16.   *Check NMI.* The NMI is checked to be sure it is active. A problem here often indicates trouble with the CMOS chip, but could also reflect problems in the BIOS ROM, PIC chip, or CPU.

17.   *Check the keyboard.* The keyboard buffer and controller are checked.

18.   *Check the mouse.* BIOS initializes the mouse (if present) through the keyboard controller. A fault is usually caused in the mouse adapter circuit.

19.   *Check system RAM.* All remaining system RAM is tested in 64KB blocks. Trouble usually means a defective memory module.

20.   *Test disk controller.* Fixed and floppy disk controllers are checked using standard BIOS calls. Problems here are usually the result of defective controllers or faulty drives. If the controllers are installed on expansion boards, you can try replacing the respective expansion board.

21.   *Set shadow RAM areas.* The system looks at CMOS to find which ROM(s) will be shadowed into RAM. Problems here are often due to a faulty adapter ROM, or problems in RAM.

22. *Check extended ROMs.* BIOS looks for signatures of 55AAh in memory, which indicate the presence of additional ROMs. The system then performs a checksum test on each ROM. A problem with this step generally indicates trouble with the extended ROM or related adapter circuitry.

23. *Test cache controller.* The external cache controller chip is tested. A problem is usually due to a fault in the cache controller chip itself or a defect in cache memory.

24. *Test CPU cache.* The internal cache present in the CPU is tested. A problem here is almost always due to a CPU fault.

25. *Check hardware adapters.* BIOS proceeds to check the high-level subsystems such as the video system, floppy disk, hard disk, I/O adapters, serial ports, and parallel ports. Problems usually reflect a fault with the respective adapter or an invalid CMOS Setup.

26. *Load the OS.* At this point, BIOS triggers INT 19h, which is the routine that loads an operating system. An error here generally results in an error message such as "Non-system disk."

BIOS Shortcomings and Compatibility Issues

No matter how much time and effort are put into BIOS code development, there are still many times when BIOS can come up short (especially in the newest, state-of-the-art systems). Before you start troubleshooting, you should have an understanding of the places where BIOS is weakest.

DEVICE DRIVERS

As you might expect, no BIOS can possibly address every piece of hardware in the PC marketplace or keep pace with the rapid advances of those devices that a BIOS does support. As a result, PC designers have devised a way to augment BIOS through the use of *device drivers*. Traditional CD-ROMs are an excellent example. There are a number of CD-ROM designs in use today—each CD-ROM and its corresponding controller board use their own circuitry to operate the drive and interface it to the PC bus. Neither the CD-ROM application, DOS, nor BIOS are capable of identifying the drive or interface. To get around this, a low-level device driver is loaded into conventional memory from disk once the PC initializes. The low-level device driver translates a set of standard DOS calls into the instructions necessary to operate the adapter and drive. An extension of DOS (MSCDEX for MS DOS–based systems) is also loaded into memory after the low-level driver. The DOS extension works seamlessly with MSDOS.SYS to provide applications with a standard set of software interrupt CD-ROM services. Generally speaking, device drivers all interface hardware to the operating system and serve to supplement the BIOS. Video, SCSI, and network adapters all make use of device drivers at some level.

The newest BIOS versions do identify and support bootable CD-ROM drives that adhere to the El Torito standard.

"FLASH" LAZINESS

The broad acceptance of "flash" memory allows BIOS to be reprogrammed "in-system" through the use of a downloadable program. There is no need to open the PC, or to exchange BIOS chips. This offers BIOS makers a great deal of versatility in the development of new BIOS, but it can also foster an attitude of laziness. Given the astounding speed at which new developments are proliferating, BIOS makers are under a great deal of pressure to create ever-more-powerful and diverse BIOS. With traditional BIOS, programmers needed to create solid, well-tested code—because replacing thousands of BIOS chips in the field is an expensive and cumbersome task. Now that BIOS updates can be quickly downloaded directly from the Internet, BIOS programmers can sometimes take the "release it now and patch it later" attitude. As a rule, BIOS code is still quite solid, but you should be aware that the potential for BIOS problems and oversights are now much higher than in years past.

BIOS SHADOWING

Another problem with BIOS chips is their inherently slow speed. BIOS is typically recorded onto flash ROM chips (older BIOS used conventional ROM chips, or other programmable ROM chips). These read-only devices are necessary because BIOS data must be maintained even when power is removed. Unfortunately, permanent storage chips such as these have hideously slow access times (150nS to 200nS) when compared with the fast RAM used in today's PCs (for example, 50nS to 70nS). When you consider that the services stored in a BIOS ROM are used almost continuously, it is easy to see that each delay is additive—the net result is an overall reduction in PC performance.

To overcome this limitation, it would be necessary to accelerate the access time of BIOS ROM. However, this is not too likely, given the current state of semiconductor technology, so PC designers do the next best thing—*ROM shadowing*. The process of "shadowing" basically copies ROM contents from the BIOS chip into available RAM in the *upper memory area* (UMA). Once the copy is complete, the system will work from the *copy* rather than the original. This allows BIOS routines to take advantage of faster RAM. Not only system BIOS, but all BIOS can be shadowed (video BIOS is particularly popular for shadowing). ROM shadowing can typically be turned on or off through the CMOS Setup routine.

Not all BIOS can be successfully shadowed. Shadowing problems can cause erratic system behavior and lockups. Whenever you encounter problems configuring a system, you should always try stabilizing the system by shutting down all shadowing options. You can restore shadowing options later and observe if system problems return.

DIRECT CONTROL

In the race to wring every last clock-tick of performance from a PC, even the most elegantly written BIOS is simply too slow for high-performance applications. If the application could work with PC hardware directly, system performance (especially disk and video subsystems) could be substantially improved. Writing directly to hardware is hardly new—pre-IBM PCs relied on direct application control. The use of BIOS was included by IBM to ensure that variations in PC hardware would still remain compatible with operating system and application software. As it turns out, today's PC hardware functions are remarkably standardized (even though the actual components can vary dramatically). With this broad base of relatively standard features, software developers are reviving the direct control approach and ignoring the use of BIOS services in favor of drivers or routines written into the application. For example, a powerful 3D accelerator such as the 3Dfx Voodoo 3 works with drivers only and does not involve any BIOS routines. The trouble with this approach is that direct hardware control may not work on all system configurations, and any changes to the system hardware (for example, upgrade or replacement parts) may cause the PC to malfunction when the particular application or driver is executed.

BIOS BUGS

As with all software-based products, BIOS code is subject to accidental errors or omissions (software bugs). When BIOS is developed, it is replicated by the thousands and purchased by motherboard manufacturers who incorporate the BIOS into their motherboards. If a bug is present in the BIOS, the system will typically lock up or crash unexpectedly, or during a certain operation. Since the same BIOS may be used in several motherboards, the bug may not manifest itself in all cases. As one example, some users of AMI BIOS (dated 04/09/90 or earlier) reported problems with the keyboard controller when running Windows or OS/2. As you can imagine, BIOS bugs are particularly frustrating. If an application contains a bug, you can turn the application off. Unfortunately, you cannot turn off the BIOS, so the only way to correct a bug in BIOS is to update the BIOS chip, flash the BIOS with an updated BIOS file, or replace the entire motherboard.

When investigating a customer complaint for a PC, you may wish to check with the BIOS manufacturer (through technical support, fax-back service, or their Internet Web site). Find if there have been any problems with the BIOS when used in the particular motherboard. For example, a given Phoenix BIOS version may exhibit a peculiar symptom when used in a particular Intel motherboard. If your symptoms match other symptoms that have been reported, a quick BIOS upgrade may save the day for your customer.

BIOS Troubleshooting

You've got to be familiar with the myriad error messages that a system can generate. Each time you start the PC, the power-on self-test (POST) initiates a comprehensive series of tests to verify the computer's hardware. Traditionally, the POST generates two types of error messages: beep codes and POST codes. Beep codes are generated through the PC speaker before the video system has properly initialized. POST codes are single-byte hexadecimal characters written to I/O port 80h (or other I/O port) as each POST test is started. You can read the POST code using a POST reader card. By matching the beep code or POST code to your particular BIOS, you can determine the exact fault.

The problem with beep codes and POST codes is their cryptic nature—you need a detailed code listing in order to match the code to the fault. However, current generations of BIOS and operating systems are starting to employ more user-friendly error messages. By displaying complete error messages (rather than simple codes), a great deal of guesswork is removed from the troubleshooting process. Remember that BIOS error messages are designed to enhance (rather than replace) beep and POST codes. You should also note that unlike beep codes and POST codes, many BIOS error messages are not fatal—that is, the system will continue to run after the error has been generated.

GENERAL SYMPTOMS

The BIOS can report myriad useful error messages during the POST, and most can be traced to memory, setup, and drive problems. The following symptoms represent a range of possible errors that you may encounter across many system versions.

SYMPTOM 7-1   **GA20 Error**   This may also appear as "8042 Gate—A20 Error." There is a fault using gate A20 when switching to the protected mode (accessing memory over 1MB). One or more SIMMs/DIMMs may be loose, or the *keyboard controller* (KBC) may have failed. Check that each of the SIMMs/DIMMs is installed securely. Try replacing the keyboard controller (if possible), or replace the entire motherboard if necessary.

SYMPTOM 7-2   **Address line short**   There is a serious problem with the memory address decoding circuitry on your motherboard. In some cases, this may be a spontaneous error that can be cleared by turning the system off for a few seconds and rebooting. If the problem persists, you should replace the motherboard.

SYMPTOM 7-3   **BIOS ROM checksum error—System halted**   The checksum of the BIOS code in the BIOS chip is incorrect—this is a *fatal* problem indicating that the BIOS code may have become corrupt. If your BIOS includes a "boot block," you may be able to boot to a floppy disk and try "reflashing" the BIOS. If your system is unable to boot, you'll need to replace the motherboard BIOS chip (or replace the motherboard) before the system will initialize.

SYMPTOM 7-4   **C: (or D:) drive error**   You may also see this presented as "Pri/Sec Master/ Slave—ATAPI Incompatible." The system cannot detect the designated drive(s). The hard disk "type" is probably set incorrectly in the CMOS Setup, or the disk may not be connected or formatted properly. Check the CMOS Setup, recheck the drive jumpers, and reconnect the drive(s). You may need to repartition and reformat the drive.

SYMPTOM 7-5   **C: (or D:) drive failure**   The drive was detected, but it failed to respond properly. This is more serious than an error and generally means that the drive is defective. Double-check the drive signal cable, and replace the drive if necessary.

SYMPTOM 7-6   **Cache memory bad, do not enable cache**   POST has determined that your L2 cache memory is defective. Do *not* attempt to enable the cache in your system. You should replace the cache RAM at your earliest opportunity. Until then, you may notice a decline in system performance. If you're using a Pentium II/III/4 or similar CPU where the L2 cache is integrated into the CPU cartridge itself, try replacing the CPU.

SYMPTOM 7-7   **CMOS battery failed**   The CMOS battery is no longer functional. You will need to replace the CMOS battery as soon as possible. If you haven't yet lost CMOS contents, take a PRINTSCREEN of each CMOS Setup page immediately to record the setup configuration, and then power-down the system and install a new battery.

SYMPTOM 7-8   **CMOS battery state low**   The CMOS battery power is getting low. Make it a point to record your CMOS settings as soon as possible, and then replace the CMOS battery promptly.

SYMPTOM 7-9   **CMOS checksum error—defaults loaded**   CMOS RAM has become corrupt, so the CMOS checksum is incorrect. The system usually loads the default equipment configuration in an effort to ensure that the system can start. A weak battery may have caused this error. Check the CMOS backup battery and replace if necessary. If a new battery will not correct the trouble, the CMOS RAM may have failed, and you will need to replace the motherboard.

SYMPTOM 7-10   **CMOS display type mismatch**   The video type indicated in CMOS RAM is not the one detected by the BIOS. Check your CMOS Setup and make sure the correct video type is selected (usually VGA). Remember to save your changes before exiting and rebooting. Also verify that there is no conflict between an integrated video adapter (on the motherboard) and a video adapter card in your system.

SYMPTOM 7-11   **CMOS memory size mismatch**   The amount of memory recorded in the CMOS Setup configuration does not match the memory detected by the POST. If you have added new memory, start your CMOS Setup and make the appropriate corrections (or simply save changes and reboot even though you change nothing). If you've made no changes to the system, try rebooting the computer. If the error appears again, some of your memory may have failed. Try a systematic replacement to locate the defective SIMM/DIMM.

SYMPTOM 7-12   **CMOS system options not set**   You may also see this reported as "CMOS settings wrong." The values stored in CMOS RAM are either corrupt or nonexistent. Check your CMOS backup battery and replace it if necessary. Enter the CMOS Setup routine and reload any missing or corrupted entries. Remember to save your changes before exiting and rebooting.

SYMPTOM 7-13   **CPU at "nnn"**   This displays the running speed of the CPU (where "nnn" is the speed in MHz). This is not an error, but a measurement. If the displayed speed is known to be different from the actual clock speed, you should check the motherboard's clock settings and multipliers, or suspect an error in BIOS speed detection. (You may need to update the BIOS to achieve an accurate measurement.)

SYMPTOM 7-14   **Data error**   The floppy disk or hard drive that you are accessing cannot read the data. One or more sectors on the disk(s) may be corrupted. If you are using DOS, run the CHKDSK or ScanDisk utility to check the file structure of the floppy disk or hard disk drive. If you find errors, rerun the utility to correct those errors. Keep in mind that it may be necessary to reload any applications or data files that were subject to file structure problems.

SYMPTOM 7-15   **Decreasing available memory**   An error has been detected in memory, and the available memory is being reduced below the point at which the fault was detected. Either a SIMM/DIMM has failed, or one or more SIMMs/DIMMs may be improperly seated. Try reinstalling your memory modules, or replace them.

SYMPTOM 7-16   **Diskette drive 0 (or 1) seek failure**   Your floppy drive was unable to seek to the desired track. A cable may be loose, or the CMOS Setup information may not match your actual floppy drive hardware. Check and correct your CMOS Setup, check your signal cable, and replace the floppy drive if necessary.

SYMPTOM 7-17   **Diskette read failure**   This may also be displayed as a "Diskette boot failure." The system was unable to read from a floppy disk. This is usually due to dirty read/write heads, a loose signal cable, or a defective floppy disk. Try cleaning the read/write heads, try a different floppy disk, check/replace the floppy signal cable, and replace the floppy drive if necessary.

SYMPTOM 7-18   **Diskette subsystem reset failed**   The PC was unable to access the floppy drive system. The disk drive controller may be faulty. Make sure that the drive controller is seated properly in its bus slot (if you're using a stand-alone drive controller) and that all cables are attached securely. Try the drive controller in another slot, and replace the drive controller if necessary.

SYMPTOM 7-19   **Display switch is set incorrectly**   Some older motherboards provide a display switch that can be set to either monochrome or color. This message indicates the switch is set to a different setting than indicated in CMOS Setup. Determine which video setting is correct, and then either turn off the system and change the motherboard jumper, or enter CMOS Setup and change the video selection.

SYMPTOM 7-20   **DMA (or DMA #1 or DMA #2) error**   A serious fault has occurred in the DMA controller system of your motherboard. In virtually all cases, the motherboard will have to be replaced (unless you can replace the DMA controller).

SYMPTOM 7-21   **DMA bus time-out**   A device has driven the bus signal for more than 7.8 microseconds. This may be a random fault, but chances are that a DMA-dependent device in the PC has failed (such as your sound card or Ultra-DMA drive controller). Reboot the computer and see if the problem clears. If not, try removing expansion devices first. Otherwise, replace the motherboard.

SYMPTOM 7-22   **Drive not ready**   No floppy disk is in the drive. Make sure that the valid disk is secure in the drive before continuing. Try another known-good disk.

SYMPTOM 7-23   **EISA CMOS checksum failure**   The checksum for your EISA CMOS RAM is bad. This means the CMOS RAM is defective or the backup battery is exhausted. Try replacing the backup battery first. If the problem persists, replace the CMOS RAM chip (or replace the entire motherboard).

SYMPTOM 7-24   **EISA CMOS not operational**   A read/write failure occurred in extended CMOS RAM. Either the CMOS RAM backup battery has died, or the CMOS RAM chip itself has failed. Try replacing the CMOS backup battery. If the problem persists, replace the CMOS RAM chip (or replace the entire motherboard).

SYMPTOM 7-25   **EISA configuration is not complete**   The slot configuration information stored in the EISA CMOS RAM is incomplete. When this error appears, the system will boot in ISA mode, which allows you to run the *EISA Configuration Utility* (ECU). Run the system's ECU (normally on a floppy disk that accompanied the system) and finish configuring the system; then save your changes and reboot.

SYMPTOM 7-26   **Enable/disable expansion board**   One of your EISA expansion boards suffered a *nonmaskable interrupt* (NMI). You can press E to enable that board, or press D to disable it—this allows the system to finish booting. Try rebooting the system and see if the problem clears. If the problem persists, try replacing the suspect expansion board.

SYMPTOM 7-27   **Expansion board not ready at slot "X"**   Your EISA BIOS cannot find the expansion board assigned to slot "X." Verify that the expansion board is in the correct slot and is seated properly. If the problem persists, try replacing the expansion board or moving it to (and reconfiguring it for) another available slot.

SYMPTOM 7-28   **Floppy disk controller failure**   This may also be reported as an "FDC Error." There is a problem with the floppy drive system—either the floppy drive or drive controller has failed. Check the floppy drive controller first, and make sure it's seated properly in its bus slot. Try a different bus slot. Check that all the drive cables are secure. Make sure that the floppy drive is receiving power. Try a new drive controller, and try a different floppy drive if necessary.

SYMPTOM 7-29   **Floppy disk(s) fail**   You may also see this reported as an "A: Drive Error." The PC cannot find or initialize the floppy drive controller or the floppy drive itself. Make sure the drive controller is installed correctly. (You might try a different expansion slot.) If no floppy drives are installed, be sure the "Diskette Drive" entries in CMOS Setup are set to "none" or "not installed." Otherwise, verify that the floppy drive is listed correctly in the CMOS Setup, and then replace the floppy disk drive if necessary.

SYMPTOM 7-30   Hard disk configuration error   The system could not initialize the hard drive in the expected fashion. This is often due to an incorrect configuration in the CMOS Setup. Make sure that the correct hard drive geometry is entered for the drive (or try autodetecting and autoconfiguring the drive). If the drive was originally partitioned in another system with different parameters, you may need to duplicate those parameters in order to access the drive. If the problem persists, try repartitioning and reformatting the drive, or replace the hard drive.

SYMPTOM 7-31   Hard disk controller failure   This may also be reported as an "HDC Error." There is a problem with the hard drive system—either the hard drive or drive controller has failed. Check the drive controller first, and make sure it's seated properly in its bus slot. Try a different bus slot. Check that all the drive cables are secure. Make sure that the hard drive is spinning up. Try a new drive controller, and try a different hard drive if necessary.

SYMPTOM 7-32   Hard disk(s) diagnosis fail   Your BIOS may run specific disk diagnostic routines. This type of message appears if one or more hard disks return an error when those diagnostics are run. In most cases, the drive itself is installed improperly or is defective. Check the drive installation, and replace the drive if necessary.

SYMPTOM 7-33   Hard disk failure   The hard drive failed initialization, which usually suggests that the drive has failed. Make sure that the drive signal cable is attached properly, and see that the drive spins up. Replace the hard drive if necessary.

SYMPTOM 7-34   Hard disk drive read failure   The drive cannot read from the hard drive, which usually suggests that the drive has failed. Make sure that the drive signal cable is attached properly, and see that the drive spins up. Replace the hard drive if necessary.

SYMPTOM 7-35   Incompatible Processor: CPU0 (or CPU1) is B0 step or below
You have installed an old version of a CPU that is not supported by the BIOS. In a single-microprocessor system, CPU0 refers to the system board microprocessor; in a dual-microprocessor system, it refers to the secondary microprocessor on the add-in card. The CPU1 message appears only on a dual-microprocessor system and always refers to the system board microprocessor. Replace the microprocessor with a current version of the microprocessor.

SYMPTOM 7-36   Incompatible Processor: Cache sizes different   This message appears for a dual-microprocessor system if the CPUs use differing L2 cache sizes. Replace one of the microprocessors to make the L2 cache sizes match.

SYMPTOM 7-37   Insert Bootable Media   You may also see this reported as "No boot device available." The BIOS cannot find a bootable media. Insert a bootable floppy disk or bootable CD, or switch to a known-good bootable drive.

SYMPTOM 7-38   INTR #1 (or INTR #2) error   A serious fault has occurred with your *programmable interrupt controller* (PIC) on the motherboard. In virtually all cases, the motherboard will have to be replaced entirely.

SYMPTOM 7-39   Invalid Boot Diskette   The BIOS can read the disk in floppy drive A, but cannot boot the system from it. Use another known-good boot disk, or try booting from a different drive.

SYMPTOM 7-40   **Invalid configuration information—please run SETUP program**
The system configuration information in your CMOS Setup does not match the hardware configuration detected by the POST. Enter the CMOS Setup program, and correct the system configuration information. Remember to save your changes before exiting and rebooting.

SYMPTOM 7-41   **Invalid configuration information for slot "X"**   The configuration information for the EISA board in slot "X" is not correct, which usually means that the system has been reconfigured without running the *EISA Configuration Utility* (ECU). Run the ECU, being sure to configure the system properly and save your changes before exiting.

SYMPTOM 7-42   **I/O Card Parity Error at xxxxx**   An expansion card has failed. If the address can be determined, it is displayed as "xxxxx." If not, the message is "I/O Card Parity Error ????". In either case, you'll need to find and reconfigure the offending device, or replace the defective expansion card.

SYMPTOM 7-43   **Keyboard clock line failure**   The BIOS has not detected the keyboard clock signal when testing the keyboard. Often, the keyboard connector is loose, or the keyboard is defective. Check the keyboard cable, and try another keyboard if necessary. If the problem persists, the *keyboard controller* (KBC) may have failed. Try replacing the keyboard controller chip, or replace the entire motherboard.

SYMPTOM 7-44   **Keyboard controller failure**   This may also be denoted as a "Keyboard interface error." The keyboard controller on the motherboard is not responding as expected. Start by checking the keyboard connection, and try a different keyboard. If the problem persists, the *keyboard controller* (KBC) may have failed. Try replacing the keyboard controller chip, or replace the entire motherboard.

SYMPTOM 7-45   **Keyboard data line failure**   The BIOS has not detected the keyboard data signal when testing the keyboard. Often, the keyboard connector is loose, or the keyboard is defective. Check the keyboard cable, and try another keyboard if necessary. If the problem persists, the keyboard controller may have failed. Try replacing the *keyboard controller* (KBC) chip, or replace the entire motherboard.

SYMPTOM 7-46   **Keyboard error or no keyboard present**   The system cannot initialize the keyboard. Make sure the keyboard is attached correctly, and see that no keys are pressed during POST. To purposely configure the system without a keyboard (for example, if you're setting up a server), you can configure the CMOS Setup to ignore the keyboard.

SYMPTOM 7-47   **Keyboard is locked out—unlock the key**   If your system comes fitted with a key lock switch, make sure that the switch is set to the "unlocked" position. If there is no key lock switch (or the switch is set properly), one or more keys may be pressed or shorted on the keyboard. Try a new keyboard.

SYMPTOM 7-48   **Keyboard stuck key failure**   In almost all cases, this is a keyboard problem. POST has determined that one or more keys on the keyboard are stuck. Make sure that nothing is resting on the keyboard, and see that no paper clips or staples may have fallen into the keyboard. Try a different keyboard.

SYMPTOM 7-49   Memory address line failure at <address>, read <value> expecting <value>   An error has occurred in the address decoding circuitry used in memory. In many cases, one or more SIMMs/DIMMs may be improperly seated. Check that all SIMMs/DIMMs are installed correctly. If the problem continues, try systematic replacement to locate a defective memory module. If you cannot find a defective SIMM/DIMM, there is likely a problem elsewhere on the motherboard. Replace the motherboard.

SYMPTOM 7-50   Memory data line failure at <address>, read <value> expecting <value>   An error has been encountered in memory. In virtually all cases, one or more SIMMs/DIMMs may be faulty or improperly seated. Make sure that every SIMM/DIMM is seated correctly, and try a systematic replacement to locate a defective memory module.

SYMPTOM 7-51   Memory double word logic failure at <address>, read <value> expecting <value>   An error has been encountered in memory. In virtually all cases, one or more SIMMs/DIMMs may be faulty or improperly seated. Make sure that every SIMM/DIMM is seated correctly, and try a systematic replacement to locate a defective memory module.

SYMPTOM 7-52   Memory odd/even logic failure at <address>, read <value> expecting <value>   An error has been encountered in memory. In virtually all cases, one or more SIMMs/DIMMs may be faulty or improperly seated. Make sure that every SIMM/DIMM is seated correctly, and try a systematic replacement to locate a defective memory module.

SYMPTOM 7-53   Memory parity failure at <address>, read <value> expecting <value>   An error has been encountered in memory. In virtually all cases, one or more SIMMs/DIMMs may be faulty or improperly seated. Make sure that every SIMM/DIMM is seated correctly, and try a systematic replacement to locate a defective memory module.

SYMPTOM 7-54   Memory size changed   You may also see this as "Memory size increased" or "Memory size decreased." If you have not altered the memory configuration of your system, chances are that one or more memory devices have failed. Make sure that every SIMM/DIMM is seated correctly, and try a systematic replacement to locate a defective memory module. If the memory checks properly, try entering the CMOS Setup and simply "exit saving changes" (even if you made no changes). This may help the system reset its detection of the available RAM.

SYMPTOM 7-55   Memory write/read failure at <address>, read <value> expecting <value>   An error has been encountered in memory. In virtually all cases, one or more SIMMs/DIMMs may be faulty or improperly seated. Make sure that every SIMM/DIMM is seated correctly, and try a systematic replacement to locate a defective memory module.

SYMPTOM 7-56   Memory size in CMOS invalid   The amount of memory recorded in the CMOS Setup configuration does not match the memory detected by the POST. If you have added new memory, start your CMOS Setup and make the appropriate corrections. If you've made no changes to the system, try rebooting the computer. If the error appears again, some of your memory may have failed. Try a systematic replacement to locate a defective SIMM or DIMM.

SYMPTOM 7-57   Memory verify error at <address>   This suggests an error verifying a value already written to memory and almost always indicates a bad memory device. Use the <address>

location along with your system's memory map to locate the defective memory devices, or systematically replace your SIMMs/DIMMs until the defective memory device is found.

SYMPTOM 7-58   **No boot device available**   The computer cannot find a viable floppy disk or hard drive—typically because the drives have not been entered properly into CMOS. Enter the CMOS Setup program and configure the proper drive information. You should also verify that your floppy disk or hard drive has been prepared as "bootable." You may need to repartition and/or reformat the hard drive.

SYMPTOM 7-59   **No boot sector on hard disk drive**   The PC is refusing to boot from the hard drive. This is usually because the drive is not configured properly. Check the CMOS Setup and verify that the correct drive information has been entered (or select autodetect). Also make sure to partition the drive with an active bootable partition, and format it as a bootable device. If the problem continues, try replacing the hard drive.

SYMPTOM 7-60   **No timer tick interrupt**   The interrupt timer on the motherboard has failed. This is a fatal error that will probably require you to replace the motherboard.

SYMPTOM 7-61   **Non-system disk or disk error**   The floppy disk in drive A or your hard drive does not have a bootable operating system installed on it. If you're booting from a floppy drive, make the disk bootable. If you're booting from a hard drive, make sure that the drive is partitioned and formatted for bootable operation.

SYMPTOM 7-62   **Not a boot diskette**   There is no operating system on the floppy disk. Boot the computer with a disk that contains an operating system.

SYMPTOM 7-63   **Off-board parity error**   There is a parity error in memory installed in an expansion slot (for example, a SIMM on the video adapter). The format is OFF BOARD PARITY ERROR ADDR (HEX) = (XXXX), where XXXX is the hex address where the error occurred. Chances are that the memory installed at the error address has failed. Try replacing the suspect memory, or replace the device in the affected expansion slot.

SYMPTOM 7-64   **On-board parity error**   There is a parity error in memory installed on the motherboard in one of the SIMM/DIMM slots. The format is ON BOARD PARITY ERROR ADDR (HEX) = (XXXX), where XXXX is the hex address where the error occurred. Chances are that the memory installed at the error address has failed. Use a systematic approach to isolate and replace the suspect memory.

SYMPTOM 7-65   **Override enabled—defaults loaded**   If the system cannot boot using the current CMOS configuration for any reason, the BIOS can override the current configuration using a set of defaults designed for the most stable, minimal-performance system operations. The CMOS may be ignored if the CMOS RAM checksum is wrong, or if a critical piece of CMOS information is missing that would otherwise cause a fatal error.

SYMPTOM 7-66   **Parity error**   A parity error has occurred in system memory at an unknown address. Chances are that a memory module has failed. Try a systematic "check and replace" approach to isolate and replace the defective memory component.

SYMPTOM 7-67   **Plug-and-play configuration error**   The system has encountered a problem in trying to configure one or more (usually PCI) expansion cards. Start the CMOS Setup routine, and check that any PnP options have been set correctly. If configuration utilities are included with your particular system, try running those utilities to resolve any configuration issues.

SYMPTOM 7-68   **Press TAB to show POST screen**   Some system OEMs (such as Acer) may replace the normal BIOS POST display with their own proprietary display—usually a graphic logo. When the BIOS displays this message, the operator is able to switch between the OEM display and the default POST display. This can be helpful for troubleshooting purposes.

SYMPTOM 7-69   **Primary master hard disk fail**   POST detects an error in the primary ("master") hard drive on the primary drive controller channel. Double-check the drive's installation, jumpering, and cable connections. Otherwise, replace the drive.

SYMPTOM 7-70   **Primary slave hard disk fail**   POST detects an error in the secondary ("slave") hard drive on the primary drive controller channel. Double-check the drive's installation, jumpering, and cable connections. Otherwise, replace the drive.

SYMPTOM 7-71   **Resuming from disk**   Award BIOS (and now many other BIOS versions) offers a save-to-disk feature for notebook computers (usually referred to as *hibernation*). This message may appear when the operator restarts the system after a save-to-disk shutdown. You will almost never find this type of message on a desktop or tower system.

SYMPTOM 7-72   **Secondary master hard disk fail**   POST detects an error in the primary ("master") hard drive on the secondary drive controller channel. Double-check the drive's installation, jumpering, and cable connections. Otherwise, replace the drive.

SYMPTOM 7-73   **Secondary slave hard disk fail**   POST detects an error in the secondary ("slave") hard drive on the secondary drive controller channel. Double-check the drive's installation, jumpering, and cable connections. Otherwise, replace the drive.

SYMPTOM 7-74   **Should be empty but EISA board found**   A valid EISA board ID was found in a slot that was configured as having no board installed. This is normally due to an improper system configuration, so run the *EISA Configuration Utility* (ECU) and reconfigure the system properly. Remember to save any changes and reboot the system.

SYMPTOM 7-75   **Should have EISA board but none found**   The board installed in a given EISA slot is not responding to the expected ID request. (Or no board ID has been found in the indicated slot.) This is normally due to an improper system configuration, so run the *EISA Configuration Utility* (ECU) and reconfigure the system properly. Remember to save any changes and reboot the system. If the problem persists, the board in the suspect slot may be defective.

SYMPTOM 7-76   **Shutdown failure**   There is a serious fault on the motherboard—usually associated with the CMOS RAM/RTC function. In most cases, you'll need to replace the motherboard.

SYMPTOM 7-77   **System halted—Press CTRL-ALT-DEL to reboot**   This error indicates the current boot attempt has been aborted, and the system must be rebooted. In most cases, the system files on the boot drive have been damaged, or the boot drive itself has failed. Try booting from another drive (for example, a floppy disk). You may need to repartition and reformat the boot drive as a bootable device, or replace the boot drive.

SYMPTOM 7-78 **Terminator/processor card not installed** This is an error that occurs with dual-CPU systems when neither a "terminator" card nor a secondary microprocessor card is installed in the secondary card connector. Make sure either a terminator card or a secondary microprocessor card is installed in the connector. Install the appropriate card and start the system again.

SYMPTOM 7-79 **Time of day clock stopped** The *real-time clock* (RTC) has stopped. The CMOS battery may be dead (or almost dead). Enter the CMOS Setup and correct the date and time. If the trouble continues, try replacing the CMOS backup battery.

SYMPTOM 7-80 **Time or date in CMOS is invalid** The time or date displayed in the CMOS Setup does not match the system clock. This can happen often under Windows 98/Me or other operating systems that can "desynchronize" the system clock. Enter the CMOS Setup utility and correct the date and time. If the problem reoccurs, you may be able to determine a specific application that is causing the problem.

SYMPTOM 7-81 **Timer chip counter 2 failed** There is a serious fault on the mother-board—probably due to a failure of a *programmable interrupt timer* (PIT). In most cases, you'll need to replace the motherboard.

SYMPTOM 7-82 **Unexpected interrupt in protected-mode** An interrupt has occurred unexpectedly. Loose or poorly inserted SIMMs/DIMMs can cause such a problem, so start by checking and reinstalling the SIMMs/DIMMs. A faulty *keyboard controller* (KBC) can also result in interrupt problems. Try replacing the keyboard controller if possible, or replace the entire motherboard.

SYMPTOM 7-83 **Warning—Thermal Probes failed** This error is usually found in Pentium Pro systems with one or two thermal probes. At system startup, the BIOS has detected that one or both of the thermal probes in the computer are not operational. You can continue to use the system, but be aware that the temperature probe(s) are disabled—a processor overheat condition will not shut down the system. You will probably have to replace the motherboard to correct this fault.

The Pentium Pro has a built-in thermocouple that halts microprocessor operation if the CPU exceeds its rated temperature.

SYMPTOM 7-84 **Warning—Temperature is too high** During system startup, the BIOS has detected that one or both microprocessors are overheated. This can happen if you try to restart the system too soon after a thermal shutdown. After displaying this message, the BIOS halts the processes and turns off the system. Let the system cool down before attempting to restart it.

SYMPTOM 7-85 **Wrong board in slot "X"** This is typically an EISA system error when the board's ID does not match the ID stored in the EISA nonvolatile memory. Run the EISA Configuration Utility to reconfigure your device layout and save any system changes.

PCI SYMPTOMS

In addition to general error detection and reporting, most modern BIOS versions can now detect and report problems associated with the PCI bus and devices. The following symptoms are generally caused by problems with PCI devices or the motherboard's PCI bus architecture. In some cases, you may need to update the motherboard's bus master drivers or enable IRQ steering to correct these issues.

SYMPTOM 7-86 **Bad PnP serial ID checksum** The serial ID checksum of a plug-and-play card is invalid. Try reconfiguring or replacing the offending expansion card.

SYMPTOM 7-87 **Floppy disk controller resource conflict** The floppy disk controller has requested a resource that is already in use by another device. Try reconfiguring or freeing the resources that are requested by the PnP system.

SYMPTOM 7-88 **NVRAM checksum error, NVRAM cleared** The *extended system configuration data* (ESCD) was reinitialized because of an NVRAM checksum error. Try rerunning the *ISA Configuration Utility* (ICU). If the problem persists, replace the NVRAM chip, or replace the motherboard entirely.

SYMPTOM 7-89 **NVRAM cleared by jumper** The "Clear CMOS" jumper on the motherboard has been moved to the "Clear" position, and the system has been initialized. CMOS RAM and ESCD have been cleared and now must be reconfigured/reloaded with the necessary data.

SYMPTOM 7-90 **NVRAM data invalid, NVRAM cleared** Invalid data has been found in the ESCD (which may mean that you have changed devices in the system). When this message is displayed, the BIOS has already rewritten the ESCD with current configuration data. Try rebooting the system once again, or enter the CMOS Setup and "exit saving changes," even though you may not change anything.

SYMPTOM 7-91 **Parallel port resource conflict** The parallel port requested a resource that is already in use by another device. Try reconfiguring or freeing the resources requested by the PnP system.

SYMPTOM 7-92 **PCI error log is full** More than 15 PCI conflict errors have been detected, and no additional PCI errors can be logged. Deal with the PCI errors already contained in the log in order to reduce the total number of errors, and address subsequent errors as they occur.

SYMPTOM 7-93 **PCI I/O port conflict** Two devices have requested the same I/O address, resulting in a conflict. Try reconfiguring or freeing the I/O resources needed to allow both devices to be configured properly.

SYMPTOM 7-94 **PCI IRQ conflict** Two devices have requested the same IRQ, resulting in a conflict. Try reconfiguring or freeing the IRQs needed to allow both devices to be configured properly.

SYMPTOM 7-95 **PCI memory conflict** Two devices have requested the same memory range resources, resulting in a conflict. Try reconfiguring or freeing the memory ranges needed to allow both devices to be configured properly.

SYMPTOM 7-96   **Primary boot device not found**   The designated primary boot device (for example, a hard disk drive, floppy disk drive, or CD-ROM drive) could not be found. Check the installation and configuration of each possible boot device.

SYMPTOM 7-97   **Primary IDE controller resource conflict**   The primary IDE controller has requested a resource that is already in use by another device. Try reconfiguring or freeing the resources that are needed to allow the IDE controller to operate.

SYMPTOM 7-98   **Primary input device not found**   The designated primary input device such as the keyboard or mouse (or other device if input is redirected) could not be found. Check the installation and configuration of all your input devices. Make sure that the input devices are also enabled in the CMOS Setup.

SYMPTOM 7-99   **Secondary IDE controller resource conflict**   The secondary IDE controller has requested a resource that is already in use by another device. Try reconfiguring or freeing the resources that are needed to allow the IDE controller to operate.

SYMPTOM 7-100   **"Static device resource conflict" or "System board device resource conflict"**   A non–plug-and-play (or legacy) ISA card has requested a resource that is already in use. Try reconfiguring the ISA card to use other resources, or try freeing the resources needed by the ISA card.

OTHER BIOS SYMPTOMS

In actual practice, you cannot "fix" a BIOS chip, but you must be able to identify possible problems with BIOS versions and incompatibilities (especially when trying to use the newest operating systems and hardware). When you find such a problem, you'll need to flash the BIOS with an updated version or to replace the troublesome BIOS chip. This part of the chapter highlights a number of common BIOS-related problems that you may encounter.

SYMPTOM 7-101   **Norton Utilities 8 reports poor disk performance with MR BIOS**
You may notice that Norton 8 identifies changes in the disk controller and suggests that disk performance may measure artificially high, but you find that disk performance is reported with a much lower result. This is a problem with the way Norton 8 interacts with certain versions of MR BIOS. Version 3.2 and later use slightly different coding that corrects this reporting problem. You may consider upgrading your version of MR BIOS, or update your version of Norton Utilities.

SYMPTOM 7-102   **Norton Utilities 9 reports problems on the disk when using MR BIOS**
After installing some versions of MR BIOS, there have been a few reports that NDD95 will misdiagnose your disk with a problem (even though ScanDisk reports the drive to be working perfectly). If this occurs, do *not* use NDD95 to correct the problem—this may damage your disk's file system. Instead, uninstall and reinstall Norton Utilities.

According to Microid Research, most NDD95 problems have been traced to the CMOS date being reset after running the flash loader utility. The flash loader intentionally clears the CMOS RAM to assure a clean startup with the newly installed MR BIOS. Be sure to reenter the date (especially the century part of the year) after flashing MR BIOS into the computer. Beginning with version 3.26, the MR BIOS flash loader carefully avoids clearing the CMOS date.

SYMPTOM 7-103   **After partitioning and formatting a drive under MR BIOS, the drive is not recognized on other systems**   You may also find this problem when reflashing the original system BIOS back over the MR BIOS that you're using. This is not a problem with MR BIOS. Instead, the trouble is with the version of FDISK included with Windows 95. The latest version of FDISK supplied with Windows 95 (or a later version of Windows such as 98/Me) supports three new partition types that are written to partition table entries on the hard disk:

- **Type 0Eh**   The same as type 06h (primary DOS), but uses BIOS INT13 extensions to get hard disk parameters.
- **Type 0Fh**   The same as type 05h (extended DOS), but uses BIOS INT13 extensions to get hard disk parameters.
- **Type 0Ch**   A FAT32 partition using BIOS INT13 extensions to get hard disk parameters.
- **Type 0Bh**   A FAT32 partition that does *not* use BIOS INT13 extensions to get hard disk parameters.

MR BIOS supports INT 13h extensions, and when you partition your hard drive under MR BIOS, FDISK will use type 0Eh or 0Fh as a partition type. When you boot from the drive, the OS reads this partition type byte and uses the BIOS INT 13 extensions to get the hard disk parameters. As long as you don't change this setup, everything works fine. However, if you use this partitioned hard drive with another BIOS which does *not* support INT 13 extensions, the operating system expects to access the hard disk parameters using the BIOS INT 13 extensions. Since your other version of the BIOS does not support this, the operating system cannot boot. According to Microid Research, this is not a problem with MR BIOS only—they claim to have re-created this problem on motherboards using BIOS from other vendors besides MR BIOS.

The recommended solution is to boot from a floppy disk, switch to the hard drive, back up the hard drive, and then repartition the drive using FDISK from the system where you intend to use the hard drive. You can also use Windows 95 FDISK with the **/X** switch, which forces FDISK to use older partition types (or update to a later version of Windows). After you repartition and reformat the drive, reload your operating system and restore your files.

SYMPTOM 7-104   **You cannot use two PCI devices simultaneously in slots 1 and 5**
This is a known issue with Tyan S1470 Titan XV motherboards and MR BIOS. The problem is generally not the BIOS, but rather the device drivers used to communicate with the PCI devices in slots 1 and 5. This problem is due to the PCI bus architecture that only provides four IRQ pins on the PCI bus. In the case of two PCI cards in slots 1 and 5, both slots are hardwired to use the same PCI IRQ. The BIOS is properly configuring both PCI cards to use the same IRQ—unfortunately, many device drivers are not properly written to handle the sharing of a PCI IRQ between different devices. You should contact the manufacturer of the PCI cards involved in order to obtain the latest drivers. If the problem persists after installing updated drivers, you may be able to work around the problem by rearranging the PCI cards. You may be able to place lower priority devices in slot 5.

SYMPTOM 7-105   **You notice that you frequently get memory/stack errors when using Windows with certain BIOS versions**   This was known to occur particularly with older versions of Windows 95. In virtually all cases, this problem is caused by odd memory timings in your particular BIOS version. It may be possible to update the BIOS to a more current version, but you may be able to work around the problem by adjusting the CMOS Setup with the following value(s).

Under the Cache menu:

- Set WaitStates to **1**
- Set SRAM Burst to a "3-1-1" pattern

Under the Chipset menu:

- Set I/O Recoverys to **1**
- Set VLB-XXX's to **1**

Under the PCI Bus menu:

- Set Latency to **64** (or as close as possible)

Your particular CMOS Setup may offer other or additional options. If you have trouble making the adjustments just mentioned, try selecting the BIOS Defaults or Startup Defaults for your CMOS Setup. This should establish the maximum system reliability, though performance may be degraded a bit.

SYMPTOM 7-106   Windows will not boot with Intel Advanced/MN (Morrison) motherboards when using MR BIOS   In other cases, the motherboard's Crystal 4232 sound system may not function. This is a known problem (especially with Windows 95) on some HP Pavilion systems that use the Advanced/MN motherboard. Microid Research reports that certain OEM versions of Windows 95 may not boot properly, and the integrated sound system may not function properly with retail versions of Windows 95. You'll need to correct this problem by updating the BIOS with a later version that contains the initialization code for the Crystal 4232 sound system. You can identify such a motherboard with the Intel BIOS ID such as 1.00.xx.BT0x. Also check for the presence of an integrated sound system by verifying that the speaker cables attach to the motherboard rather than a sound card in an expansion slot.

If you still have trouble with the sound system, try installing the latest drivers for the Crystal 4232 sound system. You can get the Windows 95 drivers from **ftp://ftp.cirrus.com/pub/drivers/ audio/b95us250.zip**, but later versions may also be available at this time. Other drivers can be found at **www.cirrus.com/drivers/audiodrv**.

SYMPTOM 7-107   You cannot use MR BIOS with the Adaptec 2940 1.2 BIOS
You notice that the adapter works on other systems. This is a problem with older versions of MR BIOS. All MR BIOS versions prior to version 3.20 are incompatible with the BIOS used with Adaptec's AHA 2940 controller using v.1.2 BIOS. MR BIOS generates an incorrect adapter ROM image in shadow RAM, which causes the system to crash. MR BIOS version 3.20 (and later) now overcomes this problem. Update your MR BIOS to the latest version, or avoid the use of Adaptec 2940 cards with that v.1.2 BIOS.

SYMPTOM 7-108   You encounter warm-boot problems with MR BIOS systems using Adaptec 2940 1.21 BIOS   All MR BIOS versions prior to ver 3.22 may have spurious warm-boot (CTRL-ALT-DEL) failures when the system includes an Adaptec 2940 card using the AHA 2940 v.1.21 BIOS. While trying to fix a memory-related bug in v.1.20, the Adaptec v.1.21 BIOS searches for a clear 128KB block of memory before performing its initialization. If it cannot find such a region, it generates a memory error on the monitor and the system halts. In most cases, it's best to update the Adaptec BIOS to a later version, or replace the SCSI adapter with another model.

SYMPTOM 7-109   **The parallel port fails diagnostics when in the bidirectional mode**
In most cases, this type of problem occurs with the National Semiconductor Super I/O chip's parallel port (though it may occur with other I/O chip makers), and it is usually due to the way BIOS handles the port's setup. This is a known issue with National's Super I/O chip and MR BIOS versions prior to 3.19. In the *Standard Parallel Port* (SPP) mode, you should have pseudo-bidirectional capability, but instead it is strictly an output port. If your application requires bidirectional capability, you'll need to change its mode to that particular setting through the CMOS Setup. You'll need to update your MR BIOS version to 3.19 or later where all four parallel port modes (SPP, Bidirectional, EPP, and ECP) have been made available in the CMOS Setup.

BIOS Upgrades

You might wonder why it would be necessary to bother with an upgrade. Ideally, a BIOS ROM should be viable for the life of a PC. While this is true in a majority of situations, there are two compelling reasons to undertake a BIOS upgrade. First, a newer BIOS can add support for drives and devices that are not currently supported (or that now require device drivers or TSRs). Two examples of this are the addition of bootable CD-ROM drives (using the El Torito standard) and the addition of bootable LS-120 drives. Placing support on a BIOS ROM means that there is one less device driver demanding space in your conventional memory. This factor used to be considered most important for older systems (i386 and slower i486-based PCs), but with the addition of so many new hardware devices, even new PCs are prime candidates for BIOS upgrades.

Second (and maybe even more important), BIOS ROM is fundamentally a piece of software. Like all software, there are sometimes defects or oversights (bugs) that cause problems with system operations. This is especially true when the same core BIOS code is "OEMed" into a variety of motherboards. For example, some motherboards may require a BIOS upgrade to better support the main chipset in use or to properly identify non-Intel CPUs. Bugs and compatibility problems virtually demand a BIOS upgrade.

RECOGNIZING BIOS PROBLEMS

Unfortunately, diagnosing a BIOS bug is not a simple task. There are no diagnostics to check BIOS operations. BIOS manufacturers rarely publicize their errors, so there is no centralized index of symptoms that you can refer to that suggest a faulty BIOS or incompatibility. However, BIOS problems tend to fall into several categories that might alert you to the possibility of BIOS trouble. You can then address the symptoms with the system or motherboard manufacturer directly.

■ *There is trouble with Windows 3.1/95/98/Me.* This is a problem typically found on older systems that appeared before the broad introduction of Windows 3.x and is usually related to drive access or keyboard operation problems. Some versions of BIOS intended to enhance Windows can cause certain older motherboard designs to crash or hang up intermittently. When the drives and keyboard check properly (and work just fine under DOS), a BIOS upgrade may be in order. You may also have to replace the keyboard controller chip. Note that BIOS upgrades may no longer be available for older systems. When this occurs, you'll need to upgrade the motherboard.

■ *There is trouble with floppy disk support.* Random disk errors may occur when a 720KB floppy disk is used in a 1.44MB drive, or the 1.44MB drive may be unable to format 1.44MB floppy disks. Once again, this symptom is seen most frequently on older PCs (1988–1991) when 1.44MB floppy drives were becoming commonplace in PCs. Floppy drive problems may be coupled to the mouse configuration.

- *There is trouble with ATA (IDE) support.* The ATA drive interface standard (also known as *Integrated Drive Electronics* or IDE) came to prominence in late 1989 and early 1990. Due to their unique timing requirements, early IDE devices were susceptible to such errors as data corruption, failure to boot, and so on. By Q2 of 1990, most BIOS versions had streamlined their IDE support. When you encounter difficulties installing an ordinary IDE drive in an older PC, check its BIOS date. If the date is 1989 or earlier, consider a BIOS upgrade.

- *There is no ATA-2 (EIDE) or Ultra-ATA (Ultra-DMA/33/66/100) support.* The mid-1990s saw hard drives move beyond 528MB and employ advanced data transfer modes. The use of large, fast hard drives using the ATA-2 interface standard (called *Enhanced IDE* or EIDE) required a BIOS that could "translate" more than 1024 cylinders and employ Logical Block Addressing when accessing the hard drive. Systems sold prior to the Pentium 133 MHz processor (before 1995) will need a BIOS upgrade to support large hard drives, though new drive controllers will often provide their own onboard BIOS to overcome this problem. It is also possible to use "overlay software" such as Disk Manager or EZ-Drive to correct this issue.

Current PCs provide support for Ultra-ATA hard drives that can support burst data transfer modes of 33MB/s, 66MB/s, or 100MB/s (called Ultra-DMA/33/66/100, respectively). The hard drive, drive controller, and BIOS must be capable of supporting Ultra-ATA in order to wring the highest performance from the drive. Otherwise, performance will fall back to lower data transfer speeds. If your current system does not support Ultra-ATA, you may be able to use a BIOS upgrade to support an Ultra-ATA hard drive, or upgrade the drive controller to one with a suitable onboard BIOS.

- *You can't successfully support hard drive partitions over 2GB, 4GB, or 8GB.* This is a symptom indirectly related to drive controller support. Even though ATA-2 supports hard drives beyond 8GB in size using *Logical Block Addressing* (LBA), many BIOS makers have cut corners—limiting their BIOS to supporting only far smaller hard drives. There seem to be two distinct generations of this problem. The first seems to kick in around 2GB, and the second seems to occur around the 4GB or 8GB point. In many cases, the drive will seem to partition properly, but the system will hang up during the reboot after using FDISK. You will need a BIOS upgrade (or a new drive controller) to correct this problem.

- *There is trouble with network support.* In some circumstances, the PC will not work properly when integrated into a Novell NetWare system (or other network). This is often due to the inability of older Novell versions to work with PC "user-defined" drive types. ROM shadowing usually has to be enabled to allow user-defined drive types—unfortunately, not all older motherboard chipsets supported ROM shadowing. BIOS versions later than 1990 have generally corrected this problem.

- *There is trouble with one or both serial ports.* Older BIOS problems often manifest themselves as COM port difficulties under DOS or Windows (often when a mouse is installed). If the serial port circuitry checks properly under diagnostics, suspect a BIOS bug. Check with the BIOS manufacturer to find if an upgrade or patch file is available.

- *You cannot disable onboard features to employ upgraded expansion devices.* Most current PC designs typically incorporate a number of key features (such as a video adapter and drive controller) directly on the motherboard. This provides the user with a distinct cost savings. To upgrade that existing controller, you'd need to disable it on the motherboard before installing the upgraded device—otherwise a hardware conflict would result. Unfortunately, there are many older motherboards in the marketplace that do not properly disable existing controllers. The result is that you cannot upgrade the particular feature. In some cases, a BIOS upgrade will be adequate to correct this problem. In other cases, this is a flaw in the design of the motherboard that will require you to replace the motherboard.

■ *The system does not identify the particular CPU or bus speed properly.* Classic 486 motherboards used a jumper to "select" the installed CPU, but Pentium and later systems use the CPUID feature incorporated into most new CPUs. In many cases, a BIOS is released before the motherboard has been tested with non-Intel CPUs (such as AMD or Cyrix chips). When these non-Intel CPUs are employed on the motherboard, the BIOS cannot identify them, or it identifies them incorrectly as Intel CPUs. When the system does not identify the CPU or bus speed at startup, chances are you need a BIOS upgrade.

■ *Key system features are not supported.* This often occurs in the very latest motherboard designs when the BIOS does not adequately support the features handled in the chipset. Typical examples of this are USB problems, SDRAM support or performance issues, or plug-and-play trouble. A BIOS upgrade should usually correct the problem, but be sure to check with the motherboard or system maker first to verify that a BIOS upgrade will be enough to correct the problem by itself.

■ *You see BIOS checksum errors in the POST.* Normally, the POST scans all BIOS chips located in the memory space and calculates a checksum for each one. That unique checksum is then compared against the checksum stored in the BIOS chip itself. If the two checksums match, the BIOS is assumed good, and the boot process can continue. Otherwise, an error is flagged. A BIOS checksum is almost always fatal, and a new BIOS chip is required to correct the problem.

There is no need to upgrade a BIOS indiscriminately—only attempt a BIOS upgrade to correct a specific problem, or to facilitate features that are not previously supported.

GATHERING INFORMATION

The BIOS upgrade process is not terribly difficult, but success depends on obtaining the correct replacement or upgrade. To ensure that you order (or download) the proper BIOS, it is important to collect some information about the system. In most cases, locating the following five items should help ensure an accurate upgrade:

■ PC make and model.

■ Motherboard manufacturer and CPU (motherboard chipset also if possible).

■ Make and version of existing BIOS (shown on the display during initialization).

■ Part number of the ROM chip itself (you may have to peel back the ROM label).

■ Make, model, and part numbers of main motherboard chipset(s) (if any).

When you consider how closely BIOS is related to PC hardware, you can understand why this information is necessary. Today, virtually all PC BIOS is recorded on flash chips, which can be reprogrammed in the field. If you find that you must replace the actual BIOS chip (due to a BIOS failure or corrupted flash process), upgrades can usually be purchased from a BIOS maker, or the original system manufacturer. For your protection, though, place orders only with firms that offer a reasonable return policy (in the event that the new BIOS does not work as expected).

PERFORMING AN UPGRADE

There are several methods of incorporating a BIOS upgrade into your PC, and in all cases, the proper solution will rely on an understanding of the options available to you. For the purposes of this book, there are four upgrade solutions available to a technician: (1) using a BIOS patch, (2) replacing the BIOS chip, (3) "burning" a new EPROM, and (4) "flashing" the BIOS. The solution you choose will depend on the age of the particular machine.

Using a BIOS Patch

As distracting and unsettling as a BIOS problem may be, few BIOS problems are fatal. Since device drivers and TSRs can serve to supplement a BIOS, they can also support shortfalls in BIOS operation. By adding a corrective file to CONFIG.SYS, AUTOEXEC.BAT, or your Windows 98/Me system, many BIOS problems can at least be abated without opening the PC enclosure. As just one example, an AMI BIOS error concerning a problem with COM2 can be corrected by adding the FIFO-OFF.COM file to AUTOEXEC.BAT. Another example is the use of a driver to enable the cache in a Cyrix CPU to enhance its performance. While this tactic will not repair the problem entirely, a corrective routine can at least allow the system to work until a suitable BIOS upgrade becomes available. To find patches and corrective files for a BIOS, you will need to search the online resources for your particular BIOS manufacturer. This solution is usually best for the oldest systems, for which BIOS upgrades cannot be obtained.

Replacing the BIOS Chip

Replacing the BIOS chip(s) is the classic solution for many older PC designs. Traditional ROMs are 28- or 32-pin *dual inline package* (DIP) devices, and IBM PC/XT (8088), PC/AT (286), 386-, and many 486-based motherboards used traditional DIP ROM chips. Late-model 486 and Pentium-based motherboards often used a socket-mounted *plastic-leaded chip carrier* (PLCC) chip for BIOS. While today's PCs and expansion products make extensive use of surface-mount chips and other components, BIOS devices are the single remaining element still implemented in DIP or PLCC sockets. You may be able to obtain updated ROM chips from the motherboard's manufacturer or from one of the BIOS vendors listed at the end of this chapter. (In a few cases, you may be able to obtain updates directly from the BIOS manufacturer.)

BIOS chip replacements are becoming ever more rare as the rapid advances in PC technology continue. If you cannot replace a physical BIOS chip, consider a motherboard upgrade.

Before proceeding with a BIOS upgrade, remove all power from the PC and disconnect the AC line cord. Remove the outer enclosure and locate the BIOS ROM(s) on the motherboard. Remember to use an antistatic wrist strap to prevent accidental static discharge from damaging the motherboard. Pay particular attention to the orientation (or *keying*) of pin 1. When more than one chip is involved, also note which ROM is "even" and which one is "odd." Remove DIP chips very carefully. You can use a DIP removal tool, or rock the chip gently from its socket using the wide edge of a regular screwdriver. Be extremely careful when removing DIP chips—you may have to put them back if things go wrong. *Gentle* is definitely better here. A specialized removal tool will be needed to remove PLCC chip devices.

You should be equally cautious when installing new DIP chips. If those 28 or 32 little pins are not inserted evenly and straight, they will bend—and break. PLCCs are a bit more forgiving since there are no leads to bend, but make sure to install the chips completely. Before restoring power, make sure the chips are inserted in their proper orientation. If the chips are installed in an orientation opposite from the one intended, you may damage the ROM. If the system fails to initialize, the chip(s) may not be inserted completely, or you may have transposed the "even" and "odd" ROMs. Double-check your work if necessary. Depending on your particular upgrade, you may also find yourself replacing the motherboard's keyboard controller chip.

Burning New EPROMS

If you handle a large number of BIOS upgrades and have access to PC-based EPROM programming equipment, you can program (or *burn*) your own ROMs. The term EPROM stands for *erasable programmable read-only memory,* so given the proper BIOS data, you can translate the contents of a BIOS disk file to a physical chip. (You might call this the "BIOS-while-u-wait" method.) EPROM programming equipment is not terribly expensive and can be obtained from any full-service electronics catalog store, but a good model with PC compatibility can easily run over $500. As you might expect, this kind of workbench BIOS requires a bit of technical skill and is certainly not a worthwhile endeavor for the occasional PC hobbyist.

However, the ability to burn your own EPROMs does offer some unique advantages for an enterprising technician. Knowledgeable technicians versed in machine language can actually customize the BIOS (for example, adding new hard drive parameters to the hard drive table). You can also create backup copies of older BIOS for systems that may no longer be in production, as well as other BIOS for video or drive systems. Of course, modifying a BIOS can have unforeseen consequences for a system—mistakes and errors will disable or crash the PC. Fortunately, you are not altering the *original* BIOS ROM, so you can always restore the original chip.

It is a simple matter to back up your BIOS contents to a disk file. All you need is the DOS DEBUG utility on a simple bootable floppy disk. *Altering or duplicating BIOS code may violate the copyright of the BIOS manufacturer.* A BIOS should *only* be duplicated or modified for the benefit of your individual customers. The typical DEBUG BIOS backup procedure is illustrated next:

```
C:\> DEBUG                ;start the DEBUG utility
- N BIOSBACK.ROM          ;name the backup file
- R BX                    ;alter the CPU's BX register
BX 0000                   ;from zero
:1                        ;to one (this indicates a 64KB file)
- M F000:0 FFFF CS:0      ;move BIOS data in preparation for recording
- W 0                     ;write the file from offset 0
Writing 10000 bytes       ;10000h = 64KB
- Q                       ;quit DEBUG
```

This procedure will save the entire 64KB data segment from F000:0000h to F000:FFFFh as a disk file. If the BIOS in your particular system is 128KB (usually starting at E000:0000h), replace the starting address in the "move" command. You can also back up other ROMs to disk, but you must know the starting address and size of the ROM. For example, a ROM that starts at D400:0000h and is 16KB long can be backed up with a procedure such as:

```
C:\> DEBUG                ;start the DEBUG utility
- N TEST.ROM              ;choose a name for the file
- R CX                    ;alter the CPU's CX register (for short transfers)
CX 0000                   ;from zero
:4000                     ;to 4000h (16KB)
- M D400:0 3FFF CS:0      ;move BIOS data in preparation of recording
- W 0                     ;write the file from offset 0
Writing 04000 bytes       ;4000h = 16KB
- Q                       ;quit DEBUG
```

Flashing the BIOS

Flash BIOS represents the current and most popular class of BIOS ROM chips, which have typically been included in PCs since the era of fast i486 systems, so your Pentium/MMX-, Pentium II-, or Pentium III/4-based PCs will almost certainly have a flash BIOS chip. A flash BIOS is essentially an *electrically erasable programmable read-only memory* (EEPROM)—that is, the chip can be erased and reprogrammed right on the motherboard. Rather than worry about warehousing and shipping new BIOS chips, a BIOS or motherboard manufacturer can provide the updated BIOS code and flash loader utility as a downloadable file.

The name of the file is typically coupled to only a particular motherboard. For example, updating the flash BIOS on an Intel VC820 Pentium II/III motherboard requires a file named **VC82010A.86A.0040.P17**. If this file name is not used, the BIOS will not be reprogrammed. The Soyo SY-7ISA+ Pentium III motherboard requires the file name **7SAP4AA2.BIN**, and so on. When attempting a flash procedure, use the following points as a guideline. (But be sure to check the documentation for your particular system.)

1.   You *must* have a flash BIOS chip in the computer (refer back to Table 7-6). If the chip does not use flash technology, you won't be able to reprogram it.

2.   Make a complete backup of your system hard drive(s) *first*—just in case there are drive problems with the new BIOS after the flash process is complete.

3.   Make a complete record of all CMOS Setup settings *before* flashing the BIOS. Since the flash loader utility will often clear the CMOS RAM anyway, you'll need to restore or tweak the CMOS Setup again after performing the flash upgrade. Pay particular attention to the hard drive geometry settings and other drive configurations.

4.   Record the current BIOS version number and/or release date, and verify that you do not already have this version running on your system (it's pointless to try flashing your system with the same BIOS version).

5.   When downloading the flash file (usually several BIOS data files, a flash loader utility, and brief documentation all compressed into a single ZIP file), be certain to only download the flash package for your exact PC make and model. If you're not sure, verify the proper file with the motherboard or system manufacturer.

Downloading and flashing the INCORRECT BIOS upgrade can render your computer unbootable—forcing you to restore the original BIOS or replace the physical BIOS chip.

6.   Create a clean, bootable floppy disk with any version of DOS, or as a Windows 98/Me startup disk.

7.   Copy the downloaded ZIP file containing your flash package to the floppy disk, and decompress the ZIP file into its constituent files (usually an EXE file as the flashing utility, a BIN or ROM file as the new BIOS data file, and one or more TXT files as the documentation). In some cases, you may need to download a generic EXE flash loader, then download the new BIN file separately.

Never attempt to flash a BIOS by running the flash utility from a hard drive. Proceed from the floppy drive only.

8. You may need to set the "Flash Enable" jumper on your particular motherboard. If so, turn off the PC, locate this jumper (refer to the documentation for your system), and set it to the "program" position.

9. Reboot the PC and start your CMOS Setup to verify that the PC will boot from the floppy drive first. This is usually indicated as a "Boot Order" or "Boot Sequence" of A:/C:.

10. Once the PC boots clean from the bootable floppy disk, start the flash loader utility with a command such as

```
A:\> awdflash          <Enter>
```

11. When the flash loader program starts, it may ask you for the name of the BIN or ROM file you wish to use as an upgrade. Type in the exact name of this file when prompted to do so. In some cases, the flash utility will automatically use the only available source file.

12. Many flash loader utilities will ask you to back up your current BIOS. If you have this opportunity, please do make a backup copy of the current BIOS to floppy disk before proceeding. Enter the file name to save, and proceed. In some cases, the flash loader program will assign a backup file name automatically (for example, BACKUP.BIN).

13. You will then be asked if you are sure you wish to continue; answer Yes.

14. Once the flash process begins, you'll usually see a progress indicator at the bottom of the display that will keep track of the flashing process.

It is critical that you do *not* power-down or reset the PC while the flash process is proceeding. Doing so will interrupt the flash process and leave your BIOS corrupt and perhaps even unrecoverable.

15. When the progress indicator has stopped (or the flash process has otherwise concluded), you'll probably see a message such as "Please cycle power or reset this machine."

16. Turn your computer completely off. Your new BIOS is installed and is ready to use.

17. If you had to set a "Flash Enable" jumper on the motherboard, reset it now to the "protected" position before restoring power to the PC.

18. Remove the bootable floppy disk from the system.

19. Restart the computer now. The new BIOS version will be shown on the display screen. You're done with the BIOS upgrade.

20. In virtually all cases, you'll need to enter your CMOS Setup immediately and restore your CMOS Setup parameters (for example, your drive types) before you can utilize the PC. You can often just restore the BIOS defaults to get your system running quickly, then tweak the settings later.

If there is an error at any point in the reprogramming process, you may hear one or more beeps. Table 7-7 outlines the beeps and descriptions for AMI flash BIOS. These are *not* beep codes in the classical sense, but flash BIOS procedural errors. Keep in mind that the flash BIOS procedures outlined here may vary for your particular system.

TABLE 7-7	AMI FLASH PROGRAMMING BEEP MESSAGES
BEEPS	**MEANING**
None	No error—successful completion.
Continuous single beep	No floppy disk in drive A.
Five beeps	Needed ROM program not present on floppy disk.
Seven beeps	Floppy read error.
Six beeps	BIOS file size error.
Eight beeps	The expected flash EEPROM is not present.
Continuous two beeps	Problem erasing the flash EEPROM.
Continuous three beeps	Problem programming the flash EEPROM.
Continuous four beeps	BIOS is not able to reset the CPU.

UPGRADING MODEM FIRMWARE

As PC communication pushes the limits of classical telephone system technologies, modem makers often release modems before new standards are finalized. When new standards finally emerge, users can often make use of enhanced speeds and modem capabilities by updating the modem's firmware. For example, many K56flex or X2 (both 56Kbps modems) can be updated to the ITU V.90 standard. You can use a technique similar to that used for your motherboard's BIOS to update your modem's firmware.

Before you upgrade a modem, make sure that your Internet Service Provider (ISP) has upgraded their servers to V.90 before you upgrade your modem. If your ISP has not upgraded their servers to V.90, do not upgrade your modem. If you upgrade before your ISP does, you will be limited to modem speeds of 33.6Kbps and below—if this happens, reflash your modem to the previous version.

Download the complete flash update kit for your exact modem model from the manufacturer's Web site—you may need to check your modem's firmware version first. For example, you'd update a Diamond Multimedia SupraExpress 56I SP modem with the V90_208X.EXE file. Open (unzip) the flash update kit, and review the specific instructions according to your operating system. In most cases, you can update the modem's BIOS through Windows 98/Me without having to leave the Windows environment. You can use the following procedure to check your modem firmware through Windows 98/Me:

1.   Click Start, highlight Programs, select Accessories, and choose HyperTerminal. If you're using Windows 98, try clicking Start, highlight Programs, select Accessories, choose Communications, and then select HyperTerminal.

2.   Click the HYPERTRM icon.

3.   When you're asked to enter a name, type **TEST** and click OK.

4.   When you're asked for a phone number, type **1234** (it doesn't matter what this number is). Make sure the correct modem is selected in the "Connect using" box, and then click OK.

5.   When the Connect screen appears, click Cancel.

6.   Now at the terminal screen, type **ATZ** and press ENTER. You should see a response of "OK."

7. Type **ATi92** and press ENTER, and you will see an entry such as "SUPxxxx"—this would be your modem's model number.

8. Type **ATi3** and press ENTER—this should display the modem's firmware version.

9. Exit HyperTerminal (it's OK to close the connection).

UPDATING VIDEO FIRMWARE

Video systems are not typically updated, but it's not uncommon to find firmware updates that correct hardware incompatibilities or firmware bugs in the very newest generations of video and 3D accelerators. For example, the Diamond Multimedia Viper V550 can be updated with BIOS version 195CBIOS.EXE. You can use a technique similar to that used for your motherboard's BIOS to update your video card's firmware:

1. Make a bootable floppy.

2. Insert the blank floppy in the A drive.

3. At the DOS command prompt, type **FORMAT A: /S**.

4. Extract all files from the 195CBIOS.EXE file to your A drive.

5. Reboot using the floppy disk. This will start the flash loader and begin the update process.

6. When the process is complete, remove the floppy disk and reboot the system.

UPGRADING DRIVE FIRMWARE

It's rather rare to update the firmware in a drive (for example, a CD, DVD, or hard drive), but there are times when a firmware update may be necessary to correct a firmware bug or to tweak a drive's performance or features. For example, Western Digital has developed a firmware update to reduce the mechanical noise associated with Western Digital's "wear leveling" feature. This firmware update is applicable to WD Caviar models AC11200, AC22000, AC22500, AC33200, AC34000, AC34300, and AC35100. The firmware update will only reduce the noise associated with wear leveling and will not affect the performance of the wear leveling feature.

1. Download the firmware update file (that is, download the **WDOVRLY4.EXE** utility for the WD update mentioned earlier).

2. Copy the firmware update file to a bootable floppy disk.

3. Restart the system with the floppy disk in the drive, and run the utility from your A: prompt.

4. Once the firmware update software starts, it will detect which drives are available—and whether they need to be updated. Allow the utility to update any drives that require service.

5. Turn off your system after the upgrade is complete. Then restart the system to allow the new firmware to take effect.

BOOT BLOCK RECOVERY

Not every BIOS upgrade goes as well as expected. You may flash the wrong version, power may be interrupted, or you may encounter problems with other drivers or TSRs running on the system. So what happens when there's a problem? Normally, a bad BIOS upgrade will leave your system unbootable, and this would require you to replace the BIOS chip. More recently, system BIOS has been designed with a boot block area that is protected from being overwritten during a flash process. If the flash process is interrupted, you can use the boot block to at least start the system. Once the system boots from the boot block, you can restore the original BIOS file, or try reloading the BIOS upgrade. The boot block recovery procedure for an Intel Classic R motherboard is shown next.

Before recovering the boot block, you'll need a *recovery disk* for your BIOS. In most cases, a recovery disk is made before the flash process is started. If you do not have a recovery disk, you'll need to create one using an image file from the BIOS maker's Web site. For example, you can use the INTELRD.EXE file for the Classic R motherboard from **www.firmware.com/support/recovery**. If there is a working BIOS present, the system can also be booted from this floppy disk to flash the BIOS on this disk into the flash chip.

1. Turn off and unplug the system.

2. Move the "boot block" jumper to the enable position. You may also need to set the flash chip's "write-protect" jumper.

3. Insert the recovery disk. If you did not create a recovery disk when you tried flashing the BIOS, check for a recovery "image file" from the BIOS maker.

4. Turn on the system.

5. After a few seconds, the floppy drive's light will come on.

6. About 20 or 30 seconds later, the speaker will beep once to indicate that the flash process has started.

7. The disk access light will remain on, but there will be nothing on the display.

8. After another 45 to 60 seconds, the speaker will beep twice to indicate that the process has finished. The floppy disk drive light may remain on.

9. Turn the system off and remove the disk.

10. Reset the system's "boot block" jumper (and the flash chip's "write protect" jumper if necessary).

11. Turn on the system and enter the CMOS Setup to restore the system's configuration.

If you encounter more than two beeps (for example, four long low beeps), there may be no floppy disk in the drive (or the disk drive is not installed properly). If any disk besides a valid recovery disk is used, no action will be taken.

BIOS UPGRADE TROUBLESHOOTING

Ideally, a BIOS upgrade can be accomplished quickly and easily, and upgrades are rarely plagued by problems. However, BIOS upgrade problems can and do occur—and can be quite serious under the right circumstances. This part of the chapter looks at a series of common BIOS upgrade symptoms and solutions.

SYMPTOM 7-110   **The flash loader utility refuses to run**   This is a known problem with BIOS flash utilities that have been customized for particular motherboards. Chances are that the flash loader was designed to run on a different motherboard. For example, the MR BIOS ZIP file includes a flash loader that was specifically customized for certain Intel motherboards. The file name of that flash loader will resemble the BIOS image file name (with the .BIO extension)—but other generic motherboards will typically use ZIP files that contain either 29C010.EXE or 28F010.EXE (or both) flash loaders.

In most cases, the flash loader (whether it's custom or generic) attempts to qualify the flash ROM in your computer as a type that it's able to program. If not, an error message to that effect is displayed, and the flash loader aborts. When this happens, you should check that a "flash-protect" jumper is set correctly to permit flash operations. If your motherboard is set for flashing but the flash loader utility refuses to run, chances are that you're trying to install a BIOS upgrade that is not intended for your specific motherboard. Verify that you've downloaded the correct BIOS update and flash loader utility. Do *not* attempt to "force" a flash update by using other flash loader utilities.

SYMPTOM 7-111   **You receive an "erase chip failure" when trying to run a flash loader**
The flash BIOS chip must be erased *before* the new BIOS code can be programmed into the chip. The flash loader program is reporting that it cannot erase the flash chip, which may be due to several reasons.

The flash chip's voltage setting may be set to a different voltage than the chip requires. For example, most flash BIOS chips are 12 volts, but some manufacturers deliberately set the flash voltage setting on the motherboard to 5 volts. This acts like a "write protect" for the BIOS chip, which means you cannot reprogram the BIOS without first setting the voltage jumper back to 12 volts. This also protects you from certain viruses such as the CIH Virus that would try to erase the BIOS and effectively "kill" your computer. Consult your motherboard's manual for the location and settings of your "flash voltage" and "write protect" jumpers.

In other cases, the motherboard's manufacturer may have installed a flash BIOS chip that the flash loader cannot erase. Verify that you've downloaded the correct flash loader and BIOS update file for your particular motherboard. You may need to download and use a different flash loader. If there is no alternate flash loader utility for your motherboard, it will be necessary to replace the BIOS chip.

SYMPTOM 7-112   **You receive a "flash chip not supported" error when trying to run a flash loader**   The flash loader utility must first check the type of flash chip that is currently installed on the motherboard, then determine whether the flash loader can read and write to the flash chip safely. When you encounter this error, the flash loader is indicating that it does not recognize the type of flash chip currently installed on the motherboard. Verify that you've downloaded the correct flash loader and BIOS update file for your particular motherboard. You may need to download and use a different flash loader. If there is no alternate flash loader utility for your motherboard, it will be necessary to replace the BIOS chip.

SYMPTOM 7-113   **After installing a new BIOS, the system now asks for a password**
Your BIOS stores the configuration data for your system in the CMOS RAM/real-time clock chip that is installed on the motherboard. The data values for the new BIOS (and the way that data is arranged) may differ from your original BIOS data configuration since new commands and features are added to newer versions of the BIOS. The first time you turn on the computer after installing the new BIOS, your new BIOS is reading the old data configuration and mistakenly thinks that a password is set.

To correct this problem, you must clear the old configuration data from your CMOS RAM chip. Some motherboards offer a "Clear CMOS" or "Clear Password" jumper located near the CMOS RAM/RTC chip. When this jumper is set and the system is booted, you can erase the CMOS data (or just the password, depending on which jumper is available to you). Turn off the PC and reset those jumpers to their original positions; then restart the system directly to the CMOS Setup and reconfigure each of the system's setup values. (Or simply select the BIOS Defaults option to load a set of basic parameters into your CMOS Setup.)

SYMPTOM 7-114   **After flashing the BIOS and reloading the system setup, the system refuses to recognize your drives**   This is almost always due to unforeseen motherboard updates that the BIOS was not designed for. During the course of a production run, a motherboard manufacturer may make a design change that may be as simple as a wiring trace change, or as complex as changing the components used on the motherboard. For example, when the Super I/O chip of the motherboard has been changed, the BIOS can no longer initialize and "talk" to the IDE controllers—in effect, this "cuts off" your hard drives. In most cases, you'll need to contact the motherboard maker and determine whether a new BIOS chip is available to replace the existing BIOS chip.

SYMPTOM 7-115   **After installing a new BIOS, you cannot print under DOS or Windows**   Chances are that the new BIOS has defaulted the printer port to "standard" mode (SPP), which is inadequate for your particular printer. You'll need to enter the CMOS Setup and change the parallel port mode setting to EPP or ECP, and verify that your LPT1 port is set to address 378h. Save your changes and reboot the system.

SYMPTOM 7-116   **You cannot flash a MR BIOS version on a Super Micro motherboard**   Super Micro motherboards normally use a 28F001 flash chip that contains a boot block loader. The boot block loader not only functions as a boot loader for BIOS recovery, but also contains the standard jump vector used during normal boot-up. To use MR BIOS on this type of motherboard, you must overwrite this boot block with MR BIOS boot code. However, the boot block portion of the flash chip is write protected and cannot be flashed. You are able to update the flash chip using the Super Micro flash loader because it only updates the non–boot block portion of the flash chip. To update the motherboard to MR BIOS, you'll need to use the new flash loader from MR BIOS that is specifically designed work around this boot block issue:

1.   Run the MRSUPER2 flash loader.
2.   Select the Backup option to create a backup copy of the original BIOS code.
3.   When your backup is complete, select the Update option and specify the correct MR BIOS flash update. Allow the update to proceed.
4.   After updating, power-off the system and set jumper J37 to 2-3. This jumper should remain in this position even when updating the flash to future revisions of MR BIOS.

To restore your original Super Micro BIOS from a backup file after MR BIOS is installed:

1.   Run the MRSUPER2 flash loader.
2.   Select the Update option and specify the appropriate file name for the Super Micro backup BIOS file. Allow the update to proceed.
3.   After updating, power-off the system and set jumper J37 to 1-2.

SYMPTOM 7-117   **The PC does not boot after upgrading the BIOS**   This is a classic problem that frequently haunts technicians. When you've replaced the physical BIOS chip(s), double-check the chip(s) for proper orientation and installation. Make sure that all of the pins are inserted into the socket, and that none of the DIP pins have been bent under the chip's body. If you're replacing "even and odd" BIOS chips, make sure that you have not accidentally transposed the even and odd chip locations. If the problem persists, try replacing the original BIOS chips—if the original chips work, you may have defective or improper replacement chips.

If you've flashed the BIOS, chances are that your problem is a little stickier. You've either flashed the wrong BIOS version, or the flash process failed for some reason. In either case, there's nothing you can do except replace the BIOS chip (you'll need to contact the system or motherboard manufacturer for a replacement) or restore the original BIOS from the boot block.

SYMPTOM 7-118 **You accidentally reset or power-down the PC during a BIOS flash, and now the PC won't start** The great weakness of flash BIOS is that it cannot be interrupted once the flash process is under way—otherwise, the BIOS will be left partially programmed and totally corrupted. Your only course of action here is to replace the BIOS chip (you'll need to contact the system or motherboard manufacturer for a replacement) or restore the original BIOS from the boot block.

SYMPTOM 7-119 **The BIOS upgrade proceeded properly, but now the system behaves erratically, or other errors appear** There are several potential causes here. Most of the time, you've either flashed the wrong BIOS version (probably for a system using an almost identical motherboard), or the BIOS became corrupted during the flash process. If you made a backup copy of the original BIOS file during the flash process, repeat the process and restore the original BIOS version. If the system works, you can verify that you downloaded the correct flash file (and repeat the upgrade if possible). If you cannot restore the original BIOS, or the problems persist, replace the BIOS chip. If the problem occurs when replacing physical chips, chances are that you've installed the BIOS for the wrong PC or motherboard, and you'll need to replace the original BIOS chip(s) until you get the proper replacements.

SYMPTOM 7-120 **The BIOS upgrade proceeded properly, but system performance seems poor** This is a frequent (but little-discussed) complaint with BIOS upgrades. In many cases, a new BIOS will require you to restore or tweak your CMOS Setup for proper performance. If you recorded your original CMOS Setup contents before attempting your upgrade, you can enter the CMOS Setup and compare the current settings to the original ones. Chances are that one or more performance-oriented settings have been disabled. Here are some points for quick tweaking. (Remember that not all of these features may be available in all BIOS versions.) For fastest booting:

- Set the "Boot Sequence" to C:/A:.
- Set the "Boot Up Floppy Drive Seek" to DISABLED.
- Set the "Boot Up System Speed" to HIGH.
- Set the "Quick Power-on Self Test" to ENABLED.

For highest overall system performance:

- Enable all shadowing unless you are using an adapter that absolutely requires that shadowing be disabled for a specified address. Video shadow will increase the video speed.
- Set "Auto Configuration" to DISABLE.
- Reduce all of the memory timings to their minimum values.
- Enable the "Turbo Read Lead Off."
- Enable the "Speculative Lead Off."

- Enable the "Turn Around Insertion."
- Increase the ISA Speed by setting *ISA Clock* to **PCICLK/3**.
- Lower 8- and 16-bit recovery times to **1** (one) each.
- Set the "System BIOS Cacheable" to ENABLE.
- Set the "Video BIOS Cacheable" to ENABLE.
- L2 Cache Cacheable Size—If you're installing 64MB of RAM or more, set to **512MB** (64MB is the default).
- Pipeline Cache Timing—Set to FASTEST if there is only 256KB total pipeline cache (FASTER is the default).

When tweaking BIOS settings in the CMOS Setup, be sure to change only one parameter at a time; retest the system's performance each time.

SYMPTOM 7-121   **You see a message such as "Update ESCD Successfully" on boot-up**   This is not really an error, but more of an informational message. The ESCD (*extended system configuration data*) is a method that the BIOS uses to store resource information for both PnP and non-PnP devices. The reason it shows this message is because the system has at least one ISA card in it, and it is running Windows 98/Me. The ESCD boot-up sequence arranged by Windows 98/Me is different from the ESCD boot-up sequence arranged by the BIOS. So on boot-up, the system BIOS will attempt to update the ESCD. This will in no way affect system performance.

SYMPTOM 7-122   **You just upgraded the BIOS and now can't boot from the A drive**   Otherwise, the A drive seems to be working normally. In virtually all cases, the updated BIOS defaulted the CMOS Setup to a "Boot Sequence" of C:/A: instead of A:/C:, so the system isn't even checking the floppy drive at startup. Start your CMOS Setup and tweak the "Boot Sequence" to A:/C:, and then save your changes and try the system again. Also verify that you actually have a working bootable floppy disk in the drive.

SYMPTOM 7-123   **You get a message saying: "Incompatible BIOS translation detected—unable to load disk overlay"**   This typically happens when you upgrade a BIOS to support *Logical Block Addressing* (LBA), but the hard drive in your system is already using overlay software such as Disk Manager. Since overlay software and LBA are usually incompatible, you'll need to either disable LBA in the CMOS Setup, or remove the overlay software from the hard drive. Since you probably upgraded the BIOS to support LBA anyway, chances are that you'll want to remove the overlay software:

1. Back up the hard drive before proceeding.
2. Boot the system from a bootable floppy disk.
3. Run FDISK and delete all partitions on the hard drive.
4. Reboot and check with FDISK to be sure that all the partitions on the drive have been removed.
5. You can repartition and reformat the drive, then restore your files from a backup.

If you cannot remove all partitions from the hard drive with FDISK, you can use the following procedure to erase the *master boot record* (MBR) on the hard drive. You'll need the DEBUG utility on your bootable floppy disk before proceeding.

```
A:\> debug
F 200 L200 0
a 100
mov ax,301
mov bx,200
mov cx,1
mov dx,0080                   ;Note: use 0081 for second fixed disk
int 13
int 3
(enter a blank line here)
G=100
q
```

The drive should now have no partitions on it. Reboot and use FDISK to partition the drive, and FORMAT to reformat each partition. You can then restore the operating system, and recover files from your backup.

Further Study

American Megatrends www.megatrends.com
Award www.award.com
IBM SurePath BIOS page www.surepath.ibm.com/
Micro Firmware www.firmware.com
Microid Research (MR BIOS) www.mrbios.com/
Phoenix Technologies www.phoenix.com/
SystemSoft www.systemsoft.com
Unicore www.unicore.com
Wim's BIOS page www.ping.be/bios/bios.shtml

8

BUSSES

When it was first introduced, the IBM PC was no gem. It was a slow, clunky contraption with virtually no system resources (memory, interrupts, DMA channels, and so on). Yet, the IBM PC ushered in the personal computer era that we know today. Certainly, it was not speed or efficiency that brought IBM systems to the forefront of technology. Instead, it was a revolutionary (and rather risky) concept called *open architecture.* Rather than designing a computer and being the sole developer of proprietary add-on devices (as so many other computer manufacturers were at the time), IBM chose to incorporate only the essential processing elements on the motherboard and leave many of the other functions to add-on devices (a.k.a. expansion boards) that could be plugged into standardized bus connectors. The use of expansion busses made the PC extraordinarily versatile, because a system could be configured according to the devices that were added. This chapter is intended to familiarize you with the three major bus types found in modern IBM-type PCs: ISA, PCI, and AGP.

Industry Standard Architecture (ISA)

The venerable *Industry Standard Architecture* (ISA), shown in Figure 8-1, is the first open system bus architecture used for IBM-type personal computers. Any manufacturer was welcome to use the architecture for a nominal licensing fee. Since no restrictions were placed on the use of ISA busses (also referred to

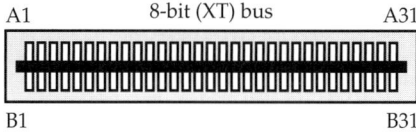

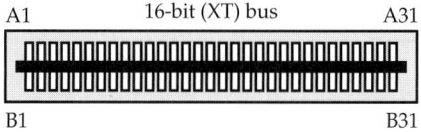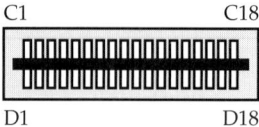

FIGURE 8-1   Diagram of 8-bit and 16-bit ISA bus slots

simply as "PC busses"), they were duplicated in every IBM-compatible clone that followed. The use of a standardized bus not only paved the way for thousands of manufacturers to produce compatible PCs and expansion devices, but also helped to support the use of standardized operating systems and applications software. Both an 8-bit and 16-bit version of the ISA bus are available, although all motherboards manufactured since the mid-1980s have abandoned the 8-bit XT version in favor of the faster, more flexible 16-bit AT version.

8-BIT ISA

Use of the 8-bit XT bus started in 1982. The 8-bit ISA bus consists of a single card edge connector with 62 contacts. The bus provides 8 data lines and 20 address lines, which allow the board to reside within the XT's 1MB of conventional memory. The bus also supports connections for six interrupts (IRQ2–IRQ7) and three DMA channels (DMA0–DMA2). The XT bus runs at the system speed of 4.77 MHz. Although the bus itself is relatively simple, IBM failed to publish specific timing relationships for data, address, and control signals. This ambiguity left early manufacturers to find the proper timing relationships by trial and error.

Although each connector on the bus is supposed to work the same way, early PCs designed with eight expansion slots required any card inserted in the eighth slot (the slot closest to the power supply) to provide a special "card selected" signal on pin B8. Timing requirements for the eighth slot are also tighter. Contrary to popular belief, the eighth slot has nothing to do with the IBM expansion chassis. The demands of slot 8 were to support a keyboard/timer adapter board for IBM's special configuration called the 3270PC. Most XT clones did not adhere to this "eighth slot" peculiarity.

Knowing the XT Signals

Table 8-1 shows the pinout for both an XT and AT ISA bus configuration. The Oscillator pin provides the 14.3 MHz system oscillator signal to the expansion bus, while the Clock pin supplies the 4.77 MHz system clock signal. When the PC needs to be reset, the RESET DRV pin drives the whole system into a reset state. The 20 address pins (0–19) connect an expansion board to the system's address bus; when address signals are valid, the Address Latch Enable (ALE) signal indicates that the address may now be decoded. The eight data lines (0–7) connect the board to the system's data bus.

 Signal labels marked with a minus sign (-), such as - REFRESH, indicate what's known as *active low logic,* where the signal is true when the logic level is low.

TABLE 8-1   ISA 8-BIT (XT) BUS PINOUT

SIGNAL	PIN	PIN	SIGNAL
Ground	B1	A1	- I/O Channel Check
Reset	B2	A2	Data Bit 7
+5 Vdc	B3	A3	Data Bit 6
IRQ 2	B4	A4	Data Bit 5
-5 Vdc	B5	A5	Data Bit 4
DRQ 2	B6	A6	Data Bit 3
-12 Vdc	B7	A7	Data Bit 2
- Card Selected	B8	A8	Data Bit 1
+12 Vdc	B9	A9	Data Bit 0
Ground	B10	A10	I/O Channel Ready
- SMEMW	B11	A11	AEN
- SMEMR	B12	A12	Address Bit 19
- I/O W	B13	A13	Address Bit 18
- I/O R	B14	A14	Address Bit 17
- DACK 3	B15	A15	Address Bit 16
DRQ 3	B16	A16	Address Bit 15
- DACK 1	B17	A17	Address Bit 14
DRQ 1	B18	A18	Address Bit 13
- REFRESH	B19	A19	Address Bit 12
Clock (4.77 MHz)	B20	A20	Address Bit 11
IRQ 7	B21	A21	Address Bit 10
IRQ 6	B22	A22	Address Bit 9
IRQ 5	B23	A23	Address Bit 8
IRQ 4	B24	A24	Address Bit 7
IRQ 3	B25	A25	Address Bit 6
- DACK 2	B26	A26	Address Bit 5
T/C	B27	A27	Address Bit 4
BALE	B28	A28	Address Bit 3
+5 Vdc	B29	A29	Address Bit 2
Oscillator (14.3 MHz)	B30	A30	Address Bit 1
Ground	B31	A31	Address Bit 0

The - I/O Channel Check (-IOCHCK) line flags the motherboard when errors occur on the expansion board. Note that the minus sign (-) preceding the signal indicates that the signal uses active low logic. The I/O Channel Ready is active when an addressed expansion board is ready. If this pin is logic 0, the CPU will extend the bus cycle by inserting wait states. Six hardware interrupts (IRQ2 to IRQ7) are used by the expansion board to demand the CPU's attention. Interrupts 0 and 1 are not available to the bus since they handle the highest priorities of the timer chip and keyboard. The - I/O Read (-I/O R) and - I/O Write (-I/O W) lines indicate that the CPU or DMA controller wants to transfer data to or from the data bus. The - Memory Read (-MEMR) and - Memory Write (-MEMW) signals tell the expansion board that the CPU or DMA controller is going to read or write data to main memory.

The XT bus supplies three DMA Requests (DRQ1 to DRQ3) so that an expansion board can transfer data to or from memory. DMA requests must be held until the corresponding - DMA Acknowledge

(-DACK1 to -DACK3) signals become true. If the Address Enable (AEN) signal is true, the DMA controller is controlling the bus for a data transfer. Finally, the Terminal Count (T/C) signal provides a pulse when the DMA transfer is completed.

16-BIT ISA

The limitations of the 8-bit ISA bus were soon obvious. With a floppy drive and hard drive taking up two of the six available interrupts, COM 3 and COM 4 taking up another two interrupts (IRQ 3 and IRQ 4), and an LPT port taking up IRQ 7, competition for the remaining interrupt was fierce. Of the three DMA channels available, the floppy and hard drives take two, so only one DMA channel remains available. Only 1MB of address space is addressable, and 8 data bits form a serious bottleneck for data transfers. It would have been a simple matter to start from scratch and design an entirely new bus, but that would have rendered the entire installed base of XT expansion cards obsolete.

The next logical step in bus evolution came in 1984/85 with the introduction of the 80286 processor in IBM's PC/AT. System resources were added to the bus while still allowing XT boards to function in the expanded bus. The result became what we know today as the 16-bit AT bus. Instead of a different bus connector, the original 62-pin connector was left intact, and an extra 36-pin connector was added, designated "C" and "D," as shown in Table 8-2 (the pin assignments for the 32-pin A/B connector are identical to Table 8-1). An extra 8 data bits were added to bring the total data bus to 16 bits. Five interrupts and four DMA channels were included. Four more address lines are also provided, in addition to several more control signals. Clock speed is increased on the AT bus to 8.33 MHz. It is important to note that although XT boards *theoretically* should work with an AT bus, not all older XT expansion boards will work on the AT bus.

Knowing the AT Signals

The - System Bus High Enable (-SBHE) is active when the upper 8 data bits are being used. If the upper 8 bits are not being used (an XT board is in the AT slot), -SBHE will be inactive. If the expansion board

TABLE 8-2   ISA 16-BIT (AT) BUS PINOUT

SIGNAL	PIN	PIN	SIGNAL
- MEM CS16	D1	C1	- SBHE
- I/O CS16	D2	C2	Address Bit 23
IRQ 10	D3	C3	Address Bit 22
IRQ 11	D4	C4	Address Bit 21
IRQ 12	D5	C5	Address Bit 20
IRQ 15	D6	C6	Address Bit 19
IRQ 14	D7	C7	Address Bit 18
- DACK 0	D8	C8	Address Bit 17
DRQ 0	D9	C9	- MEM R
- DACK 5	D10	C10	- MEM W
DRQ 5	D11	C11	Data Bit 8
- DACK 6	D12	C12	Data Bit 9
DRQ 6	D13	C13	Data Bit 10
- DACK 7	D14	C14	Data Bit 11
DRQ 7	D15	C15	Data Bit 12
+5 Vdc	D16	C16	Data Bit 13
- MASTER	D17	C17	Data Bit 14
Ground	D18	C18	Data Bit 15

requires 16-bit access to memory locations, it must return an active -MEM CS16 signal. If the expansion board requires 16-bit access to an I/O location, it must make the -I/O CS16 signal active. The - Memory Read (-MEMR) and - Memory Write (-MEMW) signals provided by an expansion board tell the CPU or DMA controller that memory access is needed up to 16MB. The -SMEMR and -SMEMW signals only indicate memory access for the first 1MB. The -MASTER signal can be used by expansion boards that are able to take control of the bus through use of a DMA channel. It is interesting to note that small, highly integrated AT systems are available for embedded systems and dedicated applications.

Mixing 8-Bit and 16-Bit ISA Boards

ISA 16-bit architecture was developed on the foundation of IBM's original 8-bit XT bus. By extending the original XT bus rather than redesigning an expansion bus from scratch, IBM was able to develop its AT so that it would accommodate new, more sophisticated 16-bit expansion boards while still being backward compatible with the installed base of 8-bit boards. For the most part, this strategy worked quite well—the ISA bus remained a prominent feature of PCs for many years. However, there is a potential problem with the ISA bus when inserting 8-bit and 16-bit adapters that both use ROM residing in the same memory region. Such a problem generally results in trouble with the 8-bit board.

To understand how this problem arises, you should be familiar with the ISA bus pinouts shown in Tables 8-1 and 8-2. There is an initial 62-pin connector (A1 through A31 and B1 through B31), followed by the extended 36-pin connector (C1 through C18 and D1 through D18). Notice that Address Bits 17, 18, and 19 are repeated on pins C8, C7, and C6. When a 16-bit board is inserted in the system, those repeated address lines indicate that a memory access is about to occur somewhere within 128KB of the address signals on A17, A18, and A19. The lower 17 address lines (A0 to A16) specify *exactly* where in that 128KB range the access will take place. If a 16-bit expansion board has memory (such as a video BIOS ROM or hard drive controller ROM) within the 128KB range about to be accessed, it uses the -MEM CS16 or -I/O CS16 line to tell the system that its memory is ready for access in 16-bit transfers. If the system receives no response from either of these lines, data is transferred in 8-bit sections.

The problem here is that 8-bit boards may also have memory within that 128KB range, but since they cannot detect the three extra address lines, the board cannot respond to the system. If a 16-bit board tells the system to proceed with a 16-bit data transfer, but there is also an 8-bit board in that same address range, the 8-bit board will be forced to receive 16-bit data transfers. As you might expect, this is quite impossible for an 8-bit board, so the 8-bit board will appear to malfunction. Since most expansion boards reserve their ROM addresses for the 128KB block between 768KB to 896KB (C0000h to DBFFFh, sometimes called the *ROM Reserve*), this is where most problems reside.

It is important for you to understand that this problem does not refer to a hardware conflict. The ROM locations of the 8-bit and 16-bit boards certainly *cannot* overlap at any point. As you might realize, however, it is possible to have several different ROMs contained within the same 128KB of system memory. If one such ROM is on a 16-bit board and one is on an 8-bit board, the 8-bit board will likely malfunction due to the way in which 16-bit boards handle ISA bus operation. Correcting such a problem is generally a matter of replacing the 8-bit board with a 16-bit version. It might also be possible to disable the 8-bit ROM using an onboard jumper, and then use the motherboard BIOS ROM instead.

ISA Retirement

Today, the ISA bus architecture is virtually obsolete in the face of more versatile expansion slots like PCI or AGP. Some current motherboard designs forego the use of ISA bus entirely, though many motherboards continue to provide one or two ISA slots for backward compatibility with "legacy" devices.

Peripheral Component Interconnect (PCI)

By the late 1980s, the proliferation of 32-bit CPUs and graphics-intensive operating systems made it painfully obvious that the 8.33 MHz ISA bus was no longer satisfactory. The PC industry began to develop alternative architectures for improved performance. Two architectures emerged: VL and PCI. While the VL bus seemed more straightforward, it had some serious limitations to overcome. Perhaps most important is the VL bus dependence on CPU speed. Another problem is that the VL standard is voluntary, and not all manufacturers adhere to VESA specifications completely. In mid-1992, Intel and a comprehensive consortium of manufacturers introduced the *Peripheral Component Interconnect* (PCI) bus. Whereas the VL bus was designed specifically to enhance PC video systems, the 188-pin PCI bus looked to the future of CPUs (and PCs in general) by providing a bus architecture that also supports peripherals such as hard drive controllers, network adapters, and so on. This part of the chapter shows you the layout and operations of the PCI bus.

PCI BUS CONFIGURATION AND SIGNALS

PCI is a 33 MHz fixed-frequency bus architecture capable of transferring data at 132MB/sec—a great improvement over the 5MB/sec transfer rate of the standard ISA bus. Another key advantage of the PCI bus is that it has automatic configuration capabilities for switchless/jumperless peripherals. Autoconfiguration (the heart of plug-and-play) will take care of all addresses, interrupt requests, and DMA assignments used by a PCI peripheral. The PCI bus specification version 2.1 calls for expandability to 64 bits and 66 MHz speed, and this would quadruple bandwidth over the current design. In practice, the 64-bit PCI bus has yet to be implemented on the PC, though it does exist in numerous server platforms (and the speed is limited to 33 MHz in most 64-bit PCI bus designs—probably for compatibility reasons). Current PCI bus features include the following:

- Data bursting as normal operating mode (both read and write)
- Linear burst ordering
- Concurrency support (deadlock, buffering solutions)
- Low latency guarantees for real-time devices
- Access-oriented arbitration (not time slice)
- Support for multiple loads (PCI boards) at 33 MHz
- Error detection and reporting
- Multimaster and peer-to-peer communication
- 32-bit multiplexed, processor-independent operation
- Synchronous 132MB/sec operation
- Variable length, linear bursting (both read and write)
- Parity on address, data, and command signals
- Concurrency/pipelining support
- Initialization hooks for autoconfiguration

■ Arbitration support

■ 64-bit extension transparently compatible with 32-bit

■ CMOS drivers, TTL voltage levels

■ 5-V and 3.3-V compatible

The PCI bus supports *linear bursts,* which is a method of transferring data that ensures the bus is continually filled with data. The peripheral devices expect to receive data from the system main memory in a linear address order. This means that large amounts of data are read from or written to a single address, which is then incremented for the next byte in the stream. The linear burst is one of the unique aspects of the PCI bus since it will perform both burst reads and burst writes. In short, it will transfer data on the bus *every* clock cycle. This doubles the PCI throughput compared to buses without linear burst capabilities.

The devices designed to support PCI have low *access latency,* reducing the time required for a peripheral to be granted control of the bus after requesting access. For example, an Ethernet controller card connected to a LAN has large data files from the network coming into its buffer. Waiting for access to the bus, the Ethernet is unable to transfer the data to the CPU quickly enough to avoid a buffer overflow—forcing it to temporarily store the file's contents in extra RAM. Since PCI-compliant devices support faster access times, the Ethernet card can promptly send data to the CPU.

The PCI bus supports *bus mastering*, which allows one of a number of intelligent peripherals to take control of the bus to accelerate a high-throughput, high-priority task. PCI architecture also supports *concurrency,* a technique that ensures the microprocessor operates simultaneously with these masters, instead of waiting for them. As one example, concurrency allows the CPU to perform floating-point calculations on a spreadsheet while an Ethernet card and the LAN have control of the bus. Finally, PCI was developed as a dual-voltage architecture. Normally, the bus is a +5 Vdc system like other busses. However, the bus can also operate in a +3.3 Vdc (low-voltage) mode.

PCI BUS LAYOUT

The layout for a PCI bus slot is shown in Figure 8-2. Note that there are two major segments to the +5 Vdc-version connector. A +3.3 Vdc-version connector adds a key in the 12/13 positions to prevent accidental insertion of a +5 Vdc PCI board into a +3.3 Vdc slot. Similarly, the +5 Vdc slot is keyed in the 50/51 position to prevent placing a +3.3 Vdc board into a +5 Vdc slot. The pinout for a PCI bus is shown in Table 8-3.

As you will see in Chapter 12, devices cannot use the same system resources. Otherwise, a hardware conflict will result. The PCI bus is an exception to this rule because it supports a technique called IRQ steering that allows IRQs to be dynamically held and reassigned as needed. To facilitate this form of IRQ sharing, the PCI bus uses its own internal interrupt system for dealing with requests from the cards on the bus. These PCI interrupts are often called #A, #B, #C, and #D, to avoid confusion with the normal system

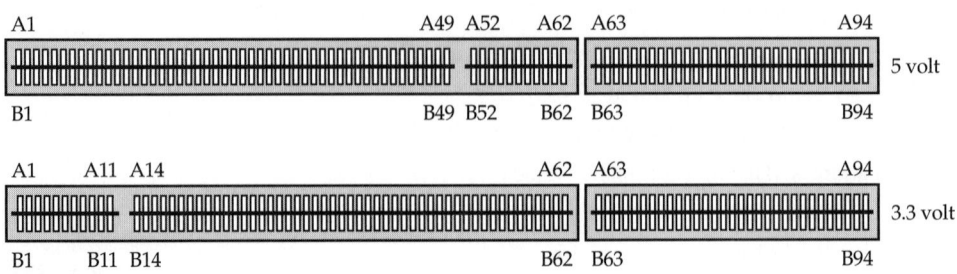

FIGURE 8-2 PCI expansion bus diagrams

TABLE 8-3   PCI BUS PINOUT—5 VOLT AND 3.3 VOLT

5 VOLT	3.3 VOLT	PIN	PIN	3.3 VOLT	5 VOLT
-12 Vdc	-12 Vdc	B1	A1	- TRST	- TRST
TCK	TCK	B2	A2	+12 Vdc	+12 Vdc
Ground	Ground	B3	A3	TMS	TMS
TDO	TDO	B4	A4	TDI	TDI
+5 Vdc	+5 Vdc	B5	A5	+5 Vdc	+5 Vdc
+5 Vdc	+5 Vdc	B6	A6	- INTA	- INTA
- INTB	- INTB	B7	A7	- INTC	- INTC
- INTD	- INTD	B8	A8	+5 Vdc	+5 Vdc
- PRSNT1	- PRSNT1	B9	A9	Reserved	Reserved
Reserved	Reserved	B10	A10	+3.3 Vdc (I/O)	+5 Vdc
- PRSNT2	- PRSNT2	B11	A11	Reserved	Reserved
Ground	Key	B12	A12	Key	Ground
Ground	Key	B13	A13	Key	Ground
Reserved	Reserved	B14	A14	Reserved	Reserved
Ground	Ground	B15	A15	- RST	- RST
Clock	Clock	B16	A16	+3.3 Vdc	+5 Vdc
Ground	Ground	B17	A17	- GNT	- GNT
- REQ	- REQ	B18	A18	Ground	Ground
+5 Vdc	+3.3 Vdc	B19	A19	Reserved	Reserved
Adr/Dat 31	Adr/Dat 31	B20	A20	Adr/Dat 30	Adr/Dat 30
Adr/Dat 29	Adr/Dat 29	B21	A21	+3.3 Vdc	+5 Vdc
Ground	Ground	B22	A22	Adr/Dat 28	Adr/Dat 28
Adr/Dat 27	Adr/Dat 27	B23	A23	Adr/Dat 26	Adr/Dat 26
Adr/Dat 25	Adr/Dat 25	B24	A24	Ground	Ground
+5 Vdc	+3.3 Vdc	B25	A25	Adr/Dat 24	Adr/Dat 24
C/ - BE3	C/ - BE3	B26	A26	IDSEL	IDSEL
Adr/Dat 23	Adr/Dat 23	B27	A27	+3.3 Vdc	+5 Vdc
Ground	Ground	B28	A28	Adr/Dat 22	Adr/Dat 22
Adr/Dat 21	Adr/Dat 21	B29	A29	Adr/Dat 20	Adr/Dat 20
Adr/Dat 19	Adr/Dat 19	B30	A30	Ground	Ground
+5 Vdc	+3.3 Vdc	B31	A31	Adr/Dat 18	Adr/Dat 18
Adr/Dat 17	Adr/Dat 17	B32	A32	Adr/Dat 16	Adr/Dat 16
C/ - BE2	C/ - BE2	B33	A33	+3.3 Vdc	+5 Vdc
Ground	Ground	B34	A34	- FRAME	- FRAME
- IRDY	- IRDY	B35	A35	Ground	Ground
+5 Vdc	+3.3 Vdc	B36	A36	- TRDY	- TRDY
- DEVSEL	- DEVSEL	B37	A37	Ground	Ground
Ground	Ground	B38	A38	- STOP	- STOP
- LOCK	- LOCK	B39	A39	+3.3 Vdc	+5 Vdc
- PERR	- PERR	B40	A40	SDONE	SDONE
+5 Vdc	+3.3 Vdc	B41	A41	- SBO	- SBO
- SERR	- SERR	B42	A42	Ground	Ground
+5 Vdc	+3.3 Vdc	B43	A43	PAR	PAR
C/ - BE1	C/ - BE1	B44	A44	Adr/Dat 15	Adr/Dat 15
Adr/Dat 14	Adr/Dat 14	B45	A45	+3.3 Vdc	+5 Vdc
Ground	Ground	B46	A46	Adr/Dat 13	Adr/Dat 13

TABLE 8-3   PCI BUS PINOUT—5 VOLT AND 3.3 VOLT *(CONTINUED)*

5 VOLT	3.3 VOLT	PIN	PIN	3.3 VOLT	5 VOLT
Adr/Dat 12	Adr/Dat 12	B47	A47	Adr/Dat 11	Adr/Dat 11
Adr/Dat 10	Adr/Dat 10	B48	A48	Ground	Ground
Ground	Ground	B49	A49	Adr/Dat 9	Adr/Dat 9
Key	Ground	B50	A50	Ground	Key
Key	Ground	B51	A51	Ground	Key
Adr/Dat 8	Adr/Dat 8	B52	A52	C/ - BE0	C/ - BE0
Adr/Dat 7	Adr/Dat 7	B53	A53	+3.3 Vdc	+5 Vdc
+5 Vdc	+3.3 Vdc	B54	A54	Adr/Dat 6	Adr/Dat 6
Adr/Dat 5	Adr/Dat 5	B55	A55	Adr/Dat 4	Adr/Dat 4
Adr/Dat 3	Adr/Dat 3	B56	A56	Ground	Ground
Ground	Ground	B57	A57	Adr/Dat 2	Adr/Dat 2
Adr/Dat 1	Adr/Dat 1	B58	A58	Adr/Dat 0	Adr/Dat 0
+5 Vdc	+3.3 Vdc	B59	A59	+3.3 Vdc	+5 Vdc
- ACK64	- ACK64	B60	A60	- REQ64	- REQ64
+5 Vdc	+5 Vdc	B61	A61	+5 Vdc	+5 Vdc
+5 Vdc	+5 Vdc	B62	A62	+5 Vdc	+5 Vdc
Key	Key	Key	Key	Key	Key
Key	Key	Key	Key	Key	Key
Reserved	Reserved	B63	A63	Ground	Ground
Ground	Ground	B64	A64	C/ - BE7	C/ - BE7
C/ - BE6	C/ - BE6	B65	A65	C/ - BE5	C/ - BE5
C/ - BE4	C/ - BE4	B66	A66	+3.3 Vdc	+5 Vdc
Ground	Ground	B67	A67	PAR64	PAR64
Adr/Dat 63	Adr/Dat 63	B68	A68	Adr/Dat 62	Adr/Dat 62
Adr/Dat 61	Adr/Dat 61	B69	A69	Ground	Ground
+5 Vdc	+3.3 Vdc	B70	A70	Adr/Dat 60	Adr/Dat 60
Adr/Dat 59	Adr/Dat 59	B71	A71	Adr/Dat 58	Adr/Dat 58
Adr/Dat 57	Adr/Dat 57	B72	A72	Ground	Ground
Ground	Ground	B73	A73	Adr/Dat 56	Adr/Dat 56
Adr/Dat 55	Adr/Dat 55	B74	A74	Adr/Dat 54	Adr/Dat 54
Adr/Dat 53	Adr/Dat 53	B75	A75	+3.3 Vdc	+5 Vdc
Ground	Ground	B76	A76	Adr/Dat 52	Adr/Dat 52
Adr/Dat 51	Adr/Dat 51	B77	A77	Adr/Dat 50	Adr/Dat 50
Adr/Dat 49	Adr/Dat 49	B78	A78	Ground	Ground
+5 Vdc	+3.3 Vdc	B79	A79	Adr/Dat 48	Adr/Dat 48
Adr/Dat 47	Adr/Dat 47	B80	A80	Adr/Dat 46	Adr/Dat 46
Adr/Dat 45	Adr/Dat 45	B81	A81	Ground	Ground
Ground	Ground	B82	A82	Adr/Dat 44	Adr/Dat 44
Adr/Dat 43	Adr/Dat 43	B83	A83	Adr/Dat 42	Adr/Dat 42
Adr/Dat 41	Adr/Dat 41	B84	A84	+3.3 Vdc	+5 Vdc
Ground	Ground	B85	A85	Adr/Dat 40	Adr/Dat 40
Adr/Dat 39	Adr/Dat 39	B86	A86	Adr/Dat 38	Adr/Dat 38
Adr/Dat 37	Adr/Dat 37	B87	A87	Ground	Ground
+5 Vdc	+3.3 Vdc	B88	A88	Adr/Dat 36	Adr/Dat 36
Adr/Dat 35	Adr/Dat 35	B89	A89	Adr/Dat 34	Adr/Dat 34
Adr/Dat 33	Adr/Dat 33	B90	A90	Ground	Ground

TABLE 8-3   PCI BUS PINOUT—5 VOLT AND 3.3 VOLT *(CONTINUED)*

5 VOLT	3.3 VOLT	PIN	PIN	3.3 VOLT	5 VOLT
Ground	Ground	B91	A91	Adr/Dat 32	Adr/Dat 32
Reserved	Reserved	B92	A92	Reserved	Reserved
Reserved	Reserved	B93	A93	Ground	Ground
Ground	Ground	B94	A94	Reserved	Reserved

IRQs (for example, IRQ 7), though they are sometimes called #1 through #4 instead. These PCI interrupt levels are not generally seen by the user, but can be accessed in the system's CMOS Setup routine, where they can be adjusted to control how PCI cards operate. If interrupts are needed by PCI cards in the slots, the PCI interrupts are mapped to regular interrupts (normally IRQ 9 through IRQ 12). The PCI slots in most systems can be mapped to at most four regular IRQs. In systems that have more than four PCI slots, or that have four slots and a USB controller (which uses PCI), two or more of the PCI devices share an IRQ.

KNOWING THE PCI SIGNALS

The PCI bus clock is usually derived from the front side bus speed. In an *asynchronous* configuration, the speed of a PCI bus can be set independently of the FSB speed, though this is rare in all but the latest motherboards. In a *synchronous* configuration (used by most PCs), the 33 MHz PCI speed is divided from the FSB. For example, if the FSB is 66 MHz, a divisor (usually in the form of a CMOS Setup entry or motherboard jumper) divides the FSB to achieve 33 MHz. More recent motherboards with faster FSB speeds use additional divisors. Synchronous PCI clocking can become very important in overclocking, because overclocking the FSB will cause PCI peripherals to be overclocked as well, often leading to system stability problems.

To reduce the number of pins needed in the PCI bus, data and address lines are multiplexed together (Adr./Dat 0 to Adr./Dat 63). It is also interesting to note that PCI is the first bus standard designed to support a low-voltage (+3.3 Vdc) logic implementation. On inspection, you will see that +5 Vdc and +3.3 Vdc implementations of the PCI bus place their physical key slots in different places so that the two implementations are *not* interchangeable. The Clock (CLOCK) signal provides timing for the PCI bus only, and can be adjusted from DC (0 Hz) to 33 MHz. Asserting the -Reset (-RST) signal will reset all PCI devices. Since the 64-bit data path uses 8 bytes, the Command/ -Byte Enable signals (C/ -BE0 to C/ -BE7) define which bytes are transferred. Parity across the Address/Data and Byte Enable lines is represented with a Parity (PAR) or 64 Bit Parity (PAR64) signal. Bus mastering is initiated by the -Request (-REQ) line and granted after approval using the -Grant (-GNT) line.

When a valid PCI bus cycle is in progress, the -Frame (-FRAME) signal is true. If the PCI bus cycle is in its final phase, -Frame will be released. The -Target Ready (-TRDY) line is true when an addressed device is able to complete the data phase of its bus cycle. An -Initiator Ready (-IRDY) signal indicates that valid data is present on the bus (or the bus is ready to accept data). The -FRAME, -TARGET READY, and -INITIATOR READY signals are all used together. A -Stop (-STOP) signal is asserted by a target asking a master to halt the current data transfer. The ID Select (IDSEL) signal is used as a chip select signal during board configuration read and write cycles. The -Device Select (-DEVSEL) line is both an input and an output. As an input, -DEVSEL indicates whether a device has assumed control of the current bus transfer. As an output, -DEVSEL shows that a device has identified itself as the target for the current bus transfer.

There are four interrupt lines (-INTA to -INTD). When the full 64-bit data mode is being used, an expansion device will initiate a -64 Bit Bus Request (-REQ 64) and await a -64 Bit Bus Acknowledge (-ACK64) signal from the bus controller. The -Bus Lock (-LOCK) signal is an interface control used to ensure use of the bus by a selected expansion device. Error reporting is performed by -Primary Error (-PERR) and -Secondary Error (-SERR) lines. Cache memory and JTAG support are also provided on the PCI bus.

Accelerated Graphics Port (AGP)

One of the remarkable advantages of the PC is its ability to "visualize" information. Whether you're graphing out your spreadsheet data for a corporate report or slashing your way through the latest virtual dungeon, the PC's video system continues to improve in color depth, resolutions, and a wide range of visual effects. All of this video information requires a tremendous amount of data. This data not only requires memory, but also needs a lot of bandwidth to pass that data to the video card. AGP opens a freeway for graphics information that is especially well suited for 3D applications.

For example, the fast floating-point performance of today's CPUs can smooth the drawing of 3D meshes and animation effects and add depth to a 3D scene. The next step is to add lifelike realism. To do this, the PC must render a 3D image by adding textures, alpha-blended transparencies, texture mapping, lighting, and other effects. AGP technology accelerates graphics performance by providing a dedicated high-speed bus for the movement of large blocks of 3D texture data between the PC's graphics controller and system memory. In practice, AGP enables a hardware-accelerated graphics controller to execute texture maps directly from system RAM (instead of caching them in the relatively limited local video memory). It also helps speed the flow of decoded video from the CPU to the graphics controller. In addition, off-loading this tremendous data overhead from the PCI bus leaves PCI free to handle drive data transfers and other controllers.

High bandwidth is the key to AGP's power. The 66 MHz AGP interface is positioned between the PC's chipset and graphics controller, as shown in Figure 8-3. This architecture significantly increases the bandwidth available to a graphics accelerator. In its basic form, AGP offers a bandwidth of 266MB/s (twice the bandwidth of PCI). This is referred to as "AGP 1X." With advanced data handling techniques, 2 bytes can be passed on every AGP clock for a bandwidth of 532MB/s (known as "AGP 2X"). Further refinements to AGP data handling and the introduction of new chipsets allow 4 bytes to be passed on every AGP clock for a bandwidth of more than 1GB/s (called "AGP 4X"). Today, the computer industry is refining the specifications for an AGP bus offering bandwidths greater than 2GB/s (dubbed "AGP 8X"). You can learn more about this emerging AGP 8X standard at **developer.intel.com/technology/agp/agp_draft9.htm**.

AGP SIMILARITIES TO PCI

The 32-bit AGP bus gets its roots in the PCI local bus specification, but makes some significant improvements and additions intended to optimize AGP for high-performance 3D graphics. The most notable difference is the clock speed. PCI uses a fixed 33 MHz bus, but AGP ups the clock speed to 66 MHz. Other major differences include the following:

■ Deeply pipelined memory read and write operations. This hides memory access latency.

■ Demultiplexing of address and data on the bus, allowing almost 100 percent bus efficiency.

■ New AC timing for the 3.3V electrical specification that provides for one (AGP 1X) or two (AGP 2X) data transfers per 66 MHz clock cycle, allowing for real data throughput in excess of 500MB/s.

■ A new low-voltage electrical specification that allows four (AGP 4X) data transfers per 66 MHz clock cycle, providing real data throughput of over 1GB/s.

■ The bus slot defined for AGP uses a new connector body (for electrical signaling reasons) that is not compatible with the PCI connector, so PCI and AGP boards are not mechanically interchangeable.

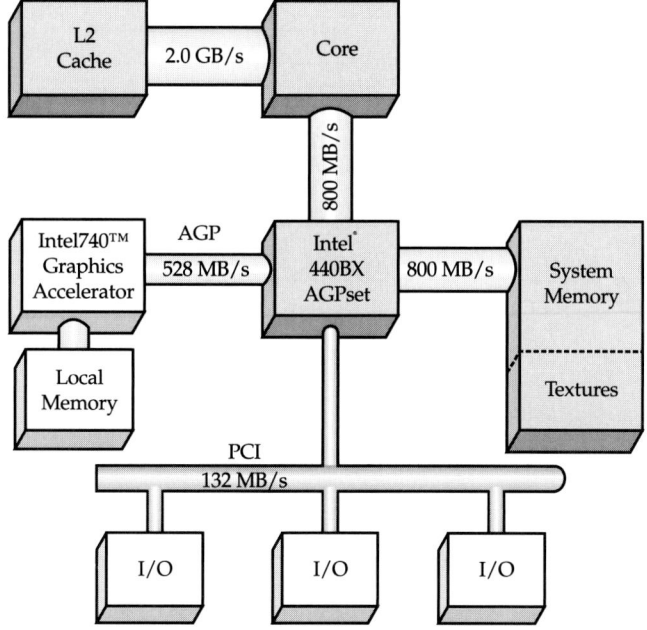

FIGURE 8-3   Block diagram of the AGP interface (Courtesy of Intel Corporation)

AGP LAYOUT

The AGP bus is a low-profile 132-pin connector intended to be used on ATX- and NLX-style mother-boards (though many current AT and baby AT motherboards will include an AGP bus). There are three variations of the AGP bus: 3.3V (Figure 8-4), Universal (Figure 8-5), and 1.5V (Figure 8-6). The signal layout (Table 8-4) is very similar between all three versions, but the key locations are different. As a result, 3.3V and 1.5V AGP cards are not interchangeable.

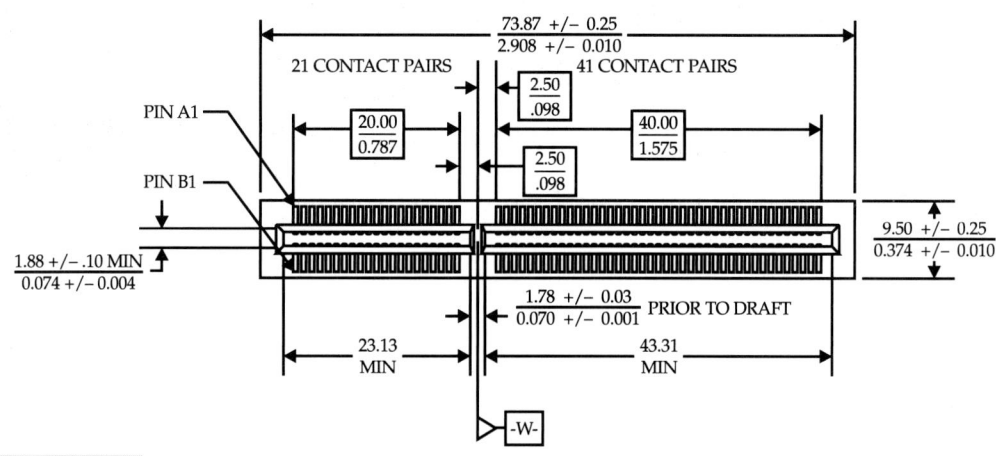

FIGURE 8-4   3.3V AGP bus connector

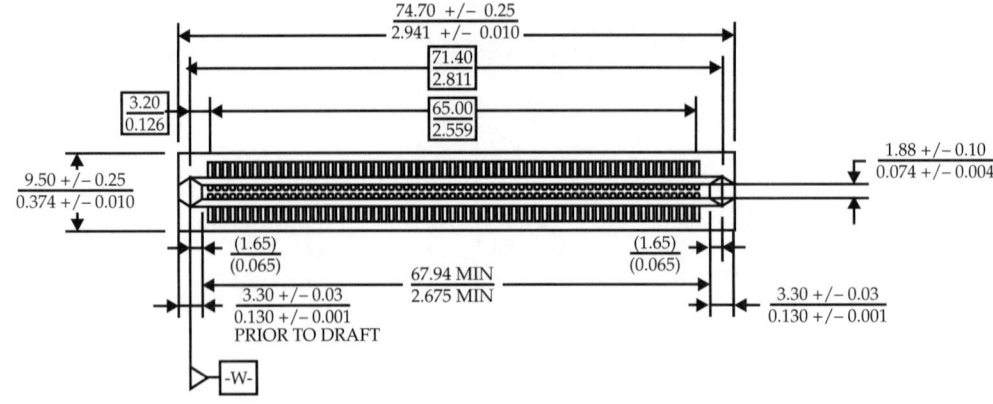

FIGURE 8-5   Universal AGP bus connector

 The AGP connector is not hot unpluggable. Be sure that the system and motherboard power is off. Unplugging an AGP card with power at the connector may cause irreparable damage to the card and/or system boards.

KNOWING THE AGP SIGNALS

The PIPE# request is asserted by the current master to indicate that a full width request is to be queued by the target. The master queues one request with each rising edge of CLK while PIPE# is asserted. When PIPE# is deasserted, no new requests are queued across the AD bus. The SideBand Address port (SBA[7 through 0]) provides an additional bus to pass requests (address and command) to the target from the master. SBA[7 through 0] are outputs from the master, and an input to the target. This port is ignored by the target until enabled.

The Read Buffer Full signal (RBF#) indicates whether the master is ready to accept previously requested low-priority read data. When RBF# is asserted, the arbiter is not allowed to initiate the return of

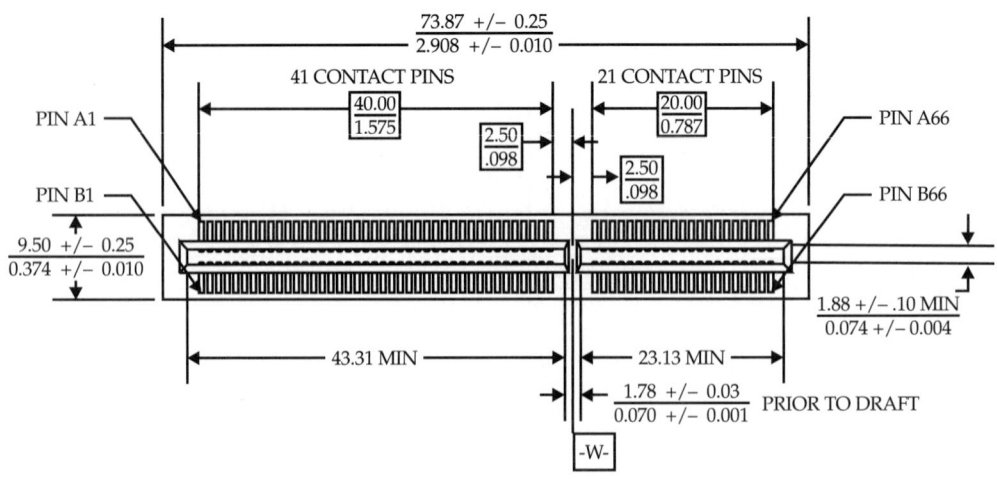

FIGURE 8-6   1.5V AGP bus connector

TABLE 8-4   AGP BUS PINOUT—3.3V, UNIVERSAL, AND 1.5V

Pin	3.3 VOLT B	3.3 VOLT A	UNIVERSAL B	UNIVERSAL A	1.5 VOLT B	1.5 VOLT A
1	OVRCNT#	12V	OVRCNT#	12V	OVRCNT#	12V
2	5.0V	TYPEDET#	5.0V	TYPEDET#	5.0V	TYPEDET#
3	5.0V	Reserved	5.0V	Reserved	5.0V	Reserved
4	USB+	USB-	USB+	USB-	USB+	USB-
5	GND	GND	GND	GND	GND	GND
6	INTB#	INTA#	INTB#	INTA#	INTB#	INTA#
7	CLK	RST#	CLK	RST#	CLK	RST#
8	REQ#	GNT#	REQ#	GNT#	REQ#	GNT#
9	VCC3.3	VCC3.3	VCC3.3	VCC3.3	VCC3.3	VCC3.3
10	ST0	ST1	ST0	ST1	ST0	ST1
11	ST2	Reserved	ST2	Reserved	ST2	Reserved
12	RBF#	PIPE#	RBF#	PIPE#	RBF#	PIPE#
13	GND	GND	GND	GND	GND	GND
14	Reserved	Reserved	Reserved	WBF#	Reserved	WBF#
15	SBA0	SBA1	SBA0	SBA1	SBA0	SBA1
16	VCC3.3	VCC3.3	VCC3.3	VCC3.3	VCC3.3	VCC3.3
17	SBA2	SBA3	SBA2	SBA3	SBA2	SBA3
18	SB_STB	Reserved	SB_STB	SB_STB#	SB_STB	SB_STB#
19	GND	GND	GND	GND	GND	GND
20	SBA4	SBA5	SBA4	SBA5	SBA4	SBA5
21	SBA6	SBA7	SBA6	SBA7	SBA6	SBA7
22	KEY	KEY	Reserved	Reserved	Reserved	Reserved
23	KEY	KEY	GND	GND	GND	GND
24	KEY	KEY	3.3Vaux	Reserved	3.3Vaux	Reserved
25	KEY	KEY	VCC3.3	VCC3.3	VCC3.3	VCC3.3
26	AD31	AD30	AD31	AD30	AD31	AD30
27	AD29	AD28	AD29	AD28	AD29	AD28
28	VCC3.3	VCC3.3	VCC3.3	VCC3.3	VCC3.3	VCC3.3
29	AD27	AD26	AD27	AD26	AD27	AD26
30	AD25	AD24	AD25	AD24	AD25	AD24
31	GND	GND	GND	GND	GND	GND
32	AD_STB1	Reserved	AD_STB1	AD_STB1#	AD_STB1	AD_STB1#
33	AD23	C/BE3#	AD23	C/BE3#	AD23	C/BE3#
34	Vddq3.3	Vddq3.3	Vddq	Vddq	Vddq1.5	Vddq1.5
35	AD21	AD22	AD21	AD22	AD21	AD22
36	AD19	AD20	AD19	AD20	AD19	AD20
37	GND	GND	GND	GND	GND	GND
38	AD17	AD18	AD17	AD18	AD17	AD18
39	C/BE2#	AD16	C/BE2#	AD16	C/BE2#	AD16
40	Vddq3.3	Vddq3.3	Vddq	Vddq	Vddq1.5	Vddq1.5
41	IRDY#	FRAME#	IRDY#	FRAME#	IRDY#	FRAME#
42	3.3Vaux	Reserved	3.3Vaux	Reserved	KEY	KEY
43	GND	GND	GND	GND	KEY	KEY
44	Reserved	Reserved	Reserved	Reserved	KEY	KEY
45	VCC3.3	VCC3.3	VCC3.3	VCC3.3	KEY	KEY

TABLE 8-4 AGP BUS PINOUT—3.3V, UNIVERSAL, AND 1.5V (CONTINUED)

Pin	3.3 VOLT B	A	UNIVERSAL B	A	1.5 VOLT B	A
46	DEVSEL#	TRDY#	DEVSEL#	TRDY#	DEVSEL#	TRDY#
47	Vddq3.3	STOP#	Vddq	STOP#	Vddq1.5	STOP#
48	PERR#	PME#	PERR#	PME#	PERR#	PME#
49	GND	GND	GND	GND	GND	GND
50	SERR#	PAR	SERR#	PAR	SERR#	PAR
51	C/BE1#	AD15	C/BE1#	AD15	C/BE1#	AD15
52	Vddq3.3	Vddq3.3	Vddq	Vddq	Vddq1.5	Vddq1.5
53	AD14	AD13	AD14	AD13	AD14	AD13
54	AD12	AD11	AD12	AD11	AD12	AD11
55	GND	GND	GND	GND	GND	GND
56	AD10	AD9	AD10	AD9	AD10	AD9
57	AD8	C/BE0#	AD8	C/BE0#	AD8	C/BE0#
58	Vddq3.3	Vddq3.3	Vddq	Vddq	Vddq1.5	Vddq1.5
59	AD_STB0	Reserved	AD_STB0	AD_STB0#	AD_STB0	AD_STB0#
60	AD7	AD6	AD7	AD6	AD7	AD6
61	GND	GND	GND	GND	GND	GND
62	AD5	AD4	AD5	AD4	AD5	AD4
63	AD3	AD2	AD3	AD2	AD3	AD2
64	Vddq3.3	Vddq3.3	Vddq	Vddq	Vddq1.5	Vddq1.5
65	AD1	AD0	AD1	AD0	AD1	AD0
66	Reserved	Reserved	Vrefcg	Vrefgc	Vrefcg	Vrefgc

low-priority read data to the master. A Write Buffer Full signal (WBF#) indicates whether the master is ready to accept data from the core logic. When WBF# is asserted, the core logic arbiter is not allowed to initiate a transaction to provide data.

The Status bus (ST[2 through 0]) provides information from the arbiter to the master on what it may do. ST[2 through 0] signals only have meaning to the master when its GNT# is asserted. When GNT# is deasserted, these signals have no meaning and must be ignored. The master may queue AGP requests by asserting PIPE# or start a PCI transaction by asserting FRAME#. ST[2 through 0] signals are always output from the core logic and input to the master.

The AD Bus Strobe 0 signal (AD_STB0) provides timing for the 2x data transfer mode on address lines AD[15 through 00]. The agent that is providing data drives this signal. The AD Bus Strobe 0 compliment (AD_STB0#, along with AD_STB0) provides timing for the 4x data transfer mode on address lines AD[15 through 00]. The agent that is providing data drives this signal. The AD Bus Strobe 1 signal (AD_STB1) provides timing for the 2x data transfer mode on address lines AD[31 through 16]. The agent that is providing data drives this signal. The AD Bus Strobe 1 compliment (AD_STB1#, along with AD_STB1) provides timing for the 4x data transfer mode on address lines AD[31 through 16]. The agent that is providing data drives this signal.

The SideBand Strobe signal (SB_STB) provides timing for SBA[7 through 0] (when supported) and is always driven by the AGP master. When the SideBand Strobes have been idle, a synch cycle needs to be performed before a request can be queued. The SideBand Strobe compliment (SB_STB#, along with SB_STB#) provides timing for SBA[7 through 0] signals (when supported) when 4x timing is supported and is always driven by the AGP master.

Clock (CLK) provides timing for AGP and PCI control signals. The USB Positive Differential Data Line (USB+) is used to send USB data and control packets to external peripheral devices. The USB Negative Differential Data Line (USB-) is used to send USB data and control packets to external peripheral devices. The USB Overcurrent Indicator (OVRCNT#) is low when too much current has been taken from the 5-volt power supply (Vbus) line on the bus connector. Otherwise, the line is at a level between 2.4 volts and Vddq. The Power Management Event signal (PME#) is not used by the AGP protocol, but is used by the PCI target interface when being power managed by the operating system. The Type Detect signal (TYPEDET#) indicates whether the interface is 1.5 volt or 3.3 volt.

CONFIGURING AN AGP SYSTEM

The AGP bus requires a 66 MHz clock. This clock is developed from the motherboard's front side bus clock (noted "FSB" or the "CPU clock"). When the motherboard is operated at 66 MHz, your AGP bus can use this clock directly. When the motherboard is operated at 100 MHz or higher, it will have to be divided down to achieve 66 MHz. Normally, you can adjust this divisor (1:1 or 2:3) using a jumper on the motherboard, or directly through the CMOS Setup. Be sure that you configure the system correctly depending on the clock speed. If the divisor is set to 2:3 when the system clock is 66 MHz, you will be *underclocking* the AGP bus. On the other hand, if the divisor is set to 1:1 when the system clock is 100 MHz, you will be *overclocking* the AGP bus. With today's motherboards supporting a wider range of FSB speeds, you will usually find a greater variety of clock divisors available, or the AGP bus will run asynchronously of the FSB.

General Bus Troubleshooting

In most cases, you will not be *troubleshooting* a bus—after all, the bus is little more than a passive connector. However, the major signals that exist on a bus can provide you with important clues about the system's operation. The most effective bus troubleshooting tool available to you is a POST board. Many POST boards are equipped with a number of LEDs that display power status, along with important timing and control signals. If one or more of those LEDs is missing, a fault has likely occurred somewhere on the motherboard. Keep in mind that the vast majority of POST boards are designed for the ISA bus. You can plug a POST board (with a built-in logic probe capable of 33 MHz operation or more) into an ISA connector, and then use the logic probe to test key signals. The following tips may help you isolate basic bus problems:

- **Voltage**   Use your multimeter and check each voltage level on the PCI bus. You should be able to find -12 Vdc and +5 Vdc regardless of whether the bus is standard or low voltage. For a low-voltage bus, you should also be able to find a +3.3 Vdc supply. If any of these supply levels is low or absent, troubleshoot or replace the power supply.

- **Clock**   The Clock signal provides timing signals for the expansion device. It can be adjusted between DC (0 Hz) and 33 MHz (or higher). If this signal is absent, the expansion board will probably not run. Check the clock generating circuitry on the motherboard, or replace the motherboard outright.

- **Reset**   The Reset line can be used to reinitialize the expansion device. This line should not be active for more than a few moments after power is applied or after a warm reset is initiated.

PCI and AGP busses are highly dependent on numerous settings in the CMOS Setup. Always check for proper CMOS configuration whenever you encounter trouble with PCI or AGP devices or bus performance.

Bus slot versions may also play a role in performance or compatibility issues. For example, a PCI card designed around version 2.1 of the PCI interface may not be fully functional if it's installed in an older motherboard using a version 2.0 PCI bus slot. As another example, an AGP 4X video card will not operate at 4X speeds if it's installed in an AGP 2X bus slot. Always make sure that your devices are designed for (or compatible with) the bus slots that they're intended for.

Another point to consider is that bus connectors are mechanical devices; as a result, they do not last forever. If you or your customer is in the habit of removing and inserting boards frequently, it is likely that the metal "fingers" providing contact will wear, eventually resulting in unreliable connections. Similarly, inserting a board improperly (or with excessive force) can break the connector. In extreme cases, even the motherboard can be damaged. The first rule of board replacement is *always try removing and reinserting the suspect board.* It is not uncommon for oxides to develop on board and slot contacts, which may eventually degrade signal quality. By removing the board and reinserting it, you can wipe off any oxides or dust and possibly improve the connections.

The second rule of board replacement is *always try a board in another expansion slot before replacing it.* This way, a faulty bus slot can be ruled out before absorbing the expense of a new board. Keep in mind that many current motherboards have a limited number of ISA slots and only one AGP slot—the remainder are PCI slots. If a bus slot proves defective, there is little that a technician can do except:

- Block the slot and inform the customer that it is damaged and should not be used.
- Replace the damaged bus slot connector (a tedious and time-consuming task) and pass the labor expense on to the customer.
- Replace the motherboard outright (also a rather expensive option).

Further Study

AGP   www.agpforum.org/
CompactPCI Home Page   www.compactpci.com/
Intel's AGP interface specification   ftp://download.intel.com/technology/agp/downloads/agp20.pdf
Intel's AGP site   developer.intel.com/technology/agp/index.htm
PCI Special Interest Group Home Page   www.pcisig.com/
Small PCI   www.pcisig.com/current/smallpci/

9

CD-ROM, CD-R,
AND CD-RW DRIVES

The *compact disc* (or CD) first appeared in the commercial marketplace in early 1982. Sony and Philips developed the CD as a joint venture and envisioned it as a reliable, high-quality digital replacement for aging analog phonograph technology. With the introduction of the audio CD, designers demonstrated that huge amounts of information could be stored simply and very inexpensively on common, non-magnetic media. Unlike previous recording media, the CD recorded data in *digital* form through the use of physical "pits" and "lands" in the disc. The digital approach allowed excellent stereo sound quality that does not degrade each time the disc is played. This optical storage technology also found its way into the PC and has evolved into a complete family of reliable high-volume storage devices: the CD-ROM, CD writer (or CD-R), and CD rewriter (or CD-RW). This chapter examines the basics of these technologies, offers some handy installation guidelines, and covers a wealth of troubleshooting issues.

The CD-ROM Drive

The CD-ROM drive that we know today (Figure 9-1) has its origins in digital audio recording, but it was quickly adapted for the PC by designers who saw CDs as a natural solution for storing all types of computer information (such as text, graphics, programs, video clips, audio files, and so on). While the CD-ROM drive can only *read* data—it cannot write—the CD-ROM is known for its low cost, good reliability, and broad media (disc) compatibility. In fact, the CD-ROM proved so popular that it quickly became standard equipment on both desktop and mobile PC systems. This part of the chapter outlines the elements of CD-ROM drives and technologies that a technician should be familiar with.

CD MEDIA

Commercial CDs are mass-produced by stamping the pattern of pits and lands onto a molded polycarbonate disc (known as a *substrate*). It is this stamping process (much like the stamping used to produce vinyl records) that places the data on the disc. But the disc is not yet readable—there are finish steps that must be performed to transform a clear plastic disc into viable, data-carrying medium. The clear polycarbonate disc is given a silvered (reflective) coating so that it will reflect laser light. Silvering coats all parts of the disc side (pits and lands) equally. After silvering, the disc is coated with a tough, scratch-resistant lacquer that seals the disc from the elements (especially oxygen, which will oxidize and ruin the reflective coating). Finally, a label can be silk-screened onto the finished disc before it is tested and packaged. Figure 9-2 illustrates each of these layers in a cross-sectional diagram.

The word *disc* is not a spelling error—the PC industry uses the term "disk" to refer to magnetic media (such as a floppy disk), but the term "disc" refers to optical media (such as a rewritable disc).

FIGURE 9-1   An external CD-R drive (Courtesy of Smart and Friendly)

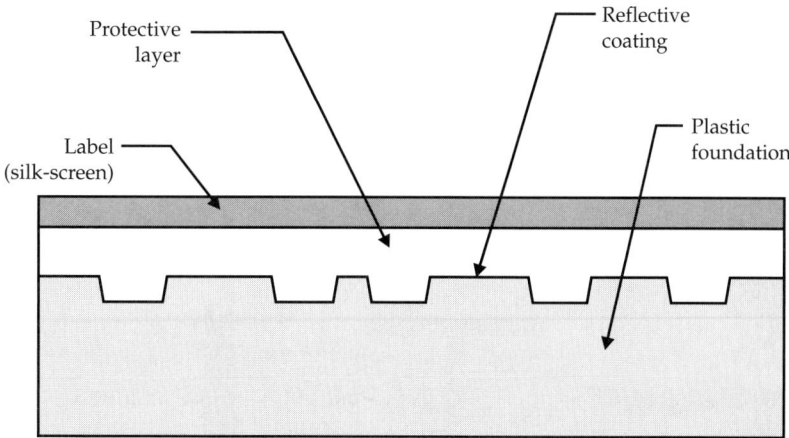

FIGURE 9-2   Cross-section of a common CD disc

CD DATA

Unlike magnetic media, such as floppy disks or hard drives, CDs are not segregated into concentric tracks and sectors. Instead, CDs are recorded as a single, continuous spiral track running from the spindle (inner) to the lead-out (outer) area. Figure 9-3 shows an example of the spiral pattern as it might be recorded on a CD. The inset illustrates the relationship between the pits and lands. Each pit is about $0.12\mu m$ (micrometers) deep and $0.6\mu m$ wide. Pits and lands may range from $0.9\mu m$ to $3.3\mu m$ in length. There are approximately $1.6\mu m$ between each iteration of the spiral. Given these microscopic dimensions, a CD-ROM disc offers about 16,000 tracks per inch (tpi).

During playback, CDs use a highly focused laser beam and laser detector to sense the presence or absence of pits. Figure 9-4 illustrates the reading behavior. The laser/detector pair is mounted on a carriage that follows the spiral track across the CD. A laser is directed at the underside of the CD, where it penetrates more than 1mm of clear plastic before shining on the reflective surface. When laser light strikes a land, the light is reflected toward the detector, which, in turn, produces a very strong output signal. As laser light strikes a pit, the light is slightly out of focus. As a result, most of the incoming laser energy is scattered away in all directions, so very little output signal is generated by the detector. As with floppy and

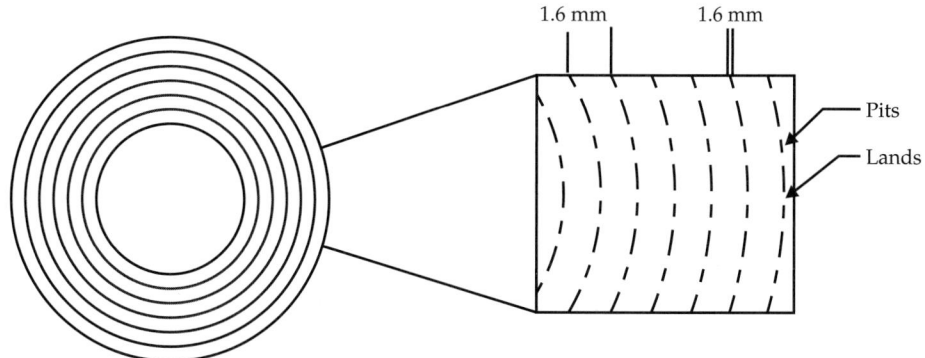

FIGURE 9-3   Close-up of a CD spiral track pattern

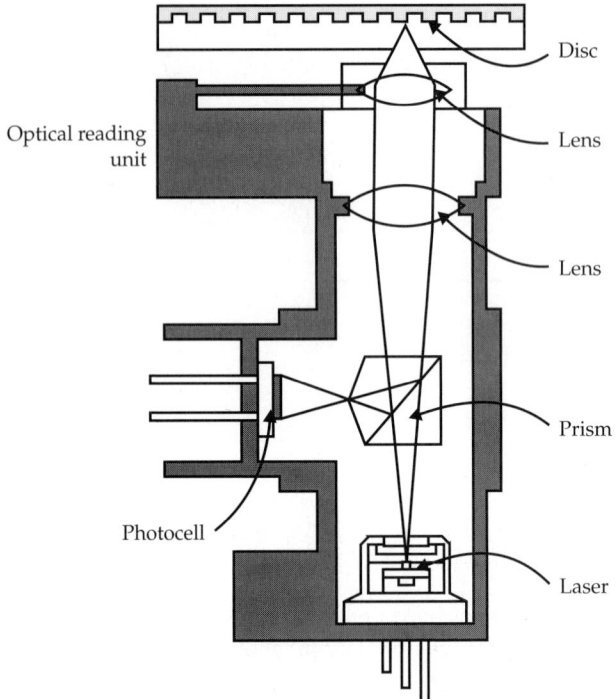

FIGURE 9-4   Reading a typical compact disc

hard drives, it is the *transition* from pit to land (and back again) that corresponds to binary levels, *not* the presence or absence of a pit or land. The analog light signal returned by the detector must be converted to logic levels and decoded, which is accomplished in a process described next.

EFM Basics

A complex decoding process is necessary to convert this arcane sequence of pits and lands into meaningful binary information. The technique of *eight-to-fourteen modulation* (EFM) is used with CD-ROMs. For hard disk drives, techniques such as *2,7 RLL encoding* can be used to place a large number of bits into a limited number of flux transitions. CDs using EFM have this same ability, and user data, error correction information, address information, and synchronization patterns can all be contained in a bit stream represented by pits and lands.

Magnetic media encodes bits as flux *transitions—not* the discrete orientation of any magnetic area. The same concept holds true with CD-ROMs, where binary 1's and 0's do not correspond to pits or lands. A binary 1 is represented wherever a *transition* (pit-to-land or land-to-pit) occurs. The *length* of a pit or land represents the number of binary 0's. Figure 9-5 illustrates this concept. The eight-to-fourteen encoding technique

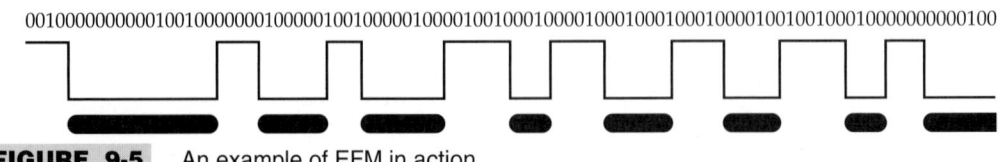

FIGURE 9-5   An example of EFM in action

TABLE 9-1   A SAMPLE OF 8-TO-14 MODULATION CODES

NUMBER	BINARY PATTERN	EFM PATTERN
0	00000000	01001000100000
1	00000001	10000100000000
2	00000010	10010000100000
3	00000011	10001000100000
4	00000100	01000100000000
5	00000101	00000100010000
6	00000110	00010000100000
7	00000111	00100100000000
8	00001000	01001001000000
9	00001001	10000001000000
10	00001010	10010001000000

equates each byte (eight bits) with a fourteen bit sequence (called a *symbol*), where each binary 1 must be separated by at least two binary 0's. Table 9-1 shows part of the eight-to-fourteen conversion. Three bits are added to merge each 14-bit symbol together.

Data Storage

A CD-ROM *frame* is composed of 24 synchronization bits, 14 control bits, 24 of the 14-bit data symbols you saw previously, and 8 complete 14-bit–error correction (EC) symbols. Keep in mind that each symbol is separated by an additional three merge bits, bringing the total number of bits in the frame to 588. Thus, 24 bytes of data is represented by 588 bits on a CD-ROM, expressed as a number of pits and lands. There are 98 frames in a data *block*, so each block carries [98×24] 2,048 bytes (2,352 with error correction, synchronization, and address bytes). The basic CD-ROM can deliver 153.6KB of data (75 blocks) per second to its host controller.

Remember that the CD-ROM disc is recorded as one continuous spiral track running around the disk, so ordinary sector and track ID information that we associate with magnetic disks does not apply very well. Instead, information is divided in terms of 0 to 59 *minutes*, and 0 to 59 *seconds* recorded at the beginning of each block. A CD-ROM (like an audio CD) can hold up to 79 *minutes* of data. However, many CD-ROMs tend to limit this to 60 minutes, because the last 14 minutes of data are encoded in the outer 5mm of disc space, which is the most difficult to manufacture and keep clean in everyday use. There are 270,000 blocks of data in 60 minutes. At 2,048 data bytes per block, the disc's capacity is 552,950,000 bytes (553MB). If all 79 minutes are used, 681,984,000 bytes (681MB) will be available in 333,000 blocks. Most CD-ROMs run between 553 and 650MB in normal production.

CARING FOR COMPACT DISCS

A compact disc is a remarkably reliable long-term storage medium (conservative expectations place the life estimates of a current CD at about 100 years). However, the longevity of a CD is affected by its storage and handling—a faulty CD can cause file and data errors that you might otherwise interpret as a defect in the drive itself. Here are some tips to help protect and maintain the disc itself:

- *Don't bend the disc.* Polycarbonate is a forgiving material, but you risk cracking or snapping (and thus ruining) the disc.

- *Don't heat the disc.* Remember, the disc is plastic. Leaving it by a heater or on the dashboard of your car will cause melting.

■ *Don't scratch the disc.* Laser wavelengths have a tendency to "look past" minor scratches, but a major scratch can cause problems. Be especially careful of circular scratches (ones that follows the spiral track). A circular scratch can easily wipe out entire segments of data, which would then be unrecoverable.

■ *Don't use chemicals on the disc.* Chemicals containing solvents such as ammonia, benzene, acetone, carbon tetrachloride, or chlorinated cleaning solvents can easily damage the disc's plastic surface.

Eventually, a buildup of excessive dust or fingerprints can interfere with the laser beam enough to cause disc read errors. When this happens, the disc can be cleaned easily using a dry, soft, lint-free cloth. Hold the disc from its edges and wipe radially (from hub to edge). Do not wipe in a circular motion! For stubborn stains, moisten the cloth in a bit of fresh isopropyl alcohol (do not use water). Place the cleaned disc in a caddie or jewel case for transport and storage.

CD STANDARDS AND CHARACTERISTICS

Like so many other PC peripheral devices, the early CD-ROM faced a serious problem of industry standardization. Just recording the data to a CD is not enough—the data must be recorded in a way that any CD-ROM drive can read. Standards for CD-ROM data formats were developed by consortiums of influential PC manufacturers and interested CD-ROM publishers. Ultimately, this kind of industry-wide cooperation made the CD-ROM one of the most uniform and standardized peripherals in the PC market. Because of the broad introduction of CD recorders and rewriters into the marketplace, it is also important for you to understand the major concepts and operations of CD recorders. This part of the chapter explains many of these key ideas and standards.

High Sierra

In 1984 (before the general release of CD-ROM), the PC industry realized that there must be a standard method of reading a disc's VTOC (Volume Table of Contents)—otherwise the CD-ROM market would become extremely fragmented as various (incompatible) standards vied for acceptance. PC manufacturers, prospective CD publishers, and software developers met at the High Sierra Hotel in Lake Tahoe, California to begin developing just such a uniform standard. By 1986, the CD-ROM standard file format (dubbed the *High Sierra* format) was accepted and approved. High Sierra remained the standard for several years, but it has since been replaced by ISO 9660.

ISO 9660

High Sierra was certainly a workable format, but it was primarily a domestic U.S. development. When placed before the *International Standards Organization* (ISO), High Sierra was tweaked and refined to meet international needs. After international review, High Sierra was absorbed (with only few changes) into the *ISO 9660* standard. Although many technicians refer to High Sierra and ISO 9660 interchangeably, you should understand that the two standards are *not* the same. For the purposes of this book, ISO 9660 is the current CD-ROM and CD-R file format. All CD-ROM, CD-R, and CD-RW drives can read ISO 9660 discs, and all CD-R/RW drives are capable of recording a CD-R disc in the ISO 9660 format (though rewritable drives use the later UDF format when working with CD-RW media).

By adhering to ISO 9660, CD-ROM drive makers can write software drivers (and use MSCDEX under DOS) to enable a PC to read the disc's VTOC. ISO 9660 also allows a CD-ROM disc to be accessed by any computer system or CD-ROM drive that follows the standard. Of course, just because a disc is recognized does not mean that it can be used. For example, an ISO 9660-compliant Mac can access a ISO 9660 MPC disc, but the files on the disc cannot be used by the Mac.

CD-ROM Standards ("Books")

When Philips and Sony defined the proprietary standards that became CD audio, CD-ROM, and so on, the documents were bound in different colored covers. By tradition, each color now represents a different level of standardization. *Red Book* (a.k.a. *Compact Disc Digital Audio Standard*: CEI IEC 908) defines the media, recording and mastering process, and the player design for CD audio. This is sometimes dubbed CD-DA (for CD Digital Audio). When you listen to your favorite audio CD, you are enjoying the benefits of the Red Book standard. CDs conforming to Red Book standards will usually have the words "digital audio" printed below the disc logo. Today, Red Book audio may be combined with programs and other PC data on the same disc.

The Yellow Book standard (ISO 10149:1989) makes CD-ROM possible by defining the additional error-correction data needed on the disc and specifying detection hardware and firmware needed in the drive. When a disc conforms to Yellow Book, it will usually be marked "data storage" beneath the disc logo. Mode 1 Yellow Book is the typical operating mode that supports computer data. *Mode 2* Yellow Book (also known as the *XA format*) supports compressed audio data and video/picture data. The Yellow Book standards build on the Red Book, so virtually all CD-ROM drives are capable of playing back CD audio discs.

The *Orange Book* (a.k.a. *Recordable Compact Disc Standard*) is the key to recordable (CD-R) and rewritable (CD-RW) drives and serves to extend the basic Red and Yellow Book standards by providing specifications for recordable products such as (Part 1) *magneto-optical* (MO) drives and (Part 2) *write-once CD-R* drives. The *Green Book* standard defines an array of supplemental standards for data recording and provides an outline for a specific computer system that supports CD-I (compact disc-interactive). Interactive kiosks and information systems using CD-I discs are based on Green Book standards. *Blue Book* is the standard for laser discs and their players. The *White Book* standards define CD-ROM video.

Digital Audio Extraction (DAE)

With the introduction of recordable CDs, it didn't take long for audio enthusiasts to express an interest in creating their own music CDs and compilations. This process typically involved recording the CD audio in the form of .WAV files to the system hard drive—those files could then be post-processed and organized for recording on a CD-R. However, this procedure presented a unique problem for CD drives. While most CD drives are capable of playing digital audio, they often prove to be a poor solution for recording that audio on the hard drive in the form of .WAV files. While just about every CD-ROM/R/RW drive will *play* standard Red Book digital audio, *not* every drive will allow you to read and *record* the digital audio data directly—a process sometimes called *CD-DA extraction*, or *digital audio extraction* (DAE).

If you're looking to create your own music CDs from existing audio CDs, you will need to use a CD drive that is suitable for good quality DAE (a specification or notation usually added to the drive box or spec sheet). A drive that is not well suited for DAE will cause artifacts such as pops, clicks, or gaps in the recorded .WAV file. Technicians should be aware of this problem and that the solution to poor-quality DAE is often to upgrade the CD drive that is reading the original music CD (the *source drive*).

Keep in mind that it is *illegal* to duplicate music or other CD contents that have been copyrighted. You cannot duplicate copyrighted materials without permission from the copyright holder.

The Multi-Speed Drive

The Red Book standard defines CD audio as a stream of data that flows from the player mechanism to the amplifier (or other audio manipulation circuit) at a rate of 150 KB/sec. This data rate was chosen to take music off the disc for truest reproduction. When the Yellow Book was developed to address CD-ROMs, this basic data rate was carried over. Designers soon learned that computer data can be transferred *much* faster than Red Book audio information, so the *multi-speed* drive was developed to work with Red Book audio at the normal 150 KB/sec rate, while running faster for Yellow Book data in order to improve the effective data throughput.

The first common multi-speed drives available were 2x drives. By running at two times the normal data transfer speed, data throughput can be doubled from 150 KB/sec to 300 KB/sec. CD-ROM drives with 4x transfer speed (600 KB/sec) can transfer data four times faster than a Red Book drive. If Red Book audio is encountered, the drive speed drops back to 150 KB/sec. Today, you can find CD-ROM drives with reading speeds up to 50x (50×150 KB/s) or 7.5 MB/s. At 50x, a CD with 650MB of data can be read in (650 / 7.5) 86.7 seconds—about a minute and a half! As you see, increased data transfer rates make a real difference in CD-ROM performance—especially for data-intensive applications such as audio/video clips.

Today, the term "multi-speed" is rarely used because it is redundant—virtually all CD drive types operate at some multiple of the original Red Book speed. For example, it is not uncommon to find CD-RW drives with 16x recording speed (CD-R), 10x rewriting speed (CD-RW), and 40x reading speed (CD-ROM).

MPC

One of the most fundamental problems writing software for PCs is the tremendous variability in the possible hardware and software configurations of individual machines. The selection of CPUs, motherboard chipsets, operating system versions, available memory, graphics systems, drive space, and other peripherals makes the idea of a "standard" PC almost meaningless. Most software developers in the PC market establish a baseline (or minimal) PC configuration to ensure that a product will run properly in a minimal machine. CD-ROM multimedia products have intensified these performance issues because of the unusually heavy demands posed by real-time audio and graphics. In the early 1990s, Microsoft assembled some of the largest PC manufacturers to create the *Multimedia Personal Computer* (or MPC) standard. By adhering to the MPC specification, software developers and consumers can anticipate the minimal capacity needed to run multimedia products.

Today, the MPC standard has been largely replaced by the broader system standards such as PC99 and later (shown in Appendix B).

MMC

The problem with advanced drives like today's CD-ROM, CD-R, and CD-RW drives is that each one tends to use its own unique "command set"—a language that defines each function or feature of the drive. Traditionally, each manufacturer of CD drives used a different command set (even varied the commands with each new drive model). This practice caused a real struggle for programmers who had to write drivers and recording software that would be compatible with a growing number of drives—each with its own diverse command set. The resulting recording software packages often took a long time to develop and were huge in size.

To combat this proliferation of command sets, some CD drive developers embraced a common command set called MMC (Multi Media Command). Since MMC-compliant drives use a common command set, software developers could write a set of drivers and writing software for one MMC-compliant recorder that would be able to run other MMC-compliant drives. CD writing software can run just about any MMC-compliant drive, so you don't need to update or mix software packages when you add or replace drives. In actual practice, MMC compliance is a nice benefit, but it is not essential because virtually all CD drives ship with suitable software and drivers anyway. You should first select a drive for its speed, format compatibility, and other features. If MMC-compliance happens to be one of those features, that's great, but don't sacrifice important features for MMC compliance.

CD-ROM Caching

One limiting factor of a CD-ROM is its data transfer rate. Even a fast multi-speed CD-ROM takes a fairly substantial amount of time to load programs and files into memory, causing system delays during CD-ROM access. If the PC could *predict* the data needed from a CD and load that data into RAM or virtual memory (that is, the hard drive) during background operations, the *effective* performance of a CD-ROM drive would be enhanced dramatically. CD-ROM caching utilities provide a "look-ahead" ability that enables CD-ROMs to continue transferring information in anticipation of use.

Real-mode (DOS) CD-ROM caching is a mixed blessing. The utilities required for caching (such as SmartDrive) must reside in conventional memory (or be loaded into upper memory). In systems that are already strained by the CD-ROM drivers and the other device drivers that have become so commonplace on PC platforms, adding a cache may prohibit some large DOS programs from running. Keep this in mind when evaluating CD-ROM caches for yourself or your customers.

By comparison, Windows 9x/Me discontinues the use of SmartDrive in favor of its own internal protected-mode caching features. If you're using Windows 9x/Me, you may optimize the CD-ROM cache through the File System Properties dialog:

1. Click on Start, Settings, Control Panel.

2. Double-click on the System icon.

3. Select the Performance tab and click the File System button.

4. Select the CD-ROM tab.

You can then optimize the CD-ROM cache size and access pattern for your drive, as in Figure 9-6.

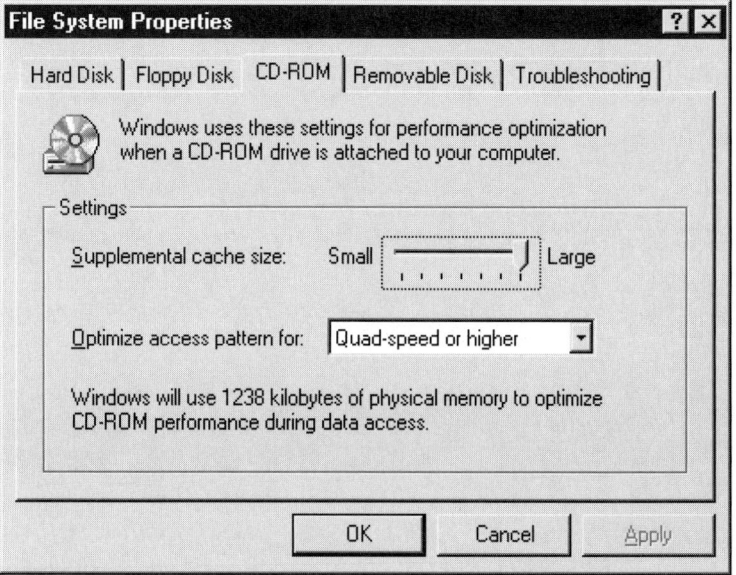

FIGURE 9-6   Adjusting the CD-ROM cache settings under Windows 98/SE

Bootable CD-ROM (El Torito)

Traditionally, CD-ROM/R/RW drives have *not* been bootable devices. Since the CD drives need software drivers, the PC always had to boot *first* in order to load the drivers. This process invariably required a bootable hard drive or floppy drive. When building a new system, this required you to boot from a floppy disk, install DOS and the CD-ROM drivers, and *then* pop in your Windows Installation CD for setup. In early 1995, the El Torito standard was finalized, which provided the hardware and software specifications needed to implement a *bootable* CD-ROM. Virtually all CD drives meet El Torito requirements today, so most CD drives (even CD-R and CD-RW drives) can be installed and recognized as CD-ROM drives under Windows 9x/Me. This gives you immediate CD-ROM functionality for the drive (allowing you to read discs) without installation of a single driver. Of course, you'll need to install drivers and other software to take full advantage of CD-R and CD-RW drives. You need three elements to implement a bootable CD-ROM:

■ A bootable CD-ROM drive mechanism (almost always fitted with a UDMA or EIDE interface).

■ A BIOS version that supports the bootable CD-ROM (now standard on almost all new motherboards)—you'll find that the CMOS Setup provides an option for CD-ROM in the Boot Order.

■ A CD with boot code and an operating system on it. If you don't already have a bootable (or system) CD, see "Creating a Bootable CD" later in this chapter.

CD Compatibility Notes

Given the staggering array of CD drive types and vintages, it is sometimes difficult to determine just which disc type is compatible with what drive type. Table 9-2 compares a variety of drive types with disc

TABLE 9-2			**GENERAL COMPATIBILITY GUIDELINES FOR CD DRIVE AND DISC TYPES**						
TYPE OF DRIVE	**CD-DA**	**CD-ROM**	**CD-ROM XA**	**BRIDGE CD**	**CD-I**	**VIDEO CD**	**PHOTO CD**	**CD-R**	**CD-RW**
Audio CD Player	Play	No	No	No	No	No	No	Single Session	No
Standard (Older) CD-ROM Drive	Play (some DAE)	Yes	No	No	No	No	No	Single Session	No
(Newer) CD-ROM XA Drive	Play, (some DAE)	Yes	Yes	Yes	No	Some	Some	Single Session	No
Multi-Session CD-ROM XA Drive	Play and DAE	Yes	Yes	Yes	No	Yes	Yes	Multi-Session	Some
CD-I Player	Play	No	No	Yes	Yes	Yes	Yes	Single Session	No
CD-R Drive	Play and DAE	Yes	Yes	Yes	Yes	Yes	Yes	Multi-Session	Some
CD-RW Drive	Play and DAE	Yes	Yes	Yes	Yes	Yes	Yes	Multi-Session	Yes

compatibility. For example, a Standard (older) CD-ROM Drive can play CD-DA discs, but only some drives can handle DAE. The drive can also handle CD-ROM discs, but usually just single-session CD-R discs (ISO 9660).

CD-ROM CONSTRUCTION

Now that you know the essentials of CD-ROM media and standards, it is time to review a typical drive in some detail. CD-ROM, CD-R, and CD-RW drives are impressive pieces of engineering. The drive must be able to accept standard-sized disks from a variety of sources (each disk may contain an assortment of unknown surface imperfections). The drive must then spin the disk at a *constant linear velocity* (CLV)—that is, the disk speed varies inversely with the tracking radius. As tracking approaches the disk edge, disk speed slows—and vice versa. Keep in mind that CLV is different from the *constant angular velocity* (CAV) method, used by floppy and hard drives, under which the media moves at a constant speed. The purpose of CLV is to ensure that CD data is read at a constant *rate*. A drive must be able to follow the spiral data path on a spinning CD-ROM accurately to within less than $1\mu m$ along the disk's radius. The drive electronics must be able to detect and correct any unforeseen data errors in real time, operate reliably over a long working life, and be available for the low price that computer users have come to expect.

CD-ROM Mechanics

You can begin to appreciate how a CD drive achieves its features by reviewing the exploded diagram of Figure 9-7. At the center of the drive is a cast aluminum or rigid stainless steel *frame assembly*. As with other drives, the frame is the single primary structure for mounting the drive's mechanical and electronic components. The *front bezel*, *lid*, *volume control*, and *eject button* attach to the frame, providing the drive with its clean cosmetic appearance and offering a fixed reference slot for CD insertion and removal. Keep in mind that many drives use a sliding tray, so the front bezel (and the way it is attached) will not be the same for every drive.

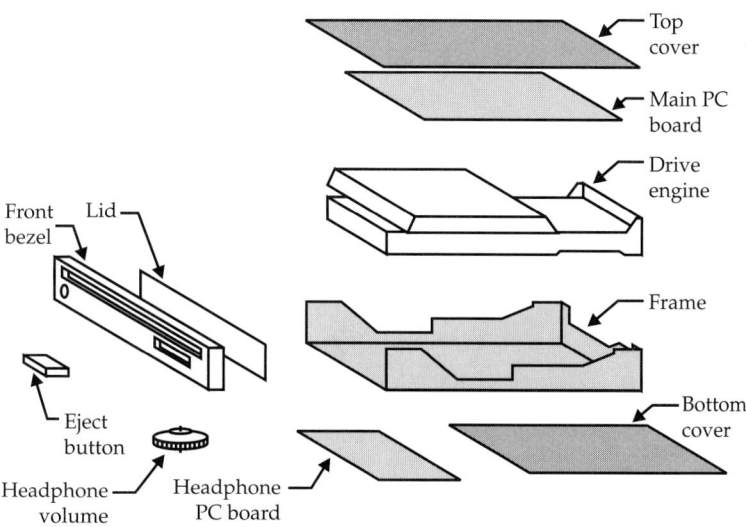

FIGURE 9-7   Exploded diagram of a basic CD drive

Although the laser type and drive electronics are somewhat different, the physical descriptions and electronic details for CD-ROM drives are also generally true for CD-R and CD-RW drives.

The drive's electronics package has been split into several PC board assemblies: the *main PCB*, which handles drive control and interfacing, and the *headphone PCB*, which simply provides an audio amplifier and jack for headphones. The bulk of the drive's actual physical work, however, is performed by a main CD subassembly called a *drive engine*. These are often manufactured by only a few companies. As a result, many of the diverse CD-ROM drives on the market actually use identical "engines" to hold/eject, spin, and read the disk. This interchangeability is part of the genius of CD-ROM drives—a single subassembly performs 80 percent of the work. Sony, Philips, and Toshiba are the major manufacturers of CD-ROM engines, but other companies such as IBM and Ikka have also been known to produce engines.

A typical drive engine is shown in Figure 9-8. The upper view of the engine features a series of mechanisms that accept, clamp, and eject the disk. The foundation of this engine is the *BC-7C assembly*. It acts as a sub-frame which everything else is mounted to. Notice that the sub-frame is shock-mounted with four *rubber feet* to cushion the engine from minor bumps and ordinary handling. Even with such mounting, a CD-ROM drive is a delicate and fragile mechanism. The *slider assembly*, *loading chassis assembly*, and the *cover shield* provide the mechanical action needed to accept the disk and clamp it into place over the drive spindle as well as to free the disk and eject it on demand. A number of levers and oil dampers serve to provide a slow, smooth mechanical action when motion takes place. A *motor/gear assembly* drives the load/unload mechanics.

The serious work of spinning and reading a disk is handled *under* the engine, as shown in Figure 9-9. A *spindle motor* is mounted on the sub-frame and connected to a *spindle motor PC board*. A *thrust retainer* helps keep the spindle motor turning smoothly. The most critical part of the CD engine is the *optical device* containing the 780nm (nanometer) 0.6mW gallium aluminum arsenide (GaAlAs) laser diode and detector, along with the optical focus and tracking components. The optical device slides along two guide rails and shines through an exposed hole in the sub-frame. This combination of device mounting and guide rails is called a *sled*.

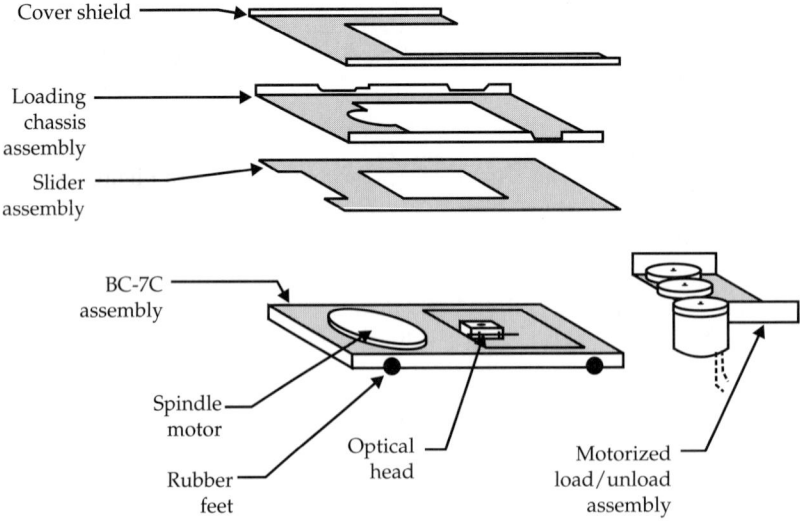

Cover shield

Loading chassis assembly

Slider assembly

BC-7C assembly

Spindle motor

Optical head

Rubber feet

Motorized load/unload assembly

FIGURE 9-8   Exploded diagram of a CD drive engine

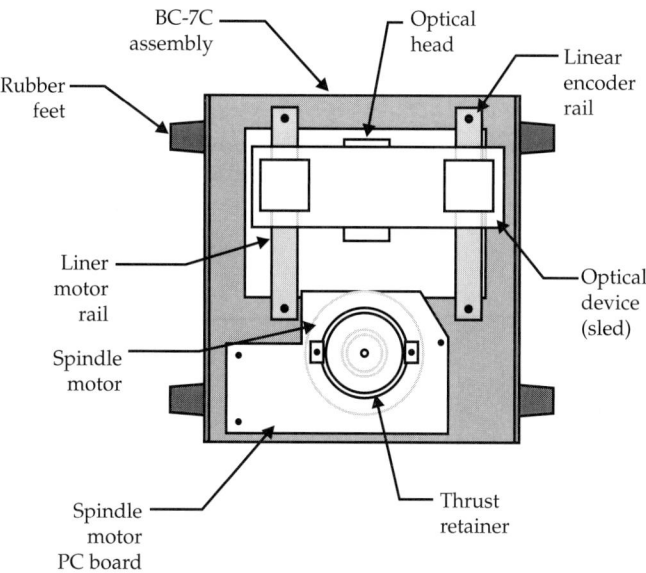

FIGURE 9-9 Underside view of a typical BC-7C assembly

CD-R and CD-RW drives will typically use lasers with different characteristics, though you may not be able to distinguish between a CD-ROM, CD-R, or CD-RW engine at first glance.

A sled must be made to follow the spiral data track along the disk. While floppy disks (using clearly defined concentric tracks) can easily make use of a stepping motor to position the head assembly, a CD drive ideally requires a *linear motor* to act much like the voice coil motor used to position hard drive R/W heads. By altering the signal driving a sled motor and constantly measuring and adjusting the sled's position, a sled can be made to track very smoothly along a disk—free from the sudden, jerky motion of stepping motors. Some CD drives still use stepping motors with an extremely fine-pitch lead screw to position the sled. The drive's main PC board is responsible for managing these operations.

CD-ROM Electronics

The electronics package used in a typical CD-ROM drive is illustrated in Figure 9-10. The electronics package can be divided into two major areas: the *controller* section and the *drive* section. The controller section is dedicated to the peripheral interface—its connection to the drive controller board. Much of a CD-ROM's electronic sophistication can be traced to the controller section. Notice that the controller circuitry shown in Figure 9-10 is dedicated to handling a SCSI interface, though most CD-ROM drives today offer a UDMA or EIDE drive interface, which will support a CD-ROM right along with your existing hard drive(s). This arrangement allows the unit's "intelligence" to be located right in the drive itself. You need only connect the drive to a system-level interface board such as a SCSI host adapter or IDE-type drive controller (that is, an IDE, EIDE, or UDMA controller) and set the drive's device identification to establish a working system.

The *drive section* electronics will manage the CD-ROM's physical operations (load/unload, spin the disk, move the sled, and so on), as well as data decoding (EFM) and error correction. Drive circuitry converts an analog output from the laser diode into an EFM signal, which is, in turn, decoded into binary data

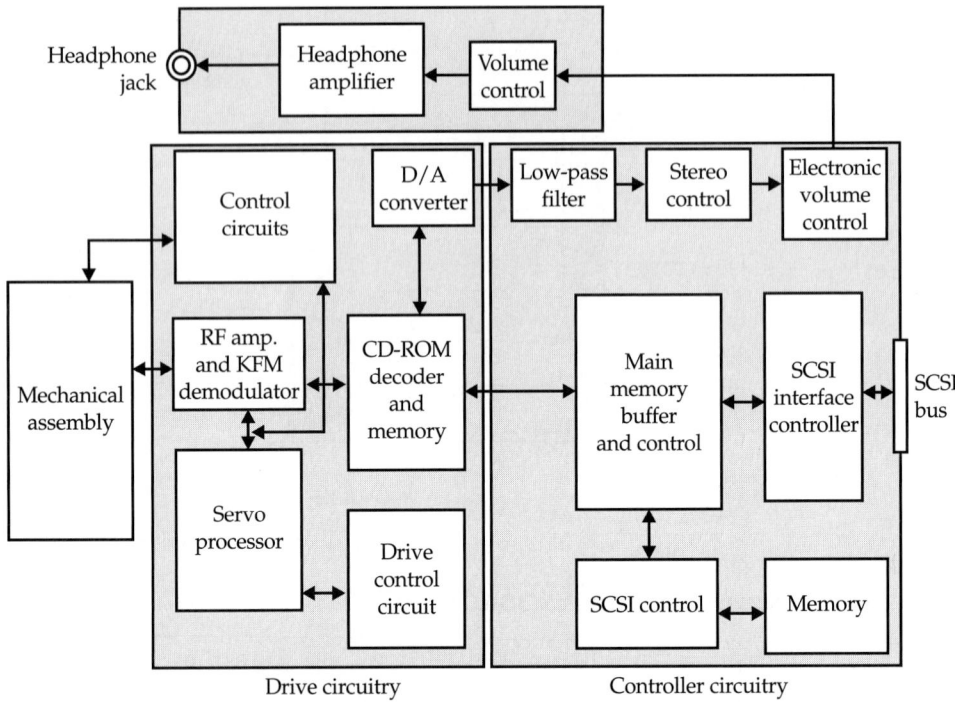

FIGURE 9-10   Electronic block diagram for a typical CD drive

and CIRC (Cross-Interleaved Reed-Solomon Code) information. A drive controller chip and servo processor chip are responsible for directing laser focus, tracking, sled motor control (and feedback), spindle motor control (and feedback), and loading/unloading motor control.

When it comes to CD drive electronics, you should certainly treat the diagram of Figure 9-10 as a guideline rather than as an absolute. There are quite a few different iterations of drive electronics and interfaces: some manufacturers use SCSI interfaces, but most systems use the UDMA or EIDE system-level interface, and a very few manufacturers implement proprietary interfaces (in some cases, these are often subtle, non-standard variations of SCSI or IDE interfaces). Obtain manufacturer's service data wherever possible for specific information on your particular drive.

CD-ROM SOFTWARE

Hardware alone is not enough to fully support a CD-ROM, CD-R, or CD-RW drive. In an ideal world, BIOS would provide the software support to handle the drive (as it does for hard drives), but, in practice, the variations between CD-ROM designs and interfaces make it impractical to provide low-level BIOS services for every possible CD drive design. Though the El Torito standard *does* allow the BIOS to provide basic bootability for a wide range of CD drives, device drivers are still required to support the drive after the system has finished booting. Manufacturers provide a hardware-specific device driver used to communicate with the CD-ROM and interface. An MS-DOS extension (MSCDEX) provides file handling and logical drive letter support. This part of the chapter explains the operations and features of real-mode CD-ROM device drivers and MSCDEX.

This software discussion deals with real-mode software operating under DOS. If you're using a CD-ROM under Windows 9x/Me, you can skip these discussions. Windows 9x/Me does not use MSCDEX, and will install a protected-mode driver for the CD-ROM (either a "native" Windows driver or one directly from the drive maker).

Device Drivers

A low-level device driver allows programs to access the CD-ROM, CD-R, or CD-RW drive properly at the register (hardware) level. Since most drives are designed differently, they require similar (but often different) device drivers. If you change or upgrade the drive at any point, the device driver must be upgraded as well. A typical real-mode device driver uses a .SYS extension and is enabled by adding its command line to the PC's CONFIG.SYS file, such as:

```
DEVICE=HITACHIA.SYS /D:MSCD000 /N:1 /P:300
```

The DEVICE command may be replaced by the DEVICEHIGH command if you have available space in the upper memory area (UMA).

A CD device driver will typically have three command line switches associated with it. These parameters are needed to ensure that the driver installs properly. For the example command line shown earlier, the **/D** switch is the name used by the driver when it is installed in the system's device table. This name must be unique and matched by the **/D** switch in the MSCDEX.EXE command line (covered later). The **/N** switch is the number of CD-ROM drives attached to the interface card. The default is 1 (which is typical for most general purpose systems). Finally, the **/P** switch is the I/O port address the drive's adapter card resides at. As you might expect, the port address should match the port address on the physical interface. If there is no **/P** switch, the default is 0300h.

There's an additional wrinkle when using SCSI-based CD drives. SCSI support also means that the PC must be fitted with a SCSI host adapter and configured with a real-mode ASPI driver in order to allow the SCSI adapter to interface to the drive (this is also true if you're using other SCSI drives and devices). Again, if the SCSI drive is being enabled under Windows 9x/Me, you'll use a protected-mode driver to run the SCSI host adapter. However, you may still need a real-mode driver for the SCSI host adapter if you're using the SCSI adapter to operate other devices under DOS. A typical real-mode ASPI driver entry might appear in CONFIG.SYS as:

```
DEVICE=C:\SCSI\ASPIPPA3.SYS /L=001
```

If there are no SCSI hard drives in the system, the SCSI adapter's onboard BIOS ROM can usually be disabled.

MSCDEX.EXE

Because MS-DOS was developed in a time when no one anticipated that large files would be accessible to a PC, it is severely limited in the file sizes that it can handle. With the development of CD-ROMs, Microsoft created a DOS extension that allows software publishers to access 650MB CDs in a standard fashion—the *Microsoft CD-ROM Extensions* (or MSCDEX). As with most software, MSCDEX offers some vital features (and has a few limitations), but it is required by a vast majority of CD-ROM, CD-R, or CD-RW products when you're working in DOS. Obtaining MSCDEX is not a problem—it is generally provided on the same disk or CD containing the CD drive's low-level device driver. New versions of MSCDEX can be obtained from the Microsoft web site (**www.microsoft.com**).

In actual operation, MSCDEX is loaded in the AUTOEXEC.BAT file. It should be loaded *after* any mouse driver, and loaded *before* any MENU, SHELL, DOSSHELL, or WIN line. It should also be loaded *before* any .BAT file is started. Keep in mind that if a .BAT file loads a network, MSCDEX must be included in the batch file *after* the network driver. Further, MSCDEX must be loaded after that network driver with the **/S** (share) switch in order to hook into the network driver chain. If you want to use the MS-DOS drive caching software (SmartDrive) to buffer the CD-ROM drive(s), load MSCDEX *before* SmartDrive. The MSCDEX **/M** (number of buffers) switch can be set to 0 when using SmartDrive. If you find that SmartDrive is interfering with MPC applications like Video for Windows, you can load SmartDrive *before* MSCDEX. and set the **/M** switch for at least 2. When loading MSCDEX, remember that the MSCDEX **/D** switch *must* match the **/D** label used in the low-level driver. Otherwise, MSCDEX will not load. If SETVER is loaded in the CONFIG.SYS file, be sure to use the latest version of MSCDEX.

Although the vast majority of CD drive bundles include installation routines that automate the installation process for the low-level driver and MSCDEX, you should understand the various command line switches (shown in Table 9-3) that make MSCDEX operate. Understanding these switches may help you to overcome setup problems.

CD-ROM INSTALLATION AND REPLACEMENT

CD-ROM drives are generally easy devices to install or replace. Most are installed as *master* devices located on the secondary IDE/EIDE/UDMA drive controller channel, though a few will coexist as *slave* devices along-side a hard drive or other drive device. The most important issue to remember is that the BIOS will not support the CD-ROM directly (even if the BIOS identifies the CD-ROM at boot time, and even if El Torito support allows you to boot from the CD)—you'll need real-mode drivers for the CD-ROM under DOS, or protected-mode drivers for the CD-ROM under Windows. This part of the chapter covers the guidelines needed to install a basic internal IDE-type CD-ROM.

TABLE 9-3	COMMAND LINE SWITCHES FOR MSCDEX	
SWITCH	**NAME**	**DEFINITION**
/D:x	Device Name	The label used by the low-level device driver when it loads. MSCDEX must match this label for the device driver and MSCDEX to work together. A typical label is MSCD000.
/M:x	Buffers Allocated	The number of 2KB buffers allocated to the CD-ROM drives. There are typically 8 buffers (16KB) for a single drive, and 4 buffers for each additional drive. This number can be set to 1 or 2 when conventional memory space is at a premium.
/L:x	Drive Letter	This is the optional drive letter for the CD-ROM. If this is not specified, the drive will be automatically assigned to the first available letter (usually D:). There must be a LASTDRIVE= entry in CONFIG.SYS to use a letter higher than the default letter. When choosing a letter for the LASTDRIVE entry, do not use Z—otherwise, network drives may not install after MSCDEX.
/N	Verbose Option	This switch forces MSCDEX to show memory usage statistics on the display each time the system boots.
/S	Share Option	This switch is used with CD-ROM installations in network systems.
/K	Kanji Option	Instructs MSCDEX to use Kanji (Japanese) file types on the CD if present.
/E	Expanded Mem.	Allows MSCDEX to use expanded memory for buffers. There must be an expanded memory driver running (EMM386.EXE) with enough available space to use it.

Set Jumper Configurations

An IDE-type CD-ROM drive may be installed as a *master* or *slave* device on any hard drive controller channel. These master/slave settings are handled through one or two jumpers located on the rear of the drive (right next to the 40-pin signal cable connector). One of your first decisions when planning an installation should be to decide the drive's configuration:

■ If you're installing the CD-ROM as the first drive on the secondary drive controller channel, it must be jumpered as the "master" device.

■ If you're installing the CD-ROM drive along side another drive (on either the primary or secondary drive controller channel), the CD-ROM must be jumpered as the "slave" device.

 Refer to the documentation that accompanies your particular CD-ROM drive in order to determine the exact "master/slave" jumper settings. If you do not have the drive documentation handy, check the drive manufacturer's Web site for online information.

A SCSI drive is frequently identified by setting a SCSI ID between 2 and 6. Once again, you must set the ID using a series of jumpers on the rear of the drive, and the ID must be unique for the drive (SCSI devices cannot share IDs).

Attach Cables and Mount the Drive

Follow these steps:

1. Turn off and unplug the PC, then remove the outer cover to expose the computer's drive bays.

2. For an IDE-type drive, attach one end of the 40-pin drive interface cable to the drive controller connector on your motherboard (or drive controller card). For a SCSI drive, attach a 50- or 68-pin SCSI cable to the SCSI host controller. Remember to align pin 1 on the cable (the side of the cable with the blue or red stripe) with pin 1 on the drive controller connector.

3. Locate an available drive bay for the CD drive. Remove the plastic housing covering the drive bay, then slide the drive inside. Locate the four screw holes needed to mount the drive. In some cases, you may need to attach mounting rails to the drive so that the drive will be wide enough to fit in the drive bay. In virtually all cases, you should mount a tray-driven CD drive horizontally (though caddy-loaded CD-ROM drives may sometimes be mounted vertically).

4. Attach the signal cable and the 4-pin power connector to the new drive, then bolt the drive securely into place. Do not overtighten the screws since this may damage the drive. If you do not have an available 4-pin power connector, you may use an appropriate Y adapter if necessary to split power from another drive (preferably the floppy drive).

5. Attach the small 4-pin CD audio signal cable from the CD drive to the CD audio input connector on your sound card. This connection allows you to play music CDs directly through your sound card. Verify that the CD audio cable is compatible with your sound card (otherwise you may need a special cable from the sound card's manufacturer).

Configure the CMOS Setup

Although the CD-ROM *does* require driver support, most current motherboard designs can identify the ATAPI IDE CD-ROM drive in BIOS, so if possible you should configure your computer's BIOS to accept the drive (through the CMOS Setup):

1. Turn the computer on. As your computer starts up, watch for a message that describes how to run the CMOS Setup (for example, Press F1 for Setup). Press the appropriate key to start the CMOS Setup program.

2. Select the basic setup where you can specify hard drive settings and choose the drive location occupied by the CD-ROM drive (that is, primary slave, secondary slave, or secondary master—depending on how you've physically jumpered and installed the drive).

3. Select *automatic drive detection* if available—this option will automatically identify the new drive. If your BIOS does *not* provide automatic drive detection, select NONE or NOT INSTALLED for the CD-ROM, and rely on drivers ONLY.

4. Save the settings and exit the CMOS Setup program. Your computer will automatically reboot.

Reassemble the Computer

Double-check all of your signal and power cables to verify that they are secure, then tuck the cables gently into the computer's chassis. Check that there are no loose tools, screws, or cables inside the chassis. Now reattach the computer's outer housing(s).

Install the Software

In order to complete your CD drive installation, you'll need to install the software drivers and applications software that accompanied the drive on disk or CD. Windows 9x/Me systems will generally detect the presence of the new CD drive and prompt you for the protected-mode drivers (or select appropriate drivers automatically). Under DOS, you may need to run an "installer" routine to add the real-mode drivers to your system and to update your CONFIG.SYS and AUTOEXEC.BAT files to load those drivers. If there's no real-mode "installer," you'll need to update your startup files manually (see "CD-ROM Software" earlier in the chapter). After you install the drivers and reboot the system, the CD-ROM should be identified, assigned a drive letter, and ready for use.

The CD-R Drive

While CD-ROM drives bring a great deal of reliable storage potential to the PC, it has only recently been possible to *record* CDs on the desktop—the technology required to create audio and computer CDs has traditionally been terribly complex and expensive, and limited by PC computing power of the day. Since the early 1990s, recordable CD (or CD-R) technology has steadily become more reliable and economical. CD recorders allow huge files, databases, and multimedia presentations to be developed and distributed with ease. Today, virtually any Pentium PC (or later) with a SCSI or UDMA interface and 1GB or more of hard drive space can support a CD-R drive for under $300. This part of the chapter explores the fundamentals of CD-R drives and explains the issues of CD-R technology and media.

CD-R MEDIA VARIATIONS

The appearance of recordable media is very similar to that of the "pressed" CD media illustrated in Figure 9-2—but with two important variations. First, the polycarbonate CD-R substrate is pre-formed with a track spiral into which data will be written during the recording process. The substrate is then coated with a greenish or bluish translucent layer and backed with a reflective layer of gold, and finally a protective lacquer is applied over the gold layer. These translucent and gold layers allow the recorded pits and lands to be read back after the recording is complete. It is important to note that CD-R media can only be written *once* and cannot be erased (though additional data can be written to a CD-R disc in subsequent sessions). Writing errors will render the disc unusable.

Orange Book Certified Media

The Orange Book (Part II) is the primary specification for CD-R media, and all CD-R media should meet the Orange Book criteria for recordability and playback. Philips and Sony (the originators of the Orange Book specification) provide Orange Book certification of CD-R media. If you want best media compatibility and reliability, CD-R media that is *not* "Orange Book certified" should generally be avoided.

High-Speed Media

It takes a finite amount of time to write information to CD-R or CD-RW discs—the faster a drive can write, the less time it will take to complete the operation. For example, a 16x drive can write a disc faster than a 10x drive. The problem is that there is often trouble with ordinary CD-R/CD-RW media writing at speeds above 4x. If you try ordinary media in faster drives (above 4x), you'll usually see an error such as a *media error* or *writing error*. This is why most drive makers will suggest that you try lowering the writing speeds when you see errors. To keep pace with today's faster writing speeds, you can use "high speed" media. CD-R discs are often rated for their top writing speed (for example, "certified to 12x writing speeds"). CD-R discs are also generally backward-compatible, so CD-R media rated for higher speeds should work in slower drives. If you have a fast CD-R drive, be sure to use suitable high-speed media.

However, things are a little bit different for high-speed CD-RW discs. The high-speed CD-RW media format *prevents* older 1x to 4x CD-RW drives from writing to it. Trying to write high-speed discs in older CD-RW drives may result in a variety of errors seemingly unrelated to the media, so you'll need a drive with 4x or faster writing speeds in order to use high-speed CD-RW media (you can't upgrade an older drive to be compatible with high-speed media). However, you can still read high-speed CD-RW media in 1x to 4x drives (and other Multi-Read drives). These CD-RW compatibility factors led to the introduction of a new CD-RW system, complete with a proprietary and separately licensed logo, known as "Compact Disc Re-Writable, High Speed." You can look for this logo to verify that your CD-RW disc is high-speed media. Similarly, you can record only high-speed media with CD-RW drives showing the high-speed CD-RW logo.

MULTISESSION CDS

One of the problems with recording early CDs is that once the CD was written, it could not be appended. This means if 123MB of data is written to a 650MB disc, the remaining 527MB of storage potential on the disc is lost. CD developers sought a means of adding new data to a CD which has been previously recorded (but still has unused space available). This *multisession* capability means that a CD is written in "sessions," with subsequent sessions linked to previous sessions—allowing the CD to be systematically filled.

A CD-R recorder that supports multisession recording can write a disc that will have multiple sessions linked together—each session containing its own lead-in, program, and lead out areas. In effect, each session is treated as a different CD. Any multisession-capable CD drive can access the data in any session. By comparison, a pressed CD-ROM or a CD-R written in Disc At Once mode contains only one lead-in area, program area, and lead-out area.

Multisession Problems

Multisession technology is clearly important because it allows you to add data to a CD-R disc incrementally (a bit at a time) as needed. This makes it possible to eventually utilize the entire disc. However, there are two general problems reading multisession discs: either you can read data only in the first session, or you can read data only in the last session.

If you can read data only in the *first* session of the disc, there is probably a compatibility issue between the disc and the drive. For example, you may have recorded the disc in standard Yellow Book CD-ROM (Mode 1) format, while your multisession CD-ROM drive works only with CD-ROM XA (Mode 2) multisession discs. In other cases, the CD-ROM drive may be too old to support multisession discs at all. Try the disc on several current drives and see if another drive will read subsequent sessions. If so, you may need to upgrade your drive to ensure multisession compatibility.

If you can only read data in the last session of the disc, the disc may have been recorded improperly. For example, you may have forgotten to link your new data (the last session) with data previously recorded on the disc. Often, you would need to re-record this disc and verify that all sessions are linked. However, some of the later CD pre-mastering software (such as Easy CD Creator Deluxe Edition at **www.roxio.com/en/products/ecdc/index.html**) will allow you to switch to different sessions using a "session selector" feature. When the selected session is *enabled*, it can be read from the CD drive as if it were the only session on the disc (any files linked from previous sessions on the same disc will still be readable). Check your own CD-R software to see if it supports such a feature.

FIXATION VS. FINALIZATION

Each session written to a disc (whether multisession or single session) must be *fixed* before the session can be read. *Fixation* is the process of writing the session's lead-in and lead-out information to the disc. This process finishes a writing session and creates a table of contents. Fixation is *required* before a CD-ROM or CD audio player can play the disc. Discs that are "fixated for append" can have additional sessions recorded later (each with their own session lead-in and lead-out) creating a multisession disc. When a disc is *finalized*, the absolute lead-in and lead-out for the entire disc are written, along with information that tells the drive not to look for subsequent sessions. This final table of contents (TOC) conforms to the ISO 9660 file standard.

DISC-AT-ONCE

Disc-at-Once is a CD writing mode that requires data to be written continuously, without any interruptions, until the entire data set is transferred to the CD-R. The complete lead-in, program, and lead-out are written in a single writing process. All of the information to be recorded needs to be staged on the computer's hard disk prior to recording in the Disc-at-Once mode. Recording in the Disc-at-Once mode eliminates the linking, run-in, and run-out blocks associated with multisession and packet recording (a.k.a. DirectCD) modes (which often are interpreted as uncorrectable errors during the glass mastering process).

The Disk-at-Once mode is usually preferred for discs that are sent to a CD-ROM replication facility when CD-R is the source media.

TRACK-AT-ONCE

The Track-at-Once writing mode is the key to multisession capability, and allows a session to be written in a number of discrete write events, called *tracks* because the written sessions contain complete "tracks" of information. The disc may be removed from the writer and read in another writer (given the proper software) before the session is fixated.

Track-at-Once writing is a form of incremental write that mandates a minimum track length of 300 blocks and a maximum of 99 tracks per disc. A track written "at once" has 150 blocks of overhead for run-in, run-out, pre-gap, and linking purposes. On the other hand, *packet write* is a method where several write events are allowed *within* a track, thus reducing the demands of overhead data. Each writing "packet" is bounded by seven blocks of data: four for run-in, two for run-out, and one for linking.

CARING FOR RECORDABLE CDS

As a rule, recordable CDs are as rugged and reliable as ordinary "pressed" CDs. Still, you should exercise some additional rules in the careful handling and storage of recordable media:

- *Maintain a comfortable environment.* Don't expose recordable discs to sunlight or other strong light for long periods of time. Also, avoid high heat and humidity, which can damage the physical disc. Always keep blank or recorded media in clean jewel cases for best protection.

- *Don't write on the disc.* Don't use alcohol-based pens to write on discs—the ink may eventually eat through the top (lacquer) surface and damage your data. Also don't use ball-point or other sharp-tipped pens because you may scratch right through the lacquer surface and damage the reflective gold layer (and ruin your data).

- *Don't use labels on the disc.* Don't put labels on discs unless they are *expressly* designed for recordable CDs. The glue may eat through the lacquer surface just as some inks do, or the label may unbalance the disc and cause problems in reading it back or recording subsequent sessions. Never try to remove a label—you might tear off the lacquer and some of the reflecting surface.

- *Watch your media quality.* Many different brands of recordable CD media are now available in the marketplace. Quality varies from brand to brand (and even from batch to batch within a given brand). If you have repeated problems that can be traced to the blank media you are using, try using a different brand or even a different batch of the same brand.

- *Don't use Kodak Photo CDs.* Avoid the use of Kodak Photo CDs on everyday CD recorders (unless the drive is specifically listed as supporting Photo CDs). Kodak Photo CDs are designed to be used only with Kodak Photo CD professional workstations. Although the discs are inexpensive, they have a protection bit that prevents them from being written on many CD recorders. When you attempt to write these discs on the recorders that recognize the protection bit, you will receive an error message.

CREATING A BOOTABLE CD

When the hard drive fails to boot a PC, technicians have traditionally been forced to deal with boot disks. While doing this could certainly start a system to the A: prompt, there was hardly any opportunity for sophisticated diagnostics, and diagnostics with an operating system such as Windows was out of the question. With the adoption of the El Torito standard, BIOS support made it possible to boot from the CD drive. This opened many possible applications for "bootable CDs" and allowed the creation of powerful recovery CDs that could boot and restore a crippled system to its original state—most commercial PCs sold today come with one or more *recovery CDs* for just this purpose. Creating a bootable CD allows you to combine operating systems with boot and diagnostic features to test defective systems or to automate the process of new system setups. The problem is that placing bootable code on a CD has generally been a cumbersome, time consuming, and error-prone process. Let's examine a more modern approach that will allow you to create a fully bootable CD for your system.

Checking for Support

Of course, a bootable CD won't do much good unless the PC supports it. Start your CMOS Setup and check the Boot Order entry. In most cases, the order is set as "A: then C:," but you will probably be able to select the particular device(s) used to boot the system. If you can select CD-ROM as a boot device, your BIOS supports bootable CDs. Most systems manufactured after 1996 will support bootable CDs. If you're dealing with an older system that does not allow the CD-ROM as a boot device, a BIOS upgrade or motherboard replacement may be needed to update the system.

The Boot Record

When a bootable CD is created, a *boot record* is put at the very beginning of the disc (just as it is with a bootable floppy or hard disk). This record specifies whether the CD is to emulate a floppy or hard disk drive and contains a pointer to the location of the actual boot image file. The El Torito specification was designed to be completely compatible with the ISO 9660 CD standard, and it adds to the ISO 9660 specification by requiring a boot record at sector 11 of the last session on the CD. The boot record contains an absolute sector number that points to the "boot catalog," but there is no restriction on the location of the boot catalog. The catalog contains a list of entries describing all the "boot images" present on the CD. Again, there is no restriction on where the boot images can be on the CD. There can be any number of them, but they fall into three different types:

- *Bootable emulation* causes the image to be mapped to drive A: or C:—resembling (or emulating) a conventional bootable storage device.

- *Non-bootable emulation* maps the image as a conventional storage device, and allocates the last drive letter to it.

- *No emulation* is a special mode that loads the image into memory and executes it directly—extremely useful when developing copy protection or "smart" CDs designed for a variety of systems. For example, the "no emulation" mode is used in the Windows NT operating system CDs.

In addition, system vendors can create multi-image CDs where the boot image is selected dynamically by the system BIOS, but doing this requires a lot of manual assembling and editing (and is beyond the scope of this book).

A CD can be configured to boot as drive A: or C:. To boot as drive A:, the boot image must be made in the same format as a 1.2MB, 1.4MB, or 2.88MB floppy disk. The first floppy disk drive (if present) will become the B: drive. If the system has a second floppy disk drive, it will not be accessible. In effect, the bootable disc will "take the place of" the emulated drive. If the CD is set to boot as the C: drive, it replaces the normal hard disk drive C: and has no size limit other than that of the CD itself. However, the source drive image must have only one partition. This partition must be both the first entry in the partition table and a standard DOS partition.

A Basic Bootable CD

Most current CD-R publishing packages are capable of reading a floppy disk and creating a boot image from it. With the appropriate menu choices made, the recording software will automatically "apply" the boot image to the CD image. With this method, it is extremely easy to make a bootable CD. Some of the more advanced packages (like Nero) can create a bootable CD from any disk image as well as allow fine-tuning of parameters such as the emulation type and startup message. The basic process for making a bootable CD from a floppy disk is described next.

1. Create a bootable floppy disk that has all of the required driver and startup software on it (such as a Windows 98/Me Startup Disk with generic CD-ROM support). Remember that you'll need a CD driver in order to use the CD in a conventional manner once the system has finished booting. It is wise to use a generic CD driver if you plan on using the finished CD in a few different systems.

2. Make sure that any path names in the CONFIG.SYS and AUTOEXEC.BAT files do *not* specify drive letters.

3. Verify that your boot process does *not* attempt to write to the disk. Set the read-only flag on all files and write-protect the disk if possible. If your system tries to write to the CD on boot-up, the system will crash.

4. Test this disk thoroughly in whatever PC environment(s) you plan to use it.

5. Once you're happy with the bootable disk, create the CD with your CD-R publishing package. Selecting the "bootable" option will usually prompt for the floppy disk. Put any other data (for example, diagnostics or an operating system) onto the CD in the *same* session.

Tips for Bootable CDs

Bootable CDs aren't particularly difficult to create, but there are some nuances that you should be aware of. Here are several important tips to keep in mind as you develop your arsenal of bootable CDs:

- A CD-RW drive is an extremely useful tool when experimenting with bootable CDs. Although your test CD-RW may be unusable in some standard CD drives, it can be used on the mastering system if the CD-RW drive is set as the primary CD, and this is enough for general test purposes. If you're planning on making a variety of bootable CDs (or just experimenting), CD-RW has the obvious advantage of media cost savings because you're not wasting CD-R discs trying to get things right.

- When making hard drive image CDs, an old hard disk drive around 650MB in size makes a useful addition to your mastering system. Since hard disk images have certain partitioning requirements, it's much easier to have a whole disk to use for your layout if you are doing this type of work.

- Under Windows NT, you'll need to have administrative rights if you are creating hard disk images (this requires access to all disk sectors).

- It is possible that you will encounter older CDs that start to boot, fail immediately, and hang your system. They do this because there was no initial standard for the first few sectors of CDs. Some may contain a correct "validation entry" without any of the other required boot files. Such CDs should be discarded.

Recording Software

Until fairly recently, bootable CDs had to be made manually with a combination of low-level tools (for instance, hex editors). Utility programs such as BOOTISO and DISKIMG were used to read bootable disks and write images to disk files. These disk images were then hex edited and manually added to the CD layout. Now that most current CD writing software is able to make bootable CDs from floppy or hard disk images, the process of bootable CD creation has become much easier.

Notable software packages include Easy CD Creator, Win-On-CD, CDRWIN, HyCD, and Nero. Generally speaking, Nero is an extremely powerful tool that offers complete control of the CD writing process and that can create bootable CDs for many platforms. It can also create *oversized* CDs that can be used to gain a small amount of copy protection. Many of these software products are available in demo, shareware, or evaluation versions, so you can try each product to see if it suits your needs *before* making a purchase.

Using Easy CD Creator

You can see how recording software has matured to support bootable CDs by examining a typical CD creation process with a product like Adaptec's Easy CD Creator (**www.roxio.com**):

1. Create a bootable DOS disk with FORMAT A: /S.

2. Copy the real-mode CD-ROM device driver, MSCDEX.EXE, SYS.COM, and XCOPY.EXE to the floppy.

3. Create a simple CONFIG.SYS file with the following lines:

   ```
   lastdrive=z
   device=my_CDrom_driver.sys /d:restore
   ```

   (where *my_Cdrom_driver.sys* is the name of your CD-ROM driver).

4. Create a simple AUTOEXEC.BAT file with the line:

   ```
   MSCDEX.exe /d:restore /l:z
   ```

   (where *z* is the drive letter of the CD).

5. Now copy your startup files to the boot disk.

6. Launch Easy CD Creator.

7. Add all of your hard drive's contents to the Data CD layout page. Doing this will allow you to do things like including your operating system and diagnostics on the CD. In practice, you may want to add only selected contents to the Data CD layout.

8. Select File, CD Layout Properties, and Data Settings.

9. Check the Bootable CD box.

10. Select ISO 9660 and click on the Properties button. Select Any MS-DOS 8+3 name.

11. Proceed with creating the CD. You will be asked to insert a bootable disk—insert the disk you created at the beginning of this process.

If you wish, you can add the keyboard files you need for your particular country. Copy the same entries you find in the C: drive CONFIG.SYS and AUTOEXEC.BAT (without any paths) to the new disk's CONFIG.SYS and AUTOEXEC.BAT files, along with the referenced files. You might also want to include FDISK.EXE and FORMAT.COM to clear up or modify the partition (especially useful after a virus attack).

If you're using SCSI CD drivers, you'll need to include the SCSI host adapter driver and its reference in your startup file(s). Keep in mind that not all SCSI controllers and motherboards can be used to boot from CD-ROM.

Test the Bootable CD

For an IDE-type CD drive, you just have to change the setting of booting sequence in BIOS to CDROM, C:, A:, then reboot the PC with the bootable CD in CD drive. For SCSI CD-ROM drives, the booting sequence of the motherboard BIOS should be changed to SCSI, IDE. If the BIOS doesn't have this option, you'll just have to temporarily set all the IDE HDD entries to None or Not Installed. Next, enter the BIOS setting of your SCSI card. For example, in Adaptec's AHA 2940U, go into Advanced Configuration

Options and enable the options: Host Adapter BIOS (Configuration Utility Reserve BIOS Space) and BIOS Support for Bootable CD-ROM. Then reboot the PC with the bootable CD in the drive.

UPGRADING CD-R/CD-RW FIRMWARE

You may be able to update the firmware used in your CD-R or CD-RW drive. Doing this may be necessary to correct bugs or fix drive compatibility problems with the system. The following steps offer a guideline that you can refer to when upgrading CD-R/CD-RW firmware.

The upgrade steps are based on an internal Plextor SCSI CD-R drive. You should always refer to the Web page or README file that accompanies the new firmware download. Be sure to download the correct firmware version for your drive—installing the wrong firmware can permanently disable the drive.

1. Power off your system completely.

2. Locate the CD-R drive and place its "flash" jumper in the flash upgrade position.

3. Make sure the power cable and the signal cable (SCSI or IDE) are still connected.

4. Power on your system and boot "clean" to a command-line prompt.

5. Make sure that the CD-R appears in "program mode." For an internal Plextor SCSI CD-R, you'll see that all four LEDs on the front panel of the drive are blinking.

6. When the system comes up, execute the new firmware program (FIRM412.EXE), which you may receive or download from the manufacturer, and use the new firmware (*.BIN) file.

7. When the .EXE applications starts, specify the location of the .BIN file.

8. Click the Update button to begin the flash process.

9. When the Update button becomes highlighted again, the flash process is complete.

10. Power off the system and reset the CD-R drive's "flash" jumper to its original position.

11. Power on the system normally.

The CD-RW Drive

CD recording offers a powerful tool for backing up important files or archiving completed work. Recording also makes it possible to distribute projects or multimedia presentations on simple and inexpensive media. The problem with CD recording is that it's a one-time deal—once the media is written, it cannot be erased or rewritten. Within the last several years, *rewritable* CD technology (or CD-RW) has developed a lot of interest by allowing specialized optical CD media to be written, erased, then rewritten as easily as for a floppy disk. Such capability allows CD rewriters to be used for large local file storage (rather than simple archiving). Almost any Pentium PC (or later) with a SCSI or UDMA interface can support a CD-RW drive. This part of the chapter outlines the important points of CD-RW technology and media.

BURNPROOF TECHNOLOGY

BurnProof technology is licensed from Sanyo and is employed by a growing number of CD-R/RW drive manufacturers as a means of "failsafe" disc writing. When a CD-R/RW drive performs a write operation, it demands a constant, uninterrupted flow of data to operate the writing laser. If the flow of data stops, the write operation fails, and the disc (namely the writable disc) is ruined. To prevent this kind of interruption, every CD-R/RW drive has a buffer—which is simply RAM that serves as a temporary storage area. However, the buffer can be emptied quickly (especially when you write at high speeds). It can also empty if you use other applications in the background (such as playing games or watching movies) while writing, or if your source drive cannot read data fast enough. Any of these factors can produce a "buffer underrun error."

BurnProof technology is able to turn off the writing laser if a buffer underrun occurs and to "remember" where the writing stopped on the disc. Once data is available again, the drive picks up where it left off, and the writing process continues. Using a drive with BurnProof technology (such as the Plextor 16x10x40 CD-RW) allows you to work on other tasks in the background without worrying about buffer underruns and ruined discs. It's a worthwhile technology that should be seriously considered when selecting a fast new CD-R/RW drive.

UDF CONCEPTS

The ISO 9660 file system has long been the established standard in CD-ROM and CD recording (Mac systems use the HFS approach). In fact, ISO 9660 is one of the key elements that propelled CD-ROM drives to the status of "standard equipment" on the PC by the early 1990s. With the broad introduction of CD-RW drives, however, ISO 9660 has been replaced by the *Universal Data Format* (UDF) file system. This section of the chapter offers some essential background on UDF and explains how the use of UDF affects the compatibility of CD-RW discs with existing CD-ROM and CD-RW drives.

Let's start with some perspective on ISO 9660. As you saw earlier in the chapter, the ISO 9660 file system grew out of the original High Sierra file system of the late 1980s. All the files read on your CD-ROM or recorded on your CD-R use the ISO 9660 format. Both Windows and Mac operating systems can read ISO 9660 discs because they provide built-in ISO 9660 readers—the "reader" is totally transparent to the end user. While ISO 9660 is just fine for existing CD-ROM and CD-R drives, it is really not sufficient to support the new generation of CD-RW drives or the emerging DVD drives. CD-RW drives require that files be added incrementally (one file at a time), *without* a waste of overhead space, and that individual files can be erased "at will" to make room on a disc. In addition, DVD drives require a file system that can support drives at least 4GB in size. These demands are well beyond the scope of ISO 9660.

UDF addresses all of these concerns by providing a format that can add and erase individual files as needed as well as support the large disc space promised by DVD. Another advantage of UDF is its "cross-platform" compatibility—a UDF disc can be read by both a Mac and Windows platform. For example, a file could be written using a Mac, then read back on a Windows PC. The UDF file format is also able to maintain Mac file attributes (for example, icons, resource forks, and file types), while ISO 9660 cannot.

Working with UDF

The *DirectCD* technology used with CD-RW drives reads and writes to the CD-RW disc using the UDF format. If you're working on a PC with a CD-RW drive (or plan on installing one yourself), chances are that you'll be using a DirectCD applet to invoke UDF on that disc. There are currently two versions of UDF. UDF 1.02 is the version used on current DVD-ROM and DVD-Video discs. UDF 1.5 is a superset of 1.02 that adds support for CD-R and CD-RW drives. If you're using DirectCD under Windows 9x/Me today, chances are that you're using UDF 3.0x or later. You can learn about the history of DirectCD at **www.roxio.com/en/support/dcdwin/dcdwinvhist.html**.

Disc Capacity Under UDF

An important issue to keep in mind when using DirectCD is that you never get the same data capacity from a CD-RW disc that you do from a CD-R disc under ISO 9660. Traditional CD-Rs under ISO 9660 can provide a full 650MB from a blank 74 minute disc. DirectCD formats CD-RW discs in fixed-length packets that support the random erase feature. This requires more space on disc than variable-length packets (which vary in length to fit the size of the data), so it's normal to have about 550MB left for writing after formatting.

DirectCD also uses a technique called *sparing*. If you were to erase and write to the same spot on CD-RW media over and over, that hot spot would eventually wear out (after a few thousand writes)—even if the rest of the disc was still unused. Sparing is a technique that writes data evenly over the disc, significantly extending its life. However, sparing also requires significant overhead.

The situation is a little different for CD-R discs formatted with DirectCD. Since CD-R media does not require random erase (CD-R is write-once media and can not be erased), fixed packet writing and sparing is not required, so CD-R discs have over 600MB of free space after being formatted for DirectCD.

UDF and Disc Compatibility

There's only one little problem with UDF—Windows 95 does not support it natively. The DirectCD drivers installed with a CD-RW drive will allow Windows 95 to read UDF discs in a CD-RW drive, but using DirectCD (UDF) discs in other drives is a little trickier. When DirectCD begins writing data to a disc, it opens a session. Before any CD-ROM drive can read a disc, the session must be closed. When you eject a disc from a CD-RW drive using the DirectCD applet, you can choose to close the disc to ISO 9660. If you do *not* close the disc to ISO 9660 when you eject it, you cannot read it on a CD-ROM drive—you must read it on a CD-R or CD-RW drive fitted with DirectCD. This is a limitation of CD-ROM drives, not the DirectCD software. As a rule, you can expect a ISO 9660 CD-R disc to play on any CD-R or CD-RW drive. On the other hand, a CD-RW disc will usually *not* play on an older CD-R drive and might not play on a newer CD-R drive without a UDF Reader utility.

Windows 98/SE (and subsequent versions of Windows) with DVD support should fully support UDF.

If you close the disc to UDF, you can still read the UDF format, but you'll need a "multi-read" CD-ROM drive and a UDF Reader utility. For example, when you install Adaptec's UDF Reader in your system, you should be able to read your closed session CD-R and CD-RW discs on CD-ROM drives regardless of whether they are ISO 9660 or UDF.

Multi-Read CD-ROM Drives

UDF reader utilities are designed to support the new generation of Multi-Read CD-ROM drives. Multi-Read is a specification developed and endorsed by the Optical Storage Technology Association (OSTA) and accepted by the industry at large. Most new CD-ROM drives on the market today (manufactured after mid-1997) are Multi-Read-compatible. To be Multi-Read compliant, a CD-ROM drive must be able to:

■   read CD-RW discs

■   read packet-written discs (both CD-R and CD-RW)

■   support the operating system to utilize UDF 1.5 (or later)

There are some non-Multi-Read CD-ROM drives that can read UDF formatted CD-R media (but not CD-RW media) using an appropriate UDF Reader utility.

UDF Readers

A UDF reader enables Multi-Read CD-ROM drives to read closed-session UDF formatted CD-R and CD-RW media under Windows 9x/Me and the Macintosh operating system. The UDF reader for Windows is called UDF Reader Driver, and the UDF Reader for Mac OS is called UDF Volume Access. UDF readers are particularly useful if you're using DirectCD to *record* data to a CD-RW disc, because you will then be able to read the CD-RW disc in a Multi-Read CD-ROM drive. Without a UDF reader, you could read the UDF disc only in another CD-RW drive using DirectCD. Since UDF is designed to be a cross-platform file format, UDF Readers also allow you to interchange UDF-formatted discs between Mac and Windows systems.

Most companies that develop DirectCD software (such as Adaptec) already offer UDF Reader utilities free of charge. You can download the Adaptec UDF Reader from the Adaptec Web site at **www.adaptec.com** or more directly from their patch/upgrade site at **www.adaptec.com/worldwide/ support/driverindex.html**. For more information, you could also send e-mail to Adaptec at **udfreader@adaptec.com**.

UDF Reader Compliance
Since UDF is intended to provide a universal file interchange format, any UDF Reader utility *should* be able to read all UDF 1.5 formatted media (media formatted with DirectCD). However, there is no independent third-party organization to test for UDF compliance, so there is no guarantee that all media claiming to be "UDF formatted" will be readable by every UDF Reader under all conditions. If you have trouble reading a UDF disc with one particular reader utility, you might wish to try another reader utility.

UDF and Audio CDs
A popular use of CD-R and CD-RW discs has been to record music for playback on an ordinary CD player (for example, copying old vinyl LPs to CD). While this is a tried and true process for CD-R discs recorded under ISO 9660, this will *not* work with UDF discs recorded with DirectCD. Audio files recorded under UDF will *not* work when played back in a commercial CD player. But audio files played back on a CD-R or CD-RW drive under DirectCD should work normally.

Windows 98 and UDF
While Windows 95 does not provide direct support for UDF, Windows 98/SE/Me will support UDF 1.02 for DVD-ROM and DVD Video discs. However, Windows 98 doesn't provide native support for UDF 1.5, so DirectCD software and UDF readers may still be required after Windows 98 is installed. Windows 98/SE and Windows Me do not require a separate UDF reader.

USING DIRECTCD
There are some simple rules to follow when preparing and working with CD-RW drives. Preparing new discs, writing data, adding data, erasing data, ejecting the disc, and recovering damaged discs are the most typical procedures that you'll need to master. This part of the chapter outlines these essential steps—though you should refer to your CD-RW user's manual for specific information.

Preparing a Data CD
Use the following steps to start DirectCD and prepare a blank CD-RW disc for reading and writing data:

1. Start the computer and insert a blank CD-RW disc in the CD-RW drive. After a few seconds, a screen will appear with the message: "Please select the type of CD you wish to create." If the DirectCD Disc Ready window appears, the disc has already been prepared and you can start writing data to it immediately. (If no screen appears after about 15 seconds, the disc may not be blank, or it may have an unreadable format—or the Auto Insert Notification option may be disabled.)

2. Select the option: "Click here to create a data CD that will be accessible through a drive letter" (that is, as you would use a floppy drive). The Format Disc screen appears.

3. If you're formatting a CD-R disc, click Next on the Format Disc screen.

4. If you're formatting a CD-RW disc, you can choose between two formatting options—click the Advanced button that appears on the Format Disc screen. When the next screen appears, select either Fast Format or Full Format and click OK.

It's often easier to select the Fast Format option, which lets you start writing to the CD-RW disc almost immediately (while the disc is formatted in the background). A Full Format requires you to wait about an hour until the formatting is complete before you can write to the disc.

5. When the Name Your Disc screen appears, type a name for the disc and click Finish. Disc formatting begins—when the DirectCD Disc Ready window appears, the formatting is complete.

6. Click OK. The DirectCD disc is ready for you to write data to it.

Writing Data to a DirectCD Disc

Once your CD is formatted as a DirectCD disc, you can write data to it in several different ways:

- Drag and drop files from Windows Explorer right onto the CD-RW icon.
- Select Save As from a Windows 98/Me/NT application File menu, then select the drive letter of your CD-RW.
- Use the Send To command.
- Use the MS-DOS command prompts from a DOS window in Windows 98/Me/NT.

Ejecting a DirectCD Disc

DirectCD gives you several formatting options when you eject a DirectCD disc from the CD-RW drive. The options depend on what kind of disc DirectCD detects in the drive and how you want to use the disc. Follow these steps to eject a DirectCD disc:

1. Push the Eject button on the front of the CD-RW drive or right-click on the CD icon on the taskbar and select Eject from the drop-down list box—the Eject Disc screen appears.

2. Carefully read the text that appears on the screen and (if options are presented) select the option you require.

3. Click Finish to eject the disc from the CD-RW drive.

Erasing a DirectCD Disc

If you're using CD-RW discs, you can actually erase files from the disc and use the recovered space to write new files. However, if you "delete" files from a CD-R disc, the files become invisible to the file system (that is, Windows Explorer) but the space they occupy is *not* made available for other files. So "deleting" files from a CD-R disc will *not* increase the available free space on the disc. Follow these steps to erase the contents of a DirectCD disc:

1. While in Windows Explorer, select the file(s) you want to erase.

2. Select Delete from the File menu.

3. Click Yes to confirm that you want to erase the files from the disc.

4. DirectCD erases the selected file(s) from the disc.

Fixing an Unreadable Disc

If no window appears on the screen (after about 15 seconds) when you insert a disc in the CD-RW drive, the disc may have an unreadable format. DirectCD has a ScanDisc application that may be able to recover data on the disc and allow you to write to it and read from it again. Follow these steps to use ScanDisc:

1. Double-click the CD icon on the right side of the Windows taskbar. If the disc is unreadable, the ScanDisc window will appear.

2. Read the text in the window, then click the ScanDisc button.

3. Wait while ScanDisc repairs the disc. A message will appear on the screen when ScanDisc is finished.

Disabling DirectCD

Ideally, DirectCD should load each time Windows 98/Me starts and provide your CD-RW drive with UDF support for CD-R and CD-RW discs. There are times, however, when DirectCD may suffer compatibility problems that affect system stability and performance. If you suspect trouble with DirectCD, you can disable the utility by disabling the DirectCD drivers in your Automatic Skip Driver agent (under the System Information utility)—once you reboot, the DirectCD drivers should not load. If you need to resolve the trouble on a more permanent basis, it's usually a good idea to uninstall DirectCD through the Add/Remove Programs wizard (then install an updated version of DirectCD later).

CARING FOR REWRITABLE CDS

As a rule, rewritable CDs are as rugged and reliable as ordinary "pressed" CDs. Still, you should exercise some rules in the careful handling and storage of rewritable media:

■ *Maintain a comfortable environment.* Don't expose rewritable discs to sunlight or other strong light for long periods of time. Also avoid high heat and humidity, which can damage the physical disc. Always keep blank or recorded media in clean jewel cases for best protection.

■ *Don't write on the disc.* Don't use alcohol-based pens to write on discs—the ink may eventually eat through the top (lacquer) surface and damage your data. Also don't use ball-point or other sharp-tipped pens, because you may scratch right through the lacquer surface and damage the reflective gold layer (and ruin your data).

■ *Don't use labels on the disc.* Don't put labels on discs unless they are *expressly* designed for rewritable CDs. The glue may eat through the lacquer surface just as some inks do, or the label may unbalance the disc and cause problems in reading it back or recording subsequent sessions. Never try to remove a label—you might tear off the lacquer and some of the reflecting surface.

■ *Watch your media quality.* Many different brands of rewritable CD media are now available in the marketplace. Quality varies from brand to brand (and even from batch to batch within a given brand). If you have repeated problems that can be traced to the blank media you are using, try using a different brand or even a different batch of the same brand.

■ *Don't use Kodak Photo CDs.* Avoid the use of Kodak Photo CDs on everyday CD recorders. Kodak Photo CDs are designed to be used only with Kodak Photo CD professional workstations. Although the discs are inexpensive, they have a protection bit that prevents them from being written on many CD recorders. When you attempt to write these discs on the recorders that do not recognize the protection bit, you will receive an error message.

■   *Be careful about power.* If you lose power while writing to your CD-RW (or if you exit an application or press CTRL-ALT-DEL) while writing to CD, you may be able to salvage your rewritable CD. Leave the CD in the drive—do *not* open the tray. Turn the machine off, then turn it back on. Reenter the application you were using. Once the application tries to access the CD-RW drive, the recovery operation will make it appear that the last session is there. However, only a part of the CD's directory may be there—your rewritable CD is still usable if you can read that directory. Repeat the entire copy operation to make sure that your files are copied successfully.

Troubleshooting CD Drives

CD drives typically install and operate with a minimum of difficulty, but compatibility issues, poor media quality, outdated driver versions, conflicting software applets, and even operating system versions can cause problems with CD drives. As a technician, you should understand the common symptoms and solutions that occur most frequently. This part of the chapter focuses on the troubleshooting procedures for CD-ROM, CD-R, and CD-RW drives.

CHANGING DRIVE LETTERS

Windows 9x/Me will assign a drive letter to each CD drive in the system at start time. Although the initial assignment is automatic, you can adjust the drive letter if necessary. Use the following steps to change a CD drive letter:

1.   Click Start, highlight Settings, and then click Control Panel.
2.   Double-click the System icon, then click the Device Manager tab.
3.   Highlight the CD-ROM drive you want to change, then click the Properties button.
4.   Click the Settings tab (Figure 9-11).
5.   In the Reserved Drive Letters section, set Start Drive Letter and End Drive Letter to the drive letter you want the CD-ROM drive to use. Click OK until you return to Control Panel.
6.   Restart the computer for your changes to take effect.

AUTO INSERT NOTIFICATION

You may notice that the CD drive light blinks every few seconds. This may occur even if there is no read operation in progress and even if there is no disc in the drive. This is usually a normal side-effect of the Auto Insert Notification (AIN) feature of Windows 9x/Me, which allows a disc to be automatically detected and launched when inserted in the drive. Normally, the AIN is a harmless feature, but there may be some performance-sensitive programs that are affected by AIN. Follow these steps to disable AIN:

1.   Open the Control Panel and double-click the System icon.
2.   Click the Device Manager tab, double-click CD-ROM, and then double-click the desired CD drive.
3.   Click the Settings tab (as in Figure 9-11), then click the Auto Insert Notification check box to clear it.
4.   Click the Close button. Restart your computer when prompted to do so.

If your computer contains a SCSI controller, Windows polls the SCSI bus periodically to determine the status of the bus and installed devices. On some computers, the disk drive access light on the front

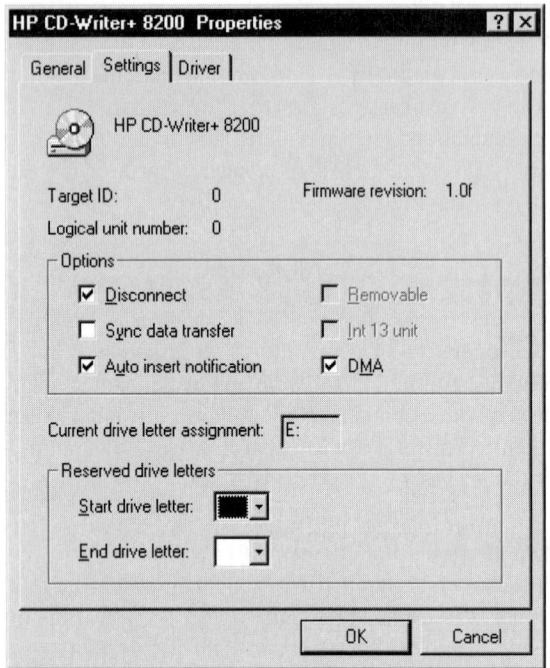

FIGURE 9-11   Changing the CD drive letter through the drive's Properties dialog

panel turns on when any SCSI device (or the SCSI bus itself) is accessed. If the computer contains a SCSI CD-ROM drive, the CD-ROM access light may blink in conjunction with the disk drive access light. Keep in mind that this blinking of the SCSI CD-ROM access light is independent of the AIN feature, and the steps listed previously will *not* prevent the CD-ROM light from blinking.

CD DRIVE PERFORMANCE

When you run a program that accesses a CD drive, you may notice that the program is not performing as well as it could. For example, you notice slow data transfers in a business or reference program. You may also find that the audio and video in a multimedia program is slow or seems to skip. This trouble can occur when the Supplemental Cache Size and Optimize Access Pattern For settings are not configured properly for your CD drive. You can optimize the CD drive settings as described here:

1. Click Start, highlight Settings, click Control Panel, and then double-click the System icon.

2. On the Performance tab, click File System.

3. Click the CD-ROM tab (as in Figure 9-6).

4. Move the Supplemental Cache Size slider to the right to allocate more system RAM for caching data from the CD drive, or to the left to allocate less RAM for caching data.

 Many multimedia programs perform better with a *smaller* cache because these program tend not to reuse data.

5. When reading continuous data (such as .AVI files), use a higher setting in the Optimize Access Pattern For box. When reading random data, increase the Supplemental Cache Size setting and decrease the Optimize Access Pattern For setting.

6. Click OK and then click Close. Restart your computer when prompted to do so.

These settings are for Windows only and will have no effect when using real-mode drivers for your CD drive.

ENABLING DMA FOR CD DRIVES

DMA (*direct memory access*—also referred to as *bus mastering*) is a technique that some PC devices use to transfer data directly to and from memory *without* passing through the processor. As a result, DMA reduces CPU overhead by providing a mechanism for data transfers that do not require monitoring by the CPU. If your PC is configured to support bus mastering operation, you can usually enable DMA drive support to improve the data transfer performance for your CD drives. Use these steps to enable DMA:

If your version of Windows (such as Windows 95) does not include DMA support, obtain and install the most current bus master motherboard driver for your computer—or install any version of Windows 98 or Windows Me for DMA support.

1. Click Start, highlight Settings, click Control Panel, and then double-click the System icon.

2. On the Device Manager tab, double-click the CD-ROM branch to expand it and then double-click the desired CD drive.

3. On the Settings tab (as in Figure 9-11), click the DMA check box to select it and then click OK.

4. Restart your computer, then test to determine if your CD drive is working properly. If your CD drive does not work properly with DMA enabled, disable DMA by clearing the DMA check box.

CD-ROM SYMPTOMS

Though the vast majority of CD-ROM problems are due to software or setup problems, the drives themselves are delicate and unforgiving devices. Considering that their prices have plummeted to the point where they are virtually disposable devices, there is little economic sense in attempting a lengthy repair. When a fault occurs in the drive or in its adapter board, your best course is typically to replace the defective drive outright.

SYMPTOM 9-1   **The drive has trouble accepting or rejecting a CD**   This problem is typical of motorized CD-ROM drives where the disc is accepted into a slot, or placed in a motorized tray—you don't see this issue in "caddy-type" CD-ROM drives. Before performing any disassembly, check the assembly through the CD tray for any obvious obstructions. If there is nothing obvious, expose the assembly and check each linkage and motor drive gear very carefully. Carefully remove or free any obstruction. Be gentle when working around the load/unload assembly. Notice how it is shock mounted in four places. If the problem persists, there is most likely a problem in the tray motor or mechanism. Your best course is to replace the CD-ROM drive outright.

SYMPTOM 9-2   **Optical read head does not seek (a drive "seek" error)**   An optical head is used to identify pits and lands along a CD-ROM and to track the spiral data pattern as the head moves across the disk. The optical head must move very slowly and smoothly to ensure accurate tracking.

Head movement is accomplished using a linear stepping motor (or *linear actuator*) to shift the optical assembly in microscopic increments—head travel appears perfectly smooth to the unaided eye. Check the drive for any damaged parts or obstructions. When the optical head fails to seek, the easiest and fastest fix is simply to replace the CD-ROM mechanism outright.

SYMPTOM 9-3   **Disc cannot be read**   This type of problem may result in a DOS level "sector not found" or "drive not ready" error. Check the CD itself to ensure that it is the right format, inserted properly, and physically clean. Cleanliness is very important to a CD. While the laser will often "look past" any surface defects in a disc, the presence of dust or debris on a disc surface can produce serious tracking (and read) errors. Try a different disc to confirm the problem. If a new or different disc reads properly, the trouble may indeed be in (or *on*) the original disc itself. Not only must the disc be clean, but the head optics must also be clear. Gently dust or clean the head optics as suggested by your drive's particular manufacturer.

Examine the power connector and signal cable between the drive and its controller board. Be sure that the cable is connected correctly and completely. Either the drive's optical head or electronics are defective. Your best course here is to try replacing the drive. If problems persist on a drive with a proprietary interface, replace the adapter board.

SYMPTOM 9-4   **The disc does not turn**   You may not hear the disc "spin up" for access. The disc must turn at a *constant linear velocity* (CLV), which is directed and regulated by the spindle motor. If the disc is not spinning during access, check to be sure that the disc is seated properly and is not jammed or obstructed. Before beginning a repair, review your drive installation and setup carefully to ensure that the drive is properly configured for operation on your system. If the computer does not recognize the CD drive ("invalid drive specification"), there may be a setup or configuration problem (either the low-level device driver or MSCDEX may not have loaded properly). If your particular drive provides you with instructions for cleaning the optical head aperture, perform that cleaning operation and try the drive again—a fouled optical head can sometimes upset spindle operation. Finally, if the drive's Activity LED comes on when drive access is attempted but the disc still doesn't turn (you may also see a corresponding DOS error message), the drive spindle system is probably defective, so replace the drive outright.

SYMPTOM 9-5   **The optical head can not focus its laser beam**   To compensate for the minute fluctuations in disc flatness, the optical head mounts its objective lens into a small focusing mechanism, which is little more than a miniature voice coil actuator—the lens does not have to move very much at all to maintain precise focus. If focus is out or not well maintained, the laser detector may produce erroneous signals. This may result in DOS drive error messages. If random but consistent DOS errors appear, check the disc to be sure that it is *optically* clean—dust and fingerprints can result in serious access problems. Try another disc. If a new disc continues to perform badly, try cleaning the optical aperture with clean (photography-grade) air. When problems persist, the optical system is probably damaged or defective. Finally, try replacing the CD-ROM drive mechanism outright.

SYMPTOM 9-6   **Audio is not being played by the sound card**   In most cases, there is a problem with the CD audio connection or system mixer setting. Start with your disc and verify that the CD you're trying to play actually contains Red Book audio (don't try to "play" data CDs). Next, try playing the music CD with a set of headphones attached to the CD-ROM drive directly. If there is no audio from the headphone jack, adjust the volume control. If there is still no music, the drive is probably defective and should be replaced.

Try playing .WAV or MIDI files through the sound card (for example, try the Sounds icon in the Control Panel) and verify that the card's volume setting is adequate. If you cannot play any sounds at all, there may be a problem with the sound card or its drivers rather than with the CD-ROM drive. Open the sound card's mixer applet and verify that the CD audio channel volume is enabled and turned up to an appropriate level. Finally, verify that the CD audio cable is appropriate for your sound card and CD-ROM drive and see that it's attached securely at both ends. Try another CD audio cable.

SYMPTOM 9-7   **There is no audio being generated by the drive**   Normally you can listen to CD audio using the drive's headphone jack. Check your headphones on another stereo and see that the headphones are working. Also adjust the headphone volume using the small dial located on the front of the CD-ROM drive. If the problem persists and *no* audio is being generated, the headphone amplifier circuit in the CD-ROM is probably defective and should be replaced.

SYMPTOM 9-8   **You see a "Wrong DOS version" error message when attempting to load MSCDEX**   You are running MS-DOS 4, 5, or 6 with a version of MSCDEX that does not support it. The solution is to change to the correct version of MSCDEX. The version compatibility for MSCDEX is listed here:

■ v1.01 14,913 bytes (No ISO9660 support—High Sierra support only)

■ v2.00 18,307 bytes (High Sierra and ISO9660 support for DOS 3.1-3.3)

■ v2.10 19,943 bytes (DOS 3.1-3.3 and 4.0—DOS 5.x support provided with SETVER)

■ v2.20 25,413 bytes (same as above with Win 3.x support—changes in audio support)

■ v2.21 25,431 bytes (DOS 3.1-5.0 support with enhanced control under Win 3.1)

■ v2.22 25,377 bytes (DOS 3.1-6.0 & higher with Win 3.1 support)

■ v2.23 25,361 bytes (DOS 3.1-6.2 and Win 3.1 support—supplied with MSDOS 6.2)

When using MS-DOS 5.x to 6.1, you will need to add the SETVER utility to CONFIG.SYS in order to use MSCDEX v2.10 or v2.20 properly (**device = c:\dos\setver.exe**). SETVER is used to tell programs that they are running under a different version of DOS than DOS 5.0. This is important since MSCDEX (v2.10 and v2.20) refuses to work with DOS versions higher than 4.0. SETVER is used to fool MSCDEX into working with higher versions of DOS. In some versions of DOS 5.0 (such as Compaq DOS 5.0), you will need to add an entry to SETVER for MSCDEX (that is, SETVER MSCDEX.EXE 4.00). This entry modifies SETVER without changing the file size or date.

SYMPTOM 9-9   **The PC halts when copying large amounts of data from a CD-ROM drive**   The protected-mode Windows CD-ROM file system includes a read-ahead feature designed to provide smoother video playback with faster and more efficient data streaming. Unfortunately, the read-ahead feature can cause the CD-ROM drive controller to be driven faster than it was intended to be, and doing this can lock up the system. Try the following steps to fix the trouble:

1. Click the Start button, highlight Settings, then click Control Panel.

2. Double-click the System icon.

3. On the Performance tab, click File System.

4. Click the CD-ROM tab (as in Figure 9-6).

5. In the Optimize Access Pattern For box, click the setting that matches the CD-ROM drive you are using. Click OK, then restart the computer when prompted.

If this doesn't solve the problem, repeat the steps, but in the Optimize Access Pattern For box, click No Read Ahead. Click OK, then restart the computer when prompted.

SYMPTOM 9-10   **You cannot access the CD-ROM drive letter under DOS**   The drive is probably available under Windows 9x/Me. You may see an error message such as *Invalid drive specification*. This is typically a problem with the CD-ROM drivers. The MS-DOS extension MSCDEX has probably not loaded. Switch to the DOS sub-directory and use the MEM /C function to check the loaded drivers and TSRs. If you see the low-level driver and MSCDEX displayed in the driver list, check the CD-ROM hardware. Make sure that the signal cable between the drive and drive controller is inserted properly and completely. If problems persist, try replacing the drive controller.

If you do *not* see the low-level driver and MSCDEX shown in the driver list, inspect your CONFIG.SYS and AUTOEXEC.BAT files. Check that the drivers are included in the startup files to begin with. Make sure that the label used in the **/D** switch is the same for both the low-level driver and MSCDEX. If the label is not the same, MSCDEX will not load. If you are using MS-DOS 5.0, be sure the SETVER utility is loaded. You could also try updating MSCEDX to v2.30 or later.

SYMPTOM 9-11   **You see an error when trying to load the low-level CD-ROM driver**
Check that you are using the proper low-level device driver for your CD-ROM drive. If you are swapping the drive (or proprietary drive controller board), you probably need to load a new driver. If the driver fails to load with original hardware, the drive controller board may have failed, or its jumper settings may not match those in the driver's command line switches. Check the signal cable running between the drive and adapter board. If the cable is crimped or scuffed, try replacing the cable. Next, try replacing the adapter board. If problems persist, try replacing the CD drive mechanism itself.

SYMPTOM 9-12   **You see an error such as "Not ready reading from drive D:"**
Check that a suitable disc is inserted in the drive and that the drive is closed properly. Make sure that the low-level device driver and MSCDEX are loaded correctly. If the drivers do not load, there may be a problem with the drive controller board (or drive mechanism itself). Also check that the data cable between the drive and adapter is connected properly and completely. If problems persist, suspect a weakness in the PC power supply (especially if the system is heavily loaded or upgraded or if there is a Y Adapter cable feeding the CD-ROM). Try a larger supply in the system, or connect the CD drive directly to the supply. If problems persist, replace the CD-ROM drive. If a new drive does not correct the problem, try a different drive controller.

SYMPTOM 9-13   **SmartDrive is not caching the CD-ROM properly in DOS**   The version of SmartDrive supplied with DOS 6.2x provides three forms of caching, although older forms of SmartDrive (such as the ones distributed with Windows 3.1, DOS 6.0 and 6.1) will *not* adequately cache CD-ROM drives. The BUFFERS statement also does *not* help caching. So if you are looking to SmartDrive for a CD-ROM cache, you should be using the version distributed with DOS 6.2x. You should also set **BUFFERS=10,0** in the CONFIG.SYS file, and the SmartDrive command line should come *after* MSCDEX. When using SmartDrive, you can change the buffers setting in the MSCDEX command line (**/M**) to 0—this allows you to save 2KB per buffer.

SmartDrive is *not* used by Windows 9x/Me, which employs its own CD caching scheme. Try disabling SmartDrive when running under Windows.

SYMPTOM 9-14 **After installing the CD-ROM drivers, system reports significantly less available RAM** This is usually a caching issue with CD-ROM driver software, and you may need to adjust the CD-ROM driver software accordingly. This type of problem has been documented with Teac CD-ROM drives and CORELCDX.COM software. If the software offers a command line switch to change the amount of XMS allocated, reduce the number to 512 or 256. Check with tech support for your particular drive for the exact command line switch settings.

SYMPTOM 9-15 **The CD-ROM drivers will not install properly on a drive using compression software** This is usually because you booted from a floppy disk and attempted to install drivers *without* loading the compression software *first*. Before doing anything else, check the loading order—allow your system to boot from the hard drive *before* installing the CD-ROM drivers. This allows the compression software to assign all drive letters. As an alternative, boot from a compression-aware floppy disk. If you *must* boot the system from a floppy disk, make sure the disk is configured to be fully compatible with the compression software being used.

SYMPTOM 9-16 **You see an error indicating that the CD-ROM drive is not found** This type of problem may also appear as loading problems with the low-level driver. There are several possible reasons why the drive hardware cannot be found. Power and signal problems are likely culprits. Make sure the 4-pin power connector is inserted properly and completely. If the drive is being powered by a Y adapter, make sure any interim connections are secure. Use a voltmeter and measure the +5 volt (pin 4) and +12 volt (pin 1) levels. If either voltage (especially the +12 volt supply) is unusually low or absent, replace the power supply. See that the drive's signal interface cable is connected securely at both the drive and controller. If the cable is visibly worn or damaged, try a new one.

Inspect the drive controller card (especially if it's a proprietary controller) and make sure that the adapter's IRQ, DMA, and I/O address settings are correct. They must also match with the command line switches used with the low-level driver. If the controller is for a CD-ROM alone, you may also try installing the controller in a different bus slot. If your CD-ROM uses a SCSI interface, make sure that the SCSI bus cable is properly terminated at both ends. If problems persist, replace the drive controller first, then replace the CD-ROM drive if necessary.

SYMPTOM 9-17 **In a new installation, the driver fails to load successfully for the proprietary interface card** In almost all cases, the proprietary interface card (or *drive controller*) has been configured improperly. Check the drive controller card first and verify that the interface card is configured with the correct IRQ, DMA, and I/O address settings, then check for hardware conflicts with other devices in the system. In some cases, you may simply enter the drive maker (for example, Teac) as the interface type during driver installation. Make sure that the interface is set properly for the system and your particular drive. Check the driver's command line next—the driver's command line switches should correctly reflect the drive adapter's configuration.

SYMPTOM 9-18 **The CD-ROM driver loads, but you see an error such as: "CDR101" (drive not ready), or: "CDR103" (CDROM disk not HIGH SIERRA or ISO)** You are using a very old version of the low-level driver or MSCDEX. Check your driver version (it may be outdated). Contact the drive manufacturer's tech support (or Web site) and see that you have the very latest version of their low-level driver. For very old drives, there may also be a later generic driver available. Check your version of MSCDEX next. Since low-level drivers are often bundled with MSCDEX, you may also be stuck with an old version of MSCDEX. You can usually download a current version of MSCDEX from the same place you get an updated low-level driver, or download it from Microsoft at **www.microsoft.com**.

SYMPTOM 9-19   You're having trouble setting up more than one CD-ROM drive
This raises concerns about both hardware and software issues. Check the drive controller first and make sure that the drive controller will support more than one CD-ROM on the same channel (most standard or nonproprietary controllers should). If it won't, you will have to install another drive controller to support the new CD-ROM drive. Low-level drivers present another problem, since you will need to have *another* copy of a low-level driver loaded in CONFIG.SYS—one copy for each drive. Make sure that the command line switches for each driver match the hardware settings of the corresponding drive adapter. Finally, check your copy of MSCDEX. You need only one copy of MSCDEX in AUTOEXEC.BAT, but the **/D:** switch must appear twice—once for *each* drive ID.

SYMPTOM 9-20   Your CD-ROM drive refuses to work with an IDE port   It may very well be that the drive uses a nonstandard or proprietary port (other than IDE). You must connect the CD-ROM drive to a compatible drive adapter, so try replacing the drive adapter board with the correct type. If the drive is proprietary, it will *not* interface to a regular IDE port. It may be necessary to purchase a drive adapter *specifically* for the CD-ROM drive. As an alternative, you might choose to upgrade the CD-ROM drive to a model that *will* use a standard IDE-type controller.

SYMPTOM 9-21   You cannot get the CD-ROM drive to run properly when mounted vertically   CD-ROM drives with motorized drive trays generally cannot be mounted vertically—disc tracking simply will not work correctly. The only CD-ROM drives that can be mounted vertically are those with caddys, but you should check with those manufacturers before proceeding with vertical mounting.

SYMPTOM 9-22   The SCSI CD-ROM drive refuses to work when connected to an Adaptec SCSI interface   Other SCSI drives are working fine in this situation. This is a common type of problem among SCSI adapters, particularly with Adaptec boards because of their great popularity. In most cases, the Adaptec drivers are the wrong version for your adapter or they're corrupted. Try turning off *Sync Negotiations* on the Adaptec SCSI interface and rebooting the system. Your SCSI drivers may also be buggy or outdated. Check with Adaptec technical support (**www.adaptec.com**) to determine if there are later drivers that you should use instead. You may need to uninstall the current drivers and reinstall the new host adapter drivers from scratch.

SYMPTOM 9-23   You see a "No drives found" error when the CD-ROM driver line is executed in CONFIG.SYS   In most cases, the driver command line switches do not match the hardware configuration of the drive controller, or your low-level driver may be missing or corrupt. Start by checking the CD driver. Open CONFIG.SYS in a word processor and see that the low-level driver has a complete and accurate command line. See that any command line switches are set correctly. Also verify that the driver referenced in the command line is actually present on the hard drive. Next, open AUTOEXEC.BAT in a word processor and see that the MSCDEX command line is accurate and complete. Also confirm that any MSCDEX command line switches are set correctly. You might try updating your version of MSCDEX.

If you are using SmartDrive with DOS 6.0 or later, try adding the **/U** switch to the end of your SmartDrive command line in AUTOEXEC.BAT. Finally, make sure that there are no other hardware devices in the system that may be conflicting with the CD-ROM drive controller. If problems persist, replace the drive controller or, if necessary, replace the CD-ROM drive.

SYMPTOM 9-24   The LCD on your CD-ROM displays an error code   Even without knowing the particular meaning of *every* possible error message, you can be assured that most CD-based error messages can be traced to the following causes (in order of ease of fixes):

■ **Bad caddy**   The CD caddy is damaged or inserted incorrectly. The CD may also be inserted into the caddy improperly. With a motorized tray, the CD may be inserted improperly.

■ **Bad mounting**   The drive is mounted improperly, or mounting screws are shorting out the drive's electronics.

■ **Bad power**   Check the +12 and +5 volts powering the CD-ROM drive. Low power may require a new or larger supply. Remove any Y-splitter that may be tapping the drive's power.

■ **Bad drive**   Internal diagnostics have detected a fault in the CD-ROM drive. Try replacing the drive.

■ **Bad drive controller**   Drive diagnostics have detected a fault in the drive controller. Try replacing the drive controller or SCSI adapter (whichever interface you're using).

SYMPTOM 9-25   **When a SCSI CD-ROM drive is connected to a SCSI adapter, the system hangs when the SCSI BIOS loads**   In most cases, the CD-ROM drive supports plug-and-play, but the SCSI controller's BIOS does not. Disable the SCSI BIOS through a jumper on the controller (or remove the SCSI BIOS chip entirely) and use a SCSI driver in CONFIG.SYS instead. You may need to download a low-level SCSI driver from the adapter manufacturer. If there are other SCSI drives on the adapter that rely on the SCSI BIOS (for example, SCSI hard drives), it may not be possible to disable the SCSI BIOS. In that case, a separate SCSI controller may be needed.

SYMPTOM 9-26   **You see an error such as "Unable to detect ATAPI IDE CD-ROM drive, device driver not loaded"**   You have a problem with the configuration of your IDE/EIDE controller hardware. Check the signal cable first and make sure that the 40-pin signal cable is attached properly between the drive and controller. IDE CD-ROM drives are typically installed on a secondary 40-pin IDE port. Make sure that there is no device in the system using the same IRQ or I/O address as your secondary IDE port. Finally, make sure that any command line switches for the low-level driver in CONFIG.SYS correspond to the controller's hardware settings.

SYMPTOM 9-27   **The CD-ROM drive door will not open once the 40-pin IDE signal cable is connected**   You should need power only to operate the drive door. If the door stops when the signal cable is attached, there are some possible problems to check. Power and signal cabling are likely culprits, so make sure that both +5 and +12 volts are available at the power connector. See that the power connector is attached securely to the back of the CD-ROM drive. The 40-pin signal cable is probably reversed at either the drive or controller. Try a different signal cable. Also make sure that the 40-pin IDE drive is plugged into a true IDE port—not a proprietary (non-IDE 40-pin) port. If problems persist, try a known-good IDE-type CD-ROM drive.

SYMPTOM 9-28   **You are using an old CD-ROM and can play CD audio, but you cannot access directories or other computer data from a CD**   Older proprietary CD-ROM drives often used *two* low-level drivers (one for audio, and one for data). You probably only have one of the drivers installed. Check your low-level drivers first and see that any necessary low-level drivers are loaded in the CONFIG.SYS file. Also see that any command line switches are set properly. Some older sound boards with integrated proprietary CD-ROM drive controllers may not work properly with the drivers required for your older CD-ROM drive. You may have to alter the proprietary controller's IRQ, DMA, or I/O settings (and update the driver's command-line switches) until you find a combination where the driver and controller will work together. If the problems persist, consider an upgrade to a modern ATAPI IDE CD-ROM drive.

SYMPTOM 9-29 **An IDE CD-ROM is not detected on a 486 PCI motherboard** This is a known problem when using Aztech CD-ROM drives and 486 PCI motherboards with SIS 82C497 chipsets. The motherboard bus noise is far too high and results in the misinterpretation of the IDE interface handshaking signals (namely the DASP and PDIAG signals). As a consequence, the CD-ROM drive is sometimes (or always) not detected. You may be able to resolve this problem by connecting the IDE CD-ROM drive as a slave device to the hard disk—though you may need to slow the hard drive's data transfer mode (through the CMOS Setup) to accommodate the slower CD-ROM drive.

SYMPTOM 9-30 **You notice that Matsushita CD-ROM drives are mis-detected as "Matshita"** This occurs under Windows 95, Windows 95 OSR2, and Windows 98. This is a problem with the CD-ROM drive itself—they return "Matshita" (instead of "Matsushita") as the device description when they're enumerated by Windows. You'll need to check with Matsushita for a firmware upgrade, driver fix, or other corrective options. You may also choose to replace the CD-ROM drive outright.

SYMPTOM 9-31 **An IDE CD-ROM is not detected when slaved to an IBM hard drive** This is a known problem with Aztech IDE CD-ROM drives and IBM Dala 3450 hard drives. The pulse width for the drive detection (DASP) signal is not long enough for the CD-ROM to identify itself properly. This results in the improper detection of an Aztech IDE CD-ROM. You should make the CD-ROM drive a master device on its own IDE channel or (if possible) upgrade the CD-ROM drive's firmware to utilize more reliable timing. If the CD-ROM manufacturer has no firmware upgrades available, and you cannot reconfigure the CD-ROM on another IDE channel, you'll need to replace the CD-ROM or the hard drive.

SYMPTOM 9-32 **The CD-ROM drive will not read or run CD Plus or Enhanced CD titles** This is a known problem with Acer CD-ROM models; 625A, 645A, 655A, 665A, 525E, 743E, 747E, and 767E. The CD Plus (or *Enhanced CD*) titles use a nonstandard data format released and supported by Sony. The new format is for interactive CD titles that incorporate video clips and music, and the data structures on these CDs cannot be recognized by these CD-ROM drive models. In this situation, you'll need to upgrade the CD-ROM drive outright to a newer model which CAN accommodate newer file types.

SYMPTOM 9-33 **You notice that the LED indicator on the CD-ROM is always on** The drive seems to be otherwise working properly. This is not necessarily a problem. Some CD-ROM drive models (such as the Acer 600 series) use the LED indicator as a READY light instead of as a BUSY light. Whenever a CD is loaded in the drive, the LED will be lit, and it will remain lit whether the drive is being accessed or not. This feature tells the user whether or not a CD-ROM disc is currently loaded in the drive by simply checking the LED. There may be a jumper on the CD-ROM drive that allows you to switch the indicator light from Ready mode to Busy mode.

SYMPTOM 9-34 **The drive vibrates or makes a great deal of noise with certain CD and CD-R discs** This is almost always due to an unbalanced disc in high-speed (that is, 12x and faster) CD-ROM drives. A disc may become unbalanced from improper silk-screening or the application of an adhesive label. When that unbalanced disc is rotated at high speeds, the entire drive tends to vibrate (often this vibration resonates inside the case, making the sound seem even louder). Make sure that each disc used in the drive is evenly marked or labeled. If the problem seems to occur on all discs, verify that the drive itself is mounted securely to the chassis.

SYMPTOM 9-35 **The system locks up when using a Panasonic "Big 5" CD-ROM drive under Windows 95** This trouble is known to occur if you're using IDE bus-mastering drivers with the Panasonic "BIG 5" 5-disc CD-ROM changer (model SQ-TC510N). The Panasonic drive will require new firmware to overcome this problem, so contact Panasonic to update the device with the latest firmware revision. To avoid this problem in the meantime, remove the CD-ROM changer from your system.

SYMPTOM 9-36 **The front panel controls of your SCSI CD-ROM drive do not appear to work under Windows 9x/Me** Those same controls appear to work fine in DOS. Windows 9x/Me uses SCSI commands to poll removable media devices every two seconds in order to see if there has been a change in status. Since SCSI commands to the CD-ROM generally have higher priority than front panel controls, the front panel controls may appear to be disabled under Windows. Try pressing the front panel controls repeatedly. You may be able to correct this by disabling the CD-ROM polling under Windows.

SYMPTOM 9-37 **You cannot change the CD-ROM drive letter under Windows 9x/Me** You need to change the drive's settings under the Device Manager:

1. Open the Control Panel and select the System icon.

2. Once the System Properties dialog opens, click on the Device Manager page.

3. Locate the entry for the CD-ROM and expand the list of CD-ROM devices.

4. Double-click on the desired CD-ROM.

5. Once the CD-ROM drive's Properties dialog appears, choose the Settings tab.

6. Locate the current drive letter assignment box and enter the new drive designation. Multiple letters are needed only when a SCSI device is implementing LUN addressing (such as multidisc changers).

7. Click on the OK button to save your changes.

8. Click on the OK button to close the Device Manager.

9. A System Settings Change window should appear. Click on the Yes button to reboot the system so that the changes can take effect, or click on the No button so that you can make more changes to other CD-ROMs before rebooting the system. Changes will not become effective until the system is rebooted.

SYMPTOM 9-38 **You installed Windows from a CD-ROM disc using DOS drivers, but when you removed the real-mode CD-ROM drivers from CONFIG.SYS, the CD-ROM no longer works** You need to enable protected-mode drivers by running the Add New Hardware wizard from the Control Panel:

1. Boot Windows 9x/Me using the real-mode drivers for your CD-ROM and its interface.

2. Open the Control Panel and select the Add New Hardware icon.

3. Proceed to add new hardware, but do *not* let Windows attempt to *auto-detect* the new hardware. Use the disk with protected-mode drivers for the new installation.

4. When the new software is installed, Windows will tell you that it must reboot before the hardware will be available—do *not* reboot yet.

5. Open a word processor such as Notepad and edit the CONFIG.SYS and AUTOEXEC.BAT files to REMark out the real-mode drivers for your CD and the reference to MSCDEX.

6. Shut down Windows 9x/Me, then power down the system.

7. Check to be sure that the CD-ROM interface is set to use the resources assigned by Windows (not necessary if the interface is PnP or a standard IDE-type controller).

8. Reboot the system—your protected-mode drivers should now load normally.

SYMPTOM 9-39   **Your CD-ROM drive's "parallel port-to-SCSI" interface worked with Windows 3.1x, but does not work under Windows 9x/Me**   This problem is typical of the NEC CD-EPPSCSI01 interface and is usually due to a problem with the driver's assessment of your parallel port type (that is, bi-directional, unidirectional, or enhanced parallel port). Try shutting down and restarting the PC—since typical "parallel port-to-SCSI" interfaces get their power from the SCSI device, the external drive must be powered up *first*. Start your CMOS Setup routine and see what mode your parallel port is set to operate in. Make sure it is set to a mode that is compatible with your parallel port drive.

Drivers may also be a problem, so update your version of MSCDEX if necessary. Change the MSCDEX command line in AUTOEXEC.BAT to load from the C:\WINDOWS\CONTROL\ directory and remove the /L:x parameter from the end of the MSCDEX command line (if present). If you're using real-mode drivers for the interface, place a switch at the end of the interface's command line that tells the driver what mode your parallel port is operating in. For example, the Trantor T358 driver (MA358.SYS) uses the following switches (yours will probably be different):

- **/m02**   For unidirectional mode (also known as *standard* or *output only*)
- **/m04**   For bi-directional mode (also known as *PS/2 mode*)
- **/m08**   For enhanced mode

Try disabling the real-mode drivers—remove or REMark-out any references to the interface's real-mode drivers in CONFIG.SYS, then remove or disable the MSCDEX command line in AUTOEXEC.BAT. Start Windows 9x/Me, open the Control Panel, select the System icon, then choose the Device Manager page. Find the SCSI adapter settings and expand the SCSI Controllers branch of the device tree. Select the device identification line for your "parallel port-to-SCSI" interface, then click on the Properties button. Click on the Settings page. In the Adapter Settings dialog box, type in the same parameter that you would have used if you were using real-mode drivers. Click on the OK buttons to save your changes, then select Yes to reboot the system. If problems persist, check the technical support for your parallel port-to-SCSI adapter and see if there are any known problems with your particular setup or any updated drivers available for download.

SYMPTOM 9-40   **You see a message such as: "CD-ROM can run, but results may not be as expected"**   This simply means that Windows 9x/Me is using real-mode drivers—the drive is running in MS-DOS Compatibility Mode. If protected-mode drivers are available for the CD-ROM drive, you should use those instead. You may download and install protected-mode drivers from the CD-ROM manufacturer's Web site.

SYMPTOM 9-41   **The CD-ROM works fine in DOS or Windows 3.1x, but sound or video appears choppy under Windows 9x/Me**   There are several factors that can affect CD-ROM performance under Windows. Windows performance (and stability) is severely degraded by real-mode drivers, so start by removing or disabling any real-mode drivers. Try installing the protected-mode drivers for your CD-ROM drive instead. If protected-mode drivers are not available for your drive, you may consider upgrading the CD-ROM hardware. Real-mode applications that are run under Windows 9x/Me can cripple a system's performance. Try exiting any DOS or Windows 3.1x applications that may be running on the Windows 9x/Me desktop. Also exit unneeded Windows applications since additional applications take a toll on processing power. Finally, try rebooting the system to ensure that Windows 9x/Me has the maximum amount of resources available before running your CD-ROM application.

SYMPTOM 9-42   **You can't read a Video CD-I disc in Windows 95 using any ATAPI/IDE CD-ROM drive**   The built-in ATAPI driver in Windows 95 cannot read raw data in 32-bit disk access mode. Note that such symptoms can also happen to any ATAPI/IDE-compatible CD-ROM as long as it is using the built-in ATAPI driver in Windows 95. You should update the CD-ROM's ATAPI driver to a current manufacturer-specific version, or you should update your version of Windows. As another alternative, you can use the following procedure:

1. Disable the 32-bit disk access feature of Windows 95.

2. On the Windows 95 desktop, click Start and choose Settings and Control Panel.

3. Click on the System icon and select the Performance option.

4. Choose File System and select the Troubleshooting option.

5. At the Troubleshooting dialog, click on Disable All 32-Bit Disk Access.

6. Edit AUTOEXEC.BAT and append the following line (where <path> is the path name of your Windows 95 software):

```
C:\<path>\COMMAND\MSCDEX.EXE /D:MSCD000
```

SYMPTOM 9-43   **You cannot play CD audio on a particular CD-ROM under Windows 95**   Replacing the CD-ROM resolves the problem. This is a known incompatibility issue with Acer 525E CD-ROM drives and Windows 95 (this does not affect the integrity of programs and data). Windows 95 will mute the CD audio on this and many other brands of double speed and faster IDE CD-ROMs. If you cannot obtain a patch directly from Microsoft or the CD-ROM manufacturer, your only real alternative is to replace the CD-ROM drive.

SYMPTOM 9-44   **After upgrading to Windows 98 or later, you notice multiple CD-ROM letters**   For example, you may see up to four CD-ROM drives displayed in My Computer or Windows Explorer, even though you have only *one* CD-ROM drive in the computer. This problem is known to occur with NEC 4X4, 4X6, 4X8, and 4X16 CD-ROM drives if you've installed the NEC Single CD tool in your previous version of Windows. To correct the problem, simply reinstall the NEC Single CD tool under Windows 98/Me using the disk included with your NEC 4x CD-ROM drive. You may also wish to download and install the latest versions of that software (and the CD-ROM drivers) from the manufacturer.

SYMPTOM 9-45   **After upgrading to Windows 98, you encounter problems with the CD-ROM and hard drive**   Once the upgrade to Windows 98 is complete, you cannot access your CD-ROM drive, hard disks connected to the IDE-type controller are forced to use MS-DOS Compatibility Mode, or another drive appears in My Computer or Windows Explorer that is about 13MB in size.

This is a known problem when Helix Hurricane for Windows 95 (by Helix Software) is installed on your computer. To correct this problem, you'll need to remove Hurricane using its uninstall tool (you may be able to patch or update Hurricane, but you'll need to contact the program manufacturer). Restart your computer and use the Startup Menu to boot to the Windows 98 Safe Mode Command Prompt Only. Run the uninstall tool in the folder where Hurricane is installed. If the uninstall tool is not available, you can disable Hurricane manually:

1. Use a text editor (such as Notepad) to open the AUTOEXEC.BAT file.

2. Disable the line containing **QWATCH.COM** in the AUTOEXEC.BAT file by REMarking-out that command line.

3. Save and close the AUTOEXEC.BAT file.

4. Use a text editor to open the SYSTEM.INI file.

5. Disable the following lines in the [386Enh] section of SYSTEM.INI by placing a semicolon (;) at the beginning of each line, such as:

    ```
    device=<path>\arpl.386
    device=<path>\Winsa.386
    device=<path>\Winguard.386
    device=<path>\vxmsems.386
    device=<path>\windrv.386
    device=<path>\vcache16.386
    device=<path>\vsectd.386
    device=<path>\heapx.386
    ```

6. Now change the following lines in the [Boot] section of System.ini from **system .drv=<path>\sysdrv.drv** to **system.drv=System.drv**, and from **display .drv=<path>\winsa256.drv** to **display.drv=Pnpdrvr.drv**.

> If your original display driver was not PNPDRVR.DRV, start Windows in the Safe Mode and change the display driver to the appropriate version.

7. Save and close the SYSTEM.INI file, then reboot the computer.

SYMPTOM 9-46   **Your CD-ROM changer doesn't work after upgrading to Windows 98/Me**   This is a known problem with the AST Advantage 828 computer with a CD-ROM changer—after upgrading to Windows 98/Me, a single CD-ROM drive may be displayed in Device Manager (and the CD-ROM changer may be displayed as Unknown Hardware under the Other Devices entry). This problem will occur if the SmartCD Manager software is installed on an AST system with a Torisan (Sanyo) CDR-C36 6X 3 disc CD-ROM changer. The SCDMGRT3.VXD file located in the \Windows\System\Iosubsys folder will typically prevent Windows 98/Me from detecting the CD-ROM changer. To correct this problem, you'll need to move the SCDMGRT3.VXD file into a different folder. You may also check for an updated version of SCDMGRT3.VXD from AST or Sanyo.

SYMPTOM 9-47   **Your SmartCD Manager software does not work under Windows 98/Me**   After upgrading to Windows 98/Me, you may find that your Torisan (Sanyo) 3 disc CD-ROM drive now has three separate drive letters assigned to it. This problem may occur even though the SmartCD Manager program has assigned only one drive letter to this device. The problem occurs because Windows 98/Me replaces the CDVSD.VXD and TORISAN3.VXD files included with the SmartCD

Manager program—the updated versions of these files are *not* compatible with your SmartCD Manager software. To correct this problem, simply reinstall the SmartCD Manager program.

SYMPTOM 9-48   **The auto insert notification feature prevents a system's suspend mode from working**   Most current computers now include power management features that place the computer in a power-down mode (suspend) after a given period of inactivity. If the Auto Insert Notification (AIN) option is enabled for IDE-type CD-ROM drives when power management is also enabled, the computer may not suspend automatically. This typically occurs because some IDE-type CD-ROM drives use the ATA GET MEDIA STATUS command method for polling. But a power management system will detect the action as "drive activity." Since a drive then appears to be in use, the power management system will not power-down the system (this is a known issue with Windows 95 OSR2). You can work around this issue by disabling the Auto Insert Notification option for affected drives.

As a more permanent fix, you may also download and install the REMIDEUP.EXE file from Microsoft's Web site. This update will install the following file update: ESDI_506.PDR version 4.00.956 (dated 5/14/96)—of course, later versions of the file should also work, and you may also consider upgrading your version of Windows.

SYMPTOM 9-49   **The computer locks up while browsing a CD-ROM**   This often occurs under Windows 95/98 after installing a Hewlett-Packard CD-RW drive in some Compaq Deskpro computers. Your computer may halt when you try to use My Computer or Windows Explorer to view the CD-RW drive. In most circumstances, this type of problem is driver-related. Compaq systems use a custom device driver file named CPQDFVS.VXD. This file, located in the \Windows\System\Iosubsys folder, can lock up the computer when you try to read from the CD-RW drive. To work around this problem for the Compaq, delete or rename the CPQDFVS.VXD file. To correct this issue on a more permanent basis, contact Compaq for a patch or update to the CPQDFVS.VXD file.

SYMPTOM 9-50   **You cannot read Rock Ridge CD-ROM extensions under Windows** This occurs because Windows 95, 98, and later are simply not designed to support the Rock Ridge CD-ROM extensions. Rock Ridge is a means of storing POSIX file system extensions on a CD-ROM, but Windows 9x/Me uses the Joliet file system (which allows for deep subdirectories and long file names) instead of the Rock Ridge CD-ROM format. If you need to read Rock Ridge-formatted CD-ROMs in Windows, configure real-mode driver support for the CD-ROM using the Windows version of MSCDEX.EXE in AUTOEXEC.BAT and the DOS device drivers (provided by the CD-ROM drive manufacturer) in CONFIG.SYS.

SYMPTOM 9-51   **Under Windows 98, an Alps DC544 CD-ROM changer appears as four individual CD-ROM drives in My Computer or Windows Explorer**   This problem occurs because the ALPSTRAY.EXE program does not work correctly in Windows 98. To work around this issue, use the Alps DC544 CD-ROM changer as if it were four different CD-ROM drives. As a more permanent fix, check with Alps for an updated ALPSTRAY.EXE file.

SYMPTOM 9-52   **The Pioneer DR-UA124X CD-ROM drive disables your IDE channel under Windows 9x/Me**   You may see a yellow exclamation point next to an IDE port in your Device Manager. This problem frequently occurs when you have a Pioneer CD-ROM drive (for example, the DR-UA124X) installed on your computer and you cannot access the CD-ROM drive connected to that IDE port. The Pioneer DR-UA124X CD-ROM drive's *firmware* causes this issue. You'll need to re-enable real-mode support for the drive. Use any text editor (Notepad, for example) to open the AUTOEXEC.BAT file. Find the MSCDEX command line and remove the REM statement at the beginning of that line. Save your changes and restart the computer. As an alternative, you may contact Pioneer for a firmware update or exchange.

SYMPTOM 9-53   **Your Toshiba Tecra 750 locks up when Windows 98 starts**   This is a known issue with Toshiba Tecra PCs with CD-ROM drives and can occur if all of these conditions exist:

■ The computer uses an IDE-type CD-ROM drive.

■ The IDE controller that is operating the CD-ROM drive is using the driver shipped with Windows 98.

■ You enable direct memory access (DMA) support for the CD-ROM drive.

This problem is caused by the IDE chipset used in Toshiba Tecra 750 computers. You may be able to correct this trouble by installing the Toshiba drivers rather than using the native Windows drivers:

1. Turn off the computer.

2. Physically remove the CD-ROM drive from the computer.

3. Restart the computer.

4. Install the Toshiba drivers for the IDE controller (if you don't have the drivers on a floppy disk already, download them from Toshiba's Web site).

5. Shut down the computer.

6. Put the CD-ROM drive back into the computer.

7. Restart your computer.

8. Windows should start normally and redetect the CD-ROM drive.

SYMPTOM 9-54   **When loading an audio CD in the drive, you receive a "no disc loaded" error**   This problem can occur under Windows 9x/Me and is typically caused when the MCI CD audio driver is not installed. You'll need to verify that the CD audio device driver is enabled:

1. Open the Control Panel and double-click on the Multimedia icon.

2. On the Advanced or Devices tab, double-click Media Control Devices.

3. Double-click CD Audio Device (Media Control).

4. Verify that the Use This Media Control Device entry is selected (Figure 9-12).

If the driver is enabled and you still receive the error message, try removing and reinstalling the device. To accomplish this, click Remove on the General tab in your CD Audio Device (Media Control) properties and then follow these steps:

1. Open the Control Panel and double-click the Add New Hardware icon.

2. Click Next, click No, and then click Next.

3. In the Hardware Types box, click Sound, Video, and Game Controllers, and then click Next.

4. In the Manufacturers box, click Microsoft MCI.

5. In the Models box, click CD Audio Device (Media Control).

6. Click Next, click Finish, and then restart your computer.

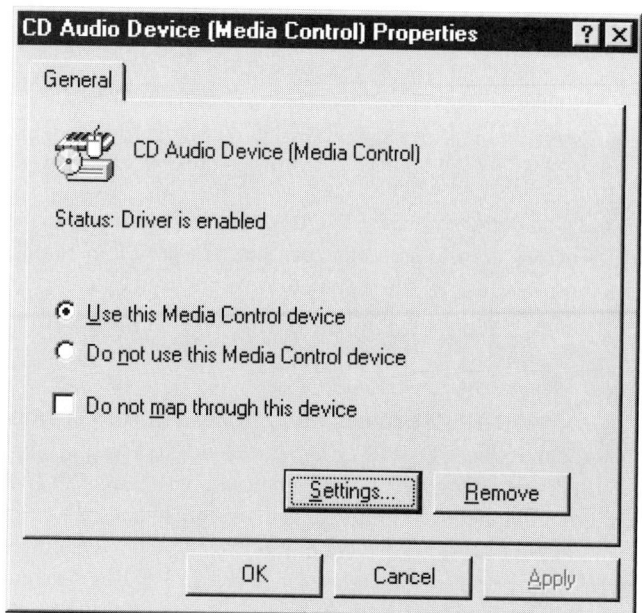

FIGURE 9-12   Enabling the CD Audio device under Windows 98/SE

SYMPTOM 9-55   **You cannot access a CD-ROM on an Acer 91 Pentium-based PC under Windows 9x/Me**   After you upgrade an Acer computer from an earlier version of Windows to Windows 9x/Me, you may find that the CD-ROM drive is not detected or that 32-bit disk and file access is not available. These problems may also occur when you upgrade an Acer computer to Windows 9x/Me. This issue occurs when the CD-ROM drive is connected to a CMD CSA-6400E PCI IDE controller—the CMD640X.SYS real-mode driver used with Acer computers is designed to work in Windows 3.1 and does *not* work in Windows 9x/Me. All Acer computer systems with a part number starting with "91.AA043" or "91.AA260" (using the CMD CSA-6400E PCI IDE controller and a Maxtor 7546AT hard disk) running Windows 9x/Me will exhibit this problem. To correct this problem, install the Windows 9x/Me version of the CMD CSA-6400E PCI IDE driver or download the updated driver file from Acer's Web site at: **www.acercm.com/drivers/storage_drivers.html**.

If you use the CMD 6400 PCI controller's protected-mode driver, 32-bit disk and file access is functional, but the CD-ROM drive is not detected. If you use the CMD 6400 PCI controller real-mode driver CMD640X.SYS, the CD-ROM drive is detected, but 32-bit disk and file access is not available.

SYMPTOM 9-56   **You cannot access a CD-ROM drive under Windows 9x/Me**   When you try to access your CD-ROM drive in Windows, you may find that you cannot run executable (.EXE) files, you cannot view complete directory listings, and you get a "Device not found" error message. These problems occur if you're using an older version of the MSCDEX.EXE file, which is *not* compatible with Windows 9x/Me. This problem commonly occurs when you install certain real-mode CD-ROM drivers—an older version of the MSCDEX.EXE file is copied to the hard disk, and the AUTOEXEC.BAT file is updated to utilize this older file. Modify the AUTOEXEC.BAT file manually to address the correct version of MSCDEX.EXE:

1. Use any text editor (such as Notepad) to open the AUTOEXEC.BAT file.
2. Locate the MSCDEX command line, then modify the line to read:

    ```
    <drive>:\<windows>\command\mscdex.exe <parameters>
    ```

    where <drive> is the drive letter where the Windows folder is located, <windows> is the name of the folder where Windows is installed, and <parameters> are the parameters from the original command line. Make sure to use all the parameters exactly as they are used in the original line.
3. Save and then close the AUTOEXEC.BAT file.
4. Restart your computer.

SYMPTOM 9-57   **A Sony CD-ROM drive is not detected during Windows 9x/Me Setup**

This problem can occur when the Sony CD-ROM drive is attached to a Media Vision sound card. Setup searches for Sony CD-ROM drives at several base I/O addresses, but a Sony CD-ROM drive attached to a Media Vision sound card is not in the range of addresses that Setup checks. As a result, Setup retains the existing real-mode drivers for the CD-ROM drive, but this often reduces system performance. You can get around this problem by setting up the Sony CD-ROM drive in Windows manually:

1. Click the Start button, highlight Settings, and click Control Panel.
2. Double-click the Add New Hardware icon, and then click the Next button.
3. Click the No option button, and then click Next.
4. Click CD-ROM Controllers, and then click Next.
5. In the Manufacturers box, click Sony. In the Models box, click Sony Proprietary CD-ROM Controller, and then click Next.
6. Click Next, and then click Finish.
7. When you are prompted to restart your computer, click No.
8. Click the Start button, highlight Settings, and then click Control Panel.
9. Double-click the System icon.
10. On the Device Manager tab, double-click the CD-ROM Controllers entry, and then double-click Sony Proprietary CD-ROM Controller.
11. Click the Resources tab.
12. In the Settings Based On box, click Basic Configuration 0.
13. Click the Use Automatic Settings check box to clear it.
14. Use the Change Settings button to modify the resources to match the CD-ROM drive's settings.
15. Click OK, then restart your computer when prompted.

 To verify that the CD-ROM drive is set up correctly, check it in Device Manager to see that no problems are reported in the Device Status box. Also, make sure that you can read a CD-ROM in the CD-ROM drive.

SYMPTOM 9-58   **Two CD-ROM drive letters appear in My Computer under Windows 9x/Me**   When you use My Computer or Windows Explorer, two CD-ROM drives may be displayed (even though you have only one CD-ROM drive in your computer). When you try to access either CD-ROM drive, your computer may lock up. This trouble can occur if you have both the real-mode CD-ROM device drivers *and* the Windows 9x/Me CD-ROM device drivers installed. To resolve this problem, use the System Configuration Editor (SYSEDIT.EXE) to disable the real-mode CD-ROM device drivers:

1. Click Start, click Run, type **sysedit** in the Open box, and then click OK.
2. Select the AUTOEXEC.BAT file, locate the line that loads the real-mode CD-ROM device drivers, and then type **rem** followed by a space at the beginning of the line. For example:

   ```
   rem c:\windows\command\mscdex.exe /d:mscd001
   ```

3. Select the CONFIG.SYS file, locate the line that loads the real-mode CD-ROM device drivers, and then type **rem** followed by a space at the beginning of the line. For example:

   ```
   rem device=c:\cdrom\cdrom.sys /d:mscd001
   ```

4. On the File menu, click Exit.
5. Click Yes when you're prompted to save the CONFIG.SYS and AUTOEXEC.BAT files.
6. Restart your computer.

SYMPTOM 9-59   **The CD-ROM refuses to run automatically under Windows 9x/Me when a disc is inserted**   This may occur even when the Auto Insert Notification feature is enabled. In most cases, the trouble is caused by an incorrect value in the registry. To resolve this problem, use Registry Editor to locate the following key:

```
HKEY_CURRENT_USER\Software\Microsoft\Windows\CurrentVersion\Policies\Explorer\NoDriveTypeAutoRun
```

Then modify the value for the NoDriveTypeAutoRun key to **0000 95 00 00 00** (or **0x95** in REGEDT32.EXE). After you make this change, quit the Registry Editor and restart your computer.

SYMPTOM 9-60   **A CD-ROM icon appears for a hard drive under Windows 95 OSR2 or Windows 98**   When you attempt to review your drives through My Computer, your hard disk icon may appear as a CD-ROM icon. If you double-click the CD-ROM icon in My Computer, you may receive an error message such as: "Cannot find autorun.exe." This problem can occur if the AUTORUN.INF file has been located in the root folder of your hard disk. To correct the problem, rename the AUTORUN.INF file to AUTORUN.OLD:

1. Click Start, point to Find, and then click Files Or Folders.
2. In the Named box, type **autorun.inf** and then click Find Now.
3. Right-click on AUTORUN.INF in the list of found files, and then click Properties.
4. Click the Read-Only check box to clear it, and then click OK.
5. Right-click on AUTORUN.INF in the list of found files, and then click Rename.
6. Type **autorun.old** and then press ENTER.
7. Restart your computer.

SYMPTOM 9-61 **You receive an error such as "CD-ROM cache acceleration file is invalid" under Windows 98** This kind of problem is typically encountered when using Quarterdeck SpeedyROM version 1.0 under Windows 98. Also, even though SpeedyROM may offer to reconstruct this file, you may continue to receive the same error message whenever you restart your computer. The trouble is generally caused when your computer's BIOS is configured to use a Fast Reboot feature. To correct this issue, disable the Fast Reboot feature in your computer's CMOS Setup.

Your BIOS may use a term other than Fast Reboot to identify the feature, so refer to your system's documentation for more CMOS Setup details.

SYMPTOM 9-62 **The drive will not read a CD correctly** As a sanity check, make sure that a CD is indeed inserted in the drive in its proper orientation (usually silk-screen side *up*). Also make sure that the CD in the drive is the right kind of disk. For example, an audio CD can not be accessed for programs and data files like a computer-compatible CD. Try accessing the disk a number of times before giving up. Try removing and reinserting the disk several times as well—inexpensive drives do not always center the disk very well.

Once you know the disk is appropriate and installed correctly, the problem may be in the adapter board or the data cable. There may be a problem with your drive's host adapter board. Turn off all power to the system, open the computer, and check again to see that the adapter board (and all available expansion boards) is inserted properly and completely. Double-check the data cable running between the drive and adapter board. If the cable is loose, or one end of the cable is reversed, data will not flow properly from drive to adapter. Double-check the adapter board's configuration to be sure that its base address, interrupt line, or DMA channel does not conflict with other devices that may be present in your system. You may have to remove the adapter board to check its configuration settings.

SYMPTOM 9-63 **The drive is recognized, but no audio is produced** Remember that a CD-ROM, CD-R, or CD-RW drive is generally a data-only device—the analog signals produced by CD audio must be routed to a sound board. Make sure that the thin, 4-wire audio cable is connected between the drive and the sound board. Adjust the sound board's volume control to achieve an adequate output. You could also plug in at the drive's headphone jack. Adjust the drive's headphone volume control for an adequate output. If your amplifier/speakers are not producing sound from the sound board, try using headphones in the drive's headphone jack. If there is sound from the headphones but none from the sound board, the sound board may be faulty, or the cable carrying the audio signal to the sound board may be disconnected or faulty. If the audio is absent under Windows 9x/Me, check to see that the necessary driver(s) is installed under the Control Panel.

SYMPTOM 9-64 **You see the following message when attempting to list a directory: Not ready reading drive [drive letter]:** There is a communication problem between the SCSI host controller and the CD-ROM, CD-R, or CD-RW drive caused by an undesirable SCSI ID for the drive or excessive bus speed at the ISA bus. Your first step should be to power-down the computer and check that the drive is connected properly to the SCSI host controller. Also make sure that the CD is inserted into the drive with the right side facing up. If problems continue, change the drive's switch settings to select a new SCSI device number. Reboot the computer and try the directory listing again. If the error message persists, you might need to try several different SCSI device ID numbers. If a new SCSI number does not correct the trouble, the bus speed of the computer may be at fault. ISA bus speed should generally not exceed 8.33MHz, so take the computer out of its "turbo" or high-speed mode and try the directory again. You may also upgrade the SCSI controller with a fully PnP adapter designed for the PCI bus.

SYMPTOM 9-65   **You see the following message when attempting to list a directory: CDROM not High Sierra or ISO 9660 format**   The cause of this error code (or of your bundled software's SCSI test program failures to detect a host adapter) is probably a memory conflict in your system—more than one device is attempting to use the same memory address(es). Conflicts are typically caused by expanded memory managers (EMM386, QEMM, 386MAX, and so on). Check your CONFIG.SYS file for the presence of a valid memory manager. You should see a device driver line such as:

```
device=c:\qemm\qemm386.sys
device=c:\dos\emm386.exe
```

Try adding parameters to your memory managers that will *exclude* the addresses used by your SCSI host adapter. You need to know the active addresses of the SCSI host adapter card from the settings of its configuration switches. Each setting should define a range of addresses (CC00 to CDFF, C800 to C9FF, DC00 to DDFF, D800 to D9FF, and so on). Refer to the documentation for your SCSI host adapter for more information. Once you know the address range of your adapter, add exclusion parameters to your CONFIG.SYS file, such as:

```
device=c:\qemm\qemm386.sys [parameters] exclude=aaaa-bbbb
device=c:\dos\emm386.exe [parameters] x=aaaa-bbbb
```

(where *aaaa* and *bbbb* are hexadecimal addresses). Reboot the computer and try the CD-ROM, CD-R, or CD-RW drive again. Other possible sources of conflict are the use of memory shadowing or disk caching, which are enabled through your system CMOS Setup program. Access your CMOS Setup and set all Disk Caching, BIOS Shadow, Shadow RAM, Video BIOS Shadow, or any Shadow options to the DISABLE condition. Reboot the computer and try the drive again.

Last-ditch sources of conflict can occur in the various computer peripherals (such as your 16-bit video card, modem card, scanner card, and so on). If your SCSI host adapter address range overlaps the address(es) of any other board, your system can encounter problems. Check the address settings of each installed peripheral and move that peripheral's address out of range of the SCSI controller and modify the address (if necessary) in the peripheral's setup or configuration program. As a check, you may wish to simply remove the peripheral to see if the problem goes away. Once you make a change, reboot the computer and try the drive again.

SYMPTOM 9-66   **You see the following message during initialization: No SCSI host adapter(s) detected**   Your system cannot find the SCSI host controller board. This may be due to faulty I/O, IRQ, or DMA settings on the host controller itself or to a memory conflict in hardware or software. Begin your investigation by powering down the computer and checking the host controller's resource settings. Use your documentation for the host controller and carefully verify each jumper or dip switch setting. A missing or improperly configured jumper can render the controller inoperative. Reset the controller board if necessary, then reboot the computer.

If the problem persists (or if you can not find faulty controller settings), you may be encountering trouble due to memory conflicts. Possible sources of conflict exist in the use of memory shadowing or disk caching which is enabled through your system CMOS Setup program. Access your CMOS setup and set all Disk Caching, BIOS Shadow, Shadow RAM, Video BIOS Shadow, or any Shadow options to the DISABLE condition. Reboot the computer and try the CD-ROM, CD-R, or CD-RW drive again.

Conflicts can also occur in various computer peripherals (your video card, modem card, scanner card, and so on). If your SCSI host adapter address range overlaps the address(es) of any other board, your system can encounter problems. Check the address settings of each installed peripheral, move that peripheral's address out of range of the SCSI controller, and modify the address (if necessary) in the peripheral's setup or configuration program. As a check, you may wish to simply remove the peripheral to see if the problem goes away. Once you make a change, reboot the computer and try the drive again. Finally, if the system simply refuses to acknowledge the SCSI controller, you may wish to try replacing the SCSI host controller.

SYMPTOM 9-67 **You see the following message during initialization: No xxxCD functions in use** This problem usually occurs with external SCSI CD-ROM drives. First, make sure the external CD-ROM, CD-R, or CD-RW drive is powered on before the computer starts to initialize. The CD drive must be available to the SCSI host controller in order for the CD-ROM/CD-R device driver MSCDEX to be loaded into memory. If the drive is turned on as expected and the MSCDEX driver will not load, check to see that the device driver in the AUTOEXEC.BAT file is listed similarly to that shown here:

```
C:\SCSI\MSCDEX /D:xxxCD /M:10 /L:[drive letter]
```

or:

```
C:\CDMENU\MSCDEX /D:xxxCD /M:10 /L:[drive letter]
```

If your AUTOEXEC.BAT file is set up as expected, check to be sure that the CD device driver (MSCDEX in this case) is actually present in the desired subdirectory. If the driver is missing (even if it is present in the wrong subdirectory), the driver will not load. Copy the driver to the appropriate subdirectory or change the path specification to the driver in the AUTOEXEC.BAT file. It is also generally recommended that your calling line appear *first* in the AUTOEXEC.BAT file. If the problem persists, try moving the calling line to the first line. Reboot the computer and try the drive again.

CD-R SYMPTOMS

CD recorders present some special problems for the typical PC. Many high-performance CD-R units use the SCSI interface in order to handle more consistent data transfer from the system to the drive. Installing a CD-R may require the addition (and expense) of a SCSI host adapter and associated driver software. CD recording demands a substantial commitment of hard drive space—perhaps as much as 1GB—in order to create an *image file* for recording (an "image file" basically converts the data to be recorded into the "pits" and "lands" that must be encoded to the blank disc). So if you're tight on drive space, you may also need another hard drive to support the CD-R. Finally, CD-Rs require a constant and uninterrupted flow of data during the recording process. If the CD-R data buffer empties, the recording process will halt, and your blank CD will be ruined (unless the drive employs BurnProof technology). This means you'll need fast hard drives and a high-performance interface (UDMA/33 or faster). This part of the chapter explains some of the problems associated with using a CD-R and illustrates a series of troubleshooting symptoms and solutions.

CD Recording Issues

Writing data to a recordable CD is a complex process that demands a great deal from your PC's hardware and software. Most of this complexity is hidden by the power of the CD authoring program, but there are a number of important factors that you should be aware of that can influence the success of CD recording:

File Sizes The sheer *amount* of data being written to the CD is less important than the individual file sizes—the recorder may have trouble locating and opening small files quickly enough to send them smoothly to the CD recorder, where fewer large files would typically record without problems.

System Interruptions Any interruption in the flow of data is fatal to CD recording, so make sure that your CONFIG.SYS and AUTOEXEC.BAT files do not load any TSR utilities that may periodically interrupt the computer's drive operations. Unneeded background applications should also be shut down. Utilities like screen savers, calendar alarms, or reminders as well as incoming faxes are just a few "features" that will interrupt disc writing. If the PC is part of a network, you should temporarily disable network sharing so that no one tries to access local files while you're trying to write the CD.

The Hard Disk The hard drive is a critical component of the CD-R system because you must transfer data from the HDD to the CD-R at a rate adequate to keep the recorder's buffer filled. There are three major issues involving your hard drive: speed, file fragmentation, and thermal calibration.

- **Speed** In order to write a virtual "image file" to a compact disc, the hard disk from which you are writing must have a transfer rate fast enough to keep the CD-R drive buffer full. This usually means an average hard disk access time of 19mS or less. It would also help to use a high-performance drive interface such as Ultra-DMA/33, Ultra-DMA/66, or SCSI-3.

- **Fragmentation** This issue is also related to speed. Searching all over a very fragmented hard disk for image file data can cause drive operations to slow down. In many cases, a badly fragmented hard drive cannot support CD-R operations. Be sure to defragment your hard drive before creating an image file.

- **Thermal calibration** All hard disks periodically perform an automatic thermal calibration to ensure proper performance. Calibration interrupts hard disk operations for as much as 1.5 seconds. Some hard disks "force" a calibration at fixed intervals (even if the disk is in use), causing interruptions that are fatal to CD writing. This problem is worse when the image file is large and the writing process takes longer. If you can select a new hard drive to support CD-R operations, choose a drive with "intelligent" thermal calibration (it postpones recalibration until the drive is idle).

CD Recorder Speed Typical CD recorders are capable of writing at 12 times the standard writing/playback speed of 150KB/s (and faster). Recording speed is simply a matter of how fast the bits are inscribed by the laser on the disc surface. It has nothing to do with how fast you read them back or how much data you can fit on the disc. However, higher recording speeds can accomplish a writing process in a shorter period of time. Faster recording speeds are certainly a time saver, but they also mean that larger recording buffers are required (and those buffers empty faster). As a consequence, faster recorders will demand a faster hard drive and interface to support data transfer. In most cases, "buffer underrun" type problems can often be corrected by slowing down the recording process rather than by upgrading the drive system.

When you write a real ISO image file from hard disk to CD, speed is rarely a problem because the image is already one gigantic file. The files and structures are already in order and divided into CD-ROM sectors, so it is necessary only to stream data off the hard drive to the CD recorder. When you write from a *virtual* image, things get trickier because a virtual image is little more than a list. The CD authoring program must consult the virtual image database to find out where each file should go in the image and where each file actually is stored on the hard disk. The authoring software must then open the file and divide it into CD-ROM sectors—all while sending data to the CD recorder in a smooth, continuous stream. Locating and opening each file is often the more time-consuming part of the recording process (which is why "on-the-fly" writing is more difficult when you have many small files).

CD Recorder Buffer   All CD recorders have a small amount of on-board buffer memory. The CD recorder's buffer helps to ensure that there is always data ready to be written because extra data is stored as it arrives from the computer. The size of the buffer is critical to trouble-free writing—a slow-down or interruption in the transfer of data from the computer will not interrupt writing so long as the buffer is not completely emptied. The larger the buffer, the greater safety margin you have in case of interruptions. If your CD recorder has a very small buffer and your hard disk is slow, you may find it difficult (or impossible) to write virtual images on-the-fly to CD. When this occurs, you can make a real ISO image file on the hard disk and record to CD from that, use a faster hard disk sub-system, or upgrade your CD recorder's buffer (if possible).

Typical Compatibility Problems

Even when CDs record perfectly, it is not always possible to read them correctly in other drives. The following notes highlight three common compatibility issues.

Problems Reading Recordable CDs   Recordable CDs frequently cannot be read in older CD-ROM drives. If the CD can be read when used on the CD-R but *not* on a standard CD-ROM drive, check the disc recording utility to make sure that the session containing the data you just wrote is *closed*—CD-ROM drives cannot read data from a session that is not closed. If your recorded disc is ejected, you receive an error message, or if you have any random problems accessing files from the recorded disc, the problem may be that your CD-ROM drive is not well calibrated to read recorded CDs. Try the disc on another CD-ROM drive or upgrade the CD-ROM drive itself. If you recorded the disc using DOS filenames, but there are difficulties in reading back the recorded CD with DOS or Windows, it may be that you have an older version of MSCDEX (before version 2.23) on your system. Check your MSCDEX version and update it if necessary.

Problems Reading Multisession CDs   If you can see only data recorded in the first session on the CD—but not in subsequent sessions—it may be that the disc was recorded in CD-ROM (Mode 1) format, while your multisession CD-ROM drive recognizes only CD-ROM XA (Mode 2) multisession CDs. If this happens, you may need to re-record the disc in the correct mode. Of course, your CD-ROM drive must support multisession operation in the first place. If you can see only data recorded in the last session, you may have forgotten to link your new data with data previously recorded on the CD. Refer to the instructions for your CD recorder and review the suggested steps required to create a multisession CD.

CD-ROM Drive Incompatibility with Recordable CDs   It may happen that you can write a CD without trouble and can read it properly on your CD-R—but when you put the disc in a standard CD-ROM drive, the disc is ejected. You may also see error messages such as "No CD-ROM" or "Drive not ready," or you have random problems accessing some files or directories. You may also find that the problems disappear when reading the CD on a different CD-ROM drive. Although you may suspect the problems stem from the original CD-ROM drive, they may actually be due to incompatibility between some CD-ROM drives (especially older ones) and recorded CDs. Some CD-ROM drive lasers are not calibrated to read recordable CDs (often the surface is different from that of factory-pressed CDs). If your CD-ROM drive reads mass-produced (silver) CDs but not recordable CDs, check with the CD-ROM drive manufacturer to determine whether this is the problem. In some cases, a drive upgrade may be available that will resolve the problem.

The combination of blank disc's brand and CD recorder can also make a difference. Use blank CD media that has been recommended by the CD-R manufacturer.

Typical Multisession CD Issues

You may encounter older CD-ROM drives that have trouble reading multisession CDs. Multisession discs are recorded according to the Orange Book (Part II) standard, which states that sessions can be written in *either* the CD-ROM or CD-ROM XA format. A fully compliant multisession CD-ROM drive should always be able to access at the last session on a disc *regardless* of its format.

Unfortunately, there have been misunderstandings and misinterpretations of the Orange Book standard, but to understand the problems, you need to know a bit of history. Multisession recording was first used by Kodak for their Photo CD initiative. Now, one roll of film does *not* fill up a Photo CD disc, so when you take your disc and a new roll of film for new Photo CD processing, the new photos are added in a "new session." This new session is linked to previous sessions so that you can see *all* the photos on the disc—no matter how many sessions they are recorded in.

Kodak chose the CD-ROM XA standard for its Photo CD disc format for reasons that had *nothing* to do with the Orange Book standard. But since Photo CD was the first reason that CD-ROM drive manufacturers had to create multisession drives, many assumed that the Kodak approach to multisession (the CD-ROM XA) was the *only* way. They accordingly wrote software drivers that assume that a multisession disc must also be XA. When one of these drivers sees a disc that is not XA, it assumes that the disc is also *not* multisession, and it tells the CD-ROM drive to read only the first session on the disc. The result is that a multisession disc is read as if it were a single-session disc, and you see only the data in the first session.

CD-ROM drive manufacturers have generally resolved this glitch in virtually all current drives and drivers (8x CD-ROM and later drives), but if you record a multisession disc in CD-ROM format you may find that some older drives—even if specified as a "multisession" drive—may not read beyond the first session on the disc. If you need to share multisession discs with others, you should test to see which format their CD-ROM drives can handle. To be on the safe side, write your disc in the CD-ROM XA format. A more permanent fix is to upgrade the older CD-ROM to a model that is fully multisession-compliant.

You cannot mix formats on the same disc—a multisession disc containing both CD-ROM and CD-ROM XA sessions would be unreadable on most drives.

Buffer Underruns

CD writing is a real-time process that must run constantly at the selected recording speed *without interruptions*. Most of the time, your computer will pass data to the CD-R faster than it is needed. This keeps CD-R's buffer constantly filled with a reserve of data waiting to be written, so small slowdowns or interruptions in the flow of data from the computer will not interrupt the writing process. The CD-R's internal buffer stores this extra data as it arrives to help maintain a steady flow of data to the writing laser.

The size of the buffer is critical to trouble-free writing. Remember that a slowdown or interruption in the transfer of data from the computer will not stop a writing cycle so long as the buffer is not *completely* emptied. The larger the buffer, the more safety margin you have in case of interruptions. A *buffer underrun* error means that for some reason the flow of data from hard disk to CD-R was interrupted long enough for the CD recorder's buffer to be emptied, and writing was halted. If this occurs during an actual write operation (rather than a pre-writing test), your recordable disc may be ruined. This checklist covers many of the typical issues that may trigger a buffer underrun:

- **"Dumb" thermal recalibration**   Disable thermal recalibration on the hard drive before writing or allow one hour or so for the system temperature to stabilize before writing.
- **Excessive file fragmentation**   Defragment the hard drive with Defrag before "burning" a CD.

■ **Insufficient free space**   The CD-R will almost certainly require some amount of "temporary" workspace on the hard drive. If there is insufficient free space on the hard drive, you may need to free additional space by offloading unneeded files or upgrading the drive itself.

■ **Too many small files**   When recording "on the fly," many small files may present too much of a load on your data transfer system, so try making an ISO "image file" first.

■ **Damaged files**   Files that are damaged or corrupted will often cause errors that will interrupt the flow of data. Run ScanDisk and Defrag to locate any possible file system problems before recording.

■ **Recording files in use**   Make sure that no files to be recorded are currently in use by any application.

■ **Slow hard drives**   Older hard drives may not support data transfer speeds high enough to keep the CD-R buffer filled. If you use slow hard drives, make an ISO "image file" first rather than writing "on the fly."

■ **Burst data transfers**   Source devices that operate in *burst* data transfer modes may have difficulty keeping the CD-R buffer filled. Try disabling the "burst" mode—while doing this may slow the overall data transfer, it may also "even out" the flow of data, making it easier to keep the recorder's buffer filled.

■ **CD-R controller configuration**   Verify that the IDE or SCSI controller operating the CD-R is configured for optimum performance (for example, use bus master drivers for UDMA controllers).

■ **Sync problems**   Certain combinations of drives and controllers may not synchronize data properly. Check that you're using the recommended hardware devices for proper CD-R operation.

■ **Outdated device drivers**   Verify that you're using the latest device drivers for the CD-R, controller, and other related devices in the system.

■ **Slow computer speed**   Systems older then 486 platforms may simply be too old to support the data transfer needs of a CD-R. Verify that your system meets the minimum system requirements for your particular CD-R model.

■ **CD-R quality**   Be sure to use good quality CD-R discs that are recommended by the CD-R manufacturer. Dirty, old, or scratched discs may not function.

■ **Memory-resident software issues**   CD-R systems may encounter buffer underrun problems when certain types of software are at work on your system:
Anti-virus
Screen saver
System agent
Scheduler
TSR (terminate and stay resident)
Network
System sounds
Animated icons or utilities
Any program that may activate on its own

■ **Insufficient virtual memory**   Adjust your Virtual Memory settings to use at least 32MB of RAM for virtual memory.

■ **Disable Auto Insert Notification**   If you have more than 16MB of RAM, disable Auto Insert Notification for the CD-ROM.

■ **Change the system's role**   If you have more than 16MB of RAM, change the hard drive's Typical Role to Network Server.

Avoiding Buffer Underruns   Although current PCs generally provide the speed and drive performance that are vital for CD recording, modern high-speed drives can empty a buffer in moments. This means buffer underruns continue to be a serious issue for technicians and end-users alike. The following tips may help you avoid buffer underruns:

- Always set audio discs to write at 1X.

- Change the UDMA transfer rate for the drive controller card being used (that is, select the fastest data transfer rate available for your system and drives).

- Defragment your hard drives at least once a week to prevent files from being scattered across the hard drive.

- Disable or remove all software in the computer *except* the operating system, the recording software, and the drivers for your source devices and CD-R.

- Disc-to-disc copying generally requires a SCSI-2, fully ASPI-compliant CD-ROM drive (at least 4x). Copying audio requires a source CD-ROM drive that supports "digital audio extraction."

- Do not record across a network—copy the desired files to your local hard drive first.

- Do not try to copy empty directories, zero byte files, or files that may be in use by the system at the time.

- For best results use SCSI-2 (or faster) source devices (preferably SCSI-3).

- In any operating system, always using the newest drivers from your SCSI controller card manufacturer.

- Log out of any networks if possible (including Windows for Workgroups and/or Microsoft Network).

- Make sure your hard drive does Smart Thermal Recalibration—it won't recalibrate if the drive is being used.

- Make sure your SCSI controller card is *fully* ASPI-compliant.

- More than 10,000 very small files should be written to an .ISO image first or recorded at 1x if possible in order to ease data transfer demands.

- Record at a slower speed (for instance, 4x rather than 8x).

- The temporary directory should always have space free for at least twice the size of the largest file you are recording.

- Try a different hard disk and/or high-quality gold recordable disc.

- With DOS 6.22 or below and a source hard disk 1GB or larger, partitions should be kept smaller than 1GB so that hard disk cluster size is 16KB instead of 32KB.

- Write an .ISO image to the hard disk first (if you have enough hard drive space).

General Symptoms

CD recorders are subject to a large number of potential errors during operation. Many typical recording errors are listed next. In most cases, the error is not terribly complex and can be corrected in just a few minutes once the nature of the problem is understood. Keep in mind that the actual error message is dependent on the CD recorder software in use, so your actual error messages may vary just a bit.

For basic CD-related issues, refer to the CD-ROM troubleshooting information earlier in this chapter.

SYMPTOM 9-68   **Absorption control error <xxx>**   This error most often means that there is a slight problem writing to a recordable disc—perhaps caused by a smear or speck of dust. It does not *necessarily* mean that your data has not been correctly recorded. A sector address is usually given so that you can (if you wish) verify the data in and around that sector. When writing is completed, try cleaning the disc (on the non-label side) gently with a lint-free cloth. If the error occurs again, try a new disc.

SYMPTOM 9-69   **Application code error**   This error typically occurs when you try to write Kodak recordable CDs (Photo CDs) on non-Kodak CD recorders. These discs have a protection bit that is recognized only by the Kodak CD-R—all other recorders will not record these discs. In this case, you'll need to use "standard" blank CDs (or use a recorder that is certified to work with Photo CDs).

SYMPTOM 9-70   **Bad ASPI open**   The CD-R ASPI driver is bad or missing, and the SCSI CD-R cannot be found. Check the installation of your CD-R drive and SCSI adapter, then check the driver installation. Try reinstalling the latest SCSI driver(s) for the drive (and the host adapter if necessary).

SYMPTOM 9-71   **Buffer underrun at sector <xxx>**   Once an image file is generated, CD writing is a real-time process that must run constantly at the selected recording speed—*without interruptions*. The CD recorder's buffer is constantly filled with data from the hard drive waiting to be written. This buffering action ensures that small slowdowns or interruptions in the flow of data from the computer do not interrupt the writing process. A *buffer underrun* message indicates that the flow of data from hard disk to CD recorder was interrupted long enough for the CD recorder's buffer to be emptied, and writing was halted. If this occurs during an actual write operation rather than a test, your CD may be damaged.

To avoid buffer underruns, you should remove as much processing load as possible from the system. For example, make sure that no screen savers or other Terminate and Stay Resident (TSR) programs are active (they can momentarily interrupt operations). Close as many open windows as possible. See that your working hard disk cannot be accessed via a network. For SCSI CD-R drives, the CD recorder's position in the SCSI chain—or the cable length between the computer and CD recorder—may cause data slowdowns. Try connecting the CD recorder as the first peripheral in the SCSI chain (if not done already), and use a shorter SCSI cable (if possible) between the CD recorder and the SCSI host adapter. Verify that the SCSI bus is terminated properly. For more information, see the earlier section "Buffer Underruns."

SYMPTOM 9-72   **Current disc already contains a closed audio session**   Under the Red Book standard for audio CDs, all audio tracks must be written in a *single* session (Disk-at-Once). If you add audio tracks in more than one session, playback results will be unpredictable. Most CD-ROM drives will play back all audio tracks on a CD even if they are recorded in several different sessions, but most home and car CD players can only play back the tracks in the *first* session. If you continue and record audio in a different session, you may have problems reading subsequent audio sessions.

SYMPTOM 9-73   **Current disc contains a session that is not closed**   In actual practice, CD-ROM drives can read back only one data track per session, so avoid recording another data track in an open session. Be sure to close the session *before* writing additional data to the disc (as a new session).

SYMPTOM 9-74   **Currently selected source CD-ROM drive or CD recorder cannot read audio in digital format**   This is more of a warning than a fault. Reading audio tracks in "digital format" is *not* the same as playing the music, and few CD-ROM drives are able to read audio tracks in digital format (only Red Book format). You may need to copy the music data from the CD to the hard drive first, then post-process the digital audio data through the application used to make the new CD. In a more contemporary setting, this type of problem indicates that the source drive cannot adequately handle digital audio extraction (DAE). You may need to upgrade the drive itself in order to achieve good DAE performance.

SYMPTOM 9-75   Data overrun/underrun   The SCSI host adapter has reported an error that is almost always caused by improper termination or a bad SCSI cable. Recheck the installation of your SCSI adapter, cabling, and termination. You may also need to reduce the processing overhead needed by unused applications. Refer to the earlier section "Buffer Underruns" for more details.

SYMPTOM 9-76   Destination disc is smaller than the source disc   This error commonly occurs when you're trying to duplicate an existing CD to the CD-R. There is not enough room on the recordable CD to copy the source CD. Try recording to a blank CD-R disc. Use 74-minute media instead of 60-minute media. Some CDs cannot be copied because of the TOC (Table of Contents) overhead in CD recorders as well as the calibration zone overhead. You may need to break up the source CD between two or more different CD-R discs.

SYMPTOM 9-77   Disc already contains tracks and/or sessions that are incompatible with the requested operation   This error appears if you're trying to add data in a format that is different from the data format already on the disc. For example, you'll see this type of error when trying to add a CD-ROM XA session to a disc that already contains a standard CD-ROM session. A disc containing multiple formats is generally *unreadable*, so you are not allowed to record the different session type.

SYMPTOM 9-78   Disc write-protected   You are attempting to write to a CD-R disc that has already been closed to further writing (finalized). Do *not* try writing to discs that are closed—instead, use a fresh blank disc for writing.

SYMPTOM 9-79   Error 175-xx-xx-xx   This error code often indicates a "buffer underrun." See the information in the earlier section "Buffer Underruns."

SYMPTOM 9-80   Error 220-01-xx-xx   This error code often indicates that some of your software cannot communicate with a SCSI device—possibly because your SCSI bus was reset. In many cases, this is caused by conflicts between real-mode and protected-mode SCSI drivers working in a Windows 9x/Me system. Try REMing out any real-mode SCSI drivers in your CONFIG.SYS file (the protected-mode drivers provided for Windows 9x/Me should be sufficient on their own). You may need to download and install updated protected-mode drivers for the SCSI host adapter and CD-R drive (as well as other SCSI devices that may be installed).

SYMPTOM 9-81   Error 220-06-xx-xx   This error code often indicates a SCSI Selection Time-Out error, which suggests a SCSI setup problem—usually with the SCSI host adapter. Contact your SCSI host adapter manufacturer for detailed installation and testing instructions. You may need to adjust the SCSI BIOS Setup or update the SCSI drivers in your system. In extreme cases, you may need to upgrade the SCSI host adapter card.

SYMPTOM 9-82   Error reading the Table of Contents (TOC) or Program Memory Area (PMA) from the disc   This recordable disc is defective or has been damaged (probably during a previous write operation, or the current write operation). Do *not* try to write to this disc. Unfortunately, there is very little you can do here except to discard the defective disc. Try a fresh, good quality disc that has been recommended by the drive manufacturer.

SYMPTOM 9-83   **General protection fault**   This type of problem has been identified with the Adaptec AHAr-152x family of SCSI host adapters and is caused by outdated driver software. You can solve this problem by upgrading to version 3.1 (or later) of Adaptec's EZ-SCSI software. If you're not using Adaptec software, check for current drivers for whatever SCSI adapter you're using.

SYMPTOM 9-84   **Invalid logical block address**   This error message usually means that the CD mastering software has requested a data block from the hard disk that either does not exist or is illegal—this may suggest a corrupted hard disk or damaged ISO file. Exit the CD mastering software and run ScanDisk and Defrag to check and reorganize your hard drive. You may need to rebuild an ISO file or reload damaged files from a backup.

SYMPTOM 9-85   **Last two blocks stripped**   This message appears when copying a track to hard disk if the track you are reading was created as multisession-compliant (following the Orange Book standard). This is because a multisession track is always followed by two run-out blocks. These are included in the count of the total size (in blocks) of the track, but they do not contain data and cannot be read back. This message appears in order to alert you just in case you notice that you have two blocks fewer than were reported for the Read Length. Don't panic—you haven't lost any data.

SYMPTOM 9-86   **MSCDEX errors are being encountered**   Early versions of MSCDEX (prior to v.2.23) had problems with file names containing "illegal" ASCII characters such as a hyphen. If a directory contains a file name with an "illegal" ASCII character, you can still see all the files by doing a directory (DIR) from DOS, or you can open the illegally named file. However, one or more files listed *after* the illegal one may not be accessible or may give errors. You should update MSCDEX to the latest available version. As an alternative, you may REM out the real-mode driver and MSCDEX command lines in your startup files and allow Windows 9x/Me to rely exclusively on protected-mode drivers.

SYMPTOM 9-87   **DOS or Windows cannot find the CD-R drive**   There are several possible reasons why the CD-R drive cannot be found by software. First, turn the computer off and wait at least 15 seconds. Make sure the IDE or SCSI adapter card is firmly seated and secured to the computer case. The IDE or SCSI adapter must also be properly configured. Check the IDE or SCSI cable and see that it is properly attached to the adapter and drive. Turn the computer on. If problems persist, make sure that the correct IDE or SCSI drivers are installed and that any command line switches are set correctly. If the problem persists, you may need to try another drive model.

SYMPTOM 9-88   **No write data (buffer empty)**   The flow of data to the CD-R drive must be extremely reliable so that its working buffer is never empty when it prepares to write a block of information to disc. This message indicates that the flow of data from the hard disk to the CD recorder has been interrupted (similar to the "Buffer Underrun" error). Ensure that there are no active no screen savers, other TSR utilities, or unneeded open windows that might momentarily interrupt operations. Your working hard disk should not be accessible over a network. Next, suspect the SCSI setup. The SCSI CD recorder's position in the SCSI chain, or the length of cabling between the SCSI adapter and CD recorder, may also cause data slowdowns. Try connecting the CD recorder as the first device in the SCSI chain (you may need to re-terminate the SCSI chain) and keeping the SCSI cable as short as possible.

SYMPTOM 9-89   **Read file error**   A file referenced by the virtual image database cannot be located or accessed on the source drive. Make sure that the suspect file is not being used by you or by someone else on a network. The file may also be damaged or corrupt, so exit the CD-R application and run ScanDisk and Defrag to check the file system for problems. You may need to reload damaged files from a backup.

SYMPTOM 9-90   **Selected disc image file was not prepared for the current disc**
This type of error message occurs if you prepared the disc image file for a blank CD, but are now trying to record it to a CD *already* containing data, or vice versa. In either case, you would wind up writing a CD that couldn't be read at all because the CD addresses calculated for the disc image are wrong for that actual CD. If you are given the option of writing anyway, select No to abort, because it is very unlikely that the writing operation would yield a readable CD. Retry the operation with a known-blank CD-R disc.

SYMPTOM 9-91   **Selected disc track is longer than the image file**   The disc verify process fails immediately because the source ISO 9660 image file and the actual ISO 9660 track on CD are not the same size—the disc track is actually longer than the image file, possibly indicating a defective CD-R drive. Retry the operation with a good quality CD-R disc. If the problem persists, you might try replacing the CD-R drive.

SYMPTOM 9-92   **Selected disc track is shorter than the image file**   The disc verify process fails immediately because the source ISO 9660 image file and the actual ISO 9660 track on CD are not the same size—the disc track is actually shorter than the image file, and could indicate a defective CD-R drive. Retry the operation with a good quality CD-R disc. If the problem persists, you might try replacing the CD-R drive with a later model.

SYMPTOM 9-93   **The "disc in" light on the drive does not blink after you turn on the computer**   In virtually all cases, there is no power reaching the CD-R drive. For internal CD-R drives, make sure the computer's 4-pin power cable is properly connected to the CD-R drive unit. For external CD-R drives, make sure the power cord is properly connected to the back of the CD-R drive unit and is plugged in to a grounded power outlet. Make sure the power switch on the back of the drive is *on*. Refer to your CD-R drive's installation guide for more detailed information.

SYMPTOM 9-94   **Write emergency**   This error occurs if the drive is interrupted during a write action. It is commonly seen when writing Red Book audio, but it can also occur with data recordings. For example, one typical reason for a write emergency is dust particles that cause the laser to jump off track. In most cases, the CD-R disc is ruined, and you'll need to retry the write process with a good quality disc.

SYMPTOM 9-95   **The CD-R is recognized by Windows 9x/Me, but it will not function as a normal CD-ROM drive**   The drive appears normally in the Windows 9x/Me Device Manager. The driver that is operating the CD-R drive may not allow the drive to function as a normal CD-ROM reader. For example, this is a known problem with the Philips CDD2000 CD-R. Check to see if there is an updated Windows 9x/Me CD-R driver that can overcome this limitation. If not, you may need to replace the CD-R drive with an upgraded model whose drivers *do* support CD-ROM–type functionality on the CD-R drive.

SYMPTOM 9-96   **You cannot read CD-R (gold) discs in some ordinary CD-ROM drives**
This is actually a very complex issue because there are a number of important factors that affect the way in which a CD is read. Laser calibration may be a factor. Some older CD-ROM drive lasers are not calibrated

to read recordable discs (whose recorded surface is slightly different from that of "pressed" discs). If your CD-ROM drive reads mass-produced (silver) CDs but not recordable CDs, check with the CD-ROM drive manufacturer to determine whether laser calibration is the problem. You may be able to return the CD-ROM drive for factory recalibration or replace the CD-ROM drive with a newer model that is better calibrated for reading both CD-ROM and CD-R discs.

Fast CD-ROM drive operations may be another problem. In order for some CD-ROM models to work as fast as they do, they must perform unconventional operations, such as a laser calibration in the lead-out area to determine the approximate position of several tracks. With some CD recorders, the session lead-out is not recorded correctly, causing problems with gold disc compatibility.

The CD-R authoring software can be a problem. Any authoring software can sometimes produce incorrect tracks due to bugs or recording glitches. A good way to check whether incompatibility problems lie with the originating software is to test the same gold disc on several CD-ROM drives. If one drive is capable of reading the gold disc back correctly, chances are that the problem was *not* in the recording process. If no drives can read the CD-R disc, then the disc may have been damaged in the recording process.

Finally, consider your version of MSCDEX. Although MSCDEX will allow non-ISO legal characters in file names, versions of MSCDEX *prior* to 2.23 have a problem in dealing with file names that contain a hyphen. If a directory contains a file name with a hyphen, although you will be able to see all the files by doing a DIR from DOS, any files listed *after* the file with the illegal name are not accessible. When trying to open them, you would get a "file not found" message. MSCDEX 2.23 (and later) appears to have fixed this bug. You may also REM-out the real-mode drivers and MSCDEX command lines in your startup files and rely on protected-mode drivers under Windows 9x/Me.

SYMPTOM 9-97   You encounter "buffer miscompare" errors when using a SCSI host adapter diagnostic utility   In many cases, you have a DMA channel conflict with another card (or device) in the system. Check the settings of every card or device that uses an IRQ, DMA channel, or I/O port address and compare these settings to the ones used for the SCSI host adapter. If there is a DMA conflict, change the DMA channel on the SCSI card to an unused channel.

Another possibility is that you're dealing with a motherboard that doesn't support bus mastering (not all PC's support bus mastering). For example, a Gateway 2000 P5-133 has only one bus mastering slot, which is normally occupied by the video adapter. If the SCSI adapter (an Adaptec AHA-1535 card, for instance) is installed in a non–bus-mastering slot in this machine, the system may freeze when trying to access a CD from the CD-R drive. It may be necessary to upgrade the motherboard to access additional bus mastering PCI slots.

SYMPTOM 9-98   You encounter a "servo tracking error" when writing a CD   A "servo tracking error" message is reported by the CD-R drive when it is unable to record to the media (the blank disc)—this is similar to when a needle "skips" on a phonograph. There is a microscopic groove imprinted on the surface of each CD-R disc that guides the laser during writing. There are a number of reasons why a "servo tracking error" might occur.

Check for defective media first. *Defective media* can include a bad disc, a bad lot of discs, or an unsupported brand of media (not all CD-R disc media work the same on all CD-R drives). For example, the Pinnacle Micro RCD-1000/5020/5040 series drives support the following disc brands: DOT, Taiyo Yuden, Mitsubishi, Sony, 3M, TDK, Verbatim, and Kodak Infoguard. Make sure that you're using a blank disc that's certified to work with your particular drive—try another disc (or disc brand) if necessary. There may be a dirty lens within the drive that prevents the laser from focusing on the surface of the media. Use a can of clean compressed air to blow out the inside of the drive through the front access door or tray.

Next, verify that the amount of data you are trying to record does not exceed the capacity of the disc. Your recording software will usually prevent you from making that mistake, but it has no way of adjusting for previously-failed sessions or bad blocks on the media—these can cause the software to make an incorrect calculation of the remaining free space, which will differ from what is *actually* free.

Finally, a servo tracking error may occur if the ambient temperature inside the drive itself is too high. If your drive is external, remove the filter from the back of the drive and use compressed air to clean it out. Confirm that the cooling fan works when the unit is powered on—if not, the drive may need to be replaced. If your drive is internal, verify that it receives enough air circulation by removing the computer's case, letting the drive cool off for a while, and then rerunning the recording session. If the problem persists, replace the drive.

SYMPTOM 9-99   **You notice frequent "pops" or "clicks" between CD audio tracks**
This is almost always a result of your particular CD recording software. The "pops" or "clicks" heard between tracks on CD digital audio (CD-DA) discs are caused when recording *without* using the Disc-At-Once option. When you select the Disc-At-Once option in the authoring software, the laser will remain powered on between each track (and run-in/run-out blocks are written without interruption). Remember that the Disc-At-Once feature is currently unavailable on a few software packages, so check the manual of your CD authoring software to see if there is a Disc-At-Once feature—if not, you may have an outdated or "lite" version, which will require an upgrade. For example, the Disc-At-Once feature is available with *Easy-CD Pro* version 1.1.409 and later, but not with *Easy-CD 95*. The *Corel CD Creator* does not support true Disc-At-Once, even as late as version 2.01.079. However, most CD recording software will offer a Disk-at-Once recording mode today.

Another possible cause for "pops" between tracks occurs when a .WAV file is created improperly (or it is corrupt). Some early shareware audio editing software had problems saving .WAV files properly, and bugs caused "pops" to occur between tracks (and at other various points throughout a song). These .WAV files were corrupted by the editing software. The most recent problem with .WAV files is the use of "extended information." Some .WAV editing software packages allow the user to save the .WAV file in an Extended .WAV Format as well as the standard .WAV format. If "extended information" is included in the .WAV file (author name, date, and so on), this will cause a "pop" to occur when played back through a standard audio CD player. Make sure you can save a .WAV file *without* this extra information to avoid the problem.

Today, pops and clicks *in* an audio track are often the result of poor digital audio extraction (DAE). You can try slowing the DAE rate in your recording software, or upgrading the drive to a model that is well suited for DAE use. (See Symptom 9-105.)

SYMPTOM 9-100   **On your home stereo, the disc will not repeat play after the last track**
When you set your home stereo CD player to Repeat Playback after the last track, the CD playback simply stops—it will not repeat. Some audio CD players cannot play back a "burned" audio disc properly if there are B0h and C0h pointers in the disc's Table Of Contents. B0h and C0h pointers are used to point to the next session and are created on discs written using the Track-At-Once (or multisession) option. CDs written using Disc-At-Once do not contain these pointers because there are no subsequent sessions. If you would like to have a disc that is fully compatible with "audio CD," use the Disc-At-Once option during recording.

SYMPTOM 9-101   **You cannot access a CD-R after upgrading to Windows 98 or later**
You may find this happens most frequently with Philips CDD200 or HO 4020I CD-R drives, and it is almost always due to problems with Corel CD Creator 2.0 being present on your system. There are two means of correcting this problem. First, uninstall Corel CD Creator and install other CD authoring software (for instance, Adaptec Easy CD Creator Pro) that should be better able to support the CD-R drive. If you cannot replace the CD authoring software, check with the CD-R maker to see of there is a firmware upgrade available for the CD-R drive.

SYMPTOM 9-102   **When upgrading to Windows 9x/Me, you receive a "fatal exception 0E" error**   While you are installing Windows and Setup restarts your computer for the last time, you may see a "blue screen" error such as:

```
A fatal exception 0E has occurred at 0028:C02A0201 in VXD IOS(04)+00001FC9
```

This problem can typically occur if Corel CD Creator 2.0 is installed on your computer. Windows 9x/Me is known to be incompatible with the CDRASPI.VXD file installed by Corel CD Creator 2.0. You can work around this problem by renaming the CDRASPI.VXD file:

1.   Start Windows 9x/Me in the Safe Mode.

2.   Click Start, highlight Find, and then click Files or Folders.

3.   In the Named box, type **cdraspi.vxd** and then click Find Now.

4.   In the list of found files, right click the CDRASPI.VXD file, and then click Rename.

5.   Type a new name for the CDRASPI.VXD file (such as **cdraspi.old**), and then press ENTER.

6.   Restart your computer normally.

SYMPTOM 9-103   **You receive a Windows Protection Error with EZ-SCSI 4.0 and Easy CD Pro 95**   After you install the Adaptec EZ-SCSI 4.0 and the Adaptec Easy-CD Pro 95 programs under Windows 98, you may receive the following error message:

```
Windows Protection Error: You need to restart your computer.
```

You may be able to use Windows, but you may not be able to use the EZ-SCSI 4.0 and Easy CD Pro 95 programs. You'll need to restart Windows in the Safe Mode and remove (uninstall) both EZ-SCSI 4.0 and Easy CD Pro 95. Check with Adaptec for updated versions of both programs.

SYMPTOM 9-104   **You receive an error when recording an audio track under four seconds**   If you try to record an audio track or .WAV file that is less than four seconds long, you will get a message indicating that a certain track cannot be written because it is less than four seconds long. Do not use .WAV files of less than four seconds. The audio standard for compact disc (Red Book) does not allow for audio files of less than four seconds. Make the audio file longer and try recording it again.

SYMPTOM 9-105   **You get poor audio quality from the CD-R**   Changes in recording speed (such as from 4x to 2x to 1x) have little or no effect on the quality of the recording. Most current CD authoring software will allow the use of IDE-style CD-ROM devices as "source drives" for copying audio CDs (Red Book or CD-DA). The Digital Audio Extraction (or DAE) test will pass, yet the copy process results in poor audio quality. Program and data CDs usually copy without problems. In virtually all cases, the problem is the source CD-ROM drive.

Use the source CD-ROM drive to extract a troublesome audio CD track to the hard disk as a .WAV file (name it CDTEST.WAV). Now use the CD-R to extract the same audio track to the hard disk as a .WAV file (name it WTEST.WAV). Play the two .WAV files from the hard drive and compare them. If the CDTEST.WAV file contains the same clicks/pops as you encountered during recording, yet the CD-R is producing clean .WAV files, then your source drive is *not* producing good quality digital audio extraction. There are three ways around this problem:

- Use the CD-R as the source *and* destination (check the CD-R manual and CD authoring software for detailed instructions on how to do this).
- Purchase a new CD-ROM drive guaranteed to support high-speed DAE.
- Use the CD authoring software settings to slow down the DAE rate. For example, in Easy CD Creator, the DAE rate is found under Tools, Options, and Advanced tab. You can experiment by extracting tracks as .WAV files after making those changes, then testing their quality by playing them from the hard drive.

CD-RW SYMPTOMS

Although UDF, DirectCD, and CD-RW drives are now well-established industry standards, there are still a number of compatibility problems and operating issues that technicians may eventually need to address. This part of the chapter examines a selection of UDF issues and CD-RW problems.

For basic CD reading and recording issues, refer to the previous parts of this chapter for CD-ROM and CD-R troubleshooting information.

Troubleshooting Tips

CD-RW drives are not terribly complicated devices to troubleshoot, but they can present some peculiar problems for technicians and do-it-yourselfers. Before you attempt to troubleshoot a CD-RW issue with your system, take a moment to work through this checklist:

- Verify that your system meets the minimum requirements for your CD-RW drive. If not, the system may fail to run properly (or not at all).
- Make sure the computer is plugged in and that each device has power. Connect any devices that are not receiving power.
- Turn off the computer's power, wait 15–20 seconds, then reboot the system. Doing this can clear some software conflicts.
- Repeat the operation with different (known good quality) CD media.
- Make sure that you're using the right type of CD for the task at hand.
- Check the README file that came with the CD-RW drive for any last-minute compatibility or performance notes that might be present with your system. Also check the CD-RW drive maker's Web site for the latest drivers and firmware upgrades.
- If the problems occur with power management, disable your PC's power management modes.

General Symptoms

Rewritable CD drives are subject to a large number of potential errors during operation, and many typical rewriting errors are covered next. In most cases, the error is not terribly difficult to understand and can be corrected in just a few minutes, once the nature of the problem is understood. Keep in mind that the actual error message is dependent on the CD recorder software in use, so your actual error messages may vary just a bit.

SYMPTOM 9-106   **The CD-ROM drive or CD audio player refuses to read CD-RW discs**
This is a common problem that is related to the age of the CD-ROM drive itself. Older CD-ROM drives (manufactured prior to mid/late-1997) are probably not Multi-Read/UDF-compatible and *cannot* read UDF formatted discs at all. CD audio players also cannot read UDF discs. If your CD-ROM is not Multi-Read–compliant, you'll need to upgrade to a Multi-Read–compliant model, or record your discs (especially audio discs) in a conventional ISO 9660 format using the CD-RW or CD-R drive.

CD-ROM drives manufactured after mid/late-1997 will probably offer Multi-Read capability, but still may not be able to read a UDF-formatted disc without the assistance of a UDF Reader utility. In most cases, you can obtain a free UDF Reader from the company providing the DirectCD software (Adaptec, for instance). Windows 98/SE/Me generally offers native UDF support for a Multi-Read drive, so a separate reader utility may not be necessary.

SYMPTOM 9-107   **A backup disc will not run properly**   DirectCD is not suitable for making backup copies of game or application discs where the application must run from the CD. This is because DirectCD uses a different method of writing data to disc (*packet writing*) than any discs produced with the ISO 9660 format. Packet-written (UDF) discs cannot be read by many standard CD-ROM drives or game machines. The only real way to work around this sort of problem is to use other recording software (such as Easy CD Creator for Windows 9x/Me or Adaptec Toast for the Mac) to make a backup copy of the disc to CD-R.

Keep in mind that some games and commercial application discs use forms of copy protection that recording software cannot work around or "break." Also remember that you cannot copy commercial software because of copyright restrictions.

SYMPTOM 9-108   **You cannot "see" a second session reading a CD-RW disc from a CD-ROM drive**   First, make sure that you're trying to read the disc on a newer Multi-Read-compatible CD-ROM drive (along with a UDF Reader utility, if necessary). Try ejecting the CD and reinserting it in the drive, then refresh the screen by selecting My Computer from inside Windows Explorer and pressing F5. Finally, try reading the disc from the CD-RW drive (or from another suitable CD-ROM drive). If another drive can read the disc, the problem is likely to be with the suspect CD-ROM drive. If the disc cannot be read in any drive, the problem is likely to be with the disc itself (try re-recording the disc).

You cannot read a multisession disc created with DirectCD under DOS or Windows 3.1x—there are no drivers to support UDF on these operating systems. If the disc was *not* recorded with DirectCD (ISO 9660) and you cannot read it under DOS or Windows 3.1x, make sure that your copy of MSCDEX (located in the AUTOEXEC.BAT file) is version 2.23. You can download the latest version of MSCDEX from the Microsoft Web site at **www.microsoft.com**.

SYMPTOM 9-109   **You receive an error such as "CD-RW is not under Direct CD control"**   You'll typically notice this problem under Windows 9x/Me when you attempt to erase, format, or copy data to a CD-RW. This type of problem is most frequently encountered when using a Ricoh

CD-RW drive and Adaptec Direct CD software. The problem can occur when the CD-RW drive uses older firmware (for example, a Ricoh CD-RW drive with v.2.03 firmware or earlier), or if you're using Adaptec DirectCD 2.0 or earlier. Try updating the drive's firmware and CD authoring software.

SYMPTOM 9-110   **The CD-RW media cannot be used when the UDF format is interrupted**   If power is lost while formatting a CD-RW disc, the disc will become unusable in any application and will fail if another format is attempted. To correct this issue, use the DirectCD Full Erase feature to wipe the disc, then try the format operation again.

SYMPTOM 9-111   **Files recorded in a second session do not appear**   If the files that you recorded in a second session do not appear when you try to read the disc in a CD-ROM drive, try the following tips:

- Try ejecting and reinserting the CD.
- Refresh the file list—select the CD-RW icon in My Computer or Windows Explorer, and then press F5.
- Check the drive. CD-RW discs can be used only in CD-RW drives or newer Multi-Read CD-ROMs.
- Try reading the CD in other CD-ROM drives. If other drives are able to read the disc, the problem is probably with the original CD-ROM drive.

SYMPTOM 9-112   **Your computer looses power while writing a CD-RW disc, now the disc is inaccessible**   If you lose power while writing to your CD (the CD-RW's drive light is on) or if you press CTRL-ALT-DELETE while writing to a CD, you'll interrupt the disc. But you may be able to salvage your disc. Leave your CD-RW disc in the drive and don't open the CD tray. Turn your computer off and cycle the power back on. Then restart the utility that you were using. Once the DirectCD utility tries to access the CD-RW drive/disc again, the recovery operation will make it appear that the last session is there, but actually only a *part* of the CD's directory may be there. Your recordable CD is still usable if you can read the directory. Just repeat the entire copy operation to make sure that your files are copied to the rewritable CD.

SYMPTOM 9-113   **You receive a "Buffer Underrun" error when you're writing in CD-R mode**   CD recordable devices require an uninterrupted data stream from the hard drive to write successfully to a CD. A "buffer underrun" message appears when the data stream is interrupted—this can occur if another program interrupts the writing process (or if the CD-RW drive's write speed is set too high for the speed at which the hard drive is running). Here are some tips to deal with buffer underrun errors (see the "Buffer Underrun" section earlier in this chapter for more detailed information):

- Use the CD authoring software's Test option to ensure that the write speed is appropriate for your computer.
- Try recording at a lower speed (such as 4x, 2x, or 1x).
- Do not use hard drive compression software—buffer underruns may be caused by this type of software.
- Exit any other background programs before writing data to the CD.
- Disable your computer's power-management feature.
- Run ScanDisk and Defrag on your hard drive—these programs improve access times to the hard drive.

■ Do not run other programs that could interrupt the writing process. Log off any networks and disable the fax modem software, screensaver, or other programs (such as TSRs) that may automatically send messages to your computer while writing data to the CD.

■ Make sure that the hard drive has enough temporary directory space—the space free should be at least twice the size of the largest file that you are recording.

■ Do not copy empty folders (files with a zero byte size) or files that are in current use.

SYMPTOM 9-114   **There is no DirectCD window after inserting a new CD-RW disc**
Verify that the CD-RW drive's DirectCD software and utilities have been installed properly. If the DirectCD window doesn't appear on the screen after you insert a new disc, follow these steps:

1. Wait a moment—it can take up to 15 seconds for the DirectCD window to appear.

2. If the rewritable disc is already formatted, you can force the window by clicking Start on the taskbar, choosing Programs, and then selecting Create a CD.

3. To prepare a CD with Easy CD Creator or DirectCD, the disc must be blank (you may have inserted a disc that is already formatted). Remove the disc and insert a good quality blank one.

4. The disc may have an unreadable format. DirectCD has a ScanDisk utility that *may* be able to recover data on the disc—simply double-click the CD icon on the Windows taskbar. Start ScanDisk and allow the process to run. A message will appear when ScanDisk is finished.

SYMPTOM 9-115   **The CD-RW drive doesn't show up in My Computer or Windows Explorer**   In effect, the drive is "disconnected" from the rest of the system. There are many possible problems that can cause this kind of behavior. If the drive doesn't appear in Explorer, click View from the top menu, then click Refresh. You might also try rebooting the computer (from a cold start) so that the PnP BIOS can recognize the CD-RW drive.

Check the drive's cabling next. Make sure that the drive's power connector is attached securely. Test the power by opening and closing the drive tray using the Eject button. Also make sure that the drive's SCSI or IDE signal cable is oriented properly and secured between the drive and drive controller. Chances are that you installed the CD-RW as a "master" IDE device. Verify that the drive jumpers are set properly and see that any other drive on that channel has been rejumpered as a "slave" drive. If you're using a SCSI CD-RW drive, see that the SCSI ID for the CD-RW is unique, and that the SCSI chain is properly connected and terminated.

Verify that the latest CD-RW drivers and utility software are installed. If problems persist, try another CD-RW drive or reconfigure the drive so that it is alone on its controller channel (that is, disconnect the "slave" IDE drive).

SYMPTOM 9-116   **The device that is sharing the IDE signal cable with your CD-RW drive no longer responds**   In most cases, that other drive was accidentally disconnected or unpowered when the new CD-RW drive was installed. Turn off and unplug your computer, then make sure that the power cables are securely attached to both drives. You can verify power to the drives by observing their power LEDs or by ejecting their disk trays. Also verify that the SCSI or IDE signal cable is oriented properly and connected securely at both drives. When using a SCSI controller, verify that the SCSI chain is properly terminated. When working with an ATAPI IDE drive, the master/slave relationship of the drives may also be an issue. If you installed the CD-RW drive as a slave device, try reconfiguring the devices so that the CD-RW drive is the master. For example, when using a CD-RW drive with Sony or Goldstar CD-ROMs, try configuring the CD-RW drive as the master and setting the CD-ROM as the slave.

Try the suspect drive by itself (disconnect the CD-RW drive). If the suspect drive returns to normal, there may be a conflict between the CD-RW drive and the other device—you may need to assign the two devices to different drive controller channels. If the problem persists, try replacing the suspect device.

SYMPTOM 9-117   **You receive an error message when double-clicking on the CD-RW icon**   There are several possible issues, which are typically caused by the drive's inability to read the disc. Here are a few things to check:

- There is no CD in the CD-RW drive. Insert a good quality CD and try reading again.

- After inserting a CD, you need to wait a moment to let the CD-RW drive read the disc information. When the LED on the front of the drive stops flashing and stays green, click on the CD-RW drive's icon again.

- The CD may be in the tray upside-down or a little off-center. Try reinserting the CD—the disc label should be facing up.

- You may be trying to read from a blank recordable CD. Copy some information to the disc and try reading it again.

SYMPTOM 9-118   **You receive an "invalid media" error when trying to boot from the CD-RW**   In many newer PC platforms, it *is* possible to boot from a CD-RW drive rather than a floppy or hard drive. An "invalid media" error from the CD-RW drive generally means that the disc doesn't contain the bootstrap files needed to begin the boot process and load your operating system. Chances are that the disc itself isn't bootable. Use a bootable CD (such as a *system rescue* disc or an OS disc such as Windows NT).

If you need to work around this problem, simply remove the disc from the CD-RW. During boot, the BIOS will skip the CD-RW and move directly to the next drive in the Boot Order (the hard drive). If you want to prevent your system from checking the CD-RW at boot time, go into the system's CMOS Setup and change the Boot Order so that the CD-RW is not included. For example, you might change the Boot Order to "A:/C:" or "C:/A:."

SYMPTOM 9-119   **You cannot copy directly from a CD-ROM drive to the CD-RW drive**
This is a very common problem that is almost always caused by inadequate hardware capabilities. The *source drive* (typically a CD-ROM) must support the extremely fast data transfers found in late-model ATAPI EIDE or SCSI-2/3 drives. If you're copying audio CDs, the source drive must be capable of digital audio extraction (or DAE). It may be necessary to upgrade the source drive or drive controller in order to support faster data transfers.

If you're using an IDE-type source and CD-RW drive, make sure that the *source* and *destination* drives are *not* on the same IDE controller channel. You may need to reconfigure your drives so that the source and destination drives are split on separate controller channels. Finally, some CDs have a copy-prevention feature (or other features) that do not allow a CD-to-CD copy. If that's the case, it may not be possible to copy that particular disc.

Make sure that you copy *only* material that belongs to you or that you have written permission to copy. Otherwise, you may be violating international copyright laws.

SYMPTOM 9-120   **Audio from the CD-RW drive is poor or absent**   Whenever you have trouble with CD audio from a CD-ROM, CD-R, or CD-RW drive, try listening to the audio using a set of headphones into the headset connector on the drive's front panel. If you cannot hear the audio (and volume adjustments don't help), then the drive is probably defective and should be replaced. If you hear the audio normally, the problem is likely in the PC's sound system. Make sure that the four-wire audio cable is completely plugged into the sound card and into the CD-RW drive. If you already have a CD-ROM or other drive providing CD audio to the sound card, you cannot connect the CD-RW's audio cable unless you either remove the current CD audio cable or use a sound card with more than one CD audio port. Make sure that the CD audio channel is not muted in the mixer software and see that the CD audio level is turned up adequately. You may need to update the sound card's drivers or application software if the sound system is not currently supporting CD audio.

If the problem is with .WAV file playback from the disc, try listening to the .WAV files from your hard drive. If the problem persists, the problem is with poor .WAV recordings (not with the CD-RW drive or sound card). If the .WAV files sound correct from the hard drive (but not from the CD), the problem may be poor recording to the CD—it may be necessary to re-record the disc using updated or alternate recording software.

SYMPTOM 9-121   **Video playback is choppy from a CD-RW drive**   This is generally *not* a problem with the CD-RW drive, but rather with the system's ability to handle streaming audio/video data from a CD. Your best solution is typically to reduce the system's processing overhead in order to provide more processing power to the video playback software (such as Windows Media Player):

- Shut down any background applications, TSRs, and screensavers.

- Reduce the size of your video playback window.

- Download and install the latest versions of DirectX, your video drivers, and your multimedia player (such as Windows Media Player).

- Many CD-RW drives tend to be rather slow (8x/6x, for example), resulting in interference with data transfers on some system configurations. Try playing the video from another faster drive, such as your system's CD-ROM drive.

- If problems persist, you may need to make one or more hardware upgrades to improve your system's multimedia playback capability (such as a faster video card, more system RAM, and a faster CPU).

SYMPTOM 9-122   **Your CD-ROM drive cannot "see" a second (or subsequent) session recorded on discs from a CD-RW drive**   There are several possible issues that can occur when reading multisession discs created on a CD-RW drive with DirectCD software. Start by ejecting and reinserting the disc. This allows the drive to redetect the disc and to read its sessions once again. You should also try refreshing the display—select the My Computer icon in Windows Explorer, then press F5.

As a rule, CD-RW discs can be used only in CD-RW drives or newer Multi-Read CD-ROMs (compatible with the UDF file system). If you're trying to read the disc on an older CD-ROM which is *not* Multi-Read–compliant, you may need to upgrade the CD-ROM to a newer version. Finally, multisession CDs created with DirectCD cannot be read in DOS or Windows 3.x. Make sure that you're in Windows 9x, Windows Me, or some other UDF-compliant operating system.

SYMPTOM 9-123 **You cannot get an application to "find" a CD in the CD-RW drive**
This is almost always a problem with the application itself rather than the drive. Many programs (such as CD-based games) look for only the first logical drive letter assigned to a CD-ROM drive or CD-RW drive. For example, if a CD-ROM drive is assigned to D: and the CD-RW drive is assigned to E:, the program will probably look for the CD *only* in drive D: and will not see the CD in drive E:. If you want to use the CD-RW drive with such programs, reassign the drive letters to make the CD-RW drive precede the CD-ROM drive:

1. For Windows 9x/Me, click Start, highlight Settings, then click Control Panel. Double-click the System icon, select the Device Manager tab, and double-click the CD-ROM entry.

2. Double-click the CD-ROM drive, then click the Settings tab. Under Reserved drive letters, select the drive letter after the existing letter (for both *start* and *end* drive letter) and click OK.

3. Now double-click the CD-RW drive entry, then click the Settings tab. Under Reserved drive letters, select the drive letter before the current one and click OK.

Further Study

Adaptec   www.adaptec.com
Creative Labs   www.creaf.com
Diamond Multimedia   www.diamondmm.com
El Torito specification   www.phoenix.com/PlatSS/products/specs.html
Hewlett-Packard   www.hp.com
HiVal   www.hival.com
NEC   www.nec.com
Pinnacle Micro   www.pinnaclemicro.com
Plextor   www.plextor.com
Roxio   www.roxio.com
Teac America   www.teac.com/DSPD/DesktopCDRW.html

10

CHIPSETS

In the early days of the PC, motherboards (and pretty much every other device) were designed and built with discrete logic gates. If you were around in the days of the PC/XT and PC/AT, you probably remember the huge motherboards packed with over 150 to 200 individual chips. Discrete chips demanded a lot of power and took up lots of room. It didn't take designers long to realize that standard functions of the PC (like floppy drive interface circuits, DMA controllers, programmable interrupt controllers, and so on) could easily be integrated into application-specific integrated circuits (or ASICs). With the use of these custom-made chips, PCs were able to drop their chip count, reduce construction costs, improve reliability, and reduce power requirements.

But there are also performance advantages to such high levels of feature integration. Combining a PC's sophisticated logic circuitry onto a few chips dramatically shortens the signal paths and allows the circuits to operate at higher speeds (these are key components of today's fastest systems). By optimizing the signal paths within the chip itself, performance could be improved even further. Designers quickly saw that they could integrate all of the core logic needed to facilitate a complete state-of-the-art PC in just a few highly integrated chips. Since these chips are specifically designed to serve as a *set* on the motherboard, they were dubbed the *chipset* (Figure 10-1).

FIGURE 10-1   The Intel 815EM chipset (courtesy of Intel Corporation)

Understanding Chipsets

Today, chipsets play a leading role in the design and fabrication of modern personal computers. Where early motherboards could use hundreds of chips, you'd be hard-pressed to find more than 20 chips on a current motherboard. In fact, chipsets are so important that new chipsets often must be developed to support each new computer technology or processor. For example, you'll find that Intel's 820 chipset supports features such as RDRAM, AGP 4X, and Ultra-DMA/66, but the venerable 440 BX Pentium II/III chipset does not. As a result, motherboards with a 440 BX chipset would have to be replaced with a motherboard using the 820 chipset before those features would be available. Ultimately, the overall features and capabilities of your PC are largely defined by the motherboard chipset (sometimes called the computer's *core logic*). This chapter is intended to identify many of the current chipsets in use today and familiarize you with their principle features.

CHIP TYPES

A chipset is an efficient and inexpensive way to bring a large number of powerful features to a PC. Figure 10-2 illustrates a typical application of an AMD 750 chipset. The 750 chipset actually consists of two devices: the AMD 751 system controller chip, and the AMD 756 peripheral bus controller chip. Obviously, other chipsets will use different numbering schemes and may employ additional chips, but the ideas here are almost identical. Let's take a look at the role each chip plays in the system.

North Bridge

In a chipset, one chip is usually responsible for interfacing (or connecting) the CPU, main memory, local bus (in this case, the AGP graphics bus), and the main system bus (the PCI bus here). This principle device is often called the *North Bridge* chip (some manufacturers simply use one word, *Northbridge*). In Figure 10-2, the AMD 751 system controller is the North Bridge chip. The 751 provides clock signal and timing support for the Athlon processors and SDRAM. In effect, the CPU and RAM communicate through the 751. This pathway between the CPU and RAM is often referred to as the *front side bus* (or FSB). In addition, the 751 provides a set of dedicated signals to handle the motherboard's Accelerated Graphics Port (AGP) bus. The video card that you install in an AGP slot will communicate directly through the 751

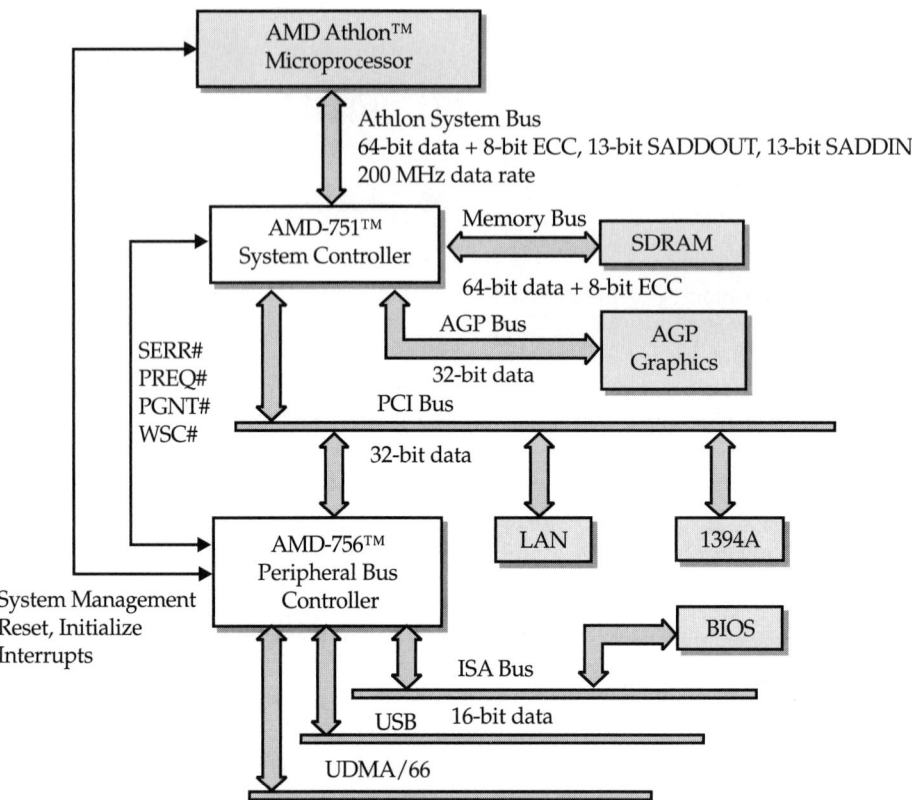

FIGURE   10-2   An application of the AMD 750 chipset

(this also allows the AGP card to quickly access main memory for video textures). Rather than an AGP slot, a designer can incorporate an AGP video chip and supply integrated AGP video capability right on the motherboard. Finally, the AMD 751 offers a direct interface to the PCI system expansion bus. You'll generally install your expansion cards (LAN cards, SCSI adapters, video capture cards, PCI sound cards, and PCI modems) into slots on this bus. As a minimum, the North Bridge chip controls the following system attributes:

- The processor types that are supported (such as Pentium II/III, Athlon, Duron, Celeron)
- The number of processors that are supported (for multiprocessing motherboards)
- The processor speeds that are supported (500 MHz, 800 MHz, 1.5 GHz, and so on)
- The front side bus speed (66 MHz, 100 MHz, 133 MHz, 200 MHz, or 266 MHz)
- The FSB multiplier needed to operate the CPU (for example, 200 MHz FSB x5 = 1 GHz CPU)
- The memory types that are supported (PC133 SDRAM or PC800 RDRAM)
- The maximum amount of memory that is supported
- The memory technologies that are supported (64Mbit or 128Mbit SDRAM)
- The type of memory error correction supported (parity or ECC)

All chipsets are not created equal, so do not underestimate the importance of the North Bridge chip. It sits squarely at the center of your PC's processing components, and a poorly designed North Bridge can result in poor system performance, even when the processor and memory are very fast. You can see this in effect when two PCs with identical CPUs and RAM are benchmarked side by side. Ideally, both PCs should benchmark the same if they're operating at the same speeds, but differing chipsets may cause profound differences in performance. This is also one of the reasons why some older PCs seem to outperform the newer systems when new (and unrefined) chipsets are employed.

South Bridge

While a North Bridge supports the bulk of the PC's raw processing power, the PC must also be able to communicate with peripheral devices in the outside world through a series of ports and other system busses. Since ports and busses generally operate at speeds that are far slower than the front side bus, system support is provided through a second chip, typically called the *South Bridge* (or *Southbridge*). As a rule, the South Bridge chip handles the system's peripheral and I/O bus operations. They go by many different names depending on the manufacturer: peripheral controller, I/O controller, integrated controller, and so on. However, South Bridge chips usually perform a very similar suite of functions.

Take another look at Figure 10-2 and you'll see the AMD 756 peripheral bus controller. The 756 interfaces directly to the system's PCI expansion bus. The chip then provides a complete ISA bus for older (legacy) devices. Since the ISA bus is also used for expansion devices, the PCI bus must be "bridged" to the ISA bus—this feature is called the PCI-to-ISA Bridge. The chip also supports a USB port and UDMA/66 controller for hard drives. Other South Bridge chips usually include serial ports, parallel ports, floppy controllers, faster UDMA/100 drive controllers, and other ports. Today, the ISA bus is being aggressively phased out of the PC platform. As a rule, expect a South Bridge chip to handle the following features:

- ISA bus support
- One or more USB ports
- One or more serial (RS-232) ports
- A parallel (IEEE 1284) port
- An infrared (IrDA) port
- Two-channel hard drive controller
- Floppy drive controller
- Power management features (APM or ACPI, DPMS, or SMM)
- Keyboard controller (KBC), including support for a PS/2 mouse

Integrated Features

On some motherboards, additional chips are included to perform some of the common functions normally found on expansion cards. This has its pros and cons. In general, incorporating built-in circuitry offers lower cost, but may limit system upgradability. If you end up adding a Sound Blaster card and a new video card because you don't like the performance of your integrated components, you aren't really saving any money. There are four popular integrated features:

- Video adapters
- Sound adapters
- Network adapter
- SCSI adapter

Intel also calls its chipsets PCIsets and AGPsets, referring to the system bus technologies that the chipsets implement.

More Information

If you're looking for detailed technical information about today's chipsets, you can usually download the complete technical manual from the chipset manufacturer's Web site (usually in Adobe Acrobat's PDF format). Table 10-1 provides the URLs for downloading many of today's chipset manuals. Table 10-2 outlines the chipsets covered in this chapter and explains their functions.

TABLE 10-1   MODERN CHIPSET INFORMATION REFERENCE

CHIPSET	COVERAGE	RESOURCE
ALi M1531	Intel, Cyrix, AMD: Socket 7	www.acerlabs.com/eng/product/core/m1531.htm
ALi M1533	South Bridge chip	www.acerlabs.com/eng/product/core/m1533.htm
ALi M1535	South Bridge chip	www.acerlabs.com/eng/product/core/m1535.htm
ALi M1535+	South Bridge chip	www.acerlabs.com/eng/product/core/m1535+.htm
ALi M1535d	South Bridge chip	www.acerlabs.com/eng/product/core/m1535d.htm
ALi M1535d+	South Bridge chip	www.acerlabs.com/eng/product/core/m1535d+.htm
ALi M1541	Intel, Cyrix, AMD: Socket 7	www.acerlabs.com/eng/product/core/m1541.htm
ALi M1543c	South Bridge chip	www.acerlabs.com/eng/product/core/m1543c.htm
ALi M1561	AMD K6-III: Socket 7	www.acerlabs.com/eng/product/core/m1561.htm
ALi M1621	Pentium II	www.acerlabs.com/eng/product/core/m1621.htm
ALi M1631	Pentium II	www.acerlabs.com/eng/product/core/m1631.htm
ALi M1632m	Pentium II/III, Celeron	www.acerlabs.com/eng/product/core/m1632m.htm
ALi M1647	AMD Athlon, Duron	www.acerlabs.com/eng/product/core/m1647.htm
ALi M1651	Pentium II/III, Celeron	www.acerlabs.com/eng/product/core/m1651.htm
AMD 640	AMD K5 and K6: Socket 7	www.amd.com/K6/k6docs/pdf/21090.pdf
AMD 750	AMD Athlon	www.amd.com/products/cpg/athlon/chipset.html
AMD 760	AMD Athlon	www.amd.com/products/cpg/athlon/760chipset.html
Intel 430 FX	Pentium	support.intel.com/support/chipsets/430FX/
Intel 430 HX	Pentium	developer.intel.com/design/chipsets/datashts/290551.htm
Intel 430 TX	Pentium	developer.intel.com/design/chipsets/datashts/290559.htm
Intel 430 VX	Pentium	support.intel.com/support/chipsets/430VX/
Intel 430 MX	Mobile Pentium	developer.intel.com/design/chipsets/440mx/index.htm developer.intel.com/design/chipsets/datashts/245052.htm
Intel 440 BX	Pentium II, III	developer.intel.com/design/chipsets/datashts/290633.htm
Intel 440 EX	Celeron	developer.intel.com/design/chipsets/datashts/290616.htm
Intel 440 MX	Celeron	developer.intel.com/design/chipsets/datashts/245052.htm
Intel 440 ZX	Pentium II, III	developer.intel.com/design/chipsets/datashts/290650.htm
Intel 440 FX	Pentium Pro	developer.intel.com/design/chipsets/datashts/290549.htm
Intel 440 GX	Pentium II, III Xeon	developer.intel.com/design/chipsets/datashts/290638.htm
Intel 440 LX	Pentium Pro	developer.intel.com/design/chipsets/440lx/ developer.intel.com/design/chipsets/datashts/290564.htm
Intel 450 GX/KX	Pentium Pro	developer.intel.com/design/chipsets/datashts/290523.htm
Intel 450 NX	Pentium II, III Xeon	developer.intel.com/design/chipsets/datashts/243771.htm
Intel 810	Celeron, Pentium III	developer.intel.com/design/chipsets/datashts/290656.htm
Intel 810E	Celeron, Pentium III	developer.intel.com/design/chipsets/datashts/290676.htm
Intel 810E2	Celeron, Pentium III	developer.intel.com/design/chipsets/datashts/290676.htm

TABLE 10-1   MODERN CHIPSET INFORMATION REFERENCE (*CONTINUED*)

CHIPSET	COVERAGE	RESOURCE
Intel 815	Celeron, Pentium III	developer.intel.com/design/chipsets/datashts/290688.htm
Intel 815E	Celeron, Pentium III	developer.intel.com/design/chipsets/datashts/290688.htm
Intel 815EP	Celeron, Pentium III	developer.intel.com/design/chipsets/datashts/290693.htm
Intel 820	Pentium III	developer.intel.com/design/chipsets/datashts/290630.htm
Intel 820E	Pentium III	developer.intel.com/design/chipsets/datashts/290630.htm
Intel 840	Pentium II, III Xeon	developer.intel.com/design/chipsets/datashts/298020.htm
Intel 850	Pentium 4	developer.intel.com/design/chipsets/datashts/290691.htm
OPTi	Chipset family (general)	ftp://ftp.opti.com/pub/chipsets/archive
SiS	Chipset family (general)	www.sis.com.tw/products/corelogic.htm
SiS 600	Pentium II	www.sis.com.tw/products/slot1/600.htm
SiS 620	Pentium II AGP chipset	www.sis.com.tw/products/slot1/620.htm
SiS 630	Pentium II	www.sis.com.tw/products/slot1/630.htm
SiS 700	AMD Athlon, Duron	www.sis.com.tw/products/slota/slota.htm
VIA VT82C597	Socket 7 North Bridge (VP3)	www.via.com.tw/pdf/productinfo/597.pdf
VIA VT8231	AMD KM133 South Bridge	www.via.com.tw/products/prodkm133.htm
VIA VT8233	Highly Integrated South Bridge: Socket 370 and Slot 1 CPUs	www.via.com.tw/datasheets/VT8233%20Southbridge%20datasheet%20overview.pdf
VIA VT82C496	Pluto chipset	www.via.com.tw/pdf/productinfo/496pluto.pdf
VIA VT82C580	Socket 7 North Bridge (VPx)	www.via.com.tw/pdf/productinfo/580vpx.pdf
VIA VT82C580VP	Socket 7 North Bridge (VP)	www.via.com.tw/pdf/productinfo/apollovp.pdf
VIA VT82C586B	Socket 7 South Bridge	www.via.com.tw/pdf/productinfo/586b.pdf
VIA VT82C595	Socket 7 North Bridge	www.via.com.tw/pdf/productinfo/595.pdf
VIA VT82C596A	Mobile PC South Bridge	www.via.com.tw/pdf/productinfo/596A.pdf
VIA VT82C596B	Socket 7 South Bridge (MVPx)	www.via.com.tw/pdf/productinfo/596b.pdf
VIA VT82C598	Socket 7 North Bridge (MVP3)	www.via.com.tw/pdf/productinfo/598.pdf
VIA VT82C601	Intel, Cyrix III North Bridge	www.via.com.tw/pdf/productinfo/dspm601brief.pdf
VIA VT82C686A	Intel, AMD South Bridge	www.via.com.tw/pdf/productinfo/686a.pdf
VIA VT82C691	Pentium II North Bridge	www.via.com.tw/pdf/productinfo/691.pdf
VIA VT82C693	Celeron Pentium II North Bridge	www.via.com.tw/pdf/productinfo/693.pdf
VIA VT82C693A	Intel, Cyrix 133 MHz North Bridge	www.via.com.tw/pdf/productinfo/693A.pdf
VIA VT82C694X	Intel, Cyrix III North Bridge	www.via.com.tw/pdf/productinfo/694X.pdf
VIA VT8363	AMD Athlon North Bridge: graphics	www.via.com.tw/pdf/productinfo/kt133.pdf
VIA VT8365	AMD Athlon North Bridge: graphics	www.via.com.tw/pdf/productinfo/dspm605brief.pdf
VIA VT8366	AMD Athlon North Bridge: DDR-SDRAM	www.via.com.tw/datasheets/KT266%20NB%20datasheet%20overview.pdf
VIA VT8371	AMD Athlon 133 MHz North Bridge	www.via.com.tw/pdf/productdm/kx133.pdf
VIA VT8501	Socket 7 North Bridge (MVP4)	www.via.com.tw/pdf/productinfo/501brief.pdf
VIA VT8605	Intel, Cyrix North Bridge: graphics	www.via.com.tw/pdf/productinfo/dspm605brief.pdf
VIA VT8633	Intel, Cyrix North Bridge: DDR-SDRAM	www.via.com.tw/products/pro266back.pdf

TABLE 10-2   SUMMARY OF MOTHERBOARD CHIPSET COMPONENTS

NOTE THAT INTEL CHIPSET CODE NAMES ARE STRICTLY UNOFFICIAL, AND INTEL DOES NOT EVEN ACKNOWLEDGE THE USE OF CODE NAMES.

CHIPSET DESIGNATION	COMPONENT	#NEEDED	FUNCTION
ALi MAGiK 1	M1647	1	System controller
	M1535D+	1	PCI/ISA/IDE/USB controller
ALi Aladdin Pro 5M	M1651	1	System controller
	M1535+	1	PCI/ISA/IDE/USB controller
ALi Aladdin Pro 4	M1641	1	System controller
	M1535	1	PCI/ISA/IDE/USB controller
ALi Aladdin TNT2	M1631	1	System controller
	M1543C	1	PCI/ISA/IDE/USB controller
ALi Aladdin Pro 2	M1621	1	System controller
	M1533	1	PCI/ISA/IDE/USB controller
ALi Aladdin 7	M1561	1	System controller
	M135D+	1	PCI/ISA/USB controller
ALi Aladdin-5	M1541	1	System controller
	M1543C	1	PCI/ISA/IDE/USB controller
ALi Aladdin 4/4+	M1531B	1	System controller
	M1533	1	PCI/ISA/IDE/USB controller
AMD 760	AMD 761	1	System controller
	AMD 766	1	Peripheral bus controller
AMD 750	AMD 751	1	System controller
	AMD 756	1	Peripheral bus controller
AMD 640	AMD 640	1	System controller
	AMD 645	1	Peripheral bus controller
Intel 850	82850	1	Memory controller hub
	82801BA	1	Integrated controller hub
	82802AB	1	Firmware hub
Intel 840	82840	1	Memory controller hub
	82803	1	Memory repeater hub RDRAM
	82804	1	Memory repeater hub SDRAM
	82806	1	64-bit PCI controller
	82801	1	Integrated controller hub
	82802	1	Firmware hub
Intel 820E	82820	1	Memory controller hub
	82820DP	1	Memory controller hub, dual processor
	82801BA	1	Integrated controller hub
	82802AB	1	Firmware hub
Intel 820	82820	1	Memory controller hub
	82820DP	1	Memory controller hub, dual processor
	82801	1	I/O controller hub
	82802	1	Firmware hub
	82380AB	1	PCI-ISA bridge

TABLE 10-2   SUMMARY OF MOTHERBOARD CHIPSET COMPONENTS *(CONTINUED)*

NOTE THAT INTEL CHIPSET CODE NAMES ARE STRICTLY UNOFFICIAL, AND INTEL DOES NOT EVEN ACKNOWLEDGE THE USE OF CODE NAMES.

CHIPSET DESIGNATION	COMPONENT	#NEEDED	FUNCTION
Intel 815EP	82815EP	1	Memory hub
	82801BA	1	Integrated controller hub
	82802AB	1	Firmware hub
Intel 815E	82815	1	Graphics/memory hub
	82801BA	1	Integrated controller hub
	82802	1	Firmware hub
Intel 815	82815	1	Graphics/memory hub
	82801AA	1	Integrated controller hub
	82802	1	Firmware hub
Intel 810E2	82810E	1	Graphics/memory hub
	82801BA	1	Integrated controller hub
	82802	1	Firmware hub
Intel 810E	82810E	1	Memory controller hub
	82801	1	Integrated controller hub
	82802	1	Firmware hub
Intel 810	82810	1	Graphics/memory controller hub
	82801	1	Integrated controller hub
	82802	1	Firmware hub
Intel 440 GX	82443GX	1	Host bridge/controller
	82371EB	1	Peripheral bus controller (PIIX4E)
Intel 440 ZX	82443ZX	1	System/AGP controller
	82371AB & EB	1	PCI ISA IDE Xcelerator (PIIX4 & E)
Intel 440 EX	82443EX	1	System AGP controller
	82371AB	1	PCI ISA IDE Xcelerator (PIIX4)
Intel 440 BX	82443BX	1	AGP host bridge controller
	82371AB	1	PCI ISA IDE Xcelerator (PIIX4)
Intel 430 VX (Triton II*)	82437VX	1	System controller
	82371SB	1	PCI ISA IDE Xcelerator (PIIX3)
	82438VX	2	Data path unit
Intel 430 TX	82439TX	1	System controller
	82371AB	1	PCI ISA IDE Xcelerator (PIIX4)
Intel 430 HX (Triton II*)	82439HX	1	System controller
	82371SB	1	PCI I/O IDE Xcelerator (PIIX3)
Intel 430 FX (Triton*)	82437FX	1	System controller
	82371FB	1	ISA bridge, PCI/ISA/IDE Xcelerator (PIIX)
	82438FX	2	Data path unit
Intel 430 MX	82437MX	1	System controller
	82438MX	2	Data path units
	82371MX	1	PCI I/O IDE Xcelerator (MPIIX)
Intel 440 FX (Natoma*)	82441FX	1	PCI and memory controller
	82442FX	1	Data bus accelerator
	82371SB	1	PCI ISA IDE Xcelerator (PIIX3)

TABLE 10-2   SUMMARY OF MOTHERBOARD CHIPSET COMPONENTS *(CONTINUED)*

*NOTE THAT INTEL CHIPSET CODE NAMES ARE STRICTLY UNOFFICIAL, AND INTEL DOES NOT EVEN ACKNOWLEDGE THE USE OF CODE NAMES.

CHIPSET DESIGNATION	COMPONENT	#NEEDED	FUNCTION
Intel 450 KX (Orion*)	82451KX	4	Memory interface component
	82452KX	1	Data path unit
	82453KX	1	Data controller
	82454KX	1 or 2	PCI bridge
Intel 450 GX (Orion*)	82451GX	4	Memory interface component
	82452GX	1	Data path unit
	82453GX	1	Data controller
	82454GX	1 or 2	PCI bridge
Intel 440 LX	82443LX	1	PCI AGP system controller
	82371AB	1	PCI ISA IDE Xcelerator (PIIX4)
VIA Apollo KT266/AMD	VT8366	1	System controller
	VT8233	1	PCI/IDE/USB controller
VIA KX133 Athlon	VT8371	1	System controller
	VT82C686A	1	PCI/ISA/IDE/USB controller
VIA Apollo KT133A	VT8363A	1	System controller
	VT82C686B	1	PCI/ISA/IDE/USB controller
VIA Apollo KT133/AMD	VT8363	1	System controller
	VT82C686A	1	PCI/ISA/IDE/USB controller
VIA ProSavage KM133 (AMD)	VT8365	1	System/graphics controller
	VT8231	1	PCI/ISA/IDE/USB controller
VIA Apollo Pro266	VT8633	1	System controller
	VT8233	1	PCI/IDE/USB controller
VIA ProSavage PM133	VT8605	1	System/graphics controller
	VT82C686A	1	PCI/ISA/IDE/USB controller
VIA Apollo Pro133A	VT82C694X	1	System controller
	VT82C596B	1	PCI/ISA/IDE/USB controller
VIA Apollo PLE133	VT8601	1	System/graphics controller
	VT82C686A	1	PCI/ISA/IDE/USB controller
VIA Apollo PM601	VT8601	1	System/graphics controller
	VT8231	1	PCI/ISA/IDE/USB controller
VIA Apollo Pro 133	VT82C693A	1	System controller
	VT82C686A	1	PCI/ISA/IDE/USB controller
VIA Apollo ProPlus	VT82C693	1	System controller
	VT82C686A	1	PCI/ISA/IDE/USB controller
VIA Apollo Pro	VT82C691	1	System controller
	VT82C686A	1	PCI/ISA/IDE/USB controller
VIA MVP4	VT8501	1	AGP system controller
	VT82C686A	1	PCI/ISA/IDE/USB controller
VIA Apollo MVP3	VT82C598AT	1	System controller
	VT82C686A	1	PCI/ISA/IDE/USB controller
VIA Apollo P6	VT82C685VP	1	System controller
	VT82C586	1	PCI/ISA/IDE/USB controller
	VT82C687	1	Memory controller
VIA Apollo VP3	VT82C597	1	System controller
	VT82C586B	1	PCI/IDE/USB controller

TABLE 10-2   SUMMARY OF MOTHERBOARD CHIPSET COMPONENTS *(CONTINUED)*

CHIPSET DESIGNATION	COMPONENT	#NEEDED	FUNCTION
VIA Apollo VP2/97	VT82C595	1	System controller
	VT82C586B	1	PCI/IDE/USB controller
VIA Apollo VPX/97	VT82C585VPX	1	System controller
	VT82C586B	1	PCI/ISA/IDE/USB controller (PC97)
	VT82C586A	1	PCI/ISA/IDE/USB controller (non-97)
	VT82C587VP	2	Share frame buffers
VIA Apollo VP-1	VT82C585VP	1	System controller
	VT82C586	1	PCI/IDE/ISA/USB controller
	VT82C587VP	2	Share frame buffers
VIA Apollo Master	VT82C575M	1	System controller
	VT82C576M	1	PCI/ISA/IDE controller
	VT82C577M	2	Frame buffers
	VT82C416	1	Support controller
SiS 735	735	1	Integrated system controller
SiS 733	733	1	Integrated system controller
SiS 730S	730S	1	Integrated system controller
SiS 635	635	1	Integrated system controller
SiS 630E	630E	1	Integrated system controller
SiS 630S	630S	1	Integrated system controller
SiS 630	630	1	Integrated system controller
SiS 620	620	1	System controller
	5595	1	Bus controller
SiS 600	600	1	System controller
	5596	1	Bus controller
SiS 540	540	1	Integrated system controller
SiS 530	530	1	System controller
	5595	1	Bus controller
SiS 5598	5598	1	Integrated system controller
SiS 5597 (Jedi)	5597	1	Integrated system controller
SiS 5596	5596	1	System controller
	5513	1	USB controller
SiS 5591	5591	1	System controller
	5595	1	Bus controller
SiS 5582	5582	1	Integrated system controller
SiS 5571 (Trinity)	5571	1	Integrated system controller
SiS 551X	5511	1	System controller
	5512	1	Bus controller
	5513	1	USB controller
SiS 85C49X (486)	85C496	1	System controller
	85C497	1	Bus controller
OPTi Discovery	82C650	1	System controller
	82C651	1	Bus controller
	82C652	1	Auxiliary PCI bus controller
OPTi Vendetta	82C750	1	Integrated system controller
OPTi Fire Star	82C700	1	Integrated system controller

There is a tremendous rivalry between the major chipset manufacturers. This chapter does not advocate the use of any given chipset (or manufacturer) over another, or attempt to make product recommendations. This chapter merely familiarizes you with the features of each chipset, and allows you to make objective assessments of system capabilities based upon the particular core logic in use.

ALi Chipsets

At one time, Acer Laboratories, Inc. (or simply ALi) had its very existence challenged by the introduction of the Intel TX chipset. The TX chipset represented Intel's entry into the low-cost/low-end chipset market—a market that provided the very foundation for manufacturers such as ALi and VIA. ALi has survived by providing less-than-cutting-edge, lower-cost chip solutions for entry-level motherboard and systems manufacturers' needs. ALi has attempted to reduce buyers' costs even further by including a video/3D graphics engine in some of its chipset products while still supporting modern features like USB, UDMA/66/100, PC100/133, and DDR-SDRAM memory.

ALI M1661 PENTIUM 4 (NORTHWOOD)

ALi is currently developing the M1661 chipset, which offers support for the Pentium 4 Northwood-series processors. It is scheduled for release sometime in late 2001, and should include support for DDR-SDRAM memory, AGP 4X, and the newest peripheral bus technologies. The chipset has not yet been released, so we won't discuss it further here.

ALI ALIMAGIK 1 AND MOBILEMAGIK

ALiMAGiK 1 features support for AMD Athlon and Duron processors. It includes support for PC1600/PC2100 DDR and 133 MHz SDRAM memory. The ALiMAGiK 1 chipset, designed for desktop PCs, includes the M1647 North Bridge and the M1535D+ South Bridge. The MobileMAGiK 1 chipset is similar to the ALiMAGiK 1 (with the addition of some power conservation features) and is designed for portable systems utilizing the Mobile AMD processors. It includes the M1647 North Bridge and the M1535+ South Bridge. Both chipsets interface with AMD's 100/133 MHz DDR front side bus. The memory controller in the M1647 supports up to 3GB of PC1600/PC2100 DDR, as well as 66/100/133 SDRAM. PC2100 DDR enables 2.1GB/s peak bandwidth between the system memory and the North Bridge. Power conservation is another important consideration.

The ALiMAGiK-series chipsets provide an integrated AC-Link host controller, hardware-based Sound Blaster Pro/16 compatibility, a host signal processing (HSP) software modem interface, Advanced Configuration and Power Interface (ACPI) support, Ultra-DMA/66/100 support, and a USB/Super-I/O controller. When used in mobile PCs, the M1647's support for AMD's PowerNow! technology allows CPU operating frequency to be changed (and even lowers the CPU voltage) to save power. The chipset supports 4X/2X/1X AGP, providing flexibility in choice of graphics controllers. Table 10-3 lists the details for ALiMAGiK chips.

ALI ALADDIN PRO 5

The Aladdin Pro 5 consists of the M1651 North Bridge combined with the M1535D+ South Bridge. It offers support for Pentium II/III and Celeron processors and can accommodate both Slot 1 and Socket 370 packages. The Aladdin Pro 5 allows the use of PC66, PC100, or PC133 SDRAM, or the latest PC200/PC266 DDR-SDRAM memory. The PC266 DDR-SDRAM memory enables 2.1GB/s peak bandwidth

TABLE 10-3   ALI ALIMAGIK 1 CHIPSET FEATURES AT A GLANCE

Supports the Athlon processor family using a host bus frequency of 100 MHz or 133 MHz double data rate (200 MHz or 266 MHz)

64-bit data bus and 32-bit addressing

Optimized buffering architecture design for CPU-to-memory, -AGP, and -PCI read/write

Supports notebook features (including FID change special cycle)

Supports back-to-back write transfers

Optimized processor commands allow scheduling and reordering

Supports synchronous/asynchronous clock between processor and memory

Supports SDRAM at 66, 100, 133 MHz, or DDR at 200, 266 MHz

Supports symmetrical and asymmetrical SDRAM/DDR addressing

Supports up to 3GB of 4, 16, 64, 128, 256, and 512Mbit SDRAM/DDR technologies

Supports memory shadowing, CAS-before-RAS, and self-refresh for SDRAM

Pipelined SDRAM/DDR cycle control with hidden precharge

Supports up to 128 entries for Graphic Address Remapping Table (GART)

AGP 66 MHz V.2.0 protocol supports AGP 1X/2X/4X modes

Supports synchronous/asynchronous clock between the processor bus and the PCI bus

32-bit address/data PCI bus using PCI bus driver technology

Supports up to 6 PCI masters (excluding the M1647 and PCI-to-ISA bridge)

Parity protection on all PCI bus signals

Fully compliant with PCI Rev. 2.2

Supports concurrent PCI bus burst data transfer at zero-wait-states

133MB/s data streaming for PCI bus-to-SDRAM/DDR access with minimum latency

Supports ACPI 1.0b and legacy power conservation schemes

between the system memory and North Bridge chip to boost system performance. This modern chipset supports the PCI 2.2 specifications and offers AGP 4X compatibility. You can learn more about the chipset in Table 10-4.

TABLE 10-4   ALI ALADDIN PRO 5 CHIPSET FEATURES AT A GLANCE

Supports the Celeron, Pentium II, and Pentium III processors using a host bus frequency of 100 or 133 MHz

64-bit data bus and 32-bit addressing

Optimized buffering architecture design for CPU-to-memory, -AGP, and -PCI read/write

Supports back-to-back write transfers

Optimized processor command scheduling and reordering

Supports synchronous/asynchronous clock mode between processor and memory

Supports SDRAM at 66, 100, 133 MHz, or DDR at 200, 266 MHz

Supports symmetrical and asymmetrical SDRAM/DDR addressing

Supports up to 3GB of 4, 16, 64, 128, 256, and 512Mbit SDRAM/DDR technologies

Supports memory shadowing, CAS-before-RAS, and self-refresh for SDRAM

Pipelined SDRAM/DDR cycle control with hidden precharge

Supports up to 128 entries for Graphic Address Remapping Table (GART)

AGP 66 MHz V.2.0 protocol supports AGP 1X/2X/4X modes

Supports synchronous/asynchronous clock between the processor bus and the PCI bus

TABLE 10-4   ALI ALADDIN PRO 5 CHIPSET FEATURES AT A GLANCE (*CONTINUED*)

32-bit address/data PCI bus using PCI bus driver technology
Supports up to 6 PCI Rev. 2.2 masters (excluding the M1651 and PCI-to-ISA bridge)
Parity protection on all PCI bus signals
Supports concurrent PCI bus burst transfer at zero-wait-states
133MB/s data streaming for PCI bus-to-SDRAM/DDR access with minimum latency
Supports ACPI 1.0b and legacy power conservation schemes

ALI ALADDIN PRO 4

The ALi Aladdin Pro 4 chipset supports Pentium II/III processors that use a 100/133 MHz FSB speed. It can also support the 66 MHz Celeron FSB setting. The Pro 4 supports PC100 and PC133 SDRAM memory. It consists of the M1641 North Bridge system controller, and either the M1535 South Bridge bus controller for desktops or the M1535D controller for mobile systems. The Pro 4 chipset offers support for UDMA/33/66, USB (four ports), and AGP 4X. Table 10-5 highlights the ALi Aladdin Pro 4 features.

ALI ALADDIN TNT2

Acer Laboratories combines the M1631 AGP/PCI/3D graphics system controller with any of four ALi South Bridge (I/O controller) chips to create the Aladdin TNT2 package. It supports the Pentium II/III or Celeron processor interface in either the Slot 1 or Socket 370 configuration, and supports system bus speeds from 66 MHz to 133 MHz (along with a built-in graphics engine and numerous multimedia enhancements). The TNT2 will also support up to 1.5GB of EDO, SDRAM, or VC SDRAM main memory.

TABLE 10-5   ALI ALADDIN PRO 4 CHIPSET FEATURES AT A GLANCE

Supports Celeron, Pentium II, and Pentium III processors using a host bus frequency of 66 or 100/133 MHz
64-bit data bus and 32-bit addressing
Optimized buffer design for CPU-to-memory read/write
Supports EDO/SDRAM/VC SDRAM
Supports symmetrical and asymmetrical DRAM addressing
64-bit data bus and additional 8-bit ECC protection under 4 RAS mode
Supports 640KB to 1MB address range shadowing
Supports up to 1.5GB of 4, 16, 64, 128, and 256Mbit DRAM technologies
Supports ECC to provide single-bit error correction and multiple-bit error detection under 4-RAS mode
CAS-before-RAS and self-refresh for SDRAM
CAS-before-RAS refresh for EDO DRAM
Pipelined DRAM cycle control with hidden precharge
Supports optional SMI memory address remapping and protection
Dynamic DRAM cooling algorithm
AGP specification 2.0 compliant with 1x/2x/4x mode support
66 MHz PCI bus protocol support
Supports up to 128 entries for Graphic Address Remapping Table (GART)
Supports synchronous clock mode between the processor bus and the PCI bus
32-bit address/data PCI bus using PCI bus driver technology

The Aladdin TNT2 is designed to improve system performance with memory and I/O throughput. The pipelined memory design helps reduce the effects of memory latency and refresh cycles. For the I/O sub-system, deep data-in/out buffers reduce the latency for PCI-initiated master reads and writes. Programmable buffer controls can be tuned to optimize the PCI-to-memory data transfer rate for different memory configurations and PCI device characteristics. The chipset is compliant with the PCI 2.2 specification (including flexible PCI latency control). This allows the PCI latency to be adjusted to achieve the best system performance. The Aladdin TNT2 can support up to five PCI masters. It is also possible to support more PCI masters, depending on the overall physical layout and design of the motherboard.

Power management features of the chipset include power-on suspend, suspend to disk, PCI bus CLKRUN, and dynamic clock stop. This provides desktop systems with very flexible power management configuration control.

The TNT2 also supports video. Its core features a 128-bit 3D pipeline that processes two pixels per clock cycle, enabling single-pass multitexturing. It offers a 32-bit color pipeline, a 32-bit Z/stencil buffer, an 8-bit stencil buffer, and per-pixel MIP mapping. The integrated graphics and host interface communicates through an AGP 2X bus, which effectively doubles AGP 2X throughout to over 1GB/s. The 128-bit graphics engine is optimized for single-cycle operation into the 64-bit SDRAM/SGRAM interface, supporting over 1GB/s throughput. Table 10-6 lists major characteristics for the TNT2.

VIA also offers a similar integrated graphics chipset for mobile systems. It uses the CyberBLADE graphics engine integrated into the M1632M North Bridge chip.

ALI ALADDIN PRO 2

The Aladdin Pro 2 is ALi's entry-level offering for the Pentium II system market. The Aladdin Pro 2 employs various techniques to improve the memory and I/O throughput to keep pace with the advanced super-scalar, super-pipelined Pentium II-class processors. It provides parity protection over the PCI bus, along with independent EC and ECC protection in memory to improve memory reliability and performance (a powerful feature for network servers). To support the 3D graphics functions, the chipset supports both a 66 MHz graphics bus and 1x/2x AGP.

TABLE 10-6   ALI ALADDIN TNT2 CHIPSET FEATURES AT A GLANCE
Supports Pentium II, III, and Celeron processors using a host bus frequency of 66, 100, or 133 MHz
Supports EDO, SDRAM, and VC SDRAM up to 1.5GB
Supports symmetrical and asymmetrical DRAM addressing
Supports 4Mbit, 16Mbit, 64Mbit, 128Mbit, and 256Mbit DRAM technologies
Supports ECC, which offers single-bit error correction and multiple-bit error detection
PCI v.2.2 bus support includes synchronous clock mode between the processor bus and PCI bus
Supports up to six PCI masters (excluding the PCI-to-ISA bridge) with parity protection on all PCI bus signals
Includes an advanced 3D/2D graphic engine with 100% hardware triangle setup and a twin-texel 32-bit graphic pipeline
Optimized Direct3D acceleration for DirectX 5.0 and DirectX 6.0, and optimized for DirectX 6.0 and OpenGL support
Video system supports both SGRAM and SDRAM
Video acceleration for DirectShow, MPEG-1, MPEG-2, and Indeo Video
Power management features include power-on suspend, suspend to disk, PCI bus CLKRUN, and dynamic clock stop

The Aladdin Pro 2 includes a data path with multiport buffers for improved data acceleration, and an external I/O controller chip to support multiple Pentium II processors (another important feature for servers). For the memory sub-system, the "pipelined" memory cycle design helps overcome latency and refresh cycle delays. As shown in Table 10-7, support for USB and UDMA/33 round out the Aladdin Pro 2 package of the M1621 system controller combined with either the M1533 or the M1543 peripheral bus controller. However, the support is missing for accepted standards such as IEEE 1394 FireWire and UDMA/66.

ALI ALADDIN 7

The Aladdin 7 is a low-cost transitional chipset designed to support both Socket 7-style processors and more recent Slot 1 Pentium II processors. Combining the M1561 North Bridge system controller with the M1535D+ South Bridge bus controller, the Aladdin 7 offers support for the standard Socket 7 features along with an integrated 2D/3D graphics engine. Table 10-8 lists the features of an Aladdin 7 chipset.

ALI ALADDIN 5

The Aladdin 5 is a fifth-generation (Pentium-class) chipset from ALi. It is also a two-chip solution that provides a combination of system performance and low system cost. The chipset is comprised of the M1541 system controller and either the M1533 or M1543 peripheral bus controller. Like the Aladdin IV, the Aladdin 5M supports all Socket 7 processors. The Aladdin 5 supports the same features as the IV with some additions and improvements, including support for AGP 2X, a 100 MHz bus speed, and power management features that support Microsoft's On Now technology. The Aladdin 5 also offers processor feature support including the Cyrix M1 and M2 "linear wrap" mode and AMD's K6 "write allocation." You can find additional details in Table 10-9.

ALI ALADDIN 4

The ALi Aladdin 4 chipset is a continuation of the venerable Aladdin series. The Aladdin 4 can be a combination of either the M1531 system controller and the M1533 peripheral bus controller, or the M1531(B) system controller and the M1543 peripheral bus controller. The main improvements in the Aladdin 4 are in the M1531(B) chip, which handles 64Mbit SDRAM support and more cacheable RAM region support. Otherwise, the features are the same for both chip combinations.

The ALi Aladdin 4 is designed as a low-cost chipset to support the Socket 7 system architecture, including support for Pentium-class Intel, Cyrix, and AMD processors at bus speeds from 50 MHz to 83.3 MHz and split voltages (for processors with MMX features). The Aladdin 4 provides the option of either

TABLE 10-7   ALI ALADDIN PRO 2 CHIPSET FEATURES AT A GLANCE
Supports all 60, 66, and 100 MHz CPU bus Pentium II processors
Includes a 256-byte buffer for CPU-to-memory write and a 128-byte buffer for CPU-to-memory read
Memory support includes FPM or EDO (up to 2GB) and SDRAM (up to 1GB)
Supports ECC to provide single-bit error correction and multiple-bit error detection
Supports mix of SDRAM, EDO DRAM, and Page Mode DRAM
Supports 4Mbit, 16Mbit, 64Mbit, 128Mbit, and 256Mbit DRAM technologies
PCI v.2.1 bus support for up to five PCI masters (excluding PCI-to-ISA bridge) and parity protection on all PCI bus signals
AGP v.1.0 support for 1X and 2X AGP modes

TABLE 10-8   ALI ALADDIN 7 CHIPSET FEATURES AT A GLANCE

128-bit data streaming architecture for highest performance SMA/UMA

PC99 compliant

100/66 MHz CPU FSB, 100 MHz ready

Standard PC100/66 SDRAM (up to 1GB) PC100 ready

33 MHz PCI 2.2 compliant I/O bus

ACPI power management

Compatible with single-chip ALi M1535D and M1543 South Bridges

First integrated North Bridge with hardware-accelerated geometry transformation & lighting (T&L)

8X Virtual AGP graphics performance and functionality

30fps DVD playback with hardware acceleration (motion compensation)

128-bit BitBLT engine, 256 raster operations

Up to 1600x1200 noninterlaced screen resolution

Up to 2.1GB/s memory interface bandwidth

Optimized driver for DirectX 7 with Direct3D, OpenGL ICD, HWMC, and GDI acceleration on Windows 98 and Windows 2000

64MB cache RAM with 8-bit tag SRAM, or 512MB cache memory with 11-bit tag SRAM. Memory type support from FPM to SDRAM (at 3.3V to 5V operation) allows some versatility in memory choice and still provides for support of faster, newer standards. The Aladdin 4 contains 8 RAS lines for up to 1GB of RAM support. Additional support for features like ACPI, USB, bus mastering, and UDMA/33 keep the Aladdin 4 chipset competitive (you can find major features summarized in Table 10-10), but this chipset is designed mainly for affordability, not performance.

TABLE 10-9   ALI ALADDIN 5 CHIPSET FEATURES AT A GLANCE

Supports all 3.3V/2.5V Socket 7 processors with bus speeds at 100 MHz, 83.3 MHz, 75 MHz, 66 MHz, 60 MHz, and 50 MHz

Supports "linear wrap" mode for Cyrix M1 and M2

Supports "write allocation" feature for AMD K6

Supports pseudo-synchronous PCI bus access

Supports pipelined-burst (PB) SRAM cache size of 256KB, 512KB, or 1MB

Cacheable memory up to 512MB with 10-bit Tag SRAM when using 512KB L2 cache, or 1GB when using 256KB L2 cache

Supports 3.3V or 5V FPM/EDO/SDRAM DIMMs

Supports 64Mbit (16M*4, 8M*8, 4M*16) technology DRAMs

Supports ECC and parity checking for DRAM

Supports four single-sided DIMMs based on x4 DRAMs

Supports four single- and double-sided DIMMs based on x8 and x16 DRAMs

Synchronous/pseudosynchronous 25/30/33 MHz 3.3V/5V tolerance PCI v.2.1 interface

Includes a PCI bus arbiter supporting five PCI masters and an AGP master

PCI-to-DRAM bandwidth up to 133MB/s

Enhanced power management including ACPI support, PCI bus CLKRUN functions, dynamic clock stop, suspend to DRAM, power-on suspend, suspend to disk, and self-refresh during suspend

Supports the AGP 1.0 interface with AGP 66 MHz PCI protocol and AGP 1X and 2X operating modes

TABLE 10-10	**ALI ALADDIN 4 CHIPSET FEATURES AT A GLANCE**

Supports all Intel, Cyrix, TI, and AMD 586-class CPUs with bus speeds of 83.3 MHz, 75 MHz, 66 MHz, 60 MHz, and 50 MHz at 3.3V/2.5V

Supports "linear wrap" mode for Cyrix M1 and M2

Supports pseudo-synchronous PCI bus access

Supports pipelined-burst (PB) SRAM cache size of 256KB, 512KB, or 1MB

Cacheable memory up to 64MB with 8-bit Tag SRAM, or up to 512MB with 11-bit Tag SRAM

Supports 3.3V or 5V FPM/EDO/SDRAM DIMMs

Supports 64Mbit (16M*4, 8M*8, 4M*16) technology DRAMs

Supports ECC and parity checking for DRAM

Fully synchronous 25/30/33 MHz 3.3V/5V-tolerant PCI v.2.1 interface

Includes a PCI bus arbiter supporting five PCI masters

PCI-to-DRAM bandwidth up to 133MB/s

Enhanced power management including ACPI support, PCI bus CLKRUN functions, dynamic clock stop, suspend to DRAM, and self-refresh during suspend

AMD Chipsets

AMD (Advanced Micro Devices) certainly is no stranger to the CPU arena, but it is a relative newcomer to the chipset market. Traditionally, AMD relied on other chipset makers to support its line of CPUs (the 5x85, K5, K6, K6-2, and K6-3). However, not all chipset makers provided the optimum support for AMD's products. As a consequence, AMD has developed the 640 chipset for use with its K6 and K6-2 CPU. In addition, the introduction of AMD's Athlon processor required AMD to develop a supporting chipset if it wanted the widest possible acceptance of the Athlon's unique architecture. The result was the AMD 750 chipset, generally regarded as one of the most stable and best-performing chipsets for the Athlon. AMD continued the practice of producing at least one chipset to support its processors with the addition of the AMD 760 chipset. The 760 chipset is for use with the newer Thunderbird core (Athlon and Duron) processors and supports DDR-SDRAM memory.

AMD 760

The AMD 760 chipset offers enhanced performance for the AMD Athlon processor and other AMD Athlon system bus–compatible processors such as the Duron. The AMD 760 chipset consists of the AMD 761 system controller (North Bridge) in a 569-pin plastic ball-grid array (PBGA) package and the AMD 766 peripheral bus controller (South Bridge) in a 272-pin PBGA package. The AMD 761 system controller supports the AMD Athlon system bus, DDR-SDRAM system memory, accelerated graphics port (AGP 4X), and the PCI bus. DDR-SDRAM is a modern memory technology that offers peak memory bandwidths up to 2.1GB/s and is designed to be competitive with RAMBUS memory. The AMD 766 peripheral bus controller features four primary functions: PCI-to-ISA/LPC bridge, OHCI USB host controller, EIDE UDMA/33/66/100 controller, and system management logic. Each function has independent access to the PCI bus, a complete set of PCI interface signals and state machines, and the capability of working independently with separate devices. You can learn more about the AMD 760 chipset in Table 10-11.

TABLE 10-11   AMD 760 CHIPSET FEATURES AT A GLANCE

Supports 100/200 MHz or 133/266 MHz double data rate (DDR) system bus

Supports 100/200 MHz or 133/266 MHz DDR memory bus

1.6GB/s peak data transfer rates at 100/200 MHz, 2.1GB/s at 133/266 MHz

PCI 2.2-compliant

Up to seven bus masters plus the AMD 766 peripheral bus controller

66 MHz AGP 2.0-compliant interface supports 1x, 2x, and 4x modes

Support for up to 4GB of DDR SDRAM

High-performance point-to-point system bus topology

Source-synchronous clocking for high-speed transfers

64-byte (cache line) data burst transfers

Concurrent processor-to-main-memory with PCI-to-main-memory

Concurrent processor-to-main-memory with AGP-to-main-memory

Concurrent processor-to-PCI with PCI-to-main-memory or AGP-to-main-memory

Memory ECC support

Supports up to two unbuffered DIMMs or four registered DIMMs

Supports 64Mbit, 128Mbit, 256Mbit, and 512Mbit technology

Supports 64-bit data width, plus 8-bit ECC paths

Supports flexible row (RAS) and column (CAS) addressing

BIOS-configurable memory timing parameters and configuration

2.5V memory interface operation with no external buffers or PLLs

Concurrent DRAM writeback and read-around-write

Burst read and write transactions

32-bit interface, compatible with 3.3-V and 5-V PCI I/O

Synchronous PCI bus operation up to 33 MHz

Automatic processor-to-PCI burst cycle detection

Zero-wait-state PCI initiator and target burst transfers

PCI-to-DRAM data streaming up to 132MB/s

Enhanced PCI command optimization, such as Memory Read Line (MRL), Memory Read Multiple (MRM), and Memory-Write-and-Invalidate (MWI)

Compliance support for both ACPI and Microsoft PC99 power management

Supports processor halt/stop grant/sleep states (ACPI C1, C2)

Supports ACPI S1 (power on suspend) and S3 (suspend to RAM) sleep states

Supports clock throttling with the processor's STPCLK#/stop grant mechanism

AMD 750

The AMD 750 is a highly integrated system chipset that offers the features and enhanced performance needed to support the AMD Athlon processor (and other Athlon-compatible processors such as the Duron). The AMD 750 chipset consists of the AMD 751 system controller and the AMD 756 peripheral bus controller.

The AMD 751 system controller includes a front side bus (FSB) that supports three 200 MHz channels, a 32-bit PCI 2.2–compliant bus interface at 33 MHz supporting up to six masters, and a 66 MHz AGP 2.0–compliant interface to support the AGP 2X data transfer mode. Currently the AMD 751 system controller is designed to support up to 768MB of PC100 SDRAM DIMMs using 16Mbit, 64Mbit, and 128Mbit memory technologies. The 200 MHz FSB includes a high-performance point-to-point system bus capability with synchronous clocking for high-speed data transfers (up to 1.6GB/s at 200 MHz). The combination of the 200 MHz system bus and the AMD 750 chipset enables high throughput between system components like CPU-to-memory, CPU-to-AGP, CPU-to-PCI, AGP-to-memory, and PCI-to-memory. This provides measurably improved performance for 3D video and multimedia applications that require high-speed data transfers and calculations.

The AMD 756 peripheral bus controller adds PCI-ISA bridge support, bus master IDE control with UDMA/33 and UDMA/66 support, and USB support, and includes the keyboard/mouse controller. Current standards for plug-and-play and power management are supplied by the AMD 756 chip. These features enable AMD 750–based systems to be Microsoft PC99-compliant. Table 10-12 lists more highlights for the AMD 750 chipset.

AMD 640

The AMD 640 chipset features two devices: the AMD 640 system controller and the AMD 645 peripheral bus controller (refer back to Table 10-2 for a comparison of chipset designations). Working together, these chips can deliver numerous high-performance features that accelerate multimedia applications (especially those designed for MMX-type processors). The AMD 640 system controller has been optimized to accelerate AMD K6 processor transactions, and it also incorporates support for modern SDRAM (Synchronous DRAM) memory. The AMD 645 peripheral bus controller features support for Ultra-DMA/33, which allows the ATA/IDE interface to provide a 33MB/s data transfer rate. System performance is further increased with "Type F" DMA, which provides a 5x improvement over standard DMA transfers. Type F DMA reduces the system bus requirements for DMA transfers, providing the CPU with greater access to the ISA bus (less of a bottleneck during data transfers). Perhaps most important for AMD, the 640 chipset is backward compatible with existing AMD and Intel CPUs.

The AMD 640 system controller (the North Bridge chip) features the 64-bit Socket 7 interface, integrated write-back cache controller, system memory controller, and PCI bus controller. The Socket 7 interface has been optimized for the AMD K6 processor, providing 3-1-1-1 transfer timing for both read and write transactions from PBSRAM (Pipeline Burst Static RAM) at 66 MHz. The memory controller features a data buffering design that uses four cache lines (16 quad words, or QW) of processor-to-DRAM or cache-to-DRAM write buffering with concurrent write-back capability to accelerate write-back and write-miss cycles. The integrated PCI bus controller features concurrent processor and PCI operation through a 5 double word (DW) posted write buffer design. PCI concurrency with DRAM or cache memory is achieved through a 48 double word posted write buffer and 26 double word prefetch buffer.

TABLE 10-12   AMD 750 CHIPSET FEATURES AT A GLANCE

Designed to be used in PC99-compliant systems

200 MHz AMD K7 (a.k.a. Athlon) host channel

Supports UDMA/66

AGP 2X

USB (four-port OHCI)

Supports up to 768MB of ECC-compliant PC100 SDRAM

PCI 2.2 compliant with support for six PCI masters

PCI-to-ISA bridge

Plug-and-play support

Advanced power management (ACPI 1.0 and APM 1.2) compliant

Includes an integrated keyboard/mouse controller

The AMD 640 design also uses byte-merging, which optimizes processor-to-PCI throughput and reduces PCI bus traffic by converting consecutive processor addresses into burst PCI cycles. The controller minimizes PCI initiator read latency and DRAM access using techniques like snoop ahead, snoop filtering, forwarding cache write-backs to the PCI initiator, and merging L1 write-backs into the PCI-posted write buffers. The integrated PCI controller supports enhanced PCI bus commands such as Memory-Read-Line, Memory-Read-Multiple, and Memory-Write-Invalidate. These features allow a PCI initiator to achieve the full 133Mbps burst transfer rate. The integrated PCI bus controller is fully compatible with the PCI Local Bus Specification (revision 2.1).

The AMD 645 peripheral bus controller (the South Bridge chip) features an integrated ISA bus controller, enhanced master mode PCI EIDE controller with Ultra-DMA/33 technology, ACPI-compatible power management unit, USB controller, PS2-compatible keyboard/mouse controller, and real-time clock (RTC) with extended 256-byte CMOS RAM. The on-chip EIDE controller has a dual-channel DMA engine with capability of interlaced dual-channel commands. High-bandwidth PCI transfers are achieved by an enhanced 16 double word data FIFO with full scatter and gather capability. The integrated USB controller features a root hub with two ports having 18-level-deep data FIFOs and built-in physical layer transceivers. The USB controller also offers backward compatibility with legacy keyboard and PS/2 mouse support. The AMD 645 peripheral bus controller meets Windows 95/98 plug-and-play requirements with steerable PCI interrupts, ISA interrupts, and DMA channels. The integrated power management unit is compliant with ACPI and APM and provides dedicated input pins for external modem ring indication and power-on, five general-purpose I/O pins with option for I^2C port, and 16 general-purpose pins that can be programmed as inputs or outputs. Table 10-13 offers the AMD 640 chipset features at a glance.

Intel Chipsets

Intel Corporation provided the 8086 CPU that went into the first PC and has often led the way in CPU development ever since. Though competitors like AMD and Cyrix are closing the performance gap (especially AMD with its Athlon and Duron processors), Intel has remained competitive with the fastest high-performance CPUs like the Pentium II, III, and 4. Since Intel is normally the first to release new CPUs, it is also ideally positioned to develop the chipsets to complement those CPUs. Intel is also a frequent collaborator with Microsoft in the proposal of new industry initiatives (such as ACPI and AGP), so it often has a powerful head start in supporting those initiatives. As you'll see in this section, Intel offers a wide range of chipsets for high-end PC platforms.

TABLE 10-13   AMD 640 CHIPSET FEATURES AT A GLANCE
Optimized for the AMD K6 processor family
Provides SDRAM, EDO RAM, and FPM RAM support
Offers PCI concurrency
Supports Ultra-DMA/33
Includes "data path units"
Includes RTC and controllers for PS/2 keyboard/mouse
Backward compatible with other AMD and non-AMD processors
Offers USB support
Supports ACPI
Includes plug-and-play support

INTEL "BROOKDALE" (Q1 2002)

Many of Intel's later 800-series chipsets rely on Rambus DRAM instead of SDRAM. No Intel chipsets support DDR SDRAM at this time. Intel has realized that support for DDR SDRAM memory will be required in at least some of its Pentium 4 chipsets. Although Rambus memory is still Intel's primary vehicle for providing the memory bandwidth needed by a Pentium 4, Intel cannot afford to ignore a segment of the market that prefers the features of DDR SDRAM.

The Intel chipset offering support for DDR SDRAM memory is currently in development (code named "Brookdale"). Other features of the chipset include support for AGP 4X, 100 MHz quad-pumped FSB (400 MHz), memory amounts up to 3GB, and UDMA/100 IDE standards. It should also offer six USB ports, and it might include integrated graphics. The design will probably rely on the current Intel hub architecture, with a graphics/memory controller hub (or GMCH), an ICH3 I/O controller hub, and a FWH firmware hub. Since the "Brookdale" chipset has not yet been released, it will not be covered further here.

INTEL 850 PENTIUM 4

The Intel 850 chipset was designed to support the Intel Pentium 4 processor and Intel NetBurst architecture. The chipset is composed of the 82850 memory controller hub (MCH) and the 82801BA I/O controller hub (ICH2). The Intel 850 chipset provides a quad-pumped 100 MHz system bus enabling a 400 MHz data bus that allows a high-bandwidth connection between the Intel Pentium 4 processor and the platform. The system bus supports dual RDRAM channels at 3.2GB/s, providing 3x the bandwidth of platforms based on Intel Pentium III processors. The Intel hub architecture delivers twice the I/O bandwidth as previous-generation North Bridge/South Bridge technology. With dedicated data paths to fully optimize the additional bandwidth, the Intel 850 chipset targets the performance PC market and provides support for future Intel NetBurst architecture-based processors.

The 82850 MCH supports dual RDRAM memory channels and the 400 MHz system bus, providing graphics support through 1.5V AGP 4X technology. The AGP 4X interface allows graphics controllers to access main memory at over 1GB/s, which is twice that of previous AGP platforms. Support for SDRAM or DDR-SDRAM memory is not available in any Pentium 4 chipsets from Intel at this time. The 850 chipset supports up to 2GB of RDRAM (Rambus) when 256Mb RDARM technology is implemented. Supported RDRAM speeds are 300 MHz and 400 MHz.

The enhanced 82801BA I/O ICH2 delivers twice the I/O bandwidth over traditional bridge architecture and provides dedicated data paths to optimize the additional bandwidth. The ICH2 makes a direct connection from the graphics and memory for faster access to peripherals. Dual Ultra-ATA/100 controllers support the fastest IDE interface for transfers to storage devices. Additional performance is gained with Intel's Storage Driver over standard ATA drivers. The ICH2 provides a 33 MHz, Rev. 2.2–compliant PCI interface for expansion devices. The ICH2 integrates a PCI arbiter that supports up to six external PCI bus masters (in addition to the internal ICH2 requests). The ICH2 supports two types of DMA (LPC and PC/PCI). DMA via LPC is similar to ISA DMA. LPC DMA and PC/PCI DMA use the ICH2's DMA controller.

The USB controller provides enhanced support for the Universal Host Controller Interface (UHCI). This includes support that allows legacy software to use a USB-based keyboard and mouse. The ICH2 is USB Rev. 1.1–compliant. The ICH2 contains two USB host controllers. Each host controller includes a root hub with two separate USB ports each, for a total of four USB ports.

AC97 audio support is also included, delivering six channels of audio for enhanced sound quality and full surround-sound capability for live broadcast and other Digital Dashboard programming. The

LAN Connect Interface (LCI) provides flexible network solutions such as home phone line, 10/100 Mbps Ethernet, and 10/100 Mbps Ethernet with LAN manageability. All three network options utilize Intel Single Driver Technology, which supports multiple products to simplify network connectivity and increase ease of deployment. Communication and Networking Riser (CNR) support allows flexibility in system configuration with a baseline feature set that can be upgraded with an audio card, modem card, or network card.

The ICH2's power management functions include enhanced clock control, local and global monitoring support for 14 individual devices, and various low-power (suspend) states (such as suspend-to-DRAM and suspend-to-disk). A hardware-based thermal management circuit permits software-independent entrance to low-power states. The ICH2 contains full support for the ACPI specification. You can compare the characteristics of Intel's 850 chipset to its 440 GX chipset in Table 10-14.

INTEL 840 PENTIUM III XEON

The Intel 840 chipset is the high-performance (workstation) member of the 800-series chipset family. In addition to the basic 82801 and 82802 support chips, the 840 utilizes the 82840 MCH. This chip provides AGP graphics 2X and 4X support, dual RDRAM memory channels, and multiple PCI segments for high-performance I/O performance. The 840 is more versatile than its 810E and 820 counterparts due to its ability to support three additional components that may be used with the standard core 800 components: the 82806, the 82803, and 82804.

The 64-bit 82806 PCI controller hub (P64H) supports 64-bit PCI slots at speeds of either 33 or 66 MHz. The P64H connects directly to the MCH using Intel's "accelerated hub architecture," providing a dedicated path for high-performance I/O. For systems requiring high RDRAM capacity, an 82803 RDRAM memory repeater hub (MRH-R) may be utilized. The MRH-R converts each memory channel

TABLE 10-14   COMPARISON OF INTEL PENTIUM 850 AND 440 GX CHIPSETS

CHIPSET	INTEL 850	INTEL 440 GX
Processor	Pentium 4	Pentium II/III Xeon
Voltage	AGTL+	GTL+
Dual CPUs	Yes	Yes
Refresh	RDRAM active	CAS-before-RAS
Memory Support	128/256Mbit	Eight rows
Max Memory Size	2GB	2GB
Memory Types	PC600 (RDRAM) PC800 (RDRAM)	PC100 SDRAM
ECC/Parity	Yes	Yes
PCI Support	PCI 2.2	PCI 2.1
Concurrent PCI	Yes	Yes
AGP	1X/2X/4X (1.5V only)	1X/2X
MTT	Yes	Yes
Bridge Type	ICH2	PIIX4E
USB Support	Yes	Yes
IDE Support	Yes (UDMA/100)	Yes (UDMA/33)
RTC	Yes	Yes
Power Mgt.	SMM & ACPI	SMM & ACPI
I/O Mgt.	SMBus & GPIO	SMBus & GPIO

into two memory channels for expanded memory capacity. For systems requiring high SDRAM capacity, an 82804 SDRAM memory repeater hub (MRH-S) may be utilized. The MRH-S efficiently translates the RDRAM protocol into SDRAM-based signals for system memory flexibility.

Chip combinations provide for SDRAM or RDRAM support, bandwidth doubling on the processor, AGP, USB, and PCI buses, and dual processor support to provide the highest possible performance. This chipset supports processors using a 133 MHz system bus, and hard drives using UDMA/66 technology. Future performance enhancements can be implemented through BIOS code changes if BIOS suppliers comply with Intel's Modular BIOS specifications. Table 10-15 compares the Intel 840 to other recent Intel chipsets.

INTEL 820(E) PENTIUM II/III

Intel continued its development of the 800-series chipset without the integrated video, and the next member of the 800 family was the Intel 820(E) chipset with features designed to support mainstream and performance systems. It includes the 800-series support for the "modular BIOS," which is flash-upgradeable as features are added to the chipset. Using the same two support chips as the Intel 810E chipset (the 82801 I/O controller hub and the 82802 firmware hub), the 820 adds either the 82820 or the 82820DP (dual processor) memory controller hub. Intended as a "long life" platform chipset solution in the rapidly changing PC market, the accelerated hub architecture of the 820 allows Intel to enhance and update components

TABLE 10-15   COMPARISON OF INTEL 840, 820, 810E, 440 BX, AND 440 ZX CHIPSETS

CHIPSET	INTEL 840	INTEL 820	INTEL 810E	440 BX	440 ZX
Processor	Pentium III/Xeon	Pentium II/III	Pentium II/III Celeron (810 only)	Pentium II/III	Pentium II/III Celeron (ZX x66 only)
Voltage	AGTL+	AGTL+	AGTL+	GTL+	GTL+
Dual CPUs	Yes	Yes	No	Yes	No
Refresh	RDRAM active	N/A	CAS-before-RAS	CAS-before-RAS	CAS-before-RAS
Memory Support	64/128/256Mbit	64/128/256Mbit	16/64/128Mbit	N/A	N/A
Max Memory Size	8GB	1GB	512MB	1GB	256MB
Memory Types	PC100 (SDRAM) PC600 (RDRAM) PC800 (RDRAM)	SDRAM	PC100 (SDRAM) RDRAM	SDRAM	SDRAM
ECC/Parity	Yes	Yes	N/A	Yes	No
PCI Support	PCI 2.2	PCI 2.1	PCI 2.2	PCI 2.1	PCI 2.1
Concurrent PCI	Yes	Yes	Yes	Yes	Yes
AGP	Yes (1X/2X/4X)	Yes (1X/2X/4X)	Yes (Integrated)	Yes (1X/2X)	Yes (1X/2X)
MTT	Yes	Yes	Dyn. Int. Arb.	Yes	Yes
Bridge Type	ICH	ICH	ICH	PIIX4E	PIIX4E
USB Support	Yes	Yes	Yes	Yes	Yes
IDE Support	Yes (UDMA/66)	Yes (UDMA/66)	Yes (UDMA/66)	Yes (UDMA/33)	Yes (UDMA/33)
RTC	Yes	Yes	Yes	Yes	Yes
Power Mgt.	SMM & ACPI	SMM & ACPI	SMM & ACPI	SMM & ACPI	SMM & ACPI
I/O Mgt.	SMBus & GPIO	SMBus & GPIO	SMBus & GPIO	SMBus & GPIO	SMBus & GPIO

without forcing system changes. The plan is to use this capability to maintain support for the fastest Pentium III processors all the way into 2001.

Although current SDRAM DIMMs are supported, achieving top performance for the 820 chipset depends on the emerging Rambus DRAM technology (delivering the potential bandwidth of 1.6GB/s needed to optimize Pentium III and AGP performance). RDRAM allows more open memory pages, increasing the opportunity for page hits and better memory access. RDRAM and the 820 chipset are designed to enable what Intel has termed "constant computing," the ability to perform numerous functions in the background without impairing foreground performance. The 820 chipset supports RDRAM technology in its current state, and provides for two memory sockets and 512MB of system memory. Continued RDRAM development should increase this amount to 1GB.

The 820 uses three integrated buses to reduce interference problems and increase data transfer rates. The Direct Rambus (memory) interface, internal hub interface, and LPC bus interface allow the doubling of bandwidth and data transfer rates. In addition, performance is improved with support for AGP 4X, UDMA/66, and a 133 MHz PCI system bus. AGP 4X graphics support offers the same direct connection to the memory controller and twice the graphics bandwidth of AGP 2X (achieving transfer rates in excess of 1GB/s). The architecture of the 820 chipset features a direct pipeline for audio and video data, and the new architecture allows for concurrent data transfer streams over the CPU, PCI, USB, and AGP buses. When the 82801BA (ICH2) I/O controller hub was produced, it was added to the 820 family, creating the 820E chipset. The ICH2 adds support for UDMA/100 and two USB host controllers for four USB ports. Table 10-16 compares features of the 820E chipset.

TABLE 10-16   COMPARISON OF INTEL 820E, 815EP, 815E, 815, AND 810E2 CHIPSETS

CHIPSET	INTEL 820E	INTEL 815EP	INTEL 815E	INTEL 815	INTEL 810E2
Processor	Pentium II/III	Pentium III/ Celeron	Pentium III/ Celeron	Pentium III/ Celeron	Pentium II/III Celeron
Voltage	AGTL+	AGTL+	AGTL+	AGTL+	AGTL+
Dual CPUs	Yes	No	No	No	No
Refresh	RDRAM active	CAS-before-RAS	CAS-before-RAS	CAS-before-RAS	CAS-before-RAS
Memory Support	64/128/256Mbit	Six rows	Six rows	Six rows	Six rows
Max Memory Size	1GB	512MB	512MB	512MB	512MB
Memory Types	PC600 (RDRAM) PC700 (RDRAM) PC800 (RDRAM)	PC100 SDRAM PC133 SDRAM	PC100 SDRAM PC133 SDRAM	PC100 SDRAM PC133 SDRAM	PC100 SDRAM
ECC/Parity	Yes	N/A	N/A	N/A	No
PCI Support	PCI 2.2	PCI 2.2	PCI 2.2	PCI 2.2	PCI 2.2
Concurrent PCI	Yes	Yes	Yes	Yes	Yes
AGP	1X/2X/4X	1X/2X/4X	1X/2X/4X	1X/2X/4X	Yes (Integrated)
MTT	Yes	Dyn. Int. Arb.	Dyn. Int. Arb.	Dyn. Int. Arb.	Dyn. Int. Arb.
Bridge Type	ICH2	ICH2	ICH2	ICH	ICH2
USB Support	Yes	Yes	Yes	Yes	Yes
IDE Support	Yes (UDMA/100)	Yes (UDMA/100)	Yes (UDMA/100)	Yes (UDMA/66)	Yes (UDMA/100)
RTC	Yes	Yes	Yes	Yes	Yes
Power Mgt.	SMM & ACPI	SMM & ACPI	SMM & ACPI	SMM & ACPI	SMM & ACPI
I/O Mgt.	SMBus & GPIO	SMBus & GPIO	SMBus & GPIO	SMBus & GPIO	SMBus & GPIO

INTEL 815 (E AND EP) PENTIUM II/III AND CELERON

The Intel 815-series chipsets are designed to meet the demands of users who require better AGP video performance than the 810-series offers, and who do not want to use Rambus memory required by the 820/840 chipsets. Intel needed a chipset with support for the newer 133 MHz FSB that also supported AGP 4X and SDRAM memory. Attempts to add SDRAM support to the Intel 820 and 840 chipsets failed. This created a situation in which Intel was not able to provide the best chipset support for its own processors. Rather than update the 440 BX chipset to support the newer IDE, AGP, PCI, and memory interfaces, Intel produced the 815-series chipsets.

The Intel 815 chipset supports the Pentium III and Celeron line of processors in the FC-PGA (flip chip PGA) package. It is a combination of the 82815 GMCH and the 82801AA ICH. It supports 32-bit system bus addressing and is limited to single-processor systems. AGTL+ bus voltage is supported at FSB speeds of 66 MHz, 100 MHz, and 133 MHz. The integrated SDRAM controller of the 815 chipset supports up to 512MB of PC100/133 SDRAM memory and allows for up to three double-sided DIMMs. It supports asymmetrical SDRAM addressing, but memory must be unbuffered (and not ECC). The chipset does allow for suspend-to-RAM power conservation operation.

Although the Intel 815 and 815E chipsets still include integrated support for AGP video, they also support a separate AGP device and meet AGP 2.0 specifications. This allows for 4X AGP data transfers, dual-mode buffers, and either 3.3V or 1.5 V AGP devices. They also provide delayed transaction support for AGP-to-SDRAM reads that cannot be immediately serviced. The 815EP member of this chipset family does not utilize the 82815 GMCH, but uses the 82815EP MCH. This eliminates any possible problems the integrated graphics support might create with a separate AGP video card. The integrated graphics support of the Intel 815 and 815E chipsets (Intel 3D with Direct AGP) can also be used in conjunction with a Graphics Performance Accelerator (GPA) card. The GPA is essentially a 4MB display cache placed on a card that is inserted into the AGP slot on the motherboard. Integrated AGP support includes a 3D hyper-pipeline, parallel data processing, precision pixel interpolation, and full 2D hardware acceleration. It supports 133 MHz system memory while running in non-CPC mode. Even with a GPA card, however, the integrated graphics of the 815 and 815E chipsets do not offer the performance of a current stand-alone AGP graphics card.

The 815 chipset utilizes the 82801AA ICH. The 815E and 815EP chipsets utilize the 82801BA (ICH2) hub. The 82801AA ICH of the 815 chipset makes a direct connection from the graphics and memory to the integrated AC97 controller, IDE controllers, dual USB ports, and PCI add-in cards. This delivers twice the bandwidth over traditional bridge architecture and provides dedicated data paths to fully optimize the additional bandwidth. The ICH supports UDMA/66 specifications for the IDE hard drive interface. It supports a maximum of six PCI slots and is compliant with PCI Rev. 2.2 specifications at 33 MHz. The Audio Modem Riser (AMR) slot is supported if the motherboard has one. It meets AC'97 Rev. 2.1 specifications. The 815 chipset's ICH supports only one host controller and two USB ports. The system management bus (SMB) offers bus master capabilities. Enhancements in the 82801BA (ICH2) hub of the 815E and 815EP chipsets include UDMA/100 support, two USB host controllers and four USB ports support, integrated LAN support, bus master and slave capabilities, and six-channel audio and telephony support. Table 10-16 compares the features of the 815/E/EP chipsets.

INTEL 810 (E AND E2) PENTIUM II/III AND CELERON

Intel began competing in the low-cost, integrated video chipset market with the introduction of the 810 chipset (dubbed the "Camino"). This is a three-chip solution including the 82810 GMCH, the 82801 ICH, and an 82802 firmware hub. The technology included in the 810 chipset is designed to enhance performance of the Intel Pentium II/III and Celeron processors. The chipset builds on the 440 BX AGP technology and includes additional features to provide improved graphics at a lower cost; 2D and 3D graphics can be optimized if software to take advantage of "Intel Graphics Technology" becomes available.

The 82810 chip is the core of the 810 chipset, with built-in control of memory and graphics that optimizes system memory arbitration in a way that is similar to AGP technology. The 82810 GMCH uses "Direct AGP" to provide 2D and 3D effects and images, and integrated "Hardware Motion Compensation" to improve soft-DVD video quality. Traditional TVs and digital flat panel displays can be used through a digital video output port. RAM memory support allows use of up to 512MB of PC100 memory. Dynamic Video Memory Technology (DVMT) provides efficient memory utilization and Direct AGP, though the operating system must use Intel software drivers and support Intel's intelligent memory arbiter to implement graphics applications.

The 82801 ICH uses the Intel accelerated hub architecture to make a direct connection from the graphics and memory to the integrated Audio Codec 97 (AC97) controller, the IDE controllers, dual USB ports, and PCI add-on cards. The accelerated hub architecture provides twice the bandwidth of the PCI bus at 266MB/s, which allows better data transfer from the I/O controller to the memory controller. True UDMA/66 and PCI Rev. 2.2 support are provided by the Intel 810 chipset.

The 82802 firmware hub (FWH) is the third member of the set. It stores system BIOS and video BIOS, eliminating a redundant nonvolatile memory component. Originally, the 810 chipset had a delayed introduction (and received some bad reviews). Intel continued development of the 800-series chipset minus the integrated AGP video system. By the time Intel was able to make the 810 chipset available, PC133 memory on a 133 MHz bus forced Intel to quickly make some improvements to the 810—dubbed the Intel 810E. The Intel 810E chipset includes all the features of the 810, with added support for faster speeds. Intel's design of the hub architecture chipset implementation enables it to easily integrate improvements in the I/O controller hub. The 82801BA (ICH2) hub was added to the 810 chipset family when it became available. This adds support for UDMA/100 and four USB ports to the core features of the 810 chipset, and is identified as the 810E2 chipset. You can compare the features of the 810E chipsets in Table 10-15, and the 810E2 chipsets in Table 10-16.

INTEL 440 GX PENTIUM II/III XEON

Optimized for the Pentium II/III Xeon processors, the Intel 440 GX chipset is otherwise much the same as the Intel 440 BX chipset. The chipset is a combination of the 82443GX host bridge controller (North Bridge) and the 82371EB (PIIX4E) peripheral bus controller. It supports the full Symmetric Multiprocessor Protocol (SMP), which allows up to two processors. A 100 MHz system bus frequency is supported along with GTL+ and AGTL+ bus driver technology. The integrated memory controller supports up to 2GB of SDRAM PC100 DIMM memory. The memory technologies supported include ECC, Registered, and Unbuffered. Up to four double-sided DIMMs (eight rows) are allowed by the Intel 440 GX chipset. SDRAM page sizes can be 2KB, 4KB, and 8KB on either 16, 64, 128, or 256Mbit RAM modules.

The Intel 440 GX includes support for PCI Rev. 2.1 standards on an interface of either 3.3V or 5V at 33 MHz. It includes PCI-to-DRAM data streaming support and allows concurrent CPU, AGP, and PCI transactions. It also provides the suspend-to-RAM feature for power conservation. The AGP, PCI, and ISA bridges are implemented through the 82371EB (PIIX4E) component of the Intel 440 GX chipset. AGP 2X support is provided in compliance with AGP Rev. 1.0. This allows for 3.3V AGP devices of up to 133 MHz (2X). It provides an AGP sideband interface for request pipelining without interfering with the data streams. The AGP support of the Intel 440 GX chipset allows for high-priority (expedite) transactions and AGP-specific data buffering.

Additional features supported by the Intel 440 GX chipset include two USB ports, UDMA/33 IDE bus speeds, enhanced DMA, and interrupt controller and timer functions. It enables a System Management Bus (SMB) with support for DIMM memory Serial Presence Detect (SPD). The USB support provided by the Intel 440 GX chipset is Rev. 1.0–compliant and allows for two USB ports with serial transfer rates of 1.5Mbit/s. It supports legacy keyboard and mouse software with USB-based devices. This follows the UHCI design guide.

The Intel 440 GX chipset provides solid, stable performance, and protects investments in SDRAM memory, but the Intel 840 chipset and Rambus (RDRAM) memory are required if the performance of UDMA/66, AGP 4X, or PCI Rev. 2.2 compliance are needed. You can learn more about 440 GX features in Table 10-14.

INTEL 440 BX PENTIUM II/III

The Intel 440 BX was the last and most powerful X-series chipset before Intel decided the new Camino chipset architecture needed a new naming method. The 440 BX consists of the 82443BX AGP host bridge controller (North Bridge) and the 82371EB (PIIX4E) PCI-ISA peripheral bus controller (South Bridge). The chipset supports both 66 MHz and 100 MHz processor bus speeds, which support a wide range of Pentium II or Pentium III processors. Dual processors are also supported with full SMP. The Intel 440 BX was the first 100 MHz chipset designed for use in Pentium II mobile systems, and the first one optimized for Pentium III performance in 3D and video applications.

Memory support is provided through an integrated DRAM controller allowing for up to four SDRAM DIMMs for a total of 1GB of memory (if registered DIMMs are used). The 440 BX enables "open page architecture" supporting multiple SDRAM pages to improve 3D performance. Additional video features include AGP 2X, AGP sideband, and AGP-specific data buffering support. The chipset enables concurrent CPU, AGP, and PCI transactions to main memory.

The PIIX4E controller in this chipset provides PC98 ACPI power management support that allows use of the 440 BX in mobile systems. The chip is PCI v.2.1–compliant to support PCI-to-ISA bridges in both 3.3V and 5V 33 MHz configurations. It includes the enhanced DMA controller, interrupt controller, and timer functions. The USB host interface has support for two USB ports, and the integrated IDE controller supports up to UDMA/33. The Intel 440 BX chipset is presented as UDMA/66-compatible, but this does not mean that the chipset supports UDMA/66. It means you can use a UDMA/66 hard drive in a 440 BX-based system, but transfer speeds will be limited to the UDMA/33 standard. Table 10-15 lists the features of an Intel 440 BX chipset.

INTEL 440 ZX PENTIUM II/III AND CELERON

Consisting of the 82443ZX system controller and 82371EB (PIIX4E) peripheral bus controller, the 440 ZX chipset was designed to be a lower-cost alternative to the 440 BX chipset (see Table 10-15). By eliminating dual processor support, cutting maximum memory support to 256MB, and dropping the support for ECC, Intel hoped this chipset would attract manufacturers producing low-cost Pentium II/III systems. Intel even included a 66 MHz version of the 440 ZX for early Celeron support. However, the ZX has not proven as popular as Intel had hoped. PC manufacturers producing a 100 MHz Pentium II/III system wanted some of the features eliminated in the 440 ZX, and instead used the 440 BX chipset. Manufacturers producing a 66 MHz Celeron system already had the respected 440 LX chipset available at a lower cost.

INTEL 430 VX PENTIUM

The Intel 430 VX chipset is found in rather late-model Pentium-based PCs designed for low-end or end-user applications (such as multimedia, games, and personal productivity software). The 430 VX chipset integrates support for the Universal Serial Bus (USB) standard, so home users can add a wide variety of plug-and-play digital input devices such as mice, keyboards, joysticks, scanners, and cameras. The 430 VX supports concurrent PCI architecture, which improves system performance with simultaneous activity on the CPU, PCI, and ISA buses. This generally enhances video and audio performance for multimedia applications and allows more high-speed peripherals in the systems without impacting the performance of the PCI bus. Improved EDO memory support, faster timing, and support for SDRAM are also included. Memory support also allows the Shared Memory Buffer Architecture (SMBA) option. The Intel 430 VX PCIset consists of the 82437VX system controller, two 82438VX data paths, and the 82371SB PCI ISA IDE Xcelerator (PIIX3).

While the 430 VX is generally considered to be a good performer, some features are noticeably absent. There is no support for multiple CPUs, and no support for ECC. The chipset will handle up to 128MB of RAM (but only 64MB are cacheable). RAM timing is also a bit slower than the 430 HX, so 430 TX systems tend to be a bit slower, even when SDRAM is installed. Table 10-17 compares the features of the 430 VX chipset.

INTEL 430 TX PENTIUM

The 430 TX chipset optimizes the capabilities of the Intel Pentium processor with MMX technology (Pentium MMX) and has found dual duty in both desktop and mobile PCs. Reduced power consumption enables new applications by delivering mobile-style power management to the desktop. The 430 TX

TABLE 10-17	COMPARISON OF INTEL 430 VX, 430 TX, 430 HX, 430 FX, AND 430 MX CHIPSETS				
CHIPSET	430 VX	430 TX	430 HX	430 FX	430 MX
Processor	Pentium	Pentium	Pentium	Pentium	Pentium
Voltage	3.3V(I/O)	3.3V(I/O)	3.3V(I/O)	3.3V(I/O)	3.3V(I/O)
Dual CPUs	No	No	Yes	No	No
Refresh	CAS-before-RAS	CAS-before-RAS	CAS-before-RAS	RAS Only	CAS-before- RAS
RAS Lines	5	6	8	5	4
64Mbit Support	No	Yes	Yes	No	No
Max Memory Size	128MB	256MB	512MB	128MB	128MB
Memory Types	SDRAM/EDO/FPM	SDRAM/EDO/FPM	EDO/FPM	EDO/SPM	EDO/SPM
SDRAM (CL=2)	6-1-1-1	6-1-1-1	N/A	N/A	N/A
EDO (66 MHz)	6-2-2-2	5-2-2-2	5-2-2-2	7-2-2-2	7-2-2-2
MA Buffers	Integrated	Integrated	Integrated	External	External
ECC/Parity	No	No	Yes	No	No
L2 Cache Type	Async, DRAM, Pburst	Pburst	Pburst	Async, Burst, Pburst	Async, Burst, Pburst
Cacheability	64MB	64MB	512MB	64MB	64MB
PCI Support	PCI 2.1	PCI 2.1	PCI 2.1	PCI 2.0	PCI 2.0
Concurrent PCI	Yes	Yes	Yes	No	No
MTT	Yes	Yes	Yes	No	No
SMBA Support	Yes	No	No	No	No
Bridge Type	PIIX3	PIIX4	PIIX3	PIIX	MPIIX
USB Support	Yes	Yes	Yes	No	No
IDE Support	BMIDE	Ultra-DMA	BMIDE	BMIDE	Normal IDE
RTC	External	Integrated	External	External	External
Power Mgt.	N/A	ACPI	N/A	N/A	SMI, APM
I/O Mgt.	N/A	SM Bus/GPIO	N/A	N/A	N/A

chipset features Dynamic Power Management Architecture (DPMA)—extending the battery life of mobile computers and enabling new power-efficient desktop models. Support for ACPI also improves power management.

The 430 TX also supports the Ultra-DMA disk drive protocol with the enhancements required for faster performance of multimedia applications. For higher memory throughput, the chipset supports SDRAM (or a mix of SDRAM and EDO RAM). Concurrent PCI support was available for the first time in a mobile PCI chipset, enabling faster and smoother video and audio performance. There is also support for USB. With the "outside the box" plug-and-play capabilities of USB, the 430 TX chipset helped the early integration of multimedia, I/O peripherals, and digital imaging devices.

The 430 TX chipset is a two-chip solution consisting of the 82439TX system controller and the 82371AB PCI ISA IDE Xcelerator. The 430 TX forms a Host-to-PCI bridge, provides second-level (L2) cache control, and offers a full 64-bit data path to main memory. The system controller integrates the cache and main memory DRAM control functions and provides bus control for transfers between the CPU, cache, main memory, and the PCI bus. The L2 cache controller supports write-back cache for cache sizes of 256KB and 512KB (cacheless designs are also supported).

The 430 TX also implements a full System Management Bus (SMBus) host controller with three-wire interface, through which the system can communicate with simple monitoring controllers. For example, "Smart Battery" devices can provide information to the power management charging system via the SMBus. Users can then be informed of the current battery state, along with an accurate prediction of the available operating time (or remaining time to fully charge the battery). Table 10-17 compares the features of the 430 TX.

INTEL 430 HX PENTIUM

The venerable 430 HX chipset (unofficially dubbed "Triton II") is perhaps the most well known and well respected Pentium chipset ever produced. With uncompromising EDO RAM timing, the 430 HX matches the performance of an asynchronous L2 cache-based system (without the cache). It supports 64Mbit DRAM and offers eight RAS lines (for up to 512MB of system memory). Memory address buffers are built into the system controller. Integrated deep-posting and FIFO buffers enable concurrent activity on both sides of the system controller and data paths for improved CPU utilization. ECC and parity memory support are integrated into the chip set, along with dual CPU support. The 430 HX supports concurrent PCI architecture and USB. The 430 HX chipset consists of the 82439HX system controller and the 82371SB PCI I/O IDE Xcelerator (PIIX3). Table 10-17 lists the features of the 430 HX.

INTEL 430 FX PENTIUM

The 430 FX chipset (or "Triton" as it is unofficially known) was the first Intel Pentium chipset to become extremely successful—so successful, in fact, that it is largely deemed to be the undoing of other competitors like ETEQ, UMC, and others. It was also the first x86-type chipset using EDO RAM (and was largely responsible for EDO emerging as a standard RAM type). Although the 430 FX is now obsolete, it is still considered to be a decent performer.

The 430 FX chipset consists of the 82437FX system controller, two 82438FX data paths, and the 82371FB PCI ISA IDE Xcelerator (or PIIX). The chipset forms a Host-to-PCI bridge, provides second-level (L2) cache control, and supports a full 64-bit data path to main memory. The system controller integrates the cache and main memory DRAM control functions and provides bus control for transfers between the CPU, cache, main memory, and the PCI bus. The L2 cache controller supports a write-back cache for cache sizes of 256KB and 512KB (cacheless designs are also supported). Cache memory can be implemented with either standard, burst, or pipelined burst SRAMs. An external Tag RAM is used for the address tag, and an internal Tag RAM handles the cache line status bits. The system controller supports up to 128MB of main memory. An optimized PCI interface allows the CPU to sustain a high bandwidth to the graphics frame buffer at all frequencies. Using the "snoop ahead" feature, the system controller allows PCI masters to achieve full PCI bandwidth. The data paths provide the connections between the CPU/cache, main memory, and PCI bus. Table 10-17 lists the specifications for the 430 FX chipset.

INTEL 430 MX MOBILE PENTIUM

The 430 MX chipset was the first of Intel's complete mobile chipset solutions for the Pentium processor. The 430 MX employed many architectural innovations developed for the 430 FX chipset designed for desktop computers, and was designed for such uses as ProShare, high-speed Ethernet, and audio/graphic-intensive applications. The 430 MX chipset was ideally suited for any application that required 25 MHz to 33 MHz bus.

The 430 MX chipset consists of the 82437MX system controller, two 82438MX data paths, and the 82371MX PCI I/O IDE Xcelerator (or MPIIX). The 430 MX forms a Host-to-PCI bridge, provides the second-level (L2) cache control, and supports a full 64-bit data path to main memory. The 82371MX MPIIX provides the bridge between the PCI bus and the ISA-like Extended I/O expansion bus. In addition, the 82371MX has an IDE interface that supports two IDE devices, providing an interface for IDE hard disks and CD-ROM drives. The MPIIX integrates many common I/O functions found in ISA-based PC systems, including a seven-channel DMA controller, two 82C59 interrupt controllers, an 8254 timer/counter, Intel SMM power management support, and control logic for NMI generation. Chip select decoding is provided for the BIOS, real-time clock, and keyboard controller. Edge/level interrupts and interrupt steering are supported for PCI plug-and-play compatibility.

The 430 MX supports EDO RAM and pipelined burst SRAM. Its architecture provides greater than 100MB/s PCI data streaming. The highly integrated Mode 4 local bus IDE controller improves the operation of fast hard drives. In addition, its integrated plug-and-play port makes systems easier to use and increases performance by transforming ISA motherboard peripherals into pseudo-PCI devices. As a mobile chipset, the 430 MX benefits from Advanced Power Management (APM) support. See Table 10-17 for detailed specifications.

INTEL 440 FX PENTIUM PRO/II

At its introduction, the 440 FX chipset (unofficially known as the "Natoma" chipset) was a highly integrated solution for supporting early Pentium II and Pentium Pro processors in mainstream business systems. This second-generation chipset optimized system performance for 32-bit application software in 32-bit operating system environments, and supported multiple CPUs. Based on concurrent PCI architecture, the 440 FX chipset included a multitransaction timer (MTT) for enhanced video transfer and higher frame rates, and a passive release mechanism for improved MPEG and audio performance. There was also enhanced write performance for full utilization of write buffers (to improve host-based processing applications) and PCI delayed transactions to ensure CPU-to-ISA write control compatibility with the PCI 2.1 specification.

The 440 FX chipset employed the 82441FX PCI and memory controller, the 82442FX data bus accelerator, and the 82371SB PCI ISA IDE Xcelerator (or PIIX3). The 440 FX chipset was intended for compact designs implemented in a four-layer board (in either the ATX, baby AT, or LPX form factors). The chipset supports up to 1GB of memory using flexible memory options, including EDO RAM. Memory was further enhanced with ECC support. The 440 FX also utilized the PIIX3, allowing motherboards to use the same I/O sub-systems as those used with the 430 HX and 430 VX. USB support allows for plug-and-play connectivity "outside the box," and Bus Master IDE (BMIDE) handles access for fast hard drives. Table 10-18 lists the features of a 440 FX chipset.

TABLE 10-18   COMPARISON OF INTEL 440 FX, 450 GX, 450 KX, AND 440 LX CHIPSETS

CHIPSET	440 FX	450 GX	450 KX	440 LX
Processor	Pentium Pro Pentium II	Pentium Pro	Pentium Pro	Pentium II
Voltage	GTL+	GTL+	GTL+	GTL+
Dual CPUs	Yes	Up to Quad Processor	Yes	Yes
Refresh	RAS only or CAS-before-RAS	CAS-before-RAS	CAS-before-RAS	CAS-before-RAS
RAS Lines	8	16	8	8
64Mbit Support	Yes	Yes	Yes	Yes
Max Memory Size	1GB	8GB	1GB	1GB EDO or 512MB SDRAM
Memory Types	EDO/FPM/BEDO	FPM	FPM	EDO/SDRAM
Memory Interleave	No	4-way, 2-way, non	2-way, non	No
ECC/Parity	Yes	Yes	Yes	Yes
PCI Support	PCI 2.1	PCI 2.0	PCI 2.0	PCI 2.1
Concurrent PCI	Yes	N/A	N/A	Yes
MTT	Yes	No	No	Yes
SMBA Support	No	No	No	No
Bridge Type	PIIX3	Not Included	Not Included	PIIX4
USB Support	Yes	N/A	N/A	Yes
IDE Support	BMIDE	N/A	N/A	BMIDE Ultra-DMA/33
RTC	External	N/A	N/A	Integrated
Power Mgt.	SMM	SMM	SMM	SMM & ACPI
I/O Mgt.	N/A	N/A	N/A	SMBus/GPIO

INTEL 440 LX PENTIUM II

The 440 LX chipset was the first in a series of AGP chipsets from Intel designed to optimize the performance of a Pentium II processor. This was seen as a major new computing platform for small business, large business, and home users alike. The 440 LX chipset with AGP extended the system bandwidth to the graphics controller and optimized the system bandwidth and concurrency with the implementation of Quad Port Acceleration (QPA). QPA provides four-port concurrent arbitration of the processor bus, graphics bus, PCI bus, and SDRAM.

The 82443LX PCI AGP system controller integrated a Host-to-PCI bridge, optimized DRAM controller and data path, and placed an AGP 1X/2X interface into a single chip. The I/O sub-system portion of the 440 LX is the 82371AB, which provided an ISA bridge, a PCI ISA IDE Xcelerator (PIIX4), and USB controller. Table 10-18 lists the features of the 440 LX chipset.

The 440 LX chipset also offered advanced power management and fast resume from powered-down states through ACPI. This enabled local power-down operation, with remote wake-up for off-hours maintenance. Application performance for 3D graphics was also improved. AGP gives PCs the capability to handle memory-intensive 3D graphics applications, providing the faster performance and enabling larger textures out of main memory, resulting in more lifelike image detail.

INTEL 450 GX/KX PENTIUM PRO

The 450 GX chipset (known unofficially as the "Orion" chipset) was designed to support Pentium Pro processor servers and scientific systems—especially those that use multiple CPUs (up to four). By comparison, the 450 KX (also sometimes referred to as "Orion") is aimed at designers of workstations and high-performance desktops with one or two CPUs. In actual practice, the 450 GX/KX chipsets are rarely used because of the many features the chipsets lack. Neither supports concurrent PCI, USB, or any form of I/O management. When compared with other contemporary chipsets, the 450 GX/KX are simply not as competitive as the 440 FX chipset. Table 10-18 highlights the features of the 450 GX/KX chipset.

VIA Chipsets

Founded in 1987, VIA is perhaps the greatest threat to Intel's dominance of the chipset market. Its line of Apollo chipsets has provided an effective alternative for the support of Intel Pentium/MMX/Pro, AMD K5 and K6, and Cyrix 6x86 and M2 CPUs. VIA chipsets are generally recognized as full-featured, high-performance solutions that are used on many motherboards. VIA also produces a selection of network and peripheral controller chips for computer applications. This part of the chapter outlines the most popular VIA motherboard chipsets available for the PC.

With the increasing acceptance and popularity of AMD Athlon and Duron processors, VIA has greatly expanded its resources supporting this line of CPUs. VIA's use of separate system and peripheral bus controllers (North Bridge and South Bridge chips) allows it to quickly update its products to support new and improved technologies such as UDMA/100 IDE data rates and DDR-SDRAM memory. An improved peripheral bus controller can be substituted for an older one and combined with existing system controllers to update an entire line of chipsets at once. The same can be done with improved system controllers and existing peripheral bus controllers. This tactic allows VIA to remain competitive in a fast-changing PC marketplace.

VIA has further diversified its product line with the addition of the VIA Cyrix line of processors. VIA is now in the position of designing processors to mate with its own chipsets, with performance enhancements integrated in both while under the control of VIA Technologies. In a joint venture, VIA Technologies and S3 Graphics have developed integrated system/graphics controller chipsets. These chipsets combine VIA's system controllers with S3's Savage4 graphics chip core technologies, and enable motherboards to include on-board graphics systems. This venture should continue to provide inexpensive, integrated chipset solutions for popular low-cost systems.

VIA APOLLO PX266

The VIA Apollo PX266 chipset should be available in the third quarter of 2001. It is intended to support Intel Pentium 4 processors in either Socket 423– or Socket 478–style packages. When it's finally released, the VIA Apollo PX266 should consist of the VT8653 North Bridge and VT8233 South Bridge chips. Also, the VPX PCI controller may be included, which provides an interface for 64-bit PCI devices. It can be configured with either an 8-bit 266MB/s V-Link bus or a 16-bit 533MB/s V-Link bus. The VT8233 is VIA's standard DDR/V-Link South Bridge device with support for ACR, six USB ports, UDMA/100, and integrated 10/100 LAN. Later, a South Bridge that is compatible with the full range of VIA DDR-SDRAM North Bridge chips will be available wtih an integrated USB 2.0 controller (this South Bridge is tentatively denoted as model number VT8235).

The PX266 chipset should support two late-model Pentium 4 processors operating in SMP (though it is not expected to support older "Willamette" Pentium 4 processors in SMP—even Willamette processors using the 478-pin package). The chipset will also support the 133 MHz bus, which Intel will be offering with late-model Pentium 4 processors. The Pentium 4's quad data rate (QDR) bus allows a 133 MHz processor bus to transfer data at an effective 533 MHz. Combined with a 64-bit data path, the 533 MHz bus delivers 4.2GB/s peak bandwidth.

Both PC100/133 and PC1600/PC2100 memory types will be supported, but PC2100 is best able to supply the memory bandwidth required for highest performance. A chipset featuring an integrated graphics core from S3 Graphics will be introduced a short time after release of the Apollo PX266 chipset. The Savage4 graphics core used in PM/KM133 and PM266/KM266 will be replaced with the Paramount graphics core, which offers improved texturing abilities and an enhanced video engine. Paramount should be a common feature in VIA chipsets with integrated graphics in the future. Table 10-19 lists the main features of the PX266 chipset.

VIA APOLLO PRO266

The VIA Apollo Pro266 supports Intel Pentium III, Celeron, and VIA Cyrix "Joshua" processor-based platforms. It supports single or dual processors and features a 266 MHz memory bus. Through its V-Link memory controller architecture, the VIA Apollo Pro266 chipset supports up to 2.0GB of DDR200/266 SDRAM (PC1600/2100) at a peak bandwidth of 2.1GB/s. DDR266 SDRAM lowers memory power consumption to 2.5 volts. The chipset also supports VCM DRAM. With its 133 MHz FSB, the VIA Apollo Pro266 chipset supports the latest Intel Pentium III processors as well as VIA's "Joshua" processor. The VIA Apollo Pro266 chipset's asynchronous bus design also supports Intel Pentium III and Intel Celeron processors running at FSB speeds of 66 and 100 MHz.

The VIA Apollo Pro266 chipset is a two-chip set consisting of the VT8633 system controller (North Bridge) and the VT8233 peripheral bus controller (South Bridge). The Apollo Pro266 also features a new high-speed V-Link bus that doubles the communication bandwidth between the North and South bridge to 266MB/s. The V-Link bus is an extension of the internal memory bus structure and further boosts performance

TABLE 10-19   VIA APOLLO PX266 CHIPSET FEATURES AT A GLANCE

Supports Intel Pentium 4 Socket 423/478 processors
Supports 100/133 MHz FSB settings (quad-pumped to 400 MHz/533 MHz)
Supports AGP Rev. 2.0 in 2X/4X modes
Supports sideband addressing (SBA) mode for nonmultiplexed address/data
200/266 MHz memory bus supports DDR200/266 (PC1600/2100)
533MB/s high-bandwidth North/South Bridge V-Link
PCI 2.2 compliant
Support for Advanced Communications Riser (ACR) card standard
Integrated six-channel AC97 Audio
Integrated MC97 modem
Integrated 10/100BaseT Ethernet controller or Home PNA
Support for UDMA/33/66/100
Support for ATAPI-compliant devices including DVD devices
PC98/99 compliant
Six USB ports (UHCI compliant)
Integrated I/O APIC for dual processor support
Integrated hardware monitoring
Supports two serial ports, IR port, parallel port, and floppy disk controller functions
ACPI v1.0 and APM v1.2 compliant

with a guaranteed transfer time and low latency. Previous chipset architectures used PCI bus standards for communication that limited transfer rates to 133MB/s. Additional features include support for six USB ports, an AC97 link for audio and modem, hardware monitoring, ACPI/OnNow power management, and integrated 10/100Mbps Ethernet. The VIA Apollo Pro266 chipset also includes an AGP 4X interface. The ATA 100 interface on the VIA Apollo Pro266 chipset provides a high-speed connection to UDMA/100 hard disk drives (delivering burst data transfer rates of 100MB/s). Features of the VIA Apollo Pro266 are listed in Table 10-20.

VIA PROSAVAGE PM133

The VIA ProSavage PM133 chipset is the result of a joint venture between VIA Technologies and S3 Graphics. The chipset supports 66 MHz, 100 MHz, and 133 MHz CPU host bus (FSB) frequencies, and supports Socket 370 (VIA Cyrix III and Intel Celeron) and Slot 1 (Intel Pentium II and III) processors. The ProSavage PM133 chipset is composed of the VT8605 integrated system/graphics controller (North Bridge) and the VT8231 peripheral bus controller (South Bridge). The VT8605 integrates VIA's VT82C694X system controller and S3's Savage4 2D/3D graphics accelerator into a single-chip package.

The ProSavage PM133 supports up to 1.5GB of system memory in six banks of DRAMs using 256Mbit DRAM technology. The DRAM controller supports standard Synchronous DRAM (SDRAM) and Virtual Channel SDRAM (VC SDRAM) in a flexible mix/match manner. The DRAM controller can run at either the host CPU bus frequency (66/100/133 MHz) or pseudosynchronous to the CPU bus frequency (66/100/133 MHz) with built-in PLL timing control.

The VT8605 system controller also supports full AGP v2.0 capability for maximum bus utilization, including 1x/2x/4x mode transfers, SBA (sideband addressing), flush/fence commands, and pipelined grants. Both Windows 95 VXD and Windows 98/2000 miniport drivers are supported for compatibility with integrated Savage4 graphics, AGP expansion card graphics, and DVD-capable multimedia accelerators.

TABLE 10-20   VIA APOLLO PRO266 CHIPSET FEATURES AT A GLANCE

Supports Intel Pentium III, Intel Celeron, & VIA Cyrix III processors
Supports 66/100/133 MHz FSB settings
Supports AGP Rev. 2.0 in 2X/4X modes
Supports sideband addressing (SBA) mode for nonmultiplexed address/data
200/266 MHz memory bus supports DDR200/266 (PC1600/2100)
Supports up to 2GB DDR200/266 SDRAM, PC133/66/100 SDRAM, Virtual Channel memory
266MB/s high-bandwidth North/South Bridge V-Link
PCI 2.2 compliant
Support for Advanced Communications Riser (ACR) card standard
Integrated 6-channel AC97 audio
Integrated MC97 modem
Integrated 10/100 BaseT Ethernet controller or Home PNA
Support for UDMA/33/66/100
Support for ATAPI-compliant devices including DVD devices
PC98/99 compliant
Six USB ports (UHCI compliant)
Integrated I/O APIC for dual processor support
Integrated hardware monitoring
Supports two serial ports, IR port, parallel port, and floppy disk controller functions
ACPI v1.0 and APM v1.2 compliant

The ProSavage PM133 supports an optional AGP interface that allows for additional AGP card integration and upgrades. The chipset's integrated Savage4 graphics accelerator provides 2D, 3D, and DVD video acceleration and supports AGP 4X and S3's DX6 texture compression (S3TC).

The ProSavage PM133 is PCI 2.2–compliant. The VT8231 (South Bridge) also includes an integrated Super-I/O interface. This includes an integrated real-time clock with extended 256-byte CMOS RAM, an integrated master mode enhanced IDE controller supporting UDMA/33/66/100 standards for 33/66/100MB/s burst transfer rates, and an integrated USB interface with root hub with two function ports supporting up to four ports. The USB controller is V.1.1- and Universal HCI V.1.1–compliant. The chipset provides distributed DMA support, an integrated AC97 link for basic audio and HSP-based modem functions, integrated hardware monitoring, and an OnNow/ACPI-compliant advanced configuration and power management interface (including suspend-to-RAM operation). Features of the VIA ProSavage PM133 chipset are listed in Table 10-21.

 Earlier versions of the VIA ProSavage PM133 chipset used the VT82C686A peripheral bus controller (South Bridge)—this combination only provided UDMA/66 IDE support.

VIA APOLLO PRO133A

The Apollo Pro133A is a newer version of the Apollo Pro133, the major difference being the added support for AGP 4X and for dual processors. The Apollo Pro133A chipset combines the VT82C694X system controller chip (North Bridge) with the versatile VT82C596B bus controller chip (South Bridge). The Apollo Pro133A chipset offers support for asynchronous FSB speeds and dual processors. This allows the chipset to be used in conjunction with a wide range of Intel and VIA processors. The Apollo Pro133A supports the 100 MHz and 133 MHz Pentium II/III and VIA "Joshua" processors. The chipset also supports the 66 MHz speed used by older Intel Celeron processors before they were upgraded to 100 MHz. The chip combination also supports UDMA/66 IDE, USB, PCI, and ISA data busses, as well as AC97 audio and MC97 modem standards, which allows for inexpensive sound and fax/modem implementation. It maintains the standard support for current memory technologies, including PC133 SDRAM and VC133 DRAM. Total memory supported is up to 4GB. Table 10-22 outlines the main features of the Apollo Pro133A chipset.

VIA APOLLO PLE133 (APOLLO PM601)

The VIA Apollo PLE133 chipset provides support for Slot 1 Intel Pentium II/III and Celeron processors, along with support for VIA Cyrix III CPUs. The VT8601 system/graphics controller (North Bridge) offers an integrated 2D/3D graphics accelerator feature. The core logic portion of the chip is based on the VIA Apollo Pro133, and the integrated graphics accelerator is based on the Trident Blade 3D graphics engine. The VT8601 system controller is combined with either the VT82C596B or the VT82C686A PCI-to-ISA South Bridge. Both South Bridge chips are PC98/PC99-compliant with integrated UDMA/33/66, four USB ports, and a complete power management feature set. The VT82C686A also integrates hardware monitoring, Super-I/O functions (floppy disk drive interface and serial/parallel ports), and an AC97 link supporting digital audio and HSP modem functions.

The Apollo PLE133 supports six banks of DRAMs for up to 1GB. The DRAM controller supports standard Fast Page Mode (FPM) DRAM, EDO DRAM, SDRAM, and VC SDRAM. The DRAM controller is optimized to run synchronous with the CPU FSB frequency of 66 MHz, 100 MHz, or 133 MHz.

The Apollo PLE133 also supports full AGP v1.0 capability with the internal 2D/3D graphics engine. The graphics controller includes a fully integrated GUI accelerator, read cache, and command FIFO that optimizes memory bandwidth and enhances graphics performance. The graphics controller, with an integrated video display and a capture engine, supports dual apertures on the PCI bus, which enables independent

TABLE 10-21   VIA PROSAVAGE PM133 CHIPSET FEATURES AT A GLANCE

Support for Slot 1 (Intel Pentium II/III) and Socket 370 (VIA Cyrix III and Intel Celeron)

66/100/133 MHz CPU FSB

64-bit advanced memory controller supporting PC100/PC133 SDRAM and VCM

DRAM interface runs in synchronous (66/66, 100/100, 133/133) mode or pseudosynchronous (66/100, 100/66, 100/133, 133/100) mode with FSB

Concurrent CPU, AGP, and PCI access

Supports standard SDRAM and VCM SDRAM memory types

Support three DIMMs or six banks for up to 1.5GB of DRAM (256Mb DRAM technology)

AGP Rev. 2.0 compliant interface supporting AGP 4x, 2x, or 1x external AGP graphics card upgrade

Supports 266 MHz 4x mode for AD and sideband addressing (SBA) signaling

AGP expansion graphics override the integrated graphics by default with no SMA frame buffer

PCI 2.2 compliant, 32-bit 3.3V PCI interface with 5V-tolerant inputs

Integrated Fast Ethernet controller with 1/10/100Mbit capability

Integrated USB controller with two root hubs and four function ports

Dual-channel Ultra-DMA/33/66/100 master mode drive controller

AC-Link interface for AC97 audio codec and PC97 modem codec

HSP modem support

Interface for optional external modem DSP

Integrated Sound Blaster Pro and DirectSound compatible digital audio controller

Supports ATAPI-compliant devices, including DVD devices

Supports PCI native and ATA compatibility modes

Two UARTs for complete serial ports

Multimode parallel port (IEEE 1284)

Floppy disk controller

Standard v1.03 or v2.1 AC97 interface with up to four AC97 codecs from multiple vendors

Supports two game ports and one MIDI port interface

Complete software driver support for Windows 95/98/2000 and Windows NT

USB v.1.1 and Intel Universal HCI v.1.1 compatible

Root hub and four function ports

Legacy keyboard and PS/2 mouse support

Five universal input channels for voltage or temperature sensing

Two fan-speed monitoring channels

Supports both ACPI and legacy (APM) power management

ACPI v1.0 and APM v1.2 compliant

PCI interrupts steerable to any interrupt channel

Steerable DMA channels for integrated floppy, parallel, and Sound Blaster Pro controllers

Microsoft Windows 2000, Windows 98 SE, Windows 98, Windows NT, Windows 95, and plug-and-play BIOS compliant

graphic and video data to be transported simultaneously to and from different memory areas, and accelerates the performance of both DirectDraw and DirectVideo APIs. The Apollo PLE133 graphics controller is integrated with a DVD video hardware block for motion compensation, gives existing PCs the ability to play DVD video in MPEG-2 format at high bandwidths with very good video quality. The graphics controller is able to use both the dedicated graphics portion and the general portion of system memory for graphics operations. As a result, DVD and 3D rendering performance and quality are improved. The graphics controller provides support of noninterlaced 1280×1024×64K, 1024×768×16M,

TABLE 10-22   VIA APOLLO PRO133A CHIPSET FEATURES AT A GLANCE

Supports dual Slot 1 and Socket 370 (Intel Pentium II/III and Celeron) processors

66/100/133 MHz CPU FSB

AGP/PCI/ISA mobile and "deep green" PC ready

Supports separately powered 3.3V (5V tolerant) interface to system memory, AGP, and PCI bus

Chipset includes Ultra-DMA/33/66, USB, and keyboard/mouse interfaces plus RTC/CMOS on chip

Sleep mode support

AGP v2.0 compliant

Supports 266 MHz 4x mode for sideband addressing (SBA) signaling

Windows 95 OSR2 VXD and integrated Windows 98/2000 miniport driver support

PCI buses are synchronous/pseudosynchronous to host CPU bus

33 MHz operation on the primary PCI bus

66 MHz PCI operation on the AGP bus

Supports up to five PCI masters

Complete steerable PCI interrupts

PCI 2.1 compliant, 32-bit 3.3V PCI interface with 5V-tolerant inputs

DRAM interface synchronous with host CPU (66/100/133 MHz) or AGP (66 MHz) for most flexible configuration

DRAM interface may be faster than CPU by 33 MHz to allow use of PC100 memory modules with 66 MHz Celeron, or use of PC133 with 100 MHz Pentium II/III

DRAM interface may be slower than CPU by 33 MHz to allow use of older memory modules with newer CPUs (PC66 modules with 100 MHz Pentium II/III)

Concurrent CPU, AGP, and PCI access

Supports FPM, EDO, SDRAM, ESDRAM, and VCM SDRAM memory types

Different DRAM types may be used in mixed combinations

Supports eight banks of DRAMs for up to 4GB

CAS-before-RAS or self-refresh

Independent clock stop controls for CPU/SDRAM, AGP, and PCI bus

Supports suspend-to-RAM operation

800×600×16M, and 640×480×16M video modes. However, the VT8601 system/graphics controller does not allow for use of optional external AGP graphics cards.

The chipset offers a USB v1.1– and Universal HCI v1.1–compliant controller. The VT82C686A includes the root hub with four function ports. Additional features include a keyboard controller with PS/2 mouse support, a real-time clock with 256-byte extended CMOS, and support for the ACPI power management standard. The Apollo PLE133 graphics controller supports four states of VESA Display Power Management System (DPMS), which decrease monitor power consumption after timeout periods. VESA DPMS power down states (ready, standby, suspend, and off) specify HSYNC and VSYNC signals to control the monitor power down state. A complete list of features is contained in Table 10-23.

The Apollo PM601 chipset is similar to the Apollo PLE133 and uses the same VT8601 system controller with the same integrated graphics engine. However, the Apollo PM601 uses the VT8231 peripheral bus controller (South Bridge) and only supports 66/100 MHz FSB settings.

VIA APOLLO PRO133

The VIA Apollo Pro133 meets the PC133 standard—increasing the speed of the system and memory buses from 100 MHz to 133 MHz. The 133 MHz memory interface supports the wide range of PC133 memory devices now on the market, and support for VCM/133 and HSDRAM technologies expands the

TABLE 10-23   VIA APOLLO PLE133 CHIPSET FEATURES AT A GLANCE

Slot 1 FSB at 66 to 133 MHz (PM601 at 66 to 100 MHz)

PC66/PC100/PC133 SDRAM memory interface (PM601 uses PC66/PC100)

DRAM interface may be faster than CPU by 33 MHz to allow use of PC100 with 66 MHz Celeron CPU, or use of PC133 with 100 MHz Pentium II/III CPU

DRAM interface may be slower than CPU by 33 MHz to allow use of older memory modules with a newer CPU

Supports FPM, EDO, SDRAM, and VCM-SDRAM memory types

Supports six banks of DRAMs for up to 1GB

CAS-before-RAS or self-refresh

PCI bus operates at 30 MHz to 33 MHz

Integrated 2D/3D GUI accelerator

AGP v1.0 compliant

AC97 link

Integrated Super-I/O features with hardware monitoring

Windows 95 OSR2 VXD and integrated Windows 98/2000 miniport driver support

PCI bus is synchronous/pseudosynchronous to host CPU bus

Supports up to five PCI masters

PCI-to-system memory data streaming up to 132MB/s

PCI 2.2 compliant, 32-bit 3.3V PCI interface with 5V-tolerant inputs

Hardware-assisted MPEG-2 architecture for DVD with AC-3

Suspend-to-RAM operation

Integrated ISA bus controller with integrated DMA, timer, and interrupt controller

Integrated keyboard controller with PS/2 mouse support

Integrated USB controller with a root hub and four function ports

USB v.1.1 and Intel Universal HCI v.1.1 compatible

Integrated Ultra-DMA/33/66 master mode drive controller with enhanced PCI bus commands

Dual-channel master mode PCI supporting four Enhanced IDE devices

Supports ATAPI-compliant devices (including DVD devices)

Supports two serial ports, IR port, parallel port, and floppy disk controller functions

Two UARTs for complete serial ports

Infrared-IrDA (HPSIR) and ASK (Amplitude Shift Keyed) IR port multiplexed on COM2

Standard mode, ECP, and EPP support with the parallel port (IEEE 1284)

Dual full-duplex Direct Sound channels between system memory and AC97 link

Standard v1.0 or v2.0 AC97 interface for single or cascaded AC97 codecs from multiple vendors

Complete software driver support for Windows 95/98/2000 and Windows NT

Supports both ACPI and legacy (APM) power management

ACPI v1.0 and APM v1.2 compliant

Microsoft Windows 98, Windows NT, Windows 95 and plug-and-play BIOS compliant

memory performance capabilities of the chipset. The VT82C693A system controller and the VT82C596B peripheral bus controller combine to provide the features of the VIA Apollo Pro133 chipset. All Slot 1 and Socket 370 Intel processors are supported. The 133 MHz FSB combines with UDMA/66 support to provide high-speed data transfers and to boost overall system performance.

The Apollo Pro133 continues support for 66/100/133 CPU bus and memory settings, and is highly scaleable. Because the Apollo Pro133 supports an asynchronous memory bus architecture, it provides the option of 66/100 or 100/133 MHz CPU and memory bus combinations. Rounding out the feature set are all currently available mainstream features, including AGP 2x, USB, ACPI, and more.

VIA APOLLO KT266

The VIA Apollo KT266 chipset is a high-performance system controller for the development of AGP/PCI desktop PC systems based on 64-bit Socket A (AMD Athlon) processors. The KT266 chip set consists of the VT8366 system controller (North Bridge) and the VT8233 V-Link peripheral bus controller (South Bridge). The VT8366 system controller provides support for communication between the CPU, DRAM, AGP bus, and the V-Link bus with pipelined, burst, and concurrent operation. The VT8233 V-Link client controller is a highly integrated PCI/LPC controller. Its internal bus structure is based on a 66 MHz PCI bus that provides 2x bandwidth compared to the previous generation of PCI/ISA bridge chips. The VT8233 also provides a 266MB/s host/client V-Link interface with V-Link-PCI and V-Link-LPC controllers. It supports five PCI slots with arbitration and decoding for all integrated functions and LPC bus.

The VT8366 supports eight banks of SDR/DDR SDRAMs for up to 4GB of system RAM. The DRAM controller supports standard SDRAM and VC SDRAM in a flexible mix/match manner, or it can be configured to support DDR SDRAM mode. The DRAM controller also supports optional ECC (single-bit error correction and multibit detection) or EC (error checking) capability, and it can run either synchronous or pseudosynchronous mode with the host CPU bus frequency (66/100/133 MHz).

The VIA Apollo KT266 chipset also supports full AGP v2.0 capability, including 2x and 4x mode transfers and SBA. Both Windows 95 VXD and Windows 98/2000 miniport drivers are supported for compatibility with major AGP-based 3D and DVD-capable multimedia accelerators. The VT8366 system controller supports two 32-bit 3.3 system buses (one AGP and one V-Link) that are synchronous/pseudosynchronous to the CPU bus. The chip also contains a built-in bus-to-bus bridge to allow simultaneous concurrent operations on each bus.

The VT8233 South Bridge supports up to five PCI slots and is PCI 2.2–compliant. It provides an integrated networking MAC controller with a standard interface for 10/100Mb BaseT Ethernet or 1/10Mb Home PNA networking. The VT8233 also includes an integrated keyboard controller with PS/2 mouse support, an integrated DS12885 style real-time clock, and an integrated master mode enhanced drive controller supporting UDMA/33/66/100. The chipset includes an integrated USB interface that is USB v1.1– and Universal HCI v1.1–compliant with root hubs and six function ports, distributed DMA support, and an OnNow/ACPI-compliant advanced configuration and power management interface. Features of the VIA Apollo KT266 chipset are listed in Table 10-24.

VIA APOLLO KT133

The popular KT133 chipset supports 64-bit Socket A (AMD Athlon and Duron) processors. It consists of the VT8363 system controller (North Bridge) and the VT82C686A peripheral bus controller (South Bridge). The VT8363 supports up to 1.5GB of memory, including standard SDRAM and VC SDRAM in a flexible mix/match manner. Memory speeds of 66/100/133 MHz are allowed. The VT8363 system controller also supports full AGP v2.0 capability for maximum bus utilization including 1x, 2x, and 4x mode transfers and SBA. Both Windows 95 VXD and Windows 98/2000 miniport drivers are supported for compatibility with major AGP-based 3D- and DVD-capable multimedia accelerators.

The VIA Apollo KT133 chipset is PCI 2.2–compliant and includes an integrated keyboard controller with PS/2 mouse support, along with an integrated real-time clock with extended 256-byte CMOS RAM. The chipset supports an enhanced IDE controller with full scatter/gather capability, and an extension to Ultra-DMA/33/66. It provides a USB interface with a root hub and four function ports, and is OnNow/ACPI-compliant. Additional features include an AC97/MC97 link, serial ports, parallel port, floppy drive interface, and game port. For power management, the KT133 provides independent clock

TABLE 10-24   VIA APOLLO KT266 CHIPSET FEATURES AT A GLANCE

Supports Socket A (Socket 462) AMD Athlon/Duron processors

100/133 MHz DDR200/266 MHz transfer on Athlon CPU address and data buses

AGP v2.0 compliant

Supports AGP sideband addressing (SBA) mode for nonmultiplexed address/data

Supports AGP 66 MHz in 1x, 2x, and 4x modes

Windows 95 OSR2 VXD and integrated Windows 98/2000 miniport driver support

Supports 66 MHz V-Link host interface with peak bandwidth of 266MB/s

V-Link operates at 2X or 4X modes

DRAM interface synchronous with host CPU (100/133 MHz) or AGP (66 MHz) for most flexible configuration

DRAM interface may be faster than CPU by 33 MHz to allow use of 133 MHz memory with 100 MHz FSB

DRAM interface may be slower than CPU by 33 MHz to allow use of 100 MHz memory with 133 MHz FSB

Supports SDR/VCM SDRAM or DDR SDRAM memory types

Supports eight banks of DRAMs for up to 4GB (512Mb x8/x16 DRAM technology) for registered SDR/DDR SDRAM modules

Supports six banks of DRAMs up to 3GB (512Mb x8/x16 DRAM technology) for unbuffered SDR/DDR SDRAM modules

Suspend-to-RAM and self-refresh operation

Integrated Fast Ethernet controller with 1/10/100Mbit capability

Integrated USB controller with three root hubs and six function ports

Dual-channel Ultra-DMA/33/66/100 master mode drive controller

AC-Link interface for AC97 audio codec and MC97 modem codec

HSP modem support

Integrated keyboard controller with PS/2 mouse support

Integrated real-time clock with extended 256-byte CMOS RAM and Day/Month Alarm for ACPI

Integrated ISA bus controller including DMA, timer, and interrupt controller

Serial IRQ for docking and nondocking applications

Supports up to five PCI masters

PCI-to-system memory data streaming up to 132MB/s (data sent to North Bridge via high speed V-Link interface)

Complete steerable PCI interrupts

PCI 2.2 compliant, 32-bit 3.3V PCI interface with 5V-tolerant inputs

Support for ATAPI-compliant devices, including DVD devices

AC-Link access to three codecs (AC97, AMC97, and MC97)

AC97 2.1 compliant

Supports both ACPI and legacy (APM) power management

ACPI v1.0 and APM v1.2 compliant

Microsoft Windows 98, Windows NT, Windows 95, and plug-and-play BIOS compliant

stop control for the CPU/SDRAM, PCI, and AGP buses for powering-down the SDRAM. Suspend-to-RAM operation is also supported. The VIA Apollo KT133 also includes a complete hardware monitoring sub-system for monitoring and control of internal and external (motherboard and system) conditions, including voltages, temperatures, fan speeds, switch open/close states, and so on. VIA Apollo KT133 features are listed in Table 10-25.

TABLE 10-25   VIA APOLLO KT133 CHIPSET FEATURES AT A GLANCE

Supports Socket A (Socket 462) AMD Athlon processors

100 MHz DDR200 MHz transfers on Athlon CPU address and data buses

Supports separately powered 3.3V (5V tolerant) interface to system memory, AGP, and PCI bus

Supports PC133 and PC100 SDRAM and Virtual Channel Memory (VCM) SDRAM up to three DIMMs

Concurrent CPU, AGP, and PCI access

Different DRAM types may be used in mixed combinations

Different DRAM timing for each bank is supported

Supports up to 1.5GB memory space (256Mb DRAM technology)

CAS-before-RAS or self-refresh

AGP v2.0 compliant

Supports sideband addressing (SBA) mode for nonmultiplexed address/data

Supports 66 MHz AGP in 1x, 2x, and 4x modes

Windows 95 OSR2 VXD and integrated Windows 98/2000 miniport driver support

Supports up to five PCI masters

PCI 2.2 compliant, 32-bit 3.3V PCI interface with 5V-tolerant inputs

Suspend-to-DRAM operation supported

Integrated ISA bus controller with integrated DMA, timer, and interrupt controller

Integrated keyboard controller with PS/2 mouse support

Integrated USB controller with a root hub and four function ports

Integrated Ultra-DMA/33/66 master mode drive controller with enhanced PCI bus commands

Distributed DMA support for ISA legacy DMA across the PCI bus

Dual-channel master mode PCI supporting four enhanced IDE devices

Support ATAPI-compliant devices (including DVD devices)

Supports two serial ports, IR port, parallel port, and floppy disk controller functions

Infrared-IrDA (HPSIR) and ASK (Amplitude Shift Keyed) IR port multiplexed on COM2

Multimode parallel port (IEEE 1284)

Integrated floppy disk controller

Dual full-duplex Direct Sound channels between system memory and AC97 link

Standard v1.0 or v2.0 AC97 interface for single or cascaded AC97 codecs from multiple vendors

Direct two game ports and one MIDI port interface

Complete software driver support for Windows 95/98/2000 and Windows NT

USB v.1.1 and Intel Universal HCI v.1.1 compatible

ACPI v1.0 and APM v1.2 compliant

Microsoft Windows 98, Windows NT, Windows 95, and plug-and-play BIOS compliant

VIA APOLLO KT133A

The VIA Apollo KT133A is an updated version of the venerable Apollo KT133 chipset. It adds support for newer, higher performance bus specifications—the most noticeable additions are support for UDMA/100 IDE data transfer speeds and for the 266 MHz FSB speeds of the newer AMD Athlon and Duron processors. The VIA Apollo KT133A combines the VT8363A system controller (North Bridge) with the VT82C686B peripheral bus controller (South Bridge). The VT8363A adds the support for the faster 266 MHz EV6 system bus, and the VT82C686B includes UDMA/100 IDE standards. The chipset adds these items to the comprehensive list of features already offered in the Apollo KT133 chipset.

VIA PROSAVAGE KM133

The VIA ProSavage KM133 chipset supports AMD Athlon and Duron superscalar processors. It is a high-performance chipset for the implementation of AGP/PCI/LPC desktop personal computer systems with 100 MHz and 133 MHz CPU host bus (FSB) frequencies. It supports DDR transfers on the EV6 CPU data and address busses for 200 MHz or 266 MHz bus speeds. The chipset includes the EV6-bus version of the Apollo ProSavage integrated graphics product line targeted at desktop PCs (developed by the VIA/S3 joint venture).

The ProSavage KM133 combines VIA's AMD Athlon/Duron system controller and S3's Savage4 2D/3D graphics accelerator into a single 552-pin BGA package—the VT8365 system/graphics controller (North Bridge). The system controller provides pipelined, burst, and concurrent operation between the CPU, DRAM, AGP bus, and PCI bus. It supports six banks of DRAMs for up to 1.5GB of system memory. The DRAM controller supports standard SDRAM and VC SDRAM in a flexible mix/match manner. The DRAM controller can run at either the host CPU bus frequency (66/100/133 MHz) or pseudosynchronous to the CPU bus frequency (66/100/133 MHz) with built-in timing control.

The VT8365 North Bridge system controller also supports full AGP v2.0 capability for maximum bus utilization, including 1x/2x/4x mode transfers and SBA. Both Windows 95 VXD and Windows 98/2000 miniport drivers are supported for compatibility with integrated Savage4 graphics, AGP expansion graphics, and DVD-capable multimedia accelerators. The ProSavage KM133 also integrates S3's Savage4 graphics accelerator into a single chip. It offers 2D, 3D, and DVD video acceleration into a cost-effective package. The chipset combines AGP 4X with S3's DX6 texture compression (S3TC) and 2Kx2K textures to deliver acceptable 3D performance and image quality for the value PC desktop market.

The VT8365 supports two 32-bit 3.3/5V system buses (one AGP and one PCI) that are synchronous/pseudosynchronous to the CPU bus. The chip also contains a built-in bus-to-bus bridge to allow simultaneous concurrent operations on each bus. The chip also supports enhanced PCI bus commands, such as Memory-Read-Line, Memory-Read-Multiple, and Memory-Write-Invalid, to minimize bus overhead. Delay-transaction and read-caching mechanisms are implemented for further improvement of overall system performance. The chip also includes an integrated Super-I/O, integrated real-time clock with extended 256-byte CMOS RAM, integrated master mode enhanced drive controller with full scatter/gather capability, and Ultra-DMA/33/66/100.

The VT8231 peripheral bus controller (South Bridge) provides support for the ISA/PCI/USB/IDE bus interfaces and is PC99-compliant. The VT8231 includes a master mode enhanced IDE controller with dual-channel DMA engine and interlaced dual-channel commands. In addition to standard PIO and DMA mode operation, the VT8231 also supports the Ultra-DMA/33, 66, and 100 standards to allow burst data transfer rates up to 100MB/s throughput. The IDE controller is SFF-8038i v1.0– and Microsoft Windows family–compliant. The chip contains an integrated LAN Fast Ethernet controller (MAC) with Media Independent Interface (MII) to external PHY. The LAN controller operates at 1/10/100Mbit/s transfer rates using either full- or half-duplex operation. It features an integrated four-port USB interface with a root hub and two function ports with built-in physical layer transceivers, distributed DMA support, an integrated AC97 link for basic audio and HSP-based modem functions, integrated hardware monitoring, and an OnNow/ACPI-compliant advanced configuration and power management interface. Table 10-26 lists the features of the VIA ProSavage KM133 chipset.

TABLE 10-26   VIA PROSAVAGE KM133 CHIPSET FEATURES AT A GLANCE

Supports Slot A, Socket A (AMD Athlon and Duron) processors

200/266 MHz CPU FSB

AGP expansion interface supporting AGP 4x, 2x, or 1x external AGP graphics card upgrades

DRAM interface runs synchronous (66/66, 100/100, 133/133) mode or pseudosynchronous (66/100, 100/66, 100/133, 133/100) mode with FSB

Concurrent CPU, AGP, and PCI access

Supports standard SDRAM and VCM SDRAM memory types

Supports three DIMMs or six banks of DRAMs for up to 1.5GB

AGP Rev. 2.0 compliant

Supports the AGP 266 MHz 4x mode

Integrated Savage4 2D/3D video accelerator

PCI 2.2 compliant, 32-bit 3.3V PCI interface with 5V-tolerant inputs

Supports up to five PCI masters

PCI-to-system memory data streaming support

Dynamic power-down of SDRAM

ACPI 1.0– and PCI Bus Power Management 1.1 compliant

Drivers for Windows 9x, Windows NT 4.0, Windows 2000, and OS/2

Integrated Fast Ethernet controller with 1/10/100Mbit capability

Integrated USB controller with two root hubs and four function ports

AC-Link interface for AC97 audio codec and MC97 modem codec

HSP modem and optional external modem DSP support

Integrated Sound BlasterPro and DirectSound compatible digital audio controller

Integrated keyboard controller with PS/2 mouse support

Dual-channel Ultra-DMA/33/66/100 master mode drive controller

Dual–channel master mode PCI supporting four Enhanced IDE devices

Supports two serial ports, IR port, parallel port, and floppy disk controller functions

Standard mode, ECP, and EPP support

USB v.1.1 and Intel Universal HCI v.1.1 compatible

Five universal input channels for voltage or temperature sensing

Supports both ACPI and legacy (APM) power management

ACPI v1.0 and APM v1.2 compliant

PCI interrupts steerable to any interrupt channel

Microsoft Windows 2000, Windows 98 SE, Windows 98, Windows NT, Windows 95, and plug-and-play BIOS compliant

VIA APOLLO KX133

The VIA Apollo KX133 is designed for use with AMD Athlon-based high-performance desktop systems. It supports current and emerging computer technologies, including AGP 4X, PC133, a 200 MHz FSB, and UDMA/66. This chipset was the first to support AGP 4X—a standard that users hope will finally show significant improvement over PCI and AGP 2X implementations. The Apollo KX133 supports the AMD Athlon 200 MHz bus, an architecture that provides twice the bus throughput of current-generation 100 MHz Pentium III-based systems.

VIA APOLLO PRO PLUS

The VIA Apollo Pro Plus is designed for Slot 1/Socket 370 mobile and desktop PC systems. To provide a high level of flexibility for motherboard and system designers, the Apollo Pro Plus incorporates the full range of core logic technologies, including advanced system power management techniques for both desktop and mobile PC applications, PC100 SDRAM, AGP 2x mode, and multiple CPU/DRAM timing configurations. The VIA Apollo Pro Plus consists of two devices. The VT82C693 North Bridge combines with the new VT82C596A South Bridge for a full set of mobile power management features for high-performance, power-conscious desktop and mobile designs. Side-by-side comparison with the VIA Apollo Pro shows the major difference in the Pro Plus is support for Socket 370 Celeron processors.

VIA APOLLO PRO

The VIA Apollo Pro is a high-performance chipset for Slot 1 mobile and desktop PC systems. The chipset is available in two configurations. For mobile and power-conscience desktop computers, the chipset combines VT82C691 system controller with the VT82C596 South Bridge chip providing a full set of mobile power management features. For cost-effective, high-performance desktop designs, the VT82C691 can also be configured with the VT82C586B South Bridge.

To provide the greatest flexibility for motherboard and system designers, the Apollo Pro incorporates a suite of core logic technologies, including advanced system power management capability for both desktop and mobile PC applications, PC100 SDRAM, AGP 2x mode, and multiple CPU/DRAM timing configurations. The Apollo Pro supports a mixing of 100 MHz and 66 MHz memory to preserve users' memory investment. Memory can be used in different speed and size configurations up to 1GB total. The chipset is AGP 1.0– and PCI 2.1–compliant and supports up to five PCI masters. Support for concurrent CPU and AGP access provides improved video performance. Disk data transfer speed support is UDMA/33.

VIA APOLLO MVP4

The Apollo MVP4 is an advanced System Multimedia Architecture (SMA) PC core logic chipset for Socket 7 systems. The VIA Apollo MVP4 is a combination of the widely successful VIA Apollo MVP3 and a high-performance 2D/3D graphics controller. The VT8501 North Bridge chip paired with the VIA VT82C686 Super South Bridge create the MVP4, which is designed to provide a low-cost, full-featured chipset for desktops and mobile PCs. System costs are also reduced by the integrated AGP 2.0–compliant 2D/3D AGP graphics controller. The controller incorporates a 64-bit 2D/3D graphics engine and video accelerator with advanced DVD video and optional TV output capability. The VIA Apollo MVP4 includes performance feature support for PC100 memory for use on a 100 MHz front side bus and UDMA/33, and UDMA/66. USB support for peripheral add-on devices and ACPI power management features round out the basic MVP4 VIA chipset.

VIA APOLLO MVP3

The aging VIA Apollo MVP3 chipset supports Socket 7–compatible processors, including Pentium, Pentium MMX, VIA Cyrix M-II, and the entire AMD K-6 processor series up to the K-6 III 533 MHz. This wide variety of processors is supported through a flexible FSB that allows speeds of 66/75/83/95/100 MHz. The Apollo MVP3 chipset combines the VT82C598AT (MVP) system controller (North Bridge) with either the VT82C686A bus controller (South Bridge) for desktop systems or the VT82C596B bus controller for mobile systems.

The chipset provides superior performance between the CPU, optional synchronous cache, DRAM, AGP bus, and PCI bus with pipelined, burst, and concurrent operation. It also provides support for PC100 SDRAM modules and allows the use of up to 768MB of memory. Other memory types supported include standard FPM DRAM, and EDO DRAM in a flexible mix/match manner. The SDRAM interface allows zero-wait-state bursting between the DRAM and the data buffers at 100 MHz. The DRAM controller also supports optional ECC or EC memory. The DRAM controller can run at either the host CPU bus frequency (66/75/83/100 MHz) or the AGP bus frequency (66 MHz).

The Apollo MVP3 chipset supports AGP v2.0 compatibility, including 2x mode transfers, SBA, flush/fence commands, and pipelined grants. Both Windows 95 VXD and Windows 98/2000 miniport drivers are supported for with major AGP-based 3D- and DVD-capable multimedia accelerators. The Apollo MVP3 chipset includes an integrated keyboard controller with PS/2 mouse support, an integrated DS12885-style real-time clock with extended 256-byte CMOS RAM, an integrated master mode enhanced IDE controller supporting UDMA/33 for 33MB/s transfer rate, and an integrated USB interface with a root hub and two USB ports. It includes distributed DMA support, and an OnNow/ACPI-compliant advanced configuration and power management interface.

VIA APOLLO P6

VIA's VT82C680 Apollo P6 is a high-performance, energy-efficient chipset for older PCI/ISA desktop and notebook PC systems based on the Intel Pentium Pro processor. The chipset supports multiple Pentium Pro configurations (based on Intel GTL+) and handles up to 66 MHz external CPU bus speeds. The chipset also supports the Pentium Pro CPU multiphase protocols for split transactions and extensive queues for optimal CPU throughput. The DRAM and PCI bus are also independently powered so that each of the buses can be run at 3.3V or 5V (the ISA bus always runs at 5V).

VIA APOLLO VP3

Although now outdated, the Apollo VP3 is a high-performance, two-chip chipset for the implementation of AGP, PCI, and ISA bus architectures in desktop and notebook PC systems based on 64-bit Socket 7 CPUs (including Intel Pentium and Pentium MMX, AMD K5 and K6, and Cyrix/IBM 6x86 and 6x86MX processors). The Apollo VP3 chipset consists of the VT82C597 system controller and the VT82C586B PCI-to-ISA bridge. The VT82C597 system controller provides superior performance between the CPU, optional synchronous cache, DRAM, AGP bus, and the PCI bus with pipelined, burst, and concurrent operation. The VT82C597 complies with the Accelerated Graphics Port Specification 1.0 and features a 66 MHz master system bus. It is interesting to note that the VP3 chipset is one of the few that provide AGP support for non-Pentium Pro processors.

VIA APOLLO VP2

Though now terribly dated, the two-chip VIA Apollo VP2/97 was the industry's most highly integrated, high-performance Socket 7–compliant chipset. With ECC, Microsoft PC97 compliance, SDRAM, 512MB DRAM, and 2MB cache support, the VP2/97 offers remarkable versatility for Intel Pentium, Pentium MMX, Cyrix/IBM 6x86 and 6x86MX, and AMD K5 and K6 MMX processors.

The Apollo VP2/97 builds on the VIA VT82C580VP Apollo VP (widely recognized as a leading Socket 7 chipset). Additional performance-related features include a fast DRAM controller with support for SDRAM, EDO, BEDO, and FPM DRAM types. Additional features include a deeper buffer with enhanced performance, an intelligent PCI bus controller with concurrent PCI master/CPU/IDE operations, and zero-wait-state PCI master and slave burst transfer rates. The Apollo VP2/97 features the VIA VT82C586B PCI-IDE controller chip, which supports ACPI/OnNow, Ultra-DMA/33, and USB technologies.

VIA APOLLO VPX/97

In its day, the VIA VT82C580VPX Apollo VPX/97 core logic chipset was a high-performance four-chip solution for Socket 7 main boards supporting Intel Pentium, Pentium MMX, Cyrix/IBM 6x86 and 6x86MX, and AMD K5 and K6 MMX processors. To enable proper implementation of the Cyrix/IBM 6x86 200+ processor, the chipset features an asynchronous CPU bus that operates at either 66 or 75 MHz speeds. Apollo VPX/97 also supports the Cyrix/IBM linear burst mode.

The Apollo VPX/97 features a fast DRAM controller with support for SDRAM, EDO, BEDO, and FPM DRAM types in mixed combinations of 32- or 64-bit data bus widths. Additional features include a deeper buffer with enhanced performance, an intelligent PCI bus controller with concurrent PCI master/CPU/IDE operations, and zero-wait-state PCI master and slave burst transfer rates. There is support for up to 2MB of L2 cache, and up to 512MB of DRAM. The VIA Apollo VPX/97 features the VIA VT82C586B PCI-IDE controller chip, which complies with the Microsoft PC97 industry standard by supporting ACPI/OnNow, Ultra-DMA/33, and USB technologies.

VIA APOLLO VP1

Now completely obsolete, the VT82C580VP Apollo VP1 is a four-chip solution for PCI/ISA desktop and notebook PCs based on Pentium, AMD K5x86, and Cyrix 6x86 CPUs. The Apollo VP1 featured functions designed to bypass conventional board-level bottlenecks including burst and normal EDO RAM, FPM RAM, and SDRAM support, burst SRAM and cache module support, and an on-board dual-channel enhanced master mode PCI IDE controller that supports up to four Enhanced IDE (EIDE) devices. The VIA Apollo VP1 chipset consists of one VT82C585VP system controller, a VT82C586 PCI/IDE/ISA/USB controller, and two VT82C587VP share frame buffers.

SiS Chipsets

SiS is another major manufacturer of chipsets that support core logic (motherboards) as well as mobile PCs and multimedia applications. Although SiS is a bit behind VIA and Intel in chipset development, it is rather unique in its inclusion of video accelerator hardware into the chipset (particularly in its later products). This makes SiS chipsets particularly appealing to entry-level PC manufacturers, where minimizing cost is very important. Since SiS products are not as widely used as other chipsets, we won't detail specific chipsets here. You can always refer to the SiS Web site for features and technical data.

Further Study

ALi   www.acerlabs.com/
AMD   www.amd.com
Intel   www.intel.com/design/chipsets/
Micron   www.micron.com/
Nvidia   www.nvidia.com/
OPTi   www.opti.com
SiS   www.sis.com.tw/products/corelogic.htm
VIA   www.via.com.tw/
VLSI (acquired by Phillips)   www.semiconductors.philips.com/

11

CMOS

With the introduction of their PC/AT computer, IBM abandoned the configuration DIP switches that had been used for the PC/XT. Rather than limit the system's configuration options, IBM chose to store the system's setup parameters in a small, low-power RAM chip called the CMOS RAM. In practice, CMOS RAM is often combined on the same chip with the *real-time clock* (RTC). In effect, the discrete switches of the XT were replaced with logical "switches" of each CMOS bit. (After all, a bit can be high or low, just as a switch can be on or off.) When a modern personal computer starts, the system attributes—stored in the CMOS RAM—are read by the BIOS, which then uses those attributes during normal system operation. As a result, it is vitally important that the correct settings be used when configuring a system. Otherwise, system problems may result. This chapter explains a broad selection of CMOS parameters in detail, then provides some guidelines for proper CMOS optimization and battery maintenance.

Many PC enthusiasts (and even experienced technicians) use the terms "BIOS" and "CMOS" inter-changeably. However, BIOS and CMOS RAM are not the same thing—though the two are intimately related. BIOS refers to the firmware instructions located on the BIOS ROM, while CMOS refers to the low-power RAM that holds the system's setup parameters. BIOS reads the CMOS RAM into main memory at start time, and provides the "Setup" routine that allows you to change the contents of CMOS, but the CMOS RAM/RTC device is a totally different chip.

The Role of CMOS

In simplest terms, CMOS RAM is nothing more than very low-power static RAM. Older CMOS RAM devices offered 64 bytes, and later implementations provide an extra 64 bytes (128 bytes total). The latest motherboards use 512 bytes or more to store the CMOS Setup along with ESCD (extended system config-uration data) information needed by the PC's *plug-and-play* (PnP) system. For the purposes of this book, we will consider a basic 128-byte CMOS system. Since RAM is naturally lost when system power is removed, a battery is added to the PC that continues to provide power to the CMOS RAM (and RTC). It is this CMOS battery backup that keeps the date, time, and system parameters intact until you turn the sys-tem on again. Of course, if the battery should fail, the system will lose its date, time, and all of its setup parameters. Many a tear has been shed trying to reconstruct lost system parameters by trial and error. You will learn about CMOS backup techniques in "Backing Up CMOS RAM," later in this chapter.

Configuring the CMOS Setup

As you might expect, CMOS data does not simply materialize out of the ether. It must be entered manually (initially by the system manufacturer, and later by you or your customers) through a setup routine. Early AT-compatible PCs relied on a disk-based setup utility. That is, you needed to boot the computer from a floppy disk containing the CMOS Setup utility. The big problem with a setup disk is that the floppy disk may fail and leave you without a setup disk, or you may lose the setup disk as the system changes hands or falls into disuse. If you find yourself with a setup disk, be sure to make a backup copy of it as soon as possible. Late-model 386 and subsequent systems abandon the use of setup disks and incorporate the setup utility onto the BIOS chip. When the setup routine resides on the system, you can usually access the setup during system initialization by pressing one or more keys simultaneously (such as DEL or CTRL-F1). This part of the chapter is intended to familiarize you with the options found in current CMOS Setup programs and to illustrate the typical defaults.

Keep in mind that the listings of CMOS Setup features found in this chapter are compiled from a num-ber of different sources. Your CMOS Setup may offer more or fewer options to choose from depend-ing on your BIOS maker and vintage.

ENTERING CMOS SETUP

The first trick in configuring your CMOS Setup is to launch the setup utility in the first place. BIOS manu-facturers are rarely consistent when it comes to accessing the setup utility. In most cases, you can only launch setup in the first few moments after the system boots—just after the memory test is finished, but before the operating system starts to load. A note on the display will usually indicate the correct key or key combination, such as:

```
Press <F1> to enter Setup...
```

Some BIOS versions allow these setup entry messages to be turned off through the CMOS Setup, so you may not see a message displayed on the monitor. However, the setup routine should still be accessible.

Unfortunately, there are about as many key combinations as there are BIOS makers, and knowing the proper key combinations for every system can be an exercise in frustration. Table 11-1 lists the known key combinations for many popular BIOS and system types. When you're stuck and cannot enter CMOS with any of the key combinations in Table 11-1, you might be able to force the CMOS Setup routine by causing a configuration change (such as removing a DIMM or two). This sometimes causes a CMOS configuration error and allows you to proceed to the setup routine.

For security purposes, some new motherboard designs allow access to CMOS Setup to be disabled through a motherboard jumper. If you absolutely cannot access the setup using a proper key combination or a forced configuration change, check the motherboard to see if the setup access jumper has been disabled.

Of course, if you've got a 286 or early 386 model PC sitting on your workbench, you'll need a setup disk to load the CMOS Setup utility. If you've actually got a setup disk for the system, consider yourself lucky. They are usually the first things to be lost. If you need a setup utility, you may be able to download a suitable third-party freeware utility from **oak.oakland.edu:/SimTel/msdos/at** or **ftp.uu.net:/systems/msdos/simtel/at**. If you find yourself working with a GRiD system, you can probably get a setup utility from **support.tandy.com/grid.html** or **http://www.ast.com/americas/files.htm**. For IBM PS/2 systems, you can get a setup utility from the IBM site at **www.pc.ibm.com/files.html**. Finally, setup utilities for Panasonic computers are available on the web at **www.panasonic.com/host/support/**.

BASIC CMOS OPTIMIZATION TACTICS

As PCs continue to evolve, the ever-increasing variety of memory types, busses, PC technology initiatives, and system architectures has forced BIOS makers to provide more and more entries in the CMOS

TABLE 11-1   TYPICAL CMOS SETUP KEY SEQUENCES

BIOS/SYSTEM	KEY OR KEY SEQUENCE
AMI BIOS	DEL key during the POST
Award BIOS	CTRL-ALT-ESC
DTK BIOS	ESC key during the POST
IBM PS/2 BIOS	CTRL-ALT-INS *after* CTRL-ALT-DEL
Phoenix BIOS	CTRL-ALT-ESC or CTRL-ALT-S
ALR PC	F2 (for PCI systems) or CTRL-ALT-ESC (for non-PCI systems)
Compaq PCs	F10
Gateway 2000 PC	F1
Sony PC	F3 while the PC is starting (you see the Sony logo), then F1

Setup. Today, there are dozens of possible setup entries in any given BIOS—each yielding hundreds of potential combinations. This variety makes it very difficult to select the optimum settings for a system. However, if you're really just interested in getting the most from your setup, the following points may come in handy:

■ *Check the basics.* Make sure that all standard CMOS settings correspond to the installed components of your system. For instance, you should verify the date, time, available memory (if possible), hard disks, and floppy disks. (See "Configuring the Standard CMOS Setup" later in this chapter.)

■ *Enable all system cache.* Make sure that all your cache memory (both internal and external) is enabled. Of course, you must have internal (L1) and external (L2) cache memory present in the system—which is always the case for systems less than five years old. (See "Configuring the Advanced CMOS Setup" later in this chapter.)

■ *Minimize RAM wait-states.* Make sure that the wait-state values used for your main system RAM are set at the minimum possible. You must be careful here because if values are too low, your system may freeze (hang up). For more information, check out "Configuring the Advanced Chipset Setup" later in this chapter.

■ *Enable ROM shadowing.* At a minimum, you should shadow your video and system ROM. On older systems, this may improve performance significantly. Newer systems (with faster "flash" ROM devices) may not benefit as much from shadowing. (See "Configuring the Advanced CMOS Setup" later in this chapter.)

■ *Enable power management.* Make sure to employ the power management features supported by your BIOS. Proper power management will conserve electricity and can extend the working life of many of the system components. (See "Configuring Power Management" later in this chapter.)

■ *Optimize drive access.* Hard disk data transfer speeds are a major bottleneck for system performance. Use the fastest data transfer protocol that your hard disk system will support (for example, Ultra-DMA/66 or Ultra-DMA/100). Remember that both the drive and drive controller must support the chosen data transfer protocol. If the hard drive system supports Bus Mastering IDE (BMIDE), you may consider using that to improve drive performance on multitasking or disk-intensive systems.

■ *Go with the BIOS Defaults.* With modern systems, it's often unnecessary to reenter every CMOS Setup parameter from scratch. Suitable default settings are now typically incorporated into the BIOS itself, so you can get a system running without messing with individual entries. (You just need to enter the drives properly.) You can find this as a Select BIOS Defaults option in your CMOS Setup main menu. BIOS defaults will generally not optimize your system's performance, but they will get you out of a tough spot when you have trouble after changing one or more settings.

HIDDEN BIOS SETTINGS

Although today's BIOS has more options than ever, there's no guarantee that you'll be able to access every available option through the CMOS Setup. In some cases, there may be hidden settings that you cannot see in the CMOS Setup (and such hidden settings cannot be altered). This can be a major impairment since many settings such as DRAM timings and cache settings can have a serious impact on PC performance. In actual practice, the settings still exist, but they are masked—often because the PC maker doesn't trust you to modify the settings. There are several tools that you can use to view and modify hidden system settings depending on the version of your BIOS.

AMI BIOS Versions

Robert Muchsel has written a program called AMI Setup (v.2.99) that will allow you to access and change the hidden settings of your AMI BIOS. The program works with AMI's High Flex BIOS versions—as well as with AMI WinBIOS. The shareware version has excellent documentation to assist you in your optimization efforts. If you need help on what a particular setting affects, take a look at the long list of BIOS options presented in the following sections. You can download AMI Setup 2.99 from **ftp://ftp.cdrom.com/pub/simtelnet/msdos/sysutl/amis2990.zip**.

Non-AMI BIOS Versions

For systems that do not use an AMI BIOS (for example, MR BIOS, Award, Phoenix), you can use the more generic CTCHIPZ utility available from **www.sysopt.com/pub/ctchip34.zip**. As with AMI Setup, the CTCHIPZ utility checks and accesses "undocumented" system settings. The one wrinkle with CTCHIPZ is that you'll need to know which chipset your system uses in order to select the correct configuration (CFG) file for your particular system. Check the documentation for CTCHIPZ in order to find the correct CFG file name. The CTCHIPZ program can be a bit tricky to comprehend and use since it's in German. You can find an English translation for the documentation at **www.sysopt.com/ctdocs.html**.

CONFIGURING THE STANDARD CMOS SETUP

The standard CMOS Setup usually comprises one screen of basic data about your system's date, time, and attached devices (primarily floppy and hard drives). It is important for you to get this data correct because the system will refuse to boot unless it is aware of all the drives installed (especially your boot hard drive, which is usually the C drive). The following alphabetic listing highlights common entries found in the standard setup menu(s):

Assign IRQ for VGA   When enabled, this option causes the system to assign an IRQ for the video card in order to speed the transfer of data between the CPU and video card. This option must be enabled if your video card requires bus mastering (such as Matrox Mystique cards with 3D graphics features). By disabling this option, you'll free up an IRQ for use elsewhere in the system.

Date and Time   Use these settings to change the date and time of the system clock.

RTC devices are notoriously inaccurate devices. Depending of the quality of the motherboard, you should expect to lose (or gain) several seconds per month. You should periodically check the date and time, and correct it as necessary.

Daylight Savings   When enabled, this feature allows the RTC to automatically adapt to the daylight saving scheme (removing one hour on the last Sunday of October and adding one hour on the last Sunday of April). As a rule, this can be enabled. Otherwise, you'll need to correct for daylight saving manually.

Error Halt   This entry determines whether the PC will stop if an error is detected during initialization (similar to Halt On later):

- ■ **No errors**   The system boot will not be stopped for any error that may be detected.
- ■ **All errors**   Whenever the BIOS detects a nonfatal error, the system will be stopped and you will be prompted.
- ■ **All, but keyboard**   The system boot will not stop for a keyboard error, but it will stop for all others.
- ■ **All, but disk**   The system boot will not stop for a disk error, but it will stop for all others.

■ **All, but disk/keyboard**   The system boot will not stop for a keyboard or disk error, but it will stop for all others.

Floppy Drive A   Set this entry to reflect the type of floppy drive installed for drive A. In most cases, the drive will be 1.44MB 3.5-inch, though a few systems may use a 2.88MB 3.5-inch floppy. Older systems may use 720KB 3.5-inch, 1.2MB 5.25-inch, or even 360KB 5.25-inch floppy drives.

Floppy Drive B   Set this entry to reflect the type of floppy drive installed for drive B. The typical selections for a floppy drive are shown for "Floppy Drive A" preceding.

Halt On   This entry tells the BIOS which errors to skip during the POST. For example, if you want the BIOS POST to continue whether or not it gets an error on a missing keyboard, set this option to "All, but keyboard" (See "Error Halt" earlier.)

Hard Disk C   This number is the BIOS drive table number of your primary (master) hard drive. In virtually all cases today, this number is 47 (User Defined), which means that you must specify the drive specs according to your hard drive manual. Otherwise, you can typically autodetect the drive parameters. SCSI drives in the C: position should be set to None or Not Installed. If you cannot autodetect the drive, there are typically six parameters that define your hard drive:

■ **Cyl**   The number of cylinders (or tracks) on your hard disk.

■ **Heads**   The number of heads in the hard disk.

■ **WPre**   This setting specifies the cylinder where Write Precompensation begins and uses additional energy to write the "compensated" cylinders. Today, WPre is essentially useless. Set it either to –1 or the maximum number of cylinders on the drive. For EIDE/IDE hard drives, it is not necessary to enter a WPre cylinder.

■ **LZ**   This setting specifies the cylinder used as the landing zone for older drives without an "autoparking" feature. Today, LZ is essentially useless. Set it either to 0 or the maximum number of cylinders on the drive.

■ **Sect/Trk**   This setting specifies the number of *sectors per track* (SPT). It is often 17 for MFM drives, and 26 for RLL drives. Modern types of drives use Zoned Recording, and the number of sectors per track will vary (increasing on the outer tracks). There is usually one translation number (63) provided for the drive.

■ **Size**   The total drive size is automatically calculated according to the number of cylinders, heads, and sectors entered earlier. The number is given in MB according to the formula (Hds*Cyl*Sect*512)/1048.

Hard Disk D   This number is the BIOS drive table number of your secondary (slave) hard drive. In virtually all cases today, this number is 47 (User Defined), which means that you must specify the drive specs according to your hard drive manual. Otherwise, you can typically autodetect the drive parameters. SCSI drives set to the D: position should be set to "none" or "not installed." If you cannot autodetect the drive, the six parameters that define your hard drive are listed under "Hard Disk C" earlier.

If your drive controller supports four hard drives, you may find an additional two hard drive entries (for example, Hard Disk E: and Hard Disk F:). These would be a "secondary master" and "secondary slave" drive.

HDD Delay   Some hard drives require several seconds in order to be identified (initialized) correctly by the BIOS. With fast boots, there may not be enough time to identify the hard drive properly. This setting allows you to artificially delay the boot-up so that the drive may be initialized. You can select from several possible time options. To keep your boot speed as fast as possible, be sure to select the lowest possible delay that ensures proper initialization.

Keyboard   This sets whether a keyboard is attached. In virtually all cases, the proper entry is installed. If not installed, the BIOS will pass the keyboard test in the POST, allowing a PC to boot without a keyboard without the BIOS producing a keyboard error (most commonly encountered in file servers, printer servers, and so on).

Memory   This category allows you to select which memory element(s) are displayed at start time. The contents are determined by the BIOS POST:

- **Base Memory**   The BIOS POST determines the amount of base (conventional) memory installed in the system.
- **Extended Memory**   The BIOS POST determines the amount of extended memory installed in the system.
- **Other Memory**   This is memory that can be allocated for different applications. The most common uses for this area are shadow RAM and AGP (video) buffer areas.
- **Total Memory**   The total memory is the sum of Base, Extended, and Other memory areas.
- **OS Select for DRAM > 64MB**   If you're using OS/2, select the OS/2 option. If you're using DOS or Windows, select Non-OS/2. Generally, Non-OS/2 is selected.

PCI/VGA Palette Snoop   This option must be enabled if any ISA card installed in the PC requires VGA palette snooping. For example, an MPEG card can be synchronized with the PCI VGA system. However, few (if any) modern cards require palette snooping, so this option is generally left disabled.

Primary Display   This entry specifies the general type of display you are using. The most frequent selection for older systems is VGA/PGA/EGA, though current systems shorten this to VGA, which is adequate for virtually all current systems. If you have an older black/white display, select Mono or Hercules. If your video adapter card is text only, select MDA.

Quick Power-On Self-Test   If you have hard drives that initialize quickly, you may be able to speed your boot time even more by selecting the Quick POST. When enabled, the BIOS will shorten or skip some items during the POST (such as no memory count). This option is normally disabled to allow the normal POST routine.

Swap Floppy Drives   This option allows you to reverse the A and B floppy drive assignments when enabled without having to physically swap the drives. Normally, this option is disabled because few systems have more than one floppy drive.

Translation Mode   IDE drives below 528MB are typically set as CHS (Cylinder Head Sector) addressing, while EIDE, Fast-ATA, and Ultra-ATA drives use LBA (Logical Block Addressing) instead.

If you alter a drive's translation mode after the drive has been partitioned and formatted, the data contained on the drive will be inaccessible. You'll need to repartition and reformat the drive.

CONFIGURING THE ADVANCED CMOS SETUP

The advanced CMOS Setup contains the settings needed to tweak your boot characteristics and to optimize the performance of memory and cache. Most of the options found here are not vital to the system's proper operation, but they can help you tailor the system to your particular tastes and needs.

Above 1MB Memory Test   Enable this feature if you want the system to check the memory above 1MB for errors. The HIMEM.SYS driver for DOS 6.2 verifies the XMS anyway, so the test would be redundant in this case. In most cases, all memory is tested by the BIOS. But for faster boot performance, leave the feature disabled.

Adapter ROM Shadow C800, 16K   This feature enables shadowing for other adapter ROMs at C800h (for example, SCSI or network controller BIOS) that may be in the system. If there are no other adapter devices in the system, keep this feature disabled.

Adapter ROM Shadow CC00, 16K   This feature enables shadowing for other adapter ROMs that may be in the system at CC00h. This feature is often disabled by default because some hard drive adapters use the CC00h address.

Adapter ROM Shadow D000, 16K   This feature enables shadowing for other adapter ROMs that may be in the system at D000h. This is the default address for most network adapters, so it should usually be disabled unless there is a network adapter in the system, or some other known device with ROM at D000h.

Adapter ROM Shadow D400, 16K   This feature enables shadowing for other adapter ROMs that may be in the system at D400h. Since some special controllers (for example, controllers that support four floppy drives) often use this space, the default is often set disabled.

Adapter ROM Shadow D800, 16K   This feature enables shadowing for other adapter ROMs that may be in the system at D800h. The default is often disabled unless there is a known ROM in the system at that address.

Adapter ROM Shadow DC00, 16K   This feature enables shadowing for other adapter ROMs that may be in the system at DC00h. The default is often disabled unless there is a known ROM in the system at that address.

Adapter ROM Shadow E000, 16K   This feature enables shadowing for other adapter ROMs that may be in the system at E000h. The default is often disabled unless there is a known ROM in the system at that address.

Adapter ROM Shadow E400, 16K   This feature enables shadowing for other adapter ROMs that may be in the system at E400h. The default is often disabled unless there is a known ROM in the system at that address.

Adapter ROM Shadow E800, 16K   This feature enables shadowing for other adapter ROMs that may be in the system at E800h. The default is often disabled unless there is a known ROM in the system at that address.

Adapter ROM Shadow EC00, 16K   This feature enables shadowing for other adapter ROMs that may be in the system at EC00h. The default is often disabled unless there is a known ROM in the system at that address. SCSI adapter BIOS ROMs are often set to this address.

Some recent forms of SCSI controllers use writable addresses and should not be shadowed or cached. Check for such warnings or cautions in the SCSI controller manual before attempting to shadow the SCSI BIOS ROM.

Boot Sector Virus Protection   This well-established feature in all current BIOS versions provides a warning whenever any software attempts to write to the disk's boot sector, which is a main target for computer viruses. You can generally keep this feature enabled unless you're installing a new operating system (like Windows 9x/Me) that needs to write to the boot sector during installation. You can disable the boot sector virus protection before installing the OS, then reenable the feature afterward.

Boot Up Floppy Seek   See "Floppy Drive Seek at Boot" later.

External Cache Memory   This feature allows you to enable or disable the external (L2) cache in the system. If there is L2 cache in the system, make sure that this feature is enabled for best performance. (Virtually all 486 and Pentium-type systems use L2 cache on the motherboard, but Pentium II/III/4 CPUs include L2 cache right in the processor cartridge.) If there is no L2 cache, keep this feature disabled. Enabling the L2 cache when there is no cache in the system may cause the PC to lock up. It may also be necessary for you to disable the L2 cache if there are system stability issues. This feature may also be presented as CPU External Cache.

Fast Gate A20 Option   This relates to the first 64KB of extended memory (A0 to A19) known as the *high memory area* (HMA). This option controls the use of the A20 address line to access memory above 1MB. Normally, all RAM access above 1MB is handled through the A20 gate in the keyboard controller chip (8042 or 8742). In virtually all cases, this option should be enabled. Disabling this option may make it impossible to access memory over 1MB.

Floppy Drive Seek at Boot   This feature selects whether a floppy drive will be checked at boot time. Keep this feature disabled for faster booting and reduced damage to floppy R/W heads. Enable this feature if you want to check for a bootable floppy disk (important for "booting clean" and running diagnostic utilities).

Disabling the floppy drive, changing the system boot sequence, and setting a CMOS password are good techniques for adding some security to a PC.

Hard Disk Type 47 RAM Area   This selection allows you to choose the location of the Type 47 HDD data area in memory. The BIOS has to place the HD type 47 data somewhere in memory. You can choose DOS memory or the I/O address space at 0:300h. DOS memory is valuable in real mode (you only have 640KB to work with), so you should try to use the I/O space instead. However, there may be some peripheral, for example, a sound card or network card, that needs this area too. Note that this feature is redundant if BIOS is shadowed (except possibly for very old BIOS).

Internal Cache Memory   This feature allows you to enable or disable the internal (L1) cache in the CPU. If there is an L1 cache in the system, make sure that this feature is enabled for best performance. (All 486-, Pentium-, and Pentium II/III/4-type CPUs use L1 cache.) If there is no L1 cache (or you have reason to believe that the CPU's L1 cache is damaged), keep this feature disabled. Enabling the L1 cache when there is no cache in the CPU may cause the PC to lock up. This feature may also be presented as "CPU Internal Cache."

Some CMOS Setup utilities combine the cache control into a single entry such as Cache Memory and allow you to select Disabled, Internal Cache Only, or Both Enabled.

Memory Parity Error Check   This feature controls the parity checking of your system's memory. Parity checking can help improve the integrity of data in memory. When enabled, parity checking will generate an error such as "PARITY ERROR AT 0AB5:00BE SYSTEM HALTED" if an error is detected. Otherwise, errors in memory will go undetected—possibly corrupting and crashing the system. If you're using parity memory on the system, go ahead and enable parity checking. If you're using any nonparity memory on your system, parity checking must be disabled.

Besides being caused by data errors, parity errors can also be caused by insufficient wait-states or by mixing slower memory with faster memory components.

Memory Test Tick Sound   When enabled, this feature generates a sequence of audible tones (or "ticks") as the memory test executes. It also provides an audible confirmation of your CPU clock speed/turbo switch setting. The idea is that an experienced user can hear if something is wrong with the system just by the tick sound pattern. However, since PCs now have much more memory than before, this setting is used infrequently. If the noise is annoying, disable the test. If you cannot hear the test when it's enabled, check the speaker.

Numeric Processor Test   This feature will test the math coprocessor. All 486DX and later CPUs use a built-in coprocessor, and this test should be enabled. (Otherwise, the coprocessor function may not be enabled.) 486SX, 486DLC, 486SLC, and all older CPUs use a separate math coprocessor, and you should set this feature depending on whether a coprocessor is present.

Password Checking Option   This option controls whether a password is used to access the system, or to access the CMOS Setup, or both. When it's enabled, you'll need to set a password, then enter the appropriate password(s) as required. Always remember to note your password(s) in a safe place, and change your passwords frequently. If you forget a password, or encounter a system with a password option in place, see the section "CMOS Password Troubleshooting" at the end of this chapter.

Shadow Memory Cacheable   *Shadowing* is the process of copying ROM to RAM. Once the ROM contents are copied into RAM, making that RAM space cacheable can often increase performance even further. You can enable this feature to cache shadow memory, or disable it to prevent caching of shadow memory. Shadow caching is usually a good idea for DOS- and Windows-based platforms and should be enabled. But Linux and other UNIX-like operating systems will not benefit from this feature, and it can remain disabled.

System Boot Sequence   This feature controls the order in which system drives are checked for an operating system. The typical sequence is A:/C:, but C:/A: can be selected for faster booting. Modern BIOS also supports booting from other items such as the CD-ROM (if it meets the El Torito bootable CD-ROM specification) and SCSI drives (even while UDMA/EIDE/IDE drives are in the system).

System Boot-Up CPU Speed   This is commonly referred to as the "turbo mode" and allows you to specify what processor speed the system will boot to. The typical settings are High and Low. High speed is recommended for best performance, but if you encounter booting problems, you should try the Low speed. Today, this setting is largely abandoned, and a PC will always attempt to boot to its maximum possible speed.

System Boot-Up Num Lock   This specifies whether you want the NUM LOCK key to be activated at boot-up. You are free to keep this feature enabled or disabled as you prefer.

System ROM Shadow F000, 64K   Memory hidden in the "I/O hole" of 0x0A0000h to 0x0FFFFFh may be used to shadow the system ROM, where the contents of the motherboard BIOS ROM are copied into RAM, and the faster RAM copy is used instead. It is generally recommended to enable this feature, though systems with faster "flash" motherboard BIOS may not see as much performance benefit. You should disable motherboard ROM shadowing if you need to update a motherboard's flash BIOS, or if you're using some memory-resident utility to shadow the BIOS. Note that motherboard ROM shadowing may also cause some operating systems (other than DOS or Windows) or applications to lock up.

Turbo Switch Function   This feature enables or disables the turbo switch. This setting is now rarely used in modern systems because PCs are always run at their top speed. (There is no need to slow down a PC artificially.) If there is a turbo switch in the system, keep this feature enabled. Otherwise, disable this feature.

Typematic Rate   This is how fast a depressed key will repeat (in characters per second or CPS). A typical setting is 15CPS, though you can adjust this rate as your taste dictates.

Typematic Rate Delay   This sets the initial delay (in milliseconds or mS) before a depressed key starts repeating. (This is how long you've got to press a key *before* it starts repeating.) A setting of 500mS (0.5s) is recommended, though you can adjust this delay as your taste dictates.

Typematic Rate Programming   This feature enables the typematic rate programming of the keyboard, which determines how a keyboard will respond if a key is held down. If enabled, a key will repeat automatically if it is held down. If disabled, the key will not repeat. This feature is often disabled.

Not all keyboards support typematic rate programming, and this feature must be disabled if the keyboard doesn't support it.

Video ROM Shadow C000, 32K   Memory hidden in the "I/O hole" of 0x0A0000h to 0x0FFFFFh may be used to shadow video ROM, where the contents of the video ROM are copied into RAM, and the faster RAM copy is used instead. It is generally recommended to enable this feature, though systems with faster "flash" video BIOS may not see as much performance benefit. You should disable video ROM shadowing if you need to update a flash video BIOS, or if you're using a memory-resident utility to shadow the video BIOS. Note that video ROM shadowing may also cause some operating systems or applications to lock up.

Virus Warning   See "Boot Sector Virus Protection" earlier.

Wait for F1 If Any Error   If enabled, the system will halt and wait for F1 keyboard input before proceeding. If disabled, the system will simply continue after displaying an error message without waiting for any keyboard input. Disable the feature if you want the system to operate as a server (without a keyboard). Otherwise, you can enable the feature.

Weitek Coprocessor   This feature is normally found on older 386 motherboards from a period when Weitek coprocessors were popular. This high-performance coprocessor has two to three times the performance of the comparable Intel coprocessors. Weitek uses some RAM address space, so memory from this region must be remapped elsewhere. If you have a 386 system with a Weitek unit, enable the feature. If you do not have a Weitek unit, disable the feature. This setting is normally found on 386 motherboards, so don't worry about it on later/current systems.

CONFIGURING THE INTEGRATED PERIPHERALS SETUP

Typical motherboards now incorporate many diverse ports, including a parallel port, serial ports, USB ports, and FDD/HDD drive controllers. Traditionally, this meant motherboard jumpers were needed to enable the ports, but now most motherboard designs use the CMOS Setup to control and configure each port.

Primary PIO   This function allows IDE drives to transfer several sectors at a time. Several modes are possible. Mode 0 means one sector at a time. Mode 1 uses no interrupts. Mode 2 means sectors are transferred in a single burst. Mode 3 means 32-bit instructions at up to 11.1MB/sec. Mode 4 offers data transfers to 16.6MB/sec. Mode 5 is an unusual mode that supports up to 20MB/sec. The standard PIO mode for most drives today is PIO mode 4. Many BIOS versions offer an automatic setting that will automatically make the best decision for your drive. Data transfer modes must be set for each drive. This setting may have no value (and may not even be used) on newer DMA-type (Ultra-DMA/33/66/100) drive controllers.

IDE DMA   Normally this is set to Auto. Enable this feature if your drives are UDMA capable (such as UDMA/33/66/100). Windows 98/SE/Me can configure this feature for you by enabling a drive's DMA feature.

On-Chip PCI IDE   This feature is used to either enable or disable your onboard IDE controllers if such controllers are integrated into your motherboard chipset. If you wish to use a stand-alone drive controller card, you may need to disable this feature. Otherwise, the onboard controllers will be enabled.

SMART Support   A growing number of BIOS versions offer the option to enable or disable a hard disk's SMART (Self Monitoring Analysis and Reporting Technology) capability. SMART is used to detect and report impending disk problems. Some utilities use this technology to make disk diagnostics. Chances are that this feature (if available) will be disabled by default. If you know that the drive supports SMART, you can try enabling the feature for improved drive system reliability.

USB Controller   Most current motherboards will offer two USB hub ports, and these hubs can be controlled through the CMOS Setup. If your computer has one or more USB ports, use this setting to enable or disable your motherboard's onboard USB controller. Disabling the ports will free an IRQ for the system.

FDD Controller   Use this feature to enable or disable your motherboard's onboard floppy disk controller. You probably want this feature enabled unless you're using a separate drive controller card and do not need the integrated floppy controller.

Serial Port(s)   This feature is used to control the motherboard's serial port(s). In many cases, you can specify the IRQ and I/O port address for the hardware in addition to simply enabling or disabling the ports outright. Normally, your serial (COM) ports are enabled, but you can disable the serial port(s) if necessary. Disabling serial ports can free the corresponding IRQ and I/O resources for the system and may be necessary if you're installing expansion hardware (such as a modem) that might conflict with serial port resources.

Parallel Port   This feature is used to disable or enable a parallel port, and to change the parallel port mode (such as standard, bidirectional, ECP, or EPP) and IRQ and I/O resources assigned to the port. Use ECP mode if possible since that will support faster data transfers between the system and other parallel port devices. Disabling parallel ports can free the corresponding IRQ and I/O resources for the system, and may be necessary if you're installing hardware that might conflict with parallel port resources. For example, a sound card often uses IRQ5, which is commonly used by LPT2.

CONFIGURING THE ADVANCED CHIPSET SETUP

The core logic (or *chipset*) is responsible for providing many of the advanced features that we take for granted in today's PCs. As a consequence, there are a tremendous number of variables involved in the proper configuration of a chipset. This part of the CMOS Setup allows you to tweak the performance of your chipset (namely memory timings, memory refresh options, data bus performance, cache enhancements, AGP setup, and so on).

The advanced chipset setup requires a more detailed understanding of chipset operation and features, and should be attempted only by experienced technicians. Incorrect chipset configurations can easily impair system performance. Remember to *always* record your original CMOS Setup settings before changing any parameters.

16-Bit I/O Recovery Time   This is an additional delay time inserted after every 16-bit operation and is sometimes needed to support older 16-bit devices. The delay value is added to the minimum delay inserted after every AT bus cycle. You may not find this parameter on current PCs—especially motherboards that have abandoned the use of ISA bus slots.

16-Bit Memory, I/O Wait-State   This entry lists the number of wait-states inserted with 16-bit memory and I/O operations. Too many wait-states will reduce bus performance, and too few wait-states can cause bus errors and system lockups. If your system uses this entry, it is normally safe to stay with the BIOS Default value.

8-Bit Memory, I/O Wait-State   This entry lists the number of wait-states inserted with 8-bit memory and I/O operations. Too many wait-states will reduce bus performance, and too few wait-states can cause bus errors and system lockups. If your system uses this entry, it is normally safe to stay with the BIOS Default value.

Alternate Bit in Tag RAM   Tag bits are used to determine the state of the information that is stored in the L2 (external) cache. The level of error determination is set with this option. If you use the Write Back caching method, use the "7+1" setting to receive best results. Otherwise, use the "8+0" setting. You will generally not find this option in Pentium II/III/4 systems where L2 cache is integrated into the processor.

AT Bus Clock Selection (or AT Bus Clock Source)   This selects a division of the CPU clock (or system clock) so it can approximate the ISA/EISA bus clock of 8.33 MHz. The settings are in terms of CLK/x (or CLKIN/x and CLK2/x), where x may have values like 2, 3, 4, or 5. CLK represents your bus processor speed. For example, 486DX33, 486DX2/66, and 486DX3/99 all use a 33 MHz bus speed and should have a divider value of 4 for an ISA speed of 8.25 MHz. For 286 and 386 processors, CLK is half the speed of the CPU. Here are some typical settings:

CLK/2	All 286 and 386 systems
CLK/3	SX/DX16, DX20, DX25, DX2/50, DX4/100
CLK/4	SX/DX33, DX2/66, DX3/99
CLK/5	DX40, DX2/80
CLK/6	DX50, DX2/100
CLK/7	60 MHz bus
CLK/8	66 MHz bus

The bus speed doesn't have to be precisely 8.33 MHz, but that's what to shoot for. An improper setting may cause significant decrease in performance. If the divider is too high, the ISA bus speed will be too low (below 8.33 MHz), and the ISA devices will perform poorly. If the divider is too low, the ISA bus speed will be too high (above 8.33 MHz), and the ISA devices may malfunction. You may not find this option on later motherboards where the ISA bus speed is asynchronous of the system clock, or on motherboards that have abandoned use of the ISA bus entirely.

AT Cycle Wait-State   This entry indicates the number of wait-states inserted whenever an operation is performed with the AT bus. You may need some additional wait-states if old ISA cards are used, especially if they are used together with fast adapter cards. Too many wait-states will reduce bus performance, and too few wait-states can cause bus errors and system lockups. When this option is available, the BIOS Default value is often the best choice.

Automatic Configuration   When enabled, this feature allows the BIOS to automatically set the settings in the advanced chipset setup (for example, clock divider, wait-states). If you're uncertain about configuring the advanced chipset features, keep this feature enabled. Disable this feature if you're going to make manual changes to the chipset setup. You may have to disable this feature when some highly specialized adapter cards are used in the system.

Burst Copy-Back Option   This caching option may be enabled or disabled. When it's enabled and a read from the memory to the processor results in a "cache miss," the chipset will try a second read (when the data transfers in burst mode). This feature is often enabled by default, but you may wish to disable this option in the event of system stability problems.

Burst Refresh   When enabled, this feature performs several refresh cycles at once. This feature can normally be enabled unless your system uses an unusual memory type or configuration. The feature should be disabled if system stability problems occur.

Burst SRAM Cycle   This feature lets you specify the timing of the burst mode read and write cycles to and from the external cache memory (L2). Typical options include 4-1-1-1 and 3-1-1-1 timings, so choose the lowest setting that works well with your system. Choosing a setting that is too low will cause problems with the cache (or system instability).

Burst Write   When enabled, the processor will write to the cache in bursts and can make caching more efficient. When disabled, the CPU will not write to the cache in bursts. Burst writing is more efficient and will generally enhance system performance.

Bus Mode   This feature selects the clock mode that is used to drive the bus. In synchronous mode, the CPU clock is used to drive the bus. In asynchronous mode, the ATCLK is used. In most cases, the synchronous mode is selected, though asynchronous mode will generally provide better compatibility for overclocked systems.

Cacheable RAM Address Range   Older chipsets usually allow memory to be cached just up to 32MB or 64MB. This is to limit the number of memory address bits that need to be saved in the cache together with its contents. Set this entry to match as much of your installed RAM as possible. For example, if you only have 32MB of RAM, select 32MB—don't enter 64MB.

Cache Read Option (Often Called the "SRAM Read Wait-State" or "Cache Read Hit Burst")   This specifies the number of clocks needed to load four 32-bit words into a CPU internal cache (typically specified as clocks per word). A timing of 2-1-1-1 indicates five clocks to load the four words and is the theoretical minimum for current high-end CPUs (486DX, Pentium, Pentium II/III, and later). This timing determines the number of wait-states for the cache RAM in normal and burst transfers (the latter for 486 systems only). Timing of 4-1-1-1 is usually recommended, but the faster timing that a computer can support, the better.

Cache Timing Control   This option sets the timing parameters on older motherboards for reading/writing to cache. The typical selections are usually fast, medium, normal, and turbo. When this feature is available, select the fastest suitable option for best performance.

Cache Wait-State   This feature is used on older motherboards to introduce additional wait-states for cache operations. Like conventional memory, fewer wait-states will result in better cache performance (but it will demand faster cache). An entry of 0 will give the optimal performance, but 1 wait-state may be required for bus speeds higher than 33 MHz.

Cache Write Option   This is the same as the Cache Read Option (see earlier), but is used to control cache write timing.

CAS-Before-RAS   When enabled, this option reduces refresh cycles and power consumption.

CAS Width in Read Cycle   This feature expresses the number of wait-states for the CPU to read DRAM. Lower figures are better for system performance.

Concurrent Refresh   This feature enables both the processor and the refresh hardware to have access to the memory at the same time. If this feature is disabled, the processor has to wait until the refresh hardware has finished, and this can slow system performance slightly. Many systems enable concurrent refresh by default.

CPU Write Back Cache   When enabled, the system will use "write back" caching. If disabled, the system will use "write through" caching.

Decoupled Refresh Option   When enabled, this feature allows the ISA bus and the RAM to refresh separately. Because refreshing the ISA bus is a slower process, separating the refresh cycles this way causes less strain on the CPU. This option is often enabled.

DMA Clock Source   This entry indicates the source of the DMA clock, which is used for DMA transfers. This setting will affect DMA performance for any peripheral (like floppy, tape, network, and SCSI adapters) using DMA. The maximum setting for traditional ISA-based PCs is 5 MHz.

DMA Wait-States   This entry lists the number of wait-states inserted before *direct memory access* (DMA) is attempted. Lower numbers (fewer wait-states) result in better DMA performance.

DRAM Burst at 4 Refresh   This is a slight variation of Burst Refresh, where the refresh is occurring in bursts of four. This feature can normally be enabled unless the RAM is not compatible with such a refresh operation.

DRAM CAS Timing Delay   DRAM is organized into rows and columns, and is accessed through strobe lines. The CPU activates a RAS (Row Access Strobe) line to find the row containing the required data, and then a CAS (Column Access Strobe) line specifies the column. As a result, RAS and CAS signals are used to identify a location in a DRAM chip. When using slow RAM, it may be necessary to introduce a delay into the CAS timing. The default is no CAS delay.

DRAM Refresh Method   This feature selects the refresh method used for RAM. The options are RAS Only and CAS-before-RAS. Most current systems use CAS-before-RAS timing by default.

E0000 ROM belongs to ATBUS   This entry indicates if the E0000h area (upper memory) belongs to the motherboard DRAM or to the AT bus. For most systems, enabled (yes) is recommended.

Extended DMA Registers   With a standard AT type of computer, DMA support is only provided for the first 16MB of system RAM. With this feature enabled, DMA support will be extended for up to 4GB of RAM. In most cases, this feature can be left disabled.

Extended I/O Decode   The normal range of I/O addresses is 0–0x3FFh using only 10 address bits. With this feature enabled, the system will support a 16-bit I/O-address bus allowing a 64KB I/O space. Most classical motherboards or I/O adapters can be decoded by only 10 address bits, so this feature can usually be left disabled.

Fast AT Cycle   When enabled, this feature may speed up data transfer rates with ISA cards (and can have an important effect on ISA video boards). You may need to disable this feature for system stability.

Fast Cache Read/Write   This allows enhanced cache performance through memory interleaving techniques, so enable this feature if you have two banks of cache (64KB or 256KB). Otherwise, leave this feature disabled.

Fast Decode Enable   This refers to some hardware that monitors the commands sent to the keyboard controller chip. The original AT used special codes not processed by the keyboard itself to control the switching of the 286 processor back from protected mode to real mode. The 286 itself had no hardware to do this, so the CPU has to be reset to switch back. PC makers added a few logic chips to monitor the commands sent to the keyboard controller chip, and when the reset CPU code was detected, the logic chips did an immediate reset. This fast decode of the keyboard reset command allowed OS/2 and Windows to switch between real and protected modes faster and enabled much better performance. You will generally find this entry on 286 and early 386 systems, since newer processors *do* have hardware instructions for switching between modes.

   If you find this entry on a current system, the "Fast Decode Enable" command is probably defined a bit differently. The design of the original AT bus made it very difficult to mix 8-bit and 16-bit RAM or

ROM within the same 128KB block of high address space. An 8-bit BIOS ROM on a VGA card forced all other peripherals using the C000h–DFFFh range to also use 8 bits. By doing an "early decode" of the high address lines along with the 8/16-bit select flag, the I/O bus could then use mixed 8- and 16-bit peripherals. In both cases, you should probably have this feature enabled.

Fast Page Mode DRAM   When enabled, this feature speeds up memory access for FPM DRAM. When memory access occurs in the same memory "page," the overhead of RAS and CAS sequences is not necessary, and memory performance is improved. This option is only found on older systems that support FPM RAM and is not used on current systems.

Hidden Refresh   This feature allows the RAM refresh memory cycles to take place in memory banks not used by your CPU at this time, instead of with the normal refresh cycles, which are executed every time the interrupt DRQ0 is called (every 15mS). There are typically three types of refresh schemes: cycle steal, cycle stretch, or hidden refresh. *Cycle steal* actually steals a clock cycle from the CPU to do the refresh. *Cycle stretch* delays a cycle from the processor to do the refresh. (Since it only occurs every 4mS or so, it's an improvement over cycle steal.) *Hidden refresh* simply refreshes idle memory banks. Most systems enable hidden refresh by default, but some memory supports hidden refresh better than others do. Try hidden refresh, but if the computer crashes or locks up, disable the hidden refresh.

Hi-Speed Refresh (or Fast Refresh)   When enabled, this feature causes refresh cycles to occur at higher frequencies in order to accomplish a refresh cycle in a shorter period. When combined with features like burst refresh, the overall system performance can improve. Not all types of memory can support Fast Refresh, and it uses more power than Slow Refresh.

IDE 32-Bit Transfer   When enabled, the read/write performance of the hard disk is faster. When disabled, only 16-bit data transfers are possible. Enable this feature if possible. It should be supported on all but the oldest systems/drives.

IDE DMA Transfer Mode   This defines the means by which DMA transfers are executed. The three typical settings are Disabled, Type B (for EISA), and Standard (for PCI). Standard is the fastest, but may cause problems with IDE CD-ROMs. The standard type is Type F.

IDE Multi-Block Mode (or IDE Block Mode)   This feature enables IDE drives to transfer several sectors per interrupt. Six modes are possible:

- Mode 0 (standard mode transferring a single sector at a time)
- Mode 1 (no interrupts)
- Mode 2 (sectors are transferred in a single burst)
- Mode 3 (speeds up to 11.1MB/s—sometimes abbreviated as "32-bit mode")
- Mode 4 (up to 16.7MB/s)
- Mode 5 (up to 20MB/s—not used in actual drive implementations)

The important attribute for block mode is the number of sectors per interrupt. The maximum number of sectors per interrupt is often (but not always) related to the drive's buffer size. If this setting is not set properly, communication with COM ports may not work. If the block size (sectors/interrupt) is set too large, you may experience serial port overruns and CRC errors. To fix this, decrease the block size, or disable block mode transfers altogether.

IDE Multiple Sector Mode   When IDE DMA Transfer Mode is enabled, this feature sets the number of sectors per burst (with a maximum of 64). Problems may occur with COM ports if this setting is configured improperly.

Interleave Mode   When enabled, the system will use an interleaved approach to access system memory. If the motherboard is not designed to support interleaved memory (or uses an advanced form of high-performance memory), this option should be disabled.

I/O Recovery Time   The I/O recovery time is the number of wait-states to be inserted between two consecutive I/O operations (generally specified as a two-number pair such as 5/3). The first number is the number of wait-states to insert for an 8-bit operation. The second is the number of wait-states for a 16-bit operation. In general, this feature can be disabled. If the AT Bus Clock is running fast (over 8.33 MHz), or you're using slow peripherals, it may be necessary to enable I/O Recovery Time starting with a value like 5/3.

A few BIOS versions specify an I/O Setup Time (or AT Bus (I/O) Command Delay). It is specified similarly to I/O Recovery Time, but is a delay before *starting* an I/O operation rather than a delay *between* I/O operations.

ISA IRQs   This entry informs the PCI cards of IRQs used by ISA cards so that the PCI cards will not attempt to assign those legacy resources. If you have no ISA devices in your system, make sure that no IRQs are reserved.

Keyboard Reset Control   This feature enables the CTRL-ALT-DEL warm reboot. As a security measure, disable this feature if you want to prohibit this kind of warm reboot. Otherwise, keep this option enabled.

Memory Read Wait-State (or DRAM Read Wait-States)   The CPU is often much faster than RAM, and it is necessary to introduce wait-states to allow the slower RAM to catch up to the CPU. Each wait-state effectively adds several nanoseconds (ns) of RAM speed. Fewer wait-states result in better system performance, and the ideal number of wait-states is 0 (though 1 wait-state is typically required). The number of wait-states necessary is approximately $(RamSpeed[ns] + 10)*Clock[MHz]/1000 - 2$. If there are too many wait-states, system performance will suffer. If there are too few wait-states, parity errors and system crashes will occur.

Memory Remapping   This feature remaps the memory used by the BIOS (A0000h to FFFFFh or 384KB) above the 1MB limit. If it's enabled, you cannot shadow video and system BIOS. In many cases, you should set this feature to disabled.

Memory Write Wait-State (or DRAM Write Wait-States)   This is the same as Memory Read Wait-State, but it applies to RAM writing. Some BIOS versions combine Memory Read/Write Wait-State options as the "DRAM Wait-States." In this case, the number of read and write wait-states must be equal.

Non-Cacheable Block-1 Base   Enter the base address of the area you don't want to cache. It must be a multiple of the Non-Cacheable Block-1 Size selected later. When this is disabled, set this to 0KB.

Non-Cacheable Block-2 Base   This is the same as Non-Cacheable Block-1 Base and is usually set to 0KB.

Non-Cacheable Block-1 Size   The non-cacheable region is intended for a memory-mapped I/O device that isn't supposed to be cached. For example, some video cards can present all video memory at 15MB to 16MB so software doesn't have to bank-switch. If the non-cacheable region covers actual RAM memory you are using, expect a significant performance decrease for accesses to that area. If the non-cacheable region covers only nonexistent memory addresses, there should be no performance hit. If you are using devices that should not be cached, enable this feature to set aside some memory from caching. Otherwise, you can leave this entry disabled.

Non-Cacheable Block-2 Size   This is the same function as Non-Cacheable Block-1 Size and is normally left disabled.

RAS Active Time   This is the amount of time a RAS signal can be kept open for multiple accesses. Higher figures will improve system performance.

RAS Precharge Time   This is the time interval during which the *Row Access Strobe* (RAS) signal to DRAM is held low for normal read and write cycles. This is the minimum interval between completing one read or write and starting another from the same (nonpage mode) DRAM. Advanced techniques such as memory interleaving or the use of page mode DRAM are often used to avoid this delay. The RAS Precharge value is typically about the same as the RAM access time. For a 33 MHz CPU, an entry of 4 is a good choice, while lower values should be selected for slower speeds.

RAS-to-CAS Delay Time   This is the amount of time a CAS is performed after a RAS. Lower figures are better for system performance, but some DRAM will not support low figures.

Refresh RAS Active Time   This is the amount of active time needed for Row Access Strobe during refresh. Lower entries are usually better.

Refresh Value   The lower this value is, the better the performance.

Single ALE Enable   *Address Latch Enable* (ALE) is an ISA Bus Signal (Pin B28) that indicates that a valid address is posted on the bus, and this bus is used to communicate with 8- and 16-bit peripheral cards. Some chipsets have the capability to support an enhanced mode in which multiple ALE assertions may be made during a single bus cycle. Single ALE Enable enables or disables this capability. Since this feature may slow the video bus if enabled, it is generally set as disabled (no).

Slow Memory Refresh Divider   If you can extend the refresh cycles of your system (using techniques like Slow Refresh), you can free more CPU time, and system performance improves. This feature allows you to select a divider that slows the refresh cycles. If you slow the refresh too much, you'll get parity errors and system crashes.

Slow Refresh   This option reduces the frequency of RAM refresh. This increases system performance slightly due to the reduced contention between the CPU and refresh circuitry, but not all RAM types necessarily support these reduced refresh rates (in which case you will get parity errors and system crashes). Many systems enable the slow refresh by default.

 Here's a tip for mobile PC users—refresh cycles take power, so using Slow Refresh to reduce the number of refresh cycles can save power.

Staggered Refresh   When enabled, refresh is performed on memory banks sequentially. This results in less power consumption and less interference between memory banks. Many systems enable Staggered Refresh by default.

Tag RAM Includes Dirty   When enabled, the cache is not replaced during cycles, simply overwritten. This results in a performance increase. However, the maximum range of cacheable memory is cut in half because a bit is needed as a "dirty bit" tag. In general, you can leave this feature disabled unless you have little system RAM.

Video BIOS Area Cacheable   This feature can enable or disable caching the video BIOS. Caching the video BIOS can often enhance video performance, but with many of today's accelerated video cards, it may be necessary to prevent caching.

CONFIGURING PLUG-AND-PLAY/PCI

Plug-and-play (PnP) and the PCI (Peripheral Component Interconnect) bus are two tightly related features designed to ease the configuration burden of PC devices. They provide modern devices with a high-performance bus capable of working directly with the CPU and main memory. However, plug-and-play and PCI features must be configured properly in BIOS in order to ensure trouble-free operation. This part of the chapter explains the options used to configure PCI slots and PnP behavior.

Action When Write Buffer Full   This feature sets the behavior of the system when the write buffer is full. By default, the system will immediately retry (rather than wait for it to be emptied).

AT/ISA Bus Clock Frequency   This is the AT bus speed in a PCI system. Select a divisor that will give you a bus speed closest to 8.33 MHz (depending on the speed of the PCI bus). In some systems, the ISA bus speed is set independently (asynchronously) from the bus clock.

Base I/O Address   This entry lists the base of the I/O address range from which the PCI device resource requests are satisfied.

Base Memory Address   This entry lists the start of the 32-bit memory address range from which the PCI device resource requests are satisfied.

Burst Copy-Back Option   When this feature is enabled, if a cache miss occurs, the chipset will initiate a second, burst cache line fill from main memory to the cache—the goal being to maintain the status of the cache.

Byte Merge Support (Sometimes Called "Byte Merging")   Eight-bit or 16-bit data traveling from the CPU to the PCI bus is held in a buffer where it is accumulated, or merged, into 32-bit data, giving faster overall performance. In this case, enabling this feature means that CPU-PCI writes are buffered.

Byte Merging   This feature allows writes to sequential memory addresses to be merged into one PCI-to-memory operation, which increases performance for older applications that write to video memory in bytes rather than words. This feature is not supported well on all PCI video cards. Enable this feature unless you encounter graphics problems.

Configuration Mode   This entry sets the method by which information about legacy cards is conveyed to the system:

- **Use ICU**   The BIOS depends on information provided by plug-and-play software (such as the Configuration Manager or ISA Configuration Utility). Only select this if you have the utilities needed.
- **Use Setup Utility**   The BIOS depends on information provided in the CMOS Setup routine—don't use configuration utilities.

CPU Burst Write Assembly   The Intel 450GX/KX Orion chipset maintains four posted write buffers. When this feature is enabled, the chipset can assemble long PCI bursts from the data held in them. By default, the feature is disabled.

CPU Dynamic-Fast-Cycle   This feature gives you faster access to the ISA bus. When the CPU issues a bus cycle, the PCI bus examines the command to determine if a PCI agent claims it. If not, then an ISA bus cycle is initiated. The Dynamic-Fast-Cycle then allows for faster access to the ISA bus by decreasing the latency (or delay) between the original CPU command and the beginning of the ISA cycle.

CPU Line Read   This feature enables or disables (default) full CPU line reads.

CPU Line Read Multiple   A line read means that the CPU is reading a full cache line. When a cache line is full, it holds 32 bytes (eight DWORDS) of data. Because the line is full, the system knows exactly how much data it will be reading and doesn't need to wait for an end-of-data signal, freeing it to do other things. When this feature is enabled, the system is allowed to read more than one full cache line at a time. The default is disabled.

CPU Line Read Prefetch   When this feature is enabled, the system is allowed to prefetch the next read instruction and to initiate the next process.

CPU Master DEVSEL# Timeout   When the CPU initiates a master cycle using an address (target) that has not been mapped to PCI/VESA or ISA space, the system will monitor the DEVSEL (device select) pin for a period of time to see if any device claims the cycle. This entry allows you to determine how long the system will wait before timing out. Choices are 3 PCICLK, 4 PCICLK, 5 PCICLK, and 6 PCICLK (default).

CPU Master Fast Interface   This entry enables or disables what is known as a "fast back-to-back" interface when the CPU operates as a bus master. When enabled, consecutive reads/writes are interpreted as the CPU high-performance burst mode.

CPU Master Post-W/R Buffer   When the CPU operates as a bus master for either memory access or I/O, this entry controls its ability to use a high-speed posted write buffer. Choices are N/A, 1, 2, and 4 (default).

CPU Master Post-W/R Burst Mode   When the CPU operates as a bus master for either memory access or I/O, this entry controls its ability to use a high-speed burst mode for posted writes to a buffer.

CPU Memory Sample Point   This feature allows you to select the cycle checkpoint, which is where memory decoding and cache hit/miss checking takes place. Each selection indicates that the check takes place at the end of a CPU cycle, with one wait-state indicating more time for checking to take place than zero wait-states. A longer check time allows for greater stability at the expense of some performance.

CPU/PCI Post Write Delay   This is the delay time before the CPU writes data into the PCI bus.

CPU/PCI Write Phase   This feature determines the turnaround between the address and data phases of the CPU master to PCI slave writes. Choices are 1 LCLK (default) or 0 LCLK.

CPU Pipelined Function   This feature allows the system controller to signal the CPU for a new memory address even before all data transfers for the current cycle are complete. This results in increased data throughput. The default is usually disabled, so pipelining is off. Enabled means that address pipelining is active.

CPU Read Multiple Prefetch   A prefetch occurs during a process (such as reading from the PCI bus or memory) when the chipset peeks at the next instruction and actually begins the next read. The Intel 450GX/KX Orion chipset has four read lines. A multiple prefetch means the chipset can initiate more than one prefetch during a process. By default, the feature is disabled.

CPU-to-PCI Burst Memory Write   When enabled, back-to-back sequential CPU memory write cycles to PCI are translated to PCI burst memory write cycles. Otherwise, each single write to PCI will have an associated FRAME# sequence. Keeping this feature enabled is best for performance, but some nonstandard PCI cards (for example, VGA adapters) may have problems.

CPU-to-PCI Post/Burst   Data from the CPU to the PCI bus can be posted (buffered by the controller) and/or burst. This entry sets the methods used:

- ■ **POST/CON.BURST**   Posting and bursting supported (default)
- ■ **NONE/NONE**   Neither supported
- ■ **POST/NONE**   Posting but not bursting supported

CPU-to-PCI Post Memory Write   This feature enables up to four double words (DW) of data to be posted to PCI. Otherwise, not only is buffering disabled, but completion of CPU writes also is limited. (The CPU write does not complete until the PCI transaction completes.) Keeping this feature enabled is best for performance.

CPU-to-PCI Read Buffer (or PCI-to-CPU Write Buffer)   When enabled, up to four double words (DW) can be read from the PCI bus without interrupting the CPU. When disabled, a write buffer is not used, and the CPU read cycle will not be completed until the PCI bus signals that it is ready to receive the data. Enabling the buffer is best for system performance.

CPU-to-PCI Read-Burst   When enabled (on), the PCI bus will interpret CPU read cycles as the PCI burst protocol, meaning that back-to-back sequential CPU memory read cycles addressed to the PCI will be translated into fast PCI burst memory cycles. Performance is improved, but some nonstandard PCI adapters (for example, VGA adapters) may experience problems.

CPU-to-PCI Read-Line   When enabled (on), more time will be allocated for data setup with faster CPUs. This feature may only be required if you add an Intel OverDrive processor to your 486-class system.

CPU-to-PCI Write Buffer   This is the same as CPU-to-PCI Read Buffer, only for writing.

CPU-to-PCI Write Posting   The Intel 450GX/KX Orion chipset maintains its own internal read and write buffers that are used to help compensate for the speed differences between the CPU and the PCI bus.

When this feature is enabled, writes from the CPU to the PCI bus will be buffered. When disabled (default), the writes will not be buffered, and the CPU will be forced to wait until the write is completed.

Delay for SCSI/HDD (or SCSI Boot Delay)   This is the length of time (in seconds) that the BIOS will wait for the SCSI hard disk to be ready for operation. If the hard drive is not ready, the PCI SCSI BIOS might not detect the hard drive correctly. The range is from 0 to 60 seconds.

DMA Line Buffer   This feature allows DMA data to be stored in a buffer so PCI bus operations are not interrupted. Disabled means that the line buffer for DMA is in single-transaction mode. Enabled allows it to operate in an 8-byte transaction mode for greater efficiency. This feature should be enabled for best system performance.

DMA Line Buffer Mode   This feature allows DMA data to be stored in a buffer so as not to interrupt the PCI bus. When the Standard mode is selected, the line buffer is in single-transaction mode. When the Enhanced mode is selected, the feature allows it to operate in 8-byte transaction mode.

E8000 32K Accessible   This 64KB area of upper memory is used for BIOS purposes on PS/2s, 32-bit operating systems, and plug-and-play. This setting allows the second 32KB page to be used for other purposes when not needed (in the same way that the first 32KB page of the F range is usable after boot-up has finished).

Enable Master   This feature enables the selected device as a PCI bus master and checks whether the card is capable of performing as a PCI master.

Fast Back-to-Back   When this feature is enabled, the PCI bus will interpret CPU read cycles as the PCI burst protocol, meaning that back-to-back sequential CPU memory read cycles addressed to the PCI will be translated into the fast PCI burst memory cycles. By default the feature is enabled.

FRAMEJ Generation   When the PCI bus bridge is acting as a PCI Master and receiving data from the CPU, a fast CPU-to-PCI buffer will be enabled if this selection is also enabled. Using the buffer allows the CPU to complete a write even though the data has not been delivered to the PCI bus. This reduces the number of CPU cycles involved and speeds overall processing:

- Normal Buffering not employed (default)
- Fast Buffer used for CPU-to-PCI writes

HCLK PCICLK   This entry allows you to set the host CLK/PCI CLK divider. The options are AUTO, 1-1, and 1-1.5.

IBC DEVSEL# Decoding   This feature allows you to set the type of decoding used by the *ISA Bridge Controller* (IBC) to determine which device to select. The longer the decoding cycle, the better chance the IBC has to correctly decode the commands. Choices are Fast, Medium, and Slow (default).

IDE Buffer for DOS and Windows   When enabled, this feature provides IDE read-ahead and posted-write buffers, so you can increase throughput to and from IDE devices by buffering reads and writes. However, this feature may actually slow older devices, so it should be disabled.

IDE Master (Slave) PIO Mode   This option changes the IDE data transfer speed to Mode 0–4 or Auto. Rather than have the BIOS issue commands to effect transfers to or from the disk drive,

PIO allows the BIOS to tell the controller what it wants, and then lets the controller and the CPU perform the complete task by themselves. Modes 1–4 are available for EIDE systems, but set to Auto for an automatic configuration.

I/O Cycle Post-Write   When this feature is enabled (default), data being written during an I/O cycle will be buffered for faster performance.

I/O Cycle Recovery   When enabled, the PCI bus will be allowed a recovery period for back-to-back I/O (which slows back-to-back data transfers). It's like adding wait-states to the PCI bus, so disable this feature (default) for best performance.

I/O Recovery Period   This feature sets the length of time for the I/O Cycle Recovery—a programmed delay that allows the PCI bus to exchange data with the slower ISA bus without data errors. The range is from 0 to 1.75 microseconds in 0.25-microsecond intervals. Typical settings include

2 BCLK	Two BCLKs (default)
4 BCLK	Four BCLKs
8 BCLK	Eight BCLKs
12 BCLK	Twelve BCLKs

IRQ 3–IRQ 15   These entries are used to list what IRQs are in use (or reserved) by ISA legacy cards. If you don't use specific IRQs, set the respective entries to Available. Otherwise, set Used by ISA Card, which means that nothing else can use it.

IRQ Line   If you have installed a device requiring an IRQ service into the given PCI slot, use this entry to inform the PCI bus which IRQ it should initiate. Choices range from IRQ 3 through IRQ 15.

ISA Linear Frame Buffer   This feature enables a buffer if you use an ISA card that features a linear frame buffer (for example, a second video card for AutoCAD). The buffer address will be set automatically.

ISA Master Line Buffer   ISA master buffers are designed to isolate the slower ISA I/O operations from the PCI bus for better performance. Keeping this feature disabled means the buffer for ISA master transaction is in single mode. Enabling this feature means it is in 8-byte mode that increases the ISA master's performance.

ISA Shared Memory Size   This option sets a block of system memory that will not be shadowed. This feature should normally be disabled unless you have an ISA card that uses the upper memory area. If you enable this feature, you'll also need to configure the ISA Shared Memory Base Address. Enter the base address—if you choose 64K, you can only choose D000h or below.

ISA VGA Frame Buffer Size (or ISA LFB Size)   This feature allows you to use a VGA frame buffer and 16MB of RAM at the same time. The system will allow access to the graphics card through a "hole" in its own memory map. In other words, access to addresses within this hole will be directed to the ISA bus instead of main memory. This feature should be set to disabled unless you're using an ISA card with more than 64KB of memory that needs to be accessed by the CPU, *and* you are not using the plug-and-play utilities. If you have less than 8MB of memory, or use MS-DOS, this feature will be ignored.

Keyboard Controller Clock   This entry sets the speed of the keyboard controller (PCICLKI = PCI bus speed). Typical options are

7.16 MHz	(Default)
PCICLKI/2	1/2 PCICLKI
PCICLKI/3	1/3 PCICLKI
PCICLKI/4	1/4 PCICLKI

Latency for CPU-to-PCI Write   This is the delay time before a CPU writes data to the PCI bus.

Latency from ADS# Status   This feature allows you to configure how long the CPU waits for the *Address Data Status* (ADS). It determines the CPU-to-PCI POST write speed. When set to 3T, this is 5T for each double word. With 2T (default), it is 4T per double word. For a quad word (Qword) PCI memory write, the rate is 7T (2T) or 8T (3T). The default should be correct, but if you add a faster CPU to your system, you may find it necessary to increase it. The choices are 3T (three CPU clocks) or 2T (two CPU clocks, the default).

Latency Timer (PCI Clocks)   This entry controls the length of time an agent on the PCI bus can hold the bus when another device has requested it. Since the PCI bus runs faster than the ISA bus, the PCI bus must be slowed during interactions with it. This setting allows you to define how long the PCI bus will delay for a transaction between the given PCI slot and the ISA bus. This number depends on the PCI master device in use, and ranges from 0 to 255. The default is often 66, but 40 is a good place to start. Smaller values result in faster access to the bus (with better response times), but bandwidth and data throughput become lower. Normally, you'd leave this setting alone unless you're working with latency-sensitive devices (for example, audio cards or network cards with small buffers).

Latency Timer Value   This is the maximum number of PCI bus clocks that the master may burst. A longer latency time gives the CPU more of a chance to control the bus.

LDEV# Check Point   You will probably not see this entry on current systems. The VESA local device (LDEV#) check point is where the VL-bus device decodes the bus commands and checks for errors within the bus cycle itself:

0	Bus cycle point T1 (default)
1	During the first T2
2	During the second T2
3	During the third T2

LDEVJ Check Point Delay   This feature allows you to select how much time is allocated for checking bus cycle commands. These commands must be decoded to determine whether a local bus device access signal (LDEVJ) is being sent, or an ISA device is being addressed. Increasing the delay increases stability (especially in the VESA subsystem) while very slightly degrading the performance of the ISA subsystem. Settings are in terms of the feedback clock rate (FBCLK2) used in the cache/memory control interface:

1 FBCLK2	One clock
2 FBCLK2	Two clocks (default)
3 FBCLK2	Three clocks

Local Memory Check Point   This entry allows you to select between two techniques for decoding and error checking local bus writes to DRAM during a memory cycle:

Slow	Extra wait-state; better checking (default)
Fast	No extra wait-state used

M1445RDYJ to CPURDYJ   This feature determines whether the PCI Ready signal is to be synchronized by the CPU clock's ready signal or bypassed (default).

Master Arbitration Protocol   This is the method by which the PCI bus determines which bus master device gains access to the bus.

Master IOCHRDY   When this feature is enabled, it allows the system to monitor for a VESA master request to generate an I/O channel ready (IOCHRDY) signal.

Master Retry Timer   This feature sets how long the CPU master will attempt a PCI cycle before the cycle is unmasked (terminated). The choices are measured in PCICLKs with the PCI timer. Values are 10 (default), 18, 34, or 66 PCICLKs.

Max. Burstable Range   This feature sets the size of the maximum range of contiguous memory that can be addressed by a burst from the PCI bus. Longer burst durations should improve performance.

Memory Hole Size   This entry defines the size of the memory hole. Options are 1MB, 2MB, 4MB, 8MB, and disabled. These are the amounts below 16MB that are assigned to the AT bus and are reserved for ISA cards.

Memory Hole Start Address   This entry defines where the memory hole starts. The selections are from 1MB to 15MB. This entry is not used if the memory hole is disabled.

Memory Map Hole Start/End Address   This entry determines where the hole starts and depends on the ISA LFB Size. If you can change it, the base address should be 16MB minus the buffer size. See "ISA VGA Frame Buffer Size" earlier.

Memory Start Address   This feature is for devices with their own memory that use part of the CPU's memory address space. It allows you to determine the starting point in memory where PCI device memory will be mapped.

Multimedia Mode   This feature enables or disables palette snooping for multimedia cards.

Onboard PCI/SCSI BIOS   You should enable this feature if your system motherboard had a built-in SCSI controller attached to the PCI bus, and you want to boot from it.

Parity   When enabled, this feature allows parity checking of PCI devices.

PCI Arbiter Mode   Devices gain access to the PCI bus through arbitration. There are two modes, mode 1 (default) and mode 2. The idea is to minimize the time it takes to gain control of the bus and move data. Generally, mode 1 should be sufficient, but try mode 2 if you encounter problems with PCI bus access.

PCI Arbit. Rotate Priority   Typically, the system manages (or arbitrates) access to the PCI bus on a first-come-first-served basis. When priority is rotated, once a device gains control of the bus, it is assigned the lowest priority, and every other device is moved up one in the priority queue. This helps to prevent any one device from monopolizing the PCI bus.

PCI Bursting   When this feature is enabled, consecutive writes from the CPU will be regarded as a PCI burst cycle. This feature should normally be enabled.

PCI Bus Parking   This is a sort of bus mastering—a device parking on the PCI bus has full control of the bus for a short time. This feature improves performance when that device is being used, but excludes others. Try enabling this feature with network cards and hard disk controllers.

PCI CLK   This feature determines whether the PCI clock is tightly synchronized with the CPU clock, or is asynchronous. If your CPU, motherboard, and PCI bus are running at multiple speeds of each other (for example, Pentium 120 MHz, 60 MHz, and 30 MHz PCI bus), choose to synchronize.

PCI Clock Frequency   This entry allows you to set the clock rate for the PCI bus, which can operate between 0 and 33 MHz. CPUCLK/3 means the PCI bus was operating at 11 MHz (33/3 = 11). The typical entries are

CPUCLK/15	CPU speed/1.5 (default)
CPUCLK/3	CPU speed/3
14 MHz	14 MHz
CPUCLK/2	CPU speed/2

PCI Concurrency   When enabled, this means that more than one PCI device can be active at a time. With Intel chipsets, it allocates memory bus cycles to a PCI controller while an ISA operation (such as bus-mastered DMA) is taking place, which normally requires constant attention. This involves turning on additional read and write buffering in the chipset. The PCI bus can also obtain access cycles for small data transfers without the delays caused by renegotiating bus access for each part of the transfer, so the feature is meant to improve performance and consistency.

PCI Cycle Cache Hit   This option defines how the cache is refreshed during PCI operation. Normal refresh will produce a cache refresh during normal PCI cycles. Fast refresh will produce a cache refresh without a PCI cycle for CAS. Fast performance is usually better.

PCI Device, Slot 1/2/3   This feature enables I/O and memory cycle decoding for PCI slots. There are three options: Enable (enables the device as a slave PCI device), Enable Master (enables the device as a master PCI device), and Use Default Latency Timer. If this is enabled (yes), you don't need to set the Latency Timer value.

PCI Dynamic Decoding   When this feature is enabled, the system can remember the PCI command that has just been requested. If subsequent commands fall within the same address space, the cycle will be automatically interpreted as a PCI command.

PCI IDE 2nd Channel   Disable this feature if you're not using the second channel on the PCI IDE card. This frees up IRQ 15. Otherwise, you will lose IRQ 15 on the ISA slots.

PCI (IDE) Bursting   This is similar to PCI Bursting, but this one enables burst mode access to video memory over the PCI bus. The CPU provides the first address, and consecutive data is transferred at one word per clock. The device must support burst mode.

PCI IDE IRQ Map To   This option allows you to configure your system to the type of IDE disk controller. An ISA device is assumed. If you have a PCI IDE controller, this setting allows you to specify which slot has the controller and which PCI INT# (A, B, C, or D) is associated with the connected hard drives. Note that this refers to the hard disk rather than individual partitions. Since each IDE controller supports two drives, you can select the INT# for each. Also note that the primary channel has a lower interrupt than the secondary channel. There are four modes:

- **PCI-Auto**   If the IDE is detected by the BIOS on one of the PCI slots, then the appropriate INT# channel will be assigned to IRQ 14.
- **PCI-Slot X**   If the IDE is not detected, you can manually select the slot.
- **Primary IDE INT#, Secondary IDE INT#**   This assigns two INT# channels for primary and secondary channels (if supported).
- **ISA**   This option assigns no IRQs to PCI slots. Use this mode for PCI IDE cards that connect IRQs 14 and 15 directly from an ISA slot using a table from a legacy paddle board.

PCI IDE Prefetch Buffers   This feature allows you to enable or disable a set of prefetch buffers in the PCI IDE controller. You may need to disable this feature with an operating system (like Windows NT) that doesn't use the BIOS to access the hard disk and that doesn't disable interrupts when completing a programmed I/O operation. Disabling also prevents errors with faulty PCI-IDE interface chips that can corrupt data on the hard disk (as can happen with true 32-bit operating systems). You can usually leave this feature disabled.

PCI I/O Start Address   The I/O devices make themselves accessible by occupying an address space. This allows you to make additional room for older ISA devices by defining the I/O start address for the PCI devices.

PCI IRQ Activated By   This lists the method by which the PCI bus recognizes an IRQ request (Level or Edge). Use the default entries unless advised otherwise by your PCI device manufacturer, or if you have a PCI device that only recognizes one of these methods.

PCI-ISA BCLK Divider   This entry allows you to set the PCI Bus CLK/ISA Bus CLK divider. The options are AUTO, PCICLK1/3, PCICLK1/2, and PCICLK1/4.

PCI Master Accesses Shadow RAM   This feature enables the shadowing of a ROM on a PCI master for better performance.

PCI Master Burst Mode   When a PCI device operates as a bus master for either memory access or I/O, this entry controls its use of a high-speed burst mode for posted writes to a buffer.

PCI Master DEVSEL# Timeout   When a PCI device initiates a master cycle using an address (target) that has not been mapped to PCI/VESA or ISA space, the system will monitor the DEVSEL (device select) pin for a period of time to see if any device claims the cycle. This entry allows you to determine how long the system will wait before timing out. Choices are 3 PCICLK, 4 PCICLK (default), 5 PCICLK, and 6 PCICLK.

PCI Master Fast Interface   This feature enables or disables what is known as a "fast back-to-back" interface when a PCI device operates as a bus master. When enabled, consecutive reads/writes are interpreted as the PCI high-performance burst mode.

PCI Master Latency   This option sets the time that a PCI master can control the bus. If your PCI master controls the bus for too long, there is less time for the CPU to control it. A longer latency time gives the CPU more time to control the PCI bus.

PCI Master Post-W/R Buffer   When a PCI device operates as a bus master for either memory access or I/O, this entry controls its use of a high-speed posted write buffer. Choices are N/A, 1, 2, and 4 (default).

PCI Master Timing Mode   This entry gives you the ability to choose between two timing modes: 0 (default) and 1.

PCI Post-Write Fast   When this feature is enabled (default), data being written during a PCI cycle will be buffered for faster performance.

PCI Preempt Timer   This entry sets the length of time before one PCI master preempts another when a service request has been pending. Typical entries are

Disabled	No preemption (default)
260 LCLKs	Preempt after 260 LCLKs
132 LCLKs	Preempt after 132 LCLKs
68 LCLKs	Preempt after 68 LCLKs
36 LCLKs	Preempt after 36 LCLKs
20 LCLKs	Preempt after 20 LCLKs
12 LCLKs	Preempt after 12 LCLKs
5 LCLKs	Preempt after 5 LCLKs

PCI Pre-Snoop   Pre-snooping is a technique by which a PCI master can continue to burst to the local memory until a 4KB page boundary is reached, rather than just a line boundary. This feature can be enabled.

PCI Slot x INTx   Use this entry to assign PCI interrupts (INT#s) to specific PCI slots:

■ **Edge/Level Select**   Once an interrupt is assigned with PCI Slot x INTx, this option programs PCI IRQs to single-edge or logic-level triggering modes. Most PCI cards use level triggering, while most ISA cards use edge triggering. However, try selecting edge triggering for PCI IDE.

PCI Streaming   Data is typically moved to and from memory and between devices in discrete chunks of limited sizes, because the CPU is involved. On the PCI bus, data can be "streamed"—that is, much larger chunks can be moved without the CPU being used. This feature should be enabled for best performance.

PCI-to-CPU Write Pending   This feature sets the behavior of the system when the write buffer is full. By default, the system will immediately retry. (But you can set it to wait for the buffer to be emptied before retrying.)

PCI-to-DRAM Buffer   When enabled, this feature improves PCI-to-DRAM performance by allowing data to be stored if a destination is busy. Buffers are needed for this feature because the PCI bus is separate from the CPU.

PCI-to-ISA Write Buffer   When enabled, the system will temporarily write data to a buffer so the CPU is not interrupted. When disabled, the memory write cycle for the PCI bus will be directed to the slower ISA bus. As a result, keeping this feature enabled is best for performance.

PCI/VGA Palette Snoop   This feature alters the VGA palette setting while graphic signals pass through the feature connector of PCI VGA card and are processed by the MPEG card. VGA snooping is used by multimedia video devices (for example, video capture boards) to look ahead at the video controller (VGA device) to see what color palette is currently in use. Enable this feature if you have MPEG connections through the VGA feature connector. (This means you can adjust PCI/VGA palettes.) Otherwise, go ahead and disable the feature.

PCI Write-Byte-Merge (or CPU-to-PCI Byte Merge)   When enabled, this allows data sent from the CPU to the PCI bus to be held in a buffer. The chipset will then write the data in the buffer to the PCI bus when appropriate.

Post Write CAS Active   This is the pulse width of the CAS# signal when the PCI master writes to DRAM.

Preempt PCI Master Option   When this feature is enabled, PCI bus operations can be preempted by certain system operations, such as DRAM refresh. Otherwise, they can take place concurrently.

Primary Frame Buffer   When this feature is enabled, the system can use unreserved memory as a primary frame buffer. Unlike the VGA frame buffer, this would reduce overall available RAM for applications. The default is usually disabled.

Residence of VGA Card   This option lists whether the VGA card resides on a PCI or VL Bus. Today, the default is PCI, though current systems will usually not include this feature because of the influence of AGP.

Slot X Using INT#   This entry selects an interrupt (INT#) channel for a PCI slot, and there are four (A, B, C, and D) for each one. That is, each PCI bus slot supports interrupts A, B, C, and D. INT#A is allocated automatically, and you would only use #B, #C, and #D if the PCI card needs to use more than one (PCI) interrupt service. For example, select #D if your PCI card needs four interrupts. Often, it is simplest to use the Auto mode.

Snoop Ahead   This feature is only applicable if the cache is enabled. When enabled, PCI bus masters can monitor the VGA palette registers for direct writes and translate them into PCI burst protocol for greater speed, which can enhance the performance of multimedia video.

Snoop Filter (or Cache Snoop Filter)   This feature saves the need for multiple inquiries to the same line if it was checked previously. When enabled, cache snoop filters ensure data integrity (cache coherency) while reducing the snoop frequency to a minimum.

State Machines   The chipset uses four state machines to manage specific CPU and/or PCI operations. Each can be thought of as a highly optimized process center designed to handle specific operations. Generally, each operation involves a master device and the bus it wishes to employ. The four state machines are CPU master to CPU bus (CC), CPU master to PCI bus (CP), PCI master to PCI bus (PP), and PCI master to CPU bus (PC). Each state machine has the following settings:

- **Address 0 WS**   This refers to the length of time the system will delay while the transaction address is decoded. When enabled, there will be no delay.
- **Data Write 0 WS**   This is the length of time the system will delay while data is being written to the target address. When enabled, there will be no delay.
- **Data Read 0 WS**   This is the length of time the system will delay while data is being read from the target address. When enabled, there will be no delay.

Stop CPU when PCI Flush   When this feature is enabled, the CPU will be stopped when the PCI bus is being flushed of data. Disabling this feature (default) allows the CPU to continue processing, giving better system performance.

Stop CPU at PCI Master   When this feature is enabled, the CPU will be stopped when the PCI bus master is operating on the bus. Disabling this feature (default) allows the CPU to continue processing, giving better system performance.

Use Default Latency Timer Value   This option determines whether the default value for the latency timer will be loaded or the succeeding latency timer value will be used. If yes is selected (default), no further programming is needed for the latency timer value.

VESA Master Cycle ADSJ   This feature allows you to increase the length of time the VESA Master has in order to decode bus commands. Typical choices are Normal (default) and Long.

VGA 128K Range Attribute   When this feature is enabled, it allows the chipset to apply features like CPU-to-PCI Byte Merge and CPU-to-PCI Prefetch to VGA memory range A0000H–BFFFFH. When enabled, the VGA receives CPU-to-PCI functions. When disabled, the system retains the standard VGA interface.

VGA Performance Mode   When this feature is enabled, the VGA memory range of A0000h–B0000h will use a special set of performance features. This feature has little or no effect using video modes beyond the standard VGA most commonly used for Windows, OS/2, UNIX, and so on, but this memory range is heavily used by games.

VGA Type   This entry is used when the video BIOS is being shadowed. The BIOS uses this information to determine which bus to use. Choices are Standard (default), PCI, and ISA/VESA.

Video Palette Snoop   This feature controls how a PCI graphics card can snoop write cycles to an ISA video card's color palette registers. Snooping essentially means interfering with a device. This is a powerful performance option, so only disable it if (1) an ISA card connects to a PCI graphics card through a VESA connector, (2) the ISA card connects to a color monitor, and (3) the ISA card uses the RAMDAC on the PCI card, and palette snooping (RAMDAC shadowing) is not operative on the PCI card.

Xth Available IRQ   This feature selects (maps) an IRQ for one of the available INT#s (A, B, C, or D). There are eleven selections (3, 4, 5, 6, 7, 9, 10, 11, 12, 14, and 15). The "1st available IRQ" means the BIOS will assign this IRQ to the first PCI slots (order is 1, 2, 3, 4), and so on. N/A means the particular IRQ has been assigned to the ISA bus and is therefore not available to a PCI slot.

CONFIGURING SECURITY

Although few employees must share a PC today, companies recognize the high cost of maintaining and troubleshooting systems that are used by everyday workers. Modern BIOS versions allow a series of passwords and protective restrictions to be applied. This can prevent unauthorized users from accessing or powering-up a system, prevent changes from being made to the CMOS Setup, and so on. Security measures can often help to prevent accidental (or malicious) changes to a system that may require time-consuming and costly labor to fix. This section outlines many of the common security features that you might encounter.

Diskette Access   When enabled, the system requires a password to boot from or access the floppy disk. This is a handy protective measure that can prevent malicious users from booting from (or introducing a virus through) a floppy disk.

Fixed Disk Boot Sector   This may be normal or write protected. In the write-protected mode, no software may write to the boot sector of a hard drive, and the drive is effectively protected from boot sector viruses. You will require a password to Format or FDISK the hard disk.

Password on Boot   When enabled, the boot process will halt and ask for the supervisor password (which must be previously set). If the supervisor password is set and this option is disabled, the BIOS assumes a user is booting.

Set Supervisor Password   This allows you to enter a password of up to about seven alphanumeric characters. Pressing ENTER displays a dialog for entering the supervisor password. In most current system designs, this password gives full access to CMOS Setup menus.

Set User Password   This allows you to enter a password of up to about seven alphanumeric characters. Pressing ENTER displays the dialog box for entering the user password. In most current system designs, this password gives limited access to CMOS Setup menus.

System Backup Reminder/Virus Check Reminder   This feature displays a message during boot-up asking (Y/N) if you have backed up the system/scanned it for viruses. The typical options for this feature are Disabled, Daily, Weekly, or Monthly. Daily displays the message on the first boot of the day, Weekly on the first boot after Sunday, and Monthly on the first boot of the month.

CONFIGURING POWER MANAGEMENT

Energy is expensive, and in a world of dwindling energy reserves and escalating energy demands, PCs are often required to work longer hours and pack in more features, yet be energy efficient. Today's PCs use far less energy than their early counterparts—largely because there are fewer components—but also because PCs employ a wide range of energy-saving techniques designed to reduce power demands as the system remains idle for a time. (These are collectively known as "green PCs.") Most power management features are selectable through the CMOS Setup. This part of the chapter illustrates how to deal with typical power management features.

Doze Timer   This feature sets the time delay before the system will reduce 80 percent of its activity. Ten to 20 minutes is usually the preferred time.

Green Timer of Main Board   This feature allows you to set the time before a CPU of an idle system will shut down. The usual options are Disabled or a time interval ranging from 1 to 15 minutes. As a rule, 5 to 10 minutes is recommended.

HDD Standby Timer   This feature sets the time after which the hard disk of an HDD idle system (no HDD access) will shut down (or spin down). Ten to 20 minutes is usually the preferred time.

Modem Use IRQ   Enter the IRQ assigned to the modem on your system (if any). If there is activity on the selected IRQ, the system will "awaken." This allows features such as "wake on ring."

PM Control by APM   If disabled, the system BIOS will ignore APM when managing the system power. When enabled, system BIOS will wait for an APM prompt before it enters any power management mode (for example, doze, standby, or suspend). If APM is installed and there is a task running (even if the timer has timed out), the APM will not prompt the BIOS to put the system into any power-saving mode.

PM Wake-Up Events   You can specify which events will wake the system and take it out of power-saving mode. When an event is disabled, the event's activity will not affect the PM timers or wake the system. When an event is enabled, the specified activity will reset the PM timers and wake the system. For example, if you have a modem on IRQ3, you can turn on IRQ3 as a wake-up event, so an interrupt from the modem can wake the system. Conversely, you may wish to turn off IRQ12 (the PS/2 mouse) as a wake-up event, so accidentally brushing the mouse does not awaken the system. By default, keyboard activity is the typical wake-up event.

Power Management Scheme   This allows you to define the amount of power management taking place in the system:

- **Disabled**   Global power management will be disabled.
- **User Define**   Users can define their own power management settings.
- **Min Saving**   Predefined timer values are used such that all timers are in their maximum value.
- **Max Saving**   Predefined timer values are used such that all timers are in their minimum value.

Standby Timer   This feature sets the time delay before the system will reduce 92 percent of its activity. Thirty to 45 minutes is usually the preferred time.

Suspend Switch   This setting is used for enabling or disabling the "hardware suspend" switch on the motherboard. If your motherboard has a hardware suspend switch, enabling this option activates the suspend switch, and disabling this option deactivates the suspend switch.

Suspend Timer   This feature sets the time after which the system goes into the most inactive state possible (which is 99 percent). Once this state is entered, the system will require a warm-up period so the CPU, hard disk, and monitor may go online. Forty-five to 60 minutes is usually the preferred time.

System Slow Down   This feature will slow the CPU clock dramatically after the timer has elapsed—reducing CPU heating and saving a great deal of power. A time anywhere from 30 to 60 minutes is usually acceptable.

Video Off Option   This selects how power management modes will turn off the display.

- **Always on**   System BIOS will never turn off the display.

- **Suspend off**   Display is off when system is in suspend mode.
- **Susp, Stby off**   Display is off when system is in standby or suspend mode.
- **All modes off**   Display is off when system is in doze, standby, or suspend mode.

Making Use of
BIOS Autoconfiguration

Virtually all current motherboards provide a default or autoconfiguration option—taking most of BIOS setup problems out of the technician's hands. In the majority of cases, an autoconfigured BIOS will work just fine. But you must remember that autoconfiguration is not an optimization of the system's setup, but rather a set of efficient settings that should ensure a working system. You will have to disable this setting if you want to tweak the CMOS Setup yourself. (Otherwise, your settings will be ignored.) If you're stuck with CMOS settings, you should be able to get the system running by using system defaults. There are two levels of default you can work with: BIOS defaults and power-on defaults.

BIOS DEFAULTS

BIOS defaults may not be (and usually aren't) tuned for your particular motherboard or chipset, but they give a reasonable chance of getting the system to boot. The BIOS default settings are also a good place to start fine-tuning your system. BIOS defaults can also recover your setup if you enter completely unacceptable values in CMOS Setup and the system refuses to boot. Of course, you'll have to start optimizing all over again.

POWER-ON DEFAULTS

When powering-up the system, the BIOS puts the system into the most conservative state possible—turbo off, all caches disabled, all wait-states set to maximum, and so on. This ensures that you can always enter CMOS Setup. This mode is particularly useful if the settings returned by BIOS defaults fail. If the system still refuses to boot, then there is a serious hardware issue with the motherboard (or elsewhere in the system) that you will need to address first.

Backing Up CMOS RAM

Taken all together, CMOS settings are hardly intuitive. Determining the proper settings for optimum system performance requires an understanding of each CMOS variable and a detailed knowledge of the individual system. Unfortunately, most end users (and even most professional technicians) are not familiar enough with the intricacies of any given PC or the meaning of each setup entry, to adequately reconstruct the CMOS Setup should the backup battery ever fail. When the battery does fail (it *will* eventually), it may take an unprepared user (or unfortunate technician) hours to rediscover settings that otherwise could be entered in a matter of minutes. This is the real tragedy—with just a few minutes of advance planning, CMOS contents can be backed up with complete safely. There are two methods of backing up CMOS contents: hard copy backup and file backup.

Today, lost CMOS settings can be recovered through the use of BIOS Defaults as mentioned earlier.

Hard copy backup is just as the name implies—CMOS contents are recorded on paper that is filed away or taped to the inside of the PC enclosure. The simplest method of hard copy backup is to connect the PC to a printer and capture a PRINTSCREEN of each data screen. This provides a fast, simple, and permanent record. On the other hand, it may take several minutes to restore the configuration.

File backup is a fairly new alternative that uses a small utility to copy CMOS RAM contents to a data file (usually on floppy disk), then restore the file to CMOS RAM addresses later as needed. Shareware utilities such as CMOS_RAM (available for download at **www.zdnet.com**) are ideal for this kind of support. When saving a CMOS RAM file, be sure to save it to a floppy disk, since losing CMOS contents will often disable the hard drive. The advantage of a backup file is speed. CMOS contents can be restored in a matter of moments.

Regardless of which technique you use to record your CMOS settings, it is important to back up the CMOS contents *each time* you alter the PC's configuration (for example, after adding a new hard drive). Otherwise, the record will no longer reflect the current state of your system.

CMOS Maintenance and Troubleshooting

Although it is very rare for CMOS RAM/RTC devices to fail, there *are* many circumstances where CMOS contents may be lost or corrupted, and system performance may be compromised by a poorly configured CMOS Setup. Beyond the traditional beep and POST codes that suggest a CMOS problem (Chapter 18), or the more recent BIOS error messages (Chapter 7), a wide range of PC symptoms can indicate an improperly or incompletely configured CMOS. This part of the chapter identifies a series of symptoms that can suggest CMOS Setup problems and offers suggestions for corrective action.

TYPICAL CMOS-RELATED SYMPTOMS

The following symptoms highlight many of the most common issues to strike the CMOS RAM/RTC portion of a system.

SYMPTOM 11-1   **Changes to CMOS are not saved after rebooting the PC**   In virtually all cases, you have exited the CMOS Setup routine incorrectly. This is a very common oversight (especially given the proliferation of different BIOS versions and CMOS Setup routines). Try making your changes again, and then be sure to "Save Then Exit and Reboot" from the Setup utility's main menu.

SYMPTOM 11-2   **The system appears to be performing poorly**   The system must be stable. If it crashes frequently, or certain devices refuse to work, you may be dealing with a system conflict in hardware or software. Use a diagnostic tool such as MSD (in DOS) or the Device Manager (in Windows 9x/Me) to help identify possible points of conflict.

If the system is free of hardware or software conflicts, you can focus on performance. Performance is often a subjective evaluation and should first be verified using a benchmark test compared to other similar PCs (identical systems if possible). If you find that your particular system is performing below its optimum level, suspect a CMOS Setup problem. In some cases, the CMOS RAM may have been loaded with its "power-on" or "autoconfiguration" defaults. While defaults will almost always allow the system to function, they will rarely offer top performance. Check the advanced CMOS and chipset setup pages (particularly the memory-, cache-, and bus speed–related entries). Refer to the "Basic CMOS Optimization Tactics" section toward the beginning of this chapter.

SYMPTOM 11-3   **CMOS mismatch errors occur**   These errors occur when the PC equipment found during the POST does not match equipment listed in CMOS. In most cases, the CMOS backup battery has failed and should be replaced. You can then load the CMOS defaults and tweak the setup as necessary to optimize the system (an easy task if you've got a record of the CMOS settings). Otherwise, refer to the "Basic CMOS Optimization Tactics" section earlier in this chapter.

If you've cleared the CMOS Setup (using a "clear" jumper on the motherboard), be sure that you've reset the jumper so as not to continue clearing the CMOS RAM.

SYMPTOM 11-4   **Some drives are not detected during boot**   This happens most often with hard drives or other devices in the Basic CMOS Setup page. In some cases, the device simply may not be listed or entered properly. (For example, you may have forgotten to enter your newly installed hard drive or floppy drive in the CMOS Setup.) In other cases, the drive may need more time to initialize at boot time. Try increasing the "boot delay" or disabling any "quick boot" feature that might be in use.

SYMPTOM 11-5   **The system boots from the hard drive, even though there is a bootable floppy disk in the drive**   Note that the system still boots and runs properly. The floppy disk is fully accessible. (If not, check the floppy drive, power, and signal cables.) This type of issue is usually not a problem, but due instead to an improper boot sequence. Most BIOS versions allow the PC to search through several different drives to locate an operating system and will boot from the first suitable drive where an operating system is found. Chances are that your boot sequence is set to "C: A:," where the C drive is checked first. Since the C drive is connected and functional, the A drive will simply be ignored. To boot from the A drive, you'll need to change the boot sequence to something like "A: C:." Remember to save any changes before exiting the CMOS Setup.

SYMPTOM 11-6   **Power management features are not available**   First, make sure that your BIOS supports power management to begin with. Modern PC power management is typically handled by a combination of BIOS and the operating system (for example, APM under Windows 95 or ACPI under Windows 98/Me). However, power management must be supported by BIOS and enabled under the CMOS Setup in order for the operating system to make use of it. If you can't use power management (or it is not available in the Windows 9x/Me Device Manager under System Devices), it probably isn't enabled in the CMOS Setup. Check the Power Management page of your CMOS Setup (or the Advanced Chipset Setup), and make sure that power management features are enabled. You may also want to review and adjust the various device timeouts as required. When you restart the operating system, you should then be able to configure the corresponding power management features.

SYMPTOM 11-7   **PnP support is not available, or PnP devices do not function properly**   First, make sure that your BIOS supports *plug-and-play* (PnP) standards. If not, you'll need to employ a DOS ISA configuration utility (or ICU) to support any PnP devices in the system. Also make sure that you're using an operating system that supports PnP (for example, Windows 9x/Me). If you can't get support for PnP devices, make sure that PnP support is enabled in the CMOS Setup, and verify that PnP-related settings (such as Configuration Mode or IRQ3-IRQ15) are all configured properly. If necessary, try loading the BIOS defaults for your CMOS Setup, which should give you baseline PnP support if your BIOS and OS support it. Be sure to record your original CMOS settings before attempting to load defaults.

SYMPTOM 11-8   **Devices in some PCI slots are not recognized or not working properly**   First, make sure that your motherboard supports PCI (Peripheral Component Interconnect) slots, and verify that there is at least one PCI adapter board in the system. There is a proliferation of PCI-related configuration settings in the PnP/PCI area of a CMOS Setup, so it is extremely difficult to suggest any one probable oversight. If you cannot get PCI devices to work (or work properly), try loading the BIOS defaults for your CMOS Setup, which should give you baseline PCI support. Be sure to record your original CMOS settings before attempting to load defaults. If your motherboard was designed early during the development of PnP, you may need a BIOS upgrade to provide adequate PnP support.

SYMPTOM 11-9   **You cannot enter CMOS Setup even though the correct key combination is used**   Make sure that you're pressing that key combination quickly enough. Many BIOS versions only allow a few moments during POST to enter CMOS Setup. Once the operating system begins to load, you'll need to reboot. Also verify that you are in fact using the correct key or key combination. It is also possible that access to CMOS Setup has been disabled through a motherboard jumper. Refer to the documentation for your particular motherboard, and locate the "CMOS access" jumper. The jumper (if it exists) should be in the position that allows access.

Careful that you don't accidentally confuse this access jumper with the "CMOS clear" jumper—the two serve completely different purposes.

SYMPTOM 11-10   **The system crashes or locks up frequently**   There are many reasons for a PC to crash or lock up. Everything from a hardware fault to a bad driver to a software bug can interfere with normal system operation. Before you check the CMOS Setup, run a DOS diagnostic to verify that the system hardware is performing properly, and check that there is no hardware conflict in the system. Then check the Device Manager and look for any signs of conflicting or inoperative devices (marked with yellow or red exclamation marks). If the system runs properly when DOS is booted clean or Windows 9x/Me is started in the Safe Mode, there may be a buggy or conflicting driver (or TSR) that is interfering with system operation.

If problems persist, there may be any of several different problems in the CMOS Setup. Typical oversights include insufficient wait-states, memory speed mismatches (for example, mixing 60ns and 70ns memory), and enabling cache (L1 or L2) when there is no such cache in the system. Review your system configuration very carefully. It is also possible that shadowing and snooping features can interfere with system operation. Try systematically disabling video ROM shadowing, motherboard ROM shadowing, and other shadowing options. Then try disabling video palette snoop, and other snooping or "pre-snoop" options.

If problems still continue, try loading the BIOS defaults into CMOS. The defaults should ensure some level of hardware stability, but you'll still need to optimize the CMOS Setup manually for best performance.

SYMPTOM 11-11   **COM ports don't work**   Assuming that the COM ports are installed and configured properly, operating problems can sometimes be traced to IDE Block Mode or IDE Multiple Sector Mode issues. Try disabling the Block Mode or Multiple Sector Mode, or scale back the block mode to a lower level. Of course, you should also check that the suspect COM ports are enabled and that their resource assignments do not conflict with other devices in the system.

SYMPTOM 11-12   **The RTC doesn't keep proper time over a month**   This is a very common problem for *real-time clock* (RTC) units. RTCs are notoriously inaccurate devices anyway—often straying by as much as several minutes per month. Some third-tier RTCs (or units burdened by heavy interrupt activity) may be off by more than several minutes (or more) per week. In practice, there is very little that can be done to correct this kind of poor timekeeping other than to replace the motherboard with one using a better-quality RTC (hardly an economical solution), or to use a "time-correcting utility" that compensates for the RTC's drift.

SYMPTOM 11-13   **The RTC doesn't keep time while system power is off**   Time seems maintained while system power is on, but the RTC appears to stop while the system is turned off. This is often a classic sign of CMOS backup battery failure. Since the RTC usually takes a bit more power than the CMOS RAM—and CMOS RAM can be maintained by a latent change—this kind of "clock stall" is often the first sign that the CMOS battery is failing. Record your CMOS Setup and replace the CMOS battery at your earliest opportunity.

SYMPTOM 11-14   **You see an "Invalid System Configuration Data" error**   This type of error often means that there is a problem with the extended system configuration data (ESCD). This is a storage space for the configuration data in a plug-and-play system. Once you have configured your system properly, the plug-and-play BIOS uses your ESCD to load the same configuration from one boot to the next. If this error message is displayed, take these steps:

1.   Go into Setup and find a field labeled Reset Configuration Data.
2.   Set this field to yes.
3.   Save and exit the CMOS Setup program. The system restarts and clears the ESCD during POST.
4.   Run whatever PnP configuration tool is appropriate for your system:

   ■ If you have Windows 9x/Me (a plug-and-play operating system), just restart your computer. Windows 9x/Me will automatically configure your system and load the ESCD with the new data.

   ■ If you don't have Windows 9x/Me, run the DOS ICU (ISA Configuration Utility) to reset the ESCD.

SYMPTOM 11-15   **You encounter "CMOS checksum" errors after updating a flash BIOS**   Flashing a BIOS chip will typically require you to clear the CMOS Setup and to reconfigure the Setup again from scratch. Most current motherboards offer a "Clear CMOS" jumper that can be used to wipe out all the CMOS settings. This is sometimes referred to as a "CMOS clear" or "CMOS NVRAM clear." Try clearing the CMOS RAM, and then load the BIOS defaults. At that point, the errors should stop, and you may need to optimize the CMOS Setup entries in order to tweak the system. If you documented the original CMOS Setup entries with PRINTSCREEN before upgrading the BIOS, you should be able to reset key entries in a matter of minutes. Remember to save your changes when exiting.

SYMPTOM 11-16   **You notice that only some CMOS Setup entries are corrupted when running a particular application**   This kind of error sometimes happens with several games and other programs on the market that access memory locations used by CMOS RAM and the *BIOS Data Area* (BDA) that are shadowed into the *Upper Memory Area* (UMA). This can alter or corrupt at least some CMOS locations. One solution is to contact the program maker and see if there is a patch or fix that will prevent CMOS access. Another solution to this problem is to exclude the C000h to CFFFh range in the EMM386 device line in your CONFIG.SYS file. This prevents programs from accessing the section of memory that the BIOS uses for shadowing. Here is an example:

```
DEVICE=C:\DOS\EMM386.EXE X=C000-CFFF
```

CMOS PASSWORD TROUBLESHOOTING

Passwords are usually regarded as a necessary evil—a means of keeping out the malicious and the curious. However, passwords also cause their share of problems. As systems are passed from person to person or department to department, passwords often become lost or forgotten. This means the system won't start. The trick with all system passwords (that is, passwords that must be entered before the operating system loads) is that they are stored in CMOS RAM along with the rest of the system's settings. If you can clear the CMOS RAM, you can effectively disable the CMOS password protection. Still, simply clearing the CMOS RAM is not always an acceptable solution because the myriad CMOS settings are almost impossible to restore without a great deal of tweaking. The following tips will help you deal with unwanted CMOS passwords:

- *Does anybody know the password?* Check with friends, colleagues, supervisors—someone just might know the password. This will save you a lot of hassle, and you can always disable the password in CMOS Setup once you're "in." If you're using an AMI BIOS and the password feature has been enabled (but no new password has been entered), try **AMI**. For Award BIOS, you can try **BIOSTAR** or **AWARD_SW**. There's no guarantee such defaults will work, but it's worth a try.

- *Check for a "Password Clear" jumper.* Open the case and take a look at the motherboard. There's probably a jumper that will clear the password without wiping out the entire CMOS Setup. In some cases, the jumper is even marked "Clear Password" (so much for security). If you can find such a jumper, set it, and then boot the system. After the system boots, power-down again and reset the jumper. Your password should now be cleared, while leaving the CMOS settings intact.

- *Force a configuration change.* Try removing a SIMM or DIMM and powering up the PC. In many cases, the BIOS will recognize the configuration change and generate an error such as "CMOS mismatch—Press F1 for Setup." This gets you into CMOS, where you can disable the password without clearing the CMOS RAM entirely. You'll have to save your changes and reboot. Keep in mind that when you finally replace that SIMM/DIMM, you'll probably see another CMOS error. Just go back into CMOS and do a quick correction. Remember that newer BIOS versions are getting smarter and may still require the password before the CMOS Setup routine will start, but it's worth a shot.

- *Clear the CMOS RAM.* There's no doubt that this is your least desirable choice. There are several ways to clear the CMOS. Look for a motherboard jumper that says "CMOS Clear" or some similar marking. Set the jumper and power-up the system. When you see a message indicating that CMOS is clear, or that default settings have been loaded, power-down the PC and reset the jumper (the password should now be gone). You can then restart the PC and reconfigure your CMOS Setup from scratch. If you're using an AMI, Award, or Phoenix BIOS (and can't find the proper jumper), you can use the DOS DEBUG utility on a clean bootable floppy disk. Start DEBUG and use the following commands for an AMI BIOS. (Don't try this through a DOS window.)

```
C:\DEBUG
-O 70 17
```

```
-O 71 17
Q
```

If you're using a Phoenix BIOS, try the following DEBUG commands:

```
C:\DEBUG
-O 70 FF
-O 71 17
Q
```

As another option, you can remove the CMOS battery and wait for the CMOS RAM to clear. As a rule, you should wait for at least 30 minutes, but I've seen CMOS RAM hold a latent charge for days. To accelerate the process, you can short a 10-kOhm resistor across the empty battery terminals. Be sure to turn the power off first. If that doesn't work, you can use the same resistor to short the CMOS RAM power pins directly, as shown in Table 11-2. Again, remember that all system power should be off before you do this. Once your CMOS RAM is clear, you will need to restore the setup (probably starting with BIOS defaults). After the CMOS is restored, be sure to take a PRINTSCREEN of each setup page and keep the copies with the PC's documentation.

CMOS BATTERY MAINTENANCE

Ordinarily, the RTC/CMOS chip requires no maintenance. However, the backup battery will need to be replaced on a fairly regular basis (often every few years). Before replacing the battery (or battery pack), be sure that you have a valid CMOS backup—either on paper or floppy disk. Turn off system power, unplug the system, and remove the battery. This will cause the CMOS RAM chip to eventually lose its contents—it may take moments, or hours, depending on the CMOS RAM chip. Recycle the original battery and install the new one according to the system manufacturer's instructions. Secure the new battery and restart the system. When the system boots, go directly to the CMOS Setup routine and restore each setting. If you have CMOS information recorded in a file, boot the system from a floppy disk, and use the CMOS backup/restore utility to restore the file. You should then be able to restart the system as if nothing had happened.

TABLE 11-2   LISTING OF COMMON CMOS RAM CHIP POWER PINS

BRAND	PART	SHORT PIN #S
Benchmarq	BQ3258S	12 and 20
Benchmarq	BQ3287AMT	12 and 21
Benchmarq	BQ3287MT	Cannot clear (replace the chip)
C&T	P82C206	12 and 32
Dallas	DS1287	Cannot clear (replace the chip)
Dallas	DS1287A	12 and 21
Dallas	DS12885S	12 and 20
Hitachi	HD146818AP	12 and 24
Motorola	MC146818AP	12 and 24
OPTi	F82C206	3 and 26
Samsung	KS82C6818A	12 and 24

Some CMOS RAM chips can retain their contents for hours on a "latent" charge and may not have to be reprogrammed after replacing the battery. However, there is no guarantee of just how long CMOS contents will remain intact. Always be prepared to restore CMOS settings.

If you're going to be storing old (replaced) motherboards for any period of time, make it a point to remove the CMOS backup battery *first*. Batteries tend to be very safe and reliable, but there are many instances where they can and *do* leak. Since batteries use an acid-based electrolyte, battery leakage can easily damage battery contacts, or spill over onto the motherboard itself—damaging circuit traces and ruining the motherboard beyond repair.

Further Study

American Megatrends   www.megatrends.com
Award BIOS   www.award.com
Dallas Semicon   www.dalsemi.com/DocControl/Overviews.web/PnP_RTC/overview.html
IBM SurePath BIOS page   www.surepath.ibm.com
MicroFirmware   www.firmware.com/catalog2.htm
MRBIOS   www.mrbios.com
Unicore   www.unicore.com
Wim's BIOS Page   www.ping.be/bios/

12

CONFLICT TROUBLESHOOTING

The incredible acceptance and popularity of the PC is largely due to the use of an *open architecture*. An open architecture allows any manufacturer to develop new devices (such as video cards, modems, sound cards, and so on) that will work in conjunction with the PC. When a new expansion card is added to the PC, the device uses various system resources to obtain CPU time and transfer data across the expansion bus. Ultimately, each device that is added to the system requires unique resources. No two devices can use the same resources—otherwise, a hardware conflict will result. Low-level software programs (such as device drivers and TSRs) that use system resources can also conflict with one another during normal operation. This chapter explains the concept of *system resources,* and then shows you how to detect and correct conflicts that can arise in both hardware and software.

Understanding System Resources

The key to mastering and eliminating conflicts is to understand the importance of each system resource that is available to you. PCs provide three typical types of resources: interrupts (or IRQs), DMA channels, and I/O areas. Many controllers and network devices also utilize BIOS, which requires memory space. Do *not* underestimate the importance of these resource areas—conflicts can occur anywhere, and carry dire consequences for a system.

INTERRUPTS

An *interrupt* is probably the most well known and understood type of resource. Interrupts are logical signals used to demand attention from the CPU. This allows a device or subsystem to work in the background until a particular event occurs that requires system processing. Such an event may include receiving a character at the serial port, striking a key on the keyboard, or any number of other real-world situations. An interrupt is invoked by asserting a logic level on one of the physical *interrupt request* (or IRQ) lines accessible through any of the motherboard's expansion bus slots. AT-compatible PCs provide 16 IRQ lines (noted IRQ 0 to IRQ 15). Table 12-1 illustrates the IRQ assignments for current AT systems. These signal lines run from pins on the expansion bus connector to programmable interrupt controllers (PICs) on the motherboard (today, PICs are normally integrated into the motherboard's chipset). The output signals generated by a PIC trigger the CPU interrupt. Keep in mind that Table 12-1 covers hardware interrupts only. A proliferation of processor- and software-generated interrupts also exists.

The use of IRQ 2 in an AT system deserves a bit of explanation. An AT uses IRQ 2 right on the motherboard, which means the expansion bus pin for IRQ 2 is now empty. Instead of leaving this pin unused, IRQ 9 from the AT extended slot is wired to the pin previously occupied by IRQ 2. In other words, IRQ 9 is being *redirected* to IRQ 2. Any AT expansion device set to use IRQ 2 is actually using IRQ 9. Of course, the vector interrupt table is adjusted to compensate for this sleight of hand.

After an interrupt is triggered, an interrupt handling routine saves the current CPU register states to a small area of memory (called the *stack*), and then directs the CPU to the *interrupt vector table,* a list of program locations in memory that correspond to each interrupt. When an interrupt occurs, the CPU will jump to the *interrupt handler* routine at the location in memory specified in the interrupt vector table and execute the routine. In most cases, the interrupt handler is a device driver associated with the board generating the interrupt. For example, an IRQ from a network card will likely call a network device driver to operate the card. For a hard disk controller, an IRQ calls the BIOS ROM code that operates the drive. When the handling routine is finished, the CPU's original register contents are "popped" from the stack, and the CPU picks up from where it left off without interruption.

TABLE 12-1	**IRQ ASSIGNMENTS FOR A TYPICAL PC**
IRQ	**FUNCTION**
0	System timer chip
1	Keyboard controller chip
2	Second IRQ controller chip
3	Serial port 2 (COM2: 2F8h-2FFh and COM4: 2E8h-2EFh)
4	Serial port 1 (COM1: 3F8h-3FFh and COM3: 3E8h-3EFh)
5	Parallel port 2 (LPT2: 378h or 278h)
6	Floppy disk controller
7	Parallel Port 1 (LPT1: 378h [color] or 3BCh [mono])
8	Real-time clock (RTC) chip
9	Unused (redirected to IRQ 2)
10	USB controller (on systems so equipped—can be disabled)
11	Windows sound system (on systems so equipped—can be disabled)
12	Motherboard mouse port (a.k.a. PS/2 mouse port)
13	Math coprocessor
14	Primary AT/IDE hard disk controller
15	Secondary AT/IDE hard disk controller (on systems so equipped—can be disabled)

As a technician, it is not vital that you understand precisely how interrupts are initialized and enabled, but you should know the basic terminology. The term *assigned* simply means that a device is set to produce a particular IRQ signal. For example, a typical hard drive controller board is assigned to IRQ 14 (primary controller) and IRQ 15 (secondary controller). Assignments are usually made with one or more jumpers or DIP switches, or are configured automatically through the use of plug-and-play (PnP) and/or the CMOS Setup. Next, interrupts can be selectively enabled or disabled under software control. An *enabled* interrupt is an interrupt where the PIC has been programmed to pass on an IRQ to the CPU. Just because an interrupt is enabled does not mean that there are any devices assigned to it. Finally, an *active* interrupt is a line where real IRQs are being generated. Note that "active" does not mean assigned or enabled.

Interrupts are an effective and reliable means of signaling the CPU, but the conventional ISA bus architecture—used in virtually all but the very latest PCs—does not provide a means of determining which slot contains the board that called the interrupt. As a result, multiple devices cannot share interrupts. In other words, no two devices can be actively generating interrupt requests on the same IRQ line at the same time. If more than one device is assigned to the same interrupt line, a hardware conflict can occur. In most circumstances, a conflict may prevent the newly installed board (or other previously installed boards) from working. In some cases, a hardware conflict can hang up the entire system. As you will see later in the chapter, IRQ steering is one established means of extending the use of interrupts in PCI bus slots, but non-PCI devices cannot share interrupts.

DMA CHANNELS

The CPU is very adept at moving data. It can transfer data between memory locations, I/O locations, or from memory to I/O and back with equal ease. However, PC designers realized that transferring large amounts of data (one word at a time) through the CPU is a hideous waste of CPU time. After all, the CPU really isn't *processing* anything during a data move—it's just shuttling data from one place to another. If there were a way to "off-load" such redundant tasks from the CPU, data could be moved more efficiently than would be possible with CPU intervention. *Direct memory access* (DMA) is a technique designed to move large amounts of data from memory to an I/O location, or vice versa, without the direct intervention by the CPU. In theory, the DMA controller chip acts as a stand-alone "data processor," leaving the CPU free to handle other tasks.

A DMA transfer starts with a DMA Request (DRQ) signal generated by the requesting device (such as the floppy disk controller board). If the channel has been previously enabled through software drivers or BIOS routines, the request will reach the corresponding DMA controller chip on the motherboard. The DMA controller will then send a HOLD request to the CPU, which responds with a Hold Acknowledge (HLDA) signal. When the DMA controller receives the HLDA signal, it instructs the bus controller to effectively disconnect the CPU from the expansion bus and allow the DMA controller chip to take control of the bus itself. The DMA controller sends a DMA Acknowledge (DACK) signal to the requesting device, and the transfer process may begin. Up to 64KB can be moved during a single DMA transfer. After the transfer is done, the DMA controller will reconnect the CPU and drop its HOLD request—the CPU then continues with whatever it was doing without interruption. This process is simply repeated for subsequent blocks of data. Table 12-2 illustrates the use of DMA channels for current AT systems.

As with interrupts, a DMA channel is selected by setting a physical jumper or DIP switch on the particular expansion board (or assigned automatically through the use of PnP). When the board is installed in an expansion slot, the channel setting establishes a connection between the board and DMA controller chip. Often, accompanying software drivers must use a command-line switch that points to the corresponding

TABLE 12-2   DMA ASSIGNMENTS FOR A TYPICAL PC

DMA	TRADITIONAL FUNCTION	CURRENT FUNCTION(S)
0	Dynamic RAM refresh	Audio system
1	Unused	Audio system or parallel port
2	Floppy disk controller	Floppy disk controller
3	Unused	ECP parallel port or audio system
4	Reserved (used internally)	Reserved (used internally)
5	Unused	Unused
6	Unused	Unused
7	Unused	Unused

hardware DMA assignment. Also, DMA channels cannot be shared between two or more devices. Although DMA sharing is possible in theory, it is extremely difficult to implement in actual practice. If more than one device attempts to use the same DMA channel at the same time, a conflict will result.

I/O ASSIGNMENTS

Both XT and AT computers provide space for 1024 I/O (input/output) ports. An I/O port acts very much like a memory address, but it's not for storage. Instead, an I/O port provides the means for a PC to communicate directly with a device—allowing the PC to efficiently pass commands and data between the system and various expansion devices. Each device must be assigned to a unique address (or address range). Table 12-3 lists the typical I/O port assignments for a recent Pentium 4-based motherboard.

TABLE 12-3   I/O ASSIGNMENTS FOR A PENTIUM 4 MOTHERBOARD

ADDRESS (HEX)	SIZE	DESCRIPTION
0000-000F	16 bytes	DMA controller
0020-0021	2 bytes	Programmable interrupt control (PIC)
0040-0043	4 bytes	System timer
0060	1 byte	Keyboard controller byte/reset IRQ
0061	1 byte	System speaker
0064	1 byte	Keyboard controller, CMD/STAT byte
0070-0071	2 bytes	System CMOS/real-time clock (RTC)
0072-0073	2 bytes	System CMOS
0080-008F	16 bytes	DMA controller
0092	1 byte	Fast A20 and PIC
00A0-00A1	2 bytes	PIC
00B2-00B3	2 bytes	APM control
00C0-00DF	32 bytes	DMA
00F0	1 byte	Numeric data processor
0170-0177	8 bytes	Secondary IDE channel
01F0-01F7	8 bytes	Primary IDE channel
0220-022F or 0240-024F	16 bytes	Audio (Sound Blaster Pro–compatible)
0228-022F	8 bytes	LPT3

TABLE 12-3   I/O ASSIGNMENTS FOR A PENTIUM 4 MOTHERBOARD (*CONTINUED*)

ADDRESS (HEX)	SIZE	DESCRIPTION
0278-027F	8 bytes	LPT2
02E8-02EF	8 bytes	COM4 or video (8514A)
02F8-02FF	8 bytes	COM2
0376	1 byte	Secondary IDE channel command port
0377	1 byte	Secondary IDE channel status port
0378-037F	8 bytes	LPT1
03B0-03BB	12 bytes	Intel 82850 memory controller hub (MCH)
03C0-03DF	32 bytes	Intel 82850 MCH
03E8-03EF	8 bytes	COM3
03F0-03F5	6 bytes	Diskette channel 1
03F6	1 byte	Primary IDE channel command port
03F8-03FF	8 bytes	COM1
04D0-04D1	2 bytes	Edge/level-triggered PIC
LPTn + 400	8 bytes	ECP port, LPTn base address + 400h
0CF8-0CFB	4 bytes	PCI configuration address register
0CF9	1 byte	Turbo and reset control register
0CFC-0CFF	4 bytes	PCI configuration data register
FFA0-FFA7	8 bytes	Primary bus master IDE registers
FFA8-FFAF	8 bytes	Secondary bus master IDE registers
Relocatable	96 bytes	I/O controller hub—ICH2 (ACPI + TCO)
Relocatable	64 bytes	D850GB (particular motherboard) board resource
Relocatable	64 bytes	Onboard audio controller
Relocatable	32 bytes	I/O controller hub—ICH2 (USB controller #1)
Relocatable	16 bytes	I/O controller hub—ICH2 (SMBus)
Relocatable	4096 bytes	Intel 82801BA PCI bridge
Relocatable	256 bytes	I/O controller hub—ICH2 Audio Mixer
Relocatable	64 bytes	I/O controller hub—ICH2 Audio Bus Mixer
Relocatable	256 bytes	I/O controller hub—ICH2 Modem Mixer
Relocatable	32 bytes	I/O controller hub—ICH2 (USB controller #2)
Relocatable	96 bytes	LPC47M102 chip

I/O assignments are generally made manually by setting jumpers or DIP switches on the expansion device itself (or automatically through the use of PnP). As with other system resources, it is vitally important that no two devices use the same I/O port(s) at the same time. If one or more I/O addresses overlap, a hardware conflict will result. Commands meant for one device may be erroneously interpreted by another. Keep in mind that while many expansion devices can be set at a variety of addresses, some devices cannot, and devices that use a range of addresses should not, overlap with the addresses (or ranges) used by other devices.

MEMORY ASSIGNMENTS

Memory is another vital resource for the PC. While early devices relied on the assignment of IRQ, DMA channels, and I/O ports, most current devices (such as SCSI controllers, network cards, video boards, modems, and so on) demand memory space for the support of each device's onboard BIOS ROM (their "firmware"). As with I/O space, no two ROMs can overlap in their addresses—otherwise, a conflict will occur. Table 12-4 lists a memory map for a modern PC.

THE ROLE OF PLUG-AND-PLAY (PNP)

Traditional PCs used devices that required manual configuration—each IRQ, DMA, I/O port, and memory address space had to be specifically set through jumpers on the particular device. If you accidentally configured two or more devices to use the same resource, a conflict would result. This would require you to isolate the offending device(s), identify available resources, and reconfigure the offending device(s) manually. Taken together, this was often a cumbersome and time-consuming process.

In the early 1990s, PC designers realized that it was possible to automate the process of resource allocation each time the system initializes. This way, a device need only be installed, and the system handles its configuration and assigns available resources without the assistance or intervention of the installer. This concept became known as "plug-and-play" (PnP), and has long been standard in the PC arena. PnP systems require three elements in order to function:

■ PnP-compliant devices (such as video boards, modems, drive controllers, and so on)

■ PnP-compliant BIOS (now used in all Pentium-class systems)

■ PnP-compliant operating systems (like Windows 95/98)

When the PnP system works properly, a PnP device can be installed in an available expansion slot on a PnP-supported motherboard (with a PnP BIOS). When Windows 98/Me starts, it recognizes the new PnP device, assigns resources, and then attempts to install the proper protected-mode driver (which could be installed from a manufacturer's floppy disk or a Windows installation CD). Thereafter, the system "remembers" the new device, and reconfigures it each time the system starts. Ideally, if the PnP device is ever removed, Windows will automatically clear the device from its "system" and free the resources for other devices.

However, if any of these elements are missing, devices will not be "autoconfigured." For example, PnP won't work under DOS (though there are DOS PnP drivers that can be used to initialize PnP devices).

TABLE 12-4	**MEMORY ASSIGNMENTS FOR A MODERN PC MOTHERBOARD**		

ADDRESS RANGE (DECIMAL)	ADDRESS RANGE (HEX)	SIZE	DESCRIPTION
1024KB–2,097,152KB	100000–7FFFFFFF	2047MB	Extended memory
960KB–1024KB	F0000–FFFFF	64KB	Runtime BIOS
896KB–960KB	E0000–EFFFF	64KB	Reserved
800KB–896KB	C8000–DFFFF	96KB	Available high-DOS memory (open to the PCI bus)
640KB–800KB	A0000–C7FFF	160KB	Video memory and BIOS
639KB–640KB	9FC00–9FFFF	1KB	Extended BIOS data (movable by memory manager software)
512KB–639KB	80000–9FBFF	127KB	Extended conventional memory
0KB–512KB	00000–7FFFF	512KB	Conventional memory

Older, jumper-configured devices (called *legacy devices*) also won't support PnP, and resources need to be reserved for legacy devices to prevent the PnP system from ignoring them entirely.

PnP "autoconfiguration" information is stored in the Extended System Configuration Data (ESCD) area, and is cleared when the CMOS RAM is cleared or lost.

CHECKING RESOURCE ASSIGNMENTS

Whether you're fixing a system problem, or just learning how your system is configured, you may need to identify any resources assigned to each device in the PC. In the early days of computing, identifying resources meant dragging out tedious manuals and checking each jumper setting by hand. Today, Windows provides convenient system tools that allow you to check resource assignments in a matter of moments using Device Manager. To open Device Manager, click Start, highlight Settings, and then click Control Panel. When Control Panel opens, double-click the System icon, and then select the Device Manager tab in the System Properties dialog box. A device tree will open, as shown in Figure 12-1.

This Device Manager tab lists all the devices that Windows "sees" in the system, and any device problems normally appear here as well. To see a summary of the system resource assignments, select the Computer entry at the top of the device tree, and then click the Properties button. The Computer Properties dialog box will appear, as shown in Figure 12-2. Click the View Resources tab (if it's not already selected). By default, the Interrupt Request (IRQ) radio button is selected, and you can scroll down the list to see what IRQ is assigned to which device. For example, you can see that the SupraMAX 56i Voice PCI

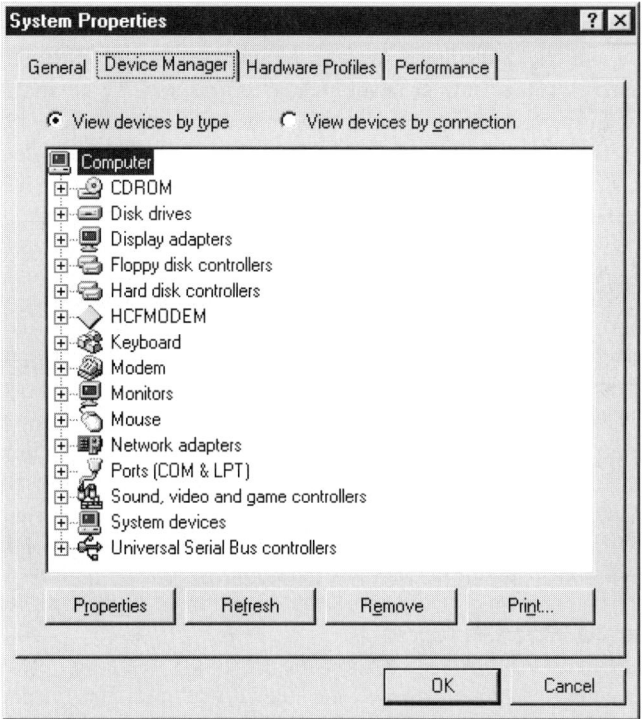

FIGURE 12-1   Checking installed devices through Device Manager

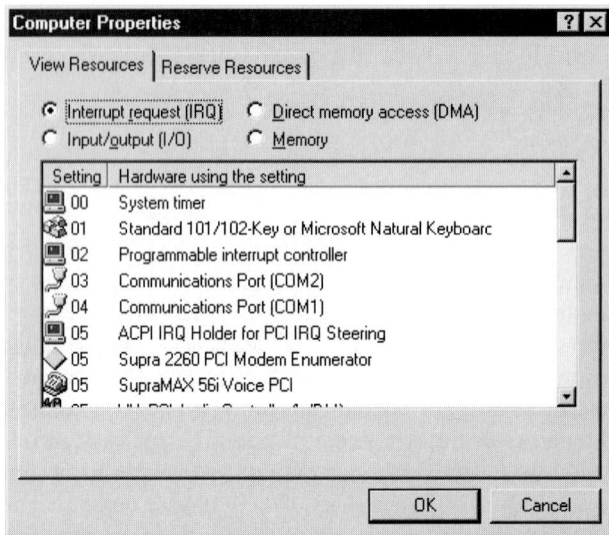

FIGURE 12-2   Checking resource assignments through the Computer Properties dialog box

modem is assigned to IRQ 5. Similarly, you can click the Input/Output (I/O), Direct Memory Access (DMA), and Memory radio buttons to reveal those resource assignments. Click Cancel when you're done checking resources.

Alternatively, you can check all the resources assigned to a given device. In Device Manager, expand the device category (for example, Display Adapters), select the desired device, and click the Properties button. The Properties dialog box for that device will appear. Select the Resources tab, as shown in Figure 12-3. You will see all the resources assigned to that device listed in the middle of the dialog box—you can simply scroll down the list to see additional resources. You can also alter any resources assigned to the device through this dialog box, but just click Cancel for now.

UNDERSTANDING IRQ STEERING

The one overriding issue about resources is that they cannot be shared—otherwise, a conflict may occur. This has been a cardinal rule of troubleshooters for more than 20 years. However, modern PCs use many different devices, and this proliferation of hardware places tremendous demands on very limited system resources (most notably IRQs). If it were possible for more than one device to use the same IRQ, a PC could support a larger number of expansion devices. Although ISA bus architectures cannot handle IRQ sharing, the PCI bus does allow IRQs to be dynamically assigned to PCI devices. This technique of dynamic IRQ assignment is known as *PCI bus IRQ steering*. IRQ steering is supported through Windows 95 OSR2, Windows 98/SE, and Windows Me. Keep in mind that the retail releases of Windows 95 and Windows 95 OSR1 do *not* provide support for PCI bus IRQ steering.

Assigning IRQs to PCI Devices

PCI bus IRQ steering gives Windows 98/SE/Me the flexibility to reprogram PCI interrupts when reconfiguring PnP PCI and ISA resources around non-PnP ISA devices. This gives Windows a very powerful tool that can automatically resolve many possible IRQ conflicts without direct intervention on the

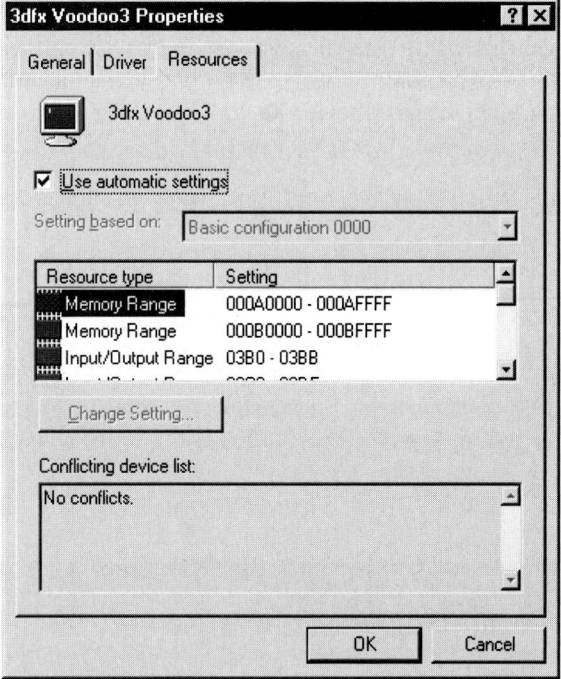

FIGURE 12-3   Checking the resources assigned to a specific device

part of the user (or technician). If PCI bus IRQ steering is *disabled* in Windows, the BIOS assigns IRQs to PCI devices. But if PCI bus IRQ steering is *enabled,* Windows will assign IRQs to PCI devices.

For example, suppose that your computer's BIOS is unaware of non-PnP ISA cards, the operating system does not support PCI bus IRQ steering, and the BIOS has set a PCI device to IRQ 10. If you then add a non-PnP ISA device that is configured for IRQ 10, you may wind up with a resource conflict. With PCI bus IRQ steering, however, the operating system can resolve this IRQ resource conflict. To correct the problem, the operating system must do the following:

1. Disable the PCI device.
2. Reprogram a free IRQ to a PCI IRQ (for example, IRQ 11).
3. Assign an IRQ holder to IRQ 11.
4. Move the PCI device to IRQ 11.
5. Reprogram IRQ 10 to be an ISA IRQ.
6. Remove the IRQ holder for IRQ 10.

When your system supports PCI bus IRQ steering, you will notice numerous *IRQ holders* when you view IRQ assignments (such as ACPI IRQ Holder for PCI IRQ Steering shown earlier in Figure 12-2). *IRQ Holder for PCI IRQ Steering* indicates that an IRQ has been programmed to PCI mode and is unavailable for ISA devices—even if no PCI devices are currently using the IRQ.

Managing IRQ Steering

As a rule, you should expect PCI bus IRQ steering to be enabled on virtually every modern PC. You can usually verify that IRQ steering is enabled by checking the IRQ assignments (as in Figure 12-2, shown earlier in the chapter). If one or more entries are marked as IRQ Holders, chances are that IRQ steering is enabled. Still, you can verify IRQ steering support using the following steps:

1. Click Start, highlight Settings, click Control Panel, and then double-click the System icon.

2. Click the Device Manager tab.

3. Expand the System Devices branch (near the bottom of the device tree).

4. Locate and double-click the PCI Bus entry, and then click the IRQ Steering tab (see Figure 12-4). You should see either IRQ Steering Enabled or IRQ Steering Disabled in the IRQ Routing Status area.

 PCI bus IRQ steering is disabled by default in Windows 95 OSR2. If you're using OSR2 and IRQ steering is disabled, verify that the Use IRQ Steering check box is selected on the IRQ Steering tab.

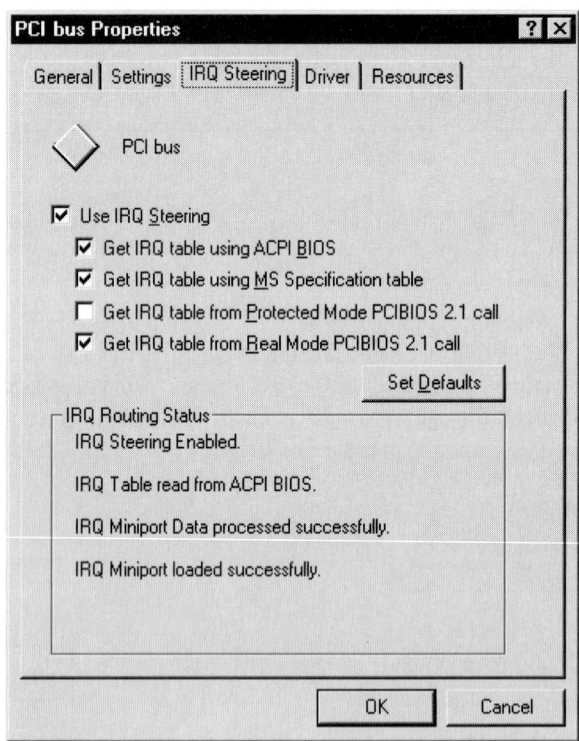

FIGURE 12-4   Checking the status of your system's IRQ steering support

The following IRQ Steering tab settings determine which routing tables Windows uses when programming IRQ steering:

■ **Get IRQ table using ACPI BIOS**   When selected, the ACPI BIOS IRQ routing table is the first table Windows tries to use to program IRQ steering. If a PCI device is not working properly, click this check box to clear it.

■ **Get IRQ table using MS Specification table**   When selected, the Microsoft Specification routing table is the second table Windows tries to use to program IRQ steering.

■ **Get IRQ table from Protected Mode PCIBIOS 2.1 call**   When selected, the Protected Mode PCIBIOS 2.1 routing table is the third table Windows tries to use to program IRQ steering.

■ **Get IRQ table from Real Mode PCIBIOS 2.1 call**   When selected, the Real Mode PCIBIOS 2.1 routing table is the fourth table Windows tries to use to program IRQ steering.

The Get IRQ Table From Protected Mode PCIBIOS 2.1 Call check box is *not* selected by default. You should only select this check box if a PCI device is not working properly.

The IRQ Steering feature is typically enabled, but may appear disabled in Device Manager for any of the following reasons:

■ The IRQ routing table that must be provided by the BIOS to the operating system is missing or contains errors. The IRQ routing table provides information about how the motherboard is configured for PCI IRQs. A BIOS upgrade may be needed to correct the trouble.

■ The Use IRQ Steering check box is not selected.

■ The Get IRQ Table From Protected Mode PCIBIOS 2.1 Call check box is not selected.

■ Your computer's BIOS does not support PCI bus IRQ steering. Contact the manufacturer of your BIOS or system for a suitable BIOS upgrade.

Follow these steps to disable PCI bus IRQ steering:

1. Click Start, highlight Settings, click Control Panel, and then double-click the System icon.
2. Click the Device Manager tab.
3. Expand the System Devices branch.
4. Double-click the PCI Bus entry, and then select the IRQ Steering tab.
5. Click the Use IRQ Steering check box to clear it, click OK, and then click OK again. Click Yes to restart your computer.

If you find that you need to disable IRQ steering, it may also be necessary to disable IRQ steering support in the CMOS Setup.

Recognizing and Correcting Conflicts

Fortunately, conflicts are almost always the result of a PC upgrade gone awry. Thus, a technician can be alerted to the possibility of a system conflict by applying the *last upgrade* rule. The rule consists of three parts:

■ A piece of hardware and/or software has been added to the system *very* recently.

■ The trouble occurred *after* a piece of hardware and/or software was added to the system.

■ The system was working fine *before* the hardware and/or software was added.

If all three of these common-sense conditions are true, chances are very good that you're faced with a hardware or software conflict (rather than a defective device). Unlike most other types of PC problems, which tend to be specific to the faulty subassembly, conflicts usually manifest themselves as much more general and perplexing problems. The following symptoms are typical of serious hardware or software conflicts:

■ The system locks up during the POST or operating system initialization.

■ The system locks up during a particular application.

■ The system locks up when a particular device (such as a TWAIN scanner) is used.

■ The system locks up randomly or without warning regardless of the application.

■ The system may not crash, but the device that was added may not function (even though it seems properly configured). Devices that were in the system previously may still work correctly.

■ The system may not crash, but a device or application that was working previously no longer seems to function. The newly added device (and accompanying software) may or may not work properly.

What makes these problems so generic is that the severity and frequency of a fault (as well as the point at which the fault occurs) depend on several factors. These factors include the particular devices that are conflicting, the resource(s) that are conflicting among the devices (for example, IRQs, DMAs, or I/O addresses), and the function being performed by the PC when the conflict manifests itself. Since every PC is equipped and configured a bit differently, it is virtually impossible to predict a conflict's symptoms more precisely.

CONFIRMING AND RESOLVING CONFLICTS

Recognizing the possibility of a conflict is one thing, but proving and correcting it is another issue entirely. However, there are some very effective tactics at your disposal. The first rule of conflict resolution is Last In First Out (or LIFO). The LIFO principle basically states that the fastest means of overcoming a conflict problem is to remove the hardware or software that resulted in the conflict. In other words, if you install board X and board Y ceases to function, board X is probably conflicting with the system, so removing board X should restore board Y to normal operation. The same concept holds true for software. If you add a new application to your system, and then find that an existing application fails to work properly, the new application is likely at fault. Unfortunately, removing the offending element is not enough. You still have to install the new device or software in such a way that it will no longer conflict in the system.

DEALING WITH SOFTWARE CONFLICTS

There are two types of software that can cause conflicts in a typical PC: TSRs and device drivers. *TSRs* (sometimes called *popup utilities*) load into memory, usually during initialization, and wait until a system event (such as a modem ring or a keyboard "hot key" combination). There are no DOS or system rules that define how such utilities should be written. As a result, many tend to conflict with application programs (and even DOS itself).

If you suspect that such a popup utility is causing the problem, find its reference in the AUTOEXEC.BAT file and disable it by placing the command REM in front of its command line, such as this:

```
REM C:\UTILS\NEWMENU.EXE /A:360 /D:3
```

The REM command turns the line into a "REMark," which can easily be removed later if you choose to restore the line. Remember to reboot the computer so that your changes will take effect.

Device drivers present another potential problem. Most hardware upgrades require the addition of one or more device drivers. Such drivers are called from the CONFIG.SYS file during system initialization (or loaded with Windows), and use a series of command-line parameters to specify the system resources that are being used. This is often necessary to ensure that the driver operates its associated hardware properly. If the command-line options used for the device driver do not match the hardware settings (or overlap the settings of another device driver), system problems can result. If you suspect that a device driver is causing the problem, find its reference in the CONFIG.SYS file and disable it by placing the command REM in front of its command line, such as in this example:

```
REM DEVICE = C:\DRIVERS\NEWDRIVE.SYS /A360 /I:5
```

The REM command turns the line into a "REMark," which can easily be removed later if you choose to restore the line. Remember that disabling the device driver in this fashion will prevent the associated hardware from working, but if the problem clears, you can work with the driver settings until the problem is resolved. Remember to reboot the computer so that your changes will take effect.

Finally, consider the possibility that the offending software is buggy or defective. Try contacting the software manufacturer. There may be a fix or undocumented feature that you are unaware of. There may also be a patch or update that will solve the problem.

Under Windows 98/SE/Me, you can use the Automatic Skip Driver agent in your System Information utility to selectively prevent suspect drivers and other Windows components from loading at start time.

DEALING WITH HARDWARE CONFLICTS

Consider an example of a hardware conflict: a PC user recently added a CD-ROM and adapter board to their system. The installation went flawlessly using the defaults—a ten-minute job. Several days later when attempting to back up the system, the user noticed that the parallel port tape backup did not respond (although the printer that had been connected to the parallel port was working fine). The user tried booting the system from a "clean" bootable floppy disk (no CONFIG.SYS or AUTOEXEC.BAT files to eliminate the device drivers), but the problem remained. After a bit of consideration, the user powered down the system, removed the CD-ROM adapter board, and booted the system from a "clean" bootable floppy disk. Sure enough, the parallel port tape backup started working again.

Stories such as this remind technicians that hardware conflicts are not always the monstrous, system-smashing mistakes that they are made out to be. In many cases, conflicts have subtle, noncatastrophic consequences. Since the CD-ROM was the last device to be added in the example, it was the first to be removed. It took about five minutes to realize and remove the problem. However, *removing* the problem is only part of conflict troubleshooting—reinstalling the device *without* a conflict is the real challenge.

Ideally, the way to correct a conflict would be to alter the conflicting setting. That's dynamite in theory, but another thing in practice. The trick is that you need to know what resources are in use and which ones are free. Unfortunately, there are only two ways to find this out under DOS. On one hand, you can track down the user manual for every board in the system, inspect each board individually to find its settings, and then work accordingly. This will work (assuming you have the documentation), but it is cumbersome and time-consuming. On the other hand, you can refer to the Device Manager under Windows.

Working with Device Manager

As you saw earlier in the chapter, determining resources is a bit easier under Windows 98/Me by using Device Manager. When you open Device Manager, double-click the Computer entry at the top of the device list. The Computer Properties dialog box will open. Select the View Resources tab (shown previously in Figure 12-2), and check the assignments for IRQs, DMA, I/O, or memory. By reviewing these entries, you can quickly determine which resources are assigned, and which are free. Device Manager is also a handy tool for identifying problem devices. Devices that are missing, disabled, conflicting, or operating in some unexpected fashion will be marked prominently in the device tree. Also, the problem device has one of the following symbols to indicate the type of problem:

- A black exclamation point (!) on a yellow field indicates that the device is not behaving as expected (usually because of a conflict). Keep in mind that the suspect device may still be functioning (though other devices may be affected).

- A problem code explaining the problem is usually displayed for the device.

- A red *X* indicates a disabled device. A disabled device is hardware that is physically present in the computer (and consuming resources), but does not have a protected-mode driver loaded. A disabled device will not function.

- A blue lowercase *i* on a white field indicates that the Use Automatic Settings feature is not selected for that device, and that those resources were manually selected. Remember that this does not necessarily indicate a malfunctioning or disabled device.

- Under Windows Me, a green question mark over a device means that a device-specific driver (in other words, a driver from the device manufacturer) for this device is not installed. Instead, a compatible driver is being used, and this may suggest the possibility that the device may not be fully functional.

It is important to note that some sound cards and video adapters do not report all of the resources they are using to Windows. This may cause Device Manager to show only one device in conflict, or show no conflicts at all. This can be verified by disabling the sound card or using the standard VGA video driver to see if the "conflict" is resolved. For example, this is a known problem with S3 video adapters and 16-bit Sound Blaster sound cards, or sound cards that are using Sound Blaster emulation for Sound Blaster compatibility.

Editing Device Resources

When you open the Properties dialog box for a device (such as shown previously in Figure 12-3), you'll see that the Resources tab allows you to adjust the resource assignments that have been made for that device. If the device is conflicting with another device in the system, an error code and explanation of the problem will appear in the Conflicting Device List at the bottom of the dialog box. Note the Use Automatic Settings check box. If Windows successfully detects a device, this check box is selected, and the device should function correctly. However, if the resource settings are based on Basic Configuration <*n*> (where <*n*> is any number from 0 to 9), it may be necessary to change the configuration by selecting a different basic configuration from the list. If the particular configuration you want for the device is not listed as a basic configuration, it may be possible to click the Change Setting button to manually adjust the resource values. For example, to edit an Input/Output Range setting:

1. Click the Use Automatic Settings check box to clear it.

2. Click the Change Setting button.

3. Click the appropriate I/O range for the device.

4. Save your changes and reboot the system.

To disable a device in Device Manager, open the Properties dialog for the device, select the General tab, and then clear the Original Configuration (Current) selection.

Device Manager Errors

When Windows detects a device problem, that error is typically presented in the device's Properties dialog box in the form of an error code (sometimes called a Device Manager Code). The major codes, their meanings, and suggested solutions are presented next.

Code 1   "This device is not configured correctly. To update the drivers for this device, click Update Driver." This code means the system has not had a chance to configure the offending device. To resolve the problem, follow the instructions in the Device Status box (usually updating the driver is an adequate solution). You may also be able to resolve this issue by removing the device in Device Manager, and then running the Add New Hardware wizard from Control Panel.

Code 2   You may see either of two different messages (depending on which device is failing). This code means that the device loader (DevLoader) did not load a device. When this device *is* a root bus DevLoader (for example, ISAPNP, PCI, or BIOS), the following message is displayed: "Windows could not load the driver for this device because the computer is reporting two <type> bus types. Contact your computer manufacturer to get an updated BIOS for your computer." The <type> entry designates ISAPNP, PCI, BIOS, EISA, or ACPI. In this case, you should check for an updated BIOS for your system.

When the device is *not* a root bus DevLoader, the following message is displayed: "The <type> device loader(s) for this device could not load the device driver." The <type> designation is the DevLoader, such as FLOP, ESDI, SCSI, and so on. To fix this trouble, click the Update Driver button to update the device driver. In addition, try removing the device from Device Manager and then running the Add New Hardware wizard to redetect the offending device.

Code 3   "The driver for this device may be bad, or your system may be running low on memory or other resources." Make sure that you have sufficient memory and drive space for the devices and software on your system. To check your system's memory and system resources, right-click My Computer on your desktop, click Properties, and then click the Performance tab. If there are adequate resources, try clicking the Update Driver button and updating the offending device's driver(s). As an alternative, try using Device Manager to remove the device, and then run the Add New Hardware wizard in Control Panel.

Code 4   "This device is not working properly because one of its drivers may be bad, or your registry may be bad." This code indicates that the .INF file for this device may be incorrect, or the Registry may be damaged. This error code is displayed if the .INF file specifies a field that should be text, but is binary instead. To update the drivers for this device, click the Update Driver button. If the problem persists, run SCANREGW.EXE to check your Registry. Alternately, you can use Device Manager to remove the device, and then run the Add New Hardware wizard to reinstall the device. If you still continue to receive this error, contact the hardware manufacturer for an updated .INF file.

Code 5   "The driver for this device requested a resource that Windows does not know how to handle." This code indicates that there was a device failure due to the lack of an "arbitrator." If a device requests a resource type for which there is no arbitrator, you'll receive this error code. To resolve this problem, update the device driver, or use Device Manager to remove the device, and then run the Add New Hardware wizard in Control Panel.

Code 6   "Another device is using the resources this device needs." This code means that there's a conflict between this device and another device. To fix this problem, shut down your computer, turn it off, and then change the resources for this device (if it must be adjusted manually). When you've finished, start Device Manager and change the resource settings for this device.

Code 7   "The drivers for this device need to be reinstalled." This code means that no configuration can be performed on the given device. The message text that is displayed for this error is specific to the driver or enumerator. To reinstall the drivers for this device, click Reinstall Driver and install the latest versions of the device drivers. If the device does not work correctly, use Device Manager to remove the device, and then run the Add New Hardware wizard in Control Panel. If you continue to receive this error code (and the device does not function properly), check with the hardware manufacturer for an updated driver.

Code 8   Several different error messages can be displayed for this error code. If the device loader (DevLoader) for a device cannot be found, you should reinstall or update the driver. As an alternative, use Device Manager to remove the device and then run the Add New Hardware wizard in Control Panel. If you continue to receive this error code, contact the hardware manufacturer for updated drivers. When the problem *is* a system DevLoader, Windows should be reinstalled, because this driver is built into the VMM32.VXD file.

Code 9   The information in the Registry for this device is invalid. If this *is* a BIOS- or ACPI-enumerated device, the following text is displayed: "This device is not working properly because the BIOS in your computer is reporting the resources for the device incorrectly." Contact your computer manufacturer to get an updated BIOS for your motherboard. If this is *not* a BIOS- or ACPI-enumerated device (for example, an add-in adapter or a device that was plugged in to the computer), the following text is displayed: "This device is not working properly because the BIOS in the device is reporting the resources for the device incorrectly". Contact the device manufacturer to get an updated firmware version for your offending device.

Code 10   "This device is either not present, not working properly, or does not have all the drivers installed." To resolve this error, make sure the device is connected to the computer correctly. For example, make sure all cables are plugged in fully and that all adapter cards are properly seated. Try upgrading the driver(s) for this device.

Code 11   "Windows stopped responding while attempting to start this device, and therefore will never attempt to start this device again." To work around this error, run the Automatic Skip Driver utility from the System Information tool. If the problem persists, contact the hardware manufacturer for updated drivers. It may be necessary to remove the offending device, its drivers, and any supporting applet software from the system.

Code 12   "This device cannot find any free <type> resources to use." This code means that one of the resource arbitrators failed. This can occur if the device is software-configurable and does not currently have an available resource (for example, all the interrupts are in use, or the device requests a resource that is currently in use by another device that will not release the resource). If you want to use this device, you must disable another device that is using the resources this device needs. To do this, click the Hardware Troubleshooter and follow the instructions in the wizard.

Code 13   "This device is either not present, not working properly, or does not have all the drivers installed." This code indicates that the device driver did not find its related hardware. To have Windows detect whether or not the device is present, click Detect Hardware. As an alternative, use Device Manager to remove the device, and then run the Add New Hardware wizard in Control Panel.

Code 14   "This device cannot work properly until you restart your computer." In many cases, this may be a temporary issue with one or more devices in the system. To resolve this error, shut down Windows, shut down your computer, and then turn the system back on.

Code 15   "This device is causing a resource conflict." This code means that the device's resources are conflicting with another device's resources—likely caused by re-enumeration. To resolve the conflict, use the process outlined in this chapter, or click Hardware Troubleshooter and follow the instructions in the wizard.

Code 16   "Windows could not identify all the resources this device uses." This code means that the device was not fully detected—when a device is not fully detected, all of its resources may not be recorded. To resolve this error code, click the Resources tab in Device Manager to manually enter the resource settings.

Code 17   "The driver information file <name> is telling this child device to use a resource that the parent device does not have or recognize." This code means that the hardware is a multiple-function device, and the .INF file for that device is providing invalid information on how to split the device's resources to the "child" devices. To resolve this error, use Device Manager to remove the device, and then run the Add New Hardware wizard in Control Panel. If you continue to receive this error code, contact the hardware's manufacturer about an updated .INF file.

Code 18   "The drivers for this device need to be reinstalled." This code means that an error has occurred, and the device (and its drivers) needs to be reinstalled. To resolve this issue, reinstall the latest drivers for this device. If you cannot use the Windows 98 Update Drivers button, try removing the device from Device Manager and then running the Add New Hardware wizard in Control Panel.

Code 19   "Your registry may be bad." This code means that your Registry returned an unknown result. To resolve this problem, click Check Registry (which will run SCANREG.EXE). If this does not correct the issue, type **scanreg /restore** from a command prompt. Finally, remove the device from Device Manager, and then redetect it using the Add New Hardware wizard in Control Panel.

Code 20   "Windows could not load one of the drivers for this device." This code means that the VxD Loader (Vxdldr) returned an unknown result—for example, there might a version mismatch between the device driver and the operating system. To resolve this issue, download the latest drivers and click Update Driver to update the drivers for this device. If that doesn't work, try removing the device from Device Manager and then redetecting it by running the Add New Hardware wizard in Control Panel.

Code 21   "Windows is removing this device." This code means that the device has a problem (usually with initialization) that may be resolved by restarting your computer. To resolve this error, shut down Windows, turn off your computer, wait several seconds, and then turn the system back on.

Code 22   There are several possible errors that may be displayed depending on your particular system configuration and operating circumstances. If the device is disabled because you disabled it using Device Manager, the following text is displayed: "This device is disabled." This code means that the device is either disabled or has not started. Simply click Enable Device to re-enable this device. If you cannot re-enable the device, it may be damaged. If the device is not started, the following text is displayed: "This device is not started." Just click Start Device to activate this device. If the device is disabled by a driver or program, the following text is displayed: "This device is disabled." However, you can't enable this device here, because it's been disabled by a Windows driver. Try removing the device in Device Manager and then redetecting it using the Add New Hardware wizard. If the problem persists, try a clean boot to rule out software interference.

Code 23   There are several possible error codes that may appear depending on your particular situation. If the offending device is a secondary display adapter, the following text appears: "This display adapter is functioning correctly. The problem is with the main display adapter." This message means that the device loader delayed the start of a device, and then did not inform Windows when it was ready to start the device. Verify the settings for the primary display adapter in Display properties. Try removing the primary and secondary display adapters from Device Manager and then rebooting to allow Windows to re-enumerate these devices. Verify that the drivers are current and installed correctly.

If the offending device is *not* a display adapter, the following text appears: "The loaders for this device cannot load the required drivers." To update the device drivers, download the latest drivers, and then click Update Driver. If that does not work, try removing the device from Device Manager and then redetecting the device using the Add New Hardware wizard.

Code 24   "This device is either not present, not working properly, or does not have all the drivers installed." Make sure the device is connected to your computer correctly. For example, make sure all cables are correctly installed, or that the adapter cards are properly seated in their slots. To have Windows detect this device, simply click Detect Hardware. If the device is PnP, you may also try upgrading the drivers for this device.

Code 25   "Windows is in the process of setting up this device." This problem typically exists only during the first and second boots after Windows Setup copies all the files. So if this code is identified, it is likely to be caused by an incomplete installation. To complete the setup, click Restart Computer to reboot the system. Reinstalling Windows may be required if the reboot does not resolve the issue.

Code 26   "Windows is in the process of setting up this device." This error means that a device did not load. There may be a problem in the device driver, or not all of the drivers were installed. Click Restart Computer to reboot the system. Hopefully, Windows will detect the device upon restart. If this does not work, use Device Manager to remove the device, and then run the Add New Hardware wizard in Control Panel. If problems persist, check with the hardware's manufacturer for an updated driver.

Code 27   "Windows can't specify the resources for this device." This error indicates that a portion of the Registry describing possible resources for a device does *not* contain valid entries (for example, the device is marked as "configurable," but the configuration information in the .INF file is set to "hardwired").

Click the Resources tab, and then select the basic configuration for the resources this device uses. You might also use Device Manager to remove the device, and then run the Add New Hardware wizard in Control Panel. If the device still does not work, consult the hardware's manufacturer for updated drivers or other assistance.

Code 28   "The drivers for this device are not installed." This message means that the device was not installed completely. To reinstall the drivers for this device, click Reinstall Driver. You may need to obtain updated drivers if the error persists.

Code 29   "This device is disabled because the BIOS for the device did not give it any resources." This error means that the device has been disabled because it does not work properly, and cannot be made to work properly with Windows. This code may also be present if the device is intentionally disabled in the BIOS. You may be able to resolve this problem by enabling or disabling the device in the computer's CMOS settings—Windows cannot override this setting. Otherwise, the offending device may be defective and need to be replaced.

Code 30   "This device is using an Interrupt Request (IRQ) resource that is in use by another device and cannot be shared. You must change the conflicting setting or remove the real-mode driver causing the conflict." This message indicates that an IRQ cannot be shared. This may occur when a PCI/EISA SCSI controller is sharing an IRQ that is also in use by a real-mode device driver that Windows cannot change. To resolve this problem, remove the real-mode driver that is using the same IRQ as this device (the real-mode driver may be loading in your CONFIG.SYS or AUTOEXEC.BAT file).

Code 31   "This device is not working properly because <device> is not working properly." This code appears when one device is dependent upon another device to be functioning correctly (this does not include devices that are enumerated by the parent device), and <device> is the dependent device that must be fixed in order for this device to work properly. The Properties button displays the properties for the other device. More than likely, the other device will also have one of these Device Manager error codes. Follow all the recommended solutions offered by the error dialog box. If the devices still do not work, remove them *both* from Device Manager, and then use the Add New Hardware wizard to redetect them. Finally, consult with the hardware manufacturer(s) for updated drivers.

Code 32   "Windows cannot install the drivers for this device because it cannot access the drive or network location that has the setup files on it." This code indicates that the installation disk or CD was not available to install the drivers (for example, the CD-ROM drive or network connection is not available). This error typically occurs during the first or second reboot after all the files are copied during Setup. To correct this problem, click Restart Computer to reboot the system. If that doesn't help, copy all the Setup files onto your local hard disk, and run Setup from there. If the problem persists, determine why the installation disk or CD is not available. Typically, these devices will also have Device Manager codes (such as the CD-ROM controller or network adapter).

Code 33   The message text that is displayed for this error is specific to the driver or enumerator. If the driver does *not* provide information as to why it did not work, the following message is displayed: "This device isn't responding to its driver." This code typically is displayed when the hardware has failed. Recheck the hardware installation, and replace the defective device if necessary.

Stack Overflow Errors

When you read about interrupts earlier in this chapter, you learned that a *stack* is a small portion of reserved memory that programs use to process hardware events. A *stack overflow* occurs when there is not enough space in memory to run the hardware interrupt routines. To resolve this trouble, you normally must increase the amount of memory space set aside for the stack (often by modifying the STACKS= line in a CONFIG.SYS file). In other cases, eliminating troublesome TSRs or correcting hardware conflicts can also resolve stack overflow problems.

Adjust CONFIG.SYS   The CONFIG.SYS startup file may not be properly configured for the Windows installation. Try reconfiguring the CONFIG.SYS file with the following values:

```
STACKS=64,512
FILES=60
BUFFERS=40
```

Also, if you're using the dual-boot capabilities of Windows, the CONFIG.SYS and AUTOEXEC.BAT files may not contain the correct configuration to run Windows. When you are dual-booting between other operating systems and Windows, these files may not have been renamed properly. Recheck the behavior of your dual-boot configuration.

Finally, examine the CONFIG.SYS file to determine if files such as HIMEM.SYS or EMM386.EXE are loaded from a folder *other* than the Windows folder. If so, boot Windows using the Safe Mode Command Prompt Only option. Rename the CONFIG.SYS file to CONFIG.DOS and the AUTOEXEC.BAT file to AUTOEXEC.DOS, and then restart your computer.

Remove Unneeded TSR(s)   Some TSRs may be interfering with Windows. Disable any nonboot device drivers in the CONFIG.SYS and AUTOEXEC.BAT files. Check the WIN.INI and SYSTEM.INI files for non-Windows-based programs or drivers that may be loading at start time.

Check Hardware Conflicts   There may be an incompatible hardware configuration. Check the port and IRQ settings of the network adapter, sound card, and modem (these are common culprits). Make sure that there are no COM2/COM4 or COM1/COM3 conflicts, and see that no devices are sharing IRQs. Disable or remove conflicting devices.

Upgrade the BIOS   The computer may need a BIOS upgrade. For example, an upgrade may be necessary to support IRQ steering and help avoid conflicts. Check the BIOS version and contact the manufacturer of your computer for information about a BIOS upgrade.

A Conflict Troubleshooting Process

One of the biggest problems with conflict troubleshooting is that every conflict situation is a bit different. Variations in PC equipment and available resources often reduce conflict troubleshooting to a "hit or miss" process. Fortunately, conflict troubleshooting can be accomplished quickly and easily by using the tools provided by Windows 98/Me (namely Device Manager). This part of the chapter provides a step-by-step process that you can use for conflict resolution under Windows 98/Me. Keep in mind that there may be other ways of resolving the troubles listed here, but these steps are often a good starting point.

The steps described next should be read like a flowchart, and you'll find many references that will take you back and forth to various steps throughout this section.

Step 1: Getting Started   Begin troubleshooting by starting Device Manager in Windows 98/Me:

1.   Click the Start button, point to Settings, and then click Control Panel.

2.   Double-click the System icon, and then click the Device Manager tab (see Figure 12-5).

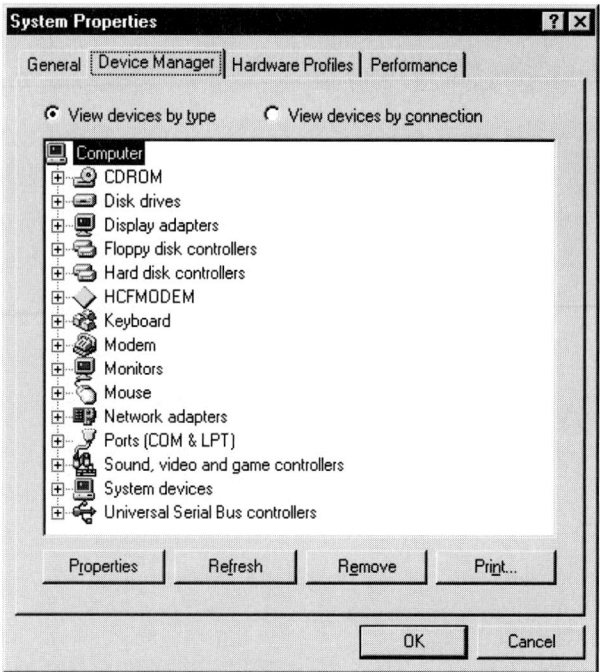

FIGURE 12-5   Starting Windows Device Manager

3.   Make sure View Devices By Type is selected.

The hardware suffering from a problem should be shown in the device list. If the troublesome hardware isn't visible in the list, click the plus sign (+) next to the type of hardware.

Check to see if the device was installed twice. Is the device you were installing (or that suffers from the conflict) listed twice in Device Manager?

■   If the device is listed only once, go to Step 2.

■   If the device is listed twice, and there's only supposed to be one such device in the system, go to Step 3.

■   If the device is listed twice, but there are supposed to be two such devices in the system, go to Step 2.

Step 2: Device Listed Only Once   If the device is listed only once, view the resource settings for the conflicting device:

1.   Double-click the hardware that shows a conflict. Its Properties dialog box should open with the General tab selected.

2.   Under Windows 98, the Disable In This Hardware Profile box should be unchecked, and the Exists In All Hardware Profiles box may be checked (see Figure 12-6).

3.   Click the Resources tab.

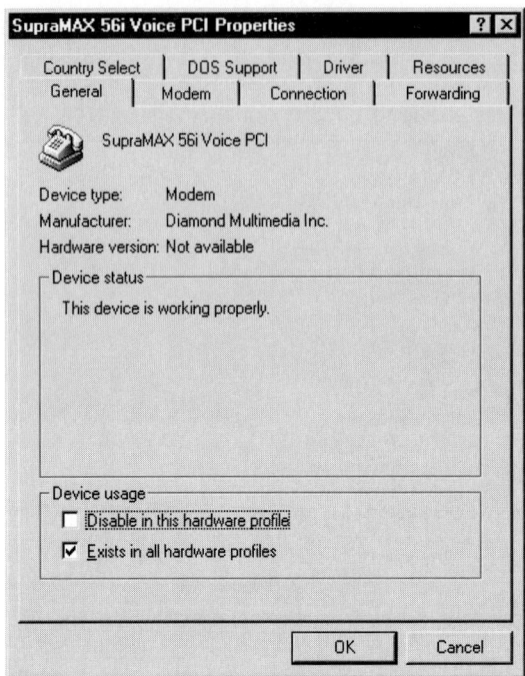

FIGURE 12-6   Checking the suspect device for usage

Do you see a box with resource settings such as in Figure 12-7? Check to see if the Conflicting Device List has any entries that indicate a problem.

■   If the box with resource settings appears, go to Step 4.

■   If the Set Configuration Manually button appears instead, go to Step 5.

■   If the device doesn't have a Resources tab, go to Step 6.

Step 3: Device Listed Twice   Remove *all* instances of the duplicated device(s), and install the device again:

1.   Remove each duplicate item from the hardware list. Click its name, and then click Remove. When you are finished, no instances of the conflicting hardware should be listed.

2.   Click OK.

3.   While still within Control Panel, double-click the Add New Hardware icon. If you see a message that you already have a wizard open, click Finish in that wizard, and then click the button in this step to start a new wizard.

4.   Click Next.

5.   Click the option to automatically detect your hardware, and then click Next. Continue until you finish with the wizard.

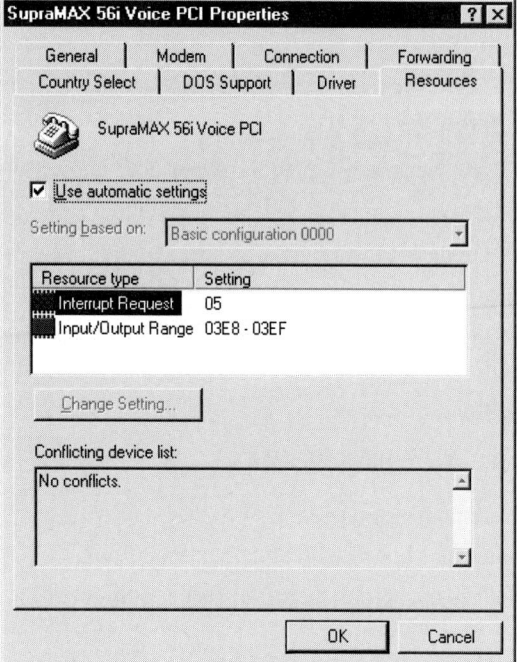

FIGURE 12-7   Checking device resources and device conflicts

You may need to reboot the system. Did this fix the problem?

■ If the conflict no longer appears, this should correct the problem, and you should be done. Exit Control Panel and restart Windows.

■ If the conflict still appears, go to Step 2.

Step 4: Resource Settings Appear   You need to identify exactly which resources are causing the conflict. In the Conflicting Device List box on the Resources tab, identify the hardware that is using conflicting resources. Determine if more than one resource conflict is listed.

■ If more than one resource conflict is listed, go to Step 7.

■ If only one conflict is listed, go to Step 8.

■ If no conflicts are listed, or if one or more indications show System Reserved as the conflict, go to Step 9.

Step 5: Manual Button Appears   Determine why the resources are not displayed:

■ If the Resources tab shows a Set Configuration Manually button, then either the device has a conflict (or other problem) and is disabled or the resource settings used by this device are working properly but don't match any of the known configurations.

■ You can tell which situation applies by reading the text above the button.

Which text message do you see?

- If you see a message that says "The device is conflicting, or the device is not currently enabled or has a problem," then go to Step 10.
- If you see a message that says "The resource settings don't match any known configurations," there is no further solution to the problem. You should probably remove the conflicting device outright.

Step 6: No Resources Tab Appears   You have probably chosen the wrong device. Select the correct device:

1. Click Cancel to return to the hardware list.
2. Carefully double-click the hardware that has a conflict. The General tab should appear.
3. Under Windows 98, the Disable In This Hardware Profile box should be unchecked, and the Exists In All Hardware Profiles box may be checked (refer to Figure 12-6).
4. Click the Resources tab.

Do you see a box with resource settings now?

- If the box with resource settings now appears, go to Step 4.
- If you see a Set Configuration Manually button, go to Step 5.
- If the resource settings still do not appear, there is no further solution to the problem. You should probably remove the conflicting device.

Step 7: More Than One Conflict Is Listed   At this point, you should determine just how many devices are listed as being *conflicting*:

- If you only see one device causing all the conflicts, go to Step 11.
- If more than one device is causing the conflicts, go to Step 12.

Step 8: Only One Conflict Is Listed   Look for a resource setting that doesn't conflict:

1. In the Resource Setting box, double-click the icon next to the resource setting that is conflicting. If you see a message that says "You must clear the Use Automatic Settings box before you can change a resource setting," click OK to close the message, and then clear the Use Automatic Settings box.
2. Scroll through the available resource settings.
3. For each setting, look at the Conflicting Device List box to see if the setting conflicts with any other hardware.
4. If you find a free setting, click OK.

Did you find a setting that doesn't conflict with any other hardware?

- If you can find a setting that does not conflict, go to Step 13.
- If you cannot find a setting that does not conflict, go to Step 14.
- If you see a message stating that the resource setting cannot be modified, go to Step 15.

Step 9: No Conflicts Are Listed   If there are no conflicts listed in the Conflicting Device List box, either you are not viewing resources for the correct device or the conflict has already been resolved (you need to restart your computer to allow Windows to configure the hardware). Look at the top of the dialog box to see if you're viewing resources for the correct device.

There is no further solution to this problem. If restarting Windows does not clear the problem, you may simply need to remove the conflicting device.

Step 10: The Device Is Conflicting   Now you need to identify which hardware is conflicting:

1. Click Set Configuration Manually. In Windows 98, clear the Use Automatic Settings box.
2. In the Conflicting Device List box, identify the other hardware that is using the conflicting resources.

Is more than one resource conflict listed?

- If more than one resource conflict is listed, go to Step 16.
- If only one resource conflict is listed, go to Step 17.
- If no conflicts are listed, go to Step 9.

Step 11: Only One Device Is Conflicting   Do you want to disable the device that is causing all the conflicts?

- If you wish to disable the conflicting device, go to Step 18.
- If you must use the hardware that is causing the conflicts, go to Step 17.

Step 12: More Than One Device Is Conflicting   Look for resource settings that don't conflict:

1. In the Resource Setting box, double-click the icon next to a resource setting that is conflicting. If you see a message that says "You must clear the Use Automatic Settings box before you can change a resource setting," click OK to close the message, and then clear the Use Automatic Settings box.
2. Scroll through the available resource setting(s).
3. For each setting, look in the Conflicting Device List box to see if the setting conflicts with any other hardware.
4. When you find a free setting, click OK.
5. Repeat steps 1 through 4 for each conflicting resource.

Did you find a free setting for each conflicting resource?

- If you do find free settings for each conflicting resource, go to Step 19.
- If some (or all) resources are still conflicting, go to Step 20.
- If you see a message indicating that the resource setting cannot be modified, go to Step 15.

Step 13: There Is a Free Setting   When a free setting is available, change the configuration:

1. Enter the new setting value.
2. Make a note of the old and new settings for later reference.
3. Click OK. If you see a message prompting you to restart your computer, click No.

Depending on the type of hardware you have, you may have to change the jumpers on your hardware card to match the new setting(s), or you may have to run a configuration utility provided by your hardware manufacturer. If the jumper settings on your card aren't set properly, your hardware will not work, even if you resolved the conflict correctly. Refer to your hardware documentation for instructions on changing jumpers.

4.   Click OK.

5.   You may see a message prompting you to restart your computer. Click No.

6.   Click the Start button, click Shut Down, and then click Yes.

7.   When Windows says it is safe to do so, turn off your computer so you can configure the hardware devices that you've changed.

This should correct the problem, and the hardware conflict should now be resolved once the PC is restarted.

Step 14: All Other Settings Conflict   Identify hardware you no longer need:

1.   Scroll through the available resource settings.

2.   When a conflict appears in the Conflicting Device List box, determine whether you still need to use the device that is causing the conflict.

Can you identify a hardware device that you no longer need to use?

■   If you can disable the conflicting device, go to Step 21.

■   If you cannot disable the conflicting device, go to Step 22.

Step 15: Resource Settings Cannot Be Modified   View the resources for the other device:

1.   In the Conflicting Device List box, make a note of which device is using the resource that cannot be modified.

2.   Click Cancel.

3.   In the hardware list, find and double-click the device that is using the resource.

Does this device have a Resources tab?

■   If a Resources tab is available, go to Step 23.

■   If a Resources tab is not available, go to Step 24.

Step 16: There Is More Than One Conflict   How many devices are listed as conflicting?

■   If only one device is causing the conflicts, go to Step 11.

■   If more than one device is causing the conflicts, go to Step 12.

Step 17: There Is Only One Conflict   Look for a resource setting that doesn't conflict:

1.   In the Resource Setting box, double-click the icon next to the resource setting that is conflicting. If you see a message that says "You must clear the Use Automatic Settings box before you can change a resource setting," click OK to close the message, and then clear the Use Automatic Settings box.

2. Scroll through the available resource settings.

3. For each setting, look in the Conflicting Device List box to see if the setting conflicts with any other hardware.

4. If you find a free setting, click OK.

Did you find a setting that doesn't conflict with any other hardware?

■ If you manage to find a setting that does not conflict, go to Step 13.

■ If you see a message indicating that the resource setting cannot be modified, go to Step 15.

■ If all other settings conflict with other hardware, there is no further solution to the problem, and you should probably remove the conflicting device.

Step 18: Disable Conflicting Hardware Determine the best way to disable the conflicting hardware:

1. On the hardware list, double-click the hardware that you want to disable. If you do not see the hardware list, click Cancel until you return to it.

2. Under Windows 98, the Disable In This Hardware Profile box should be unchecked, and the Exists In All Hardware Profiles box may be checked (refer to Figure 12-6).

3. Click the Resources tab. If there is a Set Configuration Manually button, Windows 95/98 can disable and free up resources used by this hardware without your removing its card from your computer.

Do you see a Set Configuration Manually button?

■ If the button exists, you can effectively disable the device, so go to Step 19.

■ If the button is not available, go to Step 25.

Step 19: Resources Now Set Without Conflicts Print out a report for each device you changed:

1. In the hardware list, click a device whose resource settings you changed while resolving the conflict. If you do not see the hardware list, click OK until you return to it.

2. Click Print.

3. Click the second option to print the selected class or device.

4. Click OK.

5. Repeat steps 1 through 4 for each device that you changed during this troubleshooting process.

This should correct the problem, and you should be done.

Step 20: Some Resources Are Still Conflicting Set resources to conflict with only one device:

1. Double-click a resource that is still conflicting. If you see a message that says "You must clear the Use Automatic Settings box before you can change a resource setting," click OK to close the message, and then clear the Use Automatic Settings box.

2. Scroll through the available resource settings. For each value, write down the setting and the name of the hardware it conflicts with. Then click Cancel.

3. Repeat steps 1 and 2 for each conflicting resource.

4. Looking at the list, see if you can change the resource settings so they conflict with only one device—preferably one you could disable.

Are all conflicts with one device?

■ If all the conflicts are with only one device, go to Step 11.

■ If resources still conflict with more than one device, there is no further solution to the problem, and you should probably remove the conflicting device.

Step 21: Disable the Unneeded Device   Determine whether the hardware you want to disable is PnP:

1. Select each resource setting that conflicts with the hardware you will disable, and then click OK.

2. When the message appears saying the setting conflicts with another device, click Yes to continue.

3. Click OK until you return to the hardware list.

4. Click the plus sign (+) next to the type of hardware that you want to disable.

5. Double-click the hardware that you want to disable.

6. Under Windows 98, the Disable In This Hardware Profile box should be unchecked, and the Exists In All Hardware Profiles box may be checked (refer to Figure 12-6).

7. Click the Resources tab.

8. If there is a Set Configuration Manually button, Windows 95 can disable and free up resources used by this hardware without you having to remove its card from your computer.

Do you see a Set Configuration Manually button?

■ If the button exists, you can effectively disable the device, so go to Step 19.

■ If the button is not available, go to Step 25.

Step 22: All Devices Are In Use   Write down a list of all devices using resources:

1. Scroll through the resource settings. On a piece of paper, write down the name of each piece of conflicting hardware and its setting.

2. Click Cancel until you return to the hardware list.

Rearrange resource settings for conflicting hardware:

1. On the hardware list, click the plus sign (+) next to the hardware type for the first item on your written list.

2. Double-click the hardware.

3. Click the Resources tab.

4. Double-click the resource setting that you wrote down. If you see a message that says "You must clear the Use Automatic Settings box before you can change a resource setting," click OK to close the message, and then clear the Use Automatic Settings box.

5. Scroll through the available resource settings. For each setting, look in the Conflicting Device List box to see if it conflicts with any other hardware.

6. If you find a free setting other than the one you wrote down, write down the new values, and continue.

7. If you do not find a free setting, repeat steps 1 through 5 until you run out of hardware to try or you find a free setting.

Did you find a free resource setting?

■ If you found free resources, go to Step 26.

■ If you could not locate free resources, go to Step 27.

Step 23: Resource Information Is Available   Check to see if the device can use a different resource:

1. Click the Resources tab.

2. In the Resource Setting box, double-click the resource setting that you need to free for the other device. If you see a message that says "You must clear the Use Automatic Settings box before you can change a resource setting," click OK to close the message, and then clear the Use Automatic Settings box.

3. Scroll through the available resource settings.

4. For each setting, look in the Conflicting Device List box to see if it conflicts with any other hardware.

5. If you find a free setting, click OK. If you see a message prompting you to restart your computer, click No.

Did you find a free resource setting?

■ If you found free resources, go to Step 28.

■ If you could not locate free resources (or the settings cannot be modified), go to Step 29.

Step 24: Resource Information Is Not Available   Decide which device you should disable. Because both devices need to use the same resource setting, you must decide which device you want to use. You must disable and/or remove the other device. It probably is easier to remove the device that had the original conflict. If you remove the other device, you may see a message telling you that you still have a conflict after completing the procedure. Just restart the procedure and continue resolving the conflict.
    Which device would you like to disable?

■ If you'd rather disable the original device, go to Step 30.

■ If you'd rather disable the other conflicting device, go to Step 31.

Step 25: Manual Button Not Available   Disable the conflicting hardware by removing it:

1. On the hardware list, click the plus sign (+) next to the type of hardware that you want to disable. If you do not see the hardware list, click Cancel until you return to it.

2. Click the hardware you want to disable.

3. Click Remove.

Go to Step 19.

Step 26: Free Resources Found   Change the resource settings to utilize the free resources:

1.   Save the new setting by clicking OK and then clicking OK again.

2.   If you see a message about restarting your computer, click No.

3.   Double-click the hardware that first had the conflict.

4.   Click the Resources tab.

5.   Double-click the resource that is conflicting. If you see a message that says "You must clear the Use Automatic Settings box before you can change a resource setting," click OK to close the message, and then clear the Use Automatic Settings box.

6.   Change the resource setting to the value you just freed. The Conflicting Device List box may show a conflict with the other hardware that you just changed.

7.   Click OK. If you see a message, click Yes to continue.

Go to Step 19.

Step 27: No Free Resources Available   You must disable some hardware to relieve the conflict. Do you want to disable the hardware that caused the original conflict?

■   If you want to disable the hardware that originally caused the conflict, go to Step 18.

■   If you must use *all* of the hardware in the system, there is no further solution to the problem because the conflict cannot be resolved.

Step 28: Free Setting Found   Determine whether there are any remaining conflicts:

1.   Click OK to return to the hardware list.

2.   Double-click the device that had the original conflict.

3.   Click the Resources tab.

4.   See if there are any remaining conflicts listed in the Conflicting Device List box.

If the conflict you just resolved is listed, you can ignore it. It will no longer conflict after you restart your computer later.

Are there still conflicts listed?

■   If all the resources are now set without any conflicts, go to Step 19.

■   If some or all of the resources are still conflicting, go to Step 20.

Step 29: No Free Setting Found   You must decide which device to disable. Because both devices need to use the same resource setting, you must decide which device you want to use. You must disable and remove the other device. It probably is easier to remove the device that had the original conflict at this point. If you choose to remove the other device, you may see a message telling you that you still have a conflict after you finish and restart your computer. Just restart this procedure and continue resolving the conflict.

Which device would you like to disable?

■ If you choose to disable the device with the original conflict, go to Step 30.

■ If you choose to disable the other device that it is conflicting with, go to Step 31.

Step 30: Disable Original Conflicting Device   Determine whether you have to remove the card to disable the hardware:

1. On the hardware list, double-click the hardware that you want to disable. If you do not see the hardware list, click Cancel until you return to it.

2. Under Windows 98, the Disable In This Hardware Profile box should be unchecked, and the Exists In All Hardware Profiles box may be checked (refer to Figure 12-6).

3. Click the Resources tab. If there is a Set Configuration Manually button, Windows 95 can free up resources for this hardware without you having to remove its card from your computer.

Do you see a Set Configuration Manually button?

■ If you do see that button, and there are no resource settings listed in the box, you need to restart your computer:

1. Click OK, and then click OK again.

2. You may be prompted to restart your computer. Click Yes.

■ If no button is available, you need to disable the physical hardware by removing it from the system:

1. On the hardware list, click the plus sign (+) next to the type of hardware that you want to disable. If you do not see the hardware list, click Cancel until you return to it.

2. Click the hardware you want to disable.

3. Click Remove, and then click OK.

4. You may be prompted to restart your computer. You will have to remove the card for this hardware from your computer, so you need to shut down instead of restarting. Click No.

5. Click the Start button, click Shut Down, and then click Yes. When the message says it is safe to do so, turn off your computer and remove the card from your computer.

6. Restart your PC and check if your problem has been resolved.

This should correct the conflict, and complete your troubleshooting procedure.

Step 31: Disable Other Conflicting Device   Determine whether you have to remove the card to disable the hardware:

1. On the hardware list, double-click the hardware that you want to disable. If you do not see the hardware list, click Cancel until you return to it.

2. Under Windows 98, the Disable In This Hardware Profile box should be unchecked, and the Exists In All Hardware Profiles box may be checked (refer to Figure 12-6).

3. Click the Resources tab. If there is a Set Configuration Manually button, Windows 95 can free up resources for this hardware without you having to remove its card from your computer.

Do you see a Set Configuration Manually button?

■ If you see the button, go to Step 32.

■ If you don't see the button, go to Step 33.

Step 32: Disable the Other Device   Determine whether there are any remaining conflicts:

1.   Click OK to return to the hardware list.

2.   Double-click the device that had the original conflict.

3.   Click the Resources tab.

4.   See if there are any remaining conflicts listed in the Conflicting Device List box. If the conflict you just resolved is listed, you can ignore it. It will no longer conflict after you restart your computer later.

Are there still conflicts listed?

■ If there are no further conflicts, go to Step 19.

■ If one or more conflicts are still listed, go to Step 34.

Step 33: Remove the Other Device   Disable hardware by removing it:

1.   On the hardware list, click the plus sign (+) next to the type of hardware that you want to disable. If you do not see the hardware list, click Cancel until you return to it.

2.   Click the hardware you want to disable.

3.   Click Remove.

Go to Step 19.

Step 34: There Are Still Some Conflicts   Try setting resources to conflict with only one device:

1.   Double-click a resource that is still conflicting. If you see a message that says "You must clear the Use Automatic Settings box before you can change a resource setting," click OK to close the message, and then clear the Use Automatic Settings box.

2.   Scroll through the available resource settings. For each value, write down the setting and the name of the hardware it conflicts with, and then click Cancel.

3.   Repeat steps 1 and 2 for each conflicting resource.

4.   Looking at the list, see if you can change the resource settings so they conflict with only one device—preferably one you could disable.

Are all conflicts now with one device?

■ When all the conflicts are with only one device, go to Step 11.

■ If the resources still conflict with more than one device (or cannot be changed), there is no further solution to this problem, and you should probably remove the conflicting device.

Further Study

Microsoft   www.microsoft.com
PCWiz   www.datadepo.com/datadepo.htm
Windsor Technologies   www.windsortech.com/

13

CPU IDENTIFICATION AND TROUBLESHOOTING

CHAPTER AT A GLANCE

The *central processing unit* (also called a *CPU*, *microprocessor*, or simply a *processor*) has become one of the most important developments ever realized in integrated circuit technology (Figure 13-1). On the surface, a CPU is a rather boring device—in spite of its extraordinary complexity, a typical CPU performs only three general functions: mathematical calculations, logical comparisons, and data manipulation. This isn't a very big repertoire for a device carrying well over 20 million transistors. When you look deeper, however, you realize that it is not the *number* of functions that makes a CPU so remarkable, but that each function is carried out as part of a *program* that the CPU reads and follows. By changing the *program*, the activities of a CPU could be completely rearranged without modifying the computer's physical circuitry.

Once the concept of a "generic" central processing function was born, designers realized that the same system could be used to solve an incredibly diverse array of problems (given the right set of instructions). This was the quantum leap in thinking that gave birth to the modern computer and created the two domains that we know today as "hardware" and "software." As you might have guessed, the idea of *central processing* is hardly new. The very earliest computers of the late 1940s and 1950s applied these concepts to simple programs stored on punched cards or paper tape. The mainframe and minicomputers of the 1960s and 1970s also followed the central processing concept. However, it was the integration of central processing functions onto a single silicon chip (the *microprocessor chip*) in the mid-1970s that made the first "personal" computers possible and spawned the explosive developments in CPU speed and performance that we have seen ever since.

Although a CPU can handle mathematical calculations, the CPU itself was not (until recently) designed to handle floating-point math as an internal function. Of course, floating-point math was possible through software emulation, but the performance of such an approach was unacceptable for math-intensive applications (such as CAD, scientific programs, and 3D graphic calculations). In order to deal with high-performance floating-point math in hardware, a *math co-processor* (MCP), or *numerical processing unit* (NPU), was developed to work in conjunction with the CPU. While the classical MCP was implemented as a stand-alone device (such as the Intel 8087, 80287, and 80387), newer generations of CPU incorporate the MCP's functions right into the CPU itself. You'll find that all current processors incorporate MCP features.

FIGURE   13-1   A 1.5GHz Intel Pentium 4 processor (courtesy of Intel Corporation)

The CPU is closely related to the overall speed and performance of personal computers. As a technician, you should understand the essential specifications and characteristics of CPUs. This chapter is intended to provide some insights into CPU evolution and capabilities and to illustrate some of the problems that can manifest themselves in microprocessor operation.

CPU Essentials

A typical microprocessor (such as an AMD Athlon) can be represented by a block diagram such as the one in Figure 13-2. As you can see, there are several sets of processor signals (or *busses*) that you should be familiar with: the *data* bus, the *address* bus, and the *control* bus (usually represented as individual control signals, as you see in the figure). It is these three busses that allow the CPU to communicate with the other elements of the PC and control its operations.

THE BUSSES

The *data bus* carries information to and from the CPU, and it is perhaps the most familiar yardstick of CPU performance. The number of wires in the bus represents the number of bits (or data volume) that can be carried at any point in time. Data lines are typically labeled with a "D" prefix (D0, D1, D2, Dn, and so on). The size of a data bus is typically 8, 16, 32, or 64 bits. As you might expect, larger data busses are preferred, since they allow more data to be transferred simultaneously. The Athlon processor shown in Figure 13-2 provides a 64-bit data bus to the VIA VT8366 North Bridge chip.

In order for the CPU to read or write data, it must be able to specify the precise I/O port or location in system memory. "Locations" are defined through the use of an *address bus*. The number of bits in the address bus represent the number of physical locations that the CPU can access. For example, a CPU with 20 address lines can address 2^{20} (1048576) bytes. A CPU with 25 address lines can address 2^{24} (16777216) bytes, and so on. Address lines are generally represented with an "A" prefix (A0, A1, A19, and so on).

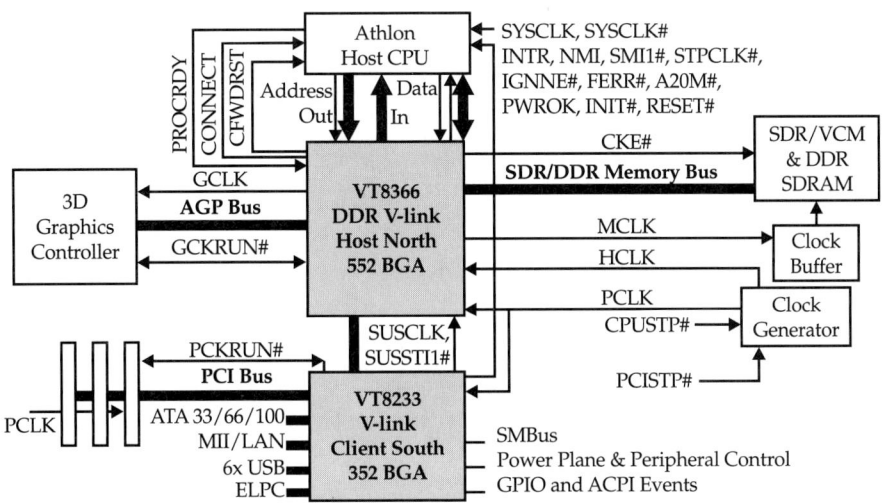

FIGURE 13-2   Diagram of an Athlon CPU with a VIA KT266 chipset (courtesy of VIA Technologies, Inc.)

Finally, *control signals* are used to synchronize and coordinate the operation of a CPU with other devices in the computer. While the number and use of each control signal varies a bit from generation to generation, most control signals fall into one of the following categories:

- Reading or writing functions (to memory or I/O locations)
- Interrupt channels
- CPU test and reset
- Bus arbitration and control
- DMA control
- CPU status
- Parity checking
- Cache operation
- Power control and management

PROCESSOR MODES

Processors are capable of operating in several different modes. The term "mode" refers to the way(s) in which a processor creates (and supports) an operating environment for itself. The processor mode controls how the processor sees and manages the system memory and the tasks that use it. Three different modes of operation have evolved for the PC: the real mode, the protected mode, and the virtual real mode. You should have a basic understanding of these three modes.

Real Mode

The original IBM PC could address only 1MB of RAM. The decisions made in those early days have carried forward, and in each new processor, the processor had to support a mode that would be compatible with the original Intel 8088 chip—this is called *real mode*. When a processor is running in real mode, it has the advantage of speed, but it otherwise accesses memory with the same restrictions of the original 8088: an addressable RAM limit of 1MB and memory access that doesn't take advantage of the 32/64-bit processing found in modern CPUs. All processors can support the real mode—in fact, the computer normally starts up in real (DOS) mode. Real mode is used by DOS and "standard" DOS applications.

Protected Mode

Starting with the IBM AT, a new processor *protected mode* was introduced. This is a much more powerful mode of operation than real mode and is used in all modern multitasking operating systems. The protected mode has numerous advantages:

- The protected mode offers full access to all of the system's memory (there is no 1MB limit in protected mode).
- The protected mode has the ability to multitask, meaning that the operating system can manage the execution of multiple programs simultaneously.
- The protected mode offers support for virtual memory, which allows the system to use the hard disk to emulate additional system RAM when needed.
- The protected mode offers faster (32/64-bit) access to memory and faster 32-bit drivers to handle I/O transfers.

Each running program has its own assigned memory locations, which are "protected" from conflicting with other programs. If a program tries to use a memory address that it isn't allowed to, a "protection fault" is generated. All of the major operating systems today use protected mode: including Windows 98/Me, Windows NT/2000, OS/2, and Linux. Even DOS (which normally runs in real mode) can access protected-mode memory using DPMI (DOS Protected Mode Interface), which is used by DOS games to break the 640KB DOS conventional memory barrier. The 386 (and later) processors can switch "on the fly" from real to protected mode, and vice-versa. Protected mode is also sometimes called *386 Enhanced Mode*, since it became mainstream with that family of processors.

Virtual Real Mode

The third mode of processor operation is actually an enhancement of the protected mode. Protected mode is normally used to run graphical multitasking operating systems, such as the various types of Windows. There is sometimes a need to run DOS programs under Windows, but DOS programs need to be run in real mode—not protected mode. *Virtual real mode* was created to solve this problem. It emulates the real mode from within the protected mode and allows DOS programs to run. A protected-mode operating system such as Windows can actually create multiple *virtual real-mode* machines—though numerous "virtual machines" can be created, each "virtual machine" acts as if it's the only one on the PC. Each virtual machine gets its own 1MB address space, an image of the real hardware BIOS routines, and so on. Virtual real mode is what is used when you use a DOS window or run a DOS game in Windows 98/Me. When you start a DOS application, Windows creates a virtual DOS machine for it to run under.

Modern CPU Concepts

There is a lot more to CPU technology than just busses and addressing modes—in fact, there are entire books written on modern microprocessors. We won't get into many of those concepts in this book, but there is a wide range of concepts that you *should* understand when working with today's PCs.

CISC VS. RISC CPUS

You may sometimes see processors referred to as "CISC" or "RISC" processors. Traditional CPUs are based on a CISC (*Complex Instruction Set Computing*) architecture. This approach allows any number of instructions to be used in the CPU, and the CPU must provide all of the internal circuitry needed to process each instruction. Since each new instruction requires many new transistors for processing, CISC offers versatility at the expense of CPU performance. CISC CPUs (such as the Intel Pentium II, III, and 4 or the AMD Athlon and Duron) are typically found in general-purpose desktop and mobile computers. By comparison, a RISC (*Reduced Instruction Set Computing*) architecture uses a limited number of very powerful instructions. This CPU type requires fewer transistors in the CPU for processing and generally results in faster CPU performance with far lower power consumption. However, RISC processors are often less versatile than their CISC counterparts. CISC CPUs appear in dedicated peripheral devices such as laser printers. Designers are still trying to develop processors that combine CISC versatility with RISC performance, though a number of RISC-type CPUs (like the DEC Alpha or MIPS Orion 4600 devices) have appeared in high-end workstations.

CIRCUIT SIZE AND DIE SIZE

The *circuit size* (or *feature size*) relates to the level of miniaturization in a processor. To make more powerful processors, more transistors are needed—this means the transistors must be made continually smaller.

Technology advancements in integrated circuit fabrication allow circuit sizes to shrink. It was once considered impossible to shrink the circuit size below 1 micron, but most recent processors use a 0.35 micron process—0.25 micron processors are commonplace, and newer chips employ a 0.18 micron process. It is now thought that fabrication technology can eventually be shrunk to as low as 0.08 microns. The issue of *heat* is important here. Packing more transistors onto a chip causes additional heat generation, so each transistor must be made smaller. The size and layout of transistors will also have an effect on die size.

By comparison, the *die size* of the processor refers to its physical surface area—the area of the "chip"—and it is typically measured in square millimeters (mm^2). Smaller die sizes allow designers to get more "chips" from a single wafer, so manufacturing costs are lower (and the resulting processor tends to be less expensive). Smaller die sizes also consume less power.

PROCESSOR SPEED

The processor's speed is a function of several critical factors. Speed is largely related to design of the processor circuit itself—the design dictates the internal timing requirements that limit the maximum speed the processor can handle. Speed is also influenced by manufacturing factors such as the circuit size and die size. In general, smaller chips can run faster because of shorter signal runs and lower power consumption. Finally, process quality (how well the manufacturer uses their equipment to make wafers) can vary, with some chips running faster than others even though they were produced with the same process (and even with the same wafer). Processors are tested and rated for their speed during the testing phase of the manufacturing process.

VERSIONS AND STEPS

A processor represents a very complex and intricate design. As with any hardware design, there are often bugs that are discovered (for instance, the "floating point" bug with early Pentium processors). This means that a given processor may exist in many different design revisions, where newer versions fix the problems encountered with older versions. Intel uses the term *stepping* to indicate a processor's revision, and the S-spec is typically marked right on the processor. AMD uses a model number to indicate the processor's revision. For example, a late-model Intel Pentium III processor may use an S-spec of "SL3WA." It is not necessary that you be able to interpret the S-spec (or other manufacturer's revision markings) on sight—you can usually find a manufacturer's table that details the processor's characteristics based on its S-spec number.

New features are generally not introduced with higher processor steps—only problems are corrected and performance issues resolved.

As a rule, the processor's revision number will have little if any impact on the system's performance, but it might. Problems may be encountered when using particular processor revisions with certain motherboard and BIOS combinations. When you encounter system reliability problems, check with the motherboard maker for possible issues with your processor step. Certain minimum step levels and step matching may also be important when using several processors on the motherboard.

PROCESSOR POWER AND MANAGEMENT

Processors consume a relatively large amount of power. In order to reduce the PC's power demands and improve performance, the traditional +5 volt operating voltages of years past have given way to processors, support chips, and expansion devices that operate at far lower voltages. The first step in this evolution was to reduce the operating voltage level to +3.3 volts. This was apparent in early Pentium processors. Newer processors (such as the Pentium MMX and Pentium II/III/4) reduce voltage levels even more using a *dual voltage* (or *split rail*) design. A split rail processor uses two different voltages. The *external* (or *I/O voltage*) is usually +3.3 volts, a level that ensures compatibility with the other chips on the motherboard. The *internal* (or *core voltage*) is somewhat lower (usually +2.5 to +2.9 volts, though +1.8 to +2.4-volt operation is appearing in the latest processors). The I/O voltage lets the processor "talk" to the motherboard, while the core voltage allows the processor to run cooler internally.

Traditionally, you'd need to set the correct operating voltage for your particular processor(s) by configuring one or more voltage regulation jumpers on the motherboard. Today, processor voltages are set automatically by voltage selection pins on the processor itself—all you need to do is plug in the processor and boot the computer.

Since the power consumption of a CPU is related to its processing speed and internal activity, Intel eventually developed power management circuitry that enables processors to conserve power (and lengthen battery life in laptop systems). Power management was originally introduced with the Intel 486SL processor (an enhanced version of the 486DX processor), and power management features were soon after standardized and incorporated into all Pentium and later processors. These power management features are referred to as System Management Mode (or SMM). SMM circuitry is integrated into the physical processor chip but operates independently to control the processor's power use based on its activity level. SMM allows the system to specify time intervals after which the CPU will be powered down partially or fully (a.k.a. *throttled back*) and also enables the suspend/resume feature that supports today's system standby and hibernate modes. SMM settings are normally controlled through the CMOS Setup.

PROCESSOR COOLING

The millions of transistors operating inside a processor all liberate a small amount of heat each time they switch on or off. When this switching action takes place hundreds of millions (even billions) of times each second, heat management becomes a serious concern. Processors have a specified "safe" temperature range that represents their limits for normal operation. If the processor overheats, serious system problems will usually result. These will usually take the form of system reboots, lockups, or crashes. An overheated processor can also manifest itself through memory errors, application errors, disk problems, or a host of other things. A severely (or repeatedly) overheated processor can also be permanently damaged—though this rarely happens. These problems can be *extremely* difficult to diagnose because they often appear to implicate other parts of the system. For example, a system crash or lockup is often associated with a software bug or hardware conflict rather than an overheated CPU.

Processors are cooled by "active" heat sinks, which are composed of a fast fan mounted to a large metal heat sink with numerous fins. The heat sink "pulls" heat away from the processor, and the fan in turn cools the heat sink. Air warmed by the heat sink is vented from the case (this is the warm air you feel exhausting from the back of the case). The problem with "active" heat sinks is that they rely on the fan. If the fan fails, the processor can overheat in a very short time. To protect the processor from an accidental fan failure, many motherboards integrate tachometers that check the fan's rotational speed and thermostats that measure the processor's case temperature. If the fan stops turning or the processor's temperature climbs over a preset limit, a warning will indicate the fault and allow you to address the trouble before a crash or other system problem occurs.

SYSTEM CLOCKS

Every modern PC uses multiple system clocks. Each clock runs at a specific frequency—normally measured in MHz. A clock *tick* is the smallest unit of time in which processing takes place and is sometimes called a *cycle*. Some types of processing work can be done in one cycle while others require many cycles.

The operation of these clocks is what drives the various circuits in the PC, and the faster they run, the more performance you can expect from your system. Original PCs had a unified system clock—a single clock drove the processor, memory, and I/O bus. A typical PC today may have as many as five different clocks. The term *system clock* generally refers to the speed of the memory bus running on the motherboard (and usually not that of the processor).

The various clocks in a modern PC are created using a single clock generator circuit (on the motherboard) to generate the "main" system clock, and then various clock multiplier (or divider) circuits create the other clock signals. System performance is tied to the speed of the system clock—this is why increasing the system clock speed is usually more important than increasing the raw processor speed. The processor spends a great deal of time waiting for information from much slower devices (especially the system busses). While a faster processor will offer better performance, the increase in speed will not add nearly as much performance if the processor is sitting idle waiting for slower parts of the system.

PROCESSOR PACKAGES

Raw chips (the small *dies*) are not used directly—they are far too fragile and sensitive. Instead, the die is placed in a *package* that will protect the die and help it to dissipate heat. That standardized package normally takes the form of a *slotted* or a *socketed* device. Each generation of CPU uses a different number of pins (and pin assignments), so a different physical socket or slot must be used on the motherboard to accommodate each new generation of processor. Slot-type processors are normally classified as "Slot 1," "Slot 2," or "Slot A." Socket-type processors are usually denoted as "Socket 370" or "Socket A."

Early CPUs were not readily interchangeable, and upgrading a CPU typically meant upgrading the entire motherboard. With the introduction of Intel's 486 CPUs, a type of "OverDrive" processor technology became popular—replacing an existing CPU with a pin-compatible replacement processor that operated at higher internal clock speeds to enhance system performance. Table 13-1 shows that the earliest "sockets" were designated Socket 1 for early 486SX and DX processors (you can see the corresponding sockets illustrated in Figure 13-3). As CPUs advanced, socket types proliferated to support an ever-growing selection of compatible processors. Today, a motherboard can typically accommodate a wide range of processor speeds in the same slot or socket design.

Though aging, Socket 7 remains a popular choice for low-budget systems. Socket 7 motherboards support most Pentium-type processors (Intel Pentium, Intel Pentium MMX, AMD K5, AMD K6, AMD K6-2, Cyrix 6x86, Cyrix 6x86MX, and Cyrix MX II). By setting the proper clock speed and multiplier, a Socket 7 motherboard can support a wide variety of Pentium-class CPUs without requiring any other hardware changes. It is this kind of versatility that has made sockets so important and that has extended the working life of current PCs by providing a viable upgrade path for future CPUs. While high-performance processors from Intel and AMD use proprietary slots and sockets, the Socket 7 scheme remains popular and available because of its versatility. You can review the evolution of Intel's processor packaging at **www.intel.com/technology/itj/q32000.htm**.

Many leading-edge processors such as the Intel Pentium II/III/4 and the AMD Athlon have (at least temporarily) shifted to a slot-based connector rather than a socket. Remember that slot-based processors are not compatible with socket-based motherboards, and vice versa. Various companies have produced adapters (such as the Abit Slotket) that allow socket-style Intel processors to be used on slot-connector style motherboards. However, the motherboard and adapter must be compatible.

THE P-RATING (PR) SYSTEM

CPUs are traditionally classified by their clock speed. For example, a 1.4 GHz Pentium 4 is generally regarded as a better performing CPU than a 900MHz Pentium III. However, a unique and perplexing marketing

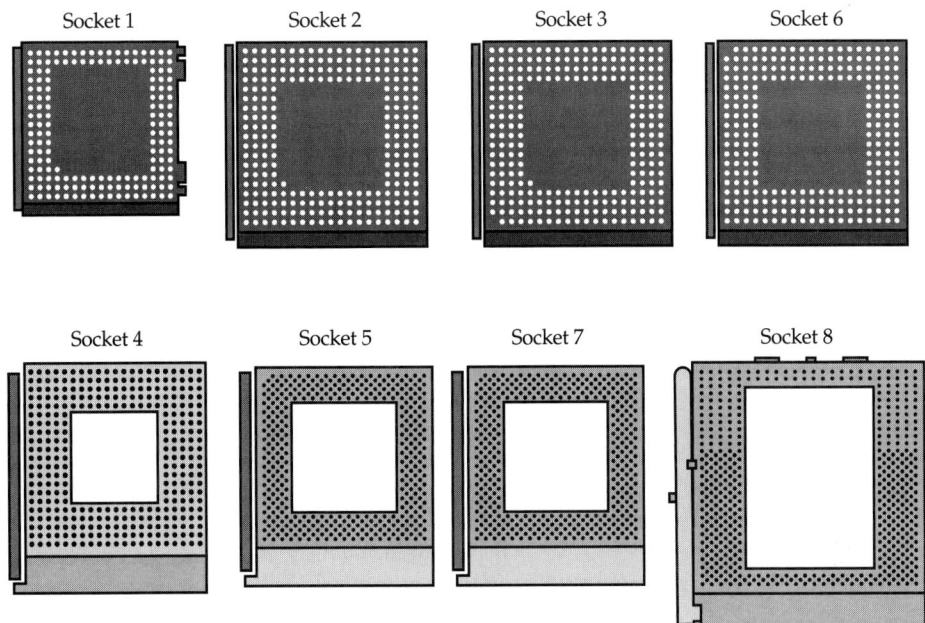

FIGURE 13-3 Comparison of traditional CPU socket styles

TABLE 13-1   COMPARISON OF MAJOR PROCESSOR PACKAGES

SOCKET	PINS	VOLTS	CPU	COMPATIBLE OVERDRIVE PROCESSOR(S)
Socket 1	169	5v	486 SX	BOXDX4ODP75, BOXDX4ODP100
			486 DX	BOXDX4ODPR75, BOXDX4ODPR100
Socket 2	238	5v	486 SX	BOXDX4ODP75, BOXDX4ODP100
			486 DX	BOXDX4ODPR75, BOXDX4ODPR100
			486 DX2	BOXPODP5V63, BOXPODP5V83
Socket 3	237	3v/5v	486 SX	BOXDX4ODP75, BOXDX4ODPR75
			486 DX	BOXDX4ODP100, BOXDX4ODPR100
			486 DX2	BOXPODP5V63, BOXPODP5V83
			486 DX4	n/a
Socket 4	273	5v	60/66MHz Pentium	BOXPODP5V133
Socket 5	320	3v	75/90/100MHz Pentium	BOXPODP3V125, BOXPODP3V150, BOXPODP3V166
Socket 6	235	3v	486 DX4	n/a
Socket 7	321	2.5/3.3v	75/90/100MHz Pentium	BOXPODP3V125, BOXPODP3V150, BOXPODP3V166
Socket 8	387	2.5v	Pentium Pro	n/a
Slot 1	242	n/a	Pentium II/III	n/a

TABLE 13-1   COMPARISON OF MAJOR PROCESSOR PACKAGES *(CONTINUED)*

SOCKET	PINS	VOLTS	CPU	COMPATIBLE OVERDRIVE PROCESSOR(S)
Slot 2	330	n/a	Pentium II/III Xeon	n/a
Socket 370	370	n/a	Pentium III/Celeron	n/a
Socket 423	423	n/a	Pentium 4	n/a
Slot A	242	n/a	AMD Athlon	n/a
Socket A	462	n/a	AMD Athlon/Duron	n/a

problem for competing CPU manufacturers was presented by the fact that a non-Intel CPU at a given clock speed can perform as well as an Intel processor at another clock speed. Although Intel continues to lead CPU development, other CPU makers like AMD and Cyrix have kept the pressure on by packing more performance into fewer clock cycles. In early 1996, Cyrix, IBM Microelectronics, and SGS Thomson (all Intel competitors) gathered to create the P-rating (or PR) system for describing their CPUs. By using a "PR" designation, a CPU can be equated to an Intel Pentium. As an example, the AMD 133MHz Am5x86 processor is marked PR75, and performs comparably to an Intel 75MHz Pentium. When the rating includes a "+" or "++" suffix (such as PR75++), it means that the CPU is delivering *better* performance than the corresponding Intel part. P-ratings are determined through a method of direct comparison:

1. The Winstone benchmark is run on a specifically configured PC system powered by an Intel processor of a given clock speed.

2. The Intel processor is removed from the system and replaced with a competing processor. The Winstone benchmark is run again and a second Winstone score is obtained from the same system now running the competing processor. The system configuration remains identical, and all peripherals are carefully documented.

3. The competing processor is assigned the highest P-rating at which it delivers Winstone scores equal to or greater than a given Pentium. For example, if an AMD K5 processor delivers performance equal to or better than a 90MHz Pentium, it receives a P-rating of 90 (that is, PR90).

It is important to note that the practice of assigning a P-rating to non-Intel processors has largely been discontinued. AMD's processors (Intel's main competitor) are now comparable to Intel models at the stated speeds, so any advantage of one manufacturer's product over another's will now depend on the specific applications the end user will be employing. You should recognize P-ratings when you see them on older Socket 7-type processors, but don't expect to see them on current AMD or VIA Cyrix processors.

ARCHITECTURAL PERFORMANCE FEATURES

The past several years have seen an explosion of technologies and techniques intended to wring more performance out of a processor. Designers have invested tremendous effort to develop the improvements that we take for granted each time we boot the system. This part of the chapter describes some of the performance enhancing features found in a modern microprocessor.

Superscalar Architecture

Program instructions are processed through circuits called e*xecution units* or *execution engines*. The term *superscalar architecture* refers to the use of multiple execution units to allow the CPU to process more than one instruction simultaneously with every clock cycle. For example, the Pentium Pro processor uses two execution "pipes" (dubbed "U" and "V"). This is a form of multiprocessing within the CPU itself, since multiple processing chores are taking place at the same time. Most modern processors are superscalar at one level or another. By combining pipelining with the multiple execution engines of a superscalar architecture, CPUs are making extremely efficient use of every clock cycle.

Pipelining

CPUs process instructions and generate results through a complex series of transistor switches inside the CPU die itself (just as any other logic chip). Early CPUs processed one instruction at a time—that is, an instruction was fetched and processed *completely*, then a new instruction was fetched. Processing could be accomplished in several clock cycles (the exact number of clock cycles depended on the particular instruction). Simple instructions could be processed in 2 or 3 clocks, while complex instructions might demand as much as 7 or 8 clocks.

The *pipelining* technique (also called *instruction pipelining*) allows a new instruction to start processing while a current instruction is still being processed. This way, a CPU can actually work on several instructions during the same clock cycle. In other words, for any given clock cycle, there may be several instructions "in the pipeline." Pipelining lets the CPU make use of execution resources that would otherwise sit idle while an instruction is being completed. Still, the CPU can only finish (generate results for) one instruction per clock cycle.

Superpipelining

As you saw previously, instructions are processed in a pipeline, with each step in the processing pipeline performing a certain amount of work on the instruction. By making the pipeline longer (with more stages), each stage performs less work, and the processor can be scaled to a higher clock frequency. This is known as *superpipelining* and is generally regarded an improvement over regular pipelining.

Speculative Execution and Branch Prediction

Some CPUs have the ability to execute multiple instructions at once. In some cases, not all of the results of the execution will be used, because changes in the program flow may mean that the given instruction should never have been executed in the first place. This often occurs in the vicinity of program branches—where a condition is tested, and the program path is altered depending on the results (for instance, an "if/then" statement). Branches represent a real problem for pipelining, because you can't always be sure that instructions will go in a linear sequence. A less sophisticated processor may stall the pipeline until the results are known, and doing this can hurt performance. More advanced processors will *speculatively execute* the next instruction anyway. The hope is that the CPU will be able to use the results if the branch goes the way it thinks it will.

Even more advanced processors combine this with *branch prediction*, where the processor can actually predict (with fairly good accuracy) which way the branch will go based on past history. Branch prediction improves the handling of branches by making use of a special small cache called the *branch target buffer* (or BTB). Whenever the processor executes a branch, it stores information about it in this area. When the processor next encounters the same branch, it is able to make an informed "guess" about which way the branch is likely to result. This helps keep the pipeline flowing and improves performance.

Dynamic (Out-of-Order) Execution

Even the fastest CPU executes instructions in the order in which they are written within the particular program. This means an improperly or inefficiently-written program can reduce the processing efficiency of the CPU. In many cases, even well-written code can become impaired during the software assembly and linking process. The *dynamic execution* technique allows the processor to evaluate the program's flow and "choose" the best order in which to process instructions. For example, instruction 2 can be executed before instruction 1 has finished. The results of the execution are "reassembled" in the correct order to ensure that the program runs correctly. When implemented properly, this "selective reordering" of instructions allows the CPU to make even better use of its processing resources—and aids overall CPU performance.

Register Renaming and Write Buffers

Register renaming is a technique used to support multiple execution paths without conflicts between different execution units trying to use the same registers. Instead of just one set of registers being used, multiple sets are put into the processor. This allows different execution units to work simultaneously without unnecessary stalls in the pipeline. *Write buffers* are used to hold the results of instruction execution until they can be written back to registers or memory locations. More write buffers allow more instructions to be executed without stalling the pipelines.

Multiprocessing

Multiprocessing is the technique of running a system with more than one processor. The idea is that you can double system performance using two processors instead of one, quadruple performance with four processors instead of one, and so on. It doesn't always work that well in actual practice, but multiprocessing can certainly result in improved performance under certain conditions. In order to employ multiprocessing effectively, the host computer must have all of the following elements in place:

- **Motherboard support**   A motherboard capable of handling multiple processors. This means additional sockets or slots for the extra CPUs and a chipset capable of handling the multiprocessor configuration.

- **Processor support**   Processors that are suitable for use in a multiprocessing system. Not all processors are suitable, and only some versions of the same processor are suitable. Be sure to check the motherboard's documentation for appropriate processor recommendations.

- **Operating system support**   An operating system that supports multiprocessing, such as Windows NT/2000 or UNIX. Other operating systems such as Windows 98 do not support multiprocessing.

Multiprocessing is most effective when used with application software designed specifically for it. Multiprocessing is managed by the operating system, which allocates different tasks to be performed by the various processors in the system. Applications designed for multiprocessing are said to be *threaded*—they are broken into smaller routines that can be run independently. This allows the operating system to let threads run on more than one processor simultaneously, and that is how multiprocessing results in improved performance. If the application isn't designed this way, it can't take advantage of multiple processors (though the operating system can still make use of the additional processors if you use more than one application at a time).

Multiprocessing can be said to be either asymmetric or symmetric. These terms indicate how the operating system divides tasks between the processors in the system. *Asymmetric* multiprocessing designates some processors to perform system tasks only, and others to run applications only. This rigid design results in poor performance during times when the computer needs to run more system tasks than user tasks, or vice versa. *Symmetric* multiprocessing (or SMP) allows *either* system or user tasks to run on any processor. It's a more flexible approach, and therefore offers better performance. SMP is what most multiprocessing PC motherboards use.

For a processor to support multiprocessing, it must support a multiprocessing protocol that dictates the way that the processors and chipset talk to each other in order to implement SMP. Intel processors typically use an SMP protocol called "APIC," and Intel chipsets that support multiprocessing are designed to work with these chips. APIC is a proprietary Intel standard, so even though AMD and Cyrix can make Intel-compatible processors, they cannot make them work in SMP configurations. AMD and Cyrix implement their own SMP standard called "OpenPIC."

Multimedia Extensions

With the growth in graphics, presentation, and other multimedia software, processor throughput often "bogged down" with the intensive calculations that were required. It became necessary to speed up certain computer-intensive processing/calculation procedures related to multimedia and communications applications. While those processes typically occupy 10 percent or less of the overall application code, they can account for up to 90 percent of the program's execution time. Intel and AMD have been locked in a bitter rivalry to provide the best "multimedia extensions" to their processors.

MMX   By 1996, Intel had introduced its MMX extensions into the Pentium processor family (dubbed "Pentium MMX") with 57 powerful new instructions. MMX instructions process multiple data elements in parallel using a technique called *Single Instruction Multiple Data* (SIMD). This technique allows processes to be performed on large amounts of data simultaneously, and reducing the overall processing required to handle the large amounts of video and audio information typically associated with multimedia. Subsequent Intel processors (such as the Pentium II/III/4 and Celeron) are compatible with the MMX instruction set. MMX provides most of its support for 2D images and audio.

3DNow   AMD also saw the need to optimize a processor's multimedia capability. But rather than focus on 2D instructions as Intel did with MMX, AMD chose to focus 21 new instructions on 3D-related features that significantly enhance the processing of 3D graphics images (as well as MPEG decoding). AMD released its 3DNow technology in 1998 (fully nine months ahead of Intel's SSE technology). Since 3DNow offered enhanced 3D processing well ahead of Intel, AMD's K6, K6-2, Athlon, and Duron processor lines presented an appealing alternative for 3D games and visualization programs. You can learn more about 3DNow at **www.amd.com/products/cpg/k623d/inside3d.html**.

SSE and SSE-II   By 1999, Intel had updated its multimedia extensions by introducing SSE (*Streaming SIMD Extensions*) for the Pentium III processor. SSE builds on MMX by adding 70 new instructions that enable advanced imaging, powerful 3D graphics (floating point) processing, streaming video and audio, speech recognition, and added Internet features. SSE features are intended for the standard end-user family of Pentium III processors. The introduction of the Pentium 4 processor added 144 new multimedia enhancement instructions, now referred to as SSE-II.

The Intel CPUs

There is little doubt that Intel Corporation has been a driving force behind the personal computer revolution. Each new generation of microprocessor represents not just mediocre improvements in processing speed, but technological leaps in execution efficiency, raw speed, data throughput, and design enhancements (such as dynamic execution and SIMD). This part of the chapter provides a historical overview of Intel microprocessors and compares their current characteristics.

8086/8088 (1978–1979)

The 29,000-transistor 8086 marked the first 16-bit microprocessor—that is, there are 16 data bits available from the CPU itself. This immediately offered twice the data throughput of earlier 8-bit CPUs. Each of the 24 registers in the 8086/8088 were expanded to 16 bits rather than just 8, and 20 address lines allowed direct access to 1,048,576 bytes (1MB) of external system memory. Although 1MB of RAM is considered almost negligible today, chip designers at the time never suspected that more than 1MB would ever be needed. Both the 8086 and 8088 (as well as many subsequent Intel CPUs) could address 64KB of I/O space (as opposed to RAM space). The 8086 was available for four clock speeds: 5MHz, 6MHz, 8MHz, and 10MHz. Three clock speeds allowed the 8086 to process 0.33, 0.66, and 0.75 MIPS (Millions of Instructions Per Second). The 8088 was available only in 5MHz and 8MHz versions (for 0.33 and 0.75 MIPS, respectively), but its rather unique multiplexing nature reduces its data bandwidth to only 2MB/s.

For all intents and purposes, the 8088 is identical to the 8086. They are exactly the same microprocessor with only one exception: the 8088 multiplexes (time-shares) 8 of the 16 address lines between the address bus and the data bus. If you look at a pinout of an 8088, you will see only 8 data lines available to the outside world (D8 to D15). During one part of a bus cycle, the lower 8 address lines serve as the lower 8 data bits (D0 to D7). During another part of the bus cycle, those 8 shared bits are used as the lower 8 bits of the address bus (A0 to A7). Both CPUs are designed to work with the 8087 math co-processor (MCP).

80186 (1980)

The 16-bit 80186 built on the x86 foundation to offer additional features such as an internal clock generator, system controller, interrupt controller, DMA (Direct Memory Access) controller, and timer/counter circuitry right on the CPU itself. No Intel CPU before or since has offered so much integration in a single CPU. The x186 was also first to abandon 5MHz clock speeds in favor of 8MHz, 10MHz, and 12.5MHz. Aside from these advances, however, the x186 remained similar to the 8086/8088 with 24 registers and 20 address lines to access up to 1MB of RAM. The x186 processors were used as CPUs in embedded applications and never saw service in personal computers. The limitations of the early x86 architecture in the PC demanded a much faster CPU capable of accessing far more than 1MB of RAM.

80286 (1982)

The 24 register, 134,000-transistor 80286 CPU (first used in the IBM PC/AT and compatibles) offered some substantial advantages over older CPUs. Design advances allow the 286 to operate at 1.2 MIPS, 1.5 MIPS, and 2.66 MIPS (for 8, 10, and 12.5MHz respectively). The 286 also breaks the 1MB RAM barrier by offering 24 address lines instead of 20 which allow it to directly address 16MB of RAM. In addition to 16MB of directly-accessible RAM, the 286 can handle up to 1GB (gigabyte) of *virtual memory*, which allows blocks of program code and data to be swapped between the 286's real memory (up to 16MB) and a secondary (or "virtual") storage location, such as a hard disk. To maintain backward compatibility with the 8086/8088 (which can address only 1MB of RAM), the 286 can operate in a real mode. One of the great failings of the 286 is that, while it can switch from real mode to protected mode, it can not switch *back* to real mode without a warm reboot of the system. The 286 uses a stand-alone math co-processor, the 80287.

80386 (1985–1990)

The next major microprocessor released by Intel was the 27,5000-transistor, 32 register, 80386DX CPU in 1985. With a full 32-bit data bus, data throughput is immediately double that of the 80286. The 16, 20, 25, and 33MHz versions allow data throughput up to 50MB/s and processing power up to 11.4 MIPS at 33MHz. A full 32-bit address bus allows direct access to a then unprecedented 4GB of RAM in addition to a staggering 64TB (terabytes) of virtual memory capacity. The 386 was the first Intel CPU to enhance processing through the use of instruction *pipelining*, which, as described earlier, allows the CPU to start working on a new instruction while waiting for the current instruction to finish. A new operating mode (called the *virtual real mode*) enables the CPU to run several real-mode sessions simultaneously under operating systems such as Windows.

Intel took a small step backward in 1988 to produce the 80386SX CPU. The 386SX uses 24 address lines for 16MB of addressable RAM and an external data bus of 16 bits instead of the full 32 bits with the DX. Correspondingly, the processing power for the 386SX is only 3.6 MIPS at 33MHz. In spite of these compromises, a significantly less expensive CPU helped to propagate the 386 family into desktop and portable computers. Aside from changes to the address and bus width, the 386 architecture is virtually unchanged from that of the 386DX.

By 1990, Intel integrated the 386 into an 855,000-transistor, low-power version called the 80386SL. The 386SL incorporated an ISA (Industry Standard Architecture)-compatible chipset along with power management circuitry that optimized the 386 for use in mobile computers. The 386SL resembled the 386SX version in its 24 address lines and 16-bit external data bus. Each member of the 386 family use stand-alone math co-processors (80387DX, 80387SX, and 80387SL). All versions of the 80386 can switch between real mode and protected mode as needed, so they will run the same software as, and are backwardly compatible with, the 80286 and the 8086/8088.

80486 (1989–1994)

The consistent push for higher speed and performance resulted in the development in 1989 of Intel's 1.2 million-transistor, 29 register, 32-bit microprocessor called the 80486DX. The 486DX provides full 32-bit addressing for access to 4GB of physical RAM and up to 64TB (terabytes) of virtual memory. The 486DX offers twice the performance of the 386DX with 26.9 MIPS at 33MHz. Two initial versions (25MHz, 33MHz) were available.

As with the 386 family, the 486 series uses pipelining to improve instruction execution, but the 486 series also adds 8KB of *cache memory* right on the chip. Cache saves memory access time by predicting the next instructions that will be needed by the CPU and loading them into the cache memory *before* the CPU actually needs them. If the needed instruction is indeed in cache, the CPU can access the information from cache without wasting time waiting for memory access. Another improvement of the 486DX is the inclusion of a floating point unit (an MCP) in the CPU itself rather than requiring a separate co-processor chip. This is not true of all members of the 486 family however. A third departure for the 486DX is that it is offered in 5 volt and 3 volt versions. The 3 volt version is intended for laptop, notebook, and other low-power mobile computing applications.

Finally, the 486DX is *upgradeable*. Up to 1989/1990, personal computers were limited by their CPU—when the CPU became obsolete, so did the computer (more specifically the *motherboard*). This traditionally forced the computer user to purchase a new computer (or upgrade the motherboard) every few years in order to utilize current technology. The architecture of the 486 is intended to support CPU upgrades where a future CPU using a faster internal clock can be inserted into the existing system. Intel dubbed this "OverDrive" technology. While OverDrive performance is not as high as that of a newer PC would be, it is much less expensive and allows computer users to protect their computer investments for a longer period of time. It is vital to note that not all 486 versions are upgradeable, and the CPU socket on the motherboard itself must be designed specifically to accept an OverDrive CPU (see the "Processor Packages" section earlier in this chapter).

The 486DX was only the first in a long line of variations from Intel. In 1991, Intel released the 80486SX and the 80486DX/50. Both the 486SX and 486DX/50 offer 32-bit addressing, a 32-bit data path, and 8KB of on-chip cache memory. The 486SX takes a small step backward from the 486DX by removing the math co-processor and offering slower versions at 16, 20, 25, and 33MHz. At 33MHz, the

486SX is rated at 20.2 MIPS. Such design compromises reduced the cost and power dissipation of the 486SX, which accelerated its acceptance into desktop and portable computers. The 486SX is upgradeable with an "OverDrive" CPU (if the computer's motherboard is designed to accept an "OverDrive" CPU), is compatible with an 80487 CPU/MCP, and is available in 5 volt and 3 volt versions. The 486DX/50 operates at a clock speed of 50MHz and performs at 41.1 MIPS. The 486DX/50 *does* integrate an onboard math co-processor, but it is not OverDrive upgradeable or available in a 3 volt version.

The first wave of OverDrive CPUs arrived in 1992 with the introduction of the 80486DX2/50 and the 80486DX2/66. The "2" along with the "DX" indicates that the chip is using an internal clock that is double the frequency of the system. The 486DX2/50 actually runs in a 25MHz system, yet the CPU performs at 40.5 MIPS. The 486DX2/66 runs in a 33MHz system, but it runs internally at 54.5 MIPS. Using a faster CPU with a slower motherboard speed allowed the CPU to work directly with existing PC motherboard designs. Both OverDrive CPUs offer onboard math co-processors and are themselves upgradeable to even faster OverDrive versions. The 486DX2/50 is available in 5 volt and 3 volt versions, while the 486DX2/66 is available only in the 5 volt version.

In 1992, Intel produced a highly integrated, low-power version of the 80486 called the 80486SL. Its 32-bit data bus, 32-bit address bus, 8KB of onboard cache, and integrated math co-processor make it virtually identical to other 486 CPUs, but the SL uses 1.4 million transistors. The extra circuitry provides a low-power management capability that optimize the SL for mobile computers. The 486SL is available in 25 and 33MHz versions and 3 volt and 5 volt designs. At 33MHz, the 486SL operates at 26.9 MIPS.

Intel rounded out its 486 family in 1993 with the introduction of three other CPU models: the 80486DX2/40, the 80486SX/SL-enhanced, and the 80486DX/SL-enhanced. The 486DX2/40 is the third OverDrive CPU intended to run in 20MHz PCs, while the CPU's internal clock runs at 40MHz and performs at 21.1 MIPS. The 486SX/SL (26.9 MIPS at 33MHz) and 486DX/SL (26.9 MIPS at 33MHz) are identical to their original SX and DX versions, but the SL enhancement provides power management capability intended to support portable computers, such as notebooks and sub-notebooks.

By 1994, Intel was finishing its 486 series with the DX4 OverDrive processors. Contrary to the DX4 designation, these 3.3V OverDrive devices are clock *triplers*—so a 486DX4/100 actually runs at a motherboard clock speed of 33MHz. It is important to note that all versions of the 80486 will run the same software and are backward compatible with all CPUs back to the 8086/8088.

PENTIUM (1993–1998)

By 1992, the 486 series had become well entrenched in everyday desktop computing, and Intel was already laying the groundwork for its next generation of CPU. While most users expected Intel to continue with its traditional numbering scheme and dub its next CPU the 80586, legal conflicts regarding trademarking forced Intel to use a name that it could trademark and call its own. In 1993, the 3.21 million-transistor Pentium microprocessor (dubbed "P5" or "P54" series) was introduced to eager PC manufacturers. The Pentium retains the 32-bit address bus width of the 486 family. With 32 address bits, the Pentium can directly address 4GB of RAM and can access up to 64TB of virtual memory. The 64-bit external data bus width can handle twice the data throughput of the 486s. At 60MHz, the Pentium performs at 100 MIPS, and 66MHz yields 111.6 MIPS (twice the processing power of the 486DX2/66). Table 13-2 shows a comparison of Pentium performance ratings in versions from 60MHz to 200MHz. All versions of the Pentium include an onboard math co-processor and are intended to be compatible with future OverDrive designs.

The original Pentium uses two 8KB caches—one for instructions and another for data (16KB total). A dual pipelining technique allows the Pentium to actually work on *more* than one instruction per clock cycle. Another substantial improvement in the Pentium's design was the inclusion of onboard power management features (similar to the 486SL line), allowing it to be used effectively in portable computers.

TABLE 13-2   COMPARISON OF INTEL PENTIUM FAMILY PROCESSORS

CHIP	MHZ	BUS SPEED	L1 CACHE	L2 CACHE	FABRICATION	TRANSISTORS	FORM FACTOR	AVAILABILITY
Pentium	60	60	16KB	---	0.8	3.1 mil	Socket 4	Obsolete
	66	66	16KB	---	0.8	3.1 mil	Socket 4	Obsolete
	75	50	16KB	---	0.6	3.3 mil	Socket 5/7	Obsolete
	90	60	16KB	---	0.6	3.3 mil	Socket 5/7	Obsolete
	100	66	16KB	---	0.6	3.3 mil	Socket 5/7	Obsolete
	120	60	16KB	---	0.6	3.3 mil	Socket 5/7	Obsolete
	133	66	16KB	---	0.35	3.3 mil	Socket 5/7	Obsolete
	150	60	16KB	---	0.35	3.3 mil	Socket 7	Obsolete
	166	66	16KB	---	0.35	3.3 mil	Socket 7	Obsolete
	200	66	16KB	---	0.35	3.3 mil	Socket 7	Obsolete
Pentium MMX	133	66	32KB	---	0.35	4.5 mil	Socket 7	Obsolete
	150	66	32KB	---	0.35	4.5 mil	Socket 7	Obsolete
	166	66	32KB	---	0.35	4.5 mil	Socket 7	Obsolete
	200	66	32KB	---	0.35	4.5 mil	Socket 7	Obsolete
	233	66	32KB	---	0.35	4.5 mil	Socket 7	Obsolete
Mobile Pentium MMX (Tillamook)	166	66	32KB	---	0.25	4.5 mil	MMO	Obsolete
	200	66	32KB	---	0.25	4.5 mil	MMO	Obsolete
	233	66	32KB	---	0.25	4.5 mil	MMO	Obsolete
	266	66	32KB	---	0.25	4.5 mil	MMO	Obsolete
	300	66	32KB	---	0.25	4.5 mil	MMO	Obsolete
Pentium Pro	150	60	16KB	256KB	0.35	5.5 mil	Socket 8	Obsolete
	166	66	16KB	256KB	0.35	5.5 mil	Socket 8	Obsolete
	166	66	16KB	512KB	0.35	5.5 mil	Socket 8	Obsolete
	180	60	16KB	256KB	0.35	5.5 mil	Socket 8	Obsolete
	200	66	16KB	256KB	0.35	5.5 mil	Socket 8	Obsolete
	200	66	16KB	512KB	0.35	5.5 mil	Socket 8	Obsolete
	200	66	16KB	1MB	0.35	5.5 mil	Socket 8	Obsolete
Pentium II (Klamath)	233	66	32KB	512KB	0.35	7.5 mil	Slot 1	Available
	266	66	32KB	512KB	0.35	7.5 mil	Slot 1	Available
	300	66	32KB	512KB	0.35	7.5 mil	Slot 1	Available
Pentium II (Deschutes)	333	66	32KB	128KB	0.25	7.5 mil	Slot 1 Socket 370	Available
	333	66	32KB	512KB	0.25	7.5 mil	Slot 1	Available
	350	100	32KB	512KB	0.25	7.5 mil	Slot 1	Available
	366	66	32KB	128KB	0.25	7.5 mil	Slot 1 Socket 370	Available
	400	66	32KB	128KB	0.25	7.5 mil	Slot 1 Socket 370	Available
	400	100	32KB	128KB	---	7.5 mil	Socket 370	Available
	400	100	32KB	512KB	0.25	7.5 mil	Slot 1	Available
	433	66	32KB	128KB	0.25	7.5 mil	Slot 1 Socket 370	Available
	450	100	32KB	128KB	---	7.5 mil	Slot 1 Socket 370	Available

TABLE 13-2   COMPARISON OF INTEL PENTIUM FAMILY PROCESSORS *(CONTINUED)*

CHIP	MHZ	BUS SPEED	L1 CACHE	L2 CACHE	FABRICATION	TRANSISTORS	FORM FACTOR	AVAILABILITY
	450	100	32KB	512KB	0.25	7.5 mil	Slot 1	Available
	466	66	32KB	128KB	0.25	7.5 mil	Socket 370	Available
	500	66	32KB	128KB	0.25	7.5 mil	Socket 370	Available
	500	100	32KB	128KB	---	7.5 mil	Socket 370	Available
	533	66	32KB	128KB	0.25	7.5 mil	Socket 370	Available
	566	66	32KB	128KB	---	7.5 mil	Socket 370	Available
	600	66	32KB	128KB	---	7.5 mil	Socket 370	Available
	633	66	32KB	128KB	---	7.5 mil	Socket 370	Available
Pentium II (Timna)	600	100	32KB	128KB	0.18	22 mil	Socket 370	Obsolete
Mobile Pentium II (Deschutes)	233	66	32KB	512KB	0.25	7.5 mil	MMO	Available
	266	66	32KB	512KB	0.25	7.5 mil	MMO	Available
	300	66	32KB	512KB	0.25	7.5 mil	MMO	Available
Mobile Pentium II - PE (Dixon)	333	66	32KB	256KB	0.25	37 mil	MMO	Available
	366	66	32KB	256KB	0.25	37 mil	MMO	Available
	400	66	32KB	256KB	0.18	37 mil	MMO	Available
Pentium II Celeron (Covington)	266	66	32KB	none	0.25	7.5 mil	Slot 1	Available
	300	66	32KB	none	0.25	7.5 mil	Slot 1	Available
Pentium II Celeron (Mendocino/ 300A)	300	66	32KB	128KB	0.25	7.5 mil	Slot 1 Socket 370	Available
	333	66	32KB	128KB	0.25	7.5 mil	Slot 1 Socket 370	Available
	366	66	32KB	128KB	0.25	7.5 mil	Slot 1 Socket 370	Available
	400	66	32KB	128KB	0.25	7.5 mil	Slot 1 Socket 370	Available
	433	66	32KB	128KB	0.25	7.5 mil	Slot 1 Socket 370	Available
	466	66	32KB	128KB	0.25	7.5 mil	Socket 370	Available
	500	66	32KB	128KB	0.25	7.5 mil	Socket 370	Available
	533	66	32KB	128KB	0.25	7.5 mil	Socket 370	Available
Pentium II Xeon	400	100	32KB	512KB 1MB	0.25	7.5 mil	Slot 2	Available
	450	100	32KB	512KB 2MB	0.25	7.5 mil	Slot 2	Available
Pentium III (Katmai)	450	100	32KB	512KB	0.25	9.5 mil	Slot 1	Available
	500	100	32KB	512KB	0.25	9.5 mil	Slot 1	Available
	533B	133	32KB	512KB	0.18	9.5 mil	Slot 1	Available
	550	100	32KB	512KB	0.25	9.5 mil	Slot 1	Available
	600	100	32KB	512KB	0.25	9.5 mil	Slot 1	Available
	600B	133	32KB	512KB	0.18 / 0.25	9.5 mil	Slot 1	Available

TABLE 13-2   COMPARISON OF INTEL PENTIUM FAMILY PROCESSORS *(CONTINUED)*

CHIP	MHZ	BUS SPEED	L1 CACHE	L2 CACHE	FABRICATION	TRANSISTORS	FORM FACTOR	AVAILABILITY
Pentium III (Coppermine)	500E	100	32KB	256KB	0.18	28 mil	Slot 1 Socket 370FC	Available
	533EB	133	32KB	256KB	0.18	28 mil	Slot 1 Socket 370FC	Available
	550E	100	32KB	256KB	0.18	28 mil	Slot 1 Socket 370FC	Available
	600E	100	32KB	256KB	0.18	28 mil	Slot 1 Socket 370FC	Available
	600EB	133	32KB	256KB	0.18	28 mil	Slot 1 Socket 370FC	Available
	650E	100	32KB	256KB	0.18	28 mil	Slot 1 Socket 370FC	Available
	667EB	133	32KB	256KB	0.18	28 mil	Slot 1 Socket 370FC	Available
	700E	100	32KB	256KB	0.18	28 mil	Slot 1 Socket 370FC	Available
	733EB	133	32KB	256KB	0.18	28 mil	Slot 1 Socket 370FC	Available
	750E	100	32KB	256KB	0.18	28 mil	Slot 1 Socket 370FC	Available
	800E	100	32KB	256KB	0.18	28 mil	Slot 1 Socket 370FC	Available
	800EB	133	32KB	256KB	0.18	28 mil	Slot 1 Socket 370FC	Available
	850E	100	32KB	256KB	0.18	28 mil	Slot 1 Socket 370FC	Available
	866EB	133	32KB	256KB	0.18	28 mil	Slot 1 Socket 370FC	Available
	933EB	133	32KB	256KB	0.18	28 mil	Slot 1 Socket 370FC	Available
	1000EB	133	32KB	256KB	0.18	28 mil	Slot 1 Socket 370FC	Available
	1133EB	133	32KB	256KB	0.18	28 mil	Slot 1/370FC	Available
(Tualatin)	1133	133 (200)	---	512KB	0.13	---	---	Q3 2001

TABLE 13-2   COMPARISON OF INTEL PENTIUM FAMILY PROCESSORS *(CONTINUED)*

CHIP	MHZ	BUS SPEED	L1 CACHE	L2 CACHE	FABRICATION	TRANSISTORS	FORM FACTOR	AVAILABILITY
	1266	133 (200)	---	512KB	0.13	---	---	Q3 2001
Mobile Pentium III (Coppermine)	400	100	32KB	256KB	0.18	28 mil	---	Available
	450	100	32KB	256KB	0.18	28 mil	---	Available
	500	100	32KB	256KB	0.18	28 mil	---	Available
(Low Voltage)	500	100	32KB	256KB	0.18	28 mil	---	Available
(Speedstep)	600/500	100	32KB	256KB	0.18	28 mil	---	Available
(Low Voltage)	600/500	100	32KB	256KB	0.18	28 mil	---	Available
(Speedstep)	650/500	100	32KB	256KB	0.18	28 mil	---	Available
(Speedstep)	700/500	100	32KB	256KB	0.18	28 mil	---	Available
(Speedstep)	750/600	100	32KB	256KB	0.18	28 mil	---	Available
(Speedstep)	800/650	100	32KB	256KB	0.18	28 mil	---	Available
(Speedstep)	850/700	100	32KB	256KB	0.18	28 mil	---	Available
	900/700	100	32KB	256KB	0.18	28 mil	---	Available
	1000/ 800	100	32KB	256KB	0.18	28 mil	---	Q2 2001
(Coppermine-T)	933	133	32KB	256KB	0.13	28 mil	---	Q2 2001
	1000	133	32KB	256KB	0.13	28 mil	---	Q2 2001
(Tualatin)	1066	133	32KB	512KB	0.13	---	---	July 2001
	1133	133	32KB	512KB	0.13	---	---	July 2001
	1200	133	32KB	512KB	0.13	---	---	Q4 2001
	1266	133	32KB	256KB	0.13	---	---	Q1 2002
Pentium III Celeron	533	66	32KB	128KB	0.25	7.5 mil	Socket 370	Available
	566	66	32KB	128KB	0.18	7.5 mil	Socket 370	Available
	600	66	32KB	128KB	0.18	7.5 mil	Socket 370	Available
	633	66	32KB	128KB	0.18	7.5 mil	Socket 370	Available
	667	66	32KB	128KB	0.18	7.5 mil	Socket 370	Available
	700	66	32KB	128KB	0.18	7.5 mil	Socket 370	Available
	733	66	32KB	128KB	0.18	7.5 mil	Socket 370	Available
	766	66	32KB	128KB	0.18	7.5 mil	Socket 370	Available
	800	100	32KB	128KB	0.18	7.5 mil	Socket 370	Available
	850	100	32KB	128KB	0.18	7.5 mil	Socket 370	Q2 2001
Pentium III Xeon (Tanner)	500	100	32KB	512KB 2MB	0.25	9.5 mil	Slot 2	Available
	550	100	32KB	512KB 2MB	0.25	9.5 mil	Slot 2	Available
	600	133	32KB	256KB	0.18	28 mil	Slot 2	Available
	700	100	32KB	1MB 2MB	0.18	28 mil	Slot 2	Available
	900	100	32KB	512KB 2MB	0.18	28 mil	Slot 2	Available
Pentium III Xeon (Cascades)	667	133	32KB	256KB	0.18	28 mil	Slot 2	Available
	733	133	32KB	256KB	0.18	28 mil	Slot 2	Available

TABLE 13-2   COMPARISON OF INTEL PENTIUM FAMILY PROCESSORS *(CONTINUED)*

CHIP	MHZ	BUS SPEED	L1 CACHE	L2 CACHE	FABRICATION	TRANSISTORS	FORM FACTOR	AVAILABILITY
	800	133	32KB	256KB	0.18	28 mil	Slot 2	Available
	866	133	32KB	256KB	0.18	28 mil	Slot 2	Available
	933	133	32KB	256KB	0.18	28 mil	Slot 2	Available
	1000	133	32KB	256KB	0.18	28 mil	Slot 2	Available
(Prestoria)	1133	133	---	256KB 512KB	0.13	---	---	Q3 2001
	1266	133	---	256KB 512KB	0.13	---	---	Q3 2001
Mobile Celeron III	400	100	32KB	128KB	0.18	22 mil	---	Available
	450	100	32KB	128KB	0.18	22 mil	---	Available
	500	100	32KB	128KB	0.18	22 mil	---	Available
	550	100	32KB	128KB	0.18	22 mil	---	Available
	600	100	32KB	128KB	0.18	22 mil	---	Available
	650	100	32KB	128KB	0.18	22 mil	---	Available
	700	100	32KB	128KB	0.18	22 mil	---	Available
	750	100	32KB	128KB	0.18	22 mil	---	Available
	800	100	32KB	128KB	0.18	22 mil	---	Q2 2001
	850	100	32KB	128KB	0.18	22 mil	---	Q3 2001
Pentium 4 (Willamette)	1300	400	20KB	256KB	0.18	42 mil	Socket 423	Available
	1400	400	20KB	256KB	0.18	42 mil	Socket 423	Available
	1500	400	20KB	256KB	0.18	42 mil	Socket 423	Available
	1700	400	20KB	256KB	0.18	42 mil	Socket 423	Available
	2000	400	20KB	256KB	0.18	42 mil	Socket 423	Q2 2001
(Prescott)	---	400	20KB	256KB	0.18	---	Socket 478	Q2 2001
(Northwood)	2000	400	20KB	512KB	0.13	---	Socket 478	2001
(Mobile P4)	1500	400	20KB	---	0.13	---	---	Q1 2002
(Xeon P4)	2000	400	---	256KB 1MB	0.13	---	Socket 603	Q4 2001

Early Pentium models started at 5 volts, but all models starting at about 100MHz (P54C) use 3.3 volts or less. Finally, the Pentium is fully backward-compatible with all software written for the 8086/8088 and later CPUs. Intel has released various versions of the Pentium up to 200MHz. Faster versions are unlikely because of more powerful processors, such as the Pentium MMX, Pentium Pro, and Pentium II/III (and the Pentium 4 line). Technicians who want the nitty-gritty details on Pentium operation can download the Pentium-family processor manuals from the Internet, as listed in Table 13-3.

The number of Pentium versions and features greatly proliferated over the years—so much so that it is *extremely* difficult to tell whether a motherboard is configured properly for a given CPU. However, you can use the S-spec rating (the engineering revision level) marked on each Pentium or Pentium MMX processor

TABLE 13-2   DETAILED PROCESSOR MANUALS AND TECHNICAL INFORMATION

PROCESSOR	MANUAL URL
Pentium Processor Manuals	developer.intel.com/design/pentium/manuals/
Pentium MMX Manuals	developer.intel.com/design/mmx/manuals/
PentiumPro Processor Manuals	developer.intel.com/design/pro/manuals/
Pentium II Manuals	developer.intel.com/design/PentiumII/manuals/
Am486DX2 Manual	www.amd.com/products/cpg/techdocs/datasheets/19200.pdf
Am486DX4 Manual	www.amd.com/products/cpg/techdocs/datasheets/19160.pdf
5x85 Manual	www.amd.com/products/cpg/techdocs/datasheets/19751.pdf
K5 Manual	www.amd.com/products/cpg/techdocs/appnotes/18524.pdf
K6 Manual	www.amd.com/K6/k6docs/pdf/20695.pdf
Cyrix MII	www.cyrix.com/products/miibrief.htm
Cyrix MII	www.cyrix.com/products/cyrtechdoc.htm
Cyrix III	www.cyrix.com/products/cyr3faq.htm

to reveal key operating characteristics of the particular CPU. Table 13-4 presents the S-specs for Pentium and Pentium MMX processors. Keep the following notes in mind when you're consulting Table 13-4:

- PPGA, TCP, and SPGA are all case styles.
- ES means "Engineering Sample."
- DP means for use in a "Dual Processor" configuration only.
- "Mobile" means the CPU was developed for mobile operation.
- MD means designed to accommodate "minimum timing."
- VR means "voltage reduced" (3.3–3.465 volts).
- VRE means the CPU uses 3.4–3.6 volts.
- VRT means the CPU uses "split voltage" (2.8V/3.3V).
- STD means "standard part" using normal timing and 3.135–3.6 volts.

TABLE 13-3   S-SPEC REFERENCE TABLE FOR PENTIUM AND PENTIUM MMX PROCESSORS

S-SPEC	MANUFACTURER'S STEP	CORE/BUS SPEED (MHZ)	COMMENTS
Q016	mxA3	150/60	ES, TCP
Q017	mxA3	166/66	ES, TCP
Q018	xA3	200/66	ES, PPGA
Q019	xA3	166/66	ES, PPGA
Q020	xA3	150/60	ES, PPGA
Q024	mcC0	150/60	TCP, VRT
Q040	mcC0	150/60	SPGA, VRT
Q0540	B1	75/50	ES
Q0541	B1	75/50	ES
Q0542	B1	90/60	STD

TABLE 13-4	S-SPEC REFERENCE TABLE FOR PENTIUM AND PENTIUM MMX PROCESSORS *(CONTINUED)*

S-SPEC	MANUFACTURER'S STEP	CORE/BUS SPEED (MHZ)	COMMENTS
Q0543	B1	90/60	DP
Q0563	B1	100/66	STD
Q0587	B1	100/66	VR
Q0601	B1	75/50	TCP, Mobile
Q0606	B3	75/50	TCP, Mobile
Q061	mxA3	150/60	ES, PPGA
Q0611	B3	90/60	STD
Q0612	B3	90/60	VR
Q0613	B1	90/60	VR
Q0614	B1	100/66	VR
Q062	mxA3	166/66	ES, PPGA
Q0628	B3	90/60	STD
Q0653	B5	90/60	STD
Q0654	B5	90/60	VR
Q0655	B5	90/60	MD
Q0656	B5	100/66	MD
Q0657	B5	100/66	VR, MD
Q0658	B5	100/66	VRE, MD
Q0666	B5	75/50	STD
Q0677	B3	100/66	VRE, MD
Q0686	mA1	75/50	VRT, TCP
Q0689	mA1	75/50	VRT, SPGA
Q0694	mA1	90/60	VRT, TCP
Q0695	mA1	90/60	VRT, SPGA
Q0697	C2	100/50 or 100/66	STD
Q0698	C2	100/50 or 100/66	VRE, MD
Q0699	C2	90/60	STD
Q0700	C2	75/50	STD
Q0704	B5	75/50	TCP, Mobile
Q0707	B5	120/60	VRE, MD
Q0708	B5	120/60	STD
Q0711	C2	120/60	VRE, MD
Q0725	C2	75/50	TCP, Mobile
Q0732	C2	120/60	VRE/MD
Q0733	C2	133/66	MD
Q0749	C2	75/50	MD
Q0751	C2	133/66	MD
Q0772	cB1	133/66	STD/no Kit
Q0773	cB1	133/66	STD
Q0774	cB1	133/66	VRE, MD (no Kit)
Q0775	C2	133/66	VRE, MD
Q0776	cB1	120/60	STD/no Kit
Q0779	mcB1	120/60	VRT, TCP
Q0783	E0	90/60	STD
Q0784	E0	100/50 or 100/66	STD

TABLE 13-4 S-SPEC REFERENCE TABLE FOR PENTIUM AND PENTIUM MMX PROCESSORS *(CONTINUED)*

S-SPEC	MANUFACTURER'S STEP	CORE/BUS SPEED (MHZ)	COMMENTS
Q0785	E0	120/60	VRE
Q0808	mcB1	120/60	3.3V, SPGA
Q0835	cC0	150/60	STD
Q0836	cC0	166/66	VRE/no Kit
Q0837	E0	75/50	STD
Q0841	cC0	166/66	VRE
Q0843	cC0	133/66	STD/no Kit
Q0844	cC0	133/66	STD
Q0846	E0	75/50	TCP, Mobile
Q0848	mA4	75/50	VRT, TCP
Q0849	mA4	90/60	VRT, TCP
Q0850	mA4	100/66	VRT, TCP
Q0851	mA4	75/50	VRT, SPGA
Q0852	mA4	90/60	VRT, SPGA
Q0853	mA4	100/66	VRT, SPGA
Q0878	cC0	150/60	STD, PPGA
Q0879	mcC0	120/60	TCP, VRT
Q0880	mcC0	120/60	SPGA, 3.1V
Q0881	mcC0	133/66	TCP, VRT
Q0882	mcC0	133/66	SPGA, 3.1V
Q0884	mcB1	100/66	VRT, TCP
Q0886	cC0	166/66	VRE, PPGA
Q0887	mcC0	100/66	TCP, VRT
Q0890	cC0	166/66	VRE, PPGA
Q0906	mcC0	150/60	TCP, 3.1V
Q0949	cC0	166/66	VRE, PPGA
Q0951	cC0	200/66	VRE, PPGA
Q0951F	cC0	200/66	VRE, PPGA
Q115	mxB1	166/66	ES, TCP
Q116	mxB1	150/60	ES, TCP
Q124	xB1	200/66	ES, PPGA
Q125	xB1	166/66	ES, PPGA
Q126	xB1	166/66	ES, SPGA
Q127	mxB1	166/66	ES, PPGA
Q128	mxB1	150/60	ES, PPGA
Q129	mxB1	133/66	ES, PPGA
Q130	mxB1	133/66	ES, TCP
Q146	myA0	200/66	TCP
Q147	myA0	233/66	TCP
Q230	mxB1	120/60	ES, TCP
Q250	myA0	266/66	TCP
Q251	myA0	266/66	TCP
Q252	myA0	166/66	TCP
Q255	myA0	166/66	TCP
Q430	xB1	200/66	SPGA

TABLE 13-4   S-SPEC REFERENCE TABLE FOR PENTIUM AND PENTIUM MMX PROCESSORS *(CONTINUED)*

S-SPEC	MANUFACTURER'S STEP	CORE/BUS SPEED (MHZ)	COMMENTS
Q586	mxB1	200/66	PPGA
Q695	myA0	266/66	TCP
Q766	myB2	266/66	TCP
Q767	myB2	266/66	TCP
Q768	myB2	300/60	TCP
S106J	cB1	133/66	STD/no Kit
SK079	C2	75/50	TCP Mobile
SK086	C2	120/60	VRE, MD
SK089	mA1	75/50	VRT, TCP
SK090	mA1	90/60	VRT, TCP
SK091	mA1	75/50	VRT, SPGA
SK092	mA1	90/60	VRT, SPGA
SK098	C2	133/66	MD
SK106	cB1	133/66	STD/no Kit
SK107	cB1	133/66	STD
SK110	cB1	120/60	STD/no Kit
SK113	mcB1	120/60	VRT, TCP
SK118	mcB1	120/60	VRT, TCP
SK119	mA4	75/50	VRT, TCP
SK120	mA4	90/60	VRT, TCP
SK121	mA4	100/66	VRT, TCP
SK122	mA4	75/50	VRT, SPGA
SK123	mA4	90/60	VRT, SPGA
SK124	mA4	100/66	VRT, SPGA
SL22F	mxA3	166/66	TCP
SL22G	mxA3	150/60	TCP
SL22M	cC0	120/60	STD
SL22Q	cC0	133/66	STD
SL239	xA3	166/66	SPGA
SL23M	myB2	266/66	TCP
SL23P	myB2	266/66	TCP
SL23R	xA3	166/66	PPGA
SL23S	xA3	200/66	PPGA
SL23T	xA3	166/66	SPGA
SL23V	xB1	166/66	PPGA
SL23W	xB1	200/66	PPGA
SL23X	xB1	166/66	SPGA
SL23Z	mxA3	166/66	PPGA
SL246	mxA3	150/60	PPGA
SL24Q	cC0	200/66	VRE, PPGA, no Kit
SL24R	cC0	166/66	VRE, no Kit
SL25H	cC0	200/66	VRE, PPGA
SL25J	cC0	120/60	STD
SL25L	cC0	133/66	STD
SL25M	xA3	166/66	PPGA

TABLE 13-4   S-SPEC REFERENCE TABLE FOR PENTIUM AND PENTIUM MMX PROCESSORS (CONTINUED)

S-SPEC	MANUFACTURER'S STEP	CORE/BUS SPEED (MHZ)	COMMENTS
SL25N	xA3	200/66	PPGA
SL26H	xA3	166/66	PPGA
SL26J	xA3	200/66	PPGA
SL26Q	xA3	200/66	PPGA
SL26T	mxB1	166/66	TCP
SL26U	mxB1	150/60	TCP
SL26V	xA3	166/66	SPGA
SL274	xA3	200/66	PPGA
SL27A	mxB1	166/66	PPGA
SL27B	mxB1	150/60	PPGA
SL27C	mxB1	133/66	PPGA
SL27D	mxB1	133/66	TCP
SL27H	xB1	166/66	PPGA
SL27J	xB1	200/66	PPGA
SL27K	xB1	166/66	SPGA
SL27S	xB1	233/66	PPGA
SL28P	myA0	200/66	TCP
SL28Q	myA0	233/66	TCP
SL293	xB1	233/66	PPGA
SL2BM	xB1	233/66	PPGA
SL2FP	xB1	166/66	PPGA
SL2FQ	xB1	200/66	PPGA
SL2HU	xA3	166/66	SPGA
SL2HX	xB1	166/66	SPGA
SL2N5	myA0	266/66	TCP
SL2N6	myA0	166/66	TCP
SL2RY	xB1	200/66	SPGA
SL2S9	xB1	200/66	SPGA
SL2WK	mxB1	200/66	PPGA
SL2WW	E0	90/60	STD
SL2ZH	myA0	266/66	TCP
SL34N	myB2	300/66	TCP
SU031	C2	90/60	STD
SU032	C2	100/50 or 100/66	STD
SU033	C2	120/60	VRE, MD
SU038	cB1	133/66	STD/no Kit
SU070	C2	75/50	STD
SU071	cC0	150/60	STD
SU072	cC0	166/66	VRE, no Kit
SU073	cC0	133/66	STD/no Kit
SU097	E0	75/50	STD
SU098	E0	75/50	STD
SU099	E0	100/50 or 100/66	STD
SU100	E0	120/60	STD
SU110	E0	100/50 or 100/66	STD

TABLE 13-4   S-SPEC REFERENCE TABLE FOR PENTIUM AND PENTIUM MMX PROCESSORS (CONTINUED)

S-SPEC	MANUFACTURER'S STEP	CORE/BUS SPEED (MHZ)	COMMENTS
SU114	cC0	200/66	VRE, PPGA
SU122	cC0	150/60	STD
SX874	B1	90/60	DP, STD
SX879	B1	90/60	STD
SX885	B1	90/60	MD
SX886	B1	100/66	MD
SX909	B1	90/60	VR
SX910	B1	100/66	VR, MD
SX921	B3	90/60	MD
SX922	B3	90/60	VR
SX923	B3	90/60	STD
SX942	B3	90/60	DP, STD
SX943	B3	90/60	DP, VR
SX944	B3	90/60	DP, MD
SX951	B3	75/50	TCP, Mobile
SX957	B5	90/60	STD
SX958	B5	90/60	VR
SX959	B5	90/60	MD
SX960	B3	100/66	VRE, MD
SX961	B5	75/50	STD
SX962	B5	100/66	VRE, MD
SX963	C2	100/50 or 100/66	STD
SX968	C2	90/60	STD
SX969	C2	75/50	STD
SX970	C2	100/50 or 100/66	VRE, MD
SX975	B5	75/50	TCP, Mobile
SX994	C2	120/60	VRE, MD
SX998	C2	75/50	MD
SX999	mcB1	120/60	3.3V, SPGA
SY005	E0	75/50	STD
SY006	E0	90/60	STD
SY007	E0	100/50 or 100/66	STD
SY009	E0	75/50	TCP, Mobile
SY015	cC0	150/60	STD
SY016	cC0	166/66	VRE, no Kit
SY017	cC0	166/66	VRE
SY019	mcC0	133/66	TCP, VRT
SY020	mcC0	100/66	TCP, VRT
SY021	mcC0	120/60	TCP, VRT
SY022	cC0	133/66	STD
SY023	cC0	133/66	STD/no Kit
SY027	mcC0	120/60	SPGA, 3.1V
SY028	mcC0	133/66	SPGA, 3.1V
SY029	mcB1	100/66	VRT, TCP
SY030	mcC0	120/60	SPGA, 3.3V

TABLE 13-4   S-SPEC REFERENCE TABLE FOR PENTIUM AND PENTIUM MMX PROCESSORS (CONTINUED)

S-SPEC	MANUFACTURER'S STEP	CORE/BUS SPEED (MHZ)	COMMENTS
SY033	E0	120/60	STD
SY037	cC0	166/66	VRE, PPGA
SY043	mcC0	150/60	TCP, 3.1V
SY044	cC0	200/66	VRE, PPGA
SY045	cC0	200/66	VRE, PPGA
SY046	mcC0	100/66	SPGA, 3.1V
SY055	cC0	166/66	VRE/no Kit
SY056	mcC0	75/50	TCP, VRT
SY058	mcC0	150/60	SPGA, VRT
SY059	xA3	166/66	PPGA
SY060	xA3	200/66	PPGA
SY061	mcC0	150/60	TCP, VRT
SY062	cC0	120/60	STD
SZ951	B3	90/60	STD
SZ977	B5	75/50	STD
SZ978	B5	90/60	STD
SZ994	C2	75/50	STD
SZ995	C2	90/60	STD
SZ996	C2	100/50 or 100/66	STD

PENTIUM PRO (1995–1999)

Even though the Pentium has proven adept at handling 16-bit and 32-bit operating systems, designers continued to seek ways to optimize the Pentium for 32-bit performance—especially for operating systems like Windows NT and the then-emerging Windows 95. The Pentium Pro (dubbed "P6" or "PPro") evolved as an "optimized" Pentium intended to support "business systems," such as high-end desktop workstations and network servers. The P6 processors range from 150MHz to 200MHz and can handle multiprocessing in systems up to four CPUs.

The Pentium Pro uses dynamic execution to improve its performance and employs two separate 8KB L1 caches—one for data, and one for instructions. Another major improvement in the Pentium Pro is its use of up to 1MB of onboard L2 cache. This maximizes the P6's performance without relying on the motherboard to supply L2 cache. You can see the use of L1 and L2 cache and Pentium Pro family performance in Table 13-2.

While not as prolific as the "classic" Pentium and Pentium MMX, there are still a number of Pentium Pro versions and features to contend with—this variety can make it difficult to determine the proper motherboard configuration for a given P6. However, you can use the "S-spec" rating marked on each Pentium Pro processor to reveal key operating characteristics of the particular CPU. Table 13-5 presents the S-specs for Pentium Pro processors. Keep the following notes in mind when you're consulting Table 13-5:

Note 1: L2 Cache refers to the silicon revision of the 256KB or 512KB on-chip L2 cache.

Note 2: The sA0 step is logically equivalent to the C0 step, but on a different manufacturing process.

Note 3: The VID pins are not supported on these parts.

Note 4: These are engineering samples only.

Note 5: The VID pins are functional but not tested on these parts.

Note 6: These sample parts are equipped with a pre-production 512KB L2 cache.

Note 7: These components have additional specification changes associated with them:

Primary voltage = 3.5V ± 5%

Max. Thermal Design Power = 39.4W @ 200MHz

Current = 11.9A

The VID pins are not supported on these parts.

T9 = Minimum GTL+ Input Hold Time = 0.9ns

Minimum Non-GTL+ Input High Voltage = 2.2V

TABLE 13-5   S-SPEC REFERENCE TABLE FOR PENTIUM PRO PROCESSORS

S-SPEC	MANUFACTURER'S STEP	L2 SIZE (KB)	CORE/BUS SPEED (MHZ)	COMMENTS
Q008	sB1	512	166/66	note 4
Q009	sB1	512	166/66	note 4
Q010	sB1	512	200/66	note 4
Q011	sB1	512	200/66	note 4
Q033	sB1	256	180/60	note 4
Q034	sB1	256	200/66	note 4
Q035	sB1	256	180/60	note 4
Q036	sB1	256	200/66	note 4
Q076	sA1	256	200/66	note 7
Q0812	B0	256	133/66	notes 3, 4
Q0813	B0	256	150/60	notes 3, 4
Q0815	B0	256	133/66	notes 3, 4
Q0816	B0	256	150/60	notes 3, 4
Q0822	C0	256	150/60	notes 3, 4
Q0825	C0	256	150/60	note 4
Q0826	C0	256	150/60	note 4
Q083	sB1	256	200/66	note 7
Q084	sB1	256	200/66	note 7
Q0858	sA0	256	180/60	notes 2, 4
Q0859	sA0	256	200/66	notes 2, 4
Q0860	sA0	256	180/60	notes 2, 4, 5
Q0861	sA0	256	200/66	notes 2, 4, 5
Q0864	sA0	512	166/66	notes 2, 4, 6
Q0865	sA0	512	200/66	notes 2, 4, 6
Q0871	sA1	256	180/60	note 4
Q0872	sA1	256	200/66	note 4
Q0873	sA0	256	180/60	notes 2, 4
Q0874	sA0	256	200/66	notes 2, 4
Q0907	sA1	256	180/60	note 4
Q0908	sA1	256	200/66	note 4
Q0909	sA1	256	200/66	note 4
Q0910	sA0	256	180/60	note 2
Q0918	sA1	512	166/66	notes 4, 6
Q0920	sA1	512	200/66	notes 4, 6

TABLE 13-5   S-SPEC REFERENCE TABLE FOR PENTIUM PRO PROCESSORS (CONTINUED)

S-SPEC	MANUFACTURER'S STEP	L2 SIZE (KB)	CORE/BUS SPEED (MHZ)	COMMENTS
Q0924	sA1	512	200/66	notes 4, 6
Q0929	sA1	512	166/66	note 4
Q932	sA1	512	200/66	note 4
Q935	sA1	512	166/66	note 4
Q936	sA1	512	200/66	note 4
SL22S	sB1	256	180/60	---
SL22T	sB1	256	200/66	---
SL22U	sB1	256	180/60	---
SL22V	sB1	256	200/66	---
SL22X	sB1	512	166/66	---
SL22Z	sB1	512	200/66	---
SL23L	sB1	256	180/60	---
SL23M	sB1	256	200/66	---
SL245	sA1	256	200/66	note 7
SL247	sA1	256	200/66	note 7
SL254	sB1	256	200/66	note 7
SL255	sB1	256	200/66	note 7
SU103	sA1	256	180/60	---
SU104	sA1	256	200/66	---
SY002	B0	256	150/60	note 3
SY010	C0	256	150/60	---
SY011	B0	256	150/60	---
SY012	sA0	256	180/60	note 2
SY013	sA0	256	200/66	note 2
SY014	B0	256	150/60	---
SY031	sA1	256	180/60	---
SY032	sA1	256	200/66	---
SY034	sA1	512	166/66	---
SY039	sA1	256	180/60	---
SY040	sA1	256	200/66	---
SY047	sA1	512	166/66	---
SY048	sA1	512	200/66	---

PENTIUM MMX (1997–1999)

The data processing demands imposed by multimedia applications continue to be a burden to most PCs—especially for graphics-intensive games and other video applications. In 1997, Intel released an important enhancement to the Pentium known as *multimedia extensions* (or MMX). By streamlining and improving the existing Pentium architecture and adding 57 new MMX instructions, the Pentium MMX was poised as the premier mid-range CPU into the late 1990s. With speeds from 133MHz to 233MHz, the Pentium MMX can typically execute existing software 10–20 percent faster than "classic" Pentium processors at the same clock speed. When using software written specifically for MMX instructions, the PC can deliver higher color depths and higher resolutions while still maintaining high frame rates for rendering and video playback.

The Pentium MMX doubled the code and data caches to 16KB each. Larger and separate internal caches improve performance by reducing the average memory access time and providing fast access to recently used instructions and data. The data cache supports a write-back (or write-through on a line-by-line basis) policy for memory updates. Pentium MMX processors also employ improved dynamic branch prediction to boost performance by predicting the most likely set of instructions to be executed.

There are many other features included in the Pentium MMX line. The superscalar architecture is capable of executing two integer instructions in parallel in a single clock cycle for improved integer processing performance. A pipelined floating point unit (FPU) supporting 32-bit, 64-bit, and 80-bit formats is capable of executing two floating-point instructions in a single clock. An additional instruction pipe was added to further improve instruction processing. A pool of four write buffers is shared between the dual pipelines to improve memory write performance. There is also a multiprocessor interrupt controller on-chip that allows low-cost symmetric multiprocessing (SMP), and there are SL technology power management features for efficient power control. Table 13-4 lists the S-spec numbers for Pentium MMX processors.

PENTIUM II (1997–CURRENT)

With the Pentium MMX and Pentium Pro processors firmly entrenched in the PC community, Intel sought to combine the best features of both—the software performance of the Pentium Pro and the multimedia performance of the Pentium MMX. The result appeared in 1997 as the "Pentium II" (or "P II," previously dubbed the "Klamath"). As with the Pentium Pro, the Pentium II is optimized for use with 32-bit operating systems and software (such as Windows 98/Me or Windows NT). Yet the P II also includes the architecture and 57 new instructions needed to handle MMX applications. At 266MHz, the Pentium II processor can provide from 1.6 to over 2 times the performance of a 200MHz Pentium processor.

The Pentium II also employs the dynamic execution technology used in the Pentium Pro. Dynamic execution uses multiple branch prediction to predict the flow of the program through several branches (accelerating the flow of work to the processor). A data flow analysis then creates an optimized (reordered) schedule of instructions by analyzing the relationships between instructions. And, finally, speculative execution carries out the instructions "speculatively" (assuming the execution order to be correct) on the basis of this optimized schedule. Dynamic execution keeps the processor's superscaler "execution engines" busy and boosts overall performance.

The Pentium II uses a 32KB L1 cache—this allows a 16KB cache for data, and a 16KB cache for instructions. It also provides 512KB of L2 cache right in the CPU package to maximize the processor's performance without relying on the motherboard for cache. The P II supports up to 64GB of physical RAM and allows dual processors—so motherboards can be designed for basic symmetric multiprocessing (SMP). A pipelined floating point unit (FPU) supporting 32-bit, 64-bit, and 80-bit formats is capable of executing two floating-point instructions in a single clock and of sustaining over 300 million floating-point instructions per second at 300MHz. Table 13-2 outlines the performance comparison for Pentium II processors from 233MHz to 450MHz.

One of the most noticeable departures from previous CPUs was the package style. Intel abandoned the use of Socket 7 (Pentium) and Socket 8 (Pentium Pro) packages and adopted a "cartridge style" package known as the "Single Edge Contact" (or "SEC") cartridge. We generally know this as the "Slot 1" style of connector. While not quite as prolific as the "classic" Pentium, the Pentium MMX, or even the Pentium Pro, there are still a large number of Pentium II versions and features to contend with. This variety can make it difficult to determine the proper motherboard configuration for a given P II. However, you can use the S-spec rating marked on each Pentium II processor to reveal key operating characteristics of the particular CPU. Table 13-6 presents the S-specs for Pentium II processors.

TABLE 13-6   S-SPEC REFERENCE TABLE FOR PENTIUM II PROCESSORS

S-SPEC	MANUFACTURER'S STEP	L2 SIZE (KB)	TAG RAM STEP	MEMORY SUPPORT	CORE/BUS SPEED (MHZ)
SL264	C0	512	T6/B0	non-ECC	233/66
SL265	C0	512	T6/B0	non-ECC	266/66
SL268	C0	512	T6/B0	ECC	233/66
SL269	C0	512	T6/B0	ECC	266/66
SL28K	C0	512	T6/B0	non-ECC	233/66
SL28L	C0	512	T6/B0	non-ECC	266/66
SL28R	C0	512	T6/B0	ECC	300/66
SL2HA	C1	512	T6/B0	ECC	300/66
SL2HC	C1	512	T6/B0	non-ECC	266/66
SL2HD	C1	512	T6/B0	non-ECC	233/66
SL2HE	C1	512	T6/B0	ECC	266/66
SL2HF	C1	512	T6/B0	ECC	233/66
SL2K9	dA0	512	T6P/A3	ECC	266/66
SL2KA	dA0	512	T6P/A3	ECC	333/66
SL2KE	TdB0	512	C6C/A3	ECC	333/66
SL2MZ	C0	512	T6/B0	ECC	300/66
SL2QA	C1	512	T6/B0	non-ECC	233/66
SL2QB	C1	512	T6/B0	non-ECC	266/66
SL2QC	C1	512	T6/B0	ECC	300/66
SL2QF	dA0	512	T6P/A3	ECC	333/66
SL2QH	dA1	512	T6P-e/A0	ECC	333/66
SL2S5	dA1	512	T6P-e/A0	ECC	333/66
SL2S6	dA1	512	T6P-e/A0	ECC	350/100
SL2S7	dA1	512	T6P-e/A0	ECC	400/100
SL2SF	dA1	512	T6P-e/A0	ECC	350/100
SL2SH	dA1	512	T6P-e/A0	ECC	400/100
SL2TV	dB0	512	T6P-e/A0	ECC	333/66
SL2U3	dB0	512	T6P-e/A0	ECC	350/100
SL2U4	dB0	512	T6P-e/A0	ECC	350/100
SL2U5	dB0	512	T6P-e/A0	ECC	400/100
SL2U6	dB0	512	T6P-e/A0	ECC	400/100
SL2U7	dB0	512	T6P-e/A0	ECC	450/100
SL2VY	dA1	512	T6P-e/A0	ECC	300/66
SL2W7	dB0	512	T6P-e/A0	ECC	266/66
SL2W8	dB0	512	T6P-e/A0	ECC	300/66
SL2WB	dB0	512	T6P-e/A0	ECC	450/100
SL2WZ	dB0	512	T6P-e/A0	ECC	350/100
SL2YK	dB0	512	T6P-e/A0	ECC	300/66
SL2YM	dB0	512	T6P-e/A0	ECC	400/100
SL2ZP	dA1	512	T6P-e/A0	ECC	333/66
SL2ZQ	dA1	512	T6P-e/A0	ECC	350/100
SL33D	dB0	512	T6P-e/A0	ECC	266/66
SL356	dB0	512	T6P-e/A0	ECC	350/100
SL357	dB0	512	T6P-e/A0	ECC	400/100
SL358	dB0	512	T6P-e/A0	ECC	450/100

TABLE 13-6	**S-SPEC REFERENCE TABLE FOR PENTIUM II PROCESSORS** *(CONTINUED)*				

S-SPEC	MANUFACTURER'S STEP	L2 SIZE (KB)	TAG RAM STEP	MEMORY SUPPORT	CORE/BUS SPEED (MHZ)
SL35V	dA1	512	T6P-e/A0	ECC	300/66
SL36U	dB1	512	T6P-e/A0	ECC	350/100
SL37F	dB0	512	T6P-e/A0	ECC	350/100
SL37G	dB0	512	T6P-e/A0	ECC	400/100
SL37H	dB0	512	T6P-e/A0	ECC	450/100
SL38M	dB1	512	T6P-e/A0	ECC	350/100
SL38N	dB1	512	T6P-e/A0	ECC	400/100
SL38Z	dB1	512	T6P-e/A0	ECC	400/100
SL3D5	dB1	512	T6P-e/A0	ECC	400/100
SL3EE	dB0	512	T6P-e/0	ECC	400/100
SL3F9	dB0	512	T6Pe/A0	ECC	400/100
SL3FN	dB0	512	T6P-e/0	ECC	350/100
SL3J2	dB1	512	T6P-e/A0	ECC	350/100

PENTIUM II OVERDRIVE (1998–CURRENT)

Two Pentium II OverDrive processors have been produced for upgrading Pentium Pro (Socket 8) processors. One OverDrive replaces the 150–180MHz Pentium Pro's (60MHz bus speed) and provides a performance increase to 300MHz. The other OverDrive replaces the 166–200MHz (66MHz bus speed) Pentium Pro processors and increases performance to 333MHz. The integrated on-die L2 cache design of the Socket 8 package style also provides a performance increase by allowing the L2 cache to operate at full core speed. Pentium II OverDrive processors for Socket 8 systems are generally rather rare today.

PENTIUM II/III CELERON (1998–CURRENT)

Commonly known as just the "Celeron," this CPU was introduced by Intel in April of 1998. It was originally manufactured as a "stripped down" version of the Pentium II. The Intel Celeron uses the same P6 core and provides the same features as the Pentium Pro and Pentium II. It has 32KB L1 cache (16KB for data and 16KB for instructions). It includes MMX features, pipelined floating point unit, and dynamic execution architecture, and it is constructed with the same 0.25 micron process to reduce heat production. Current Celerons use the "Coppermine" Pentium III core and are manufactured using a 0.18 micron process.

Most noticeably *missing* from the first Celerons was the presence of an L2 cache. This cost-cutting move was intended to increase competition against the low cost CPUs being produced by AMD and Cyrix, while maintaining the selling power of the "Intel Inside" mystique. Additional cost reductions were achieved by eliminating the fancy Pentium II plastic cover creating the Single Edge Processor Package (SEPP or Slot 1) style Celeron, and adding a PPGA (Plastic Pin Grid Array) style case for use in Socket 370 connectors. The latest Socket 370-compatible Celeron processors are available in the popular FC-PGA (Flip Chip-Pin Grid Array) style package, which offers better cooling for the processor.

Not all Socket 370 motherboards will support both PPGA and FC-PGA style processors. Be sure the selected package style is supported by the motherboard.

The lack of built-in L2 cache severely limited the performance of Intel's early Celerons. Less expensive competing processors *included* L2 cache, and they out-performed Celerons of the same or similar clock speeds. Beginning with the Celeron 300A model, Intel returned 128KB of built-in cache to the Celeron processors. For the Celeron PPGA and FC-PGA, Intel integrated the L2 cache directly on the processor die. This integration allows the L2 cache speed to scale (or "match") processor speed and improves performance even further. In fact, 128KB of integrated L2 Celeron cache running *at* the processor speed is said to match the performance of the Pentium II 512KB off-die L2 cache running at half the processor speed.

There were other Pentium II features missing in the Celeron. For example, there is no support for dual processors or for streaming SIMD extensions, limiting the Celeron's versatility in multimedia applications. There is also a lower front side bus (FSB) speed—66MHz compared to 100MHz. This feature allows computer manufacturers to use lower-cost, lower-performance parts and thereby reduce overall system cost. Fortunately, the rapid cost reductions in 100MHz-compatible components (along with severe competition from AMD) finally forced Intel to add 100MHz FSB support to the Celeron processor line. Celeron processor speeds of 800MHz and up support the 100MHz FSB.

Today, Intel has settled on the FC-PGA package for the Celeron processor. This provides for lower cost, better cooling, and integrated L2 cache. Also, motherboard redesign costs are less expensive (because of the Socket 370 style attachment)—the changes needed to go from a Socket 7 to a Socket 370 are fewer and less expensive than redesigning a motherboard for a Slot 1 connector. Third parties make an adapter (referred to as a "Slot-Ket") that allows Socket 370 Celerons to be used in Slot 1 motherboards. Celerons from 266MHz to 433MHz are available in the Single Edge Processor Package (SEPP) style, while Celerons from 300MHz and up are available in both the Plastic Pin Grid Array (PPGA) and the Flip Chip-Pin Grid Array (FC-PGA) style package. The differences in cache and package styles make for an interesting variety, as you can see in Table 13-2. For additional information, you can use the S-spec rating marked on each Celeron processor to reveal key operating characteristics of the particular CPU, as shown in Table 13-7.

TABLE 13-7   S-SPEC REFERENCE TABLE FOR CELERON PROCESSORS

S-SPEC	MANUFACTURER'S STEP	CORE/BUS SPEED (MHZ)	NOTES
SL2QG	dA1	266/66	SEPP Rev. 1
SL2SY	dA0	266/66	SEPP Rev. 1
SL2TR	dA1	266/66	SEPP Rev. 1
SL2WM	mA0	300A/66	SEPP Rev. 1
SL2WN	mA0	333/66	SEPP Rev. 1
SL2X8	dA1	300/66	SEPP Rev. 1
SL2Y2	dA1	300/66	SEPP Rev. 1
SL2Y3	dB0	266/66	SEPP Rev. 1
SL2Y4	dB0	300/66	SEPP Rev. 1
SL2YN	dA0	266/66	SEPP Rev. 1
SL2YP	dA0	300/66	SEPP Rev. 1
SL2Z7	dA0	300/66	SEPP Rev. 1
SL32A	mA0	300A/66	SEPP Rev. 1
SL32B	mA0	333/66	SEPP Rev. 1
SL35Q	mB0	300A/66	PPGA
SL35R	mB0	333/66	PPGA
SL35S	mB0	366/66	PPGA
SL36A	mB0	300A/66	PPGA
SL36B	mB0	333/66	PPGA

TABLE 13-7   S-SPEC REFERENCE TABLE FOR CELERON PROCESSORS *(CONTINUED)*

S-SPEC	MANUFACTURER'S STEP	CORE/BUS SPEED (MHZ)	NOTES
SL36C	mB0	366/66	PPGA
SL376	mA0	366/66	SEPP Rev. 1
SL37Q	mA0	366/66	SEPP Rev. 1
SL37V	mA0	400/66	SEPP Rev. 1
SL37X	mB0	400/66	PPGA
SL39Z	mA0	400/66	SEPP Rev. 1
SL3A2	mB0	400/66	PPGA
SL3BA	mB0	433/66	PPGA
SL3BC	mA0	433/66	SEPP Rev. 1
SL3BS	mB0	433/66	PPGA
SL3EH	mB0	466/66	PPGA
SL3FL	mB0	466/66	PPGA
SL3FY	mB0	500/66	PPGA
SL3FZ	mB0	533/66	PPGA
SL3LQ	mB0	500/66	PPGA
SL3PZ	mB0	533/66	PPGA
SL46S	cB0	533A/66	FC-PGA
SL3W6	cB0	533A/66	FC-PGA
SL46T	cB0	566/66	FC-PGA
SL3W7	cB0	566/66	FC-PGA
SL4PC	C0	566/66	FC-PGA
SL4NW	C0	566/66	FC-PGA
SL46U	cB0	600/66	FC-PGA
SL3W8	cB0	600/66	FC-PGA
SL4PB	C0	600/66	FC-PGA
SL4NX	C0	600/66	FC-PGA
SL3VS	cB0	633/66	FC-PGA
SL3W9	cB0	633/66	FC-PGA
SL4PA	C0	633/66	FC-PGA
SL4NY	C0	633/66	FC-PGA
SL48E	cB0	667/66	FC-PGA
SL4AB	cB0	667/66	FC-PGA
SL4P9	C0	667/66	FC-PGA
SL4NZ	C0	667/66	FC-PGA
SL48F	cB0	700/66	FC-PGA
SL4EG	cB0	700/66	FC-PGA
SL4P8	C0	700/66	FC-PGA
SL4P2	C0	700/66	FC-PGA
SL4P7	C0	733/66	FC-PGA
SL4P3	C0	733/66	FC-PGA
SL4P6	C0	766/66	FC-PGA
SL4QF	C0	766/66	FC-PGA
SL4TF	C0	800/100	FC-PGA
SL55R	C0	800/100	FC-PGA

PENTIUM III (1999–CURRENT)

First made available in February of 1999, the Intel Pentium III continues to use the same basic P6 core as the Pentium Pro and the Pentium II (so the main features of the line remain unchanged). Later Pentium III models use a 0.18 micron manufacturing process (compared to the standard 0.25 micron process), which helps lower processor operating temperatures. Processor heat is also addressed with the use of a new SECC 2 (Single Edge Contact Cartridge) package, which covers only one side of the chip—this approach decreases weight, lowers cost, and allows for a more efficient attachment of the heat sink assembly. Realizing the advantages of a "socket" connector with the Pentium III (as well as the Celeron), Intel began to produce the Pentium III in an FC-PGA (Flip Chip-Pin Grid Array) package. Some public statements suggest that Intel will gradually move all processors to the socket style and end its development of edge-connected processors.

The overall performance of the Pentium III continues to improve with the introduction of higher processor speeds and the ability to utilize a 133MHz front side bus (FSB). You can see the proliferation of Pentium III models in Table 13-2. Intel's Streaming SIMD Extensions (SSE) technology (introduced in the Pentium III) added new registers and instructions to the processor chip—bringing the total number of transistors in the core logic to over 9.5 million. As with MMX extensions, applications must be specifically written to take advantage of these SSE instructions and thereby produce any increase in 3D/graphics performance. Other performance features include a 32KB L1 cache, 4GB addressable memory with ECC, and dual processor support.

The earliest Pentium III processors (manufactured using a 0.25 micron process) use the "Katmai" core. These processors come in speeds from 450MHz to 600MHz and offer 512KB of L2 cache. The cache is located on a separate die from the processor and runs at one-half the core processor speed. The later Pentium III processors use a 0.18 micron manufacturing process. This core was named "Coppermine" and comes in speeds of 500MHz and up. The improved manufacturing process allows for the inclusion of 256KB of L2 cache on the same die as the processor. This smaller L2 cache runs at the same speed as the core processor, so performance is not impaired.

The different versions of the Pentium III can be identified by the presence or absence of several letters in the speed part of the name. If an "E" is part of the name (such as 600E), the processor includes 256KB of L2 cache. If a "B" is part of the name (such as 600B), the processor uses a FSB speed of 133MHz. Pentium III processors without any added letters offer 512KB of slower L2 cache and use an FSB speed of 100MHz. So, versions may be available with no letters, with an "E," with a "B," or with "EB" added to the name. The latest Pentium IIIs all include the "EB" suffix, offering 256KB of high-speed, on-die L2 cache designed to run at a 133MHz FSB speed.

Intel introduced the integrated "processor serial number" (or "PSN") with the Pentium III. This number allows individual processors (and possibly entire systems) to be identified remotely over a network. Identification can even take place over the Internet. Seen by Intel as a security enhancement for online transactions, this feature was viewed as an invasion of privacy by a large segment of users. Public pressure first forced Intel to make it possible to disable this feature, and finally to ship Pentium IIIs with this feature *disabled* by default. End users can still enable processor serial number identification if they wish.

There are a large number of Pentium III versions and features to contend with, and this can make it difficult to determine the proper motherboard configuration for a given P III. However, you can use the S-spec rating marked on each Pentium III processor to reveal key operating characteristics of the particular CPU. Table 13-8 presents the S-specs for the Pentium III processor family.

PENTIUM II/III XEON (1999–CURRENT)

The Xeon processor is the high-performance model of the Pentium II/III family. It is intended for demanding workstation and server environments. The Pentium Xeon's expanded features include support for up

TABLE 13-8   S-SPEC REFERENCE TABLE FOR PENTIUM III PROCESSORS

S-SPEC	MANUFACTURER'S STEP	L2 SIZE (KB)	TAG RAM STEP	MEMORY SUPPORT	CORE/BUS SPEED (MHZ)
SL35D	kC0	512	T6P-e/A0	ECC	450/100
SL35E	kC0	512	T6P-e/A0	ECC	500/100
SL364	kB0	512	T6P-e/A0	ECC	450/100
SL365	kB0	512	T6P-e/A0	ECC	500/100
SL37C	kC0	512	T6P-e/A0	ECC	450/100
SL37D	kC0	512	T6P-e/A0	ECC	500/100
SL38E	kB0	512	T6P-e/A0	ECC	450/100
SL38F	kB0	512	T6P-e/A0	ECC	500/100
SL3BN	kC0	512	T6P-e/A0	ECC	533B/133
SL3CC	kB0	512	T6P-e/A0	ECC	450/100
SL3CD	kB0	512	T6P-e/A0	ECC	500/100
SL3E9	kC0	512	T6P-e/A0	ECC	533B/133
SL3F7	kC0	512	T6P-e/A0	ECC	550/100
SL3FJ	kC0	512	T6P-e/A0	ECC	550/100
SL3H6	cA2	256	N/A	ECC	600E/100
SL3H7	cA2	256	N/A	ECC	600EB/133
SL3JM	kC0	512	T6P-e/A0	ECC	600/100
SL3JP	kC0	512	T6P-e/A0	ECC	600B/133
SL3JT	kC0	512	T6P-e/A0	ECC	600/100
SL3JU	kC0	512	T6P-e/A0	ECC	600B/133
SL3KV	cA2	256	N/A	ECC	650/100
SL3KW	cA2	256	N/A	ECC	667/133
SL3N6	cA2	256	N/A	ECC	533EB/133
SL3NA	cA2	256	N/A	ECC	600E/100
SL3NB	cA2	256	N/A	ECC	600EB/133
SL3ND	cA2	256	N/A	ECC	667/133
SL3NR	cA2	256	N/A	ECC	650/100
SL3Q9	cA2	256	N/A	ECC	500E/100
SL3QA	cA2	256	N/A	ECC	550E/100
SL3R2	cA2	256	N/A	ECC	500E/100
SL3R3	cA2	256	N/A	ECC	550E/100
SL3S9	cA2	256	N/A	ECC	700/100
SL3SB	cA2	256	N/A	ECC	733/133
SL3SX	cA2	256	N/A	ECC	533EB/133
SL3SY	cA2	256	N/A	ECC	700/100
SL3SZ	cA2	256	N/A	ECC	733/133
SL3VF	cA2	256	N/A	ECC	533EB/133
SL3VH	cA2	256	N/A	ECC	600E/100
SL3VJ	cA2	256	N/A	ECC	650/100
SL3VK	cA2	256	N/A	ECC	667/133
SL3VL	cA2	256	N/A	ECC	700/100
SL3VM	cA2	256	N/A	ECC	733/133
SL3VN	cA2	256	N/A	ECC	750/100
SL3WA	cA2	256	N/A	ECC	800EB/133

TABLE 13-8   S-SPEC REFERENCE TABLE FOR PENTIUM III PROCESSORS *(CONTINUED)*

S-SPEC	MANUFACTURER'S STEP	L2 SIZE (KB)	TAG RAM STEP	MEMORY SUPPORT	CORE/BUS SPEED (MHZ)
SL3WC	cA2	256	N/A	ECC	750/100
SL3Z6	cA2	256	N/A	ECC	800/100
SLVG	cA2	256	N/A	ECC	600EB/133
SL3VA	cA2	256	N/A	ECC	533EB/133
SL3NL	cA2	256	N/A	ECC	600E/100
SL3VB	cA2	256	N/A	ECC	600EB/133
SL3NM	cA2	256	N/A	ECC	650/100
SL3T2	cA2	256	N/A	ECC	667/133
SL3T3	cA2	256	N/A	ECC	700/100
SL3T4	cA2	256	N/A	ECC	733/133
SL3VC	cA2	256	N/A	ECC	750/100
SL3WB	cA2	256	N/A	ECC	800EB/133
SL3VE	cA2	256	N/A	ECC	800EB/133
SL3X4	cA2	256	N/A	ECC	800/100
SL3VD	cA2	256	N/A	ECC	800/100
SL444/SL446	cB0	256	N/A	ECC	500E/100
SL45R	cB0	256	N/A	ECC	500E/100
SL3XS	cB0	256	N/A	ECC	500EB/133
SL45S	cB0	256	N/A	ECC	533EB/133
SL44G	cB0	256	N/A	ECC	550E/100
SL45T	cB0	256	N/A	ECC	550E/100
SL3XT	cB0	256	N/A	ECC	600EB/133
SL45V	cB0	256	N/A	ECC	600EB/133
SL3XU	cB0	256	N/A	ECC	600E/100
SL45U	cB0	256	N/A	ECC	600E/100
SL3XV	cB0	256	N/A	ECC	650/100
SL45W	cB0	256	N/A	ECC	650/100
SL3XW	cB0	256	N/A	ECC	667/133
SL45X	cB0	256	N/A	ECC	667/133
SL3XX	cB0	256	N/A	ECC	700/100
SL45Y	cB0	256	N/A	ECC	700/100
SL45Z	cB0	256	N/A	ECC	733/133
SL3XY	cB0	256	N/A	ECC	733/133
SL3XZ	cB0	256	N/A	ECC	750/100
SL462	cB0	256	N/A	ECC	750/100
SL3Y2	cB0	256	N/A	ECC	800EB/133
SL464	cB0	256	N/A	ECC	800EB/133
SL3Y3	cB0	256	N/A	ECC	800/100
SL463	cB0	256	N/A	ECC	800/100
SL43H	cB0	256	N/A	ECC	850/100
SL49G	cB0	256	N/A	ECC	850/100
SL43J	cB0	256	N/A	ECC	866/133
SL49H	cB0	256	N/A	ECC	866/133
SL44J	cB0	256	N/A	ECC	933/133

TABLE 13-8   S-SPEC REFERENCE TABLE FOR PENTIUM III PROCESSORS *(CONTINUED)*

S-SPEC	MANUFACTURER'S STEP	L2 SIZE (KB)	TAG RAM STEP	MEMORY SUPPORT	CORE/BUS SPEED (MHZ)
SL49J	cB0	256	N/A	ECC	933/133
SL4CM	cC0	256	N/A	ECC	600E/100
SL4CL	cC0	256	N/A	ECC	600EB/133
SL4CK	cC0	256	N/A	ECC	650/100
SL4CJ	cC0	256	N/A	ECC	667/133
SL4CH	cC0	256	N/A	ECC	700/100
SL4M7	cC0	256	N/A	ECC	700/100
SL4CG	cC0	256	N/A	ECC	733/133
SL4M8	cC0	256	N/A	ECC	733/133
SL4CF	cC0	256	N/A	ECC	750/100
SL4M9	cC0	256	N/A	ECC	750/100
SL4CE	cC0	256	N/A	ECC	800/100
SL4MA	cC0	256	N/A	ECC	800/100
SL4CD	cC0	256	N/A	ECC	800EB/133
SL4MB	cC0	256	N/A	ECC	800EB/133
SL4CC	cC0	256	N/A	ECC	850/100
SL4MC	cC0	256	N/A	ECC	850/100
SL4CB	cC0	256	N/A	ECC	866/133
SL4MD	cC0	256	N/A	ECC	866/133
SL4C9	cC0	256	N/A	ECC	933/133
SL4ME	cC0	256	N/A	ECC	933/133
SL4C8	cC0	256	N/A	ECC	1GHz/133
SL4MF	cC0	256	N/A	ECC	1GHz/133
SL3V5	cA2	256	N/A	ECC	550E/100
SL3N7	cA2	256	N/A	ECC	550E/100
SL3V6	cA2	256	N/A	ECC	750/100
SL3V7	cA2	256	N/A	ECC	800/100
SL3V8	cA2	256	N/A	ECC	800EB/133
SL4G7	cA2	256	N/A	ECC	800EB/133
SL3XG	cB0	256	N/A	ECC	533EB/133
SL44W	cB0	256	N/A	ECC	533EB/133
SL3XH	cB0	256	N/A	ECC	550E/100
SL44X	cB0	256	N/A	ECC	550E/100
SL43E	cB0	256	N/A	ECC	600E/100
SL44Y	cB0	256	N/A	ECC	600E/100
SL3XJ	cB0	256	N/A	ECC	600EB/133
SL44Z	cB0	256	N/A	ECC	600EB/133
SL3XK	cB0	256	N/A	ECC	650/100
SL452	cB0	256	N/A	ECC	650/100
SL3XL	cB0	256	N/A	ECC	667/133
SL453	cB0	256	N/A	ECC	667/133
SL3XM	cB0	256	N/A	ECC	700/100
SL454	cB0	256	N/A	ECC	700/100
SL3XN	cB0	256	N/A	ECC	733/133

TABLE 13-8   S-SPEC REFERENCE TABLE FOR PENTIUM III PROCESSORS *(CONTINUED)*

S-SPEC	MANUFACTURER'S STEP	L2 SIZE (KB)	TAG RAM STEP	MEMORY SUPPORT	CORE/BUS SPEED (MHZ)
SL455	cB0	256	N/A	ECC	733/133
SL3XP	cB0	256	N/A	ECC	750/100
SL456	cB0	256	N/A	ECC	750/100
SL3XQ	cB0	256	N/A	ECC	800EB/133
SL458	cB0	256	N/A	ECC	800EB/133
SL3XR	cB0	256	N/A	ECC	800/100
SL457	cB0	256	N/A	ECC	800/100
SL43F	cB0	256	N/A	ECC	850/100
SL47M	cB0	256	N/A	ECC	850/100
SL43G	cB0	256	N/A	ECC	866/133
SL47N	cB0	256	N/A	ECC	866/133
SL448	cB0	256	N/A	ECC	933/133
SL47Q	cB0	256	N/A	ECC	933/133
SL4FP	cB0	256	N/A	ECC	1GHz/133
SL48S	cB0	256	N/A	ECC	1GHz/133
SL4C7	cC0	256	N/A	ECC	600E/100
SL4C6	cC0	256	N/A	ECC	600EB/133
SL4C5	cC0	256	N/A	ECC	650/100
SL4C4	cC0	256	N/A	ECC	667/133
SL4C3	cC0	256	N/A	ECC	700/100
SL4C2	cC0	256	N/A	ECC	733/133
SL4KD	cC0	256	N/A	ECC	733/133
SL4FQ	cC0	256	N/A	ECC	733/133
SL4BZ	cC0	256	N/A	ECC	750/100
SL4BY	cC0	256	N/A	ECC	800/100
SL4KF	cC0	256	N/A	ECC	800/100
SL4BX	cC0	256	N/A	ECC	800EB/133
SL4G7	cC0	256	N/A	ECC	800EB/133
SL4KG	cC0	256	N/A	ECC	800EB/133
SL4BW	cC0	256	N/A	ECC	850/100
SL4KH	cC0	256	N/A	ECC	850/100
SL4BV	cC0	256	N/A	ECC	866/133
SL4KJ	cC0	256	N/A	ECC	866/133
SL4BT	cC0	256	N/A	ECC	933/133
SL4BR	cC0	256	N/A	ECC	1GHz/100
SL4KL	cC0	256	N/A	ECC	1GHz/100
SL4BS	cC0	256	N/A	ECC	1GHz/133
SL4HH	cC0	256	N/A	ECC	1.13GHz/133

to eight processors, L2 cache speed *equal* to core processor speed, and an increased choice of L2 cache size. The Xeon processor is available with L2 cache amounts of 512KB, 1MB, and 2MB. The physical size of larger cache prohibits placing the cache directly on the processor die—instead, it must be in a separate package next to the core processor. Intel has overcome the cache speed problems associated with the separate core-cache location, thus enabling the Xeon cache to run at core processor speeds. The increased physical size created by this arrangement also means the Pentium Xeon cannot use the Slot 1 motherboard connector. The Slot 2 connector was developed to accommodate the Xeon's increased size. You can see the S-spec details for Pentium II/III Xeon processors in Table 13-9.

TABLE 13-9   S-SPEC REFERENCE TABLE FOR PENTIUM II/III XEON PROCESSORS

S-SPEC	MANUFACTURER'S STEP	L2 SIZE (KB)	TAG RAM STEP	CORE/BUS SPEED (MHZ)
SL2XU	B0	512	C6C-B0	500/100
SL2XV	B0	1024	C6C-B0	500/100
SL2XW	B0	2048	CK1-B1	500/100
SL3C9	B0	512	C6C-B0	500/100
SL3CA	B0	1024	C6C-B0	500/100
SL3CB	B0	2048	CK1-B1	500/100
SL3FK	C0	512	CK2-B2	550/100
SL3D9	C0	512	C6C-B0	500/100
SL3DA	C0	1024	C6C-B0	500/100
SL3DB	C0	2048	CK1-B1	500/100
SL3AJ	C0	512	CK2-B1	550/100
SL3CE	C0	1024	CK1-B1	550/100
SL3CF	C0	2048	CK1-B1	550/100
SL3TW	C0	1024	CK1-B1	550/100
SL3Y4	C0	512	CK2-B2	550/100
SL3FR	C0	512	CK2-B2	550/100
SL385	C0	512	C6C-B0	500/100
SL386	C0	1024	C6C-B0	500/100
SL387	C0	2048	CK1-B1	500/100
SL3LM	C0	512	CK2-B2	550/100
SL3LN	C0	1024	CK1-B1	550/100
SL3LP	C0	2048	CK1-B1	550/100
SL3BJ	A2	256	N/A	600/133
SL3BK	A2	256	N/A	600/133
SL3BL	A2	256	N/A	667/133
SL3DC	A2	256	N/A	667/133
SL3SF	A2	256	N/A	733/133
SL3SG	A2	256	N/A	733/133
SL3V2	A2	256	N/A	800/133
SL3V3	A2	256	N/A	800/133
SL3SS	A2	256	N/A	600/133
SL3ST	A2	256	N/A	667/133
SL3SU	A2	256	N/A	733/133
SL3VU	A2	256	N/A	800/133
SL3WM	B0	256	N/A	600/133
SL3WP	B0	256	N/A	667/133
SL3WQ	B0	256	N/A	667/133
SL3WR	B0	256	N/A	733/133
SL3WS	B0	256	N/A	733/133

TABLE 13-9 **S-SPEC REFERENCE TABLE FOR PENTIUM II/III XEON PROCESSORS**
(CONTINUED)

S-SPEC	MANUFACTURER'S STEP	L2 SIZE (KB)	TAG RAM STEP	CORE/BUS SPEED (MHZ)
SL3WT	B0	256	N/A	800/133
SL3WU	B0	256	N/A	800/133
SL3WV	B0	256	N/A	866/133
SL3WW	B0	256	N/A	866/133
SL3WX	B0	256	N/A	933/133
SL3WY	B0	256	N/A	933/133
SL4H6	C0	256	N/A	733/133
SL4H7	C0	256	N/A	733/133
SL4H8	C0	256	N/A	800/133
SL4H9	C0	256	N/A	800/133
SL4HA	C0	256	N/A	866/133
SL4HB	C0	256	N/A	866/133
SL4PZ	B0	256	N/A	866/133
SL4HC	C0	256	N/A	933/133
SL4HD	C0	256	N/A	933/133
SL4R9	C0	256	N/A	933/133
SL4HE	C0	256	N/A	1GHz/133
SL4HF	C0	256	N/A	1GHz/133
SL3U4	A0	1024	N/A	700/100
SL3U5	A0	1024	N/A	700/100
SL3WZ	A0	2048	N/A	700/100
SL3X2	A0	2048	N/A	700/100
SL4GD	A0	1024	N/A	700/100
SL4GE	A0	1024	N/A	700/100
SL4GF	A0	2048	N/A	700/100
SL4GG	A0	2048	N/A	700/100
SL49P	A1	1024	N/A	700/100
SL49Q	A1	1024	N/A	700/100
SL49R	A1	2048	N/A	700/100
SL49S	A1	2048	N/A	700/100
SL4RZ	A1	1024	N/A	700/100
SL4R3	A1	2048	N/A	700/100

PENTIUM 4 (2000–CURRENT)

As the Pentium II/III family pushes the 1GHz speed range, the inherent limitations in the traditional P6 core architecture begin to limit the performance improvements that can be achieved. Intel has responded to this by introducing its newest Pentium 4 processors sporting a redesigned "NetBurst" micro-architecture. The NetBurst micro-architecture delivers a number of new and innovative features, including Hyper Pipelined Technology, a 400MHz System Bus, Execution Trace Cache, and a Rapid Execution Engine. Other enhanced features include an Advanced Transfer Cache, Advanced Dynamic Execution, an Enhanced Floating-Point and Multimedia Unit, and the next generation of Streaming SIMD Extensions (known as SSE2). At current operating speeds of 1.3GHz to 1.5GHz, the Pentium 4 is supported by the Intel 850 chipset and is streamlined to support a wide range of multimedia and communications-focused tasks. These applications include Internet audio and streaming video, image processing, video content creation, speech, 3D, CAD, games, and multitasking user environments.

The 42 million transistor Pentium 4 is produced in a socket style package, currently known as PGA 423-pin socket for the Intel Pentium 4 Processor in an Olga on Interposer (OOI) package. It is possible that future Pentium 4s will be produced in a 428-pin package (requiring a new socket). This may limit the ability to upgrade current Pentium 4 systems. The first 428-pin Pentium 4 will use the Prescott core and became available in early 2001. A few of the more notable features of the Pentium 4 are outlined next, and Table 13-10 lists the available S-spec numbers for current Pentium 4 models.

- **Additional SIMD instructions**   The existing SSE extensions have been augmented with 144 new or improved SIMD extensions (known as SSE2). SSE2 allows the Pentium 4 to utilize 128 bits of data at once for greatly improved data handling. These additional instructions are designed to improve multimedia performance, including streaming video, speech recognition, and 3D operations.

- **Hyperpiplining and Rapid Execution**   Hyperpipelining technology doubles the pipeline depth of the older P6 architecture. For example, the Branch Prediction/Recovery pipeline in the P6 architecture is 10 stages deep, but hyperpipelining increases this to 20 stages deep. A Rapid Execution engine—actually two arithmetic logic units (or ALUs) running at two times the frequency of the core processor—is also added. This allows simple number functions (Add, Subtract, Logical And, Logical Or, and so on) to require only 1/2 clock cycle. This means the Rapid Execution Engine of the 1.5GHz Pentium 4 effectively runs at 3GHz.

- **Advanced Level 2 cache**   The improved L2 cache design of the Pentium 4 is a 256-bit (32-byte) interface that transfers data on each core clock cycle. The cache is located on-die and operates at the same speed as the core processor. For the 1.5GHz Pentium 4, this means cache data transfer rates of 48GB/s (32 bytes×1 data transfer per clock×1.5GHz) compared to only 16GB/s for a 1.0GHz Pentium III.

- **Advanced Dynamic Execution**   This feature is an expanded speculative execution engine that allows the Pentium 4 to view 126 instructions (and handle up to 48 loads and 24 stores) in the pipeline. It also provides enhanced branch prediction abilities, reducing the number of branch misses by about 33 percent over the Pentium III and other P6 core architecture processors. This means the Pentium 4 is better at "guessing" where the next piece of needed data will be and is able to store a larger number of possible pieces of data.

- **400MHz System Bus**   The Pentium 4 uses a scheme named "Quad-Pumping" that allows for a sustained effective data transfer rate of 400MHz on a 100MHz system bus. This delivers 3.2GB of data per second into and out of the processor, compared to 1.06GB/s in a 133MHz Pentium III. This 3.2GB/s data transfer speed of the Pentium 4 also requires dual pipelined Rambus (RDRAM) memory and is supported by the 850 chipset. RDRAM provides the necessary 1.6GB/s transfer rate per pipeline.

Unfortunately, early releases of the Pentium 4 have not provided the stunning performance improvements that Intel had hoped for. Intel had to abandon or scale back certain features that have compromised the overall performance of the Pentium 4. Original plans called for 16KB of L1 cache and two fully functional floating point units (FPUs). Also missing is the proposed addition of 1MB of a new, external L3 cache. These shortfalls all contribute to numerous performance problems recorded at many popular Internet sites that review computer hardware. AMD processors running at 900MHz and 1GHz currently outperform the fastest 1.5GHz Pentium 4. However, Pentium 4 performance is expected to improve dramatically as Intel updates and refines the design.

TABLE 13-10   S-SPEC REFERENCE TABLE FOR PENTIUM 4 PROCESSORS

S-SPEC	MANUFACTURER'S STEP	L2 SIZE (KB)	MEMORY SUPPORT	CORE/BUS SPEED (MHZ)
SL4SF	B2	256KB	RDRAM	1.30GHz/400MHz
SL4SG	B2	256KB	RDRAM	1.40GHz/400MHz
SL4SC	B2	256KB	RDRAM	1.40GHz/400MHz
SL4SH	B2	256KB	RDRAM	1.50GHz/400MHz
SL4TY	B2	256KB	RDRAM	1.50GHz/400MHz

Another factor that has impaired the acceptance of the Pentium 4 is the increased cost from the required use of expensive Rambus (RDRAM) memory. At this time, support for DDR-SDRAM is not implemented in the only chipset (Intel 850) compatible with the Pentium 4. Intel is expected to release a chipset supporting DDR-SDRAM with the Pentium 4 *after* Rambus memory has achieved a secure place in the market. Table 13-10 lists the S-spec characteristics for current Pentium 4 releases.

ITANIUM (MID 2001–FUTURE)

Scheduled for release sometime in mid-2001, the Intel Itanium will be the first 64-bit processor. Intel's IA-64 architecture combines a number of innovative features to address the performance limitations of traditional processor types. The Itanium architecture is based on "next generation" performance features, such as Explicit Parallelism, Predication, and Speculation, producing superior processing efficiency and increased instructions per cycle (IPC). This added processing power will help address future demanding requirements of Internet, high-end server, and workstation applications. In addition, the IA-64 architecture provides headroom and scalability for continued future growth. Unexpected problems have forced Intel to continually push the release date of the Itanium back again and again. Intel has stopped advertising or promising any specific expected release date for the Itanium.

The AMD CPUs

Advanced Micro Devices (AMD), once Intel's ally, has become its single biggest competitor. AMD is known for providing well-designed and highly compatible "alternative" processors to the PC industry and has been active in processor manufacturing and marketing since the days of the 386 (when one of its processors was the AMD Am386). Although AMD had tended to lag just a little behind the release of new Intel CPUs, that gap is now closed. With the release of AMD's newest processors (such as the Athlon and Duron), AMD is actually pushing a bit ahead in terms of processor performance and operating speeds in some benchmarks. The Pentium 4 put Intel slightly ahead in some 3D and network benchmarks (for a time at least), but the battle of the processors is a bitter one. This means that choosing the fastest processor will greatly depend on what applications you are using on your system. This part of the chapter will examine the characteristics and highlights of major AMD offerings.

AM486DX SERIES (1994–1995)

The Am486 series was AMD's answer to Intel's 486 clock doubling and tripling OverDrive processors of the early 1990s. They incorporate write-back cache and enhanced power management features: including 3 volt operation, SMM (system management mode), and clock control (appealing for Energy Star-compliant "green" desktop systems and portable PCs). Available as Am486DX4/75, Am486DX4/100, and Am486DX4/120, the AMD 486 line saw service in many late-model, low-cost 486-compatible platforms. These processors are now totally obsolete today, and chances are that you will not see them in service unless you're retrofitting an older system.

AM5X86 (1995–1999)

This is really the processor that put AMD on the map. With the appearance of Intel's Pentium line, PC users were faced with the choice of upgrading their motherboard to accommodate a "true" Pentium CPU or of using an expensive Pentium OverDrive processor in a 486 system. AMD rose to the challenge by developing the Am5x86 (or simply the "5x86") as an alternative to Intel's Pentium OverDrive processors. The Am5x86 achieves Pentium-level performance by running "clock quadrupled" at 133MHz (using the 33MHz bus speed of a 486 motherboard). This native 33MHz speed also supported the then-emerging 33MHz PCI bus perfectly. Additional features such as a unified 16KB cache using write-back technology further improved the 5x86's performance. In actual practice, Am5x86 microprocessors provided greater performance than a Pentium 75MHz while costing far less. The 5x86 became the *standard* CPU upgrade for 486 owners who wanted to utilize Pentium-class software without a major hardware upgrade.

The 5x86 also offered integrated power management features, including 3 volt operation, SMM, and clock control. This allowed the 5x86 to consume less power and run cooler than Pentium 75MHz or 486DX4/100 processors. Both desktop and mobile PCs benefited from these features. The 5x86 is totally obsolete today, though you may encounter them when retrofitting older 486-based systems.

K5 SERIES (1996–1999)

Although the Am5x86 proved to be an extremely popular processor, it was not a "true" Pentium alternative. It was not until 1996, when AMD released its *K5* series to the PC industry, that it offered a true Pentium alternative. The K5 is fully compatible with Socket 7 (Pentium) motherboards—a drop-in replacement chip. At most, the K5 might require a motherboard BIOS upgrade for proper identification and support with the motherboard's chipset. But the K5 is fully compatible with all x86 operating systems and software.

The K5 series is rated using the P-rating (or PR) system (see the "The P-Rating (PR) System" earlier in the chapter). Rather than using iCOMP or Spec benchmarks to categorize the processor's performance, each K5 is assigned a PR number that corresponds to an Intel Pentium operating at the given clock speed. For example, a K5 PR120 performs equivalently to a true Pentium at 120MHz. Table 13-11 lists a comparison of K5 performance figures.

TABLE 13-11   COMPARISON OF AMD FAMILY PROCESSORS

CHIP	MHZ	BUS SPEED	L1 CACHE	L2 CACHE	FABRICATION	TRANSISTORS	FORM FACTOR	AVAILABILITY
AMD K5.x Family								
K5.0 - P75 (no MMX)	75	50	24KB	---	0.35	4.3 mil	Socket 7	Obsolete
K5.0 - P90	90	60	24KB	---	0.35	4.3 mil	Socket 7	Obsolete
K5.0 - P100	100	66	24KB	---	0.35	4.3 mil	Socket 7	Obsolete
K5.1 - P120	90	60	24KB	---	0.35	4.3 mil	Socket 7	Obsolete
K5.1 - P133	100	66	24KB	---	0.35	4.3 mil	Socket 7	Obsolete
K5.2 - P166	116	66	24KB	---	0.35	4.3 mil	Socket 7	Obsolete

TABLE 13-11   COMPARISON OF AMD FAMILY PROCESSORS *(CONTINUED)*

CHIP	MHZ	BUS SPEED	L1 CACHE	L2 CACHE	FABRICATION	TRANSISTORS	FORM FACTOR	AVAILABILITY
AMD K6 Family (classic with MMX)								
K6-166	166	66	64KB	---	0.35	8.8 mil	Socket 7	Obsolete
K6-200	200	66	64KB	---	0.35	8.8 mil	Socket 7	Obsolete
K6-233	233	66	64KB	---	0.35/0.25	8.8 mil	Socket 7	Obsolete
K6-266	266	66	64KB	---	0.25	8.8 mil	Socket 7	Obsolete
K6-300	300	66/100	64KB	---	0.25	8.8 mil	Super 7	Obsolete
K6 Mobile-233	233	66	64KB	---	0.25	9.3 mil	Socket 7	Obsolete
K6 Mobile-266	266	66	64KB	---	0.25	9.3 mil	Socket 7	Available
K6 Mobile-300	300	66	64KB	---	0.25	9.3 mil	Socket 7	Available
AMD K6-2 Family (Chompers or "K6 3D MMX")								
K6-2/266	266	66	64KB	---	0.25	9.3 mil	Socket 7	Obsolete
K6-2/300	300	66/100	64KB	---	0.25	9.3 mil	Socket 7 Super 7	Obsolete
K6-2/333	333	95	64KB	---	0.25	9.3 mil	Super 7	Obsolete
K6-2/350	350	100	64KB	---	0.25	9.3 mil	Super 7	Obsolete
K6-2/366	366	66	64KB	---	0.25	9.3 mil	Socket 7	Obsolete
K6-2/380	380	95	64KB	---	0.25	9.3 mil	Super 7	Obsolete
K6-2/400	400	100/66	64KB	---	0.25	9.3 mil	Super 7	Obsolete
K6-2/450	450	100	64KB	---	0.25	9.3 mil	Super 7	Available
K6-2/475	475	95	64KB	---	0.25	9.3 mil	Super 7	Available
K6-2/500	500	100	64KB	---	0.25	9.3 mil	Super 7	Available
K6-2/533	533	133	64KB	---	0.25	9.3 mil	Super 7	Available
K6-2/550	550	100	64KB	---	0.25	9.3mil	Super 7	Available
AMD K6-2/P (Mobile K6-2 Family)								
K6-2P/266	266	66	64KB	---	0.25	9.3 mil	Socket 7	Obsolete
K6-2P/300	300	100	64KB	---	0.25	9.3 mil	Super 7	Available
K6-2P/333	333	66	64KB	---	0.25	9.3 mil	Socket 7	Available
K6-2P/350	350	100	64KB	---	0.25	9.3 mil	Super 7	Available
K6-2P/366	366	66	64KB	---	0.25	9.3 mil	Super 7	Available
K6-2P/380	380	95	64KB	---	0.25	9.3 mil	Super 7	Available
K6-2P/400	400	100	64KB	---	0.25	9.3 mil	Super 7	Available
K6-2P/433	433	66	64KB	---	0.25	9.3 mil	Super 7	Available
K6-2P/450	450	100	64KB	---	0.25	9.3 mil	Super 7	Available
K6-2P/475	475	95	64KB	---	0.25	9.3 mil	Super 7	Available
AMD K6-2+ Family								
K6-2+/450	450	100	64KB	128KB	0.18	---	Super 7	Available
K6-2+/475	475	100	64KB	128KB	0.18	---	Super 7	Available
K6-2+/500	500	100	64KB	128KB	0.18	---	Super 7	Available
K6-2+/533	533	133	64KB	128KB	0.18	---	Super 7	Available
K6-2+/550	550	100	64KB	128KB	0.18	---	Super 7	Availability
AMD K6-3 Family (Sharptooth or K6+ 3D MMX)								
	400	100/66	64KB	256KB	0.25	21.3 mil	Super 7	Available
	450	100	64KB	256KB	0.25	21.3 mil	Super 7	Available
AMD K6-3/P (Mobile K6-3 Family)								
K6-3P/350	350	100	64KB	256KB	0.25	21.3 mil	---	Available
K6-3P/366	366	66	64KB	256KB	0.25	21.3 mil	---	Available

TABLE 13-11   COMPARISON OF AMD FAMILY PROCESSORS *(CONTINUED)*

CHIP	MHZ	BUS SPEED	L1 CACHE	L2 CACHE	FABRICATION	TRANSISTORS	FORM FACTOR	AVAILABILITY
K6-3P/380	380	95	64KB	256KB	0.25	21.3 mil	---	Available
K6-3P/400	400	100	64KB	256KB	0.25	21.3 mil	---	Available
K6-3P/433	433	---	64KB	256KB	0.25	21.3 mil	---	Available
K6-3P/450	450	---	64KB	256KB	0.25	21.3 mil	---	Available
AMD K7 (Standard Athlon Family)								
K7/500	500c (a)	200	128KB	512KB	0.25 (0.18)	22 mil	Slot A	Available
K7/550	550c (a)	200	128KB	512KB	0.25 (0.18)	22 mil	Slot A	Available
K7/600	600c (a)	200	128KB	512KB	0.25 (0.18)	22 mil	Slot A	Available
K7/650	650c (a)	200	128KB	512KB	0.25 (0.18)	22 mil	Slot A	Available
K7/700	700c (a)	200	128KB	512KB	0.25 (0.18)	22 mil	Slot A	Available
K7/750	750	200	128KB	512KB	0.18	22 mil	Slot A	Available
K7/800	800	200	128KB	512KB	0.18	22 mil	Slot A	Available
K7/850	850	200	128KB	512KB	0.18	22 mil	Slot A	Available
K7/900	900	200	128KB	512KB	0.18	22 mil	Slot A	Available
K7/950	950	200	128KB	512KB	0.18	22 mil	Slot A	Available
K7/1000 (Copper)	1000	200	128KB	512KB	0.18	22 mil	Slot A	Available
AMD K7 (Athlon "Ultra" or Thunderbird Family)								
	650	200	128KB	256KB	0.18	22 mil	Slot A Socket A	Available
	700	200	128KB	256KB	0.18	22 mil	Slot A Socket A	Available
	750	200	128KB	256KB	0.18	22 mil	Slot A Socket A	Available
	800	200	128KB	256KB	0.18	22 mil	Socket A	Available
	850	200	128KB	256KB	0.18	22 mil	Socket A	Available
	900	200	128KB	256KB	0.18	22 mil	Socket A	Available
	950	200	128KB	256KB	0.18	22 mil	Socket A	Available
	1000	200	128KB	256KB	0.18	22 mil	Socket A	Available
	1100	200	128KB	256KB	0.18	22 mil	Socket A	Available
	1200	200	128KB	256KB	0.18	22 mil	Socket A	Available
AMD Athlon-C	1000	266	128KB	256KB	0.18	22 mil	Socket A	Available
	1133	266	128KB	256KB	0.18	22 mil	Socket A	Available
	1200	266	128KB	256KB	0.18	22 mil	Socket A	Available
	1333	266	128KB	256KB	0.18	22 mil	Socket A	---
	1400	266	128KB	256KB	0.18	22 mil	Socket A	---
AMD Athlon (Palomino)	1000	266	128KB	256KB	0.18	---	Socket A	Available
	1133	266	128KB	256KB	0.18	---	Socket A	Available
	1266	266	128KB	256KB	0.18	---	Socket A	Available
	1333	266	128KB	256KB	0.18	---	Socket A	Available
	1500	266	128KB	256KB	0.18	---	Socket A	Q2 2001
	1700	266	128KB	256KB	0.18	---	Socket A	Q4 2001

TABLE 13-11   COMPARISON OF AMD FAMILY PROCESSORS *(CONTINUED)*

CHIP	MHZ	BUS SPEED	L1 CACHE	L2 CACHE	FABRICATION	TRANSISTORS	FORM FACTOR	AVAILABILITY
Thoroughbred	2000	266	128KB	256KB	0.13	---	Socket A	2002
AMD K7 Mobile (Mobile Athlon Family)								
Palomino	733	266	128KB	256KB	0.18	---	Socket A	Available
	800	266	128KB	256KB	0.18	---	Socket A	Available
AMD Standard Duron Family								
Spitfire	600	200	128KB	64KB	0.18	22 mil	Socket A	Available
	650	200	128KB	64KB	0.18	22 mil	Socket A	Available
	700	200	128KB	64KB	0.18	22 mil	Socket A	Available
	750	200	128KB	64KB	0.18	22 mil	Socket A	Available
	800	200	128KB	64KB	0.18	22 mil	Socket A	Available
	850	200	128KB	64KB	0.18	22 mil	Socket A	Available
Morgan	900	200	128KB	64KB	0.18	---	Socket A	---
	1000	200	128KB	64KB	0.18	---	Socket A	---
Appaloosa	1500	266	128KB	64KB	0.13	---	Socket A	2002
AMD Mobile Duron Family								
Spitfire	600	200	128KB	64KB	0.18	---	Socket A	Available
	700	200	128KB	64KB	0.18	---	Socket A	Available
Morgan	800	200	128KB	64KB	0.18	---	Socket A	Q2 2001

K6 SERIES (1997–CURRENT)

The K6 processor closed much of the "performance gap" between AMD and Intel processors. Based on AMD's RISC86 superscalar micro-architecture, the K6 was touted as being competitive with Intel's Pentium II processor in terms of performance. The K6 also incorporates a full suite of support for MMX instructions and should be fully compatible with all x86 operating systems and software (as well as software designed for MMX enhancements). Since the K6 continues to use the well-established Socket 7 architecture, it should serve as a drop-in replacement for K5 and Pentium CPUs to provide MMX capability. At most, the K6 may require an upgrade to the motherboard BIOS for proper identification and support with the motherboard chipset. Table 13-11 lists the major K6 variations.

The K6 incorporates seven parallel "execution engines" and employs two-level branch prediction. When coupled with speculative and full out-of-order execution techniques, the 166-300MHz K6 family presented a serious challenge to Intel's Pentium MMX and early Pentium II processors. A large 64KB L1 cache provides 32KB for data and 32KB for instructions. The IEEE 754-compatible floating point unit (FPU) provides performance at least equivalent to the Pentium MMX, and full support for SMM (system management mode) ensures excellent power control. Mobile versions of the K6 have been optimized for use in laptop PC systems.

K6-2 AND K6-3 (1998–CURRENT)

AMD introduced an improved K6 processor in 1998. The *2* in K6-2 is earned with the addition of higher clock speeds and higher bus speeds with the K6 core. Bus speeds up to 100MHz are supported on Super 7 (Socket 7 with AGP support) motherboards. A significant addition to the K6-2 was the introduction of AMD's 3DNow technology. 3DNow is a set of 21 multimedia instructions increasing performance in 3D, multimedia, and floating-point–intensive applications. It is an extension to MMX using SIMD (Single Instruction Multiple Data) technology—3DNow technology is also employed by IDT/Centaur and Cyrix in their newer processors. The use of 3DNow, a large L1 cache, integrated "core speed" L2 cache, and Socket 7 compatibility are a few of the features that help the K6-2 to maintain its popularity and achieve its high performance. The K6-3 is merely a K6-2 with 256KB of full core speed on-die L2 cache. The K6-2 and K6-3 are AMD's answer to Intel's Pentium II/III (and competing with the Pentium name is as important as competing with Pentium performance). Table 13-11 lists the available K6-2 and K6-3 processors.

AMD's K6 processors get a boost in the competitive performance arena by being able to run as close to their upper limits as possible. Compatible motherboards must be capable of supplying the required split voltages at *very* close tolerances. A list of truly compatible and tested motherboards is kept at the AMD Web site (**www.amd.com**). The upper limit operation of the K6 processors requires that close attention be paid to heat dissipation. Heat sinks and fans must be securely attached, and thermal grease should generally be used. System airflow should provide for maximum CPU cooling. When working on an AMD system exhibiting erratic behavior, both these areas should be examined closely.

If you plan to upgrade your system from a K6-2 to a K6-3 processor, you may need a BIOS upgrade to fully support the K6-3.

ATHLON (1999–CURRENT)

With the introduction of the AMD Athlon, competition in the high-performance processor market reached a new level. First produced at 500MHz, the Athlon's current speeds are over 1.2GHz. The AMD Athlon and Intel's Pentium 4/Itanium initiatives basically eliminated any other manufacturer's ability to compete in this market. AMD's constantly improving ability to compete head-to-head with Intel in the Socket 7 style processors is thought to be part of the reason Intel changed to a Slot style connector. Rather than developing a compatible Slot 1 processor, AMD decided it was time to implement its own ideas on how a processor should be integrated in a system. AMD accepted the slot form factor so that motherboard manufacturers would not have to completely redesign the layout of their motherboards to accept the Athlon, but shape and pin count are the only constants. AMD's slot connector is named Slot A. While both utilize a 242-pin interface, Slot A and Slot 1 processors are not interchangeable.

AMD, along with Intel, quickly realized the shift to a slot type processor connection was a mistake. A socket style connector allows for simpler and less expensive manufacturing processes and better heat dissipation characteristics. Newer manufacturing techniques also allowed AMD and Intel to integrate sizable L2 cache directly on the main processor die. This allowed for smaller, less expensive L2 cache while at the same time maintaining (or even improving) processor performance. Even though AMD and Intel agree on the best style of connector for high-performance CPUs, the sockets (Socket A - 462 Pin, Socket 370, Socket 423, and so on) are not in any way compatible. It seems that AMD and Intel processors will never again be interchangeable in the same system.

The Athlon is optimized for high clock frequencies featuring a super-pipelined, super-scalar micro-architecture. It contains a total of nine execution pipelines: three for address calculations, three for integer calculations, and three for executing x87 (floating point), 3DNow, and MMX instructions. AMD specifically addressed its floating point and gaming image problem with the first fully pipelined superscalar floating-point engine and enhanced 3DNow technology. According to some tests, the floating-point performance of the AMD Athlon is more than 35 percent higher than an equally clocked Pentium III Xeon processor.

Enhanced 3DNow adds 24 new instructions—there are 19 instructions to improve MMX integer math calculations and to enhance data movement for Internet streaming applications, and there are 5 DSP extensions for soft modem, soft ADSL, Dolby Digital, and MP3 applications. The Pentium III does not support this new DSP functionality of the AMD Athlon. L1 cache on the Athlon is 128KB, and the 64-bit backside L2 cache controller supports L2 cache sizes from 256KB to 8MB. The cache design utilizes the processor's high-performance system bus and minimizes bottlenecks caused by bus bandwidth limitations. The L2 cache for Slot A style Athlon processors is located off-die, is 512KB in size, and runs at only 1/2, 2/5, or 1/3 core speed. The L2 cache for Socket A style Athlons is 256KB, is on-die, and runs at full core processor speed.

AMD's claim that the Athlon is a seventh generation (7x86) processor is based on the implementation of an entirely different system bus architecture than that utilized by the Intel Pentium family of CPUs. AMD licensed the Alpha EV-6 bus technology from Digital Equipment Corporation. The Athlon system bus operates at 200MHz or 266MHz with a bandwidth capable of 1.6GB/second data transfer speeds. With multiple processors, the system bus can scale up to 3.2GB/sec at 400MHz. It includes such advanced technology as point-to-point topology, source-synchronous packet based transfers, and low-voltage signaling. You can compare the 500MHz-1.4GHz Athlon models in Table 13-11.

The AMD Athlon processor bus architecture is designed to support scalable multiprocessing. The number of AMD Athlon processors in a multiprocessor system is a function of chipset implementation and not the AMD Athlon processor design. Forthcoming optimized chipsets are planned to enable multiprocessor system designs based on two, four, or eight or more AMD Athlon processors. Although supporting chipsets were scarce at first, all major motherboard manufacturers are now producing models supporting the AMD Athlon, with a choice of chipsets from AMD, VIA, or ALi.

Continued development of the AMD Athlon core and further improvements in memory technologies (DDR-SDRAM) should keep AMD competitive with Intel for the foreseeable future. AMD is currently working on a 64-bit processor line, code named "Hammer," to compete with the Intel Itanium series.

DURON (2000–CURRENT)

The AMD Duron processor is a scaled-down version of the Athlon designed to compete with the Intel Celeron in low-cost systems. The Duron uses the same core as the Athlon and offers most of the standard Athlon features, including the high-speed system bus, superscalar floating point unit (FPU), enhanced 3DNow functions, and 0.18 micron manufacturing process. The main difference in the Duron series is reduced cache. The Duron contains the same 128KB L1 cache as the Athlon, but it has only 64KB of on-die L2 cache. The cache architecture on AMD processors is designed so that the same information is not duplicated in L1 and L2 cache. For the Duron, this means performance is similar to a full 192KB of cache memory. The fact that the AMD Duron is little different from the Athlon has made the processor a favorite of "overclockers." Currently available in speeds from 600MHz to 950MHz (Table 13-11), the Duron should be available in GHz + speeds by the time you read this book.

While AMD has been able to eliminate the competitive gap with Intel for the desktop market, it still has work to do to compete with Intel for the mobile system processor market. AMD processors use significantly more power than Intel's. AMD has released a version of its Duron series for the mobile market, but the 700MHz mobile Duron uses 24 watts of power—a comparable Intel Pentium III uses only 14 watts. AMD will likely continue to develop more competitive mobile processors in the future.

The VIA Cyrix CPUs

Cyrix emerged as a major "alternative" processor manufacturer first in 1992 with the release of the Cyrix 486SLC and, later in 1993, with the 486DX4. By 1995, the Cyrix 5x86 (the M1sc) presented the only serious competition to the AMD 5x86. Based in no small part on its relationship with IBM, Cyrix established itself in the PC industry behind Intel and AMD but was unable to overcome the technology and performance gap that plagued some of its later processor offerings. In 1999, the Cyrix name, assets, and product research were purchased by VIA Technologies, the well-known chipset designer and manufacturer. A short time later, VIA also purchased Centaur Technology. Centaur was started in 1995 and had manufactured the processor known as the WinChip. These two acquisitions gave VIA important access to the processor market.

VIA continued development of a high-performance processor based on the newest Cyrix technologies, code-named "Joshua." The Cyrix III, based on the Cyrix-VIA Joshua core, was made available for review but was never put into large-scale production. VIA has also continued development of the Centaur core, and it was this design that was chosen for the actual public release of the Cyrix III processor. The performance and cost of the Joshua chip simply was not competitive in the low-cost processor market. The Centaur-based Cyrix III was developed under the code name "Samuel."

6X86 SERIES (1995–1999)

Cyrix introduced its 6x86 (dubbed the "M1"—later versions were called "M1R") in 1995 as an answer to the Intel Pentium and was optimized for both 16-bit and 32-bit software. The 6x86 Socket 7 processor achieves its performance through the use of two optimized super-pipelined integer units and an on-chip FPU. The integer and floating point units are tailored for maximum instruction throughput by using such techniques as register renaming, out-of-order completion, data dependency removal, branch prediction, and speculative execution. It includes a 16KB unified write-back cache. In most respects, the 6x86 uses many of the same techniques found in other Pentium-class processors.

The 6x86 series uses "P-rating" (or PR) figures instead of iCOMP or Spec numbers to indicate relative performance. For example, a Cyrix PR150+ processor will perform as well as a Pentium processor running at 150MHz. You'll find PR120+, PR133+, PR150+, PR166+, and PR200+ versions of the 6x86 available (the "+" indicates performance *better* than the corresponding Pentium). Table 13-12 outlines the various characteristics for each version.

TABLE 13-12   COMPARISON OF VIA CYRIX FAMILY PROCESSORS

CHIP	MHZ	BUS SPEED	L1 CACHE	L2 CACHE	FABRICATION	TRANSISTORS	FORM FACTOR	AVAILABILITY
Cyrix 6x86 (M1) Family								
6x86-P120	100	50	16KB	---	0.6	3 mil	Socket 7	Obsolete
6x86-P133	110	55	16KB	---	0.6	3 mil	Socket 7	Obsolete
6x86-P150	120	60	16KB	---	0.6	3 mil	Socket 7	Obsolete
6x86-P166	133	66	16KB	---	0.6	3 mil	Socket 7	Obsolete
6x86-P200	150	75	16KB	---	0.6	3 mil	Socket 7	Obsolete
Cyrix MediaGX/MediaPC Family								
	120	60	16KB	---	0.45	---	---	Obsolete
	133	66	16KB	---	0.45	---	---	Obsolete
	150	60	16KB	---	0.45	---	---	Obsolete
	166	66	16KB	---	0.35	---	---	Obsolete
	180	60	16KB	---	0.35	---	---	Obsolete
	200	60	16KB	---	---	---	---	Obsolete
	233	66	16KB	---	---	---	---	Obsolete
	266	66	16KB	---	---	---	---	Obsolete
	300	66	16KB	---	---	---	---	Obsolete

TABLE 13-12   COMPARISON OF VIA CYRIX FAMILY PROCESSORS *(CONTINUED)*

CHIP	MHZ	BUS SPEED	L1 CACHE	L2 CACHE	FABRICATION	TRANSISTORS	FORM FACTOR	AVAILABILITY
Via/Cyrix 6x86MX (M2) Family								
166-PR	150/133	60/66	64KB	---	0.35	---	Socket 7	Obsolete
200-PR	160/150	66/75	64KB	---	0.35	---	Socket 7	Obsolete
233-PR	188/166	75/83	64KB	---	0.35	---	Socket 7	Obsolete
266-PR	208	83	64KB	---	0.30	---	Socket 7	Obsolete
300-PR	233	66	64KB	---	0.30	---	Socket 7	Available
333-PR	250	83	64KB	---	0.30	---	Socket 7	Available
366-PR	250	100	64KB	---	0.25	---	Super 7	Available
400-PR	266	100	64KB	---	0.18	---	Super 7	Available
433-PR	300	100	64KB	---	0.18	---	Super 7	Available
466-PR	333	100	64KB	---	0.18	---	Super 7	Discontinued
Via "Joshua" (a.k.a. Gobi/Jedi/MII+) Family								
PR400	---	133	64KB	256KB	0.18	---	Socket 370	Discontinued
PR450	---	133	64KB	256KB	0.18	---	Socket 370	Discontinued
PR500	---	133	64KB	256KB	0.18	---	Socket 370	Discontinued
Cyrix Mojave (a.k.a. Jalapeno/MIII) Family								
	1200	---	---	256KB	0.18	---	Socket 370	Discontinued
Cyrix Mxi Family								
	466	---	64KB	---	0.18	---	---	Discontinued
	500	---	64KB	---	0.18	---	---	Discontinued
VIA Cyrix III Family								
	500	66/100/133	128KB	0KB	0.18	---	Socket 370	Available
	533	66/100/133	128KB	0KB	0.18	---	Socket 370	Available
	600	66/100/133	128KB	0KB	0.18	---	Socket 370	Available
	650	66/100/133	128KB	0KB	0.18	---	Socket 370	Available
	667	66/100/133	128KB	0KB	0.18	---	Socket 370	Available
	700	66/100/133	128KB	0KB	0.18	---	Socket 370	Available
VIA Samuel II Family								
	600	66/100/133	128KB	64KB	0.15	15 mil	Socket 370	Discontinued
	650	66/100/133	128KB	64KB	0.15	15 mil	Socket 370	Discontinued
	700	66/100/133	128KB	64KB	0.15	15 mil	Socket 370	Discontinued
	750	66/100/133	128KB	64KB	0.15	15 mil	Socket 370	Q1 2001

TABLE 13-12   COMPARISON OF VIA CYRIX FAMILY PROCESSORS *(CONTINUED)*

CHIP	MHZ	BUS SPEED	L1 CACHE	L2 CACHE	FABRICATION	TRANSISTORS	FORM FACTOR	AVAILABILITY
	800	66/100/ 133	128KB	64KB	0.15	15 mil	Socket 370	Q1 2001
	850	66/100/ 133	128KB	64KB	0.15	15 mil	Socket 370	Q1 2001
	900	66/100/ 133	128KB	64KB	0.15	15 mil	Socket 370	2001
	950	66/100/ 133	128KB	64KB	0.15	15 mil	Socket 370	2001

There are two drawbacks to the common Cyrix 6x86. First, the floating point unit (FPU) does not per-form as well as those of similar Intel and AMD processors. While this does not really affect most basic software and operating systems, math-intensive programs (especially 3D computer games) can suffer reduced performance. There is little that can be done with this issue in the 6x86 family, though subsequent processor versions (like the M2) do provide a better FPU. The second drawback to the 6x86 has been excessive heating. In practice, 6x86 processors produce more heat than their AMD or Intel counterparts. Cyrix has addressed this issue by releasing the 6x86L (or M1R) series in 1996. The "L" designation means "low power." More specifically, the 6x86L uses a split voltage of 3.3 volts to handle I/O operations with other chips and 2.8 volts to run the core of the CPU itself. Traditional 6x86 processors use 3.3 volts or 3.52 volts only. In order to support a 6x86L, a motherboard must provide split voltages, or a voltage regulator module must be added between the CPU socket and processor.

The split voltage operation of a 6x86L uses the same voltage levels as an MMX processor. However, the 6x86L is *not* an MMX-compatible processor. These split voltages were chosen so that the 6x86L would be compatible with split-voltage motherboards and could be later replaced with an MMX-com-patible device, such as the 6x86MX (or M2).

MEDIAGX (1996–1999)

Traditional PCs need stand-alone media-related devices, such as a video card and a sound card. These increase the overall cost of a PC and create the potential for hardware conflicts. The Cyrix MediaGX pro-cessor incorporates the features of audio and video, along with many other conventional motherboard components. This high level of integration provided the basis for low-cost entry-level systems that still offer good performance. The 3.3–3.6 volt MediaGX system actually consists of two chips: the MediaGX processor itself and the MediaGX Cx5510 companion chip.

The MediaGX processor is a 64-bit device with a proven x86-compatible processor core. The CPU directly interfaces to a PCI bus and DRAM memory. High-quality SVGA graphics are provided by an advanced graphics accelerator right on the MediaGX processor. The graphics frame buffer is stored in main memory and avoids the performance degradation associated with traditional Unified Memory Architecture (UMA) through the Display Compression Technology (DCT) approach. The processor is available from 120 to 300MHz (Table 13-12). It includes a 16KB unified L1 cache, a floating point unit, and enhanced system management mode (SMM) features. The PCI controller handles fixed, rotating, hybrid or ping-pong bus arbitration. It supports four masters (three on PCI bus). It uses a synchronous

CPU/PCI bus frequency and supports concurrent CPU and PCI operations. The video system supports up to 1280x1024x8, and 1024x768x16 display modes. The MediaGX also works with EDO RAM and supports up to 128MB of RAM in four banks.

The MediaGX Cx5510 companion chip represented a new generation of integrated, single-chip controllers for Cyrix's line of MediaGX-compatible processors. The Cx5510 bridges the MediaGX processor over the PCI bus to the ISA bus, performs traditional chip set functions, and supports a sound interface compatible with industry-standard sound cards, such as the Creative Labs Sound Blaster.

The key issue to keep in mind with the MediaGX series is that it is *not* Socket 7-compatible. The MediaGX and companion chip are a surface-mounted solution designed for dedicated motherboards. This means that MediaGX motherboards are *not* upgradeable to other Socket 7 processors. While the MediaGX line is considered to be obsolete, VIA is reportedly developing a new "System on a Chip" processor design—code-named "Matthew." It will combine the current Cyrix III with VIA's Pro-133X controller and Savage 4 graphics chipsets. The Matthew chip is reportedly scheduled for release sometime in late 2001.

6X86MX (1997–1999)

The 6x86MX (referred to as the "M2") was the Cyrix response to MMX processors like the AMD K6 and Intel Pentium MMX. The 6x86MX design quadruples the original 6x86 internal cache size to 64KB and increases the operating frequency to 200MHz and beyond. Additionally, it features the 57 new MMX instructions that speed up the processing of certain computing-intensive loops found in multimedia and communication applications. The 6x86MX processor also contains a scratch-pad RAM feature and supports performance monitoring. It delivers optimum 16-bit and 32-bit performance while running Windows 95/98, Windows NT, OS/2, DOS, UNIX, and other x86 operating systems. The 6x86MX processor features a super-pipelined architecture and advanced techniques, including register renaming, out-of-order completion, data-dependency removal, branch prediction and speculative execution.

You'll usually find 6x86MX processors available in 150MHz (PR166), 166MHz (PR200), 188MHz (PR233), 225MHz (PR266), and 250MHz (PR300) versions. Current Cyrix M2 processors are produced at speeds up to 333MHz (PR466). As with other Cyrix processors, performance is rated using the P-rating (or PR) nomenclature. For example, a Cyrix 6x86MX at 160MHz performs at a level equal to an Intel Pentium processor at 200MHz (Table 13-12).

VIA/CYRIX III (1999–CURRENT)

The Cyrix III processor is the latest offering from VIA Technologies in the continuing development of the Centaur WinChip core (dubbed "Samuel" by VIA). Produced specifically for the low-cost segment of the computer market, the Cyrix III uses the standard Socket 370 interface. Because of licensing agreements, it is also able to utilize the P6 Intel system bus. This helps keep costs down and allows for easy integration into existing platforms.

Available in speeds from 500MHz to 700MHz, the Cyrix III offers 128KB of full speed L1 cache. It does not offer any L2 cache, which limits performance in demanding 3D and graphics applications. Performance is also limited by a floating point unit operating at only 1/2 core processor speed. It does support AMD's 3DNow and Intel's MMX technology, and it operates at modern front side bus (FSB) speeds of 66MHz, 100MHz, or 133MHz. Table 13-12 outlines the attributes of each version.

The Cyrix III is manufactured using a 0.18 micron process and uses only 10 watts of power at full speed. This keeps heat production low and may make the processor an attractive choice for portable systems. The release of the Cyrix III also saw the end of using the PR system to determine processor performance—the Cyrix III is designed to be a full-speed competitive processor.

VIA SAMUEL II (2001–FUTURE)

Intended to be a possible successor to the Cyrix III, the main difference between the VIA Cyrix III and the Samuel II is the addition of 64KB of L2 cache and a floating point unit (FPU) running at full clock speed. The Cyrix III with optimized L1 cache (even with 128KB) was not able to compete with comparable Intel Celeron processors. VIA hopes to reach speeds in excess of 1GHz with the Samuel II line. The first generation Samuel II processors using the C5B core should be manufactured with a 0.15 micron process. The advanced C5C core with a 0.13 micron fabrication process should soon follow.

The VIA Cyrix III processor uses a core voltage of 1.5V which allows the VIA Cyrix CPU to run virtually cold. VIA Cyrix III CPUs can be run in a system without the need for a fan on the processor; this means you can have your computer running virtually silent. With these attractive features, the VIA Cyrix III may emerge as a mobile solution in the future. VIA also continues development of a C5X core (dubbed "Ezra"). It reportedly will include an even larger L2 cache (256KB), along with support for the latest Intel SSE2 multimedia extensions. The VIA roadmap calls for introducing this processor in the first quarter of 2002, and early speeds should be in the 1.2GB range.

CPU Overclocking

PC evolution is often a race for performance, and designers are constantly struggling to make the most of every last clock tick. Many factors are involved in computer performance, but CPU speed is one of the most important—faster and better CPUs have been a driving force in computer development, and older CPUs are frequently upgraded with new ones in order to wring evermore performance from current systems. While outright CPU replacements are common, they can also be expensive. As an alternative to CPU replacement, PC users and enthusiasts alike often turn to *overclocking* as a means of maximizing the performance of an existing CPU. This part of the chapter offers a comprehensive set of guidelines and procedures that can help you make informed overclocking decisions.

Overclocking is basically the practice of reconfiguring a PC to operate a CPU at a *higher* clock speed (or *bus speed*) than the particular CPU has been specified for. A system can be reconfigured to overclock a CPU in a matter of minutes simply by changing one or two jumpers on the motherboard. Ideally, this higher clock speed should increase the CPU's performance *without* damaging the CPU or reducing its working life. The economics of overclocking can be compelling. In most cases, overclocking can be accomplished with most modern CPUs for less than $30 for a new cooling unit—as opposed to $300–$800 or more for a new CPU.

Overclocking carries inherent risks to the CPU, which include permanent damage to the CPU itself, and should *never* be undertaken without careful consideration of the consequences. CPU overclocking is *not* encouraged as a regular practice, and can be *illegal* if an overclocked system is sold without informing the buyer!

OVERCLOCKING REQUIREMENTS

The most important factor to grasp about CPU overclocking is that it is *not a universally successful technique*. In many cases, your efforts to overclock a PC will fail. There are four critical elements of any PC that influence overclocking: the CPU, the motherboard, system RAM, and CPU cooling. Trouble in any one of those elements will result in overclocking problems.

CPU Issues

CPUs manufactured by Intel (especially the Celerons) seem to be the most successful at overclocking—usually because AMD and VIA Cyrix CPUs are often running very close to their rated limits already in an effort to compete with their Intel counterparts. However, not all Intel CPUs are so suitable. For example, CPUs marked with the SY022 and SU073 S-spec numbers are often limited to clock multipliers of more than x2. Also check for "faked" CPUs (which have been re-marked and resold at higher clock speeds already). Re-marked CPUs have been reported as a frequent practice in Europe, but it's always worth a check of the CPU first before proceeding. As a rule, if you can peal off any stickers underneath the CPU, it is re-marked, and most likely running over its originally rated speed anyway.

Some current CPU's have *locked* clock multipliers. The manufacturers claim that this is both to protect the end user from re-marked CPUs and to assure the integrity of performance claims. The overclocking community thinks that locked multipliers are implemented in order to force the purchase of a new CPU to improve performance.

Motherboard Issues

Even if your CPU seems perfect for overclocking, the motherboard may not be. Signal reflections and other electrical limitations with its bus signals can cause the system to crash or hang. Overclocked CPUs are also more sensitive to unstable signals from the bus and will crash if the motherboard can't deliver "clean" signals. Brand-name motherboards such as Tyan (**www.tyan com**) or Supermicro (**www.supermicro.com**) will *tend* to support CPU overclocking better than cut-priced no-name motherboards. As a result, you may find that some PCs can be overclocked easily, while others suffer severe performance problems (or will not operate at all after overclocking). Motherboard makers Abit (**www.abit-usa.com**), AOpen (**www.aopen.com**), and Asus (**www.asus.com.tw**) have also become well known for the overclocking versatility of their motherboards.

Motherboard bus speeds can present another wrinkle. Most classic motherboards support bus speeds only up to 66 or 100MHz, but more recent motherboard designs can operate at 112MHz, 133MHz, 143MHz, 150MHz, and up. These higher bus speeds will greatly affect the clock multiplier ratio when configuring your overclocking strategy, so be sure to understand the clock speed limits and multipliers for your particular motherboard. A few motherboards allow changing bus speeds in increments of 5MHz or less.

Finally, the motherboard should also support a wide range of CPU supply voltages. For example, a STD voltage of 3.3V and a VRE voltage of 3.45V are common with Pentium-class systems. If you use an MMX-type CPU (such as the P55C, the 6x86MX, or the K6) you'll need access to "split voltage" support (2.8V and 3.3V are typical). Late model Athlon or Duron processors may operate with voltages down to 1.6V. This may not sound so important because you're not "changing" the CPU. But in some cases, you may need to boost the CPU supply voltage just a bit to support overclocking. Today, you'll find that Slot 1/Slot A motherboards set their CPU voltages automatically when the CPU is installed, so don't panic if you have trouble locating CPU voltage jumpers (you may still be able to tweak CPU voltages through the system's CMOS Setup).

RAM Issues

System RAM can also be a problem in overclocked systems with bus speeds that exceed 66MHz—you'll require high-end EDO RAM or SDRAM. As a rule, EDO RAM works best with 66MHz motherboards, while low-end SDRAM tends to be best with 75MHz and 83MHz motherboards. Well-established bus speeds of 100MHz and 133MHz require high-end SDRAM, memory certified for PC100 (100MHz) and PC133 (133MHz) bus speeds, respectively. Emerging DDR-SDRAM and Rambus (RDRAM) memory support even faster speeds. Keep this in mind when planning to tweak the FSB speed.

Cooling Issues

Perhaps the most overlooked problem with CPU overclocking is insufficient cooling. CPUs draw current with each clock tick. The more clock cycles in a given period, the more current is required—and the more heat is generated. Most current CPUs run hot to begin with, but when overclocked, a CPU can easily overheat and crash (or perhaps suffer permanent damage). As a consequence, you should *never* attempt to overclock a CPU without making accommodations for better cooling. Consider a high-capacity, top-quality heat sink/fan assembly with a reliable ball-bearing fan offering a K/W (Kelvin per Watt) value of 1K/W or less. You may need to go to a hobby electronics store or full-featured computer store to find a *good* heat sink/fan. When installing the cooling unit, make sure that it fits to the CPU tightly without any air gaps, and use a thin layer of thermal grease between the CPU and heat sink. Serious overclocking enthusiasts may even employ a piezoelectric or liquid-cooled chilling unit for the CPU.

POTENTIAL PITFALLS

Before we actually get into the techniques of CPU overclocking, there are some potential hazards that you should be aware of. There are three typical failures associated with CPU overclocking: intermittent operation, shortened life span, and outright failure. All three faults are heat related.

- **Intermittent operation**   The added heat produced in the CPU can result in internal signal errors (a lost bit or shift of signal timing), which can easily cause the PC to crash—forcing you to power down the system until the CPU cools.

- **Shortened life span**   This is another heat-related problem. Rather than an immediate failure, excessive heat can shorten a CPU's life through a process of *electromigration*. Rather than a CPU working for ten years, it may work for only two years or five years (it's impossible to say for certain).

- **Outright failure**   A CPU is designed to operate from -25 to 80 degrees C. If the CPU is not cooled properly, the CPU die can exceed its maximum working temperature and fail. Though there are millions of transistors on a modern CPU, it only takes the failure of one or two to destroy a CPU.

OVERCLOCKING THE SYSTEM

At this point, you're ready to try some overclocking yourself. Generally speaking, overclocking requires three basic steps: change the bus speed, change the multiplier, and change the supply voltage. Note that you do *not* always have to change all three settings in order to successfully overclock a CPU. The general steps in overclocking a CPU are outlined next. To give you an idea of what may change, Tables 13-13 and 13-14 list some generic overclocking suggestions for older 486 and Pentium-class systems:

1. Turn off the computer. Open it up and get your motherboard manual.

2. Check the markings on the top and bottom of your CPU, write them down, and reinstall the CPU (this helps to ensure that the CPU is "real" and not re-marked).

3. Check the current clock speed and multiplier jumper settings on your motherboard, compare them with your manual, and write them down. On "jumperless" motherboards, you can usually find this information in the CMOS Setup.

4. Check the supply voltage jumper settings on your motherboard, compare them with the manual and your CPU marking, and write them down. On "jumperless" motherboards, you can usually find this information in the CMOS Setup.

5. Inspect the cooling unit on your CPU, and upgrade the cooling unit (if necessary).

6.   Change the jumper settings for clock speed and/or multiplier according to your target overclocked level. On "jumperless" motherboards, you can usually alter these settings through the CMOS Setup.

7.   Double-check that the new settings are configured as expected.

8.   Start the computer and allow it to boot to the CMOS Setup.

9.   Does it boot or reach the CMOS Setup? (If "yes," go to step 12; if "no," continue with step 10.)

10.   Turn off the computer and change the CPU voltage jumper to a *slightly* higher voltage (if possible).

11.   If you still can't boot or reach the CMOS Setup, return the voltage setting to its original value. You cannot overclock at this desired speed. Return the clock speed and multiplier settings to their original values and quit, or repeat step 6 with a lower bus/multiplier combination.

12.   Tweak your CMOS Setup settings to optimum performance values as required (this may not be necessary). In some cases, you may need to adjust RAM or bus timings to accommodate the changes to your processor settings.

13.   Does the system boot to a full working operation system? (If "no," check your cooling unit and repeat step 11; if "yes," continue with step 14.)

14.   Start testing with a utility like Winstone 99 and allow the system to "burn-in" thoroughly. Check for any crashes or other intermittent system operation. If the system proves unstable, you cannot overclock at this level. Return the clock speed and multiplier settings to their original values and quit, or repeat step 6 with a lower bus/multiplier combination.

15.   If everything works well—congratulations! Otherwise, check your cooling unit and repeat step 11.

Operating systems such as Windows 98/Me are reputed to be *very* sensitive to overclocking. This means you may not be able to overclock a system with Windows 98/Me, even though the system may overclock fine under DOS or another operating system—the best solution is to experiment and see what happens.

Change the Bus Speed

The *internal* clock of a CPU runs at a different speed than the *external* clock (or "front side bus speed"). The external clock is the speed at which the cache and the main memory run—and is usually divided down to yield suitable clock signals for the AGP bus, PCI bus, and other bus architectures in the system. There are only three different "official" bus speeds used by the Pentium, Pentium Pro, and the AMD K5: 50, 60, and 66MHz. The Cyrix/IBM 6x86 uses five bus speeds: 50, 55, 60, 66, and 75MHz. There are also new motherboards available that support the unofficial bus speeds of 83MHz to 148MHz. Typical Pentium II/III motherboards run at speeds between 66 and 133MHz. Athlon processors use 200MHz and 266MHz speeds.

TABLE 13-13   GENERIC 486 OVERCLOCKING SUGGESTIONS

CLOCK RATE (MHZ)	PROBABLE SUCCESS AT (MHZ)	POSSIBLE SUCCESS AT (MHZ)
16	20	---
20	25	33
25	33	40 or even 50
33	40	50
40	50	---
66	80	---
100	120	---

TABLE 13-14   GENERIC PENTIUM/6x86 OVERCLOCKING SUGGESTIONS

CLOCK RATE (MHZ)	PROBABLE SUCCESS AT (MHZ)	POSSIBLE SUCCESS AT (MHZ)
60	66	---
75	90	100 to 133
90	100	120 to 133
100	120	133
120	133	---
133	150	166 to 180
150	166	---
166	180	187.5
200	225	---

To change the bus speed, look in your motherboard manual for something like "Clock Speed," "CPU External (BUS) Frequency Selection," or "Front Side Bus (FSB)"—these are the jumpers you will have to change. You will probably have to change several different jumpers to establish each new bus speed. If you are lucky and happen to have a motherboard with "SoftMenu" (jumperless) technology, you can change the bus speed settings in the CMOS Setup menu without even opening the case. Only increase the bus speed one step at a time (that is, go from 60MHz to 66MHz, not 60MHz to 75MHz or 66MHz to 133MHz). This is usually the most successful way to overclock.

Change the Multiplier

The CPU's internal clock is controlled by an internal clock multiplier in each CPU, which is programmed via CPU pins. Intel Pentium CPUs support the following multipliers: x1.5, x2, x2.5, and x3. Intel Pentium Pro CPUs support x2.5, x3, x3.5, and x4. The 6x86 CPUs support only x2 and x3, but the upcoming M2 will support x2, x2.5, x3, and x3.5. Current Pentium II/IIIs support multipliers from x3.5 up to x7 and more. To change the multiplier setting, find a set of jumpers marked with a designation such as "Clock Multiplier" or "CPU to BUS Frequency Ratio Selection" in your motherboard manual. There are usually several jumpers used to change these settings. Again, you can do all of this in the CMOS Setup menu if you have a SoftMenu (jumperless) motherboard, such as the newer Abit motherboards (**www.abit.com.tw**).

Change the Supply Voltage

There are some circumstances when boosting the CPU supply voltage (from 3.3V STD to 3.45V VRE) may be necessary to make the CPU run reliably at a higher bus speed to account for the bigger voltage difference between the digital "high" and "low" conditions. The bigger difference results in "cleaner" signals for the CPU and other motherboard devices. If you can't run your CPU reliably at one particular clock speed, it's always worth considering jumping to the higher supply voltage. However, more voltage will produce more heat, so you must be *very* careful about cooling. If you cannot stabilize an overclocked system by tweaking the voltage, be sure to return the voltage setting to its original value in order to prevent undue processor heating.

Special Notes for Higher Bus Speeds

Many traditional Pentium-class motherboards handle clock speeds up to 66MHz, but later model Pentium/MMX motherboards operate up to 75MHz, and even 83MHz. There are some precautions to keep in mind when using these older motherboards with enhanced bus frequencies:

■ **PCI bus issues**   The PCI bus is taken from the clock speed. At 60 or 66MHz, the PCI bus speed is 30 or 33MHz (this is the recommended speed for PCI). However, at 75 or 83MHz, the PCI bus runs at 37.5 or 41.6MHz, respectively. This faster speed can lead to problems with some PCI devices such as SCSI controllers, video cards, and network cards. Often, SCSI controllers and network cards refuse to work at the faster speed, and some video boards just get much hotter than usual (though some video cards like the Diamond Stealth 64 aren't affected at all by higher bus speeds). Fast, modern motherboards often make the expansion bus speed independent (*asynchronous*) of the FSB, so this may not be an issue on new motherboards.

■ **EIDE bus issues**   The speed of an EIDE interface is not only determined by the PIO or DMA modes, but it is also highly dependent on the PCI clock. This is one reason why an EIDE interface is always slower in systems with 60MHz bus speeds or less. However, the EIDE interface will be faster when you are running at 75 or 83MHz bus speeds. This sounds fine at first, but either the interface or the hard disk is often not up to the faster bus speeds. For example, I've seen HDDs work fine at 75MHz bus speeds, but at 83MHz, I've had to scale back to PIO mode 2. This failure to work at faster bus speeds also applies to EIDE CD-ROM drives and could very well be the culprit if you're running into strange lockups under Windows. Again, modern motherboards with Ultra-DMA drive interfaces are often immune to such speed-related issues.

■ **ISA bus issues**   In some cases, the ISA bus speed is divided directly from the PCI bus. If the PCI bus is running faster, the ISA bus may also be running faster. This condition can cause some serious problems for ISA boards (especially older ISA boards). For example, I've heard AWE32 soundboards make strange whistling sounds when being run at a fast bus speed. You can sometimes correct for ISA speed problems by introducing ISA wait states in the CMOS Setup.

These speed issues generally do *not* relate to today's Pentium II/III/4 or Athlon/Duron motherboards, which reach 100 to 133MHz and higher.

As standard FSB speeds have increased, currently to 100MHz and 133MHz, chipsets have been developed to include dividers that maintain peripheral bus speeds at the specification's limits. PCI specifications call for 33MHz, and the AGP bus is designed to operate at 66MHz. Some modern chipsets (such as the Intel 440BX) offer only the 1/1 and 2/3 AGP bus settings. This is fine for 66MHz and 100MHz FSB speed systems but does not provide for current 133MHz FSB speed processors.

■ **AGP bus issues**   The AGP bus is designed to operate at 66MHz and is usually set as a fraction of the system bus speed. On a 100MHz or 133MHz system bus, the AGP bus speed would be set at 2/3 or 1/2, respectively, in the CMOS Setup. A 66MHz system, the Intel Celeron for instance, would be set to 1/1. This means overclocking the system bus can also overclock the AGP bus, and this can lead to system stability problems if the AGP video card does not support the higher bus speed. Some motherboards may offer more than the 2/3 or 1/2 fraction option for the AGP bus speed. You may be able to find an option that keeps the AGP bus speed at or below 66MHz. Remember, anything below 66MHz will hinder graphics performance. Be sure to monitor your video card for overheating symptoms when experimenting with higher clock settings.

The latest chipsets include a wider selection of peripheral bus settings, and many high-end AGP video cards will operate at speeds higher than the standard 66MHz.

OVERCLOCKING THE INTEL PENTIUM

Intel's Pentium and Pentium MMX processors have traditionally been regarded as some of the easiest CPUs to overclock. This can be attributed to the increased quality demands that Intel put in place after its early floating-point flaw disaster with the 60 and 66MHz Pentiums. For example, a Pentium MMX 200 seems to run fine with 2.8V at 208/83MHz and 225/75MHz. For 250/83MHz, you may need to increase the voltage to 2.9V. Table 13-15 lists some typical options for Pentium overclocking.

OVERCLOCKING THE INTEL CELERON

With the addition of L2 cache, the Intel Pentium II Celeron has become an overclocker's favorite. The Pentium core, lower price, and high production quality combined to attract users looking for performance gains through overclocking. Intel sought to limit the Celeron's use in overclocking with a locked multiplier *and* a locked bus speed of 66MHz. Some motherboard makers have not complied with the locked bus speed implementation, providing an avenue to overclock Celerons through higher bus speeds. Common motherboard bus speeds higher than 66MHz are 75MHz, 83MHz, 100MHz, and 133MHz.

With the implementation of locked multipliers, half of the processor speed setting capability has been eliminated for overclocking. Overclockers have had to depend more on motherboard features and their own ingenuity to achieve higher speeds. Many motherboard manufacturers have responded with additional front side bus (FSB) and processor voltage settings. They have seen how product reviewers focus on the ability of a motherboard to remain stable when overclocked. The trend, then, has been for modern motherboards to include numerous FSB settings covering a wide range of possible settings. They also include an increased number of voltage settings that can be easily altered in small steps.

To make it even easier for the novice to experiment with different FSB and voltage settings, most motherboards have moved control of these settings from hardware to software. Older motherboards used jumpers on the motherboard to set clock multipliers, bus speed options, and voltage settings. Many current motherboards have these options included in the CMOS Setup routine. You do not have to disconnect everything and open the case just to increase CPU voltage or up the FSB. It is also easy to increase the number of available settings when the options are selected with a click of a mouse or press of a key, instead of having to figure out if six to eight jumpers are in the correct on/off positions.

TABLE 13-15	GENERIC PENTIUM OVERCLOCKING OPTIONS			
PENTIUM AT...	**1ST CHOICE:**	**2ND CHOICE:**	**3RD CHOICE:**	**4TH CHOICE:**
75MHz	112.5MHz (1.5x75MHz)	100MHz (1.5x66MHz)	90MHz (1.5x60MHz)	83MHz (1.5x55MHz)
90MHz	125MHz (1.5x83MHz)	112.5MHz (1.5x75MHz)	100MHz (1.5x66MHz)	---
100MHz	125MHz (1.5x83MHz)	112.5MHz (1.5x75MHz)	---	---
120MHz	125MHz (1.5x83MHz)	133MHz (2x66MHz)	112.5MHz (1.5x75MHz)	---
133MHz	166MHz (2x83MHz)	150MHz (2x75MHz)	166MHz (2.5x66MHz)	---
150MHz	166MHz (2x83MHz)	187.5MHz (2.5x75MHz)	200MHz (3x66MHz)	150MHz (2x75MHz)
166MHz	208MHz (2.5x83MHz)	166MHz (2x83MHz)	187.5MHz (2.5x75MHz)	200MHz (3x66MHz)
200MHz	250MHz (3x83MHz)	225MHz (3x75MHz)	208MHz (2.5x83MHz)	---

Consider the following example for a 600MHz Celeron processor where the clock multiplier is locked at 6x. Since the multiplier cannot be changed, the motherboard maker has provided fine control that allows you to adjust the FSB in 5MHz increments:

- 6×100MHz = 600MHz (Standard)
- 6×105MHz = 630MHz (Overclocked)
- 6×110MHz = 660MHz
- 6×115MHz = 690MHz
- 6×125MHz = 750MHz
- 6×133MHz = 798MHz

Of course, even this is a very limited example. Modern motherboards offer FSB settings from 66MHz to 170MHz, often in increments of 3–5MHz. Though specified to operate on a 66MHz system bus, Celerons will usually operate at the standard Pentium III system bus speed of 100MHz. This choice is made even easier by the fact that all other components (i.e. memory, AGP video, and so on), are typically designed to operate at 100MHz. For example, a Celeron 566, which normally runs with settings of 8.5×66MHz, usually operates at 850MHz (8.5×100MHz) without any other changes. Keep in mind that higher FSB speeds can affect memory and bus timing, so you might need SDRAM memory rated for 150MHz, along with motherboards that support compatible PCI and AGP bus speeds—even at a 150MHz FSB.

The ability to successfully overclock a Celeron CPU may also depend on the availability of higher voltages. It sometimes takes a little more voltage to reach a faster signal speed. Modern motherboards again satisfy this requirement by offering a wide range of possible core voltage settings. Due to the fact that AMD and Intel processors are no longer interchangeable, motherboards would only have to support a limited number of voltages. The reality is that most motherboard manufacturers have enabled setting the CPU voltage higher than the standard voltage required by the CPU installed. This is also an option added to the CMOS Setup routine—though some motherboards still require that the voltage be set using jumpers located on the motherboard. If you find that your system will not boot after increasing the FSB setting, try slowly increasing the core voltage setting. Keep a very close watch on your CPU temperature when doing this. Any system instability or failure means you have gone too far. You should overclock only to a point where your system remains completely stable and reliable. Table 13-16 highlights numerous overclocking options and voltage settings for Celeron processors.

TABLE 13-16   GENERIC CELERON OVERCLOCKING OPTIONS

PROCESSOR	OVERCLOCKING SETTINGS	CORE VOLTAGE SETTINGS
Celeron 300A	100MHz×4.5 = (450MHz)	2.1v
	92MHz×4.5 = (414MHz)	2.0v
Celeron 333	100MHz×5 = (500MHz)	2.0v/2.1v
	92MHz×5 = (460MHz)	2.1v/2.2v
	83MHz×5 = (416MHz)	2.0v
Celeron 366	92MHz×5.5 = (506MHz)	2.2v/2.1v
	83MHz×5.5 = (458MHz)	2.1v
Celeron 400	92MHz×6 = (552MHz)	2.2v/2.1v
	83MHz×6 = (500MHz)	2.1v/2.0v

TABLE 13-16   GENERIC CELERON OVERCLOCKING OPTIONS *(CONTINUED)*

PROCESSOR	OVERCLOCKING SETTINGS	CORE VOLTAGE SETTINGS
Celeron 433	92MHz×6.5 = (598MHz)	2.3v/2.2v
	83MHz×6.5 = (542MHz)	2.2v/2.1v
	75MHz×6.5 = (487MHz)	2.1v/2.0v
Celeron 466	83MHz×7 = (583MHz)	2.2v
	75MHz×7 = (525MHz)	2.0v
Celeron 500	83MHz×7.5 = (625MHz)	2.3v
	75MHz×7.5 = (563MHz)	2.2v/2.1v
Celeron 500A	115MHz×7.5 = (863MHz)	1.5v
Celeron 533	75MHz×8 = (600MHz)	2.3v/2.2v
Celeron 533A	105MHz×8 = (840MHz)	1.7v
	100MHz×8 = (800MHz)	1.65v
	106MHz×8 = (848MHz)	1.5v
Celeron 566	100MHz×8.5 = (850MHz)	1.7v/1.65v
Celeron 600	100MHz×9 = (900MHz)	1.75v/1.7v
	92MHz×9 = (828MHz)	1.7v/1.65v
Celeron 633	100MHz×9.5 = (950MHz)	1.8v/1.75v
	92MHz×9.5 = (874MHz)	1.75v
Celeron 667	100MHz×10 = (1GHz)	1.8v/1.75v
	92MHz×10 = (920MHz)	1.8v/1.75v
	83MHz×10 = (830MHz)	1.75v/1.7v
Celeron 700	92MHz×10.5 = (966MHz)	1.8v/1.75v
	83MHz×10.5 = (875MHz)	1.8v/1.75v/1.7v

OVERCLOCKING THE INTEL PENTIUM II/III

Early Pentium II (a.k.a. "Klamath") processors were manufactured using a 0.35 micron process and were available in speeds from 233MHz to 300MHz using a 66MHz front side bus (FSB). Intel then moved to a 0.25 micron process for Pentium II ("Deschutes") processors at speeds of 333MHz to 450MHz. The 333MHz Pentium II still used the 66MHz FSB, but from 350MHz up, the FSB was increased to 100MHz. The first Pentium III processors were manufactured using the 0.25 micron process ("Katmai") and were available in speeds from 450MHz to 600MHz. Intel then produced the Pentium III using a 0.18 micron process ("Coppermine"). These Pentium IIIs are available in speeds from 500MHz and up.

Since August 1998, Intel has been locking the clock multiplier on its CPUs, so it probably will not be possible to change the multiplier when overclocking a 350MHz, 400MHz, 450MHz Pentium II, or any Pentium III or Pentium 4. If you try, the CPU will either refuse to boot the machine or boot it up at 1/3 its proper speed. To get around this limitation, a Pentium II overclocker's primary option is to increase the speed of the front side bus. Increasing the speed of the FSB also increases the speed of the PCI and AGP busses, so errors might result from some older components refusing to run properly at the higher bus speeds. For instance, overclocking a 100MHz FSB to 112MHz results in the PCI bus being overclocked to 37MHz (instead of 33MHz), and the AGP bus being overclocked to 74MHz (instead of 66MHz). Since newer PCI and AGP cards are being designed with greater tolerances, however, such differences are becoming less of a problem.

Depending on the model of Pentium II that you're attempting to overclock, you'll need to be able to adjust the clock multiplier, front side bus speed, and/or core voltage. You will also need to examine the effectiveness of your CPU cooling arrangement and improve the cooling if possible. Installing some kind of CPU temperature monitor is highly recommended. Many of the most current motherboards have a wide range of settings for multipliers, FSB speeds, and voltages—some even include integrated temperature monitors. Table 13-17 lists some popular options for Pentium II overclocking. The rules should also hold true for Pentium III overclocking (the main difference being the Pentium III's use of SSE). The one thing that you will notice is that Pentium II/III processors—especially the faster models—are not nearly as tolerant of overclocking as Celeron units. However, you can still tinker even if you don't see your particular processor in the table—just remember to test in very small increments.

To run reliably with a 100MHz FSB, you need to have 100MHz SDRAM (PC100 RAM) installed in your system. The same restriction applies when overclocking a standard 100MHz system (you may need 133MHz /PC133 SDRAM) or 133MHz system (you may need 150MHz /PC150 SDRAM). In many of the cases listed here, increasing the FSB speed requires you to *lower* the clock multiplier on your system.

OVERCLOCKING THE CYRIX 6X86

Generally speaking, the older Cyrix 6x86 CPUs are much more difficult to overclock than comparable Intel CPUs. There are two reasons for this. First, Cyrix CPUs (even the later production steps) produce tremendous amounts of heat. Overclocking them would produce so much heat that it would be difficult to remove it all without huge heat sink/fans or powered Peltier coolers. Second, 6x86 CPUs support only two multiplier settings (x2 and x3), so there are far fewer overclocking options available. Try a Cyrix P120+ (100MHz) as a P133+ (110MHz). Try a P133+ (110MHz) as a P150+ (120MHz). Finally, try a P150+ (120MHz) as a P166+ (133MHz).

TABLE 13-17   GENERIC PENTIUM II/III OVERCLOCKING OPTIONS

FSB SPEED	CLOCK MULTIPLIER	OVERCLOCKED SPEED	CHIPSET
233MHz and 266MHz Pentium II (66MHz FSB)			
75MHz	4.0	300MHz	440LX
100MHz	3.0	300MHz	440BX
112MHz	3.0	336MHz	440BX
300MHz Pentium II (66MHz FSB)			
75MHz	4.5	338MHz	440LX
100MHz	3.5	350MHz	440BX
112MHz	3.5	392MHz	440BX
100MHz	4.0	400MHz	440BX
333MHz Pentium II (66MHz FSB)			
100MHz	3.5	350MHz	440BX
75MHz	5.0	375MHz	440BX
112MHz	3.5	392MHz	440BX
100MHz	4.0	400MHz	440BX
350MHz to 450MHz Pentium II (100MHz FSB)			
112MHz	3.5	392MHz	---
112MHz	4.0	448MHz	---
112MHz	4.5	504MHz	---

You'll generally achieve the best success with 2.7 or 3.7 stepped 6x86 CPUs—they are more stable and produce less heat.

OVERCLOCKING THE AMD K5

AMD has put itself on the map with its 5x86/133MHz CPU and earned a lot of respect with the K5. However, the older PR75, PR90, and PR100 versions of the K5 do not seem to tolerate overclocking very well—probably because those CPUs were running at their performance limits already. By comparison, the later K5 versions (such as the PR120, PR133, PR150, and PR166) and the newer K6 and K6-2 seem to be much more tolerant of overclocking. When selecting an overclocking level, choose the next level up. For example, if you have a K5 PR120, try configuring it as a PR133, and so on.

OVERCLOCKING THE AMD K6-2

The AMD K6-2 series processors use various core revisions, including the AFR, AFQ, AFX, AHX, and AGR revisions. These processors are already using comparatively high voltages and require good cooling even at rated speeds. The AMD K6-2 series offers only limited overclocking options, and even minor increases will require additional cooling. Table 13-18 shows some possible overclocking options that are available if the FSB speed settings are supported by the motherboard.

TABLE 13-18   GENERIC AMD K6-2 OVERCLOCKING OPTIONS

CPU	VOLTAGE	MULTIPLIER	FSB SPEED	SPEED (MHZ)	CPU CORE
380MHz	2.20V	4	95	380	AFR
		4	100	400	AFR
		4.5	95	428	AFR
		4	112	448	AFR
		4.5	100	450	AFR
400MHz	2.20V	4	100	400	AFQ, AFR
		4	112	448	AFQ, AFR
		4.5	100	450	AFQ, AFR
		5	95	475	AFQ, AFR
		5	100	500	AFQ, AFR
		4.5	112	504	AFQ, AFR
450MHz	2.40V	4.5	100	450	AHX, AFX
	2.20V	5	95	475	AHX, AFX
		5	100	500	AHX, AFX
		4.5	112	504	AFX
475MHz	2.40V	5	95	475	AHX, AFX
	2.20V	5	100	500	AFX
		4.5	112	504	AFX
500MHz	2.20V	5	100	500	AFX
		4.5	112	504	AFX
		5.5	97	533	AFX
		5.5	100	550	AFX
		5	112	560	AFX
		6	95	570	AFX
		6	100	600	AFX

TABLE 13-18   GENERIC AMD K6-2 OVERCLOCKING OPTIONS *(CONTINUED)*

CPU	VOLTAGE	MULTIPLIER	FSB SPEED	SPEED (MHZ)	CPU CORE
		5.5	112	617	AFX
533MHz	2.20V	5.5	97	533	AFX
		5.5	100	550	AFX
		5	112	560	AFX
		6	95	570	AFX
550MHz	2.30V	5.5	100	550	AGR
		5	112	560	AGR
		6	95	570	AGR
		6	100	600	AGR
		5.5	112	617	AGR

OVERCLOCKING THE AMD ATHLON AND DURON

AMD now uses the same core (the "Thunderbird") for both the Athlon and Duron line of processors. The major differences are a smaller L2 cache and lower core voltage for the Duron series; this makes the Duron very attractive to overclockers. The trouble with Athlon/Duron overclocking is the FSB speed—Athlon and Duron processors use an identical standard front side bus speed of 200MHz (100MHz×2) because of their use of the EV6 system bus. Current Athlons support a FSB setting of 266MHz (133MHz×2). Given these very fast speeds, it is difficult to use altered FSB speeds to overclock AMD processors. The EV6 bus can be dependably raised only 10 to 15 percent over the default speed. This means a maximum FSB speed of 112MHz to 115MHz for the 100MHz bus, and 145MHz to 153MHz for the 133MHz bus.

Fortunately, AMD has made it fairly easy to unlock the locked multiplier. For the early cartridge-style Athlons, you had to make a device to unlock the multiplier and then remove the cartridge's outer case to install it. Obviously, this was well beyond the abilities of casual users, but prefabricated devices with installation instructions were soon available from commercial sources. These products were dubbed "GFDs" (or "Golden Finger Devices"), referring to the gold contacts on the edge connector that are used to unlock the multiplier. For the Socket A-style Athlon and Duron processors, AMD made it even easier to unlock the multiplier—all you really need is a lead (graphite) pencil. The entire operation consists of drawing a heavy line across a small gap between gold contacts on top of the processor. You can see this for the AMD processor in Figure 13-4. There are several Internet sites that discuss this matter in great detail, including **www.motherboards.org/articlesd.html?articleid=44&pagenum=1** and **www4.tomshardware.com/cpu/00q3/000711/index.html**. Once the processor has been unlocked, overclocking is as simple as increasing the multiplier to a number higher than the default multiplier for that specific processor.

You will also need to increase the core voltage setting for an overclocked Athlon or Duron processor. The maximum voltage for both processors that can be chosen is 1.85V. This means the Athlon Thunderbird core can be increased only 0.15V above its default voltage of 1.7V (less than a 10 percent increase). The Duron fares a little better—you can add up to 0.35V to the 1.5V default voltage, which should be more than enough for most attainable clock speeds. Table 13-19 highlights the results of an overclocked Athlon 700 and Duron 600 processor. You should notice how important it is to have motherboard support for numerous FSB, multiplier, and voltage settings. You can also see how even the slight increase in FSB speed can provide significant performance improvements.

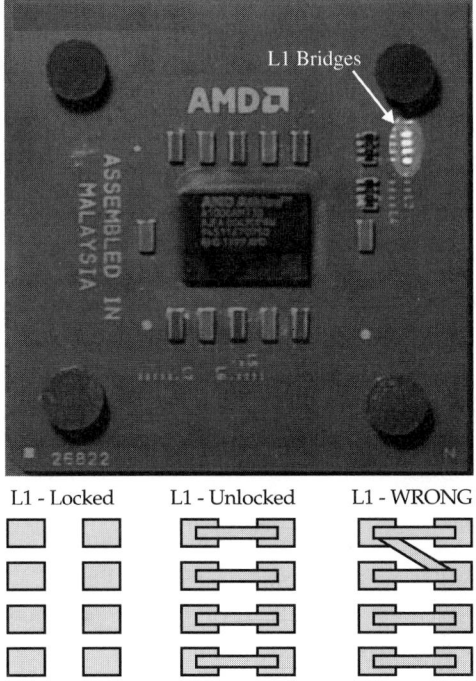

FIGURE 13-4   Unlocking an AMD Socket A processor's multiplier

TABLE 13-19   EXAMPLES OF AMD ATHLON/DURON OVERCLOCKING

SPEED	MULTIPLIER	FSB SPEED	CORE VOLTAGE	CPUMARK 99
AMD Athlon 700				
700	7	100	1.7V	64.7
770	7	110	1.7V	71.2
784	7	112	1.7V	72.5
800	8	100	1.75V	71.8
824	8	103	1.8V	74.5
825	7.5	110	1.8V	75.4
840	8	105	1.8V	Failed to boot
840	7.5	112	1.8V	Failed to boot
AMD Duron 600				
600	6	100	1.5V	51.4
650	6.5	100	1.5V	55.0
672	6	112	1.5V	57.8
683	6.5	105	1.5V	57.4
690	6	115	1.5V	59.4
700	7	100	1.5V	57.6
715	6.5	110	1.5V	60.2

TABLE 13-19   EXAMPLES OF AMD ATHLON/DURON OVERCLOCKING *(CONTINUED)*

SPEED	MULTIPLIER	FSB SPEED	CORE VOLTAGE	CPUMARK 99
748	6.5	115	1.5V	63.2
770	7	110	1.6V	63.5
800	8	100	1.6V	63.2
840	8	105	1.6V	66.7
850	8.5	100	1.65V	65.8
880	8	110	1.7V	69.9
893	8.5	105	1.7V	69.4
896	8	115	1.7V	71.2
900	9	100	1.75V	68.3
910	8.5	107	1.75V	70.9
927	9	103	1.75V	Failed to boot
935	8.5	110	1.75V	Failed to boot

Like the Intel Celeron with respect to the Pentium II/III, the AMD Duron is often a better candidate for overclocking than is the Athlon. It provides a wider range of settings and overclocking options, mainly as a result of its lower default core voltage of 1.5V. The AMD Athlon, even with its more limited overclocking options, still outperforms the Duron at comparable speeds. The larger L2 cache of the Athlon provides this performance advantage.

Overclocking immediately voids any processor warranty. Adequate preparation and precautions are an absolute requirement before attempting to overclock any processor. You should have a dependable method of monitoring processor temperature, along with additional cooling resources, installed on the system.

Troubleshooting CPU Problems

The term *"microprocessor troubleshooting"* is not the misnomer it once was. Early CPUs such as the 8088 carried only 29,000 transistors. When one of those transistors failed, it would usually result in a complete system failure—the PC would crash or freeze entirely. Further, the system would subsequently fail to boot at all. However, CPUs have become far more complex in the last 20 years or so, and new generations such as the Pentium 4 are exceeding *40 million* transistors. With so many more transistors, the probability of an immediate *catastrophic* fault is far less. Of course, *any* CPU fault is *very* serious, but there are now many cases where a system may boot, but crash when certain *specific* CPU functions are attempted (for instance, trying to execute protected-mode instructions). These kinds of errors may give the impression that a piece of software is corrupt or that one or more expansion devices may be faulty. This part of the chapter looks at a selection of CPU failure modes and offers some tactics to help resolve the problems.

TIPS FOR CONTROLLING HEAT

Heat remains the greatest enemy of overclocking (even normal processor operations), so managing that heat is an important priority. Try some of the following remedies to help you overcome CPU heating issues:

■   Use a good-quality heat sink/fan that is more than adequately rated for your particular CPU.

■ Use a thin layer of heat-sink compound to improve heat transfer between the CPU case and heat sink (available at Radio Shack; Cat. No. 276-1372).

■ For extremely hot CPUs, try a Peltier cooler or similar refrigeration unit (see "Further Study" at the end of this chapter for contacts).

■ Select reliable ball-bearing–type fans with extended service lifetimes.

■ Fold and tie cables away from areas requiring free air circulation (such as the vicinity of the CPU fan). Clear away any obstructions.

■ Make sure the CPU heat sink/fan is in close thermal contact with the processor surface (using heat-sink compound if needed). It should attach securely to the CPU or the CPU and socket. If it doesn't, get a new heat sink/fan.

■ Use a CPU cooler with an audio alarm system that will alert you in case of either fan malfunction or excessive CPU temperature.

■ If you are overclocking your CPU, compensate for the increased heat generated by using an "upsized" heat sink/fan, Peltier active cooler, or other effective chilling device.

■ Clean fan blades, fan support struts, and power supply louvers of accumulated dirt at least annually. Canned compressed air and vacuum sweeper brushes work well.

■ Increase air circulation in and out of your computer case by using an auxiliary fan.

GENERAL SYMPTOMS

When you encounter trouble starting or running the PC, check for the following symptoms as possible explanations and corrective actions.

SYMPTOM 13-1   **The system is completely dead (the system power LED lights properly)**   CPU faults are *never* subtle. When a CPU problem manifests itself, the system will invariably crash. Consequently, systems that do not boot (or freeze without warning during the boot process) stand an excellent chance of suffering from a CPU fault. The frustration with this kind of symptom is that the PC typically does not run long enough to execute its POST diagnostics, nor does the system boot to run any third-party DOS diagnostics. As a result, such "dead" systems require a bit of blind faith on the part of a technician.

Before considering a CPU replacement, you should use a multimeter and check the power supply outputs very carefully. Even though the power LED is lit, one or more outputs may be low or absent. Excessively low outputs can easily result in logic errors that will freeze the system. If this problem occurred *after* adding an upgrade, the supply may be overloaded—try removing the upgrade. If system operation returns, consider upgrading the power supply. If an output is low or absent and there has been no upgrade (or the problem continues after removing the upgrade), try replacing the power supply.

Next, strip the system of its peripherals and expansion boards, then try the system again. If operation returns, one of the expansion devices is interrupting system operation. Reinstall one device at a time and check the system. The last expansion device to be installed when the PC fails is the culprit. Replace the defective device. If the failure persists, try a new CPU. Remember to shut down and unplug the PC before continuing. When removing the original CPU, be *extremely* careful to avoid bending any of the pins (you may want to reinstall the CPU later). Use care when installing the new CPU as well—bent pins will almost always ruin the chip. If a new CPU fails to correct the problem, replace the motherboard outright.

SYMPTOM 13-2   **You get a beep code or I/O POST code indicating a possible CPU fault**
The system will almost always fail to boot. When the POST starts, it will test each of the key motherboard components (including the CPU). If a CPU fault is indicated during the POST (usually a single-byte hexadecimal code written to port 80h and read with a POST card), check each output from the system power supply. If one or more outputs is low or absent, there may be a problem in the supply. Try a new supply. If all supply outputs measure properly, try a new CPU. If a new CPU does not resolve the problem, replace the motherboard.

SYMPTOM 13-3   **The system boots with no problem, but crashes or freezes when certain applications are run**   It may seem as if the application is corrupt, but try a diagnostic such as AMIDIAG from AMI or The Troubleshooter by AllMicro. Run repetitive tests on the CPU. While the CPU may work in real mode, diagnostics can detect errors running protected-mode instructions and perform thorough register checking. AMIDIAG stands out here because of the very specific error codes that are returned. Not only will it tell you if the CPU checks bad, but it will also tell you the specific reason *why*. When an error code is returned suggesting a CPU fault, try another CPU. If a CPU fault is not detected, expand the diagnostic to test other portions of the motherboard. If the entire system checks properly, you may indeed have a corrupt file in your application.

SYMPTOM 13-4   **The system boots with no problem, but crashes or freezes after several minutes of operation**   This happens regardless of the application being run. You will also probably note that no diagnostic indicates a CPU problem. If you shut the system off and wait several minutes, the system will probably boot fine and run for several more minutes before stopping again—this is typical of thermal failure. When the system halts, check the CPU for heat. *Use extreme caution when checking for heat—you can easily be burned!* Your CPU may not be fitted with a heat sink, or its cooling fan is disconnected (or failed). As a rule, all Pentium-class and later processors (such as the Pentium MMX, Pentium II/III/4, Athlon, and Duron) require a heat sink/fan assembly for adequate cooling. Replace any defective cooling fan.

Make sure that the system cooling fan is working and that there is an unobstructed path over the CPU. If not, consider applying a heat sink with an adequate helping of thermal compound. If the CPU is already fitted with a heat sink, make sure that there is an ample layer of thermal compound between the CPU case and heat sink base. In many cases, the compound is omitted, ruining the transfer of heat and allowing the CPU to run much hotter. If you find that there is no thermal compound, allow the PC to cool, then add thermal compound between the CPU case and heat sink.

SYMPTOM 13-5   **The system BIOS mis-identifies the processor**   This frequently happens after a processor upgrade and is almost always due to a problem with the BIOS. Most BIOS versions will query the CPU with a CPUID instruction, then identify the CPU through a look-up table in the BIOS. If the CPU does not have an entry in the BIOS, it will not be identified (or will be identified incorrectly). The general way to correct this problem is to upgrade the motherboard BIOS to a later version or upgrade the motherboard outright.

SYMPTOM 13-6   **An older system refuses to run properly when the CPU's internal (L1) cache is enabled**   This type of symptom occurred frequently with older processors (such as the AMD Am486) and can almost always be traced to a configuration issue. The processor may fail if run at an incorrect bus speed (for instance, overclocking), so check and correct the motherboard bus speed to accommodate the CPU. This symptom can also occur when running the CPU at an incorrect operating voltage. Check the voltage level and reconfigure the motherboard for the correct voltage (if necessary). Finally, the motherboard must be compatible with the L1 cache type on the CPU. For example, installing a CPU with a write-back cache on a motherboard that doesn't support write-back cache can cause problems.

SYMPTOM 13-7 **You cannot run a 3.45V CPU in a 5V motherboard, even though an appropriate voltage regulator module is being used** Double-check the voltage regulator module (VRM). The VRM must have adequate current handling capacity to support the CPU's power demands. Otherwise, the VRM will be overloaded and fail to provide adequate power. Check with the CPU manufacturer for its VRM recommendations. You might also try the CPU/VRM in another 5V motherboard. If the CPU/VRM fails in another 5V motherboard, chances are that the VRM is underrated or has failed. If the CPU/VRM does work on another 5V motherboard, it is possible that the original motherboard's BIOS could not support the particular requirements of the new CPU. Check with the motherboard manufacturer to see if there is an updated BIOS (either flash or ROM chip) available for the system.

SYMPTOM 13-8 **A system malfunctions under HIMEM.SYS or DOS4GW.EXE after installing a new CPU** This type of symptom occurred frequently with older CPUs and could generally be traced to errors in the motherboard CPU voltage and type settings (opposed to the newer bus speed/multiplier configurations). Check the motherboard's CPU configuration jumpers. Also, running a 3.45V CPU at 5V or running a non-SL enhanced CPU as an SL enhanced part can cause these types of problems to occur. So make sure that the correct part is being used and see that the CPU voltage is correct (use a voltage regulator module if necessary).

SYMPTOM 13-9 **The system runs fine, but it reports the wrong type of CPU** In virtually all cases, the motherboard BIOS was not written to support the particular CPU directly. Start by checking the motherboard's CPU configuration jumpers to see that it is set properly for the particular CPU. If the problem persists, you'll probably need a BIOS upgrade (either a flash file or ROM IC) to accommodate the processor. Check with the motherboard or system maker to determine whether an appropriate BIOS upgrade is available.

SYMPTOM 13-10 **L2 cache fails after upgrading to a Pentium OverDrive processor** Installing an OverDrive-type processor can sometimes result in the secondary (L2 or "external") cache being disabled. This is usually due to a BIOS version that is not compatible with the OverDrive processor. You may need to leave the L2 cache disabled until you can upgrade the motherboard BIOS. In a few cases, a patch utility may be available for the motherboard that can be run from the CONFIG.SYS or AUTOEXEC.BAT file and that will re-enable the L2 cache as the system boots.

SYMPTOM 13-11 **Some software locks up on systems running 5x86 processors** This is a frequent problem with high-end software such as AutoDesk's 3D Studio. Often, programs like 3D Studio use software timing loops in the code. The 5x86 processor executes these loop instructions faster than previous x86 CPUs, thereby interfering with timing-dependent code inside the program. In most cases, the software manufacturer will offer a patch for the offending program. For 3D Studio, you can download the FSTCPUFX.EXE file from Kinetix (**ftp://ftp.fh-merseburg.de/pub/hardware/mainboard/asus/FSTCPUFX.EXE**). Run the executable patch file and follow the instructions. The patch alters the 3D Studio executable file.

Another prime example of software-related problems is with Clipper applications. Clipper inserts software timing loops into the applications when the code is compiled, and this also interferes with timing-dependent code in the program. For Clipper, you can download the PIPELOOP.EXE file (**ftp://ftp.ascod.ru/SOFT/Cyrix/pipeloop.exe**) and put it in your AUTOEXEC.BAT file.

SYMPTOM 13-12   **The Windows 95 Device Manager identifies the CPU incorrectly**
In many cases, the CPU is mis-identified as a 486 or other older CPU. This mistake is due to an issue with Windows 95. The algorithm used in Windows 95 to detect the CPU was likely completed before the particular CPU was released, and therefore the CPU responds to the algorithm just as a 486 does. Use a diagnostic, which *will* identify your particular CPU correctly, or check with the CPU maker for a Windows 95 patch that will support proper identification. This problem happens often with Cyrix 6x86 CPUs and can be corrected by downloading a patch such as 6XOPT074.ZIP (see the "Performance enhancement software" bullet under the upcoming "Cyrix 6x86 Symptoms" section).

SYMPTOM 13-13   **The heat sink/fan will not secure properly**   It is not tight against the surface of the CPU. This can be a serious problem for the system because a loose heat sink/fan will *not* cool the processor correctly. There are three classical solutions to this issue. First, make sure that you have the heat sink/fan model that is recommended for your particular CPU (a common error when building a new PC). Second, make sure that the heat sink attaches to either the CPU chip itself or the ZIF socket that the CPU mounts in. Third, verify that the CPU has not been altered or faked. Faked CPUs are often ground down to remove their original markings, then new markings are placed on the CPU. The grinding process reduces the package thickness and can prevent the heat sink/fan from being secure (faked CPUs have been reported as a common occurrence in Europe).

CYRIX 6X86 SYMPTOMS

From a technological standpoint, the Cyrix 6x86 (or "M1" as it used to be called) is a strong competitor to the Intel Pentium—in a properly configured system, the 6x86 has been reported actually to outclass the classic Pentium in some areas. In addition, the 200MHz version of the 6x86 uses a bus speed of 75MHz (replacing the established 66MHz bus speed). However, there are some special circumstances and symptoms to keep in mind when working on Cyrix-based platforms:

■ **Bus speed**   This is where Cyrix's problems start, since the higher bus speeds demand very fast memory technologies and advanced motherboard chipsets. You can't run the P200 chip in a Triton FX or HX motherboard because those chipsets don't support a bus speed of 75MHz. In practice, the 6x86 P200 runs at a clock speed of 150MHz by multiplying the 75MHz motherboard bus speed by 2. If you were to try running the P200 at a bus speed of 50MHz and a multiplier of 3, you would loose any performance benefit due to the slow bus speed. For the P166, P150, and P120 versions, motherboard compatibility is much better.

■ **Excess heating**   Heat is an important issue with every leading-edge CPU, but while similar Intel and AMD processors will typically run hot, the 6x86 runs *extremely* hot. Excess heat can cause data corruption, system crashes, and even shorten the working life of the CPU. In the worst cases, excess heat can destroy the CPU. Such reliability issues force the use of good-quality heat sink/fan assemblies with *all* 6x86 models. The release of 6x86L (low-voltage) versions promise to help combat the issues of heating by using a "split voltage" architecture of 2.8 volts and 3.3 volts—the same voltages used by MMX processors. Cyrix expects that the "L" series will reduce power demands by more than 25 percent. If you must replace a 6x86, go for a version 2.7 of the 6x86, or a 6x86L version (with proper voltage regulation) if you can.

- **FPU issues**   Another concern for 6x86 users is that the floating-point capability of a 6x86 is measurably below that of similar Pentiums. For example, the FPU performance of a 6x86 P166 is rated equivalent to only a Pentium 90MHz unit. There is no real solution for the current 6x86 versions, but the M2 from Cyrix appears to correct these performance problems.

- **Performance under Windows NT**   Here's another serious problem that plagued earlier 6x86 versions. The CPU is *so* sensitive to signal reflections from the CPU busses that NT would often switch off the L1 cache in the 6x86. This, in turn, caused performance degradation. Cyrix has resolved many of these issues in the version 2.7 releases as well as the 6x86L CPUs, but you may continue to see NT performance problems in systems with older 6x86 versions.

- **Performance enhancement software**   Given the various limitations of the Cyrix 6x86, there are a number of utilities available to enhance the 6x86. 6XOPT074.ZIP is a 6x86 optimizer written by Mikael Johansson. It configures 6x86 CPU registers to increase performance, and it allows Windows 95 to "see" the 6x86 CPU in the Device Manager. DIRECTNT.ZIP enables the 6x86 cache under Windows NT 4. Both of these utilities (and more) can be obtained from **compunet .hypermart.net/hardware.htm**.

SYMPTOM 13-14   **The Cyrix 6x86 system crashes or freezes after some period of operation**   This is almost always a heat-related problem caused by inadequate cooling of the 6x86. If you're not using a heat sink/fan, install one before continuing (be sure to use a thin layer of thermal grease to improve heat transfer between the CPU and heat sink). Make sure that you are using a good-quality heat sink/fan with *plenty* of capacity and see that it is securely attached to the CPU. Also see that the CPU itself is securely seated in its socket.

You might also consider installing a different 6x86 model. The Type C028 version uses 3.52 volts, and the Type C016 uses 3.3 volts, so just changing models can reduce power demands. You might also try installing a version 2.7 or later 6x86, which is better able to deal with heat. Best yet, install a 6x86L CPU (and regulator). A third possible cause of intermittent system operation is a poorly designed BIOS. Check with the motherboard maker or system manufacturer and see if there is a BIOS upgrade to better support Cyrix CPUs.

SYMPTOM 13-15   **The Cyrix 6x86 system crashes and refuses to restart**   This is another classic heat-related problem and may often indicate that the CPU or its associated voltage regulator has failed. Check the voltage regulator—regulators are more susceptible to failure with Cyrix 6x86 CPUs because of the higher current demands. If the voltage regulator checks out, replace the CPU itself (perhaps with a lower-power model, as mentioned in Symptom 13-14).

SYMPTOM 13-16   **You notice poor Cyrix 6x86 performance under Windows NT 4.0** In virtually all cases, NT has detected the 6x86 and has elected to shut down the write-back L1 cache completely. This results in the performance hit. Fortunately, there are several ways to address this problem. First, you can download the DIRECTNT.ZIP patch from **compunet.hypermart.net/hardware.htm**; this patch re-enables the L1 cache under NT 4.0. This fix brings performance back up, but it also can cause instability for NT. A more practical resolution is to replace the CPU with a 6x86 version 2.7 or higher, or a 6x86L (and suitable voltage regulator), as mentioned in Symptom 13-14. Keep in mind that VIA Technologies does *not* provide any support for older, obsolete Cyrix processors.

SYMPTOM 13-17   **Applications do not perform well**   For example, you can't get Quake (or other graphics-intensive program) to run nearly as well on a Cyrix 6x86 system as it does with a similar Pentium system. This is an issue involving Cyrix FPU performance. There is no real resolution for the problem at this time—later 6x86 versions do not correct the FPU. You may replace the CPU with an AMD or Intel model, or you can check the performance offered by the Cyrix 6x86MX (M2), if you could still find one available.

SYMPTOM 13-18   **A Cyrix 6x86 CPU won't work on your motherboard**   There   are several possible problems when upgrading to any non-Intel CPU. First, check the motherboard's chipset and make sure that the chipset and other attributes such as bus speed are compatible with the 6x86. As you saw earlier, some 6x86 iterations require unusual bus speeds in order to function. Motherboard settings are always important when installing a CPU. You will probably need to set a new clock speed to accommodate the 6x86. In some cases, you may also need to specify a CPU type. Finally, you'll need to set the CPU voltage (if your motherboard provides a "switchable" voltage regulator). Otherwise, you'll need to install a voltage regulator with enough power capacity to handle a 6x86 adequately. If you select an underrated regulator, the regulator can overheat and burn out. The last issue to consider is your BIOS. Often the BIOS must detect a CPU correctly and make slight variations in BIOS routines to use the new CPU most effectively. If the BIOS does not support your 6x86, you'll need to get a BIOS upgrade from the motherboard maker or system manufacturer.

If all else fails, try slowing down the clock speed to the next level. If the CPU runs properly then, there is probably an incompatibility between your motherboard and the 6x86. Check with the motherboard manufacturer (or system maker) and see if there are any compatibility issues that have been identified (and if there is a fix available).

SYMPTOM 13-19   **You notice performance degradation when using a Cyrix 6x86 under Windows 3.1x or Windows 95**   In many cases, performance problems when using non-Intel CPUs is related to BIOS support. Often the BIOS must identify a CPU, and adjust to accommodate any particular nuances. If the BIOS is not supporting the CPU correctly, overall performance problems can result. Check with the motherboard maker or system manufacturer for any BIOS upgrades that will better support your new CPU.

Clock speed and cache are two other issues that can affect system performance. Check the motherboard jumpers and verify that the clock speed is set correctly for your Cyrix CPU. Also check for cache jumpers and see that any cache settings are correct. You may also verify that Internal (L1) and External (L2) caching are enabled in BIOS.

OVERCLOCKING SYMPTOMS

The process of CPU overclocking is hardly a perfect one. There are many variables involved, such as the CPU type, motherboard quality, and available clock speed and multiplier settings. There are many cases when overclocking results in system problems. Some of the more common problems are identified next.

SYMPTOM 13-20   **The system does not boot up at all after reconfiguring the system for overclocking**   This is a common problem that almost always means that you *cannot* overclock the CPU at the level you have chosen. Try bumping up the processor voltage a bit. If that fails, scale back the clock speed or the multiplier until the system starts up, or return the clock and multiplier to their original values.

SYMPTOM 13-21   **The system starts after overclocking, but locks up or crashes after some short period of time**   Overclocking causes substantial heating of the CPU, and cooling must be improved to compensate for this additional heat—otherwise, the overheated CPU can lock-up and crash the system. Check the heat sink/fan and see that it is attached correctly and has a thin layer of thermal grease between the CPU and heat sink. It may be necessary to "up-size" the heat sink/fan or use a Peltier cooler.

SYMPTOM 13-22   **You see memory errors after increasing the bus speed for overclocking**
Memory performance is tightly coupled to bus speed (or "FSB speed"). For example, most 60ns RAM
types will work fine up to 66MHz, but you may need high-end 50ns EDO RAM or 50ns SDRAM when
pushing the bus speed to 75MHz or 83MHz. Overclocking a 100MHz FSB may require PC133 (133MHz)
SDRAM, and overclocking a 133MHz FSB may demand PC150 (150MHz) SDRAM. Try some faster
memory in the PC (or do not attempt to overclock the system).

SYMPTOM 13-23   **After reconfiguring for overclocking, the system works, but you see
a rash of CPU failures**   Chances are that the CPU is running far too hot and is resulting in premature
CPU failures. Check the cooling unit and see that it is securely attached and that there is a thin layer of
thermal grease between the CPU and heat sink. It may be necessary to "up-size" the heat sink/fan or use a
Peltier cooler.

SYMPTOM 13-24   **After reconfiguring for overclocking, you find that some expansion
board or other hardware is no longer recognized or working**   Since AGP, PCI, and ISA
bus clocks are often tied to the FSB speed, increasing the FSB speed will also increase the AGP, PCI, and
ISA clocks. This can upset the operation of some sensitive adapter boards. Check your CMOS
Setup—there may be provisions to adjust divisors that will set the correct speeds. For example, when you
go from an FSB of 100MHz to 133MHz, you may need to set the AGP divisor from 2/3 to 1/2 so that the
AGP bus will stay as close to 66MHz as possible. Similar settings may be available for the PCI bus. In
some motherboard designs, the bus clocks may be independent of the FSB. You may also be able to
replace the suspect hardware with a more tolerant adapter, but it is often safer to return the clock speed and
multiplier settings to their original values if you cannot tweak them yourself.

SYMPTOM 13-25   **After reconfiguring for overclocking, you notice that a number of
recent files are corrupt, inaccessible, or missing**   In effect, the system is not stable. Check for
excessive processor heat first. Otherwise, you should *not* overclock this particular system. Try scaling back
the overclocking configuration or return the clock speed and multiplier settings to their original values.

SYMPTOM 13-26   **The CPU core voltage is set at 1.7V, but PC Health and VHM give a
reading of 1.74V**   This is not necessarily a problem. Voltage output fluctuations can be caused by
your power supply unit, but a core voltage deviation of 0.05V is safe with AMD CPUs. For more serious
deviations, you may need to tweak the voltage setting so that your measuring tools report an acceptable
level. Remember that there is always a little tolerance between the ideal value represented by a setting and
the actual value that occurs as the result of that setting—this is normal in the real world—however, the tolerance should be very small.

SYMPTOM 13-27   **The system will not boot when a Duron 600 is set at 500MHz after
loading the fail-safe or optimized default option**   This is usually an issue with the processor's
information in the CMOS Setup. If you experience a 600MHz Duron failing to boot when set to 500MHz
(either manually or by fail-safe/optimized default loading), clear the CMOS via the "Clear CMOS"
jumper and manually set the CPU to the correct frequency (600MHz).

SYMPTOM 13-28   **A Pentium III 600B is being detected as a Pentium III 450**   Pentium
III processors are multiplier locked. For example, the Pentium III 600B is locked at 4.5x with the 133MHz
BUS. If your motherboard does not support the 133MHz BUS, then it will run at 100MHz, causing the
processor to run at 450MHz. Some motherboards state that the BUS will run at 133MHz, but this is not

supported by the manufacturer and may interfere with the AGP and PCI bus speeds causing problems. Unless your motherboard supports the 133MHz BUS and processors from the manufacturer, your supported speed will only be 100MHz. Reconfigure the motherboard to the proper FSB speed or replace the motherboard outright.

Further Study

AMD   www.amd.com
AMI   www.megatrends.com or www.ami.com/ (AMIDIAG)
ARM   www.arm.com/
Athlon Overclocking   www.athlonoc.com
Compaq   www.compaq.com/
CPU Central   www.cpu-central.com/
Cyrix   *See* VIA Technologies
DEC Alpha   *See* Compaq
Hardware Central   www.hardwarecentral.com/hardwarecentral/subjects/75/
IBM PowerPC   www.chips.ibm.com/products/powerpc/
Intel   www.intel.com
MIPS   www.mips.com/
Motherboard HomeWorld   www.motherboards.org/docoverclock.html
Overclockers.com   www.overclockers.com/home.asp
Overclockers Online   www.overclockersonline.com/
Sharky Extreme   www.sharkyextreme.com/hardware/celeron_oc/l.shtml
Texas Instruments   www.ti.com/
Tom's Hardware   www.tomshardware.com
VIA Technologies   www.viatech.com/

14

DATA RECOVERY TECHNIQUES

It's almost ironic that the value of a PC's hardware is often insignificant when weighed against the data that PC contains. Recent history is replete with examples of businesses that have suffered terrible financial hardship—even gone out of business—after losing vital data files. While the consequences are not nearly as severe for home offices or casual PC users, damaged files, accidental deletions, and hard drive failures are always difficult. This chapter is intended to provide some guidance that will help to protect your drive from failure and to offer some procedures that will help you recover lost or damaged data. The one thing to keep in mind here is that the drive hardware must be working. If the drive should fail outright, you may not be able to recover anything.

If you must recover data from a damaged hard drive, there are numerous "data recovery" businesses (listed at the end of this chapter) that might be able to help. Recovering data from a damaged drive is expensive and is usually only worthwhile for large corporations and government organizations. Backups are the best protection from data loss due to hardware faults.

Understanding Data Loss

The first step in overcoming data loss is to know its causes. Data is extremely vulnerable and may be damaged by many different factors. This part of the chapter explains the major causes of data loss and offers some suggestions to minimize the dangers.

HARDWARE AND SYSTEM FAILURES

By far, hardware faults are the leading cause of data failure—accounting for at least 44 percent of all data loss. Hardware failures can occur from such events as an electrical failure (or shutting down the PC improperly), a disk drive head crash, or an outright failure of the drive circuitry or electromechanical mechanisms. You'll see hardware problems indicated by error messages (for example, an error message stating that the device is "not recognized" or "not available"). You may also notice that previously accessible data is suddenly gone. In many cases, the hard drive may not even spin, or you may hear a scraping or rattling sound coming from the hard drive.

You can usually work to prevent hardware and system failures by keeping the system in a clean, temperature- and humidity-controlled environment. Protect against power surges and other types of electrical failures by employing an *Uninterruptible Power Supply* (UPS). For mission-critical data—such as an important network server—use a *Redundant Array of Independent Disks* (RAID) system to mirror your main data drive(s). RAID will often allow you to re-create the data lost on a drive.

As a rule, never open a hard drive in other than a Class 100 (or better) cleanroom environment. Otherwise the accumulation of dust and debris in everyday air can render the drive unusable. If you must reclaim data from a failed drive, send it to a company that has the specialized cleanroom facilities to attempt a hard drive repair (such as those listed at the end of this chapter). Do not attempt to operate a hard drive that you suspect may have hardware or system failure. The failure may continue to corrupt data on the drive and exacerbate the data loss. Finally, never use software recovery utilities (such as Norton Disk Doctor), to recover data in a hardware failure situation. These utilities assume that the hardware is functional, and can cause further damage to the data.

HUMAN ERROR

Contrary to popular belief, human error ranks second (about 32 percent) as the cause of all data loss. In most cases when the system seems to work properly, but previously accessible data is suddenly gone, chances are that human error is responsible at some level. For example, letting your young nephew poke around on your system without supervision is a great way to lose important data. It may be as simple as an accidental deletion of a file, or as serious as impact damage caused by accidentally dropping a drive or tape.

Human error can be prevented by keeping regular and up-to-date data backups of your current work. Also, you should avoid attempting any installations, repairs, or system operations with which you do not have previous experience. Fortunately, files and folders that are accidentally deleted can usually be recovered with the "undelete" feature included with most operating systems such as DOS (or the Recycle Bin of Windows 98/Me). If you must bring in another individual to help recover your data, make sure that the individual has the experience needed to recover files successfully.

SOFTWARE BUGS

Improper software design accounts for roughly 14 percent of all data loss. We typically refer to these as bugs in the software. Bugs are usually caused by improper software design and testing on the part of the software maker. Even when software is working perfectly, the software may have unforeseen effects on particular system platforms or combinations of hardware. In many cases, you'll notice software bugs as error messages stating that the data is inaccessible or corrupted. (The problem usually occurs after installing new software.) You may also see memory errors or other PC errors. You'll need to identify the software responsible for your data loss, and contact the software maker for the appropriate patches or upgrades.

COMPUTER VIRUSES

While the popular media seems to focus on computer viruses as a primary cause of data loss, viruses really only account for about 7 percent of all data loss (though that percentage is growing a bit with the popularity of Internet downloads). Thousands of computer viruses are currently known to exist, and that number grows daily, but viruses still have had a limited impact on data. In most cases, you'll see a virus infection broadcast with a message on the display (for example, "Your computer is now stoned"), though there may be many other strange or unpredictable behaviors that accompany the data loss.

Your best defense against computer viruses is to use a *current* antivirus tool, and to scan all incoming floppy disks and CDs for viruses. (This includes packaged software, software carried on-site by other users, and software downloaded from the Internet.) Also, do not accept e-mail file attachments from people you do not know, and virus-check any attachments that you do receive before opening them. Data is usually accessible after the virus has been removed, but be sure to remove the virus first. Also, avoid reformatting your hard drive or floppy disk as a means of eliminating viruses—this doesn't always work.

THEFT AND MALICIOUS DAMAGE

Data loss can also be traced to the occurrence of theft or malicious damage. Computers are notoriously easy to transport and sell, so they are often the target of home or office break-ins. Of course, once the PC disappears, any data that was in it goes as well. Even if the system is eventually recovered, any data probably will have been wiped clean by the system's new user. This is a prime example of where off-site backups (either in a physical safe or online via the Internet) can save the day.

If you've worked in business for any length of time, you've probably seen more than one coworker terminated or laid off. Some folks vent their anger and frustration by erasing files, loading viruses, and even physically damaging their system (though there is certainly criminal liability for such actions). If you're the boss and find yourself handing out pink slips, remember to change a user's password first.

NATURAL DISASTERS

Fire, flood, earthquake, lightning strikes—all the forces of nature account for just 3 percent of all data loss. While there is little you can do to prevent the physical destruction of your system in the face of a natural disaster, your best protection is to keep a current backup of your data stored off-site in another protected water/fire-proof location.

Protecting Drives and Data

Sooner or later, your hard drive is going to fail. It is not a question of whether, it is a question of when. While this may sound gloomy, there is absolutely no reason why a hard drive should not perform perfectly throughout its entire normal working life. Just as people can improve the quality of their life by eating right and exercising regularly, drive life can be lengthened (and your data protected) by taking some fairly common-sense precautions. The following pointers can reduce downtime and are sure ways to win a customer's loyalty.

HANDLE HANG-UPS GRACEFULLY

Virtually every computer system will stop from time to time—programs cease running, and the system won't respond to commands. We usually say the system is frozen, halted, or hung up. A system can halt for many reasons (including hardware faults), but buggy software is usually the problem. The trick is correcting the problem and regaining control of the system. As a rule, never turn off the system power. Windows usually has numerous files open. When the system hangs, those files are left open, so try to clear the problem before taking drastic action:

- *Close other programs and tasks.* If you can access other items on your task bar (for example, the Start button or other background programs), make sure to close any other programs or tasks that may be open. When one application fails, it can often destabilize your entire PC, so minimize the potential for damage if you can. Use the Windows Shut Down dialog to reboot the system.

- *Try to clear the failed process first by pressing CTRL-ALT-DEL.* This should open the Close Program dialog (go ahead, try it). If the dialog opens and you see that one or more applications are not responding, you can highlight them and click the End Task button. In many cases, this will terminate the problem software with a minimum of fuss and allow you to regain control of the system (at least enough to reboot in an orderly fashion).

- *Use the Shut Down button.* If you can open the Close Program dialog, but cannot regain control of the system, try the Shut Down button. This is a "back door" that allows you to turn the system off in an emergency. You may lose some unsaved data, but it can prevent serious Windows problems.

- *Reboot the system.* If the system remains "stuck," things get a little more serious. You're now forced to reboot the PC and will certainly lose any unsaved data. Check your hard drive activity LED. If the LED is out (and you don't hear the drive working), try pressing the PC's Reset button on the front panel. Windows should reboot, though it will probably run ScanDisk automatically to check for file problems. Avoid pressing the Reset button if the drive activity LED is on or flashing (indicating that drive activity is taking place).

- *Press the Power button.* In rare circumstances, the Reset button may fail to reboot the system. This indicates a serious problem, though not unrecoverable. In this case, you'll need to press the Power button. With most systems, you may need to hold in the Power button for several seconds (perhaps up to 5 or 6 seconds) until the power supply turns off. Wait a few seconds after the PC shuts down, and then try powering-up the system again. Windows will probably run ScanDisk automatically to check for file problems. As with the Reset button, avoid using the Power button if the drive activity LED is on or flashing (indicating that drive activity is taking place).

CHILDPROOF THE SYSTEM

Children have a heartwarming sense of curiosity, but when it comes to computers, you need to take special precautions to protect your data from prying eyes and mischievous fingers. As always, backups are handy tools to prevent data loss, but there are other more useful tactics that may help reduce the threat of accidental data loss:

- *Employ system passwords to prevent unauthorized access to the system.* This will keep curious children off the system until you're around to supervise. You can use either the BIOS password (invoked through the CMOS Setup) or the Windows logon password. If you are frequently away from your system and it is idle, use a screen-saver password to prevent a child from casually playing on the keyboard when you've got your back turned. Of course, this doesn't prevent access to files and directories once the PC is unlocked.

- *Employ file passwords to prevent access to sensitive files.* Many applications will let you encrypt their data files with a password. For example, most word processors allow you to do this. Of course, be careful not to lose the password, or you will lock yourself out of your own files.

- *Set file attributes to limit the access to important files or directories.* You can set the hidden and/or read-only file attributes of sensitive files or directories to make them harder to find or delete. This is a simple preventative tactic that will work in many cases to protect against accidental damage, though it certainly isn't a high-security option.

- *Try aftermarket program shells or navigators.* Most operating systems have special programs available that are specifically designed to provide a customized environment for kids to use on the PC. When loaded, the program sits on top of the operating system as a special user environment that allows the user to access only programs and data that have been set up and authorized for use. This can in many ways be the best solution (especially for young kids) since these shells not only protect the system, but also often provide a much more kid-friendly way for young users to access their educational programs, games, and so on.

- *Consider a dedicated PC for the kids.* With the price of PCs falling rapidly, it is not very expensive to get a slightly older PC and set it up as a machine for the kids to use. Some people do this when they upgrade—they get a new box and use the older one for the kids.

- *Don't forget to educate your children about important computing issues.* Children readily learn how computers work, so teaching your children about what they can use and what they should (and should not) touch can help avoid problems. Very young children should always be supervised when using the PC.

KEEP THE DISK(S) CLEAN

With today's huge operating systems, multi-megabyte Internet downloads, and powerful creativity programs, it's surprisingly easy to fill even a large hard drive. Cache files, temporary files, and unemptied Recycle Bins can also leave unneeded information on the drive. As a rule, you should periodically run tools to clean and maintain your disks:

- *Uninstall unneeded applications.* Many programs today can be absolutely huge (especially games). If you're finished or bored with applications on the system, uninstall them according to the publisher's recommendations. You can always reinstall them later if you want.

- *Clean up the disk with the Disk Cleanup tool in your System Tools folder.* Disk Cleanup will remove Internet cache data, temporary files, and other clutter that frequently creeps up on your available disk space.

- *Check the disk with ScanDisk.* Here's another tool in your System Tools folder that can be an invaluable aid in verifying the integrity of your files and disk media. ScanDisk can check for cross-linked files and lost allocation units—revealing the presence of potentially damaged files. ScanDisk can also perform a test of the drive platters and can alert you to possible media issues.

- *Defragment the disk with Disk Defragmenter.* This is the third tool in your System Tools folder that you should use after scanning your disks. Disk Defragmenter (or simply "Defrag") will reorganize your files so that the clusters of each file are contiguous. This type of reorganization should help to keep your disk running at peak efficiency, and reduce wear and tear that could compromise its working life.

If you want to delete something but aren't sure if it's really needed by the system, try renaming it first to another name. To the software, it is the same as if you deleted the file, since any software that needs it will be unable to find it with the new name (and will cause an error if this is the case). Since you haven't actually deleted it, you can restore the original name later if necessary. If you rename it and after a few weeks no application seems to need it, you can probably delete it permanently.

CHECK THE POWER QUALITY

Hard drives tend to be quite sensitive to variations in AC power—especially voltage spikes caused by lightning or inductive equipment (for example, motors) sharing the same AC circuit in your home or office. If there is a lot of motorized equipment or high-energy equipment in the same area as the PC, consider having a new AC line installed exclusively for the computer, or consider investing in an *Uninterruptible Power Supply* (UPS) with ample surge and spike protection.

CHECK THE DRIVE ENVIRONMENT

The way hard drives are mounted and used can have a profound impact on their overall reliability. Noise, vibrations, and handling are just a few of the issues to be concerned with:

- **Noise**   Hard drives often make a little bit of whirring noise when spinning up, and subtle clicking as the heads move from track to track—this is perfectly normal. However, drives that make loud clacking or grinding noises may be close to failure. You should back up and replace such suspect drives at your earliest opportunity before they fail. If such a noisy drive cannot be accessed, it may have already failed.

- **Smoke**   Cigar and cigarette smoke can be detrimental to a hard drive. Although the air drawn into a hard drive is passed through an extremely fine filter, any smoke particles that do manage to penetrate the drive housing are much larger than the spacing between a R/W head and platter. A single smoke particle caught between the head and platter can be dragged along the disk, eventually resulting in media damage.

- **Mounting screws**   In spite of their rigid enclosure, hard drives can be warped just slightly when tightly secured by four mounting screws. In some cases, this effect is just enough to throw out a drive's alignment and cause data problems. If you encounter drive problems after moving or remounting the drive, try loosening one or more of the screws (you need not remove them). Just taking the pressure off will usually eliminate the problem.

- **Drive handling**   If you must remove the drive for any reason (for example, during an upgrade), be very careful to handle the drive gently, and rest it on a soft, antistatic foam surface. You should avoid any impacts or hard surfaces. When re-installing the drive, be certain to use only the correct screws. Screws that are too long will warp the drive. Worse, excessive force can crack the cast enclosure, allowing dust and smoke to enter the drive freely, precipitating a rapid drive failure. Also be sure to use an antistatic wrist strap whenever working inside a PC or handling a drive outside of the system.

■ **Vibration**   Hard drives are very sensitive to vibration. Shocks and impacts can cause R/W heads to mark platter surfaces. If the drive is not secured properly, a pattern of regular vibrations may set up in the mechanical assemblies. While such subtle vibrations will rarely damage the drive outright, they can certainly shorten the drive's working life. Be sure to mount the drive evenly with four screws—do not leave screws out.

DRIVE FORMATTING

Since the drive works in terms of microscopic dimensions, the effects of gravity and thermal expansion play a role in the accuracy of head positioning. Make sure that the drive is at a running temperature (perhaps 15 minutes or more) before partitioning and formatting it. Also see that the drive is oriented correctly (horizontally or vertically) prior to partitioning and formatting. If you've moved a drive from one place to another, be sure to let the drive adjust to its new environment (that is, temperature and humidity) for at least 24 hours before using it.

AVOID HEAD PARKING

In the early days of hard drives, designers realized that head impact could damage the media. Drive designers allowed for a landing zone—an unused track where heads could be positioned before power-down. With a landing zone, it did not matter if heads contacted the platter since there was no data there to lose. A utility could "park" the heads over the landing zone. However, virtually all drives are now designed to autopark. Before the drive spins down, heads are automatically positioned over the landing zone based on CMOS Setup data. Parking programs are no longer needed and can even position the heads incorrectly before power-down (a common problem with older IDE drives that operate in translation mode). Also, most drives are dynamically loaded, so R/W heads are removed from the platters once power is removed. Avoid using parking utilities unless the utility is intended specifically for your particular drive model.

BACK UP, BACK UP, BACK UP

Regular, complete system backups are generally regarded as the best, most reliable protection against drive failures. No matter what happens to the drive, you can't really lose anything as long as you have a copy of it. In addition to applications and data files, however, you should also make it a point to back up the partition table, autoconfigure record, file allocation table, and root directory. Utilities such as DrivePro from MicroHouse can create backup copies of these critical areas. If you have a proper low-level formatter utility for your particular drive, you might try backing up the drive completely, performing a fresh low-level format to rewrite track and sector IDs, then repartitioning, reformatting, and restoring data to the drive.

CHECK FOR VIRUSES

You should aggressively protect against possible infection of a drive by using a *current* antivirus program. Run the virus checker regularly, and be sure to check new software, file attachments, and file downloads before executing them. Update the virus checker's signature files regularly to ensure that you have the latest protection.

Recovering Files and Folders

Sooner or later, you're going to delete a file (or folder) that you actually needed. While this is frustrating, it's almost always possible to recover your deleted file(s). In most cases, you can recover files and folders simply by using the Windows 95/98 Recycle Bin:

1. On the desktop, double-click the Recycle Bin icon.
2. The Recycle Bin dialog will open (Figure 14-1).
3. Scroll through the list of files in the Recycle Bin.
4. Highlight the file(s) or shortcut(s) to retrieve, click File, and then click Restore.
5. If you wish to restore several files at once, hold down the CTRL key and click each desired file; then click File and Restore.

This should return the file to its original location on the drive. If you restore a file that was originally located in a deleted folder, the folder is re-created, and that file is restored in the folder. If you're working under DOS 6.2x, you can use the UNDELETE command (derived from the old Central Point PC Tools package) to recover your deleted file(s):

1. From a command prompt, switch to the directory that contained your deleted file(s).
2. Type **undelete** to start the Undelete utility. Table 14-1 lists the command-line switches for Undelete.
3. DOS will list the deleted file(s) that it finds and prompt you for which ones you want to recover.
4. When you see the file(s) you want, simply answer yes.

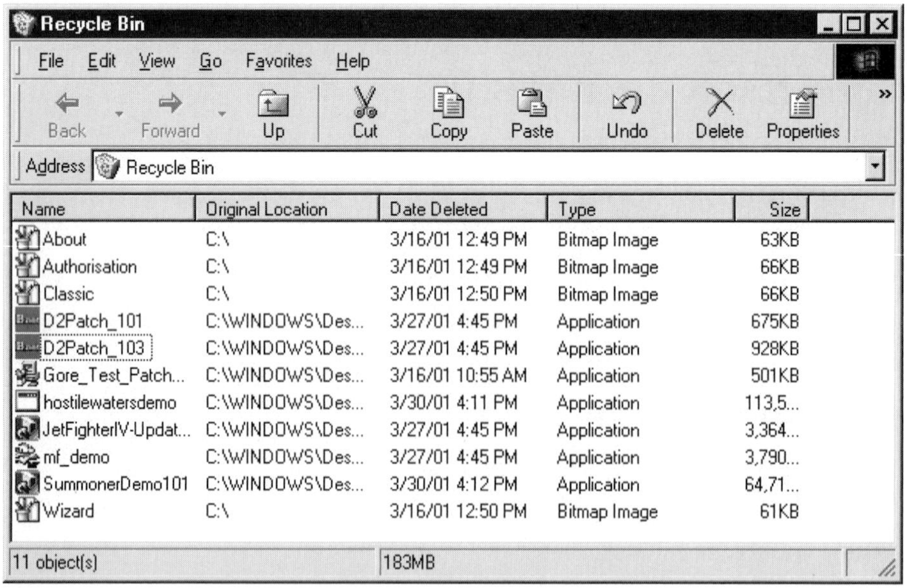

FIGURE 14-1   Using the Windows 98/SE Recycle Bin

TABLE 14-1	COMMAND-LINE SWITCHES FOR DOS 6.2X UNDELETE
SWITCH	**MEANING**
/ALL	Causes Undelete to recover everything possible using the best possible recovery method.
/DS	Uses Undelete Sentry mode for recovery.
/DT	Uses Undelete Tracking mode for recovery.
/LIST	Lists the deleted files in the current directory, but does not recover them.
/LOAD	Loads Undelete into memory (making Undelete a TSR).
/PURGE[drive]	Cleans the contents of your Undelete Sentry directory. You can no longer recover those files, but you'll protect yourself from anyone who might try to recover your private erased file(s).
/S[drive]	Enables Undelete Sentry mode to protect the drive indicated. For example, **undelete /SC** enables the Undelete Sentry for drive C:.
/STATUS	Shows the current status of Undelete.
/T[drive][-entries]	Enables Undelete Tracking mode to protect the drive indicated, and defines the number of files that will be tracked (1 to 999 files). For example, to track 50 file deletions on drive C: you'd use **undelete /TC-50**.
/U	Unloads Undelete from memory (if it's been placed in memory).

You must remember here that Windows 98/Me uses the Recycle Bin as its Undelete function, and there is no real-mode Undelete feature under Windows 98/Me. This means if you empty the Recycle Bin or delete files under DOS, you *cannot* restore those files without a third-party data recovery tool such as Ontrack's EasyRecovery. If you have access to an older DOS 6.2x system with Undelete on it (and your current system is using FAT16), you may be able to use Undelete copied onto your boot floppy disk.

The most important issue in file recovery is to restore your file(s) *as soon as possible* after deletion. Remember that "deleted" files are not wiped out—their clusters are simply marked as "free." If you go on and save new files, you may overwrite some or all of the clusters containing your deleted file(s), and this may render them unrecoverable.

Recovering FAT and Directory Damage

Many drives eventually develop file structure problems because of viruses, age, and even normal every-day operation. DOS and Windows 98/Me provide tools that allow you to check the disk's condition and (to some extent) define and repair problems with the directory structure and *File Allocation Table* (FAT). The CHKDSK utility is a basic DOS disk "fix" utility that you can use, and ScanDisk is a somewhat more powerful tool that you should be familiar with.

UNDERSTANDING CHKDSK

Although it's rather crude compared with ScanDisk or third-party software tools, CHKDSK allows you to perform several important disk operations. First, CHKDSK processes the disk to provide a detailed disk space and available memory report. The disk report is what most users think of when they consider CHKDSK, but its real function is to inspect directories and FATs to see if any discrepancies are found. Keep in mind that CHKDSK does not actually check *individual* files. CHKDSK can also check files for contiguity. Contiguous files occupy adjacent clusters on a disk. This makes the files much faster to load and save. When files become noncontiguous (fragmented), not only does disk access take longer, but also portions of the fragmented file may become lost or disassociated. CHKDSK can identify and recover such lost clusters (also known as *allocation units*).

Running CHKDSK

The generic DOS command line for CHKDSK is **CHKDSK *drive:\path filename* /F /V**. The *drive* parameter specifies which logical drive is to be analyzed. By default, the current drive will be examined, but if you boot from the A: drive, you should specify C:\ as the drive and path. If you wish to check specific files for fragmentation (in addition to the full drive analysis), you should include the appropriate entries for the *path* and *filename* parameters. The /F switch allows CHKDSK to fix any problems that it finds with directories or FATs. Keep in mind that if the /F switch is removed, CHKDSK is *prohibited* from writing to the disk. This allows you to run CHKDSK at your discretion without the danger of accidental file corruption. You are advised to always run CHKDSK in this read-only mode until you understand the nature and extent of any problems. The /V switch forces CHKDSK to display the results of its testing "verbatim," which will list all files in a disk's directories and (in some cases) provide details of any errors encountered.

The CHKDSK utility should also be available in the real mode under Windows 98/Me. For Windows 98, click Start, highlight Programs, and then click MS-DOS Prompt. For Windows Me, Click Start, highlight Programs, point to Accessories, and then click MS-DOS Prompt. Type the CHKDSK command line (such as **chkdsk**), and then press ENTER.

When you're finished with CHKDSK in the real mode, type **exit** at the command prompt, and then press ENTER to return to Windows.

Interpreting a CHKDSK Report

By itself, the report (such as the one shown in Figure 14-2) is pretty straightforward. The first five lines indicate the overall drive size, how much of that space is consumed by files, and how much space is left. If there were bad sectors on the disk, a sixth report line would be added to show the number of bytes in bad sectors. Keep in mind that a bad sector report poses no danger and does not reflect a faulty drive. Virtually all drives have some bad sectors, which are marked in the FAT so that DOS will never attempt to use those bad areas. Most IDE-type drives are able to map out such elements entirely so that DOS does not even have to deal with such problems. You may not see a bad sector report, but even the best drives have bad sectors.

The next three lines indicate the size of each cluster (or allocation unit), the total number of clusters, and the remaining clusters. For this particular drive, you see that each cluster is 2KB. You also see that there are 63307 available allocation units on the disk. (63307×2048 = 129652736 bytes, or 130MB, which is the total disk space shown in line 1.) The last two lines indicate the total amount of DOS memory available and the amount of free DOS memory.

If you were to add a path and filename to the CHKDSK command line, one or more lines would be added to the report indicating the files' contiguity. If the file was contiguous, you would see "All specified file(s) are contiguous." If there are one or more noncontiguous file blocks, you would see a report similar to "*filename* contains *xxx* non-contiguous blocks" where the *filename* is the name of the file being tested, and *xxx* corresponds to the number of noncontiguous blocks found. If disk errors are detected, one or more error messages will be produced.

```
129652736  bytes total disk space
   282624  bytes in 3 hidden files
   409600  bytes in 156 directories
126298112  bytes in 3930 user files
  2662400  bytes available on disk

     2048  bytes in each allocation unit
    63307  total allocation units on disk
     1300  available allocation units on disk

   655360  total bytes memory
   517088  bytes free
```

FIGURE 14-2   A typical diagnostic report generated by CHKDSK

USING CHKDSK

Simply stated, CHKDSK is a directory checker and patcher. CHKDSK compares the drive's directory tree with the FAT to ensure that they match. When a discrepancy is detected between the FAT and directory structure, a corresponding error message is generated. As a result of this operation, most problems that CHKDSK reports are software related rather than a drive hardware fault. Four types of errors are reported most commonly: lost allocation units, allocation errors, cross-linked files, and invalid allocation units. Of these four categories, CHKDSK will only help you resolve lost allocation units and cross-linked files.

Recovering Lost Allocation Units

Lost allocation units are usually generated when a program stops running unexpectedly without saving or deleting temporary files. Over time, lost allocation units can accumulate and take up valuable file space. When lost allocation units are detected, CHKDSK will alert you with an error message such as:

```
10 lost allocation units found in 3 chains.
Convert lost chains to files?
```

If you answer yes, lost allocation units will be converted to files with filenames such as FILE0000.CHK. You can then delete these files to free the recovered space for reuse. It's a great idea to use CHKDSK to recover lost allocation units before running a defragmenter or compression utility such as DoubleSpace.

> It's important for you to realize that this is the only type of problem that CHKDSK can actually fix effectively. Any other errors reported by CHKDSK cannot be fixed with CHKDSK. This is why it is so important that CHKDSK be run without the /F switch until you are aware of any particular problems. Allowing CHKDSK to fix a disk indiscriminately can do more harm than good.

Freeing Cross-Linked Files

Cross-linked files are generated when two or more files or directories are listed in the FAT as using the same disk space. (One or more allocation units are overlapping.) When cross-linked files are detected, you will see an error message similar to:

```
JOHNSON.TXT is cross linked on allocation unit 11234
```

CHKDSK cannot fix a cross-linked file. It has no way to separate the overlap in allocation units. You should erase the original file(s), run Disk Defragmenter, and then copy the file(s) specified in the error message back onto the drive (so they will use different allocation units). Keep in mind that some information in the cross-linked files may be corrupt, and you may have to restore any such damaged files from a backup.

Limitations of CHKDSK

There are a number of instances where CHKDSK may not operate properly (if at all). CHKDSK will not process drives—or portions of drives—that have been created using SUBST, ASSIGN, or JOIN commands. CHKDSK also does not work on network drives. SUBST creates a "virtual" volume, which is little more than a subdirectory under the original volume that uses a different logical drive name. To use CHKDSK in a subdirectory created using SUBST, you must use the TRUENAME function to specify the actual path to the desired files. Note that TRUENAME is only available in DOS 4.0 and later. Suppose you used the SUBST function to create a virtual volume such as:

```
C:\> subst e: c:\tests\diagnostics
```

When you switch to the E: drive, you are actually switching to the C:\TESTS\DIAGNOSTICS subdirectory. If you do not know what the actual subdirectory is, use the TRUENAME function:

```
E:\> truename e:
```

The system would respond with:

```
C:\TESTS\DIAGNOSTICS
```

You can then use the CHKDSK function on the true directory listing:

```
E:\> chkdsk c:\tests\diagnostics\*.*
```

To use CHKDSK on an ASSIGNed drive, you must first "unassign" the drive. For example, if you assign a drive, such as ASSIGN A=B, you will have to unassign the drive, such as ASSIGN A=A. You can then run CHKDSK. After CHKDSK is complete, you can reassign the drive. There is no known way to use CHKDSK on a JOINed drive, which is basically a directory tree created by the JOIN command. JOIN adds one disk volume to another disk volume as a subdirectory. Only the portion that is JOINed is skipped—all other portions of the drive are checked. To run CHKDSK on a network drive, you must reach the desired PC with the drive to be tested, and suspend or disable any sharing of the drive while CHKDSK is executed.

In actual practice, it is unlikely that you will deal with such limitations on modern computers, but this may be handy reference information when faced with the repair or resurrection of an older PC.

UNDERSTANDING SCANDISK

More recent versions of DOS and Windows 98/Me have basically paired the older CHKDSK utility with ScanDisk. In most respects, ScanDisk performs all of the same functions found in CHKDSK, such as checking the directory structure, locating and recovering lost allocation units, and identifying cross-linked files. However, ScanDisk not only provides additional checking and media surface scan features that can help to identify a wider array of potential problems, but also can mark out sectors on the drive that may be failing. Today, you can use ScanDisk for all the features found in older versions of CHKDSK.

Running ScanDisk

ScanDisk is primarily a protected-mode (Windows 98/Me) tool that you launch by clicking Start, high-lighting Programs, selecting Accessories, highlighting System Tools, and then clicking ScanDisk. The main ScanDisk dialog will appear, as in Figure 14-3. From this dialog, you can select the partition to be tested and invoke a thorough surface scan of the media. If you wish ScanDisk to fix any errors that it finds, simply select the "Automatically fix errors" check box. Clicking the Advanced button opens the ScanDisk Advanced Options dialog (Figure 14-4), where you can tailor the behavior of ScanDisk—especially the way it deals with lost file fragments and cross-linked files.

Do not use an older version of ScanDisk (for example, FAT16) on a newer FAT32 partition. Older versions of ScanDisk can report a great deal of erroneous information, and even result in extensive file corruption if left to "fix errors" automatically.

When you allow ScanDisk to run a complete cycle, it generates a report remarkably similar to CHKDSK (Figure 14-5), including any errors that may have been detected on the disk. If ScanDisk does detect lost file fragments or cross-linked files on the disk, you may need to erase the files involved, defragment the disk, and then recopy the offending file(s) to their proper directory from your most current backup.

Performing a surface scan of the drive may take a considerable amount of time, especially for large drives partitioned and formatted under FAT32.

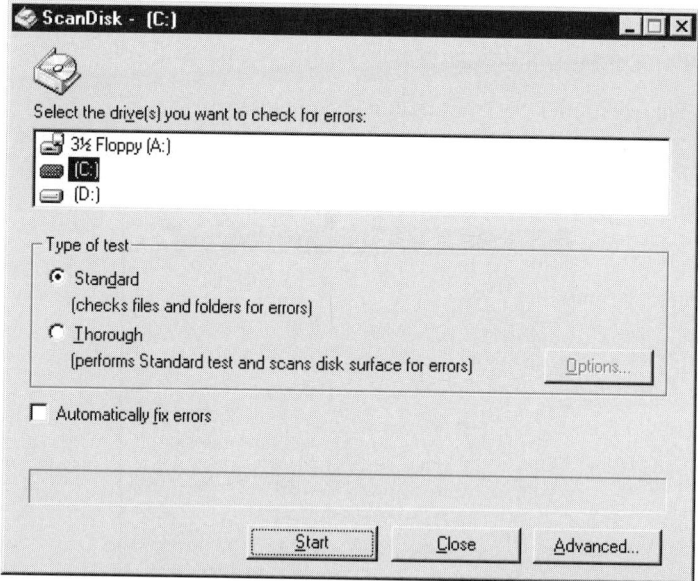

FIGURE 14-3   The main ScanDisk dialog

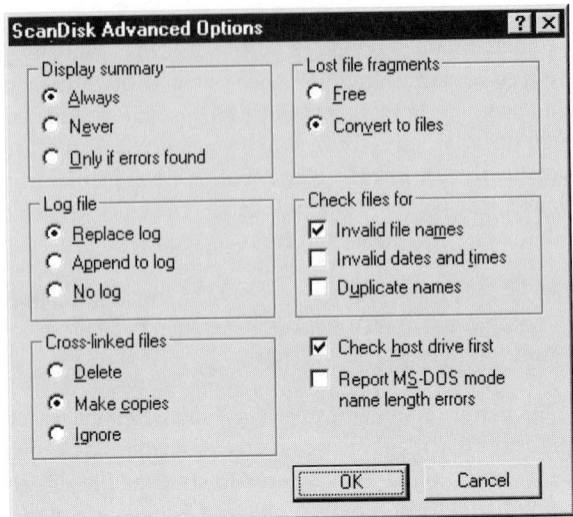

FIGURE 14-4   Configuring advanced settings under ScanDisk

Using ScanDisk at Startup

Although Windows should run ScanDisk at start time in the event of an incorrect shutdown, you may wish to place ScanDisk in a system's Startup folder so that it will run each time the system starts. This can be helpful when diagnosing persistent disk problems. To add ScanDisk to your Startup folder:

1. On the task bar, right-click the Start button and click Open.

2. Highlight the Programs folder, and then click the Startup folder.

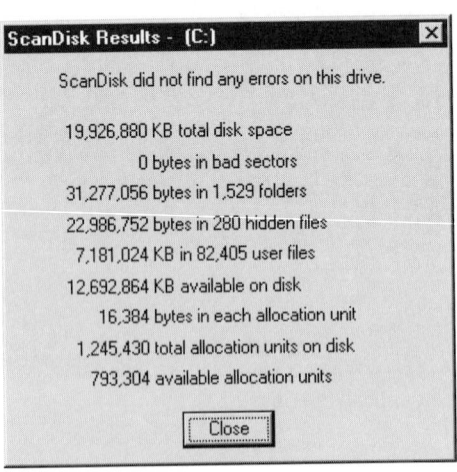

FIGURE 14-5   A typical report generated by ScanDisk

3. On the File menu, highlight New, and then click Shortcut.

4. In the "Command line" entry, type

    `scandskw.exe`

5. Click Next.

6. In the "Select a name for the shortcut" line, type

    `ScanDisk`

7. Click Finish.

You can also configure ScanDisk with certain features each time the system starts:

1. In your Startup folder, right-click ScanDisk.

2. Click Properties.

3. On the Shortcut tab, type one or more of the switches in Table 14-2 after the text that appears in Target.

For example, to check drive D and start and quit ScanDisk automatically, type in the Target entry:

`c:\windows\scandskw.exe d: /n`

To check all hard disks but prevent ScanDisk from correcting any errors it finds, type in the Target entry:

`c:\windows\scandskw.exe /a /p`

Recovering the MBR

The partition table (the *master boot record* or MBR) is the single most important sector on your hard drive. This one sector (512 bytes) contains specifications for up to four logical partitions, but it also provides instructions for starting the operating system. Without a viable MBR, the system will not even recognize the presence of the drive—let alone boot from it. Unfortunately, when the MBR is lost, it is extremely difficult to reconstruct (without losing access to all the data on the hard drive). There are several tools available for rebuilding these critical files. You can use third-party tools (such as Norton Utilities) under Windows 98/Me, you can use MIRROR and UNFORMAT under DOS 6.2x (and FAT16), or you can also use FDISK as a last-resort means of rebuilding a damaged MBR.

TABLE 14-2 COMMAND-LINE SWITCHES FOR SCANDISK	
TYPE...	**TO...**
x: (substitute drive letter for *x*)	Specify the drive you want to check
/a	Check all your local hard disks
/n	Start and quit ScanDisk automatically
/p	Prevent ScanDisk from correcting any errors it finds

USING MIRROR AND UNFORMAT

Prevention is always faster and easier than a cure—the same is true of data recovery. If you are using DOS 5.0 or later, you have access to two DOS utilities that will allow you to back up and restore the master boot record: MIRROR.EXE and UNFORMAT.COM. Before the hard drive fails, type

```
MIRROR /PARTN
```

MIRROR will start and prompt you for a drive. Place a bootable floppy disk in drive A: (or B:), and let MIRROR copy the partition table to the floppy drive. If you do this regularly (say, twice a year), you will have a good emergency backup in the event of drive trouble. When trouble occurs, simply boot from the floppy disk (which should contain a copy of UNFORMAT and the partition backup file), and then type

```
UNFORMAT /PARTN
```

UNFORMAT will ask for the location of the backup file (usually named PARTNSAV.FIL). Reference drive A: or B: (whichever drive contains the file) and continue. If the partition information looks appropriate, you can confirm the restoration, then reboot the system from the hard drive. Assuming a faulty MBR was the only problem, the hard drive should now work properly.

USING FDISK /MBR

Earlier, you read that FDISK should not be used for data recovery since it made changes that would render your data inaccessible—that is not entirely true. There is an undocumented feature of FDISK that restores the startup code at the beginning of the MBR without touching the partition table itself. When the MBR cannot be rebuilt or restored by any other means, it may be possible to use FDISK /MBR and attempt to rebuild part of the MBR. When FDISK is run in this way, it is virtually automatic. You will not even see the FDISK menu—it will simply restore the startup code and return to the DOS prompt. Given the touchy nature of FDISK, you should attempt this undocumented function only as a last resort. FDISK /MBR should not render your data inaccessible, but it might, so be sure to back up as much of your drive as possible before proceeding.

 When using FDISK, be sure to use the version that corresponds to your operating system. For example, if you're using Windows 98, be sure to use the version of FDISK that's placed on a Windows 98 Startup Disk.

USING RESCUE PROFESSIONAL

So what happens when you need the data on a hard drive, but the partition data is lost and unrecoverable, or you see an error such as "Track 0 bad, disk unusable"? Rescue Professional by AllMicro is a self-booting data-recovery tool that is designed to interact directly with drive hardware and recover individual files or entire subdirectories. Unlike other procedures covered in this chapter that attempt to restore some sort of functionality to the drive, Rescue Professional makes no attempt to correct lost partition tables or DOS boot records. Its sole job is to operate the hard drive (if physically possible) and recover as many files as it can locate.

RECOVERING AN ACCIDENTAL REFORMAT

A high-level format process is invoked with the FORMAT command, and this rewrites the boot sector, FAT, and root directory of your disk. Formatting also checks each cluster to map out any damaged or unreadable ones in the FAT. Normally, formatting is destructive to your data. The data itself is not over-written, but formatting renders it inaccessible. This means that if you accidentally format the wrong partition on your drive, the data on it can be lost. Windows 98/Me offers no native tools for recovering from an accidental format, but there are third-party tools that will save a copy of that critical data and use it to reconstruct the partition lost during an accidental format. If you're working under DOS 6.2x, you can use the Unformat command (also a relative of the old Unformat tool with Central Point's PC Tools package) to recover your disk. For example:

```
unformat c:
```

The important thing to remember here is that you must Unformat *immediately* after formatting. Once the format process is finished, the FAT is cleared, so writing new files to the disk may upset the Unformat process and prevent some (or all) of your files from being recovered.

USING EASYRECOVERY

When a hard drive physically fails, you'll need to send the disk to a professional data recovery house, and let them try to resurrect the unit just long enough to wring your data from it. If the drive hardware is still working, however, you can often use software tools such as Ontrack's EasyRecovery utility to search out and rescue inaccessible data. EasyRecovery is a do-it-yourself data recovery tool that is capable of capturing lost or inaccessible data from your drive and reconstructing the file system (including partitions larger than 8.4GB). EasyRecovery does not attempt to repair corruption on the drive itself and never writes to the suspect drive. Instead, it rebuilds the file table in memory to allow safe transfer of data to another device (such as another hard drive). This part of the chapter offers some practical data recovery tips by examining some of the features and attributes of EasyRecovery.

Obtaining EasyRecovery

EasyRecovery is not located on the companion CD. A free demo version of the software (which will identify all recoverable files and recover up to five files) can be downloaded from Ontrack at **www.ontrack.com/ freesoftware/**. If you find the software useful, you can purchase it online directly from Ontrack.

About EasyRecovery

The interesting thing about EasyRecovery is that it's a nondestructive and read-only tool that does not place any data onto the suspect (crashed) drive. Instead, data that's read from the drive is placed in memory and written to another drive (for example, another hard drive, floppy disk, or network). EasyRecovery can recover data from drives without readable boot sectors, readable FATs, or readable directories. It can also handle drives that are no longer recognized by the operating system. This type of operation makes EasyRecovery particularly handy for disks that have been damaged by a computer virus, formatted, partitioned, crashed with a power failure, or damaged by rogue software (bugs).

EasyRecovery automatically creates a "virtual drive" in memory and offers access to the files through an ordinary-looking file manager applet. You can see the lost directories and files from your crashed drive. Files and directories can be viewed and copied to a safe medium (another drive), where the software's pattern recognition technology allows the various pieces of a recovered file to be assembled properly.

Like virtually all software data recovery tools, EasyRecovery is not intended to operate a defective drive unit. If you experience drive damage (for example, you hear strange grinding noises), turn off the PC immediately. You may require the services of a data recovery house.

EasyRecovery works from a DOS command line to recover files from DOS, Windows 98/Me, Windows NT, or Novell. It is not recommended that EasyRecovery be used in a DOS window from within Windows 98/Me. There are several different versions of EasyRecovery that can be downloaded based on your particular system requirements. The Personal Edition recovers files from DOS; Windows 3.x, 95, 98, and Me; IDE/ATA/EIDE hard drives; SCSI hard drives; system disks; floppy disks; and Zip and Jaz removable media. The Professional Edition recovers files from DOS; Windows 3.x, 95, 98, Me, 2000, and NT; IDE/ATA/EIDE hard drives; SCSI hard drives; floppy disks; and Zip and Jaz removable media, and provides advanced data recovery options such as:

■ Configure system inputs with advanced tuning options to achieve better and faster data recovery results.

■ View the contents of any file in both ASCII and hex format to find the data you need.

■ Specify criteria to select recovered files and/or folders for backup using advanced tagging options to pinpoint specific data.

■ Generate reports to document files selected for backup for your records.

Using EasyRecovery

In most cases, data recovery consists of booting the system with EasyRecovery on a bootable floppy disk, selecting the drive to be recovered, then allowing EasyRecovery to process the selected drive (Figure 14-6). When EasyRecovery finishes its analysis, you'll see a listing of the virtual drive, and you can select and copy desired files/folders to the recovery drive. Of course, there are numerous features and options that can be selected within the EasyRecovery program, but you'll need to refer to the documentation files for complete explanations. You may start, stop, and resume the recovery (or copying) processes at any point. EasyRecovery allows you to find missing or corrupt volumes on your system using partition finder options to improve the speed and success of your recovery. You can also monitor the status of your recovery using the recovery progress option to check the remaining time, or the number and names of files recovered.

Depending on your system's speed, the size of your drive, and the number of files on the drive, EasyRecovery can take from 15 minutes to several hours to complete its task. EasyRecovery may require up to 24 hours to analyze the partition of an NTFS or Novell drive.

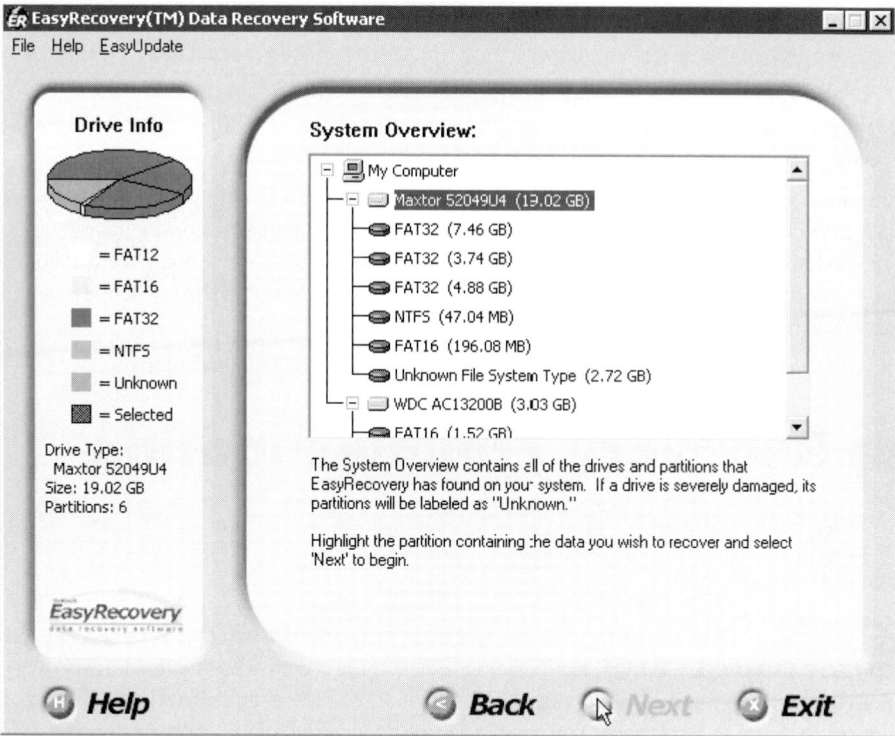

FIGURE 14-6   Analyzing the system with EasyRecovery

Data Recovery Tips

In most cases, data recovery is a fairly automatic process. You recover the file(s) or you don't. However, there are numerous tips that may help you get the most from your data recovery process:

■ The most important data recovery tip is to always keep a current backup of your work in progress. Even if you have to reinstall an operating system and applications from scratch, you can easily restore the backup of your work and keep going. If you have no backup, and you're unable to recover the data, you may need to start from scratch.

■ Always make sure that the suspect drive is specified correctly in the CMOS Setup. Changing a drive's geometry can render the drive inaccessible (until the original drive geometry settings are restored).

■ Don't mix and match data recovery tools. For example, don't use CHKDSK before running EasyRecovery. More advanced tools may misinterpret the disk recovery efforts of more basic tools like CHKDSK.

■ Select a recovery drive in advance (such as another hard drive, network drive, Jaz drive, or Zip drive). This is where the recovery program will place your recovered data, so make sure that there is ample space on the recovery drive, or see that you have ample Zip/Jaz media available.

■ Select as much RAM as possible for your swap area (where recovered data is held before writing to the recovery drive). If you can create swap space on a drive, make sure that there is ample space available on that drive, and never swap to the suspect drive.

■ Data recovery routines can take quite some time to run, so be sure to allow plenty of time to run your data recovery software.

■ Before using any data recovery software, verify that it's compatible with your partition type (FAT16, FAT32, or NTFS) and partition size (25GB versus 8GB). If the software cannot handle your partition type or size, running the software will probably destroy any chance of ever recovering your lost data. In fact, the software may make things worse. Make sure that you obtain the latest updates and patches for your data recovery software before running it.

■ Use a UPS to prevent the system from crashing during data analysis and recovery.

Data Recovery Troubleshooting

Whether you use EasyRecovery or some other data recovery tool, you may encounter errors and problems during the process of your recovery. This part of the chapter examines a few typical troubles that often plague data recovery efforts.

SYMPTOM 14-1 **The system stops responding, and the data recovery software seems to have crashed** If there is no error message, it may simply be that the data recovery process is still running. It can take many hours to fully analyze a disk. Be patient and allow up to 24 hours for a data recovery cycle to run. Data recovery software often performs analysis in conventional memory, then swaps the results out to extended memory (or a disk file). If there is severe data corruption, or a large number of small files, there may not be enough conventional or extended memory (or disk space) available. There are a few tricks that might help (depending on your software's particular options):

■ Try recovering only a part of the drive at a time. This can be accomplished by selecting a range of sectors on the drive to be analyzed.

■ Try lowering the threshold where a file is considered "bad" (a "Bad File Acceptance Setting").

■ Try swapping the analysis out to a disk file (on a known-good drive) rather than extended memory.

If the problem persists, you may need to try another data recovery tool, or send the drive out for professional data recovery techniques.

SYMPTOM 14-2 **The data recovery software reports the wrong drive size** Check the drive size as reported by the data recovery software, and verify that it accurately reflects the size of the drive you're trying to recover. If the software takes an incorrect drive size from your system BIOS, you will not get reliable data recovery results. Check the following issues:

■ Check the CMOS Setup and verify that the drive geometry is accurate for your drive. If not, enter the correct values. If you've entered exact values, try to let the BIOS autodetect the drive. Check with the drive's manufacturer to see if there's an acceptable "translation geometry" that you can use instead.

■ If the drive has "disk overlay" software installed (for example, Disk Manager or MaxBlast), the CMOS Setup may not contain the appropriate drive values. You may need to use a boot disk that enables the DDO first before booting and launching the data recovery software.

■ Check the LBA mode; drives bigger than 528MB should have it enabled in the CMOS Setup.

■ Check the drive's reported values. Some huge drives report their geometry as 16,383×16×63 regardless of their actual size. This may mean you'll need a BIOS upgrade or new drive controller to adequately support the suspect drive.

SYMPTOM 14-3   **Your data recovery software returns invalid results because it could not recognize the correct drive structure**   If your data recovery software supports automatic drive structure recognition, you should try turning that feature off, then running the recover operation again. Without automatic identification, the software should present its interpretation of the drive structure for your approval (for example, cluster size [number of sectors in a cluster], data start cluster, and data end cluster). Since the size of your partition (in KB) is roughly defined by:

```
([data end cluster-data start cluster] * [cluster size * 512]) / 2
```

if the result is equal to the partition size that you're trying to recover, you can try proceeding with the recovery. If you're not satisfied with the results, you can search again and look for the correct structure. If you simply cannot find an appropriate structure, make sure that you're using the data recovery software that's right for your file system. (For example, using software for FAT32 may show structure errors if you're using a FAT16 drive.)

SYMPTOM 14-4   **The data recovery software does not recover all missing files or directories**   This may often occur if the software's recognition routine is too loose. Try tightening the recognition routine—the recovery process may take longer, but it may catch more directories and files.

SYMPTOM 14-5   **The hard drive is making loud scraping noises, or there is clanking during disk access**   All disks make a little bit of noise as the platters spin and the disk is accessed—this is perfectly normal. But when a drive makes loud or "damaged-sounding" noises, it probably is damaged. If the drive is accessible, back up as much data as possible, and replace the drive before it fails. If the drive has already failed, do not attempt to use data recovery software. Instead, send the drive out for professional data recovery, or replace the drive outright and restore your most recent backup.

Further Study

CBL Data Recovery   www.cbltech.com
Data Recovery Group   www.datarecoverygroup.com
Data Recovery Labs   www.actionfront.com/
Data Recovery Software   www.istonline.com/recovery.htm
Easy Recovery   www.ontrack.com/easyrecovery/
Norton Utilities   www.symantec.com/sabu/n2000r/index.html
Ontrack   www.ontrack.com
Ontrack Data Advisor   www.ontrack.com/op/op_1.asp
Reynolds Utilities   www.data-recovery.com/reynolds/
Symantec (Norton Ghost 2001)   www.symantec.com
TechParts   www.recoverdata.com

15

DRIVE ADAPTERS AND RAID BASICS

Drives are generally considered to be peripheral devices This means they must be interfaced to the host system so that the drive and system may communicate with one another. Integrated Drive Electronics (IDE) has proven to be an extremely versatile and cost-effective interface scheme that can support hard drives, CD-ROM drives, DVD-ROM drives, and almost any other drive device. IDE has also proven its longevity by enduring numerous upgrades and improvements through the years. The latest iteration of IDE (referred to as Ultra-DMA/100) offers burst data transfer rates of up to 100MB/s, and this puts IDE data transfers on par with many general-purpose SCSI implementations. In addition, Redundant Array of Independent Disks (RAID) technology is growing in popularity as users seek more powerful and inexpensive ways to protect their valuable data. This chapter outlines the important issues of IDE and RAID, discusses controller installation issues, and offers a suite of controller troubleshooting procedures.

Understanding the IDE Family

From a historical perspective, the Integrated Drive Electronics interface developed in 1988 in response to an industry push to create a standard software interface for SCSI peripherals. That industry consortium, known as the Common Access Method Committee (or CAMC), attempted to originate an AT Attachment (ATA) interface that could be incorporated into low-cost AT-compatible motherboards. CAMC completed its specification, which was later approved by ANSI. The term *ATA interface* generally refers to the controller interface, while IDE refers to the drive. Today, IDE simply refers to an interface type and can be applied to either the drive or controller. For example, an IDE drive requires an IDE controller.

> Even though there are numerous iterations of the IDE family today (such as EIDE, UDMA/33, UDMA/66, and UDMA/100), the family is still commonly referred to as "IDE-type."

IDE/ATA

IDE and ATA are basically one and the same thing—a scheme designed to integrate controlling electronics onto the drive itself instead of relying on a stand-alone controller board, as older MFM and RLL drives did. This approach reduces interface costs and makes drive firmware implementations easier. IDE proved to be a low-cost, easily configured system—so much so that it created a boom in the disk drive industry. Although the terms IDE and ATA are sometimes used interchangeably, ATA is the formal standard that defines the drive and how it operates, while IDE is really the "trade name" that refers to the 40-pin interface and drive controller architecture designed to implement the ATA standard.

Classic IDE Features and Architecture

IDE drives are typically intelligent—that is, almost all the functions relegated to a separate controller board in older drives are now integrated onto the drive itself. Data is transferred through a single cable attached to a relatively straightforward *adapter board* (a simple controller board that is often little more than a buffer) attached to the system's ISA or PCI expansion bus. Exterior circuitry is so limited that virtually all motherboard chipsets provide a dual-channel IDE controller, eliminating the need for an expansion card controller. Today, classical IDE drives are fairly slow, offering data transfer rates rarely exceeding 10Mbits/s. "Classic" IDE is also limited to supporting drives up to 528MB (EIDE and later iterations of the IDE interface break the traditional 528MB barrier and can support drives larger than 60GB at this time). While IDE lacks the flexibility and expandability of SCSI, IDE is relatively inexpensive to implement. Thus, it is often the choice for simple, inexpensive, low-to-mid-range PCs that are not expected to expand much. More recently, the use of an IDE interface has extended beyond only hard drives to include such devices as CD-ROMs, DVD-ROMs, Zip drives, and tape drives through the use of the AT Attachment Packet Interface (or ATAPI) interface protocol (more on ATAPI a little later in the chapter).

A great deal of discussion has concentrated on IDE intelligence. The *intelligence* of an IDE system is determined by the capabilities of the onboard controller. For the purposes of this book, intelligent IDE drives are capable of the following functions. First, intelligent IDE drives support *drive translation*—the feature that allows CMOS drive parameters to be entered in any combination of cylinders, heads, and sectors that add up to equal or less than the true number of sectors on the drive. This is particularly handy when the actual number of cylinders exceeds 1024 (as all modern IDE-type drives do). Nonintelligent IDE drives were limited to physical mode, where CMOS parameters were entered to match physical parameters. Intelligent drives also support a number of enhanced commands that are an optional part of the original ATA specification.

Another advancement of intelligent IDE technology is *zoned recording,* which allows a variable number of sectors per track. This allows an overall increase in the number of sectors on each platter and adds to the drive's overall capacity. However, BIOS can only deal with a fixed number of sectors per track, so the zoned IDE drive must always run in translation mode. When running IDE drives in translation mode, you cannot alter interleave or sector skew factors, and you cannot change factory defect information.

A typical IDE-type controller layout is shown in Figure 15-1. The physical interface for a standard IDE device consists of a 40-pin data/control cable (old IBM implementations used either a 44-pin or 72-pin cable). This *signal cable* is responsible for carrying data and control signals between the drive and controller board. IDE-type drives also use terminating resistors to ensure reliable signal characteristics, but terminating resistors are usually fixed and cannot be removed. In most cases, two IDE-type drives can work together with terminating resistors in place. While there will be several jumpers on the drive, a set of *drive select* jumpers allow, the drive to be set as the primary (master) or secondary (slave) drive.

The signal cable for an IDE-type drive is typically a 40-pin insulation displacement connector (IDC) cable, as shown in Table 15-1. Unlike the obsolete ST506/412 or ESDI interfaces, the IDE family uses both the even- and odd-numbered wires as signal-carrying lines. Also note that most of the signal labels have dashes beside their names, indicating that the particular signal is *active low*—that is, the signal is *true* in the logic 0 state instead of being true in the logic 1 state. All signal lines on the IDE interface are fully TTL compatible where a logic 0 is 0.0 to +0.8 Vdc, and a logic 1 is +2.0 to Vcc.

Data points and registers in the IDE-type drive are addressed using the Drive Address Bus lines DA0 to DA2 (pins 35, 33, and 36, respectively) in conjunction with the -Chip Select Drive inputs -CS1FX and -CS3FX (pins 37 and 38). When a true signal is sent along the *-Drive I/O Read* (-DIOR, pin 25) line, the drive executes a read cycle, while a true on the -Drive I/O Write (-DIOW, pin 23) line initiates a write cycle. The IDE interface provides TTL-level input and output signals. Where older interfaces were serial, the IDE interface provides 16 bidirectional data lines (DD0 to DD15, pins 3 to 18) to carry data bits into or out of the drive. Once a data transfer is completed, a -DMA Acknowledge (-DMACK, pin 29) signal is provided to the drive from the hard disk controller IC. Finally, a true signal on the drive's Reset line (pin 1) will restore the drive to its original condition at power-on. A Reset is sent when the computer is first powered on or rebooted.

An IDE-type physical interface also provides a number of outputs back to the motherboard. A Direct Memory Access Request (DMARQ, pin 21) is used to initiate the transfer of data to or from the drive. The direction of data transfer is dependent on the condition of the -DIOR and -DIOW inputs. A -DMACK

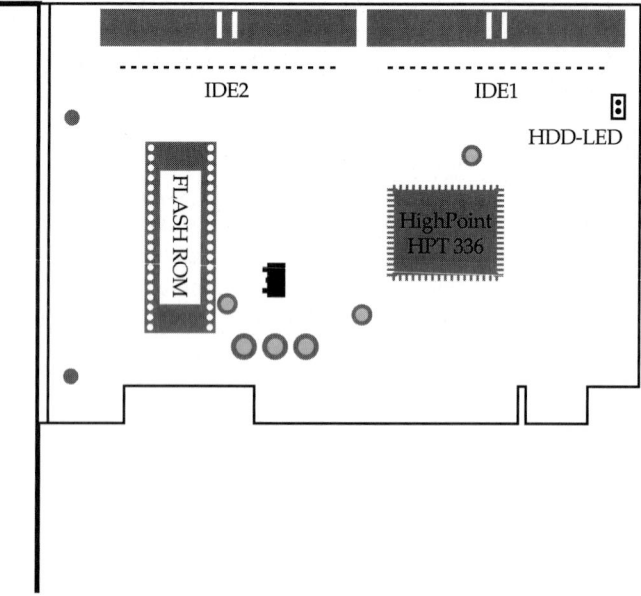

FIGURE 15-1   A typical dual-port Ultra-DMA controller card

TABLE 15-1   PIN ASSIGNMENTS FOR A TYPICAL IDE-TYPE SIGNAL CABLE

PIN	NAME	PIN	NAME
1	Reset	2	Ground
3	DD7	4	DD8
5	DD6	6	DD9
7	DD5	8	DD10
9	DD4	10	DD11
11	DD3	12	DD12
13	DD2	14	DD13
15	DD1	16	DD14
17	DD0	18	DD15
19	Ground	20	Key (slot only)
21	DMARQ	22	Ground
23	-I/O Write Data (-DIOW)	24	Ground
25	-I/O Read Data (-DIOR)	26	Ground
27	-I/O Channel Ready (-IORDY)	28	unused
29	-DMA Acknowledge (-DMACK)	30	Ground
31	Interrupt Request (INTRQ)	32	-Host 16-bit I/O (-IOCS16)
33	DA1	34	-Passed Diagnostics (-PDIAG)
35	DA0	36	DA2
37	-Host Chip Select 0 (-CS1FX)	38	-Host Chip Select 1 (-CS3FX)
39	-Drive Active (-DASP)	40	Ground

signal is generated in response when the DMARQ line is asserted (made true). -IORDY (pin 27) is an -I/O Channel Ready signal that keeps a system's attention if the drive is not quite ready to respond to a data transfer request. A drive Interrupt Request (INTRQ, pin 31) is asserted by a drive when a drive interrupt is pending (the drive is about to transfer information to or from the motherboard). The -Drive Active line (DASP, pin 39) becomes logic 0 when any hard drive activity is occurring. A -Passed Diagnostic (PDIAG, pin 34) line provides the results of any diagnostic command or reset action. When PDIAG is logic 0, the system knows that the drive is ready to use. Finally, the 16 bit -I/O Control line (IOCS16, pin 32) tells the motherboard that the drive is ready to send or receive data. Notice that there are several return (ground) lines (pins 2, 19, 22, 24, 26, 30, and 40), and a key pin (20) that is removed from the male connector.

Cabling the IDE-type Interface

The ATA IDE interface is intended to support up to two drives on the same cable (or channel) in a daisy-chain fashion. A typical IDE controller cable is illustrated in Figure 15-2. Although tradition dictates that drive 0 be attached to the end connector (as the primary, or master, drive) and a second drive be attached to the middle connector (as a secondary, or slave, drive), it is important to note that IDE supports either drive in either location. For the purposes of IDE, you need only set the proper drive jumpers to select a drive as a master or slave. The 40-pin ribbon cable (IBM uses 44-pin or 72-pin cables) should not exceed 61 cm (24 inches) in length. Since IDE-type drives rely on distributed termination as a means of signal conditioning, it is not necessary to install or remove terminating resistors.

However, you may encounter problems when running two IDE drives together. Older IDE drives did not fully adhere to the CAMC ATA IDE specification. When trying to run older drives together (especially drives from different manufacturers), they may not respond to their master/slave relationship properly, and

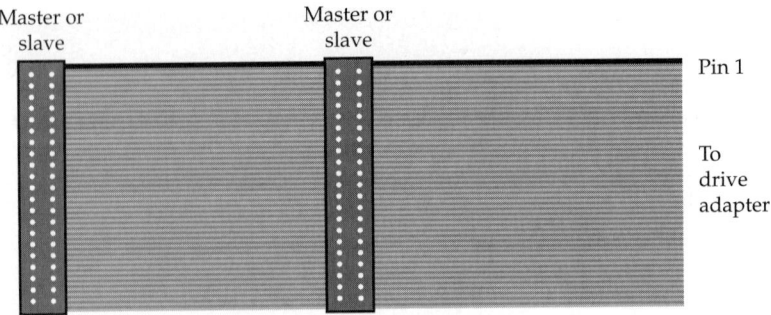

FIGURE 15-2   General signal cabling for an IDE-type drive

conflicts will result—in many cases, such problems will disable both drives. When planning a dual-IDE installation, try to use newer drives that are both from the same manufacturer. If you cannot match drives, try reversing the master/slave relationship between the drives.

BIOS Support of the IDE Family

Unlike SCSI controllers, which use an expansion ROM to provide supplemental BIOS, the firmware needed to provide IDE support is written into the motherboard's BIOS. Although systems manufactured since about 1990 are fully compatible with ATA IDE drives, adding an IDE drive to an older PC often resulted in problems. After the broad introduction of IDE, it was discovered that IDE drive operations placed different timing demands on the PC, which frequently caused disk errors such as data corruption and failure to boot. BIOS makers quickly found a solution to this timing problem, and it was incorporated into BIOS that appeared after early 1990. If you encounter a PC with pre-1990 BIOS, you should consider upgrading it before adding an IDE drive, or if the current IDE drive is exhibiting problems. Today, you may also need to upgrade a motherboard's BIOS if the drive controller cannot support the full size of a given drive (32GB, 40GB, 60GB, and so on).

ATAPI

One of the major disadvantages of ATA is that it was designed for hard drives only. With the broad introduction of CD-ROM drives in the late 1980s, designers needed a means of attaching CD-ROMs (and other devices such as tape drives) to the existing ATA (IDE) interface—rather than employing a stand-alone (proprietary) controller card. The ATA Packet Interface is an extension of the ATA (IDE) interface that's designed to allow devices other than hard drives to plug into an ordinary ATA (IDE) port. Whereas hard drives enjoy ATA (IDE) support through BIOS, ATAPI devices require a device driver to support them. Booting from an ATAPI CD-ROM is only possible with an El Torito CD-ROM and more recent motherboard BIOS versions.

ATA-2, FAST-ATA, AND EIDE

By the early 1990s, it became clear that the classic ATA architecture would soon be overwhelmed by advances in hard drive technology. The hard drive industry responded by developing the ATA-2 standard as an extension of ATA. ATA-2 is largely regarded as a significant improvement to ATA. It defines faster PIO (Programmed I/O) and DMA (Direct Memory Access) data transfer modes, adds more powerful drive commands (such as the "Identify Drive" command to support autoidentification by the BIOS), adds support for a second drive channel, handles block data transfers (Block Transfer Mode), and defines a new means of addressing sectors on the hard drive using Logical Block Addressing (LBA). LBA has proven to be a very effective vehicle for overcoming the traditional 528MB hard drive size limit. Yet ATA-2 continues to use the same 40-pin physical interface used by ATA, and the interface scheme is backward compatible with ATA (IDE) drives.

Along with ATA-2, you'll probably find two additional terms: EIDE (Enhanced IDE) and Fast-ATA. These are not standards—merely different implementations of the ATA-2 standard. EIDE represents the more popular Western Digital implementation of ATA-2 that builds upon both the ATA-2 and ATAPI standards. This has been so effective that EIDE has become the generic term. Seagate and Quantum have thrown their support behind the Fast-ATA implementation of the ATA-2 standard. However, Fast-ATA builds on ATA-2 only. For all practical purposes, there is no significant difference between ATA-2, EIDE, and Fast-ATA, and you'll probably see these three terms used interchangeably (though this is not technically correct).

Understanding the 528MB IDE Limit

The 528MB IDE limit, probably the most important and compelling limitation to IDE architecture, is the result of a simple lack of planning between the developers of BIOS and the developers of the WD1003 drive controller architecture. To understand the limitations of drive size, you must understand how IDE drives are addressed. The classic addressing scheme is known as Cylinder Head Sector (CHS) addressing. Simply stated, you place the cylinder number, head number, and sector number you need to get to into the WD1003 controller registers and then call the Int 13 routine in BIOS, which runs the drive to the desired location for reading or writing.

This works just fine in theory, but a problem exists in practice because the limiting values for cylinders, heads, and sectors are not the same in both the BIOS and the WD1003 architecture. Table 15-2 illustrates these values, and you can see their impact on drive size. BIOS specifies a maximum of 1024 cylinders, 255 heads, and 63 sectors per track. If you multiply these together, and then multiply 512 bytes/sector, you get 8,422,686,720 bytes (or 8.4GB) of theoretical capacity. For the WD1003 controller, you should be able to have 65,536 cylinders, 16 heads, and 255 sectors per track. When this is multiplied by 512 bytes per sector, you get a whopping 1.36899_{10}^{11} bytes (or 136.9GB) of theoretical capacity.

The problem is that you can only use the lowest common number for each approach. Therefore, the maximum number of cylinders you can use is 1024, the maximum number of heads is 16, and the maximum number of sectors of 63. When you multiply these out, and then multiply times 512 bytes/sector, you only get 528MB. The real tragedy here is that if BIOS designers and WD1003 designers has sat down and come up with the same numbers, we could easily have had IDE drives with capacities up to 136.9GB, and this entire issue would be moot. But instead, a traditional IDE hard drive can only address up to 528MB.

This explains why IDE worked so well with drives up to 528MB—but not more. Of course, there are ways to work around this limitation. Since BIOS is essentially software, the easiest and most economical

TABLE 15-2   CHS VALUES VS. DRIVE SIZE

	BIOS	WD1003	RESULTING LIMIT
Cylinders	1024	65536	1024
Heads	255	16	16
Sectors	63	255	63
Max. Capacity	8.4GB	136.9GB	528MB

way to overcome the 528MB barrier is to "augment" the BIOS Int 13 routine by introducing a driver when the PC is initialized. Int 13 enhancements allow the support of drive sizes up to 40GB and more. For example, Maxtor's MaxBlast and Ontrack's Disk Manager are two popular drive-overlay utilities. They allow the PC to access the entire space of a large IDE drive—not just 528MB.

EIDE and UDMA modes can work with such overlay software, and Disk Manager (or one of its similar cousins) is frequently bundled with today's huge hard drives. However, there are some compelling reasons why overlay drivers are not desirable. First, drivers take memory space—typically precious space within the first 640KB of RAM. Few systems have space remaining in the upper memory area for an overlay driver. Second, older overlay drivers don't always accommodate Windows 98/Me very well at all, so using large hard drives with overlay software under Windows can sometimes be a problem. Third, the overlay driver may conflict with other device drivers and TSRs that may be on your PC.

Ultimately, the preferred method of large drive support for EIDE and UDMA modes is to update the BIOS itself with a version that contains the necessary Int 13 enhancements. AMI and Micro Firmware were early entrants into the EIDE-compatible BIOS arena, but EIDE support quickly became standard in all BIOS and drive controller versions. Today, UDMA/66 and UDMA/100 support is common, but this is fully backward compatible with EIDE and IDE. Although upgrading a BIOS is a bit more involved than adding a driver, the rewards (more free memory and better OS compatibility) are almost always worth it. As an effective alternative to the trials of a motherboard BIOS upgrade, you can choose to upgrade your current drive controller with a new drive adapter containing onboard BIOS extensions for Int 13.

Understanding LBA

Another source of great confusion in the use of EIDE and UDMA modes is the need for Logical Block Addressing. Where traditional CHS addressing requires the specification of a discrete cylinder, head, and sector, an LBA address simply requires the specification of a sector (for example, "go to sector 324534"). The LBA algorithm (implemented in BIOS) will translate the sector to the appropriate CHS equivalent. FAT-based operating systems such as DOS and Windows *require* the use of LBA addressing. As a consequence, you'll need to update your motherboard BIOS or use an EIDE/UDMA controller with onboard BIOS. On the other hand, non-FAT operating systems (such as OS/2 and Novell Netware) do *not* require LBA addressing. When you actually have an EIDE controller in hand, you may note that the controller provides a jumper that allows you to enable or disable LBA addressing. If you are using DOS (or Windows), keep this jumper *enabled*.

Current UDMA-compliant controllers will forego a physical jumper for an entry in the CMOS Setup. Locate the "LBA" entry and verify that it's enabled.

An important consideration in choosing CHS or LBA addressing is the format of your hard drive(s). If you choose to invoke LBA addressing, you'll need to repartition and reformat your hard drive(s). You must also remember that once a hard drive is formatted for LBA, the drive will be recognized *only* by PCs that support LBA. As a result, if you take an LBA-formatted drive (UDMA) and install it into a PC whose BIOS does not support LBA (such as an older IDE-supported system), the drive will simply not be recognized, and you will have to repartition and reformat the drive again. In all cases, remember to perform a *complete* backup of your hard drive(s) before implementing UDMA on your system.

Drive Support

One of the main advantages of SCSI has traditionally been its ability to support up to seven varied devices on the same bus (hard drives, CD-ROMs, tape drives, and so on). This approach went a long way toward eliminating the proliferation of proprietary controllers and system configuration problems that remain prevalent in non-SCSI systems. Although a classic IDE controller allows two drives (master and slave) to reside on the same controller port (1F0h) and interrupt (IRQ 14), it does not support any other devices. EIDE and UDMA modes seek to overcome this limitation by adding a second channel to the EIDE/ UDMA controller.

Be careful when evaluating a controller with two channels. While the primary channel will normally support the fastest devices, the secondary channel may not. For example, it was common for EIDE controllers to fully support EIDE on the primary channel, but only support ATAPI IDE on the secondary channel. Today, it's not uncommon for a UDMA/100 controller to support up to two UDMA/100 devices on the primary channel, but only support UDMA/66 (or slower) devices on the secondary channel. Check the specifications for each channel before you start attaching devices.

In theory, an older IDE drive will work on an EIDE or UDMA channel, but you may run into trouble when mixing faster and slower devices on the same controller channel. A classic example of this is on systems that use a new fast UDMA hard drive, and then add on an IDE ATAPI CD-ROM as the slave device. In many cases, the slower CD-ROM may interfere with the UDMA drive, thereby reducing the drive's maximum data transfer rates and slowing drive performance. In more pronounced cases, the CD-ROM may not even be recognized. In extreme cases, the hard drive (and perhaps the CD-ROM also) may not be recognized, and the system won't even boot. Reconfiguring the hardware to make the slower CD-ROM a master device on the other (secondary) controller channel will almost always correct this type of problem.

Today's UDMA/100 and UDMA/66 drive controllers are somewhat more "intelligent" and are better able to adjust the data transfer speeds to accommodate devices of differing speeds on the same channel. Still, speed compatibility issues can come into play. For example, you may find that using a UDMA/100 hard drive and a non-UDMA/100 device together on the same channel may cause the maximum data transfer to fall to UDMA/66 or UDMA/33 levels.

As a rule, keep the faster devices on the primary controller channel and use the slower devices on the secondary controller channel.

ATA-3

A more recent implementation of the ATA standard is ATA-3. It does not define any new data transfer modes, but it does improve the reliability of PIO mode 4. It also offers a simple password-based security scheme, more sophisticated power management features, and Self-Monitoring Analysis and Reporting Technology (SMART). ATA-3 is also backward compatible with ATA-2, ATAPI, and ATA devices. Since no new data transfer modes are defined by ATA-3, you may also see the generic term "EIDE" used interchangeably (though this also is not technically correct).

ULTRA-ATA/33

The push for ever-faster data transfer rates is a never-ending one, and the Ultra-ATA standard represents an implementation of ATA/ATAPI-4 providing high-performance bus mastering at burst data rates up to 33MB/s using DMA data transfers. The implementation of Ultra-ATA is usually called Ultra-DMA/33 (or UDMA/33). You'll need an Ultra-ATA drive, controller, and BIOS to support an Ultra-ATA drive system, but it is fully backward compatible with previous ATA standards. You can use ordinary 40-pin IDE-type cables for UDMA/33 unless any of the following issues occur:

- The standard cable is low quality, damaged, or weakened by many installs/removals.
- The system suffers from excessive signal noise—these systems may have multiple drives, dual power supplies, or an integrated CRT.

■   The system is overclocked (or otherwise configured beyond the manufacturer's supported specifications).

ULTRA-ATA/66

The Ultra-ATA standard for ATA/ATAPI-4 was upgraded to support an even faster high-performance bus mastering with burst data rates up to 66MB/s using DMA data transfers. This more recent implementation of Ultra-ATA is usually called Ultra-DMA/66 (or UDMA/66). You'll need an Ultra-ATA/66 drive, controller, cable, and BIOS to support an Ultra-ATA/66 drive system, but it is fully backward compatible with previous ATA standards. Unlike the Ultra-ATA/33 approach, you cannot use ordinary 40-pin IDE-type cables to connect drives and controllers. Instead, you'll need a specially designed 40-pin/80-conductor cable (typically provided with UDMA/66 drives). Also keep in mind that the operating system (such as Windows 98/Me) must be enabled for DMA transfers.

Common UDMA/66 Issues

The move to Ultra-DMA/66 and Ultra-DMA/100 should be fairly trouble-free, but some common troubles plague new installations or upgrades. Take a moment to familiarize yourself with the following issues:

■   Make sure that the signal cable is Ultra-ATA/66 or Ultra-ATA/100 capable. An Ultra-ATA/ 66/100-compliant cable is a 40-pin/80-conductor cable with a black connector on one end, a blue connector on the other end, and a gray connector in the middle. In addition, pin 34 on the cable should be notched or cut (though this may be difficult to see at first glance).

■   Make sure the system board (motherboard) controller is capable of supporting Ultra-ATA/66 or Ultra-ATA/100. An Ultra-ATA/66/100-capable controller has a detect circuit that can detect whether line 34 is missing on the cable. If there is no detect circuit, the system can wrongly detect the presence of an Ultra-ATA/66/100 cable and try to configure the device for a higher transfer rate.

■   Some system board (motherboard) controllers may not successfully handle Ultra-ATA/66 or Ultra-ATA/100 on both the primary and secondary channels. If you have difficulty with a UDMA/66/100 device on the secondary controller channel, consider troubleshooting with the device in the primary master position.

■   If you have trouble getting a UDMA/66 or UDMA/100 system configured properly, contact the system board or controller card manufacturer for the latest BIOS upgrade (and any Ultra-ATA/66/100 device drivers or patches).

■   Make sure the operating system is DMA capable, and verify that the DMA mode is activated. For Windows 98/Me, check the drive's Properties dialog box in the Device Manager (Figure 15-3).

■   Make sure the Ultra-ATA/66- or Ultra-ATA/100-capable drive has been configured to run at Ultra-ATA/66 or Ultra-ATA/100 transfer rates, respectively. Some drives ship with the UDMA/66 or UDMA/100 mode disabled by default, and require a jumper change and/or software utility in order to activate the UDMA/66/100 mode.

ULTRA-ATA/100

With the growing dependence on huge files and data-intensive multimedia streams (such as video and audio), hard drive data transfer rates are still under pressure to increase. By late 2000, the PC industry embraced the move to Ultra-ATA/100 drives (also called Ultra-DMA/100 or UDMA/100) that are capable of 100MB/s data burst rates. Based on the original protocols introduced with earlier Ultra-ATA interfaces, UDMA/100 also incorporates the same 40-pin/80-conductor cables and connectors that were used with

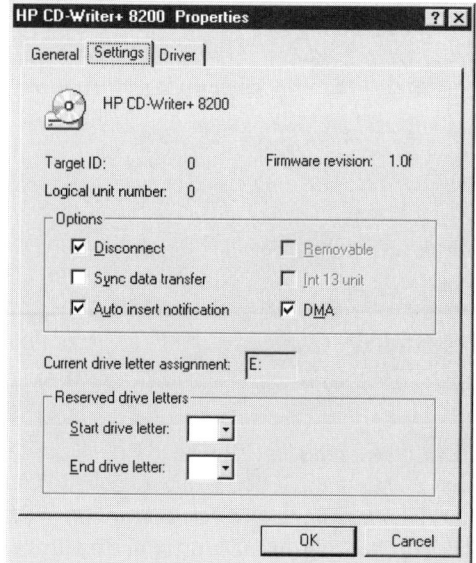

FIGURE 15-3   Checking the DMA mode in a drive's Properties dialog box

Ultra-ATA/66. Yet UDMA/100 remains fully backward compatible with existing EIDE/UDMA hard drives, removable media drives, and CD-ROM/R/RW drives.

DATA TRANSFER RATES

Data transfer rates play a major role in drive performance. In practice, there are two measures of data transfer: the rate at which data is taken from the platters, and the rate at which data is passed between the drive and controller. The internal data transfer between the platters and drive buffer is typically the slower rate, often considered to be the "sustained" data transfer rate. Older drives could run around 5MB/sec, but newer Ultra-ATA drives, such as the Maxtor DiamondMax 2160, run at 14MB/s. The external data transfer between the drive and controller (the *interface rate*) is normally the faster rate, but often can be sustained only for short durations (or bursts). Older drives provided between 5 and 8MB/sec, but ATA-2 (EIDE) drives can operate up to 16MB/sec in PIO mode 4. Ultra-DMA/66 drives can burst data at 66MB/s, and Ultra-DMA/100 drives can handle burst data transfers of 100MB/s. The modern standards of IDE external data transfer are listed in Table 15-3 as PIO and DMA modes.

TABLE 15-3   A COMPARISON OF DATA TRANSFER SPEEDS

PIO MODE	CYCLE TIME (NS)	TRANSFER RATE (MB/S)	NOTES
0	600	3.3	The old ATA (IDE) modes
1	383	5.2	
2	240	8.3	
3	180 IORDY	11.1	Newer ATA-2 (EIDE) modes
4	120 IORDY	16.6	

TABLE 15-3   A COMPARISON OF DATA TRANSFER SPEEDS *(CONTINUED)*

DMA MODE	CYCLE TIME (NS)	TRANSFER RATE (MB/S)	NOTES
Single Word 0	960	2.1	Also in ATA
Single Word 1	480	4.2	
Single Word 2	240	8.3	
Multiword 0	480	4.2	Also in ATA
Multiword 1	150	13.3	
Multiword 2	120	16.6	
Multiword 3	---	33.0	Ultra-DMA/33
Multiword 4	---	66.0	Ultra-DMA/66
Multiword 5	---	100.0	Ultra-DMA/100

You may notice that the EIDE-specific modes (PIO-3 and PIO-4) use the IORDY hardware flow control line. This means that the drive can use the IORDY line to slow down the interface when necessary. Interfaces without proper IORDY support may cause data corruption in the fast PIO modes (so you'd be stuck with the slower modes). When choosing an EIDE drive and controller, always be sure to check that the IORDY line is being used.

By comparison, DMA data transfers mean that the data is transferred *directly* between the drive and memory without using the CPU as an intermediary (as is the case with PIO). In true multitasking operating systems like OS/2, Windows NT, or Linux, DMA transfers leave the CPU free to do something useful during disk transfers. In a DOS or Windows environment, the CPU will have to wait for the transfer to finish anyway, so in these cases, DMA transfers don't offer that much of a multitasking advantage. There are two distinct types of DMA: ordinary DMA and bus-mastering DMA. Ordinary DMA uses the DMA controller on the system's motherboard to perform the complex task of arbitration, grabbing the system bus, and transferring the data. With bus-mastering DMA, all of this is done by logic in the drive controller itself.

Unfortunately, the DMA controller on traditional ISA bus systems is slow—out of the question for use with a modern hard disk. Only EISA- and PCI-based interfaces make non-bus mastering DMA viable: EISA type "B" DMA will transfer 4MB/s, and PCI type "F" DMA will transfer between 6 and 8MB/s. Today, the proper software support for DMA is relatively rare (as well as the interfaces supporting it). Still, the DMA data transfer modes are listed in Table 15-3.

Controller Installation

In many cases, you'll find that the motherboard will provide a primary and secondary drive controller channel that will suit a wide variety of drives in the market at the time the system was manufactured. Over time, new drive types, larger drive capacities, and enhanced data transfer modes may require you to upgrade the motherboard's controller feature. It may also be necessary to install a new controller in the event that an existing controller fails. This part of the chapter highlights the major points involved in controller preparation and installation.

PREPARING FOR A NEW CONTROLLER

Although a new drive controller should work with your existing drives, there may be some circumstances where a new controller may cause problems. This happens most frequently when the old controller is not removed or disabled properly, or the new controller uses an addressing scheme that is not compliant with the drive's current setup. Before you unwrap that new controller, take some time to prepare your system:

- *Back up the drive(s).* Before performing any type of drive-related work, protect your valuable data by creating a complete backup of the drive(s) on your system to tape, CD-R, Iomega Jaz, or other suitable media. Boot to the CMOS Setup and record the geometry settings for each drive (you may need to reenter them later).

- *Ready your software.* You should have your Windows 98/Me CD handy in the event you need to reinstall the operating system or load new drivers when the controller is installed. If there are drivers with the new controller, you should also have that disc on hand (or download the newest driver versions from the controller's manufacturer).

- *Review your current controller.* Eventually, you'll need to remove or disable the current controller, so take a moment to review the documentation for your system and understand the required methods for disabling the current controller. If the controller is currently integrated into your motherboard, it can typically be disabled through the CMOS Setup. (Older motherboards may use a jumper instead.) Controllers that are implemented on stand-alone expansion cards can usually just be removed.

- *Preconfigure your new controller.* Study the documentation that comes with your new controller card. If the controller offers a number of controller features (a floppy controller, game port, COM ports, or other features), you should make it a point to disable any features that are not going to be used. Remember that each feature will demand system resources, so don't allow those extra features to remain enabled and conflict with similar features still operating on the motherboard.

- *Check the BIOS version.* It's not uncommon for firmware updates to change frequently. Check with the new controller's manufacturer to see if there's a new firmware version that should be updated after you've installed the new controller.

INSTALLING THE NEW CONTROLLER

There's certainly no magic to successfully installing a new controller card, but there are a few minor wrinkles that you should be aware of:

1. Turn off and unplug the system, and then unbolt the outer housing and remove it. Set the housing and screws aside in a safe place.

2. Locate the old drive controller and gently disconnect the 40-pin cables from the controller end, but leave them connected to the drive(s). You may choose to label the signal cable(s) so that you can easily locate the primary and secondary channels.

3. Remove the old controller card (if there is one), and insert the new controller card into its expansion slot. Otherwise, unbolt the bracket from another appropriate expansion slot and insert the new controller there (use the bracket to cover up the unused slot). Bolt the new controller card to the chassis. If the original controller is integrated onto the motherboard, there is nothing to remove, but you will need to disable the controller though a motherboard jumper or the system's CMOS Setup once you reboot the system again.

4. If your computer case offers a "hard drive activity" LED, you can generally connect this cable to the small "activity" header on the new controller card. However, this is generally optional, and you may leave the activity LED connected to a drive if you wish.

5.   Locate the new drive controller headers. The primary channel may be labeled "Pri-IDE" or "IDE 0." The secondary channel may be labeled "Sec-IDE" or "IDE 1." Connect the primary and secondary drive cables to their corresponding headers on the controller.

 Remember that UDMA/66 and UDMA/100 drives and controllers must be connected via a 40-pin/80-conductor cable specially intended for UDMA/66/100 use. If you're upgrading drives along with the controller, be sure to use this cable.

CONFIGURING THE NEW CONTROLLER

Once the new controller is secure and connected, it's time to start the computer and make any necessary configuration changes to use the new controller and avoid system conflicts. Leave the computer's housing off for the time being and follow these tips:

■ *Adjust the motherboard's CMOS Setup.* Boot the system directly to the CMOS Setup. If your old controller was integrated into the motherboard, you may need to disable the controller(s). However, since we're not changing drives in this exercise, you should verify the drive geometry settings, or reenter them if necessary. No changes are needed for CD-ROM (or other ATAPI) drives that are attached to the controller. The motherboard will automatically assign the IRQ and I/O resources to the new controller. Save your changes and reboot the system.

■ *Access the new controller's BIOS.* Since virtually all drive controller cards use their own onboard BIOS chip, chances are that you'll see a BIOS banner for the controller's BIOS. If you press the key listed in the controller's BIOS banner while rebooting the system, you can access the controller's BIOS and configure specific attributes of the controller's operation. Refer to the controller's manual for specific options and suggested settings. Most installations work just fine with default settings, and you never need to change the controller's internal configuration.

SOFTWARE INSTALLATION

The new controller's onboard BIOS should fully support normal system operation in the real mode (DOS). However, Windows 98/Me will probably require the installation of numerous drivers to support the controller (especially the UDMA/66 or UDMA/100 DMA drivers). The following steps highlight a general installation scenario:

1.   Try booting the system to DOS, and then check each drive letter. Try taking a directory of each drive. If you can access all of the drives that you could before installing the new controller, you can be confident that the hardware portion of your installation was successful. If you cannot access one or more drives, recheck the motherboard's CMOS Setup and verify that all of the drive-related settings are identical to those used for the old controller. If you cannot emulate the LBA translation characteristics of the original controller, you may need to repartition and reformat the drive(s).

2.   Reboot the system and allow Windows 98/Me to boot normally. Chances are that you'll see "New Hardware Detected" as a "PCI Mass Storage Controller" (the exact hardware found will depend on your version of Windows).

3.   In most cases, the Add New Hardware wizard will appear, informing you that the new device has been found. Click Next.

4.   Select "Search for a better driver than the one your device is using now" then click Next.

5. Click Browse, insert the floppy or CD with the controller's device drivers, and then browse to the folder containing the drivers. Click Next.

6. When the driver location is found, click Next.

7. When the installation is complete, click Finished.

8. It is common for modern controllers to install twice—once for the primary channel and once for the secondary channel. Do *not* reboot the computer after installing the primary channel. Finish the secondary channel (generally, repeat these steps for the second "PCI Mass Storage Device") and then reboot the PC.

9. When the new controller is installed properly, you'll see the entries listed under Hard Disk Controllers or SCSI Controllers in your Device Manager.

UPGRADING THE CONTROLLER'S BIOS

From time to time, you may need to upgrade the drive controller's firmware in order to correct bugs, streamline features, or improve compatibility with various systems and devices. When you see that a suitable BIOS update is available, download the update and then follow these guidelines:

1. Create a bootable floppy disk, and then copy the flash utility (for example, PTIFLASH.EXE) and the new BIOS file (for example, ULBIOS.BIN) to the disk.

2. Reboot the system from the floppy disk (you'll see the A: command prompt).

3. Launch the flash loader program (for example, type **ptiflash** and press ENTER). A main menu should appear.

4. Select the option to save a backup copy of the controller's firmware to the floppy disk.

5. Once the firmware backup is finished, select the option to update the BIOS from a file.

6. A dialog box will appear. Enter the path and name of the new BIOS file (for example, **a:\ulbios.bin**). If you see an error indicating that the file was not found, double-check your path and file name.

7. The utility will update the controller's firmware, and you will see a message when the process is complete.

8. Remove the disk and reboot the system.

9. When the controller's BIOS banner appears, make sure that the BIOS version is in fact the new version.

RAID Primer

Traditionally, the most common means of protecting valuable data has been to perform routine and consistent backups to tape or other media. While this has proven to be a tried-and-true method, it often is not implemented properly. Backups are frequently forgotten or performed inconsistently. Even automated backup schemes require human interaction at some level. All too often, some data is lost during a disk failure. Designers realized that if a controller could write data to *one* drive, then the data could be written to *two* drives just as easily. One or more drives can be made to "mirror" a master drive in real time—if the main drive were to fail, the data would be accessed from a secondary drive. This is the basic premise behind a Redundant Array of Independent Disks (RAID).

The problem with RAID is that it costs money to implement. You'll need a drive controller that supports RAID (such as the Promise FastTrack100 for UDMA/100 drives) and an additional drive for each drive that you need to mirror. The extra drives don't give you more storage space, they simply mimic the original drive(s), and you need additional power and drive space for the RAID drives. End users don't often choose to spend their money on such protection, but it's common on servers and busy workstations. This part of the chapter highlights several basic RAID concepts and explains some setup options that you may encounter.

DISK ARRAY

A *disk array* is formed from a group of two or more disk drives that appear to the system as a single drive. The advantage of an array is to provide better performance and data fault tolerance. Better performance is accomplished by sharing the data transfer workload in parallel among multiple physical drives. Fault tolerance is achieved through data redundant operation, where if one (or more) drives should fail (or suffer a sector failure), a mirrored copy of the data can be found on another drive(s). For optimal results, select identical drives for installation in disk arrays. The drives' matched performance allows the array to function better as a single drive. The individual disk drives in an array are called *members*. Each member of a specific disk array is coded in its reserved sector with configuration information that identifies the drive as a member of the given array.

DISK ARRAY ADAPTER (DAA)

The generic term used for the RAID controller is the *disk array adapter*—the device that supports your mirrored drive(s), which is generally termed the disk array. Most RAID controllers are implemented using the SCSI interface, but Promise Technologies offers the FastTrack100, which support RAID functions for UDMA/100 hard drives. The controller will virtually always incorporate a BIOS that fully supports the drive operations (such as UDMA/100) and provide a setup feature (similar to the CMOS Setup) that will allow you to configure the RAID controller's features.

RESERVED SECTOR

Vital information is saved in a special location on each disk member called the *reserved sector*. This area contains array configuration data about the drive and other members in the disk array. If reserved data on any member of the array becomes corrupt or lost, the redundant configuration data on the other members can be used for rebuilds. As a rule, disk array members do not have specific drive positions. This allows drives to be placed on different RAID controller connectors or cards within the system without reconfiguring or rebuilding the array.

DISK ARRAY TYPES

A typical RAID controller supports four general operating modes: striping, mirroring, striping/mirroring, and spanning. The choice of RAID mode will affect your drive capacity, drive performance, or fault tolerance. To appreciate the versatility of RAID, you should understand a little more about each of these RAID modes.

Remember that all disk members in a formed disk array are recognized as a single physical drive to the host system.

Striping (RAID 0)

In striping mode, sectors of data are interleaved between multiple drives, effectively forming one large drive from two or more smaller ones. Striping is regarded as a performance enhancement rather than fault tolerance.

Performance is better than a single drive because the read/write workload is duplicated between the array members, and this array type is encountered in high-performance systems. Identical drives are recommended for performance (as well as data storage efficiency). The disk array data capacity is equal to the number of drive members times the smallest member capacity. For example, one 1GB and three 1.2GB drives will form a 4GB (4×1GB) disk array. The weakness with RAID 0 is that it provides no redundancy—when any disk member fails, it affects the entire array because some portion of the overall "drive" is lost.

Mirroring (RAID 1)

The mirroring approach writes duplicate data onto a pair of drives, while reads are performed in parallel (improving read performance). IDE-type RAID 1 is fault tolerant because data is duplicated, and each drive of a mirrored pair is installed on separate connectors. The RAID controller (such as FastTrack66 or FastTrack100) performs reads using data handling techniques that distribute the workload in a more efficient manner than using a single drive. When a read request is made, the controller selects the drive positioned closest to the requested data, and then looks to the idle drive to perform the next read access.

If one of the mirrored drives suffers a mechanical failure (such as a spindle failure) or does not respond, the remaining drive will continue to function (this is called fault tolerance). If one drive has a physical sector error, the mirrored drive will also continue to function. On the next reboot, the RAID software utility will display an error in the array and recommend replacing the failed drive. Users may choose to continue using their PC; however, it's often best to replace the failed drive as soon as possible.

Due to redundancy, the drive capacity of the array is half the total drive capacity. For example, two 1GB drives that have a combined capacity of 2GB would have 1GB of usable storage. With drives of different capacities, there may be unused capacity on the larger drive.

Spare Drive   Under a RAID 1 configuration, an extra *hot spare* drive can be attached to the RAID controller, but cannot be assigned to the array. In this case, the spare drive is put on standby. This drive will be activated to replace a failed drive that is part of the mirrored array. In most cases, a rebuild is performed automatically in the background to mirror the good drive onto the spare. At a later time, the system can be powered off, and the failed drive can be physically removed and replaced. Spare drives must be the same or larger capacity than the smallest array member.

Striping/Mirroring (RAID 0+1)

Striping/mirroring is a combination of the striping and mirroring array types. It can increase performance by reading and writing data in parallel while protecting data with duplication. A minimum of four drives needs to be installed. With a four-drive disk array, two pairs of drives are striped, and each pair mirrors the data on the other pair of striped drives. The data capacity is similar to a standard mirroring array with half of the total capacity dedicated for redundancy.

Spanning (JBOD)

A spanning disk array (also aptly named "JBOD" for "just a bunch of drives") is equal to the sum of all drives when the drives used are of different capacities. Spanning stores data onto a drive until it is full, and then proceeds to store files onto the next drive in the array. There are no major performance or fault tolerance array features in this mode. When any disk member fails, the failure affects the entire array.

Spanning may be considered for performance in certain instances. With striping, array performance is affected directly by the stripe block size. Block size should be tailored to the typical I/O on the drive, whether it is generally more random or sequential. However, if there is no predictability of the type of I/O access, and both random and sequential I/O occur unpredictably, the performance of a striped array will fluctuate. In the end, this may result in no overall performance gain. With spanning, the performance factor simply reflects a single drive's performance level. This offers a more predictable transfer rate and allows the use of mismatched drives.

Troubleshooting a Drive Adapter

A properly configured drive adapter will rarely cause problems in a PC because BIOS, IRQ, and I/O assignments are very strongly established in the PC industry. However, a variety of problems can plague drive adapter replacements and upgrades. This part of the chapter looks at troubleshooting for IDE-type drive systems.

SYMPTOM 15-1   **You cannot get the drive adapter software to install properly**
When installing or upgrading drive controller software, it is not uncommon to encounter problems, usually due to the many advanced features of the drive controller itself. If you cannot get new software installed, try the following steps to overcome the problem. First, start the CMOS Setup and disable the high-performance features usually related to drive controllers, such as IDE Block Mode, Multi-Sector Transfer, and 32-bit Disk Access. If there are other options for the secondary drive controller channel, try disabling them as well. You might also try moving the controller BIOS address range (for example, change the address range from C800h to CF00h).

If you still cannot get the controller software installed, there may also be trouble with overlay software (such as Disk Manager or MaxBlast software) used to partition and format a drive. You may need to uninstall the overlay software and update the CMOS Setup by enabling LBA support for the drive. If you can't uninstall the overlay software, you can run FDISK /MBR to overwrite the overlay software. Once the overlay software is removed, repartition and reformat the drive. If you cannot wipe the drive clean, check with the drive manufacturer for such a utility. You should now be able to install the new drive software.

This step is destructive to any data on the drive. Be sure to make a complete system backup (and have a bootable disk on hand) before removing the overlay software.

SYMPTOM 15-2   **The controller will not support a drive with more than 1024 cylinders**
This often happens when building a new system or piecing together a system from used parts. To support a drive with more than 1024 cylinders, the controller must support LBA (discussed earlier in the chapter), and the feature must be enabled. The controller's onboard BIOS should support LBA, but you may need to install a driver for the controller in order to support LBA. (For example, a Promise Technologies controller needs the DOSEIDE.SYS driver to support LBA.) If the controller is integrated onto the motherboard, the motherboard BIOS must support LBA. If it is not integrated, you'll need to upgrade the motherboard BIOS or install a drive adapter with an LBA-aware BIOS. Second, the hard drive itself must support LBA. Make sure the drive is an EIDE or UDMA-type hard drive. Finally, check the CMOS Setup and verify that the drive is using the LBA mode rather than the older CHS mode. You may need to repartition and reformat the hard drive.

SYMPTOM 15-3   **Loading a disk driver causes the system to hang or generate a "Bad or missing COMMAND.COM" error**   This is a known problem with some versions of the DTC DTC22XX.SYS or DOSEIDE.SYS drivers, but frequently occurs with other controllers that use disk drivers. The controller is probably transferring data *too fast* to the drive. When the disk driver loads, it obtains information from the drive, including drive speed. Sometimes the drive reports that it can support PIO mode 4 or PIO mode 3 when in actuality it cannot. In many cases, the original drivers are outdated, and the immediate solution is to slow down the data transfer rate manually. Download and install the newest drivers—until then, you may be able to add a command-line switch to the disk driver. For example, DTC recommends adding a switch to its DOSEIDE.SYS driver as in the following (where x is the drive designation):

```
DOSEIDE.SYS /v /dx:m0 /dx:p0
```

If your problems started after loading the disk drivers "high" (into the upper memory area), adjust CONFIG.SYS to load the drivers into conventional memory. Some drive adapters have reported better success with driver software when the Hidden Refresh feature is enabled in CMOS Setup (in the Advanced CMOS Setup area). This alters the way in which the system timing refreshes RAM and may better support the disk drivers. Also try disabling advanced controller options such as IDE Block Mode, Multi-Sector Transfer, and 32-bit Disk Access. Finally, if you're using overlay software (such as Disk Manager or MaxBlast), the disk driver may not work with the overlay software. You'll then need to remove the overlay software and repartition and reformat the drive before the disk driver will work.

SYMPTOM 15-4   **Drive performance is poor—data transfer rates are slow**   This often happens when installing a replacement drive controller. First, make sure that you're not running any antivirus software. Antivirus utilities that load at boot time can degrade drive performance. If the controller uses a "speed" jumper, make sure you have properly configured the jumper settings on the card to match the speed of the IDE drive and processor (this is a known issue with DTC's 2278VL and 2270 controllers). Also make sure that the highest possible data transfer rate is selected in the CMOS Setup (PIO mode 4 for older setups, or UDMA/33, UDMA/66, or UDMA/100 in newer systems). If the drive adapter uses a disk driver for optimum performance, make sure that the correct disk driver software is loaded, and that any necessary command-line switches are entered. Finally, remove any third-party software (such as Disk Manager or MaxBlast) that may have shipped with the drive itself.

SYMPTOM 15-5   **The PC refuses to boot after a drive adapter is installed**   There are many possible reasons for this kind of problem. First make sure that the drive adapter is installed properly and completely into its bus slot, and then verify that the drive signal cables are oriented and attached properly. If the drive adapter uses jumpers to match the drive and processor speeds (such as the DTC 2278VL or 2270), make sure that the adapter is configured correctly. Verify that the drive itself is properly jumpered as a master or slave. Finally, check the CMOS Setup and confirm that the proper drive parameters are being used. Try disabling advanced features like IDE Block Mode and 32-bit Disk Access. If the problem still persists, try repartitioning and reformatting the drive.

SYMPTOM 15-6   **Windows generates a "Validation Failed 03,3F" error**   This type of problem most frequently occurs after loading the Windows disk driver, and is almost always due to a 1024-cylinder limit in the drive system. Make sure that the drive and drive controller are able to support more than 1024 cylinders (both EIDE or UDMA). Check the CMOS Setup and verify that the LBA mode is selected. Once the proper hardware is configured correctly, try reinstalling the disk driver.

SYMPTOM 15-7   **Windows hangs or fails to load files after loading the controller's driver**   In most cases, Windows hangs, or every file after the offending driver is unable to load. In some cases, you may see an error message such as: "Cannot find KRN.386". Load SYSTEM.INI into a text editor and move the controller's driver (such as WINEIDE.386) to the last line in the [386enh] section. Also make sure that the classic WDCTRL driver is commented out, such as in the following:

```
;device=*WDCTRL
```

If problems persist, the controller's driver may be old or buggy. Download and install the newest disk driver version from the controller maker. If all else fails, disable the block mode and mode speed using the driver's internal switches or setup routine. For example, the WINEIDE.386 driver provides the switch WINEIDESWITCH that you can use, as shown next:

```
device=wineide.386
wineideswitch= /dx:m0 /dx:p0
```

SYMPTOM 15-8   **The controller misidentifies the drive**   For example, the UDMA/100 controller detects the UDMA/100 (DMA mode 4) drive as UDMA/33 (DMA mode 2). Generally speaking, there are only two reasons why the drive controller's BIOS won't detect a UDMA/66- or UDMA/100-capable hard drive properly. First, some drives (such as many WD ATA/100 drives) require you to run a utility to enable UDMA/100 support. These utilities can be obtained directly from the drive manufacturer. Cabling is another issue. Only a certain type of IDE cable can support data transfers of up to 100MB/s. These 80-wire/40-pin cables (a suitable cable is usually included with new drives) have twice as many ground wires as traditional IDE cables. This dramatically decreases the electrical signal noise that a 40-wire/40-pin IDE cable would otherwise produce when attempting UDMA/100 transfers. If the cable is damaged or unsuitable for UDMA/66 or UDMA/100 operation, the controller will automatically "downshift" itself to UDMA/33. Enable the UDMA/66 or UDMA/100 mode, or replace the signal cable.

SYMPTOM 15-9   **You cannot play DVD movies with a UDMA/100 controller installed**   This is a known issue with the Promise Technologies Ultra100 drive controller and is normally related to the SMART driver. DVD playback problems may be related to a bug that was discovered in the v1.42 Ultra100 SMART driver. The latest driver can be downloaded from **ftp://ftp.promise.com/Controllers/ IDE/Ultra100/**. However, SMART's function is to notify you of any hard drive problems that may occur during the drive's life, and thus is not performance-related; a temporary solution is to rename the SMART driver. For example, the Ultra100 SMART driver should be located in the c:\windows\system\iosubsys directory. Rename the PU100VSD.VXD file to **PU100VSD.PTI** and reboot the system.

SYMPTOM 15-10   **Drives over 65GB are not reported correctly in the controller's banner**   For example, the Promise Technologies Ultra100 does not display the correct size of hard drives with more than 65GB in the BIOS banner. In virtually all cases, this is an issue with the controller's BIOS. According to Promise Technologies, this problem is purely cosmetic and does not interfere with the operating system's use of the drive. The operating system will still use the full storage space of the disk. The display problem has been fixed in the Ultra100 v2.00 BIOS (build 12 and above), but the problem still exists in the Ultra66 BIOS.

SYMPTOM 15-11   **After replacing a drive adapter with a different model, the hard drive is no longer recognized**   This can happen frequently with all types of IDE drives and controllers. You will find that the new controller probably is not using the same translation geometry used when the drive was originally partitioned. Verify that the drive geometry and LBA settings are as close as possible to the settings used on the older controller. You may need to use "user-defined" settings rather than "autodetect" to ensure that the geometry settings are identical. In order for the new drive adapter card to recognize an existing drive, you'll have to repartition and reformat the drive with FDISK and FORMAT. Reinstall the original controller and perform a complete system backup before continuing.

SYMPTOM 15-12   **You cannot enable 32-bit Disk Access under Windows**   In most cases, you're using the wrong protected-mode driver, or the driver should be upgraded with a newer version. Download and install the latest disk drivers for your drive adapter. Before installing the new driver(s), be sure to disable advanced data transfer features such as IDE Block Mode and 32-bit Disk Access (if enabled). Load SYSTEM.INI into a text editor. Make sure that the protected-mode disk driver is installed under the [386enh] section, and verify that the WDCTRL driver is remarked out. Note that many Windows drivers will not support an IBMSLC2 processor or Ontrack's Disk Manager, and will *not* work with 32-bit disk access.

SYMPTOM 15-13   **The IDE-type drive adapter's secondary port refuses to work**   If the drive adapter has a secondary drive channel, that secondary channel is not working. In many cases, this type of problem occurs when the drive adapter relies on a disk driver for proper operation. The secondary channel often must be enabled specifically through the disk driver's command line in CONFIG.SYS, such as:

```
DEVICE=DOSEIDE.SYS /V /2
```

Make sure that the drive attached to the secondary channel is jumpered as the master drive, and verify that the signal cable between the drive and controller is oriented properly. Also remember that a secondary drive channel requires a unique interrupt (usually IRQ 15). Make sure there is no hardware conflict between the secondary port's IRQ and other devices in the system. Try disabling advanced data transfer features in the CMOS Setup like IDE Block Mode and 32-bit Disk Access. If your hard drive is an older IDE drive, it may not support Multi-Sector Transfer. Try disabling this feature in the CMOS Setup, or add the necessary command-line switch to the disk driver command line in CONFIG.SYS, such as:

```
DEVICE=DOSEIDE.SYS /V /2 /D0:M0
```

SYMPTOM 15-14   **The drive adapter's BIOS doesn't load**   First, make sure that the BIOS is enabled (usually through a jumper on the drive adapter), and see that the BIOS chip is seated correctly and completely in its socket on the drive adapter. If problems persist, try changing the BIOS address—it's probably conflicting with another BIOS in the system. Also check the IRQ and I/O port assignments for the drive adapter for possible conflicts. If all else fails, try another drive controller.

SYMPTOM 15-15   **The drive adapter BIOS loads, but the system hangs up**   First, make sure that the drive parameters are set properly in the CMOS Setup. Inexperienced users frequently mistake the parameters for a second drive in CMOS with a drive on the secondary channel. When no drive is in the primary slave position, the second drive should be "none" or "not installed." If you have an onboard drive controller, make sure to disable it; otherwise, you'll have a hardware conflict between the two drive controllers. Check the individual drives attached to the controller and verify that each drive is jumpered as a unique master or slave device (try reversing the drive order or working with only one drive). Finally, try disabling some of the advanced drive performance parameters in CMOS, such as IDE Block Mode.

SYMPTOM 15-16   **The ATAPI CD-ROM is not recognized as the slave device vs. an IDE master**   First, verify that the CD-ROM is in fact ATAPI compatible and suitable for use on an IDE-type interface. Second, make sure that the proper low-level ATAPI driver for the CD-ROM drive is in use. If the driver is old, try downloading and installing the newest version of the driver. If problems persist, the trouble is probably due to a fast IDE-type device coexisting with a slower IDE ATAPI device. Reconfigure the CD-ROM as the master device on the secondary drive controller channel. You may need to update the ATAPI driver command line in CONFIG.SYS.

SYMPTOM 15-17   **Hard drives are not recognized on the secondary drive controller channel**   Make sure that all the hard drives are jumpered correctly. If only one drive is on the secondary channel, it should be configured as the single or master drive. If two drives are on the secondary channel, verify that the drives are jumpered as master and slave. If the drive adapter uses a disk driver to support EIDE or secondary channel operation, make sure that the command line in CONFIG.SYS uses the correct switch(es) to enable the secondary drive channel. For example, the Promise Technologies 2300 would add an /S switch to the command line such as:

```
device=c:\eide2300\eide2300.sys /S
```

Check that your system's power management features are not enabled on IRQ 15 (and confirm that no other devices are conflicting with IRQ 15). If the drive is set to "autoconfigure" in the CMOS Setup, try entering the drive's parameters specifically. The drive may be too old to understand the IDC (Identify Drive Command) needed for autoconfiguration. Finally, try booting the system clean (with just disk driver software if necessary) to see if there are any other driver or TSR conflicts.

SYMPTOM 15-18   **The drive adapter can only support 528MB per disk**   First, make sure that the LBA mode is enabled. This is often accomplished through the CMOS Setup, but it may also be necessary to enable an LBA support jumper on some older EIDE drive adapters. If problems persist, the drive adapter's BIOS is probably too old and should be upgraded to a new version. If you cannot upgrade the drive adapter's BIOS, install a new drive adapter outright.

SYMPTOM 15-19   **You get a "code 10" error relative to the drive adapter**   You notice that Windows 98/Me is running in MS-DOS Compatibility Mode, and the system only boots in Safe Mode. You'll probably find one or more devices (including the drive adapter) marked with a yellow exclamation point. Disk overlay software (such as Disk Manager, EZ-Drive, or MaxBlast) will often cause problems when used in conjunction with drive adapters that use their own disk driver software. The disk overlay must be removed *before* installing the adapter's disk drivers. Remove the overlay software, or simply repartition and reformat the drive (remember to do a complete backup *before* repartitioning). Next, remove or disable any 32-bit disk drivers previously installed under Windows. With Promise Technologies drive adapters, you'll probably see the following under SYSTEM.INI.

```
[386enh]
device=*int13
;device=*wdctrl
;device=c:\windows\system\eide2300.386 (for eide2300plus)
;device=ontrackw.386
;device=c:\windows\system\pti13.386 (for the 4030)
;device=c:\windows\system\ptictrl.386 (for the 4030)
;device=wdcdrv.386
;device=c:\windows\system\maxi13.386 (for the eidemax)
;device=c:\windows\system\maxctrl.386 (for the eidemax)
32bitdiskaccess=off
```

When first installing the disk driver (such as the Promise Windows 95 driver), follow these steps. (Note that some EIDE drive adapters—especially new ones—do not require special drivers.)

1. Open the Control Panel and double-click the System icon.

2. Choose Device Manager, and double-click on Hard Disk Controller.

3. Click once on the driver (standard IDE/ESDI driver), and click on Remove.

4. Reboot the computer.

5. Reopen the Control Panel and start the Add/New Hardware wizard.

6. Answer No when prompted for Windows to autodetect the device(s).

7. Select Hard Disk Controller, and click on Have Disk.

8. Either insert the floppy disk, or choose Browse and move to the subdirectory where the disk drivers are located.

9. Follow the prompts and choose Finish, but do not reboot the computer yet.

10. Open the Control Panel and double-click the System icon.

11. Choose Device Manager and double-click on Hard Disk Controller. Click once on the installed driver and choose Properties. Select the Resource tab. If you see Basic Configuration of 1, IRQ 15, change this to Basic Configuration of 0, IRQ 14.

12. Reboot the computer so that your changes can take effect.

There may also be a DMA conflict. Some drive adapters take advantage of DMA when the parallel port is in the ECP mode (the conflict occurs most often with the soundboard). To find out which devices use DMA, open the Control Panel, double-click on the System icon, select Device Manager, and double-click on Computer. Choose Direct Memory Access. You can then either switch the controller's use of DMA or disable it altogether. You may need to alter the DMA setting on the drive controller itself, and then switch the parallel port's mode to EPP.

SYMPTOM 15-20 **You encounter mouse problems after changing the drive adapter**
This is a known problem with Logitech pointing devices or standard pointing devices using Logitech drivers. In most cases, you can correct the problem by downloading and installing version 7.0 or later Logitech drivers, or switch to the Windows native serial mouse driver:

1. Open the Control Panel and double-click on the System icon.

2. Select Device Manager and double-click on the Mouse.

3. Click once on Logitech and choose Remove.

4. Start the Add/New Hardware wizard in the Control Panel.

5. Choose No when Windows prompts to autodetect the device.

6. Select Mouse. Click on Standard Serial Mouse. Click on Finish.

7. Reboot the computer.

Another solution may be to disable the COM port's FIFO buffer. Open the Control Panel and choose the System icon. Click on Device Manager. Double-click on Ports [COM & LPT]. Choose the communications port that the mouse uses (for example, COM 1) by clicking on it once, and then click on Properties. Select Port Settings and choose Advanced. Uncheck the box next to "Use FIFO buffers" and then click OK.

SYMPTOM 15-21 **You cannot run Norton AntiVirus with Promise drive adapters**
This appears to be an issue with the Norton AntiVirus (NAV) software itself. According to Symantec (**www.symantec.com**), a patch has been released that corrects this problem.

SYMPTOM 15-22 **The system hangs after counting through system memory** You may also receive error messages such as "Get Configuration Failed!" or "HDD Controller Failure." First, make sure that you have at least one hard drive attached to the controller, and see that the signal cable is oriented properly at both ends. It is also possible that you may have a problem when more than one drive is connected. Make sure that the drives are jumpered in the desired master and slave relationship. Try working with only one drive or reverse the drive relationship. In all cases, verify that the CMOS Setup entries accurately reflect the drives that are connected. If your drive adapter uses onboard RAM, the RAM may be bad. Try replacing the controller's onboard RAM.

SYMPTOM 15-23   **There are errors reading or writing to floppies after replacing/ upgrading a drive adapter**   This is almost always due to a hardware conflict between the floppy adapter on the new controller and another floppy adapter elsewhere in the system. Disable the floppy adapter port on the new drive controller card. If you're using the new floppy port, disable the floppy port already in the system.

If you cannot successfully disable a current or preexisting floppy controller, you'll need to remove the new drive controller and install a controller without a floppy port (or one that can be disabled properly).

SYMPTOM 15-24   **Your drive controller won't function with a 75 MHz bus speed** This occurs because the odd bus speed results in a PCI speed of about 37.5 MHz (which is higher than the 33 MHz that the PCI bus is designed for). This effectively "overclocks" the PCI bus, and can often result in unstable or erratic operation for sensitive PCI devices such as the drive controller. The best solution here is to drop the bus speed to 66 MHz so that the clock can be divided down to 33 MHz for the PCI bus, or reset the PCI bus divisor speed to an appropriate level for 100 MHz or 133 MHz motherboards.

SYMPTOM 15-25   **You cannot use APM with hard drives operated from a new drive controller**   This is a known issue with high-end controllers such as the Promise FastTrack66. In most cases, this symptom occurs because the system sees the new controller card as a SCSI controller. Using IDE commands for APM will not work because the card is seen as a SCSI card. SCSI commands for APM will not work because the drives are IDE. You will need to replace the controller with a model suitable for APM use, or forego the use of APM modes.

SYMPTOM 15-26   **You can't boot from a new IDE controller if you have a SCSI card in the system already**   Chances are that you'll need to tweak the setup of your new IDE controller (such as Ultra100) and existing SCSI card. If you have an actual SCSI controller in the system, the computer will attempt to boot from whichever controller is recognized first. To get one controller to be recognized before another, you must get its BIOS to load first. Manipulating the BIOS address that the card is set to use normally takes care of this.

However, virtually all IDE controllers are fully PnP, which means that only the PnP BIOS on the motherboard can control which resources the card uses. Generally, the PCI slot with the highest priority will be assigned the lowest BIOS address. On most motherboards, the PCI slot with the highest priority is PCI slot 1. If you cannot assign a specific memory address or loading order to your PCI devices through the CMOS Setup, try inserting the IDE drive controller so that it's in PCI slot 1.

SYMPTOM 15-27   **EMM386 fails to load after installing a new IDE controller**   This is a known issue with some Promise IDE controllers (such as the FastTrack66) and is caused by the way the motherboard handles memory. There is no work-around for this problem at the moment, but check for an updated controller BIOS from the manufacturer. If there is no update available, you'll need to disable the use of EMM386 (which should be unneeded under Windows anyway).

SYMPTOM 15-28   **You cannot get QuickBooks 5.0 to start with an IDE controller in the system**   This is a known issue with some Promise controllers such as the Ultra33 and is caused by the controller's driver. I have found that if you use the Ultra33 driver version 1.33 and set it to Business mode with the UltraTune utility, QuickBooks will start. You can download this driver version from **ftp://ftp.promise.com/Controllers/IDE/U33_133.zip**.

SYMPTOM 15-29   **You find that your IDE controller is conflicting with the USB controller**   This is a BIOS problem with the IDE controller itself. Check to see if a new BIOS version is available for your controller. For a Promise Ultra66, a new BIOS has been released to fix the conflict. You can download the BIOS from **ftp://ftp.promise.com/Controllers/IDE/Ultra66/U66_0628.zip**.

Further Study

Adaptec   www.adaptec.com
Connect.Com   www.connectcom.net/
DTC   www.datatechnology.com
Promise Technologies   www.promise.com

16

DVD DRIVES

The *compact disc* opened up a whole new world of possibilities for the PC. These simple, mass-produced plastic discs could hold up to an hour of stereo music, or 650MB (or more) of computer programs and data. Software makers quickly found the CD-ROM to be an outstanding medium for all types of multimedia applications, large databases, and interactive games. But today, the CD-ROM is showing its age, and a single CD no longer provides enough storage for the increasing demands of data-intensive applications. A new generation of high-density optical storage called *DVD* is now widely available for the desktop PC (Figure 16-1). "DVD" stands for "digital versatile disc" (because it can hold programs and data as well as video and sound). But whatever you call it, DVD technology promises to supply up to 17GB of removable storage on your desktop PC. This chapter covers the background and workings of a DVD package, shows you the steps for DVD installation, and offers a series of basic troubleshooting solutions.

FIGURE 16-1   A Creative Labs DVD-ROM drive

The Potential of DVD

The argument for DVD is a compelling one because having gigabytes of removable storage to work with opens up some exciting possibilities for entertainment and software development. As DVD continues to work its way into the marketplace, you will probably notice two distinct designations: DVD-Video and DVD-ROM. *DVD-Video* is the approach used to store movies on the disc (analogous to the way audio is placed on CDs). Eventually, DVD-Video is expected to replace videotape players in home entertainment. *DVD-ROM* refers to computer-based software and data recorded on the disc. Where audio CDs can be played on CD-ROM drives, DVD-Video discs will be playable on DVD-ROM drives in your PC. Understandably, there are a lot of players looking to make the most of what DVD has to offer:

- Hollywood has been a major factor in the development of DVD-Video—placing full-length movies, sound tracks, and even multilingual subtitling on a single disc. Since all DVD discs are read by laser, there is no physical contact between the disc and its player. The result is that the disc won't wear out like VHS videotapes.

- Business presentations, education, and professional training will also benefit from DVD technology. Animations, charts, and interactive applets can be integrated with real-time video. This offers a truly immersive training experience that CD-ROM technology has only scratched the surface of.

- Applications for archiving are limitless. Mapping programs, telephone directories, and encyclopedias—any software that now spans several CDs can be concentrated on one DVD disc and dramatically expanded to offer unprecedented detail.

- Any data-intensive computer software (especially 3D and other interactive games) will get a real boost from the sheer storage volume offered by DVD-ROM technology.

Specifications and Standards

The next step in exploring DVD is to understand the various specifications "on the box" and to become familiar with the specifications that make DVD work and with what a DVD will support. You don't need a lot of technical details, but you should recognize the most important points that you'll probably run across while reading documentation.

ACCESS TIME

The access time is the time required for the drive to locate the required information on a disc. Optical drives like CD and DVD drives are relatively slow and can demand up to several hundred milliseconds (mS) to access information. The older Toshiba DVD drive bundled with Diamond Multimedia's Maximum DVD Kit quotes a DVD access time of only 200 mS (compared to about 100 mS for CDs). However, DVD drives have become considerably faster over the last few years, and today's DVD drives are easily on par with CD-ROM access times. For example, the recent Creative Labs Encore 12X DVD drive lists an access time of only 130 mS.

DATA TRANSFER RATES

Once data has been accessed, it must be transferred off of the disc to the system. The data transfer rate measures how fast data can be read from the disc. There are two typical means of measuring the data rate. First is the speed at which data is read into the drive's onboard buffer (the *sequential* or sustained data transfer rate). Second is the speed at which data is transferred across the interface to the drive controller (the *buffered* or burst data transfer rate). The typical rate used for comparison is the burst transfer rate. The Creative Labs Encore 12X DVD drive offers a buffered data transfer rate of up to 16.2MB/s (PIO Mode 4). As a result, virtually all current DVD-ROM drives are compatible with most EIDE and UDMA drive controllers in the marketplace today.

ASPECT RATIOS

Aspect ratio refers to the width-to-height ratio of a television image. Traditional television sets have always conformed to the 4:3 ratio (roughly square in appearance). Wide-screen displays with a 16:9 or 20:9 ratio (similar to theater screens) appear more rectangular. DVD technology brings more versatility to on-screen viewing by incorporating four different display capabilities. Video can be stored on a DVD disc in a standard TV 4:3 format or 16:9 wide screen. DVD players can output video in four different ways:

- Full frame 4:3 video (for 4:3 display)
- Letterbox 16:9 video (for 4:3 display)
- Pan and scan 16:9 video (for 4:3 display)
- Wide screen 16:9 video (for 16:9 display)

Full Frame
Full frame video is generally normal television footage converted for storage on DVD disc. This would include most television shows on the market today and movies that have been converted for television viewing.

Letterbox
When showing a movie in letterbox mode, the player adds black bars to the top and bottom of the image. The image is then filtered so that the remaining area of the screen is filled in—allowing the viewer to see the movie in the same aspect as it appeared in the theater. With NTSC titles, this results in an image consisting of 360 lines of resolution. The image still contains a third more viewable lines than VHS tape, which consists of 242 viewable lines.

Pan and Scan
Pan and scan can either be automatic or manual sideways-panning in a movie. Automatic pan and scan will change the camera view based upon a prerecorded selection made by the producer of the DVD disc. Manual pan and scan allows viewers to choose between different camera viewpoints at their leisure. As with other features (such as language selection), the publisher of the disc must incorporate the feature for it to be available to the viewer.

Zooming (often confused with pan and scan) is a feature where the hardware will store a portion of the screen in memory and then allow a user to dynamically enlarge that portion of the screen. Usually, the zoomed image will be enhanced so that it does not appear grainy when enlarged. Zooming is *not* a feature supported by the DVD standard.

Wide Screen

The wide-screen mode is often compared to letterbox mode when viewed on a computer monitor or television, but it's not the same thing. TVs and monitors are designed to a standard 4:3 ratio, and the displayed image will be put into a letterbox when displayed on the screen. Look carefully at the top and bottom of a wide-screen image. There will be a few extra black lines added. The black lines were added when the movie was mastered to DVD because movie film does not exactly match the 16:9 screen ration of wide screen. (Movies are slightly wider.)

Unlike letterbox images, wide-screen movies do not sacrifice vertical resolution to fill the display area. On a high-resolution computer monitor, it would be easy to see the crispness of the image compared with a letterboxed image. If the player did not letterbox the image (and the image were allowed to fill the whole screen), the characters in the movie would seem stretched to appear very tall and skinny. As wide-screen digital television becomes more available, wide-screen movies will be able to play back to their full height and width without the letterbox.

BOOKS AND STANDARDS

As you saw in Chapter 9, CD technology is defined by a set of accepted standards. We have come to know these as *books*. Since each CD book was bound in a different color jacket, each standard is dubbed by color. For example, the standard that defines CD audio is called Red Book. Similarly, DVD technology is defined by a set of books such as those outlined in Table 16-1. You can also find DVD books described in the DVD Forum at **www.dvdforum.org/tech-dvdbook.htm**.

DATA FORMATS

All DVD discs must use a data format that describes how data is laid out. Data formats are critical because they outline data structures on the disc such as volumes, files, blocks, sectors, CRCs, paths, records, file allocation tables, partitions, character sets, time stamps, as well as methods for reading and writing. The format used by most books is called the *UDF Bridge*. The UDF Bridge is a combination of the UDF (Universal Data Format) created by OSTA (Optical Storage Technology Association) and the established ISO-9660 format used for CDs. You may see the UDF referred to as standard ISO/IEC 13346. The UDF is a very flexible format that has been adapted to CD-RW and DVD, and has been made backward compatible to existing ISO-9660 operating system software (such as Windows 98/Me). Actual utilization of this disk system on DVD discs will depend largely on what Microsoft dictates as the future operating system standard. Stand-alone DVD movie players are supposed to use UDF. With the release of Windows 98, the UDF Bridge has been abandoned in favor of full UDF support.

Audio and Video Standards

Even with the huge data capacities offered by DVD, an entire movie's worth of real-time audio and video would never fit on a DVD without some form of compression. Both audio and video must be extensively compressed, and MPEG (Moving Pictures Experts Group) compression has been the scheme of choice. Video compression uses fixed data rate MPEG-1 (ISO/IEC 1117-2) at 30 frames per second with resolutions of 352×240, or variable data rate MPEG-2 (ISO/IEC 13818-2) at 60 frames per second with resolutions of 720×480. Audio compression uses MPEG-1 (ISO/IEC 1117-3) stereo, MPEG-2 (ISO/IEC 13818-3) 5.1

TABLE 16-1   SUMMARY OF CONTEMPORARY DVD STANDARDS

DVD Specifications for Read-Only Disc	
DVD-ROM	Part 1: Physical Specifications Ver. 1.0 Part 2: File System Specifications Ver. 1.0
DVD-Video	Part 3: Video Specifications Ver. 1.1 Jacket Picture Format Ver. 1.0 IEC958 (to convey non-PCM encoded audio bitstreams) Ver. 1.0
DVD-Audio	Part 4: Audio Specifications Ver. 1.0 (with version information from 1.0 to 1.1 and 1.1 to 1.2) Packed PCM: MLP Reference Information Ver. 1.0
DVD Specifications for Recordable Disc	
DVD-R (3.9G)	Part 1: Physical Specifications Ver. 1.0 Part 2: File System Specifications Ver. 1.0
DVD-R for General Use	Part 1: Physical Specifications Ver. 2.0 Part 2: File System Specifications Ver. 2.0
DVD-R for Authoring Use	Part 1: Physical Specifications Ver. 2.0 Part 2: File System Specifications Ver. 2.0
DVD Specifications for Rewritable Disc	
DVD-RAM (2.6G)	Part 1: Physical Specifications Ver. 1.0 Part 2: File System Specifications Ver. 1.0 (with version information from 1.0 to 1.1)
DVD-RAM (4.7G)	Part 1: Physical Specifications Ver. 2.0 (with version information from 2.0 to 2.1) Part 2: File System Specifications Ver. 2.0
DVD Specifications for Re-recordable Disc	
DVD-RW	Part 1: Physical Specifications Ver. 1.0 (with version information from 1.0 to 1.1) Part 2: File System Specifications Ver. 1.0
DVD Specifications for DVD-RAM/DVD-RW/DVD-R for General Discs	
DVD Video Recording	Part 3: Video Recording Ver. 1.0 (with version information from 1.0 to 1.1)
DVD Stream Recording	Part 5: Stream Recording Ver. 0.9

and 7.1 surround sound, or Dolby AC-3 5.1 surround and stereo. MPEG-2 and AC-3 audio compression allow 48,000 samples per second, where MPEG-1 allows only 44,100 samples per second. MPEG-2 compression is typically regarded as the preferred scheme for DVD.

The audio designations "5.1" and "7.1" indicate five (or seven) signal channels, plus one subwoofer channel.

CD Compatibility

One of the most important aspects of any technology is backward compatibility—how well the new device will support your existing media. The same issue is true for DVD drives. Since DVD technology is designed as an improvement over existing CD-ROMs, the DVD was designed to replace the CD-ROM rather than coexist with it. Ideally, you'd remove your CD-ROM and replace it with a DVD-ROM drive.

This means the DVD must be compatible with as many existing CD-ROM standards as possible. Older DVD-ROM drives supported only a limited number of formats such as CD-Audio, CD-ROM, CD-I, CD Extra, CD-ROM/XA, and Video CD formats. Multisession (such as Photo CD) and CD-R discs were a bit more problematic. Today's drives such as the Creative Labs Encore 12X support a full suite of disc formats including CD-Audio, CD-I, CD Extra, CD-ROM, CD-ROM/XA, Photo CD, CD-R, CD-RW, Video CD, DVD-Video, and even DAE (digital audio extraction).

If you discover that an older DVD drive refuses to support Photo CD and CD-R discs, it may be necessary to upgrade the drive's firmware (or the entire drive mechanism) in order to handle more recent formats.

Content Protection

One of the problems with electronic media is that it's easy to transfer and manipulate. Copyright laws prohibit the unauthorized use of electronic media, but with the ease of electronic data transfers, companies are constantly devising new ways to protect and control the distribution of their intellectual property. There are several approaches in place to manage content protection.

REGION CODE CONTROL

Motion picture studios want to control the home release of movies in different countries because theater releases are not simultaneous. Therefore, they have required that the DVD standard include codes that can be used to prevent playback of certain discs in certain geographical regions. Each player is given a code for the region in which it's sold. The player will refuse to play discs that are not allowed in that region. This means that discs bought in one country may not play on players bought in another country. Table 16-2 lists the code numbers and the regions each number covers. Keep in mind that region codes are entirely optional, and discs without codes will play on any player in any country.

More recent DVD drives are actually sold without a region code assigned. The code is assigned when a disc is inserted and can typically be changed up to four or five times before being fixed by the drive's firmware.

Region Codes and Windows

Under Windows 98/Me, the initial default DVD region is chosen during setup when you select a country in the Establishing Your Location dialog. If you choose None for a country location, the default region selection is based on the country code and time zone. The first time a DVD movie is placed in the drive,

TABLE 16-2	STANDARD DVD REGION CODES
CODE	REGION
1	Canada, United States, and U.S. territories
2	Japan, Europe, South Africa, Middle East (including Egypt)
3	Southeast Asia, East Asia (including Hong Kong)
4	Australia, New Zealand, Pacific Islands, Central America, South America, Caribbean
5	Former Soviet Union, Indian Subcontinent, Africa (also North Korea, Mongolia)
6	China

Windows 98/Me compares the disc's region with the region selected during setup. If the DVD disc and setup region entries are different, the Windows default is changed to match the DVD movie.

Once the selected region has been used to watch a movie, you can change it up to four more times (for a total of five possible settings). If the disc is from a region other than the default, a dialog appears to tell you that the disc is from a different region. That dialog then displays the region for the current movie disc and the current player region—along with a list of new player regions and countries you can select (if possible). If you then select a new region, a warning appears stating the number of region changes remaining before the change is written permanently. The DVD drive itself will enforce the changes. Each time the region is changed, the new region is written to the drive's firmware. When the region change limit is reached, the DVD firmware locks out further attempts until the drive unit is replaced or reset by the manufacturer.

MACROVISION

Macrovision (for example, Macrovision 7) is a proprietary piracy protection scheme that utilizes the signal in the nondisplayed region of a video signal to prevent copying. Macrovision varies the signal controlling the automatic gain control (AGC) of a recording deck, thereby washing out and darkening the recording signal of a tape or DVD disc being recorded.

COPY GENERATION MANAGEMENT SYSTEM (CGMS)

DVD-Video discs may contain information that can be used to prevent copying of the disc on equipment (such as a VCR) if the VCR is equipped with a *Copy Generation Management System* (CGMS). Several video recorder manufacturers have adopted CGMS, which works by embedding a signal in the video image in an area of the screen not normally seen by viewers. CGMS does not work unless both the player and recorder allow the signal to be present during playback.

CONTENT SCRAMBLING SYSTEM (CSS)

To protect its movie titles from being copied in perfect digital fidelity, the motion picture industry endorses a key-based data encryption system called *Content Scrambling System* (CSS). Operation involves authentication of the device, the exchange of keys, and decryption of the DVD content. Some PC-DVD solutions include hardware decryption integrated within the decoder board.

DIGITAL VIDEO EXPRESS (DIVX)

Digital Video Express (Divx) is a proprietary encoding scheme principally sponsored by consumer electronics retailer Circuit City and the law firm of Ziffren, Brittenham, Branca, and Fischer. This scheme requires users to have a Divx player for playback and a dial-up connection. Divx players are more expensive than DVD players (costing nearly $100 more than a standard DVD player) and did not reach the market until February 1998.

A Divx DVD disc—suggested retail price, $4.99—will play back for a 48-hour period starting when the disc is inserted in the drive. Once the 48 hours have passed, the player will no longer play the disc. Not only will the disc be unplayable, the player automatically registers the disc online when it's inserted in the player. Disconnecting the Divx player from the phone line renders the player unusable until it's reconnected to the Divx online service. The disc also may not be played in any other player unless the user chooses to connect and buy more time (a.k.a. "pay for view"), or the user pays to completely unlock the disc.

Regular DVD players are unable to access a Divx disc because the access coding method directs playback first to an embedded instruction that is not recognized by normal DVD players. The normal DVD player will display an error indicating that there are no playable files on the disc.

The Divx scheme has largely been abandoned today because of continuing problems involving Divx disc and player compatibility, as well as immense pressure from inexpensive DVD players and poor overall industry support.

DVD Media

At its core, DVD technology is identical to classical CD-ROMs. Data is recorded in a spiral pattern as a series of pits and lands pressed into a plastic substrate. The actual size and dimensions of a DVD are identical to our current compact discs. However, there are some key differences that give DVD its advantages. First, data is highly concentrated on the disc. Where classical CDs use spiral tracks that are 1.6μm apart, DVD tracks are only 0.74μm apart. A typical pit on a classic CD is 0.83μm, but DVD pits are just 0.4μm. Table 16-3 compares the specifications for DVD and CD media. In short, the data on a DVD is much denser than on a regular CD. Figure 16-2 illustrates the differences between DVDs and CDs. To detect these smaller geometries, the laser used in a DVD operates at a much shorter wavelength (a short-wavelength red laser).

Second, DVD can employ multiple layers of pits and lands (each in their own reflective layer), so one physical disc can hold several layers' worth of data. The DVD drive's laser focus control can select which layer to read. Finally, a regular CD only uses one side of the disc, but both sides of the DVD can be used. Combined with this multilayer technique, the DVD can theoretically supply up to four layers of data to a

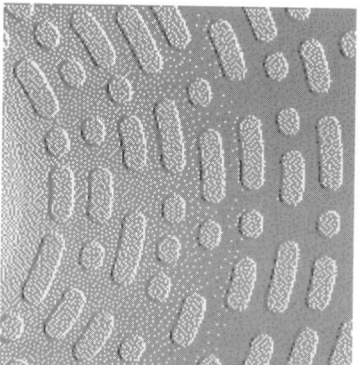

An example of DVD pits and lands

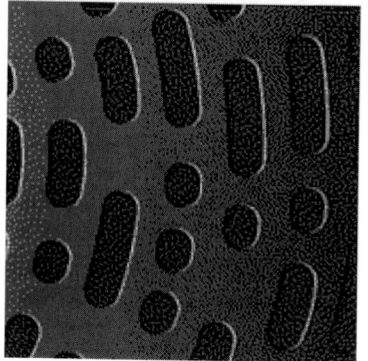

An example of ordinary CD pits and lands

FIGURE 16-2   Comparison of DVD and CD data density

TABLE 16-3	COMPARISON OF DVD AND CD MEDIA SPECIFICATIONS	
SPECIFICATION	**DVD**	**CD-ROM**
Diameter (mm)	120	120
Disc thickness (mm)	1.2	1.2
Substrate thickness (mm)	0.6	1.2
Track pitch (μm)	0.74	1.6
Minimum pit size (μm)	0.4	0.83
Wavelength (nm)	635/650	780
Single-layer capacity (GB)	4.7	0.65

DVD drive (Figure 16-3). In actual practice, DVD-ROM discs will likely only use one side of the disc—at least for a while. What all this means is that a DVD disc can offer up to 8.5GB of storage for a single-sided double-layer disc, or up to 17GB of storage for a double-sided double-layer disc.

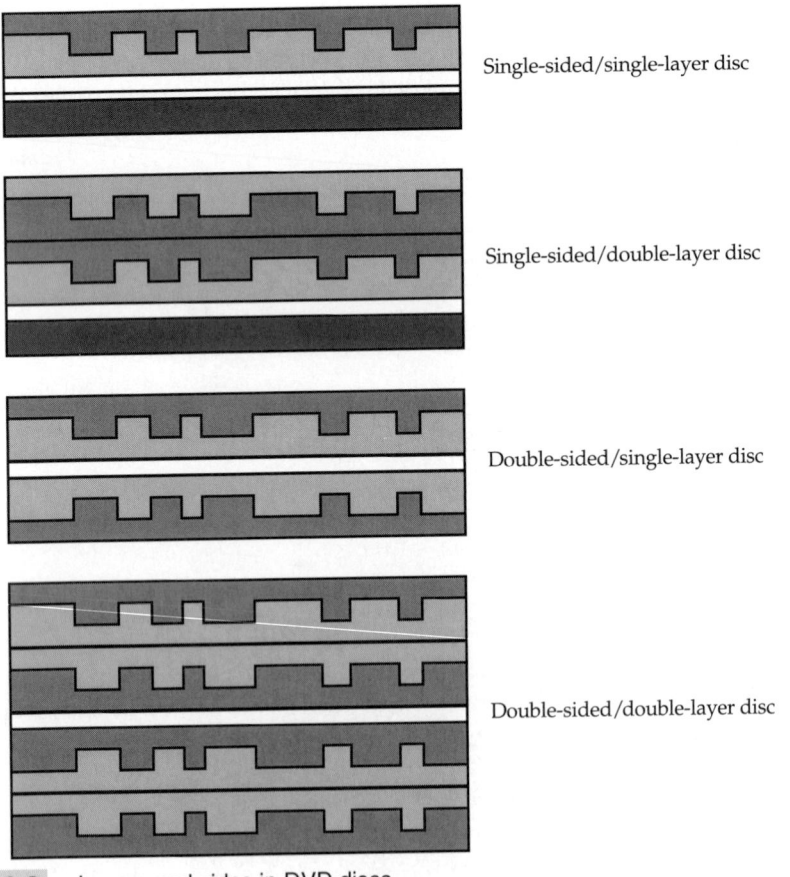

Single-sided/single-layer disc

Single-sided/double-layer disc

Double-sided/single-layer disc

Double-sided/double-layer disc

FIGURE 16-3   Layers and sides in DVD discs

CARING FOR A DVD DISC

As with CDs, a DVD disc is a remarkably reliable long-term storage media. (Conservative estimates of the life of a DVD disc are about 100 years.) However, the longevity of an optical disc is affected by its storage and handling. A faulty CD can cause file and data errors that you might otherwise interpret as a defect in the drive itself. You can get the most life out of your optical disc by obeying the following rules:

- *Don't bend the disc.* Polycarbonate is a forgiving material, but you risk cracking or snapping (and thus ruining) the disc.

- *Don't heat the disc.* Remember, the disc is plastic. Leaving it by a heater or on the dashboard of your car will cause melting.

- *Don't scratch the disc.* Laser wavelengths have a tendency to "look past" minor scratches, but a major scratch can cause problems. Be especially careful of circular scratches (ones that follow the spiral track). A circular scratch can easily wipe out entire segments of data that would be unrecoverable.

- *Don't use chemicals on the disc.* Chemicals containing solvents such as ammonia, benzene, acetone, carbon tetrachloride, or chlorinated cleaning solvents can easily damage the plastic surface.

Eventually, a buildup of excessive dust or fingerprints can interfere with the laser beam enough to cause disc errors. When this happens, the disc can be cleaned easily using a dry, soft, lint-free cloth. Hold the disc by its edges and wipe radially (from hub to edge). Do not wipe in a circular motion. For stubborn stains, moisten the cloth in a bit of fresh isopropyl alcohol. *Do not use water or ammonia.* Place the cleaned disc in a caddy or jewel case for transport and storage.

Contrary to popular belief, DVD discs are not more sensitive to scratches or dust than ordinary CDs.

The DVD Drive and Decoder

A DVD drive looks almost identical to a CD-ROM drive in size, shape, and layout. In fact, if not for the "DVD" logo on the tray, you'll probably mistake a DVD-ROM drive for a CD-ROM, CD-R, or CD-RW drive. The front of a DVD drive (Figure 16-4) carries all of the standard features that you'd find on any CD-ROM. A motorized disc tray loads and unloads the disc. You can close or open the tray by toggling the Load/unload (or Eject) button. Most current DVD-ROM drives won't eject a disc that is "locked" by a software application (such as a running movie). You will need to close your DVD application before ejecting the locked disc. The drive activity LED (or Busy indicator) lights whenever data is being read from the drive. Since the DVD drive also supports CD audio, you can connect headphones to the headphone jack and adjust volume right from the front panel.

Much of the rear of a DVD-ROM will also probably look familiar (Figure 16-5). Power is connected through a 4-pin Molex connector, so you can use any suitable power connector from your power supply. The signal connector, which is typically either EIDE/UDMA (40-pin) or SCSI (50- or 68-pin), connects the drive directly to your existing drive adapter. Unlike early CD-ROM drives, DVD-ROM drives do not use proprietary drive controllers. A series of small jumpers allows you to set the drive's identity. For SCSI-type drives, you can set the SCSI ID (usually ID2 through ID6). For EIDE or UDMA-type drives, you will set the drive as either a primary (master) or secondary (slave) drive. If you're running an EIDE/UDMA DVD-ROM along with a hard drive, the hard drive would typically be the master device, and the DVD-ROM drive would be the slave device. If you're running the DVD-ROM drive alone, set it as the master device. Finally, there are two audio output connectors: a 4-pin CD audio connector that

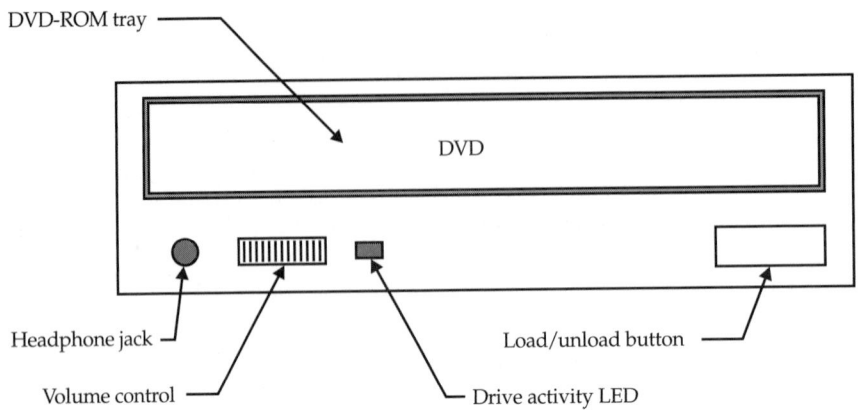

DVD-ROM tray

DVD

Headphone jack

Load/unload button

Volume control

Drive activity LED

FIGURE 16-4   Front view of a typical DVD-ROM drive

attaches to a sound board, and a 2-pin digital audio connector that supplies sound to a *digital audio tape* (DAT) or other digital recording system (though this output is rarely used).

 Since DVD drives almost always use EIDE/UDMA interfaces rather than older IDE interfaces, they may be used along with fast EIDE/UDMA hard drives on the same controller channel with no (or negligible) degradation in hard drive performance.

INSIDE THE DRIVE

Things get a little more interesting when you look inside the DVD-ROM drive (Figure 16-6). Looking in from the top of the drive, you'll see the major subassemblies needed to operate the drive. That black circular wheel near the tray is the *spindle motor* that turns the disc. You can also see the laser assembly and the *laser sled* that the laser rides back and forth on. A small motor drives a screw that runs the sled. The load/unload mechanics run the disc tray in and out (though the mechanical parts are obscured below the plastic tray). The main electronics deck is mounted on the underside of the drive (Figure 16-7). This is a single printed circuit board that contains all of the circuitry needed to run the drive interface, load/unload motor, audio amplifiers, spindle motor, laser, and laser sled.

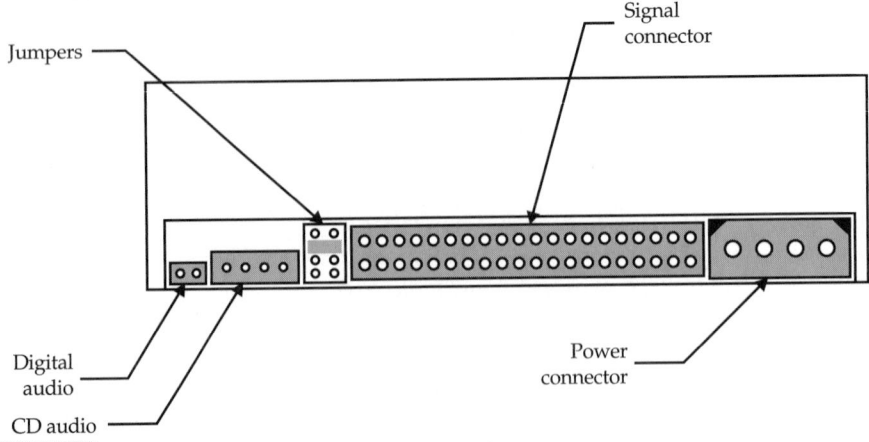

Jumpers

Signal connector

Digital audio

CD audio

Power connector

FIGURE 16-5   Rear view of a typical DVD-ROM drive

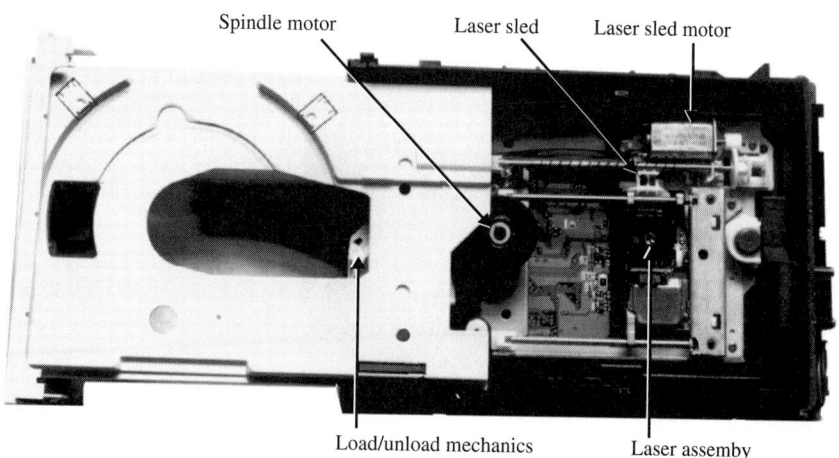

Spindle motor   Laser sled   Laser sled motor

Load/unload mechanics   Laser assemby

FIGURE 16-6   Looking into the top of a typical DVD-ROM drive

Drive firmware and
region control chip

FIGURE 16-7   Looking at the bottom of a typical DVD-ROM drive

REGION CODE CONTROL

One item of particular interest in Figure 16-7 is the removable chip. This chip contains firmware for the drive, as well as the unit's region codes. As you saw earlier in the chapter, motion picture studios want to control the home release of movies in different countries because theater releases are not simultaneous. Therefore, they have required that the DVD standard include codes that can be used to prevent playback of certain discs in certain geographical regions. Each player is given a code for the region in which it's sold (or can be assigned a code based on the first few discs that are played in it). Once a region code is fixed, the drive will refuse to play discs that are not allowed in that region. This means that discs bought in one country may not play on players bought in another country. Table 16-1 earlier in the chapter lists the code numbers and the regions each number covers. Keep in mind that region codes are entirely optional, and discs without codes will play on any player in any country.

THE MPEG-2 DECODER

Although a DVD disc can easily provide over 4GB of storage, that is still not nearly enough space to hold the audio and video data required for an average-length Hollywood movie. Movie data must be highly compressed before being recorded on the disc. (Compression usually follows the MPEG-2 standard.) This presents some unique problems for the PC during playback. The compressed movie audio and video data is passed along the SCSI or EIDE/UDMA cable to the drive controller. However, the overhead processing needed to decode the sound and picture can easily bog down all but the fastest systems. This can result in poor playback performance, such as broken audio and dropped video frames.

To ensure smooth, real-time playback of the DVD movie, a hardware-based MPEG-2 decoder card (Figure 16-8) is normally added to an available PCI slot, and connected directly to the monitor. (Video output from the graphics accelerator is passed through the decoder card to the monitor.) The decoder card takes over the job of decompressing the MPEG-2 information—relieving a tremendous amount of work from the system processor. Decoded audio from the movie is also passed from the decoder card to the sound card using a CD audio connection.

In the early days of DVD, MPEG decoders were a necessity. Today's fast processors can often handle the decoding process without aid of a decoder card (though it's still recommended).

FIGURE 16-8   A typical MPEG-2 decoder card for DVD video and audio playback

A LOOK AT MPEG-2

When the original video source is recorded for DVD, MPEG-2 analyzes the video picture for redundant data. Over 95 percent of the digital data that represents a video signal is redundant and can be compressed without visibly harming the picture quality (also referred to as *loss-less compression*). By eliminating redundant data, MPEG-2 achieves excellent video quality at far lower bit rates.

MPEG-2 encoding for DVD is a two-stage process. The original signal is first evaluated for complexity. Then higher bit rates are assigned to complex pictures, and lower bit rates are assigned to simple pictures. This allows for an adaptive variable bit-rate process. The DVD-Video format uses compressed bit rates with a range of up to 10Mbits/s. Although the average bit rate for digital video is often quoted as 3.5Mbits/s, the actual figure will vary according to movie length, picture complexity, and the number of audio channels required. With MPEG-2 compression, a single-layer, single-sided DVD disc has enough capacity to hold 2 hours and 13 minutes of video and audio on a 12cm disc. At the nominal average data rate of 3.5Mbits/s, this still leaves enough capacity for discrete 5.1 channel digital sound in three languages, plus subtitles in four additional languages.

SOFTWARE DVD DECODERS

While a hardware decoder card is highly recommended, it is not always required. Decoding can be accomplished using software applications. The advantage of software decoding is simplicity. DVD upgrades are easier since you don't need the hardware decoder card. However, considering the amount of processing power required for real-time MPEG-2 decoding, you will need a very fast Pentium III/4 platform in order to sustain an adequate DVD-Video frame rate. Slower PCs (or other processing overhead such as running background applications) may not be able to support software-only decoding. This may manifest itself as choppy video, lost frames, and/or distorted audio. Make certain that your PC meets the minimum system requirements (preferably the recommended system configuration) for DVD decoding software.

If your PC does not meet the minimum requirements for decoding software, you may wish to update your video card to a model that offers motion compensation, or other types of DVD playback assistance. For example, various ATI graphics chips (including the Rage 128, Rage PRO, and Rage LT PRO) contain DVD-processing hardware that can assist in decoding DVD without the need for a full hardware decoder card. Still, if you need to consider a video card upgrade, it is often more efficient to leave the video device in place and add a full hardware decoder card instead.

NOTES ON DOLBY AC-3

Dolby AC-3 (also called Dolby Surround AC-3 or Dolby Digital) is another method of encoding DVD audio besides MPEG-2 audio. With five channels and a common subwoofer channel (known as "5.1"), you get the effects of 3D surround sound with right, left, center, left ear, right ear, and common subwoofer speakers. AC-3 runs at 384Kbits/s. In actual practice, DVD products sold in North America and Japan will include Dolby AC-3 sound on the accompanying MPEG-2 board, while DVD products sold in Europe will likely use the MPEG-2 audio standard.

DECODER BOARD CONNECTIONS

There are five major connections on the MPEG-2 decoder board, as shown in Figure 16-9: an analog input jack, an analog output jack, a digital output jack, a monitor connector, and a video input connector. The analog input is rarely (if ever) used in normal operations, but it may be handy for mixing-in an auxiliary audio signal to the decoder board. The analog output signal provides the master audio signal that is fed to

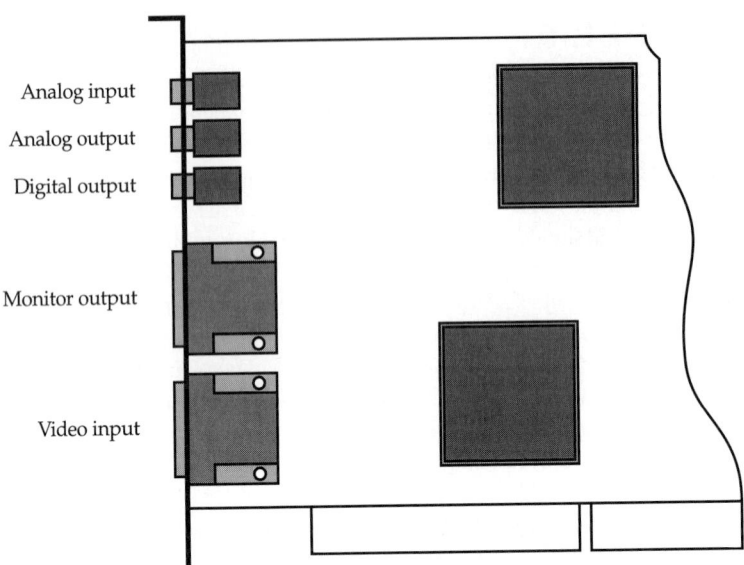

Analog input

Analog output

Digital output

Monitor output

Video input

FIGURE 16-9   Common decoder board connections

the line input of your existing sound board. The advantage of using a line input is that you don't need a volume control on the decoder board. Instead, you can set the line input volume through your sound board's mixer applet. When you play a DVD video, any audio will continue to play through your sound board and speakers. The digital output is intended to drive an external Dolby Digital device, so you will probably not be using the digital output in most basic PC setups.

The MPEG-2 decoder board will now drive your VGA/SVGA monitor through the monitor connector. This is important because the decoded video stream is converted to RGB information and fed to the monitor directly. This avoids having to pass the video data across the PCI/AGP bus to your video card. The normal output from your video card is looped from your video board to the decoder card; so while the decoder board is idle, your normal video signal is just "passed through" the MPEG-2 board to the monitor.

DVD-ROM Installation and Replacement

DVD-ROM drives are generally easy devices to install or replace. Most are installed as master devices located on the secondary EIDE/UDMA drive controller channel, though many will coexist as slave devices alongside a hard drive or other drive device. The most important issue to remember is that the BIOS will not support the DVD-ROM playback directly (even if the BIOS identifies the DVD-ROM at boot time and recognizes the drive as a CD-ROM. You'll need real-mode drivers for the DVD-ROM under DOS or protected-mode drivers for the DVD-ROM under Windows 9x/Me. Keep in mind that real-mode (DOS) drivers for DVD-ROM drives are extremely rare, so be sure that your particular DVD offers real-mode drivers (if that's what you need) before making a purchase. This part of the chapter covers the guidelines needed to install a basic internal ATAPI IDE-type DVD-ROM.

Before beginning the installation, be sure to set the Display mode to 640×480×16 (60Hz refresh rate) or other default video mode as suggested by the DVD maker's installation instructions. Once the DVD drive is installed and running, you can readjust the video mode to an appropriate resolution, color depth, and vertical refresh rate.

SELECT JUMPER CONFIGURATIONS

An IDE-type DVD-ROM drive may be installed as a master or slave device on any current hard drive controller channel. These master/slave settings are handled through one or two jumpers located on the rear of the drive (right next to the 40-pin signal cable connector). One of your first decisions when planning an installation should be to decide the drive's configuration:

■ If you're installing the DVD-ROM as the first drive on the secondary drive controller channel, it must be jumpered as the master device.

■ If you're installing the DVD-ROM drive alongside another drive (on either the primary or secondary drive controller channel), the DVD-ROM must be jumpered as the slave device.

Refer to the documentation that accompanies your particular DVD-ROM drive to determine the exact master/slave jumper settings. If you do not have the drive documentation handy, check the drive manufacturer's Web site for online information.

ATTACH CABLES AND MOUNT THE DRIVE

Once the DVD drive is configured the way you want it, it's time to install the drive in your system. The following steps outline a general installation process:

1. Turn off and unplug the PC, and then remove the outer cover to expose the computer's drive bays.

2. Attach one end of the 40-pin drive interface cable to the drive controller connector on your motherboard (or drive controller card). Remember to align pin 1 on the cable (the side of the cable with the blue or red stripe) with pin 1 on the drive controller connector.

3. Locate an available drive bay for the DVD-ROM drive. Remove the plastic housing covering the drive bay, and then slide the drive inside. Locate the four screw holes needed to mount the drive. In some cases, you may need to attach mounting rails to the drive so that the drive will be wide enough to fit in the drive bay. In virtually all cases, you should mount a tray-driven DVD-ROM drive horizontally (though caddy-loaded drives may be mounted vertically).

4. Attach the 40-pin signal cable and the 4-pin power connector to the new drive, and then bolt the drive securely into place. Do not overtighten the screws since this may damage the drive. If you do not have an available 4-pin power connector, you may use an appropriate Y-adapter if necessary to "split" power from another drive (preferably the floppy drive).

5. Attach the small 4-pin digital audio (or CD audio) signal cable from the DVD-ROM to the CD audio input connector on your sound card. This connection allows you to play music CDs directly from the DVD-ROM through your sound card. Verify that the CD audio cable is compatible with your sound card. (Otherwise you may need a specialized cable from the sound card's manufacturer.)

If you already have a CD-ROM drive in the system providing CD audio to the sound card, you may choose to use the DVD-ROM instead, or leave the CD-ROM's audio cable alone. If your sound card has a second CD audio connector, you may be able to wire the DVD-ROM's audio to your sound card too.

INSTALLING THE DECODER CARD

Locate an open PCI card slot, and install the PnP MPEG-2 decoder card into the slot. In most cases, you simply need to disconnect the monitor from the video output, attach the monitor to the decoder card's monitor output port, and then use a short pass-through cable to connect the video output to the decoder card's video input connector. This ties in the decoder card with the video system.

If you'll be using a software decoder, you may not need to install a hardware decoder card, and this part of the installation may be omitted.

CONFIGURING THE CMOS SETUP

Although the DVD-ROM does require driver support for playback, recent motherboard designs can identify the ATAPI IDE DVD-ROM drive in BIOS and allow the drive to boot the system or serve as a basic CD-ROM. You should configure your computer's BIOS to accept the drive if possible (through the CMOS Setup).

1. Turn the computer on. As your computer starts up, watch for a message that describes how to run the CMOS Setup (for example, "Press F1 for Setup"). Press the appropriate key to start the CMOS Setup program.

2. Select the "hard drive settings" menu, and choose the drive location occupied by the DVD-ROM drive (such as the "primary slave," "secondary slave," or "secondary master" depending on how you've physically jumpered and installed the drive).

3. Select "Automatic drive detection" if available. This option will automatically identify the new drive. If your BIOS does not provide automatic drive detection, select "none" or "not installed" for the DVD-ROM, and rely on drivers only.

4. Save the settings and exit the CMOS Setup program. Your computer will automatically reboot.

REASSEMBLE THE COMPUTER

Double-check all of your signal and power cables to verify that they are secure, and then tuck the cables gently into the computer's chassis. Check that there are no loose tools, screws, or cables inside the chassis. Now reattach the computer's outer housing(s).

INSTALL THE SOFTWARE

To complete your DVD-ROM installation, you'll need to install the software drivers that accompanied the drive on floppy disk or CD. Windows 98/Me systems will generally detect the presence of the new DVD-ROM (and hardware decoder if appropriate), and prompt you for the protected-mode drivers automatically. After you install the drivers and reboot the system, the DVD-ROM should be ready for use. Before you can play DVD movie discs, you'll also need to install the DVD player software (for example, Zoran SoftDVD) and other utilities from the drive's installation disc.

Many DVD-ROM drives will not support real-mode (DOS) drivers, so they will only work under Windows 95/98.

UPGRADING DVD-ROM FIRMWARE

You may be able to update the firmware used in your DVD-ROM drive. This may be necessary to correct bugs or fix drive compatibility problems with the system. The following steps offer a guideline that you can refer to when upgrading DVD-ROM firmware.

> You should always refer to the Web page or README file that accompanies the new firmware download. Be sure to download the correct firmware version for your drive. Installing the wrong firmware can permanently disable the drive.

1. Power-off your system completely.
2. Locate the DVD-ROM drive, and place its "flash" jumper in the flash upgrade position. If there is no flash jumper, it may not be possible to upgrade the drive's firmware.
3. Make sure the power cable and the signal cable (SCSI or IDE) are still connected.
4. Power-on your system and boot clean to a command-line prompt.
5. Make sure that the DVD-ROM appears in program mode. You'll need to refer to the documentation for your particular drive in order to identify the correct program mode.
6. When the system comes up, execute the new firmware program (such as FIRM412.EXE), which you may receive or download from the manufacturer, and use the new firmware (*.BIN) file.
7. When the EXE applications starts, specify the location of the BIN file.
8. Click the Update button to begin the flash process.
9. When the Update button becomes highlighted again, the flash process is complete.
10. Power-off the system and reset the DVD-ROM drive's flash jumper to its original position.
11. Power-on the system normally.

Troubleshooting DVD-ROM Drives

Even though a DVD-ROM package should install with an absolute minimum of muss and fuss, and run with all the reliability of a CD-ROM, there are times when things just don't go according to plan. Both software and hardware problems can interrupt your DVD-ROM system. This part of the chapter provides a series of guidelines and tips to resolve a wide range of problems and covers some of the most common troubleshooting issues.

INITIAL SETUP AND TIPS

When installing or correcting problems on a DVD-ROM system, it may help to set the DVD system configuration to a default state using the criteria outlined next:

■ **Video configuration** Regardless of the amount of video RAM provided by your video adapter, try setting the display to 640×480 using 16-bit color (the high-color mode). You might also try setting the monitor type to standard VGA.

■ **DirectX installation** If you're not yet using Windows 95 OSR2 (4.00.950 B), or do not have any Windows 95 games installed, chances are that you don't have DirectX installed (or you're using a very old version). Though DirectX versions 2.0 and higher should support DVD, using the latest version may increase your system's video performance (since it also includes newer DirectDraw drivers for your video card). Check for the latest version of DirectX (for example, DirectX 8.0a) at **www.microsoft.com/directx**.

■ **DVD drivers**   Drivers are being updated regularly to provide better hardware compatibility, so you should check for the latest Cinemaster drivers and the latest release of DVD Player from Quadrant International: **www.qi.com/**. Of course, you can also check for drivers directly from the DVD manufacturer.

■ **Video drivers**   Many video drivers are also updated regularly for better video performance and compatibility. Check the Web page for your video card vendor for updated video drivers. This may be especially important if you're using a video card with motion compensation or other DVD video decoding features instead of a full hardware decoder card.

■ **IDE controller compatibility**   There is also a lingering issue with the IDE controllers on some motherboards (depending on which version of Windows you're using). If you have trouble with your IDE controllers, check the Intel Developer's Page for more details and fixes at **developer .intel.com/design/motherbd/IDEINFUP.HTM**. Late versions of Windows 95 and Windows 98/Me should have no problems with IDE controller identification and setup.

DVD SOFTWARE AND WINDOWS 98

Although Windows 98 is supposed to offer full support for DVD systems, you may find that DVD systems refuse to install properly (or cease working) once Windows 98 is installed. If this is the case, check the DVD manufacturer's Web site for updated DVD-ROM drivers and software applets. Microsoft supports DVD discs within Windows 98 using SCSI and ATAPI-compliant DVD-ROM drives. Playing movies (DVD-Video) is supported only with the following decoder adapters:

Windows 98/SE and Windows Me should offer superior compatibility for DVD hardware.

■ Toshiba DVD decoder adapters used with Toshiba Infinia DVD systems with either S3 or ATI display adapters.

■ Quadrant Cinemaster C rev. 1.2 decoder adapters included with Dell XPS–series computers. Note that updated Quadrant Cinemaster decoder drivers are available on the Windows 98 CD-ROM in the drivers\dvd\quadrant folder.

■ Windows 98 DVD player is designed to work with the Windows 98 decoder drivers, so the option to add or remove a DVD player is not available until a supported DVD decoder adapter is installed and detected.

■ Once a DVD decoder card is detected and the Windows 98 drivers are installed, a shortcut for DVD player is added to the Entertainment menu. The option to add or remove a DVD player becomes available under Multimedia on the Windows Setup tab (in the Add/Remove Programs tool). After being installed, the DVD player software can be removed and reinstalled without having to reinstall the decoder drivers.

If an appropriate DVD decoder card is used, but has third-party drivers installed, Windows 98 will not install the Windows 98 drivers or DVD player software until the third-party drivers are removed using Device Manager.

DVD SYMPTOMS

If the preceding tips don't help you to resolve the problem, you can check the following symptoms for specific issues and corrective action.

SYMPTOM 16-1   **The DVD drivers refuse to install**   This is almost always because Windows 9x/Me is having a problem with one or more INF files on your driver installation disk(s). Check with your DVD vendor to confirm whether you need to delete one or more entries in your OEM*xx*.INF file(s) (where *xx* is any suffix). If you're using an MKE DVD kit, you may also need to delete one or more entries from a MKEDVD.INF file. The INF files are typically contained in the C:\WINDOWS\INF\OTHER directory. Once you've corrected the appropriate INF file(s), you can reinstall the DVD drivers:

1.   Click Start, select Settings, and then click on Control Panel. Double-click the System icon.

2.   Click on the Device Manager tab, and then select Sound, Video, and Game Controllers or CD-ROM.

3.   Select the DVD driver(s), and then click Remove (Figure 16-10).

4.   Exit the Device Manager and reinstall the drivers again.

SYMPTOM 16-2   **The DVD drive isn't detected**   There are several possible reasons why a DVD drive may not be detected. Check the power connector attached to the drive, and make sure that the drive isn't being powered from a Y-splitter power cable. Check the signal cable next. Both SCSI and EIDE signal cables must be attached securely to the drive. SCSI interfaces are complicated a bit by termination, so verify that any SCSI bus is properly terminated. Make sure that the drive is jumpered properly for its SCSI ID or EIDE/UDMA master or slave relationship. Finally, make sure that the DVD drivers are installed and running. Check the drivers under the Sound, Video, and Game Controllers (or CD-ROM) entry of your Device Manager.

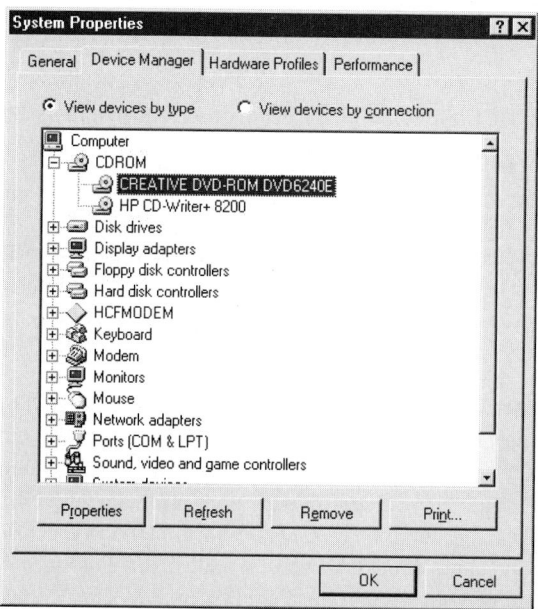

FIGURE 16-10   Locating the DVD driver in Windows 98/SE Device Manager

SYMPTOM 16-3   **You see an error message that the drive is not fully compatible with the software**   You may also see this as a message that no DVD drive is found. This frequently occurs when installing a DVD-ROM drive in conjunction with Zip, Jaz, tape, or CD-ROM drives. The DVD drive will need to be the next available drive letter after any IDE or SCSI hard drives. Alphabetically, there should be no other drives (such as Zip, Jaz, tape, or CD-ROM drives) with drive letters *before* that of the DVD drive.

To change the drive letter assignment in your system, power-down and disconnect all the affected drives except the DVD drive, and then boot to Windows 9x/Me Safe Mode and remove the drives (including the DVD drive) from Device Manager. Restart to normal mode, and the DVD drive will be reassigned the lowest available drive letter. Next, power-down again and reconnect the other drives. Restart the system, and they will automatically be redetected and assigned drive letters higher than the DVD drive.

SYMPTOM 16-4   **You see an error indicating the DVD device driver could not be loaded**   You'll need to check the DVD driver installation, or manually install the drivers. To do this, you will need to open the Control Panel, open System Properties, and then select the Device Manager tab. In the category of Other Devices, select PCI Multimedia Device and click on Properties. In the Properties dialog, select the Driver tab and click on Change Driver. Browse to the DVD Drivers Installation Disk and click OK. Click OK again, select the proper MPEG board (such as MKE DVD-AV Decoder Board), and click OK again. Exit the PCI Multimedia Device Properties by clicking OK again, and Windows 9x/Me will copy over the proper drivers. You will then need to restart the machine.

SYMPTOM 16-5   **DVD players may not work under Windows**   This is known to happen with first-generation Creative DVD kits (or MKE DVD kits) under Windows 98/Me. For example, you may no longer be able to write to your DVD-RAM drive. This problem occurs because the older kits rely on the *Compact Disc File System* (CDFS), but Windows 98/Me loads the UDF file system for DVD drives. To work around this issue, disable UDF for the DVD drives:

1. Click Start, click Run, type **msconfig** in the Open box, and then click OK.
2. Click Advanced (Figure 16-11).
3. Select the "Disable UDF file system" check box (second entry from the bottom), and then click OK.
4. Click OK again and click Yes when prompted to restart the computer.
5. When your computer restarts, UDF is disabled and the DVD kit should work.

SYMPTOM 16-6   **You see an error such as "Cannot open <filename>, video and audio glitches may occur"**   This type of error almost always indicates a fault with the driver installation, and you should rerun the setup utility that accompanied your the DVD drive product. You may also wish to check for driver bug fixes or patches from the drive maker.

SYMPTOM 16-7   **There is no audio when playing an audio CD**   This is a common problem—especially during new DVD-ROM drive installations. Chances are that you did not connect the 4-wire CD audio cable between the DVD-ROM drive and the sound board. If so, the cable may be reversed (or defective). Of course, if you're still using your original CD-ROM drive and the CD-ROM is connected to the sound board, there will be no CD audio from the DVD-ROM drive. There is no way to "parallel" or "gang" the sound cable. If the DVD-ROM audio cable is connected to the sound board, make sure that the CD audio input of your sound board's mixer applet is turned up to a reasonable level.

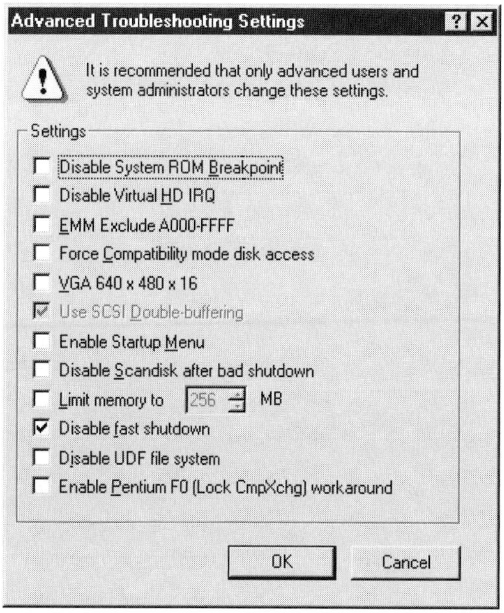

FIGURE 16-11   Disabling UDF support under Windows 98/SE

If you wish to continue using an existing CD-ROM drive as the CD audio drive, you can still use audio from the DVD-ROM drive by using a patch cable to feed the headphone output signal from the drive to the sound card's line in jack. Then adjust the sound card's line in mixer so that you can hear audio from the DVD-ROM headphone. Alternately, you can upgrade the sound card to a model that provides two different CD audio channel inputs.

SYMPTOM 16-8   **The system will not restart to normal mode after DVD-ROM drive installation**   This problem sometimes occurs when installing the DVD on a system with the USB Supplement for Windows 95 (OSR2). You may need to uninstall the USB Supplement or consider an upgrade to Windows 98/Me. Boot into Windows 95 Safe Mode, and open the Add/Remove Programs applet from Control Panel. If the Universal Serial Bus Supplement is listed, highlight it and click the Add/Remove button. This will uninstall the supplement, and you will be prompted to restart the system.

Next, the DVD system's MPEG-2 decoder card should be assigned a unique *interrupt request* (IRQ). Open the System applet from Control Panel, click on the Device Manager tab, and double-click on Computer. Here you'll see a list of IRQs and the name of the device using each IRQ. If the decoder card is not listed (or its IRQ is being shared with any device other than the IRQ holder for PCI steering), assign a unique IRQ to the card. This can usually be accomplished through the BIOS of your computer, or possibly by moving the decoder card to another PCI slot.

Finally, you may need to change the memory range used by the MPEG-2 decoder card. Open the System applet from Control Panel, click on the Device Manager tab, and then double-click on Sound, Video and Game Controllers. Finally, double-click on the MPEG-2 decoder card (Figure 16-12). Click on the Resources tab and remove the check mark next to "Use automatic settings." Finally, double-click on the Memory Range entry and enter **D1000000-D10FFFFF**. Click OK and restart the PC for your changes to take effect.

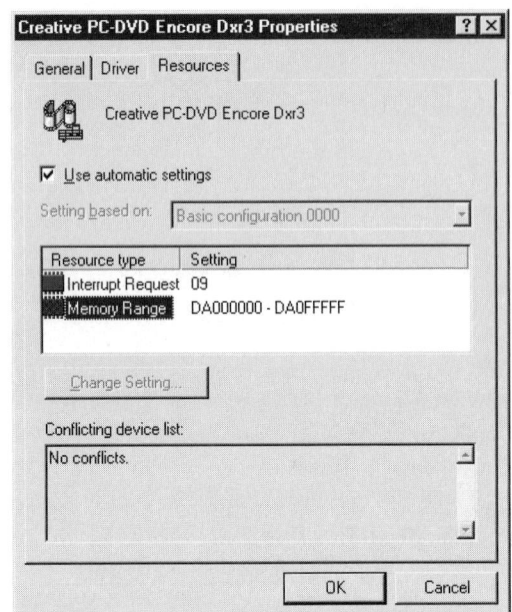

FIGURE 16-12   Adjusting the decoder card's address range under Windows 98/SE

SYMPTOM 16-9   **You experience error messages or system lockups during DVD software installation**   Movies play, but white lines appear randomly on the screen. In virtually all cases, the problem is being caused by an IRQ or memory range conflict. Open the System applet from Control Panel, click on the Device Manager tab, and double-click on Computer. Here you'll see a list of IRQs and the name of the device using each IRQ. If the decoder card is not listed (or its IRQ is being shared with any device other than the IRQ holder for PCI steering), assign a unique IRQ to the card. This can usually be accomplished through the BIOS of your computer, or possibly by moving the decoder card to another PCI slot.

You may need to change the memory range used by the MPEG-2 decoder card. Open the System applet from Control Panel, click on the Device Manager tab, and then double-click on Sound, Video and Game Controllers. Finally, double-click on the MPEG-2 decoder card. Click on the Resources tab, and remove the check mark next to "Use automatic settings." Finally, double-click on the Memory Range entry and enter **D1000000-D10FFFFF**. Click OK and restart for the changes to take effect.

SYMPTOM 16-10   **Your DVD-ROM will not autoconfigure using the automatic configuration utility provided with the drive**   In many cases, this is a problem caused by an unusually high video refresh rate. DVD systems seem to operate best at video refresh rates of 60Hz or so. Try lowering your video refresh rate to 75Hz or lower through the video card's Properties dialog or Display control settings.

SYMPTOM 16-11   **You can play DVD-based games, but the system hangs up when inserting a DVD-Video**   When the system hangs, the video window either stays black, or the DVD logo comes up—and then the machine freezes. This is often a surprisingly simple issue. Frequently setting the video adapter's settings to the default values will correct the problem. Although your current video settings may work wonderfully with static images (even through other player software), the unique demands of your DVD decoder board may cause too much information to be directed at your video card at once. Start with your basic video default settings, and then systematically increase resolution and color depth to an acceptable quality level.

As an alternative, you might try setting the drive letter for the DVD-ROM drive to be the first "CD-ROM" in the system. This is a particularly useful tactic when playing back CD-I and Video CD movies with software (such as Xing), but it also helps the DVD player software utilize the DVD-ROM drive.

SYMPTOM 16-12   **Movies appear bright (then dim) when watching a DVD-Video from the video card's TV output**   This problem only occurs when a VCR is connected between the "TV output" of the video adapter and the TV set. Video display adapters with TV output capability will enable Macrovision copy protection during DVD movie playback. The Macrovision-encoded video signal will effectively prevent a VCR from recording a watchable movie.

If you videotape a Macrovision-encoded movie and then play it back, you'll typically see occasional glimpses of the movie interspersed with 20 to 30 seconds of no picture (or possibly just a blue screen). Even if you're not actually recording, the VCR attempts to compensate for the Macrovision-encoded signal, and this generally leads to the symptom described. To resolve this symptom, simply connect the video card's TV output directly to the TV set using either the "composite" or "S-Video" connections.

Remember that sound connections are completely independent of video connections, and if you wish to hear the DVD movie through the TV set, you will also need to connect the audio output of the PC to the TV set.

SYMPTOM 16-13   **When playing DVD-Video, the image appears distorted (often described as a "spaghetti western")**   This type of issue is often associated with Matrox Millennium or Mystique video cards, but can also occur with other types of video cards. In virtually all cases, the trouble is with your video drivers. They may be old, buggy, or incompatible with the DVD drivers and video player software at work on your system. Download and install the latest video drivers, and try flashing the video card's BIOS (if possible). If the problem persists, disable DirectDraw for Overlays, and resize the screen to the default sizes recommended.

SYMPTOM 16-14   **You cannot resize the movie display to full screen (or select any display size other than the default)**   This is particularly associated with Matrox video cards, but may occur with other video cards. These video cards probably don't support the hardware-based video scaling required for DVD. Try upgrading the video drivers, and flash the video card's BIOS (if possible). Otherwise, you have little alternative except to upgrade the video card or to continue using the smaller screen size.

SYMPTOM 16-15   **You receive a "display overlay not available" error message when launching the DVD player software**   This is a known issue with the ATI DVD player 1.2 software, but similar problems can occur with other players. Chances are that the DVD player software requires additional display adapter memory (beyond what is used by the current display mode). If the current display mode uses most of the display adapter's memory, there's no memory left over for the DVD player, and the error message will occur.

This message is most likely to occur when the display adapter has only 4MB of display memory, and 1152×864 at 32 *bits per pixel* (bpp) is selected as the display mode. This display mode consumes almost 4MB of display memory just to paint the Windows desktop. To resolve this problem, simply select a lower color depth or (lower resolution). For example, if you're running at 32bpp, try 16bpp. This will consume only half as much display memory and should leave an adequate amount for the display overlay and other DVD functions.

If the error message persists after reducing the display resolution (and/or color depth), it may be the result of interference by other video-related processes. Check for "WebTV" or "WaveTop" background tasks. These are normally visible in the task bar. Right-click the icons for these tasks, and select Pause, Suspend, Quit, or Exit to disable them. Then try the DVD player software again.

SYMPTOM 16-16 **You encounter a "card required" error when installing SoftDVD player software** This is a known problem with ATI video cards and Zoran SoftDVD player software (you may see "ATI AGP card required") and is almost always due to inadequate system requirements. The SoftDVD player has several major system requirements:

- An appropriate video card must be present.
- AGP support must be enabled at the operating system level.
- An Intel Pentium II processor (or later) is required.
- Only a 16bpp color depth (65K colors) is supported.
- The sound drivers must be DirectX compliant.

To resolve this problem, ensure that all requirements of the SoftDVD player are met.

SYMPTOM 16-17 **The decoder card is not recognized by Windows Me** When you attempt to use the Windows Me DVD Player, you may receive an error message such as:

```
To use the DVD player, you need to install either a software DVD decoder, or
a hardware DVD decoder.
```

For example, this problem can occur if you use a Sigma Designs Hollywood Plus DVD decoder or a Creative Labs Dxr3 decoder card. In virtually all cases, the current device drivers for the decoder card are not compatible with the Windows DVD Me Player. Contact the manufacturer of your decoder card for any Windows Me device driver updates.

SYMPTOM 16-18 **You cannot restart or resume a DVD movie** When using Microsoft DVD Player under Windows 98/Me, you cannot resume the movie. Some DVD movies require that you use the movie's menu rather than the DVD Player program's menu. Try using the movie's menu displayed in the viewing window while you're playing the DVD movie. You can also try updating the DVD Player software.

SYMPTOM 16-19 **Cinemaster DVD decoding software causes the PC to freeze** When you use a Cinemaster software-based DVD decoder utility with the Windows Me DVD Player, your computer may stop responding. Chances are that an outdated version of the Cinemaster software decoder is installed on your computer. You can generally correct the problem by updating the Cinemaster decoder at **www.qi.com**.

SYMPTOM 16-20 **You cannot change resolutions with DVDExpress software** When you play a DVD under Windows Me using the Mediamatics/Compaq DVDExpress DVD player, you may receive an error message such as:

```
Cdvdplay has caused an error in QDVD.DLL. Cdvdplay will now close.
```

In virtually all cases, the problem is with the DVDExpress software and can generally be corrected by updating the software through the software maker's Web site. You can easily work around this problem by not changing resolutions while the DVDExpress software is running.

SYMPTOM 16-21   **You get "blue screen" errors when ejecting a DVD**   The error occurs when manually ejecting a DVD under Windows Me DVD Player software, and you'll normally see an error message such as:

```
Error Reading CD-ROM in drive X:
```

Not all drives exhibit this behavior, but it is known to occur on the TORiSAN DRD-U424 due to the way that the DVD movie is stopped. Quit the DVD Player software before manually ejecting the DVD movie, or click Eject in the program to eject the DVD.

SYMPTOM 16-22   **You get audible static when playing a DVD movie under Windows Me**   This issue is known to occur when using a Yamaha DS1 WDM driver while playing a DVD movie with WinDVD 2000 or PowerDVD version 2.55. This problem is caused by the Yamaha DS1 WDM driver under Windows Me. Verify the presence of WDM drivers:

1. Click Start, point to Settings, and then click Control Panel.
2. Double-click the System icon.
3. Click the Device Manager tab.
4. Scroll down to the Sound, Video and Game Controllers option, and then expand the entry.

The Yamaha Native DS1 WDM driver is listed when you have the WDM drivers installed. Simply install the Yamaha VXD drivers from the original manufacturer, or download the generic driver from Yamaha's Web site at **www.yamaha.com/lsi/dindex.htm**.

SYMPTOM 16-23   **A hardware DVD decoder doesn't handle zoom functions**   This is a known issue when using a Creative Dxr2 decoder card under Windows Me. If you have the Creative WDM drivers installed for the Creative Dxr2 DVD decoder card, you cannot use the Zoom In/Out command while playing a DVD title using Microsoft's DVD Player. This is almost always an issue with the Creative Dxr2 DVD decoder, so check the Creative Labs Web site (**www.creaf.com**) for driver updates.

SYMPTOM 16-24   **The DVD-ROM reads data as audio tracks**   You're not able to run an application or a DVD movie from the CD or DVD. This is an issue with drives such as the Pioneer DVD-303R under Windows Me. In virtually all cases, the trouble is due to incorrect jumper settings on the DVD drive itself. Verify the jumper settings on the DVD drive. For example, set the DVD drive byte setting at 2048 instead of 512.

SYMPTOM 16-25   **You cannot change the size of a DVD playback window**   When you run the Windows Me DVD Player utility in a window and right-click the DVD icon on the task bar, the Size command is unavailable. This is an issue with Windows Me. To adjust the size of the DVD Player window, use the mouse pointer to drag the window borders to the size that you want, or click the DVD icon in DVD Player, and then click Size.

SYMPTOM 16-26   **You get pink lines when switching from DVD Player to a full-screen MS-DOS session under Windows Me**   For example, if you press ALT-TAB to switch between a DVD movie and a full-screen MS-DOS session, you may see pink lines on both sides in DVD Player. This problem is known to occur if you're using a Cinemaster DVD hardware decoder and an ATI Rage Pro video adapter. This is a problem with Windows Me. To avoid this problem, do not switch between DVD movies and a full-screen MS-DOS session, or exit your DVD player software before using DOS sessions.

SYMPTOM 16-27   **The DVD motorized tray won't open or close**   The most common issue here is the DVD application itself. Some DVD applications (such as DVD-Video player applications) will lock the disc tray closed while a video DVD disc is playing. Try closing all open applications. If the tray still won't open, try restarting the PC. This should clear any software lock. If the tray still refuses to open or close, the drive itself may be defective. You can force the tray open using a straightened paper clip in the emergency-eject hole in the front of the drive.

SYMPTOM 16-28   **There is no DVD audio while playing a movie or other multimedia presentation**   Here's another common oversight during new DVD installations. Check the external audio cable attached between the MPEG-2 decoder board and the line in jack of your sound board. The cable may be plugged into the wrong jack(s), or the cable may simply be defective. Also check the sound board's mixer applet, and see that the line in volume control setting is turned up to an acceptable level. If you're connecting the DVD-ROM's CD audio cable to the sound card, verify that the cable is attached securely, and see that the cable is compatible with the drive and the sound card.

SYMPTOM 16-29   **Video quality appears poor**   MPEG-2 compression is well respected for its ability to reproduce high-quality images. The problem of poor image quality is almost always because of your video configuration. Your color depth or resolution is too low. DVD-Video playback is best at resolutions of 800×600 or higher, and color depths of 16-bits (High Color) or higher (for example, 24-bit True Color). In most cases, 256 colors will result in a dithered image.

SYMPTOM 16-30   **The video image is distorted when trying to play an MPEG file**   Other video operations probably seem fine. A full or partially distorted MPEG image can be the result of two problems. First, the video connections on the back of the card could be loose. Verify that all connections to the MPEG-2 decoder card are secure. Another common cause of distorted playbacks is that the refresh rate on your video card is set too high. It is recommended that the video refresh rate be kept *below* 85Hz when running MPEG files. Try adjusting the vertical refresh rate to 72Hz, or even 60Hz.

SYMPTOM 16-31   **The picture is beginning to occasionally pixelize or "break apart"**   The audio may also seem periodically distorted. It is highly likely that the DVD disc needs to be cleaned. Clean the DVD disc properly and try it again, or try another disc. Also try closing any unused applications running in the background. If the problem persists with another DVD disc as well (and both discs are in good condition), try reinitializing the drive by powering down and rebooting the system. If the problem still persists, the internal optics of the DVD-ROM drive may need to be cleaned with a bit of photography-grade compressed air. Otherwise, try replacing the DVD-ROM drive.

SYMPTOM 16-32   **You notice the DVD-ROM light flashing regularly without a disc inserted**   System performance may be reduced. This is often because the DVD-ROM drive's properties are set for "Auto insert notification" under Windows 9x/Me. Start the Device Manager, highlight the DVD-ROM drive, and click the Properties button. You'll see the DVD-ROM Properties dialog. In the Options area of the Properties dialog, locate the "Auto insert notification" check box and uncheck it. Save your changes. (You might need to reboot the system.) This should stop the drive's constant checking for a disc.

SYMPTOM 16-33   The DVD drive's "busy" indicator flashes slowly once a disc is inserted   The drive is not recognizing the disc. In most cases, the disc is simply dirty. Try cleaning the disc in a radial motion (from the hub to the edge, like the spokes of a wheel). Try another disc. If the drive cannot recognize other discs, the drive's optical reader may be dirty. Try using a can of photography-grade compressed air to clean any accumulations of dust from the drive. If the drive's "busy" indicator is on all the time (and doesn't recognize any discs), the drive may be defective.

SYMPTOM 16-34   You see an error message that says "Disk playback unauthorized" The region code on the DVD disc does not match the code embedded into the drive. There isn't much that can be done when this error occurs. Note that region code limitations are only applied to DVD-Video movie releases. Programs and data discs are generally not marked with region codes.

SYMPTOM 16-35   You receive an "authentication error" when playing DVD movies with a Zoran SoftDVD player   The error suggests that the region code for the DVD disc is not supported by the player software. This problem normally occurs when the DVD disc is designed for a different region than the player being used. For example, the error message would appear when attempting to play a "region 2" DVD disc on a "region 1" version of SoftDVD software. However, there are rare reports of this error occurring in situations where the DVD region codes are correct. The following suggestions may help to correct region problems with the Zoran SoftDVD player:

■ Ensure that the DVD title being played is designed for the appropriate region. Today, the SoftDVD player is designed for the playback of region 1 DVD titles. You may need to upgrade the player software.

■ If you're using SoftDVD with a SCSI DVD drive, ensure that the most recent ASPI driver is installed for the SCSI controller.

■ Panasonic A01 F/W 1.12 DVD drives will yield authentication errors when attempting to play DVDs with Zoran SoftDVD software. This appears to be an issue with the DVD drive itself, and no solution exists with that specific drive.

■ Toshiba SM-M1002 DVD drives using a firmware version prior to 3426 should be updated to the current firmware revision.

■ For Matsushita SR-852 DVD drives, the following DVD-ROM driver files should be used: MKEATAPI.MPD and MKEVSD.VXD (on the SR-8582 installation disc) MKEUPD.VXD (on the SR-8581 installation disc)

SYMPTOM 16-36   You get an error message when inserting a DVD movie   This is known to occur with Cinemaster WDM DVD drive software under Windows 98/Me. When you insert a DVD movie, you may receive an error message such as:

```
The software DVD isn't supported, you need to install the proper decoder.
```

If you check the Device Manager, you may notice an exclamation point (!) next to the drive (such as the "Cinemaster C WDM DVD drive"), and it may display a status of Code 28. This can occur if the PnP OS setting in the computer's CMOS Setup is set to yes. Change the PnP OS setting in the CMOS Setup to No. Reinstall the DVD drivers:

1.   Click Start, highlight Settings, click Control Panel, and then double-click the System icon.

2. Click the Device Manager tab, double-click the DVD branch to expand it, click the drive (such as "Cinemaster C WDM DVD drive"), and then click Properties.

3. On the Driver tab, click Update Driver, click Next, click "Search for a better driver than the one your device is using now," and then click Next.

4. Insert your Windows CD, click to select the "Specify a location" check box, type the path to your DVD-ROM drive, and then click Next.

5. Click Next, click Finish, and then click Close.

SYMPTOM 16-37 **The display turns magenta (red) when attempting to adjust the DVD video overlay feature** When adjusting the video overlay, you may have some trouble finding the video window. It often helps to change your background to magenta so you can see where the video window is. To do this, right-click on your background, and select Properties. Select the Background tab and select "none" as both the Pattern and the Wallpaper. Then select the Appearance tab, and select Magenta as the color of the desktop. Click OK to finish changing your background color to magenta. It should now be easier to locate the video window while adjusting the overlay.

SYMPTOM 16-38 **The DVD drive cannot read CD-R or Photo CD discs** This is not an error—most first-generation DVD drives will not read CD recordable or Photo CD (Kodak) discs. In some cases, it is even possible to damage CD recordable discs due to the laser wavelength and energy used in the DVD drive. Do not attempt to read CD-R or Photo CD discs in the DVD unless the drive specifications specifically state that the drive is compatible with those types of discs. Chances are that you'll need to update the older DVD drive's firmware (or replace the DVD drive completely) to correct the problem.

SYMPTOM 16-39 **You experience difficulties with a particular DVD movie title even though others play normally** If most movies play normally, chances are that the problem movie is an older edition (version). Some older DVD-ROM movie releases contained mastering problems that cause playback errors. Try exchanging the movie for a later edition. If the problem persists (or you cannot play most movies properly), you may need updated DVD-ROM drivers. Download the latest drivers from the DVD manufacturer's Web site and install them. The following instructions explain a driver upgrade for a Creative Labs DVD-ROM drive:

1. Create a directory called DVDNEW in the root directory of the boot drive.

2. Download file DVDEW95.EXE into this directory.

3. Click on Start, Programs, and select MS-DOS Prompt.

4. Change to the DVDNEW directory you created (for example, C:\DVDNEW), and then type **DVDEW95 -D** and press ENTER.

5. The file will extract and create a SETUP subdirectory within C:\DVDNEW.

6. Follow the instructions in the README.1ST file to install the new drivers and programs.

SYMPTOM 16-40 **You experience difficulties with the DVD software's Parental Control feature** The Parental Control is not working properly or is causing user problems. This is often because the Parental Control feature is not working properly in the DVD software, and you'll need to uninstall and reinstall the DVD software to disable Parental Control.

First, uninstall the DVD software. To do this, open the Add/Remove Programs applet from Control Panel. Highlight the particular DVD software (such as Encore software) and click on Add/Remove. After the uninstall is complete, reinstall the software choosing the option for a custom install. Make sure there is not a check mark next to "Parental Control" in the select list. This will reinstall the software without the Parental Control feature. A later release of the DVD software (or a patch) may address this problem and allow you to resume using the Parental Control feature.

SYMPTOM 16-41   **When playing some DVD-Video titles, you encounter a "blue screen" error that mentions Parental Control**   You notice the Parental Control feature is set to "kids" and will not retain any other settings. The problem is outdated Ravisent driver/player software. This issue has been corrected in the Ravisent driver/player software released after December 23, 1997. You must go to Ravisent's Web site (**www.qi.com/**), and then download the latest player and the drivers from the "S Series 2.x" Cinemaster section.

These drivers are only for the S Series 2.3 version of the card. If you have the 2.2 version of the card, use the links that point to the last updates for the 2.2 cards.

SYMPTOM 16-42   **Your screen saver turns on while playing a DVD title**   Since a screen saver is activated after some period of inactivity, leaving the keyboard/mouse untouched while watching a DVD movie can allow the screen saver to activate. Screen savers do not check for the presence of DVD activity, so you'll need to disable the screen saver (through the Display icon in the Control Panel) before using the DVD-ROM drive to watch movies.

SYMPTOM 16-43   **You notice a reddish tint when playing movies with the DVD-ROM drive**   This is typically an end-user issue that can easily be corrected by reducing contrast or by adjusting the tint setting through the DVD player application software.

SYMPTOM 16-44   **You find that MPEG-1 files play back fine on your DVD player software, but there is no sound**   However, MPEG-2 files and DVD-Video (movies) play back correctly with sound. This is generally a problem with the DVD player software that may require a patch or upgrade. (Check with the player software's manufacturer.) As a temporary work-around, use a generic MPEG file player (such as Windows Media Player) to run MPEG-1 files until the DVD player can be upgraded or replaced.

SYMPTOM 16-45   **You cannot play a DVD or CD in the DVD drive, or certain types of discs cannot be read in the drive**   There are many possible (often simple) issues that can prevent a disc from playing in an optical drive. First, the disc may be placed upside-down in the disc tray, or the disc may be dirty. Recheck the disc orientation, and clean the disc if necessary. If the disc is warped or seriously damaged, it may need to be replaced.

The drive's optical reader may be dirty. This can happen on older drives, or drives that are operated in dusty/dirty environments. Use a can of photography-grade compressed air to gently blow dust out of the drive. Finally, DVD movie discs are released with a region code that must correspond to the code contained in the drive. If the codes are different, the DVD disc will not play. You may need to obtain a disc with the correct region code.

SYMPTOM 16-46   **When attempting to play a disc, you receive a message such as "Disc does not contain DVD-Video data"**   DVD player software cannot find the title track and/or information files on the disc. If you're trying to use a DVD disc, the disc may be scratched or damaged. Clean the disc if possible, or replace the damaged disc. If you're simply trying to play MPEG video from an ordinary CD, click OK to close the error dialog. The disc may still play.

SYMPTOM 16-47   **You receive an error message such as "Unable to locate DVD-ROM drive—assume drive D:—Error1"**   The DVD drive may not have been properly configured by Windows 9x/Me or may be disconnected. Verify that the DVD drive is jumpered properly, and see that its power and signal cables are oriented and secured. Try another signal cable if necessary, or try the DVD drive as the only device on the drive controller. Reboot the PC from a cold start, and see if Windows will redetect the DVD drive. If not, run the Windows 9x/Me Add New Hardware wizard to "force" Windows to detect the hardware. If the Add New Hardware wizard fails to detect the DVD drive, you may need to specify the drive make and model manually. In all cases, be sure to have the latest DVD drivers on hand.

SYMPTOM 16-48   **During the DVD video configuration process, you receive an error such as "Auto Alignment failed"**   This error almost always suggests that the hardware MPEG-2 decoder card cable may not be properly connected. Check the cable connection on the hardware decoder card (particularly "VGA In" and "VGA Out"), and see that the cable is secure. Try another cable if possible. Start the DVD player software, press the Settings button, and select Video Configuration. Press the Auto button to have the video automatically configured.

SYMPTOM 16-49   **After connecting an MPEG-2 decoder card, the video image seems blue (or contains a blue tint)**   This is generally due to the improper connection or setup of the MPEG-2 card. The VGA loopback cable between the video card and the MPEG-2 decoder card is not connected correctly. Check the loopback cable, and try reseating the connector if possible. DVD video alignment may not be set correctly. Open the Video Configuration utility and set the video alignment. Try using the Auto feature to automatically configure the video. If automatic configuration does not work, try making minor adjustments manually.

Your color key value may not be set correctly. Change the color scheme of your Windows 9x/Me desktop. Right-click on the Windows 9x/Me desktop and click Properties. In the Display Properties dialog, click the Appearance tab. Then select Desktop in the Item list, and select a different color scheme from the list. Click OK to accept the changes.

SYMPTOM 16-50   **The DVD-ROM drive cannot play a DVD disc, or certain other types of disc media (such as CD-plus)**   There are several possible issues that might cause this type of problem. First, make sure that the entire suite of drivers has been installed for your drive. Check for the latest drivers and download any available patches or updates. You also may not have the correct player software for your drive, so make sure to download and install the latest version of your player software. Also verify that the DVD disc is the correct format for the type of system that you're using. For example, a PC should use an ISO9660-compatible format, rather than an Apple/Mac HFS disc or UNIX disc format. Finally, your DVD drivers/software may have been corrupted by a virus. Run a virus scan program, and then remove/reinstall any damaged software.

SYMPTOM 16-51   **After upgrading the video card, DVD movies will not play**   Chances are that your new video card is neither defective nor incompatible. Instead, the problem is that the link(s) between your video and DVD drivers have been broken. When new video cards are installed, they change entries in the Registry that associate MPEG playback with video card drivers. The new video card's MPEG drivers are probably not DVD compliant, but since they took precedence over the MPEG drivers of the older DVD system, this is likely to be the problem. Try reinstalling the video card from scratch, and then reinstall the DVD drivers and software. This should reinstall the proper DVD MPEG-ready drivers and correct the problem.

SYMPTOM 16-52   **DVD-Video movies will play only on the primary monitor** When using DVD player software installed in a multimonitor Windows 98/Me system, DVD movies will only play on the primary monitor. If the DVD player window is moved to the secondary monitor, no picture appears. This is a limitation of secondary displays under Windows 98/Me. The primary display has a full complement of 3D and video acceleration features, but a secondary display does not. To correct this problem, move the DVD player window back to the primary monitor.

SYMPTOM 16-53   **Windows 98/Me halts or reboots when running a software DVD player designed for Windows 95** This is an issue most frequently associated with the Zoran SoftDVD player, but may occur with other software products. In most cases, the system halts immediately after the Play button is clicked, but this may also occur at other points within the player software. In some instances, the system may reboot or report an "Unrecoverable Application Error." Generally, the SoftDVD player may successfully play a single DVD movie or file, and then report an error (such as "your computer is not configured to start DVD") when attempting to play a second movie. Chances are that the subtle design changes between Windows 95 and Windows 98/Me are causing a problem with the player software (tailored for Windows 95). Try the following:

- Remove and reinstall the DVD player application.
- Check to see if a patch or update is available for your DVD player.
- Experiment with different video resolutions, color depths, and refresh rates.
- Try an alternate or updated video driver.

SYMPTOM 16-54   **Even when a DVD system is properly configured under Windows 95, you get no sound from the speakers** This is almost always due to an old (original) release of Windows 95. The use of old Windows 95 drivers was corrected in Windows 95 OSR2 and is not an issue with Windows 98/Me. If you cannot upgrade your operating system to Windows 95 OSR2 or Windows 98/Me, check with the DVD package manufacturer for updated drivers and patches that might correct the problem. Keep in mind that the DVD drive will still read data DVD discs and other CDs properly.

SYMPTOM 16-55   **You receive a "media error" when using Windows Explorer to eject a DVD movie** This issue has been reported with Toshiba DVD players. When you use Windows Explorer to eject a DVD movie that is currently being played by a Toshiba DVD player, you receive the following "blue screen" error message:

```
Re-insert the media and press any key to continue.
```

When you insert the DVD movie back into the player and press a key, you may receive the same error message (and the movie may be automatically ejected). This problem may occur if you press a key before the DVD movie is fully spun up. To resolve the problem, insert the DVD movie into the player, but wait to press a key until the light on the Toshiba DVD player is turned off. This indicates that the DVD movie is fully spun up.

SYMPTOM 16-56   **You cannot capture a DVD video image with the PRINTSCREEN key under Windows 98/Me** If you try to capture a still image of a DVD movie with the PRINTSCREEN key, and then paste the image into a program, only a blue or black box may be pasted into the program. This is the normal design of your DVD system. The DVD data stream is decoded by the DVD decoder card, and then redirected back to the video adapter. When the computer uses an external patch cable, the video stream is sent from the video adapter to the DVD decoder card, and then directly to the monitor as an "overlay." This is done to improve the playback performance of DVD video by bypassing slower portions of the computer. Since the DVD data stream does not pass through the Windows API layer, the video output cannot be captured, and you only capture the playback area in which the movie is displayed.

SYMPTOM 16-57   You encounter problems when using a SoftDVD player in Windows 98/Me   When you view a DVD movie using the SoftDVD player program included with some computers, you may experience various playback problems. In most cases, you can correct these types of problems by modifying the player's INI file:

1. Click Start, select Find, and then click Files or Folders.
2. In the Named box, type **SOFTDVD.INI** and then click Find Now.
3. In the list of "found files," double-click the SOFTDVD.INI file.
4. Type the following lines in the SOFTDVD.INI file:

    ```
    [dvdfs]
    AlignedAccess=0
    ```

 Be sure to insert a blank line above and below these two lines.

5. In the File menu, click Save, and then click Exit.
6. Restart your computer when prompted to do so.

SYMPTOM 16-58   The screen appears clipped when playing a DVD movie   This is a known issue when using Cinemaster 1.2 drivers under Windows 98/Me. Both sides of the screen may appear "clipped." This is caused by an aspect ratio bug in the DVD player software. You'll need to contact Microsoft or the maker of your DVD player software to obtain the correct patch or software update for your DVD player. For example, Microsoft offers an update for the DVDPLAY.EXE file (09/29/98, 9:43a, 125,440 bytes), which should correct this aspect ratio problem. Keep in mind that you may also need to update your DirectX components (for example, DirectX 8.0a) before updating the DVD player software.

SYMPTOM 16-59   You encounter problems with the DVD/TV tuner unit after upgrading Windows   After you upgrade a Toshiba Infinia 72xx laptop PC to Windows 98/Me, a yellow exclamation point may be displayed next to the DVD/TV Tuner device in the Device Manager. Your DVD/TV Tuner device may not work correctly (if at all). This problem can occur if your computer is configured to use the Toshiba TV/FM version 2.13B2 device driver. This driver is not totally compatible with Windows 98/Me. Contact Toshiba to obtain an upgraded driver for your PC.

SYMPTOM 16-60   A Creative Labs DXR2 DVD drive will not work under Windows 98/Me   After upgrading your computer to Windows 98/Me, your Creative Labs Encore DXR2 DVD drive may no longer work correctly. This problem occurs because the Windows setup process updates the DLL files used by the DVD drive. Those new files may not be compatible with the Creative Labs DXR2. There are two methods of correcting the problem.

First, contact Creative Labs to obtain updated drivers designed specifically for Windows 98/Me. You can download drivers from Creative Labs at **www.creaf.com/pcdvd/support/drivers/**. You can also try renaming WINASPI.DLL, WNASPI32.DLL, and APIX.VXD, and then extract new copies of WINASPI.DLL, WNASPI32.DLL, and APIX.VXD from your original Windows 98/Me CD. Under Windows 98, the WINASPI.DLL and WNASPI32.DLL files are in the WIN98_40.CAB file, and the APIX.VXD file is in the WIN98_47.CAB file.

SYMPTOM 16-61 **Windows 98 may lock up if the DVD drive tray is left open at boot time** If your portable computer includes a DVD drive, and the nonmotorized drive tray is left open during and after the Windows 98 startup, you may find that Windows 98 locks up several minutes after Windows is started. This problem is known to occur with the Toshiba Tecra 8000 DVD under Windows 98 and is usually caused because the DVD drive or CD-ROM drive supports *Media Event Status Notification* (MESN) according to the PC98 specification. Since those portable drives have nonmotorized trays, the trays are not closed automatically when Windows boots, so Windows fails because of false reporting from the MESN feature.

First, close the drive tray while Windows is starting (or within one minute after it starts). You should generally keep the DVD drive or CD-ROM drive tray closed—except when you're inserting or removing discs. This policy also reduces the risk of drive problems due to dust buildup (or damage from striking the opened tray). Another option is to disable DMA support for the DVD drive or CD-ROM drive:

1. Click Start, highlight Settings, and then click Control Panel.
2. Double-click the System icon, and then click the Device Manager tab.
3. Click the CD-ROM branch to expand it, click your CD-ROM drive or DVD drive, and then click Properties.
4. Click the Settings tab.
5. Click the DMA check box to clear it, and then click OK.
6. Click OK, and then restart your computer when prompted to do so.

Finally, you can try disabling the auto insert notification feature for the DVD drive or CD-ROM drive:

1. Click Start, highlight Settings, and then click Control Panel.
2. Double-click the System icon, and then click the Device Manager tab.
3. Click the CD-ROM branch to expand it, click your CD-ROM drive or DVD drive, and then click Properties.
4. Click the Settings tab.
5. Click the Auto Insert Notification check box to clear it, and then click OK.
6. Click OK, and then restart your computer when prompted to do so.

For more information on Media Event Status Notification (MESN), review the SFF8090 (a.k.a. Mt. Fuji) specification available from **ftp://fission.dt.wdc.com/pub/standards/SFF/specs/**.

SYMPTOM 16-62 **You receive a "fatal exception in CDVSD" when starting Windows 98** When starting the computer, you encounter the following "blue screen" error message:

```
An exception 0E has occurred at 0028:C143EADA in VXD CDVSD(01) + 00001CFA. This
was called from 0028:C18413E8 in VXD voltrack(04)+ 00000A18. It may be possible
to continue normally.
```

This problem is reported to occur with the Agate Technologies AGAATAPI.MPD and Intel IDEATAPI.MPD miniport drivers, and can generally occur if a disc is not in the DVD drive (or when a disc is ejected from the DVD drive) while you're using a third-party SCSI miniport driver. An incorrect communication method is used when an IOS "VSD" is installed between the CDVSD and SCSIPORT layers, and the DVD drive supports Group 2 timeout commands. Check with Microsoft (or your DVD drive maker) to see if an updated version of CDVSD.VXD is available.

Further Study

Creative Labs www.creaf.com
Diamond Multimedia www.diamondmm.com
DVD Forum www.dvdforum.org
Hitachi www.hitachi.com
Matsushita www.panasonic.com/office/storage/stor.html
Panasonic www.panasonic.com
Toshiba www.toshiba.com/taecdpd/

17

ENHANCING SYSTEM PERFORMANCE

PC users receive the best return on their system investment when it's operating at peak efficiency. However, new hardware isn't always the answer. Even with state-of-the-art hardware, there are many important operating system and setup factors that will affect the performance of a system. Swap file problems, inadequate memory, and poor system settings are just a few of the issues that can reduce the system's effectiveness. This chapter is intended to help you identify the key performance areas of a typical Windows 98/Me PC and offers a set of handy guidelines that will help you get the most from a system.

Checking Performance Under Windows 98/Me

The first step in improving your system's performance is to investigate the current performance level of your system. If you're using Windows 98/Me, you can get an overview of the system's performance through the System Properties dialog. This will give you a broad overview of the system's key resources and the way in which Windows perceives them. You can access this dialog through the System icon:

1. Click Start, highlight Settings, and then click Control Panel.

2. Once the Control Panel opens, double-click the System icon.

3. Click the Performance tab (Figure 17-1).

UNDERSTANDING THE RESOURCES

The Performance tab will list six major parameters that will affect your system performance. You should understand how to interpret each of these settings:

■ **Memory** This specifies the amount of physical memory (RAM) in your computer that's recognized by Windows. If this value is less than the amount reported by BIOS during the POST memory count, you may have a problem with the way Windows recognizes or handles your RAM. This is also a quick way to tell how much RAM is in your customer's system. At a minimum, there should be enough RAM to properly support the operating system installed.

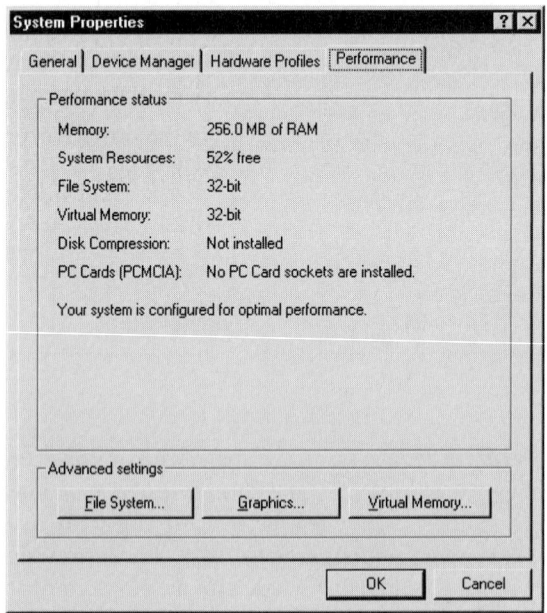

FIGURE 17-1   Getting an overview of the system through the System Properties dialog

- **System Resources**   This indicates the percentage of free system resources (generally taken to mean "free RAM"). If this number is too low, your computer may perform slowly due to excessive use of virtual memory. You can correct this by closing unused background applications, or by adding more RAM to the system. A system that has too little RAM may perform poorly due to extensive disk swapping.

- **File System**   This entry specifies the type of file system that you're using (for example, MS-DOS or 32-bit), and this will affect the efficiency with which files are read from or written to your system drives. Your disk's performance will be slower if you're using the DOS Compatibility Mode, and this may mean that there's one or more drives in the system that are using the incorrect drivers, or are configured improperly. Windows will perform best using the 32-bit file system.

- **Virtual Memory**   Virtual memory is hard disk space that is used as extra RAM. This entry indicates whether virtual memory is enabled (using 32-bit or DOS Compatibility Mode) or disabled. If virtual memory is enabled in the DOS Compatibility Mode, the disk being used for virtual memory is also using that mode. The same is true for the 32-bit virtual memory mode. A disk using DOS Compatibility Mode is slower than a disk using 32-bit mode, and system performance will suffer accordingly.

- **Disk Compression**   This specifies whether you've installed any disk compression software on your computer (for example, DriveSpace 3). If not, the entry will state "Not installed." If you do use compression software, the 32-bit version will yield optimal performance. Real-mode (DOS Compatibility Mode) compression software will run more slowly and impair overall system performance.

- **PC Cards (PCMCIA)**   This entry indicates if you have a PC (a.k.a. PCMCIA) card slot enabled and is most commonly used with laptop systems. If there are no socket services installed, the entry will note "No PC Card sockets are installed." Otherwise, the entry will list either 32-bit software (for optimum performance) or DOS Compatibility Mode (real-mode) software. With 32-bit Windows PC Card support, you can insert and remove PC Cards while your computer is running.

Ideally, your system should offer ample memory and utilize 32-bit protected-mode drivers for all of the features installed on your system. This will generally offer the best overall performance, and the system will typically display a message such as "Your system is configured for optimal performance" below the PC Cards entry (such as in Figure 17-1). If you're missing a protected-mode driver, or there's a device installed in the system that Windows doesn't recognize, it will almost always "fall back" to suitable real-mode (DOS Compatibility Mode) drivers instead. If your computer's performance status is not optimal, a description of the performance problem(s) will appear below the PC Cards line. For more information on a given problem, click an item, and then click Details.

System Monitor and Performance

System Monitor is a Windows tool that measures the performance of hardware, software services, and applications. (The version included with Windows 98/Me will also log performance over time.) When you make changes to the system configuration, System Monitor shows the effect of your changes on overall system performance. This offers you a powerful tool that can help determine the effect of system upgrades, or help find the cause of problems on a local or remote computer. For example, logging memory allocation while using a specific application could be helpful in detecting programs with memory leaks or unexpected processing overhead. As another example, you could measure system performance before making a configuration change, and changes in performance may help you identify performance bottlenecks.

INSTALLING SYSTEM MONITOR

If System Monitor is not currently installed on your system, you may easily install System Monitor using the Add/Remove Programs wizard, as shown next:

1. Click Start, highlight Settings, and then click Control Panel.

2. Once the Control Panel is open, select the Add/Remove Programs icon.

3. Click the Windows Setup tab.

4. Select System Tools, and then click Details.

5. Click System Monitor, and then click OK (Figure 17-2). This will install System Monitor on your system. If Windows CAB files are not installed on your system, you may need the Windows installation CD to install System Monitor.

USING SYSTEM MONITOR

System Monitor is considered to be a diagnostic tool and is normally not installed under Windows 98. Fortunately, it's very easy to install. Before attempting to install it, check to see if it's already on your system:

1. Click Start, highlight Programs, and click Accessories.

2. Select System Tools.

3. If System Monitor is installed, it will appear near the bottom of the System Tools menu. If it's present, you can start System Monitor simply by clicking on the menu entry.

4. By default, the System Monitor display appears as shown in Figure 17-3, and the charting will start automatically.

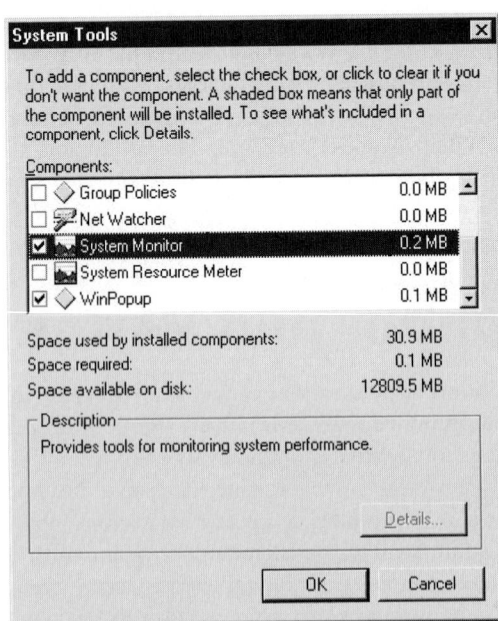

FIGURE 17-2   Installing System Monitor

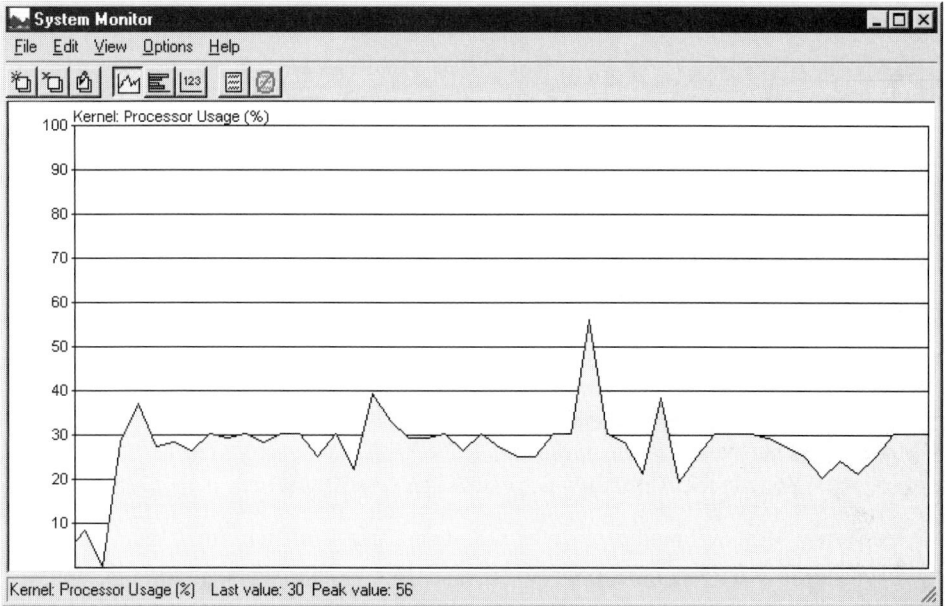

FIGURE 17-3   Starting System Monitor in its default mode

Adjusting the Chart Format

By default, System Monitor uses a "strip-chart" format (as in Figure 17-3), but it also offers bar charts or numeric charts, depending on how you'd prefer to view the information. Once System Monitor is running, you can click View, then select the desired chart format. There are also shortcut buttons below the main menu.

Adjusting the Chart Appearance

You can control the color and update frequency under System Monitor. To adjust a color, click Edit, and then select Edit Item. Choose the item you want to adjust, and the Chart Options dialog will appear. For example, you can change the color and scale of Kernel Processor Usage in Figure 17-4. If you need to adjust the update frequency, click the Options menu, click Chart, and adjust the update slider accordingly.

Logging System Performance

System Monitor offers the capability to log any of the parameters that it's measuring. You can then use the log information to analyze performance issues later on. To begin a logging session:

1. Start System Monitor (if it's not already running).

2. Click File, and then select Start Logging.

3. Enter a file name for the log file, and then click Save.

4. On the File menu, click Stop Logging to halt the log process.

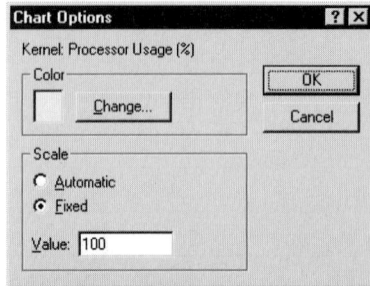

FIGURE 17-4   Adjusting chart characteristics

Configuring System Monitor

System Monitor uses the dynamic data information in the Windows registry to report on the state of many different processes. You can select exactly which of those processes must be displayed in System Monitor:

1. With System Monitor running, click the Edit menu, and then click Add Item.

2. In the Category list, click the resource that you want to monitor. System Monitor will work with seven major categories, which are outlined in Table 17-1.

3. In the Item list, select one or more resources that you want to monitor.

4. When you've selected an item, you may click Explain for more information about a selected resource.

5. Click OK. You'll see the performance chart of that resource added to System Monitor.

6. If you wish to remove an item later, simply click Edit, select Remove Item, highlight the item to be removed, and then click OK.

TABLE 17-1   SYSTEM MONITOR PARAMETERS

DIAL-UP ADAPTER SETTINGS

Setting	Measurement
Alignment errors	Serial port alignment errors.
Buffer overruns	Serial port buffer overrun errors.
Bytes received/second	Number of bytes received per second.
Bytes transmitted/second	Number of bytes transmitted per second.
Connection speed	Connection speed in bits per second.
CRC errors	Number of frames with CRC errors.
Frames received/second	Number of good frames received per second.
Frames transmitted/second	Number of frames transmitted per second.
Framing errors	Serial port framing errors.
Incomplete frames	Number of incomplete frames received.
Overrun errors	Serial port overrun errors.
Timeout errors	Serial port timeout errors.

TABLE 17-1   SYSTEM MONITOR PARAMETERS *(CONTINUED)*

DIAL-UP ADAPTER SETTINGS

Total bytes received	Total number of bytes received.
Total bytes transmitted	Total number of bytes transmitted.

DISK CACHE SETTINGS

Setting	Measurement
Cache buffers	Number of active buffers in a cache, including any and all compressed buffers.
Cache hits	Number of times data found in the cache, resulting in I/O requests.
Cache misses	Number of times data not found in the cache, resulting in I/O requests.
Cache pages	Current number of disk cache pages.
Failed cache recycles	Number of times a recycling request (either least recently used [LRU] or random) has failed. This can happen in low memory situations or when all cache buffers are currently in use.
LRU cache recycles	Number of times the cache is sequentially searched for a buffer to recycle, beginning with the oldest data. This happens when new data needs to be added to the cache, or when memory manager needs to borrow memory from the cache.
Maximum cache pages	Maximum number of disk cache pages.
Minimum cache pages	Minimum number of disk cache pages.
Random cache recycles	Number of times the cache is randomly searched for a buffer to recycle. This can happen whenever the cache becomes filled with data not used lately.

FILE SYSTEM SETTINGS

Setting	Measurement
Bytes read/second	The number of bytes read from the file system each second.
Bytes written/second	The number of bytes written by the file system each second.
Dirty data	The number of bytes waiting to be written to the disk. Dirty data is stored in cache blocks, so the number reported might be larger than the actual number of bytes waiting.
Reads/second	The number of read operations delivered to the file system each second.
Writes/second	The number of write operations delivered to the file system each second.

KERNEL SETTINGS

Setting	Measurement
Processor usage (%)	The approximate percentage of time the processor is busy.
Threads	The current number of threads present in the system.
Virtual machines	The current number of virtual machines present in the system.

MEMORY MANAGER VMM32 SETTINGS

Setting	Measurement
Allocated memory	The total amount in bytes of other memory and swappable memory. If this value is changing when there is no activity on the computer, it indicates that the disk cache is resizing itself.
Discards	The number of pages discarded from memory each second. (The pages are not swapped to the disk because the information is already on the disk.)
Disk cache size	The current size, in bytes, of the disk cache.
Instance faults	The number of instance faults each second.
Locked memory	The amount of allocated memory that is locked.
Locked non-cache pages	Number of non-cache locked pages.

TABLE 17-1   SYSTEM MONITOR PARAMETERS (CONTINUED)

MEMORY MANAGER VMM32 SETTINGS

Setting	Measurement
Maximum disk cache size	The largest size possible for a disk cache. This is a fixed value loaded at system startup.
Mid-disk cache size	The mid-disk cache size. This is a fixed value loaded at system startup.
Minimum disk cache size	The smallest size possible for a disk cache. This is a fixed value loaded at system startup.
Other memory	The amount of allocated memory not stored in the swap file, for example, code from Win32 *dynamic link libraries* (DLLs) and executable files, memory mapped files, nonpageable memory, and disk cache pages.
Page faults	The number of page faults each second.
Page-ins	The number of pages swapped into memory each second, including pages loaded from a Win32-based executable file or memory-mapped files. This value does not necessarily indicate low memory.
Page-outs	The number of pages swapped out of memory and written to disk each second.
Pages mapped from cache	Used to monitor MapCache/WinAlign changes. The swap file size in use at the same time as this setting should be monitored for differences after running the WinAlign tool.
Swap file defective	The number of bytes in the swap file that are found to be physically defective on the swap medium. Because swap file frames are allocated in 4096-byte blocks, a single damaged sector causes the whole block to be marked as defective.
Swap file in use	The number of bytes being used in the current swap file.
Swap file size	The size, in bytes, of the current swap file.
Swappable memory	The number of bytes allocated from the swap file. Locked pages still count for the purpose of this value. This includes code from 16-bit applications and DLLs, but not code from Win32 DLLs and executable files.
Unused physical memory	Amount of physical memory (RAM) not currently in use.

MICROSOFT NETWORK CLIENT SETTINGS

Setting	Measurement
Bytes read/second	The number of bytes read from the redirector each second.
Bytes written/second	The number of bytes written to the redirector each second.
Number of nets	Number of networks currently running.
Open files	Number of open files on the network.
Resources	Number of resources.
Sessions	Number of sessions.
Transactions/second	The number of server message block (SMB) transactions managed by the redirector each second.

MICROSOFT NETWORK SERVER/ NETWARE SETTINGS

Setting	Measurement
Buffers	The number of buffers used by the server.
Bytes read/sec	The total number of bytes read from a disk.
Bytes written/sec	The total number of bytes written to a disk.
Bytes/sec	The total number of bytes read from and written to a disk.
Memory	The total memory used by the server.
NBs	Server network buffers.
Server threads	The current number of threads used by the server.

To select more than one item, press CTRL while clicking the items that you want to select. To select several items in a row, click the first item, and then hold down SHIFT while clicking the last item.

Troubleshooting with System Monitor

System Monitor is a versatile program that can measure a variety of important system parameters, but you'll need to have some idea of just what you're looking for in order to interpret the data that's displayed. This section offers some guidelines for basic performance troubleshooting.

Memory Leaks   If you suspect that an application might not be freeing memory when finished using it (sometimes called *memory leaks*), you should monitor the value of Kernel/Threads over time. This will indicate whether the application is starting threads and not reclaiming them later. Windows 98/Me should automatically remove such threads when the application closes, but if you identify a leak while the application is running, you may decide to restart the application periodically.

Insufficient Memory   If the values for Memory Manager/Discards and Memory Manager/Page-outs indicate a great deal of activity, performance problems might be related to system memory "stress." These values might indicate a need for more physical memory (RAM) in the system.

Poor Overall Performance   If a computer seems slow, check the values reported by Kernel/Processor Usage (%), by Memory Manager/Page Faults, and by Memory Manager/Locked Memory, and then interpret them using the following guide:

- If values for Kernel/Processor Usage (%) are high even when the user is not working, check to see which application(s) might be keeping it busy. To do this, press CTRL-ALT-DEL to see the list of tasks running in the Close Program dialog.

- If the values for Memory Manager/Page Faults are high, the application(s) being used might have memory needs beyond the computer's capabilities, so you may need to add more RAM to the system.

- If the Memory Manager/Locked Memory statistics continually assume a large portion of the Memory Manager/Allocated Memory value, inadequate free memory might be affecting performance. Also, you might be running an application that locks memory unnecessarily. ("Locked memory" indicates the portion of memory used that cannot be paged out.) Check your application(s) first to verify they're not locking memory, and then try adding more RAM to the system.

Graphics Performance

Graphics adapter technology is advancing in leaps and bounds—especially in the area of graphics "acceleration." Powerful 2D and 3D acceleration schemes speed the opening of screens and dialog boxes, or vastly increase the frame rate in your favorite 3D "shooter." Unfortunately, graphics acceleration techniques are not always standard, and Windows 98/Me may sometimes assume that a particular accelerator feature is present when it is not. You might see such problems ranging anywhere from small display irregularities to random system crashes. Windows 98/Me allows control over your graphics accelerator in order to isolate possible accelerator-related problems. This allows you to continue using Windows until the driver can be updated (or the adapter can be replaced).

ADJUSTING GRAPHICS ACCELERATION

You can manage the level of graphics acceleration used on your system through the Advanced Graphics Settings dialog and slider:

1. Click Start, highlight Settings, and then select Control Panel.

2. When the Control Panel opens, click the Performance tab.

3. Click the Graphics button in the Advanced Settings area.

4. The Advanced Graphics Settings dialog will appear (Figure 17-5).

Note the slider's current position in case you want to return the slider to this starting point later. You can alter the level of hardware acceleration by moving the slider left or right:

- The default setting is Full. This turns on all graphics hardware acceleration features available in the display driver.

- The first notch from the right (75%) can often be set to correct mouse pointer display problems. This setting disables hardware cursor support in the display driver by adding the SwCursor=1 entry to the [Display] section of SYSTEM.INI.

- The second notch from the right (50%) can be set to correct certain display errors. This setting prevents some bit block transfers from being performed on the display card and disables memory-mapped I/O for some display drivers. This setting adds the SwCursor=1 and Mmio=0 entries to the [Display] section of SYSTEM.INI, and the SafeMode=1 setting to the [Windows] section of WIN.INI.

- The last notch from the right (None) can be selected to correct problems if your computer frequently stops responding to input or suffers other severe problems. This setting adds the SafeMode=2 entry to the [Windows] section of WIN.INI, which removes all driver acceleration support and causes Windows 98 to use only the *device-independent bitmap* (DIB) engine rather than bit block transfers for displaying images.

As an example, an error message at system startup stating that an application caused "an invalid page fault in module <unknown>" might indicate a problem between the display driver and the Windows 98 DIB engine. In such cases, the None setting should correct the problem until you're able to update the display driver or replace the video card.

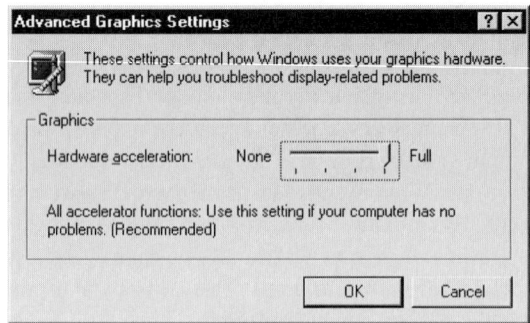

FIGURE 17-5   Adjusting the graphics hardware acceleration level

CHECKING AND ADJUSTING DISPLAY SETTINGS

Video performance will also be affected by the Display settings of your video system. Often, reducing resolutions or selecting a smaller color palette can improve display frame rates (at least until the video driver or adapter card can be upgraded). To check the current Display configuration:

1. Click Start, highlight Settings, and then select Control Panel.
2. When the Control Panel opens, click the Display tab.
3. Select the Settings tab (Figure 17-6).
4. Note the Display description (that is, "Plug and Play Monitor on Voodoo 3 AGP").
5. The color depth is listed in the Colors drop-down list, while the resolution is shown by the Screen area slider. You can adjust the color depth and resolution as needed, then apply those changes to your display system.

 Your monitor must be capable of displaying the resolution that you select. Make sure that you do not increase the resolution above the monitor's capability. Otherwise, the screen image will be terribly distorted, and you may damage the monitor.

Limited Resolution and Color Depth

If you notice that you cannot select resolutions higher than 640×480 or cannot select color depths higher than 16 colors, chances are that the display driver for your video card has not been installed (or is installed

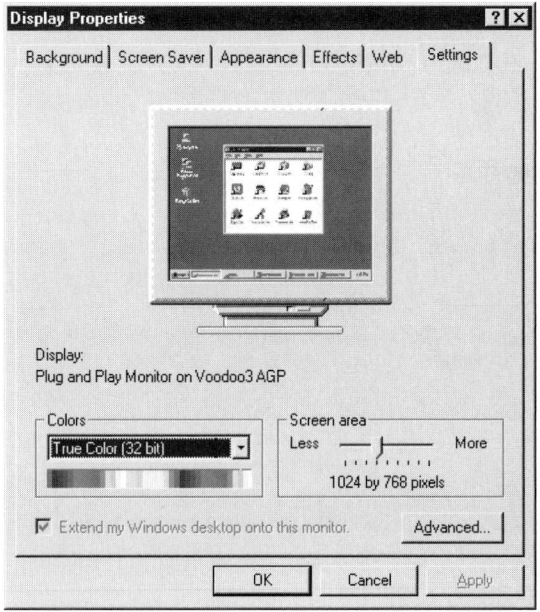

FIGURE 17-6 Checking the display settings

incorrectly). This happens frequently after reinstalling Windows or replacing the video adapter. You can almost always correct this problem by upgrading the display driver. As an alternative, you can remove the video adapter entry in the Device Manager, reboot the computer, and then allow Windows 98/Me to redetect the adapter so that you may install the correct drivers at that time.

Checking DirectX

Modern Windows platforms rely on the use of Microsoft's DirectX APIs to provide the complex suite of video, sound, and input device support that is required for many current games and multimedia software packages. If you're playing games or just viewing an occasional video clip, it's important that you install the latest version of DirectX on your system. You can download DirectX from Microsoft's Web site at **www.microsoft.com/directx**. (DirectX 8a is the latest version available for the PC.) Before installing or upgrading DirectX, you should check the version (if any) currently installed on your system:

1. Click Start and then click Run.

2. In the Open dialog, type **dxdiag** and click OK (Figure 17-7).

3. Select the System tab (if it's not already selected), and look at the System Information area. The DXDIAG utility reveals several pieces of information about your system and lists the installed DirectX version at the bottom, such as "DirectX 7.0 (4.07.00.0716)."

4. Click Exit when you're done checking the version.

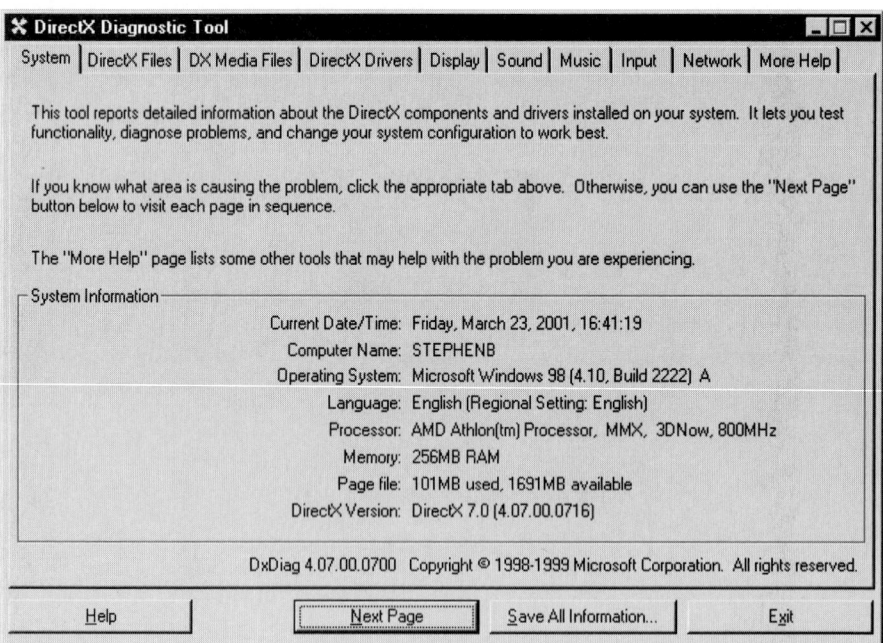

FIGURE 17-7   The DXDIAG diagnostic dialog for DirectX

Memory Performance

Memory interacts very closely with the CPU, and memory performance can have a profound impact on overall system performance. You must install an adequate amount of memory with the right characteristics, then configure the system to utilize that memory in the best possible way. You should also be concerned with system cache, and verify that it's properly enabled. The following points highlight the memory issues that you should be aware of:

■ **Memory amount**   You should install enough physical memory to adequately support your operating system and the application(s) that you intend to run. Generally, 32MB is considered to be the minimum amount of memory for Windows 95/98 and most general applications, but most systems today with Windows 98/Me are fitted with 128MB of RAM or more. More memory is helpful for graphics, multimedia, and other memory-intensive applications (such as 3D computer action games). If there is not enough memory to support your system, you'll see a great deal of hard drive activity as data is passed back and forth to the swap file, and overall system performance will suffer.

Cache and memory are related. Since cache can only support a limited amount of RAM, any memory access that takes place outside of the cached memory range will be slowed. This will also impair overall system performance. When selecting RAM for your system, be sure that you do not exceed the Maximum Cacheable RAM specification listed for your motherboard. If you must add more RAM, check to see if you must add more cache to support the additional RAM, or else disable caching entirely.

■ **Memory characteristics**   When selecting RAM for your system, choose RAM with the optimum characteristics for your particular motherboard. Consider the memory type first. SDRAM is generally considered to be the fastest memory type and is supported by most Pentium II/III/4 motherboards. Use PC133 (133 MHz) SDRAM wherever possible. An alternative to SDRAM is Rambus DRAM (RDRAM), which uses dedicated high-speed channels to exchange data between the CPU and memory. PC800 RDRAM is typical today and is widely supported on many motherboards using Intel's 800 series chipsets. Also consider the memory speed, since faster memory will respond better than slower memory. For example, SDRAM uses 12ns, 10ns, or 8ns "Cycle Time." The 8ns SDRAM will be faster. Also select SDRAM with a "CAS Latency" of 2 rather than 3 (if possible).

Error checking features such as parity or ECC generally do not affect memory performance, so you may select RAM with or without such features.

■ **Avoid "SIMM/DIMM Stackers"**   As DIMM slots became commonplace on motherboards, some manufacturers developed adapters that allowed you to "stack" several smaller SIMMs/DIMMs into a single device that would fit in a DIMM slot. This technology worked fine, but upsets the RAM timing because of the added distance between the RAM and the motherboard (introduced by the SIMM adapter). This can degrade the RAM's performance. You may need to add a wait state in the system's CMOS Setup in order to compensate for this added delay. As a rule, forgo memory adapters, and use suitable RAM devices that are appropriate for your system's speed.

■ **Optimize the CMOS Setup**   You can often wring a bit more performance from your memory by manually optimizing the memory settings in your CMOS Setup (usually under the Advanced Chipset

Setup menu). The trick is to keep wait states and latencies as low as possible, while keeping memory access techniques at a level that is appropriate for the memory type that you're using. Pushing the RAM too far will cause errors and may prevent the system from even booting. You should refer to the manual that accompanies your motherboard for detailed information regarding your CMOS Setup (or refer to Chapter 11).

Drive Performance

To improve the performance of a hard drive, you must first understand the factors that influence drive performance. The two most important factors are time-related: the amount of time it takes to locate a file, and the rate at which data can be passed back and forth between the drive and system. Every other concern is intimately related to those two issues.

SEEK TIME AND LATENCY

Since read/write heads are mechanical devices, it takes a finite amount of time to move them across a disk platter. The time required to accomplish this move depends on the size of the drive and the type of mechanism moving the heads. Newer drives are typically quite small, so the distances that must be traversed are short. Smooth and efficient voice-coil actuators are the head drive mechanism of choice, so movement is also enhanced. The combination of these factors has drastically reduced seek time over the last 20 years, but seek time is still a major part of overall drive delays.

Unfortunately, *seek time* is a rather generic term—different manufacturers each measure seek time as a slightly different parameter. The best-case seek time is referred to as *track-to-track seek time,* where the R/W heads only need to step in or out to the next adjacent track (or cylinder). This time is typically only a few hundred microseconds. If the best-case seek time is the time required to step between two adjacent tracks, the worst-case seek time is the time needed to step from the outermost track to the innermost track (or vice versa). Few manufacturers actually use this time since it seems so large. Instead, most drive manufacturers use an *average seek time,* which is the time needed to step halfway across the disk surface. Today, most drives offer average seek times between 6ms and 12ms. There is no way to accelerate seek times other than to simply upgrade the drive to a newer model with a smaller seek time specification.

Another part of drive performance is *latency.* Latency refers to the time it takes for the drive platters to rotate under the read/write heads once they've stepped into position. As with seek time, there are several different ways of measuring latency. *Maximum latency* is the time it takes for the platters to make one full turn, while *average latency* (more commonly used) is the time for one half turn. Average latency seems to run about 4ms for today's 7200 rpm drives. Once again, there is no way to reduce latency without upgrading to a faster physical drive.

DATA TRANSFER RATES

Once the drive's R/W heads and platters have moved into position, data can flow to or from the drive. The rate at which data can flow is known as the *data transfer rate.* Data transfer is generally given in Mbits/s. If you divide this figure by 8, you will get MB/s. A more practical measure of data transfer is the data rate between the hard drive and the drive controller (across the interface). EIDE hard drives can support burst data transfer rates up to 16MB/s, though Ultra-ATA hard drives can reach bursts of 100MB/s (66MB/s for

Ultra-DMA/66, or 33MB/s for Ultra-DMA/33). This is comparable with fast SCSI-2 drive configurations, as shown in Table 17-2. In virtually all cases, you can speed the performance of your hard drive system by upgrading the drive and controller to newer models (for example, an Ultra-DMA/100 drive and compatible PCI-based controller card if necessary).

Data transfer rates are a key part of drive delay. Most of the hesitation and pauses you see in the everyday operation of DOS or Windows 98/Me are largely because the operating system is waiting for the drive to catch up. The operating system typically must wait for a file to be loaded or saved before any other operations can continue. The faster a file's data can be transferred to or from the drive, the shorter those delays would be. Today, "apparent" drive performance is enhanced through the aggressive use of caching, where drive data is cached to RAM so the system may continue, then written to the drive as time allows.

FILE FRAGMENTATION

The interaction of operating systems also affects drive performance. When a drive is high-level formatted with an operating system, the drive's space is segregated into sets of adjacent sectors (called *clusters*). The size of a cluster depends on the size of the drive, but today's large, multi-gigabyte drives usually use 32KB to 64KB clusters under FAT16, or 4KB to 8KB clusters under FAT32. The cluster approach was designed to simplify file "housekeeping"—easing file storage tracking requirements while keeping wasted space minimal. Although the system is less than ideal, it works, and has been in use since DOS was able to

TABLE 17-2   COMPARISON OF HARD DRIVE DATA TRANSFER RATES

DATA TRANSFER MODE	BURST DATA RATE	NOTES
Single Word DMA 0	2.1MB/s	Old ATA (IDE) drives
PIO Mode 0	3.3MB/s	IDE drives
Single Word DMA 1	4.2MB/s	IDE drives
Multi Word DMA 0	4.2MB/s	IDE drives
SCSI-1	5.0MB/s	8-bit SCSI
PIO Mode 1	5.2MB/s	IDE drives
PIO Mode 2	8.3MB/s	IDE drives
Single Word DMA 2	8.3MB/s	IDE drives
Fast SCSI-2	10.0MB/s	16-bit SCSI
Wide SCSI-2	10.0MB/s	16-bit SCSI
PIO Mode 3	11.1MB/s	Newer ATA-2 (EIDE) drives
Multi Word DMA 1	13.3MB/s	EIDE drives
PIO Mode 4	16.6MB/s	EIDE drives
Multi Word DMA 2	16.6MB/s	EIDE drives
Fast/Wide SCSI-2	20.0MB/s	16-bit SCSI
Fast-20 SCSI-3	20.0MB/s	8-bit SCSI
Multi Word DMA 3	33.0MB/s	Ultra-ATA (Ultra-DMA/33) drives
Wide/Fast-20 SCSI-3	40.0MB/s	16-bit SCSI
Fast-40 SCSI-3	40.0MB/s	8-bit SCSI
Multi Word DMA 4	66.0MB/s	Ultra-ATA (Ultra-DMA/66) drives
Wide/Fast-40 SCSI-3	80.0MB/s	16-bit SCSI
Multi Word DMA 5	100MB/s	Ultra-ATA (Ultra-DMA/100) drives

support hard drives. The problem with cluster-based file storage is that files are stored wherever clusters are available. Ideally, all of the clusters that compose a file should be contiguous (adjacent to one another), but that is a rare occurrence in actual practice. As a drive fills and old files are erased, clusters are filled and reclaimed throughout the drive.

As a result, changing files gradually become scattered across the drive as DOS searches for any available clusters. This scattering behavior is called *file fragmentation*, and it is a natural side effect of DOS. The problem with file fragmentation is that each time the continuity of a file is broken, the drive's R/W heads have to be repositioned before another cluster can be read. If a file uses four clusters, and each cluster is several tracks apart, the heads will have to be repositioned four times to read or write that file. These additional seek times prolong the loading or saving of a file. In addition to these delays, the extra mechanical demands of R/W head positioning can eventually lead to premature drive failure.

Managing File Fragmentation

DOS and Windows 98/Me offer the Disk Defragmenter tool (often called Defrag), which should be used periodically to reorganize the disk clusters so that all clusters related to a particular file are made contiguous. Once your related clusters are relocated together, the drive doesn't have to work as hard to load or save files. This often makes your drive access seem faster. You can find Defrag in your Windows System Tools menu:

1. Click Start, highlight Programs, choose Accessories, and select System Tools.

2. Click on Disk Defragmenter. The Defrag window will open (Figure 17-8).

3. You can select the drive(s) to be defragmented, and then start the process by clicking OK.

4. It may take a while for Defrag to finish—depending on the size of the drive, the number of files it contains, and the extent of fragmentation. FAT32 drives can take much longer to finish because there are many more clusters for Defrag to work with.

If you're using Windows 98/Me, you can also configure Defrag to help your applications start faster. Select the Settings option in your Defrag dialog. The Disk Defragmenter Settings dialog will

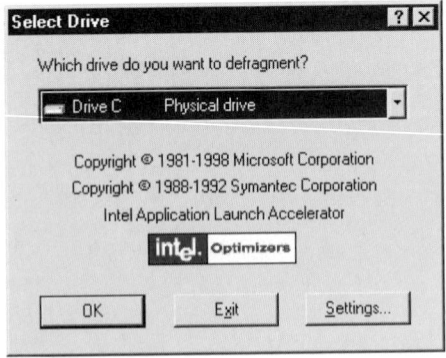

FIGURE 17-8   Defragmenting the selected hard drive

appear (Figure 17-9). Check the "Rearrange program files so my programs start faster" box so that Defrag will rearrange your applications for faster boot-up. If you do not select this option, Defrag will simply group your file clusters without any consideration of startup speed.

USING FAT32

Windows 98/Me offers full support for FAT32 partitions. FAT32 uses smaller clusters than FAT16 and allows drives over 2GB to be partitioned as a single logical volume. Windows 98 provides a Drive Converter (FAT32) utility that can convert your existing FAT16 partition(s) to FAT32. Since clusters are smaller, "slack space" can be reduced dramatically—freeing up as much as several hundred MB on your drive. Windows 98 also uses FAT32 partitions far more efficiently, which allows fast disk access (and fast application loading in conjunction with Disk Defragmenter). You can start Drive Converter by clicking Start, highlighting Programs, pointing to Accessories, selecting System Tools, and then clicking Drive Converter. The converter will start and allow you to convert your selected drive(s). However, there are some important tips to remember before you use the converter:

- Once you convert a partition to FAT32 format using Drive Converter, you cannot return to the FAT16 format unless you repartition and reformat the FAT32 drive. If you converted the drive on which Windows 98 is installed, then you must reinstall Windows 98 after repartitioning the drive as FAT16.

- Older disk compression software (including DriveSpace 3) is not compatible with FAT32. If your drive is already compressed, you may not be able to convert to FAT32.

- If you convert a removable disk to FAT32, and use that disk with an operating system that is not FAT32-compatible, you cannot access the disk when running the other operating system.

- If your computer has a "hibernate" feature, the conversion process may turn this feature off. You may need to reenable this feature manually.

- Because previous versions of Windows are not compatible with FAT32, you cannot uninstall Windows 98 after converting.

- Some disk utilities that depend on FAT16 may not work with FAT32 drives. You will be prompted if you're running one of these utilities. Contact your disk utility manufacturer to see if there is an updated version that is compatible with FAT32.

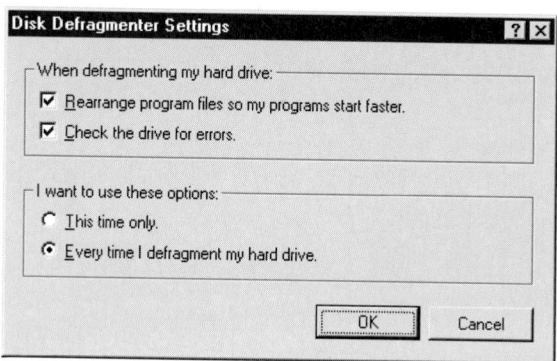

FIGURE 17-9   Improving application startup speed with Defrag

■ If you convert your hard drive to FAT32 using Drive Converter, you can no longer use dual boot to run earlier versions of Windows (that is, Windows 95 [Version 4.00.950], Windows NT 3.x, Windows NT 4.0, or Windows 3.x).

 FAT32 drives may perform slower on disk-intensive operations when your computer is running in DOS mode, or when you're running Windows in Safe Mode. If you use the DOS mode with FAT32 drives, you may find that performance is improved significantly if you load the SmartDrive disk-caching program.

CHECKING FOR DISK ERRORS

You can use the ScanDisk utility to check the disk for file problems such as lost allocation units and cross-linked files. Such file problems are quite common with FAT-based operating systems, and file damage can corrupt an application, driver, or data file. You should run ScanDisk periodically and allow it to correct any problems that it finds. If you detect damaged file(s), be sure to defragment the drive, then reinstall the damaged file(s) from a backup or the original installation disks. You can run ScanDisk from DOS by simply exiting Windows to DOS, switching to the drive that you need to test, then typing

```
C:> SCANDISK          <Enter>
```

You can then follow the on-screen directions to correct any error that's encountered. For a deeper test, select Yes to perform a surface test on the drive. (This may take anywhere from several minutes to several hours.) Finally, select View Log to review any actions and results taken by ScanDisk. If you're having trouble starting Windows, use the DOS version of ScanDisk. Otherwise, use ScanDisk through Windows:

1. Click Start, highlight Programs, select Accessories, highlight System Tools, and click System Tools.

2. Click ScanDisk. The ScanDisk dialog will open (Figure 17-10).

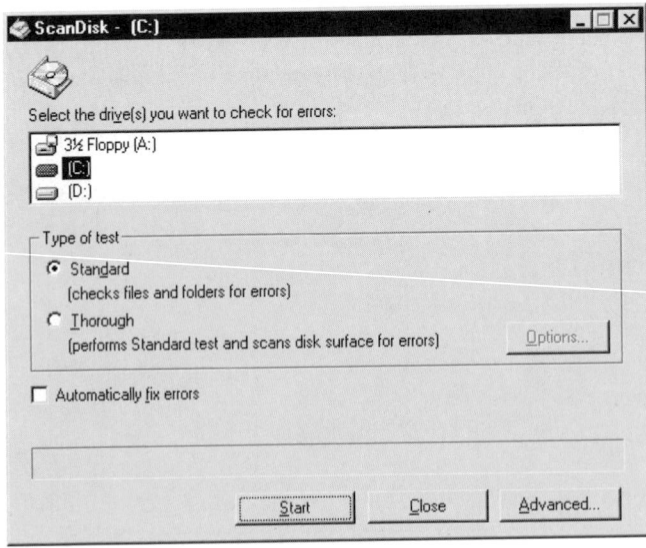

FIGURE 17-10   Checking and correcting disk problems with ScanDisk

3. You can select the drive to be tested, along with a surface scan or other advanced options.

4. In most cases, you should run ScanDisk to test for errors first, but do not allow ScanDisk to fix errors automatically until you've identified the errors.

Be very careful with ScanDisk versions. If you're using a FAT32 partition, be sure to use the Windows 98/Me version of ScanDisk. Using an older version of ScanDisk on a FAT32 partition may cause file damage.

32-BIT DRIVERS

Ideally, Windows 98/Me will apply a 32-bit protected-mode driver to every drive in the system—this ensures optimum performance. You can verify the use of 32-bit drivers by reviewing the File System entry in your Performance tab under the System icon. By default, 32-bit disk access is always enabled unless Windows 98/Me detects a real-mode disk driver that does not have a protected-mode replacement. This could be an older Stacker driver, a hard-disk security or encryption driver, or other legacy driver for a hard drive. To prevent the performance loss that occurs when Windows 98/Me is forced to use a real-mode disk driver, upgrade to a protected-mode replacement for the offending driver.

If you need to determine why a real-mode disk driver was installed under Windows, check the IOS.LOG file.

BUS MASTERING

Traditionally, a *bus* is simply a means of allowing devices access to system resources, and this was almost always accomplished under the direction of a master device—the system CPU. This meant that most data transfers between the drive controller and host system were accomplished through *Programmed I/O* (PIO) modes (see Table 17-2). With the introduction of "intelligent" bus architectures such as PCI, individual devices on the bus could assume control and initiate data transfers without the direct intervention of the CPU. This technique is generally called *Direct Memory Access* (DMA). There's nothing really new about DMA, and PCs have offered DMA channels since the early IBM PCs. The difference is that today's busses allow high-performance DMA transfers by devices that temporarily assume control of that bus. Such *bus mastering* requires the use of bus master drivers.

If your system has bus mastering drivers installed (and devices that support DMA data transfers), you'll see a DMA check box in the Options area of the Properties dialog for that device, such as in Figure 17-11. By default, the DMA check box is usually unselected. If you select the DMA check box, the drive will attempt to use DMA data transfers. Be extremely careful when enabling DMA data transfers. If your system hardware does not fully support bus mastering (or the bus master drivers are old or corrupt), you may find that drive performance actually decreases—or the system may even become unstable. Try installing the latest bus master drivers for your motherboard/chipset before enabling DMA data transfers.

OPTIMIZING THE SWAP FILE

Windows 98/Me uses a special file on your hard disk called a *virtual memory swap file* (also called a *paging file*). When using virtual memory under Windows 98/Me, some of your program code and data are kept in memory (system RAM), while other information is swapped temporarily to virtual memory. When that information is required again, Windows 98/Me pulls it back into RAM (and swaps other information to virtual memory if necessary). This activity is transparent to the end user, though you might notice that your hard disk is working. Virtual memory allows you to run more programs at one time than the computer's existing RAM would normally allow. The Windows 98/Me swap file is dynamic, so it can shrink

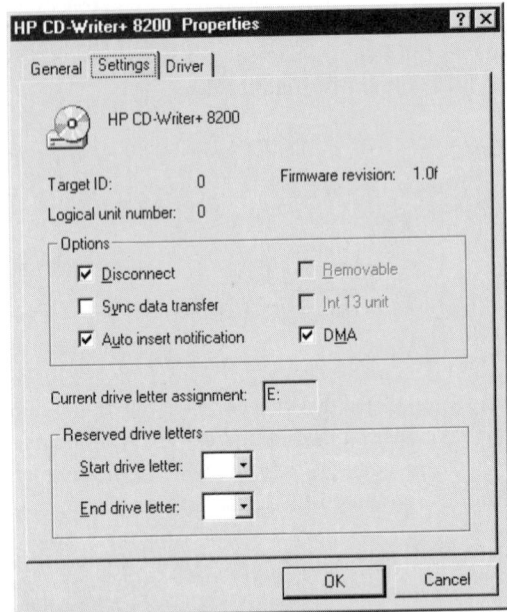

FIGURE 17-11   Enabling DMA data transfers through the device's Properties dialog

or grow as needed based on the tasks at hand and available disk space. It can also occupy a fragmented region of the hard disk with no substantial performance penalty.

> The best way to ensure good swap file performance is to ensure that the drive containing your swap file has ample free space. This way, the swap file size can shrink and grow as needed.

Although your system's default settings usually provide good overall swap file performance, you can manually adjust the parameters used to define the swap file. For example, to optimize swap file performance on a computer with multiple hard drives, you can override the default location of the Windows swap file. As a rule, the swap file should be placed on the drive with the fastest performance. If you've placed the swap file on a drive that's extremely busy, performance might be boosted by relocating the swap file to another one of the drives that's not as busy. To adjust your virtual memory swap file size:

1. Open the Control Panel, double-click the System icon, click the Performance tab, and then click Virtual Memory. The Virtual Memory dialog appears, as in Figure 17-12.

2. By default, the "Let Windows manage my virtual memory settings" option is selected.

3. To specify a different hard disk, click the "Let me specify my own virtual memory settings" option, and then specify the new disk in the Hard disk box. As an alternative, type values (in KB) in the Minimum or Maximum box, and then click OK.

If you set the maximum swap file size in the Virtual Memory dialog to use the amount of free space currently on a drive, Windows 98/Me assumes that it can increase the swap file beyond that size if more free disk space becomes available. If you want to impose a fixed limit on the swap file size, make sure that the limit you choose is less than the current maximum drive space.

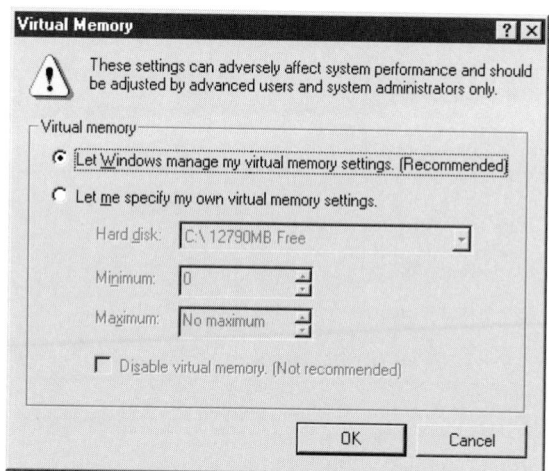

FIGURE 17-12   Configuring virtual memory settings for the PC

OPTIMIZING THE HARD DRIVE FILE SYSTEM

In Windows 98/Me, file system and drive performance can be controlled based on how the computer is used in most situations. The option for configuring file system performance is controlled only by the user. None of these settings is affected by other configuration changes that might be made in Windows 98/Me (such as installing file and printer sharing services). To optimize file system performance, open the Control Panel, double-click the System icon, click the Performance tab, click File System, and then select the Hard Disk tab (Figure 17-13). You can adjust cache optimizations by moving the Read-Ahead Optimization slider. In the "Typical role of this computer" entry, select the most common role for this computer, and then click OK. Each role is outlined next:

■ **Desktop computer**   This is a normal computer acting primarily as a network client, or an individual computer with no networking. This configuration assumes that there is more than the minimum required RAM and that the computer is running on AC power (rather than the battery).

■ **Mobile or docking system**   This is usually any computer with limited memory. This configuration assumes that RAM is limited, and the computer is commonly running on battery power, so the disk cache should be flushed frequently.

■ **Network server**   This is a computer used primarily as a peer server for file or printer sharing. This configuration assumes that the computer has adequate RAM and frequent disk activity, so the system is optimized for a large amount of disk access.

The time to launch an application often depends on cluster size (therefore, the particular file system). Smaller cluster sizes allow applications to launch faster—a 4KB cluster size (FAT32) is best, but larger cluster sizes (for example, FAT16) give less of a performance boost.

Each disk performance profile adjusts the values of the following file system settings in your registry:

■ PathCache specifies the size of the cache that the *virtual file allocation table* (VFAT) can use to save the locations of the most recently used directory paths. This cache improves performance by reducing

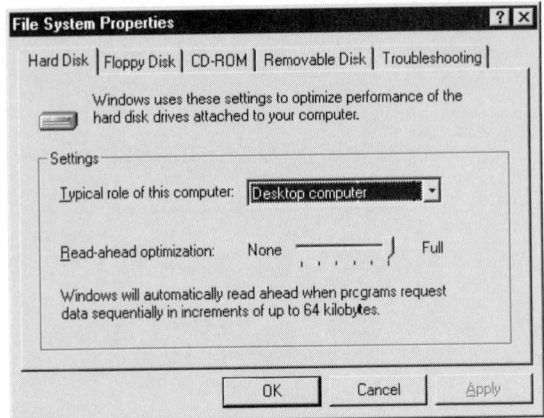

FIGURE 17-13   Setting system file properties for the hard drive(s)

the number of times the file system must seek paths by searching the file allocation table. There are 32 paths for the Desktop profile, 16 paths for Mobile or docking system, and 64 paths for Network server.

- NameCache stores the locations of the most recently accessed file names. The use of PathCache and NameCache together means that VFAT never searches the disk for the location of cached file names. Both PathCache and NameCache use memory out of the general system heap. There are about 677 file names (8KB) for the Desktop computer profile, 337 file names (4KB) for Mobile or docking system, and 2729 file names (16KB) for Network server.

- The BufferIdleTimeout, BufferAgeTimeout, and VolumeIdleTimeout settings control the time between when changes are placed in the buffer and when they are written to the hard disk.

The values assigned to each disk performance profile are stored in the following registry key:

HKEY_LOCAL_MACHINE\Software\Microsoft\Windows\CurrentVersion\FSTemplates

The following subkey contains the actual settings for the profile currently used:

HKEY_LOCAL_MACHINE\System\CurrentControlSet\Control\FileSystem

An additional performance setting in the FileSystem subkey can be used to change the size of the contiguous space that VFAT searches for when allocating disk space. Under DOS, the file system began allocating the first available space found on the disk. This caused a great deal of disk fragmentation and related performance problems. Under Windows 98, VFAT first tries to allocate space in the first contiguous 0.5MB of free space, and then returns to the DOS method if it cannot find at least this much contiguous free space. This optimizes performance for both the swap file and multimedia applications. In some cases, you might choose to set a smaller value in the registry (for example, when you're not running demanding applications). A smaller value for ContigFileAllocSize can lead to more fragmentation on the disk and more disk access for the swap file.

OPTIMIZING THE CD-ROM FILE SYSTEM

The CD-ROM cache is separate from the cache used for disk file and network access because the performance characteristics of the CD-ROM are different. The cache can be paged to disk (the file and network cache cannot). This reduces the work for Windows 98/Me, but still allows better CD-ROM performance. When

Windows 98/Me is retrieving data from a compact disc, it's still faster to read a record from the cache—even if it's been paged to disk—since the disk-access time is much faster than the CD-ROM access time.

A small CD-ROM cache makes a big difference in streaming performance, but a much larger cache does not pay off as significantly unless the cache is large enough to contain entire multimedia streams.

To set the supplemental cache size for your Windows 98 CD file system:

1. Open the Control Panel, double-click the System icon, click the Performance tab, and then click File System.
2. Click the CD-ROM tab and then drag the slider to set the Supplemental Cache Size (Figure 17-14).
3. Move the Supplemental Cache Size slider to the right to allocate more RAM for caching data from the CD-ROM drive, or to the left to allocate less RAM for caching data. Note that many multimedia programs perform better with a smaller cache because they tend not to reuse data.
4. In the "Optimize access pattern for" box, select a setting based on your computer's CD-ROM drive speed.
5. Click OK; then shut down and restart the computer.

OPTIMIZING REMOVABLE DISK PERFORMANCE

Windows 98/Me gives you the option to use write-behind caching to improve the performance of removable disk drives, such as the Zip or Jaz drive. To set write-behind caching for removable disk drives:

1. Open the Control Panel, double-click the System icon, click the Performance tab, click File System, and then click the Removable Disk tab.
2. Select the "Enable write-behind caching on all removable disk drives" check box, and then click OK.
3. If this causes a problem with disk operations, repeat the first step, then clear the "Enable write-behind caching on all removable disk drives" check box, and click OK.

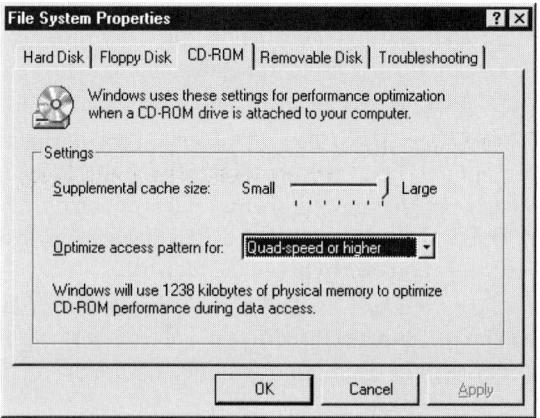

FIGURE 17-14   Setting system file properties for the CD-ROM drive(s)

FILE SYSTEM TROUBLESHOOTING TIPS

The System option in Control Panel presents a set of options for changing file system performance. You can use these options when you experience rare hardware or software compatibility problems. To display the file system troubleshooting options:

1. Open the Control Panel, double-click the System icon, and then click the Performance tab.
2. Click File System and then click the Troubleshooting tab.

Enabling any of these file system troubleshooting options will seriously degrade system performance. Enable these options only if necessary, and disable them as soon as possible.

You can then select one or more troubleshooting options. Each option is highlighted next:

- *Disable new file sharing and locking semantics.* This option alters the internal rules for file sharing and locking on hard disks (governing whether some processes can access open files in certain share modes). This option should be selected if a DOS-based application has problems with sharing under Windows. (This sets SoftCompatMode=0 in the registry.)

- *Disable long name preservation for old programs.* This option turns off the "tunneling" feature, which preserves long file names when files are opened and saved by applications that do not recognize long file names. This option should be checked when an important legacy program is not compatible with long file names. (This sets PreserveLongNames=0 in the registry.)

- *Disable protected-mode hard disk interrupt handling.* This option prevents Windows from terminating interrupts from the hard disk controller and bypassing the BIOS routine that handles these interrupts. Some hard disk drives might require this option to be checked in order for interrupts to be processed correctly. If this option is checked, the BIOS routine handles the interrupts, slowing system performance. (This sets VirtualHDIRQ=1 in the registry, but this setting is off by default in Windows 98.)

- *Disable synchronous buffer commits.* The "file commit" function is used to guarantee the integrity of user data being written to a disk. Normally, the function is used by applications to ensure that critical data is written to the disk before returning from a call made to the file commit function. Choosing this option disables this feature. Data is still written to disk, but it is written to disk in the background—at the discretion of the file system. Keep in mind that choosing this option can compromise data written to disk by an application should the system crash before the data is actually written.

- *Disable all 32-bit protected-mode disk drivers.* This option ensures that no 32-bit disk drivers are loaded in the system (except the floppy driver). Typically, you'd check this option if the computer does not start because of disk peripheral I/O problems. If this option is enabled, all I/O will go through real-mode drivers or the BIOS. In this case, all disk drives that are visible only in protected mode will no longer be visible. (This sets ForceRMIO=1 in the registry.)

- *Disable write-behind caching for all drives.* This option ensures that all data is flushed continually to the hard disk, removing any performance benefits gained from disk caching. This option should be checked if you're performing risky operations and must ensure prevention of data loss. (This sets DriveWriteBehind=0 in the registry.)

Remove Real-Mode Caching

Cache serves a vital role in the PC by holding frequently used program code and data in memory, rather than having to constantly refer to the disk. This can substantially speed your apparent drive performance on the system. In Windows 98/Me, the disk cache system is dynamic, so you do not need to configure its size as part of your normal system configuration. This means certain settings used for Windows 3.x are not required in Windows 98/Me and should be removed from your startup files:

- Share and SmartDrive entries should be removed from AUTOEXEC.BAT.
- SmartDrive double-buffer entries should be removed from CONFIG.SYS.

Windows 98/Me aggressively writes the contents of "dirty" memory pages (pages that contain changes) during system idle time, even if it does not need the memory at that point. This activity causes more disk action during idle times, but speeds up future memory allocations by doing some of the work while the system is idle.

RECOVERING LOST DISK SPACE

Your hard drive serves as a repository for many types of information. Some of this information is essential (for example, work files and important applications), but a great deal of information may be nonessential. Internet files (Web pages that have been cached to your PC), downloaded program files, items lingering in the Recycle Bin, and other temporary files can eventually take up a substantial amount of disk space. You can recover this lost disk space by using the Disk Cleanup tool under Windows 98/Me. Click Start, Programs, Accessories, System Tools, and Disk Cleanup. Select the drive you'd like to clean, and a dialog will appear with an analysis of the space that may be recovered (Figure 17-15). You can select any items to be kept or simply select OK to recover this wasted disk space.

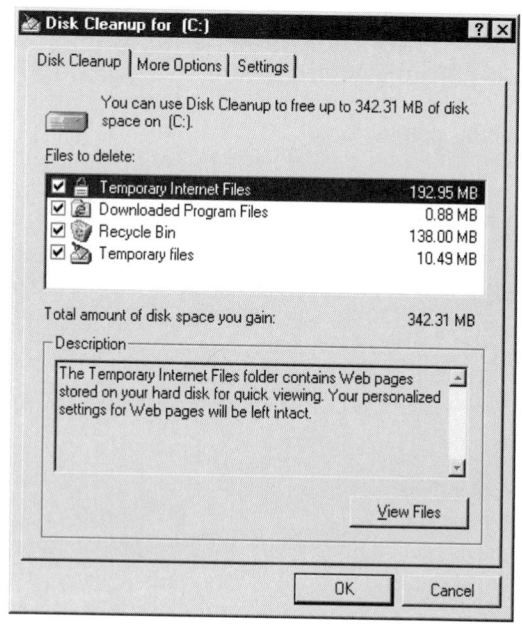

FIGURE 17-15   Recovering wasted disk space with the Disk Cleanup wizard

Managing the Registry

The Windows 98/Me registry is a critical part of your Windows platform that maintains a great deal of information about your system. When problems occur with the registry, your system may become unstable or fail to start in extreme circumstances. Windows offers several tools that allow you to manage and maintain your registry. This part of the chapter offers a series of handy tips for RegClean (Registry Clean), and ScanReg (Registry Checker).

UNDERSTANDING REGCLEAN

When you install, uninstall, and reinstall programs on your computer, you'll find that registry entries (or *keys*) are created, modified, and deleted. Over time, your computer's registry may begin to contain corrupted, unused, and unnecessary registry keys—especially if unneeded keys are not removed when you uninstall a program. As a result, you may eventually experience problems when using important Windows features (for example, OLE to embed objects, or automation to control other programs). The RegClean utility is designed to clean up unnecessary entries in your registry.

Running RegClean

If you do not have RegClean installed on your system, download it from the Microsoft Web site and install it. Double-click the RegClean icon to start the utility. RegClean displays a progress dialog. While the progress dialog box is displayed, RegClean loads a copy of the parts of the registry that it's going to check and then performs the actual scanning. Depending on how much information is in your registry (and the speed of your CPU), the scanning process takes from about 30 seconds to as much as 30 minutes. Once these progress meters have disappeared, you will be prompted for the next action.

 If you have many entries in your registry, RegClean might sometimes appear to have stopped working. RegClean might appear completely halted whenever it is checking remote or removable drives. Don't worry about this; simply allow RegClean to finish its cycle.

You can do two things at this point:

- *Exit RegClean.* If RegClean did not find any errors in your registry (or if you don't want RegClean to fix the errors that it may have found), click Cancel.

- *Allow RegClean to fix the errors that it found.* Click Fix Errors to prompt RegClean to remove any entries containing errors that may have been found in the registry. A progress meter is displayed while RegClean does this. When the progress meter disappears, RegClean is done. Click Exit to close RegClean.

Clicking Fix Errors also creates an UNDO.REG file in the folder where you ran RegClean. The file will have the following title:

```
UNDO <computer> yyyymmddhhmmss.REG
```

where <computer> is the name of your computer, yyyymmdd is the date, and hhmmss is the time. If you'd like to undo or replace what RegClean removed from your registry at any point, double-click the UNDO.REG file.

RegClean does not fix every known problem with the registry. It does not fix a "corrupt" registry. It is limited to fixing problems with normal registry entries located in HKEY_CLASSES_ROOT. RegClean will generally leave any entries in the registry that it does not understand or that could possibly be correct. Consequently, it is very possible that RegClean will not correct a problem that you have encountered.

When You Cannot UNDO

Normally, you should be able to undo changes made by RegClean simply by double-clicking on the UNDO.REG file. If Windows displays several error message boxes when you try to double-click the UNDO.REG file, chances are that you have a problem with the associated program(s) or REG files (rather than the UNDO file itself). Try correcting the problem as shown next:

1. Open an Explorer window, click the View menu, and select Options.

2. In the Options dialog box, select the File Types tab.

3. Scroll down in the Registered File Types list until you find Registration Entries.

4. Double-click this item, or click the Edit button.

5. In the Edit File Type dialog box, select Merge, and either double-click this item or click the Edit button.

6. In the "Editing action for type: Registration Entries" dialog, make sure that the text in the "Application used to perform action" field has the following entry (including the double quotes):

    ```
    regedit.exe "%1"
    ```

7. Click the OK buttons to close all three dialog boxes.

8. You should be able to double-click on the UNDO.REG file.

UNDERSTANDING SCANREG

When you start your computer successfully, the Registry Checker (SCANREG.EXE) automatically creates a backup of system files and registry configuration information (including user account information, protocol bindings, software program settings, and user preferences) once daily. Files that the Registry Checker backs up include SYSTEM.DAT, USER.DAT, SYSTEM.INI, and WIN.INI. ScanReg automatically scans the system registry for invalid entries and empty data blocks each time it's started. If invalid registry entries are detected, it will restore the previous day's backup. If no backups are available, ScanReg tries to make repairs to the registry. If the registry contains more than 500KB of empty data blocks, ScanReg automatically optimizes it. Finally, Windows Setup runs ScanReg to verify the integrity of the existing registry before it performs an upgrade. (If it detects registry damage, ScanReg tries to fix the damage automatically.) This part of the chapter describes how to run ScanReg and customize ScanReg by manually editing the SCANREG.INI file.

Using ScanReg

You can start ScanReg through the Windows System Information utility. Simply click Start, highlight Programs, point to Accessories, select System Tools, and then click System Information. On the Tools menu, click Registry Checker. You can also start ScanReg from the Windows Run command line. Simply click Start, click Run, type **SCANREGW.EXE** (or **SCANREG.EXE** for the real-mode version) in the Open box, and then click OK.

To restore individual files, follow these steps:

1. Click Start, select Find, and click Files or Folders.

2. In the Named box, type **rb0*.cab**, and then click Find Now.

3. Double-click on the "cabinet file" that has the correct registry file to be restored.

4. Right-click the file you want to restore, click Extract, and then choose the folder where the new file is to be placed.

 To use ScanReg with the /restore parameter, it *must* be run from a command prompt running outside of Windows (for example, from a command prompt booted from your emergency startup floppy disk). You can choose up to five registry backup files listed for you to restore.

Editing SCANREG.INI

The SCANREG.INI file contains all of the settings used to run SCANREG.EXE (or the protected-mode version of ScanReg called SCANREGW.EXE). You can edit SCANREG.INI by loading it into any text editor such as Notepad. The typical entries for SCANREG.INI (and their meanings) are outlined next:

■ **Backup**   A value of 1 (default) causes a backup copy of your registry to be made the first time you start your computer on any given day (determined by the system clock). A value of 0 disables this automatic registry backup. Note that disabling the registry backup is not recommended.

■ **Optimize**   A value of 1 (default) automatically optimizes your current registry if it contains 500KB of unused space. A value of 0 disables this automatic optimization process.

■ **MaxBackupCopies**   A value of 5 (default) saves the last five registry backups in the \Windows\ Sysbckup folder. In practice, you can set this value between 0 and 99. Note that when you restore a registry backup using ScanReg for DOS, only the five earliest backups are displayed.

■ **BackupDirectory**   By default, this entry does not contain a value, and registry backups are automatically saved in the \Windows\Sysbckup folder. To change the location where registry backups are saved, type the full path to the folder. For example, if you want to save registry backups in the c:\registry\ backups folder, change the BackupDirectory line to read

```
BackupDirectory=c:\registry\backups
```

More Windows Performance Tips

Of course, there are numerous other tactics that you can use to improve the performance of your Windows platform. Just a few of the more common recommendations are covered next.

USE WINDOWS UPDATE

It's hard to know when you need to update important Windows files on your computer. Windows 98/Me provides a resource site on the Web (called "Windows Update") that you can use to identify new updates and patches that might help your computer run better. Windows Update can automatically review the system software on your computer, and then recommend when you need to install updates specific to your computer. To use Windows Update while you're online, click Start, and then click Windows Update.

CHECK YOUR REGISTRY

Since the registry often loads drivers and other programs at start time, you should periodically run ScanReg or RegClean to inspect the registry for unused or "faulty" entries that can waste time and valuable RAM loading unneeded elements on your Windows platform. Use these steps to launch Registry Checker:

1. Click Start, highlight Programs, select Accessories, and then highlight System Tools.
2. Click System Information.
3. Click Tools from the menu bar and then click Registry Checker.

DISABLE DESKTOP ANIMATIONS

Animations may seem pretty and interesting, but they can demand a surprising amount of memory and processing power. You can free these resources by turning off your desktop animations:

1. Right-click your desktop, select Active Desktop, and click Customize My Desktop.
2. Click the Effects tab.
3. Clear the "Animate windows, menus, and lists" and "Show window contents while dragging" options.
4. Save your changes and reboot the system if necessary.

DISABLE POWER CONSERVATION

Power-saving techniques often spin down the hard drive and power-off the monitor during periods of inactivity. Make sure that your idle periods are suitable for the way in which you use the system. If your idle periods are too short, you may find yourself waiting for the display to reappear, or the drive to spin up for disk access. If you cannot determine more suitable idle time settings, disable your power saving modes.

REMOVE DISK COMPRESSION

Disk compression utilities (such as DriveSpace 3) slow the drive performance a bit due to their use of on-the-fly compression. You can reconfigure DriveSpace to only compress files if drive space drops below some preset amount, or disable/remove the compression utility outright. This will reduce your free drive space, but speed the drive's performance.

Further Study

Maxtor www.maxtor.com
Microsoft www.microsoft.com
Quantum www.quantum.com
Seagate www.seagate.com
Western Digital www.wdc.com

18

ERROR CODES

Most computers are remarkably adept at testing their own hardware and reporting serious errors during start time. They do this through the Power-On Self-Test (POST) routine written into BIOS. Since BIOS is written expressly for a particular processor, chipset, and other motherboard hardware, the BIOS is an ideal choice for startup diagnostics. However, startup diagnostics pose a unique problem—it's hard to report an error when the system isn't fully functional. BIOS reports POST errors through the use of audible signals (called *beep codes*) as well as through hexadecimal codes (called *POST codes*) that are written to established I/O addresses. This chapter presents the most popular beep and POST codes used on today's PCs.

Beep Codes

When a fault is detected *before* the video system is initialized, errors are indicated with a series of beeps (the beep codes). Since each BIOS is a bit different, the accuracy, precision, and quality of error detection and reporting varies from BIOS to BIOS. While most POST routines today follow a remarkably similar pattern, the reporting style can vary greatly. Some routines (such as AMI) generate a continuous string of beeps, while other routines (such as Phoenix) create short beep sequences. This part of the chapter is intended to help you understand and interpret the beep codes produced by major BIOS makers:

 If your BIOS isn't listed below, assume that beep codes are related to video, RAM, or power issues—in that order.

AMI (American Megatrends)	Table 18-1
Dell (PowerEdge)	Table 18-2
Compaq (AlphaServer)	Table 18-3
IBM desktop (Aptiva)	Table 18-4
Phoenix Technologies	Table 18-5

TABLE 18-1   AMI BEEP CODES

BEEPS	ERROR MESSAGE
1s	System RAM Refresh Failure. The programmable interrupt timer (PIT) or programmable interrupt controller (PIC) has probably failed. Replace the motherboard.
2s	Memory Parity Error. A parity error has been detected in the first 64KB of RAM. The RAM is probably defective. Replace the memory or motherboard.
3s	Base 64KB Memory Failure. A memory failure has been detected in the first 64KB of RAM. The RAM is probably defective. Replace the memory or motherboard.
4s	System Timer Failure. The system clock/timer chip has failed.
5s	CPU Failure. The system CPU has failed. Try replacing the CPU or motherboard.
6s	Gate A20 Failure. The keyboard controller chip has failed, so Gate A20 is no longer available to switch the CPU into protected mode. Replace the keyboard controller or motherboard.
7s	Exception Error. The CPU has generated an exception error due to a fault in the CPU or some combination of motherboard conditions. Replace the motherboard.
8s	Video Memory Read/Write Error. The system video adapter is missing or defective. Try replacing the video adapter.
9s	ROM Checksum Error. The contents of the system BIOS ROM do not match the expected checksum value. The BIOS ROM is probably defective and should be replaced.
10s	CMOS Shutdown Register Read/Write Error. The shutdown register for the CMOS memory has failed. Try replacing the RTC/CMOS chip.
11s	Cache Error/L2 Cache Bad. The L2 cache is faulty. Replace the L2 cache or integrated L2 cache hardware device.
1l-3s	Memory Test Failure. A fault has been detected in memory over 64KB. Replace the memory or the motherboard.
1l-8s	Display Test Failure. The display adapter is missing or defective. Replace the video adapter board. If the video adapter is on the motherboard, try replacing the motherboard.

TABLE 18-2   DELL BEEP CODES (POWEREDGE FAMILY)

BEEPS	ERROR MESSAGE
1-1-3	NVRAM write/read failure. The CMOS RAM has probably failed. Replace the main board.
1-1-4	BIOS checksum failure. The BIOS chip has probably failed. Replace the main board.
1-2-1	Programmable interval-timer failure. Replace the main board.
1-2-2	DMA initialization failure. Replace the main board.
1-2-3	DMA page register write/read failure. Replace the main board.
1-3-1	Main-memory refresh verification failure. Remove and reseat the DIMMs. If the problem persists, replace the memory module(s).
1-3-2	No memory installed. Remove and reseat the DIMMs and reboot the system. If the problem persists, replace the memory module(s).
1-3-3	Chip or data line failure in the first 64 KB of main memory. Remove and reseat the DIMMs and reboot the system. If the problem persists, replace the memory module(s).

TABLE 18-2 DELL BEEP CODES (POWEREDGE FAMILY) *(CONTINUED)*

BEEPS	ERROR MESSAGE
1-3-4	Odd/even logic failure in the first 64 KB of main memory. Remove and reseat the DIMMs and reboot the system. If the problem persists, replace the memory module(s).
1-4-1	Address line failure in the first 64 KB of main memory. Remove and reseat the DIMMs and reboot the system. If the problem persists, replace the memory module(s).
1-4-2	Parity failure in the first 64 KB of main memory. Remove and reseat the DIMMs and reboot the system. If the problem persists, replace the memory module(s).
2-1-1 to 2-4-4	Bit failure in the first 64 KB of main memory. Remove and reseat the DIMMs and reboot the system. If the problem persists, replace the memory module(s).
3-1-1	Slave DMA-register failure. Replace the main board.
3-1-2	Master DMA-register failure. Replace the main board.
3-1-3	Master interrupt-mask register failure. Replace the main board.
3-1-4	Slave interrupt-mask register failure. Replace the main board.
3-2-4	Keyboard-controller test failure. Check the keyboard cable and connector for proper connection. If the problem persists, replace the main board.
3-3-1	CMOS RAM failure. Replace CMOS/RTC chip or the main board.
3-3-2	System configuration check failure. Replace the main board.
3-3-3	Keyboard controller not detected.
3-3-4	Screen initialization failure. Verify that the monitor cable is correctly connected. If the problem persists, replace the main board.
3-4-1	Screen-retrace test failure. Ensure that the monitor cable is correctly connected. If the problem persists, replace the main board.
3-4-2	Video ROM detection failure. Replace the main board or install another video card.
4-2-1	No timer tick. Replace the main board.
4-2-2	Shutdown failure. Replace the main board.
4-2-3	Gate A20 failure. Replace the main board.
4-2-4	Unexpected interrupt in protected mode. Verify that all expansion cards are properly seated, and then reboot the system.
4-3-1	Improperly seated or faulty DIMM, DIMMs not installed in sets, or a faulty or improperly seated memory module. Be sure that the DIMMs are installed in sets, if necessary, and in the proper sockets for each memory bank in use. If this does not resolve the problem, remove and reseat the DIMMs. If the problem persists, replace the DIMMs or the memory module(s).
4-3-3	Defective system board. Replace the main board.
4-3-4	Time-of-day clock stopped. Replace the battery. If the problem persists, replace the main board.
4-4-1	Faulty I/O chip or Super I/O controller failure. The system board is defective, so replace the system board.
4-4-2	Parallel-port test failure. The system board is defective, so replace the system board.
4-4-3	Math co-processor failure. This means a defective microprocessor, so replace the microprocessor.
4-4-4	Cache test failure. This means a defective microprocessor, so replace the microprocessor.

TABLE 18-3 COMPAQ BEEP CODES (ALPHASERVER FAMILY)

BEEPS	ERROR MESSAGE
1	No error.
1-3	VGA monitor not plugged in. Graphics option card different from the one shipped with the system.
1-1-2	A ROM data path error was detected while loading SRM/AlphaBIOS console code.
1-1-4	The SROM code is unable to load the console code, or an FROM header area or checksum error detected.

TABLE 18-3 COMPAQ BEEP CODES (ALPHASERVER FAMILY) *(CONTINUED)*

BEEPS'	ERROR MESSAGE
1-1-7	No boot block on floppy device.
1-2-1	TOY NVRAM failure.
1-2-4	B-cache error.
1-3-3	No usable memory detected.
3-3-1	Generic system failure.
3-3-3	Failure of onboard SCSI controller.

TABLE 18-4 IBM BEEP CODES (APTIVE 2173 SERIES)

BEEPS	ERROR MESSAGE
1-1-3	CMOS read/write error. The system may be configured improperly. Run the system setup routine.
1-1-4	ROM BIOS checksum error. Replace the main board.
1-2-X	DMA controller error. Replace the main board.
1-3-X	Memory module error. Check, reinstall, or replace the memory module(s) or replace the main board.
1-4-4	Keyboard error. Check the keyboard and its installation. Replace the keyboard, or replace the main board.
1-4-X	Error detected in first 64 KB of RAM. One or more memory modules may have failed. Try reseating the memory module(s), replace the memory module(s), and then replace the main board.
2-1-1	System board fault. Run the system setup routine or replace the main board.
2-1-2	System board fault. Run the system setup routine or replace the main board.
2-1-X	Error detected in first 64 KB of RAM. One or more memory modules may have failed. Try reseating the memory module(s), replace the memory module(s), and then replace the main board.
2-2-2	Video adapter fault. The onboard video system has failed. Install a stand-alone video card or replace the main board.
2-2-X	Error detected in first 64 KB of RAM. One or more memory modules may have failed. Try reseating the memory module(s), replacing the memory module(s), and then replacing the main board.
2-3-X	Memory module error. Check, reinstall, or replace the memory module(s) or replace the main board.
2-4-X	Memory module error. Check, reinstall, or replace the memory module(s) or replace the main board.
3-1-X	DMA register failed. Replace the main board.
3-2-4	Keyboard controller chip failed. Replace the main board.
3-3-4	Screen initialization failed. The video system has failed. Replace the video adapter, or replace the main board if the video system is integrated into the main board.
3-4-1	Screen retrace test error. The video system has failed. Replace the video adapter, or replace the main board if the video system is integrated into the main board.
3-4-2	Cannot locate video ROM. The video system has failed. Replace the video adapter or replace the main board if the video system is integrated into the main board.
4	Video adapter fault. The onboard video system has failed. Install a stand-alone video card or replace the main board.
1l-1s	Base 640 KB memory error or shadow RAM error. Replace the defective memory module(s) or replace the motherboard.
1l-2s	Video adapter fault. The onboard video system has failed. Install a stand-alone video card or replace the main board.

TABLE 18-4   IBM BEEP CODES (APTIVE 2173 SERIES) *(CONTINUED)*

BEEPS	ERROR MESSAGE
1l-3s	Video adapter fault. The onboard video system has failed. Install a stand-alone video card or replace the main board.
3s	Memory failure. Check, reinstall, or replace the memory module(s) or replace the main board.
Continuous	System board failure. Replace the motherboard.
Repeating	Stuck key on the keyboard, keyboard cable detached or damaged, or main board failure. Clean or replace the keyboard, or replace the motherboard.

TABLE 18-5   PHOENIX BIOS BEEP CODES

BEEPS	ERROR MESSAGE
1-1-2	CPU Register Test Failure. The CPU has likely failed. Replace the CPU.
Low 1-1-2	System Board Select Failure. The motherboard is suffering from an undetermined fault. Try replacing the motherboard.
1-1-3	CMOS Read/Write Failure. The RTC/CMOS IC has probably failed. Try replacing the RTC/CMOS chip.
Low 1-1-3	Extended CMOS RAM Failure. The extended portion of the RTC/CMOS IC has failed. Try replacing the RTC/CMOS chip.
1-1-4	BIOS ROM Checksum Error. The BIOS ROM has probably failed.
1-2-1	Programmable Interval Timer (PIT) Failure. The PIT has probably failed.
1-2-2	DMA Initialization Failure. The DMA controller has probably failed.
1-2-3	DMA Page Register Read/Write Failure. The DMA controller has probably failed.
1-3-1	RAM Refresh Failure. The refresh controller has failed.
1-3-2	64KB RAM Test Disabled. The test of the first 64KB of system RAM could not begin. Try replacing the motherboard.
1-3-3	First 64KB RAM or Data Line Failure. The first RAM chip/module has failed.
1-3-4	First 64KB Odd/Even Logic Failure. The first RAM control logic has failed.
1-4-1	Address Line Failure 64KB of RAM.
1-4-2	Parity Failure First 64KB of RAM. The first RAM chip/module has failed.
1-4-3	EISA Failsafe Timer Test Fault. Replace the motherboard.
1-4-4	EISA NMI Port 462 Test Failure. Replace the motherboard.
2-1-1	Bit 0 First 64KB RAM Failure. This data bit in the first RAM chip has failed.
2-1-2	Bit 1 First 64KB RAM Failure.
2-1-3	Bit 2 First 64KB RAM Failure.
2-1-4	Bit 3 First 64KB RAM Failure.
2-2-1	Bit 4 First 64KB RAM Failure.
2-2-2	Bit 5 First 64KB RAM Failure.
2-2-3	Bit 6 First 64KB RAM Failure.
2-2-4	Bit 7 First 64KB RAM Failure.
2-3-1	Bit 8 First 64KB RAM Failure.
2-3-2	Bit 9 First 64KB RAM Failure.
2-3-3	Bit 10 First 64KB RAM Failure.
2-3-4	Bit 11 First 64KB RAM Failure.
2-4-1	Bit 12 First 64KB RAM Failure.
2-4-2	Bit 13 First 64KB RAM Failure.
2-4-3	Bit 14 First 64KB RAM Failure.

TABLE 18-5   PHOENIX BIOS BEEP CODES (CONTINUED)

BEEPS	ERROR MESSAGE
2-4-4	Bit 15 First 64KB RAM Failure.
3-1-1	Slave DMA Register Failure. The DMA controller has probably failed.
3-1-2	Master DMA Register Failure. The DMA controller has probably failed.
3-1-3	Master Interrupt Mask Register Failure. The interrupt controller has probably failed.
3-1-4	Slave Interrupt Mask Register Failure. The interrupt controller has probably failed.
3-2-2	Interrupt Vector Loading Error. BIOS is unable to load the interrupt vectors into low RAM. Replace the motherboard.
3-2-3	Reserved.
3-2-4	Keyboard Controller Test Failure. The keyboard controller has failed.
3-3-1	CMOS RAM Power Bad. Try replacing the CMOS backup battery. Try replacing the RTC/CMOS chip. Replace the motherboard.
3-3-2	CMOS Configuration Error. The CMOS configuration has failed. Restore the configuration. Replace the CMOS backup battery. Replace the RTC/CMOS chip. Replace the motherboard.
3-3-3	Reserved.
3-3-4	Video Memory Test Failed. There is a problem with the video memory. Replace video memory or replace the video adapter board.
3-4-1	Video Initialization Test Failure. There is a problem with the video system. Replace the video adapter.
4-2-1	Timer Tick Failure. The system timer chip has failed.
4-2-2	Shutdown Test Failure. The CMOS chip has failed.
4-2-3	Gate A20 Failure. The keyboard controller has probably failed.
4-2-4	Unexpected Interrupt in Protected Mode. There is a problem with the CPU.
4-3-1	RAM Test Address Failure. System RAM addressing circuitry has failed.
4-3-3	Interval Timer Channel 2 Failure. The system timer chip has probably failed.
4-3-4	Time of Day Clock Failure. The RTC/CMOS chip has failed.
4-4-1	Serial Port Test Failure. A fault has developed in the serial port circuit.
4-4-2	Parallel Port Test Failure. A fault has developed in the parallel port circuit.
4-4-3	Math Co-processor Failure. Try replacing the math co-processor.

POST Codes

During initialization, the POST performs a self-diagnostic routine designed to check key areas of the motherboard (and common peripherals) for major faults. When an error is detected early in the test cycle, you'll probably hear a series of one or more beep codes, as described above. BIOS makers came to realize that most beep code sequences are not terribly specific, and a beep code can often represent any one of a number of possible failures. In order to make more specific information available to technicians, POST procedures are designed to output a single hexadecimal byte to I/O port 80h (or other suitable I/O address) as each step in the initialization is started or completed. If the PC should fail at any point during startup, the code at port 80h represents the *last* step to be successfully completed. By knowing the full sequence of I/O POST codes generated by a BIOS, a technician can quickly determine the test step that failed and thus pinpoint the fault with reasonable confidence. This part of the chapter presents the POST sequences for popular PC BIOS versions.

INTERPRETING POST CODES

When working with POST codes, it is important to understand that not all codes are the direct result of a test. Many codes simply indicate that a CPU is attempting to initialize various areas of the PC. These types of codes are known as *checkpoints*—they simply show that certain initialization steps are being completed. Just because you see a hexadecimal code does not *necessarily* mean that anything has failed.

Also remember that few listings of BIOS codes are actually complete. With the exception of publicly available code lists (for the IBM PC, XT, and AT), most BIOS manufacturers are generally unwilling to release the full context of their POST codes. As a result, POST code indexes such as those in this book are often compilations of data extracted from a number of different sources. If you encounter a POST code that is not covered in this book, your best course is usually to contact the BIOS manufacturer directly for specific details.

Another area of confusion can arise (particularly for the novice technician) over when the POST process starts and ends. When a system is first started with a POST board installed, the POST display is typically blank—this is *normal* for the initial moments after PC power is applied. After that, codes should begin flashing across the seven-segment LEDs. If the LEDs remain blank, you can assume that no data is reaching the card. In that event, make sure that your system produces POST codes (a few systems do *not*), and see that the POST board's I/O address is set properly (some systems use I/O ports other than 80h). After the POST is complete, a system will attempt to boot an operating system. Ordinarily, the last code on the display is 00h or FFh, so don't worry if either of these codes remain on the seven-segment display. In some cases—depending on the particular BIOS—some *other* code may be left in the display. If the system appears to boot normally, you rarely need to worry about this. Also keep in mind that not all tests are performed in numerical order. You will find that the POST code sequences in many of the following tables are a bit mixed, so look over each table carefully:

All of the POST codes presented in the following tables are "hexadecimal" (or "h") numbers. For example, a POST code of 13 would be "13h" (or "hex").

Acer	Table 18-6
AMI (prior to 04/1990)	Table 18-7
AMI (04/1990–02/1991)	Table 18-8
AMI (02/1991–12/1991)	Table 18-9
AMI (06/1992–08/1993)	Table 18-10
AMI WinBIOS (12/1993+)	Table 18-11
AMI version 2.2x	Table 18-12
AMI Plus BIOS	Table 18-13
AMI Color BIOS	Table 18-14
AMI EZ-Flex BIOS	Table 18-15
Award AT BIOS v.3.0	Table 18-16
Award AT BIOS v.3.0-3.03	Table 18-17
Award AT BIOS v.3.1	Table 18-18
Award AT BIOS 3.3	Table 18-19
Award AT ISA/EISA BIOS 4.0	Table 18-20
Award EISA BIOS	Table 18-21
Award PnP BIOS (4–5.x)	Table 18-22
Award non-PnP BIOS (4–5x)	Table 18-23
Compaq BIOS (general)	Table 18-24
Dell BIOS	Table 18-25
Hewlett-Packard Vectra	Table 18-26

IBM PC/AT BIOS	Table 18-27
IBM PS/2 BIOS	Table 18-28
Microid Research 1.0A BIOS	Table 18-29
Microid Research (modern)	Table 18-30
Microid Research 3.4x BIOS	Table 18-31
Phoenix ISA/EISA/MCA BIOS	Table 18-32
Phoenix BIOS Plus (v.1.0)	Table 18-33
Phoenix UMC chipset BIOS	Table 18-34
Phoenix PCI BIOS	Table 18-35
Phoenix BIOS 4.0 BIOS	Table 18-36

TABLE 18-6   ACER BIOS POST CODES

CODE	DESCRIPTION
04	POST Start
08	Shutdown Condition 0
0C	Testing the BIOS ROM checksum
10	Testing the CMOS RAM shutdown byte
14	Testing the DMA controller
18	Initializing the system timer
1C	Testing the memory refresh system
1E	Determining the memory type
20	Testing the low 128KB of memory
24	Testing the 8042 keyboard controller IC
28	Testing the CPU descriptor instruction
2C	Testing the 8259 interrupt controller IC
30	Setting up a temporary interrupt
34	Configure the BIOS interrupt vectors and routines
38	Testing the CMOS RAM
3C	Determining the memory size
40	Shutdown Condition 1
44	Initializing the video BIOS ROM
45	Setting up and testing RAM
46	Testing cache memory and controller
48	Testing memory
4C	Shutdown Condition 3
50	Shutdown Condition 2
54	Shutdown Condition 7
58	Shutdown Condition 6
5C	Testing the keyboard and auxiliary I/O
60	Setting up BIOS interrupt routines
64	Testing the real-time clock
68	Testing the floppy disk drive
6C	Testing the hard drive
70	Testing the parallel port
74	Testing the serial port
78	Setting the time of day
7C	Detect and invoke any optional ROMs
80	Checking for the math co-processor

TABLE 18-6   ACER BIOS POST CODES (*CONTINUED*)

CODE	DESCRIPTION
84	Initializing the keyboard
88	Initializing the system (step 1)
8C	Initializing the system (step 2)
90	Boot the operating system
94	Shutdown Condition 5
98	Shutdown Condition A
9C	Shutdown Condition B

TABLE 18-7   AMI BIOS POST CODES (PRIOR TO APRIL 1990)

CODE	DESCRIPTION
01	NMI is disabled and the i286 register test is about to start
02	i286 register test has passed
03	ROM BIOS checksum test (32KB from F8000h) passed OK
04	8259 PIC has initialized OK
05	CMOS interrupt disabled
06	Video system disabled and the system timer checks OK
07	8253/4 programmable interval timer test OK
08	Delta counter channel 2 OK
09	Delta counter channel 1 OK
0A	Delta counter channel 0 OK
0B	Parity status cleared
0C	The refresh and system timer check OK
0D	Refresh check OK
0E	Refresh period checks OK
10	Ready to start 64KB base memory test
11	Address line test OK
12	64KB base memory test OK
13	System interrupt vectors initialized
14	8042 keyboard controller checks OK
15	CMOS read/write test OK
16	CMOS checksum and battery OK
17	Monochrome video mode OK
18	CGA color mode configured properly
19	Attempting to pass control to video ROM at C0000h
1A	Returned from video ROM
1B	Display memory R/W test OK
1C	Display memory R/W alternative test OK
1D	Video retrace test OK
1E	Global equipment byte set for proper video operation
1F	Ready to initialize video system
20	Video test OK
21	Video display OK
22	The power-on message is displayed

TABLE 18-7   AMI BIOS POST CODES (PRIOR TO APRIL 1990) *(CONTINUED)*

CODE	DESCRIPTION
30	Ready to start the virtual mode memory test
31	Virtual memory mode test started
32	CPU has switched to virtual mode
33	Testing the memory address lines
34	Testing the memory address lines
35	Lower 1MB of RAM found
36	Memory size computation checks OK
37	Memory test in progress
38	Memory below 1MB is initialized
39	Memory above 1MB is initialized
3A	Memory size is displayed
3B	Ready to test the lower 1MB of RAM
3C	Memory test of lower 1MB OK
3D	Memory test above 1MB OK
3E	Ready to shutdown for real-mode testing
3F	Shutdown OK—now in real mode
40	Ready to disable gate A20
41	A20 line disabled successfully
42	Ready to start DMA controller test
4E	Address line test OK
4F	System still in real mode
50	DMA page register test OK
51	Starting DMA controller 1 register test
52	DMA controller 1 test passed, starting DMA controller 2 register test
53	DMA controller 2 test passed
54	Ready to test latch on DMA controller 1 and 2
55	DMA controller 1 and 2 latch test OK
56	DMA controller 1 and 2 configured OK
57	8259 PIC initialized OK
58	8259 PIC mask register check OK
59	Master 8259 PIC mask register OK
5A	Ready to check timer interrupts
5B	Timer interrupt check OK
5C	Ready to test keyboard interrupt
5D	ERROR detected in timer or keyboard interrupt
5E	8259 PIC controller error
5F	8259 PIC controller OK
70	Start of keyboard test
71	Keyboard controller OK
72	Keyboard test OK
73	Keyboard global initialization OK
74	Floppy setup ready to start
75	Floppy controller setup OK
76	Hard disk setup ready to start
77	Hard disk controller setup OK

TABLE 18-7 AMI BIOS POST CODES (PRIOR TO APRIL 1990) *(CONTINUED)*

CODE	DESCRIPTION
79	Ready to initialize timer data
7A	Verifying CMOS battery power
7B	CMOS battery verified OK
7D	Analyzing CMOS RAM size
7E	CMOS memory size updated
7F	Send control to adapter ROM
80	Enable the SETUP Routine if DELETE is pressed
81	Return from adapter ROM
82	Printer data initialization is OK
83	RS-232 data initialization is OK
84	80x87 check and test OK
85	Display any soft-error message
86	Give control to ROM at E0000h
87	Return from system ROM
00	Call the INT19 boot loader

TABLE 18-8 AMI BIOS POST CODES (APRIL 1990 TO FEBRUARY 1991)

CODE	DESCRIPTION
01	NMI disabled and 286 register test about to start
02	286 register test passed
03	ROM BIOS checksum (32K at F800:0) passed
04	Keyboard controller test with and without mouse passed
05	Chipset initialization over; DMA and Interrupt controller disabled
06	Video disabled and system timer test begins
07	CH-2 of 8254 initialization half way
08	CH-2 of timer initialization over
09	CH-1 of timer initialization over
0A	CH-0 of timer initialization over
0B	Refresh started
0C	System timer started
0D	Refresh link toggling passed
10	Refresh on and about to start 64K base memory test
11	Address line test passed
12	64K base memory test passed
15	Interrupt vectors initialized
17	Monochrome mode configured
18	Color mode configured
19	About to look for optional video ROM at C000 and give control to ROM if present
1A	Return from optional video ROM
1B	Shadow RAM enable/disable completed
1C	Display memory read/write test for display type as set in the CMOS setup program
1D	Display memory read/write test for alternate display type complete if main display memory read/write test returns error

TABLE 18-8	**AMI BIOS POST CODES (APRIL 1990 TO FEBRUARY 1991)** *(CONTINUED)*

CODE	DESCRIPTION
1E	Global equipment byte set for proper display type
1F	Video mode configured, call for mono/color begins
20	Video mode configuration completed
21	ROM type 27256 verified
23	Power-on message displayed
30	Virtual mode memory test about to begin
31	Virtual mode memory test started
32	Processor executing in virtual mode
33	Memory address line test in progress
34	Memory address line test in progress
35	Memory below 1MB calculated
36	Memory above 1MB calculated
37	Memory test about to start
38	Memory below 1MB initialized
39	Memory above 1MB initialized
3A	Memory size display initiated. Will be updated when BIOS goes through memory test
3B	About to start below 1MB memory test
3C	Memory test below 1MB completed; about to start above 1MB test
3D	Memory test above 1MB completed
3E	About to go to real mode (shutdown)
3F	Shutdown successful and processor in real mode
40	Cache memory on and about to disable A20 address line
41	A20 address line disable successful
42	486 internal cache turned on
43	About to start DMA controller test
50	DMA page register test complete
51	DMA unit-1 base register test about to start
52	DMA unit-1 base register test complete
53	DMA unit-2 base register test complete
54	About to check F/F latch for unit-1 and unit-2
55	F/F latch for both units checked
56	DMA unit 1 and 2 programming over; about to initialize 8259 interrupt controller
57	8259 initialization over
70	About to start keyboard test
71	Keyboard controller BAT test over
72	Keyboard interface test over; mouse interface test started
73	Global data initialization for keyboard/mouse over
74	Display SETUP prompt and about to start floppy setup
75	Floppy setup over
76	Hard disk setup about to start
77	Hard disk setup over
79	About to initialize timer data area
7A	Timer data initialized and about to verify CMOS battery power
7B	CMOS battery verification over
7D	About to analyze POST results
7E	CMOS memory size updated

TABLE 18-8 AMI BIOS POST CODES (APRIL 1990 TO FEBRUARY 1991) *(CONTINUED)*

CODE	DESCRIPTION
7F	Look for DEL key and get into CMOS setup if found
80	About to give control to optional ROM in segment C800 to DE00
81	Optional ROM control over
82	Check for printer ports and put the addresses in global data area
83	Check for RS232 ports and put the addresses in global data area
84	Co-processor detection over
85	About to display soft error messages
86	About to give control to system ROM at segment E000
00	System ROM control at E000 over. Now give control to Int 19h boot loader

TABLE 18-9 AMI BIOS POST CODES (FEBRUARY 1991 TO DECEMBER 1991)

CODE	DESCRIPTION
01	Processor register test about to start and NMI to be disabled
02	NMI is disabled—power-on delay starting
03	Power-on delay complete. Any initialization before keyboard BAT is in progress
04	Initialization before keyboard BAT complete. Reading keyboard SYS bit to check soft reset/power-on
05	Soft reset/ power-on determined. Going to enable ROM (that is, disable shadow RAM/cache)
06	ROM enabled, calculating ROM BIOS checksum, waiting for KB controller input buffer to be free
07	ROM BIOS checksum passed (KB controller I/B free) going to issue BAT command to keyboard controller
08	BAT command to keyboard controller issued. Going to verify BAT command
09	Keyboard controller BAT result verified. Keyboard command byte to be written next
0A	Keyboard command byte code issued. Going to write command byte data
0B	Keyboard controller command byte written. Going to issue Pin 23 & 24 blocking/ unblocking command
0C	Pin 23 & 24 of keyboard controller is blocked/unblocked. NOP command of keyboard controller to be issued next
0D	NOP command processing done. CMOS shutdown register test to be done next
0E	CMOS shutdown register R/W test passed. Going to calculate CMOS checksum and update DIAG byte
0F	CMOS checksum calculation is done. DIAG byte written. CMOS initialization to begin (If "INIT CMOS IN EVERY BOOT" is set)
10	CMOS initialization done (if any). CMOS status register about to initialize for Date and Time
11	CMOS Status register initialized. Going to disable DMA and Interrupt controllers
12	DMA Controller #1 & #2, interrupt controller #1 & #2 disabled. About to disable video display and initialize port-B
13	Video display disabled and port-B initialized. Chipset initialization/auto memory detection about to begin
14	Chipset initialization/auto memory detection over, 8254 timer test about to start
15	CH-2 timer test halfway, 8254 CH-2 timer test to be complete
16	Ch-2 timer test over, 8254 CH-1 timer test to be complete
17	CH-1 timer test over, 8254 CH-0 timer test to be complete
18	CH-0 timer test over. About to start memory refresh

**TABLE 18-9   AMI BIOS POST CODES (FEBRUARY 1991 TO DECEMBER 1991)
(CONTINUED)**

CODE	DESCRIPTION
19	Memory Refresh started. Memory refresh test to be done next
1A	Memory Refresh line is toggling. Going to check 15 microsecond ON/OFF time
1B	Memory refresh period 30 microsecond test complete. Base 64KB memory test about to start
20	Base 64KB memory test started. Address line test to be done next
21	Address line test passed. Going to do toggle parity
22	Toggle parity over. Going for sequential data R/W test
23	Base 64KB sequential data R/W test passed. Setup before Interrupt vector initialization about to start
24	Setup before vector initialization complete. Interrupt vector initialization about to begin
25	Interrupt vector initialization done. Going to read I/O port of 8042 for turbo switch (if any)
26	I/O port of 8042 is read. Going to initialize global data for turbo switch
27	Global data initialization is over. Any initialization after interrupt vector to be done next
28	Initialization after interrupt vector is complete. Going for monochrome mode setting
29	Monochrome mode setting is done. Going for Color mode setting
2A	Color mode setting is done. About to go for toggle parity before optional ROM test
2B	Toggle parity over. About to give control for any setup before optional video ROM check
2C	Processing before video ROM control is done. About to look for optional video ROM and give control
2D	Optional video ROM control done. About to give control to do any processing after video ROM returns control
2E	Return from processing after the video ROM control. If EGA/VGA not found, then do display memory R/W test
2F	EGA/VGA not found. Display memory R/W test about to begin
30	Display memory R/W test passed. About to look for retrace checking
31	Display memory R/W test/retrace check failed. About to do alternate display memory R/W test
32	Alternate display memory R/W test passed. About to look for alternate display retrace checking
33	Video display checking over. Verification of display with switch setting and card to begin
34	Verification of display adapter done. Display mode to be set next
35	Display mode configuration complete. BIOS ROM data area about to be checked
36	BIOS ROM data area check over. Going to set cursor for power-on message
37	Cursor setting for power-on message ID complete. Going to display the power-on message
38	Power-on message display complete. Going to read new cursor position
39	New cursor position read and saved. Going to display the reference string
3A	Reference string display is over. Going to display the "Hit Esc" message
3B	"Hit ESC" message displayed. Virtual mode memory test about to start
40	Preparation for virtual mode test started. Going to verify from video memory
41	Returned after verifying from display memory. Going to prepare the descriptor tables
42	Descriptor tables prepared. Going to enter in virtual mode for memory test
43	Entered in the virtual mode. Going to enable interrupts for diagnostics mode
44	Interrupts enabled (if diagnostics switch is on). Going to initialize data to check memory wrap around at 0:0
45	Data initialized. Going to check for memory wrap around at 0:0 and finding the total system memory size
46	Memory wrap around test done (memory size calculation over). About to go for writing patterns to test memory
47	Pattern to be tested written in extended memory. Going to write patterns in base 640KB

TABLE 18-9 **AMI BIOS POST CODES (FEBRUARY 1991 TO DECEMBER 1991)**
(CONTINUED)

CODE	DESCRIPTION
48	Patterns written in base memory. Going to determine amount of memory below 1MB
49	Amount of memory below 1MB found and verified. Going to determine amount of memory above 1MB
4A	Amount of memory above 1MB found and verified. Going for BIOS ROM data area check
4B	BIOS ROM data area check over. Going to check Esc and clear memory below 1MB for soft reset
4C	Memory below 1MB cleared (soft reset). Going to clear memory above 1MB
4D	Memory above 1MB cleared (soft reset). Going to save the memory size
4E	Memory test started (no soft reset). About to display the first 64KB memory test
4F	Memory size display started(this will be updated during memory test). Going for sequential and random memory test
50	Memory test below 1MB complete. Going to adjust memory size for relocation/shadow
51	Memory size adjusted for relocation/shadow. Memory test above 1MB to follow
52	Memory test above 1MB complete. Preparing to go back to real mode
53	CPU registers are saved including memory size. Going to enter real mode
54	Shutdown successful (CPU in real mode). Going to restore registers saved during preparation for shutdown
55	Registers restored. Going to disable gate A20 address line
56	A20 address line disable successful. BIOS ROM data area about to be checked
57	BIOS ROM data area check halfway. BIOS ROM data area check to be complete
58	BIOS ROM data area check over. Going to clear "Hit Esc" message
59	"Hit Esc" message cleared and "WAIT" message displayed. About to start DMA and interrupt controller test
60	DMA page register test passed. About to verify from display memory
61	Display memory verification over. About to go for DMA #1 base register test
62	DMA #1 base register test passed. About to go for DMA #2 base register test
63	DMA #2 base register test passed. About to go for BIOS ROM data area check
64	BIOS ROM data area check halfway. BIOS ROM data area check to be completed
65	BIOS ROM data area check over. About to program DMA unit 1 and 2
66	DMA unit 1 and 2 programming over. About to initialize 8259 interrupt controller
67	8259 initialization over. About to start keyboard test
80	Keyboard test started (clearing output buffer, checking for stuck key). About to issue keyboard reset
81	Keyboard reset error/stuck key found. About to issue keyboard controller interface test command
82	Keyboard controller interface test over. About to write command byte and initialize circular buffer
83	Command byte written. Global data initialization done. About to check for lock-key
84	Lock-key checking over. About to check for memory size mismatch with CMOS
85	Memory size check done. About to display soft error; check for password or bypass setup
86	Password checked. About to do programming before setup
87	Programming before setup complete. Going to CMOS setup program
88	Returned from CMOS setup and screen cleared. About to do programming after setup
89	Programming after setup is complete. Going to display power-on screen message
8A	First screen message displayed. About to display "WAIT" message
8B	"WAIT" message displayed. About to perform main and video BIOS shadow
8C	Main/Video BIOS shadow successful. Setup options programming after CMOS setup about to start

TABLE 18-9 **AMI BIOS POST CODES (FEBRUARY 1991 TO DECEMBER 1991)**
(CONTINUED)

CODE	DESCRIPTION
8D	Setup options are programmed, mouse check and initialization to be done next
8E	Mouse check and initialization complete. Going for hard disk floppy reset
8F	Floppy check returns that floppy is to be initialized. Floppy setup to follow
90	Floppy setup is over. Test for hard disk presence
91	Hard disk presence test over. Hard disk setup to follow
92	Hard disk setup complete. About to go for BIOS ROM data area check
93	BIOS ROM data area check halfway. BIOS ROM data area check to be completed
94	BIOS ROM data area check over. Going to set base and extended memory size
95	Memory size adjusted due to mouse support hdisk type 47. Going to verify from display memory
96	Returned after verifying from display memory. Going to do any initialization before C800 option ROM control
97	Any initialization before C800 option ROM control is over. Option ROM check and control next
98	Option ROM control is done. About to give control to do any required processing after option ROM returns control
99	Any initialization required after option ROM test over. Going to set up timer data area and printer base address
9A	Return after setting timer and printer base address. Going to set the RS-232 base address
9B	Returned after RS-232 base address. Going to do any initialization before co-processor test
9C	Required initialization before co-processor is over. Going to initialize the co-processor next
9D	Co-processor initialized. Going to do any initialization after co-processor test
9E	Initialization after co-processor test complete. Going to check extended keyboard and ID and Num Lock
9F	Extended keyboard check done and ID flag set. Num Lock on/off. Keyboard ID command to be issued
A0	Keyboard ID command issued. Keyboard ID flag to be reset
A1	Keyboard ID flag reset. Cache memory test to follow
A2	Cache memory test over. Going to display any soft errors
A3	Soft error display complete. Going to set the keyboard typematic rate
A4	Keyboard typematic rate set. Going to program memory wait states
A5	Memory wait states programming over. Screen to be cleared next
A6	Screen cleared. Going to enable parity and NMI
A7	NMI and parity enabled. Going to do any initialization required before giving control to optional ROM at E000
A8	Initialization before E000 ROM control over. E000 ROM to get control next
A9	Returned from E000 ROM control. Going to do any initialization required after E000 optional ROM control
AA	Initialization after E000 optional ROM control is over. Going to display system configuration
00	System configuration is displayed. Giving control to INT 19h boot loader

TABLE 18-10 **AMI BIOS POST CODES (JUNE 1992 TO AUGUST 1993)**

CODE	DESCRIPTION
01	Processor register test about to start and NMI to be disabled
02	NMI is disabled. Power-on delay starting
03	Power-on delay complete. Any initialization before keyboard BAT is in progress next

TABLE 18-10 AMI BIOS POST CODES (JUNE 1992 TO AUGUST 1993) *(CONTINUED)*

CODE	DESCRIPTION
04	Any initialization before keyboard BAT is complete. Reading keyboard SYS bit, to check soft reset/power-on
05	Soft reset/power-on determined. Going to enable ROM (disable shadow RAM/cache) if any
06	ROM is enabled. Calculating ROM BIOS checksum and waiting for 8042 keyboard controller input buffer to be free
07	ROM BIOS checksum passed. KB controller input buffer free. Going to issue BAT command to the keyboard controller
08	BAT command to keyboard controller is issued. Going to verify the BAT command
09	Keyboard controller BAT result verified. Keyboard command byte to be written next
0A	Keyboard command byte code is issued. Going to write command byte data
0B	Keyboard controller command byte is written. Going to issue Pin 23 & 24 blocking/unblocking command
0C	Pin 23 & 24 of keyboard controller is blocked/unblocked. NOP command of keyboard controller to be issued next
0D	NOP command processing is done. CMOS shutdown register test to be done next
0E	CMOS shutdown register R/W test passed. Going to calculate CMOS checksum and update DIAG byte
0F	CMOS checksum calculation is done and DIAG byte written. CMOS initialization to begin (if "INIT CMOS IN EVERY BOOT" is set)
10	CMOS initialization done (if any). CMOS status register about to initialize for Date and Time
11	CMOS Status register initialized. Going to disable DMA and interrupt controllers
12	DMA controller #1 & #2, interrupt controller #1 & #2 disabled. About to disable video display and initialize port-B
13	Disable video display and initialize port B. Chipset initialize/auto memory detection about to begin
14	Chipset initialization/auto memory detection complete. 8254 timer test about to start
15	CH-2 timer test halfway. 8254 CH-2 timer test to be completed
16	CH-2 timer test over. 8254 CH-1 timer test to be completed
17	CH-1 timer test over. 8254 CH-0 timer test to be completed
18	CH-0 timer test over. About to start memory refresh
19	Memory refresh started. Memory refresh test to be done next
1A	Memory refresh line is toggling. Going to check 15 microsecond ON/OFF time
1B	Memory refresh period 30 microsecond test complete. Base 64KB memory test about to start
20	Base 64KB memory test started. Address line test to be done next
21	Address line test passed. Going to do toggle parity
22	Toggle parity over. Going for sequential data R/W test
23	Base 64KB sequential data R/W test passed. Any setup before interrupt vector initialization about to start
24	Setup required before vector initialization complete. Interrupt vector initialization about to begin
25	Interrupt vector initialization done. Going to read I/O port of 8042 for turbo switch (if any)
26	I/O port of 8042 is read. Going to initialize global data for turbo switch
27	Global data initialization is over. Any initialization after interrupt vector to be done next
28	Initialization after interrupt vector is complete. Going for monochrome mode setting
29	Monochrome mode setting is done. Going for Color mode setting
2A	Color mode setting is done. About to try toggle parity before option ROM test
2B	Toggle parity over. About to give control for any setup required before option video ROM check
2C	Processing before video ROM control is done. About to look for optional video ROM and give control

TABLE 18-10   AMI BIOS POST CODES (JUNE 1992 TO AUGUST 1993) *(CONTINUED)*

CODE	DESCRIPTION
2D	Option video ROM control done. About to give control for processing after video ROM returns control
2E	Return from processing after video ROM control. If EGA/VGA not found, do display memory R/W test
2F	EGA/VGA not found. Display memory R/W test about to begin
30	Display memory R/W test passed. About to look for the retrace checking
31	Display memory R/W test or retrace checking failed. About to do alternate display memory R/W test
32	Alternate display memory R/W test passed. About to look for the alternate display retrace checking
33	Video display checking over. Verification of display type with switch setting and actual card to begin
34	Verification of display adapter done. Display mode to be set next
35	Display mode setup complete. BIOS ROM data area about to be checked
36	BIOS ROM data area check over. Going to set cursor for power-on message
37	Cursor setting for power-on message complete. Going to display power-on message
38	Power-on message display complete. Going to read new cursor position
39	New cursor position read and saved. Going to display the reference string
3A	Reference string display over. Going to display the "Hit ESC" message
3B	"Hit ESC" message displayed. Virtual mode memory test about to start
40	Preparation for virtual mode test started. Going to verify from video memory
41	Returned after verifying from display memory. Going to prepare descriptor tables
42	Descriptor tables prepared. Going to enter in virtual mode for memory test
43	Entered in virtual mode. Going to enable interrupts for diagnostics mode
44	Interrupts enabled (if "diags" switch on). Going to initialize data to check memory wrap around at 0:0
45	Data initialized. Going to check for memory wrap around at 0:0 and find total memory size
46	Memory wrap around test done (size calculation finished). About to go for writing patterns to test memory
47	Pattern to be tested written in extended memory. Going to write patterns in base 640KB memory
48	Patterns written in base memory. Going to find out amount of memory below 1MB
49	Amount of memory below 1MB found and verified. Going to find amount of memory above 1MB
4A	Amount of memory above 1MB found and verified. Going for BIOS ROM data area check
4B	BIOS ROM data area check over. Going to check ESC and clear memory below 1MB for soft reset
4C	Memory below 1MB cleared (soft reset). Going to clear memory above 1MB
4D	Memory above 1MB cleared (soft reset). Going to save memory size
4E	Memory test started (no soft reset). About to display first 64KB memory test
4F	Memory size display started (this will be updated during memory test). Going for sequential and random memory test
50	Memory test below 1MB complete. Going to adjust memory size for relocation/shadow
51	Memory size adjusted for relocation/shadow. Memory test above 1MB to follow
52	Memory test above 1MB complete. Preparing to go back to real mode
53	CPU registers saved including memory size. Going to enter real mode
54	Shutdown successful (CPU in real mode). Going to restore registers saved during prep for shutdown
55	Registers restored. Going to disable gate A20 address line
56	A20 address line disable successful. BIOS ROM data area about to be checked
57	BIOS ROM data area check halfway. BIOS ROM data area check to be completed
58	BIOS ROM data area check over. Going to clear "Hit ESC" message
59	"Hit ESC" message cleared and "WAIT" message displayed. About to start DMA and PIC test
60	DMA page register test passed. About to verify from display memory
61	Display memory verification over. About to go for DMA #1 base register test

TABLE 18-10   AMI BIOS POST CODES (JUNE 1992 TO AUGUST 1993) *(CONTINUED)*

CODE	DESCRIPTION
62	DMA #1 base register test passed. About to go for DMA #2 base register test
63	DMA #2 base register test passed. About to go for BIOS ROM data area check
64	BIOS ROM data area check halfway. BIOS ROM data area check to be completed
65	BIOS ROM data area check over. About to program DMA unit 1 and 2
66	DMA unit 1 and 2 programming over. About to initialize 8259 interrupt controller
67	8259 initialization over. About to start keyboard test
80	Keyboard test started (clearing output buffer, and checking for stuck key). About to issue keyboard reset
81	Keyboard reset error/stuck key found. About to issue keyboard controller interface command
82	Keyboard controller interface test over. About to write command byte and initialize circular buffer
83	Command byte written and global data initialization done. About to check for lock-key
84	Lock-key checking over. About to check for memory size mismatch with CMOS
85	Memory size check done. About to display soft error and check for password or bypass setup
86	Password checked. About to do programming before setup
87	Programming before setup complete. Going to CMOS setup program
88	Returned from CMOS setup program, screen is cleared. About to do programming after setup
89	Programming after setup complete. Going to display power-on screen message
8A	First screen message displayed. About to display "WAIT" message
8B	"WAIT" message displayed. About to do main and video BIOS shadow
8C	Main/video BIOS shadow successful. Setup options programming after CMOS setup about to start
8D	Setup options programmed. Mouse check and initialization to be performed next
8E	Mouse check and initialization complete. Going for hard disk and floppy reset
8F	Floppy check indicates that floppy is to be initialized. Floppy setup to follow
90	Floppy setup is over. Test for hard disk presence to be performed
91	Hard disk presence test over. Hard disk setup to follow
92	Hard disk setup complete. About to go for BIOS ROM data area check
93	BIOS ROM data area check halfway. BIOS ROM data area check to be completed
94	BIOS ROM data area check over. Going to set base and extended memory size
95	Memory size adjusted due to mouse support and hard disk type 47. Going to verify from display memory
96	Returned after verifying from display memory. Going to do any initialization before C800 option ROM control
97	Any initialization before C800 option ROM control is over. Option ROM check and control will be done next
98	Option ROM control is done. About to give control to do any required processing after option ROM returns control
99	Any initialization required after option ROM test is over. Going to set up timer data area and printer base address
9A	Return after setting timer and printer base address. Going to set the RS-232 base address
9B	Returned after RS-232 base address. Going to do any initialization before co-processor test
9C	Required initialization before co-processor is over. Going to initialize the co-processor next
9D	Co-processor initialized. Going to do any initialization after co-processor test
9E	Initialization after co-processor test is complete. Going to check extended keyboard and keyboard ID and NUMLOCK
9F	Extended keyboard check is done, ID flag set, NUMLOCK on/off. Keyboard ID command to be issued
A0	Keyboard ID command issued. Keyboard ID flag to be reset

TABLE 18-10   AMI BIOS POST CODES (JUNE 1992 TO AUGUST 1993) *(CONTINUED)*

CODE	DESCRIPTION
A1	Keyboard ID flag reset. Cache memory test to follow
A2	Cache memory test over. Going to display soft errors
A3	Soft error display complete. Going to set keyboard typematic rate
A4	Keyboard typematic rate set. Going to program memory wait states
A5	Memory wait states programming over. Screen to be cleared next
A6	Screen cleared. Going to enable parity and NMI
A7	NMI and parity enabled. Going to do any initialization before giving control to option ROM at E000
A8	Initialization before E000 ROM control over. E000 ROM to get control next
A9	Returned from E000 ROM control. Going to do any initialization after E000 option ROM control
AA	Initialization after E000 option ROM control is over. Going to display the system configuration
00	System configuration is displayed. Giving control to INT 19h boot loader

TABLE 18-11   AMI WINBIOS POST CODES (DECEMBER 1993 AND LATER)

CODE	DESCRIPTION
01	Processor register test about to start. Disable NMI next
02	NMI is disabled. Power-on delay starting
03	Power-on delay complete (to check soft reset/power-on)
05	Soft reset/power-on determined. Going to enable ROM (disable shadow RAM cache if any)
06	ROM is enabled. Calculating ROM BIOS checksum
07	ROM BIOS checksum passed. CMOS shutdown register test to be done next
08	CMOS shutdown register test done. CMOS checksum calculation next
09	CMOS checksum calculation done. CMOS diagnostic byte written, and CMOS initialization to begin
0A	CMOS initialization done (if needed). CMOS status register to initialize Date and Time
0B	CMOS status register initialization done. Initialization before keyboard BAT to be done next
0C	KB controller I/B free. Going to issue the BAT command to keyboard controller
0D	BAT command to keyboard controller is issued. Going to verify the BAT command
0E	Keyboard controller BAT result verified. Any initialization after KB controller BAT next
0F	Initialization after KB controller BAT done. Keyboard command byte to be written next
10	Keyboard controller command byte is written. Going to issue Pin 23 & 24 blocking/unblocking command
11	Keyboard controller Pin 23 & 24 blocked/unblocked. Check for INS key during power-on
12	Checking for INS key during power-on finished. Going to disable DMA/IRQ controllers
13	DMA controller #1 and #2 and IRQ controller #1 and #2 disabled. Video display disabled, and port B initialized—chipset initialization/auto memory detection next
14	Chipset initialization/auto memory detection over. Uncompress the POST code if using a compressed BIOS
15	POST code is uncompressed. 8254 timer test about to start
19	8254 timer test over. About to start memory refresh test
1A	Memory refresh line is toggling. Going to check 15 microsecond ON/OFF time
20	Memory refresh 30 microsecond test complete. Base 64KB memory/address line test about to start
21	Address line test passed. Going to try toggle parity
22	Toggle parity finished. Going for sequential data R/W test on base 64KB memory
23	Base 64KB sequential data R/W test passed. Going to set BIOS stack and do any setup before Interrupt

TABLE 18-11   AMI WINBIOS POST CODES (DECEMBER 1993 AND LATER) (*CONTINUED*)

CODE	DESCRIPTION
24	Setup required before vector initialization complete. Interrupt vector initialization about to begin
25	Interrupt vector initialization done. Going to read input port of 9042 for turbo switch (if any) and clear password if POST diagnostic switch is ON
26	Input port of 8042 is read. Going to initialize global data for turbo switch
27	Global data initialization for turbo switch is over. Any initialization before setting video mode to be done next
28	Initialization before setting video mode is complete. Testing mono mode and color mode setting
2A	Monochrome and color mode settings done. About to toggle parity before option ROM test
2B	Toggle parity is finished. About to give control for any setup required before option video ROM check
2C	Processing before video ROM control is finished. About to look for option video ROM and give system control
2D	Option video ROM control is finished. About to give control for any processing after video ROM returns control
2E	Return from processing after video ROM control. If EGA/VGA not found, do display memory R/W test
2F	EGA/VGA not found. Display memory R/W test about to begin
30	Display memory R/W test passed. About to look for the retrace checking
31	Display memory R/W test or retrace checking failed. About to do alternate display memory R/W test
32	Alternate display memory R/W test passed. About to look for the alternate display retrace checking
34	Video display checking over. Display mode to be set next
37	Display mode setup. Going to display the power-on message
39	New cursor position read and saved. Going to display the "Hit DEL" message
3B	"Hit DEL" message displayed. Virtual mode memory test about to start
40	Going to prepare the descriptor tables
42	Descriptor tables prepared. Going to enter in virtual mode for memory test
43	Entered in virtual mode. Going to enable interrupts for diagnostics mode
44	Interrupts enabled (if diagnostic switch is on). Going to initialize data to check memory wrap around at 0:0
45	Data initialized. Going to check for memory wrap around at 0:0 and find total system memory size
46	Memory wrap around test done (memory size calculation over). About to go for writing patterns to test memory
47	Pattern to be tested written to extended memory. Going to write patterns in base 640KB memory
48	Patterns written to base memory. Going to find amount of memory below 1MB
49	Amount of memory below 1MB found and verified. Going to find out amount of memory above 1MB
4B	Amount of memory above 1MB found and verified. Check for soft reset. Going to clear memory below 1MB for soft reset next (if power-on, go to POST step 4Eh)
4C	Memory below 1MB cleared (soft reset)
4D	Memory above 1MB cleared (soft reset). Save memory size next (go to POST step 52h)
4E	Memory test started (not soft reset). Display first 64KB memory size next
4F	Memory size display started (this will be updated during memory test). Sequential and random memory test next
50	Memory testing/initialization below 1MB complete. Going to adjust displayed memory size for relocation/shadow
51	Memory size display adjusted for relocation/shadow. Memory test above 1MB to follow
52	Memory testing/initialization above 1MB complete. Going to save memory size information
53	Memory size information is saved, and CPU registers are saved. Going to enter real mode
54	Shutdown successful (CPU in real mode). Disable gate A20 line next
57	A20 address line disable successful. Going to adjust memory size depending on relocation/shadow

TABLE 18-11   AMI WINBIOS POST CODES (DECEMBER 1993 AND LATER) (*CONTINUED*)

CODE	DESCRIPTION
58	Memory size adjusted for relocation/shadow. Going to clear "Hit DEL" message
59	"Hit DEL" message cleared, and "WAIT" message displayed. About to start DMA and interrupt controller test
60	DMA page register test passed. About to go for DMA #1 base register test
62	DMA #1 base register test passed. About to go for DMA #2 base register test
65	DMA #2 base register test passed. About to program DMA unit 1 and 2
66	DMA unit 1 and 2 programming over. About to initialize 8259 interrupt controller
67	8259 initialization finished. About to start keyboard test
80	Keyboard test started. Clear output buffer, check for stuck key, and issue reset keyboard command next
81	Keyboard reset error/stuck key found. About to issue keyboard controller interface test command
82	Keyboard controller interface test over. About to write command byte and initialize circular buffer
83	Command byte written and global data initialization done. Check for lock-key next
84	Lock-key checking finished. About to check for memory size mismatch with CMOS
85	Memory size check done. About to display soft error and check for password or bypass setup
86	Password checked. About to do programming before setup
87	Programming before setup complete. Uncompress SETUP code and execute CMOS setup
88	Returned from CMOS setup and screen is cleared. About to do programming after setup
89	Programming after setup complete. Going to display power-on screen message
8B	First screen message displayed, and "WAIT" message displayed. About to do main/video BIOS shadow
8C	Main and video BIOS shadow successful. Setup options programming after CMOS setup about to start
8D	Setup options are programmed. Mouse check and initialization next
8E	Mouse check and initialization complete. Going for hard disk controller reset
8F	Hard disk controller reset done. Floppy setup to be done next
91	Floppy setup is complete. Hard disk setup to be done next
94	Hard disk setup is complete. Going to set base and extended memory sizes
96	Memory size adjusted due to mouse support and hard disk type 47. Any initialization before C800 done. Option ROM control next
97	Initialization before C800 option ROM control is finished. Option ROM check and control next
98	Option ROM control finished. About to give control for any required processing after option ROM returns control next
99	Any initialization required after option ROM test over. Going to set up timer data area and printer base address
9A	Return after setting timer and printer base address. Going to set the RS-232 base address
9B	Returned after RS-232 base address. Going to do any initialization before co-processor test
9C	Required initialization before co-processor is finished. Going to initialize the co-processor next
9D	Co-processor initialized. Going to do any initialization after co-processor test
9E	Initialization after co-processor test complete. Going to check extended keyboard and test keyboard ID and NUMLOCK
9F	Extended keyboard check is done and ID flag is set. NUMLOCK on/off. Issue keyboard ID command next
A0	Keyboard ID command issued. Keyboard ID flag to be reset
A1	Keyboard ID flag reset. Cache memory test to follow
A2	Cache memory test over. Going to display any soft errors
A3	Soft error display complete. Going to set the keyboard typematic rate

TABLE 18-11 AMI WINBIOS POST CODES (DECEMBER 1993 AND LATER) (*CONTINUED*)

CODE	DESCRIPTION
A4	Keyboard typematic rate set. Going to program memory wait states
A5	Memory wait state programming over. Going to clear the screen and enable parity/NMI
A7	NMI and parity enabled. Going to do any initialization required before giving control to option ROM at E000
A8	Initialization before E000 ROM control over. E000 ROM to get control next
A9	Returned from E000 ROM control. Going to do required initialization
AA	Initialization after E000 option ROM control is finished. Going to display the system configuration
B0	System configuration is displayed. Going to uncompress SETUP code for hot-key setup
B1	Uncompressing of SETUP code is complete. Going to copy any code to specific area
00	Copying of code to specific area done. Giving control to INT 19h boot loader
F0	Initialization of I/O cards in slots is in progress (EISA)
F1	Extended NMI sources enabling is in progress (EISA)
F2	Extended NMI test is in progress (EISA)
F3	Display any slot initialization messages
F4	Extended NMI sources enabling in progress

TABLE 18-12 AMI BIOS POST CODES (VERSION 2.2X)

CODE	DESCRIPTION
00	Flag test (the CPU is being tested)
03	Register test
06	System hardware initialization
09	Test BIOS ROM checksum
0C	Page register test
0F	8254 timer test
12	Memory refresh initialization
15	8237 DMA controller test
18	8237 DMA controller initialization
1B	8259 PIC initialization
1E	8259 PIC test
21	Memory refresh test
24	Base 64KB address test
27	Base 64KB memory test
2A	8742 keyboard test
2D	MC146818 CMOS IC test
30	Start the protected-mode test
33	Start the memory sizing test
36	First protected-mode test passed
39	First protected-mode test failed
3C	CPU speed calculation
3F	Reading the 8742 hardware switches
42	Initializing the interrupt vector area
45	Verifying the CMOS configuration
48	Testing and initializing the video system
4B	Testing unexpected interrupts

TABLE 18-12   AMI BIOS POST CODES (VERSION 2.2X) *(CONTINUED)*

CODE	DESCRIPTION
4E	Starting second protected-mode test
51	Verifying the LDT instruction
54	Verifying the TR instruction
57	Verifying the LSL instruction
5A	Verifying the LAR instruction
5D	Verifying the VERR instruction
60	Address line A20 test
63	Testing unexpected exceptions
66	Starting the third protected-mode test
69	Address line test
6A	Scan DDNIL bits for null pattern
6C	System memory test
6F	Shadow memory test
72	Extended memory test
75	Verify the memory configuration
78	Display configuration error messages
7B	Copy system BIOS to shadow memory
7E	8254 clock test
81	MC46818 real-time clock test
84	Keyboard test
87	Determining the keyboard type
8A	Stuck key test
8D	Initializing hardware interrupt vectors
90	Testing the math co-processor
93	Finding available COM ports
96	Finding available LPT ports
99	Initializing the BIOS data area
9C	Fixed/Floppy disk controller test
9F	Floppy disk test
A2	Fixed disk test
A5	Check for external ROMs
A8	System key lock test
AE	F1 error message test
AE	System boot initialization
B1	Call Int 19 boot loader

TABLE 18-13   AMI BIOS POST CODES (AMI PLUS FAMILY)

CODE	DESCRIPTION
01	NMI disabled
02	CPU register test complete
03	ROM checksum tests OK
04	8259 PIC initialization OK
05	CMOS interrupt disabled

TABLE 18-13   AMI BIOS POST CODES (AMI PLUS FAMILY) *(CONTINUED)*

CODE	DESCRIPTION
06	System timer (PIT) OK
07	PIC channel 0 test OK
08	Delta count channel (DMA) 2 test OK
09	Delta count channel (DMA) 1 test OK
0A	Delta count channel (DMA) 0 test OK
0B	Parity status cleared (DMA/PIT)
0C	Refresh and system time check OK (DMA/PIT)
0D	Refresh link toggling OK (DMA/PIT)
0E	Refresh period on/off 50% OK (RAM or address line)
10	Ready to start 64KB base memory test
11	Address line test OK
12	64KB base memory test OK
13	Interrupt vectors initialized
14	8042 keyboard controller test
15	CMOS read/write test OK
16	CMOS checksum and battery test
17	Monochrome mode setup OK (6845 chip)
18	CGA mode setup OK (6845 chip)
19	Checking video ROM
1A	Optional video ROM checks OK
1B	Display memory R/W test OK
1C	Alternate display memory checks OK
1D	Video retrace check OK
1E	Global byte setting for video OK (video adapter)
1F	Mode setting for mono/color OK (video adapter)
20	Video test OK
21	Video display OK
22	Power-on message display OK
30	Ready for virtual mode memory test
31	Starting virtual mode memory test
32	CPU now in virtual mode
33	Memory address line test
34	Memory address line test
35	Memory below 1MB calculated
36	Memory size computation OK
37	Memory test in progress
38	Memory initialization below 1MB complete
39	Memory initialization above 1MB complete
3A	Display memory size
3B	Ready to start memory below 1MB
3C	Memory test below 1MB OK
3D	Memory test above 1MB OK
3E	Ready to switch to real mode
3F	Shutdown successful
40	Ready to disable A20 gate (8042 chip)

TABLE 18-13   AMI BIOS POST CODES (AMI PLUS FAMILY) *(CONTINUED)*

CODE	DESCRIPTION
41	A20 gate disabled (8042 chip)
42	Ready to test DMA controller (8237 DMA chip)
4E	Address line test OK
4F	CPU now in real mode
50	DMA page register test OK
51	DMA unit 1 base register OK
52	DMA unit 1 channel OK
53	DMA unit 2 base register OK
54	DMA unit 2 channel OK
55	Latch test for both DMA units OK
56	DMA units 1 and 2 initialized OK
57	8259 PIC initialization complete
58	8259 PIC mask register OK
59	Master 8259 PIC mask register OK
5A	Check timer and keyboard interrupt
5B	PIT timer interrupt OK
5C	Ready to test keyboard interrupt
5D	ERROR...timer/keyboard interrupt
5E	8259 PIC error
5F	8259 PIC test OK
70	Start the keyboard test
71	Keyboard test OK
72	Keyboard test OK
73	Keyboard global data initialized (8042 chip)
74	Ready to start floppy controller setup
75	Floppy controller setup OK
76	Ready to start hard drive controller setup
77	Hard drive controller setup OK
79	Ready to initialize timer data
7A	Verifying CMOS battery power
7B	CMOS battery verification complete
7D	Analyze test results for memory
7E	CMOS memory size update OK
7F	Check for optional ROM at C0000h
80	Keyboard checked for SETUP keystroke
81	Optional ROM control OK
82	Printer ports initialized OK
83	Serial ports initialized OK
84	80x87 test OK
85	Ready to display any soft errors
86	Send control to system ROM E0000h
87	System ROM E0000h check complete
00	Call Int. 19 boot loader

TABLE 18-14   AMI BIOS POST CODES (AMI COLOR FAMILY)

CODE	DESCRIPTION
01	CPU flag test
02	Power-on delay
03	Chipset initialization
04	Hard/soft reset
05	ROM enabled
06	ROM BIOS checksum
07	8042 KBC test
08	8042 KBC test
09	8042 KBC test
0A	8042 KBC test
0B	8042 protected-mode test
0C	8042 KBC test
0D	8042 KBC test
0E	CMOS checksum test
0F	CMOS initialization
10	CMOS/RTC status OK
11	DMA/PIC disable
12	DMA/PIC initialization
13	Chipset and memory initialization
14	8254 PIT test
15	PIT channel 2 test
16	PIT channel 1 test
17	PIT channel 0 test
18	Memory refresh test (PIT chip)
19	Memory refresh test (PIT chip)
1A	Check 15µS refresh (PIT chip)
1B	Check 30µS refresh (PIT chip)
20	Base 64KB memory test
21	Base 64KB memory parity test
22	Memory read/write test
23	BIOS vector table initialization
24	BIOS vector table initialization
25	Check of 8042 KBC
26	Global data for KBC configured
27	Video-mode test
28	Monochrome-mode test
29	CGA-mode test
2A	Parity enable test
2B	Check for optional ROMs in the system
2C	Check video ROM
2D	Reinitialize the main chipset
2E	Test video memory
2F	Test video memory
30	Test video adapter
31	Test alternate video memory

TABLE 18-14	**AMI BIOS POST CODES (AMI COLOR FAMILY)** *(CONTINUED)*
CODE	**DESCRIPTION**
32	Test alternate video adapter
33	Video-mode test
34	Video mode setup
35	Initialize the BIOS ROM data area
36	Power-on message display
37	Power-on message display
38	Read cursor position
39	Display cursor reference
3A	Display SETUP start message
40	Start protected-mode test
41	Build descriptor tables
42	CPU enters protected mode
43	Protected-mode interrupt enabled
44	Check descriptor tables
45	Check memory size
46	Memory read/write test
47	Base 640KB memory test
48	Check 640KB memory size
49	Check extended memory size
4A	Verify CMOS extended memory
4B	Check for soft/hard reset
4C	Clear extended memory locations
4D	Update CMOS memory size
4E	Display base RAM size
4F	Perform memory test on base 640KB
50	Update CMOS RAM size
51	Perform extended memory test
52	Resize extended memory
53	Return CPU to real mode
54	Restore CPU registers for real mode
55	Disable the A20 gate
56	Recheck the BIOS vectors
57	BIOS vector check complete
58	Display the SETUP start message
59	Perform DMA and PIT test
60	Perform DMA page register test
61	Perform DMA #1 test
62	Perform DMA #2 test
63	Check BIOS data area
64	BIOS data area checked
65	Initialize DMA chips
66	Perform 8259 PIC initialization
67	Perform keyboard test
80	Keyboard reset
81	Perform stuck key and batch test (keyboard)

TABLE 18-14 AMI BIOS POST CODES (AMI COLOR FAMILY) *(CONTINUED)*

CODE	DESCRIPTION
82	Run 8042 KBC test
83	Perform lock key check
84	Compare memory size with CMOS
85	Perform password/soft-error check
86	Run CMOS equipment check
87	CMOS setup test
88	Reinitialize the main chipset
89	Display the power-on message
8A	Display the wait and mouse check
8B	Attempt to shadow any option ROMs
8C	Initialize XCMOS settings
8D	Rest hard/floppy disks
8E	Compare floppy setup to CMOS
8F	Initialize the floppy disk controller
90	Compare hard disk setup to CMOS
91	Initialize the hard disk controller
92	Check the BIOS data table
93	BIOS data table check complete
94	Set memory size
95	Verify the display memory
96	Clear all interrupts
97	Check any optional ROMs
98	Clear all interrupts
99	Setup timer data
9A	Locate and check serial ports
9B	Clear all interrupts
9C	Perform the math co-processor test
9D	Clear all interrupts
9E	Perform an extended keyboard check
9F	Set the NUMLOCK on the keyboard
A0	Keyboard reset
A1	Cache memory test
A2	Display any soft errors
A3	Set typematic rate
A4	Set memory wait states
A5	Clear the display
A6	Enable parity and NMI
A7	Clear all interrupts
A8	Turn over system control to the ROM at E0000
A9	Clear all interrupts
AA	Display configuration
00	Call Int. 19 boot loader

TABLE 18-15   AMI BIOS POST CODES (AMI EZ-FLEX FAMILY)

CODE	DESCRIPTION
01	NMI disabled...starting CPU flag test
02	Power-on delay
03	Chipset initialization
04	Check keyboard for hard/soft reset
05	ROM enable
06	ROM BIOS checksum
07	8042 KBC test
08	8042 KBC test
09	8042 KBC test
0A	8042 KBC test
0B	8042 protected-mode test
0C	8042 KBC test
0D	Test CMOS RAM shutdown register
0E	CMOS checksum test
0F	CMOS initialization
10	CMOS/RTC status OK
11	DMA/PIC disable
12	Disable video display
13	Chipset and memory initialization
14	8254 PIT test
15	PIT channel 2 test
16	PIT channel 1 test
17	PIT channel 0 test
18	Memory refresh test (PIT chip)
19	Memory refresh test (PIT chip)
1A	Check 15µS refresh (PIT chip)
1B	Test 64KB base memory
20	Test address lines
21	Base 64KB memory parity test
22	Memory read/write test
23	Perform any setups needed prior to vector table initialization
24	BIOS vector table initialization in lower 1KB of system RAM
25	Check of 8042 KBC
26	Global data for KBC setup
27	Perform any setups needed after vector table initialization
28	Monochrome-mode test
29	CGA-mode test
2A	Parity enable test
2B	Check for optional ROMs in the system
2C	Check video ROM
2D	Determine if EGA/VGA is installed
2E	Test video memory (EGA/VGA not installed)
2F	Test video memory
30	Test video adapter
31	Test alternate video memory

TABLE 18-15   AMI BIOS POST CODES (AMI EZ-FLEX FAMILY) *(CONTINUED)*

CODE	DESCRIPTION
32	Test alternate video adapter
33	Video-mode test
34	Video mode setup
35	Initialize the BIOS ROM data area
36	Set cursor for power-on message display
37	Display power-on message
38	Read cursor position
39	Display cursor reference
3A	Display SETUP start message
40	Start protected-mode test
41	Build descriptor tables
42	CPU enters protected mode
43	Protected-mode interrupt enable
44	Check descriptor tables
45	Check memory size
46	Memory read/write test
47	Base 640KB memory test
48	Find amount of memory below 1MB
49	Find amount of memory above 1MB
4A	Check ROM BIOS data area
4B	Clear memory below 1MB for soft reset
4C	Clear memory above 1MB for soft reset
4D	Update CMOS memory size
4E	Display base 64KB memory test
4F	Perform memory test on base 640KB
50	Update RAM size for shadow operation
51	Perform extended memory test
52	Ready to return to real mode
53	Return CPU to real mode
54	Restore CPU registers for real mode
55	Disable the A20 gate
56	Recheck the BIOS data area
57	BIOS data area check complete
58	Display the SETUP start message
59	Perform DMA page register test
60	Verify display memory
61	Perform DMA #1 test
62	Perform DMA #2 test
63	Check BIOS data area
64	BIOS data area checked
65	Initialize DMA chips
66	Perform 8259 PIC initialization
67	Perform keyboard test
80	Keyboard reset
81	Perform stuck key and batch test (keyboard)

TABLE 18-15   AMI BIOS POST CODES (AMI EZ-FLEX FAMILY) *(CONTINUED)*

CODE	DESCRIPTION
82	Run 8042 KBC test
83	Perform lock key check
84	Compare memory size with CMOS
85	Perform password/soft-error check
86	Run CMOS equipment check
87	Run CMOS setup if selected
88	Reinitialize the main chipset after setup
89	Display the power-on message
8A	Display the wait and mouse check
8B	Attempt to shadow any option ROMs
8C	Initialize system per CMOS settings
8D	Rest hard/floppy disks
8E	Compare floppy setup to CMOS
8F	Initialize the floppy disk controller
90	Compare hard disk setup to CMOS
91	Initialize the hard disk controller
92	Check the BIOS data table
93	BIOS data table check complete
94	Set memory size
95	Verify the display memory
96	Clear all interrupts
97	Check any optional ROMs
98	Clear all interrupts
99	Setup timer data
9A	Locate and check serial ports
9B	Clear all interrupts
9C	Perform the math co-processor test
9D	Clear all interrupts
9E	Perform an extended keyboard check
9F	Set the NUMLOCK on the keyboard
A0	Keyboard reset
A1	Cache memory test
A2	Display any soft errors
A3	Set typematic rate
A4	Set memory wait states
A5	Clear the display
A6	Enable parity and NMI
A7	Clear all interrupts
A8	Turn over system control to the ROM at E0000
A9	Clear all interrupts
AA	Display configuration
00	Call Int. 19 boot loader

TABLE 18-16   AWARD BIOS POST CODES (AT BIOS VERSION 3.0)

CODE	DESCRIPTION
01	Test CPU flag registers
02	Power-up check...initialize motherboard chipset
03	Clear the 8042 KBC
04	Reset the 8042 KBC
05	Test the keyboard
06	Disable video system, parity, and DMA controller
07	Test CPU registers
08	Initialize CMOS/RTC IC
09	Perform BIOS ROM checksum
0A	Initialize the video interface
0B	Test the 8254 timer channel 0
0C	Test the 8254 timer channel 1
0D	Test the 8254 timer channel 2
0E	Test CMOS RAM shutdown byte
0F	Test extended CMOS RAM (if present)
10	Test the 8237 DMA controller channel 0
11	Test the 8237 DMA controller channel 1
12	Test the 8237 DMA controller page registers
13	Test the 8741 KBC interface
14	Test the memory refresh and toggle circuits
15	Test the first 64KB of system memory
16	Set up the interrupt vector tables in low memory
17	Set up video I/O operations
18	Test MDA/CGA video memory unless an EGA/VGA adapter is found
19	Test the 8259 PIC mask bits channel 1
1A	Test the 8259 PIC mask bits channel 2
1B	Test the CMOS RAM battery level
1C	Test the CMOS RAM checksum
1D	Set system memory size from CMOS information
1E	Check base memory size 64KB at a time
1F	Test base memory from 64KB to 640KB
20	Test stuck interrupt lines
21	Test for stuck NMI
22	Test the 8259 PIC
23	Test the protected mode and A20 gate
24	Check the size of extended memory above 1MB
25	Test all base and extended memory found up to 16MB
26	Test protected-mode exceptions
27	Initialize shadow RAM and move system BIOS (and video BIOS) into shadow RAM
28	Detect and initialize 8242 or 8248 chip
2A	Initialize the keyboard
2B	Detect and initialize the floppy drive
2C	Detect and initialize serial ports
2D	Detect and initialize parallel ports
2E	Detect and initialize the hard drive

TABLE 18-16 **AWARD BIOS POST CODES (AT BIOS VERSION 3.0)** *(CONTINUED)*

CODE	DESCRIPTION
2F	Detect and initialize the math co-processor
31	Detect and initialize any adapter ROMs
BD	Initialize the cache controller if present
CA	Initialize cache memory
CC	Shutdown the NMI handler
EE	Test for unexpected processor exception
FF	Call the Int. 19 boot loader

TABLE 18-17 **AWARD BIOS POST CODES (VERSION 3.0 TO 3.03 C.1987)**

CODE	DESCRIPTION
01	Processor test part 1: processor status verification—tests following CPU status flags: set/clear carry zero sign and overflow (fatal)—infinite loop if failed or continue test if OK
02	Determine type of POST test—fails if keyboard interface buffer filled with data—infinite loop if failed or continue test if OK
03	Clear 8042 keyboard interface—send verify TEST_KBRD command (AAh)—continue test if OK
04	Reset 8042 keyboard controller—verify AAh return from 03
05	Get 8042 keyboard controller manufacturing status—read input port via keyboard controller to determine manufacturing or normal mode operation
06	Initialization chips on board LSI chips—disable color/mono video, parity, and DMA (8237A)—reset co-processor, initialize (8254) timer 1, clear DMA page registers and CMOS shutdown byte
07	Processor test #2: read/write verify SS/SP/BP registers with FFh and 00h data pattern
08	Initialize CMOS chip
09	EPROM checksum for 32 KB
0A	Initialize video interface
0B	Test 8254 channel 0
0C	Test 8254 channel 1
0D	Test 8254 channel 2
0E	Test CMOS date and timer
0F	Test CMOS shutdown byte
10	Test DMA channel 0
11	Test DMA channel 1
12	Test DMA page registers
13	Test 8741 keyboard controller
14	Test memory refresh toggle circuits
15	Test 1st 64KB of system memory
16	Set up interrupt vector table
17	Set up video I/O operations
18	Test video memory
19	Test 8259 channel 1 mask bits
1A	Test 8259 channel 2 mask bits
1B	Test CMOS battery level
1C	Test CMOS checksum
1D	Set up configuration byte from CMOS

TABLE 18-17 AWARD BIOS POST CODES (VERSION 3.0 TO 3.03 C.1987) *(CONTINUED)*

CODE	DESCRIPTION
1E	Sizing system memory & compare w/CMOS
1F	Test found system memory
20	Test stuck 8259 interrupt bits
21	Test stuck NMI (parity or I/O check) bits
22	Test 8259 interrupt functionality
23	Test protected mode and A20 gate
24	Sizing extended memory above 1MB
25	Test found system/extended memory
26	Test exceptions in protected mode
27	Reserved
2A	POST_KEYBOARD present during reset. Keyboard before boot has no relationship to POST 19
2B	POST_FLOPPY present during initialization of floppy controller and drive(s)
2C	POST_COMM present during initialization of serial cards
2D	POST_PRN present during initialization of parallel cards
2E	POST_DISK present during initialization of hard disk controller and drive(s)
2F	POST_MATH present during initialization of math co-processor—result remains after DOS boot; left on the port 80 display
30	POST_EXCEPTION present during protected-mode access or when processor exceptions occur—a failure indicates that protected-mode return was not possible
CC	POST_NMI present when selecting the F2 system halt option

TABLE 18-18 AWARD BIOS POST CODES (AT BIOS VERSION 3.1)

CODE	DESCRIPTION
01	Test CPU flag registers
02	Power-up check...initialize motherboard chipset
03	Clear the 8042 KBC
04	Reset the 8042 KBC
05	Test the keyboard
06	Disable video system, parity, and DMA controller
07	Test CPU registers
08	Initialize CMOS/RTC chip
09	Perform BIOS ROM checksum
0A	Initialize the video interface
0B	Test the 8254 timer channel 0
0C	Test the 8254 timer channel 1
0D	Test the 8254 timer channel 2
0E	Test CMOS RAM shutdown byte
0F	Test extended CMOS RAM (if present)
10	Test the 8237 DMA controller channel 0
11	Test the 8237 DMA controller channel 1
12	Test the 8237 DMA controller page registers
13	Test the 8741 KBC interface
14	Test the memory refresh and toggle circuits

TABLE 18-18   AWARD BIOS POST CODES (AT BIOS VERSION 3.1) *(CONTINUED)*

CODE	DESCRIPTION
15	Test the first 64KB of system memory
16	Set up the interrupt vector tables in low memory
17	Set up video I/O operations
18	Test MDA/CGA video memory unless an EGA/VGA adapter is found
19	Test the 8259 PIC mask bits channel 1
1A	Test the 8259 PIC mask bits channel 2
1B	Test the CMOS RAM battery level
1C	Test the CMOS RAM checksum
1D	Set system memory size from CMOS information
1E	Check base memory size 64KB at a time
1F	Test base memory
20	Test stuck interrupt lines
21	Test for stuck NMI
22	Test the 8259 PIC
23	Test the protected mode and A20 gate
24	Check the size of extended memory above 1MB
25	Test all base and extended memory found up to 16MB
26	Test protected-mode exceptions
27	Initialize shadow RAM and move system BIOS (and video BIOS) into shadow RAM
28	Detect and initialize 8242 or 8248 chip
2A	Initialize the keyboard
2B	Detect and initialize the floppy drive
2C	Detect and initialize serial ports
2D	Detect and initialize parallel ports
2E	Detect and initialize the hard drive
2F	Detect and initialize the math co-processor
31	Detect and initialize any adapter ROMs at C8000h to EFFFFh (and F0000h to F7FFFh)
39	Initialize the cache controller if present
3B	Initialize cache memory
CA	Detect and initialize alternate cache controller
CC	Shutdown the NMI handler
EE	Test for unexpected processor exception
FF	Call the INT 19 boot loader

TABLE 18-19   AWARD BIOS POST CODES (AT BIOS VERSION 3.3)

CODE	DESCRIPTION
01	Test 8042 KBC
02	Test 8042 KBC
03	Test 8042 KBC
04	Test 8042 KBC
05	Test 8042 KBC
06	Initialize any system chipsets
07	Test the CPU flags

TABLE 18-19   AWARD BIOS POST CODES (AT BIOS VERSION 3.3) *(CONTINUED)*

CODE	DESCRIPTION
08	Calculate the CMOS checksum
09	Initialize the 8254 PIT
0A	Test the 8254 PIT
0B	Test the DMA controller
0C	Initialize the 8259 PIC
0D	Test the 8259 PIC
0E	Test ROM BIOS checksum
0F	Test extended CMOS
10	Test the 8259 PIT chip
11	Test the 8259 PIT chip
12	Test the 8259 PIT chip
13	Test the 8259 PIT chip
14	Test the 8259 PIT chip
15	Test the first 64KB of RAM
16	Initialize the BIOS interrupt vector tables
17	Initialize the video system
18	Check video memory
19	Test 8259 PIC 1 mask
1A	Test 8259 PIC 2 mask
1B	Check CMOS battery level
1C	Verify the CMOS checksum
1D	Verify the CMOS/RTC chip
1E	Check memory size
1F	Verify memory in the system
20	Initialize DMA
21	Initialize PIC
22	Initialize PIT
24	Check extended memory size
25	Test all extended memory detected
26	Enter the protected mode
27	Initialize the shadow RAM and cache controller
28	Test the shadow RAM and cache controller
2A	Initialize the keyboard
2B	Initialize the floppy drive controller
2C	Check and initialize serial ports
2D	Check and initialize parallel ports
2E	Initialize the hard drive controller
2F	Initialize the math co-processor
31	Check for any option ROMs in the system
FF	Call the Int. 19 boot loader

TABLE 18-20	AWARD BIOS POST CODES (AT BIOS VERSION 4.0)

CODE	DESCRIPTION
01	Processor test 1: Verify CPU status flags—set, test, clear, and test the carry, zero, sign, overflow flags (fatal)
02	Processor test 2: Write/read/verify all CPU registers, except SS, SP, and BP with data patterns FF and 00
03	Calculate BIOS EPROM and sign-on message checksum—fail if not 0
04	Test CMOS RAM interface and verify battery power is available
05	Initialize chips: Disable NMI, PIE, AIE, UEI, SQWV; disable video, parity checking, and DMA; reset math co-processor, clear all page registers and CMOS RAM shutdown byte. Initialize timers 0, 1 and 2, and set EISA timer to a known state; initialize DMA controllers 0 and 1; initialize interrupt controllers 0 and 1; initialize EISA registers
06	Test memory refresh toggle to ensure memory chips can retain data
07	Set up low memory—initialize chipset early—test presence of memory—run OEM chipset initialization routines, clear lower 256KB of memory—enable parity checking and test parity in lower 256KB, then test lower 256KB of memory
08	Set up interrupt vector table and initialize first 120 interrupt vectors with SPURIOUS_INT_HDLR and initialize INT 00-1F according to INT_TBL
09	Test CMOS RAM checksum and load default if checksum is bad.
0A	Initialize keyboard—detect type of keyboard controller (optional) and set NUMLOCK status
0B	Initialize video interface—read CMOS RAM location 14 to find out type of video in use; detect and initialize the video adapter
0C	Test video memory and write sign-on message to screen
0D	OEM specific
0E	Reserved
0F	Test DMA controller 0 with AA, 55, FF, 00 pattern
10	Test DMA controller 1 with AA, 55, FF, 00 pattern
11	DMA page registers—use I/O ports to test address circuits
12-13	Reserved
14	Test 3254 timer 0 counter 2
15	Verify 8259 interrupt controller channel 1 by toggling interrupt lines off/on
16	Verify 8259 interrupt controller channel 2 by toggling interrupt lines off/on
17	Test stuck 8259 interrupt bits—turn interrupt bits off and verify no interrupt mask register is on
18	Test 8259 functionality—force an interrupt and verify the interrupt occurred
19	Test stuck NMI bits (parity I/O check)—verify NMI can be cleared
1A-1E	Reserved
1F	Set EISA mode—if EISA non-volatile memory checksum is good, execute EISA initialization—if not, execute ISA tests and clear EISA mode. Test EISA configuration, memory checksum, and communication ability
20	Initialize and enable EISA slot 0 (system board)
21-2F	Initialize and enable EISA slots 1-15
30	Size base memory from 256-640KB and test with various patterns
31	Test extended memory above 1MB using various patterns—press ESC to skip
32	If EISA mode flag set, test EISA memory found during slot initialization—press ESC to skip
33-3B	Reserved
3C	Verify CPU can switch in/out of protected, virtual 86. and 8086 page modes
3D	Detect if mouse is present, initialize it, and install interrupt vectors
3E	Initialize cache controller according to CMOS RAM setup

TABLE 18-20   AWARD BIOS POST CODES (AT BIOS VERSION 4.0) *(CONTINUED)*

CODE	DESCRIPTION
3F	Enable shadow RAM according to CMOS RAM setup or if MEM TYPE is SYS in the EISA configuration information
40	Reserved
41	Initialize floppy disk drive controller and any drives
42	Initialize hard disk drive controller and any drives
43	Detect and initialize serial ports
44	Detect and initialize parallel ports
45	Detect and initialize math co-processor
46	Print Setup message ("press CTRL-ALT-ESC to enter Setup") at bottom of the screen and enable setup
47	Set speed for boot
48-4D	Reserved
4E	Reboot if manufacturing POST loop pin is set—otherwise, display any messages for non-fatal POST errors—enter setup if user pressed CTRL-ALT-ESC
4F	Security check (optional)—ask for password
50	Write all CMOS RAM values back to CMOS RAM, and clear the screen
51	Pre-boot enable—enable parity, NMI, cache before boot
52	Initialize ROMs between C80000-EFFFF—when FSCAN enabled, initialize from C80000 to F7FFF
53	Initialize time value at address 40 of BIOS RAM area
55	Initialize DDNIL counter to NULLs
63	Boot attempt—set low stack and boot by calling INT 19
B0	Spurious interrupt occurred in protected mode
B1	Unclaimed NMI—if unmasked NMI occurs, display "Press F1 to disable NMI, F2 to boot"
BF	Program chipset—called by POST 7 to program chipset from CT table
C0	OEM specific—turn on/off cache
C1	OEM specific—test for memory presence and size on-board memory
C2	OEM specific—initialize board and turn on shadow and cache for fast boot
C3	OEM specific—turn on extended memory DRAM select and initialize RAM
C4	OEM specific—handle display/video switch to prevent display switch errors
C5	OEM specific—fast gate A20 handling
C6	OEM specific—cache routine for setting regions that are cacheable
C7	OEM specific—shadow video/system BIOS after memory proven good
C8	OEM specific—handle special speed switching
C9	OEM specific—handle normal shadow RAM operations
D0-DF	Debug—available POST codes for use during development
E0	Reserved
E1-EF	Set up pages: E1 = page 1, E2 = page 2, and so on
FF	If no error flags such as memory size are set, boot via INT 19—load system from drive A: or C: and display error message if boot device not found

 EISA codes may be sent to I/O port 300h. Be sure to set your POST reader card to the address that's appropriate for your system.

TABLE 18-21	AWARD BIOS POST CODES (EISA BIOS FAMILY)

CODE	DESCRIPTION
01	Test the CPU flags
02	Test the CPU registers
03	Initialize the DMA controller, PIC, and PIT
04	Initialize memory refresh
05	Initialize the keyboard
06	Test BIOS ROM checksum
07	Check CMOS battery level
08	Test lower 256KB of RAM
09	Test cache memory
0A	Configure the BIOS interrupt table
0B	Test the CMOS RAM checksum
0C	Initialize the keyboard
0D	Initialize the video adapter
0E	Test video memory
0F	Test DMA controller 0
10	Test DMA controller 1
11	Test page registers
14	Test the 8254 PIT chip
15	Verify 8259 PIC channel 1
16	Verify 8259 PIC channel 2
17	Test for stuck interrupts
18	Test 8259 functions
19	Test for stuck NMI
1F	Check extended CMOS RAM (if available)
20	Initialize and enable EISA slot 0
21-2F	Initialize and enable EISA slots 1 to 15
30	Check memory size below 256KB
31	Check memory size above 256KB
32	Test any EISA memory found during slot initialization
3C	Enter protected mode
3D	Detect and initialize mouse
3E	Initialize the cache controller
3F	Enable and test shadow RAM
41	Initialize floppy disk drive controller
42	Initialize hard disk drive controller
43	Detect and initialize serial ports
45	Detect and initialize math co-processor
47	Set speed for boot
4E	Display any soft errors
4F	Ask for password (if feature is enabled)
50	Check all CMOS RAM values and clear the display
51	Enable parity, NMI, and cache memory
52	Initialize any option ROMs present from C8000h to EFFFFh or F7FFFh
53	Initialize time value at address 40 of BIOS RAM area
63	Call Int. 19 for boot loader

TABLE 18-21   AWARD BIOS POST CODES (EISA BIOS FAMILY) *(CONTINUED)*

CODE	DESCRIPTION
B0	NMI still in protected mode (protected mode failed)
B1	Disable NMI
BF	Initialize any system-specific chipsets
C0	Cache memory on/off
C1	Check memory size
C2	Test base 256KB RAM
C3	Test DRAM Page Select
C4	Check video modes
C5	Test shadow RAM
C6	Configure cache memory
C8	Check system speed switch
C9	Test shadow RAM
CA	Initialize OEM chipset
FF	Call Int. 19 boot loader

TABLE 18-22   AWARD BIOS POST CODES (PNP BIOS VERSION 4-5.X)

CODE	DESCRIPTION
C0	Turn off OEM specific cache, shadow RAM. Initialize all the standard devices with default values.
C1	Auto detection of onboard DRAM & cache.
C3	Test the first 256K DRAM. Expand the compressed codes into temporary DRAM area, including the compressed system BIOS & Option ROMs.
C5	Copy the BIOS from ROM into E000-FFFF shadow RAM so that POST will go faster.
01-02	Reserved
03	Initialize EISA registers (EISA BIOS only).
04	Reserved
05	Keyboard Controller Self-Test. Enable Keyboard Interface.
06	Reserved
07	Verifies CMOS's basic R/W functionality.
BE	Program defaults values into chipset.
09	Program the configuration register of Cyrix CPU. OEM specific cache initialization.
0A	Initialize the first 32 interrupt vectors. Initialize INTs 33 to 120. Issue CPUID instruction to identify CPU type. Early Power Management initialization.
0B	Verify the RTC time is valid. Detect bad battery. Read CMOS data into BIOS stack area. Perform PnP initializations (PnP BIOS only). Assign IO & Memory for PCI devices (PCI BIOS only).
0C	Initialization of the BIOS data area (40:00-40:FF).
0D	Program some of the chipset's value. Measure CPU speed for display. Video initialization including MDA, CGA, EGA/VGA.
0E	Initialize the APIC (Multi-Processor BIOS only). Test video RAM (if monochrome display device found). Show startup screen message.
0F	DMA channel 0 test.
10	DMA channel 1 test.

TABLE 18-22   AWARD BIOS POST CODES (PNP BIOS VERSION 4-5.X) (CONTINUED)

CODE	DESCRIPTION
11	DMA page registers test.
12-13	Reserved
14	Test 8254 timer 0 counter 2.
15	Test 8259 interrupt mask bits for channel 1.
16	Test 8259 interrupt mask bits for channel 2.
17	Reserved
19	Test 8259 functionality.
1A-1D	Reserved
1E	If EISA NVM checksum is good, execute EISA initialization (EISA BIOS only).
1F-29	Reserved
30	Get base memory & extended memory size.
31	Test base memory from 256K to 640K. Test extended memory from 1M to the top of memory.
32	Display the Award Plug & Play BIOS extension message (PnP BIOS only). Program all onboard super I/O chips (if any) including COM ports, LPT ports, FDD port, and so on.
33-3B	Reserved
3C	Set flag to allow users to enter CMOS setup utility.
3D	Initialize keyboard. Install PS/2 mouse.
3E	Try to turn on level 2 cache.
3F-40	Reserved
BF	Program the rest of the chipset.
41	Initialize floppy disk drive controller.
42	Initialize hard drive controller.
43	If it is a PnP BIOS, initialize serial & parallel ports.
44	Reserved
45	Initialize math co-processor.
46-4D	Reserved
4E	If there is any error, show all the error messages on the screen & wait for user to press F1.
4F	If password is needed, ask for password. Clear the Energy Star logo (Green BIOS only).
50	Write all the CMOS values currently in the BIOS stack areas back into the CMOS.
51	Reserved
52	Initialize all ISA ROMs. Later PCI initializations (PCI BIOS only). PnP initializations (PnP BIOS only). Program shadow RAM according to setup settings. Program parity according to setup setting. Power Management initialization.
53	If it is not a PnP BIOS, initialize serial & parallel ports. Initialize time in BIOS data area.
54-5F	Reserved
60	Set up virus (boot sector) protection.
61	Try to turn on level 2 cache. Set the boot up speed according to setup setting. Last chance for chipset initialization. Last chance for Power Management initialization. Show the system configuration table.
62	Set up daylight savings according to setup values. Program the NUMLOCK, type rate & type speed according to setup setting.
63	If there is any changes in the hardware configuration, update the ESCD information (PnP BIOS only). Clear memory areas that have been used. Boot system via INT 19h.
FF	System booting. This means that the BIOS already passed control to the operating system.

TABLE 18-23   AWARD BIOS POST CODES (NON-PNP BIOS VERSION 4-5.X)

CODE	DESCRIPTION
C0	Turn Off Chipset. OEM Specific Cache control.
01	Processor Test 1. Processor Status (1FLAGS) Verification.
02	Processor Test 2. Read/Write/Verify all CPU registers.
03	Initialize Chipset. Disable NMI, PIE, AIE, UEI, SQWV. Disable video, parity checking, DMA. Reset math co-processor. Clear all page registers and CMOS shutdown byte. Initialize DMA controllers 0 and 1. Initialize interrupt controllers 0 and 1.
04	Test Memory Refresh Toggle. RAM must be periodically refreshed to keep the memory from decaying. This function ensures that the memory refresh function is working properly.
05	Blank video and initialize keyboard. Keyboard controller initialization.
06	Reserved
07	Test CMOS Interface and Verify Battery Status. CMOS is working correctly, detects bad battery.
BE	Chipset Default Initialization. Program chipset registers with power-on BIOS defaults.
C1	Memory Presence Test. OEM Specific-Test to size on-board memory.
C5	Early Shadow. OEM Specific-Early Shadow enable for fast boot.
C6	Cache Presence. External cache size detection test.
08	Set up Low Memory. Early chipset initialization. Memory presence test. OEM chipset routines. Clear low 64K of memory. Test first 64K memory.
09	Early Cache Initialization. Cyrix CPU initialization and cache initialization.
0A	Set up Interrupt Vector Table. Initialize first 120 interrupt vectors.
0B	Test CMOS RAM Checksum. Test checksum—if bad, or INSERT key pressed, load defaults.
0C	Initialize Keyboard. Detect type of keyboard controller.
0D	Initialize Video Interface. Detect CPU clock. Read CMOS location 14h to find the type of video in use. Detect and initialize video adapter.
0E	Test Video Memory. Write sign-on message to screen. Set up shadow RAM.
0F	Test DMA Controller 0. BIOS checksum test. Keyboard detect and initialization.
10	Test DMA Controller 1.
11	Test DMA Page Registers.
12-13	Reserved
14	Test Timer Counter 2.
15	Test 8259-1 Mask.
16	Test 8259-2 Mask.
17	Test Stuck Keys.
18	Test 8259 Interrupt Functionality.
19	Test Stuck NMI Bits.
1A	Display CPU clock.
1B-1E	Reserved
1F	Set EISA Mode. If EISA non-volatile memory checksum is good, execute EISA initialization. If not, execute ISA tests and clear EISA mode flag.
20	Enable Slot 0. Initialize slot 0 (System Board).
21-2F	Enable Slots 1-15. Initialize slots 1 through 15.
30	Size Base and Extended Memory. Size base memory from 256K to 640K and extended memory above 1MB.
31	Test Base and Extended Memory. Test base memory from 256K to 640K and extended memory above 1MB using various bit patterns.
32	Test EISA Extended Memory. If EISA flag is set, then test EISA memory found in slots.
33-3B	Reserved

TABLE 18-23   AWARD BIOS POST CODES (NON-PNP BIOS VERSION 4-5.X) (*CONTINUED*)

CODE	DESCRIPTION
3C	Set up Enabled.
3D	Initialize and Install Mouse. Detect if mouse is present; initialize and install interrupt vectors.
3E	Set up Cache Controller.
3F	Reserved
BF	Chipset Initialization. Program chipset registers with Setup values.
40	Display "Virus Protect" Disable or Enable.
41	Initialize Floppy Drive and Controller.
42	Initialize Hard Drive and Controller.
43	Detect and Initialize Serial/Parallel Ports.
44	Reserved
45	Detect and Initialize Math Co-processor.
46	Reserved
47	Reserved
48-4D	Reserved
4E	Manufacturing POST Loop or Display Messages.
4F	Security Password.
50	Write CMOS. Write all CMOS values back to RAM and clear screen.
51	Pre-boot Enable. Enable parity checker. Enable NMI. Enable cache before boot.
52	Initialize Option ROMs. Initialize any option ROMs present from C8000h to EFFFFh.
53	Initialize Time Value.
60	Set up Virus Protect.
61	Set Boot Speed.
62	Set up NUMLOCK.
63	Boot Attempt.
B0	Spurious. If interrupt occurs in protected mode.
B1	Unclaimed NMI. If unmasked NMI occurs, display "Press F1 to disable NMI, F2 reboot."
E1-EF	Set up Pages.
FF	Call Boot Loader.

TABLE 18-24   COMPAQ BIOS POST CODES (GENERAL) (*CONTINUED*)

CODE	DESCRIPTION
00	Initialize flags
01	Read manufacturing jumper
02	8042 Received Read command
03	No response from 8042
04	Look for ROM at E000
05	Look for ROM at C800
06	Normal CMOS reset code
08	Initialize 8259
09	Reset code in CMOS byte
0A	Vector via 40:67 reset function
0B	Vector via 40:67 with E01 function
0C	Boot reset function
0D	Test #2 8254 Counter 0

TABLE 18-24 COMPAQ BIOS POST CODES (GENERAL) (*CONTINUED*)

CODE	DESCRIPTION
0E	Test #2 8254 Counter 2
0F	Warm boot
10	PPI disabled
11	Initialize VDU controller
12	Clear Screen; turn on video
13	Test time 0
14	Disable RTC interrupts
15	Check battery power
16	Battery has lost power
17	Clear CMOS diagnostics
18	Test base memory (first 128KB)
19	Initialize base memory
1A	Initialize VDU adapters
1B	The system ROM
1C	CMOS checksum
1D	DMA controller/page registers
1E	Test keyboard controller
1F	Test 286 protected mode
20	Test real and extended memory
21	Initialize time-of-day
22	Initialize 287 co-processor
23	Test the keyboard and 8042
24	Reset A20
25	Test floppy disk subsystem
26	Test fixed disk subsystem
27	Initialize parallel printer
28	Perform search for optional ROMs
29	Test valid system configuration
2A	Clear screen
2B	Check for invalid time and date
2C	Optional ROM search
2D	Test timer 2
2F	Write to diagnostic byte
30	Clear first 128KB bytes of RAM
31	Load interrupt vectors 70-77
32	Load interrupt vectors 00-1F
33	Initialize MEMSIZE and RESETWD
34	Verify CMOS checksum
35	CMOS checksum not valid
36	Check battery power
37	Check for game adapters
38	Check for serial ports
39	Check for parallel printer ports
3A	Initialize port and communication timeouts
3B	Flush keyboard buffer

TABLE 18-24   COMPAQ BIOS POST CODES (GENERAL) (*CONTINUED*)

CODE	DESCRIPTION
40	Save RESETWD value
41	Check RAM refresh
42	Start write of 128KB RAM test
43	Rest parity checks
44	Start verify of 128KB RAM test
45	Check for parity errors
46	No RAM errors
47	RAM error detected
50	Check for dual frequency in CMOS
51	Check CMOS VDU configuration
52	Start VDU ROM search
53	Vector to VDU option ROMs
54	Initialize first display adapter
55	Initialize second display adapter
56	No display adapters installed
57	Initialize primary VDU mode
58	Start of VDU test (each adapter)
59	Check existence of adapter
5A	Check VDU registers
5B	Start screen memory test
5C	End test of adapter
5D	Error detected on an adapter
5E	Test the next adapter
5F	All adapters successfully tested
60	Start of memory tests
61	Enter protected mode
62	Start memory sizing
63	Get CMOS size
64	Start test of real memory
65	Start test of extended memory
66	Save size memory (base)
67	128KB option installed CMOS bit
68	Prepare to return to real mode
69	Back in real mode attempt successful
6A	Protected-mode error during test
6B	Display error message
6C	End of memory test
6D	Initialize KB "OK" string
6E	Determine size to test
6F	Start MEMTEST
70	Display XXXXXKB "OK"
71	Test each RAM segment
72	High order address test
73	Exit MEMTEST
74	Parity error on bus

TABLE 18-24   COMPAQ BIOS POST CODES (GENERAL) (*CONTINUED*)

CODE	DESCRIPTION
75	Start protected mode test
76	Prepare to enter protected mode
77	Test software exceptions
78	Prepare to return to real mode
79	Back in real mode successful
7A	Back in real mode not successful
7B	Exit protected test
7C	High order address test failure
7D	Entered cache controller test
7E	Programming memory cache
7F	Copy system ROM to high RAM
80	Start of 8042 test
81	Do 8042 self-test
82	Check result received
83	Error result
84	OK 8042
86	Start test
87	Got acknowledge
88	Got result
89	Test for stuck keys
8A	Key seems to be stuck
8B	Test keyboard interface
8C	Got result
8D	End of test
90	Start of CMOS test
91	CMOS seems to be OK
92	Error on CMOS read/write test
93	Start of DMA controller test
94	Page registers seem OK
95	DMA controller is OK
96	8237 initialization is complete
97	Start of NCA RAM test
A0	Start of floppy disk tests
A1	FDC reset active (3F2h bit 2)
A2	FDC reset inactive (3F2h bit 2)
A3	FDC motor on
A4	FDC timeout error
A5	FDC failed reset
A6	FDC passed reset
A8	Start to determine drive type
A9	Seek operation initiated
AA	Waiting for FDC seek status
AF	Floppy disk tests completed
B0	Start of fixed disk drive tests
B1	Combo board not found—exit

TABLE 18-24   COMPAQ BIOS POST CODES (GENERAL) (*CONTINUED*)

CODE	DESCRIPTION
B2	Combo controller failed—exit
B3	Testing drive 1
B4	Testing drive 2
B5	Drive error (error condition)
B6	Drive failed (failed to respond)
B7	No fixed drives—exit
B8	Fixed drive tests complete
B9	Attempt to boot from floppy disk
BA	Attempt to boot fixed drive
BB	Boot attempt failed FD/HD
BC	Boot record read, jump to boot record
BD	Drive error, retry booting
BE	Weitek co-processor test (386, 386/xxe, 386&486/33L, P486c)
C0	Disable NMI
C1	Turn off hard disk subsystem
C2	Turn off video subsystem
C3	Turn off floppy disk subsystem
C4	Turn off hard disk/modem subsystems
C5	Go to standby
C6	Update BIOS time of day
C7	Turn on hard disk/modem subsystems
C8	Turn on floppy disk subsystem
C9	Turn on video subsystem
CB	Flush keyboard input buffer
CC	Re-enable MNI
D0	Entry to clear memory routine
D1	Ready to go to protected mode
D2	Ready to clear extended memory
D3	Ready to reset back to real mode
D4	Back in real mode, ready to clear
D5	Clear base memory, CLIM register initialization failure (SLT/286)
D7	Scan and clear DDNIL bits
D9	4-way cache detect
DD	Built-in self-test failed
E0	Ready to replace E000h ROM
E1	Completed E000h ROM replacement
E2	Ready to replace EGA ROM
E3	Completed EGA ROM replacement
E8	Looking for serial external boot ID (Deskpro 2/386N, 386s/20)
E9	Receiving for serial external boot sector (2/386N, 386s/20)
EA	Looking for parallel external boot ID (2/386N, 386s/20)
EB	Receiving parallel external boot sector (2/386N, 386s/20)
EC	Boot record read, jump to boot record (2/386N, 386s/20)

TABLE 18-25   DELL BIOS POST CODES (GENERAL)

CODE	DESCRIPTION
01	CPU register test in progress
02	CMOS R/W test failed
03	BIOS ROM checksum bad
04	8254 PIT test failed
05	DMA controller initialization failed
06	DMA page register test failed
08	RAM refresh verification failed
09	Starting first 64KB RAM test
0A	First 64KB RAM or data line bad
0B	First 64KB RAM odd/even logic bad
0C	First 64KB address line bad
0D	First 64KB parity error
10	Bit 0 bad in first 64KB
11	Bit 1 bad in first 64KB
12	Bit 2 bad in first 64KB
13	Bit 3 bad in first 64KB
14	Bit 4 bad in first 64KB
15	Bit 5 bad in first 64KB
16	Bit 6 bad in first 64KB
17	Bit 7 bad in first 64KB
18	Bit 8 bad in first 64KB
19	Bit 9 bad in first 64KB
1A	Bit 10 bad in first 64KB
1B	Bit 11 bad in first 64KB
1C	Bit 12 bad in first 64KB
1D	Bit 13 bad in first 64KB
1E	Bit 14 bad in first 64KB
1F	Bit 15 bad in first 64KB
20	Slave DMA register bad
21	Master DMA register bad
22	Master interrupt mask register bad
23	Slave interrupt mask register bad
25	Loading interrupt vectors
27	Keyboard controller test failed
28	CMOS RAM battery bad
29	CMOS configuration validation in progress
2B	Video memory test failed
2C	Video initialization failed
2D	Video retrace failure
2E	Searching for a video ROM
30	Switching to video ROM
31	Monochrome operation OK
32	Color (CGA) operation OK
33	Color operation OK
34	Timer tick interrupt in progress (or bad)
35	CMOS shutdown test in progress (or bad)

TABLE 18-25   DELL BIOS POST CODES (GENERAL) (*CONTINUED*)

CODE	DESCRIPTION
36	Gate A20 bad
37	Unexpected interrupt in protected mode
38	RAM test in progress or high address line is bad
3A	Interval timer channel 2 bad
3B	Time of day test bad
3C	Serial port test bad
3D	Parallel port test bad
3E	Math co-processor test bad
3F	Cache memory test bad

TABLE 18-26   HP BIOS POST CODES (VECTRA FAMILY)

CODE	DESCRIPTION
01	LED test
02	Processor test
03	System (BIOS) ROM test
04	RAM refresh timer test
05	Interrupt RAM test
06	Shadow the system ROM BIOS
07	CMOS RAM test
08	Internal cache memory test
09	Initialize the video card
10	Test external cache
11	Shadow option ROMs
12	Memory subsystem test
13	Initialize EISA/ISA hardware
14	8042 self-test
15	Timer 0/Timer 2 test
16	DMA Subsystem test
17	Interrupt controller test
18	RAM address line independence test
19	Size the extended memory
20	Real-mode memory test (first 640KB)
21	Shadow RAM test
22	Protect-mode RAM test (extended RAM)
23	Real time clock (RTC) test
24	Keyboard test
25	Mouse test
26	Hard disk test
27	LAN test
28	Flexible disk controller subsystem test
29	Internal numeric co-processor test
30	Weitek co-processor test
31	Clock speed switching test
32	Serial port test
33	Parallel port test

TABLE 18-27   IBM BIOS POST CODES (AT-TYPE)

CODE	DESCRIPTION
01	CPU flag and register test
02	BIOS ROM checksum test
03	CMOS shutdown byte test
04	8254 PIT test—bits on
05	8254 PIT test—bits on
06	8237 DMA initialize registers test 0
07	8237 DMA initialize registers test 1
08	DMA page register test
09	Memory refresh test
0A	Soft reset test
0B	Reset 8042 KBC
0C	KBC reset OK
0D	Initialize the 8042 KBC
0E	Test memory
0F	Get I/P buffer switch settings
DD	RAM error
11	Initialize protected mode
12	Test protected-mode registers
13	Initialize 8259 PIC #2
14	Setup temporary interrupt vectors
15	Establish BIOS interrupt vectors
16	Verify CMOS checksum and battery OK
17	Set the defective CMOS battery flag
18	Ensure CMOS set
19	Set return address byte in CMOS
1A	Set temporary stack
1B	Test segment address 01-0000 (second 64KB)
1C	Decide if 512KB or 640KB installed
1D	Test segment address 10-0000 (over 640KB)
1E	Set expansion memory as contained in CMOS
1F	Test address lines 19-23
20	Ready to return from protected mode
21	Successful return from protected mode
22	Test video controller
23	Check for EGA/VGA BIOS
24	Test 8259 PIC R/W mask register
25	Test interrupt mask registers
26	Check for hot (unexpected) interrupts
05	Display 101 error (system board error)
27	Check the POST logic (system board error)
28	Check unexpected NMI interrupts (system board error)
29	Test timer 2 (system board error)
2A	Test 8254 timer
2B	System board error
2C	System board error
2D	Check 8042 KBC for last command

TABLE 18-27   IBM BIOS POST CODES (AT-TYPE) (*CONTINUED*)

CODE	DESCRIPTION
2F	Go to next area during a warm boot
30	Set shutdown return 2
31	Switch to protected mode
33	Test next block of 64KB
34	Switch back to real mode
F0	Set data segment
F1	Test interrupts
F2	Test exception interrupts
F3	Verify protected-mode instructions
F4	Verify protected-mode instructions
F5	Verify protected-mode instructions
F6	Verify protected-mode instructions
F7	Verify protected-mode instructions
F8	Verify protected-mode instructions
F9	Verify protected-mode instructions
FA	Verify protected-mode instructions
34	Test keyboard
35	Test keyboard type
36	Check for "AA" scan code
38	Check for stuck key
39	8042 KBC error
3A	Initialize the 8042
3B	Check for expansion ROM in 2KB blocks
40	Enable hardware interrupts
41	Check system code at segment E0000h
42	Exit to system code
43	Call boot loader
3C	Check for initial program load
3D	Initialize floppy for drive type
3E	Initialize hard drive
81	Build descriptor table
82	Switch to virtual mode
90-B6	Memory and bootstrap tests
32	Test address lines 0-15
44	Attempt to boot from fixed disk
45	Unable to boot...go to BASIC

TABLE 18-28   IBM BIOS POST CODES (PS/2-TYPE)

CODE	DESCRIPTION
00	CPU flag test
01	32-bit CPU register test
02	Test BIOS ROM checksum
03	Test system enabled

TABLE 18-28   IBM BIOS POST CODES (PS/2-TYPE) (CONTINUED)

CODE	DESCRIPTION
04	Test system POS register
05	Test adapter setup port
06	Test RTC/CMOS RAM shutdown byte
07	Test extended CMOS RAM
08	Test DMA and page register channels
09	Initialize DMA command and mode registers
0A	Test memory refresh toggle
0B	Test keyboard controller buffers
0C	Keyboard controller self-test
0D	Continue keyboard controller self-test
0E	Keyboard self-test error
0F	Set-up system memory configuration
10	Test first 512KB RAM
11	Halt system if memory test occurs
12	Test protested-mode instructions
13	Initialize interrupt controller 1
14	Initialize interrupt controller 2
15	Initialize 120 interrupt vectors
16	Initialize 16 interrupt vectors
17	Check CMOS/RTC battery
18	Check CMOS/RTC checksum
19	CMOS/RTC battery bad
1A	Skip memory test in protected mode
1B	Prepare for CMOS shutdown
1C	Set up stack pointer to end of first 64KB
1D	Calculate low memory size in protected mode
1E	Save the memory size detected
1F	Set up system memory split address
20	Check for extended memory beyond 64MB
21	Test memory address bus lines
22	Clear parity error and channel lock
23	Initialize interrupt 0
24	Check CMOS RAM validity
25	Write keyboard controller command byte
40	Check valid CMOS RAM and video system
41	Display error code 160
42	Test registers in both interrupt controllers
43	Test interrupt controller registers
44	Test interrupt mask registers
45	Test NMI
46	NMI error has been detected
47	Test system timer 0
48	Check stuck speaker clock
49	Test system timer 0 count
4A	Test system timer 2 count
4B	Check if timer interrupt occurred
4C	Test timer 0 for improper operation (too fast or too slow)

TABLE 18-28   IBM BIOS POST CODES (PS/2-TYPE) (*CONTINUED*)

CODE	DESCRIPTION
4D	Verify timer interrupt 0
4E	Check 8042 keyboard controller
4F	Check for soft reset
50	Prepare for shutdown
51	Start protected-mode test
52	Test memory in 64KB increments
53	Check if memory test done
54	Return to real mode
55	Test for regular or manufacturing mode
56	Disable the keyboard
57	Check for keyboard self-test
58	Keyboard test passed
59	Test the keyboard controller
5A	Configure the mouse
5B	Disable the mouse
5C	Initialize interrupt vectors
5D	Initialize interrupt vectors
5E	Initialize interrupt vectors
60	Save DDNIL status
61	Reset floppy drive
62	Test floppy drive
63	Turn floppy drive motor off
64	Set up serial ports
65	Enable real-time clock interrupt
66	Configure floppy drives
67	Configure hard drives
68	Enable system CPU arbitration
69	Scan for adapter ROMs
6A	Verify serial and parallel ports
6B	Set up equipment byte
6C	Set up configuration
6D	Set keyboard typematic rate
6E	Call Int. 19 boot loader

TABLE 18-29   MR BIOS POST CODES (MICROID RESEARCH VERSION 1.0A)

CODE	DESCRIPTION
01	Chipset problem
02	Disable NMI and DMA
03	Check BIOS ROM checksum
04	Test DMA page register
05	Keyboard controller test
06	Initialize the RTC, 8237, 8254, and 8259
07	Check memory refresh
08	DMA master test

TABLE 18-29   MR BIOS POST CODES (MICROID RESEARCH VERSION 1.0A) (*CONTINUED*)

CODE	DESCRIPTION
09	OEM-specific test
0A	Test memory bank 0
0B	Test PIC units
0C	Test PIC controllers
0D	Initialize PIT channel 0
0E	Initialize PIT channel 2
0F	Test CMOS RAM battery
10	Check video ROM
11	Test RTC
12	Test keyboard controller
13	OEM-specific test
14	Run memory test
15	Keyboard controller
16	OEM-specific test
17	Test keyboard controller
18	Run memory test
19	Execute OEM memory test
1A	Update RTC contents
1B	Initialize serial ports
1C	Initialize parallel ports
1D	Test math co-processor
1E	Test floppy disk
1F	Test hard disk
20	Validate CMOS contents
21	Check keyboard lock
22	Set number lock on keyboard
23	OEM-specific test
29	Test adapter ROMs
2F	Call Int. 19 boot loader

TABLE 18-30   CONTEMPORARY MR BIOS BEEP AND POST CODES (MICROID RESEARCH)

BEEP	CODE	DESCRIPTION
LH-LLL	03	ROM-BIOS checksum failure
LH-HLL	04	DMA page register failure
LH-LHL	05	Keyboard controller self test failure
LH-HHL	08	Memory refresh circuitry failure
LH-LLH	09	Master (16 bit) DMA controller failure
LH-HLH	09	Slave (8 bit) DMA controller failure
LH-LLLL	0A	Base 64K pattern test failure
LH-HLLL	0A	Base 64K parity circuitry failure
LH-LHLL	0A	Base 64K parity error
LH-HHLL	0A	Base 64K data bus failure
LH-LLHL	0A	Base 64K address bus failure

TABLE 18-30	CONTEMPORARY MR BIOS BEEP AND POST CODES (MICROID RESEARCH) (*CONTINUED*)

BEEP	CODE	DESCRIPTION
LH-HLHL	0A	Base 64K block access read failure
LH-LHHL	0A	Base 64K block access write failure
LH-HHHL	0B	Master 8259 failure
LH-LLLH	0B	Slave 8259 failure
LH-HLLH	0C	Master 8259 interrupt address failure
LH-LHLH	0C	Slave 8259 interrupt address failure
LH-HHLH	0C	8259 interrupt address error
LH-LLHH	0C	Master 8259 stuck interrupt error
LH-HLHH	0C	Slave 8259 stuck interrupt error
LH-LHHH	0C	System timer 8254 CH0/IRQ0 failure
LH-HHHH	0D	8254 channel 0 (system timer) failure
LH-LLLLH	0E	8254 channel 2 (speaker) failure
LH-HLLLH	0E	8254 OUT2 (speaker detect) failure
LH-LHLLH	0F	CMOS RAM read/write test failure
LH-HHLLH	0F	RTC periodic interrupt / IRQ8 failure
LH-LLHLH	10	Video ROM checksum failure
None	11	RTC battery discharged or CMOS contents corrupt
LH-HLHLH	12	Keyboard controller failure
None	12	Keyboard error—stuck key
LH-LHHLH	14	Memory parity error
LH-HHHLH	14	I/O channel error
None	14	RAM pattern test failed
None	15	Keyboard failure or no keyboard present
LH-LLLHH	17	A20 test failure due to 8042 timeout
LH-HLLHH	17	A20 gate stuck in disabled state
None	17	A20 gate stuck in asserted state
None	18	Parity circuit failure
None	19	Data bus test failed, or address line test failed, or block access read failure, or block access read/write failure, or banks decode to same location
LH-LHLHH	1A	Real time clock (RTC) is not updating
None	1A	RTC settings are invalid
None	1E	Diskette CMOS configuration invalid, or diskette controller failure, or diskette drive A: failure, or diskette drive B: failure
None	1F	FDD CMOS configuration invalid, or fixed disk C: failure, or fixed disk D: failure
None	20	Fixed disk configuration change, or diskette configuration change, or serial port configuration change, or parallel port configuration change, or video configuration change, or Memory configuration change, or co-processor configuration change
None	21	System key is in locked position
None	29	Adapter ROM checksum failure

In Table 18-30, L=low tone and H=high tone.

TABLE 18-31   MR BIOS POST CODES (MICROID RESEARCH VERSION 3.4X)

CODE	DESCRIPTION
00	Cold Start, output EDX register to I/O ports 85h, 86h, 8Dh, 8Eh for later use
01	Initialize any Custom KBD controller, disable CPU cache, cold initialize onboard I/O chipset, size & test RAM, size cache
02	Disable critical IO (monitor, DMA, FDC, I/O ports, speaker, NMI)
03	Checksum the BIOS ROM
04	Test page registers
05	Enable A20 Gate, issue 8042 Self-test
06	Initialize ISA I/O
07	Warm initialize custom KBD controller, warm initialize onboard I/O chipset
08	Refresh toggle test
09	Test DMA Master registers, test DMA Slave registers
0A	Test 1st 64K of base memory
0B	Test Master 8259 mask, test Slave 8259 mask
0C	Test 8259 Slave, test 8259 slave's interrupt range, initialize interrupt vectors 00–77h, initialize KBD buffer variables
0D	Test Timer 0, 8254 channel 0
0E	Test 8254 Ch2, speaker channel
0F	Test RTC, CMOS RAM read/write test
10	Turn on monitor, show any possible error messages
11	Read and checksum the CMOS
12	Call video ROM initialization routines, show Display sign-on message, show ESC Delay message
13	Set 8MHz AT bus
14	Size and test the base memory, stuck NMI check
15	No KB and PowerOn: Retry KB initialization
16	Size and test CPU cache
17	Test A20 OFF and ON states
18	Size and test external memory, stuck NMI check
19	Size and test system memory, stuck NMI check
1A	Test RTC time
1B	Determine Serial ports
1C	Determine parallel ports
1D	Initialize numeric co-processor
1E	Determine floppy disk controllers
1F	Determine IDE controllers
20	Display CMOS configuration changes
21	Clear screens
22	Set/reset NUMLOCK LED, perform security functions
23	Final determination of on-board serial/parallel ports
24	Set KB typematic rate
25	Initialize floppy controller
26	Initialize ATA disks
27	Set the video mode for primary adapter
28	Cyrix WB-CPU support, Green PC: purge 8259 slave, relieve any trapped IRQs before enabling PwrMgmt, set 8042 pins, CTRL-ALT-DEL possible now, Enable CPU features
29	Reset A20 to OFF, install Adapter ROMs
2A	Clear Primary Screen, convert RTC to system ticks, set final DOS timer variables

TABLE 18-31   MR BIOS POST CODES (MICROID RESEARCH VERSION 3.4X) (*CONTINUED*)

CODE	DESCRIPTION
2B	Enable NMI and latch
2C	Reserved
2D	Reserved
2E	Fast A20: Fix A20
2F	Purge 8259 slave; relieve any trapped IRQs before enabling Green-PC. Pass control to INT 19 boot
32	Test CPU Burst
33	Reserved
34	Determine 8042, set 8042 warm-boot flag STS.2
35	Test HMA Wrap, verify A20 enabled via F000:10 HMA
36	Reserved
37	Validate CPU: CPU Step NZ, CPUID Check. Disable CPU features
38	Set 8042 pins (Hi-Speed, Cache-off)
39	PCI Bus: Load PCI; Processor Vector initialized, BIOS Vector initialized, OEM Vector initialized
3A	Scan PCI bus
3B	Initialize PCI bus with intermediate defaults
3C	Initialize PCI OEM with intermediate defaults, OEM bridge
3D	PCI bus or Plug and Play: Initialize AT Slotmap from AT bus CDE usage
3E	Find phantom CDE ROM PCI-cards
3F	PCI bus: final Fast Back-to-Back state
40	OEM POST Initialization, Hook Audio
41	Allocate I/O on PCI bus, logs-in PCI-IDE
42	Hook PCI-ATA chips
43	Allocate IRQs on the PCI bus
44	Allocate/enable PCI memory/ROM space
45	Determine PS/2 mouse
46	Map IRQs to PCI bus per user CMOS, enable ATA IRQs
47	PCI-ROM install, note user CMOS
48	If Setup conditions: execute Setup utility
49	Test F000 Shadow integrity, transfer EPROM to Shadow-RAM
4A	Hook VL ATA Chip
4B	Identify and spin-up all drives
4C	Detect Secondary IRQ, if VL/AT-Bus IDE exists but IRQ not known yet, then auto-detect it
4D	Detect/log 32-bit I/O ATA devices
4E	ATAPI drive M/S bitmap to Shadow-RAM, Set INT13 Vector
4F	Finalize Shadow-RAM variables
50	Chain INT 13
51	Load PnP, Processor Vector initialized, BIOS Vector initialized, OEM Vector initialized
52	Scan Plug and Play, update PnP Device Count
53	Supplement IRQ usage—AT IRQs
54	Conditionally assign everything PnP wants
58	Perform OEM Custom boot sequence just prior to INT 19 boot
59	Return from OEM custom boot sequence. Pass control to 1NT 19 boot
5A	Display MR BIOS logo
88	Dead motherboard and/or CPU and/or BIOS ROM
FF	BIOS POST finished

TABLE 18-32 PHOENIX BIOS POST CODES (ISA/EISA/MCA BIOS)

CODE	DESCRIPTION
01	CPU register test
02	CMOS R/W test
03	Testing BIOS ROM checksum
04	Testing 8253 PIT chip
05	Initializing the 8237 DMA controller
06	Testing the 8237 DMA page register
08	RAM refresh circuit test
09	Test first 64KB of RAM
0A	Test first 64KB RAM data lines
0B	Test first 64KB RAM parity
0C	Test first 64KB RAM address lines
0D	Parity failure detected for first 64KB RAM
10-1F	Data bit (0-15) bad in first 64KB RAM
20	Slave DMA register faulty
21	Master DMA register faulty
22	Master PIC register faulty
23	Slave PIC register faulty
25	Initializing interrupt vectors
27	Keyboard controller test
28	Testing CMOS checksum and battery power
29	Validate CMOS contents
2B	Video initialization faulty
2C	Video retrace test failed
2D	Search for video ROM
2E	Test video ROM
30	Video system checks OK
31	Monochrome video mode detected
32	Color (40 column) mode detected
33	Color (80 column) mode detected
34	Timer tick interrupt test
35	CMOS shutdown byte test
36	Gate A20 failure (8042 KBC)
37	Unexpected interrupt
38	Extended RAM test
3A	Interval timer channel 2
3B	Test time-of-day clock
3C	Locate and test serial ports
3D	Locate and test parallel ports
3E	Locate and test math co-processor
41	System board select bad
42	Extended CMOS RAM bad

TABLE 18-33   PHOENIX BIOS BEEP AND POST CODES (PLUS VERSION 1.0)

BEEP	CODE	DESCRIPTION
none	01	CPU register test in progress
1-1-3	02	CMOS write/read failure
1-1-4	03	ROM BIOS checksum failure
1-2-1	04	Programmable interval timer failure
1-2-2	05	DMA initialization failure
1-2-3	06	DMA page register write/read failure
1-3-1	08	RAM refresh verification failure
none	09	1st 64KB RAM test in progress
1-3-3	0A	1st 64KB RAM chip or data line failure multi-bit
1-3-4	0B	1st RAM odd/even logic failure
1-4-1	0C	Address line failure 1st 64K RAM
1-4-2	0D	Parity failure 1st 64K RAM
2-1-1	10	Bit 0 1st 64KB RAM failure
2-1-2	11	Bit 1 1st 64KB RAM failure
2-1-3	12	Bit 2 1st 64KB RAM failure
2-1-4	13	Bit 3 1st 64KB RAM failure
2-2-1	14	Bit 4 1st 64KB RAM failure
2-2-2	15	Bit 5 1st 64KB RAM failure
2-2-3	16	Bit 6 1st 64KB RAM failure
2-2-4	17	Bit 7 1st 64KB RAM failure
2-3-1	18	Bit 8 1st 64KB RAM failure
2-3-2	19	Bit 9 1st 64KB RAM failure
2-3-3	1A	Bit A(10) 1st 64KB RAM failure
2-3-2	1B	Bit B(11) 1st 64KB RAM failure
2-4-2	1C	Bit C(12) 1st 64KB RAM failure
2-4-2	1D	Bit D(13) 1st 64KB RAM failure
2-4-3	1E	Bit E(14) 1st 64KB RAM failure
2-4-4	1F	Bit F(15) 1st 64KB RAM failure
3-1-1	20	Slave DMA register failure
3-1-2	21	Master DMA register failure
3-1-3	22	Master interrupt mask register failure
3-1-4	23	Slave interrupt mask register failure
none	25	Interrupt vector loading in progress
3-2-4	27	8042 keyboard controller test failure
none	28	CMOS power failure/checksum calculation in progress
none	29	CMOS configuration validation in progress
3-3-4	2B	Screen memory test failure
3-4-1	2C	Screen initialization failure
3-4-2	2D	Screen retrace test failure
none	2E	Search for video ROM in progress
none	30	Screen believed running with video ROM
none	31	Mono monitor believed operable
none	32	Color monitor (40 column) believed operable
none	33	Color monitor (80 column) believed operable
4-2-1	34	Timer tick interrupt test in progress or failed (non-fatal)

TABLE 18-33   PHOENIX BIOS BEEP AND POST CODES (PLUS VERSION 1.0) (*CONTINUED*)

BEEP	CODE	DESCRIPTION
4-2-2	35	Shutdown failure (non-fatal)
4-2-3	36	Gate A20 failure (non-fatal)
4-2-4	37	Unexpected interrupt in protected mode (non-fatal)
4-3-1	38	Memory high address line fail at 01000-0A000 (non-fatal)
4-3-2	39	Memory high address line fail at 100000-FFFFFF (non-fatal)
4-3-3	3A	Timer chip counter 2 failed (non-fatal)
4-3-4	3B	Time-of-day clock stopped
4-4-1	3C	Serial port test
4-4-2	3D	Parallel port test
4-4-3	3E	Math co-processor test
low 1-1-2	41	System board select bad
low 1-1-3	42	Extended CMOS RAM bad

TABLE 18-34   PHOENIX BIOS POST CODES (UMC CHIPSET/PCI BUS)

CODE	DESCRIPTION
02	Verify real mode
04	Get CPU type
06	Initialize system hardware
08	Initialize chipset registers with initial POST values
09	Set in-POST flag
0A	Initialize CPU registers
0C	Initialize cache to initial POST values
0E	Initialize I/O
10	Initialize power management
11	Load alternate registers with initial POST values
12	Jump to User Patch 0
14	Initialize keyboard controller
16	BIOS ROM checksum
18	8254 timer initialization
1A	8237 DMA controller initialization
1C	Reset PIC
20	Test DRAM refresh
22	Test 8742 keyboard controller
24	Set ES segment register to 4GB
26	Enable Address Line A20
28	Autosize DRAM
2A	Clear 512KB base RAM
2C	Test 512KB base address lines
2E	Test 512KB base memory
30	Test base address memory
32	Test CPU bus clock frequency
34	Test CMOS RAM

TABLE 18-34	PHOENIX BIOS POST CODES (UMC CHIPSET/PCI BUS) (*CONTINUED*)
CODE	**DESCRIPTION**
35	Test chipset register initialized
36	Test check resume
37	Reinitialize the chipset
38	Shadow system BIOS ROM
39	Reinitialize the cache
3A	Autosize the cache
3C	Configure advanced chipset registers
3D	Load alternate registers with CMOS values
3E	Read hardware configuration from keyboard controller
40	Set initial CPU speed
42	Initialize interrupt vectors
44	Initialize BIOS interrupts
46	Check ROM copyright notice
47	Initialize manager for PCI option ROMs
48	Check video configuration against CMOS
49	Initialize PCI bus and devices
4A	Initialize all video adapters
4C	Shadow video BIOS ROM
4E	Display copyright notice
50	Display CPU type and speed
52	Test keyboard
54	Set key click if enabled
56	Enable keyboard
58	Test for unexpected interrupts
5A	Display prompt "Press F2 to Enter Setup"
5C	Test RAM between 512KB and 640KB
5E	Test base memory
60	Test expanded memory
62	Test extended memory address lines
64	Jump to User Patch 1
66	Configure advanced cache registers
68	Enable external and CPU caches
69	Set up power management
6A	Display external cache size
6C	Display shadow message
6E	Display non-disposable segments
70	Display error messages
72	Check for configuration errors
74	Test RTC
76	Check for keyboard errors
7A	Enable keylock
7C	Set up hardware interrupt vectors
7E	Test co-processor if present
80	Disable onboard I/O ports
82	Detect and install external RS232 ports

TABLE 18-34   PHOENIX BIOS POST CODES (UMC CHIPSET/PCI BUS) (*CONTINUED*)

CODE	DESCRIPTION
84	Detect and install external parallel ports
86	Reinitialize onboard I/O ports
88	Initialize BIOS data area
8A	Initialize extended BIOS data area
8C	Initialize floppy controller
8E	Hard disk "auto-type" configuration
90	Initialize hard disk controller
91	Initialize local bus hard disk controller
92	Jump to User Patch 2
94	Disable A20 address line
96	Clear huge ES segment register
98	Search for option ROMs
9A	Shadow option ROMs
9C	Set up power management
9E	Enable hardware interrupts
A0	Set time of day
A2	Check key lock
A4	Initialize typematic rate
A8	Erase F2 prompt
AA	Scan for F2 key stroke
AC	Enter Setup
AE	Clear in-POST flag
B0	Check for errors
B2	POST done
B4	One beep
B6	Check password (optional)
B8	Clear global descriptor table
BC	Clear parity checkers
BE	Clear screen (optional)
BF	Check virus and backup reminders
C0	Try to boot with INT 19
D0	Interrupt handler error
D2	Unknown interrupt error
D4	Pending interrupt error
D6	Initialize option ROM error
D8	Shutdown error
DA	Extended Block Move
DC	Shutdown 10 error
E2	Initialize the chipset
E3	Check for Forced Flash
E5	Check HW status of ROM
E6	BIOS ROM is OK
E7	Do a complete RAM test
E8	Do OEM initialization
E9	Initialize interrupt controller

TABLE 18-34   PHOENIX BIOS POST CODES (UMC CHIPSET/PCI BUS) (*CONTINUED*)

CODE	DESCRIPTION
EA	Read in the bootstrap code
EB	Initialize all vectors
EC	Boot the flash program
ED	Initialize the boot device
EE	Boot code was read OK

TABLE 18-35   PHOENIX BIOS POST CODES (PCI BUS)

CODE	DESCRIPTION
02	If the CPU is in protected mode, turn on A20 and pulse the reset line, forcing a shutdown
04	On a cold boot, save the CPU type-information value in the CMOS
06	Reset DMA controllers, disable videos, clear pending interrupts from RTC, and set up port B register
08	Initialize chipset control registers to power-on defaults
0A	Set a bit in the CMOS that indicates POST—used to determine if the current configuration causes the BIOS to hang
0C	Initialize I/O module control registers
0E	External CPU caches are initialized and cache registers are set to default
10/12/14	Verify response of 8742
16	Verify BIOS ROM checksums to zero
18	Initialize all three of 8254 timers
1A	Initialize DMA command register and initialize 8 DMA channels
1C	Initialize 8259 interrupt controller and cascade and edge-triggered mode
20	Test DRAM refresh by polling refresh bit in port B
22	Test 8742 keyboard controller and send self-test command to 8742—also read the switch inputs from the 8742 and write the keyboard controller command byte
24	Set ES segment register to 4GB
26	Enable Address Line A20
28	Autosize DRAM
2A	Clear first 64KB of RAM
2C	Test RAM address lines
2E	Test first 64KB bank of memory consisting of a chip address line test and a RAM test
30/32	Find true MHz value
34	Clear CMOS diagnostic byte, check RTC, and verify battery has not lost power—checksum the CMOS and verify it has not been corrupted
36/38/3A	External cache is autosized and its configuration saved for enabling later in POST
3C	Configure advanced cache features and configure external cache's configurable parameters
3E	Read hardware configuration from keyboard controller
40	Set system power-on speed to the rate determined by the CMOS—if the CMOS is invalid use a conservative speed
42	Initialize interrupt vectors 0-77h to the BIOS general interrupt handler

TABLE 18-35   PHOENIX BIOS POST CODES (PCI BUS) (CONTINUED)

CODE	DESCRIPTION
44	Initialize interrupt vectors 0-20h to proper values from the BIOS interrupt table
46	Check copyright message checksum
48	Check video configuration
4A	Initialize both monochrome and color graphics video adapters
4C/4E	Display copyright message
50	Display CPU type and speed
52	Test for the self-test code if a cold start—when powered by the keyboard, performs a self-test and sends an AA if successful
54	Initialize keystroke clicker during POST
56	Enable keyboard
58	Test for unexpected interrupts
5A	Display prompt "Press F2 to Enter Setup"
5C	Determine and test the amount of memory available
5E	Perform address test on base memory
60	Determine and test the amount of extended memory available
62	Perform an address line test on A0 to the amount of memory available
68	External and CPU caches are enabled (if present) and non-cacheable regions are configured if necessary
6A	Display cache size onscreen if non-zero
6C	Display BIOS shadow status
6E	Display the starting offset of the non-disposable section of the BIOS
70	Check flags in CMOS and in the BIOS data area to see if any errors have been detected during POST—if so, display error messages onscreen
72	Check status bits for configuration errors—if so, display error messages onscreen
74	Test RTC if the battery has not lost power
76	Check status bits for keyboard errors—if so display error messages onscreen
78	Check for stuck keys on the keyboard—if so display error messages onscreen
7A	Enable keylock
7C	Set up hardware interrupt vectors
7E	Test co-processor if present
80-82	Detect and install RS232 ports
84	Detect and install parallel ports
86-88	Initialize timeouts/key buffer/soft reset flag
8A	Initialize extended BIOS data area and initialize the mouse
8C	Initialize both floppy disks and display an error message if failure was detected
8E	Hard disk autotype configuration
90	If the CMOS RAM is valid and intact and fixed disks are defined, call the fixed disk routine to initialize the fixed disk system and take over the appropriate interrupt vectors
92-94	Disable A20 address line
96-98	Scan for ROM BIOS extensions
9E	Enable hardware interrupts
A0	Set time of day
A2	Set up NUMLOCK indicator and display a message if key switch is locked
A4	Initialize typematic rate
A6	Initialize hard disk autoparking
A8	Erase F2 prompt

TABLE 18-35 PHOENIX BIOS POST CODES (PCI BUS) *(CONTINUED)*

CODE	DESCRIPTION
AA	Scan for F2 key strokes
AC	Check to see if SETUP should be executed
AE	Clear ConfigFailedBit and InPostBit in CMOS
B0	Check for POST errors
B2	Set/clear status bits to reflect POST complete
B4	One beep
B6	Check for password before boot
B8	Clear global descriptor table (GDT)
BA	Initialize the screen saver
BC	Clear parity error latch
BE	Clear screen
C0	Try to boot with INT 19
D0-D2	If an interrupt occurs before interrupt vectors have been initialized, this interrupt handler will try to see if the interrupt caused was an 8259 interrupt
D4	Clear pending timer and keyboard interrupts and transfer control to the double word address located at RomCheck
D6-D8-DA	Return from extended block move

TABLE 18-36 PHOENIX BIOS POST CODES (VERSION 4.0)

BEEP	CODE	DESCRIPTION
1-1-1-3	02	Verify real-mode operation
1-1-2-1	04	Get the CPU type
1-1-2-3	06	Initialize system hardware
1-1-3-1	08	Initialize chipset registers with POST values
1-1-3-2	09	Set POST flag
1-1-3-3	0A	Initialize CPU registers
1-1-4-1	0C	Initialize cache to initial POST values
1-1-4-3	0E	Initialize I/O
1-2-1-1	10	Initialize Power Management
1-2-1-2	11	Load alternate registers with POST values
1-2-1-3	12	Jump to UserPatch0
1-2-2-1	14	Initialize keyboard controller
1-2-2-3	16	BIOS ROM checksum
1-2-3-1	18	8254 timer initialization
1-2-3-3	1A	8237 DMA controller initialization
1-2-4-1	1C	Reset Programmable Interrupt Controller
1-3-1-1	20	Test DRAM refresh
1-3-1-3	22	Test 8742 Keyboard Controller
1-3-2-1	24	Set ES segment to register to 4 GB
1-3-3-1	28	Auto-size DRAM
1-3-3-3	2A	Clear 512K base RAM
1-3-4-1	2C	Test 512 base address lines
1-3-4-3	2E	Test 512K base memory

TABLE 18-36   PHOENIX BIOS POST CODES (VERSION 4.0) (CONTINUED)

BEEP	CODE	DESCRIPTION
1-4-1-3	32	Test CPU bus-clock frequency
1-4-2-4	37	Reinitialize the motherboard chipset
1-4-3-1	38	Shadow system BIOS ROM
1-4-3-2	39	Reinitialize the cache
1-4-3-3	3A	Autosize cache
1-4-4-1	3C	Configure advanced chipset registers
1-4-4-2	3D	Load alternate registers with CMOS values
2-1-1-1	40	Set initial CPU speed
2-1-1-3	42	Initialize interrupt vectors
2-1-2-1	44	Initialize BIOS interrupts
2-1-2-3	46	Check ROM copyright notice
2-1-2-4	47	Initialize manager for PCI Options ROMs
2-1-3-1	48	Check video configuration against CMOS
2-1-3-2	49	Initialize PCI bus and devices
2-1-3-3	4A	Initialize all video adapters in system
2-1-4-1	4C	Shadow video BIOS ROM
2-1-4-3	4E	Display copyright notice
2-2-1-1	50	Display CPU type and speed
2-2-1-3	52	Test keyboard
2-2-2-1	54	Set key click if enabled
2-2-2-3	56	Enable keyboard
2-2-3-1	58	Test for unexpected interrupts
2-2-3-3	5A	Display prompt "Press F2 to enter SETUP"
2-2-4-1	5C	Test RAM between 512 and 640k
2-3-1-1	60	Test expanded memory
2-3-1-3	62	Test extended memory address lines
2-3-2-1	64	Jump to UserPatch1
2-3-2-3	66	Configure advanced cache registers
2-3-3-1	68	Enable external and CPU caches
2-3-3-3	6A	Display external cache size
2-3-4-1	6C	Display shadow message
2-3-4-3	6E	Display non-disposable segments
2-4-1-1	70	Display error messages
2-4-1-3	72	Check for configuration errors
2-4-2-1	74	Test real-time clock
2-4-2-3	76	Check for keyboard errors
2-4-4-1	7C	Set up hardware interrupts vectors
2-4-4-3	7E	Test co-processor if present
3-1-1-1	80	Disable onboard I/O ports
3-1-1-3	82	Detect and install external RS232 ports
3-1-2-1	84	Detect and install external parallel ports
3-1-2-3	86	Re-initialize onboard I/O ports
3-1-3-1	88	Initialize BIOS data area
3-1-3-3	8A	Initialize extended BIOS data area
3-1-4-1	8C	Initialize floppy controller

TABLE 18-36   PHOENIX BIOS POST CODES (VERSION 4.0) (CONTINUED)

BEEP	CODE	DESCRIPTION
3-2-1-1	90	Initialize hard-disk controller
3-2-1-2	91	Initialize local-bus hard-disk controller
3-2-1-3	92	Jump to UserPatch2
3-2-2-1	94	Disable A20 address line
3-2-2-3	96	Clear huge ES segment register
3-2-3-1	98	Search for option ROMs
3-2-3-3	9A	Shadow option ROMs
3-2-4-1	9C	Set up Power Management
3-2-4-3	9E	Enable hardware interrupts
3-3-1-1	A0	Set time of day
3-3-1-3	A2	Check key lock
3-3-3-1	A8	Erase F2 prompt
3-3-3-3	AA	Scan for F2 key stroke
3-3-4-1	AC	Enter SETUP
3-3-4-3	AE	Clear in-POST flag
3-4-1-1	B0	Check for errors
3-4-1-3	B2	POST done—prepare to boot operating system
3-4-2-1	B4	One beep
3-4-2-3	B6	Check password (optional)
3-4-3-1	B8	Clear global descriptor table
3-4-4-1	BC	Clear parity checkers
3-4-4-3	BE	Clear screen (optional)
3-4-4-4	BF	Check virus and backup reminders
4-1-1-1	C0	Try to boot with INT 19
4-2-1-1	D0	Interrupt handler error
4-2-1-3	D2	Unknown interrupt error
4-2-2-1	D4	Pending interrupt error
4-2-2-3	D6	Initialize option ROM error
4-2-3-1	D8	Shutdown error
4-2-3-3	DA	Extended Block Move
4-2-4-1	DC	Shutdown 10 error
4-3-1-3	E2	Initialize the motherboard chipset
4-3-1-4	E3	Initialize refresh counter
4-3-2-1	E4	Check for forced Flash
4-3-2-2	E5	Check HW status of ROM
4-3-2-3	E6	BIOS ROM is OK
4-3-2-4	E7	Do a complete RAM test
4-3-3-1	E8	Do OEM initialization
4-3-3-2	E9	Initialize interrupt controller
4-3-3-3	EA	Read in bootstrap code
4-3-3-4	EB	Initialize all vectors
4-3-4-1	EC	Boot the Flash program
4-3-4-2	ED	Initialize the boot device
4-3-4-3	EE	Boot code was read OK

The POST Reader Card

Although virtually all current PC BIOS versions make use of port 80h, the port itself is merely a repository for that information. In order for you to read the contents of port 80h, you will need a POST board (such as the Micro2000 *Post-Probe* shown in Figure 18-1), which should be installed in an open slot prior to troubleshooting and then removed once troubleshooting is completed. *Remember to turn the PC off before installing or removing a POST card.* Essentially, the design of a POST board is quite simple. It reads the byte at the POST I/O port, and displays the hexadecimal code in the two seven-segment displays. However, many POST boards today provide a technician with a much more powerful troubleshooting tool. As an example, the Post-Probe supplies a series of LEDs that check for main voltages (+12Vdc, –12Vdc, +5Vdc, and –5Vdc) and the presence of key signals on the expansion bus (address latch, I/O read, I/O write, memory read, memory write, system clock, and so on). Even an on-board logic probe attachment is provided.

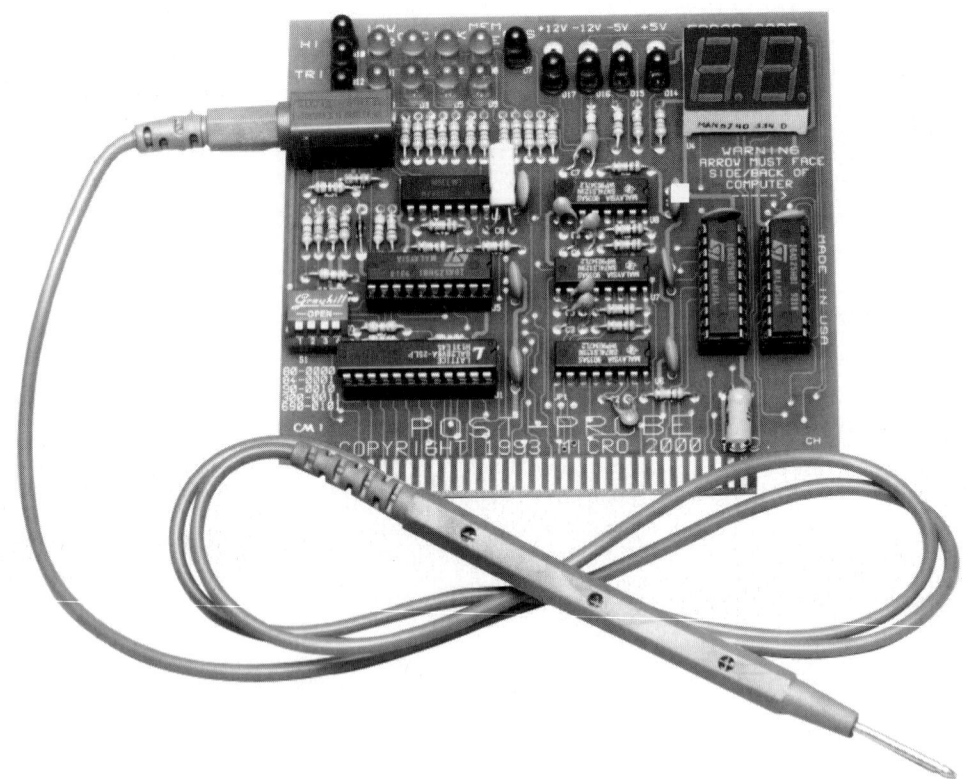

FIGURE 18-1   The PostProbe card from Micro2000 (Courtesy of Micro2000, Inc.)

I/O PORTS

While most traditional ISA-based PCs make use of port 80h, not all PCs follow this rule. The Compaq PC outputs codes to port 84h, and PS/2 models 25 and 30 send codes to port 90h. PS/2 model 20-286 sends codes to port 190h. Even most EISA-based PCs use port 80h, but Compaq PCs continue to use port 84h. EISA machines with Award BIOS use port 300h. Systems with a micro channel bus architecture (MCA) use port 680h. Take note that some PS/2 models, Olivetti, early AT&T, some NCR, and a few AT clones will send POST codes to a printer port at 3BCh, 278h, or 378h. The current generation of POST boards typically provides a DIP switch or jumper array for selecting the active port location. Before choosing a POST board, make sure that it can read the *proper* port address for your system.

Another issue to keep in mind is that *not all* PCs produce POST codes. The original IBM PC, the AMI XT, and some systems using HP, DTK, and ERSO BIOS do not send out POST codes during initialization. If you are testing such a system, you will be unable to see hexadecimal codes using the POST card (but power and signal indicators should still work).

INTERPRETING THE LEDS

Before working with the various POST codes in detail, you should have an understanding of the many discrete signal LEDs that accompany current POST boards. These individual signals can be a great asset when interpreted in conjunction with the POST code. Keep in mind that each POST card will offer a different selection of LEDs, so your own POST card *may not* have all of the indicators shown here:

- **Power LEDs**   The PC will not work correctly (if at all) if any power supply voltage is low or absent. Typical POST cards provide four LEDs that light when +5Vdc, +12Vdc, –5Vdc, and –12Vdc are available. If any of those LEDs are dim or out, there may be a problem with the power supply or its connection to the motherboard. If problems occur after upgrading the system, the power supply may be overloaded. In any case, power LEDs help you to identify power problems quickly and effectively.

- **ALE**   The *Address Latch Enable* signal is generated by the CPU and is used by virtually all devices in the PC that must capture address signals (such as BIOS). When this LED is on, address generation by the CPU is probably working fine. If this LED is out, there is a problem manipulating addresses in the system. You should then suspect the CPU, DMA controller, Bus Buffer/Controller, or Clock Generator/System Controller chip. This alert can be very helpful for technicians who choose to troubleshoot to the component level.

- **I/OW**   An *I/O Write* LED will generally light whenever BIOS attempts to write data to an I/O device such as a floppy disk. The BIOS will then attempt to read what was written to confirm that that portion of the system is working as expected. If the I/OW LED stays out, you should suspect a fault in either the BIOS or the system's DMA controller chip.

- **I/OR**   An *I/O Read* LED will generally light whenever BIOS attempts to read data back from an I/O device after data has been written. If this LED remains out, you should suspect a fault in either the BIOS or the system's DMA controller chip.

- **MR/W**   During POST, the BIOS will attempt to write various data patterns into memory, then read those patterns back to verify memory integrity. The *Memory R/W* LED will light during both the read and write operations (it will flicker a bit). If the MW/R LED does not light, there is likely to be a problem with the BIOS, DMA Controller, Memory Controller, or System Controller chip.

- **Reset**   When the system is first turned on, the reset line will be asserted. This keeps the CPU neutralized until the *Power Good* signal is received from the power supply. At this point, the reset line should be released, and the *Reset* LED should go out—the initialization process will begin. The reset line should not light again unless the PC's Reset button is pressed. If the Reset LED stays lit, it could indicate a problem with the Power Good signal at the supply or motherboard. The reset line may also be shorted—in which case you may have to replace the motherboard.

- **CLK**   The *clock* LED(s) light to indicate the presence of synchronizing signals generated by the PC's clock generator chip. If these signals are not being generated, the CPU simply will not function. If the clock indicator(s) do not light, you should suspect a fault in the system time base crystal or the clock generator chip. Keep in mind that micro channel systems do not supply clock signals to the bus.

- **OSC**   The *oscillator* LEDs indicate the presence of a 14.138MHz signal. XT systems used this signal for all internal timing, but AT systems use the oscillator only as a color burst signal for the video adapter. If the oscillator indicator(s) do not light, you should suspect a fault in the color burst crystal or the clock generating circuitry.

Further Study

American Megatrends (AMI)   www.megatrends.com
Data Depot   www.datadepo.com
Micro2000   www.micro2000.com
Phoenix Technologies   www.phoenix.com/
TriniTech Omni Analyzer   www.pcanalyzer.com/Eng_omni.htm
Ultra X Post Cards   www.uxd.com/products.html

19

FANS AND
COOLING DEVICES

When electrical power is applied to a circuit, the circuit uses that power to perform work. In the case of a PC, *work* would be the myriad processing operations that go on throughout the computer every moment. For computers (as with all machines), the conversion of power into work is not a perfect one—a portion of power is dissipated in the form of *heat*. Over time, an excessive buildup of heat will cause a chip (and thus the PC) to fail prematurely. As a result, it is very important that a computer system be properly outfitted to deal with heat. This chapter is intended to illustrate the various methods used to cool a PC, explain the effects that inhibit cooling, and show you how to deal with cooling problems.

The Importance of Heat Management

You might wonder why heat is taken so seriously—after all, the vast majority of chips and passive components found in a PC dissipate very little heat at all. Unfortunately, it is the few components that do produce heat that cause most problems: drive motors, power supply regulating circuits, the CPU(s), and graphics processors. Heat affects the reliability of all electronic devices, and manufacturers of processors and other computer components specify a maximum operating temperature for their products. Most devices are not certified to function properly beyond 50°C–80°C (122°F–176°F). However, in a loaded PC with only standard cooling, operating temperatures can easily exceed the limits. The result can be memory errors, hard disk read-write errors, faulty video, and other problems not commonly recognized as heat related.

If we look at this in more mathematical terms, the life of an electronic device is directly related to its operating temperature. Each 10°C (18°F) temperature rise reduces component life by 50 percent. Engineers and scientists may recognize that this is based on the Arrhenius equation, which states that time to failure is a function of $e^{-Ea/kT}$, where Ea is activation energy of the failure mechanism being accelerated, k is Boltzmann's constant, and T is absolute temperature. Fortunately, we don't need to actually work this equation—we just need to appreciate that heat kills electronic devices. Conversely, each 10°C (18°F) temperature reduction increases component life by 100 percent. In actual practice, it is recommended that computer components be kept as cool as possible (within an acceptable noise level) for maximum reliability, longevity, and return on investment. As a technician, you must take the steps that are necessary to cool critical PC devices, and manage the overall operating temperature of the system.

COOLING METHODOLOGIES

To understand how various cooling devices work, you must understand some basic principles about heat transfer. First, heat tends to travel from places of *more* heat to places of *less* heat. If you don't believe this, apply a hot soldering iron to one end of a wire and see how long it takes the other end to get warm. While this is a tremendous oversimplification, you get the basic idea. There are three general modes of heat transfer: convection, conduction, and radiation.

Convection is the transfer of heat through air currents. A heat source warms nearby air, which rises. The warmer rising air is replaced by cooler air, which is then heated. Eventually, a circulating airflow develops. This is the basic principle behind the radiators that heat your home in the winter. It is also an essential element of PC cooling. You might ask how heating and cooling can be the same thing. Well, as heat is transferred to the air, the device providing the heat is cooled. When a CPU heats up, it tends to heat the surrounding air. Unfortunately, such *static convection* has limited effect in a PC. Static convection does not remove enough heat to cool a very hot device (such as a CPU). Static convection also relies on a circulating flow of air, which is difficult to establish in the close quarters of a highly obstructed PC. A way to multiply the effect of convection is to force an airflow across the heated device. Fans are used to force air through the PC. This *forced convection* provides much more effective cooling and can be directed to specific areas around the PC. Most of the cooling methods covered in this chapter rely on forced convection.

Conduction is the transfer of heat through physical contact. The radiator system in your car works this way. By circulating cooler liquid around a warmer surface, the cooler liquid picks up the surface heat, thus cooling the surface. The liquid, now warmed, is circulated to a chilling assembly, which is intended to take away any heat picked up by the liquid so that the liquid is kept cooled. In a car, this is the front radiator, which is cooled by the forced air of a large fan. Although conduction is a much more effective means of cooling than convection, conduction can only cool the areas of contact, whereas convection can cool large areas. Some CPU cooling devices use circulating liquid, but these *chillers* are relatively rare and expensive. As a consequence, you will rarely find conductive cooling techniques in PCs.

Finally, *radiation* is the transfer of heat through infrared emission. For example, the warmth you feel from sunlight or a sun lamp is due to the effects of infrared radiation. Since there are no significant infrared emission sources in a PC, radiation will not be discussed further. At this point, you can see how these heat transfer principles are employed in a PC environment.

Natural Convection

Natural (or static) convection is the cooling technique employed in most computer monitors. Take a look at the rear enclosure on your monitor and notice the open slots along the top and bottom of the enclosure.

The openings beneath the monitor are for air intake, and the upper slots allow air to escape. These slots provide a free flow of air through the monitor. Yet, this process works without the benefit of a fan. You can easily see how this process works. Let the monitor run for a while, and place your hand over the upper slots—you can feel hot air rising. The warm circuitry inside the running monitor heats the surrounding air, which rises up and out. As warm air is displaced, new cooler air is drawn in from the bottom slots. Although monitor circuits will heat up (especially the power supply), none of the components becomes hot enough to require forced convection.

As you might expect, the success of this method depends on an unobstructed air path. If "Fluffy" the cat curls up on top of the monitor, the exhaust vents will be blocked. This interrupts the flow of air, and temperatures inside the monitor will increase. Eventually, you may notice the display rolling or shifting position—an initial warning that the monitor circuits are overheating. If the blockage continues for an extended period, the monitor may fail prematurely. Besides monitors, dot-matrix and ink jet printers typically rely on convection to cool their circuits.

Heat Sinks

Another rule of heat transfer is that the effectiveness with which heat is transferred depends on the amount of surface area that is exposed. Check out the radiator in your car—each of those tiny fins adds a small amount of surface area to the overall radiating surface. This is the principle behind *heat sinks*. By adding a heat sink to a heated component, you increase the effective surface area of the component's case that is open to the air. Since more air can flow over a larger surface (through natural or forced convection), more heat is carried away and the component stays cooler. For components that become inordinately hot during normal operation (such as voltage regulator chips, graphics processors, or CPUs), a heat sink is a very simple and inexpensive way to enhance cooling (see Figure 19-1). Of course, heat sinks are not just for chips. Take a look at the print head of a dot matrix printer. You'll find a set of cast aluminum fins set right into the head assembly. Many different production methods are used to create heat sinks for processors and other chips. A few of the more popular production methods are described here:

- **Extrusion**   The most popular production method for heat sinks, it is inexpensive and can result in very fine structures (for example, see Figure 19-1). In most cases, liquid aluminum is pressed through a form so that a long stick with the shape of the heat sink is created. After this extruded stick has cooled down, it is cut into pieces as needed. However, not all heat sink types can be made with extrusion.

- **Folded fin**   Produces heat sinks that are made of a thin metal plate, which is folded and bonded onto a base plate. The radiator in your car uses this design. The advantage is that the fins are hollow, so they have a bigger surface and allow better airflow (and thus better cooling). Folded fin heat sinks are light, compact, and very efficient. However, heat sinks with folded fins are more expensive to produce, and only a few manufacturers offer coolers using this design.

- **Bonded fin**   Produces heat sinks that are very similar to the folded fin design, but instead of folding a long continuous piece of metal, this method bonds many smaller metal plates onto the base plate. The advantages and disadvantages are the same as for the folded fin method.

- **Die casting**   A production method that gives the designer a lot of freedom, and allows for certain heat sink shapes that cannot be produced using extrusion. Die casting also allows for highly integrated cooling. For example, the heat sinks used on dot matrix print heads are almost always extruded. However, the fins of a die cast heat sink cannot be very fine, and this may limit the amount of surface area handled by the casting.

FIGURE 19-1   Attaching a heat sink to a typical cartridge-style processor (Courtesy of
Intel Corporation)

■ **Cold forging**   A relatively exotic and expensive production method for heat sinks. However, it is
used for heat sinks with many small pin fins, and high-end coolers such as the Alpha PFH6035MUC
are produced using this approach.

■ **Milling**   Also a very unusual and expensive production method for heat sinks. Milling is used when
it's necessary to create relatively large and very complex cooling units such as the heat sinks by HP
PolarLogic. The heat sinks used for chillers are often milled.

Heat Sink Compound   The surface of a chip or a heat sink is never entirely flat. If you place a heat sink
directly on a CPU or other chip, tiny (microscopic) gaps will exist between the two surfaces. Since air conducts
heat poorly, these gaps will slightly impair the heat transfer from the chip to the heat sink. Therefore, an interface material with a high thermal conductivity is needed to fill these gaps, and thus improve heat conductivity.

The most commonly used interface material in electronics cooling is *thermal grease* (also called heat
sink compound). This is a white, sticky, acrid-smelling paste applied directly on the heat sink or CPU. A
good-quality thermal grease will provide the best possible cooling performance. However, thermal grease
is quite messy to handle. For this reason, most heat sink manufacturers ship their heat sinks with a *thermal
pad,* which is supposed to replace thermal compound. Cheap heat sinks usually come with silver/gray
graphite pads. Graphite pads are inexpensive, but provide poor performance unless a high pressure is
applied to the pad, and this is not the case when a CPU and heat sink are installed in a typical way. A graphite pad is better than no interface material at all, though. Today, far more advanced thermal pads are available, made by companies such as Power Devices, Bergquist, or Chomerics, to name a few. These pads
come very close to thermal compound in terms of performance.

If you have a heat sink with a thermal pad and you would like to use thermal compound, you should
scratch off the thermal pad. Under no circumstances should you use both.

When using thermal grease, you should apply a very thin (paper thin) layer on the heat sink with your finger before installing it. Don't use too much—thinner layers are better. Then, secure the heat sink firmly to the CPU. Thermal grease does not get hard, so you could even reuse it when you buy a new CPU. Standard silicone-based thermal compound can be purchased at almost any electronics store including Radio Shack (Cat. No.: 276-1372) for about $2. High-end thermal compounds with even better thermal performance are available from specialized heat sink retailers.

You may notice that the heat sink gets a bit hotter after using thermal grease. This does not mean that the CPU is getting hotter—it means that more heat is being removed from the CPU, which is therefore a bit cooler.

Fans

There are limits to what convection can do, and the heat liberated by devices in a PC will usually build up within the system. Fans are commonly used to produce strong local airflow. When attached to a heat sink (Figure 19-2), a fan can force air across the many fins and keep the processor or graphics chip significantly cooler than can a heat sink alone. Of course, the heated air removed from a heat sink can be evacuated from a chassis through the use of one or more large fans.

Two kinds of fans are being used on CPU heat sinks: ball bearing and sleeve bearing fans. *Sleeve bearing* fans are usually less expensive and often quieter, but are often unreliable over the long term. Poor-quality sleeve bearing fans are known to fail in six months or less. The cheapest kind of sleeve bearing fan simply consists of a ring made of a porous material that has been dipped in a lubricant. The fan motor's shaft rotates inside this ring and is lubricated by the lubricant stored inside the porous material. *Ball bearing* fans use a rotating shaft that is surrounded by tiny balls, which allow smooth rotation with hardly any wear and tear. These fans are a bit more expensive (and sometimes a little louder), but they are generally far more reliable. Keep in mind that a few fans use Teflon sleeve bearings, which can be just as reliable as ball bearing fans, and the Teflon sleeves may be quieter.

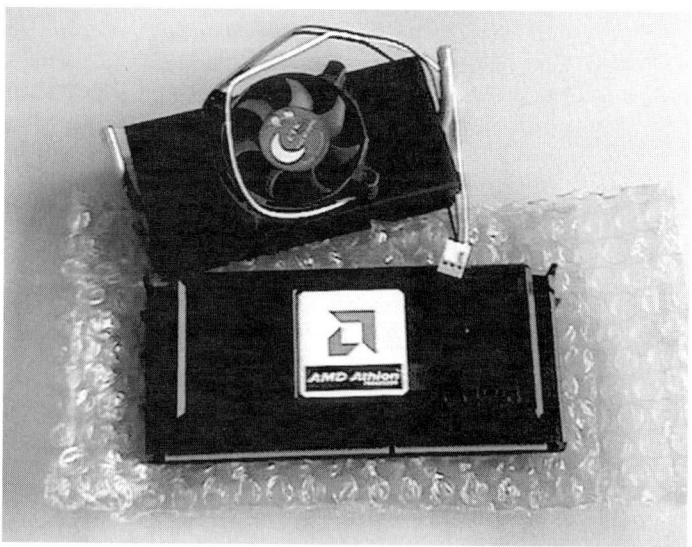

FIGURE 19-2   A typical heat sink/fan unit

If a sticker on the fan says "Ball Bearing," you're typically getting a fan that uses both ball bearings and sleeve bearings. A fan needs two bearings, and the popular 50x10mm "ball bearing" fans that come with many heat sinks are usually fans with one ball bearing and one sleeve bearing. Larger fans (60x25mm and up) sometimes have two ball bearings, and these are often referred to as *two ball bearing* or *dual ball bearing* fans.

High airflow always creates noise, a reality that cannot be avoided. For this reason, even a very high-quality fan can be quite loud. With a good fan, however, most of the noise that is created comes from air turbulence, *not* from the fan motor itself. In fact, fan vibrations are a sign of poor quality. If you hold the fan in your hand, you should not feel any significant vibrations. In actual practice, a larger fan that spins at a lower speed will be less noisy than a smaller fan spinning at a high speed, even if the two provide the same amount of airflow. So bigger fans are usually better.

The most common unit for specifying airflow is cubic feet per minute (or CFM). The metric equivalent is cubic meters per minute (or m^3/min). Table 19-1 shows the conversions between typical units. For example, 1 CFM equals 0.47 liters/sec. Common 50x10mm CPU fans usually move up to 10 CFM. High-speed 50x10mm fans with 6000 rpm can move even more air. Many 60x25mm fans can move between about 20 and 30 CFM, 80x25mm fans handle around 30 to 40 CFM, and 120mm fans can pass over 100 CFM of air. When buying a fan, remember that you'll always have to chose between high performance and low noise. The goal is to find a good compromise for your system.

Chassis Fans   Natural convection is fine for cooling monitors and printers, but PCs are too cramped and obstructed to establish a consistent airflow. As a result, heated air must be evacuated from the enclosure. This is usually accomplished with one or more axial or radial fans positioned in the system. By positioning the fans blowing out of the enclosure, cooler air can be vacuumed into the system through strategically located intake slots in the housing. Some systems use a second fan blowing into the enclosure from the front chassis. This kind of push-pull cooling develops a very strong airflow.

According to the ATX form factor specification, a power supply fan should blow air into the case, through the power supply, and toward the motherboard. Since the CPU is located on the motherboard just beyond the power supply fan, the idea is that the CPU benefits from this more direct airflow. However, as the power supply gets hot, the fan would blow warm air toward the CPU (which usually isn't a good idea). So, many case manufacturers are ignoring the ATX specifications and ship their cases with a power supply fan that blows air out of the system.

If your power supply fan blows air in, it might sometimes be beneficial to reverse the fan. Remember that you must reverse the entire fan unit. Reversing polarity won't work, and might even damage your fan.

TABLE 19-1   CONVERTING BETWEEN AIR HANDLING UNITS

CONVERT FROM		CFM	M³/MIN	M³/HOUR	L/S	L/MIN
Cubic feet/minute	1 CFM =	1	0.028	1.7	0.47	28.3
Cubic meter/minute	1 m³/min =	35.28	1	60	16.67	1000
Cubic meter/hour	1 m³/h =	0.588	0.017	1	0.28	16.67
Liter/second	1 l/s =	2.12	0.06	3.6	1	60
Liter/min	1 l/s =	0.035	0.001	0.06	0.017	1

The rule of thumb is that when more than one fan is used, the fans should be blowing in the *same* direction. For example, if the power supply fan is evacuating air out of the unit, a second fan (usually located in the front of the chassis) should be blowing air into the system. Having fans compete with each other (both directing air into or out of the system) can actually decrease the effective airflow and impair effective cooling. Another issue to consider is vent holes. If there are ventilation holes in your case right next to the secondary fan, or other openings such as an open card slot or I/O panel opening, it can sometimes be helpful to close these holes to ensure proper airflow.

Finally, consider the connectors on your chassis fans. If there is a free fan connector on your motherboard, then you'll probably want a fan with a three-pin connector. This allows the motherboard to regulate the fan and measure rpm (so the system is able to report stalled fans). Otherwise, you'll need to use fans with standard Molex-type drive power connectors, and the fans will run at full duty while the system is on.

Fan Duct   Traditionally, the CPU was just about the only major heat source inside a computer case. Today, times have changed, and graphics chips, chipsets, and memory chips run hot as well. These additional devices often require special heat sinks or even fans. In the future, you might end up with three to five fans inside your system, which would be extremely noisy, and also expensive for system integrators. Intel has introduced a new cooling methodology called *fan duct* (Figure 19-3). The fan duct system will distribute air from a single fan to all parts of the system that require cooling. This way, all components will get fresh cool air from outside the case (even without their own fan).

The fan duct approach provides cooler air in the system chassis and provides air directly to the core components that need it most. This is accomplished by mounting a fan directly over these key components, including the processor, memory, and chipset configurations. The fan duct also supplies cooling to an

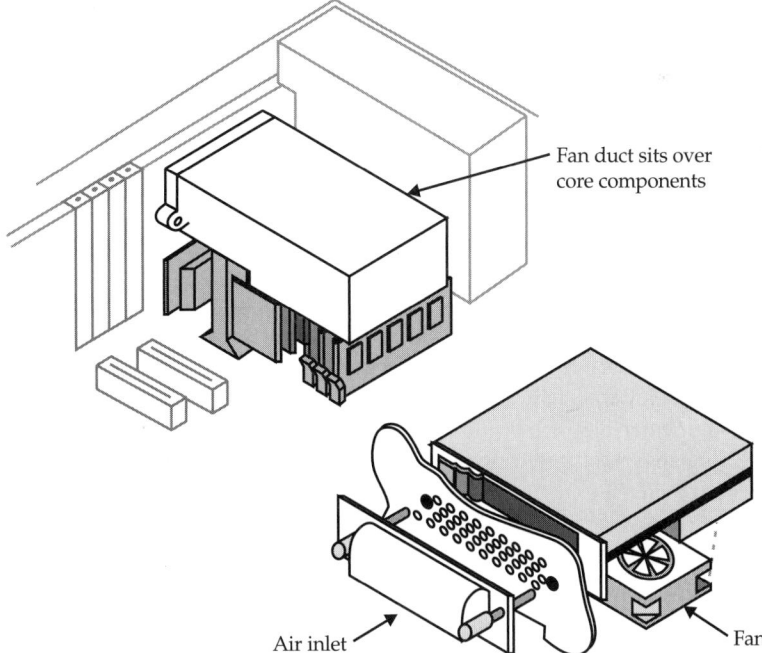

Fan duct sits over core components

Air inlet

Fan

FIGURE 19-3   Example of a fan duct system (Courtesy of Intel Corporation)

AGP expansion card (even though the fan is not mounted over the card). In addition, the fan duct solution employs a tube that draws in fresh air from the outside and spreads it around the entire core of the system, instead of merely cooling the processor. As an open specification, Fan Duct 1.0 provides a universal solution across the industry that enables OEMs of all sizes to provide cost-effective system cooling. You can learn more about Fan Duct 1.0 at **developer.intel.com/ial/sdt/fanduct.htm**.

Fan Cards   Even with good-quality chassis-mounted fans, some high-performance systems require an extra measure of cooling, especially in the CPU area. An ongoing trend in PC cooling is the use of a *fan card*—a standard-sized ISA or PCI expansion board with one or two +12 Vdc fans mounted to it. This allows you to place the fan card in the immediate vicinity of a CPU or drive to improve the local airflow. However, there are some limitations to fan cards that you should be aware of. First, many expansion boards are full-sized boards, so the chances are very good that at least one side of the fan card will be somewhat obstructed by another full-slot expansion board. As long as the fan card is blowing *away* from the adjacent expansion board, this should not present a problem. If the fan card is blowing *toward* the adjacent expansion board, a region of turbulent air will be produced, which reduces the fan card's overall effectiveness.

Another concern is EMI produced by the fan motors. As inductive devices, fans are notorious for producing unwanted electromagnetic interference. If the fan card is placed in close proximity of a sensitive device such as a drive controller or video capture board, the electrical noise produced by the fans can degrade the other device's performance or cause operating errors. There is also the possibility that electrical noise from the fans may travel back along the +12 Vdc voltage line and interfere with other devices in the system that are using +12 Vdc. It is always wise to approach fan cards with a certain amount of suspicion, especially if you have problems with a device after the fan card is installed.

The vibrations produced by fan cards are also notorious for rocking the fan card right out of its slot, so be sure to bolt the fan card into its slot using the expansion card bracket.

CPU Fans   CPUs have always run hot, and the reason is readily understandable—a single microscopic transistor dissipates virtually no heat, but the combined heat from over 20 million+ transistors crammed into a wafer the size of a fingernail becomes *extreme*. The surface temperature of a Pentium processor can easily exceed 70°C (Pentium II/III/4 processors can run even higher). With such a strong concentration of heat, even forced air through a heat sink can leave a CPU running hot. To manage heat in the latest Athlon and Pentium III/4 processors, a CPU fan can be employed. Basically, a CPU fan mounts a small, high-speed fan that blows down into a heat sink assembly. The in-rushing air cools the heat sink (and thus the CPU) very effectively. Table 19-2 lists the typical operating temperatures for popular CPUs.

Unfortunately, there are some disadvantages to the CPU fan. First, the added height of a heat sink/fan combination can obstruct full-length expansion boards. This is typical of poorly designed AT-style motherboards (though ATX and NLX motherboards position the CPU well away from expansion slots). Similarly, if your particular motherboard places the CPU under a low-hanging drive or other chassis obstruction, a CPU fan may not fit. Before using a CPU fan, make sure that you have several cubic inches of available space *over* the CPU.

The CPU fan also requires power. Check that you have a power connector available from the power supply, or make sure that the CPU fan assembly comes with a built-in Y-connector. Today, the power management and cooling features provided by most motherboards allow you to plug the fan(s) directly into connectors on the motherboard. This allows the motherboard to regulate fan speed and measure rpm to detect failing or stalled fans.

TABLE 19-2   TYPICAL CPU CASE TEMPERATURES

AMD ATHLON AND DURON

Socket A CPUs (Athlon, Duron), up to 1 GHz	90°C
Socket A CPUs (Athlon), 1.1 GHz or more	95°C
All Slot A CPUs (Athlon classic, Athlon Thunderbird)	70°C

AMD K6 SERIES

All K6 CPUs (166-300 MHz) and most K6-2/K6-III CPUs	70°C
K6-2/K6-III CPUs with model name ending with X (K6-2-450AFX)	65°C
K6-2-400AFQ (uncommon)	60°C
K6-2+, K6-III+, and most mobile K6/K6-2 CPUs	85°C
Mobile K6/K6-2 models ending with K (mobile K6-2-P-400AFK)	80°C

INTEL PENTIUM 4

Pentium 4, 1.3 GHz	69°C
Pentium 4, 1.4 GHz	70°C
Pentium 4, 1.5 GHz	72°C

INTEL PENTIUM III

Pentium III Socket 370, 500-866 MHz	80-85°C
Pentium III Slot 1 (first generation, OLGA), 550-600 MHz	80-85°C
Pentium III Slot 1 (Coppermine), 500-866 MHz	80-85°C
Pentium III Socket 370 and Slot 1, 933 MHz	75°C
Pentium III Slot 1, 933 MHz	60°C
Pentium III Slot 1 1 GHz	60-70°C
Pentium III Slot 1, 1.13 GHz (first version)	62°C

INTEL CELERON

Celeron 266-433 MHz	85°C
Celeron 466-533 MHz (0.25μ)	70°C
Celeron 533-600 MHz (Coppermine)	90°C
Celeron 633 and 667 MHz	82°C
Celeron 700 MHz and higher	80°C

INTEL PENTIUM II

Pentium II (1st generation and Klamath)	72-75°C
Pentium II (2nd generation, 2.0V core), 266-333 MHz	65°C
Pentium II (350-400 MHz)	75°C
Pentium II (450 MHz)	70°C

INTEL PENTIUM PRO

Pentium Pro, 256 or 512K L2 cache	85°
Pentium Pro, 1MB L2 cache	80°C

Another possible problem involves vibration. Since the fan is now physically coupled to the CPU, there is a bit of debate over what (if any) damage is done to the CPU by fan vibrations over the long term. The best defense against vibration and premature failure is to use a good-quality ball bearing fan unit. There are three attributes to consider when selecting a processor cooling unit:

■ Large heat sink area for extra heat dissipation area

■ Long-life and low-noise ball bearing fan (or Teflon sleeve)

■ Convenient and well-designed clips to ease installation at the CPU

> If you must use a Y-splitter cable to power a CPU heat sink/fan, *never* split power from a hard drive or other critical drive. Split power from a floppy drive instead.

Liquid Cooling (The "Heat Pipe")

CPU cooling can also be accomplished through conductive devices generally known as heat pipes. A small number of liquid-cooling devices are available for CPUs, most of which are used in Pentium II/III notebook systems that do not have the space for heat sinks or CPU fans. The drawback to a liquid-cooled system is clear enough—a breach in the cooling loop can deposit liquid onto the motherboard and result in real damage. Extra expense is another consideration.

The basic principles behind the heat pipe are well known among refrigeration professionals, but are not all that intuitive to computer technicians. Basically, a vacuum-tight tube is filled with a low boiling point fluid. The tube is run through a small heat sink fitted over the CPU. The advantage here is that since heat does not have to dissipate to the air, the heat sink can be quite thin.

This CPU heat sink is known as the *evaporator*, since the fluid running through it is evaporated ("flashed" to vapor) by the CPU's heat. Since the process of evaporation is a cooling process, heat is transferred from the CPU to the evaporated fluid, which then travels back up through the tube where it runs through a somewhat larger metal plate known as the *condenser*. The condenser is usually located under the notebook's keyboard assembly where there is enough empty space for the heat to dissipate and allow the fluid to return to its liquid state. Once the liquid returns to its liquid state, it is free to recirculate back to the heat sink. Two of the most interesting elements of the heat pump are that it requires absolutely no electricity and has no moving parts. So long as the evaporator remains in good contact with the CPU, the heat pump should continue operating indefinitely. Circulation is driven by the natural phase changes of the liquid.

Although the heat pump is a relatively simple and reliable mechanism, it poses some unique problems for small computer assemblies. If you upgrade or repair mobile computers at all, you will need to know the important issues for heat pipe assembly and installation:

- *Be careful of liquid.* Remember that you are basically dealing with a delicate liquid vessel mounted in the bowels of your mobile computer. As a result, you must be extremely careful during disassembly and reassembly procedures. Crimping the tube at any point will reduce the pipe's effectiveness. Breaking the heat pipe can result in chemicals being spilled into the main board.

- *Be careful of dust and debris.* As you saw, the evaporated liquid sheds its heat in the condenser, which is located under the keyboard. But just like convection heating in the home, heat will have trouble leaving the condenser if it is "insulated"—covered with dust and debris accumulated from long periods of use. If you find yourself working on a mobile PC using a heat pipe, be sure that the condenser is clean and free of dust. You may choose to blow away any dust and debris with compressed air.

- *Be careful of contact.* As far as the CPU is concerned, the heat pipe's evaporator is just another heat sink. Like any heat sink, there must be good physical contact between the CPU and the evaporator in order for proper cooling to occur. If the evaporator is left loose (or otherwise mounted incorrectly), the heat pipe will be ineffective.

Piezoelectric Coolers

Piezoelectric devices (called *Peltier coolers*) mount a layer of piezoelectric material over the CPU. As the crystal layer vibrates, a temperature differential develops through it, which actually results in a cooler surface (applied against the CPU). This means the elements actually have a "hot" side and a "cold" side. To accomplish this, the Peltier element uses power (a lot of power). So, in addition to *pumping* heat, a Peltier element will actually *produce* heat. Overall, the system will run hotter, but the Peltier element will cool the CPU where it is needed. The problem with piezoelectric chillers is their expense, as well as the yet-unclear potential for CPU damage from long-term exposure to vibration. Though a Peltier cooler can be a perfect thermal solution, poorly designed or improperly installed fans can be dangerous. Here are a few Peltier-related dangers:

> Good Peltier coolers cool significantly better than conventional heat sinks, making them suitable for overclocking. It is important to note that the heat sink of a Peltier cooler will get hotter than the heat sink of a conventional cooler, because of the heat the Peltier element produces.

- **Overheating** Peltier coolers come with a heat sink and fan. If the fan dies, the additional heat of the Peltier element may damage your CPU. Also, you must ensure proper airflow through the system. A Peltier cooler will add heat to the system, so other heat-sensitive devices like hard disks must be properly ventilated or cooled. Make sure that there are no cables that disturb the airflow or even cover the fan. As with all other heat sink units, you should use thermal grease.

- **Electric problems** The Peltier will draw a lot of power, possibly more than your power supply can cope with. This is especially a problem at boot-up—while your hard disk(s) is spinning up, it uses more power. If the Peltier starts drawing its power immediately, it may overload the supply. Good Peltier coolers solve this problem by turning on the Peltier element only after a certain time (when the CPU gets warm). Peltier wiring can be another problem. If the gauge of the wiring is too small (a common issue on some cheap Peltiers), the wiring may overheat due to the current. As a rule, the Peltier cooler should have a dedicated power connector from the power supply—don't let your Peltier share a line with a hard disk or floppy drive.

- **Water condensation** This is a particular problem when you use your computer in a damp location. When your CPU runs very cool (in the time just after turning on your computer), it might become chilled below room temperature, and this can cause condensation on the CPU, the socket, and under the socket. The hotter and the more humid the air inside your computer case is, the more likely you are to experience condensation problems. Good Peltier coolers solve this problem by turning on the Peltier element only *after* the CPU has reached a preset temperature. In actual practice, short circuits due to condensation are very unlikely.

- **Peltier sizing** The Peltier element must have the right size. If the Peltier element is bigger than the part of the CPU it covers (sometimes a problem with CPUs that have a smaller metal plate in the middle, such as the Pentium 200/MMX), then condensation might occur. On the other hand, if the Peltier element is too small (a problem with the K6, which has a big metal plate on the top), then cooling might be inadequate.

Advanced Configuration and Power Interface (ACPI)

Today's PCs are extremely power-conscious in order to comply with the growing trends of global power conservation. ACPI is a power conservation feature supported by the system BIOS and operating system. ACPI systems can power-down to several different levels, eventually using as little as 5W of power in a "hibernation" mode. ACPI enables a PC to measure temperatures of critical components within its system. Temperature-sensing circuits can then be read by the BIOS and operating system, and critical temperature triggers can be programmed to cause alarm events. Alarms then initiate systematic power-saving modes that will cool corresponding elements of the system.

A system is generally divided into thermal zones (processor, memory and chipset), so different power management regimes may be applied to the various zones independently. Cooling policies may be either passive or active. In a *passive* policy, device performance is limited to reduce heat generation. In an *active* policy, fan speed and on/off controls are used to limit temperature as heat increases. Cooling policies may be mixed and can be used in any order. For example, suppose that the processor's temperature starts to rise. The operating system senses a critical temperature and downshifts the processor's clock speed to limit power dissipation. If temperature continues to rise, a cooling fan is switched on (slow). Further increases in temperature cause the operating system to increase the fan speed. If the fan speed maximum is reached and the temperature continues to rise, the system shuts down entirely to prevent damage to the processor.

Cooling Problems

Cooling is often the most overlooked and neglected features of a PC. In many basic off-the-shelf systems, cooling is sufficient. But over time, constant use, environmental factors, and upgrades, the cooling plan may need to be reviewed or revised. As with so many other elements of PC service, successful troubleshooting means knowing where to look. This part of the chapter shows you the factors to consider when evaluating PC cooling and cooling problems.

FAN WEAR

Fans don't last forever. They are electromechanical devices, and eventually the motor or rotating shaft will wear out and fail. Normally, PC cooling fans are very quiet devices—they have to be, since loud operation in a home or office environment would quickly become maddening. The first sign of fan failure is excessive *noise*. A persistent buzz or grinding sound immediately points to a fan problem. The fan motor may also be unusually hot. In extreme cases, the fan will hang up and stop altogether (it may start again if you nudge it gently). The best way to deal with a cranky fan is to replace it outright. A new fan must have the same three major characteristics of the original fan: (1) physical mounting dimensions, (2) operating voltage—usually +12 Vdc, and (3) airflow rate.

BAD HEAT SINK CONTACT

In order for a heat sink to be effective, it must have a strong physical connection to the host chip that it's cooling. This ensures that the maximum amount of heat is transferred from the chip to the heat sink/fan. The better that contact is, the more efficiently that heat is transferred into the heat sink—and the cooler the chip runs. There are a variety of ways to secure a heat sink/fan, but clipping the chip and heat sink together has been easiest and most popular. However, not all heat sink clips are tight, and even a tight clip does not guarantee good contact. Check to see that the heat sink is attached securely, and be sure to add a layer of thermal grease between the chip and heat sink. Thermal grease fills in any air space between the chip and heat sink, so heat transfer is enhanced. Suspect heat sink problems when the system locks up randomly for no apparent reason or the CPU suffers chronic failures.

 Thermal grease is toxic and can stain clothing. When using thermal grease, be sure to work carefully, and avoid getting it on hands and clothing.

One of the more recent trends in heat sink marketing is the use of stick-on heat sinks—just peel off an adhesive backing and stick the heat sink in place. It sounds terrific in principle, but adhesive is often more of a thermal insulator than a thermal conductor. As a general rule, go with the clip-on heat sinks wherever possible.

CPU VIBRATION FAILURE

CPU heat sink/fans are generally regarded as one of the most effective CPU cooling devices available, but there is a certain amount of debate over the effect of long-term fan vibration on the CPU. Some manufacturers argue that since the fan is physically attached to the heat sink (and CPU), the fan's vibrations will be carried directly into the CPU, which will shorten the CPU's working life. However, there are no studies available to prove or disprove that possibility. As a result, you should rely on your own experience when checking or recommending CPU heat sinks. Normally, it is reasonable to expect that the cooler CPU should run longer and more reliably. So if you find that the CPU fails frequently when fitted with a CPU fan, try a large heat sink or high-quality heat sink/fan instead.

SUNLIGHT

Anyone who has ever been in the sunlight understands how warming it can be. This natural warming can be magnified through glass, so sunlight indoors can feel even warmer. When a PC sits exposed to sunlight for prolonged periods, the metal enclosures tend to pick up much of that heat (and heat the air inside). Although sunlight alone rarely provides enough heating to endanger the system, it can intensify the cooling demands while the system is operating. As a general rule, do not expose the PC and its peripherals to direct sunlight for extended periods of time.

THERMAL CYCLING

Turn it off or leave it on? This is the perennial PC question and one that continues to be a hotbed of debate among technicians. The best way to answer this question is to approach it both theoretically and practically. Theoretically, each time material heats up, it expands. When the material cools down again, it contracts. Thus, every time a PC is turned on, the chips, solder joints, and wiring tend to expand until the system reaches a stable operating temperature. When the PC is turned off, it gradually cools down and its components contract until the PC returns to room temperature. Over time, this "accordion effect" of expansion and contraction (referred to as *thermal cycling*) is known to cause material to fatigue and fracture—a chip breaks down, or a solder joint becomes intermittent—you get the idea. As a consequence of this effect, long-time PC veterans argue that the PC should be left on constantly. This allows the system to achieve a stable temperature, so thermal cycling is eliminated.

From a practical standpoint, however, the view is a bit different. First, the damaging effect of thermal cycling is dependent on the *amount of temperature difference*. Frankly, today's PCs just don't get that hot (although CPUs and graphics processors can fail if not properly cooled). Cooler PCs are affected less by thermal damage. Drive wear is also another nonissue, with current, cool-running designs exhibiting MTBFs of over 300,000 hours. The other consideration is the rising cost of power, which is wasted by simply leaving the PC on overnight. On the other hand, there is no reason to power down the PC each time you get up for a coffee. Ultimately, the current thinking is to go ahead and turn the PC off overnight, or whenever you must leave the system for more than a few hours. If your system offers power conservation support (such as "standby" and "hibernation" modes), you should employ those techniques to lower the system's total power demands.

EXCESSIVE DEVICES

Many PCs are eventually upgraded with more RAM, more drives, new CPUs, and so on. Each new device added to the system contributes to its overall heat production. For heavily expanded systems, it may be necessary to augment cooling with a supplemental exhaust fan or inlet fan at the chassis. The general yard-stick for judging the need for extra cooling is to feel the air exhausting from the system. If the air feels comfortable or somewhat warm, chances are that cooling is adequate. If the air feels hot, it's time to add a new fan. True, this is a rather subjective means of measurement, but it is accurate enough for most situations.

DUST

Perhaps the most significant problem of reliable, long-term PC cooling is *dust*, which is always present in everyday air. For the purposes of this book, "dust" includes other contaminants too, such as pet hair and cigarette smoke. Dust has two effects on the PC. First, dust collects on the fan blades and intake vents or filters. This interrupts and limits airflow into and out of the system. Second, dust can collect on a printed circuit board where airflow is limited. The dust acts as a *thermal blanket* that prevents normal convective cooling. When upgrading or servicing a PC, make it a point to vacuum any accumulations of dust in or around the system.

AC POWER PROBLEMS

Power supplies can be serious sources of heat, especially in the regulator portion of the supply, which is designed to maintain a stable voltage output as AC input levels and load demands change. If AC climbs over its nominal value, the regulator must work harder to maintain a constant output. This results in excessive power supply heating. Lagging AC levels result in larger amounts of current being drawn to keep the power output steady, which also causes extra heating. Persistent power supply failures or unusually hot operation may suggest problems with AC (or an overloaded system power supply).

PCs in regions with chronic power distribution problems may benefit from the use of Uninterruptible Power Supply (UPS) systems between the AC outlet and system.

BLOCKED VENTS

Air needs a clear path into and out of the system, which is usually accommodated through vent slots located around the enclosure. If the vent slots are obstructed or blocked, airflow may be interrupted. (This is especially detrimental to devices relying on natural convection for cooling.) You can see the importance of proper ventilation by reviewing the installation guidelines for almost any piece of consumer electronics. Most guidelines recommend that you leave several inches of free space on each side of the enclosure. Make sure that vent slots are unobstructed and clear of dust or debris. Keep in mind that more openings are not necessarily better. Unexpected openings in the chassis (open expansion slots or missing I/O panel covers, for example) may allow air to enter or leave the chassis unexpectedly, and this may impair proper airflow and cooling through the system.

EXCESSIVE CPU VOLTAGE

Not all CPUs use the same voltage. Intel, AMD, and Cyrix CPUs use slightly different voltage levels for proper operation (usually between +2.4 Vdc and +3.6 Vdc). If the CPU voltage is tweaked a bit too high for the particular CPU, it will generate excessive heat. Another typical oversight comes with the use of Pentium MMX (or compatible) processors that use dual voltages (approximately +2.8 Vdc and +3.3 Vdc) for reduced power and lower heating. Again, if the CPU voltage is set too high, excessive heating will result, which can shorten the CPU's working life. Devices like Autotime's Processor Protector (Figure 19-4) are tools that you can use to quickly and efficiently verify the CPU voltage(s).

FIGURE 19-4   Checking CPU voltages with the Processor Protector (Courtesy of Autotime)

Troubleshooting Cooling Problems

Cooling problems manifest themselves in a variety of ways—usually through intermittent system operation and frequent failures. This part of the chapter is intended to illustrate some of the more perplexing cooling problems that you should be aware of.

HEAT DETECTORS

To deal with system heat problems, you should know when excessive heating occurs. Today, the power management and cooling systems of most motherboards incorporate hardware monitoring that will report cooling fan speeds and (if properly equipped) indicate the CPU temperature. You can then set alarm points that will alert you if a cooling fan stops or CPU temperature exceeds your preset value. If you're working with older systems (or systems that do not incorporate such hardware monitoring features), you can use after-market heat detectors (such as the 110 Alert unit from PC Power & Cooling) to alert you to excess heat.

Devices like the 110 Alert monitor interior case temperature and processor cooler fan rotation inside any computer. At 110°F (40°C), a loud audible alarm will sound. The 110 Alert also monitors electrical current to the processor's cooling fan, so the audible alarm will sound when the cooling fan slows by 30 percent or more. To install a device such as the 110 Alert, connect a spare power lead to the connector labeled "110 Alert," and then connect the opposite end directly to the processor's cooling fan power connector. (Power for the processor cooling fan must be supplied by the 110 Alert; otherwise, the alarm may sound continuously.) Remove the protective backing from the mounting tape, and mount the unit on a smooth, clean surface in a convenient location within the top third of the computer.

Do not locate the heat detector near the CPU or other high heat source, because this may result in a nuisance alarm.
Also, do not connect a Y-splitter between a 110 Alert and the processor cooling fan. You cannot split the power to the processor cooling fan and another device such as a hard disk drive. This will cause intermittent nuisance alarms because the 110 Alert is sensing the current of both devices.

GENERAL SYMPTOMS

SYMPTOM 19-1   **The fan is producing an unusual amount of noise, but it seems to be working properly**   This can often happen after replacing a fan and is typically the result of fan vibrations being introduced to the PC chassis. While this is rarely harmful to the system, it can become quite annoying. Check the way in which the new fan is mounted, and be sure that any damping material is in place. Otherwise, you may try adding small standoffs of foam around each mounting screw to damp vibration. Of course, if the fan is original equipment, it may be wearing out and need to be replaced. Try a new fan.

SYMPTOM 19-2   **The fan has stopped turning**   First, check to see if the fan is the type that works intermittently by means of a small internal thermostat. If so, the fan may simply have stopped normally. You should see it start and stop as required. However, most fans turn continuously, so if the fan has stopped, it may have become disconnected or it may have failed. Check the fan's power connection. If the problem persists, try a new fan.

SYMPTOM 19-3   **The CPU freezes intermittently**   This is a classic sign of CPU overheating. While overheating will not necessarily destroy a CPU immediately, prolonged or repeated overheating can precipitate a permanent failure. Check the heat sink or CPU fan attached to the CPU.

Be sure to let the system cool before touching the heat sink. If the cooling device is loose, reattach it securely (be sure to use thermal compound). If the heat sink is secure, but overheating continues, try a more aggressive device such as a CPU fan.

SYMPTOM 19-4   **You are experiencing frequent CPU failures**   Chronic CPU failures are rare occurrences and can often be traced to insufficient cooling. If the CPU does not have a heat sink, try adding one. If a heat sink is already attached, try a larger heat sink or CPU fan. However, if a CPU fan is already in use, there may be a vibration problem, which shortens the CPU's working life. Try "downgrading" to a regular heat sink, or use an alternative cooling device such as a Peltier cooler.

SYMPTOM 19-5   **You are experiencing frequent drive failures**   This is typical of the hard drive in an overloaded system. When replacing the hard drive, take careful note of the exhaust heat and the overall number of devices in the system. If the exhaust is unusually warm, or there are many adjacent drives in the system, try mounting the replacement drive by itself away from other drives—maybe in a rear drive bay. If possible, try mounting the drive vertically. If it is impossible to relocate the offending drive, try adding a supplemental fan, or a fan card, to improve airflow over the drive.

Further Study

Autotime   www.autotime.com
CoolerGuys   www.coolerguys.com/
PC Power & Cooling   www.pcpowercooling.com
The Heat Sink Guide   www.heatsink-guide.com/

20

FLOPPY AND LS-120 DRIVES

The ability to interchange programs and data between various compatible computers is a fundamental requirement of almost every computer system. It is just this kind of file exchange compatibility that helped rocket IBM PC/XTs into everyday use and spur the personal computer industry into the early 1980s. A standardized operating system, file structure, and recording media also breathed life into the fledgling software industry. With the floppy disk, early software developers could finally distribute programs and data to a mass market of compatible computer users. The mechanism that allowed this quantum leap in compatibility is the floppy disk drive (Figure 20-1). Although floppy drives are quite inexpensive and reliable, they are also very limited in their storage space—allowing only up to 1.44MB on a traditional disk. The LS-120 is an ultra-high-density floppy system (compatible with all 3.5-inch disks) that can support up to 120MB on a single LS-120 disk. This chapter examines the operating concepts, installation guidelines, and troubleshooting issues for both conventional floppy drives and LS-120 devices.

The Floppy Drive

A venerable floppy disk drive (FDD) is one of the least expensive and most reliable forms of mass storage ever used in computer systems. Virtually every one of the millions of personal computers sold each year incorporates at least one floppy drive. Most notebook and laptop computers also offer a single floppy drive.

FIGURE 20-1   NEC FD1138H floppy drive (NEC Technologies, Inc.)

Not only are floppy drives useful for transferring files and data between various systems, but the advantage of removable media—the floppy disk itself—makes floppy drives an almost intuitive backup for your important data files. Although floppy drives have evolved through a number of iterations from 8 inches to 5.25 inches to 3.5 inches, their basic components and operating principles have changed very little.

MAGNETIC STORAGE CONCEPTS

Magnetic storage media has been attractive to mainframe and minicomputer designers for many years—long before the personal computer had established itself in homes and offices. This popularity is primarily due to the fact that magnetic media is *nonvolatile*. Unlike system RAM, no electrical energy is needed to maintain the information once it is stored on magnetic media. Although electrical energy is used to read and write magnetic data, magnetic fields do not change on their own, so data remains intact until other forces (such as another floppy drive) act upon it. It is this smooth, straightforward translation from electricity to magnetism and back again that has made magnetic storage such a natural choice. To understand how a floppy drive works and why it fails, you should have an understanding of magnetic storage. This part of the chapter describes the basic storage concepts used for floppy drives.

Magnetic Media

For the purposes of this book, *media* is the physical material that actually holds recorded information. In a floppy disk, the media is a small Mylar disk coated on both sides with a precisely formulated magnetic material often referred to as the *oxide* layer. Every disk manufacturer uses their own particular formula for magnetic coatings, but most coatings are based on a naturally magnetic element (such as iron, nickel, or cobalt) that has been alloyed with nonmagnetic materials or rare earth. This magnetic material is then compounded with plastic, bonding chemicals, and lubricant to form the actual disk media coating.

The fascinating aspect of these magnetic layers is that each and every particle of the media acts as a microscopic magnet. Each magnetic particle can be aligned in one orientation or another under the influence of an external magnetic field. If you have ever magnetized a screwdriver's steel shaft by running a permanent magnet along its length, you have already seen this magnetizing process in action. For a floppy disk, microscopic points along the disk's surfaces are magnetized in one alignment or another by the precise forces applied by read/write (or R/W) heads. The shifting of alignment polarities would indicate a logic 1, while no change in polarity would indicate a logic 0. (You will see more about data recording and organization later in this chapter.)

In analog recording (such as audio tapes), the magnetic field generated by read/write heads varies in direct proportion to the signal being recorded. Such linear variations in field strength cause varying amounts of magnetic particles to align as the media moves. On the other hand, digital recordings such as floppy disks save binary 1's and 0's by applying an overwhelming amount of field strength. Very strong magnetic fields *saturate* the media—that is, *so much* field strength is applied that any further increase in field strength will not cause a better alignment of magnetic particles at that point on the media. The advantage to operating in saturation is that 1's and 0's are remarkably resistant to the degrading effects of noise that eventually appear in analog magnetic recordings.

Although the orientation of magnetic particles on a disk's media can be reversed by using an external magnetic field, particles tend to resist the reversal of polarity. *Coercitivity* is the strength with which magnetic particles resist change. Higher coercitivity material has a greater resistance to change, so a stronger external field will be needed to cause changes. High coercitivity is generally considered to be desirable (up to a point) because signals stand out much better against background noise, and signals will resist natural degradation caused by age, temperature, and random magnetic influences. As you might expect, a highly coercive media requires a more powerful field to record new information.

Another advantage of increased coercitivity is greater "information density" for media. The greater strength of each media particle allows more bits to be packed into less area. The move from 5.25-inch to 3.5-inch floppy disks was possible due largely to a superior (more coercitive) magnetic layer. This coercitivity principle also holds true for hard drives. To pack more information onto ever-smaller platters, the media must be more coercive. Coercitivity is a common magnetic measurement with units in *oersteds* (pronounced "or-steds"). The coercitivity of a typical floppy disk can range anywhere from 300 to 750 oersteds. By comparison, hard drive and magneto-optical (MO) drive media usually offer coercitivities up to 6000 oersteds or higher.

The main premise of magnetic storage is that it is *static* (once recorded, information is retained without any electrical energy). Such stored information is presumed to last forever, but in actual practice, magnetic information begins to degrade as soon as it is recorded. A good magnetic media will reliably "remember" (or retain) the alignment of its particles over a long period of time. The ability of a media to retain its magnetic information is known as *retentivity*. Even the finest, best-formulated floppy disks degrade eventually (although it could take many years before an actual data error materializes).

Ultimately, the ideal answer to media degradation is to refresh (or write over) the data and sector ID information. Data is rewritten normally each time a file is saved, but sector IDs are only written once when the disk is formatted. If a sector ID should fail, you will see the dreaded "Sector Not Found" disk error, and any data stored in the sector cannot be accessed. This failure mode also occurs in hard drives. There is little that can be done to ensure the integrity of floppy disks other than maintaining one or more backups on freshly formatted disks. However, some commercial software is available for restoring disk data (especially hard drives).

Magnetic Recording Principles

The first step in understanding digital recording is to see how binary data is stored on a disk. Binary 1's and 0's are *not* represented by discrete polarities of magnetic field orientations as you may have thought. Instead, binary digits are represented by the presence or absence of flux *transitions,* as illustrated in Figure 20-2. By detecting the *change* from one polarity to another instead of simply detecting a discrete polarity itself, maximum sensitivity can be achieved with very simple circuitry.

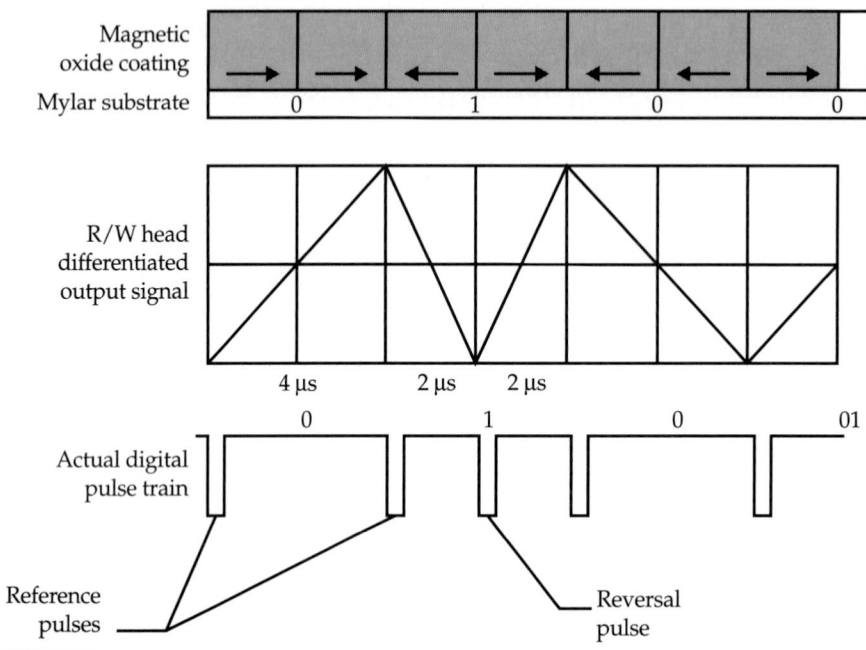

FIGURE 20-2   Flux transitions in floppy disks

In its simplest form, a logic 1 is indicated by the presence of a flux reversal within a fixed time frame, while a logic 0 is indicated by the absence of a flux reversal. Most floppy drive systems insert artificial flux reversals between consecutive 0's to prevent reversals from occurring at great intervals. You can see some example magnetic states recorded on the media of Figure 20-2. Notice that the direction of reversal does not matter at all—it is the reversal event that defines a 1 or 0. For example, the first 0 uses left-to-right orientation, while the second 0 uses a right-to-left orientation, but both can represent 0's. The second trace in Figure 20-2 represents an amplified output signal from a typical read/write head. Notice that the analog signal peaks wherever there is a flux transition—long slopes indicate a 0, and short slopes indicate a 1. When such peaks are encountered, peak detection circuits in the floppy drive cause marking pulses in the ultimate data signal. Each bit is usually encoded in about 4 μs.

Often, the most confusing aspect of flux transitions is the artificial reversals. Why reverse the polarities for consecutive 0's? Artificial reversals are added to guarantee synchronization in the floppy disk circuitry. Remember that data read or written to a floppy disk is serial, and without any clock signal, such serial data is *asynchronous* of the drive's circuitry. Regular flux reversals (even if added artificially) create reference pulses that help to synchronize the drive and data without use of clocks or other timing signals. This approach is loosely referred to as the *modified frequency modulation* (MFM) recording technique. Early hard drives (such as ST506/412 drives) also employed MFM recording.

The ability of floppy disks to store information depends upon being able to write new magnetic field polarities on top of old or existing orientations. A drive must also be able to sense the existing polarities on a disk during read operations. The mechanism responsible for translating electrical signals into magnetic signals (and vice versa) is the R/W head. In principle, a *head* is little more than a coil of very fine wire wrapped around a soft, highly permeable core material, as illustrated in Figure 20-3.

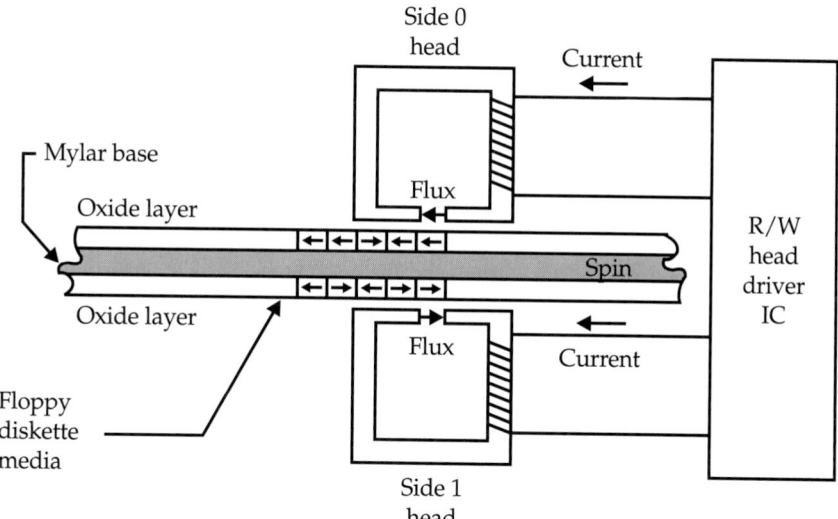

FIGURE 20-3   Floppy drive recording principles

When the head is energized with current flow from a driver chip, a path of magnetic flux is established in the head core. The direction (or orientation) of flux depends on the direction of energizing current. To reverse a head's magnetic orientation, the direction of energizing current must be reversed. The small head size and low current levels needed to energize a head allow very high frequency flux reversals. As magnetic flux is generated in a head, the resulting, tightly focused magnetic field aligns the floppy disk's particles at that point. In general practice, the current signal magnetizes an almost microscopic area on the media. R/W heads actually contact the media while a disk is inserted into a drive.

During a read operation, the heads are left unenergized while the disk spins. Just as varying current produces magnetism in a head, the reverse is also true—varying magnetic influences cause currents to be developed in the head(s). As the spinning media moves across a R/W head, a current is produced in the head coil. The direction of induced current depends on the polarity of each flux orientation. Induced current is proportional to the flux density (how closely each flux transition is placed) and the velocity of the media across each head. In other words, signal strength depends on the rate of change of flux versus time.

Data and Disk Organization

Another important aspect of drive troubleshooting is to understand how data is arranged on the disk. You cannot place data just *anywhere*. The drive would have no idea where to look for the data later on, and wouldn't even be able to determine whether the data is valid. For a disk to be of use, information must be sorted and organized into known, standard locations. Standardized organization ensures that a disk written by one drive will be readable by another drive in a different machine. Table 20-1 compares the major specifications of today's popular drive types.

It is important to note that a floppy disk is a two-dimensional entity possessing both height and width (depth is irrelevant here). This two-dimensional characteristic allows disk information to be recorded in concentric circles, which creates a random-access type of media. *Random access* means that it is possible to move around the disk almost instantly to obtain a desired piece of information. This is a much faster and more convenient approach than a sequential recording medium such as magnetic tape.

TABLE 20-1 COMPARISON OF GENERAL FLOPPY DRIVE SPECIFICATIONS

SPECIFICATION	5.25 INCH (360KB)	5.25 INCH (1.2MB)	3.5 INCH (720KB)	3.5 INCH (1.44MB)	3.5 INCH (2.88MB)
Bytes per sector	512	512	512	512	512
Sectors per track	9	15	9	18	36
Tracks per side	40	80	80	80	80
Sectors per cluster	2	1	2	1	2
FAT length (sectors)	2	7	3	9	9
Number of FATs	2	2	2	2	2
Root directory length	7 sectors	14 sectors	7 sectors	14 sectors	15 sectors
Max. root entries	112	224	112	224	240
Total sectors on disk	708	2371	1426	2847	5726
Media base	Ferrite	Ferrite	Cobalt	Cobalt	Cobalt
Coercitivity (oersteds)	300	300	600	600	720
Media descriptor byte	FDh	F9h	F9h	F0h	F0h
Encoding format	MFM or FM	MFM or FM	MFM	MFM	MFM
Data rate (KB/sec)	250 or 125	500 or 250	500	500	500

Floppy disk organization is not terribly complicated, but there are several important concepts that you must be familiar with. The disk itself is rotated in one direction (usually clockwise) under read/write heads that are perpendicular (at right angles) to the disk's plane. The path of the disk beneath a head describes a circle. As a head steps in and out along a disk's radius, each step describes a circle with a different circumference—rather like lanes on a roadway. Each of these concentric "lanes" is known as a *track*. A typical 3.5-inch disk offers 160 tracks—80 tracks on each side of the media. Tracks have a finite width that is defined largely by the drive size, head size, and media. When a R/W head jumps from track to track, it must jump precisely the correct distance to position itself in the middle of another track. If positioning is not correct, the head may encounter data signals from two adjacent tracks. Faulty positioning almost invariably results in disk errors. Also notice that the circumference of each track drops as the head moves toward the disk's center. With less space and a constant rate of spin, data is densest on the innermost tracks (79 or 159 depending on the disk side) and least dense on the outermost tracks (0 or 80). A track is also known as a *cylinder*.

Every cylinder is divided into smaller units called *sectors*. There are 18 sectors on every track of an 3.5-inch disk. Sectors serve two purposes. First, a sector stores 512 bytes of data. With 18 sectors per track and 160 tracks per disk, an 8.89cm disk holds 2,880 sectors [18×160]. At 512 bytes per sector, a formatted disk can handle about (2,880×512) 1,474,560 bytes of data. In actual practice, this amount is often slightly less, to allow for boot sector and file allocation information. Sectors are referenced in groups called *clusters* or *allocation units*. While hard drives can group 16 or more sectors into a cluster, floppy drives only use 1 or 2 sectors in a cluster.

Second, and perhaps more important, a sector provides housekeeping data that identifies the sector, the track, and error-checking results from cyclical redundancy check (CRC) calculations. The location of each sector and housekeeping information is set down during the format process. Once formatted, only the sector data and CRC results are updated when a disk is written. Sector ID and synchronization data is never rewritten unless the disk is reformatted. This extra information means that each sector actually holds more than 512 bytes, but you only have access to the 512 data bytes in a sector during normal disk read/write operations. If sector ID data is accidentally overwritten or corrupted, the user data in the afflicted sector becomes unreadable.

The format process also writes a bit of other important information to the disk. The boot record is the first sector on a disk (sector 0). It contains several key parameters that describe the characteristics of the disk. If the disk is bootable, the boot sector will also run the files (IO.SYS and MSDOS.SYS) that load DOS. In addition to the boot record, a File Allocation Table (FAT) is placed on track 00. The FAT acts as a table of contents for the disk. As files are added and erased, the FAT is updated to reflect the contents of each cluster. As you might imagine, a working FAT is critical to the proper operation of a disk. If the FAT is accidentally overwritten or corrupted, the entire disk can become useless. Without a viable FAT, the computer has no other way to determine what files are available or where they are spread throughout the disk. The very first byte in a FAT is the *media descriptor* byte, which allows the drive to recognize the type of disk that is inserted.

Media Problems

Magnetic media has come a long way in the last decade or so. Today's high-quality magnetic materials, combined with the benefits of precise, high-volume production equipment, produce disks that are exceptionally reliable over normal long-term use in a floppy disk drive. However, floppy disks are removable items. The care they receive in physical handling and the storage environment where they are kept will greatly impact a disk's life span.

The most troubling and insidious problem plaguing floppy disk media is the accidental influence of magnetic fields. Any magnetized item in close proximity to a floppy disk poses a potential threat. Permanent magnets such as refrigerator magnets or magnetic paper clips are prime sources of stray fields. Electromagnetic sources like telephone ringers, monitor or TV degaussing coils, and all types of motors will corrupt data if the media is close enough. The best policy is to keep all floppy disks in a dedicated container placed well away from stray magnetic fields.

Disks and magnetic media are also subject to a wide variety of physical damage. Substrates and media are manufactured to very tight tolerances, so anything at all that alters the precise surface features of a floppy disk can cause problems. The introduction of hair, dirt, or dust through the disk's head access aperture, wild temperature variations, fingerprints on the media, or any substantial impact or flexing of the media can cause temporary loss of contact between media and head. When loss of contact occurs, data is lost and a number of disk errors can occur. Head wear and the accumulation of worn oxides also affect head contact. Once again, storing disks in a dedicated container located well out of harm's way is often the best means of protection.

DRIVE CONSTRUCTION

At the core of a floppy drive (Figure 20-4) is a frame assembly (15). It is the single, main structure for mounting the drive's mechanisms and electronics. Frames are typically made from die-cast aluminum to provide a strong, rigid foundation for the drive. The front bezel (18) attaches to the frame to provide a clean, cosmetic appearance, and to offer a fixed slot for disk insertion or removal. For 3.5-inch drives, bezels often include a small colored lens, a disk ejection button hole, and a flap to cover the disk slot when the drive is empty. A spindle motor assembly (17) uses an outer-rotor DC motor fabricated onto a small PC board. The motor's shaft is inserted into that large hole in the frame. A disk's metal drive hub automatically interlocks to the spindle. For 5.25-inch disks, the center hole is clamped between two halves of a spindle assembly. The halves clamp the disk when the drive lever is locked down. The disk activity LED (20) illuminates through the bezel's colored lens whenever spindle motor activity is in progress. Figure 20-5 shows the spindle motor assembly from the underside of the drive.

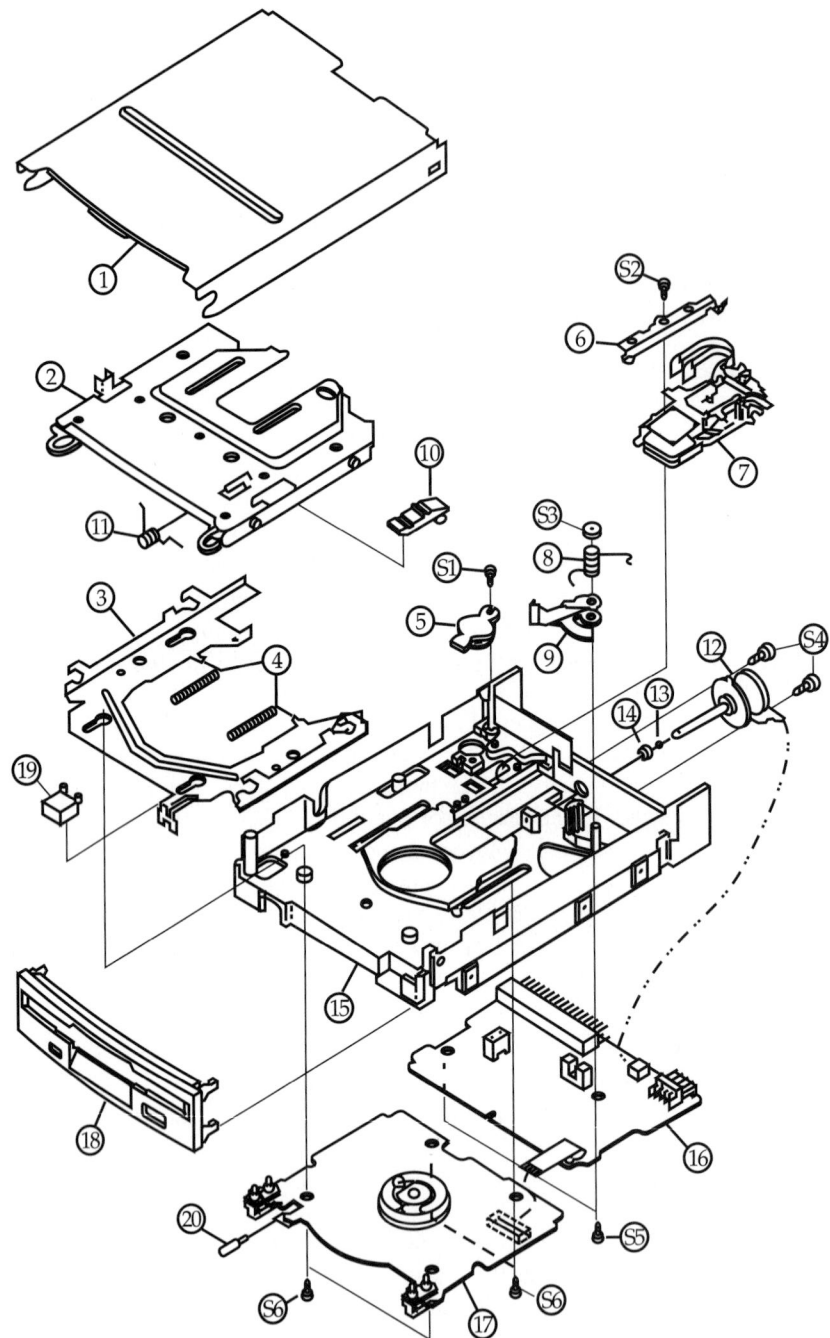

FIGURE 20-4 Exploded diagram of a floppy disk drive assembly (Teac America, Inc.)

Fixing screws

A — PCBA spindle motor servo

Connector J5 (CN61)

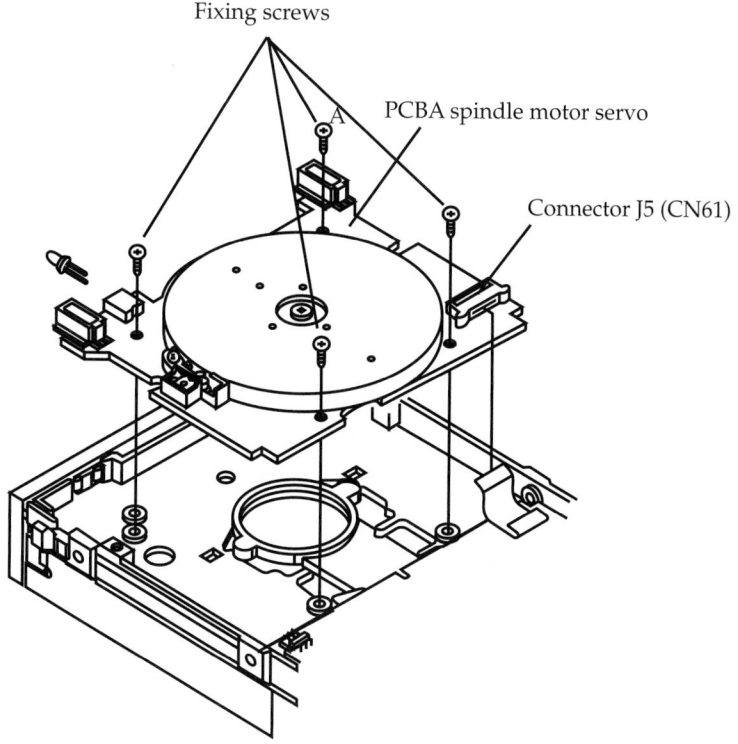

FIGURE 20-5 Underside view of a floppy drive spindle motor assembly (Teac America, Inc.)

Just behind the spindle motor is the drive's control electronics (16 on Figure 20-4). It contains the circuitry needed to operate the drive's motors, R/W heads, and sensors. A standardized interface is used to connect the drive to a floppy drive controller. Figure 20-6 shows a close-up of a drive's control board (note the optoisolator just below U1). The read/write head assembly (7 on Figure 20-4), also sometimes called a head carriage assembly, holds a set of two R/W heads. Head 0 is the lower head (underside of the disk), and head 1 is on top. A head stepping motor (12) is added to ensure even and consistent movement between tracks. A threaded rod at the motor end is what actually moves the heads. A mechanical damper (5) helps to smooth the disk's travel into or out of the drive. Figure 20-7 shows a close-up of the R/W heads and stepping motor.

When a disk is inserted through the bezel, the disk is restrained by a disk clamp assembly (2 in Figure 20-4). To eject the disk, you would press the ejector button (19), which pushes a slider mechanism (3). When the ejector button is fully depressed, the disk will disengage from the spindle and pop out of the drive. For 5.25-inch drives, the disk is released whenever the drive door is opened. Your particular drive may contain other miscellaneous components. Finally, the entire upper portion of a drive can be covered by a metal shield (1).

Drive Electronics

Proper drive operation depends on the intimate cooperation between magnetic media, electromechanical devices, and dedicated electronics. Floppy drive electronics is responsible for two major tasks: controlling

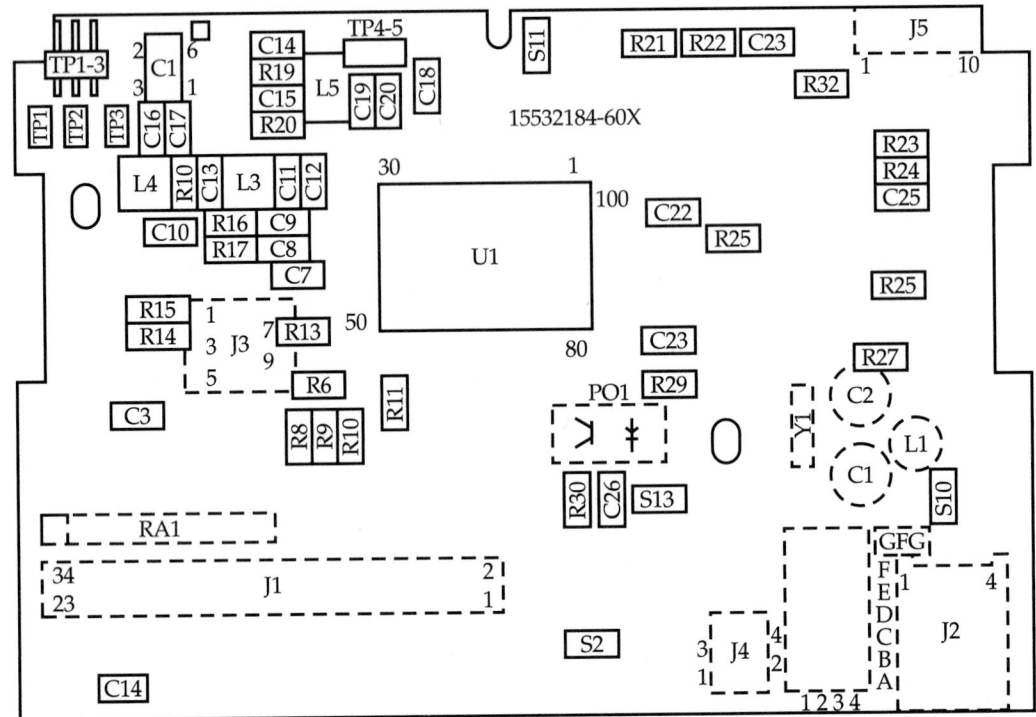

FIGURE 20-6   Typical floppy drive main logic/interface board (Teac America, Inc.)

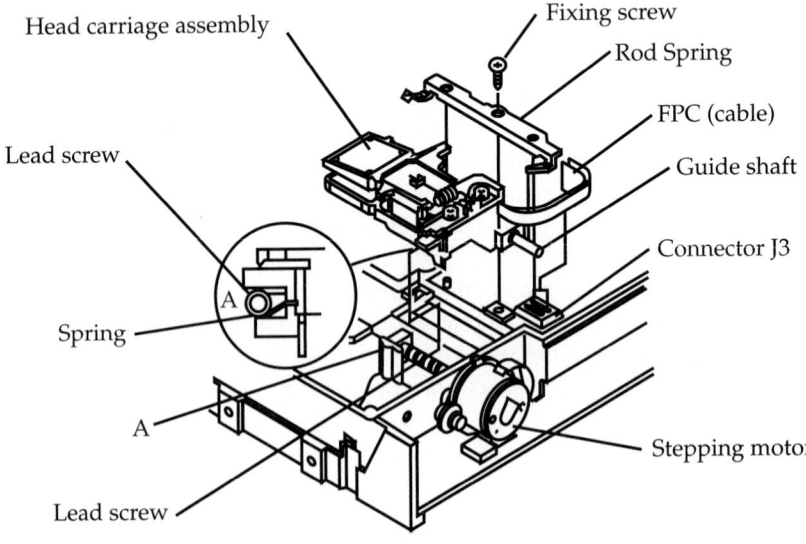

FIGURE 20-7   Detailed view of a R/W head and stepping motor (Teac America, Inc.)

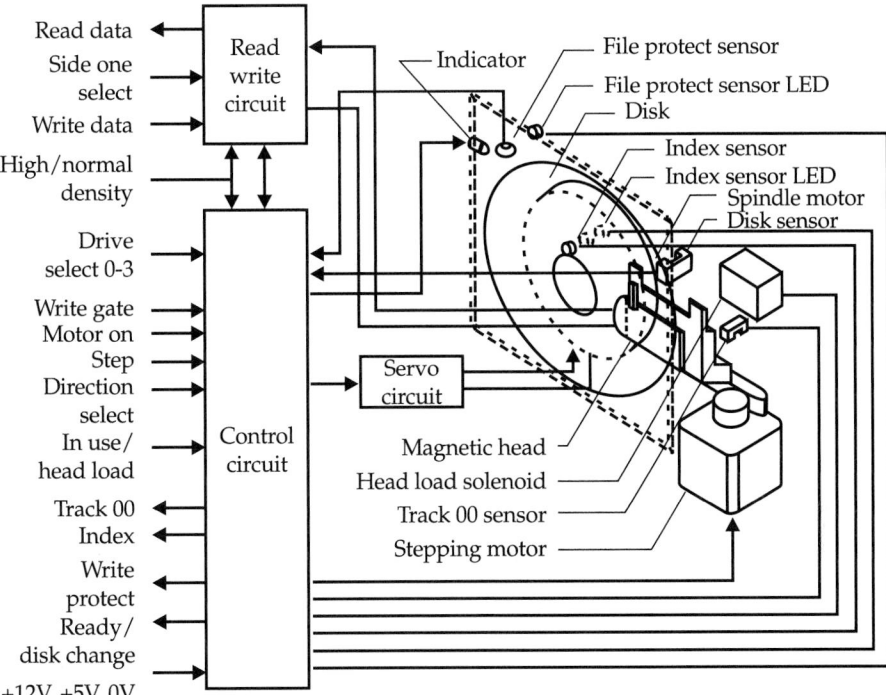

Read data
Side one select
Write data
High/normal density
Drive select 0-3
Write gate
Motor on
Step
Direction select
In use/ head load
Track 00
Index
Write protect
Ready/ disk change
+12V, +5V, 0V

Read write circuit

Control circuit

Servo circuit

Indicator
File protect sensor
File protect sensor LED
Disk
Index sensor
Index sensor LED
Spindle motor
Disk sensor

Magnetic head
Head load solenoid
Track 00 sensor
Stepping motor

FIGURE 20-8   Block diagram of a floppy drive

the drive's physical operations and managing the flow of data into or out of the drive. These tasks are not nearly as simple as they sound, but the sleek, low-profile drives in today's computer systems are a far cry from the clunky, full-height drives found in early systems. Older drives needed a large number of chips spanning several boards that had to be fitted to the chassis. However, the drive in your computer right now is probably implemented with only a few highly integrated chips that are neatly surface mounted on two small, opposing PC boards. This part of the chapter discusses the drive's operating circuits. A complete block diagram for a Teac 3.5-inch floppy drive is illustrated in Figure 20-8 (shown with a floppy disk *inserted*).

Write-protect sensors are used to detect the position of a disk's file-protect tab. For 3.5-inch disks, the write-protect notch must be covered to allow both read and write operations. If the notch is open, the disk can only be read. Optoisolators are commonly used as write-protect sensors, because an open notch will easily allow light through, while a closed notch will cut off the light path.

Before the drive is allowed to operate at all, a disk must be inserted properly and interlocked with the spindle. A disk-in-place sensor detects the presence or absence of a disk. Like the write-protect sensor, disk sensors are often mechanical switches that are activated by disk contact. If drive access is attempted without a disk in place, the sensor causes the drive's logic to induce a DOS "Disk Not Ready" error code. It is not unusual to find an optoisolator acting as a disk-in-place sensor.

The electronics of a 3.5-inch drive must be able to differentiate whether the disk contains normal (double) density or high-density media. A high-density sensor looks for the hole that is found near the top of all high-density disk bodies. A mechanical switch is typically used to detect the high-density hole, but a separate LED/detector pair may also be used. When the hole is absent (a double-density disk), the switch is activated upon disk insertion. If the hole is present (a high-density disk), the switch is not actuated. All switch conditions are translated into logic signals used by the drive electronics.

Before disk data can be read or written, the system must read the disk's boot sector information and FAT. Programs and data can be broken up and scattered all over a disk, but the FAT must always be located at a known location so that the drive knows where to look for it. The FAT is always located on track 00—the first track of disk side 0. A track 00 sensor provides a logic signal when the heads are positioned over track 00. Each time a read or write is ordered, the head assembly is stepped to track 00. Although a drive "remembers" how many steps should be needed to position the heads precisely over track 00, an optoisolator or switch senses the head carriage assembly position. At track 00, the head carriage should interrupt the optoisolator or actuate the switch. If the drive supposedly steps to track 00 and there is no sensor signal to confirm the position (or the signal occurs *before* the drive has finished stepping), the drive assumes that a head-positioning error has occurred. Head step counts and sensor outputs virtually always agree unless the sensor has failed or the drive has been physically damaged.

Spindle speed is a critically important drive parameter. Once the disk has reached its running velocity (300 or 360 RPM), the drive must maintain that velocity for the duration of the disk access process. Unfortunately, simply telling the spindle motor to move is no guarantee that the motor is turning—a sensor is required to measure the motor's speed. This is the *index sensor*. Signals from an index sensor are fed back to the drive electronics, and spindle speed is adjusted to maintain a constant rotation. Most drives use optoisolators as index sensors. They work by detecting the motion of small slots cut in a template or the spindle rotor itself. When a disk is spinning, the output from an index sensor is a fast logic pulse sent along to the drive electronics. Keep in mind that some index sensors are magnetic. A magnetic sensor typically operates by detecting the proximity of small slots in a template or the spindle rotor, but the pulse output is essentially identical to that of the optoisolator.

Floppy Drive Interface

The drive must receive control and data signals from the computer and deliver status and data signals back to the computer as required. The series of connections between a floppy disk PC board and the floppy disk controller circuit is known as the *physical interface*. The advantage to using a standard interface is that various drives made by different manufacturers can be mixed and matched by computer designers. A floppy drive working in one computer will operate properly in another computer regardless of the manufacturer as long as the same physical interface scheme is being used.

Floppy drives use a physical interface that includes two cables: a power cable and a signal cable. Both cable pinouts are illustrated in Figure 20-9. The classical power connector is a 4-pin Molex connector, although many low-profile drives used in mobile computers (laptops or notebooks) may use much smaller connector designs. Floppy drives require two voltage levels: +5.0 Vdc for logic and +12.0 Vdc for motors. The return (ground) for each supply is also provided at the connector. The signal connector is typically a 34-pin *insulation displacement connector* (IDC) cable. Notice that all odd-numbered pins are ground lines, while the even-numbered pins carry active signals. Logic signals are all TTL-level signals.

In a system with more than one floppy drive, the particular destination drive must be selected before any read or write is attempted. A drive is selected using the appropriate "drive select" line (drive select 0 to 3) on pins 10, 12, 14, and 6 respectively. For notebook or sub-notebook systems where only one floppy drive is used, only drive select 0 is used. The remaining select inputs may simply be disconnected. The spindle motor servo circuit is controlled through the "motor on" signal (pin 16). When pin 16 is logic 0, the spindle motor should *spin up* (approach a stable operating speed). The media must be spinning at the proper rate before reading or writing can take place.

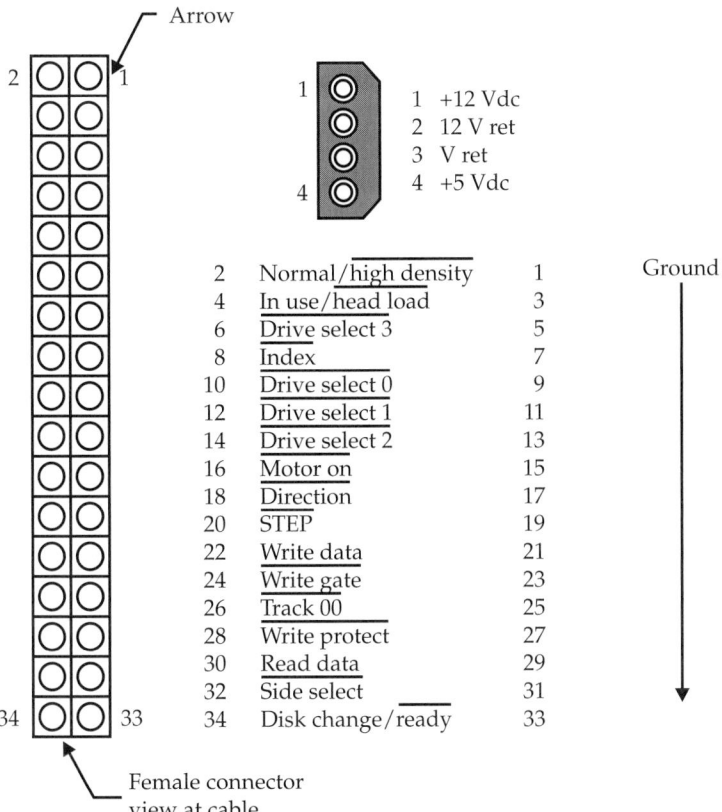

Arrow

1	+12 Vdc	
2	12 V ret	
3	V ret	
4	+5 Vdc	

2	Normal/high density	1	Ground
4	In use/head load	3	
6	Drive select 3	5	
8	Index	7	
10	Drive select 0	9	
12	Drive select 1	11	
14	Drive select 2	13	
16	Motor on	15	
18	Direction	17	
20	STEP	19	
22	Write data	21	
24	Write gate	23	
26	Track 00	25	
28	Write protect	27	
30	Read data	29	
32	Side select	31	
34	Disk change/ready	33	

Female connector
view at cable

FIGURE 20-9   Pin assignments for a standard 34-pin floppy drive interface

To move the R/W heads, the host computer must specify the number of steps a head carriage assembly must move, and the direction in which steps must occur. A "direction select" signal (pin 18) tells the coil driver circuit whether the heads should be moved inward (toward the spindle) or outward (away from the spindle). The "step" signal (pin 20) provides the pulse sequence that actually steps the head motor in the desired direction. The combination of step and direction select controls can position the R/W heads over the disk very precisely. The "side select" control pin (pin 32) determines whether head 0 or head 1 is active for reading or writing—only one side of the disk can be manipulated at a time.

Two signals are needed to write data to a disk. The "write gate" signal (pin 24) is logic 0 when writing is to occur, and logic 1 when writing is inhibited (or reading). After the write gate is asserted, data can be written to the disk over the "write data" line (pin 22). When reading, the data that is extracted from the disk is delivered from the "read data" line (pin 30).

Each of the drive's sensor conditions are sent over the physical interface. The "track 00" signal (pin 26) is logic 0 whenever the head carriage assembly is positioned over track 00. The "write protect" line (pin 28) is logic 0 whenever the disk's write-protect notch is in place. Writing is inhibited whenever the write protect signal is asserted. The "index" signal (pin 8) supplies a chain of pulses from the index sensor. Media type is indicated by the "normal/high-density" sensor (pin 2). The status of the disk-in-place sensor is indicated over the "disk change ready" line (pin 34).

FLOPPY DRIVE INSTALLATION AND REPLACEMENT

Unlike many of the various peripherals and drives that are now available for a PC, floppy drives are almost universal in their design and features, meaning you usually have very little to consider because the drives are all the same. However, you must concern yourself with the following three issues. After you've selected the drive, installation should be very straightforward.

- **Drive bay space**   The trend toward smaller, low-profile enclosures has put a lot of pressure on available drive space. Given that many systems are already fitted with a floppy drive, hard drive, and CD-ROM/R/RW drive, rarely is a fourth bay available for even a second hard drive. One of the first problems when planning for a new floppy drive is to locate an external drive bay. If you do not have an external drive bay available, you may be able to move a hard drive to an internal drive bay. This relocates the hard drive and frees an external drive bay for another floppy drive. If you cannot free a drive bay for another floppy drive, you may need to consider a larger case (one with more external drive bays), use an external "parallel port" floppy drive, or remove another unneeded drive to make space for the floppy.

- **BIOS compatibility**   One problem with PC/AT (i286) and early i386 systems was that their BIOS often did not support the high-density 3.5-inch drive format. The drive could be read from and written to properly, but the BIOS would only allow disks to be formatted to 720KB (instead of 1.44MB). The solution to this incompatibility has been either to upgrade the BIOS (to a version later than 11/85) or to use the DRIVER.SYS utility in DOS to explicitly specify the physical drive as a high-density device. If you suspect that DRIVER.SYS is needed to support a 3.5-inch high-density floppy drive on an older PC, open your CONFIG.SYS file and try a command line such as:

```
device=c:\dos\driver.sys /D:1 /F:7
```

This command line creates a new "logical" floppy drive that is actually the same physical floppy drive specified by the /D switch (0=A:, 1=B:). The /F switch determines the type of drive to be created. In this case, a value of 7 indicates a 3.5-inch 1.44MB drive. Check your DOS manual for additional parameters. This problem has been completely eliminated in virtually all subsequent BIOS releases after late 1985 and early 1986, but it can cause some confusion when dealing with very old PCs.

- **Power connections**   A power supply only offers a limited number of drive power connectors. Small systems may not have a free drive power connector for another floppy drive. When this occurs, you may use a Y-splitter cable to add another power connector. However, place the Y cable in with the existing floppy drive (never split power from critical drives such as the hard drive). If you're simply replacing a defective floppy, just reuse the existing power connector.

Typical Installation

In most cases, installing a second floppy drive is a three-step process: configure the drive jumper(s), mount and cable the drive, and configure the new drive in CMOS. Although a floppy drive installation is often a quick and painless procedure—even for a novice—there are a few nuances that you should be aware of. When followed carefully, this process can typically be completed in under 30 minutes. If you're simply replacing an old or defective floppy drive, remove the old drive first, and then follow the procedures outlined next.

It's normally a good idea to perform a complete system backup of your hard drives before attempting any kind of drive work. Although floppy drive installation should not affect your hard drives in any way, backups will protect your data and system configuration from accidental data loss.

Prepare the System   Turn the system off and unplug it from the AC receptacle before proceeding. Remove the screws holding the outer cover and place them aside in a safe place. Gently remove the PC's outer cover and set it aside (out of the path of normal floor traffic). You should now be able to look into the PC and observe the open drive bay, the motherboard, and any expansion boards and drives that are installed.

Remember to use an antistatic wrist strap whenever working inside a PC. This will prevent accidental static discharge, which can damage the computer's delicate electronics.

Prepare the Drive Bay   Now that the outer cover is removed, you should open the desired drive bay. In many cases, this is as simple as just removing the plastic bezel that covers an empty bay (the bezel will usually pop right out). If you must relocate an existing drive, things get a bit more complicated. First, decide where the drive (almost always a hard drive) will be relocated—often to an internal bay in the rear of the PC. You can then remove the mounting screws, disconnect the power and signal cables from the hard drive, and slide the hard drive out of the bay. Remount the hard drive in the internal bay, and gently secure each screw into place. (Be careful not to overtighten the screws.) Reattach the power and signal cables to the hard drive. Pay particular attention when connecting the signal cable. If the cable is installed backward, the hard drive will not function. The red or blue stripe along one side of the ribbon cable always marks pin 1.

The procedure is a bit different when replacing an existing floppy drive. Unbolt the existing drive, disconnect the power and signal cables, and slide the old drive out of the bay and set it aside carefully. If you have a good-quality antistatic bag available, seal the old drive in the antistatic bag. At this point, you should have an open drive bay. Take a quick inventory and make sure that you have a floppy signal cable and power connector available. You may need a Y-splitter connector to tap power from another drive.

When using a Y-splitter to tap power from another drive, never split power from a hard drive. This can cause erratic drive (and system) operation.

Set the Floppy Jumpers   Before installing the new drive, remove it from any protective packaging and locate any jumpers or DIP switches on the drive. A manual will be important here. It will be necessary to set at least four conditions: the drive select jumper, the disk change jumper, the media sensor jumper, and the terminating resistors.

The drive select (or DS) jumper allows the drive to be set as drive 0, 1, 2, or 3. Although most XT and AT controllers support four floppy drives, each cable supports only two. As a general rule, you will set both the drives as B: (you'll see why below). However, interpreting the jumper selections is not always intuitive, because different manufacturers mark the jumpers differently. For example, instead of 0, 1, 2, and 3, a drive may be labeled 1, 2, 3, and 4. Other variations include DS0 and DS1, or DS1 and DS2. As a rule of thumb, the lowest designation is generally considered to be drive A:, the next highest digit is considered drive B:, and so on. Since just about all floppy drive cables use a twist between the two floppy drive connectors, both floppy drives can be set to the second jumper position (drive B:). As a consequence, the twist will automatically swap the endmost drive to A:. If in doubt, and there's a twist in the cable, set the drive select jumpers to B:. Now, if there is no twist in the floppy cable (a very rare occurrence), be sure to set the endmost drive to A:, and set the middle drive to B:. (Since this is a daisy-chain configuration, you could actually reverse this order, but it is not traditional.)

Terminating resistors add another wrinkle to the drive setup. As with many other daisy-chain cable applications, terminating resistors are used at both ends of the signal cable to establish ideal signal characteristics. Normally, floppy drives come equipped with terminating resistors installed. Since most systems use a single drive installed at the end of the cable (as drive A:), this is generally a good default. When installing a single drive, be sure that the drive has terminating resistors installed. When installing a second floppy drive as drive A:, be sure it has terminating resistors in place, and check that the second drive (in the middle cable position) has no terminating resistors. When installing a second floppy drive as drive B:, be sure that the terminating resistors are removed.

Although the "middle" (B:) floppy drive should have its terminating resistors removed or disabled, this is not always necessary because of the low-frequency signals on the floppy drive cable. In most cases, you could leave the middle (B:) floppy drive with its terminating resistors in place.

The disk change jumper is a vital part of almost all contemporary drives. This signal tells the PC when a disk is removed so that when a new disk is inserted and read, the directory information will be cached in the system. The disk change signal should be enabled on all drives except for old 5.25-inch 360KB drives. Finally the media sensor (on 1.44MB and 2.88MB drives) jumper should be enabled wherever possible. The sensor allows the drive to detect whether a 760KB, 1.44MB, or 2.88MB disk is installed.

Mount the New Floppy Drive   Now that the floppy drive is configured, slide it gently into the open drive bay. Line up the four mounting holes and screw the drive in carefully. Be sure not to tighten the mounting screws excessively, which can warp the drive's frame and cause R/W problems or premature drive failure. Make it a point to use screws of the proper size and length to do the job.

Connect Power and Signal Cables   Once the drive is installed and mounted securely, connect the power and signal cables as required. The 4-pin power cable is relatively foolproof because of its keyed shape. For the signal cable, however, take care to install the card edge or IDC-type connector in the correct orientation. If the signal cable is installed backward, the drive will not work (the system may not even boot). The red or blue stripe along one side of the ribbon cable always represents pin 1.

Update CMOS Settings   If the steps are performed correctly, the new floppy drive should now be fully installed. Before you can actually use the drive, you must update the system's CMOS Setup entries to accommodate the new drive. Make sure that any tools or extra hardware are removed from the system, reattach the AC cord to the power supply, and then reboot the computer. As the system boots, start the CMOS Setup routine and adjust the configuration as needed for your new floppy drive. You'll need to specify whether a 5.25-inch 360KB, 5.25-inch 1.2MB, 3.5-inch 720KB, 3.5-inch 1.44MB, or 3.5-inch 2.88MB floppy drive is installed. If you have updated or replaced an old drive, make sure that the drive parameters reflect the new device. If you've added a second drive, enter the appropriate parameters for that new drive. When the settings are correct, save the system CMOS and reboot the system so that your changes can take effect.

Test the Drive   Insert a known-good disk in the drive. If the installation is correct, you should see the new drive designator under DOS, as an available option under the Windows Explorer, or as a new drive entry when double-clicking on My Computer on the Windows 9x/Me desktop. Try writing and reading a few files from the drive. You might also try formatting a blank disk in the new drive. If these tests are successful, you can be confident that the new drive is working properly. Be sure to remove any tools or hardware from the system, and then reinstall the system's outer housings. Do not use excessive pressure to tighten the screws. Try the drive one more time, and return the system to service.

Reversing Floppy Drive Assignments

Reversing the letter assignments of your floppy drives sometimes is necessary. This often happens when you wish to boot from a floppy drive that is not in a boot order supported by the BIOS. For example, you may want to change the boot order if you have a 5.25-inch drive as A: and a 3.5-inch drive as B:, and the boot order doesn't support booting from the B: drive. Fortunately, you can easily reverse the drive order by reversing the drives physically and logically. Remember to power-down and unplug the computer before beginning.

Leave the Drive Jumpers in Place   Remember that for most PCs, both floppy drives are jumpered as B:. (It is the "flip" in the floppy drive cable that turns the end-most drive to A:.) If your floppy drive cable does indeed have a flip, you can leave the floppy drives jumpered the way they are. The only time you'll need to reverse the drive's ID jumpers is when there is no flip in the cable, and each drive must be jumpered with a unique ID.

Exchange the Floppy Cable Connections   Reconnect the floppy drive cable by placing the middle drive at the end, and the endmost drive at the middle. Depending on the way each drive is arranged in your system's case (and the amount of slack in the floppy cable), it may be necessary to actually exchange the floppy drives in the drive bays also. If this is the case, you should disconnect the power cables from the floppy drives, unbolt each drive, reinstall each drive in the opposite drive bay, and then reattach the power and signal cables. Now is also a good time to check all connections of the floppy signal cable. If the cable is loose or appears damaged, it should be replaced.

If the middle drive had terminating resistors disabled, you may need to enable those terminating resistors when you place that drive at the end of the cable (A:), and disable the terminating resistors on the drive that you swapped to the middle of the cable (B:).

Reverse the Drive Assignments in CMOS   When you first reapply power to the PC, you will probably receive an error message indicating that the equipment detected does not match the equipment specified in the CMOS Setup. This error occurs because the physical drives are now reversed, but the CMOS still "expects" to find the floppy drives in their original positions. You'll need to start the CMOS Setup and reverse the floppy drive assignments. For example, if you had a 5.25-inch 1.2MB floppy as A: and a 3.5-inch 1.44MB floppy as B:, you'll need to assign a 3.5-inch 1.44MB floppy as A: and a 5.25-inch 1.2MB floppy as B: after you make the physical drive swap. Save your changes and reboot the computer so that your changes can take effect. Test both drives to verify that each is working.

The LS-120 Drive

With multimegabyte text, image, multimedia, and CAD files now commonplace, the traditional 1.44MB disk is falling into disuse because today's huge files often don't fit on them. The LS-120 drive is intended to offer higher storage capacities (up to 120MB) on magneto-optical disks, while still providing full backward compatibility with existing floppy disks. The LS-120 also employs an ATAPI IDE interface (the same class of interface used by CD-ROMs and hard drives), so its performance is far better than the traditional 300KB/s found with floppy drives. This part of the chapter explains the LS-120 capabilities, highlights a typical LS-120 installation, and covers many of the most persistent troubleshooting problems.

LS-120 DRIVE LAYOUT AND CHARACTERISTICS

The LS-120 drive uses both magnetic and optical reading/writing techniques. This makes an LS-120 something of a cross between a floppy drive and a CD-ROM. Using these "hybrid" technologies, the LS-120 can offer storage capacities of 120MB (equivalent to about 83 floppy disks) on specially designed and formatted SuperDisks. (SuperDisk LS-120 disks by Imation are usually recommended.) At the same time, it is fully backward compatible with existing 1.44MB disks (so any existing floppy disks are still usable). The LS-120 also provides much faster data transfers, at up to 750KB/s (five times the rate of a standard floppy). Unlike ordinary floppy drives, the LS-120 uses an ATAPI IDE interface, so the drive can be installed alongside existing hard drives and CD-ROM/R/RW drives. The standard 3.5-inch form factor means that the LS-120 can be installed in any existing drive bay as a floppy disk replacement. In fact, you might not even notice the difference between a floppy and LS-120 drive at first glance.

Disk Compatibility and Cleaning

Since the LS-120 is designed to work with 120MB and 1.44MB disks, there is often some confusion as to how disks may be interchanged. Here are the basic rules for disks:

- The LS-120 can read and write 120MB, 1.44MB, and 720KB disks. You can even format 1.44MB and 720KB disks on the LS-120 (though you may need the latest LS-120 driver to ensure compatibility).

- Disks of 1.44MB and 720KB can't be formatted to 120MB in the LS-120 (only specially designed magneto-optical disks can work at 120MB).

- LS-120 disks can't be read on 1.44MB floppy drives. You must have an LS-120 drive in the system.

Imation (and other LS-120 clone makers) generally recommends that the drive heads be cleaned after 40 to 80 hours of operation, depending on the cleanliness of the operating environment. As with floppy drive head cleaning, this regular maintenance offers an easy, practical, and thorough method for safely removing error-causing dust and debris from magnetic recording heads. As a rule, you should use a head-cleaning kit designed specifically for an LS-120 drive. Ordinary floppy head-cleaning disks can be too abrasive for an LS-120.

LS-120 DRIVE INSTALLATION AND REPLACEMENT

The LS-120 drive offers higher storage capacities and faster performance, as well as bootable operation. However, you'll need to verify several important elements of your PC before installation can begin. As a minimum, you should check the following points.

- **Computing power**   The LS-120 drive typically requires a *minimum* of a 486DX2/66 MHz processor, 8MB of RAM, and 5MB of free hard drive space. Although modern PCs easily meet these requirements, older systems should be evaluated carefully before planning an LS-120 installation.

- **Power connections**   A power supply only offers a limited number of drive power connectors. Small systems may not have a free drive power connector for another drive device. When this occurs, you may use a Y-splitter cable to add another power connector. However, place the Y cable in with the existing floppy drive. (Never split power from critical drives such as the hard drive.) If you're using the LS-120 to replace an existing floppy, just reuse the existing power connector.

- **Drive bay space**   The trend toward smaller, low-profile enclosures has put a lot of pressure on available drive space, so one of the first problems when planning for a new LS-120 drive is to locate an external drive bay. If you do not have an external drive bay available, you may be able to move a hard drive to an internal drive bay. This relocates the hard drive and frees an external drive bay for the LS-120 drive. If you're using the LS-120 as a replacement for your existing floppy drive, it's a matter of removing the existing floppy drive and then installing the LS-120 in that drive space.

If you're planning to replace a floppy with the LS-120, be sure to copy the LS-120 driver disk to your hard drive before you remove the floppy drive.

■ **Drive controller space**   Remember that the LS-120 drive uses your hard drive controller rather than the floppy drive controller. This means that you'll need an open connector on either your primary or secondary IDE drive controller channels. If you do not have an available signal connector (for example, your system has two HDDs, a CD-ROM, and a DVD-ROM drive), you may not be able to install the LS-120 drive without removing one of those existing drives first. Also, the LS-120 requires the Logical Block Addressing (LBA) mode for proper operation, so your drive controller should be an EIDE or Ultra-DMA type. Also keep in mind that the LS-120 will not operate from a tertiary IDE controller such as the IDE controller integrated onto a sound card.

■ **BIOS compatibility**   If you plan to use the LS-120 as a secondary storage device and not as a bootable drive, you'll probably continue to use your existing floppy drive, and no BIOS adjustments are needed. The LS-120 will be enabled *solely* by device drivers. If you plan to use the LS-120 as a bootable drive, remember that you'll need to check the system BIOS for compatibility. The boot order entry in your CMOS Setup should include the option for an LS-120 drive. (Your BIOS may use another designator such as UHD Floppy, Floptical, Removable Drive.) If your BIOS does not provide such support, you may need to upgrade the BIOS before installing the LS-120 drive. Once the drive is installed and the old floppy drive is removed, remember to disable the floppy controller and change the boot order so that the system will boot from the LS-120.

IBM MicroChannel PCs do not support bootable LS-120 drives.

Typical Installation of the LS-120

Installing an LS-120 drive is often a three-step process: configure the drive jumper(s), mount and cable the drive, and configure the new drive in CMOS. Although most LS-120 installations are quick and painless procedures, you need to be aware of a few nuances. When followed carefully, this process typically can be completed in under 30 minutes. If you're replacing an existing floppy drive, remove the floppy drive and its cable first, and then follow the procedures below.

It's normally a good idea to perform a complete system backup of your hard drives before attempting any kind of drive work. Although LS-120 installation should not affect your hard drives in any way, backups will protect your data and system configuration from accidental data loss.

Prepare the System   Turn the system off and unplug it from the AC receptacle before proceeding. Remove the screws holding down the outer cover and place them aside in a safe place. Gently remove the PC's outer cover and set it aside (out of the path of normal floor traffic). You should now be able to look into the PC and observe the open drive bay, the motherboard, and any expansion boards and drives that are installed.

Remember to use an antistatic wrist strap whenever working inside a PC. This will prevent accidental static discharge, which can damage the computer's delicate electronics.

Prepare the Drive Bay   Now that the outer cover is removed, you should open the desired drive bay. This is as simple as removing the plastic bezel covering an empty bay (the bezel will usually pop right out). If you must relocate an existing drive, things get a bit more complicated. First, decide where the drive (almost always a hard drive) will be located—often an internal bay in the rear of the PC. You can then remove the mounting screws, disconnect the power and signal cables from the hard drive, and slide the hard drive out of the bay. Remount the hard drive in the internal bay and gently secure each screw into place (be careful not to overtighten the screws). Reattach the power and signal cables to the hard drive. Pay particular attention when connecting the signal cable. If the cable is installed backward, the hard drive will not function. The red or blue stripe along one side of the ribbon cable always marks pin 1.

The procedure is a bit easier when replacing an existing floppy drive. Unbolt the existing drive, and then disconnect the power and signal cables. Slide the old drive out of the bay and set it aside carefully. If you have a good-quality antistatic bag available, seal the old drive in the antistatic bag. Also remove the floppy drive cable from the system. At this point, you should have an open drive bay. Take a quick inventory and make sure that you have an available IDE signal cable and power connector available.

When using a Y-splitter to tap power from another drive, never split power from a hard drive. This can cause erratic drive (and system) operation.

Set the LS-120 Jumpers   In almost all cases, the LS-120 drive will be connected as the slave device to an existing master device (such as a CD-ROM drive) on the secondary drive controller channel. Check the LS-120 jumpers and verify that the LS-120 drive is configured as a slave device. If there are currently no devices on the secondary channel (for example, the system has only one HDD and CD-ROM—both on the primary channel), you may need to use the LS-120 jumpers to reconfigure the drive as a master device. This allows the LS-120 to exist by itself on the secondary channel. Of course, you should refer to the documentation enclosed with your LS-120 drive for specific jumper arrangements and precautions.

Mount the LS-120 Drive   Now that the LS-120 drive is configured, slide it gently into the open drive bay. Line up the four mounting holes and screw the drive in carefully. Be sure not to tighten the mounting screws excessively, which can warp the drive's frame and cause R/W problems or premature drive failure. Make it a point to use screws of the proper size and length to do the job. If you're placing the LS-120 into a larger 5.25-inch drive bay, be sure to premount the drive into its extended frame (or attach drive rails) before sliding the complete assembly into the drive bay.

Connect Power and Signal Cables   Once the drive is installed and mounted securely, connect the power and signal cables as required. The 4-pin power cable is relatively foolproof because of its keyed shape. For the signal cable, however, take care to install the 40-pin signal cable connector in the correct orientation. If the signal cable is installed backward, the drive will not work (the system may not even boot). The red or blue stripe along one side of the ribbon cable always represents pin 1. As long as the drive is jumpered properly, you may place the LS-120 in either the middle or endmost IDE connector. *Do not use the 34-pin floppy drive signal cable.*

Update CMOS Settings   If you're using the LS-120 as a supplemental drive rather than as a bootable drive (and the old floppy is still in place), skip this step. Otherwise, you must update the system CMOS entries to accommodate the new drive. Make sure that any tools or extra hardware are removed from the system, reattach the AC cord to the power supply, and then reboot the computer. As the system boots, start the CMOS Setup routine and adjust the configuration as needed to disable the old floppy drive and floppy controller. Check to make sure that the LS-120 drive is identified properly along with your other IDE drive devices. Also configure the boot order to select the LS-120 as the first boot device. With the floppy removed and the LS-120 set as a boot device, the LS-120 should become the new A: drive. When the settings are correct, save the system CMOS and reboot the system so that your changes can take effect.

Test the Drive To test for bootability, insert a blank disk into the LS-120 and restart the PC. If you get a "non-system disk" error, the system has tried to boot from the LS-120. Now try booting the system from a known-good bootable disk such as a Windows 9x/Me startup disk. You should wind up at the A: command prompt. Try writing and reading a few files from the drive. You might also try formatting a blank disk in the new drive. If these tests are successful, you can be confident that the new drive is working properly. Be sure to remove any tools or hardware from the system, and then reinstall the system's outer housings. Do not use excessive pressure to tighten the screws.

Driver Installation

You do not need separate drivers when using the LS-120 under Windows Me, Windows 98/SE, Windows 95 (OSR2), Windows NT 4.0, or Windows NT 3.51 with Service Pack 5. These operating systems should automatically detect your LS-120 drive. The drive shows up as the logical A: drive (3.5-inch floppy) under My Computer. If you have other peripheral devices such as hard drives or CD-ROMs, they are automatically assigned the next available drive letter. If your operating system is Windows NT 4.0 or NT 3.51 (with SP5), you do not need to change your system settings. However, you will need drivers under DOS, Windows 3.1/3.11, Windows NT 3.51 (without SP5), and Windows 95/95A.

 Because it's normal for an LS-120 installation to shift your CD-ROM (and other drive) letters, you may have trouble running certain applications that expect to see the original drive letter. You may need to reinstall those applications.

DOS/Windows 3.1x Driver Installation Use the following guidelines to install the real-mode drivers for an LS-120 drive. Your own drive may be slightly different, so be sure to check the installation instructions for specific steps and precautions.

1. For Windows 3.1x, select the Run option. Enter the path to the LS-120 drivers (for example, **a:\install** or **c:\temp\install**) and press ENTER.

2. After the installer starts, select Express Install for the quickest install process, and then press ENTER.

3. Remove the driver disk (if you used one) and reboot the PC.

4. The system modifies your CONFIG.SYS file and saves a backup of the original file. Your system displays this message to verify the installation:

    ```
    ID 2: LS- 120 Ver 4 420 Direct Access Device (removable)
    ID 2 Drive Letter is D LS- 120
    LS-120 driver(s) connected
    LS-120 driver installed
    ```

5. If these messages do not appear, check your operating system type and version and then reinstall the device driver again.

Windows 95/95A/NT 3.51 (without SP5) Driver Installation Use the following guidelines to install the protected-mode drivers for an LS-120 drive. Your own drive may be slightly different, so be sure to check the installation instructions for specific steps and precautions.

1. Click Start and select Run. Enter the path to the LS-120 drivers (for example, **a:\setup** or **c:\temp\setup**) and press ENTER.

2. A menu-driven installation program guides you through the installation process. This process automatically updates the system's registry with the appropriate drivers.

3. When the installation process is complete, remove the driver disk (if you used one) and reboot the PC.

Windows NT 4.0/NT 3.51 (with SP5) Driver Installation   Use the following guidelines to install the protected-mode drivers for an LS-120 drive under NT 4.0 or later. Your own drive may be slightly different, so be sure to check the installation instructions for specific steps and precautions.

1. From the Control Panel, double-click the System icon, and then click Device Manager. A list of all the drivers used by the system appears.

2. Select the ATAPI device driver and change its setting to "Started at boot."

3. Restart your computer. The LS-120 drive is now recognized as the logical A: or B: drive within My Computer.

For new NT installations, install the LS-120 drive before installing Windows NT. As you install Windows NT, your system automatically identifies the LS-120 drive and loads the appropriate drivers. After you restart your computer, the system recognizes the LS-120 drive as the logical A: or B: drive.

Uninstalling the Device Driver

When you remove the LS-120 drive, you'll also need to remove the drivers that accompany it. This is not a problem under Windows 98/Me and other newer operating systems (you can use the Add/Remove Programs wizard to handle software removal), but you'll need to address the issue manually under Windows 95 and DOS.

■ Under Windows 95, restart the SETUP.EXE install program and check the Uninstall SuperDisk Device Driver & Utility button. Run the deinstallation process as you would an installation, as described above.

■ Under DOS or Windows 3.1x, search for these lines in the CONFIG.SYS file: c:\atlas\atapimgr.sys and c:\atlas\mkels120.sys. REMark out these lines everywhere they occur—your own installation may use different utilities. Then reboot the system.

Changing the LS-120 Drive Letter

Occasionally, you may to change the LS-120 drive letter from its default setting. For example, this may be important if you need to adjust the letter assignments of other drives. Follow these steps to adjust the drive letter:

1. Click Start, select Settings, and then click Control Panel.

2. In the Control Panel, double-click the System icon.

3. Click on the Device Manager tab.

4. Click on Disk Drives, and then double-click on the LS-120 drive.

5. Click on Settings, and set the desired drive letter.

6. Restart your computer when prompted.

LS-120 CONSIDERATIONS AND ISSUES

Ideally, you should be able to install and boot from an LS-120 drive with an absolute minimum of fuss. But the LS-120 is a relatively new class of bootable drive, and a system must meet several minimum requirements in order to support the drive. There are also several potential system compatibility problems that you should be aware of.

Booting and System BIOS

Perhaps the most interesting aspect of the LS-120 is that it's bootable in both 120MB and 1.44MB modes, so you boot from either size of disk. However, you'll need a motherboard or drive controller BIOS that is designed to accommodate the LS-120 (you'll see "LS-120" as a boot option in the CMOS Setup "Boot Order" entry). If your BIOS does not recognize the LS-120, you may need to upgrade the BIOS before installing the drive. The following three BIOS versions are known to support LS-120 technology:

- Award BIOS version 4.51PG or later
- AMI BIOS version 6.26.02 or later
- Phoenix BIOS version 6.0 or later

Booting and Operating Systems

Although the LS-120 will work in DOS and in all versions of Windows, only Windows 95 release B (4.00.950B) and *later* will treat the LS-120 as bootable. Older versions of Windows only support the drive as a removable and nonbootable disk that will not be assigned to drive letter A: or B:. Make sure that the LS-120 disk has been formatted to be bootable. This will be available as a check box item when formatting in Windows, or as a command-line switch when formatting from a DOS prompt (adding the traditional /S switch to the Format command line). As an example, if formatting the A: drive (which is your LS-120) to be bootable, type

```
FORMAT A: /S
```

Also, the LS-120 does work under Windows NT, but you must pay particular attention to several things during installation. NT 4.0 and NT 3.51 (SP5) have built-in support for the LS-120 and require no special drivers. Other versions of NT require running the SETUP.EXE utility from the Windows directory on the LS-120 driver disk. Remember to have the ATAPI service set to "ENABLED AT BOOT."

Compatibility with System Manufacturers

You may encounter problems installing the retail version of an LS-120 drive on some systems built by major system houses such as Packard Bell or Compaq. Many major system houses use their own OEM version of the LS-120, which must be installed instead of the retail version. If you encounter such difficulties, check with technical support for the system manufacturer to find out whether any known problems with retail LS-120 compatibility exist, or whether driver updates/patches may be necessary.

Compatibility with System Utilities

The LS-120 is not fully compatible with all system utilities—most notably antivirus programs, some backup software, and drive utilities such as Norton Utilities. When the LS-120 is installed with such software, the drive (or the software) may fail to function normally. If you encounter read/write difficulties while using any such system utilities, try disabling or temporarily uninstalling them to determine if the problem goes away.

LS-120 Device Conflicts

Although the LS-120 is an IDE device, it is known to experience problems when installed in conjunction with certain other device configurations. In most cases, the LS-120 (or the other IDE device on the ribbon cable) may not be detected. This type of problem is usually fixed by reversing the drive positions on the ribbon cable, or reversing the master/slave jumper relationship of the two devices. For example, if your LS-120 is connected to the secondary IDE port and jumpered as the master device, and an IDE CD-ROM is also connected to the secondary IDE port as a slave device, and now the CD-ROM is not functioning properly, change the jumpering on the two devices so that the LS-120 is now the slave and the CD-ROM is the master.

In other cases, the LS-120 drive is not seen on the secondary IDE port regardless of the jumper settings. This is often because the motherboard chipset is not recognized properly by Windows 95, and the secondary IDE port is left disabled. If the IDE port you are connecting to is listed in the Device Manager as a "Standard ESDI/IDE PORT," you'll need to contact your motherboard maker for the updated .INF file for Windows 95. If your motherboard uses an Intel chipset, you can search on Intel's Developer page (**developer.intel.com/design/motherbd/ideinfup.htm**) for the INF file to update Windows 95.

Finally, the LS-120 may be misidentified as a CD-ROM by the BIOS during system boot. If this occurs, you'll need to update your system BIOS from the system maker or motherboard manufacturer. Ideally, the drive should be identified as an LS-120 or UHD Floppy (Ultra High Density).

Drive Overlay Software

Numerous types of drive overlay software are in use today, such as Disk Manager, EZ-Drive, MaxBlast, and more. This overlay software is used to partition and prepare hard drives when the system BIOS will not support the drive's full size. In practice, overlay software can also affect other IDE drives (such as the LS-120) and result in performance problems.

If you're having trouble using the LS-120 and drive overlay software is installed on the hard drive, you may need to remove the overlay software from the hard drive. If your system hardware will not support the full size of a given hard drive, you may need to upgrade the system BIOS or drive controller BIOS first to accommodate the drive. Then you can remove the overlay software.

 Removing the overlay software will normally require you to change the drive geometry in the CMOS Setup, and then repartition and reformat the drive completely using FDISK and FORMAT. Be sure to perform a complete system backup before attempting to remove the overlay software.

Driver Support Under Windows 95 "A"

Reports have erroneously stated that driver support for the LS-120 is already available in the "A" version of Windows 95. This oversight occured because some utility program(s) installed *after* Windows 95 has changed the dates of certain files from your original Windows 95 install, or has changed the generic IDE driver for Windows 95 to a newer one in order to support another piece of hardware you have installed. To fix this, you need to use the RegEdit utility located in your Windows directory.

 Improper editing of your registry can make your system fail to boot, result in a loss of data, or force you to reinstall Windows 95. Changes should be made only under the direction of an experienced technician or someone experienced at editing the registry. Be sure to make a backup copy of your registry files before proceeding.

Find the following section in your registry:

```
HKey_Local_Machine\System\CurrentControlSet\Services\Class\HDC
```

Find the entries under this section which refer to ATAPI.MPD. Change all ATAPI.MPD entries to ESDI_506.PDR. Exit your registry editor and save your changes. If you have problems restarting Windows 95 after editing the registry, you can always reboot from a rescue disk and reload your backup copy of the registry.

Floppy and LS-120 Troubleshooting

In most cases, floppy and LS-120 drives (and their media) should provide long and reliable service. However, there are circumstances when a drive installation or replacement doesn't go as planned, or you're faced with a faulty drive on a customer's system. This part of the chapter examines some troubleshooting guidelines for floppy and LS-120 drives, and offers some solutions for a range of specific symptoms.

CREATING A WINDOWS ME STARTUP DISK

When troubleshooting a PC, it is often necessary to boot a system from the floppy drive in order to run real-mode diagnostics. Windows normally allows you to create a boot disk (a startup disk) automatically, though you can create a startup disk manually. Windows Me does not have a command-line startup disk creation utility, but you can create the Windows Me startup disk manually. The following procedure shows you how to create a Windows Me startup disk.

Windows Me must be installed, and the \Windows\Command\Ebd folder must be present on the hard disk.

1. Start the computer using a Windows 98 startup disk.
2. Click to select Start Computer Without CD-ROM Support.
3. Type the following command at a command prompt, and then press ENTER:

    ```
    format a: /s
    ```
4. Insert the blank disk when prompted.
5. When the disk has finished formatting, with the newly formatted disk still in the drive, type the following commands, and then press ENTER (after each command):

    ```
    attrib -h -s -r *.*
    del *.*
    copy c:\windows\command\ebd\*.*
    ```

FLOPPY TROUBLESHOOTING GUIDELINES UNDER WINDOWS 9X

Today, a great deal of everyday work takes place under Windows 95/98. As a result, floppy drive problems are often first noticed under Windows. When Windows reports trouble reading a floppy drive, try the steps below to identify and resolve the issue through Windows.

Check the Floppy Controller in Safe Mode

Start Windows in Safe Mode and try to access the floppy drive. To start Windows in Safe Mode, restart the computer, and then press the F8 key when you see the message "Starting Windows." Then choose Safe Mode from the Startup menu. To start Windows 98 in Safe Mode, restart your computer, press and hold down the CTRL key after your computer completes the power-on self-test (POST), and then choose Safe Mode from the Startup menu. If you can access the floppy drive in Safe Mode, follow these steps:

1. Right-click the My Computer icon from your desktop and click Properties.
2. Click the Device Manager tab, and then double-click the Floppy Disk Controllers entry.
3. Highlight the floppy disk controller for the drive you are having problems with, and then click Properties.
4. In Windows 95, click the Original Configuration (Current) check box to clear it. In Windows 98, click the Disable In This Hardware Profile check box to select it. This disables the Windows protected-mode driver for the floppy disk drive controller.
5. Click OK and restart Windows normally.

If you can now access the floppy disk drive successfully after following the procedure above, you may be faced with one or more of the following conditions:

1. The floppy disk drive controller may not be supported in protected mode.
2. There are drivers loading in the CONFIG.SYS or AUTOEXEC.BAT file that may be necessary for protected-mode access.
3. There are drivers loading in the CONFIG.SYS or AUTOEXEC.BAT file that may be causing conflicts in Windows and need to be disabled.

If you still cannot access the floppy disk drive, follow these steps to redetect the floppy drive controller:

1. Right-click the My Computer icon from your desktop and click Properties.
2. Click the Device Manager tab, and then double-click the Floppy Disk Controllers entry.
3. Highlight the floppy disk controller, click Remove to remove the controller, and then click OK.
4. Open your Control Panel, and then double-click the Add New Hardware icon.
5. Click Next, and then click Yes to allow Windows to detect the hardware in your computer.
6. When the Add New Hardware wizard is finished, restart the computer and try the floppy drive again.

Redetecting the floppy disk controller should correct addressing problems with the controller by detecting the correct address range. If the floppy disk controller is not detected correctly, there may be a problem with the floppy disk controller. If the floppy disk controller is redetected, but you still cannot access the floppy drive, there may be a problem with the disk itself.

Suspect Your Disk(s)

One or more of your disks may be damaged. Use a disk utility (such as ScanDisk) to test the disk for damage, or try a known-good, high-quality disk.

Never use a disk utility that is not compliant with your version of Windows. Noncompliant disk utilities can damage DMF (compressed) disks. The Windows ScanDisk tool recognizes DMF disks and does not damage them.

You may also try the following command from a DOS command prompt:

```
C:\> copy a:\*.* nul          <Enter>
```

For example, if you are having problems with drive A:, insert a disk you are having problems with in drive A: and type the command. This command copies the files on the disk to a null device. If there is a problem copying the files, error messages appear on the screen, and that disk is probably defective.

Suspect Your Tape Backup

Floppy problems are known to occur under Windows when using an Irwin tape backup unit under Windows 9x. Windows 9x setup should remove the following statement from the [386Enh] section of the SYSTEM.INI file:

```
device=<path>\VIRWT.386
```

If you reinstall the Irwin tape backup software after you install Windows 95/98, this statement is placed in the SYSTEM.INI file again, and can cause conflicts with floppy disk access in Windows. When this occurs, you must comment-out that line in SYSTEM.INI.

Check the CMOS Setup

Reboot your computer and verify that the floppy drive entries in your CMOS Setup are correct. If not, Windows will not be able to recognize your floppy drive hardware. If you must make changes to your CMOS Setup, remember to save your changes as you exit.

Check for Device Conflicts

Device conflicts (reported by the Device Manager) can cause problems reading from and writing to floppy disks. You can generally resolve device conflict problems by changing or removing the resources from Device Manager that are causing the conflict. Typical conflicts occur with hard drive controller cards, video cards, or COM ports.

FLOPPY SYMPTOMS

Floppy drives will usually give you years of reliable service, but there are some cases when the drive, controller, media (and even the system's configuration) can cause problems. When trouble occurs, you can refer to the symptoms below to help you isolate and correct the problem.

SYMPTOM 20-1   **The floppy drive is completely dead**   The system boots, but the disk does not even initialize when inserted. This behavior can be caused by a number of important problems, so consider each possibility carefully before acting.

■ *Check the floppy disk.* Make sure the disk is properly inserted into the floppy drive assembly. If the disk does not enter and seat just right within the drive, disk access will be impossible. Try several different disks to ensure that the test disk is not defective. It may be necessary to partially disassemble the computer to access the drive and see the overall assembly. Free or adjust any jammed assemblies or linkages to correct disk insertion. If you cannot get disks to insert properly, replace the floppy drive.

■ *Check the drive power.* Loose connectors or faulty cable wiring can easily disable a floppy drive. Use your multimeter to measure DC voltages at the power connector. Place your meter's ground lead on pin 2 and measure +12 Vdc at pin 1. Ground your meter on pin 3 and measure +5 Vdc at pin 4. If either or both of these voltages is low or missing, troubleshoot your computer power supply or replace the supply outright.

■ *Check the signal cable.* Verify that the drive's 34-pin ribbon cable is attached securely at the drive(s) and at the drive controller. Reattach the signal cable if it's loose, and try another signal cable if necessary.

■ *Replace the floppy drive.* If the problem persists, chances are that the floppy drive is defective (perhaps the disk-in-place sensor has failed). Try replacing the floppy drive with a known-good drive from another system.

■ *Replace the floppy drive controller.* If a new floppy drive still does not resolve the problem, you may have a defective floppy drive controller circuit. If so, you may also receive a floppy drive or controller error from the system BIOS at boot time. Try disabling the existing floppy controller and install an expansion card controller (with only the floppy controller portion enabled).

SYMPTOM 20-2   **The floppy drive rotates a disk, but will not seek to the desired track**
This type of symptom generally suggests that the head-positioning stepping motor is inhibited or defective, but all other floppy drive functions are working properly.

■ *Check the drive for obstructions.* Carefully inspect the head-positioning assembly to be certain that there are no broken parts or obstructions that could jam the read/write heads. You may wish to examine the mechanical system with a disk inserted to be certain that the trouble is not a disk alignment problem that may be interfering with head movement. Gently remove any obstructions that you may find. Be careful not to accidentally misalign any linkages or mechanical components in the process of clearing an obstruction.

■ *Check the drive power.* Remove any disk from the drive and reconnect the drive's signal and power cables. Apply power to the computer and measure drive voltages with your multimeter. Ground your multimeter on pin 2 of the power connector and measure +12 Vdc at pin 1. Move the meter ground to pin 3 and measure +5 Vdc on pin 4. If either voltage is low or absent, troubleshoot your computer power supply or replace the supply outright.

■ *Check the signal cable.* Verify that the drive's 34-pin ribbon cable is attached securely at the drive(s) and at the drive controller. Reattach the signal cable if it's loose, and try another signal cable if necessary.

■ *Replace the floppy drive.* If the problem persists, chances are that the floppy drive is defective (perhaps the head-positioning system has failed). Try replacing the floppy drive with a known-good drive from another system.

■ *Replace the floppy drive controller.* If a new floppy drive still does not resolve the problem, you may have a defective floppy drive controller circuit. If so, you may also receive a floppy drive or controller error from the system BIOS at boot time. Try disabling the existing floppy controller and install an expansion card controller (with only the floppy controller portion enabled).

SYMPTOM 20-3   **The floppy drive heads seek properly, but the spindle does not turn**
This symptom suggests that the spindle motor is inhibited or defective, but all other floppy drive functions are working properly.

■ *Check the drive for obstructions.* Power-down the computer and remove the floppy drive. Carefully inspect the spindle motor, drive belt (if used), and spindle assembly. Make certain that there are no broken parts or obstructions that could jam the spindle. If there is a belt between the motor and spindle, make sure the belt is reasonably tight—it should not slip. You should also examine the floppy drive with a disk inserted to be certain that the disk's insertion or alignment is not causing the problem. Double-check your observations using several different disks. Gently remove any obstruction(s) that you may find. Be careful not to cause any accidental damage in the process of clearing an obstruction. Do not add any lubricating agents to the assembly, but gently vacuum or wipe away any significant accumulations of dust or dirt.

■ *Check the drive power.* Remove any disk from the drive and reconnect the drive's signal and power cables. Apply power to the computer and measure drive voltages with your multimeter. Ground your multimeter on pin 2 of the power connector and measure +12 Vdc at pin 1. Move the meter ground to pin 3 and measure +5 Vdc on pin 4. If either voltage is low or absent, troubleshoot your computer power supply or replace the supply outright.

■ *Check the signal cable.* Verify that the drive's 34-pin ribbon cable is attached securely at the drive(s) and at the drive controller. Reattach the signal cable if it's loose, and try another signal cable if necessary.

■ *Replace the floppy drive.* If the problem persists, chances are that the floppy drive is defective (perhaps the spindle motor control system has failed). Try replacing the floppy drive with a known-good drive from another system.

■ *Replace the floppy drive controller.* If a new floppy drive still does not resolve the problem, you may have a defective floppy drive controller circuit. If so, you may also receive a floppy drive or controller error from the system BIOS at boot time. Try disabling the existing floppy controller and install an expansion card controller (with only the floppy controller portion enabled).

SYMPTOM 20-4 **The floppy drive will not read from/write to the disk**   All other operations appear normal. This type of problem can manifest itself in several ways, but your computer's operating system will usually inform you when a disk read or write error has occurred.

■ *Check the disk.* Begin by trying a known-good, properly formatted disk in your suspect drive. A faulty disk can generate some very perplexing read/write problems.

■ *Clean the floppy drive.* If a known-good disk does not resolve the problem, try cleaning the read/write heads thoroughly. Do not run the drive with a head-cleaning disk inserted for more than 30 seconds at a time, or you risk damaging the heads with excessive friction.

■ *Check the signal cable.* Verify that the drive's 34-pin ribbon cable is attached securely at the drive(s) and at the drive controller. Reattach the signal cable if it's loose, and try another signal cable if necessary.

■ *Replace the floppy drive.* If the problem persists, chances are that the floppy drive is defective (perhaps the head read/write system has failed). Try replacing the floppy drive with a known-good drive from another system.

■ *Replace the floppy drive controller.* If a new floppy drive still does not resolve the problem, you may have a defective floppy drive controller circuit. If so, you may also receive a floppy drive or controller error from the system BIOS at boot time. Try disabling the existing floppy controller and install an expansion card controller (with only the floppy controller portion enabled).

SYMPTOM 20-5   **The drive is able to write to a write-protected disk**   When this kind of problem occurs, it is almost always the drive itself that is defective.

■ *Check the disk.* Remove and examine the disk itself to verify that it is actually write protected. If the disk is not write protected, write-protect it appropriately, and try the disk again. You might also try a different disk.

■ *Clean the floppy drive.* Try cleaning the drive by blowing clean compressed air into the drive (pay particular attention to cleaning off the write-protect sensor).

■ *Replace the floppy drive.* If the problem persists, chances are that the floppy drive is defective—perhaps the write-protect sensor or onboard drive electronics has failed. Try replacing the floppy drive with a known-good drive from another system.

SYMPTOM 20-6   **The drive can only recognize either high- or double-density media, but not both**   This type of problem usually appears in 3.5-inch drives during the disk format process when the drive must check the media type.

■ *Check the disk.* Verify that you're using the correct disk type. (This is actually a common oversight, because many generic disks are unmarked.)

■ *Clean the floppy drive.* Try cleaning the drive by blowing clean compressed air into the drive (pay particular attention to cleaning off the "media type" sensor).

■ *Check the signal cable.* Verify that the drive's 34-pin ribbon cable is attached securely at the drive(s) and at the drive controller. Reattach the signal cable if it's loose, and try another signal cable if necessary.

■ *Replace the floppy drive.* If the problem persists, chances are that the floppy drive is defective—perhaps the media-type sensor or onboard drive electronics has failed. Try replacing the floppy drive with a known-good drive from another system.

SYMPTOM 20-7   **When a new disk is inserted in the drive, a directory from a previous disk appears**   You may have to reset the system in order to get the new disk to be recognized. This is the classic "phantom directory" problem and is usually due to a drive or cable fault.

■ *Check the signal cable.* Verify that the drive's 34-pin ribbon cable is attached securely at the drive(s) and at the drive controller. Reattach the signal cable if it's loose, and try another signal cable if necessary.

■ *Check the driver's jumpers.* If this is a new drive installation, check the floppy drive's jumpers. Some floppy drives allow the DISK CHANGE signal to be enabled or disabled. Make sure that the DISK CHANGE signal is enabled.

■ *Replace the floppy drive.* If the problem persists, chances are that the floppy drive is defective—perhaps the disk change logic has failed in the drive's electronics. Try replacing the floppy drive with a known-good drive from another system.

If you suspect a phantom directory problem, do not initiate any writing to the disk. Its FAT table and directories could be overwritten, rendering the disk's contents inaccessible without careful data recovery procedures.

SYMPTOM 20-8   **Double-density (720KB) 3.5-inch disks are not working properly when formatted as high-density (1.44MB) disks**   This is a common problem when double-density disks are pressed into service as high-density disks. In practice, double-density disks use a lower-grade media than high-density disks, which makes double-density disks unreliable when used in high-density mode. Some good-quality disks will tolerate this misuse better than other lower-quality disks. As a general rule, do not use double-density disks as high-density disks.

SYMPTOM 20-9   **Your 3.5-inch high-density floppy disk cannot format high-density disks**   You can read and write to them just fine. This is a problem that plagues older computers (i286 and i386 systems) with after-market high-density drives added. The problem is a lack of BIOS support for high-density formatting—the system is just too old. In such a case, you have a choice. First, you can upgrade your motherboard BIOS to a version that directly supports 3.5-inch high-density disks. You could also use the DRIVER.SYS utility—a DOS driver that allows an existing 3.5-inch drive to be "redefined" as a new logical drive providing high-density support. A typical DRIVER.SYS command line would appear in CONFIG.SYS similar to this:

```
device = c:\dos\driver.sys /D:1
```

SYMPTOM 20-10   **The A: drive appears in My Computer even though no drive is installed**   When you double-click My Computer on a Windows 9x/Me system with no floppy disk drive installed, a removable disk (A:) appears. When you view the drives in Device Manager, no floppy disk drive is listed because none exists on the computer. This occurs because DOS always creates drive A: on a computer. When Windows starts, this information is sent to the real-mode manager (RMM). Unfortunately, this issue occurs by design, and no workaround is available.

SYMPTOM 20-11   **The floppy drive runs randomly while using the system**   This problem usually arises when a folder that includes a PIF file that references a program file on a floppy disk drive is opened. For example, if you have a PIF file with a command line such as a:\edit.com in the \Windows\Temp folder, your floppy disk drive may be active when you start the PC. Change the command-line reference in the Properties of the shortcut, or delete the shortcut:

1.   Click Start, point to Find (or Search in Windows Me), and then click For Files Or Folders.

2.   In the Named box (or Search For Files Or Folders Named in Windows Me), type ***.lnk**, click the location you want to search in the Look In box, and then click Find Now.

3.   Right-click a shortcut on the list of found files, click Properties, and then click the Program tab.

4.   Delete any reference to drive A: or drive B: on the Command box or Working section, and then click OK. For example, if the command line reads a:\edit.com, simply change the line to read **edit.com**.

5.   Repeat the last two steps until you have corrected all the shortcuts, and then quit the Find tool.

This problem can also occur on other removable media besides floppy disks.

SYMPTOM 20-12   **You can't access the hard drive after booting from a disk**   After you start your Windows 9x/Me computer from a floppy disk for troubleshooting purposes (or to install an operating system), you may see an "Invalid Drive Specification" error message when changing to the hard disk—even though the hard disk is correctly partitioned and formatted. This error usually means that you have a drive overlay program installed, and you did not follow the proper procedures to boot from a floppy disk. When a drive overlay program is loaded, you cannot boot directly from a floppy disk if you want to be able to access the hard disk. You must first load the drive overlay program and then boot from the floppy disk. Check the documentation included with your drive overlay software for information about how to boot from a floppy disk and access the hard disk.

SYMPTOM 20-13   **The floppy controller prevents system hibernation or standby**
When your Windows Me system has been idle long enough to enter standby mode (or if you try to use standby mode manually), your computer refuses to enter standby mode or returns from standby mode immediately. You may also receive an error message such as this:

```
Your computer cannot hibernate or standby because the standard floppy disk
controller cannot enter into low-power state.
```

If you then check the SUSFAIL.TXT log, you see an entry such as this:

```
The devnode 'standard floppy disk controller' (BIOS\*PNP0700\00) denied the
suspend.
```

This issue is known to occur when Iomega Ditto Tools are installed on your computer. Ditto Tools installs drivers that prevent you from using suspend mode. To correct this problem, contact Iomega (**www.iomega.com**) to inquire about software updates and patches. To work around this issue temporarily, disable all power management features when you are using Ditto Tools.

SYMPTOM 20-14   **There are no jumpers available on the floppy disk, so it is impossible to change settings**   This is not a problem as much as it is an inconvenience. Typically, you can expect "unjumpered" floppy disks to be set to the following specifications:

Drive select	1 (B: drive)
Disk change (pin 34)	enabled
Frame ground	enabled

This configuration supports traditional single and dual (1.44MB) floppy drive systems using twisted floppy cables.

SYMPTOM 20-15   **When using a combination floppy drive (called a "combo drive"), one of the drives does not work, but the other works fine**   This problem is often caused by a drive fault. First, check the power connector. Make sure that both +5 volts and +12 volts are adequately provided to the drive through the 4-pin "mate-n-lock" connector. If the drive is receiving the proper power, the drive itself has almost certainly failed—try a new drive.

SYMPTOM 20-16   **DOS reports an error such as "Cannot read from drive A:"**   A disk is fully inserted in the drive, and the drive LED indicates that access is being attempted.

- ■ *Check the disk.* Begin by trying a known-good, properly formatted disk in your suspect drive. A faulty disk can generate some very perplexing read/write problems.

- ■ *Clean the floppy drive.* If a known-good disk does not resolve the problem, try cleaning the read/write heads thoroughly. Do not run the drive with a head-cleaning disk inserted for more than 30 seconds at a time, or you risk damaging the heads with excessive friction.

- ■ *Check the drive for obstructions.* Carefully inspect the spindle motor, drive belt (if used), and read/write head assembly. Make certain that there are no broken parts or obstructions that could jam the heads. You should also examine the floppy drive with a disk inserted to be certain that the disk's insertion or alignment is not causing the problem. Double-check your observations using several different disks. Gently remove any obstruction(s) that you may find. Be careful not to cause any accidental damage in the process of clearing an obstruction.

■ *Check the signal cable.* Verify that the drive's 34-pin ribbon cable is attached securely at the drive(s) and at the drive controller. Reattach the signal cable if it's loose, and try another signal cable if necessary.

■ *Replace the floppy drive.* If the problem persists, chances are that the floppy drive is defective (perhaps the head read/write system has failed). Try replacing the floppy drive with a known-good drive from another system.

■ *Replace the floppy drive controller.* If a new floppy drive still does not resolve the problem, you may have a defective floppy drive controller circuit. If so, you may also receive a floppy drive or controller error from the system BIOS at boot time. Try disabling the existing floppy controller and install an expansion card controller (with only the floppy controller portion enabled).

SYMPTOM 20-17   You cannot upgrade an XT-class PC with a 3.5-inch floppy disk
XT systems support up to four double-density 5.25-inch floppy disk drives. They will not support 3.5-inch floppy disks at all. To install 3.5-inch floppy disks, you should check your DOS version (you need to have DOS 3.3 or later installed). Next, you'll need to install an 8-bit floppy drive controller board (remember to disable any existing floppy controller in the system first). The floppy controller will have its own onboard BIOS to support floppy disk operations. Finally, take a look at the XT configuration switches and see that any entries for your floppy drives are set correctly. If you're using a stand-alone floppy controller, you may need to set the motherboard jumpers to "no floppy drives."

SYMPTOM 20-18   The floppy drive activity LED stays on as soon as the computer is powered up   This is a classic signaling problem that occurs after changing or upgrading a drive system. In virtually all cases, one end of the drive cable has been inserted backward. Make sure that pin 1 on the 34-pin cable is aligned properly with the connector on both the drive and controller. If problems remain, the drive controller may have failed. This is rare, but try a new drive controller.

SYMPTOM 20-19   You are unable to swap floppy drives so that A: becomes B:, and B: becomes A: This often happens on older systems when users want to make their 3.5-inch after-market B: drive into their A: drive, and relegate their aging 5.25-inch drive to B: instead.

■ *Check the signal cable.* For floppy cables with a wire twist, the endmost connector is A:, and the connector prior to the twist is B:. Reverse the connectors at each floppy drive to reverse their identities.

■ *Check the drive jumpers.* If the cable has no twist (this is rare), reset the jumper ID on each drive so that your desired A: drive is set to DS0 (Drive Select 0), and your desired B: drive is jumpered to DS1. If you accomplish this exchange, but one drive is not recognized, try a new floppy signal cable.

■ *Check the CMOS settings.* You'll need to reverse the floppy drive entries for your A: and B: drives, and then reboot the system.

SYMPTOM 20-20   The new drive does not work, or the system does not recognize the new drive   This classic problem of the system not recognizing the newly installed drive is typically the result of incorrect or overlooked CMOS settings.

■ *Check the CMOS settings.* Reboot the system and start the CMOS Setup routine. Verify the floppy drive parameters against the actual physical drives in the system, and then make sure that the correct data is entered in CMOS. You may have forgotten to save the data initially. Save the new data correctly and try the system again.

■ *Check the signal cables.* Inspect the power and signal cables at the drive. Loose or incorrectly attached cables can effectively disable the drive. Install each cable carefully and try the system again.

■ *Replace the floppy drive.* If the problem persists, chances are that the new floppy drive is defective. Try replacing the floppy drive with a known-good drive from another system.

SYMPTOM 20-21   **You cannot boot the system from the new floppy drive**   If the drive is recognized properly and operates as expected, the failure to boot actually may not be a failure—rather, the boot order established in your CMOS Setup may not be set to include the new drive. Often, the boot order is A: then C:, or C: then A:. If you installed a new floppy as B:, the system will not attempt to boot because it is not included in the boot order. Restart the CMOS Setup routine and adjust the boot order to address your new floppy drive first (for example, B:/C:, or A:/B:/C:).

SYMPTOM 20-22   **After the second floppy is installed, there are a lot of signal problems, such as read or write errors**   Chances are that you left the terminating resistors in place on the second (middle) floppy drive, resulting in signal errors. You should have a terminating resistor pack on the drive at the *end* of the daisy-chain cable. Check that the terminating resistors are in place on drive A:, and remove the terminating resistors from the middle drive (B:). Also check that the signal cables are installed securely on both drives. Loose or damaged cables can cause signal problems.

SYMPTOM 20-23   **The floppy drive light comes on even when there is no disk in the drive**   This may happen at any time, or particularly during shutdown or reboot of the system. When floppy drive access seems to occur during shutdown or reboot, it may be that you have antivirus software (such as McAfee's VirusScan or Norton AntiVirus AutoProtect) set to check the floppy drive automatically. You'll need to disable autochecking of the floppy drive. For McAfee's VirusScan, right-click its icon from the task bar and select Properties. Under the Scan Floppies On entry in the Detection tab, uncheck the Shutdown box. Remember to save your changes. For Norton AntiVirus AutoProtect, right-click its icon from the task bar and select Options. Click the Advance button and, under the Check Floppies entry, uncheck the Check Floppies When Reboot Computer box. Remember to save your changes.

SYMPTOM 20-24   **You cannot create a Windows startup Disk**   There are many possible problems that may prevent Windows from properly creating a startup disk, but the following points outline the most common issues.

■ *Check the disk.* The disk itself may have ten or more bad sectors, or the first sector may be damaged. Try a known-good disk (preferably a high-quality or premium-grade disk). Also, Windows 9x/Me generally requires a high-density (1.44MB) floppy disk to create a startup disk.

■ *Check your antivirus software.* Many antivirus tools can interfere with floppy disk operations. Disable or uninstall your antivirus software according to the manufacturer's instructions.

■ *Check the CMOS settings.* Reboot the system and start the CMOS Setup routine. Verify the floppy drive parameters against the actual physical drives in the system, and then make sure that the correct data is entered in CMOS. You may have forgotten to save the data initially. Save the new data correctly and try the system again.

■ *Disable/remove floppy tape devices.* Some older tape backup devices utilizing the floppy controller may prevent you from gaining access to the floppy drive. To work around this behavior, disconnect the tape backup device from the floppy controller before you attempt to create a Windows 9x/Me startup disk, or disable the tape backup driver.

■ *Replace the floppy drive.* If the problem persists, chances are that the new floppy drive is defective. Try replacing the floppy drive with a known-good drive from another system.

LS-120 SYMPTOMS

LS-120 drive systems had enjoyed a surge in popularity as a versatile, high-capacity alternative to floppy disks. Unfortunately, the 120MB drive lost ground to the more aggressive removable media alternatives such as 250MB Zip drives, 2GB Jaz drives, and CD-R/RW drives. Although Imation no longer produces the internal SuperDisk drives, it continues to support the drive, and you'll find numerous symptoms and solutions outlined below.

SYMPTOM 20-25 **You cannot eject USB floppy or LS-120 drives** When you right-click a USB external floppy disk drive or a USB external LS-120 drive in the Windows Me My Computer window (or in Windows Explorer) and then click Eject, the disk in the drive may not be ejected. This occurs because the external USB floppy disk drive or LS-120 drive attached to the computer does not support this "soft eject" feature. To eject the disk, simply press the Eject button on the drive.

SYMPTOM 20-26 **After installing a parallel port LS-120 drive, you cannot access programs protected by a parallel port hardware key (a "dongle")** This is almost always a limitation of the "dongle" itself. Those hardware keys must generally be connected to the parallel port first (then other parallel port devices can be added). If the LS-120 drive is installed before the dongle, the dongle may not respond properly, and software that uses it may refuse to work. Try connecting the dongle first.

SYMPTOM 20-27 **You cannot boot from the LS-120 drive using a DOS 6.22, Windows 95, or Windows 95A (OSR1) boot disk** In order to boot from an LS-120 device, both your operating system and motherboard BIOS must support the LS-120.

■ *Check your operating system.* Only Windows 98, Windows 95 (OSR2), and Windows NT 4.0 allow you to boot from either a 1.44MB or 120MB disk. If your operating system is too old to support the LS-120 as a boot device, you'll need to upgrade your operating system.

■ *Check the CMOS settings.* Examine the available options under your boot order. If you see an option such as SuperDisk, Floptical, LS-120, UHD Floppy, Removable Device, or Removable Drive, be sure to select that device as the first drive in your boot order. If there are no such entries to choose from, your BIOS may not fully support the LS-120 drive as a boot device, and a BIOS upgrade may be in order. If you cannot obtain a BIOS upgrade from the original system or motherboard maker, you can probably obtain a suitable upgrade from Unicore at **www.unicore.com** or 800-800-BIOS.

SYMPTOM 20-28 **After you install an LS-120 drive, your CD-ROM (or other IDE-type device) does not work properly** A number of typical installation issues may cause the new LS-120 drive to interfere with your existing drive(s).

■ *Check your drive jumpers.* One drive must be set as the master device, and the other must be set as the slave device. Make sure that the drives are not both set the same way, or try reversing the master/slave relationship.

■ *Check the signal cable.* Verify that the LS-120 is cabled properly. The signal cable should be secure and inserted in the proper orientation.

■ *Try a different channel.* In a few cases, the LS-120 drive may not be compatible with the other drive on that same channel. You might try moving the drive to a different IDE channel, or disconnect the other drive from that channel and see if the LS-120 drive will operate normally by itself. If so, you might want to replace that drive with one from another manufacturer.

SYMPTOM 20-29 **After installing the LS-120 device drivers, you can no longer play music CDs** This is a problem that sometimes occurs when the LS-120 drivers do not interact properly with the CD-ROM drivers. In many cases, this type of issue can be corrected by updating both the LS-120 and CD-ROM drives to their very latest protected-mode (Windows 9x/Me) drivers.

SYMPTOM 20-30 **The install program aborts after stating your system already has support for the LS-120** When running a SETUP.EXE program to install the LS-120 device drivers, you find an error message stating that your system already has support for the drive. The install program then aborts without finishing the install, but your LS-120 drive does not work. This can occur because the last step performed by the install program is to look at the date stamp of the ESDI_506.PDR file. If the file is *newer* than July 1995, the install program aborts. Edit the registry to change that entry from ESDI_506.PDR to **ATAPI.MPD**. Once you've renamed that entry, the setup program should operate normally and complete your installation.

SYMPTOM 20-31 **The CD-ROM drive letter shifts after installing the LS-120 drive** For example, the CD-ROM was D:, but after installing the LS-120, the LS-120 is now D:, and the CD-ROM is now E:. This is normal if the LS-120 drive is not made bootable (A:) in the CMOS Setup. When the LS-120 is not bootable, the LS-120 drivers are typically loaded first, and take precedence over the CD-ROM when drive letters are assigned. This condition is normal. Do not try to reverse the CD-ROM and LS-120 drive letters (although you can do this through the drive's Properties dialog boxes under Windows). Doing so may cause one or both of the drives to be unreadable. If you have installed something from CD-ROM and it will not run now, try reinstalling the application on top of the older installation so that it updates the drive letter for the new configuration.

SYMPTOM 20-32 **The LS-120 drive letter is greater than C:, but you cannot boot from the LS-120 because the floppy drive (that you removed from the system) still appears as A:** Several important oversights may account for this type of problem:

■ *Check the CMOS settings.* Make sure that you have altered the boot order in your CMOS Setup such that the LS-120 drive is selected as the first boot device.

■ *Upgrade the BIOS.* If you find that the LS-120 (or other similar entry such as UHD Floppy or Floptical) drive is not listed in your available boot options, you may need to update your motherboard's BIOS and then adjust the boot order as outlined above.

■ *Replace the floppy drive.* Use this as an interim measure so that you can boot from a disk.

SYMPTOM 20-33 **After physically installing the LS-120 drive, it is not detected as an ATAPI IDE device** This problem frequently occurs when trying to install the LS-120 with an older drive controller. The LS-120 requires LBA (Logical Block Addressing)—the same mode used for newer hard drives. This requires an EIDE or newer Ultra-DMA drive controller. In some cases, you may be able to upgrade the system BIOS in order for the existing drive controller to support the LBA mode. If this is not possible, you may need to replace the existing drive controller with a newer drive controller card (incorporating its own onboard BIOS).

SYMPTOM 20-34   **After plugging in the USB LS-120 drive, you don't see an icon appear on the desktop**   There are several possible reasons why the LS-120 drive might not appear after making the USB connection:

■ Make sure a properly formatted LS-120 disk is in the drive.

■ Make sure you are using the cables that came with the drive, and see that all cables are securely connected.

■ Make sure the computer and drive both have power (or that the USB hub controlling the drive is powered).

If problems persist, eject the disk and power-down the drive. Unplug and reseat the USB connection on the drive end. Plug the drive back into the power source (or hub), reconnect the USB cable at the computer end, and reinsert the disk into the drive. If you still cannot get the USB LS-120 drive to work, try another drive.

SYMPTOM 20-35   **You disconnected the LS-120 drive while the PC was in suspend ("sleep") mode, but now it doesn't work right after connecting it to another PC**   In virtually all cases, the LS-120 disk may be corrupted. You cannot disconnect the drive or eject the disk while files are open on the LS-120 disk. If there were files open when you disconnected the drive, the file (and perhaps the entire disk) may be corrupted. Try rebooting the PC and see if you can access any of the files on the disk.

SYMPTOM 20-36   **When copying files to/from a USB LS-120 drive, the computer froze when you disconnected the cable**   Even though USB devices are physically "hot pluggable," they cannot be connected or disconnected while data transfer is taking place. The USB device must be idle before it's disconnected. In the future, be sure that the LS-120 drive's activity LED is out before disconnecting the USB cable.

SYMPTOM 20-37   **You cannot format a 1.44MB disk in an LS-120 drive**   Virtually all LS-120 drives should be able to format older 720KB and 1.44MB disks. If you cannot get the disk to format properly, chances are that you're using an older SuperDisk driver. For the Imation SuperDisk LS-120, you need driver version 1.2.5 or later. Check with the LS-120 drive maker to see if a driver patch or update is available for download.

SYMPTOM 20-38   **You cannot format a 1.44MB disk in an LS-120 drive on a Windows NT platform**   This is almost always caused by a problem with NT 4.0 using Service Pack 3. There are several possible solutions to this problem:

■ Replace the ATAPI.SYS driver from Service Pack 2 (follow the procedure outlined in Microsoft's Knowledge Base article Q170572).

■ Install Microsoft Post SP3 hot fixes (ATA-FIXI.EXE and IDE-FIXI.EXE) available from **ftp://ftp.microsoft.com/bussys/winnt/winnt-public/fixes/usa/nt40/hotfixes-postSP3/**.

■ Upgrade your version of Windows NT to Service Pack 4.

SYMPTOM 20-39   **You find one or more phantom drives with the LS-120**   A *phantom drive* is a condition in which an extra drive designation appears, but neither the drive you are accessing nor the "extra" drive are readable.

■ *Check your drivers.* You may be loading the driver for the LS-120 in DOS, as well as a DOS CD-ROM driver. If this is the case, REM out the line loading MSCDEX in your AUTOEXEC.BAT file. You may also need to manually set the drive letter for the CD-ROM in the Device Manager.

■ *Check the CMOS settings.* If you removed your A: drive (intending to use your LS-120 as your boot drive), but now you have a "removable disk" and a floppy drive that don't display in My Computer (or the Device Manager), the problem is likely that your CMOS Setup may still have a drive type set for drive A:. If the LS-120 is replacing your old A: drive, set the DRIVE TYPE for drive A: to "none" or "not installed." If the phantom drive still appears, make sure you have enabled the option to boot from the LS-120 drive.

SYMPTOM 20-40   **You cannot read or format LS-120 media**   This happens most frequently under Windows 3.1x and the initial release (the "A" version) of Windows 95. In this case, you probably need to have the DOS version of the LS-120 driver installed. Run the LS-120 setup disk from a DOS window and install the DOS driver support.

If you are using the "B" version of Windows 95, do not load the DOS driver support for the LS-120 (LS120.SYS). When active in the background, this DOS driver can cause data corruption.

This is also a known problem on some platforms that use the FMTLS120.EXE utility included with the Imation LS-120 SuperDisk drive. Do not use this utility. Remove it from the system. Use the standard DOS or Windows FORMAT function. The media formatted with the FMTLS120 utility may now be corrupt and unrecoverable.

SYMPTOM 20-41   **You find that the LS-120 drive is running very slowly when using Windows 98**   The LS-120 is supported natively under Windows 98, but you may need to make some changes to the disk setup. Right-click on My Computer, select Control Panel, and then select System. The System Properties dialog box will appear. Select the Performance tab, and click on the File System button. You should then see a Removable Disk tab. Select that tab, and then enable Write-Behind Caching On All Removable Drives. Restart the PC if necessary. Intermittent slowdowns may indicate a dirty drive. Use a disk cleaning kit certified for LS-120 drives to clean your LS-120 read/write heads.

SYMPTOM 20-42   **The LS-120 drive is running in the "DOS Compatibility Mode"**   You'll need some new drivers to overcome this problem. Go to Microsoft's Web site at **support . microsoft.com/support/downloads** and download the files REMIDEUP.EXE and IOSUPD.EXE. After you install these new files, the LS-120 drive should be able to run in protected mode.

SYMPTOM 20-43   **The LS-120 drive's LED is constantly on after inserting a new disk in the drive**   This almost always means that the LS-120 disk is damaged. Carefully eject the disk and insert a new LS-120 disk into the drive. If the new disk works properly, the disk that you removed should be reformatted or discarded.

SYMPTOM 20-44   **The LS-120's drive power indicator never flashes, or it remains lit continuously**   This is almost always a problem with the drive's connections to your system. If the power LED *never* comes on at all, chances are that the drive is not receiving power. Check the 4-pin power connector to the LS-120 drive. Reseat the power connector securely if necessary. If the power LED remains on *continuously*, a problem with the signal cable probably exists—one end of the cable may be reversed or loose. Verify that the IDE cable is oriented properly, and see that it's secure. Reseat the signal cable (or try a new signal cable) if necessary.

SYMPTOM 20-45   **After installing the LS-120 drive, you find that the drive isn't responding, and has no icon under Windows**   There are several possible issues for you to consider.

- *Check the desktop.* The icon may simply be hidden—this is a common oversight. Autoarranging the icons on your desktop should reveal any icons that may have been hidden under one another.

- *Check the physical installation.* The drive may not be installed properly. Recheck the power and signal cables attached to the drive. See that they're secure and oriented properly. Also verify that the IDE port you've installed the LS-120 drive on is enabled (you can usually enable an IDE port through the CMOS Setup). If another device is on the same IDE channel, temporarily disconnect that device and try the LS-120 drive by itself, or move the LS-120 drive to another IDE channel.

- *Update your bus mastering devices.* Bus mastering can adversely affect the LS-120 drive. If you're using bus mastering, obtain and install the updated drivers for your system. If you cannot locate updated bus mastering drivers, use Microsoft's default drivers. Get the READIMDE.EXE file from **ftp://ftp.microsoft.com/bussys/winnt/winnnt-public/fixes/usa/hotfixes-postSP3**.

SYMPTOM 20-46   **The system crashes with "blue screen" errors each time the LS-120 drive is accessed**   This is a known problem when using antivirus software. If you're running McAfee's VirusScan software (or other antivirus software), disable the Scan Floppies On Access option, or any "removable disk" option that scans the LS-120 drive. This scanning process takes a great deal of time and can seriously bog down the drive's performance.

SYMPTOM 20-47   **When copying large files, the copy process is eventually interrupted with a "blue screen" error**   In virtually all cases, this indicates a defective disk. The error occurs when the copy process encounters bad sectors on the 120MB disk. Try a new or known-good disk to see if the problem goes away. If you find that the 120MB disk is bad, you may be able to run ScanDisk (in the media test mode) in an effort to map out the bad sectors. This may make the bad disk usable again, though its reliability cannot be guaranteed.

This may also be an operating system problem. If you're using an older version of Windows 95 (the original release or OSR1 version), you'll need to install the latest device drivers for the LS-120 drive so that Windows 95 will support the LS-120 properly. You may also upgrade Windows to a later version.

SYMPTOM 20-48   **A disk is stuck in the LS-120 drive**   This can happen on rare occasions when a poorly made disk fails, or when foreign matter interferes with the disk eject mechanism. Carefully insert a pin or paper clip into the emergency eject hole located on the Eject button. Press the pin or clip in the hole gently until the disk ejects from the slot. You can then replace the disk or clean the drive as necessary.

SYMPTOM 20-49   **You encounter "insufficient disk space" messages when using an LS-120 disk**   You may also see this kind of problem with an error such as "cannot create file or folder." An LS-120 disk will hold up to 120MB of files, so "disk space" warnings often mean that the disk is either full or has too many files in its directory.

■ *Check the free space.* Verify that adequate free space is left on the LS-120 media. If the disk has been used previously, it may already contain files that take up a considerable amount of space. If files already are on the disk, use a fresh disk, or delete unneeded files from the disk.

■ *Check the file count.* Note the number of files listed in the root directory. FAT-based file systems impose a limit of 253 files in the root directory. If 253+ files already are in the root directory, try creating subdirectories on the disk and storing additional files there, or use a fresh LS-120 disk.

SYMPTOM 20-50   **You find that you cannot "quick format" an LS-120 disk under Windows 9x**   This is a common problem when using an LS-120 drive under Windows. Windows 95 and Windows 98 do not natively support the LS-120's "quick format" option. Right-click on your LS-120 drive icon and select Format to perform a full format. After the first disk has been fully formatted, subsequent quick formats should work fine.

SYMPTOM 20-51   **You cannot use the DiskCopy command with an LS-120 drive**   This is a known limitation of the DOS DiskCopy command. It will not support disks larger than 32MB. If you need to copy 120MB disks, use the utility suite that accompanies your LS-120 drive.

SYMPTOM 20-52   **Microsoft Backup does not eject the first LS-120 disk when asking for the second disk**   This is a known issue with older versions of Microsoft Backup under Windows 95. You should upgrade to Windows 98/SE/Me (or switch to a new third-party backup utility), which will properly support the LS-120 as a removable media drive.

SYMPTOM 20-53   **You cannot use Microsoft Backup to back up to an LS-120 drive**   Although Microsoft Backup will work with an LS-120 drive, the software does not support disks larger than 32MB. Microsoft will likely address the Backup issue in its next release of the utility. In the meantime, Imation has a software toolkit for the LS-120 drive. The SuperDisk Tools Kit is available from **store.imation.com** and includes the following utilities:

■ CA Backup for fast and easy data protection

■ CA InnocuLAN Anti-Virus to protect your files with virus detection

■ Disk Consolidator, which combines multiple 3.5-inch disks on a single 120MB disk

■ Copy Disk to duplicate LS-120 disks

 NovaStor offers a downloadable trial version of its NovaDisk backup program, which works with the LS-120MB disks. You can obtain the program directly from **www.novastor.com**.

Further Study

Imation   www.imation.com
Mitsumi   www.mitsumi.com
Sony   www.storagebysony.com/categories/categorymain.asp?id=1#
Teac   www.teac.com/DSPD/floppy.html

21

HARD DRIVES

The *hard disk drive* (or HDD) evolved to answer the incessant demands for permanent, high-volume, high-speed file and data storage in the PC (Figure 21-1). Early floppy disks provided simple and inexpensive storage, but they are slow, and programs quickly became far too large to store adequately on them. Switching between multiple floppy disks also proved to be a cumbersome proposition. By the early 1980s, hard drives had become an important part of PC architecture and helped to fuel further OS and applications development—today, the hard drive is an absolutely indispensable element of the modern PC. The hard drive holds the operating system that boots the system, stores the multi-megabyte applications and files we rely on, and even provides "virtual memory" for systems lean on RAM. Hard drive performance also has a profound effect on overall system performance. As you might imagine, hard drive problems can easily cripple a system. This chapter presents some essential principles of hard disk drives and file systems and provides you with some guidelines for drive testing and troubleshooting.

Basic Drive Concepts

The first step in understanding hard drives is to learn the basic concepts involved. Many of the essential ideas discussed with floppy drives also apply to hard drives, but the additional performance requirements and operating demands placed on hard drives have resulted in an array of important new concepts. In principle, a hard disk drive is very similar to a floppy drive—a magnetic recording media is applied to a substrate material that is then spun at a high rate of speed. Magnetic read/write heads in close proximity to the media can step rapidly across the spinning media to detect or create flux transitions as required. When you look closely, however, you can see that there are some major physical differences between floppy and hard drives.

PLATTERS AND MEDIA

While floppy disks use magnetic material applied over a thin, flexible substrate of mylar (or some other plastic), hard drives use rugged, solid substrates called *platters*. You can clearly view the platters of a hard drive in Figure 21-2. A platter was traditionally made of aluminum because aluminum is a light material,

FIGURE 21-1   A contemporary hard drive unit (NEC Technologies, Inc)

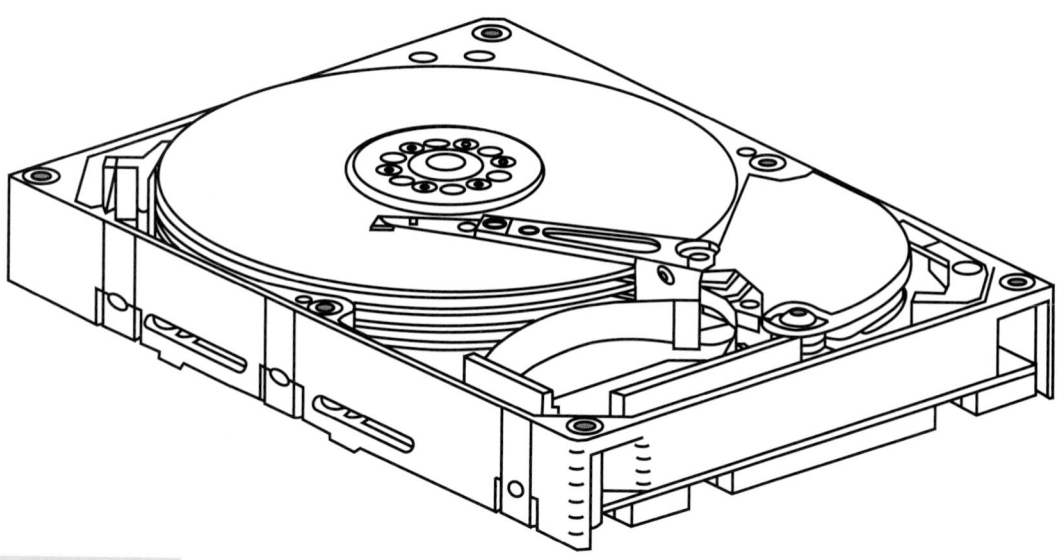

FIGURE 21-2   Maxtor hard drive (Maxtor Corporation)

it is easy to machine to desired tolerances, and holds its shape under the high centrifugal forces that occur at high rotation rates. But today, most platters are made from ceramic composite materials—these light, strong materials have a *very* low thermal expansion (so there are fewer media problems) and can withstand higher centrifugal forces than can aluminum. A major advantage of a hard drive is speed, and ceramic platters are rotated at about 7,200 RPM to as much as 10,000 RPM (compared to older hard drives that ran at 3,600 to 5,400 RPM). A hard drive generally uses two or more platters, though extremely small drive assemblies may use only one platter.

Hard drives must be capable of tremendous recording densities—well over 10,000 bits per inch (BPI). To achieve such substantial recording densities, platter *media* is far superior to the oxide media used for floppy disks. First, the media must have high coercitivity, so that each flux transition is well defined and easily distinguishable from every other flux transition. Coercitivity of hard drive media typically exceeds 1,400 oersteds. Second, the media must be *extremely* flat across the entire platter surface to within microscopic tolerances. Hard drive R/W heads do not actually contact the media, as floppy drives do, but ride within a microscopic flow of air over the platter surfaces. A miniscule surface defect or foreign matter (such as a dust particle) can collide with a head and scratch the media. Such a *head crash* is often a catastrophic defect that requires hard drive replacement. You'll see more about head flight and surface defects later in this chapter.

Media today is a thin-film that has long since replaced magnetic oxides. Thin-film media is a microscopic layer of pure metal (or a metal compound) that is bonded to the substrate surface through an interim layer. The media is then coated with a protective layer to help in surviving head crashes. Thin-film media also tends to be very flat, so R/W heads *can* be run at microscopic distances from the platter surfaces.

AIRFLOW AND HEAD FLIGHT

Read/write heads in a hard disk drive must travel extremely close to the surface of each platter, but they can *never* actually contact the media while the drive is running. The heads could be mechanically fixed, but fixed-altitude flight does not allow for shock or natural vibration that is always present in a drive assembly. Instead, R/W heads are made to float above a platter surface by suspending the heads on a layer of moving air. Figure 21-3 illustrates the typical airflow in a hard drive. Disk (platter) rotation creates a slight cushion that elevates the heads. You may also notice that some air is channeled through a fine filter that helps to remove any particles from the drive's enclosure.

It is important to note that *all* hard drives seal their platter assemblies into an airtight chamber. The reason for such a seal is to prevent contamination from dust, dirt, spills, or strands of hair. Contamination that lands on a platter's surface can easily result in a *head crash*. A head crash can damage the head, the media, or both—and any physical damage can result in an unusable drive. Consider the comparison shown in Figure 21-4. During normal operation, a hard drive's R/W head flies above the media at microscopic distances. Many technical professionals relate this to a jumbo jet flying 30 feet above the ground at 600 miles per hour. It follows then that any variation in surface flatness due to platter defects or contaminants can have catastrophic effects on head height. Even an average particle of smoke is ten times *wider* than this flying height. With such proportions, you can understand why it's critically important that the platter compartment remain sealed at all times. The platter compartment can be opened only in a *cleanroom* environment (a small, enclosed room where the air is filtered to remove any contaminants larger than 3 microns). Hard drive assemblers wear gloves and cleanroom suits that cover all but their faces—masks cover their mouth and nose to prevent breath vapor from contaminating the platters.

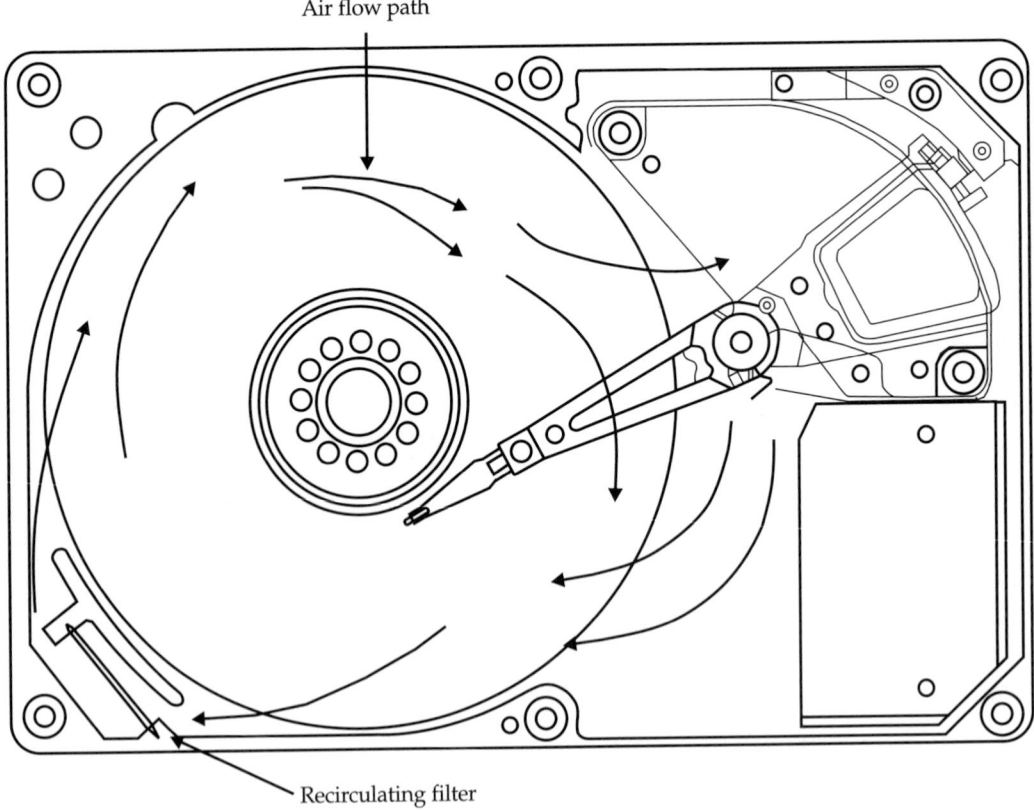

FIGURE 21-3   Airflow patterns in a hard drive (Maxtor Corporation)

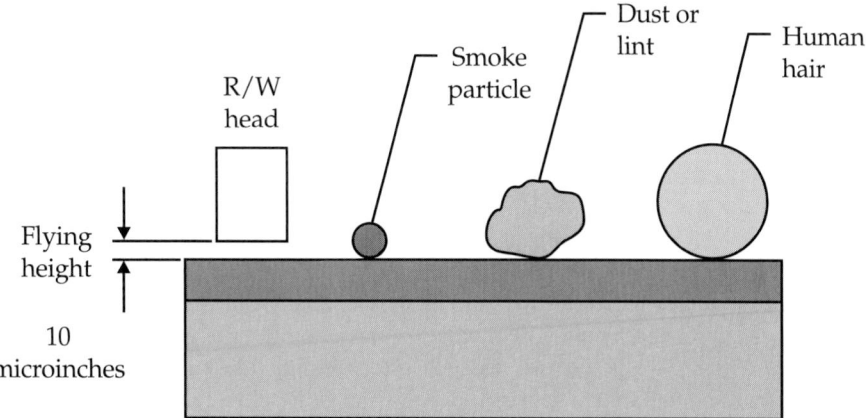

FIGURE 21-4   Comparison of foreign objects on a hard drive platter

DATA DENSITY CHARACTERISTICS

It is desirable to pack as much information as possible in the media of hard drive platters. The *areal density* of a media describes this maximum amount of capacity in terms of megabytes per square inch (sometimes noted as "MBSI" or "MB/in^2"). Today's hard drives used in most computers use media supporting over 2500 MBSI (with early PC hard drives, this figure was more like 400 to 800 MBSI). As you might imagine, physically smaller platters must hold media with a higher areal density to offer storage capacities similar to larger drives.

There are several major factors that affect a real density. First, the actual size of magnetic particles in the media places an upper barrier on areal density—smaller particles allow higher areal densities. Larger coercitivity of the media and smaller R/W heads with tighter magnetization fields allow higher areal densities. Finally, head height (the "altitude" of a R/W head over the platter surface) affects density. The closer a R/W head passes to its media, the higher areal densities can be. As heads fly further away, magnetic fields spread out, resulting in lower densities. Surface smoothness is then another major limiting factor in areal density, since smoother surfaces allow R/W heads to fly closer to the media.

There are other factors that define the way in which data can be packed onto a drive, most of which are related to areal density. *Track density* indicates the number of tracks per inch (TPI). The track density is also influenced by the precision of the R/W head positioning system—finer precision allows more tracks to be defined. *Flux density* indicates the number of individual magnetic flux transitions per linear inch of track space and is rated as flux changes per inch—termed "FCI" or "KFCI" (for "thousands of FCI"). Finally, you'll probably see references to *recording density*, which is basically the number of bits per linear inch of track space and is specified as bits per inch—termed "BPI" or "KBPI" (for "thousands of BPI").

LATENCY AND SEEK

As fast as a hard drive is, it cannot work instantaneously. There is a finite period of delay between the moment that a read or write command is initiated over the drive's physical interface and the moment that desired information is available (or placed). This delay is known as *latency*. More specifically, latency refers to the time it takes for needed bytes to pass under a R/W head. If the head has not quite reached the desired location, latency can be quite short. If the head has just missed the desired location, the head must wait almost a full rotation before the needed bits are available again, so latency can be rather long. In general, a disk drive is specified with *average latency* that (statistically) is time for the spindle to make half of a full rotation. For a disk rotating at 5,400 RPM (or 60 rotations per second), a full rotation is completed in 11.1ms [1/60]. Average latency would then be 5.6ms [11.1/2]. Disks spinning at 7,200 RPM offer an average latency of 4.2ms, and so on. As a rule, the faster a disk spins, the lower its latency will be. Ultimately, disk speed is limited by centrifugal forces acting on the platters.

The time it takes to step the R/W heads between tracks adds yet another delay to hard drive performance, and this is known as *seek time*. There are numerous ways of listing seek time. *Track-to-Track Seek* is the time needed to step between two adjacent tracks on the platter and is usually very short (roughly 2ms). *Full Stroke Seek* is the time needed to step from the innermost to the outermost tracks, and is relatively long (about 20ms). The *Average Seek* is usually taken as half of the Full Stroke seek (10ms for this example).

Seek and latency work together when loading and saving files. For example, when loading a file, it takes a certain amount of seek time to locate the track containing the start of your file. There is also some latency while the platter rotates around to the necessary sector. The disk may read several sectors in rapid succession but then need to jump to another track to continue reading—this imparts more seek time and additional latency while the disk looks for that next desired sector. And so it goes until the file is completely read.

You can imagine that if the head tries to step directly from the end of one track to the beginning of another, the head will arrive too late to catch the new track (because the disk has spun too much by the time the heads arrive). This means the drive will have to wait almost an entire rotation to pick up the start of that track. By offsetting the start points of each successive track, as in Figure 21-5, head travel time can be compensated for. This *cylinder skewing* technique is intended to improve hard drive performance by reducing the disk time lost during normal head steps. A head should be able to identify and read the desired information from a track within one disk rotation.

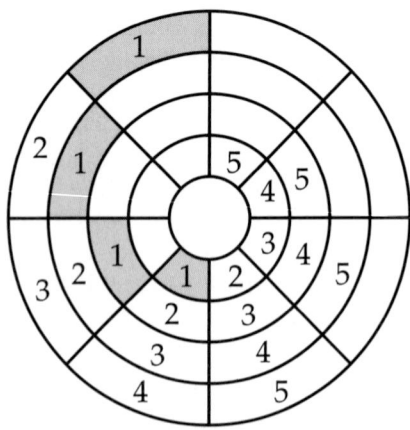

FIGURE 21-5   An example of cylinder skewing

TRACKS, CYLINDERS, AND SECTORS

As with floppy drives, you cannot simply place data anywhere on a hard drive platter—the drive would have no idea where to look for data or whether the data is even valid. The information on each platter must be sorted and organized into a series of known, standard locations. Each platter side can be considered as a two-dimensional field possessing length and width. With this sort of geometry, data is recorded in sets of concentric circles running from the disk spindle to the platter edge. A drive can move its R/W heads over the spinning media to locate needed data or programs in a matter of milliseconds. Every concentric circle on a platter is known as a *track*.

While each surface of a platter is a two-dimensional area, the number of platter surfaces involved in a hard drive (four, six, eight, or more) brings a third dimension (height) into play. Since each track is located directly over the same tracks on subsequent platters, each track in a platter assembly can be visualized as a *cylinder* that passes through every platter. The number of cylinders is equal to the number of tracks on one side of a platter. Thus, the terms "track" and "cylinder" are used interchangeably. Figure 21-6 shows data organization on a simple platter assembly. Note that only one side of the three platters is shown.

A typical platter physically contains many thousands of tracks—for example, the Maxtor DiamondMax 80GB drive provides 158,816 physical tracks (though you would enter only 16,383 *logical* tracks in the CMOS Setup, because Logical Block Addressing (LBA) drive translation handles the conversion in the BIOS). Consider what happens with the 80GB Maxtor drive when you enter 16,383 cylinders, 16 heads, and 63 sectors per track (at 512 bytes per sector)—the result is only 8,455,200,768 bytes (8.4GB), which is the CHS (cylinder/head/sector) limit for BIOS. Obviously, this cannot be right, even though that's what you enter in the CMOS Setup. If you substitute the actual number of cylinders for the drive, you get 81,964,302,336 bytes (81.96GB) which *is* exactly what Maxtor specifies for the drive's capacity.

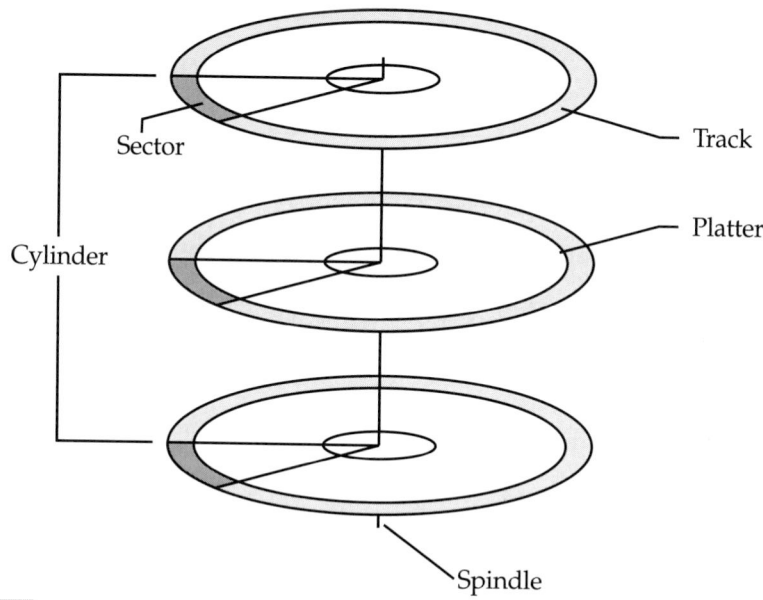

FIGURE 21-6   Data organization on a hard drive

In most cases, you do *not* need to know the actual number of drive cylinders because the BIOS will use LBA to translate the common 16,383x16x63 entry into the correct geometry without your direct intervention.

Tracks are broken down even further into small segments called *sectors*. As with DOS floppy disks, a sector holds 512 bytes of data, along with error-checking and housekeeping data that identifies the sector, track, and results calculated by cyclical redundancy checking (CRC). The location and ID information for each sector is developed when the drive is low-level formatted at the factory. After formatting, only sector data and CRC bytes are updated during writing. If sector ID information is accidentally overwritten or corrupted, the data recorded in the afflicted sector becomes unreadable.

Figure 21-7 shows the layout for a typical sector on a Maxtor SCSI drive. As you can see, there is *much* more than just 512 bytes of data. The start of every sector is marked with a pulse. The pulse signaling the first sector of a track is called the *index pulse*. There are two portions to every sector: an address area and data area. The *address area* is used to identify the sector. This is critically important because the drive must be able to identify precisely which cylinder, head, and sector location is about to be read from or written to. This location information is recorded in the *address field* and is followed by two bytes of cyclical redundancy check (CRC) data. When a drive identifies a location, it generates a CRC code that it compares to the CRC code recorded on the disk. If the two CRC codes match, the address is assumed to be valid, and disk operation can continue. Otherwise, an error has occurred and the entire sector is considered invalid. This failure usually precipitates a catastrophic DOS error message.

After a number of bytes are encountered for drive timing and synchronization, up to 512 bytes can be read from or written to the *data field*. The data is processed to derive eleven bytes of ECC error-checking code using Reed Solomon encoding. If data is being read, the derived ECC is compared to the recorded ECC. When the codes match, data is assumed to be valid and drive operation continues. Otherwise, a data

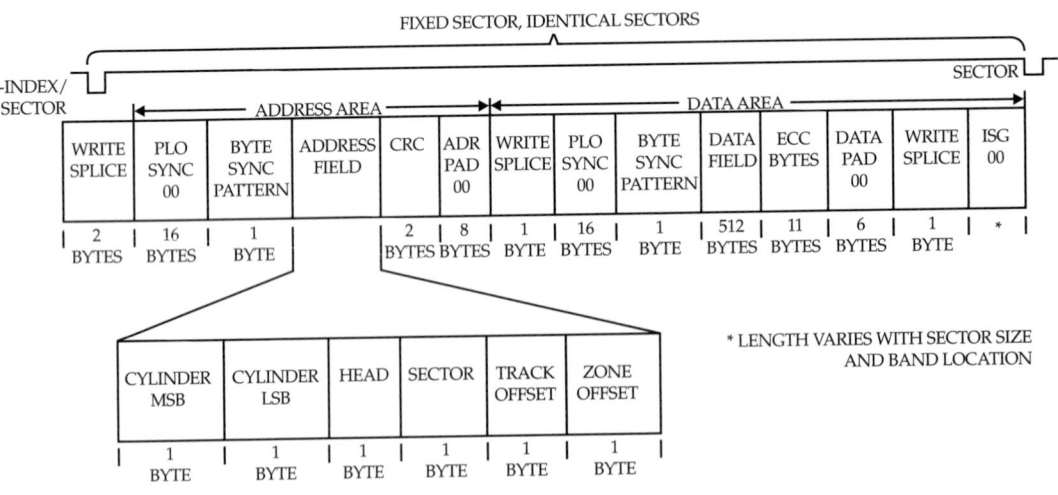

FIGURE 21-7   A typical hard drive sector layout (Maxtor Corporation)

read error is assumed. During writing, the old ECC data is replaced with the new ECC data derived for the current data. It is interesting to note that only the data and ECC fields of a sector are written after formatting. All other sector data remains untouched until the drive is reformatted. If a retentivity problem eventually causes one or more bits to become corrupt in the address area, the sector will fail.

ZONED RECORDING

In the early days of hard drives, every track had the same 63 sectors (unusually numbered 1 through 63). This worked well, but designers realized that for a constant angular velocity (CAV) drive, the data was recorded more densely on the inner tracks where the circumference is smaller than on the outer tracks where the circumference is larger. A feature known as *zoned recording* was added to the drive, which allows a *variable* number of sectors per track. The total number of tracks is divided up into several areas, or *zones* (usually 16 zones) across the platter. All of the tracks within a given zone use the same number of sectors, but inner zones use fewer sectors, while outer zones use more sectors. Zoned recording lets hard drives make the most efficient use of their storage space. Zoned recording is managed by the drive itself, so you still enter a fixed number in the "Sectors per Track" entry under the CMOS Setup (usually 63). Typical hard drives can run from 195 to 312 physical sectors per track.

63 sectors per track is still used in CMOS Setup even though the actual number may vary across the platter—LBA will again translate the geometry for the drive.

SECTOR SPARING

Not all sectors on a hard drive are useable. When a drive is formatted, bad sectors must be removed from normal use. The *sparing* process is a form of defect management and works to ensure that each track has access to the appropriate number of working sectors. When sparing is performed *in-line* (as a drive is being formatted), faulty sectors cause all subsequent sectors to be shifted up one sector. In-line sparing is not widely used. *Field defect* sparing (after the format process is complete) assigns (or remaps) faulty sectors to other working sectors located in spare disk tracks that are reserved for that purpose. For example, EIDE/UDMA hard drives use field defect sparing. It reserves a full 16 tracks for spare sectors (often referred to as the *defect management zone*). Faulty sectors are typically marked for reallocation when the disk is formatted.

The only place where faulty sectors are *absolutely* not permitted is on track 00. Track 00 is used to hold a hard drive's partition and FAT information. If a drive cannot read or write to track 00, the entire drive is rendered unusable. If a sector in track 00 fails during operation, reformatting the drive to lockout the bad sector will not necessarily recover the drive's operation. Track 00 failures usually necessitate reformatting the drive from scratch or replacing it entirely.

LANDING ZONE

The R/W heads of a hard drive fly at only a microscopic distance from their respective platter surfaces—held aloft with faint air currents produced by the spinning platters. When the drive is turned off, however, the platters slow to a halt. During this *spindown* period, airflow falls rapidly and heads can literally "crash" into the platter surfaces. Whenever a head touches a platter surface, data can be irretrievably destroyed. Even during normal operation, a sudden shock or bump can cause one or more heads to skid across their surfaces. Although a drive can usually be reformatted after a head crash, data and programs would have to be reloaded from scratch.

In order to avoid a head crash during normal startup or spindown cycles, a cylinder is reserved (either the innermost or outermost cylinder) as a *landing zone* (LZ). No data is stored on the landing zone, so any surface problems caused by head landings are harmless. All hard drives today will automatically move the head assembly over the landing zone before spindown (known as *parking the head*), then gently lock the heads into place until power is restored. Locking helps to ensure that random shocks and vibrations do not shake the heads onto adjacent data-carrying tracks and cause damage while power is off. Older hard drives required a specific "landing zone" entry in the CMOS Setup. But today, the process is automatic, so you can usually just enter "0" for the LZ or allow the system to autodetect the LZ with the rest of the drive geometry.

INTERLEAVE

The *interleave* of a hard drive refers to the order in which sectors are numbered on a platter. Interleave was a critical factor in older desktop computer systems where the core logic (CPU and memory) was relatively slow compared to drive performance. It was necessary to create artificial delays in the drive to allow core logic to catch up. Delays were accomplished by physically separating the sectors (numbering contiguous sectors out of order). This ordering forced the drive to read a sector, then skip one or more sectors to reach the next subsequent sector. The "interleaved" drive would have to make several rotations before all sectors on a track could be read.

The ratio of a sector's length on the platter to the distance between two sequential sectors is known as the *interleave factor*. For example, if a drive reads a sector and skips a sector to reach the next sequential sector, the interleave factor would be 1:3, and so on. The greater the interleave, the more rotations that would be needed to read all the sectors on a track, and the slower the drive would be. To achieve highest disk performance, interleave should be eliminated. Since drive and interface logic today is so much faster than even the fastest hard drive, the issue of interleave is largely irrelevant now. Drives no longer interleave their sectors, so all sectors are in sequential order around the track, and the interleave factor is 1:1—all data on a track can ideally be read in one disk rotation. An interleave factor of 1:1 yields optimal drive performance.

As a rule, *never* allow any drive utility to adjust or "optimize" the drive interleave. Changing the interleave not only destroys existing data, but it can also seriously impair drive performance.

WRITE PRECOMPENSATION

As you have already seen, a hard drive spins its platter(s) at a constant rate (such as 7,200 RPM)—its constant angular velocity (CAV). While constant rotation requires only a very simple motor circuit, extra demands are placed on the media. Tracks closer to the spindle are physically shorter than tracks toward the platter's outer edge. Shorter tracks result in shorter sectors. For inner sectors to hold the same amount of data as outer sectors, data must be packed more densely on the inner sectors—each magnetic flux reversal is actually closer together. Unfortunately, smaller flux reversals produce weaker magnetic fields in the R/W heads during reading.

If the inner sectors are written with a stronger magnetic field, flux transitions stored in the media will be stronger. When the inner sectors are then read, a clearer, better-defined signal will result. The use of increased writing current to compensate for diminished disk media response is known as *write precompensation* (WP). The track where write precompensation is expected to begin is specified in the drive's parameter table in CMOS Setup. Write precompensation filled an important role in early drives that used oxide-based media. Today's thin-film media and very small drive geometries (combined with

Zoned Recording techniques) result in low signal differences across the platter area, so write precompensation (although still specified in the drive geometry) is rarely meaningful anymore. In most cases, you can enter "0" for WP, or allow the system to autodetect the WP.

START TIME

Booting a computer can take about 30 seconds—often more. Some of this time is an artificial delay needed to initialize the hard drive(s) from a cold start. From the moment power is applied to the hard drive, it can take anywhere from 7 to 10 seconds for the drive's onboard controller to start and initialize the drive so that it can be recognized by the system POST. This period is known as the drive's *start time*. Boot problems with a new hard drive are frequently caused by an insufficient start time. The BIOS attempts to check for the presence of a hard drive that has not yet had time to initialize. When you find that drives are not recognized at boot time, but are readable once the system boots, adding several seconds to the drive's start time (or power-on boot delay) in the CMOS Setup may correct the problem.

DRIVE POWER MODES

Modern hard drives are not simply "on" or "off." They operate in any one of several modes, and each mode makes different power demands on the host system. This characteristic is particularly important because today's PCs are becoming ever more power conscious, so the ability to control drive power is an integral part of PC power conservation systems. Typical hard drives operate in any of five different power modes that are controlled by the operating system (such as Windows 9x/Me):

- **Spin-up**   The drive is spinning up following initial application of power and has not yet reached full speed. This demands about 14W and is particularly demanding of the power supply (if the supply is marginal or overloaded, the hard drive may not spin-up properly).
- **Seek**   This is a random access operation by the disk drive as it tries to locate the required track for reading or writing. This demands about 8.5–9.0W.
- **Read/Write**   A seek has been completed, and data is being read from or written to the drive. This uses about 5.0W.
- **Idle**   This is a basic power conservation mode where the drive is spinning and all other circuitry is powered on, but the head actuator is parked and powered off. This drops power demands to about 4W, yet the drive is capable of responding to read commands within 40ms.
- **Standby**   The spindle motor is not running (the drive "spins down"). This is the main power conservation mode that requires just about 1W. It may take up to several seconds for the drive to leave this mode (or spin-up) upon receipt of a command that requires disk access.

SERVO TECHNIQUES

Modern hard drives use voice coil actuators to position the R/W heads over the desired track. However, drives need to verify that the heads are positioned correctly *before* reading or writing can take place. The drive needs feedback to tell it where the heads actually are (versus where the drive thinks the heads are). If the heads are positioned incorrectly, the drive can make the necessary adjustments. Think of driving a car in a 50 mph zone. You step on the accelerator to make the car move, but you need to check the speedometer to see what the actual speed is. If the speed is still too slow, you can give the car more gas. If the speed is too fast, you can apply less gas (or the brake if needed). This constant feedback is called a *servo loop*.

For the hard disk, feedback information is provided from the platters themselves, using special codes (called *servo codes*) written on the disk that let the drive know where the heads are as the actuator moves. Servo codes are read by the heads and fed back to the actuator control logic. By putting different codes on each track of the disk, the actuator can always figure out which track the heads are on. There are three different ways to implement a hard disk servo mechanism:

■ **Wedge Servo**   Servo information is recorded in a wedge of each platter (like a slice out of a pie). The remainder of the platter contains data. The problem is that the servo information is in only one location on the hard disk. To position the heads, a lot of waiting must be done for the servo wedge to rotate around to where the heads are, and these delays make the positioning performance of such drives painfully slow. This technique is used in older drives and is now considered obsolete.

■ **Dedicated Servo**   This approach was found on many drives through the 1990s. An entire surface of one disk platter is dedicated for servo information, and no servo information is recorded on the other surfaces. One head is constantly reading servo information—this allows very fast servo feedback and eliminates the delays associated with wedge servo designs. Unfortunately, an entire surface of the disk is wasted because it can contain no user data. There are other problems; for example, the heads where data is recorded may not always line up exactly with the head that is reading the servo information, so adjustments must be made to compensate. Also, since the servo platter may be warmer or cooler than the data platters, these drives are notorious for needing frequent thermal recalibration. Dedicated servo drives usually have an odd number of heads.

■ **Embedded Servo**   The newest servo technique intersperses servo information with data across the entire surface of all of the hard disk platter surfaces. This means servo information and data are read by the same heads, and the heads never have to wait for the disk to rotate the servo information into place (as with wedge servo). This method doesn't provide the constant positioning information available with a dedicated servo, but it also doesn't cause an entire surface to be wasted on servo overhead. The need for constant thermal recalibration is also greatly reduced, since the servo information and data are the same distance from the center of the disk and will expand or contract together. All modern hard disks now use embedded servo.

In all cases, the servo codes are written to the disk surfaces at the time the hard disk is manufactured. This process requires special, complex, and expensive equipment, and servo codes are intended to last the life of the drive. Servo codes cannot be rewritten without returning the drive to the factory. Remember that the disk heads themselves are locked out at the hardware level (by the drive's electronics) from writing to any areas where servo information is written. The creation of this precise servo information is part of the *low-level formatting* of a modern drive—which is now always a factory process. Modern IDE-type hard drives do *not* need low-level formatting, and traditional BIOS routines to invoke low-level formatting are largely ignored by the drive.

 Do *not* attempt to low-level format any type of IDE drive—doing this can damage the drive's servo information and render the drive unusable.

THERMAL RECALIBRATION

When hard drives operate, heat naturally produced by the electronics, spindle motor, and voice coil actuator causes the drive media to expand. This gradually changes the location of each track, and the drive must periodically adjust for such changes. As designers continued to pack more tracks on a platter (and the number of tracks per inch increases), it became more important than ever to allow for thermal expansion—especially with *dedicated servo* drives. For servo information and data on different platters, adjustments were necessary to ensure that servo and user data did not become misaligned. Such adjustments are known as *thermal recalibration.*

To address this problem, most drives manufactured in the mid-1990s include a thermal recalibration feature. Every few minutes, the heads are moved and the distance between tracks measured. This information is recorded in the drive's memory, and is used to help position the heads for reading or writing. When the recalibration occurs, you can hear the disk operate as if you were accessing it (even if you're not). The problem with thermal recalibration is that disk access is delayed until the recalibration process is complete. This process doesn't cause data to be lost, but it can affect operations that depends on real-time drive access (such as video captures, CD-R creation, or digital audio extraction). Drive makers responded to thermal recalibration problems by allowing the recalibration to be put off until the drive was idle. Such drives were frequently advertised as audio/visual (A/V) drives in the late 1990s. Today, thermal recalibration is still required, but its need has been greatly reduced with embedded servo drives. Embedded servo drives almost eliminate the interruptions to "real-time" disk access, and thermal recalibration can even be disabled on some newer embedded servo drive models.

IDE Drive Standards and Features

IDE hard drive technology has come a long way since its introduction in the late 1980s. In fact, IDE technology has come *so* far that it's difficult to keep all of the terminology straight. Let's start this part of the chapter by examining the important concepts and evolution of IDE technology.

BINARY MEGABYTES VS. DECIMAL MEGABYTES

Most folks know that hard drive sizes are measured in megabytes (MB) and gigabytes (GB)—however, beginners and experienced technicians alike are often confused by the difference between *binary megabytes* and *decimal megabytes* (as well as gigabytes). For example, you'll notice that when you install a new 4GB hard drive, utilities like the CMOS Setup, FDISK, and Windows Explorer will report only about 3.72GB, but other utilities like CHKDSK report about 4GB. This difference is often confusing, but it's due to the way in which manufacturers and software makers calculate drive capacity. Technically, hard drive capacity is calculated by multiplying the number of cylinders, sectors, and heads times 512, such as this:

```
Capacity = Cylinders x Heads x Sectors x 512 (bytes per sector)
```

So, if you're using an AC2850 drive with 1654 cylinders, 16 heads, and 63 sectors, you'd wind up with:

```
1654 x 16 x 63 x 512 = 853,622,784 bytes
```

By comparison, an AC34000 drive with 7752 cylinders, 16 heads, and 63 sectors would yield:

```
7752 x 16 x 63 x 512 = 4,000,776,192 bytes
```

The problem is that hard drive manufacturers use the notion of *decimal megabytes* (or decimal gigabytes) to determine the size of their hard drives. To calculate drive sizes in decimal megabytes, just divide the drive size by 1,000,000 (or 1,000,000,000 for GB). For the AC2850, you'd get

```
853,622,784 / 1,000,000 = 853.6MB
```

For the AC34000, you'd get

```
4,000,776,192 / 1,000,000,000 = 4.0GB
```

Makes sense, right? Unfortunately, many software makers will use *binary megabytes* (or binary giga-bytes) to calculate drive sizes. A binary megabyte is 1,048,576 bytes, and a binary gigabyte is 1,073,741,824 bytes, so here's how a lot of software will report the AC2850:

```
853,622,784 bytes / 1,048,576 = 814MB
```

And here's the calculation for the AC34000:

```
4,000,776,192 bytes / 1,073,741,824 = 3.72GB
```

These are simply two slightly different ways of representing the same drives, so *both* methods are correct. The important issue here is to recognize the difference and to *not* mistake that difference as being a problem with the drive.

IDE/ATA

IDE (*Integrated Drive Electronics*) and ATA (*AT Attachment*) are basically one and the same thing—a disk drive scheme designed to integrate the controller onto the drive mechanism itself, instead of relying on a stand-alone controller board as older MFM and RLL drives did. This approach reduces interface costs and makes drive firmware implementations easier. IDE proved to be a low-cost, easily configured system—so much so that it created a boom in the disk drive industry. Although the terms "IDE" and "ATA" are sometimes used interchangeably, ATA is the formal standard that defines the drive and how it operates, while IDE is really the "trade name" that refers to the 40-pin interface and drive controller archi-tecture designed to implement the ATA standard.

The AT Attachment interface was submitted to the American National Standards Institute (ANSI) for approval in 1990, and it was finally published in 1994 as ANSI standard X3.221-1994, titled *AT Attach-ment Interface for Disk Drives*. This standard is sometimes called *ATA-1* to distinguish it from its suc-cessors. The original IDE/ATA standard defines the following features and transfer modes:

■ The specification calls for a single channel in a PC, shared by two devices that are configured as mas-ter and slave.

■ ATA includes support for PIO modes 0, 1, and 2.

■ ATA includes support for single-word DMA modes 0, 1, and 2 and multiword DMA mode 0.

ATA does not include support for enhancements such as ATAPI support for non–hard-disk IDE/ATA devices, block mode transfers, logical block addressing, Ultra-DMA modes, or other advanced features. The ATA-1 standard is now completely obsolete, and drives developed to meet this standard are no longer made. At the recommendation of the T13 Technical Committee, ATA-1 was withdrawn as an official ANSI standard in 1999.

ATAPI

Originally, the IDE/ATA interface was designed to work only with hard drives. Other devices such as CD-ROMs and tape drives used proprietary interfaces (often implemented on sound cards), the floppy disk interface (which is slow and cumbersome), or SCSI. In the early 1990s, designers realized that there would be enormous advantages to using the standard IDE/ATA interface to support devices other than hard drives. The intention was not to replace SCSI, but rather to eliminate proprietary interfaces and the slow floppy interface for tape drives.

Unfortunately, given the ATA command structure, it wasn't possible to put non–hard drive devices on the IDE channel and expect them to work. A special protocol was developed called the *AT Attachment Packet Interface*, or *ATAPI*. The ATAPI standard is used for devices like CD, tape, and removable media drives. It enables them to use the standard IDE cable used by IDE/ATA hard drives and to be configured as master or slave, just like a hard drive. When you see a CD-ROM or other non-HDD peripheral denoted as an "IDE device," it is really using the ATAPI protocol. Internally, the ATAPI protocol is not at all similar to the standard ATA command set used by hard drives. The name "packet interface" suggests that commands to ATAPI devices are sent in groups called *packets*. In some ways, ATAPI resembles SCSI more than IDE in terms of its command set and operation. The first ATAPI standard document was called SFF-8020 (later renamed INF-8020), which is now quite old and obsolete. In the late 1990s, the T13 Technical Committee took over control of the ATAPI command set and protocol, combining it with ATA into the ATA/ATAPI-4 standard.

A special ATAPI driver is used to communicate with ATAPI devices—this driver must be loaded into memory before the device can be accessed (though most newer operating systems such as Windows support ATAPI internally and load their own drivers for the interface). The actual data transfers use regular PIO or DMA modes—just like hard disks—though support for the various modes differs widely by device. For the most part, ATAPI devices will coexist with IDE/ATA devices. From the user's perspective, ATAPI devices behave as if they are regular IDE/ATA disks on the channel. Newer BIOS versions will even allow the system to boot from ATAPI CD-ROM drives.

ATA-2, FAST-ATA, AND EIDE

By the early 1990s, it became clear that ATA architecture would soon be overwhelmed by advances in hard drive technology. The ATA interface committee responded by developing the ATA-2 standard, which essentially combined the features and attributes defined by marketing programs created at Seagate, Quantum, and Western Digital. This standard was published in 1996 as ANSI standard X3.279-1996, called the *AT Attachment Interface with Extensions*. ATA-2 is largely regarded as a significant improvement to ATA-1. It defines faster PIO (Programmed I/O) and DMA (Direct Memory Access) data transfer modes, adds more powerful drive commands (such as the "Identify Drive" command to support auto-identification in CMOS), adds support for a second drive channel, handles block data transfers (Block Transfer Mode), and defines and new means of addressing sectors on the hard drive using Logical Block Addressing (LBA). LBA has proven to be a very effective vehicle for overcoming the traditional 528MB hard drive size limit. Yet ATA-2 continues to use the same 40-pin physical interface used by ATA-1, and it is backward compatible with ATA (IDE) drives.

Along with ATA-2, you'll probably find two additional terms: EIDE (*Enhanced IDE*) and *Fast-ATA*. These are not standards—merely different implementations of the ATA-2 standard. EIDE represents the Western Digital implementation of ATA-2, which builds upon both the ATA-2 and ATAPI standards. This has been *so* effective that *EIDE* has become the "generic" term. Seagate and Quantum have thrown their support behind the Fast-ATA implementation of the ATA-2 standard. However, Fast-ATA builds on ATA-2 only. For all practical purposes, there is no significant difference between ATA-2, EIDE, and Fast-ATA, and you'll probably see these three terms used interchangeably (though this is not *technically* correct).

ATA-3

A more recent implementation of the ATA standard is ATA-3, which was published in 1997 as ANSI standard X3.298-1997 called *AT Attachment 3 Interface*. It does not define any new data transfer modes, but it does improve the reliability of PIO Mode 4. It also offers a simple password-based security scheme, more sophisticated power management features, and "Self-Monitoring Analysis and Reporting Technology" (SMART). ATA-3 is also backward compatible with ATA-2, ATAPI, and ATA devices. Since no new data transfer modes are defined by ATA-3, you may also see the generic term "EIDE" used interchangeably (though this is also not technically correct).

You may see a "PIO Mode 5" described in some places with the claim that it was introduced in ATA-3. This mode was suggested by some controller manufacturers but never approved and never implemented. It is not defined in any of the ATA standards and exists only in some BIOS versions.

ATA-3 does *not* define any of the Ultra-DMA modes—these were first defined with the ATA/ATAPI-4 standard. ATA-3 is also not the same as ATA-33 (ATA-33 is often used as a slang term for Ultra-DMA/33).

ATA/ATAPI-4 (ULTRA-ATA/33)

The next significant enhancement to the ATA standard saw the ATA Packet Interface (ATAPI) feature set merged with the conventional ATA command set and protocols to create ATA/ATAPI-4. This standard was published by ANSI in 1998 as NCITS 317-1998, *AT Attachment with Packet Interface Extensions*. Aside from combining ATA and ATAPI, this standard defined several other significant enhancements and changes:

■ High-speed Ultra-DMA modes 0, 1, and 2 were created, defining transfer rates of 16.7, 25, and 33.3 MB/s.

■ A 40-pin/80 conductor IDE cable was first defined in this standard. It was thought that the higher-speed Ultra DMA modes would require the use of this cable in order to eliminate signal problems caused by the higher speed. The use of this cable was left optional for this standard, though it became mandatory under the faster UDMA modes defined in ATA/ATAPI-5.

■ Cyclical Redundancy Checking (CRC) was added to ensure the integrity of data sent using the faster Ultra DMA modes.

■ The command set was cleaned up, several older and obsolete commands were removed, and special command queuing and overlapping protocols were defined.

Obviously, the Ultra-DMA (UDMA) modes were the most exciting part of this new standard. Ultra-DMA modes 0 and 1 were never really implemented by hard disk manufacturers, but UDMA mode 2 made a real impression since it doubled the throughput of the fastest transfer mode then available to 33.3MB/s. Ultra-DMA mode 2 was quickly dubbed "Ultra-DMA/33," and drives conforming to ATA/ATAPI-4 are often called "Ultra-ATA/33" drives (which is technically inaccurate).

In actual practice, you'll need an Ultra-ATA drive, controller, and BIOS to support an Ultra-ATA drive system, but it is fully backward compatible with previous ATA standards. You can use ordinary 40-pin IDE-type cables for UDMA/33 unless any of the following issues occur:

■ The standard cable is of low quality, damaged, or weakened by many installations.

- The system suffers from excessive signal noise—these systems may have multiple drives, dual power supplies, or an integrated CRT.

- The system is overclocked (or otherwise configured beyond the manufacturer's supported specifications).

ATA-ATAPI-5 (ULTRA-ATA/66)

With the rapid adoption of ATA/ATAPI-4, the T13 committee immediately began work on its next generation of interface standard dubbed ATA/ATAPI-5. This standard was published by ANSI in 2000 as NCITS 340-2000, the *AT Attachment with Packet Interface—5*. The changes defined in ATA/ATAPI-5 include

- More high-speed Ultra-DMA modes 3 and 4, defining transfer rates of 44.4 and 66.6 MB/s, respectively.

- The 40-pin/80-conductor IDE cable that was optional in ATA/ATAPI-4 is made mandatory for UDMA modes 3 and 4. ATA/ATAPI-5 also defines a method by which a host system can detect if an 80-conductor cable is in use, so it can determine whether or not to enable the higher-speed transfer modes.

- Numerous interface commands were changed, and some old ones were deleted.

As with ATA-3, not that many changes were made in ATA/ATAPI-5. However, the main change was certainly important—another doubling of the throughput of the interface to 66.6 MB/s. Many companies quickly labeled ATA/ATAPI-5 drives running Ultra-DMA mode 4 as "Ultra-ATA/66." During late 1999 and early 2000, new IDE/ATA drives conforming to this standard began appearing on the market.

You'll need an Ultra-ATA/66 drive, controller, and BIOS to support an Ultra-ATA/66 drive system, but it is fully backward compatible with previous ATA standards. Unlike the Ultra-ATA/33 approach, you'll need a specially designed 40-pin/80-conductor cable (typically provided with UDMA/66 drives). Also keep in mind that the operating system must also be enabled for DMA transfers. Keep the following issues in mind when implementing a UDMA/66 system:

- Make sure that the signal cable is Ultra-ATA/66-capable. An Ultra-ATA/66-compliant cable is a 40-pin, 80-conductor cable with a black connector on one end, a blue connector on the other end, and a gray connector in the middle. In addition, pin 34 on the cable should be notched or cut (though this may be difficult to see with the human eye).

- Make sure the system board (motherboard) controller is capable of supporting Ultra-ATA/66. An Ultra-ATA/66 capable controller has a detect circuit that can detect missing line 34 on the cable. If there is no detect circuit, the system can wrongly detect the presence of an Ultra-ATA/66 cable and try to configure the device for a higher transfer rate.

- Some system board (motherboard) controllers may not successfully handle Ultra-ATA/66 on both the primary and secondary channels. If you have difficulty with a UDMA/66 device on the secondary controller channel, consider troubleshooting with the device in the primary master position.

- If you have trouble getting a UDMA/66 system configured properly, contact the system board (motherboard) or controller card manufacturer for the latest BIOS upgrade (and any Ultra-ATA/66 device drivers or patches).

- Make sure the operating system is "DMA-capable," and verify that the DMA mode is activated. For Windows 9x/Me, check the drive's Properties dialog in the Device Manager.

- Make sure the Ultra-ATA/66-capable drive has been configured to run at Ultra-ATA/66 transfer rates. Some drives ship with the UDMA/66 mode disabled by default and require a jumper change and/or software utility in order to activate the UDMA/66 mode.

ATA/ATAPI-6 (ULTRA-ATA/100)

At the time this edition is being written, the T13 Technical Committee is working on the next version of the ATA standard, the ATA/ATAPI-6. It is likely that this standard will be completed in 2001 and published sometime late in that year or early in 2002. Since this standard is still in development, it is impossible to say exactly what features and changes it will include. One addition to the standard will almost certainly be the new Ultra-DMA mode 5, which increases transfer throughput to 100MB/s (now available in drives dubbed UDMA/100). Some possible new features for the next standard include the following:

■ LBA address size would be expanded to overcome the traditional 28-bit LBA scheme (limiting drive sizes to 137GB—a possible size barrier in the next year or two). An addressing mode will probably be included in ATA/ATAPI-6 that expands the address width from 28-bits to either 48 or 64 bits.

■ Hard drive noise reduction (acoustic management) may be included that allow the mechanics of the drive to be modified under software control—allowing the user choose between higher performance or quieter operation.

■ Additional ATA commands may be added to support audio and video streaming (or other multimedia operations).

Ultra-DMA/100 drives are currently available and may be standardized with the release of ATA/ATAPI-6.

DATA TRANSFER MODES

Data transfer rates play a major role in drive performance. In practice, there are two measures of data transfer: the rate at which data is taken from the platters and the rate at which data is passed between the drive and controller. The *internal* data transfer between the platters and drive buffer is typically the slower rate. Older Ultra-ATA drives like the Maxtor DiamondMax 2160 run at 14MB/s, but their newer DiamondMax 80 (UDMA/100) drives can move information between the buffer and media at up to 46.7MB/s. The *external* data transfer between the drive and controller (the "interface rate") is often the *faster* rate. Older ATA-2 (EIDE) drives can operate up to 16MB/s using PIO mode 4, but Ultra-DMA/66 drives can burst data from the buffer to the interface at 66MB/s, and Ultra-DMA/100 drives can handle burst data transfers of 100MB/s.

The modern standards of external data transfer are listed as PIO (or *Programmed I/O*) and DMA (*Direct Memory Access*) modes. PIO modes are managed by the system processor. The PIO mode specifies how fast data is transferred to and from the drive, as shown in Table 21-1.

TABLE 21-1	**DATA TRANSFER SPEED FOR PIO MODES**		
PIO MODE	**CYCLE TIME (NS)**	**TRANSFER RATE (MB/S)**	**NOTES**
0	600	3.3	These are the old ATA (IDE) modes.
1	383	5.2	
2	240	8.3	
3	180 IORDY	11.1	These are the newer ATA-2 (EIDE) modes.
4	120 IORDY	16.6	

You may notice that the EIDE-specific modes (PIO-3 and PIO-4) use the IORDY hardware flow control line. This means that the drive can use the IORDY line to slow down the interface when necessary. Interfaces without proper IORDY support may cause data corruption in the fast PIO modes (so you'd be stuck with the slower modes). When choosing an EIDE drive and controller, always be sure to check that the IORDY line is being used.

By comparison, DMA data transfers mean that the data is transferred *directly* between the drive and memory without using the CPU as an intermediary (as is the case with PIO). In true multitasking operating systems like OS/2, Windows NT, or Linux, DMA transfers leave the CPU free to do something useful during disk transfers. In a DOS or Windows environment, the CPU will have to wait for the transfer to finish anyway, so in these cases DMA transfers don't offer that much of a multitasking advantage. There are two distinct types of direct memory access: ordinary DMA and bus-mastering DMA. *Ordinary DMA* uses the DMA controller on the system's motherboard to perform the complex task of arbitration, grabbing the system bus, and transferring the data. With *bus-mastering DMA*, all this is done by logic in the drive controller itself. DMA transfer modes are listed in Table 21-2.

BLOCK MODE TRANSFERS

Traditionally, an interrupt (IRQ) is generated each time a read or write command is passed to the drive. This causes a certain amount of overhead work for the host system and CPU. If it were possible to transfer *multiple* sectors of data between the drive and host without generating an IRQ, data transfer could be accomplished much more efficiently. *Block mode* transfers allow up to 128 sectors of data to be transferred at a single time and can improve transfers as much as 30 percent. However, block mode transfers are not terribly effective on single-tasking operating systems like DOS—any improvement over a few percent usually indicates bad buffer cache management on the part of the drive. Finally, the block size that is optimal for drive throughput isn't always the best for system performance. For example, the DOS FAT file system tends to favor a block size equal to the cluster size.

BUS MASTERING DMA

Conventional DMA is called third-party DMA, which means that the DMA controllers on the motherboard coordinate the DMA transfers (the third party is the DMA controller itself). Unfortunately, these DMA controllers are old and very slow—basically unchanged since the earliest days of the PC. They are

TABLE 21-2   DATA TRANSFER SPEED FOR DMA MODES

DMA MODE	CYCLE TIME (NS)	TRANSFER RATE (MB/S)	NOTES
Single Word 0	960	2.1	also in ATA
1	480	4.2	
2	240	8.3	
Multi Word 0	480	4.2	also in ATA
1	150	13.3	
2	120	16.6	
3	--	33.0	Ultra-DMA/33
4	--	66.0	Ultra-DMA/66
5	--	100.0	Ultra-DMA/100

also tied to the old ISA bus, which has been all but abandoned for performance reasons. When multiword DMA modes 1 and 2 became popular, so did the use of the high-speed PCI bus for IDE/ATA controller cards. At that point, the old method of DMA transfers had to change.

Modern IDE/ATA hard disks use first-party DMA transfers. The term *first-party* means that the peripheral device itself does the work of transferring data to and from memory, with no external DMA controller involved—this is also called *bus mastering* because the transferring device becomes the "master of the bus." Bus mastering IDE (or BM IDE) allows the hard disk and memory to work without relying on the old DMA controller built into the system or needing any support from the CPU. It requires the use of the PCI bus and achieves the efficient transfer of data to and from the hard disk and system memory. Bus mastering DMA keeps CPU utilization *low*.

While there are obvious advantages to bus mastering DMA, the use of bus-mastering multiword DMA mode 2 never really caught on—primarily due to the poor state of support for the technology for the first couple of years. PIO modes required no work and were very simple, but DMA was not even supported by the first version of Windows 95 (special drivers had to be used). Problems with implementing bus mastering DMA on systems between 1996 to 1998 included buggy drivers, software the didn't work properly, CD-ROM drives that wouldn't work with the drivers, and so on. Thus, DMA didn't offer much incentive to make the switch.

Bus mastering DMA finally took off when the industry moved to Ultra-DMA. Once Ultra-DMA/33 doubled the interface transfer rate, DMA had an obvious speed advantage over PIO (in addition to its other efficiency improvements). Support for DMA was also cleaned up and made native in Windows 9x/Me, and most of the problems with the old drivers were eliminated. Today, the use of Ultra-DMA data transfers are standard in the industry, and you rarely (if ever) encounter IDE-type hard drives using PIO data transfers. To make the most of bus master performance, your system must have *all* of the following elements:

■ The motherboard (drive controller) must be bus master IDE (BM IDE)-compliant.

■ The motherboard BIOS must support bus mastering.

■ You need a multitasking operating system (OS) such as Windows 9x/Me.

■ A bus mastering device driver is needed for the operating system.

■ And you need a bus mastering-compatible IDE device (disk drive, CD-ROM) that supports "DMA multi-word" modes.

You *can* use bus master IDE and non-bus master IDE devices in the same system, but the non-bus master IDE devices may reduce the overall performance of the bus mastering devices. Still, bus mastering IDE is not a cure-all for system performance problems. In fact, bus mastering will probably not benefit the system significantly if you run DOS applications, work with only single applications at a time, or use multiple applications that are not disk-intensive.

Windows Bus Master IDE Drivers

As mentioned previously, you'll need a bus master driver to support your operating system (namely Windows 9x/Me). The initial release of Windows 95 offered only a generic solution (ESDI_506.PDR), and the version released with OSR2 is still quite basic. The bus master drivers shipped with Windows 98 and later will generally offer better performance. For top performance, you should use the bus master driver that accompanies your motherboard (or other bus master-compliant drive controller). You can check Drivers Headquarters at **www.drivershq.com** for current bus master drivers.

Bus Master Driver Issues

While bus mastering can clearly enhance the drive performance of a busy multitasking system, it is not without its problems. As it turns out, bus master driver issues are the most prevalent problems. The two most common issues are

■ The CD-ROM or IDE-type HDD on the secondary drive channel disappears after installing the bus master driver.

■ Windows 9x/Me takes a long time to boot after bus master drivers are installed.

In both cases, you'll notice that the secondary controller channel (IDE) no longer appears in the Device Manager. This is because bus master drivers do not support ATA (IDE) controllers correctly. You'll need to install the bus master driver for the primary (EIDE) drive channel and leave the PIO driver in place to support the secondary (IDE) drive channel. Install the bus master driver, then alter the Registry to manually redirect the secondary IDE drive channel to use a standard IDE driver again:

Altering the Windows Registry can have a profound effect on your system and even prevent the system from booting. Always make a backup copy of the original Registry files (SYSTEM.DAT and USER.DAT) before attempting to edit them.

1. Start REGEDIT, load the Registry file, and find the entry

    `HKEY_LOCAL_MACHINE/System/CurrentControlSet/control/Services/Class/hdc`

2. There should be four sub-directories: 0000-0003

3. Find the one where DriverDesc reads something like "Primary Bus Master IDE controller" or "Secondary Bus Master IDE controller," according to the port you want to change (should be 0002 or 0003). You'd most likely want to change the secondary entry.

4. In this subdirectory, change PortDriver from "ESDI_506.PDR" (or whatever bus master driver you're using) to "IDEATAPI.MPD."

5. You can also change the DriverDesc to something like "Standard IDE/ESDI controller"—this will produce a more familiar entry when viewed in the Device Manager.

6. Save your changes and reboot the computer.

Your secondary (IDE) drive controller channel should now be using a standard IDE driver, and the IDE devices on that channel (such as the CD-ROM) should now appear normally. Here's another trick that may shorten the startup time—start Windows 9x/Me in Safe Mode and delete all drives in Device Manager. Then reboot the PC and allow Windows to re-detect all the drives automatically.

Some technicians have suggested that configuring an ATAPI CD-ROM as the "slave" device when it's the only device on the secondary (IDE) drive channel might work when using bus master drivers. Normally, the only IDE device would be jumpered as the master. Please note that this suggestion won't damage the CD-ROM or drive controller, but it has *not* been tested to verify whether it actually works. Given the proliferation of bus master hardware and software, there may circumstances where this suggestion may or may not work. Consider it a last resort.

UNDERSTANDING SMART TECHNOLOGY

SMART (Self-Monitoring Analysis and Reporting Technology) is a *self-diagnostic* system that enables the PC to predict the impending failures of devices such as disk drives. With a given failure prediction, the user or system manager can back up key data, replace a suspect device *prior* to data loss, and avoid undesired downtime. SMART is a key for improving data integrity and data availability of the PC.

SMART goes by a variety of names in the computer industry. The term *Predictive Failure Analysis (PFA)* was given to SMART technology by its inventor, IBM. PFA is implemented in all of IBM's mainframe computer systems. Compaq was one of the first companies to implement SMART in its hard drives, and the feature was dubbed *Drive Failure Prediction (DFP)*. The initial Compaq Computer SMART specification was modified and submitted for general industry consideration by the Small Form Factor Committee. SMART is now being standardized by ANSI in the ATA-4 (ANSI X3T13 ATA\ATAPI-4) specification.

To implement SMART, the host computer must have BIOS or device driver support that is capable of sending SMART commands to and from the ATA interface registers. SMART technology is growing in popularity, and all current Maxtor drives are SMART-ready. You can learn more about SMART from Maxtor at **www.maxtor.com/products/DiamondMax/techsupport/misc/smart.html**. You can also check with StorageSoft at **www.storagesoft.com/deskUtils.asp** for detailed information on its EZ-SMART utility.

DRIVE CACHING

All modern hard disks contain an integrated cache, also called a *buffer*. The purpose of this cache is similar to other caches in the PC, though it's not normally considered part of the PC cache hierarchy. Cache acts as a buffer between a fast device and a slow one. For hard drives, the cache holds the results of recent disk reads and fetches information that is likely to be requested (for example, the sector or sectors immediately after the one just requested). Cache improves the performance of any hard drives by reducing the number of physical accesses to the disk, and allows data to stream uninterrupted from the disk when the bus is busy. Most modern hard drives have between 512KB and 2MB of internal cache, though some high-performance SCSI drives have as much as 16MB.

Cache Operation

Hard drive cache helps to correct for the speed difference between the drive and the interface. Finding a piece of data on the hard drive involves random positioning and incurs a penalty of *milliseconds* as the head actuator is moved and the disk rotates on the spindle. On a typical IDE/ATA hard disk, transferring a 4KB block of data from the disk's internal cache is over 100 times *faster* than actually finding it and reading it from the platters.

The basic principle behind cache operation is relatively simple. Reading data from the drive is generally done in blocks of various sizes (not just one 512-byte sector at a time). The cache is broken into segments, each of which can contain one block of data. When a request is made for data from the drive, the cache is first queried to see if the data is present in any cache segments. If it is, the cache data is passed to the interface without accessing the drive. If the data is not in the cache, it's read from the drive, passed to the interface, and then placed into the cache in the event that it's asked for again. Since cache is limited in size, there is only a limited amount of data that can be held before the segments must be recycled.

Typically the oldest piece of data is replaced with the newest one. This is called circular, first-in/first-out (*FIFO*), or wrap-around caching. To improve performance, most drive manufacturers today have implemented enhancements to their cache management circuitry, such as:

- **Adaptive Segmentation**   Conventional cache is chopped into a number of equal-sized segments. Since requests can be made for data blocks of different sizes, this can cause some of the cache data to be left over—and thus wasted. Many newer drives dynamically resize their cache segments based the space required for each access. It can also change the number of segments. This is more complex to handle than fixed-size segments and can result in waste if the space isn't managed properly.

- **Pre-Fetch**   The drive's cache logic (based on analyzing access and usage patterns of the drive), attempts to load cache data that has not been requested yet, but that it *anticipates* will be requested soon. This usually means loading additional data beyond that which was just read. When done correctly, this will improve performance a bit.

- **User Control**   High-end drives have implemented a set of commands that allow detailed control of the drive's cache operation—this includes letting the user enable or disable caching, set the size of segments, control adaptive segmentation and pre-fetch, and so on.

Cache helps very little if you're doing a lot of random data access in different parts of the disk. If the disk has not loaded a piece of data recently, it won't be in the cache. The cache is also poor help if you're reading a large amount of data from the disk (normally it's pretty small). For example, when copying a 10MB file on a typical disk with a 512KB buffer, 5 percent of the file could be in the buffer at most—the rest must be read from the disk itself. This means cache doesn't have as much impact on overall system performance as you might think. Figure 21-8 illustrates the caching algorithm used by Quantum Corporation for some of their ProDrive hard drives.

Write Caching

With no write caching, every write to the hard drive involves a performance hit while the system waits for the hard disk to access the correct location on the drive and write data. This takes at least 10ms on most drives and really slows down performance as the system waits for the hard drive. This mode of operation is called *write-through caching*—the data written is actually put into the cache in case it needs to be read again later, but the write occurs at the same time. When write caching is enabled, the system writes to the drive, but the drive holds the data in its cache and immediately sends an acknowledgement to the operating system. The rest of the system can then continue without having to wait for the actuator to position and the disk to spin. This is called *write-back caching* because the data is stored in the cache and written back to the platters only later on. Write-back caching improves performance, but it puts data at risk because power failures or other system problems that occur before the cached data is actually written can cause data corruption. Due to this risk, write caching is not used at all in some situations—especially for applications where high data integrity is critical.

Drive Construction

Now that you have a background in major hard drive concepts and operations, it is time to take a drive apart and show you how all the key pieces fit together. While it's extremely unlikely that you will ever need to disassemble a hard drive, the understanding of each part and its placement will help you to appreciate drive testing and the various hard drive failure modes. An exploded diagram for a Quantum hard

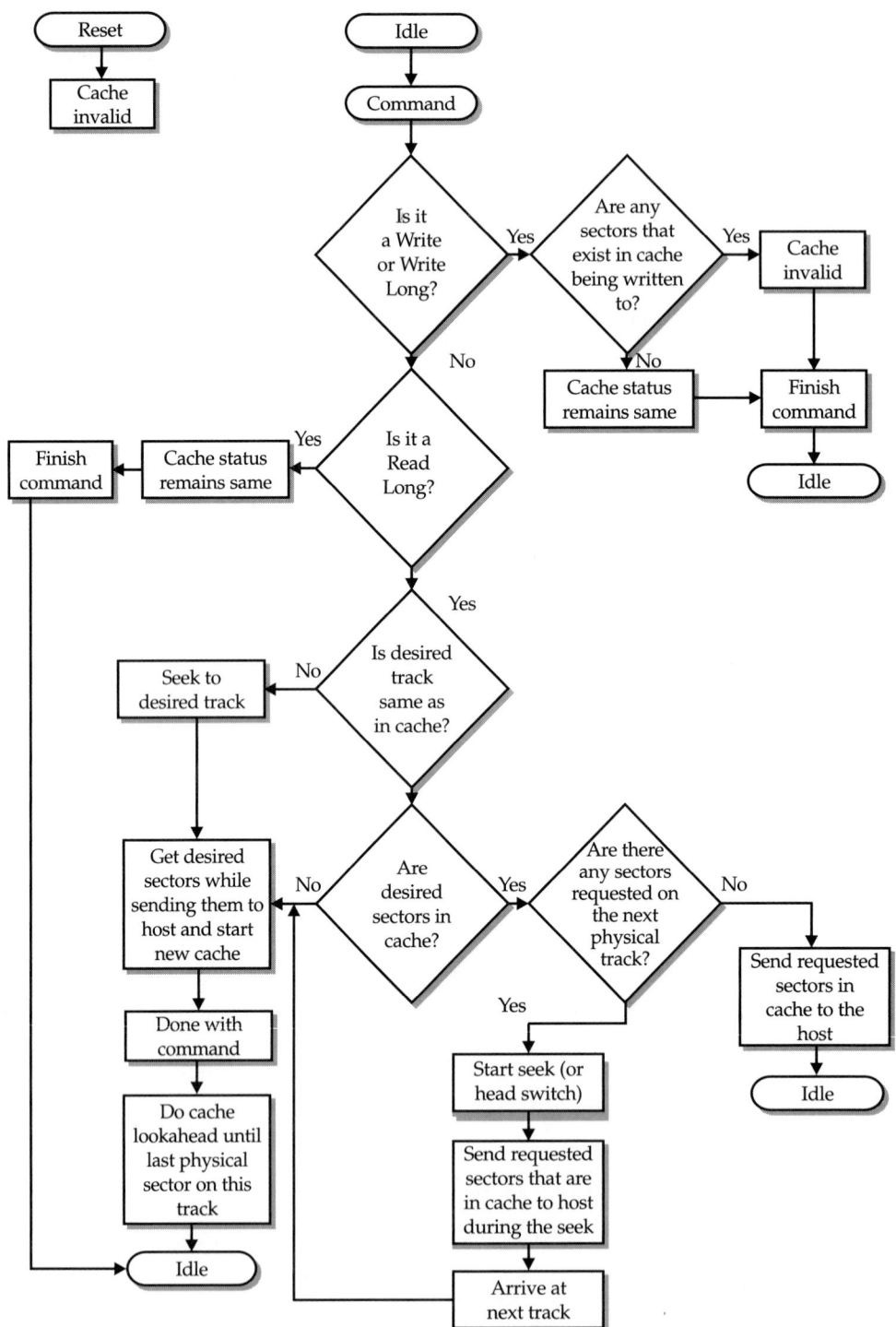

FIGURE   21-8   A cache control algorithm (Maxtor Corporation)

drive is illustrated in Figure 21-9. There are six areas that this chapter concentrates on: the frame, platters, R/W heads, head actuators, spindle motor, and electronics package. Let's look at each area.

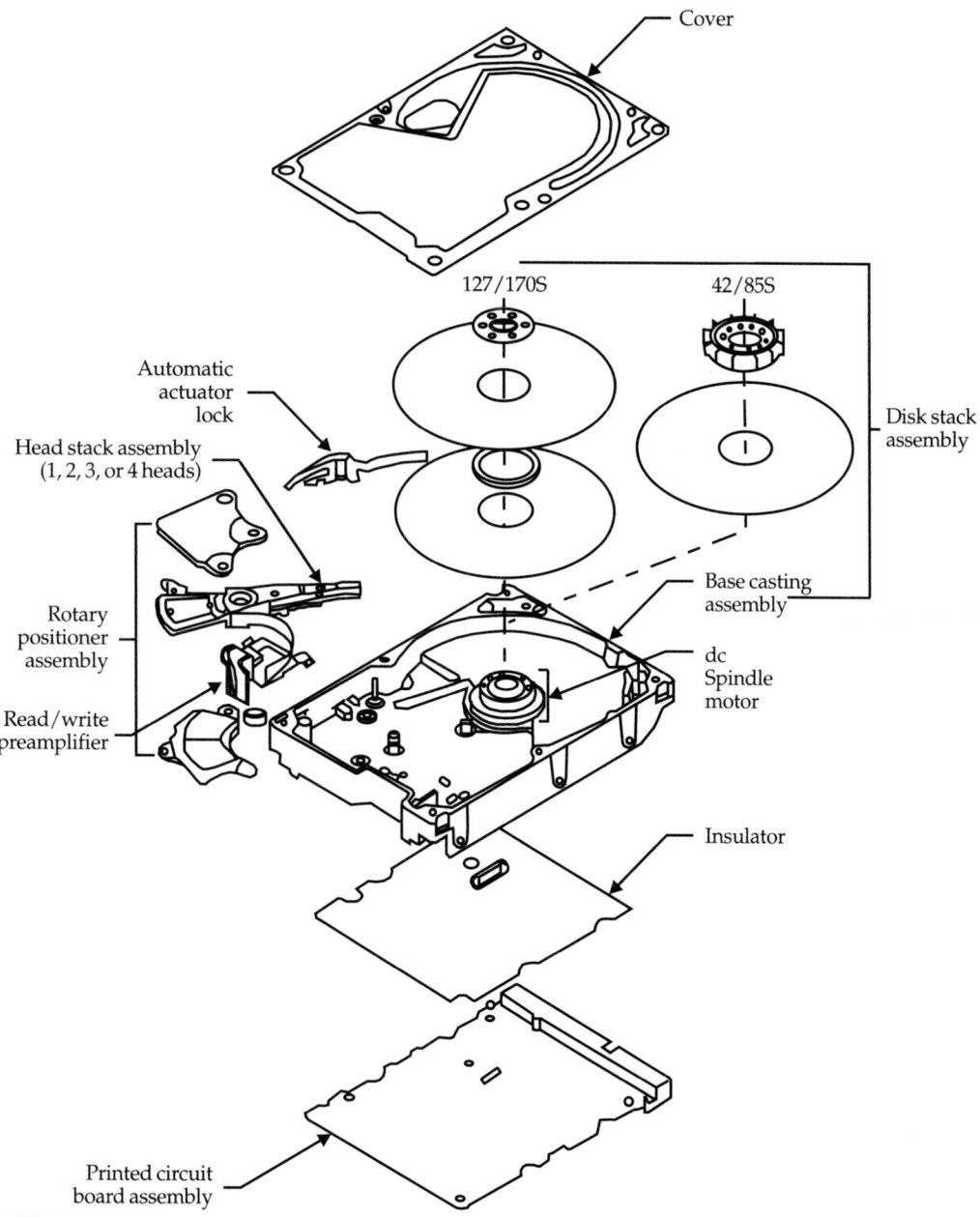

Cover

127/170S

42/85S

Automatic actuator lock

Head stack assembly (1, 2, 3, or 4 heads)

Disk stack assembly

Rotary positioner assembly

Base casting assembly

dc Spindle motor

Read/write preamplifier

Insulator

Printed circuit board assembly

FIGURE 21-9   An exploded diagram of a Quantum hard drive (Quantum Corporation)

FRAME

The mechanical *frame* (1) is remarkably important to the successful operation of a hard drive. The frame (or *chassis*) affects a drive's structural, thermal, and electrical integrity. A frame must be rigid and provide a steady platform for mounting the working components. Larger drives typically use a chassis of cast aluminum, but the small drive in your notebook or sub-notebook computer may use a plastic frame. The particular frame material really depends on the *form factor* (dimensions) of your drive.

PLATTERS

As you probably read earlier in this chapter, *platters* (2) are relatively heavy duty disks of aluminum, glass, or ceramic composite material. Platters are then coated on both sides with a layer of magnetic material (the actual media) and covered with a protective layer. Finished and polished platters are then stacked and coupled to the *spindle motor* (3). Note that some drives may only use one platter. Before the platter stack is fixed to the chassis, the *R/W head assembly* (4) is fitted in between each disk. There is usually one head per platter side, so a drive with two platters should have three or four heads. During drive operation, the platter stack spins at 5,400 RPM or higher (up to 10000 RPM).

READ/WRITE HEADS

As with floppy drives, read/write (R/W) heads form the interface between a drive's electronic circuitry and magnetic media. During writing, a head translates electronic signals into magnetic flux transitions that saturate points on the media where those transitions take place. A read operation works roughly in reverse. Flux transitions along the disk induce electrical signals in the head that are amplified, filtered, and translated into corresponding logic signals. It is up to the drive's electronics to determine whether a head is reading or writing.

Early R/W heads generally resembled floppy drive heads: soft iron cores with a core of 8 to 34 turns of fine copper wire. Such heads were physically large and relatively heavy, limiting the number of tracks available on a platter surface and presenting more inertia to be overcome by the head positioning system. Virtually all current hard drive designs have abandoned classical "wound coil" heads in favor of thin-film R/W heads. Thin-film heads are fabricated in much the same way as chips or platter media using photochemical processes. The result is a very flat, sensitive, small, and durable R/W head, but even thin-film heads use an air gap and 8 to 34 turns of copper wire. The small size and light weight allow for smaller track widths (large drives today can use over 16000 tracks) and faster head travel time. The inherent flatness of thin-film heads helps to reduce flying height to only 5 microns or so.

In assemblies, the heads themselves are attached to long metal arms that are moved by the head actuator motor(s), as shown in Figure 21-10. Read/write "preamp" chips are typically mounted on a small PC board that is attached to the head/actuator assembly. The entire subassembly is sealed in the platter compartment and is generally inaccessible unless opened in a cleanroom environment. The compartment is sealed with a *metal lid/gasket assembly* (6).

HEAD ACTUATORS

Unlike floppy motors that step their R/W heads in and out, hard drives *swing* the heads along a slight arc to achieve radial travel from edge to spindle. Many hard drives use *voice coil motors* (also called *rotary coil motors* or *servos*) to actuate head movement. Voice coil motors (5) work using the same principle as analog meter movements: a permanent magnet is enclosed within two opposing coils. As current flows through the coils, a magnetic field is produced that opposes the permanent magnet. Head arms are

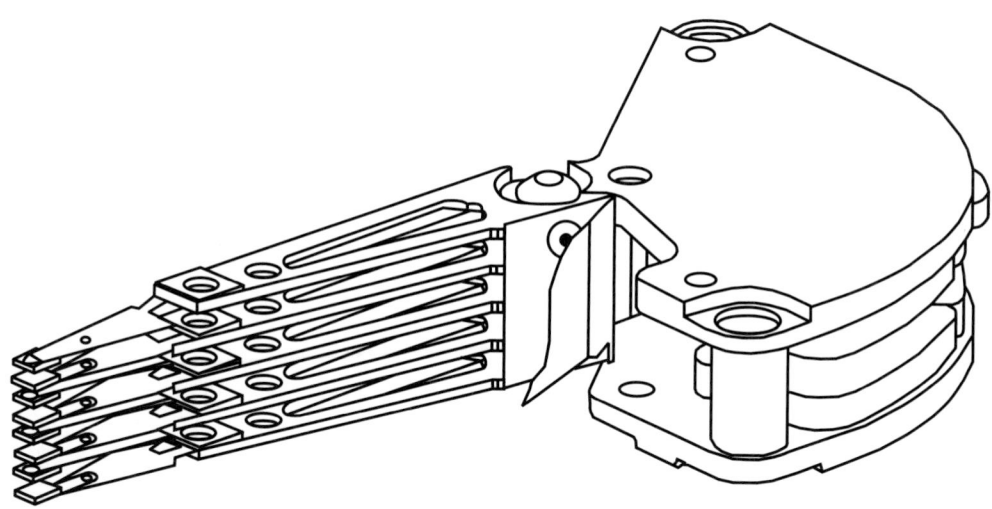

FIGURE 21-10   Close-up of a head actuator assembly (Maxtor Corporation)

attached to the rotating magnet, so the force of opposition causes a deflection that is directly proportional to the amount of driving current. Greater current signals result in greater opposition and greater deflection. Cylinders are selected by incrementing the servo signal and maintaining the signal at the desired level. Voice coil motors are very small and light assemblies that are well suited to fast access times and small hard drive assemblies.

The greatest challenge to head movement is to keep the heads centered on the desired track. Otherwise, aerodynamic disturbances, thermal effects in the platters, and variations in voice coil driver signals can cause head-positioning error. Head position must be constantly checked and adjusted in real time to ensure that desired tracks are followed exactly. The process of track-following is called *servoing* the heads. Information is required to compare the heads' expected position to their actual position—any resulting difference can then be corrected by adjusting the voice coil signal. Servo information is placed somewhere on the platters using a variety of techniques. The servo system uses the phase shift of pulses between adjacent tracks to determine whether heads are centered on the desired track or drifting to one side or another. This book will not be concerned with the particular tracking techniques—only that tracking information must be provided to keep the heads in proper alignment.

SPINDLE MOTOR

One of the major factors that contribute to hard drive performance is the speed at which the media passes under the R/W heads. Media is passed under the R/W heads by spinning the platter(s) at a high rate of speed (at least 3600 RPM and to as high as 10000 RPM). The *spindle motor* is responsible for spinning the platter(s). A spindle motor is typically a brushless, low-profile DC motor (similar in principle to the spindle motors used in floppy disk drives). An *index sensor* (10) provides a feedback pulse signal that detects the spindle as it rotates. The drive's *control electronics* (8) uses the index signal to regulate spindle speed as precisely as possible. Today's drives typically use magnetic sensors that detect iron tabs on the spindle shaft, or optoisolators that monitor holes or tabs rotating along the spindle. The spindle motor and index sensor are also sealed in the platter compartment.

Older hard drives used a rubber or cork pad to slow the spindle to a stop after drive power is removed, but virtually all IDE drives use a technique called *dynamic braking*. When power is applied to a spindle motor, a magnetic field is developed in the motor coils. When power is removed, the magnetic energy stored in the coils is released as a reverse voltage pulse. Dynamic braking channels the energy of that reverse voltage to stop the drive faster and more reliably than physical braking.

DRIVE ELECTRONICS

Hard drives are controlled by a suite of remarkably sophisticated circuitry. The drive electronics board mounted below the chassis contains all of the circuitry necessary to communicate control and data signals with the particular physical interface, maneuver the R/W heads, read or write as required, and spin the platter(s). Each of these functions must be accomplished to high levels of precision. In spite of the demands and complexity involved in drive electronics, the entire circuit can be fabricated on a single PC board responsible for the following functions:

- Controlling the spindle motor and ensuring that the spindle runs at the correct speed
- Controlling the head actuator's positioning to various tracks (and handles servoing)
- Managing all read/write operations
- Implementing power management features
- Handling the geometry translation from *logical* (entered in the CMOS Setup) to *physical* (on the drive platters)
- Managing the internal cache and optimization features (such as pre-fetch)
- Coordinating other functions such as the flow of data over the interface, optimizing multiple requests, converting data to and from the read/write heads, and so on
- Implementing all advanced performance and reliability features (such as SMART)

A practical hard drive is illustrated in the block diagram of Figure 21-11. You should understand the purpose of each part. The heart of this drive is a microcontroller (μC). A μC is basically a customized version of a microprocessor that can process program instructions as well as provide a selection of specialized control signals that are not available from ordinary microprocessors. A μC can be considered an application-specific chip (ASIC). The program that operates this drive is stored in a small programmable read-only memory (PROM) chip. The microcontroller provides signals to the voice-coil driver chip, read/write preamplifier chip, read/write ASIC, and disk controller/ interface ASIC. A controller/interface ASIC works in conjunction with the μC by managing data and control signals on the physical interface. For the drive shown, the ASIC is designed to support a SCSI interface, but variations of this model can use interface ASICs that support IDE interfaces.

The primary activity of the controller/interface ASIC is to coordinate the flow of data into or out of the drive. The controller determines read or write operations, handles clock synchronization, and organizes data flow to the read/write ASIC. The controller also manages the local cache memory (located on the drive itself). Commands received over the physical interface are passed on to the μC for processing and response. The frequency synthesizer helps to synchronize the controller and read/write ASIC. Finally, the disk controller ASIC is responsible for selecting the head position and controlling the spindle and motor driver.

The read/write ASIC is another major chip on the drive's PC board. A R/W ASIC accepts data from the controller chip and translates data into serial signals that are sent to the write driver for writing. The R/W ASIC also receives signals amplified by the read preamp and translates serial signals into parallel

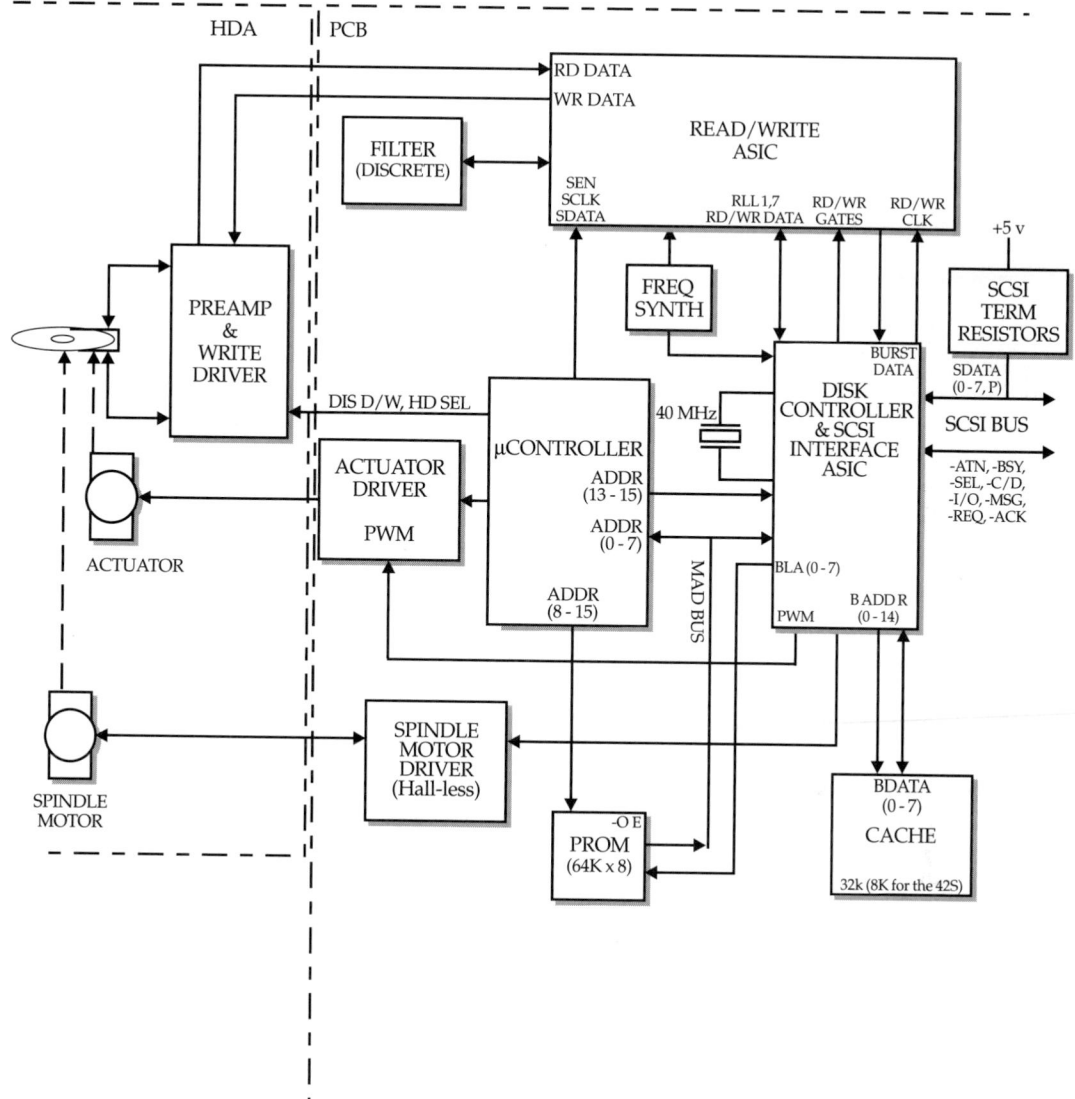

FIGURE 21-11   Block diagram of a Quantum drive electronics system (Quantum Corporation)

digital information available to the controller ASIC. A discrete filter affects the way in which analog signals are handled. R/W heads are connected directly to the read preamplifier/write driver chip, which is little more than a bi-directional amplifier chip.

The actuator driver accepts a logic enable signal from the µC and a proportional logic signal from the controller ASIC. The actuator driver then produces an analog output current that positions the R/W heads by driving a voice coil motor. The spindle motor driver is turned on and off by a logic enable signal from the controller ASIC. Once the spindle motor driver is enabled, it will self-regulate its own speed using feedback from an index sensor. All components within the dotted area marked "HAD" are located within the sealed platter compartment, while other components in the area marked "PCB" are located on the drive PC board. Most of the drive's *intelligence* is contained in the µC, controller ASIC, and R/W ASIC.

Drive Preparation Concepts

You can imagine a disk drive as being a big file cabinet. When the drive is first installed, the "file cabinet" is completely empty—there are no dividers or folders or labels of any kind to organize information. In order to make the drive useful, it must be prepared for use. There are two steps needed to prepare a drive: partitioning and formatting. *Partitioning* divides the physical drive into one or more logical volumes (which receive a drive letter), and *formatting* allows the drive to store files that are suitable to the operating system. As you might imagine, these steps are critically important for the proper operation of a drive. This part of the chapter outlines the essentials of drive preparation and file systems.

PARTITIONING

Partitioning the drive is the process of dividing the physical drive space into pieces (called *partitions* or *logical volumes*). This is one of the first things done when setting up a new hard drive, because partitions are one of the major disk structures that define how the disk is laid out. In fact, you *must* partition a drive even if you're only putting all of the space into a single volume. Partitioning is important because partition size and type will have an important impact on both performance and disk space efficiency.

There are several file systems in service today, but operating systems like DOS and Windows 9x/Me continue to use the file allocation table (FAT) system. The main criticism of the FAT is that sectors are grouped and assigned as *clusters*—and this can be a wasteful use of drive space (especially for large drives where up to 64 sectors—32KB—may be in a single cluster). One of the newly created partitions will be assigned as the boot partition, and a *master boot record* (MBR) containing special boot code and a partition table will be written to the first sector. The MBR is often referred to as the *master boot sector* (MBS). FDISK is the DOS/Windows utility used for drive partitioning. Different operating systems carry their own partitioning limitations:

■ Versions of MS-DOS and PC-DOS after 3.30 (but before 4.0) have a 32MB per partition limit.

■ All versions of DOS have a 1024 cylinder limitation. To access more cylinders, you'll need a device driver or a controller card that offers a "translate mode" (for example, LBA).

■ DOS and Windows 95 are limited to 2.1GB per partition.

■ Versions of Windows NT 4.0 and earlier are limited to a 4.2GB boot partition.

■ Windows 95 OSR2 and Windows 98 use FAT32 partitions that can support up to 2TB partitions.

There are a few third-party partitioning tools such as Partition Magic by PowerQuest.

Understanding the "Master Boot Record"

As you've seen, the master boot record (or MBR) is information that is normally stored in the first sector of the hard drive. This information is simply a small data structure that identifies where an operating system (OS) is located on the drive so that the OS can be loaded into the system's memory (RAM) at boot time. The MBR contains two elements; executable code (a "program") and a *partition table*, which identifies each partition residing on the hard drive. The MBR executable code begins the boot process by looking up the partition table to determine what partition holds the operating system. It then loads the boot sector of the partition containing the OS into RAM, and transfers execution of the "program" to the partition boot sector. The partition boot sector then finishes loading the operating system files into RAM.

Creating/Restoring the MBR In actual practice, the MBR is created during the partition process (using FDISK). If the MBR is corrupted or damaged, you can often restore the MBR using FDISK with the /MBR switch, such as:

```
C:\> FDISK /MBR                      <Enter>
```

Remember to back up as much of the drive *before* attempting this command. It should not corrupt the drive partitions or its data, but it *could*—any changes to the boot information can render the data on your drive inaccessible.

The MBR and "Drive Overlays" When a system BIOS or drive controller will not support the full size of a drive, you typically have the option of upgrading the BIOS (and/or drive controller) or using "drive overlay" software, such as EZ-Drive, MaxBlast, Data Lifeguard Tools, or other products. The use of "overlay" software will effect the way an MBR is configured. When drive overlay software (EZ-Drive in this discussion) controls a hard drive, the MBR is stored on the *second* sector of the hard drive—the first sector contains EZ-Drive code (also known as EZ-BIOS). Sectors 3 through 17 also contain EZ-Drive code that is referred to as the "INT13 Handler" (INT13 deals with hard disk services). When the system is powered on, it looks at the first sector of the hard drive for boot instructions. In this case, the boot sequence is as follows:

- ■ EZ-Drive code loads from sector 1 on the drive.
- ■ EZ-Drive loads the "INT13 Handler" located in sectors 3 through 17, and uses this information to set up the hard drive for proper access at its full capacity.
- ■ EZ-Drive loads the regular Master Boot Record found on sector 2, which in turn loads the operating system.

Viruses and the MBR A common type of virus is one that replaces the MBR with its own code. Each time a computer is started, the code in the MBR is loaded into memory. If the MBR contains a virus, the virus code is loaded every time a system starts up, making this type of virus *very* dangerous. Some MBR viruses do little more than display a message on your screen, while others can destroy your data. An MBR virus usually enters a system through a floppy disk that the system accessed either at startup or while the system was on. If your BIOS supports an "MBR protection" feature (often referred to as *boot sector virus protection*), this prevents new information from being written to the MBR, so make sure that this feature is *enabled* in the CMOS Setup.

FORMATTING

Even after partitioning, an operating system cannot store files on a drive. A series of data structures must be written to the drive. A *volume boot sector* (VBS), two copies of the *file allocation table* (FAT), and a *root directory* are written to each logical partition. High-level formatting also checks and locks out bad sectors so that they will not be used during normal operation. FORMAT is the DOS utility used for high-level formatting. It is interesting to note that the FORMAT utility will perform both low-level and high-level formatting for a floppy disk, but *not* for a hard drive.

FAT BASICS

Microsoft DOS and Windows 9x/Me use a file allocation table (FAT) approach to organize files on the drive. Individual sectors are organized into groups called *clusters*, and each cluster is assigned a number. Floppy drives and some early hard drives used a 12-bit number known as FAT12, but hard drives typically used a 16-bit number (called FAT16). The newest releases of Windows 95 (OSR2) and Windows 98/Me assign a 32-bit number to each cluster (called FAT32). By assigning each cluster its own number, it is possible to store files in any available (unused) clusters throughout the drive without worrying about the file's size. As files are erased, those clusters become available for re-use. Overall, the FAT system has proven to be a versatile and reliable file management system.

The problem with the FAT system is that you can have only as many clusters as can be specified by the number of bits available. For a 12-bit FAT, you can only have 4,096 (2^{12}) clusters. For a 16-bit FAT, you can have 65,536 (2^{16}) clusters. If the drive is 120MB, each cluster must then be about 1.8KB (120MB / 65,536)—2KB in actual practice. If the drive were 500MB, each cluster must be about 7.6KB (540MB / 65,536)—8KB in actual practice. Since only *one* file can be assigned to any given cluster, the entire space for that cluster is assigned (even if the file is very small). So if you were to store a 2KB file in an 8KB cluster, you'd waste 6KB (8KB-2KB)! This wasted space is known as *slack space*. Of course, the FAT12 system was abandoned while hard drives were still about 32MB, but you get the idea that very large drives can waste a serious amount of space when using a FAT system.

Another frequent complaint about FAT file systems is the phenomenon of *file fragmentation*. Since clusters are all independent and clusters are assigned wherever they can be found, a file requiring more than one cluster can be scattered anywhere on the disk. For example, suppose you're editing a large image (it can take several MBs). The file may use the 20 available clusters on track 345, two more available clusters on track 1012, 50 available clusters on track 2011, and so on all across the disk. In theory, fragmentation is simply a harmless side effect of the FAT system. But in practice, badly fragmented files can force the hard drive to work unusually hard chasing down the various clusters associated with the file. Not only does this slow the drive's effective performance, but the extra work required of the drive may ultimately shorten its working life. The best way to correct this issue is to periodically *defragment* the disk with a utility like *Disk Defragmenter*. Defragmenting the disk will rearrange all the clusters so that all of the clusters for any given file will be contiguous.

FAT16

DOS (including the DOS under Windows 9x/Me) uses the FAT16 file system to store data. The FAT16 system uses 16-bit-cluster address numbers, which allow up to 65,536 clusters. Under FAT16, a cluster can be as big as 32KB, which translates into a maximum partition size of 2,147,483,648 bytes (2.1GB—65,536 × 32,768). While a 16-bit cluster number is much more efficient than a 12-bit cluster number, every file *must* take up at least one cluster—even if the file size is much smaller than the cluster. For the very large drives we have today, the correspondingly large clusters can result in a significant amount of slack space. If the physical drive is larger than 2.1GB, you must create subsequent logical partitions to utilize the additional space. For example, if you have a 3.1GB drive, you can create one 2.1GB partition, than create a second 1.0GB partition. One way to reduce *slack space* is to create a larger number of smaller logical partitions—doing this results in smaller clusters and creates more drive letters (one for each partition on the drive).

Partitioning Large Hard Drives

Chances are that you're already familiar with the DOS FDISK partitioning utility and have used it at one time or another to partition older hard drives. However, large hard drives (over 2GB) present an unusual wrinkle for technicians—DOS and Windows 95 support partitions only up to 2GB. When you install a hard drive that's larger than 2GB, you need to create multiple partitions on the drive. Otherwise, you won't be able to take advantage of the full drive capacity. The procedure below offers a step-by-step guide for partitioning large drives.

Partitioning Large Drives with FAT16 FDISK   If you're working with large hard drives under DOS or an early version of Windows, follow the procedure below to partition hard drives using the FAT16 version of FDISK:

1. At the FDISK Options menu, select "4. Display partition information" and press ENTER. If the partition information display indicates that there are existing partition(s) on the drive, these partitions must be deleted *before* proceeding (select "3. Delete partition information" on the FDISK Options menu to remove any existing partitions).

2. At the FDISK Options menu, select "1. Create DOS partition or Logical DOS drive" and press ENTER. The "Create DOS partition or Logical DOS Drive" menu is displayed. Select "1. Create Primary DOS partition" and press ENTER.

3. The message "Do you wish to use the maximum available size for a Primary DOS Partition and make the Partition active (Y/N)" is displayed. Press N and press ENTER.

When this message is displayed, you *must* respond with N. If you reply Y, a primary partition of 2.048GB will be created, and the system will not be able to access the remainder of the drive's capacity unless the partition is deleted.

4. Type in the size of the Primary Partition (in MB). This value can be anywhere from 1MB to 2,048MB (default). Then press the ENTER key. The message "Primary DOS Partition created" is displayed. Press ESC to continue.

5. At the FDISK Options menu, select "1. Create DOS partition or Logical DOS drive" and press ENTER. The "Create DOS partition or Logical DOS Drive" menu is displayed. Select "2. Create Extended DOS partition" and press ENTER.

6. The "Create Extended DOS Partition" screen is displayed. Press ENTER to place the remaining available space on the drive into the Extended DOS partition.

If all of the remaining drive space is not placed into the Extended DOS partition, the total capacity of the hard drive will not be available to the system.

7. Press ESC to continue when the FDISK message "Extended DOS Partition created" appears on the monitor. FDISK will now prompt you to create logical drives for the Extended DOS partition. The message "Enter logical drive size in megabytes or percent of disk space (%)..." is displayed.

8. Type the value desired for the capacity value of the logical drive size (up to 2,048MB) and press ENTER. If you choose a value less than the displayed total size, you must continue entering drive sizes until all of the available space has been assigned logical drive letters.

Remember that each logical DOS drive created represents a drive letter to the operating system (such as C:, D:, E:, or F:).

9. Press ESC to continue when the FDISK message "All available space in the Extended DOS Partition is assigned to logical drives" appears.

10. If the drive is going to be the primary boot drive, select "2. Set active partition" and press ENTER at the FDISK Options menu. The "Set Active Partition" screen is displayed and the message "Enter the number of the partition you want to make active" is displayed. Press 1, then press ENTER. The message "Partition 1 made active" is displayed. Press ESC.

11. Press ESC to exit FDISK. Exiting FDISK under DOS will cause the system to reboot. Under Windows 95, the system may return to the **c:\windows\command>** prompt, and the user will have to reboot the system manually.

12. After the system reboots, each drive letter assigned to the partitioned hard drive must be formatted with FORMAT. You should now be able to use the drive.

There have been a number of problems reported with the Windows 95 version of FDISK. As a rule, use the DOS 6.22 version of FDISK or the 16-bit version of FDISK included with OSR2.

FAT32

Obviously, the limitations of FAT16 present a serious issue with hard drives over 8GB. Since FDISK can create only four partitions of 2GB each, any space above 8GB may be inaccessible (not to mention the large number of drive letters). Microsoft responded by developing a 32-bit FAT system implemented in a service release of Windows 95 (called *OSR2*) and now standard in Windows 98/Me. The upper four bits are reserved, so the system will actually access 268,435,456 (2^{28}) clusters (over 256 million clusters). This allows single partitions of 8GB with clusters only 4KB in size—the maximum size of any given partition is 2TB (yes, *terrabytes*—thousands of gigabytes). FAT32 also eliminates the fixed size for a root directory, so you can have as many files and directories in the root as you want.

On the surface, this probably sounds like a great deal, but there are some issues that you'll need to consider before updating to FAT32. First, DOS applications (without being rewritten) can access only files up to 2GB, and Win32 applications can work with files up to 4GB. By itself, that's not so bad, but FAT32 partitions are accessible only through FAT32-aware operating system versions, such as the OSR2-enhanced Windows 95 and Windows 98/Me and their corresponding versions of DOS 7.X—no other operating system can read the partitions (including Windows NT). Also, any disk utilities written for FAT16 won't work for FAT32 (and using them can seriously damage your data).

Even though the OSR2 release ships with FAT32 versions of FDISK, FORMAT, SCANDISK, and DEFRAG, the version of DriveSpace 3 will *not* support FAT32. So, if you're using drive compression, you may need to remove the compression support before moving to FAT32. Further, there are older APIs (application programming interfaces) in service that simply won't support FAT32, so some programs may refuse to work outright until the software is recompiled with FAT32-compliant APIs. DOS device drivers (such as those needed to support SCSI devices) will also have to be updated for FAT32. In other words, you may lose some SCSI device functionality until suitable drivers become available. Finally, the OSR2 version of Windows 95 appears to *decrease* FAT32 drive performance (though that's not really an issue under Windows 98/Me).

Partitioning and Formatting for FAT32

Before you make the decision to use FAT32, you'll need to become familiar with the issues involved in partitioning and formatting. The basic steps in drive preparation are the same as for FAT16, but FAT32 introduces a few wrinkles that you should be aware of. This part of the chapter describes the general process used to partition and format the drive under FAT32. First, a FAT32 partition can be created (with Windows 95 OSR2 or Windows 98/Me) only under the following circumstances:

- The hard drive *must* be greater than 528MB in *total* capacity.
- The partition size must be greater than 528MB.
- You need an OSR2 Setup Disk or OSR2 Startup Disk made from another OSR2-configured PC (or a suitable Windows 98/Me Startup Disk).
- When the OSR2/98 FDISK prompts "Do you wish to enable large disk support? Y or N," you'll need to answer Y. If you answer N, a FAT16 partition will be created.

Partitioning Large Hard Drives with FAT32 FDISK   If you're working with large hard drives under a later version of Windows (or its corresponding DOS version), follow the procedure below to partition hard drives using the FAT32 version of FDISK:

1. Boot the PC with the Windows 95 OSR2 (or Windows 98/Me) Startup Disk.

2. At the "Welcome to Setup" screen, press the F3 key twice—doing this will terminate the execution of the Setup program and take you to the A: prompt.

If you have a Startup Disk from another PC, you can boot from that disk instead and avoid the hassle of exiting the OSR2 "Setup" routine.

3. Type **FDISK** and press ENTER. You'll be prompted with "Do you wish to enable large disk support? Y or N."

4. Press Y to create a FAT32 partition and press ENTER. At this point, the FDISK Options menu will appear on the screen. If there is more than one hard drive in the system, use option "5. Change current fixed drive" to select the desired drive to partition. Be careful—partitioning the wrong drive will render any existing data on that drive inaccessible.

5. Select option "4. Display Partition Information" and press ENTER. For a brand new hard drive, FDISK should respond: "No Partitions Defined." Any preexisting partitions (FAT16 partitions) must be *deleted* before continuing. Remember, this will delete *all* existing data on the hard drive.

6. Press the ESC key to return to the FDISK Options menu, then select option "1. Create DOS partition or Logical DOS drive" and press ENTER. Next, select option "1. Create Primary DOS Partition" and press ENTER.

7. After FDISK verifies the drive integrity, it will prompt you with "Do you wish to use the maximum available size for a Primary DOS Partition and make the Partition active (Y/N)?" Press Y and press ENTER.

8. Exit FDISK by pressing the ESC key until you see the message "You must restart the system for changes to take effect." Press the ESC key to exit FDISK and remove the floppy disk in drive A:. Reboot the computer using CTRL-ALT-DEL if necessary.

Formatting Large Hard Drives with FAT32 FORMAT   If you're working with large hard drives under a later version of Windows (or its corresponding DOS version), follow the procedure below to format hard drive partitions using the FAT32 version of FORMAT:

1. Boot the PC with the Windows 95 OSR2 (or Windows 98/Me) Startup Disk.

2. At the "Welcome to Setup" screen, press the F3 key twice—doing this will terminate the execution of the Setup program and take you to the A: prompt.

> If you have an OSR2 Startup Disk from another PC, you can boot from that disk instead and avoid the hassle of exiting the OSR2 "Setup" routine.

3. Type **FORMAT** *<drive letter >***:** and press ENTER to start formatting (such as **FORMAT D:**). After FORMAT starts, you'll see the message: "WARNING all data on non removable disk drive <letter:> will be lost proceed with format? Y/N."

4. Press Y and press ENTER. The FORMAT utility will then prepare the selected hard drive partition for use with FAT32.

Using the FAT32 "Drive Converter"

Windows 98 provides a "drive converter" that allows you to convert FAT16 partitions to FAT32 format. After you convert your hard disk to FAT32, you *cannot* convert back to the original FAT system. Before you convert to the FAT32 file system, uninstall any utilities or tools that protect or encrypt the MBR or partition table (for example, uninstall Bootlock included with Symantec Norton Your Eyes Only). The simplest method is to just type **cvt** *<drive>***: /cvt32** and then press ENTER. Remember that *<drive>* is the drive that you want to convert to the FAT32 file system. Another step-by-step approach is listed below:

1. Click Start, select Programs, highlight Accessories, choose System Tools, click Drive Converter (FAT32), and then click Next.

2. In the Drives box, click the drive that you want to convert to the FAT32 file system.

3. Click Next, then click OK.

4. Click Next, click Next, and then click Next again.

5. Allow the conversion process to complete.

6. When the conversion is complete, click Finish and reboot the PC if necessary.

> The FAT32 converter may fail if your hard drive is less than 512MB or has bad sectors (often resulting in data corruption).

Drive Capacity Limits

Capacity limitations are encountered whenever a computer system BIOS (and operating system) is unable to identify (or *address*) physical locations on a hard drive. This is *not* a problem with the design or structure of the hard drive itself, but rather a limitation of the system's BIOS or operating system. For the BIOS, it is not capable of translating the addresses of the sectors beyond a certain number of cylinders—thus limiting the capacity of the hard drive to less that its full amount. For the operating system, the file structure—the File Allocation Table—is limited in the number of physical locations (or addresses) that can be entered in the FAT. Drive manufacturers first encountered BIOS limitations in 1994 with the release of

540MB (ATA-2/EIDE) hard drives. Operating system limitations were discovered with the release of hard drives larger than 2.1GB. Your exact limitations vary depending on your BIOS version and the operating system. Today, you'll probably encounter BIOS with limitations at 2.1GB, 4.2GB, 8.4GB, and 32GB levels. FAT16 operating systems like DOS and Windows 95 have a 2.1GB partition size limitation. Windows NT has a 4.2GB partition size limit. Windows 95 OSR2 and Windows 98/Me can access much larger drives using the FAT32 file system. This part of the chapter is intended to help you understand and correct these drive size limitations.

TYPICAL CAPACITY LIMITS

One of the most common problems with hard drives (especially when trying to add a new disk to an older system) is finding that not all of the drive is actually accessible. This is almost always due to BIOS and operating system issues that result from the shortsighted planning of the designers who invented hard disk structures, access routines, and operating systems many years ago. In some cases, they are due to actual hardware or software bugs that are not detected until hard drives grow beyond a certain size. Fortunately, there are now solutions to most of these problems. This section examines many of these issues so you can understand and get beyond these limitations.

1024 Cylinders (528MB)

The 528MB limitation for standard IDE/ATA hard disks started showing up in systems starting around 1994. This limitation caused a hard disk with a size *over* 528MB to appear as having only 528MB under some circumstances. This problem resulted from the geometry-specification limitations of the IDE/ATA standard and the BIOS Int 13h standard. Since only the lowest common denominator of both standards can be used, the maximum drive size that the BIOS can "see" is 1,024 cylinders×16 heads×63 sectors×512 bytes/sector, which equals 528,482,304 bytes (528MB). The best way to correct this problem is to upgrade the BIOS to a version that supports translation—logical block addressing (LBA)—or to install overlay software.

 This limit is referred to as the 504MB or the 528MB barrier—depending on whether you're looking at binary or decimal MB.

4,096 Cylinders (2.1GB)

As you saw above, the basic problem with BIOS-related capacity limits is that the normal BIOS on older PCs is not designed to handle hard drives with over 1,024 cylinders. Every hard disk made today uses far more than 1,024 cylinders, causing a drastic reduction in available capacity. Systems with enhanced BIOS can employ LBA translation to get around the 1,024-cylinder limitation and support larger drives. Some BIOS versions (even supporting translation) from around 1996 fail with more than 4,095 cylinders. This essentially causes the same problems at the 528MB barrier to occur all over again at the 2.1GB level.

It takes 12 bits to represent up to 4,096 cylinders, but due to poor BIOS code writing on some systems, only 12 bits of the cylinder number are available. Since it takes a 13th bit to handle numbers above 4,096 and only 12 bits are available, the BIOS is unable to "see" more than 2.1GB on the disk. On some BIOS, 4,097 cylinders may show up as only 1 cylinder if the 13th bit is just ignored and the lower-order 12 bits are used by themselves. The best way to correct this problem is to upgrade the BIOS to a version that supports more than 4,096 cylinders or to install overlay software.

 Don't confuse this problem with the FAT16 limitation of 2.1GB shown below—they are separate issues.

FAT16 Partition Limit (2.1GB)

This 2.1GB capacity barrier is a file system problem that has nothing to do with the BIOS and is a limitation on disk volumes in the FAT16 file system. Given the way that disks use clusters, it is not possible to have more than 2.1GB in a single partition under the DOS or Windows 3.x/95A operating systems. Under Windows NT, the limit is 4GB rather then 2.1GB with FAT partitions (NTFS partitions do not have this limitation). If you install a drive over 2GB into a machine using regular FAT16, you may use the entire disk (assuming that you aren't limited by one of the other BIOS-related barriers). However, to access the full capacity of the disk, you must partition it into sections. Since this limitation is a function of the operating system, it affects IDE/ATA and SCSI hard disks equally.

This limitation does *not* apply to disks formatted using FAT32 introduced in Windows 95 OSR2. It is also not a problem in Windows 98, Windows Me and Windows 2000. There is also the NTFS file system, supported by Windows NT and Windows 2000, which uses a completely different set of structures and can have enormous partitions. The best solution to this issue is to repartition and reformat the drive using FAT32 utilities, then install a FAT32-aware operating system such as Windows Me.

6,322 Cylinders (3.26GB)

This is one of the most obscure size limitations that you may encounter—affecting only a small percentage of systems. It appears that the BIOS cannot handle drive geometry with more than 6,322 cylinders. Attempting to set a higher cylinder value than 6,322 may cause the PC to hang. This typically limits the capacity on such systems to about 3.26GB (6,322 cylinders×16 heads×63sectors×512 bytes/sector). The best way to correct this problem is to upgrade the BIOS to a version that supports more than 6,322 cylinders or install overlay software.

 The significance of 6,322 cylinders is unclear, so there is no apparent reason why this limitation exists.

Phoenix BIOS 4.0x Limit (3.28GB)

This is another obscure size limitation due specifically to a programming error in a few types of systems made in the mid-to-late 1990s. Some systems that use Phoenix BIOS (notably versions 4.03 or 4.04) have a problem with the BIOS routine that calculates the size of hard disk drives. This problem is also odd because the barrier actually isn't a single consistent level—it seems to vary with the geometry parameters, and behavior can be different based on the values entered.

Assuming standard IDE head and sector values of 16 and 63, respectively, the cylinder field can have a maximum value of 6,349 without any problems, resulting in a maximum capacity of 3.28GB. If a cylinder value of 6,350 to 8,322 is used, the CMOS Setup program may lock up. Cylinder values of 8,323 to 14,671 apparently work, but the displayed drive size is incorrect. Subsequent versions of this Phoenix BIOS code have corrected this bug, which occurred several years ago. If you still have a system exhibiting this problem, you may be able to get a BIOS upgrade to correct the problem.

 BIOS code is initially written by the BIOS maker and is subsequently tailored by specific system or motherboard manufacturers. This means that some implementations of these BIOS versions may not have this bug while others will.

8,192 Cylinders (4.22GB)

The normal way of circumventing cylinder limitations is to use BIOS geometry translation. Basically, translation works by dividing the hard disk's number of cylinders by a binary number, such as 2, 4, 8, or 16, and then multiplying the number of heads by the same number. This lets the number of cylinders that the BIOS "sees" remain below the Int 13h limit of 1,024. However, this translation causes a problem in some systems when using a hard disk over about 4GB in size.

When the number of cylinders on the drive is between 8,192 and 16,383, the number typically used for translation is 16. This *should* actually work because it overcomes the BIOS issues and results in geometry that falls within acceptable limits. But a problem was discovered when drives first exceeded 8,192 cylinders around 1997—DOS and early versions of Windows failed when presented with a drive that had (effectively) 256 heads. This is actually a barrier caused by both the operating system and the system BIOS. The operating system should have been able to handle 256 heads, but the BIOS was creating the problem due to its translation.

When this problem surfaced, the easiest way to deal with it was to change the way the BIOS did translation so that BIOS stopped creating translated geometries that used 256 heads. One common way that this was done was to use 15 as the translation factor instead of 16. To help avoid some of these problems, many hard disk manufacturers also changed their geometries to use only 15 heads instead of 16. So instead of a drive being specified with 12,496 cylinders, 16 heads, and 63 sectors, it might use 13,329 cylinders, 15 heads, and 63 sectors. If you have a BIOS that suffers from this 256 head problem, you will need to upgrade the BIOS or install drive overlay software.

240 Head Limit (7.93GB)

The BIOS Int 13h interface normally restricts some drives to 8.46GB, given the limits of 1,024 cylinders, 256 heads, and 63 sectors. In some systems, however, the Int 13h interface restriction results in a smaller limit of 7.93GB. As with the 8,192 cylinder limit, DOS and some Windows versions cannot handle translated geometry that specifies 256 heads. To get around this, some BIOS versions have changed their translation method so that only 240 heads are presented to the operating system. This fixes the 256 head problem, but shaves some capacity off the Int13h limit. The 1,024 cylinder and 63 sector restrictions remain, but with only 240 heads the maximum drive capacity becomes 1,024 cylinders×240 heads×63 sectors×512 bytes/sector = 7,927,234,560 bytes. If you find that you're not getting full capacity from an 8GB drive, a BIOS upgrade is probably in order.

The Int 13 Limit (8.46GB)

Often just called the *8GB Barrier*, this limit is one of the most important for hard drives. Now that disk capacities have exceeded 60–80GB, this gets the attention that the old 528MB limit got in the mid-to-late 1990s. Many people run into this particular barrier as they attempt to upgrade systems originally purchased in the late 1990s with hard disks originally between 1GB and 8GB in size. This issue is also based on a BIOS limitation, but with this particular barrier, we are actually faced with the traditional limits of how hard disks are used in the PC.

The Int 13h interface standard used by the BIOS allocates 10 bits for the cylinder number (thus a maximum of 1,024 cylinders), 8 bits for the head number (maximum of 256 heads), and 6 bits for the sector number (maximum of 63 sectors, since the number 0 is not used). Multiplying these together with 512 bytes per sector, you get a maximum of 8,455,716,864 bytes (8.45GB). This is the *largest* hard disk size that can be addressed using the *standard* Int 13h interface. Unlike the old 528MB limit, there is *no* translation that can work around this because it isn't caused by a *combination* of limitations like the 528MB barrier is. To overcome this limit, there must be a change in the *way* hard disks are accessed. This means leaving Int 13h behind and using Int 13h extensions.

Int 13h extensions require support from *both* the BIOS and the operating system. Some older operating systems do not support Int13h extensions. For example, all versions of non-Windows DOS (6.22 and earlier) and Windows NT version 3.5 will not support Int 13h extensions and cannot use hard disks over 8.4 GB in size. Windows 98/Me should have no trouble supporting Int 13h extensions with a suitable BIOS.

The Windows 95 Limit (32GB)

Microsoft officially announced in 1999 that Windows 95 does not support hard disks over 32GB in size. While the cause for this limitation is unclear (Microsoft does not seem to document the underlying cause), upgrading the operating system to Windows 98/Me should correct the trouble.

65,536 Cylinders (33.8GB)

Dubbed the *32GB Barrier*, this is a relatively recent hard drive limit (it showed up in early 1999) and is yet another in a long series of limits caused by the inability of a BIOS version to handle a particular number of cylinders (much like previous smaller barriers). In this case, some versions of Award BIOS cannot handle drives that have more than 65,535 cylinders. Since hard disk parameters usually use 16 heads and 63 sectors, this works out to a capacity of about 33.8GB before trouble occurs. As of about June 1999, this problem had been corrected, so it is most likely to show up on systems purchased before that time. As a BIOS issue, the best corrective action is usually to upgrade the BIOS from the system or motherboard manufacturer.

The ATA Limit (137GB)

To circumvent past hard disk barriers, most modern hard disks are addressed using logical block addressing and a sector number. Even when we're not faced with discrete cylinder, sector, and head limits, the number of bits that define the sector number will eventually become a problem. In the case of the ATA interface, 28 bits are used for the sector number interface between the operating system, BIOS, and hard drive. This means a drive can have a maximum of 2^{28} sectors. At 512 bytes per sector, that's approximately 137.4GB. There aren't any ATA hard disks that large now, but given the rapid improvements in drive capacity, we may be faced with 137GB drive issues by late 2002 and into 2003. This may become the great "barrier" of the future.

To overcome this issue, fairly significant changes must be made to the interface between the hard disk and the rest of the system. The T13 technical committee is already working on several different proposals for expanding ATA addressing from 28 bits to either 48 or 64 bits—either of which would allow monstrous hard disk sizes. Even the 48-bit proposal would result in drive sizes a million times larger than the current limit.

HOW BIOS HANDLES LIMITS

When you install a hard drive into a system where the BIOS is unable to handle its size, the system can react in a number of different ways. The exact response will depend on the system, the age of the BIOS, and the integrity of the BIOS routines. But in just about all cases, the problems are normally caused by more cylinders than the BIOS supports. There are four typical ways in which a BIOS can fail to support the cylinder count:

■ **Truncation**   When presented with a logical geometry containing more cylinders than it can handle, the BIOS may simply *truncate* the total to the maximum it supports. This is usually seen in older BIOS versions that does not support more than 1,024 or 4,096 cylinders and is also common in systems that do not support Int 13h extensions. Generally, truncation wastes some space on the drive but is still preferable to the other possible responses.

■ **Wrap Around**   Some old BIOS versions assume that the number of cylinders will always be 1,024 or below and look only at the bottom 10 bits of the cylinder number coming from the hard disk. As a result, the BIOS counts up to 1,024 and then wraps around to zero again and starts over. So if you tried to use a drive with 3,500 cylinders, the BIOS would "see" only 428 cylinders, because it would count up 1,024 three times (to yield 3,072), wrap around three times, and then end up with 428 cylinders (3,500 minus 3,072). The same thing can happen to a BIOS that support only 4,096 cylinders—it may look only at the bottom 12 bits. This means that in some cases you can put a 2.5GB drive into your system and end up with only about 400 MB of usable space showing up.

■ **Incorrect Reporting**   Some BIOS reports the true number of logical cylinders that the drive has, suggesting that your system supports the full size of the hard disk. However, the BIOS has no real perception of the number. When you try to partition and format the hard disk, you will be stuck with the 1,024 or 4,096 limit. This is a BIOS issue that has confused and frustrated even the best technicians.

■ **System Failure**   Some BIOS versions will totally lock up if you try to use them with a disk larger than they can support. While this behavior is relatively rare, it is seen more frequently with larger and more obscure drive limits. If the system locks up when you try to autodetect or enter drive geometry, it's time for a BIOS upgrade.

OVERCOMING CAPACITY LIMITS

As hard drive capacity has reached and exceeded each size limit, various hardware and software techniques have evolved to support these larger disks. Some of these solutions are simpler and more elegant than others—some are based on *fixing* the BIOS problem, while others are oriented more towards *working around* it. In general, the simpler solutions have met with the best results. More complex solutions (especially with software drivers) tend to suffer more incompatibilities and other issues. There are typically four solutions to overcome capacity limits:

■ **BIOS upgrades**   These are usually the most reliable and elegant solutions, and with the advent of flash BIOS, the upgrade can usually be downloaded and installed for free (often without ever opening the system). BIOS upgrades are considered to be the most effective long-term solutions for most capacity problems.

■ **BIOS expansion cards**   Basically these are just BIOS chips on an expansion card that installs in a motherboard slot to supplement (replace) the motherboard's BIOS for the IDE/ATA controllers. The new BIOS code takes over for the hard disk controller code, and lets you get around most size barriers—you continue to use the IDE/ATA connectors on your existing motherboard or controller card.

■ **Controller upgrades**   Rather than just install a BIOS card, the entire drive controller can be replaced as an expansion card (along with its own onboard BIOS code). You'd then move your drives to the new controller and disable the motherboard's drive controller in the CMOS Setup. Controller upgrades are very popular because they also allow for the newest drive technologies. For example, a UDMA/100 drive controller card can replace an aging EIDE controller and allow for much larger drives.

■ **Overlay software**   Also called *dynamic drive overlays* (DDOs), this software overrides some of the BIOS code in your motherboard or hard disk controller, allowing access to the full size of a new hard disk on an older system. The software must be loaded immediately when the machine is booted to ensure that the driver is in place before any other piece of software tries to access the disk. Otherwise, the disk will not work properly. While such software is usually distributed free with new drives, there are often compatibility and interoperability issues that can result in problems. Overlay software should generally be used as a last resort when no BIOS upgrades are available and it's not possible to upgrade the controller.

Drive Installation/Replacement Guidelines

Hard drives must be installed when building new PCs, adding supplemental drives to an existing system, or replacing outdated or failed drives. The installation process is not terribly complicated, but it can be a bit confusing to the novice. This part of the chapter offers some basic guidelines for IDE-type drive installation.

SELECT JUMPER CONFIGURATIONS

An IDE-type drive may be installed as a master or slave device on any hard drive controller channel. These master/slave settings are handled through one or two jumpers located on the rear of the drive (right next to the 40-pin signal cable connector). One of your first decisions when planning an installation should be to decide the drive's configuration:

■ If you're installing only one hard drive in the system, it must be jumpered as the master device. Note that the master drive on the primary drive controller channel will be the boot drive (that is, the drive C:).

■ If you're installing a second hard drive alongside the first, that second drive must be jumpered as the slave device.

■ If you're installing a second hard drive on the second drive controller channel, it should be jumpered as the master device (any other device should be reconfigured as a slave device).

Refer to the documentation that accompanies your particular hard drive in order to determine the exact master/slave jumper settings. If you do not have the drive documentation handy, check the drive manufacturer's Web site for online information.

ATTACH CABLES AND MOUNT THE DRIVE

The next phase of installation is to slide the drive into a bay, connect the power and signal cables, then secure the drive in place:

1.   Turn off and unplug the PC, then remove the outer cover to expose the computer's drive bays.

2.   Attach one end of the 40-pin drive interface cable to the drive controller connector on your motherboard (or drive controller card). Remember to align pin 1 on the cable (the side of the cable with the blue or red stripe) with pin 1 on the drive controller connector.

A 40-pin/80-conductor cable is *required* to run in Ultra-DMA/66 or Ultra-DMA/100 mode. Attach the blue end of the connector to the drive controller end, the black connector to the master (or single) drive, and the gray connector (if there is one) to the slave drive.

3. Locate an available drive bay for the hard drive. Remove the plastic housing covering the drive bay, then slide the drive inside. Locate the four screw holes needed to mount the drive. In some cases, you may need to attach "mounting rails" to the drive so that the drive will be wide enough to fit in the drive bay. You may mount the drive horizontally (usually with the circuit board down) or vertically.

4. Attach the 40-pin signal cable and the 4-pin power connector to the new drive, then bolt the drive securely into place. Do not overtighten the screws since this may damage the drive. If you do not have an available 4-pin power connector, you may use an appropriate Y-adapter if necessary to "split" power from another drive (preferably the floppy drive).

CONFIGURE THE CMOS SETUP

Before you attempt to partition or format your new drive, you must configure your computer's BIOS to accept the drive (through the CMOS Setup).

1. Turn the computer on. As your computer starts up, watch for a message that describes how to run the CMOS Setup (such as "Press F1 for Setup"). Press the appropriate key to start the CMOS Setup program.

2. Select the basic configuration menu with hard drive settings. To set the drive parameters, choose the *primary master* or *primary slave* (or *secondary master/slave* depending on how you've physically installed the drive).

3. Select Automatic Drive Detection (Auto) if available—this option automatically configures the computer for your new drive. If your BIOS does not provide automatic drive detection, select User-Defined drive settings and enter the appropriate geometry values from the drive documentation. As a rule, Write Precomp and Landing Zone parameters are set to zero.

4. Verify that the LBA Mode is enabled for your drive. Many BIOS versions use the logical block addressing (LBA) mode to access drives with capacities greater than 528MB. Most BIOS will automatically set this mode during the autodetection process.

5. Enable the Ultra-DMA mode if it is available (and both the drive and controller support it).

6. Save the settings and exit the CMOS Setup program. Your computer will automatically reboot.

FINISH THE DRIVE PREPARATION

Boot the system with a Windows 9x/Me Startup Disk containing FDISK and FORMAT, which will be used to partition and format the drive, respectively. Partition the disk with FDISK. If you use a FAT16 version of FDISK, you cannot create partitions greater than 2.1GB. If you use the FAT32 version of FDISK, you can create extremely large partitions. Now use FORMAT to prepare each partition on the drive for your operating system. Again, use the version of the FORMAT utility appropriate to the FAT system you plan on using. (You can find detailed instructions in the "Partitioning and Formatting for FAT32" section above.) After partitioning and formatting, you should be able to access the new drive's letter and to read and write files to it.

REASSEMBLE THE COMPUTER

Double-check all of your signal and power cables to verify that they are secure, then tuck the cables gently into the computer's chassis. Check that there are no loose tools, screws, or cables inside the chassis. Now reattach the computer's outer housing(s).

Drive Testing and Troubleshooting

Fortunately, not all hard drive problems are necessarily fatal. True, you may lose some programs and data (back up your hard drive frequently), but many drive problems are recoverable without resorting to drive replacement. Instead of focusing on repairing a hard drive's electronics or mechanics, today's repair tactics focus on repairing a drive's *data*. By reconstructing or relocating faulty drive information, it is often possible to recover from a wide variety of drive problems—if doing so fails to correct problems, the drive (and/or its controller) must be replaced. Before you begin any sort of drive troubleshooting, you should take the following steps:

- Gather a DOS boot disk or Windows 9x/Me Startup Disk. If you don't have a boot disk on hand, you should make one now *before* continuing.

- Gather your DOS installation disk(s) or Windows 9x/Me Installation CD—if you need to reinstall the operating system or any of its components at some point, these will be invaluable.

- Gather any hard drive/controller diagnostics that you'll need.

- Back up as much as you can from your hard drive(s) before attempting any sort of drive service.

GENERAL TROUBLESHOOTING GUIDELINES

Although most drive installations and replacements will proceed flawlessly, there are many times when problems will crop up. If you've installed a hard drive and it does not function properly, perform the following basic checks before examining specific symptoms:

- *Be careful for power and static discharge.* Always turn off and unplug the computer before changing jumpers or unplugging cables and cards. Wear an antistatic wrist strap (or use other antistatic precautions) while working on your computer or handling a drive.

- *Verify compatibility.* Verify that the drive controller and drive are appropriately matched to each other (and to your computer). For example, an Ultra-DMA/100 drive will not run at top speed on an Ultra-DMA/33 controller.

- *Check all cards.* Verify that all expansion cards (including the drive controller card) are seated in their slots on the motherboard, and are secured with mounting screws. Often one or more cards may be displaced when a PC is transported or opened for service.

- *Check all connectors and cables.* Make sure that all ribbon and power cables are securely connected. Ribbon cables are easily damaged (especially at the connectors). Try a new cable that you know is good. Make sure no connector pins are bent. Verify that pin 1 on the interface cable is aligned with pin 1 on the drive and the controller.

- *Verify drive jumper settings.* Review the instructions in your drive's manual (and in your host adapter installation guide) and see that all appropriate jumpers are installed—or removed—as necessary. Incorrect or duplicated jumper settings (such as two master drives on the same channel) can easily interfere with drive operation.

- *Check your power supply capacity.* Each time you add a new device to your computer, make sure your computer's power supply can support the total power demand. Install a larger (higher wattage) power supply if necessary.

■ *Verify the drive settings in your CMOS Setup.* The drive settings in the CMOS Setup must not exceed the physical specifications of your drive. Also, the settings must not exceed the limitations set by the operating system and BIOS. Try the CMOS Setup's autodetect feature to identify the drive, or consider upgrading the BIOS and/or drive controller.

■ *Check for viruses.* Before you use an unknown disk in your system for the first time, scan it for viruses. Also scan the system for viruses periodically.

POTENTIAL PROBLEMS WITH Y-ADAPTERS

On rare instances, you may find that a drive will not function—or is damaged outright—when using a Y power adapter (Y-adapter). This can happen because a number of Y-adapters on the market are incorrectly wired. Y-adapters consist of a clear plastic plug with four metal prongs on an end that attaches to an existing power connector from the power supply. There are also two sets of wires leading to two plugs with female connections on the other ends, which are attached to internal devices such as hard drives, CD-ROM drives, and so on. The problem with some of these newer connectors is that the wires are attached incorrectly on one of the female connectors.

Examine both female connectors—make certain that both of the female connectors are lined up with the two rounded corners facing up that and both of the squared corners are facing down. The four wires attached to the female connectors should now be in the following order (from left to right):

Yellow (+12Vdc)**, Black** (ground)**, Black** (ground)**, and Red** (+5Vdc)

If this order is reversed on one of the connectors, then your Y-adapter is faulty and should *not* be used. As a rule, you should never split power from the hard drive under any circumstances.

POTENTIAL PROBLEMS WITH BUS SPEEDS ABOVE 66MHZ

Many Pentium and later motherboards offer an adjustable system bus clock that may be set either by the system BIOS or with jumpers. This "bus speed" setting allows you to increase the system bus clock above 66MHz—usually to 75MHz or 83MHz. Most drives have no problem with the higher bus clock speeds, but some problems may result because of the way that some motherboards handle the interaction between the higher bus speeds (above 66MHz) and the IDE-type interface.

On some motherboards, when the system clock is increased above 66MHz, the PCI bus (ideally 33MHz) is also increased—this higher speed reduces the PCI bus I/O Cycle Time. This change in the I/O Cycle Time violates the IDE specification and may cause disruptions in the communications between the hard drive and the PCI bus. This is *not* a faulty hard drive or drive design. When the PCI bus speed is forced over 33MHz because of higher bus speed settings, you may see drive operation problems such as data loss, data corruption, and failure of the system to recognize the hard drive on boot-up. Higher bus speeds will not cause any kind of permanent hard drive failure, and returning the system bus speed to 66MHz can usually eliminate the problem(s). The best solution to this problem is to either return the motherboard to a 66MHz bus speed or upgrade the motherboard with a model where the PCI bus speed is "asynchronous" of the bus speed. The latter fix allows you to increase the bus speed, but the PCI clock will remain fixed at 33MHz.

Current Pentium II, III, and 4 motherboards designed to operate up to 100MHz or higher are almost *all* asynchronous and should not pose a problem. But this issue may crop up when working with slightly older motherboards or systems.

TROUBLESHOOTING "DOS COMPATIBILITY MODE" PROBLEMS

One of the great advantages enjoyed by Windows 9x/Me is that it operates in the protected-mode—drivers and software can be executed beyond the traditional real-mode RAM limit of 1MB. By comparison, DOS is a real-mode environment. DOS programs and drivers can be executed only within the first 640KB of RAM (the conventional memory area). If Windows 9x/Me cannot establish protected-mode operation for a drive, it will fall back on real-mode driver support—this is known as *DOS Compatibility Mode*. Unfortunately, real-mode support often impairs system performance. If you notice that one or more of the hard drives in a system is using DOS compatibility mode—there may be an error message such as "Compatibility Mode Paging reduces overall system performance"—you'll need to track down and correct the cause. In general, Windows 9x/Me may invoke the DOS compatibility mode for any of the following reasons:

■ A questionable device driver, TSR, or computer virus has hooked the INT 21h or INT 13h chain before Windows 9x/Me loaded.

■ The hard disk controller in your computer was not detected by Windows 9x/Me.

■ The hard disk controller was removed from the current configuration in Device Manager.

■ There is a resource conflict between the hard disk controller and another hardware device.

■ The Windows 9x/Me protected-mode driver is missing or damaged.

■ The Windows 9x/Me protected-mode driver detected incompatible or unsupportable hardware.

You can use the following procedure to isolate and correct the cause of DOS Compatibility Mode problems:

1. Open the Control Panel, double-click the System icon, then choose the Performance tab in the System Properties dialog. You can identify which drive is using DOS compatibility mode and why.

2. If the driver name listed as causing the DOS Compatibility Mode is **MBRINT13.SYS**, your computer may be infected with a boot-sector virus, or you are running real-mode disk overlay software (for an IDE hard disk with more than 1024 cylinders) that is *not* compatible with Windows 9x/Me protected-mode disk drivers.

   ■ Run a current antivirus program to detect and remove boot sector viruses (such as Norton Anti-Virus or McAfee VirusScan). You may need to rewrite your boot sector using a DOS command such as **FDISK /MBR**.

   ■ If you cannot detect any virus activity, check any drive overlay software. For example, if you're using Disk Manager, make sure that you're using Disk Manager 7.0 or later—use Disk Manager 7.04 if you're running DriveSpace 3 (included with the Microsoft Plus! pack). You may need to make similar updates if you're running other drive overlay software.

3. If the driver name that is listed in step 2 is *also* in the CONFIG.SYS file, contact the driver's manufacturer to determine whether there is a more recent version of the driver that allows protected-mode operation in Windows 9x/Me. You may be able to download and install the latest driver version from the driver manufacturer's Web site.

4. If *no* driver is listed on the Performance tab, check to make sure that the hard disk controller is listed in the Device Manager. If it's not, install it through the Add New Hardware wizard. If the wizard cannot detect the controller automatically, run the wizard again but do not let it attempt to

detect the hardware in your computer—instead, select the controller specifically from the hardware list. If your particular controller is not listed, contact the manufacturer of the disk controller to obtain a Windows 9x/Me protected-mode disk driver (or a Windows 3.1x 32-bit disk access "FastDisk" driver if available).

If the hard disk controller *is* listed in Device Manager but has a red *X* over it, it has been removed from the current hardware profile. Click Properties for the controller in Device Manager and then click the check box corresponding to the current hardware profile under Device Usage.

5.   If the hard disk controller *is* listed in the Device Manager, but has a yellow "!" over it, there is a resource conflict (IRQ, I/O, DMA, or BIOS address range) with another device, the protected-mode driver is missing or damaged, or the "Disable all 32-bit protected-mode disk drivers" check box has been selected in File System properties.

■   Double-click the System icon in the Control Panel, click the Performance tab, and then click File System. Select the Troubleshooting tab and see that the "Disable all 32-bit protected-mode disk drivers" check box has *not* been selected.

■   Resolve any resource conflicts with other devices in the system.

■   Make sure that the protected-mode driver is in the **\Windows\SYSTEM\IOSUBSYS** directory and is loading properly. To find which driver is providing 32-bit disk access, click Properties for the disk controller in Device Manager and click the Driver tab to see which driver files are associated with the controller. For most IDE, EIDE, and ESDI disk controllers, 32-bit disk access is provided by the **ESDI_506.PDR** driver. For SCSI controllers, Windows 95 often uses **SCSIPORT.PDR** and a "mini port" (or .MPD) driver. Restart Windows 9x/Me, press F8 when the "Starting Windows" message appears, then select a Logged (BOOTLOG.TXT) start. If the 32-bit driver is listed as loading properly, you're all set. Otherwise, the driver may be missing or damaged—try reinstalling the 32-bit drivers.

6.   Load SYSTEM.INI into a text editor and check to see if the **MH32BIT.386** driver is being loaded (check for a line that reads **device=mh32bit.386**). This driver is installed by MicroHouse EZ-Drive software and is *not* compatible with the Windows 9x/Me protected-mode disk drivers. Unfortunately, this driver is not removed by Windows 9x/Me Setup, so you'll need to disable the line manually, save your changes, and reboot the PC.

7.   If all else fails, you may be able to achieve protected-mode support from the disk controller by disabling any of the controller's advanced features (such as caching or fast or "turbo" modes) and reducing data transfer rates. You may also try systematically disabling advanced IDE controller features in the CMOS Setup.

8.   If problems persist, you may have to replace the drive controller with a model that better supports protected-mode operation.

DETECTING A DDO

A Dynamic Drive Overlay (or DDO) is used to support access to a large hard drive when the system BIOS or drive controller is unable to do so. Since the DDO can sometimes cause problems with drive access and system performance, it must be detected before removal. You can use the telltale signs below to identify the presence of a DDO on a Windows 9x/Me system:

- **DDO startup message**   When you boot your computer, a message may be displayed on the screen that shows the DDO manufacturer's name (or prompts you to press a key to boot to a floppy disk). Current versions of drive overlay software may not display this message by default.

- **BIOS revision date**   Computers made before 1994 generally do not support LBA. If your BIOS shows an early revision date, it will probably need a DDO in order to support hard drives over 528MB.

- **FDISK "/status" switch**   Boot your computer with a Windows 9x/Me Startup Disk and type **fdisk /status** from the command prompt. Verify that the sum of the existing partitions is *larger* than the total hard disk space. If so, a DDO is at work.

- **Windows Startup Disk**   Reboot your computer with the Windows 9x/Me Startup Disk (this will prevent the DDO program from loading), and then boot to a command prompt. Check to see if files on the C: drive are accessible. If not, the drive is inaccessible because a DDO has not been loaded for the hard drive.

- **Verify file names**   Some drive overlay files use an .OVL or a .BIN extension. At the command prompt, type **dir /a *.bin** or **dir /a *.ovl** to check for the existence of files other than DRVSPACE.BIN and DBLSPACE.BIN. If there are other such files, a DDO is probably installed.

- **Check CONFIG.SYS**   Drive overlay software may be loaded from the CONFIG.SYS file in order to access drives *other* than the active boot partition of the master drive on the primary IDE controller. If there is DDO software called in CONFIG.SYS, disable it there if necessary.

REMOVING A DDO

When you install a drive overlay utility like EZ-Drive or MaxBlast (or other similar software), there may be a point where it's necessary to remove it. You may need to do this when upgrading the BIOS and/or drive controller, making the dynamic drive overlay (or DDO) software no longer required. In most cases, you can remove your DDO without losing any data—as long as you have an alternative means of accessing the drive (such as an updated BIOS or drive controller). The example below illustrates the removal of Disk Manager (other utilities follow a similar process).

 Before you remove a DDO, make a complete backup copy of all the data on your hard drive. Also run CHKDSK or ScanDisk (or a third-party equivalent) to detect and repair any damaged files. If the DDO removal program encounters a serious file problem (or is interrupted by a power loss or hardware failure), the removal will fail and your data *can* be lost.

1. Boot the computer to drive C:, then insert your DiscWizard disk (or CD).

2. Type **DM** to start Disk Manager, then choose the Select Installation Options Menu.

3. Select the Maintenance Menu.

4. Select Migrate Dynamic Drive. This option moves the data on your drive so that it can be accessed without the DDO. Remember that this conversion may take up to an hour to complete (depending on the size of your drive).

5. When the conversion has finished, exit Disk Manager, remove the disk, and reboot the computer.

6. Enter your CMOS Setup program and configure the hard drive with the appropriate number of cylinders, heads, and sectors as specified for your drive model (or autodetect).

7. Save your changes in the CMOS Setup and reboot again.

8. When your computer has rebooted, insert the DiscWizard disk into drive A:.

9. Type **A:\DM** to start Disk manager, then choose the Maintenance Menu.

10. Select Uninstall Disk Manager.

11. Select the correct drive to uninstall from and allow the process to complete.

12. When the uninstall is complete, exit Disk Manager and reboot the system.

Disk Manager can also remove a drive overlay placed by the EZ-Drive program. Simply select Convert Drive Format from the Maintenance Menu.

DRIVE NOT RECOGNIZED BY OPERATING SYSTEM

There are some circumstances when a hard drive is recognized correctly by the BIOS (for example, the drive is properly autodetected), but it is not properly identified by the operating system. In virtually all cases, the problem can be traced to installation issues or drive software. Check the essential installation points first:

1. Check the parameters in the CMOS Setup and verify that the drive parameters *and* translation mode (such as LBA) are set correctly.

2. Contact the system or motherboard manufacturer to verify potential BIOS capacity limitations. For example, you may need a BIOS upgrade to accommodate the drive sizes that you're using.

3. Ensure that newly installed drive controller cards do not conflict with the existing system BIOS. You may need to disable the motherboard's existing drive controller channel(s) through the CMOS Setup before the new controller card will be recognized by the OS.

4. Systematically step down the enhanced features of your BIOS (for example, systematically disable block mode, multisector transfers, 32-bit transfers, PIO mode settings, and so on) to their minimum values, or disable the features entirely. You may also try the BIOS Default settings in your CMOS Setup.

5. If your motherboard uses ISA bus slots, check AT BUS Clock speed in your CMOS Setup and verify that it's set from 8 to10MHz (ideally 8.33MHz). Doing this may not be necessary if there are no ISA cards in the system.

6. Increase the boot process time in your CMOS Setup—you can enable Floppy Seek At Boot, Test Memory Above 1MB, and/or set the Boot Order to "A: then C:."

7. Set Boot Speed to its slowest value in the CMOS Setup, and/or set the Boot Delay entry (if present) to its highest value.

8. Double-check your partitions using FDISK. If the drive was not previously partitioned, create a Primary DOS partition on the drive. Use option 2 to set the partition "active." Exit FDISK and reboot. Format the new partition and install the system files. If the drive was previously partitioned, make sure the first partition is PRI DOS and its Status is "A." Compare the sum of all partition sizes to the Total Disk Space—they should be the same to within about 1MB. If the total is different, correct the drive parameters or translation mode in CMOS Setup and repartition the drive.

If the drive was previously partitioned, but no partitions are currently seen in FDISK, do *not* attempt to create new partitions if data on the drive is to be saved.

9. Double-check the master/slave jumpers on all drives using the primary controller.

10. Install (set) the jumper for I/O Channel Ready on the drive (if that option is present).

11. If you're using a SCSI drive, verify that the Parity jumper is installed.

12. Check all of your cable connections and try a shorter replacement cable (or connect the drive to the middle cable connector).

13. Replace the drive controller card.

14. Remove the slave drive (if present) to determine the presence of any master/slave drive compatibility issues.

15. You may also need to check for data corruption or errors on the drive.

16. Clean-boot the system with a boot disk and execute **FDISK /MBR** and **SYS C:**. Make sure the DOS version on the floppy disk is the *same* version as on the hard drive before using the SYS command.

17. Bypass CONFIG.SYS and AUTOEXEC.BAT to check for problems in your startup files. If this works, use the "step-by-step" boot mode in the Windows Startup Menu to walk through each step of these files until the problem is found, then edit both the CONFIG.SYS and AUTOEXEC.BAT files and "comment out" the statement(s) causing the problem.

18. Check for drive compression and try removing the compression drivers if there is no important data on the drive.

19. Delete the partition using FDISK, then repartition and reformat the drive.

20. Replace the hard drive.

CHECKING FOR FAT16 AND FAT32

It may be necessary for you to identify the presence of a FAT16 or FAT32 partition *before* using disk utilities, backup software, or other applications. Doing this will prevent accidental loss of data from using an incompatible software version (such as using a FAT16 version of ScanDisk on a FAT32 partition).

■ Under Windows 98, double-click the My Computer icon on your desktop, then right-click the drive you're interested in. Click Properties from the drop-down menu. Look at the General tab on the line marked "File system." A FAT16 partition will simply say "FAT," while a FAT32 partition will specify "FAT32."

■ Try the **ver** (version) command from a DOS prompt, such as:

```
Windows 95A. [Version 4.00.950]
Windows 95B. [Version 4.00.1111]
Windows 98. [Version 4.10.1998]
```

■ If you need a FAT32 version of FDISK, check to see that FDISK asks, "Do you wish to enable large disk support (Y/N)." If it does *not* ask this question, it's probably a FAT16 version.

■ You can also check the partition type using a FAT32 version of FDISK. Select option 4 to display the partition information. The System field will read "FAT32" if the partition is FAT32 or "FAT16" if the partition is FAT16. If the partition has not been formatted, the System field will read "Unknown."

DEALING WITH DRIVE NOISE

All hard drives make a certain amount of noise during normal operation, and the noise level will vary depending on whether the drive is spinning or accessing. However, a drive making substantial or abnormal noises may indicate an impending failure. The trick here is to tell the "normal" noises from the "abnormal" noises. A drive makes three basic sounds:

■ A "whining" noise during the drive spin-up (and a mild "whir" while the system is on).

■ Regular clicking or tapping sounds during drive access (the R/W heads stepping across the platters).

■ Hard clicks when the drive heads park before power off.

You should develop a keen ear for abnormal drive sounds such as:

■ A high-pitched whining sound (such as a screech or squeal) can be an indication of problems.

■ Noises (vibrations) caused by mounting issues. These noises are due to either a high-frequency vibration in the mounting hardware or a potential drive failure.

■ Repeated and regular tapping, grinding, or beeping. When the hard drive is suspect, it is always important to make an immediate backup of your data.

To isolate the drive further, disconnect the drive's signal cable and power the system up. If the noise persists, the drive should be backed up and replaced at your earliest convenience. If the noise stops, there may be an issue with the cable or controller that you should investigate further.

DEALING WITH SPIN PROBLEMS

All hard drives must spin their platters at a constant rate of speed, so any spin problems can render the drive inaccessible. Spin problems can usually be broken down into three types:

■ *Drive does not spin at all.* When a system is turned on, the characteristic hard drive wind-up sounds are not present. This can also occur if the hard drive spins down (without cause) after working for a period of time.

■ *Drive spins up and spins down again.* This normally occurs during the initial power up. The hard drive will start spinning and then slow down (or it cycles up to a point and ceases to spin).

■ *Drive spins down following period of inactivity.* The hard drive fails to spin up when access is attempted.

The first things to check for are installation errors:

■ Check the jumper settings on all hard drives attached to the same interface cable. For example, check the master/slave jumpers on each drive, then check for "energy management" or "deferred spinup" jumpers. Most SCSI (and a few IDE) hard drives contain one or both jumper options.

■ Check all of the power supply cable connections.

■ Check the interface (ribbon) cable connections.

■ Check system software for power management and disable or uninstall that software if necessary.

Next, check for "green" or "power management" features that might be set improperly:

■ Disable your drive-related power management features in the CMOS Setup.

- Disable the power management jumper on your hard drive (if present).

- Some overlay software has the ability to set power management features. For example, you can disable power management under Maxtor's MaxBlast software (versions 7.04–7.12) by removing the **/E** switch. Clean-boot the system if other power management software is the suspected culprit.

- Windows 9x/Me can enable power management. This feature will need to be disabled through the operating system's Power Management icon in the Control Panel.

Finally, check for hardware failures with the drive and/or its controller:

- Try installing the drive in another system—doing this will verify the problem is with the drive, *not* the system.

- Use a different power supply plug.

- Use a different interface (ribbon) cable.

- Use a different drive controller (for example, try a PCI drive controller card).

- Disconnect the ribbon cable from the drive.

- Replace the drive outright.

HARDWARE SYMPTOMS

Now that you've seen some general troubleshooting guidelines, it's time to review some specific problems and solutions. The important notion here is that a hard drive *problem* does not necessarily mean a hard drive *failure*. The failure of a sector or track does not automatically indicate physical head or platter damage—this is why software tools have been so successful at restoring operation (and even recovering data). Remember, though, that drive troubleshooting has the potential of destroying any data on the drive(s). Before attempting to troubleshoot hard drive problems, be sure to back up as much of the drive as possible. If there is no backup available, do not repartition or reformat the drive unless *absolutely* necessary and all other possible alternatives have been exhausted.

The term "*IDE-type drive*" is taken to mean any drive using a 40-pin IDE-style interface. This includes IDE, EIDE, ATAPI IDE, Ultra-DMA/33, Ultra-DMA/66, and Ultra-DMA/100 (using the 40-pin/80-conductor cable). Specific drive types or exceptions will be noted in the section on symptoms.

SYMPTOM 21-1   **The hard drive is completely dead**   The drive does not spin up, the drive light does not illuminate during power-up, or you see an error message indicating that the drive is not found or ready. Make sure the 4-pin power connector is inserted properly and completely. If the drive is being powered by a Y-adapter, make sure any interim connections are secure. Use a voltmeter and measure the +5 volt (pin 4) and +12 volt (pin 1) levels. If either voltage (especially the +12 volt supply) is unusually low or absent, replace the power supply. Also check your signal cable. See that the drive's signal interface cable is connected securely at both the drive and controller ends. For IDE-type drives, this is the 40-pin ribbon cable. If the cable is visibly worn or damaged, try a new cable.

The PC cannot use a hard drive that it doesn't recognize, so enter the CMOS Setup routine and see that all of the parameters entered for the drive are correct. Heads, cylinders, sectors per track, landing zone, and write precompensation must all correct—otherwise, POST will not recognize the drive. If you have an autodetect option available, try that also. Remember to save your changes in CMOS and reboot the system.

If problems continue, the hard drive itself may be defective. Try a known-good hard drive. If a known-good drive works as expected, your original drive is probably defective and should be replaced. If a known-good hard drive fails to operate, replace the drive controller with a new expansion board.

SYMPTOM 21-2   You see drive activity, but the computer will not boot from the hard drive   In most cases, this is due to drive failure, boot sector failure, or DOS/Windows file corruption. Make sure that the drive's signal cable is connected securely at both the drive and controller. If the cable is visibly worn or damaged, try a new one. Check the CMOS Setup and verify that all of the parameters entered for the drive are correct. Heads, cylinders, sectors per track, landing zone, and write precompensation must all correct—otherwise, POST will not recognize the drive. If the BIOS provides an option to autodetect the drive, try that as well.

Boot from a floppy disk and try accessing the hard drive. If the hard drive is accessible, chances are that the boot files are missing or corrupt. Try a utility such as DrivePro's Drive Boot Fixer. You might also try running **FDISK /MBR**, which will rebuild the drive's master boot record (*the FDISK /MBR command may render the files on your drive inaccessible*).

You may have a problem with your drive system hardware. If you cannot access the hard drive, run a diagnostic such as Windsor Technologies' *PC Technician*. Test the drive and drive controller. If the controller responds but the drive does not, try repartitioning and reformatting the hard drive. If the drive still doesn't respond, replace the hard drive outright. If the controller doesn't respond, replace the hard drive controller.

SYMPTOM 21-3   There are errors during drive reads or writes   Magnetic information does not last forever, and sector ID information can gradually degrade to a point where you encounter file errors. Start by checking for any file structure problems on the drive. Use a utility such as ScanDisk to examine the drive and search for bad sectors. If a failed sector involves part of an .EXE or .COM file, that file would be corrupt and should be restored from a backup. If there are no problems detected with the file structure, replace the drive signal cable (try a UDMA/66/100 cable). Otherwise, replace the suspect drive outright.

SYMPTOM 21-4   Hard drive performance appears to be slowing down over time   In virtually all cases, diminishing drive performance can be caused by file fragmentation. To a far lesser extent, you may be faced with a computer virus. Start the PC with a "clean" boot disk and make sure there are no TSRs or drivers being loaded. After a clean boot, run your antivirus checker and make sure that there are no memory-resident or file-based viruses. If the system checks clean for computer viruses, you should check for file fragmentation next. Start your defragmentation utility (such as Defrag) and check to see the percentage of file fragmentation. If there is more than 10 percent fragmentation, you should consider running the defragmentation utility under Windows 9x/Me. This process could take from several minutes to several hours, depending on the size of your drive. Once defragmentation is complete, reboot the system normally.

SYMPTOM 21-5   You can access the hard drive correctly, but the drive light stays on continuously   A continuous LED indication is not *necessarily* a problem as long as the drive seems to be operating properly. Check the drive and drive controller for drive LED jumpers—examine the drive itself for any jumper that might select *latched* mode instead of *activity* mode. If there are no such jumpers on the drive, check the drive controller or motherboard. Set the jumper to *activity* mode to see the drive light during access only. Next, consider the possibility of drive light *error messages*. Some drive types (especially SCSI drives) use the drive activity light to signal drive and controller errors. Check the drive and controller documents to determine if there is any error indicated by the light remaining on.

SYMPTOM 21-6 **You cannot access the hard drive, and the drive light stays on continuously** This usually indicates a reversed signal cable, and is most common when upgrading or replacing a drive system. In virtually all cases, one end of the signal cable is reversed. Make sure that *both* ends of the cable are installed properly (remember that the red or blue stripe on one side of the cable represents pin 1). If problems persist, replace the drive controller. It is rare for a fault in the drive controller to cause this type of problem, but if trouble persists, try a known-good drive controller board.

SYMPTOM 21-7 **You see a "No Fixed Disk Present" error message on the monitor** This kind of problem can occur during installation or at any point in the PC's working life. Make sure the 4-pin power connector is inserted properly and completely. If the drive is being powered by a Y-adapter, make sure any interim connections are secure. Use a voltmeter and measure the +5 volt (pin 4) and +12 volt (pin 1) levels. If either voltage (especially the +12 volt supply) is unusually low or absent, replace the power supply. Make sure the drive's signal cable is connected securely at *both* the drive and controller. If the cable is visibly worn or damaged, try a new one.

Enter the CMOS Setup and see that all of the parameters entered for the drive are correct. Heads, cylinders, sectors per track, landing zone, and write precompensation must all correct—otherwise, POST will not recognize the drive. You might also try autodetecting the drive. Also verify that there are no other expansion devices in the system using the same IRQs or I/O addresses used by your drive controller. If there are, change the resources used by the conflicting device. If your drive system uses a SCSI interface, make sure that the SCSI cable is terminated properly. If problems continue, try a known-good hard drive. If a known-good drive works as expected, your original drive is probably defective. If problems persist with a known-good hard drive, replace the drive controller board.

SYMPTOM 21-8 **Your drive spins up, but the system fails to recognize the drive** Your computer may flag this as a *"hard-disk error"* or *"hard-disk controller failure"* during system initialization. Make sure that the interface signal cable is inserted properly and completely at the drive and controller. Try a new signal cable. See that a first drive is configured as *master*, and a second drive is configured as *slave*. For SCSI drives, see that each drive has a unique ID setting and check that the SCSI bus is terminated properly.

Enter the CMOS Setup routine and see that all of the parameters entered for the drive are correct. Heads, cylinders, sectors per track, landing zone, and write precompensation must all correct—otherwise, POST will not recognize the drive. Try using the autodetect feature if it is available. If the CMOS is configured properly, you should suspect a problem with the partition. Boot from a floppy disk and run FDISK to check the partitions on your hard drive. Make sure that there is at least one DOS partition. If the drive is to be your boot drive, the primary partition must be active and bootable. Repartition and reformat the drive if necessary.

Try another hard drive or controller. If a known-good drive works as expected, your original drive is probably defective. If a known-good hard drive fails to work as expected, replace the drive controller. If problems persist with a known-good floppy drive, replace the drive controller board.

SYMPTOM 21-9 **Your IDE drive spins up when power is applied, then rapidly spins down again** The drive is defective, or it is not communicating properly with its host system. Make sure the 4-pin power connector is inserted properly and completely into the drive. Also see that the interface signal cable is inserted properly and completely at the drive and controller. Try a new signal cable. The first drive should be configured as *master*, and a second drive should be configured as *slave*. For SCSI drives, see that each drive has a unique ID setting and check that the SCSI bus is terminated properly. If problems persist, try a known-good hard drive. If a known-good drive works as expected, your original drive is probably defective.

SYMPTOM 21-10   **You see a "Sector not found" error message**   This problem usually occurs after the drive has been in operation for quite some time and is typically the result of a media failure. Fortunately, a bad sector will affect only one file. Use a utility such as SpinRite from Gibson Research (or another data recovery utility) and attempt to recover the damaged file. Be aware that you may be unsuccessful and have to restore the file from a backup later. Next, use a disk utility (such as ScanDisk) to evaluate the drive, then locate and map out any bad sectors that are located on the drive. If ScanDisk maps out bad sectors, you may need to restore those files from a backup.

SYMPTOM 21-11   **You see a "1780 or 1781 ERROR" on the system**   The classical 1780 error code indicates a *Hard Disk 0 Failure,* while the 1781 error code marks a *Hard Disk 1 Failure.* Start the PC with a clean boot disk and make sure there are no TSRs or drivers being loaded. If you haven't done so already, run your antivirus checker and make sure that there are no memory-resident or file-based viruses. If you can access the hard drive once your system is booted, chances are that the boot files are missing or corrupt. Try a utility such as DrivePro's Drive Boot Fixer to recover the boot files or recopy the boot files with SYS and re-create the master boot record with **FDISK /MBR**. Otherwise, you will need to repartition and reformat the disk, then restore disk files from a backup.

    If you cannot access the hard drive, run a diagnostic such as Windsor Technologies' PC Technician. Test the drive and drive controller. If the controller responds but the drive does not, try repartitioning and reformatting the hard drive. If the drive still doesn't respond, replace the hard drive outright. If the controller doesn't respond, replace the hard drive controller.

SYMPTOM 21-12   **You see a "1790 or 1791 ERROR" on the system**   The classical 1790 error code indicates a *Hard Disk 0 Error,* while the 1791 error code marks a *Hard Disk 1 Error.* Make sure that the interface signal cable is inserted properly and completely at the drive and controller. Try a new signal cable. Next, boot from a floppy disk and run FDISK to check the partitions on your hard drive. Make sure that there is at least one DOS partition. If the drive is to be your boot drive, the primary partition must be active and bootable. Repartition and reformat the drive if necessary. Finally, replace the hard drive or controller. If a known-good drive works as expected, your original drive is probably defective. If problems persist with a known-good floppy drive, replace the drive controller board.

SYMPTOM 21-13   **You see a "1701 ERROR" on the system**   The 1701 error code indicates a hard drive POST error—the drive did not pass its POST test. Make sure the 4-pin power connector is inserted properly and completely. If the drive is being powered by a Y-adapter, make sure any interim connections are secure. Use a voltmeter and measure the +5 volt (pin 4) and +12 volt (pin 1) levels. If either voltage (especially the +12 volt supply) is unusually low or absent, replace the power supply. Enter the CMOS Setup routine and see that all of the parameters entered for the drive are correct. Heads, cylinders, sectors per track, landing zone, and write precompensation must all correct—otherwise, POST will not recognize the drive. Try autodetecting the drive.

SYMPTOM 21-14   **The system reports random data, seek, or format errors**   Random errors rarely indicate a permanent problem, but identifying the problem's source can be a time-consuming task. Make sure the 4-pin power connector is inserted properly and completely. If the drive is being powered by a Y-adapter, make sure any interim connections are secure. Use a voltmeter and measure the +5 volt (pin 4) and +12 volt (pin 1) levels. If either voltage (especially the +12 volt supply) is unusually low, replace the power supply. Make sure that the interface signal cable is inserted properly and completely at the drive and controller. Try a new signal cable. Also try re-routing the signal cable away from the power supply or "noisy" expansion devices.

If problems occur after remounting the drive in a different orientation, you may need to repartition and reformat the drive or return it to its original orientation. Try relocating the drive controller away from cables and "noisy" expansion devices. If your system has a turbo mode, your ISA drive controller may have trouble operating while the system is in turbo mode. Take the system out of turbo mode. If the problem disappears, try a new drive controller. The disk media may also be defective. Use a utility such as ScanDisk to check for and map out any bad sectors. Once bad sectors are mapped out, you may need to restore some files from your backup.

Try the hard drive and controller in another system. If the drive and controller work in another system, there is probably excessive noise or grounding problems in the original system. Reinstall the drive and controller in the original system and remove all extra expansion boards. If the problem goes away, replace one board at a time and retest the system until the problem returns. The last board you inserted when the problem returned is probably the culprit. If the problem persists, there may be a ground problem on the motherboard. Try replacing the motherboard as an absolute last effort.

SYMPTOM 21-15   **You see an "Error reading drive C:" error message**   Read errors in a hard drive typically indicate problems with the disk media, but may also indicate viruses or signaling problems. Start with the signal cable and make sure that the interface signal cable is inserted properly and completely at the drive and controller. Try a new signal cable. Start the PC with a clean boot disk and make sure there are no TSRs or drivers being loaded. If you haven't done so already, run your antivirus checker and make sure that there are no memory-resident or file-based viruses.

If problems occur after remounting the drive in a different orientation, you may need to repartition and reformat the drive, or return it to its original orientation. Use a utility such as ScanDisk to check for and map out any bad sectors. Once bad sectors are mapped out, you may need to restore some files from your backup. Try another hard drive. If a known-good drive works as expected, your original drive is probably defective and should be replaced.

SYMPTOM 21-16   **You see a "Track 0 not found" error message**   A fault on track 00 can disable the entire drive, since track 00 contains the drive's file allocation table (FAT). This can be a serious problem that may require you to replace the drive. Examine the drive signal connector and verify that the interface signal cable is inserted properly and completely at the drive and controller. Try a new signal cable. Boot from a floppy disk and run FDISK to check the partitions on your hard drive. Make sure there is at least one DOS partition. If the drive is to be your boot drive, the primary partition must be active and bootable. Repartition and reformat the drive if necessary. Finally, try a known-good hard drive. If a known-good drive works as expected, your original drive is probably defective.

SYMPTOM 21-17   **You see a "Hard Disk Controller Failure" or a large number of defects in last logical partition**   This is typically a CMOS Setup or drive controller problem. Enter the CMOS Setup routine and see that all of the parameters entered for the drive are correct. If the geometry specifies a larger drive, the system will attempt to format areas of the drive that don't exist—resulting in a large number of errors. If CMOS is configured correctly, there may be a problem with the hard drive controller. Try a new hard drive controller. If a new drive controller does not correct the problem, the drive itself is probably defective and should be replaced.

SYMPTOM 21-18   **An IDE drive under 528MB does not partition or format to full capacity**   When relatively small hard drives do not realize their full capacity, the CMOS Setup is usually at fault. The drive parameters entered into CMOS must specify the *full* capacity of the drive, using a geometry setup that is acceptable. If you use parameters that specify a smaller drive, any extra capacity will be ignored. If there are over 1,024 cylinders, you must use an alternative "translation geometry" to realize the drive's full potential. The drive's maker can provide you with the right translation geometry. Also check your DOS version—older versions of DOS use a partition limit of 32MB. Upgrade your older version of DOS to 6.22 (or MS-DOS 7.0 with Windows 9x/Me).

SYMPTOM 21-19   **An IDE-type drive over 528MB does not partition or format to full capacity**   This type of problem may also be due to a CMOS Setup error, but it is almost always due to poor system configuration. Check the CMOS Setup first—the drive parameters entered into CMOS must specify the *full* capacity of the drive. If you use parameters that specify a smaller drive, any extra capacity will be ignored. If there are over 1,024 cylinders, you must use an alternative "translation geometry" to realize the drive's full potential. The drive's maker can provide you with the right translation geometry. Also check the CMOS Setup for LBA. EIDE drives need Logical Block Addressing to access over 528MB. Make sure that there is an entry such as "LBA Mode" in CMOS. Otherwise, you may need to upgrade your motherboard BIOS to have full drive capacity.

The BIOS may be at fault. If you cannot upgrade an older motherboard BIOS, install an EIDE drive controller with its own controller BIOS—doing this will supplement the motherboard BIOS. If neither your motherboard nor controller BIOS will support LBA mode, you will need to install drive overlay software (such as EZ-Drive or Drive Manager).

SYMPTOM 21-20   **You see "Disk Boot Failure," "non system disk," or "No ROM Basic—SYSTEM HALTED" error message**   There are several possible reasons for these errors. Check the signal connector first and make sure that the interface signal cables are inserted properly and completely at the drive and controller. Try some new signal cables. Next, start the PC with a clean boot disk and make sure there are no TSRs or drivers being loaded that might interfere with drive operation. If you haven't done so already, run your antivirus checker and make sure that there are no memory-resident or file-based viruses.

Enter the CMOS Setup routine and see that all of the parameters entered for the drive are correct. Heads, cylinders, sectors per track, landing zone, and write precompensation must all be entered accurately. Now boot from a floppy disk and run FDISK to check the partitions on your hard drive. Make sure that there is at least one DOS partition. If the drive is to be your boot drive, the primary partition must be active and bootable. Finally, it is possible that the hard drive itself is defective. Try a known-good hard drive. If a known-good drive works as expected, your original drive is probably defective. If problems persist with a known-good floppy drive, replace the drive controller.

SYMPTOM 21-21   **The hard drive in a PC is suffering frequent breakdowns (every 6 to 12 months)**   When drives tend to fail within a few months, there are some factors to consider. Power may be an issue. If the AC power supplying your PC is "dirty" (that is, lots of spikes and surges), power anomalies can often make it through the power supply and damage other components. Remove any high-load devices such as air conditioners, motors, or coffee makers from the same AC circuit used by the PC, or try the PC on a known-good AC circuit. You might also consider a good UPS to power your PC.

Excessive drive use may be another factor. If the drive is being worked hard by applications and swap files, consider upgrading RAM, adding cache, or disabling virtual memory to reduce dependency on the drive. Periodically run a utility like DEFRAG to reorganize the files. Doing this reduces the amount of "drive thrashing" that occurs when loading and saving files. Finally, consider the environment. Constant low-level vibrations, such as those in an industrial environment, can kill a hard drive. Smoke (even cigarette smoke), high humidity, very low humidity, and caustic vapors can ruin drives. Make sure the system is used in a stable office-type environment.

SYMPTOM 21-22 **A hard drive controller is replaced, but during initialization the system displays error messages such as "Hard Disk Failure" or "Not a recognized drive type"**   The PC may also lock-up. Some drive controllers may be incompatible in some systems. Check with the controller manufacturer and see if there have been any reports of incompatibilities with your PC. If so, try a different drive controller board.

SYMPTOM 21-23 **A new hard drive is installed, but it will not boot, or a message appears such as "HDD controller failure"**   The new drive has probably not been installed or prepared properly. Make sure the 4-pin power connector is inserted properly and completely. If the drive is being powered by a Y-adapter, make sure any interim connections are secure. Use a voltmeter and measure the +5 volt (pin 4) and +12 volt (pin 1) levels. If either voltage (especially the +12 volt supply) is unusually low or absent, replace the power supply. Also make sure the drive's signal interface cable is connected securely at both the drive and controller. If the cable is visibly worn or damaged, try a new one.

Enter the CMOS Setup routine and see that all of the parameters entered for the drive are correct. Heads, cylinders, sectors per track, landing zone, and write precompensation must all correct—otherwise, POST will not recognize the drive. The drive also might not be prepared properly. Run FDISK from a bootable disk to partition the drive, then run FORMAT to initialize the drive. Then run SYS C: to make the drive bootable.

SYMPTOM 21-24 **The drive will work as a primary drive, but not as a secondary (or vice versa)**   In most cases, the drive is simply jumpered incorrectly, but there may also be timing problems. Check the drive jumpers first. Make sure that the drive is jumpered properly as a primary (single drive), primary (dual drive), or secondary drive. The drive signal timing may also be off. Some IDE-type drives (especially older models) may not work as primary or secondary drives with certain other drives in the system. Reverse the primary/secondary relationship. If the problem persists, try the drives separately. If the drives work individually, there is probably a timing problem, so try a different drive as the primary or secondary.

SYMPTOM 21-25 **You install a Y-adapter that fails to work**   Some Y-adapters that are incorrectly wired can cause severe damage to any device attached to them. Examine the power connector first. Make certain that both of the female connectors are lined up with the two chamfered (rounded) corners facing up and both of the squared corners facing down. The four wires attached to the female connectors should now be in the following order from left to right: **Yellow** (+12Vdc), **Black** (ground), **Black** (ground), **Red** (+5Vdc). If this order is reversed on one of the connectors, then your Y power adapter is faulty and should *not* be used.

SYMPTOM 21-26 **During the POST, you hear a drive begin to spin-up and produce a sharp noise** This problem can be encountered with some combinations of drives, motherboards, and motherboard BIOS versions. It can easily result in data loss (and media damage). Check the motherboard BIOS version first; then contact the PC system manufacturer and see if a BIOS upgrade is necessary. Try an upgrade if necessary; oherwise, replace the drive controller. Often a new drive controller may resolve the problem if the motherboard BIOS cannot be replaced. If you cannot correct this issue through BIOS, the drive itself may be defective and require replacement.

SYMPTOM 21-27 **You're using an Ultra-DMA hard drive, but there is no "DMA" check box available in the drive's Properties dialog** If the "DMA" checkbox is unavailable, there is a possibility that Windows does not view the drive as Ultra-DMA capable. This could be a driver issue, or your hard drive (or motherboard drive controller) does not support Ultra-DMA. Assuming the drive and motherboard both support Ultra-DMA operation, make sure that you are running the latest bus-mastering drivers (these are installed by default if your motherboard supports them)—you may need to download the latest bus-mastering drivers from the drive controller maker or from the motherboard manufacturer. Once the proper drivers are installed, Windows 98/Me will automatically handle all transfer rates that the drive and motherboard support. You may need to enable DMA mode transfers through the drive's Properties dialog.

SYMPTOM 21-28 **After installing a large HDD (unpartitioned), you cannot access the floppy drive** This will effectively hang the system and prevent you from completing the hard drive's installation. In most cases, this is due to an issue with the drive size. Some BIOS versions cannot perform the proper translation on an 8.4GB (or larger) drive and will hang the system as a result. Try setting the drive up using the following parameters:

- Cylinders: 1023
- Heads: 16
- Sectors: 63

Of course, this setting represents a small IDE drive, and the system will tell you that this is a 504MB or 528MB drive. If you are then able to boot to a floppy disk, then you may either upgrade the BIOS or drive controller to support the large hard drive natively or install drive overlay software such as Disk Manager or MaxBlast. Be sure to restore the drive's proper CMOS Setup parameters after upgrading the BIOS (or installing drive overlay software).

SYMPTOM 21-29 **After configuring a drive with the correct parameters (such as 16383 x 16 x 63), the system still indicates that the drive is only 504MB or 528MB** Keep in mind that 528MB (or 504MB) is the limitation of the original Cylinder/Head/Sector (CHS) translation method used on IDE drives. This problem was resolved with the LBA translation technique. Make sure that the CMOS Setup is configured to use Logical Block Addressing (LBA) if it is available. If it is not, you may need to upgrade the BIOS (or drive controller) or install drive overlay software such as Disk Manager or MaxBlast.

SYMPTOM 21-30 **When replacing or repartitioning certain Compaq systems, you can no longer access the system's setup** This occurs because you removed the "diagnostic partition." Some Compaq computers store the system BIOS information in a non-DOS, or "diagnostic," partition on the hard drive, instead of storing it on a chip on the motherboard as most other systems do. If you have such a Compaq model and you install the new drive as a master, you will need to copy or reinstall the diagnostic partition onto the new drive. If you don't, you will not be able to access your CMOS Setup upon boot up. If you install the new drive as a slave or non-boot drive, you do not need to reinstall this partition. In addition, if you're planning to install the drive with an older version of Western Digital's EZ-Drive, you must use version 9.06w or later.

If you install the new drive as a master, you can use drive overlay software to copy the diagnostic partition and your data from the old drive to the new one. If you're concerned only about the diagnostic partition, you can use the drive overlay software to transfer the data, then reformat the drive. As long as you do this under the DDO's control (assuming EZ-BIOS installed itself), it will not affect the diagnostic partition. Just boot to C:, insert the startup disk, then start formatting. If you have more than one partition, make sure you format the correct drive letters corresponding to the other partitions.

When trying to access the "diagnostic partition," you may encounter an error message that refers to a memory conflict. This is a known issue and you will need to contact Compaq directly for detailed instructions should this occur.

SYMPTOM 21-31   You detect hard drive errors caused by damaged data or physical damage   You may receive one of the following error messages when you are starting or using your computer:

```
Serious Disk Error Writing Drive <X>
Data Error Reading Drive <X>
Error Reading Drive <X>
I/O Error
Seek Error - Sector not found
```

These error messages indicate either damaged data or physical damage on the hard disk. Run ScanDisk to examine the hard drive. Running ScanDisk with the "Thorough" option selected examines the drive for physical damage—if damaged data is detected, ScanDisk allows you to save the damaged data to a file (or discard the data). Keep in mind that ScanDisk's "surface scan" may take a considerable amount of time on large hard disks. If ScanDisk is unable to repair damaged data (or indicates that the drive suffers from physical damage), you'll need to replace the drive.

SYMPTOM 21-32   You find that a PC using an Ultra-DMA controller/drive may lock up when running Windows 95 (OSR2)   The lockup occurs when the drive is being accessed. This problem occurs when there's a hardware error while data is being read from the hard drive. When the error happens during an Ultra-DMA data transfer, the Windows device driver does not successfully recover from the error and retry the operation—so the system halts. This is a known issue with Windows 95 OSR2, and an update file (REMIDEUP.EXE) is available for download from the Microsoft Web site. The updated file ESDI_506.PDR version 4.00.1116 (dated 8/25/97 or later) should fix the problem under Windows 95 OSR2. You may also upgrade the operating system to Windows 98/Me, which should offer far better native UDMA support.

SYMPTOM 21-33   You encounter errors accessing a hard drive with its "spin-down" feature enabled   This frequently occurs under Windows 95 (and OSR2), and you may find that incorrect data is read from or written to the drive, or you may encounter GPFs. This type of problem is known to occur under Windows 95 (and OSR2) if the drive requires more than 7.5 seconds to "spin-up"—an error is then generated in the Windows 95 driver, resulting in incorrect data being read from the drive (which can result in GPFs). You can work around this problem by disabling hard disk spin-down on the Disk Drives tab using the Power tool in the Control Panel. An update file (REMIDEUP.EXE) is available for download from the Microsoft Web site. The updated file ESDI_506.PDR version 4.00.1113 (dated 12/6/96 or later) should fix the problem under Windows 95 (and OSR2). For Windows 95, the VOLTRACK.VXD version 4.00.954 (dated 3/6/96 or later) file is also installed. You may also correct this problem by upgrading the operating system to Windows 98/Me.

SYMPTOM 21-34   **One or more subdirectories appear lost or damaged**   Both the root directory of a drive and its FAT contain references to subdirectories. If data in either the root directory or file allocation table is corrupt, one or more subdirectories may be inaccessible by the drive. Try repairing the drive's directory structure. Use ScanDisk (with DOS 6.2 or later) to check the disk's directory structure for problems, then correct any problems that are reported.

SYMPTOM 21-35   **The hard drive's root directory is damaged**   A faulty root directory can cripple the entire disk, rendering *all* subdirectories inaccessible. You may be able to recover the root directory structure. Use a utility like DISKFIX (with PC Tools) to reconstruct the damaged FATs and directories. If you have been running MIRROR, DISKFIX should be able to perform a very reliable recovery. You may also try other recovery/corrective utilities, such as DrivePro or ScanDisk. However, if you cannot recover the root directory reliably, you'll need to reformat the drive, then restore its contents from a backup.

SYMPTOM 21-36   **You see a "Bad or Missing Command Interpreter" error message**   This is a typical error that appears when a drive is formatted in one DOS version but loaded with another. Compatibility problems occur when you mix DOS versions. Start by booting the PC with a "clean" boot disk and make sure there are no TSRs or drivers being loaded. If you haven't done so already, run your antivirus checker and make sure that there are no memory-resident or file-based viruses. Finally, make sure that the drive is partitioned and formatted with the version of DOS you intend to use. Also be sure to use FORMAT with the **/S** switch or use **SYS C:** in order to transfer system files to the drive.

SYMPTOM 21-37   **You see an "Incorrect DOS version" error**   You attempted to execute an external DOS command (such as FORMAT) using a version of the utility that is *not* from the same DOS version as the COMMAND.COM file currently running. Reboot with a corresponding version of COMMAND.COM or get a version of the utility that matches the current version of COMMAND.COM.

SYMPTOM 21-38   **The hard drive is infected by a bootblock virus**   You may detect the presence of a bootblock virus (a virus that infects the MBR) by running an antivirus utility or receiving a warning from the BIOS bootblock protection feature. In every case, you should attempt to use the antivirus utility to eradicate the virus. You may also remove a bootblock virus by using **FDISK /MBR** (though doing so could render the contents of your disk inaccessible). If you're using drive overlay software such as Disk Manager, you can usually rewrite the code through the "Maintenance Menu" within the Disk Manager utility itself.

SYMPTOM 21-39   **You see a "File Allocation Table Bad" error**   The operating system has encountered a problem with the FAT. Normally, there are two copies of the FAT on a drive—chances are that one of the copies has become damaged. It may also be possible that there is no partition on the drive to begin with. Run ScanDisk—doing this may be able to correct the problem by allowing you to select which copy of the FAT you wish to use. If the problem continues, you'll need to back up as many files as possible and reformat the drive.

SYMPTOM 21-40   **DOS requires you to "Enter Volume Label," but the label is corrupt**
Some versions of DOS (for instance, DOS 3.x) require you to enter the volume label when formatting a hard drive or deleting a logical drive partition using the FDISK command. However, if the volume label is corrupt (or was changed by a third-party utility to contain lowercase letters), this is impossible to do. To correct this problem, use the LABEL command to delete the volume label, then use FORMAT or FDISK. When you are prompted for the volume label, press ENTER (which indicates *no* volume label). If LABEL doesn't successfully delete the volume label, you can use the following debug script to erase the first sector of the drive and make it appear unformatted, then repartition and reformat the drive. Start DEBUG, then type the following:

```
-    F 100 L 200 0       ;Create a sector of zeros at address 100
-    W 100 2 0 1          ;Write information at address 100 to sector 0 of drive 2
-    Q                    ;Quit DEBUG
```

For DOS versions 5.x and later, you can use the following command to handle the problem:

```
format /q /v:VOLUME x:
```

where *VOLUME* is the new volume name you want to assign to the hard disk drive, and *x:* is the drive letter you want to format.

SYMPTOM 21-41   **You cannot empty the Recycle Bin under Windows 9x/Me**   There are several possible issues. When you right-click the Recycle Bin, the "Empty Recycle Bin" command may be unavailable (or the Properties command may be unavailable). You may also find that files you delete may be permanently deleted—rather than simply "moved" to the Recycle Bin. In virtually all cases, this problem is caused when your fixed hard disk is marked as a removable drive. You'll have to "unmark" the hard drive:

1. Click Start, select Settings, and then double-click Control Panel.
2. Double-click the System icon.
3. Click the Device Manager tab.
4. Double-click the Disk Drives branch to expand it.
5. Click your hard disk, then click Properties.
6. On the Settings tab, click the Removable check box to clear it.
7. Click OK, then click OK again.
8. Restart your computer.

 You cannot use this procedure on a *true* removable drive. If the drive is removable, the Removable option is reset when you restart the computer.

SYMPTOM 21-42   **Software diagnostics indicate an average access time that is longer than specified for the drive**   The average access time is the average amount of time needed for a drive to reach the track and sector where a needed file begins. Review your drive specifications and verify the timing specifications for your particular drive—its timing may be correct. Before you replace a drive,

try testing several similar drives for comparison. If only the suspect drive measures incorrectly, you may not *need* to replace the drive itself just yet, but you should at least maintain frequent backups in case the drive is near failure.

Also keep in mind that different software packages measure access time differently. Make sure that the diagnostic subtracts system overhead processing from the access time calculation. Try one or two other diagnostics to confirm the measurement. Start your defragmentation utility (such as Disk Defragmenter) and check to see the percentage of file fragmentation. If there is more than 10 percent fragmentation, you should consider running the defragmentation utility.

SYMPTOM 21-43   **Software diagnostics indicate a slower data transfer rate than specified**   This is often due to less-than-ideal data transfer rates rather than an actual hardware failure. Review your drive specifications and verify the timing specifications for your particular drive—its timing may be correct. Also keep in mind that different software packages measure access time differently. Make sure that the diagnostic subtracts system overhead processing from the access time calculation. Try one or two other diagnostics to confirm the measurement.

Next, enter the CMOS Setup routine and verify that any enhanced data transfer modes are enabled (such as PIO Mode 4 or DMA mode 4 or 5). Doing that can increase data transfer rate substantially. Start your defragmentation utility (such as Disk Defragmenter), and check to see the percentage of file fragmentation. If there is more than 10 percent fragmentation, you should consider running the defragmentation utility. Finally, if the drive is a SCSI type, make sure the SCSI bus is terminated properly—poor termination can cause data errors and result in re-transmissions that degrade overall data transfer rates.

SYMPTOM 21-44   **The FDISK procedure hangs up or fails to create or save partition records for the drive(s)**   You may also see an error message such as "Runtime error." This type of problem often indicates a problem with track 00 on the drive. Make sure that the interface signal cables are inserted properly and completely at the drive and controller. Try some new signal cables if necessary. Next, enter the CMOS Setup routine and see that all of the parameters entered for the drive are correct. Heads, cylinders, sectors per track, landing zone, and write precompensation must all be appropriate. Check with the drive maker and see if there is an alternative "translation geometry" that you can enter instead. If the BIOS supports autodetection, try autodetecting the drive.

Check your version of FDISK. The version of FDISK you are using must be the same as the DOS version on your boot disk—older versions may not work. Now run FDISK and see if there are any partitions already on the drive. If so, you may need to erase any existing partitions, then create your new partition from scratch. *Remember that erasing a partition will destroy any data already on the drive.*

If partitions are not the problem, use a utility such as ScanDisk to check the media for physical defects—especially at track 00. If there is physical damage in the boot sector, you should replace the drive. Check for software from the manufacturer. Some drive makers provide low-level preparation utilities that can rewrite track 00. For example, Western Digital provides the WD_CLEAR.EXE utility. If problems still persist, replace the defective hard drive.

SYMPTOM 21-45   **After using FDISK to partition a large hard drive, the system hangs when booting from a floppy disk**   This is almost always an issue with a system BIOS (or drive controller) that cannot properly support a large (8.4GB+) drive. Some BIOS versions are confused when they encounter an 8.4GB or larger hard drive, and they assign it 0 heads by mistake. Under these conditions, you'll be able to partition the drive with FDISK, but the partition table that it creates will contain invalid information. When you boot to a floppy disk, the operating system on that floppy disk attempts to access the partition table on the hard drive. The invalid information created by FDISK causes the OS to hang. The solution is to upgrade the system BIOS (or the drive controller) to support the large drive natively or to install drive overlay software such as Disk Manager or MaxBlast.

SYMPTOM 21-46   **FDISK reports an error such as "no space to create partition" or "disk is write protected"**   There are several possible issues that may cause this type of behavior. Check the CMOS Setup first. Chances are that your BIOS has enabled virus protection for the master boot record (also referred to as "Boot Sector Write Protect"). You must go into the system's CMOS Setup and disable that feature before partitioning a drive (or installing/upgrading an operating system). Now check the drive jumpers. Some hard drives also require the use of two jumpers rather than just one. Verify that your drive is jumpered properly for its place in your particular drive configuration (such as single master, master with slave, or slave). If the problem persists, the BIOS may not be able to support your drive properly. Check for a BIOS upgrade (or upgrade the drive controller) or install drive overlay software such as Disk Manager or MaxBlast.

SYMPTOM 21-47   **FDISK refuses to partition the drive and hangs the system or returns a "runtime error"**   In many cases, track 00 on the drive has been corrupted. If you can perform a low-level format of the drive, try using the disk manufacturer's LL formatting (or "drive preparation") utility to reconstruct track 00. For example, Western Digital's "Data Lifeguard Tools" utility (**www.wdc.com/service/ftp/drives.html#dlgtools**) can be used to perform a "pseudo" LL format on Western Digital drives. From the main menu, choose Diagnostics, select the correct drive, and choose "Write Zeros." After the operation completes, run FDISK again. Your particular drive manufacturer may offer other similar utilities. If this does not resolve the problem, the drive itself may need to be replaced.

SYMPTOM 21-48   **The high-level (DOS) format process takes too long**   In almost all cases, long formats are the result of older DOS versions. Check your DOS version. MS-DOS version 4.x tries to recover hard errors—which can consume quite a bit of extra time. You will probably see a number of "Attempting to recover allocation units" messages. Your best course is to upgrade the DOS version to 6.22 (or MS-DOS 7.x with Windows 9x/Me). Later versions of DOS abandon hard error retries.

SYMPTOM 21-49   **You install Disk Manager to a hard drive, then install DOS, but DOS formats the drive back to 528MB**   After Disk Manager is installed, you must create a rescue disk to use in conjunction with your DOS installation. There are two means of accomplishing this. First, you can do the following:

1. Create a "clean" DOS-bootable disk.

2. Copy two files from the original Disk Manager disk to your bootable disk: XBIOS.OVL and DMDRVR.BIN.

3. Create a CONFIG.SYS file on this bootable disk with these three lines:

```
DEVICE=DMDRVR.BIN
FILES=35
BUFFERS=35
```

4. Remove the bootable disk and reboot the system.

5. When you see "Press space bar to boot from diskette," do so—the system will halt.

6. Insert the rescue disk in drive A:, then press any key to resume the boot process.

7. At the A: prompt, remove your rescue disk, insert the DOS installation disk, then type **setup**.

8. You will now install DOS files without overwriting the Disk Manager files.

Or you may use an alternative approach:

1. Create a "clean" DOS-bootable disk.

2. Insert the original Disk Manager disk in the A: drive and type:

    ```
    DMCFIG/D=A:
    ```

3. You will prompted to inert a bootable floppy in drive A:.

4. You will need to remove and insert the bootable disk a few times as Drive Manager files are copied.

5. Remove the floppy and reboot the system.

6. When you see "Press space bar to boot from diskette," do so—the system will halt.

7. Insert the rescue disk in drive A:, then press any key to resume the boot process.

8. At the A: prompt, remove your rescue disk, insert the DOS installation disk, then type **setup**.

9. You will now install DOS files without overwriting the Disk Manager files.

SYMPTOM 21-50   **ScanDisk reports some bad sectors, but cannot map them out during a surface analysis**   You may need a surface analysis utility for your particular drive that is provided by the drive maker. For example, Western Digital provides the WDATIDE.EXE utility for its Caviar series of drives. It will mark all "grown" defects and compensate for lost capacity by utilizing spare tracks.

These types of surface analysis utilities are typically destructive. Make sure to have a complete backup of the drive before proceeding. Also, the utility may take a very long time to run if your drive's capacity is large.

SYMPTOM 21-51   **ScanDisk reports an "Out of Memory" error after copying data from a smaller drive to a larger one**   The data seems to copy successfully, but when you run ScanDisk you get an "Out of Memory" error (or you have a problem using Defrag). Chances are that you've copied data from a smaller drive to a larger drive that uses FAT32 (you're running Windows 95 OSR2 or Windows 98/Me) with a utility that can copy the contents of one hard drive to another. The utility may have created an image of the drive that was copied to the other, or it copied data sector by sector from one drive to the other.

If you used an older utility (or version of EZ-Drive) to copy the data, the clusters were probably not correctly resized for the new FAT32 partition. When a partition becomes formatted, it is divided into clusters—or small blocks. These clusters are used to store data, and the size of a cluster is determined by the size of the partition. Older copy utilities often do not support FAT32 properly and will incorrectly size the cluster on the new FAT32 partition when they transfer data from the old drive to the new one. You can verify that this has occurred by running CHKDSK from a DOS prompt. The correct cluster sizes for FAT32 partitions are listed here:

512MB to 8.2GB = 4KB cluster size

8.2GB to 16.4GB = 8KB cluster size

16.4GB to 32.8GB = 16KB cluster size

32.8GB and higher = 32KB cluster size

If CHKDSK reports an incorrect cluster size for your partition, you need to erase the data and copy it using an updated utility.

SYMPTOM 21-52   **You cannot get 32-bit access to work under Windows 3.1x**   Y o u are probably not using the correct hard drive driver. Check your EIDE BIOS. If your motherboard (or drive controller) BIOS supports LBA, obtaining a driver should be easy. The drive maker either provides a 32-bit driver on a floppy disk accompanying the drive, or a driver can be downloaded from the drive maker's Web site. If the motherboard (or drive controller) does not support LBA directly, you can install drive overlay software such as Ontrack's Disk Manager (7.0 or later) and run DMCFIG to install the 32-bit driver software.

SYMPTOM 21-53   **Drive diagnostics reveal a great deal of wasted space on the drive** You probably have a large drive partitioned as one or more FAT16 logical volumes. If you deal with large numbers of small files, it may be more efficient to create multiple smaller partitions utilizing smaller clusters. As an alternative, you may choose to repartition the drive using FAT32, which supports much larger partitions (while allowing for smaller clusters).

SYMPTOM 21-54   **After installing a new hard drive, Windows 98/Me detects the drive only if it's noted as "removable" in the Device Manager**   Chances are that you missed one or two steps and neglected to partition and format the drive. All hard disk drives must be partitioned before they can be formatted—even if the drive is only going to have a single partition. Windows 98/Me incorrectly allows you to format an unpartitioned drive *if* you designate the drive as "removable." Using a drive this way will almost certainly result in data loss. The solution is to back up any data on the drive, then remove the checkmark from the "removable" box in the Windows 98 Device Manager. Next, use FDISK to create at least one primary and active partition. Reboot the system, then format the partition(s) with FORMAT. This process will destroy any data on the drive, but should correct the recognition issue.

SYMPTOM 21-55   **When upgrading Windows 95 OSR2 to Windows 98, you see an "SU0013" error**   When drive C: is configured as a "removable media" device and using the FAT32 file system, you may see an error such as; "SU0013—Setup cannot create files on your startup drive and cannot set up Windows 98." To circumvent this issue, you'll need to run Setup from DOS:

1. Boot your computer with a Windows 98 Startup Disk.

2. On the Startup menu, choose "Start Computer with CD-ROM Support," and then press ENTER.

3. At the A: prompt, type *<drive>*:\win98\setup, where *<drive>* is the drive letter assigned to your CD-ROM drive, and then press ENTER.

4. Follow the instructions shown to finish the Setup process and complete the upgrade.

SYMPTOM 21-56   **You find that the System Configuration Utility will not work under Windows 98**   When you run the System Configuration Utility, the following items may not work:

- Diagnostic Startup—Interactive Load
- Enable Startup Menu
- Disable Scandisk After bad shutdown
- Disable SCSI Double-Buffering

This problem occurs if you use any version of the DriveSpace disk compression software to compress your hard disk in place (that is, you compressed the entire hard disk). When you compress a hard disk in place, DriveSpace swaps hard disk letters after the initialization of the compressed volume file (CVF). Because the System Configuration Utility is not aware of the drive letter swap, it edits the MSDOS.SYS file on the CVF instead of the MSDOS.SYS file on the host drive. This is a problem with Windows 98. To correct this problem, edit the MSDOS.SYS file on the host drive (usually drive H:) after DriveSpace is loaded. Note that DriveSpace hides the host drive by default. To make the host drive visible, follow these steps:

1. Click Start, highlight Programs, select Accessories, select System Tools, and then click DriveSpace.

2. Click the compressed drive (where the hidden drive is a host drive), then click Properties on the Drive menu.

3. Click the Hide Host Drive check box to clear it.

4. Click OK.

Now start a word processor such as EDIT and load the MSDOS.SYS file for the host drive, then adjust the MSDOS.SYS file as follows (if the appropriate line does not exist, create it in the [Options] section):

■ To enable "diagnostic startup," edit or add the line **orig_diag_BootMenu=1**. To disable the option, remove the line or change the value from **1** to **0**.

■ To enable the "Startup Menu," edit or add the line **BootMenu=1**. To disable the option, change the value from **1** to **0**.

■ To disable "automatic ScanDisk after an incorrect shutdown," edit or add the line **AutoScan=0**. To enable the option, change the value from **0** to **1**.

■ To enable "SCSI double-buffering," edit or add the line **DoubleBuffer=1**. To disable SCSI double-buffering, change the value from **1** to **0**.

SYMPTOM 21-57 **You encounter an "invalid command line" error when using NAI Nuts & Bolts DiskMinder** This problem occurs when recovering after an improper shutdown under Windows 98 if you are using the NAI Nuts & Bolts DiskMinder program instead of ScanDisk as your disk repair program. NAI Nuts & Bolts DiskMinder is unable to correctly interpret the **/simpleui** switch used with ScanDisk in the WIN.COM file. To work around this problem, simply ignore the error message, and DiskMinder can continue normally. Check with the program maker to see if a patch or update is available.

SYMPTOM 21-58 **Norton DiskDoctor refuses to run after an improper shutdown under Windows 9x/Me** After you upgrade Windows 95 to Windows 98/Me (or reinstall Windows), the Norton DiskDoctor utility (included with Symantec Norton Utilities 2.0s or 3.0x) doesn't run automatically after an improper shutdown of Windows—ScanDisk for DOS is used instead. Norton Utilities updates the WIN.COM file to run the Norton DiskDoctor utility (NDD.EXE) when Windows is shut down incorrectly. When you upgrade Windows 95 to Windows 98/Me (or reinstall Windows), the WIN.COM file is replaced, and ScanDisk is then used as the default disk utility. You can correct this problem simply by reinstalling Norton Utilities again. You could also create an alternative utility file for DiskDoctor. At a command prompt (from within Windows), enter the following commands:

```
cd\windows\command
copy ndd.exe scandisk.alt
```

This creates a copy of the Norton DiskDoctor utility named SCANDISK.ALT. When Windows 9x/Me is shut down improperly, the SCANDISK.ALT file (now the Norton DiskDoctor utility) is run automatically.

SYMPTOM 21-59   **ScanDisk incorrectly reports hard drive problems under Windows 98** When you upgrade from Windows 3.x to Windows 98, Setup may quit and recommend you run ScanDisk to repair your hard disk—but no errors are found after you run ScanDisk. This is a known problem with Windows 98 and occurs when your Windows 3.x-based computer is configured to use a network server for virtual memory. To work around this issue, run Windows 98 Setup with the **/is** parameter (Setup runs normally, but skips ScanDisk) such as:

```
setup /is
```

SYMPTOM 21-60   **When running CHKDSK.EXE from a command prompt, you receive an "F parameter not specified" error**   This issue may occur under Windows 9x/Me, and the entire error message usually appears as such:

```
Errors found, F parameter not specified. Corrections will not be written to disk.
CHKDSK cannot check the validity of this drive because the following path is too
long:
```

This problem typically occurs when the command line you type contains more than 67 characters. To get around this issue, use ScanDisk instead of CHKDSK to check your hard disk for errors.

SYMPTOM 21-61   **While using APC PowerChute, Defrag locks up the system after selecting a disk to defragment**   This problem occurs when you're using APC PowerChute Plus 5.0 or 5.0.1 under Windows 98—these versions of PowerChute Plus are designed for Windows 95 only. To work around this problem, quit PowerChute Plus before using Defrag:

1. Press CTRL-ALT-DEL to open the Close Program dialog box.
2. Click PowerChute Plus, and then click End Task.
3. Do the same thing for Iconclnt.
4. Now run Defrag normally.

To restart PowerChute Plus after Defrag is completed, simply reboot the computer. For a more permanent fix to this problem, obtain updated software from APC.

SYMPTOM 21-62   **Defrag causes a GPF in USER.EXE under Windows 9x/Me**   When you try to run Defrag from System Agent or Task Scheduler, you may receive a General Protection Fault (or GPF) in USER.EXE. This may occur if the task information for Defrag has become damaged. Delete the Defrag task from System Agent or Task Scheduler, and then create a new task.

SYMPTOM 21-63   **You cannot place a FAT32 partition on a drive**   The trick to establishing a FAT32 partition on a drive is to partition the drive correctly. Try the following steps to partition a drive:

1. In the Windows 9x/Me Device Manager, select the drive and click on Properties.
2. Click Settings, then click the Int13 Unit check box to select it.
3. Quit the Device Manager and restart Windows.

4.   Once Windows is restarted, open an MS-DOS session and use the FDISK command to partition the drive (be careful not to partition an existing drive accidentally).

5.   Restart Windows again. You should be able to format the drive and use the FAT32 file system.

SYMPTOM 21-64   **After moving a FAT32 SCSI hard drive from one controller to another, you cannot read or write reliably to the SCSI drive**   This is because SCSI drives are highly controller-dependent to begin with, and you should be prepared to repartition and reformat SCSI drives *whenever* changing the SCSI host controller. This behavior is particularly evident when you partition and format a hard disk using a SCSI controller that fully supports Int 13 extensions, and you then move the hard disk to a controller that does *not* fully support Int 13 extensions. To move a drive using the FAT32 file system to a different controller, you must verify that *both* controllers fully support Int 13 extensions in the same manner—if they do not, data loss will most likely occur.

SYMPTOM 21-65   **When you try to compress a drive with DriveSpace or DriveSpace 3, you receive the following error message: "Drive C cannot be compressed because it is a FAT32 drive"**   This is because DriveSpace was designed to work with the FAT12 and FAT16 file systems and cannot be used on drives with the FAT32 file system. Unfortunately, there is no correction for this problem, and Microsoft is considering an update for a future release. In the meantime, your only options are to avoid using drive compression or to use a third-party drive compression tool that is FAT32 compatible. Check out the Stacker site (**www.stac.com**).

SYMPTOM 21-66   **When booting from a floppy disk, you cannot access your FAT32 hard drive partition(s)**   The system boots fine from the hard drive. This is an issue with the boot disk. Boot disks made with older versions of DOS or Windows are not "FAT32-aware" and cannot support access to your FAT32 hard drive partition(s). For example, you cannot access your Windows 98 FAT32 drive when booting from a Windows 95a Startup Disk. Create a Windows 98/Me Startup Disk in order to boot your FAT32 system.

SYMPTOM 21-67   **You encounter an error message such as: "Setup found a compressed volume or a disk cache utility"**   This can occur if you try to install a retail version of Windows 95 over an OSR2 version of Windows 95. There are actually a number of problems that can crop up when installing an older version of Windows 95. The initial error usually appears like:

```
Setup found a compressed volume or a disk-cache utility on your computer.
Quit setup and check your compressed volume with your disk-compression
software or remove the disk-cache utility. Then run Setup again.
```

If you continue trying to install Windows 95 on a hard disk using the FAT32 file system, you may receive the following error message:

```
SU-0013
```

If you are installing the retail version of Windows 95 over OSR2 on a hard disk using the FAT16 file system, Setup continues but experiences numerous file version conflicts that generate the following message:

```
A file being copied is older than the file currently on your computer. It is
recommended that you keep your existing file.
```

If you click Yes to keep the newer files, Setup finishes, but when you restart the computer, the system may stop responding (hang up) at the logo screen, or you see an error message such as: "Fatal Exception 0D has occurred at 0117:00007E1F." Starting Windows 95 in Safe mode may also generate the following error message:

```
Fatal Exception 0D has occurred at 0117:00007E1F
```

To verify the version you are installing, type **ver** at a command prompt. Version 4.00.950 (files dated 7-11-95) is the retail version and OEM (non-OSR2) version. Version 4.00.1111 (files dated 8-24-96) indicates the Windows 95 OEM Service Release 2 (OSR2). Do *not* install the retail or OEM (non-OSR2) version of Windows 95 into an existing Windows 95 OSR2 folder. If you are installing to a hard disk using the FAT16 file system, install to a *different* folder.

> Do *not* install the retail or OEM version of Windows 95 on a hard disk using the FAT32 file system.

You should reinstall OSR2 using the OSR2 CD provided by your OEM. If an OSR2 CD-ROM was not provided to you by your OEM, the OSR2 files may have been provided in a folder on your hard disk. To locate this folder, type the following command at a command prompt:

```
dir *.cab /s
```

To reinstall OSR2, run SETUP.EXE from the folder containing the OSR2 cabinet (.CAB) files. If you cannot reinstall ORS2, contact your OEM (the company that sold the system) for assistance. Installing a more recent version of Windows 98/Me should also relieve the problem.

SYMPTOM 21-68   **You cannot use SHARE.EXE in Windows 95**   The SHARE.EXE utility is not supported in the OSR2 release of Windows 95. In order to support the FAT32 file system, SHARE.EXE support has been disabled in the real-mode MS-DOS kernel regardless of whether or not you have any drives using the FAT32 file system. Instead, file sharing and locking capabilities are provided by VSHARE.VXD in OSR2 and are not supported in MS-DOS mode. This means you may not be able to install or run some MS-DOS-based programs or 16-bit Windows-based programs that require SHARE.EXE.

Some programs (such as Microsoft Word version 6.0 for Windows and Quattro Pro version 6.0 for Windows) do not require SHARE.EXE to be loaded in order to start. Instead, they simply look for a file named SHARE.EXE in either the root folder or the DOS folder. This file can be a zero-byte file created with a text editor like EDIT or Notepad. Other programs may simply look for the string "share" in the AUTOEXEC.BAT file.

SYMPTOM 21-69   **The system may hang up when certain drive software is used under FAT32**   After installing the drive software (such as PC Tools Pro 9.0), the computer will probably hang up during startup after you see the following message:

```
Analyzing drive C:
Reading system areas
```

In virtually all cases, this occurs because your drive software is *not* compatible with the FAT32 file system in Windows 95 OSR2 (or Windows 98/Me). You can contact the software maker (such as Symantec for PC Tools Pro 9.0 at **www.symantec.com**) for a FAT32-aware version of the software. As a work-around, you can use a text editor (such as EDIT or Notepad) to edit the AUTOEXEC.BAT file and disable the command line that starts the software. For PC Tools Pro 9.0, you'd REM-out its line such as:

```
REM call pctools.bat
```

SYMPTOM 21-70   **You encounter errors using IBM antivirus utilities on a FAT32 file system**   In actual practice, you'll probably encounter either of the following symptoms:

- When you're installing IBM Anti-Virus, the Setup program offers to scan for viruses. If you choose to scan, you may receive an error message stating that the master boot record could not be read.

- When you're scanning for viruses on a drive using the FAT32 file system, IBM Anti-Virus may report that errors occurred while it was checking for viruses. The error log may contain information such as: "Errors during virus checking: unexpected error code 18."

Older versions of IBM Anti-Virus are *not* written to work with the new FAT32 file system included with OSR2 and Windows 98/Me. There is no work-around for this, and you'll need to obtain an updated version of IBM software or use a different antivirus tool that is FAT32-aware.

SYMPTOM 21-71   **When using Defrag on a FAT32 system, you encounter an error message such as "DEFRAG0026 Make sure disk is formatted"**   You may also see an error such as:

```
Windows cannot defragment this drive. Make sure the disk is formatted and
free of errors. Then try defragmenting the drive again.
```

This error can be caused when running an earlier version of DEFRAG.EXE than the version included with Windows 95 OSR2 (or Windows 98/Me). To resolve this problem, extract a new copy of the DEFRAG.EXE file from your original Windows 95 OSR2 (or Windows 98/Me) CD:

1.   Open an MS-DOS prompt in Windows.

2.   Change to the Windows folder and then type the following line:

```
ren defrag.exe defrag.xxx
```

3.   Insert the OSR2 CD, OSR2 disk 6, or Windows 98/Me CD in the appropriate drive. If you are using the CD-ROM, type the following line:

```
extract <x>:\win95\win95_05.cab defrag.exe /l <z>:\windows
```

where *<x>* is the CD-ROM drive letter and *<z>* is the drive containing the Windows folder. If you are using disk 6, type the following line:

```
extract <x>:\win95_06.cab defrag.exe /l <z>:\windows
```

where *<x>* is the drive containing disk 6 and *<z>* is the drive containing the Windows folder.

SYMPTOM 21-72   **You see an "Invalid Media" error message when formatting a FAT32 partition**   When you try to format a FAT32 file system partition larger than 8025MB (8GB) from within Windows 9x/Me, you may receive the following error message:

```
Verifying <xxx.xx>M
Invalid media or track 0 bad-disk unusable
Format terminated
```

where *<xxx.xx>* is the size of the partition. This error occurs if there is a non-DOS partition preceding the extended DOS partition *and* the primary DOS partition has been formatted using the real-mode FORMAT.EXE command. To correct this problem, you'll need to reformat the volume using the following steps:

1. Click the Start button, click Shut Down, click "Restart The Computer In MS-DOS Mode," and then click Yes.

2. Type the following command and then press ENTER:

    ```
    format <drive>:
    ```

    where *<drive>* is the drive letter for the partition you want to format.

3. When the partition is formatted, type **exit** to restart Windows.

SYMPTOM 21-73 **Opening a folder seems to take a very long time** When you open a folder in Microsoft Explorer on a drive using the FAT32 file system, it may seem to take an unusually long time before the window is accessible, or the "The Working in Background" mouse pointer may be present for a long time. This problem occurs because the total space used by all directory entries in the folder exceeds 32KB. To resolve this issue, move some files to a different folder.

SYMPTOM 21-74 **You find that your FAT32 system works in "Compatibility Mode" when using Ontrack Disk Manager** After you install FAT32 on a drive that uses Ontrack Disk Manager (version 6.03 or 7.04), all drives use MS-DOS compatibility mode, or the computer seems to take an unusually long time to boot. This happens because the Dynamic Drive Overlay (or DDO) is unable to find files in the root folder that it needs to start correctly. A Dynamic Drive Overlay makes calculations for the starting root folder cluster based on FAT12 and FAT16 volumes and returns a value of zero for FAT32 volumes (it does this because of changes made in the root directory structure). The overlay software searches all possible clusters in the root folder for its overlay files. You'll need to configure Disk Manager to avoid searching the root folder for overlay files.

Configuring Disk Manager software to avoid searching the root folder causes Disk Manager not to hook the DOS interrupt chain—forcing Disk Manager to load low in conventional memory.

SYMPTOM 21-75 **The OSR2 version of Windows 95 will not allow dual-booting with Windows 3.1x** If you try to dual-boot Windows version 3.x on a computer running Windows 95 OSR2, you'll receive one of the following error messages:

- This version of Windows does not run on MS-DOS 6.x or earlier.

- You started your computer with a version of MS-DOS incompatible with this version of Windows. Insert a Startup diskette matching this version of Windows and then restart.

- The system has been halted. Press CTRL-ALT-DELETE to restart your computer.

- This version of Windows cannot be run on this version of DOS.

Beginning with OSR2, dual-booting with Windows 3.x is *not* supported in Windows 95. To dual-boot between Windows 3.x and Windows 95, you'll need to install the retail version of Windows 95. If you have FAT32 drives, you need to remove the FAT32 partitions and create FAT16 partitions with the Windows 95 or MS-DOS 6.x version of FDISK.EXE.

Neither MS-DOS 6.x nor the early retail version of Windows 95 will recognize a FAT32 volume.

SYMPTOM 21-76   After you install Windows 98/Me (or convert a partition to FAT32), Windows 98/Me reports "DOS Compatibility Mode"   This can occur when the drive controller has not been detected properly under Windows 98/Me. Try rebooting the PC and see if Windows will redetect the drive controller (you may need to remove the drive controller entry from the Device Manager before rebooting the system). For specific details about resolving Compatibility Mode problems, refer to the DOS Compatibility Mode troubleshooting guide at the start of this section.

SYMPTOM 21-77   After converting a drive to FAT32, you notice that tools like ScanDisk and Defrag take much longer to run   This is an undesired side effect of the FAT32 file system. It takes Defrag and ScanDisk the same amount of time to examine a single cluster, regardless of the cluster's size. Since FAT32 uses smaller clusters, there are many times more clusters, and such utilities take considerably longer than they had before conversion. Microsoft compensates for this by including the Tune Up Wizard, which allows you to schedule such tasks to take place when you're away from the computer.

SYMPTOM 21-78   The FAT32 conversion utility crashed after reporting that it found bad sectors   This is a side effect of ScanDisk. If ScanDisk has marked any sectors bad, the FAT32 converter will refuse to run, even if the sectors are fixed by third-party disk utilities (such as Data Lifeguard Tools). ScanDisk uses the FAT table to keep track of bad sectors. But even if third-party utilities remap bad sectors at the hardware level, ScanDisk is not aware of those changes. One solution is to wipe the hard drive clean and start over (in which case you'd just partition the drive using FAT32 to begin with). Here's an easier workaround when there are only a few bad sectors:

1.   Before using the FAT32 conversion utility, perform a complete backup of your hard drive.

2.   Run your third-party disk utility software (such as Data Lifeguard Tools) to make sure that any bad sectors have been re-mapped.

3.   Open a DOS window and type:

    ```
    cvt x: /cvt32
    ```

    where *x* is the drive letter you wish to convert.

4.   The converter will then run, disregarding any sectors that have previously been marked bad by ScanDisk.

SYMPTOM 21-79   The FAT32 converter under Windows 98 cannot locate the drive partition to be converted   When using the Windows 98 "drive converter" tool to convert a drive from FAT16 to FAT32, you may receive an error message such as: "Drive converter unable to find the drive partition." This problem can occur if you try to convert a FAT16 logical drive that begins above the 8.0GB mark. For example, if you have a 10GB hard disk with five 2.0GB FAT16 partitions, you may have trouble converting the fifth drive (drive G:) to FAT32. To work around this problem, delete all of your partitions above the 8.0GB mark and then re-create your partitions:

All data on the specific partition or drive will be deleted, so back up your data before you perform the following steps.

1. Click Start, select Programs, then click MS-DOS Prompt.

2. At the command prompt, type **FDISK**, press Y when you're prompted to "enable large disk support," and then press ENTER.

3. Press 4, and then press ENTER.

4. Press Y, and then press ENTER. Note the partition information for all of the drives listed on this screen, and then press ESC.

5. Press 3, press ENTER, press 3, then press ENTER again.

6. Press the letter that corresponds to the last drive listed in the extended partition, then press ENTER. For a 10.0GB drive with five 2.0GB partitions, the fifth "drive" would be G: (the only one remaining in FAT16 format).

7. Type the "volume label" displayed to the left of the drive letter exactly as it appears, then press ENTER.

8. Press Y, press ENTER, press ESC, then press ESC again.

9. Press 1, press ENTER, press 3, then press ENTER again.

10. You're prompted to use all of the remaining available drive space—press Y and then press ENTER.

11. Press ESC to exit FDISK, type **exit**, and then press ENTER.

12. Restart your computer so that your changes will take effect.

13. Double-click My Computer, right-click drive G:, then click Format.

14. Click Full, click Start, then click OK.

Further Study

Maxtor   www.maxtor.com
MicroHouse   www.microhouse.com
PowerQuest   www.powerquest.com
Quantum   www.quantum.com
Seagate   www.seagate.com
StorageSoft, Inc.   www.storagesoft.com
Symantec   www.symantec.com
Western Digital   www.wdc.com

JOYSTICKS
AND GAME PORTS

Few peripheral devices have come to represent PC entertainment like the *joystick* (Figure 22-1). Although it is one of the simplest peripherals available for a PC, the joystick allows a user to bring an element of hand-eye coordination to interactive programs (for example, flight simulators and 3D "walk-through" games) that would simply be impossible with a keyboard or mouse. The joystick interfaces to the host PC through a basic connection called the *game port adapter* (or simply the game port). This chapter discusses the joystick and game port, then covers a selection of troubleshooting issues.

Understanding the Game Port System

The typical game port uses a relatively simple interface to the PC. Only the lower 8 data bits are used (which explains why so many older game ports used the older 8-bit XT card style rather than switching to a 16-bit AT ISA card type). Also, only the lower 10 address bits are needed. Since the game port is an I/O device, the card uses I/OR and I/OW control signals. On virtually all PCs, port 201h is reserved for the game port. Figure 22-2 illustrates a typical game port system.

INSIDE THE JOYSTICK

Each analog joystick is assembled with two separate potentiometers (these are adjustable resistors, which are typically 100 kOhms) arranged perpendicularly to one another. One potentiometer represents the X axis,

FIGURE 22-1   A Thrustmaster TopGun Fox 2 joystick

while the other potentiometer represents the Y axis. Both potentiometers are linked together mechanically and attached to a movable stick. As the stick is moved left or right, one potentiometer is moved. As the stick moves up or down, the other potentiometer is moved. Of course, the stick can be moved in both the X and Y axes simultaneously, with the proportions of resistance reflecting the stick's position. The stick itself is normally tensioned with a series of springs so that it will return to the center position when released. You can see the wiring scheme for a standard 15-pin dual joystick port in Figure 22-3. Standard game ports use a DB-15 (15-pin) female connector, and the pinout for a standard joystick port is listed in Table 22-1.

Don't be fooled by the fancy plastic molding, contoured grips, and "techno" appearance of today's joysticks. They may look fancy, but virtually all analog joysticks are internally identical.

Detecting the stick's X and Y position is not an intuitively obvious process. Ultimately, the analog value of each potentiometer must be converted to a digital value that is read by the game application software. This

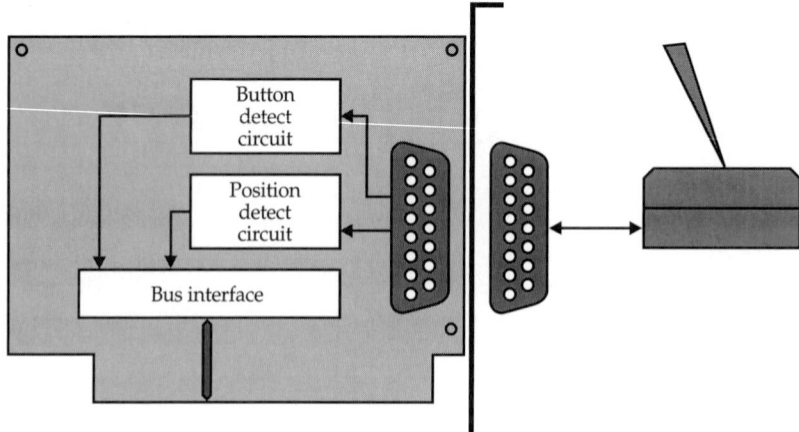

FIGURE 22-2   Simplified diagram of a game port system

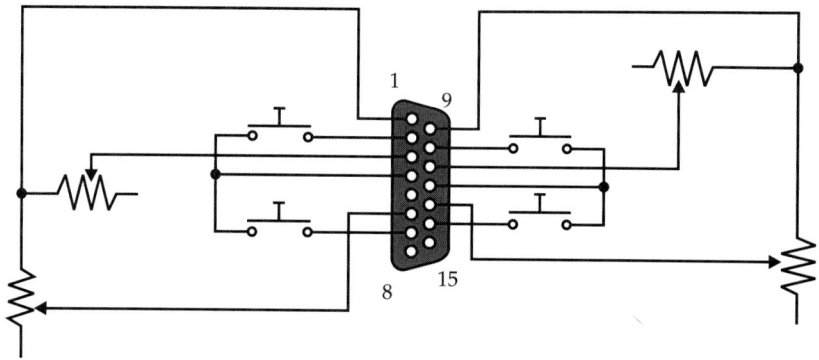

FIGURE 22-3   Wiring diagram for a conventional dual joystick port

is an important wrinkle—since the game port does not generate an interrupt, it is up to the particular *application* to interrogate the joystick port regularly. You might imagine that such a conversion would use an *analog-to-digital converter* (ADC). However, an ADC provides much greater resolution than is needed, and its conversions require a relatively long time. Current game port conversion circuits use a "multivibrator" element.

Ultimately, the resistance of each potentiometer is determined indirectly by measuring the amount of time required for a charged capacitor to discharge through the particular potentiometer. If a certain axis is at 0 ohms, the multivibrator's internal capacitor will discharge in about $24.2\mu S$, while at 100 kOhms, the multivibrator's capacitor will discharge in about $112\mu S$. Since this is a relatively linear relationship, the discharge time can easily be equated to potentiometer position. (An actual routine to accomplish this requires only about 16 lines of assembler code.) The multivibrator technique also simplifies the circuitry needed on the game port adapter. It is really the application (the game itself) that is doing the work.

TABLE 22-1   **PIN ASSIGNMENTS FOR A STANDARD 15-PIN JOYSTICK PORT**

PIN	JOYSTICK
1	XY1 (Joystick 1 +5V supply)
2	Switch 1
3	Potentiometer X1 signal
4	Ground (for switch 1 & 2)
5	Ground (for switch 2)
6	Potentiometer Y1 signal
7	Switch 2
8	N.C. (or +5V)
9	XY2 (Joystick 2 +5V supply)
10	Switch 3
11	Potentiometer X2 signal
12	Ground (for switch 3 & 4)
13	Potentiometer Y2 signal
14	Switch 4
15	N.C. (or +5V)

A joystick also has one or two buttons. As you see from Figure 22-3, the buttons are typically open, and their closed state can be detected by reading the byte at I/O port 201h. Since the game port is capable of supporting two joysticks simultaneously (each with two buttons), the upper four bits of I/O port 201h indicate the on/off status of all four buttons.

Windows 98/Me supports a joystick as a game controller through an icon in the Control Panel. You can access, add, delete, and modify your joysticks through that properties dialog (Figure 22-4). Unlike DOS applications, Windows provides joystick support to all applications, so you need only identify and calibrate the joystick once.

ADAPTING A SECOND JOYSTICK

While the typical game port can support two joysticks, most joystick products only connect a single joystick. This means only half the game port is being utilized. You can purchase a joystick Y-adapter from any computer store, or construct a Y-adapter using the pinout in Table 22-2. You'll need a DB-15 (15-pin) male connector to attach to the game port and two DB-15 female connectors to attach to each of the two joysticks.

Some types of game port boards provide a separate 15-pin connector for each joystick. Some cut-price game port boards only provide one connector and the circuitry for one joystick. Verify the capabilities of your game port before using or replacing a joystick Y-adapter.

JOYSTICK CALIBRATION

Unfortunately, the values of time versus resistance that you saw earlier are not the same for every system. Variations in joystick potentiometers, game port adapter circuits, and computer speed will all affect the relationship of time versus resistance. Even variations in component temperature as the PC warms up can

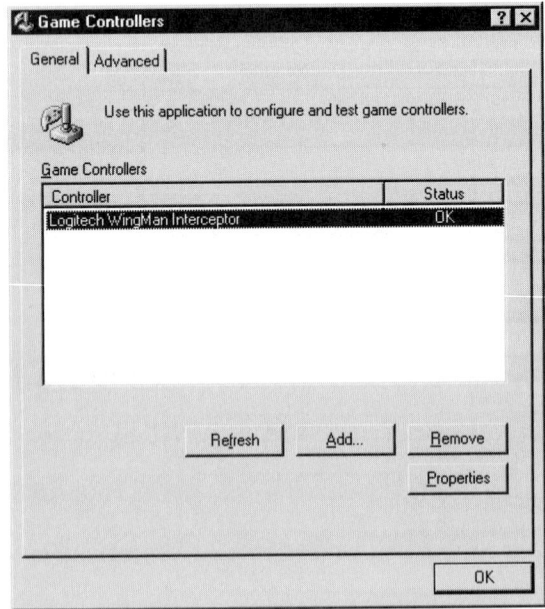

FIGURE 22-4   Identifying a joystick through the Windows Game Controllers properties dialog

TABLE 22-2   PIN ASSIGNMENTS FOR A JOYSTICK Y-ADAPTER

GAME PORT (DB-15 MALE)		JOYSTICK 1 (DB-15 FEMALE)	JOYSTICK 2 (DB-15 FEMALE)
Pin	Definition	Pin	Pin
1	XY1 (Joystick 1 +5V supply)	1	
2	Switch 1	2	
3	Potentiometer X1 signal	3	
4	Ground (for switch 1 & 2)	4	
5	Ground (for switch 2)	5	
6	Potentiometer Y1 signal	6	
7	Switch 2	7	
8	N.C. (or +5V)	8	
9	XY2 (Joystick 2 +5V supply)		1
10	Switch 3		2
11	Potentiometer X2 signal		3
12	Ground (for switch 3 & 4)		4 and 5
13	Potentiometer Y2 signal		6
14	Switch 4		7
15	N.C. (or +5V)		8

cause changes in resistance interpretation. This is why each application program that uses a joystick (or the Windows Game Controllers icon) comes with a *calibration* routine. Calibration allows a given application to measure values for center and corner positions. With this data as a base, the application can extrapolate all other joystick positions.

Take it slowly when calibrating. This is most important when you're setting up the controller in a game. The game will ask you to supply it with specific information about your controller. If you do not provide the correct information, or do not follow the calibration process, it cannot correctly interpret the controller signals during game play. There are several types of calibration that you should be familiar with: *corner-to-corner* calibration, *low and high axis value* calibration, *full circle* calibration, and *invisible* calibration.

Corner-to-Corner Calibration

This type of software calibration teaches the software what values your controller uses for these three requested locations. The software can then make calculations based on these positions to determine where the joystick is at any time. The main difficulty with this type of calibration is that many joysticks don't have "corners" that a game player can feel (for example, many joysticks use circular openings rather than square ones). To position the joystick in a corner, you'd need to know where the electrical corners are located, or make your best guess. Some games ask you to move your controller like this:

■ Move the controller to the upper-left corner and press a button.

■ Move the controller to the lower-right corner and press a button.

■ Center the controller and press a button.

 Make sure that you hold the joystick handle in position until after you have pressed the button. If you release the handle before you press the button, it will self-center and the game will read the wrong values.

Low and High Axis Value Calibration

This type of software calibration teaches the software the extreme positions of each axis for your joystick. The software can then make calculations based on these positions to determine where the joystick is at any time. This is often a more comprehensive and reliable means of calibration. You may be asked to perform controller movements like these:

- Move the controller to the left and press a button.
- Move the controller to the right and press a button.
- Move the controller forward and press a button.
- Move the controller back and press a button.
- Center the controller and press a button.

Full-Circle Calibration

Other calibration programs ask you to move the controller around in a full circle. After you have completed the requested movements, a button press or keystroke allows the software to determine the minimum and maximum values for the horizontal and vertical axes of the controller. Software calibration programs like this sometimes display a graph of the controller axes. This is a particularly useful approach when you're using a joystick with a circular housing opening.

Invisible Calibration

There could be several reasons why you may not notice any kind of calibration program when you begin some games. Some games "remember" the calibration from a previous session, so if you're having problems controlling a craft or character, look at the manual (or the game's online help) for a keystroke that will allow you to recalibrate the joystick. Some games assume that the readings from a controller at game startup represent the joystick's center position. If your controller was not centered at game startup, you may experience problems. Once again, it may be necessary to recalibrate the joystick manually.

Another reason why you may not see any prompt to calibrate a joystick at the beginning of a game is because the game is defaulting to the mouse or keyboard. You will need to locate an option in the game that will let you select the correct input device. Look for a "configure" menu, or an installation or setup program. Choosing "joystick or game pad" as an input device should activate the calibration program.

JOYSTICK DRIFT

The term *drift* (rolling) is used to indicate a loss of control by the joystick. There are several possible reasons for this. As a technician, you should understand why drift occurs and how to correct such problems. First, drift may be the result of a system conflict. Since the game port does not generate an interrupt, conflicts rarely result in system crashes or lockups, but another device feeding data to port 201h can easily upset joystick operation. If you have sound boards or multiport I/O boards in your system equipped with game ports, be sure to disable any unused ports. (Check with the user instructions for individual boards to disable extra game ports.)

Another possible cause of drift is heat. Once PCs are started up, it is natural for the power used by most components to be dissipated as heat. Unfortunately, heating tends to change the value of components. For logic circuits, this is typically not a problem, but for analog circuits, the consequences can be much more pronounced. As heat changes the values of a multivibrator circuit, timing (and thus positional values) will shift. As the circuit warms up, an error creeps into the joystick. Well-designed game port adapters will use high-quality, low-drift components that minimize the effects of heat-related drift. It is interesting to note that the joystick itself is rarely the cause of drift. If you can't compensate for drift by periodically recalibrating the joystick, try a better-quality game port adapter board.

Finally, the quality of calibration is only as good as the calibration routine itself. A poor or inaccurate routine will tend to calibrate the joystick incorrectly. Try another application. If another application can calibrate and use the joystick properly, you should suspect a bug in the particular application. Try contacting the application manufacturer to find if there is a patch or fix available.

CLEANING JOYSTICKS

Ordinarily, the typical joystick should not require routine cleaning or maintenance. Most joysticks use reasonably reliable potentiometers that should last for the life of the joystick. The two major enemies of a joystick are wear and dust. Wear occurs during normal use as potentiometer sliders move across the resistive surface—it can't be avoided. Over time, wear will affect the contact resistance values of both potentiometers. Uneven wear will result in uneven performance. When this becomes noticeable, it is time to buy a new joystick. Joysticks endure violent movements during game play, and this can also shorten their working life.

Dust presents another problem. The open aperture at the top of a joystick is an invitation for dust and other debris. Since dust is conductive, it can adversely affect potentiometer values and interfere with slider contacts. If the joystick seems to produce a jumpy or nonlinear response to the application, it might be worth trying to clean the joystick rather than scrapping it. Turn off the computer and disconnect the joystick. Open the joystick, which is usually held together by two screws in the bottom housing. Remove the bottom housing and locate the two potentiometers. Most potentiometers have small openings somewhere around their circumference. Dust out the joystick area with compressed air, and spray a small quantity of good-quality electrical contact cleaner into each potentiometer. Move the potentiometer through its complete range of motion a few times, and allow several minutes for the cleaner to dry. Reassemble the housing and try the joystick again. If problems persist, replace the joystick.

JOYSTICKS AND WINDOWS 95/98

Games have traditionally been a domain of DOS, so there has been little support for joysticks under older Windows versions. However, now that games are routinely using Windows 98/Me (taking advantage of features like DirectX and Direct3D), you can install and calibrate a variety of joysticks under Windows. Open your Control Panel and look for the Game Controllers joystick icon. If a joystick icon appears in your Control Panel, joystick support is already installed, and you can skip to the Game Controller setup. If you have not yet added your PC game port as New Hardware in the Windows Control Panel, you should do this first:

1.   Click the Start button.

2.   Select Settings, then Control Panel.

3.   In the Control Panel, look for a joystick icon. If it's there, skip to the Game Controller setup. If not, double-click the Add New Hardware icon to start the Add New Hardware wizard.

4.   When prompted to have Windows search for new hardware, select No. Click Next to continue.

5.   Select Sound, Video and Game Controllers and then click Next.

6.   Select the manufacturer and game port joystick (or other appropriate model). This will add the game port as a device. Click Next.

7.   If resource settings are given as 0201-0201, click Next. Windows will look for the required files. If it can't find these files, it will ask you to insert your Windows installation CD.

8.   When the files have been installed, click Finished.

9.   Shut down your computer, and restart Windows 98/Me to enable your game port support.

Once your game port driver has been added, a joystick icon appears in your Control Panel. Use this to set up and calibrate your joystick:

1.   Double-click the Game Controllers icon in the Control Panel.

2.   In the Game Controllers section, choose the appropriate joystick type from the list, and then click Properties.

3.   The Game Controller properties dialog will appear and provide you with a basic calibration dialog. For advanced joysticks, you may see an actual representation of the device, as in Figure 22-5. In either case, test the joystick's range of motion and buttons, and then save your calibration.

4.   You should now be able to use the joystick under any Windows 98/Me game or other joystick-aware application.

Troubleshooting Joysticks and Game Ports

The unique advantage to troubleshooting this area of a PC is that there is surprisingly little to actually go wrong. In virtually all cases, problems reside in the joystick, the game port adapter, or the application software—that's about it. This part of the chapter provides you with some handy troubleshooting issues and examines some perplexing joystick problems.

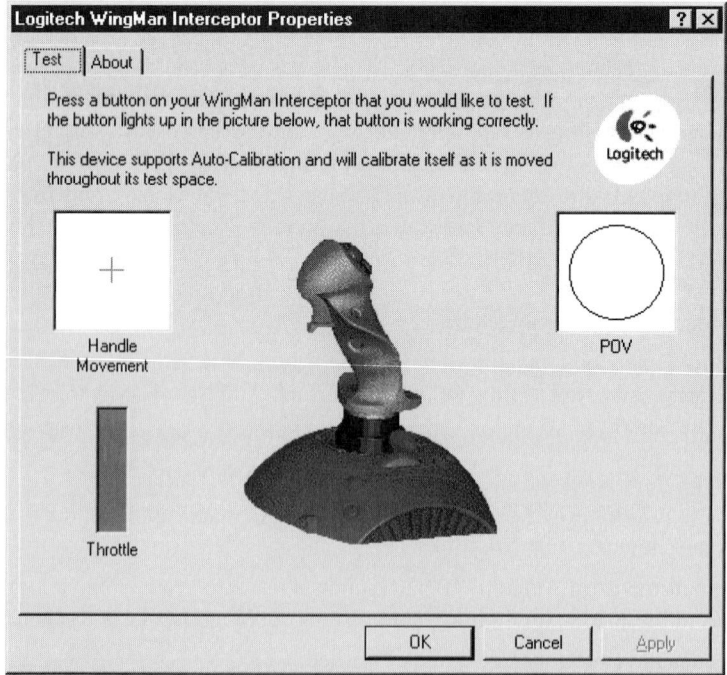

FIGURE 22-5   Calibrating the joystick through the Game Controller properties dialog

JOYSTICK ELIMINATOR PLUG

From time to time, you may find yourself testing a game port, but have no joystick handy. (Or it might be too much of a hassle to "borrow" a joystick already connected to a working PC.) You can construct a very simple circuit with two resistors (Figure 22-6) that can fool the game port into thinking that a real joystick is attached. This "joystick eliminator" plug simply places the cursor in a far corner of the display.

ADAPTING "HEADER" CONNECTIONS

Some multi-I/O boards implement the game port as a 16-pin "header" (ribbon cable) connector—assuming that you'll use a DB-15 connector "plate" in another open card slot and simply connect the DB-15 plate to the multi-I/O card using a 16-pin ribbon cable. The pin assignments are all identical (pin 16 of the IDC connector is just left unused), but remember that the pin *order* is different between header and DB-style connectors. For example, the top row of a DB-15 connector runs pins 9 through 15, but the top row of a ribbon cable uses pins 2, 4, 5, 6, 10, 12, 14, and 16.

SOUND CARDS AND Y-ADAPTER PROBLEMS

You will probably encounter difficulties when connecting commercial joystick Y-adapters to the game port on a sound board. This is because many sound card manufacturers (such as Creative Labs) have replaced pin 12 (normally the ground for joystick 2 switches 3 and 4) and pin 15 (typically N.C. or +5V) with specialized MIDI interface pins. The problem doesn't surface using a single joystick because pins 12 and 15 are normally unused. But when a second joystick is added through a Y-adapter, the second joystick will probably fail to function. Table 22-3 illustrates a simple correction to enable a commercial Y-adapter. Essentially, you must disconnect pins 12 and 15 at the game port (sound board) end, then cross-wire pin 12 to pin 5 (ground), and cross-wire pin 15 to pin 9 (+5V). If you want to make your own sound board–compatible Y-adapter, follow the pinout in Table 22-4.

Do *not* attempt to connect a MIDI device to the sound card while this modified Y-adapter is in place. Doing so can easily damage the MIDI device or the sound card's MIDI/game port.

BASIC JOYSTICK/CONTROLLER TROUBLESHOOTING GUIDELINES

There may be instances where your new game port or joystick is not detected or fails to respond. When this happens, try the following guidelines before attempting to research specific symptoms. The guidelines can help you isolate problems with analog, USB, and serial device detection.

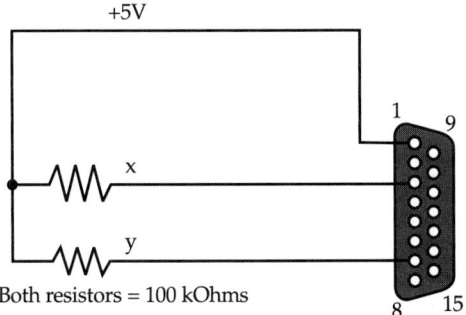

FIGURE 22-6   A simple "joystick eliminator" plug for game port testing

TABLE 22-3   PIN ASSIGNMENTS FOR A SOUND BOARD JOYSTICK CABLE ADAPTER

DB-15 MALE (TO GAME PORT) WIRE PIN...	DB-15 FEMALE (TO JOYSTICK Y-ADAPTER) TO PIN(S)...
1	1
2	2
3	3
4	4
5	5 and 12
6	6
7	7
8	8
9	9 and 15
10	10
11	11
12 unused	To pin 5
13	13
14	14
15 unused	To pin 9

It is important to discern if the issue is a *detection* issue or a *game setup* issue. Click Start, highlight Settings, click Control Panel, and then click the Game Controllers icon. If the manufacturer's gaming device is listed under Game Controllers, and its status is listed as OK, you'll know that the hardware is being detected properly by the system, and the device *should* work in the Control Panel if you try to calibrate it. (Go ahead and test this.) If it *does* work properly, the issue lies within the setup of the game, and

TABLE 22-4   PIN ASSIGNMENTS FOR A SOUND BOARD–COMPATIBLE JOYSTICK Y-ADAPTER

GAME PORT (DB-15 MALE) WIRE PIN...	JOYSTICK 1 (DB-15 FEMALE) TO PIN...	JOYSTICK 2 (DB-15 FEMALE) AND TO PIN...
1—XY1 (Joystick 1 +5V supply)	1	1
2—Switch 1	2	—
3—Potentiometer X1 signal	3	—
4—Ground (for switch 1 & 2)	4	4
5—Ground (for switch 2)	5	5
6—Potentiometer Y1 signal	6	—
7—Switch 2	7	—
8—N.C. (or +5V)	8	—
9—XY2 (Joystick 2 +5V supply)	—	8
10—Switch 3	—	2
11—Potentiometer X2 signal	—	3
12—MIDI	—	Unused
13—Potentiometer Y2 signal	—	6
14—Switch 4	—	7
15—MIDI	—	Unused

not in your hardware. However, if the gaming device is not listed under Game Controllers (or shows that the status is Not Connected), you should follow the troubleshooting steps next.

Dealing with Analog Devices

Chances are that you're using a traditional analog-type joystick, wheel, or other controller. If you're using an analog game controller device, try the guidelines suggested here.

Check Hardware Connections   Examine the connectors on both the joystick cable and ports on the computer, and look for bent pins or other damage. Ensure that the connector on the joystick's cable is completely seated in the game port on the computer. If the device is attached through a switch box or Y-adapter, try connecting *directly* to the computer.

Also verify that you've connected the 15-pin connector to a game port rather than a MIDI port. If your 15-pin port can serve as either a game port or MIDI port, see that the port is configured as a game port.

Check Game Port   Verify that the game port is enabled and that it is the only game port enabled on the system. Two active ports can cause an address conflict. In some cases, a game port is integrated into the motherboard of the computer, and when a game card is installed into the system, it conflicts with the preexisting port. Disable or remove any conflicting game port hardware.

Check Joystick Properties   Make sure that the proper device has been activated in the Windows 98/Me Joystick Properties tab—it should be set as Joystick 1. This will also reinitialize the device driver:

1. Click Start, highlight Settings, and then click Control Panel.

2. Double-click the Game Controllers icon.

3. For the Joystick Configuration entry, select None and click Apply.

4. Reselect your particular gaming device and click Apply.

Change Game Port Address   Verify that the game port is using the correct resources and that they do not conflict with other devices in the system:

1. Click Start, highlight Settings, and then click Control Panel.

2. Double-click the System icon, and then click the Device Manager tab.

3. Click the plus (+) next to Sound, Video and Game Controllers.

4. Double-click on the game port entry to bring up its properties dialog.

5. Click the Resources tab, and uncheck the Use Automatic Settings box.

6. Select Input/Output Range under Resource Type, click on Change Setting (if the game port allows you to), and select either 0200-0207 or 0201-0201.

7. Click OK until the system asks to restart the computer, and answer Yes or OK.

If the problem persists, skip ahead to the "Check for Software Problems" section.

Dealing with Digital (USB) Devices

USB game controllers have been growing in popularity over the last few years due to the appeal of their advanced features and their ease of connection/disconnection. If you're using a digital (USB) game controller device, try the guidelines suggested here.

Check Hardware Connections   Connect the gaming device directly to the computer's USB port. If a USB port hub is being used, try connecting the device directly to the USB port on the computer. If the device works correctly when directly connected to the computer, contact the manufacturer of the USB hub for assistance or replacement. For some advanced joysticks (such as the Logitech WingMan Force or the WingMan Formula Force), make sure the adapter is plugged in and connected to the gaming device. Many early USB systems (with motherboards using the PIX 3 chip) shipped with the USB ports disabled. These systems must have their USB ports enabled through the CMOS Setup before a USB device will be detected and function properly.

Do not connect a gaming device to the serial and USB ports at the same time. Connecting a gaming device to both ports simultaneously can cause detection problems or erratic joystick behavior.

Check USB Port Configuration   Your PC's USB port should be enabled and supported under Windows 98/Me. Use the Device Manager to verify that the USB port is correctly configured:

1. Click Start, highlight Settings, and then click Control Panel.
2. Double-click the System icon, and then click the Device Manager tab.
3. Verify that you have an entry called Universal Serial Bus Controller. If this entry does not exist, you'll need to contact your USB hardware vendor to correctly configure the USB controller.
4. Open the Universal Serial Bus Controller entry by clicking on its plus (+) sign. Verify that there is a USB Root Hub entry and an entry for the USB Port. If either of these icons is missing (or has an exclamation point or red *X* on it), contact your USB hardware vendor to correctly configure the USB controller.

Check Game Port Driver   Most USB gaming devices will function on computers without game ports or sound cards. However, DirectX requires a game port entry in the Sound, Video and Game Controllers section of the Device Manager in order for gaming devices to be added in the Control Panel. Check for the presence of a game port driver:

1. Click Start, highlight Settings, and then click Control Panel.
2. Double-click the System icon, and then click the Device Manager tab.
3. Click the plus (+) sign next to Sound, Video and Game Controllers, and verify there is a listing for Game Port Joystick. If there is no listing, you'll need to add a game port driver.

If the problem persists, skip ahead to the "Check for Software Problems" section.

Dealing with Serial Devices

Some game controller devices use serial ports rather than game or USB ports. In some cases, advanced joystick or wheel controllers may use a game port and a serial port. If your game controller device uses a serial port, follow the guidelines given here.

Check Hardware Connections   Examine the connectors on both the joystick cable and serial ports on the computer, and look for bent pins or other damage. Ensure that the connector on the joystick is completely seated in the serial port on the computer. If the gaming device came with a power supply (such as a Logitech WingMan Force), see that the AC adapter is connected to the gaming device. If the device is attached to the serial port through a switch box or Y-adapter, try connecting it *directly* to the computer.

Check Game Port Driver   Most serial gaming devices will function on computers without game ports or sound cards. However, DirectX requires a game port entry in the Sound, Video and Game Controllers section of the Device Manager in order for gaming devices to be added in the Control Panel. Check for the presence of a game port driver:

1.   Click Start, highlight Settings, and then click Control Panel.

2.   Double-click the System icon, and then click the Device Manager tab.

3.   Click the plus (+) sign next to Sound, Video and Game Controllers, and verify there is a listing for Game port joystick. If there is no listing, you'll need to add a game port driver.

Check Serial Port Configuration   Ensure that the serial port is correctly configured. Most serial gaming devices do not have a preset address or IRQ. They will assume the settings of the port they are connected to, such as:

■   COM1: IRQ4 Address 03F8h

■   COM2: IRQ3 Address 02F8h

■   COM3: IRQ4 Address 03E8h

■   COM4: IRQ3 Address 02E8h

For example, if you attach the joystick to COM 3 and another device in the system is using COM 1, an IRQ conflict will arise between these two devices. To correct this, connect the joystick to another serial port (if available). Also, verify that Windows 98/Me has the correct settings for the serial ports:

1.   Click Start, highlight Settings, and then click Control Panel.

2.   Double-click the System icon, and then click the Device Manager tab.

3.   Double-click on the Ports, COM and LPT entry.

4.   Select the COM port where the gaming device is attached, and then click the Properties button.

5.   Click on the Resources tab, and verify the I/O Address and IRQ entries are set to the proper settings.

6.   Disable Use Automatic Settings.

7.   Check the conflicting device list for possible conflicts if everything appears to be OK.

If the serial ports appear to be configured correctly, it's possible that a modem or other internal card in the system may be interfering with the serial port the joystick is attached to. Try removing these cards to see if the conflict is eliminated.

Check for Software Problems
Software conflicts can interfere with the communications between the computer and the gaming device. If the hardware seems to be working properly, try temporarily eliminating any programs running in the background and retesting the gaming device.

Clear the Startup Folder   Programs in the Startup folder load and stay in memory and may interfere with the detection of the gaming device. To determine if there is a conflicting application in the Startup group, remove the icons from the Startup folder and restart Windows. To do this, click on Start, Settings, and then Taskbar. Click the Start Menu Programs button, and then click on Advanced. Click the plus (+) sign next to Programs, and then click on the Startup folder. Drag all the program icons onto the desktop area. This will prevent them from loading automatically when the computer boots. Restart the system and see if the issue has been resolved. If so, drag the program icons back into the Startup group, one by one, and see where the problem returns.

Clear the Registry Run Folder   The Run folder of your registry is another place where programs are automatically executed when the system is started. Programs starting from this area may also interfere with the detection of your gaming device. Launch the Registry Editor by clicking Start, and then select Run. In the Open line, type **C:\WINDOWS\REGEDIT.EXE** and click the OK button. The Run folder is located in the following key:

```
HKEY_LOCAL_MACHINE\Software\Microsoft\Windows\CurrentVersion\Run
```

Once Run is highlighted, click on Registry and choose Export. Give the file a name, and save it to the desktop. This procedure makes a backup of the Run folder that can be restored by double-clicking on the REG file you saved to the desktop. When Run is highlighted, the contents of the Run folder will be displayed. Check this folder to see what else may be launched during the boot process. Only Explorer and Systray are necessary to the system. Start removing other programs, one by one, rebooting between each removal. If the problem goes away, the last program removed from the Run folder may be the conflicting software.

Editing the registry incorrectly may stop Windows from booting. Be sure to make complete backups of the registry to your Startup Disk before proceeding.

Clear the WIN.INI File   Software programs may also be loaded from the "Load=" and "Run=" lines of your WIN.INI file and may also interfere with the detection of your gaming device. To check for these programs, click Start and select Run. In the Open line, type **WIN.INI**, and then click the OK button. The WIN.INI file should be opened in Notepad. Place a semicolon (;) in front of the following two lines (if present), as shown here:

```
[Windows]
;Load=
;Run=
```

Putting a semicolon at the beginning of these lines will prevent any programs listed in these lines from being loaded. Save the changes and restart Windows. If this resolves the conflict, then remove the semicolons, one by one, from the "Run=" and "Load=" lines, and restart Windows each time to see if the symptom is corrected.

Reinstall/Update DirectX   Most Windows 98/Me software today requires the latest version of DirectX in order for pointing and gaming devices to operate properly. If an earlier version of DirectX is installed (or if the installed version is damaged), the gaming device properties will show the device as Not Connected under the Game Controllers icon in your Control Panel. Try reinstalling DirectX, or download and install the latest version from Microsoft at **www.microsoft.com/directx**.

Install New Game Controller Driver   In some cases, installing an HID-compliant game controller driver will resolve some detection issues:

1.   Click Start, highlight Settings, and then click Control Panel.

2.   Double-click the Game Controllers icon.

3.   Click Add and then click Add Other.

4.   On the left side of the window, select Standard Game Device.

5.   On the right side of the window, select HID-Compliant Game Controller.

6.   Click Next and then click Finish.

7.   Close the Game Controllers properties dialog and restart the system.

"FORCE FEEDBACK" TROUBLESHOOTING GUIDELINES

The idea of *force feedback* adds yet another level of realism to computer gaming. Imaging feeling the "rat-tat-tat" of a virtual submachine gun, or the tremor when your fighter takes a direct hit. Computer games written to take advantage of the force feedback protocols in DirectX will be able to transfer such real-world signals to your force feedback–compliant joystick, such as Microsoft's SideWinder Force Feedback Pro. The SideWinder Force Feedback Pro (and other force-compliant joysticks) uses MIDI signals to transmit force feedback effects. If the MIDI features of your sound card are not functioning properly, the force feedback effects will not be felt. If your game supports force feedback, but you do not feel those effects through the joystick, you can use this guide to help you isolate the problem.

Test the Force Feedback System

If you have a force feedback game controller device installed, you can use the Windows Control Panel to check the force feedback operation of your joystick and to determine if it and the MIDI port on your sound card are operating correctly:

1.   Click Start, highlight Settings, and then click Control Panel.

2.   Double-click the Game Controllers icon.

3.   In the list of game devices, select your joystick (for example, SideWinder Force Feedback Pro) and click Properties.

4.   If your joystick is not listed in the Controller column, click Add, select the joystick, and then click OK.

5.   Click the Test Forces tab.

6.   Grasp the joystick handle and press several buttons on the joystick that correspond to the types of forces you want to feel.

If the forces work correctly in this test mode, chances are that it's the game configuration that's not set properly, so see the "Check the Game Configuration" section next. If the test mode does not work, see the "Check the Force Feedback LED" section.

Check the Game Configuration

If force feedback effects are working in test mode, then the joystick and MIDI/game port are working. Since your joystick and software are working correctly, the lack of force feedback effects in your game is most likely caused by one (or both) of the following:

■   Your game is not force feedback enabled.

■   An incorrect setting or option was chosen in your force feedback game (for example, forces were disabled).

To resolve these problems, review the manual that came with your game, and note any special instructions that refer to enabling force feedback. Also, you may need to reinstall your game (paying particular attention to any selections that have to do with the type of sound card in your computer).

Check the Force Feedback LED

The LED on the front of the joystick must remain lit. If it's blinking, it indicates that the joystick is not properly connected to its AC adapter (there's no power for forces), and no force feedback effects will be felt. Connect the AC adapter. The LED should be lit and not blinking. Also make sure that the joystick is connected directly to the game port on the computer (rather than to a Y-adapter or switch box) before you continue.

If the LED is now on continuously, test the forces again. If the LED was on and it's still not responding to force signals, you should remove the device from your Device Manager, download the latest version of the joystick force feedback drivers from the manufacturer, and then reinstall the joystick drivers from scratch.

Check the MIDI Port

Make sure that the MIDI port is enabled on the sound card, and verify that it's using a valid MIDI address. The MIDI port supplied on your sound card must be enabled in order for force feedback to work with your joystick:

1. Click Start, highlight Settings, and then click Control Panel.

2. Double-click the Multimedia icon, and then click the Advanced tab.

3. In the Multimedia Devices area, double-click MIDI Devices and Instruments to display the list of MIDI ports installed on your computer.

4. Click the entry in the list that identifies your MIDI port (such as MIDI for External MIDI Port, MIDI for MPU-401, MIDI for Sound Blaster, or MPU-401 Compatible).

5. Click Properties and click the General tab. Make sure that the Use MIDI Features On This Device option is selected.

If the forces on your joystick still seem sluggish or intermittent, try selecting the MIDI for FM Synthesis option. If you have two external MIDI ports listed (for example, you have both MIDI for External MIDI Port and MIDI for MPU-401), then your computer has two external MIDI ports. If you enable one of the external MIDI ports and your joystick doesn't provide force feedback, enable the other external MIDI port and try the joystick again.

No MIDI Port Available   If there is no MIDI port listed, your MIDI port is not enabled. There are two possible reasons for this:

■ Your sound card driver is installed but the MIDI port is not configured properly. (Use the Windows Device Manager to check the configuration of your external MIDI port.)

■ The incorrect driver is installed (or not set up properly) for your external MIDI port. (Install the correct driver for your sound card, and then test the forces again.)

You can usually install the correct driver by either reinstalling the sound card software from your original CD or floppy disks, or by downloading the latest driver from your sound card manufacturer's Web site. After reinstalling the sound card software (or installing new sound card drivers), check the sound card manual (or any instructions that accompanied the new drivers) to learn how to enable the external MIDI/game port.

Configure the MIDI Port   If no MIDI port is available, you'll need to configure your computer's external MIDI port before using force feedback devices:

1. Click Start, highlight Settings, and then click Control Panel.

2. Double-click the System icon, and then click the Device Manager tab.

3. Make sure the View Devices By Type option is selected.

4. Scroll down the list and double-click Sound, Video and Game Controllers.

5. Click the MIDI entry in the list that corresponds to your exact sound card.

6. Click Properties, and then click the Resources tab.

7. Scroll down the Resource Settings list until you see a listing for Input/Output Range. There may be more than one entry. For the external MIDI port to operate, there must be one Resource Type entry in the list with one of the following Setting values:

```
0300 - 0301
0310 - 0311
0320 - 0321
0330 - 0331
```

Enable Your MIDI Port   Find a configuration from the preceding listing that enables the MIDI port. If the Use Automatic Settings box is not checked, select it and then click OK. Windows will attempt to configure your sound card for all available resources. It may be necessary to restart Windows to complete the process. Check new configuration settings as shown in the previous section.

Try a "Basic Configuration"   If you still have trouble getting the MIDI port to respond, try a new "basic configuration" for the sound card:

1. Clear the Use Automatic Settings check box.

2. Select Basic Configuration 0000 from the Setting Based On list box.

3. Check the Resource Settings list again to see if the necessary Resource Type and Setting are listed. Look for one of the following four values:

```
0300 - 0301
0310 - 0311
0320 - 0321
0330 - 0331
```

4. If none of the values matches, select the next configuration setting in the Setting Based On list (that is, Basic Configuration 1, Basic Configuration 2, and so on). Repeat this process until you find a Resource Type and Setting that contains one of the four required values.

5. If you find the proper Resource Type and Setting, but a device conflict message appears in the Conflicting Device list, resolve the problem with the Windows Hardware Conflict Troubleshooter.

If none of the basic configurations have the necessary Resource Type and Setting, your sound card is not set up properly (its external MIDI port is not installed). In this case you should run the installation/setup procedure that came with your sound card again. If your computer came with the sound card already installed, look for the installation floppy disk or CD for the sound card that came with your computer. It's also possible that you do not have an external MIDI port that is compatible with the joystick. In this case, you'll need to purchase a compatible sound card, equipped with an MPU-401 compatible port, before you can use the joystick.

Checking for "Unknown Devices"
Check for your sound card in the Unknown Devices section of Device Manager. If your sound or MIDI device is listed here, it may not operate properly. If your sound card is listed here, you may need to remove

it and reinstall it following the directions provided by the sound card's manufacturer. You may also need to obtain an updated sound card driver from the manufacturer.

Checking for Multiple Ports and Connections

Check your computer for more than one game port. Examine the back of your computer for an adapter that has 15-pin game ports mounted on it. If you have an adapter that contains two 15-pin game ports, you'll probably need to remove this adapter from your computer for the game port on your sound card to work properly. Also see that the joystick is connected *directly* to the sound card's MIDI port. Verify that there is no extension cable or Y-adapter connected to the joystick—this is very important. Some extension cables do not transmit MIDI, and some are too long to support the MIDI signal. For best joystick communications, you should have the joystick directly connected to the computer.

Checking for "Single Mode DMA"

If the joystick seems sluggish or intermittent (or even stops responding) while playing your game—especially when music is playing—you may have a sound card that requires single mode DMA:

1. Click Start, highlight Settings, and then click Control Panel.

2. Double-click the Multimedia icon, and then click the Advanced tab.

3. In the Multimedia Devices area, double-click Audio Devices.

4. Select the listed audio device, click Properties, and then click Settings.

5. If the Settings button is unavailable (shaded), there is no Use Single-Mode DMA option on your computer. If there is a Use Single-Mode DMA check box, select it and reboot the system if necessary.

Close Background Software

If problems persist, other software running on the computer may be interfering with the force feedback system. Try closing other programs that might be running in the background. Use the Task Manager (CTRL-ALT-DEL) to systematically shut down everything but Explorer and Systray.

SYMPTOMS

If you've followed the preceding basic troubleshooting guidelines but find that your joystick or game port is still not responding, use the following symptoms to isolate the specific problem.

SYMPTOM 22-1   **The joystick does not respond**   Make sure that the joystick is plugged into the game port correctly. When the game port has more than one connector, be sure that the joystick is plugged into the correct connector (joystick 1 or joystick 2). If the game port is running through a sound board, make sure that the sound board is configured to use the port as a game port instead of a MIDI port, and see that any joystick Y-adapter is wired properly. Refer to the application and see that it is configured to run from the joystick. (If mouse or keyboard control is selected, the joystick will not function.) Now that many new joysticks are appearing with supplemental functions (for example, hat switches, throttle controls, and so on), make sure that the application is written to take advantage of the particular joystick. If problems persist, make sure that the game port is set for the proper I/O address. (Most are fixed at 210h, but check the user documentation to be sure.) Try a known-good joystick with the game port. If a known-good joystick works, the original joystick is defective and should be replaced. If another joystick is not the problem, try a different game port board.

SYMPTOM 22-2   Joystick performance is erratic or choppy   Start by checking the joystick to be sure that it is connected properly. Try another joystick. When a new joystick works properly, the original joystick is probably damaged and should be replaced. If a new joystick fails to solve the problem, the game port board may be too slow for the system. Remember that many game ports still use XT board types. An older board design may not be able to process joystick signals fast enough to provide adequate signaling to the system. Not only should you try another game port adapter, but you also should use a speed-adjusting game port.

SYMPTOM 22-3   The joystick is sending incorrect information to the system—the joystick appears to be drifting   First, check the application to be sure that the joystick is calibrated correctly. If you cannot calibrate the joystick, the application may not support the joystick properly—try another application. Make sure that there are no other active devices in the system (such as other game ports) using I/O port 201h. If this happens, data produced on those other boards will adversely affect the game port you are using. If all unused game ports are disabled, check the active game port. Poor-quality game ports can drift. Try a newer, low-drift or speed-adjusting game port board.

SYMPTOM 22-4   The basic X/Y, two-button features of the joystick work, but the hat switch, throttle controls, and supplemental buttons do not seem to respond   In virtually all cases, the joystick is configured wrong. Check the application first. Many new applications provide numerous joystick options and allow you to define the particular use of each feature from within the application itself.

Check the joystick definition files next. Your joystick probably requires a supplemental driver or definition file (for example, an FCS file) in order to use all of the joystick's particular features. Finally, check the game port type. You may need a dual-port game port adapter rather than an inexpensive single-port game port adapter. Some enhanced joysticks use both joystick positions. (For example, the XY axis and fire buttons make up one joystick, while the throttle and other buttons take up the other position.) You may need to install a dual-port game port card.

SYMPTOM 22-5   You see an error such as "Joystick not connected" under Windows 98/Me   Windows doesn't recognize the game port hardware. Check the game port driver first. Use the Device Manager under Windows 98/Me to examine the resources assigned to the game port driver. Typically, the resource range should be set to 201h through 201h (only one address location). If the game port entry has a yellow icon next to it, there is a hardware conflict in the system, and other hardware is also trying to use the same I/O location.

Next, check the game port hardware for proper configuration. The game port card should be installed properly in its bus slot. Make sure that the game port is enabled. (Game ports integrated onto sound cards or multi-I/O cards may need to be enabled using a jumper.) If a sound card enables you to switch a 15-pin port between MIDI and joystick, see that the jumper is set to the "joystick" position. Make sure the joystick cable is not cut or damaged anywhere, and see that it is attached securely to the game port. Finally, test a known-good joystick on the system. If a new joystick works as expected, the original joystick is probably suffering from internal wiring damage.

SYMPTOM 22-6   The joystick drifts frequently and requires recalibration   This type of symptom is usually the result of problems with the game port adapter. Try a different game port adapter, and see if the problem persists. If problems disappear, you simply need a better-quality or speed-adjusting game port. Otherwise, test a known-good joystick on the system. If a new joystick works as expected, the original joystick is probably suffering from internal wiring damage and should be replaced.

SYMPTOM 22-7   **The joystick handle has lost tension—it no longer "snaps" back to the center**   This problem may be accompanied by a rattling sound within the joystick. In most cases, a spring has popped out of place inside the joystick. Check the joystick for internal damage. Open the joystick and see if any springs or clips have slipped out of place. Replace any springs or clips (if possible). Some joysticks also employ mechanical latches that can enable or disable the spring action of the X and Y axis. Check to see that any such latches are enabled. If you cannot locate or correct the problem, simply replace the joystick.

SYMPTOM 22-8   **The joystick responds, but refuses to accept a calibration**   In virtually all cases, the problem is with your game port adapter. Check the hardware setup. Make sure that there are no other devices in the system using the I/O address assigned to your game port (for example, 201h). If more than one adapter in your system has game port capability, see that only one game port is enabled. Replace the game port, or enable a different game port in the system. If drift issues continue with different applications, you may need to replace the game port adapter with a low-drift or speed-adjusting model.

SYMPTOM 22-9   **The hat switch and buttons on a joystick work only intermittently (if at all)**   This problem also applies to stand-alone pedals. In most cases, erratic behavior of a joystick's enhanced features is a symptom of game port speed problems. Check the joystick first. Try a known-good joystick. If the problems disappear, the original joystick may be defective. If the problems persist, you have a game port problem. Make sure that there are no other devices in the system using the I/O address assigned to your game port (201h). If more than one adapter in your system has game port capability, see that only one game port is enabled. If drift issues continue with different applications, you may need to replace the game port adapter with a low-drift or speed-adjusting model.

SYMPTOM 22-10   **When downloading FCS (or "calibration") files to a joystick, the line saying "put switch into calibrate" doesn't change when the download switch is moved**   This is a typical problem with advanced joysticks. In most cases, the joystick needs to be cleared. To clear the joystick, rock the download switch back to "analog," then to "calibrate." This should clear the joystick for a new calibration download. Try downloading the FCS file again. Under Windows 98/Me, you may simply need to update the driver file(s) for your joystick, wheel, or other controller. If problems persist, the actual switch may be defective. Try a known-good joystick instead.

SYMPTOM 22-11   **You need to fiddle with the download switch**   To download a calibration file, you need to rock the red switch back and forth a number of times (or press the ENTER key a number of times) to get it to 100%. This is virtually always the result of a keyboard controller (keyboard BIOS) compatibility problem. Upgrade the keyboard controller (keyboard BIOS). Some advanced joystick products do not interact well with the host computer's keyboard controller. For example, Thrustmaster's Mark II experiences known microcode problems with a few of the keyboard controller chips on the market. These include AMI versions (D, B, 8, 0), Acer, and Phoenix. You may need to replace the keyboard controller or system BIOS with a later version.

SYMPTOM 22-12   **You cannot use a joystick on a PC using a sound card with an ESS or OPTi chipset**   The joystick may stop responding while using an application, or report a "not connected" status in the Game Controllers area of the Control Panel. This is a known problem with the ESS and OPTi sound chipsets. Use the following steps to set Single Mode DMA to use the joystick.

1.   Click Start, select Settings, and then click Control Panel.

2.   Double-click the Multimedia icon.

3.   On the Advanced tab, double-click the Audio Devices entry to expand it.

4.   Click the "Audio for..." entry that corresponds to your particular sound card, and then click Properties.

5.   Click Settings.

6.   Select the Use Single Mode DMA check box.

7.   Click OK until you return to Windows, and then restart the PC.

SYMPTOM 22-13   **The joystick port is not removed when the sound card is removed**
The entry for your game port will still be visible in the Windows 98/Me Device Manager. This is not really a problem. Windows does not recognize the game port as being part of the sound card, so removing the sound card doesn't automatically disable the game port. Also, the virtual joystick device driver (VJOYD.VXD) cannot detect whether the game port or joystick is installed, so the driver is always active. You'll need to manually remove the game port in Device Manager:

1.   Use the right mouse button to click My Computer, and then click Properties on the menu.

2.   Click the Device Manager tab.

3.   Double-click the Sound, Video and Game Controllers entry to expand it.

4.   Click the joystick port, and then click Remove.

5.   Return to Windows 98/Me and restart the system.

SYMPTOM 22-14   **You cannot disable a "jumperless" joystick port**   This is an issue that frequently crops up with newer sound boards like the Ensoniq VIVO, and jumperless boards that are controlled exclusively through drivers. The VIVO also uses drivers to disable certain functions like the joystick port. Use the following steps to disable the VIVO's joystick port. (The specific command lines for your own sound board may be different, but the idea is very similar.)

1.   Exit Windows and enter the DOS mode.

2.   Edit the SNDSCAPE.INI file in the \Windows directory. Change the line JSEnable=true to JSEnable=false. (Check your particular sound board's documentation for the correct command line.)

3.   Save the file and reboot the system. The joystick will now be disabled.

SYMPTOM 22-15   **Your joystick doesn't work with a Sound Blaster Live card**   This is an issue with the Sound Blaster Live card. It's an excellent sound card, but the game port on the card is very slow. This means any fast analog device that is used with the Sound Blaster Live card will have trouble being "seen" by Windows. In this instance, your best solution is to disable the sound card's game port and install a fast game port card instead.

SYMPTOM 22-16   **The cross-hair on your axis is off center**   This is a frequent issue with digital joysticks such as the Gravis Blackhawk Digital. Chances are that you're dealing with a Windows 98/Me shadow driver problem:

1.   Restart your system in the Safe Mode.

2.   Open your Control Panel, double-click the System icon, and then choose the Device Manager tab.

3.   Click on the (+) in front of the Sound, Video and Game Controllers entry to expand the list. You can only have one driver that contains "game port" or "joystick" in its name.

4.   Make sure you have the Windows installation CD (or other disc containing your game port driver), and then remove all listings that refer to your game port or joystick.

5.   When you restart the computer, it should detect new hardware, and may ask for the installation CD. If it tells you that it is recommended to keep your newer driver, select No and install the drivers from your disc(s).

6.   Save the changes and reboot the system if necessary. Your joystick should now be on center.

SYMPTOM 22-17   **You get a "fatal exception" error when you open the Gaming Devices wizard in the Control Panel**   For example, you may see an error such as:

```
A Fatal Exception Error 0E occurred at 0028:58C10F3F
```

This error can usually occur if the game port is conflicting with another device. Use the Device Manager to see whether another device is conflicting with the game port. If Device Manager reports that there's a problem with the configuration of the game port, reconfigure the game port so that it uses resources that are not already in use by another device. If the game port is a PnP device and is conflicting with another device, you must disable the device before attempting to change the resource settings. Use the following steps under Windows 95/98:

1.   Open the Control Panel, and double-click the System icon.

2.   Click the Device Manager tab, and double-click Sound, Video and Game Controllers.

3.   Double-click the Gameport Joystick entry.

4.   In the Gameport Joystick Properties dialog, click the General tab, clear the Original Configuration check box, and then click OK. Under Windows 98, check the box Disable in This Hardware Configuration.

SYMPTOM 22-18   **The joystick's throttle or slider control does not work in certain games**   For example, when you use the SideWinder 3D Pro joystick, the throttle or slider control may not work in one or more of your games. This is because the throttle works only while the joystick is emulating a more basic model. For the SideWinder 3D Pro, the mode switch should be in position one. This position causes the SideWinder 3D Pro to emulate a CH Flightstick Pro. Make sure that the switch is set in this position, and calibrate the SideWinder as a CH Flightstick Pro joystick. This should correct the problem. You may also be able to correct the problem by patching or upgrading your offending game(s) to a version that supports your specific joystick type directly.

SYMPTOM 22-19   **The Game Controllers tool switches between "OK" and "Not Connected"**   When you use the Game Controllers tool in Control Panel to check the status of a USB game controller, the game controller status may toggle between OK and Not Connected. In addition, you may see random buttons light up on the screen when you use the Game Controllers tool to test a USB game controller. This problem occurs when the USB game controller is connected to the game port on your computer, and the game port on your computer is not working correctly. To correct this problem, connect the USB game controller to the USB port on your computer, or install a working game port in your computer. If there is no USB port on your computer, you may be able to resolve this problem by contacting the manufacturer of your sound (or game port) card to obtain updated drivers. This may correct problems or incompatibilities with the sound card's game port controller and allow the joystick to function properly.

Further Study

Advanced Gravis   www.gravis.com
CH Products   www.chproducts.com/
Logitech   www.logitech.com
Thrustmaster   www.thrustmaster.com

23

KEYBOARDS

Keyboards are the classical input device for computers (Figure 23-1). By manipulating a matrix of individual electrical switches, commands and instructions can be entered into the computer one character at a time. If you've used computers or typewriters to any extent, you already have an excellent grasp of keyboard handling. However, keyboards certainly present their share of drawbacks and limitations. Although today's keyboard switches are not mechanically complex, they have a number of important moving parts. When you multiply this number of moving parts times the 80 to 100+ keys on a typical keyboard, you are faced with a substantial number of moving parts. A jam or failure in any one of these many mechanical parts results in a keyboard problem. Most keyboard failures are hardly catastrophic, but they can certainly be inconvenient. This chapter gives you the information needed to understand and repair computer keyboards.

Keyboard Basics

To understand a keyboard, you must first understand the kinds of switches that are used. In general, there are two types of switches that you should be concerned with: mechanical switches and membrane switches. Both switches are used extensively throughout the computer industry, but any single keyboard will use only one type of switch.

FIGURE 23-1   A Cherry G83-3000 keyboard (Cherry Electrical Products)

A *mechanical key switch* is shown in Figure 23-2. Two tempered bronze contacts are separated by a plastic actuator bar. The bar is pushed up by a spring in the switch base. When the key cap is depressed, the actuator bar slides down. This action compresses the spring and allows the gold-plated contacts to touch. Since gold is a soft metal and an excellent conductor, a good, low-resistance electrical contact is developed. When the key cap is released, the compressed spring expands and drives the plastic actuator bar between the contacts once again. The entire stroke of travel on a mechanical switch is little more than 3.56mm (0.140 inch), but an electrical contact (a *make* condition) can be established in as little as 1.78mm (0.070 inch). Mechanical switches are typically quite rugged—many are rated for 100 million cycles or more.

A *membrane key switch* is illustrated in Figure 23-3. A plastic actuator rests on top of a soft rubber boot. Inside, the rubber boot is coated with a conductive silver-carbon compound. Beneath the rubber boot are two open PC board contacts. When the key cap is depressed, the plastic actuator collapses the rubber boot. Collapse forces the conductive material across both PC board contacts to complete the switch. When the key cap is released, the compressed rubber boot breaks its contact on the PC board and returns to

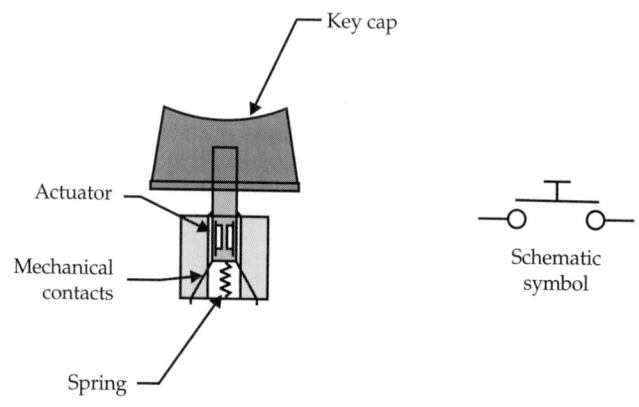

Key cap

Actuator

Mechanical
contacts

Schematic
symbol

Spring

FIGURE 23-2   Mechanical switch assembly

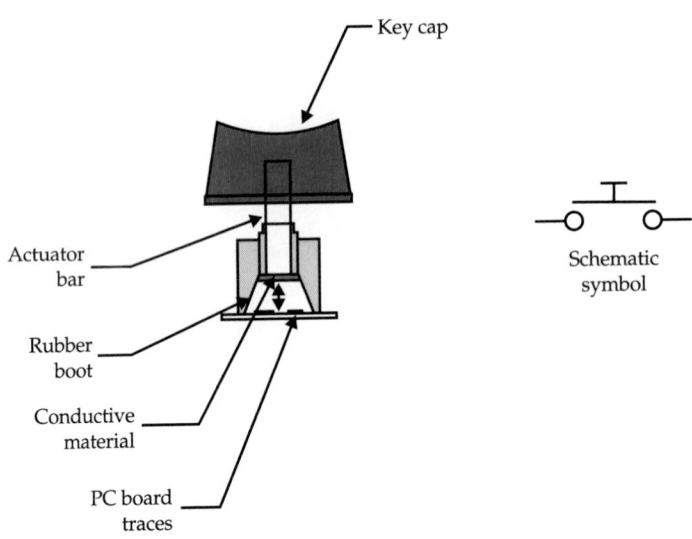

FIGURE 23-3   Membrane switch assembly

its original shape. The full travel stroke of a membrane key switch is about 3.56mm (0.140 inch)—roughly the same as a mechanical switch. An electrical contact is established in about 2.29mm (0.090 inch). Membrane switches are not quite as durable as mechanical switches. Most switches are rated for 20 million cycles or less.

Mechanical and membrane switches offer a number of unique advantages and disadvantages. Mechanical switches tend to be highly reliable and provide a good tactile feedback when typing (that clicking noise usually associated with offices). On the other hand, mechanical keyboards are more expensive to manufacture and can be extremely sensitive to spills and foreign matter. Membrane switches are not quite as reliable, and tend to offer a softer, "mushier" feel when typing (some people prefer this feel). Due to the membrane cover used in the keyboard, membrane switches seem to withstand spills and foreign matter better than mechanical switches.

The next step in understanding a keyboard is to learn about the *key matrix*. Keys are not interpreted individually—that is, each switch is not wired directly to the motherboard. Instead, keys are arranged in a matrix of rows and columns, as shown in Figure 23-4. When a key is pressed, a unique row (top to bottom) and column (left to right) signal is generated to represent the corresponding key. The great advantage of a matrix approach is that a huge array of keys can be identified using only a few row and column signals. Wiring from the keyboard is vastly simplified. An 84-key keyboard can be identified using only 12 column signals and 8 row signals.

KEY CODES

When a key is pressed, the row and column signals that are generated are interpreted by a *keyboard interface* chip (typically located on the keyboard assembly itself). The keyboard interface converts the row and column signals into a single-byte code (called a *key code* or *scan code*). Two unique scan codes are produced during a keystroke cycle. When the key is depressed, a *make code* byte is sent along to the system. When the key is released, a *break code* byte is generated. Both codes are transmitted to the host computer in a serial fashion. For example, a make code of 1Eh is sent when the *A* key is pressed. A 9Eh code is sent

Row signals

Column signals

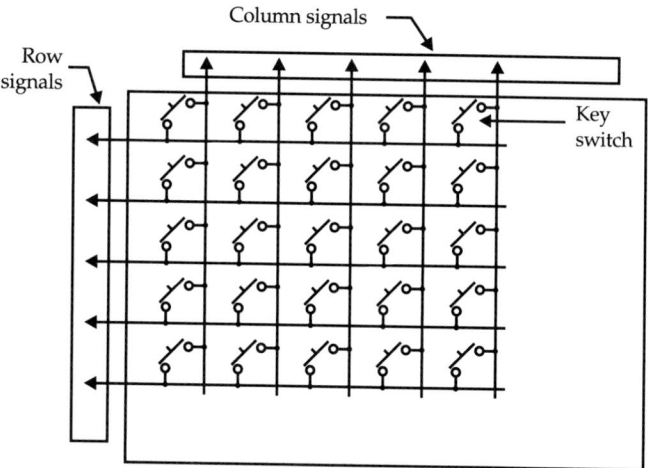

Key switch

FIGURE 23-4 Simplified diagram of a keyboard matrix

when the *A* key is subsequently released. By using two individual codes, the computer can determine when a key is held down, or when keys are held down in combinations. Just about every key on a keyboard is *typematic*—that is, it repeats automatically if it is held down for more than 500mS or so. Typematic settings can usually be adjusted in the CMOS advanced settings for your system.

Most computers today are prepared for multinational operation. To accommodate the special characters and punctuation used in various different countries, keyboard controllers (KBCs) can be configured to provide scan codes for different languages. Table 23-1 illustrates the make and break codes for conventional keyboards used in the domestic United States.

TABLE 23-1   STANDARD SCAN CODES FOR U.S. KEYBOARDS

KEY	MAKE CODE	BREAK CODE	KEY	MAKE CODE	BREAK CODE
A	1E	9E	B	30	B0
C	2E	AE	D	20	A0
E	12	92	F	21	A1
G	22	A2	H	23	A3
I	17	97	J	24	A4
K	25	A5	L	26	A6
M	32	B2	N	31	B1
O	18	98	P	19	99
Q	10	90	R	13	93
S	1F	9F	T	14	94
U	16	96	V	2F	AF
W	11	91	X	2D	AD
Y	15	95	Z	2C	AC
0/)	0B	8B	1/!	02	82
2/@	03	83	3/#	04	84
4/$	05	85	5/%	06	86

TABLE 23-1   STANDARD SCAN CODES FOR U.S. KEYBOARDS (CONTINUED)

KEY	MAKE CODE	BREAK CODE	KEY	MAKE CODE	BREAK CODE
6/^	07	87	7/&	08	88
8/*	09	89	9/(	0A	8A
./>	29	A9	-/_	0C	8C
=/+	0D	8D	[	1A	9A
]	1B	9B	;/:	27	A7
'/"	28	A8	,/<	33	B3
//?	35	B5	Left SHIFT	2A	AA
Left CTRL	1D	9D	Left ALT	38	B8
Right SHIFT	36	B6	Right ALT	E0 38	E0 B8
Right CTRL	E0 1D	E0 9D	CAPS LOCK	3A	BA
BACKSPACE	0E	8E	TAB	0F	8F
SPACEBAR	39	B9	ENTER	1C	9C
ESC	01	81	F1	3B	BB
F2	3C	BC	F3	3D	BD
F4	3E	BE	F5	3F	BF
F6	40	C0	F7	41	C1
F8	42	C2	F9	43	C3
F10	44	C4	F11	57	D7
F12	58	D8	UP ARROW	E0 48	E0 C8
DOWN ARROW	E0 50	E0 D0	LEFT ARROW	E0 4B	E0 CB
RIGHT ARROW	E0 4D	E0 CD	INSERT	E0 52	E0 D2
HOME	E0 47	E0 C7	PAGE UP	E0 49	E0 C9
DELETE	E0 53	E0 D3	END	E0 4F	E0 CF
PAGE DOWN	E0 51	E0 D1	SCROLL LOCK	46	C6

Note: All make and break codes are given in hexadecimal (hex) values.
Alphabetic characters represent both upper- and lowercase

KEYBOARD INTERFACES

Once a key is pressed and the keyboard interface converts the key matrix signals into a suitable scan code, that code must be transmitted to the KBC on the host computer's motherboard. Once key data reaches the KBC, the KBC converts it to parallel data, which in turn generates an interrupt that forces the system to handle the key. The actual transfer of scan codes between the keyboard and PC is accomplished *serially* using one of the interfaces shown in Figure 23-5.

Note that there are really three important signals in a keyboard interface: the keyboard clock (KBCLOCK), the keyboard data (KBDATA), and the signal ground. Unlike most serial communication, which is asynchronous, the transfer of data from keyboard to controller is accomplished *synchronously*—data bits are returned in sync with separate clock signals. As you might expect, the signal ground provides a common reference for the keyboard and system. The keyboard is powered by +5 Vdc, which is provided through the keyboard interface. It is also important to note that most XT-style systems are designed with a unidirectional data path (from keyboard to system). AT-style keyboard interfaces are bidirectional. This feature allows AT keyboards to be controlled and programmed from the PC.

IBM PC/XT/AT configuration

6 pin mini-DIN connector

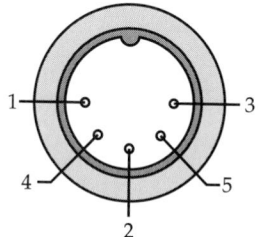

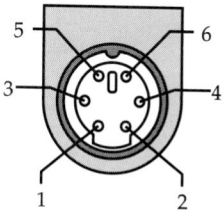

1 KBCLOCK
2 KBDATA
3 nc
4 Ground
5 +5 Vdc (pr +3.0 or +3.3 Vdc)

1 KBDATA
2 nc
3 Ground
4 +5 Vdc (pr +3.0 or +3.3 Vdc)
5 KBCLOCK
6 nc

FIGURE 23-5   Keyboard interface connectors

DVORAK KEYBOARDS

Virtually all technicians are familiar with QWERTY-style keyboards, the standard format for typewriters that was adopted in the late 1800s. A popular alternative to the QWERTY keyboard is the *Dvorak keyboard*. Mechanically and electronically, the Dvorak keyboard is identical to conventional keyboards. Only the key order is different. All of the vowels are located on the left side of the home row (the middle row of letters) in the pattern AOEUIDHTNS.

Dvorak keyboards claim several advantages over QWERTY models. Most letters typed (roughly 70 percent) are on the home row, so finger (and wrist strain) is reduced. With less reach to deal with, typing can be accomplished faster and with fewer errors. On a Dvorak keyboard, the majority of words require both hands for typing, whereas thousands of words demand one-handed typing for QWERTY keyboards. The Dvorak keyboard spreads out the strain on your hands more evenly.

Converting to Dvorak Keyboards

There are two classical methods of implementing Dvorak keyboards: dedicated keyboards and keyboard conversions. Dedicated keyboards, just as the name implies, are ready-made Dvorak keyboards that you buy and plug in. Although the keys are located in different places, the key codes are the same, so your PC doesn't know the difference. As a result, you can interchange QWERTY and Dvorak keyboards at will without any changes to the PC or operating system. You can also convert your existing QWERTY keyboard to Dvorak under Windows 98/Me:

1. Open the Control Panel and double-click on the Keyboard icon.

2. Select the Language page (Figure 23-6) and double-click on the English (United States) entry (or your own default entry for a different country).

3. Select United States–Dvorak from the list that appears.

4. Save your changes. You may need to install a floppy disk with the proper drivers to support Dvorak operation.

5. It may be necessary to reboot the system.

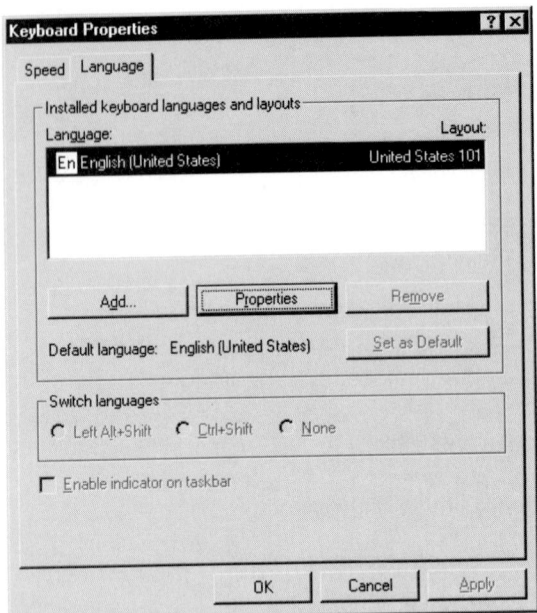

FIGURE 23-6   Controlling language in the Keyboard Properties dialog box

Under DOS, you will need a DOS TSR to handle the conversion. For MS-DOS 5.0 through 6.22, you can find the Dvorak TSR on the MS-DOS Supplemental Disk. You can obtain the driver files from Microsoft's FTP or Web site (**www.microsoft.com**), or from the Microsoft forum on CompuServe (GO MSDOS). Download the file DOS62S.EXE.

If you do download and extract these supplemental DOS files, make very sure to extract them to a new or temporary directory. Under no circumstances should you allow DOS files to overwrite files in the DOS directory or in any of your Windows directories.

Once the software conversion is made, you need to exchange the keys on your QWERTY keyboard. Figure 23-7 illustrates the comparison between a QWERTY key layout and a Dvorak key layout. You can use a key-pulling tool to physically exchange the key caps, or use key stickers or overlays from Hooleon Corporation at (602) 634-7515 or Keytime at (206) 522-8973. You can also obtain more detailed information directly from Dvorak International at (802) 287-2434.

Keyboard Maintenance and Troubleshooting

Keyboards are perhaps the most abused part of any computer, yet they are often ignored until serious problems develop. With some regular cleaning and maintenance, however, a keyboard can easily last for the lifetime of a computer. This part of the chapter shows you some practical techniques for keyboard service.

QWERTY
```
Q   W   E   R   T   Y   U   I   O   P
A   S   D   F   G   H   J   K   L   ;   '
Z   X   C   V   B   N   M   ,   .   /
```

Dvorak
```
"   ,   .   P   Y   F   G   C   R   L   /
A   O   E   U   I   D   H   T   N   S   -
;   Q   J   K   X   B   M   W   V   Z
```

FIGURE 23-7   QWERTY vs. Dvorak keyboard layouts

CORRECTING PROBLEM KEYBOARDS

Virtually all computer keyboards are open to the air. Over time, everyday dust, pet hair, air vapor, cigar/ciga-rette smoke, and debris from hands and ordinary use settles into the keyboard. Eventually, accumulations of this foreign matter cause keys to stick or prevent keys from making proper contact (for example, a key may not work every time it is pressed). In either case, keyboard problems will develop. Fortunately, correcting a finicky keyboard is a relatively straightforward process. First, remove the key caps of the offending keys. Be sure to note where each key is placed before starting your disassembly—especially if the keyboard is a DVORAK-type or unusual ergonomic design. To remove a key cap, bend an ordinary paper clip into the shape of a narrow U, and bend in small tabs at the tip of the U shape. Slip the small tabs under the key cap and pull up gently. Do not struggle with the key cap. If a cap will not come off, remove one or more adjacent caps. If there is a substantial accumulation of foreign matter in the keyboard, you should consider removing all of the key caps for a thorough cleaning, but this requires more time.

Avoid removing the SPACEBAR unless it is absolutely necessary, since the SPACEBAR is often much more difficult to replace than ordinary keys.

Flip the keyboard upside down and rap gently on the case. This will loosen and dislodge any larger, heavier foreign matter and allow it to fall out of the keyboard. A soft-bristled brush will help loosen the debris. Return the keyboard to an upright position. Use a can of compressed air (available from almost any electronics or photography store) to blow out the remainder of foreign matter. Since this tends to blow dust and debris in all directions, you may wish to use the compressed air outside or in an area away from your workbench. A medium- or firm-bristled brush will help loosen any stubborn debris.

Now that the keyboard is cleaned out, squirt a small amount of good-quality electronics-grade contact cleaner (also available from almost any electronics store) into each key contact, and work the key to distrib-ute the cleaner evenly. Allow a few minutes for the contact cleaner to dry completely, and test the keyboard again before reinstalling the key caps. If the problems persist, the keyboard may be damaged, or the individ-ual key(s) may simply be worn out beyond recovery. In such an event, replace the keyboard outright.

VACUUM CLEANERS AND KEYBOARDS

There is an ongoing debate as to the safety of vacuum cleaners with computer equipment. The problem is static discharge. Many vacuum cleaners, especially small, inexpensive models, use cheap plastic and syn-thetic fabrics in their construction. When a fast air flow passes over those materials, a static charge is developed (just like combing your hair with a plastic comb). If the charged vacuum touches the keyboard, a static discharge may have enough potential to damage the KBC chip or even travel back into the mother-board for more serious damage.

If you do choose to use a vacuum for keyboard cleaning, take these three steps to prevent damage. First, make sure that the computer is powered down and disconnect the keyboard from the computer before starting service. If a static discharge does occur, the most that would be damaged is the keyboard itself. Second, use a vacuum cleaner that is made for electronics work and certified as "static-safe." Third, try working on an antistatic mat (such as the mat shown in Figure 23-8) that is properly grounded. This will tend to "bleed off" static charges before they can enter the keyboard or PC.

REPLACING THE SPACEBAR

Of all the keys on the keyboard, replacing the SPACEBAR is probably the most difficult. The SPACEBAR is kept even by a metal wire that is inserted into slots on each leg of the plastic bar key. However, you have to get the wire into the slots *without depressing the wire*. If you push the wire down, you compress the wire and installation becomes impossible. As a general rule, do not remove the SPACEBAR unless absolutely necessary. If you must remove the SPACEBAR, remove several surrounding key caps also. This will let you get some tools under the SPACEBAR wire later on. Once the SPACEBAR is reinserted, you can easily replace any of the other key caps.

PREVENTING PROBLEMS

Keyboard problems do not happen suddenly (unless the keyboard is dropped or physically abused). The accumulation of dust and debris is a slow process that can take months (sometimes years) to produce serious, repetitive keyboard problems. By following a regimen of regular cleaning, you can stop problems before they manifest themselves in your keyboard. In normal office environments, keyboards should be cleaned once every four months. Keyboards in home environments should be cleaned every two months. Keyboards in harsh or industrial environments should be cleaned even more frequently.

Turn your keyboard upside down and use a soft-bristled brush to clean between the keys. This prevents debris that may already be on the keys from entering the keyboard. Next, run the long, thin nozzle of your compressed air can between the key spaces to blow out any accumulations of dust. Since compressed air tends to blow dust in all directions, you may consider doing this outside or in an area away from your workbench. Instead of compressed air, you may use a static-safe vacuum cleaner to remove dust and debris.

DEALING WITH LARGE OBJECTS

Staples and paper clips pose a clear and present danger to keyboards. Although the odds of a staple or paper clip finding its way into a keyboard are generally slight, foreign objects can jam the key, or short it

FIGURE 23-8 A Curtis antistatic keyboard mat (Curtis, a division of Rolodex, Secaucus, NJ)

out. If the keyboard is moved, the object can wind up in the keyboard's circuitry where serious damage can occur. When a foreign object falls into the keyboard, *do not* move the keyboard. Power-down the PC, locate the object, and find the nearest key. Use a paper clip bent in a U shape with the ends of the U angled inward to remove the nearest key cap. Use a pair of nonconductive tweezers or needle-nose pliers to remove the object. Gently replace the key cap.

DEALING WITH SPILLS

Accidental spills are probably the most serious and dangerous keyboard problem. Coffee, soda, and even tap water is highly conductive (even corrosive). Your keyboard will almost certainly short circuit. Immediately shut down your computer (you may be able to exit your application using a mouse) and disconnect the keyboard. The popular tactic is simply to let the liquid dry. The problem with this tactic is that most liquids contain minerals and materials that are corrosive to metals. Your keyboard will never be the same unless the offending liquid is *removed* before it dries. Also, liquids tend to turn any dust and smoke film into a sticky glue that will just jam the keys when dry (not even considering the sticky sugar in most sodas).

Disassemble the keyboard's main housings and remove the keyboard printed circuit assembly. As quickly as you can after the incident, rinse the assembly thoroughly in clean, room-temperature, demineralized water (available from any pharmacy for contact lens maintenance). You can clean the plastic housings separately. *Do not use tap water.* Let the assembly drip dry in air. Do not attempt to accelerate the drying process with a hair dryer or other such heat source. The demineralized water should dry clean without mineral deposits or any sticky, conductive residue. Once the assembly is dry, you may wish to squirt a small amount of good-quality, electronics-grade contact cleaner into each key switch to ensure no residue remains on the contacts. Assuming that the keyboard's circuitry was not damaged by the initial spill, you should be able to reassemble the keyboard and continue using it without problems. If the keyboard behaves erratically (or not at all), replace the keyboard outright.

DISABLING A KEYBOARD

Keyboards are an essential peripheral for all computers except servers. There are many cases where network administrators would prefer to restrict direct access to the server, and prevent potential tampering. Traditional PCs did not allow you to disable the keyboard, but newer systems do offer a CMOS Setup entry that can enable or disable the keyboard. When the keyboard is disabled through CMOS, the PC will boot without suffering "Keyboard not found" errors. Before starting service on a server, it may be necessary to reattach and reenable the keyboard.

KEYBOARD SYMPTOMS

Although their appearance may seem daunting at first glance, keyboard systems are not terribly difficult to troubleshoot, primarily because of their modularity—if all else fails, replacing a keyboard outright is a simple matter. The keyboard's great weakness, however, is its vulnerability to the elements. Spills, dust, and any other foreign matter that finds its way between the key caps can easily ruin a keyboard. The keyboard's PC board is also a likely candidate to be damaged by impacts or other physical abuse. The following procedures address many of the most troublesome keyboard problems.

SYMPTOM 23-1   **During initialization, you see an error message indicating that no keyboard is connected**   Check your keyboard cable and see that it is inserted properly and completely into the PC connector. Remember that you have to reboot your system to clear this error message. Try another compatible keyboard. If a new keyboard assembly works properly, there is probably a wiring fault in the original keyboard. Given the very low price of new keyboards, it is usually most economical simply to replace a defective keyboard. If you're working on a file or network server, see that the CMOS Setup has enabled the keyboard.

If a known-good keyboard fails to function, try the original keyboard on a known-good PC to verify that the keyboard itself is indeed operational. If it is, your trouble lies in the PC. Check the wiring between the PC keyboard connector and the motherboard. Check the connector pins to make sure that none of them has been bent or pushed in (resulting in a bad connection). You might also want to check the soldering connections where the keyboard connector attaches to the motherboard. Repeated removals and insertions of the keyboard may have fatigued the solder joints. Reheat any defective solder joints. If the keyboard connector is intact, the KBC chip likely has failed. Try booting the PC with a POST board installed. A KBC failure usually is indicated by the system stopping on the appropriate POST code. You can attempt to replace the KBC, or replace the motherboard outright. If a POST board indicates a fault other than a KBC (such as the programmable interrupt controller that manages the KBC's interrupt), you can attempt to replace that component, or simply exchange the motherboard anyway.

SYMPTOM 23-2   During initialization, you see an error message indicating that the keyboard lock is on   In many cases, the detection of a "locked" keyboard will halt system initialization. Make sure that the keyboard lock switch is set completely to the "unlocked" position. If the switch is unlocked, but the system detects it as locked, the switch may be defective. Turn off and unplug the system, then use a multimeter to measure continuity across the lock switch. (You may need to disconnect the lock switch cable from the motherboard.) In one position, the switch should measure as an open circuit. In the opposing position, the switch should measure as a short circuit. If this is not the case, the lock switch is probably bad and should be replaced. If the switch measures properly, there is probably a logic fault on the motherboard (perhaps the KBC). Your best course is to try another motherboard.

SYMPTOM 23-3   The keyboard is completely dead—no keys appear to function at all All other computer operations are normal. This symptom assumes that your computer initializes and boots to its DOS prompt or other operating system as expected, but the keyboard does not respond when touched. Keyboard status LEDs may or may not be working properly. Your first step in such a situation is to try a known-good keyboard in the system. *Note that you should reboot the system when a keyboard is replaced.* If a known-good keyboard works, the fault is probably on the keyboard interface chip. You can attempt to replace this chip if you wish, but it is often most economical to simply replace the keyboard outright.

If another keyboard fails to correct the problem, use a multimeter and check the +5V supply at the keyboard connector (refer to Figure 23-5). If the +5V signal is missing, the female keyboard connector may be broken. Check the connector's soldering junctions on the motherboard. Reheat any connectors that appear fatigued or intermittent. Many motherboards also use a "pico-fuse" to protect the +5V supply feeding the keyboard connector. If your +5V is lost, locate and check the keyboard connector fuse. If problems continue, replace the motherboard.

SYMPTOM 23-4   The keyboard is acting erratically. One or more keys appear to work intermittently, or are inoperative   The computer operates normally and most keys work just fine, but one or more keys do not respond when pressed. Extra force or repeated strikes may be needed to operate the key. This type of problem can usually range from a minor nuisance to a major headache. Chances are that your key contacts are dirty. Sooner or later, dust and debris works into all key switches. Electrical contacts eventually become coated and fail to make contact reliably. This symptom is typical of older keyboards, or keyboards that have been in service for prolonged periods of time. In many cases, you need only vacuum the keyboard and clean the suspect contacts with a good-quality electronics-grade contact cleaner.

Begin by disconnecting the keyboard. Use a static-safe, fine-tipped vacuum to remove any accumulations of dust or debris that may have accumulated on the keyboard's PC board. You may wish to vacuum your keyboard regularly as preventive maintenance. Once the keyboard is clean, gently remove the plastic key cap from the offending key(s). The use of a key cap removal tool is highly recommended, but you may also use a modified set of blunt-ended tweezers with their flat ends (just the tips) bent inward. Grasp the key cap and pull up evenly. You can expect the cap to slide off with little resistance. Do not *rip* the key cap off—you stand a good chance of marring the cap and causing permanent key switch damage.

Use a can of good-quality electronics-grade contact cleaner and spray a little bit of cleaner into the switch assembly. When spraying, attach the long narrow tube to the spray nozzle—this directs cleaner into the switch. Work the switch in and out to distribute the cleaner. Repeat once or twice to clean the switch thoroughly. Allow residual cleaner to dry thoroughly before retesting the keyboard. *Never use harsh cleaners or solvents.* Industrial-strength chemicals can easily ruin plastic components and housings. Reapply power and retest the system. If the suspect key(s) responds normally again, install the removed key cap and return the system to service. As a preventive measure, you might wish to go through the process of cleaning every key.

Membrane keys must be cleaned somewhat differently from mechanical keys. You need to remove the rubber or plastic boot to clean the PC board contacts. Depending on the design of your particular membrane switch, this may not be an easy task. If you are able to see the contact boot, use a pick or tweezers to gently lift the boot. Spray a bit of cleaner under the boot, and then work the key to distribute the cleaner. If the boot is confined within the individual key, you may have to remove the suspect key before applying cleaner.

If cleaning does not work, your next step should be to disassemble the keyboard and replace the defective key switch(es). Observe the board closely for cracks or fractures. Many key switch designs still utilize through-hole soldering technology, but you should exercise extreme care when desoldering and resoldering. Extra care helps prevent accidental damage to the PC keyboard. You also have the more economical option of replacing the entire keyboard assembly outright.

SYMPTOM 23-5   **The keyboard is acting erratically. One or more keys may be stuck or repeating**   Suspect a shorted or jammed key. Short circuits can be caused by conductive foreign objects (such as staples and paper clips) falling into the keyboard and landing across PC board contacts. Remove all power and disassemble the keyboard housing assembly. Once the keyboard is exposed, shake out the foreign object or remove it with a pair of needle-nose pliers or sharp tweezers.

Accumulations of dirt or debris can work into the key actuator shaft and restrict its movement. Apply good-quality electronics-grade contact cleaner to the key, and work the key in and out to distribute the cleaner evenly. If the key returns to normal, you may reassemble the computer and return it to service. Keys that remain jammed should be replaced. If you cannot clear the jammed key, simply replace the entire keyboard assembly outright. If you elect to replace the keyboard assembly, retain the old assembly for parts. Key caps, good switches, and cable assemblies can be scavenged for use in future repairs.

SYMPTOM 23-6   **You see "KBC Error" (or a similar message) displayed during system startup**   When your computer initializes (either from a warm or cold start), it executes a comprehensive self-test routine that checks the key chips in the system (the CPU, memory, drive controllers, and so on). As part of this power-on self-test (POST) routine, the computer looks for the KBCLK signal, along with a series of test scan codes generated by the KB controller chip. You can see the keyboard LEDs flash as the controller sequences through its codes. If either the keyboard clock or keyboard data signals are missing, the POST knows that either the keyboard is disconnected or the KBC has failed. If you are using a POST board, it will probably display a code corresponding to a KBC error. Unless you have the tools and inclination to replace a KBC controller chip, your best course is simply to replace the motherboard outright.

SYMPTOM 23-7   **You cannot clear macros from a programmable keyboard**   In most cases, you need to use the correct key combination to clear the macros. If the keyboard has a REMAP key, press that first (a Program light or other LED will start blinking). Press the CTRL key twice to map the key to itself. Press ALT twice to map the key to itself. Press the SUSPEND MACRO key (the Program light should stop blinking). Press the CTRL and ALT keys while pressing SUSPEND MACRO. This will clear all of the keyboard's programming. The key sequence used for your keyboard may be different, so be sure to check the procedure for your own keyboard. If problems persist, replace the keyboard.

SYMPTOM 23-8   **The keyboard keys are not functioning as expected**   Pressing a key causes unexpected results or a series of operations that ordinarily would not be attributed to that key. Chances are that the keyboard has been programmed with macros, and you'll need to clear those macros to restore normal keyboard operation. If the keyboard has a REMAP key, press that first (a Program light or other LED will start blinking). Press the CTRL key twice to map the key to itself. Press ALT twice to map the key to itself. Press the SUSPEND MACRO key (the Program light should stop blinking). Press the CTRL and ALT keys while pressing SUSPEND MACRO. This will clear all of the keyboard's programming. The key sequence used for your keyboard may be different, so be sure to check the procedure for your own keyboard. If problems persist, replace the keyboard.

SYMPTOM 23-9   **The PC freezes when you press "volume" hot keys on the keyboard**   This type of trouble is known to happen with multifunction keyboards, such as Microsoft IntelliType, Natural, and Internet keyboards, and can usually be traced to the use of RealPlayer software. For example, Microsoft keyboards can suffer this trouble if the IntelliType Pro software is installed while RealPlayer is running on the computer, or if you're running a version of RealPlayer that is earlier than RealPlayer G2 version 6. You may be able to resolve this problem by removing RealPlayer, clean-booting your computer, and then reinstalling the IntelliType Pro software:

1.   Click Start, highlight Settings, and then click Control Panel.
2.   Double-click the Add/Remove Programs icon.
3.   In the list of installed programs, click RealPlayer.
4.   Click Add/Remove and then follow the instructions on the screen to finish removing RealPlayer.

Now clean-boot the computer. Follow the steps below for Windows 98:

1.   Click Start, highlight Programs, select Accessories, point to System Tools, and then click System Information.
2.   On the Tools menu, click System Configuration Utility.
3.   On the General tab, click Selective Startup, and then click to clear the following check boxes:
      Process Config.sys File
      Process Autoexec.bat File
      Process Winstart.bat File (if available)
      Process Win.ini File
      Load Startup Group Items

4. Click OK and restart the computer when prompted.

To restore your original configuration, click Normal Startup on the General tab in the System Configuration Utility tool.

When the system has been cleanly rebooted, reinstall the keyboard's applet software (for example, Microsoft's IntelliType Pro software), and then download and install the latest version of RealPlayer software from **www.realplayer.com**. Finally, reboot the system normally and test the keyboard's operation.

SYMPTOM 23-10 **Some keys on a programmable keyboard will not remap to their default state** This can happen with some Gateway 2000 (AnyKey) keyboards—as well as other programmable keyboards—and you may have to "force clear" the keyboard at boot time. Power-down the system. While holding down the SUSPEND MACRO key, turn the system power back on. Continue booting with the SUSPEND MACRO key depressed until the Program light (or similar LED) quits flashing. This light will stay lit until you depress and release it.

For Gateway 2000 AnyKey keyboards, if there is an "AnykeyXX T" line in the AUTOEXEC.BAT file, this will terminate any programming function of the keyboard. If there is an "AnykeyXX A" line in the AUTOEXEC.BAT file, this will activate the programming function.

SYMPTOM 23-11 **A wireless keyboard types random characters** You'll need to reset both ends of the wireless system. First, take a look at the DIP switch settings controlling the RF channel for the wireless transmitter and receiver (usually under the battery cover at the keyboard). Make sure that the transmitter and receiver are both set for the same channel. Find the "reset" button on both the transmitter and receiver. Press the RF receiver reset button first, and then press the RF transmitter button immediately after (usually within 15 seconds of one another). If the problem persists, reboot the system and try the reset process again.

SYMPTOM 23-12 **The wireless keyboard beeps while typing** In virtually all cases, the batteries in the wireless keyboard are running low. Replace the batteries and try the wireless keyboard again—the beeping should stop.

SYMPTOM 23-13 **The wireless keyboard isn't responding** You notice that the infrared light on the module isn't on, and the problem persists even after replacing the batteries. It may be that the keyboard's ID codes have gotten out of synch. Position the keyboard about 1.5 feet away from the IR module and make sure that the keyboard is in low power mode (the middle power switch setting). While the keyboard is pointing directly at the IR module, press and hold down the F10 and F12 keys simultaneously with the 1 key on the top row. If the IR light stays on, then it's in sync. If the LED doesn't stay on, release the keys, wait a few seconds, and repeat the F10-F12 sequence with the 2 key. If this still doesn't work, repeat this process with the 3 through 6 keys (there are six ID codes, 1 through 6). Review the instructions for your particular keyboard for specific reset/synchronization instructions.

SYMPTOM 23-14 **Typed characters do not appear, but the cursor moves** This issue is a result of the color scheme being used. Some of the applications reported as suffering this problem are MSWORKS 4.0, CASHGRAF, MSBOB (address book and letter writer), and MSPUBLISHER. Check the color scheme selected by right-clicking on the desktop. Click on Properties and then the Appearance tab. Set the scheme to Windows Standard. Click on OK to return to the desktop. The text should now appear normal. This solution can generally be attempted with any application.

SYMPTOM 23-15   **Some function keys and Windows keys may not work on some PC configurations**   For example, this is a known problem with Toshiba 8500 desktop systems and the Microsoft Natural Keyboard. In virtually all cases (including the Toshiba 8500), the PC keyboard controller BIOS recognizes the keyboard during the POST, but it does not recognize some of the keys—including certain function keys and Windows-specific keys. You'll need to try a generic keyboard, or upgrade the system's KBC BIOS.

SYMPTOM 23-16   **One or more Windows-specific keys don't work**   This is almost always a limitation of the KBC BIOS. For example, a Jetkey KBC BIOS (v.3.0) will not recognize the right Windows key on a Microsoft Natural Keyboard. You'll need to try a generic keyboard, or upgrade the system's KBC BIOS.

SYMPTOM 23-17   **The PC freezes when you press the "sleep" hot key on the keyboard** This is a known issue with certain high-end multifunction keyboards, such as the Microsoft IntelliType, Natural, and Internet keyboards, and is almost always due to a system configuration problem. To correct this trouble, you should use the Device Manager to troubleshoot possible device conflicts or disabled devices on the system.

SYMPTOM 23-18   **Remote control programs don't work after installing keyboard drivers**   Many PC "remote control" programs (such as PC Anywhere, ReachOut, and Carbon Copy) use keyboard and mouse drivers that simply are not compatible with the keyboard's native drivers. For example, the remote control programs listed above will not work when IntelliType software is installed for the Microsoft Natural Keyboard. You'll need to disable the remote control software, install patches for the remote control software that will properly support the keyboard, or replace the keyboard with a more generic model.

SYMPTOM 23-19   **Function keys do not respond, and the keyboard is incorrectly identified as an 84-key keyboard**   This is a known issue with high-end multifunction keyboards such as the Microsoft Natural Keyboard Elite, and is usually due to interference by software utilities such as Attachmate software. To resolve this issue, add the OverrideKeyboardType DWORD value to the following registry key:

```
HKEY_LOCAL_MACHINE\SYSTEM\CurrentControlSet\Services\i8042prt\Parameters
```

and then change the value data of this entry from 0 to 4. Be sure to make a complete backup of your registry to a bootable floppy disk before attempting any changes to your registry.

SYMPTOM 23-20   **On an IBM PS/2 system, you encounter keyboard errors, even though the keyboard driver loads successfully**   Often, you'll see an error like "Keyboard error: keyboard not found," and you cannot access the keyboard. This type of problem is known to occur on PS/2 systems when the IBM ROM BIOS patch file (DASDDRVR.SYS) is loaded *after* the keyboard driver in CONFIG.SYS. Rearrange the CONFIG.SYS file to load the DASDDRVR.SYS file before the keyboard driver. Make sure you are loading the patch driver (DASDDRVR.SYS) that is designed for your *specific* computer (for example, you cannot use the DASDDRVR.SYS file that ships with an IBM PS/2 Model 80 on a PS/2 Model 70 computer). This device driver can normally be found on the setup disk that you received with your IBM PS/2. Otherwise, you can obtain it from IBM (**www.ibm.com**).

SYMPTOM 23-21 **Assigned key sounds do not work** When you assign sounds to keystrokes (under the Options tab in the Keyboard tool in your Control Panel), the sounds may play when you press the assigned keys. This problem is known to occur with some programmable keyboards when HiJaak Pro or HiJaak 95 Graphics Suite installed on your computer. These products may load a device driver named "Runner" that disables programmable keyboard sounds. You may be able to work around the problem by closing the "Runner" task:

■ Press CTRL-ALT-DEL to open the Close Program dialog box.

■ If "Runner" is listed, click Runner, and then click End Task.

SYMPTOM 23-22 **You cannot use Windows-specific keys to start task-switching software other than TASKSW16.EXE** You *can* start the desired task-switching software using CTRL-ESC or by double-clicking the desktop. Chances are that your Windows-specific key will not start any other task-switching utility if TASKSW16.EXE can be found on the path. You'll need to update the task-switching program reference in SYSTEM.INI. Load SYSTEM.INI into any text editor, and modify the line that reads:

```
TASKMAN=TASKSW16.EXE
```

to read

```
TASKMAN=<task manager>
```

where <task manager> is the name of the executable file you want to start when you press the Windows key. Rename the TASKSW16.EXE file (for example, to TASKSW16.OLD), or move it to a directory that is not in the path. Save and close the SYSTEM.INI file, and then restart the computer.

SYMPTOM 23-23 **The NumLock feature may not activate when the NUM LOCK key is pressed** This can happen with some programmable keyboards when pen software is installed on the system. You should be able to correct the problem by disabling the pen device:

1. Click Start, select Settings, then click Control Panel.
2. Double-click the System icon and select the Device Manager tab.
3. Double-click the Ports entry to expand it.
4. Double-click the port to which the pen (or touch-screen) device is connected.
5. In the Device Usage area on the General tab, click the Original Configuration (Current) check box to clear it. (If you're using OSR2, click the Disable In This Hardware Profile check box to select it.)
6. Click OK, and then restart the system when prompted.

To reenable your pen device, repeat the steps above, but reselect (or re-clear) the check box in step 5.

SYMPTOM 23-24 **The "Language" section of the Keyboard tool is disabled under Windows 98/Me** When you're using the Keyboard tool in Control Panel, you may encounter the following symptom(s): a message may say "Old-Style Keyboard detected, pane disabled," or the language list may be blank (and you may not be able to change any language settings). This problem can occur if the keyboard registry key is damaged or missing:

```
HKEY_LOCAL_MACHINE\System\CurrentControlSet\control\keyboard layouts
```

To resolve this problem, reinstall Windows 98/Me into the same folder as the original installation.

SYMPTOM 23-25   **You encounter keyboard problems when using IE 4.0x/5 and an Adobe Acrobat (PDF) file under Windows 98**   If you have a PDF file open in Internet Explorer, you may lose some keyboard functionality. Keys that may not work include the PAGE UP, PAGE DOWN, and arrow keys. To work around this problem, minimize and restore the IE window, use the Zoom buttons on the Adobe Acrobat toolbar, or use the mouse to scroll through the file.

SYMPTOM 23-26   **You have problems using a real-mode keyboard driver with an international code page**   If an international code page is installed in conjunction with a real-mode keyboard driver (such as KEYBOARD.SYS), you may find that console programs cannot detect extended character keystrokes (such as INSERT, DELETE, HOME, and so on). Console programs that don't work directly with the console API may not recognize extended keystrokes. When a real-mode keyboard driver is installed, the current character in the keyboard buffer is sent to the console program. With an international code page loaded, the data returned through the console API is slightly different than that in Windows 98/Me. This problem has been corrected in Windows 98 SE and later, but for older versions of Windows, you can download the patch (a new version of CONAGENT.EXE) from **www.microsoft.com/support/supportnet/overview/overview.asp**.

SYMPTOM 23-27   **You find two keyboards listed in the Windows Device Manager**   When you restart your computer after installing a USB keyboard, both the USB keyboard device and the Standard 101/102-Key or Microsoft Natural Keyboard device are listed in the Keyboard branch of your Device Manager. This occurs because USB keyboards may still require the Standard 101/102-Key or Natural Keyboard driver to work properly (if your BIOS does not fully support USB in the real mode). This may seem awkward, but it's perfectly normal. If you disable the Standard 101/102-Key or Microsoft Natural Keyboard device in Device Manager and restart your computer, the USB keyboard will not work—Windows 98/Me automatically installs the device again. You might try a system BIOS upgrade to better support the USB ports on your motherboard.

SYMPTOM 23-28   **The new USB keyboard does not operate properly under Windows 98 after installation**   You know that your system should fully support USB devices. This problem can occur when you install a new USB keyboard while your system is off, and your computer is set up to have you log on when you start it. USB keyboards are not enumerated until *after* you log on to your computer. To correct this problem, click Cancel when you're prompted to log on, click Start, click Log Off <user name>, click Yes, and *then* log on to your computer.

SYMPTOM 23-29   **You notice that the keyboard language unexpectedly changes to a "default" language**   When you start a program under Windows 98/Me (or when a program is started using OLE), your keyboard may revert to the "default" language—regardless of the language you're currently using. For example, when you start a program, you'll see the Language icon on the taskbar change to indicate that the default language is being used (but when a program is started using OLE, the language icon may not change). To work around this problem, simply change the keyboard driver to the desired language after you start the program. Click the Language icon on the taskbar, and then click the language that you want. Now press the appropriate shortcut key combination for switching keyboard layouts (by default, this is LEFT ARROW-ALT-SHIFT).

SYMPTOM 23-30   **The "automatic repeat" feature doesn't work for USB keyboards after returning from suspend mode under Windows 98 SE**   This is a known problem with Windows 98 SE, but a patch is available from Microsoft at **www.microsoft.com/support/ supportnet/overview/overview.asp**. The English version of this patch should have the following file attributes (or later):

```
KBDHID.VXD   10/04/99   05:32p          4.10.2223      16,666KB
```

SYMPTOM 23-31   **After upgrading to Windows 98, your custom keyboard layout may be lost**   This problem occurs when user profiles are enabled in Windows 95 and a custom keyboard layout option is selected in a user profile (rather than the default profile). Since Windows 98 setup only parses the settings for a default user during the upgrade to Windows 98, the keyboard setting changes to the default user profile during the upgrade. To correct this problem, log on to the computer using a user profile *other* than the default, and then modify the keyboard layout in Windows 98:

1. Click Start, highlight Settings, and then click Control Panel.
2. Click Keyboard, click Language, click Properties, and then click the layout you want to use in the Keyboard Layout box.
3. Click OK, click OK again, and then restart the computer.

SYMPTOM 23-32   **Your laptop does not detect a PS/2 keyboard**   This is a known problem with configurations such as the IBM ThinkPad and Natural Keyboard Elite. For example, when you connect the Natural Keyboard Elite to the PS/2 port on an IBM ThinkPad laptop, the keyboard may not be detected. This problem generally occurs because the PS/2 port on the IBM ThinkPad does not detect any PS/2 keyboard without the correct adapter cable or docking station. To correct this problem, you must connect the keyboard to an appropriate docking station.

SYMPTOM 23-33   **Your particular keyboard doesn't work with a Compaq DeskPro 4000 system**   For example, the Natural Keyboard Elite is known to have trouble with the Compaq DeskPro 4000. When you connect the keyboard to your computer, the keyboard may be detected the first time you start the system, but the keyboard may not be detected during subsequent starts. In virtually all cases, the keyboard device you're using will not operate on systems using the VIA UHCI chipset. Try a different (basic model) keyboard.

SYMPTOM 23-34   **You find that you cannot use the USB Natural Keyboard Elite in the DOS mode**   For example, when you start the computer (or restart your computer) in DOS mode, the Natural Keyboard Elite may not function properly. You may also receive either of the following error messages:

```
Keyboard Error
```

or

```
Keyboard Not Present
```

This problem can occur if you connect the Natural Keyboard Elite to your computer using a USB adapter, but your computer's BIOS doesn't fully support USB keyboards. Your system BIOS must support USB devices in order for any type of USB keyboard to work in DOS. You should upgrade the system

BIOS with a version that supports USB devices. To work around this issue temporarily, shut down Windows and turn off the computer. Disconnect the keyboard from the USB port, and then remove the USB adapter. Connect another keyboard to a PS/2 port on the computer, and then restart the system normally.

SYMPTOM 23-35   **Keyboard lights do not illuminate in the DOS mode**   This is a known problem when using the Natural Keyboard Elite with a Compaq Presario system under DOS. The LED lights on the keyboard may remain unlit in DOS, but may work properly under Windows. This is an issue with the Compaq system (rather than the keyboard), but no features are lost in the DOS mode.

SYMPTOM 23-36   **Your keyboard does not work properly on an IBM Aptiva system** For example, when you connect a Natural Keyboard or Natural Keyboard Elite to an IBM Aptiva computer, the keyboard may not work properly. This problem may occur if you have IBM Rapid Access Keyboard software running on the Aptiva system. To correct this issue, remove the IBM Rapid Access Keyboard software (this software is not needed if you use another keyboard, such as the Natural Keyboard family):

1. Click Start, highlight Settings, and then click Control Panel.
2. Double-click the Add/Remove Programs icon.
3. In the list of installed programs, click IBM Rapid Access Keyboard, and then click Add/Remove.
4. Follow the instructions on the screen to remove the IBM Rapid Access Keyboard software.

The EZ-Button program is a component of the IBM Rapid Access Keyboard software, so this program is also removed when you remove the IBM Rapid Access Keyboard software.

SYMPTOM 23-37   **Your Natural Keyboard does not work properly on certain Toshiba laptops** For example, when you use a Natural Keyboard Elite attached to the PS/2 port on one of the following Toshiba laptops, the keyboard may not function properly:

- Satellite 110C
- Satellite Pro 400C
- Tecra 720CDT
- Tecra 500CDT

This problem can occur because plug-and-play hardware detection on the PS/2 port times out *before* the computer enumerates the keyboard. This is a problem with the keyboard. To get around this issue, use the USB adapter included with the keyboard to connect the keyboard to the USB port on the laptop (if one is available). If a USB port is not available on your computer, you'll need to return the keyboard for an updated model that operates properly on the Toshiba family of laptops.

Further Study

Chicony   www.chicony.com/
Keytronic   www.keytronic.com
Microsoft   www.microsoft.com/catalog/navigation.asp?subid=22&nv=9
Mitsumi   www.mitsumi.com
NMB Technologies   www.nmbtech.com/

24

MEMORY
TROUBLESHOOTING

Memory holds the program code and data that is processed by the CPU, and it is this intimate relationship between memory and the CPU that forms the basis of computer performance. Larger and faster CPUs are constantly being introduced, and more complex software is regularly developed to take advantage of the processing power. In turn, the more complex software demands larger amounts of faster memory. With the explosive growth of Windows (and more recently Windows 98/Me), the demands made on memory performance are more acute than ever. These demands have resulted in a proliferation of memory types that go far beyond the simple, traditional DRAM. Pipeline-burst cache, video memory (VRAM), fast synchronous DRAM (SDRAM), flash BIOS, and emerging memory types (such as Rambus) now compete for the attention of PC technicians. These new forms of memory also present some new problems. This chapter will provide an understanding of memory types, configurations, installation concerns, and troubleshooting solutions.

Essential Memory Concepts

The first step in any discussion of memory is to understand how solid-state memory works, what the important technologies are, and how memory is organized in the PC. If you already have a good grasp of memory basics, feel free to skip this part of the chapter. Otherwise, you may find the following information to be a good overview of memory basics.

MEMORY ORGANIZATION

All memory is basically an *array* of individual storage elements organized into rows and columns, as shown in Figure 24-1. Each row is known as an *address*—there may be 1 million, 2 million, 4 million (often more) addresses on a single memory chip. The columns represent *data bits*—an older memory chip may only have one column of bits, but more recent high-density memory chips may have two or four columns of bits.

As you can see in Figure 24-1, the intersection of each column and row is an individual memory bit (known as a *cell*). This is important because the number of components that make up a cell—and the way those components are fabricated onto the memory chip—will have a profound impact on memory performance. For example, a classic *dynamic RAM* (DRAM) cell is a single MOS transistor, while *static RAM* (SRAM) cells often pack several transistors and other components onto the chip's die for every bit. Although you don't have to be an expert on chip design, you should realize that the internal fabrication of a memory chip has more to do with its performance than just the way it is soldered into your computer.

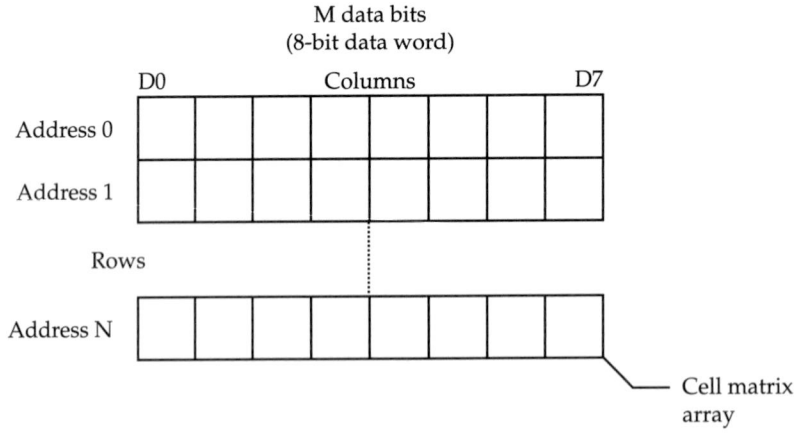

FIGURE 24-1   Simplified diagram of a memory array

MEMORY SIGNALS

The array of memory bits communicates with the "outside world" through three sets of signals: address lines, data lines, and control lines. Figure 24-2 illustrates these signal types. *Address lines* define which row of the memory array will be active. In actual practice, the address is specified as a binary number, and conversion circuitry inside the memory chip translates the binary number into a specific row signal. *Data lines* carry the data bits back and forth to the storage cells (columns) at the defined address. *Control lines* are used to operate the memory chip. For example, a Read/-Write (R/-W) line defines whether data is being read from the specified address, or written to it. A -Chip Select (-CS) signal makes a memory chip active or inactive. (This ability to "disconnect" from a circuit is what allows a myriad of memory chips to share common address and data signals in the computer.) Some memory types require additional signals such as row address-select (RAS) and column address-select (CAS) for refresh operations. More exotic memory types may require additional control signals, but you get the general idea.

Memory Packages and Structures

Ultimately, the memory die is mounted in a package just like any other chip. The completed memory packages can then be soldered to your motherboard, or attached to plug-in structures such as SIMMs, DIMMs, and RIMMs. There are really only five package styles normally used for memory devices:

■ **DIP (Dual Inline Package)**   This is the classical "chip" package used for through-hole mounting (prior to surface-mount technology). The advantage of DIP packages is their compatibility with sockets, which

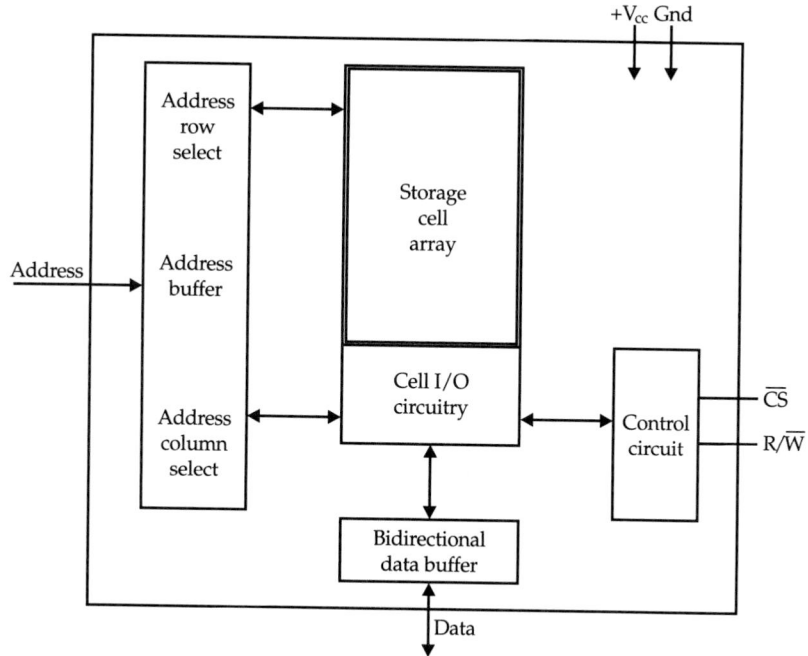

FIGURE 24-2   Simplified diagram of a basic memory chip

allows chips to be inserted or removed as required. Unfortunately, the long metal pins can bend and break if the chip is inserted or removed incorrectly. Also, the overall size of the package demands extra space. DIP chips can be found in older PCs (such as 286 and earlier systems) and older VGA/SVGA video boards. DIPs are still sometimes used on motherboards to hold cache RAM or BIOS chips.

- **SIP (Single Inline Package)** This type of package is rarely used today—there are simply not enough pins. However, they did make a short appearance with memory devices in late-model 286 and early 386 systems that flirted with proprietary memory expansions. Long-time technicians may remember NEC using such devices in a 2MB add-on module for their 386SX/20, and you needed to add that module *before* you added even more memory in the form of proprietary SIMMs. SIPs can be troublesome because they are difficult to find replacements for, so expect replacement memory modules that use them to cost a premium.

- **SOJ (Small-Outline "J" Lead)** This is the contemporary package style for surface-mount circuits. The leads protrude from the package like a DIP, but are bent around just under the package in the form of a "*j*". There are sockets for SOJ packages, which are often employed for replaceable memory chips like the BIOS ROM, but most SOJ RAM devices are soldered directly to the motherboard as system memory (or a video board as video RAM). Memory modules often use SOJ-type memory components.

- **TSOP (Thin, Small-Outline Package)** Like the SOJ, a TSOP is also a surface-mount package style. However, rather than bending pins under the package, the pins extend away (almost horizontally). Its small, thin body makes TSOP memory ideal for narrow spaces. Expect to find such devices serving as memory in notebook/sub-notebook systems, or PCMCIA cards (a.k.a. PC Cards).

- **CSP (Chip Scale Package)** Unlike other forms of packaging, CSP doesn't use pins to connect the chip to its circuit. Instead, the package uses a series of surface-mount contact pads on the underside of the chip (similar to a ball grid array or BGA package style). Rambus memory chips typically utilize this kind of packaging to create Rambus modules (RIMMs).

MEMORY MODULES

In the early days of PC design, memory chips were soldered to the motherboard. This gave the PC a fixed amount of RAM, but also made it terribly inconvenient to add more RAM. To expand the amount of RAM on a system, designers began to incorporate memory chips onto specialized memory modules that could be added later if needed. This way, an inexpensive system could be sold with a minimum amount of "base memory" on the motherboard, and then the memory could be upgraded later using one or more modules. Today, standard memory modules are used exclusively. This greatly simplifies the process of memory troubleshooting because all RAM modules can be removed and replaced if necessary. You will generally encounter three types of memory modules: SIMMs, DIMMs, and RIMMs.

Proprietary Add-On Modules

Once Intel's 286 processor opened the door for more than 1MB of memory, PC makers scrambled to fill the void. However, the rush to more memory resulted in a proliferation of nonstandard (and incompatible) memory modules. Each new motherboard came with a new add-on memory scheme, which invariably led to a great deal of confusion among PC users and makers alike. You will likely find proprietary memory modules in 286 and early 386 systems, though no current desktop system uses proprietary memory modules.

SIMM

By the time 386 systems took hold in the PC industry, proprietary memory modules had been largely abandoned in favor of the 30-pin *Single In-line Memory Module* (SIMM). A SIMM is light, small, and can hold anywhere between 1MB and 16MB of RAM (depending on the module's vintage). Later SIMM versions were physically larger, with 72 pins, and able to hold as much as 32MB of RAM.

SIMMs are placed into special sockets on the motherboard. The sockets are specifically designed to ensure that once inserted, the SIMM will be held in place tightly. SIMMs are secured in their sockets by inserting them at an angle (usually about 60 degrees from the motherboard) into the base of the socket, and then tilting them upward until they are perpendicular to the motherboard. Special metal clips on either side of the socket snap in place when the SIMM is inserted correctly. The SIMM is also keyed with a notch on one side, so it cannot be installed backwards.

Perhaps the greatest advantage of a SIMM is *standardization*: using a standard pin layout, a SIMM from one PC can be installed into almost any other compatible PC. The 30-pin SIMM (Table 24-1) provides 8 data bits and generally holds up to 4MB of RAM. The 30-pin SIMM proved its worth in 386 and early 486 systems, but fell short when providing more memory to later-model PCs. The 72-pin SIMM (Table 24-2) replaced the 30-pin SIMM version by providing 32 data bits, and may hold up to 32MB (or

TABLE 24-1   PIN ASSIGNMENTS FOR A STANDARD 30-PIN SIMM

PIN	NAME	DESCRIPTION
1	VCC	+5 Vdc
2	-CAS	-Column Address Strobe
3	DQ0	Data 0
4	A0	Address 0
5	A1	Address 1
6	DQ1	Data 1
7	A2	Address 2
8	A3	Address 3
9	GND	Ground
10	DQ2	Data 2
11	A4	Address 4
12	A5	Address 5
13	DQ3	Data 3
14	A6	Address 6
15	A7	Address 7
16	DQ4	Data 4
17	A8	Address 8
18	A9	Address 9
19	A10	Address 10
20	DQ5	Data 5
21	-WE	-Write Enable
22	GND	Ground
23	DQ6	Data 6
24	n/c	Not connected
25	DQ7	Data 7
26	QP	Data Parity Out
27	-RAS	-Row Address Strobe
28	-CASP	-Parity Control
29	DP	Data Parity In
30	VCC	+5 Vdc

TABLE 24-2 PIN ASSIGNMENTS FOR A STANDARD 72-PIN SIMM

PIN	NON-PARITY	PARITY	DESCRIPTION
1	VSS	VSS	Ground
2	DQ0	DQ0	Data 0
3	DQ18	DQ18	Data 18
4	DQ1	DQ1	Data 1
5	DQ19	DQ19	Data 19
6	DQ2	DQ2	Data 2
7	DQ20	DQ20	Data 20
8	DQ3	DQ3	Data 3
9	DQ21	DQ21	Data 21
10	VCC	VCC	+5 Vdc
11	n/c	n/c	Not connected
12	A0	A0	Address 0
13	A1	A1	Address 1
14	A2	A2	Address 2
15	A3	A3	Address 3
16	A4	A4	Address 4
17	A5	A5	Address 5
18	A6	A6	Address 6
19	A10	A10	Address 10
20	DQ4	DQ4	Data 4
21	DQ22	DQ22	Data 22
22	DQ5	DQ5	Data 5
23	DQ23	DQ23	Data 23
24	DQ6	DQ6	Data 6
25	DQ24	DQ24	Data 24
26	DQ7	DQ7	Data 7
27	DQ25	DQ25	Data 25
28	A7	A7	Address 7
29	A11	A11	Address 11
30	VCC	VCC	+5 Vdc
31	A8	A8	Address 8
32	A9	A9	Address 9
33	-RAS3	-RAS3	-Row Address Strobe 3
34	-RAS2	-RAS2	-Row Address Strobe 2
35	n/c	PQ26	Parity 26 (3rd)
36	n/c	PQ8	Parity 8 (1st)
37	n/c	PQ17	Parity 26 (3rd)
38	n/c	PQ35	Parity 35 (4th)
39	VSS	VSS	Ground
40	-CAS0	-CAS0	-Column Address Strobe 0
41	-CAS2	-CAS2	-Column Address Strobe 2
42	-CAS3	-CAS3	-Column Address Strobe 3
43	-CAS1	-CAS1	-Column Address Strobe 1
44	-RAS0	-RAS0	-Row Address Strobe 0
45	-RAS1	-RAS1	-Row Address Strobe 1
46	n/c	n/c	Not connected

TABLE 24-2   PIN ASSIGNMENTS FOR A STANDARD 72-PIN SIMM *(CONTINUED)*

PIN	NON-PARITY	PARITY	DESCRIPTION
47	-WE	-WE	Read/-Write
48	n/c	n/c	Not connected
49	DQ9	DQ9	Data 9
50	DQ27	DQ27	Data 27
51	DQ10	DQ10	Data 10
52	DQ28	DQ28	Data 28
53	DQ11	DQ11	Data 11
54	DQ29	DQ29	Data 29
55	DQ12	DQ12	Data 12
56	DQ30	DQ30	Data 30
57	DQ13	DQ13	Data 13
58	DQ31	DQ31	Data 31
59	VCC	VCC	+5 Vdc
60	DQ32	DQ32	Data 32
61	DQ14	DQ14	Data 14
62	DQ33	DQ33	Data 33
63	DQ15	DQ15	Data 15
64	DQ34	DQ34	Data 34
65	DQ16	DQ16	Data 16
66	n/c	n/c	Not connected
67	PD1	PD1	Presence Detect 1
68	PD2	PD2	Presence Detect 2
69	PD3	PD3	Presence Detect 3
70	PD4	PD4	Presence Detect 4
71	n/c	n/c	Not connected
72	VSS	VSS	Ground
Size: (presence detect lines)			
PD2	PD1	Size	
GND	GND	4 or 64MB	
GND	NC	2 or 32MB	
NC	GND	1 or 16MB	
NC	NC	8MB	
Access Time: (presence detect lines)			
PD4	PD3	Access time	
GND	GND	50ns, 100ns	
GND	NC	80ns	
NC	GND	70ns	
NC	NC	60ns	

more). Table 24-3 outlines a variation of the standard 72-pin SIMM, highlighting the use of Error Correction Code (ECC) instead of parity.

SIMMs are generally available as *single-sided* or *double-sided*—referring to whether DRAM chips are found on only one side or both sides of the SIMM. The 30-pin SIMMs are almost always single-sided; 72-pin SIMMs are either single-sided or double-sided. Some double-sided SIMMs are also constructed as

TABLE 24-3   A STANDARD 168-PIN PC133 SDRAM DIMM

PIN	ECC	OPTIMIZED	DESCRIPTION
1	VSS	VSS	Ground
2	DQ0	DQ0	Data 0
3	DQ1	DQ1	Data 1
4	DQ2	DQ2	Data 2
5	DQ3	DQ3	Data 3
6	DQ4	DQ4	Data 4
7	DQ5	DQ5	Data 5
8	DQ6	DQ6	Data 6
9	DQ7	DQ7	Data 7
10	VCC	VCC	+5 Vdc
11	PD5	PD5	Presence Detect 5
12	A0	A0	Address 0
13	A1	A1	Address 1
14	A2	A2	Address 2
15	A3	A3	Address 3
16	A4	A4	Address 4
17	A5	A5	Address 5
18	A6	A6	Address 6
19	n/c	n/c	Not connected
20	DQ8	DQ8	Data 8
21	DQ9	DQ9	Data 9
22	DQ10	DQ10	Data 10
23	DQ11	DQ11	Data 11
24	DQ12	DQ12	Data 12
25	DQ13	DQ13	Data 13
26	DQ14	DQ14	Data 14
27	DQ15	DQ15	Data 15
28	A7	A7	Address 7
29	DQ16	DQ16	Data 16
30	VCC	VCC	+5 Vdc
31	A8	A8	Address 8
32	A9	A9	Address 9
33	n/c	n/c	Not connected
34	-RAS1	-RAS1	-Row Address Strobe 1
35	DQ17	DQ17	Data 17
36	DQ18	DQ18	Data 18
37	DQ19	DQ19	Data 19
38	DQ20	DQ20	Data 20
39	VSS	VSS	Ground
40	-CAS0	-CAS0	-Column Address Strobe 0
41	A10	A10	Address 10
42	A11	A11	Address 11
43	-CAS1	-CAS1	-Column Address Strobe 1
44	-RAS0	-RAS0	-Row Address Strobe 0
45	-RAS1	-RAS1	-Row Address Strobe 1
46	DQ21	DQ21	Data 21

TABLE 24-3   A STANDARD 168-PIN PC133 SDRAM DIMM *(CONTINUED)*

PIN	ECC	OPTIMIZED	DESCRIPTION
47	-WE	-WE	Read/-Write
48	-ECC	-ECC	-Error Correction Control
49	DQ22	DQ22	Data 22
50	DQ23	DQ23	Data 23
51	DQ24	DQ24	Data 24
52	DQ25	DQ25	Data 25
53	DQ26	DQ26	Data 26
54	DQ27	DQ27	Data 27
55	DQ28	DQ28	Data 28
56	DQ29	DQ29	Data 29
57	DQ30	DQ30	Data 30
58	DQ31	DQ31	Data 31
59	VCC	VCC	+5 Vdc
60	DQ32	DQ32	Data 32
61	DQ33	DQ33	Data 33
62	DQ34	DQ34	Data 34
63	DQ35	DQ35	Data 35
64	n/c	DQ36	Data 36
65	n/c	DQ37	Data 37
66	n/c	DQ38	Data 38
67	PD1	PD1	Presence Detect 1
68	PD2	PD2	Presence Detect 2
69	PD3	PD3	Presence Detect 3
70	PD4	PD4	Presence Detect 4
71	n/c	DQ39	Data 39
72	VSS	VSS	Ground

composite SIMMs. Internally, composite SIMMs are wired as if they were actually two single-sided SIMMs back to back. This doesn't affect the characteristics or capacity of the module, but some motherboards cannot handle composite SIMMs because they are slightly different electrically. For example, 72-pin SIMMs that are 1MB, 4MB, and 16MB in size are normally single-sided, while 2MB, 8MB, and 32MB SIMMs are generally double-sided. This is why there are so many motherboards that will only work with 1MB, 4MB, and 16MB SIMMs. You should always check your motherboard to see what SIMM sizes are required. Composite SIMMs will *not* work in a motherboard that doesn't support them.

DIMM

The *Dual In-line Memory Module* (DIMM) closely resembles SIMMs, as shown in Figure 24-3, but are physically larger. The 168-pin module accommodates a 64-bit data bus width. Where a SIMM ties each pin together between the front and back, a DIMM keeps all electrical signals separate. This provides for many more pins without making the module much larger. The added size and pin count of the modern DIMM easily supports 64MB, 128MB, and 256MB of RAM—allowing a substantial amount of RAM with only one or two modules. Table 24-4 lists the pinout for an unbuffered DRAM DIMM, and Table 24-5 presents the pinout for an unbuffered SDRAM DIMM.

FIGURE 24-3   A standard 168-pin PC 133 SDRAM DIMM

TABLE 24-4   PIN ASSIGNMENTS FOR A STANDARD 168-PIN UNBUFFERED DRAM DIMM

PIN	NON-PARITY	PARITY	72 ECC	80 ECC	DESCRIPTION
1	VSS	VSS	VSS	VSS	Ground
2	DQ0	DQ0	DQ0	DQ0	Data 0
3	DQ1	DQ1	DQ1	DQ1	Data 1
4	DQ2	DQ2	DQ2	DQ2	Data 2
5	DQ3	DQ3	DQ3	DQ3	Data 3
6	VCC	VCC	VCC	VCC	+5 Vdc or +3.3 Vdc
7	DQ4	DQ4	DQ4	DQ4	Data 4
8	DQ5	DQ5	DQ5	DQ5	Data 5
9	DQ6	DQ6	DQ6	DQ6	Data 6
10	DQ7	DQ7	DQ7	DQ7	Data 7
11	DQ8	DQ8	DQ8	DQ8	Data 8
12	VSS	VSS	VSS	VSS	Ground
13	DQ9	DQ9	DQ9	DQ9	Data 9
14	DQ10	DQ10	DQ10	DQ10	Data 10
15	DQ11	DQ11	DQ11	DQ11	Data 11
16	DQ12	DQ12	DQ12	DQ12	Data 12
17	DQ13	DQ13	DQ13	DQ13	Data 13
18	VCC	VCC	VCC	VCC	+5 Vdc or +3.3 Vdc
19	DQ14	DQ14	DQ14	DQ14	Data 14
20	DQ15	DQ15	DQ15	DQ15	Data 15
21	n/c	CB0	CB0	CB0	Parity/Check Bit Input/Output 0
22	n/c	CB1	CB1	CB1	Parity/Check Bit Input/Output 1
23	VSS	VSS	VSS	VSS	Ground
24	n/c	n/c	n/c	CB8	Parity/Check Bit Input/Output 8
25	n/c	n/c	n/c	CB9	Parity/Check Bit Input/Output 9
26	VCC	VCC	VCC	VCC	+5 Vdc or +3.3 Vdc

TABLE 24-4   PIN ASSIGNMENTS FOR A STANDARD 168-PIN UNBUFFERED DRAM DIMM
(CONTINUED)

PIN	NON-PARITY	PARITY	72 ECC	80 ECC	DESCRIPTION
27	-WE0	-WE0	-WE0	-WE0	Read/-Write Input
28	-CAS0	-CAS0	-CAS0	-CAS0	-Column Address Strobe 0
29	-CAS1	-CAS1	-CAS1	-CAS1	-Column Address Strobe 1
30	-RAS0	-RAS0	-RAS0	-RAS0	-Row Address Strobe 0
31	-OE0	-OE0	-OE0	-OE0	-Output Enable
32	VSS	VSS	VSS	VSS	Ground
33	A0	A0	A0	A0	Address 0
34	A2	A2	A2	A2	Address 2
35	A4	A4	A4	A4	Address 4
36	A6	A6	A6	A6	Address 6
37	A8	A8	A8	A8	Address 8
38	A10	A10	A10	A10	Address 10
39	A12	A12	A12	A12	Address 12
40	VCC	VCC	VCC	VCC	+5 Vdc or +3.3 Vdc
41	VCC	VCC	VCC	VCC	+5 Vdc or +3.3 Vdc
42	DU	DU	DU	DU	Don't Use
43	VSS	VSS	VSS	VSS	Ground
44	-OE2	-OE2	-OE2	-OE2	-Output Enable 2
45	-RAS2	-RAS2	-RAS2	-RAS2	-Row Address Strobe 2
46	-CAS2	-CAS2	-CAS2	-CAS2	-Column Address Strobe 2
47	-CAS3	-CAS3	-CAS3	-CAS3	-Column Address Strobe 3
48	-WE2	-WE2	-WE2	-WE2	Read/-Write Input 2
49	VCC	VCC	VCC	VCC	+5 Vdc or +3.3 Vdc
50	n/c	n/c	n/c	CB10	Parity/Check Bit Input/Output 10
51	n/c	n/c	n/c	CB11	Parity/Check Bit Input/Output 11
52	n/c	CB2	CB2	CB2	Parity/Check Bit Input/Output 2
53	n/c	CB3	CB3	CB3	Parity/Check Bit Input/Output 3
54	VSS	VSS	VSS	VSS	Ground
55	DQ16	DQ16	DQ16	DQ16	Data 16
56	DQ17	DQ17	DQ17	DQ17	Data 17
57	DQ18	DQ18	DQ18	DQ18	Data 18
58	DQ19	DQ19	DQ19	DQ19	Data 19
59	VCC	VCC	VCC	VCC	+5 Vdc or +3.3 Vdc
60	DQ20	DQ20	DQ20	DQ20	Data 20
61	n/c	n/c	n/c	n/c	Not connected
62	DU	DU	DU	DU	Don't Use
63	n/c	n/c	n/c	n/c	Not connected
64	VSS	VSS	VSS	VSS	Ground
65	DQ21	DQ21	DQ21	DQ21	Data 21
66	DQ22	DQ22	DQ22	DQ22	Data 22
67	DQ23	DQ23	DQ23	DQ23	Data 23
68	VSS	VSS	VSS	VSS	Ground
69	DQ24	DQ24	DQ24	DQ24	Data 24
70	DQ25	DQ25	DQ25	DQ25	Data 25
71	DQ26	DQ26	DQ26	DQ26	Data 26

TABLE 24-4   PIN ASSIGNMENTS FOR A STANDARD 168-PIN UNBUFFERED DRAM DIMM
(CONTINUED)

PIN	NON-PARITY	PARITY	72 ECC	80 ECC	DESCRIPTION
72	DQ27	DQ27	DQ27	DQ27	Data 27
73	VCC	VCC	VCC	VCC	+5 Vdc or +3.3 Vdc
74	DQ28	DQ28	DQ28	DQ28	Data 28
75	DQ29	DQ29	DQ29	DQ29	Data 29
76	DQ30	DQ30	DQ30	DQ30	Data 30
77	DQ31	DQ31	DQ31	DQ31	Data 31
78	VSS	VSS	VSS	VSS	Ground
79	n/c	n/c	n/c	n/c	Not connected
80	n/c	n/c	n/c	n/c	Not connected
81	n/c	n/c	n/c	n/c	Not connected
82	SDA	SDA	SDA	SDA	Serial Data
83	SCL	SCL	SCL	SCL	Serial Clock
84	VCC	VCC	VCC	VCC	+5 Vdc or +3.3 Vdc
85	VSS	VSS	VSS	VSS	Ground
86	DQ32	DQ32	DQ32	DQ32	Data 32
87	DQ33	DQ33	DQ33	DQ33	Data 33
88	DQ34	DQ34	DQ34	DQ34	Data 34
89	DQ35	DQ35	DQ35	DQ35	Data 35
90	VCC	VCC	VCC	VCC	+5 Vdc or +3.3 Vdc
91	DQ36	DQ36	DQ36	DQ36	Data 36
92	DQ37	DQ37	DQ37	DQ37	Data 37
93	DQ38	DQ38	DQ38	DQ38	Data 38
94	DQ39	DQ39	DQ39	DQ39	Data 39
95	DQ40	DQ40	DQ40	DQ40	Data 40
96	VSS	VSS	VSS	VSS	Ground
97	DQ41	DQ41	DQ41	DQ41	Data 41
98	DQ42	DQ42	DQ42	DQ42	Data 42
99	DQ43	DQ43	DQ43	DQ43	Data 43
100	DQ44	DQ44	DQ44	DQ44	Data 44
101	DQ45	DQ45	DQ45	DQ45	Data 45
102	VCC	VCC	VCC	VCC	+5 Vdc or +3.3 Vdc
103	DQ46	DQ46	DQ46	DQ46	Data 46
104	DQ47	DQ47	DQ47	DQ47	Data 47
105	n/c	CB4	CB4	CB4	Parity/Check Bit Input/Output 4
106	n/c	CB5	CB5	CB5	Parity/Check Bit Input/Output 5
107	VSS	VSS	VSS	VSS	Ground
108	n/c	n/c	n/c	CB12	Parity/Check Bit Input/Output 12
109	n/c	n/c	n/c	CB13	Parity/Check Bit Input/Output 13
110	VCC	VCC	VCC	VCC	+5 Vdc or +3.3 Vdc
111	DU	DU	DU	DU	Don't Use
112	-CAS4	-CAS4	-CAS4	-CAS4	-Column Address Strobe 4
113	-CAS5	-CAS5	-CAS5	-CAS5	-Column Address Strobe 5
114	-RAS1	-RAS1	-RAS1	-RAS1	-Row Address Strobe 1
115	DU	DU	DU	DU	Don't Use
116	VSS	VSS	VSS	VSS	Ground

TABLE 24-4   PIN ASSIGNMENTS FOR A STANDARD 168-PIN UNBUFFERED DRAM DIMM (CONTINUED)

PIN	NON-PARITY	PARITY	72 ECC	80 ECC	DESCRIPTION
117	A1	A1	A1	A1	Address 1
118	A3	A3	A3	A3	Address 3
119	A5	A5	A5	A5	Address 5
120	A7	A7	A7	A7	Address 7
121	A9	A9	A9	A9	Address 9
122	A11	A11	A11	A11	Address 11
123	A13	A13	A13	A13	Address 13
124	VCC	VCC	VCC	VCC	+5 Vdc or +3.3 Vdc
125	DU	DU	DU	DU	Don't Use
126	DU	DU	DU	DU	Don't Use
127	VSS	VSS	VSS	VSS	Ground
128	DU	DU	DU	DU	Don't Use
129	-RAS3	-RAS3	-RAS3	-RAS3	-Column Address Strobe 3
130	-CAS6	-CAS6	-CAS6	-CAS6	-Column Address Strobe 6
131	-CAS7	-CAS7	-CAS7	-CAS7	-Column Address Strobe 7
132	DU	DU	DU	DU	Don't Use
133	VCC	VCC	VCC	VCC	+5 Vdc or +3.3 Vdc
134	n/c	n/c	n/c	CB14	Parity/Check Bit Input/Output 14
135	n/c	n/c	n/c	CB15	Parity/Check Bit Input/Output 15
136	n/c	CB6	CB6	CB6	Parity/Check Bit Input/Output 6
137	n/c	CB7	CB7	CB7	Parity/Check Bit Input/Output 7
138	VSS	VSS	VSS	VSS	Ground
139	DQ48	DQ48	DQ48	DQ48	Data 48
140	DQ49	DQ49	DQ49	DQ49	Data 49
141	DQ50	DQ50	DQ50	DQ50	Data 50
142	DQ51	DQ51	DQ51	DQ51	Data 51
143	VCC	VCC	VCC	VCC	+5 Vdc or +3.3 Vdc
144	DQ52	DQ52	DQ52	DQ52	Data 52
145	n/c	n/c	n/c	n/c	Not connected
146	DU	DU	DU	DU	Don't Use
147	n/c	n/c	n/c	n/c	Not connected
148	VSS	VSS	VSS	VSS	Ground
149	DQ53	DQ53	DQ53	DQ53	Data 53
150	DQ54	DQ54	DQ54	DQ54	Data 54
151	DQ55	DQ55	DQ55	DQ55	Data 55
152	VSS	VSS	VSS	VSS	Ground
153	DQ56	DQ56	DQ56	DQ56	Data 56
154	DQ57	DQ57	DQ57	DQ57	Data 57
155	DQ58	DQ58	DQ58	DQ58	Data 58
156	DQ59	DQ59	DQ59	DQ59	Data 59
157	VCC	VCC	VCC	VCC	+5 Vdc or +3.3 Vdc
158	DQ60	DQ60	DQ60	DQ60	Data 60
159	DQ61	DQ61	DQ61	DQ61	Data 61
160	DQ62	DQ62	DQ62	DQ62	Data 62
161	DQ63	DQ63	DQ63	DQ63	Data 63

TABLE 24-4   PIN ASSIGNMENTS FOR A STANDARD 168-PIN UNBUFFERED DRAM DIMM (CONTINUED)

PIN	NON-PARITY	PARITY	72 ECC	80 ECC	DESCRIPTION
162	VSS	VSS	VSS	VSS	Ground
163	CK3	CK3	CK3	CK3	
164	n/c	n/c	n/c	n/c	Not connected
165	SA0	SA0	SA0	SA0	Serial Address 0
166	SA1	SA1	SA1	SA1	Serial Address 1
167	SA2	SA2	SA2	SA2	Serial Address 2
168	VCC	VCC	VCC	VCC	+5 Vdc or +3.3 Vdc

TABLE 24-5   PIN ASSIGNMENTS FOR A 168-PIN UNBUFFERED SDRAM DIMM

PIN	NON-PARITY	72 ECC	80 ECC	DESCRIPTION
1	VSS	VSS	VSS	Ground
2	DQ0	DQ0	DQ0	Data 0
3	DQ1	DQ1	DQ1	Data 1
4	DQ2	DQ2	DQ2	Data 2
5	DQ3	DQ3	DQ3	Data 3
6	VDD	VDD	VDD	+5 Vdc or +3.3 Vdc
7	DQ4	DQ4	DQ4	Data 4
8	DQ5	DQ5	DQ5	Data 5
9	DQ6	DQ6	DQ6	Data 6
10	DQ7	DQ7	DQ7	Data 7
11	DQ8	DQ8	DQ8	Data 8
12	VSS	VSS	VSS	Ground
13	DQ9	DQ9	DQ9	Data 9
14	DQ10	DQ10	DQ10	Data 10
15	DQ11	DQ11	DQ11	Data 11
16	DQ12	DQ12	DQ12	Data 12
17	DQ13	DQ13	DQ13	Data 13
18	VDD	VDD	VDD	+5 Vdc or +3.3 Vdc
19	DQ14	DQ14	DQ14	Data 14
20	DQ15	DQ15	DQ15	Data 15
21	n/c	CB0	CB0	Parity/Check Bit Input/Output 0
22	n/c	CB1	CB1	Parity/Check Bit Input/Output 1
23	VSS	VSS	VSS	Ground
24	n/c	n/c	CB8	Parity/Check Bit Input/Output 8
25	n/c	n/c	CB9	Parity/Check Bit Input/Output 9
26	VDD	VDD	VDD	+5 Vdc or +3.3 Vdc
27	-WE	-WE	-WE	Read/-Write
28	DQMB0	DQMB0	DQMB0	Byte Mask signal 0
29	DQMB1	DQMB1	DQMB1	Byte Mask signal 1
30	-S0	-S0	-S0	-Chip Select 0
31	DU	DU	DU	Don't Use
32	VSS	VSS	VSS	Ground
33	A0	A0	A0	Address 0

TABLE 24-5   PIN ASSIGNMENTS FOR A 168-PIN UNBUFFERED SDRAM DIMM
(CONTINUED)

PIN	NON-PARITY	72 ECC	80 ECC	DESCRIPTION
34	A2	A2	A2	Address 2
35	A4	A4	A4	Address 4
36	A6	A6	A6	Address 6
37	A8	A8	A8	Address 8
38	A10/AP	A10/AP	A10/AP	Address 10
39	BA1	BA1	BA1	Bank Address 1
40	VDD	VDD	VDD	+5 Vdc or +3.3 Vdc
41	VDD	VDD	VDD	+5 Vdc or +3.3 Vdc
42	CK0	CK0	CK0	Clock signal 0
43	VSS	VSS	VSS	Ground
44	DU	DU	DU	Don't Use
45	-S2	-S2	-S2	-Chip Select 2
46	DQMB2	DQMB2	DQMB2	Byte Mask signal 2
47	DQMB3	DQMB3	DQMB3	Byte Mask signal 3
48	DU	DU	DU	Don't Use
49	VDD	VDD	VDD	+5 Vdc or +3.3 Vdc
50	n/c	n/c	CB10	Parity/Check Bit Input/Output 10
51	n/c	n/c	CB11	Parity/Check Bit Input/Output 11
52	n/c	CB2	CB2	Parity/Check Bit Input/Output 2
53	n/c	CB3	CB3	Parity/Check Bit Input/Output 3
54	VSS	VSS	VSS	Ground
55	DQ16	DQ16	DQ16	Data 16
56	DQ17	DQ17	DQ17	Data 17
57	DQ18	DQ18	DQ18	Data 18
58	DQ19	DQ19	DQ19	Data 19
59	VDD	VDD	VDD	+5 Vdc or +3.3 Vdc
60	DQ20	DQ20	DQ20	Data 20
61	n/c	n/c	n/c	Not connected
62	Vref,NC	Vref,NC	Vref,NC	
63	CKE1	CKE1	CKE1	Clock Enable Signal 1
64	VSS	VSS	VSS	Ground
65	DQ21	DQ21	DQ21	Data 21
66	DQ22	DQ22	DQ22	Data 22
67	DQ23	DQ23	DQ23	Data 23
68	VSS	VSS	VSS	Ground
69	DQ24	DQ24	DQ24	Data 24
70	DQ25	DQ25	DQ25	Data 25
71	DQ26	DQ26	DQ26	Data 26
72	DQ27	DQ27	DQ27	Data 27
73	VDD	VDD	VDD	+5 Vdc or +3.3 Vdc
74	DQ28	DQ28	DQ28	Data 28
75	DQ29	DQ29	DQ29	Data 29
76	DQ30	DQ30	DQ30	Data 30
77	DQ31	DQ31	DQ31	Data 31
78	VSS	VSS	VSS	Ground

TABLE 24-5 **PIN ASSIGNMENTS FOR A 168-PIN UNBUFFERED SDRAM DIMM** *(CONTINUED)*

PIN	NON-PARITY	72 ECC	80 ECC	DESCRIPTION
79	CK2	CK2	CK2	Clock signal 2
80	n/c	n/c	n/c	Not connected
81	n/c	n/c	n/c	Not connected
82	DAS	DAS	DAS	Serial Data
83	CLS	CLS	CLS	Serial Clock
84	VDD	VDD	VDD	+5 Vdc or +3.3 Vdc
85	VSS	VSS	VSS	Ground
86	DQ32	DQ32	DQ32	Data 32
87	DQ33	DQ33	DQ33	Data 33
88	DQ34	DQ34	DQ34	Data 34
89	DQ35	DQ35	DQ35	Data 35
90	VDD	VDD	VDD	+5 Vdc or +3.3 Vdc
91	DQ36	DQ36	DQ36	Data 36
92	DQ37	DQ37	DQ37	Data 37
93	DQ38	DQ38	DQ38	Data 38
94	DQ39	DQ39	DQ39	Data 39
95	DQ40	DQ40	DQ40	Data 40
96	VSS	VSS	VSS	Ground
97	DQ41	DQ41	DQ41	Data 41
98	DQ42	DQ42	DQ42	Data 42
99	DQ43	DQ43	DQ43	Data 43
100	DQ44	DQ44	DQ44	Data 44
101	DQ45	DQ45	DQ45	Data 45
102	VDD	VDD	VDD	+5 Vdc or +3.3 Vdc
103	DQ46	DQ46	DQ46	Data 46
104	DQ47	DQ47	DQ47	Data 47
105	n/c	CB4	CB4	Parity/Check Bit Input/Output 4
106	n/c	CB5	CB5	Parity/Check Bit Input/Output 5
107	VSS	VSS	VSS	Ground
108	n/c	n/c	CB12	Parity/Check Bit Input/Output 12
109	n/c	n/c	CB13	Parity/Check Bit Input/Output 13
110	VDD	VDD	VDD	+5 Vdc or +3.3 Vdc
111	-CAS	-CAS	-CAS	-Column Address Strobe
112	DQMB4	DQMB4	DQMB4	Byte Mask signal 4
113	DQMB5	DQMB5	DQMB5	Byte Mask signal 5
114	-S1	-S1	-S1	-Chip Select 1
115	-RAS	-RAS	-RAS	-Row Address Strobe
116	VSS	VSS	VSS	Ground
117	A1	A1	A1	Address 1
118	A3	A3	A3	Address 3
119	A5	A5	A5	Address 5
120	A7	A7	A7	Address 7
121	A9	A9	A9	Address 9
122	BA0	BA0	BA0	Bank Address 0
123	A11	A11	A11	Address 11

**TABLE 24-5   PIN ASSIGNMENTS FOR A 168-PIN UNBUFFERED SDRAM DIMM
(CONTINUED)**

PIN	NON-PARITY	72 ECC	80 ECC	DESCRIPTION
124	VDD	VDD	VDD	+5 Vdc or +3.3 Vdc
125	CK1	CK1	CK1	Clock signal 1
126	A12	A12	A12	Address 12
127	VSS	VSS	VSS	Ground
128	CKE0	CKE0	CKE0	Clock Enable Signal 0
129	-S3	-S3	-S3	-Chip Select 3
130	DQMB6	DQMB6	DQMB6	Byte Mask signal 6
131	DQMB7	DQMB7	DQMB7	Byte Mask signal 7
132	A13	A13	A13	Address 13
133	VDD	VDD	VDD	+5 Vdc or +3.3 Vdc
134	n/c	n/c	CB14	Parity/Check Bit Input/Output 14
135	n/c	n/c	CB15	Parity/Check Bit Input/Output 15
136	n/c	CB6	CB6	Parity/Check Bit Input/Output 6
137	n/c	CB7	CB7	Parity/Check Bit Input/Output 7
138	VSS	VSS	VSS	Ground
139	DQ48	DQ48	DQ48	Data 48
140	DQ49	DQ49	DQ49	Data 49
141	DQ50	DQ50	DQ50	Data 50
142	DQ51	DQ51	DQ51	Data 51
143	VDD	VDD	VDD	+5 Vdc or +3.3 Vdc
144	DQ52	DQ52	DQ52	Data 52
145	n/c	n/c	n/c	Not connected
146	Vref,NC	Vref,NC	Vref,NC	
147	n/c	n/c	n/c	Not connected
148	VSS	VSS	VSS	Ground
149	DQ53	DQ53	DQ53	Data 53
150	DQ54	DQ54	DQ54	Data 54
151	DQ55	DQ55	DQ55	Data 55
152	VSS	VSS	VSS	Ground
153	DQ56	DQ56	DQ56	Data 56
154	DQ57	DQ57	DQ57	Data 57
155	DQ58	DQ58	DQ58	Data 58
156	DQ59	DQ59	DQ59	Data 59
157	VDD	VDD	VDD	+5 Vdc or +3.3 Vdc
158	DQ60	DQ60	DQ60	Data 60
159	DQ61	DQ61	DQ61	Data 61
160	DQ62	DQ62	DQ62	Data 62
161	DQ63	DQ63	DQ63	Data 63
162	VSS	VSS	VSS	Ground
163	CK3	CK3	CK3	Clock signal 3
164	n/c	n/c	n/c	Not connected
165	SA0	SA0	SA0	Serial address 0
166	SA1	SA1	SA1	Serial address 1
167	SA2	SA2	SA2	Serial address 2
168	VDD	VDD	VDD	+5 Vdc or +3.3 Vdc

Today, DIMMs are the standard module type and are used to support high-performance SDRAM and DDR SDRAM memory.

DIMMs are also placed into special sockets on the motherboard that will hold the modules tightly in place. Unlike SIMMs, a DIMM is inserted vertically and locked into place in the vertical position. Special plastic clips on either end of the socket snap in place when the DIMM is inserted correctly. The DIMM is also keyed with a series of notches (depending on type and operating voltage), so it cannot be installed backwards. Although DIMMs have largely standardized the installation of RAM in a computer, there are several other factors to consider such as voltage, buffering, and module technology.

- **Voltage**   The voltage levels used on memory modules keep decreasing in order to increase performance and manage heat. Classical computer systems used to operate at a standard of +5 volts, but most modern PCs use +3.3 volt and +2.5 volt logic circuitry. DIMMs are available in +5 and +3.3 volt models, but +3.3 volt is certainly the most common.

- **Registers and Buffers**   Registers and buffers improve memory operation by "redriving" signals in the memory chips. They can be external to the memory module, or they can be located on the module itself. Having registers and buffers placed directly on the memory module enables a system to support a greater quantity of modules. Buffering is normally used with older FPM and EDO RAM where buffers simply redrive the signals. Buffering allows more DIMMs to be installed on the motherboard. Most DIMMs are unbuffered because a tremendous amount of RAM can still be installed using unbuffered RAM. When installing or upgrading memory, unbuffered and buffered (or registered) modules cannot be mixed. Registering is used with more recent SDRAM. Registering is similar to buffering, but the data is clocked in and out of the register by the system clock. Registered modules are slightly slower than nonregistered modules, because the registering process takes one clock cycle. You will normally find registered DIMMs in network servers or other high-end PCs that demand a lot of RAM.

In actual practice, the term buffer is used with all types of RAM, though this is technically incorrect. For example, you'll see "unbuffered SDRAM," even though it should technically be "unregistered SDRAM."

- **Composite vs. Noncomposite**   *Composite* and *noncomposite* are terms first used by Apple Computer to explain the difference between modules of the same capacity that use a different number of chips. For example, you can have a memory module with 8 of the new high-density chips, or 32 of the old density chips (even though both modules may offer the same capacity). The module using the latest technology and fewer chips is referred to as noncomposite, and the module using earlier technology and additional chips is called composite. Most PC users are better served to buy the more recent noncomposite modules.

RIMM

The *Rambus In-line Memory Module* (RIMM) looks almost identical to DIMMs, but is slightly bigger (with several keys between the metal contact fingers). Also called the Direct Rambus Memory Module, these advanced memory devices transfer data in 16-bit chunks along dedicated memory channels. Early RIMM implementations used 168 pins, but the 600 MHz (PC600), 711 MHz, and 800 MHz (PC800) RIMMs available today use 184 pins. Rambus modules also include a long heat sink (or *heat spreader*) used to manage the elevated operating temperatures encountered with RDRAM chips. You'll see more about Rambus DRAM later in the chapter.

Logical Memory Organization

The way a computer's memory is organized and used represents the result of evolution over several computer generations. Memory access and timing support is taken care of by your system's microprocessor and chipset. So as CPUs and chipsets improve, memory-handling capabilities have improved as well. Today's microprocessors (such as the Intel Pentium II, Pentium III, and Pentium 4) are capable of addressing more than 4GB of system memory—well beyond the levels of contemporary software applications. Unfortunately, the early PCs were not nearly so powerful. Older PCs could only address 1MB of memory due to limitations of the 8088 microprocessor.

Since backward compatibility is so important to computer users, the drawbacks and limitations of older systems had to be carried *forward* into newer computers instead of being eliminated. Newer systems overcome their inherent limitations by using memory in different ways, along with the hardware and software needed to access the memory. This part of the chapter describes the typical classifications of computer memory use: conventional, extended, and expanded memory. This chapter also describes high memory concepts. Note that these memory types have nothing to do with the actual memory chips in your system, but the way in which system software *uses* the memory.

CONVENTIONAL MEMORY

Conventional memory is the traditional 640KB assigned to the DOS Memory Area (10000h to 9FFFFh, as shown in Figure 24-4). The original PCs used microprocessors that could only address 1MB of memory (called *real-mode memory* or *base memory*). Out of that 1MB, portions of the memory must be set aside for basic system functions. BIOS code, video memory, interrupt vectors, and BIOS data are only some of the areas that required reserved memory. The remaining 640KB became available to load and run your application, which can be any combination of executable code and data. The original PC only provided 512KB for the DOS program area, but computer designers quickly learned that another 128KB could be added to the DOS area while retaining enough memory for overhead functions; so 512KB became 640KB.

Every IBM-compatible PC still provides a 640KB "base memory" range, and most DOS application programs continue to fit within that limit to ensure backward compatibility with older systems. However, the drawbacks to the 8088 CPU were soon apparent. More memory had to be added to the computer for its evolution to continue. Yet, memory had to be added in a way that did not interfere with the conventional memory area.

EXTENDED MEMORY (XMS)

The 80286 processor introduced in IBM's PC/AT was envisioned to overcome the 640KB barrier by incorporating a *protected mode* of addressing. The 80286 can address up to 16MB of memory in protected mode, while its successors (the 80386 and later) can handle 4GB of protected-mode memory. Today, virtually all computer systems provide several MB of *extended memory* (called XMS). Besides an advanced microprocessor, another key element for extended memory is software. Memory management software must be loaded in advance for the computer to access its extended memory. Microsoft's later DOS versions (up to MS-DOS 6.22) provide an extended memory manager utility (HIMEM.SYS), but there are other off-the-shelf utilities as well—Windows 98/Me/NT/2000 supplies its own memory manager tools.

Unfortunately, DOS itself cannot make use of extended memory. You may fill the extended memory area with data, but the executable code that constitutes the program remains limited to the original 640KB of base memory. Some programs written with DOS extenders can overcome the 640KB limit, but the

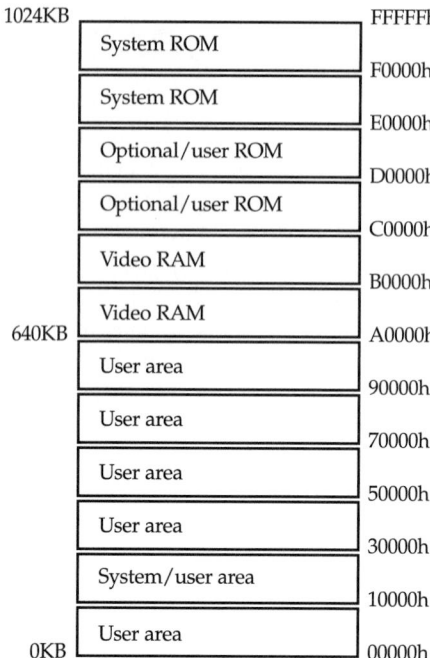

FIGURE 24-4   Conventional and upper memory in a typical PC

additional code needed for such "DOS extenders" can make such programs a bit clunky. A *DOS extender* is basically a software module containing its own memory management code that is compiled into the final application program.

The DOS extender loads a program in real-mode memory. After the program is loaded, it switches program control to the protected-mode memory. When the program in protected mode needs to execute a DOS (real-mode) function, the DOS extender converts protected-mode addresses into real-mode addresses, copies any necessary program data from protected- to real-mode locations, switches the CPU to real-mode addressing, and carries out the function. The DOS extender then copies any results (if necessary) back to protected-mode addresses, switches the system to protected-mode once again, and the program continues to run. This back-and-forth conversion overhead results in less than optimum performance compared to strictly real-mode programs, or true "protected-mode" programs.

With multiple megabytes of extended memory typically available, it is possible (but unlikely) that any one program will utilize all of the extended memory. Multiple programs that use extended memory must *not* attempt to utilize the same memory locations. If conflicts occur, a catastrophic system crash is almost inevitable. To prevent conflicts in extended memory, memory manager software can make use of three major industry standards: the *Extended Memory Specification* (XMS), the *Virtual Control Program Interface* (VCPI), or the *DOS Protected-Mode Interface* (DPMI). This chapter will not detail these standards, but you should know where they're used.

EXPANDED MEMORY (EMS)

Expanded memory (EMS) is another popular technique used to overcome the traditional 640KB limit of real-mode addressing. Expanded memory uses the same "physical" RAM chips, but differs from extended memory in the way that physical memory is used. Instead of trying to address physical memory locations outside of the conventional memory range as extended memory does, expanded memory blocks are switched into the base memory range where the CPU can access it in real mode. The original expanded memory specification (called the Lotus-Intel-Microsoft: *LIM*, or *EMS* specification) used 16KB blocks of memory that were mapped into a 64KB range of real-mode memory existing just above the video memory range. Thus, four "blocks" of expanded memory could be dealt with simultaneously in the real mode.

Early implementations of expanded memory utilized special expansion boards that switched blocks of memory, but later CPUs that support memory mapping allowed expanded memory managers (EMMs or LIMs) to supply software-only solutions for i386, i486, Pentium, and later machines. EMS/LIM 4.0 is the latest version of the expanded memory standard that handles up to 32MB of memory. An expanded memory manager (such as the DOS utility EMM386.EXE) allows the extended memory sitting in your computer to emulate expanded memory. For most practical purposes, expanded memory is more useful than extended memory because its ability to map directly to the real mode allows support for program multitasking. To use expanded memory, programs must be written specifically to take advantage of the function calls and subroutines needed to switch memory blocks. Functions are completely specified in the LIM/EMS 4.0 standard.

UPPER MEMORY AREA (UMA)

The upper 384KB of real-mode memory is not available to DOS because it is dedicated to handling memory requirements of the physical computer system. This is called the *High DOS Memory Range* or *upper memory area* (UMA). However, even the most advanced PCs do not use the *entire* 384KB, so there is often a substantial amount of unused memory existing in your system's real-mode range. Late model CPUs like the i386 and i486 can remap extended memory into the range unused by your system. Since this "found" memory space is not contiguous with your 640KB DOS space, DOS application programs cannot use the space, but small independent drivers and TSRs *can* be loaded and run from this UMA. The advantage of using this high DOS memory is that more of the 640KB DOS range remains available for your application program. Memory management programs (such as the utilities found with DOS 5.0 and higher) are needed to locate and remap these memory "blocks."

HIGH MEMORY

There is a peculiar anomaly that occurs with CPUs supporting extended memory—they can access one *segment* (about 64KB) of extended memory beyond the real-mode area. This capability arises because of the address line layout on late model CPUs. As a result, the real-mode operation can access roughly 64KB *above* the 1MB limit. Like high DOS memory, this "found" 64KB is not contiguous with the normal 640KB DOS memory range, so DOS cannot use this high memory to load a DOS application, but device drivers and TSRs can be placed in high memory. DOS 5.0 is intentionally designed so that its 40–50KB of code can be easily moved into this high memory area. With DOS loaded into high memory, an extra 40–50KB or so will be available within the 640KB DOS range.

Memory Considerations

Memory has become far more important than just a place to store bits for the microprocessor. It has proliferated and specialized to the point where it is difficult to keep track of all the memory options and architectures that are available. This part of the chapter reviews established memory types, then explains some of the current memory architectures and the major issues surrounding them.

MEMORY SPEED AND WAIT STATES

The PC industry is constantly struggling with the balance between price and performance. Higher prices usually bring higher performance, but low cost makes the PC appealing to more people. In terms of memory, cost cutting typically involves using cheaper (slower) memory devices. Unfortunately, when slower memory is used, the CPU must be made to wait until memory can catch up. All memory is rated in terms of speed—specifically access time. *Access time* is the delay between the time that data in memory is successfully addressed, to the point at which the data has been successfully delivered to the data bus. For PC memory, access time is measured in nanoseconds (ns), and traditional memory offers access times of 50–60ns, whereas 70ns memory is extremely common in older i486 systems. SDRAM is an exception to this rule, and is typically rated in terms of cycle time rather than access time. *Cycle time* is the minimum amount of time needed between accesses. Cycle time for SDRAM averages around 12ns, with 10ns, 8ns (and faster) SDRAM devices available.

 Today's high-performance memory is rated in terms of system speed (megahertz) rather than access or cycle times. For example, PC133 SDRAM is used in systems with a 133 MHz front side bus (FSB). As another example, PC800 RDRAM transfers data on both sides of a 400 MHz Rambus channel clock.

It is almost always possible to use *faster* memory than the manufacturer recommends. The system should continue to operate normally, but there's rarely ever a performance benefit. As you'll see in the following sections, memory and architectures are typically tailored for specific performance. Using memory that is faster should not hurt the memory, or impair system performance, but it costs more, and will not produce a noticeable performance improvement—simply because the system is not equipped to employ the faster memory to its best advantage. The only time such a tactic would be advised is when your current system is almost obsolete, and you would want the new memory to be usable on a new, faster motherboard if you choose to upgrade the motherboard later on.

A *wait state* orders the CPU to pause for one clock cycle in order to give memory additional time to operate. Typical PCs use one wait state, though very old systems may require two or three. The latest PC designs with high-end memory or aggressive caching may be able to operate with no (zero) wait states. As you might imagine, a wait state is basically a waste of time, so more wait states result in lower system performance. Zero wait states allow optimum system performance. Wait states let the system support old, slow memory (but the resulting system performance would be so poor that there would be little point in using the system in the first place).

There are three classical means of selecting wait states. First, the number of wait states may be fixed (common in old XT systems). Wait states may be selected with one or more jumpers on the motherboard (typical of i286 and early i386 systems). Midrange and later systems (such as i486, Pentium, and Pentium II/III/4 computers) place the "wait state" or "memory speed" control in the CMOS Setup routine—or it is selected automatically. You may have to look in an "advanced settings" area to find the appropriate entry. When optimizing a computer, you should be sure to set the minimum number of wait states.

 Setting too few wait states can cause the PC to behave erratically, or even prevent the system from starting.

DETERMINING MEMORY SPEED

During troubleshooting, or when selecting replacement parts, it's often necessary to check memory modules for proper memory speed (that is, "access time" or "cycle time" for SDRAM). Unfortunately, it can be very difficult to determine memory speed accurately based on part markings. Speeds are normally marked cryptically by adding a number to the end of the part number. For example, a traditional part number ending in -6 often means 60ns, a -7 is usually 70ns, and a -8 can be 80ns. SDRAM often uses markings such as -12 for 12ns cycle time, or -10 for 10ns cycle time. Still, the only means of being absolutely certain of the memory speed is to cross-reference the memory part number with a manufacturer's catalog, and read the speed from the catalog's description (for example, 4Mx32 50ns EDO).

MEGABYTES AND MEMORY LAYOUT

Now is a good time to explain the idea of bytes versus megabytes. Very simply, a *byte* is 8 bits (binary 1's and 0's), and a *megabyte* is one million of those bytes (1,048,576 bytes to be exact—but manufacturers often round down to the nearest million or so). The idea of megabytes (MB) is important when measuring memory in your PC. For example, if a SIMM is laid out as 1M by 8 bits, it has 1MB. If the SIMM is laid out as 4M by 8 bits, it has 4MB. Unfortunately, memory has not been laid out as 8 bits since the IBM XT.

More practical memory layouts involve 32-bit memory (for 486 and OverDrive processors) or 64-bit memory (for Pentium II/III/4 processors). When memory is "wider" than 1 byte, it is still measured in MB. For example, a 1Mx32-bit (4 bytes) SIMM would be 4MB. That is, the *capacity* of the device is 4MB. A 4Mx32-bit SIMM would be 16MB. So when you go shopping for an 8MB 72-pin SIMM, chances are you're getting a 2Mx32-bit memory module. Table 24-6 provides you with an index to help identify common 72-pin SIMMs and 168-pin DIMMs based on the number and type of RAM chips onboard. You can see the relationship between memory layout and overall capacity. Table 24-7 outlines standard part numbers for common memory modules.

TABLE 24-6   SIMM/DIMM IDENTIFICATION GUIDELINES

168-PIN SYNCHRONOUS DIMMS

Type of Component	Number of Chips Onboard	Module Type	DIMM Capacity
2x8 TSOP SDRAM	8	2MBx64	16MB
2x8 TSOP SDRAM	16	4MBx64	32MB
4x4 TSOP SDRAM	32	8MBx64	64MB
8x8 TSOP SDRAM	8	8MBx64 (Noncomposite)	64MB
8x8 TSOP SDRAM	9	8MBx72 (Noncomposite)	64MB
8x8 TSOP SDRAM	16	16MBx64 (Noncomposite)	128MB
8x8 TSOP SDRAM	18	16MBx72 (Noncomposite)	128MB

168-PIN PC DIMMS

Type of Component	Number of Chips Onboard	Module Type	DIMM Capacity
4x4 SOJ/TSOP DRAM	16	4MBx64	32MB
4x4 SOJ/TSOP DRAM	18	4MBx72 ECC	32MB
4x4 SOJ/TSOP DRAM	32	8MBx64	64MB
4x4 SOJ/TSOP DRAM	36	8MBx72 ECC	64MB
8x8 SOJ/TSOP DRAM	16	16MBx64	128MB

72-PIN SIMM MODULES

Type of Component	Number of Chips Onboard	Module Type	SIMM Capacity
1x4 SOJ	8	1MBx32	4MB
1x16 SOJ	2	1MBx32	4MB
1x4/1x1 SOJ	8/4	1MBx36	4MB
1x4 SOJ	16	2MBx32	8MB

TABLE 24-6   SIMM/DIMM IDENTIFICATION GUIDELINES *(CONTINUED)*

168-PIN SYNCHRONOUS DIMMS

1x16 SOJ	4	2MBx32	8MB
1x4/1x1 SOJ	16/8	2MBx36	8MB
4x4 SOJ/TSOP	8	4MBx32	16MB
4x4/4x1 SOJ/TSOP	8/4	4MBx36	16MB
4x4 SOJ	16	8MBx32	32MB
4x4/4x1 SOJ	16/8	8MBx36	32MB
16x1 SOJ	32	16MBx32	64MB
16x1 SOJ	36	16MBx36	64MB

Legend:

TSOP: Thin Small-Outline Package

SOJ: Small-Outline "J"-Lead Package

ECC: Error Correction Code (a more powerful form of parity)

x8, x32, x64: Non-parity RAM

x9, x36, x72: Parity or ECC RAM

TABLE 24-7   TYPICAL PART NUMBERS FOR COMMON MEMORY MODULES

168-PIN STANDARD DIMMS

	ECC		Non-ECC	
EDO	**Buffered**	**Non-Buffered**	**Buffered**	**Non-Buffered**
16MB	KTM2x72VN82-60EG	KTM2x72VN44-60EG	----	KTM2x64VN61-60EG
32MB	KTM4x72V82-60EG	KTM4x72VN44-60EG	----	KTM4x64VN42-60EG
64MB	KTM8x72V84-64EG	KTM8x72VN84-60EG	----	KTM8x64VN84-60EG
128MB	KTM16x72V44-60EG	KTM16x72VN84-60EG	----	KTM16x64VN84-60EG
256MB	KTM32x72V44-60EG	----	----	----
	ECC		**Non-ECC**	
FPM	**Buffered**	**Non-Buffered**	**Buffered**	**Non-Buffered**
16MB	KTM2x72V82-60G	----	----	----
32MB	KTM4x72V44-60G	----	----	----
64MB	KTM8x72V84-60G	----	----	----
128MB	KTM16x72V48-60G	----	----	----
	ECC		**NON-ECC**	
SDRAM	**66MHz**	**100MHz**	**66MHz**	**100MHz**
16MB	KTM66x72/16	----	KTM66x64/16	----
32MB	KTM66x72/32	KGM100x72C#/32	KTM66x64/32	KGM100x64C#/32
64MB	KTM66x72/64	KGM100x72C#/64	KTM66x64/64	KGM100x64C#/64
128MB	KTM66x72/128	KGM100x72C#/128	KTM66x64/128	KGM100x64C#/128

Note: For 100 MHz SDRAM DIMMs, substitute either a 2 or 3 for the # to indicate CAS latency speed. The modules are interchangeable and can be mixed, but the system will run at the slower CAS Latency 3 speed.

72-PIN STANDARD SIMMS

	60 nanoseconds		70 nanoseconds	
EDO	**Non-Parity**	**Parity**	**Non-Parity**	**Parity**
8MB (Tin leads)	KTM2x32L-60ET	KTM2x36L-60ET	KTM2x32L-70ET	----
8MB (Gold leads)	KTM2x32L-60EG	KTM2x36L-60EG	KTM2x32L-70EG	----

TABLE 24-7   TYPICAL PART NUMBERS FOR COMMON MEMORY MODULES *(CONTINUED)*

72-PIN STANDARD SIMMS

EDO	60 nanoseconds		70 nanoseconds	
	Non-Parity	Parity	Non-Parity	Parity
16MB (Tin leads)	KTM4x32L-60ET	KTM4x36L-60ET	KTM4x32L-70ET	----
16MB (Gold leads)	KTM4x32L-60EG	KTM4x36L-60EG	KTM4x32L-70EG	----
32MB (Tin leads)	KTM8x32L-60ET	KTM8x36L-60ET	KTM8x32L-70ET	----
32MB (Gold leads)	KTM8x32L-60EG	KTM8x36L-60EG	KTM8x32L-70EG	----
64MB (Tin leads)	KTM16x32LA-60ET	----	----	----
64MB (Gold leads)	KTM16x32LA-60EG	----	----	----
128MB (Tin leads)	KTM32x32LA-60ET	----	----	----
128MB (Gold leads)	KTM32x32LA-60EG	----	----	----

FPM	60 nanoseconds		70 nanoseconds	
	Non-Parity	Parity	Non-Parity	Parity
8MB (Tin leads)	KTM2x32L-60T	KTM2x36L-60T	KTM2x32L-70T	KTM2x36L-70T
8MB (Gold leads)	KTM2x32L-60G	KTM2x36L-60G	KTM2x32L-70G	KTM2x36L-70G
16MB (Tin leads)	KTM4x32L-60T	KTM4x36L-60T	KTM4x32L-70T	KTM4x36L-70T
16MB (Gold leads)	KTM4x32L-60G	KTM4x36L-60G	KTM4x32L-70G	KTM4x36L-70G
32MB (Tin leads)	KTM8x32L-60T	KTM8x36L-60T	KTM8x32L-70T	KTM8x36L-70T
32MB (Gold leads)	KTM8x32L-60G	KTM8x36L-60G	KTM8x32L-70G	KTM8x36L-70G
64MB (Tin leads)	KTM16x32L-60T	KTM16x36L-60T	KTM16x32L-70T	KTM16x36L-70T
64MB (Gold leads)	KTM16x32L-60G	KTM16x36L-60G	KTM16x32L-70G	KTM16x36L-70G
128MB (Tin leads)	KTM32x32L-60T	KTM32x36L-60T	----	----
128MB (Gold leads)	KTM32x32L-60G	KTM32x36L-60G	----	----

PRESENCE DETECT (PD)

Another feature of modern memory devices is a series of physical signals known as the Presence Detect lines. By setting the appropriate conditions of the PD signals, it is possible for a computer to immediately recognize the characteristics of the installed memory devices, and configure itself accordingly. Presence Detect lines typically specify two operating characteristics of memory: size (device layout) and speed. Table 24-8 highlights many of the most commonly used signal combinations.

TABLE 24-8   BASIC INDEX OF PRESENCE DETECT (PD) SIGNALS

72-PIN SIMM		PIN 67 (PD1)	PIN 68 (PD2)	PIN 69 (PD3)	PIN 70 (PD4)	PIN 71 (PD5)
Size (parity pinout)	256Kx32/36	GND	N/C	--	--	--
	512Kx32/36	N/C	GND	--	--	--
	1Mx32/36	GND	GND	--	--	--
	2Mx32/36	N/C	N/C	--	--	--
	4Mx32/36	GND	N/C	--	--	N/C
	8Mx32/36	N/C	GND	--	--	N/C
Size (ECC pinout)	256Kx32/36	GND	N/C	--	--	N/C
	512Kx32/36	N/C	GND	--	--	N/C
	1Mx32/36	GND	GND	--	--	N/C
	2Mx32/36	N/C	N/C	--	--	N/C

TABLE 24-8   BASIC INDEX OF PRESENCE DETECT (PD) SIGNALS *(CONTINUED)*

72-PIN SIMM		PIN 67 (PD1)	PIN 68 (PD2)	PIN 69 (PD3)	PIN 70 (PD4)	PIN 71 (PD5)
	4Mx32/36	GND	N/C	--	--	GND
	8Mx32/36	N/C	GND	--	--	GND
Speed (parity/ECC pinout)	60ns	--	--	N/C	N/C	--
	70ns	--	--	GND	N/C	--
	80ns	--	--	N/C	GND	--
	100ns	--	--	GND	GND	--
	120ns	--	--	N/C	N/C	--

MEMORY REFRESH

The electrical signals placed in each DRAM storage cell must be replenished (or *refreshed*) periodically every few milliseconds. Without refresh, DRAM data will be lost. In principle, refresh requires that each storage cell be read and rewritten to the memory array. This is typically accomplished by reading and rewriting an entire row of the array at one time. Each row of bits is sequentially read into a sense/refresh amplifier (part of the DRAM chip), which basically recharges the appropriate storage capacitors, then rewrites each row bit to the array. In actual operation, a row of bits is automatically refreshed whenever an array row is selected. The entire memory array can be refreshed by reading each row in the array every few milliseconds.

The key to refresh is in the way DRAM is addressed. Unlike other memory chips that supply all address signals to the chip simultaneously, a DRAM is addressed in a two-step sequence. The overall address is separated into a row (low) address and a column (high) address. Row address bits are placed on the DRAM address bus first, and the -Row Address Select (-RAS) line is pulsed to logic 0 to multiplex the bits into the chip's address decoding circuitry. The low portion of the address activates an entire array row and causes each bit in the row to be sensed and refreshed. Logic 0's remain logic 0's, and logic 1's are recharged to their full value.

Column address bits are then placed on the DRAM address bus, and the -Column Address Select (-CAS) is pulsed to logic 0. The column portion of the address selects the appropriate bits within the chosen row. If a read operation is taking place, the selected bits pass through the data buffer to the data bus. During a write operation, the read/write line must be logic 0, and valid data must be available to the chip before -CAS is strobed. New data bits are then placed in their corresponding locations in the memory array.

Even if the chip is not being accessed for reading or writing, the memory must still be refreshed to ensure data integrity. Fortunately, refresh can be accomplished by interrupting the microprocessor to run a refresh routine, which simply steps through every row address in sequence (column addresses need not be selected for simple refresh). This row-only (or -RAS only) refresh technique speeds the refresh process. Although refreshing DRAM every few milliseconds may seem like a constant aggravation, the computer can execute quite a few instructions before being interrupted for refresh. Refresh operations are generally handled by the chipset on your motherboard. Often, memory problems (especially "parity errors") that cannot be resolved by replacing a SIMM can be traced to a refresh fault on the motherboard.

CLOCK LINES

SDRAM memory requires either two or four clock signal lines between the system clock and the memory module. Modules with two clock lines (called two-clock SDRAM) are usually found with older SDRAM modules. For example, the first Intel designs were two-clock because there were only eight chips on the module. Modules with four clock lines (called four-clock SDRAM) are generally employed on newer SDRAM modules. The four-clock designs allow for fewer chips per clock line, which decreases the signal load on each line and enables a quicker data interface.

CAS LATENCY

Latency is normally a delay. With SDRAM, CAS latency refers to the number of clock cycles it takes before a column can be addressed on the memory chip. SDRAM with a latency of CL2 indicates a two-clock cycle delay. SDRAM with a latency of CL3 indicates a three-clock cycle delay. Smaller numbers result in better memory performance. When SDRAM chips first came out, it was difficult to produce chips with a CAS latency as low as CL2. Although some specifications called for CL2, many modules worked fine at a CAS latency of CL3. Today, virtually all SDRAM uses a CAS latency of CL2 for best performance.

BURSTING AND PIPELINING

PC designers try to make the most of every memory access. Traditionally, only one piece of data is handled with every memory access cycle. Burst access (or *bursting*) is a performance improvement that lets the processor retrieve a block of information from consecutive memory addresses (rather than a single piece of information from one address). This provides the CPU with additional data from memory based on the likelihood that it will be needed. The CPU gets the instructions it needs without having to send an individual request for each one. In actual practice, bursting can work with many different types of memory and can function when reading or writing data.

Pipelining is a processing technique in which a task is divided into a series of stages, with some of the work completed at each stage. By dividing a larger task into smaller, overlapping tasks, pipelining is used to significantly improve system performance. Once the flow through a pipeline is started, the execution rate of instructions is high regardless of the number of stages through which they progress.

Bursting and pipelining techniques first became popular at about the time that EDO memory technology became available. EDO chips that featured these functions were called "Burst EDO" or "Pipeline Burst EDO" chips.

UNBUFFERED, BUFFERED, AND REGISTERED

Memory modules may be "unbuffered," "buffered," or "registered." This distinction is defined by the way in which electrical signals are handled by the memory module, and your choice of module will affect the maximum amount of RAM that can be installed on the motherboard. An *unbuffered* memory module contains only memory devices—data passed between the memory chips is not boosted by buffers on the module itself. Unbuffered modules are fast because there is no buffering circuitry to slow the signals, and their slightly lower cost makes them ideal for use in everyday PCs. Unfortunately, unbuffered electrical signals are prone to attenuation, so only a few unbuffered modules (usually one or two) can be used at a time.

By adding *buffers* or *registers* to the memory module, the electrical signals entering and leaving the memory module are strengthened. This slows the module's performance by a few nanoseconds, but allows the use of additional memory modules—thus the motherboard can support much more memory.

(This is particularly important for memory-hungry systems such as network servers.) For EDO and FPM memory modules, the process of redriving memory signals is called *buffering*. For SDRAM memory modules, the process of redriving memory signals is called *registering*. Registering is similar to buffering, but registering clocks data into and out of the module using the system's clock. The motherboard's memory controller chip determines the type of memory modules required, so you cannot use unbuffered and buffered (or registered) modules together on the same system. (They're also keyed differently so that you cannot use them on an incompatible motherboard.)

MEMORY TYPES

In order for a computer to work, the CPU must take program instructions and exchange data directly with memory. As a consequence, memory must keep pace with the CPU (or make the CPU wait for it to catch up). Now that processors are so incredibly fast—and getting faster every few months—traditional memory architectures are being replaced by specialized memory devices that have been tailored to serve specific functions in the PC. As you upgrade and repair various systems, you will undoubtedly encounter some of the memory designations explained next (listed alphabetically).

BEDO (Burst Extended Data Output RAM)

This powerful variation of EDO RAM reads data in a burst, which means that after a valid address has been provided, subsequent data addresses can be read in only one clock cycle each. The CPU can read BEDO data in a 5-1-1-1 pattern (five clock cycles for the first address, then one clock cycle for subsequent addresses. While BEDO offers an advantage over EDO, it is only supported currently by the VIA chipsets: 580VP, 590VP, 680VP. Also, BEDO seems to have difficulty supporting motherboards over 66 MHz. All forms of EDO RAM are considered obsolete today.

CDRAM (Cached DRAM)

As with EDRAM, the CDRAM from Mitsubishi incorporates cache and DRAM on the same memory chips. This eliminates the need for an external (or L2) cache, and has the extra benefit of adding cache whenever RAM is added to the system. The difference is that CDRAM uses a "set-associative" cache approach that can be 15–20 percent more efficient than the EDRAM cache scheme. On the other hand, EDRAM appears to offer better overall performance. CDRAM never received much attention from the PC industry and is now considered obsolete.

DDR SDRAM

One limitation of SDRAM is that the theoretical limitation of the design is 125 MHz (though technology advances may allow up to 133 MHz and 150 MHz operation), but bus speeds will need to increase well beyond that in order for memory bandwidth to keep up with future processors. There are several competing standards on the horizon, but most of them require special pinouts, smaller bus widths, or other design considerations. First introduced in 2000, double data rate SDRAM (DDR SDRAM) allows output operations to occur on both the rising and falling edge of the system clock. Currently, only the rising edge signals an event to occur, so the DDR SDRAM design can effectively double the speed of operation up to at least 200 MHz or 266 MHz (a prime candidate for AMD Athlon motherboards). There are already numerous AMD-based chipsets that support DDR SDRAM, and even Intel Pentium 4 chipsets will be supporting DDR SDRAM in the future.

DRAM (Dynamic Random Access Memory)

DRAM was first utilized in early personal computers. It achieves a good mix of speed and density, while being relatively simple and inexpensive to produce—only a single transistor and capacitor is needed to hold a bit. Unfortunately, DRAM contents must be refreshed every few milliseconds, or the contents of each bit location will decay. DRAM performance is also limited because of relatively long access times. Today, only a few low-end video boards continue to use DRAM chips to supply video memory. DRAM remains the most recognized and common form of computer memory, and we often use the term "DRAM" to refer to other types of RAM (though that's technically inaccurate).

A typical DRAM memory access would occur as follows: The row address bits are placed onto the address pins. After a period of time, the RAS signal falls, which activates sense amps and causes the row address to be latched into the row address buffer. When the RAS signal stabilizes, the selected row is transferred onto the sense amps. Next, the column address bits are set up and then latched into the column address buffer when CAS falls. At that point, the output buffer is also turned on. When CAS stabilizes, the selected sense amp feeds its data to the output buffer.

EDO RAM (Extended Data Out RAM)

Introduced in 1995, EDO RAM is a well-established variation of DRAM that extends the time in which output data is valid—thus the data's presence on the data bus is "extended." This is accomplished by modifying the DRAM's output buffer, which prolongs the time in which *read data* is valid. The data will remain valid until a motherboard signal is received to release it. This eases timing constraints on the memory and allows a 15–30 percent improvement in memory performance with little real increase in cost. Because a new external signal is needed to operate EDO RAM, the motherboard must use a chipset designed to accommodate EDO. Intel's Triton chipset was one of the first to support EDO, though most chipsets of that vintage were quickly updated to support EDO. You should realize that EDO RAM can be used in non-EDO motherboards, but there will be no performance improvement. Today, EDO RAM is completely obsolete when compared to SDRAM, DDR SDRAM, and Rambus DRAM memory technologies.

EDRAM (Enhanced DRAM)

This is another, lesser-known variation of the classic DRAM developed by Ramtron International and United Memories. First demonstrated in August 1994, the EDRAM eliminates an external cache by placing a small amount of static RAM (cache) into each EDRAM device itself. In essence, the cache is distributed *within* the system RAM, and as more memory is added to the PC, more cache is effectively added as well. The internal construction of an EDRAM allows it to act like page-mode memory—if a subsequent read requests data that is in the EDRAM's cache (known as a *hit*), the data is made available in about 15ns—roughly equal to the speed of a fair external cache. If the subsequent read requests data that is not in the cache (called a *miss*), the data is accessed from the DRAM portion of memory in about 35ns, which is still much faster than ordinary DRAM. EDRAM is obsolete today.

FPM DRAM (Fast-Page Mode DRAM)

This is a popular twist on conventional DRAM. Typical DRAM access is accomplished in a way that is similar to reading a book—a memory "page" is accessed first, and then the contents of that "page" can be located. The problem is that every access requires the DRAM to relocate the "page." The *fast-page mode* overcomes this delay by allowing the CPU to access multiple pieces of data on the same "page" without having to relocate the "page" every time. As long as the subsequent read or write cycle is on the previously located "page," the FPDRAM can access the specific location on that "page" directly.

During the early 1990s, FPM became the most widely used access method for DRAMs, and is still used on many older systems. The general benefit of FPM memory is reduced power consumption (because sense and restore current is not necessary during page-mode access). Though FPM was a major innovation, there are still some drawbacks. The most significant limitation is that the output buffers turn off when

CAS goes high. Also, the minimum cycle time is 5ns before the output buffers turn off, which essentially adds at least 5ns to the cycle time.

Today, FPM memory is one of the least desirable forms of memory. You should only consider using FPM if your system does not support any of the later memory types (such as a 486-based system). Typical timings are 6-3-3-3 (initial latency of three clocks, with a three-clock page access). Due to the limited demand, you may find that FPM is actually more expensive than most of the faster memory technologies now available.

PC100/PC133 SDRAM

When Intel decided to officially implement a 100 MHz system bus speed, they understood that most of the early SDRAM modules available at that time would not operate properly above 83 MHz. In order to support 100 MHz bus speeds, Intel introduced the PC100 specification as a guideline to manufacturers for building modules that would function properly on their 100 MHz chipsets (such as the 440BX). With the PC100 specification, Intel laid out a number of guidelines for trace lengths, trace widths and spacing, the number of printed circuit layers, EEPROM programming specs, and so on.

There is still quite a bit of confusion regarding what a "true" PC100 module actually consists of. While the chip speed rating is used most often to determine the overall performance of the chip, a number of other timings are very important: tRCD (RAS to CAS delay), tRP (RAS precharge time), and CAS latency all play a role in determining the fastest bus speed the module will operate on to still achieve a 4-1-1-1 timing. PC100 SDRAM on a 100 MHz (or faster) system bus will provide a performance boost for Socket 7 systems of between 10 percent and 15 percent, since the L2 cache is running at system bus speed. Pentium II/III systems will not see as big a boost because the L2 cache is running at half the processor speed (with the exception of the cacheless Celeron chips of course). Pentium 4 and Athlon processors require the faster PC133 SDRAM for a 133 MHz motherboard, or 200/266 MHz DDR SDRAM.

RDRAM (Rambus DRAM)

Most of the memory alternatives so far have been variations of the same basic DRAM architecture. Rambus, Inc. (joint developers of EDRAM) has developed a relatively new memory architecture called the Rambus Channel. A CPU or specialized controller chip is used as the "master" device, and the RDRAMs are used as "slave" devices. Blocks of data are then sent back and forth across the Rambus channel. With a 400 MHz clock, the Rambus Channel can transfer data on both edges of the clock. This results in 16-bit data transfer rates approaching 800 MHz (called PC800 RDRAM), and offers 1.6GB/s of data bandwidth. Earlier implementations of RDRAM used a 300 MHz clock, resulting in PC600 RDRAM. By late 2000, Intel had embraced Rambus completely, and the current generation of 850 chipset (for the Pentium 4 processor) supports Rambus exclusively.

SDRAM (Synchronous or Synchronized DRAM)

Typical memory can only transfer data during certain portions of a clock cycle. Introduced in late 1996, the SDRAM modifies memory operation so that outputs can be valid at *any* point in the clock cycle. By itself, this is not really significant, but SDRAM also provides a "pipeline burst" mode that allows a second access to begin before the current access is complete. This "continuous" memory access offers effective access speeds as fast as 10ns, and can transfer data at up to 100MB/s. SDRAM is now quite popular on current motherboard designs, and is supported by the Intel VX (and later) chipsets, as well as VIA 580VP, 590VP, and 680VP (and later) chipsets. Like BEDO, SDRAM can transfer data in a 5-1-1-1 pattern, but it can support motherboard speeds up to 100 MHz and 133 MHz that are so vital for Pentium II/III systems (see "PC100/PC133 SDRAM" earlier).

SGRAM (Synchronous Graphics RAM)

SGRAM is a video-specific extension of SDRAM that includes graphics-optimized read/write features. SGRAM also allows data to be retrieved and modified in blocks instead of individually—this reduces the number of reads and writes that memory must perform, and increases the performance of the graphics controller by making the read/write process more efficient.

SRAM (Static Random Access Memory)

The SRAM is also a classical memory design that is even older than DRAM. SRAM does not require regular refresh operations, and can be made to operate at access speeds that are much faster than DRAM. However, SRAM uses six transistors or more to hold a single bit. This reduces the density of SRAM and increases its power demands (which is why SRAM was never adopted for general PC use in the first place). Still, the high speed of SRAM has earned it a place as the PC's L2 (or external) cache. You'll probably encounter three types of SRAM cache schemes: Asynchronous, Synchronous Burst, and Pipeline Burst.

Asynchronous Static RAM (Async SRAM or ASRAM) is the "traditional" form of L2 cache introduced with i386 systems. There's really nothing too special about ASRAM except that its contents can be accessed much faster (20ns, 15ns, or 12ns) than DRAM. ASRAM does not have enough performance to be accessed synchronously and has long since been replaced by better types of cache. *Synchronous Burst Static RAM* (Sync SRAM or SBSRAM) is largely regarded as the best type of L2 cache for intermediate speed motherboards (~60–66 MHz). With access times of 8.5ns and 12ns, the SBSRAM can provide synchronous bursts of cache information in 2-1-1-1 cycles (two clock cycles for the first access, then one cycle per access—in time with the CPU clock). However, as motherboards pass 66 MHz (such as 75 MHz and 83 MHz designs), SBSRAM loses its advantage to Pipelined Burst SRAM. *Pipelined Burst Static RAM* (PB SRAM) is the fastest form of high-performance cache now available for 75 MHz+ motherboards (with speeds of about 4.5ns to 8ns). PBSRAM requires an extra clock cycle for "lead off," but then can sync with the motherboard clock (with timing such as 3-1-1-1) across a wide range of motherboard frequencies.

VRAM (Video Random Access Memory)

DRAM has been the traditional choice for video memory, but the ever-increasing demand for fast video information (as in high-resolution SVGA displays) requires a more efficient means of transferring data to and from video memory. Originally developed by Samsung Electronics, video RAM achieves speed improvements by using a "dual data bus" scheme. Ordinary RAM uses a single data bus—data enters or leaves the RAM through a single set of signals. Video RAM provides an "input" data bus and an "output" data bus. This allows data to be read from video RAM at the same time new information is being written to it. You should realize that the advantages of VRAM will only be realized on high-end video systems such as 1024x768x256 (or higher), where you can get up to 40 percent more performance than a DRAM video adapter. Below that, you will see no perceivable improvement with a VRAM video adapter. Today, high-performance video adapters use SDRAM or DDR SDRAM.

WRAM (Windows RAM)

Samsung Electronics has introduced WRAM as a new video-specific memory device. WRAM uses multiple bit arrays connected with an extensive internal bus and high-speed registers that can transfer data almost continuously. Other specialized registers support attributes such as foreground color, background color, write-block control bits, and true-byte masking. Samsung claims data transfer rates of up to 640MB/s—about 50 percent faster than VRAM—yet WRAM devices are cheaper than their VRAM counterparts. While WRAM has received some serious consideration in the last few years, it has been largely ignored in favor of SDRAM for video systems.

MEMORY TECHNIQUES

Rather than incur the added expense of specialized memory devices, PC makers often use inexpensive, well-established memory types arranged in unique architectures designed to make the most of existing memory technologies. There are four popular architectures that you will probably encounter in almost all systems: paged memory, interleaved memory, memory cache, and shadow memory.

Paged Memory

The paged memory approach basically divides system RAM into small groups (or "pages") from 512 bytes to several KB long. Memory management circuitry on the motherboard allows subsequent memory accesses on the same "page" to be accomplished with zero wait states. If the subsequent access takes place outside of the current "page," one or more wait states may be added while the new "page" is found. This is identical in principle to fast-page mode DRAM explained earlier. You will find page-mode architectures implemented on high-end i286, PS/2 (model 70 and 80), and many i386 systems.

Interleaved Memory

Simply put, *interleaved* memory combines two banks of memory into one. This technique provides better performance than paged memory. The first portion is "even," while the second portion is "odd"—so memory contents are alternated between these two areas. This allows a memory access in the second portion to begin before the memory access in the first portion has finished. In effect, interleaving can substantially improve memory performance. The traditional problem with interleaving is that you must provide memory as matched pairs. For example, you'd need to install two SIMMs, and one SIMM would be accessing while the second is being read. Today, memory such as SDRAM can be logically divided into cell banks on the DIMM itself.

Memory Cache

Perhaps the most recognized form of memory enhancement technique is memory cache (Figure 24-5). *Cache* is a small amount (anywhere from 8KB to 1MB) of very fast memory such as SRAM that forms an interface between the CPU and ordinary DRAM. The SRAM typically operates on the order of 5ns to 15ns, which is fast enough to keep pace with a CPU using zero wait states. A *cache controller* chip on the motherboard keeps track of frequently accessed memory locations (as well as predicted memory locations) and copies those contents into cache. When a CPU reads from memory, it checks the cache first. If the needed contents are present in the cache (called a *cache hit*), the data is read at zero wait states. If the needed contents are not present in the cache (known as a *cache miss*), the data must be read directly from DRAM at a penalty of one or more wait states. A small quantity of very fast cache (called *Tag RAM*) acts as an index, recording the various locations of data stored in cache. A well-designed caching system can achieve a hit ratio of 95 percent or more—in other words, memory can run *without* wait states 95 percent of the time.

There are two levels of cache in the contemporary PC. CPUs from the i486 onward have a small "internal cache"—known as *L1 cache*—while "external cache" (SRAM installed as DIPs or COAST modules on the motherboard) is referred to as *L2 cache*. The i386 CPUs have no internal cache (though IBM's 386SLC offers 8KB of L1 cache). Most i486 CPUs provide an 8KB internal cache. Early Pentium processors are fitted with two 8KB internal caches—one for data and one for instructions. Today's Pentium II/III/4 Slot 1 CPU incorporates 256–512KB of L2 cache into the processor cartridge itself (so there is no L2 cache on those motherboards).

Shadow Memory

ROM devices (whether the BIOS ROM on your motherboard or a ROM chip on an expansion board) are frustratingly slow, with access times often exceeding several hundred nanoseconds. ROM access then

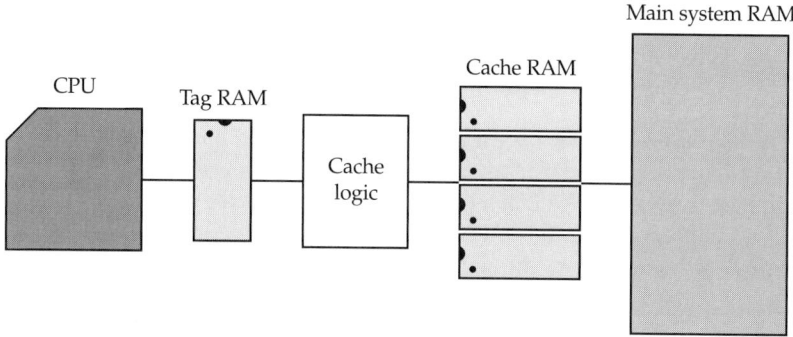

FIGURE 24-5   Major cache system components

requires a large number of wait states, which slow down the system's performance. This problem is compounded because the routines stored in BIOS (especially the video BIOS ROM on the video board) are some of the most frequently accessed memory locations in your computer.

Beginning with the i386-class computers, some designs employed a memory technique called *shadowing*. ROM contents are loaded into an area of fast RAM during system initialization, and then the computer maps the fast RAM into memory locations used by the ROM devices. Whenever ROM routines must be accessed during run time, information is taken from the faster "shadowed ROM" instead of the actual ROM chip. The ROM performance can be improved by at least 300 percent.

Shadow memory is also useful for ROM devices that do not use the full available data bus width. For example, a 16-bit computer system may hold an expansion board containing an 8-bit ROM chip. The system would have to access the ROM not once but twice to extract a single 16-bit word. If the computer is a 32-bit machine, that 8-bit ROM would have to be addressed four times to make a complete 32-bit word. You may imagine the hideous system delays that can be encountered. Loading the ROM to shadow memory in advance virtually eliminates such delays. Shadowing can usually be turned on or off through the system's CMOS Setup routine.

Parity

As you might imagine, it is vital that data and program instructions remain error free. Even one incorrect bit due to electrical noise or a component failure can crash the PC, corrupt drive information, cause video problems, or result in a myriad of other faults. PC designers traditionally approached the issue of memory integrity by employing a technique known as *parity* (the same technique used to check serial data integrity for your modem).

PARITY PRINCIPLES

The basic idea behind parity is simple—each byte written to memory is checked, and a 9th bit is added to the byte as a checking (or *parity*) bit. When a memory address is later read by the CPU, memory checking circuitry on the motherboard will calculate the *expected* parity bit and compare it to the bit actually *read* from memory. In this fashion, the PC can continuously diagnose system memory by checking the integrity of its data. If the read parity bit matches the expected parity bit, the data (and indirectly the RAM) is assumed to be valid, and the CPU can go on its way. If the read and expected parity bits do not match, the system registers an error and halts. Every byte is given a parity bit, so for a 32-bit PC, there will be 4 parity bits for every address. For a 64-bit PC, there are 8 parity bits, and so on.

Even vs. Odd

There are two types of parity—even and odd. With *even parity*, the parity bit is set to 0 if there are an even number of 1's already in the corresponding byte (keeping the number of 1's even). If there is not an even number of 1's in the byte, the even parity bit will be 1 (making the number of 1's even). With *odd parity*, the parity bit is set to 0 if there is an odd number of 1's already in the corresponding byte (keeping the number of 1's odd). If there is not an odd number of 1's in the byte, the odd parity bit will be 1 (making the number of 1's odd).

Although even and odd parity work opposite to one another, both schemes serve exactly the same purpose, and have the same probability of catching a bad bit. The memory device itself does not care at all about what type of parity is being used—it just needs to have the parity bits available. The use of parity (and the choice of even or odd) is left up to the motherboard's memory control circuit.

Parity Problems

While parity has proven to be a simple and cost-effective means of continuously checking memory, there are two significant limitations. First, though parity can detect an error, it cannot correct the error because there is no way to tell *which* bit has gone bad. This is why a system simply halts when a parity error is detected. Second, parity is unable to detect multibit errors. For example, if a 1 accidentally becomes a 0 and a 0 accidentally becomes a 1 within the same byte, parity conditions will still be satisfied. Fortunately, the probability of a multibit error in the same byte is extremely remote.

CIRCUMVENTING PARITY

Over the last few years, parity has come under fire from PC makers and memory manufacturers alike. Opponents claim that the rate of parity errors due to hardware (RAM) faults is very small, and that the expense of providing parity bits in a memory-hungry marketplace just isn't justified anymore. There is some truth to this argument, considering that the parity technique is over 20 years old and has serious limitations.

As a consequence, some motherboard makers have begun removing parity support from their low-end motherboards, and others are providing motherboards that will function with or without parity (usually set in CMOS or with a motherboard jumper). Similarly, some memory makers are now providing non-parity and "fake" parity memory as cheaper alternatives to conventional parity memory. *Non-parity* memory simply forgoes the 9th bit. For example, a non-parity SIMM would be designated x8 or x32 (for example, 4Mx8 or 4Mx32). If the SIMM supports parity, it will be designated x9 or x36 (for example, 4Mx9 or 4Mx36). *Fake parity* is more devious—the 9th bit is replaced by a simple (and dirt cheap) parity generator chip that "looks" like a normal DRAM chip. When a read cycle occurs, the parity chip on the memory module provides the proper parity bit to the motherboard all the time. In effect, your memory is "lying" to the motherboard.

While there's a cost savings, your memory is left with no means of error checking at all. It's a little like driving a car without a speedometer—you could go for miles without a problem, but sooner or later you'll cross a speed trap. In actual practice, you can go indefinitely without parity, but when an error *does* occur, having parity in place can save you immeasurable frustration. Unless the "lowest cost" is your absolute highest priority, it is recommended that you spend the extra few dollars for parity RAM.

 Most motherboards can be operated with non-parity RAM. It is also usually possible to mix parity and non-parity memory in the same system. But in either case, you will need to disable all parity checking features for the RAM.

Abuse and Detection of Fake Parity

Another potential problem with "fake" parity memory is fraud. There have been numerous instances where memory was purchased as "parity" at full price—only to find that the parity memory chips were actually parity generator chips. This was determined by dissecting the chip packages and finding that the chip die in the parity position did not match the chip dies in the other bit positions. The buyer doesn't know because parity generators are packaged to look just like memory chips, and there's no other obvious way to tell just by looking at the memory module or other memory device. System diagnostic software also cannot detect the presence of parity memory versus fake memory.

There are really only two ways to protect yourself from fake memory fraud. First, industry experts indicate that many fake parity chips (the parity generators) are marked with designations such as "BP," "VT," "GSM," or "MPEC." If you find that one out of every nine chips on your memory module carries such a designation (or any other designation not matching the first eight), you may have a fraud situation. Of course, the first step in all justice is a "benefit of the doubt;" so contact the organization you purchased the memory from—they may simply have sent the wrong modules.

Second, you can check the chip dies themselves. Unfortunately, this requires you to carefully dissect several chip packages on the memory module and compare the chip dies under a microscope—resulting in the destruction of the memory device(s). If the ninth die looks radically different (usually much simpler) than the other eight, you've likely got fake parity. A nondestructive way to check the module is to use a SIMM/DIMM checker (if you have access to one) with a testing routine specially written to test parity memory. If the module works but the parity chip test fails (the tester cannot *write* to the parity memory), chances are you've got fake parity.

If you determine that you have been sold fake parity memory in place of real parity memory, and you cannot get any satisfaction from the seller, you are encouraged to inform the Attorney General in the seller's state. After all, if you're being defrauded, chances are that a lot of other people are too—and they probably don't know it.

ALTERNATIVE ERROR CORRECTION

Although I support the use of parity, I also recognize its old age. In the world of personal computing, parity is an *ancient* technique. Frankly, it could easily be replaced by more sophisticated techniques such as Error Correction Code (ECC) or ECC-on-SIMM (EOS). ECC (which is already being employed in high-end PCs and file servers) uses a mathematical process in conjunction with the motherboard's memory controller, and appends a number of ECC bits to the data bits. When data is read back from memory, the ECC memory controller checks the ECC data read back as well.

ECC has two important advantages over parity. It can actually *correct* single-bit errors "on-the-fly," without the user ever knowing there's been a problem. In addition, ECC can successfully detect 2-bit, 3-bit, and 4-bit errors, which makes it an incredibly powerful error detection tool. If a rare multibit error is detected, ECC is unable to correct it, but it will be reported and the system will halt.

It takes 7 or 8 bits at each address to successfully implement ECC. For a 32-bit system, you'll need to use x39 or x40 SIMMs (for example, 8Mx39 or 8Mx40). These are relatively new designations, so you should at least recognize them as ECC SIMMs if you encounter them. As an alternative, some 64-bit systems use two 36-bit SIMMs for a total of 72 bits—64 bits for data and 8 bits (which would otherwise be for parity) for ECC information.

EOS is a relatively new (and rather expensive) technology that places ECC functions on the memory module itself, but provides ECC results as parity—so while the memory module runs ECC, the motherboard continues to "see" parity. This is an interesting experiment, but it is unlikely that EOS will gain significant market share. Systems that use parity can be fitted with parity memory much more cheaply than with EOS memory.

Selecting and Installing Memory

Installing memory is not nearly as easy as it used to be. Certainly, today's memory modules just plug right in, but deciding which memory to buy, how much (or how little) to buy, and how to use existing memory in new systems presents technicians with a bewildering variety of choices. This part of the chapter illustrates the important ideas behind choosing and using memory.

GETTING THE RIGHT AMOUNT

"How much memory do I need?" This is an age-old question that has plagued the PC industry ever since Intel's 80286 CPU broke the 1MB memory barrier. With more memory, additional programs and data can be run by the CPU at any given time, which indirectly helps to improve the productivity of the particular PC. The problem is cost. Today's SDRAM is running around $2/MB, compared with about 1.25 cents/MB (about $12.50/GB) for hard drive space. Consequently, memory is far more expensive than hard drive space; so the goal of good system configuration is to install *enough* memory to support the PC's routine tasks. Installing *too much* memory means that you've spent money for PC resources that just remain idle. Installing *too little* memory results in programs that will not run, or suffer diminished system performance because of extensive swap file use (typical under Windows).

So how much memory *is* enough? The fact of the matter is that "enough" is an ever-changing figure. DOS systems of the early 1980s (8088/8086) worked just fine with 1MB. By the mid-1980s (80286), DOS systems with 2MB were adequate. Into the late 1980s (80386), Windows 3.0 and 3.1 needed 4MB. As the 1990s got under way (80486), Windows systems with 8MB were common (even DOS applications were using 4–6MB of EMS). Today, with Pentium II/III/4 systems and Windows 98, 32MB is considered to be an absolute minimum requirement, and 64–128MB systems are readily available. For today, 64MB is the minimum benchmark that you should use for general-purpose home and office systems, but 128MB systems are readily available. And this is not to say that 128MB systems are the pinnacle of performance. Today's file servers and industrial-strength design packages are employing 256–512MB of RAM, and motherboard chipsets can often support up to 1GB of RAM or more.

FILLING BANKS

Another point of confusion is the idea of a "memory bank." Traditional memory devices are installed in sets (or *banks*). The amount of memory in the bank can vary depending on how much you wish to add, but there must always be enough data bits in the bank to fill each bit position. Table 24-9 illustrates a relationship between data bits and banks for the range of typical CPUs. For example, the 8086 is a 16-bit microprocessor (2 bytes). This means that 2 extra bits are required for parity, giving a total of 18 bits. Thus, one bank is 18 bits wide. You may fill the bank by adding eighteen 1-bit DIPs, or two 30-pin SIMMs. As another example, an 80486DX is a 32-bit CPU, so 36 bits are needed to fill a bank (32 bits plus 4 parity bits). If you use 30-pin SIMMs, you will need four to fill a bank. If you use 72-pin SIMMs, only one is needed. For a newer Pentium III/4 CPU, you can fill a "bank" with only one 168-pin DIMM. Note that the size of the memory in MB does not really matter, so long as the *entire* bank is filled.

Bank Requirements

There is more to filling a memory bank than just installing the right number of bits. Memory amount, memory matching, and bank order are three additional considerations. First, you must use the proper *memory amount* that will bring you to the expected volume of total memory. Suppose a Pentium system has 8MB already installed in Bank 0, and you need to put another 8MB into the system in Bank 1. Table 24-9 shows

TABLE 24-9   CPU VS. MEMORY "BANK" SIZE

CPU	DATA WIDTH (W/PARITY)	XMB BY 1 DIPS	30-PIN SIMMS	72-PIN SIMMS	168-PIN DIMMS
8088	9 bits	9	1	-	-
8086	18 bits	18	2	-	-
80286	18 bits	-	2	1 (2 banks)	-
80386SX, SL, SLC	18 bits	-	2	1 (2 banks)	-
80386DX	36 bits	-	4	1	-
80486SLC, SLC2	18 bits	-	2	1 (2 banks)	-
80486DX, SX, DX2, DX4	36 bits	-	4	1	-
Pentium (Socket 7)	64 bits	-	8	2	1
Pentium II/III (Slot 1)	64 bits	-	-	-	1

that two 72-pin SIMMs are needed to fill a bank, but each SIMM need only be 1M. Remember from the discussion of megabytes that a 1Mx36-bit (w/parity) device is 4MB. Since two such SIMMs are needed to fill a bank, the total would be 8MB. When added to the 8MB already in the system, the total would be 16MB.

How about another example? Suppose the same 8MB is already installed in your Pentium system, and you want to add 16MB to Bank 1 rather than 8MB (bringing the total system memory to 24MB). In that case, you could use two 2M 72-pin SIMMs where 2Mx36 is 8MB (w/parity) per SIMM. Two 8MB SIMMs yield 16MB, bringing the system total to (16MB + 8MB) or 24MB.

Now for a curve. Suppose you want to outfit that Pentium as a network server with 128MB of RAM. Remember that there's already 8MB in Bank 0, which means there's only Bank 1 available. Since the largest commercially available SIMMs are 8Mx36 (32MB w/parity), you can only add up to 64MB to Bank 1 (for a system total of 72MB). To get around this, you should *remove* the existing 1Mx36 SIMMs in Bank 0 and fill both Bank 0 and Bank 1 with 8Mx36 SIMMs, which would put 64MB in Bank 0 and 64MB in Bank 1—yielding 128MB in total. You can review many of the recommended SIMM/DIMM combinations for a basic Pentium motherboard in Table 24-10. The important thing to remember is that there are often several different ways to implement the amount of RAM that you need.

TABLE 24-10   MEMORY MODULE COMBINATIONS FOR A BASIC PENTIUM MOTHERBOARD

MEMORY SIZE	SIMM 1	SIMM 2	SIMM 3	SIMM 4	SIMM 5	SIMM 6	DIMM 1	DIMM 2
8MB	1Mx32	1Mx32	-	-	-	-	-	-
8MB	-	-	-	-	-	-	1Mx64	-
16MB	2Mx32	2Mx32	-	-	-	-	-	-
16MB	1Mx32	1Mx32	1Mx32	1Mx32	-	-	-	-
16MB	-	-	-	-	-	-	2Mx64	-
16MB	-	-	-	-	-	-	1Mx64	1Mx64
24MB	1Mx32	1Mx32	2Mx32	2Mx32	-	-	-	-
24MB	1Mx32	1Mx32	1Mx32	1Mx32	1Mx32	1Mx32	-	-
24MB	-	-	-	-	-	-	1Mx64	2Mx64
32MB	4Mx32	4Mx32	-	-	-	-	-	-

TABLE 24-10 **MEMORY MODULE COMBINATIONS FOR A BASIC PENTIUM MOTHERBOARD (CONTINUED)**

MEMORY SIZE	SIMM 1	SIMM 2	SIMM 3	SIMM 4	SIMM 5	SIMM 6	DIMM 1	DIMM 2
32MB	2Mx32	2Mx32	2Mx32	2Mx32	-	-	-	-
32MB	1Mx32	1Mx32	1Mx32	1Mx32	2Mx32	2Mx32	-	-
32MB	-	-	-	-	-	-	4Mx64	-
32MB	-	-	-	-	-	-	2Mx64	2Mx64
40MB	1Mx32	1Mx32	4Mx32	4Mx32	-	-	-	-
40MB	-	-	-	-	-	-	1Mx64	4Mx64
48MB	2Mx32	2Mx32	4Mx32	4Mx32	-	-	-	-
48MB	1Mx32	1Mx32	1Mx32	1Mx32	4Mx32	4Mx32	-	-
48MB	2Mx32	2Mx32	2Mx32	2Mx32	2Mx32	2Mx32	-	-
48MB	-	-	-	-	-	-	2Mx64	4Mx64
64MB	8Mx32	8Mx32	-	-	-	-	-	-
64MB	4Mx32	4Mx32	4Mx32	4Mx32	-	-	-	-
64MB	2Mx32	2Mx32	2Mx32	2Mx32	4Mx32	4Mx32	-	-
64MB	-	-	-	-	-	-	8Mx64	-
64MB	-	-	-	-	-	-	4Mx64	4Mx64
72MB	1Mx32	1Mx32	8Mx32	8Mx32	-	-	-	-
72MB	-	-	-	-	-	-	1Mx64	8Mx64
80MB	2Mx32	2Mx32	8Mx32	8Mx32	-	-	-	-
80MB	1Mx32	1Mx32	1Mx32	1Mx32	8Mx32	8Mx32	-	-
80MB	-	-	-	-	-	-	2Mx64	8Mx64
96MB	4Mx32	4Mx32	8Mx32	8Mx32	-	-	-	-
96MB	2Mx32	2Mx32	2Mx32	2Mx32	8Mx32	8Mx32	-	-
96MB	4Mx32	4Mx32	4Mx32	4Mx32	4Mx32	4Mx32	-	-
96MB	-	-	-	-	-	-	4Mx64	8Mx64
128MB	16Mx32	16Mx32	-	-	-	-	-	-
128MB	8Mx32	8Mx32	8Mx32	8Mx32	-	-	-	-
128MB	4Mx32	4Mx32	4Mx32	4Mx32	8Mx32	8Mx32	-	-
128MB	-	-	-	-	-	-	8Mx64	8Mx64
136MB	1Mx32	1Mx32	16Mx32	16Mx32	-	-	-	-
144MB	2Mx32	2Mx32	16Mx32	16Mx32	-	-	-	-
144MB	1Mx32	1Mx32	1Mx32	1Mx32	16Mx32	16Mx32	-	-
160MB	4Mx32	4Mx32	16Mx32	16Mx32	-	-	-	-
160MB	2Mx32	2Mx32	2Mx32	2Mx32	16Mx32	16Mx32	-	-
192MB	8Mx32	8Mx32	16Mx32	16Mx32	-	-	-	-
192MB	4Mx32	4Mx32	4Mx32	4Mx32	16Mx32	16Mx32	-	-
192MB	8Mx32	8Mx32	8Mx32	8Mx32	8Mx32	8Mx32	-	-
256MB	32Mx32	32Mx32	-	-	-	-	-	-
256MB	16Mx32	16Mx32	16Mx32	16Mx32	-	-	-	-
256MB	8Mx32	8Mx32	8Mx32	8Mx32	16Mx32	16Mx32	-	-
256MB	-	-	-	-	-	-	16Mx64	16Mx64

Another bank requirement demands *memory matching*—using modules of the same size and speed within a bank. For example, when adding multiple SIMMs to a bank, each SIMM must be rated for the same access speed and share the same memory configuration (for example, 2Mx36). This issue is not quite so critical with DIMMs, where only one device is needed to constitute a "bank." Still, most DIMM-based systems have their own special requirements:

- DIMMs must meet the required guidelines for your motherboard (such as 100 MHz SDRAM in 32MB, 64MB, or 128MB modules using 64Mbit or 128Mbit technology). If the DIMM does not use the correct speed, memory type, memory size, or RAM chip technology, the system may act erratically or fail to recognize the DIMM.

- If you have two identical DIMMs—that is, DIMMs of the same speed, type, size, chip technology, and both are single sided (or both double sided)—then you may install them in either Bank 0 or Bank 1.

- If you have two DIMMs of different sizes (a 64MB and 128MB DIMM, for example), install the larger DIMM in Bank 0 and the smaller DIMM in Bank 1.

- If you have two DIMMs of the same size, and one is single sided and one is double sided, install the single-sided DIMM in Bank 0 and the double-sided DIMM in Bank 1.

Finally, you should generally follow the *bank order*. The rule is that you'd fill Bank 0 first, then Bank 1, then Bank 2, and so on. Otherwise, memory will not be contiguous within the PC, and CMOS will not recognize the additional RAM. Keep in mind that most current motherboards will support DIMMs in almost any bank (following the DIMM guidelines); so you may not need to fill DIMM banks in a given order, but that's usually the safe way to go if you don't have documentation handy.

Memory Troubleshooting

Unfortunately, even the best memory devices fail from time to time. An accidental static discharge during installation, incorrect installation, a poor system configuration, operating system problems, and even outright failures due to old age or poor manufacture can cause memory problems. This part of the chapter looks at some of the troubles that plague memory systems and offers advice on how to deal with them.

MEMORY TEST EQUIPMENT

If you're working in a repair-shop environment, or plan to be testing a substantial number of memory devices, you should consider acquiring some specialized test equipment. A memory tester, such as the SIMCHECK from Innoventions, Inc. (Figure 24-6), is a modular microprocessor-based system that can perform a thorough, comprehensive test of various memory modules and indicate the specific chip that has failed (if any). The system can be configured to work with specific modules by installing an appropriate adapter module like the one shown in Figure 24-7. Intelligent testers work automatically and show the progress and results of their examinations on a multiline LCD. Guesswork is totally eliminated from memory testing.

Single chips such as DIPs and SIPs can be tested using a single chip plug-in module. The static RAM checker illustrated in Figure 24-8 is another test bed for checking high-performance static RAM components in a DIP package. Both Innoventions test devices work together to provide a full-featured test system. Specialized tools can be an added expense, but no more so than an oscilloscope or other piece of useful test equipment. The return on your investment is less time wasted in the repair and fewer parts to replace.

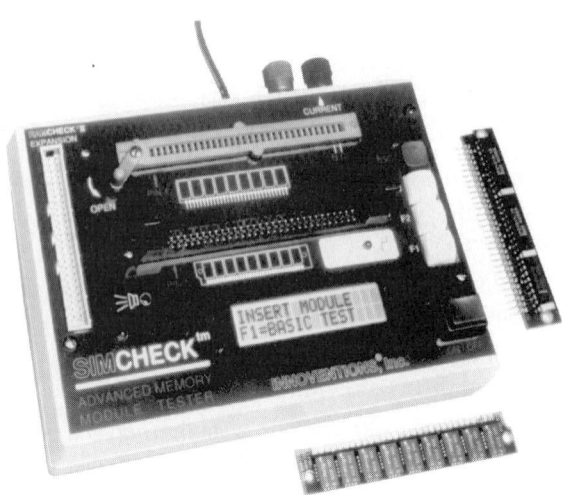

FIGURE 24-6 The SIMCHECK main unit (Innoventions, Inc.)

REPAIRING SIMM/DIMM/RIMM SOCKETS

If there is one weak link in the architecture of a SIMM, DIMM, or RIMM, it is the socket that connects it to the motherboard. Ideally, the memory module should sit comfortably in the socket, then gently snap in—held in place by two clips on either side of the socket. In actual practice, you really have to push that module to get it into place. Taking it out again is just as tricky. As a result, it is not uncommon for a socket to break from excessive force and render your extra memory unusable.

The best (that is, the *textbook*) solution is to remove the damaged socket and install a new one. Clearly there are some problems with this tactic. First, removing the old socket will require you to remove the

FIGURE 24-7 The SIMCHECK PS/2 SIMM adapter (Innoventions, Inc.)

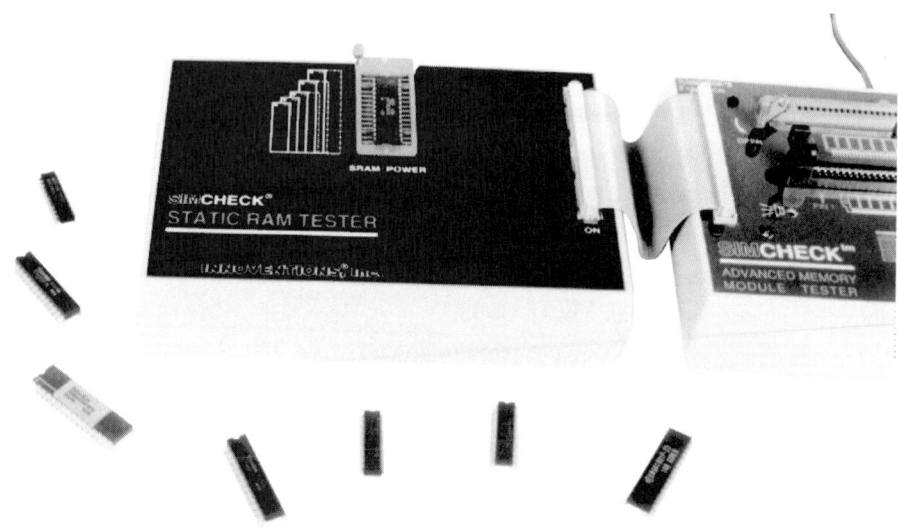

FIGURE 24-8   The SIMCHECK static RAM adapter (Innoventions, Inc.)

motherboard, desolder the broken socket, and then solder in a new socket (which you can buy from a full-service electronics store such as DigiKey). In the hands of a skilled technician with the right tools, this is not so hard. But the printed circuit runs of a computer motherboard are *extremely* delicate, and the slightest amount of excess heat can easily destroy the sensitive, multilayer connections—ruining the motherboard entirely.

Fortunately, there are some tricks that might help you. If either of the socket's clips have been bent or broken, you can usually make use of a medium-weight rubber band that is about one inch shorter than the socket. Wrap the rubber band around the module and socket, and the rubber band should do a fair job holding the memory module in place. If any part of the socket should crack or break, it can be repaired (or at least reinforced) with a good-quality epoxy. If you choose to use epoxy, be sure to work in a ventilated area, and allow plenty of time for the epoxy to dry. This does not "fix" the problem, but it may contain the damage and allow the motherboard to serve a long and reliable working life.

CONTACT CORROSION

Corrosion can occur on a memory module's contacts if the module's contact metal is not the same as the socket's contact metal. This will eventually cause contact (and memory) problems. As a rule, check that the metal on the socket contact is the same as the module's contacts (usually tin or gold). You may be able to get around the problem in the short term by cleaning corrosion off the contacts manually using a cotton swab and good electronics-grade contact cleaner. In the meantime, if you discover that your memory and connectors have dissimilar metals, you may be able to get the memory seller to exchange your memory modules.

PARITY/ECC ERRORS

Parity/ECC errors constitute many of the memory faults that you will see as a technician. As you saw earlier in this chapter, parity and ECC are important parts of a computer's self-checking capability. Errors in memory will cause the system to halt rather than continue blindly along with a potentially catastrophic error. But it is not just faulty memory that causes parity or ECC errors. Parity and ECC can also be influenced by your system's configuration. Here are the major causes of parity/ECC problems:

- One or more memory bits that are intermittent or have failed entirely
- Poor connections between the memory module and its socket
- Too few wait states entered in BIOS (memory is too slow for the CPU)
- An intermittent failure or other fault in the power supply
- A bug, computer virus, or other rogue software
- A fault in the memory controller chip or BIOS
- A loose or missing RIMM heat spreader, resulting in an overheated Rambus chip

When you're faced with a parity/ECC error after a memory upgrade, you should suspect a problem with wait states or memory type settings in the CMOS Setup routine, so check them first. If the wait states or other memory settings are correct, systematically remove each module, clean the contacts, and reseat each module. If the errors continue, try removing one bank of memory modules at a time. (Chances are that the memory is bad.) You may have to relocate memory so that Bank 0 remains filled. When the error disappears, the memory you removed is likely to be defective.

 Some full-service PC shops may have a memory tester unit available. If so, they may be persuaded to test your suspect memory module(s) for a nominal cost (perhaps even for free).

When parity/ECC errors occur spontaneously (with no apparent cause), you should clean and reinstall each memory module *first* to eliminate the possibility of bad contacts. Next, check the power supply outputs—low or electrically "noisy" outputs may allow random bit errors. You may have to upgrade the supply if it is overloaded. Try booting the system "clean" from a write-protected floppy disk to eliminate the possibility of buggy software or computer viruses. If the problem persists, suspect a memory defect in the memory module.

CONTEMPORARY MEMORY SYMPTOMS

With the rapid advances in computer technology, specific numerical (or "bank and bit") error codes have long-since been rendered impractical in newer systems where tens of megabytes can be stored in just a few chips. The i486, Pentium, Pentium II, and today's Pentium III/4 computers use a series of generic error codes. The *address* of a fault is always presented, but there is no attempt made to correlate the fault's address to a physical chip. Fortunately, today's memory systems are so small and modular that trial-and-error isolation can often be performed rapidly on just a few memory modules. The following symptoms highlight many of the most common memory problems encountered in "contemporary" systems.

SYMPTOM 24-1   The number "164" appears on the monitor   This is a generic "memory size error"—the amount of memory found during the POST does not match the amount of memory listed in the system's CMOS Setup. Run the CMOS Setup routine and make sure that the listed memory amount matches the actual memory amount. If memory has been added or removed from the system, you will have to adjust the figure in the CMOS Setup to reflect that configuration change. If CMOS Setup parameters do not remain in the system after power is removed, try replacing the CMOS backup battery or CMOS/RTC chip.

The latest CMOS Setup routines do not actually list the amount of RAM—it is detected automatically. However, you may simply have to enter the CMOS Setup, then immediately "save changes and exit" to reset the amount of detected RAM in your system.

SYMPTOM 24-2 **You see an "Incorrect Memory Size" error message**   This message can be displayed if the CMOS system setup is incorrect, or if there is an actual memory failure that is not caught with a numerical 200-series or "164" code. Start by checking your CMOS Setup. If the CMOS Setup is not updated to reflect memory additions (or removals), or the overall memory size changes because of a memory failure, you may need to adjust or resave your CMOS Setup. If the error persists, there is probably a failure in some portion of RAM.

If the trouble persists, you'll need to locate the defective memory device(s). Remove all memory modules from the system, alter the CMOS Setup to reflect base memory (system board) only, and retest the system. If the problem disappears, the fault is in some portion of expansion memory. If the problem persists, you know the trouble is likely in your base (system board) memory. Take a known-good memory module and systematically swap devices until you locate the defective device. If you have access to a repair shop with a memory tester, the process will be much faster.

SYMPTOM 24-3 **You see a "ROM Error" message displayed on the monitor**   This may also appear as a "207" error on some systems. To guarantee the integrity of system ROM, a checksum error test is performed as part of the POST. If this error occurs, one or more ROM locations may be faulty. Your only alternative here is to replace the system BIOS ROM(s) and retest the system. (You cannot flash older AT-class ROMs.)

SYMPTOM 24-4 **New memory is installed, but the system refuses to recognize it** New memory installation has always presented some unique problems since different generations of PCs deal with new memory differently. The oldest PCs require you to set jumpers or DIP switches in order to recognize new blocks of memory. The vintage i286 and i386 systems (such as a PS/2) use a setup disk to tell CMOS about the PC's configuration (including new memory). More recent i386 and i486 systems incorporate an "installed memory" setting into a CMOS Setup utility in BIOS that must be updated after the memory is installed or removed. Late-model i486, Pentium, and Pentium II/III/4 systems actually "autodetect" installed memory each time the system is booted (so it need not be entered in the CMOS Setup, though Setup may need to "autodetect" the new RAM amount on first boot). Make sure that your memory is identified according to the vintage of your particular system.

Also check that a correct bank has been filled properly. The PC may not recognize any additional memory unless an entire bank has been filled and the bank is next in order (Bank 0, then Bank 1, and so on). You may wish to check the PC's user manual for any unique rules or limitations in the particular motherboard. Keep in mind that many late-model Pentium II/III/4 motherboards do *not* need banks filled in order, though that's usually the safest policy to follow when upgrading or troubleshooting any PC.

SYMPTOM 24-5 **New memory has been installed or replaced, and the system refuses to boot** Memory installations often proceed flawlessly, but when boot problems occur, you can usually narrow the problem down to several key areas. Always start by checking AC power, the system power switch, and power connections to the motherboard. Check that none of the system cabling was dislodged during the memory installation. Also see that all expansion boards and cables are inserted evenly and completely. Flexing the motherboard during memory installation may have pried one or more boards slightly out of their slots.

Your memory modules may not be inserted correctly. Take the modules out and seat them again—making sure the locking arm is holding the module securely in place. If the problem continues, you probably do not have the right memory module for that particular computer. Make sure the memory module is the correct part that is compatible with your PC. Finally, check for any particular "device order" that may be required by the motherboard. Certain systems require that memory be installed in pairs or in descending order by size. Refer to the system or motherboard manual for specific details on your exact system. If all else fails, replace the memory module(s).

SYMPTOM 24-6   You see an "XXXX Optional ROM Bad, Checksum = YYYY" error message   Part of the POST sequence checks for the presence of any other ROMs in the system. When another ROM is located, a checksum test is performed to check its integrity. This error message indicates that an external BIOS ROM (such as a SCSI adapter BIOS or video card BIOS) has checked "bad," or its address conflicts with another device in the system. In either case, system initialization cannot continue.

Check the ROM address setting first. If you have just installed a new peripheral device when this error occurs (such as a SCSI controller board), try changing the new device's ROM address jumpers to resolve the conflict. Next, check the new device itself. Remove the peripheral board, and the fault should disappear. Try the board on another PC. If the problem continues on another PC, the adapter (or its ROM) may be defective. If this error has occurred spontaneously, remove one peripheral board at a time and retest the system until you isolate the faulty board; then replace the faulty board (or just replace its ROM if possible).

SYMPTOM 24-7   You see a general RAM error with fault addresses listed   In actual practice, the error message may appear as any of the examples here depending on the specific fault, where the fault was detected, and the BIOS version reporting the error.

```
Memory address line failure at <XXXX>, read <YYYY>, expecting <ZZZZ>
Memory data line failure at <XXXX>, read <YYYY>, expecting <ZZZZ>
Memory high address failure at <XXXX>, read <YYYY>, expecting <ZZZZ>
Memory logic failure at <XXXX>, read <YYYY>, expecting <ZZZZ>
Memory odd/even logic failure at <XXXX>, read <YYYY>, expecting <ZZZZ>
Memory parity failure at <XXXX>, read <YYYY>, expecting <ZZZZ>
Memory read/write failure at <XXXX>, read <YYYY>, expecting <ZZZZ>
```

Each of the errors shown is a general RAM error message indicating a problem in base or extended/expanded RAM. The code "XXXX" is the failure segment address—an offset address may be included. The word "YYYY" is what was read back from the address, and "ZZZZ" is the word that was expected. The difference between these read and expected words is what precipitated the error.

In general, these errors indicate that at least one RAM chip (if you have RAM soldered to the motherboard) or at least one memory module has failed. A trial-and-error approach is usually the least expensive route in finding the problem. First, reseat each memory module and retest the system to be sure that each module is inserted and secured properly. Rotate a known-good memory module through each occupied SIMM/DIMM/RIMM socket in sequence. If the error disappears when the known-good module is in a slot, the old device that had been displaced is probably the faulty one. You can go on to use specialized module troubleshooting equipment to identify the defective chip, but such equipment is rather expensive unless you intend to repair a large volume of modules to the chip level.

If the problem remains unchanged, even though every module has been checked, the error is probably in the motherboard RAM or RAM support circuitry. Run a thorough system diagnostic if possible, and check for failures in other areas of the motherboard that affect memory (such as the interrupt controller, cache controller, DMA controller, or memory management chips). If the problem prohibits a software diagnostic, use a POST board and try identifying any hexadecimal error code. If a support chip is identified, you can replace the defective chip, or replace the motherboard outright. If RAM continues to be the problem, try replacing the motherboard RAM (or replace the entire motherboard), and retest the system.

SYMPTOM 24-8   You see a "Cache Memory Failure—Disabling Cache" error   The cache system has failed. The tag RAM, cache logic (motherboard chipset), or cache memory on your motherboard is defective. Your best course is to replace the cache RAM chip(s) or COAST (Cache-on-a-Stick) module. If the problem persists, try replacing the cache logic or tag RAM (or replace the entire motherboard). You will probably need a schematic diagram or a detailed block diagram of your system in order to locate the cache memory chip(s), so refer to the system or motherboard manual for detailed information.

SYMPTOM 24-9   You see a "Decreasing Available Memory" error message   This is basically a confirmation message that indicates a failure has been detected in extended or expanded memory, and that all memory *after* the failure has been disabled to allow the system to continue operating (although at a substantially reduced level). Your first step should be to reseat each memory module and ensure that they are properly inserted and secured. Next, take a known-good memory module and step through each occupied slot until the problem disappears—the device that had been removed is probably the faulty one. Keep in mind that you may have to alter the system's CMOS Setup parameters as you move memory around the machine. (An incorrect setup can cause problems during system initialization.)

SYMPTOM 24-10   You are encountering a memory error with HIMEM.SYS under DOS   In many cases, this is a compatibility problem with system memory. For example, the Intel Advanced/AS motherboard is incompatible with two specific Texas Instruments EDO SIMMs (part numbers TM124FBK32S-60 and TM248GBK32S-60). Other EDO SIMMs from TI and other vendors will not cause this error. Try a SIMM from a different manufacturer. Also make sure that you're using the latest version of HIMEM.SYS.

SYMPTOM 24-11   Memory devices from various vendors refuse to work together   The system experiences a "memory failure" during the memory count at start time. This is a very "machine-specific" problem. For example, Gateway Solo PCs can suffer this problem when customers use the same size memory modules (4MB, 8MB, or 16MB) made by *different* vendors. Try matching the memory modules from the same manufacturer (including part number and speed).

SYMPTOM 24-12   Windows 9x/Me Protection Errors occur after adding memory modules   Windows 9x/Me stalls with Windows Protection Errors during boot, or randomly crashes with "Fatal Exception Errors" when opening applications. This is a known problem with the Intel Thor motherboard using the 1.00.01.CNOT BIOS after installing 32MB of RAM. This issue is usually due to certain third-party SIMMs operating at speeds faster or slower than 60ns. The motherboard probably has tight memory specifications, and SIMMs that operate at the correct speed are required (not faster or slower, even though the SIMMs are "marked" properly). Some SIMM manufacturers mark the SIMMs at 60ns, but the SIMMs actually run at 45ns. Try some SIMMs from a different manufacturer. It is also possible that a BIOS upgrade may loosen timing enough to make the SIMMs usable.

SYMPTOM 24-13   **Windows returns a fault in the MS-DOS extender**   This kind of error can occur in Windows 9x/Me, and usually happens in either of two formats: "Bad fault in MS-DOS extender" or "Fault outside of MS-DOS extender." You may also see a "stack dump" with a format such as

```
Raw fault frame:
EC=0344 CS=031F IP=85E2 AX=001D BX=0005 CX=1800 DX=155F
SI=0178 DI=0178 BP=016E DS=027F ES=027F SS=027F SP=0166
```

An error such as "Bad fault in MS-DOS extender" generally occurs when the fault handler in DOSX.EXE (the DOS extender) generates another cascaded fault while trying to handle a protected-mode exception. This error is usually caused by one of the following factors:

■ HIMEM.SYS is unable to control the A20 line (which may indicate a motherboard problem).

■ DOS=HIGH is not functioning properly (perhaps HIMEM.SYS is not loaded or corrupt).

■ Your RAM may be defective. You might try a RAM diagnostic to isolate any memory problems.

■ You are not running MS-DOS (your system is running DR DOS, for example).

■ The third-party memory manager (such as 386MAX) is not configured correctly.

■ A "EMM386.EXE NOEMS x=A000-EFFF" command line is missing from the CONFIG.SYS file.

■ You have an old, out-of-date BIOS ROM that isn't supporting the DOS extender properly.

■ Your memory-related CMOS Setup configuration is incorrect.

■ Your Windows files are old or corrupted. Run ScanDisk to test for file problems, and then reinstall Windows if necessary.

■ Your system is infected with a computer virus (for example, Form, Forms, Noint, or Yankee Doodle are known to cause this type of problem). Check the system with a current antivirus utility.

If you see an error such as "Standard mode fault outside MS-DOS extender," the Windows kernel may be generating a processor exception during initialization (before it has installed its own exception handlers), or when the kernel determines that it cannot handle an exception. The underlying causes are almost always the same as just outlined. The portion of the error display labeled "Raw fault frame" contains information generated by the 80286 or 80386 processor in response to the original fault.

SYMPTOM 24-14   **Windows returns a "General Protection Fault" (or GPF)**   There are several possible causes behind general protection faults under Windows 9x/Me. An x86-type CPU (from 80286 to Pentium III/4 processors) can detect when a program encounters a problem. The most common problems include stack faults, invalid instructions (such as software bugs), divide errors (divide by zero or "math" errors), and general protection faults. These generally indicate nonstandard code in a Windows application, in Windows itself, or in a Windows device driver.

■ **Stack Fault (a.k.a. Interrupt 12)**   There are several possible reasons for a "stack fault." An instruction may try to access memory beyond the limits of the current Stack segment, or load the "SS" register with invalid information (though that shouldn't happen under Windows 95/98). Stack faults are always fatal to the current application in Windows, but Windows may not crash completely.

■ **Invalid Instruction (a.k.a. Interrupt 6)**   The CPU detects most invalid instructions and generates a software interrupt to report them. Invalid instructions are always fatal to the application. This should never happen, but is usually caused by coding errors that accidentally execute data instead of code.

- **Divide Error (a.k.a. Interrupt 0)**   This error is caused when the CPU's intended destination register cannot hold the result of a divide operation—it could be divide by zero, or divide overflow. In either case, the problem is almost always due to a problem with the program.

- **General Protection Fault (a.k.a. Interrupt 13)**   Any protection violations that do not cause another exception cause a "general" protection exception because one of the following conditions is true:

  - Exceeding a segment limit when using the CS, DS, ES, FS, GS memory segments. This is a very common bug in programs—usually caused by miscalculating how much memory is required in an allocation.

  - Transferring program execution to a segment of memory that is not executable (for example, jumping to a location that contains garbage).

  - Writing to a read-only or a code segment of memory.

  - Loading a bad value into a segment register.

  - Using a null pointer. A value of 0 is defined as a null pointer. In protected mode, it is always invalid to use a segment register that contains 0.

In virtually all cases, the solution to a "protection fault" is to try reloading the suspect program, driver, or Windows module. (Run ScanDisk to check the disk file system for errors.) If the suspect program or driver is buggy, it may be necessary to download and install a patch file to correct potential programming errors.

SYMPTOM 24-15   **You see a memory error such as "Unable to control A20 line"**
This error is almost always related to the HIMEM.SYS driver. The A20 line controls access to the first 64KB of extended memory (known as the *high memory area*, or "HMA"). The HIMEM.SYS device driver must control the A20 line in order to manage extended memory. The error message is reported by HIMEM.SYS if it incorrectly identifies the extended memory handling mechanism of the computer, or if the handling method in your PC's BIOS is unknown.

There are two workarounds for this problem. First, you can set the "machine" switch. Add the "/M:x" (the "machine type") switch to the HIMEM.SYS command line in your CONFIG.SYS file (where "x" is the "machine number" between 1 and 14 or 16). Shut down and then restart your computer. For example:

```
DEVICE=C:\DOS\HIMEM.SYS /M:1
```

An incorrect A20 machine handler may hang the system at boot-up. You should have an MS-DOS version 5.0 (or Windows 9x/Me) bootable floppy disk available to boot from before you experiment with different machine switches.

Check the BIOS version next. It may be necessary to upgrade your machine's BIOS, or contact your system vendor for assistance in modifying your CMOS settings—you may need to disable a FastGate (or similar) option.

SYMPTOM 24-16   **You see a memory error such as "Cannot setup EMS buffer" or "Unable to set page frame base address"**   This is a known problem with many Dell Inspiron 7000 computers under Windows 98, and appears when starting a DOS-based program that requires Expanded Memory (EMS) page frames. EMS page frames normally require 64KB of upper memory, but Dell Inspiron 7000-series computers can only provide 54K of upper memory. This is an issue with the Dell system design, and generally cannot be corrected unless you turn off the program's use of EMS page frames (or run the program on another system).

SYMPTOM 24-17   **Memory contents are corrupted (or the PC halts) when entering a CPU power-down state under Windows 98**   If your system's power management settings are configured to allow the processor to enter a "C3" power state on a computer supporting the "Advanced Configuration and Power Interface" (ACPI) standard, you may encounter symptoms such as corrupted memory after several minutes of inactivity, or the computer may stop responding after several minutes of inactivity.

This problem is due to an issue with the Intel 440BX chipset under Windows 98 (caused by Windows 98 itself), which may allow memory contents to be corrupted when a CPU enters or leaves its power-down state. If that motherboard uses the Intel PIIX4-E IDE controller chipset, the computer might hang (known to occur if a bus mastering operation occurs while in the power-down state). Until a patch is available for Windows 98, you can work around this issue by preventing the CPU from entering the C3 power state. To accomplish this, exit Windows and reboot the computer. Enter your CMOS Setup and set the "lvl3_latency" entry to a value greater than 0x3E8h (1000 decimal). If "lvl3_latency" is greater than 0x3E8h, the Windows 98 ACPI driver does not enter the C3 state. You'll need to save your changes and reboot the PC for those changes to take effect.

SYMPTOM 24-18   **Windows 98 appears unstable after disabling virtual memory (the "swap file")**   There is not enough RAM in the system. This can occur if you disable virtual memory with only 16MB of RAM. Windows 98 has higher memory requirements than Windows 95, so while 16MB may be the "theoretical" minimum for Windows 98, 32MB of RAM or more would result in better system performance and stability. To resolve this problem, install more RAM in your computer, enable virtual memory, or both. To enable virtual memory:

1.   Restart your computer and hold down the CTRL key until the Windows 98 Startup menu appears.

2.   Choose Safe Mode from the Startup menu.

3.   Click Start, highlight Settings, and then click Control Panel.

4.   Double-click System, click the Performance tab, and then click Virtual Memory.

5.   Click the option labeled "Let Windows manage my virtual memory settings."

6.   Click OK, click Close, and then click Yes when you are prompted to restart your computer.

SYMPTOM 24-19   **You encounter a Windows 98 "protection error" involving NTKERN**   This problem occurs when installing Windows 98 and restarting for the first time. You may see an error message such as

```
While initializing device NTKERN: Windows Protection Error. You need to
restart your computer.
```

Or you may receive an error message after the Windows 98 Setup is completed, such as

```
Invalid VxD Dynamic Link Call to Device 3 Service B
```

or

```
While Initialing Device <filename> Windows Protection Error. You need to
restart your computer.
```

If you try to start in the Safe Mode, you may receive a message like this:

```
HIMEM.SYS Has Detected Unreliable XMS Memory at <address>.
```

In virtually every case, there is defective memory (RAM) in your computer. You'll need to systematically remove or replace the SIMM(s), DIMM(s), or RIMM(s) in your computer to eliminate any bad memory. If your computer has over 16MB of memory, it may be possible to configure your computer to use only 16MB of memory (factoring out any RAM above 16MB).

1. Use Notepad to open the SYSTEM.INI file in the \Windows folder.

2. Add the following line to the [386enh] section of the SYSTEM.INI file:

    ```
    MaxPhysPage=01000
    ```

3. Save this file and quit Notepad.

4. Restart the computer, and then restart the Windows 98 Setup utility.

 If you can't start in the Safe Mode, restart your computer and hold down the CTRL key until the Windows 98 Startup menu appears; then choose Command Prompt Only. Use a DOS text editor like EDIT to update the \Windows\System.ini file as just shown.

You can also limit RAM through System Configuration. Use the System Configuration tool to limit the amount of memory (RAM) available to Windows 98 by following these steps:

1. Restart your computer, hold the CTRL key until the Windows 98 Startup menu appears, and choose the Safe Mode.

2. Click Start, highlight Programs, select Accessories, select System Tools, and then click System Information.

3. On the Tools menu, click the System Configuration utility.

4. On the General tab, click Advanced.

5. Click the "Limit Memory To <n> MB" check box (where <n> is a number) to select it, and then set the memory limit value to "16MB."

6. Click OK, click OK again, and then restart your computer.

SYMPTOM 24-20   **The Windows 95/98 system slows or locks up when playing MIDI files continuously**   When a MIDI (*musical instrument digital interface* or .MID) file is played repeatedly or continuously, your computer may lock up, or the computer may seem sluggish for a short time after you stop playing the MIDI file. Screen savers and games that use repeated MIDI playback are typically susceptible to this problem. The problem is caused by the Windows MIDI sequencer (MCISEQ.DRV), which loses a small amount of memory for each successive playback of a MIDI file. This is a known problem with the MIDI sequencer in Windows 95 and Windows 98; so until a suitable update or patch file becomes available to correct the MIDI sequencer, you should avoid using the screen saver or game, or disable MIDI playback. Note that closing and then reloading a MIDI file releases the lost memory.

SYMPTOM 24-21   **After installing Windows 98, the Device Manager may show a yellow exclamation mark next to the PC Card (PCMCIA) network adapter**   You may also see a status message such as "Error Code 10" in the adapter's Properties. This is known to occur on laptops such as the DEC HiNote Ultra II when the PC Card network adapter uses memory that the computer's BIOS has reserved. Windows 98 determines a free range of memory, and then assigns that range to the network adapter for use; but the network adapter driver may not be able to use the assigned range if it is reserved by

904   CHAPTER 24: MEMORY TROUBLESHOOTING

the BIOS. To get around this problem, try excluding the memory range that is being reserved by the BIOS so that Windows 98 will not use it.

1. Click Start, highlight Settings, and click Control Panel.

2. Double-click the System icon.

3. Double-click Computer on the Device Manager tab.

4. Click the Reserve Resources tab, and then click Memory.

5. Click Add, type **CA000** in the Start Value box; then type **CB000** in the End Value box.

6. Click OK, and click OK again.

7. Click the PC Card network adapter to highlight it, and then click Remove.

8. Click OK, and then click Close.

9. Restart your computer. The network adapter will be redetected and reinstalled by Windows 98.

SYMPTOM 24-22   **You notice that Windows 98 system resources remain lower after quitting a program**   This is often referred to as "memory leakage," when memory is not freed by a program after it quits. Restart the PC—rebooting the PC from scratch should return any "leaked" memory. You can use this trick as a temporary workaround. Memory leakage can also occur if you start a program, and then quit before it has completely started. Do not quit a program before it has completely started. Memory leakage is often caused by poorly coded or buggy software rather than Windows itself. If you notice "leakage" with a particular program, check with the software maker's Web site to see if there is a downloadable patch or update that will correct the memory leakage.

SYMPTOM 24-23   **You see an error message such as "Insufficient memory to initialize Windows," even though there is plenty of RAM**   The problem may be "too much" RAM. When attempting to install or start Windows 9x/Me with over 768MB of RAM (perhaps 1GB or more), the system may return an erroneous "insufficient memory" message. This is generally regarded as a problem with Windows 9x/Me, but you can work around the problem by limiting the amount of RAM that Windows can use to 768MB.

1. Use Notepad to edit the SYSTEM.INI file.

2. Add the following line in the [386Enh] section of the SYSTEM.INI file:

   ```
   MaxPhysPage=30000
   ```

3. Save the SYSTEM.INI file, and then restart your computer.

If this problem occurs during Windows Setup, start the system to the command prompt (a.k.a. DOS) mode and use the DOS-based EDIT utility to modify the SYSTEM.INI file. When you save the edited SYSTEM.INI file and reboot the PC, the Windows Setup should continue.

SYMPTOM 24-24   **When trying to format a hard drive under Windows 98, you see an error message such as "Insufficient memory to load system files"**   The format process will terminate. This error occurs if you attempt to format your hard disk using the **format c: /q /u /s /v** command at a command prompt, but there is not enough free conventional memory to use the **/s** switch. This error may also occur if you start your computer using the Windows 98 startup disk, and then attempt to format your hard disk. This is a problem with Windows 98, but there are ways to work around the problem.

First, do not use the **/s** switch with the **format** command—after the format process is finished, transfer the system files to the hard disk using the **SYS C:** command. If you're restarting your computer using the Windows 98 startup disk, choose "Start Computer With CD-ROM Support" on the Windows 98 Startup menu, and then use the **format** command to format your hard disk.

SYMPTOM 24-25   **Your Windows 9x/Me system returns an "internal stack overflow" error**   "*Stacks*" are small sections of reserved memory that programs use for processing hardware events. A "stack overflow" occurs when there is not enough space in memory to run the hardware interrupt routines. When Windows shows an "internal stack overflow" error, there is not enough space in memory (either set aside, or available to handle the calls being made to the system hardware).

The CONFIG.SYS file may not be properly configured for the Windows installation. Try the following values: STACKS=64,512 (this is the maximum allowed), FILES=60, and BUFFERS=40. Also check for old memory managers. Examine the CONFIG.SYS file to determine whether files such as HIMEM.SYS or EMM386.EXE are being loaded from a folder other than the Windows folder. If so, boot Windows using the Safe Mode Command Prompt Only (DOS) option. Rename the CONFIG.SYS file to CONFIG.DOS, and the AUTOEXEC.BAT file to AUTOEXEC.DOS, and then restart the computer.

Some TSRs may be interfering with Windows. Disable any non-boot device drivers in the CONFIG.SYS and AUTOEXEC.BAT files. If you are installing from Windows 3.x and getting a stack overflow error, check the WIN.INI and SYSTEM.INI files for non-Windows-based programs or drivers that may be loading. Also check for resource conflicts—there may be an incompatible hardware configuration. Check the port and IRQ settings of any network card, sound card, and/or modem. Make sure that there are no COM2/COM4 or COM1/COM3 conflicts, and that no devices are sharing IRQs. Disable or remove conflicting devices. Finally, the computer may need a BIOS upgrade. Check the BIOS version and contact the manufacturer of your computer for information about a BIOS upgrade.

SYMPTOM 24-26   **You encounter random "fatal exception" errors under Windows 9x/Me**   You may also notice that there are more "fatal exception" errors under Windows 9x/Me than under Windows 3.1x. The most common cause for these error messages is faulty physical memory (RAM) on the computer. Try starting the system in Safe Mode. If the "fatal exception" errors disappear, the problem may be with one or more buggy or corrupted drivers loading in the normal mode. You may then need to systematically disable background software and drivers in order to isolate the offending software.

Check the CMOS Setup next. In some circumstances it may be possible to adjust the CMOS settings (such as changing memory wait states, or disabling the motherboard's L2 cache) to stabilize Windows 9x/Me successfully. Finally, check/replace the RAM. To resolve "fatal exception" errors, it is often necessary to isolate and replace the defective RAM. In rare cases, the problem may be on the motherboard.

SYMPTOM 24-27   **An error indicates that there is not enough memory to start Windows 9x/Me (or an application)**   This problem can occur if there is not enough real and virtual memory to start the Windows shell (or the particular program). Start your computer to the DOS prompt and free some space on the hard disk containing your swap file (virtual memory). Once you free some space on your hard disk, restart Windows normally and try to run the program again. If the problem persists (or you cannot free more space on the drive), try adding RAM to the system.

If you try to start a program on a PC with only 4MB of free RAM, and less than 8MB of free space on the hard disk with a swap file, you may not be able to shut down and restart your computer normally. You must press CTRL-ALT-DEL to open the Close Program dialog box, and then click Shut Down to shut down Windows.

SYMPTOM 24-28 **EMM386 refuses to load after installing Windows 98** This issue can occur if you load EMM386.EXE using the /Highscan switch. The /Highscan switch can interfere with hardware detection during setup, so it is disabled by Windows 98 Setup. You can reenable EMM386 using the following steps:

1. Use Notepad to open the CONFIG.SYS file.

2. Locate the line that loads EMM386.EXE, and remove the following text from the beginning of the line:

   ```
   rem -- by Windows 98 setup -
   ```

3. Save and close the CONFIG.SYS file.

4. Restart the computer.

SYMPTOM 24-29 **General protection faults are generated after restarting a program in Windows 95/98** If you close a 16-bit program that is marked as "not responding" in the Close Program dialog box, and then restart the program, you may receive a general protection fault (GPF) error. This happens because of the way the offending program was originally closed. When a program is closed normally, its dynamic link libraries (DLLs) are unloaded from memory. When you use the Close Program dialog to close a program that is not responding, the program's DLLs are not unloaded (and are not reinitialized when you restart the program later). The only real solution here is to shut down the computer, and then restart it from scratch.

SYMPTOM 24-30 **You find that you cannot use 256MB DIMMs that contain 64Mbit RAM components** You should double-check the manufacturer's recommendations for your motherboard and verify the type of DIMM sizes and technologies best suited to the particular motherboard. Some motherboard models (such as Intel's JN440BX motherboard) cannot use such sophisticated RAM components on a DIMM of that capacity. This can cause the motherboard to produce invalid timing signals and cause unpredictable system behavior. Try smaller DIMM(s), or use DIMM(s) with less dense memory components on board.

Further Study

Autotime   www.autotime.com
CST, Inc.   www.simmtester.com
Innoventions   www.simcheck.com
Kingston   www.kingston.com
PNY   www.pny.com

25

MICE AND TRACKBALLS

As software packages evolved beyond simple menus and began to make use of the powerful graphics systems coming into popular use during the mid-1980s (EGA and VGA graphics), ever-larger amounts of information were presented in the user interface. Simple, multilayered text menus were aggressively replaced with striking *graphical user interfaces* (GUIs). System options and selections were soon represented with symbols (graphic "buttons" or "icons") instead of plain text. Using a keyboard to maneuver through such visual software soon became a cumbersome (if not impossible) chore.

Peripheral designers responded to this situation by developing a family of *pointing devices* (Figure 25-1). Pointing devices use a combination of hardware and software to produce and control a graphical screen *cursor*. A software device driver generates the cursor and reports its position. As the pointing device is moved around, hardware signals from the pointing device are interpreted by the device driver, which moves the cursor in a like manner. By positioning the cursor over a graphic symbol and activating one, two, or three of the buttons on the pointing device, it is now possible to select (click or double-click) and manipulate (a.k.a. drag) options in the application program instead of using a keyboard.

There are three factors needed to make a pointing device work: the physical signal-generating hardware itself, a software driver (the device driver), and the application program, which must be written to make use of the device driver. If any of these three items is missing, the pointing device will not work. This

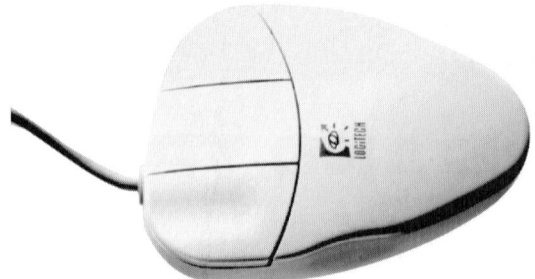

FIGURE 25-1   A Logitech MouseMan (Logitech, Inc.)

chapter looks at the technology, maintenance, and troubleshooting of two popular pointing devices: the mouse and the trackball.

The Mouse

Although the development of computer pointing devices has been ongoing since the early 1970s, the first commercial pointing device for IBM-compatible systems was widely introduced in the early 1980s. The device was small enough to be held under your palm, and your fingertips rested on its button(s). A small, thin cord connects the device to the host computer. The device's small size, long tail-like cord, and quick scurrying movements around the desk immediately earned it the label of "mouse."

Every mouse needs at least one button. By pressing the button, you indicate that a selection is being made at the current cursor location. Many mouse-compatible software packages only make use of a single mouse button even to this day. A two-button mouse is more popular (reflecting the endurance of the mouse design) because a second button can add more flexibility to the mouse. For example, one button can work to select an item, while the second button can be used to deselect that item again, or to activate other menus and options. Windows 98/Me use the right-click to bring up a context-sensitive menu for icons, files, and folders. A few mouse designs use three buttons, but the third button is rarely supported by application programs other than CAD or high-end art applications.

MOUSE GESTURES

The first mouse gesture is called *clicking,* which is little more than a single momentary press of the left mouse button (on a two-button mouse). Clicking is the primary means of making a selection in the particular application program. The second common gesture is *double-clicking,* which is simply two single clicks in immediate succession. A double-click also represents selection, but its exact use depends upon the application program—under Windows 98/Me, a double-click will launch a selected application or open a desired data file. The third type of mouse gesture is the *drag,* where a graphical item can be moved around the display. Dragging is almost always accomplished by pressing and holding the left mouse button while the cursor is over the desired item, then (without releasing the button) moving the item to its new location. When the item has moved to its new position, releasing the left mouse button will "drop" the item in that location.

Interestingly, pen gestures are interpreted by the computer's operating system, but mouse movements and button conditions are handled by the actual application program (such as a word processor or game). Thus, the same mouse gestures can be made to represent different actions depending on which program is executing.

MOUSE CONSTRUCTION

A mouse is a relatively straightforward device consisting of four major parts: the plastic housing, the mouse ball, the electronics PC board, and the signal cable. Figure 25-2 illustrates a typical mouse assembly. The housing assembly will vary a little depending on the manufacturer and vintage of your particular mouse (just walk through a computer store and look at the variety of mouse styles available on the shelf), but the overall scheme is almost always identical. The mouse ball is a hard rubber ball situated up inside the mouse body just below a small PC board. When the mouse is positioned on a desktop, the ball contacts two actuators that register the mouse ball's movement in the X (left-to-right) and Y (up-to-down) directions. Both sensors generate a series of pulses that represent movement in both axes. Pulses equate to mouse movement—more pulses mean more movement. The pulses from both axes are amplified by the mouse circuit board and sent back to the computer along with information on the condition of each mouse button. Figure 25-3 shows an older Suncom CrystalMouse, which allows you to see the internal mouse construction.

The mouse device driver must be loaded before the mouse will work. Under DOS, the real-mode driver is loaded in CONFIG.SYS or AUTOEXEC.BAT. Under Windows 98/Me, the protected-mode mouse driver is loaded as Windows boots. Once the driver is loaded, it interprets the pulses generated by the mouse and translates them into X and Y screen locations where the visible mouse cursor is positioned. As the mouse moves left and right or up and down, pulses are added or subtracted from the cursor's X and Y screen coordinates by the device driver. The application program can then call for the X and Y coordinates, as well as button states. The key to a working mouse is its sensor devices. Sensors (or actuators)

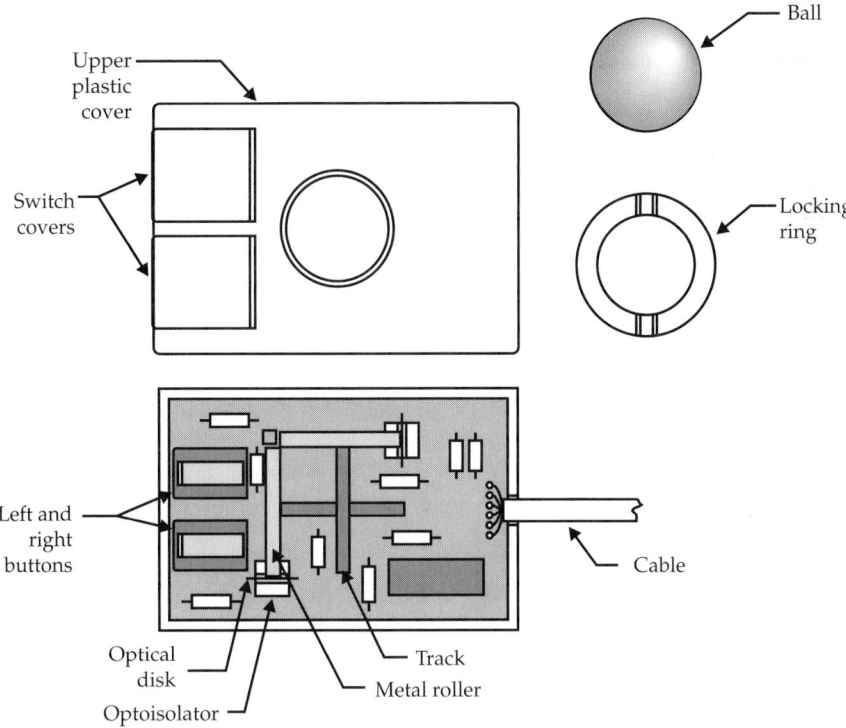

FIGURE 25-2   Internal construction of a basic mouse

FIGURE 25-3   The CrystalMouse from Suncom Technologies (Suncom Technologies)

must be responsive enough to detect minute shifts in mouse position and generate pulses accordingly, yet be reliable enough to withstand wear, abuse, and environmental effects. There are two general types of sensors: mechanical and optomechanical.

Mechanical Sensors

The greatest challenge in mouse design (and the largest cause of failures) is the reliable and repeatable conversion of mouse movement into serial electrical pulses. Early mouse versions used purely mechanical sensors to encode the mouse ball's movements. As the mouse ball turned against a roller (or shaft), copper contacts on the shaft would sweep across contacts on the mouse PC board—much like commutating rings and brushes on a DC motor. Each time a roller contact touches a corresponding contact in the mouse, an electrical pulse is generated. Since a mouse must typically generate hundreds of pulses for every linear inch of mouse movement, there are several sets of contacts for each axis.

It is important to note that mouse pulses can be positive or negative depending on the relative direction of the mouse in an axis. For example, moving the mouse right may produce positive pulses, while moving the mouse left may produce negative pulses. Similarly, moving the mouse down along its Y axis may produce positive pulses, while moving the mouse up may produce negative pulses. All pulses are then interpreted and tracked by the host computer.

Although mechanical sensors are simple, straightforward, and very inexpensive to produce, there are some significant problems that can plague the mechanical mouse. Mechanical mouse designs are not terribly reliable. The metal-on-metal contact sets used to generate pulses are prone to wear and breakage. Dust, dirt, hair, and any other foreign matter carried into the mouse by the ball can also interfere with contacts. Any contact interference prevents pulses from being generated. This condition results in a frustratingly intermittent "skip" or "stall" of the cursor while you move the mouse. Fortunately, it is often a simple matter to disassemble and clean the contacts.

Optomechanical Sensors

The next generation of mouse designs replaced the mechanical contacts with an *optoisolator* arrangement, as illustrated in Figure 25-4. A hard rubber mouse ball still rests against two perpendicularly opposed metal or plastic actuator rollers, but instead of each roller driving an array of contacts, the rollers

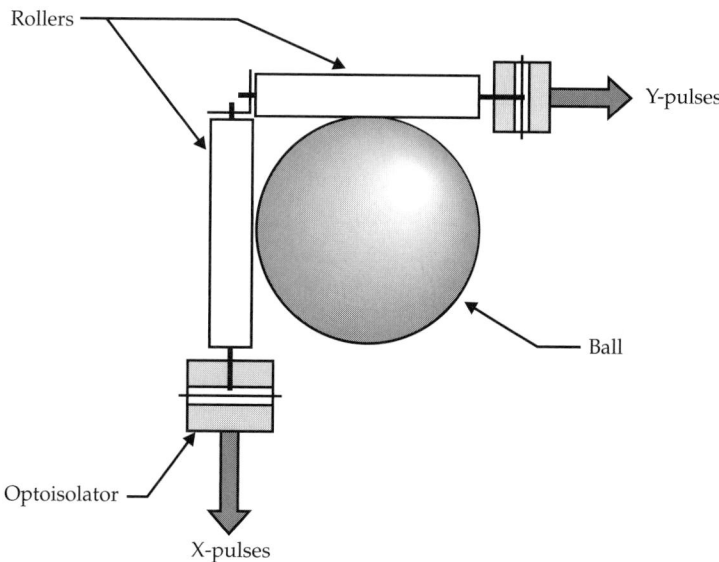

FIGURE 25-4   Sensor layout for an optomechanical mouse or trackball

rotate slotted wheels that are inserted into optoisolators. An optoisolator shines LED light across an air gap where it is detected by a photodiode or phototransistor. When a roller (and slotted wheel) spins, the light path between LED and detector is alternated or "chopped." This causes the detector's output signal to oscillate—thus, pulses are generated. The pulse frequency is dependent on mouse speed. As with the mechanical mouse, the optomechanical mouse produces both positive and negative serial pulses, depending on the direction of mouse movement.

The optomechanical mouse is a great improvement over the plain mechanical approach. By eliminating mechanical contacts, wear and tear on the mouse is significantly reduced, resulting in much longer life and higher reliability. However, the mouse is still subject to the interference of dust and other foreign matter that invariably finds its way into the mouse housing. Regular cleaning and internal dusting can prevent or correct instances of cursor skip or stall. Most mouse models in production today use optomechanical sensors.

The Trackball

The *trackball* is basically an inverted mouse. Instead of using your hand to move a mouse body around on a desk surface, you move a trackball in a stationary housing. Your hand or fingertips move the ball itself, which is mounted through the top of the device. The advantage to a trackball is that it does not move. As a result, trackballs can be incorporated into desktop keyboards or added to your work area with a minimum of required space. Such characteristics have made trackballs extremely popular with laptop and notebook computers. Today, most notebook computers incorporate pointing devices directly.

In spite of its advantages, however, a trackball is not quite as easy to use as a mouse. The successful use of a mouse is largely a matter of hand-eye coordination—a flick of the wrist and a click or two can maneuver you through a program at an impressive rate. Since you can move the mouse and manipulate its buttons simultaneously, dragging is a very intuitive gesture. Trackballs are usually turned with only your thumb. This positions the rest of your hand such that you can only reach one trackball button. That is a fine arrangement as long as you're only clicking a single button, but you often have to move your hand around completely to get to the second button (or you must at least let go of the ball). Dragging is also typically a cumbersome effort. Even a clumsy trackball is better than none at all, so you should be as familiar with trackballs as with a mouse.

TRACKBALL CONSTRUCTION

Virtually all trackballs use the same optomechanical sensor technology that is used with mice. Instead of the mouse PC board resting over the ball, a trackball sits on top of a PC board. The hard rubber ball sits at the intersection of a set of small plastic rails (or *tracks*)—thus, the term "trackball." The rails position the ball between two perpendicularly oriented metal or plastic rollers. Each roller drives a slotted wheel, which, in turn, runs between the LED and detector of an optoisolator. As the ball and rollers are made to turn, the slotted wheels cause the respective optoisolator's light path to alternate and generate signal pulses. Pulse frequency is dependent on the relative movements of each roller. Pulses are read and interpreted just as they are with a mouse.

During initialization, your computer must load a device driver designed to read the proper port, interpret any signals generated by the trackball, and make switch and roller information available to whatever program calls for it. Given the similarities of mice and trackballs, many mouse-compatible applications are capable of accessing trackball data and responding just like a mouse. Even the trackball device driver is virtually identical to a mouse driver. (Trackball drivers are usually "adopted" mouse drivers that simply compensate for the inversion of the ball.) Since the technologies and construction techniques of mice and trackballs are essentially the same, the remainder of this chapter will treat a mouse and trackball as interchangeable devices.

Cleaning a Pointing Device

Pointing devices are perhaps the simplest peripheral available for your computer. While they are reasonably forgiving to wear and tear, trackballs and mice can easily be fouled by dust, debris, and foreign matter introduced from the ball. Contamination of this sort is almost never damaging, but it can cause some maddening problems when using the pointing device. A regimen of routine cleaning will help to prevent contamination problems. You can use prefabricated mouse cleaning kits (Figure 25-5) to speed the cleaning process. Turn your computer off and disconnect the mouse from the system before performing any cleaning procedures:

1. *Remove the ball.* A ball is held in place by a retaining ring. For a mouse, the retaining ring is on the bottom. For a trackball, the ring is in the top. Rotate the ring (usually counterclockwise) and remove it gently—the ball will fall out. Place the retaining ring in a safe place.

2. *Clean the ball.* Wash the ball in warm, soapy water, and then dry it thoroughly with a clean, lint-free towel. Place the ball in a safe place with the retaining ring.

3. *Blow out the dust.* Use a can of photography-grade compressed air to blow out any dust or debris that has accumulated inside the pointing device. You may want to do this in an open or outdoor area.

4. *Clean the rollers.* Notice that there are three rollers in the mouse/trackball: an X roller, a Y roller, and a small pressure roller that keeps the ball pressed against the X and Y rollers. Use a cotton swab dipped in isopropyl alcohol to clean off any layer of gunk that may have accumulated on the rollers. If any gunk falls off the rollers, you'll need to remove it.

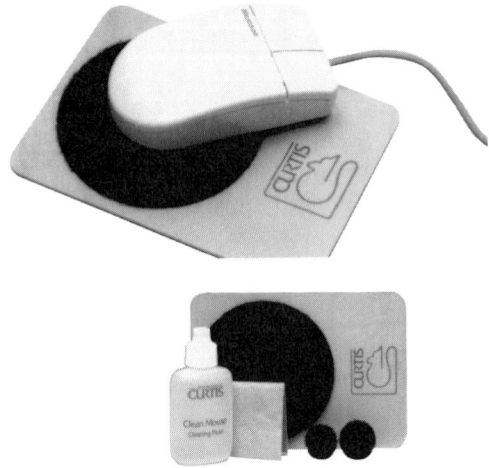

FIGURE 25-5   A Curtis mouse cleaning kit (Curtis, a division of Rolodex, Secaucus, NJ 07094)

5. *Reassemble and test.* Allow everything to dry completely. Then replace the ball and secure the retaining ring (usually by turning it clockwise again). You should then reconnect and test the pointing device to be sure that it is performing as expected.

Do not use harsh solvents, wood alcohol, or chemicals inside the pointing device or on the ball. Chemicals can easily melt the plastic and result in permanent damage to the pointing device.

Troubleshooting a Pointing Device

The weakest link in a pointing system is the peripheral pointing device itself. Few peripheral devices are subjected to the wear and general abuse of trackballs or mice. They are dropped, yanked, and moved constantly from place to place. Damage to the device's circuit board, cabling, and connector is extremely common due to abuse. Accumulations of dust and debris can easily work into the housing and create havoc with the rubber ball, tracks, and rollers. Hardware conflicts and driver configuration issues can also result in frequent problems. This part of the chapter guides you through some simple troubleshooting techniques for your trackball and mouse.

MOUSE/TRACKBALL INTERFACES

From time to time, you may need to check the physical interface on a mouse or trackball. At its core, the mouse is a simple serial device—that is, it can pass serial data back and forth with the host computer using communication protocols managed by the mouse driver. There are four types of mouse interfaces commonly found in the field: serial mice, bus mice, PS/2 mice, and USB mice. This part of the chapter highlights the pinouts for each interface type.

Serial Mice

A serial mouse connects to an existing RS-232 serial port at the PC (usually COM1 or COM2) using a standard DB-9F (9-pin female) or DB-25F (25-pin female) connector. Table 25-1 lists the pinout for a Logitech Type M, V, or W serial mouse connector.

TABLE 25-1   PIN ASSIGNMENTS FOR A SERIAL PORT MOUSE (LOGITECH)

DB-9F 9 PIN	DB-25F 25 PIN	WIRE NAME	COMMENTS
shell	1	Protective Ground	
3	2	Receive Data	Serial data from host to mouse
2	3	Transmit Data	Serial data from mouse to host (for power only)
7	4	RTS	Request to Send
8	5	CTS	Clear to Send
6	6	DSR	Data Set Ready
5	7	Signal Ground	
4	20	DTR	Data Terminal Ready

Bus Mice

There are many circumstances when it is not possible to use a serial mouse on an open COM port, and the older PC is not fitted with a PS/2 port. In this case, it may be necessary to use a bus mouse, which basically involves using a stand-alone mouse controller board (a bus mouse controller) and mouse fitted with a bus mouse connector. This is usually a male subminiature D-type connector or a miniature male DIN (circular) connector. Be careful not to mistake the 9-pin DIN connector of a bus mouse for the 6-pin circular connector of a PS/2 mouse. Table 25-2 lists the pinout for a Logitech bus mouse.

PS/2 Mice

Most current computers are fitted with one or two PS/2 ports. (These are often called PIX ports because the motherboard's PIX controller(s) can manage the ports directly.) PS/2 ports are basic serial interfaces that are ideal for keyboards and mice. PS/2 mice use a 6-pin DIN (barrel) connector, as shown in Table 25-3. Bidirectional data transmission is controlled by the CLK and DATA lines. Both are fed by an "open collector" device that lets either the host or mouse control the lines. During nontransmission, CLK is at logic "1," and DATA is at logic "0" or "1." The PC can inhibit mouse transmission by forcing CLK to logic "0."

TABLE 25-2   PIN ASSIGNMENTS FOR A BUS MOUSE PORT (LOGITECH)

WIRE COLOR	MINI-DIN PIN	LOGITECH P-SERIES SIGNAL	MICROSOFT INPORT SIGNAL
Black	1	+5V	+5V
Brown	2	X2	XA
Red	3	X1	XB
Orange	4	Y1	YA
Yellow	5	Y2	YB
Green	6	Left	SW1
Violet	7	Middle	SW2
Gray	8	Right	SW3
White	9	GND	Logic GND
SHIELD	shell	Chassis	Chassis

TABLE 25-3   PIN ASSIGNMENTS FOR A PS/2 MOUSE PORT (LOGITECH)

PIN	WIRE NAME
1	DATA
2	Reserved
3	Ground
4	+5V Supply
5	CLK
6	Reserved
Shield	Chassis

USB Mice

Most current computers are fitted with one or two USB (Universal Serial Bus) connections and can accommodate a USB mouse/trackball. The advantage of USB ports is their convenience. You can connect and disconnect USB devices with the system running, and the device will automatically be identified and enumerated under Windows 98/Me. USB also allows you to "mix and match" many different types of USB devices on the same port, so you can connect a USB mouse directly to the computer's main USB port, or to a connector on any USB hub attached to the system. The simple 4-pin USB connection follows this layout:

- Pin 1: Power
- Pin 2: Data –
- Pin 3: Data +
- Pin 4: Ground

MOUSE DRIVER SOFTWARE ISSUES

Device drivers are often underrated when it comes to mouse/trackball troubleshooting. The driver plays a vital role in mouse performance, and any driver bugs or incompatibilities will have direct consequences on mouse operation. Mouse drivers are also surprisingly versatile programs that can be extensively configured through the use of command-line switches. For example, Table 25-4 lists the command-line switches for Microsoft's real-mode Mouse driver 9.0x. When dealing with any kind of mouse issue, always start by checking that the correct driver is installed, that the driver is the latest version, and that it is using any necessary command-line switches to adapt itself to the particular PC. (Default settings are not always adequate.)

MOUSEKEYS UNDER WINDOWS 9X

Windows 98/Me traditionally relies on a mouse for clicking and dragging, but there is a little-known feature of Windows 98/Me called "MouseKeys" that allows you to use the numeric keypad to move the mouse around the screen, click, double-click, and drag. MouseKeys can be helpful if you're caught without a mouse (or troubleshooting a defective mouse system), and you need to navigate the Windows 98/Me environment.

The MouseKeys feature is activated through the Accessibility properties under the Control Panel. Click on Start, select Settings, and then open the Control Panel. Double-click on the Accessibility icon and select the Mouse tab (Figure 25-6). You can enable or disable MouseKeys by checking or clearing the check box. Once MouseKeys is enabled, you can further optimize its settings (Figure 25-7) by clicking the Settings button. If you check the Use shortcut box, you can turn MouseKeys on and off by toggling LEFT ALT-LEFT SHIFT-NUM LOCK.

TABLE 25-4	COMMAND-LINE SWITCHES FOR MICROSOFT MOUSE DRIVER 9.0X
SWITCH	**EXPLANATION**
ON	Enable mouse
OFF	Disable mouse
/B	Bus mouse type
/C<n>	Serial mouse on COM1 or COM2
/E	Load mouse in low memory
/F	Find pointing device
/H<n>	Horizontal sensitivity (5–100)
/I<n>	InPort mouse type (1 or 2)
/KP<n>	Small button selection (P = Primary, S = Secondary)
/K<n>	ClickLock (/KC = ON, /K = OFF)
/M<n>	Enable default cursor (/M1 = ON, /M = OFF)
/N<n>	Cursor delay (0–10)
/O<n>	Rotation angle (0–359)
/P<n>	Active acceleration profile
/Q	Load mouse quietly (no startup messages; only in 9.01)
/R<n>	Interrupt rate
/S<n>	Horizontal and vertical sensitivity (5–100)
/V<n>	Vertical sensitivity (5–100)
/Y	Disable hardware cursor
/Z	PS/2 mouse type

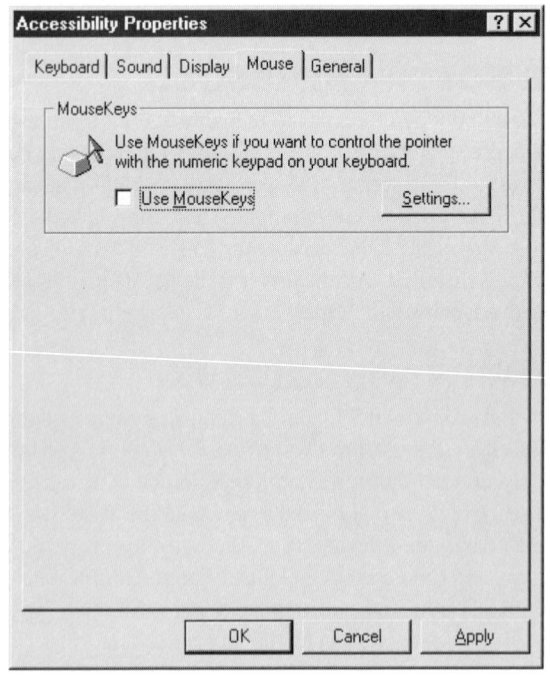

FIGURE 25-6   Controlling the Windows MouseKeys feature

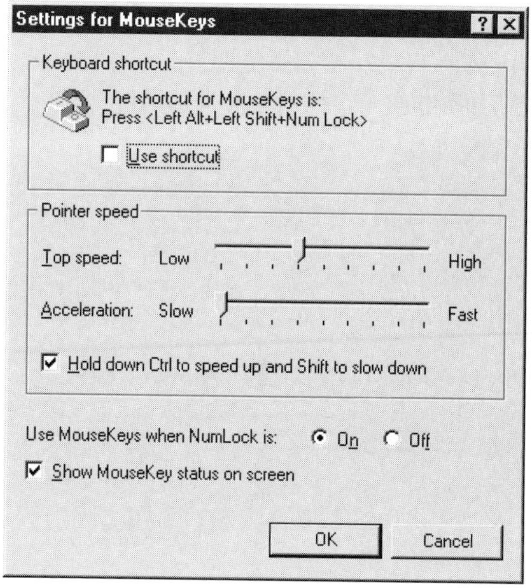

FIGURE 25-7   Adjusting MouseKeys for best performance

Once the MouseKeys feature is turned on, move the cursor by pressing the arrow keys on the numeric keypad. Use the HOME, END, PAGE UP, and PAGE DOWN keys to move the mouse cursor diagonally. You can left-click by pressing the 5 key on the numeric keypad. To left-double-click, press the + key on the numeric keypad. To right-click, press the – button on the numeric keypad first, and then press 5 to click or + to double-click. To click as if you were using both mouse buttons at once, press the * key on your numeric keypad, and then press 5 to click or + to double-click. If you want to switch back to standard clicking, press / on your numeric keypad.

You'll also need to be able to drag using MouseKeys. Make sure that the MouseKeys feature is turned on, and then move the mouse pointer over the desired object. Press INS on the numeric keypad to hold down the mouse button and grab the object. Move the mouse pointer over the new desired area, and then press DEL on the numeric keypad to drop the object.

ADJUSTING MOUSE PROPERTIES

To use a mouse comfortably and successfully, the mouse must be adjusted for your personal preferences. You'd be surprised at how many people get frustrated because they can't double-click, only to find that the "Double-click speed" property for the mouse is set too high. You can tailor the mouse to your own tastes through the Mouse Properties dialog (Figure 25-8). Click Start, highlight Settings, and then click Control Panel. When the Control Panel is open, double-click the Mouse icon. You can select the "handedness" of the mouse, its double-click speed (sensitivity), its pointer format, movement sensitivity, and cursor "trails" (very handy in older LCD laptop displays).

COMMON MOUSE DETECTION ISSUES

When installing, replacing, or upgrading a pointing device, you may encounter a Windows 98/Me error such as "Mouse Not Detected." If Windows starts, you will be forced to use keyboard shortcuts to navigate

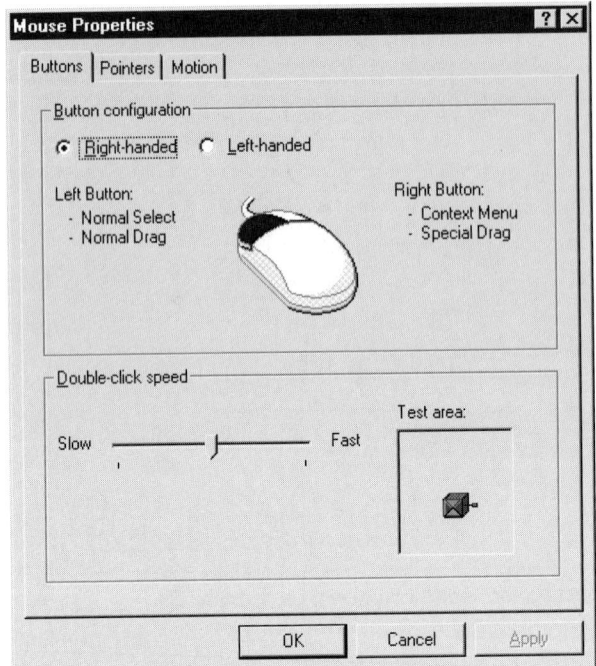

FIGURE 25-8   The Mouse Properties dialog under Windows

around and exit Windows again. If you're faced with a mouse detection problem, use the following check-list to isolate the most common hardware issues:

■ A port-specific pointing device has been connected to the wrong port. (A serial-only mouse has been connected to a PS/2 mouse port using an adapter.)

■ The port being used by the mouse/trackball is disabled, defective, or incorrectly configured.

■ You're using an incompatible bus mouse adapter card. For example, when using a Logitech bus mouse, Logitech bus adapters must be used. Verify that any third-party bus mouse adapters have been removed from the system.

■ The port being used by the mouse/trackball is experiencing a hardware conflict with another device in the system (for example, an IRQ or I/O address conflict).

■ You're inserting an extension cable or switch box between the pointing device and the system. Most pointing devices do not support the use of extension cables or switch boxes. If a switch box or extension cable is being used, remove it and connect the pointing device *directly* to the system.

■ The pointing device is defective. Verify this by trying the device on another system. Replace the defective pointing device if necessary.

■ The pointing device is incompatible with your system. Verify this by trying another pointing device connected to the same system and port. If another pointing device fails on the same port, the problem may be with that system or port. Otherwise, try a different pointing device.

MOUSE ISSUES WITH VIDEO DRIVERS

Installing some third-party video drivers can cause the Windows 98/Me mouse pointer to behave erratically (or not move at all). It may also cause odd types of "video corruption." (For example, the mouse pointer destroys screen elements.) Since the mouse driver uses video driver information to generate the screen cursor, some video drivers may not operate properly with your particular mouse driver. Try changing the video mode to a lower resolution or color depth (such as the "standard VGA" mode), and see if the problem disappears. If it does, you should try updating the video driver or the mouse driver. Otherwise, you may need to update the video card's firmware, or use a different pointing device.

USB MOUSE TROUBLESHOOTING TIPS

USB ports offer a surprising amount of versatility when connecting external devices to the system. While USB ports should be well supported under Windows 98/Me, there are numerous issues that may impair USB operation and mouse performance:

- *Check the OS versions.* Generally speaking, USB mice require Windows 98/Me. Windows 95 and OSR2.x with the USB supplement are not supported.

- *Check the driver versions.* Connecting a USB pointing device to a USB port on your system should result in the device being detected by the system (and the default USB drivers being installed). This may require the Windows 98/Me CD, so insert the CD when prompted by Windows. You may use the default USB drivers that ship with Windows 98/Me. But to utilize the enhanced features of your mouse, the very latest mouse driver versions for your mouse are needed. In most cases, you can obtain the latest mouse drivers directly from the manufacturer's Web site. Uninstall any older version(s) of the pointing device software from your system before installing the version that shipped with your current device.

- *Check the product version.* Verify that your USB mouse/trackball is using the latest firmware. Initial product releases or prerelease (evaluation) units may not function reliably.

- *Enable the USB controller.* Many early USB (PIX3) systems shipped with the USB ports disabled. These systems must have their USB ports enabled before the mouse will be detected and function properly. These USB ports are generally enabled through the CMOS Setup. If a USB add-on card is being used, please be sure that it is a *retail* version. Prerelease versions of USB cards may not function correctly with current USB hardware. Check with the USB card's manufacturer for new drivers or firmware updates.

- *Check the USB host controller.* For a USB pointing device to function properly on the USB port, the USB Host Controller must be identified correctly by Windows 98/Me. Click Start, highlight Settings, and then click Control Panel. Double-click the System icon, and select the Device Manager tab. Verify that there is an entry called "Universal Serial Bus Controller." If this entry is missing, the controller may not be enabled or detected properly.

- *Check the mouse entry in Device Manager.* Click Start, highlight Settings, and then click Control Panel. Double-click the System icon, select the Device Manager tab, and then click the Mouse entry. Verify that there is a mouse entry that reads "HID-compliant mouse" and another entry that states the name of your USB device. If there are any errors reported on these icons (by exclamation points or red *X*s), highlight these icons and click the Remove button. Once these icons have been removed, click the Refresh button and allow Windows 98 to redetect the pointing device. Open the Mouse entry again, and verify that there are no errors reported. Power-down the computer and restart Windows, and then test the USB device to see if it's working.

■ *Check your external hubs.* If two external hubs are daisy-chained together, at least one must be powered (connected to AC). If you're using two or more unpowered hubs, there may not be enough current in the second hub to properly power the USB devices connected to it. If this occurs, connect the pointing device to the first hub and test it. (Or try connecting the mouse directly to the USB port instead of a hub.)

■ *Check your USB hardware detection.* If the USB pointing device is not detected by Windows 98/Me after plugging in the device and installing the drivers, try the following:

1. Shut down the system, allow it to power-off, and then restart it.

2. Try connecting the pointing device to a second USB port (if your system has one).

3. Try connecting the mouse to a second system with a working USB port to verify the USB mouse hardware is working. Any Windows 98/Me system equipped with a USB port should detect the mouse.

4. Try connecting another USB device into the same USB port. If the second device is detected correctly, the mouse may be defective. If the second device is also not detected correctly, the USB port may be disabled or malfunctioning.

5. If you're using a USB hub to connect the mouse, try connecting the mouse directly to the USB port on your system.

■ *Check for software issues.* Windows 98/Me includes a system configuration utility that can boot your system without resident programs loading from the Windows registry, the StartUp folder, and system files. Use this tool to isolate possible software conflicts:

1. Click Start and select Run. In the Open command line, type **msconfig** and click OK. The system configuration utility should appear.

2. On the General tab, click Selective Startup. Click on the WIN.INI tab, and then click on the plus (+) sign next to the [windows] section. Check for the presence of the "LOAD=" and "RUN=" lines. If there are programs loading from either of these lines, remove the check marks from those entries. This will prevent anything in those lines from loading upon startup.

3. Click on the Startup tab, and remove the check mark from every box except the entry for "System Tray (SysTray.Exe)." This will prevent memory resident programs from loading from the Run folder and other startup folders of the registry.

4. Click the OK button, and Windows should prompt you to reboot. After rebooting, test the device to see if the problem has disappeared. If it has, one of the programs loading at startup is causing the issue. Re-add each item systematically (one at time, rebooting between each addition). When you find the problem application, contact that program's manufacturer for more information or a possible work-around.

SYMPTOMS

If you cannot correct mouse problems with the preceding general guidelines, it's time to look for specific symptoms. This part of the chapter highlights a wide selection of symptoms that normally occur.

SYMPTOM 25-1   **The mouse cursor appears, but it only moves erratically as the ball moves (if at all)**   This symptom may occur in either the horizontal or vertical axis. This symptom suggests that there is an intermittent condition occurring somewhere in the pointing device. You should not have to disassemble your computer at all during this procedure. Start your investigation by powering down the computer. Check the device's cable connector at the computer. Make sure the connector is tight and inserted properly. If you are in the habit of continually plugging and unplugging the mouse/trackball, excessive wear can develop in the connector pins. If the connector does not seem to fit tightly in the computer, try a new pointing device.

A more likely problem is that the device's rollers are not turning, or turning only intermittently. In most cases, roller stall is due to a dirty or damaged ball, or an accumulation of dirt blocking one or both sensors. Clean the ball and blow out any dust or debris that may have settled into the mouse/trackball housing. Refer to the preceding section on cleaning, and try to clean the device thoroughly. *Never use harsh solvents or chemicals to clean the housings or ball.*

If you have the mouse connected to a standard serial communication port (a COM port), you should check that there are no other devices using the same interrupt (IRQ). For example, COM1 and COM3 use the same IRQ, while COM2 and COM4 share another IRQ. If you have a mouse on COM1 and a modem on COM3, there will almost invariably be a hardware conflict. If possible, switch the mouse (or conflicting device) to another port and try the system again.

If there is no hardware conflict, and cleaning does not correct an intermittent condition, remove the device's upper housing to expose the PC board, and use your multimeter to check continuity across each wire in the connecting cable. Since you probably will not know which connector pins correspond to which wires at the sensor PC board, place one meter probe on a device's wire and "ring-out" each connector pin until you find continuity. Make a wiring chart as you go. Each time you find a wire path, wiggle the cable to stimulate any possible intermittent wiring. Repair any intermittent wiring if possible. If you can not find continuity or repair faulty wiring, simply replace the pointing device.

SYMPTOM 25-2   **One or both buttons function erratically (if at all)**   Buttons are prone to problems from dust accumulation and general contact corrosion. Your first step should be to power-down your computer and disconnect the pointing device. Remove the ball and upper housing to expose the PC board and switches. Spray a small amount of electronics-grade contact cleaner into each switch, and then work each switch to circulate the cleaner.

If cleaning does not improve intermittent switch contacts, you may wish to check continuity across the connecting cable. With the ball and housing cover removed, use your multimeter to check continuity across each wire in the connecting cable. Since you probably do not know which connector pins correspond to which wires at the device, place one meter lead on a device wire and "ring-out" each connector pin until you find continuity. Once you find continuity, wiggle the cable to stimulate any possible intermittent wiring. Repair any intermittent wiring if you can, or simply replace the pointing device.

SYMPTOM 25-3   **The screen cursor appears on the display, but it does not move**
If the cursor appears, the device driver has loaded correctly and the application program is communicating with the driver. Your first step should be to suspect the serial connection. If there is no serial connection, however, there will be no pulses to modify the cursor's position. If you find a bad connection, power-down your computer before reattaching the device's serial connector, and then restore power and allow the system to reinitialize.

If the device is attached correctly to its proper serial port, the problem probably exists in the pointing device's wiring. Remove the ball and upper housing to expose the PC board, and then use your multimeter to check continuity across each wire in the connecting cable. Since you probably do not know which connector pins correspond to which wires in the device, place one meter lead on a device wire and "ring-out" each connector pin until you find continuity. Once you find continuity, wiggle the cable to stimulate any possible intermittent wiring. Repair any intermittent or open wiring if you can, or simply replace the pointing device.

SYMPTOM 25-4   **The mouse/trackball device driver fails to load**   The device driver is a short program that allows an application program to access information from a pointing device. Most computer users prefer to load their device drivers during system initialization by invoking the drivers in the CONFIG.SYS or AUTOEXEC.BAT files. Most drivers are written to check for the presence of their respective device first. If the expected device does not respond, the driver will not be loaded into memory. Other drivers load blindly regardless of whether the expected device is present.

If the device driver fails to load during initialization, your pointing device may not have been detected. Power-down your computer and check the connection of your pointing device. Ensure the device is securely plugged into the proper serial port (or other mouse port). If the device is missing or incorrectly inserted, install or resecure the pointing device and allow the system to reinitialize. If you see a "File Not Found" error message displayed at the point your device driver was supposed to load, the driver may have been accidentally erased, may be corrupted, or may be located in a subdirectory where the CONFIG.SYS or AUTOEXEC.BAT files are not looking. Try reinstalling a valid copy of your mouse device driver, and ensure that the driver is located where your calling batch file can access it. Reboot your system.

Most well-designed application programs check for the presence of a pointing device through the device driver during initial program execution. If the application program aborts or fails to execute because of a "No Mouse Found" or "No Mouse Driver" error, return to the preceding paragraphs and recheck the device and driver installation.

SYMPTOM 25-5   **You see a "General Protection Fault" after installing a new mouse and driver under Windows**   First, this is probably not a hardware fault. (Although it would be helpful to check any mouse driver command-line switches in CONFIG.SYS or AUTOEXEC.BAT.) It is more likely that the new mouse driver is conflicting with one or more applications. Try several different applications—most will probably work just fine. Check with the mouse manufacturer to see if there are any other reported problems, and find if any patches are planned. If you have an older version of the mouse driver available, try replacing that one. An older driver may not work as well as a newer one, but it may not suffer from this kind of compatibility problem. If there are no older drivers available, and no patches that you can use, you may be forced to change the mouse and mouse driver to something completely different in order to eliminate the problem.

SYMPTOM 25-6   **You see the error "This pointer device requires a newer version"**   In virtually all cases, you have the wrong driver installed on the system for your driver. Check the driver and make sure that the driver you are using is appropriate for the particular mouse. For example, a Logitech or Genius mouse selected in Windows setup can cause this kind of problem if you have a Microsoft mouse on the system. Change the mouse type under Windows. Under Windows 98/Me, you'll need to remove the old mouse reference from the Device Manager, and then use the Add New Hardware wizard to install the new mouse manually.

SYMPTOM 25-7   **You see the error "Mouse port disabled or mouse not present"**   This is almost always a connection problem or a setup problem. Check the signal connector first. Make sure the mouse cable is not cut or damaged anywhere, and see that it is attached securely to the serial or PS/2 port. Many newer system BIOS versions now provide an option in the CMOS Setup for a mouse port. Check the CMOS Setup, and see that any entries for your mouse are enabled properly.

SYMPTOM 25-8   **The mouse works for a few minutes, then stops**   When the computer is rebooted, the mouse starts working again. This is a problem that often plagues cut-price mice and is almost always due to buildups of static in the mouse. The static charges are interfering with the mouse circuitry and causing the mouse to stop responding (though charges are not enough to actually damage the mouse). There are generally three ways to resolve the problem: (1) spray the surrounding carpet and upholstery with very dilute fabric softener to dissipate static buildup; (2) hire an electrician to ensure that the computer and house wiring are grounded properly; or (3) replace the mouse with a more static-resistant model.

SYMPTOM 25-9   **You attempt a double-click but get quadruple-click, or you attempt a single-click and get a double-click**   This is a phenomenon called "button bounce" and is the result of a hardware defect (broken or poorly buffered mouse buttons). You may be able to clean the mouse buttons by spraying in some good-quality electronic-grade contact cleaner. Otherwise, you'll need to replace the mouse.

SYMPTOM 25-10   **A single mouse click works, but double-click doesn't**   When this problem occurs, it is almost always because the "double-click speed" is set too high in the Windows 98/Me mouse control panel. Try setting it lower. Click Start, select Settings, and then open the Control Panel. Double-click the Mouse icon, and adjust the "Double-click speed" slider under the Buttons tab.

SYMPTOM 25-11   **A PS/2 mouse is not detected by a notebook PC under Windows**   There is a known problem with PS/2 mouse detection on a Toshiba portable computer under Windows 95. You can usually correct the problem by taking the following steps:

1. Shut down the computer entirely, and physically disconnect the PS/2 mouse from the PS/2 port.

2. Restart the PC to the DOS mode, and create backup copies of your CONFIG.SYS and AUTOEXEC.BAT files.

3. Restart Windows (reboot the PC if necessary).

4. Click Start, select Settings, open the Control Panel, and double-click on the System icon.

5. Select the Device Manager tab, and double-click the Mouse entry.

6. Select the mouse entry that is not being detected (for example, "Toshiba AccuPoint"), and click Remove.

7. Select and remove any other mouse entries.

8. Shut down the computer and reconnect the mouse, and then turn the PC back on.

9. When the system reboots, it should detect the mouse and attempt to reinstall the appropriate drivers.

If this doesn't fix the problem, a hardware issue could exist. Try a different PS/2 mouse (preferably from a manufacturer other than the current one). If a different make and model PS/2 mouse does not work, the PS/2 port may require service.

SYMPTOM 25-12   **Mouse pointer options are not saved**   This is a known problem when you use the "extra points" features in the Mouse Manager program included with the Microsoft Mouse driver. The pointer options are not saved or written to the MOUSE.INI file when you are running a virus-protection program such as Microsoft Anti-Virus (MSAV) or Norton AntiVirus (NAV). To correct this problem, remove the CHKLIST.MS or CHKLIST.CPS file in the directory that contains the mouse files. To determine the location of that directory, type **set** at the MS-DOS command prompt. It will return a list of locations of various files and memory strings. Look for the "MOUSE=" line, and then go to that directory and delete the CHKLIST.MS or CHKLIST.CPS file. Reboot the system and try saving options again.

SYMPTOM 25-13   Clicking the right mouse button doesn't start the default context menus of Windows   If the mouse manager software you're running is using an assignment set for the right button, this assignment will override the Windows default setting of "context menus." Open the mouse management software utility, and change the assignment for the right button to "Unassigned." Save your changes. The right mouse button will now access the default context menus.

SYMPTOM 25-14   The system's "Fast Media" device no longer functions after installing a pointing device under Windows   The Fast Media device is an infrared remote control device (typical of Packard Bell systems) that allows you to control the mouse pointer as well as a CD player, TV tuner, modem, radio card, and other items. This device only works with native Microsoft drivers. When you install pointing device drivers, the Fast Media device no longer functions. This happens because the Fast Media software installs some virtual drivers that only communicate with the native Microsoft drivers.

Unfortunately, you may need to choose between the Fast Media system (and forgo the advanced features of your new pointing device), or disable the Fast Media system in order to use all of the features of your pointing device. You may also check with Packard Bell to see if there is an update to the Fast Media drivers that is more compliant with other device drivers.

SYMPTOM 25-15   Your system only detects a basic two-button mouse after plugging it into a "Media Select" unit   This is a problem that plagues some Packard Bell systems with Media Select units. The Packard Bell Media Select is a box that fits underneath the monitor and plugs into the PS/2 port of the computer system. This Media Select device also has a PS/2 port for a PS/2-style mouse. It seems that the Media Select unit uses a pass-through PS/2 port connection that causes detection problems for some pointing devices. In most cases, cleaning up the registry and removing unneeded entries can clear this problem:

Never attempt to edit your registry without first creating a complete registry backup on your boot floppy disk. Incorrectly editing the registry may prevent the system from booting.

1. Click Start and select Run.

2. On the Open line, type **c:\windows\regedit.exe** and press ENTER.

3. Open the following key:

    `Hkey_Local_Machine\System\CurrentControlSet\Services\Class\Mouse\xxxx`

    where xxxx is an incremental 4-digit number starting at 0000.

4. Click on each folder under the Mouse folder, and delete them until there are no 000X folders remaining.

5. Save your changes and exit the registry editor.

6. Remove the FMEDIA reference from the Windows Startup group or WIN.INI file as necessary.

7. Save any changes, shut down, and then restart the system normally.

8. Open the properties dialog or applet for your pointing device to verify the correct detection.

If this does not correct the detection issue, you'll need to connect the pointing device *directly* to the computer system's PS/2 port (bypassing the Media Select box). You may also use the serial port if the pointing device is a PS/2-serial combination unit. This will allow you to keep the Media Select and achieve correct detection if the serial port is working properly.

SYMPTOM 25-16   **The mouse pointer does not move after installing a Logitech "First Mouse" on a system**   Windows will generally not indicate any problems with mouse detection. There is a known compatibility problem with some Packard Bell computers and Logitech's two-button First Mouse (version M/N:M34). You can use the keyboard to invoke a basic work-around:

1.   Press CTRL-ESC to open the Start menu.

2.   Use the arrow keys to highlight Settings, then Control Panel, and press ENTER.

3.   Move the arrow key over to the Mouse icon and press ENTER. This will open the Mouse Properties dialog box.

4.   Using the TAB key, tab over to the Quick Setup tab, and then use the RIGHT ARROW key to open the Devices tab.

5.   On the Devices tab, tab over to the Add Mouse button and press ENTER.

The pointing device applet should now detect the two-button serial mouse, and the pointer should move properly. However, you'll need to perform this procedure each time you restart the system. If your Packard Bell system has a dedicated PS/2 mouse port, another option is to contact the pointing device maker to see if you can exchange the serial version for a PS/2 version.

SYMPTOM 25-17   **After installing a three-button mouse, you receive an error such as "pointing device on unknown port"**   You may also find that the device is only shown as a two-button mouse. In most cases, there are older mouse traces in the registry that must be removed before the new pointing device can be properly detected:

Do not attempt to edit your registry without first creating a complete registry backup on your boot floppy disk. Incorrectly editing the registry may prevent the system from booting.

1.   Click Start and select Run.

2.   On the Open line, type **c:\windows\regedit.exe** and press ENTER.

3.   Open the following key:

    Hkey_Local_Machine\System\CurrentControlSet\Services\Class\Mouse\xxxx

    where xxxx is an incremental 4-digit number starting at 0000.

4.   Click on each folder under the Mouse folder, and delete them until there are no 000X folders remaining.

5.   Save your changes and exit the registry editor.

6.   Open the properties dialog or applet for your pointing device to verify the correct detection.

SYMPTOM 25-18   **When installing a three- or four-button PS/2 pointing device on a laptop with its own pointing device, the new device only shows up as a two-button mouse**   There are several possible solutions to this issue depending on what laptop and pointing device you're using. Try disabling the internal pointing device. Some systems may require that you disable the internal pointing device first (usually through the CMOS Setup) in order to detect a new pointing device on the external mouse port. You may also wish to contact the system manufacturer to see if there is a BIOS update available, or any further information about using external pointing devices on the system.

SYMPTOM 25-19   **You receive a "KBC error" when connecting a pointing device to certain laptop PS/2 ports**   For example, this is a known compatibility issue between the Toshiba 400 series notebook and Logitech PS/2 "combo" pointing devices. These Toshiba systems have a single PS/2 connector on the back that may accept either a mouse or keyboard, and the problem is caused by a BIOS oversight. Toshiba has a BIOS upgrade that resolves this issue. (Version v.5.40 or later can be obtained by contacting Toshiba America.) If a BIOS upgrade is not available, you may connect the Logitech "combo" pointing device to the serial port instead (use only Logitech adapters).

SYMPTOM 25-20   **After installing the applets for your pointing device, you receive an "0E Exception" error on a blue screen**   You may also find that you can press ENTER and still access Windows, but this error appears on each boot. This problem is often encountered on IBM systems. IBM has found a problem with version 1.10 of their "TrackPoint" drivers. This error produces a blue screen on boot-up if the mouse drivers are changed. The work-around for this trouble is to uninstall the IBM TrackPoint software through the Add/Remove Programs icon in the Windows Control Panel. You may then need to reinstall the drivers for your new pointing device.

SYMPTOM 25-21   **The pointing device (or system) freezes when the system wakes from its suspend mode**   Many current mouse drivers have the ability to perform a search for mice when a system wakes from its suspend mode. (For Windows 98/Me, this is defined by a key in the Windows registry.) This registry setting defines the action that the driver will perform upon power management suspend/resume commands. If the mouse stops working after a resume, this parameter should be set to Off, as described next:

 Do not attempt to edit your registry without first creating a complete registry backup on your boot floppy disk. Incorrectly editing the registry may prevent the system from booting.

1.   Click Start and select Run.

2.   On the Open line, type **regedit.exe** and press ENTER.

3.   Click the plus (+) sign next to HKEY_LOCAL_MACHINE.

4.   Click the plus (+) sign next to SOFTWARE.

5.   Click the plus (+) sign next to your pointing device maker (for example, Logitech).

6.   Click the plus (+) sign next to the software name (for example, MouseWare).

7.   Click the plus (+) sign next to CurrentVersion.

8.   Single-click on the Technical folder, and information should be displayed on the right side of the registry editor screen.

9.   Under the Name column, double-click on the APMMode entry; an Edit String dialog should appear.

10.   Modify the Value Data line to read **Off**, and click the OK button. The full line should now read

    `HKEY_LOCAL_MACHINE\SOFTWARE\Logitech\MouseWare\CurrentVersion\Technical\APMMode="Off"`

11.   Exit the Registry Editor and restart your system. Then test the computer again to see if it resumes without freezing.

If you still experience APM issues, try uninstalling the mouse applet(s) using the Add/Remove Programs icon in the Control Panel. This will restore the system to the native drivers supplied by Windows. Now test your system again to see if it resumes correctly. If it still fails, try another mouse in the same port.

SYMPTOM 25-22   **When running a DOS program from Windows 98/Me, the mouse cursor moves very slowly compared to native Windows applications**   There are several possible issues to consider here. If the problem only occurs under one DOS application (and not in others), the problem may be with the particular application. You may need a patch or update for that application, or you may want to try installing the very latest mouse driver. Also try shutting down to DOS and running the program from the native DOS mode (rather than through a DOS window).

SYMPTOM 25-23   **The modem won't start after installing new mouse management software**   For example, this is a known problem when installing Logitech's MouseWare 6.60 or later under Windows 95. Sometimes the mouse drivers may detect the modem as a second mouse and try to initialize it. This can cause the modem to go into a busy state. However, you can prevent the mouse drivers from searching the serial port that the modem is using:

Do not attempt to edit your registry without first creating a complete registry backup on your boot floppy disk. Incorrectly editing the registry may prevent the system from booting.

1.   Download the current mouse driver for Windows 95.

2.   Edit the Windows 95 registry by clicking on the Start menu and selecting Run.

3.   Type **c:\windows\regedit.exe** on the Open line.

4.   Click OK. The registry editor will start.

5.   Double-click on the HKEY_LOCAL_MACHINE folder.

6.   Double-click on the SOFTWARE folder.

7.   Double-click on the manufacturer's folder (that is, Logitech).

8.   Double-click on the manufacturer's driver folder (that is, MouseWare).

9.   Double-click on the CurrentVersion folder.

10.   Click on the Global folder.

11.   Let's assume the mouse is on COM1 and the modem is on COM2. On the right side of the screen, there will be a list of value data strings. Double-click on the "PortSearchOrder" string. An Edit String dialog will appear. The Value Data line will read

        COM1, COM2

12.   Remove the space, the comma, and "COM2" so the line reads

        COM1

13.   If you only plan to use one mouse on the system, change the "MaximumDevices" Value Data line to "1" using the same steps as earlier. This will tell the driver to stop searching for additional mice after the primary mouse has been found.

If you are not using a serial mouse, remove "Serial" from the "SearchOrder" Value Data line so that no serial devices are searched for at all. In general, remove any reference to the port the modem is using.

14.   Click OK, and the values under the data value section on the right side of the screen should change. Exit the registry editor (saving is automatic). Shut down the computer and reboot from a cold start so that your changes can take effect.

SYMPTOM 25-24   **The mouse pointer moves only vertically**   The mouse is connected to a PS/2 port under Windows 95. If the mouse works along one axis but not the other, it's usually due to a hardware problem—the mouse either needs cleaning or repair. However, in some cases a software configuration problem can occur when the mouse driver (for example, Mouse Power v9.5) is installed on a system with plug-and-play BIOS running Windows 95, and the mouse is connected to the PS/2-style mouse port. As soon as you touch the mouse, the pointer darts over the right edge of the screen, and then will move only up and down.

 Do not attempt to edit your registry without first creating a complete registry backup on your boot floppy disk. Incorrectly editing the registry may prevent the system from booting.

1.   To regain control over your computer, reboot in Safe Mode.

2.   Click Start, then Run, then type **regedit**, and press ENTER.

3.   Open the HKEY_LOCAL_MACHINE\Enum folder and see if "BIOS" is listed under Enum. If it is, then you know the software configuration problem is causing the issue.

4.   Open HKEY_LOCAL_MACHINE\Enum\BIOS*PNP0F13, and look for a key (usually "05" or "07") under "*PNP0F13." Click on this key to highlight it. The key under "*PNP0F13" should now be highlighted, and the corresponding values should be displayed on the right side of the window. Note that there are "string values" with an "ab" icon next to them, and "binary values" with a "011" icon next to them.

5.   Compare your values to those shown next. Edit your entries until all your values shown on the screen match the values shown next:

```
ab  Class     "Mouse"
011 ConfigFlags 00 00 00 00
ab  DeviceDesc  "Mouse Systems v2.18"
ab  Driver      "Mouse\0000"
ab  HardwareID  "*PNP0F0C"
ab  Mfg         "Mouse Systems"
```

6.   Open HKEY_LOCAL_MACHINE\System\CurrentControlSet\Services\Class\Mouse. There should be multiple keys under Mouse (such as "0000" and "0001"). All but one are to be deleted. Carefully determine which one pertains to your current mouse (by looking at the values associated with each key), and delete all keys under Mouse except the related one.

7.   Make sure the one remaining key under Mouse is labeled "0000" (rename it if necessary).

8.   Click on the X box in the far upper-right corner of the registry editor to close it.

9.   Reboot the computer from a cold start. The computer should reboot in normal mode, and the problem with the mouse and keyboard should be gone.

SYMPTOM 25-25   **The new serial mouse is not detected by Windows**   For example, Windows may not detect your serial PnP mouse, EasyBall, or IntelliMouse, and using the Add New Hardware wizard cannot correct the trouble. In virtually all cases, this occurs because the registry entries for your previous pointing device were not properly removed from the registry. This problem is known to occur with Microsoft, Microsoft-compatible, or Logitech mouse models. Try the following steps to work around the problem:

Do not attempt to edit your registry without first creating a complete registry backup on your boot floppy disk. Incorrectly editing the registry may prevent the system from booting.

1. Click Start, then Run, then type **regedit**, and press ENTER.

2. Locate and remove the following registry key:

    HKEY_LOCAL_MACHINE\System\CurrentControlSet\Services\Class\Mouse\<nnnn>

    where <nnnn> is an incremental four-digit number starting at 0000.

3. Locate and remove the following registry keys (if they exist):

    HKEY_LOCAL_MACHINE\Enum\Root\Mouse\<nnnn>

    where <nnnn> in an incremental four-digit number starting at 0000.

4. Locate and remove all registry keys under the following registry key (if they exist):

    HKEY_LOCAL_MACHINE\Enum\Serenum

5. Locate and remove the following registry key (if it exists):

    HKEY_LOCAL_MACHINE\Software\Logitech\Mouseware

6. Right-click My Computer, and then click Properties.

7. On the Device Manager tab, click each serial pointing device, and then click Remove.

8. Click OK and restart Windows.

9. When you restart Windows, the attached pointing device is detected, and the appropriate drivers should be installed.

SYMPTOM 25-26   **USB pointing devices do not work in Safe Mode**   After you try to start your computer in Safe Mode, your computer may not respond to any keyboard commands, or you may receive an error message such as "Windows did not detect a mouse attached to a computer. You can safely attach a serial mouse now." The problem occurs if you're using a USB keyboard or mouse, but your system BIOS does not support USB devices in the real mode. Windows 98 and Windows 95 do not support the use of a USB keyboard or mouse in Safe Mode or in real mode unless the computer's BIOS supports these devices. To work around this problem, use a standard keyboard or mouse instead of a USB keyboard or mouse. To correct the trouble permanently, upgrade the motherboard's BIOS to a version that provides real-mode USB support.

SYMPTOM 25-27   **The serial mouse is not listed in the Device Manager under Windows Me**   After installing Windows Me (or exchanging the pointing device), the mouse is not listed in Device Manager—though it works correctly. Even clicking Refresh in the Device Manager will not update the device listing for the mouse. In most cases, you will need to force legacy hardware detection:

1. Click Start, click Settings, and then click Control Panel.

2. Double-click the Add New Hardware wizard.

3. In the first wizard window that opens, click Next.

4. Click Next again to search for plug-and-play (PnP)–compatible devices.

5. After the PnP search is finished, click Yes, and then click Next. Windows then detects hardware that is not PnP compatible.

6.   After the hardware detection is complete, click Finish to quit the Add New Hardware wizard.

7.   Reboot the system if necessary, and recheck the Device Manager to see that the pointing device is listed.

SYMPTOM 25-28   **A Logitech MouseMan is misidentified under Windows Me**   For example, when you install a pointing device such as a Logitech MouseMan (Wheelmouse) under Windows Me, it is identified as a Microsoft IntelliMouse. This occurs because the PnP identification reported by the Logitech mouse is identical to the information provided by the IntelliMouse. You can work around this problem by installing Logitech MouseWare 8.3 and setting up the mouse as a Wheelmouse2 (PS/2) in Device Manager. However, if the mouse is removed and redetected, Windows Me automatically defaults to the Microsoft IntelliMouse drivers. To correct this problem permanently, check with Logitech to see if a new INF file is available for the mouse. If Logitech obtains its own vendor ID information and incorporates that into an updated INF, the mouse can be uniquely identified and installed with the correct drivers.

SYMPTOM 25-29   **The USB mouse causes the web browser's "Back" button to go back two pages**   This is known to occur under Windows 98/Me. When you click the left button on a USB mouse once to use the Back button of Internet Explorer, IE goes back two web pages when it should go back just one page. In virtually all cases, the trouble is caused by an older version of the mouse software (or selecting the incorrect mouse when installing the mouse drivers). For example, you can see this problem when installing or using an older version of Microsoft IntelliPoint software, or by selecting the incorrect mouse when first installing the Microsoft IntelliPoint software. You will need to remove the older software and reinstall the newer software:

1.   Click Start, highlight Settings, and then click Control Panel.

2.   In Control Panel, double-click the Add/Remove Programs wizard.

3.   Click the Install/Uninstall tab, click the mouse software (such as Microsoft IntelliPoint), and then click the Add/Remove button.

4.   When prompted, restart the computer.

5.   Reinstall the mouse software (for example, IntelliPoint), and choose the correct mouse.

SYMPTOM 25-30   **The mouse pointer moves erratically when pointer speed is set high**   This is a known issue with Windows Me when the mouse pointer speed is set above level 5 and the mouse is moved rapidly. The best way to correct this trouble is to open the Mouse Properties dialog, select the Pointers Options tab, and adjust the pointer movement to level 5 or lower.

Further Study

Genius   www.genius-kye.com/
Logitech   www.logitech.com
Microsoft   www.microsoft.com
Mitsumi   www.mitsumi.com
Mouse Systems   www.mousesystems.com/
Mouse Trak   www.mousetrak.com/
No Hands Mouse   www.footmouse.com/

26

MODEMS AND FAX CARDS

Long before computers ever became *personal*, the mainframe and minicomputers of the 1960s and 1970s needed to communicate over large geographic distances—sometimes across town, sometimes around the world. Designers faced the problem of wiring the computers together—stringing a cable across even a few miles represents a serious logistical challenge. Instead of installing a network of *new* cabling, computer designers realized that they already had a sophisticated, worldwide wiring system in place: the *public switched telephone network* (PSTN). By enabling one computer to "call" another and exchange data, computers could communicate over telephone lines anywhere a telephone jack is available (or even using cellular facilities).

Of course, computers cannot work *directly* on your telephone line. The digital information processed by computers must be translated (or *modulated*) into audible sounds that are carried across telephone lines to a remote location. The sound signals coming from the telephone lines must be converted back into digital information (or *demodulated*) for the computer. A device called a MOdulator/DEModulator (MODEM, or commonly "modem") performs this continuous process of modulation and demodulation between a computer and telephone line. As the number of personal computers has grown into the millions, the demand for faster and more reliable modem communication has resulted in impressive speed and performance. Today's modems have also enabled entirely new developments such as facsimile and voice-over-data capabilities. This chapter is intended to explain the operations, standards, and connections of today's modems as well as to provide you with a compendium of modem symptoms and solutions.

Modem Construction and Operation

In order to know how a modem works (and what to do when things go wrong), you should be familiar with the typical sections of a modem circuit. Most modems today can be fabricated with only a few specialized chips and discrete parts, and virtually all computer communication systems contain the same essential parts. First, data must be translated from parallel into serial form and back again. Serial data being transmitted must be converted into an audio signal, then placed on an ordinary telephone circuit. Audio signals received from the telephone line must be separated from transmitted signals, then converted back into serial data. All of these activities must take place under the direction of a controller circuit. Finally, a modem uses nonvolatile RAM (NVRAM) to maintain a lengthy list of setup parameters (or *S registers*). For the purposes of this book, there are two types of modems: internal and external.

INTERNAL MODEMS

The *internal* modem is fabricated as a stand-alone board that plugs directly into an ISA or PCI expansion bus. You can see each major modem function detailed in the block diagram of Figure 26-1. The internal modem contains its own *universal asynchronous receiver/transmitter* (UART)—it is the UART that is responsible for manipulating data into and out of serial form. A UART forms the foundation of a serial port, and its improper setting in installation of the modem can cause a serious hardware conflict for your PC. When installing an internal modem, be sure that the IRQ line and I/O address chosen for the UART "serial port" do not conflict with other serial ports (a.k.a. COM ports) already in the system. It may be necessary to disable conflicting ports.

Before being transmitted over telephone lines, serial data must be converted into audio signals. A *modulator* circuit carries out this process. The modulated audio is then coupled to the telephone line using a circuit very similar to that used by ordinary telephones to couple voice signals. Audio signals pass through a single RJ11-type (*telephone jack*) connector at the rear of the modem to the telephone line. (Many modems provide a second RJ11 jack for a telephone—this allows you to check the line and make calls while the modem is idle.) Signals received from the telephone line must be translated back into serial data. The *telephone interface* separates received signals and passes them to the *demodulator*. After demodulation, the resulting serial data is passed to the UART, which in turn converts the serial bits into parallel words that are placed on the system's data bus.

Besides combining and separating modulated audio data, the telephone interface generates the dual-tone multi-frequency (DTMF) dialing signals needed to reach a remote modem—in much the same way as a touch-tone telephone works. When a remote modem dials in, the telephone interface detects the incoming ring and alerts the UART to begin negotiating a connection. Finally, the telephone interface drives

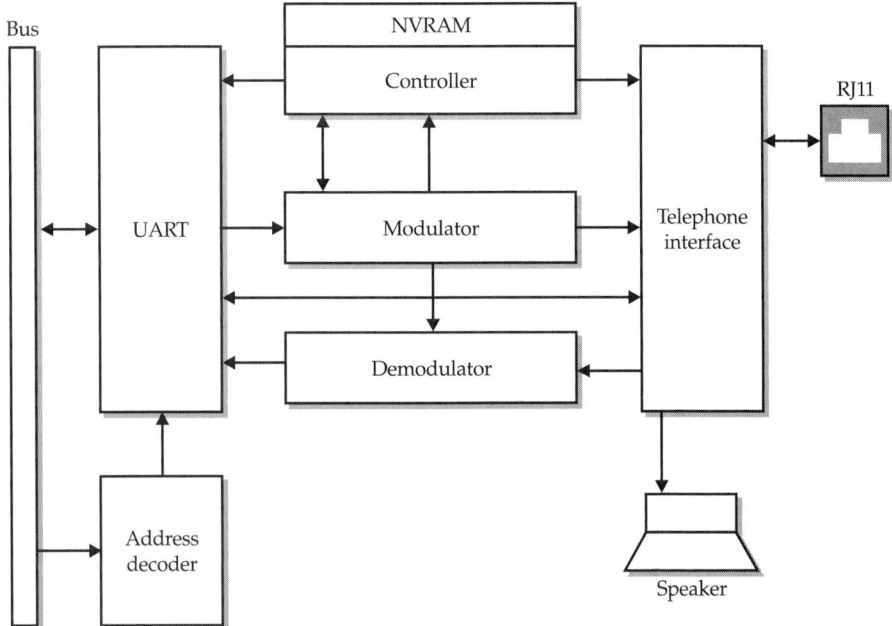

FIGURE 26-1   Basic block diagram of an internal modem

a small speaker. During the first stages of modem operation, the speaker is often used to hear a dial tone, dialing signals, and audio negotiation between the two modems (that high-pitched squeal that we normally associate with fax or modem connections). Once a connection is established, the speaker is usually disabled.

A *controller* circuit manages the overall operation of the modem, but, in a more general sense, it switches the modem between its *control* and *data* operating modes. The controller accepts commands from the modulator that allow modem characteristics and operating parameters to be changed. In the event of power loss or reset conditions, default modem parameters can be loaded from NVRAM. Permanent changes to modem parameters are stored in NVRAM.

EXTERNAL MODEMS

For all intents and purposes, the *external* modem provides virtually all of the essential functions offered by an internal modem. As you can see by the block diagram of Figure 26-2, many of the external functions are identical to those of an internal modem. The major difference between modems is that the external modem does *not* include a built-in UART to provide the serial port. Instead, the external modem relies on an existing serial port (or COM port) already configured in the PC. A 9-pin or 25-pin serial cable connects the PC serial port to the modem. This often makes external modem setup faster and easier than internal modems, since you need not worry about interrupt lines and I/O address settings—hardware conflicts are rare with external modems.

The other practical difference in an external modem is the way it is powered. Where internal modems are powered directly from the expansion bus, external modems must be powered from a small AC adapter (or batteries). In locations where AC outlets are scarce, this may be a problem. On the plus side, external modems provide a series of signal status LEDs. The LEDs allow you to easily check the state of serial communications.

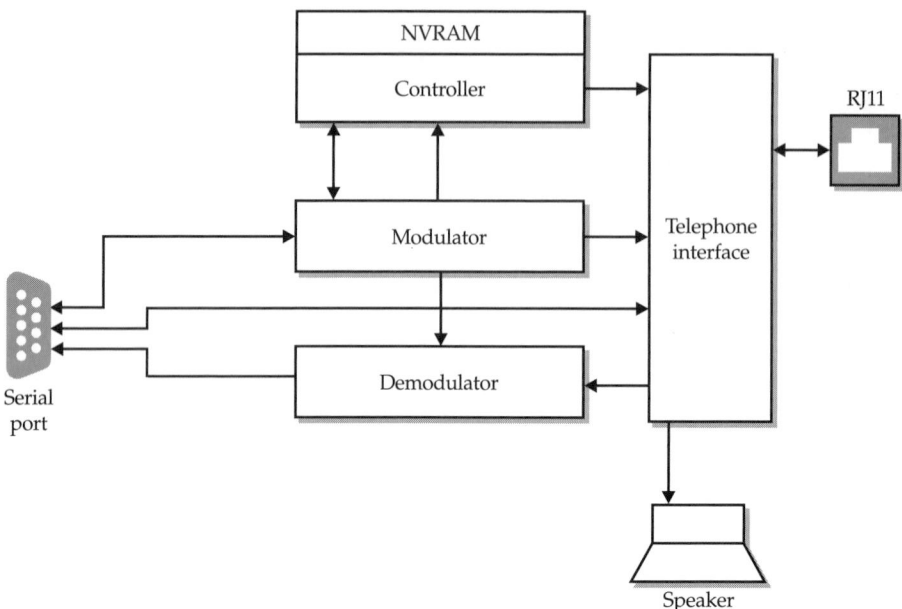

FIGURE 26-2   Basic block diagram of an external modem

ADVANCED MODEM FEATURES

Today's modems do far more than just exchange data between computers. There are myriad advanced features built into current modems that you should be aware of—a few of the more notable advancements are listed next.

x2 Technology

Although the term "x2" is trademarked by US Robotics, x2 is often used generically to refer to high-speed modem technology employed for early 56 Kbps modems. The x2 technology was a relatively early protocol developed for 56 Kbps downloads from the Internet, corporate networks, and online services over regular phone lines. While x2 doesn't support 56 Kbps uploads or 56 Kbps transfers between modems, it does offer a powerful enhancement for PC users seeking more speed from the Internet or other online services. You need three elements to support x2 at 56 Kbps downloads: an ISP or other remote "x2 compatible" modem at the server, an analog loop between your home/office and the local central office, and an x2 modem (such as a US Robotics Sportster). However, x2 technology is very sensitive to telephone line issues, and it must have close to ideal conditions to achieve top-speed downloads. When uploading or communicating with other modems, an x2 modem typically runs at 28.8 Kbps.

K56flex

Lucent Technologies and Rockwell Semiconductor Systems co-authored the K56flex protocol, which allows Lucent's and Rockwell's modem chip sets to interoperate. Lucent Technologies and Rockwell had to introduce their own version of 56 Kbps-capable technology in order to remain competitive. Their version was named *K56flex* and was *not* compatible with x2 modems at speeds over 33.6 Kbps. Internet Service Providers wanting to provide 56 Kbps support had to choose between these two competing technologies.

Users desiring high-speed access had to first check with their ISP to determine which version was implemented at the provider's end, then purchase a compatible modem. All this was happening even while the ITU was in the process of finalizing a universal standard for 56 Kbps (now dubbed V.90—formerly called V.pcm).

K56flex technology uses a pure digital "downstream" connection to achieve its high-speed data transfer to your computer. In this way, K56flex technology is different from other modem technologies because the "downstream" data is digitally encoded instead of modulated. This method of data transfer eliminates one analog loop, lowers noise levels, and allows the higher transmission rates. This is an *asymmetrical* technique, so "upstream" transmissions (mostly keystroke and mouse commands from your computer, which require less bandwidth) continue to flow at the slower V.34 rate. The upstream direction remains slower because an analog to digital conversion must still be made at the client end.

In order to maintain sales (and alleviate customer's fears of buying a modem that would shortly become obsolete), all modem manufacturers try to guarantee that their modems would be upgradable through a software patch (a "firmware" upgrade) to meet almost any universal standard. If it turned out that the modem could *not* be upgraded through software, the modem would have to be replaced. Both the firmware and replacement options are provided at no cost to the consumer.

V.90

The finalized ITU standard for 56 Kbps modem transmission speeds was introduced in February of 1998. The working name of this standard was *V.pcm* (pulse code modulation) with a final release name of *V.90*. This standard continues to enable high-speed downstream data transfers by digitally encoding all downstream data. Upstream transmissions continue to run at the conventional rates of up to 33.6 Kbps (that is, upstream data—data sent from your modem—is sent as an analog signal that mirrors the V.34 standard).

Since the existing telephone network infrastructure cannot support data speeds faster than 56 Kbps, V.90 and V.92 (which added a few tweaks) will almost certainly be the *final* analog modem speed standards. Analysts predict that modem sales will grow to about 75 million modems sold per year, and almost all of these will be V.90. In order to support higher data transfer speeds, computer users will need to move to more performance-oriented communication technologies such as *cable modem* and *digital subscriber line* (DSL) services.

DSVD

In addition to simply sending and receiving data, some modern modems incorporate a feature called *dual simultaneous voice and data* (or DSVD). The modem can carry your analog voice as well as computer data. In effect, the modem becomes a "speakerphone" able to transfer real-time voice and data at the same time (though the bandwidth needed to transfer voice information reduces the available bandwidth for data transfers). Note that the DSVD feature can be used only between two DSVD modems. To use DSVD, you need a soundboard with a microphone (to digitize your voice) as well as a set of speakers (to play the voice from the other end). DSVD has found a small but powerful niche among online computer gamers who wish to communicate in real-time as they play.

Voice Mail

Some modern modems are providing advanced voice mail features that essentially allow the modem (and PC) to serve as an intelligent answering machine or digital information system. When installed and configured properly, voice mail allows you to create mailboxes, record voice greetings/announcements for each mailbox, record messages to each mailbox, access each mailbox remotely, and even support "fax-on-demand." Voice mail features are particularly popular with small businesses or small-office home-office (SOHO) environments looking to automate messaging and information distribution.

Autodetection/Auto-Switching

Virtually all current modems can detect the difference between a voice call, a modem call, and an incoming fax. The modem can then inform the system of the call and automatically employ the proper software tools to record the voice message (used with voice mail systems), start BBS or other electronic messaging software to communicate with the calling modem (ideal for remote access software), or record the fax image to the hard drive.

Distinctive Ring

Many local phone service areas now support the *distinctive ring* feature that allows several phone numbers to be assigned to the same *physical* telephone line—each assigned number rings with a different ringing pattern (called a *cadence*). Modems that are compatible with distinctive ring can be placed on the same physical phone line with other devices, but will answer only when a certain ringing pattern is detected.

Caller ID

Modern modems are also able to detect the caller's originating telephone number, which is transmitted to the receiving end of the communications link. In its simplest form, *caller ID* simply provides an onscreen display of the caller's telephone number (used most often when you're receiving calls with the modem in "speakerphone" mode). In its most enhanced form, database software can trap the caller ID number, then automatically pull up contact information, notes of past phone conversations, or a wide range of other caller-related information. This is an ideal feature for sales or help desk services.

Modem on Hold

This feature is found in the latest dial-up V.90/V.92 modems intended to integrate the suite of calling services from your local phone company, such as Call Waiting, Caller ID, and Voice Mail services. The modem software will alert you to incoming calls while you're online and tell you who is calling in a small popup dialog. If you choose to take the call, the modem *suspends* your online session during your conversation and lets you resume it afterwards *without* redialing. If you ignore the call, it will be routed to your voice mail (available through most local phone companies today).

Quick Connect

During dial-up connections, a modem usually has to test the line conditions in order to learn the best connection available. A quick connect feature reduces the time it takes to make a connection to your service provider. The modem remembers the line conditions from the previous connection, so it can bypass portions of its negotiation sequence and get you online faster.

V.pcm Upstream

Even though V.90 communication allows for downstream data transfers up to about 56 Kbps, the upstream transfers rarely exceed 28 Kbps. V.pcm technology allows the modem's upstream communication to reach much faster speeds of 48 Kbps. You choose whether to maintain the fastest possible downstream speed or to balance your connection for somewhat slower downstream (but faster upstream) communication.

ISDN Modems

Integrated Services Digital Network (or ISDN) technology is a system of digital phone connection that has been available for over a decade. The ISDN system allows data to be transmitted in purely *digital* form. Since ISDN is completely digital, data transfers can be extremely fast—up to 128 Kbps. There are two basic types of ISDN service: the *Basic Rate Interface* (BRI), and the *Primary Rate Interface* (PRI). BRI consists of two 64 Kbps "B" channels and one 16 Kbps "D" channel for a total of 144 Kbps. This basic service is intended to meet the needs of most individual users.

For a Basic Rate Interface ISDN line equipped with two B channels, one (or both) of the 64 Kbps B channels are connected in a virtual permanent circuit. Home and business users who install ISDN adapters in place of their modems can see complex graphic Web pages arriving very quickly (up to 128 Kbps). ISDN requires adapters at *both* ends of the transmission, so your Internet service provider also needs an ISDN adapter. To access BRI service, it's necessary to subscribe to an ISDN phone line. The customer must also be within 18,000 feet (about 3.4 miles or 5.5 km) of the telephone company's central office for BRI service—beyond that, expensive repeater devices are required, or ISDN service may not be available at all. Customers will also need special equipment to communicate with the phone company switch and with other ISDN devices. These devices include ISDN Terminal Adapters (sometimes called "ISDN Modems," though that is technically incorrect) and ISDN Routers. ISDN is generally available from your phone company in most urban areas in the United States and Europe.

DSL Modems

The *Digital Subscriber Line* (called DSL, ADSL, or xDSL) is the next generation of PC communication technology that allows for the transmission of voice, video, and data over existing copper telephone lines at very high speeds. DSL provides dedicated bandwidth that can be up to 143 times faster than a 56 Kbps modem, and 62 times faster than ISDN. DSL uses your ordinary phone line, but doesn't tie it up—you can access the Internet while you're using the same phone line for a conversation (or faxing) in addition to the permanent Internet connection.

The copper telephone lines are often referred to as the *local loop*—that last mile from the telephone company's central office (CO) to the end-user's home or business.

There are several variations of DSL technologies, but the best known of these technologies are *Asymmetric Digital Subscriber Line* (ADSL) and *ADSL Lite* (dubbed "Splitterless ADSL," "Universal ADSL," or "G.lite"). Standard ADSL service is often referred to as "Full Rate ADSL" or "G.dmt," and is now also known by the ITU standard *G.992.1*. This supports up to 8 Mbps bandwidth downstream and up to 1 Mbps upstream. The asymmetrical aspect of ADSL technology makes it ideal for Internet/Intranet surfing, video-on-demand, and remote local area network (LAN) access, since these users typically download more information than they send. ADSL requires a voice/data splitter—commonly called a *POTS Splitter* (for "Plain Old Telephone Service")—to be installed at the consumer's home or business location. This device separates voice from data transmissions. For simultaneous use of the telephone and data access, additional phone wires may need to be installed at the location. Full Rate ADSL supports service up to a maximum range of 18,000 feet (about 3.4 miles or 5.5 km) from the telephone company's central office to the end-user.

ADSL Lite technology does *not* require a POTS splitter to be installed at the consumer's home or business, but its performance is slower. ADSL Lite provides a downstream bandwidth up to 1.5 Mbps and an upstream bandwidth up to 512 Kbps. It also supports service up to a maximum range of 18,000 feet (about 3.4 miles or 5.5 km) from the central office. ADSL Lite has also been approved as a separate standard by the ITU.

With DSL, telephone companies are competing with cable companies and their cable modem services, and it is thought that quite a few telephone companies will replace their ISDN services with DSL in most areas. Consequently, ADSL services (and other forms of DSL) are expected to become more widely available in 2002 and beyond.

WinModems

Over the last few years, the PC industry has seen a trend away from conventional hardware fax/modem devices and toward simpler, less expensive software modems (dubbed *Windows Modems* or *WinModems*). A hardware-based modem (such as a fax/modem) contains a *controller*, *data pump*, and *phone network circuit*—all integrated into the hardware of the modem device itself. The host computer simply sends data to the modem, and the modem does the rest. By comparison, a software modem eliminates both the controller and data pump portions of a modem and relies on the host computer's CPU to handle those functions instead. As a result, WinModems are the simplest and least expensive modem type (generally found in low-end PCs), but they make the greatest demands on system processing power.

It is important for you to realize that most modern WinModem designs are quite reliable, but they will work *only* under Windows 9x/Me and other operating systems supported by the WinModem drivers. If you use DOS programs that require modem access, you'll need to replace the WinModem with a conventional fax/modem device.

MODEM COMMANDS

Modems used to be "dumb" devices. It was almost impossible for them to do things like answer the ringing telephone line, dial a number, set speaker volume, and so on. Hayes Microcomputer Products developed a product called a *Smartmodem* that accepted high-level commands in the form of ASCII text strings. This was dubbed the *Hayes AT command set* (now simply called the *AT command set*), and it has been the de-facto standard for modem commands since its inception. As a consequence, virtually every modem that is *Hayes-compatible* is capable of using the AT command set. Ultimately, the AT commands go a long way to simplifying the interface between a modem and communication software. Table 26-1 provides an extensive index of the AT commands—this resource can be particularly helpful when trying to interpret command strings.

> Settings with an underline (such as F0) are the default settings for an entry.

Interpreting Commands

Virtually all AT command strings start with the prefix "AT" (attention). For example, the command string **ATZE1Q0V1** contains five separate commands: attention (**AT**), reset the modem to its power-up defaults (**Z**), enable the command echo to send command characters back to the sender (**E1**), send command result codes back to the PC (**Q0**), and select text result codes, which causes words to be used as result codes (**V1**).

TABLE 26-1 GENERAL INDEX OF THE AT COMMAND SET	
BASIC AT COMMANDS	
(A/)	Repeat Last Command
(A)	Answer
(Bx)	CCITT or Bell Modulation
B0	CCITT operation at 300 or 1200 bps
B1	BELL operation at 300 or 1200 bps
B2	V.23 originate mode: receive 1200 bps, transmit 75 bps; answer mode: receive 75 bps, transmit 1200 bps
B3	V.23 originate mode: receive 75 bps, transmit 1200 bps; answer mode: receive 1200 bps, transmit 75 bps
B15	Selects V.21 when the modem is at 300 bits/s
B16	Selects Bell 103J when the modem is at 300 bits/s (default)
(Cx)	Carrier Control. The modem will accept the C1 command without error in order to assure backward compatibility with communications software that issues the C1 command. The C0 command may instruct some modems not to send carrier (that is, it puts them in a receive-only mode).
C0	Transmit carrier always off
C1	Normal transmit carrier switching

TABLE 26-1   GENERAL INDEX OF THE AT COMMAND SET *(CONTINUED)*

BASIC AT COMMANDS

(Dx) Dial. The valid dial string parameters are described next. Punctuation characters may be used for clarity, with parentheses, hyphen, and spaces being ignored:

0-9 DTMF digits. The numbers 0 to 9

The "star" digit (tone dialing only)

The "pound" digit (tone dialing only)

! Flash. The modem will go on-hook for a time defined by the value of S29

, Dial pause. The modem will pause for a time specified by S8 before dialing the digits following ","

; Return to command state. Added to the end of a dial string, this causes the modem to return to the command state after it processes the portion of the dial string preceding the ";". This allows the user to issue additional AT commands while remaining off-hook. The additional AT commands may be placed in the original command line following the ";" or may be entered on subsequent command lines. The modem will enter call progress only after an additional dial command is issued without the ";" terminator. Use "H" to abort the dial in progress and go back on-hook.

^ Enable calling tone. Applicable to current dial attempt only. The calling tone is a 1800 Hz tone every three to four seconds that alerts recipient of automatic calling equipment (as defined in CCITT V.25).

> Ground pulse. If enabled by country specific parameter, the modem will generate a grounding pulse on the EARTH relay output.

@ Wait for silence. The modem will wait for at least five seconds of silence in the call progress frequency band before continuing with the next dial string parameter. If the modem does not detect these five seconds of silence before the expiration of the call abort timer (S7), the modem will terminate the call attempt with a NO ANSWER message. If busy detection is enabled, the modem may terminate the call with the BUSY result code. If answer tone arrives during execution of this parameter, the modem handshakes.

$ List. Displays a list of dial commands or "Bong Tone" detection.

A-D DTMF letters A, B, C, and D

J Fastest speed. Perform MNP 10 link negotiation at the highest supported speed for this call only.

K Power adjustment. Enable power level adjustment during MNP 10 link negotiation for this call only.

L Re-dial last number. The modem will re-dial the last valid telephone number. This command must be used immediately after the "D" with all the following characters ignored.

P Select pulse dialing. Pulse dial the numbers that follow until a "T" is encountered. Affects current and subsequent dialing.

R Delay. This command will cause the modem to wait 10 seconds after dialing then go into answer mode. This command must be placed at the end of the dial string.

T Select tone dialing. Tone dial the numbers that follow until a "P" is encountered. Affects current and subsequent dialing.

W Wait for dial tone. The modem will wait for a dial tone before dialing the digits following "W". If no dial tone is detected within the time specified by S6, the modem will abort the rest of the sequence, return on-hook, and generate an error message.

(Ex) Command Echo

E0 Disables command echo
E1 Enables command echo

(Fx) Select Line Modulation

F0 Selects autodetect mode—all connect speeds are possible
F1 Selects V.21 or Bell 103 according to the "B" setting
F2 Not supported (some modems use this setting for 600 bps)
F3 Originator is at 75 bps and answerer is at 1200 bps
F4 Selects V.22 1200 bps or Bell 212A according to the "B" setting
F5 Selects V.22bis as the only acceptable line modulation
F6 Select V.32bis 4800 bps or V.32 4800 bps as the only acceptable line modulation
F7 Selects V.32bis 7200 bps as the only acceptable line modulation

TABLE 26-1 GENERAL INDEX OF THE AT COMMAND SET *(CONTINUED)*

BASIC AT COMMANDS

F8 Selects V.32bis 9600 bps or V.32 9600 bps as the only acceptable line modulation
F9 Selects V.32bis 12,000 bps as the only acceptable line modulation
F10 Selects V.32bis 14,400 bps as the only acceptable line modulation

(Hx) Disconnect [Hangup]

H0 The modem will release the line if the modem is currently online and will terminate any test (AT&T) that is in progress.
H1 If on-hook, the modem will go off-hook and enter command mode. The modem will return on-hook after a period of time determined by S7.

(Ix) Identification

I0 Reports product code
I1 Reports pre-computed checksum from ROM
I2 Modem will respond OK
I3 Reports firmware revision
I4 Reports modem identifier string
I5 Reports Country Code parameter (for example, "022")
I6 Reports modem data pump model and internal code revision

(Lx) Speaker Volume

L0 Low speaker volume
L1 Low speaker volume
L2 Medium speaker volume
L3 High speaker volume

(Mx) Speaker Control

M0 Speaker is always off.
M1 Speaker is on during call establishment, but off when receiving carrier.
M2 Speaker is always on.
M3 Speaker is off when receiving carrier and during dialing, but on during answering.

(Nx) Automode Enable

N0 Automode detection is disabled
N1 Automode detection is enabled

(Ox) Return to OnLine Data Mode

O0 Enters online data mode without a retrain
O1 Enters online data mode with a retrain before returning to online data mode
O3-14 Forces the modem to a new rate that is user defined (defined in S62)

(P) Set Pulse Dial Default

(Qx) Quiet Results Codes

Q0 Enables result codes to the DTE
Q1 Disables result codes to the DTE

(Sn) Read/Write S-Registers

n=v Sets S-register "n" to the value "v"
n? Reports the value of S-register "n"

(T) Set Tone Dial Default

(Vx) Result Code Form

V0 Enables short-form (terse) result codes
V1 Enables long-form (verbose) result codes

(Wx) Error Correction Message Control

W0 Upon connection, the modem reports only the DTE speed.

TABLE 26-1   GENERAL INDEX OF THE AT COMMAND SET *(CONTINUED)*

BASIC AT COMMANDS

W1 Upon connection, the modem reports the line speed, the error correction protocol, and the DTE speed respectively.
W2 Upon connection, the modem reports the DCE speed.

(Xx) Extended Result Codes

X0 Sends only OK, CONNECT, RING, NO CARRIER, ERROR, and NO ANSWER result codes
X1 Sends only OK, CONNECT, RING, NO CARRIER, ERROR, NO ANSWER, and CONNECT XXXX
X2 Sends only OK, CONNECT, RING, NO CARRIER, ERROR, NO DIAL TONE, NO ANSWER, and CONNECT XXXX
X3 Sends only OK, CONNECT, RING, NO CARRIER, ERROR, NO ANSWER, CONNECT XXXX, and BUSY
X4 Enables monitoring of busy tones; sends all messages

(Yx) Long Space Disconnect

Y0 Disables long space disconnect
Y1 Enables long space disconnect

(Zx) Soft Reset and Restore Profile

Z0 Soft reset and restore stored profile 0
Z1 Soft reset and restore stored profile 1

AT "&" COMMANDS

(&Bx) Autoretrain

&B0 Hang up on a poor received signal
&B1 Retrain on a poor received signal; hang up if the condition persists
&B2 Do not hang up; do not retrain (that is, tolerate any line)

(&Cx) RLSD (DCD) Option

&C0 RLSD remains ON at all times
&C1 RLSD follows the state of the carrier

(&Dx) DTR Option

&D0 DTR drop is interpreted according to the current &Q setting as follows:
(&Q0, 5, 6)   DTR is ignored (assumed ON). Allows operation with DTEs that don't provide DTR.
(&Q1, 4)   DTR drop causes the modem to hang up; auto-answer is not affected.
(&Q2, 3)   DTR drop causes the modem to hang up; auto-answer is inhibited.

&D1 DTR drop is interpreted according to the current &Q setting as follows:
(&Q0, 1, 4, 5, 6)   DTR drop is interpreted by the modem as if the asynchronous escape sequence had been entered. The modem returns to asynchronous command state without disconnecting.
(&Q2, 3)   DTR drop causes the modem to hang up; auto-answer is inhibited.

&D2 DTR drop is interpreted according to the current &Q setting as follows:
(&Q0-6)   DTR drop causes the modem to hang up; auto-answer is inhibited.

&D3 DTR drop is interpreted according to the current &Q setting as follows:
(&Q0, 1, 4, 5, 6)   DTR drop causes the modem to perform a soft reset as if the "Z" command were received. The &Y setting determines which profile is loaded.
(&Q2, 3)   DTR drop causes the modem to hang up; auto-answer is inhibited.

(&Fx) Restore Factory Configuration

&F0 Restore factory configuration 0
&F1 Restore factory configuration 1

(&Gx) Select Guard Tone

&G0 Disables Guard Tone
&G1 Disables Guard Tone
&G2 Selects 1800 Hz guard tone

TABLE 26-1 **GENERAL INDEX OF THE AT COMMAND SET** *(CONTINUED)*

AT "&" COMMANDS

(&Hn)	Sets Transmit Data (TD) flow control (see also &Rn)
&H0	Flow control disabled
&H1	Hardware flow control; Clear to Send (CTS) (default)
&H2	Software flow control, XON/XOFF
&H3	Hardware and software flow control
(&In)	Sets Receive Data (RD) software flow control (see also &Rn)
&I0	Software flow control disabled (default)
&I1	XON/XOFF signals to your modem and remote system
&I2	XON/XOFF signals to your modem only
(&Jx)	Telephone Jack Type
&J0	RJ11 telephone jack
&J1	RJ12 or RJ13 telephone jack
(&Kx)	Flow Control
&K0	Disables flow control
&K3	Enables RTS/CTS flow control
&K4	Enables XON/XOFF flow control
&K5	Enables transparent XON/XOFF flow control
&K6	Enables both RTS/CTS and XON/XOFF flow control
(&Lx)	Dial Up/Lease Line Option
&L0	Dial line
&L1	Leased line
(&Mx)	Asynchronous/Synchronous Mode Selection
&M0	Selects direct asynchronous operation
&M1	Selects synchronous connect mode with asynchronous offline command mode
&M2	Selects synchronous connect mode with asynchronous offline command mode
&M3	Selects synchronous connect mode
&M4	Hayes AutoSync mode
(&Nn)	Sets connect speed
&N0	Variable rate (default)
&N1	300 bps
&N2	1200 bps
&N3	2400 bps
&N4	4800 bps
&N5	7200 bps
&N6	9600 bps
&N7	12,000 bps
&N8	14,400 bps
&N9	16,800 bps
&N10	19,200 bps
&N11	21,600 bps
&N12	24,000 bps
&N13	26,400 bps
&N14	28,800 bps
&N15	31,200 bps
&N16	33,600 bps
&N17	33,333 bps
&N18	37,333 bps
&N19	41,333 bps

TABLE 26-1   GENERAL INDEX OF THE AT COMMAND SET *(CONTINUED)*

AT "&" COMMANDS

&N20	42,666 bps
&N21	44,000 bps
&N22	45,333 bps
&N23	46,666 bps
&N24	48,000 bps
&N25	49,333 bps
&N26	50,666 bps
&N27	52,000 bps
&N28	53,333 bps
&N29	54,666 bps
&N30	56,000 bps
&N31	57,333 bps

(&Px) Dial Pulse Ratio

&P0 Make=39%, break=61% (at 10 pps for the US)
&P1 Make=33%, break=67% (at 10 pps for Europe)
&P2 Make=33%, break=67% (at 20 pps for Japan)

(&Qx) Sync/Async Mode

&Q0 Selects direct asynchronous operation
&Q1 Selects synchronous connect mode with async offline command mode
&Q2 Selects synchronous connect mode with async offline command mode
&Q3 Selects synchronous connect mode
&Q4 Selects AutoSync operation
&Q5 Modem will try to negotiate an error-corrected link
&Q6 Selects asynchronous operation in normal mode (speed buffering)
&Q8 MNP error control mode. If an MNP error control protocol is not established, the modem will fallback according to the current user setting in S36.
&Q9 V.42 or MNP error control mode. If neither error control protocol is established, the modem will fallback according to the current user setting in S36.

Starting AutoSync Set registers S19, S20, and S25 to the desired values before selecting AutoSync operation with &Q4. After the CONNECT message is issued, the modem waits the period of time specified by S25 before examining DTR. If DTR is on, the modem enters the synchronous operating state; if DTR is off, the modem terminates the line connection and returns to the asynchronous command state.

Stopping AutoSync AutoSync operation is stopped upon loss of carrier or the ON-to-OFF transition of DTR. Loss of carrier will cause the modem to return to the asynchronous command state. An ON-to-OFF transition of DTR will cause the modem to return to the asynchronous command state and either not terminate the line connection (&D1 active) or terminate the line connection (any other &Dn command active).

(&Rx) RTS/CTS Option

&R0 In Sync mode, CTS tracks the state of RTS; the RTS-to-CTS delay is defined by S26. In Async mode, CTS acts according to V.25bis handshake.
&R1 In Sync mode, CTS is always ON (RTS transitions are ignored). In Async, CTS will drop only if required by flow control.
&R2 Received data to computer only on RTS

(&Sx) DSR Override

&S0 DSR will remain ON at all times.
&S1 DSR will become active after answer tone has been detected and inactive after the carrier has been lost.

TABLE 26-1   GENERAL INDEX OF THE AT COMMAND SET *(CONTINUED)*

AT "&" COMMANDS

(&Tx)	Test and Diagnostics
&T0	Terminates the test in progress; clears S16
&T1	Initiates local analog loopback, V.54 Loop 3
&T2	Returns an ERROR message
&T3	Initiates local digital loopback, V.54 Loop 2
&T4	Enables digital loopback acknowledgment for remote request
&T5	Disables digital loopback acknowledgment for remote request
&T6	Initiates remote digital loopback
&T7	Remote digital with self-test and error detector
&T8	Initiates local analog loopback, V.54 Loop 3, with self-test
(&Un)	Sets floor connect speed
&U0	Disabled (the default)
&U1	300 bps
&U2	1200 bps
&U3	2400 bps
&U4	4800 bps
&U5	7200 bps
&U6	9600 bps
&U7	12,000 bps
&U8	14,400 bps
&U9	16,800 bps
&U10	19,200 bps
&U11	21,600 bps
&U12	24,000 bps
&U13	26,400 bps
&U14	28,800 bps
&U15	31,200 bps
&U16	33,600 bps
&U17	33,333 bps
&U18	37,333 bps
&U19	41,333 bps
&U20	42,666 bps
&U21	44,000 bps
&U22	45,333 bps
&U23	46,666 bps
&U24	48,000 bps
&U25	49,333 bps
&U26	50,666 bps
&U27	52,000 bps
&U28	53,333 bps
&U29	54,666 bps
&U30	56,000 bps
&U31	57,333 bps
(&Vx)	Display Current Configuration and Stored Profiles
&V0	View active file, stored profile 0, and stored phone numbers
&V1	View active file, stored profile 1, and stored phone numbers
(&Wx)	Store Current Configuration
&W0	Store the current configuration as profile 0
&W1	Store the current configuration as profile 1

TABLE 26-1 GENERAL INDEX OF THE AT COMMAND SET *(CONTINUED)*

AT "&" COMMANDS

(&Xx) Sync Transmit Clock Source Option

&X0 The modem generates the transmit clock.
&X1 The DTE generates the transmit clock.
&X2 The modem derives the transmit clock.

(&Yx) Designate a Default Reset Profile

&Y0 The modem will use profile 0.
&Y1 The modem will use profile 1.

(&ZL?) Displays the last executed dial string

(&Zn?) Displays the phone number stored at position "n" (n = 0-3)

(&Zn=x) Store Telephone Number

&Zn=x (n = 0 to 3, and x = dial string)

AT "%" COMMANDS

(%BAUD) Bit Rate Multiplier

(%Cx) Enable/Disable Data Compression

%C0 Disables data compression; resets S46 bit 1
%C1 Enables MNP 5 data compression negotiation; resets S46 bit 1
%C2 Enables V.42bis data compression; sets S46 bit 1
%C3 Enables both V.42bis and MNP 5 data compression; sets S46 bit 1

(%CCID) Enable Caller ID

(%CD) Carrier Detect Lamp

(%CDIA) Display last DIAG

(%CIDS) Store ID Numbers

(%CRID) Repeat Last ID

(%CSIG) Store SIG Numbers

(%CXID) XID Enable

(%Dx) V.42bis Dictionary Size

%D0 Dictionary set to 512
%D1 Dictionary set to 1024
%D2 Dictionary set to 2048
%D3 Dictionary set to 4096

(%Ex) Enable/Disable Line Quality Monitor and Auto-Retrain Fallback/Fall Forward

%E0 Disable line quality monitor and auto-retrain
%E1 Enable line quality monitor and auto-retrain
%E2 Enable line quality monitor and fallback/fall forward
%E3 Enable line quality monitor and auto-retrain, but hang-up when EQM reaches threshold

(%Gx) Auto Fall Forward/Fallback Enable

%G0 Disabled
%G1 Enabled

(%L) Line Signal Level

(%Mx) Compression Type

%M0 Compression disabled
%M1 Transmit compression only
%M2 Receive compression only
%M3 Two-way compression

(%P) Clear Encoder Dictionary

(%Q) Line Signal Quality

TABLE 26-1   GENERAL INDEX OF THE AT COMMAND SET *(CONTINUED)*

AT "%" COMMANDS

(%Sx)	Set Maximum String Length in V.42bis
(%SCBR)	Call Back Reference Outgoing Calls
(%SKEY)	Store Authentication Key Outgoing Call
(%SPRT)	Security Mode—Outgoing Calls
(%SPNP)	Serial Plug and Play Control
(%SPWD)	Password Outgoing Calls
(%SSPW)	Supervisor Password Outgoing Calls
(%SUID)	User ID Outgoing Calls
(%TTx)	PTT Testing Utilities
%TT00-%TT09	DTMF tone dial digits 0 to 9
%TT0A	DTMF digit *
%TT0B	DTMF digit A
%TT0C	DTMF digit B
%TT0D	DTMF digit C
%TT0E	DTMF digit #
%TT0F	DTMF digit D
%TT10	V.21 channel no. 1 mark (originate) symbol
%TT11	V.21 channel no. 2 mark symbol
%TT12	V.23 backward channel mark symbol
%TT13	V.23 forward channel mark symbol
%TT14	V.22 originate (call mark) signaling at 600 bps (NOT SUPPORTED)
%TT15	V.22 originate (call mark) signaling at 1200 bps
%TT16	V.22bis originate (call mark) signaling at 2400 bps
%TT17	V.22 answer signaling (guard tone if PTT required)
%TT18	V.22bis answer signaling (guard tone if required)
%TT19	V.21 channel no. 1 space symbol
%TT20	V.32 9600 bps
%TT21	V.32bis 14,400 bps
%TT1A	V.21 channel no. 2 space symbol
%TT1B	V.23 backward channel space symbol
%TT1C	V.23 forward channel space symbol
%TT30	Silence (online), that is, go off-hook
%TT31	V.25 answer tone
%TT32	1800 Hz guard tone
%TT33	V.25 calling tone (1300 Hz)
%TT34	Fax calling tone (1100 Hz)
%TT40	V.21 channel 2
%TT41	V.27ter 2400 bps
%TT42	V.27ter 4800 bps
%TT43	V.29 7200 bps
%TT44	V.29 9600 bps
%TT45	V.17 7200 bps long train
%TT46	V.17 7200 bps short train
%TT47	V.17 9600 bps long train
%TT48	V.17 9600 bps short train
%TT49	V.17 12,000 bps long train
%TT4A	V.17 12,000 bps short train
%TT4B	V.17 14,400 bps long train
%TT4C	V.17 14,400 bps short train

TABLE 26-1   GENERAL INDEX OF THE AT COMMAND SET *(CONTINUED)*

AT "\" COMMANDS

(\Ax)   Select Maximum MNP Block Size

\A0   64 characters
\A1   128 characters
\A2   192 characters
\A3   256 characters
\A4   Max 32 characters (for ETC-enhanced throughput cellular)

(\Bx)   Transmit Break to Remote

\B1-\B9   Break length in 100 mS units (default = 3—non-error–corrected mode only)

(\Cx)   Set Autoreliable Buffer

\C0   Does not buffer data
\C1   Buffers data on the answering modem for four seconds
\C2   Does not buffer data on the answering modem

(\Ex)   Optimize Local Echo

(\Gx)   Modem-to-Modem Flow Control (XON/XOFF)

\G0   Disables modem-to-modem XON/XOFF flow control
\G1   Enables modem-to-modem XON/XOFF flow control

(\Jx)   Constant DTE Speed Option

\J0   DCE and DTE rates are independent.
\J1   DTE rate adjusts to DCE connection rate after online.

(\Kx)   Break Control. If the modem receives a break from the DTE when the modem is operating in data transfer mode:

\K0   Enter online command mode, no break sent to the remote modem
\K1   Clear data buffers and send break to remote modem
\K2   Same as **\K0**
\K3   Send break to remote modem immediately
\K4   Same as **\K0**
\K5   Send break to remote modem in sequence with transmitted data

If the modem is in the online command state (waiting for AT commands) during a data connection, and the **\B** command is received in order to send a break to the remote modem:

\K0   Clear data buffers and send break to remote modem
\K1   Clear data buffers and send break to remote modem (same as **\K0**)
\K2   Send break to remote modem immediately
\K3   Send break to remote modem immediately (same as **\K2**)
\K4   Send break to remote modem in sequence with data
\K5   Send break to remote modem in sequence with data (same as **\K4**)

If there is a break received from a remote modem during a non-error–corrected connection:
\K0   Clears data buffers and sends break to the DTE
\K1   Clears data buffers and sends break to the DTE (same as **\K0**)
\K2   Send a break immediately to DTE
\K3   Send a break immediately to DTE (same as **\K2**)
\K4   Send a break in sequence with received data to DTE
\K5   Send a break in sequence with received data to DTE (same as **\K4**)

(\Lx)   MNP Block/Stream Mode Select

\L0   Use stream mode for MNP connection
\L1   Use interactive block mode for MNP connection

(\Nx)   Operating Mode

\N0   Selects normal speed buffered mode

TABLE 26-1 GENERAL INDEX OF THE AT COMMAND SET *(CONTINUED)*

AT "×" COMMANDS

\N1	Selects direct mode
\N2	Selects reliable (error correction) mode
\N3	Selects auto reliable mode
\N4	Selects LAPM error correction mode
\N5	Selects MNP error correction mode
(\O)	Originate Reliable Link Control
(\Qx)	DTE Flow Control Options
\Q0	Disables flow control
\Q1	XON/XOFF software flow control
\Q2	CTS flow control to the DTE
\Q3	RTS/CTS hardware flow control
(\S)	Report Active Configuration
(\Tx)	Set Inactivity Timer
n=0	Disable the inactivity timer
n=1-90	Length in minutes
(\U)	Accept Reliable Link Control
(\Vx)	Protocol Result Code
\V0	Disable protocol result code (CONNECT 9600)
\V1	Enable protocol result code (CONNECT 9600/LAPM)
(\Xx)	Set XON/XOFF Pass-through Option
\X0	If XON/XOFF flow control enabled, do not pass XON/XOFF to remote modem or local DTE.
\X1	Always pass XON/XOFF to the remote modem or local DTE.
(\Y)	Switch to Reliable Operation
(\Z)	Switch to Normal Operation

AT "-" COMMANDS

(-Jx)	Set V.42 Detection Phase
-J0	Disables the V.42 detection phase
-J1	Enables the V.42 detection phase
(-Kx)	MNP Extended Services
-K0	Disables V.42 LAPM to MNP 10 conversion
-K1	Enables V.42 LAPM to MNP 10 conversion
-K2	Enables V.42 LAPM to MNP 10 conversion; inhibits MNP Extended Services
(-Qx)	Enable Fallback to V.22 bis/V.22
-Q0	Disables fallback to 2400 bps (V.22bis) and 1200 bps (V.22); fallback only to 4800 bps
-Q1	Enables fallback to 2400 bps (V.22bis) and 1200 bps (V.22)
(-SDR=n)	Distinctive Ring Reporting
-SDR=1	Type 1 Distinctive Ring Detect
-SDR=2	Type 2 Distinctive Ring Detect
-SDR=3	Type 1 and Type 2 Distinctive Ring Detect
-SDR=4	Type 3 Distinctive Ring Detect
-SDR=5	Type 1 and Type 3 Distinctive Ring Detect
-SDR=6	Type 2 and Type 3 Distinctive Ring Detect
-SDR=7	Types 1, 2, and 3 Distinctive Ring Detect

TABLE 26-1   GENERAL INDEX OF THE AT COMMAND SET *(CONTINUED)*

AT "=" COMMANDS

Distinctive Ring Types:

Type	On	Off	ON	Off	On	Off	Sound
1	2.0	4.0					Rinnnnnnnnnng
2	0.8	0.4	0.8	4.0			Ring Ring
3	0.4	0.2	0.4	0.2	0.8	4.0	Ring Ring Rinnng

(-SEC=n)   LAPM and MNP Link Control

-SEC=0   Disable LAPM or MNP10; EC transmit level set in register S91
-SEC=1, 0-30   Enable LAPM or MNP10; EC transmit level set to value after comma (0 to 30)

(-SKEY)   Program Key

(-SPRT)   Remote Security Mode

(-SPWD)   Program Password

(-SSE)   Simultaneous Voice Data

(-SSG)   Set DSVD Receive Gain

(-SSKY)   Program Supervisor Key

(-SSP)   Select DVSD Port

(-SSPW)   Supervisor Password

(-SUID)   Program User ID

(-V)   Display Root Firmware Version Number

AT " COMMANDS

("Hx)   V.42bis Compression Control

"H0   Disable V.42bis
"H1   Enable V.42bis only when transmitting data
"H2   Enable V.42bis only when receiving data
"H3   Enable V.42bis for both directions

("Nx)   V.42bis Dictionary Size

"N0   512 bytes
"N1   1024 bytes
"N2   1536 bytes

("Ox)   Select V.42bis Maximum String Length

n=6–64
n=32

AT "~" COMMANDS

(~Dx)   Factory Configured Operating Profile

~D0   Disable (No Error Correction, No Data Compression)
~D1   MNP4
~D2   MNP5
~D3   V.42
~D4   V.42bis

AT "~~" COMMANDS

(~~Lx)   Digital Line Current Sensing On/Off

~~L0   Turn off digital line current sensing
~~L1   Turn on digital line current sensing

(~~S=m)   Digital Line Over-Current Sense Time Set

m=0 through 9
m=4

TABLE 26-1   GENERAL INDEX OF THE AT COMMAND SET *(CONTINUED)*

AT "~~" COMMANDS

(~~S?)   Display Line Over-Current Sense Time Display

AT "+" FAX COMMANDS

Some modems support fax commands conforming to EIA standard 578. These commands are given here with short descriptions—they also typically support error correction and V.17terbo at 19.2KB.

(+FAA)   Auto Answer Mode Parameter

(+FAXERR=x)   Fax Error Value Parameter

(+FBOR=x)   Phase C Data Bit Order Parameter

(+FBUF?)   Read the Buffer Size

(+FCLASS?)   Service Class Indication

+FCLASS?   000 if in data mode; 001 if in fax class 1

(+FCLASS=x)   Service Class Capabilities

+FCLASS=?   0—modem is set up for data mode
            0,1—modem is capable of data and fax class I services

(+FCLASS=n)   Service Class Selection

+FCLASS=0   Select data mode
+FCLASS=1   Select fax class 1

(+FCR)   Capability to Receive

(+FDCC=x)   Modem Capabilities Parameter

(+FDCS=x)   Current Session Results

(+FDIS=x)   Current Session Negotiation Parameters

(+FDR)   Begin or Continue Phase C Receive Data

(+FDT=x)   Data Transmission

(+FET=x)   Transmit Page Punctuation

(+FK)   Terminate Session

(+FLID=x)   Local ID String Parameter

(+FMDL?)   Request Modem Model

(+FMFR?)   Request Modem IC Manufacturer

(+FPHCTO)   Phase C Time Out

(+FPTS=x)   Page Transfer Status

(+FREV?)   Request Modem Revision

(+FRH=?)   FAX SDLC Receive Capabilities

(+FRH=n)   Modem Accept Training (SDLC)

(+FRM=?)   FAX Normal Mode Receive Capabilities

(+FRM=n)   Modem Accept Training

(+FRS=?)   FRS Range Capabilities

(+FRS=n)   Receive Silence

+FRS=4   That is, wait 40 mS for silence

(+FTH=?)   FAX SDLC Mode Transmit Capabilities

(+FTH=n)   Modem Initiate Training (SDLC)

(+FTM=?)   FAX Normal Mode Transmit Capabilities

(+FTM=n)   Modem Initiate Training

(+FTS=?)   FTS Range Capabilities

(+FTS=n)   Transmission Silence

+FTS=5   That is, fax transmission silence for 50 ms

TABLE 26-1   GENERAL INDEX OF THE AT COMMAND SET *(CONTINUED)*

AT "+" COMMANDS

(+VCID)   Caller ID Service

OTHER AT COMMANDS

(_+BRC+_)   Remote Escape into BRC State (from Host Online Data Mode)

($BRC)   Enable/Disable Host

(#CID)   Enable Caller ID Detection

(:E)   Compromise Equalizer Enable

:E0   Disables the equalizer
:E1   Enables the equalizer

($GIVEBRC)   Enter BRC State (from Target Online Command State)

(*Hx)   Link Negotiation Speed

*H0   Link negotiation occurs at the highest supported speed
*H1   Link negotiation occurs at 1200 bps
*H2   Link negotiation occurs at 4800 bps

()Mx)   Enable Cellular Power Level Adjustment

)M0   Disables power level adjustment during MNP 10 link negotiation
)M1   Enables power level adjustment during MNP 10 link negotiation

(@Mx)   Initial Cellular Power Level Setting

@M0   -26 dBm
@M1   -30 dBm
@M2   -10 dBm
@M26   -26 dBm

While this may seem like a mouthful, a typical modem can accept command strings up to 40 characters long. The term *result codes* refers to the messages that the modem generates when a command string is processed. Table 26-2 outlines a series of typical result codes. Either numbers (default) or words (using the **V1** command) can be returned. When a command is processed correctly, a result code **OK** is produced, or **CONNECT** when a successful connection is established.

TABLE 26-2   LIST OF TYPICAL MODEM RESULT CODES

RESPONSE CODE	VERBOSE	DEFINITION
0	OK	The OK code is returned by the modem to acknowledge execution of a command line.
1	CONNECT	Sent alone when speed is 300 bps
2	RING	The modem sends this result code when incoming ringing is detected on the line.
3	NO CARRIER	No modem carrier signal is detected.
4	ERROR	Generated from AT command string errors, if a command cannot be executed or if a parameter is outside of range
5	CONNECT 1200	Connection at 1200 bps
6	NO DIAL TONE	No dial tone was received from the local line.
7	BUSY	A busy tone has been detected.

TABLE 26-2   LIST OF TYPICAL MODEM RESULT CODES *(CONTINUED)*

RESPONSE CODE	VERBOSE	DEFINITION
8	NO ANSWER	The remote modem does not answer properly.
9	CONNECT 600	Connection at 600 bps
10	CONNECT 2400	Connection at 2400 bps
11	CONNECT 4800	Connection at 4800 bps
12	CONNECT 9600	Connection at 9600 bps
13	CONNECT 14400	Connection at 14,400 bps
14	CONNECT 19200	Connection at 19,200 bps
15	CONNECT 16800	Connection at 16,800 bps
16	CONNECT 19200	Connection at 19,200 bps
17	CONNECT 38400	Connection at 38,400 bps
18	CONNECT 57600	Connection at 57,600 bps
22	CONNECT 1200TX/75RX	Connection at 1200 bps/75 bps
23	CONNECT 75TX/1200RX	Connection at 75 bps/1200 bps
24	CONNECT 7200	Connection at 7200 bps
25	CONNECT 12000	Connection at 12000 bps
26	CONNECT 1200/75	Connection at 1200 bps/75 bps (V.23)
27	CONNECT 75/1200	Connection at 75 bps/1200 bps (V.23)
28	CONNECT 38400	Connection at 38,400 bps
29	CONNECT 21600	Connection at 21,600 bps
30	CONNECT 24000	Connection at 24,000 bps
31	CONNECT 26400	Connection at 26,400 bps
32	CONNECT 28800	Connection at 28,800 bps
33	CONNECT 115200	Connection at 115.2 Kbps
35	DATA	Modem data is present.
40	CARRIER 300	A V.21 or Bell 103 carrier has been detected on the line.
42	CARRIER 75/1200	A V.23 backward channel carrier has been detected on the line.
43	CARRIER 1200/75	A V.23 forward channel carrier has been detected on the line.
44	CARRIER 1200/75	A V.23 forward channel carrier has been detected on the line.
45	CARRIER 75/1200	A V.23 backward channel carrier has been detected on the line.
46	CARRIER 1200	The high or low channel carrier in either V.22 or Bell 212 mode has been detected on the line.
47	CARRIER 2400	The high or low channel carrier in V.22bis or V.34 mode has been detected on the line.
48	CARRIER 4800	The channel carrier in V.32, V.32bis, or V.34 has been detected on the line.
49	CARRIER 7200	The channel carrier in V.32bis or V.34 has been detected on the line.
50	CARRIER 9600	The channel carrier in V.32, V.32bis, or V.34 mode has been detected on the line.
51	CARRIER 12000	The channel carrier in V.32bis or V.34 mode has been detected on the line.
52	CARRIER 14400	The channel carrier in V.32bis or V.34 mode has been detected on the line.
53	CARRIER 16800	The channel carrier in V.32terbo or V.34 mode has been detected on the line.

TABLE 26-2 LIST OF TYPICAL MODEM RESULT CODES *(CONTINUED)*

RESPONSE CODE	VERBOSE	DEFINITION
54	CARRIER 19200	The channel carrier in V.32terbo or V.34 mode has been detected on the line.
55	CARRIER 21600	The channel carrier in V.34 mode has been detected on the line.
56	CARRIER 24000	The channel carrier in V.34 mode has been detected on the line.
57	CARRIER 26400	The channel carrier in V.34 mode has been detected on the line.
58	CARRIER 28800	The channel carrier in V.34 mode has been detected on the line.
66	COMPRESSION: CLASS 5	The modem has connected with MNP class 5 data compression.
67	COMPRESSION: V.42bis	The modem has connected with V.42bis data compression.
69	COMPRESSION: NONE	The modem has connected without data compression.
70	PROTOCOL: NONE	The modem has connected without any form of error correction.
76	PROTOCOL: NONE	The modem has connected without any form of error correction.
77	PROTOCOL: LAP-M	The modem has connected with V.42 LAPM error correction.
80	PROTOCOL: MNP	The modem has connected with MNP error correction.
81	PROTOCOL: MNP 2	The modem has connected with MNP error correction.
82	PROTOCOL: MNP 3	The modem has connected with MNP error correction.
83	PROTOCOL: MNP 2, 4	The modem has connected with MNP error correction.
84	PROTOCOL: MNP 3, 4	The modem has connected with MNP error correction.
100	CONNECT 28000 EC*	Connection at 28,000 bit/s (V.90 mode) (Lucent Technologies)
101	CONNECT 29333 EC*	Connection at 29,333 bit/s (V.90 mode) (Lucent Technologies)
102	CONNECT 30666 EC*	Connection at 30,666 bit/s (V.90 mode) (Lucent Technologies)
103	CONNECT 33333 EC*	Connection at 33,333 bit/s (V.90 mode) (Lucent Technologies)
104	CONNECT 34666 EC*	Connection at 34,666 bit/s (V.90 mode) (Lucent Technologies)
105	CONNECT 37333 EC*	Connection at 37,333 bit/s (V.90 mode) (Lucent Technologies)
106	CONNECT 38666 EC*	Connection at 38,666 bit/s (V.90 mode) (Lucent Technologies)
107	CONNECT 41333 EC*	Connection at 41,333 bit/s (V.90 mode) (Lucent Technologies)
108	CONNECT 42666 EC*	Connection at 42,666 bit/s (V.90 mode) (Lucent Technologies)
109	CONNECT 45333 EC*	Connection at 45,333 bit/s (V.90 mode) (Lucent Technologies)
110	CONNECT 46666 EC*	Connection at 46,666 bit/s (V.90 mode) (Lucent Technologies)
111	CONNECT 49333 EC*	Connection at 49,333 bit/s (V.90 mode) (Lucent Technologies)
112	CONNECT 50666 EC*	Connection at 50,666 bit/s (V.90 mode) (Lucent Technologies)
113	CONNECT 53333 EC*	Connection at 53,333 bit/s (V.90 mode) (Lucent Technologies)
114	CONNECT 54666 EC*	Connection at 54,666 bit/s (V.90 mode) (Lucent Technologies)
151	CONNECT 31200	Connection at 31,200 bps.
152	CONNECT 31200/ARQ	Connection at 31,200 bps with Automatic Repeat Request
153	CONNECT 31200/V34	Connection at 31,200 bps with fallback to 28.8KB (V.34)
154	CONNECT 31200/ARQ/V34	Connection at 31,200 bps with ARQ and fallback to 28.8KB
155	CONNECT 33600	Connection at 33,600 bps.
156	CONNECT 33600/ARQ	Connection at 33,600 bps with Automatic Repeat Request
157	CONNECT 33600/V34	Connection at 33,600 bps with fallback to 28.8KB (V.34)
158	CONNECT 33600/ARQ/V34	Connection at 33,600 bps with ARQ and fallback to 28.8KB
180	CONNECT 33333	(3COM—USR Modem)
184	CONNECT 37333	(3COM—USR Modem)
188	CONNECT 41333	(3COM—USR Modem)
192	CONNECT 42666	(3COM—USR Modem)
196	CONNECT 44000	(3COM—USR Modem)

TABLE 26-2   LIST OF TYPICAL MODEM RESULT CODES *(CONTINUED)*

RESPONSE CODE	VERBOSE	DEFINITION
200	CONNECT 45333	(3COM—USR Modem)
204	CONNECT 46666	(3COM—USR Modem)
208	CONNECT 48000	(3COM—USR Modem)
212	CONNECT 49333	(3COM—USR Modem)
216	CONNECT 50666	(3COM—USR Modem)
220	CONNECT 52000	(3COM—USR Modem)
224	CONNECT 53333	(3COM—USR Modem)
228	CONNECT 54666	(3COM—USR Modem)
232	CONNECT 56000	(3COM—USR Modem)
236	CONNECT 57333	(3COM—USR Modem)

* **Note:** EC appears only when the extended result codes configuration option is enabled. "EC" is replaced by one of the following symbols, depending upon the error-control method used:

- **V42bis**   V.42 error control and V.42bis data compression
- **V42**   V.42 error control only
- **MNP 5**   MNP class 4 error control and MNP class 5 data compression
- **MNP 4**   MNP class 4 error control only

Controlling Attributes

Many attributes of the Hayes-compatible modem are programmable. To accommodate this feature, each parameter must be held in a series of memory locations (called *S-registers*). Each S-register is described in Table 26-3. For example, the default escape sequence for the AT command set is a series of three plusses: "**+++**". You could change this character by writing an new ASCII character to register S2. Default S-register values are fine for most work, but you can often optimize the modem's operation by experimenting with the register values. Since S-register contents must be maintained after power is removed from the modem, the registers are stored in nonvolatile RAM (NVRAM).

TABLE 26-3   INDEX OF S-REGISTER ASSIGNMENTS

REGISTER	FUNCTION	RANGE	UNITS	DEFAULT
S0	Rings to Auto-Answer	0–255	Rings	0
S1	Ring Counter	0–255	Rings	0
S2	Escape Character	0–255	ASCII	43
S3	Carriage Return Character	0–127	ASCII	13
S4	Line Feed Character	0–127	ASCII	10
S5	Backspace Character	0–255	ASCII	8
S6	Wait Time for Dial Tone	2–255	seconds	4
S7	Wait for Carrier	1–255	seconds	50
S8	Pause Time for (,) Comma	0–255	seconds	2
S9	Carrier Detect Response Time	1–255	1/10 sec	6
S10	Carrier Loss Disconnect Time	1–255	1/10 sec	14
S11	Touch Tone (DTMF) Duration	50–255	1/1000 sec	95

TABLE 26-3   INDEX OF S-REGISTER ASSIGNMENTS (CONTINUED)

REGISTER	FUNCTION	RANGE	UNITS	DEFAULT
S12	Escape Code Guard Time	0–255	2/100 sec	50
S13	Reserved	---	---	---
S14	General Bit Mapped Options	---	---	138 (8Ah)
S15	Reserved	---	---	---
S16	Test Mode Bit Map Options (&T)	---	---	0
S17	Reserved	---	---	---
S18	Test Timer	0–255	seconds	0
S19	Auto-Sync Bit Map Register	---	---	0
S20	AutoSync HDLC Address or BSC Sync Character	0–255	---	0
S21	V.24/General Bit Map Options	---	---	4 (04h)
S22	Speaker/Results Bit Map Options	---	---	118 (76h)
S23	General Bit Map Options	---	---	55 (37h)
S24	Sleep Inactivity Timer	0–255	seconds	1
S25	Delay to DTR Off	0–255	1/100 sec	5
S26	RTS-to-CTS Delay	0–255	1/100 sec	1
S27	General Bit Map Options	---	---	73 (49h) with ECC 74 (4Ah) without ECC
S28	General Bit Map Options	---	---	0
S29	Flash Dial Modifier Time	0–255	10 ms	70
S30	Disconnect Activity Timer	0–255	10 sec	0
S31	General Bit Map Options	---	---	194 (C2h)
S32	XON Character	0–255	ASCII	17 (11h)
S33	XOFF Character	0–255	ASCII	19 (13h)
S34	Reserved	---	---	---
S35	Reserved	---	---	---
S36	LAPM Failure Control	---	---	7
S37	Line Connection Speed	---	---	0
S38	Delay Before Forced Hangup	0–255	seconds	20
S39	Flow Control	---	---	3
S40	General Bit Map Options	---	---	105 (69h) No MNP 10 107 (6Bh) MNP 10
S41	General Bit Mapped Options	---	---	131 (83h)
S43	Auto Fallback Character for MNP Negotiation	0–255	---	13
S44	Data Framing	---	---	---
S46	Data Compression Control	---	---	136 (no compression) 138 (with compression)
S46*	Automatic Sleep Timer	0–255	100 mS	100
S47	Forced Sleep Timer with Power-down Mode in PCMCIA	0–255	100 mS	10
S48	V.42 Negotiation Control	---	---	7
S49	Buffer Low Limit	---	---	---
S50	Buffer High Limit	---	---	---
S50*	FAX/Data Mode Selection	---	---	0 (data mode) 1 (fax mode)

TABLE 26-3   INDEX OF S-REGISTER ASSIGNMENTS *(CONTINUED)*

REGISTER	FUNCTION	RANGE	UNITS	DEFAULT
S53	Global PAD Configuration	---	---	---
S55	AutoStream Protocol Request	---	---	---
S56	AutoStream Protocol Status	---	---	---
S57	Network Options Register	---	---	---
S58	BTLZ String Length	6–64	bytes	32
S59	Leased Line Failure Alarm	---	---	---
S60	Leased Line Failure Action	---	---	---
S61	Leased Line Retry Number	---	---	---
S62	Leased Line Options	---	---	---
S62*	DTE Rate Status	0–17	---	16 (57600 bps)
S63	Leased Line Transmit Level	---	---	---
S64	Leased Line Receive Level	---	---	---
S69	Link Layer k Protocol	---	---	---
S70	Max Number of Retransmissions	---	---	---
S71	Link Layer Timeout	---	---	---
S72	Loss of Flag Idle Timeout	---	---	---
S72*	DTE Speed Select	0–18	---	0 (last autobaud)
S73	No Activity Timeout	---	---	---
S74	Minimum Incoming LCN	---	---	---
S75	Minimum Incoming LCN	---	---	---
S76	Maximum Incoming LCN	---	---	---
S77	Maximum Incoming LCN	---	---	---
S78	Outgoing LCN	---	---	---
S79	Outgoing LCN	---	---	---
S80	X.25 Packet Level N20 Parameter	---	---	---
S80*	Soft Switch Functions	---	---	1
S81	X.25 Packet Level T20 Parameter	---	---	---
S82	LAPM Break Control	---	---	128 (40h)
S84	ASU Negotiation	---	---	---
S85	ASU Negotiation Status	---	---	---
S86	Call Failure Reason Code	0–255	---	---
S87	Fixed Speed DTE Interface	---	---	---
S91	PSTN Xmit Attenuation Level	0–15	-dBm	10
S92	Fax Xmit Attenuation Level	0–15	-dBm	10
S92*	MI/MIC Options	---	---	---
S93	V.25bis Async Interface Speed	---	---	---
S94	V.25bis Mode Control	---	---	---
S95	Result Code Messages Control	---	---	0
S97	V.32 Late Connecting Handshake Timing	---	---	---
S99	Leased Line Transmit Level	0–15	-dBm	10
S101	Distinctive Ring Reporting	0–63	---	0
S105	Frame Size	---	---	---
S108	Signal Quality Selector	---	---	---
S109	Carrier Speed Selector	---	---	---
S110	V.32/V.32bis Selector	---	---	---

TABLE 26-3   INDEX OF S-REGISTER ASSIGNMENTS *(CONTINUED)*

REGISTER	FUNCTION	RANGE	UNITS	DEFAULT
S113	Calling Tone Control	---	---	---
S116	Connection Timeout	---	---	---
S121	Use of DTR	---	---	---
S122	V.13 Selection	---	---	---
S141	Detection Phase Timer	---	---	---
S142	Online Character Format	---	---	---
S143	KDS Handshake Mode	---	---	---
S144	Autobaud Group Selection	---	---	---
S150	V.42 Options	---	---	---
S151	Simultaneous Voice Data Control	---	---	---
S154	Force Port Speed	---	---	---
S157	Timeout Result Code	---	---	---
S201	Cellular Transmit Level (MNP 10)	10–63	---	58 (3Ah)
S202	Remote Access Escape Character	0–255	ASCII	170

*Note: The register may be used for different purposes by some modems.

MODEM INITIALIZATION STRINGS

One of the most difficult steps in configuring a new modem (or new modem software) involves the proper use of initialization strings. *Initialization strings* (or *init strings* as they are sometimes called) are vital to setting up the modem properly before each use—if the setup is not done correctly, the modem will not behave as expected (if it works at all). Years ago, you'd need to configure a modem with a specific initialization string yourself. Today, Windows 9x/Me drivers provide all of the modem support, so you don't need to worry about the initialization string (just use the latest driver). However, you may still need to enter a string to optimize modem operation or to configure DOS modem software. Keep in mind that initialization strings are not absolute—except for the "AT" at the start of each line, you can modify each string as required for your own system and telephone line.

You may notice that many AT command strings are so long that they seem to "run over" onto a second line. When you enter strings into communication software, you should be sure to enter all of the commands *without* spaces or carriage returns—initialization strings are always one continuous line.

At first glance, an initialization string may seem quite daunting. But if you take a moment to examine the string in detail (and refer to the AT Command Set listed in Table 26-1), you should be able to decode even the longest command strings in just a few moments. Let's try a few basic examples. The command string

```
ATS0=0&B1&H1&W
```

tells the modem to not answer an incoming call (S0=0), use CTS flow control (&B1), use a fixed DTE rate (&H1), and store this adjusted configuration in the modem's internal memory called NVRAM (&W). Similarly, the command string

```
ATS0=0&K3&W
```

tells the modem to *not* answer an incoming call (S0=0), use hardware flow control (&K3), and store this adjusted configuration in the modem's internal memory (&W). As you can see, an initialization string is merely a list of individual commands that enable, disable, or adjust specific operating parameters for a given modem. Most modem manufacturers attempt to use basic default values so that the modem will still operate without any alteration through the initialization string, but some amount of tailoring is usually required for optimum performance. If you cannot find the appropriate initialization string for your particular modem, you should check with the modem's manufacturer.

Initialization Strings and Windows 9x/Me

Modem initialization strings in Windows 9x/Me and Windows Dial Up Networking can be adjusted in the system Registry or through the Modem icon in the Control Panel. When a modem is installed on a Windows 9x/Me system, the default initialization string is written to the Registry by the modem's .INF driver file. The key containing the default string is

```
HKEY_LOCAL_MACHINE\System\CurrentControlSet\Services\Class\Modem\0000\Init
```

(Systems with multiple modems may have modem IDs of 0000, 0001, 0002 and so on.) You can use this entry in the Registry to adjust the modem's initialization string manually with the Registry Editor (REGEDIT). However, most users are uncomfortable with editing the Registry, since errors to the Registry can cause serious problems and prevent Windows 9x/Me from booting. The safer and faster method of adjusting the modem's initialization string is through the Modem icon:

1. Open your Control Panel and double-click the Modem icon.
2. Highlight your modem and click the Properties button.
3. Select the Connection tab, then click the Advanced button.
4. The Advanced Connection Settings dialog appears (Figure 26-3).
5. Enter your new command string in the Extra settings box. When using this box, you do *not* need to preface your new command string with "AT."

You can try this yourself. Enter **S11=40** in the Extra settings box. Click the OK button to save your changes and exit the Modem icon, and then try connecting to the Internet. Register S11 determines the amount of time (in milliseconds) between the tones of a phone number. The default setting is usually 70 ms. By entering "40" (milliseconds), you should hear a definite decrease in the time it takes to dial a number.

Just below the Extra settings text box is the "Append to log" check box. If you select this option, Windows will keep a running log of the commands sent and received during a modem session. You can confirm that the correct commands are being sent. The combination of the Sent and Received commands may help you determine if a problem is caused by the system's software or hardware—or even by the Service Provider.

 Be sure to check for an updated modem driver if you're experiencing modem problems or when you check for driver updates for other system components. The new modem driver may contain a different (and better) default initialization string.

MODEM MODES

The modem is always in one of *two* primary modes: the command mode or the data mode. When first switched on (or reset), the modem starts up in *command mode*. In this mode, the controller circuit (sometimes called a *command processor*) is constantly checking to see if you have typed a valid AT command.

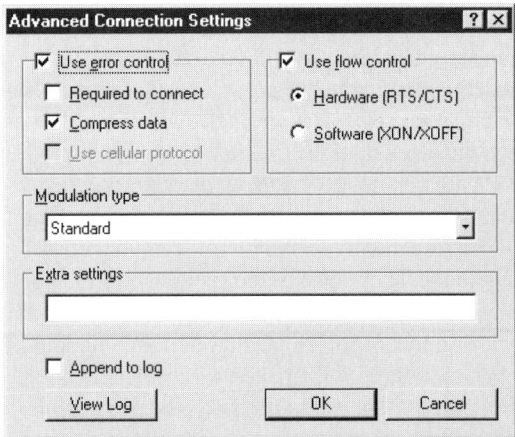

FIGURE 26-3   The Advanced Connection Settings dialog under Windows 98/SE

When the modem receives a valid command, it executes that command for you. While your modem is in the command mode, you can instruct it to answer the telephone, change an S-Register value, hang up or dial the telephone, and perform any number of other command functions.

The other mode is the *data mode*. In the data mode, your modem is transmitting all of the data it receives from your computer or terminal along the telephone line to the remote modem. Your modem is constantly checking the state of the *Data Carrier Detect* (DCD) and *Data Terminal Ready* (DTR) signals (depending on the system configuration). It is also watching the local data stream for a command mode escape sequence. The default escape sequence the AT command set is "**+++**". When the proper escape sequence (or a change in the state of the DCD or DTR signal) occurs, the modem returns to a command mode where it waits for the next AT command.

MODEM NEGOTIATION

Now that you have seen the essential elements of a modem and learned about modem signaling, you can use that background to form a picture of how the modem works in actual practice. You see, modem communication is not an event—it is a *process* whose success depends not only on your modem, but also on the modem and PC you are trying to communicate with. This part of the chapter is intended to familiarize you with an operating session for a typical modem.

Communication begins when you instruct the communication software to establish a connection. Control signals sent to the selected serial port cause the UART to assert the Data Terminal Ready (DTR) signal. This tells the attached modem that the PC is turned on and ready to transmit. The modem responds by asserting the Data Set Ready (DSR) line. The serial port receives this signal and tells the software that the modem is ready—both DTR and DSR *must* be present for communication to take place.

The communication software then sends an AT initialization string to the COM port (which forwards the string to the modem). In the command mode, the controller circuit interprets the initialization string that tells the modem to go off hook (get dial tone), then dial the telephone number of the destination modem. Dialing may take place in pulse (rotary) or tone (DTMF) mode, depending on the initialization string. The modem transmits an acknowledgment back to the COM port—this is often displayed right on the communication software window. The line at the destination end begins to ring. If configured properly and running communication software of its own, the remote modem will pick up the ringing line, and a complete wiring path will be established between the two modems.

When the destination modem picks up the line, your local modem sends out a standard tone (a *carrier* tone). The carrier lets the remote modem know it's being called by another modem. If the remote modem recognizes the carrier, it sends out an even higher pitched tone. You can often hear these squealing tones when your modem is equipped with a speaker. Once your modem recognizes the remote modem, it sends a Carrier Detect (CD) signal to the serial port. These mutual carriers will be modulated to exchange data.

OK, both modems know they are talking to another modem, but now there has to be a mutual agreement on *how* they'll exchange data. They must agree on transmission speed, the proper size of a data packet, the signaling bits on each end of the data packet, whether or not parity will be used, and whether the modems will operate in half-duplex or full-duplex mode. Both modems must settle on these parameters or the data exchanged between them will make no sense. This process is known as *negotiation*. Assuming that the negotiation process is successful, both modems can now exchange data.

When the communication software attempts to send data, it tells the serial port to assert the Request to Send (RTS) signal. This checks to see if your modem is free to receive data. If the PC is busy doing something else (such as disk access), it will disable the RTS signal until it is ready to resume sending. When the modem is ready for data, it will return a Clear to Send (CTS) signal to the serial port. The PC can then begin sending data to the modem and receiving data returned from the remote end. If the modem gets backed up with work, it will drop the CTS line until it is ready to resume communication. Since a standard system of tones is used, both modems can exchange data simultaneously.

When the time comes to terminate the connection, the communication software will send another AT command string to the serial port that causes it to break the connection. If the connection is broken by the remote modem, the local modem will drop the Carrier Detect line. The communication software will interpret this as a *Dropped Carrier* condition. That is basically all the phases involved in modem communication.

V.22bis Connections

The following steps detail the connection sequence for a V.22bis modem:

1. **Pickup**   The receiving modem picks up the ringing line (goes *off-hook*). It then waits at least two seconds. This is known as a *billing delay* and is required by the telephone company to ensure that the connection has been properly established. No data transfer is allowed during the billing delay.

2. **Answer Tone**   The receiving modem transmits an *answer tone* back to the network. A 2100 Hz tone lasts for about 3.3 seconds. An answer tone serves two purposes. First, you can hear this tone in the receiving modem's speaker, so manual modem users know when to place their modem into data mode. Even more important, the answer tone is used by the telephone network to disable echo suppressers in the connection in order to allow optimum data throughput. If echo suppressers remain active, data transfer will be half-duplex (one direction at a time). The answering modem then goes silent for about 75 ms to separate the answer tone from data.

3. **The USB1 Signal**   The receiving modem then transmits alternating binary 1's at 1200 bps (known as the *USB1* signal—*not* to be confused with the Universal Serial Port). This results in the static sound you hear just after the answer tone. The sending modem detects the USB1 signal in about 155 ms, then falls silent for about 456 ms.

4. **The S1 Signal**   After the 456 ms silence, the sending modem transmits double digits (00 and 11) at 1200 bps for 100 ms (the *S1* signal). An older Bell 212 or V.22 modem does not send the S1 signal, so if the S1 signal is absent, the receiving V.22bis modem will fall back to 1200 bps. The receiving modem (still generating a USB1 signal) receives the S1 signal. It responds by sending a

100 ms burst of S1 signal so that the sending modem knows the receiving modem can handle 2400 bps operation. At this point, both modems know whether they will be operating in 1200 bps or 2400 bps mode.

5. **The SB1 Signal**   At this point, the sending modem sends scrambled 1's at 1200 bps (the SB1 signal). The scrambling-effect creates white noise that checks power across the whole audio bandwidth. The receiving modem then replies with the SB1 signal for 500 ms.

6. **Ready to Answer**   After 500 ms, the receiving modem starts sending scrambled 1's at 2400 bps for 200 ms. A full 600 ms after getting the SB1 signal from the receiving modem, the sending modem also sends scrambled 1's at 2400 bps for 200 ms. After both modems have finished their final 200 ms transmissions, they are ready to pass data.

V.32 Connections
The following steps detail the connection sequence for a V.32 modem:

1. **Pickup**   The receiving modem picks up the ringing line (goes *off-hook*). It then waits at least two seconds. This is known as a *billing delay* and is required by the telephone company to ensure that the connection has been properly established. As with the V.22bis modem, no data transfer is allowed during the billing delay.

2. **Answer Tone**   The receiving modem transmits an *answer tone* back to the network. A V.25 answer tone (a 2100 Hz tone with a duration of about 3.3 seconds) is returned to the calling modem. However, the V.32 modem uses a modified answer tone where the signal phase is reversed every 450 ms—this sounds like little clicks in the signal. An answer tone serves two purposes. First, you can *hear* this tone in the receiving modem's speaker, so manual modem users know when to place their modem into data mode. Even more important, the answer tone is used by the telephone network to disable echo suppressers in the connection in order to allow optimum data throughput. The modems themselves will handle echo suppression.

3. **Signal AA**   The sending modem waits about 1 second after receiving the answer tone, then generates an 1800 Hz tone (known as Signal AA). When the receiving modem interprets this signal, it knows (quite early on) that it is communicating with another V.32 modem.

4. **The USB1 Fall Back**   If the answering modem heard signal AA, it will immediately try establishing a connection—otherwise, it will reply to the sending modem with a USB1 signal (alternating binary 1's at 1200 bps). This causes the connection to "fall back" to a V.22bis connection. This fall back attempt will continue for three seconds. If the sending modem does not respond to the USB1 signal within three seconds, the receiving modem will continue trying the connection as a V.32.

5. **Signal AC and CA**   During a V.32 connection, the receiving modem sends Signal AC (a mixed 600 Hz and 3000 Hz tone signal) for at least $1/2400^{\text{th}}$ of a second, then it reverses the signal phase—creating Signal CA.

6. **Signal CC**   When the sending modem detects the phase change in Signal AC/CA, it reverses the phase of its own Signal AA—creating a new signal (called Signal CC).

7. **Echo Canceller Configuration**   Once the answering modem receives the phase-changed signal CC, it again changes the phase of CA—returning it to signal AC. This multitude of phase changes may seem like a ridiculous waste of time, but this exchange between the two modems is vital for approximating the round-trip (propagation) delay of the communication circuit so that the modem's echo canceller circuitry may be set properly.

8.   **Agreeing on Specifics**   Once the exchange of phase changes sets the echo cancellers, both modems exchange data in half-duplex mode in order to set up adaptive equalizers, test the phone line quality, and agree on an acceptable data rate. In actual practice, the answering modem sends first (from 650 ms to 3525 ms). The sending modem responds, but leaves the signal on while the answering modem sends another burst of signals (this is when the final data rate is established).

9.   **Passing Data**   Once the data rate is established, both modems proceed to send scrambled binary 1's for at least $1/1200^{th}$ of a second (a brief white-noise sound), then they are ready to pass data.

READING THE LIGHTS

One of the appealing attributes of external modems is the series of lights that typically adorns the front face. By observing each light and the sequence in which they light, you can often follow the progress of a communication—or quickly discern the cause of a communication failure. The following markings are typical of many modems, but keep in mind that your particular modem may use fewer indicators (or be marked differently):

- **HS** (High Speed)   When this indicator is lit, the modem is operating at its very highest transfer rate.

- **AA** (Auto Answer)   When illuminated, your modem will answer any incoming calls automatically. This feature is vital for unattended systems such as bulletin boards.

- **CD** (Carrier Detect)   This lights whenever the modem detects a carrier signal and means it has successfully connected to a remote computer. This LED will go out when either one of the modems drops the line.

- **OH** (Off Hook)   This LED lights any time the modem takes control of the telephone line—equivalent to taking the telephone off-hook.

- **RD** (Receive Data)   Also marked **Rx**. This LED flickers as data is received by the modem from a remote modem.

- **SD** (Send Data)   Also marked **Tx**. This LED flickers as data is sent from your modem to the remote modem.

- **TR** (Terminal Ready)   This light illuminates when the modem detects a DTR signal from the communication software.

- **MR** (Modem Ready)   A simple power-on light that indicates the modem is turned on and ready to operate.

Understanding Signal Modulation

Once the modem accepts a bipolar signal from an RS-232 port, the carrier signal being generated on the telephone line must be modulated to reflect the logic levels being transmitted. Several different means of signal modulation have been developed through the years to improve the efficiency of data transfers. This part of the chapter gives you a brief explanation of each scheme. As you would expect, modems on both ends of the connection must be capable of the same modulation scheme.

BPS VS. BAUD RATE

In the early days of modem communication, each audio signal *transition* represented a single bit. Each audio signal is known as a *baud*, and the *baud rate* naturally equaled the transmission rate in bps (or bits-per-second). Unlike those early modems, newer modem schemes can encode 2, 3, or 4 or more bits into every audio signal transition (or baud). This means that modem throughput now equals 2x, 3x, or 4x the baud rate being carried across the telephone line.

For example, a modem operating at 2400 baud (2400 audio signal transitions per second) can carry 4800 bps if 2 bits are encoded onto every baud. The same 2400 baud modem could also carry 9600 bps if 4 bits are encoded onto every baud. Today, the modem's baud rate *rarely* matches the modem's throughput in bps unless a very old signaling standard is being used. If the modem were operating at 4800 baud and used 3-bit encoding, the modem would be handling 14,400 bps (14.4 Kbps). The concept of *encoding* is different from *data compression*, since encoding transfers *all* original data bits from system to system, while data compression replaces repeating sequences of bits with much shorter bit sequences (known as *symbols* or *tokens*). You will see much more about encoding schemes and data compression later in this section.

MODULATION SCHEMES

To discuss modulation, you must first understand a *sinusoidal* waveform. There are basically three physical characteristics to any waveform: amplitude, frequency, and phase. Each of these characteristics can be adjusted to represent a bit. *Amplitude* is simply the magnitude of the wave (usually measured in volts peak-to-peak or volts RMS). Amplitude represents how far above and below the zero axis that waveform travels. *Frequency* indicates the number of times that a single wave will repeat over any period of time—measured as cycles-per-second: (Hertz, or Hz). An 1800 Hz signal repeats 1800 times per second. The signal also has a time reference known as *phase*. Phase is measured in degrees where 90 degrees is the time to travel 25 percent of a wave, 180 degrees is the time to travel 50 percent of the wave, 270 degrees is the time to travel 75 percent of a wave, and so on. Since phase can take on any one of four states (degrees), phase shifts can be made to represent 2 bits simultaneously. Data between modems is commonly modulated by altering the amplitude, frequency, and phase of a carrier signal.

Frequency Shift Keying (FSK) is very similar to frequency modulation (FM), where only the frequency of a carrier is changed, and is one of the oldest modulation schemes. FSK sends a logic 1 as one particular frequency (usually 1750 Hz), and a logic 0 is sent as another discrete frequency (often 1080 Hz). Frequencies are typically sent at 300 baud, and each baud can carry 1 bit, so FSK can send 300 bps. This early technique resulted in the classical "baud = bps" confusion that is still prevalent today.

Phase Shift Keying (PSK) is a close cousin of FSK, but the phase timing of a carrier wave is altered while the carrier's frequency stays the same. By altering the carrier's phase, a logic 1 or 0 is represented. Since phase can be shifted in several precise increments (that is, 0, 90, 180, or 270 degrees), PSK can encode 1, 2, or 3 or more bits bit per baud. For example, a 1200 baud modem using PSK can transmit 2400 bps over an 1800 Hz carrier. PSK can also be used in conjunction with FSK to encode even more bits per baud.

Quadrature Amplitude Modulation (QAM) uses both phase and amplitude modulation to encode up to 6 bits onto every baud, although 4 bits are usually reserved for data. Not only can four phase states represent 2 bits, but also four levels of amplitude can represent another 2 bits. Most QAM modems use a 1700 Hz or 1800 Hz carrier and a base rate of 2400 baud, so they carry up to 9600 bps.

Trellis Coded Quadrature Amplitude Modulation (TCQAM or TCM) also uses an 1800 Hz carrier at a 2400 baud base rate, but uses the full 6-bit encoding capability of QAM to handle 14,400 bps. Most newer modems using TCM offer high speed and excellent echo cancellation circuitry. TCM is a most popular modulation scheme for mid-performance modems, since data can be checked on the fly with much better reliability than by using a parity bit.

Pulse Code Modulation (PCM) a sampling technique for digitizing analog signals, especially audio signals. PCM samples the signal 8000 times a second: each sample is represented by 8 bits for a total of 64 Kbps. There are two standards for coding the sample level: Mu-Law and A-Law. The Mu-Law standard is used in North America and Japan, while the A-Law standard is used in most other countries. PCM was originally used with high-performance T-1 and T-3 carrier systems. These carrier systems combine the PCM signals from many lines and transmit them over a single cable or other medium. Today, however, PCM is the basis for our V.90 and V.92 56Kbs analog modem standards.

Signaling Standards

Now that you have covered serial concepts and modulation techniques, you can see how modulation is used in conjunction with the many communications standards (or *protocols*) that have appeared. This part of the chapter details each of the major standards for modems, data compression, and error correction that are now in force today. Most data sent between modems contains some amount of repetitive or redundant information. If the redundant information is located and replaced by a small token during transmission—the data is *compressed*. A token could be passed much faster than the redundant data, and the receiving modem can accurately recreate the original data based on the token. *Data compression* has become an important technique that allows modems to increase their data throughput without increasing the baud rate or bps. Data compression can occur only when the two communicating modems support the same compression protocol. If modems support more than one type of compression, the communicating modems will use the most powerful technique common to both.

Modem *error correction* is the ability of some modems to detect data errors that may have occurred in transit between modems, then automatically resend the faulty data until a correct copy is received. As with modulation standards, both modems must be using the same error correction standard in order to operate together. However, there are few error correction standards, and most modem manufacturers adhere closely to the few that are available.

BELL STANDARDS

The old "Bell System" largely dictated North American telecommunications standards before the company was broken up into AT&T and seven regional operating companies in 1984. Before that time, two major standards were developed that set the stage for future modem development:

- **BELL103** was the first widely accepted modem standard using simple FSK modulation at 300 baud. This is the *only* standard where the data rate matches the baud rate. It is interesting to note that some modems today *still* support BELL103 as a lowest common denominator when all other modulation techniques fail.

- **BELL212A** represents a second widely accepted modem standard in North America using PSK modulation at 600 baud to transmit 1,200 bps. Many European countries ignored BELL212A in favor of the similar (but not entirely identical) European standard called V.22.

ITU (CCITT) STANDARDS

After the Bell System breakup, AT&T no longer wielded enough clout to dictate standards in North America—and certainly not to the international community, which had developed serious computing interest. It is at this time that the ITU (*International Telecommunications Union*, formally the CCITT) gained prominence and acceptance in the U.S. leading to the conformance of all U.S. modems to ITU standards. ITU specifications are characterized by the letter "V" (as in V.17). The "V" simply means *standard* (rather like the "RS" in RS-232). The number following simply denotes the particular standard. Some standards also add the term "bis," which means the *second version* of a particular standard. You may also see the term "ter" or "terbo," which indicates the *third version* of a standard. The following list provides a basic outline of ITU standards. Only the standards that appear in **boldface** relate to modems in particular, but *all* are related to communications. This index may aid you in understanding the broad specifications that are required to fully characterize the computer communications environment:

- V.1 is a very early standard that defines binary 0/1 bits as space/mark line conditions and voltage levels.

- V.2 limits the power levels (in decibels or dB) of modems used on phone lines.

- V.4 describes the sequence of bits within a character as transmitted (the data frame).

- V.5 describes the standard synchronous signaling rates for dial-up lines.

- V.6 describes the standard synchronous signaling rates for leased lines.

- V.7 provides a list of modem terms in English, Spanish, and French.

- V.8 describes the initial handshaking (negotiation) process between modems and forms the basis for call "autodetection" or "auto-switching" (voice/fax/modem).

- V.10 describes unbalanced high-speed electrical interface characteristics (RS-423).

- V.11 describes balanced high-speed electrical characteristics (RS-422).

- V.13 explains simulated carrier control (with a full-duplex modem used as a half-duplex modem).

- V.14 explains the procedure for asynchronous to synchronous conversion.

- V.15 describes the requirements and designs for telephone acoustic couplers. This is largely unused today since most telephone equipment is modular and can be plugged into telephone adapters directly rather than loosely attached to the telephone handset.

- **V.17** describes an application-specific modulation scheme for Group 3 fax, which provides two-wire half-duplex trellis-coded transmission at 7200, 9600, 12,000, and 14,400 bps. In spite of the low number, this is a fairly recent standard.

- V.19 describes early DTMF modems using low-speed parallel transmission. This standard is largely obsolete.

- V.20 explains modems with parallel data transmission. This standard is largely obsolete.

- **V.21** provides the specifications for 300 bps FSK serial modems (based upon BELL103).

- **V.22** provides the specifications for 1200 bps (600 baud) PSK modems (similar to BELL212A).

- **V.22bis** describes 2400 bps modems operating at 600 baud using QAM.

- V.23 describes the operation of a rather unusual type of FM modem working at 1200/75 bps. That is, the host transmits at 1200 bps and receives at 75 bps. The remote modem transmits at 75 bps and receives at 1200 bps. V.23 is used in Europe to support some videotext applications.

- V.24 this is known as EIA RS-232 in the US. V.24 defines *only* the functions of the serial port circuits. EIA-232-E (the current version of the standard) also defines electrical characteristics and connectors.

- V.25 defines automatic answering equipment and parallel automatic dialing. It also defines the answer tone that modems send.

- V.25bis defines serial automatic calling and answering, which is the ITU (CCITT) equivalent of AT commands. This is the current ITU standard for modem control by computers via serial interface. The Hayes AT command set is used primarily in the U.S.

- **V.26** defines a 2400 bps PSK full-duplex modem operating at 1200 baud.

- **V.26bis** defines a 2400 bps PSK half-duplex modem operating at 1200 baud.

- **V.26terbo** defines a 2400/1200 bps switchable PSK full-duplex modem operating at 1200 baud.

- **V.27** defines a 4800 bps PSK modem operating at 1600 baud.

- **V.27bis** defines a more advanced 4800/2400 bps switchable PSK modem operating at 1600/1200 baud.

- **V.27terbo** defines a 4800/2400 bps switchable PSK modem commonly used in half-duplex mode at 1600/1200 baud to handle Group 3 fax rather than computer modems.

- V.28 defines the electrical characteristics and connections for V.24 (RS-232). Where the RS-232 specification defines all necessary parameters, the ITU (CCITT) breaks the specifications down into two separate documents.

- **V.29** defines a 9600/7200/4800 bps switchable PSK/QAM modem operating at 2400 baud. This type of modem is often used to implement Group 3 fax rather than computer modems.

- **V.32** defines the first of the truly modern modems as a 9600/4800 bps switchable QAM full-duplex modem operating at 2400 baud. This standard also incorporates trellis coding and echo cancellation to produce a stable, reliable, high-speed modem.

- **V.32bis** a fairly new standard extending the V.32 specification to define a 4800/7200/9600/12,000/14,400 bps switchable TCQAM full-duplex modem operating at 2400 baud. Trellis coding, automatic transfer rate negotiation, and echo cancellation made this type of modem one of the most popular and least expensive for everyday PC communication.

- **V.32terbo** continues to extend the V.32 specification by using advanced techniques to implement a 14,400/16,800/19,200 bps switchable TCQAM full-duplex modem operating at 2400 baud. Unlike V.32bis, V.32terbo is not widely used because of the rather high cost of components.

- **V.32fast** this is the informal name to a standard that the ITU has used for older high-speed modems. A V.32fast modem generally replaces V.32bis with speeds up to 28,800 bps. It is anticipated that this will be the last *analog* protocol—eventually giving way to all-digital protocols as local telephone services become entirely digital. V.32fast will probably be renamed V.34 on completion and acceptance.

- **V.33** defines a specialized 14,400 bps TCQAM full-duplex modem operating at 2400 baud.

- **V.34** defines the standard for modem communication at 2400 through 28,800 bps.

- **V.34+** is an update to V.34 outlining the enhancements needed for modem communication at 33,600 bps.

- **V.36** defines a specialized 48,000 bps *group* modem that is rarely (if ever) used commercially. This type of modem uses several conventional telephone lines.

- **V.37** defines a specialized 72,000 bps *group* modem that combines several telephone channels.

- **V.42** is the only ITU error correcting procedure for modems using V.22, V.22bis, V.26ter, V.32, and V.32bis protocols. The standard is also defined as a *Link Access Procedure for Modems* (LAPM) protocol. ITU V.42 is considered very efficient and is about 20 percent faster than MNP4. If a V.42 connection cannot be established between modems, V.42 automatically provides fallback to the MNP4 error correction standard.

- **V.42bis** uses a Lempel-Ziv–based data compression scheme for use in conjunction with V.42 LAPM (error correction). V.42bis is a data compression standard for high-speed modems that can compress data by as much as 4:1 (depending on the type of file you send). Thus, a 9600 baud modem can transmit data at up to 38,400 bps using V.42bis. A 14.4 Kbps modem can transmit up to a startling 57,600 bps.

■ V.50 sets standard telephony limits for modem transmission quality.

■ V.51 outlines required maintenance of international data circuits.

■ V.52 describes apparatus for measuring data transmission distortion and error rates.

■ V.53 outlines impairment limits for data circuits.

■ V.54 describes loop test devices for modem testing.

■ V.55 describes impulse noise measuring equipment for line testing.

■ **V.56** outlines the comparative testing of modems.

■ V.57 describes comprehensive test equipment for high-speed data transmission.

■ **V.90** is a standard for 56 Kbps modems approved by the International Telecommunication Union (ITU) in February 1998.

■ **V.92** is an update of the 56 Kbps standard that uses PCM to improve the upstream data transfer rates up to 48 Kbps.

■ V.100 describes the interconnection techniques between PDNs (Public Data Networks) and PSTNs (Public Switched Telephone Networks).

MNP STANDARDS

The *Microcom Networking Protocol* (MNP) is a complete hierarchy of standards developed during the mid-1980s that are designed to work with other modem technologies for error correction and data compression. While most ITU standards refer to modem data transfer, MNP standards concentrate on providing error correction and data compression when your modem is communicating with another modem that supports MNP. For example, MNP class 4 is specified by ITU V.42 as a backup error control scheme for LAPM in the event that V.24 can not be invoked. Out of nine recognized MNP levels, your modem probably supports the first five. Each MNP class has all the features of the previous class plus its own:

■ **MNP class 1 (block mode)**   This is an old data transfer mode that sends data in only one direction at a time—about 70 percent as fast as data transmissions using no error correction. This level is now virtually obsolete.

■ **MNP class 2 (stream mode)**   This is an older data transfer mode that sends data in both directions at the same time—about 84 percent as fast as data transmissions using no error correction.

■ **MNP class 3**   The sending modem strips start and stop bits from a data block before sending it, while the receiving modem adds start and stop bits before passing the data to the receiving computer. About 8 percent faster than data transmissions using no error correction. The increased throughput is realized only if modems on both ends of the connection are operating in a *split speed* (or *locked COM port*) fashion—that is, the rate of data transfer from computer to modem is *higher* than the data transfer rate from modem to modem. Also, data is being transferred in big blocks (such as 1KB) or continuously (by using the Zmodem file transfer protocol, for example).

■ **MNP class 4**   This is a protocol (with limited data compression) that checks telephone connection quality and uses a transfer technique called *Adaptive Packet Assembly*—on a noise-free line, the modem sends larger blocks of data. If the line is noisy, the modem sends smaller blocks of data (less data will have to be resent). This means more successful transmissions on the first try. About 20 percent faster than data transmissions using no error correction at all, so most current modems are MNP4 compatible.

- **MNP class 5**   This is classical MNP data compression. MNP5 provides data compression by detecting redundant data and recoding it to fewer bits, thus increasing effective data throughput. A receiving modem decompresses the data before passing it to the receiving computer. MNP5 can speed data transmissions up to 2x over using no data compression or error correction (with the kind of data being a determinant factor in level of increased speed). In effect, MNP5 gives a 2400 bps modem and effective data throughput of as much as 4800 bps and a 9600 bps system as much as 19,200 bps.

- **MNP class 6**   This standard uses *Universal Link Negotiation* to let modems get maximum performance out of a line. Modems start at low speeds, then move to higher speeds until the best speed is found. MNP6 also provides *Statistical Duplexing* to help half-duplex modems simulate full-duplex modems.

- **MNP class 7**   This standard offers a much more powerful data compression process (Huffman encoding) than does MNP5. MNP7 modems can increase the data throughput by as much as 3x in some cases. Although MNP7 is more efficient than MNP5, not all modems are designed to handle the MNP7 protocol. Also, although MNP7 is faster than MNP5, MNP7 is still generally considered slower than the ITU's V.42bis.

- **MNP class 9**   This standard reduces the data overhead (the housekeeping bits) encountered with each data packet. MNP9 also improves error correction performance because only the data that was in error has to be re-sent instead of resending the entire data packet.

- **MNP class 10**   This standard uses a set of protocols known as *Adverse Channel Enhancements* to help modems overcome poor telephone connections by adjusting data packet size and transmission speed until the most reliable transmission is established. This is a more powerful version of MNP4.

FILE TRANSFER PROTOCOLS

Even with powerful data transfer, compression, and correction protocols, the way in which data is packaged and exchanged is still largely undefined by ITU and MNP standards. You see, a typical modem has no way of knowing the difference between a keyboard stroke or data being downloaded from a hard drive—the modem does not understand a file. Instead, it only works with bytes, bits, timing, and tones. As a consequence, the modem relies on communications software to manage file characteristics such as filename, file size, and content. The software routines that bundle and organize data between modems are called *file transfer protocols*. Errors that occur during file transfer are automatically detected and corrected by file transfer protocols. If a block of data is received incorrectly, the receiving system sends a message to the sending system and requests the retransmission. This process is automatic and essentially transparent to the computer users (except perhaps for a display in the communication software's file transfer status window). The following are some of the more traditional transfer protocols:

The transfer protocols outlined next were used mainly with dial-up modem connections to BBS facilities. Modern file transfers over the Internet generally use more sophisticated networking protocols, such as File Transfer Protocol (FTP), or e-mail protocols, such as Mime.

- **ASCII**   This protocol is designed to work with ASCII text files only. Be aware that you do *not* have to use this protocol when transferring text files. The ASCII protocol is useful for uploading a text file when you are composing e-mail online.

- **Xmodem**   This is one of the most widely used file transfer protocols. Introduced in 1977 by Ward Christensen, this protocol is slow, but reliable. The original Xmodem protocol used 128-byte packets and a simple *checksum* method of error detection. A later enhancement, Xmodem-CRC, uses a more secure *Cyclic Redundancy Check* (CRC) method for error detection. Xmodem protocols always attempt to use CRC first. If the sender does not acknowledge the requests for CRC, the receiver shifts to the checksum mode and continues its request for transmission. Mismatching the two variants of Xmodem during file transfers is usually the reason for transfer problems, although many communication systems can now detect the differences automatically.

■ **Xmodem-1K**   The Xmodem-1K protocol is essentially Xmodem CRC with 1KB (1,024 bytes) packets. On some systems and bulletin boards, it may also be referred to as Ymodem. Some communication software programs (most notably Procomm Plus 1.x) also list Xmodem-1K as Ymodem. Procomm Plus 2.0 no longer refers to Xmodem-1K as Ymodem.

■ **Ymodem**   A Ymodem protocol is little more than a version of Xmodem-1K that allows multiple-file batch transfer (sending/receiving several files one after another unattended). On some systems it is listed as Ymodem Batch (and is sometimes called *true Ymodem*). Ymodem offers a faster transmission rate than Xmodem and better data security through a refined CRC checksum method.

■ **Ymodem-g**   The Ymodem-g protocol is a variant of basic Ymodem designed for use with modems that support error correction. This protocol does not provide software error correction or recovery itself, but expects the *modem* to provide the service. It is a streaming protocol that sends and receives 1K packets in a continuous stream until instructed to stop. It does not wait for positive acknowledgment after each block is sent, but rather sends blocks in rapid succession. If any block is unsuccessfully transferred, the entire transfer is canceled.

■ **Zmodem**   This is generally the best protocol to use if the electronic service you are calling supports it. Zmodem has two significant features: it is extremely efficient, and it provides automatic *crash* recovery. Like Ymodem-g, Zmodem does not wait for positive acknowledgment after each block is sent, but rather sends blocks in rapid succession. If a Zmodem transfer *crashes* (is canceled or interrupted for any reason), the transfer can be resurrected later and the previously transferred information need *not* be re-sent. Zmodem can detect excessive line noise and automatically drop to a shorter, more reliable data packet size when necessary. Data integrity and accuracy is assured by the use of reliable 16-bit CRC (cyclic redundancy check) methods rather than less reliable CRC checking of Ymodem and Xmodem.

■ **Kermit**   The Kermit protocol was developed at Columbia University. It was designed to facilitate the exchange of data among very different types of computers (mainly minicomputers and mainframes). You probably will not need to use Kermit unless you are calling a minicomputer or mainframe at an educational institution.

■ **Sealink**   The Sealink protocol is a variant of Xmodem. It was developed to overcome the transmission delays caused by satellite relays or packet-switching networks. However, Sealink is rarely used today.

Installing an Analog Modem

Both internal and external analog modem devices are typically PnP devices that are designed for automatic detection and resource assignments. Still, most modem (especially WinModem) problems *start* when the card is first installed in the system—problems that are usually due to inadequate or incorrect installation of the hardware and software. This part of the chapter offers an overview of the installation process so that you can check for missing steps. When replacing the modem, remember that the initialization and operating strings often vary slightly between modem manufacturers—be sure to alter any AT command strings in the communication software to accommodate the new modem or remove the old modem and its application software *before* exchanging the modem.

Always use proper static precautions (such as an antistatic wrist strap) when working inside a system with sensitive devices—such as the modem card.

INTERNAL HARDWARE INSTALLATION

Installing an internal modem requires a bit of care because you'll need to open the system and work inside of it. The following steps outline the general process, but be sure to reference the manufacturer's instructions for particular precautions.

1.   Shut down Windows 9x/Me, then turn off and unplug the computer.

2.   Unbolt the outer case, then remove the housing and set it (and the screws) aside in a safe place.

3.   If you're replacing an existing modem with a newer, faster model, you'll need to remove the old modem first. Disconnect the telephone line cord (and other telephone cords) from the modem. Unbolt the old modem card bracket from the chassis and remove the old modem from its expansion slot. Be sure to set the old modem aside on a static-safe surface or in an antistatic bag.

4.   Locate a slot for the new modem card. Older modem card devices will require an ISA slot, though most current modem cards (V.90/V.92 56 Kbps and later) will need a PCI slot. Find an available slot that's appropriate for your modem card. Remove the cover for the slot you intend to use (if it's not already removed) and save the screw for the mounting bracket.

5.   Insert the modem card. Push the card in firmly and evenly until it's fully seated in the slot. Replace the screw to secure the bracket of your modem card to the computer's chassis.

6.   Reconnect the modem to the telephone wall jack using the modem's LINE or TELCO jack.

 The phone jack you use *must* be for an *analog* phone line (the type found in most homes). Many office buildings have digital phone lines (a.k.a. PBX lines). Be sure you know which type of line you have. The modem may be damaged if you use a digital phone line.

7.   If you wish to use a phone on the same line that the modem is using (when the modem is not in use), plug your phone's line cord into the modem's PHONE jack.

8.   If your modem model supports "simultaneous voice and data," you may need a microphone to support that feature. If so, plug the microphone into the MIC jack on the modem or soundcard, depending on the design of your modem.

9.   If your modem offers full-duplex speakerphone capabilities, plug a set of powered external speakers (not included) into the SPEAKER jack on the modem. Some modem designs may simply play back sound through the soundcard's speakers, so additional speakers may not be required.

SOFTWARE INSTALLATION

Now that the physical hardware for your new modem card has been installed, it's time to install the modem drivers and application software that you'll need to identify the device under Windows 9x/Me and use advanced features (such as a voice mail system). Leave the computer's housing off for now, but reconnect the AC cord to the computer and prepare to start the system again.

 Always refer to the README file on the modem card's driver disc to obtain the very latest feature descriptions and software installation guidelines for your particular card.

1. When Windows restarts, it should detect the modem automatically. If the modem is not PnP-com-pliant (or you're using an old version of Windows), you may need to use the Add New Hardware wizard to run the modem installation process.

2. Click "Driver from disk provided by hardware manufacturer." Then click OK.

3. Insert the driver CD into the CD-ROM, then select the CD-ROM drive letter.

4. Click OK. Windows will load the modem's drivers.

5. Once Windows finishes loading the information from the driver CD, you should verify that the modem installation was a success. When your desktop returns, click Start, highlight Settings, then click Control Panel.

6. Double-click the Modems icon.

7. In the Modems Properties dialog, you should see a suitable description for your modem (Figure 26-4). If so, your modem installed properly.

8. Now you should test your modem. Click the Diagnostics tab. Select the modem (or the COM port that your modem is on), then click the More Info button.

9. After a few moments, you should see the More Info dialog (Figure 26-5), which lists the modem's Port Information as well as a series of standard modem commands.

10. If the modem responds to each of the commands, the modem should be working, and you're ready to try the modem online. You can reattach the computer's outer housing and return the system to normal service. If the modem does *not* respond or an error is generated, you should double-check the modem's installation and verify that the modem has been properly identified.

11. Once the modem is working, you can install any other applications or support software (such as voice mail or fax software) that accompany your modem.

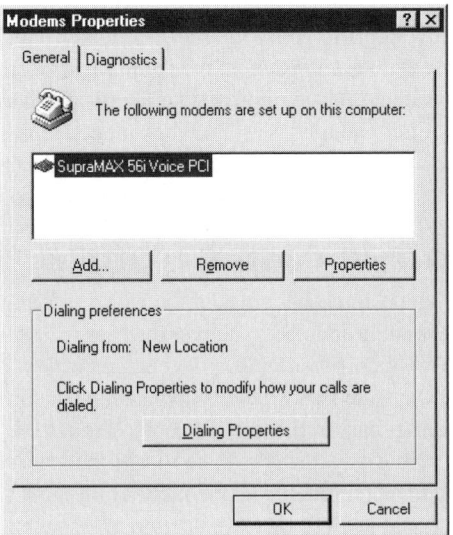

FIGURE 26-4   Checking your modem in the Modem Properties dialog under Windows 98/SE

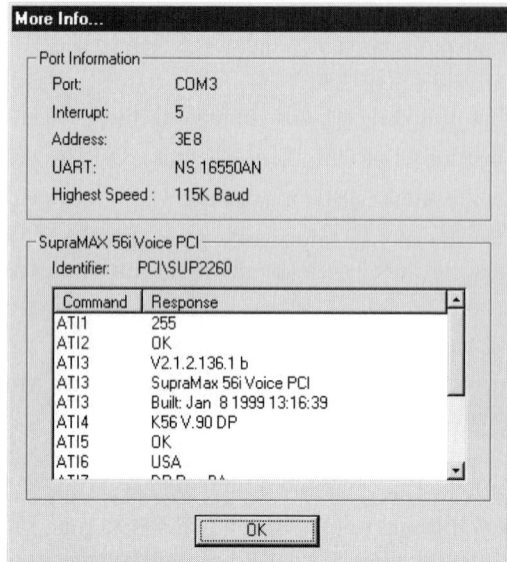

FIGURE 26-5   Verifying the modem's operation under Windows 98/SE

Installing a Cable Modem

Over the last few years, the Internet has exploded with content. Not only can you view text and images, but you can now access real-time audio and video broadcasting, Java applets, ShockWave multimedia presentations, and so much more. The intense growth in Internet use and the increasing complexity of Internet media have placed a strain on the bandwidth offered by Internet Service Providers (ISPs). There are simply too many users trying to access gobs of data-intensive information. Most Internet connections are dial-up, and while conventional modems have continued to improve in order to pass more data across the existing global telephone network, that is no longer enough. With 56 Kbps modems pushing the capabilities of today's phone network, another large network is positioning for the Internet—the cable television system. This part of the chapter presents the essential requirements and installation steps for typical cable modems.

UNDERSTANDING THE CABLE MODEM

In most regions of the United States (and other areas of the world offering cable television access), cable television (or CATV) systems are being adapted to deliver Internet access. Local cable companies offering Internet access can serve as ISPs—incorporating Internet charges with your existing cable television bill. Early cable modems were "one way" devices, so they supplemented a conventional analog modem with a high-speed "cable modem". Internet data in those systems was requested "upstream" via your phone line (using an existing modem in much the way that you do now), and that data was sent "downstream" from the Internet via the CATV network to a computer's "cable modem" at burst rates of up to 38 Mbps. Current cable modems are fully bidirectional devices that can operate independently of analog modems, network cards, or other devices. In fact, it's not uncommon to find USB/Ethernet external cable modems. A typical cable modem kit will contain:

Before installing a cable modem, contact your local cable service provider to verify the availability of cable service in your area and arrange for cable Internet access. In many cases, a cable technician will need to check the cable outlet that you intend to use prior to connecting the modem.

■ Cable modem device

■ Cable modem power adapter (or AC cord)

■ Instruction guide(s)

■ Driver/applet software CD

■ Universal Serial Bus (USB) cable and/or Ethernet cable (depending on how you're connecting the modem)

   As a rule, your PC must meet the following requirements:

■ Pentium processor or equivalent (Pentium 166 or higher recommended).

■ An active two-way cable line installed by your cable service provider.

■ A length of coaxial cable (which may be provided by your cable service).

■ Your original Windows 95, Windows 98, Windows Me, Windows 2000, or Windows NT 4.0 installation CD.

   If you plan to connect the cable modem through the PC's USB port, you'll need a PC running Windows 98, Windows Me, or Windows 2000, along with an active USB port on your computer.

   If you plan to connect the cable modem to an existing Ethernet port on your PC's network card, you'll need a PC running Windows 95, Windows 98, Windows Me, Windows NT 4.0, or Windows 2000. You'll also need to have the TCP/IP protocol and active Ethernet port or network interface card (NIC) installed in your computer.

USB HARDWARE INSTALLATION

If you do not have a network card available (or don't want the hassle of a NIC installation first), use the following steps to connect the USB/Ethernet cable modem to a USB port on your system:

1. Power on the computer.

2. Connect the coaxial cable to the cable modem's CATV cable connector and to the wall cable outlet.

3. Connect the USB cable to the modem and to the computer's USB port.

4. Plug the cable modem's power supply into a surge protector or into an electrical outlet.

5. Within a few minutes, the computer detects the cable modem.

USB Software Installation

After the computer detects the cable modem, insert the driver CD and follow the onscreen prompts to install the necessary driver file(s) and other software. The actual process varies a bit depending on your operating system.

   For **Windows 98**:

1. The Add New Hardware wizard appears when the modem is detected.

2. Select "Search for the best driver for your device (Recommended)" and click Next.

3. Check the CD-ROM drive check box and click Next to search for the necessary driver files.

4. Select the correct driver. For a 3Com modem, you'd choose "The updated driver (Recommended) 3Com HomeConnect TM Cable Modem External with USB" and then click Next.

5. When Windows locates the driver files, click Next to automatically install the necessary files.

6. When prompted, insert the Windows 98 CD into the CD-ROM drive and click OK.

7. After Windows copies the driver files, click Finish. The System Settings Change dialog box appears.

8. Click Yes to reboot your computer.

The process is a bit simpler under **Windows Me**:

1. The Add New Hardware wizard screen appears when the modem is detected.

2. Select "Automatic search for a better driver (Recommended)" and click Next.

3. When Windows locates the driver files, click Next to install the necessary files.

4. Click Finish. The System Settings Change dialog box appears.

5. Click Yes to reboot your computer.

Windows 2000 offers a few wrinkles:

1. The Found New Hardware wizard screen appears when the modem is detected.

2. Select "Search for a suitable driver for my device (recommended)" and click Next.

3. Check the CD-ROM drives check box and click Next to search for the necessary driver files.

4. When the Found New Hardware wizard displays the search results, click Next to install the necessary driver files.

5. If the Digital Signature Not Found screen appears, click Yes to continue the installation.

6. When the Found New Hardware wizard completes the installation, click Finish.

Check the LEDs
When the modem is operating properly, the Link Status and Power LEDs on the front of the modem are illuminated and *not* blinking. If you're powering up the cable modem for the first time, allow up to 15 minutes for the Link Status LED to stop blinking while the modem calibrates itself for your cable connection.

ETHERNET HARDWARE INSTALLATION
If you have an Ethernet network (or Ethernet NIC available) under Windows 9x/Me/NT4/2000, use the following guidelines and steps to connect the USB/Ethernet cable modem to an Ethernet port on your system.

Verify the TCP/IP Protocol Configuration
Before installing the cable modem using the Ethernet setup, you must verify that your computer has the TCP/IP protocol installed (if not, you'll need to install it before connecting the modem).

For **Windows 9x/Me**:

1. Right-click the Network Neighborhood icon (or the My Network Places icon under Windows Me) on the Windows desktop and click Properties (Figure 26-6).

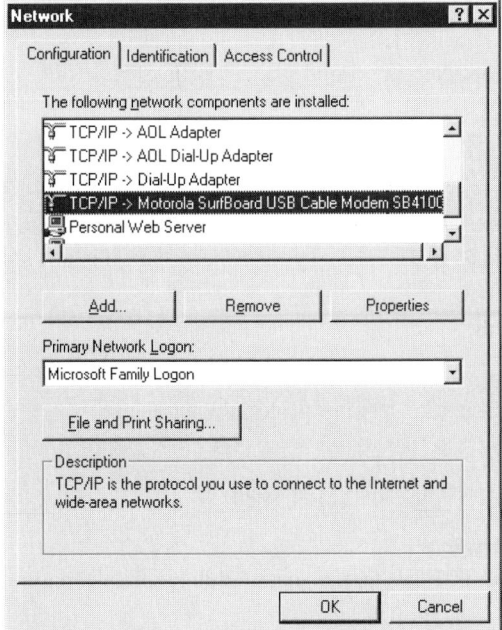

FIGURE 26-6   Checking for TCP/IP support under Windows 98/SE

2.   Look for an entry named TCP/IP. If you see TCP/IP listed next to your Ethernet hardware device, you can now skip down and install the cable modem hardware. If TCP/IP is not listed, you must complete the following steps.

3.   Click Add.

4.   Click Protocol, then click Add.

5.   Click Microsoft in the Manufacturers list and Click TCP/IP in the Network Protocols list.

6.   Click OK.

7.   Click Yes when prompted to restart your computer (recheck for TCP/IP). You can now skip to the instructions for installing the cable modem hardware.

   Windows 2000 uses the same basic process, but there are a few minor differences that you should be aware of:

1.   Right-click the My Network Places icon on the Windows desktop.

2.   Right-click Local Area Connection and click Properties. Look for an entry named TCP/IP. *If you see TCP/IP listed next to your Ethernet hardware device, you can skip down and install the cable modem hardware*. If TCP/IP is not listed, complete the following steps.

3.   Scroll to the Interne/t Protocol (TCP/IP) option.

4.   Click to place a check mark in the Internet Protocol check box.

5.   Click OK. You can now install the cable modem hardware.

Windows NT 4.0 presents even a few more wrinkles, so here is the general process:

1. Right-click the Network Neighborhood icon and click Properties.

2. Click the Bindings tab.

3. Select All Protocols from the Show bindings for drop-down list.

4. Look for an entry named TCP/IP. If you see TCP/IP listed, double-click it to search for your Ethernet card. *If you see your Ethernet card listed, you can skip to the instructions for installing the cable modem hardware.* If TCP/IP or your Ethernet card is not listed, you must complete the following steps.

5. Click the Protocols tab.

6. Click Add.

7. Click TCP/IP protocol in the Network protocol list.

8. Click OK.

9. Click Yes when prompted to restart your computer.

Install the Cable Modem

Once you've verified that the TCP/IP stack is installed on your system, you can proceed to connect the modem hardware:

1. Power-off the computer.

2. Connect the coaxial cable to the cable modem's CATV cable connector and to the cable outlet.

3. Connect the Ethernet cable between the Ethernet port and the cable modem.

4. Plug the cable modem's power adapter into the cable modem's power jack and into a wall outlet or surge protector.

5. Power-on the computer—doing this should start the hardware detection process.

Check the LEDs

When the modem is operating properly, the Link Status and Power LEDs on the front of the modem are illuminated and *not* blinking. If you're powering up the cable modem for the first time, allow up to 15 minutes for the Link Status LED to stop blinking while the modem calibrates itself for your cable connection.

Modem Troubleshooting

Okay, the modem is installed (or replaced), the drivers are installed, the communication software is loaded, the telephone line is connected—and nothing happens. This is an all-too-common theme for today's technicians and computer enthusiasts. Although the actual failure rate among ordinary modems is quite small, it turns out that modems (and serial ports, as you will see later in the book) are some of the more difficult and time-consuming devices to set up and configure. As a consequence, proper setup from the start can simplify troubleshooting significantly. When a modem fails to work properly, there are a number of conditions to explore:

■ **Incorrect hardware resources**   An internal modem must be set with a unique IRQ line and I/O port. If the assigned resources are also used by another serial device in the system (such as a mouse), the modem or the conflicting device (or perhaps both) will not function properly. Remove the modem and use a diagnostic to check available resources. Under Windows 9x/Me, you can use the Device Manager to investigate devices and examine their configurations. Reconfigure the internal modem to clear the conflict or use the CMOS Setup to disable the conflicting COM port so that the modem can use its resources. External modems make use of existing COM ports.

■ **Defective telecommunication resources** All modems need access to a telephone line in order to establish connections with other modems. If the telephone jack is defective or hooked up improperly, the modem may work fine but no connection is possible. Remove the telephone line cord from the modem and try the line cord on an ordinary telephone. When you lift the receiver, you should draw dial tone. Try dialing a local number—if the line rings, chances are good that the telephone line is working. Check the RJ11 jack on the modem. One or more bent connector pins can break the line even though the line cord is inserted properly.

■ **Improper cabling** An external modem must be connected to the PC serial port with a cable. Traditional serial cables were 25-pin assemblies. Later, 9-pin serial connectors and cables became common—out of those 9 wires, only three are really vital. As a result, quite a few cable assemblies may be incorrect or otherwise specialized. Make sure that the serial cable between the PC and modem is a "straight-through" type cable (rather than a *null modem* cable). Also check that both ends of the cable are intact (installed evenly, no bent pins, and so on). Try a new cable if necessary.

■ **Improper power** External modems must receive power from batteries or from an AC eliminator. Make sure that any batteries are fresh and installed completely. If an AC adapter is used, see that it is connected to the modem properly.

■ **Incorrect software settings** Both internal and external modems must be initialized with an AT ASCII command string before a connection is established. If these settings are absent or incorrect, the modem will not respond as expected (if at all). Check the communication software and make sure that the AT command strings are appropriate for the modem being used—different modems often require slightly different command strings. Be sure that you're using the latest driver version designed specifically for your modem model.

■ **Suspect the modem itself** Modems are typically quite reliable in everyday use. If there are jumpers or DIP switches on the modem, check that each setting is placed correctly. Perhaps their most vulnerable point is the telephone interface, which is particularly susceptible to high-voltage spikes that might enter through the telephone line. If all else fails, try another modem.

CHECK THE COMMAND PROCESSOR

The "command processor" is the controller that manages the modem's operation in the command mode, and it is the command processor that interprets AT command strings. When the new modem installation fails to behave as it should, you should first check the modem command processor using the following procedure. Before going too far with this, make sure you have the modem's user guide on hand (if possible). When the command processor checks out, but the modem refuses to work under normal communication software operations, the software may be refusing to save settings such as COM port selection, speed, and character format:

1. Make sure the modem is installed properly and connected to the desired PC serial port. Of course, if the modem is internal, you will need to worry only about IRQ and I/O port settings. Check the Device Manager to see that the internal modem's COM port setting is not conflicting with an existing COM port on the PC.

2. Start the communication software and select a "direct connection" to establish a path from your keyboard to the modem (this is sometimes referred to as "terminal mode"). You will probably see a dialog box appear with a blinking cursor. If the modem is working and installed properly, you should now be able to send commands directly to the modem.

   For example, under Windows 9x/Me, you can use the HyperTerminal applet under Start, Programs, Accessories, and HyperTerminal. Once the HyperTerminal folder opens, double-click the Hypertrm icon, and type **Test1** in the Connection Description dialog. Click OK. When you're asked to enter a phone number, enter your own number and click OK. When the Connect dialog asks to dial the number, just click Cancel. A text window appears, as in Figure 26-7. Type **AT** (you may not see the letters as you type them) and press ENTER. You should see an "OK" response.

3. Type the command **AT** and then press ENTER. The modem should return an "OK" result code. When an "OK" is returned, chances are that the modem is working correctly. If you see double characters being displayed, try the command **ATE0** to disable the command mode echo. If you do not see an "OK," try issuing an **ATE1** command to enable the command mode echo. If there is still no response, commands are not reaching the modem or the modem is defective. Check the connections between the modem and serial port. If the modem is internal, check that it is installed correctly and that all jumpers are placed properly.

4. Try resetting the modem with the **ATZ** command and then pressing ENTER. Doing this should reset the modem. If the modem now responds with "OK," you may have to adjust the initialization command string in the communication software, the Registry, or the Extra settings line in your modem's properties.

5. Try factory default settings by typing the command **AT&F**, then pressing ENTER. Doing this should restore the factory default values for each S-register. You may also try the command **AT&Q0** and ENTER to deliberately place the modem into asynchronous mode. You should see

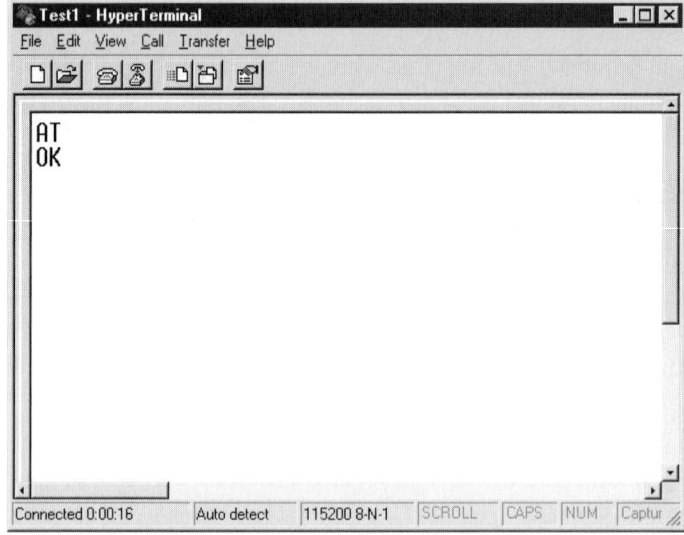

FIGURE 26-7   Testing the modem's command processor with HyperTerminal

"OK" responses to each attempt, indicating the modem is responding as expected—it may be necessary to update the modem's initialization command string. If the modem still does not respond, the communication software may be incompatible or the modem may be defective.

CHECK THE DIALER AND TELEPHONE LINE

After you've demonstrated that the modem's command processor is responding properly, you can also check the telephone interface by attempting a call—doing this also can verify an active telephone line. When the telephone interface checks out but the modem refuses to work under normal communication software operations, the software may be refusing to save settings such as COM port selection, speed, and character format:

1. Make sure the modem is installed properly and connected to the desired PC serial port. Of course, if the modem is internal, you will need to worry only about IRQ and I/O port settings. Check that there is no conflict between the modem's COM port and the system's COM port(s).

2. Start the communication software and select a "direct connection" to establish a path from your keyboard to the modem (this is sometimes referred to as "terminal mode"). You will probably see a dialog box appear with a blinking cursor. If the modem is working and installed properly, you should now be able to send commands directly to the modem. See the previous HyperTerminal.

3. Dial a number by using the **DT** (dial using tones) command followed by the full number being called—for example, **ATDT15085551212** followed by pressing ENTER . If your local telephone line supports only rotary dialing, use the modifier **R** after the **D**. If calling from a PBX, be sure to dial 9 or other outside-access codes. Listen for a dial tone, followed by the tone dialing beeps. You should also hear the destination phone ringing. When these occur, they ensure that your telephone interface dials correctly and that the local phone line is responding properly.

4. If there is no dial tone, check the phone line by dialing with an ordinary phone. Note that some PBX systems must be modified to produce at least 48 volts DC for the modem to work. If there is no dial tone but the modem attempts to dial, the telephone interface is not grabbing the telephone line correctly (the dialer is working). If the modem draws dial tone but no digits are generated, the dialer may be defective. In either case, try another modem.

TYPICAL COMMUNICATION PROBLEMS

Even when the modem hardware is working perfectly, the serial communication process is *anything* but flawless. Problems ranging from accidental loss of carrier to a catastrophic loss of data regularly plague computer communication. To make your online time as foolproof as possible, this section of the chapter shows you how to deal with some of the most pernicious communication problems.

■ **Modem settings** Modem settings are critically important to inter-modem communication. The number of data bits, use of parity, number of stop bits, and data transfer speed must be set *precisely* the same way on both modems. Otherwise, the valid data leaving one modem will be interpreted as complete "junk" at the receiving end. Normally, this should not happen when modems are set to auto-answer—negotiation should allow both modems to settle at the same parameters. The time that incompatible settings really become a factor is when negotiation is unsuccessful or when communication is being established manually. A typical example is an avid BBS user with communication software set to 8 data bits, no parity bit, and 1 stop bit trying to use a network which runs at 7 data bits, even parity, and 2 stop bits. The aspect that stands out with incompatible settings is that virtually *nothing* is intelligible—and the connection is typically lost.

■ **Modems and UART types**   The UART is clearly the heart of a modem system. It is the modem that converts bus data into serial data (and vice versa), but the UART must be able to keep pace with the modem's data transfer rate. As modem speeds have increased, UARTs have become faster also. When installing a new external modem on an older PC, an older PC's serial port may simply not be fast enough to deal with the modem. The result is often limited modem performance (if the modem works at all). Today, the 16550A UART is the device of choice. Table 26-4 compares the major UART types. When faced with an older UART, it may be possible to replace the UART chip outright—otherwise, it is a simple matter to *disable* the existing serial port and install a newer serial adapter card incorporating a new UART.

■ **Line noise**   While faulty settings can load a transmission with trash, even a properly established connection can lose integrity periodically. Remember that serial communication is made possible by a global network of switched telephone wiring. Each time you dial the same number, you typically get a different set of "wiring." Faulty wiring at any point along the network, electrical storms, wet or snowy weather, and other natural or man-made disasters can interrupt the network momentarily or cut communication entirely. Most of the time, brief interruptions can result in small patches of garbled text. This type of behavior is most prominent in real-time online sessions (such as typing in a chat message). When uploading or downloading files, file transfer protocols can usually catch such anomalies and correct errors or request new data packets to overcome the errors. When you have trouble moving files or notice a high level of "junk" online, try calling back—when a new telephone line is established, the connection quality might be better.

■ **Transmit and receive levels**   Other factors that affect both leased and dial-up telephone lines are the transmit and receive levels. These settings determine the signal levels used by the modem in each direction. Some Hayes-compatible modems permit these levels to be adjusted. The range and availability of these adjustments is in large part controlled by the local telephone system. For example, the recommended settings and ranges are different for modems sold in the UK than for those sold in the US. See the documentation accompanying the modem to determine whether this capability is supported.

■ **System processor limitations**   Some multi-tasking operating systems can occasionally lose small amounts of data if the computer is heavily loaded and cannot allocate processing time to the

TABLE 26-4   COMPARISON OF POPULAR UART TYPES

UART	DESCRIPTION
8250	This is the original PC/XT serial port UART. There are several minor bugs in the UART, but the original PC/XT BIOS corrected for them. The 8250 was replaced by the 8250B.
8250A	This slightly updated UART fixed many of the issues in the 8250, but it would not work in PC/XT systems because the BIOS was written to circumvent the 8250's problems. In either case, the 8250A will not work adequately over 9600 bps.
8250B	The last of the 8250 series reinserted the bugs that existed in the original 8250 so that PC/XT BIOS would function properly. The 8250B also does not run above 9600 bps.
16450	This higher-speed UART was the desired choice for AT (i286) systems. Stable at 9600 bps, the 16450 laid the groundwork for the first "high-speed" modems. However, the 16450 will not work in PC/XT systems. This chip should be replaced by the 16550A.
16550	The 16550 was faster than the 16450, allowing operation above 9600 bps, but its performance was still limited by internal design problems. This chip should be replaced by the 16550A.
16550A	The fastest of the UARTs, a 16550A eliminates many of the serial port problems encountered when using a fast modem.

communications task frequently enough. In this case, the host computer itself corrupts data. This could also cause incomplete data transmission to the remote system. Host processor capabilities should be a concern when choosing software for data communications when the line speed is greater than 9,600 bps and the modem-to-DTE connection is 19,200 bps or higher (for example, when data compression is used). The modem will provide exact transmission of the data it receives, but if the host PC cannot "keep up" with the modem because of other tasks or speed restrictions, precautions should be taken when writing software or when adding modems with extra high speed capabilities.

One way to avoid the problem of data loss caused by the host PC is the use of an upgraded serial port such as a Hayes Enhanced Serial Port card, or a newer modem with a 16550 UART. Such advanced modems are powerful enough to take some of the load off of the PC processor. When processor time is stretched to the limit, try shutting down any unnecessary applications to reduce load on the system. Processor loading can become a notable issue with today's WinModem devices.

■ **Call waiting**   The *call-waiting* feature now available on most dial-up lines momentarily interrupts a call. This interruption causes a click that informs voice call users that another call is coming through. While this technique is dynamite for voice communication, it is also quite effective at interrupting a modem's carrier signal—and may cause some modems to drop the connection. One way around this is to set S-register S10 to a higher value so the modem tolerates a fairly long loss of carrier signal. Data loss may still occur, but the connection will not drop. Of course, the remote modem must be similarly configured. When originating the call, a special prefix (usually ***70**) can be issued as part of the dialing string to disable call waiting for the duration of the call. The exact procedure varies from area to area, so contact your local telephone system for details.

■ **Automatic timeout**   Some Hayes-compatible modems offer an automatic *timeout* feature. Automatic timeout prevents an inactive connection from being maintained. This "watchdog" feature prevents undesired long-distance charges for a connection that was maintained for too long. This inactivity delay can be set or disabled with S-register S30.

■ **System lock up**   There are situations where host systems *do* lock up, but in many cases it is simply that one or the other of the computers has been *flowed off*—that is, the character that stops data transfer has been inadvertently sent. This can happen during error-control connections if the wrong kind of local flow control has been selected. In addition, the problem could be the result of incompatible EIA 232-D/ITU V.24 signaling. When systems seem to cease transmitting or receiving without warning but do not disconnect, perform a thorough examination of flow control and try a different flow control method if possible.

■ **Modem initialization strings**   As you saw earlier in this chapter, modems rely on initialization strings for proper configuration at start time or when new communication software is initialized. The initialization string *must* be correct for your particular modem in order to utilize all of the modem's features and achieve optimum performance. You may be able to use "generic" initialization strings but not get full functionality from the modem (for example, you may be able to use a Hayes-compatible initialization string, but Caller ID may not work). Check the modem's initialization string, try a new driver, or enter the preferred string in the *Extra settings* line of the modem's properties dialog.

MODEM TROUBLESHOOTING IN WINDOWS 98

Even with the versatility and support provided by Plug-and-Play, many modem setups are still plagued by installation, configuration, and performance problems—especially when used under a Windows platform such as Windows 98/SE. This part of the chapter is intended to offer a basic troubleshooting guide for when your modem fails to dial-out under Windows 98/SE.

Verifying Your Modem

Begin by checking the modem's status in your Windows system. It should be identified correctly and installed with the proper device drivers. Use the following steps to verify your modem under Windows 98/SE:

1. Click Start, highlight Settings, and then click Control Panel.

2. Double-click the Modems icon.

3. Select the General tab, then verify that the modem listed in that entry is correct (Figure 26-8).

If there is *no* modem listed or an incorrect modem is listed (even though Windows reported that a modem was detected), you should download the very latest driver for your modem, *Remove* the current modem reference(s), then update the modem drivers:

1. Click Start, highlight Settings, and then click Control Panel.

2. Double-click the System icon.

3. Select the Device Manager tab.

4. If a Modem entry exists, double-click the Modem branch to expand it. If the entry does not exist, look for an Other Devices branch, then double-click to expand that branch.

5. Double-click your modem entry, click the Driver tab, and then click the Update Driver button.

Your Windows 98 Update Device Driver wizard will then search for the best driver (or display a list from which you can select the appropriate driver). If you use the Update Device Driver wizard to search for a driver, you can also specify a location for the driver. Drivers for some additional modems are

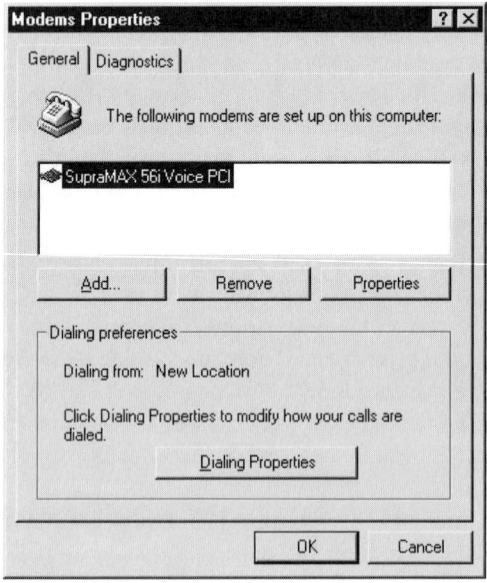

FIGURE 26-8   Verifying the modem entry in your system under Windows 98/SE

included in the \Drivers\Modem folder on the Windows 98 CD, but if you've downloaded a new set of modem drivers from the manufacturer's web site, you may need to look for the new drivers in your \Temp or \Download directories. After the modem drivers are updated, reboot the system and verify that the correct drivers are listed, then try using your modem again. If the correct driver appears in your Device Manager, but the modem still refuses to operate properly, you may need to troubleshoot further. Follow the appropriate steps given next for your *WinModem* or *standard modem*.

WinModem Issues   A *WinModem* (also called a *Windows-only modem* or *software modem*) depends on drivers that are specific to the operating system in order to function. This means that your modem *must* be recognized by the operating system *before* any troubleshooting can be performed. Windows 98/Me should normally detect the presence of a WinModem and add it to the Device Manager properly. If a WinModem is *not* detected, you should expect one of three possible causes:

- The WinModem has previously been detected (even though the correct drivers may not have been installed for it). In this case, the WinModem should be listed in your Device Manager, and the driver can be updated using the procedure in the previous "Verifying Your Modem" section.

- The WinModem drivers were installed and then removed, but some Registry entries remain. The Registry entries need to be removed before the WinModem can be detected again. For example, 3Com/US Robotics modems use the WMREGDEL.EXE tool included on your Windows installation CD to clear all WinModem-related Registry entries and then restart your computer. The WMREGDEL.EXE tool is located in the \Drivers\Modem\3com-usr\Winmodem folder. If Windows 98/Me still does not detect your WinModem, the WMREGDEL.EXE tool may not have removed all the necessary Registry entries. If this occurs, you may need to contact the particular modem maker in order to obtain a specific fix or workaround instructions (for example, there may be a specific Registry entry that needs to be deleted manually).

- The last option is to consider an actual WinModem defect—something may be wrong with the actual WinModem device. Try another WinModem (perhaps one from a different manufacturer) or check with your WinModem maker for specific testing instructions.

WinModem Driver Notes   If there are no default Windows 98/Me drivers for your WinModem, Windows prompts you to search for drivers. Suitable drivers may exist in the \Drivers\Modem folder on your Windows installation CD. If no drivers are located for your particular WinModem, Windows adds the device under the Other Devices branch of your Device Manager. You can then use the Device Manager to update the existing drivers with new drivers provided by your WinModem manufacturer. If your WinModem still does not work after installing and/or updating the drivers, there may be a resource conflict or an issue specific to your particular WinModem. Use the following sections of this discussion to troubleshoot further.

Given the dependence of a WinModem on operating system drivers, you *cannot* perform any troubleshooting outside of the operating system. For example, you *cannot* test a Windows 98/Me WinModem at a command prompt in the DOS mode.

Standard Modem Issues   A standard fax/modem does not offload important tasks to the host system or rely on the operating system for direct support. This means you may test the modem in DOS—even if it isn't detected by Windows. One of the easiest means of modem testing is to check direct communications with the modem port (COM port). Open a DOS windows under Windows 98/Me, type the following command, then press ENTER:

```
echo ATM1L3X0DT12345 > COM1
```

or replace "COM1" with the serial port number to which the modem is connected (such as COM2 or COM3). The first command, **AT** (attention), signals that the modem is about to receive information. **M1** is a universal command to turn the modem's speaker on (if it is off by default). **L3** is a universal command to raise the modem's speaker volume to the maximum level (if it is at the lowest by default). **X0** signals the modem to run the command without waiting for a dial tone—this is useful if modem and voice calls use the same phone line. Finally, the **DT12345** command instructs the modem to dial the digits **12345**. To hang up the modem again, simply type

```
echo ATH0 > COM1
```

then press ENTER. If your modem is on a port other than COM1, replace "COM1" with the serial port number to which the modem is connected (such as COM2 or COM3).

 To place your computer in DOS mode, click Start, click Shut Down, click "Restart In MS-DOS Mode," and then click OK. To quit MS-DOS mode, type **exit** at the command prompt and then press ENTER.

If the modem does *not* respond with a dial tone or communication signal in DOS mode, there may be something physically wrong with either the modem or the COM port. Verify that the modem's COM port is configured as expected or reconfigure the modem manually. If there is a resource conflict between the COM port and another device in the system, you may need to resolve the conflict in order to enable the modem. Otherwise, try a new modem. If the modem does *not* respond with a dial tone or communication signal in Windows 98/Me but *does* respond in DOS mode, Windows 98/Me itself may not be communicating correctly with your COM port. This trouble can occur for several reasons:

- The COM port has not been detected. Click Start, highlight Settings, click Control Panel, double-click Add New Hardware, and then follow the instructions on your screen to detect and install the COM port.

- The serial port device drivers are corrupt. Use the System File Checker (or SFC) tool to verify the integrity of the SERIAL.VXD, VCOMM.VXD, and SERIALUI.DLL serial port drivers. To access the System File Checker, click Start, highlight Programs, highlight Accessories, point to System Tools, then choose the System Information utility. Once the System Information utility starts, click Tools on the main menu, then select the System File Checker. You may need to reinstall or update any damaged files.

- Finally, there is a resource conflict between your COM port and another device in the system. You'll need to resolve the conflict using the Device Manager, as shown in the next section of this chapter.

RESOLVING RESOURCE CONFLICTS

A COM port requires the use of an interrupt (or IRQ) signal and an I/O port address. If you're using a WinModem, you should also plan on using a direct memory access (or DMA) channel. Normally, devices should use unique resources, and no two devices in the system can share the same resources. When the same resources are used by two or more devices, a *resource conflict* is said to occur. Conflicts may prevent one or both conflicting devices from functioning until the conflict is identified and resolved. In virtually all cases, you can manage resources and resolve conflicts using the Device Manager:

1. Click Start, highlight Settings, and then click Control Panel.

2. Double-click the System icon, then select the Device Manager tab.

If there is a resource conflict that prevents one device from working, an exclamation point in a yellow circle is displayed for the device. However, a WinModem that conflicts with another device *might not* have an exclamation point in a yellow circle—in this case, you must determine if there is a conflict yourself. Follow these steps to view the resource settings used by your modem:

3. On the Device Manager tab, double-click the Modem branch to expand it.

4. Double-click your modem, then click the Resources tab (Figure 26-9).

If a Resources tab does not exist, your modem's resources cannot be configured by Windows 98—to determine the resources your modem is using, consult the documentation included with your modem.

5. Write down the resource settings used by your modem, then click OK.

6. Double-click Computer (at the top of your Device Manager hardware list) to view all the resource settings in use on your computer. Click each resource setting to determine if there is another device using any of the same settings your modem is using.

Any hardware using the "IRQ Holder For PCI Steering" setting can be disregarded—this does *not* cause a resource conflict.

If there is another device using any of the settings in use by your modem, you'll need to change the setting for that device (or your modem). If the device is Plug-and-Play–compliant, you may be able to do this through the Resources tab in Device Manager (although some devices may require you to change jumper

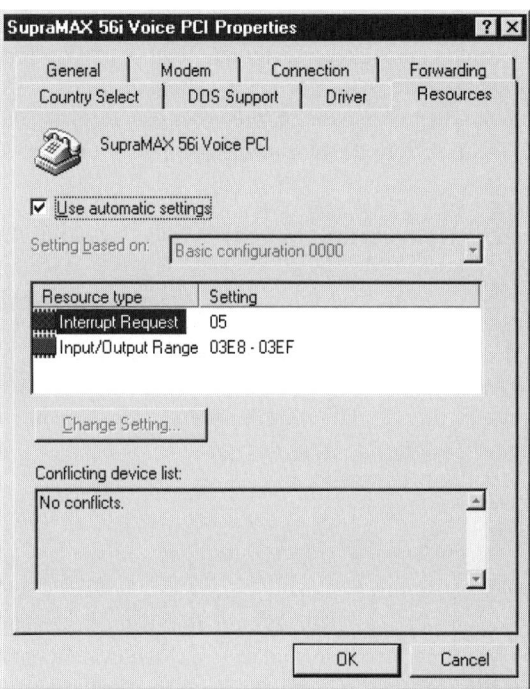

FIGURE 26-9   Checking and adjusting modem resources under Windows 98/SE

pins or dip switches on the device itself). Since WinModems are invariably Plug-and-Play devices, you should be able to change the settings for the modem through your Device Manager:

1.   Double-click the Modem branch to expand it, then double-click your WinModem entry.

2.   On the Resources tab, click the Use Automatic Settings check box to clear it.

3.   In the Setting Based On box, click a basic configuration with settings that do *not* conflict with any other device.

If *none* of the available basic configurations have settings that do not conflict with any other device, you may need to change some resource settings manually. Click the last available basic configuration, and then double-click the resource setting you need to change. If you still cannot clear the conflict, you may need to remove the other conflicting device (at least temporarily).

OTHER ISSUES

The general instructions covered in this discussion are designed to provide the essential troubleshooting guidelines for most common modem problems. Still, there are many other specific modem issues under Windows 98/Me that a technician should be aware of.

US Robotics WinModems

Some US Robotics WinModems may *not* be detected properly during the Windows 98/Me upgrade process—this may occur even if the WinModem was working perfectly under Windows 95. If your US Robotics WinModem is not detected when Windows 98/Me starts and is not listed in the Device Manager (either under the Modem or Other Devices branch), use the WMREGDEL.EXE tool included on the Windows installation CD to clear all WinModem-related Registry entries, then restart your computer. The WMREGDEL.EXE tool is located in the \Drivers\Modem\3com-usr\Winmodem folder on the Windows installation CD. If Windows 98/Me still does not detect your US Robotics WinModem, the WMREGDEL.EXE tool may not have removed all the necessary Registry entries—try an updated version of the WMREGDEL.EXE tool from the 3Com/US Robotics FTP site.

Sound4 WinModems

Packard Bell systems typically incorporate the Sound4 WinModems, but these modems might *not* be detected properly during the Windows 98 upgrade process. If the WinModem stops working properly after upgrading to Windows 98, you'll need to contact Packard Bell technical support for a suitable workaround (depending on your system model).

WinModem Not Found

After you upgrade to Windows 98, then double-click the WinModem icon in your Control Panel, you may receive an error such as:

```
Error: There is no WinModem found in your computer, but some corrupted files
were found and they have been cleaned.
```

If you view your WinModem in Device Manager, you may also notice multiple WinModem entries. This problem will typically occur if your WinModem is not using the most current setup information (.INF) file or device driver. You'll need to delete all of your WinModem entries, erase any WinModem references from the Registry, then redetect/reinstall the WinModem using the very latest .INF and driver files available from the modem maker.

Port Errors

When you try to use your modem, you may receive an error message such as:

```
Could not open port
```

This type of hardware error message is generally the result of a resource conflict between the modem and another device (or a program is loading in the Startup folder that opens a COM port for some use other than the modem). If you'd like to weed out any possible resource conflicts, refer to the guidelines covered in the previous "Resolving resource conflicts" section. If you'd like to check for possible Startup folder issues, you can use these steps to temporarily disable programs in the Startup folder:

1. Click Start, highlight Programs, select Accessories, highlight System Tools, and then click System Information.

2. On the Tools menu, select the System Configuration Utility.

3. Click the Startup tab.

Identify any programs that may control your modem, then click that program's check box to clear it. If you're unsure whether or not a specific program should be disabled, clear *all* of the check boxes *except* for the following utilities:

- ScanRegistry
- SystemTray
- LoadPowerProfile
- TaskMonitor

After you save your changes, you'll need to reboot the system and see if your changes have cleared the problem. If they did not, try disabling other non-essential files in the Startup folder.

DUN Error 630

When you attempt to use Dial-Up Networking (or DUN) services, you may receive an error message such as:

```
Error 630: The computer is not receiving a response from the modem. Check
that the modem is plugged in. Turn the modem off, and then turn it back on.
```

This error message will occur if the modem is using an serial port assignment that was adjusted when new devices are installed by Windows 98 hardware detection. In these cases, change the properties of your Dial-Up Networking (DUN) connection to use the new modem settings (rather than wrestle with tweaking the modem's settings).

Certain programs in the Startup folder can also cause this error message. Systematically disable programs in the Startup folder as outlined in the previous "Port Errors" section.

DUN Error 633

When you attempt to use Dial-Up Networking (or DUN) services, you may receive an error message such as:

```
Error 633: The modem is not installed or configured for Dial-Up Networking. To
check your modem configuration, double-click the Modems icon in Control Panel.
```

In many cases, you may need to delete and reconfigure the DUN settings for your modem. In other cases, this error message can occur if the TELEPHON.INI file is missing or damaged.

DUN Error 745

When you attempt to use Dial-Up Networking (or DUN) services, you may receive an error message such as:

```
Error 745: An essential file is missing. Re-install Dial-Up Networking.
```

This error message typically occurs when a Dial-Up Networking dynamic-link library (.DLL) file is missing or damaged. You may need to remove DUN support from Windows 98 Setup, then reinstall the support from the Windows 98 installation CD.

TAPI Issues

Check the modem's diagnostics by clicking Start, highlighting Settings, and then clicking Control Panel. Double-click the Modems icon and then select the Diagnostics tab. Click the More Info button to test the modem. When the modem passes its diagnostic tests but is not available in HyperTerminal, Phone Dialer, or Dial-Up Networking (DUN), there may be a problem with the computer's Telephony Application Programming Interface (TAPI) setup, or the TELEPHON.INI file may be missing or damaged. You may need to reinstall TAPI support, or remove and reinstall the damaged TELEPHON.INI file.

CHECKING MODEM FIRMWARE

Today, it is common for modems to sport a "flash" BIOS (firmware) that can be updated as new firmware versions are made available. Many late-model 33.6 Kbps and x2 and K56flex 56 Kbps modems offered such upgradeable firmware in preparation for the V.90 standard. If you're considering a modem firmware upgrade, you'll need to check the current firmware version on your modem. You can use HyperTerminal to determine the firmware version of your modem:

1. Click Start, highlight Programs, select Accessories, and choose HyperTerminal.

2. Double-click the Hyperterm icon.

3. When the program starts, type **TEST** for a name, and proceed.

4. When you're asked for a telephone number, just type **1234** and make sure that the correct modem device is selected from the Connect Using drop down menu. Click OK to proceed.

5. Now click Cancel (don't actually try connecting)—this will bring you to the terminal window.

6. Type in **ATE1** (even if you don't see it appear on the screen) and press ENTER. The modem should respond with "OK."

7. Now you can type any AT commands you wish. Try typing **ATi3** or **ATi92**—these two AT commands will tell you the exact firmware version and type of modem that you're using. For example, my modem responds:

    ```
    U.S. Robotics Sportster 33600 Fax V4.3.185
    ```

Once you find the firmware version, you can compare it with the new version available for download, and upgrade your firmware if the online version is newer. To determine if your modem supports the V.90 standard, follow these steps:

1. Click Start, select Settings, click Control Panel, then double-click the Modems icon.

2. On the Diagnostics tab, click the correct modem and then click More Info.

3. After a few moments, a series of AT commands and responses will appear in the information box.

4. Locate the line that begins with "ATI7." If your modem supports the V.90 standard, "V.90" should be listed beside that command.

5. Click OK.

GENERAL SYMPTOMS

Many of the problems that you will encounter with modem/fax boards are related to their physical and software configuration. The host PC also plays an important role in the modem's overall performance and reliability. Modems themselves are rarely at fault—although they are hardly invulnerable. This part of the chapter presents you with an index of potential problems and troubleshooting solutions. When you determine that the modem itself is at fault, you should replace the modem outright. When replacing the modem, remember that the initialization and operating strings often vary slightly between modem manufacturers—be sure to alter any AT command strings in the communication software to accommodate the new modem or remove the old modem and its application software before exchanging the modem.

SYMPTOM 26-1   **The PC (or communication software) refuses to recognize the modem**   First, verify that the modem is turned on (external modems only)—for internal modems, see that the modem is installed correctly and completely in its expansion slot. Check your CMOS settings and verify that the COM port for your external modem is enabled. There may be a COM port (IRQ) conflict in the system. Check the configuration of your internal modem (try the Windows Device Manager) and verify that there are no hardware conflicts. If you have trouble running the modem in "terminal mode" (the modem doesn't respond to AT commands), make sure that you're entering everything in either uppercase (AT) or lowercase (at) format—mixing cases can sometimes confuse a modem.

SYMPTOM 26-2   **Your 33.6 Kbps modem is detected as a 28.8 Kbps modem**   This can happen if your version of Windows 9x/Me doesn't supply hardware information about the faster modem that you're trying to use. In virtually every case, you'll need to supply a suitable Windows 9x/Me driver for the modem in the form of an .INF file that accompanied the modem device or is available for download from the modem manufacturer's Web site.

SYMPTOM 26-3   **The modem appears to be functioning properly, but you can't see what you're typing**   There are two types of duplex, *full* and *half*. Half-duplex systems simply transmit to and receive from each other. Full-duplex systems do that also, plus they "receive" what they transmit—echoing the data back to the sender. Since half-duplex systems do not echo, what is being sent is typically not shown on the screen. Most terminal programs have an option to enable LOCAL ECHO so that what is transmitted is also displayed. You can often enable the modem's local echo by typing the **ATE1** command during a direct connection or adding the **E1** entry to the modem's initialization string. When local echo is not an option, switching to full-duplex mode will often do the same thing. Customer complaints that they can't see what they are typing are solved by turning on local echo or switching to full-duplex.

SYMPTOM 26-4   **The modem appears to be functioning properly, but you see double characters print while typing**   By their nature, full-duplex modem connections produce an echo. If local echo is enabled in addition, you'll see not only what you are transmitting but also that characters are being echoed, creating a double display—for example, when you hit **ABC**, you'll see "AABBCC". This can be annoying, but is otherwise totally harmless. Customer complaints of double letters are solved by turning off local echo by entering the **ATE0** command during direct connection or adding the **E0** command to the modem's initialization string.

SYMPTOM 26-5 **Your 32-bit TAPI-compliant programs cannot detect your modem**
Even though you have a modem installed under Windows 9x/Me, a 32-bit TAPI program may not be able to access the modem. The TAPI program may even start the Install New Modem wizard. For example, the Install New Modem wizard may start when you launch the Make New Connection wizard in Dial-Up Networking—even though a modem is already installed. The following error message may appear after you attempt to dial a connection:

```
Error 633 The modem is not installed or configured for dial up networking.
To check your modem configuration, double click on the modems icon in the
Control Panel.
```

In virtually all cases, this fault will occur if the "Unimodem TAPI Service Provider" file (UNIMDM.TSP) is missing or damaged. To correct the fault, extract a new copy of the UNIMDM.TSP file from your original Windows disks or CD to the \Windows\System folder. For Windows 95, the UNIMDM.TSP file is located in the WIN95_03.CAB cabinet file. For Windows 98, the UNIMDM.TSP file is located in the WIN98_63.CAB cabinet file. For Windows 98 Second Edition, the UNIMDM.TSP file is located in the WIN98_69.CAB cabinet file.

SYMPTOM 26-6 **Your modem diagnostics feature cannot access the modem under Windows 98** When you attempt to run modem diagnostics on the modem (such as a 3Com Megahertz 10/100 LAN+56K Modem PC Card) after resuming your laptop from standby mode, you may receive the following error:

```
Couldn't open port.
```

This problem can occur if you try running the modem diagnostics before the computer goes into standby mode, and modem diagnostics leaves the modem's communication port open. If the port is open when your computer goes into standby mode, it remains open after you resume your computer. This is a problem with Windows 98, and a patch is now available from Microsoft. The English version of this patch contains the following attributes:

```
VCOMM.VXD       6/25/99      12:51:29p       4.10.2017       Windows 98
```

SYMPTOM 26-7 **You have trouble with a Sierra Semiconductor 33.6 Kbps modem**
When you try to use a Sierra Semiconductor 33.6 Kbps modem under Windows 98, you may encounter an "Error 630" message, and your modem may not connect successfully. This problem may not occur with every program that uses your modem. This trouble can occur because the Sierra Semiconductor 33.6 modem driver is *not* fully compatible with Windows 98. To correct this issue, update the modem driver to a version that's fully compliant with Windows 98/Me. To work around this issue, you can configure your modem to use the "Sierra 28800 PnP SQ3456" modem driver (though this will operate the modem at a slower speed than normal):

1. Click Start, highlight Settings, click Control Panel, then double-click the System icon.
2. Click the Device Manager tab, double-click the Modem entry, click your Sierra modem, then click Properties.

3. Click the Driver tab, click Update Driver, and then click "Display a list of all the drivers in a specific location, so you can select the driver you want."

4. In the Manufacturer's box, click Sierra Semiconductor.

5. In the Models box, click "Sierra 28800 PnP SQ3456."

6. Click Next, then follow the instructions on the screen to finish installing the driver.

SYMPTOM 26-8   **When creating a connection, your modem is missing from the "Select A Device" box**   If you try to use an existing connection under Windows 98/Me, you may receive an error such as:

```
Error 633: The modem is not installed or configured for Dial-Up Networking.
To check your modem configuration, double-click the Modems icon in Control
Panel
```

If you test your modem by clicking More Info on the Diagnostics tab under the Modems icon in your Control Panel, your modem may respond normally—and appear to be working correctly. This problem can occur if the "TAPI service provider" entry in your Registry is missing (or corrupted) or if the TELEPHON.INI file is missing or damaged. Access the system Registry and use REGEDIT to view the following key:

```
HKEY_LOCAL_MACHINE\Software\Microsoft\Windows\Current Version\
Telephony\Providers
```

Set the value of the **ProviderFilename0** to **TSP3216L.TSP**. Save the changes, quit the Registry Editor, then restart your computer. If the TELEPHON.INI file is missing or damaged, you'll need to recreate it:

1. Click Start, highlight Find, then click Files Or Folders.

2. In the Named box, type **telephon.ini**, then click Find Now.

3. If you do *not* find the TELEPHON.INI file, skip the next step. If you *do* find the TELEPHON.INI file, right-click the file, click Rename, type **telephon.old**, then press ENTER.

4. Quit the Find tool, click Start, click Run, type **tapiini.exe**, then press ENTER.

5. Restart your computer.

SYMPTOM 26-9   **You encounter trouble with a PhoebeMicro 56 Kbps modem under Windows 98/SE**   The modem may refuse to dial out. It may also hang up and crash the communication software with an error such as:

```
The modem failed to respond. Make sure it is properly connected and turned
on. If it is an internal modem or is connected, verify that the interrupt
for the port is properly set.
```

In virtually every case, the problem is due to faulty or outdated modem drivers accompanying the device. Contact the modem manufacturer to obtain the very latest drivers, or try default drivers on the Windows 98/SE CD.

SYMPTOM 26-10   **Your modem refuses to dial out when using a TAPI program**
When you use a TAPI program under Windows 9x/Me (such as Dial-Up Networking, Phone Dialer, or HyperTerminal), you may receive an error message such as:

```
There is no dialtone. Make sure your modem is connected to the phone line.
```

In most cases, this error occurs when you're trying to dial using a calling card and you have enabled the "Wait for dial tone before dialing" option. You must disable the "Wait for dial tone before dialing" option:

1. Click Start, highlight Settings, and then click Control Panel.
2. Double-click the Modems icon.
3. Select your modem, then click Properties.
4. On the Connection tab, click the "Wait for dial tone before dialing" check box to clear it.
5. Click OK, then click OK again.
6. It may be necessary to restart the computer.

SYMPTOM 26-11   **Your modem properties are not available through the Modems icon in your Control Panel**   When you modify your modem's properties under Windows 9x/Me, the Configure button may be unavailable in HyperTerminal or Dial-Up Networking. Also, when you click your modem and then click Properties in the Modems tool under the Control Panel, you may receive an error message such as:

```
The modem properties cannot be displayed because the modem information is
corrupt. Remove this modem by clicking Remove and add it again.
```

However, you find that removing and reinstalling the modem does *not* correct the problem. In a few cases, this problem can occur if an incorrect version of the UMDM16.DLL file is installed in the \Windows\System folder. If this occurs, rename the UMDM16.DLL file and extract a new copy of the file from your original Windows CD. In the vast majority of cases, this problem will occur if the MODEMUI.DLL file is damaged. To correct this problem, use Windows Explorer or My Computer to rename the MODEMUI.DLL file in the \Windows\System folder to MODEMUI.OLD, then extract a new copy of the MODEMUI.DLL file from your Windows CD to your \Windows\System folder.

SYMPTOM 26-12   **Your faxes are garbled when using a class 2 fax/modem**   When you open the fax in a Windows 9x/Me application such as Fax Viewer, the output may resemble a bar code or contain blank pages. This is almost always a problem with the fax/modem, since some class 2 fax/modems reverse the bit order of incoming faxes. To correct this problem, switch the "bit order" of incoming faxes for each of your affected fax/modems by editing the Registry:

1. Exit your fax/modem software, then launch your Registry Editor (REGEDIT).
2. Locate the following Registry key:

   ```
   Hkey_Local_Machine\Software\Microsoft\At Work Fax\Local Modems\
   TAPI0001<xxxx>
   ```

   where <xxxx> is a unique TAPI identifier for the fax/modem), then add the string value **CL2SWBOR** to that Registry key.
3. Set the string value for CL2SWBOR to **1**.
4. Save your changes and quit the Registry Editor, then restart your computer.

SYMPTOM 26-13   Your V.34 internal 28.8 Kbps modem is not detected properly
When you run the Add New Hardware wizard under Windows 9x/Me, the V.34 modem may be detected as a "standard modem," even though the modem is included in the hardware list. This problem occurs because the V.34 modem included in the hardware list is not a 28.8 Kbps modem, but the actual installed modem is a 28.8 Kbps modem. To install the modem correctly, you'll need to provide the manufacturer's drivers:

1. Click Start, highlight Settings, and then click Control Panel.

2. Double-click the Modems icon.

3. Click Add.

4. Click the "Don't detect my modem; I will select it from a list" check box to select it, then click Next.

5. Click Have Disk.

6. In the "Copy Manufacturer's File From" box, type the path to the disk containing the manufacturer's driver files, then click OK.

7. Follow the instructions on the screen to complete the installation.

SYMPTOM 26-14   You cannot dial phone numbers over 32 characters long   When you try to dial a long phone number (over 32 characters) under Windows 98, your modem may not respond or dial out. This is typically a driver issue and is usually caused when using a controller-less modem with a "standard" (or "generic") modem driver instead of the driver that is specifically designed for your particular modem. To resolve this issue, you should obtain and install the most current modem driver for your particular modem.

SYMPTOM 26-15   You cannot initialize your modem properly when using pcANYWHERE under Windows 98   When you use Symantec's pcANYWHERE 7.0 to dial out by modem and establish a connection, you may receive an "Error initializing modem" error message. The modem then continues to dial out, and the connection *is* established. The performance of pcANYWHERE is not affected, but the error message may appear every time you dial out with a modem to establish a pcANYWHERE connection. This problem is known to occur with version 7.0 of this software, and you will need to upgrade to pcANYWHERE 7.5 or later in order to correct the problem.

SYMPTOM 26-16   The modem is detected on the wrong COM port on your PC   The modem may not respond or work correctly and may appear to be using COM3 even if you've configured your modem to use COM1. This is a known issue with systems such as the Acer Aspire and is caused by an issue with the system's BIOS. For example, this problem can occur if COM1 is disabled in your computer's BIOS, but the system incorrectly reports the disabled status of COM1—Windows 9x/Me still detects COM1, and may assign your modem to COM3 to avoid resource conflicts. The proper long-term fix is to upgrade the system BIOS. But you may work around the issue by disabling COM1 in the Device Manager:

1. Right-click My Computer, click Properties, and then click the Device Manager tab.

2. Double-click the Ports (COM & LPT) branch to expand it, click Communications Port (COM1), and then click Properties.

3. Click to select the "Disable in this hardware profile" check box, then click OK.

4. Double-click the Modems branch to expand it, click your modem, click Remove, click OK, and then restart your computer.

5.   When your computer restarts, follow the instructions on the screen to reinstall your modem.

SYMPTOM 26-17   **You encounter an "Error 630" when dialing out with your modem**
When you attempt to dial out under Windows 98, you may receive an error message such as:

```
Error 630: The computer is not receiving a response from the modem. Check
that the modem is plugged in, and if necessary, turn the modem off, and then
turn it back on.
```

You may also see an error indicating that the communication port is invalid or busy. This fault can occur if you have the "Support SerialKey devices" Accessibility option configured to use the same COM port where your modem is connected. You'll need to disable or reconfigure the "Support SerialKey devices" option:

1.   Click Start, highlight Settings, click Control Panel, then double-click Accessibility Options.

2.   On the General tab, either click to clear the "Support SerialKey devices" check box or click Settings, click a different COM port in the Serial port box, then click OK.

3.   Click OK.

SYMPTOM 26-18   **You cannot get CU-SeeMee videoconferencing to work with ADSL under Windows 98/SE**   When you try to establish a CU-SeeMe videoconference with an Internet Connection Sharing (or "ICS") host over an Asymmetric Digital Subscriber Line (ADSL) connection, you may be unable to connect to any Internet conference site. If you *are* able to initialize a conference, it may time out. You should disable ICS on the host computer:

1.   Click Start, highlight Settings, click Control Panel, then double-click Internet Options.

2.   Click the Connections tab, then click Sharing.

3.   Click to clear the "Enable Internet Connection Sharing" check box, then click OK.

4.   Use CU-SeeMe on the ICS host.

SYMPTOM 26-19   **The modem will not answer at the customer's site, but it works fine in the shop**   Since deregulation of the original Bell Telephone Company, customers have been allowed to attach devices to phone lines with the proviso that they notify the phone company of each device's FCC registration and ringer equivalence number (REN). While few customers make it a point of informing their local telephone company how many phones and gadgets are connected to the telephone line, there is a good reason for doing so—you see, the amount of *ringing voltage* supplied to a site is fixed. If you load down the line beyond its maximum rating, not enough voltage will be available to ring all of the bells. The *ringer equivalence* is the amount of load that the device will place on the line. Modems have to be able to detect a ring signal before they know to pick up. If the ringing signal is too weak, the modem will not detect it properly and initiate an answer sequence.

    Have the customer remove some other equipment from the phone lines and see if the problem disappears. With today's fax machines, modems, multiple extension phones, and answering machines all plugged into the same line, it would be easy to overload the ringing voltage. The customer should also take a listing of the registration numbers and ringer equivalence numbers on *all* devices connected to phone lines and notify the local phone company of them. The phone company can then boost the ringer voltage to compensate for the added loads.

As a precaution, make sure that your customer is starting the communication software properly before attempting to receive a modem call—the modem will not pick up a ringing line unless the proper software is running and the modem is in an "auto-answer" mode.

SYMPTOM 26-20 **Your modem is receiving or transmitting garbage, or is having great difficulty displaying anything at all** Serial communication is totally dependent on the data frame settings and transfer rate of the receiver and the transmitter being an exact match. The baud rate, word bits, stop bits, and parity must all match exactly or errors will show up. These errors can show as either *no* data or as *incorrect* data (garbage) on screen. You'll see this one crop up a lot when customers switch from calling a local BBS to CompuServe. Local BBS's are usually set for 8-bit words, no parity, and one stop bit. CompuServe, on the other hand, uses 7-bit words, even parity, and 2 stop bits. The terminal software must be reconfigured to match the settings of each service being called. Most programs allow for these differences by letting you specify a configuration for each entry in the dialing directory. Also check the method of flow control being used (such as XOFF/XON, DTR/DSR, or CTS/RTS) and make sure that it is set properly.

Baud rate mismatches most often result in what looks like a dead modem—often, nothing is displayed on either end. Modems will automatically negotiate a common baud rate to connect at without regard to the terminal settings. The modems will normally connect at the highest baud rate available to the slowest modem, so if a 14,400 bps modem connects to a 2400 bps modem, both will set themselves to 2400 bps. If the software on the higher speed modem is still set for the higher speed, you'll typically get large amounts of garbage or nothing at all.

If the problem is a result of being connected to a service such as a BBS, call the SYSOP and find out the settings. You can also let the modem tell you what transfer rate it connects at. Before dialing, set a direct connection and send the command **ATQ0V1** to the modem. This tells the modem to send result codes in plain English. When connected, you'll see a message similar to "CONNECT 2400." The actual number you see is the bps rate, and you can reconfigure your software accordingly. Working out the word, stop, and parity bits may be a process of trial and error, but almost all BBS installations use 8 data bits, no parity, and 1 stop bit. If you are forced to attempt trial and error, target one item to get right at a time. First get the baud rates to match. Next get word bits settled down and then go for parity and stop bits. If you make more than one change you'll never know which change made the difference. It may *seem* slower, but your overall service time will be cut.

SYMPTOM 26-21 **The modem is connected and turned on, but there is no response from the modem** The communication software's configuration must match the port settings of the modem. Check to make sure that any modem parameters are entered and saved properly. Establish a direct connection with the modem and enter the **ATZ** command. Doing this will reset the modem. The modem should respond "OK" or "0" (the numerical equivalent of OK). If that doesn't work, change to COM2 and try again, then COM3 and COM4. If none of the combinations work, check the DIP switches or jumpers on the modem for the correct configuration. Finally, try the modem on another PC or replace the suspect modem outright.

SYMPTOM 26-22 **The modem will not pick up the phone line** The modem is not able to initiate a call or answer an incoming call. Most modems today come with two RJ11 telephone line connectors for the phone lines: one labeled "LINE" (where the outside line enters the modem) and the other labeled "PHONE" (where an extension telephone can be plugged in). Check that the outgoing telephone line is plugged into the LINE jack. Leave the PHONE connector disconnected while the modem is in use.

Test the modem manually by establishing a direct connection and typing a dial command such as **ATDT15083667683**. When you enter this command string, the modem should go off hook, draw dial tone, and dial the numbers. If this happens as expected, you can be reasonably sure that the modem is working properly—and the communication software is at fault. Check the modem initialization strings or try a new communication package. If the modem does not respond during a direct connection, check that the modem is installed and configured properly. You may need to try a new modem.

SYMPTOM 26-23   **The modem appears to work fine, but prints garbage whenever it's supposed to show IBM text graphics, such as boxes, or ANSI graphics**   Your terminal emulation mode is wrong. The communication software is probably set for 7-bit words. The IBM text graphic character set starts at ASCII 128 and has to have the eighth bit. Adjust the communication software configuration to handle 8-bit words. You may also be using an unusual ASCII character set during the connection—try setting the character set emulation to ANSI BBS or TTY.

SYMPTOM 26-24   **You frequently see strange character groups like "[0m" appearing in the text**   These are ANSI control codes attempting to control your display. Popular among BBS software, ANSI codes can be used to set colors, draw ASCII boxes, clear the screen, move the cursor, and so on. DOS provides an ANSI screen driver called ANSI.SYS that can be loaded into the CONFIG.SYS when the computer is rebooted. Most of today's terminal software will offer a setting for this as well. If you are able to select character set emulation in your communication software, try setting to ANSI BBS.

SYMPTOM 26-25   **The modem makes audible "clicking" noises when hooked to phone line**   There is probably a short in the phone line. The "clicking" is the noise of the modem trying to pick up when it sees the short and hang up when the short clears. Try replacing the line cord going from the modem to the telephone wall jack—line cords don't last very long under constant use and abuse. If problems continue, try using a different telephone line—the physical wiring may be defective between the wall jack and telephone pole. Contact your local telephone company if you suspect this to be the case. Next, try establishing a direct connection to the modem and enter an **AT&F** command, which will restore the modem's factory default settings. If that clears the problem, the modem's initialized state may not be fully compatible with the current telephone line characteristics. Check each modem setting carefully and adjust parameters to try and settle its operation down. If factory default settings do not help and the telephone line seems reliable, there may be a problem with the modem's telephone interface circuit—try replacing the modem.

SYMPTOM 26-26   **The modem is having difficulty connecting to another modem**   The modem is powered and connected properly. It dials the desired number and you can hear the modems negotiating, but they never quite seem to make a connection. This is a classic software configuration problem. You may often see a "NO CARRIER" message associated with this problem. Check each parameter in your communication software—especially the modem's AT initialization string. Make sure that each entry in the string is appropriate for your modem. If the string looks correct, try disabling the modem's MNP5 protocol. You will have to refer to the modem's manual to find the exact command, but many modems use **AT\N0**. If your modem is using MNP5 and the destination modem does not support it, the negotiation can hang up. If problems persist, try lowering the modem's data transfer rate. While most modems can set the proper transfer rate automatically, some modems that do not support it may also cause the negotiation to freeze.

Another problem may be that your modem is not configured to wait long enough for carrier from the remote modem. You can adjust this delay by entering a larger number for S-register S7. Start the communication software, establish a direct connection (terminal mode), type **ATS7?**, and press ENTER. Doing this will return the current value of register S7. You can then use the command **ATS7=10** to enter a larger delay (in this case, 10 seconds). That should give the destination modem more time to respond. If all else fails, try a modem from a different manufacturer.

SYMPTOM 26-27   **The modem starts dialing before it draws a dial tone**   As a result, one or more of the numbers are lost during dialing, making it difficult to establish a connection. Chances are that the modem is working just fine, but the modem does not wait long enough for dial tone to be present once it goes off hook. The solution is to increase the time delay *before* the modem starts dialing. This can be done by changing the value in S-register S6. To find the current value, start the communication software and establish a direct connection (terminal mode), then type **ATS6?** followed by pressing ENTER. Doing this queries the S-register. You can then enter a new value such as **ATS6=10** (which would provide a 10-second delay).

SYMPTOM 26-28   **The modem has trouble sending or receiving when the system's power saving features are turned on**   This type of problem is most prevalent with PCMCIA modems running on a notebook PC. The power conservation features found on many notebook systems often interferes with the modem's operation—proper modem operation typically relies on full processing speed, which is often scaled back when power conservation is turned on. Ultimately, the most effective resolution to this problem is simply to turn the power conservation features off while you use the modem (you can reset the power features later). However, it may be possible to correct these types of problems using a BIOS upgrade for the mobile PC or an updated modem driver.

SYMPTOM 26-29   **You see an error such as: "Already on line" or "Carrier already established"**   These types of errors often arise when you start a communications package while the modem is already online. You might also find this problem when the Carrier Detect (CD) signal is set *always on* (using a command string such as **AT&C0**). To make sure that the CD signal is on only when the modem makes a connection, use a command string such as **AT&C1&D2&W**. The **&W** suffix loads the settings into nonvolatile RAM. If this problem arises when you hang up the connection without signing off the modem, you will have to reboot the system to clear the CD signal—**AT&F** and **ATZ** will *not* clear the signal.

SYMPTOM 26-30   **The modem refuses to answer the incoming line**   First, make sure to set the communication software to answer the calling modem—or set the modem to auto-answer mode (set S-register S0 to **1** or more). On external modems, you will see the "AA" LED lit when the auto-answer mode is active. Problems can also occur if your external modem does not recognize the DTR signal generated by the host PC. The command **AT&D** controls how the modem responds to the computer's DTR signal. An external modem turns on the TR light when it is set to see the DTR signal. If the TR light is out, the modem will not answer (regardless of whether the auto-answer mode is enabled or not). Use the **AT&D0** command if your serial port does not support the DTR signal or if your modem cable does not connect to it. Otherwise, you should use the **AT&D2** command.

SYMPTOM 26-31   **The modem switches into the command mode intermittently**   When this problem develops, you may have to tweak the DTR arrangement. To correct this fault, try changing the modem's DTR setting using the command **AT&D2&W**.

SYMPTOM 26-32   **Your current modem won't connect at 2400 bps with a 2400 bps modem**   This is a compatibility issue between vastly different generations of hardware. The modem you're trying to connect with is almost certainly an older model that doesn't support error control (MNP protocols). You can disable error control on your modem by entering the command **AT&M0** and pressing ENTER; then try placing the call to the modem again. When you're finished, reset your modem with the **ATZ** command to reenable the error control features.

SYMPTOM 26-33   The communications software is reporting many cyclic redundancy check (CRC) errors and low characters per second (CPS) transfers   This may simply be a matter of a poor phone connection established through the telephone network. Try making the call again—chances are that the call will be routed differently, resulting in a more reliable connection. Next, check the flow control scheme (XOFF/XON, CTS/RTS, and so on) to verify that it is optimum, or type **AT&F1** from the terminal mode to load the optimum flow control setting. The serial port rate in your communications software may be set too high for your modem's UART or your area's phone lines. Try lowering the serial port rate in your communications software to 38,400 bps or 19,200 bps (or lower for slower modems). The remote site you are dialing into may have trouble with the file transfer protocol you've selected. Try using a different file transfer protocol (such as Ymodem-g rather than Zmodem). Do not use Xmodem if other protocols are available. Finally, there may be a TSR program running in the background and interfering with data communications. Disable any TSR programs running in the background and try the communication again.

SYMPTOM 26-34   Errors are constantly occurring in your V.17 fax transmissions As a rule, sending fax transmissions over a modem should present no special problems for a PC, but there are some issues to keep in mind. First, your modem initialization string could be insufficient or incomplete for fax transmissions. Enter the correct initialization string (determined by your particular modem) for fax support, such as **AT&H3&I2&R2S7=90**. You could also have a disruptive TSR program running in the background. Disable any TSR programs and try the communication again. There could be an outdated communications driver on your system. Load the communications driver that came with your fax software (this may require you to reinstall your internal modem). Finally your baud rate may be set too high. Try a lower baud rate of 9600 bps.

SYMPTOM 26-35   Your 32-bit communications programs may report a slower speed than your 16-bit communications programs   For example, if your 16-bit programs report that they are communicating at 38,400 bits per second (bps), your 32-bit Windows 9x/Me programs may report that they are communicating at 14,400 bps. The problem here is a difference in the way 16-bit and 32-bit programs report communication speeds.

A 32-bit communication program designed for Windows 9x/Me reports the modem *line speed* when reporting the speed at which the program is communicating. The modem line speed is the speed between your modem and the modem you're connected to (the speed at which data is transmitted over the telephone line). By comparison, most 16-bit communications programs that are designed for DOS/Windows 3.x report the *port speed* when reporting the speed at which the program is communicating. The port speed is the speed between your modem and your computer (the speed between the serial port that your modem is connected to and your computer). Since port speed is typically faster than modem line speed, 16-bit programs generally report a faster speed than 32-bit programs. You can use the following workaround to correct the issue:

1.   Click Start, highlight Settings, and then click Control Panel.

2.   Double-click Modems.

3.   Click your modem, and then click Properties.

4.   On the Connection tab, click Advanced.

5.   In the Extra Settings box, type **S95=0**, then click OK.

6.   Click OK, then click Close.

SYMPTOM 26-36   **During installation, a modem setup program cannot find the internal modem**   In virtually all cases, you have a hardware conflict between the modem and another device in the system. Check the hardware installation first. For internal modems, make sure the IRQ and I/O address are set correctly and see that there are no other devices using the same IRQ or I/O space as your modem. Under Windows 9x/Me, the Device Manager can usually display any conflicting devices with yellow icons (exclamation marks). Next, make sure that the modem is inserted properly into its bus slot. If any of the card's gold "fingers" appear corroded or soiled, clean the fingers gently with a pencil eraser. Try the modem in another bus slot. Finally, check the modem switches. Most external modems use a series of DIP switches to configure their various features. Refer to the modem's documentation and see that any modem switches are set properly.

SYMPTOM 26-37   **After installing a new internal modem, the system mouse driver no longer loads, or the mouse behaves erratically**   In virtually all cases, there is a hardware conflict between the new modem and the existing mouse port. Check the hardware installation. If the mouse is connected to a COM port, make sure that your internal modem is set to use a different COM port. You may need to disable COM2 on the motherboard or I/O controller and set up the modem as COM2. Under Windows 9x/Me, the Device Manager can usually display any conflicting devices with a yellow icon (exclamation mark).

SYMPTOM 26-38   **After installing modem driver software, Windows locks up or crashes**   This is almost always the result of a defective or outdated modem driver. Check the software installation. Make sure that the modem driver software you have installed is the proper version for the particular modem *and* your version of Windows (3.1, 3.11, 95, 98, Me, and so on). You can usually check the driver version on the modems manufacturer's Web site. If you do find that the modem driver is incorrect, run any "uninstall" utility that accompanied the software in order to remove the driver cleanly—otherwise, you'll have to remove the modem driver references from SYSTEM.INI manually. Under Windows 9x/Me, you can often remove a device from the Device Manager, then allow Windows to re-detect the modem during the next boot (and reinstall the new drivers at that point).

SYMPTOM 26-39   **DOS communication software works fine, but Windows communication software will not**   You may also see Windows error messages suggesting that certain files are missing. In most cases, the modem drivers (and any required parameters) have not been loaded properly. Check the software installation and make sure that the modem driver software you have installed is the proper version for the particular modem *and* your version of Windows (such as 3.1, 3.11, 95, 98, Me, and so on). Try uninstalling the modem drivers (if possible), then reload the drivers from scratch—making sure that they are set up properly for your system configuration. Next, check the manufacturer's Web site for any adjustments or workarounds that may be required for your particular modem and drivers. You may need to make manual adjustments to SYSTEM.INI and WIN.INI files as well as the Windows 9x/Me Registry files.

SYMPTOM 26-40   **You cannot get the modem's "distinctive ring" feature to work**   Some new modems support the "distinctive ring" service provided by many telephone companies. This allows the modem to reside on the same physical telephone line as other devices, but only answer when the proper ringing pattern is received. Improper modem configuration is the most common problem. Try calling the distinctive ring numbers associated to your telephone line and see that each number rings with the required pattern. Note that the "distinctive ring" service is not available from all telephone companies and service areas. Next, check the initialization string for **S101.** Modems supporting "distinctive ring" usually control the feature through register **S101**. A typical AT command string may appear such as "**AT&FS101=60**". A typical setting list is shown here:

S101=0	Detect all ringing cadences and report them with RING result code
S101=1	Enables the RING result codes; all ringing types will be reported
S101=30	Report only unidentified ring types
S101=46	Report only ring type D
S101=54	Report only ring type C
S101=58	Report only ring type B
S101=60	Report only ring type A
S101=62	Disables *all* ringing detection—the modem will not answer any ring

To specify a particular ring type, you must *disable* the other ring types with this register.

Next, check the initialization string for **-SDR**. Rather than using S-register 101, some modems use the **-SDR** command to configure "distinctive ring" operation. A typical AT command string may appear such as **AT&F-SDR=1**. A setting list is shown here:

-SDR=0	Disables the distinctive ring function
-SDR=1	Enables distinctive ring type 1
-SDR=2	Enables distinctive ring type 2
-SDR=3	Enables distinctive ring type 1 and 2
-SDR=4	Enables distinctive ring type 3
-SDR=5	Enables distinctive ring type 1 and 3
-SDR=6	Enables distinctive ring type 2 and 3
-SDR=7	Enables distinctive ring type 1,2, and 3

SYMPTOM 26-41   **You cannot get the modem's Caller ID feature to work**   Some new modems support the Caller ID service provided by many telephone companies. This allows the modem to identify the telephone number and caller to the computer's communication software when the ringing line is answered. Improper modem configuration is the most common problem. Before you do anything else, check the Caller ID service. Connect any Caller ID-compatible telephone or phone box to the telephone line and make sure that the ID service is working properly. Note that the Caller ID service is not available from all telephone companies and service areas. Also, remove other Caller ID devices. It is possible that other caller ID compatible telephones of phone boxes may be interfering with the modem. Try removing any other devices from the phone line. Check the initialization string for %CCID. Modems supporting Caller ID usually control the feature through a %CCID command. A typical AT command string may appear such as **AT&F%CCID=1**. A setting list is shown here:

%CCID=0	Turns Caller ID off
%CCID=1	Gives Caller ID data using a formatted output
%CCID=2	Gives Caller ID data using an unformatted output

Finally, check the initialization string for **#CID**. Rather than using the **%CCID** command, some modems support Caller ID using the **#CID** command. A typical command string may appear such as **AT&F#CID=1**. A setting list is shown here:

AT#CID=0	Turns Caller ID off
AT#CID=1	Gives Caller ID data using a formatted output
AT#CID=2	Gives Caller ID data using an unformatted output

There are two special messages that may be sent instead of Caller ID information. "O" means that the caller is *Out* of the Caller ID service area—usually a long distance call. "P" is for *Private* and will be displayed for callers who have made arrangements with their phone company to have their numbers blocked.

SYMPTOM 26-42   **You cannot recall previous Caller ID data**   This assumes that normal Caller ID features are proven to be working correctly. In most cases, your communication software is not sending the correct AT command to your modem. Check the Caller ID feature and make sure that Caller ID is enabled using the **%CCID** or **#CID** commands as in the previous symptom. Caller ID *must* be enabled first before data can be recalled. Check the initialization string for **%CRID**. Caller ID data can typically be recalled using the **%CRID** command such as **AT%CRID=0** (recall formatted data) or "**AT%CRID=1**" (recall unformatted data).

SYMPTOM 26-43   **The modem will not provide synchronous communication**
Modems are typically asynchronous devices, but most can be configured for synchronous communication with host systems such as mainframe computers. If your modem will not work in synchronous mode, chances are that the modem is not configured properly. You must configure *both* the originating modem and the answering modem. The originating modem will be configured for synchronous originate mode and will dial a stored number when a connection is attempted. You will need a dumb terminal or terminal emulation software to configure the modem:

1. Attach the modem to a serial port on a PC or dumb terminal using a standard RS-232 cable.
2. Configure the *port speed* setting in the dumb terminal or the terminal emulation software to match the speed that will be used on the synchronous port.
3. Configure the software for *direct connect* or *terminal mode* and open the connection to the port.
4. Type **AT&F&W** and press ENTER. The modem should respond with "OK". If double characters appear, type **ATE0** and press ENTER to disable local character echo.
5. Type **AT&Q2&S2&W** and press ENTER. The modem should respond with "OK."
6. Type **AT&Z0=T[phone number to store]** and press ENTER. The modem should respond with "OK."
7. Type **AT&D2&W** and press ENTER. The modem should respond with "OK."
8. Type **AT&C1E0Q1&W** and press ENTER. The modem should *not* respond with "OK" because character echo and result-code reporting have been disabled.

Next, configure the answering modem. The answering modem must be configured for synchronous answer mode. Although the answering modem is usually attached to the mainframe host system, you will first need to connect it to a dumb terminal for configuration. To configure the answering modem:

1. Attach the modem to a serial port on a PC or dumb terminal using a standard RS-232 cable.

2. Configure the *port speed* setting in the dumb terminal or the terminal emulation software to match the speed that will be used on the synchronous port.

3. Type **AT** and press ENTER. The modem should respond with "OK." If double characters appear, type **ATE0** and press ENTER to disable local character echo.

4. Type **AT&F&W** and press ENTER. The modem should respond with "OK."

5. Type **AT&Q1&S2&W** and press ENTER. The modem should respond with "OK."

6. Type **ATS0=1** (or the number of rings you want the modem to answer on) and press ENTER. The modem should respond with "OK."

7. Type **AT&D2&W** and press ENTER. The modem should respond with "OK."

8. Type **AT&C1E0Q1&W** and press ENTER. The modem should *not* respond with "OK" because character echo and result-code reporting have been disabled.

Now, disable command recognition. After each modem has been configured properly, the command recognition should be disabled as follows:

1. Turn the modems off.

2. Locate the DIP switches that define modem operations.

3. Move the proper DIP switch to turn *command recognition* off. If the modem is internal, move the appropriate jumper. The particular DIP switch or jumper will depend on your specific modem, so check the modem's documentation.

4. Turn the modems on.

Finally, establish a synchronous connection. Attach the originating modem to the SDLC or synchronous port and turn the power on. When a connection is attempted, the modem will automatically dial the stored number and attempt to connect to the other modem. Attach the answering modem to the synchronous port on the host system. The modem will answer incoming calls in **&Q1** synchronous mode.

SYMPTOM 26-44   **The modem appears to be set up and configured properly, but it is experiencing data loss**   Such symptoms may appear as excessive file transfer errors, missing text or characters, and jumbled ASCII text. Though modern modems are capable of data rates up to 230,400 bps, data rates over 19,200 bps can cause problems for older PCs because of inadequate serial port hardware. Check the UART first—your serial ports should be using 16550A UARTs for optimum performance. If the UART is older, data throughput will be limited. If you cannot upgrade the UART chip directly, you can often disable the existing serial port and install an upgraded I/O board. Any diagnostic program such as MSD can identify the UARTs in your system. Check your modem drivers and make sure that the modem driver software is up to date and optimized for your particular version of Windows (3.1, 3.11, 95, 98, Me, and so on). Finally, reduce your data rates. If you cannot resolve the problem through a driver or new UART, try reducing the modem's data rate in your communication software.

SYMPTOM 26-45   **When running modem software, you see an error such as "Can't run on a Plug and Play ready system"**   In most cases, the PCMCIA modem is incompatible with a PC's PnP architecture. Check your PnP driver. You may need to load an alternative PnP driver for your modem. Check with the modem manufacturer's BBS, CompuServe forum, or Web site to obtain any updated driver software. You may need to disable the existing DOS PnP driver in CONFIG.SYS.

SYMPTOM 26-46   **The modem appears to be set up and configured properly, but it regularly connects at slower speeds than it is capable of**   There are several different factors that can account for such a problem. First, modems can connect only at the maximum speed of the slowest modem. If the remote modem is slower than yours, your connection speed will be limited. Try connecting to a faster BBS or other online connection. Check the modem initialization string next—there may be one or more important commands missing from the command string. Look for the recommended initialization string in the modem's documentation. Also see that the correct modem is selected in the communication software.

Check the modem's firmware version. Use the **ATI3** command to check the modem's ID information (including the firmware revision). If the firmware is old, it may need to be updated. If the firmware is very new, it may contain a bug that the manufacturer should be made aware of. Finally, try a different phone line. Faulty or noisy telephone connections can reduce effective communication speed. Also, try the call at an "off time."

SYMPTOM 26-47   **Windows 9x/Me insists on assigning the modem to COM5**
You will need to reconfigure the modem's port assignment through the Control Panel. First, you'll need to remove any unused modem entries. Software that has been loaded for previous modems may interfere with the current modem's software. Under Windows 98/SE, remove unused modem hardware references through the Device Manager:

1. Select My Computer, double-click on Control Panel, and then choose Modems.
2. Highlight any modems that are no longer in the system and press the Remove button.
3. If there are multiple entries for the same modem, remove all entries for the modem, restart the system, and then reinstall the software.

Next, verify the modem on COM5. Check to see that the modem is identified and checks properly before continuing:

1. Select My Computer, double-click on Control Panel, and then choose Modems.
2. Select the Diagnostics tab.
3. Highlight COM5 and press the More Info button.
4. Verify that the modem responds to the **ATI3** command with its proper ID information.
5. Click OK.

Now find an unused COM port. Check the Diagnostics screen and examine the COM ports in use—any ports not in use are available. Next, use REGEDIT.EXE to edit the Windows 9x/Me Registry. You can change the COM port assignment by adjusting the Registry:

1. Click on the Start button, then select Run.
2. Type **regedit** and click OK.
3. Select the Edit/Find option, and then type **COM5**.
4. Click Find Next—this should highlight PORTNAME under a Registry key.
5. Double-click on PORTNAME.

6. Enter the new COM port, such as "COM2."

7. Click OK, then close REGEDIT.

8. Shut down and restart Windows.

Before attempting to edit a Windows Registry file, make sure to have a complete backup of the registry files SYSTEM.DAT and USER.DAT.

Finally, check the updated configuration and verify that the modem now works on new COM port:

1. Select My Computer, double-click on Control Panel, and then choose Modems.

2. Select the Diagnostics tab.

3. Select the new COM port that you selected for the modem.

4. Press the More Info button.

5. Verify that the modem responds to the **ATI3** command with its proper ID information.

6. Click OK.

SYMPTOM 26-48   **You cannot get the modem to work with a Winsock, but conventional BBS or CompuServe connections work fine**   In almost all cases, an error with the modem can be traced to one or more command strings in your Internet connection configuration files. First, make sure that you are using the Winsock version that is appropriate for your particular Internet connection software (such as Windows Dial-Up Networking). Next, check the configuration file. Contact your modem manufacturer to check on any fixes or workarounds. Some modems may not work with the default command strings provided with their Internet software. For example, the Motorola Power 14.4 PCMCIA modem will not work with Trumpet Winsock because of an error in the LOGIN.CMD file—the **$modemsetup=** string is wrong.

SYMPTOM 26-49   **You are having trouble configuring the modem for hardware and software flow control**   This is usually due to invalid command strings. Try some generic command strings. The following two AT command strings can configure most Hayes-compatible modems for hardware or software flow control. Keep in mind that you may need to add additional commands in order to configure the modem completely.

■ Software flow control (XON/XOFF)   **AT&F1&C1&D2**

■ Hardware flow control (CTS/RTS)   **AT&F1&C1&D2\Q3**

Under Windows, you can also set error correction and flow control options through the modem's Advanced Connection Settings dialog, as in Figure 26-3.

SYMPTOM 26-50   **The modem will not establish a connection through a cellular telephone**   In most cases, the modem is not configured properly. Check the SCM setting first—make sure that the *Station Class Mark* (SCM) level is set correctly. Try resetting the modem with an **AT&F1** command. Check the phone type. Make sure that the telephone is set to *analog* mode—the digital mode may interfere with modem operation.

SYMPTOM 26-51   **The modem will not fax properly through a cellular telephone**
In most cases, the modem is not configured properly. Check the modem's initialization string first and

make sure that the initialization string is set correctly. A basic command string may be **AT&F1E1V1&C1&D2\Q3S7=90S10=60** (though this may not work on all modems). Check the *data rate* next. For faxing, see that the data rate is set to 4800. You may use the command **AT%B4800**.

SYMPTOM 26-52   **Windows 95/98 recognizes the modem, but 16-bit communications software will not see it**   Windows 95/98 may not have updated the SYSTEM.INI file to reflect changes to the COM port settings. Check the SYSTEM.INI file. Your COM port base address and IRQs are defined in the [386Enh] section of your SYSTEM.INI file. Check these settings to make sure that they match your modem settings. The following lines need to be added to your SYSTEM.INI file in the [386enh] section:

```
com1irq=4
com1base=03f8
com2irq=3
com2base=02f8
com3irq=4
com3base=03e8
com4irq=3
com4base=02e8
```

SYMPTOM 26-53   **DOS ICU software is installed, but it will not allow configuring the modem on COM1 or COM2**   The ICU software may be inappropriate for your particular modem and system configuration. Check with the modem manufacturer and see if there is a replacement DOS PnP driver or other workaround. If there is alternate PnP software available, you may need to remove the installation of ICU before proceeding:

1.   Delete the ESCD.RF file from the root directory of c:\.

2.   In the CONFIG.SYS file, delete the line that says: **device=c:\plugplay\...** and save your changes.

3.   In the [386Enh] section of SYSTEM.INI, delete the lines that start with **device=c:\plugplay...** and save your changes.

4.   In the [windows] section of WIN.INI, the RUN= entry should have no reference to ICU or PLUGPLAY after the equal sign. Save your changes if any were made.

5.   Delete the **c:\plugplay** directory.

6.   Exit windows and reboot your system.

SYMPTOM 26-54   **The modem's flash ROM update will not install because it cannot recognize the modem's current firmware version**   This is invariably a problem with the flash ROM update software itself. Check the software source. Contact the manufacturer to see if there is a corrected update available or see if there is a workaround to the problem. There may be one or more command line switches that can override the update's firmware autodetection.

SYMPTOM 26-55   **The modem establishes connections properly, but it frequently drops connections**   Both hardware and software issues can cause this kind of trouble. Problems with the telephone connection itself can cause connection problems. Try connecting to various different places. If problems seem to occur more frequently in one connection over another, the remote location may be suffering from communications problems. Also try using a different local telephone line. Next, check the modem's initialization string and make sure that the modem is set up properly for data compression and error correction.

Finally, check the Windows driver. If you are using Windows-based communications software, it must be able to support high speed. The standard Windows drivers will not support 28.8 Kbps operation unless third-party communications software modifies it (though Windows 98 drivers are more current). To find out what communications driver you are currently using, review the [Boot] section of your SYSTEM.INI file.

SYMPTOM 26-56   **When selecting a modem in your communication software, your particular modem is not listed**   You will need to obtain the proper driver supplements from the modem manufacturer (or software maker). Try running the modem as a Hayes-compatible—virtually all modems will function as generic Hayes-compatible modems **AT&F&C1&D2**.

SYMPTOM 26-57   **It seems to take the modem an unusually long time to hang up**
The carrier delay time is probably set too long. Check the carrier delay time. Modems can be set to wait (often as long as 25 seconds) after a carrier is lost to see whether it comes back—if you frequently encounter poor signal quality, this feature can be quite convenient. After a legitimate hang-up, however, the modem may continue to wait. In this case, you may want to set the value of the S10 register to a low number—10 or less.

SYMPTOM 26-58   **The modem is configured as COM4 (IRQ3) under Windows 9x/Me, but the modem refuses to work**   There may be a hardware acceleration issue. Go into the Windows 9x/Me Control Panel, double-click the System icon, select Performance, and then click Graphics. Set Hardware Acceleration to "None" and try the modem again. Some advanced modem manufacturers have found an addressing conflict with certain graphics accelerator cards. If you configure your Windows graphics driver to basic VGA and find the modem works at that setting, then the problem is probably an addressing conflict with your graphics card. You may want to try using one of the more commonly used COM port and IRQ settings, such as:

COM 1	IRQ 4
COM 2	IRQ 3
COM 3	IRQ 5 (if not used by your sound card)

SYMPTOM 26-59   **When autodetect tries to add a new modem at COM2, Windows 95/98 locks up**   Open the Control Panel (System Settings) and deselect COM2. This can be accomplished by selecting COM2 under System Settings, then choosing Properties. There should be a red "X" in a box down towards the bottom of the Properties screen. Click once on the red "X" and it should clear. This disables the COM port in Windows. Click OK, then restart the machine. When Windows 9x/Me restarts, it should now find the COM port. This technique can apply to all available COM ports.

SYMPTOM 26-60   **HyperTerminal works using PCMCIA support under Windows 9x/Me, but no 16-bit communication programs work**   Using a text editor, edit the SYSTEM.INI file in your Windows directory. Under the [386Enh] section of your SYSTEM.INI file, change the COMM.DRV line back to its original COMM.DRV. This line should read **comm.drv=comm.drv**. Also check that there is a line that states **device=*vcd**. If your SYSTEM.INI has a line that reads **device=*vrdd**, place a semicolon (;) in front of it. Your 16-bit applications should now work.

SYMPTOM 26-61   **A WinModem installed correctly and responds to AT commands fine, but whenever you call out, the modem makes a 9600 V.34 connection**   This is typically due to a problem with the current communications driver. Adding the following line:

```
ForceBridgeOrRouter=TRUE
```

to the SYSTEM.INI file may correct this problem by bypassing the current communications driver and going directly to the WinModem driver. You should also make sure that your Port Rate is set to 19,200 in your Control Panel (Port Settings) in Windows 3.1x and to 38,400 or higher in Windows 9x/Me.

SYMPTOM 26-62   **Windows 9x/Me doesn't detect the WinModem**   First, make sure that the system has a free COM port or IRQ to use. If the WinModem was previously installed on the system with Windows 3.1x running, you'll need to search the SYSTEM.INI and WIN.INI files and remove all WinModem settings so that Windows 9x/Me can detect the WinModem properly. Under Windows 9x/Me, make sure that the modem is not listed in the Device Manager under Other Devices. If it is, delete the reference and reinstall. Next, make sure the WinModem's key (such as "USR1001" for the USR WinModem) is not in the Registry—if it is, remove the reference(s) from the Registry.

SYMPTOM 26-63   **You have difficulty using a WinModem after upgrading to Windows 98**
If you double-click the WinModem icon in Control Panel, you may receive the following error message:

```
Error: There is no WinModem found in your computer, but some corrupted files
were found and they have been cleaned.
```

If you view your modem in the Device Manager, you may also notice more than one WinModem entry. This problem generally occurs because your WinModem is *not* using the most current .INF file or device driver. To correct this problem, uninstall the WinModem drivers, remove the multiple WinModem entries in Device Manager, then reinstall the most current WinModem drivers:

1. Click Start, highlight Settings, click Control Panel, double-click the WinModem icon, then click Uninstall. This should uninstall the WinModem drivers.

2. See if the WinModem icon is still in the Control Panel. If the WinModem icon is gone, the uninstall process was successful. If the WinModem icon is still available, the uninstall process was not successful, and you will need to contact the modem manufacturer for detailed removal instructions.

3. Now remove the WinModem entries in Device Manager. Right-click My Computer, click Properties, then click the Device Manager tab.

4. Double-click the Modem branch to expand it, click a WinModem entry, and then click Remove. Repeat this until *all* WinModem entries are removed, then click OK.

5. Reinstall the most current WinModem drivers.

SYMPTOM 26-64   **The WinModem is repeatedly detected when you start Windows 98**
For example, after you uninstall a WinModem and restart your computer, Windows 98 may try to install the modem and prompt you to restart your computer. After you restart your computer, Windows may prompt you to restart your computer again, and this behavior may continue indefinitely. This problem can occur if you uninstall the WinModem by using Device Manager (or the Modems tool in your Control Panel) instead of using the WinModem utility provided by the modem's manufacturer. To fix this problem, use the WinModem utility to uninstall your WinModem *instead* of using the Device Manager or the Modems tool:

1. Restart your computer and start Windows 98 in the Safe Mode.

2. Click Start, highlight Settings, and then click Control Panel.

3. Use the WinModem utility to uninstall your WinModem. For detailed information about how to use the WinModem utility to uninstall your WinModem, review the documentation included with your particular modem.

4. Restart your computer normally

5. If you're prompted to install your WinModem again, use the software included with your modem to do so.

SYMPTOM 26-65   The cable modem is installed, but it doesn't work
Your cable modem may have been installed with an IRQ conflict. Right-click the My Computer icon on your desktop and then click Properties. Click the Device Manager tab at the top of the "System Properties" dialog and look for a yellow exclamation point over the cable modem's entry (for example, "3Com U.S. Robotics Cable Modem") in the Network Adapters section. If the modem has a yellow exclamation point, it suffers from a resource conflict. Uninstall the modem by highlighting it and then clicking the Remove button. You will be asked if you wish to uninstall the device. Click OK. Next, you need to free an IRQ for the modem.

Double-click the Computer icon at the top of the Device Manager screen. In the Setting column, look for numbers between 3 and 15 that *aren't* listed—these are IRQs available for use by the cable modem. If none are available, choose an unneeded device to be removed or disabled (you might consider disabling any serial or COM ports that are not in use). Once you have freed the necessary IRQ, restart your computer and try reinstalling the cable modem again. Some versions of Windows will not support *both* the cable modem and a network interface card (such as an Ethernet card) at the same time. You may need to uninstall or disable any existing network interface cards in your computer before installing the cable modem card.

SYMPTOM 26-66   When the PC comes out of "power save" mode, my system is frozen
If the upstream (analog modem) connection is active when a computer goes into its power save mode, the computer may freeze when coming out of power save mode again. Either hang up the analog modem *before* your computer goes into power save mode or disable the power save features on your PC. If you choose to disable the power save mode, disable it in *both* the Windows 9x/Me Control Panel and the system's CMOS Setup. To disable power save in Windows 98/SE, click Start, select Settings, and click Control Panel. Double-click the Power icon, and select OFF in the Power Management box. Now click Apply. You may need to reboot the PC for your changes to take effect.

SYMPTOM 26-67   The cable modem scans for an active channel, pauses on an active channel, but instead of locking on to it, continues to scan for active channels   Your cable modem may be assigned to IRQ 12—this is often a problem. although Windows 9x/Me will not report it as a problem. IRQ 12 is normally reserved as the interrupt for a system's PS/2 (mouse) port. Right-click the My Computer icon on your desktop and then click Properties. Click Device Manager and then click Network Adapters. Double-click the entry for your cable modem (for example, "3Com Cable Modem") and then click Resources. Look for "Interrupt Request" in the Resource Type column. If the number listed to the right is "12," you will need to move the cable modem to a different IRQ.

SYMPTOM 26-68   The cable modem scans for an active channel, but never locks on to one   Check the cable and connections between your cable modem and the CATV jack at the wall—make sure the connections are reasonably tight. Try rebooting the PC and see if the cable modem will re-scan and achieve a good channel lock. If the problem persists, the signal from your cable company's equipment may be too weak. Call your cable company to determine whether or not this may be the problem.

SYMPTOM 26-69   **During registration, you receive a "DHCP offer receive" error**
This type of error generally means that the cable modem is encountering difficulties obtaining an IP address. Click on the "Register again" button—registration may proceed in spite of this error. Start by checking the network adapter. Click Start, select Settings, and click Control Panel. Double-click the Network icon. In the list of installed network components that appears, highlight the "TCP/IP -> Dial-Up Adapter" entry and then click Properties. In the "TCP/IP Properties" dialog that appears, click the IP Address tab. Make sure the "Obtain an IP address automatically" option is checked. Click OK and close all open windows. Reboot the PC and try the cable modem again.

Check the IP configuration. Click Start and then click Run. Type **winipcfg.exe** and press ENTER. When the "IP Configuration" dialog appears, make sure the values in the "IP Address" and "Default Gateway" fields *are* identical and *do not* equal zero. If they *are not* identical or *are* equal to zero, contact the cable modem manufacturer for technical support. Check the CMCC software. In your CMCC application, click Options, click Preferences, and then click "DHCP IP Address". Make sure "Auto Detect" is enabled unless your cable company recommends against it. If problems persist, check with the cable company for additional support or suggestions.

SYMPTOM 26-70   **During registration, you receive a "TFTP Error code =4 (timeout)"**
This type of error generally means that the cable modem is having troubles with the system's TCP/IP stack. Click on the "Register again" button—registration may proceed in spite of this error. Check the TCP/IP stack next. Click Start, select Settings, and click Control Panel. Double-click the Network icon. In the list of installed network components, highlight the "TCP/IP -> Dial-Up Adapter" entry and then click Properties. In the "TCP/IP Properties" dialog that appears, click the IP Address tab. Make sure the "Obtain an IP address automatically" option is checked. Click OK and close all open windows. Reboot your computer and try again. If registration fails again after rebooting the system, contact your cable company for additional support or suggestions.

SYMPTOM 26-71   **My cable modem setup does not use the analog modem to dial the cable company's server**   This generally indicates an issue with the analog modem or your telephone line. Check for dial tone at the telephone line (no dial tone may mean the line is dead). Also double-check the access number for your cable company's server. You will not be able to access the Internet with your cable modem until your analog modem connects properly. If the problem persists, you may need to troubleshoot or replace the analog modem.

Further Study

Boca Research   www.bocaresearch.com
Diamond Multimedia   www.diamondmm.com
ITU   www.itu.int
Lucent Technologies   www.lucent.com/micro/
ModemHelp   www.modemhelp.com/index3.html
Motorola   www.mot.com
US Robotics   www.3com.com/56k/index.html
Zoom Telephonics   www.zoomtel.com

27

MONITOR TROUBLESHOOTING

From its humble beginnings as a basic monochrome text display, the monitor (Figure 27-1) has grown to provide real-time photorealistic images of unprecedented quality and color. Monitors have allowed real-time video playback, stunning graphics, and information-filled illustrations to replace the generic "command-line" user interface of just a few years ago. In effect, monitors have become our virtual window into the modern computer. With many millions of computers now in service, the economical maintenance and repair of computer monitors represents a serious challenge to technicians and hobbyists alike. Fortunately, the basic principles and operations of a computer monitor have changed very little since the early days of terminal displays. This chapter explains the basic concepts behind today's computer monitors and provides a cross-section of handy troubleshooting procedures.

FIGURE 27-1   A CTX EX910 color monitor (CTX International, Inc.)

Monitor Specifications and Characteristics

PCs are defined by a set of fairly well-understood specifications such as RAM size, hard drive space, and clock speed. However, monitor specifications describe a whole series of physical properties that PCs never deal with. With this in mind, perhaps the best introduction to monitor troubleshooting is to discuss each specification in detail and to show you how each specification and characteristic affects a monitor's performance.

CRT

The *cathode ray tube* (CRT) is essentially a large vacuum tube. One end of the CRT is formed as a long, narrow neck, while the other end is a broad, almost-flat surface. A precise coating of colored phosphors is applied inside the CRT along the front face. The neck end of the CRT contains an element (called the *cathode*) that is energized and heated to very high temperatures (much like an incandescent lamp). At high temperatures, the cathode liberates electrons. When a very high positive voltage potential is applied at the front face of the CRT, electrons liberated by the cathode (which are negatively charged) are accelerated toward the front face. When the electrons strike the phosphor on the front face, light is produced. Magnetic force is used to direct the stream of electrons across the front face, and a visible image is produced. Of course, there are other elements needed to control and direct the electron stream, but this is CRT operation in a nutshell. CRT face size (or *screen size*) is generally measured as a *diagonal* dimension—that is, a 43.2cm (17") CRT is 43.2cm (17") between opposing corners. Larger CRTs are more expensive, but produce larger images, which are usually easier on the eyes.

PIXELS AND RESOLUTION

The picture element (*pixel*) is the very smallest point that can be controlled on a CRT. For monochrome displays, a pixel may simply be turned on or off. For a color display, a pixel may assume any number of different colors. Pixels are combined in the form of an array (rows and columns). It is the size of that overall pixel array that defines the display's *resolution*. Thus, resolution is the total number of pixels in *width* by the total number of pixels in *height*. For example, a typical VGA resolution is 640 pixels wide by 480 pixels high (a total of 307,200 pixels). Typical *Super VGA* (SVGA) resolution is 800 pixels wide by 600 pixels high (a total of 480,000 pixels). Today's monitors can easily support a resolution 1280 pixels wide by 1024 pixels high (1,310,720 pixels) or even 1600 pixels wide by 1200 pixels high (a whopping 1,920,000 pixels). Resolution is important for computer monitors since higher resolutions allow finer image detail.

TRIADS AND DOT PITCH

While monochrome CRTs use a single, uniform phosphor coating (usually white, amber, or green), color CRTs use three color phosphors (red, green, and blue) arranged as triangles (or *triads*). Figure 27-2 illustrates a simple series of color phosphor triads. On a color monitor, each triad represents *one* pixel (even though there are three *dots* in the pixel). By using the electron streams from three electron guns—one gun for red, one for blue, and another for green—to excite each dot, a broad spectrum of colors can be produced. The three dots are placed so close together that they appear as a single point to the unaided eye.

 It's important to remember that electrons themselves are invisible—they have no color. Color is produced when the invisible electron strikes a colored phosphor.

The quality of a color image is related to just how close the three dots are to one another. The closer together they are, the purer the image appears. As the dots are spaced farther apart, the image quality degrades because the eye can begin to discern the individual dots in each pixel. This results in lines that no longer appear straight and colors that are no longer pure. *Dot pitch* is a measure of the distance between two adjacent phosphor dots of the same color on the display. This is also the same dimension for the distance between openings in a shadow mask. Displays with a dot pitch of 0.31mm or less generally provide adequate image quality, though a dot pitch of 0.28mm or less is preferred.

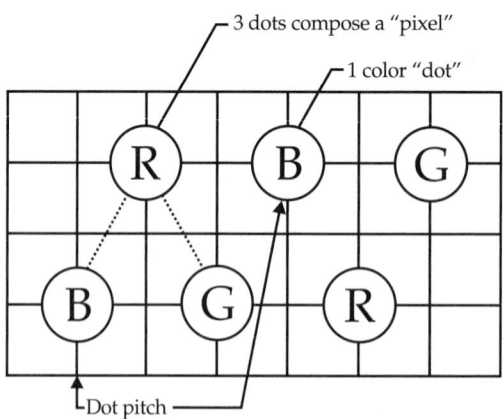

FIGURE 27-2   Arranging color phosphors in a CRT

SHADOW AND SLOT MASKS

The *shadow mask* is a thin sheet of perforated metal that is placed in the color CRT just behind the phosphor coating. Electron beams from each of the three electron guns are focused to converge at each hole in the mask—not at the phosphor screen (Figure 27-3). The microscopic holes act as apertures that let the electron beams through only to their corresponding color phosphors. In this way, any stray electrons are *masked,* and color is kept pure. Some CRT designs substitute a shadow mask with a *slot mask* (also called an *aperture grille*), which is made up of vertical wires behind the phosphor screen. The "dot pitch" for CRTs with slot masks is defined as the distance between each slot. Keep in mind that monochrome CRTs do not need a shadow mask at all since the entire phosphor surface is the same color.

CONVERGENCE

Remember that three electron guns are used in a color monitor. The electrons themselves are invisible, but each gun excites a particular color phosphor. All three electron beams are tracking around the screen simultaneously, and the beams converge at holes in the shadow mask. This *convergence* of electron beams is closely related to color purity in the screen image. Ideally, the three beams converge perfectly at all points on the display, and the resulting color is perfectly pure throughout (such as pure white). If one or more beams do not converge properly, the image color will not be pure. In most cases, poor convergence will result in colored shadows. For example, you may see a red, green, or blue shadow when looking at a white line. Serious convergence problems can result in a blurred or distorted image. Monitor specifications usually list typical convergence error as *misconvergence* at both the display center and the overall display area. Typical center misconvergence runs approximately 0.45mm, while overall display area misconvergence is about 0.65mm. Larger numbers result in poorer convergence. Fortunately, monitor convergence can be calibrated—often with the monitor's own onboard adjustments.

PINCUSHION AND BARREL DISTORTION

The front face of most CRTs is slightly convex (bulging outward). However, digital images are perfectly square (that is, two dimensional). When a flat (2D) image is projected onto a curved (3D) surface, distortion results. Ideally, a monitor's raster circuits will compensate for this screen shape so that the image

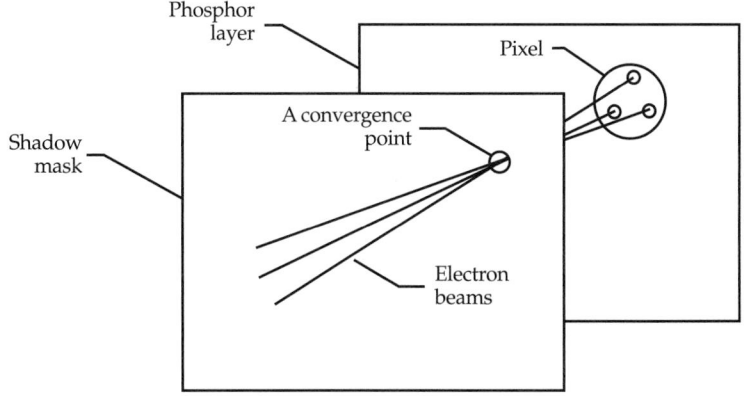

Sizes and distances are not shown to scale

FIGURE 27-3   The importance of convergence in a color monitor

appears flat when viewed at normal distances. In actual practice, however, the image is rarely flat. The sides of the image (top to bottom) and (left to right) may be bent slightly inward, or slightly outward. Figure 27-4 illustrates an exaggerated view of these effects. *Pincushioning* occurs when sides are bent inward making the image's border appear concave. *Barreling* occurs when the sides are bent outward, making the image's border appear convex. In most cases, these distortions should be just barely noticeable (no more than 2.0mm or 3.0mm). Keep in mind that many technicians refer to barrel distortion as *pincushioning* as well, though this is not technically correct.

HORIZONTAL AND VERTICAL SCANNING, RASTER, AND RETRACE

To understand what *scanning* is, you must first understand how a monitor's image is formed. A monitor's image is generated one horizontal line of pixels at a time starting from the upper-left corner of the display (Figure 27-5). As the beams travel horizontally across the line, each pixel in the line is excited based on the video data contained in the corresponding location of video RAM on the video adapter board. When a line is complete, the beam turns off (known as *horizontal blanking*). The beam is then directed horizontally (and slightly lower vertically) to the beginning of the next subsequent line. A new horizontal line can then be drawn. This process continues until all horizontal lines are drawn and the beam is in the lower-right corner of the display. When this image "page" is complete, the beam turns off (called *vertical blanking*) and is redirected back to the upper-left corner of the display to start all over again.

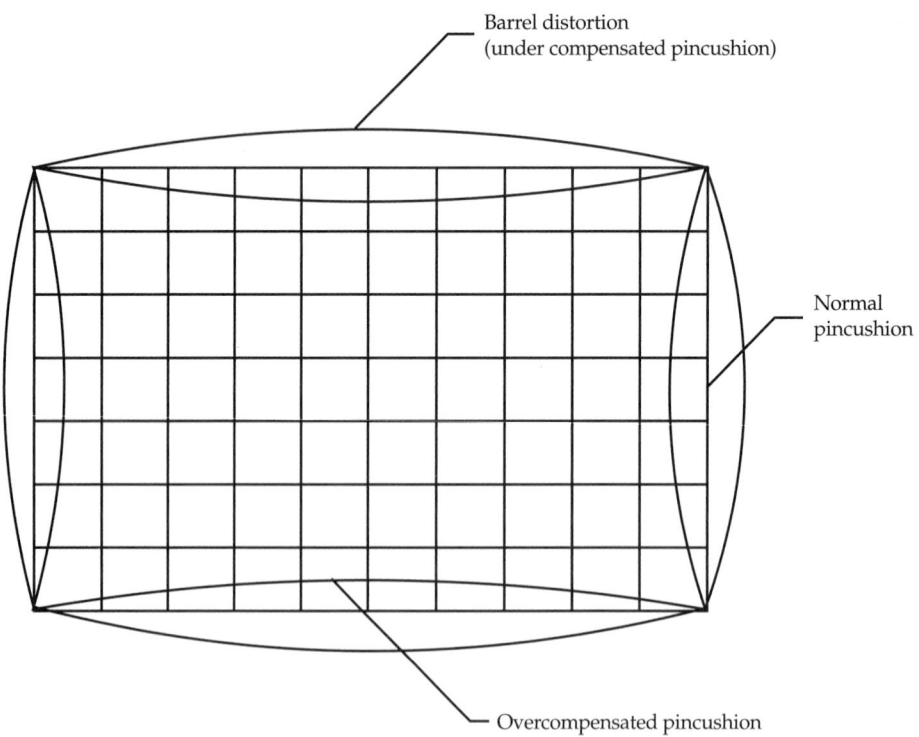

FIGURE 27-4   The effects of pincushion and barrel distortion

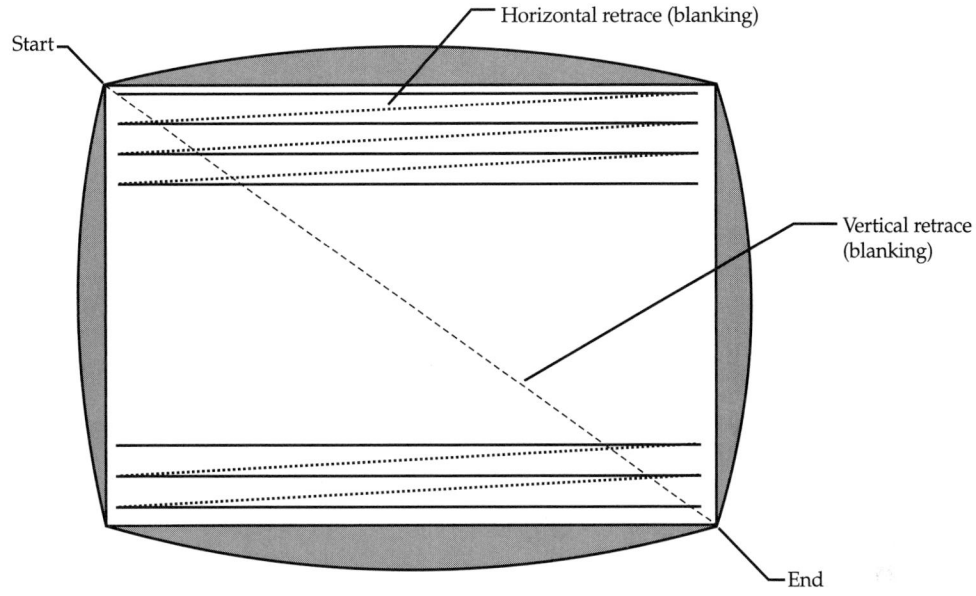

FIGURE 27-5   Forming a screen image on a CRT

The rate at which horizontal lines are drawn is known as the *horizontal scanning rate* (sometimes called *horizontal sync rate*). The rate at which a complete page of horizontal lines is generated is known as the *vertical scanning rate* (or *vertical sync rate*). Both the horizontal and vertical blanking times are known as *retrace times* since the deactivated beams are "retracing" their path before starting a new trace. A typical horizontal retrace time is 5μS, while the typical vertical retrace time is 700μS. This continuous horizontal and vertical scanning action is generally referred to as the *raster*.

We can easily apply numbers to scanning rates to give you an even better idea of their relationship. A typical VGA monitor with a resolution of 640×480 pixels uses a horizontal scanning rate of 31.5 kHz. This means that 31,500 lines can be drawn in 1 second, or a single line of 640 pixels can be drawn in 31.7μS. Since there are 480 horizontal lines to be drawn in one page, a complete page can be drawn in (480×31.7μS) 15.2mS. If a single page can be drawn in 15.2mS, the screen can be refreshed 65.7 times per second (65.7 Hz). This is roughly the vertical rate that will be set for VGA operation at 640×480 resolution. In actual practice, the vertical scanning rate will be set to a whole number such as 60 Hz, which leaves a lot of spare time for blanking and synchronization. It was discovered early in TV design that vertical scanning rates under 60 Hz resulted in perceivable flicker that causes eyestrain and fatigue. You can see that horizontal scanning rates are not chosen arbitrarily. The objective is to select a horizontal frequency that will cover a page's worth of horizontal pixel lines for any given resolution at about 60 times per second (or even higher for reduced flicker). Table 27-1 compares typical monitor resolutions and scan rates.

INTERLACING

Images are "painted" onto a display one horizontal row at a time, but the sequence in which those lines are drawn can be *noninterlaced* or *interlaced.* As you see in Figure 27-6, a noninterlaced monitor draws all of the lines that compose an image in one pass. This is preferable since a noninterlaced image is easier on your eyes. The entire image is refreshed at the vertical scanning frequency, so a 60-Hz vertical scanning

TABLE 27-1   TYPICAL SCAN RATES VS. MONITOR RESOLUTION

RESOLUTION	HORIZONTAL SCAN	VERTICAL SCAN	MONITOR
720×348	18.43 kHz	50 Hz	MDA
320×200	15.85 kHz	60.5 Hz	CGA
640×350	21.8 kHz	60 Hz	EGA
640×350	31.5 kHz	70 Hz	MCGA
640×480	31.5 kHz	60 Hz	VGA-G
640×480	37.5 kHz	75 Hz	EVGA
640×480	43.3 kHz	85 Hz	VESA
720×400	31.5 kHz	70 Hz	VGA-Text
720×400	37.9 kHz	85 Hz	VESA
800×600	37.9 kHz	60 Hz	SVGA
800×600	46.9 kHz	75 Hz	ESVGA
800×600	53.7 kHz	85 Hz	VESA
832×624	49.7 kHz	75 Hz	Macintosh 16" Color
1024×768	48.4 kHz	60 Hz	VESA
1024×768	56.5 kHz	70 Hz	VESA
1024×768	60.0 kHz	75 Hz	EUVGA
1024×768	60.2 kHz	75 Hz	Macintosh 19" Color
1024×768	68.7 kHz	85 Hz	VESA
1152×864	67.5 kHz	75 Hz	VESA
1152×870	68.7 kHz	75 Hz	Macintosh 21" Color
1280×960	60.0 kHz	60 Hz	VESA
1280×960	85.9 kHz	85 Hz	VESA
1280×1024	64.0 kHz	60 Hz	VESA
1280×1024	80.0 kHz	75 Hz	VESA
1280×1024	91.1 kHz	85 Hz	VESA
1600×1200	75.0 kHz	60 Hz	VESA
1600×1200	81.3 kHz	65 Hz	VESA
1600×1200	87.5 kHz	70 Hz	VESA
1600×1200	93.8 kHz	75 Hz	VESA

rate will update the entire image 60 times in 1 second. A noninterlaced display draws an image as two passes. Once the first pass is complete, a second pass fills in the rest of the image. The effective image refresh rate is only half the stated vertical scanning rate. The typical 1,024×768 SVGA monitor offers a vertical scanning rate of 87 Hz, but since the monitor is interlaced, effective refresh is only 43.5 Hz—screen flicker is much more noticeable.

BANDWIDTH

In the very simplest terms, the *bandwidth* of a monitor is the absolute maximum rate at which pixels can be sent to the monitor. Typical VGA displays offer a bandwidth of 30 MHz. That is, the monitor could generate up to 30 million pixels per second on the display. Consider that each scan line of a VGA display uses 640 pixels and the horizontal scan rate of 31.45 kHz allows 31,450 scan lines per second to be written. At that rate, the monitor is processing (640 pixels/scan line × 31,450 scan lines/second) 20,128,000 pixels/second—

Noninterlaced   Interlaced

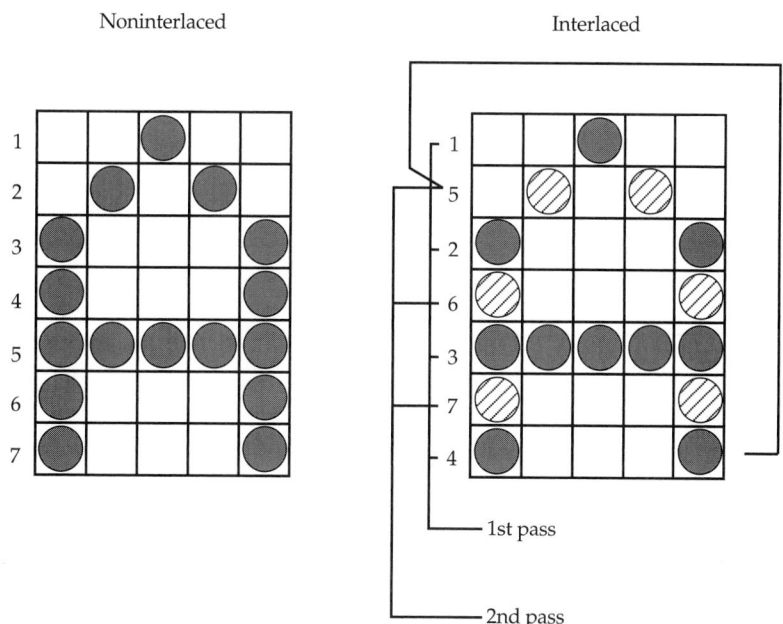

FIGURE 27-6   Interlaced vs. noninterlaced scanning

well within the monitor's 30-MHz bandwidth. The very newest color monitors offer bandwidths of 135 MHz. Such high-resolution 1280×1024 monitors with scanning rates of 79 kHz would need to process at least (1280 pixels/scan line × 79,000 scan lines/second) 101,120,000 pixels/second (101.12 MHz), so enhanced bandwidth is truly a necessity for high resolutions.

SWIM, JITTER, AND DRIFT

The electron beam(s) that form an image are directed around a display using variable magnetic fields generated by separate vertical and horizontal *deflection coils* mounted around the CRT's neck. The analog signals that drive each deflection coil are produced by horizontal and vertical deflection circuitry. Ideally, deflection circuitry should steer the electron beam(s) precisely the same way in each pass. This would result in an absolutely rock-solid image on the display. In the real world, however, there are minute variations in the placement of images over any given period. *Jitter* is a term used to measure such variation over a 15-second period. *Swim* (sometimes called *wave*) is a measure of position variation over a 30-second period. *Drift* is a measure of position variation over a one-minute period. Note that all three terms represent essentially the same problem over different amounts of time. Swim, jitter, and drift may be expressed as fractions of a pixel or as physical measurements such as millimeters.

VIDEO SIGNAL

This specification lists signal levels and characteristics of the analog video input channel(s). In most cases, a video signal in the 0.7-Vpp (peak to peak) range is used. Circuitry inside the monitor amplifies and manipulates these relatively small signals. A related specification is input impedance, which is often at 75 ohms. Older monitors using digital (on-off) video signals typically operate with signals up to 1.5 volts.

SYNCHRONIZATION AND POLARITY

After a line is drawn on the display, the electron beams are turned off (blanked) and repositioned to start the next horizontal line. However, no data is contained in the retrace line. For the new line to be in sync with the data for that line, a *synchronization* pulse is sent from the video adapter to the monitor. There is a separate pulse for horizontal synchronization and vertical synchronization. In most current monitors, synchronization signals are edge-triggered TTL (transistor-transistor logic) signals. *Polarity* refers to the edge that triggers the synchronization. A *falling* trigger (marked "–" or "positive/negative") indicates that synchronization takes place at the high-to-low transition of the sync signal. A *leading* trigger (marked "+" or "negative/positive") indicates that synchronization takes place on the low-to-high transition of the sync signal.

Color Circuits

To fully understand color monitors, it is best to start with a block diagram. The block diagram for a VGA monitor is shown in Figure 27-7. Three complete video drive circuits are needed (one for each primary color—red, green, and blue). While early color monitors used logic levels to represent video signals, current monitors use analog signals, which allow the intensity of each color to be varied. The CRT is designed to provide three electron beams, which are directed at corresponding color phosphors. By varying the intensity of each electron beam, virtually any color can be produced. For practical purposes, the color monitor can be considered in three subsections: the video drive circuits, the vertical drive circuit, and the horizontal drive circuit (including the high-voltage system).

VIDEO DRIVE CIRCUITS

The schematic diagram for a typical RGB (red, green, and blue) drive circuit is shown in Figure 27-8. This schematic is actually part of a Tandy VGM-220 analog color monitor. You will see that there are three separate video drive circuits. Components with a 5*xx* designation (such as IC501) are part of the red video drive circuit. The 6*xx* designation (such as Q602) shows a part in the green video drive circuit. A 7*xx* marking (such as C704) indicates a component in the blue video drive circuit. Other components marked with 8*xx* designations (such as Q803) are included to operate the CRT control grid. Let's walk through the operation of one of these video circuits.

The red analog signal is filtered by the small array of F501. The ferrite beads on either side of the small filter capacitor serve to reduce noise that may otherwise interfere with the weak analog signal. The video signal is amplified by transistor Q501. Potentiometer VR501 adjusts the signal *gain* (the amount of amplification applied to the video signal). Collector signals are then passed to the differential amplifier circuit in IC501. Once again, noise is a major concern in color signals, and differential amplifiers help to improve signal strength while eliminating noise. The resulting video signal is applied to a "push-pull" amplifier circuit consisting of Q503 and Q504, then fed to a subsequent push-pull amplifier pair of Q505 and Q506. Potentiometer VR502 controls the amount of DC bias used to generate the final output signal. The output from this final amplifier stage is coupled directly to the corresponding CRT video control grid. The remaining two drive circuits both work the same way.

Problems with the video circuits in color monitors rarely disable the image entirely. Even if one video drive circuit should fail, there are still two others to drive the CRT. Of course, the loss of one primary color will severely distort the image colors, but the image should still be visible. You can tell when one of the video drive circuits fails; the faulty circuit will either saturate the display with that color, or cut that color out completely. For example, if the red video drive circuit should fail, the resulting screen image will either be saturated with red, or red will be absent (leaving a greenish-blue or cyan image).

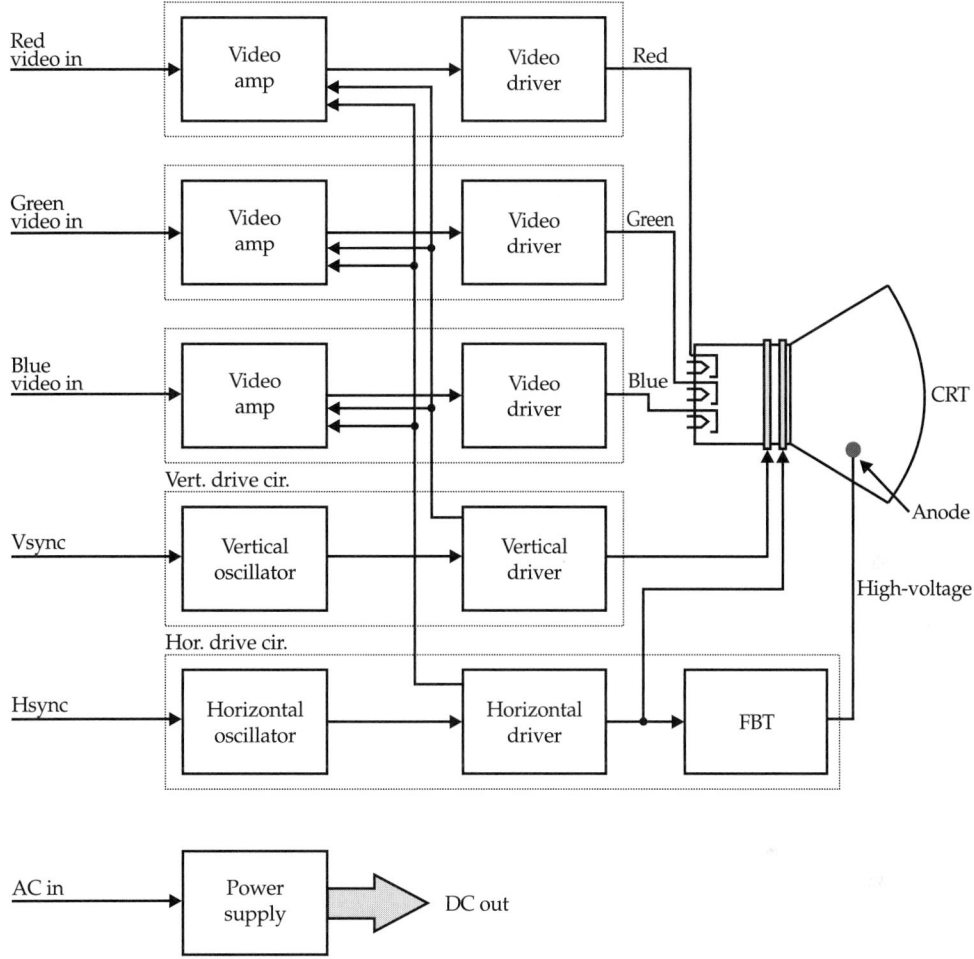

FIGURE 27-7   Block diagram of a color (VGA) monitor

VERTICAL DRIVE CIRCUIT

The vertical drive circuit is designed to operate the monitor's *vertical deflection yoke* (V-DY). To give you a broad perspective of vertical drive operation and its interrelation to other important monitor circuits, Figure 27-9 illustrates the vertical drive, horizontal drive, high-voltage, and power supply circuits all combined in the same schematic. This schematic is essentially the main PC board for the Tandy VGM-220 monitor. Components marked with 4*xx* numbers (such as IC401) are part of the vertical drive system.

The vertical sync pulses enter the monitor at connector CH202 (the line marked "V"). A simple exclusive-OR gate (IC201) is used to condition the sync pulses and select the video mode being used. Since the polarity of horizontal and vertical sync pulses will be different for each video mode, IC201 detects those polarities and causes the digitally controlled analog switch (IC401) to select one of three vertical size (V-SIZE) control sets that is connected to the vertical sawtooth oscillator (IC402). This mode-switching circuit allows the monitor to autosize the display.

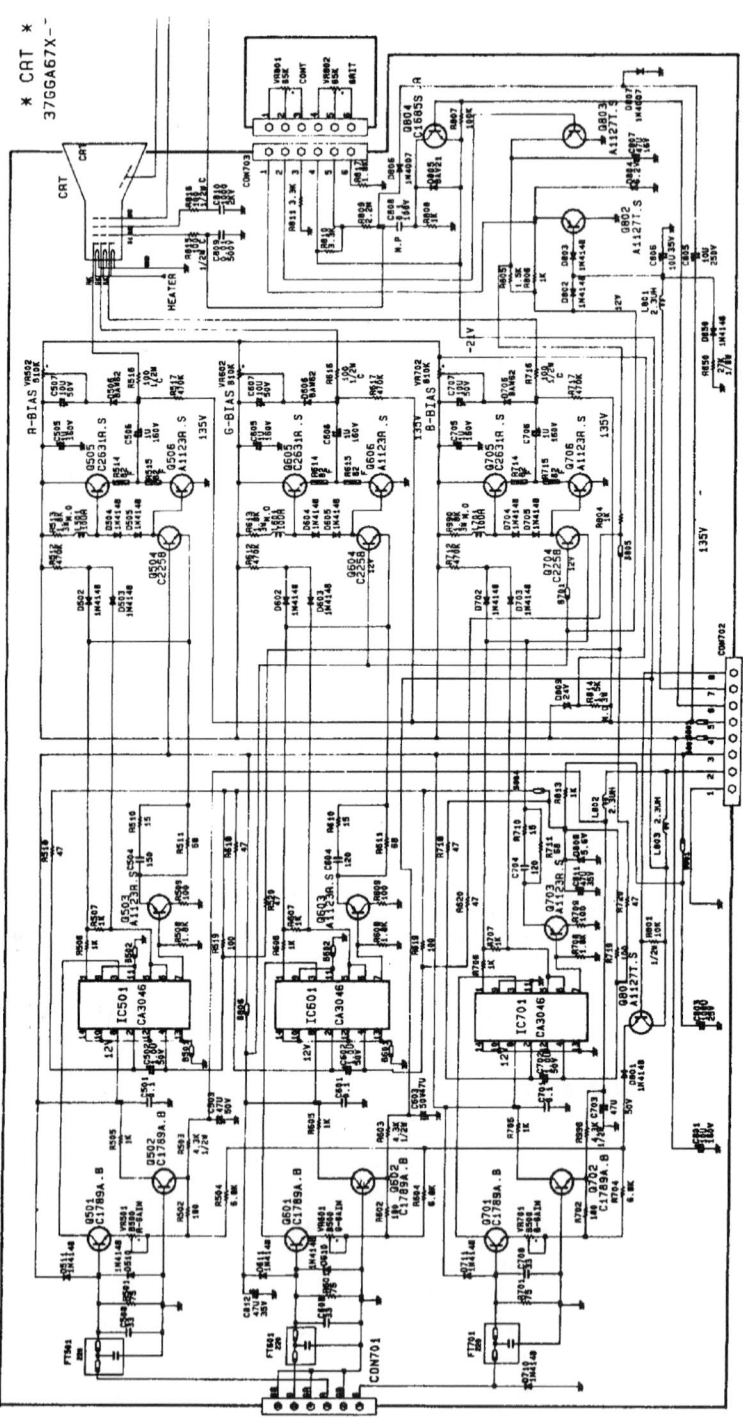

FIGURE 27-8   Schematic of a VGM-220 video circuit (Tandy Corporation)

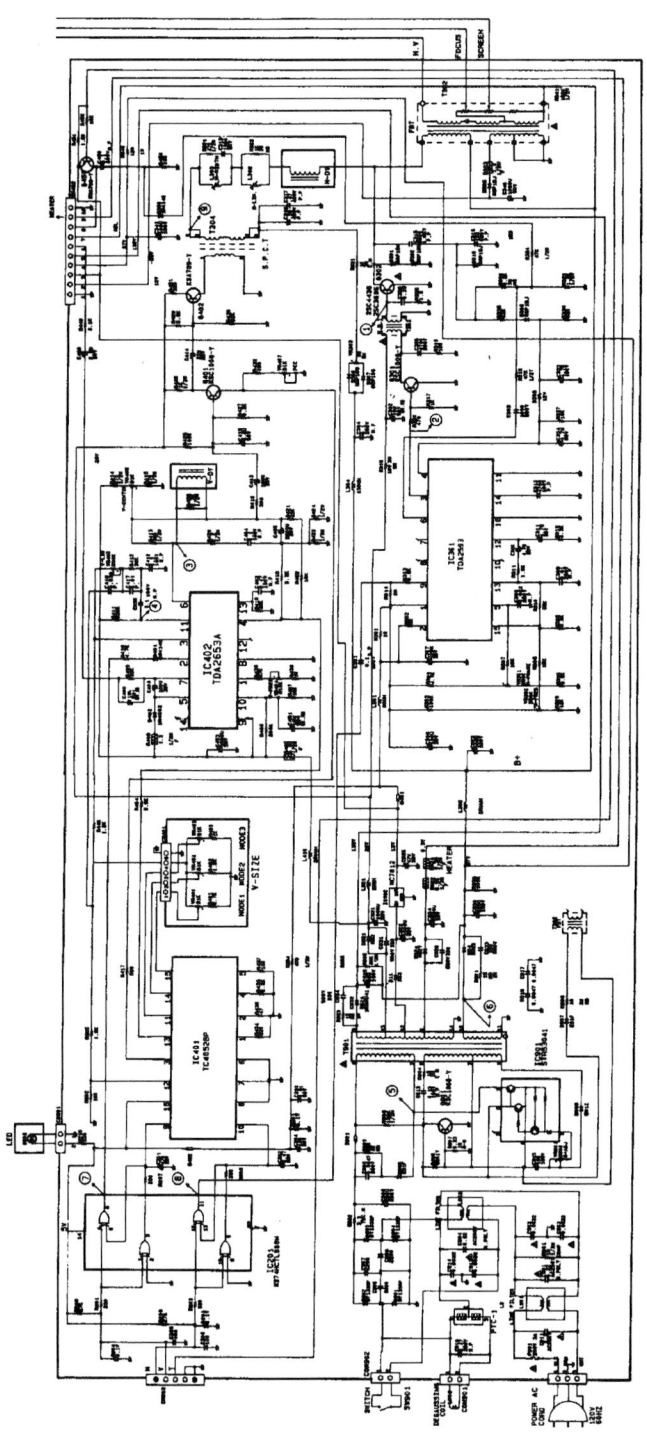

FIGURE 27-9 Schematic of a VGM-220 main (raster) circuit (Tandy Corporation)

The vertical sync pulse fires the vertical sawtooth oscillator on pin 2 of IC402. The frequency of the vertical sweep is set to 60 Hz, but can be optimized by adjusting the vertical frequency control (V-FREQ) VR404. It is highly recommended that you *not* attempt to adjust the vertical frequency unless you have an oscilloscope available. Vertical linearity (V-LIN) is adjusted through potentiometer VR405. Vertical centering (V-CENTER) is controlled through VR406. Linearity and centering adjustments should only be made while displaying an appropriate test pattern. It is interesting to note that there are no discrete power amplifiers needed to drive the vertical deflection yoke. IC402 pin 6 drives the deflection yoke directly through an internal power amplifier.

The pincushion circuit forms a link between the vertical and horizontal deflection systems through the pincushion transformer (T304). Transistors Q401 and Q402 form a compensator circuit that slightly modulates horizontal deflection. This prevents distortion in the image when projecting a flat, two-dimensional image onto a curved surface (the CRT). Potentiometer VR407 provides the *pincushion control* (PCC). As with other alignments, you should not attempt to adjust the pincushion unless an appropriate test pattern is displayed.

Problems that develop in the vertical amplifier will invariably affect the appearance of the CRT image. A catastrophic fault in the vertical oscillator or amplifier will leave a narrow horizontal line in the display. The likeliest cause is the vertical drive chip (IC402) since that component handles both sawtooth generation and amplification. If only the upper or lower half of an image disappears, only one part of the vertical amplifier in IC402 may have failed. However, any fault on the PC board that interrupts the vertical sawtooth will disable vertical deflection entirely. When the vertical deflection is marginal (too expanded or too compressed), suspect a fault in IC402, but its related components may also be breaking down. An image that is overexpanded will usually appear "folded over" with a whitish haze along the bottom. Note that vertical drive problems do not affect display colors.

HORIZONTAL DRIVE CIRCUIT

The horizontal drive circuit is responsible for operating the *horizontal deflection yoke* (H-DY). It is this circuit that sweeps the electron beams left and right across the display. To understand how the horizontal drive works, you should again refer to the schematic of Figure 27-9. All components marked with 3*xx* numbers (such as IC301) relate to the horizontal drive circuit. Horizontal sync signals enter the monitor at connector CH202 (the line marked "H") and are conditioned by the executive-OR gates of IC201. Conditioned sync pulses fire the horizontal oscillator (IC301). Horizontal frequency should be locked at 31.5 kHz, but potentiometer VR302 can be used to optimize the frequency. Do not attempt to adjust horizontal frequency unless you have an oscilloscope available. Horizontal phase can be adjusted with VR301. You should avoid altering any alignments until a suitable test pattern is displayed.

IC301 is a highly integrated device that is designed to provide precision horizontal square wave pulses to the driver transistors Q301 and Q302. IC301 pin 3 provides the horizontal pulses to Q301. Transistor Q301 switches on and off, causing current pulses in the horizontal output transformer (T303). Current pulses produced by the secondary winding of T303 fire the horizontal output transistor (Q302). Output from the HOT (Horizontal Output Transistor circuit) drives the horizontal deflection yoke (H-DY). The deflection circuit includes two adjustable coils to control horizontal linearity (H-LIN; L302) and horizontal width (H-WIDTH; L303). You will also notice that the collector signal from Q302 is directly connected to the *flyback transformer* (FBT). Operation of the high-voltage system is covered in the next section.

Problems in the horizontal drive circuit can take several forms. One common manifestation is the loss of horizontal sweep, leaving a vertical line in the center of the display. This is generally due to a fault in the horizontal oscillator (IC301) rather than the horizontal driver transistors. The second common symptom is a loss of image (including raster) and is almost always the result of a failure in the HOT. Since the HOT also operates the flyback transformer, a loss of horizontal output will disrupt high-voltage generation, and the image will disappear.

THE FLYBACK CIRCUIT

The presence of a large positive potential on the CRT's anode is needed to accelerate an electron beam across the distance between the cathode and CRT phosphor. Electrons must strike the phosphor hard enough to liberate visible light. Under normal circumstances, this requires a potential of 15,000 to 30,000 volts. Larger CRTs need higher voltages because there is a greater physical distance to overcome. Monitors generate high voltage through the *flyback circuit.*

The heart of the high-voltage circuit is the *flyback transformer* (FBT), as shown in Figure 27-9. The FBT's primary winding is directly coupled to the horizontal output transistor (Q302). Another primary winding is used to compensate the high-voltage level for changes in brightness and contrast. Flyback voltage is generated during the horizontal *retrace* (the time between the end of one scan line and the beginning of another) when the sudden drop in deflection signal causes a strong voltage spike on the FBT secondary windings. You will notice that the FBT in Figure 27-9 provides one multitapped secondary winding. The topmost tap from the FBT secondary provides high-voltage to the CRT anode. A high-voltage rectifier diode added to the FBT assembly forms a half-wave rectifier. Only positive voltages reach the CRT anode. The effective capacitance of the CRT anode will act to filter the high-voltage spikes into DC. You can read the high-voltage level with a high-voltage probe. The CRT needs additional voltages in order to function. The lower tap from the FBT secondary supplies voltage to the focus and screen grid adjustments. These adjustments, in turn, drive the CRT directly.

Trouble in the high-voltage circuit can render the monitor inoperative. Typically, a high-voltage fault manifests itself as a loss of image and raster. In many cases where the HOT and deflection signals prove to be intact, the flyback transformer has probably failed, causing a loss of output in one or more of the three FBT secondary windings. The troubleshooting procedures in the next section of this chapter will cover high-voltage symptoms and solutions in more detail.

CONSTRUCTION

Before jumping right into troubleshooting, it would be helpful to understand how the circuits shown in Figure 27-9 are assembled. A wiring diagram for the Tandy VGM-220 is shown in Figure 27-10. There are two PC boards: the video drive PC board and the main PC board. The main PC board contains the raster circuits, power supply, and high-voltage circuitry. The video drive PC board contains red, green, and blue video circuits. Video signals, focus grid voltage, screen grid voltage, and brightness and contrast controls connect to the video drive board. The video PC board plugs into the CRT at its neck (although the diagram of Figure 27-10 may not show this clearly). A power switch, power LED, and CRT degaussing coil plug into the main PC board. There are also connections at the main PC board for the AC line cord and video sync signals.

Troubleshooting a CRT

In spite of its age, the *cathode ray tube* (CRT) continues to play an important role in modern computer monitors. There are some very important reasons for this longevity. First, the CRT is relatively inexpensive to make, and it needs only simple circuitry in order to operate. Second, the CRT is extremely rugged and reliable. Typical working lives can extend to ten years or more. It is this combination of low cost, ease of operation, and long-term reliability that has allowed the CRT to keep pace with today's personal computers.

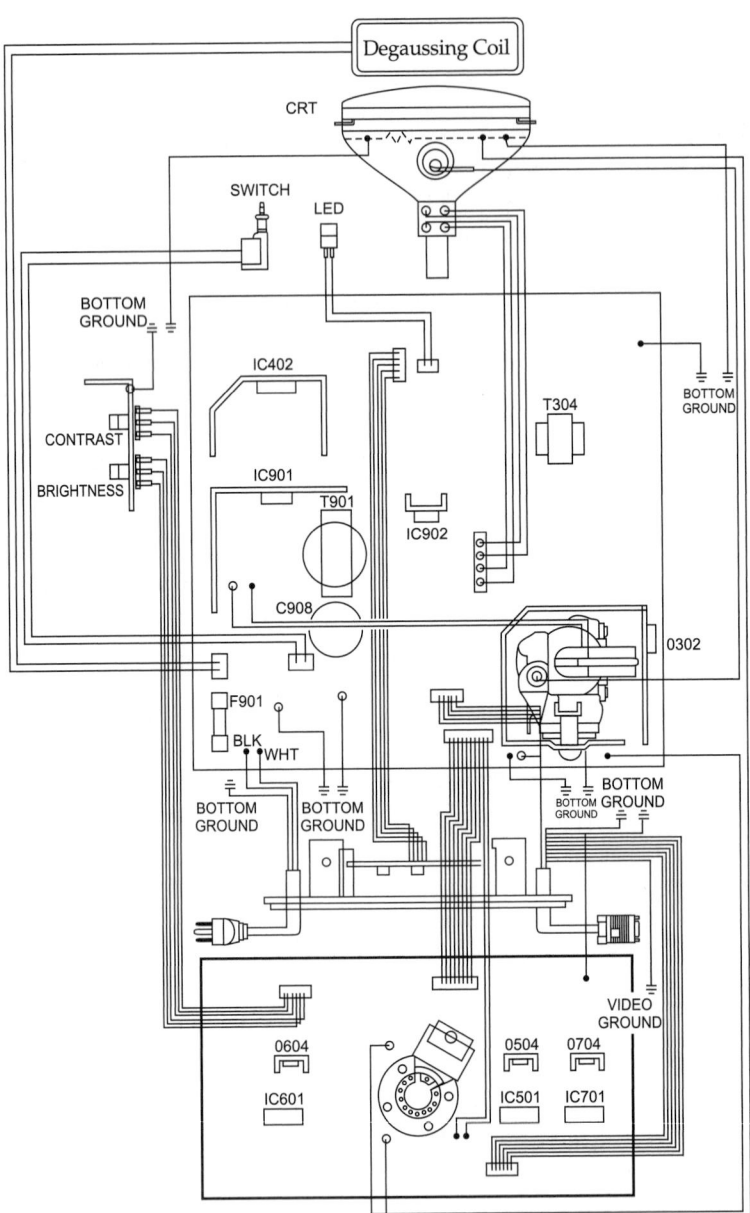

FIGURE 27-10   Wiring diagram for the VGM-220 monitor (Tandy Corporation)

However, CRTs are certainly not perfect devices. The delicate assemblies within the CRT used to generate and direct electron beams can eventually open, short-circuit, or wear out. And like most classical vacuum tubes, CRT failures often occur slowly over a period of weeks or months. This part of the chapter shows you the assemblies in a typical color CRT, explains the faults that often occur, and offer some alternatives for dealing with CRT problems.

INSIDE THE CRT

Before we discuss CRT problems, you should have an understanding of the color CRT itself. Figure 27-11 shows a cross-section of a typical color CRT. To produce an image, electron beams are generated, concentrated, and directed across a phosphor-coated face. When electron beams (which are invisible) strike phosphor, light is liberated. This is the light you see from the CRT. The color of light is determined by the particular phosphor chemistry. You will note that there are three electron guns in the color CRT: a beam for red, a beam for green, and a beam for blue.

Electron beams start with a heater wire. When energized, the heater becomes extremely hot. (This is the glow you see in the CRT neck.) The heat from a heater warms its corresponding cathode, and a barium tip on the cathode begins "boiling off" electrons. Ordinarily, electrons would simply boil off into a big, clumsy cloud. But since electrons are negatively charged, they will be attracted to any large positive potential. A moderate positive potential (+500 volts or so) on the screen grid starts accelerating the electrons down the CRT's neck, while the control grid voltage limits the electrons—effectively forcing the unruly cloud into a beam. Once electrons pass the screen grid, a high positive potential on the CRT anode (anywhere from 15 to 30 kV) rockets the electrons toward the CRT face. The beam is still rather wide, so a focus grid applies another potential that works to concentrate the beam.

All this is very effective at generating narrow, high-velocity electron beams. But unless you want to watch a big, bright spot in the middle of the CRT, there has to be some method of tracing the beams around the CRT's face. Beam tracing is accomplished through the use of deflection magnets placed around the

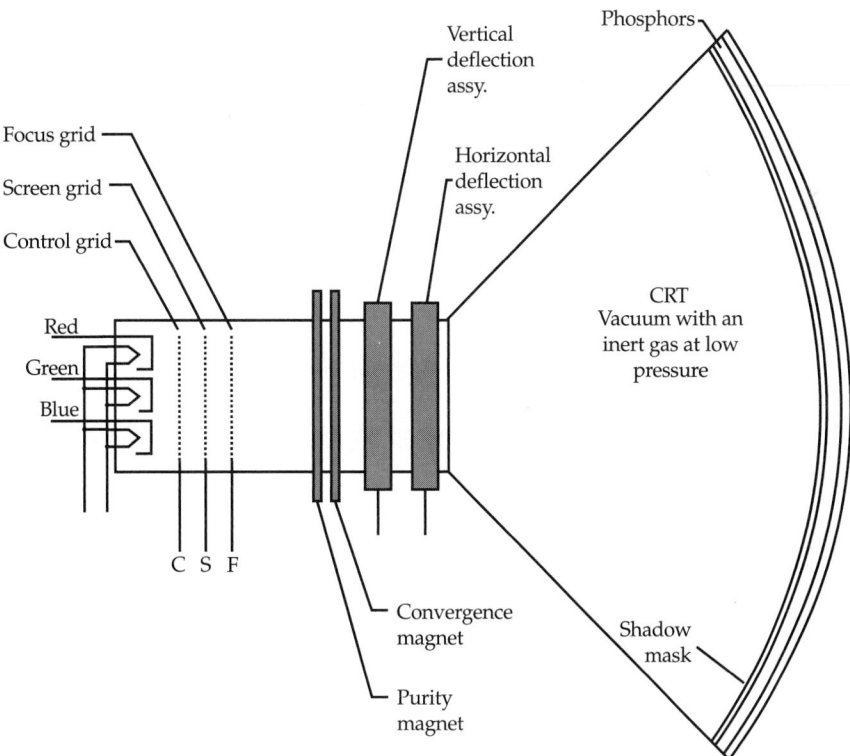

FIGURE 27-11   Cross-section of a basic color CRT

CRT neck. You will see these magnets (actually electromagnets) as heavy coils of wire where the CRT funnel meets the neck. There are actually four electromagnets in this deflection assembly: two opposing electromagnets direct the beam in the vertical direction, while another set of opposing magnets direct the beam in the horizontal direction. Using electrical signals from the monitor's raster circuits, an electron beam can traced across the entire CRT face.

Another element of the CRT that you should understand is called the shadow mask. A shadow mask is basically a thin metal sheet with a series of small holes punched into it. Some CRTs use a mask of rectangular openings referred to as an aperture grille or slot mask. Both types of mask fulfill the same purpose—to ensure that electron beams strike only the color phosphors of the intended pixel. This is a vital element of a color monitor. In a monochrome monitor, the CRT is coated with a single homogenous layer of phosphor. If stray electrons strike nearby phosphor particles, a letter or line may simply appear to be a bit out of focus. For a color CRT, however, stray electrons can cause incorrect colors to appear on nearby pixels. Masks help to preserve color purity. Color purity is also aided by a purity magnet, which helps correct fine beam positioning. A convergence magnet helps ensure that all three electron beams meet (or converge) at the shadow mask.

Of course, grids, heaters, and cathodes are all located inside the glass CRT vessel. Electrical connections are made through a circular arrangement of sealed pins in the neck. Table 27-2 explains the designations for each pin. Keep in mind that the high-voltage anode is attached directly to the CRT in the top-right part of the glass funnel. Also remember that some CRT designs may use additional pins.

CORRECTING SHORTS

You can probably guess that short circuits within a CRT can be maddening. There is just no way to get to them. However, most shorts are not held in place by anything more than gravity, or a slight arc during contact. As a result, it may be possible to dislodge the short by turning the monitor over and gently rapping on the CRT neck with the plastic end of a screwdriver. Obviously, this is also a prime way to shatter the CRT, so be *very* careful if you attempt to dislodge a suspected short. If a few light taps don't do the job, quit while the CRT is still in one piece.

CRT TESTERS/REJUVENATORS

Since shorts are small fragments of conductive material, they can be burned away using a surge of electricity. This is much safer than the "tap-and-pray" method just mentioned. Devices such as Sencore's CR70 Universal CRT Restorer/Analyzer can help check the CRT for shorts and opens. Such devices can

TABLE 27-2	TYPICAL CRT PIN DESIGNATIONS
DESIGNATION	**DESCRIPTION**
G1	Control grid voltage
G2	Screen grid voltage
G3 or F	Focus grid voltage
KG	Green video signal
KR	Red video signal
KB	Blue video signal
H1	Heater voltage in
H2	Heater voltage out

also burn out a wide variety of shorts and (in many cases) rejuvenate weak elements. As another advantage, a tester can usually check and rejuvenate a CRT without having the whole monitor available. Most CRT test equipment can perform four major operations: color balance testing, emission testing, removing shorts, and beam rejuvenation:

■ **Color balance testing**   To produce pure white (and all other true colors), all three electron guns must be able to run at the same intensity. A color balance test can compare the strongest gun to the weakest gun. If there is a variation of more than 55 percent, the weakest gun will be displayed as "bad." But it is possible to recover a portion of the weaker beam's operation through a "Beam Builder" or "Beam Rejuvenator" function on the tester.

■ **Emission testing**   A cathode must be able to "emit" electrons—that is the basis of all vacuum tubes. As the cathode ages, ions generated from air in the CRT gradually block the cathode's ability to produce electrons. This is *ion poisoning,* which results in weakened electron beams. A rejuvenator function can usually overcome low-emission problems.

■ **Removing shorts**   Generally speaking, a decent CRT tester/rejuvenator can remove shorts between the control grid and the cathode or the screen grid. In practice, you may see such a function marked "Remove G1 Short" or some similar nomenclature. However, few testers attempt to remove heater-to-cathode shorts because the energy needed to clear a short there would usually burn out the heater element entirely.

■ **Beam rejuvenation**   The purpose of rejuvenation is basically to restore the emission of weak electron guns. This is usually accomplished by boosting the heater voltage (making the cathode extremely hot), then passing a 100-mA to 150-mA current through the cathode. The effect of rejuvenation exposes fresh emitting material, which in turn adds new life to weakened guns. A current meter measures beam current. When beam current reaches its nominal range during rejuvenation, the electron gun is restored.

CRT SYMPTOMS

CRTs enjoy a long, reliable working life because there are really no moving parts—merely a set of stationary metal elements. However, the grids and cathodes are located very close to one another. Physical shocks can dislodge elements and cause sudden short circuits. Eventually, regular use will alter the physical dimensions of cathodes and grids (resulting in the development of a slower, more gradual short circuit). The stress of regular wear can also cause open circuits in the heater, cathode, or grid. Let's take a look at some of the typical problems that manifest themselves in a CRT.

When considering a CRT replacement, remember that the CRT is typically the most expensive part of the monitor. For larger monitors, the CRT becomes an even larger percentage of the monitor's overall cost. In many cases, the cost for a replacement CRT approaches the original cost of the entire monitor. As a consequence, you should carefully evaluate the economics of replacing the CRT versus buying a new monitor outright.

SYMPTOM 27-1   **Heater opens in the CRT**   Each time the heater runs, it expands. When the CRT turns off, the heater cools and contracts again. This regular thermal expansion and contraction may eventually fatigue the heater and cause it to open. You will see this as a complete loss of the corresponding color. Since heaters are all tied together electrically, there is no way to measure a particular heater directly; but you may see only two glowing heaters in the CRT neck instead of three. An open heater cannot be recovered, and the only available alternative is to replace the CRT itself.

SYMPTOM 27-2   **Heater shorts to a cathode in the CRT**   This is not as strange as it might seem at first. To heat a cathode effectively, the heater must be *extremely* close to the cathode—especially to the barium element that actually liberates the electrons. Over time, the heater may develop accumulations of corrosion, which might eventually cause the heater to contact the cathode. In theory, this should never happen because the inert low-pressure gasses inside the CRT should prevent this. But in actual practice, some small amount of oxygen will still be present in the CRT, and oxidation may occur. A shorted heater will cause the electron gun to fire at full power—in effect, the electron gun will be stuck "on." The image will appear saturated with the color of the defective electron gun. For example, if the blue heater shorts to the cathode, the image will appear saturated with blue. You will also likely see visible retrace lines in the image.

You can verify this problem by removing all power from the monitor, removing the video drive board from the CRT's neck, and measuring the resistance between a heater wire and the suspect cathode. For the CRT pinout listed in Table 27-2, you could check the blue cathode by measuring resistance between the KB and H1 (or H2) pins. Ideally, there should be infinite resistance between the heaters and cathodes. If there is measurable resistance (or a direct short circuit), you have found the problem. If the resistance measures infinity as expected, you may have a defect on the video drive board.

SYMPTOM 27-3   **Cathode shorts to the control grid in the CRT**   A cathode can also short-circuit to the control grid. Often, corrosion flakes off the cathode and comes in contact with the control grid. When this happens, the control grid loses its effectiveness, and the corresponding color will appear saturated. In practice, this symptom will appear very much like a heater short. Fortunately, you should be able to verify this problem with your meter by measuring resistance between the control grid and the suspect cathode. Ideally, there should be infinite resistance between the control grid and all cathodes. If you read a measurable resistance (or a direct short circuit), chances are good that you're facing a cathode-to-control grid short.

SYMPTOM 27-4   **One or more colors appear weak**   This is a common symptom in many older CRTs. Over time, the barium emitter in your cathodes will wear out or develop a layer of ions (referred to as *cathode poisoning*), which inhibits the release of electrons. In either case, the afflicted cathode will lose efficiency, resulting in weakened screen colors. Typically, you might expect all three cathodes to degrade evenly over time (and they will), but by the time the problem becomes serious enough for service, you will usually notice one color weaker than the others. Try increasing the gain of the afflicted signal on the video drive board. If the cathode is indeed afflicted, increasing signal gain should *not* have a substantial effect on the color brightness, and you should consider replacing the CRT.

SYMPTOM 27-5   **CRT phosphors appear aged or worn**   Phosphors are specially formulated chemicals that glow in a particular color when excited by a high-energy electron beam. Typically, phosphors will last for the lifetime of the monitor, but age and normal use will eventually reduce the sensitivity of the phosphors. For old CRTs, you may see this as dull, low-contrast colors. Perhaps a more dramatic problem occurs with *phosphor burn,* which occurs when a monitor is left on, displaying the same image for a very long period. If you turn the monitor off, you can see the latent image burned onto the CRT as a dark shadow. In both cases, there is no way to rejuvenate phosphors, so the CRT will have to be replaced. You can advise customers to prolong the life of their CRT by keeping the brightness at a minimum and using a screen-saver utility if an image will sit unchanging for a long time.

SYMPTOM 27-6   **The CRT suffers from bad cutoff (a.k.a. bad gamma)**   On a CRT, color linearity is a function of the cathode's ability to adjust the level of electron emission. In other words, beam intensity must be linear across the entire range of the video signal (such as 0 to 20 volts or 0 to 50 volts).

As cathodes age, however, they tend to become nonlinear. When this happens, images tend to be too "black and white" rather than display a smooth transition of colors. Technicians often refer to this as a "gassy" CRT, which is actually a CRT gamma problem. In addition to cathode wear, control grid failure can adversely affect beam intensity.

SYMPTOM 27-7 **Open control grid in the CRT** The control grid is used to limit the beam intensity produced by a cathode by applying a potential on the grid. Occasionally, you will find that a control grid might open. In that case, there is no longer a potential available to control the beam intensity, and the beam will fire at full intensity. At first glance, you might think this is a cathode-to-control grid short or a heater-to-cathode short. But if you can't find a short with your multimeter, the control grid is probably open, and the CRT will have to be replaced.

SYMPTOM 27-8 **Open screen grid in the CRT** The screen grid plays an important role in image brightness by accelerating the electron beam toward the CRT phosphors. If the screen grid opens, there will be no potential available to begin accelerating the beam. This will result in a very dark image—even with the screen voltage at maximum. You might think this is a control-to-screen grid short, but if you can't find the short with your multimeter, the screen grid is probably open, and the CRT will have to be replaced.

SYMPTOM 27-9 **Open focus grid in the CRT** A focus grid assembly serves to concentrate electron beams into narrow pinpoints by the time the beam reaches the shadow mask. There is typically a focus control located around the flyback transformer. If the focus grid fails, the image will appear highly distorted, and the focus adjustment will have no effect. When a focus grid fails, the entire CRT will have to be replaced.

SYMPTOM 27-10 **Control grid shorts to screen grid in the CRT** The same flakes of oxidation that can short a cathode to the control grid can also short the control grid to the screen grid. The screen grid starts accelerating the electrons toward the CRT face. If the screen grid is shorted, it will reduce the energy imparted to the electrons. In effect, a shorted screen grid will significantly reduce the overall image brightness (even with the brightness at maximum). In extreme cases, the image may disappear entirely. You can measure the screen grid voltage at G2, which typically runs from 250 volts to 750 volts in normal operation. If the voltage is low (even with the screen grid control at maximum), power-down the monitor, remove the video drive board from the monitor's neck, restart the monitor, and measure the screen voltage again. If the screen voltage returns to normal, you can be confident that the screen grid is shorted. If screen voltage remains low, you may have a fault in the screen voltage circuit. You can also verify a short between the control and screen grids by powering-down the monitor and measuring resistance between the G1 and G2 pins on the CRT neck. Ideally, there should be infinite resistance.

Troubleshooting a Color Monitor

Any discussion of monitor troubleshooting must start with a reminder of the dangers involved. Computer monitors use very high voltages for proper operation. *Potentially lethal shock hazards exist within the monitor assembly—both from ordinary AC line voltage and from the CRT anode voltage developed by the flyback transformer. You must exercise extreme caution whenever a monitor's outer housings are removed.* If you are uncomfortable with the idea of working around high voltages, defer your trouble-shooting to an experienced technician.

WRAPPING IT UP

When you finally get your monitor working again and are ready to reassemble it, be very careful to see that all wiring and connectors are routed properly. No wires should be pinched or lodged between the chassis or other metal parts (especially sharp edges). After the wiring is secure, make sure that any insulators, shielding, or protective enclosures are installed. This is even more important for larger monitors with supplemental X-ray shielding. Replace all plastic enclosures and secure them with their full complement of screws.

POSTREPAIR TESTING AND ALIGNMENT

Regardless of the problem with your monitor or how you go about repairing it, a check of the monitor's alignment is always worthwhile before returning the unit to service. Your first procedure after a repair is complete should be to ensure that the high-voltage level does not exceed the maximum specified value. Excessive high-voltage can liberate X-radiation from the CRT. Over prolonged exposure, X rays can present a serious biohazard. The high-voltage value is usually marked on the specification plate glued to the outer housing, or recorded on a sticker placed somewhere inside the housing. If you cannot find the high-voltage level, refer to service data from the monitor's manufacturer. Once high voltage is correct, you can proceed with other alignment tests. When testing (and realignment) is complete, it is wise to let the monitor run for 24 hours or so (called a *burn-in test*) before returning it to service. Running the monitor for a prolonged period helps ensure that the original problem has indeed been resolved. This is a form of quality control. If the problem resurfaces, there may be another more serious problem elsewhere in the monitor.

MONITOR SYMPTOMS

When problems can clearly be traced to a faulty monitor, you can use the following symptoms to identify and correct the issues.

SYMPTOM 27-11   **The image is saturated with red or appears greenish-blue (cyan)**
If there are any user color controls available from the front or rear housings, make sure those controls have not been accidentally adjusted. If color controls are set properly (or not available externally), the red video drive circuit has probably failed. Refer to the example circuit of Figure 27-8. Use your oscilloscope to trace the video signal from its initial input to the final output. If there is no red video signal at the amplifier input (the base of Q501), check the connection between the monitor and the video adapter board. If the connection is intact, try a known-good monitor. If the problem persists on a known-good monitor, replace the video adapter board. As you trace the video signal, you can compare the signal to characteristics at the corresponding points in the green or blue video circuits. The point at which the signal disappears is probably the point of failure, and the offending component should be replaced. If you do not have the tools or inclination to perform component-level troubleshooting, try replacing the video drive PC board entirely.

If the video signal measures properly all the way to the CRT (or a new video drive PC board does not correct the problem), suspect a fault in the CRT itself. The corresponding cathode or video control grid may have failed. If you have access to a CRT tester/rejuvenator, test the CRT. If the CRT measures bad (and cannot be recovered through any available rejuvenation procedure), it should be replaced. Keep in mind that a color CRT is usually the most expensive component in the monitor. As with any CRT replacement, you should carefully consider the economics of the repair versus buying a new or rebuilt monitor.

SYMPTOM 27-12   **The image is saturated with blue or appears yellow**   If there are any user color controls available from the front or rear housings, make sure those controls have not been accidentally adjusted. If color controls are set properly (or not available externally), the blue video drive circuit has probably failed. Refer to the example circuit of Figure 27-8. Use your oscilloscope to trace the video signal from its initial input to the final output. If there is no blue video signal at the amplifier input (the base of Q701), check the connection between the monitor and the video adapter board. If the connection is intact, try a known-good monitor. If the problem persists on a known-good monitor, replace the video adapter board. As you trace the video signal, you can compare the signal to characteristics at the corresponding points in the green or red video circuits. The point at which the signal disappears is probably the point of failure, and the offending component should be replaced. If you do not have the tools or inclination to perform component-level troubleshooting, try replacing the video drive PC board entirely.

If the video signal measures properly all the way to the CRT (or a new video drive PC board does not correct the problem), suspect a fault in the CRT itself. The corresponding cathode or video control grid may have failed. If you have access to a CRT tester/rejuvenator, test the CRT. If the CRT measures bad (and cannot be recovered through any available rejuvenation procedure), it should be replaced. Keep in mind that a color CRT is usually the most expensive component in the monitor. As with any CRT replacement, you should carefully consider the economics of the repair versus buying a new or rebuilt monitor.

SYMPTOM 27-13   **The image is saturated with green or appears bluish-red (magenta)**
If there are any user color controls available from the front or rear housings, make sure those controls have not been accidentally adjusted. If color controls are set properly (or not available externally), the green video drive circuit has probably failed. Refer to the example circuit of Figure 27-8. Use your oscilloscope to trace the video signal from its initial input to the final output. If there is no green video signal at the amplifier input (the base of Q601), check the connection between the monitor and the video adapter board. If the connection is intact, try a known-good monitor. If the problem persists on a known-good monitor, replace the video adapter board. As you trace the video signal, you can compare the signal to characteristics at the corresponding points in the red or blue video circuits. The point at which the signal disappears is probably the point of failure, and the offending component should be replaced. If you do not have the tools or inclination to perform component-level troubleshooting, try replacing the video drive PC board entirely.

If the video signal measures properly all the way to the CRT (or a new video drive PC board does not correct the problem), suspect a fault in the CRT itself. The corresponding cathode or video control grid may have failed. If you have access to a CRT tester/rejuvenator, test the CRT. If the CRT measures bad (and cannot be recovered through any available rejuvenation procedure), it should be replaced. Keep in mind that a color CRT is usually the most expensive component in the monitor. As with any CRT replacement, you should carefully consider the economics of the repair versus buying a new or rebuilt monitor.

SYMPTOM 27-14   **Raster is present, but there is no image**   When the monitor is properly connected to a PC, a series of text information should appear as the PC initializes. We can use this as our baseline image. Isolate the monitor by trying a known-good monitor on your host PC. If the known-good monitor works, you prove that the PC and video adapter are working properly. Reconnect the suspect monitor to the PC and turn up the brightness (and contrast if necessary). You should see a faint white haze covering the display. This is the raster generated by the normal sweep of an electron beam. Remember that the PC must be on and running. Without the horizontal and vertical retrace signals provided by the video adapter, there will be no raster.

For a color image to fail completely, all three video drive circuits will have to be disabled. You should check all connectors between the video adapter board and the monitor's main PC board. A loose or severed wire can interrupt the voltage(s) powering the board. You should also check each output from your power supply. A low or missing voltage can disable your video circuits as effectively as a loose connector. If you find a faulty supply output, you can attempt to troubleshoot the supply, or you can replace the power supply outright. For monitors that incorporate the power supply onto the main PC board, the entire main PC board would have to be replaced.

If supply voltage levels and connections are intact, use an oscilloscope to trace the video signals through their respective amplifier circuits. Chances are that you will see all three video signals fail at the same location of each circuit. This is usually due to a problem in common parts of the video circuits. In the example video drive board of Figure 27-8, such common circuitry involves the components marked with 8*xx* numbers (such as Q801). If you do not have the tools or inclination to perform such component-level troubleshooting, replace the video drive PC board. You should also suspect a problem with the raster blanking circuits. During horizontal and vertical retrace periods, video signals are cut off. If visible raster lines appear in your image, check the blanking signals. If you are unable to check the blanking signals, try replacing the video drive PC board. If a new video drive board fails to correct the problem, replace the main PC board.

If you should find that all three video signals check correctly all the way to the CRT (or replacing the video drive circuit does not restore the image), you should suspect a major fault in the CRT itself. There is little else that can fail. If you have a CRT tester/rejuvenator available, you should test the CRT thoroughly for shorted grids or a weak cathode. If the problem cannot be rectified through rejuvenation (or you do not have access to a CRT tester), try replacing the CRT. Keep in mind, however, that a CRT is usually the most expensive part of the monochrome monitor. If each step up to now has not restored your image, you should weigh the economics of replacing the CRT versus scrapping it in favor of a new or rebuilt unit.

SYMPTOM 27-15   **A single horizontal line appears in the middle of the display**   The horizontal sweep is working properly, but there is no vertical deflection. A fault has almost certainly developed in the vertical drive circuit (refer to Figure 27-9). Use your oscilloscope to check the sawtooth wave being generated by the vertical oscillator/amplifier chip (pin 6 of IC402). If the sawtooth wave is missing, the fault is almost certainly in the chip. For the circuit of Figure 27-9, try replacing IC402. If the sawtooth wave is available on IC402 pin 6, you should suspect a defect in the horizontal deflection yoke itself, or one of its related components. If you are not able to check signals to the component level, simply replace the monitor's main PC board.

SYMPTOM 27-16   **Only the upper or lower half of an image appears**   In most cases, there is a problem in the vertical amplifier. For the example circuit of Figure 27-9, the trouble is likely located in the vertical oscillator/amplifier chip (IC402). Use your oscilloscope to check the sawtooth waveform leaving IC402 pin 6. If the sawtooth is distorted, replace IC402. If the sawtooth signal reads properly, check for other faulty components in the vertical deflection yoke circuit. If you do not have the tools or inclination to check and replace devices at the component level, replace the monitor's main PC board. When the image is restored, be sure to check vertical linearity.

SYMPTOM 27-17   **A single vertical line appears along the middle of the display** The vertical sweep is working properly, but there is no horizontal deflection. However, to even see the display at normal brightness, there must be high voltage present in the monitor. The horizontal drive circuit must be working (refer to Figure 27-9). The fault probably lies in the horizontal deflection yoke. Check the yoke and all wiring connected to it. It may be necessary to replace the horizontal deflection yoke or the entire yoke assembly.

If horizontal deflection is lost as well as substantial screen brightness, there may be a marginal fault in the horizontal drive circuit. If there is a problem with the horizontal oscillator pulses, the switching characteristics of the horizontal amplifier will change. In turn, this affects high-voltage development and horizontal deflection. Use your oscilloscope to check the square wave generated by the horizontal oscillator IC301 pin 3, as shown in Figure 27-9. You should see a square wave. If the square wave is distorted, replace the oscillator chip (IC301). If the horizontal pulse is correct, check the horizontal switching transistors (Q301 and Q302). Replace any transistor that appears defective. If the collector signal at the HOT is low or distorted, there may be a short circuit in the flyback transformer primary winding. Try replacing the FBT. If you do not have the tools or inclination to check components to the component level (or the problem persists), replace the monitor's main PC board. When the repair is complete, check the horizontal linearity.

SYMPTOM 27-18   **There is no image and no raster**   When the monitor is properly connected to a PC, a series of text information should appear as the PC initializes. We can use this as our baseline image. Isolate the monitor by trying a known-good monitor on your host PC. If the known-good monitor works, you prove that the PC and video adapter are working properly. Reconnect the suspect monitor to the PC, and turn up the brightness (and contrast if necessary). Start by checking for the presence of horizontal and vertical synchronization pulses. If pulses are absent, no raster will be generated. If sync pulses are present, there is likely a problem somewhere in the horizontal drive or high-voltage circuits.

Always suspect a power supply problem, so check every output from the supply (especially the 20-Vdc and 135-Vdc outputs, as shown in Figure 27-9). A low or absent supply voltage will disable the horizontal deflection and high-voltage circuits. If one or more supply outputs are low or absent, you can troubleshoot the power supply circuit or replace the power supply outright. (When the power circuit is combined on the monitor's main PC board, the entire main PC board would have to be replaced.)

If the supply outputs read correctly, suspect your horizontal drive circuit. Use your oscilloscope to check the horizontal oscillator output at the base of Q301, as shown in Figure 27-9. You should see a square wave. If the square wave is low, distorted, or absent, replace the horizontal oscillator chip (IC301). If a regular pulse is present, the horizontal oscillator is working. Since Q301 is intended to act as a switch, you should also find a pulse at the collector of Q301. If the pulse output is severely distorted or absent, Q301 is probably damaged (remove Q301 and test it). If Q301 reads as faulty, it should be replaced. If Q301 reads good, check the horizontal coupling transformer (T303) for shorted or open windings. Try replacing T303. (There is little else that can go wrong in this part of the circuit.)

Check the HOT (Q302) next by removing it from the circuit and testing it. If Q302 reads faulty, it should be replaced with an exact replacement part. If Q302 reads good, the fault probably lies in the flyback transformer. Try replacing the FBT. If you do not have the tools or inclination to perform these component-level checks, simply replace the monitor's main PC board outright.

In the event that these steps fail to restore the image, the CRT has probably failed. If you have access to a CRT tester/rejuvenator, you can test the CRT. When the CRT measures as bad (and cannot be restored through rejuvenation), it should be replaced. If you do not have a CRT test instrument, you can simply replace the CRT. Keep in mind, however, that a CRT is usually the most expensive part of a color monitor. If each step up to now has not restored your image, you should weigh the economics of replacing the CRT versus scrapping it in favor of a new or rebuilt unit. If you choose to replace the CRT, perform a full set of alignments.

SYMPTOM 27-19   **The image is too compressed or too expanded**   A whitish haze may appear along the bottom of the image. Start by checking your vertical size control to be sure that it was not adjusted accidentally. Since vertical size is a function of the vertical sawtooth oscillator, you should suspect the vertical oscillator circuit. A sawtooth signal that is too large will result in an overexpanded image, while a signal that is too small will appear to compress the image. Use your oscilloscope to check the vertical sawtooth signal. For the vertical drive circuit of Figure 27-9, you should find a sawtooth signal on IC402 pin 6. If the signal is incorrect, try replacing IC402. You may also wish to check the PC board for any cracks or faulty soldering connections around the vertical oscillator circuit. If the problem persists, or you do not have the tools or inclination to perform component-level troubleshooting, simply replace the monitor's main PC board outright.

SYMPTOM 27-20 **The displayed characters appear to be distorted** The term "distortion" can be interpreted in many different ways. For our purposes, we will simply say that the image (usually text) is difficult to read. Before even opening your toolbox, check the monitor's location. The presence of stray magnetic fields close to the monitor can cause bizarre forms of distortion. Try moving the monitor to another location. Remove any electromagnetic or magnetic objects (such as motors or refrigerator magnets) from the area. If the problem persists, it is likely that the monitor is at fault.

If only certain areas of the display appear affected (or affected worse than other areas), the trouble is probably due to poor linearity (either horizontal, vertical, or both). If raster speed varies across the display, the pixels in some areas of the image may appear too close together, while the pixels in other areas of the image may appear too far apart. You can check and correct horizontal and vertical linearity. If alignment fails to correct poor linearity, your best course is often simply to replace the monitor's main PC board. If the image is difficult to read because it is out of focus, you should check the focus alignment. If you cannot achieve a sharp focus using controls either on the front panel of the monitor or on the flyback transformer assembly, there is probably a fault in the flyback transformer. Try replacing the FBT. If the problem persists, your best course is often simply to replace the monitor's main PC board.

SYMPTOM 27-21 **The display appears wavy** There are visible waves appearing along the edges of the display as the image sways back and forth. This is almost always the result of a power supply problem. One or more outputs are failing. Use your multimeter to check each supply output. If you find a low or absent output, you can proceed to troubleshoot the supply, or you can simply replace the supply outright. If the power supply is integrated onto the main PC board, you will have to replace the entire main PC board.

SYMPTOM 27-22 **The display is too bright or too dim** Before opening the monitor, be sure to check the brightness and contrast controls. If the controls had been accidentally adjusted, set contrast to maximum, and adjust the brightness level until a clear, crisp display is produced. When front panel controls fail to provide the proper display (but focus seems steady), suspect a fault in the monitor's power supply. Refer to the example schematic of Figure 27-9. If the 135-Vdc supply is too low or too high, brightness levels controlling the CRT screen grid will shift. If you find one or more incorrect outputs from the power supply, you can troubleshoot the supply or replace the supply outright. For those monitors that incorporate the power supply on the main PC board, the entire main PC board will have to be replaced.

SYMPTOM 27-23 **You see visible raster scan lines in the display** The very first thing you should do is check the front panel brightness and contrast controls. If contrast is set too low and/or brightness is set too high, raster will be visible on top of the image. This will tend to make the image appear a bit fuzzy. If the front panel controls cannot eliminate visible raster from the image, chances are that you have a problem with the power supply. Use your multimeter and check each output from the supply. If one or more outputs appear too high (or too low), you can troubleshoot the supply or replace the supply outright. If the supply is integrated with the monitor's main PC board, the entire PC board will have to be replaced.

If the power supply is intact, you should suspect a problem with the raster blanking circuits. During horizontal and vertical retrace periods, video signals are cut off. If visible raster lines appear in your image, check the blanking signals. If you are unable to check the blanking signals, try replacing the video drive PC board. If a new video drive board fails to correct the problem, replace the main PC board.

SYMPTOM 27-24 **Colors bleed or smear** Ultimately, this symptom occurs when unwanted pixels are excited in the CRT. However, this can be caused by several different problems. Perhaps the most common problem is a fault in the video cable between the video board and the monitor. Electrical noise (sometimes called *crosstalk*) in the cable may allow signals representing one color to accidentally be picked up in another color signal wire. This can easily cause unwanted colors to appear in the display. Although the video cable is designed to be shielded and carefully filtered, age or poor installation can precipitate this type of problem. Try wiggling the cable. If the problem stops, appears intermittent, or shifts around, you have likely found the source of the problem. Replace the cable with a proper replacement assembly.

If the video cable appears intact, suspect failing capacitors in the video amplifier circuits. You can see these capacitors in the schematic of Figure 27-8. Capacitors such as C505 and C506 are typically low-value, high-voltage components, so they tend to degrade rather quickly. Fortunately, such capacitors are easy to spot on the video amplifier board. If the color problem appears intermittent (or occurs when the monitor warms up), try a bit of liquid refrigerant on each capacitor. If the problem disappears, the one you froze is probably defective. Otherwise, you can turn off and unplug the monitor, then check each capacitor individually. When replacing capacitors in the video amplifier circuit, be sure to replace them with the same type and voltage rating.

If capacitors are not at fault, suspect the amplifier transistors on the video amplifier board (such as Q504, Q505, or Q506). Turn off and unplug the monitor, and then try checking each transistor. Chances are that your readings will be inconclusive, so try comparing readings from each transistor to find a device that gives the most unusual readings. Try replacing any defective or questionable amplifier transistors. If you do not have the time or inclination to troubleshoot the video amplifier board, try replacing the board outright.

SYMPTOM 27-25 **Colors appear to change when the monitor is warm** Either colors will appear correctly when the monitor is cold, then change as the monitor warms up, or vice versa. In both cases, there is likely to be some kind of thermal problem in the video amplifier circuits. Turn off and unplug the monitor, and then start by checking the video cable—especially its connection to the raster board inside the monitor. If this connection is loose, it may be intermittent or unreliable. Tighten any loose connections, and try the monitor again. Also check the cable that connects the video amplifier board to the raster board.

If the connections appear tight, often your best course of action is to remove the video amplifier board and try resoldering each of the junctions. Chances are that age or thermal stress has fatigued one or more connections. By resoldering the connections, you should be able to correct any potential connection problems. You might also try resoldering the connector that passes video data from the raster board to the video amplifier board. If your problems persist, try replacing the video amplifier board.

SYMPTOM 27-26 **An image appears distorted in 350- or 400-line mode** In most cases, the distortion is an image that appears excessively compressed. As you probably read earlier in this book, different screen modes have a different number of horizontal lines (that is, a 640×480 display offers 480 horizontal traces of 640 pixels each). When the screen mode changes, the number of lines changes as well (such as to a 320×200 mode). As you might expect, the "size" of each pixel has to be adjusted when the screen mode changes in order to keep the image roughly square—otherwise the image simply "shrinks." Monitors detect the screen mode by checking the polarity of the sync signals. You can see this function in the schematic of Figure 27-9.

Typically, each screen mode size can be optimized by an adjustment on the raster board. However, if a mode adjustment is thrown off (or the sync sensing circuit fails), an image can easily appear with an incorrect size. If you notice this kind of distortion without warning, suspect a problem with the sync sensing circuit. If the sync sensing circuit is incorporated into a single chip (such as IC201), replace the chip outright.

If you notice a size problem after aligning the monitor, you may have accidentally upset a size adjustment. Readjust the size controls to restore proper image dimensions.

SYMPTOM 27-27   **The fine detail of high-resolution graphic images appears a bit fuzzy**   At best, this kind of symptom may not appear noticeable without careful inspection, but it may signal a serious problem in the video amplifier circuit. High resolutions demand high bandwidth. A video amplifier must respond quickly to the rapid variations between pixels. If a weakness in the video amplifier(s) occurs, it can limit bandwidth and degrade video performance at high resolutions. The problem will likely disappear at lower resolutions. The particular problem with this symptom is that it is almost impossible to isolate a defective component—the video amplifier board *is* working. As a result, your best course of action is to check all connectors for secure installation first. Nicked or frayed video cables can also contribute to the problem. If the problem remains, replace the video amplifier board.

SYMPTOM 27-28   **The display changes color, flickers, or cuts out when the video cable is moved**   Check the video cable's connection to the video adapter at the PC. A loose connection will almost certainly result in such intermittent problems. If the connection is secure, there is an intermittent connection in the video cable. Before replacing the cable, check its connections within the monitor itself. When connections are intact, replace the intermittent video cable outright. Do not bother cutting or splicing the cable. Any breaks in the signal shielding will cause crosstalk, which will result in color bleeding.

SYMPTOM 27-29   **The image expands in the horizontal direction when the monitor gets warm**   One or more components in the horizontal retrace circuit are weak—and are changing value a bit once the monitor gets warm. Turn off and unplug the monitor. You should inspect any capacitors located around the *horizontal output transistor* (HOT). The problem is that thermal problems such as this can be extremely difficult to isolate because you can't measure capacitor values while the monitor is running, and after the monitor is turned off, the parts will cool too quickly to catch a thermal problem. It is often most effective to simply replace several of the key capacitors around the HOT outright. If you don't want to bother with individual components, replace the raster board.

SYMPTOM 27-30   **The image shrinks in the horizontal direction when the monitor gets warm**   This is another thermal-related problem, which indicates either a weakness in one or more components, or a mild soldering-related problem. Turn off and unplug the monitor. Start by checking for a poor solder connection—especially around the horizontal deflection yoke wiring, the *horizontal output transistor* (HOT), and the flyback transformer. If nothing appears obvious, you might consider resoldering all of the components in the HOT area of the raster board. If problems continue, suspect a failure in the HOT itself. Semiconductors rarely become marginal—they either work or they don't. Still, semiconductor junctions can become unstable when temperatures change, which can result in circuit characteristic changes. You could also try replacing the HOT outright.

It is also possible that one or more midrange power supply outputs (such as 12 or 20 volts) are sagging when the monitor warms up. Use a voltmeter and measure the outputs from your power supply. If the 12 or 20 volt outputs appear to drop a bit once the monitor has been running for a while, you should troubleshoot the power supply.

SYMPTOM 27-31   **High-voltage fails after the monitor is warm**   There are many possible causes behind this problem, but no matter what permutation you find, you will likely be dealing with soldering problems, or thermal-related failures. Turn off and unplug the monitor. Inspect the HOT's heat sink assembly. There may be a bad solder connection on the heat sink ground. There may also be an open solder connection on one or more of the flyback transformer pins. If you cannot locate a faulty soldering connection, you may simply choose to resolder all of the connections in the flyback area.

If the problem persists, you should suspect that either your HOT or flyback transformer is failing under load (after the monitor warms up). One possible means of isolating the problem is to measure pulses from the HOT output with your oscilloscope. If the pulses stop at the same time your high voltage fails, you can suspect a problem with your HOT or other horizontal components. Try replacing the HOT. If high voltage fails but the HOT pulses remain, your flyback transformer has likely failed. Replace the flyback transformer. If you do not have an oscilloscope, try replacing the HOT first since that is the least-expensive part, and then replace the flyback transformer if necessary.

In the unlikely event that both a new HOT and flyback transformer do not correct the problem, you should carefully inspect the capacitors in the HOT circuit. One or more might be failing. Unfortunately, it is very difficult to identify a marginal capacitor (especially one that is suffering from a thermal failure). You may try replacing the major capacitors in the HOT circuit, or replace the raster board entirely.

SYMPTOM 27-32   **The image blooms intermittently**   The amount of high voltage driving the CRT is varying intermittently. Since high voltage is related to the HOT circuit and flyback transformer, you should concentrate your search in those two areas of the raster board. Examine the soldering of your HOT and FBT connections—especially the ground connections if you can identify them. You may try resoldering all of the connections in those areas. (Remember to turn off and unplug the monitor before soldering.) There may also be a ground problem on the video amplifier board that allows all three color signals to vary in amplitude. When this happens, the overall brightness of the image changes, and the image may grow or shrink a bit in response. Try resoldering connections on the video amplifier board.

If the problem remains (even after soldering), your FBT may be failing—probably due to an age-related internal short. High-end test equipment such as Sencore's monitor test station provides the instrumentation to test a flyback transformer. If you do not have access to such dedicated test equipment, however, try replacing the FBT assembly. If you do not have the time or inclination to deal with component replacement, go ahead and replace the raster board outright. In the unlikely event that your problem persists, suspect a fault in the CRT itself. If you have access to a CRT tester/rejuvenator, you can check the CRT's operation. Some weaknesses in the CRT may be corrected (at least temporarily) by rejuvenation. If the fault cannot be corrected, you may have to replace the CRT.

SYMPTOM 27-33   **The image appears out of focus**   Before suspecting a component failure, try adjusting the focus control. In most cases, the focus control is located adjacent to the flyback transformer. Keep in mind that the focus control should be adjusted with brightness and contrast set to optimum values. Excessively bright images may lose focus naturally. If the focus control is unable to restore a proper image, check the CRT focus voltage. In Figure 27-9, you can find the focus voltage off a flyback transformer tap. If the focus voltage is low (often combined with a dim image), you may have a failing FBT. It is possible to test the FBT if you have the specialized test instrumentation. Otherwise, you should just replace the FBT outright. If you lack the time or inclination to replace the FBT, you can simply replace the raster board.

If a new FBT does not resolve your focus problem, suspect a fault in the CRT—probably in the focus grid. You can use a CRT tester/rejuvenator to examine the CRT, and it may be possible to restore normal operation (at least temporarily). If you do not have such equipment, you will simply have to try a new CRT.

SYMPTOM 27-34   **The image appears to flip or scroll horizontally**   There is a synchronization problem in your horizontal raster circuit. Begin by checking the video cable to be sure that it is installed and connected securely. Cables that behave intermittently (or that appear frayed or nicked) should be replaced. If the cable is intact, suspect a problem in your horizontal circuit. If there is a horizontal sync (or "horizontal hold") adjustment on the raster board, adjust it in small increments until the image snaps back into sync. If there is no such adjustment on your particular monitor, try resoldering all of the connections in the horizontal processing circuit. If the problem persists, replace the horizontal oscillator chip, or replace the entire raster board.

SYMPTOM 27-35   **The image appears to flip or scroll vertically**   There is a synchronization problem in your vertical raster circuit. Begin by checking the video cable to be sure that it is installed and connected securely. Cables that behave intermittently (or that appear frayed or nicked) should be replaced. If the cable is intact, suspect a problem in your vertical circuit. If there is a vertical sync (or "vertical hold") adjustment on the raster board, adjust it in small increments until the image snaps back into sync. If there is no such adjustment on your particular monitor, try resoldering all of the connections in the vertical processing circuit. If the problem persists, replace the vertical oscillator chip, or replace the entire raster board.

SYMPTOM 27-36   **The image appears to shake or oscillate in size**   This may occur in bursts, but it typically occurs constantly. In most cases, this is due to a fault in the power supply—usually the 135-volt (B+) output. Try measuring your power supply outputs with an oscilloscope, and see if an output is varying along with the screen size changes. If you locate such an output, the filtering portion of that output may be malfunctioning. Track the output back into the supply, and replace any defective components. If you are unable to isolate a faulty component, replace the power supply. When the power supply is integrated onto the raster board, you may have to replace the raster board entirely.

If the outputs from your power supply appear stable, you should suspect a weak capacitor in your horizontal circuit. Try resoldering the FBT, HOT, and other horizontal circuit components to eliminate the possibility of a soldering problem. If the problem remains, you will have to systematically replace the capacitors in the horizontal circuit. If you do not have the time or inclination to replace individual components, replace the raster board outright.

Here's an unusual problem. The shaking you see may be related to a problem in the degaussing coil located around the CRT funnel. Ordinarily, the degaussing coil should unleash most of its energy in the initial moments after monitor power is turned on. Thermistors (or posistors) in the power supply quickly diminish coil voltage—effectively cutting off the degaussing coil's operation. A fault in the degaussing coil circuit (in the power supply) may continue to allow enough power to the coil to affect the image's stability. Try disconnecting the degaussing coil. If the problem remains, the degaussing coil is likely operating properly. If the problem disappears, you have a fault in the degaussing coil circuit.

Further Study

Acer   www.aci.acer.com.tw
CTX   www.ctxintl.com
Hitachi   www.hitachi.com
Magnavox   www.magnavox.com
NEC   www.nec.com
Sony   www.sony.com
Viewsonic   www.viewsonic.com

MOTHERBOARD TROUBLESHOOTING

The *motherboard* is the heart of any personal computer (Figure 28-1). It is the motherboard that provides system resources (such as IRQ lines, DMA channels, I/O locations), supports the core components such as the CPU, chipset(s), and *real-time clock* (RTC), and handles all system memory—including SDRAM, BIOS ROM, and CMOS RAM. Indeed, most of a PC's capabilities are defined by motherboard components. This chapter provides a guided tour of contemporary motherboards and shows you how to translate error information and symptoms into motherboard repairs.

Active, Passive, and Modular

Before going any further, you should understand the difference between a motherboard and a backplane. For the purposes of this book, a *motherboard* is a printed circuit board containing most of the processing components required by the computer. This is certainly the most common form of motherboard that you will encounter as a technician. PC purists often refer to a motherboard as an *active backplane*. The term "active" is used because there are sophisticated chips running on the board. The advantage of a motherboard is its comprehensive nature—the motherboard virtually *is* the PC. Unfortunately, the motherboard has disadvantages. Namely, it is difficult to upgrade. Aside from plugging in an upgraded CPU or adding RAM, the only real way to upgrade a motherboard is to replace it with a newer one. For example, the only way to add PCI bus slots to an all-ISA motherboard is to replace the motherboard with one containing PCI slots. Obviously, this is a time-consuming and error-prone process.

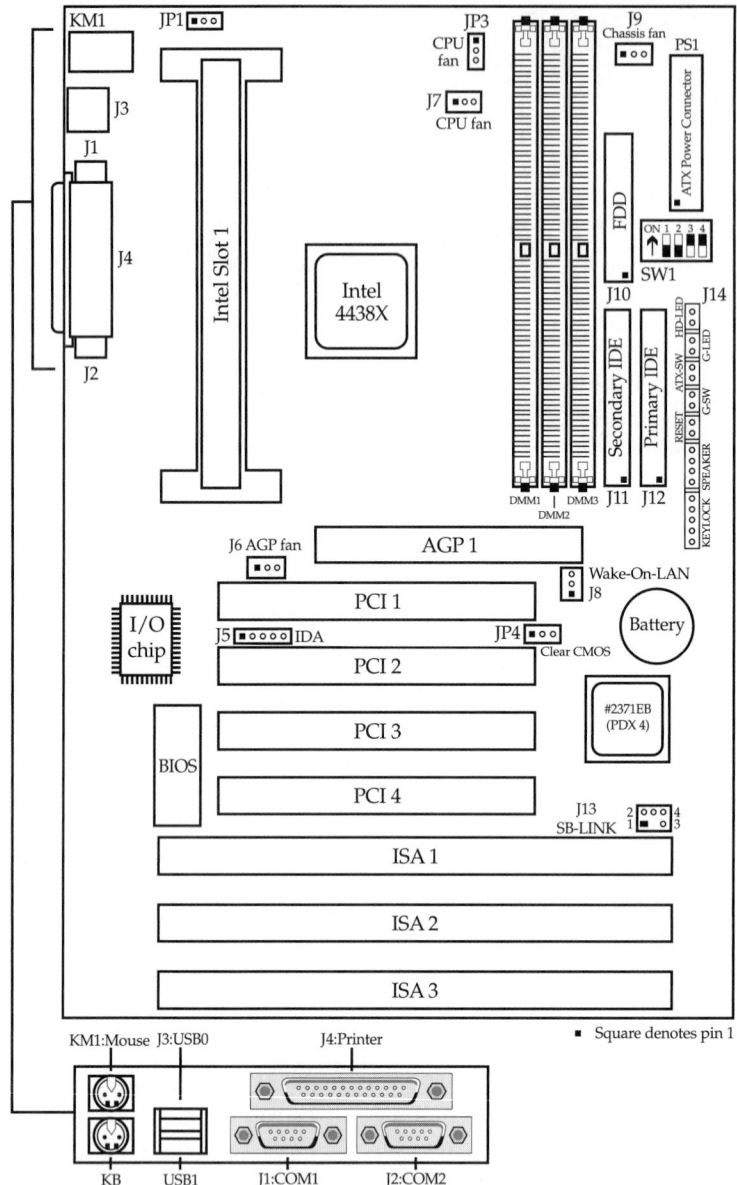

FIGURE 28-1   A contemporary ATX Slot 1 motherboard design

On the other hand, a backplane (also referred to as a *passive backplane*) is little more than a board containing interconnecting slots. There are no major chips on the backplane (except perhaps some power supply regulating circuitry). The CPU, system RAM, BIOS ROM, and other central processing components are fabricated onto a board that simply plugs into one of the backplane slots. Other expansion devices (such as a video board, drive controller, sound board, and so on) just plug into adjacent slots. The PS/2 was one of the first PCs to use a backplane design. Backplane systems range from easy to somewhat easier to troubleshoot.

Unlike traditional motherboards that require the entire system to be disassembled, a processor board can be removed and replaced as easily as any other board, so it is also a simple matter to upgrade the PC by installing a new processor board. The great limitation to backplane-based systems is the bus. Where traditional motherboards can optimize a system with different busses, the backplane is limited to a single bus style that interconnects the various cards (usually ISA or MCA). High-performance bus architectures like PCI or AGP are not readily available.

In an effort to provide a motherboard that is more upgradable and serviceable, manufacturers often experiment with *modular* motherboards. The modular motherboard places the CPU, math coprocessor, and key support chips on a replaceable card, which plugs into a motherboard that in turn holds the BIOS ROM, CMOS RAM, system RAM, other system controllers, and bus interfaces. The modular approach allows a motherboard to be upgraded far more than a traditional motherboard without having to replace it outright. The replacement processing card is much cheaper than a new motherboard. However, today's PC architectures can usually support a variety of CPU versions and an extensive amount of RAM on the original motherboard, so "modular" motherboards have never become a very popular approach.

Contrary to popular belief, expansion bus connectors are not needed to make a motherboard. You can see this in any laptop or notebook computer motherboard. The devices that traditionally demanded expansion slots (such as video and drive controllers) are easily fabricated directly onto the motherboard. Even the motherboards used in most desktop and tower PCs over the last few years integrate video and drive controller circuits. If upgrades are needed in the future, the motherboard-based circuits can be disabled with jumpers, and replacement subsystems are plugged into expansion slots.

Understanding Active Motherboards

Before you can troubleshoot a motherboard effectively, it's important that you know your way around and be able to identify most of the common components. Although each motherboard is designed differently, this process of identification is not nearly as difficult as it might sound. This part of the chapter will familiarize you with the essential functions and components that you'll find on a modern motherboard.

SOCKETS AND SLOTS

When examining a motherboard, you'll probably find it described with a slot or socket designation. Typical designations include Socket 7, Socket 8, Slot 1, Socket 360, Slot 2, or Slot A, Socket A, Socket 432. These popular classifications refer to the type(s) of CPU that a particular motherboard will support:

- **Socket 7**   These motherboards are generally designed for Pentium and Pentium MMX CPUs, as well as AMD K6-2, K6-3, or Cyrix MIII processors. You may also see these motherboards designated as Super 7 when there is an AGP slot available.

- **Socket 8**   These motherboards are made for Pentium Pro CPUs. You won't find many Socket 8 motherboards still in use, and those that you do encounter will mainly be in older network servers or workstations.

- **Slot 1**   These motherboards use a Single Edge Cartridge (SEC) processor box rather than a pin grid array chip (a conventional "chip") and are intended for Pentium II and Pentium III systems.

- **Socket 360**   These motherboards are intended for later model Pentium III and most Celeron versions of the Pentium processor. These socket-mounted processors are often easier to cool and have fewer issues with installation and retention.

- **Slot 2**   These motherboards are also intended for SEC processors, but these accommodate the slightly advanced Pentium II/III Xeon processors. In virtually all cases, Slot 2 motherboards are used in high-end network server and workstation systems, so you'll rarely (if ever) find Slot 2 motherboards in the hands of home or small-business users.

■ **Slot A** These motherboards are intended for the AMD Athlon processor—AMD's answer to the Intel Pentium III/4. While a Slot 1 and Slot A connector may appear identical at first glance, they are incompatible, so you must use a Slot A motherboard when building or working on an Athlon-based system.

■ **Socket A** These motherboards are designed for later model AMD Athlon and most AMD Duron processors. As with other socket-based designs, there are fewer installation, cooling, and retention issues. However, Socket A is not compatible with other socket types.

■ **Socket 432** These motherboards (such as Intel's D850GB) are intended for socket versions of the Pentium 4 processor. Socket 432 is not compatible with other socket types.

The important thing to remember here is that motherboard sockets/slots have distinct limitations. A given socket or slot type is not only limited in the type of processors that it can accept, but it is also limited in the processor speeds that can be used. For example, a DFI P2XBL (440BX chipset-based) motherboard can support Slot 1 (Pentium II) processors from 233 MHz to 500 MHz. By comparison, the newer Intel VC820 (i820 chipset-based) motherboard can support Slot 1 (Pentium III) processors from 450 MHz to 733 MHz. Both motherboards use the Slot 1 processor connector, but a different range of processors. Just because a motherboard offers a particular slot or socket, don't just assume that a corresponding processor type will work—it may not. Always check the system or motherboard documentation to verify the compatible processors for a given motherboard model.

THE POWER OF CHIPSETS

The next thing you'll notice about most modern motherboards is the general absence of chips. There are perhaps two or three large chips on the whole motherboard. That's because virtually all of the motherboard's many functions are handled by a suite of powerful interrelated chips (known as the *chipset,* detailed in Chapter 10). The chipset forms the "glue" that connects your processor and memory with your drive controllers (the FDD and HDD controllers), expansion busses (ISA, PCI, and AGP), I/O ports (serial, parallel, PS/2, USB), and sometimes even a video controller and sound controller. Figure 28-2 illustrates the importance of chipsets on the Intel D850GB Pentium 4 motherboard.

This block diagram places the 850 chipset squarely at the center of the motherboard's functionality. The *82850 Memory Controller Hub* (MCH) is responsible for interfacing to the processor, system memory, and AGP bus. (This is not a mistake since AGP makes use of system RAM, so a direct connection is needed through the chipset.) The *82801BA I/O Controller Hub* (ICH2) manages the UDMA/33/66/100 drive controllers, USB ports, hardware monitor, PCI bus, and a sound subsystem (eliminating the need for a separate sound card). There is also an *SST49LF004A Firmware Hub* (FWH), which basically manages the system firmware (the BIOS) and CMOS RAM/RTC functions. A powerful *LPC I/O Controller* chip provides the floppy drive interface and all of your I/O ports. Other than a few other buffer and voltage regulator chips, that's it—that's your computer.

The block diagram of Figure 28-2 serves as a recent example for the purposes of this discussion. Your own motherboard may use a very different selection of chips and features.

EXPANSION SLOTS

Of course, our motherboard is rather incomplete by itself. There are numerous other features and functions (such as a video adapter, SCSI host controller, network card, and many other devices) that may be added to the system depending on your particular needs. These *expansion* devices are added through the

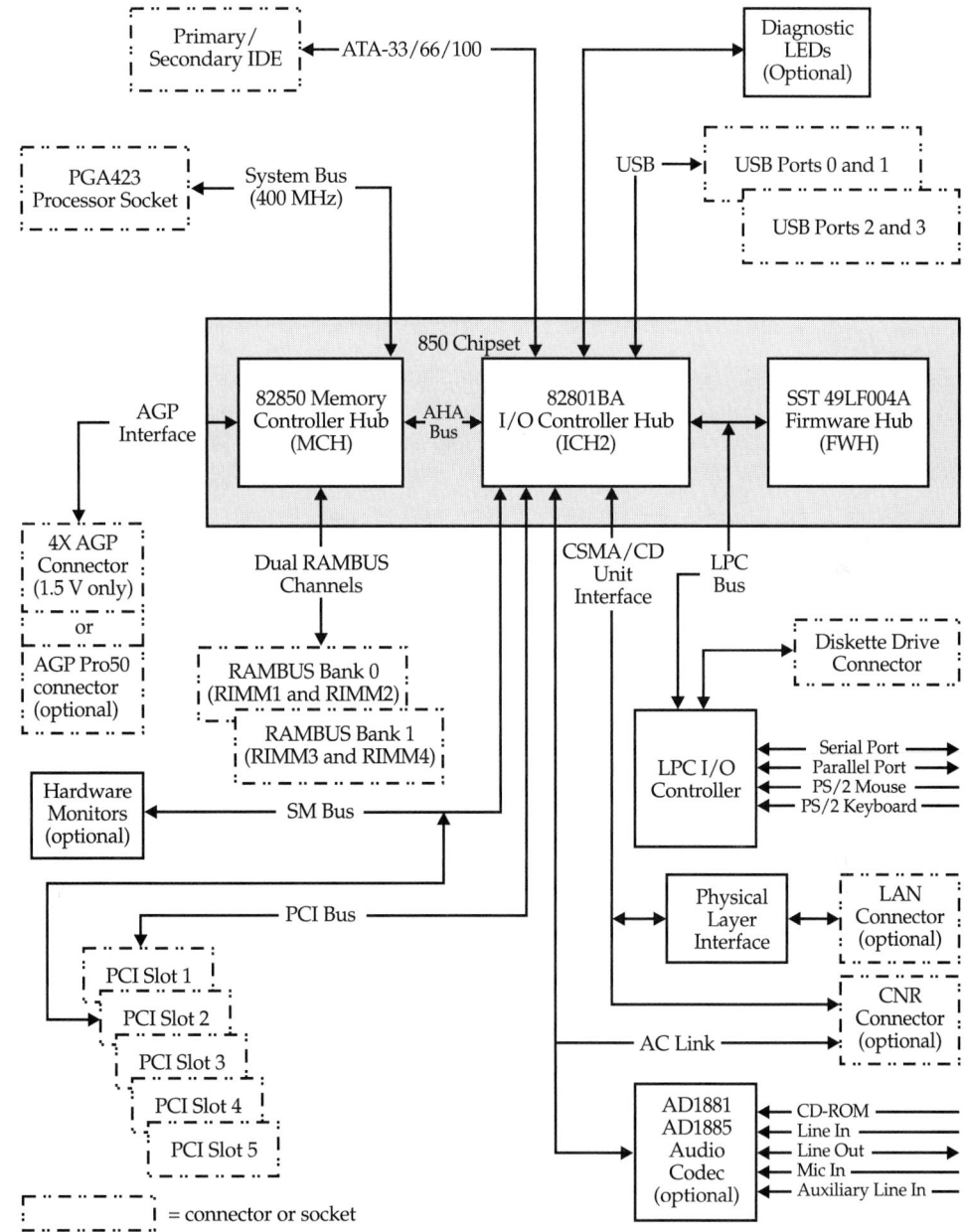

FIGURE 28-2   A block diagram of the Intel D850GB Pentium 4 motherboard
(Courtesy of Intel Corporation)

use of expansion slots on the motherboard. There are three general types of expansion slots (detailed in Chapter 8): ISA, PCI, and AGP.

■ **ISA**   The *Industry Standard Architecture* bus is the "granddaddy" of expansion slots, and is rapidly falling into disuse. (You'll note that there are none on the D850GB motherboard.) You might use an

ISA slot to accommodate a low-bandwidth device such as a legacy modem or sound card, but most contemporary data-intensive devices are better served by the newer expansion slots.

■ **PCI**   The *Peripheral Component Interconnect* scheme is a versatile, high-speed, "intelligent" bus. It is the preferred bus architecture for today's demanding devices such as SCSI host adapters, video capture cards, and network interface cards. The D850GB offers five PCI slots that are all handled by the ICH2 component of the chipset.

■ **AGP**   Although you can use PCI video adapters, the *Accelerated Graphics Port* is intended to provide a high-speed data path directly between the graphics card and system memory—allowing improved frame rates for 3D games, visualization programs, and other "calculation intensive" graphics work. There is only one 1.5V AGP slot on the motherboard.

Expansion slots are a vital consideration during a motherboard upgrade because existing expansion cards must typically be added to the new motherboard. If the new motherboard doesn't offer a suitable number of appropriate slots, you may have to select alternate expansion devices—raising the cost and complexity of the upgrade.

MEMORY SLOTS

Today, motherboards generally do not include "base RAM," so all memory in the system must be added through DIMM/RIMM slots. The Intel VC820 motherboard was one of the first to offer the new generation of RIMM (Rambus inline memory module) slots for high-speed memory access, and this emphasis on RIMM is continued on the D850GB motherboard. The problem with DIMM/RIMM slots is that there are few of them—perhaps only two or three. DIMM/RIMM units can supply lots of memory, so it's easy to stuff a motherboard with RAM, but it's harder to upgrade your RAM. With only a few memory slots, you may find yourself replacing existing memory modules with larger ones (rather then just adding more modules like you could in the "good old days" of SIMM modules). With memory prices on the rise, replacing a DIMM/RIMM with a larger model may add an unforeseen expense to the system. It's important for you to familiarize yourself with the location of the memory slots on your motherboard. Understand the memory characteristics that are required, and learn just what size combinations are acceptable. For example, the D850GB supports from 128MB to 2GB of fast PC800 and PC600 Rambus memory (RDRAM).

THE CMOS BATTERY

Your CMOS RAM contents are maintained through a small coin cell on the motherboard. Normally you don't need to mess with the battery, but when you're upgrading or replacing the motherboard, you may need to install the battery (or remove protective material between the battery and holder). The battery should sit properly and securely in its holder. Similarly, if you're taking an older motherboard out of service, remember to remove the battery and place it in a safe plastic container. Leaving a battery in place for a prolonged period can eventually allow the battery to leak, and acids from the battery may damage the motherboard.

FORM FACTOR

Another important classification that you must be familiar with is the motherboard's form factor. In simplest terms, the *form factor* is little more than the dimensions of the board and its mounting hole positions, as well as the general layout and placement of key components such as the CPU, memory modules, expansion slots, and I/O ports. Today, there are three major form factors to consider: AT, ATX, and NLX. It is important for you to understand that form factors do not directly influence performance. A "baby AT" motherboard and an NLX motherboard can offer exactly the same performance characteristics. Form factor is most important in system assembly and access for service or upgrading.

AT-Style Motherboards

The AT-style motherboards really represent the classic approach to component placement, as shown in the Tyan S1590 Trinity 100 AT motherboard of Figure 28-3. AT-style motherboards are typically available in two variations: the baby AT and the full AT. Both variations simply affect the overall dimensions of the motherboard. (Full AT motherboards are larger.) You can usually identify an AT-style motherboard

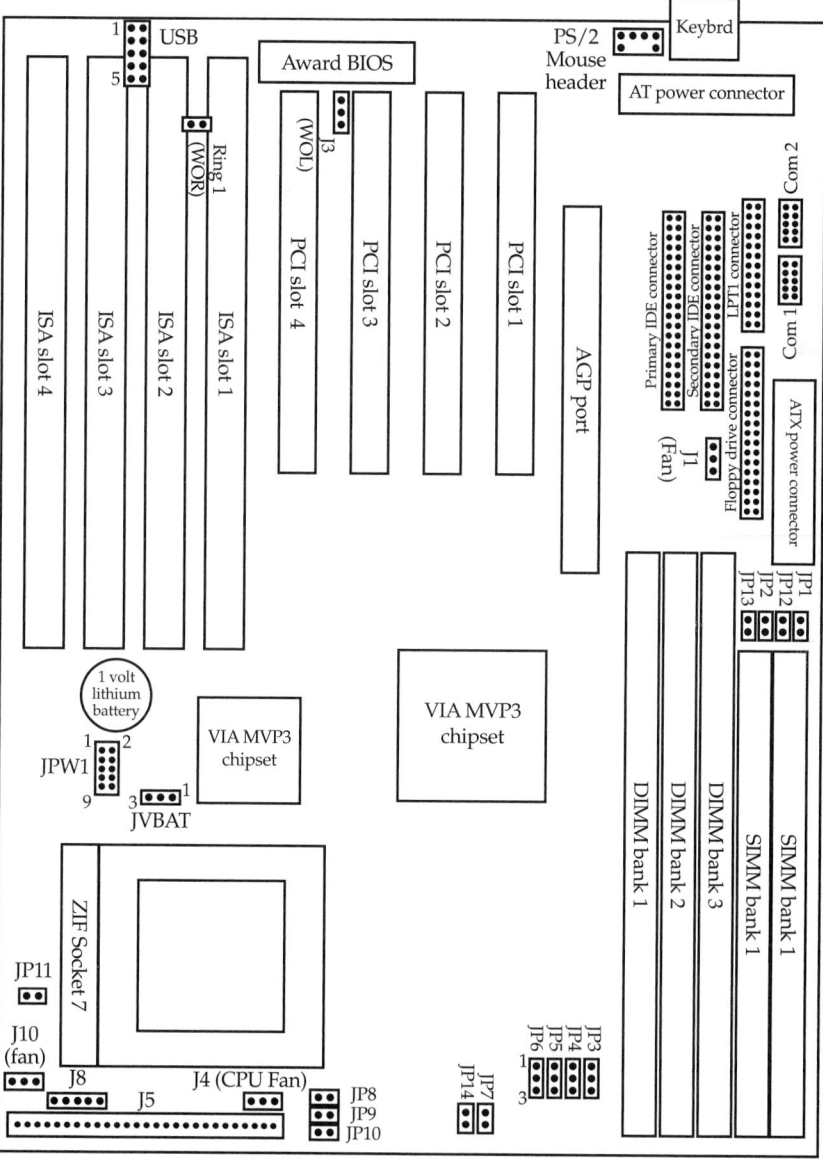

The tiny number "1"s next to jumpers of 3 pins or more indicate the position of pin 1 for that jumper.

FIGURE 28-3   The Tyan S1590 Trinity 100 AT-style motherboard layout (Courtesy of Tyan Computer Corporation)

based upon three distinctions. First, look at the power connectors where the power supply attaches. An AT-style motherboard uses two sets of 6-pin inline connectors usually designated "P8" and "P9." Second, the CPU is usually positioned in line with one or more of the ISA bus slots (almost always obstructing full-length ISA cards). Third, the I/O ports of an AT motherboard (such as COM ports, LPT ports, PS/2 ports, USB ports, and so on) are often spread out along the back panel of the chassis.

ATX-Style Motherboards

The ATX-style motherboards are the result of the first serious industry push to standardize the dimensions, device layouts, and connection schemes of a PC motherboard such as the Intel D850GB ATX Socket 432 (Pentium 4) motherboard shown in Figure 28-4. As with an AT layout, an ATX motherboard is distinguished by three points. First, all I/O port connectors (such as COM ports, LPT ports, USB ports, PS/2 ports, and so on) are concentrated into a single I/O panel located at the rear of the motherboard. Second, the ATX motherboard uses a 20-pin power connection from the power supply (and perhaps a supplemental 8-pin connection). Third, the CPU is located clear and away from all expansion bus slots—eliminating any interference with full-slot expansion cards. ATX motherboards can be found supporting all current CPU types (Socket/Super 7, Socket 360, Socket A, Socket 432, Slot 1, Slot 2, and Slot A CPUs).

NLX-Style Motherboards

While ATX motherboards represented a good effort at standardization, they still retain all the assembly problems of AT-style motherboards—namely that the motherboard is cumbersome to install and

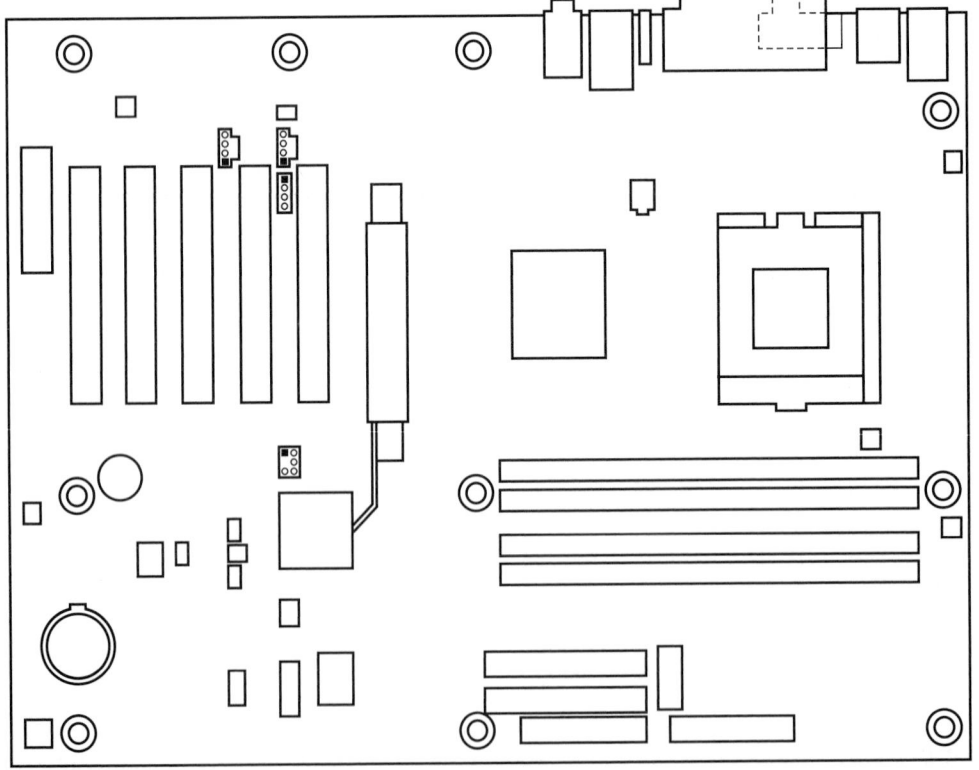

FIGURE 28-4   The Intel D850GB ATX-style motherboard layout (Courtesy of Intel Corporation)

time-consuming to upgrade or replace. The NLX-style motherboards (such as the Intel JN440BX NLX motherboard of Figure 28-5) overcome this disadvantage by making the motherboard a replaceable (also referred to as a *dockable*) device. All expansion slots and connection headers (such as speaker connector,

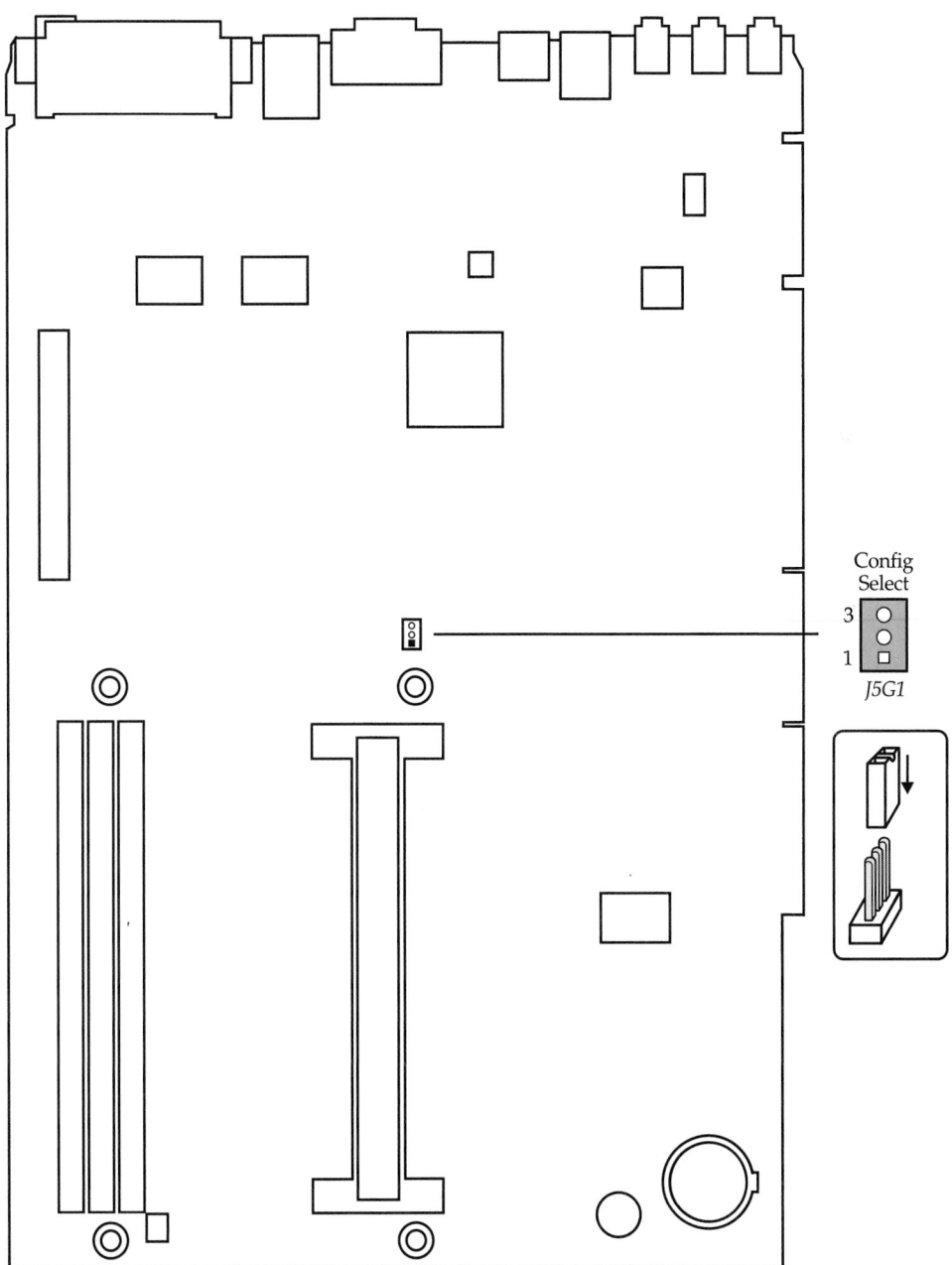

Config
Select

3

1

J5G1

FIGURE 28-5 Simplified view of the Intel JN440BX NLX-style motherboard layout (Courtesy of Intel Corporation)

power switch connector, and so on) are then moved to a *riser card*. The NLX motherboard itself then plugs into the riser card. Note the long card edge connector along the right side of the board that interfaces with the riser. In this fashion, the motherboard can quickly and easily be removed from the system to change jumpers, add memory, or install a replacement motherboard.

LEARNING YOUR WAY AROUND

Now that you've seen some essential motherboard attributes, it's time to actually look up close at a current motherboard and identify the critical parts that you should expect to find. For the purposes of this book, we'll use the Intel D850GB ATX Socket 432 motherboard shown again in Figure 28-6. Other motherboards and form factors will appear a bit different, but the basic parts are the same.

The chipset and other components discussed next are presented for example purposes only. Your motherboard will undoubtedly use different chips (and chipsets)—each offering their own set of characteristics.

A.   *AD1881/AD1885 audio codec.* This optional chip can support audio features directly on the motherboard—eliminating the need to install a separate sound board.

B.   *AGP bus connector.* This is your 1.5V AGP bus slot for the connection of your high-performance video adapter/accelerator.

C.   *82850 Memory Controller Hub chip.* This is the core "front side" processing chip that interfaces the CPU, memory, and AGP bus.

D.   *I/O panel connections.* These are the serial, parallel, USB, and PS/2 ports (and so on) that you'll use to connect peripheral devices to the system. Figure 28-7 illustrates the I/O port layout for a D850GB. The number of ports and their relative location may vary from model to model, but this figure is a good overall example.

ITEM	DESCRIPTION	ITEM	DESCRIPTION
A	PS/2 mouse port	F	Serial port 0
B	PS/2 keyboard port	G	LAN connector (optional)
C	USB port 0	H	Audio line input
D	USB port 1	I	Audio line output
E	Parallel port	J	Microphone input

E.   *+12V power connector (ATX12V).* This is an auxiliary power connector providing +12 Vdc to the motherboard. This may be needed to handle telephony, LAN, or other features of the motherboard.

F.   *Socket 432 processor connector.* This is the 432-pin connector for your Pentium 4 processor. Be sure that the processor is secure in the socket, and that the cooling unit attaches properly to the processor housing.

G.   *Hardware monitor.* This optional feature provides low-cost instrumentation capabilities including internal ambient temperature sensing, remote thermal diode sensing for direct monitoring of processor temperature, power supply monitoring (such as +5V, +3.3V, +2.5V, 3.3 VSB, and Vccp) to detect levels above or below acceptable values, and SMBus interface support.

H, I.   *RIMM sockets 1 through 4.* These four sockets support two banks of two *Rambus inline memory modules* (RIMMs). If these were DIMM sockets, you'd probably be using SDRAM or DDR SDRAM DIMMs.

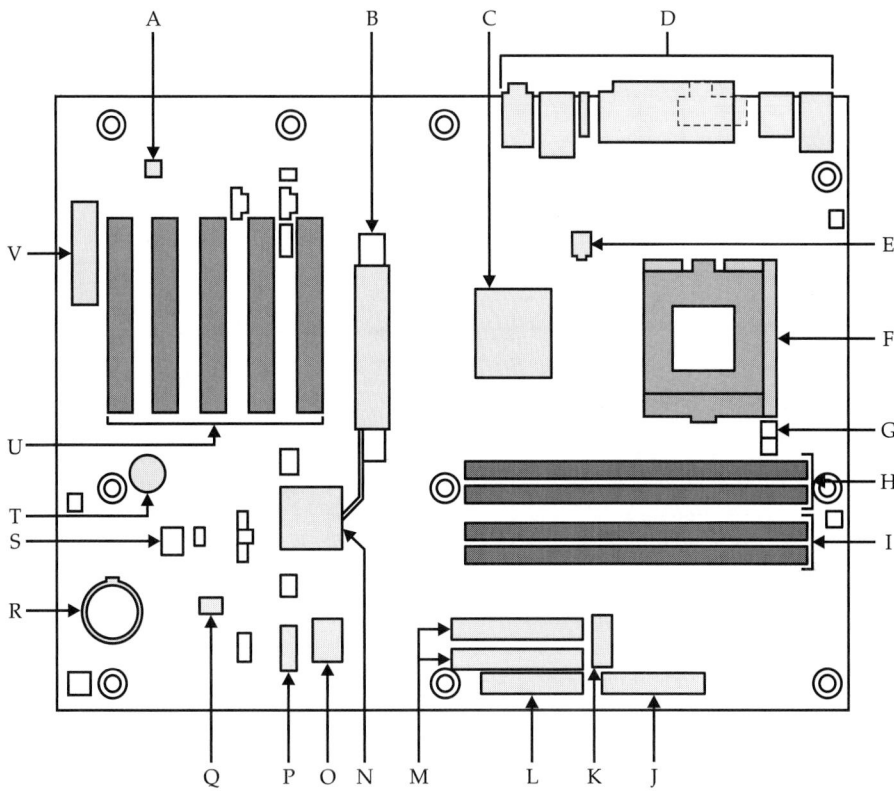

FIGURE 28-6   Identifying the major elements of a motherboard (Courtesy of Intel Corporation)

A   AD1881/AD1885 audio codec (optional)
B   AGP connector (AGP Pro 1.5V connector optional)
C   Intel 82850 Memory Controller Hub (MCH)
D   Back panel connectors
E   +12V power connector (ATX12V)
F   Pentium 4 Processor socket
G   Hardware monitor
H   RAMBUS Bank 0 (RIMM1 and RIMM2)
I   RAMBUS Bank 1 (RIMM3 and RIMM4)
J   Power connector
K   Auxiliary Power connector
L   Diskette drive connector
M   IDE connectors
N   Intel 82801BA I/O Controller Hub (ICH2)
O   SMSC LPC47M102 I/O Controller
P   Front panel connector
Q   Enhanced thermal monitor and fan control device
R   Battery
S   SST 49LF004A 4 Mbit Firmware Hub (FWH)
T   Speaker
U   PCI bus add-in card connectors
V   Communication and Networking Riser (CNR) connector (optional)

J, K.   *ATX power connectors.* Connector J is the standard 20-pin ATX power connector provided by the power supply, and connector K is the 6-pin supplemental ATX power port. Not all motherboards will use the auxiliary 6-pin connector.

L.   *Floppy connector.* This is the standard 34-pin floppy controller port.

M.   *IDE connectors.* These are the primary and secondary 40-pin IDE controller ports for your hard drives and other ATAPI devices like CD-ROM or DVD-ROM drives. This system supports Ultra-DMA/66 and Ultra-DMA/100.

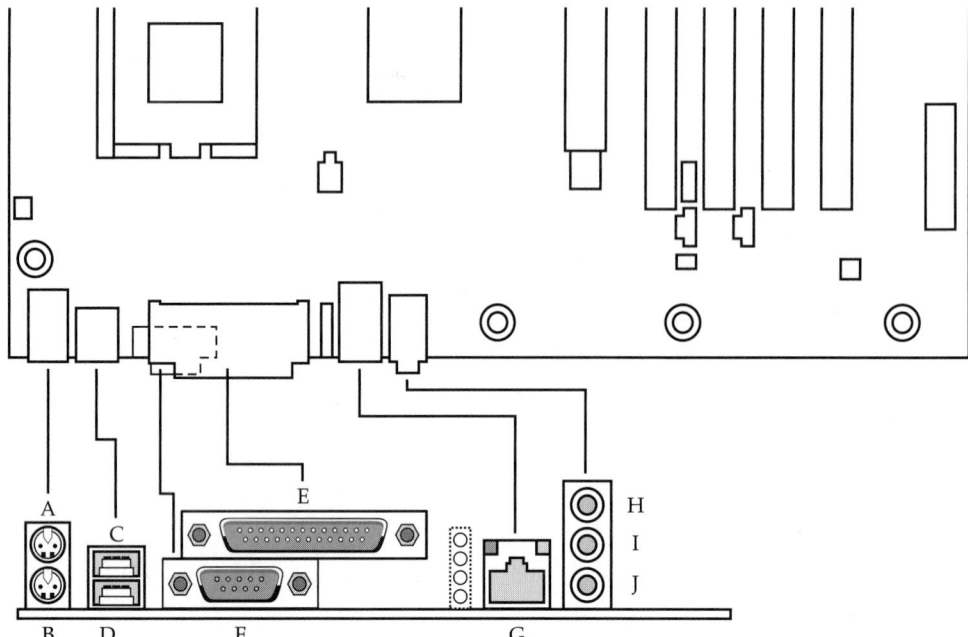

FIGURE 28-7   I/O connector layout for the D850GB motherboard (Courtesy of Intel Corporation)

N.   *82801BA I/O Controller Hub chip.* This ICH2 chip is a highly integrated controller that supports your HDD controller channels, USB ports, PCI bus, and audio system.

O.   *SMSC LPC47M102 I/O Controller chip.* This chip handles all of the I/O ports in the system, as well as the floppy controller function.

P.   *Front panel connector.* This header provides the pins that connect to the case wires (such as the power LED, power switch, key lock, reset switch, and so on).

Q.   *Thermal monitor and fan control.* This device monitors temperatures in the system and regulates fan speeds for optimum cooling.

R.   *CMOS battery.* This is the coin cell that maintains your CMOS RAM contents. Be sure to replace the battery with an identical type.

S.   *SST 49LF004A 4Mbit Firmware Hub chip.* This is the 4Mbit controller (FWH) that handles your BIOS and CMOS RAM.

T.   *Speaker.* Normally the speaker serves little purpose except to handle beep codes generated by the BIOS POST.

U.   *PCI bus connectors.* These are your main expansion slots for other devices in the system.

V.   *Communications and Networking Riser (CNR).* This connector supports the relatively new Intel CNR standard for modem/networking devices. Recent motherboards provided an Audio/Modem Riser (AMR) connector instead. This connector type is rarely used in actual practice.

Audio Connectors

There are also numerous smaller audio connectors on the motherboard that you should be familiar with, and you can see several of them illustrated in Figure 28-8. Your particular motherboard may offer more or different connectors, but the D850GB supplies the following:

A. *Auxiliary line input.* This is a sound channel that allows you to mix in an auxiliary audio signal. The pinout is shown next:

PIN	SIGNAL NAME
Pin 1	Left auxiliary signal
Pin 2	Ground
Pin 3	Ground
Pin 4	Right auxiliary signal

B. *ATAPI CD audio connector.* This is a slightly different CD audio connector scheme using differential signaling. The presence of this second connector also lets you mix audio from a second compliant CD-ROM drive. The pinout is as follows:

PIN	SIGNAL NAME
Pin 1	Left audio signal
Pin 2	Differential ground
Pin 3	Differential ground
Pin 4	Right audio signal

C. *"Legacy" CD audio connector.* This serves as the conventional audio connector found on most sound cards. Since the D850GB offers onboard sound support, you can feed the audio from a CD to this connector. The legacy pinout is as follows:

PIN	SIGNAL NAME
Pin 1	CD ground
Pin 2	Audio left channel
Pin 3	CD ground
Pin 4	Audio right channel

D. *PC/PCI connector.* This is a serial interface to the PCI bus that can be used with several PCI-based devices that do not necessarily use a PCI bus. The pinout for this connector is listed next:

PIN	SIGNAL NAME
Pin 1	PCI data in
Pin 2	Ground
Pin 3	No connection
Pin 4	PCI request out
Pin 5	Ground
Pin 6	Serial IRQ out

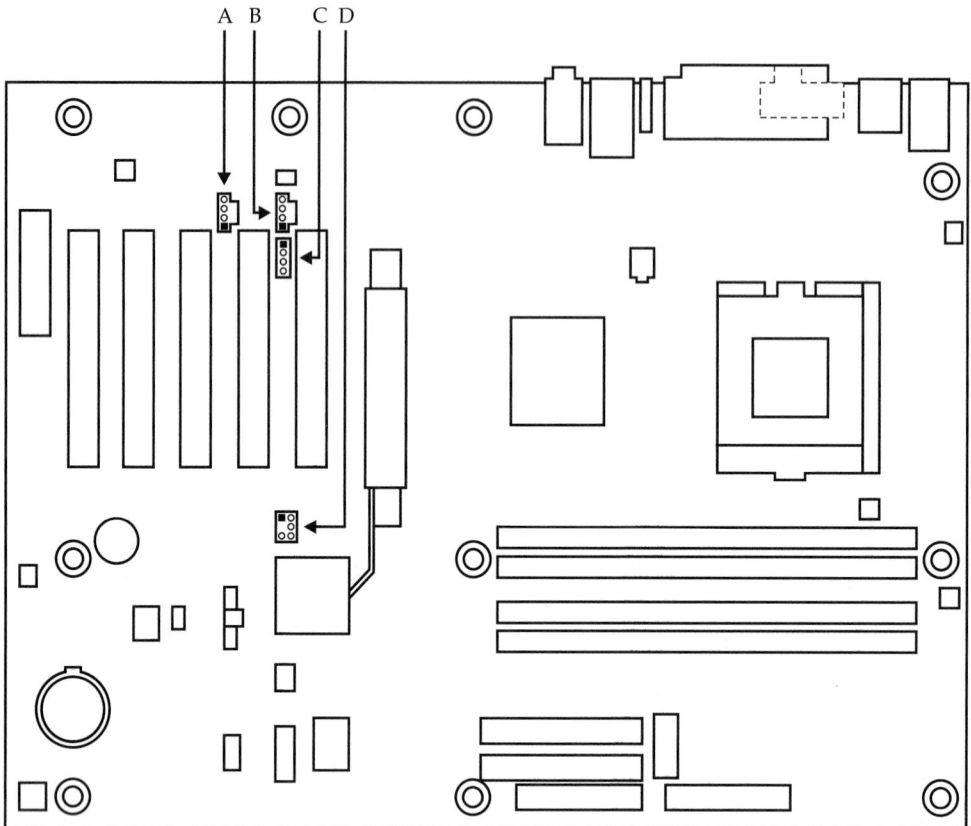

FIGURE 28-8 Identifying audio-based motherboard connectors (Courtesy of Intel Corporation)

Power and Control Connectors

There are numerous hardware control and power connections on the motherboard, as shown in Figure 28-9. These connectors are used to attach the power supply, operate fans, and manage "wake" devices. These features are vital for proper cooling and effective power management, and the D850GB offers the following connections:

A. *ATX12V Power connector.* If the power supply provides this 4-pin connector, you can use this feature to supply additional current for +12V devices in the system. The pin assignments are shown next:

PIN	SIGNAL NAME
Pin 1	Ground
Pin 2	Ground
Pin 3	+12V
Pin 4	+12V

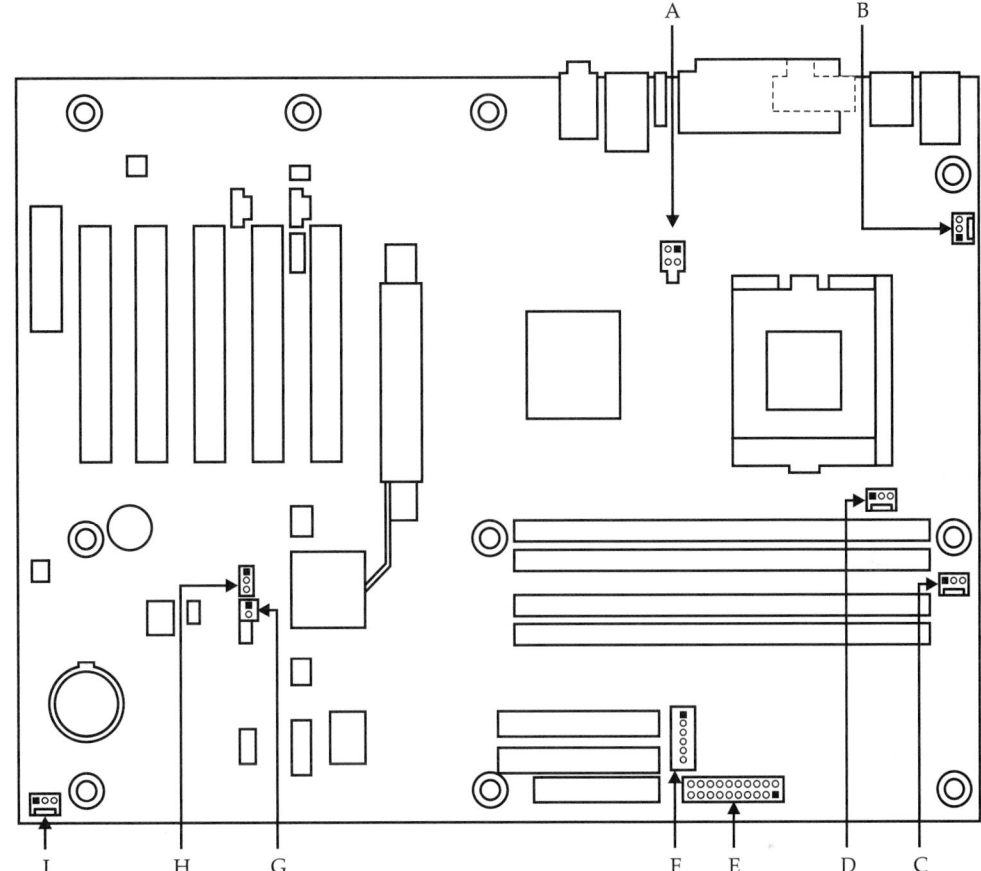

FIGURE 28-9   Identifying power and control connections (Courtesy of Intel Corporation)

B.   *Processor Voltage Regulator Fan connector (FAN4).* This is a 3-wire fan cable that provides power to the +12 Vdc processor voltage regulator fan. The third wire is grounded, so there is no tachometer control over the fan.

C.   *RIMM Fan connector (FAN2).* This is a 3-wire fan cable that provides power to the +12 Vdc RIMM cooling fan used to cool the Rambus modules. The third wire provides a tachometer signal to the motherboard that the motherboard can use to monitor the fan's performance.

D.   *Processor Fan connector (FAN3).* This is a 3-wire fan cable that provides power to the +12 Vdc processor cooling fan. The third wire provides a tachometer signal to the motherboard that the motherboard can use to monitor the fan's performance.

E.   *Main Power connector.* The ATX power supply attaches to the motherboard at this 20-pin connection (item J in Figure 28-7). It is vital that this cable be securely attached to the motherboard connector. Otherwise, power may cut out erratically. Data loss and damage to the motherboard may result. The pinout for this connector is listed next:

CONNECTOR	SIGNAL NAME	CONNECTOR	SIGNAL NAME
Pin 1	+3.3V	Pin 11	+3.3V
Pin 2	+3.3V	Pin 12	−12V
Pin 3	Ground	Pin 13	Ground
Pin 4	+5V	Pin 14	PS-ON# (power supply remote on/off)
Pin 5	Ground	Pin 15	Ground
Pin 6	+5V	Pin 16	Ground
Pin 7	Ground	Pin 17	Ground
Pin 8	PWRGD (Power Good)	Pin 18	TP_PWRCONN_18
Pin 9	+5V (Standby)	Pin 19	+5V
Pin 10	+12V	Pin 20	+5V

F. *Auxiliary Power.* If the power supply provides a supplemental 6-pin power connector, it should be attached to the motherboard at this point. This connector provides additional +3.3V and +5V sources to support a larger number of onboard features. The pin assignments are listed next:

PIN	SIGNAL NAME
Pin 1	Ground
Pin 2	Ground
Pin 3	Ground
Pin 4	+3.3V
Pin 5	+3.3V
Pin 6	+5V

G. *Wake On Ring connector.* This two-pin connector allows you to attach a device that will "wake" the system from a modem when an incoming ring is detected. The two signals are Ground and Ring.

H. *Wake On LAN connector.* This connector allows you to attach a device that will "wake" the system from a LAN when a system is in the power-down state. The three pins are listed next:

PIN	SIGNAL NAME
Pin 1	+5 Vdc (standby)
Pin 2	Ground
Pin 3	Wake On LAN signal

I. *Chassis Fan connector (FAN1).* This is a 3-wire fan cable that provides power to the +12 Vdc chassis cooling fan. The third wire provides a tachometer signal to the motherboard that the motherboard can use to monitor the fan's performance.

Front Panel Connector

Ultimately, you'll need to connect front panel cables to the motherboard to control power, reset, and so on. Figure 28-10 illustrates the front panel connector for an Intel VC820 motherboard, and the pin assignments for an Intel D850GB front panel connector (item P in Figure 28-6) are shown next:

PIN	SIGNAL NAME	PIN	SIGNAL NAME
Pin 1	HD_PWR: Hard disk LED pull-up to +5V	Pin 9	+5V: IR Power
Pin 2	HDR_BLNK_GRN: Front panel green LED	Pin 10	N/C
Pin 3	HAD#: Hard disk active LED	Pin 11	Reserved
Pin 4	HDR_BLNK_YEL: Front panel yellow LED	Pin 12	Ground

PIN	SIGNAL NAME	PIN	SIGNAL NAME
Pin 5	Ground	Pin 13	Ground
Pin 6	FPBUT_IN: Power switch	Pin 14	N/C (pin removed)
Pin 7	FP_RESET#: Reset switch	Pin 15	Reserved
Pin 8	Ground	Pin 16	+5V: Power

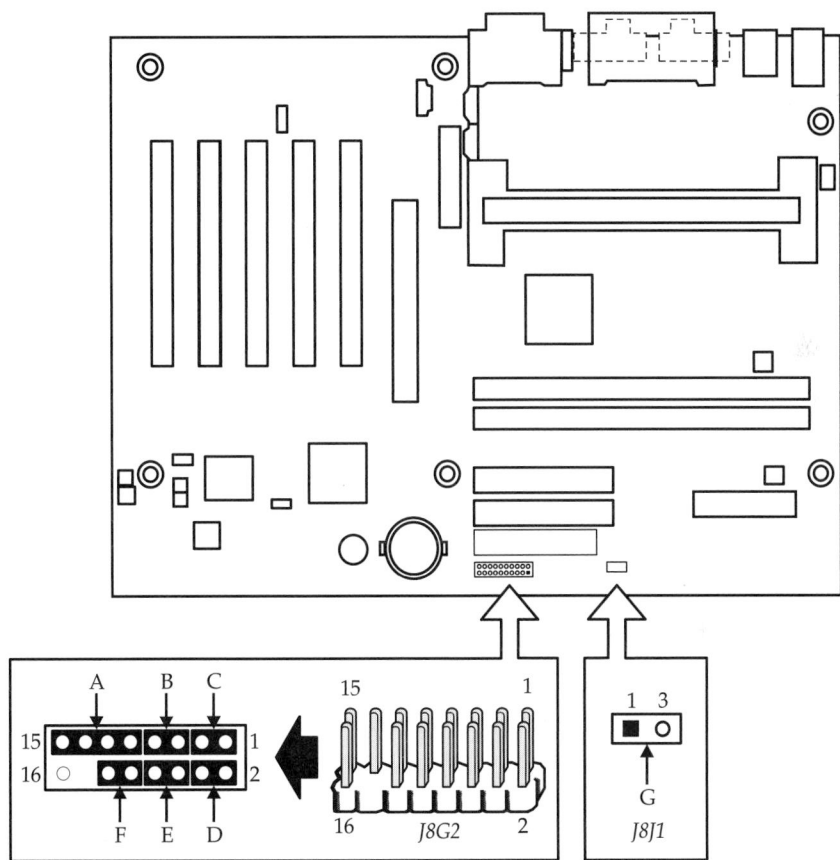

Item	Pins	Description
Front Panel Connector	A	9, 11, 13 and 15	Infrared port
	B	5 and 7	Reset switch
	C	1 and 3	Hard drive activity LED
	D	2 and 4	Power / Sleep / Message waiting LED
	E	6 and 8	Power switch
	F	10 and 12	No connect
Auxiliary Front Panel Power LED connector	G	1 and 3	Auxiliary Power LED connector (Pin 2 keyed)

FIGURE 28-10   Identifying front panel connections on the VC820 motherboard (Courtesy of Intel Corporation)

MAKING SOME COMPARISONS

If you'd like to see how easily motherboards could vary from model to model, let's take another look at that Tyan motherboard in Figure 28-3. There are some striking similarities, but here are a few of the differences that should stand out against a motherboard like the D850GB:

- *The CPU connector is different.* The Tyan "Super 7" motherboard accommodates a Socket 7 processor rather than a Socket 432 processor for the D850GB. This means you'd need to stick with an AMD or Cyrix Socket 7 processor rather than a Pentium 4 socket-based processor. If the D850GB used a Slot 1 connector, you'd need to use a Pentium II/III processor.

- *The expansion slot layout is different.* The Tyan sports four ISA slots, four PCI slots, and an AGP slot. This should not pose a problem unless you have no ISA cards and need more than four PCI slots.

- *The chipset is different.* The Tyan uses a VIA MVP3 chipset rather than Intel's i820 chipset. (See Chapter 10 for details on the MVP3.)

- *I/O ports are almost nonexistent.* Look closely at Figure 28-3, and you'll find connections for USB, PS/2 mouse, COM ports, and printer (LPT) ports. The problem is that these are "headers" rather than actual connectors. This means you'll need to purchase the port connectors on expansion card brackets using small ribbon cables that plug into those headers—an inconvenient and error-prone approach, especially when you're shuffling expansion cards around.

- *The memory configuration is different.* Where the D850GB uses new Rambus memory, the Tyan motherboard offers both 72-pin SIMM and 168-pin DIMM slots for memory modules. Immediately, this means the memory used for the D850GB is not compatible with the Tyan motherboard.

Upgrading a Motherboard

As a PC ages, it is the motherboard that limits the system's upgradability. True, you can add RAM and upgrade a CPU, and while these tactics can prolong the working life of older systems, they have a limited impact on the overall performance of a motherboard (especially older i486 and Pentium/MMX motherboards). As PC technology surges ahead and the price of advanced motherboards continues to drop, replacing an outdated motherboard outright is becoming an increasingly cost-effective upgrade option. This part of the chapter illustrates the most important concerns when planning a motherboard upgrade, walks you through an upgrade process, and shows you how to deal with typical upgrade problems.

CONSIDERING THE UPGRADE

Upgrading a motherboard is not particularly difficult, but it *is* a time-consuming, detail-oriented process. As a result, advance planning can be a substantial benefit. The following tips cover some important points to keep in mind when planning a motherboard upgrade. As with any upgrade, make it a point to call around and find the best price and delivery terms. Given the added expense of a motherboard, you should find a vendor with a liberal return policy just in case you accidentally obtain an incorrect or defective ("dead-out-of-the-box") replacement.

Compare Features
All motherboards are not created equal, so check the specifications closely before making a choice. BIOS plays a vital role in such advanced features as plug-and-play, APM, Ultra-ATA/100 support, USB support, boot sector virus protection, and so much more. The move toward PC power conservation (referred

to as "green" PCs) is resulting in features like ACPI. The number and type of I/O slots define system expandability. Most modern motherboards provide onboard features like drive controllers, video adapters, sound devices, and COM/LPT ports. If your major interest is enhanced video/multimedia performance, a Pentium III/4 motherboard with a single AGP bus slot will probably do the trick.

Check Dimensions and Mounting

You cannot overlook the nuts and bolts involved in a motherboard upgrade. Unfortunately, this is often the most difficult (and neglected) consideration. First, the physical dimensions of the motherboard must fit within the space currently available in your PC. A smaller motherboard is generally not a problem, but a larger (or oddly shaped) motherboard will invariably encounter interference from drives and the power supply. The other issue is mounting holes. Chances are very good that mounting holes on the new motherboard will not match the original mounting holes.

The use of ATX and NLX motherboards and cases goes a long way to easing the problems of dimensioning. Since ATX and NLX form-factor motherboards, cases, and power supplies are all designed to be interchangeable, moving to these form factors can greatly ease the upgrade problems associated with physical motherboard mounting.

If you elect to replace a full AT or baby AT motherboard with an ATX or NLX motherboard, you *must* also upgrade the case and power supply as well.

Check CPU and Slot Locations

Check the sales literature or online product documentation for the new motherboard, and find the location of the new CPU relative to the expansion slots. Since it is assumed that you will be upgrading your system to a Pentium III/4 or AMD compatible motherboard, the use of a CPU heat sink will be mandatory. As a result, the CPU/heat sink combination could easily interfere with the installation of one or more expansion boards. This could be a real problem if your current system is heavily loaded. (You can see how the CPU socket would interfere with full-length ISA cards in Figure 28-3.) Try to pick a motherboard that places the CPU out of the way of expansion boards. For ATX and NLX motherboards, the CPU's placement normally does not interfere with the expansion slots.

Consider Collateral Upgrades

Before finally committing to a new motherboard, take a moment to evaluate the other subassemblies found in the PC, and anticipate any other immediate upgrade needs. Will your old EIDE hard drive really take advantage of the new motherboard's Ultra-DMA/100 drive controller? Do you need a new memory type (such as DDR SDRAM DIMMs rather than EDO SIMMs)? Will your old PCI video accelerator be retired in favor of a high-performance AGP 3D graphics card? Each of these extras will boost the ultimate cost of the upgrade that much higher, so it is always worthwhile to compare this adjusted cost against the purchase price of a similar PC available off the shelf. In some cases, it may be in your customer's best interest to simply buy or build a new PC.

Check the Costs

Choose your new motherboard carefully, using a balance between price and cutting-edge features. New motherboards are not terribly expensive, but you can usually find a great deal if you look 6 to 12 months back. For example, a new Pentium 4 motherboard (with the Pentium 4 installed) can easily run over $600, while a recent Pentium III motherboard (plus CPU) can be had for well under $300. The idea is that you can save a bundle of money if you can make do with upgrades that are just slightly off the cutting edge.

Perhaps even more important, make sure you are aware of any hidden costs with the motherboard. For example, make sure that you know whether the new motherboard comes with current BIOS, a CPU, and CMOS backup battery. If you plan to be running software that demands MMX or SSE capability, see that the CPU is suitable. Also find out how much RAM is on the motherboard, and see if your current RAM is compatible. You might find yourself buying 64MB to 128MB (or more) of new SDRAM DIMMs or RIMMs because you can't transfer the EDO SIMMs from the old motherboard to the new one. This will bump up the cost of the upgrade by at least several hundred dollars.

Pros and Cons of Traditional Upgrades

Motherboard upgrades provide a much more sweeping and comprehensive improvement in system performance than changing any one element on the original motherboard itself. A new motherboard not only supports better and faster processors, but it also provides better caching, space, and support for larger amounts of faster RAM (such as DDR SDRAM or Rambus DRAM), advanced bus slots for added system performance, and superior data-handling through the use of current BIOS and streamlined, highly integrated chipsets. Such upgrades can also consume a fair amount of time (easily an hour or more) depending on the amount of mechanical disassembly that is required. The other disadvantage is that of physical incompatibility. If the mounting holes on a new motherboard do not align with the original mounting standoffs, new mounting holes will have to be created (or the case will have to be replaced).

Pros and Cons of Daughtercard Upgrades

The two great drawbacks to motherboard replacement are price and time. Some companies like Compaq addressed these disadvantages by designing a *modular motherboard*—a unit that mounts the CPU, cache, and often the system RAM on a readily accessible module referred to as a *daughtercard*. The daughtercard can be replaced in only a few minutes, with no real disassembly required. Since the daughtercard is specifically designed to carry the core processing components, an upgrade can easily yield a 100 percent to 600 percent performance improvement. These are compelling advantages, especially when many systems need to be upgraded. The problem with daughtercards is that they are proprietary devices that must be designed to mate with a specific motherboard. As a result, a daughtercard is generally quite expensive—sometimes more than a conventional motherboard. Daughtercard upgrades also prevent new bus architectures from being introduced to the system.

Pros and Cons of Processor Card Upgrades

Older bus-mastering systems (such as the PS/2) have found another alternative to motherboard upgrades. Instead of taking the time to replace the main motherboard assembly, MicroChannel systems allow a supplemental CPU board (called a *processor card*) to be installed in any available expansion slot. Since the MicroChannel architecture allows bus mastering, the processor card can take over system control from the CPU resident on the motherboard—effectively shutting down the original CPU—and provide a CPU enhancement of 200 percent or more. As with any expansion board, the processor card can be configured and installed in a matter of minutes. On the downside, a processor card is still rather pricey when compared to another CPU itself, and more expensive than a conventional motherboard. Although processor cards are generally more standardized than daughtercards, they are generally limited to MCA systems. ISA and PCI systems typically do not incorporate this design philosophy. Processor cards also do not support the introduction of new bus architectures into a system.

PERFORMING THE UPGRADE

Unlike CPU or expansion card upgrades, replacing an entire motherboard is a rather involved process that requires a substantial amount of care to be accomplished successfully. This part of the chapter covers the essential steps and precautions that you will need to remember during the upgrade. Before starting the upgrade, it is a good idea to run a benchmarking program and note the system performance benchmark figure. This gives you something to measure the system against once the upgrade is finished. You are also strongly urged to perform a complete system backup before proceeding. *Collateral system damage during an upgrade is a serious possibility.*

Static Precautions

Virtually all of the chips used in today's computers are fabricated with technologies that make them *extremely* sensitive to *electrostatic discharge* (ESD). To ensure the safe handling of motherboards and other system components during the upgrade, make it a point to take the following precautions. First, invest in an antistatic mat that is large enough to cover a majority of your work area. See that the antistatic mat is properly cabled and attached to a reliable earth ground. *Under no circumstances* should you allow a motherboard to rest on a synthetic or static-prone surface. Second, use an antistatic wrist strap whenever handling components or tools inside the PC. Cable the wrist strap to the antistatic mat or to another reliable earth ground. Third, always try to handle printed circuit boards by their edges. Avoid touching the individual chip pins or printed wiring. Fourth, have a supply of good-quality antistatic bags on hand to hold the system's expansion boards as they are temporarily removed. Finally, excessively dry environments tend to allow substantial buildups of static charges in objects, clothing, and bodies. If it is possible, try to work in an environment with at least 40 percent humidity.

Save Your CMOS

Before starting your upgrade, make it a point to obtain a current record of your CMOS settings. You can do this by taking PRINTSCREEN shots of each CMOS setup page. You should be particularly interested in the hard drive setup information, since you will certainly need to load that data into the new motherboard's CMOS before the system will recognize your boot drive and other devices. Once you have the CMOS information, set it aside in a safe place.

> Most current BIOS versions allow you to enter "BIOS Defaults" in the CMOS Setup, which should establish a working system baseline with a minimum of fuss, but you may still need to identify your hard drives manually.

Prepare the System

At this point, you can prepare the system for its upgrade. A word of caution is in order here: *be especially careful of screwdriver blades when working inside the PC.* If you should slip, the blade can easily gouge the motherboard and result in broken traces. It pays to be careful and gentle when upgrading a motherboard. *Before opening the PC cover, turn the system off, and unplug it from the AC receptacle.* This helps to ensure your safety by preventing the PC from being powered accidentally while you are working on it.

Remove the screws holding down the outer cover, and place those screws aside in a safe place. Gently remove the PC's outer cover and set it aside (out of the path of normal floor traffic). You should now be able to look into the PC and observe the motherboard, along with any expansion boards and drives that are installed. Now that you are looking at the complete PC, this is the time for you to *label* things. Clearly marked labels will help you remember the purpose of each cable (such as power, drives, key lock, speaker, drive light, and so on) and show you where each item went on the original motherboard or on various expansion boards. *Don't be afraid to label things.* Labels need not be fancy—a roll of masking tape and an indelible marker are all that's required. Remember that you'll have to take this all apart, so anything that will help you remember where things go will be a help.

Remove the Original Motherboard

At this point, you should begin clearing the obstructions to the motherboard. Start by removing each expansion board. Place each board into an antistatic bag, and set each bag aside on the antistatic mat. Next, remove any cables that are attached to the motherboard (such as the key lock or speaker cables). If there are floppy drive and hard drive cables connected to the motherboard, remove them as well. Finally, disconnect the power cable(s). For AT-style motherboards, you'll find two 6-pin power connectors from the power supply. For ATX motherboards, you'll find a single 20-pin power connector. If there are any drives or chassis assemblies interfering with the motherboard, remove them now, and set them aside carefully.

NLX motherboards do not carry any of the burden found in AT-style or ATX motherboards. All of that peripheral equipment is attached to the NLX riser card. You need only detach and unplug the NLX motherboard from its riser card.

You should now have an unobstructed view of the motherboard. Locate and remove each of the screws holding the motherboard in place. In many cases, there may be at least six (sometimes eight or more). Once each of the screws has been removed, gently lift out the motherboard and lay it aside onto the antistatic mat—preferably in its own antistatic bag. (The whole board should fit on the mat.) The motherboard should lift out without difficulty. If the motherboard does not budge or lift out easily, you may have overlooked a screw, nylon standoff, or cable. *Do not force the motherboard!* Often, there may be one or more white nylon standoffs that are still clipping the motherboard in place. Patiently locate the obstruction(s), and carefully clear each one.

After you remove the original motherboard, you should also remove the CMOS backup battery and place it into a heavy-gauge plastic bag before storing the original motherboard. This will prevent an aging CMOS backup battery from rupturing and damaging the original motherboard with leaking electrolyte.

Install the New Motherboard

You can now place the new motherboard into the chassis and see that each I/O port and mounting hole line up properly. Secure it into place. Do not use excessive force when tightening the screws. Excessive force can cause the motherboard to warp and result in failure. When securing the board, check that there are no metal brackets or standoffs that might touch the new motherboard and cause a short circuit. It is usually recommended for you to use a thin, nonconductive washer between each standoff and the motherboard. Once the new motherboard is installed mechanically, you can start reassembling the other devices that you stripped from the system.

Refer to the user's guide that accompanies the new motherboard, and check each jumper or DIP switch. This is a particularly important step because many contemporary motherboards provide services right onboard that have traditionally been assigned to expansion boards (such as video adapters and drive controllers). For example, if you used a dual serial port board with your original motherboard, but your new motherboard provides two serial ports, you won't need the dual serial port board. If you need to use that board, you will have to set motherboard jumpers to disable the onboard serial ports.

The same thing is true of video adapters. If a video port is available on the new motherboard, but you have a 3D graphics accelerator board on hand, you will have to disable the onboard video port to prevent a hardware conflict. If the new motherboard provides a floppy and IDE controller, you can abandon that drive controller board and plug the drives right into the appropriate connectors on the motherboard. In that case, check the drive control jumpers to be sure they are enabled. Be sure to review each available jumper carefully. Also verify that the motherboard's bus speed, clock multiplier, and CPU voltage settings are all configured properly for the CPU.

Reassemble the System

Once the motherboard jumpers are set, you can install the CPU, system RAM, and power/case cables. CPU installation should go easily, but be aware that a socket-based CPU must be oriented properly in the socket relative to pin 1. Slot-based processors will generally only insert in one orientation. Chances are that the CPU will require a heat sink/fan, so be sure to install it securely if needed (along with thermal compound to improve heat transfer between the CPU and heat sink/fan assembly). If you need to install the BIOS chip(s), you may do that next. Be careful to orient each BIOS ROM properly relative to pin 1. If there is more than one BIOS ROM, be sure to install the chips in their proper places. Reversing the BIOS ROM locations should not damage them, but the system will probably not boot. The new motherboard will need a backup battery to support the CMOS/RTC chip. If there is not a battery already on the new motherboard, install a new battery (or reconnect the original battery pack).

Make sure that each SIMM, DIMM, or RIMM snaps gently into place. If they do not, they may be inserted improperly. When inserting cables, note that the red strip on each ribbon cable is pin 1. Make sure that pin 1 on the cable is matched to pin 1 on the corresponding connector. Inserting a ribbon cable backward is rarely damaging, but it may prevent the system from booting. Reconnect the power cables. Finally, install the expansion boards that you will need in the system. Remember that you may not need all of the adapter boards you started with if the motherboard will be taking over particular functions. If you had disassembled any drives or chassis subassemblies before removing the original motherboard, be sure to reassemble those items now, and check that their power and signal cabling are secure. Reconnect any ancillary devices such as the mouse, keyboard, and monitor.

Testing the System

At last, you will face the moment of truth. If things have gone well, this procedure should have taken no more than an hour or so. Once the components and cabling are all secure, it will be time to reconnect the AC line cord and to try applying power to the system. Make sure that your hands and any tools are clear of the PC. Turn on the monitor, double-check your power cable installation one more time, and then go ahead and press the power switch.

After a moment or two, you should see a BIOS message appear on the monitor. This is a good sign. When the POST displays its message asking to start the setup procedure (usually by pressing F1), go ahead and start it. Review each screen in the setup routine, and restore as many CMOS settings as possible (especially the memory amount, floppy drive types, and hard drive configuration). Chances are that there will be several setup variables that were not in the original system. Just leave these in their default states for now. You can always optimize them later. Save the CMOS Setup and reboot the computer. Your upgraded system should now complete its POST successfully and boot to the operating system.

When booting to Windows 9x/Me, the Windows platform will automatically identify the new device(s) and try installing the appropriate drivers for them. You may need to have your Windows installation CD handy. Once Windows has reconfigured itself for the new hardware, install any patches from the motherboard's installation CD (if needed). Finally, check the Device Manager for any hardware problems or conflicts. Congratulations, you have completed your motherboard upgrade.

 If you cannot adequately reconfigure the CMOS Setup, select the BIOS Defaults option, which should apply the variables necessary to get the PC working. You can then tweak the CMOS values later to improve system performance.

When the system boots as expected, the last step should be to power-down the computer and reassemble the outer housing. You can then run your benchmarking program again to determine the new benchmarks for your PC. You can see the relative improvement in performance over that of the original system.

Troubleshooting a Motherboard

Since motherboards contain the majority of system processing components, it is likely that you will encounter a faulty motherboard sooner or later. The BIOS POST is written to test each subsection of the motherboard each time the PC is powered-up, so most problems are detected well before you ever see the DOS prompt. Errors are reported in myriad ways. Beep codes and POST codes (Chapter 18) provide indications of fatal errors that occur before the video system is initialized. Still, there are plenty of symptoms that can elude the initial testing at start time. This part of the chapter digs in and presents a lengthy selection of motherboard symptoms for you to reference.

REPAIR VS. REPLACE

This is the perennial troubleshooting dilemma. The problem with motherboard repair is not so much the availability of replacement parts (although that *can* be a challenge) as it is the use of *surface-mount soldering* (SMT). A surface-mounted chip cannot be desoldered with conventional tools. To successfully desolder a surface-mounted chip, you need to heat each of the chip's pins (often in excess of 200) simultaneously, then lift the chip off the board. It's then a simple matter to clean up any residual solder. Unfortunately, specialized surface-mount soldering equipment is required to do this. The equipment is readily available commercially, so it's easy to buy. But you can invest $1000 to $2000 to equip your workbench properly.

As you can imagine, the "repair vs. replace" decision is an economic one. It makes little sense for the part-time PC enthusiast to make such a substantial investment to exchange a defective chip (which usually cost under $20). It is generally better to replace the motherboard outright, which is only a fraction of the cost of such SMT equipment. On the other hand, professionals who intend to pursue PC repair as a living are well served with surface-mount equipment. The customer's cost for labor, part(s), and markup is typically much less than that for purchasing a new motherboard (especially the high-end boards such as Pentium III/4 motherboards).

START WITH THE BASICS

Since motherboard troubleshooting does represent a significant expense, you should be sure to start any motherboard repair by inspecting the following points in the PC. *Remember to turn all power off before performing these inspections.*

- *Check all connectors.* Connector problems can happen easily when the PC is serviced or upgraded, and you accidentally forget to replace every cable (or the cable is installed incorrectly). Start with the power connector, and inspect each cable and connector attached to the motherboard. Frayed cables should be replaced. Loose or detached cables should be reattached properly.

- *Check all socket-mounted chips.* Some chips in the computer (especially the CPU) get hot during normal operation. It is not unheard of for the repetitive expansion and contraction encountered with everyday use to eventually "rock" a chip out of its socket. The CPU, BIOS ROM, and often the CMOS/RTC module are socket mounted, so check them carefully.

- *Check power levels.* Low or erratic AC power levels can cause problems in the PC. Use a multimeter to check AC at the wall outlet. Be very careful whenever dealing with AC. Take all precautions to protect yourself from injury. If the AC is low or is heavily loaded by motors, coffeemakers, or other highly inductive loads, try the PC in another outlet running from a different circuit. If AC checks properly, use your multimeter (or a measurement tool such as PC Power Check from Data Depot) to check the power supply outputs. If one or more outputs are low or absent, you should repair or replace the supply.

- *Check the motherboard for foreign objects.* A screw, paper clip, or free strand of wire can cause a short circuit that may disable the motherboard. Examine the motherboard carefully, and use ample lighting.

- *Check that all motherboard DIP switches and jumpers are correct.* For example, if the motherboard provides a video port, and you have a video board plugged into the expansion bus, the motherboard's video circuit will have to be disabled through a switch or jumper. Otherwise, a hardware conflict can result that may interfere with motherboard operation. You will need the user manual for the PC in order to identify and check each jumper or switch. Today, virtually all motherboard configuration issues (including clock speeds and multipliers) are handled through the system's CMOS Setup, so jumper settings are no longer as critical as they used to be.

- *Check for intermittent connections and accidental grounding.* Inspect each of the motherboard's mounting screws, and see that they are not touching nearby printed traces. Also check the space under the motherboard, and see that there is nothing that might be grounding the motherboard and chassis. As an experiment, you may try loosening the motherboard mounting screws. If the fault goes away, the motherboard may be suffering from an intermittent connection—when all screws are tight, the board is bent just enough to let the intermittent appear. Unfortunately, intermittent connections are almost impossible to find.

GENERAL MOTHERBOARD SYMPTOMS

The general guidelines just covered should help you to identify and correct many of the more common problems that you may encounter. If you're stuck with a particular issue, refer to the following symptoms for specific solutions.

SYMPTOM 28-1   **The Slot 1 retention mechanism is not holding the Slot 1 processor securely in place**   You find that there is "play," which allows the processor to move (and possibly fall out of its slot). In virtually all cases, this means the retention mechanism is not mounted securely on the motherboard. It's probably sitting too high, and allowing the CPU to "float." You'll need to check the installation of that retention mechanism. Support the motherboard so that it will not bend while the retention mechanism is being pressed into the mounting holes. (But do not place the motherboard on a hard surface to install the retention mechanism.) If the retention mechanism push pins are not secured properly, the retention mechanism can become loose, causing the processor to fall out of the motherboard. To install a retention mechanism with captive brass fasteners, simply use a medium Phillips screwdriver to screw the fasteners into the preinstalled brass Pemstuds. To install the retention mechanism with plastic fasteners:

1. Leave space below each mounting hole so that the fastener can protrude through the hole.
2. Find the Slot 1 connector on the motherboard.
3. Position the retention mechanism on the motherboard next to the slot 1 connector.
4. Push down on the retention bracket until the black plastic fasteners are correctly seated and the retention mechanism fits *snugly* against the board.
5. Push each white retainer pin into its respective black fastener until the head of each pin is seated onto the head of each fastener. This should keep the retention mechanism securely in place.

SYMPTOM 28-2   **After removing a hard drive or other IDE device, the system seems to boot slowly, but seems fine otherwise**   Chances are that the BIOS still expects an IDE device to respond, and it is waiting for the device that you removed. This is what causes the delay. If you remove a secondary drive on the primary channel, or any drive on the secondary channel, you should check the CMOS Setup and set that corresponding drive position to "none" or "not installed." Save your changes and reboot the system. You should see that the BIOS is no longer waiting for devices that you marked out in the CMOS Setup.

SYMPTOM 28-3   You notice that your system automatically powers back on after a power failure   This is probably the result of a CMOS Setup configuration rather than a hardware fault, and it occurs on standard Intel-manufactured motherboard products that use a Phoenix BIOS and use either the Intel 430TX PCIset or the Intel 440LX PCIset (or later chipset). You'll probably find a feature in the BIOS setup utility (usually under Boot Menu) that controls the action of the computer following a power failure. These options include Stay Off, Last State (to restore the previous power state—either on or off—before AC power was lost), or Power On (so the system will always power back on). If you check this setting in the CMOS Setup, you'll probably notice that it's set to Power On or Last State. If you'd prefer the system to remain off after a power failure, set this entry to Stay Off.

In all cases, the computer powers-up for 300mS when AC power is restored, reads the current setup boot values, and goes to the appropriate state (on or off).

SYMPTOM 28-4   You receive a "static device resource conflict" error message   A "static device resource conflict" warning message while booting Windows 9x/Me may be generated from numerous (and often unrelated) situations. The majority of technicians reporting this problem have a Pro Audio Spectrum 16 card installed. The Windows 9x/Me registration for this card includes both 10-bit I/O addresses (201H and 388H) and 16-bit aliases to these addresses (A201H and F388H). The BIOS detects that the 10-bit address will also overlap with the 16-bit address and flags this as a resource conflict. Since it is a single card requesting both these resources, the warning can be ignored if that is the case. There are also reports of other configurations causing "static resource conflict" warnings. Some of these instances appear to be corrected by clearing the ESCD area in NVRAM. This can be accomplished by performing a CMOS clear:

1. Note your current settings.
2. Turn power off.
3. Set the CMOS Clear jumper or switch to the Clear position (see the product documentation).
4. Turn power on.
5. After approximately 30 seconds, turn the power off.
6. Set the CMOS Clear jumper or switch to the Off or Normal position.
7. Turn your system on, and enter the CMOS Setup to change settings as you require (hard drive, etc.).

SYMPTOM 28-5   You cannot operate or boot from an LS-120 "floptical" drive   In virtually all cases, this is a limitation of the motherboard's BIOS. For example, Intel motherboards that have a Phoenix BIOS and use either the Intel 430TX, 440LX, 440BX, or 440EX chipsets support booting from an LS-120 floppy drive. Most other motherboards with a Pentium MMX–compliant (or later) chipset will support LS-120 drives. If you have trouble recognizing or booting from the LS-120, check with the motherboard or system maker for a BIOS upgrade.

SYMPTOM 28-6   When upgrading the motherboard, the system won't boot when using an older CPU, but it boots fine with a newer CPU   You find that the older CPU runs fine on another system. This generally means that the newer motherboard contains a "lockout" that prevents

66-MHz bus speeds. This forces the motherboard to use 100-MHz or 133-MHz bus speeds. If a 66-MHz front side bus processor is installed, the motherboard will not boot. If this is the case, there is no way around the problem except to use an appropriate processor model.

SYMPTOM 28-7   **The system displays PC100 memory even though PC133 memory is installed**   First, verify that your system bus is actually set to 133 MHz. If the bus is set to 100 MHz, the memory speed may be reported incorrectly. This error may also sometimes occur when the DRAM Clock entry in your CMOS Setup is set incorrectly. Try setting the DRAM Clock to Host CLK in the Chipset features section of your CMOS Setup.

SYMPTOM 28-8   **The motherboard's COM port(s) won't work**   In almost every case, an inability to use a COM port is a result of *not* using the supplied header cables, or the COM ports are disabled in the CMOS Setup. To ensure that the motherboard is recognizing and initializing the COM ports correctly, boot the system and check the CMOS Setup. Locate the settings that control your COM ports. Verify that the COM ports are enabled. You should also see that the IRQs and I/O addresses are configured properly for each port. Now examine your COM port header cables closely. See that the header is fit over every pin and is oriented properly (look for "pin 1"). Since many motherboard makers use different pin assignments for COM port headers, make sure that you're using the header cable that's specifically intended for your particular motherboard model.

One other point—if your system has internal modems or other serial devices (such as a multi-I/O card with one or more COM ports), see that those other serial devices are *not* conflicting with the motherboard's COM port(s). You may need to reconfigure or remove the conflicting device(s).

SYMPTOM 28-9   **The system halts during boot and displays an "Incompatible ATAPI Device" error**   This may occur after installing a new ATAPI device or upgrading the motherboard while reusing an existing ATAPI device(s). This is a known issue with the Pioneer 32X CD-ROM and an AMI BIOS and can also occur with other incompatible BIOS versions and ATAPI devices. In almost every case, the solution is to upgrade the motherboard's BIOS to a newer version. Of course, you could try a different ATAPI device instead.

SYMPTOM 28-10   **The system will not turn off when you press the power button**
This is an issue with the motherboard's power management settings. In many cases, the power button is designed to turn off the system *only* when you press and hold the power button for more than 5 seconds. You may be able to reconfigure the power button for "instant off" through the CMOS Setup. If you cannot reconfigure the power button for instant off, you may need a BIOS upgrade.

SYMPTOM 28-11   **You discover the "Wake On LAN" device has damaged your power supply**   This is probably because your power supply did not provide adequate standby current. You need to use an ATX power supply with 800 mA provided through the +5-Vsb (standby) power line. This is required by most "Wake On LAN" network cards, which require +5V @ 750 mA in sleep mode. Try an ATX power supply with minimum 800 mA at the +5-Vsb output to avoid over-current damage to the power supply. This may require a power supply upgrade.

SYMPTOM 28-12   **You encounter a "Serial Presence Detect" error at boot time**
This is a problem with the system RAM being properly identified to the BIOS. If "non-SPD" memory is detected during the POST, or the BIOS cannot determine that the memory installed meets SPD 100-MHz requirements, the BIOS will display this error message:

```
SERIAL PRESENCE DETECT (SPD) device data missing or inconclusive
Properly programmed SPD device data is required for reliable operation
Do you wish to continue?
Y/N Type [Y] to continue, [N] to shut down
```

While "non-SPD" memory remains present on the system, subsequent boots will display the following message:

```
SERIAL PRESENCE DETECT (SPD) device data missing or inconclusive
100MHz memory assumed
```

If SPD 100-MHz memory cannot be confirmed during POST, the BIOS will provide this information to the user and offer the option to run the system with memory that may not meet the full 100-MHz operating requirements. If the system will be used in a mission-critical application where data integrity is vital, the system should be shut down, and SPD 100-MHz memory should be installed before operation.

SYMPTOM 28-13 **After installing one or more RIMM modules in the system, you get a repeating beep code and no video** This is often a problem with the way you installed your new Rambus DRAM. Chances are that the beep code indicates a problem during detection of the RIMM modules. If a RIMM socket is not populated with memory, ensure it is populated with a *Continuity RIMM* (C-RIMM). Also check to ensure that system memory is securely installed, and that any RIMMs in use have been specifically recommended by the motherboard manufacturer. For example, do not use PC600 RIMMs when PC800 RIMMs are required.

SYMPTOM 28-14 **You find that IRQ9 is not available to assign an ISA device** Chances are that this is an issue related to your particular motherboard's power management system. For example, IRQ9 is not available to ISA devices on the Intel JN440BX motherboard because it is dedicated to the power management function on the motherboard's PIIX4 controller. This is also true for other motherboards that utilize the PIIX4 controller chip. You may free the IRQ by disabling the motherboard's power management features, or select another available IRQ for the device.

SYMPTOM 28-15 **Windows 98/Me reports insufficient memory with 32MB installed** This is a known issue on motherboards that use the VIA MVP4 chipset (such as the AOpen MX59 Pro motherboard). The MVP4 chipset supports shared memory between system RAM and the video system; 8MB of system RAM is assigned to the onboard graphics controller by default. If this is the case, you may actually only have 24MB of RAM for Windows 98/Me, and this may not be enough. You can add more RAM to the system. You may also enter the CMOS Setup and reduce the Frame Buffer Size value from 8MB to 2MB in order to keep more of the 32MB available for Windows 98/Me. If you *do* reduce the Frame Buffer Size, be sure to also reduce the color depth and resolution under Windows 98/Me.

SYMPTOM 28-16 **The system runs fine with Setup defaults, but is unstable with Turbo defaults** This is because the Turbo defaults generally use more aggressive settings that wring more performance out of the motherboard. In some cases, certain hardware combinations may not respond well to Turbo settings and result in system instability. Check your hardware list against the requirements for the Turbo default settings. If you identify an item that is not appropriate (such as slow RAM), you can upgrade that hardware. Otherwise, you may simply need to select the Setup defaults and stick with an acceptable level of system performance.

SYMPTOM 28-17   **A motherboard failure is reported, but goes away when the PC's outer cover is removed**   There is likely to be an intermittent connection on the motherboard. When the housing is secured, the PC chassis warps just slightly. This may be enough to precipitate an intermittent contact. When the housing is removed, the chassis relaxes and hides the intermittent connection. Replace the outer cover and gently retighten each screw with the system running. Chances are that you will find one screw that triggers the problem. You can leave that screw out, but it is advisable to replace the motherboard as a long-term fix.

SYMPTOM 28-18   **The POST (or your software diagnostic) reports a CPU fault**   This is a fatal error, and chances are that system initialization has halted. CPU problems are generally reported when one or more CPU registers do not respond as expected or have trouble switching to the protected mode. In either case, the CPU is probably at fault. Fortunately, the CPU is socket/slot mounted and should be very straightforward to replace. Be sure to remove all power to the PC, and make careful use of static controls when replacing a CPU. Mark the questionable CPU with indelible ink before replacing it.

Zero-insertion force (ZIF) sockets are easiest, since the processor will be released simply by lifting the metal lever at the socket's side. Slide out the original CPU, and insert a new one. Secure the metal lever, and try the PC again. However, many CPUs are mounted in *pin grid array* (PGA) sockets, and a specialized PGA removal tool is strongly suggested for proper removal. You should also be able to use a small, regular screwdriver to gently pry up each of the four sides of the CPU. But be very careful to avoid cracking the chip, the socket, or the motherboard—never use excessive force. When the processor is free, install the new CPU with close attention to pin alignment, and then gently press the new CPU into place. If you're working with slot-based processors (such as Slot 1 or Slot A), you'll need to release the processor's retention mechanism before removing the processor from its slot.

A word about heat sink/fans—most Pentium MMX and later CPUs are equipped with a metal heat sink (or heat sink/fan) assembly. It is vital to the proper operation of your system that the heat sink be reinstalled correctly. Otherwise, the new CPU will eventually overheat and lock up or fail. Be sure to use good-quality thermal compound to ensure proper heat transfer to the heat sink. (Remember that a sound mechanical connection does not guarantee a good thermal connection.)

SYMPTOM 28-19   **The POST (or your software diagnostic) reports a problem with the floating point unit**   Math coprocessor (also called the *floating point unit* or FPU) problems are generally reported when one or more MCP registers do not respond as expected. Fortunately, MCP faults are not always fatal. It is often possible to remove the MCP or disable the MCP availability through the CMOS Setup. Of course, programs that depend on the MCP will no longer run, but at least the system can be used until a new one is installed. On older systems that use separate MCP chips, the device is socket mounted and should be very straightforward to replace. Be sure to remove all power to the PC, and make careful use of static controls when replacing an MPC. Mark the questionable MPC with indelible ink before replacing it. When the MCP function is integrated into the CPU (such as 486DX, Pentium, Pentium II/III/4, and later CPUs), the process is a bit more expensive. You'll need to replace the entire CPU, but the replacement process is no more difficult. (Remember to remount any heat sink/fan assembly properly.)

SYMPTOM 28-20   **The POST (or your software diagnostic) reports a BIOS ROM checksum error**   The integrity of your system BIOS ROM is verified after the CPU is tested. This is necessary to ensure that there are no unwanted instructions or data that might easily crash the system during POST or normal operation. A checksum is performed on the ROM contents, and that value is compared with the value stored in the ROM itself. If the two values are equal, the ROM is considered good and initialization continues. Otherwise, the BIOS is considered defective and should be replaced.

Traditionally, BIOS ROM is implemented as one or two chips that are plugged into DIP or PLCC sockets. They can be removed easily with the blade of a regular screwdriver, as long as you pry the chip up slowly and gently. (Be sure to pry the chip evenly from both ends.) When installing new DIP chips, you may have to straighten their pins against the surface of a table or use a DIP pin-straightening tool. Ultimately, the DIP pins will fit nicely into each receptacle in the DIP socket. You can then ease the chip evenly down into the socket. Alignment is critical to ensure that all pins are inserted. If not, one or more pins may be bent under the chip and ruin the new ROM. Also, be sure to insert the new chip(s) in the proper orientation. If they are accidentally installed backward, they may be damaged.

Current BIOS chips use flash ROM technology, which allows the device to be erased and reprogrammed in the field without having to replace the entire BIOS ROM chip outright. When a flash BIOS fails its checksum test, it also has probably failed. Since flash BIOS devices are often fabricated as PLCC chips, it is a bit easier to replace them, but you will need a PLCC removal tool to take the original chip out of its socket. There simply is not enough room for a screwdriver.

SYMPTOM 28-21   The POST (or software diagnostic) reports a timer (PIT) failure, an RTC update problem, or a refresh failure   The PIT is often an 8254 or compatible device. Ultimately, one or more of its three channels may have failed, and the PIT should be replaced. It is important to realize that many modern motherboards incorporate the PIT functions into a system controller or other chipset device. (Refer to the chipset chapter for a listing of chipsets and functions.) Since the PIT is typically surface mounted, you can attempt to replace the device or replace the motherboard entirely.

SYMPTOM 28-22   The POST (or software diagnostic) reports an interrupt controller (PIC) failure   The PIC is often an 8259 or compatible device, and there are two PICs on the typical AT motherboard. (PIC 1 handles IRQ0 through IRQ7, and PIC 2 handles IRQ8 through IRQ15.) Of the two, PIC 1 is more important since the lower interrupts have a higher priority, and the lowest channels handle critical low-level functions such as the system timer and keyboard interface. Generally, a diagnostic will reveal which of the two PICs has failed. Make sure that there are no interrupt conflicts between two or more system devices. You can then replace the defective PIC. In all current systems, both PICs are integrated into a system controller chip or chipset device. You can replace the defective chip if you have the appropriate surface-mount equipment available, or replace the motherboard entirely.

SYMPTOM 28-23   The POST (or software diagnostic) reports a DMA controller (DMAC) failure   The DMAC is often an 8237 or compatible device, and there are two DMACs on the typical AT motherboard. (DMAC 1 handles channel 0 through channel 3, and DMAC 2 handles channel 4 through channel 7.) Of the two, DMAC 1 is more important since channel 2 runs the floppy disk controller. Generally, a diagnostic will reveal which of the two DMACs has failed. Make sure that there are no DMA conflicts between two or more system devices. You can then replace the defective DMAC. In many current systems, both DMACs are integrated into a system controller chip or chipset device. You can replace the defective chip if you have the appropriate surface-mount equipment available, or replace the motherboard entirely.

SYMPTOM 28-24   The POST (or software diagnostic) reports a KBC fault   The *keyboard controller* (KBC) is often either an 8042 or an 8742. Since the KBC is a microcontroller in its own right, diagnostics can usually detect a KBC fault with great accuracy. The KBC may be either a socket-mounted PLCC device or (in rare cases) a surface-mounted chip. Remember to remove all power and mark the old KBC before you remove it from the PC. You'll probably need a PLCC-removal tool to take out the old KBC. If you cannot exchange a defective KBC, you'll need to replace the motherboard.

SYMPTOM 28-25 **A keyboard error is reported, but a new keyboard has no effect**
The keyboard fuse on the motherboard may have failed. Many motherboard designs incorporate a small fuse (called a *pico-fuse*) in the +5Vdc line that drives the keyboard. If this fuse fails, the keyboard will be dead. Use your multimeter and measure the +5 Vdc line at the keyboard connector. If this reads 0 Vdc, locate the keyboard fuse on the motherboard and replace it. (You may have to trace the line back to the fuse that looks almost exactly like a resistor.) Otherwise, you'll need to replace the entire motherboard.

SYMPTOM 28-26 **The POST (or software diagnostic) reports a CMOS or RTC fault**
With either error, it is the same device that is usually at fault. The CMOS RAM and RTC are generally fabricated onto the same device. RTC problems indicate that the real-time clock portion of the chip has failed or is not being updated. CMOS RAM failure can be due to a dead backup battery or a failure of the chip itself. When dealing with a CMOS or setup problem, first try a new backup battery and reload the CMOS Setup variables. If a new battery does not resolve the problem, the CMOS/RTC chip should be replaced. Often, the CMOS/RTC chip is surface mounted and will have to be replaced (or the motherboard will have to be replaced). However, there is a growing trend toward making the chip socket-mounted and including the battery in a single replaceable module (such as the Dallas Semiconductor-type devices). Modules are typically replaceable DIP devices.

SYMPTOM 28-27 **The POST (or software diagnostic) reports a fault in the first 64KB of RAM** The first RAM page is important since it holds the *BIOS data area* (BDA) and interrupt vectors. The system will not work without it. When a RAM error is indicated, your only real recourse is to replace the motherboard RAM. On older motherboards, if the diagnostic indicates which bit has failed and you can correlate the bit to a specific memory chip, you can sometimes replace the defective chip (typically surface mounted). Otherwise, you'll need to systematically locate and replace all of the motherboard RAM, or replace the motherboard entirely. Newer motherboards utilize DIMMs (and sometimes RIMMs) for *all* system memory, so it should be a relatively simple matter to cycle through each memory module with a known-good unit to isolate the defective memory module.

SYMPTOM 28-28 **The MCP does not work properly when installed on a motherboard when external (L2) caching is enabled** This is an issue that you might encounter when resurrecting older motherboards. Some non-Intel math coprocessors (a.k.a. floating point units) work in areas that must be non-cached. For example, a Cyrix EMC87 MCP with an AMI Mark IV i386 motherboard has been known to cause this type of problem. When MCP problems arise (especially during upgrades), try disabling the external (L2) cache through CMOS Setup. As another alternative, try a different math coprocessor.

SYMPTOM 28-29 **A "jumperless motherboard" receives incorrect CPU Soft Menu settings and now refuses to boot** This may occur on a motherboard such as the Abit IT5V and is usually due to accidental settings during system configuration. Fortunately, this type of problem can be corrected by removing power from the motherboard. Try turning off the system and unplugging it for several minutes. When you restore power to the system, the CPU Soft Menu will automatically reset the CPU frequency for the lowest setting and allow the motherboard to boot. You can then go back into the CPU Soft Menu and correct any speed setting errors. If this were a jumpered motherboard, you would need to find the CPU speed jumper and set it correctly.

SYMPTOM 28-30 **When installing two 64MB SIMMs, only 32MB of RAM are displayed when the computer powers-up** This tends to be a chipset-related problem. The motherboard is probably using a 430VX (or similar) chipset, which—though supporting 128MB of RAM—will not support 64MB memory devices. For example, the 430VX only supports the following memory devices:

■ 512K×32-bit (2MB)

■ 1M×32-bit (4MB)

■ 2M×32-bit (8MB)

■ 4M×32-bit (16MB)

The layout for a 64MB SIMM is 16M×32-bit, which isn't in the list just shown. When you install two 64MB SIMMs, the system will use the 4M×32-bit specification to calculate the memory, thus displaying 32MB. Unfortunately, this is a limitation of the motherboard and cannot be corrected without upgrading the motherboard (or using smaller memory modules).

SYMPTOM 28-31   A Creative Labs PnP sound board refuses to work on one motherboard, but the board works just fine on another motherboard This is an issue where the PnP BIOS is usually at fault. Check with the motherboard manufacturer to see if there is a BIOS update to correct PnP problems. If not, you may need to disable the sound card's PnP compatibility and configure the card manually (as a legacy device). If that's not possible, you may need to select another sound card for the system.

SYMPTOM 28-32   The system CD-ROM drive refuses to work once an IDE bus master driver is installed This is almost always caused by a driver that is not interacting properly with the IDE/EIDE bus controller on the motherboard. In almost all cases, you should contact the motherboard or system manufacturer and update the IDE bus master driver(s), or disable bus mastering completely under Windows 98/Me.

SYMPTOM 28-33   You cannot get an AMD 5x86 133-MHz CPU to run on your motherboard This is a symptom found when upgrading older 486-vintage motherboards. Check your voltage first. The AMD 5x86 runs on 3.3V, so you may need a voltage regulator in the CPU socket. (The AMD CPU may already be damaged.) Also check your BIOS version. You may need an updated BIOS to support the AMD CPU properly. Check your jumper settings next. The speed or CPU type selection is almost always set wrong. If you cannot jumper the motherboard correctly (such as 33-MHz bus speed), then the motherboard itself is limited. It cannot enable the 4x internal CPU clock for the AMD 5x86. In this case, you will need to use a different CPU or replace the motherboard outright.

SYMPTOM 28-34   You cannot get a Cyrix 5x86 CPU to run on your motherboard Check your voltage first. The Cyrix 5x86 uses 3.3V, so you may need a voltage regulator in the CPU socket (the Cyrix CPU may already be damaged). Also check your BIOS version. You may need an updated BIOS to support the Cyrix CPU properly. Check your jumper settings next. The speed (33 MHz) or CPU type selection is almost always set wrong. If problems persist, you may need a different CPU or motherboard.

SYMPTOM 28-35   You see the error message "System Resource Conflict" on the AMI BIOS POST display This is an error generated by AMI PnP BIOS (though other PnP BIOS may produce similar errors) and is generated when the BIOS detects a resource conflict during initialization. You may try to force the BIOS to reconfigure the conflicting resource by pressing INSERT during POST. If problems continue, you may need a BIOS update, which may be able to resolve assignment conflicts more intelligently. Otherwise, you may need to try reconfigure the conflicting resource manually (disabling its PnP support) or remove the offending device entirely.

SYMPTOM 28-36 **The system hangs after using MEMMAKER under DOS** This is most prevalent with AMI's WinBIOS that cannot support the "highscan" option used with EMM386.EXE. Make sure to disable the highscan option from EMM386 before running MEMMAKER. You may also choose to upgrade the system BIOS to a more recent version that may be more robust when testing memory. As an alternative, discontinue the use of DOS in favor of Windows 98/Me.

SYMPTOM 28-37 **Your Power Management icon does not appear in the Windows 9x/Me Control Panel** This occurs even though the APM parameter under the BIOS Power Management Setup is enabled. This problem occurs if you do not enable the APM function before you install Windows 9x/Me. If you have already installed Windows 9x/Me, you should reinstall it. Before doing so, however, make sure that the APM function is enabled.

SYMPTOM 28-38 **Systems with a Western Digital 1.6GB HDD fail to boot even though BIOS recognizes the presence of HDD** This is a typical problem with large hard drives that often need additional time to start up after powering the system. Check the Advanced Setup menu of your CMOS Setup, and increase the Power-on Delay time. This should correct the problem. This problem may reoccur if CMOS default values are reloaded or CMOS contents are lost.

SYMPTOM 28-39 **After installing Windows 95, the system can no longer find the CD-ROM drive on the secondary IDE channel** You may also find that the IDE drives are running in DOS compatibility mode. This problem occurs often with motherboards using the Intel 430HX chipset. For example, Windows 95 doesn't recognize the Intel 82371SB drive controller on the motherboard, and this causes BIOS to disable the secondary IDE channel. Devices on the secondary channel are not being detected after the system is rebooted. In most cases, you can upgrade the BIOS to correct this problem or move the IDE devices to a separate IDE controller. You may also be able to download a patch to update the MSHDC.INF file, which will force Windows 95 to recognize the 82371SB controller. As an alternative, you can upgrade to Windows 98/Me, which should overcome this trouble.

SYMPTOM 28-40 **The system hangs up or crashes when the chipset-specific PCI-IDE DOS driver is loaded** This is a known problem with Micro-Star motherboards using a VIA VP1 chipset and Award BIOS 4.50PG. The problem is with the BIOS version and its interaction with the PCI controller portion of the VIA chipset. Upgrading the BIOS version should resolve the problem. Otherwise, it may be necessary to upgrade the motherboard.

SYMPTOM 28-41 **You notice that your Pentium motherboard is unusually picky about which SIMMs it will accept** This occurs even though the SIMMs are all within the proper type and rating. There are several possible problems to consider. First, Intel chipsets are very discriminating when it comes to memory speed, so make sure that the memory speed is well within the required range (usually 70nS or faster). Second, try changing the Wait States in the CMOS Setup to a lower speed (such as 4-4-4-4). If your system works under this low speed, then increase the speed (such as 3-3-3-3, 3-2-2-2, 3-1-1-1, and so on), and keep trying till the best number has been reached. Finally, the memory itself may be of questionable quality. Try good-quality memory bought from a reputable vendor. Make sure the vendor offers a liberal return policy so that you can return questionable memory easily.

SYMPTOM 28-42 **You experience a problem with pipeline burst cache** This is a recognized problem with UMC pipeline burst cache (especially on an Amptron motherboard). The problem can usually be solved by adjusting the cache control to 4-4-4-4. (The default in CMOS is typically 2-3-3-3.) This will reduce performance, but should stabilize cache operations.

SYMPTOM 28-43 **You get no display, or the system refuses to boot because of the keyboard controller** Note that the video adapter proves out fine in another system. This is a problem with the VIA 82C41 24-pin keyboard controller (especially on the Amptron PM-7600 motherboard). A fault with the KBC may cause a "no display" or "fail to boot" condition. The VIA 82C41 is extremely sensitive to damage from power supply surges/spikes and ESD damage. Replace the KBC, or replace the motherboard with a more robust model.

SYMPTOM 28-44 **Your customers forget their BIOS password** The PC password is stored in the CMOS RAM located in either the motherboard chipset or the *real-time clock* (RTC) chip. If it is stored in the chipset, the CMOS memory is backed up by a coin-shaped lithium battery (or other battery). If it is stored in the RTC chip, it has an internal battery to back up the CMOS RAM. For the external battery, first make a complete backup of the CMOS settings. Turn off the system, and then remove the battery for at least two hours. This should clear the CMOS setting and erase the password. For the RTC battery, determine which RTC chip you have. There are five different kinds of real-time clock CMOS chips:

- Dallas DS 12887 Real Time
- Benchmarc
- Dallas DS 12B887
- Dallas DS 12887A
- BQ3287A

For the Dallas DS 12887 and Benchmarc RTC chips, if you can boot to the A: prompt, flash the BIOS chip with the same boot block record but different BIOS revision. For example, if you have a P/I P55TP4XE motherboard with BIOS revision 0202, flash the BIOS chip to BIOS revision 0115. A BIOS checksum error will be generated. Enter the CMOS Setup screen, reload setup defaults, and then save and exit. At this point, the password has been cleared. You can flash the BIOS back to the original revision. If you can't boot to the A: prompt, turn off the system, remove the BIOS chip, and insert another with the same boot block record but different BIOS revision. Power-on the system. A BIOS checksum error will be generated. Turn off the system. Reinstall the original BIOS. Power-on the system again, and press DEL to enter the BIOS setup screen. Reload the setup defaults, and then save and exit.

For the Dallas DS 12887A, there is a jumper on the motherboard that clears the CMOS. Please check your manual for the location of this jumper, which will vary among motherboards. Shorting this jumper should erase the system configuration information (including password) stored in the CMOS. To clear the CMOS, make sure the system is off. Short the jumper for a moment and then remove it. *Do not leave this jumper shorted.* After clearing the CMOS, the password should be erased. For the BQ3287A and Dallas DS12B887 RTC chips, short the same jumper as in the previous section, but make sure to power the system on and off *before* removing the jumper.

SYMPTOM 28-45 **You encounter problems with Western Digital hard drives (the drives work on other systems)** This type of problem has been identified with ASUS motherboards using Award BIOS with older Western Digital (~1.6GB) drives. Note that problems do not appear in newer Western Digital drives. There are several means of addressing the problems. First, disable the Quick Power-on Self Test in your CMOS Setup, and enable the Floppy Seek option. This will increase the time that the drive gets to spin up. If your CMOS offers a Power-on Delay Time instead, try increasing that time. Also avoid using Disk Defragmenter, or the disk surface scan feature of ScanDisk with these older Western Digital drives. Both have been reported to increase the number of bad blocks on the disk.

Next, consider a BIOS upgrade (especially if you're using a motherboard with the Intel 430FX chipset). Some BIOS versions use a "park head" command that can cause problems with Western Digital hard drives. Finally, check the Western Digital Web site (**www.wdc.com**) for any drive firmware patches that might be currently available. If all else fails, you might replace the drive outright or upgrade the drive controller.

SYMPTOM 28-46   **You encounter memory parity errors at boot-up**   If you're using nonparity memory devices (such as a 32-bit device instead of a 36-bit device), you will need to disable DRAM ECC or parity checking through the CMOS Chipset Features settings. This problem can occur if you reload default CMOS settings, which restores parity/ECC on a system with nonparity memory. Also keep in mind that the Triton chipset does not support parity, so even if you use parity RAM, you should try disabling parity checking. If the system is configured properly, you may actually have a memory failure, and you'll need to isolate the memory fault.

SYMPTOM 28-47   **You flash a BIOS, but now you get no video**   When you flash a BIOS, the old CMOS settings are usually left useless. This means you'll have to restore the proper CMOS settings before the system may run properly. Clear your CMOS RAM and reload the proper settings (or choose the BIOS Defaults for a good system baseline). The BIOS chip itself may also be troublesome. There are some problems when flashing an Intel flash ROM chip. Make sure that there are no warnings or cautions in the system documentation or from the manufacturer's Web site before flashing a particular BIOS chip. Try restoring the original BIOS if possible, or contact the manufacturer for a replacement BIOS.

SYMPTOM 28-48   **You are trying to use a PnP sound card and PnP modem together on the same system, but you get hardware conflicts**   This is an all-too-common problem with PnP systems. In general, the modem should take COM2 (2F8h and IRQ3), and the sound card should take 220h, IRQ5, and DMA 1. Try adding the cards one at a time. For example, install the sound card first, and let Windows 9x/Me detect it. Add the modem next. If problems persist, configure one or both cards manually (that is, disable their PnP support) if possible, or try alternative cards.

SYMPTOM 28-49   **After the DRAM speed is set to 70nS in the Advanced Chipset Setup, the system crashes or refuses to boot**   Chances are that you have the incorrect number of wait-states set for your memory configuration; 70nS RAM typically requires at least one wait-state. Disable any Auto Configure DRAM Timing feature, and then set the number of wait-states to 1. That should clear up the problem.

SYMPTOM 28-50   **There is 32MB (or more) of memory, and the BIOS counts it all during POST, but you only see 16MB in the CMOS Setup screen**   This is a problem that has been identified with some Award BIOS versions. To correct the problem, make sure that the "memory hole" option in the Advanced Chipset Setup area is disabled. The memory hole option assumes a maximum of 16MB of physical RAM in the system. You may also try disabling the system's shadow RAM or BIOS shadow option.

SYMPTOM 28-51   **You move a working IDE drive from an older 386/486 system to your new Pentium (or later) system, but the system no longer works**   In most cases, the data transfer mode is set improperly for the old IDE hard drive (for example, using LBA mode when the IDE drive requires CHS mode). Find the Peripheral Setup screen in your CMOS Setup, and make sure to change all the PIO mode settings to Mode 0. (Chances are the settings are currently at Automatic and are configuring the data transfer incorrectly.) The idea is to ensure that the drive is configured exactly the same way as it was on its original system. If you cannot duplicate the original BIOS configuration, get the settings as close as you can, and then repartition and reformat the drive in order to use it on a different (older) controller.

SYMPTOM 28-52 **Windows 95 locks up when you install a Diamond Stealth Video 3200 board and an Intel EtherExpress Pro 10/100 network card** However, you verify that both cards work fine on other systems. Problems begin when you load the Intel network driver. This is a problem that has been identified with Premio motherboards and is due to a problem in the system BIOS. Upgrade the Premio BIOS to the latest version, or upgrade the entire motherboard.

SYMPTOM 28-53 **You install a Pentium P55C (MMX) 200-MHz CPU and set the CPU speed jumper(s) for 200 MHz, but the system still reports 166 MHz** In virtually all cases, you have set the speed jumper(s) incorrectly. Take another look at the documentation for your motherboard, and see that the speed is indeed set correctly. (Double-check possible documentation errors with the motherboard manufacturer.) If problems persist, the BIOS may not recognize the higher CPU speed correctly, so try upgrading the motherboard BIOS. As an additional check, verify that the CPU is not fake or mismarked.

SYMPTOM 28-54 **The system frequently locks up or crashes after installing a Cyrix 6x86 CPU** In most cases, the Cyrix 6x86 is not being cooled properly and is overheating. Make sure that you have a heat sink/fan assembly attached properly to the Cyrix, and see that the fan is running. Also, the Cyrix 6x86 P166+ is a 3.52V CPU. Check your voltage regulator and see that it is set to provide 3.45 to 3.6 volts.

SYMPTOM 28-55 **After installing a Pentium 120-MHz motherboard, you get registry corruption or "out of memory" errors from Windows 95** This happens most often with slightly older Pentium motherboards (~100–120 MHz), and is almost always a BIOS version problem, which causes the motherboard to misbehave under Windows 95. You will need to update the BIOS version for your particular motherboard or to upgrade the motherboard entirely.

SYMPTOM 28-56 **The motherboard fails to autodetect the hard drive parameters** This is a known problem on Data Expert EXP8551S motherboards and is due to a problem with Windows 95 in recognizing the PCI/ISA/I/O controller portion of the chipset. You can use the following procedure to force Windows 95 to recognize the chipset properly:

1. Boot up the Windows 95 system normally.
2. Change the directory to /WINDOWS/INF.
3. Edit the hidden file MSHDC.INF.
4. Search for all lines with the "1230" device ID. Copy the lines and replace "1230" with "7010" (the correct device ID).
5. Save the file MSHDC.INF.
6. Remove the Standard IDE/ESDI Hard Disk Controller entry from the Device Manager.

7. Restart the computer, and then choose the Windows default driver following the instructions shown on the screen.

You should make a backup copy of the MSHDC.INF file before editing the file. That way, you can easily restore the original file if necessary.

If the problem persists, try entering the specific hard drive parameters for your particular drive into the CMOS Setup. As an alternative, you may be able to upgrade the motherboard's BIOS or upgrade the motherboard entirely.

SYMPTOM 28-57   **The motherboard refuses to detect the SCSI controller during boot-up**   This problem has been identified with the Data Expert EXP8551 motherboard, but may occur on many different types of PCI motherboards. In most cases, you will have to change the configuration of your PCI slots on the motherboard. For example, if the SCSI controller is installed on Slot 2, you will need to configure the PCI Slot 2 in CMOS Setup.

SYMPTOM 28-58   **You find that you cannot run a Cyrix 6x86 CPU on a particular motherboard**   This is a problem that has been identified on Eurone/Matsonic motherboards and is usually the result of an incompatible motherboard clock generator. Some clock generators support the Cyrix 120-, 133-, and 166-MHz models, but exempt the 200-MHz model. Other clock generators support the 120-, 150-, 166-, and 200-MHz models, but exempt the 133-MHz model. So if you're using a 133-MHz or 200-MHz Cyrix CPU, you may be using the wrong clock generator. You will have to replace the CPU with a speed suitable to the particular clock generator, or change the motherboard to one that will accommodate the particular CPU speed.

SYMPTOM 28-59   **The system can count up to and recognize only 8MB of RAM though the system can accommodate even more**   This is often a problem identified with Freetech 586F61x motherboards using Award BIOS version D or earlier. You can duplicate the problem by initiating a software reset with CTRL-ALT-DEL, then pressing the hardware reset. BIOS will only count memory up to 8MB. You will need to update the Award BIOS to version E or later. Freetech provides the BIOS patch on their Web site. Otherwise, you can upgrade the motherboard entirely.

SYMPTOM 28-60   **When four 8MB SIMMs are installed in the system (32MB), the system only counts up to 24MB**   This is a known problem with Giga-Byte motherboards (typically the GA-586ATE, ATM, and AP ver 1.x). The motherboard does not support double-sided SIMMs (such as 2MB, 8MB, 32MB, or 128MB) in the center bank. Install the SIMMs in bank 0 and bank 2—leaving bank 1 empty.

Some motherboards require the banks to be filled in sequential order or allow you to change the bank order with jumpers.

SYMPTOM 28-61   **Gold-plated modules do not work properly in tin-plated sockets**
As a general rule, you should avoid mixing metal types when choosing memory modules. The metal in the SIMM/DIMM/RIMM socket must be the same as the metal on the module itself. Otherwise, tin debris will transfer to the gold surface and oxidize. This will eventually result in memory failures that suggest faulty memory modules (even though the modules may be fine).

SYMPTOM 28-62   **Even though all peripherals in the system are SCSI, Windows 95 will continue to detect the PCI IDE controller**   You notice that this occurs even though the controller was disabled in the CMOS Setup. This is a known problem with the Iwill P54TS motherboard. Normally, Windows 95 will try to recognize and enable I/O devices, but should not enable devices that are deliberately disabled in CMOS. This is typically a BIOS problem. (The onboard IDE controllers were not properly disabled.) Try upgrading your BIOS to the latest version, or upgrade the motherboard outright.

SYMPTOM 28-63   **You get an "EISA CMOS Configuration Error" when the system starts up**   For EISA systems, you must run the *EISA configuration utility* (ECU) in order to properly set up the system. Without this step, the system will not be able to detect any possible resource conflicts. This type of problem is most common when installing a new EISA motherboard, when CMOS contents are lost, or when devices (such as memory) are added or removed.

SYMPTOM 28-64   **The SMP (dual processor) mode refuses to run in Windows NT**   The most common problem is an incompatibility with the SMP HAL shipped with Windows NT (versions prior to 3.51) and the motherboard's chipset. If you are upgrading from an older version of NT (prior to 3.51), first install NT as a standard PC (single processor kernel), and then install NT with the default multiprocessor kernel it provides. (NT will not recognize your dual CPUs if you upgrade straight to a multiprocessor configuration.)

SYMPTOM 28-65   **When attempting to upgrade your flash BIOS, you encounter an "insufficient memory" error**   In most cases, you simply don't have enough conventional memory available to execute the flash program. Most flash programs require about 560KB of conventional RAM. Try booting clean with a DOS floppy disk (without any CONFIG.SYS or AUTOEXEC.BAT files), and then run the flash upgrade utility.

SYMPTOM 28-66   **You see a prolonged system message saying "Updating ESCD" each time the system boots**   The *extended system configuration data* (ESCD) area is part of a PnP system, and those contents are stored in an area of the CMOS RAM. One or more PnP devices are attempting to update your BIOS settings. To stop this from occurring, set the BIOS to program mode. This message is perfectly normal when the system's hardware configuration changes, but should not occur repeatedly.

SYMPTOM 28-67   **You notice a yellow exclamation over your USB port in the Device Manager**   Windows 9x/Me indicates that it has detected an unknown PCI device (though this problem is far more common with older versions of Windows without full USB support). In virtually all cases, the proper driver for the USB on your system has not been installed, and Windows 9x/Me cannot recognize the USB hardware. You can usually correct this problem by updating your system BIOS to a newer version that supports the USB hardware better under Windows. In some cases, you may also need to upgrade Windows to a more robust version such as Windows 98/Me.

SYMPTOM 28-68   **The Device Manager under Windows 95 indicates four COM ports (at unusual IRQs and I/O addresses), but there are only two physical ports on the motherboard**   This problem has been identified with the Ocean Rhino motherboard while running a very old Award BIOS. The Award BIOS has since been upgraded to provide full support for Windows 9x/Me, so download the newest BIOS version from the motherboard manufacturer, or upgrade the motherboard outright.

SYMPTOM 28-69   The performance of a motherboard with an AMD K5 CPU seems extremely poor   This is almost always because of the motherboard BIOS. Chances are the BIOS was released before the AMD K5 was widely introduced, so there may be problems providing proper AMD support. Make sure that you are using the very latest BIOS, which supplies adequate AMD support, or upgrade the motherboard outright.

SYMPTOM 28-70   The system hangs after installing a Cyrix 6x86 CPU   There is probably a problem with the utilization of system cache, which is causing the system to hang. Try disabling the internal (L1) and external (L2) cache through the CMOS Setup. Upgrade the BIOS to provide better 6x86 support, or upgrade the motherboard outright.

SYMPTOM 28-71   When attempting to upgrade the BIOS version, you cannot use a key sequence such as CTRL-HOME to reboot the PC in order to start the flash process   The current BIOS version does not support such key sequences. To flash the BIOS, start the flash program manually from the DOS prompt. For example:

```
A:\> AMIFL PAIV17.ROM    <Enter>
```

SYMPTOM 28-72   You find that a particular SVGA board refuses to work on a particular motherboard   However, the video board proves out fine on other systems. In most cases, this is a compatibility problem between the video chipset and the motherboard. There may be a BIOS upgrade for the motherboard or video board that can overcome the problem. You may simply have to use a different video board.

SYMPTOM 28-73   When the onboard printer port is set to 3BCh (and EPP/SPP mode) and another parallel port add-on card is set to 378h or 278h, the BIOS only recognizes the add-on card   Port 3BCh seems to disappear. This may be a configuration problem with the Winbond chipset, which specifies that LPT1 on the motherboard should be set at 378h (EPP or SPP), while add-on parallel ports should be set at 278h or 3BCh. The Winbond chip was designed this way for Windows 95. Check with the motherboard manufacturer for any available BIOS upgrades that can correct this issue.

SYMPTOM 28-74   With 32MB of RAM on the motherboard, Checkit 3.0 causes the system to reboot when performing DRAM tests   This is because Checkit 3.0 will not perform memory testing over 16MB. This is an issue with Checkit—not the motherboard. Upgrade to a later version of Checkit, or switch to an alternate system diagnostic utility.

SYMPTOM 28-75   The IBM Blue Lighting CPU will not run on a motherboard that should support it   In most cases, the problem is an older BIOS version. Make sure that you are running the latest version of BIOS before installing the IBM Blue Lightning (basically a Cyrix processor). Also check to make sure that any CPU type and speed jumpers are set properly for the CPU.

SYMPTOM 28-76   When using a benchmark program such as SYSINFO, the overall performance rating of a Pentium 100 system marks better than a Pentium 120 system   This is because of the PCI bus speed. For a 100-MHz system, the PCI bus speed is 33 MHz. For a 120-MHz system, the bus speed is 30 MHz because of the way bus speed is divided. The slightly faster PCI system will register a bit better system performance.

Always make sure that your benchmark and diagnostic programs are updated for the CPUs and other hardware that you are testing.

SYMPTOM 28-77   **You cannot get parallel port devices to work on your motherboard** In most cases, you must set the proper parallel port mode (such as SPP/ECP/EPP) for the particular device you plan to use. Often, setting the port to Compatibility Mode will work for many common peripherals, but not for more advanced printers or interactive devices. Parallel port modes are selected through the CMOS Setup—usually under Integrated Peripherals or some similar heading.

SYMPTOM 28-78   **You notice that some configurations of memory provide less performance than others** This type of problem is most noted on motherboards with 440FX chipsets and is usually the result of a BIOS problem. Try updating your BIOS to the latest available version, or upgrade the motherboard entirely.

SYMPTOM 28-79   **You see no performance improvement when enabling PCI/IDE bus mastering** The problem often is that you are using an older (or buggy) driver. Make sure that you have installed the most recent bus mastering driver file for your particular motherboard. (For example, Triton I, Triton II, and Natoma chipsets may use the same driver.)

SYMPTOM 28-80   **The BIOS banner displayed on power-on is showing the wrong motherboard model** In virtually all cases, this is a problem with the BIOS version where it cannot identify the correct hardware platform. Get the latest update for your motherboard BIOS.

SYMPTOM 28-81   **The Pentium P55CM BIOS shows a 150-MHz CPU even though the CPU is a 166-MHz model** This is almost always due to a BIOS fault. You should upgrade to the very latest BIOS version for your particular motherboard. If you cannot flash the BIOS, replace the BIOS chip outright.

SYMPTOM 28-82   **You see a "Static Device Resource Conflict" error message after the system memory count when using the P55CM CPU** This is usually a problem with the PCI bus system. Press and hold the INSERT key before turning on the computer. Release the INSERT key when the video comes up. This forces the system to reassign PCI resources. If the error message still appears, remove all PCI cards (except for the video card) and try again. Reinsert one PCI card at a time until the problem returns—that is where the problem is.

SYMPTOM 28-83   **The motherboard is installed, but the system won't boot** This is a classic sign of installation problems (especially after an upgrade). Start with the basics. Check all of the cables and connectors—especially the power connectors. Also make sure that there are no metal standoffs or brackets shorting the motherboard from underneath. Next, check for any wiring or cables that may be installed backward. While this will rarely keep a PC from booting, it is possible. Be sure that pin 1 on each cable aligns with pin 1 of each connector. Finally, double-check the socket-mounted chip such as the CPU, BIOS ROM(s), and memory modules. They should all be aligned properly and inserted evenly and completely. If you locate an incorrectly installed chip, it may or may not be damaged. Remove it from the motherboard, check it for bent or broken pins, reinsert it correctly, and try the motherboard again. If the chip is damaged, it should be replaced.

SYMPTOM 28-84 **The motherboard starts, but it will not boot from the hard drive or recognize the correct amount of RAM in the system** You may see an error message such as "CMOS Error; press F1 to run SETUP." This error generally indicates that the motherboard is working, but the system CMOS contains incorrect information. Either you forgot to enter the new CMOS variables, you forgot to save the settings when you updated them, or the backup battery is not installed and CMOS contents were lost after the system was powered-down. Check the backup battery first. If the battery is a coin cell, see that it is inserted properly and completely into its holder. If the battery is a "pack type," check to see that it is plugged into the proper motherboard connector in the right polarity. If the battery is installed correctly, try a new one. Run the CMOS Setup utility, and check each drive and memory setting. If you entered a drive parameter or RAM amount improperly, correct the settings and save CMOS again. Reboot the PC. If new CMOS settings are lost after the PC is powered-down, the backup battery has failed—try a new battery.

SYMPTOM 28-85 **The system boots and runs, but it locks up unpredictably** This is another issue that crops up frequently after a motherboard upgrade or replacement. Make sure that the CPU and all system RAM are installed correctly and securely. Try reseating the RAM. Check the system CPU for excessive heat. An overheated CPU can lock up without warning. If the CPU is fitted with a heat sink, make sure that the heat sink is securely attached and that you have used ample amounts of thermal compound to aid heat transfer. If the CPU runs hot and there is no heat sink, try adding one.

Also consider the possibility of controller conflicts. For example, if there is a video port on the new motherboard, but you also have a video board installed in an expansion slot, you will have to set jumpers to disable the motherboard's video port. The same thing is true for drive controller conflicts, as well as serial or parallel port conflicts. Take another close look at the expansion boards in your system, and make sure that the board functions do not conflict with the functions provided on the motherboard.

SYMPTOM 28-86 **You cannot get SSE2 features to work with the Pentium 4 processor** This is almost always because you're using an older version of DirectX. While DirectX 7.0a will work fine with the Pentium 4, it does not support SSE2. Upgrade to DirectX 8.0a or later from Microsoft (**www.microsoft.com/directx**).

SYMPTOM 28-87 **The system won't power-on** If you find that your system cannot power-on on its own—requiring you to unplug and replug the power each time—clear the CMOS jumper to remove any garbage CMOS data, and reset the BIOS settings to their defaults. First, turn off the system. Then move the CMOS jumper from its default location to the Clear position for several seconds before moving it back. (Or power-on the system briefly before powering-down and moving the jumper back.) Turn on the system and press DEL to enter the CMOS Setup screen. Set the correct CPU speed, and then save and exit the setup screen.

Further Study

Abit Computer Corp. www.abit.com.tw
Acer America Corp. www.acer.com
American Megatrends (AMI) www.megatrends.com
ASUS www.asus.com
Biostar Microtech Intl. www.biostar.net

CompuTrend Systems, Inc. (Premio)   www.premiopc.com

Data Expert Corp.   www.dataexpert.com

Diamond Flower, Inc. (DFI)   www.dfiusa.com

Elitegroup Computers, Ltd. (ECS)   www.ecs.com.tw

Famous Technology Co., Ltd.   www1.magic-pro.com.hk/famous/index.html

First International Computer, Inc. (FIC)   www.fica.com

Fong Kai Industrial Co. (FKI)   www.fkusa.com

Gemlight Computer Ltd.   www.gemlight.com.hk

Genoa Systems Corp.   www.genoasys.com

Giga-Byte Technology Co., Ltd.   www.giga-byte.com

Intel Corp.   www.intel.com

Iwill Computer   www.iwill.com.tw

Jbond   www.jbond.com

J-Mark Computer Corp.   www.j-mark.com

Micronics Computers, Inc.   www.micronics.com

Microway   www.microway.com

Micro Star International Co., Ltd. (MSI)   www.msi.com.tw

PC Chips Manufacturing Ltd.   www.pcchips.com

Pine Technology Ltd.   www.pinegroup.com

Shuttle Computer International   www.shuttlegroup.com

Soyo Computer Inc.   www.soyo.com.tw

Supermicro Computer Inc.   www.supermicro.com

Tekram Technology   www.tekram.com

Tyan Computer   www.tyan.com

29

PARALLEL PORT
TROUBLESHOOTING

Even after more than two decades of intense computer development, the *parallel port* (also called the *LPT port*, *Centronics port*, or *printer port*) remains one of the most versatile and reliable printer connection techniques in the computer industry. By sending an entire byte of data from computer to printer port simultaneously, and managing the flow of data with discrete handshaking signals, the circuitry required to bundle and decode data and control signals (such as that needed by serial ports) is virtually eliminated. The longevity of parallel ports has been due largely to the their simplicity and good overall performance, but today's parallel ports are not invulnerable to failure. Cable problems, static discharge damage, and spontaneous hardware faults can easily disable printer communication. Additional parallel port problems can arise from the new generation of high-performance printers and other parallel port devices, and from port sharing. This chapter explains the pin assignment and operation of conventional parallel ports, explains the advances that have taken place, and presents a series of troubleshooting procedures intended to help you isolate and correct port problems.

Understanding the Parallel Port

The parallel port interface is one of the simplest and most straightforward circuits that you will encounter in a PC. Figure 29-1 illustrates a typical bidirectional port. A parallel port is composed of three separate registers: the data register, the status register, and the control register. Address bits A0 to A9 are decoded

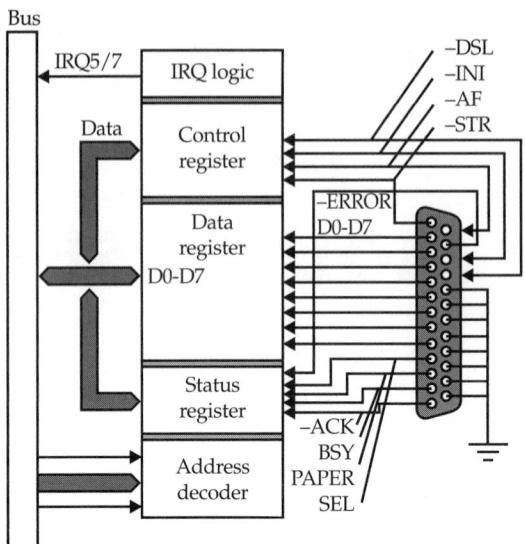

FIGURE 29-1   Block diagram of a basic bidirectional parallel port

to determine which of the three registers is active. The use of -I/OR (-I/O Read) and -I/OW (-I/O Write) lines determine whether signals on the data bus (D0 to D7) are being read from or written to the respective register. When the port is ready to accept another character, handshaking line conditions will trigger an interrupt to request a new character.

The heart of a parallel port is the *data register*. In older PCs, the data register could only be written to (which renders the port unidirectional). But virtually all PCs since the release of 386 systems provide data registers that can be read and written (which makes the port bidirectional). To access a printer, the system CPU simply loads the port data register with the value to be passed. The bidirectional *control register* manages the behavior of the port and sets the conditions under which new characters are requested from the CPU. For example, the control register is typically set up to generate an interrupt whenever the printer is ready to accept another character (for example, IRQ7 for LPT1, and IRQ5 for LPT2). Finally, the *status register* is read to determine the printer's status (extracted from the logic conditions of several printer handshaking lines). All that remains is the port connector itself, which is a female 25-pin subminiature D-type connector.

ADDRESSES AND INTERRUPTS

As previously mentioned, the conventional parallel port in a PC is implemented through a series of three registers. One register simply buffers the 8 data bits, while the other two registers handle the port's handshaking lines. Whereas older BIOS versions supported only two or three parallel ports, today's PCs use BIOS written to support up to four complete parallel ports designated LPT1, LPT2, LPT3, and LPT4. The base addresses allocated for each port are 0378h (LPT1), 0278h (LPT2), 03BCh (LPT3), and 02BCh (LPT4). The base address of each port corresponds to the data register. The status register of a respective port is accessed from the base address with an offset of 01h (that is, 0379h, 0279h, 03BDh, and 02BDh), and the control register is accessed with an offset of 02h (that is, 037Ah, 027Ah, 03BEh, and 02BEh).

Although a typical PC can theoretically support four LPT ports, it is extremely rare for a PC to offer more than two ports. Even then, the IRQ for LPT2 (IRQ5) often conflicts with the IRQ assigned to sound functions.

During initialization, ports are checked in the following order: 03BCh, 0378h, 0278h, and 02BCh. LPT designations are assigned depending on what ports are found, so keep in mind that LPT addresses may be exchanged in a manner depending on your particular system. The specific I/O addresses for each port are kept in the BIOS data area of RAM starting at 0408h. As you might expect, only one LPT port can be assigned to a base address. If more than one parallel port is assigned to the same address, system problems will almost certainly occur.

The use of interrupts gets a bit complicated. There are basically two modes of requesting new characters for the printer: polling and interrupt-driven. *Polling,* the most popular method, occurs when the BIOS polls (or checks) the respective port's status register to see if it is ready to accept another character—no interrupts are generated. An *interrupt-driven* interface is much more efficient, but can bog down other important operations during printing.

For technicians who work on older machines, keep in mind that address 03BCh was originally reserved for a parallel port located on the IBM Monochrome Display Adapter (MDA). If you are servicing an older system with *no* video support on the motherboard, the address 03BCh may be reserved in the event that you, for some reason, want to install an IBM MDA card. For newer systems with video support located on the motherboard, address 03BCh is usually the first parallel port address.

Always begin your service examination by checking the number of parallel ports in your system. Adding parallel ports to various expansion cards is so easy that you can exceed the limit of four parallel ports without even knowing it. If more than four ports are active, a hardware conflict can result and crash the system—you will have to remove or disable the extra ports.

PARALLEL PORT SIGNALS

IBM and compatible PCs implement a parallel port as a 25-pin subminiature D-type female connector similar to the one shown in Figure 29-2. The parallel connection at the printer uses a 36-pin Centronics-type connector (Amphenol type 57-30360). The exact reasoning for this rather specialized connector is not clear, since 11 pins of the Centronics connector will remain unused. There are three types of signals to be concerned with in parallel connections: data lines, control (or *handshaking*) lines, and ground lines. Table 29-1 identifies the name and description of each pin. The following section describes each signal. The pin numbers at both the PC and printer ends are listed for your reference. Also remember that all signals on the parallel port are compatible with conventional TTL (5-volt logic) signal levels.

Data lines

The *data lines* are the actual data-carrying conductors that carry information from the parallel port to or from the printer or other peripheral. There are eight data lines (D0 to D7), located on pins 2 through 9. To reduce the effects of signal noise on parallel cables, each data line is given a corresponding *data ground* line (pins 20 to 27). Ground lines also provide a common electrical reference between the computer and peripheral. The remainder of a parallel port is devoted to handshaking.

Initialize and Select

To ensure that the printer starts in a known initialized state, an -Initialize signal (-INI on pin 16) sent from the computer is used to reset a printer to the state it powered up in. Initializing the peripheral has the same effect as turning it off and then turning it on again. The -Initialize line is active-low, so the printer must

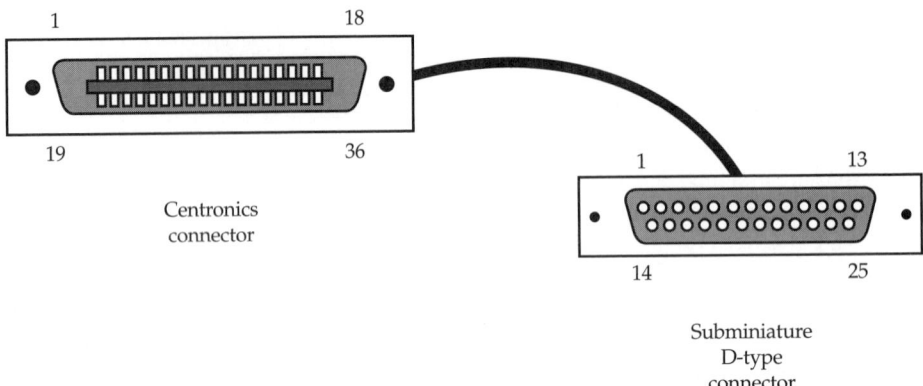

FIGURE 29-2 A typical parallel (printer) port cable assembly

apply a logic 0 to trigger an initialization. The Select line (SEL on pin 13) tells the waiting computer that the peripheral is online and ready to receive data. Select is an active-high logic signal, so a logic 1 indicates that a device is online and ready, while a logic 0 indicates that the printer is not ready to receive data.

TABLE 29-1   PIN ASSIGNMENTS FOR A PARALLEL PORT INTERFACE

SIGNAL NAME	LABEL	SIGNAL PIN			GROUND PIN		
		D-sub IEEE 1284A	Centronics IEEE 1284B	IEEE 1284C	D-sub IEEE 1284A	Centronics IEEE 1284B	IEEE 1284C
Data bit 0	D0	2	2	6	19	20	24
Data bit 1	D1	3	3	7	19	21	25
Data bit 2	D2	4	4	8	20	22	26
Data bit 3	D3	5	5	9	20	23	27
Data bit 4	D4	6	6	10	21	24	28
Data bit 5	D5	7	7	11	21	25	29
Data bit 6	D6	8	8	12	22	26	30
Data bit 7	D7	9	9	13	22	27	31
Error (Fault)	S3	15	32	4	23	29	22
Select	S4	13	13	2	24	28	20
PaperEnd	S5	12	12	5	24	28	23
Acknowledge	S6	10	10	3	24	28	21
Busy	S7	11	11	1	23	29	19
Strobe	-C0	1	1	15	18	19	33
AutoLF	-C1	14	14	17	25	30	35
Init	C2	16	31	14	25	30	32
SelectIn	-C3	17	36	16	25	30	34
HostLogic High				18			18
PeriphLogic High			36				36

The computer will not send data when the select line is logic 0. You can usually determine the Select line's general condition from the printer's front panel "online" light.

Strobe, Busy, and Acknowledge

Once a computer has placed 8 valid bits on the parallel data lines, the peripheral must be told that the data is ready. A -Strobe signal (-STR on pin 1) is applied to the peripheral from the computer just after data is valid. The brief -Strobe signal causes the peripheral to accept the byte and store it in the printer's internal buffer for processing.

Under ideal circumstances, parallel printer ports can achieve data rates of up to 500,000 characters per second. With such a tremendous throughput, the printer needs some method of coordinating data transfer—the computer must wait between characters until the printer is ready to resume accepting new characters. Printers use the Busy signal (BSY on pin 11) to delay the computer until the printer is ready. Peripherals drive the Busy line to logic 1 any time a -Strobe signal is received. The Busy signal remains logic 1 for as long as it takes the peripheral to prepare for the next byte. It is important to note that a Busy signal can delay the computer indefinitely if a serious peripheral error has occurred (for example, paper exhausted or ribbon jammed).

When the peripheral has received a byte and dealt with it, the peripheral must then request another character from the waiting computer. The printer drops the Busy line and initiates a brief -Acknowledge pulse (-ACK on pin 10). -Acknowledge signals are always active-low logic signals, and a typical acknowledge pulse lasts about 8μS. It is this interaction of data, -Strobe, Busy, and -Acknowledge signals, that handles the bulk of data transfer in a parallel port.

Auto Feed

Some printers make the assumption that a carriage return signal (or CR) will automatically advance the paper to the next line, while other printers simply return the carriage to the beginning of the existing line without advancing the paper. Many printers make this feature selectable through the use of a DIP switch in the printer, but an -Auto Feed signal (-AF on pin 14) from the computer can control that feature. A TTL logic 0 from the computer causes the printer to feed one line of paper automatically when a carriage return command is detected. A TTL logic 1 from the computer allows only a carriage return (paper would have to be fed manually). Most computer parallel ports keep this line at logic 0.

Device Select

The -Device Select line (-DSL on pin 17) allows the computer to bring the peripheral online and offline remotely. Many parallel ports leave this signal as a logic 0 so that peripherals will automatically accept data. A logic 1 on this line would inhibit printer operation.

Error

The -Error signal (-ERROR on pin 15) generated by a printer (or other peripheral) tells the computer that trouble has occurred, but is not specific about the exact problem. A variety of problems can cause an error—it depends on your particular peripheral and what it is capable of detecting. The error line uses active-low logic, so it is normally logic 1 until an error has occurred. An -Error signal can typically indicate an "Out of Paper," "Printer Offline," or "General Printer Fault" error condition.

PORT OPERATION

This part of the chapter describes a standard sequence of events in a basic parallel port. The parallel data transfer begins by placing the printer online. -Strobe and -Acknowledge must be TTL logic 1, while Busy must be logic 0. In this state, the peripheral can now accept a byte of data. When printing is attempted, the CPU polls the desired LPT port and checks its status register. If the post is ready, a byte is written to the data register and passed to the peripheral.

Data must be valid for at least 0.5μS *before* the computer initiates a logic 0 -Strobe. The printer responds by returning a logic 1 Busy signal, which changes the port's status. Subsequent polling of the status register will indicate that the port is unavailable. The -Strobe pulse must last at least 1.0μS. Data must be held valid at least 0.5μS *after* the -Strobe pulse passes. This timing ensures that the peripheral has enough time to receive the data. Since Busy is now logic 1, communication stops until the data byte has been processed. Processing can take 1mS if the printer's buffer is not full. If the printer's buffer is full, communication may be halted for a second or more. After the data byte has been processed, Busy is dropped to logic 0 and the printer sends a 5.0μS logic 0 -Acknowledge pulse to request another data byte from the waiting computer. Once the -Acknowledge line returns to a TTL logic 1 condition, the interface is ready to begin a new transfer. The status register then indicates the port is ready, and when the port is next polled, a new byte can be written. Figure 29-3 illustrates this relationship—one complete cycle can take a bit over 1mS.

ADVANCED PARALLEL PORTS

The appeal of a parallel port is easy to understand—it is *simple*. While serial devices struggle with baud rates, stop bits, and parity (problems that continue to this day), parallel devices just plug into the 25-pin D-type connector, and away you go. The parallel port offered "plug-and-play" convenience long before the term ever came in vogue. Although the parallel port has been a staple of PC communication, it certainly has not gone unchanged over the last 15 years. If you've been shopping for new computers or I/O boards over the last year or two, you've probably noticed the terms Enhanced Parallel Port (EPP) and

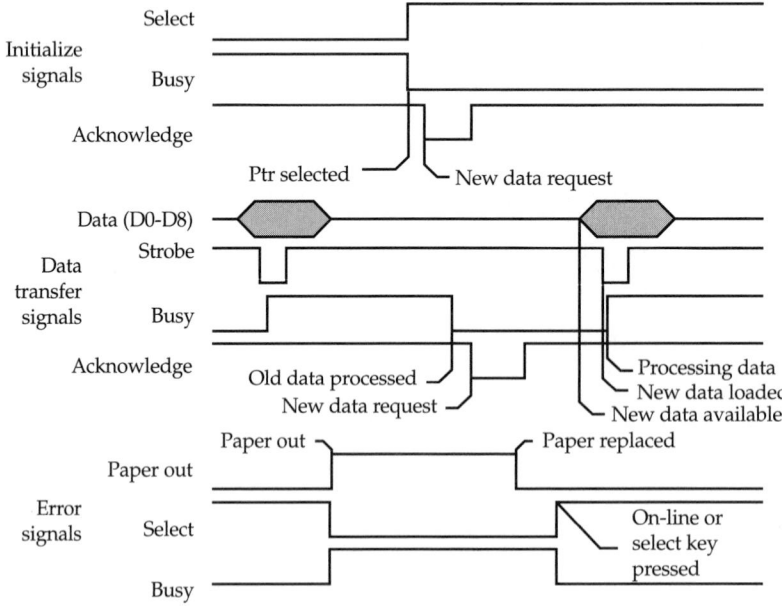

FIGURE 29-3   Typical parallel port timing diagram

Enhanced Capabilities Port (ECP) associated with the parallel port. With the IEEE 1284 parallel port standard developed by the Institute of Electrical and Electronic Engineers (IEEE), the PC industry has finally moved past the "classical" parallel port architecture and embraced a truly improved parallel port. This part of the chapter compares the various parallel port modes.

Unidirectional ports

The original PC utilized a unidirectional parallel port. That is, the port sent data only one way (from the PC to the peripheral device, which was almost always a printer). For the time, unidirectional communication was adequate for general-purpose PCs, and the parallel port became synonymous with "printer port." Unidirectional ports reigned in the PC market until 1987 (around the time of the 386).

"Type 1" bidirectional ports

By 1987, IBM had launched its PS/2 line. Among the other technological advances in the PS/2, IBM incorporated a bidirectional parallel port. Bidirectional ports were hardly a breakthrough (older hobby-type PCs had used similar ports), but IBM was really the first to use a bidirectional port in a commercial PC. The bidirectional port was really not any faster or better than a unidirectional port, but the ability to send data back to the PC opened up the parallel port to other devices besides printers (for example, parallel port tape drives and so on). Clone PC manufacturers jumped on the improvement, and bidirectional ports became common in almost all subsequent clones.

"Type 3" bidirectional ports

One of the problems with bidirectional parallel ports is that they are CPU-intensive, requiring relatively large amounts of CPU attention in order to manage the transfer of data. Later models of the PS/2 (the 57, 90, and 95) made an attempt to increase the throughput of a parallel port by using Direct Memory Access (DMA) techniques. The DMA approach allows the CPU to define a block of memory (for example, printer ASCII characters) to be sent. A DMA controller takes over control from the CPU and transfers the data without CPU intervention—generally resulting in faster data transfer. This approach also worked when receiving data. In practice, Type 3 bidirectional ports are rarely used because today's high-performance CPUs can transfer data much faster than a DMA process.

IEEE 1284 MODES

By the end of the 1980s, it was becoming clear that conventional bidirectional parallel ports were simply not adequate to handle the new generations of faster peripherals that were appearing for the parallel port (such as CD-ROMs, tape drives, and laser printers). The 150 KB/s parallel transfer rates that were once considered speedy were now severely limiting the performance of new peripherals. In 1991, a group of major PC manufacturers—including IBM, Lexmark, and Texas Instruments—formed the Network Printing Alliance (NPA) in an attempt to develop a new parallel port architecture. In 1994, the IEEE (in conjunction with the NPA) released the Standard Signaling Method for a Bi-Directional Parallel Peripheral Interface, also known as IEEE standard 1284.

The IEEE 1284 does not define a single parallel approach, but instead outlines *five* different operational modes for the parallel port: compatibility mode, nibble mode, byte mode, ECP mode, and EPP mode. All five modes offer some amount of bidirectional capability (known under IEEE 1284 as *back channel communication*). When the 1284-compliant parallel port is initialized, it checks to see which operating mode is most appropriate.

Currently, the only operating systems that have built-in support for IEEE 1284 are Windows 95/98/Me/2000, and Solaris. They have support for IEEE 1284 negotiation (a.k.a. "parallel port plug-and-play") and fast printing in ECP mode. To take advantage of this capability, you must have a printer and a parallel port with ECP capability. In addition, the parallel port must be configured in the Windows Device Manager as an "ECP Printer Port" with an IRQ and DMA channel configured. You can determine your parallel port's configuration in the Device Manager (as shown in Figure 29-4). If you don't have these settings configured (but *do* have an ECP-capable printer), the driver will "fall back" to Fast Centronics mode. If neither of these conditions is met, the driver stays in the old "slow" mode.

Compatibility Mode

This mode defines the basic protocol used by most PCs to transfer data to a simple printer. It's commonly called Centronics mode, and is the method commonly associated with the standard parallel port. In this mode, data is placed on the port's data lines, the printer status is checked for errors and busy conditions, and then a data strobe is generated by the software that clocks the data to the printer. To output one byte of data, this port requires four I/O instructions (and at least as many additional instructions). This type of operation limits the bandwidth capabilities at the port to about 150 KB/s. This bandwidth is sufficient for communicating with dot matrix, ink jet, and many older laser printers, but it's a serious limitation when communicating with LAN adapters, removable disk drives, and the newest generation of laser printers.

Many of the integrated IEEE 1284 I/O controller chips have implemented a mode that uses a FIFO (First In/First Out) buffer to transfer data with the compatibility mode protocol—this mode is referred to as Fast Centronics (or Parallel Port FIFO) mode. When this mode is enabled, data written to the FIFO port will be transferred to the printer using hardware generated strobes for the handshaking. Since there is very little latency between transfers, and the software does not have to do any of the strobing or handshake checking, data rates over 500 KB/s are achievable with some systems. Remember that this mode is *not* an IEEE 1284–defined mode.

 Whenever problems are encountered with the operation of parallel port devices, try setting the parallel port to compatibility mode in the system's CMOS Setup. You may loose data transfer speed, but you should gain compatibility with older devices.

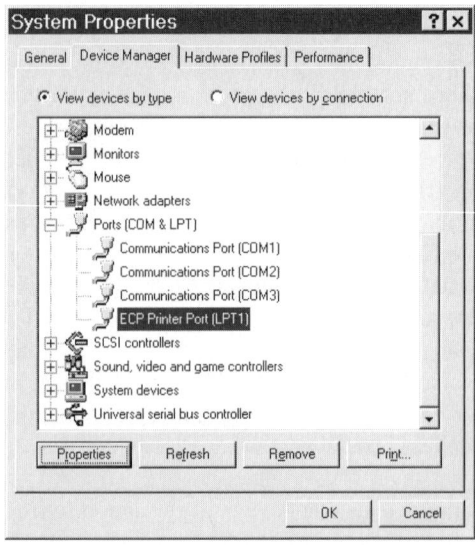

FIGURE 29-4   Checking the parallel port mode in Device Manager

Nibble Mode

Nibble mode is the most common way to get "reverse" channel data back from a printer or other peripheral. This mode is usually combined with compatibility mode (or a proprietary forward channel mode) to create a complete bidirectional data channel. All standard parallel ports provide five lines from the peripheral to the PC that can be used for external status indications. Using these lines, a peripheral can send a byte of data (8 bits) by sending 2 "nibbles" (4 bits per "nibble") of information to the PC in two data transfer cycles.

Nibble mode (like compatibility mode) requires that the software drive the protocol by setting and reading lines on the parallel port. Nibble mode is the most software-intensive mode for reverse channel data communication. For this reason, a *severe* bandwidth limitation of approximately 50 KB/s applies for this type of data transfer. The major advantage of this approach is the ability to operate on all PCs that have a parallel port. The performance limitations don't have much effect on low-bandwidth peripherals such as printers, but can be intolerable when used with other bidirectional devices.

Byte Mode

With later implementations of the parallel port interface, some manufacturers (led by IBM on its PS/2 parallel port) added the capability to disable the drivers used for driving the data lines and allowed the data port to become an "input" data port. This enables a peripheral to send an entire byte of data to the PC in one data transfer cycle by using the eight data lines (rather than the two cycles required using nibble mode). This approach enables the byte mode for reverse channel data transfer that can be used to provide data rates *into* the PC approaching that of compatibility mode (which sends data *from* the PC). This type of port is sometimes referred to as an enhanced bidirectional port and is often mistaken for an Enhanced Parallel Port (EPP)—the two port types are not the same thing.

ECP Mode

The Extended Capability Port (ECP) protocol was proposed by Hewlett-Packard and Microsoft as an advanced mode for communication with printer and scanner-type peripherals. Like the EPP protocol described next, ECP provides a high-performance bidirectional communication path between the host system and the peripheral. When the ECP protocol was proposed, a standard register implementation was also proposed (this can be found in the document "The IEEE 1284 Extended Capabilities Port Protocol and ISA Interface Standard," available from Microsoft).

The many features of ECP include Run Length Encoding (RLE) data compression for the host system's LPT port, FIFO buffers for both the forward and reverse channels, DMA channel use, and programmed I/O (PIO). The RLE feature enables real-time data compression that can achieve compression ratios up to 64:1, which is particularly useful for printers and scanners that are transferring huge amounts of data that has large strings of repetitive information. In order for the RLE mode to be enabled, both the host *and* the peripheral must support it.

Channel addressing is a scheme used to address multiple logical devices within a single physical device. For example, in a multifunction device such as a fax/printer/modem, a single parallel port is attached to a printer, fax, and modem. Using ECP channel addressing to access each of these devices, you could receive data from the modem device while the printer data channel is busy processing a print image. With the compatibility mode protocol, if the printer gets too busy, no more communication can occur until the printer data channel is free, whereas with ECP, the software driver simply addresses another channel, and communication can continue.

With the EPP scheme described next, a software driver may intermix read and write operations without any overhead or protocol handshaking. With the ECP protocol, however, changes in the data direction must be negotiated. The host must request a "reverse channel transfer" by asserting a request, and then wait for the peripheral to acknowledge the request by asserting an acknowledge signal. Only then can a reverse channel data transfer take place. Since the previous transfer may have been DMA-driven, the host software must either wait for the DMA transfer to complete or interrupt the DMA, backflush the FIFO (to determine the exact transferred byte count), and then request the reverse channel.

EPP Mode

The Enhanced Parallel Port (EPP) protocol was originally developed by Intel, Xircom, and Zenith Data Systems as a means of providing a high-performance parallel port link that would still be compatible with the standard parallel port. This protocol was originally implemented by Intel in its 386SL chipset (the 82360 I/O chip). This was prior to the establishment of the IEEE 1284 committee and the associated standards work. The EPP protocol offered many advantages to parallel port peripheral manufactures, and it was quickly adopted by many manufacturers as an optional data transfer method. A loose association of around 80 interested manufacturers was formed to develop and promote the EPP protocol. This association became the EPP Committee, which was instrumental in helping to get this protocol adopted as an IEEE 1284 advanced mode. Since EPP-capable parallel ports were available *prior* to the release of the IEEE 1284 standard, there is a small difference between the pre-1284 EPP ports and established 1284 EPP protocol.

One of the most important features to note here is that the entire data transfer occurs within one ISA I/O cycle. The effect is that, by using the EPP protocol for data transfer, a system can achieve transfer rates between 500 KB/s and 2 MB/s. This means that parallel port peripherals can operate at *close* to the same performance levels as an equivalent ISA plug-in card (the performance level from a parallel port device is one of the major features of the EPP protocol). Data transfer will take place at the speed of the slowest part of the interface (the host adapter or the peripheral device), but this speed-adaptive property is transparent to both the host and peripheral. The EPP controller will generate the necessary handshake signals and strobes to transfer the data using an EPP Data Write cycle, and will run exactly like a standard parallel port.

The ability to transfer data to or from the PC by the use of a single instruction is what enables EPP mode parallel ports to transfer data at ISA-type bus speeds. Rather than having the software implement an I/O-intensive software loop, a block of data can be transferred with a single instruction. Depending upon the host adapter port implementation and the capability of the peripheral, an EPP port can transfer data from 500 KB/s to nearly 2 MB/s. This data transfer rate is more than enough to enable data-intensive devices such as network adapters, CD-ROM drives, tape backups, and other peripherals. The EPP protocol provides a high degree of coupling between the peripheral driver and the peripheral, meaning that the software driver is always able to determine and control the state of communication to the peripheral at any given time. Mixing the read and write operations (as well as block transfers) can be accomplished easily.

ECP/EPP CABLE QUALITY

Conventional parallel ports are limited to cable lengths of about 10 feet (about 3 meters). Beyond that, cross-talk in the parallel cable can result in data errors. Ideally, high-quality, well-shielded cable assemblies can extend that range even more, but the cheap, mass-produced cable assemblies that you often find in stores are rarely suited to support communication over more than 6 feet (about 2 meters). To support the high-speed communication promised by IEEE 1284, a new cable specification also had to be devised. This is hardly a trivial concern, especially considering that IEEE 1284 seeks to extend parallel port operation to as much as 30 feet (about 10 meters). Be sure to use an appropriate high-quality cable approved for IEEE 1284 when configuring a parallel port in ECP or EPP modes.

IEEE 1284 ISSUES

Unfortunately, while the potential and promise of IEEE 1284 offers a lot of appeal, some serious considerations are involved in configuring an enhanced port arrangement. Specifically, you will require an IEEE

1284–compliant parallel port, cable, and peripheral (printer, tape drive, hard drive, and so on) to take full advantage of enhanced capabilities.

Installing an IEEE 1284 parallel port is certainly not a problem. Virtually all current multi-I/O boards and motherboards now provide IEEE 1284–compliant ports. The trouble is that using a $5 printer cable with your old Panasonic KX-P1124 dot-matrix printer won't provide any advantages. To start benefiting from an IEEE 1284 port, you need at least an IEEE 1284 cable and a device with significant memory capacity (such as a laser printer). At that point, you may start to see some speed improvements, but the additional speed will still fall far short of the projected figures. Ultimately, you need to install IEEE 1284–compliant peripherals that will provide ID information to the port and allow optimum performance.

Troubleshooting the Parallel Port

While the typical parallel port is a rather simple I/O device, it presents some special challenges for the technician. Older PCs provided their parallel ports in the form of 8-bit expansion boards. When a port failed, it was a simple matter to replace the board outright. Today, however, virtually all PCs provide at least one parallel port directly on the motherboard—a feature usually supported by an I/O controller component of the motherboard's main chipset. When a problem is detected with a motherboard parallel port, a technician often has three choices:

- Replace the South Bridge chip that supports the parallel port(s). Doing this requires access to surface-mount soldering tools and replacement chips, and can be quite economical in volume. But this is a totally impractical solution for end-user troubleshooting.

- Set the motherboard jumpers (if possible) to *disable* the defective parallel port, and install an expansion multi-I/O board to take the place of the defective port. This assumes there is an available expansion slot. This solution uses an expansion slot, but offers a cheap, fast fix for a defective parallel port. Remember to disable all other unused ports of the multi-I/O board.

- Replace the motherboard. This is a simple tactic that requires little overhead equipment, but can be rather expensive—a general solution of last resort if you confirm that the parallel port is defective.

If a diagnostic cannot identify the presence of a physical parallel port (a loopback plug may need to be attached), you can usually consider the port to be defective.

PREVENTING PARALLEL PORT TROUBLE

Parallel ports are generally not complex devices, but some common issues show up regularly. Before you check out the symptoms later in this chapter, consider the following points:

- **Cable**   You'd be surprised how many parallel port problems are caused by loose, cheap, or damaged printer cables. Make sure the cable is 6 feet or less in length and that it is secure at *both* ends. Try a different cable, or try the suspect cable in place of a known-good one. In many cases, using a good-quality IEEE 1284–approved cable will resolve many difficulties.

- **Port mode**   Remember that modern parallel ports can operate in several different modes such as compatibility, ECP, or EPP. Not all parallel port devices work properly with ECP or EPP modes. If you have trouble with a printer or other parallel port device, try setting the parallel port to compatibility mode or standard mode in the system's CMOS Setup. In other cases, you may need to configure the port as ECP or EPP to get full functionality from a high-end printer or multipurpose parallel port device.

■ **Hardware conflicts**   LPT ports use IRQ7 and IRQ5. For systems with a second LPT port (LPT2), it is common for IRQ5 to have a conflict, because it is almost always used by sound boards. If you must use two or more LPT ports on your system, it may be necessary to reconfigure the sound board to use another IRQ or to remove the sound board entirely.

■ **Printer driver conflicts**   This is a problem that often arises with parallel port devices such as Iomega Zip drives or SyQuest SyJet drives. The drive software sends special reserved, nonprintable characters to the parallel port; this signals the drive that the next data being placed on the parallel port cable is for that drive (not the printer). Color printers and multiple-font printers may also be using some of these special characters for their printer setups. This situation can cause conflicts between the two drivers and make each unit (the printer and the parallel port drive) look defective to the system. Many printer companies, such as Hewlett-Packard, are in the process of rewriting printer drivers to stay clear of these reserved nonprintable characters, but some drivers still use these characters and will cause conflicts that cannot be resolved. The only way to correct this problem is to use one LPT port for the parallel port drive and another LPT port for the printer (or use a switch box to isolate the devices). You should contact the printer manufacture to see if it has updated drivers that will not interfere with the parallel port device.

■ **Printer monitoring software**   Another form of driver conflicts happens with printer monitoring software. Some companies, such as HP, have status drivers that monitor the printer's status. If you have these printers connected to the pass-through port of a parallel port drive, these printer monitoring drivers should be disabled. These drivers can also cause data corruption and system problems. Disabling status communications does not affect the printing.

WINDOWS CONFIGURATION TROUBLESHOOTING

Windows has long displaced DOS as the predominant PC operating system, so the vast majority of troubles with printers and other parallel port devices will show up under Windows. This part of the chapter highlights the most common issues when configuring a parallel port device under Windows 98/Me. Configuration problems usually fall into one of the following categories:

■ **Cabling problems**   Make sure that you're using a suitable cable between the PC's parallel port and the device. If there is a switch box or other pass-through-type device between the port and device, try connecting the device directly to the port. If you have another parallel port device besides the printer, consider setting up an additional parallel port on your computer to accommodate both devices.

■ **Port disabled or IRQs reserved**   Reboot the PC to the CMOS Setup and check the status of the parallel port(s). Make sure that the LPT port is actually enabled (most can be disabled through the CMOS Setup). Also verify that an appropriate IRQ is assigned to the port (for example, IRQ 7 for LPT1, or IRQ 5 for LPT2)—some PnP BIOS versions may automatically reserve those IRQs.

■ **Port configured improperly**   While you're in the CMOS Setup, also check the parallel port mode. In most cases, compatibility mode or standard mode is fine for basic printers, but high-end printers and other parallel port devices may need ECP or EPP mode to operate properly. Some systems may also provide nonstandard or custom port modes that are incompatible with the device being attached.

■ **Disable any status monitors**   Printer monitoring software and other printer-related TSRs are notorious for interfering with parallel port devices. Try disabling or uninstalling any kind of status monitoring software on the system. Check the Windows Startup folder and Automatic Skip Driver Agent in the System Information utility to see just what's starting at boot time. DOS TSRs and other real-mode software can be disabled by REMarking out the offending command line in CONFIG.SYS or AUTOEXEC.BAT.

■ **Parallel port device set to the wrong mode**   Make sure that the printer or other parallel port device (for example, a SyQuest drive) is not set to plug-and-play mode. Check the documentation that accompanies your device to see whether any alternate modes (for example, a legacy mode) may be used instead.

■ **Check and correct any IRQ conflicts**   Check the Device Manager and verify that no other devices are using the IRQ(s) allocated to your parallel port(s). This is usually not a problem with IRQ 7, but may be a problem with sound boards and IRQ 5. Reconfigure or remove the conflicting device(s). For example, consider a SyQuest drive. If you have no SCSI controllers listed (or a SyQuest Parallel Port Drive is listed under SCSI Controllers but is marked with a yellow exclamation point), that usually indicates that an IRQ conflict is preventing the SyQuest Windows driver from loading.

■ **Check and remove any similar device drivers**   If you've upgraded or switched to a different parallel port device, the old drivers may still be on your system, and this may cause interference with the new device driver(s). For example, if your system has another removable media device (such as a tape backup) running a device driver in Windows, these devices may compete with SyQuest Windows drivers and prevent the SyQuest drive from installing properly under Windows. Take a moment to remove or uninstall any drivers and applet software related to the old parallel port device(s), and then reinstall the new device's drivers if necessary.

SYMPTOMS

SYMPTOM 29-1   **You hear a beep code or see a POST error indicating a parallel port error**   The system initialization may or may not halt depending on how the BIOS is written. Low-level initialization problems generally indicate trouble in the computer's hardware. If the computer's beep code sequence is indistinct, you could try rebooting the computer with a POST analyzer card installed. The BIOS POST code displayed on the card can be matched to a specific error explanation in the POST card's documentation. Once you have clearly identified the error as a parallel port fault, you can proceed with troubleshooting.

Start with the system as a whole and remove any expansion boards that have parallel ports available. Retest the computer after removing each board. If the error disappears after removing a particular card, then that card is likely at fault. You can simply replace the card with a new one or attempt to repair the card to the component level. If there is only one parallel port in the system, it is most likely built into the motherboard.

For older systems, the fault is probably in one or more of the discrete I/O chips or latches directing the port's operation. You need to refer to the schematic(s) for your particular system motherboard to determine exact signal flows and component locations. Newer system motherboards enjoy a far lower component count, so all parallel port circuitry is usually integrated onto the motherboard's chipset (usually the South Bridge chip). A schematic would still be valuable to determine signal paths, but you could probably trace the parallel port connector directly to its controlling chip. Replace any defective components or replace the motherboard outright.

SYMPTOM 29-2   **You see a 9xx parallel adapter displayed on your XT or early AT system**   BIOS has not located any parallel circuit defects on initialization, but has been unable to map LPT labels to the appropriate hardware-level ports. As in Symptom 29-1, the 9xx series error codes usually indicate a hardware fault in the computer. Follow the procedures in Symptom 29-1 to isolate and resolve the problem, or replace the motherboard outright.

SYMPTOM 29-3   **The computer initializes properly, but the peripheral (printer) does not work**   Your applications software may indicate a "printer timeout" or "general printer" error. Before you even open your toolkit, you must determine whether the trouble lies in your computer or your peripheral. When your printer stops working, run a self-test to ensure the device is at least operational. Check all cables and connectors (perhaps try a different cable). If the peripheral offers multiple interfaces, such as serial and parallel, make sure the parallel interface is activated in the peripheral. Also be sure to check the software package being used (word processor, painting package, system diagnostic, and so on) to operate the printer. Ensure that the software is configured properly to use the appropriate LPT port, and that any necessary printer driver is selected. If no software is available, you can try printing from the DOS command line using the SHIFT and PRINTSCREEN keys. This key sequence will dump the screen contents to a printer.

Disconnect the printer at the computer and install a parallel loopback plug. Run a diagnostic to inspect each available parallel port. Take note of any port that registers as defective. Locate the corresponding parallel port. If the port is installed as an expansion board, replace the defective expansion board. If the port is on the motherboard, you can replace the defective port controller chip, install an alternate expansion board to take the place of the defective port, or replace the motherboard outright.

SYMPTOM 29-4   **The peripheral (printer) will not go online**   Before data can be transferred across a parallel port, proper handshaking conditions must exist: the Busy (pin 11) and Paper Out (pin 12) lines must be TTL logic 0, and the Select (pin 13) and -Error (pin 15) lines must be TTL logic 1. All four signals are outputs from the peripheral. You can examine these levels with an ordinary logic probe. If any of these signals is incorrect, the peripheral will not be online. First, try a new communication cable. An old or worn cable may have developed a fault in one or more connections. Next, try the computer with a different peripheral. If a new peripheral *does* come online, the error exists in the original peripheral's parallel port circuitry.

If a different peripheral does not operate properly, there is a problem with the computer's parallel port. Examine and alter the computer configuration to ensure that there is no conflict between multiple parallel ports. Disconnect the printer at the computer and install a parallel loopback plug. Run a diagnostic to inspect each available parallel port. Take note of any port(s) that registers as defective. Locate the corresponding parallel port. If the port is installed as an expansion board, replace the defective expansion board. If the port is on the motherboard, you can replace the defective port controller chip, install an alternate expansion board, or replace the motherboard outright.

SYMPTOM 29-5   **Data is randomly lost or garbled**   Your first step should be to check the communication cable. Make sure the cable is intact and properly secured at both ends. The cable should also be less than 2 meters (about 6 feet) long. Very long cables can allow cross-talk to generate erroneous signals. If the cable checks properly, either the port or peripheral is at fault. Start by suspecting the parallel port. Disconnect the printer at the computer and install a parallel loopback plug. Run a diagnostic to inspect each available parallel port. Take note of any port that registers as defective. Locate the corresponding parallel port. If the port is installed as an expansion board, replace the defective expansion board. If the port is on the motherboard, you can replace the defective port controller chip, install an alternate expansion board, or replace the motherboard outright.

If you cannot test the computer's parallel port directly, test the port indirectly by trying the peripheral on another known-good computer. If the peripheral works properly on another computer, the trouble is probably in the original computer's parallel port circuitry. Replace any defective circuitry or replace the motherboard. If the peripheral remains defective on another computer, the peripheral itself is probably faulty.

SYMPTOM 29-6 You see a continuous "paper out" error even though paper is available and the printer's paper sensor works properly Try another printer. If another printer works, the problem is in your original printer and not in the parallel port. Use a logic probe and check the Paper Out signal at the computer. Try removing and reinserting paper while the printer is running. You should see the Paper Out signal vary between a TTL logic 0 (paper available) and a TTL logic 1 (paper missing). If the signal remains TTL logic 1 regardless of paper availability, the printer's sensor or communication circuits are probably defective. If the Paper Out signal correctly follows the paper availability, the trouble is probably in your computer's communication circuitry.

When you suspect that the problem is in the parallel port, disconnect the printer at the computer and install a parallel loopback plug. Run a diagnostic to inspect each available parallel port. Take note of any port that registers as defective. Locate the corresponding parallel port. If the port is installed as an expansion board, replace the defective expansion board. If the port is on the motherboard, you can replace the defective port controller chip, install an alternate expansion board, or replace the motherboard outright.

Further Study

ECP Technical Document www.fapo.com/files/ecp_reg.pdf
Hewlett-Packard www.hp.com
IEEE 1284 www.fapo.com/ieee1284.htm
LPT ports and parallel drives syquest.com/support/papers.html

30

PLUG-AND-PLAY CONFIGURATION AND TROUBLESHOOTING

One of the key appeals of the IBM-type personal computer architecture is its functional modularity—its ability to accept a variety of expansion devices such as modems, video controllers, drive adapters, video capture/TV boards, and so on. Each device that is added to a system needs to be configured in order to utilize unique IRQ, DMA, and I/O resources. Traditionally, devices were configured manually using a series of jumpers on the device. While this proved to be a straightforward approach, it also opened the way for many configuration conflicts (that is, devices accidentally configured to use overlapping resources). Reporting utilities are also imprecise, making conflict resolution somewhat of a tedious, hit-and-miss process. Current operating systems typically provide better tools for conflict resolution (see Chapter 12), but resolving conflicts still demands a certain amount of patience and expertise.

Designers have long sought to automate the device configuration process and remove the error-prone task of device configuration from the hands of end users and busy technicians. The result of this automatic configuration technology has become known as *plug-and-play* (PnP). First introduced with late-model 486 systems, PnP has long since been a standard technology implemented in all current PCs. Although

PnP simplifies much of the configuration problems with new systems, there are still many situations where PnP doesn't work perfectly (especially when running devices under DOS, or using pre-PnP devices in a PnP system). This chapter describes the requirements for PnP, outlines the special requirements for implementing PnP under DOS, and provides a wide selection of troubleshooting issues.

Understanding PnP Under Windows 98/Me

The first step in troubleshooting PnP is to understand the issues involved in making it run. PnP is not one particular technology, but rather it is a combination of features brought together into a single approach. There are three components involved in a PnP system: PnP devices, PnP BIOS, and a PnP-compliant operating system—each part must be PnP compatible.

PNP DEVICES

A PnP system requires one or more devices—the modems, video adapters, chipsets, drive adapters, and myriad other hardware elements in the PC. Ideally, every device in the PC will be PnP compatible, and today's systems do contain virtually all PnP devices. PnP devices are capable of identifying themselves and their resource requirements to the rest of the system. The only wrinkles occur when non-PnP (*legacy*) devices are mixed into the system hardware.

PNP BIOS

A PnP system requires a PnP BIOS—especially at boot time. Since PnP devices initialize in the inactive state by default, the PnP BIOS is needed to initialize the core PnP devices (such as the video adapter and boot drive) in order to complete the POST and launch the operating system. Also note that the original version of PnP BIOS (version 1.0) was finalized in May 1994. By October 1994 (version 1.0a), additional clarifications were added. As a consequence, older PnP systems are not fully compliant with the current specification. PnP support problems on older systems can usually be corrected with a BIOS upgrade. System PnP support can typically be enabled or disabled through the CMOS Setup routine.

PNP OPERATING SYSTEM

The PnP OS takes over where the PnP BIOS leaves off by identifying and configuring the remaining PnP devices in the system, then loading the appropriate drivers needed to initialize and operate each respective device. The OS also must keep resources aside for non-PnP (legacy) devices and report any changes to the hardware complement in the system. Windows 98 and Windows Me are generally regarded as the premier PnP operating systems for end users and general-purpose PCs, while Windows NT and Windows 2000 provide PnP support for networked and business systems.

AN OVERVIEW OF PNP BEHAVIOR

Now that you've seen the essential elements of PnP, it's time to look at how it all works. A PnP system must be robust enough to handle several important functions. The major functions that must be handled by these three PnP components can be summarized as follows:

- **Identification of installed devices**   The PnP system must be able to identify each installed device. This requires the device to have a certain amount of onboard intelligence.

■ **Determination of device resource requirements**   Based on the device identification, the PnP system must be able to determine the kinds of resources (IRQ, DMA, I/O addresses, or BIOS space) required to support the device.

■ **Creation of a complete system configuration, eliminating all resource conflicts**   After all devices have been identified, and their resource needs evaluated, the PnP system must allocate the required resources to each device every time the system initializes (without causing a resource conflict).

■ **Loading of device drivers**   After the operating system starts, it must load the appropriate device drivers needed to support every device in the system.

■ **Notification of configuration changes**   Each time a PnP device is added or removed from the PC, the PnP system reports the configuration change. When a device is added, the PnP system attempts to identify it and install the appropriate device drivers. When a device is removed, the PnP system attempts to remove all traces of the device and its drivers.

The PnP system starts with the BIOS at boot time. A certain amount of configuration must first be performed by the system BIOS during system initialization. For the system to boot, the PnP BIOS must configure a display device, input device, and initial boot device (such as video adapter, keyboard, and floppy/hard drives). Then, the PnP BIOS must pass the information about each of these devices to the operating system (Windows 98/Me) for additional configuration of the remaining system devices.

The operating system continues the configuration process by identifying every device in the system and gathering their respective resource requirements. Each nonboot device (such as modems and video capture devices) must be inactive upon power-up so that the operating system can identify any conflicts between the resource requirements of different devices before configuring them. When different devices require the same resources, the devices must be able to provide information to the operating system about alternative resource requirements. The operating system then uses initial or alternative requirements to assemble a working system configuration. Once any resource conflicts have been resolved, the operating system automatically programs each hardware device with its working configuration and then stores all configuration information in the central database contained in *extended system configuration data (ESCD) memory, which is part of the CMOS RAM space. Finally, the operating system loads the device drivers for each device and notifies these drivers of each resource assignment.*

If a change occurs to the system configuration during operation (for example, a device is installed or removed), the hardware must be able to notify the operating system of the event so that the operating system can configure the new device. Additionally, applications must be able to respond to configuration changes to take advantage of new devices and to cease calling devices that have been removed. Such dynamic configuration events might include the insertion of a PC Card, the addition or removal of a peripheral such as a mouse, CD-ROM drive, or printer, or a docking/undocking event for a notebook computer.

In most cases, configuration changes are made before boot time while system power is off. Only PC Card and laptop designs support "hot" insertion and removal.

Device Types and Identification

The PnP system is designed to support a wide variety of devices across a number of different bus architectures. In general, there are nine classifications of PnP devices:

■ ISA bus cards

■ PCI bus cards

■ MicroChannel Architecture (MCA) bus cards

- VESA Local Bus (VLB) cards
- IDE devices (for hard drives and CD-ROM drives)
- SCSI controllers and devices
- PC Card devices
- Serial port devices (such as modems)
- Parallel port devices (such as printers and parallel port drives)

For the PC to recognize and configure a PnP device, each device must be able to identify itself and its resource requirements to the system. Even motherboard busses and devices must be able to identify themselves. Identification is accomplished through a seven-character code. Each manufacturer is assigned a three-character prefix, the following character identifies the device type, and the remaining three characters identify the particular device. For example, the PnP code "PNP0907" identifies a "Western Digital VGA" device adapter. Microsoft reserves the code "PNP" for itself, but other manufacturers are assigned their own codes (for example, Creative Labs uses the "CTL" prefix). The advantage of Microsoft's prefixes is that they are "generic," and you can usually identify a device adequately by utilizing the Microsoft generic equivalent. Table 30-1 lists some of the generic PnP identification categories and codes used by Microsoft.

TABLE 30-1   AN EXAMPLE OF MICROSOFT'S GENERIC PNP ID CODES

SYSTEM DEVICES—PNP0XXX—INTERRUPT CONTROLLERS	
PNP0000	AT interrupt controller
PNP0001	EISA interrupt controller
PNP0002	MCA interrupt controller
PNP0003	APIC
PNP0004	Cyrix SLiC MP interrupt controller
SYSTEM DEVICES—PNP0XXX—TIMERS	
PNP0100	AT timer
PNP0101	EISA timer
PNP0102	MCA timer
SYSTEM DEVICES—PNP0XXX—DMA	
PNP0200	AT DMA controller
PNP0201	EISA DMA controller
PNP0202	MCA DMA controller
SYSTEM DEVICES—PNP0XXX—KEYBOARDS	
PNP0300	IBM PC/XT keyboard controller (83-key)
PNP0301	IBM PC/AT keyboard controller (86-key)
PNP0302	IBM PC/XT keyboard controller (84-key)
PNP0303	IBM Enhanced (101/102-key, PS/2 mouse support)
PNP0304	Olivetti keyboard (83-key)
PNP0305	Olivetti keyboard (102-key)
PNP0306	Olivetti keyboard (86-key)
PNP0307	Microsoft Windows keyboard
PNP0308	General Input Device Emulation Interface (GIDEI) legacy
PNP0309	Olivetti keyboard (A101/102 key)
PNP030A	AT&T 302 keyboard
PNP030B	Reserved (by Microsoft)

TABLE 30-1   AN EXAMPLE OF MICROSOFT'S GENERIC PNP ID CODES *(CONTINUED)*

PNP0320	Japanese 106-key keyboard A01
PNP0321	Japanese 101-key keyboard
PNP0322	Japanese AX keyboard
PNP0323	Japanese 106-key keyboard 002/003
PNP0324	Japanese 106-key keyboard 001
PNP0325	Japanese Toshiba desktop keyboard
PNP0326	Japanese Toshiba laptop keyboard
PNP0327	Japanese Toshiba notebook keyboard
PNP0340	Korean 84-key keyboard
PNP0341	Korean 86-key keyboard
PNP0342	Korean enhanced keyboard
PNP0343	Korean enhanced keyboard 101b
PNP0343	Korean enhanced keyboard 101c
PNP0344	Korean enhanced keyboard 103
SYSTEM DEVICES—PNP0XXX—PARALLEL DEVICES	
PNP0400	Standard LPT printer port
PNP0401	ECP printer port
SYSTEM DEVICES—PNP0XXX—SERIAL DEVICES	
PNP0500	Standard PC COM port
PNP0501	16550A-compatible COM port
PNP0502	Multiport serial device (non-intelligent 16550)
PNP0510	Generic IRDA-compatible device
PNP0511	Generic IRDA-compatible device
SYSTEM DEVICES—PNP0XXX—DISK CONTROLLERS	
PNP0600	Generic ESDI/IDE/ATA compatible hard disk controller
PNP0601	Plus Hardcard II
PNP0602	Plus Hardcard IIXL/EZ
PNP0603	Generic IDE supporting Microsoft Device Bay Specification
PNP0700	PC standard floppy disk controller
PNP0701	Standard floppy controller supporting MS Device Bay Spec.
SYSTEM DEVICES—PNP0XXX—EARLY SOUND SYSTEMS	
PNP0802	Microsoft Sound System device (now obsolete—use PNPB0xx instead)
SYSTEM DEVICES—PNP0XXX—DISPLAY ADAPTERS	
PNP0900	VGA Compatible
PNP0901	Video Seven VRAM/VRAM II/1024i
PNP0902	8514/A Compatible
PNP0903	Trident VGA
PNP0904	Cirrus Logic Laptop VGA
PNP0905	Cirrus Logic VGA
PNP0906	Tseng ET4000
PNP0907	Western Digital VGA
PNP0908	Western Digital Laptop VGA
PNP0909	S3 Inc. 911/924
PNP090A	ATI Ultra Pro/Plus (Mach 32)
PNP090B	ATI Ultra (Mach 8)
PNP090C	XGA Compatible
PNP090D	ATI VGA Wonder

TABLE 30-1   AN EXAMPLE OF MICROSOFT'S GENERIC PNP ID CODES *(CONTINUED)*

PNP090E	Weitek P9000 Graphics Adapter
PNP090F	Oak Technology VGA
PNP0910	Compaq QVision
PNP0911	XGA/2
PNP0912	Tseng Labs W32/W32i/W32p
PNP0913	S3 Inc. 801/928/964
PNP0914	Cirrus Logic 5429/5434 (memory mapped)
PNP0915	Compaq Advanced VGA (AVGA)
PNP0916	ATI Ultra Pro Turbo (Mach64)
PNP0917	Reserved (by Microsoft)
PNP0918	Matrox MGA
PNP0919	Compaq QVision 2000
PNP091A	Tseng W128
PNP0930	Chips & Technologies Super VGA
PNP0931	Chips & Technologies Accelerator
PNP0940	NCR 77c22e Super VGA
PNP0941	NCR 77c32blt
PNP09FF	Plug and Play Monitors (VESA DDC)

SYSTEM DEVICES—PNP0XXX—PERIPHERAL BUSSES

PNP0A00	ISA Bus
PNP0A01	EISA Bus
PNP0A02	MCA Bus
PNP0A03	PCI Bus
PNP0A04	VESA/VL Bus
PNP0A05	Generic ACPI Bus
PNP0A06	Generic ACPI Extended-IO Bus (EIO bus)

SYSTEM DEVICES—PNP0XXX—REAL-TIME CLOCK, BIOS, MOTHERBOARD DEVICES

PNP0800	AT-style speaker sound
PNP0B00	AT Real-Time Clock
PNP0C00	Plug-and-play BIOS
PNP0C01	System Board
PNP0C02	General ID for reserving resources required by PnP motherboard registers
PNP0C03	Plug-and-play BIOS Event Notification Interrupt
PNP0C04	Math Coprocessor
PNP0C05	APM BIOS (Version independent)
PNP0C06	Reserved for identification of early plug-and-play BIOS implementation
PNP0C07	Reserved for identification of early plug-and-play BIOS implementation
PNP0C08	ACPI system board hardware
PNP0C09	ACPI Embedded Controller
PNP0C0A	ACPI Control Method Battery
PNP0C0B	ACPI Fan
PNP0C0C	ACPI power button device
PNP0C0D	ACPI lid device
PNP0C0E	ACPI sleep button device
PNP0C0F	PCI interrupt link device
PNP0C10	ACPI system indicator device

TABLE 30-1 AN EXAMPLE OF MICROSOFT'S GENERIC PNP ID CODES *(CONTINUED)*

PNP0C11	ACPI thermal zone
PNP0C12	Device Bay Controller
PNP0C13	Plug-and-play BIOS (used when ACPI mode cannot be used)
SYSTEM DEVICES—PNP0XXX—PCMCIA CONTROLLER CHIPSETS	
PNP0E00	Intel 82365-Compatible PCMCIA Controller
PNP0E01	Cirrus Logic CL-PD6720 PCMCIA Controller
PNP0E02	VLSI VL82C146 PCMCIA Controller
PNP0E03	Intel 82365-compatible CardBus Controller
SYSTEM DEVICES—PNP0XXX—MICE	
PNP0F00	Microsoft Bus Mouse
PNP0F01	Microsoft Serial Mouse
PNP0F02	Microsoft InPort Mouse
PNP0F03	Microsoft PS/2-style Mouse
PNP0F04	Mouse Systems Mouse
PNP0F05	Mouse Systems 3-Button Mouse (COM2)
PNP0F06	Genius Mouse (COM1)
PNP0F07	Genius Mouse (COM2)
PNP0F08	Logitech Serial Mouse
PNP0F09	Microsoft BallPoint Serial Mouse
PNP0F0A	Microsoft Plug-and-Play Mouse
PNP0F0B	Microsoft Plug-and-Play BallPoint Mouse
PNP0F0C	Microsoft-compatible Serial Mouse
PNP0F0D	Microsoft-compatible InPort-compatible Mouse
PNP0F0E	Microsoft-compatible PS/2-style Mouse
PNP0F0F	Microsoft-compatible Serial BallPoint-compatible Mouse
PNP0F10	Texas Instruments QuickPort Mouse
PNP0F11	Microsoft-compatible bus Mouse
PNP0F12	Logitech PS/2-style Mouse
PNP0F13	PS/2 Port for PS/2-style Mice
PNP0F14	Microsoft Kids Mouse
PNP0F15	Logitech bus mouse
PNP0F16	Logitech SWIFT device
PNP0F17	Logitech-compatible serial mouse
PNP0F18	Logitech-compatible bus mouse
PNP0F19	Logitech-compatible PS/2-style Mouse
PNP0F1A	Logitech-compatible SWIFT Device
PNP0F1B	HP Omnibook mouse
PNP0F1C	Compaq LTE Trackball PS/2-style Mouse
PNP0F1D	Compaq LTE Trackball Serial Mouse
PNP0F1E	Microsoft Kids Trackball Mouse
PNP0F1F	Reserved (by Microsoft Input Device Group)
PNP0F20	Reserved (by Microsoft Input Device Group)
PNP0F21	Reserved (by Microsoft Input Device Group)
PNP0F22	Reserved (by Microsoft Input Device Group)
PNP0F23	Reserved (by Microsoft Input Device Group)
PNP0FFF	Reserved (by Microsoft Systems)

TABLE 30-1   AN EXAMPLE OF MICROSOFT'S GENERIC PNP ID CODES *(CONTINUED)*

SYSTEM DEVICES—PNP8XXX—NETWORK ADAPTERS

PNP8001	Novell/Anthem NE3200
PNP8004	Compaq NE3200
PNP8006	Intel EtherExpress/32
PNP8008	HP EtherTwist EISA LAN Adapter/32 (HP27248A)
PNP8065	Ungermann-Bass NIUps or NIUps/EOTP
PNP8072	DEC (DE211) EtherWorks MC/TP
PNP8073	DEC (DE212) EtherWorks MC/TP_BNC
PNP8078	DCA 10Mb MCA
PNP8074	HP MC LAN Adapter/16 TP (PC27246)
PNP80C9	IBM Token Ring
PNP80CA	IBM Token Ring II
PNP80CB	IBM Token Ring II/Short
PNP80CC	IBM Token Ring 4/16Mbs
PNP80D3	Novell/Anthem NE1000
PNP80D4	Novell/Anthem NE2000
PNP80D5	NE1000 Compatible
PNP80D6	NE2000 Compatible
PNP80D7	Novell/Anthem NE1500T
PNP80D8	Novell/Anthem NE2100
PNP80DD	SMC ARCNETPC
PNP80DE	SMC ARCNET PC100, PC200
PNP80DF	SMC ARCNET PC110, PC210, PC250
PNP80E0	SMC ARCNET PC130/E
PNP80E1	SMC ARCNET PC120, PC220, PC260
PNP80E2	SMC ARCNET PC270/E
PNP80E5	SMC ARCNET PC600W, PC650W
PNP80E7	DEC DEPCA
PNP80E8	DEC (DE100) EtherWorks LC
PNP80E9	DEC (DE200) EtherWorks Turbo
PNP80EA	DEC (DE101) EtherWorks LC/TP
PNP80EB	DEC (DE201) EtherWorks Turbo/TP
PNP80EC	DEC (DE202) EtherWorks Turbo/TP_BNC
PNP80ED	DEC (DE102) EtherWorks LC/TP_BNC
PNP80EE	DEC EE101 (Built-In)
PNP80EF	DECpc 433 WS (Built-In)
PNP80F1	3Com EtherLink Plus
PNP80F3	3Com EtherLink II or IITP (8- or 16-bit)
PNP80F4	3Com TokenLink
PNP80F6	3Com EtherLink 16
PNP80F7	3Com EtherLink III
PNP80F8	3Com Generic Etherlink Plug-and-Play Device
PNP80FB	Thomas Conrad TC6045
PNP80FC	Thomas Conrad TC6042
PNP80FD	Thomas Conrad TC6142
PNP80FE	Thomas Conrad TC6145
PNP80FF	Thomas Conrad TC6242

TABLE 30-1   AN EXAMPLE OF MICROSOFT'S GENERIC PNP ID CODES *(CONTINUED)*

PNP8100	Thomas Conrad TC6245
PNP8105	DCA 10MB
PNP8106	DCA 10MB Fiber Optic
PNP8107	DCA 10MB Twisted Pair
PNP8113	Racal NI6510
PNP811C	Ungermann-Bass NIUpc
PNP8120	Ungermann-Bass NIUpc/EOTP
PNP8123	SMC StarCard PLUS (WD/8003S)
PNP8124	SMC StarCard PLUS With On Board Hub (WD/8003SH)
PNP8125	SMC EtherCard PLUS (WD/8003E)
PNP8126	SMC EtherCard PLUS With Boot ROM Socket (WD/8003EBT)
PNP8127	SMC EtherCard PLUS With Boot ROM Socket (WD/8003EB)
PNP8128	SMC EtherCard PLUS TP (WD/8003WT)
PNP812A	SMC EtherCard PLUS 16 With Boot ROM Socket (WD/8013EBT)
PNP812D	Intel EtherExpress 16 or 16TP
PNP812F	Intel TokenExpress 16/4
PNP8130	Intel TokenExpress MCA 16/4
PNP8132	Intel EtherExpress 16 (MCA)
PNP8137	Artisoft AE-1
PNP8138	Artisoft AE-2 or AE-3
PNP8141	Amplicard AC 210/XT
PNP8142	Amplicard AC 210/AT
PNP814B	Everex SpeedLink /PC16 (EV2027)
PNP8155	HP PC LAN Adapter/8 TP (HP27245)
PNP8156	HP PC LAN Adapter/16 TP (HP27247A)
PNP8157	HP PC LAN Adapter/8 TL (HP27250)
PNP8158	HP PC LAN Adapter/16 TP Plus (HP27247B)
PNP8159	HP PC LAN Adapter/16 TL Plus (HP27252)
PNP815F	National Semiconductor Ethernode *16AT
PNP8160	National Semiconductor AT/LANTIC EtherNODE 16-AT3
PNP816A	NCR Token-Ring 4Mbs ISA
PNP816D	NCR Token-Ring 16/4Mbs ISA
PNP8191	Olicom 16/4 Token-Ring Adapter
PNP81C3	SMC EtherCard PLUS Elite (WD/8003EP)
PNP81C4	SMC EtherCard PLUS 10T (WD/8003W)
PNP81C5	SMC EtherCard PLUS Elite 16 (WD/8013EP)
PNP81C6	SMC EtherCard PLUS Elite 16T (WD/8013W)
PNP81C7	SMC EtherCard PLUS Elite 16 Combo (WD/8013EW or 8013EWC)
PNP81C8	SMC EtherElite Ultra 16
PNP81E4	Pure Data PDI9025-32 (Token Ring)
PNP81E6	Pure Data PDI508+ (ArcNet)
PNP81E7	Pure Data PDI516+ (ArcNet)
PNP81EB	Proteon Token Ring (P1390)
PNP81EC	Proteon Token Ring (P1392)
PNP81ED	Proteon ISA Token Ring (1340)
PNP81EE	Proteon ISA Token Ring (1342)

TABLE 30-1   **AN EXAMPLE OF MICROSOFT'S GENERIC PNP ID CODES** *(CONTINUED)*

PNP81EF	Proteon ISA Token Ring (1346)
PNP81F0	Proteon ISA Token Ring (1347)
PNP81FF	Cabletron E2000 Series DNI
PNP8200	Cabletron E2100 Series DNI
PNP8209	Zenith Data Systems Z-Note
PNP820A	Zenith Data Systems NE2000-Compatible
PNP8213	Xircom Pocket Ethernet II
PNP8214	Xircom Pocket Ethernet I
PNP821D	RadiSys EXM-10
PNP8227	SMC 3000 Series
PNP8228	SMC 91C2 controller
PNP8231	Advanced Micro Devices AM2100/AM1500T
PNP8263	Tulip NCC-16
PNP8277	Exos 105
PNP828A	Intel '595 based Ethernet
PNP828B	TI2000-style Token Ring
PNP828C	AMD PCNet Family cards
PNP828D	AMD PCNet32 (VL version)
PNP8294	IrDA Infrared NDIS driver (Microsoft-supplied)
PNP82BD	IBM PCMCIA-NIC
PNP82C2	Xircom CE10
PNP82C3	Xircom CEM2
PNP8321	DEC Ethernet (All Types)
PNP8323	SMC EtherCard (All Types except 8013/A)
PNP8324	ARCNET Compatible
PNP8326	Thomas Conrad (All Arcnet Types)
PNP8327	IBM Token Ring (All Types)
PNP8385	Remote Network Access Driver
PNP8387	RNA Point-To-Point Protocol Driver
PNP8388	Reserved (for Microsoft Networking components)
PNP8389	Peer IrLAN infrared driver (Microsoft-supplied)
PNP8390	Generic network adapter
SYSTEM DEVICES—PNPAXXX—SCSI AND PROPRIETARY CD ADAPTERS	
PNPA002	Future Domain 16-700 compatible controller
PNPA003	Panasonic proprietary CD-ROM adapter (SBPro/SB16)
PNPA01B	Trantor 128 SCSI Controller
PNPA01D	Trantor T160 SCSI Controller
PNPA01E	Trantor T338 Parallel SCSI controller
PNPA01F	Trantor T348 Parallel SCSI controller
PNPA020	Trantor Media Vision SCSI controller
PNPA022	Always IN-2000 SCSI controller
PNPA02B	Sony proprietary CD-ROM controller
PNPA02D	Trantor T13b 8-bit SCSI controller
PNPA02F	Trantor T358 Parallel SCSI controller
PNPA030	Mitsumi LU-005 Single Speed CD-ROM controller + drive
PNPA031	Mitsumi FX-001 Single Speed CD-ROM controller + drive
PNPA032	Mitsumi FX-001 Double Speed CD-ROM controller + drive

TABLE 30-1   AN EXAMPLE OF MICROSOFT'S GENERIC PNP ID CODES *(CONTINUED)*

SYSTEM DEVICES—PNPBXXX—SOUND, VIDEO CAPTURE, AND MULTIMEDIA	
PNPB000	Sound Blaster 1.5–compatible sound device
PNPB001	Sound Blaster 2.0–compatible sound device
PNPB002	Sound Blaster Pro–compatible sound device
PNPB003	Sound Blaster 16–compatible sound device
PNPB004	Thunderboard-compatible sound device
PNPB005	Adlib-compatible FM synthesizer device
PNPB006	MPU401 compatible
PNPB007	Microsoft Windows Sound System–compatible sound device
PNPB008	Compaq Business Audio
PNPB009	Plug-and-Play Microsoft Windows Sound System Device
PNPB00A	MediaVision Pro Audio Spectrum (Trantor SCSI enabled, Thunder Chip disabled)
PNPB00B	MediaVision Pro Audio 3D
PNPB00C	MusicQuest MQX-32M
PNPB00D	MediaVision Pro Audio Spectrum Basic (No Trantor SCSI, Thunder Chip enabled)
PNPB00E	MediaVision Pro Audio Spectrum (Trantor SCSI enabled, Thunder Chip enabled)
PNPB00F	MediaVision Jazz-16 chipset (OEM Versions)
PNPB010	Auravision VxP500 chipset—Orchid Videola
PNPB018	MediaVision Pro Audio Spectrum 8-bit
PNPB019	MediaVision Pro Audio Spectrum Basic (no Trantor SCSI, Thunder chip disabled)
PNPB020	Yamaha OPL3-compatible FM synthesizer device
PNPB02F	Joystick/Game port
SYSTEM DEVICES—PNPCXXX-DXXX—MODEMS	
PNPC000	Compaq 14400 modem
PNPC001	Compaq 2400/9600 modem

Detection vs. Enumeration

Detection is the process that Windows 98/Me uses during its search for legacy (or non–plug-and-play), devices on a computer. Detection is used during Windows setup and any time that you use the Add New Hardware wizard to search for new hardware installed in your computer. Detection does not take place each time you start Windows 98/Me. During the detection process, Windows creates a file called DETLOG.TXT in the root directory of the boot drive. You can use this file as a basic troubleshooting tool in order to determine which devices were detected or if any errors are encountered.

By comparison, *enumeration* is the process that Windows 98/Me uses to identify the PnP devices in your computer—including those devices on PnP busses such as ISAPNP, PCI, and PCMCIA (PC Card) devices. Enumeration occurs each time Windows 98/Me starts and whenever Windows 98/Me receives notification that a change has occurred in the computer's hardware configuration (such as when you remove a PCMCIA card).

Extended System Configuration Data (ESCD)

While the BIOS is certainly able to assign resources to each PnP device in the system, it usually does not. After all, most people only change their system hardware on rare occasions. This saves precious time during each boot, but it also prevents the BIOS from making different assignment decisions each time the system starts. When BIOS alone assigns resources, you might find resource settings changing even when the hardware remains unchanged. To ensure that PnP resources remain consistent each time the system boots, assignments are retained in the extended system configuration data (ESCD) area. The ESCD is a small amount of *nonvolatile RAM* (NVRAM)—similar to the CMOS RAM—that holds configuration information for the PnP hardware in your system. At boot time, the BIOS checks this area of memory. If no changes have occurred since the last boot, nothing needs to be reconfigured, and the POST can skip that portion of the boot process.

The ESCD also serves as a link between the BIOS and the operating system. Both use the ESCD area to read the current status of PnP hardware devices and to record changes. Windows 98/Me reads the ESCD to see if hardware has been changed and reacts accordingly (for example, by reporting the detection of a new device and launching the Add New Hardware wizard). Windows also allows users to override PnP resource assignments by manually changing resources in the Device Manager. This information is recorded in the ESCD area so the BIOS knows about the changes during subsequent boots and doesn't try to change the assignment back again.

Problems Updating the ESCD   Normally, you'll see the message "Updating ESCD" only once after hardware has been changed. However, there are relatively rare cases where you'll see the message each time the system boots (even though the hardware has not changed). This is often caused by an incompatibility between how Windows 98/Me and the BIOS use the ESCD. There are several ways to address this message:

- If the system displays "Updating ESCD…Success" after adding or removing hardware on the next boot-up only, then this is normal for most BIOS versions. No action is required on your part.

- If the system displays this message every time the PC boots, then there may be a conflict between the BIOS and the operating system. The ESCD information is managed by both the BIOS and by Windows 98/Me to allow for PnP resource allocation. However, some BIOS versions record hardware configuration information in a way that is subtly different from Windows. When this happens, Windows will change the ESCD area back to the way it "expects" it to be on each boot. When you then reboot the system, the BIOS will see this change made by Windows and change the data back again. This tug-of-war will continue to happen each time the system is booted. Generally speaking, this does not damage the system, but a BIOS upgrade may be necessary to correct the problem.

- If the system displays a message like "Updating ESCD…" but then stalls the boot process (either with or without displaying the word "Success"), there is a problem with updating the ESCD. This can usually be traced to a problem with an expansion card—usually the one you just added to the machine. It could also be a problem with the motherboard itself.

Legacy Devices

Another issue to consider when working with PnP systems is the support of non-PnP devices (legacy devices). These are the traditional "jumpered" devices that need to be configured manually. Under DOS, legacy devices run just fine and require no special support, but they can cause a problem under Windows 98/Me. Remember that a PnP system relies on the ability to automatically identify every device in the system. Since legacy devices are not designed to communicate their configuration to the operating system, there is no way for Windows 98/Me to detect the device—much less assign resources for it. This means Windows 98/Me can assign resources to a PnP device that are already in use by a legacy device. Windows circumvents this problem by requiring you to "register" legacy devices using the Add New Hardware wizard under the Control Panel. Once a legacy device is installed and the system is rebooted, use the Add New Hardware wizard to "tell" Windows 98/Me about the new device and install the proper drivers for it.

Enabling PnP Under DOS

Now that PnP devices are essentially standard, a new problem has developed for technicians—PnP support under DOS. While Windows 98/Me is a natural platform for PnP devices, DOS cannot automatically identify and configure PnP devices without additional real-mode software drivers. This makes it difficult to use many PnP devices under DOS. But with a proliferation of DOS games and other applications still in service, PnP support is often a necessity. In other cases, older hardware platforms may lack the support to fully implement a PnP system (such as older BIOS). This part of the chapter examines the techniques used to implement PnP support under DOS and Windows 3.1x.

If you do not have access to a PnP operating system (that is, you're using DOS or Windows 3.1x), you will need to install a PnP configuration driver in CONFIG.SYS that will perform resource allocation and configuration for a PnP device. A PnP *configuration driver* determines the resource settings of all your system devices and legacy cards, configures PnP cards, and provides relevant configuration information to other drivers or applications that access your PnP cards. By contrast, a PnP *configuration utility* allows you to view, enter, or change the resource settings of the PnP and legacy cards in your system. The new or changed settings are then used by the PnP configuration driver to configure new PnP cards. For example, the PnP driver for an Ensonique SoundScape board is DWCFGMG.SYS entered into a CONFIG.SYS command line. The corresponding PnP utility for that Ensonique board is SSINIT.EXE, which is entered into an AUTOEXEC.BAT command line.

THE PNP CONFIGURATION DRIVER

A PnP driver is loaded in the CONFIG.SYS file. For example, the Creative Labs PnP Configuration Manager (for Creative Labs PnP devices) would load the driver CTCM.EXE in a command line such as:

```
device=c:\ctcmdir\ctcm.exe
```

where c:\ctcmdir is the directory where you have installed CTCM. This CTCM statement will be placed before all the statements that load other low-level device drivers (such as CTSB16.SYS and SBIDE.SYS) so that your Creative PnP cards will be configured before these device drivers try to use them. For an Ensonique SoundScape sound board, the PnP driver would be installed such as:

```
device=c:\plugplay\drivers\dos\dwcfgmg.sys
```

In most cases, an automated installation routine will copy the PnP files to your hard drive and make any necessary changes to your CONFIG.SYS file. But if you have to install the software manually, make sure to place the driver command lines for each PnP device *after* the PnP configuration manager.

THE PNP CONFIGURATION UTILITY

A PnP utility is loaded in the AUTOEXEC.BAT file. It is this utility that actually configures and initializes the PnP device. For Creative Labs PnP devices, the utility CTCU is entered in an AUTOEXEC.BAT command line(s) such as:

```
set CTCM=C:\ctcmdir
C:\ctcmdir\CTCU /S /W=C:\windows
```

where c:\ctcmdir and c:\windows are the directories where your CTCM, CTCU, and Windows 3.x files are respectively installed. For an Ensonique SoundScape sound board, a typical entry would appear similar to:

```
set sndscape=c:\sndscape
lh c:\sndscape\ssinit /I
```

Once again, most PnP products will come with an automated installation routine on floppy disk. But when you are troubleshooting a defective installation or performing a manual installation, the format just shown can help you avoid problems.

BLASTER VARIABLES

When configuring a PnP sound board, you will usually have to deal with a BLASTER variable in the AUTOEXEC.BAT file. For legacy sound cards, the BLASTER variable includes fixed settings for address, interrupt, and DMA information such as:

```
set BLASTER=A220 I5 D1 T1
```

With a PnP installation, however, the BLASTER variable is redefined to "X out" the interrupt and DMA entries, as illustrated here:

```
set BLASTER=A220 IXX DX T1
```

The actual values for interrupt and DMA will be entered when the PnP configuration utility runs.

PROBLEMS WITH GENERIC PNP CONFIGURATION SOFTWARE

There are a number of generic PnP driver/utility sets designed to support a wide range of PnP devices under DOS or Windows 3.1x. One of the most popular sets is the *Intel Configuration Manager* (ICM) and *ISA Configuration Utility* (ICU)—both developed by Intel Corporation. In fact, this software may already be installed on your PC (or bundled with PnP cards). While the idea of generic PnP software is an appealing one, such generic software is not necessarily compatible with all types of PnP boards. When the software and hardware are incompatible, you will see one of the following error messages:

- Failed NVS write
- Failure to detect PnP BIOS machine
- Failure to assign new configuration to PnP card
- ICM may not be able to configure your PnP card properly

As a general rule, you should use the manufacturer-specific software that accompanies a PnP device rather than generic PnP software.

PROBLEMS WITH MANUFACTURER'S PNP SOFTWARE

While manufacturer-specific PnP software will generally provide excellent service, there are some potential limitations to keep in mind. When you use a non-PnP operating system like DOS or Windows 3.1x (and you do not have a PnP BIOS), your PnP card works like a software-configurable card. In such a situation, the PnP driver needs to know which resources have been reserved by each legacy card, PnP card, and system device in your system before it can allocate conflict-free resources to your new PnP card. Normally, the PnP driver can "see" all the resource settings, but you may need to use the PnP utility to enter the resource settings of all the legacy cards in your PC.

You may still encounter hardware conflicts if the resource settings specified through a PnP utility are incomplete or wrong. If this happens, use the configuration utility to select a different group of resources for the PnP card that caused the conflict. You may need to try a few combinations until you find one that works. This can be tedious, but it is easier than the traditional method of changing DIP switches or jumpers.

HANDLING PNP CONFIGURATION ISSUES UNDER DOS

DOS PnP software allows you to use PnP devices in the DOS environment. In many cases, DOS support for PnP works adequately, but there are several issues that can arise when you do the following:

■ *Choose between the PnP BIOS, PnP software, or PnP OS.* There are a number of PC setups that allow you to configure a PnP device based on the PnP BIOS, the PnP driver/utility software, or the PnP operating system. When you are faced with such a choice, it is often better to use the PnP software or operating system rather than the BIOS. Set the BIOS so that it will not configure PnP devices. The reason is that a BIOS does not have any way of knowing how legacy devices are configured, so allowing the BIOS to configure a mixed system (with legacy and PnP devices) introduces an excellent chance for hardware conflicts.

For "pure" system configurations (containing all PnP devices) you can choose to let the PnP BIOS configure PnP devices.

■ *Upgrade a PnP system to Windows 98/Me.* You may have a system with PnP devices that is running with PnP driver and utility software under DOS or Windows 3.1x. When Windows 98/Me is installed, it should recognize the PnP device(s) during the hardware detection phase of the installation, then install the proper software for dealing with the device(s) under Windows 98/Me. At the same time, Windows should REMark out the real-mode driver and utility software entries under CONFIG.SYS and AUTOEXEC.BAT. This loss of real-mode drivers can cause a problem when returning to the DOS mode later.

■ *Replace generic PnP software with manufacturer-specific software.* If there is already generic software used to initialize and run your PnP device(s), that software should be disabled before installing manufacturer-specific software. You can do this by placing the REM statement before the generic software's command lines in CONFIG.SYS and AUTOEXEC.BAT. It is not necessary to remove generic PnP software files from the system.

■ *The system hangs or reboots whenever the driver software loads.* The upper memory area of your PnP BIOS machine is probably mapped by EMM386 using the HIGHSCAN option (and thus can get corrupted easily). When it does, CTCM (or other DOS PnP software) will not work properly. Your system may then hang or reboot whenever you load CTCM. To resolve this problem, remove the HIGHSCAN option in the EMM386 statement in the CONFIG.SYS file. For example, change the statement:

```
device=c:\dir\emm386.exe highscan
```

to

```
device=c:\dir\emm386.exe
```

where C:\dir is the directory in which your EMM386 utility is installed.

Managing and Troubleshooting PnP Devices

Plug-and-play technology provides technicians and end users with a powerful configuration tool that takes much of the guesswork and trial-and-error out of hardware installations and upgrades. Still, PnP platforms are far from perfect, and managing the mix of PnP and legacy devices in many of today's systems takes a bit of care. This part of the chapter provides some tips for working with PnP and legacy devices under Windows 98/Me, then examines a series of PnP troubleshooting procedures.

INSTALLING PNP DEVICES

Ideally, you simply need to install the physical device in the system. When Windows 98/Me starts, it should recognize the new device automatically and install the appropriate drivers for it. If Windows cannot locate an appropriate driver already on board, it will prompt you to provide a floppy disk, CD, or path containing the correct driver.

INSTALLING LEGACY DEVICES

Remember that legacy devices are configured manually and cannot report their configuration to Windows 98/Me automatically. When installing new legacy hardware in the system, you must run the Add New Hardware wizard to register the device with Windows 98/Me and add the appropriate driver:

1. In the Control Panel, double-click the Add New Hardware icon.
2. In the Add New Hardware wizard, click Next, and then select "Automatically detect installed hardware."
3. Allow Windows 95/98 to detect the new device, and then follow the instructions to configure the driver.

There are some cases where the Add New Hardware wizard cannot detect the new device. When this occurs, select "Install specific hardware." You'll need to specify the new device type, manufacturer, and model, and then install the driver.

UPDATING DEVICE DRIVERS

All devices installed under Windows 98/Me (both PnP and legacy) are heavily dependent on drivers. Over time, drivers often need to be updated to resolve bugs with the driver, streamline the performance of the particular device, or overcome incompatibilities with other devices or drivers. An important part of device management under Windows 98/Me involves driver updates. In some cases, new drivers are provides on a "maintenance disk" sent by the manufacturer. In other cases, the new driver is downloaded from the manufacturer's tech support Web site. But in either case, all drivers must be properly installed—usually through the Add New Hardware wizard. The following steps outline the process for installing a new driver:

1. In the Control Panel, double-click the Add New Hardware icon.
2. Click Next, click No, and then click Next (do not let the wizard autodetect devices).
3. Click the type of hardware for which you are installing the driver, and then click Next.
4. Click Have Disk.

5. Type the path for the driver you are installing and click OK, or click Browse and locate the driver manually. You must type the path for or locate the OEMSETUP.INF file from the manufacturer.

6. In the dialog box listing the INF file, click OK. Click OK to continue.

7. Click the correct driver and then click OK.

8. Click Finish.

For Windows 98 systems, drivers can typically be updated just by clicking the Update Driver button on the Driver tab in the device's Properties dialog (Figure 30-1). That will start the Update Device Driver wizard (Figure 30-2), which will automatically walk you through the driver update process. However, you can still use the Add New Hardware wizard to update device drivers if necessary.

INSTALLING MODEMS MANUALLY

With the popularity of online resources such as AOL and the Internet, most current PCs are equipped with a modem. While modem installation is very similar to other device installations, modems offer some peculiar wrinkles that often demand a slightly different installation approach. (They are also not always detected with 100 percent reliability.) These steps outline a modem installation:

1. In the Control Panel, double-click the Modems icon.

2. If this is to be the first modem installed in the computer, the Install New Modem wizard starts automatically (Figure 30-3). If not, click Add on the General tab.

3. If you want Windows 98 to autodetect your modem, click Next. If not, click the "Don't detect my modem…" check box to select it, and then click Next.

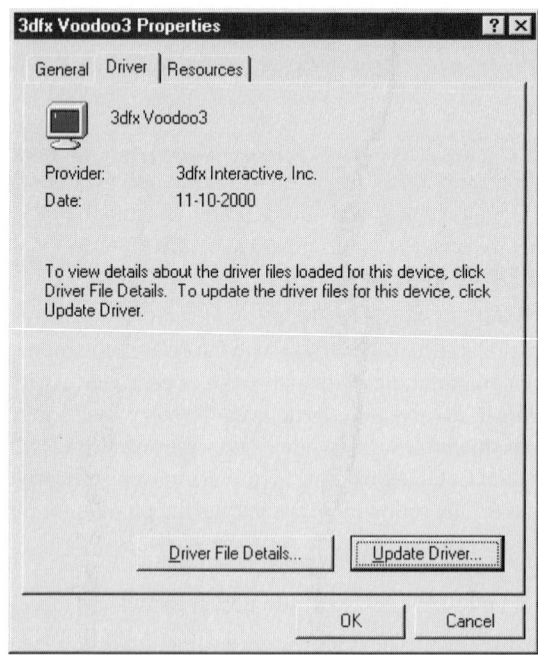

FIGURE 30-1 Using the Update Driver button under Windows 98/SE

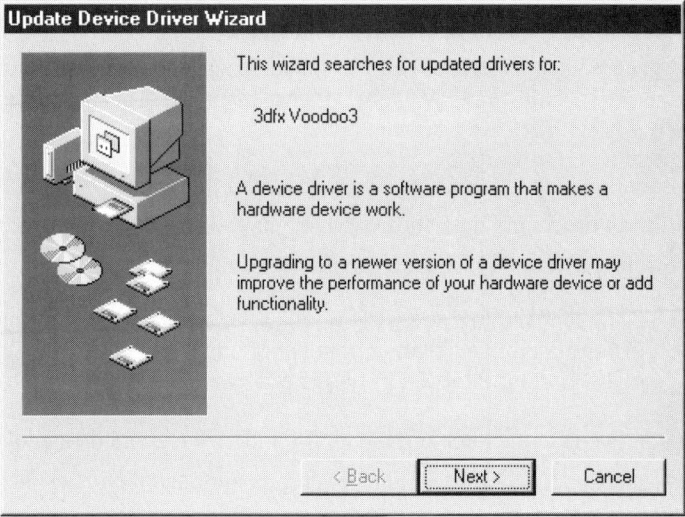

FIGURE 30-2   Starting the Update Device Driver wizard

4. If you chose to have Windows 98 detect your modem, Windows queries the serial ports on your computer looking for a modem. If Windows detects an incorrect modem, click Change, and select the appropriate manufacturer and model. Click Next, and then continue with Step 7.

5. If you chose to select your modem manually, click the appropriate manufacturer and model, and then click Next.

6. Click the appropriate communications port, and then click Next.

7. Click Finish.

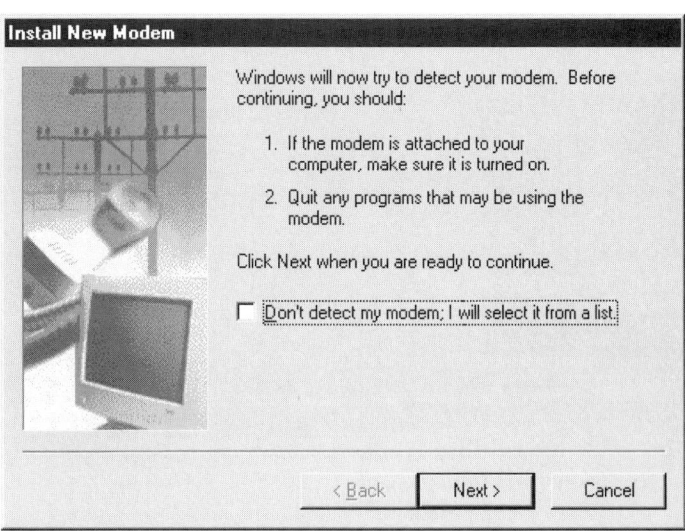

FIGURE 30-3   Starting the Install New Modem wizard

INSTALLING PRINTERS MANUALLY

Although the newest generation of printers are PnP compatible and can be identified automatically, most traditional printers must be specified under Windows 98/Me manually. This is accomplished through the Printers icon as specified next:

1. Click the Start button, point to Settings, and then click Printers.

2. Double-click Add Printer, and then click Next (Figure 30-4).

3. Click Local Printer or Network Printer as appropriate, and then click Next.

If you click Network Printer, you are prompted for the network path for the printer. If you do not know the correct path, click Browse, or check with your network administrator. Click either Yes or No as appropriate in the "Do you print from MS-DOS-based programs?" area, and then click Next.

4. Click the appropriate manufacturer and model for your printer, and then click Next.

5. If you chose to install a local printer, click the correct port, and then click Next.

6. Type a name for the printer (or accept the default name), and then click either Yes or No in the "Do you want your Windows-based programs to use this printer as the default printer?" area. Click Next.

7. To print a test page, click Yes, and then click Finish.

DISABLING A DEVICE

Ordinarily, Windows 98/Me identifies devices, assigns resources, and loads drivers for all the devices it finds. From time to time (especially during troubleshooting), it may be necessary to disable a device. In effect, disabling a device prevents Windows 98/Me from loading drivers or allocating resources associated

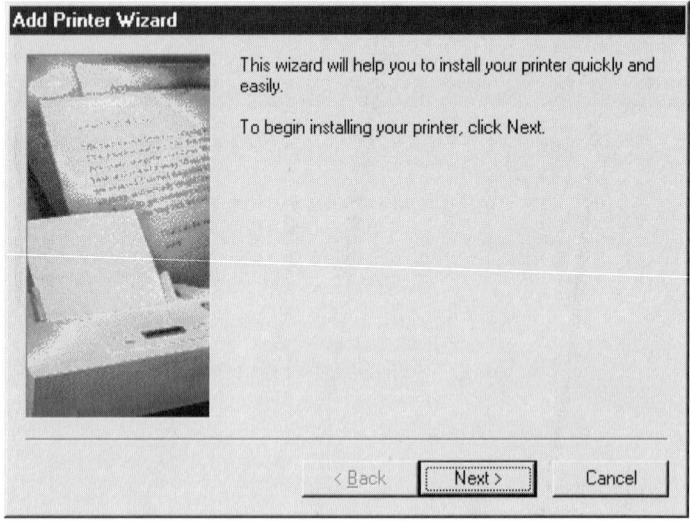

FIGURE 30-4   Starting the Add Printer wizard

with the device, but does not remove the device from the system. This is a particularly handy trick when checking for resource assignment problems:

1. Click the Start button, point to Settings, and then click Control Panel.

2. Double-click the System icon.

3. On the Device Manager tab, click the device you want, and then click Properties.

4. On the General tab, click the "Original configuration (current)" check box to clear it, and then click OK. Under Windows 98, you should check the box marked "Disable in this hardware profile," and then click OK.

5. You may need to reboot the system in order to free the resources, but the neutralized device should no longer be available.

REMOVING A DEVICE

There will be times (especially during troubleshooting) where it may be necessary to remove a device entirely from the Windows 98/Me platform in order to free resources otherwise assigned to the device. Normally, Windows should free the resources of a PnP device simply by disabling it (see "Disabling a Device" preceding), or when the device is physically removed. But legacy cards may need to be removed manually before their assigned resources can be freed. To free resource settings used by disabled hardware:

1. Click Start, Settings, and Control Panel. Click the System icon, and select the Device Manager tab.

2. In the hardware list, click the plus sign (+) next to the type of hardware, and then click the device that is disabled.

3. Click Remove, and then click OK.

4. Click the Start button, and then click Shut Down. Click OK. When the message appears saying it is safe to do so, turn off and unplug your computer, and then remove the physical hardware device from inside the computer.

 PnP device resources are freed automatically when you disable or remove a device. To see if resources are free after the device is disabled but before removing the device, double-click the device in the hardware list in Device Manager, and then click the Resources tab.

SYMPTOMS

As a rule, a computer's PnP system runs in the background, and you will rarely need to work with it directly (other than to tweak a conflicting resource or disable a device). However, when problems do arise, you can usually correct trouble by referring to the following symptoms.

SYMPTOM 30-1   Windows Setup crashes on first boot after configuring PnP devices
This problem can occur if *all* the following conditions exist: (1) your computer has a PCI bus with PCI adapters, (2) there is an ISA adapter (such as a sound card) in your computer, (3) the ISA adapter was not configured (or was not running in real mode) before you ran Setup, and (4) you have not changed any of your computer's CMOS settings. If all of these conditions are true, chances are that one hardware device in the computer may be conflicting with another. When this occurs, Windows may hang up or crash.

For example, if you have a PCI-based computer with a PCI video card, PCI SCSI adapter, and ISA sound card, Setup runs its hardware detection and finds the ISA device. When Setup is finished, your computer is restarted, and the sound card driver is loaded. When Windows enumerates the PCI bus and its adapters, it finds that the BIOS has set the IRQ for one of the PCI devices to the same IRQ as the sound card—causing the conflict.

There are several possible techniques to correct this problem. First, try reserving the IRQ for your ISA devices in the CMOS Setup—this prevents the BIOS from assigning the IRQ to another device such as the PCI system. You can try removing the ISA device(s) until the computer is completely configured to run Windows 98/Me, and then reinstall the device(s). After you reinstall each ISA adapter, run the Add New Hardware wizard to configure the device. Third, if the ISA device is software configurable, you may be able to assign nonconflicting resources using your Device Manager:

1. Reboot your computer. When you see the "Starting Windows" message, press F8, and then choose Safe Mode from the Startup menu.

2. Click Start, highlight Settings, and then click Control Panel.

3. Double-click the System icon, and then click the Device Manager tab.

4. Highlight the offending ISA device, and then click Properties.

5. Click the "Original configuration (current)" check box to clear it, and then click OK. Under Windows 98, select the "Disable in this hardware profile" check box. Now restart Windows.

6. If Windows 98 starts and finishes the setup configuration, click Start, highlight Settings, and then click Control Panel.

7. Double-click the System icon, and then click the Device Manager tab.

8. Click the offending ISA device, and then click Properties.

9. Click the Resources tab. On the Resources tab, select a nonconflicting resource for the ISA device (if one is available). If you do not have a suitable resource available, you may need to reconfigure another device to free up the appropriate resources (or remove the offending ISA device).

10. Restart the system again if necessary.

SYMPTOM 30-2   **Selecting a "None of the above" hardware profile under Windows 95/98 may reset your device configurations**   When you have multiple hardware profiles configured on your system, an option labeled "None of the above" is included in the list of available hardware profiles when you start the computer. If you select "None of the above," plug-and-play enumeration occurs, and *some* devices may be reset to configurations that the drivers cannot support. When this occurs, you may have to manually reload the original device drivers. This problem is corrected the following updated file(s):

■ For Windows 95 version 4.00.950 (retail release) and 4.00.950 A (Service Pack 1), use the update:

```
IO.SYS       dated 12/22/97     5:53pm           223,230 bytes
```

■ For Windows 95 version 4.00.950 B (OSR 2 and 2.1) and 4.00.950 C (OSR 2.5), use the update:

```
IO.SYS       dated 12/22/97     6:10pm           214,918 bytes
```

■ For Windows 98 version 4.10.1998 (retail release), use the update:

```
IO.SYS       dated 05/21/99     05:13p           222,456 bytes
```

SYMPTOM 30-3   **The Energy Star check box is not available for your monitor**
When you check the Monitor tab in the Display Properties dialog box under Windows 98, the "Monitor is Energy Star compliant" check box may not be available. This trouble can occur if Windows 98 is configured to automatically detect plug-and-play monitors. You must disable the automatic detection of any plug-and-play monitor(s):

1. Click Start, highlight Settings, click Control Panel, and then double-click Display.

2. Click the Settings tab, and then click Advanced.

3. Click the Monitor tab, clear the "Automatically detect Plug & Play monitors" check box, click OK, and then click OK again.

4. Restart the computer.

SYMPTOM 30-4   **After upgrading to Windows 98/SE, the ES1869 sound device is disabled**   When you review the ES1869 Plug-and-Play AudioDrive sound card in Device Manager, you'll notice a yellow exclamation point and a status of "Code 10" for the sound card. This problem occurs after you upgrade your Windows 95/98 system to Windows 98 Second Edition (SE) or higher. To fix this problem, you'll need to remove and reinstall the ES1869 Plug-and-Play sound card:

1. Click Start, highlight Settings, click Control Panel, and then double-click the System icon.

2. Click the Device Manager tab, click the "ES1869 Plug and Play AudioDrive" sound card, click Remove, click OK, and then click OK again.

3. Click Yes when you're prompted to restart your computer.

4. After your computer restarts, the ES1869 Plug-and-Play AudioDrive sound card should be detected and installed properly.

SYMPTOM 30-5   **The system crashes when you run the Add New Hardware wizard under Windows 98/Me**   This issue may be caused by the incorrect interpretation of data stored in the computer's CMOS RAM (set up by the BIOS). On certain motherboards, Windows 98/Me may not be able to successfully complete the plug-and-play detection process. You can probably resolve this issue by upgrading the system BIOS.

SYMPTOM 30-6   **You encounter an error when updating the Crystal PnP Audio Codec Driver under Windows 98**   After you update the "Crystal Plug and Play Audio Codec" driver in your Device Manager, you may receive an error message such as:

```
Crystal PnP Audio CODEC
Setup cannot upgrade the existing driver for this device. Press OK to
continue.
```

This problem can occur if Windows 98 cannot safely upgrade the driver that's already installed. The problem might also occur if such an upgrade might disable a feature that the current driver provides, or if the information (INF) file for the driver is missing.

SYMPTOM 30-7   **You find that a joystick port is not removed when you remove the sound card**   When you remove a sound card from your computer, and remove the sound card in the Windows 98/Me Device Manager, the joystick (game port) on the sound card continues to appear in

Device Manager. This trouble occurs because there is no parent-child relationship between the sound card and the joystick port. The virtual joystick device driver (VJOYD.VXD) is unable to detect whether the joystick port has been removed (or the joystick port is present but has no joystick attached), so the driver is always active. When you remove the sound card in Device Manager, the joystick port is not automatically removed. You'll need to remove the game port device manually:

1. Right-click the My Computer icon on your desktop, and then click Properties.

2. Click the Device Manager tab.

3. Click the plus sign (+) next to "Sound, video, and game controllers" to expand the branch.

4. Click the Gameport Joystick device to highlight it, and then click Remove.

SYMPTOM 30-8   **You notice more than one instance of the same port in the Windows 98/Me Add New Hardware wizard**   When you're manually installing new hardware (such as a modem) using the Add New Hardware wizard, multiple instances of COM or LPT ports may appear as options in the port selection dialog. This trouble can occur when there are duplicate entries for a COM or LPT port in the registry. Duplicate entries can occur if the computer does not contain a plug-and-play BIOS. You can generally correct this problem by editing the redundant registry entries manually:

Editing the registry incorrectly may prevent the system from booting. Before you edit the registry, you should first make a backup copy of the registry files (SYSTEM.DAT and USER.DAT) to your boot disk. Both are hidden files in the \Windows folder.

1. In the Registry Editor (REGEDIT), export the appropriate registry keys (for backup purposes):

```
HKEY_LOCAL_Machine\Enum\Bios\*PNP0400 (or *PNP0401) for duplicate LPT ports
HKEY_LOCAL_Machine\Enum\Bios\*PNP0500 (or *PNP0501) for duplicate COM ports
```

2. Now delete the appropriate registry keys:

```
HKEY_LOCAL_Machine\Enum\Bios\*PNP0400 (or *PNP0401) for duplicate LPT ports
HKEY_LOCAL_Machine\Enum\Bios\*PNP0500 (or *PNP0501) for duplicate COM ports
```

3. Quit the Registry Editor, and then shut down and restart your computer normally.

4. Click Start, highlight Settings, click Control Panel, and then double-click Add New Hardware.

5. Click Next, click Yes, and then click Next again. Windows automatically locates the installed ports and re-creates the correct entries in the registry without duplicates.

SYMPTOM 30-9   **You cannot select a higher display resolution in the Windows 98/Me Display Properties dialog**   When you try to increase the screen resolution in the Display Properties dialog, you may be unable to choose a higher resolution than the video system is capable of. For example, your monitor may support a maximum resolution of 1600×1200 pixels, but this setting may be missing from the Screen Area box. In virtually all cases, the system's ESCD contains incorrect information about your particular monitor. You'll need to install your monitor manually:

1. Click Start, highlight Settings, click Control Panel, and then double-click Display.

2. Click the Settings tab, and then click Advanced.

3. Click the Monitor tab, click the "Automatically detect Plug & Play monitors" check box to clear it, and then click Apply.

4.   Click Change, click Next, click "Display a list of all the drivers in a specific location, so you can select the driver you want", and then click Next.

5.   Click "Show all hardware," and then follow the instructions on the screen to finish installing your specific monitor.

SYMPTOM 30-10   **You see wavy lines when using a MAG DX-1795 monitor under Windows 98/Me**   This problem may be caused if your video adapter is configured for 1600×1200 resolution, and the "Automatically detect Plug & Play monitors" check box is selected on the Monitor tab in the Display Properties dialog. To correct this problem, you'll need to reinstall your monitor manually:

1.   Click Start, highlight Settings, click Control Panel, and then double-click Display.

2.   Click the Settings tab, and then click Advanced.

3.   On the Monitor tab, click the "Automatically detect Plug & Play monitors" check box to clear it, and then click Change.

4.   Click Next, click "Display a list of all the drivers in a specific location, so you can select the driver you want," and then click Next.

5.   Click Show All Hardware.

6.   In the Manufacturers box, click "MAG Technology Co., Ltd.," and then click MAG DX-1795 in the Models box.

7.   Click Next, and then follow the instructions on your screen to finish installing the monitor.

SYMPTOM 30-11   **The PC powers-down when you shut down Windows 98/Me**
When you use the Shut Down command on the Start menu to shut down Windows, your computer may automatically power-down after displaying the message "Please wait while your computer shuts down." This behavior is a normal *Advanced Power Management* (APM) feature. There is no way to change this action—the hardware powers-down in response to a software request. However, this occurs only on computers with a PnP BIOS that supports APM features.

SYMPTOM 30-12   **You have trouble restarting the PC when a device uses IRQ 12**
When you try to restart your computer under Windows 98/Me using the Restart option in your Shut Down dialog box, your computer may hang up. This is often a problem on computers with a BIOS that "expects" IRQ 12 to be used by a PS/2-style mouse port—but instead it is used by a software-configurable hardware device such as a PnP expansion card. To work around this problem, reserve IRQ 12 in Device Manager (or change the IRQ for the software-configurable device in Device Manager). You may also consider upgrading the BIOS in your computer to a later version. To reserve an IRQ with Device Manager:

1.   Open the Control Panel, and then double-click the System icon.

2.   On the Device Manager tab, double-click the Computer entry.

3.   Click the Reserve Resources tab, click the Interrupt Request (IRQ) option, and then click Add.

4.   In the Value box, click the IRQ you want to reserve (IRQ 12).

5.   Click OK until you return to the Control Panel.

6.   Reboot the PC if necessary.

SYMPTOM 30-13   **The "volume control" tool may not be installed with some sound cards under Windows 98/Me**   Tools such as Volume Control are installed based on the hardware detected during the installation of Windows. If the computer contains an ISA PnP device that is not enabled by the BIOS, the device is not detected until after Windows is installed. There are two ways around this. If you're just installing Windows 98/Me now, use the Custom Setup option. When you're prompted to select the components you want, select Volume Control in the Multimedia section. If Windows is already installed, follow these steps to install Volume Control:

1.   Open the Control Panel, and then double-click the Add/Remove Programs icon.

2.   Click the Windows Setup tab, click Multimedia, and then click Details.

3.   Select the Volume Control check box.

4.   Click OK, and then click OK again.

5.   Reboot the PC if necessary.

SYMPTOM 30-14   **The ES1788 or ES688 sound device is not detected when it's installed under Windows 98**   This happens because the device is not fully PnP compliant. You'll need to install the device manually using the Add New Hardware wizard:

1.   Click Start, highlight Settings, and then click Control Panel.

2.   Double-click the Add New Hardware icon, click Next, and then click Next again.

3.   Click "No, I want to select the hardware from a list," and then click Next.

4.   In the Manufacturers box, click "ESS Technology, Inc."

5.   In the Models box, click "ESS AudioDrive," click Next, and then click Next again.

6.   Restart Windows when you're prompted to do so.

SYMPTOM 30-15   **After reinstalling Windows 98 on a multimonitor system, you have to reconfigure some monitors after setup is completed**   This is a known problem with some ATI video adapters. Windows 98 disables PnP functionality for ATI video adapters because they do not handle plug-and-play correctly. To work around this problem, manually configure each monitor connected to an ATI video adapter:

1.   Click Start, highlight Settings, and then click Control Panel.

2.   Double-click the Display icon, and then click the Settings tab.

3.   In the Display box, click the adapter you want, and then click Advanced.

4.   On the Monitor tab, click Change.

5.   Click Next, click "Display a list of all the drivers in a specific location, so you can select the driver you want," and then click Next.

6.   Click Show All Hardware.

7.   Click the appropriate manufacturer and model of your monitor, click Next, and then click Finish.

8.   Click Close, click OK, and then reboot the system if necessary.

SYMPTOM 30-16   **After upgrading Windows, the Display Adapters entry is missing in the Device Manager**   This problem is known to occur when your video adapter uses the Nvidia Riva 128 chipset and is unable to secure an IRQ during the PnP detection portion of Windows 98 setup. One solution is to assign an IRQ to the video system using the "Assign IRQ to VGA" option in your CMOS Setup (if available). Another option is to disable PCI bus IRQ steering in the Device Manager.

SYMPTOM 30-17   **You see an error such as "CTSOUND1008: Invalid /BLASTER=A:xxxx argument"**   When you upgrade Windows 3.x to Windows 98/Me on a computer with a Creative Labs Sound Blaster 16 sound card installed, you may receive the following error when your computer restarts:

```
Error CTSOUND1008: Invalid "/BLASTER=A:xxx" argument
```

or

```
Error: DIGN8002 The BLASTER environment settings are invalid
```

This problem will generally occur if the PnP configuration drivers for your Sound Blaster 16 sound card are being loaded from the AUTOEXEC.BAT and CONFIG.SYS files. To correct this problem, you'll need to open your start-up files in a text editor and REMark out the command lines related to your sound card. For example, in AUTOEXEC.BAT:

```
REM c:\vibra16\diagnose /s /w=c:\windows
```

and under CONFIG.SYS:

```
REM device=c:\vibra16\drv\vibra16.sys /unit=0 /blaster=a:220 i:10 d:3 h:7
```

Save your changes and reboot the system.

SYMPTOM 30-18   **Windows 98 locks up when using a Diamond Stealth II S220 video adapter**   This problem occurs most frequently when you start the Add New Hardware wizard while the Windows 98 default drivers for the Diamond Multimedia Stealth II S220 are installed—your computer may crash. If the "standard VGA" video driver is installed, the Add New Hardware wizard runs successfully. This is almost always due to a driver problem, so be sure to obtain and install the most current version of driver for this display adapter.

SYMPTOM 30-19   **You find a "Code 8" is shown for a PnP BIOS device after upgrading to Windows 98/Me**   After upgrading, a yellow exclamation point may be displayed next to the "Plug-and-Play BIOS" device in Device Manager. If you view the Properties for the Plug-and-Play BIOS device, the following message may appear:

```
This device is not working properly because the file (BIOS.VXD) that loads
the drivers for this device is bad (Code 8). To fix this problem, click
Update Driver to update the driver for this device.
```

If you then click the Update Driver button and attempt to search for a better driver, you may receive a message saying that the best driver is already installed. In virtually all cases, the Windows 95 version of the BIOS.VXD file is in the \Windows folder, and you'll need to correct this:

1.   Click Start, select Find, and then click Files Or Folders.

2.   In the Named box, type **bios.vxd**, and then click Find Now.

3.   In the Look in box, click the drive on which the \Windows folder is located.

4. In the list of found files, right-click the BIOS.VXD file located in the \Windows folder, click Delete, and then click Yes.

5. Quit the Find tool, and restart your computer.

SYMPTOM 30-20 **Windows 95 fails to recognize the computer as plug-and-play**
This type of problem often occurs with older Intel OEM motherboards. Windows 95 does not recognize the computer as a plug-and-play platform—even though you receive a message during start up such as "Intel PnP BIOS Extensions Installed." Intel has developed some OEM motherboards that are equipped with a PnP BIOS that does not contain the run-time services necessary to configure motherboard devices. An example of such a motherboard is the Intel P5/90. Gateway 2000 (and possibly other OEMs) ship computers with the P5/90 motherboard. You'll need to upgrade the system BIOS to comply with the plug-and-play BIOS version 1.0a specification or later.

SYMPTOM 30-21 **You notice IRQ conflicts with PCI display adapters** When you install a PCI video adapter that is configured to use a particular interrupt (IRQ), Windows may configure it to use another IRQ that is already in use by another device. While PCI devices can share PCI IRQs, Windows does not support sharing PCI IRQs with other non-PCI devices (such as an IDE controller). Use the Device Manager to resolve the conflict by assigning a different IRQ to one of the conflicting devices (usually the new PCI video adapter).

This kind of behavior does not occur with ISA or VESA Local Bus VLB display adapters.

SYMPTOM 30-22 **The resources for disabled devices are not freed** Even though you disable a device in your computer's CMOS Setup, Windows 98/Me reenables the device and allocates its resources. Windows may also reinstall a device that is removed from Device Manager. This happens because Windows 98/Me detects PnP devices regardless of the CMOS Setup. To prevent Windows from reactivating disabled hardware, you must disable the hardware in the computer's CMOS Setup and remove it from the current configuration in Windows 98/Me. This frees the device's resources for other devices to use:

1. Click the Start button, point to Settings, and then click Control Panel.

2. Double-click the System icon.

3. Click the Device Manager tab, and then double-click the device you want to disable.

4. Click the General tab, and then click the "Original configuration (current)" check box to clear it. Under Windows 98, check the box marked "Disable in this hardware profile."

5. Click the OK button.

6. Restart Windows when prompted.

7. Immediately start the CMOS Setup routine, and disable the device in the CMOS Setup.

8. Save the changes to CMOS, and allow the system to boot normally.

When you disable a device in Device Manager, you must restart your computer before you can reassign the device's resources to another device.

SYMPTOM 30-23 **An AST PnP BIOS is not registered as PnP** The AST plug-and-play BIOS is not registered as plug-and-play capable under Windows 95/98. This is usually because the AST

PnP BIOS contains incorrect information in its 16-bit protected-mode entry point. When Windows 95/98 detects this incorrect code in the AST BIOS, it will not recognize the BIOS as plug-and-play capable. You'll need to contact AST for a BIOS upgrade.

SYMPTOM 30-24   **A PnP ISA adapter is not recognized automatically**   If you insert a PnP ISA adapter in a computer whose motherboard does not contain PCI slots, Windows 98/Me may not recognize the new ISA adapter automatically. The Device Manager may also display a "PCI bus" entry with an exclamation point in a yellow circle, with the status "No Plug and Play ISA bus was found. (Code 29)." This problem is typically caused by a PnP BIOS that is not supported by Windows on computers that have a PCI BIOS, but not a PCI bus. On PCI computers, it is usually the PCI driver that starts the PnP ISA driver. If the PCI driver fails, the ISA driver is not loaded, and therefore PnP ISA adapters are not automatically recognized or configured. To add a PnP adapter so that Windows 98/Me automatically recognizes it, enable the ISA PnP bus manually:

1. In Control Panel, double-click the Add New Hardware icon, and then click Next.
2. Click No, and then click Next.
3. Click System Devices, and then click Next.
4. Click "ISA Plug And Play Bus," and then click Next.
5. Click Finish.
6. Restart your computer when you are prompted to do so.

You may also want to contact your computer manufacturer to see about obtaining an updated PnP BIOS that is better supported by Windows 98/Me.

SYMPTOM 30-25   **The computer no longer operates properly after docking or undocking**   As an example, the keyboard or mouse may stop working. "Hot docking" and "hot undocking" refer to inserting the computer in a docking station or removing it from the docking station while the computer is running at full power. By contrast, "warm docking" refers to docking or undocking the computer while it is in suspend mode. Laptop or portable computers with a PnP BIOS can be hot or warm docked or undocked. In virtually all cases, the computer does not have a suitable PnP BIOS. (This is mandatory for hot or warm docking and undocking.) To correct this problem on a permanent basis, you'll need to upgrade the laptop's BIOS to a version that better supports PnP. In the meantime, you can work around this problem by turning the computer off before you dock or undock it.

SYMPTOM 30-26   **Serial PnP devices are not recognized when an adapter is used to connect them**   For example, when you use a 9-pin to 25-pin serial adapter with a serial PnP device, the device may not be enumerated by the configuration manager at start up. This is caused by the adapter. Some 9-pin to 25-pin serial adapters do not connect the lines that pass the PnP initialization string (including adapters made by Microsoft before the release of Windows 95). Try another (more current) serial adapter. If the problem persists, add the device manually using the Add New Hardware wizard in the Control Panel.

SYMPTOM 30-27   **Windows 98/Me Setup hangs up when detecting SCSI controllers** This often happens with Adaptec SCSI controllers on the first reboot while PnP devices are being detected. It is known to happen when a SCSI hard disk is supported by an Adaptec AHA 2940, Adaptec 2940AU, or Adaptec 2940W controller. You can work around this problem by disabling the SCSI controller and allowing Setup to finish the PnP device detection:

1. Enable PnP SCAM support in the Adaptec SCSI controller BIOS Setup.

2. Disable BIOS Support For Int13 Extension in the Adaptec SCSI controller BIOS Setup.

3. Restart Windows 98/Me, press F8 when you see the "Starting Windows" message, and then choose Safe Mode from the Startup menu.

4. In Control Panel, double-click the System icon, click the Performance tab, click File System, and then click the Troubleshooting tab.

5. Enable the following two options: "Disable protect-mode hard disk interrupt handling" and "Disable all 32 bit protect-mode disk drivers."

6. Click OK, and then click OK again.

7. When you are prompted to restart your computer, click Yes to continue with Setup.

8. After Windows is installed, disable the options you enabled in Step 5.

SYMPTOM 30-28   **After installing an HP OfficeJet 300 printer, you encounter a "Fatal Exception Error" each time you run the Add New Hardware wizard**   You'll typically see Exception Errors 06, 0E, 0C, or 0D. This is because the HP OfficeJet Series 300 Device Manager contends with Windows for control of the PnP system. The HP installation process sets up a shortcut in the Startup folder that runs HPOJDMAN.EXE /AUTOPROMPT. This causes HPOJDMAN.EXE to run in the background. Start the Close Program dialog box by pressing CTRL-ALT-DEL. Click HPOJDMAN in the list of tasks, and then click End Task. Check with HP (**www.hp.com**) for updated printer software utilities.

SYMPTOM 30-29   **The PS/2 mouse is disabled after installing an ISA PnP device** For example, installing a Sound Blaster 16 "value" sound card disables the PS/2 mouse. This problem can occur on computers where the PnP BIOS (rather than Windows) assigns resources to ISA PnP devices. The PnP BIOS may assign IRQ 12 to the IDE drive and disable the mouse port. To correct this problem, disable the BIOS PnP support in the computer's CMOS Setup to allow Windows 98/Me to configure the hardware instead.

SYMPTOM 30-30   **When running the Add New Hardware wizard, it doesn't detect a device that has been removed in Device Manager on a multiple-profile system**   This is because removing a PnP device from one profile and leaving it in another causes a flag to be set in the registry to prevent the device from being enumerated on the next start up. This may also cause the Add New Hardware wizard to bypass the device. The flag exists only in the profile in which the device was removed. To prevent this type of problem from occurring, disable the device in Device Manager instead of removing it. To disable a device, click the "Disable in this hardware profile" check box for the device in Device Manager. To restore (or redetect) the device, remove it from all profiles, and then run the Add New Hardware wizard.

SYMPTOM 30-31   **An extra serial port is displayed in the Device Manager**   When you are using Windows 95 OSR 2 or 2.1, you may see an extra communications port in Device Manager. There is an exclamation point in a yellow circle next to the port. If you remove the port, it is redetected again the next time you restart your computer. The computer's PnP BIOS is probably reporting (incorrectly) that the COM ports are not using resources—though they were detected during setup. This is a problem with Windows 95. Check with Microsoft (**www.microsoft.com**) for any available upgrades or patches, or upgrade to a later version of Windows.

SYMPTOM 30-32 **You cannot set up Windows 98/Me with a PnP program active**
When you try to install Windows 98/Me, you may receive the following error message:

```
A fatal exception OE has occurred at 0028:xxxxxxxx in VxD VMM(06) + xxxxxxxx
```

Or, you may receive a Vwin32 error message displayed on a blue screen, a registry error message, or a *general protection* (GP) fault error message. This problem can occur if you have a PnP program active in memory when you try to install Windows. To work around this issue, install Windows from a command prompt. Restart the computer. When you see the "Starting Windows" message, press F8, and then choose Command Prompt Only from the Startup menu. At the command prompt, type:

```
<drive>:\setup.exe
```

where <drive> is the drive containing your original Windows installation CD.

SYMPTOM 30-33 **An IBM ThinkPad doesn't support PnP under Windows 95/98**
Chances are that the ThinkPad required a BIOS update. The following IBM ThinkPad models are known to need specific BIOS versions:

■ **ThinkPad 750 family**   750/360/755 System Program Service Diskette version 1.20 or later

■ **ThinkPad 755C/Cs and 360/355 family**   750/360/755 System Program Service Diskette version 1.20 or later

■ **ThinkPad 755CE/CD, ThinkPad 755CX/CV, ThinkPad 755CDV**   755 System Program Service Diskette version 1.30 or later

■ **ThinkPad 701C**   701C System Program Service Diskette version 3H or later

■ **ThinkPad 340CSE and 370C**   340 System Program Service Diskette version 1.10 or later

The following ThinkPad models require APM BIOS 1.1 or later and PnP BIOS 1.0a or later in order for these features to work correctly with Windows 95/98:

■ ThinkPad 755C/Cs

■ ThinkPad 360/355 family

■ ThinkPad 755CE/CD/CX/CV/CDV

■ ThinkPad 340CSE

■ ThinkPad 370C

■ ThinkPad 701C

■ ThinkPad 530CS

The following ThinkPad models require APM BIOS version 1.0 to work correctly with Windows 95/98. There is no PnP BIOS support for these models:

■ ThinkPad 750 family

■ ThinkPad 340 monochrome display system

■ ThinkPad 230Cs

To obtain an updated BIOS or System Program Service Diskette for an IBM ThinkPad computer, please contact IBM (**www.ibm.com**).

SYMPTOM 30-34   **A PnP pointing device is not detected**   When you connect a PnP point-ing device (such as Microsoft PnP serial mouse, Microsoft EasyBall, or Microsoft IntelliMouse), the new device may not be detected by Windows 98/Me. Running the Add New Hardware wizard does not correct the problem. This is almost always because the registry entries for your previous pointing device were not properly removed from the registry. This problem is known to occur when your previous pointing device was a Microsoft, Microsoft-compatible, or Logitech mouse. To work around this problem, use the Registry Editor (REGEDIT) to remove the registry entries for your previous pointing device. Remove the following registry keys:

```
Hkey_Local_Machine\System\CurrentControlSet\Services\Class\Mouse\<nnnn>
```

where <nnnn> is an incremental 4-digit number starting at 0000. Also remove the following registry keys (if they exist):

```
Hkey_Local_Machine\Enum\Root\Mouse\<nnnn>
```

where <nnnn> in an incremental 4-digit number starting at 0000. Remove all registry keys under the fol-lowing registry keys (if they exist):

```
Hkey_Local_Machine\Enum\Serenum
```

Remove the following registry key (if it exists):

```
Hkey_Local_Machine\Software\Logitech\Mouseware
```

Right-click My Computer, and then click Properties on the menu that appears. Click the Device Manager tab. Click each serial pointing device, and then click Remove. Click OK, and then restart Windows 95/98. When you restart Windows, the attached pointing device will be detected, and the appropriate drivers will be installed.

Editing the registry incorrectly may prevent the system from booting. Before you edit the registry, you should first make a backup copy of the registry files (SYSTEM.DAT and USER.DAT) to your boot disk. Both are hidden files in the \Windows folder.

SYMPTOM 30-35   **The PnP printer is redetected every time Windows 95/98 starts**
This occurs even when the printer is already installed. When you start Windows 95/98, the following message may be displayed:

```
New Hardware Found
<device>
Windows has found new hardware and is installing the software for it
```

This problem is known to occur with Hewlett-Packard 4L and Hewlett-Packard DeskJet 660C PnP print-ers and is usually caused by damage to the following registry key:

```
Hkey_Local_Machine\Enum\Lptenum
```

Remove the registry key and then restart your computer. When Windows restarts, it will detect the printer and install support for it. Once the printer is installed, it will no longer be detected each time you start Windows 95/98.

 Editing the registry incorrectly may prevent the system from booting. Before you edit the registry, you should first make a backup copy of the registry files (SYSTEM.DAT and USER.DAT). Both are hidden files in the \Windows folder.

SYMPTOM 30-36 **After installing Windows 95/98, none of the APM features were installed** You may also note that there is no "battery meter" for laptops. Some computers and BIOS revisions have known incompatibilities with the APM 1.1 specification. You are probably running Windows 95/98 on such a computer. As a result, the hardware "suspend" functions of your computer should still function correctly, but you cannot use the Windows 95/98 APM features. Windows 95 turns off APM support completely on the following computers:

- AMIBIOS 07/08/1994
- AMIBIOS 07/08/94
- Any Gateway ColorBook >1.0 w/SystemSoft BIOS
- Any Gateway ColorBook with APM 1.0
- AST Ascentia 900N
- Canon Innova 150C
- DECpc LPv+ 1.00
- DECpc LPv+ 1.01
- DECpc LPv+ 1.02
- NCR/AT&T 3150
- Ultra laptop 486sx33
- Wyse Forte GSV 486/66
- Zenon P5/90

Windows 95 turns off power status polling (so you do not see a battery meter) on the following computers:

- IBM ThinkPad 500
- LexBook
- WinBook

Windows 95 uses APM 1.0 mode on NEC Versa and AT&T Globalyst systems with APM 1.1 BIOS and no plug-and-play BIOS. The following IBM ThinkPad computers support APM 1.1:

- ThinkPad 755C
- ThinkPad 360/355 Family
- ThinkPad 755CE/CD/CX/CV/CDV
- ThinkPad 340CSE

■ ThinkPad 370C

■ ThinkPad 701C

■ ThinkPad 530CS

The following IBM ThinkPad computers work with Windows 95, but only APM BIOS 1.0 is supported:

■ ThinkPad 750 family

■ ThinkPad 340 (monochrome)

■ ThinkPad 230Cs

The ASUS PCI/I P55SP4 motherboard with a SiS 5511/5512/5513 chipset and an Award BIOS has been known to exhibit similar problems. (The battery meter may appear on the task bar when it should not.) This problem should be fixed with PnP BIOS version 0110 (11/21/95) for revision 1.2 and 1.3 motherboards. Revision 1.4 motherboards have this fix using PnP BIOS version 0303 (11/21/95).

SYMPTOM 30-37 **The Device Manager reports a "PCI-to-ISA Bridge Conflict"** The Device Manager displays a PCI-to-ISA bridge entry with an exclamation point in a yellow circle—indicating that there is a resource conflict. This problem is typically caused by a PnP BIOS that reports both a PCI and an ISA bus, but only an ISA bus is present, so there is no actual conflict. You'll need to update the PnP BIOS to a version with better detection and reporting capability.

SYMPTOM 30-38 **The PnP BIOS is disabled on a laptop or notebook computer** When you install Windows 98/Me on a dockable notebook computer with a PnP BIOS, you see no "Eject PC" command on the Start menu when the notebook computer is docked in a docking station. Also, no PnP BIOS node is displayed in System Devices under the Device Manager. This problem was known to occur on IBM ThinkPad (360/750/755 series) dockable notebook computers with a PnP BIOS and occurs because early versions of dockable notebook computers with PnP BIOS are not fully compatible with Windows. When a PnP BIOS is disabled in Windows 98/Me, certain features (such as warm docking) no longer work. To make your dockable notebook computer compatible with Windows, contact the manufacturer of your notebook computer and obtain the most recent PnP BIOS.

In general, a PnP BIOS dated after 7/1/95 is compatible with Windows 95/98/Me.

SYMPTOM 30-39 **The sound device on a DEC HiNote Ultra isn't working** When you install Windows 98/Me over an existing Windows for Workgroups 3.1x or Windows 3.1x installation on a DEC HiNote Ultra computer with a PnP BIOS, the sound device no longer works properly. Also, the wrong sound device is installed in Windows. This is a PnP BIOS problem—early versions of the DEC HiNote Ultra shipped with a PnP BIOS are not compatible with Windows 98/Me. Contact DEC and obtain the most recent PnP BIOS for the DEC HiNote Ultra.

SYMPTOM 30-40 **Device resources are not updated in a "forced" configuration** You'll notice that an exclamation point appears over a resource icon in Computer properties in Device Manager, or that changes you make to the resources assigned to a PnP device in the computer's CMOS Setup are not reflected in the Settings column in Computer properties under Device Manager. This is because the device is using a forced configuration instead of an automatic configuration. To remove a forced configuration and allow the PnP device to be fully configurable by the computer's BIOS and Windows, set the device to use automatic settings:

1.   Double-click the System icon in Control Panel.

2.   Click the Device Manager tab.

3.   Double-click the device, and then click the Resources tab.

4.   Click the "Use automatic settings" check box to select it.

5.   Click OK.

> A "forced" configuration overrides any BIOS or ROM settings (even if Windows knows the device is currently consuming a different set of resources). If you move a device to a different set of resources, you must update the forced configuration manually. When you are diagnosing hardware problems, it is a good idea to look for forced configurations and remove them.

SYMPTOM 30-41   **Restarting the computer causes the PC to hang**   This often happens when you try to restart your computer using the "Restart the computer" option in the Shut Down Windows dialog. This problem can occur on computers with a BIOS that expects IRQ 12 to be used by a PS/2-style mouse port, but instead have a software-configurable hardware device (such as a PnP adapter) using IRQ 12. To work around this problem, reserve IRQ 12 in Device Manager, or change the IRQ for the software-configurable device in Device Manager. You may also want to consider upgrading the BIOS in the computer to a later version. To reserve an IRQ with Device Manager:

1.   In the Control Panel, double-click the System icon.

2.   On the Device Manager tab, double-click Computer.

3.   On the Reserve Resources tab, click the Interrupt Request (IRQ) option, and then click Add.

4.   In the Value box, click the IRQ you want to reserve.

5.   Click OK until you return to Control Panel.

SYMPTOM 30-42   **Adding a PCI device to a Dell Dimension causes the system to hang in Windows 95/98**   The BIOS in the Dell computer has probably configured the new PCI device to use IRQ 10, but another legacy device installed in the system is already configured to use IRQ 10. Although Windows 95/98 is designed to recognize resource conflicts such as this, this particular conflict causes the computer to hang before the Windows Configuration Manager recognizes that the conflict exists. The PCI bus is normally a PnP-compatible bus, but the BIOS in Dell Dimension computers statically allocates IRQ 10 to a new PCI device. There is no way to disable this behavior. To work around this problem, configure the existing legacy device to use an IRQ other than IRQ 10.

SYMPTOM 30-43   **You cannot configure disabled devices in the Device Manager**   When you're using a PnP BIOS, you may not be able to configure (through Device Manager) a device that has been disabled in the BIOS—even though the BIOS supports configuring devices for the next time the computer starts. When you click the device in Device Manager and then click Properties, you see a message such as:

```
The device has been disabled in the hardware. In order to use this device,
you must re-enable the hardware. See your hardware documentation for details
(Code 29).
```

This is a problem with Windows 95. You'll need to enable the device in the BIOS *before* you try to configure it in Device Manager.

SYMPTOM 30-44   **A Toshiba T4900 laptop doesn't switch from LCD to external monitor**   If you place a Toshiba T4900 computer into its docking station while Windows 95/98 is running (a "warm dock" operation), the display may not switch from the LCD screen to the external monitor. Toshiba's PnP BIOS does not switch the display properly between the LCD screen and an external monitor. For a short-term work around, press F5 to manually toggle the display between the LCD screen and the external monitor. In the meantime, contact Toshiba for a PnP BIOS upgrade.

SYMPTOM 30-45   **A third port is detected with a CMD PCI dual-port IDE controller**
When using a CMD PCI Dual Port IDE controller (with at least *one* device on both the primary and secondary port), the Device Manager displays a third port. This "false" third port is displayed with an exclamation point inside a yellow circle. This happens because the PnP BIOS in your computer is erroneously reporting that a third port is present. Windows 95/98 does not allocate any resources to the third port, and the existence of the third port in Device Manager should not cause any problems. However, if you want to disable the third port, follow these steps:

1.   Right-click My Computer, and then click Properties on the menu that appears.

2.   Click the Device Manager tab.

3.   Click the third port, and then click Properties. Note that you may need to expand a branch of the hardware tree by double-clicking the branch, or by clicking the plus sign (+) to the left of the branch, before you can click the port.

4.   Click the "Original configuration (current)" check box to clear it, and then click OK. With Windows 98, click the "Disable in this hardware profile" box to select it, and then click OK.

Further Study

Microsoft's plug-and-play page   www.microsoft.com/hwdev/specs/pnpspecs.htm
Microsoft PnP technology   www.microsoft.com/hwdev/PlugnPlay/
Intel's plug-and-play page   developer.intel.com/ial/plugplay/index.htm

31

POWER PROTECTION

Power is one of those issues that's often taken for granted (or at least treated as an afterthought). Surges, spikes, and other power anomalies that occur in commercial power systems every day can damage the PC's power supply, and they often can affect the drives and motherboard circuitry as well. Even when no serious damage occurs to the system, power failures can result in wasted time and lost data for any office or organization. This chapter is intended to explain the concepts of power protection and show you the four major types of power protection devices that are available. As a PC technician, you can use this information to help your customers develop adequate and reliable power protection plans that will suit their needs and budgets. Proper power protection improves system reliability and reduces downtime.

Understanding Power Problems

Generally speaking, we have all come to take power for granted. In most cases, we simply tend to plug a device in the nearest available outlet and turn it on, *assuming* that an appropriate amount of voltage and current is available. If the device fails to function as expected, the natural assumption is that the *device* is at fault. In truth, this is not always the case. Computers and peripherals need certain minimum amounts of current and voltage at the AC line. If either value is too high or too low, the computer may behave erratically (or not work at all).

Commercial power is generated as a sinusoidal (called *alternating current,* or AC) wave similar to the one shown in Figure 31-1. The amplitude of the wave represents *voltage*, and the rate at which the wave repeats represents *frequency*. Voltage and frequency characteristics vary in different regions of the world. Regardless of region, however, the AC signal should be perfectly smooth and regular. In practice, AC can suffer from a variety of ills: blackouts, brownouts, surges, and spikes.

BLACKOUTS

A *blackout* is a complete loss of electrical power where voltage and current drop to a very low value (typically zero). Blackouts are usually caused by a physical interruption in the local power network due to accidental damage by a person or act of nature. The interruption may affect an area as small as a street or as large as an entire region, depending on the point in the power distribution network where damage occurs.

Unless backup power is available, the loss of AC will invariably shut down the computer in a matter of milliseconds. In most cases, simply loosing power does not damage a PC—memory is simply lost (along with any unsaved information), often just an inconvenience for casual home users. For business users, however, loosing power can mean the loss of valuable data, representing hours of lost productivity. In extremely rare cases, a sudden and complete power loss can corrupt a hard drive's file structure and possibly damage files. The best and least expensive means of protection against a rare blackout is to save work regularly—every 30 minutes to an hour. By taking this precaution, no more than an hour of work could be lost if power fails. For remote areas or regions that are subject to frequent power outages, a fast-switching backup power supply (BPS) or a reliable uninterruptible power supply (UPS) is highly recommended.

BROWNOUTS

Perhaps more dangerous than a sudden, complete power loss is the *brownout* (or *sag*), an undervoltage condition caused by questionable electrical wiring or excessive electrical load on an AC circuit.

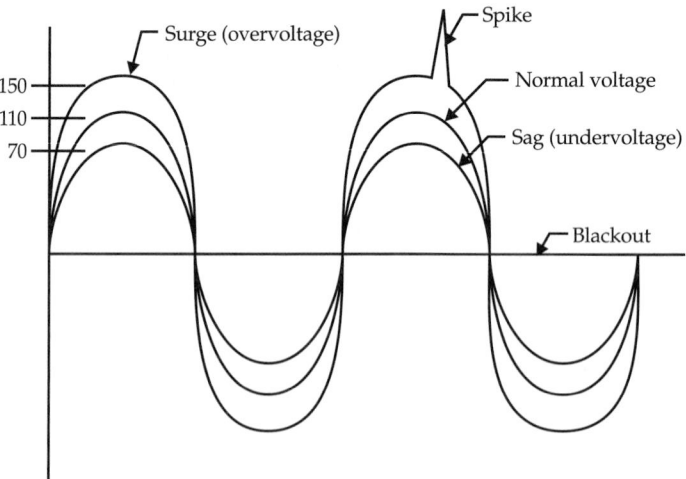

FIGURE 31-1   Comparison of AC sine waves during typical power problems

High-load items (like air conditioners, coffee pots, fan motors, overhead projectors, photocopiers, and so on) draw so much current that the AC voltage level drops. PC supplies are *regulated,* which means the DC output provided to the computer circuitry will be constant over a range of AC input conditions. However, when AC conditions fall outside of that tolerable range, the supply will fall out of regulation, resulting in intermittent system operation (the system mysteriously freezes, random memory errors occur, files may be lost or corrupted on the hard drive, and so on).

Undervoltage conditions can also damage the power supply. Since the PC's power supply responds to low AC voltages by drawing excessive current, serious undervoltage conditions can cause unusual heating that will eventually damage a PC power supply. If your customers complain of unusual system problems such as those just described, ask them to try their system on another circuit. Although one circuit may be loaded down, other circuits are probably not. If your customer cannot find a lightly used circuit (or does not have access to one), ask your customer to try disconnecting high-load devices in their area, such as air conditioners, fans, and heaters. If the problems disappear, advise your customer to have a new AC circuit installed from the circuit breaker (make it very clear that the new AC circuit should be from another line phase). Urban areas suffer from summer brownouts that affect entire areas. Such regional brownouts are usually due to the massive air conditioner load that is common in the summer season.

It is difficult to overcome brownout conditions, since most BPSs do not engage until voltage levels drop below brownout levels (usually 85 to 95 Vac). However, a UPS will prevent unpleasant surprises since the computer runs from the UPS normally anyway. Brownouts and blackouts do not interrupt UPS operation.

SURGES AND SPIKES

Basically, spikes and surges are the same villain—they just take different forms. *Surges* are small overvoltage conditions (140 Vac or more) that take place over relatively long periods (usually more than 1 second). To regulate power to a desired level, excess energy must be switched (in switching power supplies) or thrown away (in linear power supplies). In either case, excessive voltage creates overheating in the supply, and will eventually destroy it. Some power supplies are designed to shut down in the event of voltage or thermal overloads, but you cannot always count on this feature in today's proliferation of inexpensive clone PCs.

A *spike* is a large overvoltage condition (perhaps as much as 2,500 volts) that occurs in the space of milliseconds. Lightning strikes and high-energy switching can cause spikes on the AC line. Heavy equipment like drill presses, welders, grinders, and other highly motorized devices can produce tremendous power spikes during normal operation or when switched on and off. If your PC is on the same AC circuit as that heavy equipment, the spikes can damage the power supply. While some supplies are designed with surge suppression components (transformers, capacitors, gas discharge tubes, and metal oxide varistors, or MOVs), spikes that pass through surge suppression can damage the supply regulator or pass through the supply to damage many portions of the motherboard. Also bear in mind that spikes can also pass along the telephone line and damage your modem.

SYMPTOMS OF POWER PROBLEMS

Before you run out and invest hard-earned money in power protection equipment, you first should have some indication of power problems. Power problems are often difficult to measure because the power "event" occurs too quickly to measure without very specialized power monitoring equipment. Still, there are some situations that may suggest chronic power problems:

- The lights tend to flicker or periodically vary in intensity.
- There are frequent or regular errors in data transmission between network nodes.

- The PC stalls, crashes, or reboots for no apparent reason.
- You suffer chronic or frequent component failures (for example, modems don't seem to last long).
- You suffer chronic or frequent hard drive failures or file access problems.
- The CMOS RAM or modem NVRAM periodically looses its contents or becomes corrupted.
- The PC behaves erratically when other high-energy devices are turned on.
- The modem regularly looses its connection, or fails data transfers.
- The monitor display flickers or waves.
- You encounter frequent or chronic write errors to disks.

These symptoms do not guarantee the existence of a power problem, but they should alert you to their possibility.

Protection Devices

A well-designed power supply is built to withstand many of the ills found in urban and suburban AC power distribution. Unfortunately, the never-ending push to reduce component count and cost in clone systems has meant that compromises have been made in the PC supply. You cannot always count on the presence of effective spike or overvoltage protection in original or replacement supplies. Therefore, you should understand the various options that are available to you and your customer.

SURGE AND SPIKE SUPPRESSERS

Surge suppressers, such as the Best SpikeFree shown in Figure 31-2, are simple and relatively inexpensive devices ($20 to $200) that are designed to absorb high-voltage transients produced by lightning and other high-energy equipment. Protection is accomplished by clamping (or shunting) voltages above a certain level (usually above 200 volts). MOVs are often included that can respond quickly and clamp voltages as high as 6000 volts. However, powerful surges such as direct lightning strikes can blow right through an MOV. Also, MOVs degrade with each spike. Once they have passed a number of surges, they are destroyed and must be replaced. There is no way to know whether or not the MOV is working, so there is no way to really tell if a surge suppresser is actually protecting the system.

Many protectors show a neon lamp or LED that goes out when the MOV has blown or when the protector is no longer active. Good suppressers also incorporate a circuit breaker rather than a fuse. This feature is a great convenience, because a circuit breaker can be reset, whereas many fused units must be disassembled to replace the fuse (or the unit must be replaced outright). If possible, select a surge suppresser approved under UL1449 (or an international equivalent). Remember that, as a rule, surge/spike protectors are the simplest and least expensive power protection devices—they are also the most limited.

Modems and fax boards are also susceptible to damage from spikes present on everyday telephone lines. When recommending protection schemes, do not forget to include telephone line spike protection as well. Several of the Best SpikeFree devices shown in Figure 31-2 also provide data line protection along with AC line protection.

LINE POWER CONDITIONERS

Line conditioners perform all the functions that a surge suppresser does, but they also provide some additional power protection. Whereas surge suppressers are passive devices (functioning only when a surge is

FIGURE 31-2   The SpikeFree product line from Best Power (Best Power Technology, Inc.)

present), line conditioners (such as the Best Citadel line conditioners shown in Figure 31-3) use transformers and capacitors for power isolation and high-frequency RF noise filtering. This results in a larger and more expensive—but more effective—power protection scheme. Another advantage of line conditioners is their tolerance to brief brownout conditions. Since transformers and capacitors are energy storage components, those components will continue to provide energy to the power supply during short brownouts (on the order of several milliseconds).

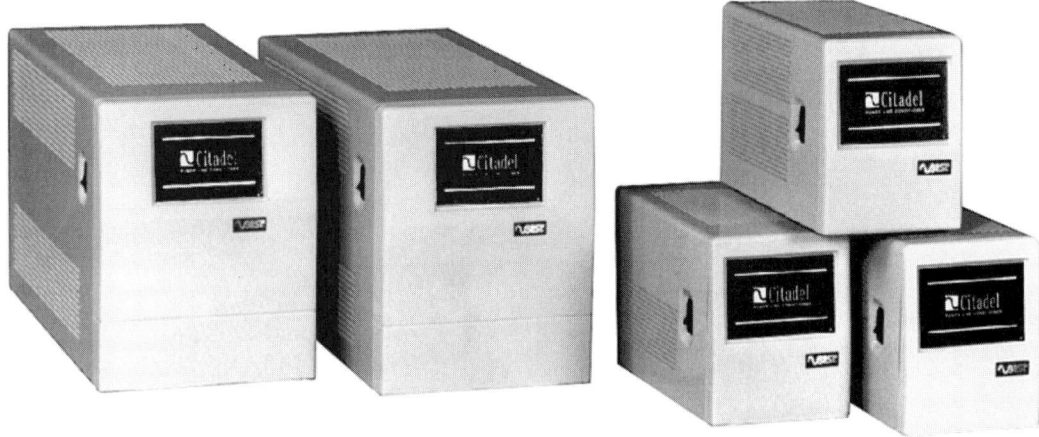

FIGURE 31-3   The Citadel product line from Best Power (Best Power Technology, Inc.)

BACKUP POWER

Surge suppressers and line conditioners will take your customers only so far. Those devices can protect a computer from brief power anomalies and keep their systems off your workbench until it is time to upgrade. Sooner or later, though, power *will* fail. When your customer cannot afford to be in the dark (literally), you should recommend a supplemental power system. A *backup power supply* (BPS) is an offline power system that provides power to your computer *only* when main AC power fails. Power is supplied from a series of batteries that are kept charged while AC power is available. When AC fails, the DC battery power is modulated into AC and switched inline to provide power to the system. Any decent BPS (like the Best Patriot backup supply shown in Figure 31-4) can provide power for 15 to 60 minutes, depending on the amount of load attached to it—plenty of time to save any work in progress and shut down in an orderly fashion.

The problem with some bargain-priced BPS units is their *switching time*. It many take several milliseconds to detect the loss of power and actually initiate the switch-over to battery power. In that few milliseconds, a PC may brownout or reboot anyway and defeat the point of having backup power in the first place. If a customer is having problems with power switch-over, ask them to lighten the load on the BPS. Instead of trying to back up four machines with a BPS, try one or two and experiment a bit. A lighter load may allow the BPS to switch faster and preserve the PC's operation. If operation is acceptable with a lighter load, the prescription might be more BPS installations. If problems persist, find a better BPS for your customer. A BPS that offers a *ferroresonant transformer* (FRT) is often a good bet, since an FRT can provide energy for several milliseconds to smooth the transfer to battery power.

Another problem to remember is that a BPS may not offer any significant level of power protection. Since battery power is free of AC anomalies, inexpensive BPS designs may omit surge suppression or line conditioning features for the direct AC circuit. If power protection devices are already available, the problem is moot. However, if your customer is not yet using power protection devices, recommend a BPS (such as the Best Patriot) that incorporates surge/spike protection.

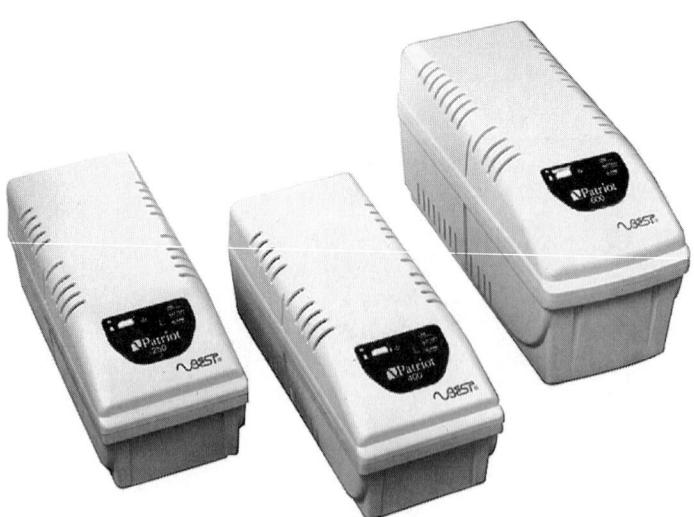

FIGURE 31-4   The Patriot BPS power line from Best Power (Best Power Technology, Inc.)

UNINTERRUPTIBLE POWER SUPPLIES

The *uninterruptible power supply* (UPS) is probably the best all-around form of power protection available. It is also the most expensive. Whereas a BPS provides modulated power only when AC fails, a UPS is designed to provide modulated DC continuously—the PC runs from battery power *all the time*. AC keeps the batteries charged, but line AC does not power the PC directly. As a result, the PC is isolated from even the worse line power anomalies. Like a BPS, a UPS provides power only for a limited time after AC fails (depending on the attached load), allowing the user to save data and shut down. However, there are no switching problems to contend with. High-end UPS systems, such as the Best Fortress UPS shown in Figure 31-5, provide an excellent combination of uninterruptible power, brownout correction, and surge and spike protection.

One thing to consider when recommending a UPS is the type of modulation provided by the modulator. Inexpensive UPS devices modulate DC battery power into an AC square wave. This is "technically" AC, but remember that some PCs and peripherals do not work well with square waves. It is preferable to recommend a UPS with a power *inverter* circuit. The inverter produces a precise sine wave (rather than a square wave), which is compatible with all PCs and peripherals.

SIZING A BPS/UPS

As you might expect, the batteries in a UPS cannot power a load forever. This means a UPS can only power certain pieces of equipment for a limited amount of time. The exact amount of time depends on the *load* (the amount of equipment) that you've attached to the UPS and the size (or capacity) of the UPS itself. For a UPS of any given capacity, a higher load will result in shorter running time. Lightening the load (or using a larger-capacity UPS) will increase the running time. The real trick is to determine your running time by checking the load that you're planning to attach.

All UPS systems are rated in terms of volt amperes (VA), which is a more technical indication of power (usually measured in watts, or W). The power requirements of your equipment should be less than or equal to the VA capacity of the UPS. For example, an IBM OfficePro 700 UPS provides 700VA capacity. A VA capacity will generally operate a load at that level for about 8–10 minutes. That means the 700VA

FIGURE 31-5 The Fortress UPS product line from Best Power (Best Power Technology, Inc.)

UPS should power 700VA worth of PC equipment for about 10 minutes. If you're using half the load (350VA), the UPS should operate for twice as long (16–20 minutes). If you're using a quarter of the load (175VA), the UPS should operate for four times as long (35–40 minutes), and so on. In practice, the actual amount of running time will be a bit longer if the load is measurably lower than the UPS capacity (in other words, the UPS is overrated for the load).

The real trick is to calculate the load that you're attaching. All PC equipment makers list a load rating for their devices. This rating is usually listed on the nameplate or label near the line cord on the rear of the device. The rating may be in VA, in watts (W), or in amps (A). Ideally, all loads should be denoted in VA so that the loads can simply be added together. If a load is in watts, convert to VA by multiplying W × 1.4. If a load is in amps, convert to VA by multiplying A × 120 (for a 120V device) or A × 230 (for a 230V device). Suppose you want to use a UPS to run a monitor, PC, and tape drive. A typical example may be as follows:

Computer VA	=	120V×2A	=	240VA
Monitor VA	=	100W×1.4	=	140VA
Tape drive VA	=	120V×1A	=	120VA
Total			=	**500VA**

In this example, a 500VA UPS will run this load for about 8–10 minutes, or a 1000VA UPS will run this equipment for about 20 minutes. Table 31-1 compares basic load and runtimes for several common UPS capacities.

Do not connect laser printers to a UPS! The power requirements of a typical laser printer are much larger than the requirements of other computer peripherals, and may trip the UPS system's protective circuit breaker. Plug laser printers into a quality surge suppressor. Print jobs can always be requeued when the power is restored.

TABLE 31-1   TYPICAL COMPARISON OF UPS RUNTIME VS. LOAD

LOAD	250VA	400VA	450VA	600VA	900VA	1250VA
50VA	37min	100min	120min	145min	220min	270min
75VA	29min	72min	88min	105min	155min	210min
100VA	23min	47min	65min	79min	110min	160min
150VA	14min	30min	41min	54min	83min	115min
200VA	8min	19min	32min	41min	65min	92min
250VA	5min	13min	24min	31min	47min	75min
300VA	--	9min	18min	22min	40min	64min
350VA	--	7min	14min	17min	35min	54min
400VA	--	5min	11min	13min	29min	46min
450VA	--	--	8min	10min	24min	40min
500VA	--	--	--	7min	20min	34min
550VA	--	--	--	6min	17min	29min
600VA	--	--	--	5min	15min	25min
700VA	--	--	--	--	13min	22min
800VA	--	--	--	--	11min	17min
900VA	--	--	--	--	10min	13min
1000VA	--	--	--	--	--	10min
1250VA	--	--	--	--	--	9min

Backup, Backup, Backup

A strange fact of today's society is that the *information* contained in a computer is often more valuable than the computer system itself. Serious power interruptions can damage a computer, but even more important is the loss of vital data from memory or the hard drive. Power protection devices are intended to protect the PC from damage and keep the system operating in the face of poor or absent AC—at least until the system can be shut down safely. However, power protection devices are not foolproof. Regular backups of memory and disk files are vital to any protection plan.

Advise your customers to save their work religiously. Saving every 30 to 60 minutes is usually prudent (more often in a busy office environment)—it is also *free*. If your customers do not have a tape backup to support their hard drive files, strongly recommend a tape drive. System backups once a day (even once a week) can preserve vital data in the rare event that a hard drive is damaged by a spike or brownout.

Troubleshooting Power Protection Devices

Power protection devices (especially BPS and UPS systems) are often ignored once they are installed. In fact, power systems require a certain level of regular attention and are themselves subject to a wide array of problems that can affect the reliability of your PC or network. This part of the chapter examines many of the common problems that can affect BPS/UPS systems and offers some suggestions for corrective action.

VERIFYING ELECTRICAL SAFETY

Before we discuss troubleshooting specifically, it would be wise to review the overall electrical power and interconnection scheme used by the PC. Electrical power "events" can be conducted by any long cable connected to your computer, LAN, or modem. The following tips can help you protect your equipment from potential damage:

- Use a UPS or surge suppresser to protect all AC operated PC equipment—especially the main system (desktop or tower) and monitor.

- Verify that your AC power receptacles are properly wired (you may need the services of a licensed electrician for this). Even though PC equipment may appear to operate properly under normal conditions, operating computer equipment from improperly wired outlets can pose a shock hazard.

- Plug in all power protection and/or PC equipment line cords to the same AC circuit wherever possible. This basically means that power to all the PC equipment is controlled by the same building fuse or circuit breaker.

- RS-232 serial interface ports on computers, terminals, printers, plotters, and modems are especially sensitive to damage from electrical transients because they use the computer chassis ground as a single common ground. Protect both ends of an RS-232 serial interface cable longer than 5 feet (1.5 meters) with good-quality serial port protection devices specifically designed for that purpose. Do not attempt to run RS-232 links between equipment in separate buildings—use good-quality short-haul modems instead.

■ Use good-quality network protection devices to protect your Ethernet network interface cards (NICs) and other LAN equipment at each end of a network's 10Base-T UTP or coaxial Thinnet cable. Thinnet (10Base2) networks are especially susceptible to intersystem ground noise when the cable shields are inadvertently grounded at more than one location. Verify your system's true single ground point and check to be sure that T-connectors or any exposed connector barrels are not touching the metal chassis of your computer.

■ Use good-quality network protection devices to protect your 4 and 16 Mbps Token Ring NICs and other LAN equipment at each end of a network's UTP cable.

■ Protect the telephone port of your telecommunications equipment (modem, fax, telex, answering machine, and so on) from damage due to nearby lightning activity with a good-quality lightning or surge arrestor designed specifically for telecommunications equipment.

TESTING BPS/UPS BATTERIES

Batteries are electrochemical devices, meaning they all will fail eventually. BPS/UPS backup batteries are certainly no exception. If there is trouble with your BPS/UPS system (or as part of regular maintenance on the power system), you should be able to test the batteries in a BPS or UPS for integrity. The following steps outline testing for +12 Vdc batteries:

1. Make sure that your BPS or UPS is connected correctly, and has at least 50 percent of its total load devices plugged in (desktop unit, monitor, scanner, and so on).

2. Turn on the system and its attached peripherals, and allow the PC to boot normally.

3. Simulate a power outage by disconnecting the BPS or UPS line cord.

4. Use a standard digital voltmeter and measure each individual battery voltage.

5. Each +12 Vdc battery should read between +11.5 Vdc and +12.5 Vdc. Any battery measuring outside of that range should be considered defective and should be replaced.

6. All batteries should measure about the same. Any battery that differs more than 0.4 volt from the rest of the batteries should be considered bad and replaced.

7. Wait about 5 minutes and repeat the test (looking for one weak battery to discharge faster than the others). If any battery appears to be discharging faster than the others, it should be considered bad and replaced.

UPS BATTERY REPLACEMENT

Another result of batteries being electrochemical devices is that after an ample number of charge and discharge cycles, they'll eventually wear out and need to be replaced. As a rule of thumb, you can expect to change your BPS/UPS batteries every three to five years under normal use. Other circumstances such as bad commercial power sources, elevated temperatures where the batteries are stored, and improper maintenance procedures can all reduce the working life of a battery. You should suspect battery problems when they cannot hold a charge (short run times and "low battery" alarms even after ample charging time).

If you find that battery replacement is required, you can use the following guidelines to replace the UPS batteries. Remember that you *must* replace batteries with the exact same make and model as the original batteries or use a suitable substitute recommended by the particular UPS manufacturer. If you must substitute batteries, it may be necessary to replace *all* of the batteries in that UPS (even if only one is weak). Be sure to consult with the UPS manufacturer for its recommendations. As a rule, UPS systems allow for cold (UPS off) and warm (UPS on) battery substitution.

Preparing for Cold Substitution

The safest way to replace UPS batteries is through *cold* substitution—powering down the UPS and all load devices, and then replacing the batteries. Use the following steps as a basis for cold substitution:

1. Shut down all load devices (the server, monitor, printer, and so on).

2. Take the UPS out of its operate mode (press the Standby button on the UPS). The ON LED goes out, and power to the load receptacles stops.

3. Disconnect the UPS from utility (AC) power.

4. Wait at least 60 seconds for the UPS internal circuitry to discharge.

Preparing for Warm Substitution

In general, UPS batteries may be replaced without powering off the UPS (*hot-swapped*) if the UPS is *not* currently charging the batteries and is not supplying battery power to load devices—that is, normal AC power is available. To determine whether warm substitution is safe, be sure to check the UPS indicators to verify that the batteries are fully charged and that the UPS is supplying utility power rather than battery power.

Older batteries may register as fully charged but still be incapable of providing adequate backup for load devices. This means the battery charge LEDs may indicate the batteries are fully charged, while the UPS diagnostics have determined that the batteries need to be replaced.

Removing the Battery Pack

Use the following steps as a general guideline to remove the old battery pack from the UPS (your own UPS may be different, so check with the manufacturer for its specific recommendations):

1. Open the UPS cabinet to access the battery pack. The exact procedure may vary between UPS models, so be sure to review the procedures for your own UPS system. In many cases, you must remove several screws holding a faceplate, and then detach the faceplate to reveal the LED display cable.

2. Disconnect the LED display cable from the faceplate, and then set the faceplate aside. Take care to avoid damaging the printed circuit board behind the LED display.

3. Remove the screws that are retaining the battery pack.

4. Slide the battery pack partially out of the UPS chassis to access the battery terminals.

5. Disconnect the negative (black) battery pack terminal connections.

6. Disconnect the positive (red) battery pack terminal connections.

7. Slide the battery pack out to access the battery cable retainer bracket. Remove the screw and battery cable retainer bracket.

8. Carefully slide the battery pack out until the plastic handle(s) is accessible.

9. Remove the battery pack and set it aside for proper disposal.

Remember that UPS battery packs are generally quite heavy and can often exceed 60 pounds. Get some help when transporting the battery pack, and be sure that there is a safe location to set the pack once it's removed.

Installing the New Battery Pack

With the old battery pack removed, use the following steps as a guideline to install the new batteries in a UPS (your own UPS may be different, so check with the manufacturer for its recommendations):

1. Slide the new battery pack into the chassis, leaving room to replace the battery cable retainer bracket.

2. When installing the bracket, position the cables to lie flat and to run under the plastic handling strap(s).

3. Reconnect the positive (red) battery pack terminal connections.

4. Reconnect the negative (black) battery pack terminal connections.

5. Reinstall the screw(s) holding the battery pack to the UPS chassis.

6. Reinstall the display faceplate, if necessary. Attach the LED display cable to the LED display.

7. Replace the screw(s) holding the faceplate to the chassis.

Testing the Battery Pack

After the new battery pack is installed, run a UPS self test or diagnostic (press the Test/Alarm Reset button). Refer to the documentation that accompanied your specific UPS for self test or diagnostic instructions. Remember that most UPS systems will not invoke a self test until the new batteries are 90 percent charged or more, so you may need to wait a little while until the new battery pack is charged. If there are problems with the new installation, one or more battery warning displays (battery service indicators) will light. You may need to go back and check your terminal connections.

Disposing of Old Batteries

Due to the dangerous and caustic chemicals used in batteries, it is virtually impossible to discard used batteries with ordinary trash because it's illegal in most parts of the US (and the world). When you replace UPS batteries, most vendors will also provide instructions and suitable packaging for you to ship the batteries to an appropriate disposal facility. If the vendor does not provide adequate disposal options, check your local yellow pages for a recycling center that meets all local environmental protection standards.

UPS LOCATION TIPS

While the physical location of a UPS may not be critical, there are some tips that may help prevent backup power problems:

- Install the UPS as close as possible to the equipment that it will protect. If this distance is more than 25 feet (7.6 meters), transient noise can appear in the electrical distribution system.

- If the UPS batteries are in a separate cabinet, the battery cabinet should be as close to the UPS as possible. If the batteries will be farther away from the unit than the standard cables allow, you may need to replace the battery cables with a larger gauge wire to reduce voltage losses across the line.

- The UPS should be in a flat location in a controlled, indoor environment. Do not install the UPS next to open windows.

- Keep the UPS away from heat sources, direct sunlight, moisture, or corrosive gas.

- Do not place any objects on top of the UPS and do not install it in any type of enclosure. Do not operate the UPS or batteries in a sealed room or container.

UNDERSTANDING LINE LOAD INDICATORS

During normal operation, a UPS rectifies the AC input, and then uses it to charge the batteries and feed the inverter circuit. If your UPS provides a Line Load indicator, this will show the amount (percentage) of UPS power that your system is actually using. Remember that a UPS can provide only a limited amount of power, so you should verify that the line load power being provided to your PC equipment is *less than* 100 percent of the total UPS capacity—otherwise, you'll overload the UPS. A Line Load indicator that's approaching 100 percent means that the UPS is in danger of overloading, and you'll need to reduce the number of devices demanding power from the UPS (or replace the UPS with a larger model).

If the Line Load indicator flashes and the UPS cuts out the AC source power, chances are that the AC feeding the UPS is too high or too low. You'll need a licensed electrician to "buck" or "boost" the AC power within a range that's appropriate for the UPS.

UNDERSTANDING BATTERY POWER INDICATORS

When the UPS runs on battery backup power (the *inverter*), the Battery and Inverter indicators are typically illuminated—this commonly happens during a power outage or when AC input power is not acceptable to the UPS (too high or too low). If your UPS provides a Battery Charge indicator, this will show the amount of battery charge that's left in the UPS. As the UPS runs on battery power, the amount of charge (and the amount of time the UPS can continue running on battery) will decrease, and the display will generally show this decrease in operating time. It's important that main AC power be restored (or the system be shut down) before the battery charge drops out. If the Battery indicator starts flashing, the battery voltage is low and shutdown of the UPS is imminent.

UNDERSTANDING THE BYPASS INDICATOR

Ideally, the UPS is providing power through its inverter, so AC is never *directly* connected to the system. However, if your UPS is equipped with a Bypass button and indicator, you can sometimes bypass the UPS and run the system from AC power. This happens if there is a UPS overload, if the UPS cannot run on battery power (for example, because of an inverter failure), or if you press the Bypass button. If the cause of the bypass is an overload, the UPS can automatically transfer back to normal operation after the overload has been removed.

UNDERSTANDING THE ALARM INDICATOR

When the UPS detects a problem, you'll generally see a flashing Alarm indicator or a seven-segment error number display (often in conjunction with an alarm beep or tone). You can typically silence the audible alarm by pressing an Alarm button, but the flashing indicator (or message display) will still display a problem until it's corrected. If you don't see a solution listed in the following sections, refer to the UPS manual or manufacturer's technical support.

UPS QUICK CHECKLIST

Many of the common problems that occur with UPS systems usually fall into one of the following general categories:

■ *The UPS is on but is not supplying power to the equipment.* The output circuit breaker on the back of the UPS may have been tripped. Reset the breaker.

■ *No UPS indicators are on, and no alarm is sounding.* The UPS is not operating. Input power might not be available to the UPS (for example, an extended power outage may have occurred) or the input circuit breaker on the back of the UPS may have been tripped. Check the AC input power supply, and then reset the breaker and restart the UPS.

■ *The green Line indicator is not on even though AC line input seems to be available, and the UPS beeps every few seconds.* Input power might not be available to the UPS. The output circuit breaker on the back of the UPS may have been tripped. Check the AC input power supply, and then reset the breaker and restart the UPS.

■ *The amount of UPS battery run time is less than the rating.* The battery may not be fully charged or may be bad, or the charger may have failed. Recharge the battery for at least ten hours by connecting the UPS to a source of AC line input, and then retest the battery backup time. If the problem persists, the batteries may need to be replaced, or the charger may need to be repaired or replaced.

■ *The yellow Battery indicator is flashing.* The battery voltage is low. Recharge the battery for at least ten hours by connecting the UPS to a source of AC line input. If the problem persists, the batteries may need to be replaced, or the charger may need to be repaired or replaced.

DEALING WITH COMMON ALARM CONDITIONS

Many of the current generation of BPS and UPS systems incorporate a certain amount of "intelligence" that oversees features such as battery charging and self-diagnostics. When important conditions are not met or errors are detected, the BPS/UPS will produce an alarm. Although the actual means used to present the alarm (for example, beeps, seven-segment codes, or alphanumeric LCD readouts) can vary quite a bit, you should understand the essential alarm meanings and know how to respond quickly.

■ **Batteries Disconnected** The BPS/UPS batteries are not properly connected. Verify the connection of all batteries in the BPS/UPS. The UPS will *not* protect your system until this fault is corrected.

■ **Batteries Undercharged** The PC is receiving power, but the batteries have an insufficient charge and will not protect your system for long. See that the batteries are allowed ample time to charge. If this is a persistent problem, you may wish to inspect each of the batteries.

■ **Check Battery** The BPS/UPS has detected a possible problem with its batteries. Verify that all of your batteries are properly connected in the BPS/UPS. You should test and replace any defective batteries.

■ **Check Fan** The cooling fan inside the BPS/UPS is not functioning properly. The fan may need to be replaced, or the BPS/UPS may require factory service or replacement.

■ **Check Fuse Board** The BPS/UPS has detected a possible problem with an internal fuse board. It may be possible to check/replace the fuse board, but this usually means that the BPS/UPS has failed and is in need of factory service or replacement.

■ **Check Inverter** The BPS/UPS has detected a possible problem with its inverter circuit (the circuit that actually turns battery DC back into AC for the computer). This usually means that the BPS/UPS has failed and is in need of factory service or replacement.

■ **Check MOVs** The BPS/UPS has detected a problem with a MOV inside the unit. This usually means that the BPS/UPS has failed and is in need of factory service or replacement.

■ **Check Power Supply** The unit has detected a possible problem with the unit's internal power supply (which powers the BPS/UPS microprocessor controls). This type of problem usually means that the BPS/UPS has failed and is in need of factory service or replacement.

- **Circuit Breaker Warning/Shutdown**   There is high output current being provided by the BPS/UPS. This usually occurs because excessive PC equipment is overloading the BPS/UPS. Shut down all of the PC equipment and reset the BPS/UPS. Then disconnect the extra PC equipment that is overloading the BPS/UPS.

- **High AC Out/Shutdown**   The BPS/UPS is generating an unusually high AC output voltage, and will shut down to prevent damaging the PC equipment. This usually means that the BPS/UPS has failed and is in need of factory service or replacement.

- **High Ambient Temperature**   The temperature inside the BPS/UPS is too high. Make sure that the BPS/UPS is placed where room temperature is within the system's recommended range (high-temperature industrial environments are typically bad). Also, make sure that nothing is blocking the cooling vents in the BPS/UPS.

- **High Battery**   The battery voltage in the BPS/UPS is high. There may be a problem with the battery charger settings, the charging circuit itself, or one or more batteries. This condition usually means that the BPS/UPS has failed and is in need of factory service or replacement.

- **Low AC Out/Shutdown**   The BPS/UPS is generating an unusually low AC output voltage, and will shut down to prevent damaging the PC equipment. This condition usually means that the BPS/UPS has failed and is in need of factory service or replacement.

- **Low Battery**   Battery voltage is too low for the BPS/UPS to operate on battery power, and the unit will subsequently shut down. In most cases, you should see a low runtime error first. If the batteries are too low even while the BPS/UPS is operating from AC, there may be a problem with the charging circuit or batteries in the unit.

- **Low Runtime**   The PC is running on battery power, and the amount of battery time remaining is low (usually two minutes or less). Do an orderly shutdown of your PC equipment immediately. In most cases, you do not need to shut off the BPS/UPS (when AC power returns, the BPS/UPS can automatically restart and begin to recharge its batteries).

- **Memory Error**   On startup, the BPS/UPS unit has failed its automatic memory validity test (usually in "intelligent" microprocessor-based BPS/UPS units). This usually means that the BPS/UPS has failed and is in need of factory service or replacement.

- **Output Short Circuit**   This problem is usually signaled by a continuous error tone, and typically indicates an overload condition when the UPS unit it turned on. Check the wiring and verify that you're not loading down the UPS with excessive equipment. (Similar to "Overload," described next).

- **Overload**   The PC equipment is drawing more power than the BPS/UPS is designed to provide. This condition can seriously reduce battery runtime. You'll need to shut down extra PC equipment (scanners, printers, and so on) until the error stops.

- **Replace Batteries**   This error is typically generated as one or more beep patterns from the UPS and suggests that one or more batteries in the unit will not hold a proper charge. You should check each battery in the UPS and replace any questionable batteries at your earliest convenience.

- **UPS Fault**   A serious error has occurred in the UPS. The UPS will probably not protect your system during this error condition until the fault is cleared or the UPS is replaced.

SYMPTOMS AND SOLUTIONS

If you have trouble with a power protection device that is not addressed in the preceding general guidelines, refer to the following symptoms for specific solutions to a few common problems.

SYMPTOM 31-1   **The BPS/UPS will not turn on**   This is usually indicated when the power light doesn't come on or the unit doesn't beep. Check that the AC power is available at the outlet and see that the AC line cord is connected to the BPS/UPS properly. If the unit has a circuit breaker or fuse, check to see if it has tripped. Reset the circuit breaker or replace the fuse as necessary. Also make sure that the unit is not overloaded with excessive PC equipment (which can draw excess current and pop the fuse or circuit breaker).

SYMPTOM 31-2   **A "site wiring fault" is indicated (usually while the BPS/UPS is powering loads)**   This condition is most likely due to a building wiring error (such as a missing ground), an overload on the neutral wiring, or polarity reversal between the hot and the neutral wires. There may be a "cheater" plug or adapter installed onto the unit's line cord plug—resulting in no connection to ground. You'll need a licensed electrician to check and correct the building wiring as needed.

SYMPTOM 31-3   **The BPS/UPS is on, but the PC equipment is not receiving power (the unit's circuit breaker may or may not be tripped)**   In most cases, this condition is accompanied by a loud tone or error message indicating an overload. The problem is that the BPS/UPS has shut down because too much PC equipment is plugged in (such as a laser printer). Shut off the PC equipment and disconnect any "excess" devices—you may place them on a simple surge suppresser on a different AC outlet. Then reset the BPS/UPS (reset the circuit breaker if necessary).

SYMPTOM 31-4   **The BPS/UPS indicates a power failure, even though AC power has not failed**   This often happens if the unit's AC line cord has become loose. Make sure the line cord is installed properly. If the unit's circuit breaker has tripped, the BPS/UPS may be overloaded by too much PS equipment. Disconnect excessive devices and plug them into ordinary surge suppressers instead.

SYMPTOM 31-5   **The BPS/UPS beeps (kicks in) occasionally, but the PC equipment operates normally**   This symptom typically indicates that the BPS/UPS is noting brief lapses in AC or other power anomalies. In most cases, this kind of operation is perfectly normal and indicates that the BPS/UPS is busy protecting the PC equipment from power problems. If there is an audible tone that is distracting, you can often disable the audible alarm on most BPS/UPS systems.

SYMPTOM 31-6   **The BPS/UPS beeps (kicks in) frequently (often several times each hour), even though the PC equipment operates normally**   This symptom almost always indicates that the AC line voltage powering the BPS/UPS is low to begin with or heavily loaded by other devices drawing current elsewhere. First, have the line voltage checked by a licensed electrician, and corrected if necessary. You might also reduce the sensitivity of the BPS/UPS by reducing the "transfer voltage" (the voltage at which the unit kicks in) by several volts (not all BPS/UPS systems provide this feature). Finally, try removing any unnecessary devices that may be loading down the AC line voltage (such as coffee pots or air conditioners).

SYMPTOM 31-7   **The BPS/UPS does not provide the expected runtime**   First, check whether there is an excessive load on the BPS/UPS (such as a laser printer). Disconnect any excess devices and plug them into ordinary surge suppressers elsewhere. If the problem persists, the batteries in the BPS/UPS itself may be weak from age or abuse or may not have been charged completely after a prior use. Make sure that the BPS/UPS is given ample time to charge. Otherwise, test and replace weak batteries as needed.

SYMPTOM 31-8 **The computer reboots when the BPS/UPS kicks in** This condition occurs because the PC equipment does not have enough "ride-through time" until the BPS/UPS can react. In most cases, there is an excessive load on the BPS/UPS. Remove excessive PC equipment from the BPS/UPS and try the system again. If the problem persists, you may need to replace the BPS/UPS with one offering a faster switch-over time.

Further Study

APC www.apcc.com
Best Power (Invensys) www.bestpower.com/
TrippLite www.tripplite.com

32

POWER SUPPLIES AND POWER MANAGEMENT

Power supplies play a vital role in the operation of PCs and their peripherals. A power supply converts commercial AC into one or more levels of DC that can be used by electronic and electromechanical devices inside the computer. This may not sound very glamorous, but a faulty or low-quality supply can cause serious system problems, stability issues, data loss, and (in extreme cases) can damage your motherboard or drives. Every technician should understand the operation of a *switching power supply* and know the important characteristics to consider when replacing or upgrading a supply.

But over the last few years, "power" has become more important than just plugging in a little silver box. Global concerns about limited natural resources and "greenhouse" gasses have focused attention on the tens of millions of PCs that consume power around the world. Not only must a power supply operate correctly, but modern computers must also employ aggressive power management techniques to significantly reduce the system's power consumption during idle periods. This chapter will explain the operation of a typical switching power supply, offer reliable guidelines for selecting and upgrading a supply, and cover solutions for the most common power supply problems. You'll also review the major power management schemes for desktop and mobile PCs, see how to use those schemes, and learn how to troubleshoot many of the more troublesome power management problems.

Understanding Switching Supplies

The great disadvantage to ordinary *linear* power supplies is their tremendous waste. At least half of all power provided to a linear supply is thrown away as heat. Most of this waste occurs in the regulator portion of the supply. Ideally, if there was just enough energy supplied to the regulator to achieve and maintain a stable output voltage, regulator waste could be reduced almost entirely, and supply efficiency would be vastly improved. This is the concept behind a switching power supply.

CONCEPTS OF SWITCHING REGULATION

Instead of throwing away extra input energy, a switching power supply creates a feedback loop. A feedback circuit senses the output voltage provided to a load, then switches the AC primary (or secondary) voltage on or off as needed to maintain steady levels at the output. In effect, a switching power supply is constantly turning on and off in order to keep the output voltage(s) steady. A block diagram of a typical switching power supply is shown in Figure 32-1. There are various possible configurations, but Figure 32-1 illustrates one classical design approach.

Raw AC line voltage entering the supply is immediately converted to pulsating DC, then filtered to provide a *primary DC* voltage. Notice that unlike a linear supply, AC is not transformed before rectification, so primary DC can easily reach levels exceeding 170 volts. Remember that AC is 120 volts RMS. Since capacitors charge to the peak voltage (peak = RMS×1.414), DC levels can be higher than your AC voltmeter readings.

Keep in mind that high-voltage pulsating DC can be as dangerous as AC line voltage and should be treated with *extreme* caution.

On start up, the switching transistor is turned on and off at a high frequency (usually 20 kHz to 40 kHz) and a long duty cycle. The switching transistor acts as a *chopper,* which breaks up this primary DC to form

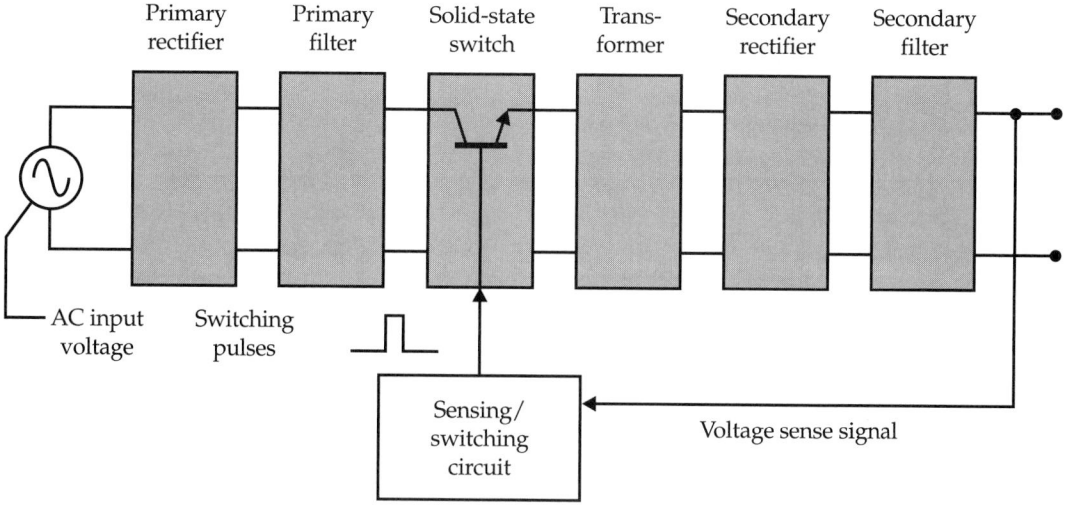

FIGURE 32-1   Block diagram of a switching power supply

chopped DC that can now be used as the primary signal for a step-down transformer. The duty cycle of chopped DC will affect the AC voltage level generated on the transformer's secondary winding (output). A long duty cycle means a larger output voltage (for heavy loads), and a short duty cycle means lower output voltage (for light loads). *Duty cycle* itself refers to the amount of time that a signal is "on" compared to its overall cycle. The duty cycle is continuously adjusted by the sensing/switching circuit. You can use an oscilloscope to view switching and chopped DC signals. Figure 32-2 illustrates a more practical representation for a switching supply.

AC voltage produced on the transformer's secondary winding (typically a step-down transformer) is *not* a pure sine wave, but it alternates regularly enough to be treated as AC by the remainder of the supply. Secondary voltage is re-rectified and refiltered to form a *secondary DC* voltage that is actually applied to the load. Output voltage is sensed by the sensing/switching circuit, which constantly adjusts the chopped DC duty cycle. As load increases on the secondary circuit (more current is drawn by the load), output voltage tends to drop. This is perfectly normal, and the same thing happens in every unregulated supply. However, a sensing circuit detects this voltage drop and increases the switching duty cycle. In turn, the duty cycle for chopped DC increases, which increases the voltage produced by the secondary winding. Output voltage climbs back up again to its desired value—output voltage is regulated.

The reverse will happen as load decreases on the secondary circuit. (Less current is drawn by the load.) A smaller load will tend to make output voltage climb. Again, the same actions happen in an unregulated supply. The sensing/switching circuit detects this increase in voltage and reduces the switching duty cycle. As a result, the duty cycle for chopped DC decreases, and transformer secondary voltage decreases. Output voltage drops back to its desired value. Output voltage remains regulated.

Consider the advantages of a switching power circuit. Current is only drawn in the primary circuit when its switching transistor is on, so very little power is wasted in the primary circuit. The secondary circuit will supply just enough power to keep load voltage constant (regulated), but very little power is wasted by the secondary rectifier, filter, or switching circuit. Switching power supplies can reach efficiencies higher than 85 percent (35 percent more efficient than most comparable linear supplies). More efficiency means less heat is generated by the supply, so components can be smaller and packaged more tightly.

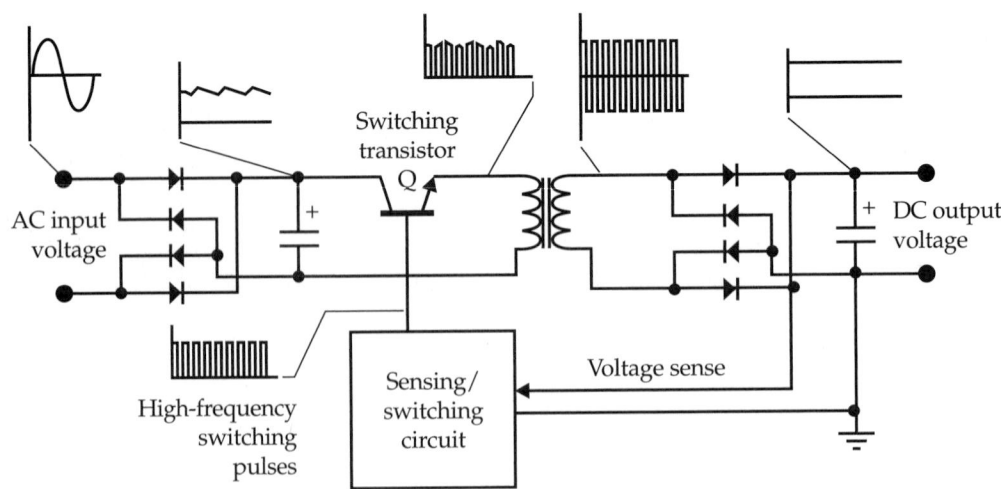

FIGURE 32-2   Simplified diagram of a switching power supply

Unfortunately, there are several disadvantages to switching supplies that you must be aware of. First, switching supplies tend to act as radio transmitters. Their 20-kHz to 40-kHz operating frequencies can wreak havoc on radio and television reception, not to mention the circuitry within the PC or peripheral itself. This is why you will see most switching supplies somehow covered or shielded in a metal casing. It is critically important that you replace any shielding removed during your repair. Strong *electromagnetic interference* (EMI) can easily disturb the operation of a logic circuit. Second, the output voltage will always contain some amount of high-frequency ripple. In many applications, this is not enough noise to interfere with a load. In fact, most of the noise is filtered out in a carefully designed supply. Finally, a switching supply often contains more components and is more difficult to troubleshoot than a linear supply. This is often outweighed by the smaller, lighter packaging of switching supplies. In virtually all cases today, a defective power supply unit is simply replaced.

In actual practice, sensing and switching functions can be fabricated right onto an integrated circuit. Chip-based switching circuits allow simple, inexpensive circuits to be built as shown in Figure 32-3. AC line voltage is transformed (usually stepped down), and then it is rectified and filtered before reaching a switch-regulating chip. The chip chops DC voltage at a duty cycle that will provide adequate power to the load. Chopped DC from the switching regulator is filtered by the combination of choke and output filter capacitor to reform a steady DC signal at the output. The output voltage is sampled back at the switching chip, which constantly adjusts the chopped DC duty cycle.

CONNECTING A POWER SUPPLY

PC power supplies operate the motherboard directly, as well as a number of internal drives. This part of the chapter presents the typical connection schemes for AT, ATX, and NLX power supplies and highlights the major signals that you should be familiar with.

AT-Style Power Connections

The AT-style power supply is largely considered to be the classic connection scheme for IBM-compatible PCs. An AT-style supply provides four voltages to the motherboard (+5 Vdc, –5 Vdc, +12 Vdc, and –12

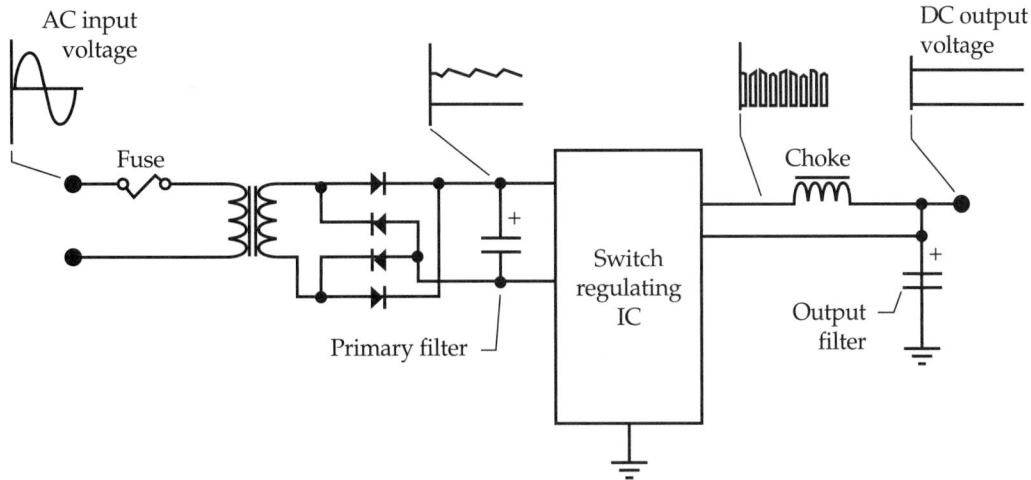

FIGURE 32-3 Simplified schematic of a chip-based switching power supply

Vdc) through a series of two heavy 6-pin connectors, as shown in Figure 32-4. You may notice that there are several wires for Ground and other voltage signals such as +5 Vdc. There is no difference between these like-colored wires. The extra wires are provided simply because the additional wire is needed to help carry the required current.

If you can't remember the orientation of P8 and P9 connectors, just remember that the black ends of each connector go together.

The only discrete signal in the AT-style power connector is the Power Good (PwrGood or PG) signal. This signal is typically tied to the CPU's Reset pin. When the PC is first powered-up, this signal is logic 0, and the CPU is forced into a continuous Reset mode. After the power supply outputs are stable (usually about 0.5 second from the time you flip the power switch), this signal rises to a logic 1. This releases the Reset signal, and the CPU can begin processing—starting the POST and boot process.

Drive Power Connections

The internal drives of a PC (such as floppy drives, hard drives, CD-ROM drives, and so on) must also be powered. Since drives are electromechanical devices that typically demand a substantial amount of current, they are powered directly from the power supply rather than from their respective interfaces. Drives traditionally use a heavy-duty 4-wire connector to provide +12 Vdc and +5 Vdc to each drive. The +12

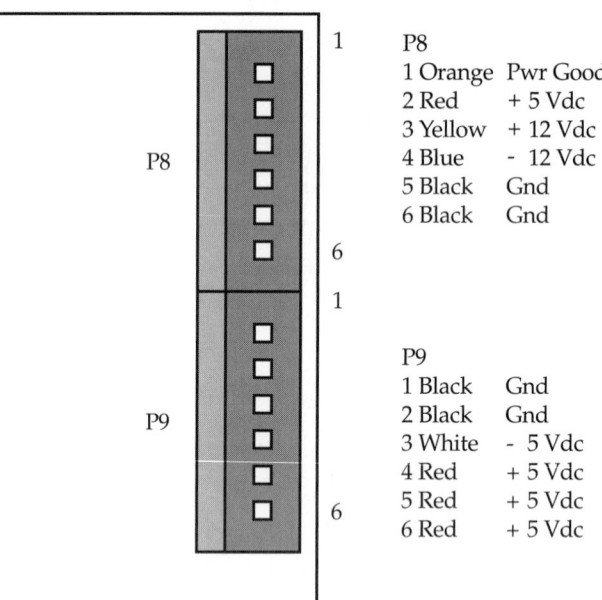

FIGURE 32-4   AT-style motherboard power connections

Vdc signal powers the drive's motor(s), while the +5 Vdc signal operates the drive's logic circuits. The wire colors are identified as follows:

Yellow	+12 Vdc
Black	Ground
Black	Ground
Red	+5 Vdc

As a rule, there should be one drive power connector for each drive in the system. Higher-capacity power supplies typically offer more drive power connectors. If you do not have enough drive power connectors to power all of the drives in your system, you may be able to use a Y-adapter cable to transform one power connector into two. However, you should be *extremely* judicious in the use of Y-adapters. Inadequate power connectors may suggest that you're pushing the power supply beyond its capacity, and erratic system behavior can result (if the system boots at all). Also, *never* split the power connector operating a hard drive. The power diverted from a hard drive may result in erratic HDD performance and data corruption.

ATX/NLX-Style Power Connections

While ATX and NLX form-factor systems now constitute virtually all new systems entering service today, their power requirements are remarkably similar. The ATX/NLX power supply provides five voltages to the motherboard (+5 Vdc, –5 Vdc, +12 Vdc, –12 Vdc, and +3.3 Vdc) through a 20-pin connector, as shown in Figure 32-5. The +3.3 Vdc supply is added to support the broad use of low-voltage logic that is now standard in the PC. Older AT-style motherboards also incorporate low-voltage logic, but required an onboard voltage regulator to supply the +3.3 Vdc rather than the power supply. The ATX/NLX signals can be identified by their unique wire colors:

Black	Ground
Blue	–12 Vdc
Brown	3.3V sense
Gray	Power OK
Green	PS-ON (the "soft power" control signal)
Orange	+3.3 Vdc
Purple	5VSB ("standby" voltage for power-managed devices)
Red	+5 Vdc
White	–5 Vdc
Yellow	+12 Vdc

In addition to the actual DC voltages feeding the motherboard, there are also several important logic signals used to control the power system:

PS-ON   PS-ON is an active-low signal received from the motherboard that turns on all of the main power outputs (+3.3 Vdc, +5 Vdc, –5 Vdc, +12 Vdc, and –12 Vdc). When this signal is held high (logic 1) or left open-circuited, the power supply outputs should be *off*. In effect, this is the signal that allows "soft control" of the system power (such as automatic power-down when shutting down Windows 98/Me).

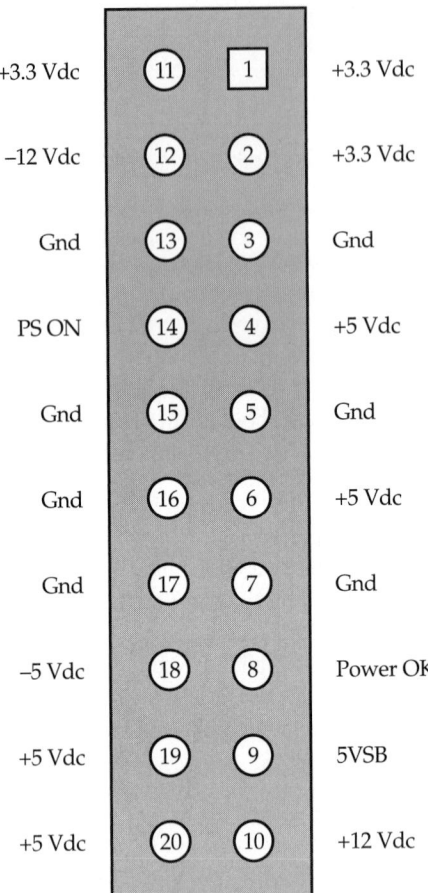

+3.3 Vdc	(11) [1] +3.3 Vdc
−12 Vdc	(12) (2) +3.3 Vdc
Gnd	(13) (3) Gnd
PS ON	(14) (4) +5 Vdc
Gnd	(15) (5) Gnd
Gnd	(16) (6) +5 Vdc
Gnd	(17) (7) Gnd
−5 Vdc	(18) (8) Power OK
+5 Vdc	(19) (9) 5VSB
+5 Vdc	(20) (10) +12 Vdc

FIGURE 32-5   ATX/NLX-style motherboard power connector

5VSB   5VSB is a standby voltage source that may be used to "tickle" power-managed devices that require power input during the powered-down state. The 5VSB pin should deliver 5 Vdc (+/− 5 percent) at a minimum of 10mA for devices to operate.

PW-OK   PW-OK (Power OK) is a Power Good signal and should be set at logic 1 by the power supply to indicate that the +5 Vdc and +3.3 Vdc outputs are above the undervoltage thresholds of the power supply. Once this signal is received from the supply, the motherboard can begin its POST and boot process.

Optional ATX/NLX-Style Power Connector
The ATX and NLX form-factor specifications also provide for an optional 6-pin power connector such as the one illustrated in Figure 32-6. Each signal adds a certain amount of versatility to the ATX/NLX system. You can identify the optional power connector signals by their wire colors:

White	FanM
White/Blue stripe	FanC
White/Brown stripe	3.3V sense
White/Red stripe	1394V
White/Black stripe	1394R

FanM Signal   The FanM (Fan Monitor) signal is an open-collector, 2-pulse-per-revolution tachometer signal from the power supply fan. This signal allows the system to monitor the power supply for fan speed or failures. If this signal is not implemented on the motherboard, it should not affect the power supply function.

FanC Signal   The FanC (Fan Control) signal is an optional fan speed and shutdown control signal. The fan speed and shutdown are controlled by a variable voltage on this pin. This signal allows the system to request control of the power supply fan from full speed to off. The control circuit on the motherboard should supply voltage to this pin from +12 Vdc to 0 Vdc for the fan control request.

3.3V Sense Line   A remote 3.3V sense line can be added to the optional connector to allow for accurate control of the 3.3 Vdc line directly at motherboard loads.

1394V Pin   This pin on the optional connector allows for implementation of a segregated voltage supply rail for use with unpowered IEEE-1394 (FireWire) solutions. The power derived from this pin should be used to power *only* 1394 connectors (unregulated anywhere from 8 to 40 volts).

1394R Pin   The 1394R pin provides an isolated ground path for unpowered IEEE-1394 (FireWire) implementations. This ground should be used *only* for 1394 connections and should be fully isolated from other ground planes in the system.

Voltage Tolerances

If you pursue power supply testing or troubleshooting at any level, you're going to need to test the output voltages. One important aspect of voltage measurements that is often overlooked by novice technicians is the idea of *voltage tolerance.* Voltage outputs are rarely exact and may vary from their rated value by as much as 5 percent (often 3–4 percent for the +3.3 Vdc output). For example, a +5 Vdc output may actually

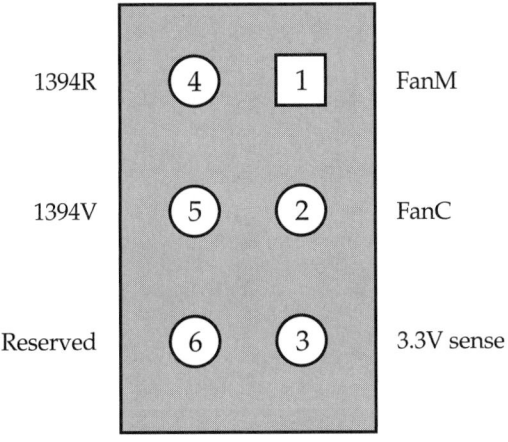

FIGURE 32-6   Optional ATX/NLX-style motherboard power connector

read from +4.75 Vdc to +5.25 Vdc, while a +12 Vdc output may read from +11.4 Vdc to +12.6 Vdc. As long as the measured voltage is within a reasonable tolerance, the output should be considered good. If the measured voltage strays outside of this reasonable tolerance (usually to the low side), chances are that excessive devices are overloading the output. If the output measures extremely low (or is absent), chances are that the output (and the power supply) is defective. You can then choose to repair or replace the power supply as you see fit.

Upgrading a Power Supply

Power is the lifeblood of every PC. Each element of a PC—from hard drives and memory, to video boards, motherboards, and modems—demands energy from the power supply. Many of today's IBM-compatible clones cut costs by using power supplies that provide enough power to run the basic system, but not much else. When you upgrade or refit such a PC, you can often run into system problems such as random lock-ups, error messages, and a variety of other strange behaviors. This part of the chapter shows you how to recognize potential power problems and upgrade the supply if needed. *Use extreme caution whenever working with power systems.* AC at the wall outlet (and inside the power supply itself) can be very danger-ous in the hands of untrained personnel. If you're uncomfortable dealing with the hazards of AC, refer the actual testing and upgrade procedures shown here to more experienced individuals.

RECOGNIZING POTENTIAL POWER PROBLEMS

As with most PC problems, the key to recognizing power problems is proper diagnosis. Diagnosing a failed power supply is a relatively simple process. First, a supply malfunction will typically prevent a PC from booting—a fairly obvious symptom. A low or absent power output registered on a multimeter or POST board offers a direct indication of the problem. After you identify a failed supply, it becomes a mat-ter of troubleshooting the supply or replacing it. Unfortunately, many power problems are intermittent. The power supply has not necessarily failed, but it is not able to supply enough power to keep the system running properly. The following chronic problems can often help you navigate this gray area:

■ *The computer freezes intermittently.* Just because your system locks up does not necessarily mean that you should call the power company. Most computers are prone to freeze due to software application and configuration errors (which are never due to power problems), especially after you install a new application. The time you should suspect power problems is when your system (that has been working fine for some time) suddenly starts freezing for no reason at all (and regardless of the operating system or applications being used). Not just once, but several times a day, and maybe even several times an hour. If the system tends to freeze when it is moved to a new location (running on a different power circuit), power problems may also be to blame.

■ *There are random memory errors.* As with system lockups, an occasional memory error message does not necessarily indicate a power problem, especially if you have just added a new application or device driver. If you suddenly see a rash of memory errors (or have just finished upgrading the sys-tem), it's time to check your power. When memory errors occur after moving the PC to another loca-tion, power problems are likely at fault.

■ *Data is lost or corrupted on the hard drive.* Hard drive problems can be the result of several fac-tors—everything from a loose data cable to operator error. Check the drive carefully to be sure that it is connected securely. If the drive seems to be having difficulty reading or writing the disk, check power first before attempting to back up the disk or run any disk-based diagnostics. If you attempt to defragment or test the disk with power problems present, subsequent problems can do even more damage. This symptom also suggests that the supply may be overloaded. This may be the case if problems developed after you installed another drive or a power-hungry expansion board into your system. If power checks correctly, you can proceed with disk diagnostics.

■ *There is trouble communicating with modems or peripherals.* You may see a rash of communication errors when trying to use a modem or mouse. (You may see other communication driver error messages.) Make sure that the peripherals connected to your system are installed and configured properly. Established systems that suddenly have trouble staying online or interacting with the printer may be suffering from a power problem. In some cases, the loss of –5V from the power supply can disable the modem (and cause odd connection sounds) without causing any other system problems.

■ *The system suffers from chronic hardware failures.* Such a problem is characterized by a fault that seems to reoccur after a few days or a week. For example, you see a memory error, replace the memory, and the fault goes away, but the same fault returns a few days later. This type of problem suggests that power spikes (brief, high-voltage surges of electricity) are entering the system from the AC line. Many economy power supplies omit even the most rudimentary spike and surge suppression circuitry, so power anomalies often pass through the supply to the motherboard and drives with little (if any) protection at all. In most cases, a power anomaly will crash the system, but does not result in any real damage. In extreme cases, a strong power anomaly can actually damage one or more chips on the motherboard, expansion board(s), or drive(s).

DEALING WITH POWER PROBLEMS

Now that you have an idea how power problems tend to manifest themselves in the PC, you can take some decisive steps to isolate and rectify the problem. Regardless of what symptoms your particular system may be exhibiting, you should not automatically assume that your system (or power supply) is at fault. Before you even think about opening the PC, you should check the AC line voltage.

Checking the AC

Even the most forgiving power supply needs a stable source of AC in order to function correctly. Industrial devices such as motors and heaters can draw so much power that there is insufficient AC voltage remaining to power the computer. Commercial and domestic appliances such as air conditioners, stoves, coffee makers, and refrigerators can also result in low or unsteady AC levels. Appliances are also notorious for their introduction of voltage spikes that can easily result in circuit damage.

For the most part, it is rather pointless to look for power problems with ordinary test instruments. Multimeters are good for testing overall AC levels, but they are usually too slow to catch rapidly changing power levels such as spikes. Even most surges will go undetected. Oscilloscopes are too expensive for casual 50/60-Hz measurements, and they rarely save any anomalies that are detected. Once the problem is displayed, it is gone. As a result, you are forced to sit and watch the oscilloscope until a problem occurs. Serious power observations require a dedicated power test instrument with data logging or long-term chart recording capabilities. Such equipment is available, but is far too expensive for ordinary users (though technicians may consider the PC Power Check board from Data Depot). Fortunately, there are some trial-and-error steps that can be taken to test the problem.

First, you need to make sure that your AC outlet is providing the right amount of voltage. Use a multimeter to measure the output at your wall outlet. Domestic U.S. voltage levels should be between 110 and 130 Vac. If voltage is too low (or too high), the objective is to find out if there is anything on the circuit that might be causing the voltage problem. Check to see if there are any high-energy devices on the same circuit (such as coffee makers or air conditioners). If so, try turning those devices off. If the AC at your computer's outlet returns to a normal value, try your system now. That may have been the problem. Eventually, you will need to turn your air conditioner or coffee maker back on, so be sure to shut down your system until you can have a new line installed or find another line for the computer.

If there are no other devices on the line (or the line voltage fails to return to a normal level), your next step should immediately be to find an outlet with the proper voltage level. If an outlet with a proper voltage cannot be found, an electrician should be consulted to install a proper AC line. An electrician should also be able to ensure that the AC line is properly grounded. When the AC line voltage seems correct, suspect the computer supply itself.

Suspect the Supply

When the AC input seems correct, you should suspect the computer supply. If the system is suffering from chronic hardware problems, try putting a good-quality surge protector between the AC wall outlet and computer AC cord. It also would be acceptable to try the system on another AC line that may be free of surges or spikes. Open the computer and use a multimeter to check the voltage level at each supply output against the pin assignments shown in Table 32-1. The +12 Vdc and +5 Vdc levels should be correct. The power LEDs on a PC Power Check (or suitably equipped POST board) will also give you an approximation of supply output levels.

If any supply output level is low, the supply may be overloaded by too many devices in the system. If you have just upgraded the system with a new drive or expansion board, try removing or disabling the upgrade, and see if DC voltages climb to their normal levels. If they do, the supply is overloaded and should be upgraded as shown next. If levels do not return to normal (or either or both of the voltages are high), the supply may be defective. If you determine the supply to be defective, you may troubleshoot or replace the supply at your discretion.

UPGRADING THE POWER SUPPLY

It is not uncommon for power supplies to become overloaded by upgrades and peripherals or to fail after prolonged use or repeated voltage spikes. When most consumers buy a PC, the power supply capacity is often the last specification on their minds. It is the more exciting specifications such as CPU speed and hard drive capacity that get all the attention. Few people worry about upgrading a brand-new system. As a technical professional, the best advice you can give consumers is very simple: "Don't skimp on power." If

TABLE 32-1   INDEX OF TYPICAL POWER SUPPLY WIRE ASSIGNMENTS

WIRE COLOR	VOLTAGE OR DESIGNATION
Black	Ground
Blue	−12 Vdc
Brown	+3.3V Sense (ATX and NLX supplies)
Gray	Power OK (~ +5 Vdc in ATX and NLX supplies)
Green	Power Supply ON ("soft control signal" for ATX and NLX supplies)
Orange	+3.3 Vdc (ATX and NLX supplies)
Orange	Power Good (~ +5 Vdc in AT-style supplies)
Purple	+5 Vdc Standby (ATX and NLX supplies)
Red	+5 Vdc
White	−5 Vdc
Yellow	+12 Vdc

you buy a new system, get one with a supply capacity that will be big enough to support a few typical upgrades like a video capture board, an additional hard drive, a CD-R/RW drive, an internal modem, more memory, and so on. You need not invest in the biggest and best supply (unless you're building a network server, or you have a lot of expansion devices from a previous system), but don't trap yourself by getting the smallest (cheapest) one either.

Choosing a Supply

When you determine that your supply has failed (or needs to be upgraded), there are two important factors that you need to consider: the power capacity of the new supply, and its physical dimensions. The *capacity* of a power supply is measured in *watts* (W). This is the maximum amount of power that can be supplied to a load (the computer) safely. Today's PC power supplies range from about 50W to 300W or more. Choosing the proper power rating for an upgraded supply is often a matter of approximation. You can usually calculate a safe upgrade by adding 50W to the original supply rating. For example, a fair upgrade for an IBM AT supply (usually 192W) would be the next closest rating to (192 +50) 242W. The actual supply might be 230W or 260W or something in that range, but at least you're in an acceptable range of ratings.

Before you finally choose a replacement supply, you will need to consider its physical dimensions. The new supply must be able to fit within the space allotted inside the PC. The new supply must be bolted into place, so its mounting holes should align properly with the holes in the original supply. This problem is largely taken care of with the new generation of ATX and NLX form-factor power supplies that are specifically designed to be readily interchangeable with ATX/NLX cases and motherboards.

A new supply must also have a connector scheme that is compatible with the motherboard. The 4-pin mate-n-lock connectors are standard for powering the drives in a PC (such as hard drives and CD-ROM drives), but motherboard power connectors can vary a bit from model to model. Figure 32-4 illustrates a typical "AT-style" motherboard power connector set, while Figure 32-5 shows an ATX/NLX motherboard power connector. Be sure to get a supply with the correct connector configuration for your motherboard. If you cannot find a compatible third-party supply, contact the PC's manufacturer. Some computer enthusiasts might be tempted to splice a power supply into the old motherboard connector. Avoid this at all costs. A new power supply is typically warranted for 90 days to one year. Splicing its wiring immediately voids any warranty.

Test the Upgrade Carefully

When installing a new supply, be sure that it is unplugged and turned off. Locate the line voltage selector switch (110/220), and verify that it is set appropriately for your region of the world. Before firing up the supply for the first time, remove any optional or noncritical expansion boards until you can verify that the PC is working correctly. You can then power-down the PC again, reinstall any additional boards or peripherals, and burn-in the system for at least 48 hours before returning it to service.

Troubleshooting Switching Power Supplies

Troubleshooting a switching power supply can be a complex and time-consuming task. Although the operation of rectifier and filter sections is reasonably straightforward, sensing/switching circuits can be complex oscillators that are difficult to follow without a schematic. Subassembly replacement of DC switching supplies is quite common.

POWER SUPPLY SERVICE TIPS

Power and power supply problems can manifest themselves in a stunning variety of ways, but the following tips should help you to stay out of trouble:

- Power supply cooling is important. Keep the vent openings and cooling fan blades clean.
- Make sure that the *line voltage switch* (120/220 Vac) is set correctly for your region.
- Verify that the power supply connectors are attached to the motherboard and drives securely.
- Remember that for AT-style power connections, *the black wires go together.*
- Do not use a Y-adapter to split power from an HDD. (Avoid Y-adapters entirely if possible.)
- Some Y-adapters are wired improperly. If you have trouble with a device after installing a Y-adapter, check the splitter, or try powering the device directly.
- Voltage tolerances are usually +/– 5 percent (+/– 3 percent for 3.3 Vdc), so be sure each output is within tolerance.
- Erratic system behavior after adding a new device can be the result of an overload. Try removing the device. If the system stabilizes, consider a power supply upgrade.

AN EXAMPLE POWER SUPPLY

For the purposes of this troubleshooting discussion, consider the chip-based switching supply of Figure 32-7. The STK7554 is a switching regulator chip manufactured as a 16-pin SIP (single in-line package). It offers a dual output of 24 Vdc and 5 Vdc. Notice that *both* output waveforms from the STK7554 are 38-volt square waves, but it is the *duty cycle* of those square waves that sets the desired output levels. The square wave's amplitude simply provides energy to the filter circuits. Filters made from coils (or "chokes") and high-value polarized capacitors smooth the square wave input (actually a form of pulsating DC) into a steady source of DC. There will be some small amount of high-frequency ripple on each DC output. Smaller, nonpolarized capacitors on each output act to filter out high-frequency components of the DC output. Finally, note the resistor-capacitor-diode combinations on each output. These form a surge and flyback protector that prevents energy stored in the choke from reentering the chip and damaging it. Refer to Figure 32-7 for the following symptoms.

SYMPTOMS

Let's start off by troubleshooting "hard" faults with your power supply itself. The following two symptoms highlight most of the most common problems associated with power and power supply failures.

SYMPTOM 32-1   **The PC or peripheral is completely dead—no power indicators are lit**
Check the AC line voltage entering the PC before beginning any major repair work. Use your multimeter to measure the AC line voltage available at the wall outlet powering your computer or peripheral. *Use extreme caution whenever measuring AC line voltage levels.* Normally, you should read between 105 and 130 Vac to ensure proper supply operation. If you find either very high or low AC voltage, try the device in an outlet that provides the correct amount of AC voltage. Unusual line voltage levels may damage your power supply, so proceed cautiously.

If AC line voltage is normal, suspect the main power fuse in the supply. Most power fuses are accessible from the rear of the computer near the AC line cord, but some fuses may only be accessible by disassembling the device and opening the supply. Unplug the system and remove the fuse from its holder. You

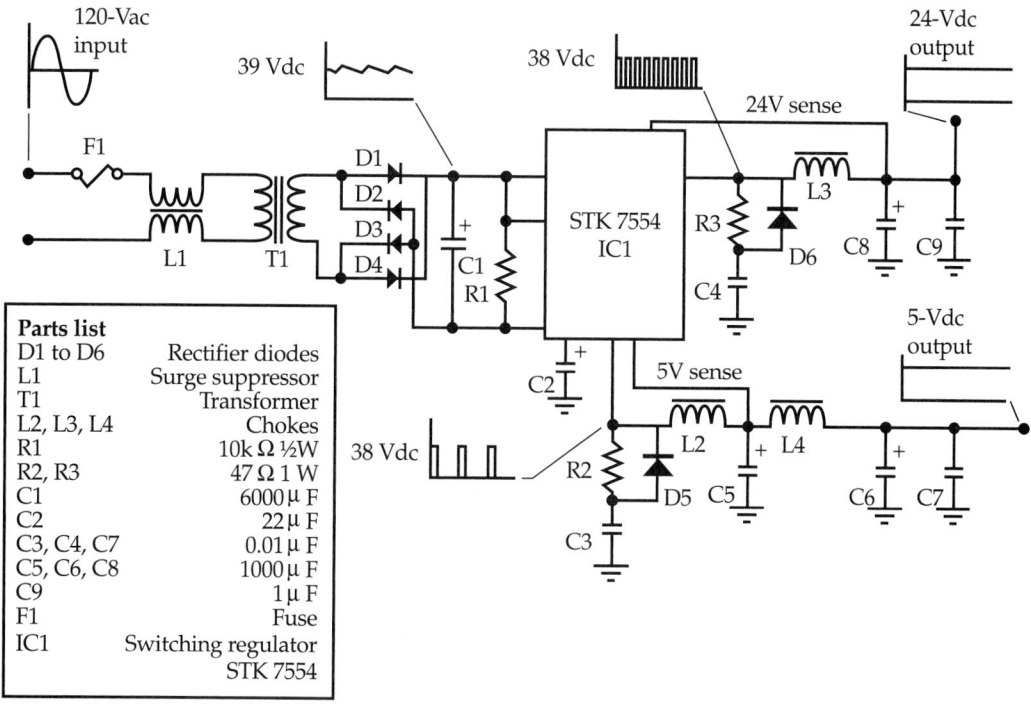

FIGURE 32-7   A complete chip-based switching power supply

should find the fusible link intact, but use your multimeter to measure continuity across the fuse. A good fuse should measure as a short circuit (0 ohms), while a failed fuse will measure as an open circuit (infinity). Replace any failed fuse and retest the PC. If the fuse continually fails, there is a serious defect elsewhere within the power supply or other computer/peripheral circuits. If your supply has an AC selector switch that sets the supply for 120 Vac or 240 Vac operation, be sure that switch is in the proper position for your region of the world. (An improperly set AC switch can disable the entire system.)

Unplug the computer and disassemble it enough to expose the power supply clearly. Restore power to the PC, and measure each DC output with your multimeter or oscilloscope. (You can usually find a power connector at the motherboard or other main board.) Make sure that any power cables are securely attached. If each output measures correctly, then your trouble lies outside of the supply. A key circuit has failed elsewhere in the device. You can try a POST board or diagnostic to trace the specific problem further. A low output voltage suggests a problem within the supply itself. Check each connector and all interconnecting wiring leading to or from the supply. Remember that many switching supplies must be attached to a load for proper switching to occur. If the load circuit is disconnected from its supply, the voltage signal could shut down or oscillate wildly.

When supply outputs continue to measure incorrectly with all connectors and wiring intact, chances are that your problem is inside the supply. For the sake of discussion, measure the primary AC voltage applied across the transformer (T1). Use *extreme caution* when measuring high-voltage AC. You should read approximately 120 Vac for Figure 32-7. If voltage has been interrupted in that primary circuit, you will read 0 Vac. Check the primary circuit for any fault that might interrupt power. Measure secondary AC voltage supplying the rectifier stage. It should read higher than the highest output voltage that you expect. For the example of Figure 32-7, the highest expected DC output is 24 volts, so AC secondary voltage should be several volts higher than this. The example shows this as 28 Vac. If primary voltage reads correctly and secondary voltage does not, you may have an open circuit in the primary or secondary transformer winding. Try replacing the transformer.

Next, check the preswitched DC voltage supplying the switching chip. Use your multimeter or oscilloscope to measure this DC level. You should read approximately the peak value of whatever secondary AC voltage you just measured. For Figure 32-7, a secondary voltage of 28 Vac should yield a DC voltage of about [28 Vac RMS×1.414] 39 Vdc. If this voltage is low or nonexistent, unplug AC from the supply, and check each rectifier diode. Then inspect the filter capacitor.

Use an oscilloscope to measure each chopped DC output signal. You should find a high-frequency square wave at each output (20 kHz to 40 kHz) with an amplitude approximately equal to the preswitched DC level (38 to 39 volts in this case). Set your oscilloscope to a time base of 5 or 10 μS/DIV, and start your VOLTS/DIV setting at 10 VOLTS/DIV. Once you have established a clear trace, adjust the time base and vertical sensitivity to optimize the display.

If you do not read a chopped DC output from the switching chip, either the chip is defective, or one (or more) of the polarized output filter capacitors may be shorted. Unplug the PC and inspect each questionable filter capacitor. Replace any capacitors that appear shorted. As a general rule, filter capacitors tend to fail more readily in switching supplies than in linear supplies because of high-frequency electrical stress and the smaller size of most switching supply components. If all filter capacitors check out correctly, replace the switching chip. Use care when desoldering the old regulator. Install a socket for the chip (if possible) to prevent repeat soldering work; then just plug in the new chip. If you do not have the tools to perform the work just outlined (or the problem persists), replace the power supply.

SYMPTOM 32-2   **Supply operation is intermittent—device operation cuts in and out with the supply**   Begin by inspecting the AC line voltage into your printer. Be sure that the AC line cord is secured properly at the wall outlet and printer. Make sure that the power fuse is installed securely. If the PC/peripheral comes on at all, the fuse has to be intact. Unplug the system and expose your power supply. Inspect every connector or interconnecting wire leading into or out of the supply. A loose or improperly installed connector can play havoc with the system's operation. Pay particular attention to any output connections. In almost all cases, a switching power supply must be connected to its load circuit in order to operate. Without a load, the supply may cut out or oscillate wildly.

In many cases, intermittent operation may be the result of a PC board problem. PC board problems are often the result of physical abuse or impact, but they can also be caused by accidental damage during a repair. *Lead pull-through* occurs when a wire or component lead is pulled away from its solder joint, usually through its hole in the PC board. This type of defect can easily be repaired by reinserting the pulled lead and properly resoldering the defective joint. *Trace breaks* are hairline fractures between a solder pad and its printed trace. Such breaks can usually render a circuit inoperative, and they are almost impossible to spot without a careful visual inspection. *Board cracks* can sever any number of printed traces, but they are often very easy to spot. The best method for repairing trace breaks and board cracks is to solder jumper wires across the damage between two adjacent solder pads. You may also simply replace the power supply outright.

Some forms of intermittent failures are time or temperature related. If your system works just fine when first turned on, but fails only after a period of use, then spontaneously returns to operation later on (or after it has been off for a while), you may be faced with a thermally intermittent component. That is, a component may work when cool, but fail later on after reaching or exceeding its working temperature. After a system quits under such circumstances, check for any unusually hot components. *Never touch an operating circuit with your fingers—injury is almost certain.* Instead, smell around the circuit for any trace of burning semi-conductor or unusually heated air. If you detect an overheated component, spray it with a liquid refrigerant. Spray in short bursts for the best cooling. If normal operation returns, then you have isolated the defective component. Replace any components that behave intermittently. If operation does not return, test any other unusually warm components. If problems persist, replace the entire power supply.

Understanding Power Management

As millions of new PCs enter service each year, power conservation has become a matter of increasing global importance. By designing PCs that use less power and employ comprehensive power-down techniques during periods of nonuse, a computer can actually be left on all the time, yet use only about 5W of power in its deepest power-saving state (less than most nightlights). This also reduces electric bills and lowers the cost of running your PC(s). Power conservation is also important for mobile PCs (laptops and notebooks) in order to get the longest possible working time from each battery charge. For the purposes of this book, *power management* is achieved when a system's BIOS, chipset, operating system, and devices all cooperate to reduce the power demands of an idle computer. This part of the chapter explains the basic concepts of popular power management techniques and covers a suite of power management problems for desktop and mobile systems.

POWER MANAGEMENT AND WINDOWS 98/ME

Several important elements are required to support power management: the BIOS, chipset, devices, and operating system. The operating system provides the controls and dialogs needed for selecting your power management strategy, and it runs the various drivers needed to control each piece of power managed hardware. Windows 98 and Windows Me are largely considered to be the premier operating systems for power management, and you can configure just about any power-managed part of the PC through Windows' Power Management Properties dialog. The dialog for Windows 98 is shown in Figure 32-8.

Power management under Windows begins by selecting a *power scheme.* This basic categorization uses predefined settings that control the power-down timing of your hardware devices. However, you can also tailor the settings of a given scheme to suit your tastes. There are three classic power-saving modes that you should be familiar with:

- **Basic conservation** You can turn off your monitor (or LCD backlight) and hard drive(s) automatically after a given period of inactivity (conserving a great deal of power while the rest of the system may be running normally).

- **Standby** You can put the computer into a standby mode when it's idle. While in standby mode, your monitor and hard drive(s) turn off, and some computer devices are powered-down. When you want to use the computer again, it comes out of standby mode quickly, and your desktop (along with your important work) is restored exactly as you left it. Standby is particularly handy for saving battery power in laptop computers.

- **Hibernation** You can put your computer into hibernation mode after longer periods of inactivity (such as you leave your office for the day). Power management's hibernate feature turns off your monitor and hard drive(s) first. (That is, it enters the standby mode first.) If idle time continues, the system will save everything in memory on disk, then turn off your computer. When you restart your computer, your computer's last state is restored to memory from the disk, and your desktop is restored exactly as you left it.

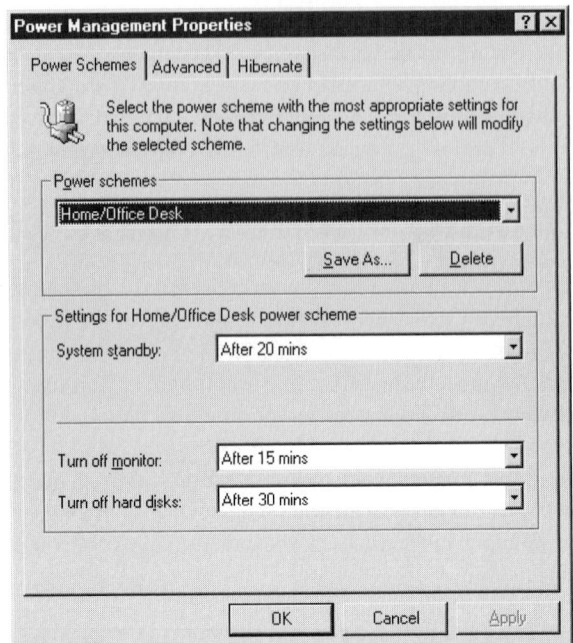

FIGURE 32-8   The Power Management Properties dialog under Windows 98/SE

The following sections outline a number of techniques that you can use to control power management under Windows 98/SE.

Selecting a Power Scheme   To enable the system's standby mode and take advantage of your computer's power management features, you first need to select a power scheme. Click Start, highlight Settings, click Control Panel, and then double-click the Power Management icon. The Power Management Properties dialog will appear (Figure 32-8). Click the Power schemes drop-down menu, and select from the available choices that loosely define how the PC is used:

- Always On
- Home/Office Desk
- Portable/Laptop

When you select a scheme, you'll notice that the settings for that power scheme ("System standby," "Turn off monitor," and "Turn off hard disks") will be updated to their default values. If you wish to tweak the default timer values (for example, you want to add more time before the system drops into standby mode), you can simply click on the respective timer and select the desired time value from the drop-down list. Using these timer entries, you can configure the monitor, hard drive, and standby delays according to your own preferences. Be sure to Apply your changes before clicking OK.

If you're using a laptop computer, you can specify a different standby delay for battery power, and a different setting for AC power.

Saving/Deleting a Power Scheme   If you've made changes to your power scheme's timer value(s), you can save all of those settings as a unique power scheme. Once you have your timer settings the way you want them, simply click Save As, and then enter the name for your new scheme. The new scheme is added to the Power schemes drop-down list. If you no longer wish to save a particular power scheme on your system, simply select the scheme from the Power schemes drop-down list and click Delete.

Manually Invoking the Standby Mode   The easiest way to place your PC in the standby mode is to use the Shut Down Windows dialog (Figure 32-9). You can also configure the system to let you use the standby mode whenever you press the Power button on your system (or whenever you close the lid on your laptop). Click Start, highlight Settings, click Control Panel, and then double-click the Power Management icon. The Power Management Properties dialog will appear. Click the Advanced tab (Figure 32-10). Locate the entry "When I press the power button on my computer," and then click Standby. If you're using a laptop, locate the entry "When I close the lid of my portable computer," and then click Standby. Click Apply (or OK), and then turn off the power or close the laptop's lid.

It's a good idea to save your work before putting a computer into standby mode. While the computer is in standby, information in RAM is not saved to your hard drive. If there's an interruption in power, the information in memory can easily be lost.

Manually Invoking the Hibernation Mode   When you put your computer in hibernation, everything in the computer's memory is saved on your hard disk. When you turn the computer back on, all programs and documents that were open when you put the PC into hibernation are restored on the desktop. Click Start, highlight Settings, click Control Panel, and then double-click the Power Management icon. The Power Management Properties dialog will appear. Click the Hibernate tab and select the check box (Figure 32-11). Click the Advanced tab (Figure 32-10). Locate the entry "When I press the power button on my computer," and then click Hibernate. If you're using a laptop, locate the entry "When I close the lid of my portable computer," and then click Standby. Click Apply (or OK), and then turn off the power or close the laptop's lid.

If the Hibernate tab is not displayed, your computer does not support this feature.

Incoming Calls in Standby Mode   Normally, a PC in standby mode will wake when the modem answers an incoming call. You must start the program that you use to answer the telephone (that is, your

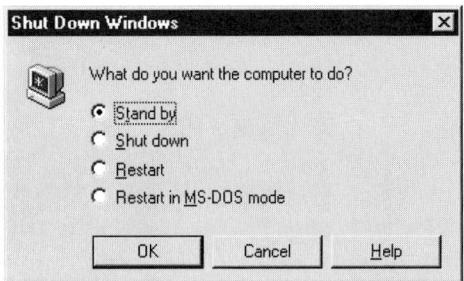

FIGURE 32-9   Using the "Stand by" feature of the Shut Down Windows dialog

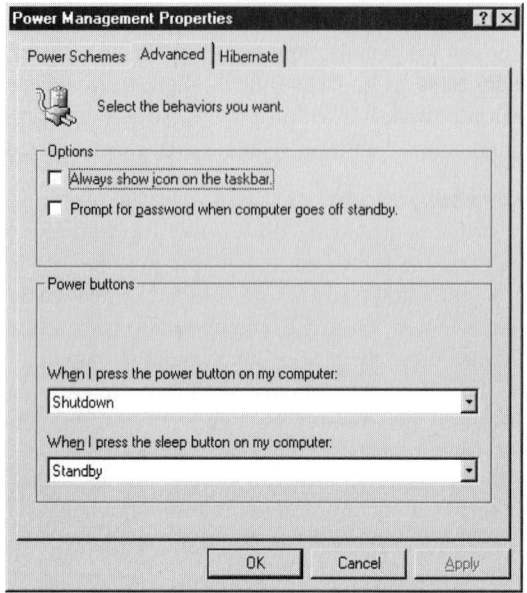

FIGURE 32-10   The Advanced Power Management Properties dialog under Windows 98/SE

modem's communication software) and make sure that your external modem is turned on. After the PC enters its standby mode, it should come out of standby for the duration of the call, then return to standby automatically.

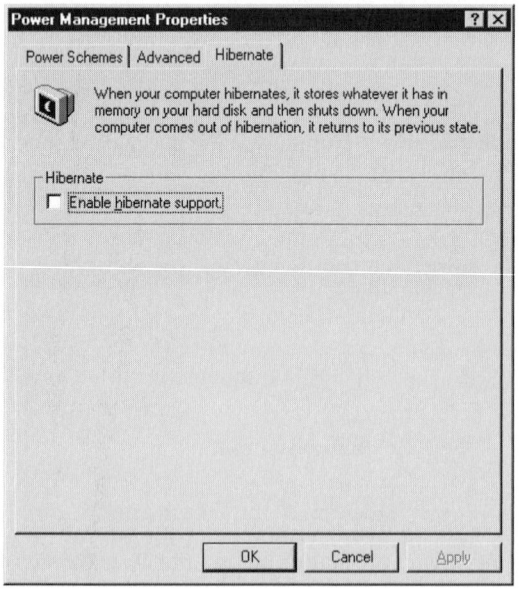

FIGURE 32-11   Enabling the Hibernate power saving mode under Windows 98/SE

Configuring Battery Warnings   You can configure your laptop system to produce warnings for "low" and "critical" battery conditions and instruct the PC how to respond to such alarms. Click Start, highlight Settings, click Control Panel, and then double-click the Power Management icon. The Power Management Properties dialog will appear. Click the Alarms tab (*not* shown in Figure 32-8). For both the "Low battery alarm" and "Critical battery alarm" entries, you can specify the settings you want by dragging the slider to the appropriate level. Click the Alarm Actions entry to select the type of alarm notification and power level you want. For example, if you want your computer to shut down when an alarm occurs, click "When the alarm goes off, the computer will" in the Alarm Actions dialog.

Passwords in Standby or Hibernation   To prevent anyone from moving a mouse or pressing a key to bring your system out of standby or hibernation, you can use passwords to protect your system on waking. Click Start, highlight Settings, click Control Panel, and then double-click the Power Management icon. The Power Management Properties dialog will appear. Click the Advanced tab, and then click "Prompt for password when computer goes off standby." You use your Windows password for both standby and hibernation. Remember that you are not required to use a password, but it does afford a certain amount of security since your system will be running while you're away from it.

ADVANCED POWER MANAGEMENT (APM)

APM represents the first major industry effort to establish a standardized power conservation method on the PC. Although APM concepts were in place with later versions of DOS and Windows 3.1x, APM was really first embraced as a "systemwide" standard with the introduction of Windows 95. Today, APM support is implemented in virtually every BIOS, chipset, and device in production and is carried through into Windows 98/Me. APM provides you with a mechanism for shutting down major power-consuming devices such as the monitor (or laptop's LCD backlight), spinning down the system hard drive(s), and "throttling back" the CPU during idle periods. APM can also query the battery to obtain its current charge information and report remaining battery life with great accuracy.

You can check for the presence of APM support by opening your Control Panel and double-clicking the System icon, and then selecting the Device Manager tab. Double-click the System devices entry, and look for the "Advanced Power Management support" line, as in Figure 32-12. If your system has not installed APM, you may install it manually:

1.   Open the Control Panel, and double-click the Add New Hardware wizard.
2.   Click Next.
3.   Click Yes (Recommended), and then click Next.
4.   Click Next.

Now verify that APM support has been enabled as explained in the preceding paragraph. Remember that if you do not see references to APM, but you do see references to ACPI (explained in the next section), your system is likely using the more advanced ACPI instead of the older APM scheme. This is fine, and you do not need to install APM. Simply skip to the following section on ACPI.

There are several different versions of APM, but version 1.2 is one of the most recent. Some computers conform to the APM specification 1.0; others use APM 1.1 or 1.2. Although Windows 98/Me works with all of these specifications, there are advantages to using APM 1.2. Version 1.1 is designed to give the operating system more control over power management than APM 1.0 permitted. For example, if a computer is using APM 1.2, the operating system can force the BIOS to wait until it has prepared the running

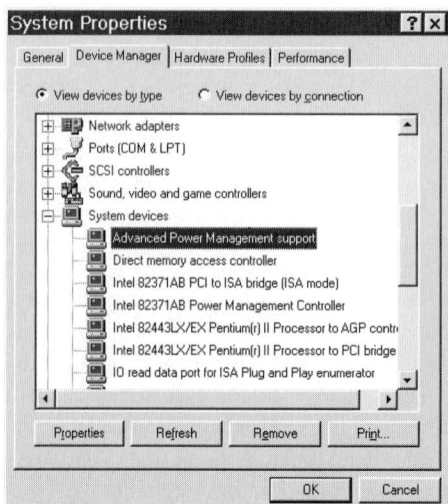

FIGURE 32-12   Checking the Device Manager for APM support

programs and drivers for suspend mode. Also, a computer using APM 1.2 allows the operating system to reject the request for suspend mode. However, there may be instances where your system does not fully support APM 1.1 or 1.2, and you may need to "force" Windows to use the initial APM 1.0 system. You can do this by double-clicking the "Advanced Power Management support" entry in your Device Manager, and then clicking the Settings tab (Figure 32-13). Simply click the "Force APM 1.0 mode" check box. If the system stabilizes, you'll know that one or more devices (or drivers) are having trouble with APM 1.1 or 1.2 on your system, and you can isolate and update the offending device(s) accordingly.

ADVANCED CONFIGURATION AND POWER INTERFACE (ACPI)

ACPI has largely been introduced under Windows 98/SE and builds on the basics of APM by allowing much more comprehensive control of each device in the power-managed state. For example, an ACPI system can turn off (or "throttle back") a wider range of devices such as CD-ROMs, DVD-ROMs, modems, network devices, and so on. ACPI also allows the system to "wake" and perform predetermined tasks based upon real-world events. For example, an ACPI system may wake when the modem receives a call, connect and exchange data, and then return to a standby or hibernate state after the call is completed. Current PCs use ACPI 2.0 introduced in July 2000.

In addition to enabling OS-controlled power management, ACPI provides a generic system event mechanism for plug-and-play and an OS-independent interface for device configuration control. This means your ACPI system can actually manage device configuration as well as power. In effect, ACPI is a marriage of PnP and APM that offers much more precise and versatile control over a system's devices.

Hibernate modes are known to have trouble on some FAT32 systems. If you use the hibernate mode, you may need to use FAT16 partitions. Newer systems are overcoming this limitation.

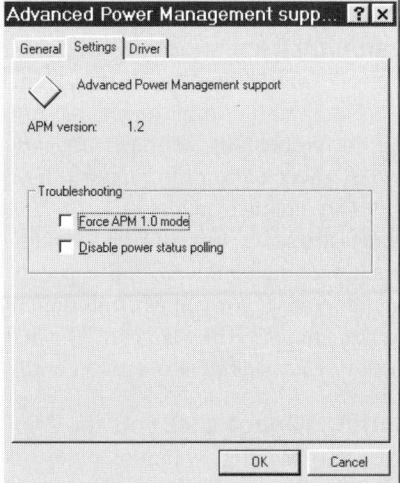

FIGURE 32-13   Forcing the APM 1.0 mode through the APM Settings tab

If you do not have ACPI support already in place when you install Windows 98, you can add ACPI support by reinstalling Windows 98 with the **/p j** command-line switches. This adds the **ACPIOption** string value with a value data of 1 to the registry. To run Windows 98 Setup using the **/p j** switches, click Start, click Run, type the following command in the Open box, and then click OK:

```
setup /p j
```

Reinstalling Windows 98 is the best way to ensure that all devices are configured correctly.

To enable ACPI support in Windows 98 or later, you must first have an ACPI-compatible mother-board and an ACPI 1.0–compliant BIOS.

Troubleshooting Power Management

Power management offers some compelling advantages for the PC. Systems can be extremely responsive, yet use very little power in the idle state. Ideally, the BIOS, chipset, devices, and operating system must work together seamlessly to avoid system crashes and data corruption. Unfortunately, this doesn't always happen (especially with older systems). BIOS incompatibilities, buggy drivers, and noncompliant hardware devices are just some of the issues that can result in power management problems. This part of the chapter explores a range of power management symptoms and solutions.

ACPI SYMPTOMS

The *Advanced Configuration and Power Interface* (ACPI) is now the standard power management technology employed by current PCs. While ACPI offers more comprehensive and versatile control over the many devices in a system, there is also far more latitude for problems to occur. The following symptoms offer a cross-section of common ACPI issues that you should be familiar with.

SYMPTOM 32-3   **The Windows 98 system with ACPI BIOS and UDMA-compliant device(s) will crash when resuming from suspend mode**   If an ATAPI storage device requires the use of a Get Task File (or _GTF) method to resume from the suspend mode on a computer with an ACPI BIOS, the computer may crash during the resume process. Most *Ultra-DMA* (UDMA) CD-ROM and optical drives cause this problem on computers that attempt to suspend and then resume. This error occurs because Windows 98 (Second Edition) supports the optional ACPI _GTF technique for IDE hard disks *only*. ATAPI devices are not well supported.

The best solution to this problem is to update your BIOS to a version that supports the _GTF technique for ATAPI IDE devices. Until then, try changing the ACPI Sleep state to S1 instead of S3 (if your computer's BIOS allows you to do so). Otherwise, you can work around this problem by disabling the DMA support (disable the UDMA mode) on your ATAPI device(s). This will reduce the performance of such device(s), but allow for smoother power management operation until you can update the BIOS.

SYMPTOM 32-4   **When starting Windows 98, you see ACPI errors against a red screen** ACPI error messages on a red screen are generated by the computer's BIOS, so this problem occurs most frequently when your computer has a hardware or BIOS problem. To correct this issue, contact your system or BIOS manufacturer to download a BIOS upgrade that may fix this problem. If a hardware device is mentioned in the error, check for updated drivers or firmware for the suspect hardware device. You can usually determine the precise error using these guidelines:

- A *1xxx* error code on a red (or blue) background indicates an error during the initialization phase of the ACPI driver and usually means the driver cannot read one or more of the ACPI devices.

- A *2xxx* error code usually indicates an *ACPI machine language* (AML) interpreter error.

- A *3xxx* error code indicates an error within the ACPI driver event handler—usually when the event handler is running as the result of a *general-purpose event* (GPE).

- A *4xxx* error code indicates a thermal management error.

- A *5xxx* error code typically suggests an error with a particular piece of ACPI-compliant hardware.

SYMPTOM 32-5   **The Windows 98 low battery alarm does not play the alarm sound or display the low battery message**   There are two possible variations to this problem depending on how you've configured your laptop. If you've set up a low (or critical) battery alarm to play a sound and display a warning message, you may find that the message is displayed, but the sound is not played. Instead, the sound may be played when you click OK to close the message window, or when the window closes automatically after a five-minute delay. Alternately, if you set up the battery alarm to perform an action (such as enter the standby mode) in addition to playing a sound or displaying a warning message, you may notice that the standby/shutdown action is performed, but the sound may not be played and the warning message may not be displayed.

In virtually all cases, this fault occurs on computers that fully conform to the ACPI specification if any action is configured for the battery alarm *in addition to* notification through a sound. This is a known problem with Windows 98 and may have a patch or update available at the Microsoft "Update Windows" site. You can work around this problem in the meantime. To receive audible notification for a low or critical battery alarm, simply do not configure any other type of notification or action in addition to the sound alarm.

SYMPTOM 32-6   **When a standby mode is invoked under Windows 98, the ACPI computer enters the hibernate mode instead**   This problem may take three different forms depending on how you try to enter the standby mode. If you select the standby action for the Power button on the Advanced tab of the Power Management tool in your Control Panel, and you press the Power button, the computer may hibernate instead of entering the standby mode. Second, if you select the standby mode when the laptop computer lid is closed, the computer may also hibernate instead of standing by when the lid is closed. Finally, if you click Start, select Shut down, and then click Stand by, the computer may hibernate instead of standing by.

This problem is common on ACPI systems when the "Enable hibernate support" option is enabled on the Hibernate tab in your Power Management Properties dialog. With this setup, Windows 98 causes the computer to hibernate instead of entering standby mode. This is a problem with Windows 98 (corrected in Windows 98/SE and later), and Microsoft has developed a patch that should correct the issue. The English patch should have the following file attributes or later:

```
6/29/98   9:01pm   4.10.2101   115,665   CONFIGMG.VXD
6/29/98   9:01pm   4.10.2101   37,523    VPOWERD.VXD
7/21/98   9:02pm   4.10.2102   194,494   NTKERN.VXD
```

The Hibernate tab appears in Power Management Properties only if the computer is configured to support hibernation.

SYMPTOM 32-7   **When resuming from suspend or standby mode and running a Windows 98 DirectX6 program, the PC may crash**   This is a known problem with Windows 98 (reported to be fixed in Windows 98/SE) and is known to occur on Compaq Presario 5720 systems. This problem can occur if *all* of the following conditions exist on your system:

■   Your computer uses ACPI for power management.

■   Your computer contains an AGP-based video adapter.

■   You run a program that uses DirectX6 (or later) after you resume your computer.

Microsoft has developed a patch that should correct the issue. You should contact Microsoft for the patch or download it from the Microsoft Web site. The patch should have the following file attributes or later:

```
Pci.vxd     4.10.2017  11/6/98   6:28pm   65,919 bytes
Pcimp.pci   4.10.2017  11/6/98   6:33pm   16,240 bytes
```

SYMPTOM 32-8   **One or more ACPI devices report Device Manager problems under Windows 98**   After you start Windows 98 on an ACPI-compliant computer, one or more hardware devices may not function properly (if at all). They may appear to have the following problems in Device Manager:

■   This device is not working properly because the BIOS in your computer is reporting the resources for the device incorrectly (Code 9).

■   This device is not present, not working properly, or does not have all the drivers installed (Code 10).

■   The drivers for this device are not installed (Code 28).

■   This device is causing a resource conflict (Code 15).

In virtually all cases, the Windows 98 ACPI driver (ACPI.SYS) does not properly release the ACPI GlobalLock feature, even though it's been explicitly released by *ACPI Source Language* (ASL) code. This is a problem with Windows 98. GlobalLock is a feature of ACPI that allows the protection of resources between ASL code executed by the operating system, and the legacy BIOS/SMI environment. The original release of Windows 98 does not release this feature. This causes a number of problems—including exclamation points on all the devices that require access to a resource that's "jammed" by GlobalLock. You can download and install a new version of ACPI.SYS from Microsoft. The version should have the following file attributes:

```
ACPI.SYS  4.10.2000  11/23/98  7:51pm  80,256 bytes
```

SYMPTOM 32-9   **You find the Sleep button disabled after waking an ACPI computer under Windows 98**   This often happens when you press the Sleep button while the system is waking. This is a known problem with Windows 98, and there's a patch available from Microsoft. The English version of this fix should have the following file attributes (or later):

```
12/13/99  11:32p  4.10.2103  194,518  NTKERN.VXD
```

SYMPTOM 32-10   **A Packard Bell system restarts continuously under Windows 98/SE**   After you enable ACPI support on a Packard Bell Multimedia 4350 computer, the system may restart continuously. This fault can occur if you have a Yamaha DS-XG sound card installed in your computer, and both the sound card and the ACPI system attempt to use interrupt IRQ9. To resolve this issue, modify the IRQ used for your sound card:

1. Start your system in the Safe Mode.

2. Click Start, highlight Settings, and then click Control Panel.

3. Double-click the System icon, and then click the Device Manager tab.

4. Double-click the entry for Sound, Video and Game Controllers, and then double-click the "Legacy sound controller."

5. On the Resources tab, clear the Use Automatic Settings check box, and click Interrupt Request.

6. In the Resource Type column, click Change Setting.

7. In the Value box, click or type a number of an available IRQ that does not conflict with any other device in your computer, and then click OK until you return to the Control Panel.

8. Close the Control Panel and reboot the computer if prompted to do so.

SYMPTOM 32-11   **You cannot use ACPI properly under Windows 98 with Asus P2B-type motherboards**   After you install Windows 98/SE on a computer with an Asus P2B-type motherboard, the computer may not wake up after it has been suspended. This is a known problem with P2B-series motherboards using BIOS version 1008. This version may not function properly with ACPI. You'll need to use a BIOS version that corrects the problem. You can fall back to version 1007 or try upgrading to a later version.

SYMPTOM 32-12   **Your system prompts you twice for a hardware profile when ACPI is enabled under Windows 98/SE**   This is a known issue with certain laptop models. When you start a system that uses ACPI power management, you may be prompted for a hardware profile twice. If you create more than one hardware profile and restart your computer, you may receive a message such as

"Windows cannot determine what configuration your computer is in." This problem occurs when the computer's BIOS supports both ACPI and plug-and-play. The real-mode boot process detects the PnP BIOS and prompts for the profile, and then the protected-mode boot process detects ACPI support, but a "blue screen" error requests the profile again.

To work around this issue temporarily, read each prompt carefully, and then select the same hardware profile during the first and second prompt. Microsoft has a patch available for Windows 98/SE that should address this problem. The English version of the Windows 98 patch should have the following file attributes (or later):

```
08/18/99 12:30p  4.10.2103    222,670 WINBOOT.SYS
12/13/99 11:01p               115,689 CONFIGMG.VXD
```

The English version of the Windows 98 SE patch should have the following attributes (or later):

```
09/13/99 05:45p  4.10.2223    222,670 WINBOOT.SYS
08/18/99 11:51a               125,081 CONFIGMG.VXD
```

SYMPTOM 32-13   **A system entering the ACPI S4 mode locks up when a USB device is attached**   This is a problem with Windows 98/SE. When the computer tries to enter the ACPI S4 (suspend to disk) mode, the USB Host controller is removed. When in the S4 mode, Windows is unable to cancel requests previously made to the USB devices. This is a problem with Windows 98/SE, and Microsoft has a fix that should correct the trouble. The English version of this patch should have the following file attributes (or later):

```
09/08/99 03:46p 4.10.2224   18,928 USBD.SYS
```

SYMPTOM 32-14   **You notice that some legacy devices may not respond after resuming from a power-saving state under Windows 98/SE**   This can happen when you resume an ACPI system, and legacy (non-PnP) devices stop functioning. The *Virtual Communications Device* (VCOMM) doesn't attempt to put LPT ports into the D0 power state (full power) when the port is opened. It is assumed to always be powered-on. The problem is that VCOMM puts the LPT port into the D3 power state (powered-off) when you suspend your computer, but does not return it to the D0 state after you resume your computer. This issue can be traced to Windows 98/SE, and Microsoft has a patch that can be installed. The English version of this patch should have the following file attributes (or later):

```
9/27/99  11:06pm  4.10.2018  33,107  VCOMM.VXD
```

PnP printers that do not turn on before the computer starts may also stop working. This problem affects any device that's connected to a parallel (LPT) port on a computer running Windows 98 and Windows 98 SE.

SYMPTOM 32-15   **Windows 98 does not support the passive cooling mode in ACPI**   The ACPI specification defines two categories of cooling: active and passive. Active cooling methods may include running one or more fans to provide increased airflow and improve the dissipation of heat from active components. Passive cooling methods may include slowing down (throttling down) the computer's CPU so that it generates less heat. The problem is that Windows 98 only supports the active cooling mode.

In active cooling mode, the computer first uses active cooling methods to control the temperature of the computer. If the system's temperature continues to rise when the active cooling methods are in use, the computer uses passive cooling methods to cool overheated components. In passive cooling mode, the computer first uses passive cooling methods to control the temperature of the computer. If the computer's temperature continues to rise when the passive cooling methods are in use, the computer uses active cooling methods to cool overheated components. In either cooling mode, if the temperature continues to rise to critical levels, the computer may shut down or go to some other nonoperating, lower-power state. This is to help prevent thermal damage to components.

The computer's cooling mode is controlled by a temperature *set point,* the temperature at which each cooling method is activated. For example, if the set point for the active cooling method is lower than the set point for the passive cooling method, the active method is employed first, and the computer goes to active cooling mode. If the set point for the passive cooling method is lower than the set point for the active cooling method, the passive method is employed first, and the computer goes to passive cooling mode. Windows 98 configures the computer to operate only in active cooling mode and does not provide an interface for changing the active and passive cooling set points to operate in passive cooling mode.

SYMPTOM 32-16 **The Windows 98 system may hang up when you connect and disconnect a laptop's AC power cord** If you connect and then disconnect the power cord on a battery-powered ACPI-compliant computer, one of the following symptoms may occur: either the computer will hang up, or you'll receive a Fatal Exception 0E error. This is a problem with Windows 98 and has been reported with IBM ThinkPad 600 systems. Your computer may seem to retain some amount of functionality (including the ability to shut down or restart the system), but certain ACPI functions (such as thermal management) may be disabled. In some circumstances, this may result in the computer's internal temperature reaching dangerously high levels without Windows 98 activating the appropriate cooling methods to reduce the temperature.

To get around this problem temporarily, shut down and restart your computer normally. If you're unable to shut down Windows properly, you may have to turn your computer off and then back on. To prevent this problem from occurring again, do not connect and disconnect the power cord repeatedly in rapid succession.

SYMPTOM 32-17 **The system is slow to resume from the hibernate mode on certain systems** This is a known problem on systems such as the Toshiba Tecra 8000 or Portege 7020 and generally results as a slow boot when the system resumes. This problem typically occurs when the Battery Mode setting in the computer's CMOS Setup is set to Full Power. This is incorrect in the BIOS. This setting actually enables the PCI Clock Run power-saving feature, which causes all PCI peripherals not to run at full capacity until an ACPI-aware operating system is booted. When the computer resumes from its hibernate mode, the slow boot takes place because the boot loader is not ACPI aware. If you cannot update the BIOS to correct this misrepresentation, you can generally work around it by setting the following CMOS Setup options:

1. Set the Battery Mode or BIOS Power Management option to User Setting instead of Full Power.

2. Change the CPU Sleep Mode option to Disable.

3. Change the Processing Speed option to High.

4. Change the Cooling Method option to Performance.

The CPU speed may still be slower than expected, even if you change all of the settings just listed. For example, the Portege 7020 has a built-in power-saving feature that slows down the CPU when the remaining battery power is less than 50 percent (until an ACPI-aware operating system overrides the setting).

SYMPTOM 32-18 **You see a "System Halted" error** When you try to shut down Windows Me, you may receive an error such as:

```
Your computer failed to reboot. You need to power off the computer, wait a
few seconds and power it back on. System Halted.
```

This problem almost always occurs because the system's power-management driver is not compliant with the ACPI specification for rebooting a legacy-free computer. Microsoft has a patch that can be installed. The English version of this patch should have the following file attributes (or later):

```
12/22/2000   03:06p   4.90.3004   50,223   Vpowerd.vxd
```

To work around this problem, use the Reset or Power button on the computer to restart the computer.

SYMPTOM 32-19 **Your ECP parallel port prevents hibernation** When you try to place your computer in hibernation mode (for example, click Start, click Shut Down, and then click Hibernate), the computer may not enter hibernation mode—or it may return from hibernation mode right away. If you check the SUSFAIL.TXT file, you'll see a message such as:

```
ECP printer port (lpt1) (bios\*pnp0401\00) denied the suspend.
```

In most cases, this problem can occur if a multipurpose device (such as a printer/fax device) is attached to an ECP port and is active. (For example, the device is monitoring the port for an incoming fax.) To work around this problem, disable the active fax or multipurpose device before placing the computer in hibernation mode. You may also try changing the parallel port mode, though this may impair the performance of your multifunction device.

SYMPTOM 32-20 **The PC hangs instead of entering standby mode** This is a known issue with systems like the Dell XPS B533R under Windows Me. The trouble usually occurs because the computer (originally shipped in ACPI mode) has been changed to APM mode. On the Dell XPS, this issue is known to occur with an A01 BIOS dated 1-06-2000. To get around this issue, put the computer in ACPI mode. This is its default configuration as shipped, and this is the configuration that supports standby or suspend mode. You can typically adjust the power management mode through the CMOS Setup.

SYMPTOM 32-21 **You cannot get the system to hibernate when disk space is low** When your ACPI-enabled computer attempts to hibernate under Windows Me, hibernation may not work, and you may not receive any error messages to indicate that there is a problem. However, pop-up notification of low disk space may be displayed from a hard disk icon that is on the right side of the task bar. This problem occurs because there is not enough free hard disk space available on your computer for the hibernate file. When you enable hibernation on a computer that is compliant with ACPI, space for the hibernate file is not allocated immediately, but rather created when the hibernate command is issued. Microsoft has a patch that can be installed. The English version of this patch should have the following file attributes (or later):

```
10/05/2000   06:15p   4.90.0.3002   203,994   Ntkern.vxd
10/05/2000   04:46p   4.90.0.3001   471,048   Vmm.vxd
10/05/2000   05:38p   4.90.0.3001   50,223    Vpowerd.vxd
```

In the meantime, there are several ways to work around this problem. First, you can create additional free space on the hard drive that contains the Windows folder. (The easiest way to do this is with the Disk Cleanup utility.) Second, if your computer has multiple hard disks, partitions, or removable media, you may be able to move data and programs to drives that contain more free space—freeing space on the drive with your Windows folder.

APM SYMPTOMS

Before the introduction of ACPI, *Advanced Power Management* (APM) was the standard for PC power management. While APM is falling into disuse, many older systems continue to employ APM, and even newer systems will "fall back" to APM when trouble arises with ACPI. The following symptoms offer a selection of common APM problems that you should be familiar with.

SYMPTOM 32-22   **Your computer hangs while you try to shut it down**   After you click the "Shut down the computer" option in the Shut Down Windows dialog, the computer may halt (or display a black screen) after you see the "Please wait while your computer shuts down" message. In many cases, this problem is caused by an incompatibility between the Windows APM system and the APM BIOS in your computer. If the BIOS in your computer instructs the system to suspend (rather than shut down), Windows cannot shut down correctly. As a temporary fix, disable your APM support by double-clicking the Power icon in your Control Panel, then setting the Power Management option to Off. To correct the problem more permanently, you'll probably need to upgrade the system BIOS.

SYMPTOM 32-23   **You receive errors when using EMM386 under DOS on laptops with suspend/resume features**   If you're using EMM386 v. 4.45, you may receive an error such as "Serious disk error has occurred" or "Segment Load Failure" (in Windows-based applications). In virtually all cases, this error is caused by a faulty interaction between the laptop power manager feature and EMM386.EXE. To work around this problem, try the following:

■   First, try removing EMM386.EXE to see if the problem is related to using EMM386.EXE. If the problem remains after disabling EMM386, you may need to update the system BIOS.

■   Try to determine if there is a region that needs to be excluded from the system's *upper memory area* (UMA) to allow the laptop's power management to work with EMM386.EXE (4.45). This information may be available in your laptop manual. As an alternative, you can try excluding the A000h–EFFFh memory range to test for a UMA conflict such as:

```
device=c:\dos\emm386.exe noems x=a000-efff
```

■   If the problem occurs only with EMM386.EXE version 4.45 and cannot be corrected with the previous tips, use the version of EMM386.EXE that came with the laptop. Remember that using a different (OEM) version of EMM386 may prevent you from using MemMaker.

SYMPTOM 32-24   **You find that a laptop PC in a docking station may not offer APM support under Windows 95**   When you use Windows 95 on a mobile computer with APM, you see that the suspend command does not appear on the Start menu. (And the APM icon does not appear in Control Panel.) You may also find that the Windows 95 Setup program does not correctly detect APM support on an APM-capable computer. However, this should not affect the DOS real-mode APM support

(POWER.EXE), which should continue to function properly. This problem occurs if your computer disables APM functionality while it is in a docking station.

Some systems (such as the Zenith 420s and 425s) will disable APM when in a docking station, and this will prevent access to the APM features in Windows 95. This is simply part of the individual system's design, and APM support on these computers is not available while they're docked. You may be able to upgrade the system's BIOS to correct this issue, but in the meantime, you'll simply need to add APM support back into Windows 95 after you remove the machine from its docking station.

SYMPTOM 32-25   You cannot use APM 1.1 on certain systems under Windows 95/98
This is a known problem with the AST Ascentia 900N laptop. You cannot use APM features with this system. In virtually all cases, this is a BIOS problem. For example, the Ascentia 900N computer supports APM version 1.1, but the BIOS installed in this system returns an unexpected value when Windows 95/98 makes function calls. Therefore, the Windows protected-mode APM driver (VPOWERD.VXD) is unable to load, and APM support is not provided. A BIOS upgrade should correct the problem. In the meantime, you may be able to use APM 1.0 instead of 1.1:

1. Right-click on My Computer, and then click Properties on the menu that appears.
2. Click the Device Manager tab.
3. Click "Advanced Power Management support," and then click Properties. You may need to expand the "System devices" branch of the hardware tree by double-clicking the branch before you can select APM Support.
4. Click the Settings tab.
5. Click the "Force APM 1.0 mode" check box to select it.
6. Click OK, and reboot the system if necessary.

SYMPTOM 32-26   Your system reboots shortly after resuming to Windows 95/98
This is a known problem with certain laptops such as the Toshiba 4500. If you shut down Windows in suspend mode (or close the lid), Windows appears to shut down successfully. But when you resume Windows, the computer reboots after a short time. This occurs because those systems (Toshiba 4500) require an additional driver file to successfully implement APM features. The APM features do not function correctly without that driver. For the Toshiba 4500, that driver is WRESUME.386. You'll need to obtain that additional driver file, then add it to the SYSTEM.INI file. Let's use the Toshiba 4500 as an example:

1. Open a text editor (such as Notepad or WordPad), and load the SYSTEM.INI file into the editor.
2. In the [386Enh] section of the file, add the following line:

    ```
    device=<path>\wresume.386
    ```

    where <path> is the path to the WRESUME.386 file. For example, if the WRESUME.386 file is located in the \Windows folder on drive C:, add the following line:

    ```
    device=c:\windows\wresume.386
    ```

3. Save your changes to the SYSTEM.INI file and exit the text editor.
4. Shut down Windows and restart your computer normally. The system should wake properly without rebooting.

SYMPTOM 32-27   The Suspend option appears on the Windows 95/98 Start menu, but it doesn't work   When you're using Windows 95/98 on a computer that supports APM, you may find that nothing happens when you click the Suspend option on the Start menu. This trouble is known to occur on numerous systems including the Compaq Summit 60 system. In virtually all cases, the system simply doesn't support the suspend feature (though it does support APM). Windows cannot detect whether a particular computer supports the suspend feature, so the Suspend command is always on the Start menu when APM is enabled.

To correct this problem, you should consider a BIOS upgrade to a newer version that will properly support the suspend function under APM. In the meantime, you can disable the suspend feature on the Start menu:

1. Click Start, highlight Settings, and then click Control Panel.

2. Double-click the Power icon.

3. In the "Show Suspend command on Start menu" box, click the Never option.

4. Apply or save your changes, and then reboot the system if necessary.

SYMPTOM 32-28   You find that your system is constantly suspending and resuming
If you click Suspend on the Start menu, and then press the Suspend button on your system before it goes completely to sleep, the computer continually suspends and resumes. You need to reboot the PC to stop the loop. This is a known issue on systems such as the Compaq Elite under Windows 95. This occurs because the APM BIOS in the Compaq Elite computer has trouble processing a software suspend request and a hardware suspend request at the same time. You may be able to correct this issue by upgrading the system's BIOS. When you need to suspend your Compaq Elite system in the meantime, use either the Suspend command on the Start menu, or the Suspend button on the computer itself. Wait for the suspend procedure to finish before you perform any other operation.

SYMPTOM 32-29   Your system does not shut down after periods of inactivity (even though you've configured the APM features properly)   This is a known problem on systems such as the Compaq Contura Aero under Windows 95. The computer's hard disk may stop spinning to save power during periods of inactivity and then start spinning again two seconds later. In virtually all cases, this is a problem with the system's BIOS when running under Windows, and it can be corrected by updating the system's BIOS.

SYMPTOM 32-30   Your laptop may not suspend automatically under Windows 95/98
This problem often occurs on certain Toshiba laptops under Windows. The computer may not automatically go into its low-power suspend mode. This happens because some laptop computers (such as the Toshiba T1910, T2100, T2400, and T4850) monitor the system IRQ lines to determine if the system is busy. Any hardware interrupt (other than IRQ0) resets the auto-suspend timer. Windows generates interrupts that prevent these computers from going into their low-power suspended mode. A BIOS upgrade may correct this problem. In the meantime, you can suspend the computer manually by clicking Start and then clicking Suspend, or by using the hardware Suspend switch.

SYMPTOM 32-31   Your display (monitor) does not wake after an Energy Star shutdown under Windows 95   When you try to wake your computer after APM has shut down the display, the monitor may remain in its sleep mode. To reactivate the monitor, you must turn the computer off and back on. This problem is known to occur with several different Compaq computers (and other systems) using the Cirrus Logic 54xxx video chipset. There is a conflict between the Windows APM and the computer's BIOS. The Compaq Presario 520, 522, 524, 526, 528, and Prolinea 466 are known to exhibit this problem. There are generally four options for dealing with this type of problem:

- Do not enable APM in the computer's CMOS Setup.
- Do not inform Windows 95/98 that the monitor is Energy Star compliant.
- Disable APM in the Device Manager under Windows 95/98.
- Obtain an APM-compliant BIOS upgrade for the system (perhaps the best solution if possible).

SYMPTOM 32-32   **You cannot install APM on a system under Windows 95/98**
When you install Windows 95/98 on a system (such as the Midwest Micro Elite Soundbook), the APM features are not installed, and you cannot add Windows 95/98 APM support using the Add/Remove Programs wizard. In virtually all cases, the Windows 95/98 APM drivers do not work correctly with the BIOS in that particular system, so APM support cannot be installed. To use APM features in Windows 95/98, you must install the OEM-version APM drivers that came with the particular computer. If you don't have such drivers handy, check with the system manufacturer for driver patches or updates.

SYMPTOM 32-33   **You encounter a system error when trying to suspend a computer under Windows 95**   Some systems (such as the Global Dynamic 466 computer) will produce a system error message on a blue screen when you select the Suspend command on the Start menu under Windows 95. This is almost always a BIOS problem. For example, the APM BIOS in the Global Dynamic 466 computer is defective and does not support the suspend process correctly. The best solution is to upgrade the system BIOS to a version that provides better APM support. In the meantime, do not use the Suspend command. You should remove the Suspend command from your Start menu:

1. Click Start, highlight Settings, and then click Control Panel.
2. In Control Panel, double-click the Power icon.
3. In the Power Properties dialog, click the "Never show Suspend command in Start menu" option.

SYMPTOM 32-34   **The display flashes when the system tries to use APM features under Windows 95**   This type of problem is reported to occur with some AMI BIOS versions. A number of "green" computer systems that have built-in power management support may experience a constant flashing of the display. The display may start flashing as soon as Windows 95 starts, after a long period of inactivity on the computer, or after you attempt to suspend the computer. Also, the mouse cursor may jump to the center of the screen, and the system may respond so slowly that you're unable to use it.

This happens when Windows 95 APM polls the BIOS for APM events, and the BIOS returns a Resume from Suspend command. This causes Windows 95 to reinitialize some software and hardware (such as the display and the mouse), resulting in the display flashing, the mouse centering, and the system delays. You must disable power management support under Windows 95:

1. Click Start, highlight Settings, and then click Control Panel.
2. In Control Panel, double-click the System icon.
3. In the System Properties dialog, click the Device Manager tab, and then double-click "System devices."
4. Double-click "Advanced Power Management support."

5. Click the Settings tab.

6. Make sure that the box to "Enable Power Management support" is not checked.

7. Click the OK button, shut down the computer, and then restart Windows 95 normally.

SYMPTOM 32-35   **Systems using APM 1.0 may not restore all necessary hardware states under Windows 95**   If you're faced with one or more of the following conditions, your system may lose certain functions when returning from the suspend mode:

■ A DOS session was active when you suspended the system.

■ You activated the suspend mode with a hardware switch (such as a Suspend button on the computer).

■ The computer contains an APM 1.0–compliant BIOS version.

For example, if you're playing a DOS-based game with sound when you suspend the system, sound support may not function when the system resumes. In most cases, the problem is related to the hardware switch. When you suspend the system using a hardware switch, your APM 1.0 BIOS may process the suspend request too quickly for Windows 95 to save the current hardware settings. This means Windows 95 may not be able to reinitialize all the hardware devices properly when the system resumes. To work around this problem, use the Suspend feature on the Start menu to suspend the system instead of using a hardware switch.

APM 1.1 (and later) systems do not have this problem because Windows 95 can request that the hardware wait until the operating system is ready to be suspended.

SYMPTOM 32-36   **Using the hardware suspend button crashes your computer under Windows 95**   For example, when Windows 95 APM features are enabled, the PC will halt when you press the Suspend button. Turning the computer off and then back on does not correct the problem. In most situations, there is a mismatch between the system BIOS and the Windows APM version. For example, this problem is known to occur on systems such as the AcerNote 782 laptop. Windows 95 uses APM version 1.1, but the AcerNote 782 does not reliably support APM 1.1. To circumvent this problem, configure Windows 95 to use APM version 1.0:

1. Open your Control Panel, and double-click the System icon.

2. On the Device Manager tab, double-click the System branch, and then double-click "Advanced Power Management support."

3. On the Settings tab, select the "Force APM 1.0 mode" check box.

4. Click OK until you return to the Control Panel.

5. Restart your computer when prompted to do so.

SYMPTOM 32-37   **You cannot suspend a Canon NoteJet II 486C computer under Windows 95**   When you click the Suspend command on the Start menu of a Canon NoteJet II 486C computer, the computer does not suspend. When you use the computer's Suspend button to suspend the computer, the system suspends, but it will not resume. This happens because the APM BIOS on the Canon NoteJet II 486C does not support the Suspend option in Windows 95. Do not suspend the Canon NoteJet II 486C when you're running Windows 95. Try removing the Suspend command from the Start menu:

1. Click Start, highlight Settings, and then click Control Panel.

2. In Control Panel, double-click the Power icon.

3. In the Power Properties dialog, click the "Never show Suspend command in Start menu" option.

4. Apply the changes and reboot the system if necessary.

SYMPTOM 32-38   **You cannot use APM with an NEC Image P90 system and Matrox MGA PCI video adapter under Windows 95**   With this combination of hardware and operating system, the system may crash when you try the Suspend command on the Start menu. There was no way to use APM features reliably on a NEC Image P90 computer with a Matrox MGA PCI display adapter. (There may be BIOS updates or other suitable patches at this time.) You'll need to disable APM on the system:

1. Open the Control Panel, and double-click the System icon.

2. On the Device Manager tab, double-click the "System devices" entry to expand it.

3. Double-click "Advanced Power Management support."

4. On the Settings tab, clear the "Enable Power Management support" check box.

5. Click OK until you return to Control Panel, and reboot the system if necessary.

SYMPTOM 32-39   **The computer will not suspend when a DOS session is running under Windows 95**   You find that an APM-compliant computer is not suspended when a DOS session (or virtual machine) is active. When no screen saver is selected and the "Shut off monitor" option is enabled, the monitor is not shut off when a DOS session is running. To get around this problem, simply enable a screen saver:

1. Open your Control Panel, and then double-click the Display icon.

2. Click the Screen Saver tab.

3. Click a screen saver in the Screen Saver box, and then click OK.

SYMPTOM 32-40   **When installing Windows, you receive an "Exception 0E in VPOWERD" message when the system first boots**   The VPOWERD driver may cause a page fault ("Fatal Exception error 0E") on the first reboot during Windows Setup on certain computer models that support APM. The best fix for this problem is to upgrade the system's BIOS version to one that offers better APM/ACPI support. Otherwise, you can circumvent this problem by disabling APM during the Windows Setup process:

■ If you're not using Automated Setup, click the Custom button in the Setup Options screen, and then clear the Advanced Power Management check box.

■ If you are using Automated Setup, add the following line to the [System] section of the MSBATCH.INF file such as:

```
"Power"="No APM"
```

You *must* include the quotation marks. Remember that this method disables all APM functions in Windows.

As an alternative, Microsoft reports that they have a Windows fix for this problem. Check with Microsoft at **www.microsoft.com** for an appropriate patch file.

SYMPTOM 32-41   Your laptop system continues to drain power even when in the suspend mode under Windows 95/98   This type of problem is known to occur on a number of Gateway 2000 laptop systems (such as the ColorBook 4SX25, 4SX33, 4DX33, Liberty, and Solo), and is always caused by a BIOS problem. You should contact the system manufacturer for a current BIOS upgrade.

SYMPTOM 32-42   You encounter a "Fatal Exception 0E" error when the system is performing a suspend process   On an APM-compliant system under Windows 95/OSR1, a "Fatal Exception 0E" error may occur in VPOWERD module if a "critical suspend" event takes place while the computer is already in the process of suspending normally. This happens because your Windows 95 power management driver does not properly handle the new critical suspend request while it is processing a normal suspend request.

For example, this error may crop up if you manually suspend the computer when the computer's battery is critically low. The low-battery condition could cause a critical suspend request to be issued by the system BIOS. The critical suspend request is issued while Windows 95 is already processing the normal suspend request—and then the problem can occur. This trouble is corrected by the following update for Windows 95 (and does not occur under Windows 98 or later):

```
VPOWERD.VXD 4.00.952   11/13/96    19,693 bytes
```

This patch does not work properly with Windows 95 OSR 2 or later.

SYMPTOM 32-43   You notice that the Windows 95 clock loses time when APM is enabled   When you enable APM on a computer running Windows 95, the clock may slow down or stop when the computer switches to suspend mode. However, the system clock continues to keep the correct time, and you can reset the clock to the correct time by restarting the computer. This problem can occur if you enabled APM in the computer's CMOS settings after Windows 95 was installed, or if your computer's BIOS supports an older version of APM. If APM was enabled in CMOS after installing Windows 95, it may be that the Windows APM features may not have been installed. Reinstall Windows 95 to install APM support. To verify that APM support is enabled:

1. Open the Control Panel and double-click the System icon.

2. Click the Device Manager tab, and then double-click the "System devices" branch to expand it.

3. Double-click "Advanced Power Management support."

4. On the Settings tab, verify that the "Enable Power Management support" check box is selected.

If APM support is installed, you can suspend the system by clicking the Start button, then clicking Suspend before the computer switches into its suspend mode. If the trouble is that your system's BIOS supports older version(s) of APM, you may be able to correct the problem by upgrading the computer's BIOS.

SYMPTOM 32-44   **You see that the Windows 98 shutdown display appears before the system powers-off**   If your system is configured to automatically power-off when you shut down Windows 98, the message "It's now safe to turn off your computer" may be displayed briefly on your monitor before your computer powers-off. When you shut down Windows 98 on a computer that supports APM, the Windows 98 shutdown display (LOGO.SYS) is displayed at the same time APM procedures are being processed. This behavior is a normal result of the new Fast Shutdown functionality in Windows 98.

SYMPTOM 32-45   **You receive an error indicating that your system cannot enter standby mode**   When your attempt to put Windows 98/SE in standby mode, you may see an error message such as:

```
Your computer cannot go on standby because a device driver or program won't allow
it. Close all programs and try again.
```

However, if you close all programs and attempt to put Windows 98 into standby mode again, you'll receive the same error message. This error can occur if a program, driver, or other hardware device is preventing Windows 98 from going into standby mode. (This is sometimes referred to as a *veto* of the suspend command.) To isolate this problem, use the Power Management Troubleshooter (PMTSHOOT.EXE) tool to determine just where the trouble is.

SYMPTOM 32-46   **Your system will not suspend if the Deluxe CD Player utility is running under Windows 98**   With Deluxe CD Player running on a laptop, the computer's APM software may not activate the suspend mode. To work around this issue, quit the Deluxe CD Player before trying to suspend the system. This is a known problem with the Windows 98 Plus pack, so check with Microsoft for a patch or update for the CD player utility.

SYMPTOM 32-47   **Your Windows 98 system does not wake to run the task you asked it to**   When you use the "Wake the computer to run this task" option for a given task in the Task Scheduler, your computer may not resume from its suspend state to run the scheduled task at the required time. This problem can occur if your computer's BIOS does not support APM version 1.2 or later. Unfortunately, the "Wake the computer to run this task" check box is available on any computer—even though this feature only works on computers that support APM 1.2 or later. To fix this problem, upgrade your computer's BIOS to a version that supports APM version 1.2 (or later).

SYMPTOM 32-48   **When your display is turned off by APM under Windows 98, you cannot resume the display**   This is a known problem with Windows 98, and trouble can crop up if any of the following situations is true:

- The 3D Maze screen saver is currently running. Shut down and restart the system, and then disable the screen saver (or select another one).

- Your display resolution is set to 800×600 or higher. Shut down and restart the system, open the Control Panel, select the Display icon, and choose a lower (or higher) display resolution.

- You're using a Matrox MGA Impression Lite, Plus, Plus 220, or Ultima video adapter and driver. Check with Matrox for an updated driver or firmware, or remove the Matrox card and install another display adapter.

SYMPTOM 32-49   **You find that the APM device in the Windows 98 Device Manager shows a code of 10**   When you view the Advanced Power Management support device in your Device Manager, you see a yellow exclamation point displayed on the device, along with the following status message:

```
This device is not present, not working properly, or does not have all the
drivers installed (Code 10).
```

This problem can occur if APM support is disabled in the computer's BIOS (or if your computer does not support Microsoft's implementation of APM). Enable APM support in the computer's CMOS Setup. If APM is enabled, but the status remains unchanged, it may be necessary to upgrade the system's BIOS to a later version that offers better APM support. In extreme cases, you may need to upgrade the system's motherboard.

SYMPTOM 32-50   **The computer cannot enter its suspend mode in Windows 98**
When your computer has been inactive long enough for it to go to standby mode, it may not enter the standby mode properly. You may also receive a message saying that your computer will stand by in 15 seconds, but the standby mode is not invoked. This problem is known to occur if a Windows 98 screen saver is currently active, such as 3D Flower Box, 3D Flying Objects, 3D Maze, 3D Text, or Channel Screen Saver. This problem only applies to computers that support APM or the ACPI specification and is a known problem in Microsoft Windows 98, but there are several ways to work around the problem:

■   Use a different screen saver.

■   Disable the screen saver.

■   Reduce the screen saver's complexity.

SYMPTOM 32-51   **You find that the Windows 95/98/SE task bar clock seems to be losing time**   There are several ways that this problem may manifest itself. First, when you use the Date/Time tool to select a different year, the clock may stop until you click Apply or OK, and the clock does not compensate for the length of time it was stopped. When you use the Date/Time tool to select a different month or date, the time may be decreased by 5–10 seconds. Finally, when you leave your computer on for an extended amount of time, the time may lose from two minutes up to an hour per day.

■   Check your APM settings. Disable APM in the CMOS Setup, and configure Windows to manage APM.

■   Disable third-party programs and utilities such as antivirus, screen saver, and system utilities.

■   Use a clean boot to isolate possible driver or software issues.

■   Check for a weak CMOS backup battery. Open a DOS window and use the TIME function to check time under DOS. Compare the DOS and Windows time entries. If the times are the same, try a new battery. If the times are not the same, there may be a hardware or configuration problem under Windows that is unsetting the time under Windows.

    The CMOS *does* keep the correct time, and if you restart the computer, the Windows clock is updated. Also, if you start your computer in Safe Mode, Windows *does not* lose time.

SYMPTOM 32-52 **The hard drive appears to remain active even after Windows 98 shuts down**   You may notice that the system's hard drive appears to be active even after you see the message "It's now safe to turn off your computer." On newer computers that use ACPI features, APM features make it possible for you to put your computer in standby or hibernate mode to save power resources. The OnNow feature allows only the devices that need to be active to "wake up." In certain situations, the OnNow feature may continue to activate the hard disk even though the computer has shut down. This problem may be caused by the APM features in Windows 98 and does not cause any problem or loss of features.

SYMPTOM 32-53 **When Windows 95/98 resumes from suspend mode, one or more hard drives seem to be missing**   This is a known issue with some Toshiba laptops. After you resume your laptop computer from suspend mode, hard drives attached to the AMD SCSI controller may be missing in My Computer and Windows Explorer. This problem occurs when you suspend and resume your computer while it's in its docking station, though the APM BIOS used by Toshiba laptop computers does support suspending and resuming while the computer is docked. To prevent this problem from occurring, you'll need a patch for the laptop. For the Toshiba systems, obtain the TAP utility from Toshiba's Web site. (The TAP utility prevents the computer from going into suspend mode while it is docked.)

SYMPTOM 32-54 **You encounter a write data error when using a CD-RW under Windows 98**   When you try to format a blank disc with a CD-RW drive, you may receive the following error message:

```
Error: Write Data
Illegal Start Block Address (0x4000004b)
```

You will not be able to read or write to the disc. In virtually all cases, this problem can occur if APM is enabled on your computer. You can try disabling the APM permanently:

1. Click Start, highlight Settings, click Control Panel, and then double-click the Power Management icon.

2. In the "System standby" box, click Never, click Never in the "Turn off monitor" box, and then click Never in the "Turn off hard drive" box.

3. Click Apply, click OK, and then restart your computer.

If you don't want to permanently disable APM, you can temporarily disable it, use your CD-RW drive, and then reenable APM:

1. Click Start, highlight Settings, click Control Panel, and then double-click the Power Management icon.

2. In the "System standby" box, click Never, click Never in the "Turn off monitor" box, and then click Never in the "Turn off hard drive" box.

3. Click Apply, click OK, and then restart your computer.

4. Use your CD-RW drive, and then restart your computer normally.

5. Click Start, highlight Settings, click Control Panel, and then double-click the Power Management icon.

6. In the "System standby," "Turn off monitor," and "Turn off hard drive" boxes, click the appropriate time settings that you want to use.

7. Click Apply, click OK, and then restart your computer.

SYMPTOM 32-55   The computer halts when you try to shut down Windows 98 (not SE)
This problem can occur if your computer uses ACPI and the "Fast shutdown" feature is disabled. This issue is a problem with Windows 98 that is known to affect the following computers:

- Compaq Deskpro EN Series 6350
- Compaq Presario 7234 5680, 5670, 5690, 5686, 5695, 5680
- Toshiba Tecra 750
- Generic computer with AMD P233 K6 CPU and Award BIOS version 4.51PG (1995)
- IBM Aptiva 2137

You can install a patch from Microsoft that should address this problem. The English version of this fix should have the following file attributes (or later):

```
ACPI.SYS  4.10.2000  11/23/98  7:51pm  80,256 bytes
```

To work around this problem temporarily, enable the "Fast shutdown" feature:

1. Click Start, highlight Programs, point to Accessories, select System Tools, and then click System Information.
2. On the Tools menu, click the System Configuration Utility.
3. On the General tab, click Advanced.
4. Click the "Disable fast shutdown" check box to clear it, click OK, and then click OK again.
5. Click Yes when you're prompted to restart your computer.

SYMPTOM 32-56   The monitor turns off while your DVD movie is playing under Windows 98/SE   This problem can crop up if you're using APM, and the DVD player program you're using is not designed to work with APM. To resolve this problem, contact the manufacturer to see if there's an APM-aware version of your DVD player program, or disable APM for your monitor. If there is no player update, you should try disabling APM:

1. Click Start, point to Settings, click Control Panel, and then double-click the Power Management icon.
2. On the Power Schemes tab, click Never in the "Turn off monitor" box.
3. Click OK and reboot the PC if necessary.

SYMPTOM 32-57   Windows 98/SE doesn't shut down or restart properly in the DOS mode   After you install Windows 98/SE, you may not be able to use the "Shut down" or "Restart in MS-DOS mode" options successfully. This problem can occur if your video adapter requires an IRQ in the DOS mode, but your computer's BIOS doesn't assign one to it. Windows 98/SE includes updates for ACPI, OnNow, and APM and may require the latest BIOS upgrade. To resolve this problem:

- Check your computer's BIOS for a setting to assign an IRQ to the video adapter.
- Check for an updated video adapter BIOS (firmware).
- Check for an updated system BIOS.

SYMPTOM 32-58   **Your Windows 98/SE system reports low drive space after the system exits its standby mode**   This issue can occur if CyberWarner software is running when the computer enters its standby or suspend modes. CyberWarner is a program designed to protect system files from replacement or damage by backing up the files. On computers that support APM, CyberWarner may make multiple backups of the same files when the computer is in standby or suspend mode. To work around this problem, quit the CyberWarner software before the computer enters standby or suspend mode.

SYMPTOM 32-59   **You notice that the laptop's battery drains faster when a USB device is attached**   This may happen under Windows 95/98/SE. Battery-powered computers that use APM or ACPI may experience increased power consumption leading to an increased drain of battery power when a USB device is attached. This happens because the bus activity required to maintain communications with the USB device prevents the CPU from switching to a "C3" (Clock-Stopped) power state. When a USB device is not connected, the CPU can spend a significant amount of time in the C3 state, which reduces power consumption and extends battery life significantly. Try to conserve battery power; disconnect all USB devices if you're not using them. As an alternative, use the Power Management tool in Control Panel to adjust the power scheme settings. This allows you to use shorter timeout values for turning off the monitor and hard drives and for placing the computer in a system standby state.

Further Study

ACPI Specification   www.teleport.com/~acpi/spec.htm
ACPI Web site   www.teleport.com/%7Eacpi/
Amtrade   www.amtrade.com
Astec   www.astec.com/
Data Depot (PC Wiz)   www.datadepo.com/index.htm
Intel's Instantly Available PC site   developer.intel.com/technology/iapc/
Microsoft's ACPI and OnNow site   www.microsoft.com/hwdev/onnow.htm
PC Power and Cooling   www.pcpowercooling.com
TUV (German Standards)   www.tuv.com/
UL (Underwriter's Laboratories)   www.ul.com/

33

REMOVABLE MEDIA DRIVES

Perhaps the single most important complaint about hard drives has been that they are not portable—you can't just slide out one drive and pop in a new one. Hard drives are traditionally permanent installations. When that drive fills up, you must physically add another hard drive or replace the existing hard drive with a larger model. Both options require an invasive and time-consuming upgrade procedure (and then the drive must be partitioned and formatted before use). High-capacity *removable media drives* overcome this limitation—the drive hardware remains in the PC, but the media (or the disks) can be inserted and removed as needed.

With a removable media drive (such as the Iomega Zip, Iomega Bernoulli, Iomega Jaz, SyQuest EZ-Flyer, or SyQuest SyJet), you can finally achieve *limitless* storage simply by exchanging data cartridges. If you need to use files on another PC, you can just pop out a cartridge and take it with you to another PC with a compatible drive. Although removable media drives are not quite as fast as hard drives, they are solid performers, and you can usually start programs (or even boot the PC) right from that drive. This chapter highlights a series of troubleshooting procedures for the Iomega Zip, Bernoulli, and Jaz drives.

Traditional removable media drives are under a tremendous amount of pressure from today's versatile CD-R and CD-RW drives and their very inexpensive media. Consequently, Iomega and SyQuest type removable media drives are gradually becoming obsolete.

Iomega Zip Drives

In order for removable media to be popular, it must follow three basic guidelines: it must record quickly, it must hold a lot of data on a single cartridge (or other media), and it must be portable between drives. Floppy drives are very portable, but they hold only a little data. Tapes hold a lot of data, but they are slow and not very portable between drives. Hard drives are quite fast and hold a great deal of data, but they simply are not portable. The search for reusable, high-capacity media that is transportable between inexpensive, readily available drives has led Iomega to produce its Zip drive.

The Zip drive has become perhaps the single most popular nonstandard drive in production today. In fact, Zip drives are so popular that some PC makers include them as standard equipment in new systems. Zip drives offer relatively fast seek times at 29mS, and can sustain data rates of 300 KB/s across the parallel port (or 1 MB/s via SCSI or ATAPI IDE interfaces). Each cartridge can hold up to 250MB (only 100MB in older drive versions), which is large enough to hold huge illustrations, CAD layouts, and even small multimedia presentations. When used with a SCSI interface and a properly configured Adaptec SCSI controller, you may even boot your system from the Zip drive. Zip drives are available in internal ATAPI and SCSI versions, as well as external parallel port and USB versions. This part of the chapter offers some installation guidelines for Zip drives, provides some tips for using them most effectively, and covers a collection of troubleshooting procedures.

ZIP DRIVE INSTALLATION AND REPLACEMENT

Zip drives generally are not too difficult to install, but there are some important guidelines that might help smooth possible problems. This part of the chapter highlights the installation sequence for parallel port, USB port, and ATAPI IDE drives.

Parallel Port

Follow these steps to set up and install an external Iomega Zip drive on a conventional PC parallel port:

1. Unpack the Zip drive and verify that all the software and accessories are in the box.
2. Turn off the computer and all of its peripherals.
3. Connect the cable between the Zip drive and the computer's parallel port. Secure the cable but do not overtighten it. If there is a printer connected to the parallel port, disconnect it now.
4. Connect the drive's power supply.

You can use a Universal Power Supply—the supply included with your Zip drive can be used worldwide. It works at any voltage from 100 to 240 volts. All you need is the appropriate plug adapter.

5. Power-up the Zip drive.

When you want to power-down your Zip drive, first eject any disk from the drive, and then push the power button to power-down the drive.

6. Boot the PC and allow Windows to fully load.
7. After Windows starts, place the Zip software CD in the CD-ROM drive; the setup program should start automatically. If you don't have a CD-ROM drive, you can download and install the software from the Iomega Web site.

8.   Follow the instructions to complete the software's installation. You'll need to restart the PC (and the setup utility) to finish the installation.

You'll see a Guest window that allows you to choose the drive letters you want to use for your Zip drive (and other removable drives). If installing the Zip drive causes your CD-ROM drive letter to change, you should change it back. This prevents having to reinstall applications or games.

9.   As an option, you may run the Iomega Parallel Port Accelerator utility, which can help to optimize the data transfer rate for your drive.

10.   If you have a printer, you can try connecting it to the Zip drive using a standard printer cable.

   This completes the general installation of a parallel port Zip drive.

USB Port

Follow these steps to set up and install an external Iomega Zip drive on a standard PC Universal Serial Bus (USB) port:

1.   Unpack the Zip drive and verify that all of the software and accessories are in the box.

2.   Boot the PC and allow Windows 98/Me to fully load. You must be using Windows 98/Me for proper USB support.

3.   After Windows 98/Me starts, place the Zip software CD in the CD-ROM drive; the setup program should start automatically. If you don't have a CD-ROM drive, you may be able to download and install the software from the Iomega Web site.

4.   Follow the instructions to complete the software's installation. You'll need to restart the PC (and the setup utility) to finish the installation.

You'll be installing the drivers before connecting your USB Zip drive. This is typical of many USB devices.

5.   Connect the USB cable between the Zip drive and the computer's USB port. Do not use USB extension cables with the Zip drive—data loss may result.

6.   Connect the drive's power supply. Although USB is supposed to supply power to many devices, high-power devices such as drives require the use of a supplemental power supply. The drive's power LED will come on.

You can use a Universal Power Supply—the supply included with your Zip drive can be used world-wide. It works at any voltage from 100 to 240 volts. All you need is the appropriate plug adapter.

7.   Insert a new Zip disk into the drive. You will see the Zip drive icon in My Computer or Windows Explorer. Double-click the Zip drive icon to access your Zip disk.

   This completes the general installation of a parallel port Zip drive.

ATAPI IDE Port

Follow these steps to set up and install an internal Iomega Zip drive on a system using an ATAPI IDE-type controller channel:

1. Evaluate your system requirements. You need an empty 3.5-inch or 5.25-inch drive bay and an open position on your primary or secondary hard drive controller (preferably EIDE or Ultra-DMA) to support an internal ATAPI IDE Zip drive.

 A Zip drive meets the latest ATAPI specifications. However, some computers with early ATAPI support may not meet these specifications and may not work correctly with removable ATAPI drives like the Zip. If the computer locks up or fails to boot correctly after the Zip drive is installed, you may need to update your system BIOS and/or drive controller to a later model.

2. Unpack the Zip drive and verify that all of the software and accessories are in the box.

3. Turn off and unplug the computer, and then remove the outer cover. On some computers (especially tower models), you may need to remove a plastic face plate as well to access an available drive bay.

4. Identify your drive configuration. Examine the drive(s) currently connected to your primary and secondary hard drive controller ports. Based on the current configuration, you can decide on the best way to install and configure the new Zip drive.

   ■ If your hard drive and CD-ROM are connected to different controller channels, try installing the Zip drive as the slave drive on the secondary drive controller port.

   ■ If your hard drive and CD-ROM are connected to the same controller channel, try installing the Zip drive as the master drive on the secondary drive controller port.

5. Locate your secondary IDE connector. Find the wide, flat ribbon cable on the back of the CD-ROM drive and follow it. If the cable also connects to a hard drive, follow the cable back to the motherboard's connector (usually marked "pri IDE"), and then locate the secondary drive controller (often marked "sec IDE"). If the cable does not also connect to the hard drive, follow the cable back to the motherboard's connector (which is often the secondary controller).

To install the Zip drive as a slave device:

1. Check the jumpers. The Zip drive is configured as the slave device by default. This makes it the second device on the secondary drive controller channel. Double-check to verify that the drive is jumpered as "slave." Also verify that the jumper on the first (master) device is in fact set to "master."

2. Locate an available drive bay. Select a 5.25-inch or 3.5-inch drive bay to install the Zip drive. If you select a 3.5-inch bay, you may need to remove the Zip drive's mounting rails. Since there is a limited amount of cable length between the first (master) drive and the Zip drive, try selecting a drive bay as close as possible to the master device (such as the CD-ROM drive).

3. Insert the drive into a drive bay. Be sure that the drive is level and oriented properly.

4. Remove the original IDE cable. Locate the wide ribbon cable attached between the first (master) device and the drive controller. Note the orientation of pin 1 (the red or blue stripe in the cable), and then disconnect the cable from the drive and controller, and set the cable aside.

5. Connect the new IDE cable. Connect the "long end" (the end furthest from the middle connector on the cable) to the secondary IDE port on the motherboard. Connect the middle connector to the first drive (such as the CD-ROM), and then connect the other end of the cable to the Zip drive. Be sure to verify the orientation of the cable.

6. Connect power to the Zip drive. Locate an available drive power connector from the power supply, and connect it securely to the Zip drive.

7. Bolt down the Zip drive. Use the original mounting screws and bolt the Zip drive into place. Do not overtighten the screws.

8. Recheck the cables to be sure that nothing has been accidentally loosened, and then reattach the computer's outer cover.

9. Reconnect the AC power cord, turn the PC on, and allow Windows to load.

10. After Windows starts, place the Zip software CD in the CD-ROM drive; the setup program should start automatically. If you don't have a CD-ROM drive, you may be able to download and install the software from the Iomega Web site.

11. Follow the instructions to complete the driver and utility software installation. You'll need to restart the PC (and the setup utility) to finish the installation.

To install the Zip drive as a master device:

1. Check the jumpers. The Zip drive is configured as the slave device by default. This normally makes it the second device on the secondary drive controller channel. Set the jumper so that the Zip drive is configured as the master device.

2. Locate an available drive bay. Select a 5.25-inch or 3.5-inch drive bay to install the Zip drive. If you select a 3.5-inch bay, you may need to remove the Zip drive's mounting rails. Since there is a limited amount of cable length between the controller and the Zip drive, try selecting a drive bay as close as possible to the drive controller.

3. Insert the drive into a drive bay. Be sure that the drive is level and oriented properly.

4. Connect the new IDE cable. Connect the "long end" (the end furthest from the middle connector on the cable) to the secondary IDE port on the motherboard. Connect the other end of the connector to the Zip drive. Be sure to verify the orientation of the cable so that pin 1 (the blue or red stripe) is aligned with pin 1 on the drive and controller.

5. Connect power to the Zip drive. Locate an available drive power connector from the power supply, and connect it securely to the Zip drive.

6. Bolt down the Zip drive. Use the original mounting screws and bolt the Zip drive into place. Do not overtighten the screws.

7. Recheck the cables to be sure that nothing has been accidentally loosened, and then reattach the computer's outer cover.

8. Reconnect the AC power cord, turn the PC on, and allow Windows to load.

9. After Windows starts, place the Zip software CD in the CD-ROM drive—the setup program should start automatically. If you don't have a CD-ROM drive, you may be able to download and install the software from the Iomega Web site.

10. Follow the instructions to complete the driver and utility software installation. You'll need to restart the PC (and the setup utility) to finish the installation.

USING THE ZIP DRIVE

The Zip drive is generally simple and straightforward to use, but if you're new to the Zip drive family, this part of the chapter covers some important nuances that you should be familiar with to achieve the best operation from the drive.

Accessing a Zip Drive

To use the Zip drive, insert a Zip disk, and then select the drive letter assigned to the Zip drive in My Computer (Windows 9x/Me or Windows NT 4.0) or File Manager (Windows NT 3.51 or Windows 3.1). You can now read, write, or copy files to and from the Zip drive using the same techniques used with other drives on your system.

> The green power/eject button will flash when the Zip drive is transferring data, or when a Zip disk is inserted or ejected.

Inserting a Zip Disk

Push the disk gently into the drive slot—similar to inserting a floppy disk. The green activity light will flash momentarily, and then glow continuously. If the activity light continues to blink slowly, push the eject button to eject the Zip disk, and then reinsert it carefully. Remember that drive power should be connected before inserting a Zip disk.

Ejecting a Zip Disk

There are two general means of ejecting a Zip disk: use the eject button, or use the Iomega software "eject" command. Remember that you should remove a Zip disk when the drive is not in use, and remove a disk *before* disconnecting power or moving the Zip drive. If you need to eject a disk during a power failure, disconnect the power supply from the Zip drive, and gently push a straightened paper clip into the emergency disk eject hole on the back of the drive. The disk mechanism should release the disk.

Powering the Zip Drive

The Zip drive generally requires that power be available to it *before* your operating system starts to load—otherwise, Windows may not detect the drive at start time. Iomega usually suggests that you connect your PC, Zip drive, and printer (or other parallel port device) to a power strip so that all three devices are powered simultaneously.

Powering Down the Zip Drive

The power/eject button on the 250MB Zip drive allows you to power-down the drive when it is not in use. In power-down mode, the drive uses a very small amount of power that is needed to support data pass-through (when a printer or scanner is connected to the Zip drive).

The Zip drive also has an automatic sleep mode that spins down a Zip disk after 15 minutes of inactivity. This feature minimizes power consumption when the Zip drive is not being accessed. During a "drive sleep," the green power light remains on, and the Zip disk automatically spins up again when it needs to be accessed. You can use the Iomega software to change the drive sleep setting.

Zip Disk Compatibility

The 250MB Zip drive is fully backward compatible, which allows you to read and write 100MB Zip disks. But due to the design of the 250MB Zip drive, its performance when writing to a 100MB Zip disk is significantly reduced. The time required to write information to a 100MB Zip disk in a 250MB parallel port Zip drive may be more than twice that needed to write the same information to a 250MB Zip disk. To get top performance from your 250MB Zip drive, you should use 250MB Zip disks whenever you want to store new information. Here are some important guidelines when using Zip disks:

■ If you write data to a 100MB Zip disk using a 250MB Zip drive, and later find that the disk cannot be read by a 100MB Zip drive, try reading the disk again in your 250MB Zip drive.

■ If the 250MB Zip drive locks up when you're writing to a 100MB Zip disk, you can verify that the drive is operating correctly by checking that the green activity light is blinking irregularly. A slow, steady blink may indicate a serious problem with the drive. If there is a slow, steady blink, try ejecting the disk and reinserting it.

■ You can use the Iomega Short Format option only if you need to format a 100MB Zip disk in a 250MB Zip drive—the Long Format option is not supported for 100MB Zip disks in a 250MB Zip drive.

■ A 250MB Zip disk cannot be used in a 100MB Zip drive. The 100MB Zip drive will automatically reject a 250MB disk.

ZIP DISK GUIDELINES

Iomega Zip disks are rather delicate and sensitive, and must be treated with care to avoid damage to the disk or drive, or loss of your important data. Here are some practical guidelines that can help you get a longer working life from your disks:

■ Always make sure the power supply is connected to the drive before inserting a Zip disk. Otherwise, you might damage your drive.

■ Never *force* a Zip disk into or out of the drive. If the eject button doesn't work, power-down the drive and try the emergency eject feature.

■ Never use ordinary 3.5-inch floppy disks or floppy head-cleaning disks in your Zip drive. Such media is not compatible with the heads on a Zip drive and thus may cause severe damage to the drive mechanism.

■ Keep your Zip drive on a level surface. Avoid moving the drive when a Zip disk is inserted and in use.

■ Always remove the Zip disk from the drive when you are transporting your Zip drive, even if it's just across the room.

■ Return the Zip disk to its protective case when it's not in the drive.

■ Avoid exposing the Zip drive or Zip disks to dust, direct sunlight, high temperature, moisture, and magnetic fields (such as from monitors and some speakers). Otherwise, you may eventually experience data loss or drive damage.

■ If you have a printer connected through a Zip drive, make sure the power supply is connected (even if you're not using the Zip drive). Power to the drive is required for correct data pass-through.

■ Before connecting or disconnecting your Zip drive, always shut down the computer and disconnect power from the Zip drive.

ZIP DRIVE SOFTWARE CONSIDERATIONS AND TESTING

Getting the most from a Zip drive requires that you keep drivers and applications software up to date, and install/uninstall those drivers manually if necessary. You'll also need to know how to adjust the Zip drive letter and how to format and write-protect your Zip media. This part of the chapter offers a series of essential Zip drive procedures.

Obtaining Updated Zip Software

New drivers and applications software can help overcome performance problems and compatibility issues. The latest drivers for your Zip drive may be downloaded from Iomega's FTP site at **www.iomega.com/software/index.html**. Once you locate the proper page, choose the operating system you're using (such as Windows 9x/Me, Windows NT, Windows 3.1x/DOS, and so on). A listing describing each file available for download will guide you through the process. You may also order the latest Iomega software by calling 1-800-MY-STUFF (though there's a nominal charge when you order the software by phone).

Manually Install Zip Parallel Port Drivers

If you cannot install the Zip software automatically (there is no autorun from the CD), you can use the following steps to install the drivers manually under Windows 9x/Me. Start by uninstalling the existing Zip parallel port driver:

1. Click Start, highlight Settings, and click Control Panel.
2. In the Control Panel, double-click the System icon.
3. In the System Properties dialog box, choose the Device Manager tab.
4. Under Device Manager, click on the plus (+) symbol next to SCSI Controllers.
5. If the Iomega Parallel Port Interface is listed, highlight the entry and click Remove.

If no SCSI controllers are listed in Device Manager, or the Iomega Parallel Port Interface is not listed within SCSI controllers, the drive has not been installed yet.

Now manually install the Zip drivers for your parallel port:

1. Insert the IomegaWare CD into your CD-ROM drive.

If the installation begins automatically, cancel the manual installation process.

2. Click on Start, highlight Settings, and then click Control Panel.
3. In the Control Panel, double-click Add New Hardware.
4. Click the Next button to begin the installation process.
5. If you're prompted to have Windows search for new hardware, choose No.
6. In the Hardware Types list, choose SCSI Controllers, and then click Next.
7. In the next screen, choose Have Disk.
8. At the Install From Disk prompt, click the Browse button.
9. From the Drives drop-down list, choose the drive letter of your CD-ROM drive.
10. In the Folders list, double-click the w9xstuff folder and click OK twice.
11. In the Models list, choose the Iomega Parallel Port Zip Interface, click Next, and click Finish.
12. Restart your computer. Your driver is now installed.

Uninstalling Zip Software

If you need to remove the Zip software (such as Iomega Tools) from your Windows 9x/Me platform, use the Add/Remove Programs wizard in your Control Panel to remove the Iomega Tools for Windows 9x entry:

1. Click Start, highlight Settings, and select Control Panel.
2. In the Control Panel, double-click the Add/Remove Programs icon.
3. Select Iomega Tools for Windows 9x in the Installed Program list box, and click Add/Remove.
4. Follow the program removal screens that appear.

5. Click OK to close the Add/Remove Programs window.

6. Restart Windows 9x.

Changing the Zip Drive Letter

It may be necessary for you to change the drive letter assignment of your Zip drive if you encounter drive problems or issues with other software-driven drives like CD-ROMs. Use the following steps to adjust the drive letter(s):

1. Right-click the My Computer icon on your desktop, and then choose Properties.

2. Select the Device Manager tab.

3. Click on the + next to the CD-ROM or Disk Drives icon, and choose the Settings tab.

4. Choose Start Drive Letter and assign the drive letter you need from the drop-down menu.

5. Choose the same letter for End Drive Letter.

6. Click OK and allow your system to reboot for changes to take effect.

7. Repeat the preceding steps by clicking the + next to Disk Drives, and assign a different drive letter to your Iomega drive.

Formatting Zip Disks with Iomega Software

The Iomega software that's installed with the Zip disk offers the facility for reformatting Zip disks if the need arises. Before you format a disk, remember that all the information on it will become inaccessible, so use caution to avoid accidental data loss:

1. Right-click the Zip drive icon on your Windows desktop.

2. Select Format from the drive shortcut menu, and choose the format type.

    ■ Use Short Format if you want to quickly erase all data on a disk so you can reuse it.

    ■ Use Long Format With Surface Verify if you are formatting a disk for which you have forgotten the password, or if you need to repair a disk that has developed read/write errors due to bad sectors.

3. Click Start to begin formatting the Zip disk.

Formatting Zip Disks with Windows 9x/Me

You can also use the conventional FORMAT utility under Windows 9x/Me to format a Zip disk:

1. Double-click the My Computer icon on your desktop.

2. Right-click the Iomega drive icon where you'd like to format your Zip disk.

3. Select Format, and specify the format type.

4. Click Start to proceed with the format.

Formatting Zip Disks with DOS

If you'd prefer to work under DOS, use the following steps to format your Zip disk:

If you're in Windows, be sure to exit to DOS. Make note of your Iomega drive letter.

1. Click Start and select Shut Down.

2. Select Restart Your Computer In MS-DOS Mode.

3. Click Yes.

4. Insert the disk that you would like to format into your Iomega drive.

5. At the DOS prompt, type **format** *x***:** (where *x* is the letter of your Zip drive), and then press ENTER.

6. Type **Y** for yes to proceed with the format.

Protecting Zip Disks

Iomega includes a special read/write-protect feature that allows you to write-protect a disk through software instead of with a mechanical write-protect switch. You can write-protect a disk (and assign a password that must be used to remove the write protection). You can also add read/write protection to a disk so that it cannot be written to (or read from), without a password. Use the following steps to protect your disks:

1. Insert the disk you want to protect into your Zip drive.

2. Right-click the Zip drive icon on your Windows desktop.

3. Select Protect from the drive shortcut menu.

4. Choose the protection option you want to use.

Although Zip disk protection options are set by using Iomega's software, the actual protection mechanism is part of the drive hardware. The disk protection cannot be bypassed using other software programs.

Zip Drive Troubleshooting

Even though your Zip drive may be installed and configured properly, numerous problems can plague a drive. If you cannot correct drive problems with the previous guidelines, review the following symptoms for detailed corrective action.

SYMPTOM 33-1 **Zip drive operation seems erratic, or you experience data transfer problems**   In virtually all cases, this is a problem with the Zip drive's cabling. For external drives, check that the parallel port cable or USB cable is attached securely. See that any screws or clips are holding the cables in place. For internal drives, verify that the 40-pin IDE cable or 50/68-pin SCSI signal cable is attached securely. (SCSI cable chains must also be terminated properly.) If problems persist, there may be a problem with the controller operating your drive (the parallel port, USB port, IDE controller card, or SCSI adapter). Double-check the controller's configuration and see that each drive is jumpered (identified) properly.

SYMPTOM 33-2 **A Zip disk is automatically ejected after you insert it into the drive**   The problem here is almost always the disk itself. You may be using a 250MB Zip disk in a 100MB Zip drive, or using a non-Zip disk in the drive. Check the disk and verify that you're using the proper Zip media for your drive. If the problem persists and the disk operates in other Zip drives, the drive itself may be at fault.

SYMPTOM 33-3 **The Zip drive refuses to work with software "dongles" or other pass-through devices**   This is a common problem because there is no single parallel port specification. There are some parallel port devices (such as multi-I/O adapters, scanners, printers, software dongles, and so on) that are not fully compatible with a Zip drive.

■ *Remove the devices.* The easiest way to check compatibility is to remove the dongle or other parallel port device. If the Zip drive works directly, you know the other device is at fault, and it may be necessary to update the dongle or other device.

■ *Add a parallel port.* If you cannot replace, remove, or tweak your existing parallel port devices, it may be necessary to add another parallel port to the system to support the Zip drive (or swap the drive type to USB or an internal model).

SYMPTOM 33-4   There is no drive letter for the SCSI Zip drive under Windows 9x/Me
The drive does not appear to respond. In virtually all cases, the SCSI driver has not loaded properly.

■ *Check the device driver(s).* Open the Device Manager, expand the SCSI Controllers entry, and then check the Iomega Adapter line beneath it. If there is a yellow symbol with an exclamation mark on it, the Windows 9x/Me driver did not load. Check the controller next by highlighting that Iomega Adapter line and selecting Properties. Click the Resources page, and then verify that your I/O Range and IRQ options are set correctly. They must match the jumper settings on your adapter board. If you must update the resource settings manually, make sure the Automatic Settings box is not checked (and remember to save any changes). If you allocated new resources, you may have to shut off the PC and change jumper settings on the controller board itself to match the resources allocated in the Device Manager. Restart the computer. Once the system reboots, the Windows 9x/Me driver should load normally.

■ *Check the cables.* If problems persist, check the signal connector (especially for SCSI adapters). Make sure the SCSI cable is intact and connected to the drive properly. If problems continue, your SCSI adapter is probably installed correctly, but the bus may be terminated improperly. Make sure that you terminate both ends of the SCSI bus properly.

SYMPTOM 33-5   There is no drive letter for the parallel port Zip drive under Windows 9x/Me   Parallel port drive problems can almost always be traced to faulty connections, port configuration issues, or driver problems.

■ *Check the cables.* Check the external power connector first. Parallel port drives are powered externally. Make sure that the power pack is working, and see that the power cable is connected properly to the drive. If the drive does not appear to power-up, try a different power pack or drive. Check the signal cable next, and make sure that you are using a good-quality, known-good parallel port cable that is attached securely at the PC and drive. The Zip drive is very sensitive to devices such as copy protection modules (or *dongles*), and other pass-through devices. Try connecting the drive directly to the parallel port. Also disconnect any printers on the parallel port.

■ *Check the parallel port.* The parallel port setup may be incorrect. Reboot the PC and enter CMOS Setup. Check to see that the parallel port is configured in EPP or bidirectional mode. If the problem continues in EPP mode, try configuring the parallel port for compatibility mode.

■ *Check the host controller.* For SCSI installations, check the SCSI host controller. There is a known incompatibility between the Iomega Zip drive and the Adaptec 284x adapter. The Iomega PPA3 driver does not work with the Adaptec 284x controller. Check with Iomega for an updated driver.

■ *Check your driver(s).* Open the Device Manager and find the SCSI Controllers entry (even though it is a parallel port device). If there is no such entry, the driver is not installed. If you expand the SCSI Controllers section, there should be an entry for the Iomega Parallel Port Zip Interface. If there is not, the driver is not installed. Check for hardware conflicts. If the Device Manager entry for the Iomega Parallel Port Zip Interface has a yellow circle with an exclamation mark on it, the interface is configured improperly and is conflicting with other devices. Also check for device properties. Highlight the Iomega Parallel Port Zip Interface entry, click Properties, and then select the Settings page. Find the box marked Adapter Settings, and then type:

```
/mode:nibble /speed:1
```

Save your changes and reboot the system. If that fails, try reinstalling the drivers. Highlight the Iomega Parallel Port Zip Interface and select Remove. Then reinstall the drivers from scratch. Next, try running in DOS. Start the PC in DOS mode (command prompt only), and then install the Iomega installation disk and type:

```
a:\guest
```

If the Zip drive still does not receive a drive letter, the parallel port may be faulty or incompatible with the drive. Try the drive on another system. If this tactic works on another system, the problem is definitely related to your original PC hardware. If the problem follows the drive, the fault is likely in the drive. Try another drive.

SYMPTOM 33-6   **An Iomega Zip drive displays a floppy disk icon under Windows 9x/Me**   However, the drive appears to operate properly. This is almost always due to the use of a real-mode DOS driver to support the Iomega drive and adapter. You need to update the real-mode driver to an appropriate protected-mode driver for Windows 9x/Me. For SCSI adapters, you need to find the protected-mode SCSI driver for your particular SCSI adapter and install it through the Add New Hardware wizard in the Control Panel. After the protected-mode driver is installed, you can remove the obsolete real-mode driver from CONFIG.SYS. For native Iomega SCSI adapters, get the protected-mode drivers directly from Iomega. For parallel port Zip drives, uninstall the old drive software and install the new Windows 9x/Me driver software.

SYMPTOM 33-7   **The Zip drive takes over the CD-ROM drive letter in Windows 9x/Me**
You may simply need to switch drive letters between the Zip drive and CD-ROM drive:

1.   Open Device Manager and double-click the Disk Drives entry.

2.   Highlight the Iomega Zip drive entry and click Properties.

3.   Click the Settings page.

4.   In the Reserved Drive Letters section, you will see a Start Drive Letter and an End Drive Letter setting. Enter the desired drive letter for the Zip drive in both start and end drive entries. (Be sure to use the same drive letter for both start and end.) Click on OK.

5.   Double-click the CD-ROM entry.

6.   Highlight your CD-ROM Drive entry and click Properties.

7.   Click the Settings page.

8.   In the Reserved Drive Letters section, you will see a Start Drive Letter and an End Drive Letter setting. Enter the desired drive letter for the CD-ROM drive in both start and end entries. (Be sure to use the same drive letter for both start and end.) Click OK.

9.   Click OK to close Device Manager, and then restart the computer.

SYMPTOM 33-8 **You encounter Zip drive letter problems under DOS** The drive letters following C: may change unexpectedly when Iomega drivers are installed to support a new device. This can interfere with applications that look at specific drives or with access to network resources. You need to relocate the drives before installing Iomega software. Since the GUEST.EXE utility loads at the end of AUTOEXEC.BAT, the Iomega drive will be assigned the last drive letter. DOS assigns letters to network drives alphabetically after assigning letters to any internal or external drives connected to the computer. When a new drive is added, the network drive may be "pushed down" one letter (for example, from E: to F:). Applications that reference specific drive letters may then fail to work correctly unless they are reinstalled or adjusted for the drive letter change. If you use a batch file to connect to a network, it will need to be updated to the new drive letter. A network login script may also need to be revised.

Use the DOS LASTDRIVE= command to relocate your first network drive letter farther down the alphabet. This insulates your network drive letter assignment from future changes if you add other drives to your system. For example, you can make your network drive N: by adding the following line to the end of CONFIG.SYS. This would allow you to add ten drives (D: through M:) to a system without pushing down your network drive letter.

```
LASTDRIVE=M
```

Do not set your last drive to Z:, or you will be unable to access any network drive. If you use multiple network drives, do not set your last drive to a letter late in the alphabet (such as X: or Y:) since that will limit the number of network drives you can use simultaneously.

Check your CD-ROM drive letters. CD-ROM drives have a specific drive letter determined by the /L option of MSCDEX in AUTOEXEC.BAT (for example, /L:E assigns the CD-ROM as drive E:). When a new drive is installed, DOS may assign the CD-ROM drive letter to the new drive, and the CD-ROM drive may seem to disappear. Change the drive letter for the CD-ROM to a letter not assigned to another drive. You may want to relocate your CD-ROM drive several letters down the alphabet so that you do not have to relocate it each time you add a new drive to your system. You must have a LASTDRIVE statement in CONFIG.SYS that sets the last drive equal to or later than the CD-ROM letter. Finally, check the overall system configuration. When DOS *does* reassign drive letters, be sure to check each of the following points:

- Edit the PATH statement in AUTOEXEC.BAT to correctly reference new drive letters.
- Edit any batch files (including AUTOEXEC.BAT) to correctly reference new drive letters.
- Edit all Windows INI files and Windows groups to correctly reference new drive letters.
- Check other application setup files and rerun the application's setup if drive letters cannot be edited.
- For networks, check your user login script for references to specific network drive letters.
- Reboot the computer and check major applications. Those that do not work with the new drive letter may need to be reinstalled.

SYMPTOM 33-9 **You encounter duplicate Zip drive letters** You notice that the Zip drive (or another drive) has been assigned a duplicate drive letter. In most cases, the problem can be traced to a third-party SCSI adapter and drivers that conflict with Iomega SCSI drivers. *Do not use any drive before correcting this problem.* Open your CONFIG.SYS file and examine each driver that scans the SCSI bus to assign drive letters. Chances are very good that you have a third-party driver that is assigning a letter to the Zip drive, as well as an Iomega-specific driver assigning another letter to the Zip drive. Use a command-line switch with the third-party SCSI driver to limit the number of IDs that will be assigned.

SYMPTOM 33-10   **The GUEST utility cannot find an available drive letter**   If all drive letters are in use, GUEST will not be able to assign a drive letter to the Zip drive. Change the last drive designation. Use the DOS LASTDRIVE command in the end of CONFIG.SYS to increase the number of available drive letters. Do not use a letter near the end of the alphabet.

SYMPTOM 33-11   **The system hangs when installing drivers for Windows 9x/Me**
System hang-ups during installation are usually the result of hardware conflicts or problems. Check the signal cable first, and make sure that you are using a good-quality, known-good cable that is attached securely at the PC and drive. Open the Device Manager and find the SCSI Controllers entry. If there is no such entry, the driver is not installed. If you expand the SCSI Controllers section, there should be an entry for the Iomega Parallel Port Zip Interface. If there is not, the driver is not installed.

Check for hardware conflicts. If the Device Manager entry for the Iomega Parallel Port Zip Interface has a yellow circle with an exclamation mark on it, the interface is configured improperly and is conflicting with other devices. Highlight the Iomega Parallel Port Zip Interface entry, click Properties, and then select the Settings page. Find the box marked Adapter Settings, and then type

```
/mode:nibble /speed:1
```

Save your changes and reboot the system. If problems continue, try running in DOS. Start the PC in DOS mode (command prompt only), and then install the Iomega installation disk and type:

```
a:\guest
```

If the Zip drive still does not receive a drive letter, the parallel port may be faulty or incompatible with the drive. Try the drive on another system. If this tactic works on another system, the problem is definitely related to your original PC hardware. If the problem follows the drive, the fault is likely in the drive. Try another drive.

SYMPTOM 33-12   **After installing a Zip drive, you find the other drives in the system are using the DOS compatibility mode**   This is almost always the result of the GUEST.EXE program. The real-mode GUEST.EXE program supplied by Iomega is designed to allow you to access the Zip drive in DOS and Windows 9x/Me, and this causes the other drives in your system to use the DOS compatibility mode. (You may also notice a decline in drive or system performance.) Try installing the protected-mode drivers for the Iomega drive:

1. In the Control Panel, double-click the Add New Hardware icon.
2. Click Next, click the No button, and then click Next.
3. Click Other Devices, and then click Next.
4. In the Manufacturers box, click Iomega, and then click Have Disk.
5. Install the files from the Windows 9x/Me CD by inserting the CD in the drive, typing the following line in the Copy Manufacturer's Files From box, and then clicking Next:

    ```
    <drive>:\drivers\storage\iomega
    ```

    Replace <drive> with the drive letter of the CD-ROM drive.
6. After the files are copied, click Finish.
7. Restart the computer when prompted to do so.

SYMPTOM 33-13   **A Zip guest locks up or cannot locate the drive or adapter**
Chances are that an ASPI manager referenced in the GUEST.INI file is conflicting with hardware in the PC. This often happens in systems with two SCSI adapters (and parallel ports). Try editing the GUEST.INI file. Open the GUEST.INI file on your Iomega install disk and specify which ASPI manager needs to load in order to access the Zip drive. Remember to make a backup copy of the GUEST.INI file before editing it. As an alternative, choose the Iomega SCSI adapter driver. If you are using a native Iomega SCSI adapter, choose the ASPI manager that applies to the adapter, as shown in Table 33-1. Once you've identified the proper ASPI manager for your adapter, REMark out all the other ASPI lines in GUEST.INI except for the one that you need.

If you're using a non-Iomega SCSI adapter, you will need to add the complete path and file name for the driver to GUEST.INI, and REMark out all the other ASPI drivers. Once the GUEST.INI file is updated, save your changes and reboot the system; then run GUEST from the drive and directory containing the updated GUEST.INI file. If problems persist, try the drive on another system, or try a new drive on the suspect system.

SYMPTOM 33-14   **System recovery fails after the Zip Tools setup process is complete**
If the Zip Tools software for your Zip drive fails to install properly (or if the system hangs or was powered down), the Windows Startup group will have a Zip setup icon that will attempt to run each time Windows is started. Delete the Zip icon in your Startup group, and then reinstall the Zip software.

SYMPTOM 33-15   **The Zip drive setup could not find a Zip Tools disk for Zip parallel port drives**   This is usually an issue with the GUEST.INI file, which needs to be edited for proper operation. Start the system from a clean floppy disk, insert the Iomega installation disk, and then try running the GUEST utility. If a drive letter is assigned, there may be a driver in CONFIG.SYS or AUTOEXEC.BAT that is conflicting with the Zip drive. If GUEST fails to assign a Zip drive letter from a clean boot, open the GUEST.INI file in a text editor, locate the ASPI=ASPIPPA3.SYS line, and then add the switches; /MODE=1 /SPEED=1. This makes the complete command line appear as follows:

```
ASPI=ASPIPPA3.SYS SCAN /INFO SL360=NO SMC=NO /MODE=1 /SPEED=1
```

Reboot the PC and run the GUEST utility again. If GUEST does run but you still cannot read the Zip Tools disk, make sure that the signal cables are secure between the drive and system. If problems persist, try the Zip drive on another PC. If GUEST works on another PC, the original PC is using an incompatible parallel port. If the drive still refuses to work, try another Zip drive.

TABLE 33-1   NATIVE IOMEGA ASPI DRIVERS

IOMEGA ADAPTER	ASPI MANAGER
Zip Zoom SCSI Accelerator	ASPIPC16.SYS
Jaz Jet SCSI Accelerator	ASPI2930.SYS
Parallel Port Zip Drive	ASPIPPA3.SYS or ASPIPPM1.SYS
PPA-3 Adapter	ASPIPPA3.SYS
PC1616	ASPIPC16.SYS
PC800	ASPIPC8.SYS
PC2	ASPIPC2.SYS
PC4	ASPIPC4.SYS

SYMPTOM 33-16   You see error messages such as "Can't Find Zip Tools Disk" or "No Drive Letters Added" when using Zip parallel port drives   In most cases, you will have to manually assign the proper ASPI driver by editing your GUEST.INI file. Open the GUEST.INI file on your Iomega install disk. Highlight the ASPI driver line that reads ASPIPPA3.SYS, and then add the following commands: /MODE=1 /SPEED=1. Remember to make a backup copy of the GUEST.INI file before editing it. The final command line should look like this:

```
ASPI=ASPIPPA3.SYS SCAN /INFO SL360=NO SMC=NO /MODE=1 /SPEED=1
```

Save your changes to GUEST.INI, and then run GUEST from the drive and directory that contains your edited GUEST.INI file. GUEST should now assign a drive letter to the Zip drive. Reboot the PC, start Windows, and then run the Iomega setup routine from the drive and directory that contains your edited GUEST.INI file. The Windows installation should now proceed normally.

Next, check the signal connector, and make sure that the parallel port or SCSI cable is connected properly between the drive and system. Try a known-good working signal cable. If problems persist, boot the system from a clean disk and try running GUEST. If a drive letter is assigned properly, then a driver loading in CONFIG.SYS or AUTOEXEC.BAT conflicts with the Zip drive. You have to systematically locate the offending driver. Finally, try the Zip drive on another PC. If GUEST works on another PC, the original PC is using an incompatible parallel port. If the drive still refuses to work, try another Zip drive.

SYMPTOM 33-17   Windows allows the network drive letter to conflict with the Zip drive letter   You may see this as a "No Zip Tools Disk Detected" message. The drive may also no longer be accessible from the File Manager or DOS prompt. The problem is that Windows allows GUEST to assign a drive letter that is already used by a network drive. Remap the shared volume. Since GUEST is typically run first, you need to alter the network drive letter under Windows.

SYMPTOM 33-18   You cannot print while using a Zip drive   The Iomega parallel port Zip drive works as a pass-through device, and the software allows the drive to share a parallel port with printers. However, some printers require two-way communication between the printer and parallel port, and this conflicts with the Zip software. This can cause data corruption and system lockups. In many cases, disabling the bidirectional communication features of the printer will clear the problem. Work-arounds for Canon, Okidata, Lexmark, and Hewlett-Packard are covered here.

Canon Printers   Several Canon printers use a driver that is incompatible with the Zip drive. The drivers need exclusive access to the parallel port for proper operation of the printer. To work around this problem temporarily, you can disable the drivers for that printer:

■   **Canon BJ-610**   Insert two semicolons (;;) in front of the following lines in the [386Enh] section of the SYSTEM.INI file:

```
DEVICE=WPSRCOM.386
DEVICE= WPSCREM.386
DEVICE=CANON BJ-610, WPSCR, LPT1
```

■   **Canon BJC-610**   Insert two semicolons (;;) in front of the following lines in the [386Enh] section of the SYSTEM.INI file:

```
DEVICE=WPSRCOM.386
DEVICE= WPSCREM.386
DEVICE=WPSRBND.386
```

In the WIN.INI file, insert two semicolons (;;) in front of the following lines:

```
LOAD=WPSLOAD.EXE
DEVICE=CANON BJC-610, WPSCR, LPT1
```

■ **Canon BJC-620**   Insert two semicolons (;;) in front of the following lines in the [386Enh] section of the SYSTEM.INI file:

```
DEVICE=WPSRCOM.386
DEVICE= WPSCREM.386
DEVICE=WPSRBND.386
```

In the WIN.INI file, insert two semicolons (;;) in front of the following lines:

```
LOAD=WPSLOAD.EXE
DEVICE=CANON BJC-620, WPSCR, LPT1
```

 After these lines have been REMarked out, the Zip drive will function, but the printer will not. To restore printer capability, remove the semicolons from the WIN.INI and SYSTEM.INI files and restart Windows.

 Rather than disable the printers, you can install the drivers for the Canon BJC-600e (if you are using the Canon BJC-610 or BJ-610). If you are using the BJC-620 printer, install the Canon BJC-210 drivers. This allows access to both the Zip drive and the printer—though at a reduced resolution.

■ **Canon Multi-Pass 1000**   You cannot use this printer and the parallel port Zip drive at the same time. The only way to make the printer and drive compatible is to change the output of the printer to "File" when you need to use the Zip drive, and then back to "LPT1" when you want to use the printer. Use the following procedure to toggle the output from File to LPT1 under Windows 9x:

1. Double-click My Computer.
2. Double-click Properties.
3. Right-click the Canon Printer.
4. Click Details.
5. Click the down arrow button in the window labeled "Print to the following port."
6. Click FILE (to switch back, choose LPT1).
7. Click OK at the bottom of your screen.

Okidata Printers   The Okidata 600e also exhibits port problems when used with a Zip drive. To enable the Zip drive, insert two semicolons in front of the following line in the [BOOT] section of the SYSTEM.INI file:

```
COMM.DRV=INSYTHCOMM.DRV
```

Just below that line, add the following line:

```
COMM.DRV=COMM.DRV
```

In the [386Enh] section of SYSTEM.INI, insert two semicolons in front of the following line:

```
DEVICE=OKIPORT.386
```

In the WIN.INI file, insert two semicolons in front of these lines:

```
LOAD=C:\WINDOWS\SYSTEM\STATMON.EXE
DEVICE=OL600E, OKIGDI, LPT1
```

Lexmark Printers   Most Lexmark printers can work with the Zip drive's bidirectional support disabled. Under Windows 9x/Me, you can disable bidirectional support by using the following steps:

1. Right-click the My Computer icon, and then double-click the Printers icon.

2. Right-click the Lexmark printer icon, and then select Properties.

3. Choose Details, select Spool settings, and then choose Disable Bidirectional support.

4. Save your changes and reboot the PC if necessary.

Hewlett-Packard Printers   Hewlett-Packard printers are known for their extensive use of the parallel port, so it is quite common to encounter problems between recent HP printers and other parallel port devices, such as the Zip drive. Fortunately, some work-arounds are available for most HP models.

■ **Hewlett Packard 4S, 4+, 4V, 4SI, 4L, 4P, and 5P**   You need to disable the bidirectional communication between the printer and system. This can be accomplished by executing the following command from the RUN command line:

```
c:\windows\dinstall -fdinstall.ins
```

You can also use the following steps:

1. Bring up the WIN.INI file through either SYSEDIT (in Windows) or EDIT (in DOS).

2. In the first section of this file, you should see a line that reads LOAD=HPSW.EXE. You need to disable this line by inserting a semicolon (;) at the beginning of the line.

3. Scroll down to the section labeled [Spooler] and insert a semicolon (;) at the beginning of the line that reads QP.LPT1=HPLJ4QP.DLL.

4. Save the WIN.INI file, exit Windows, and restart the system.

You can now use the HP printer and Zip drive together. These changes will not affect the printer; they just disable the status windows that may pop up to report the current status of the printer.

■ **Hewlett Packard 5L**   If you installed your printer using the HOST option, you will need to uninstall the printer, and then reinstall it using the PCL option:

1. Disconnect the printer from the computer or the Zip drive.

2. Click Start, select Settings, and then select the Printers icon.

3. Click the HP 5L Printer icon and press DEL. When the system asks to delete files that were only used by this printer, choose Yes (or OK).

4. Reboot the computer with the printer still disconnected.

5. When the computer reboots, use the 5L installation disks to reinstall the drivers. When prompted for a Custom or Express Installation, choose Custom and select PCL Mode.

If the problem persists, disable the WIN.INI line that reads LOAD=HPLJ5W.EXE by placing two semicolons at the beginning of the line. You will need to do the same with the line that reads QP.LPT1=??? in the [Spooler] section of your WIN.INI file.

■ **HP 5P, 5M, 6P, 6M, DeskJet 600c, and HP DeskJet printers**   The Status Monitor utility (HPPROPTY.EXE) loaded with these printers must be disabled. There are two ways to disable the HPPROPTY.EXE utility that will disable the Status Monitor without disabling the printer. The quick fix is to press CTRL-ALT-DEL, choose HPPROPTY, and then choose End Task. This closes the Status Monitor, but you need to remember to do this each time you boot the PC. For a more permanent fix, right-click the My Computer icon. Open the Windows folder, and then the SYSTEM folder. Right-click the file HPPROPTY.EXE and rename this file **HPPROPTY.BAK**. You may need to reboot the PC so that your changes will take effect.

SYMPTOM 33-19   **You encounter problems installing a Zip SCSI drive**   In virtually all cases, SCSI problems can be traced to hardware problems or driver issues. Make sure that power is provided to the drive (see that the drive power light comes on). See that the SCSI signal cable is intact and connected securely between the drive and SCSI adapter. Try a new signal cable. Both ends of the SCSI bus must be terminated properly. Make sure that terminators are installed in the correct places. Ensure that the Zip SCSI drive is assigned to a SCSI ID that is not in use by any other SCSI device. Finally, check the drivers. The drivers for your SCSI adapter and drive must be correct, must use the right command-line switches, and must be the very latest versions. Also check for conflicts between SCSI drivers or other drivers in the system.

SYMPTOM 33-20   **The drive letter is lost each time the PC is turned off**   In many cases, the GUEST utility does not load properly because it is at the end of AUTOEXEC.BAT. Relocate the GUEST command line by opening the AUTOEXEC.BAT file and moving the GUEST command line to a point earlier in the file. Ideally, the GUEST command line should be the entry immediately following the MSCDEX command line. Save your changes and reboot the computer. The GUEST utility should now load each time the system is rebooted.

SYMPTOM 33-21   **When installing IomegaWare software for your Zip drive, a virus checker reports a virus**   The typical report may indicate a "Romeo & Juliet" virus. This is often an error made by the virus checker when its virus definitions mistake the IomegaWare as a virus. Disable the antivirus software before attempting to install the software. If the IomegaWare software installs without error, you may reenable the antivirus program after the installation is complete. If not, you may need to obtain an updated version of the antivirus software.

SYMPTOM 33-22   **You see an error message such as "Drive X does not exist"**   There are several different reasons for this kind of problem. Check the disk first. You must use a PC-formatted disk—a Mac-formatted disk will not work in a PC. Try several different disks. If the error message occurs on only one disk, try reformatting that disk. (Remember that formatting the disk will remove all data from the disk.) If you're receiving the error while using more than one disk (or the disk will not format), the drive may be defective and should be replaced. Finally, there may be a driver or TSR interfering with the Zip drive. Try a clean DOS boot to eliminate the use of real-mode drivers and TSRs, and try the drive again.

SYMPTOM 33-23 **Your Windows 98 system locks up when using a USB Zip drive**
The most common problems occur when you connect or use the USB Zip drive in the wrong way. Verify
that you're following the proper guidelines:

1. Power-up your USB Zip drive at the same time you turn on your computer (or immediately after).

2. Wait at least 30 seconds before reconnecting your USB Zip drive to your computer (if you remove
your USB Zip drive while your computer is on).

3. Confirm that your computer meets the USB 1.1 specification. If it does not, do not combine your
USB Zip drive with other low-speed devices (such as a USB keyboard or mouse).

4. Use only USB hubs that have an independent power supply. If you connect the USB Zip drive to a
non-powered hub, your computer may lock up. The USB Zip drive may not transfer data correctly
or may not be recognized by your computer.

SYMPTOM 33-24 **When installing a USB Zip drive under Windows 9x/Me, you see an
error such as "No Iomega drives found"** This error occurs when the Iomega Tools software
fails to assign a drive letter to your Zip drive. The problem is with your software. Iomega Tools is an older
version of software that shipped with Zip and Jaz drives. IomegaWare is the latest version of the software.
Iomega recommends that you obtain the most current version of the IomegaWare software from
www.iomega.com/software/.

Download the IomegaWare package onto your system, and then double-click the icon to begin the
installation process. Once you've downloaded and installed the software, you should no longer receive
the error message. If you now have a drive letter, the updated software resolved your problem, and you can
now use your drive.

SYMPTOM 33-25 **You notice that USB Zip drive performance is poor** Other USB devices running at the same time as the USB Zip drive can affect performance. Digital cameras, page scanners,
and other USB devices that process large amounts of data may affect performance. Here are some tips to
tweak performance:

■ Disconnect all USB devices from your computer, and then reconnect the USB Zip drive. Try the USB
Zip alone and test performance again.

■ Make sure that you are using the cable that came with your USB Zip drive.

■ Close all open applications through the Task Manager.

SYMPTOM 33-26 **The system locks up when connecting other USB devices to your
existing USB Zip drive** Computers that are not compliant with USB hub specification 1.10 may
lock up when a device (such as a USB keyboard, mouse, or joystick) is plugged in while the USB Zip drive
is connected. Contact your computer manufacturer to verify that your USB hub is version 1.10 compliant.
If it is not, you will continue to experience lockups. To correct the problem, you may want to consider
upgrading your USB hub. If the hub is compliant, you may need to update the USB drivers, your Windows
version, or stick with the USB Zip drive only.

SYMPTOM 33-27 **You see an error such as "Disk in drive X not formatted"** There
are several different reasons for this kind of error. Check the disk first. You must use a PC-formatted
disk—a Mac-formatted disk will not work in a PC. Try several different disks. If the error message occurs
on only one disk, try reformatting that disk. (Remember that formatting the disk will remove all data from

the disk.) If you're receiving the error using more than one disk (or the disk will not format), the drive may be defective and should be replaced. Finally, a driver or TSR may be interfering with the Zip drive. Try a clean DOS boot to eliminate the use of real-mode drivers and TSRs, and try the drive again.

SYMPTOM 33-28   **When formatting a Zip disk, the Iomega format software returns a fatal exception error**   This type of formatting error is almost always because of problems with outdated or corrupted Zip drivers. Such an error may appear as follows:

```
"A fatal exception 0E has occurred at 0028:C3C64C51 in VXD IOMEGA (01) +
00000CB5. The current application will be terminated. Pressing any key
closes the Explorer window."
```

You'll need to update the Zip driver(s). Check the Iomega Web site at **www.iomega.com** and obtain a new IOMEGA.VXD file. Click Start, highlight Find, and then click Files or Folders. Find the old IOMEGA.VXD file and replace it with the newer version.

SYMPTOM 33-29   **The Zip drive's green power light does not illuminate**   The green light on a Zip drive indicates that the drive is plugged in and receiving power. If the light is not on, then the drive is either turned off or not plugged in, or there is a physical problem with the drive.

- *Check the power button.* If no disk is in the drive, press the eject button once. The eject button doubles as a power button, so pressing it will turn the drive on and off. Inserting a disk will also turn the drive on automatically. If there is already a disk in the drive, the button functions as an eject button, and the disk should be removed before turning off the power.

- *Unplug the drive.* Disconnect the drive from power and the computer. Take the drive to another outlet and plug the power cable in. If the light comes on, there may be a problem with the first power outlet. If the light does not come on, the drive and/or power supply needs to be replaced.

SYMPTOM 33-30   **You see an error such as "Cannot create or replace, make sure the disk is not full or write protected"**   There are several different reasons for this kind of error. Check the disk first. You must use a PC-formatted disk—a Mac-formatted disk will not work in a PC. Try several different disks. If the error message occurs on only one disk, try reformatting that disk. (Remember that formatting the disk will remove all data from the disk.) If you're receiving the error using more than one disk (or the disk will not format), the drive may be defective and should be replaced. Finally, there may be a driver or TSR interfering with the Zip drive. Try a clean DOS boot to eliminate the use of real-mode drivers and TSRs, and try the drive again.

SYMPTOM 33-31   **You encounter a fatal exception error when using the Iomega Copy Machine software**   This kind of problem is typically due to an issue with the Zip drive's automatic spin-down/eject feature used when doing a multiple disk copy. It may be necessary for you to disable the auto spin-down/eject function. Start the Copy Machine software by choosing its icon within the Iomega Tools folder. Next, select Options and then Runtime. Deselect the Auto Spin-Down/Eject option by removing the check from the box. Finally, choose OK to accept the changes, and reboot the PC if necessary. When performing subsequent multiple disk copies, you'll be prompted to eject each disk by pressing the eject button on the front of your Zip drive.

SYMPTOM 33-32   You encounter an error such as "General failure reading drive X"
There are several different problems that can cause this kind of error. Check the disk first. You must use a
PC-formatted disk—a Mac-formatted disk will not work in a PC. A driver or TSR may be interfering with
the Zip drive. Try a clean DOS boot to eliminate the use of real-mode drivers and TSRs, and try the drive
again. Finally, try several different disks. If the error message occurs on only one disk, try reformatting that
disk. (Remember that formatting the disk will remove all data from the disk.) If you're receiving the error
using more than one disk (or the disk will not format), the drive may be defective and should be replaced.

SYMPTOM 33-33   You encounter an error such as "Insufficient disk space"   You may
also see this error as "Disk is full" or "Destination is full." This error message may be caused by several
possible problems—the disk is full, is exceeding the operating system's file limit, or is bad.

■ *Check the disk space.* Use a tool like Windows Explorer to verify that enough free space exists on the Zip
disk to contain the file(s) you need. If there is not enough, try copying fewer files, or use a fresh Zip disk.

■ *Check the number of files.* Make sure that you have not exceeded the file limit of your operating system. Remember that DOS will not allow you to have more than 511 files in the root directory. Use
Windows Explorer (or the DOS DIR command) to list the files on your Zip disk. The number of files
on the root director should be less than 511. If the number of files is 511, you'll have to move some
files into other directories to reduce the number of files on the root directory.

■ *Cycle power to the system.* If the error persists, try shutting down the computer and Zip drive, and then
repower the system in the correct order.

■ *Try several different disks.* If the error occurs on only one disk, try reformatting that disk. (Remember
that formatting the disk will remove all data from the disk.) If you're receiving the error while using
more than one disk (or the disk will not format), the drive may be defective and should be replaced.

**SYMPTOM 33-34   When using Iomega Tools or other Zip drive software, you see an
error such as "Program performed an illegal operation"**   In virtually all cases, there is a conflict between the Zip software and another program running on your system. You'll need to reboot the system and isolate the offending software.

■ *Reboot the system.* This will clear the error from memory and allow you to check other software. When
you reboot the system, make sure to turn off the power to the drive and then turn it back on again.

■ *Close all open programs.* Open the Close Program dialog box by pressing CTRL-ALT-DEL at the same
time. Close open programs by highlighting a program and then clicking the End Task button (do not
close Explorer). As you close one application at a time, try your Zip drive again. Once the problem is
resolved, the last application that was closed is the one causing the conflict. Once you have determined which application is causing the conflict, either discontinue use of that application when using
your Zip drive, or obtain an updated version from the software maker (if possible).

■ *Reinstall the Zip software.* If the problem persists, delete and then reinstall the Iomega Tools software.

**SYMPTOM 33-35   When using Microsoft Backup under Windows 95, you receive an
error such as "The disk is full—disk linking is not supported"**   This problem occurs because
Microsoft Backup cannot back up over multiple disks (a.k.a. "disk spanning"). Instead of using Microsoft
Backup, install the backup software intended for use with the Zip disk (such as "1-Step Backup").

To install Iomega Tools for Windows 95, put the Zip installation floppy in the A: drive. From the Start menu, select Run. In the Open dialog box, type **A:\guest95** and then click OK. Guest95 should find a drive letter for your Zip drive. Now put your Zip Tools disk into the Zip drive. Double-click the My Computer icon, and then double-click the Zip drive icon. You should see a folder called W95stuff. Double-click the W95stuff folder, and double-click setup95.exe. Follow the screen instructions to complete the installation.

SYMPTOM 33-36   When using Iomega Tools software under Windows 9x/Me, you see an error message such as "No Iomega drives found"   This occurs when the Iomega Tools software fails to assign a drive letter to your Zip drive, and is often a fault of old software. Iomega Tools is an older version of software that shipped with Zip drives. IomegaWare is the latest version of the software and should be updated in every possible case before troubleshooting. You can download the various components of IomegaWare from the Iomega site at **www.iomega.com/software**. Start by downloading the Core IomegaWare Tools package onto your desktop, and then double-click the icon to begin the installation process. Once you have downloaded and installed the Core IomegaWare Tools software, you should no longer receive the error message.

SYMPTOM 33-37   When installing IomegaWare software under Windows 98, you see an error such as "ISINST30 caused a general protection fault"   When you attempt to install the IomegaWare software, you may receive the following error message:

```
ISINST30 caused a general protection fault in module _INS0433._MP at <address>
```

This error is caused by the Microsoft MSWHEEL.EXE wheel-mouse driver software. To resolve this error, you'll need to disable the wheel-mouse software, install the Zip software, and then reenable the wheel-mouse software. Start by disabling the MSWHEEL.EXE program:

1. Click Start, point to Programs, Accessories, System Tools, and click System Information.
2. Click the System Configuration utility on the Tools menu.
3. Click the Setup tab.
4. Click the check box next to MSWHEEL.EXE to clear the box.
5. Click File and choose Exit.
6. Restart your computer when prompted.

Install the IomegaWare software. Insert the IomegaWare CD into your CD-ROM drive, and installation should start automatically. If you need a later version of IomegaWare, you can download it from **www.iomega.com/software**. Now reenable the MSWHEEL.EXE program:

1. Click Start, point to Programs, Accessories, System Tools, and click System Information.
2. Click the System Configuration utility on the Tools menu.
3. Click the Setup tab.
4. Click the check box next to MSWHEEL.EXE to add a check mark.
5. Click File and choose Exit.
6. Restart your computer when prompted.

SYMPTOM 33-38   **When using a Zip drive, you see an error such as "X:\is not accessible. The device is not ready"**   When the drive refuses to respond, there are several points to check.

■ *Check the Zip disk.* Verify that a Zip disk is in the drive. If a disk is not in the drive (or if the disk is ejected after restarting your computer), Windows will display the error message. Place a disk into your Zip drive, wait a few seconds, and click the Retry button.

■ *Check/disable read/write protection.* Read/write protection is a security feature that requires a password, and it should be reserved for highly sensitive data. If your Zip disk is read/write-protected, you'll get the error message when trying to access a protected disk. The following steps should remove read/write protection:

1. Double-click the My Computer icon.

2. Right-click the icon that represents your Zip drive, and choose the Protect option.

3. The Present Disk Status dialog box will indicate whether your disk is read/write-protected.

4. If your disk is write-protected, you must remove the read/write protection by selecting the Remove Protection button before accessing the disk.

You'll need to enter the correct password in order to remove read/write protection. If you do not have the correct password, you won't be able to remove that protection from the disk.

■ *Check the cables.* Shut down the drive and computer, disconnect the data cable from the Zip drive, and carefully examine both ends of the cable for bent or broken pins. If the cable is damaged, it should be replaced. If it is not, reconnect it securely. Restart your computer to Windows, place a Zip disk in the drive, and try accessing the disk again.

■ *Try the drive on another PC.* Install your Zip drive on a different computer and see if you can read the disk on that system. If you can, there may be a problem with the original computer's interface. If the problem persists, the drive may be defective and require replacement.

SYMPTOM 33-39   **When using a Zip drive under Windows 9x/Me, you see an error such as "The disk in drive X: is not formatted"**   This kind of behavior is almost always caused by incompatible formatting or software conflicts.

■ *Check the disk format.* You must use a PC-formatted Zip disk—a disk formatted for a Macintosh computer will not work. Zip disks come preformatted for either Macintosh or PC. A disk that is formatted for a Mac will have a small dot located on the lower-left corner of the disk label. If you have a Mac-formatted disk and you wish to reformat it for use on your PC (remember that formatting will permanently remove all data from that disk), follow these steps:

1. Insert the Zip disk into the drive.

2. If you receive a message such as "The disk in drive X: is not formatted. Do you want to format it now?" choose No.

3. Double-click the My Computer icon, and then right-click the Zip drive's icon.

4. Select Format.

5. Select Long Format With Surface Verify.

6. Click Start and allow the process to complete.

■ *Try the disk in a clean environment.* Boot to DOS and see if you can access the disk. If you can, there may be a software conflict. If you cannot, the trouble may be with the disk itself.

1. Restart your computer with a blank bootable disk in drive A:.

2. When you get a "non-system disk" error message, eject the floppy disk from the A: drive and press the F8 key twice.

3. From the Windows Startup Menu, choose Safe Mode Command Prompt Only.

4. At the DOS prompt type **progra~1\iomega\tools\guest** to obtain a drive letter for your Zip drive.

5. Insert the Zip disk into the Zip drive.

6. At the DOS prompt, type **dir x:** (where x is the drive letter assigned to your Zip drive) and read the directory of files on your Zip disk.

■ *Try another Zip disk.* If the error occurs on only one disk, try reformatting that disk. If you're receiving the error message with more than one disk (or the disk will not format), the drive is probably defective and should be replaced.

■ *Try another parallel port setting.* If problems persist, try setting another parallel port mode such as bidirectional, standard, ECP, or EPP. In many cases, "downgrading" the parallel port mode will correct hardware issues, but it will reduce drive performance.

SYMPTOM 33-40   **You see an error such as "Cannot create or replace—make sure the disk is not full or write protected"**   In most cases, this problem is caused by exceeding the file limit imposed by the operating system (such as 511 files under DOS).

■ *Check the disk space.* Use a tool like Windows Explorer to verify that enough free space exists on the Zip disk to contain the file(s) you need. If not enough exists, try copying fewer files, or use a fresh Zip disk.

■ *Check the number of files.* Make sure that you have not exceeded the file limit of your operating system. Remember that DOS will not allow you to have more than 511 files in the root directory. Use Windows Explorer (or the DOS DIR command) to list the files on your Zip disk. The number of files on the root director should be less than 511. If the number of files is 511, you'll have to move some files into other directories to reduce the number of files on the root directory.

SYMPTOM 33-41   **You see an error message such as "No drives are supported by Iomega Tools"**   The trouble is with your version of the Zip drive's software. Iomega Tools is an older version of IomegaWare software. To correct this error, you should download and install the latest version of IomegaWare software from Iomega's Web site at **www.iomega.com/software**. Install the IomegaWare software by double-clicking the file you have downloaded to your computer. This will begin the installation process.

SYMPTOM 33-42   **The Zip drive is clicking continuously**   A click is perfectly normal when inserting or removing a disk, but *continuous* clicking indicates a serious problem. This problem is often referred to as the "click of death" and is often a problem related to a fault in the Zip drive (especially older versions of the Zip drive). Check the disk first. Try another Zip disk in the drive. (Make sure that the disk is blank, to prevent damaging good disks.) If the problem persists, the drive is almost certainly defective and should be replaced. Iomega recommends the following precautions for Zip disks:

■ Eject disks prior to transporting any Zip drive. This forces the drive heads (which read and write to the disks) to park safely.

■ Avoid dropping your drive. It will almost certainly damage internal structures.

■ Make it a point to transport and store Zip disks in approved disk cases.

Iomega also offers a utility that tests the integrity of the drive heads and Zip media. If you're uncertain about the reliability of your Zip drive or disks, running the diagnostics could help isolate the problem. (Use a blank formatted disk while running these tests.)

1.   Open My Computer or Windows Explorer.

2.   Right-click the Zip drive icon in My Computer or Windows Explorer.

3.   Choose Properties from the menu.

4.   Click the Diagnostics tab.

5.   Click the Diagnose Now button to start the test.

The diagnostic will report "Passed" or "Failed." If the diagnostic reports "Failed," you should contact Iomega to repair or replace the drive.

SYMPTOM 33-43   **The Zip drive's LED flashes continuously**   This almost always indicates a problem with the drive. When you insert or eject a disk (or copy files to or from your Zip drive), the light on the Zip drive will normally blink several times. If the light flashes continuously, there is a problem.

■ *Check the disk.* Try ejecting and reinstalling the Zip disk. (Be sure to use a blank disk to avoid accidental data loss.) You may also wish to try a different disk. If a new disk corrects the problem, the original disk is defective and should be replaced or discarded.

■ *Cycle the drive.* Power-down the computer and Zip drive, and then restart the system properly. After restarting the system, try the Zip disk(s) again. If the problem persists, the drive is probably defective and should be replaced. Otherwise, the drive simply needed to be cycled.

If the Zip drive is an external model, unplug the power cord from the drive, wait at least five seconds, and plug the power cord back into the drive.

SYMPTOM 33-44   **You cannot eject a Zip disk from a drive**   This is a frequent problem reported with parallel port Zip drives. If the Zip disk won't eject from the drive (either when pushing the eject button or using the software "eject" feature), there may be a hardware failure or an incorrect software setting.

■ *Close your open applications.* Press CTRL-ALT-DEL to open the Close Program dialog box. Close all open applications one at a time (except Explorer and Systray) by highlighting an application and choosing the End Task button. Once all applications are closed (except Explorer and Systray), try to eject the disk from the Zip drive using the eject button on the front of the drive. If the disk ejects, there is a software application problem.

■ *Cycle the drive.* Power-down the computer and Zip drive, and then restart the system properly. After restarting the system, try ejecting the Zip disk(s) again. If the problem persists, the drive is probably defective and should be replaced. Otherwise, the drive simply needed to be cycled.

■ *Try another disk.* Insert a different blank formatted Zip disk into the drive (without connecting the data cable to the computer). If the disk ejects, the original disk is defective. If the disk still does not eject, the drive is probably defective and should be replaced.

■ *Try the emergency eject button.* Remove the power cord from your Zip drive. Straighten out a paper clip and insert it into the emergency eject hole located on the back of the drive (above the right-hand cable connector). If the disk still refuses to eject, the drive is probably defective and should be replaced.

SYMPTOM 33-45   You cannot format a 100MB Zip disk in a 250MB Zip drive   This is known to be a problem under Windows 3.1x. If you try to format a 100MB disk in a 250MB drive in Windows 3.1x, an error message indicates that the format has failed. This is an erroneous error—the format was successful, and files *can* be copied to and from the disk correctly. The disk and drive are working properly (no damage has occurred), but an incorrect message is being displayed.

SYMPTOM 33-46   The Zip drive refuses to spin up   There are a variety of possible problems that might contribute to this symptom.

■ *Try another disk.* Insert a different blank formatted Zip disk into the drive. If the new disk works properly, the original disk is defective. If the problem persists, the trouble is with conflicting software or Zip drive problems.

■ *Try a clean boot.* Real-mode drivers and TSRs can sometimes interfere with the Zip drive. Start the PC from a bootable DOS disk. If the drive spins up, there is an issue with your startup files (CONFIG.SYS and AUTOEXEC.BAT). Try systematically REMarking out any files that might interfere with the Zip drive.

■ *Check the parallel port.* If you're using a parallel port Zip drive, change the mode of your parallel port to SPP, EPP, standard, or bidirectional.

■ *Replace the drive.* If problems persist, the drive is probably defective and should be replaced.

SYMPTOM 33-47   You notice poor performance with a parallel port 250MB Zip drive
Zip drive performance depends on the performance of your LPT port. Optimum performance requires a parallel port running in EPP mode—a parallel port in ECP or unidirectional mode may cause erratic performance. Access your system's CMOS Setup to reconfigure the parallel port. Once you have located the parallel port settings, choose either EPP, bidirectional, SPP, standard, AT, PS/2, or fast mode. Save your changes and reboot the system.

Your BIOS may not allow you to change the parallel port mode (especially older systems). In this case, you may be able to change the parallel port mode through a jumper setting on the motherboard.

If you're using a SCSI Zip drive, check your cable length and optimize the chain. The combined SCSI chain length (the total of all cables in the SCSI chain) should not exceed 6 meters (about 19.6 feet), though it should ideally be much shorter. This includes both internal and external SCSI devices. The fastest device should be the last (or farthest) from the computer.

SYMPTOM 33-48   There is no power light on the external Zip drive   The green light on an external Zip drive indicates that the drive is plugged in and receiving power. Check that all the connections are tight. If the problem persists and the light still does not come on, try another power supply to determine whether the first one is defective. Also, plug the power supply into another outlet to determine whether the first outlet is the problem. If there is still no response, the drive is probably defective and should be replaced.

SYMPTOM 33-49   **The computer locks up after running the parallel port accelerator utility**   In some cases, a system lockup may occur after installing the parallel port driver and then running the Parallel Port Accelerator. Sometimes, running the Parallel Port Accelerator utility will cause the drive to stop running (or even cause the system to lock up during boot). Disconnect the Zip drive and reboot the computer. Remove the modifications made by the Parallel Port Accelerator:

1. Right-click the My Computer icon and select Properties.
2. Click the Device Manager tab.
3. Click the plus sign (+) next to SCSI Controllers.
4. Double-click Iomega Parallel Port Interface.
5. Click the Settings tab.
6. Remove all the information from the Adapter settings box.
7. Click OK and then click OK again.
8. Click Yes to restart your computer.
9. Reconnect the Zip parallel port drive and try it again.

SYMPTOM 33-50   **The computer locks up when running an open application and trying to eject a Zip disk**   If a file or application that resides on your Zip disk is open or in use, and you try to eject that disk, the computer may lock up. Before you eject your Zip disk, make certain that you close any files or applications that may be open (or in use).

SYMPTOM 33-51   **There is a Zip disk read failure on the Zip drive under Windows 9x/Me**   In virtually all cases, the problem is a defective Zip disk. Using an improperly formatted Zip disk in the drive may also cause a problem.

■ *Check the disk.* Use a different Zip disk and see if another disk resolves the problem (or try the original disk on another Zip drive). Make sure to use a blank Zip disk so that you won't loose any critical data.

■ *Try reformatting the disk.* If a different disk works, and the original disk seems to have a problem, try reformatting the original Zip disk:

1. Double-click the My Computer icon on your desktop.
2. Right-click the Zip drive icon and select Format.
3. Select Long Format With Surface Verify.
4. Click Start, and click Start again.
5. When the disk has finished formatting successfully, click OK.

If you cannot format the Zip disk successfully, the disk is almost certainly defective and should be replaced.

■ *Try the drive on another system.* If the disk can be read after moving the Zip drive to another PC, there may be a problem with the PC or with the way the drive was connected to that system.

■ *Suspect the drive.* If no disks can be read on the Zip drive, double-check the drive's installation and setup. If the problem persists, then the drive itself may be defective and should be replaced.

SYMPTOM 33-52 **You see a "fatal exception error" when using an ATAPI IDE Zip drive** This is a known issue under Windows 95 (and OEM2), but was fixed under Windows 98. This problem occurs when you're using an Intel motherboard and AMI (or Intel) BIOS. The Zip drive may also be installed on the secondary IDE channel. The error may also occur when you start the computer without a disk in the drive, or you eject the disk from the Zip drive. This is a problem with Windows 95, but can be corrected by obtaining the latest update files for Windows:

```
ESDI_506.PDR version 4.00.956 (dated 5/14/96) and later

VOLTRACK.VXD version 4.00.954 (dated 3/6/96) and later
```

To install this update, download the REMIDEUP.EXE file from the Microsoft Software Library to an empty folder. In My Computer or Windows Explorer, double-click the REMIDEUP.EXE file, and then follow the instructions on the screen. The following files are installed by REMIDEUP.EXE:

```
ESDI_506.PDR        4.00.1116   8/25/97    11:16a          24,426

VOLTRACK.VXD        4.00.954    3/6/96     9:54a           18,518
```

SYMPTOM 33-53 **You encounter "Windows Protection" errors at startup (the Windows logo screen) when using an HP printer and parallel port Zip drive** This issue can occur if you have an HP 4000 or 8000 series printer attached to a Zip drive, and the Zip drive is attached to the parallel port. To work around this problem, disable bidirectional support in your computer's CMOS Setup (or in the properties of your printer). To disable bidirectional support:

1. Click Start, highlight Settings, and click Printers.
2. Right-click your printer (such as HP 4000 or HP 8000), and then click Properties.
3. Click the Details tab, click Spool Settings, click Disable Bidirectional Support For This Printer, click OK, and then click OK again.

Iomega Bernoulli and Jaz Drives

The Bernoulli disk is a variation of fixed disk technology. Conventional hard drives rotate rigid disks that force read/write heads to ride on the resulting cushion of air. By comparison, the Bernoulli disk uses a flexible platter that is forced to flex beneath a fixed read/write head. At first glance, you probably would not know the difference between a fixed-platter cartridge (such as a SyQuest or Iomega Jaz cartridge) and a Bernoulli cartridge.

Bernoulli disks have been around for years, and have been through 20MB, 35MB, 44MB, 65MB, 90MB, 105MB, 150MB, and 230MB incarnations. The Iomega Bernoulli 230 drive will operate with all of the previous disk sizes (except 20MB and 44MB) with only a negligible performance hit. Bernoulli drives are traditionally SCSI devices, but Iomega offers a parallel port-to-SCSI adapter to allow operation with a PC parallel port. When used on a SCSI system, you can use the Iomega PC2x, PC4x, PC90, PC800, PC1600, and PC1616 SCSI adapters. Other SCSI adapters can also be used as long as they are ASPI compatible and an ASPI driver is provided by the adapter vendor.

By contrast, the Iomega Jaz family uses more conventional "rigid disks" that suspend the read/write heads under a thin layer of air (the same approach used in hard drives). The Jaz is also a more recent development, offering faster drive performance and storage capacities of 1GB and 2GB per cartridge.

READ/WRITE-PROTECTING JAZ DISKS

Read/write protection prevents data from being written to (or read from) the disk. Jaz disks are protected electronically rather than by a traditional mechanical write-protect tab. Jaz disk protection is available from Iomega SCSI utilities 2.2 for DOS, and in the Windows version of Iomega Tools. Protection features include four options:

■ Write protection

■ Read/write protection

■ "Unprotect" until ejection

■ Remove protection

Note that password protection is optional for write protection, but is required for read/write protection. When set, this password must be used to access the disk (or change protection options). Keep in mind that no one can recover data from a read/write-protected disk—should you forget the password. If the password is forgotten, you'll have to reformat the Jaz disk using a "surface verify" option. Reformatting the disk will destroy all the data on it. You cannot use DOS FORMAT (or any other type of disk management software) to remove the password protection. To unprotect a Jaz disk, you must run the Iomega SCSI utilities (or use the Iomega Tools program):

1. Double-click the My Computer icon.

2. Read/write-protect the Iomega disk by right-clicking the disk icon and choosing the Protect option. (If a disk is not inserted in the drive, the Protect option will not be available.)

3. Use the same processes to remove the read/write protection.

UNPROTECTING THE JAZ SOFTWARE DISK

During a normal successful install from the Jaz Tools disk, the unused partition is removed and the disk becomes formatted for the platform that the software is installed on. Until this process is performed (or the software reclaims the disk), the disk will remain write-protected. Use the following steps to remove the write partition and reclaim the disk. To reclaim the Tools disk, double-click the My Computer icon, and then double-click the Jaz drive icon. In the Jaz drive folder, open the w95stuff folder, and then run RECLAIM. Once reclaimed, the write protection should be removed. If this does not reclaim the disk properly, try the following DOS procedure:

1. Start the PC to the Startup menu.

2. From the Startup menu, choose Command Prompt Only.

3. Place the Jaz software floppy disk into your A: drive.

4. At the C:\ prompt, type **A:\GUEST** and press ENTER.

5. Once GUEST assigns a drive letter, insert the Tools disk into the Jaz drive.

6. Type *x:* (where *x* is the drive letter for the Jaz drive) and press ENTER.

7.   At the *x:* prompt, type **cd\dosstuff** and press ENTER.

8.   Type **RECLAIM** and press ENTER to reclaim the Tools disk.

REMOVING IOMEGA TOOLS FROM THE STARTUP GROUP

Programs located in the Startup folder are automatically executed when Windows is loaded. During installation, Iomega Tools places several programs in this group. If a program icon is moved or deleted from the Startup group, the program will no longer start automatically when Windows starts (the program will have to be started manually). To move or remove items from the Startup group:

1.   Open the Iomega Tools folder by double-clicking it from My Computer.

2.   Click Start, highlight Settings, and then click the Taskbar entry.

3.   Choose the Start Menu Programs tab, and then click the Advanced button.

4.   Click the plus (+) symbol next to Programs, and then double-click the Startup folder.

5.   To move the contents, highlight all the icons to be moved, and then drag them to the open Iomega Tools folder. To delete the icons instead, highlight the icons and press DEL.

Once icons have been removed from the Startup folder, the Iomega Tools software must be reinstalled to reinsert them into the Startup group.

UNINSTALLING JAZ TOOLS SOFTWARE

You may need to remove the Jaz software to upgrade it or resolve possible software/driver conflicts. Use the following steps to remove the Iomega Tools software under Windows:

1.   Click Start, point to Settings, and click Control Panel.

2.   From the Control Panel, open the Add/Remove Programs wizard.

3.   Highlight Iomega Tools for Windows 9x/NT and click Add/Remove.

4.   Restart your computer when prompted to do so.

If you need to remove Iomega Tools software under DOS:

1.   From the C:\ prompt, type **edit autoexec.bat** and press ENTER.

2.   Remove the following lines:

```
@SET SCSI_DRIVER=C:\IOMEGA
@SET SCSI_UTILITY=C:\IOMEGA
```

3.   From the File menu, select Exit and save the changes when prompted.

4.   From the C:\ prompt, type **edit config.sys** and press ENTER.

5.   Remove the following lines:

```
DEVICE=C:\IOMEGA\SCSICFG.EXE
DEVICE=C:\IOMEGA\SCSIDRVR.SYS
```

6.   From the File menu, select Exit and save the changes when prompted.

7.   From the C:\ prompt, type **deltree iomega** and press ENTER.

8.   Reboot the computer.

GENERAL DRIVE INSTALLATION AND REPLACEMENT

Removable media (or RM) drives are generally easy devices to install or replace. Most are installed as master devices located on the secondary IDE drive controller channel, though a growing number will coexist as slave devices alongside a hard drive or other drive device. The most important issue to remember is that the BIOS will not support an RM drive directly (even if the BIOS identifies the RM drive at boot time). You'll need real-mode drivers for the RM drive under DOS, or protected-mode drivers for the RM drive under Windows. In most cases, you'll also install a set of software utilities for disk cartridge partitioning, formatting, R/W protection, and so on. This part of the chapter covers the guidelines to follow to install a basic internal IDE-type RM drive.

Select Jumper Configurations

An IDE-type RM drive may be installed as a master or slave device on any hard drive controller channel. These master/slave settings are handled through one or two jumpers located on the rear of the drive (right next to the 40-pin signal cable connector). One of your first decisions when planning an installation should be to decide the drive's configuration:

- If you're installing the RM drive as the first drive on the secondary drive controller channel, it must be jumpered as the master device.

- If you're installing the RM drive alongside another drive (on either the primary or secondary drive controller channel), the RM drive must be jumpered as the slave device.

Refer to the documentation that accompanies your particular RM drive to determine the exact master/slave jumper settings. If you do not have the drive documentation handy, check the drive manufacturer's Web site for online information.

Preinstall Any Software

Some RM drive designs require that you preinstall one or more software utilities prior to installing the physical drive. This ensures that Windows will "find" the drive after installation (especially true for exotic USB devices). If your particular RM drive suggests that you insert a software CD and install software prior to the drive's physical installation, you should handle that software installation now. After the required software is installed, you can power-down the PC and begin the actual drive installation.

Attach Cables and Mount the Drive

At this point, you'll need to connect the physical drive and secure it to the chassis, as explained for an internal ATAPI IDE-type drive here:

1. Turn off and unplug the PC, and then remove the outer cover to expose the computer's drive bays.

2. Attach one end of the 40-pin drive interface cable to the drive controller connector on your motherboard (or drive controller card). Remember to align pin 1 on the cable (the side of the cable with the blue or red stripe) with pin 1 on the drive controller connector.

3. Locate an available drive bay for the RM drive. Remove the plastic housing covering the drive bay, and then slide the drive inside. Locate the four screw holes needed to mount the drive. In some cases, you may need to attach "mounting rails" to the drive so that the drive will be wide enough to fit in the drive bay. In virtually all cases, you should mount an RM drive horizontally (though some RM drive models may be mounted vertically).

4. Attach the 40-pin signal cable and the 4-pin power connector to the new drive, and then bolt the drive securely into place. Do not overtighten the screws, because doing so may damage the drive. If you do not have an available 4-pin power connector, you may use an appropriate Y-splitter if necessary to split power from another drive (preferably the floppy drive).

Configure the CMOS Setup

Although virtually all RM drives require real- or protected-mode driver support, recent motherboard designs can identify the ATAPI IDE RM drive in BIOS, so you should configure your computer's BIOS to accept the drive if possible (through the CMOS Setup):

1. Turn on the computer. As your computer starts, watch for a message that describes how to run the CMOS Setup (such as "Press F1 for Setup"). Press the appropriate key to start the CMOS Setup program.

2. Select the basic configuration menu, and choose the drive location occupied by the RM drive (for example, primary slave, secondary slave, or secondary master, depending on how you've physically jumpered and installed the drive).

3. Select Automatic Drive Detection, if available. This option will automatically identify the new drive. If your BIOS does not provide automatic drive detection, select none or not installed for the RM drive, and rely on drivers only.

4. Save the settings and exit the CMOS Setup program. Your computer will automatically reboot.

Reassemble the Computer

Double-check all of your signal and power cables to verify that they are secure, and then tuck the cables gently into the computer's chassis. Check that no loose tools, screws, or cables are inside the chassis. Now reattach the computer's outer housing(s).

Since the operating system will assign a drive letter only to a partitioned and formatted disk cartridge, you should be sure to insert an appropriate disk cartridge into the drive before rebooting the system. If you do not insert a disk cartridge, the drive may not receive a drive letter at boot time.

Install the Software

To complete your RM drive installation, you need to install the software drivers and utilities that accompanied the drive on floppy disk or CD. If you've preinstalled any software prior to installing the drive, you'll likely need to complete the software installation now. Windows 9x/Me systems generally will detect the presence of the new RM drive and prompt you for the protected-mode drivers automatically. After you install the drivers and reboot the system, the RM drive should be ready for use.

BERNOULLI DRIVE TROUBLESHOOTING

Today, Bernoulli drives are falling into disuse, so you will probably not encounter these drive types or media frequently. However, the following symptoms can help to correct trouble with Bernoulli installations.

SYMPTOM 33-54   **The Bernoulli drive has a "floppy" icon in Windows 9x/Me**   This is usually the result of running a real-mode driver to support the Bernoulli drive and adapter under Windows 9x/Me. Check the Bernoulli driver. You may need to disable the real-mode driver (in CONFIG.SYS) and install the latest protected-mode driver under Windows 9x/Me. The Iomega software bundle typically provides protected-mode drivers for Jaz Jet, Zip Zoom, PC1600, PC1616, PC800, PC2x, PPA-3, and parallel port devices. If you're using a different drive adapter, you may need to upgrade and update the driver accordingly. If you are using a non-Iomega adapter (such as a SCSI adapter), you'll need protected-mode drivers from the particular SCSI adapter vendor (such as Adaptec). However, Windows does have a comprehensive library of generic protected-mode drivers already available.

SYMPTOM 33-55   **A Bernoulli SCSI drive does not have a drive letter in Windows 9x/Me**   The drive does not appear to respond. In virtually all cases, the SCSI driver has failed to load.

■ *Check the SCSI driver.* Open the Device Manager and expand the SCSI Controllers entry, and then check the Iomega Adapter line beneath it. If there is a yellow symbol with an exclamation mark on it, the Windows 9x/Me driver did not load. Highlight that Iomega Adapter line and select Properties. Click the Resources page, and then verify that your I/O Range and IRQ options are set correctly. They must match the jumper settings on your SCSI adapter board. If you must update the resource settings manually, make sure the Automatic Settings box is not checked. Remember to save any changes. If you allocated new resources, you may have to shut off the PC and change jumper settings on the controller to match the resources allocated in the Device Manager. Restart the computer. Once the system reboots, the Windows 9x/Me driver should load normally.

■ *Check the connections.* If the driver checks out properly, you'll need to check the device connections. Check the SCSI signal connector first, and make sure the SCSI cable is intact and connected to the drive properly.

■ *Check SCSI termination and ID assignments.* If problems persist, your SCSI adapter is probably installed correctly, but the bus may be terminated improperly. See that you terminate both ends of the SCSI bus properly. Finally, make sure that the SCSI ID for your drive does not conflict with the ID of other SCSI devices in the system.

SYMPTOM 33-56   **The Bernoulli drive takes over the CD-ROM's drive letter in Windows 9x/Me**   You may simply need to switch drive letters between the Bernoulli drive and CD-ROM drive:

1.   Open Device Manager and double-click the Disk Drives entry.

2.   Highlight the Iomega Bernoulli drive entry and click Properties.

3.   Click the Settings page.

4.   In the Reserved Drive Letters section, there is a Start Drive Letter and an End Drive Letter setting. Enter the desired drive letter for the Bernoulli drive in both start and end drive entries. (Be sure to use the same drive letter for both start and end.) Click OK.

5.   Double-click the CD-ROM entry.

6.   Highlight your CD-ROM Drive entry and click Properties.

7.   Click the Settings page.

8.   In the Reserved Drive Letters section, there is a Start Drive Letter and an End Drive Letter setting. Enter the desired drive letter for the CD-ROM drive in both start and end entries. (Be sure to use the same drive letter for both start and end.) Click OK.

9.   Click on OK to close Device Manager, then shut down and restart the computer.

SYMPTOM 33-57   **You encounter an "Invalid Drive Specification" error after installing an Iomega SCSI drive**   Your system automatically boots into Windows, and it will not return to the installation program. The error occurs when you try to access the Iomega drive. In most cases, you need to install the Iomega SCSI software from the DOS prompt. Boot the system from a clean disk, and then try installing the Iomega SCSI software again.

SYMPTOM 33-58   **You encounter SCSI communication problems**   In virtually all cases, SCSI problems can be traced to hardware problems or driver issues. Check the power connector first, and see that power is provided to the drive (the drive power light should be on). Make sure that the SCSI cable is intact and connected securely between the drive and SCSI adapter. Try a new signal cable if possible. Termination may also be a problem. Both ends of the SCSI bus must be terminated properly. Make sure that terminators are installed in the correct places on your SCSI chain. The Bernoulli SCSI drive must be assigned to a SCSI ID that is not in use by any other SCSI device. Finally, check the drivers. Make sure that the drivers for your SCSI adapter and drive are correct, use the right command-line switches, and verify that you're using the very latest versions. Also check for conflicts between SCSI drivers or other drivers in the system.

SYMPTOM 33-59   **Your IDE Bernoulli drive receives two drive letters**   Your plug-and-play (PnP) BIOS is detecting the Bernoulli drive as a fixed drive and assigning one drive letter, but the Iomega drivers detect the Bernoulli drive *again*—assigning a second drive letter. PnP support for the Bernoulli drive may be a problem. Enter your system's CMOS Setup and disable the PnP support for the Bernoulli drive. Save your changes and reboot the system. If you cannot disable BIOS support for the Bernoulli drive, power-up the system with the Bernoulli disk removed. This causes BIOS to overlook the drive, but the Iomega drivers will still assign the drive letter properly.

SYMPTOM 33-60   **The compressed removable media drive(s) are not automatically mounted on startup**   This problem can occur under Windows 9x if the computer has two floppy disk drives and the following settings exist in the DRVSPACE.INI file:

```
MaxRemovableDrives=2
AutoMount=1
```

To resolve this issue, you'll need to increase the value of the MaxRemovableDrives= setting to match the total number of removable media drives in the computer. For example, if your computer has two floppy disk drives and a double Bernoulli drive, use MaxRemovableDrives=4 (two floppy disk drives plus two Bernoulli drives). Edit the DRVSPACE.INI file as follows:

1.   Locate the DRVSPACE.INI file using Windows Explorer (it should be in the root directory). Right-click the file, and then click Properties.

2.   Click the Read-only check box to clear it, and then click OK.

3.   Double-click the DRVSPACE.INI file to open it.

4.   Change the value of the MaxRemovableDrives= setting to match the total number of removable media drives, or set the AutoMount= entry to the drive letters assigned to the removable media drives. For example, if you have a double Bernoulli drive with drive letters D: and E: assigned to the drive, use the setting AutoMount=DE.

5.   Save and close the file, and then reboot Windows 9x.

 When you use an Iomega RCD driver with a double Bernoulli drive, you may receive a "General Failure" error message the first time you access the second drive. This causes automatic activation and automatic mounting to fail. Use an Iomega OAD or SCSI driver to resolve the problem.

Jaz/Bernoulli Drive Troubleshooting

Even though your Jaz/Bernoulli drive may be installed and configured properly, there are numerous problems that can plague a drive (and adapter). If you cannot correct drive problems with the preceding guidelines, review the following symptoms for detailed corrective action.

SYMPTOM 33-61   **You encounter an error such as "chipset error 0x8" when using a Jaz Jet PCI card**   When starting the computer, you find that the Jaz Jet PCI card will display the error, and the computer may lock up. This error is usually caused by a bad connection in the PCI slot.

■ *Check the PCI card.* Make sure the SCSI adapter card is seated properly. Shut down your computer and disconnect the power supply. Disconnect the Jaz drive from the Jaz Jet SCSI adapter card. Remove the case from your computer and locate your SCSI adapter card. Reinsert the card in the *same* slot, pressing firmly on the edge of the card to ensure proper connections. Be sure to bolt the card securely into place. If the error disappears after you restart the computer, you may reconnect the Jaz drive and continue using it normally.

■ *Exchange the slot or card.* If the error persists, try the card in another slot. If this corrects the problem, the slot is defective. This will not damage the card, but you may need to replace or upgrade the motherboard at another point in the future. If the card still refuses to work in another slot, the card may be defective, so try another card.

SYMPTOM 33-62   **Using an Iomega PC2X 8-bit Bernoulli controller may cause the system to crash**   According to Iomega, its PC2X 8-bit Bernoulli controller cards may not function properly on 486/33 MHz and faster computers. For Windows 9x setup, you may need to run setup with the "ignore hardware detection" parameter, such as

```
SETUP /I
```

To correct this problem, you'll need to use the controller on a slower computer (rarely a practical option) or install a better Bernoulli controller card in the existing system.

SYMPTOM 33-63   **The parallel port adapter (PPA-3) does not have a drive letter in Windows 9x/Me**   Parallel port drive problems can almost always be traced to faulty connections, port configuration issues, or driver problems.

■ *Check the power/signal connections.* Parallel port drives are powered externally, so ensure that the power pack is working, and see that the power cable is connected properly to the drive. If the drive does not appear to power-up, try a different power pack or drive. Also make sure that you are using a good-quality, known-good parallel port cable that is attached securely at the PC and drive.

■ *Isolate the parallel port.* Remove any other devices on the parallel port. Parallel port drives are often very sensitive to devices such as copy protection modules (or dongles), and other pass-through devices. Try connecting the drive *directly* to the parallel port. Also disconnect any printers on the parallel port.

■ *Check the CMOS Setup.* The parallel port's setting may not be compatible with the drive. Reboot the PC and enter CMOS Setup. Check to see that the parallel port is configured in EPP or bidirectional mode.

■ *Check the SCSI controller.* There is a known incompatibility between the Bernoulli drive and the Adaptec 284x adapter. The Iomega PPA-3 driver does not work with the Adaptec 284x controller. Check with Iomega for an updated SCSI driver. You may also try contacting Adaptec for updated drivers.

■ *Check the SCSI drivers.* Open the Device Manager and find the SCSI Controllers entry (even though it is a parallel port device). If there is no such entry, the driver is not installed. If you expand the SCSI Controllers section, there should be an entry for the Iomega Adapter. If there is not, the driver is not installed. If the Device Manager entry for the Iomega Adapter has a yellow circle with an exclamation mark on it, the interface is configured improperly and is conflicting with other devices in the system.

■ *Check the host adapter configuration.* Highlight the Iomega Adapter entry, click Properties, and then select the Settings page. Find the box marked Adapter Settings, and then type

```
/mode:nibble /speed:1
```

Save your changes and reboot the system.

■ *Try reinstalling the host adapter drivers.* Highlight the Iomega Adapter and select Remove. Then reinstall the drivers from scratch.

■ *Check/replace the drive.* Try the drive on another PC. If the drive works on another system, the parallel port is incompatible (or the PPA-3 is not configured properly). If the drive does not work on another PC, try a new Bernoulli drive.

SYMPTOM 33-64   **You encounter an "Invalid Unit Reading Drive *<x>*" error**   S o f t-
ware drivers appear to load properly, and the Bernoulli drive is assigned a drive letter as expected. This often occurs under Windows 3.1x or DOS. In virtually all cases, there is a problem with the SMARTDRV statement (or other caching software) in AUTOEXEC.BAT.

■ *Check the drive controller BIOS.* There may be a conflict with the BIOS on your PC1616 controller card. If you are not booting from the PC1616, try disabling the PC1616 BIOS with the ISACFG.COM utility accompanying the PC1616 adapter. (You can also obtain the utility from Iomega at **www.iomega.com**.) Reboot the PC. The error should be corrected.

■ *Check for SmartDrive.* If you are booting from the PC1616 controller (the Bernoulli drive), leave the controller's BIOS enabled, but try loading SMARTDRV high (into the upper memory area). If you cannot load SMARTDRV high, disable its command line in AUTOEXEC.BAT, reboot the system, and then load SMARTDRV from the DOS command line once the PC initializes. If problems persist, try the new GUEST program from Iomega (make sure you're using the latest version). Once you install the GUEST.EXE and GUEST.INI files in your PC, enter the path and command line for GUEST near the end of AUTOEXEC.BAT (before Windows starts), such as

```
c:\zinstall\guest.exe
```

If these solutions fail to correct the error, then SMARTDRV cannot be loaded and will need to be REMarked out of the AUTOEXEC.BAT file entirely.

 If you use the GUEST program, you cannot compress the disks using DISKSPACE. Also, GUEST does not support the PC80 or PC90 adapter cards.

SYMPTOM 33-65   **You encounter problems using the parallel port interface (PPA-3) with a Bernoulli drive**   Problems with the PPA-3 are usually related to installation issues, but drivers can also prevent the PPA-3 from responding.

■ *Check the power/signal connections.* The external device must be turned on before powering up the computer. If the device refuses to power-up, check the power pack and its connection to the Bernoulli drive. Make sure that the signal cable is the proper length and is connected securely to the drive and system. Unusually long cables may cause read/write errors.

■ *Isolate the parallel port.* Try disconnecting the printer or other parallel port devices from the system, and try the PPA-3 as the only parallel port device attached to the parallel port.

■ *Check the drive termination.* The PPA-3 board is terminated, and the last drive attached to the PPA-3 cable must also be terminated. If the Bernoulli drive is the last device attached to the PPA-3, make sure it is terminated properly.

■ *Check the driver installation.* You need either OAD 1.3 (and higher) or Iomega SCSI 2.0 (and higher) to use the PPA-3 board. Once the drivers are installed, you should see several lines in CONFIG.SYS, such as

```
REM OAD 1.3 or later:
DEVICE=C:\OADDOS\ASPIPPA3.SYS /L=001
DEVICE=C:\OADDOS\DOSCFG.EXE /M1 /V /L=001
DEVICE=C:\OADDOS\DOSOAD.SYS /L=001
```

or

```
REM Iomega SCSI 2.0 or later:
DEVICE=C:\IOMEGA\ASPIPPA3.SYS /L=001
DEVICE=C:\IOMEGA\SCSICFG.EXE /V /L=001
DEVICE=C:\IOMEGA\SCSIDRVR.SYS /L=001
```

Try some ASPIPPA3.SYS command-line options. The ASPIPPA3.SYS driver provides several important command-line options (listed next) that can be employed to streamline its operation. If the ASPIPPA3.SYS command line generates any errors, you can decipher the errors by using Table 33-2.

/MODE=n

■ /MODE=1 is the most compatible mode.

■ /MODE=2 is the Bi-directional Transfer Mode. Your PC must have a bidirectional parallel port.

■ /MODE=3 is Enhanced Mode, which requires an Intel SL series microprocessor (such as 80386SL, 80486SL, or 82360SL) or later.

/SL360=Yes/No

■ This tells the ASPIPPA3.SYS driver whether the computer uses an Intel SL microprocessor chipset. If you're not sure (or a divide overflow occurs during loading), set to /SL360=No.

/SPEED=n

■ Values 1 to 10 are available. Start by setting /SPEED=1. If that solves the problem, continue to increase the value until the problem recurs, and then use the highest value that functioned properly. If you are still not sure which value to use, set /SPEED=1.

/SCAN

■ Forces the ASPIPPA3.SYS driver to check all parallel port addresses. There are three addresses possible: 278h, 378h, and 3BCh.

/Busy_Retry=Yes

■ Forces the driver to retry several times when a device is busy (instead of just reporting an error).

/Port=<Address>

■ Used to manually specify the port address of the parallel port.

SYMPTOM 33-66   **The Iomega PPA-3 locks up on installation**   Chances are that the ASPIPPA3.SYS driver is causing the computer to lock up, or is causing a "Divide by zero overflow" error.

■ *Check the power/signal connections.* The external device must be turned on before powering up the computer. If the device refuses to power-up, check the power pack and its connection to the Bernoulli drive. Also make sure that the signal cable is the proper length and is connected securely to the drive and system. Unusually long cables may cause read/write errors.

■ *Check the drive termination.* The PPA-3 board is terminated, and the last drive attached to the PPA-3 board must also be terminated. If the Bernoulli drive is the last device attached to the PPA-3, make sure it is terminated properly by setting the termination switch on the back of the drive to *I*. If the switch is set to *O*, turn off the drive, set the switch to *I*, turn the drive on, and reboot the PC. Update the ASPIPPA3.SYS driver. Try adding the /SL360=NO switch to the command line, such as

```
DEVICE=C:\IOMEGA\ASPIPPA3.SYS /SL360=NO
```

Save your changes to CONFIG.SYS and reboot the computer.

■ *Isolate PPA-3 problems.* Try the PPA-3 board and Bernoulli drive on another PC. If they work on another system, the original parallel port is probably incompatible. If the PPA-3 and drive do not work on another system, try another set of cables. If problems persist, try the Bernoulli drive directly on a SCSI adapter. If the drive works directly, the PPA-3 has probably failed. If the drive still does not work, it has probably failed and should be replaced.

SYMPTOM 33-67   **You have problems when running Iomega Jaz Tools under Windows 9x/Me**   When Iomega Tools for Windows is installed on your computer, the system may crash (or you may receive an error message referencing the IOMEGA.VXD file) when you attempt to use the Iomega Jaz Tools. This occurs most frequently under FAT32 partitions of OSR 2 or later. Chances are

TABLE 33-2   ASPIPPA3.SYS ERROR MESSAGES

ERROR CODE	POSSIBLE CAUSE
4001	Command-line syntax error.
4002	Adapter initialization failed—possible problem with the adapter or the parallel port.
4003	User specified a port address, and there was no adapter there.
4004	No adapter found.
4005	User pressed both SHIFT keys to bypass this driver.
4006	Current DOS version is not supported by this driver.
4100	Conflicting port address was detected in command line.
4107	Improper speed value. Acceptable range is 0 to 10 decimals.
4108	Bad value—value outside limits.

that you're using an older version of Jaz Tools for Windows 95 (earlier than version 5.0). Earlier versions of Jaz Tools are not compatible with FAT32. You'll need to uninstall the Jaz Tools package, and then install version 5.0 or later, which is FAT32-aware.

SYMPTOM 33-68   **The system runs in "DOS Compatibility Mode" when booting from a removable media drive**   When your PC is configured to boot from a removable media drive, the Performance tab in System Properties may show that the computer is using DOS Compatibility Mode for virtual memory. This is known to be a frequent problem under Windows 95 and OSR 1, and is known to occur with Zip drives, Jaz drives, and SyQuest EZ drives (and may also occur with other IDE or SCSI removable media drives). This problem does not occur with Windows 95 OSR 2 and later. To avoid this problem, upgrade Windows or configure Windows 95 so that the Windows swap file is located on a nonremovable disk:

1. In Control Panel, double-click System.
2. Click the Performance tab, and then click Virtual Memory.
3. Click "Let me specify my own virtual memory settings," click a nonremovable disk in the Hard Disk box, click OK, and then click OK again.

SYMPTOM 33-69   **The Jaz drive isn't detected when connecting it through a SCSI adapter card**   In many cases, this is a software problem. Boot clean (from a bootable floppy disk), and then run your GUEST software from the Jaz installation disk by typing

```
a:\guest
```

If the drive is detected using the GUEST utility under DOS, the problem is software related. Try removing the Jaz drivers and software utilities, and then reinstall the latest software version from scratch. If the problem is not resolved, the trouble is hardware related. Verify that no other devices are using the same IRQ as your SCSI adapter. Also make sure that your Jaz drive is correctly terminated and is not using the same SCSI ID as another SCSI device. Check all power connections to the Jaz drive. If the Jaz drive doesn't respond and the power connections are secure, the drive is probably defective and should be replaced.

Try the Jaz drive on a different computer. If the drive is detected properly on a different computer, there may be a problem with the first computer's configuration. If the Jaz drive is not detected on another computer, the Jaz drive may be defective.

SYMPTOM 33-70   **The Jaz drive isn't detected when connecting it through a Jaz Traveler**   In many cases, this is a software problem. Boot clean (from a bootable floppy disk), and then run your GUEST software from the Jaz installation disk by typing

```
a:\guest
```

If the drive is detected using the GUEST utility under DOS, the problem is software related. Try removing the Jaz drivers and software utilities, and then reinstall the latest software version from scratch. If the problem is not resolved, the trouble is hardware related. The Jaz drive must be connected directly to the parallel port. The Jaz drive will not work properly if connected through a switch box, dongle, or software key. Also verify that no other device is using IRQ 7. Check all power connections to the Jaz drive. If the Jaz drive doesn't respond and the power connections are secure, the drive is probably defective and should be replaced.

Try the Jaz drive on a different computer. If the drive is detected properly on a different computer, there may be a problem with the first computer's configuration. If the Jaz drive is not detected on another computer, the Jaz drive may be defective.

SYMPTOM 33-71   The PC locks up (or does not finish booting) when connected to a SCSI Jaz drive   Make sure that you're powering on the Jaz drive and your computer at the same time. (Try connecting both the computer and the Jaz drive to a power strip, and power the system from the power strip.)

If the computer still won't boot, there may be a problem with your system's configuration. Try the Jaz drive on a different computer. If the system boots after removing the Jaz drive, the drive may be defective. If the Jaz drive works properly on another computer, you may need to reconfigure the system (or the SCSI adapter card). If the computer locks up, boot clean and run the GUEST utility from the Jaz installation disk by typing

```
a:\guest
```

If the drive is detected using the GUEST utility under DOS, the problem is software related. Try removing the Jaz drivers and software utilities, and then reinstall the latest software version from scratch. Try isolating any conflicting software. Open the Close Program dialog box by pressing CTRL-ALT-DEL. Close open programs by highlighting a program and then clicking the End Task button (do not close Explorer or Systray). Remember to close one application at a time, and then try your Jaz drive again. Repeat this process until the problem is resolved. Once the problem is resolved, the last application that was closed is the one causing the conflict.

If the problem is not resolved, the trouble is hardware related. Verify that no other devices are using the same IRQ as your SCSI adapter. Also make sure that your Jaz drive is correctly terminated and is not using the same SCSI ID as another SCSI device. Check all power connections to the Jaz drive. If the Jaz drive doesn't respond and the power connections are secure, the drive is probably defective and should be replaced.

Try the Jaz drive on a different computer. If the drive is detected properly on a different computer, there may be a problem with the first computer's configuration. If the Jaz drive is not detected on another computer, the Jaz drive may be defective.

SYMPTOM 33-72   An incorrect icon appears for a Jaz drive   Ideally, the icon should be a green Jaz drive, so the actual problem depends on the icon that is shown in Windows Explorer.

First, the Jaz icon may look like a floppy or hard disk drive icon. Chances are that a real-mode TSR or driver is interfering with the Jaz drive. Restart your computer. When you see the message "Starting Windows," press F8. From the Startup menu, choose Step-by-Step Confirmation. As each step is processed, answer yes to every entry except "Process your startup device drivers (CONFIG.SYS)" and "Process your startup command file (AUTOEXEC.BAT)." This will prevent real-mode drivers from loading at startup. If the incorrect Jaz icon is now replaced with the correct green Jaz icon, there is a driver conflict in either your AUTOEXEC.BAT or CONFIG.SYS file. You'll need to systematically disable each real-mode command line until you identify the offending command line. If the Jaz icon is not the correct green Jaz icon, then a Windows driver is causing the problem. You may need to remove the Jaz drivers and other software and update/reinstall that software from scratch.

If the Jaz icon takes any other form, there may be a problem with Imagicon software. Open the Close Program dialog box by pressing CTRL-ALT-DEL. Highlight the Imagicon entry and then click the End Task button. Click Start, point to Programs, point to Startup, and then click Iomega Disk Icons. If the problem persists, reboot your computer and run ScanDisk. Correct any file system problems indicated by ScanDisk. If the problem still continues, delete and then reinstall the Iomega Tools software.

SYMPTOM 33-73   **The system locks up while installing Jaz Tools software**   In most cases, you'll notice lockups when launching the Iomega setup software. This is usually caused by a conflict with another driver that is loading during Windows 9x/Me startup. To determine which file is causing this conflict, close all open programs:

1. Open the Close Program dialog box by pressing CTRL-ALT-DEL.

2. Close open programs by highlighting a program and then clicking the End Task button (do not close Explorer).

3. Close one application at a time, and then try your Jaz drive again.

4. Repeat this process until the problem is resolved. Once the problem is resolved, the last application that was closed is the one causing the conflict.

5. Once you have determined which application is causing the conflict, you should discontinue the use of that application when using your Jaz drive, or obtain an updated version of that software.

SYMPTOM 33-74   **You receive an "insufficient disk space" message writing to the Jaz disk under DOS**   This error message may be caused if the disk is full, exceeds the file limit imposed by your operating system, or is defective.

■ *Check the disk space.* Verify that the disk has enough space available to hold the files you wish to copy.

■ *Check the operating system.* Make sure that you do not exceed the file limit of your operating system. DOS will not allow you to include more than 511 files in the root directory. Switch to the drive letter of your Jaz drive. From the drive prompt, type **dir** and press ENTER. The number of files in the root director should be less than 511. Otherwise, you'll have to move individual files into other directories to reduce the number of files on the root directory.

■ *Try cycling power.* If the error persists, try shutting down the computer (and Jaz drive). Then restart the system from a "cold" start.

■ *Try several different disks.* If the error message occurs on only one disk, try reformatting that disk (formatting the disk will remove all data from the disk). If reformatting the disk doesn't help, discard the disk and use a fresh one. If you're receiving the error message with more than one disk, the drive may be defective and should be replaced.

SYMPTOM 33-75   **No drives on your system are supported by Iomega Tools in DOS**
Boot the system clean, and then run GUEST from the Jaz installation disk by typing **a:\guest**. If the drive is detected using the GUEST utility under DOS, the problem is software related. Try removing the Jaz drivers and software utilities, and then reinstall the latest software version from scratch. Try isolating any conflicting software. Open the Close Program dialog box by pressing CTRL-ALT-DEL. Close open programs by highlighting a program and then clicking the End Task button (do not close Explorer or Systray). Remember to close one application at a time. Then try your Jaz drive again. Repeat this process until the problem is resolved. Once the problem is resolved, the last application that was closed is the one causing the conflict.

If the problem is not resolved, the trouble is hardware related. Verify that no other devices are using the same IRQ as your SCSI adapter. Also make sure that your Jaz drive is correctly terminated and is not using the same SCSI ID as another SCSI device. Check all power connections to the Jaz drive. If the Jaz drive doesn't respond and the power connections are secure, the drive is probably defective and should be replaced.

Try the Jaz drive on a different computer. If the drive is detected properly on a different computer, there may be a problem with the first computer's configuration. If the Jaz drive is not detected on another computer, the Jaz drive may be defective.

SYMPTOM 33-76   **The GUEST utility cannot locate the Jaz Tools disk**   Verify that the Jaz Tools disk is in your Jaz drive. If the Jaz Tools disk is already inserted into your Jaz drive, eject and then reinsert the Jaz Tools disk. You may also wish to try another Jaz Tools disk. Next, verify that your Jaz drive is assigned a drive letter. Double-click the My Computer icon. There should an icon representing the Jaz drive. If your Jaz drive is not assigned a drive letter, you'll need to connect the drive properly.

Close all open programs. Open the Close Program dialog box by pressing CTRL-ALT-DEL. Close open programs by highlighting a program and then clicking the End Task button (do not close Explorer or Systray). Close one application at a time, and then try your Jaz drive again. Repeat this process until the problem is resolved. The last application that was closed is the one causing the conflict. Once you've determined which application is causing the conflict, discontinue the use of that application while using your Jaz drive (or obtain an updated version of the software).

SYMPTOM 33-77   **No drive letters were added for the Jaz drive in DOS**   Boot the system clean, and then run GUEST from the Jaz installation disk by typing **a:\guest**. If the drive is detected using the GUEST utility under DOS, the problem is software related. Try removing the Jaz drivers and software utilities, and then reinstall the latest software version from scratch. Try isolating any conflicting software. Open the Close Program dialog box by pressing CTRL-ALT-DEL. Close open programs by highlighting a program and then clicking the End Task button (do not close Explorer or Systray). Remember to close one application at a time; then try your Jaz drive again. Repeat this process until the problem is resolved. Once the problem is resolved, the last application that was closed is the one causing the conflict.

If the problem is not resolved, the trouble is hardware related. Verify that no other devices are using the same IRQ as your SCSI adapter. Also make sure that your Jaz drive is correctly terminated and is not using the same SCSI ID as another SCSI device. Check all power connections to the Jaz drive. If the Jaz drive doesn't respond and the power connections are secure, the drive is probably defective and should be replaced.

Try the Jaz drive on a different computer. If the drive is detected properly on a different computer, there may be a problem with the first computer's configuration. If the Jaz drive is not detected on another computer, the Jaz drive may be defective.

SYMPTOM 33-78   **You see an error indicating that the Jaz disk in your drive is not formatted**   First verify that you're using a PC-formatted disk (a Mac-formatted Jaz disk will not work in a PC). Try several different Jaz disks. If the error message occurs on only one disk, try reformatting that disk. (Remember that formatting the Jaz disk will remove all data from that disk.) If you cannot format the suspect Jaz disk, it may be defective and require replacement. If you're receiving the error message with any Jaz disk (or the disk will not format on your drive), the drive may be defective and need to be replaced.

SYMPTOM 33-79   **You encounter a "general failure reading drive" message in DOS**   In many cases, this is a disk problem. First check your connections and confirm that the Jaz drive's signal and power cables are attached properly. Verify that you're using a PC-formatted disk (a Mac-formatted Jaz disk will not work in a PC), and compare results with several different Jaz disks. If the error message occurs on only one disk, try reformatting that disk. (Remember that formatting the Jaz disk will remove all data from that disk.) If you cannot format the suspect Jaz disk, it may be defective and require replacement. If you're receiving the error message with any Jaz disk (or the disk will not format on your drive), the drive may be defective and need to be replaced.

SYMPTOM 33-80   **You get a "disk full" error even though there is still space on the Jaz disk under Windows 9x/Me**   In virtually all cases, you've exceeded the file limit imposed by the operating system (though in a few cases, a defective disk may cause this error message). Verify that the Jaz disk has enough room available to contain the files you wish to copy. The number of files you see when you first open your Iomega drive cannot exceed the limit imposed by your operating system (typically 511 files under DOS and Windows 9x/Me). If the number of files exceeds this limit, you will have to move individual files into another folder (usually on your hard drive) to temporarily reduce the number of files, and make a new folder on your Jaz disk. You may then move the files back to your Iomega disk:

1. Click Start and select Windows Explorer.
2. Make a new folder on your hard drive by clicking File, New, and selecting Folder.
3. Type a name for the new folder.
4. Move two or more files from the root directory of your Jaz disk into the newly created folder.
5. Move the new folder from your hard drive to your Jaz drive.
6. Move other files from the root directory of your Jaz drive to this new folder to make additional space.

If the problem persists with a certain disk, compare results with several different Jaz disks. If the error message occurs on only one disk, try reformatting that disk. (Remember that formatting the Jaz disk will remove all data from that disk.) If you cannot format the suspect Jaz disk, it may be defective and require replacement. If you're receiving the error message with any Jaz disk (or the disk will not format on your drive), the drive may be defective and need to be replaced.

SYMPTOM 33-81   **When backing up, you receive an error indicating that "disk linking is not supported under Windows 9x/Me"**   This is a problem with Microsoft Backup. It does not support disk linking over multiple Jaz disks. Instead, you should remove Backup and install Iomega's 1-Step Backup for Zip and Jaz software (part of the Iomega Tools software bundle).
To install Iomega Tools for Windows 95/98, put the Jaz installation floppy in the A: drive. Click Start and select Run. In the Open box, type **a:\guest95** and click OK. Put your Jaz Tools disk into the Jaz drive. Double-click the My Computer icon, and then double-click the Jaz drive icon. You should see a folder called w95stuff. Double-click the w95stuff folder, and then double-click setup95.exe. Follow the screen instructions to complete the installation. Now try backing up with the Iomega software.

SYMPTOM 33-82   **You encounter a "fatal exception" error when using the Copy Machine software for your Jaz drive**   In virtually all cases, the problem is caused by the Auto Spin-Down/Eject feature in the Iomega Copy Machine software. You'll need to disable the feature under Windows 9x/Me. Start the Iomega Copy Machine software by clicking its icon in the Iomega Tools folder. Select Options, and then choose Runtime. Deselect the Auto Spin-Down/Eject option by clearing the check box. Finally, choose OK to accept the changes.

SYMPTOM 33-83   **You see an error such as "program performed an illegal operation"**
Try rebooting the system first (make sure to cycle power to the drive also). Close all open programs to clear possible conflicting software. Open the Close Program dialog box by pressing CTRL-ALT-DEL. Close

any open programs by highlighting a program and then clicking the End Task button (do not close Explorer). Close one application at a time. Then try your Jaz drive again. Repeat this process until the problem is resolved. Once the problem is resolved, the last application that was closed is the one causing the conflict. You may be able to patch or update the offending program. As an alternative, you may be able to uninstall and reinstall the Iomega Tools software.

SYMPTOM 33-84   **You receive an error such as "Cannot create or replace: make sure the disk is not full or write protected"**   You may also see this as a "General failure writing to drive" error or a "Drive does not exist" error. In most cases, the Jaz disk is formatted improperly or the disk is defective. Start by checking the disk format. You must use a PC-formatted disk (a Mac-formatted disk will not work on a PC). Try several different disks. If the error message occurs on only one disk, try reformatting that disk. (Remember that formatting the disk will remove all data from the disk.) A defective disk should be replaced. If you're receiving the error message with any disk (or the disk will not format on that drive), the drive may be defective. Try another drive.

SYMPTOM 33-85   **You receive an error such as "ASPI for Win32 not installed" when working with a SCSI Jaz drive**   This error message is known to occur while trying to install the IomegaWare software, and is caused by a conflict with the MSWHEEL application (which is part of Microsoft IntelliMouse Pro). The MSWHEEL software controls the functionality of the wheel on the mouse. Start by closing the MSWHEEL application:

1. Open the Close Program dialog box by pressing CTRL-ALT-DEL.
2. Highlight the MSWHEEL application by clicking Mswheel.
3. Click the End Task button to close the application.

Now manually install the Iomega SCSI driver in Windows 9x/Me:

1. Insert the IomegaWare CD into your CD-ROM drive. If the installation begins automatically, cancel the installation process.
2. Click Start, highlight Settings, and then click Control Panel.
3. Double-click Add New Hardware from the Control Panel.
4. Click the Next button to start the installation process.
5. If you're prompted to have Windows search for new hardware, choose No.
6. Choose SCSI Controllers from the Hardware Types list, and then click Next.
7. Choose Have Disk from the next screen.
8. From the "Install from disk" prompt, click the Browse button.
9. From the Drives drop-down list, choose the drive letter of your CD-ROM drive.
10. From the Folders list, double-click the w9xstuff folder and select OK twice.
11. In the Models list, choose the driver for the Zip or Jaz drive you are installing.
12. After highlighting the driver, select Next and click Finish.
13. Restart your computer.

Finally, install the IomegaWare software manually:

1. Click Start, and then Run.

2. Click Browse. In the Browse dialog box, highlight your CD-ROM drive by clicking it in the Look In drop-down box.

3. Highlight the file setup.exe and click the Open button.

4. In the Open box (after the path and file name), type a space and then **/N**. This will prevent GUEST from running during the installation.

5. Follow the prompts to complete the installation of your IomegaWare software.

SYMPTOM 33-86 **You receive an "INST30" error with your Jaz disk under Windows 9x/Me** When you attempt to install IomegaWare software, you may receive the following error message: "ISINST30—this application performed an illegal operation and will be shut down." In virtually all cases, the problem is due to a software conflict or corruption. Start by closing any background software. Open the Close Program dialog box by pressing CTRL-ALT-DEL. Close each application (one at a time) by highlighting an application and clicking the End Task button. Remember not to close Explorer or Systray. If the error disappears, the last program to be closed was responsible for the error. You may need to stop using that software while installing the Iomega software (or the Jaz drive). In some cases, you may be able to patch or update the offending software. If the problem persists, you may need to remove and/or reinstall the IomegaWare software from its installation CD.

SYMPTOM 33-87 **You get an error such as "Disk not in the drive" when using IomegaWare 2.0 under Windows 9x/Me** If you receive the error message "Disk not in the drive" when a disk is actually inserted in the drive, it may be that the disk has been read/write-protected. Double-check your Jaz drive to be sure a Jaz disk is inserted. Eject the disk and reinsert it to ensure that it is positioned properly. Also try several different disks. If no disks are detected, the drive may be defective. If only one disk is causing the problem (and the following steps don't help), the disk itself may be defective.

If the problem persists, check the read/write protection status on the Jaz disk. If the disk is protected, it may not respond until it is unprotected. Make sure that the Jaz disk is inserted properly in the drive. Locate and click the Iomega drive icon where the disk is inserted. If you don't have an IomegaWare shortcut on your desktop, click Start, select Programs, select Iomega, and then double-click the IomegaWare icon. From the pop-up menu, choose Properties, located at the bottom of the list. In the dialog area labeled Disk is a padlock symbol, which will indicate whether the disk has been protected or locked. If the padlock is displayed as closed (or locked), the disk has been protected using the read/write protection tool.

If you have forgotten the password, you will be given the option to perform a "long format" on the disk. Performing a long format on the Jaz disk will erase all information.

If the Jaz disk IS protected, you'll need to unlock the read/write-protected disk now. Locate and click the Iomega drive icon where the disk is inserted. If you don't have an IomegaWare shortcut on your desktop, click Start, select Programs, select Iomega, and then double-click the IomegaWare icon. From the pop-up menu, select Properties. Click the Change button in the Disk section. In the Unprotect window, type the password for the disk and click OK.

An option within the Unprotect window allows you to remove the read/write protection *temporarily*. Checking this option will allow you to access the disk in that session, but once the disk is ejected, it will be read/write-protected again.

SYMPTOM 33-88   **The Jaz drive fails to spin up**   This is a surprisingly common problem that can be caused by three issues. First check the drive's power connections. If the drive is not receiving adequate power, it will not spin up a Jaz disk. If the drive is external, you may need to replace the Jaz drive's power adapter. The disk itself may also be at fault. Make sure that the disk is inserted properly and securely (you may need to eject and reinsert the disk). Also try a new disk. If a new disk works, the original disk may be damaged or defective. Finally, boot the system clean from a floppy disk and try the drive/disk again from the GUEST utility under DOS. If the problem clears, there may be some DOS (or Windows) utility software that is conflicting with the disk. If a clean boot fails to clear the problem, the Jaz drive itself may be defective.

SYMPTOM 33-89   **The Jaz drive will not format a disk**   In many cases, this occurs when the Jaz disk is read/write-protected. So you'll need to verify that the disk is not protected. Double-click the My Computer icon, and then right-click the Jaz drive and select Protect. In the Disk Protect Options dialog box, choose Remove Protection. If the disk is password-protected you must supply the password used to initially write-protect the disk before removing the protection.

If the disk is not protected, you should try several different disks. If other unprotected Jaz disks format normally, the original disk is probably defective. If the problem continues with more than one disk, try a clean DOS boot and enable the drive using the GUEST utility. If problems disappear with other disks, you're probably getting software interference from one or more TSRs or drivers on the system. If the problem persists on any disk (even after booting the system clean), the Jaz drive may be defective.

SYMPTOM 33-90   **The computer locks up after running parallel port accelerator software**   This problem may occur after installing the parallel port driver and then running the Parallel Port Accelerator utility. Running the Parallel Port Accelerator utility will sometimes cause the drive not to work (or even cause the system to lock up during boot). Turn off the PC, disconnect the drive, and try rebooting the computer with the drive's signal cable disconnected. The system will almost certainly boot normally. Now remove the system changes made by your Parallel Port Accelerator software:

1. Right-click the My Computer icon on your desktop.
2. Select Properties from the menu.
3. Click the Device Manager tab.
4. Click the plus (+) sign next to SCSI controllers.
5. Double-click Iomega Parallel Port Interface.
6. Click the Settings tab.
7. Remove all the information from the Adapter Settings box.
8. Click OK, and then click OK again.
9. Click Yes when prompted to restart your computer.

SYMPTOM 33-91   You cannot "long format" a 1GB Jaz disk in a 2GB Jaz drive

The internal read/write heads on a 2GB Jaz drive are different from those on a 1GB Jaz drive. A short format will work correctly on the 1GB Jaz disk, but a long format will fail. Use only a 1GB Jaz drive to perform a long format on a 1GB Jaz disk.

SYMPTOM 33-92   The Jaz drive makes a grinding noise when reading or writing to a disk   This is a very serious symptom that may indicate a mechanical problem with the drive. Carefully eject and reinsert the Jaz disk. Do not try another disk in the drive. If the drive is defective, it may cause damage to other Jaz disks. Immediately eject the disk if the grinding noise begins again. If the noise returns, try the disk on another Jaz drive. If the disk is readable on another Jaz drive (and there is no grinding nose), chances are that the original Jaz drive is defective and should be replaced.

Further Study

Exabyte   www.exabyte.com
Fuji (for Zip media)   www.fujifilm.com
Imation (for disk media)   www.imation.com
Iomega   www.iomega.com
SyQuest   www.syquest.com

34

SCSI SYSTEMS AND TROUBLESHOOTING

PC designers have always sought ways to connect more devices to fewer cables, and achieve faster data transfer between the system and its peripheral devices. In the early 1980s, it became clear that a more versatile and intelligent interface would be needed to overcome the myriad proprietary interfaces appearing at the time. By 1986, PC designers responded with the introduction of the *Small Computer System Interface* (SCSI, pronounced "scuzzy"). SCSI proved to be a revolution for PC power users, because a single adapter could operate a number of unique devices simultaneously, all daisy-chained to the same signal cable. Whereas "low-end" PCs needed one adapter for hard drives, one adapter for the CD-ROM, another adapter for a tape drive, and so on, a system fitted with a SCSI adapter (such as the Adaptec card shown in Figure 34-1) could handle all of these devices (and more) and achieve data throughputs that other interfaces of the day couldn't begin to approach.

Today's PC industry has changed. Proprietary interfaces have been essentially abandoned in favor of the standardized interfaces (such as UDMA/66 and UDMA/100), and these standard interface schemes now support a variety of devices while offering low cost and performance levels rivaling traditional SCSI.

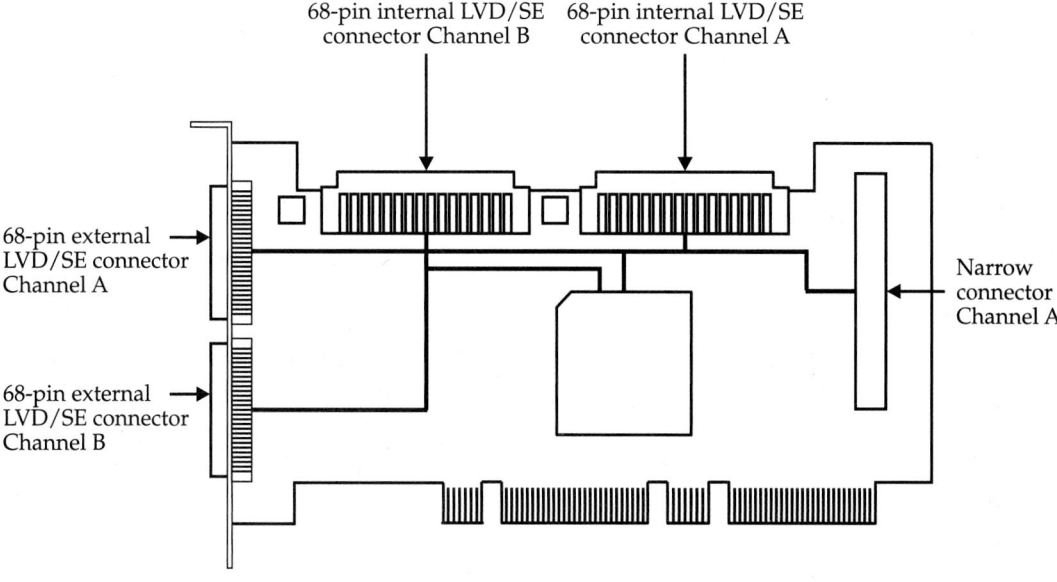

68-pin internal LVD/SE connector Channel B

68-pin internal LVD/SE connector Channel A

68-pin external LVD/SE connector Channel A

68-pin external LVD/SE connector Channel B

Narrow connector Channel A

FIGURE 34-1   A typical SCSI host adapter (Courtesy of Adaptec)

Yet, SCSI has endured and evolved, and it remains the interface of choice for multitasking, servers, and other high-end computer systems. This chapter will provide an overview of the SCSI interface, cover the essential installation and setup of a SCSI host adapter, and show you how to deal with the most important troubleshooting problems. You'll also learn about two advanced serial SCSI techniques: FireWire and FibreChannel.

Understanding SCSI Concepts

Ideally, peripheral devices should be *independent* of the microprocessor's operation. The computer should only have to send commands and data to the peripheral and then wait for the peripheral to respond. Printers work this way. The parallel and serial ports are actually *device-level* interfaces. The computer is unconcerned with *which* device is attached to the port. In other words, you can take a printer built 12 years ago and connect it to a new AMD Athlon-based system, and the printer will work just fine because only data and commands are being sent across the interface. This is a simple example of the concept behind SCSI. Computers and peripherals can be designed, developed, and integrated without worrying about hardware compatibility—such compatibility is established entirely by the SCSI interface.

DEVICE INDEPENDENCE

From a practical standpoint, SCSI is both a *bus,* an organization of physical wires and terminations, where each wire has its own name and purpose, and a *command set,* a limited set of instructions that allows the computer and peripherals to communicate over that physical bus. The SCSI bus is used in systems that want to achieve device independence. For example, all hard disk drives look alike to the SCSI interface (except for their total capacity), all optical drives look alike, all printers look alike, and so on. For any particular type of SCSI device, you should be able to replace an existing device with another device without any system modifications, and new SCSI devices can often be added to the bus with little more than a driver upgrade. Since the intelligence of SCSI resides in the peripheral device itself and *not* in the computer, the computer is able to employ a small set of standard commands to accomplish data transfer back and forth to the peripheral.

SCSI VARIATIONS

At this point, let's take a look at the evolution of the SCSI interface and examine the ways in which it has evolved and proliferated. SCSI began life in 1979 when Shugart Associates (PC "old timers" might remember it as one of the first PC hard drive makers) released its Shugart Associates Systems Interface (SASI) standard. The X3T9.2 committee was formed by ANSI in 1982 to develop the SASI standard, which was renamed SCSI. SCSI drives and interfaces that were developed under the evolving X3T9.2 SCSI standard were known as SCSI-1, though the actual SCSI-1 standard (ANSI X3.131-1986) didn't become official until 1986. SCSI-1 provided a system-level 8-bit bus (referred to as *narrow*) that could operate up to eight devices and transfer data at up to 5 MB/s. However, the delay in standardization led to a lot of configuration and compatibility problems with SCSI-1 setups. Table 34-1 compares the specifications of each SCSI standard.

Although SCSI-1 was supposed to support all SCSI devices, manufacturers took liberties with the evolving standard. This frequently led to installation and compatibility problems between SCSI-1 devices that, theoretically, should have worked together perfectly. Today, all obsolete SCSI-1 adapters should be upgraded to SCSI-3 installations.

Earlier in 1986 (even before the SCSI-1 standard was ratified), work started on the SCSI-2 standard, which was intended to overcome many of the speed and compatibility problems encountered with SCSI-1. By 1994, ANSI approved the SCSI-2 standard (X3.131-1994). SCSI-2 was designed to be back-

TABLE 34-1	COMPARISON OF SCSI CONVENTIONS				
TERMS	**NAME**	**MHZ**	**BUS WIDTH**	**MB/S**	**MBIT/S**
SCSI-1	SCSI-1	5	8	5	40
Fast SCSI	SCSI-2	10	8	10	80
Fast-Wide SCSI	SCSI-2/ SCSI-3	10	16	20	160
Ultra SCSI	SCSI-3	20	8	20	160
Ultra-Wide SCSI	SCSI-3	20	16	40	320
Ultra2 SCSI	SCSI-4	40	8	40	320
Ultra2-Wide SCSI	SCSI-4	40	16	80	640
Ultra3 SCSI	Ultra 160	40*2[1]	8	80	640
Ultra3-Wide SCSI	Ultra 160	40*2[1]	16	160	1280
Ultra4 SCSI	Ultra 320	Undefined			
Ultra4-Wide SCSI	Ultra 320	Undefined			

[1] Ultra3 features the same base frequency as Ultra2 (40 MHz), but transmits 2 bytes per data clock, thus doubling the total throughput.

ward compatible with SCSI-1, but SCSI-2 also provided for several variations. Fast SCSI-2 (or Fast SCSI) doubles the SCSI bus clock speed and allows 10 MB/s data transfers across the 8-bit SCSI data bus. Wide SCSI-2 (or Wide SCSI), which also doubles the original data transfer rate to 10 MB/s, uses a 16-bit data bus instead of the original 8-bit data bus (the SCSI clock is left unchanged). To support the larger data bus, Wide SCSI uses a 68-pin cable instead of the traditional 50-pin cable. Wide SCSI can also support up to 16 SCSI devices. Designers then combined the attributes of fast and wide operation to create Fast Wide SCSI-2 (or Fast Wide SCSI), which supports 20 MB/s data transfers across a 16-bit data bus. Whenever you see references to Fast SCSI, Wide SCSI, or Fast Wide SCSI, you're *always* dealing with a SCSI-2 implementation.

But SCSI advancement didn't stop at SCSI-2. ANSI began development of the SCSI-3 standard in 1993 (even before SCSI-2 was adopted). SCSI-3 is intended to be backward compatible with SCSI-2 and SCSI-1 devices, and many SCSI devices and controllers are using the advances offered by SCSI-3 development. These typical SCSI-3 devices are generally known as Fast-20 SCSI (or Ultra SCSI-3, also termed Ultra SCSI). Ultra SCSI uses a 20 MHz SCSI bus clock with an 8-bit data bus to achieve 20 MB/s data transfers. By using a 16-bit data bus, SCSI-3 offers Wide Fast-20 SCSI (or Ultra Wide SCSI-3, also termed Ultra Wide SCSI), which handles 40 MB/s data transfers.

SCSI development continued with the SCSI-4 implementations. The SCSI-4 standard covers Fast-40 SCSI (called Ultra2 SCSI-4 and Ultra2 SCSI) using a 40 MHz bus clock to provide 40 MB/s data transfers with an 8-bit data bus. The 16-bit data bus version is known as Wide Fast-40 SCSI (also called Ultra2 Wide SCSI-4 or Ultra2 Wide SCSI), which is supposed to support 80 MB/s data transfers. Whenever you see references to Ultra2 or Fast-40, you're almost certain to be faced with a SCSI-4 setup.

SCSI advances have continued. The Ultra3 SCSI standard (a.k.a. Ultra160) employs a 40 MHz bus clock that is "double-transitioned." This feature allows twice the effective data transfer on the same 40 MHz clock, yielding data transfers up to 80 MB/s. The Ultra3 Wide SCSI standard offers 16 data bits rather than 8. On the same double-transitioned 40 MHz clock, Ultra3 Wide SCSI can achieve data transfers up to 160 MB/s. While Ultra360 (Ultra4) SCSI standards have not yet been fully defined, you can be sure that even faster SCSI implementations are on the horizon.

Also keep in mind that SCSI has traditionally been a *parallel* bus—that is, 8 or 16 bits of data are transferred at a time across parallel data lines. SCSI-3 is proposing three new *serial* connection schemes. You'll see these referred to as Serial Storage Architecture (SSA), FibreChannel, and IEEE 1394 (a.k.a. FireWire). These serial schemes will offer faster data transfers than their parallel bus cousins offer, but they are not backward compatible with SCSI-2 or SCSI-1.

BUS LENGTH

As you're already aware, SCSI devices are daisy-chained together with a 50-pin or 68-pin cable. The total length of this cable makes up the overall SCSI bus. When there are only *internal* SCSI devices, the bus length is measured from the SCSI host adapter to the last internal SCSI device on the chain (the terminated device). When there are only *external* SCSI devices, the bus length is measured from the SCSI host adapter to the last external SCSI device on the chain (it should also be terminated). When there are *both* internal and external SCSI devices, the bus length is measured from the last external device to the last internal device. There are finite limits on the length of your SCSI bus. As SCSI implementations have become faster over the years, that effective bus length has shortened. Table 34-2 illustrates the maximum SCSI bus lengths for single-ended, differential, and low-voltage differential (LVD) signaling approaches.

TABLE 34-2	MAXIMUM SCSI BUS LENGTHS		
TERMS	**SINGLE-ENDED**	**DIFFERENTIAL**	**LVD**
SCSI-1	6m	25m	12m[2]
Fast SCSI	3m	25m	12m[2]
Fast Wide SCSI	3m	25m	12m[2]
Ultra SCSI	1.5m–3m	Up to 25m	Up to 12m
Wide Ultra SCSI	Up to 3m	Up to 25m	Up to 12m
Ultra2 SCSI	[1]	25m	12m
Wide Ultra2 SCSI	[1]	25m	12m
Ultra3 SCSI	[1]	25m	12m
Wide Ultra3 SCSI	[1]	25m	12m

[1] Single-ended and high-powered differential are not defined at Ultra2 and Ultra3 speeds.
[2] Only if all devices on the bus support LVD.

INITIATORS AND TARGETS

There are basically two types of devices on the SCSI bus: initiators and targets. An *initiator* starts communication when something has to be done, and a *target* responds to the initiator's commands. The important thing for you to understand here is that this master/slave relationship is not a one-way arrangement. An initiator may become a target at some point in the data transfer cycle, and the target may become the initiator at other points. A SCSI bus can support up to eight devices simultaneously, but there *must* be at least one initiator and one target in the system. A SCSI *host adapter* card is typically the initiator, and all other devices (such as hard drives or CD-ROMs) are usually targets, but that is not necessarily the only possible scenario.

Many kinds of computer peripherals are candidates for the SCSI bus. Each peripheral offers unique characteristics and applications, but each also requires different methods of control. By adding SCSI "intelligence" to these devices, they can all be made to share the same bus together. The SCSI nomenclature groups similar devices together into specific device types. The original SCSI standard defines six device types:

■ Random access devices (for example, hard drives)

■ Sequential access (for example, tape drives)

■ Printers

■ Processors

■ WORM (write once read many) drives

■ Read-only random access devices

The SCSI-2 interface adds five more device types to the specification:

■ CD-ROM drives

■ Scanners

■ Magneto-optical drives

■ Media changer (jukebox)

■ Communication devices

SYNCHRONOUS AND ASYNCHRONOUS

As a system-level interface, SCSI requires an operating *handshaking protocol* that organizes the transfer of data from a sending point to a requesting point. There are typically three handshaking protocols for SCSI: asynchronous, synchronous, and fast synchronous. The *asynchronous* protocol works rather like a parallel port. Each byte must be requested and acknowledged before the next byte can be sent. Asynchronous operation generally results in very reliable (but slow) performance. *Synchronous* and *fast synchronous* operations both ignore the request/acknowledge handshake for data transfer only. This allows slightly faster operation than an asynchronous protocol, but a certain fixed amount of time delay (sometimes called an *offset*) must be allowed for request and acknowledge timing. The fast synchronous protocol uses slightly shorter signals, resulting in even faster speed. An important point to remember is that SCSI systems can typically use any of these three protocols as desired. The actual protocol that is used must be mutually agreed to by the initiator and the target through their communications. SCSI systems normally initialize in an asynchronous protocol.

DISCONNECT AND RECONNECT

Allowing a target to operate offline while the initiator is occupied elsewhere would be desirable in several situations, such as at tape rewind time. An important feature of SCSI is the ability to *disconnect* two communicating devices, and then *reconnect* them again later. Disconnect and reconnect operations allow several different operations to occur simultaneously in the system, and are the main reasons why SCSI architecture is so desirable in a multitasking environment. It is up to the initiator to grant a disconnect privilege to a target.

SINGLE-ENDED AND DIFFERENTIAL

The signal wiring used in a SCSI bus has a definite impact on bus performance. There are two generally used wiring techniques for SCSI: single-ended and differential. Both wiring schemes have advantages and disadvantages.

The *single-ended* (SE) wiring technique is, as the name implies, a single wire carrying a particular signal from initiator to target. Each signal requires only one wire. Terminating resistors at each end of the cable help to maintain acceptable signal levels. A common ground (return) provides the reference for all single-ended signals. Unfortunately, single-ended circuitry is not very noise resistant, so single-ended cabling is generally limited to about 6 meters at data transfer speeds of 5 MHz or less. At higher data transfer speeds, cable length can be as short as 1.5 meters. In spite of the disadvantages, single-ended operation is popular because of its simplicity.

The *differential* (DIF) wiring approach uses two wires for each signal (instead of one wire referenced to a common ground). A differential signal offers excellent noise resistance because it does not rely on a common ground. This allows much longer cables (up to 25 meters) and higher-speed operation (10 MHz). An array of pull-up resistors at each end of the cable help to ensure signal integrity. The drawback of differential wiring is that it is more complicated than single-ended interfaces.

Low-voltage differential (LVD) SCSI is an emerging standard defined in the SPI-2 document of SCSI-3 that runs on 3.3 Vdc rather than 5 Vdc. The goal of LVD is to allow higher data rates while combining the benefits of single-ended and differential SCSI bus schemes. LVD is less sensitive to electromagnetic noise and allows high data rates at greater cable lengths than a single-ended bus. LVD is the interface specified for use with Ultra-2 SCSI and Ultra160/m specifications.

While LVD is not directly compatible with single-ended wiring, the devices will use multimode driver circuits that automatically detect the type of bus used and switch to the appropriate mode of operation. This capability allows you to use an LVD/SE device on a single-ended bus without having to set any switches or jumpers. Therefore, LVD has been introduced gradually without the loss of the current investment in single-ended devices. Still, the advantages of LVD are lost when an LVD/SE device is used in a single-ended bus—as soon as one single-ended device is connected to an LVD/SE bus, the whole bus switches to single-ended mode (with all its limitations).

TERMINATORS

When high-frequency signals are transmitted over adjacent wires, signals tend to degrade and interfere with one another over the length of the cable. This is a very normal and relatively well understood electrical phenomenon. In the PC, SCSI signal integrity is enhanced by using powered resistors at each end of the data cable to "pull up" active signals. Most high-frequency signal cables in the PC are already terminated by built-in pull-up resistors at drives and controller cards. The small resistor array is known as a *terminator*. Since there is a distinct limit to the number of devices that can be added to a floppy drive or IDE cable, designers have never made a big deal about termination—they just added the resistors, and that was it. With SCSI, however, up to eight devices can be added to the bus cable. The SCSI cable also must be terminated, but the location of terminating resistors depends on which devices are added to the bus, and *where* they are placed. As a result, termination is a much more vital element of SCSI setup and troubleshooting. Poor or incorrect termination can cause intermittent signal problems. Later on, you'll see how to determine the proper placement of terminating resistors.

Termination is typically either active or passive. Basically, *passive* termination consists of simply plugging a resistor pack into a SCSI device. Passive resistors are powered by the TERMPWR line. Passive termination is simple and effective over short distances (up to about 1 meter) and usually works just fine for the cable lengths inside a PC, but can be a drawback over longer distances. *Active* terminators provide their own regulated power sources, which makes them most effective for longer cables (such as those found in external SCSI devices like page scanners) or Wide SCSI systems. Most SCSI-2 and later implementations use active terminators. A variation on active termination is *forced perfect termination* (FPT), which includes diode clamps that prevent signal overshoot and undershoot. This makes FPT effective for long SCSI cable lengths.

SCSI IDS AND LUNS

A typical SCSI bus will support up to eight devices, called *logical units*, each of which must have its own unique ID number (0 to 7). If two devices use the same ID, a conflict will result. IDs are typically set for the SCSI adapter and each SCSI device using jumpers or DIP switches (see Figure 34-2). Typically, the SCSI adapter is set for ID7, the primary SCSI hard drive is set to ID0, and a second SCSI hard drive is set to ID1. Other devices can usually be placed anywhere from ID2 to ID6.

Logical unit numbers (LUNs) are similar to SCSI IDs because both identify SCSI devices. However, LUNs indicate devices within devices—divisions within IDs. Every SCSI ID from 0 to 7 can have up to 8 LUNs (64 LUNs in SCSI-3), or eight subdevices for every given device ID. Suppose you needed to use more than eight devices on a SCSI bus. You could cause your device to respond to a SCSI ID, and have each device using the ID respond to a different LUN. For example, if you had three hard drives E:, F:, and G:, you could have all three drives use ID2, but E: could be assigned LUN0, F: could be assigned LUN1, and G: could be assigned LUN2. This is often the case with SCSI RAID systems in which far more drives are available than SCSI IDs. Unfortunately, a SCSI user cannot arbitrarily decide to use LUN assignments—the hardware must be designed for that purpose. Also, LUNs are seldom used, and many SCSI adapters don't

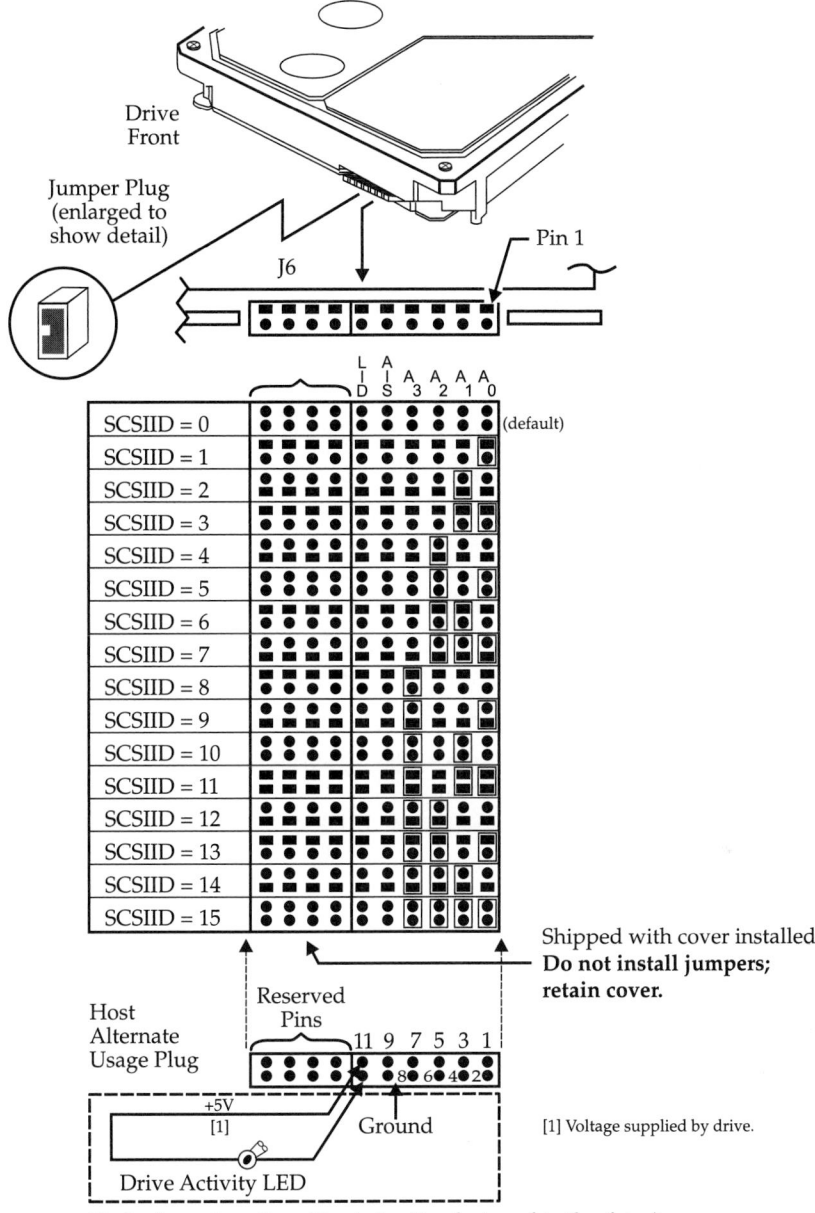

FIGURE 34-2   Setting a SCSI ID jumper (Courtesy of Seagate)

check for them. This shortcut speeds bus scanning a bit. If you have a device that uses LUNs (such as a CD jukebox), you may need to enable LUN support in the host adapter's BIOS or device driver.

BUS CONFIGURATIONS

Most common SCSI implementations currently available use single-ended cabling that supports an 8-bit data bus (known as an A-cable). An A-cable is a 50-pin assembly, as outlined in Table 34-3. The 50-pin single-ended SCSI cable has three major sections: ground wires, data signals, and control signals. You will notice that at least half of the single-ended interface carries ground lines. There are eight data lines (D0 to D7) and a data parity bit (DPAR). Note that SCSI parity is always odd. There are four terminator power lines (TERMPWR) and nine control signal wires. Each signal is explained here:

- **-C/D (Control/Data; driven by target)**   Allows the target device to select whether it will be returning a command or data to the initiator.

- **-I/O (Input/Output; driven by target)**   Allows the target device to determine whether it will be receiving or sending information along the data bus.

- **-MSG (Message; driven by target)**   Allows the target device to send coded status or error messages back to the initiator during the message portion of the SCSI bus cycle.

- **-REQ (Request; driven by target)**   A data strobe signal that allows a potential target device to obtain data on the bus.

- **-ACK (Acknowledge; driven by initiator)**   A data strobe signal sent in response to the target's REQ signal that informs the target device that it has gained use of the bus.

- **-BSY (Busy; driven by initiator or target)**   Allows a device to inform the bus that the device is currently busy.

- **-SEL (Select; driven by initiator or target)**   A signal used by an initiator to select a target device.

- **-ATN (Attention; driven by initiator)**   A signal produced by the initiator that informs the target that the initiator has a message ready. The target should switch to the message phase.

- **-RST (Reset; driven by initiator or target)**   A strobe signal that triggers a bus-wide reset of all devices. Usually, only one device produces a reset signal.

The differential SCSI interface replaces most of the ground wires with + signal leads. For example, pin 2 represents +D0, while pin 27 is -D0. These + and - signal pairs are the differential signals. Note that there are still a few ground wires, but the grounds are not related to differential signals as they are to single-ended signals. Just about all of the data and control signals in the differential interface serve an identical purpose in the single-ended interface, but you will notice that the signal locations have been rearranged, as shown in Table 34-4. There is one additional differential signal: the DIFFSENS (Differential Sense) line, which provides an active high-enable for differential drivers. Keep in mind that plugging a differential cable into a single-ended interface (or vice versa) can damage the device, the SCSI adapter, or both.

As you might imagine, Wide (16-bit) SCSI implementations will not work with A-cables. A 16-bit cable is needed. Early implementations of Wide SCSI used a second cable to provide the extra signal lines, but this approach was quickly abandoned in favor of a single cable assembly (called a P-cable). The single-ended P-cable is shown in Table 34-5. While many of the signals may look familiar, notice that there are 68 pins instead of 50—primarily to support the eight additional data lines (D8 to D15). Control lines are identical to those in the A-cable.

Table 34-6 shows the pinout for a differential 68-pin P-cable. The 80-pin implementation for a SCSI cable (called SCA-2) is listed in Table 34-7.

TABLE 34-3   PINOUT OF A STANDARD SINGLE-ENDED A-CABLE

SIGNAL	PIN	PIN	SIGNAL
Ground	1	2	Data 0
Ground	3	4	Data 1
Ground	5	6	Data 2
Ground	7	8	Data 3
Ground	9	10	Data 4
Ground	11	12	Data 5
Ground	13	14	Data 6
Ground	15	16	Data 7
Ground	17	18	Data Parity
Ground	19	20	Ground
Ground	21	22	Ground
Reserved	23	24	Reserved
Open	25	26	TERMPWR
Reserved	27	28	Reserved
Ground	29	30	Ground
Ground	31	32	-ATN
Ground	33	34	Ground
Ground	35	36	-BSY
Ground	37	38	-ACK
Ground	39	40	-RST
Ground	41	42	-MSG
Ground	43	44	-SEL
Ground	45	46	-C/D
Ground	47	48	-REQ
Ground	49	50	-I/O

TABLE 34-4   PINOUT OF A STANDARD DIFFERENTIAL A-CABLE

SIGNAL	PIN	PIN	SIGNAL
Ground	1	2	Ground
+Data 0	3	4	-Data 0
+Data 1	5	6	-Data 1
+Data 2	7	8	-Data 2
+Data 3	9	10	-Data 3
+Data 4	11	12	-Data 4
+Data 5	13	14	-Data 5
+Data 6	15	16	-Data 6
+Data 7	17	18	-Data 7
+Data Parity	19	20	-Data Parity
DIFFSENS	21	22	Ground
Reserved	23	24	Reserved
TERMPWR	25	26	TERMPWR
Reserved	27	28	Reserved
+ATN	29	30	-ATN
Ground	31	32	Ground

TABLE 34-4   PINOUT OF A STANDARD DIFFERENTIAL A-CABLE *(CONTINUED)*

SIGNAL	PIN	PIN	SIGNAL
+BSY	33	34	-BSY
+ACK	35	36	-ACK
+RST	37	38	-RST
+MSG	39	40	-MSG
+SEL	41	42	-SEL
+C/D	43	44	-C/D
+REQ	45	46	-REQ
+I/O	47	48	-I/O
Ground	49	50	Ground

TABLE 34-5   PINOUT OF A STANDARD SINGLE-ENDED P-CABLE

SIGNAL	PIN	PIN	SIGNAL
Ground	1	35	Data 12
Ground	2	36	Data 13
Ground	3	37	Data 14
Ground	4	38	Data 15
Ground	5	39	Data Parity 1
Ground	6	40	Data 0
Ground	7	41	Data 1
Ground	8	42	Data 2
Ground	9	43	Data 3
Ground	10	44	Data 4
Ground	11	45	Data 5
Ground	12	46	Data 6
Ground	13	47	Data 7
Ground	14	48	Data Parity 0
Ground	15	49	Ground
Ground	16	50	Ground
TERMPWR	17	51	TERMPWR
TERMPWR	18	52	TERMPWR
Reserved	19	53	Reserved
Ground	20	54	Ground
Ground	21	55	-ATN
Ground	22	56	Ground
Ground	23	57	-BSY
Ground	24	58	-ACK
Ground	25	59	-RST
Ground	26	60	-MSG
Ground	27	61	-SEL
Ground	28	62	-C/D
Ground	29	63	-REQ
Ground	30	64	-I/O

TABLE 34-5   PINOUT OF A STANDARD SINGLE-ENDED P-CABLE (*CONTINUED*)

SIGNAL	PIN	PIN	SIGNAL
Ground	31	65	Data 8
Ground	32	66	Data 9
Ground	33	67	Data 10
Ground	34	68	Data 11

TABLE 34-6   PINOUT OF A STANDARD DIFFERENTIAL P-CABLE

SIGNAL	PIN	PIN	SIGNAL
+Data 12	1	35	-Data 12
+Data 13	2	36	-Data 13
+Data 14	3	37	-Data 14
+Data 15	4	38	-Data 15
+Data Parity 1	5	39	-Data Parity 1
Ground	6	40	Ground
+Data 0	7	41	-Data 0
+Data 1	8	42	-Data 1
+Data 2	9	43	-Data 2
+Data 3	10	44	-Data 3
+Data 4	11	45	-Data 4
+Data 5	12	46	-Data 5
+Data 6	13	47	-Data 6
+Data 7	14	48	-Data 7
+Data Parity 0	15	49	-Data Parity 0
DIFFSENS	16	50	Ground
TERMPWR	17	51	TERMPWR
TERMPWR	18	52	TERMPWR
Reserved	19	53	Reserved
+ATN	20	54	-ATN
Ground	21	55	Ground
+BSY	22	56	-BSY
+ACK	23	27	-ACK
+RST	24	58	-RST
+MSG	25	59	-MSG
+SEL	26	60	-SEL
+C/D	27	61	-C/D
+REQ	28	62	-REQ
+I/O	29	63	-I/O
Ground	30	64	Ground
+Data	31	65	-Data
+Data	32	66	-Data
+Data	33	67	-Data
+Data	34	68	-Data

TABLE 34-7   80-PIN SINGLE-ENDED SCSI CABLE PINOUT

SIGNAL	PIN	PIN	SIGNAL
12 VOLT	1	41	12-volt GROUND
12 VOLT	2	42	12-volt GROUND
12 VOLT	3	43	12-volt GROUND
12 VOLT	4	44	12-volt GROUND
Reserved/NC	5	45	Reserved/NC
Reserved/NC	6	46	Reserved/NC
DB (11)	7	47	GROUND
DB (10)	8	48	GROUND
DB (9)	9	49	GROUND
DB (8)	10	50	GROUND
I/O	11	51	GROUND
REQ	12	52	GROUND
C/D	13	53	GROUND
SEL	14	54	GROUND
MSG	15	55	GROUND
RST	16	56	GROUND
ACK	17	57	GROUND
BSY	18	58	GROUND
ATN	19	59	GROUND
DB (P0)	20	60	GROUND
DB (7)	21	61	GROUND
DB (6)	22	62	GROUND
DB (5)	23	63	GROUND
DB (4)	24	64	GROUND
DB (3)	25	65	GROUND
DB (2)	26	66	GROUND
DB (1)	27	67	GROUND
DB (0)	28	68	GROUND
DB (P1)	29	69	GROUND
DB (15)	30	70	GROUND
DB (14)	31	71	GROUND
DB (13)	32	72	GROUND
DB (12)	33	73	GROUND
5 volt	34	74	5-volt GROUND
5 volt	35	75	5-volt GROUND
5 volt	36	76	5-volt GROUND
SYNC	37	77	ACTIVE LED OUT
RMT START	38	78	DLYD START
SCSI ID (0)	39	79	SCSI ID (1)
SCSI ID (2)	40	80	SCSI ID (3)

UNDERSTANDING SCSI BUS OPERATION

Now that you have learned about SCSI bus concepts and structure, you can see how the interface behaves during normal operation. Since bus wires are common to every device attached to the bus, a device must obtain permission from all other devices before it can take control of the bus. This attempt to access the bus is called the *arbitration phase*. Once a device (such as the SCSI controller) has won the bus arbitration, it must then make contact with the device to be communicated with. This device selection is known as the *selection phase*. When this contact is established, data transfer can take place. This part of the chapter will detail negotiation and information transfer over the SCSI bus.

Negotiation

Devices must negotiate to access and use a SCSI bus. Negotiation begins when the bus is free (BSY and SEL lines are idle). A device begins arbitration by activating the BSY line and its own data ID line (data bit D0 to D7, depending on the device). If more than one device tries to control the bus simultaneously, the device with the higher ID line wins. The winning device (an initiator) attempts to acquire a target device by asserting the SEL line and the data ID line (data bit D0 to D7) of the desired device. The BSY line is then released by the initiator, and the desired target device asserts the BSY line to confirm it has been selected. The initiator then releases the SEL and data bus lines. Information transfer can now take place.

Information

The selected target controls the data being transferred and the direction of transfer. Information transfer lasts until the target device releases the BSY line, thus returning the bus to the idle state. If a piece of information will take a long time to prepare for, the target can end the connection by issuing a *disconnect* message. It will try to reestablish the connection later with a new arbitration and selection procedure.

During information transfer, the initiator tells its target how to act on a command and establishes the mode of data transfer during the *message-out phase*. A specific SCSI command follows the message during the *command phase*. After a command is sent, data transfer takes place during the *data-in* and/or *data-out* phases. The target relinquishes control to the initiator during the command phase. For example, the command itself may ask that more information be transferred. The target then tells the initiator whether the command was successfully completed or not by returning status information during a *status phase*. Finally, the command is finished when the target sends a progress report to the initiator during the *message-in* phase. Consider this simple SCSI communication example:

1. *Bus free phase.* The system is idle.
2. *Arbitration phase.* A device takes control of the bus.
3. *Select phase.* The desired device is selected.
4. *Message-out phase.* The target sets up data transfer.
5. *Command phase.* Commands are exchanged between the target and initiator.
6. *Data-in phase.* Data is exchanged between the target and initiator.
7. *Status phase.* Results of the exchange are reported.
8. *Message-in phase.* Devices report that the exchange is complete.
9. *Bus free phase.* The system is idle.

Installing a SCSI System

Today, virtually all SCSI host adapters are PnP devices that are designed for automatic detection and resource assignment in a motherboard's PCI slot. Still, most SCSI host adapter problems *start* when the card is first installed in the system; problems are usually due to inadequate or incorrect installation of the hardware and software. This part of the chapter offers an overview of the SCSI adapter installation process and SCSI BIOS setup so that you can check your own installation for missing steps.

If your server motherboard incorporates a SCSI host adapter, you can generally skip the installation steps and focus on the SCSI setup and configuration issues.

INTERNAL HARDWARE INSTALLATION

Implementing SCSI on your server or workstation requires that you install a SCSI host adapter and at lease one SCSI device. The following steps outline the installation of a typical SCSI host adapter:

1. Shut down your system, and then turn off and unplug the computer.

2. Unbolt the outer case, and then remove the housing and set it (and the screws) aside in a safe place.

3. If you're replacing an existing SCSI host adapter with a newer, faster model, you'll need to remove the old SCSI adapter first. Disconnect the internal and external SCSI cable(s) from the SCSI adapter. Unbolt the old SCSI card bracket from the chassis and remove the old SCSI adapter from its expansion slot. Be sure to set the old SCSI adapter aside on a static-safe surface or in an antistatic bag.

4. Locate a slot for the new SCSI host adapter card. Most current SCSI host adapter devices will require a PCI slot, though some older SCSI cards will use an ISA slot. Find an available bus-mastering PCI slot that's appropriate for your SCSI adapter card. Remove the cover for the slot you intend to use (if it's not already removed) and save the screw for the mounting bracket.

5. Insert the SCSI host adapter card. Push the card in firmly and evenly until it's fully seated in the slot. Replace the screw to secure the bracket of your SCSI card to the computer's chassis.

6. If you're connecting any internal SCSI devices, plug the 50-pin or 68-pin SCSI connector on the end of the internal SCSI ribbon cable into the SCSI card's header. Make sure to align pin 1 on both connectors.

7. Connect your computer's drive activity LED cable to the appropriate connector on the SCSI card (if desired). This connection is designed to operate the front-panel LED found on most PC cabinets to indicate activity on the SCSI bus.

8. Make any external SCSI bus connections that may be required (for example, from your SCSI scanner or external SCSI drives).

The SCSI bus requires proper termination, and no duplicate SCSI IDs. Before you attempt to reboot the computer, verify the SCSI IDs for each SCSI device, and double-check the SCSI termination at the end(s) of your SCSI chain.

If your server's motherboard provides an onboard SCSI host adapter, remember that the onboard adapter may be terminated by default. If you cannot disable the onboard adapter's termination, you may be limited to using only internal or external SCSI devices, but not both. See your motherboard's documentation for specific limitations.

SOFTWARE INSTALLATION

Now that the physical hardware for your new SCSI host adapter card has been installed, it's time to install the SCSI adapter drivers and application software that you'll need to identify the device under the operating system. The following steps illustrate a typical procedure for Windows 98/Me, so check the adapter's recommendations for other operating systems. Leave the computer's housing off for now, but reconnect the AC cord to the computer and prepare to start the system again.

Always refer to the README file on the SCSI adapter card's driver disc to obtain the very latest feature descriptions and software installation guidelines for your particular card.

1. When Windows restarts, it should detect the SCSI host adapter automatically.

2. Click Driver From Disk Provided By Hardware Manufacturer. Then click OK.

3. Insert the driver CD into the CD-ROM, and then select the CD-ROM drive letter.

4. Click OK. Windows will load the SCSI adapter's drivers.

5. Once Windows finishes loading the information from the driver CD, verify that the SCSI adapter's installation was a success. When your desktop returns, click Start, highlight Settings, and then click Control Panel.

6. Double-click the System icon, and then click the Device Manager tab.

7. Double click on the SCSI Controllers branch to expand it.

8. See that your new SCSI host adapter is listed (Figure 34-3). If it is, your new SCSI host adapter is probably installed properly. You can exit the Device Manager and begin using your SCSI adapter. If it is not listed, you'll need to check the installation.

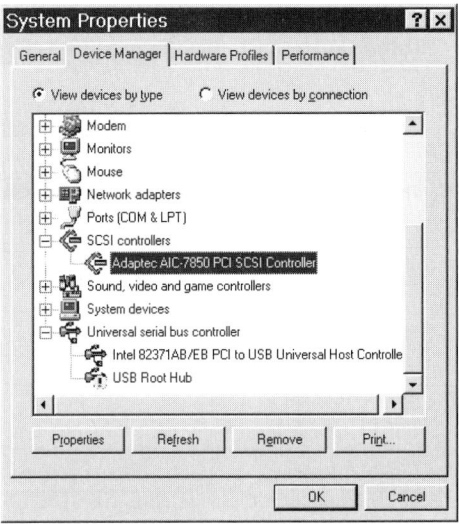

FIGURE 34-3   Checking the SCSI adapter after installation

Use the following steps to install software for Windows NT:

1. Open the Control Panel and double-click the SCSI Adapters icon.

2. The SCSI Adapters dialog box opens. Select the Drivers tab.

3. In the Install Driver dialog box, click Have Disk.

4. The Install From Disk dialog box opens and asks for the path to the drivers. If you're installing from a floppy disk, specify **a:**, and if you're installing from the HDD, specify the path to the HDD, such as **c:\advansys**.

5. The Install Driver dialog box returns and lists the drivers available for installation. Highlight the appropriate driver (such as AdvanSys Windows NT SCSI HBA Driver) and click OK. Windows NT may ask you to repeat the path to the drivers.

6. Drivers are now copied to the NT system. Remove the driver disk from the system and reboot Windows NT.

You can then confirm driver installation under Windows NT:

1. Open the Control Panel and double-click the SCSI Adapters icon.

2. The SCSI Adapters dialog box opens. Select the Devices tab.

3. One of the entries will list the SCSI driver (for example, AdvanSys Window NT SCSI HBA Driver), as shown in Figure 34-4. If you expand this entry, you should see all the active SCSI devices connected to the card.

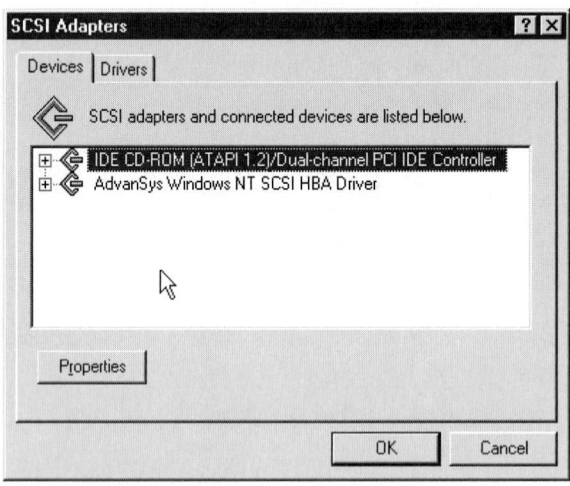

FIGURE 34-4   Checking a SCSI controller

CONFIGURING THE SCSI BIOS

Whether added as an expansion device or integrated into your server's motherboard, the vast majority of SCSI host adapters employ a BIOS (or *firmware*) to configure the adapter's various operations. In most cases, the default settings of your SCSI BIOS are adequate, and you should not need to change the default configuration of the host adapter. However, you may decide to alter these default values if there is a conflict between device settings, or if you need to optimize the system's performance. This part of the chapter outlines the default settings of a common Symbios SCSI host adapter and explains many of the SCSI BIOS settings that you may encounter. Typical default settings are listed in Table 34-8. The global settings affect your host adapter and all SCSI devices that are connected to it, but the device settings affect only individual SCSI devices.

The version number of your SCSI BIOS appears in a banner displayed on your computer monitor during boot. If a configuration utility is available, the following message (or something similar) also appears on your monitor:

```
Press Ctrl-C to start Symbios Configuration Utility...
```

This message remains on your screen for about five seconds, giving you time to start the utility. If you decide to press CTRL-C, the message changes to the following:

```
Please wait, invoking Symbios Configuration Utility...
```

After a brief pause, your computer monitor displays the Main menu of the Symbios SCSI BIOS Configuration Utility.

The SCSI BIOS Configuration Utility is a powerful tool. If you somehow disable all of your controllers while using it, pressing CTRL-A (or CTRL-E on version 4.04 or later) after memory initialization during reboot allows you to reenable the defaults and reconfigure your SCSI BIOS.

Not all devices detected by the Configuration Utility can be controlled by the BIOS. Devices such as tape drives and scanners require that a device driver specific to that peripheral be loaded. The device manufacturer provides the device drivers.

TABLE 34-8   TYPICAL DEFAULT SETTINGS FOR A SCSI HOST ADAPTER

GLOBAL DEFAULT SETTINGS	
SCAM Support	Off (applies to BIOS version 4.09 and later)
Parity Checking	Enabled
Host Adapter SCSI ID	7
Scan Order	Low to High (0 to Max)
DEVICE DEFAULT SETTINGS	
Synchronous Transfer Rate (MB/s)	40
Data Width	16
Disconnect	On
Read/Write I/O Time-out (seconds)	10
Scan for Devices at Boot Time	Yes
Scan for SCSI LUNs	Yes
Queue Tags	On

Main Menu   When you start the Symbios SCSI BIOS Configuration Utility, the Main menu appears. This menu displays a list of up to four Symbios PCI to SCSI host adapters in the system and information about each of them. To select an adapter, use only the arrow keys and the ENTER key. You can then view or change the current settings for that adapter and the SCSI devices attached to it. Select an adapter only if its Current Status is On. If any settings are altered, the system reboots upon exit from the Configuration Utility when you use the Quit option.

Change Adapter Status   This option allows you to activate or deactivate a host adapter and all SCSI devices attached to it. When this option is used to make a change, the change takes place after a reboot once you exit from the utility. To change an adapter's status, select it and press ENTER. Press the ESC key to exit from this menu and return to the Main menu.

Adapter Boot Order   This option allows you to set the order in which host adapters will boot (when more than one SCSI host adapter is in the system). When this option is selected, the Boot Order menu appears. To change an adapter's boot order, select it and press ENTER. The system prompts you to enter the new boot sequence number. To remove an adapter from the boot order, press ENTER again rather than entering a new sequence number. Only four adapters can be assigned a boot order, starting with boot sequence number zero (0). If an invalid number is entered, an error message appears. When the adapters are ordered properly, press the ESC key to exit from this menu.

Additional Adapter Configuration   This option allows you to configure an adapter that is not assigned a boot order. When this option is selected, the Adapter Configuration menu appears. Highlight the adapter to be configured and press ENTER. The message "Resetting adapter, please wait" appears, and then the system scans for devices. Finally, the Utilities menu appears and lists the available options.

Display Mode   This option determines how much information about your host adapter(s) and SCSI devices appears on the computer monitor during boot. For more complete information, choose the Verbose setting. For a faster boot, choose the Terse setting.

Mono/Color   This option allows a choice between a monochrome or color display for the SCSI BIOS Configuration Utility. Choose the Mono setting to get a more readable screen on a monochrome monitor (if necessary). In most cases, the Color option will yield the best results on color displays.

Language   When the Language option is enabled, you can select from one of several different languages (for example, English, German, French, Italian, and Spanish).

Utilities Menu   When you select a host adapter on the Main menu, the Utilities menu appears. Choose the Adapter Setup option to view and change the selected adapter settings. Choose the Device Selections option to view and change settings for the devices attached to the selected adapter. After making changes to the configuration of any host adapter or connected SCSI device, the system returns to the Utilities menu. Before you exit this menu, you're prompted to save or cancel any changes.

ADAPTER SETUP MENU

The settings in this menu are global settings that affect the selected host adapter and all SCSI devices attached to it. A choice can be selected by highlighting it and pressing ENTER:

SCAM Support   Symbios BIOS version 4.xx and above supports the SCSI PnP protocol called SCAM (SCSI Configured AutoMatically). SCAM support by default is *off* in versions 4.09 and later for the SYM53C875 controller. You may choose to turn this feature on *only* if the system drivers do not require SCAM to be off.

Parity   Symbios PCI SCSI host adapters always generate parity, but some older SCSI devices do not. You're offered the option of disabling parity checking. When disabling parity checking, it's also necessary to disable disconnects for all devices, as parity checking for the reselection phase is not disabled. If a device does not generate parity and it disconnects, the I/O cycle never completes because the reselection never finishes.

Host SCSI ID   The host adapter's SCSI ID (LUN) is a unique number used to identify the device on the SCSI bus. In general, it's suggested that you *not* change the host adapter ID from the default value of 7 (this ID gives the SCSI adapter the highest priority on the SCSI bus). Also, please note that if you have 8-bit SCSI devices (narrow), they cannot see host IDs greater than 7.

Scan Order   This option allows the user to tell the SCSI BIOS and device drivers to scan the SCSI bus from low to high (0 to Max) SCSI ID, or from high to low (Max to 0) SCSI ID. If more than one device is on the SCSI bus, changing the scan order changes the order in which drive letters are assigned by the system. Drive order may be reassigned differently in systems supporting the BIOS Boot Specification (BBS). This scan order option may conflict with operating systems that automatically assign a drive order.

Removable Media Support   This option defines the removable media support for a specific drive. When this option is selected, a window appears with three choices: None, Boot Drive Only, and With Media Installed. None indicates there is no removable media support. Boot Drive Only provides removable media support for a removable hard drive if it is first in the scan order. With Media Installed provides removable media support wherever the drive actually resides. One of these choices can be selected by highlighting it and pressing ENTER.

CHS Mapping   This option defines the cylinder head sector (CHS) values that will be mapped onto a disk without preexisting partition information. SCSI PnP Mapping is the default value. To support interchange with noncompatible systems, there is another option that can be selected by choosing CHS Mapping and then selecting Alternate CHS Mapping. Neither of these options will have any effect after the disk has been partitioned with the FDISK command. To remove partitioning, two options are available: reformat the disk using the Format Device option, and use the FDISK /MBR command at the C:\ prompt (where MBR is the master boot record). After clearing the partitions and data, it is necessary to reboot and clear memory, or the old partitioning data will be reused, thus nullifying the previous operation.

Spinup Delay (seconds)   This option allows you to stagger spinups for a longer period of time to balance the total current load. The default value is 2 seconds, with choices between 1 and 10 seconds. This is a power management technique designed to accommodate disk devices that may have heavy current loads during power-up. If multiple drives are being powered up simultaneously and drawing heavy current, this option staggers the spinups to limit startup current.

DEVICE SELECTIONS MENU

The settings in this menu affect individual SCSI devices attached to the selected host adapter. Changes made from this menu do *not* cause the system to reboot upon exit from the SCSI BIOS Configuration Utility.

Sync Rate (MB/s)   This option defines the maximum data transfer rate at which the host adapter will attempt to negotiate. The host adapter and a SCSI device must agree to a rate they can both handle.

Width (Bits)   This option defines the maximum SCSI data width at which the host adapter will attempt to negotiate. The host adapter and a SCSI device must agree to the data width they can both handle. Only host adapters that can handle 16-bit data transfers have this option enabled.

Disconnect   SCSI devices have the ability to disconnect from the initiator during an I/O transfer. This option frees the SCSI bus to allow other I/O processes. It also tells the host adapter whether or not to allow a device to disconnect. Some devices run faster with disconnects enabled (mostly newer devices), while some run faster with disconnects disabled (mostly older devices).

Read Write I/O Time-Out (Seconds)   This option sets the amount of time the host adapter waits for a read, write, or seek command to complete before trying the I/O transfer again. This option is intended to allow the system to recover if an I/O operation fails, and it is recommended that you always set the time-out to a value greater than zero. A zero value allows unlimited time for an operation to complete, and could result in the system being hung up.

Scan for Device at Boot Time   Set this option to No if there is a device that you do not want to be available to the system. On a bus with only a few devices attached, you can speed up boot time by changing this setting to No for all unused SCSI IDs.

Scan for SCSI Logical Units (LUNs)   Set this option to No if problems arise with a device that responds to all LUNs whether they are occupied or not. For example, if a SCSI device with multiple LUNs is present on your system, but you do not want all of those LUNs to be available to the system, then set this option to No. This will limit the scan to LUN 0 only.

Queue Tags   If the device driver supports this capability, this option allows you to enable or disable the issuing of queue tags during I/O requests.

Initial Boot   This option allows any device attached to the first adapter to become the boot device. It provides the users of non-BBS personal computers with some of the flexibility of a BBS machine.

Format Device   If enabled, this option allows the user to low-level format a magnetic disk drive. Low-level formatting will completely and irreversibly erase all data on the drive. Formatting will default the drive to a 512-byte sector size even if the drive had previously been formatted to another sector size.

Verify   This option allows the user to read all the sectors on a disk looking for errors. When selected, this option displays the following message: "Verify all sectors on the device. Press ESC to abort. Press any key to continue."

Restore Default Setup   This option resets all device selections back to their default settings. Select this option to restore all manufacturing defaults for the specified adapter. Note that all user-customized options will be lost upon saving after restoring the default setup.

EXITING THE SCSI BIOS

Since some changes take effect only after the system reboots, it is important that you exit this Configuration Utility properly. Return to the Main menu and exit using the Quit option. Rebooting the system without properly exiting from this utility may cause some changes to *not* take effect.

SCSI Considerations

Whether you're considering adding SCSI support to your own computer or planning an upgrade for a customer, there are four essential elements that you must consider: the SCSI peripheral(s), the SCSI host adapter, the SCSI cable assembly, and the SCSI software driver(s). If any one of these four elements is missing or ill-planned, your installation is going to run into problems.

SCSI PERIPHERALS

The first items to be considered are the SCSI peripherals themselves. You first need to know what types of devices are needed (such as a SCSI hard drive or CD-ROM). The peripheral should be compatible with the architecture of your controller (for instance, SCSI-3 or SCSI-4). You may also find a growing base of Ultra160/m-compliant adapters and peripherals. Each SCSI peripheral device should also have a wide range of available SCSI ID settings. SCSI typically handles eight IDs (0 to 7), and the peripheral should have the flexibility to run on virtually any ID. If only a few IDs are available, you may be limited when it comes time to add other SCSI devices. Peripherals should support SCSI parity.

Ideally, a SCSI-4 host adapter should support SCSI-3 and SCSI-2 devices. If you have any intention of employing SCSI-4 devices, be sure to use a SCSI-4 adapter.

SCSI devices are available in both internal and external versions. If you consider an internal peripheral, make sure that there is adequate drive space in the PC to accommodate the new peripheral. (Either a drive bay is available, or an existing device may be removed to make room.) If the peripheral is to be an external device (such as a printer or scanner), there should be two SCSI connectors on the device, to allow for daisy-chaining additional devices later. All SCSI peripherals other than hard drives will require device drivers. Make sure that the device driver is compatible with the same standard protocol used by the adapter (such as ASPI, CAM, or LADDR). Compatibility is a serious consideration since peripherals using incompatible device driver standards will not work properly. Finally, try to choose SCSI peripherals that offer built-in cable termination.

SCSI HOST ADAPTER

The next item to be considered is the SCSI host adapter (often just called a host or HA), which fits in the PC expansion bus. Make sure to choose an adapter that is compatible with the PC bus in use (either ISA or PCI). Bus-mastering 32/64-bit PCI SCSI adapters will provide superior performance if your system will support them. Like the peripheral itself, the adapter should also be designed to support the SCSI-3 standard (or SCSI-4 if possible). Although most adapters are assigned a SCSI ID of 7, the adapter should be flexible enough to work with any ID from 0 to 7. The host adapter will also require a device driver for using devices other than hard drives. Make sure that the host device driver uses the same standard as the peripheral(s) (ASPI, CAM, or LADDR). It is important to note here that the driver standard has nothing to do with the choice of SCSI-2, SCSI-3, or SCSI-4. It is only important that the peripherals and the adapter use the *same* driver standard.

SCSI CABLES AND TERMINATORS

Check that you select the proper cabling for the SCSI level you are using. Although SCSI cabling is now highly standardized, some older cables may use slight modifications for particular peripherals (typical with SCSI-1 devices). Be certain that you know of any specialized cabling requirements when choosing peripherals. Try to avoid specialized cabling if at all possible, but if you *must* use specialized cabling, you should determine what impact the cabling will have on any other SCSI peripherals that may be installed (or may be installed later). Use good-quality SCSI cables specifically intended for the SCSI level you are using (probably SCSI-3/4), and keep the cables short to minimize signal degradation.

SCSI cables must be terminated at the beginning (host adapter) and end (after the last device) of the SCSI chain. Try to choose internal peripherals that have built-in terminators. Also try to select a host adapter and peripherals that use the same type of terminator resistor network. SCSI-2 and later systems use active terminator networks. You will see much more about cabling and termination a bit later in this chapter.

Remember that SCSI host adapters integrated onto server motherboards may have fixed termination enabled, and you may not be able to run both internal and external devices from that controller.

SCSI DRIVERS

Device drivers provide the instructions that allow the SCSI host adapter to communicate with the PC, as well as with the peripherals in the SCSI chain (or the SCSI *bus*). The host adapter itself will require a device driver, as will every peripheral that is added. For example, a SCSI system with one CD-ROM will need a driver for the host adapter and a driver for the CD-ROM. Make sure that driver standards (ASPI, CAM, or LADDR) are the *same* for the host adapter and peripherals. The only exception to the device driver requirement (at this time) is the SCSI hard drive, which may be supported by the SCSI adapter's BIOS ROM.

Real-mode device drivers are added by including them in your PC's CONFIG.SYS and AUTOEXEC.BAT files. One issue to keep in mind when adding device drivers is that drivers use *conventional* memory (unless you successfully load the drivers into high memory). The more drivers that are added, the more memory that will be consumed. It is possible that a large number of device drivers may prevent certain memory-demanding DOS applications from running. To keep as much conventional memory (the first 640KB in RAM) as free as possible, use the DOS devicehigh and loadhigh features to load the drivers into upper memory (from 640KB to 1MB in RAM). Windows 9x/Me/NT avoids this problem by using protected-mode drivers for the host adapter and devices.

TIPS FOR A SMOOTH INSTALLATION

SCSI is not a terribly difficult technology to implement properly, but the subtle considerations and inconsistencies that have always been a part of SCSI implementations can result in confusion and serious delays for you and your customer. The following tips should help to ease your upgrades:

■ *Add only add one SCSI device at a time.* By adding one device at a time and testing the system after each installation, it becomes much easier to determine the point where problems occur. Imagine what happens when you add an adapter, hard drive, and CD-ROM without performing checks. If the system fails to function, you will have to isolate and check each item to locate the fault. On the other hand, by adding the adapter and testing it, adding the hard drive and testing it, and then adding the CD-ROM and testing it, installation troubleshooting becomes a much simpler matter (although it may take a bit more time overall).

■ *Record the host adapter's resources.* One of the most difficult aspects of troubleshooting is determining the configuration of a system. This determination is especially important during an upgrade since you *must* know the interrupts (IRQs), DMA channel(s), and I/O ranges used by other expansion devices in the PC. Any overlap in the use of these system resources will eventually result in a hardware conflict. When you install a SCSI host adapter, make it a point to record its IRQ, DMA, and I/O settings along with the SCSI ID settings of all devices that are installed. Tape the record to the inside of the PC's cover—next time the PC returns for service or upgrade, you'll have the information right at your fingertips.

■ *Use good-quality cabling.* Using the correct terminators and cables can have a profound effect on the performance of your SCSI installation. Good-quality cables and terminators provide electrical characteristics that support good signal transfer, resulting in good data reliability between the host controller and peripherals. If cable quality is substandard or terminators are not correct for the SCSI level being used, the cable's electrical characteristics and data transfer will be degraded.

CABLING AND TERMINATION

Once the host adapter and peripheral are configured and installed, you must connect them with a cable. Internal devices are typically connected with a 68-pin IDC (insulation displacement connector) ribbon cable (a P-cable). By placing multiple connectors along the length of cable, daisy-chaining can be achieved with a single connector on each internal device. External devices typically connect to an external 68-pin connector on the rear of the SCSI adapter, and each device offers two connectors to allow daisy-chaining to additional devices. Most commercial adapter and drive kits are packed with an appropriate cable.

The cable(s) must be terminated. There are internal and external SCSI cable terminators, along with SCSI devices that have terminating resistor networks already built in. The concept of termination is reasonably simple: achieve the desired signal cable characteristics by *loading* each end of the SCSI chain with resistors. If the chain is not terminated properly, signals will not be carried reliably (which invariably results in system errors). For technicians and end users alike, the trouble usually arises in determining where the ends are. A number of examples will help to clarify how to determine the chain ends.

For a single SCSI drive and adapter, as shown in Figure 34-5, the ends are easy to see. One end should be terminated at the host adapter (which usually has terminating resistors built in). The other end should be terminated at the SCSI hard drive (which also usually has terminating resistors built in). In this type of situation, you need only connect the cable between both devices and verify that the terminators are in place.

When a second SCSI peripheral is added, as shown in Figure 34-6, termination becomes a bit more complex. Suppose a CD-ROM is added with a SCSI ID of 6. The terminator on the existing SCSI hard drive is no longer appropriate—it should be removed, and the termination should be made on the CD-ROM, which is now the *last device* in the SCSI chain. In most cases, a terminator network can be deactivated by flipping a DIP switch or changing a jumper on the peripheral itself. If the terminator cannot be shut off, it can almost always be removed by gently easing the resistor network out of its holder using needle-nose pliers. If you remove a terminator, place it in an envelope and tape it to the inside of the PC enclosure. If it is simply impossible to remove the existing terminator on the hard drive, place the CD-ROM between the adapter and hard drive and remove the CD-ROM's terminator (rearrange the chain). The SCSI host adapter must remain terminated.

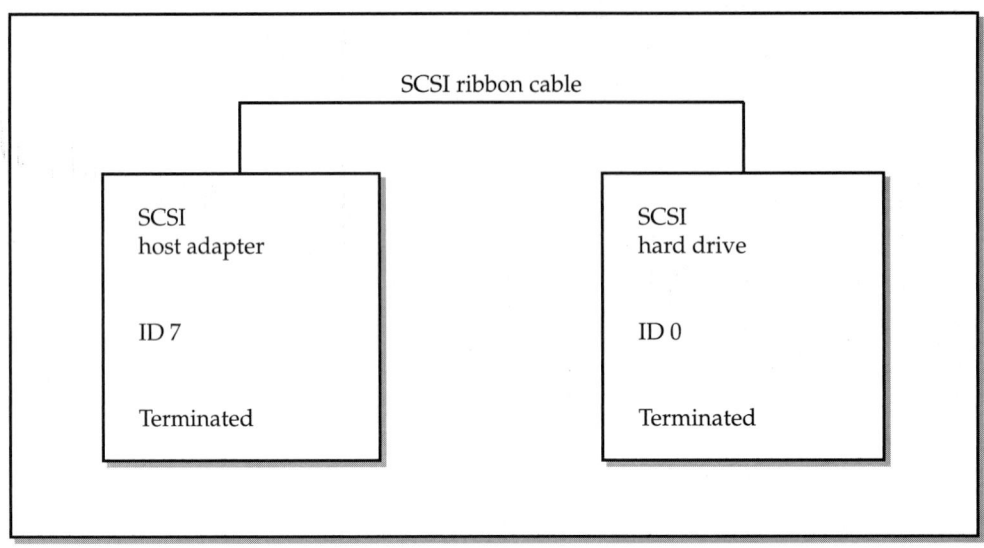

Inside the PC

FIGURE 34-5   Terminating an internal SCSI adapter and hard drive

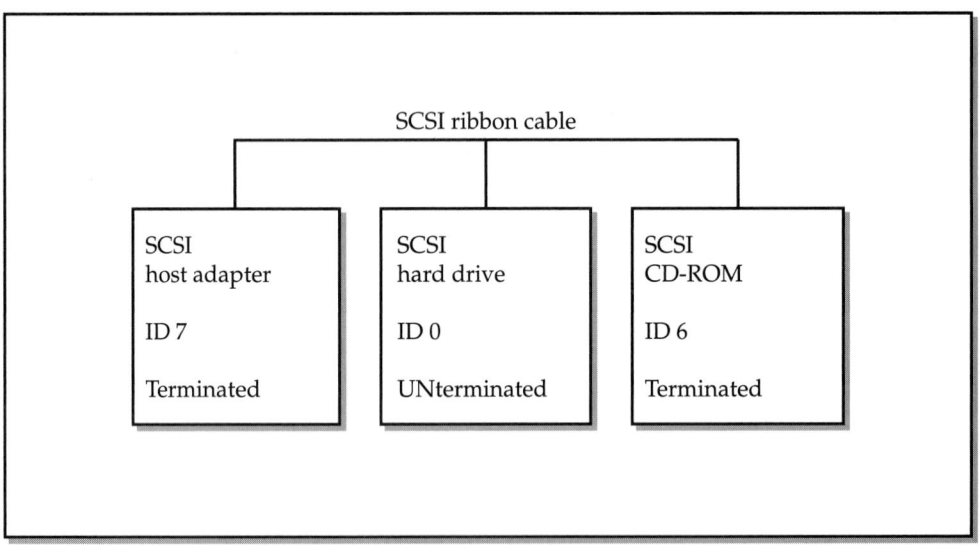

Inside the PC

FIGURE 34-6   Terminating an internal SCSI adapter, HDD, and CD-ROM

So what happens if an *external* device is used (such as a scanner), as in Figure 34-7? An external cable connects the adapter to the scanner. Since the scanner (ID 6) and adapter (ID 7) are the only two points in the chain, both are terminated. Most external devices designed for SCSI-2 compatibility allow the active terminator built into the peripheral to be switched off if necessary.

Suppose both an internal *and* an external SCSI device are being used, as shown in Figure 34-8. The SCSI host adapter (ID 7) is no longer at an end of the chain, so its terminator should be switched off or removed. It is the internal hard drive (ID 0) and external scanner (ID 6) that now form the ends, so both devices should be terminated. Since both peripherals should ideally support internal termination, nothing needs to be done except to confirm that the terminators are in place and switched on.

REAL-MODE SCSI DRIVER ISSUES

Hardware configuration and installation are only one part of the SCSI installation. Software needs to be installed to allow the hardware to interact with your system. The problem with SCSI drivers is that, prior to 1991, various drivers were rarely compatible. For example, an adapter and hard drive may have worked fine, but adding a CD-ROM would create havoc since the CD-ROM driver was not compatible with the hard drive or the host adapter driver (or both). After 1991, a set of universal driver standards appeared that created a buffer between the operating system and hardware that isolated each particular driver from the others. Drivers can now be written for each peripheral without worry of incompatibility, as long as the drivers are written to be compatible with the standard.

There are typically three competing SCSI standards: ASPI (Advanced SCSI Programming Interface), CAM (Common Access Method), and LADDR (Layered Device Driver Architecture). ASPI is certainly

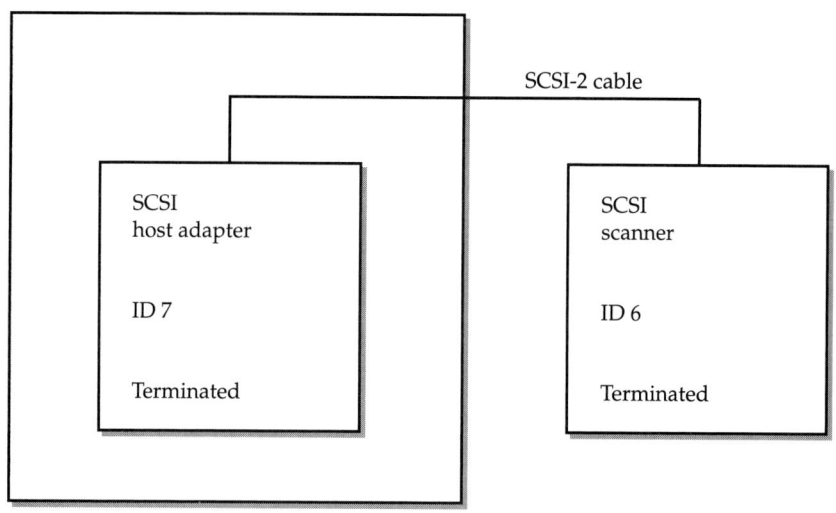

Inside the PC

FIGURE 34-7   Terminating an external SCSI device

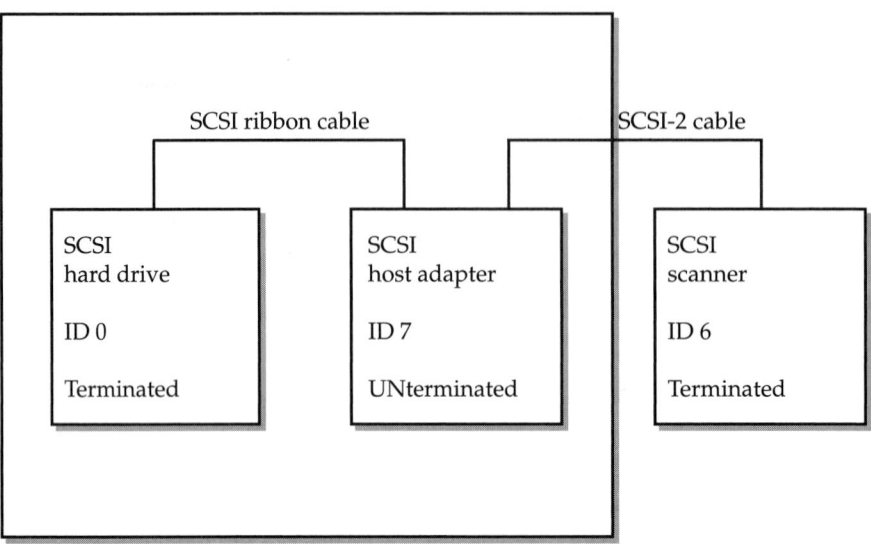

Inside the PC

FIGURE 34-8   Terminating mixed internal and external SCSI devices

the most popular of the three standards. The object of compatibility is to select a host adapter and peripherals that support the *same* standard. For example, if you select a host adapter that uses an ASPI driver, each of the peripherals that you choose must also use ASPI drivers. If you upgrade the host adapter later, you also upgrade the host's ASPI driver—full compatibility *should* be maintained.

The actual installation process varies little from other software installations. The real-mode driver files for your adapter and peripheral(s) are copied to a subdirectory on the hard drive, and then the CONFIG.SYS and AUTOEXEC.BAT files are updated to load the appropriate drivers on system startup. If your particular system commits too much conventional memory to drivers, you can manually optimize your startup files later to load as many drivers as possible into upper memory.

TIPS FOR WINDOWS SCSI DRIVERS

If you intend to use your SCSI system under Windows 98/Me/NT/2000, you'll need to install protected-mode drivers for the host adapter and devices. Contemporary SCSI host adapters (and many SCSI devices) are compliant with plug-and-play operation under Windows 98/Me/NT/2000. This means Windows typically should be able to identify the SCSI adapter (or newly installed devices) and install the appropriate protected-mode drivers for it. Ordinarily, this process should be automatic, but you may need to use the SCSI Adapters icon in the Control Panel to verify the controller's installation:

■ Verify the SCSI adapter and devices in DOS first with its real-mode drivers.

■ If Windows does *not* automatically identify the SCSI hardware, you should run the SCSI Adapters wizard to register the device(s) and install the protected-mode drivers (remember *not* to let Windows detect devices itself).

■ You can use the SCSI Adapters wizard to update existing SCSI drivers if new versions become available.

If your SCSI hardware is not listed in the SCSI Adapters wizard, you'll need to contact the hardware manufacturer(s) and download the correct protected-mode drivers. If there are no protected-mode drivers for your SCSI hardware (that would be rare today), you'll need to use the real-mode (DOS) drivers. Doing this may result in all system drives running in DOS Compatibility Mode and impair system performance.

Troubleshooting the SCSI System

As far as the *bus* is concerned, very little can go wrong—wires and connectors do not fail spontaneously. However, it never hurts to examine the wiring, connectors, and terminator network(s) to ensure that the physical connections are intact (especially after installing or configuring new devices). The most likely areas of trouble are in the installation, setup, and operation of the devices residing on the bus.

ISOLATING TROUBLE SPOTS

Assuming that your SCSI devices have been installed correctly, problem scenarios can occur during normal operation. The first indication of a problem usually comes in the form of an error message from your operating system or application program. For example, your SCSI hard drive may not be responding, or the host PC may not be able to identify the SCSI host controller board, and so on.

The advantage to SCSI architecture is that it is reasonably easy to determine problem locations using intuitive deduction. Consider a typical SCSI system with one initiator (a host controller) and one target (such as a hard drive). If the hard drive fails to function, the trouble is either in the host controller or the drive itself. When you see drive access being attempted, but an error is generated, the trouble is probably in the drive. If no drive access is attempted before an error is generated, the error is likely in the host controller. As another example, consider a setup with one initiator and two or more targets (a hard drive and CD-ROM). If *both* the hard drive and CD-ROM become inoperative, the problem is likely in the host controller card, since the host adapter controls both targets. If only *one* of the devices becomes inoperative (and the other device works just fine), the trouble is likely in the particular device itself.

USING SCSI AND IDE DEVICES

Most experienced technicians can recall trouble when mixing SCSI and IDE-type drives on the same system, resulting in boot problems and BIOS conflicts. Today, those issues have largely been resolved, so follow these points when mixing SCSI and IDE (EIDE/UDMA) support on the same PC:

- SCSI cards (such as Adaptec cards) can generally coexist with another controller (such as EIDE or UDMA) installed in the computer.

- If you have both an EIDE/UDMA hard disk drive and a SCSI hard disk drive, the IDE-type drive is typically the boot drive. In this case, disable the BIOS on the SCSI card according to the SCSI host adapter's instructions.

- If your computer supports BBS, *both* SCSI and non-SCSI disk drives can coexist and you can specify which drive to boot from. For example, you can elect to boot from a SCSI drive, even if IDE-type drives are in the system. Check your system documentation for specific instructions and limitations.

- You cannot connect an IDE-type device to a SCSI card, or a SCSI device to an IDE controller card.

- Disable the BIOS on the SCSI card if no SCSI hard disk drives are installed.

GENERAL TROUBLESHOOTING TIPS

No matter how many precautions you take, you cannot always prevent problems from striking during SCSI installations or replacements. Fortunately, if you are installing devices one by one, as suggested, you will have far fewer problem areas to check. Your first diagnostic for a SCSI installation should be the host adapter's SCSI BIOS initialization message. If you see no initialization message when the system powers up, any problem is likely to be with the host adapter itself. Either it is not installed properly or it is defective. Make sure that the adapter is set to the desired ID (usually 7). Try a new or alternate SCSI adapter. If the adapter provides its initialization message as expected, the problem is probably related to driver installation. Check the installation and any command-line switches for each device driver. When installing a SCSI hard drive instead of IDE hard drives, you must ensure that any previous hard drive references are mapped out of the CMOS Setup by selecting "none" or "not installed." If preexisting drive references are not removed, the system will try to boot from IDE drives that aren't there.

Be aware that faulty SCSI ID settings can result in system problems such as "ghost" disks—disks that the system says are there but that cannot be read from or written to. Some peripherals may also not work properly with the ID that has been assigned. If you have problems interacting with an installed device, try the device with a different ID, and make sure that no two devices are using the *same* ID. Don't be surprised to find that certain types of cables don't work properly with SCSI installations. Make sure that everything is terminated correctly. Also be sure that any external SCSI devices are powered up (if possible) before the PC is initialized. If problems persist, try different cables. The following is a quick-reference checklist:

- Check the power to all SCSI devices (make sure that the power supply has enough capacity to handle all of your attached SCSI devices).

- Check the 50/68-pin signal cable to all SCSI devices. It should be a good-quality cable that is attached securely to each device.

- Check the orientation of each connector on the SCSI cable. Pin 1 must always be in the proper orientation.

- Check the SCSI ID of each device. Duplicate IDs are *not* allowed unless you're using LUN designations, which can occur when using a large number of SCSI devices, such as a RAID system.

- Check that both ends of the SCSI cable are properly terminated and that the terminators are active.

- Check the SCSI controller's configuration (IRQ, I/O, BIOS addresses, and so on). Verify that the SCSI controller is not conflicting with other devices in the system.

- Check the SCSI host adapter BIOS. If you're not booting from SCSI hard drives, you can often leave the SCSI BIOS disabled. This will also simplify the device configuration. You may be able to upgrade the host adapter's BIOS to resolve performance problems or compatibility issues.

- Check the CMOS Setup for drive configurations. When SCSI drives are in the system and IDE/EIDE drives are not, be sure that the drive entries under CMOS are set to "none" or "not installed."

- Check the PCI bus configuration in the CMOS Setup. See that the PCI slot containing the SCSI host adapter is active and is using a unique IRQ (usually named IRQ A). PCI bus mastering should also be enabled.

- Check for the real-mode drivers under DOS. If you're working under DOS, see that any needed drivers for the host adapter and non-HDD devices are installed in the CONFIG.SYS and AUTOEXEC.BAT files.

■ Check for the protected-mode drivers under Windows 98/Me/NT/2000. If you're working under Windows, see that any needed protected-mode drivers for the host adapter and SCSI devices are installed. The SCSI host adapter should be properly identified in the SCSI Adapters wizard.

■ Try REMarking out real-mode drivers if problems occur only under Windows 98/Me/NT/2000. Real-mode SCSI drivers can sometimes interfere with protected-mode SCSI drivers. If the SCSI system works fine in DOS, but not in Windows, try temporarily disabling the DOS drivers in your startup files.

SCSI SYMPTOMS

Even the best-planned SCSI setups go wrong from time to time, and SCSI systems already in the field will not run forever. Sooner or later, you will have to deal with a SCSI problem. This part of the chapter is intended to show you a variety of symptoms and solutions for many of the problems that you will likely encounter.

SYMPTOM 34-1   **After initial SCSI installation, the system will not boot from the floppy drive**   You may or may not see an error code corresponding to this problem. Suspect the SCSI host adapter first. There may be an internal fault with the adapter that is interfering with system operation. Check that all of the adapter's settings are correct and that all jumpers are intact. If the adapter is equipped with any diagnostic LEDs, check for any problem indications. When adapter problems are indicated, replace the adapter board. If a SCSI hard drive has been installed and the drive light is always on, the SCSI signal cable has probably been reversed between the drive and adapter. Make sure to install the drive cable properly.

Check for the SCSI adapter BIOS message generated when the system starts. If the message does not appear, check for the presence of a ROM address conflict between the SCSI adapter and ROMs on other expansion boards. Try a new address setting for the SCSI adapter. If there is a BIOS wait-state jumper on the adapter, try changing its setting. If you see an error message indicating that the SCSI host adapter was not found at a particular address, check the I/O setting for the adapter.

Some more recent SCSI host adapters incorporate a floppy controller. This can cause a conflict with an existing floppy controller. If you choose to continue using the existing floppy controller, be sure to disable the host adapter's floppy controller. If you'd prefer to use the host adapter's floppy controller, remember to disable the preexisting floppy controller port.

SYMPTOM 34-2   **The system will not boot from the SCSI hard drive**   Start by checking the system's CMOS Setup. When SCSI drives are installed in a PC, the corresponding hard drive reference in the CMOS Setup must be changed to "none" or "not installed" (this assumes that you will *not* be using IDE/EIDE hard drives in the system). If you have not mapped out previous hard drive references, do so now, save the CMOS Setup, and reboot the PC. If the problem persists, check that the SCSI boot drive is set to ID 0. You will need to refer to the user manual for your particular drive to find how the ID is set.

Next, check the SCSI parity to be sure that it is selected consistently among all SCSI devices. Remember that *all* SCSI devices must have SCSI parity enabled or disabled. If even one device in the SCSI chain does not support parity, it must be disabled on *all* devices. Check the SCSI cabling to be sure that all cables are installed and terminated properly. Finally, be sure that the hard drive has been partitioned and formatted properly. If it has not, boot from a floppy disk and prepare the hard drive as required using FDISK and FORMAT.

SYMPTOM 34-3   **The SCSI drive fails to respond with an alternate HDD as the boot drive**   Technically, you should be able to use a SCSI drive as a nonboot drive (such as drive D:) while using an IDE/EIDE drive as the boot device. If the SCSI drive fails to respond in this kind of arrangement, check the CMOS setting to be sure that drive 1 (the SCSI drive) is mapped out (or set to "none" or "not installed"). Save the CMOS Setup and reboot the PC. If the problem persists, check that the SCSI drive is set to SCSI ID 1 (the nonboot ID). Next, make sure that the SCSI parity is enabled or disabled consistently throughout the SCSI installation. If the SCSI parity is enabled for some devices and disabled for others, the SCSI system may function erratically. Finally, check that the SCSI cabling is installed and terminated properly. Faulty cables or termination can easily interrupt a SCSI system. If the problem persists, try another hard drive.

Later SCSI host adapters use BIOS that allows SCSI drives to boot even with IDE/EIDE drives in the system. In such a configuration, the Boot Order entry in CMOS Setup will determine whether A:, C:, or SCSI will be the boot device.

SYMPTOM 34-4   **The SCSI drive fails to respond with another SCSI drive as the boot drive**   This typically occurs in a dual-drive system using two SCSI drives. Check the CMOS Setup and make sure that both drive entries in the setup are set to "none" or "not installed." Save the CMOS Setup. The boot drive should be set to SCSI ID 0, while the supplemental drive should be set to SCSI ID 1 (you will probably have to refer to the manual for the drives to determine how to select a SCSI ID). The hard drives should have a DOS partition and format. If not, create the partitions (FDISK) and format the drives (FORMAT) as required. Check to be sure that SCSI parity is enabled or disabled consistently throughout the SCSI system. If some devices use parity and other devices do not, the SCSI system may not function properly. Make sure that all SCSI cables are installed and terminated properly. If the problem persists, try systematically exchanging each hard drive.

SYMPTOM 34-5   **The system works erratically. The PC hangs or the SCSI adapter cannot find the drive(s)**   Such intermittent operation can be the result of several different SCSI factors. Before taking any action, be sure that the application software you were running when the fault occurred did not cause the problem. Unstable or buggy software can seriously interfere with system operation. Try different applications and see if the system still hangs. (You might also try any DOS diagnostic utilities that accompanied the host adapter.) Check each SCSI device and make sure that parity is enabled or disabled consistently throughout the SCSI system. If parity is enabled in some devices and disabled in others, erratic operation can result. Make sure that no two SCSI devices are using the same ID. Cabling problems are another common source of erratic behavior. Make sure that all SCSI cables are attached correctly and completely. Also check that the cabling is properly terminated.

Next, suspect a possible resource conflict between the SCSI host adapter and another board in the system. Check each expansion board in the system to be sure that nothing is using the same IRQ, DMA, or I/O address as the host adapter (or check the Device Manager under Windows 9x/Me). If you find a conflict, you should alter the most recently installed adapter board. If problems persist, try a new drive adapter board.

SYMPTOM 34-6   **You see an 096xxxx error code**   This is a diagnostic error code that indicates a problem in a 32-bit SCSI host adapter board. Check the board to be sure that it is installed correctly and completely. The board should not be shorted against any other board or cable. Try disabling one SCSI device at a time. If normal operation returns, the last device to be removed is responsible for the problem. (You may need to disable drivers and reconfigure termination when isolating problems in this fashion.) If the problem persists, remove and reinstall all SCSI devices from scratch or try a new SCSI adapter board.

SYMPTOM 34-7   **You see a 112xxxx error code**   This diagnostic error code indicates a problem in a 16-bit SCSI adapter board. Check the board to be sure that it is installed correctly and completely. The board should not be shorted against any other board or cable. Try disabling one SCSI device at a time. If normal operation returns, the last device to be removed is responsible for the problem. (You may need to disable drivers and reconfigure termination when isolating problems in this fashion.) Try a new SCSI host adapter board.

SYMPTOM 34-8   **You see a 113xxxx error code**   This is a diagnostic code that indicates a problem in a system (motherboard) SCSI adapter configuration. If a SCSI BIOS ROM is installed on the motherboard, be sure that it is up-to-date and installed correctly and completely. If problems persist, try replacing the motherboard's SCSI controller chip or the system board. It may be possible to circumvent a damaged motherboard SCSI controller by disabling the motherboard's controller and then installing a SCSI host adapter card.

SYMPTOM 34-9   **You see a 210xxxx error code**   There is a fault in a SCSI hard disk. Check that the power and signal cables to the disk are connected properly. Make sure the SCSI cable is correctly terminated. Try repartitioning and reformatting the SCSI hard disk. Finally, try a new SCSI hard disk.

SYMPTOM 34-10   **A SCSI device refuses to function with the SCSI adapter even though both the adapter and device check properly**   This is often a classic case of basic incompatibility between the device and host adapter. Even though SCSI-2 and later standards help to streamline compatibility between devices and controllers, there are still situations when the two just don't work together. Check the literature included with the finicky device for any notices of compatibility problems with the controller (perhaps the particular controller brand) you are using. If there are warnings, there may also be alternative jumper or DIP switch settings to compensate for the problem and allow you to use the device after all. A call to technical support at the device's manufacturer may reveal any recently discovered bugs or fixes (for example, an updated SCSI BIOS, SCSI device driver, or host adapter driver). If problems remain, try using a similar device from a different manufacturer (for example, try a Connor tape drive instead of a Mountain tape drive).

SYMPTOM 34-11   **You see a "No SCSI Controller Present" error message**   Immediately suspect that the controller is defective or installed improperly. Check the host adapter installation (including IRQ, DMA, and I/O settings) and see that the proper suite of device drivers has been installed correctly. If the system still refuses to recognize the controller, try installing it in a different PC. If the controller also fails in a different PC, the controller is probably bad and should be replaced. However, if the controller *works* in a different PC, your original PC may not support all the functions under the interrupt 15h call required to configure SCSI adapters (such as an AMI SCSI host adapter). Consider upgrading the PC BIOS ROM to a new version—especially if the PC BIOS is older. There may also be an upgraded SCSI BIOS or host adapter driver to compensate for this problem.

SYMPTOM 34-12   **The PCI SCSI host adapter is not recognized, and the SCSI BIOS banner is not displayed**   This often occurs when installing new PCI SCSI host adapters. The host computer must be PCI REV. 2.0 compliant, and the motherboard BIOS must support PCI-to-PCI Bridges (PPB) and bus mastering; this is typically a problem (or limitation) with some older PCI motherboard chipsets, and you'll probably find that the PCI SCSI adapter board works just fine on newer systems. If the system *doesn't* support PPB, it may not be possible to use the PCI SCSI adapter. You can try an ISA SCSI adapter instead or upgrade the motherboard to one with a more recent chipset.

If the system hardware *does* offer PPB support and the problem persists, the motherboard BIOS may still not support PPB features as required by the PCI 2.0 standard. In this case, try a motherboard BIOS upgrade if one is available. If the problem continues, either the board is not in a bus mastering slot or the PCI slot is not enabled for bus mastering. Configure the PCI slot for bus mastering through CMOS Setup or through a jumper on the motherboard (check your system's documentation to see exactly how to do this).

SYMPTOM 34-13   **During boot-up, you see a "Host Adapter Configuration Error" message**   In virtually all cases, this indicates a problem with the PCI slot configuration for the SCSI host adapter. Try enabling an IRQ for the SCSI adapter's PCI slot (usually accomplished through the CMOS Setup). Make sure that any IRQ being assigned to the SCSI adapter PCI slot is not conflicting with other devices in the system.

SYMPTOM 34-14   **You see an error message such as "No SCSI Functions in Use"** Even when a SCSI adapter and devices are installed and configured properly, there are several possible causes for this kind of an error. First, make sure that no hard disk drivers are installed when no physical SCSI hard disks are in the system. Also make sure that no hard disk drivers are installed (in CONFIG.SYS) when the SCSI host adapter BIOS is enabled. HDD drivers aren't needed then, but you could leave the drivers in place and disable the SCSI BIOS. Finally, this error can occur if the HDD was formatted on another SCSI controller that does not support ASPI or uses a specialized format. For example, Western Digital controllers only work with Western Digital HDDs. In this case, you should try a more generic controller.

SYMPTOM 34-15   **You see an error message such as "No Boot Record Found"** This is generally a simple problem which can be traced to several possible issues. First, chances are that the drive has never been partitioned (FDISK) or formatted as a bootable drive (FORMAT). Repartition and reformat the hard drive. If you partitioned and formatted the drive with a third-party utility (such as TFORMAT), be sure to answer "Y" if asked to make the disk bootable. A third possibility can occur if the disk was formatted on another manufacturer's controller. If this is the case, there may be little alternative but to repartition and reformat the drive again on your current controller.

SYMPTOM 34-16   **You see an error such as "Device fails to respond—No devices in use. Driver load aborted"**   In most cases, the problem is something simple such as the SCSI device not being turned on or cabled correctly. Verify that the SCSI devices are on and connected correctly. In other cases, the SCSI device is on but fails the INQUIRY command. This happens when the SCSI device is defective or is not supported by the host adapter. The device may need default jumper settings changed (for example, the drive should Spin up and Come Ready on its own). You may find that the SCSI device is sharing the same SCSI ID with another device. Check all SCSI devices to verify that each device has a separate SCSI ID. You may have the wrong device driver loaded for your particular device type. Check CONFIG.SYS to make sure the correct driver is loaded for the drive type (for example, TSCSI.SYS for a hard disk, not a CD-ROM).

SYMPTOM 34-17   **You see an error such as "Unknown SCSI Device" or "Waiting for SCSI Device"**   The SCSI hard disk has failed to boot as the primary drive. Check that the primary hard disk is set at SCSI ID 0. Make sure that the drive is partitioned and formatted as the primary drive. If necessary, boot from a floppy with just the ASPI manager loaded in CONFIG.SYS and no other drivers, and *then* format the drive. It may also be that the SCSI cable termination is not correct (or TERMPWR is not provided by the HARD DISK for the host adapter). Verify the cable terminations and TERMPWR signal.

SYMPTOM 34-18   **You see an error such as "CMD Failure XX"**   This typically occurs during the FORMAT process. The XX is a vendor-specific code, and you'll need to contact the vendor to determine what the error means. The most common problem is trying to partition a drive that is *not* low-level formatted. If this is the case, run the low-level format utility that accompanied the SCSI drive, and then try partitioning again. If you're experiencing a different error, you may need to take other action, depending on the nature of the error.

SYMPTOM 34-19   **After the SCSI adapter BIOS header appears, you see a message like "Checking for SCSI target 0 LUN 0"**   The system pauses about 30 seconds and then reports "BIOS not installed, no INT 13h device found." The system then boots normally. In most cases, the BIOS is trying to find a hard drive at SCSI ID 0 or 1, but no hard drive is available. If you do not have a SCSI hard drive attached to the host adapter, then it is recommended that you disable the SCSI BIOS.

SYMPTOM 34-20   **The system hangs when the SCSI BIOS header appears**   This is usually caused by a terminator problem. Make sure that the SCSI devices at the end of the SCSI chain (either internally or externally) are terminated. Check all device IDs to make sure that they are unique, and also check for system resource conflicts (such as BIOS address, I/O address, and interrupts). You may also need to disable the Shadow RAM feature in the CMOS Setup.

SYMPTOM 34-21   **The SCSI BIOS header is displayed during system startup, and then you get the message "Host Adapter Diagnostic Error"**   The card either has a port address conflict with another card, or has been changed to port address 140h and the BIOS is enabled. Some SCSI host adapters are able to use the BIOS under port address 140h, so check for I/O conflicts. You may need to reconfigure the SCSI host adapter.

SYMPTOM 34-22   **When installing an EISA SCSI adapter and running the EISA configuration utility, you see an "EISA configuration slot mismatch" or "Board not found in slot x" error**   This error is caused by your board not being completely seated in the EISA slot. You can verify this by booting to a floppy disk and running the DOS Debug command. After typing **debug**, you will receive the debug prompt (a dash). Then type **i Xc80**, where X is the EISA slot in which your board is physically installed. If 04 is returned, the board is correctly seated and the problem lies elsewhere. If FF is returned, the board needs to be pushed down further. Power down your system before reseating your board.

SYMPTOM 34-23   **You can't configure an EISA SCSI adapter in enhanced mode**
You get the error "Unable to initialize Host Adapter" or the system hangs after the SCSI BIOS scans the SCSI devices. These errors are usually limited to motherboards that do not support LEVEL INT triggering. These chipsets (such as the Hint and SIS) require that a few modifications be made to the host adapter's EISA configuration (.CFG) file. Make the following changes to the !ADP000X.CFG file:

```
CHOICE = "Enhanced Mode"
FREE
INT=IOPORT(1) LOC (7 6 2 1 0) 10000B
LINK
IRQ=11|12|10|15|14|9
SHARE = "AHA-1740"              (Change to: SHARE = NO)
TRIGGER = LEVEL                (Change to: TRIGGER = EDGE)
```

```
INIT=IOPORT(3) LOC(4 3 2 1 0) 10010B | 10011B | 10001B | 1010B | 10101B | 10000B
(Change first zero in each binary number to a one; Example: 10010B = 11010B)
```

Another option is to download the latest .CFG file for your SCSI adapter card (such as ASWC174.EXE). Reconfigure the card with the new .CFG file and select Edge Triggered IRQ.

SYMPTOM 34-24   **Adaptec EZ-SCSI software causes an "Invalid Page Fault" error under Windows 9x/Me**   When you reinstall the Adaptec EZ-SCSI version 4.0x software, you may receive the following error message:

```
ADPST32 caused an invalid page fault in module MSCUISTF.dll at
015f:007d1bf7.
```

After you receive this error message, the computer may hang. This problem can be caused when an Adaptec 3940UW Dual Channel SCSI adapter is installed on your computer, when you previously set the Write and Read Cache settings to Enable in SCSI Explorer (included with EZ-SCSI 4.0x), or when you uninstalled the EZ-SCSI software and then restarted the computer before attempting to reinstall the EZ-SCSI software. You should restore the firmware defaults for the SCSI BIOS:

1. Reboot the computer. When you see the SCSI BIOS banner, press CTRL-A to start the SCSI BIOS Setup program.

2. In the SCSI BIOS Setup program, press F6 (or other appropriate) to restore the factory default settings. You must do this for both channels if you're using a dual-channel SCSI host adapter.

3. Turn your computer off and back on.

4. Uninstall and then reinstall the EZ-SCSI software.

SYMPTOM 34-25   **You encounter problems with a BusLogic PCI SCSI controller**
The Windows 9x/Me Device Manager displays an exclamation point in a yellow circle next to the PCI BusLogic SCSI Controller entry, or the system performance is not as good as you expect with the PCI BusLogic SCSI controller. This fault can occur if the BusLogic card is not configured as a "true" PCI device.

To configure the BusLogic card as a "true" PCI device, remove the jumpers in the bottom-right corner of the card. If you remove the jumpers, the card can be enumerated. If you leave the jumpers on the card, the card is detected as a "legacy" device and is not enumerated by the PnP system. Also, if you leave the jumpers on, the I/O range is set to a standard address (such as 330h, 334h, 130h, or 134h) instead of a high PCI address. As a rule, if the version number in the top-right corner of the BusLogic card is -01-4.23K or later, the card is supported in true PCI mode and you should remove the jumpers. If the version is earlier than -01-4.23K, leave the jumpers on the card.

SYMPTOM 34-26   **You encounter problems with an Adaptec SCSI controller and CD-RW drive**   Your computer may hang when you start your Windows 98 computer, or your computer may run slowly when you try to access drives in your computer. This problem can occur if you're using an Adaptec AHA-2940U2W SCSI host adapter with a SCSI CD-RW drive. The AIC78U2.MPD driver file included with the Adaptec AHA-2940U2W SCSI adapter is *not* completely compatible with Windows 98. To correct this problem, download the 7800W9X.EXE file from Adaptec's Web site (**www.adaptec.com**). This self-extracting file contains updated drivers for the Adaptec AHA-2940U2W SCSI adapter.

SYMPTOM 34-27   **Windows 98 cannot locate the SCSI CD-ROM after upgrading**
When Windows 98 Setup restarts your computer for the first time, Setup may be unable to access your SCSI CD-ROM drive, and you may receive error messages stating that files cannot be found (the file names vary depending on your computer's hardware). Once Setup is completed and you attempt to start Windows 98, your computer may hang, and only a blinking cursor may be displayed on a black screen. In virtually every case, this problem will occur if the HIDE120.COM file (a file related to an LS120 drive) is being loaded from the AUTOEXEC.BAT file. Open your AUTOEXEC.BAT file and disable (that is, REM out) the HIDE120 command line, such as:

```
REM d:\lsl120\hide120.com
```

SYMPTOM 34-28   **You see an error such as "Too many devices are terminated on the SE connectors"**   The SCSI card BIOS has detected that more than two devices have been terminated on the narrow SE (single-ended) SCSI segment. Verify the termination on the devices connected to the internal and external 50-pin connectors. Terminate *only* the SCSI device at the ends of the cable. Remove or disable the terminators on the SCSI devices between the ends of the cable.

SYMPTOM 34-29   **You see an error such as "Insufficient termination detected on the SE connectors"**   The SCSI card BIOS has detected that either only one or no devices have been terminated on the narrow SE SCSI segment. Verify the termination on the devices connected to the internal and external 50-pin connectors. Terminate the SCSI devices at the ends of the cable and leave the other devices unterminated.

Understanding FireWire and FibreChannel

SCSI has traditionally been an 8-bit or 16-bit "parallel" standard allowing a wide variety of devices to communicate with the host computer at high speeds. Although designers constantly struggle to improve SCSI performance, it's clear that technical issues in cabling and controllers present some serious challenges to faster parallel SCSI. As part of today's SCSI-3 standards, designers have developed two serial SCSI approaches: FireWire (IEEE 1394) and FibreChannel (FC). This part of the chapter explores the main ideas behind FireWire and FibreChannel.

ABOUT FIREWIRE

Simply put, the IEEE 1394 interface is a remarkably fast and effective high-speed serial SCSI interface that is intended to support peripheral data transfers between demanding peripheral devices. This technology was originally developed by Apple, but was eventually adopted by the IEEE as an official industry standard. Operating at speeds up to 400 Mb/s (megabits per second), systems supporting IEEE 1394 have 30 times more bandwidth than USB (though USB is not in the SCSI family). IEEE 1394 also includes automatic configuration *without* the need for device IDs or terminators, hot swapping of peripherals, and support for up to 63 devices (on cables up to 15 feet long). This technology permits the addition of a virtually unlimited amount of data storage capacity through the use of multiple external hard drives.

Given its high speed, IEEE 1394 technology is perfectly suited for multimedia peripherals, hard drives, and printers. It's becoming the interface of choice for moving audio files and the images from video camcorders and digital cameras. More and more computer users are employing IEEE 1394 for their multimedia, home entertainment, and data processing applications. IEEE 1394 is gaining support as a solution for many applications outside of the computer industry. FireWire is offered as a standard interface on many new consumer digital devices, including camcorders, still cameras, and even the newest game consoles. When redefining the MIDI standard with MIDI 2, music manufacturers have chosen IEEE 1394 as the new-generation interface for electronic musical instruments and high-performance editing systems. A group of VCR manufacturers also has adopted IEEE 1394 as the video interface for its next generation of products. The Video Electronics Standards Association (VESA) has selected IEEE 1394 for its home-distribution network in such systems as set-top boxes and high-definition television.

Installing an IEEE 1394 Adapter

To employ IEEE 1394 devices on your computer, you need to install an IEEE 1394 adapter card. This part of the chapter explains the proper installation and setup of a typical IEEE 1394 adapter. Before you get started, make sure that your system meets the minimum requirements for an IEEE 1394 adapter:

- Pentium 200 MHz processor or better
- 32MB of RAM or more
- Available PCI card slot on the motherboard
- Windows 98 SE (Second Edition) or higher
- CD-ROM drive (for loading drivers)

Verify that you have Windows 98 SE or later installed on your system by right-clicking My Computer and selecting Properties. The General tab in System Properties should indicate Windows 98 Second Edition.

The steps that follow describe how to install the IEEE 1394 adapter card in one of your computer's PCI slots. If you don't have a PCI slot available, you need to disable and remove another PCI device, or upgrade your motherboard to a model offering more PCI slots.

1. With your computer shut down and unplugged, remove the system's outside cover.

2. Install the adapter in an open PCI slot in your computer by carefully pushing the adapter into the PCI slot, holding the card by the external edges only.

3. Secure the card into place with a single chassis screw.

4. Close your computer. Reattach the power cable, power-up the system, and allow the system to restart normally.

5. After your computer has finished rebooting, insert your Windows 98 SE CD.

6. Windows will detect that you've installed new hardware, and launch the Add New Hardware wizard. The wizard searches for new drivers for your IEEE 1394 adapter. Click Next.

7. Make sure the Search For The Best Driver For Your Device option is selected. Click Next.

8. Windows will search for the new drivers. Be sure to select the CD-ROM Drive check box, and deselect the Floppy Disk Drives check box. Click Next.

9. The Add New Hardware wizard defaults to the updated drive. Click Next.

10. Click Next again so that Windows can install the best driver for the adapter.

11. Windows finishes installing software for your adapter. Click Finish. You may need to restart the computer so that the basic adapter will be detected.

If you plan on capturing video and audio to your system, plan on at least 50 to 60MB per minute (perhaps as much as 100MB per minute). You will need a tremendous amount of storage space for digital video capture and editing.

Software Setup

Although Windows 98/Me/2000 should offer adequate support for IEEE 1394 adapters, you will probably need to install the specific drivers that accompanied the particular adapter in order to guarantee best results. Follow these steps:

1. Insert the IEEE 1394 adapter's CD into your CD-ROM drive. The Autorun program will start automatically in a few seconds.

2. The main menu appears, showing several options. Click Setup 1394 Adapter.

3. The 1394 Adapter Setup Welcome screen appears. Click Next.

4. In the Driver Update dialog box, click Next to continue. This will prepare your system to support your specific IEEE 1394 adapter.

5. Click Next again to verify that you have the latest IEEE 1394 drivers from Microsoft.

6. Under Windows 98 SE, your IEEE 1394 adapter software is ready to finalize your setup. Click Finish when you see the Congratulations screen, to update your 1394 drivers and install a safe-removal utility that allows you to safely remove any of your plug-and-play devices.

7. The Windows 98/SE Update dialog box appears. Click Yes to continue and load the update.

8. The license agreement for the Windows 98/SE Update appears. Click Yes to continue. You must restart your computer for the new settings to take effect. When prompted to restart the system, click Yes.

Windows 2000 already has the required IEEE 1394 driver support. Click Next when the FireWire device is detected. When the Congratulations screen appears, click Finish and then restart your computer.

Connecting IEEE 1394 Devices

Once your IEEE 1394 adapter is installed on a Windows 98/Me platform, it's time to connect your individual devices. In most cases, connecting IEEE 1394 devices is a simple matter, but you need to remember some rules:

■ IEEE 1394 devices can be connected in any combination of branching and chaining, as long as no loops are formed.

■ An IEEE 1394 bus can support up to 16 consecutive cable hops of 4.5 meters (14.76 feet) each.

■ There are no SCSI-style ID numbers to set, and no termination requirements.

■ To connect a digital video (DV) camcorder, digital still camera, scanner, printer, or other IEEE 1394 peripheral, simply plug the 6-pin connector on the supplied FireWire cable to the IEEE 1394 adapter, and attach the 4-pin connector to the device's IEEE 1394 port. Both connectors snap into place when properly engaged.

■ If you wish to connect two devices together (or if your device has a 6-pin IEEE 1394 port), you can obtain 6-pin to 6-pin FireWire cables at your favorite retailer.

■ If you have problems with high-bandwidth FireWire devices (such as digital video transfers), make certain that no other FireWire devices are being used at the same time.

In addition to these general guidelines, you need to keep in mind the following list of important things that you should not do:

■ Do not connect more than 63 devices at one time (including computers).

■ Do not connect devices in such a way that any two devices have more than 16 cables directly connected between them.

■ Do not connect IEEE 1394 cables in a way that forms a "ring" of devices.

■ Leave unused 1394 connections empty—there are *no* terminators for FireWire connections.

■ Connect devices that require power from an IEEE 1394 port directly to the computer—*not* to another device.

■ Do not unplug an IEEE 1394 device while it is being used. For example, do not unplug an IEEE 1394 hard drive while copying files onto it.

Working with FireWire Hard Drives

While IEEE 1394 has seen service mainly in digital video work, drive manufacturers (such as Western Digital) have recently introduced a line of external FireWire hard drives. By using the IEEE 1394 interface, FireWire hard drives can be installed quickly and easily with no real configuration issues (you don't even have to shut down the PC). Remember that FireWire hard drives are external peripherals that operate through an IEEE 1394 adapter card. Most current PCs should easily meet the minimum system requirements, but it's certainly worth a moment to verify the requirements before attaching devices.

Make sure that you have Windows 98/Me (or Windows 2000) installed on your system by right-clicking My Computer and selecting Properties. The General tab in System Properties should show Windows 98 Second Edition or later.

IEEE 1394 hard drives are precision instruments. As with any internal hard drive, they should be handled with care during unpacking and installation. FireWire drives are not intended to be portable drives, so rough handling, shock, or vibration may damage them. Do not unpack your drive until you're ready to use it.

Once you've opened your drive to install it, take a moment to record the serial number and model number from the drive mechanism. You'll need this information when setting up the drive.

Installing a FireWire Hard Drive

The installation of an IEEE 1394 hard drive is remarkably straightforward, but you need to install some supporting software for the drive. You generally need the following items to ensure a smooth installation:

■ IEEE 1394 hard drive

■ A 6-pin to 6-pin IEEE 1394 cable

■ An AC power adapter for the drive

■ IEEE 1394 hard drive's CD

You should connect your new IEEE 1394 hard drive to your computer *before* performing any setup procedures. For best results, be sure to follow these steps:

1. Connect the AC power adapter to the power socket on the IEEE 1394 hard drive, and then plug the AC adapter into an electrical outlet.

2. Turn on your IEEE 1394 hard drive (move the drive's power switch to the On position).

3. Power-up your computer.

4. Plug one end of the FireWire cable (included) into any FireWire port on your computer.

5. Plug the other end of the FireWire cable into either of the IEEE 1394 hard drive's ports (port A or port B).

If you do not follow this process, it may take longer for the PC to recognize the IEEE 1394 hard drive.

6. Once the system has booted, insert the IEEE 1394 hard drive's CD into your CD-ROM drive. The setup program will start automatically. If the program does not start automatically, open Windows Explorer, click the CD-ROM drive icon, and then double-click the SETUP.EXE file.

7. When the Main Menu dialog box appears, select Setup 1394 Hard Drive.

8. The license agreement appears. Click I Accept.

9. The Setup 1394 Device dialog box appears next, showing the drive(s) detected in your system. Check the serial number of your new IEEE 1394 hard drive and make sure it matches the serial number displayed in this dialog box.

10. Once you're sure that the program has selected your new IEEE 1394 hard drive, click Setup. This process may take several minutes.

11. After the basic installation is complete, you may be prompted to register your new IEEE 1394 hard drive. If so, click Register Now and follow the instructions.

If you're working under Windows 2000, you already have the required IEEE 1394 driver support. Follow these steps:

1. When the Congratulations dialog box appears, click Finish and you will be taken back to the Main menu.

2. Click Exit in the Main menu, and then click Close to restart your computer and have the new settings take effect.

3. If you're working under Windows 98 SE, you may need to update the Windows drivers. After registering your drive, the Driver Update dialog box prompts you to update your 1394 storage drivers. It is usually recommended that you click Finish so that you may safely unplug your 1394 hard drive from your computer later.

4. The Windows 98/SE Update dialog box appears. Click Yes to continue and complete your installation.

5. The Microsoft license agreement for the Windows 98/SE Update then appears. Click Yes to continue.

6. You must restart your computer for the new settings to take effect, so click Yes when prompted to restart the system.

If you encounter any operating system issues, check for a newer version of the IEEE 1394 drivers on Microsoft's Web site.

Disconnecting a FireWire Hard Drive

FireWire allows for hot-pluggable devices, so a hard drive may be connected or disconnected while the PC is running. However, you should follow the protocol outlined next before disconnecting your drive; otherwise, data loss may result.

1. Click the Windows Unplug Or Eject Hardware icon in your system tray (located in the bottom-right corner of your screen).

2. Click Stop Hard Drive OHCI IEEE 1394 Host Controller.

3. In the dialog box that appears, select your IEEE 1394 hard drive from the list, and then click Stop.

4. In the next dialog box, stop the IEEE 1394 hard drive and prepare it for safe removal by clicking OK.

Do not unplug your 1394 hard drive while copying files. This could result in data loss and disk damage.

FIBRECHANNEL

FibreChannel is another powerful variation of the serial SCSI-3 standards allowing for very fast data transfers between devices over a relatively simple copper or fiber cable. Bandwidth is the main advantage of FibreChannel. Remember that the peak bandwidth of UltraWide SCSI is 40 MB/s, and UltraWide2 SCSI offers a maximum bandwidth of 80 MB/s. However, FibreChannel offers a current bandwidth of 100 Mb/s, and is expected to achieve 200 Mb/s and 400 Mb/s in the future. Another significant advantage of FibreChannel is increased transmission distance. With parallel SCSI, the maximum distance between a host server and an external storage device is 12 feet (or 3.5 meters). Using fiber-optic cable, a FibreChannel interconnect can easily achieve transmission distances of about 500m. With more advanced fiber-optic equipment, FibreChannel can transfer data for distances of up to about 10km. Such huge distances allow for remote mirroring of data at very high data rates, effectively providing off-site data storage in real time. The longer communication links of FibreChannel also allow multiple systems to share the same storage facilities.

Given its speed and distance advantages, FibreChannel is expected to be a key technology for high-speed storage interconnections (such as processor-to-storage and storage-to-storage communications) and for the serial drive interface (in high-performance disk systems). FibreChannel allows for the integration of primary and secondary storage, as well as for shared storage among multiple servers. FibreChannel has also become a serious player in Gigabit Ethernet, a high-speed extension to Ethernet. It leverages the physical advantages and encoding used in FibreChannel data transfers. Gigabit Ethernet provides the high-speed local area network (LAN), while FibreChannel provides the high-speed storage area network (SAN). A FibreChannel SAN allows a client attached to a specific processor to access data in any storage device within the SAN because all storage devices are accessible to all processors.

FC Topologies

FibreChannel adapters (called *nodes*) each have one or more ports that enable external communication. Each port uses two "fibres"—one for outgoing information, and the other for incoming information. The pair of fibres is called a *link*. All the components that connect FC ports comprise an interconnect topology. The two basic topologies used today to provide connectivity between FibreChannel ports are FibreChannel-Arbitrated Loop (FC-AL) and the fabric switch. A typical FibreChannel card is shown in Figure 34-9.

FC-AL is a serial interface that creates logical point-to-point connections between ports with the minimum number of transceivers and without a centralized switch. FC-AL therefore provides a less expen-

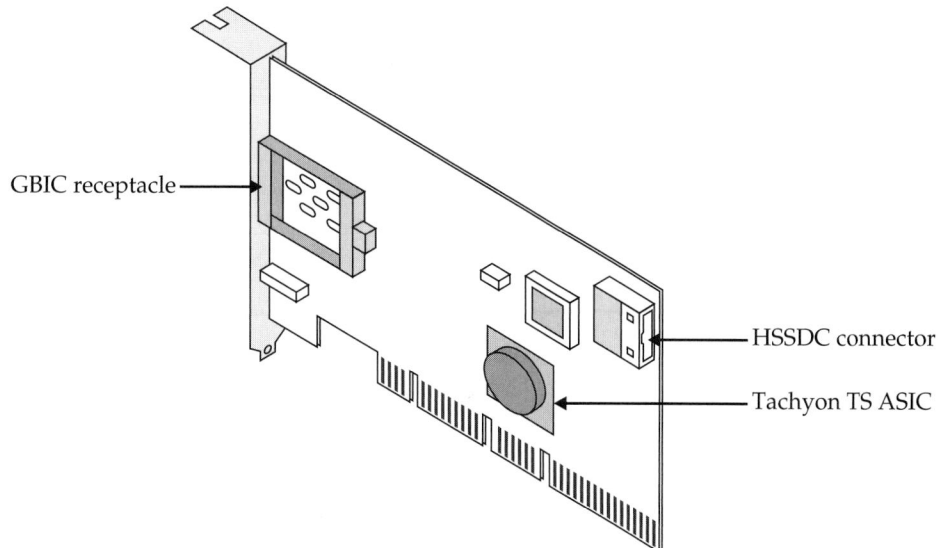

GBIC receptacle

HSSDC connector

Tachyon TS ASIC

FIGURE 34-9   A typical FibreChannel host adapter (Courtesy of Adaptec)

sive connection scheme. All ports on the loop share the bandwidth of a FibreChannel loop. A single pair of ports on the loop communicate at one time, while the other ports on the loop act as repeaters. More than 100 devices (or nodes) can be attached on a single FC-AL loop. Large subsystems of devices can be attached to nodes on expansion modules, and expansion modules can be cascaded to connect many more subsystems.

Hubs are useful in configuring FC-AL. A hub contains several ports that are internally connected in a loop. Each port is fitted with an electronic bypass switch to maintain the continuity of the loop should a controller (or device attached to the port) be powered off or malfunction. A hub port can also accept either electrical (copper) or optical (fiber) input, so the hub can support long- or short-distance communication. For example, if you want to locate the hub and controllers some distance from the server, an optical connection could be used between the server and hub, while copper connections could be used between the hub and local controllers.

By comparison, a *fabric switch* allows multiple pairs of nodes to communicate with each other simultaneously. So, as more nodes are added, the total data throughput capability can increase incrementally. A fabric switch requires a cross-point switching device (with the intelligence to make the switching connections). A pair of transceivers is required to form the link between the FC port and the port on the switch (transceivers add to the cost of the switch).

Functional Levels and Service Classes
Five functional levels are included in the FibreChannel standard, dubbed FC-0 to FC-4. You should understand the basic outline of each level:

■   **FC-0**   Defines the physical characteristics of the interface and media. The standard includes many variations to allow for maximum flexibility while employing existing media and different technologies. For example, FC-0 includes copper and fiber-optic media with speeds of 12.5 MB/s and increasing to 1.0625 Gb/s (commonly referred to as full speed). Speeds of 2 to 4 Gb/s have also been addressed by the standards working group responsible for FibreChannel development.

- **FC-1**   Defines the encoding/decoding and transmission protocol. The 8B/10B code is an 8-bit byte encoded into 10 bits for transmission, and then decoded at the receiving end. This approach has excellent transmission properties, and allows for low-cost component design, clock recovery, and error detection. Some of the unused code points are used to form special characters (such as ordered sets for signaling and frame delineation).

- **FC-2**   Defines how data is transported from one port to the next. This is the framing and signaling protocol level.

- **FC-3**   Provides common services such as striping of data or multicast operations. This level is not used in current implementations.

- **FC-4**   Outlines the mapping of upper-level protocols to the lower levels of FibreChannel. Current mappings include SCSI, Intelligent Peripheral Interface 3 (IPI-3), High Performance Parallel Interface (HIPPI), IP, IEEE 802.2, and Single Byte Command Code Set Mapping (SBCCS).

The FibreChannel standard currently describes three classes of service:

- **Class 1**   A switched circuit connection (such as those used in telephone systems). Once a connection is established, the connecting ports can use the entire bandwidth in both directions. The connection is established using a special Start of Frame (SOF), the source address, and the destination address in the frame header. The connection remains open for frame transmission until it is terminated by the End of Frame (EOF) disconnect on the last frame of transmission. This type of service accommodates the traditional channel environment, ensuring rapid, uninterrupted communication with an extremely high degree of data integrity checking and acknowledgment of frame reception.

- **Class 2**   Provides for frame switching. Frames to different recipients can be transmitted (multiplexed in time) to different recipients. Also, a recipient may receive frames from many different sources (multiplexed in time). Class 2 provides the same high degree of checking and acknowledgment of frame reception that Class 1 provides.

- **Class 3**   Identical to Class 2, but with one major difference: there is no acknowledgment of frame reception. Today's networks operate in this mode at the hardware level. Class 3 is also used for the attachment of disk storage on FC-AL. The topology of the loop ensures proper data delivery, and the SCSI protocol that is used provides acknowledgment that ensures data integrity.

Further Study

Adaptec   www.adaptec.com
Ancot   www.ancot.com
FibreChannel Association   www.Amdahl.com/ext/CARP/FCA/FCA.html
Quantum   www.quantum.com/src/
SCSI guide   www.delec.com/guide/scsi/
SCSI Trade Association   www.scsita.org
Symbios articles   www.lsilogic.com
Symbios specs   www.symbios.com/x3t10
Western Digital   www.wdc.com

35

SERIAL AND INFRARED PORT TROUBLESHOOTING

Every PC needs a means of communicating with external devices. While today's computers use USB and IEEE 1394 (a.k.a. FireWire) connections, early PCs relied solely on serial and parallel ports for their device communication. The parallel port was generally considered to be a "printer port," so another port was needed to communicate with simple low-bandwidth devices like modems and mice. The Electronics Industry Association (EIA) responded to this early need by developing a standard for *serial* communication. Instead of sending 8 bits at a time over a set of data lines (as a parallel port does), only two data lines were used—one to transmit data, and one to receive data. The EIA denoted its serial standard as *RS-232* (or simply the "serial port"). A serial port offers several distinct advantages over early parallel ports. First, the serial port was designed to be bidirectional right from the start. This made "serial" the preferred method for interactive devices such as modems, mice, tablets, and so on. Second, the serial port used fewer physical signal lines than the parallel port. This made cabling less expensive and reduced potential connector problems. Where a printer cable is generally limited to 2 meters, a serial cable can easily exceed 60 meters, which opened the way for basic local networking.

The one problem with serial communication has traditionally been the need to physically connect devices. This often required you to shut down the system, make physical connections, install drivers, and make other changes to the system before the two devices would communicate. With the advent of Windows 9x/Me, designers have introduced a means of infrared serial communication (based on the same technology used for TV remote controls) that avoids troublesome connection and configuration problems. By employing infrared serial ports adhering to Infrared Device Association (IrDA) standards, you can conveniently print or exchange files with other IrDA-compliant systems. This chapter shows you the essential concepts of serial communication and port operation, explains the setup and workings of IrDA devices, and then guides you through a series of troubleshooting procedures.

Understanding Asynchronous Communication

The serial port is not terribly difficult to grasp, but its operation is a bit more involved than that of a parallel port. To appreciate the operations and signals of a typical serial port, you need to be familiar with a variety of concepts. When a parallel port strobes a printer, the printer "knows" that all 8 bits of data are available and valid. However, a serial port must send or receive 8 data bits (one bit at a time) over a single data line. As you might imagine, this presents some serious challenges for the receiving device, which must determine where the data stream starts and ends—hardly a simple task. It is certainly possible to send a synchronizing clock signal along with the data wire. The receiving device could easily use the clock to detect each data bit. This technique is known as *synchronous* serial communication. It is reliable, but rarely used in PCs (other than the keyboard interface).

Instead of using a discrete clock signal to accompany the data, it is possible to eliminate the clock by embedding synchronization information along with the data bits. Thus, when a data stream reaches a receiving device, it can strip away the synchronization bits, leaving the original data. As a result, serial communication is not constrained by a clock. This is *asynchronous* communication—a popular and inexpensive serial technique. The remainder of this chapter deals with asynchronous communication.

THE DATA FRAME

Asynchronous communication requires that data bits be combined with *synchronization bits* before transmission. Synchronization bits provide three important pieces of information to the receiving device: where the data starts, where the data ends, and whether the data is correct. These bits, combined with the data byte, form the *data frame,* as illustrated in Figure 35-1. The first thing you should notice about serial data is that it is bipolar—that is, it has both positive and negative voltages. Contrary to what you might guess, a positive voltage represents a logic 0 (called a *space*), and a negative voltage represents a logic 1 (called a *mark*). The next thing you should note is that the serial signal line is normally idle in the logic 0 (space) state.

The first element of all asynchronous data frames is a single *start bit,* which is always logic 1 (mark). When the receiver detects logic 1, it "knows" the data frame has started. The next 5 to 8 bits are always the *data bits*. The exact number of bits (usually 8) can be set by the communication software, but must be the same at both the transmitting and receiving ends. After data, a single error-checking bit (called a *parity bit*) can be included if desired. Parity is calculated at the sending device and sent with the word. Parity is also calculated at the receiving device and checked against the received parity bit. If the two match, the

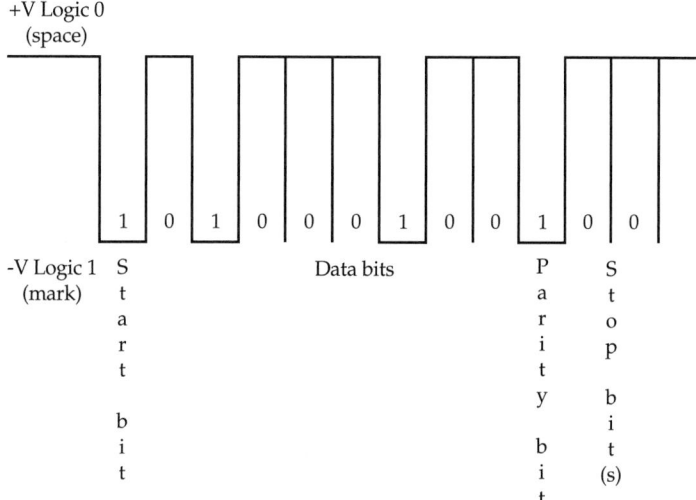

FIGURE 35-1   A typical asynchronous data frame

data is assumed to be correct. If the two do not match, an error is flagged. There are five classes of parity in serial communication:

- **None**   No parity bit is added to the word. This is typical for much of today's serial communication.
- **Even**   If the number of 1's in the data word is odd, parity is set to 1 to make the number of 1's even.
- **Odd**   If the number of 1's in the data word is even, parity is set to 1 to make the number of 1's odd.
- **Mark**   Parity is always set to 1.
- **Space**   Parity is always set to 0.

 Many communication connections today abandon the use of parity in favor of the more reliable and sophisticated cyclical redundancy check (CRC). A CRC has the same effect as a parity check, but instead of checking one byte at a time, an entire block of data is checked.

The last part of a data frame is the *stop bit(s)*—typically only one, but two can be used. Stop bits are always logic 0 (space). After the receiving device detects the stop bit(s), the line remains idle in the space condition awaiting the next subsequent start bit. Framing is usually denoted as data/parity/stop. For example, the connection to a BBS typically uses 8/N/1 framing (8 data bits/no parity bit/1 stop bit).

 One of the most important aspects of serial communication is that both the receiving and transmitting ends must be configured for the exact same data frame. If both ends are not configured identically, serial data will be misinterpreted as meaningless garbage.

SIGNAL LEVELS

Whereas the parallel port uses TTL-compatible logic signals in its communication, a serial port uses bipolar signaling (both positive and negative voltages). The advantage of bipolar signaling is that it supports very long cabling with minimum noise. A logic 0 (space) condition is represented by a positive voltage between +3 Vdc and +15 Vdc. A logic 1 (mark) condition is represented by a negative voltage between –3 Vdc and –15 Vdc. On average, you can expect to see serial ports using +/–5 Vdc or +/–12 Vdc since those voltages are already produced by the PC power supply.

BAUD VS. BPS

Another key concept of asynchronous communication is the idea of *rate*. Since data is traveling across a serial link versus time, the rate at which that data passes becomes an important variable. Although rate is not a literal part of the data frame, it is every bit as important. Simply stated, serial data rates are measured in *bits per second* (bps). This is a simple and intuitive measurement. If the serial port is delivering 2400 bits in one second, it is working at 2400 bps. At that rate, the average bit is (1/2400 bps) 417μs. When you're dealing with a serial port, you're dealing with bits and bps.

Traditionally, when the bits from a serial port are processed through a modem, the modem will modulate the data through a series of phase, frequency, or amplitude transitions. A *transition* is referred to as a *baud* (named for French mathematician J.M.E. Baudot). Older modems designed to operate with signal rates of 2400 bps or less could modulate the telephone line at the bit rate—thus baud would be the same as bps. However, this is a faulty comparison. Since later modems were restricted by the limited bandwidth of a telephone line, modems had to encode more than one bit in every transition. As a result, the effective bps of a modern modem usually exceeds its baud rate by several times. For example, a modem that can encode 4 bits in every transition can work at 2400 baud—yet be sending the equivalent of 9600 bps. See the difference? As modems evolved to encompass data compression standards, effective bps has been increased even more (yet the modem still only works at a relatively low baud rate). When you're dealing with modems, you're usually dealing with baud rates.

There's another catch you need to be aware of. Since baud refers to any transition (Baudot never said a word about modems), it is *technically* valid to measure a serial port speed in baud, although doing so can be terribly confusing. For example, today's serial port circuits can sustain data rates of 115,200 bps. Now, since every bit from the serial port is treated as a "transition" by local devices, such as printers, it becomes just as correct to say 115,200 baud. The thing to remember here is that most modems don't operate over 2400 baud (though advanced modem modulation techniques can transfer 56 Kbps). The telephone line just cannot handle faster signal transition rates. So if you see high baud rates quoted in books or specifications, the reference probably is to the performance of the serial port, not the modem.

Understanding the Serial Port

A serial port must be capable of several important operations. It must convert parallel data from the PC system bus into a sequence of serial bits, add the appropriate framing bits (which may be changed for different serial connections), and then provide each of those bits to the data line at the proper rate. The serial port must also work in reverse, accepting serial data at a known rate, stripping off the framing bits, converting the serial data bits back into bus form, and checking blocks of data for accuracy. The heart of the serial port is a single chip—the *universal asynchronous receiver/transmitter* (UART). A simplified block diagram for a serial port is illustrated in Figure 35-2.

The UART connects directly to the PC bus architecture—it is either added to the motherboard or incorporated on an expansion board. A UART chip contains all of the internal circuitry necessary to process, transmit, and receive data between the serial line and the PC bus. Since the UART is programmable, its configuration (its framing format and baud rate) can be set through DOS or Windows communication software. All data output, data input, and handshaking signals needed by the serial port are generated

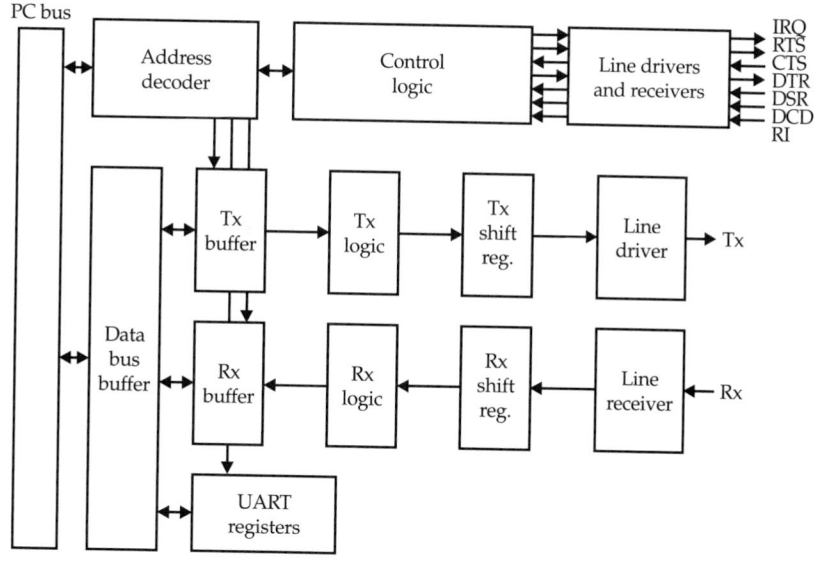

FIGURE 35-2   Simplified block diagram of a UART

within the UART itself. It is interesting to note that the UART is powered by +5 Vdc only—just like most other chips in the system. This means that data and handshaking signals entering and leaving the UART are all TTL compatible. Transmitted data is converted to bipolar signals through a line driver chip. Bipolar data that appears on the receive line is converted back to TTL levels through a line receiver chip. All that remains is the port connector itself. The original serial port design used a 25-pin male subminiature D-type connector, but newer ports have abandoned the extra handshaking signals to accommodate a 9-pin male subminiature D-type connector.

ADDRESSES AND INTERRUPTS

The UART is controlled through a series of important registers that allow the serial port characteristics to be programmed. They also shuttle the transmitted and received data as required. Older BIOS versions supported only two serial (or COM) ports, but newer BIOS releases support four COM ports (designated COM1 through COM4). MicroChannel (MCA) bus systems can support up to eight COM ports (COM1 through COM8). The typical base addresses for the COM ports are shown in Table 35-1. When a new COM port is installed in the system, it must be assigned to a valid base address and interrupt (IRQ). During actual operation, communication software deals with each port register individually. Table 35-2 lists the standard base address offsets for UART registers. Note that with no offset, both transmit and receive registers are available.

During system initialization, COM ports are checked in the following order: 03F8h, 02F8h, 03E8h, 02E8h, 03E0h, 02E0h, 0338h, and 0238h. (MCA systems use a different order.) COM designations are assigned depending on what ports are actually found, so keep in mind that the COM addresses may be exchanged depending on your particular system. In virtually all cases, COM1 is available at 03F8h. The specific I/O addresses for each COM port are kept in the BIOS data area of RAM starting at 0400h. As you might expect, only one COM port can be assigned to a base address. If more than one COM port is assigned to the same base address, system problems will almost certainly occur.

TABLE 35-1   TYPICAL SERIAL PORT ADDRESSES AND IRQ ASSIGNMENTS

BUS ARCHITECTURE	PORT	ADDRESS	IRQ
All Systems	COM1	03F8h	IRQ4
All Systems	COM2	02F8h	IRQ3
ISA	COM3	03E8h	IRQ4
ISA	COM4	02E8h	IRQ3
ISA	COM3	03E0h	IRQ4
ISA	COM4	02E0h	IRQ3
ISA	COM3	0338h	IRQ4
ISA	COM4	0238h	IRQ3
MCA	COM3	3220h	IRQ3
MCA	COM4	3228h	IRQ3
MCA	COM5	4220h	IRQ3
MCA	COM6	4228h	IRQ3
MCA	COM7	5220h	IRQ3
MCA	COM8	5228h	IRQ3

The use of interrupts in conjunction with COM ports can easily be confusing. Unlike parallel ports, which can be polled by BIOS, a serial port *demands* the use of interrupts. Since early PCs allocated space for two COM ports, only two IRQ lines were reserved (IRQ4 for COM1 and IRQ3 for COM2). Unfortunately, when PC BIOS expanded its support for additional COM ports, there were no extra IRQ lines available to assign. Thus, COM ports had to "share" interrupts. For example, COM1 and COM3 must share IRQ4, while COM2 and COM4 must share IRQ3. The problem is that no two devices can use the same IRQ at the same time—otherwise, a system conflict will result. Ultimately, though a typical PC can use four COM ports, only *two* of the four can be used at any one time (for example, COM1 and COM2, COM3 and COM4, COM1 and COM4, or COM2 and COM3). Further, the assignment of COM port address and IRQ lines must match. While COM3 and COM4 *can* be polled by BIOS, the speed and asynchronous nature of contemporary data transmission make polling very unreliable for serial ports.

Always begin a service examination by checking the number of serial ports in your system. Serial ports are so simple and easy to add to various expansion cards that you might exceed the maximum number of

TABLE 35-2   TYPICAL UART REGISTER ADDRESS OFFSETS

REGISTER	OFFSET
Receive Register	00h
Transmit Register	00h
Interrupt Enable Register	01h
Interrupt ID Register	02h
Data Frame Register	03h
UART Control Register	04h
Serialization Status Register	05h
UART Status Register	06h
General Purpose Register	07h

ports, or allow two ports to conflict, without even realizing it. Be sure to remove or disable any unused or conflicting COM ports by removing the offending port or disabling it through jumpers or DIP switches. A common oversight is to add an internal modem as COM2 while hardware support for COM2 is still enabled on the motherboard. When you encounter conflicting COM ports, you will need to disable unneeded ports to prevent conflicts.

DTE VS. DCE

As you work with serial ports and peripherals, you will often see the acronyms DTE and DCE used frequently. DTE stands for *data terminal equipment*, which is typically the computer containing the serial port. The modem, serial printer, or other serial peripheral is referred to as the *data carrier equipment* (or DCE). The distinction becomes important because the data and handshaking signals are swapped at the DCE end. For example, the Tx pin ("transmit"—usually on pin 3 of a 9-pin DTE) cannot connect directly to the same pin on the DCE; it must route to the Rx ("receive") pin instead. The DCE connector makes those swaps, so pin 3 of the DCE would be the Rx pin, and a straight-through cable can be used without difficulty.

However, suppose that two DTEs had to be connected. Since both devices carry the same signals on the same pins, a straight-through cable would cause confusion (the Tx line would connect to the Tx line on the other device, Rx would connect to Rx, and so on). As you can imagine, two DTEs cannot be connected with a straight-through cable. Of course, a specialized cable can be built that contains the proper wire swaps, but an easier alternative is simply to use a *null-modem,* which plugs into one end of the straight-through cable. The null-modem is little more than a jumper box that contains all of the proper swaps. This allows two DTEs to work as if one were a DTE and one were a DCE.

SERIAL PORT SIGNALS

IBM and compatible PCs implement a serial port as either a 25-pin or 9-pin subminiature D-type connector, similar to the ones shown in Figure 35-3. Both ends of the serial cable are identical. There are three type of signals to be concerned with in a serial connection: data lines, control (or handshaking) lines, and ground lines. Table 35-3 identifies the name and description of each conductor for both 25-pin and 9-pin serial connections. Keep in mind that all data and control signals on the serial port are bipolar.

Tx and Rx

These are simply the data lines into and out of the port. Tx is the Transmit line, which outputs serial data from the PC, and Rx is the Receive line, which accepts serial data from the serial peripheral.

RTS and CTS

The RTS (Request to Send) signal is generated by the DTE. When asserted, it tells the DCE (for example, the modem) to expect to receive data. However, the DTE can't just dump data to DCE. The DCE must be *ready* to receive the data, so after the RTS line is asserted, the DTE waits for the CTS (Clear to Send) signal back from the DCE. Once the DTE receives a valid CTS signal, it can begin transferring data. It is this RTS/CTS handshake that forms the basis for data flow control via the system hardware.

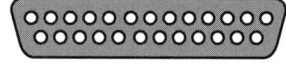 

25-pin M   9-pin M

FIGURE 35-3   Serial port connectors

TABLE 35-3 **PIN ASSIGNMENTS FOR A TYPICAL SERIAL PORT CONNECTOR**

25-PIN CONNECTOR	9-PIN CONNECTOR	SIGNAL NAME	SIGNAL DIRECTION
1	n/a	Protective Ground	n/a
2	3	Tx—Transmit Data	Output
3	2	Rx—Receive Data	Input
4	7	RTS—Request to Send	Output
5	8	CTS—Clear to Send	Input
6	6	DSR—Data Set Ready	Input
7	5	Signal Ground	n/a
8	1	DCD—Data Carrier Detect	Input
9	n/a	+ Transmit Current Loop	Output
11	n/a	– Transmit Current Loop	Output
18	n/a	+ Receive Current Loop	Input
20	4	DTR—Data Terminal Ready	Output
22	9	RI—Ring Indicator	Input
23	n/a	DSRD—Data Signal Rate Indicator	I/O
25	n/a	- Receive Current Loop	Input

DTR and DSR

When the DTE is turned on or initialized and ready to begin serial operation, the DTR (Data Terminal Ready) line is asserted. This tells the DCE (for example, the modem) that the DTE (such as the computer) is ready to establish a connection. When the DCE has initialized and is ready for a connection, it will assert the DSR (Data Set Ready) line back to the DTE. Once the DTE is ready and recognizes the DSR signal, a connection is established. This DTR/DSR handshake is established only once when the DTE and DCE devices are first initialized, and must remain active throughout the connection. If either the DTR or DSR signal should fail, the communication channel will be interrupted (and the RTS/CTS handshake will no longer have any effect).

DCD

The DCD (Data Carrier Detect) signal is particularly useful with modems. It is produced by the DCE when a carrier is detected from a remote target, and the DCE is ready to establish a communications pathway. The DCD signal is then sent back to the DTE. Once the DCD line is asserted, it will remain as long as a connection is established.

RI

The RI (Ring Indicator) signal is asserted by the DCE and is also particularly useful with modems. It is produced by the DCE when a telephone ring is detected. This becomes a vital signal if it is necessary for a remote user to call in and access your computer for remote diagnostics or other purposes. This is also an important signal when the system's power management is configured to "wake on ring."

IrDA Port Issues

A growing number of desktop and laptop PCs (and their peripherals) are being equipped with infrared serial ports (dubbed "IrDA" by the Infrared Desktop Association). IrDA ports allow PCs and peripherals to communicate serially over an infrared link rather than going through the hassle of using cables. For example, you can type a document on a laptop, move the laptop into the vicinity of an IrDA printer, and then print the document without ever attaching a cable. You can also share files between two IrDA-compliant PCs. Although IrDA ports offer some real connectivity benefits to PC users, they also present some problems with installation and configuration. This part of the chapter outlines the essential techniques to install and use IrDA devices, and offers some solid guidelines for testing and troubleshooting.

INSTALLING THE IRDA DRIVER(S)

The Infrared Communications Driver supports hardware devices that enable networking and communications over infrared media up to 115.2 Kbps. The "hardware device" can be an infrared port built into the PC or an infrared adapter connected to one of the PC's serial or parallel ports. IrDA lets you use wireless infrared links instead of serial and parallel cables. For example, you can exchange files between two computers that are equipped with an infrared device and Infrared Communications Driver 2.0 (or later), or you can print to IrDA-capable printers without the need for cable. You can also access your local area network (LAN) using IrLAN. IrLAN currently supports Access Point Mode, which enables a computer with an IrDA adapter to attach to a LAN through an access point device that acts as the network adapter for the computer. An *access point device* is hardware supporting both a LAN network interface controller (NIC) and an infrared (IrDA) transceiver.

If you already have a PC fitted with IrDA support, you simply need to use the Add New Hardware wizard to install a new set of drivers, or use the Add Infrared Device wizard from the IR icon in the Control Panel. If you'll be installing IrDA support for the first time, download the newest IR drivers from the Microsoft Web site (**www.microsoft.com**), and run SETUP.EXE:

1. When the Add Infrared Device wizard prompts to choose a manufacturer's name for the IR device, choose Standard Infrared Devices if the computer has a built-in device, or choose the name of the manufacturer and the model of the adapter if an IR adapter is attached to the computer. Click the Next button.

2. When the Add Infrared Device wizard prompts to choose the communications port that the IR device is physically connected to, click the port from the list. If you're uncertain which physical communications port the IR device is using, select the first COM port in the list (for example, COM1); then click the Next button.

3. When the Add Infrared Device wizard prompts to select the virtual COM and LPT ports, accept the default values by clicking the Next button. After the wizard copies the IR communications driver files to the hard disk, watch for the wizard to display two "New Hardware Found" messages.

4. When prompted by the Add Infrared Device wizard, click the Finish button to complete the IR device installation. (If the wizard did not display "New Hardware Found" messages, then restart the computer.)

5. Activate the IR device by double-clicking the Infrared icon in the Control Panel. If there is no Infrared icon in the Control Panel, select the Refresh option from the Control Panel View menu (or press F5) to make the Infrared icon appear.

TESTING AN IRDA LINK

The next step is to test the IR device. The easiest and quickest way to do this is to print over an IrDA link to an IR-capable printer, or exchange data between two computers using the IR link (and a communications application like LapLink).

You must always remove any previously installed version of the IrDA communications driver before installing a new driver. For example, if an early beta release of the version 2.0 driver is installed, it must be removed before installing the current version 2.0 release.

Testing an IR Link to a Printer

If you're testing an IR link to an IrDA-compliant printer (such as the HP 5P), you must first install the IR communications driver on your computer, and then try the Print option in your printing application. Make sure that you have the correct printer driver installed for your IR-capable printer, and see that you've selected the infrared printing port (the virtual LPT port) as the printer port. If the application prints correctly to your IR-capable printer, you have validated the link successfully.

Testing an IR Link Between Computers

To test a link between two computers, you must install the IR communications driver on both computers. One way to test an IR link is to use HyperTerminal on both computers, and send characters from the keyboard of each computer over the IR link:

Most applications that can communicate over a null modem cable connecting serial ports on two Windows 98/Me computers should also be able to communicate over an IR link.

1.   On both computers, click Start, highlight Settings, and then click Control Panel.

2.   Double-click the Infrared icon.

3.   Move the IR devices within three feet of each other, and make sure they're pointing at each other.

4.   When the two IR devices discover each other, the message "Available infrared devices in range" will appear on the Status tab of your Infrared Monitor interface.

5.   Make sure before you proceed that Infrared Monitor reports both IR devices have the appropriate infrared device within range. You might have to realign the IR devices so that they point right at each other, move them closer together, or change the batteries in an IR adapter (or connect AC power to an IR adapter).

6.   On one of the computers, click the Options tab in the Infrared Monitor interface and locate the information that starts with "Providing application support on...." Write down the name of the COM port you find there. This is the name of the simulated serial port that the IR link is using. In practice, the name of this virtual serial port might be COM4 or COM5, and it will differ from the name of the physical communications port that your IR device is running on (which is typically COM1 or COM2).

7.   Run HyperTerminal by clicking Start button, pointing to Programs, selecting Accessories, clicking HyperTerminal, and then double-clicking the HYPERTRM.EXE icon.

8.   In the Connection Description dialog box, type a descriptive name (such as Direct IR) for the new connection, and then click OK.

9.   In the Phone Number dialog box, use the Connect Using drop-down list to select the "Direct to Com*x*" entry (where *x* is the number of the virtual COM port that you wrote down before). Click OK, and you're ready to start using HyperTerminal on one of the computers.

10.   Repeat the last four steps on the other computer so that both systems are running HyperTerminal on their correct virtual COM port.

11. Select HyperTerminal on either computer and type any characters at the keyboard. If the characters you type appear in the HyperTerminal window on the other computer, then you've confirmed that the IR link works in that direction. Try the other computer. If the IR link works in both directions using HyperTerminal, you've confirmed successful installation of the IR driver on the two computers.

12. Disconnect the HyperTerminal direct IR connection by exiting HyperTerminal on both computers. When you are prompted to save the session, click Yes. This saves the direct IR connection setup information as an icon in the HyperTerminal main folder. You can double-click this icon to restart one side of the HyperTerminal direct IR connection at any time in the future.

The IR transceivers on the two computers do not have to be made by the same manufacturer, but both transceivers must be IrDA compliant. For example, you could have a JetEye PC Infrared PC interface (ESI-9680) attached to one desktop system, and an Adaptec AIRport (APA-9320) External Infrared Adapter attached to the other desktop, and the IR link should work.

RUNNING DCC OVER AN IRDA LINK

With a Direct Cable Connection (DCC), you can establish a direct serial or parallel cable connection between two computers, and this allows you to share the resources of the computer designated as the host. DCC can also be used over an IR link. The computer that contains the information you want to share is the host, and the other computer is the guest. You can share folder(s) on the host and grant access rights to anyone using the guest computer by following this Windows procedure:

1. Double-click the My Computer icon.

2. Double-click the icon of the drive that contains the file(s) you want to share (for example, double-click on the icon for your C: drive).

3. Right-click on the icon of the folder you want to share, and then select Properties.

4. In the folder Properties dialog box, select the Sharing tab (Figure 35-4), and then select the Shared As option. Enter a share name, enter a comment, and add user access rights (Full or Read-Only). The picture of a hand is added to the folder icon to indicate the selected folder is now a shared resource.

Check for the presence of DCC, and install it on both PCs if necessary:

1. Click Start, select Programs, and then point to Accessories. A Direct Cable Connection entry appears in this menu if it's installed on your computer. Under Windows 98, DCC is listed in the Communications submenu under Accessories. If DCC is installed, skip these steps. Otherwise, you'll need to install DCC. Be sure to check both computers, and install DCC on both systems if necessary.

2. Click Start, highlight Settings, and then click Control Panel.

3. Double-click the Add/Remove Programs icon.

4. In the Add/Remove Program Properties dialog box, click the Windows Setup tab.

5. In the Components list, click Communications, and then click the Details button.

6. In the Communications dialog box, make sure Direct Cable Connection is checked, and then click OK. Windows will install the DCC components.

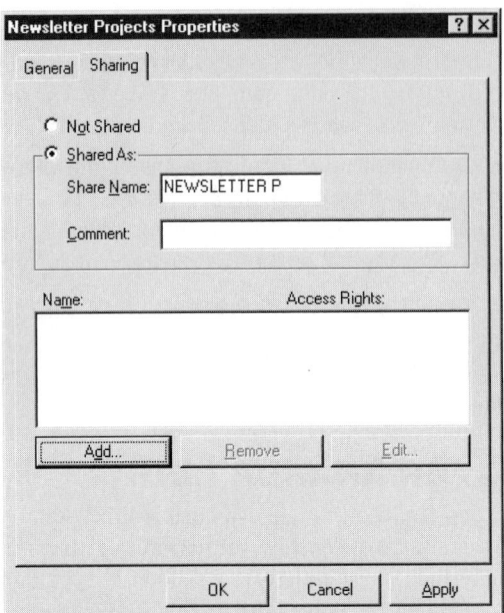

FIGURE 35-4   Sharing files through a drive Properties dialog box

Now configure and test the DCC IR link between the two computers:

If the host is connected to a network, the guest can reach shared resources on the network through a DCC connection to the host.

1.   Make sure the IR communications driver is properly installed and the IR devices are enabled. Keep in mind that you might want to limit the IR connection speed to 9600 bps for the first test of DCC over the IR link, and then increase the speed later.

2.   On the host computer, click Start, point to Accessories, and then click Direct Cable Connection. Under Windows 98, select the Communications submenu under Accessories, and then click Direct Cable Connection.

3.   Follow the steps in the Direct Cable Connection wizard to set up the host computer. When the wizard prompts you, select the Host option. When the wizard prompts you to choose a port, use the same virtual port that you used in the preceding section, "Testing an IR Link Between Computers."

4.   The wizard will also offer password protection. You do not need to establish password protection on the host for this test, but you may wish to use password protection for normal use of the IR link. When you're done with the wizard, click the Finish button. DCC will start running on the IR link and display the message "Waiting to connect via serial cable on Com*x*" (where *x* is the name of the virtual port that the IR link is using).

5.   Repeat the preceding four steps for the guest computer, but when the wizard prompts you, you must select the Guest option instead of the Host option. When you're done with the wizard, click the Finish button. The DCC connection is automatically made over the IR link, and all the shared folders on the host are displayed on the guest's screen.

6. To copy a shared folder from the host to the guest over the IR link, select the folder's icon in the window that displays all the shared folders that are on the host, and drag the icon to the desktop. To work on a shared folder on the host without copying it to the guest, just double-click on the folder in the display on the guest.

If infrared communication is interrupted, it's usually because something has moved between the infrared devices, or one device has been moved out of range. Remove the obstruction, or move the device back into range. If there's no obstruction and the devices are in range, check to see if a noninfrared device is interfering with the infrared communication. If communication is restored before the Status properties countdown ends, no data will be lost.

REMOVING THE IRDA DRIVER(S)

In some instances, it may be necessary to remove the IR communication drivers (most often when upgrading the drivers or IR adapter hardware). The IR communication drivers can be removed either by using Add/Remove Programs in the Control Panel or by using the Device Manager. Using Add/Remove Programs in the Control Panel:

1. Click the Start button and select the Settings option, and then select Control Panel.
2. Double-click Add/Remove Programs in the Control Panel.
3. When a list of software components is displayed, select the Infrared Support For Windows entry and click the Add/Remove button.
4. Restart the system when prompted to do so.

    To use the Device Manager:

1. Right-click on the My Computer icon, select the Properties option from the pop-up menu, and then click the Device Manager tab in the System Properties dialog box.
2. To display the name of the infrared device installed on the computer, make sure the View Devices By Type option is selected in the System Properties dialog box. Then click the plus sign to the left of the "Infrared device" class label. Select the infrared device name, and click the Remove button.
3. Click OK to confirm the device removal. After the Device Manager has successfully removed the infrared device installation from the computer, the "Infrared device" class label will disappear from the System Properties dialog box. Click the Close button.

The Infrared Monitor icon may still be displayed in the Windows status bar (even after the infrared device is removed). Ignore it—the Infrared Monitor cannot be used to establish an IR link after the infrared device is removed.

MAKING THE MOST OF IRDA

Infrared links are handy and efficient tools that allow you to print and exchange files without the hassle of physical connections between devices. Still, IR communication can be plagued by numerous factors, including data transfer efficiency, device range, and device detection. The following tips can help you deal with efficiency, range, and detection issues.

    If you find that your IR communication is not efficient:

■ Check for partial obstructions of infrared activity.
■ Move the infrared devices closer together.

- Clean the infrared windows.
- Shade the devices, or turn off bright lights.
- Make sure the devices are not moving or vibrating.

If you find that IR devices frequently/intermittently go out of range:

- Check for partial obstructions of infrared activity.
- Move the infrared devices closer together.
- Clean the infrared windows.
- Shade the devices, or turn off bright lights.
- Make sure the devices are not moving or vibrating.
- Recharge/replace the batteries for the IR device, or check its power supply connections.

If you find that the system cannot detect devices that should be in range:

- Verify that the system's infrared support is turned on.
- Verify that the infrared "searching" option is turned on.
- Make sure that the IR search interval is not too high.
- Move the devices closer together.
- Verify that the device is fully IrDA compliant (there should be no non-IrDA devices).
- Double check that the IrDA device is turned on (and that its batteries are fully changed).
- Verify that the infrared device on your PC is turned on.
- Make sure nothing is blocking the infrared activity.
- Make sure that no dirt or grease is on the infrared windows.
- Shield the IR windows so that direct sunlight is not shining on the infrared receiver.

IRDA TIPS

Although IR support is reasonably automatic under Windows 95/98, a number of tips can make your troubleshooting much easier. Be sure to review the following checklist carefully before you attempt to isolate IR problems on your system.

- Always remove the existing IR drivers before installing new IR drivers (or upgrading the IR adapter hardware). Preexisting drivers can sometimes interfere with new IR drivers.
- If you upgrade the IR adapter hardware on your system, you must remove the IR drivers and install new drivers.
- Be sure to select the proper virtual COM port for the IR adapter. If you select the wrong COM port during installation, the system will be unable to use the IR adapter.
- IR communication problems may require you to realign the IR devices so that they are closer together (usually three feet or less) and in a direct line of sight. You may need to try new batteries in the IR adapter.
- If an IR adapter is attached to a COM port that is using an older 8250 UART instead of a 16550A UART (or if an IR adapter is connected to a relatively slow computer such as a 386 running at 20 MHz), you might need to use the "Limit Connection Speed To…" option in the Infrared Monitor Options tab to

limit the connection speed to 19.2 Kbps. After establishing a successful IR connection at this speed, you can use the "Limit Connection Speed To…" option to experiment with higher speed connections.

■ Communication over a virtual COM port link between two computers may not be reliable if a printer's IR adapter is also within range. Be sure to move the printer's IR adapter (or any other nonessential IR adapter) out of range.

■ Do not suspend a Windows 98/Me computer while an IR connection is established. Wait until the IR link is disconnected (or force a disconnection) before putting the computer in suspend mode. For example, if an IrLAN connection is established on a laptop, you must always move the laptop out of range of the IrLAN "access point" before suspending the system (or closing the laptop lid). Otherwise, the connection remains active and can drain the battery over time.

■ Connecting and disconnecting over a low-speed IR link (or over a poor-quality link) can take a few seconds, during which time the screen will appear to be frozen. To work around this, you should use a higher-speed connection and take steps to improve the quality of the connection.

■ If you use the Windows 95 version of HyperTerminal to transfer files, you will not be able to transfer files successfully over an IR link using the Zmodem protocol as it's implemented by HyperTerminal—use a later version of Windows.

■ When you run the Windows 95 version of Direct Cable Connection (DCC) and establish the connection between the host and guest computers, the guest computer may display the message: "Direct Cable Connection was unable to display shared folders of the host computer" and prompt you to enter the host computer's name. A simple place to find the host computer's name is on the Status tab of the Infrared Monitor dialog box.

■ For IR adapters that can be powered by the serial port, AA batteries, or an external power supply, the serial port may not provide sufficient power for the adapter in some cases. This can cause reduced operating range and/or a failure to find another IR device that is nearby and aligned correctly. If you suspect such a problem, connect an AC adapter or add fresh batteries to the battery compartment in the infrared adapter.

■ If you have an ACTiSYS 220L IR adapter attached to your computer, and print to a printer that is using an Extended Systems ESI-9580 printer IR adapter (or you're printing to the HP DeskJet 340), you must use the Options tab in Infrared Monitor to limit the connection speed to 19.2 Kbps to print successfully. If you allow the IR devices to automatically negotiate the connection speed without setting this limit, they'll negotiate a higher connection speed, and your application will not be able to print.

■ The TI TravelMate 5000 and Sharp PC 3050 may communicate over an IR link only at very low speeds (such as 9600 baud).

■ If you have an HP Omnibook 4000C or an HP Omnibook 600CT, you must install a special echo-canceling serial driver in addition to the components that make up the IR communications driver. The echo-canceling driver is available from Hewlett-Packard.

■ If you use the Infrared Monitor Options tab to change the port that the IR adapter is attached to while IR communications are in progress, the IR connection is lost without prompting you to verify that it's OK to disconnect.

■ If there's a problem establishing an IR link to an IrLAN access point device when the network is also connected to a NIC in the computer, try disconnecting the LAN from the NIC. Restart the computer and make sure that the computer's IR device and the LAN access point's IR port are within range. Then use the Infrared icon in the Control Panel to activate the IR link between the computer and the LAN access point device.

■ The IPX protocol may not communicate over an IrLAN access point. This can be caused by the dial-up adapter becoming the primary IPX adapter, and no other adapter (such as the IrLAN adapter) can take over. To work around this fault, you can create a profile that does not contain the dial-up adapter, and use it when accessing the network through IrLAN.

■ If the IR connection between the computer and the IrLAN access point is disconnected during a file copy to a NetWare server running burst mode (that is, the IR beam is blocked), the file transfer cannot recover, and the computer will freeze. Turn off burst mode to recover from a disconnection. There will be performance degradation with the burst mode off.

■ Using the virtual parallel port connection to an Extended Systems ESI-9910 JetEye Net Plus IrLAN access point to send data to a printer may result in a program fault. To work around this problem, use the virtual serial port on the IrLAN access point to reach the printer.

Troubleshooting Serial and Infrared Ports

Although the typical serial port is a rather simple I/O device, it presents some special challenges for the technician. Older PCs provided their serial ports in the form of 8-bit expansion boards. When a port failed, it was a simple matter to replace the board outright. Today, however, virtually all PCs provide at least one serial port directly on the motherboard—usually integrated into a component of the main chipset. When a problem is detected with a motherboard serial port, a technician often has three choices:

■ Replace the UART (responsible for virtually all serial port failures) on the motherboard. This requires access to surface-mount soldering tools and replacement chips, and can be quite economical in volume.

■ Set the motherboard jumpers (if possible) to disable the defective serial port, and install an expansion board (such as a multi-I/O board) to take the place of the defective port. This assumes there is an available expansion slot.

■ Replace the motherboard outright. This is a simple tactic that requires little overhead equipment, but can be rather expensive.

Virtually all commercial diagnostics are capable of locating any installed serial ports and testing the ports thoroughly through a loopback plug. Now that you have reviewed the layout, signals, and operation of a typical serial port, you can take a clear look at port troubleshooting procedures.

USING MODE TO CONFIGURE A SERIAL PORT

On some systems, it may be necessary for you to make changes to the serial port's configuration while in the real-mode (DOS). You can use the MODE command to make your changes. From a command line prompt, type

```
mode comX: /<parameters>
```

where X: is the COM port that you need to tweak (such as COM2), and <parameters> represents the serial port features that are being altered (including baud rate, parity, data bits, and stop bits). For example:

```
MODE COM1: BAUD=2400 PARITY=N DATA=5 STOP=1 TO=OFF XON=ON ODSR=OFF OCTS=ON
DTR=OFF RTS=OFF IDSR=OFF
```

Table 35-4 lists the complete suite of serial port parameters that you can change with the MODE command.

SERIAL PORT CONFLICTS

Hardware and software conflicts with a system's serial ports are some of the most recurring and perplexing problems in PC troubleshooting. Although PC purists are pleased with the fact that current operating systems and BIOS support four COM ports, they cannot overcome the fact that there are still only *two* interrupts available to run the ports from. Technicians trying to upgrade a PC often encounter problems adding I/O adapters since many current PC motherboards already provide two COM ports right out of the factory. If a PC offers only one COM port (COM1), and another serial port is placed in the system (by accident or on purpose), be aware that you must choose a port and IRQ that does not conflict with the existing port (such as COM 2 or COM4). If the PC already provides two COM ports (COM1 and COM2), adding a third COM port to the system will cause a hardware conflict. You can rectify the conflict by disabling the new COM port, or by disabling one of the two existing COM ports, and jumpering the new COM port to those settings.

Serial device drivers can also be a source of problems for COM ports. Incorrectly written mouse drivers, printer drivers, or third-party interrupt handlers can leave a port inoperative or erratic. If problems develop after a new driver is installed, disable the driver's reference in CONFIG.SYS, or install an updated protected-mode driver under Windows 98/Me using the Add New Hardware wizard. TSRs (often loaded in AUTOEXEC.BAT) can cause problems as well. If problems develop after a new TSR is installed, disable the offending TSR and try the system again. Remember that drivers and TSRs can easily be disabled by adding the REM statement before the command line in CONFIG.SYS or AUTOEXEC.BAT. If the communication trouble is under Windows 98/Me, strongly suspect the Windows communication package, or the registry may need to be adjusted for an optimum modem initialization string.

MATCH THE SETTINGS

It's bad enough that you can only (practically) use two COM ports, but you also have to make sure that the port addresses and IRQ assignments match, as shown earlier in Table 35-1. For example, suppose that there is no COM1 at 03F8h, but there *is* a COM port at 02F8h. During system initialization, BIOS locates each available port and assigns a COM designation. So, since there is no port at 03F8h, the port at 02F8h

TABLE 35-4	**MODE COMMAND PARAMETERS**
PARAMETER	**DESCRIPTION**
BAUD=	Sets the data transmission rate in bits per second.
PARITY=	Sets how the system checks for transmission errors using the parity bit. The value can be one of the following: N (None), E (Even), O (Odd), M (Mark), or S (Space).
DATA=	Sets the number of data bits in a frame (5 through 8).
STOP=	Sets the number of stop bits that define the end of a frame (1, 1.5, or 2).
TO=ON|OFF	Turns the "infinite timeout processing" option on or off.
X=ON|OFF	Turns the XON/XOFF (software handshaking) protocol on or off.
ODSR=ON|OFF	Turns the output handshaking using Data Set Ready (DSR) circuit on or off.
OCTS=ON|OFF	Turns the output handshaking using Clear To Send (CTS) circuit on or off.
DTR=ON|OFF	Turns the DTR circuit on or off.
RTS=ON|OFF|HS|TG	Specifies the settings for the RTS circuit to on, off, handshake, or toggle.
IDSR=ON|OFF	Turns the DSR circuit sensitivity on or off.

(normally COM2) is the first port detected, and is assigned as COM1. However, DOS and BIOS expect COM1 to use IRQ4, but the port at 02F8h uses IRQ3. If you attempt to use BASIC or DOS for COM1, the standard interrupt handlers will not work. You would have to use communication software that talks to the port directly (and thus avoids using DOS interrupt handlers) and can be assigned with the address and IRQ setting of your choosing. As an alternative, you can switch the COM port to 03F8h and set the interrupt to IRQ4. That should restore normal COM1 operation through DOS.

FRAME IT RIGHT

The data frame and rate play very important roles in serial communication. The sending and receiving ends of the serial link must be set to the *same configuration*—otherwise, the received data will be interpreted as garbage. If you encounter such troubles, be sure to check the settings for data bits, parity bit, stop bits, and baud rate. For example, you can adjust the port settings of a serial port by highlighting the port in Device Manager and then clicking Properties to open the Properties dialog box (Figure 35-5). Change the data frame at either end of the serial link such that all devices are running with the same parameters. You may need to use the MODE command to make changes to the serial port setup.

FINDING A PORT ADDRESS WITH DEBUG

You can use the DOS Debug utility to determine the I/O addresses of a serial port. Make sure that you boot the computer in the DOS mode, and then switch to the directory containing the Debug utility (such as C:\DOS). Type

```
C:\DOS\> debug          <Enter>
```

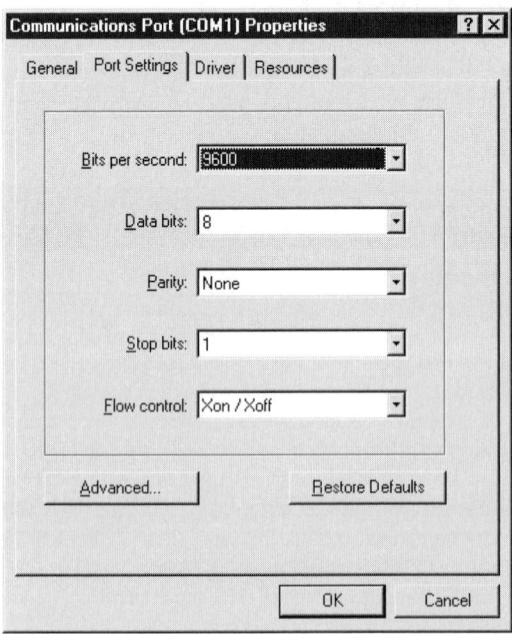

FIGURE 35-5   Adjusting the properties of a serial (COM) port through Windows 98

A hyphen will appear. This is the Debug prompt. At the Debug prompt, type the following:

```
D 40:00 09
```

A single line of text appears, such as follows:

```
0040:0000 F8 03 F8 02 00 00 00 00-78 03
```

To exit Debug, press Q (to quit), and then press ENTER to leave Debug and return to the DOS prompt. The line of interest begins 0040:0000. In this example, the F8 03 (read 03F8h) and F8 02 (read 02F8h) indicate two serial ports (COM1 and COM2). Other possibilities include E8 03 (read 03E8) and E8 02 (read 02E8), which are COM3 and COM4, respectively. A machine with four serial ports should read

```
0040:0000 F8 03 F8 02 E8 03 E8 02-78 03
```

A machine with no serial ports should read

```
0040:0000 00 00 00 00 00 00 00 00-78 03
```

The -78 03 entry is the address of the first parallel port (read 0378h).

GENERAL SYMPTOMS

SYMPTOM 35-1   **You hear a beep code or see a POST error indicating a serial port fault**
The system initialization may or may not halt, depending on how the BIOS is written. Low-level initialization problems generally indicate trouble in the computer's hardware. If the computer's beep code sequence is indistinct, you could try rebooting the computer with a POST analyzer card installed. The BIOS POST code displayed on the card could be matched to a specific error explanation in the POST card's documentation. Once you have clearly identified the error as a serial port fault, you can proceed with troubleshooting.

Start with the system as a whole and remove any expansion boards that have serial ports available. Retest the computer after removing each board. If the error disappears after removing a particular card, then that card is likely at fault. You can simply replace the card with a new one, or attempt to repair the card to the component level. If there is only one serial port in the system, it is most likely built into the motherboard. Again, you can replace the defective UART, replace the motherboard, or disable the defective motherboard port.

SYMPTOM 35-2   **You see an 11xx or 12xx serial adapter error displayed on your system**   A hardware fault has been detected in one of the COM ports. The 11xx errors typically indicate a fault in COM1, while 12xx errors suggest a problem with COM2, COM3, or COM4. In most cases, the fault is in the UART. You have the option whether to replace the UART IC, replace the motherboard, or disable the defective COM port and replace it with an expansion board.

SYMPTOM 35-3   **The computer initializes properly, but the serial peripheral does not work**   Your applications software may indicate that no device is connected. Before you even open your tool kit, you must determine whether the trouble lies in your computer or your peripheral. When your modem or printer stops working, run a self test to ensure the device is at least operational. Check all cables and connectors (perhaps try a different cable). Also be sure to check the software package being used to operate the serial port. Ensure that the software is configured properly to use the appropriate COM port and that any necessary drivers are selected.

Disconnect the peripheral at the computer and install a serial loopback plug. Run a diagnostic to inspect each available serial port. Take note of any port that registers as defective. Locate the corresponding serial port. If the port is installed as an expansion board, replace the defective expansion board. If the port is on the motherboard, you can replace the defective UART chip, install an alternate expansion board, or replace the motherboard outright.

SYMPTOM 35-4   **Data is randomly lost or garbled**   Your first step should be to check the communication cable. Make sure the cable is intact and properly secured at both ends. Try a different cable. If the cable checks properly, either the port or peripheral is at fault. Start by suspecting the serial port. Make sure that the DTE and DCE are both set to use the same data frame and data rate. Incorrect settings can easily garble data. If problems persist, disconnect the printer at the computer and install a serial loopback plug. Run a diagnostic to inspect each available serial port. Take note of any port that registers as defective. Locate the corresponding serial port(s). If the port is installed as an expansion board, replace the defective expansion board. If the port is on the motherboard, you can replace the defective port controller chip, install an alternate expansion board, or replace the motherboard outright.

If you cannot test the computer's serial port directly, test the port indirectly by trying the peripheral on another known-good computer. If the peripheral works properly on another computer, the trouble is probably in the original computer's serial port circuitry. Replace any defective circuitry or replace the motherboard. If the peripheral remains defective on another computer, the peripheral itself (such as a printer or modem) is probably faulty.

IRDA SYMPTOMS

SYMPTOM 35-5   **LapLink does not recognize the IR COM port**   When you attempt to use LapLink with virtual COM ports created by an infrared adapter, you may receive the following error message:

```
This port is unavailable: it may not be physically present in this computer.
If no other communications program is currently running, check for a mouse
or other serial device on this port.
```

This problem occurs because LapLink accesses the hardware directly to determine the status of the COM port and does not recognize virtual COM ports created using the infrared adapter. To work around this problem, you need to contact Traveling Software for a possible patch for LapLink, or discard the use of LapLink in favor of the Direct Cable Connection (DCC) tool included with Windows 98/Me.

SYMPTOM 35-6   **You encounter problems maintaining an IR connection in the daylight**   This is a common problem with all infrared devices, and is usually caused by "interference" from the natural IR component of ordinary sunlight. Try shortening the transmission distance between the transmitter and receiver (move the devices closer together), and make sure the path between the two is as straight as possible.

SYMPTOM 35-7   **You see an error message indicating that there's an "internal error on the IrDA device"**   When you double-click the Infrared icon in Control Panel, you may receive the following error message:

```
ERROR 1: There is an internal error on the IRDA device...
```

This error can occur if the infrared port is disabled in the computer's CMOS settings. Enable the Infrared port in the computer's CMOS settings.

SYMPTOM 35-8   **You receive an "internal error 45" when using the IrDA device under Windows 98**   When you double-click the Infrared tool in Control Panel, you may receive an error message such as:

```
Internal Error 45: Your infrared software has encountered an error, check
infrared software settings under network properties.
```

This error can crop up when the Fast Infrared Protocol is missing or damaged. If you install an infrared device in Windows 98, the Fast Infrared Protocol is not installed by default. You must manually add the protocol in Network Properties. To resolve this problem, remove and then reinstall the Fast Infrared Protocol:

1. Click Start, point to Settings, and then click Control Panel.

2. Double-click the Network icon.

3. In the list of installed network components, click Fast Infrared Protocol, and then click Remove.

4. Restart your computer when you are prompted to do so.

5. Click Start, point to Settings, and then click Control Panel.

6. Double-click Network.

7. On the Configuration tab, click Add.

8. Click Protocol, and then click Add.

9. In the Manufactures box, click Microsoft, click Fast Infrared Protocol in the Network Protocols box, and then click OK.

10. Click OK, and then restart your computer when you're prompted to do so.

SYMPTOM 35-9   **You receive a Windows 98 error indicating that the "recipient device is not ready to receive"**   When you try to transfer a file from one computer to another computer using an IrDA connection, you receive an error message such as:

```
The recipient device is not ready to receive. Please make sure infrared
transfer is enabled on the receiving device.
```

This error message may occur even though infrared transfer *is* enabled on the receiving computer. This fault usually means that the minimum transmission speed for the IR device on one computer is lower than the minimum transmission speed for the IR device on the other computer. For example, you may receive the error if the minimum IR transmission speed on one computer is 2400 bps, but the minimum IR transmission speed on the other computer is 9600 bps. Reconfigure your IR devices so that they are both using the same speed settings.

SYMPTOM 35-10   **Your infrared system does not search when it's enabled under Windows 98**   When you enable or disable infrared searching, you may find several possible symptoms. When you click the Search For And Provide Status For Devices Within Range check box to select it after IR communication is already enabled, searching does not *start*. When you click that same check box to clear it when IR communication is enabled, searching does not *stop*. Also, when you click that same check box, you receive an error message such as:

```
Cannot search for devices because other infrared devices are operating
nearby
```

To get around these problem, enable or disable IR communication and the Search For And Provide Status For Devices Within Range check boxes at the same time:

- Click Start, highlight Settings, and then click Control Panel.
- Double-click Infrared Monitor, and then click the Options tab.
- Click the Enable Infrared Communication check box to select it, click the "Search For And Provide Status For Devices Within Range check box to select it, and then click Apply.
- Click OK.

SYMPTOM 35-11   You cannot use DCC with an IR printer port   When you attempt to connect two computers using the DCC tool under Windows 98/Me, you may be able to select an LPT port. However, if you select an LPT port and it is an infrared port, the connection does not work, and you may receive an error message such as:

```
Waiting to connect via cable on LPT<n>. Is the host computer running?
```

or

```
Cannot connect to the host computer. Make sure you have Direct Cable
Connection on the host computer and you have connected your cable to both
computers.
```

This problem occurs because the IR port is a *unidirectional* port, but DCC requires that LPT ports be bidirectional. There is no fix, but you can work around this problem by selecting an IR COM port instead of an IR LPT port for IR communication between computers.

SYMPTOM 35-12   You see that Fast Infrared devices are not working   This is a known issue with systems such as the Gateway 2000 Solo 9100 that are upgraded to Windows 98. There may also be more than one Fast Infrared device listed in Device Manager. Unfortunately, Windows 98 setup does not detect or replace the original Fast Infrared drivers that were installed on the computer. When Windows 98 is installed, two sets of Fast Infrared drivers are installed, and this results in a conflict that prevents the IR device(s) from working. To correct this problem, remove all the Fast Infrared drivers:

1. Click Start, highlight Settings, click Control Panel, double-click the System icon, and then click the Device Manager tab.

2. Click the first infrared device listed under the Infrared Devices branch, click Remove, and then click OK. Do this for each additional device in this Infrared Devices branch.

3. Double-click the Network Adapters branch to expand it. If a Fast Infrared port is listed, highlight the Fast Infrared port, click Remove, and then click OK.

4. Click OK to close Device Manager, and then restart your computer. When the computer restarts, Windows 98 redetects the Fast Infrared device and installs the correct drivers.

SYMPTOM 35-13   **You get garbled printing or blank pages when printing to an infrared printer**   For example, this may occur when you try to print to a Canon BJC 50 printer using an IrDA link. In virtually all cases, this problem is caused by an incompatibility between the infrared ports (for example, the PC has an IrDA 1.1 port, but the printer has an IrDA 1.0 port). To correct the problem, set the computer's IrDA port mode to version 1.0 through the CMOS Setup (or upgrade the motherboard BIOS). As a workaround, limit the computer's IrDA port speed to 56 Kbps or slower (though this will cause print jobs to run more slowly):

1.   Click Start, highlight Settings, click Control Panel, and then double-click the Infrared icon.

2.   Click the Options tab, select the lower speed in the Limit Connection Speed To box, click OK, and then close the Control Panel.

3.   Reboot the PC if necessary, and try your print job again.

Further Study

ActiSys   www.actisys.com
Adaptec   www.adaptec.com
HP   www.hp.com
Sharp   www.sharp.com
TI   www.ti.com

36

SOUND BOARDS

Sound is a feature of the PC that had been largely overlooked in early systems. Aside from a simple, oscillator-driven speaker, the early PCs were mute. Driven largely by the demand for better PC games, designers developed stand-alone sound boards that could read sound data recorded in separate files, then reconstruct those files into basic sound, music, and speech. Since the beginning of the 1990s, those early sound boards have blossomed into an array of powerful, high-fidelity sound products capable of duplicating voice, orchestral soundtracks, and real-life sounds with uncanny realism (Figure 36-1). Not only have sound products helped the game industry to mature, but they have been instrumental in the development of *multimedia* technology (the integration of sound and picture) as well as Internet web phones, voice recognition and command, and other powerful communication tools. This chapter is intended to explain the essential ideas and operations of a contemporary sound board and to show you how to isolate a defective sound board when problems arise.

FIGURE 36-1   Logitech SoundMan Wave sound board (Copyright © 1995 Logitech Corporation)

Understanding Sound Boards

Before you attempt to troubleshoot a problem with a sound board, you should have an understanding of how the board works and what it must accomplish. This type of background helps you when recommending a sound board to a customer or choosing a compatible card as a replacement. If you already have a strong background in digital sound concepts and software, feel free to skip directly to the troubleshooting portion of this chapter.

THE RECORDING PROCESS

All sound starts as pressure variations traveling through the air. Sound can come from almost anywhere—a barking dog, a laughing child, a fire engine's siren, a person speaking—you get the idea. The process of recording sound to a hard drive requires sound to be carried through several manipulations, as shown in Figure 36-2. First, sound must be translated from pressure variations in the air to analog electrical signals. This is accomplished by a microphone. These analog signals are amplified by the sound card, then *digitized* (converted to a series of representative digital words, each taken at a fixed time interval). The resulting stream of data is processed and organized through the use of software, which places the data (as well as any overhead or housekeeping data) into a standard file format (such as the WAV format). The file is saved to the drive of choice—typically a hard drive, though CD-RW drives are now a popular choice for saving large data files.

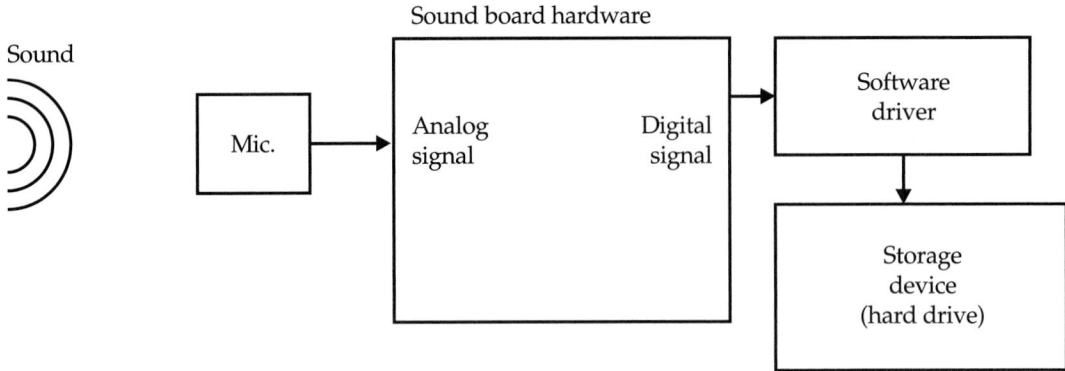

FIGURE 36-2 The sound board recording process

THE PLAYBACK PROCESS

Simply speaking, the playback process is virtually the reverse of recording (Figure 36-3). A software application opens a sound file on the hard drive (or CD drive), then passes the digital data back to the sound card. Data is translated back into equivalent analog levels. Ideally, the reconstructed shape of the analog signal closely mimics the original digitized signal. The analog signal is amplified, then passed to a speaker. If the sound was recorded in stereo, the data is divided into two channels that are separately converted back to analog signals, amplified, and sent to their corresponding speakers. Speakers convert the analog signal back into traveling pressure waves that you can hear.

THE CONCEPT OF SAMPLING

To appreciate the intricacies of a sound card's operation, you must understand the concept of *digitization*—otherwise known as *sampling*. In principle, sampling is a very straightforward concept: an

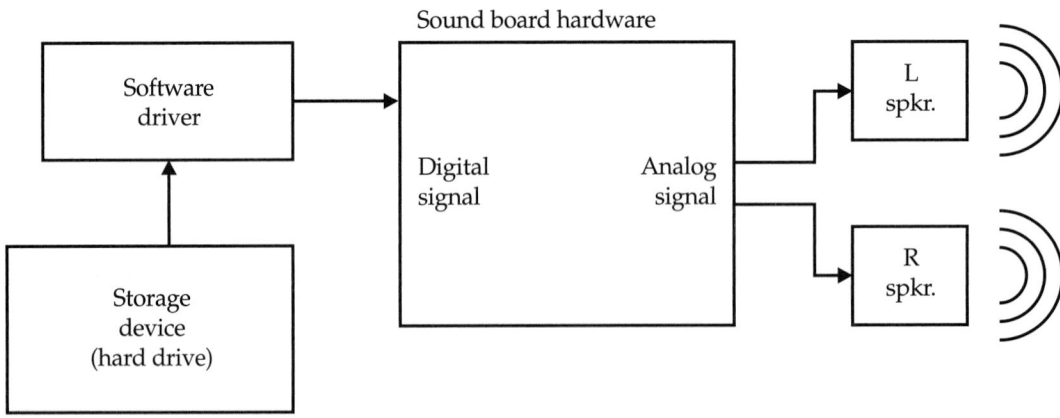

FIGURE 36-3 The sound board playback process

analog signal is measured periodically, and its voltage at each point in time is converted to a digital number. The device that performs this conversion is known as an *analog-to-digital converter* (ADC). It sounds simple enough in principle, but there are some important wrinkles.

The problem with sampling is that a digitizer circuit has to capture enough points of an analog waveform to reproduce it faithfully. The example in Figure 36-4 illustrates the importance of sampling rate. Waveforms A and B represent the same original signal. Waveform A is sampled at a relatively slow rate—only a few samples are taken. The problem comes when the signal is reconstructed with a *digital-to-analog converter* (DAC). As you can see, there are not enough sample points to reconstruct the original signal. As a result, some of the information in the original signal is lost. This is a form of distortion known as *aliasing* and results in substantial distortion during playback. By comparison, waveform B is the same signal, but it is sampled at a much higher rate. When that data is reconstructed, the resulting signal is a much more faithful reproduction of the original.

As a rule, a signal should be sampled at least twice as fast as the highest frequency contained in the signal. This is known as Nyquist's Sampling Theorem. The lowest standard sampling rate used with today's sound boards is 11 kHz. This allows fair reproduction of normal speech and vocalization (with frequency components up to about 5.5 kHz). However, most low-end sound boards can digitize signals up to 22 kHz. Unfortunately, the human range of hearing is about 22 kHz. To capture sounds reasonably well throughout the entire range of hearing, you would need a sampling rate of 44 kHz. This is often known as CD-quality sampling since it is the same rate used to record audio on CDs. The disadvantage to high sampling rates is disk space (and sound file size). Each sample is a piece of data, so the more samples taken each second, the larger and faster a file grows.

Data Bits vs. Sound Quality

Not only does the number of samples affect sound quality, but also the precision (or number of bits) of each sample. Suppose that each sample is converted to a 4-bit number. That means each sampled point can

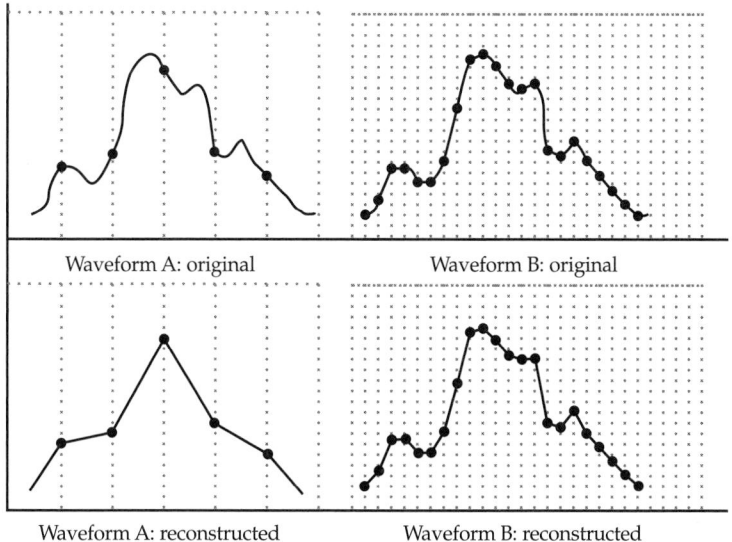

Waveform A: original   Waveform B: original

Waveform A: reconstructed   Waveform B: reconstructed

FIGURE 36-4   The concept of digital sampling

be represented by a number from 0 to 15—not much precision there. If 8 bits are used for each sample, 256 discrete levels can be supported. But the most popular configuration is 16-bit conversion that allows a sample to be represented by one of 65,536 levels. At that level of resolution, samples will form a very close replica of the original signal. Many common sound boards will capture audio as 16-bit data.

THE ROLE OF MIDI

Although most of a sound card is geared toward handling the recording and playback of sound files, the *musical instrument digital interface* (MIDI) port has become an inexpensive and popular addition to most sound card designs. MIDI is a standard protocol that is defined by hardware, software, and electrical interconnections. At the core of a MIDI interface is a synthesizer chip. Unlike a sound file that basically contains the digital equivalent of an analog waveform, a MIDI file is a set of instructions for playing musical notes. Each note is sent to the synthesizer, along with duration, pitch, and timing specifications. This means very complex MIDI musical scores can be produced using relatively small data files. The synthesizer can be made to replicate a variety of musical instruments such as a piano, guitar, harmonica, flute—you name it. High-end sound boards are capable of synthesizing a small orchestra. Since most synthesizers can process several channels simultaneously, the MIDI standard supports playing a number of "instruments" (or voices) at the same time. Thus, very high quality music can be produced with MIDI on a PC. The two most common synthesizer types are FM and Wavetable.

Figure 36-5 illustrates the kinds of things MIDI is capable of. Prerecorded MIDI files can be read from a storage device like a hard drive file or from CD-ROM. (Many games include an orchestral-quality MIDI soundtrack on the CD.) The MIDI data is passed through to the sound board's synthesizer, which reproduces the sound, and out to the amplified speakers. If you plan on composing music yourself, you can interface a MIDI instrument to the sound board's MIDI port. Using MIDI sequencer software, the notes played on the instrument will be heard through the speaker as well as recorded to the MIDI file on the hard drive. Note that you do not need a MIDI instrument to play back a MIDI file, but you need an instrument and sequencer software to create a MIDI file. Also, since MIDI is not sound (but rather sound "blueprints"), the same MIDI composition entered on a keyboard can be played back as a harp, a guitar, or a flute.

INSIDE A SOUND BOARD

Now that you're aware of the major functions a sound board must perform, you can see those functions in the context of a complete board. Figure 36-6 shows a simplified block diagram of a sound board. Note that your sound board may differ somewhat, but all contemporary boards should generally contain these subsections.

The core element of a sound board is the *digital signal processor* (DSP). A DSP is a variation of a microprocessor that is specially designed to manipulate large volumes of digital data. Like all processor components, the DSP requires memory. A ROM contains all of the instructions needed to operate the DSP and direct the board's major operations. A small quality of RAM serves two purposes: it provides a "scratch pad" area for the DSP's calculations and serves as a buffer for data traveling to or from the PC bus.

Signals entering the sound board are passed through an amplifier stage and provided to an A/D converter. When recording takes place, the DSP runs the A/D converter and accepts the resulting conversions for processing and storage. Signals delivered by a microphone are typically quite faint, so they are amplified significantly. Signals delivered to the "line" input are often much stronger (such as the output from a CD player or stereo preamplifier), so they receive less amplification.

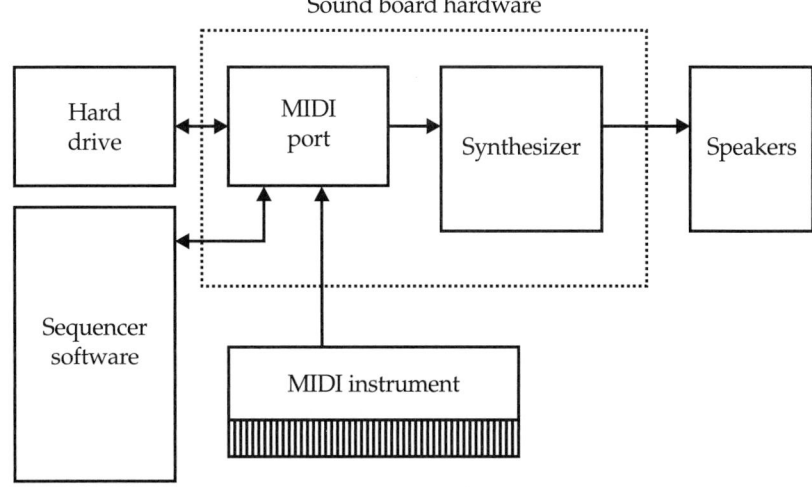

FIGURE 36-5   The basic path of MIDI signals through the PC

For signals leaving the sound board, the first (and often most important) stop is the mixer. It is the mixer that combines CD audio, DSP sound output, and synthesizer output into a single analog channel. Since virtually all sound boards now operate in a stereo mode, there will usually be two mixer channels and amplifier stages. The audio amplifier stage(s) boost the analog signal for delivery to stereo speakers.

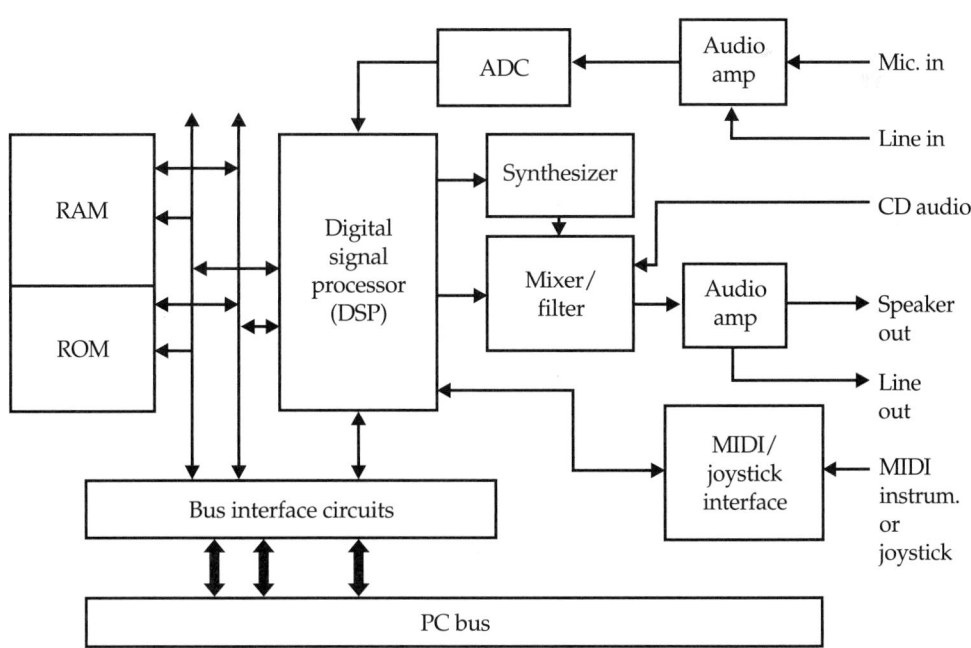

FIGURE 36-6   Simplified block diagram of a basic sound board

If the sound will be driving a stereo system, a "line" output provides a separate output. Amplifier output can be adjusted by a single master volume control located on the rear of the board, though most sound boards now use software applet(s) to adjust mixer and volume levels rather than a hardware control.

Finally, a MIDI controller is provided to accommodate the interface of a MIDI instrument to the sound board. In many cases, the interface can be jumpered to switch the controller to serve as a joystick port. That way, the sound board can support a single joystick if a MIDI instrument will not be used. MIDI information processed by the DSP will be output to the onboard synthesizer.

Understanding Audio Benchmarks

An important aspect of sound boards is their audio benchmarks. Unlike logic and processing circuitry, which is measured in terms of millions (sometimes billions) of operations per second, the benchmarks that define a sound card are very much analog. If you are an audiophile, many of the following terms may already be familiar. If most of your experience has been with logic systems, however, these concepts will appear very different from many of the other discussions in this book.

DECIBELS

No discussion of sound concepts is complete without an understanding of the *decibel* (dB). Decibels are used because they are logarithmic. Human hearing is not a linear response. That is, if you increase the power of your stereo output from 4W to 16W, the resulting sound is not four times louder—in fact, it is only twice as loud. If you increase the power from 4W to 64W, the sound is only three times as loud. In human terms, amplitude perception is measured logarithmically. As a result, very small decibel values actually relate to substantial amounts of power. The accepted formula for decibels is

$$\text{gain (in dB)} = 10 \log_{10} \frac{P_{out}}{P_{in}}$$

Don't worry if this formula looks intimidating. (Chances are that you won't actually need to work this formula.) But consider what happens when output power is greater than input power. Suppose a 1mW signal is applied to a circuit, and a 2mW signal leaves. The circuit provides a gain of +3dB. Suppose the situation is reversed: a 2mW signal is applied to the circuit, and a 1mW signal leaves it. The circuit would then have a gain of −3dB. Negative gain is a loss, also called *attenuation*. As you see, a small dB number represents a large change in signal levels.

FREQUENCY RESPONSE

Expressed simply, the *frequency response* of a sound board is the range of frequencies that the board will handle uniformly. Examine the sample graph of Figure 36-7. Ideally, a sound board should be able to output the same amount of power (0dB) across the entire working frequency range of the board (usually 20 Hz to 20 kHz). This would show up as a flat line across the graph. In actual sound cards, however, this is not practical, and there will invariably be a *rolloff* of signal strength at both ends of the operating range. A good-quality sound board will demonstrate sharp, steep rolloffs. As the rolloffs get longer and shallower at high and low frequencies, the board has difficulty producing sound power at those frequencies. The result is that bass and treble ranges may sound weak, and this affects the sound's overall fidelity. By looking at a frequency response curve, you can anticipate the frequency ranges where a sound board may sound weak.

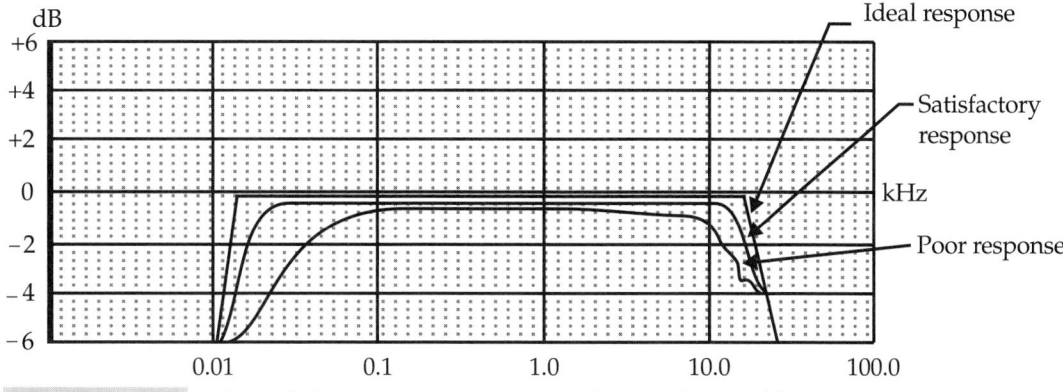

FIGURE 36-7   A simple frequency-response curve for a basic sound board

SIGNAL-TO-NOISE RATIO

The *signal-to-noise ratio* (SNR) of a sound board is basically the ratio of maximum undistorted signal power to the accompanying electronic noise being generated by the board (primarily hum and hiss) expressed in decibels. Ideally, this will be a very large dB number, which would indicate that the output signal is so much stronger than the noise signal, that for all intents and purposes, the noise is imperceptible. In actual practice, a good-quality sound board will enjoy an SNR of 85dB or higher—but these boards are difficult to find. For most current sound boards with SNR levels below 75dB, there may be audible hum and hiss present during silent periods, as well as a certain amount of sound "grit" underlying sound and music reproduction. Some very inexpensive sound boards are on the market with SNR levels as low as 41dB (noise may be noticeable and actually annoying).

You may also find the SNR value expressed as an *A-weighted* decibel number. The reason for this is that human hearing is not equal at all frequencies, so we cannot hear all noise equally. The process of A-weighting emphasizes the noise levels at frequencies we are most sensitive to. Resulting SNR values are often several dB higher (better) than non-weighted SNR values. Be careful here; a sound board with a low SNR may use the A-weighted value in the specification sheet. If this is the case, subtract about 3 or 4dB for the actual SNR figure.

TOTAL HARMONIC DISTORTION

Sound and music are rich in harmonics (overtones), which are basically integer multiples of an original frequency signal (although at much lower levels). As a consequence, harmonics are a valuable attribute of sound. The number and amplitude of harmonics provide the sound characteristics that allow you to distinguish between a guitar, flute, piano, or any other musical instrument played at the same note. Without harmonics, every instrument would just produce flat tones, and every instrument would sound exactly the same.

However, when sound is produced in an electronic circuit, other unwanted harmonics are generated that can alter the sound of the music being produced (thus the term *harmonic distortion*). The *total harmonic distortion* (THD) of a sound board is the *root-mean squared* (RMS) sum of all unwanted harmonic frequencies produced, expressed as a percentage of the total undistorted output signal level. In many cases, the RMS value of noise is added to THD (expressed as THD+N). The lower this percentage the better. THD+N values over 0.1 percent can often be heard and suggest a less than adequate sound board design.

INTERMODULATION DISTORTION

This specification is related to harmonics. When two or more tones are generated together, amplifiers create harmonics as well as tone combinations. For example, if a 1-kHz and 60-Hz tone are mixed together, *intermodulation harmonics* will be generated (such as 940 Hz, 880 Hz, 1060 Hz, 1120 Hz, and so on). It is this intermodulation that gives sound a harsh overtone. Since intermodulation is not related to sound quality, it is a form of distortion that should be kept to a very low level. Like THD, *intermodulation distortion* (IMD) is the RMS sum of all unwanted harmonic frequencies expressed as a percentage of the total undistorted output signal level. IMD should be under 0.1 percent on a well-designed board.

SENSITIVITY

While it does not directly affect the fidelity of sound reproduction, sensitivity can be an important specification. *Sensitivity* is basically the amplitude of an input signal (such as a microphone signal) that will produce the maximum undistorted signal at the output(s) with volume at maximum.

GAIN

By itself, sensitivity is hard to apply to a sound board, but if you consider the board's output power versus its input signal power and express the ratio as a decibel, you would have the *gain* of the sound board. Many sound boards offer a potential gain of up to 6dB. However, it is important to note that not all sound boards provide positive gain. Some boards actually attenuate the signal even with the volume at maximum. In practical terms, this usually forces you to keep the volume control at maximum.

3D AUDIO (A3D)

The A3D audio technology in your sound card (that is, part of a Diamond Multimedia Sonic Impact and other A3D audio systems) was developed by Aureal Semiconductor and is the result of many years of research into human hearing and digital audio reproduction. In the real world, we can close our eyes, listen to a sound, and pinpoint its direction, distance, and motion. Our ears allow us to hear 360 degrees in all directions, while our eyes cover only about 140 degrees in the direction we're facing. The eyes and ears work in close cooperation to provide us with a seamless perception of reality. When the ears hear a sound from behind, we decide to turn our head and look at an object.

A3D audio is based on the following premise: we can hear sounds in three dimensions by using only our two ears, so it's possible to create sounds from two speakers (or a set of headphones) that have the same effect. There are several listening cues that allow us to hear sounds three-dimensionally. There are split-second differences between what each ear hears when listening to a sound. Sound waves usually appear earlier and louder at the ear closest to the sound source. That same sound (originating from various locations around a listener), will sound different because of the changes in the way it gets reflected and filtered by the shoulders, face, and the outer ear before reaching the ear drum. These listening effects can be summarized in a set of audio filters called *Head Related Transfer Functions* (HRTFs).

A3D technology uses advanced signal processing algorithms and HRTF measurement techniques. This digitally re-creates these hearing cues along with the absorption, reflection, and Doppler shift effects, which affect sound waves as they travel from a sound source, through an environment, to the listener's ears. The result is a lifelike audio experience that "surrounds" the listener with sound that seems like it's in three dimensions, using only a single pair of ordinary speakers or headphones.

In practice, DirectSound and DirectSound3D are DirectX wave audio playback APIs that allow you to simultaneously play multiple wave files and move sound sources within a simulated 3D space (DirectSound3D). They take advantage of sound-accelerator hardware (found on many high-end sound cards such as the Sonic Impact A3D board) to improve performance and minimize CPU usage. You can check for the presence of D3D drivers through the DirectX diagnostic (DXDIAG), as shown in Figure 36-8.

Using Microphones

Ever-growing numbers of sound card owners are using their sound cards to record sound or to broadcast sound over the Internet through such applications as WebPhone or NetMeeting. Sound recording demands the use of microphones, and not all microphones work properly with every sound board. Often, the user mistakes a poor microphone response as being a problem with the sound card. This part of the chapter looks at some important considerations for choosing and using a microphone.

MICROPHONE TYPES

There are three types of microphones: dynamic, condenser, and electret condenser. You will find all three microphone types available for sound boards:

■ **Dynamic**   Dynamic microphones are typically hand-held or desktop units. They have a larger response range and typically sound better than condenser microphones. A dynamic microphone does not require phantom power because the diaphragm element in the microphone can create enough electric current for the sound board to use.

■ **Condenser**   Condenser microphones are the small multimedia microphones that typically come with computers. When you open a new sound board and take the microphone out of the box, it is almost always a condenser microphone. They do not have as good a response range as dynamic microphones, and they also have a smaller diaphragm. This demands phantom power for the sound board.

■ **Electret condenser**   Electret condenser microphones are basically condenser microphones with a built-in battery. They have the same response as a condenser microphone, but they do not require phantom power to operate. Some electret condenser microphones will allow you to remove this internal battery. With the battery not installed, phantom power would be required.

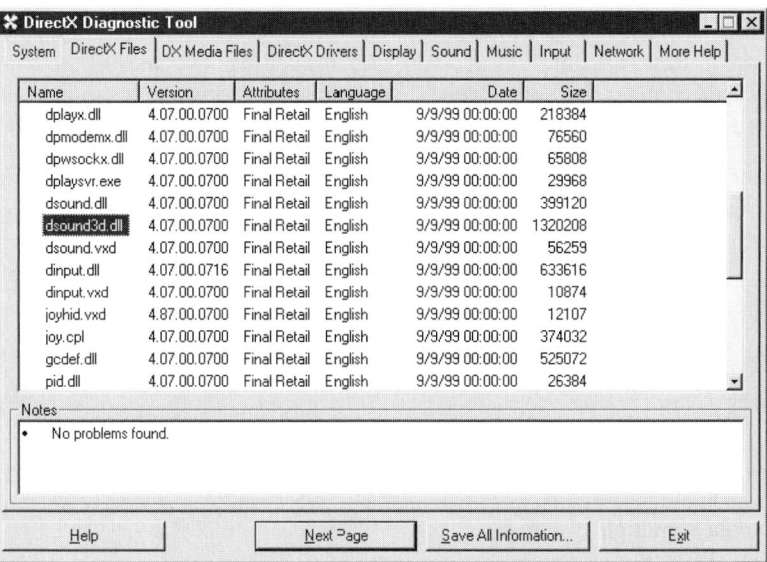

FIGURE 36-8   Checking for 3D sound support through DXDIAG

PHANTOM POWER

So the next question is, "What is phantom power?" *Phantom power* is simply a small, low-current power source on the sound board that is used to power condenser microphones. Devices like dynamic and electret microphones can produce enough current on their own to avoid the use of phantom power, but condenser microphones demand phantom power as a current source.

Here's the main problem with today's sound boards: not all of them provide switchable phantom power. Ideally, sound boards (like the Creative Sound Blaster Live 5.1 Platinum) would provide phantom power and allow you to jumper the phantom power on or off depending on which microphone type you plan to use. If you use a dynamic microphone, you'd switch phantom power off. If you use a condenser microphone, you'd switch phantom power on. When a sound board does not provide phantom power at all, you're stuck using a dynamic microphone or a powered electret condenser microphone. If a sound board provides full-time phantom power (and you cannot turn it off), you'll need to stay with a condenser microphone.

You can probably see the potential for trouble here. If you use a condenser microphone on an unpowered sound board, the microphone will not work at all (or generate little more than faint noise). On the other hand, plugging a dynamic or electret microphone into a powered sound board will usually result in severe clipping. Once again, you'll capture little more than noise.

CHOOSING A MICROPHONE

Whether you're choosing a microphone for yourself or recommending one to someone else, there are some considerations to keep in mind. Perhaps the most important issue is the application. If you just need a basic, inexpensive microphone to record a few simple voice notations, a condenser or electret microphone would work just fine, and your sound board will require a phantom power supply. If you want to record more professional vocals, or prepare a formal presentation, a dynamic microphone will generally provide the best results, and no phantom power is needed.

Installing/Upgrading a Sound Board

Fortunately, adding a sound card to a system is a remarkably straightforward procedure. The only real problem areas are in hardware conflicts and software installation. This part of the chapter covers the essential steps and precautions that you will need to remember when installing a sound card. Although the chances of a system failure during the upgrade are extremely remote, it is always a wise policy to back up any vital files or programs before opening the system.

If you're replacing an existing sound card (or disabling the sound support on your motherboard), be sure to uninstall all of the sound card's application software, and remove the existing sound card's entry in your Device Manager *first*. Then shut down the system directly and remove/disable the old sound device.

STATIC DISCHARGE PRECAUTIONS

Most of the chips used in today's expansion boards are fabricated with technologies that make them extremely sensitive to *electrostatic discharge* (ESD). To ensure the safe handling of sound boards and other system components during the upgrade, make it a point to take the following precautions. First, use an antistatic wrist strap whenever handling components or tools inside the PC. Cable the wrist strap to another reliable earth ground. Next, always try to handle expansion boards by their edges. Avoid touching the individual chip pins or printed wiring. Third, if you will be removing an old sound board, have a good-quality antistatic bag on hand to store it in. Under no circumstances should you allow a sound board (or any expansion board) to rest on a synthetic or static-prone surface. Finally, excessively dry environments tend to allow substantial buildups of static charges in objects, clothing, and bodies. If it is possible, try to work in an environment with at least 40 percent humidity.

PREPARE THE SYSTEM

At this point, you can prepare the system for its upgrade. A word of caution is in order here: *be especially careful of screwdriver blades when working inside the PC.* If you should slip, the blade can easily gouge the motherboard (or an expansion board) and result in broken traces. It pays to be careful and gentle when upgrading an expansion device. Before you even consider opening the PC cover, turn the system off, and unplug it from the AC receptacle. This helps to ensure your safety by preventing the PC from being powered accidentally while you are working on it.

Remove the screws holding down the outer cover, and place those screws aside in a safe place. Gently remove the PC's outer cover and set it aside (out of the path of normal floor traffic). You should now be able to look into the PC and observe the motherboard, along with any expansion boards and drives that are installed. If you will be replacing an existing sound board, now is the time for you to label any cables connected to it. Labels need not be fancy—a roll of masking tape and an indelible marker are all you need.

REMOVE THE OLD BOARD

If there is no sound board already in the PC, feel free to skip to the next step. Otherwise, start by disconnecting any cables that are attached to the current sound board. (Make sure each cable is labeled.) You can then remove the screw that attaches the board bracket to the chassis, and gently ease the board from its expansion slot. Be sure to handle the board by its edges. When the old board is removed, seal it in an antistatic bag and set it aside. There are several important cables to look for:

- Speaker output cable
- Microphone input cable (if a microphone is attached)
- Line input cable (if you're mixing in a source from outside of the sound board)
- CD audio cable between the CD-ROM drive and sound board
- CD-ROM drive interface cable (if there's a CD-ROM in the system using that interface)
- The 15-pin joystick or MIDI interface cable

INSTALL THE NEW BOARD

Find an open expansion slot for the new sound board. Virtually all sound boards today are 16-bit devices, so you will need a PCI slot. (Legacy sound cards may require a full ISA slot.) The card slot should also accommodate a full-length board, though most sound boards only need a half-slot space. For legacy-type sound boards, check each jumper on the new sound board, and see that none of the IRQ, DMA, or I/O settings conflicts with other devices in the system. If problems arise, this list will help isolate conflict problems. Today's PnP devices will simply configure themselves and begin driver installation once Windows starts. Ease the new board into its expansion slot, and be careful to avoid flexing the motherboard too much in the process. Once the sound card is installed properly, secure the board bracket to the PC chassis with the single screw.

CONNECT THE CABLES

Now that the new sound card is in place, reconnect the cables as required. As a minimum, you will need to connect speakers, but you may also have to connect a CD audio cable, CD-ROM drive interface cable, microphone, MIDI or joystick cable, and so on. Figure 36-9 illustrates the typical connections for a Creative Sound Blaster Live 5.1 Platinum card. After each of the cables is secured, you can reconnect AC to the computer and reboot the system.

INSTALL THE WINDOWS SOFTWARE

Once Windows 9x/Me starts, you'll need to install the proper drivers and utilities for the sound board. If the sound card is plug-and-play ready (as virtually all are now), Windows will probably identify the new sound hardware automatically and attempt to install drivers for it. If your sound board has a Windows 98/Me driver disk or CD, be sure to use the drivers from that media. (Otherwise, Windows may install older or incompatible native drivers.) In most cases, the installation wizard will guide you through the driver installation process automatically.

Even if Windows 9x/Me correctly identifies and installs the new sound board, you may need to manually remove the old card (if one was installed) from the Windows 95/98 Device Manager yourself before the new sound board will function.

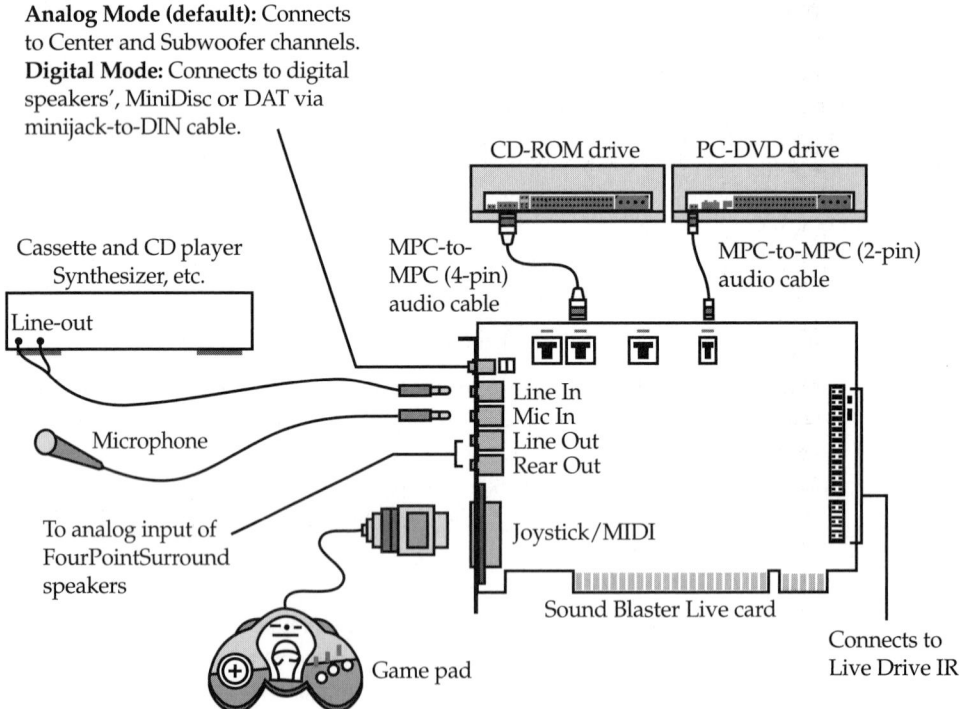

FIGURE 36-9   Connections for a modern sound board (Courtesy of Creative Labs)

INSTALL THE DOS SOFTWARE

If you're planning on using your sound board for real-mode (DOS) games, you will need to install one or more DOS files so that they will run with CONFIG.SYS and AUTOEXEC.BAT each time the system starts. Otherwise, you will have no sound support under DOS. Today, sound boards are one of the very few devices to still come with DOS drivers and utilities. This is done almost exclusively to provide backward compatibility for your favorite legacy games. This part of the chapter looks at the typical way to configure a modern sound board (such as a Sound Blaster Live) for DOS.

If you do not require sound support under DOS, you can almost always skip the installation of real-mode drivers and use Windows exclusively.

Generally, an installation routine with the sound board will automatically copy the real-mode drivers to your PC and modify your existing CONFIG.SYS and AUTOEXEC.BAT files with the appropriate command lines. Some installers will add DOS support along with the Windows drivers, while other products will keep Windows and DOS installers separate. Check the DOS support notes with your particular sound card. For the Sound Blaster Live card, the installation program adds the following three command lines to AUTOEXEC.BAT:

```
SET CTSYN=C:\WINDOWS
SET BLASTER=A220 I5 D1 H5 P330 T6
C:\PROGRA~ 1\CREATIVE\SBLIVE\DOSDRV\SBEINIT.COM
```

The first two lines prepare the environment variables for your audio card. The third line runs SBEINIT.COM, which is the required MS-DOS driver.

As with most DOS drivers, SBEINIT.COM requires that the HIMEM.SYS and EMM386.EXE files be loaded, to allow the driver to access expanded memory. If needed, the installation program adds the necessary HIMEM.SYS and EMM386.EXE lines to your CONFIG.SYS file. In rare cases where a program does not work with expanded memory, simply add the NOEMS parameter to your memory manager. For example:

```
DEVICE=C:\WINDOWS\EMM386.EXE NOEMS
```

You may load this driver into high memory in the AUTOEXEC.BAT file, even though the default is not to. For example:

```
LOADHIGH=C:\PROGRA~ 1\CREATIVE\SBLIVE\DOSDRV\SBEINIT.COM
```

As a rule, do not remove the memory manager, and do not attempt to load SBEINIT.COM into high memory when using the NOEMS option if SBEINIT.COM fails to run SBELOAD.EXE or SBECFG.EXE. If your DOS game will not work with a memory manager, you will not be able to use the Sound Blaster Live card with the game.

Environment Variables

Environment variables are basically used to pass hardware configuration information to the software in your system. For DOS, the Sound Blaster Live card includes the following:

- CTSYN environment variable
- BLASTER environment variable

The CTSYN environment variable points to the location of the CTSYN.INI file, which usually resides in the Windows directory. The syntax for this variable is as follows:

```
CTSYN=<path>
```

where <path> is the location of the CTSYN.INI file. The BLASTER environment variable specifies the base I/ O address, IRQ line, and DMA channels of the Sound Blaster interface. Its syntax is

```
BLASTER=A220 I5 D1 H5 P330 T6
```

The parameters in the command line are as follows:

- **A**xx   SB interface's base I/ O address
- **I**x   IRQ line used by the audio interface
- **D**x   First DMA channel used by the audio interface
- **H**x   Second DMA channel used by the audio interface
- **P**xx   MPU-401 UART interface's base I/ O address
- **T**x   Card type; the x value must be 6

Checking Resources for DOS

When configuring a DOS game, you will generally need to tell the game about the sound board's resource assignments (IRQ, DMA, and I/O). To find the resources assigned to a Sound Blaster Live card's emulation mode, try the following steps:

1.   Click Start, highlight Settings, and click Control Panel.

2.   In the Control Panel, double-click the System icon.

3.   In the System Properties dialog, click the Device Manager tab.

4.   Double-click Creative Miscellaneous Devices, and then double-click "Creative SB Live SB16 Emulation."

5.   Click the Resources tab, and record the information listed there.

Your sound board may also offer a DOS utility that can help identify the card's resources. For the Sound Blaster Live card, switch to the DOS driver directory where you installed the card's software, such as:

```
C:\PROGRA~ 1\CREATIVE\SBLIVE\DOSDRV
```

Now type **sbecfg** and then press ENTER.

TEST THE SOUND BOARD

When the system reboots to Windows, you'll normally hear the "Windows start-up" sound. This will tell you that the sound board is working. You may need to adjust the volume levels on your speakers and mixer/equalizer applet (such as in Figure 36-10) in order to achieve an optimum sound, but those start-up chimes will often announce a working sound board. Once you've tweaked the volume settings, try an audio CD in the drive, and see if you can hear music through the sound board and speakers. (Of course, you'll need a 4-wire CD audio cable connected between the sound board and CD drive.) If you're working under DOS, you'll need to enable the card with one or more DOS drivers and run a DOS diagnostic (or actual game) to use the card.

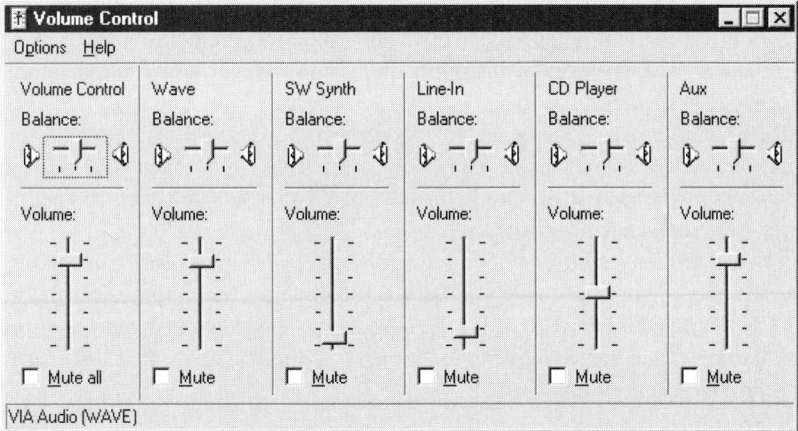

FIGURE 36-10   The standard Windows 98/SE Volume Control applet

Troubleshooting a Sound Board

Traditionally, most sound boards use many of the same chipsets and basic components, but since each board is designed a bit differently, it is very difficult for commercial diagnostic products to identify failed chip functions. For the most part, commercial and shareware diagnostics can only identify whether a brand-compatible board is responding or not. As a result, this chapter will take the subassembly replacement approach. When a sound board is judged to be defective, it should be replaced outright. This part of the chapter reviews the problems and solutions for sound boards under both DOS and Windows 9x/Me. The following tips may help you nail down a sound problem most efficiently:

- Check to see that your speakers are connected, powered, and turned on.
- Check that the speaker volume and sound board master volume (if there's a physical control knob) are both turned up to no more than 75 percent—though 50 percent is usually more than adequate.
- Check to see that the mixer volume and master volume are set properly in the Volume Control applet (or other mixer/equalizer applet).
- Make sure that the music or sound file(s) are installed properly.
- Check that all sound board and multimedia drivers are installed.
- Make sure that the sound board drivers are up to date.
- Check for resource conflicts between the sound board and other devices in the system.
- Make sure that the sound board is selected and configured properly (especially for DOS apps).
- The sound device should be enabled and configured under CMOS (for sound functions incorporated on the motherboard).

DOS DRIVERS AND DRIVER ORDER

Unlike most other expansion devices that are driven by system or supplemental BIOS, sound boards make use of small device drivers to set up their operations. Under DOS, these drivers are generally included in

CONFIG.SYS and AUTOEXEC.BAT and are called when the system is first initialized. Most sound board drivers are only used to initialize and set up the board, so they do not remain resident. This is good since it reduces the load on conventional and upper memory. However, these initialization routines vary from board to board. For example, the files installed for a Creative Labs Sound Blaster will not support a Turtle Beach MultiSound board. When you elect to replace a sound board, you must also disable any current (old) sound board drivers and include any new supporting driver files. The process is not difficult—just follow the installation instructions for the board—but this software consideration does add another wrinkle to the replacement process.

When there are problems installing or upgrading a sound board under DOS, one of the first issues to suspect is the driver loading order. Sound boards are typically multifunction devices that require several drivers in CONFIG.SYS and AUTOEXEC.BAT. If the drivers are installed in the wrong order, the sound board (or other features of the board) may not function. As a rule, the drivers should be loaded in the following order *after* your memory managers:

■   The sound board's device driver:

```
DEVICE=C:\SB16\DRV\SB16.SYS /A:220
```

■   The CD-ROM port setup driver (if the sound board is so equipped):

```
DEVICE=C:\SB16\DRV\CDSETUP.SYS /P:340
```

■   The proprietary CD-ROM driver (if the sound board is so equipped):

```
DEVICE=C:\SB16\DRV\MTMCDAE.SYS /D:MSCD001 /P:340 /A:0 /T:5 /I:11
```

FULL-DUPLEX DRIVERS

Many current sound board designs are compatible with "multimedia communication" technologies such as Internet Phone, NetMeeting, and other communication tools. These tools require full-duplex operation. That is, sound is digitized with the microphone, and received sound is played through the speakers simultaneously. This demands full-duplex drivers. If you plan to use communication tools, you'll need to install full-duplex sound card drivers that are appropriate for your particular sound board and operating system. For example, the Creative Labs SB32, AWE32, and AWE64 require the Windows 95 (or later) full-duplex driver file (SBW95UP.EXE) available from the Creative Labs Web site at **www.creaf.com**. To use those same devices for full duplex under Windows NT 4.0, you'd need the AWENT40.EXE driver file (or later). As a rule, always check with the sound board maker for their latest full-duplex drivers.

 You may find that full-duplex drivers are not available for older sound boards or for sound boards running under OS/2 or Windows NT. In that case, you cannot support full-duplex applications and may need to upgrade the sound board before you can use that communication software.

SOUNDBOARD ACCELERATION

Modern sound boards incorporate an increasingly complex range of processing functions such as EAX sound effects and 3D "positional" sound. Such features are usually handled by the sound board itself (rather than straining the system processor). This is referred to as *sound hardware acceleration*—similar in principle to the way modern video adapters include onboard acceleration features. Normally, a sound board will handle acceleration features easily and with minimum impact on system stability. In a few cases, however, sound acceleration can result in system problems. When your sound board supports onboard acceleration, you can adjust the level of acceleration through the Multimedia icon in order to test system stability:

1. Click Start, highlight Settings, and then select Control Panel.

2. Double-click the Multimedia icon, and then select the Audio tab (if it's not already selected).

3. Select Advanced Properties in the Playback area, and then click the Performance tab (Figure 36-11).

4. Move the Hardware acceleration slider to None, then Apply your changes, and reboot the system (if necessary).

Test the system again. If the system's performance stabilizes, try moving up the slider again, one step at a time, until the system destabilizes. That's the point where your trouble is occurring, and a driver update will usually correct the problem. If the system's performance does not stabilize, you have an issue with something other than sound hardware acceleration.

MULTIPLE CODECS

Windows makes extensive use of *codecs* (coders/decoders) to support the variety of multimedia applications available. For example, video capture requires numerous codecs to encode the audio and video streams being passed to the PC. As another example, audio playback requires one codec for each type of audio format. In many cases, you may find more than one copy of the same codec on the system. This can easily happen as various multimedia applications are installed and removed. When there is more than one instance of the same codec, conflicts may result that impair the performance of your multimedia applications.

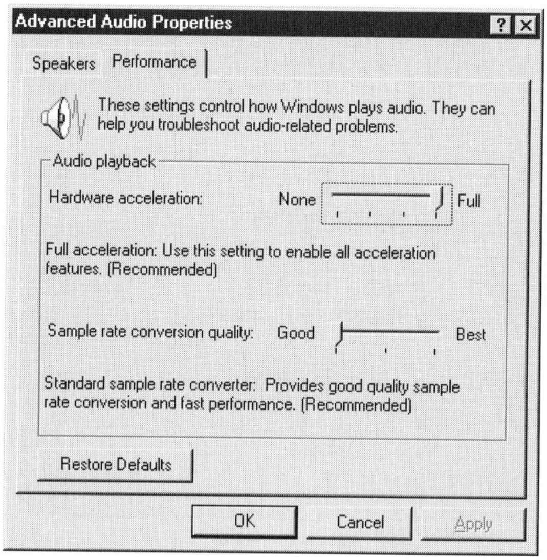

FIGURE 36-11   Adjusting sound board hardware acceleration

Whenever you encounter trouble with audio recording, playback, capture, and so on, always check for duplicate codecs under your Multimedia icon:

1.   Click Start, highlight Settings, and then select Control Panel.

2.   Double-click the Multimedia icon, and then select the Devices tab.

3.   Expand the Audio Compression Codecs entry (Figure 36-12), and look for duplicate entries.

4.   If you see duplicate entries, check the Properties for each instance, and remove the older instance.

5.   Apply your changes and reboot the system if necessary.

6.   You can check for duplicate codecs under entries as well.

WAV PLAYBACK PROBLEMS

Of all the sound board problems reported, perhaps the most common is the failure to play wave files (ordinary sound files with the .WAV extension) under Windows 98/Me. This problem usually manifests itself during the Windows start up or shutdown when the accompanying sounds are not played. A variety of issues can prevent WAV files from playing.

Program-Specific Problems

If you cannot play WAV files from a specific program that you use in Windows 98/Me, check to see if the same problem occurs when you play the file from another program. If the problem occurs *only* with one particular program, the files associated with that program may be damaged, there may be a missing codec (or duplicate codecs), or that program may not be configured correctly under Windows. If you cannot get WAV files to play under *any* application, chances are that another issue is responsible.

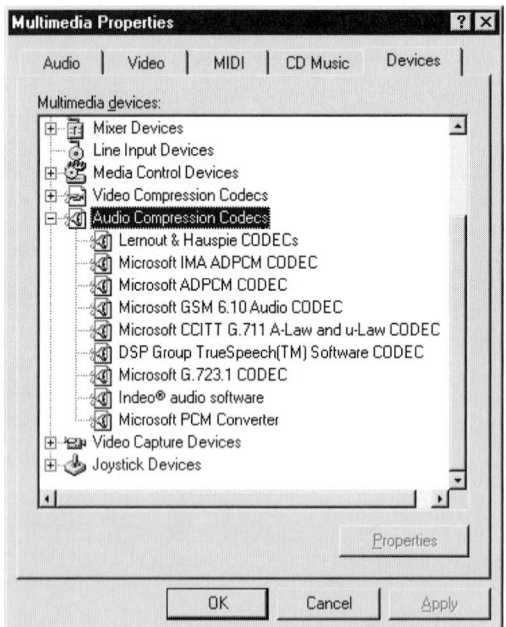

FIGURE 36-12   Checking for duplicate audio codecs on the system

Sound Device Not Configured Properly

If you cannot play any WAV files in Windows 9x/Me (or if WAV files are not played at the proper volume), you may not have a sound device selected, or the sound device that you have selected may not be configured properly. To select and configure a sound device in Windows:

1. Open the Control Panel, and double-click the Multimedia icon.

2. In the Playback area under the Audio tab (Figure 36-13), click the playback device that you want to use in the Preferred device list. Click the Playback icon and set the master volume to an adequate level (usually 50–75 percent volume is adequate).

3. In the Recording area under the Audio tab, click the playback device that you want to use in the Preferred device list. Click the Recording icon, and set the Microphone volume to an adequate level.

4. Make sure that the speakers are properly connected to the sound card and that the speakers are turned on.

Mixer Settings Not Configured Properly

If you cannot play any WAV files under Windows 9x/Me (or if WAV files are not played at the proper volume), the mixer control settings may not be configured properly. You can use the mixer control program included with Windows (see Figure 36-10) to adjust the volume for playback, recording, and voice commands. To configure mixer control settings for Windows 98/SE:

1. Click the Start button, point to Programs, point to Accessories, point to Entertainment, and then click Volume Control.

2. Make sure that the "Mute all" check box below the Volume Control slider and the Mute check box below the Wave slider are not selected, and that the Balance sliders for Volume Control and Wave are in the center of the scale.

3. Move the Volume Control and Wave sliders at least halfway to the top of the scale. You may need to adjust the current Volume Control or Wave settings to play WAV files at the volume level you want.

If the Volume Control and Wave sliders do not appear, click Properties on the Options menu, and then select the Volume Control and Wave check boxes in the "Show the following volume controls" box.

Sound Hardware Not Configured Properly

It is possible that your sound board may not be compatible with the type of WAV file you are attempting to play, or there may be a resource conflict between your sound board and another device installed in your computer. Check the Device Manager to see if there are any resource conflicts with your sound board. To determine whether your sound card supports the WAV file format you are attempting to play, contact the sound card's manufacturer.

Damaged Sound Files

If you cannot play certain WAV files in Windows 9x/Me (or if the WAV files are not played properly), the WAV files themselves may be damaged. To check if a WAV file is damaged, right-click the WAV file in Windows Explorer, click Properties on the menu, and then click the Details tab. The Audio Format line should contain information about the type of compression used to compress the file, the sound quality of the file, and whether the file is in stereo. If this information is missing, the WAV file is probably damaged and should be reinstalled or recopied to the drive.

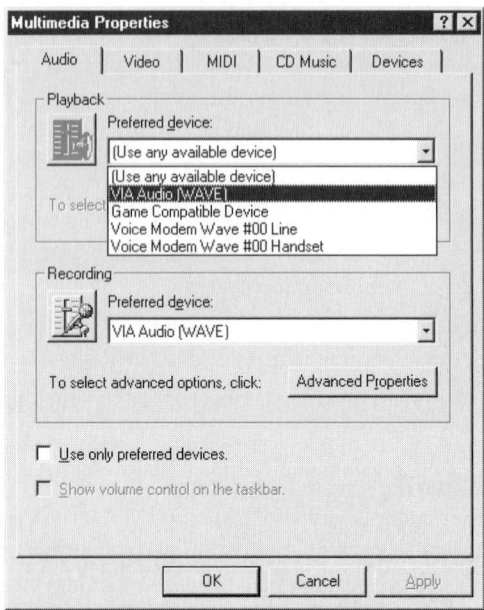

FIGURE 36-13   Selecting a playback device under Windows

If you can play other WAV files of a similar format, chances are good that the suspect file is indeed damaged. If you can play WAV files of different formats, but not WAV files of a particular format, it may be that your sound board does not support that format.

Compression-Related Problems

Windows 9x/Me includes 32-bit versions of several common codecs including *Adaptive Delta Pulse Code Modulation* (ADPCM), *Interactive Multimedia Association* (IMA) ADPCM, *Group Special Mobile* (GSM) 6.10, *Consultative Committee for International Telephone and Telegraph* (CCITT) G.711 A-Law and u-Law, and Truespeech from DSP. These 32-bit codecs are installed by default during Windows setup and are used by multimedia programs even if a 16-bit version of the same codec is available. Make sure that the WAV file format is supported by an available codec. Otherwise, you may need to install an appropriate codec.

HARDWARE SYMPTOMS

Although sound boards are reasonably reliable devices, there are many specific problems that cannot be resolved with the preceding general guidelines. When you're facing an issue with a sound device, refer to the following symptoms for possible explanations and solutions.

SYMPTOM 36-1   **A noticeable buzz or hum is produced in one or both speakers**
Low-cost speakers generally use unshielded cables. Unfortunately, strong signals from AC cords and other signal-carrying conductors can easily induce interference in the speaker wires. Try rerouting speaker cables clear of other cables in the system. If problems persist, try using higher-quality speakers with shielded cables and enclosures. In most cases, that should resolve everyday noise problems. If the noise continues regardless of what you do, there may be a fault in the sound board's amplifier. Try moving

the sound board to another bus slot away from other boards or the power supply. If that does not resolve the problem, try a new sound board.

SYMPTOM 36-2   **There is no sound from the speaker(s) when using the sound board in the real mode**   The lack of sound from a sound board can be due to any one of a wide range of potential problems. If the sound board works with some applications but not with others, it is likely that the problem is due to an improperly installed or configured application. See that the offending application is set up properly. (And make sure it is even capable of using the sound card.) Also check that the proper sound driver files (if any) are loaded into CONFIG.SYS and AUTOEXEC.BAT as required. In many cases, there are one or two sound-related environment variables that are set in AUTOEXEC.BAT. Make sure that your start-up files are configured properly.

Check your speakers next. See that they are turned on and set to a normal volume level. The speakers should be receiving adequate power and should be plugged properly into the correct output jack. If speakers have been plugged into the wrong jack, no sound will be produced. If the cable is broken or questionable, try a new set of speakers. Also see that the master volume control on the sound board is turned up most (or all) of the way. If volume is controlled through software, see that the mixer volume levels are set adequately.

If problems continue, there may be a resource conflict between the sound board and another device in the system. Examine the IRQ, DMA, and I/O settings of each device in the system. Make sure that no two devices are using the same resources. If problems persist, and no conflict is present, try another sound board.

SYMPTOM 36-3   **CD audio will not play through the sound board**   This problem can occur under both DOS and Windows. First, make sure that the sound board is actually capable of playing CD audio. (Older boards may not be compatible.) If the sound card is playing sound files, but is not playing CD audio, there are several things for you to check. First, open the PC and make sure that the CD audio cable (a thin, 4-wire cable) is attached from the CD-ROM drive to the sound board. If this cable is broken, disconnected, or absent, CD audio will not be passed to the sound board. If the cable is intact, make sure that the CD audio player is configured properly for the sound board you are using, and check the start-up files to see that any drivers and environment variable needed by CONFIG.SYS and AUTOEXEC.BAT are available. If the CD-audio fails to play under Windows 9x/Me, make sure that an MCI (multimedia control interface) CD audio driver is included in the list of Audio Compression Codecs in the Devices tab under you Multimedia icon.

SYMPTOM 36-4   **You see an error such as "No interrupt vector available"**   The DOS interrupt vectors used by the sound board's setup drivers (usually INT 80h to BFh) are being used by one or more other drivers in the system. As a consequence, there is a software conflict. Try disabling other drivers in the system one at a time until you see the conflict disappear. Once you have isolated the offending driver(s), you can leave them disabled or (if possible) alter their command-line settings so that they no longer conflict with the sound board's software.

SYMPTOM 36-5   **There is no MIDI output**   Make sure that the file you are trying to play is a valid MIDI file (usually with a .MID extension). In most cases, you will find that the MIDI Mapper under Windows is not set up properly for the sound board. Load the Windows MIDI Mapper applet from the Control Panel, and set it properly to accommodate your sound board. In some cases, you may simply need to remove the sound device from the Device Manager, and then allow Windows to redetect the device and install the latest drivers for the sound board.

SYMPTOM 36-6   **Sound play is jerky**   Choppy or jerky sound playback is typically the result of a hard drive problem. More specifically, the drive cannot read the sound file to a buffer fast enough. In many cases, the reason for this slow drive performance is excessive disk fragmentation. Try defragmenting the drive with Disk Defragmenter under Windows. If the problem persists, try reducing the sound quality or disabling special sound effects in order to reduce the sound processing load on the system.

SYMPTOM 36-7   **You see an error such as "Out of environment space"**   The system is out of DOS environment space. You will need to increase the system's environment space by adding the following line to your CONFIG.SYS file:

```
shell=c:\command.com /E:512 /P
```

This command line sets the environment space to 512 bytes. If you still encounter the error message, change the E entry to 1024 (that is, **/E:1024**).

SYMPTOM 36-8   **Regular "clicks," "stutters," or "hiccups" occur during the playback of speech**   This may also be heard as a "garbled" sound in speech or sound effects. In virtually all cases, the system CPU is simply not fast enough to permit buffering without dropping sound data. Systems with i286 and slower i386 CPUs typically suffer this kind of problem. This is often compounded by insufficient memory (especially under Windows) that automatically resorts to virtual memory. Since virtual memory is delivered by the hard drive, and the hard drive is much slower than RAM anyway, the hard drive simply can't provide data fast enough. Unfortunately, there is little to be done in this kind of situation (aside from adding RAM, upgrading the CPU, or changing the motherboard). If it is possible to shut off various sound features (such as music, voice, effects, and so on), try shutting down any extra sound features that you can live without. Make sure that there are no TSRs or other applications running in the background that may be demanding valuable system processing time.

SYMPTOM 36-9   **The joystick is not working, or not working properly on all systems**   This problem only applies to sound boards with a multifunction MIDI/joystick port being used in the joystick mode. Chances are that the joystick is conflicting with another joystick port in the system. Disable the original joystick port or the new joystick port. Only one joystick port (game adapter) can be active at any one time in the system. Since joystick performance is dependent on CPU speed, the CPU may actually be too fast for the joystick port. Disable the joystick port, or try slowing down the CPU.

SYMPTOM 36-10   **You install a sound board and everything works properly, but now the printer does not seem to work**   There is an interrupt conflict between the sound board and an IRQ line used by the printer. While parallel printers are often polled, they can also be driven by an IRQ line (IRQ5 or IRQ7). If the sound board is using either one of these interrupts, try changing to an alternative IRQ line. When changing an IRQ line, be sure to reflect the changes in any sound board files called by CONFIG.SYS or AUTOEXEC.BAT.

SYMPTOM 36-11   **You see the message "Error MMSYSTEM 337: The specified MIDI device is already in use"**   This problem often occurs with high-end sound boards such as the Creative Labs AWE64. This error is often caused by having the sound board's mixer display turned on with the wavetable synthesizer selected (for example, the LED display in the Creative Mixer turned on and Creative Wave Synthesizer selected as the MIDI playback device). You can usually correct the problem by turning the mixer display off.

SYMPTOM 36-12   You see the message "Error: Wave device already in use" when trying to play wave files while a MIDI file is playing   This problem often occurs with high-end sound boards such as the Creative Labs AWE64 and is usually the result of a device configuration problem. If full-duplex is turned on and you try to play a WAV file and a MIDI file at the same time with the wavetable synthesizer (such as the Creative Wave Synthesizer) selected as the MIDI playback device, an error will occur. To resolve this problem, you need to turn off the full-duplex mode:

1. Hold down the ALT key, and double-click on My Computer.

2. Select the Device Manager tab. There should be a listing for Sound, Video, and Game Controllers in the Device Manager; double-click on the listing to expand it.

3. You should now see a listing for the sound device (such as Creative AWE32 16-Bit Audio). Double-click on the listing, and then select the Settings tab. Uncheck the box labeled "Allow full-duplex operation." Click OK until you are back to the Control Panel.

4. Now try to play a WAV and MIDI file at the same time.

SYMPTOM 36-13   You hear pops and clicks when recording sound under Windows 9x/Me   There is insufficient cache to adequately support the recording process (or cache is improperly configured). Try the following procedure to alter the way cache is allocated:

1. Open Notepad and load SYSTEM.INI.

2. Locate the area of SYSTEM.INI labeled [vcache].

3. Add the following line below [vcache]:

    ```
    maxfilecache=2048
    ```

4. Save your changes to the SYSTEM.INI file.

5. From the desktop, right-click on My Computer, and then select Properties.

6. Select the Performance page, and then click on File System.

7. Find the slider marked "Read-ahead optimization," and then pull the slider to None.

8. Save your changes and restart Windows.

SYMPTOM 36-14   You notice high-frequency distortion in one or possibly both channels   In many cases, the AT Bus Clock is set over 8 MHz, and data is being randomly lost. This problem usually occurs in very fast systems using an ISA sound board. Enter the system's CMOS Setup, and check the AT Bus Clock under the Advanced Chipset Setup area. See that the bus clock is set as close as possible to 8 MHz. If the bus clock is derived as a divisor of the CPU clock, you may see an entry such as /4. Make sure that the selected divisor results in a clock speed as close to 8 MHz as possible. If problems still persist, try increasing the divisor to drop the bus speed below 8 MHz. (Note that this may have an adverse effect on other ISA peripherals.) Another alternative is to replace the ISA card with an updated PCI sound board.

SYMPTOM 36-15   You hear pops and clicks when playing back prerecorded files under Windows 9x/Me   There is an excessive processing load on the system that is often caused by virtual memory and/or 32-bit access. Start by disabling virtual memory. Open the Control Panel and double-click on the System icon. Select the Performance page, and click on Virtual Memory. Set the swap file to None and save your changes. Try the file playback again. If problems persist, try disabling 32-bit file access. If that still does not resolve the problem, try disabling 32-bit disk access.

SYMPTOM 36-16   You hear pops and clicks on new recordings only; preexisting files sound clean   This is often due to issues with software caching. If you are using DOS or Windows 3.1, disable SmartDrive from both CONFIG.SYS and AUTOEXEC.BAT, and then restart the computer for your changes to take effect. If problems continue (or you are using Windows 9x/Me), there may be an excessive processing load on the system due to virtual memory or 32-bit access. Follow the recommendations under Symptom 36-15.

SYMPTOM 36-17   You hear pops and clicks when playing back or recording any sound file   In most cases, there is a wiring problem with the speaker system. Check all of your cabling between the sound board and speakers. If the speakers are powered by AC, make sure that the power jack is inserted properly. If the speakers are powered by battery, make sure that the batteries are fresh. Check for loose connections. If you cannot resolve the problem, try some new speakers. If the problem persists, replace the sound board.

SYMPTOM 36-18   The sound board will play back fine, but it will not record   The board probably records fine in DOS, but not in Windows. If the sound board is using 16-bit DMA transfer (typical under Windows), there are two DMA channels in use. Chances are that one of those two DMA channels is conflicting with another device in the system. Determine the DMA channels being used under Windows, and then check other devices for DMA conflicts. If you are using Windows 98/Me, check the Device Manager and look for entries marked with a yellow icon.

SYMPTOM 36-19   A DMA error is produced when using a sound board with an Adaptec 2842 controller in the system   This is a known problem with the Digital Audio Labs "DOC" product and the Adaptec 2842. You will need to alter the controller's FIFO buffer. Go to the controller's setup by pressing CTRL-A when prompted during system start up. Select the advanced configuration option, and then select the FIFO threshold. Chances are that it will be set to 100 percent. Try setting the FIFO threshold to 0 percent, and see if this makes a difference.

SYMPTOM 36-20   A DMA error is produced when using a sound board with an Adaptec 1542 controller in the system   This is a known problem with the Digital Audio Labs "DOC" sound product and the Adaptec 1542. The problem can usually be resolved by rearranging the DMA channels. Place the Adaptec controller on DMA 7, and then place the sound board on DMA 5 for playback and DMA 6 for recording.

SYMPTOM 36-21   You encounter DMA errors using an older sound board and an Adaptec 1542   In many cases, you can clear DMA issues by slowing down the 1542 using the **/n** switch. Add the **/n** switch to the ASPI4DOS command line in CONFIG.SYS such as:

```
device=c:\aspi4dos.sys /n2
```

If slowing down the 1542 with an **/n2** switch doesn't fix the problem, then you should strongly consider upgrading the sound board. This is a known problem with the older Digital Audio Labs CardD sound board.

SYMPTOM 36-22   **The sound board will not play or record—the system locks up when either is attempted**   The board will probably not play in either DOS or Windows, but may run fine on other systems. This is a problem that has been identified with some sound boards and ATI video boards. ATI video boards use unusual address ranges that sometimes overlap the I/O address used by the sound board. Reconfigure the sound board to another I/O address (if possible), or replace the sound board with a fully PnP PCI model.

SYMPTOM 36-23   **The sound board will record, but will not play back**   Assuming that the sound board and its drivers are installed and configured properly, chances are that a playback oscillator on the sound board has failed. Try replacing the sound board.

SYMPTOM 36-24   **The sound application or editor produces a significant number of DMA errors**   This type of problem is known to occur frequently when using the standard VGA driver that accompanies Windows. The driver is poorly written and cannot keep up with screen draws. Try updating your video driver to a later, more efficient version. If the driver is known to contain bugs, try using a generic video driver written for the video board's chipset.

SYMPTOM 36-25   **The sound board will not record in DOS**   There are several possible problems that can account for this behavior. First, suspect a hardware conflict between the sound board and other devices in the system. Make sure that the IRQs, DMA channels, and I/O port addresses used by the sound board are not used by other devices. If the hardware setup appears correct, suspect a problem between DOS drivers. Try a clean boot of the system (with no CONFIG.SYS or AUTOEXEC.BAT). If sound can be run properly now, there is a driver conflict. Examine your entries in CONFIG.SYS or AUTOEXEC.BAT for possible conflicts, or for older drivers that may still be loading to support hardware that is no longer in the system.

Finally, suspect the hard drive controller. Try setting up a RAM drive with RAMDRIVE.SYS. You can install a RAM drive on your system by adding the line:

```
device=c:\dos\ramdrive.sys /e 8000
```

The 8000 is for 8MB worth of RAM. Make sure there is enough RAM in the PC. Once the RAMdrive is set up, try recording and playing from the RAM drive. (You may have to specify a new path in the sound recorder program.) If that works, the hard drive controller may simply be too slow to support the sound board, and you may need to consider upgrading the drive system.

SYMPTOM 36-26   **When recording sound, the system locks up if a key other than the recorder's "hot keys" is pushed**   This is a frequent problem under Windows 3.1x. The system sounds (generated under Windows) may be interfering with the sound recorder. Try turning off system sounds. Go to the Main icon, choose the Control Panel, and then select Sounds. There will be a box in the lower-left corner marked "Enable system sounds." Clear the check mark, and then click OK.

SYMPTOM 36-27   **After the sound board driver is loaded, Windows locks up when starting or exiting**   In virtually all cases, you have a hardware conflict between the sound board and another device in the system. Make sure that the IRQs, DMA channels, and I/O port addressed used by the sound board are not used by other devices. You may need to upgrade the sound board with a fully PnP PCI model.

SYMPTOM 36-28   **When using Windows sound editing software, the sound board refuses to enter the "digital" mode—always switching back to the analog mode**   Generally speaking, this is a software configuration issue. Make sure that your editing (or other sound) software is set for the correct type of sound board (such as an AWE32 instead of a Sound Blaster 16/Pro). If problems persist, the issue is with your sound drivers. Check the [drivers] section of the Windows SYSTEM.INI file for your sound board driver entries. If there is more than one entry, you may need to disable the competing driver. This is a known problem with the Digital Audio Labs CardDplus and is caused by incorrect driver listings. For example, the proper CardDplus driver must be entered as:

```
Wave=cardp.drv
```

and the companion driver must be listed as:

```
Wave1=tahiti.drv
```

You will need to make sure that the proper driver(s) for your sound board are entered in SYSTEM.INI. You may also need to restart the system after making any changes.

SYMPTOM 36-29   **The microphone records at very low levels (or not at all)**   Suspect the microphone itself. Most sound boards demand the use of a good-quality dynamic microphone. Also, Creative Labs and Labtec microphones are not always compatible with sound boards from other manufacturers. Try a generic dynamic microphone. Make sure that the card's phantom power is set properly for the microphone being used. Phantom power should be on for condenser microphones and off for dynamic microphones. If problems persist, chances are that your recording software is not configured properly for microphone input. Try the following procedure to set up the recording application properly under Windows 9x/Me:

1.   Open your Control Panel and double-click on the Multimedia icon.

2.   The Multimedia Properties dialog will open. Select the Audio page.

3.   See that the Preferred device and Preferred quality settings are correct.

4.   Save your changes and reboot the system if necessary.

5.   Open the Volume Control applet, and set the microphone volume to an adequate level.

SYMPTOM 36-30   **The sound card isn't working in full-duplex mode**   Virtually all current sound boards are capable of full-duplex operation for such applications as Internet phones. Check the specifications for your sound board, and verify that the board is capable of full-duplex operation. If it is, and full duplex isn't working, your driver may be inadequate, or the audio properties may be set up incorrectly:

1.   Open your Control Panel and double-click on the Multimedia icon.

2.   The Multimedia Properties dialog will open. Select the Audio page.

3.   If the Playback device and the Record device are set to the same I/O address, this is only half duplex.

4.   Change the playback device I/O address so it is different from the record device address.

5.   Click the Apply button, and then click the OK button.

6.   You should now be in full-duplex mode.

Most of the very latest sound boards (such as the Monster Sound 400) will carry full-duplex operation with the *same* playback and record device selected. You may simply need to update the sound device drivers.

SYMPTOM 36-31 **Your dynamic microphone clips terribly, and recordings are noisy and faint** This is probably due to phantom power being switched on in your sound board. Try turning the phantom power off. If you cannot turn phantom power off, try plugging the dynamic microphone into the sound board's line input jack. Remember to open the sound board's mixer applet, and set the line input level properly.

SYMPTOM 36-32 **You have trouble using Creative Labs or Labtec microphones with your (non–Creative Labs) sound board** This is a common complaint among Ensoniq sound board users. It turns out that Ensoniq sound boards are not compatible with Creative Labs or Labtec microphones. Try a generic microphone instead.

SYMPTOM 36-33 **There is static at the remote end when talking through a voice application such as WebPhone** Noise is occurring at the line input or microphone input that is being transmitted to the remote listener. Check the line input signal. You might try reducing or turning off the line input mixer level. If the problem persists, check your phantom power setting and your microphone. Try reducing the microphone level in the sound board's mixer. Try a different microphone.

SYMPTOM 36-34 **You encounter pops and cracks during recording or playback** This is a known problem with a Sound Blaster Live and Windows 98 on a VIA motherboard using either an Apollo VP3 (VT82C597) or Apollo MVP3 (VT82C598) system controller chipset and a VIA IDE bus master driver version 2.1.33 update. Follow these steps to remove the popping/cracking sound:

1. Run SETUP.EXE of the VIA IDE Bus master driver version 2.1.33 again.

2. Select the Enable/Disable (Ultra) DMA option instead, and then click the Next button.

3. Unselect/uncheck the available devices, and then click the Next button.

4. Reboot the system.

Please check the VIA Web site at **www.viatech.com** for updates on your motherboard.

SYMPTOM 36-35 **You encounter short bursts of sound when playing a WAV file** This problem happens when you're using a Sound Blaster Live card on VIA motherboard with the Apollo VP3 (VT82C597) or Apollo MVP3 (VT82C598) system controller chipset. This combination causes repeated buffering during a WAV playback on Windows 98 (Version 4.10.1998). To resolve this problem, download and install the VIA PCI IRQ Miniport driver version 1.3a Setup program. This program can be obtained from the VIA Web site **www.via.com.tw/**. Reboot the system after installing the update.

SYMPTOM 36-36 **The sound card's SB16 emulation is causing IRQ conflicts on the PC** You'll need to disable this device:

1. Click Start, highlight Settings, and click Control Panel.

2. Double-click the System icon, and then click the Device Manager tab.

3. Click the plus sign (+) next to "Creative Miscellaneous Devices."

4. Click the sound card's "SB16 Emulation" to highlight it, and then click Properties.

5. Select the "Disable in this hardware profile" check box.

6. Save your changes and reboot the system if necessary.

 This will disable your sound device in the DOS mode.

SYMPTOM 36-37 **You stop hearing sounds after the system resumes from suspend mode under Windows 98/SE** If your computer enters the suspend mode while a program using DirectSound is running, you may no longer hear sounds from the program after you resume the computer. This problem can occur if the DirectSound components of your platform (such as an older version of DirectX) do not resume properly. To correct the issue permanently, download and install the latest version of DirectX from Microsoft at **windowsupdate.microsoft.com/**. You can work around the problem and restore sound to the program by rebooting the system and not allowing the system to enter the suspend mode.

SYMPTOM 36-38 **No WAV sounds are played with Ensoniq PCI sound cards under Windows 98/SE** When you're using an Ensoniq PCI sound card, WAV files may not be played properly (or at all), even though MIDI files can be heard normally. This problem occurs if the preferred audio playback device is set to "Use any device." To hear WAV file playback, set the Ensoniq card as the preferred device:

1. Click Start, highlight Settings, and then click Control Panel.

2. Double-click the Multimedia icon.

3. Click the Audio tab.

4. In the Playback section, click Ensoniq in the Preferred device box.

5. Click OK and reboot the PC if necessary.

SYMPTOM 36-39 **Your USB speakers don't work after upgrading to Windows 98/SE** This trouble will occur if another sound card was detected as the preferred audio playback device during the installation of Windows 98/SE. To correct this problem, select the USB audio device as the preferred playback device:

1. Click Start, highlight Settings, and then click Control Panel.

2. Double-click the Multimedia icon.

3. Click the Audio tab.

4. In the Playback section, click your USB audio device in the Preferred device box.

5. Click OK and reboot the PC if necessary.

SYMPTOM 36-40 **You get no volume from Yamaha USB speakers** This is a known problem for the Yamaha YSTMS55D USB speakers under Windows 98/SE. After you install the Yamaha USB speakers, the speakers may produce little (or no) volume when you use the volume control knob on the speakers. This problem is almost always caused by an incompatible Yamaha driver. You'll need to reinstall or update the device drivers and applications software for your speakers. For the Yamaha speakers, reinstall the Windows 95/98 driver for the Yamaha USB device, the Yamaha Human Interface Device, and the Yamaha Sound Recorder from the original installation media:

1. Click Start, highlight Settings, click Control Panel, and then double-click the System icon.

2. On the Device Manager tab, double-click the Sound, Video and Game Controllers branch, and then double-click the "Yamaha USB device."

3. On the Driver tab, click the Update Driver button, click Next, click "Display a list of all the drivers in a specific location, so you can select the driver you want," and then click Next.

4. Click the appropriate Yamaha driver, click Next, click Next, click Finish, and then click Yes to restart your computer.

5. After you change the drivers, open the Volume Control tool, and move the volume settings to the highest level. You can then use the volume knob on the speakers to control the sound level.

SYMPTOM 36-41   **An Aztech 2316 sound card is mistakenly identified as a Sound Blaster Pro**   When you use the Add New Hardware wizard under Windows 98/SE to detect your Aztech 2316 sound card, it may be incorrectly identified as a Sound Blaster Pro sound card. To fix this error, use the Device Manager to install your Aztech 2316 sound card manually:

1. Click Start, highlight Settings, click Control Panel, and then double-click the System icon.

2. Click the Device Manager tab, double-click the Sound, Video and Game Controllers entry, and then double-click SoundBlaster Pro.

3. Click the Driver tab, click Update Driver, and then click Next.

4. Click "Display a list of all the drivers in a specific location…", and then click Next.

5. Click "Show all hardware," click Aztech Labs, and then click "Aztech 2316 Compatible Legacy Audio (WDM)."

6. Click Next, and then click Finish.

7. Restart your computer.

SYMPTOM 36-42   **Your sound card delivers a "DSP timeout"**   This often happens on 440GX motherboards under Windows 98, and you'll find this happens even though you switch card slots and reinstall/update the sound card's drivers. The problem is with the motherboard's chipset (usually a 440GX). You must download the .INF update utility for the GX chipset from your system or motherboard manufacturer. This motherboard is newer than Windows 98 and must have this patch installed for PCI and AGP devices to function correctly.

SYMPTOM 36-43   **You replace a legacy ISA sound card with a PCI sound card, and now you get a "virtual device driver (VxD)" error at boot time**   The problem is almost always caused by the *old* sound card drivers (not the new sound card drivers). Chances are that you did not remove or uninstall the old sound card's drivers and application software, and they're still trying to load when the system boots. Since the old card is no longer installed, the drivers show an error and refuse to load. You'll need to remove the old sound card's drivers and uninstall the old application software. In some cases, you may then need to reinstall the newest sound drivers and applets.

SYMPTOM 36-44   **You find that your speakers "sleep" or the bass is too low**   This is a known problem with Cambridge 4 Point surround speakers and is almost always caused by a driver problem. Aureal has released a set of drivers (2030_22rc or later) that should address this issue. Go to

www.a3d.com/html/download/drivers/ and download the complete drivers for the Vortex 2 chipset. These drivers will allow the bass to function normally in both stereo and quad modes.

SYMPTOM 36-45 **You cannot install a sound card's software before installing the sound card** This is a known problem with Phoenix BIOS and LiveWare 2.0 when you're installing a Sound Blaster Live card. To install the sound software, you should install the sound card and its drivers first. Install the sound board and reboot your PC. After the PC has restarted, Windows 95/98 will attempt to detect your audio card and install drivers for it. Insert the original installation disc that comes with your sound board into the CD-ROM drive. When prompted to install the drivers:

1. Choose to install the drivers provided by your hardware manufacturer (found in the installation disc).

2. Specify the location and path where the driver software is located.

3. Now run the software setup program.

SYMPTOM 36-46 **You encounter an error such as "Setup cannot detect the sound card on your system"** The sound application's setup program cannot detect the sound card hardware, so you'll need to make a few quick checks to isolate the problem:

- Check that the sound card is listed and enabled under your Device Manager.

- Use another mouse device, or disconnect it entirely.

- Restart the system to your CMOS Setup, and see that your PNP OS INSTALLED option is set to Yes.

- Try moving the card to another PCI slot.

SYMPTOM 36-47 **Your sound card's application software will not install on a Cyrix-based system** This is a known issue with LiveWare 2.0 software on Cyrix 6x86 266-MHz (and slower) systems. Check the software's maker to see if there's a patch or update that will work around this problem. Otherwise, you may not be able to use the software on that system.

SYMPTOM 36-48 **You try to play back more than one source (such as microphone and CD audio), but you cannot keep the sources unmuted at the same time in the mixer** In the sound card's application software (a.k.a. mixer), make sure that the "What you hear" option is not chosen as the Record source. Choosing another recording source will enable you to unmute multiple analog sources at the same time. However, note that "environment" audio effects can only be applied to the analog source specified as the Recording source.

SYMPTOM 36-49 **You find that the mixer settings change every time you switch to an "environment preset" in the surround (A3D) mixer** You're probably trying to maintain the same mixer settings all the time. You can achieve this by dissociating the mixer from the environment preset. To do this with software like LiveWare 2.0, click the Surround Mixer title in the upper-left corner in the Preset Deck of the Surround Mixer. The system menu appears with Dissociate Mixer Settings. To dissociate mixer settings, make sure the command is checked. To associate mixer settings, make sure the command is not checked.

SYMPTOM 36-50   You've associated an application to the "environment presets," but the "environmental audio" preset is not activated when the application is launched
Chances are that the "AutoEA" feature is not working—it must be running. This means the AutoEA icon must appear in the System Tray, or the AutoEA applet must be open. Remember that the AutoEA feature will not work if your current speaker configuration doesn't conform to the one specified in AutoEA. For example, if you specified "2 speakers" in AutoEA, it won't work if your current speaker configuration is "4 speakers."

SYMPTOM 36-51   The game's acoustics don't seem any different whether "environmental audio effects" (EAX) is enabled or not   Chances are that your EAX system is not initialized properly. For EAX to initialize correctly, you should verify that the current "environmental audio" setting is set as No Effects.

SYMPTOM 36-52   You notice slower frame rates with some games when using "environmental audio effects" (EAX) with your sound card's application software
This is a problem with the sound board's application software and not the game itself. Download and install the latest update to your sound board's drivers and application software. This should optimize the game's frame rate by streamlining its audio effect performance.

SYMPTOM 36-53   You encounter numerous problems with the sound card's application software   These problems may take several forms:

- You hear pops or clicks when using certain features in a given game (such as using the "RazorJack" weapon in Unreal Tournament).

- You can't use an in-game volume slider in some games after installing the application software.

- You cannot import game presets for your audio setup.

In all cases, the sound card's application software (such as LiveWare 2.0) is buggy or corrupted. Download and install the newest version of your sound card drivers and application software.

SYMPTOM 36-54   Your sound card's application software locks up when trying to play audio CDs   This is a known issue with software like Creative PlayCenter. The IDE bus mastering hard disk controllers on your system must support the DMA option for high-speed access to your CD-ROM drive correctly. If the hard disk controllers do not properly support this option, your software may lock up. To determine if your hard disk controller drivers need updating:

1.   Click Start, highlight Settings, and click Control Panel.
2.   Double-click the System icon, and then click the Device Manager tab.
3.   Click the plus sign (+) next to the "CD-ROM" entry.
4.   Click the first device listed under "CD-ROM" to highlight it, and then click Properties.
5.   Click the Settings tab. If there's a check box labeled "DMA," clear the box.
6.   Repeat these steps for any other devices listed under the CD-ROM entry.
7.   Save your changes and reboot the system if necessary.

If this does not solve the difficulty, you'll need to contact your motherboard manufacturer for updated bus mastering IDE hard disk controller drivers.

SYMPTOM 36-55 **When using a four-speaker system, you notice that the sound seems unbalanced in the four-speaker mode** Ensure that your speakers are properly placed so that the sound output is balanced. There is a chance that one or more of the audio devices (such as WAV, CD audio, or MIDI) are being positioned within the speaker environment in the Speaker applet—resulting in the imbalance. This could happen if your previous setting was for a Game Environment found on the Environments tab, and you continue to use this same setting for other media playback. Go to the Environments tab, and set this to No Effects (or use another neutral preset such as Multi-speaker Normal). Alternately, you can go to the Speaker applet and choose another appropriate setting.

SYMPTOM 36-56 **CD audio is not loud, even with the volume turned all the way up** If your CD audio signal is not loud enough, it is most likely because you're using the A3D reference drivers for your sound card. The A3D drivers add a new feature that allows you to pass the CD audio through an equalizer (or EQ), and your EQ is affecting the volume. Change the EQ settings, bypass the EQ, or go to A3D settings and remove "CD Audio" from the analog EQ pass-through list.

SYMPTOM 36-57 **After a new sound board is installed, the system locks up when trying to play sound and/or MIDI files** This is typical of a system hardware conflict between a legacy sound board and one or more other devices in the PC. Unfortunately, the only real way to resolve this type of problem is to remove the sound board and check its IRQ, DMA, and I/O settings against other boards in the PC. This is often a cumbersome and time-consuming process. As an alternative, try checking the Device Manager. You can compare the active resources against the sound board settings, and then adjust any settings that overlap. Also check the sound board software that is called by CONFIG.SYS and AUTOEXEC.BAT. If you have replaced an older sound board, make sure that any command-line references to the older software have been properly disabled with the REM statement.

If you're trying to use a PnP sound board under DOS, you'll need to add a DOS PnP configuration utility to your CONFIG.SYS file. The driver floppy disk that accompanied the PnP sound board should include an appropriate version of this driver. You may need to use this configuration utility to "reserve" the IRQ, DMA, and I/O resources being used by other legacy devices in the system. This will prevent the PnP BIOS from accidentally assigning the sound board to resources that are in use elsewhere.

SYMPTOM 36-58 **The system does not lock up during use, but there is no sound provided by the board** Start with the basics. Make sure that the speakers are turned on and powered properly, and then check that the speaker cable is properly plugged into the Speaker Out jack. Speakers inadvertently plugged into the Microphone In jack will not produce any sound. Next, check the sound board's volume control, and make sure it is turned up to at least 75 percent.

Under DOS, check the sound board software that is called by CONFIG.SYS and AUTOEXEC.BAT. See that the sound board software is installed properly. If you have replaced an older sound board, make sure that any command-line references to the older software have been properly disabled with the REM statement. Under Windows 95/98, see that there are no conflicts listed in the Device Manager, and verify that the correct sound board drivers are installed.

SYMPTOM 36-59   **The sound board works, but there is no CD audio under DOS**   I n
almost all cases there is no CD audio cable between the CD-ROM drive and sound board, or the cable is
damaged. Check the cable and try a new one. Some CD audio cables are wired a bit differently and will not
work with generic CD-ROM and sound board combinations. Also verify that the correct complement of
DOS sound card and CD-ROM drivers is installed to support CD audio playback. (Check to see if there is
a patch or update driver available.)

SYMPTOM 36-60   **The sound board works, but there is no CD audio under Windows
9x/Me**   The first thing you should suspect is that the CD audio cable between the CD-ROM and sound
board is absent, disconnected, or damaged. Check the cable and try a new one. If the cable checks properly, check the Device Manager to verify that the correct complement of Windows sound board and
CD-ROM drivers is installed to support CD audio playback. (Check to see if there is a patch or update
driver available.)

SYMPTOM 36-61   **There is no sound during Windows events**   Windows sounds are
selected through the Sounds dialog under the Control Panel. If there are no sounds assigned, there will be
no sounds generated during Windows events. Check the Sounds dialog, and make sure the desired sounds
are assigned. If the proper sounds are assigned (but there are still no event sounds), check for the presence
of sound board drivers in the Device Manager.

Further Study

Altec-Lansing   www.altecmm.com
Creative Labs   www.creaf.com
Diamond Multimedia   www.diamondmm.com
Ensoniq   www.ensoniq.com
Frontier Design Group   www.frontierdesign.com/
Voyetra/Turtle Beach   www.tbeach.com/

37

VIDEO ADAPTERS
AND ACCELERATORS

The monitor itself is merely an output device (a "peripheral") that translates synchronized analog or TTL (Transistor to Transistor Logic) video signals into a visual image. Of course, a monitor alone is not good for very much—except perhaps as a conversation piece or a room-heater. The next logical question is: where does the video signal come from? A video adapter circuit (Figure 37-1) produces all video signals displayed on a monitor. The term "adapter" is often used because the PC is "adapted" to the particular monitor through this circuit. In most cases, the video adapter is an expansion board that plugs into the PC's available bus slots. It is the video adapter that converts raw data from the PC into image data that is stored in the adapter's *video memory*. The exact amount of memory available depends on the particular adapter and the video modes that the adapter is designed to support. The earliest adapters offered as little as 256KB, while the latest adapters provide 64MB or more. The video adapter then translates the contents of video memory into the video signals that drive a monitor.

The actual operations of a video adapter are certainly more involved than as described, but you can begin to appreciate the critical role that the video adapter plays in a PC. If a video adapter fails, the monitor will display gibberish (or nothing at all). To complicate matters even further, many current software applications require device drivers (called *video drivers*). A video driver is a rather small program that allows an operating system (such as Windows 9x/Me) to access a video adapter's high-resolution and high-color video modes with little or no interaction from the system BIOS. Video drivers have a profound effect on your video performance and stability, and during troubleshooting it will be necessary for you to isolate display problems to either the monitor, the video adapter, or video driver before a solution can be found. This chapter explains the operation and troubleshooting of typical 2D and 3D video adapters.

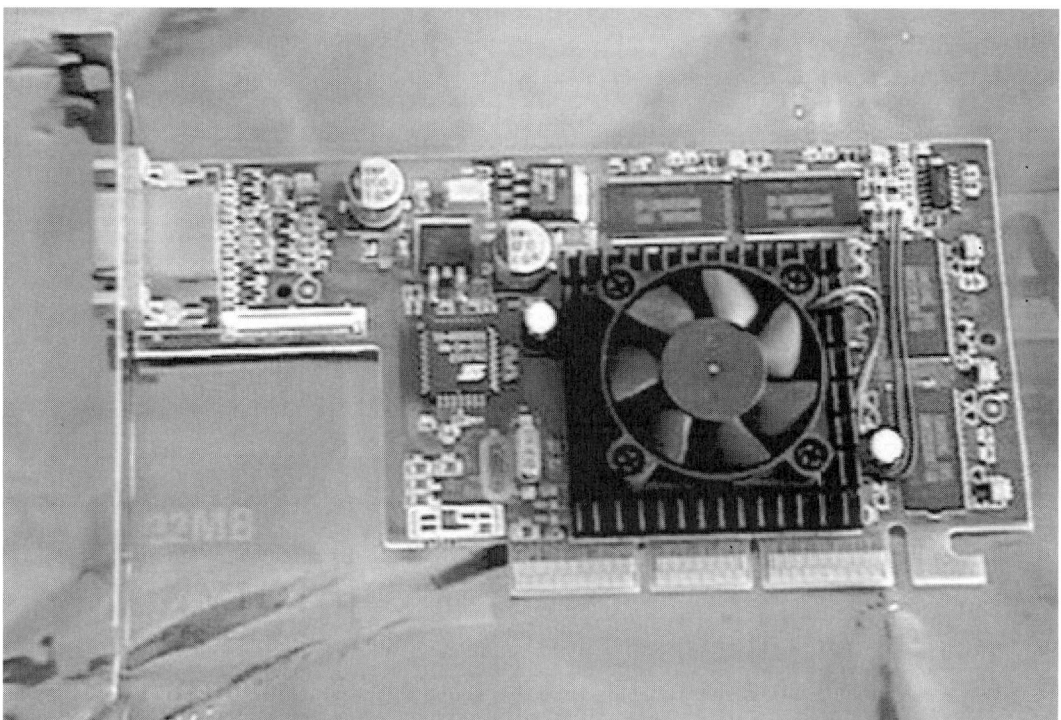

FIGURE 37-1   An ELSA ErazorX AGP graphics accelerator card

Understanding Conventional Video Adapters

The conventional frame buffer is the oldest and most well established type of video adapter. The term *frame buffer* refers to the adapter's operation—image data is loaded and stored in video memory one "frame" at a time. Frame buffer architecture (as shown in Figure 37-2) has changed very little since PCs first started displaying text and graphics. The heart of the frame-buffer video adapter is the highly integrated display controller chip (sometimes called a *CRTC* or *Cathode Ray Tube Controller*). The CRTC generates control signals and supervises adapter operation. It is the CRTC that reads video RAM (or VRAM) contents and passes those contents along for further processing. Many new video boards use specially designed chip groups (called *chipsets*) that are intended to work together. Chipsets provide fast, efficient video performance while minimizing the amount of overhead circuitry needed on a video adapter. Today, there is fierce competition between chipset designers and manufacturers to produce the fastest product with the latest features. For example, the NVIDIA GeForce3 graphics chipset contains 57 million transistors, 20 percent more than the Intel Pentium 4 processor.

TEXT VS. GRAPHICS

Video RAM also plays a vital role since it is RAM that holds the image data to be displayed. The video adapter can operate in two modes—text and graphic. In the *text* mode (for example, the DOS "command line" mode), ASCII characters are stored in video RAM. A *character ROM*, *character generator*, and *shift register* produce the pixel patterns that form ASCII screen characters. The character ROM holds a pixel pattern for every possible ASCII character (including letters, numbers, and punctuation marks). The character generator converts ROM data into a sequence of pixel bits and transfers them to a shift register. The shift register produces a bitstream. At the same time, an attribute decoder determines whether the defined ASCII character is to be displayed as blinking, inverted, high-intensity, standard text, or a text color (for color monitors). The signal generator is responsible for turning the ASCII serial bitstream from the shift register into the video and synchronization signals that actually drive the monitor. The signal generator may produce either analog or TTL video signals depending on how the particular monitor is to be operated. Today, virtually all color graphic monitors operate from analog video signals.

In the *graphic* mode (for example, the Windows 9x/Me desktop), video RAM locations will contain the color/grayscale information for each screen pixel rather than ASCII characters, so the character ROM and character-generating circuitry used in text mode is bypassed. For example, monochrome graphics uses a single bit per pixel, 16 color graphics uses 4 bits per pixel, 256 color graphics uses 8 bits per pixel, and so on. Pixel data taken from VRAM by the CRTC is passed through the character generator without any changes. Data is then sent directly to the shift register and on to the signal generator. It is the signal generator that produces analog or TTL video signals along with sync signals, as dictated by the CRTC.

ROM BIOS (Video BIOS)

There is one part of the classical video adapter that has not been mentioned yet—the *video BIOS*. The display controller requires substantial instruction changes when it is switched from text mode to any one of its available graphics modes. Since the instructions required to re-configure and direct the CRTC depend

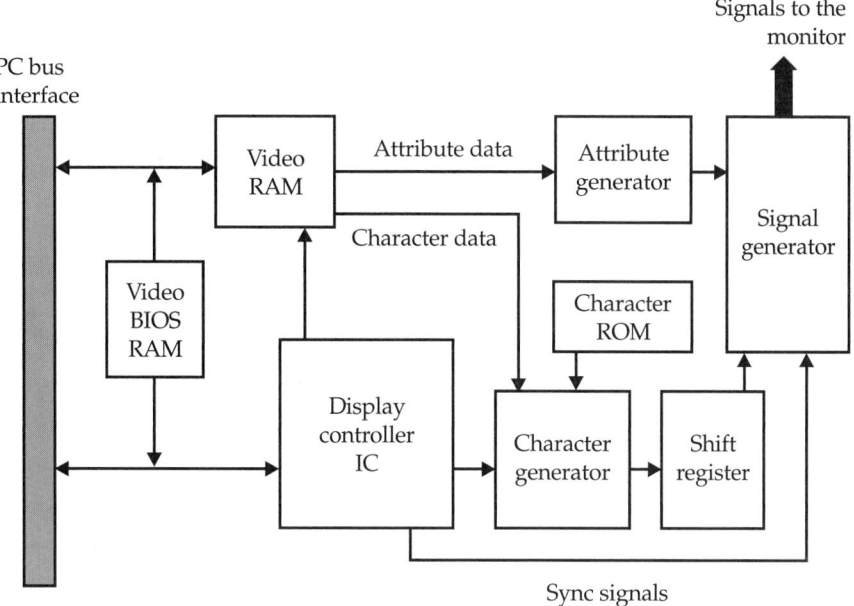

FIGURE 37-2   Block diagram of a simple frame buffer video adapter

on its particular design (and the video board design in general), it is impossible to rely on the particular software application or the PC's BIOS to provide the required software. As a result, all video adapters from EGA on use local BIOS ROM to hold the "firmware" needed by the particular display controller. Current PC architecture allocates about 128KB of space from C0000h to DFFFFh within the upper memory area. This space is reserved for devices with expansion ROMs such as hard drive controllers and video adapters. Motherboard BIOS works in conjunction with the video BIOS that is detected during the POST.

Modern video adapters often allow you to flash update the video BIOS. The procedure is similar to flashing a motherboard BIOS, but care should be taken to follow the exact directions available from various manufacturers' BIOS update Web sites.

Reviewing Video Display Hardware

The early days of PC development left users with a simple choice between monochrome or color graphics (all video adapters support text modes). In the years that followed, however, the proliferation of video adapters has brought an astonishing array of video modes and standards that you should be familiar with before upgrading a PC or attempting to troubleshoot a video system. This part of the chapter explains each of the video standards that have been developed in the last 20 plus years and shows you the video modes that each standard offers. Tables 37-1 and 37-2 provide a comprehensive listing of the standard hardware- and software-supported video modes for a 3Dfx Voodoo3 and NVIDIA GeForce 2 video accelerator.

TABLE 37-1   DISPLAY MODES FOR A 3DFX VOODOO 3 VIDEO ADAPTER

RESOLUTION	NUMBER OF COLORS	VERTICAL FREQUENCY (HZ)
320×200	256, 65K	70, 85
320×240	256, 65K	60, 70, 75, 85
400×300	256, 65K	60, 70, 75, 85
512×384	256, 65K	60, 70, 75, 85
640×200	16	70
640×350	16	70
640×400	256, 65K, 16.7M	70, 85
640×480	256, 65K, 16.7M	60, 72, 75, 85, 100, 120, 140, 160
720×480	256, 65K, 16.7M	60, 72, 85
720×576	256, 65K, 16.7M	72, 100
800×600	256, 65K, 16.7M	60, 72, 75, 85, 100, 120, 140, 160
920×760	256, 65K	60, 75, 85
1024×768	256, 65K, 16.7M	60, 70, 75, 85, 100, 120
1152×864	256, 65K, 16.7M	60, 70, 75, 85, 100, 120
1280×960	256, 65K	60, 75, 85
1280×1024	256, 65K, 16.7M	60, 70, 75, 85, 100
1600×1024	256, 65K, 16.7M	60, 76, 85
1600×1200	256, 65K, 16.7M	60, 65, 70, 75, 80, 85, 100
1792×1344	256, 65K, 16.7M	60, 75
1856×1392	256, 65K, 16.7M	60, 75
1920×1080	256, 65K, 16.7M	60, 72, 75, 85
1920×1200	256, 65K, 16.7M	60, 76, 85
1920×1440	256, 65K, 16.7M	60, 75, 85
2046×1536	256, 65K, 16.7M	60, 75

The display modes shown are *not* all necessarily supported by *all* monitors or software. Check the capabilities of your monitor and the requirements of your software before choosing a given display mode or refresh rate.

As a rule, refresh rates greater than 75Hz are generally not noticeable.

The major difference in the video modes supported by the two video accelerators is the higher refresh rates offered by the newer GeForce 2 chipset. The modern features and capabilities of the newer video accelerator are focused on improved multimedia, graphics, and gaming applications performance.

MDA (MONOCHROME DISPLAY ADAPTER–1981)

The Monochrome Display Adapter (MDA) is the oldest conventional video adapter available for the PC. Text is available in 80-column x 25-row format using 9x14-pixel characters. Being a text-only system, MDA offered no graphics capability, but it achieved popularity because of its relatively low cost, good text display quality, and integrated printer (LPT) port. Figure 37-3 shows the video connector pinout for an MDA board. The 9-pin monitor connection uses four active TTL signals: intensity, video, horizontal, and vertical. *Video* and *intensity* signals provide the on/off and high/low intensity information for each pixel. The *horizontal* and *vertical* signals control the monitor's synchronization. MDA boards have long been obsolete, and the probability of your encountering one is remote at best.

TABLE 37-2   DISPLAY MODES FOR AN NVIDIA GEFORCE 2 VIDEO ADAPTER

RESOLUTION	NUMBER OF COLORS	VERTICAL FREQUENCY (HZ)
640×480	256, 65K, 16.7M	60, 70, 72, 75, 85, 100, 120, 140, 144, 150, 170, 200, 240
800×600	256, 65K, 16.7M	60, 70, 72, 75, 85, 100, 120, 140, 144, 150, 170, 200, 240
1024×768	256, 65K, 16.7M	60, 70, 72, 75, 85, 100, 120, 140, 144, 150, 170, 200, 240 (65K)
1152×864	256, 65K, 16.7M	60, 70, 72, 75, 85, 100, 120, 140, 144 (65K), 150, 170, 200, 240 (65K)
1280×960	256, 65K, 16.7M	60, 70, 72, 75, 85, 100, 120, 140, 144 (65K), 150, 170 (65K)
1280×1024	256, 65K, 16.7M	60, 70, 72, 75, 85, 100, 120, 140, 144 (65K), 150, 170
1600×900	256, 65K, 16.7M	60, 70, 72, 75, 85, 100, 120, 140 (65K), 144 (65K), 150 (65K)
1600×1200	256, 65K, 16.7M	60, 70, 72, 75, 85, 100, 120 (65K)
1920×1080	256, 65K, 16.7M	60, 70, 72, 75, 85, 100 (65K)
1920×1200	256, 65K, 16.7M	60, 70, 72, 75, 85, 100 (65K)
1920×1440	256, 65K, 16.7M	60, 70, 72 (65K), 75, 85 (65K)
2048×1536	256, 65K	60 (16.7M), 70, 72, 75

CGA (COLOR GRAPHICS ADAPTER–1981)

The Color Graphics Adapter (CGA) was the first to offer color text and graphics modes for the PC. A 160x200 low-resolution mode offered 16 colors, but such low resolution received very little attention. A 320x200 medium-resolution graphics mode allowed finer graphic detail, but with only four colors. The highest resolution mode provides 640x200 at 2 colors (usually black and one other color). The relationship between resolution and colors is important since a CGA *frame* requires 16KB of video RAM. A 640x200 resolution results in 128,000 pixels. With 8 bits able to represent 8 pixels, 16,000 bytes (128,000/8) are adequate. A 320x200 resolution results in 64,000 pixels, but with 2 bits needed to represent 1 pixel (4 pixels/byte), 16,000 bytes (64,000/4) are still enough. You can see that video RAM is directly related to video capacity. Since there is typically much more video RAM available than is needed for an image, video boards support multiple video *pages*. Figure 37-4 shows the pinout for a typical CGA

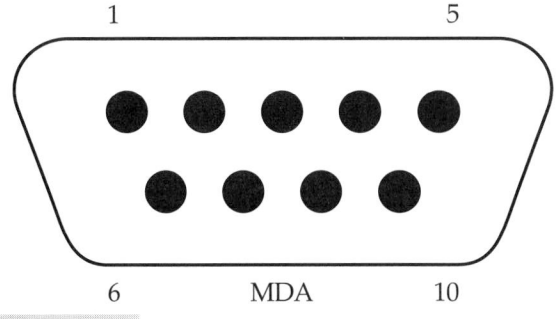

1. Ground
2. Ground
3. n/a
4. n/a
5. n/a
6. (+) Intensity
7. (+) Video
8. (+) Horizontal sync
9. (–) Vertical sync

FIGURE 37-3   Pin assignment of an MDA video connector

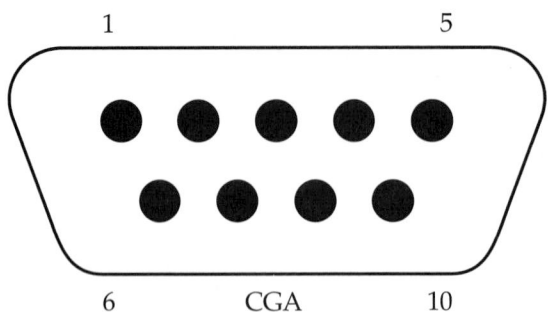

1. Ground
2. Ground
3. Red
4. Green
5. Blue
6. Intensity
7. n/a
8. Horizontal sync
9. Vertical sync

FIGURE 37-4   Pin assignment of a CGA video connector

video connector. As with the earlier MDA design, CGA video signals reserve pins 1 and 2 as ground lines, while the horizontal sync signal is produced on pin 8 and the vertical sync signal is produced on pin 9. CGA is strictly a digital display system with TTL signals used on the Red (3), Green (4), Blue (5), and Intensity (6) lines.

EGA (ENHANCED GRAPHICS ADAPTER–1984)

It was not long before the limitations of CGA became painfully apparent. The demand for higher resolutions and color depths drove designers to introduce the next generation of video adapter, known as the Enhanced Graphics Adapter (EGA). One of the unique appeals of EGA was its backward compatibility—an EGA board would emulate CGA and MDA modes on the proper monitor, as well as its native resolutions and color depths when using an EGA monitor. EGA is known for its 320x200x16, 640x200x16, and 640x350x16 video modes. More memory is needed for EGA, and 128KB is common for EGA boards (although many boards could be expanded to 256KB).

The EGA connector pinout is illustrated in Figure 37-5. TTL signals are used to provide Primary Red (3), Primary Green (4), and Primary Blue (5) color signals. By adding a set of secondary color signals (or color *intensity* signals), such as Red Intensity (2), Green Intensity (6), and Blue Intensity (7), the total of six color control signals allow the EGA to produce up to 64 possible colors. Although 64 colors are possible, only 16 of those colors are available in the palette at any one time. Pin 8 carries the horizontal sync signal, pin 9 carries the vertical sync signal, and pin 1 remains ground.

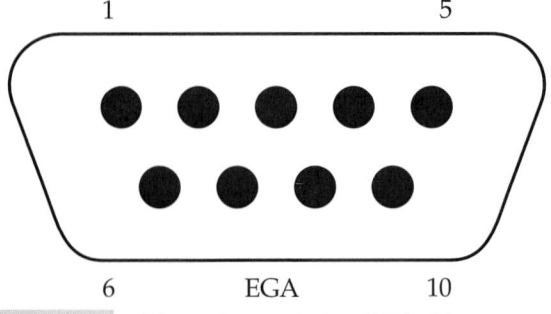

1. Ground
2. Red intensity
3. Primary red
4. Primary green
5. Primary blue
6. Green intensity
7. Blue intensity
8. Horizontal sync
9. Vertical sync

FIGURE 37-5   Pin assignment of an EGA video connector

PGA (PROFESSIONAL GRAPHICS ADAPTER–1984)

The Professional Graphics Adapter (PGA) was also introduced in 1984. This system offered a then-revolutionary display capability of 640x480x256. Three-dimensional rotation and graphics clipping was included as a hardware function, and the adapter could update the display at 60 frames per second. The PGA was incredibly expensive and beyond the reach of all but the most serious business user. In actual operation, a PGA system required two or three expansion boards, so it also represented a serious commitment of limited system space. Ultimately, PGA failed to capture any significant market acceptance. It is unlikely that you will ever encounter a PGA board—most that ever saw service in PCs have long since been upgraded.

MCGA (MULTI-COLOR GRAPHICS ARRAY–1987)

The Multi-Color Graphics Array (MCGA) had originally been integrated into the motherboard of IBM's PS/2-25 and PS/2-30. MCGA supported all of the CGA video modes and also offered several new video modes, including a 320x200x256 mode that had became a preferred mode for game software of the day. MCGA was one of the first graphic systems to use analog color signals rather than TTL signals. Analog signals were necessary to allow MCGA to produce its 256 colors using only three primary color lines (red, green, and blue, or "RGB").

IBM also took the opportunity to employ a new, high-density 15-pin subminiature "D-type" connector, as shown in Figure 37-6. One of the striking differences between the "analog" connector and older TTL connectors is the use of individual ground lines for each color. Careful grounding is vital, since any signal noise on the analog lines will result in color anomalies. If you inspect a video cable closely, you will find that one or both ends are terminated with a square metal box that actually contains a noise filter. It is important to realize that although the MCGA could *emulate* CGA modes, older TTL monitors were no longer compatible with analog RGB signal levels.

Although there were a number of notable technical improvements that went into the PS/2 design, none of them could assure broad acceptance of the PS/2 series. However, the MCGA ushered in a new age of analog display technology, and virtually all subsequent video adapters now use the 15-pin analog format shown in Figure 37-6. While MCGA adapters are also (technically) obsolete, the standard lives on in MCGA's cousins, VGA and SVGA.

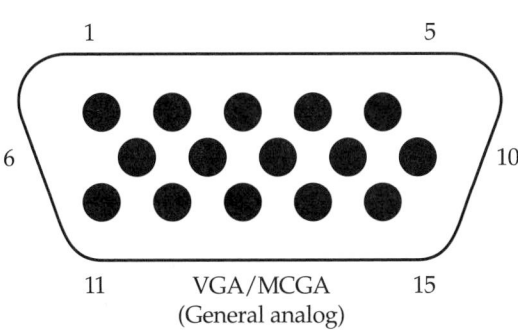

1. Red
2. Green
3. Blue
4. Ground
5. Ground
6. Red ground
7. Green ground
8. Blue ground
9. n/a
10. Ground
11. Ground
12. n/a
13. Horizontal sync
14. Vertical sync
15. n/a

FIGURE 37-6   Pin assignment of a VGA/MCGA/SVGA video connector

VGA (VIDEO GRAPHICS ARRAY–1987)

The Video Graphics Array (VGA) was introduced along with MCGA and implemented in other members of IBM's PS/2 series. The line between MCGA and VGA has always been a bit fuzzy since both were introduced simultaneously (both using the same 15 pin video connector) and VGA can handle every mode that MCGA could. For all practical purposes, we can say that MCGA is a *subset* of VGA.

It is VGA that provides the familiar 640x480x16 screen mode which has become the baseline for Microsoft Windows 9x/Me "SafeMode" displays. The use of analog color signals allows VGA systems to produce a palette of 16 colors from 262,144 possible colors. VGA also provides backward compatibility for all older screen modes. Although the PS/2 line has been discontinued, the flexibility and backward compatibility of VGA proved so successful that VGA adapters were soon developed for the PC. For a time, VGA support was considered to be "standard equipment" for all new PCs, but SVGA boards have rapidly replaced VGA systems, and most SVGA adapters offer full VGA support.

8514 (1987)

The 8514/A video adapter is a high-resolution system also developed for the PS/2. In addition to full support for MDA, CGA, EGA, and VGA modes, the 8514/A can display 256 colors at 640x480 and 1024x768 (interlaced) resolutions. Unfortunately, the 8514/A was a standard ahead of its time. The lack of available software and the demise of the PS/2 line doomed the 8514/A to extinction before it could become an accepted standard. The XGA standard (see the upcoming section "XGA (1990)") rapidly became the PC standard for high-resolution/high-color display systems on MicroChannel PC platforms.

SVGA (SUPER VIDEO GRAPHICS ARRAY)

Ever since VGA became the de facto standard for PC graphics, there has been a strong demand from PC users to move beyond the 640x480x16 limit imposed by "conventional" VGA to provide higher resolutions and color depths. As a result, new generations of extended or *super VGA* (SVGA) adapters have moved relentlessly into the PC market. Unlike VGA, which adhered to strict hardware configurations, there is no generally accepted standard on which to develop an SVGA board—each manufacturer makes an SVGA board that supports a variety of different (and not necessarily compatible) video modes. For example, one manufacturer may produce an SVGA board capable of 1024x768x65K, while another manufacturer may produce a board that reaches only 640x480x16M (more than 16 million colors).

This "mixing and matching" of resolutions and color depths has resulted in a very competitive (but very fractured) market—no two SVGA boards are necessarily capable of the same things. This proliferation of video hardware also makes it impossible for applications software to take advantage of *super* video modes without supplemental software called *video drivers*. Video drivers are device drivers (loaded before an application program is started) that allow the particular program to work with the SVGA board hardware. Video drivers are typically developed by the board manufacturer and shipped on a floppy disk with the board. Windows 9x/Me takes particular advantage of video drivers, since the Windows interface allows *all* Windows applications to use the same graphics system rather than requiring that a driver be written for every application (as DOS drivers must). Using an incorrect, obsolete, or corrupted video driver can be a serious source of performance and stability problems for SVGA installations. The one common attribute of SVGA boards is that *most* offer full support for conventional VGA (which requires no video drivers), so Windows can *always* be started "safely" in the conventional 640x480x16 VGA mode. There are only a handful of SVGA board manufacturers that have abandoned conventional VGA support.

Today, most SVGA boards offer terrific video performance, a wide selection of modes, and extremely reasonable prices. If it were not for the lack of standardization in SVGA adapters, VGA would likely be considered obsolete already. The *Video Electronics Standards Association* (VESA) has started the push for SVGA standards by proposing and supporting the VESA BIOS Extension (VBE)—a *universal* video driver. The extension (now at version 3.0) provides a uniform set of functions that allow application programs to detect a card's capabilities and use the optimum adapter configuration regardless of how the particular board's hardware is designed. Virtually all of the SVGA boards in production today support the VESA BIOS Extensions, and it is worthwhile to recommend boards that support VESA SVGA. Some SVGA boards even incorporate the extensions into the video BIOS ROM, saving the RAM space that would otherwise be needed by a video driver.

XGA (1990)

The XGA and XGA/2 are 32-bit high-performance video adapters developed by IBM to support MicroChannel-based PCs. XGA design with MicroChannel architecture allow the adapter to take control of the system for rapid data transfers. MDA, CGA, EGA, and VGA modes are all supported for backward compatibility. In addition, several color depths are available at 1024x768 resolution, and a photo-realistic 65,536 colors are available at 640x480 resolution. To improve performance even further, fast video RAM and a graphics co-processor are added to the XGA design. XGA is generally limited to high-performance applications in MicroChannel systems. The migration to ISA-based PCs has been slow because the ISA bus is limited to 16 bits and does not support bus mastering, as MicroChannel busses do. For PCs, SVGA adapters using the high-performance PCI (and now the AGP) bus will likely provide extended screen modes as they continue to grow in sophistication as graphics accelerators.

Understanding Graphics Accelerators

When screen resolutions approach 640x480 and beyond, the data needed to form a single screen image can be substantial. Consider a single 640x480x256 image. There are (640x480) 307,200 pixels. Since there are 256 colors, 8 bits are needed to define the color for each pixel. This means 307,200 bytes are needed for every frame. When the frame must be updated 10 times per second, 3,072,000 (307,200 x 10) bytes per second (3.072MB/sec) must be moved across the bus (PCI or ISA bus). If a 65,536 color mode is being used, 2 bytes are needed for each pixel, so 614,400 bytes (307,200 x 2) are needed for a frame. At 10 frames per second, 6,144,000 (614,400 x 10) bytes per second (6.144MB/sec) must be moved across the bus. This is just for video information and does not reflect the needs of system overhead operations, such as memory refresh, keyboard and mouse handling, drive access, and other data-intensive system operations. When such volumes of information must be moved across an ISA bus limited at 8.33 MHz, you can see how a serious data transfer bottleneck develops. Even the PCI bus can be strained by higher video modes (though the high-bandwidth data channel provided by AGP has eased this bottleneck). Such video data "bottlenecks" result in painfully slow screen refreshes—especially under Windows, which requires frequent refreshes.

Video designers seek to overcome the limitations of conventional video adapters by incorporating processing power onto the video board itself rather than relying on the system CPU for graphic processing. By off-loading work from the system CPU and assigning the graphics processing to local processing components, graphics performance can be improved by a factor of three or more. There are several means of acceleration, the use of which may depend on the sophistication of the board (Figure 37-7). *Fixed-function* acceleration relieves load on the system CPU by providing adapter support for a limited number of specific functions, such as BitBlt or line draws. Fixed-function accelerators were an improvement over frame-buffers, but they do not offer the performance of more sophisticated accelerators. A *graphics accelerator* uses an application-specific chip (or ASIC) that intercepts graphics tasks and processes them without the intervention of the system CPU. Graphics accelerators are perhaps the most cost-effective type of accelerator. *Graphics co-processors* are the most sophisticated type of accelerator. The co-processor acts as a CPU that is dedicated to handling image data. Older graphics co-processors, such as the TMS34010 and TMS34020, represent the *Texas Instruments Graphical Architecture* (TIGA), which is broadly used for high-end accelerators. Unfortunately, not all graphics co-processors provide increased performance to warrant the higher cost.

Figure 37-8 shows the block diagram for a basic graphics accelerator. The core of the accelerator is the graphics chip (or video chipset). The graphics chip connects directly with the PC expansion bus. Graphics commands and data are translated into pixel data and stored in video RAM. High-performance video memory offers a second data bus that is routed directly to the video board's RAMDAC (random access memory video-to-analog converter). The graphics chip directs RAMDAC operation and ensures that VRAM data is available. The RAMDAC then translates video data into red, green, and blue analog signals along with horizontal and vertical synchronization signals. Output signals generated by the RAMDAC drive the monitor. This architecture may appear simple, but such an impression is due to the extremely high level of integration provided by the chipsets being used. Table 37-3 provides a listing of many 2D and 3D graphics chipsets in use today.

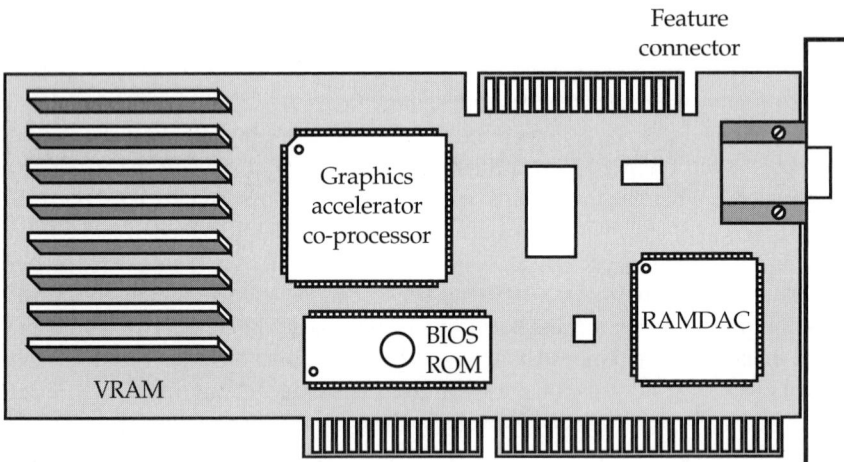

FIGURE 37-7   A typical video accelerator card

PC bus interface

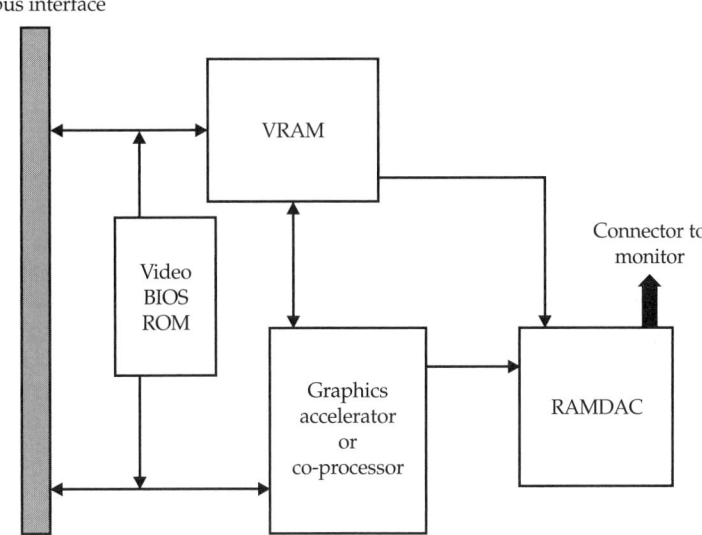

FIGURE 37-8   Basic block diagram of a video accelerator board

TABLE 37-3	INDEX OF POPULAR 2D AND 3D VIDEO CHIPSETS
MANUFACTURER	**PRODUCT**
3dfx	VSA-100 Chip (**www.3dfx.com/**)
3dfx	Voodoo Series (Voodoo Rush to Voodoo 5)
3dfx	Velocity Series (100 – 200)
3DLabs	Permedia (**www.3dlabs.com/product/card/index.htm**)
3DLabs	GLINT 300SX
3DLabs	Oxygen (VX1 - GVX1 - GMX - ACX)
3DLabs	Wildcat 4110, 4210, Wildcat II 5110
Acer Labs	ALI-M3145 (**www.acerlabs.com/**)
Acer Labs	ALI CAT-32/64
Alliance Semiconductor	ProMotion-3210 (**www.alsc.com/**)
Alliance Semiconductor	ProMotion-6410
Alliance Semiconductor	ProMotion-6422
Alliance Semiconductor	ProMotion-AT24
ARK Logic	ARK1000PV
ARK Logic	ARK2000PV
Artist Graphics	3GA Graphics Processor
Artist Graphics	Artist 3GA
Artist Graphics	Artist GPX
ATI	264VT (**www.ati.com/na/pages/products/pc/pc_index.html**)
ATI	3D RAGE
ATI	Mach32
ATI	Mach64

TABLE 37-3   INDEX OF POPULAR 2D AND 3D VIDEO CHIPSETS (*CONTINUED*)

MANUFACTURER	PRODUCT
ATI	Mach64CT
ATI	Mach8
ATI	3D XPRESSION
ATI	XPERT (98, 99, 128, 2000, At Play, At Work, etc.)
ATI	3D CHARGER
ATI	All-In-Wonder (Pro, 128, 128 Pro)
ATI	RAGE 128 (Magnum, Fury, FuryPro, Fury MAXX)
ATI	RADEON (All-In-Wonder, VE, DDR, SDRAM)
Avance Logic	ALG 2032 (**www.avance.com**)
Avance Logic	ALG 2064
Avance Logic	ALG 2302
Avance Logic	ALG 2308
Avance Logic	ALG 2364
Avance Logic	ALG 2401
Avance Logic	ALG 25128
Avance Logic	ALG 2564
Avance Logic	ALG 27000
Avance Logic	ALG 2101
Avance Logic	ALG 2228
Avance Logic	ALG 2301
Chips and Technologies	64300 (purchased by Intel)
Chips and Technologies	82C455/6
Chips and Technologies	82C452
Chromatic Research	Mpact
Cirrus Logic, Inc.	CL-GD5420 (**www.cirrus.com**)
Cirrus Logic, Inc.	CL-GD5421
Cirrus Logic, Inc.	CL-GD5422
Cirrus Logic, Inc.	CL-GD5424
Cirrus Logic, Inc.	CL-GD5425
Cirrus Logic, Inc.	CL-GD5426
Cirrus Logic, Inc.	CL-GD5428
Cirrus Logic, Inc.	CL-GD5429
Cirrus Logic, Inc.	CL-GD5430
Cirrus Logic, Inc.	CL-GD5434
Cirrus Logic, Inc.	CL-GD5434-E
Cirrus Logic, Inc.	CL-GD5436
Cirrus Logic, Inc.	CL-GD5440
Cirrus Logic, Inc.	CL-GD5446
Cirrus Logic, Inc.	CL-GD5462
Cirrus Logic, Inc.	CL-GD54M40
Cirrus Logic, Inc.	CL-GD5480
IIT (AGX)	AGX-015
IIT (AGX)	AGX-016
Intel Corp.	Intel i740 (**developer.intel.com/design/graphics/**)
Intel Corp.	Intel i810 (AGP chipset)
Intel Corp.	Intel i815 (AGP chipset)

TABLE 37-3   INDEX OF POPULAR 2D AND 3D VIDEO CHIPSETS (*CONTINUED*)

MANUFACTURER	PRODUCT
Lockheed Martin	Real3D
Matrox	MGA-1064SG (**www.matrox.com**)
Matrox	MGA-2064W
Matrox	Mystique 220
Matrox	Millennium II
Matrox	m3D
Matrox	Productiva G100
Matrox	Mystique G200
Matrox	Marvel G200
Matrox	Marvel G400
Matrox	Marvel G450 eTV
Matrox	Millennium G200
Matrox	Millennium G400
Matrox	Millennium G450
NCR	77C22E+
NCR	77C32BLT
NVIDIA/SGS-THOMSON	NV1/STG-2000 (**www.nvidia.com/**)
NVIDIA	Riva 128
NVIDIA	Riva 128ZX
NVIDIA	Vanta
NVIDIA	Riva TNT and TNT2
NVIDIA	Quadro
NVIDIA	Quadro2 (Pro, MXR)
NVIDIA	GeForce 256
NVIDIA	GeForce2
NVIDIA	GeForce3
Number Nine	Imagine 128 Series 2 (**www.nine.com/products/index.html**)
Number Nine	"Ticket To Ride"
Number Nine	"Ticket To Ride IV"
Oak Technologies Inc.	OTI-057/67 (**www.oaktech.com**)
Oak Technologies Inc.	OTI-077
Oak Technologies Inc.	OTI-087
Oak Technologies Inc.	OTI-64105/107
Oak Technologies Inc.	OTI-64111
Oak Technologies Inc.	OTI-64217
Realtek Semiconductor Corp.	RTG3105I (**www.realtek.com.tw**)
Rendition	Vérité (**www.rendition.com/**)
S3, Inc. (Now SONICblue)	Aurora64V+
S3, Inc.	S3-801 (**www.sonicblue.com**)
S3, Inc.	S3-805/805p
S3, Inc.	S3-805I
S3, Inc.	S3-864
S3, Inc.	S3-868
S3, Inc.	S3-911
S3, Inc.	S3-924
S3, Inc.	S3-928

TABLE 37-3 INDEX OF POPULAR 2D AND 3D VIDEO CHIPSETS (*CONTINUED*)

MANUFACTURER	PRODUCT
S3, Inc.	S3-964
S3, Inc.	S3-968
S3, Inc.	S3-ViRGE
S3, Inc.	S3-ViRGE/VX
S3, Inc.	Scenic/MX2
S3, Inc.	Trio32 (732)
S3, Inc.	Trio64 (764)
S3, Inc.	Trio64UV+
S3, Inc.	Trio64V+
S3, Inc.	Savage3D
S3, Inc.	Savage4
S3, Inc.	Savage2000
Sierra Semiconductor	Falcon/64
Sierra Semiconductor	SC15064
Silicon Integrated Systems	SiS6205 (**www.sis.com.tw/products/multimedia.htm**)
Silicon Integrated Systems	SiS6215
Silicon Integrated Systems	SiS6225
Silicon Integrated Systems	SiS6326
Silicon Integrated Systems	SiS6326AGP
Silicon Integrated Systems	SiS6326DVD
Silicon Integrated Systems	SiS300/301
Silicon Integrated Systems	SiS305
S-MOS	SPC1500
ST Microelectronics	Kyro II (**us.st.com/stonline/index.shtml**)
Trident Microsystems	TGUI9420/30 (**www.tridentmicro.com**)
Trident Microsystems	TGUI9440AGi
Trident Microsystems	TGUI9660/968x
Trident Microsystems	TVGA8900CL
Trident Microsystems	TVGA9000
Trident Microsystems	TVGA9200Cxr
Trident Microsystems	TVGA9400CXi
Trident Microsystems	TVGA8900C
Trident Microsystems	3Dimage 975
Trident Microsystems	3Dimage 985
Trident Microsystems	Blade 3D
Tseng Labs, Inc.	ET4000/W32
Tseng Labs, Inc.	ET4000/W32i
Tseng Labs, Inc.	ET4000/W32p
Tseng Labs, Inc.	ET4000AX
Tseng Labs, Inc.	ET6000
Tseng Labs, Inc.	VIPeR
Tseng Labs, Inc.	VPR6000
UMC	UMC 86C408
UMC	UMC 86C418
UMC	UMC 8710
Weitek	P9000

TABLE 37-3   INDEX OF POPULAR 2D AND 3D VIDEO CHIPSETS (*CONTINUED*)

MANUFACTURER	PRODUCT
Weitek	P9100
Western Digital (Paradise)	WD90C30 (**www.wdc.com**)
Western Digital (Paradise)	WD90C31
Western Digital (Paradise)	WD90C33
Western Digital	RocketCHIP

VIDEO SPEED FACTORS

There is no *one* element that defines the performance of an accelerator board. Overall performance is actually a *combination* of five major factors: the video accelerator chip(s) (a.k.a. the "chipset"), the video RAM, the video BIOS/drivers, the RAMDAC, and the expansion bus architecture. By understanding how each of these factors relates to performance, you can make the best recommendations for system upgrades or replacement boards.

Video Accelerator

Of course, the video accelerator chip itself (usually the graphics chipset being used) is at the core of the accelerator board. The type of chip (fixed-function, graphics accelerator, or graphics co-processor) loosely defines the board's capabilities. All other factors being equal, a board with a graphics accelerator will certainly perform better than a fixed-function accelerator. Companies like 3dfx, ATI, Advance Logic, Chips & Technologies, Matrox, NVIDIA, S3, and Oak Technology have developed many of the video accelerator chips in use today. Many of the older chips provided a 32-bit data bus (newer designs provide a 64-bit or 128-bit data bus), and they sustain very high data rates; however, a data bottleneck across a 16-bit (ISA) expansion bus can seriously degrade the chip's effectiveness. Therefore, you should match the recommended board to the particular system—a state-of-the-art graphics accelerator will not necessarily make your old i286 shine.

Video RAM

Video adapters rely on RAM to hold image data, and video accelerator boards are no exception. While the current amount of video RAM typically varies from 16MB to 32MB (some late-mode video adapters offer as much as 64MB), the *amount* of RAM is not so important to a video accelerator as the RAM's *speed*. Faster memory is able to read and write image data faster, so adapter performance is improved. The introduction of specialized video RAM (VRAM)—memory devices with two separate data busses that can be read from and written to simultaneously—is reputed to be superior to conventional dynamic RAM (DRAM) or EDO RAM, such as the kind used for ordinary PC memory. Recent advances in DRAM speed have narrowed that gap, while DRAMs have remained very economical.

At this point, adapters with fast DRAM or EDO RAM are just about as fast as adapters with specialized video RAM for video modes up to 1024x768x256. For higher modes and color depths found on high-end accelerators, specialized video RAM is still the way to go for optimum performance. DDR-SDRAM (Double Data Rate SDRAM) memory looks promising for both system and graphics memory. The latest video adapters utilize DDR-SDRAM memory. This memory technology was originally developed for use in high-performance video adapters, but it is now being used as main system memory on the newest motherboards. It effectively doubles its speed by using both edges of each clock cycle. Keep in mind that graphics board manufacturers are using the doubled rate in their specifications and advertising. AGP video boards are also being produced in different versions and prices depending on the type and speed of the memory provided on each adapter, and AGP video adapters can also access system RAM for certain video data storage.

Video BIOS and Drivers

Software is often considered an afterthought to adapter design, yet it plays a surprisingly important role in accelerator performance. Even the finest accelerator board hardware can bog down when run under carelessly and loosely written code. There are two classes of software that you must be concerned with: video BIOS and video drivers. The *video BIOS* is *firmware* (software that is permanently recorded on a memory device such as a ROM). Video BIOS holds the programming that allows the accelerator to interact with DOS applications software. Current adapters have *flash upgradeable* BIOS ROMs that allow the video adapter's firmware to be updated without removing the video adapter from the PC. VESA BIOS extensions are now being used almost universally as part of the video BIOS for many accelerators as well as conventional frame-buffer adapters. Adding VESA BIOS extensions to video BIOS eliminates the need to load another device driver under DOS.

However, there are compelling advantages to video drivers. Windows 9x/Me works quite well with drivers (and generally ignores video BIOS entirely). Unlike BIOS ROMs, which can be troublesome to upgrade, a video driver can change very quickly as bugs are corrected, enhancements are made, and performance is streamlined. The updated driver can be downloaded from a manufacturer's Web site on the Internet (or other online information service such as AOL) and installed on your system in a matter of minutes without the PC having to be dissembled. It is also possible for you to use third-party video drivers. Hardware manufacturers are not always adept at writing efficient software, and a third-party driver developed by an organization that *specializes* in software may actually let your accelerator perform *better* than the original driver shipped from the manufacturer.

"Reference drivers" are often available from the video chipset maker's Web site. Video board manufacturers typically customize these drivers for their specific product. Customized reference drivers often include performance improvements, but they can be unstable because they have not been tested on or written for specific video cards.

The RAMDAC

Just about every analog video system in service today is modeled after the 15-pin VGA scheme that uses three separate analog signals to represent the three primary colors. The color for each pixel must be broken down into component red, green, and blue levels, and those levels must be converted into analog equivalents. A digital-to-analog converter (or DAC) handles the conversion from digital values to analog levels. Each conversion also requires a certain amount of time. Faster DACs are needed to support faster horizontal refresh rates. Current video boards incorporate RAMDAC rated at up to 350MHz, which can support very high resolutions at reasonably high refresh rates. Remember that each video adapter uses a *palette* that is a subset of the colors that can possibly be produced. Even though a monitor may be able to produce "unlimited" colors, a VGA board can produce only 256 of those colors in any 256-color mode. Older video boards stored the palette entries in registers, but the large-palette video modes now available (64K colors through 16 million colors) require the use of RAM. Boards that incorporate a RAMDAC (Random Access Memory Digital-to-Analog Converter) are preferred, since memory integrated with DACs tends to be much faster than accessing discrete RAM elsewhere on the board. Keep in mind that the RAM on a RAMDAC is used for holding palette information—not for the actual image.

Expansion Bus Architectures

Finally, graphic data must be transferred between the PC motherboard and the adapter, as you saw early in this section. Such transfer takes place across the PC's *expansion bus*. If data can be transferred between the PC and adapter at a *faster* rate, video performance should improve. For example, a wider data bus (for instance, 32 bits rather than 16 bits) and faster bus speeds (66MHz rather than 33MHz) will support faster data transfers—or higher *video bandwidth*. Consequently, the choice of bus *architecture* has a significant impact on video performance. Video accelerators are available to support three bus architectures: ISA, PCI, and AGP.

ISA   The venerable Industry Standard Architecture (ISA) has remained virtually unchanged since its introduction with the PC/AT in the early 1980s. The ISA continues to be a mature interface standard for most IBM-compatible expansion devices. While the latest motherboards do not include support for ISA, the sheer volume of ISA systems currently in service guarantees that they will be on desktops for another few years. However, ISA's 16-bit data bus width, its lack of advanced features such as *interrupt sharing* or *bus mastering*, and its relatively slow 8.33MHz operating speed form a serious bottleneck to the incredible volume of video data demanded by Windows 9x/Me and most graphics-intensive DOS applications. ISA works—but it has long since been abandoned as the interface of choice for optimum video performance. When recommending an accelerator product, look to the newer busses for best results.

PCI   Intel's Peripheral Component Interconnect (PCI) bus was one of the most versatile and powerful bus architectures to reach the PC. The PCI bus runs at a fixed frequency of 30 or 33MHz, and offers a full 64-bit data bus that can take advantage of new 64-bit CPUs such as Intel's Pentium family (though most implementations of the PCI bus are designed for a 32-bit implementation). The PCI bus overcomes the speed and functional limitations of ISA, and the PCI architecture is intended to support *all* types of PC peripherals (not just video boards). PCI video boards easily outperform ISA bus video adapters, though today's video systems use the faster AGP bus.

AGP   Intel developed and introduced an advanced "local bus" architecture called "AGP" (the Accelerated Graphics Port—a close cousin of PCI) intended to meet the increasing demands for speed and bandwidth needed to support real-time 3D graphics. AGP is a dedicated high-speed bus that directly connects the chipset and the graphics controller. This connection creates a data channel specifically for graphics (unlike the PCI bus, which must share bandwidth and system resources among the various PCI peripherals installed in any given system). The introduction of AGP removes data-hungry 3D and video data transfers from the PCI bus. PCI device performance can also benefit since video data transfers are no longer required. The system BIOS, chipset, and operating system must all support AGP to take advantage of AGP's performance capabilities. The only operating systems that fully support AGP at this time are Windows 98/Me and Windows 2000. Windows 95 OSR 2.1 has limited AGP support, so any AGP performance benefit will be correspondingly limited. DirectDraw (part of DirectX) is constantly being updated because it is responsible for controlling AGP's use of main system memory.

While PCI specifications limit data transfer rates to a bandwidth of 132MB/sec, the 32-bit 66MHz AGP bus has a base bandwidth of 264MB/sec. The AGP 2X specification supports a bandwidth of 533MB/sec by transferring data on both the rising and falling edges of the 66MHz clock (*double-clocking*), and it also implements more efficient data transfer modes. The *timing* of data transfers is controlled by strobe signals rather than the standard method of clock cycles—strobe signals are generated by the device sending the data (either the PC or the AGP board). Generating both the data and the strobe signals allows the sending device to precisely control the timing. Separating the data transfer timing from the bus clock also allowed Intel to create an AGP 4X specification. By increasing the number of strobe signals from three to six, Intel defined a "virtual" clock speed of 264MHz (4×66), and this improvement again doubles the potential bandwidth of the AGP connection to 1.06GB/sec.

A significant AGP feature is its ability to access system memory *directly* during rendering. In this situation, system memory is referred to as "Non-Local Memory" (NLM). The operating system can reserve portions of the system's main memory for use by the graphics controller. There are two methods of using NLM supported by Intel's AGP specifications, and both require support from the operating system through an API (such as DirectDraw) to utilize NLM for texture map storage and some z-buffering. The first method is through Direct Memory Access (DMA). The DMA mode utilizes NLM only for mass storage of information such as texture data. This allows the graphic controller to keep fewer texture maps in local memory (on the video board). NLM is mainly a specification intended to reduce system cost. Non-Local Memory can be used for texture maps, thus allowing applications (for instance, games) to use larger maps—this improves game realism and image quality without sacrificing performance or requiring more, expensive local memory. Direct Memory Execute (or DiME) is the second mode used by AGP adapters to utilize NLM. In this mode—often referred to as "Execute Mode"—3D functions are actually performed in Non-Local Memory, and the end result is then transferred to the graphics adapter for display. DiME can actually *impair* performance if the graphics adapter's resources are superior to the host system's components.

AGP has 32 multiplexed address and data lines. There are eight additional lines for *sideband* addressing. These eight extra sideband address lines allow the graphics controller to issue new address and command data for read/write requests while data continues to move from previous requests on the main 32 data/address lines. An additional AGP feature is known as "Fast Write." The Fast Write feature enables the CPU to write directly to the graphics card's frame buffer *without* going through system memory. Fast Write is reported to be up to 30 percent faster than standard AGP 4X, and 2D as well as 3D applications are supposed to benefit from AGP 4X Fast Write. Fast Write also requires chipset support, which currently means an Intel i820 chipset or the newer chipsets from ALi and VIA.

Intel designed the AGP specifications for its Pentium Pro and newer CPUs, so it does not produce any chipsets to support both AGP and Socket 7 processors, such as the AMD or Cyrix CPUs. If you want to take advantage of AGP performance using a Socket 7 processor you will need to use a "Super 7" motherboard with an AGP-compliant chipset from ALi or VIA.

3D Graphics Accelerator Issues

Technically speaking, *3D graphics* is the visual representation of a scene or object along three axes of reference (height, width, and depth) to make the scene look more realistic. This technique "tricks" the PC user into seeing a 3D image on a flat (a 2D) screen. There has been an astonishing rise in the demand for 3D video from all parts of the PC industry. 3D rendering has proven to be the technique of choice for many types of high-end games, business presentations, computer-aided design, and multimedia applications. However, the use of 3D demands more of a PC than simply passing huge volumes of data across an expansion bus. 3D rendering requires complex mathematical calculations, determinations of coloring, the inclusion of special effects, and conversion of the rendered scene to a 2D plane (the display). In virtually all cases, these tasks must be accomplished in real-time (15 frames per second and faster). Today, most video systems are upgraded for the express purpose of supporting 3D animation (usually in 3D computer games such as *Quake III* or *Serious Sam*). This part of the chapter examines some of the key factors involved on 3D rendering and acceleration.

THE 3D PROCESS

To display a 3D object in real time, an object is first represented as a set of points (or *vertices*) in a 3D coordinate system consisting of x, y, and z coordinates. The *object* may be a car, a fighter plane, or a complete 3D world, and the vertices of each object are stored in system RAM and completely define the object. In order to display this object on the flat 2D monitor, the object must then be rendered.

Rendering is the act of calculating—on a "per pixel" basis—the different color and position information that tricks the viewer into perceiving depth on the 2D screen. Rendering also fills in the points on the surface of the object that were previously stored only as a set of vertices. In this way, a solid object can be drawn on the screen—even shaded with lighting, shadows, and fog for 3D effect. In order to render an object, it is necessary to determine the color and position information. To accomplish this efficiently, the vertices of the object are segmented into triangles, and these triangles (a set of three vertices) are then passed down the *3D-processing pipeline* one at a time. The general steps involved in 3D rendering are listed here:

- **Triangularize the 3D object**   This process divides the 3D object into triangles (sets of three vertices).
- **Transformation**   Translates, rotates, and zooms the object as necessary on the basis of the "camera angle." This is a mathematically intensive part of the rendering process.
- **Clipping**   Eliminates any portions of the object that fall outside of the "window" of the viewer's line of sight. Clipping also demands a fair amount of mathematical processing.
- **Lighting**   Calculates shadow or light information depending on where light sources in the 3D world are positioned. Other effects such as "fog" can also be included in this processing step.
- **Map triangles to screen**   The triangularized, transformed, clipped, and illuminated object must then be "mapped" to the 2D screen. Triangles that are farther away from the viewer's viewpoint will be smaller then those triangles that are closer.
- **Draw the triangles**   The triangles are then drawn to the screen using a variety of shading and texture mapping techniques. This time-intensive process completes the scene that you see, and the entire process must be repeated for every frame generated by the game or other application.

3D SPEED ISSUES

Higher frame rates create realism and true-to-life atmosphere in 3D games. Speed is the main factor in providing faster frame rates. If the frame rate of a game is too slow, the game becomes unplayable because the time needed to react to an action in the game will be far too long. Consider playing a flight simulator if the display was only updated once or twice per second. Since much of the graphics-processing overhead has been relieved from the system CPU, frame rate is now largely dependent on the speed of a graphics accelerator. The speed of a 3D graphics engine is typically rated in terms of "millions of *texels* (textured pixels) per second" or Mtexels/sec. It is also frequently rated in polygons (a.k.a. triangles) per second. Current 3D graphics accelerators can provide hundreds of millions of texels per second or more. For example, the relatively recent NVIDIA GeForce 2 Ultra graphics chipset can render 2 billion texels (gigatexels) (or 31 million triangles) per second.

The speed of a 3D application is dependent on many tasks, but the most daunting tasks are 3D geometry and rendering. *Geometry* is the suite of calculations used to determine an object's position and color on the screen. *Rendering* (as you saw previously) is the actual drawing of the object on-screen. A typical graphics accelerator takes the load off of the CPU so that the CPU can devote more processing power to other functions. More advanced CPUs (such as the Pentium MMX, Pentium II, Pentium III with SME technology, or Pentium 4 with SME2 technology) incorporate additional instructions that aid many of the calculation-intensive work needed in 3D environments. Three features that most often affect 3D speed are bus mastering, resolution, and color depth.

Bus Mastering

With a PCI bus master graphics accelerator, a 3D graphics engine will never incur latency (delays) during the rendering process, because once the CPU has prepared all of the triangles for rendering, the bus master will come and fetch the list of triangles asynchronously without requiring the CPU to wait. There are two different implementations of bus mastering: the basic bus master and the scatter-gather bus master. A *basic* bus master is capable of operating independently from the host CPU for short periods of time before it interrupts the host to ask for direction. During data-intensive operations like 3D, this arrangement minimizes the advantages of bus mastering. By contrast, a *scatter-gather* bus master is able to operate almost independently from the host CPU, achieving significant performance benefits. Bus mastering is eliminated if graphics are implemented through AGP, since AGP is essentially a point-to-point connection between the graphics adapter and core logic, and the graphics adapter is always considered to be the "master" device.

Resolution

Because of limitations in operating systems and graphics accelerators, most games and multimedia applications have been developed for low resolutions (such as 640×480) to achieve high-performance. Increasing resolution means displaying more pixels on the screen with every frame—which places more demand on the monitor and graphics board. Some older applications developed in 320×200 can be played at 640×400, but the extra pixels are simply a replication of existing ones, which makes the image appear "blocky." With today's standards in software and fast hardware accelerators, developers can include more unique pixel information in each frame, effectively increasing graphics detail at resolutions to 800×600, 1024×768, or even higher. This means gamers can play in high resolutions with excellent image quality.

Color Depth

Using extra colors in 3D games makes the scenes much richer and more life-like. The more colors used in a scene, the more detailed and realistic it looks, but the more calculations are needed to determine the color of each rendered pixel. With the new generation of 3D graphics accelerators, higher color depths are supported without dramatic performance loss, and developers can now use more colors in each scene. For example, developers can now use 16-bit (65K) or 24-bit (16.7M) color instead of the traditional 8-bit (256) color.

IMPROVING 3D PERFORMANCE THROUGH HARDWARE

A 3D graphics accelerator improves 3D performance by relieving the host CPU of many of the computation-intensive tasks needed to render a scene. In most cases, these tasks are performed by a graphics processor chip(s) on the 3D video accelerator itself. Today's 3D graphics accelerators have an astonishing array of features—some of which are highlighted next:

Perspective-Correct Texture Mapping

In real life, objects have details that allow us to recognize them. For example, an object made of wood is granular (you can see the dark wood grain), while steel is smooth and shimmering. In 3D applications, this kind of detail is called a *texture*. Applying two-dimensional texture images to 3D objects or scenes make them appear more realistic. For example, if you walk around a black box, you don't know what it is.

However, if you apply textures to the sides and top of that box, you can create a wooden crate, a metal safe, a control panel, a pedestal—just about anything your imagination can conceive.

In the real world, our perspective relative to an object changes as our position changes. For example, when you are walking along the side of a house, the house will have a different perspective which each step. In order to create this experience in a 3D application, texture maps must be "corrected" to fit the changing perspective. If the texture mapping is not perspective-correct, the image will be visually incorrect and filled with artifacts from previous frames. While older 3D graphics accelerators did not provide perspective correct texture mapping in hardware, virtually all of the newest 3D graphics engines offer perspective-correct textures at full rendering speed.

Texture Mapping Methods

Texture mapping is a data-intensive operation—a bitmap is wrapped onto a 3D object or polygon to add more visual details (thus enhancing realism). The original bitmap used as the texture to be mapped is also called the "source texture." There are several ways to map textures onto a 3D object with perspective correction:

- **Point sampling**   This is the most common way to map a texture on a polygon. Point sampling allows the 3D graphics engine to approximate the color value of a given pixel on the resulting texture map by replicating the value of the closest existing pixel on the source texture. Point sampling provides very good results when used in conjunction with tile-based MIP mapping, and it maintains high performance levels at a low cost.

- **Filtering**   Some source textures may need a considerable amount of warping, which may lead to a "blocky" appearance. Some graphics accelerator manufacturers use a technique called bilinear filtering to make the textures appear smoother. In bilinear filtering, four-source texel values are read, and their color values are then blended together based on proximity. The resulting values will be used for the texel to be drawn. While this technique is useful, the resulting quality is not comparable to using high-resolution source textures. 3D graphics accelerators without support for palletized textures have to scale down the textures to store them and apply filtering to map them onto polygons. Doing this results in poor quality rendering.

- **MIP mapping**   MIP-mapping is another way to improve the quality of the 3D texture mapped object. The more alterations made to a texture to "fit" an object, the less it will resemble the source texture. One way to avoid this severe deviation from the original texture is to create three copies, or MIP levels, of the same source texture (each in different sizes). MIP mapping can be implemented in four ways: tile-based MIP mapping, per-pixel MIP mapping, tri-linear MIP mapping, and the latest technique using *anisotropic* filtering to reduce distortion caused by 3D to 2D conversions.

- **Fogging**   In order to maintain high performance, developers created an arsenal of tricks to reduce the amount of rendering needed for a scene. One of these tricks is called *fogging*. It is used mostly in landscape scenes, such as flight simulators. Fogging allows the developer to "hide" the background of a scene behind a layer of "fog"—mixing the textures' color values with a monochrome color such as white. Most newer 3D graphics chips support fogging in hardware.

 Modern high-performance 3D adapters have improved methods of 3D rendering and texture mapping. These features include single-pass multi-texturing, anisotropic texture filtering, per-pixel texturing, texture compression, and fog and depth cueing.

Lighting

For greater realism in a scene, *lighting* is applied to objects to accentuate curves or create an ambiance (such as shadows). For example, if you're looking at a fireplace, the fire texture may also be treated as a light source—this will allow the "fire" to illuminate nearby objects and cast shadows (further enhancing the realistic illusion). Lighting effects are generally limited when implemented in software (otherwise the frame rate degrades). A key advantage of performing hardware-based 3D rendering is the ability to apply lighting effects to polygons while maintaining full rendering speed. Current adapters offer the ability to support up to eight hardware-based "light sources" (often more).

Texture Transparency

The technique of *texture transparency* is similar to chroma-keying in video. This technique draws one image on top of another—with each appearing to fit there naturally. Mapping complicated objects in a 3D scene (such as trees) is a challenge for the software developer. They must be able to map the tree on a transparent polygon so that the background of the scene will be shown through the "branches". Objects like trees may not be essential, but they significantly improve the overall realism of a scene. Without texture transparency, these objects are typically left out or simplified. New 3D graphics chips support texture transparency in hardware, allowing developers to add a higher level of detail while maintaining graphics performance.

Hardware z-Buffering

The use of a *z-buffer* (or *depth buffer*) is necessary when two objects are intersecting each other. The z-buffer determines which portions of the intersecting objects are visible and which are hidden. However, many software developers do not use a z-buffer for all objects in the scene. This is because the z-buffer takes up space in the off-screen memory which could be used instead to store extra source textures for greater detail. For this reason, many 3D graphics chips provide an optional z-buffer allowing the developer to decide whether to use the off-screen memory for z-buffering or texture storage. If a game using a z-buffer (such as *Quake III*) is played on a graphics accelerator that does not allow for a hardware z-buffer, the game will not run—or will run at very low frame rates—since all z-buffering will need to be done in software. This is where AGP's use of Non-Local Memory for texture storage and z-buffering helps to improve rendering performance.

ST Microelectronics (designer of the Kyro graphics chipsets) and PowerVR have developed a method of rendering pixels for only the visible portion of objects in a frame. This technology has been dubbed Tile-Based Rendering (or TBR). Standard 3D graphics accelerators draw all of the polygons that comprise a scene first, then shade and texture these polygons. A test is then run on the z-buffer to determine which of the polygons are visible. The polygons that are not visible get discarded, but only after they have run through the 3D pipeline, consuming fill rate and memory bandwidth. Early tests suggest that the TBR method may improve rendering performance in some applications.

Palletized Textures

Storing source textures of 3D games in off-screen memory is very taxing on the graphics frame buffer. Each time a new scene is created, all of its source textures need to be loaded in off-screen memory for use by the graphics chip. Memory available to store textures is limited because a 3D game accelerator generally has about 16–32MB of memory. This restricts the number of textures, effectively reducing the detail and other graphics qualities available in the scene. To compensate for this, developers can use a method of *palletized textures*, which assigns a Color Look-Up Table (or CLUT) to each texture in the scene. This technique allows the developer to use a smaller amount of colors for each texture, instead of the normal

16-bit color values (65K colors). This smaller color format (CLUT) requires less memory space than the true 65K colors, which means more colors can be saved in memory to add detail to a scene. AGP specifications also address this issue by allowing main system memory to be used for storing textures.

However, most older 3D graphics accelerators do not support palletized textures, which means the information can be stored only in full 16-bit color format in the frame buffer, utilizing all of the available off-screen memory. In such cases, the extra textures will have to be stored and retrieved from system memory, resulting in a serious hit on performance. Alternatively, textures can to be dropped from the scene by the graphics accelerator in order to maintain performance. Newer 3D graphics accelerators do provide full hardware support for palletized textures, and they allow developers to create very detailed scenes with two to four times as many textures. 3D applications are consequently given a significant performance boost, because the applications do not rely on the speed of the system to convert the information to 16-bit colors.

Alpha-Blending

Blending is a visual effect that mixes two textures on the same object. Different levels of blending can be implemented to create visual effects. The simplest method is called "screen door" or "stippling": only some pixels making up the object are rendered to produce a "see-through" effect. For example, the developer would decide that an object would be 50 percent transparent. The graphics accelerator would then draw the background image, and write only every second pixel of the object. This approach is easy to implement in hardware and delivers reasonable quality at a low cost. By contrast, true *alpha-blending* is a data-intensive operation, which involves reading the values of two source textures and performing the perspective calculations on both textures simultaneously. This effect is very taxing on performance and costly to implement, and only high-end 3D graphics cards use true alpha-blending in hardware.

Gouraud Shading

Gouraud shading (or *smooth shading*) draws smooth shadows across the face of an object. This causes the viewer's eyes to perceive depth and curvature information from the surface of the object. Gouraud shading works by reading the color information at the three vertices of a triangle and interpolating the intensities in red, green, and blue smoothly between the three vertices. Gouraud shading is the most popular algorithm used to draw 3D objects on a 2D screen. Most objects can be rendered with amazing realism in 3D by using Gouraud shading, and this feature is often available in 3D graphics accelerator hardware.

Double-Buffering

Everyone has seen the old animation trick of drawing a cartoon character on the corner of a page of paper, and altering the drawing slightly on following pages of paper. When the sheaf of paper is complete and the pages are flipped rapidly, the cartoon character appears to move smoothly. Double-buffered 3D animation on the PC works in the same way—the next position of the character is being drawn *before* the page is flipped. Viewing 3D animation without double buffering would be like looking at the animated cartoon if the character were being redrawn with every flip of the page (the animation would appear to "flicker").

Double-buffering requires having two areas reserved on the frame buffer of the 3D graphics card. Both regions need to be the size of the visible screen, and one buffer is used to render the next frame of the animation while the other displays the previously rendered animation frame on the monitor. Under Windows, double-buffering requires the use of bit-blitting to copy the animation from buffer to buffer.

Color Dithering

The number of colors that can be drawn to the visible screen depends on the number of bits-per-pixel that carry color information. For instance, with eight bits per pixel of color information, only 256 colors can exist on the desktop at any one time. Color dithering is the process of mixing these defined colors into small patterns to produce a wider spectrum of color without requiring extra video memory. This is especially important in 3D, since techniques such as Gouraud shading require many shades of each color used in each scene. If dithering were not handled in hardware, a 3D scene could contain only eight different main colors in 256-color mode (since each color would require 32 shades to be programmed into the color lookup table to roughly approximate Gouraud shading). With hardware support for color dithering, a scene with many more colors may be rendered without requiring extra video RAM.

Anti-Aliasing

Anti-aliasing is a technique for disguising the jagged edges of a curved line or a line with very low or very high slope. These jagged edges are especially visible at lower resolutions with each pixel appearing as a "stair step" rather than a smooth line. Anti-aliasing is a way to use color information to make up for a lack of screen resolution. It simulates higher resolution by using color information to trick our eye into seeing a smoother line or edge than the screen can physically allow. By adding pixels of a slightly different color next to the line or curve at the transition points the "edge" is blurred. The eye sees this blur as a smooth edge rather than a different color. Full Scene Anti-Aliasing (FSAA) is the current high-performance implementation of this feature. FSAA requires a lot of resources and may slow 3D rendering to an unacceptable level. The video adapter's adjustment/configuration utility will usually allow you to toggle this feature on and off.

Bump Mapping

Bump mapping is a relatively new technique used to add detail to an image or object without increasing the number of polygons needed to construct that image or object. This technique uses light effect calculations to create small bumps on the surface of an object—the bumps add visual textures without complicating the surface of the object. Bump mapping uses light calculations to add shadow and light to the sides of the "bump." Different methods of implementing bump mapping include: pre-calculated bump mapping, perturbed environment bump mapping, perturbed blend bump mapping, and perturbed normal bump mapping.

Understanding DirectX

When Windows first emerged as a major operating system, its focus was primarily on file management and utilities. High-performance graphics and other forms of multimedia were barely even dreamed of. It was therefore very difficult for Windows to support graphics-intensive applications that came later, such as games, DVD, PC-TV, or MPEG video (and is largely the reason why DOS lingered for so long on many PC platforms). Developers realized that in order for Windows to finally become *independent* of DOS, a standard means of supporting high-performance multimedia functions would be absolutely essential—and *DirectX* technology was born. With Windows 95, DirectX has emerged as a key element in graphics, sound, and interaction for multimedia platforms. This part of the chapter offers a basic overview of DirectX and its components.

PIECES OF A PUZZLE

Contrary to popular belief, DirectX is not *one single* piece of software. Instead, DirectX is actually a comprehensive collection of Windows 9x/Me APIs (application programming interfaces) that provide a standardized set of features for graphics, sound, input devices, multi-player interaction, and application setup. DirectX software is categorized in three layers: a foundation layer, a media layer, and a components layer.

Foundation

The *foundation* layer forms the heart and soul of DirectX. It is a set of low-level APIs that are the basis for all high-performance multimedia under Windows 9x/Me. DirectX foundation APIs provide direct access to hardware acceleration such as 3D graphics acceleration chips (in effect, allowing Windows to "talk" directly to hardware). The foundation layer uses the following APIs:

- **DirectDraw**   Providing graphics "surface" management.
- **Direct3D**   The *immediate mode* supplies low-level 3D features used in conjunction with DirectDraw.
- **DirectInput**   Supports a rich selection of input devices (including new *force feedback* joysticks).
- **DirectSound**   Provides sound and mixer effects.
- **DirectSound3D**   Offers 3D sound effects from ordinary 2D speaker arrangements.
- **DirectSetup**   Installs software and drivers automatically.

Media

The DirectX *media* layer consists of application-level APIs that take advantage of the system-level services provided by the DirectX foundation. The media-level services are device independent and include features such as animation, behaviors, and video streaming. The DirectX media layer includes six APIs:

- **Direct3D**   The *retained mode* offers a collection of 3D scene features.
- **DirectPlay**   Supports multiplayer/network play.
- **DirectShow**   Handles slide-show-type operation and features.
- **DirectAnimation**   Supplies animation support.
- **DirectModel**   Supplies 3D modeling support.
- **DirectMusic**   Provides composition and playback of message-based musical data.

Components

The *components* layer makes up the top level of the DirectX hierarchy. These are a group of application-specific modules that can draw on all features available in the media and foundation layers. DirectX components include:

- **NetMeeting**   An online whiteboard for real-time group collaboration.
- **ActiveMovie**   A set of tools for rendering full-screen MPEG video and supporting playback of a wide range of audio and video formats.
- **Netshow**   Enables live broadcast of rich multimedia content over the Internet along with the compelling 3D worlds of VRML.

MORE ON DIRECTDRAW

Most Windows programs access *drawing surfaces* indirectly through Win32 device context functions such as **GetDC**. The application then writes indirectly to the device through the graphics device interface (GDI) system. The GDI is the Windows component that provides an abstraction layer that enables all standard Windows applications to draw to the screen. The disadvantage of GDI is that it was *not* designed for high-performance graphics software. It was made to be used by business applications like word processors and spreadsheets. The GDI provides access to a video buffer in system memory (not video memory) and does not take advantage of special features that some video cards provide. As a result, the traditional GDI is great for most types of business software, but it is far too slow for multimedia or game software.

DirectDraw circumvents this limitation by providing drawing surfaces that represent actual video memory. This means that with DirectDraw, an application can write *directly* to the memory on the video card, making your graphics routines extremely fast. Surfaces are represented as contiguous blocks of memory, so it easy to perform addressing within them. DirectDraw also supports hardware-accelerated functions like bit-blitting and overlays. DirectDraw works with a wide variety of display hardware. It is designed so that applications can determine the capabilities of the underlying display hardware and then use any supported hardware-accelerated features. Any features that are not supported in hardware can then be emulated in software.

In actual practice, DirectDraw is not a high-level graphics API that draws graphics *primitives* like lines and rectangles. Instead, DirectDraw is a low-level API that operates at the graphics *surface* level—providing the essential support for higher-level 2D and 3D graphics APIs, which *do* draw and render.

MORE ON DIRECTSOUND

DirectSound is the audio component of DirectX. DirectSound enables hardware and software sound mixing, capture, and effects like 3D positioning and panning. In operation, DirectSound is essentially a sound mixing engine—the application places a set of sounds in buffers (called *secondary buffers*). DirectSound then combines these sounds and writes them into a *primary buffer* that holds the sound that the listener actually hears. DirectSound automatically creates a primary buffer that typically resides in memory on the sound card itself. The application creates the secondary buffers either in system memory or directly on the sound card. DirectSound supports pulse-code modulation (PCM) sound data, but it does not currently support compressed wave formats. DirectSound does not include functions for parsing a sound file (it is the responsibility of the developer to stream data in the correct format into the secondary sound buffers).

The DirectSound mixing engine does not simply mix several sounds together. It can also apply *effects* to a sound as it is written from a secondary buffer into the primary buffer. Although these effects are audible with standard loudspeakers, they are more obvious and compelling when the user wears headphones. Basic effects are volume/frequency control and panning (changing the relative volume between the left and right audio channels), but DirectSound can also simulate 3D positional effects through the following techniques:

- **Rolloff**   The further an object is from the listener, the quieter it sounds. This phenomenon is known as *rolloff*.

- **Arrival offset**   This is the key to positional sound. For example, a sound emitted by a source to the listener's right will arrive at the right ear slightly before it arrives at the left ear (the duration of this offset is approximately a millisecond) and vice versa.

- **Muffling**   The orientation of the ears ensures that sounds coming from behind the listener are slightly muffled compared with sounds coming from in front. In addition, if a sound is coming from the right, the sounds reaching the left ear will be muffled by the mass of the listener's head as well as by the orientation of the left ear (and vice versa).

- **Doppler shift**   DirectSound automatically creates Doppler shift effects for any buffer or listener that has a velocity. Effects are cumulative—if the listener and the sound source are both moving, the system automatically calculates the relationship between their velocities and adjusts the Doppler effect accordingly.

MORE ON DIRECTINPUT

DirectInput provides high-performance access to input devices, including the mouse, keyboard, and joystick as well as the new force-feedback (input/output) devices that are arriving on the market. DirectInput offers generalized device interfaces that support a much wider range of input and output devices than the standard Win32 API functions. DirectInput works *directly* with device drivers—bypassing the Windows message system. This results in faster and more responsive access to input devices. DirectInput also supports *force feedback devices*, which "respond" to an application with physical effects, such as kickback (when a trigger is fired), vibration, and resistance. Force feedback devices make many game and entertainment experiences much more realistic and engaging. DirectInput also supports the Universal Serial Bus for access to USB input devices.

MORE ON DIRECT3D

Direct3D is a drawing interface for 3D hardware. Using DirectDraw as a base, Direct3D actually draws and renders the 3D scenes. You can use Direct3D in either *immediate mode* or *retained mode*. The Direct3D immediate mode was developed as a low-level 3D API and is ideal for developers who need to port games and other high-performance multimedia applications to the Windows operating system. It is a device-independent way for applications to communicate with accelerator hardware at a low level. By contrast, retained mode is a high-level 3D application programmer interface (API) for programmers who require rapid development or who want the support for hierarchies and animations. Direct3D retained mode is built "on top" of immediate mode. The three components of the Direct3D device are the transform (formulas describing how to convert a coordinate in 3D space into 2D display coordinates), the state variables (defining the styles for drawing operations), and the draw engine, which actually generate the object.

MORE ON DIRECTPLAY

Applications (especially games) can be more compelling if they can be played against real players, and the PC provides a versatile platform for connections over networks or the Internet. Instead of forcing the developer to deal with the differences that each connection scheme represents, DirectPlay provides well-defined generalized communication capabilities. DirectPlay is a software interface that simplifies an application's access to communication services.

A DirectPlay *session* is a communications channel between several machines. Before an application can start communicating with other machines, it must "join a session." An application can do this in two ways: it can identify all the existing sessions on a network and join one of them, or it can create a new session and wait for other machines to join it. Once the application has joined a session, it can create a player and exchange messages with all the other players in the session. Each session has one machine that is designated as the host. The host is the owner of the session and is the only machine that can change the properties of the session.

The most essential entity within a DirectPlay session is a *player*. A player represents a logical object within the session that can send and receive messages. DirectPlay does not have any representation of a physical machine in the session. Each player is identified as being either a local player (one that exists on your machine) or a remote player (one that exists on another machine), and each machine must have at least one local player before it can start sending and receiving messages. DirectPlay supports the concept of *groups* within a session. A group is logical collection of players. By creating a group of players, an application can send a single message to the group and all the players in the group will receive a copy of the message.

DIRECTX 8.0 FEATURES

DirectX 8.0 (the current version) includes new and updated features. The major components remain much the same, but some features of previous versions have been consolidated. The five major components of DirectX 8.0 are DirectAudio, DirectGraphics, DirectInput, DirectPlay, and DirectShow.

DirectAudio

DirectAudio provides the current architecture for integrated music and sound effects playback. Its features minimize CPU usage and 3D hardware requirements. While DirectAudio includes DirectSound and DirectMusic, the distinction between them is small. DirectMusic has become the accepted API for creation of interactive sound effects. The DirectMusic synthesizer is the main sound generator for DirectAudio. This synthesizer creates all the sounds, sub-mixes them and sends the result to DirectSound buffers for processing.

DirectGraphics

The DirectGraphics module in DirectX 8.0 moves some DirectDraw features to Direct3D. These include creation of resources such as textures and vertex buffers, display mode selection, and the presentation of rendered images on the display. DirectGraphics also supports multisample rendering—this allows for full-scene anti-aliasing (FSAA) and multisample effects such as motion blur. Programmable vertex processing and programmable pixel processing allow for both general environment mapping and per-pixel environment mapping.

DirectInput

The DirectInput component of DirectX 8.0 provides a default user interface for configuring devices. This feature also enables applications to access control device images for use in their own configuration interfaces.

DirectPlay

The DirectPlay module in DirectX 8.0 updates this layer for improved performance and simplicity. It is scalable to support thousands of users in a multiplayer environment. DirectPlay Voice allows for a voice-prompted user interface with a selection of low- and high-bandwidth technologies.

DirectShow

The DirectShow component of DirectX 8.0 provides a single setup program for graphics, audio, and streaming programs. DirectShow applications will benefit from easier dependency testing. It allows real-time editing of displayed images (such as graphs). DirectShow also includes improved DVD support. It can play Karaoke as well as video discs.

DETERMINING THE DIRECTX VERSION

Since DirectX is a collection of APIs, each application that uses DirectX is written to use a particular version of DirectX—the application *needs* the correct version of DirectX (or later) components installed under Windows 9x/Me. Otherwise, the application will not work. In most cases, DirectX is backward compatible, so an application written for DirectX 3.x should work on a system with DirectX 8.0x installed. But an application written for DirectX 8.0x won't work on a system with DirectX 6.x. As a technician, you'll need to spot DirectX version issues. You can use the following procedure to check the current version of DirectX installed on a given system:

1. Using Windows Explorer or My Computer, locate the DDRAW.DLL file in the \Windows\System folder.

2. Use the right mouse button to click the DDRAW.DLL file, then click Properties on the menu that appears.

3. Click the Version tab.

4. Compare the version number on the File Version line with the following list:

- **4.02.0095**   DirectX 1
- **4.03.00.1096**   DirectX 2
- **4.04.00.0068**   DirectX 3 or 3a
- **4.05.00.0155**   DirectX 5
- **4.05.01.1721**   DirectX 5.1
- **4.05.01.1998**   DirectX 5.2 (Windows 98 and later)
- **4.06.02.0436**   DirectX 6.1
- **4.06.03.0518**   DirectX 6.1a
- **4.07.00.0700**   DirectX 7
- **4.07.00.0716**   DirectX 7a
- **4.07.01.3000**   DirectX 7.1
- **4.08.00.0400**   DirectX 8.0 (Digital Signature Date 11/4/2000)
- **4.08.00.0400**   DirectX 8.0a (Digital Signature Date 1/16/2001)

DirectX versions 3 and 3a use the same version of the DDRAW.DLL file. To determine whether you are using version 3 or 3a of DirectX, use the previous procedure to check the version of the D3DRGBXF.DLL file:

- **4.04.00.0068**   DirectX 3
- **4.04.00.0070**   DirectX 3a

If the DDRAW.DLL file does *not* exist in the \Windows\System folder, DirectX is probably not installed on your computer.

DirectX 6.1 and above include a useful utility named "DirectX Diagnostic Tool." In Windows 9x/Me, you can launch this utility from the System Information program in the System Tools menu folder under Accessories. You can also launch DirectX Diagnostic by clicking Start, selecting Run, and typing **dxdiag** in the text box. This tool (Figure 37-9) reports detailed information about the DirectX components and drivers installed on your system. It lets you test functionality, diagnose problems, and change your system configuration.

DirectX 7.0 and DirectX 8.0 each had some problems implementing USB controller devices. Version 7.0a and 8.0a were quickly made available to address these problems.

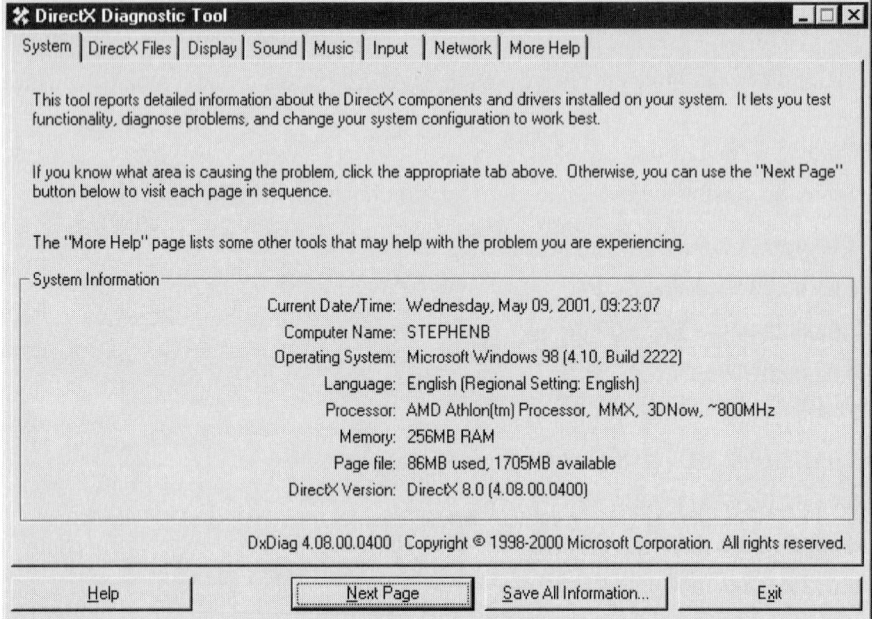

FIGURE 37-9   The DXDIAG dialog

OPENGL NOTES

Introduced in 1992, OpenGL is another popular cross-platform standard for 3D hardware acceleration. The OpenGL Architecture Review Board (an independent group) oversees the OpenGL specification. Currently the board includes representatives from ATI, Compaq, Intel, NVIDIA, Microsoft, and others. OpenGL Version 1.2, the latest release, is available for Windows, MacOS, Linux, and UNIX systems. OpenGL is used for 3D hardware acceleration in many popular games like *Quake III*, *Baldurs Gate*, *Descent 3*, and *MDK2*. OpenGL offers the same 3D rendering features described in the section on DirectX—these features include transform and lighting (T&L), clipping, and rendering. The 3D effects supported by OpenGL include real-time fog, anti-aliasing, bump mapping, 3D textures, and more.

OpenGL is also used for 3D graphics and effects in television and motion pictures. It is integral to the development of many virtual reality (or VR) environments. OpenGL popularity is also due in some part to its support for the Linux operating system. Many games have been made available in versions for play on Linux systems using OpenGL 3D hardware acceleration. OpenGL is also compatible with all Microsoft operating systems, including Windows 9x/Me, NT, and 2000.

Both the operating system and video hardware must support OpenGL. Most major video chipset makers (NVIDIA, ATI, Matrox, and others) offer support for OpenGL. The required drivers for specific video adapters are included on the adapter's installation CD or are available from the video adapters manufacturer's Web site. The OpenGL files needed for specific applications and games should be included on the program's CD along with an installation utility. You can also obtain and install OpenGL directly from the Web. The OpenGL installation utility, GLSetup, will automatically examine your hardware and install only the files required for that hardware. The complete OpenGL installation program, with support for most video chipsets, is over 85MB and would take hours to download using a 56K connection.

Microsoft did not include OpenGL run-time libraries in the original release of Windows 95. The libraries were included beginning with Windows 95 OSR2 and should be present in later versions of Windows.

Replacing/Updating a Video Adapter

Whether you're building a new PC from scratch, upgrading your system, or replacing a failed video adapter, you'll need to install a new video card with confidence. In virtually all cases, you'll need to remove references to any original video card first, replace the old card with the new one, then install the new drivers and video applet software under Windows 9x/Me. This part of the chapter highlights the general steps needed to upgrade your video system.

REMOVING OLD DEVICE DRIVERS

New video adapters can be quite sensitive to drivers and applet software from an old video device, so it's usually important for you to remove the drivers and all support software for your current video device before removing the old card and installing the new one. Of course, if you're installing a video device into a *new* system, you won't have to worry about this step. To remove the display utilities or control panels for a display card you are currently using, you must first locate and identify them. There are four main places where you should look for these items:

■ Check the user's guide, installation instructions, or owner's manual for the card you're about to remove. Any programs that would have been added to your system when you installed the card should be described in the documentation. There may also be specific instructions for uninstalling the card's software from your system—if so, you should use *those* instructions to remove the card's software suite.

■ Many video-related programs add an item under the Programs entry on your Start menu. Such an item may be listed by the name of the display card it is associated with or by the name of the company that manufactured the card. Display utilities and control applets are often given their own specific names, like the "3dfxTools" software for a new Voodoo3 card. If you find such a menu entry, look to see if there's an Uninstall option. If you find an Uninstall feature, that's probably the best way to remove the software from your system.

■ The Windows Control Panel probably contains the actual program icons for any display utilities or control applets that may have been installed with the existing video card. This may help you to identify the program you wish to remove (though it probably will *not* give you a direct method for removing it). However, the Add/Remove Programs wizard in the Control Panel can probably remove the software for you—once you know what software to remove.

■ The Windows Startup folder may contain a shortcut to a display utility or control applet for the existing video card. If so, you can simply delete the shortcut from the Startup folder to disable the program (but that will not remove the software from your system). You may also wish to use the Add/Remove Programs icon in the Control Panel to actually remove that software from your system.

Once the applet software is removed from the system, it's time to select a default video mode and remove the video adapter from your Windows Device Manager:

1. Click Start, highlight Settings, click Control Panel, then double-click the Display icon.

2. Select the Settings tab.

3. Use the Colors drop-down to select the color-depth you need (for example, "16 colors").

4. Move the Screen Area slider to a resolution of 640x480.

5. Click on the Apply button to test the selections you have made, then click OK to finalize the selections.

6. Return to the Settings tab and click on the Advanced button to open the adapter's Properties dialog.

7. Select the Adapter tab, and then click Change.

8. When the Update Device Driver wizard appears, click Next.

9. On the next screen, select "Display a list of all the drivers in a specific location, so you can select the driver you want," then click Next.

10. Select "Show all hardware," then scroll to the top of the list under "Manufacturers" and select "(Standard display types)," then select "Standard PCI Graphics Adapter (VGA)" under "Models" and click Next.

11. Windows will install the standard VGA display driver and prompt you to restart your system for the changes to take effect.

12. You should go ahead and restart your system to verify that the standard VGA display driver loads properly.

When you restart the system, the standard VGA display driver is activated for use with your current display card. This should allow you to remove the old card and install the new one without the danger of driver conflicts or incompatible video modes. Once the new card is installed, you can easily return to the Display settings and configure the desired resolution and color depth again.

EXCHANGING THE VIDEO ADAPTER

Now it's time to switch to your new video adapter. This is generally not a difficult process, but you'll need to pay attention to your particular system configuration. Remember to use an anti-static wrist strap and to keep the new video card in its protective anti-static bag until you're just ready to install it.

1. Turn off and unplug the PC, then remove the outer housing.

2. Locate the original video adapter (where the monitor cable attaches to the PC) and disconnect the monitor cable.

3. If the original video adapter is integrated into the motherboard, check the motherboard's user manual to see if there's a jumper needed to disable that adapter. If so, set the required jumper so that the onboard video adapter is disabled. (If you must disable the onboard video adapter through the CMOS Setup, doing that will be described later.)

4. If the original video adapter is simply an expansion card, unbolt the bracket from the chassis and remove the original card. Set it aside—preferably in an anti-static bag.

5. If you're replacing a PCI-based video card with an AGP-based video card, check the motherboard's user manual to see if there's a jumper to enable AGP support—older AGP motherboards often required this. If so, set the required jumper so that AGP is enabled.

6. Remove the new video card from its bag and insert it into its appropriate bus slot. Be sure that the card is seated evenly and completely and then bolt the card's bracket to the chassis.

AGP connectors are very sensitive to alignment problems. Be sure the card is completely seated and that the bracket does not move the card when the hold-down screw is tightened.

7. If there's another video/3D accelerator card in the system, you may need to attach that accelerator's feature connector to the new video card.

8. Reattach power and restart the system.

9. When the system boots for the first time, be sure to boot directly to the CMOS Setup. If you must disable the old on-board video adapter through the CMOS Setup, you must do that *now*. If you're installing an AGP video adapter in place of a PCI model, check to see if there are any AGP-related settings needed to enable AGP support on the system. Save your changes and exit the CMOS Setup.

INSTALLING NEW SOFTWARE

Once the CMOS Setup has been updated and your changes (if any) have been saved, the system will reboot once again. At this point, we'll see if the new video card is identified properly and install the appropriate drivers and support software to utilize its features.

1. Allow the system to boot normally. Since virtually all video cards are fully PnP-compliant, Windows 9x/Me should identify the new video device and query you for the appropriate drivers (typically provided on CD).

2. Place the CD into the CD-ROM drive. In most cases, the CD's autorun feature will launch a menu-driven installer that will allow you to load the card's drivers and support software (for example, 3Dfx Tools, 3Dfx TV, or 3Dfx Tweaks).

3. Install the drivers and support software and reboot the system if necessary.

CHECKING THE INSTALLATION

Once the software is installed and the system reboots, you can check for the presence of your new video adapter card, then reset the video mode to your liking.

1. From the Windows desktop, double-click My Computer, then double-click Control Panel.

2. Double-click the System icon, then select the Device Manager tab.

3. Double-click the Display Adapter entry to expand it.

4. Check the display adapter reference. You should see a reference to the new adapter that you just installed. There should be *no* yellow exclamation marks or red *X*s marking the adapter.

5. Close the Device Manager and double-click the Display icon.

6. Click the Settings tab, then click Advanced.

7. Check for tabs that mention your new display adapter (for example, 3Dfx Info, 3Dfx TV, or 3D Tweaks).

If you see the entry for your new video adapter in the Device Manager (and also in the advanced display settings dialog) and no errors are indicated, chances are that your new video adapter is working properly. You may now return to the Settings tab in your Display dialog, and set the desired resolution and color depth for your display.

AGP Overclocking

The AGP bus was designed as a 66MHz bus architecture, and this 66MHz signal is almost always derived from the motherboard's Front Side Bus (FSB) clock. When motherboards offered only a 66MHz clock, this arrangement was not a problem for AGP, since the FSB clock and the AGP clock were basically the same thing. However, when motherboards went to 100MHz and 133MHz (and faster), the AGP bus needed to be *derived* from the FSB. In many cases, the AGP clock is set from a motherboard jumper or through an entry in the CMOS Setup. You'll generally find these settings denoted as the "AGP Ratio," and you can usually select "1:1," "2:3," or "1:2," depending on the FSB speeds available. You can see an example of how this setting is used next:

■ If the FSB is 66MHz, set the AGP Ratio to 1:1, and the AGP clock will be 66MHz.

■ If the FSB is 100MHz, set the AGP Ratio to 2:3, and the AGP clock will be 66MHz.

■ If the FSB is 133MHz, set the AGP Ratio to 1:2, and the AGP clock will be 66MHz.

You can also see the potential for "overclocking":

■ If the FSB is 100MHz, setting the AGP Ratio to 1:1 will cause the AGP clock to be 100MHz.

■ If the FSB is 133MHz, setting the AGP Ratio to 2:3 will cause the AGP clock to be 88.7MHz.

As a rule, it is *unsafe* to overclock the AGP bus—especially if you're using AGP in the 2X or 4X data modes. In most cases, an overclocked AGP bus will result in unstable video and system operation. In extreme cases, the overclocked AGP card will be damaged.

AGP AND BIOS SETTINGS

The number of video BIOS settings has been increasing steadily—even before the introduction of AGP. Every video card should include a list of recommended BIOS settings with its documentation (or the setting should be available from the manufacturer's Web site), and you should see that your CMOS Setup is configured properly for your particular AGP video card. For example, Table 37-4 lists the recommended settings for a Viper II Z200 card—you get some idea of how important BIOS settings have become. You can compare these settings to the entries for an NVIDIA GeForce chipset in Table 37-5.

  Not all listed options will be available on all motherboards. Should particular setting combinations fail, try loading "BIOS Defaults" in the CMOS Setup.

VIDEO OVERCLOCKING NOTES

Although you are certainly discouraged from overclocking a video adapter, today's powerful hardware accelerators offer some unique potential for overclocking that any technician should be aware of. You should at least know that such practices exist so that you can identify and correct video problems.

In principle, overclocking a video chipset and video memory is very similar to overclocking a CPU and main system memory. In actual practice, it is often *easier* to overclock video components than it is to overclock main system components, since the speed settings for your video adapter are typically adjustable without having to open the system. Small third-party utilities for overclocking popular video chipsets

TABLE 37-4   BIOS SETTINGS FOR A TYPICAL AGP CARD

BIOS SETTINGS: PCI/AGP GENERAL

IRQ assignment	[toggle]
Boot with PnP O/S	[enable]
Pallet snooping	[disable]
PCI bursting	[disable]
PCI latency timer	[128]
Peer concurrency	[disable]
Video ROM BIOS Shadow	[disable]
Video BIOS shadowing	[disable]
Video BIOS cacheable	[disable]
Video RAM cacheable	[disable]
Byte-Merge	[disable]
Decouple Refresh	[disable]
Hidden Refresh	[disable]
USWC options	[Uncache Speculative Write Combining]
Video Memory Cache Mode	[UC]
Snoop Ahead	[disable]

BIOS SETTINGS: AGP SPECIFIC

USB	[enabled]
PCI 2.1 compliance	[enable—also may assign IRQ to VGA]
Passive release/refresh	[enabled]
Delayed transactions	[enabled/disabled—toggle, may also enable PCI 2.1 compliance]
VGA BIOS Sequence	[AGP-PCI, PCI-AGP, PCI]
AGP/Graphics aperture size	[Target 1/2 installed RAM]
Write Cache Pipeline	[disable]
Read Around Write	[disable]
Primary Frame Buffer	[disable]
VGA Frame Buffer	[disable]
Frame Buffer Posted Write	[disable]
RAS-CAS Delay	[3T]
Cache Read	[disable] (VIA Motherboards)
CPU Wait Pipeline	[disable] (VIA Motherboards)
AGP Master 1 WS Write	[enable/disable]
AGP Master 1 WS Read	[enable/disable]
AGP Ratio	[set to 2/3 instead of 1/1]
AGP Multi Trans Timer	[disable]
AGP Low Priority Timer	[disable]
AGP 2x	[disable]
AGP Turbo Mode	[disable]
AGP Bus Turbo Mode	[disable]
AGP Transfer Mode	[1x]

TABLE 37-5   BIOS SETTINGS FOR AN NVIDIA GEFORCE-BASED VIDEO CARD

UC or USWC	USWC
Fast Writes	Enabled
AGP Mode	2x or 4x (depending on whether your motherboard supports AGP4X or not)
AGP Driving Control	Auto
AGP Aperture Size	128MB RAM - Set to 64MB or 32MB
	96MB RAM - Set to 48MB or 24MB
	64MB RAM - Set to 32MB or 16MB
	48MB RAM - Set to 24MB or 12MB
	32MB RAM - Set to 24MB or 12MB
	16MB RAM - Set to 24MB or 12MB
Assign IRQ to VGA	Enabled
Video BIOS Shadow	Disabled
Video BIOS Cacheable	Disabled
C8000—XXXXX Shadow	Disabled
Peer Concurrency	Enabled
Concurrent PCI Host	Enabled
PCI Streaming	Enabled
VGA Palette Snoop	Disabled
Memory Hole (Between 15-16MB)	Enabled

are available for download from numerous Web sites, and some video adapter manufacturers provide core and memory speed controls in their native display adjustment utilities and drivers. Third-party utilities—such as TNTClock (**www.octools.com/graphics.html**) for the NVIDIA TNT chipset—are limited to adjusting only the core and the memory speed of the video adapter. Other utilities like Powerstrip from Entech (**www.entechtaiwan.com/**) offer not only the ability to adjust core and memory speeds of many different video chipset and adapters, but also offer the ability to adjust a wide range of display settings. These utilities make video overclocking possible with only a few clicks of the mouse. Unfortunately, they can also make it very easy to damage your video adapter.

As with CPU overclocking, there are limits to how far you can "push" a video adapter. Increasing clock speeds will increase heat generated by the graphics chipset, so it is important that adequate cooling (and temperature monitoring) be implemented. Additional case ventilation may also be required to exhaust heated air from the system. Most video adapters will generate corrupt frames as the thermal limit for a graphics chipset is exceeded. Images that contain "snow" or incorrect colors are often a sign that the video memory speed has been exceeded.

Once you have recorded the default operating speeds and temperatures of a video adapter, you can begin to slowly increase the core and memory speeds using the appropriate utility. The increases should be small (2–5MHz at a time), and each increase should be followed by testing the video components with a demanding game or benchmark burn-in utility. Any problems, corrupt displays, or crashes indicate that the limits of the video adapter and cooling resources have been exceeded—either return to a stable setting or increase cooling activity.

 One of the first things a technician should check for when video stability problems are reported is video overclocking by the customer or system builder.

Troubleshooting Video Adapters

A PC video system consists of four parts: the host PC itself, the video adapter/accelerator, the monitor, and the software (video BIOS and drivers). To deal with a failure in the video system, you must be able to isolate the problem to one of these four areas. When isolating the problem, your best tool is a working (or *testbed*) PC. With another PC, you can systematically exchange hardware as needed to verify each element of the video system.

BASIC PROBLEM ISOLATION

The first step is to verify the monitor by testing it on a known-good working PC. Keep in mind that the monitor *must* be compatible with the video adapter on which it is being tested. If the monitor works on another PC, the fault lies in one of the three remaining areas. If the monitor fails on a known-good machine, try the known-good monitor on the questionable machine. If the known-good monitor then works on your questionable machine, you can be certain that the fault lies in your monitor (you can refer to the appropriate chapter here for detailed troubleshooting if you wish). If the monitor checks out, suspect the video adapter. Follow the same process to check the video adapter. Try the suspect video adapter on a known-good PC. If the problem follows the video adapter, you can replace the video adapter. If the suspect video adapter works in a known-good system, the adapter is probably good. Replace the adapter in the suspect machine, but try another expansion slot and make sure that the monitor cable is attached securely.

If both the monitor and the video adapter work in a known-good PC, but the video problem persists in the original machine, suspect a problem with the PC motherboard. Try the working video adapter in another expansion slot. Either the expansion slot is faulty, or a fault has occurred on the motherboard. Run some PC diagnostics if you have some available. Diagnostics may help to pinpoint motherboard problems. You may then choose to troubleshoot the motherboard further or replace the motherboard at your discretion.

When the video system appears to work properly during system initialization but fails with a particular application (or in Windows 9x/Me), strongly suspect a problem with the selected video driver. Since almost all video adapters support VGA at the hardware level, set your application (or change the Windows setup) to run in "standard VGA" mode (for Windows 9x/Me, you can start the PC in the "Safe Mode"). If the display functions properly at that point, you can be confident that the problem is driver-related. Check with the manufacturer to see that you have the latest video driver available. Reload the driver from its original disk (or a new disk) or select a new driver. You may also check to see if a new video firmware version is available from the video adapter manufacturer. If the problem persists in VGA mode, the trouble may be in the video adapter. Problem isolation can be summarized with these points:

■ *Check the driver(s).* Video drivers are critically important in all versions of Windows. Older drivers may contain bugs or be incompatible with certain applications. Incompatibility accounts for the majority of all video problems. Obtain the latest video driver release and make sure it is properly installed on the system. If the driver is the most current, try a generic (or *reference*) video driver (usually available from the video chipset manufacturer).

■ *Check the physical installation.* See that the video board is installed properly in its expansion slot and make sure that any video card jumpers are set properly for the particular host system.

■ *Check for memory conflicts.* The memory space used by video adapters is hotly contested territory in the real-mode (DOS) upper memory area. Printer drivers, sound cards, tape backups, SCSI adapters, and scanners are just some of the devices that can step all over the memory space needed by a video board. Many of today's video boards require you to *exclude* a range of upper memory through your memory manager (often A000h through C7FFh, though particular video boards may be different). Make sure that any necessary memory exclusions are made in CONFIG.SYS at the memory manager's command line. You may also have to add an **EMMExclude=A000-C7FF** line to the [386enh] section of your SYSTEM.INI file.

■ *Suspect your memory manager.* Advanced real-mode memory managers such as QEMM or Netroom use very aggressive techniques to find available memory. Often, this interferes with video operation. Try disabling any "Stealth" or "Cloaking" mode or try disabling your real-mode memory manager.

■ *Check your system's CMOS setup.* Today's motherboards sport all manner of advanced features. Try systematically disabling such attributes as: video cache, video RAM shadow, byte-merge, palette snoop, or decouple/hidden refresh. If "PCI bus bursting" is used on the video bus, try disabling that also. If the video system requires the use of an interrupt, make sure that the IRQ is not being used by another device. If the user manual for your video card lists any special settings for your CMOS Setup, verify that you've made the appropriate changes. In many cases, you can try loading the BIOS Defaults for your CMOS Setup.

■ *Compatibility.* Check the video adapter maker's (and motherboard maker's) Web site for any known compatibility issues. Current video adapters may have minimum power requirements or use some features not supported by the motherboard's chipset. This type of checking should be done *before* purchasing a video adapter for an upgrade.

MULTIPLE DISPLAY SUPPORT GUIDE

Traditionally, only one video adapter is allowed on the system, but Windows 98/Me seeks to "extend" the desktop by supporting the use of more than one video adapter. This allows more open windows and thus provides more information to the user at any given time. However, multiple display (or "multi-monitor") support is far from perfect and must be used with the right combination of system BIOS, video adapter chipsets, and Windows 98/Me. This part of the chapter highlights some of the key hardware requirements and issues common to multi-monitor operation.

Video Adapters

All of the video adapters used in a computer with multi-monitor support *must* be Peripheral Component Interconnect (PCI) or Accelerated Graphics Port (AGP) devices using the multi-monitor compliant Windows 98/Me display drivers. Industry Standard Architecture/Extended Industry Standard Architecture (ISA/EISA) display adapters are specifically *not* supported. Keep in mind that the video adapters installed in your computer do *not* have to be identical. Each video adapter and monitor combination is separately enumerated by Windows 98/Me, and can be configured to use different screen resolutions and color depths. For example, the primary display can be set to 1024×768×256, and the secondary display can be set to 800×600×32K.

Video Chipsets/Drivers

Any combination of the following supported PCI-based video adapters can be used for multi-monitor operation. Devices in Table 37-6 will serve as primary and secondary adapters. The drivers in Table 37-6 are supported by Microsoft and are included on the Windows 98 CD.

TABLE 37-6   VIDEO CHIPSETS/DRIVERS SUITABLE FOR MULTI-MONITOR OPERATION

CARD	DRIVER	CARD	DRIVER
ATI Mach 64 GX (GX, GXD, VT) ATI Graphics Pro Turbo PCI ATI Graphics Xpression ATI WinTurbo	ATIM64.DRV	Cirrus 5446 STB Nitro 64V	CIRRUSMM. DRV
ATI Rage I, II, & II+ ATI All-In-Wonder ATI 3D Xpression+ PC2TV ATI 3D Xpression ATI 3D Xpression+	ATI_M64.DRV	S3 ViRGE ViRGE (325) ViRGE VX (988) ViRGE DX (385) ViRGE GX (385) Diamond Stealth 3D 2000 Diamond Stealth 3D 3000	S3V.DRV
ATI Rage Pro (AGP & PCI) ATI Xpert@Work (4 & 8MB) ATI Xpert@Play (4 & 8MB) ATI All-In-Wonder Pro	ATIR3.DRV	Diamond Stealth 3D 2000 Pro Number Nine 9FX Reality 332 STB Nitro 3D STB Powergraph 3D	
S3 765 (Trio64V+) * Only certain updates will work: 40, 42, 43, 44, 52, 53, & 54. If the card is one of these updates, Windows 98 will recognize the card as a Trio 64V+. Otherwise, it is recognized as a Trio 32/64. Note which Microsoft driver Windows 98 selects when you use this card.	S3MM.DRV	STB Velocity 3D STB MVP/64 STB MVP/64 3D STB WorkStation (2 & 4 output) Miro Crystal VR4000	
S3 Trio64V2(DX/GX) Diamond Stealth 64 Video 2001 STB PowerGraph 64V+ STB MVP 64 Miro TwinHead 22SD Hercules Terminator 64/Video Number Nine 9FX Reality 332 (S3 Virge) Number Nine 9FX Reality 334 (S3 Virge GX/2) Number Nine 9FX Reality 772 (S3 Virge VX) California Graphics V2/DX Videologic GraphicsStar 410	S3MM.DRV	ET6000 Hercules Dynamite 128/Video STB Lightspeed 128	ET6000.DRV
		S3 Aurora Compaq Armada	S3MM.DRV
		Trident 9685/9680/9682/9385/9382 Jaton Video - 57P	TRID_PCI.DRV
		InterGraphics Systems (IGS) CyberPro 2000A, 2MB	IGA2K.DRV
		Permedia 2 TI TVP4020, 8 meg PCI (Reference board) TI TVP4020 8 meg AGP (Reference board) Diamond Fire GL Pro 1000 PCI Diamond Fire GL Pro 1000 AGP STB (Symmetric) Glyder MAX-2 PCI	GLINT.DRV
Cirrus 5436 Cirrus Alpine	CIRRUSMM. DRV		

Matrox, NVIDIA, and ATI offer video adapters with integrated support for dual and multiple monitors, so adding another video adapter is not necessary.

Enabling Multi-monitor Support

As you saw previously, the primary requirement for multi-monitor support is that the video adapters *must* be Peripheral Component Interconnect (PCI) devices or Accelerated Graphics Port (AGP) devices. You can enable multi-monitor support with the following steps:

1. While the computer is turned off, add any additional video adapters and monitors.
2. Start Windows 98/Me. Install the video adapter and monitor drivers (as necessary), then restart your computer if you're prompted to do so.
3. Click Start, highlight Settings, then click Control Panel.
4. Double-click the Display icon, then click the Settings tab.
5. In the Display box, click the adapter you want to use, then click the "Extend my Windows desktop onto this monitor" check box to select it.
6. Click OK.

Multi-Monitor Issues

Multi-monitor display technology is fairly well established under Windows 98/Me, but there are situations where problems will arise. The easiest way to test your multi-monitor setup is to start Paint or WordPad under Windows 98/Me. When Paint or WordPad is *not* running in full-screen mode, drag the program from one monitor to the other. If you can drag the program from one monitor to the other, you'll know that multi-monitor support is working correctly. If doing this presents problems, try these tips to help isolate the trouble.

■ Disable the secondary display adapter to confirm that your program works properly on the primary display adapter:

   1. Click Start, highlight Settings, click Control Panel, then double-click the Display icon.
   2. On the Settings tab, click the secondary monitor icon.
   3. Click the "Extend my Windows desktop onto this monitor" check box to clear it, then click OK.

■ Avoid programs that do not fully comply with multi-monitor support:
   ■ Programs or drivers that modify the GDI.EXE file or the display driver.
   ■ Programs that use Adobe Type Manager.
   ■ Remote control programs such as pcANYWHERE.

■ Verify that the correct display driver is installed for the secondary display device:

   1. Click Start, highlight Settings, click Control Panel, then double-click the Display icon.
   2. On the Settings tab click Advanced, then click the Adapter tab.
   3. Verify that the installed video driver is the *correct* driver for the video adapter in your computer. If not, you should use the Update Driver wizard to install the correct driver(s).

■ Verify that the secondary monitor displays the following message when you start your computer:

```
If you can read this message, Windows has successfully initialized this
display adapter. To use this adapter as part of your Windows desktop,
open the Display option in the Control Panel and adjust the settings on
the Settings tab.
```

If this message is *not* displayed, confirm that the secondary display adapter is installed:

1. Click Start, highlight Settings, click Control Panel, then double-click the System icon.
2. On the Device Manager tab, double-click Display Adapters to confirm that all of your video adapters have been correctly installed. If they haven't, you should recheck the installation of any missing devices.

■ Verify that the secondary display adapter has a supported chip set as listed in Table 37-6.

■ If you notice that the "Extend my Windows desktop onto this monitor" box is unavailable, you can select the secondary monitor and try extending the desktop again:

1. Click Start, highlight Settings, click Control Panel, then double-click the Display icon.
2. On the Settings tab, click the secondary monitor icon. After you click the secondary monitor icon, the "Extend my Windows desktop onto this monitor" check box should become available.

MISSING DISPLAY OPTIONS

Ideally, once a video adapter is installed and configured, you should be able to select any of its available resolutions and color depths through the Windows 9x/Me Display icon. However, when you try to change the Desktop Area setting, some known options of that the video adapter may not be available. For example, a video adapter that can display to a resolution of 1024×768×256 may offer only 640×480×256 and 800×600×16 as the resolution/color options. Missing display options can occur when one or more of the following situations are present on your system:

■ The computer is a PCI system and the Monitor Timing settings in the CMOS Setup are set incorrectly. The Monitor Timing settings should match the capabilities of the monitor (screen). Check your monitor's documentation for the maximum supported resolution and then make the necessary changes to the Monitor Timing settings.

■ The Monitor Type is incorrect in your Display properties (Figure 37-10). You can open this dialog in Windows 98/SE by right-clicking the on the desktop, selecting Properties, clicking the Settings tab, clicking the Advanced button, selecting the Monitor tab, and then clicking the Change button. The Monitor Type should match the monitor brand and model that you are using. If your monitor is not listed, you can select the Generic setting that corresponds to the capabilities of your monitor.

■ The Windows video driver doesn't support the display mode you're trying to use. If you are confident that the display and video adapter are capable of a higher resolution, try setting the Adapter Type to one of the high-resolution generic (Super VGA) modes. A better solution is often to update the video driver to the latest manufacturer's version.

In virtually all cases, the full suite of video adapter resolutions and color depths should become available once you've isolated one of the common problems listed previously.

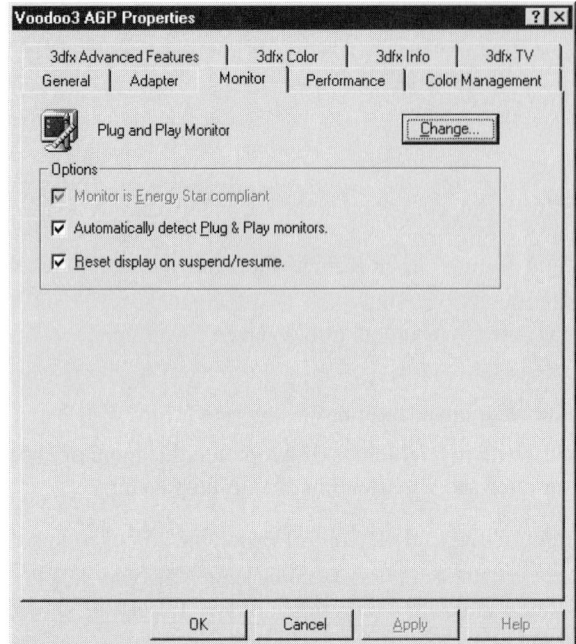

FIGURE 37-10   Changing monitor types through the Windows 98/SE Display dialog

BASIC VIDEO TROUBLESHOOTING WITH WINDOWS 9X/ME

Most video problems under Windows 9x/Me fall into one or more typical categories. This part of the chapter is intended to present a systematic approach that will allow you to isolate and correct many of the most common Windows 9x/Me video problems.

Display Drivers

If video problems occur when Windows is started normally, but do not occur when Windows is started in Safe Mode, chances are the trouble is related to the display driver that Windows is attempting to use. Given the vast number of video drivers and hardware in service, your first step should be to check the video driver:

1.   Use any text editor (such as Notepad) to open the SYSTEM.INI file in the \Windows folder.

2.   In the [Boot] section, search for the **display=** line. If this line reads anything *other* than the following, the driver was designed for Windows 3.1 (or an earlier version of Windows):

```
Display.drv=Pnpdrvr.drv
```

If the line *does* appear as shown and you're using a video driver designed for Windows 9x/Me, check the "Advanced Settings" section. Otherwise, uninstall the old driver and use the latest version of the Windows 9x/Me driver or use the standard VGA driver included with Windows 9x/Me. For Windows 95 do the following:

1.   Click Start, highlight Settings, click Control Panel, then double-click the Display icon.

2.   Click the Settings tab, then click Change Display Type.

3.   Click the Change button in the Adapter Type section, then click Show All Devices.

4.   In the Manufacturers box, click (Standard Display Types).

5.   In the Models box, click Standard Display Adapter (VGA), click OK, then click Close.

6.   Click Close and reboot the system if necessary.

If you're using Windows 98/Me:

1.   Click Start, highlight Settings, click Control Panel, then double-click the Display icon.

2.   Click the Settings tab, then click Advanced.

3.   Click the Adapter tab, then click Change.

4.   Click Next, click "Display a list of all the drivers in a specific location, so you can select the driver you want", then click Next.

5.   Click Show All Devices.

6.   In the Manufacturers box, click (Standard Display Types).

7.   In the Models box, click Standard Display Adapter (VGA), click OK, then click Next.

8.   Click Next, click Next, then click Finish.

9.   Click Close, click Close again, then click Yes to restart your computer.

Advanced Settings

Windows 9x/Me offers a built-in process for troubleshooting common video problems using an adjustable slider. This slider lets you change the way Windows uses the video card. It is a good idea to start with the setting on the right (the Full setting) and systematically move the slider one setting to the left until you find the setting that works best. Follow these steps to use the slider:

1.   Open the Control Panel and double-click the System icon.

2.   Click the Performance tab, then click the Graphics.

3.   Note that the Hardware Acceleration slider (Figure 37-11) has four settings (Full, Most, Basic, and None). Choose a setting from the Hardware Acceleration slider:

▪ **Full**   This is the default setting and allows for full hardware acceleration.

▪ **Most**   This setting adds **SWCursor=1** to the [Display] section of the SYSTEM.INI file, which disables the hardware cursor. The Most setting applies to Western Digital (WD) or S3-compatible drivers. If you have problems with the way the mouse pointer appears on the screen, try this setting.

▪ **Basic**   In addition to the setting in Most, this setting adds **SafeMode=1** to the [Windows] section of the WIN.INI file. Setting SafeMode to 1 allows for basic acceleration only (for example, pattern bit block transfers [bitblt] and screen-to-screen bitblt transfers). It also adds **MMIO=0** to the [Display] section of the SYSTEM.INI file, which disables memory-mapped I/O for S3-compatible drivers. Try the Basic setting if your computer seems to stop responding (hangs) randomly and you have an S3-compatible video driver.

▪ **None**   In addition to the settings in Basic, this setting adds **SafeMode=2** to the [Windows] section of the WIN.INI file. Setting SafeMode to 2 disables all video card acceleration (for example, the GDI calls the device-independent bitmap [DIB] engine directly for screen drawing, rather than using the display driver). Try the None setting if your computer seems to hang randomly, you have an S3-compatible video driver, and the Basic setting does not resolve the problem.

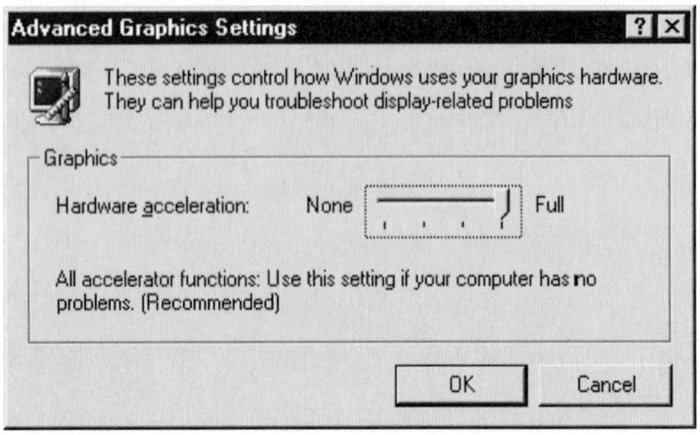

FIGURE 37-11 The graphics acceleration slider for isolating video problems

Color Depth Problems

In some cases, you may experience problems changing color depth on your computer. For example, you cannot select anything other than 256 colors (even though the video card may be capable of far more colors). Chances are that there is a problem with the display driver. Either the driver is not correct for your video card, the driver is outdated or buggy, or the driver is damaged. You can usually correct this type of problem by downloading the latest driver for your video card, removing the current video driver(s), then installing the new video driver. If the video card is not identified correctly, or the driver fails to install, the card may be conflicting with other devices in the system.

Monitor Configuration

For very best video performance, verify that your monitor is identified correctly, and is using a suitable driver. Doing this will generally help video quality and ensure proper power management in the video system. Use the following steps to verify that your monitor is selected correctly in Windows 95:

1. Click Start, highlight Settings, click Control Panel, and then double-click the Display icon.
2. Click the Settings tab, then click Change Display Type.
3. Click the Change button in the Monitor Type section, then click Show All Devices.
4. In the Manufacturers box, click the manufacturer of your monitor. If your monitor manufacturer is not listed, click (Standard Monitor Types).
5. In the Models box, click the monitor you are using, click OK, then click Close.
6. Click OK and reboot the system if necessary.

Use the following steps to verify that your monitor is selected correctly in Windows 98:

1. Click Start, highlight Settings, click Control Panel, then double-click the Display icon.
2. Click the Settings tab, then click Advanced.
3. Click the Monitor tab, then click Change.
4. In the Manufacturers box, click the manufacturer of your monitor. If your monitor manufacturer is not listed, click (Standard Monitor Types).
5. In the Models box, click the monitor you are using, click OK, then click OK again.
6. Click OK and reboot the system if necessary.

Verify the Drivers

If you suspect that one or more display drivers are missing or damaged, you can use the Windows Setup to verify the condition of your drivers. To verify drivers under Windows 95, run Windows 95 Setup again and choose the Verify option when you are prompted. The Verify option causes Windows 95 to check all files and replace any that are missing or damaged. Under Windows 98/SE, run the Windows System File Checker tool. To start the System File Checker, click Start, click Run, type **sfc.exe** in the Open box, and then click OK. You may need to have your Windows 98/SE installation disc on-hand in the event that files need to be replaced.

Display Setting Problems

If you're unable to change your display settings, the display driver may be corrupted. You can use the following procedure to check the driver installation:

1. Open the Control Panel, double-click the System icon, and then click the Hardware Profiles tab (Figure 37-12).

2. Highlight the hardware profile that is marked (current) and click copy, then enter a name for the new profile (such as **test**).

3. Reboot the computer and press F8 when you see the "Starting Windows" prompt. Choose Safe Mode from the Startup Menu.

4. You will be prompted to choose a hardware profile to boot with. Choose the new (in this example, **test**) profile and allow the computer to boot into Windows. This hardware profile will allow you to make changes to Device Manager without altering the original hardware configuration.

5. Open the System icon again and click the Device Manager tab.

6. Expand the Display Adapters entry to view the list of device drivers.

7. Click the display adapter that is listed and click the Remove button. Choose OK when you see the message "You are about to remove this device from your system". If there are multiple display drivers listed, repeat the steps for each device.

8. Close System Properties, and then reboot the computer.

9. When you receive the Hardware Profile prompt again, choose your new (**test**) profile. Windows should detect a display adapter and either prompt you to restart the computer to complete the device installation or prompt you to provide a manufacturer's disk to install the drivers.

10. When you reboot again, choose the new (**test**) profile again and try adjusting the display settings from the Settings tab of the Display icon in your Control Panel.

11. If your issue is resolved, then you may delete the new (**test**) hardware profile that you created and perform the same set of steps to remove and redetect the display driver when you reboot into your original hardware configuration.

12. If these steps do not correct the problem, remove the new (**test**) hardware profile and check with the video card's manufacturer for additional information, firmware upgrades, and so on.

VIDEO SYMPTOMS

Many common video problems can be isolated and resolved using the previous guidelines. However, when the problems persist, you can refer to the following symptoms for specific explanations and solutions.

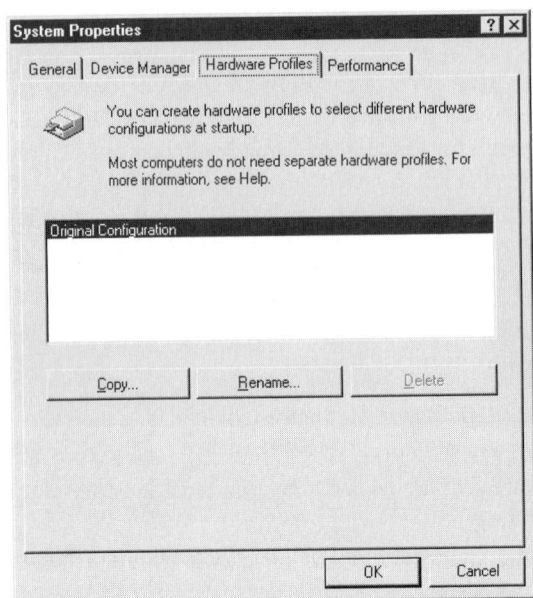

FIGURE 37-12   Adjusting the system's hardware profiles to test a video system

SYMPTOM 37-1   **The computer is on, but there is no display**   The PC seems to initialize properly. If you hear a series of beeps during system initialization, refer to Chapter 18 to determine the error. Make sure that the monitor is turned on and plugged into the video adapter properly. Also, check that the monitor's brightness and contrast controls are turned up enough (it sounds silly, but it really *does* happen). Try the monitor on a known-good PC. If the monitor works properly, suspect the video adapter. Power-down the PC and make sure the video adapter is seated properly in its expansion slot. If any of the board contacts are dirty or corroded, clean the contacts by rubbing them with an eraser. You can also use any electronics-grade contact cleaner. You may want to try the video board in another expansion slot.

Chances are that the video adapter has at least one hardware jumper or DIP switch setting. Contact the manufacturer or refer to the owner's manual for the board and check that any jumpers or DIP switch settings on the board are configured properly. If this is a new installation, check the adapter board settings against the configuration of other expansion boards in the system. When the hardware settings of one board overlap the settings of another, a hardware conflict can result. When you suspect a conflict, adjust the settings of the video adapter (or another newly installed device) to eliminate the conflict. There may also be a memory conflict. Some video adapters make unusual demands of upper system memory (the area between 640KB and 1MB). It is possible that an *EXCLUDE* switch must be added to the EMM386.EXE entry in a CONFIG.SYS file. Check with the adapter's instruction manual to see if there are any memory configuration changes or optimizations that are required.

SYMPTOM 37-2   **There is no display, and you hear a series of beeps when the PC initializes**   The video adapter failed to initialize during the system's POST. Since the video adapter is not responding, it is impossible to display information—that is why a series of beeps is used. Bear in mind that the actual beep sequence may vary from system to system depending on the type of BIOS being used. You can probably find the beep code for your BIOS in Chapter 18. In actual practice, there may be several reasons why the video adapter fails. Power-down the PC and check that the video adapter is installed properly and securely in an expansion slot. Make sure that the video adapter is not touching any exposed wiring or any other expansion board.

Isolate the video adapter by trying another adapter in the system. If the display works properly with another adapter installed, check the original adapter to see that all settings and jumpers are correct. If the problem persists, the original adapter is probably defective and should be replaced. If a new adapter fails to resolve the problem, there may be a fault elsewhere on the motherboard. Install a POST board in the PC and allow the system to initialize. Each step of the initialization procedure corresponds to a two-digit hexadecimal code shown on the POST card indicators. The last code to be displayed is the point at which the failure occurred. POST cards are handy for checking the motherboard when a low-level fault has occurred. If a motherboard fault is detected, you may troubleshoot the motherboard or replace it at your discretion.

SYMPTOM 37-3   You see large blank bands at the top and bottom of the display in some screen modes, but not in others   Multifrequency and multimode monitors sometimes behave this way. This is not necessarily a *defect*, but it can cause some confusion unless you understand what is going on. When screen resolution changes, the overall number of pixels being displayed also changes. Ideally, a multifrequency monitor should detect the mode change and adjust the vertical screen size to compensate (a feature called *auto-sizing*). However, not all multifrequency monitors have this feature. When video modes change, you are left to adjust the vertical size manually. Of course, if there is information *missing* from the display, there may be a serious problem with VRAM or the adapter's graphics controller chip. In such case, try another video adapter board.

SYMPTOM 37-4   The display image rolls   Vertical synchronization is not keeping the image steady (horizontal sync may also be affected). This problem is typical of a monitor that can not display a particular screen mode. Mode incompatibility is most common with fixed-frequency monitors, but can also appear in multifrequency monitors that are being pushed beyond their specifications. The best course of action here is to simply reconfigure your software to use a compatible video mode (or reduce the vertical refresh rate). If that is an unsatisfactory solution, you will have to upgrade to a monitor that will support the desired video mode.

If the monitor and video board are compatible, there is a synchronization problem. Try the monitor on a known-good PC. If the monitor also fails on a known-good PC, try the known-good monitor on original PC. If the known-good monitor works on the suspect PC, the sync circuits in your original monitor have almost certainly failed. If the suspect monitor works on a known-good PC, the trouble is likely in the original video adapter. Try replacing the video adapter.

SYMPTOM 37-5   An error message appears on system startup indicating an invalid system configuration   The system CMOS backup battery has probably failed, and the video type may have defaulted to EGA or MCA instead of VGA, resulting in the error. This is typically a symptom that occurs in older systems. If you enter your system setup (either through a BIOS routine or through a disk-based setup utility) and examine each entry, you will probably find that all entries have returned to a default setting—including the video system setting. Your best course is to replace the CMOS backup battery and enter each configuration setting again (hopefully you have recorded each setting on paper already, or saved the CMOS contents to floppy disk using a CMOS backup utility). Once new settings are entered and saved, the system should operate properly. If the CMOS *still* will not retain system configuration information, the CMOS RAM itself is probably defective. Use a software diagnostic to check the

RTC/CMOS chip (and the rest of the motherboard) thoroughly. If a motherboard fault is detected, you can troubleshoot the motherboard or replace it at your discretion.

SYMPTOM 37-6   **Garbage appears on the screen or the system hangs up**   There are a variety of reasons why the display may be distorted. One potential problem is a monitor mismatch. Check the video adapter jumpers and DIP switch settings and be sure that the video board will support the type of monitor you are using. It is possible that the video mode being used is not supported by your monitor (the display may also roll, as described in Symptom 37-4). Try reconfiguring your application software to use a compatible video mode. The problem should disappear. If that is an unsatisfactory solution, you will have to upgrade to a monitor that will support the desired video mode. Some older multifrequency monitors are unable to switch video modes without being turned off and then turned on again. When such monitors experience a change in video mode, they will respond by displaying a distorted image until the monitor is reset. If you have an older monitor, try turning it off, wait several minutes, then turn it on again.

Conflicts between device drivers and terminate-and-stay-resident (TSR) programs will upset the display and are particularly effective at crashing the computer. The most effective way to check for conflicts is to create a backup copy of your system startup files CONFIG.SYS and AUTOEXEC.BAT. From the root directory at the DOS prompt (or directory that contains your startup files), type

```
copy autoexec.bat autoexec.xyz
copy config.sys config.xyz
```

The extensions "xyz" suggest that you use any three letters, but avoid using "bak" since many ASCII text editors create backup file with this extension.

Now that you have backup files, go ahead and use an ASCII text editor (such as the text editor included with DOS) to REM-out each driver or TSR command line. Reboot the computer. If the problem disappears, use the ASCII text editor to reenable one REMed-out command at a time. Reboot and check the system after each command line is reenabled. When the problem occurs again, the last command enabled is the cause of the conflict. Check that command line carefully. There may be command line switches that you can add to the startup file that will load the driver or TSR without causing a conflict. Otherwise, you would be wise to leave the offending command line REMed-out. If you encounter serious trouble in editing the startup files, you can simply recopy the backup files to the working file names and start again.

Video drivers also play a big part in Windows. If your display problems are occurring in Windows, make sure that you have loaded the proper video driver and that the driver is compatible with the video board being used. If problems persist in Windows, load the standard generic VGA driver. The generic VGA driver should function properly with virtually every video board and VGA (or SVGA) monitor available. If the problem disappears when using the generic driver setup, the original driver is incorrect, corrupt, or obsolete. Contact the driver manufacturer to obtain a copy of the latest driver version. If the problem persists, the video adapter board may be defective or incompatible with Windows. Try another video adapter.

SYMPTOM 37-7   **Your video card doesn't work on a VIA- or ETEQ-based system**
This is a known issue with the Viper II Z200 and is the same on both "Super 7" and Slot 1 based systems. The Viper II Z200 card does not interact properly with the MVP3 or ETEQ chipsets. Check to see that the AGP driver and IRQ routing drivers have been installed properly before attempting to install the display

adapter. All the necessary motherboard updates can be found in a file from **www.viatech.com/drivers/ 4IN1409.exe**. This patch is supposed to work for both the MVP3 and ETEQ chipset (Super 7) as well as the VIA Apollo Pro chipset (for Pentium II systems).

SYMPTOM 37-8   **Your video card doesn't work on an ALI-based system**
This is a known issue with video cards such as the Viper V770 and is the same on both "Super 7" and Slot 1 based systems. This problem probably occurs because the ALI-based chipset requires an AGP driver in order to support AGP cards such as the V770. Ensure that the latest AGP driver from ALI has been installed from: **www.acerlabs.com/acerlabs/drivers.htm**. This patch is supposed to work for both the Aladdin V chipset (Super 7) as well as the Aladdin Pro II chipset (for Pentium II systems—also referred to as the BXPro).

SYMPTOM 37-9   **Your video card doesn't work on an AMD Athlon-based system**
This is a known issue with video cards such as the Viper II Z200 and almost always means that the Athlon motherboard requires an AGP "miniport" driver. Ensure that the latest AGP "miniport" driver has been installed from AMD: **www1.amd.com/athlon/config**.

SYMPTOM 37-10   **Selecting a screen resolution over 640x480 causes an HP Pavilion system to reboot in the Safe Mode**   This is an HP BIOS problem. HP has a main board BIOS upgrade for the Pavilion that should fix this issue. The release notes for this new BIOS indicate that it fixes a problem allocating IRQs to add-in AGP adapters (such as NVIDIA-based display adapters). Check out the HP site at **www.hp.com**.

SYMPTOM 37-11   **When booting to Windows, you find a black screen, or Windows indicates that the display adapter is not configured properly**   You may also find a yellow exclamation mark on the video card in your Device Manager. In virtually all cases, this occurs because the video card does not have an adequate IRQ assigned to it. Boot into your system to the CMOS Setup and look for an option such as "Assign IRQ for PCI VGA"—see that it's set to "enabled" or "auto." If the video card is not assigned to a suitable IRQ and the system BIOS does not have an option to assign an IRQ, you'll need to contact your motherboard manufacturer and check for a BIOS update.

SYMPTOM 37-12   **After installing 3D accelerator drivers, you find an error such as: "Invalid VxD dynamic link call from h3vddd(01)+0000 4974"**   In virtually every case, you're trying to use an AGP accelerator card under Windows 95 OSR2 *without* having proper USB support update installed. The file USBSUPP.EXE can be found on your Windows 95 CD (if the CD is labeled "With USB Support"). In addition to providing proper USB support, this file also installs a new Virtual Memory Manager (VMM) that may be required for the AGP version of your accelerator card (for instance, the Monster Fusion) in Windows 95. If you do not have that file on your CD, it can be downloaded at: **ftp://ftp.opti.com/pub/chipsets/system/861/usbsupp.exe**. Upgrading the OS to Windows 98/SE or Windows Me should also correct this issue.

SYMPTOM 37-13   **After upgrading from an older video card, you can access higher colors but cannot use resolutions over 640×480**   This type of issue is seen frequently when upgrading an older Stealth 64 card—true color modes are accessible, but resolutions above 640×480 are not. This problem is almost always due to residual entries left in the Registry. Start your Registry editor and check the following key:

```
HKEY_LOCAL_MACHINE/Config/0001/Display/Settings
```

Right next to the setting "Resolution" is an entry called **ScreenArea**. This entry was left over from a former "Virtual Desktop" and was probably set to 640x480. Remove this key, save your changes, and reboot the system.

SYMPTOM 37-14   **Windows 95 reports a memory conflict with a PCI-to-PCI bridge and the AGP graphics adapter**   This PCI-to-PCI bridge is sometimes called the Intel 82443LX or 82443BX bridge. This is not a "real" error. The memory conflict that appears between the PCI bridge and the AGP graphics adapter is a known conflict. This error is caused by the way Windows 95 reports memory usage and is not known to cause problems. Windows 98 and later will not report this problem, so you may ignore the issue or upgrade if you wish.

SYMPTOM 37-15   **There are problems with IE 5 after installing 3D accelerator drivers**
For example, you may experience problems if you install Diamond Multimedia Monster Fusion video drivers on a computer running Internet Explorer 5. In one case, you may receive the following error after installing the Monster Fusion drivers on a system with IE 5 and restarting the PC:

```
EXPLORER caused an Invalid page fault in module EXPLORER.EXE at
015f:00401f31
```

In another case, Windows may not start if you download and install Diamond video drivers from the Diamond Web site and then restart your computer. This trouble can occur because some Diamond video drivers replace the COMCTL32.DLL file with a version that is *not* totally compatible with IE 5. Update the drivers to the latest versions. For example, Diamond Multimedia now has updated drivers that address this issue at **www.diamondmm.com**. As an alternative, you may extract a new copy of the COMCTL32.DLL file:

1. Start Windows in the native DOS mode (the Safe Mode Command Prompt).
2. Rename the COMCTL32.DLL file in the \Windows\System folder to COMCTL32.OLD by typing

    ```
    ren c:\windows\system\comctl32.dll comctl32.old
    ```

    at the command prompt, and then press ENTER. Now type

    ```
    extract c:\window~1\setupw95.cab comctl32.dll /l c:\windows\system
    ```

    and then press ENTER.
3. Restart the computer normally.

SYMPTOM 37-16   **You notice a horizontal line scrolling down one side of the screen with multiple monitors under Windows 98/SE**   This problem is almost always caused when your monitors are too close to a fluorescent light source (or you're using an unshielded monitor and you place it too close to another monitor). Most early monitors are *unshielded*, so they do *not* confine the magnetic field they emit. Later monitors are *shielded* so that most of the magnetic fields they emit are confined within the monitor. If you place an unshielded monitor too close to another monitor, the magnetic field emitted by the unshielded monitor may interfere with the other monitor. Move the unshielded monitor away from any monitors or fluorescent light sources it interferes with, or place a shield (an ordinary "cookie sheet," for example) between the unshielded monitor and any monitors it interferes with. You may also choose to replace the unshielded monitor with a shielded model.

SYMPTOM 37-17   **You cannot drag a window from one monitor to another under Windows 98/SE**   This problem can occur if the window you're trying to drag is maximized or your monitors are not positioned correctly. To work around this issue, restore the window to its previous size before you drag it to a different monitor. To do this, simply click the Restore button (the middle button in the upper-right corner of a window). You should also verify your monitor's position:

1. Click Start, click Help, then click the Index tab.
2. Type **multiple display support**.
3. Double-click the "arranging monitors" topic for detailed information.

 A basic Permedia video adapter cannot currently be used as your primary video adapter (this excludes the Permedia NT and Permedia-2).

SYMPTOM 37-18   **You notice a black screen when you run a program requiring DirectX under Windows 95/98**   When you run a DirectX-based program, your monitor may display a black screen (or may display only wavy lines on a black background). This fault can occur if the DirectX-based program changes the default refresh rate that your display adapter uses with the monitor. Change the refresh rate to an acceptable level for your monitor and selected resolution (such as 60Hz or 72Hz):

1. Click Start, highlight Settings, then click Control Panel.
2. Double-click the Display icon, click the Settings tab, then click Advanced.
3. Click the Adapter tab, then click Adapter Default in the Refresh Rate box.
4. Click OK when you're prompted to test the setting.
5. If the setting is displayed correctly, click Yes to keep the setting.

   If this doesn't work, try reducing the hardware acceleration for the video adapter:

1. Click Start, highlight Settings, then click Control Panel.
2. Double-click the System icon, click the Performance tab, then click Graphics.
3. Move the Hardware Acceleration slider to one notch from the left (the Basic setting), click OK, click Close, then click Yes when you're prompted to restart your computer.

SYMPTOM 37-19   **You encounter a blank screen after installing a secondary video adapter for Windows 98**   This trouble can occur if your computer has a built-in video adapter and either your computer's BIOS does not provide support for multiple video adapters or the secondary video adapter is not supported for "multiple display" use. To resolve this behavior, update your computer's BIOS and/or obtain a different video adapter that's properly supported for Windows 98 multi-monitor service.

SYMPTOM 37-20   **You find that Riva 128 video adapters do not support multi-monitor operation**   When you add a secondary video adapter to a system that uses a Riva 128 video adapter as the *primary* video adapter, the computer may hang up. This problem is almost always caused by an incompatible driver used by the Riva 128 video adapter. Consequently, Riva 128 video adapters are *not* supported for use with the multiple display feature. If you want to use multiple monitors, you should use only video adapters that are known to work in a multiple-monitor environment (see Table 37-6). Replace the incompatible video adapter with a model that *is* compatible with multi-monitor operation.

SYMPTOM 37-21   **You have trouble using the ATI Rage II PCI video card as a second video adapter**   When you try the ATI Rage II PCI video adapter as a secondary display adapter under Windows 98, the secondary display adapter may not work properly (if at all). When you view the ATI Rage II PCI Properties dialog box in Device Manager, you may see an error message such as:

```
Multiple Display Support cannot start this device. The area of memory
normally used by video is in use by another program or device. To enable
Multiple Display Support, remove EMM386 or other memory managers from
CONFIG.SYS and restart your computer.
```

Try adding an EMMExclude entry to the SYSTEM.INI file:

1.   Open the SYSTEM.INI file using any text editor (such as Notepad).

2.   Add the following line to the [386enh] section of the SYSTEM.INI file:

```
emmexclude=c000-cfff
```

3.   Save and then close the SYSTEM.INI file.

4.   Restart your computer.

As an alternative, try adding the exclusion to the EMM386 command line of your CONFIG.SYS file:

1.   Open the CONFIG.SYS file using any text editor (such as Notepad).

2.   Add the following lines:

```
device=<windows>\himem.sys
device=<windows>\emm386.exe x=c000-cfff
```

where <windows> is the path to the folder in which Windows is installed.

3.   Save and then close the CONFIG.SYS file.

4.   Restart your computer.

SYMPTOM 37-22   **The screen image becomes distorted when changing resolutions** This is known to occur with certain monitors under Windows 98 (such as the NEC 4FG). Some video adapters (such as the Diamond Stealth 64, Video 2001, and S3 Trio 64V+) default to a refresh rate of 60Hz. NEC 4FG monitors can support only refresh rates of less than 60Hz at a resolution of 1280x1024 or higher. For example, if you're using an NEC 4FG monitor and you change the display resolution to 1280x1024 or higher, your screen may become distorted. This trouble can occur if you're using a video adapter that defaults to a refresh rate of 60Hz at such high resolutions. To correct this fault, optimize the refresh rate of your video adapter *before* you attempt change the display resolution:

1.   Click Start, highlight Settings, then click Control Panel.

2.   Double-click the Display icon.

3.   Select the Settings tab, then click Advanced.

4.   Click the Adapter tab, then click Optimal in the Refresh Rate box.

5.   Click OK and then click OK again when you receive the following message:

> Windows will now adjust the refresh rate of your display. The screen
> may flicker for a few moments while the settings are being changed. If
> the display becomes garbled or unusable, simply wait and Windows will
> restore your original settings.

6. Click Yes when you're prompted to keep this setting, then click OK.

SYMPTOM 37-23   **You see wavy lines in the monitor's display**   This is known to occur under Windows 98 with monitors such as the MAG DX-1795. This problem can occur if your video adapter is configured for 1600x1200 screen resolution *and* the "Automatically detect Plug & Play monitors" check box is selected on the Monitor tab in Display Properties. To correct this problem, manually install your monitor in Display Properties:

1. Click Start, highlight Settings, then click Control Panel.

2. Double-click the Display icon.

3. Click the Settings tab, then click Advanced.

4. On the Monitor tab, click the "Automatically detect Plug & Play monitors" check box to clear it, then click Change.

5. Click Next, click "Display a list of all the drivers in a specific location, so you can select the driver you want," then click Next.

6. Click Show All Hardware.

7. In the Manufacturers box, click "MAG Technology Co., Ltd." and then click "MAG DX-1795" in the Models box.

8. Click Next, then follow the instructions on your screen to finish installing the monitor.

SYMPTOM 37-24   **When returning to Windows from a DOS application, the Windows screen "splits" from top-to-bottom**   This is a DOS problem that is seen under Windows and indicates an obsolete or corrupted video driver (for example, using a Windows 3.0 video driver under Windows 3.1)—chances are that the video adapter is running just fine. Make sure that the proper DOS "grabber" file is installed and specified in the SYSTEM.INI file. Check with the video board manufacturer to obtain the latest assortment of drivers and grabber files. Try reinstalling the drivers from their master disk. If you do not have current drivers available, try switching to the generic VGA driver.

SYMPTOM 37-25   **The system hangs up during initialization, some characters may be missing from the display, or the screen colors may be incorrect**   These are classic symptoms of a hardware conflict between the video adapter and one or more cards in the system or area of memory. Some video boards use an area of upper memory that is larger than the "classical" video area. For example, the Impact SVGA board imposes itself on the entire address range between A0000h and DFFFFh. In this kind of situation, any other device using an address in this range will conflict with the video board. A conflict may occur when the video board is first installed, or the board may work fine until another device is added or modified.

Resolving a hardware conflict basically means that *something* has to give—one of the conflicting elements (the IRQ lines, DMA channels, or I/O addresses) must be adjusted to use unique system resources. To you as a technician, it rarely matters which of the conflicting devices you change, but remember that system startup files, device drivers, and application settings may also have to change to reflect newly selected resources. You may also be able to resolve some memory conflicts by adding the *EXCLUDE* switch to EMM386.EXE. The video adapter manual will indicate when an *EXCLUDE* switch is necessary.

SYMPTOM 37-26   Your system is generating DMA errors with a VGA board in the system and video BIOS shadowing disabled   This is a fairly rare symptom that develops only on some older i486 systems and is usually due to an 8-bit VGA board in a system equipped with a slower version of the i486 CPU (in the 25MHz range). Because 8-bit access takes so long, some DMA requests are ignored—thus an error is generated. If you find such a problem, try enabling *video ROM shadowing* through the CMOS setup to allow faster access to video instructions. Also, you may try a newer revision of the i486 CPU.

SYMPTOM 37-27   The system hangs up using a 16-bit VGA board, and one or more 8-bit controllers   This is typically a problem that arises when 8-bit and 16-bit ISA boards are used in the same system. Due to the way that an ISA bus separates the 8-bit and 16-bit segments, accessing an 8-bit board when there are 16-bit boards in the system may cause the CPU to (falsely) determine that it is accessing a 16-bit board. When this occurs, the system will almost invariably crash. Try removing any 8-bit boards from the system. If the crashes cease, you have probably nailed down the error. Unfortunately, the only real correction is to either remove the 8-bit board(s) or reconfigure the board(s) to use a higher area of memory.

SYMPTOM 37-28   You have trouble sizing or positioning the display, or you see error messages such as "Mode Not Supported" or "Insufficient Memory"   These kinds of errors may occur in newer or high-end video boards if the board is not set up properly for the monitor it is being used with. Most new video boards include an installation routine that records the monitor's maximum specifications, such as resolution (and refresh frequencies), horizontal scanning frequencies, and vertical scanning frequencies. If such data is entered incorrectly (or the monitor is changed) certain screen modes may no longer work properly. Check the video adapter's installation parameters and correct its setup if necessary.

SYMPTOM 37-29   You frequently encounter GPFs when using QuickTime for Windows 1.1   This is a notable problem with ATI Mach64 cards, but has been known to occur with other advanced video boards. Often, the problem can be corrected by making a change in the Windows SYSTEM.INI file. For the ATI Mach64, you must turn **DeviceBitmaps=off** under the [macx] section. As an alternative, start the ATI FlexDesk, type **OPT** (this starts a "hidden" window), then uncheck the DeviceBitmap entry.

SYMPTOM 37-30   The video board will not boot up when used in a particular motherboard   There are noted cases of hardware incompatibility between certain video boards and motherboards. This incompatibility usually causes a great deal of confusion because the video board may work just fine when tested in a different motherboard, and other video boards may work well in the original motherboard—the technician simply winds up chasing ghosts. A noted example of this problem is the Boca Research VGAXL1/2 refusing to work in a Micronics 486DX2/66 motherboard. The solution to this problem demands that U13 on the video board be a Texas Instruments TI-74F04. If U13 is a Motorola chip, you'll need to send the board back for rework—strange but true. For general troubleshooting purposes, if a certain video board and motherboard refuse to work together, don't waste your time chasing ghosts—contact *both* the video board maker and PC (or motherboard) maker and see if there are any reports of incompatibilities.

SYMPTOM 37-31   Diagnostics refuse to show all of the available video modes for a particular board even though all video RAM was properly detected, or the board refuses to operate in some video modes   When a video board does not respond to certain video modes (usually the higher video modes), it is usually because there is a conflict in the upper memory area, and a memory range needs to be excluded. If there is a memory manager at work (for instance, QEMM, 386MAX, or EMM386), try disabling the memory manager in CONFIG.SYS or boot the system from a clean floppy. Try your diagnostic(s) again—chances are that the problem has disappeared. To fix this problem on a more permanent basis, reenable the memory manager using an exclude command. Try **x=B100h-B1FFh** as the first parameter on the memory manager's command line. If that does not work, try **x=A000h-BFFFh**. Finally, try **x=A000h-C7FF**.

SYMPTOM 37-32   Pixels appear "dropped" behind the mouse cursor, and graphic images appear to break up under Windows   There are two major causes for this older type of problem: bad video RAM or the system ISA bus speed is too fast. Check the CMOS Setup for an entry in Advanced Setup such as "AT Bus Clock," "ISA Bus Speed," or "AT Bus Speed." The corresponding entry should be set to 8.33MHz. Otherwise, excessive speed may be resulting in "lost" video data. If the bus speed is set properly, run a diagnostic to check the integrity of video RAM (you may have to replace the video RAM, or replace the video board entirely).

SYMPTOM 37-33   You encounter video-related conflicts in Packard Bell systems   The system refuses to boot or starts with "garbage" and erratic screen displays. This symptom is encountered most frequently with Boca video boards on Packard Bell systems with video circuits already on the motherboard. Even when the onboard video has been disabled, reports indicate that the video circuitry remains active and then conflicts with the add-on video board. Packard Bell indicates that their Vxxx.16 BIOS will correct this problem, so contact Packard Bell for an appropriate BIOS upgrade.

SYMPTOM 37-34   Text appears in an odd color   For example, text that should be green appears black. This is almost always the result of a problem with the palette decoding registers on the particular video board and will typically appear when using higher color modes (for instance, 64k or 16M colors). Make sure that the video drivers are correct, complete, and up-to-date. If the problem persists, you may need to replace the video board.

Remember that you can select myriad color and text schemes under Windows 95/98. Before you conclude that color problems are caused by a faulty video card, be sure to try the "Windows Default" desktop scheme.

SYMPTOM 37-35   When an application is started (under Windows), the opening display appears "scrambled"   While this might appear to be a video memory problem at first glance, it is actually more likely to be related to a buggy video driver. Upgrade the video driver to the latest version or try a generic video driver (a "reference driver") that is compatible with your video chipset.

SYMPTOM 37-36   The display colors change when exiting from a DOS shell under Windows   This problem has been noted with older video boards such as the Diamond SpeedStar Pro and is almost always the result of a video board defect (usually a palette problem). For the Diamond board, the product must be replaced with revision A2. For other video boards, such problems can usually be corrected by replacing the video board.

SYMPTOM 37-37   **The computer locks up or crashes when starting an .AVI file**
This problem is encountered frequently as computer users first begin to try multimedia applications. Rather than being a problem with the video board specifically, the trouble is often due to using an outdated version of Video for Windows. Make sure to use Video for Windows 1.1E or later. Video for Windows can be downloaded from the Diamond Multimedia FTP site at **ftp://ftp.diamondmm.com/pub/misc/vfw11e.exe**. You may also need to edit the [DrawDib] section of the WIN.INI file and add an entry that says **DVA=0**. If no [DrawDib] section is present, you can add it. Remember to restart Windows after making any changes. You may also be able to correct this type of problem by upgrading to Windows 98/SE, which should contain many of the very latest drivers and support components.

SYMPTOM 37-38   **The computer is running very slowly (poor performance), and the hard drive light is continuously lit**   This problem is particularly apparent with Diamond Edge 3D video boards on systems with more than 16MB of RAM. The Diamond Edge 3D board comes with both 1MB and 6MB MIDI bank files. Diamond recommends that you use only the 6MB bank file on systems with over 16MB of RAM. To change the size of the MIDI bank file being used:

1.   Right-click on My Computer and choose Properties.

2.   Open the System Control Panel and click on the Device Manager tab.

3.   Click on the (+) symbol beside the Sound, Video, and Game Controller line.

4.   Highlight the Diamond EDGE 3D PCI Multimedia Device and click on Properties.

5.   Click on Settings. You will then see the 1MB and 6MB MIDI bank selection.

6.   Select the 6MB option and choose OK.

7.   Restart your computer when prompted.

SYMPTOM 37-39   **You notice that .AVI files have distorted colors or "grainy" playback**
This usually occurs when playing 8-bit .AVI files that are not supported by DCI, and it can usually be corrected by disabling the accelerated video playback features of the video board. For example, the older Diamond ViperPro Video board is noted for this problem, and you would need to edit the COPRO.INI file located in the \Windows directory. In the [VCP] area, change the **VCPEnable=** line to **off**. Save the .INI file and restart Windows.

SYMPTOM 37-40   **The PCI video board will not work under Windows unless the system's PCI SCSI devices are disconnected**   This type of problem occurs only on certain combinations of PCI system hardware. For example, this type of symptom has been documented using Phoenix BIOS 4.04 and a UMC8810P-AIO motherboard on systems with an NCR SCSI controller and SCSI devices. You can often correct such problems by correcting the Advanced System Setup in CMOS. Start the CMOS Setup, go to the Advanced System Setup, and select PCI Devices. Set up the PCI slot for the SCSI controller as IRQ9 and **LEVEL** edge select. The slot for the video board should have the IRQ set to **NONE**, and **LEVEL** edge select. Change the Base Memory Address from 0080000000 to 0081000000.

SYMPTOM 37-41   **There are boot problems when a new video board is installed**
Typical problems include no video or eight beeps when the system is turned on. This is usually the result of an outdated system BIOS, which is not capable of detecting the particular video chipset in use—the BIOS interprets this as meaning that there is no video board in the system, and an error is generated

accordingly. Contact the motherboard manufacturer (or PC maker) for an updated system BIOS. Most BIOS versions dated after the fall of 1994 should be able to detect most modern video chipsets.

SYMPTOM 37-42   There are boot problems when a PCI video board is installed
There are two common problems that account for this. First, the system BIOS did not complete the config-uration of the video board correctly, and the board has not been enabled onto the PCI bus. The video board manufacturer may have a utility available that can "remap" the video card to a new address outside of physical memory. For the Matrox Millennium, use the PCIMAP.EXE utility. Other Matrox boards use the MGABASE.EXE utility. Other PCI video board manufacturers probably offer their own utilities. The second problem is that the system BIOS has assigned a base memory address to the video board that is used by another device or that is reserved for use by the motherboard chipset. While the utilities men-tioned may often help to correct this problem, a more permanent fix is usually to update the system BIOS. Investigate a BIOS upgrade from the motherboard (or PC) manufacturer.

SYMPTOM 37-43   The monitor overscans when entering a DOS shell from Windows
This creates a highly distorted image and can (if left for prolonged periods) damage the monitor cir-cuitry. The cause of this problem is usually a bug in the video driver. For example, this type of problem is known to happen when using the older Diamond SpeedStar Pro with drivers prior to version 1.06. Obtain the latest video driver from the video board maker or try a generic video driver written by the video chipset maker.

SYMPTOM 37-44   You encounter an intermittent "Divide by Zero" error   Although there are several possible causes for this type of error, they are *all* related to flaws in software—specifi-cally, problems with the video driver or video "toolkit" that is installed with the particular video board. For example, "Divide by Zero" errors can be corrected in the Diamond Stealth 64 Video 2001 series by opening the InControl Tools package and changing a "Center to Viewport" selection to "Center to Desk-top." Similarly, the "Maximize to Viewport" selection should be changed to "Maximize to Desktop." Often, upgrading the video driver or video support tools will eliminate this problem.

SYMPTOM 37-45   During MPEG playback, the display flickers, shows low refresh rates, or appears to be in an interlaced mode   This is not necessarily an error. With some video boards (such as the Diamond MVP1100), MPEG files cannot play correctly at high refresh rates—typically over 72Hz. When an MPEG file is played, the driver will automatically switch to a 72Hz vertical refresh rate. This may result in an unexpected change in display quality during playback. After exiting from the MPEG player, the original (higher) refresh rate will be restored. If a vertical refresh rate *lower* than 72Hz was originally selected, then the vertical refresh rate will not change during MPEG play-back, so you should see no difference in the display.

SYMPTOM 37-46   You receive an error such as "There is an undetectable problem in loading the specified device driver" when starting an MPEG player or other video tool
In almost all cases, the related driver is missing, installed improperly, or corrupt. Reinstall the MPEG playback driver(s) for your particular video board and make sure to use the latest version. If problems per-sist, check for the driver under the WIN.INI or SYSTEM.INI file and see that there is only one **load=** ref-erence to the particular driver(s)—repeated references can cause conflicts or other loading problems. Similar drivers (other MPEG drivers) can also cause conflicts, so verify that the only drivers being loaded are the ones used by your current video adapter and/or playback software.

SYMPTOM 37-47   **On video boards with TV tuners, the TV window is blurry or fuzzy at 1024×768 or higher resolutions**   This symptom is particularly noted with the Diamond DVV1100. Unfortunately, this type of symptom is usually the result of limited bandwidth of the particular video board—specifically of the video chipset. The only real option is to reduce the resolution to 800x600 or 640×480 when running the TV and to lower the refresh rate to 60Hz. Contact your video board's manufacturer—there may be an RMA or other replacement/upgrade program available to correct the issue.

SYMPTOM 37-48   **On video boards with TV tuners, the reception does not appear as good as that of an ordinary TV**   This problem has been noted in conjunction with Matrox Media-TV boards, and it is usually due to the local cable company using the HRC carrier frequency instead of the standard carrier frequency. For Matrox boards, you can correct the problem by modifying the DVMCIMIL.INI file found in the \Windows directory. Under the [Carrier] section, change the **CarrierType=0** entry to **CarrierType=1**. Other video/TV boards may utilize different .INI entries or allow carrier selection through the use of an onboard jumper, but poor reception is almost always the result of an unusual cable carrier.

SYMPTOM 37-49   **You encounter errors such as "Insufficient video memory"**
There is not enough video memory on the board to handle screen images at the resolution and color depth you have selected. In most cases, the system may crash. Your immediate solution should be to select a lower resolution or smaller color palette. If you are encountering such problems when attempting to play .AVI or MPEG files, you should be able to select smaller video windows and lower color depth without altering your Windows setup. As a more long-term solution, you should consider adding more video memory or replacing the video board with one that contains more video memory.

SYMPTOM 37-50   **The PCI video board is not working properly—there is a BIOS conflict with PCI interrupt 1Ah**   The lower 32KB of the ROM BIOS has been redirected for high memory use. Disable this memory with your memory manager by adding an *EXCLUDE* command such as: **x=f000-f7ff**.

SYMPTOM 37-51   **You encounter video corruption or sporadic system rebooting when using an SLC-type motherboard**   This particular symptom has been most noted when using Number Nine video boards with Alaris SLC2 motherboards. The SLC2 microprocessor uses a 32-bit internal data bus, but the external data bus (seen by the motherboard) is 16-bit. Most of the registers on contemporary PCI video boards are mapped as 32 bits and cannot be accessed as two 16-bit registers. As a result, the video board simply cannot be used together with the particular motherboard. You will have to upgrade the motherboard or use a different video board.

SYMPTOM 37-52   **Video playback experiences long pauses while the hard drive thrashes excessively**   This is a problem that appears under Windows 95/98 and is almost always the result of disk-caching problems. Start Windows Explorer and highlight the drivers responsible for video playback (for a Motion Pixels video board, highlight MPXPLAY.EXE and MPXPLAY.PIF). Click the right mouse button and select Properties. In the Memory page, make sure that the "Protected" option has been set. Restart the video clip, or restart Windows 95/98 if necessary. Also check your CONFIG.SYS and AUTOEXEC.BAT files and verify that there are no caching utilities being loaded.

SYMPTOM 37-53   You cannot use the loop-through feature of your video board
Typical examples include the Number Nine 9FX Motion 771 VGA loop through connector with a Reel Magic board and a Number Nine driver. Unfortunately, this is often the result of a limitation with the video board's graphics processor IC (refusing to support loop-through functionality). To use loop-through, try the standard VGA driver.

SYMPTOM 37-54   Windows appears with a "black box" cursor and/or icons that fail to appear on the screen   In most cases, the problem is caused by an incompatibility with the motherboard's noncompliant PCI BIOS (the motherboard's BIOS does not comply with the PCI backward-compatibility requirement). To overcome this problem, set the video board's memory aperture manually by editing the SYSTEM.INI file located in the \Windows directory. For example, when working with a Number Nine 9GXE, find the [#9GXE] section of SYSTEM.INI, then add a command line such as: **APERTURE-BASE=0x8800** or **APERTURE-BASE=31**. Save the file and restart Windows. The actual section for your particular video board may be different.

SYMPTOM 37-55   There are video problems or the system locks up while using an antivirus program   This error occurs frequently when using memory-resident virus checking. Some video boards allow you to compensate for this by editing the SYSTEM.INI file. For the Number Nine 9GXE board, find the [#9GXE] area in SYSTEM.INI, then set the **FastMMIO=** entry to **off**. Remember to save the .INI file and restart Windows. The actual section for your particular video board may be different. As an alternative, you could also disable or remove the antivirus program or check with the antivirus maker to see if there's a patch or update that might improve the program's compatibility.

SYMPTOM 37-56   An error indicates that there is not enough memory for playback or re-sizing of the playback window   This type of problem is directly caused by a lack of system (not video) memory in the PC. If your system uses SMARTDRV (Windows 3.1x), try reducing the memory used for caching. Try unloading various unneeded programs from memory and consider disabling any RAM drives that may be active. Finally, consider adding more system RAM to the PC.

SYMPTOM 37-57   The video board refuses to accept a particular video mode
Mode problems are most frequent when attempting to use unusual palette sizes, such as 32K or 64K colors. Try setting the video board to 256 colors. If a higher color depth is needed, it may be possible to run the video board in a palletized mode or grayscale mode by adding command line switches to the video driver. Refer to the instructions that accompany the particular video board for detailed information. You may also consider a video BIOS upgrade, or an upgraded VESA driver (such as UNIVBE 5.3 from SciTech Software). Updated video drivers and/or firmware may also be available to correct the problem.

SYMPTOM 37-58   The video system cannot lock memory using QEMM and linear video memory   This is often a DOS problem with Motion Pixels video boards when using QEMM 7.04 and earlier versions. The DPMI has a bug when accessing physical memory above the DPMI's host memory. Upgrade the version of QEMM to 7.5 (or later) or play video under Windows instead.

SYMPTOM 37-59   The video system cannot lock memory under Windows, or the system hangs   This is also a problem noted most often with Motion Pixels video boards and is almost always related to the use of a WINDPMI.386 DPMI driver loaded through SYSTEM.INI. WINDPMI.386 reports the wrong amount of free lockable DPMI memory. If your Windows platform is using Borland's

WINDPMI.386, manually reduce the cache size with the **/c** option, or remove (or disable) the driver from SYSTEM.INI entirely. You might also consider upgrading WINDPMI.386 to a later version. Contact Borland technical support or the technical support department of the video board maker.

SYMPTOM 37-60   Other devices don't work properly after the PCI video card is installed   For example, the sound card output is distorted or a fast modem loses data. This can happen often with newer video adapters. Some computers require that software wait for the hardware to be ready to receive new data. Newer video board drivers are not normally set to do this because it slows them down slightly (and it's not necessary for most current computers). Under Windows 9x:

1. Right-click on the Windows desktop background.
2. Click the Properties menu item and select the video board's Settings tab.
3. Select the Advanced button, then click the Performance tab.
4. Clear the "Use automatic PCI bus retry" check box.
5. Accept your changes and reboot the computer when instructed to do so.

Under Windows 3.1x, edit the SYSTEM.INI file in your \Windows directory to add the line **PCIChipSet=1** to the particular video board's section (for instance, [mga.drv]).

SYMPTOM 37-61   A Windows 9x game doesn't start or runs slower than normal The program uses the Microsoft DirectX interface. DirectX may not be installed, or an older version of DirectX is installed. Most programs that use DirectX install it as part of their installation, but some do not. Also, some older programs may install an earlier version of DirectX (overwriting a later version). To see if DirectX is installed:

1. Right-click on the Windows 95/98 desktop.
2. Click the Properties menu item and select the video adapter's Settings tab.
3. Click the Advanced button and click the Information tab.
4. Look at the Microsoft DirectX Version label. DirectX 5.x (or later) should be the current version.

If the current version of DirectX is installed, you're finished. Otherwise, you'll need to install DirectX.

If the DirectX setup program asks if you want to replace the existing display drivers, click *No*.

SYMPTOM 37-62   You replace an older 3D accelerator with a newer one, but the new accelerator is not working properly   You often see this kind of trouble when replacing a 3Dfx Voodoo card or Monster I card with a newer card such as a Monster Fusion. You'll need to remove the original Voodoo graphics card and clean out all of the old references to the card:

3Dfx provides an .INF file to remove these references. You can download it from: **www.3dfx.com/view_io.asp?ID=96**.

1. Click Start and select Run, then type **regedit**.
2. Locate the **HKEY_LOCAL_MACHINE/Enum/PCI** key and delete the **VEN_121A&DEV** folder.

3. Locate the **HKEY_LOCAL_MACHINE/Software** key and delete the **3Dfx Interactive** folder.

4. Locate the **HKEY_LOCAL_MACHINE/Software/Diamond** key and delete the **Monster3D** folder.

5. Locate the **HKEY_LOCAL_MACHINE/Software/Microsoft/Windows/Current Version/ ControlsFolder/Display/shellex/Property Sheet Handlers** key and delete any folders pertaining to the original **Voodoo** card.

6. Save your changes to the Registry, then use Windows Explorer to open the c:\Windows\Inf\Other folder.

7. Delete any *.INF file pertaining to the **Monster3D**, **3Dfx Interactive**, the **Monster Fusion**, and so on.

8. Click Start, select Find, then choose Files and Folders. Search for any references to "glide" and delete any file references that you find.

9. Search for files such as DD3DFX.DRV, DD3DFX16.DLL, DD3DFX32.DLL, and MM3DFX*.* and delete those files that you find.

10. Search for the FXMEMMAP.VXD file and delete it as well.

11. Finally, search for SST1INIT*.* and delete it.

12. Restart the computer and reinstall the drivers for the new Monster Fusion device.

SYMPTOM 37-63   **You encounter a "Fatal Exception 0D" error when using an ATI All-in-Wonder Pro video adapter**   This problem can occur under Windows 98/Me after you install the ATI All-In-Wonder Pro video adapter drivers version 5.0 or later. Chances are that you are using a program written to use features of the Windows 3.x 16-bit video device drivers that are no longer available in the 32-bit video device drivers used in Windows 98/Me. It is also possible that you are using a program that installs an older version of a multimedia program. The best way to correct this problem is to reinstall the latest drivers and applets for the video card. You may be able to work around the trouble using the following procedure:

1. Restart your computer in the Safe Mode.

2. Click Start, click Run, type **msconfig**, and then click OK.

3. Click the SYSTEM.INI tab, double-click the [boot] branch to expand it, and then right-click **Display.drv=Pnpdrvr.drv**.

4. Click Clear, click OK, then click Yes to restart your computer.

5. Repeat steps 2 and 3.

6. Click Select, click OK, then click No when you're prompted to restart your computer.

7. Click Start, highlight Settings, then click Control Panel.

8. Double-click the Display icon, click the Settings tab, then click Advanced.

9. Click the Adapter tab, click Change, click Next, then click "Display a list of all the drivers in a specific location, so you can select the driver you want."

10. Click Next, then click the "ATI All-In-Wonder Pro dated 5/11/98."

11. Click Next, click Next again, then click Finish.

12. Click Apply, click Close, then restart your computer.

SYMPTOM 37-64   **You get a blank screen after installing a second video adapter**
This trouble can occur under Windows Me if your computer has a built-in video adapter and either your computer's BIOS does not provide support for multiple video adapters or the secondary video adapter is not supported for multiple display use. To correct this problem, update your computer's BIOS or obtain a properly supported video adapter.

SYMPTOM 37-65   **The NVIDIA TNT2 Ultra video adapter is improperly detected as an NVIDIA TNT2 video adapter**   This problem can occur under Windows Me due to an issue that is specific to the Diamond V770 Ultra (NVIDIA TNT2 Ultra) video adapter. The video BIOS for the NVIDIA TNT2 Ultra driver has the same subsystem ID as the Diamond V770 (NVIDIA TNT2) adapter. Consequently, Setup cannot determine which adapter is installed, so it installs the Nvidia TNT2 driver. You may need a firmware upgrade for the Ultra card. You can also manually reinstall the Windows Me NVIDIA TNT2 Ultra drivers or reinstall the Diamond V770 Ultra drivers.

SYMPTOM 37-66   **You encounter a "Fatal Exception 0E" error when disabling a Matrox video adapter**   When you shut down or restart your computer under Windows 98/Me, you may see an error message such as:

```
A Fatal Exception 0E has occurred at 0028:C00082CD in VxD VMM(01) +000072CD
```

This problem occurs if you have an incompatible (or early version) Matrox video driver installed on your computer. Download and install the latest Matrox video driver for your video adapter from the Matrox Web site (**www.matrox.com**).

SYMPTOM 37-67   **Your Diamond Viper V330 video adapter is identified as an NVIDIA Riva 128 card**   After installing Windows Me, you notice that your Diamond Viper V330 video adapter is detected as an NVIDIA Riva 128. The Diamond Viper V330 video adapter may not have a PnP ID that matches the PnP ID for the Windows Me driver. Since the NVIDIA Riva 128 driver is the same as the Diamond V330 driver under Windows Me, you may manually install the Windows Me Diamond V330 driver, or leave the current driver in place. If you wish to update the driver manually:

1.   Click Start, highlight Settings, click Control Panel, then double-click the System icon.

2.   Click the Device Manager tab.

3.   Click the plus sign (+) next to Display Adapters.

4.   Double-click the NVIDIA Riva 128 device.

5.   Click the Driver tab, then click Update Driver.

6.   Click "Specify the location of the driver (Advanced)," then click Next.

7.   Click "Display a list of all drivers in a specific location..." and then click Next.

8.   Click Show All Hardware.

9.   In the Manufacturers box, click Diamond.

10.   In the Models box, click Diamond Viper V330.

11.   Click Next, then finish the installation.

SYMPTOM 37-68   **You encounter a "General Protection Fault" in the SMDRV.DRV file**
This is a known issue when using a Silicon Motion EM video adapter under Windows Me. When you try to change the video resolution, you may receive an error message such as:

```
RUNDLL32 caused a GPF in SMDRV.DRV.
```

After this error message, your mouse may no longer work. This problem occurs because the Silicon Motion Lynx EM video adapter driver is not fully compatible with Windows Me. You may need to download and install an updated video driver that is optimized for Windows Me. To continue using the Lynx adapter, select the Standard Video Adapter (VGA) driver:

1. Click Start, highlight Settings, click Control Panel, then double-click the Display icon.
2. On the Settings tab, click Advanced.
3. On the Adapter tab, note the name of your current video driver and click Change.
4. Click Next, click "Display a list of all the drivers in a specific location, so you can select the driver you want," then click Next.
5. Click Show All Devices, then click (Standard Display Types) in the Manufacturers box.
6. In the Models box, click Standard Display Adapter (VGA), then click OK.
7. Click Next, click Next again, click Next again, then click Finish.
8. Click Close, then click Close again.
9. Click Yes when you're prompted to restart the computer.

SYMPTOM 37-69   **You can use only 640×480 resolution with a 3D Prophet card**
This is known to happen with the DDR version of the card (using Double Data Rate SDRAM) under Windows Me. This problem occurs because the Windows Me video card drivers are not fully compatible with the 3D Prophet DDR-DVI video card. To fix this problem, install 3D Prophet device drivers from the CD that came with the 3D Prophet DDR-DVI video card:

1. Click Start, highlight Settings, then click Control Panel.
2. Double-click the Display icon.
3. Click the Settings tab, then click Advanced.
4. Click the Adapter tab, then click Change.
5. Click the location of the driver.
6. Insert the manufacturer's CD, then click Next.
7. Follow the instructions on the computer screen to install the device driver for the video card.

SYMPTOM 37-70   **You notice poor DirectDraw operation when running in 24-bit color mode**   If you use the True Color (24-bit) mode in Windows Me, the number of frames per second (FPS) displayed on the screen may be reduced relative to other color modes. This issue occurs because most video adapter drivers do not support 24-bit DirectDraw operation. The 16-bit and 32-bit modes are faster and are typically recommended over 24-bit mode. Try changing the color mode in Windows:

1. Right-click a blank area on the desktop, then click Properties.
2. In the Display Properties dialog box, click the Settings tab.

3.   In the Colors box, click High Color (16-bit) or True Color (32-bit).

4.   Click OK.

If the High Color (16-bit) or True Color (32-bit) modes are not available in the Settings tab, your video adapter driver may be outdated. Download and install an updated video driver for Windows Me.

SYMPTOM 37-71   **You can't use Direct3D with NVIDIA GeForce drivers under Windows Me**   For example, when you run a game such as *Diablo II* on a computer with an NVIDIA GeForce video card (as well as TNT and TNT2 cards) using the Windows Me video driver, the video becomes corrupt (and the game is unplayable) when you use Direct3D mode. The video driver that ships with Windows Me causes this problem, but there is an updated video driver available from NVIDIA (**www.nvidia.com/Products/Drivers.nsf**). To work around the problem, you may also disable Direct3D acceleration:

1.   Click Start, click Run, type **dxdiag**, then click OK.

2.   Click the Display tab.

3.   Click Disable next to DirectDraw: Acceleration Enabled.

4.   Click Exit.

Disabling Direct3D acceleration slows the overall video system performance.

SYMPTOM 37-72   **Running Outlook Express causes the system to hang**   This is a known issue when using an S3 Diamond Viper V770 Ultra card under Windows Me. The trouble is related to issues with the V770 video driver, so download and install an updated video driver from S3 at **www.s3.com**.

SYMPTOM 37-73   **You don't see the VGA setting checked when using a standard VGA driver**   When you view your Windows Me display settings by clicking Advanced on the General tab of the MSCONFIG.EXE tool, the VGA 640 x 480 x 16 check box is not selected even though you're using this resolution. This is a problem with Windows Me. The MSCONFIG.EXE tool determines if the computer is in standard VGA mode by looking for the line **display.drv=vga.drv** in the [boot] section of the SYSTEM.INI file. However, the computer can also be in standard VGA mode if **display.drv=pnpdrvr.drv** is found. There is no immediate fix for this problem, but you can safely ignore this check box.

SYMPTOM 37-74   **An ArcadeFX TNT2 video accelerator causes the system to hang** This is a known issue frequently under Windows Me and is caused by a BIOS issue on the video card. To correct this problem, check for a BIOS update from Best Data at **www.bestdata.com**.

SYMPTOM 37-75   **You can't get multiple displays to work with a Matrox G400 DualHead video adapter**   When you are trying to set up multiple monitors with a Matrox DualHead video adapter under Windows 98/Me, only one monitor may work. Device Manager shows only one display adapter. Even if there is more than one monitor listed in Device Manager, the second monitor stays blank (no input signal) under Windows. In Control Panel, the Display Properties dialog box shows only the one monitor. When you click the Settings tab and then click Advanced, there is no DualHead Display tab. Both monitors are connected to the dual port Matrox display card and power is on for each monitor. In most cases, the trouble can be traced to a third-party peripheral incorrectly attached to the Matrox card—typical peripherals include non-Matrox DVD decoders, TV tuner cards, and non-Matrox video capture cards/devices. Use the following steps to resolve the problem:

1. Turn off your computer.
2. Remove the cover from the computer.
3. Remove the cable connected to the Matrox display card.
4. Restart your computer.
5. Click Start, highlight Settings, then click Control Panel.
6. Double-click the Display icon, click the Settings tab, then click Advanced.
7. Click the DualHead Display tab.
8. Select the option for multiple monitors.
9. Restart your computer.
10. In Control Panel, double-click the Display icon.
11. On the Settings tab, enable the second monitor.
12. Restart your computer.

Further Study

3Dfx   www.3dfx.com/ (Acquired by NVIDIA)
3DGPU   www.3dgpu.com/
3DLabs   www.3dlabs.com/
3DRage   www.3drage.com/
Anandtech   www.anandtech.com/index.html
ATI   www.ati.com/na/pages/na_index.html
Creative Labs   www.americas.creative.com/
Data Expert   www.dataexpert.com.tw
Diamond Multimedia   www.diamondmm.com (Purchased by S3)
DirectX Support   www.microsoft.com/directx/homeuser/support.asp
DirectX Troubleshooter   support.microsoft.com/support/DirectX/DirectX_7.0/TShooter/default.asp
DirectX   www.microsoft.com/directx/
Fast Graphics   www.fastgraphics.com/
GL Setup   www.glsetup.com/
Guillemot   www.guillemot.com/
Guru3D   www.guru3d.com/
Hercules   www.hercules.com (Division of Guillemot)
Install DirectX   support.microsoft.com/support/kb/articles/Q179/1/13.ASP
Intel AGP   developer.intel.com/technology/agp/tutorial/index.htm
Matrox   www.matrox.com
MatroxUsers   www.matroxusers.com/
Maximum3D   www.maximum3d.com/
Number Nine   www.nine.com (Ceased operation—support site only)

NVIDIA   www.nvidia.com/
Oak   www.oaktech.com (Video discontinued—legacy drivers available)
OpenGL Organization   www.opengl.org/
Trident   www.trid.com
Tweak 3D   www.tweak3d.net/
VESA Standards   www.vesa.org/
VIA Technologies   www.viatech.com/index.htm
Video Logic   www.videologic.com
Voodoo Extreme   www.voodooextreme.com/

38

VIDEO CAPTURE CARDS

Of all the expansion devices that have become available for PCs over the last decade, *video capture* boards (Figure 38-1) are certainly some of the most exciting. The ability to record sound and video on a PC has been an important element in the push toward desktop multimedia PCs. The captured data can then be edited, enhanced, and incorporated into any manner of computerized presentation. Such potential makes the video capture board ideal for applications in areas ranging from real estate to business to medicine—even Internet-based video conferencing. This chapter introduces you to basic video recorder concepts, outlines a typical installation process, and shows you how to deal with a wide range of problems that can accompany the hardware.

FIGURE 38-1   Playing a captured video file in Windows Media Player

Understanding Video Capture Boards

The first step in dealing with video capture problems is to understand the overall processes that make the board work in the first place. Figure 38-2 illustrates a multifunction video board that doubles as a capture board, a VGA video adapter, and a "video output" system (to drive things such as a TV monitor or VCR). The capture board plugs right into any available PCI slot (though many older video capture–type products used the ISA bus for basic compatibility). A few multifunction cards (that is, cards that integrate the video adapter, graphics accelerator, PC-TV, MPEG decoder, and so on) use the AGP slot rather than the PCI slot.

HOW A CAPTURE BOARD WORKS

The heart of the capture board is a *microcontroller* that directly operates the *video decoder* and *image controller* chip(s). Video signals entering the decoder are converted to analog RGB (red, green, and blue) data. The *genlock* circuit is a high-frequency clock source that is phase-locked to the horizontal sync signal of the video source. The ADC (analog-to-digital converter) circuits use the genlock signal as a basis for digitizing the video (not all video capture products offer a genlock feature). The image controller (which can be set to operate in several different color modes, such as 16-bit and 24-bit modes) directs the transfer of digitized image data into *image memory*. Image memory can then be read from a second data bus directly to a *digital multiplexer*. The multiplexer selects data from either the image memory or the

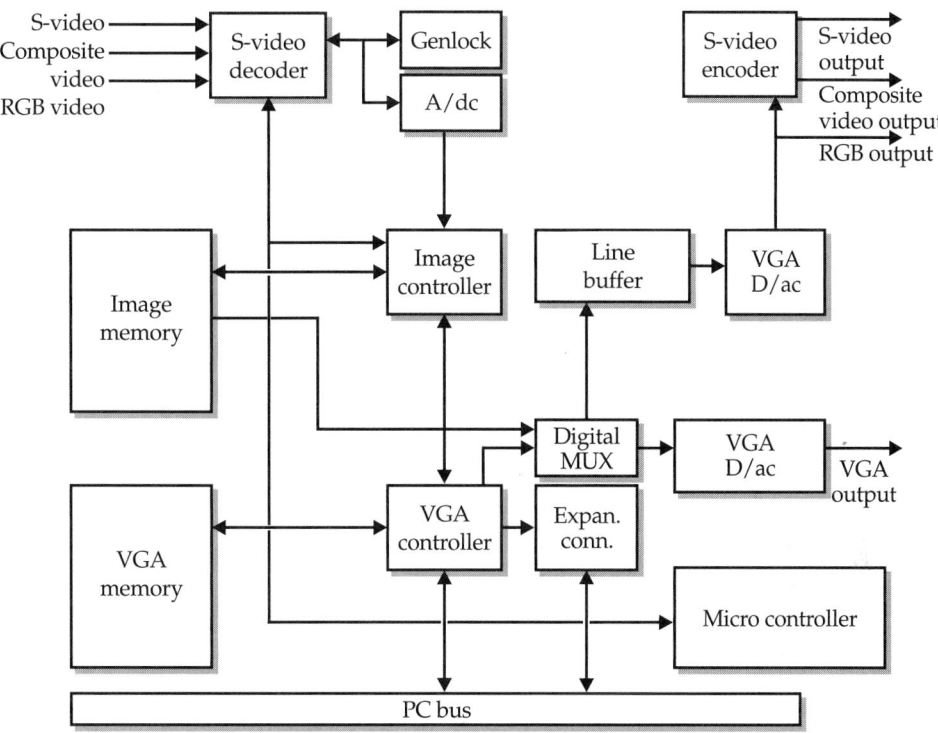

FIGURE 38-2   Block diagram of an integrated video capture/VGA board

VGA controller to be passed on to the *VGA DAC* (digital-to-analog converter), where data is converted into analog form to drive the monitor. Thus, you can see the digitized video image on the monitor while it is being recorded.

The capture board also contains a standard VGA sub-system that provides a VGA video adapter for the PC on the same board. The VGA controller chip manages the video adapter operations and stores graphics information in the *VGA memory*. The VGA controller can be addressed directly from the expansion bus. When the capture circuit is idle, the VGA controller passes data from the VGA memory on to the data multiplexer, where it is converted to analog RGB monitor signals. Not all video capture devices include an on-board video adapter—many only capture video, and use the existing video adapter for preview and playback.

The capture board in Figure 38-2 offers an added bonus—a video drive sub-system. Video data is passed through a line buffer. The line buffer (also dubbed a "scan converter") converts the data to National Television Standards Committee (NTSC) data rates, and then passes the data on to a stand-alone VGA DAC. The analog RGB signals are sent to an output port, as well as processed through an S-Video encoder, which provides an independent video source. This system is ideal for observing the VGA image on a TV or recording it to a VCR. Figure 38-3 shows the typical connector arrangement for such a multifunction capture board. As a technician, you should realize that only a few video capture boards provide built-in VGA adapter support or an independent video output.

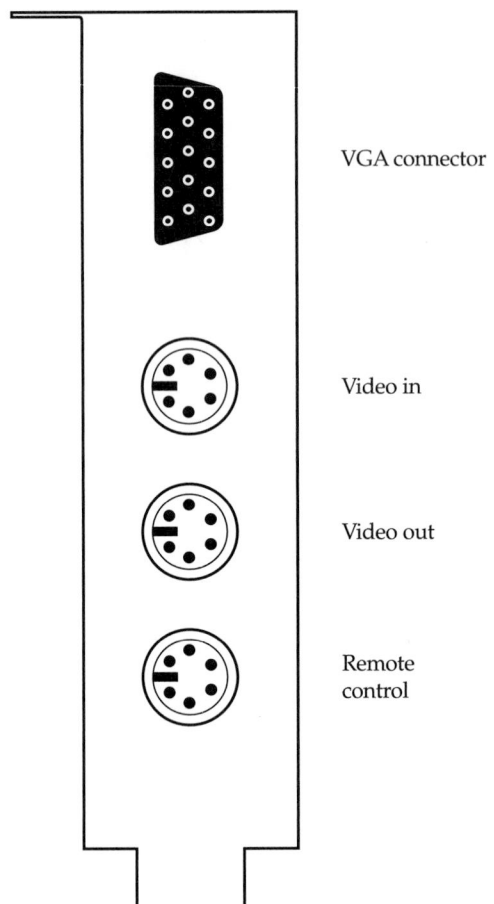

VGA connector

Video in

Video out

Remote
control

FIGURE 38-3 Typical video capture board connections

THE CAPTURE PROCESS

Now that you have some insight into how a basic video capture board works, you can understand how the video capture process works in the PC as a whole. Figure 38-4 shows a "roadmap" of audio and video data through the PC. As with all capture systems, the process begins with a *video source*. In today's PCs, the source can be virtually any video device, such as a camcorder, VCR, or DVD player. Video signals are sent to the capture board, while sound is sent to the PC's sound board.

The video capture board digitizes the video signal. Most boards—such as Intel's Smart Video Recorder (SVR) family—will process and compress the video data on-the-fly (also known as *hardware-based compression*). Data is then stored in system RAM. Audio is digitized by the sound board, and that audio data is also placed in system RAM. Sound and video data are synchronized together using software codecs like Indeo (the basis of Microsoft *Video for Windows*), and then stored on the hard drive in a standard file format, such as Audio-Video Interleave (AVI) or MPEG (MPG). While data is being moved

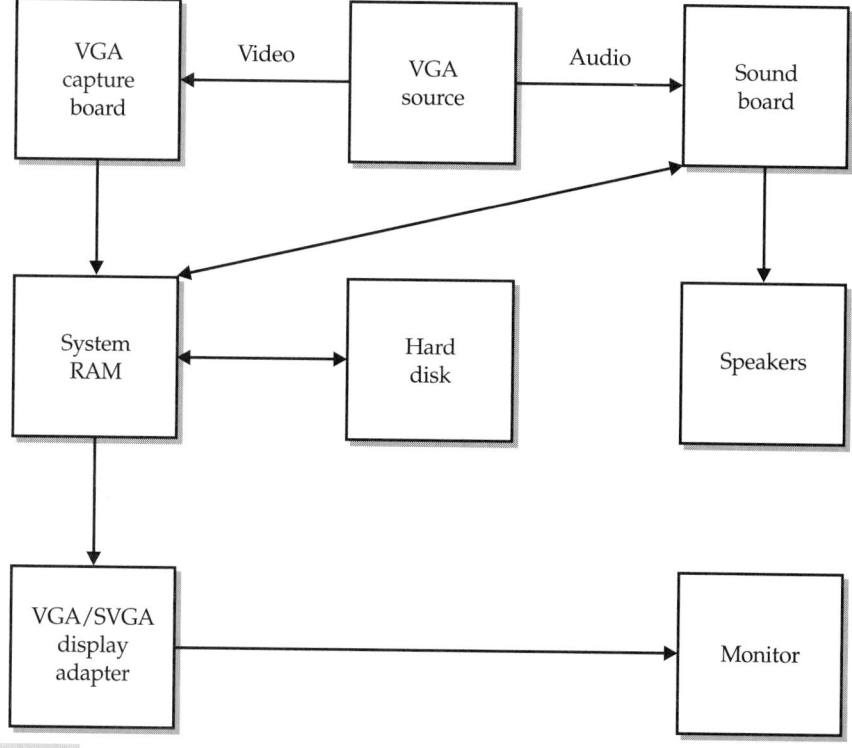

FIGURE 38-4   The audio/video capture and playback sequence

to the hard drive, additional data compression techniques (or *software-based compression*) can be applied to reduce the overall resulting file size.

During the playback process, files are read from the hard drive and expanded (if necessary, with software decompression techniques) into system RAM. Sound and video data are separated. Video data is sent to the display adapter and on to the monitor in a Windows playback dialog box. Sound data is sent to the sound board, where it is processed and passed to the speakers. Thus, sound and video can be repeated as required or used in conjunction with other computer packages (such as presentation packages).

THE ROLE OF A CODEC

Video capture produces a *tremendous* amount of data. Just consider a single 320×200 frame, which is made up of 64,000 pixels (320×200). If you're using a color depth of 65,536 colors, each pixel would need 16 bits (2 bytes), or 128KB per frame. If you are trying to capture ten complete frames per second, more than 1.28MB per second has to be channeled into system RAM—and on to the hard drive as a file. As you might imagine, it would not take more than a few seconds to use up all the available RAM in a PC. However, much of the video data captured in each frame is repetitive. It can be compressed before storing data in RAM or on the hard drive, and then decompressed during playback. As a result, the actual data stored in the system can be much less than it would be otherwise.

The *compressor/decompressor* (or *codec*) is responsible for reducing this data load. A well-designed codec can reduce this data overhead without measurably reducing the quality of an image. Codec functions can be implemented in hardware as a digital signal processor or in software as a driver. Today, there are five major codec techniques: Cinepack, Indeo, Video 1, RLE, and MPEG. Cinepack is perhaps the best codec, offering very good compression for fast action sequences (where data changes rapidly) with little loss of image quality. However, Cinepack compression is a very slow process—not really appropriate for on-the-fly compression. Intel's Indeo video is much faster than Cinepack, but is not well suited for quickly changing data such as that found in fast action sequences. Video 1 and RLE are generally used only for slow animation or palletized video. MPEG is a newer and more robust scheme that allows high levels of compression that can be handled quickly through software.

Intel Indeo Video

Indeo video is Intel's digital video capture, compression, and decompression software. The technology revolves around a software-based codec (a driver) that compresses digital video data for storage, and decompresses it for playback on a multimedia PC. In order for a computer to play files compressed with Indeo video, the Indeo video codec must be installed on the computer, using the setup program provided by Intel. You can check for the presence of Indeo video drivers using the following steps:

1. Click Start, select Settings, and then open the Control Panel.

2. Double-click the Multimedia icon.

3. Select the Devices tab.

4. Double-click Video Compression Codecs (see Figure 38-5).

5. Double-click the Indeo video drivers you see listed.

6. Click Settings. An About box appears containing the version number.

 If there are no Indeo video drivers listed, they are not installed. You can also use this same process to check for other codecs such as Cinepack, MPEG, and more.

MPEG Video

The Moving Picture Experts Group (MPEG) of the Joint ISO/IEC Technical Committee (JTC 1) on Information Technology has developed two international MPEG standards for encoding digital video information: MPEG-1 and MPEG-2. MPEG-1 is formally known as ISO/IEC 11172, and MPEG-2 is formally known as ISO/IEC 13818. MPEG has three main advantages over other video compression/decompression schemes:

■ **Universal compatibility** Unlike system-specific formats, such as AVI and QuickTime, MPEG files are system-independent, meaning many different software and hardware players can play MPEG files on a variety of different systems. Many free programs are available on the market for playing MPEG files (such as Windows Media Player), as well as inexpensive hardware video boards with hardware support for MPEG file playback.

■ **Excellent compression** MPEG offers greater compression ratios than any other format—sometimes reducing the size of the input video at ratios of up to 200:1. That means a video clip that would take 200MB of uncompressed data could require as little as just 1MB when encoded with MPEG.

■ **Highest quality**   MPEG offers multiplatform compatibility and high compression levels, with very little loss in image quality—even at high compression ratios.

MPEG-1   MPEG-1 was designed to produce reasonable-quality images and sound at low bit rates—roughly equivalent to VHS quality. The strength of MPEG-1 is its high compression ratio with relatively high quality. MPEG-1 is intended to fit the capacity of CD-ROM, Video CD, and CD-I, and is often used to transmit video over dial-up networks (such as the Internet). Most "home brew" videos are compressed using MPEG-1.

MPEG-2   MPEG-2 is an advanced scheme designed to produce higher-quality images at higher bit rates. MPEG-2 delivers true broadcast quality video at a full screen resolution of 720×480 pixels for NTSC. MPEG-2 is the standard specified for DVD, and is intended to satisfy other high-quality video applications like digital satellite TV, cable networks, and video games. Given the processing demands of MPEG-2 encoding, it is unlikely that you will work with MPEG-2 on an ordinary video capture setup.

MPEG Audio   MPEG audio for both MPEG-1 and MPEG-2 is CD-quality audio, storing two channels of 16-bit audio sampled at 32 kHz, 44.1 kHz, or 48 kHz. The two audio channels can be either single (mono), dual (two mono channels), stereo, or joint stereo (intensity stereo or m/s-stereo). MPEG-1 audio also allows for copyright marks and original/copy marks within the audio layer. MPEG-2 differs in that it supports multiple channels in the same stream.

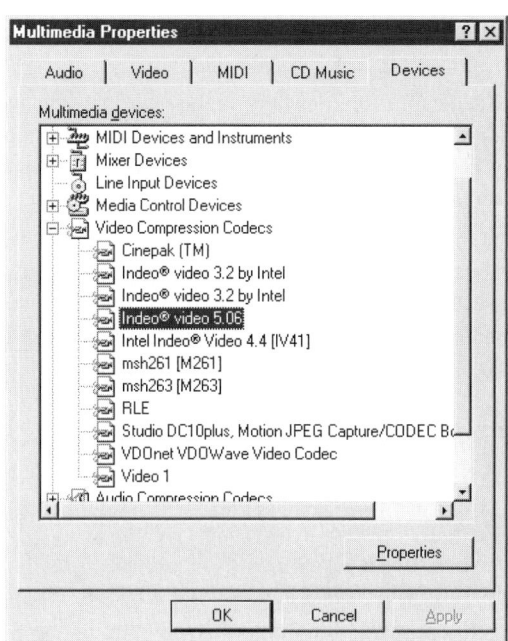

FIGURE 38-5   Checking for video compression codecs

Installing a Video Capture Card

Today's video capture devices are typically PnP devices that are designed for automatic detection and resource assignments. Still, most capture problems *start* when the card is first installed in the system. Usually, problems are due to inadequate or incorrect installation of the hardware and software. This part of the chapter offers an overview of the installation process, so that you can check for missing steps.

 Always use proper static precautions (such as an antistatic wrist strap) when working inside a system with sensitive devices such as a video capture card.

Many video capture installations begin with the installation of software. The rapid advances in video capture and processing hardware make it difficult for Windows to properly identify every possible device after installation, so installing at least some minimal software first can ensure proper detection. In many cases, the capture software should also be updated to the very latest version *before* the hardware is installed. Once the software is installed (if necessary), you can install the hardware:

1. Shut down Windows 98/Me, and then turn off and unplug the computer.

2. Unbolt the outer case, and then remove the housing and set it (and the screws) aside in a safe place.

3. Remove the old video adapter or capture device (if necessary). If your video capture card integrates the features of a video adapter and/or graphics accelerator, you may need to disconnect your monitor and remove the existing video adapter from the system first. If the video adapter is integrated onto the motherboard, you'll need to disable the video adapter through a jumper or the system's CMOS Setup. If the video capture card will exist alongside the current video adapter, you can skip this step.

4. Locate a slot for the video capture card. Many capture card devices will require a PCI slot, though some "integrated" video capture cards (those including the video adapter, MPEG-2 decoder, and so on) may need an AGP slot. Find an available slot that's appropriate for your capture card (such as a high PCI slot). Remove the cover for the slot you intend to use (if it's not already removed), and save the screw for the mounting bracket.

5. Insert the video capture card. Push the card in firmly and evenly until it's fully seated in the slot. Replace the screw to secure the bracket of your capture card to the computer's chassis. Install the capture card in a high PCI slot (such as # 1 or #2)—usually closest to the AGP video adapter. Rearrange cards if necessary. If you need to change the arrangement of add-on cards in a system, it's best to move one card at a time.

6. Make your signal connections. You'll need to connect your external devices to the video capture card. Here are just a few of the connections you may need to make (your capture card may have more or fewer connections depending on its particular features):

    ▪ **Monitor**   If your video capture card is taking the place of your existing video adapter, double-check that the monitor cable is also secure at the monitor end.

    ▪ **Video Input**   This is the primary video input (usually through an S-Video or RCA jack), which allows you to display and capture video from a VCR, camcorder signals, or ordinary TV video signals.

- **Audio Line Output (LineOut)**   Of course, you'll want to hear the captured audio through your system speakers, so connect this output to your sound card's LineIn connection (if necessary). Your capture card package will usually provide a short patch cable for this purpose.

- **Audio Line Input (LineIn)**   This is sound input: where you should connect the sound source from a VCR or video camera.

- **TV Output**   If your capture card provides an output that will drive an external TV (dubbed a "scan converter" feature), you can connect the remote TV to this jack. Remember that if your remote TV has a TV/video switch, be sure that it's set to the *video* position. Similarly, you can attach this output to a VCR, but you'll need to set the VCR's tuner/line switch to the *line* position.

The ability to handle TV input and output signals often allows you to record TV shows or prerecorded video tapes through your capture device. Keep in mind that the unauthorized recording or use of broadcast television programming, videotape, or other copyrighted material may violate copyright laws. In most cases, you cannot record from a copy-protected video source.

SOFTWARE INSTALLATION

If you have not already installed software for your video capture card, it's time to install the software now. You can then view and record your video signals and edit the captured video to an AVI or MPG file. Leave the computer's housing off for now, but reconnect the AC cord to the computer, and prepare to start the system again. Always refer to the README file on the video capture card's driver disc to obtain the very latest feature descriptions and software installation guidelines for your particular card.

In virtually all cases, the video capture system will require a recent version of DirectX. You should download and install the very latest version of DirectX before proceeding with the software installation. You may need to install DirectX to utilize all the features of your video capture device.

1. Reboot the computer. Turn on your computer and allow Windows 98/Me to boot normally. In virtually all cases, Windows will detect the VIDEO capture card automatically at start time. Windows usually reports finding a "PCI adapter" (even if you're using an AGP card).

2. Install the display drivers (if necessary). If your capture card is now serving as the video adapter, you should install the display drivers now, and then reconfigure the Display settings for a suitable resolution and color depth.

3. Install the video capture drivers. After the computer restarts, you should insert the driver/software CD in the drive. Chances are that an AUTORUN.INF file will launch the driver installation automatically. Follow the on-screen instructions to install the video capture driver files, and then restart your computer so that your changes can take effect. Doing this will probably add one or more entries for your capture card to the Sound, Video, And Game Controllers list of your Device Manager. Leave the CD in the drive.

4. Expect system tests. Once you reboot the system, there may be one or more performance tests that will evaluate the performance of your hard drive and system—any results will generally be used to limit your video capture settings. You may need to reboot the system again.

5. Test your setup. Now it's time to see that your hardware is working properly. If your installation CD offers a "diagnostic" mode, check to see that all of your connections are secure, and verify that the video capture card hardware is responding. For example, you may be able to attach a video

camera and see the picture in a "capture overlay" window. You may need to reboot the computer before proceeding.

6.   Install the applications. One of the final steps is to install the related application software that supports your video capture card (such as the capture and editing software tools). Select each utility that you want to install, and then follow the on-screen instructions to load and test each utility.

VIDCAP DRIVER NOTES

The heart of your video capture software is the video capture (VIDCAP) driver. This is the interface through which you'll select a video source, video format, capture window size, capture data rates, and other attributes. A typical VIDCAP driver will offer three setting areas: the video source, the video format, and overlay/preview settings.

Video Source

This window is where you'll select the source of the video signal to be captured (Figure 38-6). The *Video channel* area typically allows for S-Video, Composite video, and TV tuner video (cable or antenna). The dialog box in Figure 38-6 even allows you to select the channel that you want to capture from. The *Standard* area lets you select the video format that you'll be capturing. You can choose from NTSC, PAL, or SECAM, depending on your region of the world. If your capture card provides a "scan converter" to support a remote television output, you can select the Output To TV check box to enable this feature.

Video Format

The video format dialog box allows you to define the color characteristics of your captured video. The RGB mode allows you to select a basic "uncompressed" AVI video format in 8-bit color (256 shades of gray), 16-bit color (high-color mode), or 24-bit color (true-color mode). If you select MPEG or MJPEG as the video format, you'll compress the captured video into an MPG file. You can configure many of the capture characteristics in the MJPEG Settings dialog box (Figure 38-7). The MJPEG Dimensions area allows you to select the size (resolution) of the capture frames: full size, half size, CIF, and QIF. The smaller your capture window, the less data will be generated (and less storage space needed). When you're recording in MJPEG format, you can select the amount of compression to be applied in the MJPEG Quality area. Since MPEG formats use *lossy* compression techniques, "lower" quality will result in faster capture rates, but poorer image integrity. The dialog box in Figure 38-7 also illustrates the "required" and "available" hard drive data transfer rates, so that you'll be able to keep your video capture selections within the capabilities of your storage system.

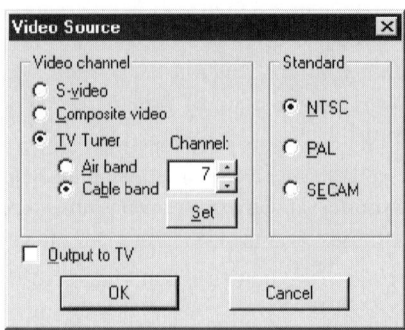

FIGURE 38-6   Configuring the source characteristics for video capture

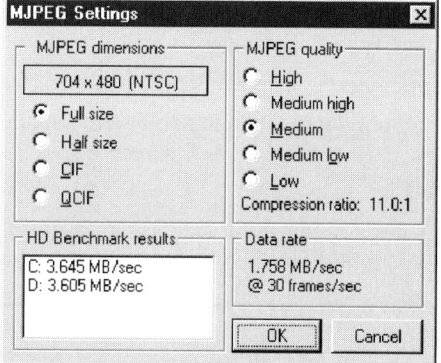

FIGURE 38-7   Configuring the capture MJPEG settings

Overlay and Preview Modes

The video capture program that you're using may give you a choice of *overlay* or *preview* modes. When the MJPEG video format is selected, overlay and preview settings have no effect. If an RGB video format is selected, overlay and preview settings affect how video is viewed or captured:

■ In the overlay mode, the video signal appears in its capture windows in real time because the video signal is not being processed through the VIDCAP algorithm. This feature is handy because you don't spend vital processing time viewing the image as if you were capturing it.

■ In the preview mode, the video signal is processed as if it were being captured. You may notice a low frame rate in the video window (the video may appear "jerky"). This is a somewhat more accurate representation of how the video capture system will handle the capture after the process starts.

Making the Most of Video Capture

Even under the best of circumstances, video capture presents a serious challenge to system processing. The challenge of video capture is to record an image of adequate quality at a window size large enough to be meaningful, while maintaining a frame rate high enough to reproduce smooth motion, and while taking up a minimum amount of storage space. High-quality video capture requires a careful balance of processing power with window size, frame rate, and original image quality. This part of the chapter outlines some issues to consider when capturing video.

IMAGE WINDOW SIZE

It takes a finite amount of time to put a pixel on the screen—the more pixels that must be generated, the more time that is required. Since larger playback windows contain more pixels, it takes more time to "draw" each playback frame. This in turn reduces the frame rate. Larger playback windows also result in larger video files. Faster machines can support larger playback windows for any given frame rate. Though more recent capture platforms support the processing ability to handle "full frame" captures, there are three classical playback window sizes:

- 320×240 is considered ideal for many multimedia applications, but is limited to slower frame rates (unless you're using a reasonably fast computer).

- 240×180 is regarded as a good intermediate window size across a range of frame rates.

- 160×120 is the smallest commonly used video window size, but allows the fastest frame rates.

IMAGE FRAME RATE

Frame rate has a significant influence on playback quality. Faster frame rates provide smoother images (especially for moving images or action shots), but they are processor-intensive and generate more data. Smaller playback windows can usually sustain a higher frame rate, and vice versa. Faster machines can support faster frame rates for any given playback window size. The most common frame rates are listed here:

- **5–10 fps**   Used for low data-rate applications like video conferencing or Internet video.

- **15 fps**   Considered satisfactory for most multimedia presentation applications.

- **24 fps**   The frame rate at which motion pictures are projected in theaters.

- **25 fps**   PAL (Europe) broadcast television frame rate.

- **30 fps**   NTSC (U.S., Japan) broadcast television frame rate.

VIDEO SOURCE QUALITY

The most important factor affecting the quality of your final video capture file is the quality of the *original* source video. Compression cannot re-create detail that wasn't present in the original image, but it can take artifacts present in the original video (such as static) and potentially make them worse. So it is important that the best video source possible be used to create compressed video files.

Compression algorithms (such as Cinepak, MPEG, or Indeo) analyze the digitized video input stream, searching for redundant or predictable data patterns that can be compressed and reconstructed later. The codec compressor interprets noise or artifacts digitized from the analog source as *nonredundant*, unpredictable data and therefore wastes valuable CPU time and file space attempting to accurately compress and store these deficiencies. That's why the quality of the original source video is so critical to the quality of the resulting compressed digital video file. Video artifacts can also look worse after compression than they did originally.

Capture your source video using a high-quality video tape format. The best source video uses S-Video rather than composite formats. S-Video signals carry separate signals for *luminance* (brightness) and *chrominance* (color)—resulting in higher bandwidth and an improved signal-to-noise ratio. Composite video sources modulate the luminance and chrominance together on one signal, which lowers both the bandwidth and the signal-to-noise ratio. Composite video signals are also subject to video artifacts, such as color bleeding. The following are the available formats (in order of image quality):

- **D1 and Digital Betacam**   D1 and Digital Betacam actually store video information digitally (rather like an audio CD). Both formats are broadcast quality but expensive, even for a professional's budget.

- **D2**   D2 is the digital composite cousin of D1 and is similar to D1 in both quality and expense.

- **Betacam SP**   Betacam SP is the most widely used analog recording format for video creation and post-production. Its high quality makes it an ideal choice for professional and semiprofessional multimedia authoring.

- **1" Type C, ¾" U-Matic**   1" and ¾" literally refer to the width of the recording tape used in each format. 1" is an open reel-to-reel format, and ¾" is a cartridge format. Both are older, professional studio formats. Both types produce better results than consumer formats, but they have been almost entirely supplanted by the newer and better Betacam SP format.

- **Videodisc/DVD**   Despite being a composite format, videodisc (also known as *laserdisc*) still provides good overall quality. Some videodisc players provide S-Video outputs, though the original signal is still composite, and low-cost electronics can sometimes make these S-Video outputs worse than the composite. For our purposes, the DVD video output is about the same quality as a videodisc.

- **Hi-8, Super-VHS**   Hi-8 and S-VHS are consumer formats, so they're inexpensive and easily available. Both produce good results for desktop and consumer use.

- **VHS**   VHS is the familiar home consumer format. Its composite signal and low-cost recording and playback mechanisms make it the lowest in quality of any available format, and is not suitable for commercial multimedia.

COLOR

As with lighting, selecting colors and arranging color in a scene can affect the overall quality of your video source. Use the following points to optimize your use of color:

- *Avoid saturated colors in the scene.* Video with highly saturated colors (especially red) can bleed or appear blocky—particularly when viewed on 8-bit (256-color) displays.

- *Avoid adjacent areas of high contrast.* For example, a white shirt with black stripes is a poor choice. Sudden changes in brightness levels can emphasize color bleeding and create edges that are more difficult to compress.

- *Avoid extremely thin horizontal or vertical lines.* Areas of fine detail are not always particularly visible after compression, especially when displayed in a small video playback window. Extremely fine lines or patterns (such as those that are one-pixel wide) can distort the source video image. Such distortion looks bad and makes the image extremely difficult to compress successfully.

LIGHTING

If you've ever snapped a photo, you've probably been concerned with lighting. Lighting is just as important with video, and can affect the overall image quality used during the capture. The following points offer some lighting tips to produce the clearest images and minimize the noise often produced in poor lighting environments:

- *Use ample light.* Adequate lighting is vital for creating high-quality video. Most consumer video cameras generate noise in low light. Random noise in an image decreases the redundant information and leads to poor compressed video quality and larger image files.

- *Avoid fluorescent light.* The "color temperature" of fluorescent light makes videos look blue-green. If you're in an office, shoot near windows to use the natural light. Place the camera between the windows and the subject (don't use the windows as a background, because doing so places your subject in a shadow).

- *Use natural light wherever possible.* The best light occurs outside on a cloudy or overcast day, because the light is evenly diffused. Direct sunlight can create areas of deep shadow where video noise can be prominent.

■ *Use a reflector to bounce light onto your subject.* Reflectors produce more even lighting and can also reduce areas of deep shadow.

CAMERA TECHNIQUES

The way in which you use the camera to record original video will also have a profound impact on the way in which the codec can compress the video during capture. The following tips can help you get the most compression potential from your camera techniques:

■ *Use a tripod.* Even the best hand-held video camera moves, and this movement is always noticed by the viewer. Also, because a camera on a tripod is steadier, more information is redundant between frames—yielding better compression.

■ *Use close-ups.* Remember that your video will probably be played within a relatively small window on a computer monitor. Close-ups work well to emphasize your visual message in this medium and reduce the small detail that may be lost during compression anyway.

■ *Don't overuse pans and zooms.* Pans and zooms limit how much can be compressed, because nearly every pixel can change between frames. Rather than zooming, break the action up into two static shots (one close-up and one long shot). Use other techniques to create visual excitement. For example, instead of centering your subject in the frame, create a more dynamic shot by placing the subject to one side of center and directing your attention to the other side of the frame.

■ *Use autofocus wisely.* The autofocus feature of most modern video cameras works well for most medium and wide shots, but don't use it in close-ups where the subject is moving, or when zooming in on a subject. The entire image gets blurry for a moment, and then sharp as the camera attempts to stay focused on the object in the center of the frame. The result is distracting and limits the effectiveness of compression because every pixel changes as the camera refocuses. Instead, lock your camera on non-autofocus, zoom in tight on the subject, and then manually focus and zoom back out to frame the shot *before* you shoot.

Troubleshooting Video Capture Cards

Like most other expansion devices, video capture products generally use highly integrated, proprietary chips. As a result, it can be extremely difficult to troubleshoot the capture board to the component level. Fortunately, a large number of capture problems can be tracked to installation, setup/configuration, software, or operational errors. When diagnostics can isolate problems to the capture board itself, it is a simple matter to replace the capture board outright.

HARDWARE CONFLICTS—VIDEO CAPTURE DEVICES

Hardware conflicts are a serious issue in today's systems. Sound boards, MPEG decoder cards, modems, drive controllers, network interface cards (NICs), and video capture boards all contribute to the congestion that fills up a system and demands its available resources. Most devices require an interrupt (IRQ), one or more I/O address settings, an occasional direct memory access (DMA) channel, and possibly some small amount of memory for a BIOS (firmware). Unfortunately, those resources are scarce in most PCs, and you must be aware of what resources are available and what is being used before adding new devices to your system. Your most effective course is to analyze the free resources available through the Device Manager before starting your installation.

All CPUs tackle only one task at a time. When a device such as the keyboard needs the CPU to perform important work that cannot wait for free CPU time, an interrupt signal is generated which forces the CPU to put aside whatever it was doing and respond to the interrupt immediately. When the device requesting the interrupt has been taken care of, the CPU can return to whatever it was doing until the next interrupt comes along. The problem is that only *one* device can use any one interrupt. If two or more devices try to use the same interrupt at the same time, one of those conflicting devices will not operate properly. In mild cases, this condition may appear simply as system hesitation. In serious cases, IRQ conflicts can crash your system. When you find that more than one device is using an interrupt, you must place one of those conflicting devices on an unused IRQ. IRQs can usually be changed through the device's Properties dialog box under Windows 9x/Me. You can recognize the effects of IRQ conflicts between a video capture board and other devices in your system from the following symptoms:

- Video frames are dropped during video capture or playback.
- The video capture or playback process is slow or jumpy.
- The system or VIDCAP software hesitates or hangs up (crashes) completely.
- The display or data file generated during capture is corrupt.
- Audio is not captured or played back properly (if at all).

An I/O address works a bit differently. Most devices require one or more addresses to exchange data and instructions between its "registers" and the system. This I/O address works in conjunction with an IRQ, although an IRQ can be changed without changing the I/O address. All devices must use a unique I/O address. Otherwise, one device may try writing data while another device tries to read data, and the operation of both devices will be affected. I/O conflicts may also result in system crashes. As with IRQs, it is important that each device be assigned to its own unique I/O address. If more than one address is needed, there can be *no* overlap of addresses at all. When more than one device attempts to use the same address, you must move one of the devices to an unused area. I/O settings can usually be changed through the device's Properties dialog box under Windows 9x/Me. You can recognize the effects of I/O conflicts between a video capture board and other devices in your system from the following symptoms:

- The video capture board installation program or device driver refuses to recognize the presence of the capture card (or initialize the capture card).
- Microsoft *Video for Windows* (or other capture drivers/applications) can't initialize the capture device.
- The video capture board works erratically or fails to respond at all.

REMOVING/DISABLING OLDER VIDEO CAPTURE DEVICES

Video capture devices can be very sensitive to the presence of other video capture devices or older drivers. Before you install a new video capture device, make it a point to remove the old video capture device (if it's still in the system) and remove all the drivers and applet software that supported the older capture device. It's normally a simple matter to remove an older video capture card and uninstall its corresponding software, but getting rid of those older codecs can be tricky unless you know where to look. Start by removing the old video capture device through the Device Manager:

1.   Click Start, highlight Settings, and then click Control Panel.
2.   Double-click the System icon.

3.   Select the Device Manager tab.

4.   Click the plus (+) sign to the left of Sound, Video And Game Controllers.

5.   Click the older capture driver that you want to remove, and then click the Remove button.

6.   Reboot your system.

When the system reboots, verify that the corresponding codec(s) have been removed:

1.   Click Start, highlight Settings, and then click Control Panel.

2.   Double-click the Multimedia icon.

3.   Select the far-right tab (in Windows 95 it's called Advanced, and in Windows 98/Me it's called Devices).

4.   Click the plus (+) sign to the left of Video Capture Devices.

5.   Click the device that you want to remove, and then click the Remove button. If the system won't let you remove the codec, it's probably still listed in the Device Manager and should be removed there first.

6.   If the codec is related to other elements of your graphics card or TV tuner (and you *cannot* remove the codec), you can select the device by clicking on it, and then clicking on the Properties button. Select "Do not use this capture device," and then click the Apply button. You may have to restart Windows for this change to take effect.

B&W ERRORS

If you notice that the color source image in your preview/overlay window is in black and white, and any captured clips are played back in black and white, there may be a setup or configuration issue that you need to correct. These problems are usually fixed by adjusting video source settings. Use either Adobe Premiere or the VIDCAP software specific to your capture device to bring up the Video Source settings screen. Check the following points:

■ *4.43 MHz color carrier (or some other unusual color model) has been selected.* Remove the check in the 4.43 MHz color carrier check box by clicking on it.

■ *The Saturation setting is set to zero (or nearly zero).* Click the Default button: brightness, contrast, sharpness, brightness, and hue will be reset to their default values.

■ *The video input Standard setting is set to PAL rather than to NTSC.* At the top of the Video Source dialog box (in the box marked Standard), set this to NTSC.

■ *If you're using S-Video cables for input/output, they may be damaged.* Try replacing the S-Video cable(s).

AUDIO/VIDEO SYNC ISSUES

When you capture audio and video simultaneously, it's important that the audio and video components of the capture remain properly synchronized. Otherwise, sounds and voices will not mesh, and the capture won't play back correctly. This part of the chapter provides some tips that may help you correct A/V synchronization issues.

Synchronization is sometimes a problem on captured clips that have yet to be made into a movie. In such cases, the capture rate is usually too high for the hard drive to play back the file. The solution is to lower the capture rate and recapture again. If frames are being dropped during the capture process, continue to lower the data rate and recapture until no frames are dropped. If the problems still occur after lowering the capture rate substantially, check and correct the "setting suggestions," as shown below. If the problems occur on clips that have been compiled (such as a completed MPEG file), the problem could be caused by numerous issues, such as:

- The computer's hardware and/or operating system settings are incorrect.
- The capture settings are incorrect.
- The MPEG file settings are incorrect.
- The original clips have dropped frames from the capture.

SUGGESTED SETTINGS

Capture quality is also influenced by the way in which your capture card is configured, and by other actions taking place on your PC platform. Try the following suggestions to streamline your capture setup:

- Check the version of your video capture driver and upgrade to the current driver if necessary.
- If you're using Adobe to develop your video, upgrade older versions of Adobe to the current versions: for Windows, use version 4.2 or later.
- Make sure that the drivers for your sound card, video adapter, and hard drive controller are all up-to-date.
- Under Windows 9x/Me, there are settings for disabling the software cache for your hard drive. Open the Control Panel, double-click the System icon, select the Performance tab, and click File System. Set Read-Ahead Optimization to "None". Go from there to Troubleshooting and put a check in the Disable Write-Behind Caching For All Drives check box.
- Device problems (such as conflicts) can play havoc with your captures. Open the Control Panel, double-click the System icon, and select the Device Manager tab. Check for exclamation marks or question marks on any devices. If there are problems, reconfigure or reinstall the offending device(s).
- Review the CONFIG.SYS and AUTOEXEC.BAT files, and disable any TSRs or old 16-bit drivers.
- Turn off any background applications to open as much conventional memory as possible:
  Turn off the wallpaper.
  Turn off the screen saver.
  Disable any real mode drivers.
  Disable MS Plus "System Agent."
  Disable any virus checker.
  Delete any unnecessary fonts.
- Change the resolution of the display adapter—reduce it to 800×600×256 (you may also try a higher color depth).
- Disable the video acceleration on your display adapter.
- Make sure that the computer is not connected to a network (if it is, log out).
- Make sure that the hard drive that is receiving the captured video has DMA data transfers enabled, and is set to 32-bit mode. Hooking up a device that uses only 16-bit drivers will cause all devices on the chain to work in 16-bit mode.

- Defrag the capture drive.

- Run ScanDisk on the capture drive.

- Make sure that compression software (such as DriveSpace) is not being used. If it is, try capturing to another uncompressed drive.

- Make sure that the hard drive you're capturing video to is a high-performance drive (such as UDMA/66, UDMA/100, or WideSCSI-2 or later).

- Try a second HDD for the video capture.

- Make sure that there is an adequate amount of RAM in the system. If you're editing a lot of clips and transitions, plan on at least 64MB to 128MB.

TROUBLESHOOTING TIPS

Although video capture and playback devices can sometimes be daunting, there is a series of fairly "standard" troubleshooting policies that can help you track down potential problem areas quickly:

- *Use the latest drivers.* Video capture devices depend heavily on drivers. Buggy or outdated drivers can easily result in errors and poor performance.

- *Run in the 8-bit (256 color) graphics mode.* Running in any "lower" mode (such as 16 color) will result in extremely poor image quality. If you have sufficient video memory and PC processing power, you should run in the 16-bit (or high-color) video mode.

- *Use care in the installation of drivers—especially with capture drivers that depend on DirectDraw and ActiveX resources under Windows 9x/Me.* You may need to update or reinstall these resources (such as update DirectX to 8.0a or later) after the capture device is installed.

- *Be sure to use a strong and clean signal for recording.* Your capture is only as good as the original signal.

- *Be sure to use good-quality cabling.* Poor cabling and connectors can easily degrade even strong video signals. Check that all of your video/audio cables are secure.

- *When using MPEG players and capture devices, use moderate video resolutions and refresh rates.* These devices normally "downshift" higher refresh rates during play, and the flicker can be quite noticeable at high resolutions.

- *Don't shift video modes while MPEG players or capture devices are in use.* The change in the video drivers can crash the computer.

- *Disable power management features such as APM when using video capture and playback devices.* The computer can crash if the system shuts down into suspend mode while these devices are in operation.

- *PCI video devices often depend on the correct configuration of a PCI bus slot. Check the slot's configuration under your CMOS Setup.* In some cases, you may need to move the PCI video capture card to a higher-priority slot (usually closet to the AGP slot).

The following points highlight a series of common problems, and their most frequent causes:

- **Capture card not found**   The capture card may be installed in an incorrect (a low priority) PCI slot, or there may be an IRQ conflict in the system. Recheck the installation of the capture card.

- **No frames captured**   The SCSI host adapter and/or capture card may be installed in an incorrect (a low priority) PCI slot, or there may be an IRQ conflict in the system. Recheck the installation of the capture card and SCSI host adapter (if there is SCSI support in the system).

■ **Dropped frames**   Close any unneeded applications and try a smaller capture window. Try capturing to a faster drive capable of high-performance data transfers (such as UDMA/100). The capture card may be installed in an incorrect (a low priority) PCI slot, or there may be an IRQ conflict in the system.

■ **Skipped frames**   The SCSI host adapter and/or capture card may be installed in an incorrect (a low priority) PCI slot, or there may be an IRQ conflict in the system. Recheck the installation of your capture card and SCSI host adapter (if there is SCSI support in the system).

■ **Poor overlay**   There is trouble with the video card driver, DirectX version, or PCI IRQ sharing. Try updating DirectX along with the video card's drivers, and then reset the display to an appropriate resolution and color depth for captures. If the problem persists, try disabling IRQ Steering on the system.

■ **No audio**   Verify that your speakers are on and properly connected to the sound card. Test the speakers on another PC if necessary. If the speakers and sound card check out, try disabling IRQ Steering on the system.

■ **Distorted audio**   Check your audio settings to see that volume levels are correct, and then check the audio cables for damage or connection problems. If the problem continues, check for possible IRQ problems between the capture card, sound card, or other devices in the system.

■ **No output to VCR or camera**   In virtually all cases, the video clip processing software (such as Adobe Premiere) is using incorrect presets or VCR input selection.

■ **Black lines in playback**   The SCSI host adapter and/or capture card may be installed in an incorrect (a low priority) PCI slot, or there may be an IRQ conflict in the system. Recheck the installation of your capture card and SCSI host adapter (if there is SCSI support in the system).

■ **Audio/video not synchronized**   This can sometimes depend on the capture frame settings. Be sure to capture at 29.97 frames per second.

SYMPTOMS

If you've reviewed and followed the preceding guidelines, but there are still problems with your video capture device, you can refer to the following symptoms for specific issues and their recommended solutions.

SYMPTOM 38-1   **When you connect a camcorder, your capture software crashes with a "fatal exception" error**   In virtually all cases, the incorrect drivers have been installed on the system. Try reinstalling the capture software and supporting files (such as updating to DirectX 8.0a or later) from the manufacturer's CD, or download any patches or updates from the manufacturer's Web site. During your reinstallation, make sure that you are installing drivers and files for the correct video capture hardware model.

SYMPTOM 38-2   **When launching your video capture software, an error indicates that the capture hardware is not found**   In most cases, you *must* run video capture software with the hardware that it was designed/optimized for. If you try to run the software with other hardware, the software will usually respond with an error. If you previously had installed some other video capture controller in your system, it's most likely that some files relating to this device are still on your hard drive, and these may be conflicting with the current video capture device. If you had (or still have) another video capture device in the system, disable it in Device Manager:

1.   Click Start, select Settings, click Control Panel, and then double-click the System icon.

2. Click the Device Manager tab.

3. Locate the "old" video capture device (usually located under Sound, Video And Game Controllers).

4. Double-click the old device reference. On the General tab under Windows 98, put a check in the box marked Disable In This Hardware Profile. Reboot your computer.

You should also verify that the correct (current) video capture device is listed in the Device Manager and that it is running without conflicts. If the problem persists, try removing the video capture device from the Device Manager and allowing Windows to redetect and reinstall the drivers for it on the next boot.

SYMPTOM 38-3   **When launching the video editing software, you receive an error such as "Cannot initialize audio playback"**   This message usually indicates that the audio sub-system (your sound card) is already in use by another application. Make sure that your CD player (or any other application that uses the sound card) is not running. Press CTRL-ALT-DELETE simultaneously to open the Close Program window. Click any individual applications listed in the Close Program window that may be tying up your sound card, and select End Task. Always be sure to leave Explorer and Systray running. Also check your Device Manager to verify that the sound device is running properly. If you notice any yellow exclamation marks or red *X*s, you may need to troubleshoot a sound hardware conflict or remove and reinstall the sound device.

SYMPTOM 38-4   **You cannot launch your video capture software by double-clicking its icon**   In virtually all cases, you must reboot the system after installing the video capture drivers and software. If you have just installed the software but have not rebooted the system, try that now. If you find that certain applications conflict with the video capture device, you may also need to reboot the system so that any such conflicts may be cleared. If the problem persists, try reinstalling the video capture software.

SYMPTOM 38-5   **Windows keeps detecting a previously installed capture device instead of your current one**   If you had a different capture card previously installed and the computer keeps trying to load these drivers, then some of the files for the *old* card are still on the system. If you have uninstalled the previous hardware and software, more than likely some INF files (or some other file) were never removed, and the old device is still being identified. To get around this problem, identify and delete any old INF files associated with the old video capture device.

SYMPTOM 38-6   **The video capture WDM driver doesn't work under Windows 98** Capture programs using the Video for Windows 1.1 (VFW) interface cannot directly communicate with analog video capture devices that use the Windows Driver Model (WDM) video capture interfaces in Windows 98. These analog capture devices may include PCI adapters with video decoder chips that use WDM drivers. This occurs because the VFW/WDM mapper files included with Windows 98 do *not* allow WDM-based analog capture devices to be used with the VFW 1.1 interface. You can download a patch file from the Microsoft Web site that should correct this problem. This patch should have the following file attributes (or later):

```
VFWWDM.DRV   4.10.2043  8/10/98  9:35pm  15,344 bytes
VFWWDM.DLL   4.10.2043  8/10/98  9:38pm  56,832 bytes
KSWDMCAP.AX  4.10.2043  8/10/98  9:29pm  51,712 bytes
```

 This problem was corrected in Windows 98 Second Edition and Windows Me.

SYMPTOM 38-7   **There are problems installing the S-Video cable**   Most video capture boards are designed to accept composite audio/video signals from either a single RCA connector or an S-Video connector. Unfortunately, the S-Video connector is not keyed to prevent incorrect insertion. An incorrectly installed connector will generally result in signals not reaching the capture board. It is possible to install the S-Video cable rotated 90 degrees from where it should be. Make sure that the arrow on the cable matches the marking on the capture board.

SYMPTOM 38-8   **Even though a valid video source is available, you see vertical multicolored lines in the capture application window**   This problem is particular to capture boards when the board itself is loose or installed improperly or the signal cabling is not secure. Check the capture board to see that it is fully inserted in the expansion slot. If there are any modules or sub-boards attached to the capture board, see that they are secure and inserted properly. Also check any connectors and cables to be sure that they are all installed correctly.

SYMPTOM 38-9   **Even though a valid video source is available, you see nothing but black in the capture application window**   There are several possible reasons for this symptom. First, check the video signal being fed to the capture board. If there is no signal, the video capture window (such as the Video for Windows VIDCAP window) will be dark. You can test the video signal by disconnecting the video cable from the capture board and connecting it to a stand-alone monitor, such as a TV set. Damaged or defective video cables and connectors should be replaced. If you are using a camcorder as a real-time video source, make sure that the camera is turned on, that the lens cover is off, and that you have selected the correct video source (composite or S-Video, for example). Also check that the capture board is inserted in the system properly and completely. Any submodules should be attached securely to the main expansion board.

Finally, there may be an IRQ conflict between your video capture board and another device in your system. If you attempt to capture a video file while the capture window is dark and receive an error such as "Wave input device not responding," there is almost certainly an IRQ problem. Run a diagnostic such as Microsoft MSD (or use the Windows Device Manager) to identify unused IRQs, and then set the video capture board to use an available IRQ. In some cases, you must run an installation routine for the capture board when changing settings. If problems persist, the capture board may have failed.

SYMPTOM 38-10   **During installation, you see the error "Unable to locate an available interrupt"**   This type of symptom occurs with an IRQ conflict or when a device driver or TSR interferes with the installation. Make sure that the capture board is configured to use an available IRQ (such as 9, 10, 11, or 12). You may have to use a diagnostic (such as Microsoft MSD or the Device Manager) to locate available interrupts. Try booting the system from a clean DOS disk to prevent any TSRs or device drivers from interfering with installation.

Unfortunately, if there is a conflict during installation, there will also probably be conflicts during actual use. So, if you suspect a TSR or device driver conflict, you will have to disable TSRs and device drivers one by one until the conflict disappears, and then work with the offending TSR or device driver configuration to eliminate the conflict. Under Windows 9x/Me, you can adjust device resources through the video capture card's Properties dialog box.

SYMPTOM 38-11 You cannot initialize the capture board because of a lack of available IRQs   On some systems, the capture board fails to initialize when launching the capture application. This problem is usually due to the lack of an available interrupt request (IRQ) for the capture board to use. To check the IRQs on your system:

1. Go to the Windows 9x/Me desktop.
2. Right-click the My Computer icon and select Properties.
3. Click the Device Manager tab.
4. Double-click Computer to display all IRQ resources.

You see each of your system's interrupts and which devices are using them. If all IRQs are already assigned to other devices, you need to free an IRQ for the video capture board. You can usually free an IRQ by removing a device no longer in use or disabling the IRQ on a feature not being used (for example, if you're not using the MIDI port of a sound board, disable it to free the IRQ).

SYMPTOM 38-12 When starting the capture utility, you see the error "Unable to initialize a capture device"   This is an error message produced by the capture utility (such as the Video for Windows VIDCAP utility) when the capture board cannot be located. For most capture boards, this probably indicates an IRQ conflict with one or more devices in the system, which can occur easily when new devices are added to the system *after* the capture board has been installed. Use a diagnostic (such as Microsoft MSD or the Device Manager) to locate unused IRQs. If new equipment has been added, change the new equipment to relieve the conflict. If the error manifested itself when the capture board was installed, change the board's IRQ to an available setting.

If interrupts check out properly, make sure the capture board is inserted properly and completely into the motherboard. If any modules or sub-boards are attached to the capture board, see that they are inserted and secured properly. You may also have installed the capture software in the wrong order. Some boards require that software be installed first, and then the hardware must be installed. If this process is reversed, the capture board's Windows drivers may not install properly. Try reinstalling the capture software. If the software is correct, try another capture board.

SYMPTOM 38-13 Your capture halts with a message that the audio data rate has changed   This is often an issue with digital video captures. Many digital video camcorders allow audio to be stored in either 12-bit or 16-bit mode (32 kHz and 48 kHz, respectively), so this message is generally produced by digital video capture software when it detects that the bit rate of your audio source has changed during the capture. To avoid this error, you should keep the same audio bit rate setting on your digital video camcorder at all times. If you have tapes that contain different bit rates, you capture each of those footage segments separately.

SYMPTOM 38-14 You only capture up to 18 minutes when capturing in a "full quality" mode   This is normally an issue with the video capture software. Some software packages place a 4GB limit on a captured file's size. A "full quality" file has a maximum length of about 18.5 minutes (18.5 minutes is 1110 seconds at a data rate of 3.6 MB/sec—this works out to approximately 4GB). The "preview quality" mode can capture much longer files, since it captures at a low data rate (normally a few hundred KB/sec—less than a tenth of the full-quality data rate). To work around this issue, keep your captures relatively short. You can always edit them together using video editing software.

SYMPTOM 38-15   When capturing, you get an error such as "Cannot capture—the data rate on C: is less than the required rate"   Many video capture packages (especially for digital video) require that the hard drive receiving the captured video be able to sustain some minimum data transfer rate (such as 4 MB/sec). This data rate is necessary in order to transfer the video from the signal source to the hard drive *without* any loss of data. Any lost data will show up as dropped frames, and video with dropped frames plays back with visible "stutter," making the captured footage unusable. Captured video that is "jerky" or "stutters" in this fashion and can be corrected only by recapturing the video until no frames are dropped.

Low data rates and data loss can be influenced by many factors (refer to the previous "Audio/Video Sync Issues" section). If your hard drives cannot support the minimum required data rate, you may not have UDMA support enabled for the drive(s). Check whether UDMA support is enabled on your hard drives:

1.   Open your Device Manager and double-click Disk Drives.

2.   Double-click the device GENERIC IDE TYPE *xx* (*xx* is some two-digit number, usually 01, 02, and so forth).

3.   Click the Settings tab.

4.   In the section marked Options, select the DMA check box. If you do *not* have a check box called DMA, then you probably do not have the UDMA driver loaded or your hard drives do not support UDMA (or both).

5.   You'll get a message stating that you may want to contact your hard drive vendor to ensure that the setting is supported. Click OK.

6.   You'll be prompted to reboot your system. Click OK.

7.   When the system reboots, recheck to see that DMA support is enabled, and run any video capture benchmarking utility again to detect the performance of your hard drive(s). If the drive(s) indicate an adequate data rate, try your capture again.

SYMPTOM 38-16   You receive the error "Unable to capture video, the video source is not stable"   In most cases, you've selected the incorrect video source format. Verify that you have the correct video standard (NTSC, PAL, or SECAM) selected for your capture device.

SYMPTOM 38-17   You receive a "copy protection" error when you try to capture video   If you've been playing a DVD video—and it has copy protection—the copy protection may not be disabled when the DVD video stops playing. So, after you play a copy-protected DVD video, you may not be able to record any video with a video recorder connected to your capture card. To disable this "accidental" copy protection, restart your computer. You may want to check for a patch to update your DVD video player so that it will properly disable the copy protection when you shut it down.

SYMPTOM 38-18   You find zero frames captured, one frame captured, or that line playback is frozen on the first frame   This is almost always an IRQ issue. The IRQ assigned to the capture card is probably assigned as "edge trigger" instead of "level trigger." Go to your CMOS Setup, select your PnP configuration menu, look for IRQ Activated By, and make sure that this is set to "level." Otherwise, check for IRQ conflicts between devices on the system, or try relocating the video capture card in a high-priority PCI slot.

SYMPTOM 38-19   **The PC capture window is displaying only part of the video clip**
In virtually all cases, you have not selected the correct video standard (for example, you've selected PAL instead of NTSC). Go to the Properties dialog box for your capture software, select the Video tab, and select the correct video standard to match your video source.

SYMPTOM 38-20   **Colors appear washed out or bleeding**   This can occur either while viewing the video image before capture or during the actual playback of an image file. If the problem manifests itself before capture, begin by checking the signal quality from your video source, such as a VCR or video camera. A loose or damaged cable or a poor-quality video source can result in signal degradation at the video capture board.

If the video signal and connections are intact (and the signal looks good on a monitor, such as a TV set), the problem may be in the Windows video driver being used. Better color depth in the video driver will result in better color quality in the video capture. In virtually all cases, a 16-color video driver (generic VGA) is totally inappropriate for video capture applications—a 256-color driver is considered to be the minimum. If you're already using a 256-color video driver, try an upgrade to a 32K, 64K, or 16M color driver. You may have to contact the manufacturer of the particular video board to obtain an advanced video driver for Windows 9x/Me.

SYMPTOM 38-21   **The video signal appears to be weak or washed out even though the video signal source is acceptable**   This is typical when a composite video signal output is being sent to the video capture board as well as to a stand-alone monitor through a Y-connector. Composite output signals are usually power balanced for *one* connection load *only*. When the load on a composite output is not balanced properly, the video signal at your capture board will not contain enough power (signal degradation will occur). Try connecting the video signal *directly* to the video capture board.

SYMPTOM 38-22   **You get a "Vertical Sync" error when trying to capture**   Chances are that you have an IRQ conflict. Check the IRQ assigned to the video card's PCI slot in the Device Manager under Windows 9x/Me. If the PCI slot that the video card is in is being used by another device, you need to reassign the PCI slot for the video board a different IRQ. This can be done through your system's CMOS Setup. If *no* IRQ is being assigned to the PCI slot the video card is in, that can also be a problem. Once again, you can assign an IRQ to the PCI slot through the CMOS Setup. There could also be an IRQ conflict with the video capture driver. To check this, look in the Control Panel under Multimedia. Click the Advanced tab and then look under Video Capture Drivers, where you'll see an entry such as Diamond Multimedia Capture Driver. Double-click it and then click the Settings option, which enables you to change the IRQ of the capture driver. Try a free IRQ, or free an IRQ.

SYMPTOM 38-23   **Up to 50 percent of small frames are being dropped (large frames appear to capture properly)**   This symptom may occur in systems using fast 32-bit SCSI adapter boards and is almost always due to the effects of double-buffering in the SMARTDRV.EXE utility. If possible, try to disable SmartDrive in the CONFIG.SYS file. If SmartDrive cannot be disabled (usually because doing so would have adverse side-effects on other devices that rely on SmartDrive's caching), try capturing video at a larger frame size, such as 320×240, *before* capturing at a small frame size. Doing this lets SmartDrive adjust to the data needs of the larger frame size, so subsequent captures at a smaller frame size should work correctly until the system is rebooted. An updated video capture driver may also provide better performance.

SYMPTOM 38-24   **When capturing video, the corresponding screen image appears broken-up or jerky**   If the image being previewed on the screen prior to capture looks smooth, and the captured video looks smooth when played back, you should suspect that the customer's hardware platform is not quite fast enough to update the screen while capturing. This is not necessarily a problem, since many video capture applications (such as Video for Windows) are designed to sacrifice screen updates for the sake of smooth captures. If you need a smooth display during capture, start by relieving any unnecessary processing loads from the system:

1. Close other Windows 9x/Me applications running in the background.
2. Close any DOS applications running through a window.
3. Make sure the Windows disk cache is set to at least 2MB (4MB if possible).
4. Set audio capture specifications to 8-bit, mono, 11 kHz sample frequency for the lowest audio processing overhead.

SYMPTOM 38-25   **The video capture board is working, but captures are occurring very slowly**   In most cases, very slow recording performance is the result of an IRQ conflict between the capture board and another device on the system. Evaluate the components in your system or run a diagnostic (such as Microsoft's MSD or the Device Manager) to locate and identify any unused interrupts in your system. If you are faced with a *jumper-only* capture board, set the jumper(s) to use a free valid IRQ. If your capture board requires a software setup, run its setup utility and choose another valid interrupt (such as 9, 10, 11, or 15).

SYMPTOM 38-26   **You find that you cannot use the Super Compressor option in Video for Windows**   This is not an actual user problem. The Super Compressor is an offline compression utility that compresses and stores video files captured at 320×240, 15 fps at the same data rate as CD-ROM (150 KB/sec). Video for Windows version 1.0 does not support the Super Compressor function when used with Indeo 3.0 device drivers. Only the Quick Compressor in the VIDEDIT utility is available. Later versions of Video for Windows use this function, and you should upgrade your version of Video for Windows at your earliest convenience. This is typically not an issue in modern video capture devices that use high-compression codecs such as MPEG.

SYMPTOM 38-27   **You can't capture more than one frame of video**   This is a problem reported with the Intel SVR III. While trying to capture video, the capture process stops after one frame, but the capture application acts as if it is still capturing and you must click Stop to exit. The YUV9 video format always seems to exhibit this problem. The RGB24 video format seems to work at lower window sizes. There are no problems capturing still images or sequences of still images. This problem appears to be related to an improper or incomplete installation of Windows 95 Direct Draw drivers. You can download and install DirectX 8.0a or later drivers from Microsoft's Web site at **www.microsoft.com/directx**.

SYMPTOM 38-28   **The color video being captured is shown as black and white**   There are two possible causes for this. First, the capture window (such as the Video for Windows VIDCAP utility) is set to receive a Composite video source, but the video signal is being fed to the capture board through its S-Video cable. Check the configuration settings under your video capture options. Make sure that the correct input type (Composite or S-Video) is selected in the video capture utility.

Another possible source of problems is a bad connection. Check that the video signal is indeed color and that a good cable is securely attached to the capture board. Try a different video source. Next, check that the capture board is inserted properly and completely in the expansion slot. If any modules or sub-boards are attached to the capture board, see that they are secured correctly. If problems persist, try another capture board.

SYMPTOM 38-29   **The video image shown in the capture window appears torn or bent at the top**   This symptom is typical of signals being supplied by VCRs (or camcorders used as VCRs) and is almost always the result of a weak video synchronization signal from the signal source. This problem often can be rectified by using a different (stronger) signal source (for example, another camcorder or VCR). If you're using a VCR signal source, make sure that the Video for Windows VCR box is checked.

Use the S-Video signal source if possible, since S-Video signals are less prone to noise and losses than are composite signals. Also make sure that the video cable feeding your capture board is not lying parallel to power cables, since the power cable can induce unwanted noise into the video signal. Try placing the video capture board in another expansion slot as far as possible from the system power supply and other expansion boards, since electrical signals generated by other boards may cause interference with the video data. As a sanity check, make sure that any modules or sub-boards for the video capture device are attached properly.

SYMPTOM 38-30   **When capturing video, you get the error "No frames captured. Confirm that vertical sync interrupts are configured and enabled"**   The Intel SVR III has some known issues, but these may also affect other capture devices:

- The Adaptec 1542B and 1542C 16-bit ISA SCSI controllers were tested with the SVR III using IRQ 11 and I/O address 330h. When the SVR III was also set to IRQ 11, the VIDCAP utility in Video for Windows returned blank video (no frames were captured) and then returned the error message. Reconfigure the system devices to avoid IRQ conflicts.

- The Media Vision Pro Audio Spectrum 16, a 16-bit sound board, was tested with the SVR III using IRQ 5, IRQ 15, and I/O addresses 220h and 388h. When the SVR III and the Pro Audio Spectrum 16 were both set to IRQ 11, the SVR III software detected a conflict, and Video for Windows returned the error message. Reconfigure the system devices to avoid IRQ conflicts.

- A Diamond VLB Speedstar Pro Video board using IRQ 2 by default can also caused this fault. Disable the use of IRQ 2 on the Diamond Video Board.

- SiS FI2 P54C motherboards using an Award BIOS also have been known to suffer this problem. You'll need to go into BIOS and tweak the chipset configuration. Change the ISA BUS Clk Frequency entry from PCI Clk Divided by 3 to PCI Clk Divided by 4.

This changes numerous settings in the chipset configuration. For example, SRAM, Read Pulse, SRAM Burst, and Refresh all switch to a slower value.

SYMPTOM 38-31   **You see artifacts when capturing video at high data rates**   When capturing at high data rates (such as when using 640×480 resolutions and 30 fps frame rates), occasional problems have been noted on some PCs—most notably with Intel SVR III or Pro capture products. *Artifacts*, which resemble black horizontal lines, may appear in your preview or capture window. Try repeating the capture (the best strategy if the problem occurs only infrequently). If the artifacts occur too frequently for you to recapture, you're probably trying to capture at too high a data rate for your computer's PCI bus to handle. Reduce PCI bus traffic by lowering the data rate of the video you're capturing:

- Use a lower frame rate.
- Use a lower window resolution.
- If you're using RGB24 as the Video Format, try using YUV9 instead.
- Use more compression (a lower-quality setting).
- Turn off the preview mode.

If you continue to find horizontal black lines in both preview and captured video (even at 320×240 resolution) when using the YUV9 Video Format, your computer's PCI chipset may be programmed to disable a feature called "host memory write-posting." When enabled, this feature allows your PCI chipset to write to memory at its maximum speed. When write-posting is disabled, your PCI bus performance can be significantly reduced. Write-posting is enabled in different ways on different systems. Some computers may permit this feature to be controlled through the CMOS Setup, while other computers may require a BIOS upgrade from the system manufacturer.

SYMPTOM 38-32   **You see artifacts when capturing video using certain PCI graphics cards**   The method used by some graphics cards and their drivers to utilize the PCI bus can sometimes cause horizontal line artifacts. For example, Intel has verified a problem using the Number Nine 9FX Motion 771 graphics card (which uses the S3 Vision968 graphics chipset) together with the SVR III. The problems seem to occur when the display color depth is 16-bit or 32-bit and when "preview" is on during the capture process. This symptom also seems to occur in files captured at 320×240 resolution at 15 fps using either the YUV9 or RGB24 video format. Try setting the graphics display to 8-bit (256-color) mode (this has no effect on the quality of the captured video—only the previewed video). You might also try disabling "preview" during the capture process.

SYMPTOM 38-33   **Systems with SiS 5596 or 5511 PCI chipsets lock up when using a video capture device**   This is a known issue with the Video Logic Captivator PCI board and similar devices. SiS has identified the problem, and a fix is available through a BIOS update. Contact the system maker or motherboard manufacturer for a BIOS update.

SYMPTOM 38-34   **Systems lock up when running video capture devices on PCs with Phoenix BIOS**   Some PCs are known to lock up with the Video Logic Captivator PCI card installed (affected products include members of the DEC Venturis family). This problem has been traced to the Phoenix v.1.6 BIOS. All PCs using Phoenix v.1.6 BIOS should be upgraded to Phoenix BIOS v.1.9 or later.

SYMPTOM 38-35   **You cannot use the capture device on a system with a SiS PCI chipset**   This is a known problem with the Intel SVR III, and is due to a driver compatibility issue. The SVR III driver 1.2 will cause the system to lock up when launching the capture utility. You can determine the current driver version by opening the README.TXT file on the SVR III CD-ROM. Download and install the version 1.3 driver or later (SVR3-14.EXE from Intel at **www.intel.com**). Otherwise, you may need to upgrade the video capture device. You can find out which PCI chipset is in your system by checking the PCI chipset in the Device Manager:

1. Click Start, Settings, and Control Panel.

2. Double-click the System icon.

3. Go to the Device Manager tab.

4. Click the plus (+) sign in front of System Devices and look for a reference to the PCI To ISA Bridge, as in Figure 38-8.

SYMPTOM 38-36   You cannot use the capture device on a system with an S3 chipset-based video card   If your system uses an Award BIOS version 4.51pg, Windows 95 Release 2 (OSR2), and an S3 968-based video graphics card, you may experience system lockups when trying to launch your capture program. This is a known problem that has been seen with the Intel SVR III and the Diamond Stealth 64, as well as with the Number Nine Motion 771. This problem arises from a memory address conflict between the Intel SVR III and the S3-based video graphics card. According to Intel, the S3 apparently requests only 32MB of virtual memory rather than the 64MB it actually requires. If the BIOS allocates the memory for the capture device (such as the SVR III) right above the S3 board's range, the system will lockup. To correct this problem, you need to change the memory address range used by the video capture device:

1. Open the Device Manager and double-click the capture device (for example, the Intel Smart Video Recorder III). Ignore the exclamation point next to it, if it has one.

2. Click the Resources tab, and then uncheck the box titled Use Automatic Settings.

3. Double-click the memory range and enter an address of **FFFBF000 - FFFBFFFF** (the spaces on each side of the "-" symbol are needed). Click OK.

4. If Windows 9x/Me returns the message "The setting you have chosen conflicts with another device," click NO, and then scroll with the up and down arrows next to the address range until no conflict is noted. Click OK.

Some installations have also noted that reinstalling Windows 95a or installing a video graphics card *not* based on the S3 968 chipset may also correct this problem.

SYMPTOM 38-37   The live video window display has a gray background   This problem sometimes happens with the Video Logic Captivator family. There are some PCs that have a problem displaying live video using Captivator Pro/TV and instead show a gray background. If the window is moved around or covered by another window, then the Windows background may show through—it's as though the live video is transparent. Verify that all cabling and software for the video/MPEG device is installed properly.

PCs using the VIA VT481/495 chipset on the motherboard are known to have this problem (such as the Unisys MPI46664-539 model 486/66 MHz). The problem is due to nonstandard ISA bus timing used by the motherboard, so sending data to the video/MPEG device (such as the Captivator Pro/TV) registers results in the card being reset by accident. There is no known workaround or patch except to use a different video/MPEG device.

SYMPTOM 38-38   The video device locks up in 8-bit (256-color) display modes
This problem is known to occur with Prolab VideoWorks, but it can also occur with other video/MPEG devices. You might experience system lockups on PCs when displaying live video in 8-bit display modes with DirectX 5 installed. This problem occurs only with graphics cards that use *color keying* rather than

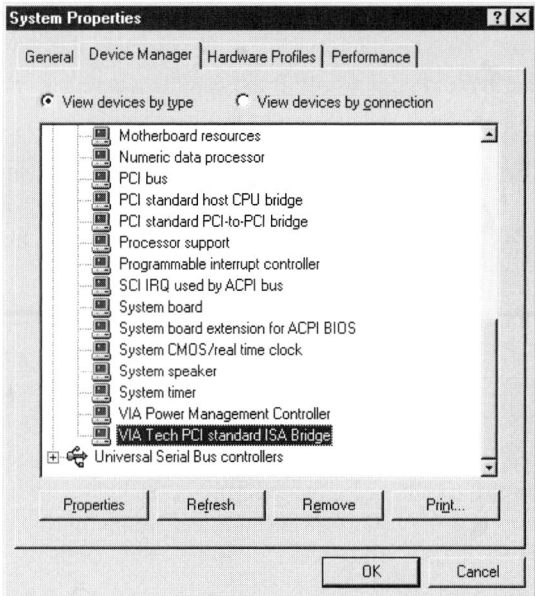

FIGURE 38-8   Locating the PCI to ISA bridge in using Device Manager

hardware overlay to display live video (for example, S3 Vision 968–based graphics cards). The only known workaround at this time is to run in a 16-bit display mode, upgrade DirectX, or replace the video device entirely.

SYMPTOM 38-39   **CU-SeeMe video software locks the system when it tries to start the video capture system**   This is a problem between CU-SeeMe software and the initialization of your VIDCAP driver. You must make sure the VIDCAP mode is set to 24-bit RGB or 16-bit RGB *before* you start CU-SeeMe. For example, suppose you're using Ulead software to capture in MJPEG format and then you exit that software—your capture settings are stored in the VIDCAP driver. The moment you start CU-SeeMe, it tries to communicate with the VIDCAP driver, but it won't work because the VIDCAP software is set to MJPEG, and CU-SeeMe understands only RGB data. You have to launch your video capture software again and set it to RGB (and also QCIF size image), and then exit; you then should be able to start CU-SeeMe.

SYMPTOM 38-40   **Your video adapter supports the "overlay surface" mode, but the video capture system diagnostics report "primary" or "not supported"**   In most cases, the problem here is related to the video adapter, its configuration, or the drivers being used. Check the following points:

■ *Change your color depth.* The color depth may be set too high or too low. Set the color depth to 16-bit in Display Properties and retry the video capture diagnostic test.

■ *Change your resolution.* The desktop area may be set too high. Set the desktop area in Display Properties to 800×600 (or lower) and retry the video capture diagnostic test.

■ *Change your driver.* You may be using a generic Windows driver or an older version of your graphics card. Your video card's driver may also be corrupt. Reinstall the latest version of your video card's driver.

■ *Check the DirectX installation.* You may not have DirectX installed properly. Download and install the latest version of DirectX (such as 8.0a or later).

SYMPTOM 38-41   **The correct overlay type is reported, but the video in your capture window is not "full motion"**   In most cases, the capture application (such as VIDCAP or Adobe Premiere) has Overlay selected, but Overlay must also be selected while recording. Look at the following two examples:

■ In VIDCAP, open the Options menu and make sure a check mark appears in front of the Overlay option. If no check mark appears, click Overlay. Next, go back to the Options menu and select Video Display. Verify that a check mark appears in front of Overlay While Recording. If no check mark is present, click the box and one will appear. Save your changes and reboot if necessary.

■ In Premiere 4.2, open a capture window and then make sure a check mark appears in front of the Overlay option in the Movie Capture menu. If there is no check mark, click Overlay and a check mark will appear. Next, go back to the Movie Capture menu and select Video Display. Verify that a check mark appears in front of Overlay While Recording. If no check mark is present, click the box and one will appear.

SYMPTOM 38-42   **The quality of your overlay image appears poor**   There are several possible issues that can have this effect on the overlay window. First, check the quality settings for the video in your overlay window. For example, if you're capturing in VIDCAP, open the Options menu and select Video Display. Set Overlay Scaling to High Resolution. If you're capturing in Premiere 4.2, open a capture window and then use the Movie Capture menu to select Video Display. In the Video Display window, set Overlay Scaling to High Resolution.

The color depth or desktop area (resolution) on your video card may be set too high. If you reduce the color depth and/or the desktop area under Display Properties, the quality of the overlay may improve. Overlay is normally somewhat grainy, and the colors are a bit washed out in comparison to the NTSC/PAL output. Remember that the quality of the overlay window does not affect the capture or playback quality. Finally, you might need to change the memory range that the video capture card is using:

1. Click Start, select Settings, and then click Control Panel.
2. Double-click the System icon.
3. Select the Device Manager tab.
4. Click the plus (+) sign next to Sound, Video And Game Controllers.
5. Double-click your video capture card listing to review its properties.
6. Select the Resources tab.
7. Disable (uncheck) the Use Automatic Settings option.
8. Highlight the Memory Range resource and click Change.
9. Select a new memory range that has a different first digit (either number or letter) from the range that was originally used. You may have to try several different ranges to find one that works.

SYMPTOM 38-43   **You get a VxD VMM error when capturing with VIDCAP**   You may have to set VIDCAP to capture to memory. As a rule, always capture to *disk* when capturing in VIDCAP. This setting is located by selecting Video on the Capture menu. The default VIDCAP setting is Capture To Disk, and that is always the recommended setting.

SYMPTOM 38-44   **You receive a GPF or IPF error during scene detection**   You're probably using a buggy or outdated driver or application software. Check whether the video capture device manufacturer has an update or patch that you can download and install to correct this type of problem. In the meantime, you may be able to work around this problem by turning off "scene detection" in your video capture software.

SYMPTOM 38-45   **The video capture software will not capture when you click the Capture button**   You're probably using a buggy or outdated driver or application software. Check whether the video capture device manufacturer has an update or patch that you can download and install to correct this type of problem.

SYMPTOM 38-46   **The hue slider won't work properly in capture mode**   You're probably using a buggy or outdated driver or application software. Check whether the video capture device manufacturer has an update or patch that you can download and install to correct this type of problem.

SYMPTOM 38-47   **The video capture software locks up when you try to capture**   You're probably using a buggy or outdated driver or application software. Check whether the video capture device manufacturer has an update or patch that you can download and install to correct this type of problem.

Check for an audio driver problem. For example, the Studio DV10plus video capture system can experience problems with the Creative Labs Sound Blaster PCI 128 (driver version 4.05.1205) and Gateway G6 computers with on-board audio that use the Creative Labs Audio PCI 64D (driver version 4.05.1135B). You can use the Device Manager to see if you have any "offending" devices. Often, updating the sound card's drivers may clear some compatibility problems.

Try capturing using the basic VIDCAP applet that accompanies your capture device. Also try disabling the audio device in Device Manager:

1.   Click Start, select Settings, click Control Panel, and then double-click the System icon.

2.   When the System Properties dialog box appears, click the Device Manager tab.

3.   Click the plus (+) sign next to Sound, Video And Game Controllers.

4.   Locate your main audio driver and double-click it.

5.   At the bottom of the General tab, select the check box labeled Disable In The Hardware Profile.

6.   If you check the Device Manager again, you'll see a red *X* indicating that the sound card is disabled.

7.   Try your capture again.

If you can capture with VIDCAP or with the sound card disabled, chances are that you have an audio capture driver problem. Check for updated audio drivers or check with the video capture manufacturer for updates or patches that might improve the compatibility with your sound card.

SYMPTOM 38-48   **You get a pink screen when testing your video input**   This is usually a video overlay or DirectX compatibility problem. Check with your video card and sound card manufacturer to make sure that you're using the latest drivers for each device. You may also need to download and install the latest version of DirectX (such as DirectX 8.0a) from Microsoft's Web site. If the trouble persists, try changing your display settings (for example, change your resolution and color depth).

SYMPTOM 38-49   **When outputting video to tape (or TV), the video window on the monitor continues to show video**   Normally, the clip window on the PC monitor should appear gray or black *without* the video playing there. In many cases, the Output To Video option is not activated in the video capture display driver. This driver is always in operation when a capture program is started (or an AVI compressed with MJPEG has been opened). This driver runs in the background after being activated and can be brought to the foreground by pressing ALT-TAB. Activate the Output To Video feature by selecting the appropriate check box in this window.

It is also possible that the AVI file to be output is *not* compressed with MJPEG. Some video capture hardware will not output a video file to tape or TV unless that file is in the correct format. You may need to rebuild the video clip so that it has been properly compressed with MJPEG, and then try the output again.

SYMPTOM 38-50   **Your audio signal drops out during the capture**   In most cases, the problem is with the video capture software rather than the hardware. For example, Studio DV software version 1.03 fixes this type of issue. If there's a README file available, review it to see what the file fixes *before* you download the file. Make sure that the video editing software is *not* running when you apply the patch.

SYMPTOM 38-51   **You can't import bitmap or still image files into the Intel DVP 4.0 application**   If you can import WAV and AVI files but can't import BMP and other static image files, you need to move three files from the DVP 4.0 directory to the \Windows\System directory: DSEQFI40.DLL, TGAFIL40.DLL, and FLIFIL40.DLL. These DLL files are copied to the DVP 4.0 directory by the DVP 4.0 setup program, and in very rare cases, the location of the files results in the error "Can't import this media type" when trying to import single-image file formats. Manually moving these DLL files to the \Windows\System directory should fix the problem.

SYMPTOM 38-52   **You get an error such as "The following entry should be in your system.ini file: [drivers] Msvideo=stlthcap.drv"**   You're then asked to click OK to add or to click Cancel to exit. This symptom means that, for some reason, the capture driver for your capture card was not installed in the SYSTEM.INI file. All you'd need to do is click OK to have the software add it for you. The driver might have been replaced if you've had another capture driver (from a different video capture board) installed recently. Click OK to reinstall the current capture software.

SYMPTOM 38-53   **Your video playback appears "jittery" after rendering the final MPEG file**   In most cases, you'll find that you've reversed the field order (A-B or B-A) during the final render of the MPEG project. You can either re-render the video clip in frame mode or use field order A (RRS) or field order B (RRG).

SYMPTOM 38-54   **The video playback appears to "tear"**   In virtually all cases, the monitor's refresh rate is too high (for example, above 60 Hz). You can usually reduce the monitor's refresh rate below 75 Hz through the Display Properties dialog box.

SYMPTOM 38-55   **You see the error "MMTASK ERROR—GPF IR30.DLL 0003:0B85" when trying to play a captured file**   You encounter this error when trying to play a captured file with a utility like Media Player or VIDEDIT, and there is video and sound in the same file (it does not occur if audio is not captured). The audio track can be played if video is not played. This problem is known to be related to drive overlay software. For example, a Western Digital 1GB drive using an overlay software is known to conflict with the IR30.DLL file. Drive overlay software is used so that DOS can read a drive with more than 1024 cylinders. If you upgrade the motherboard BIOS or drive controller to support LBA mode operation, you can eliminate the use of overlay software, and the error should disappear.

SYMPTOM 38-56   **The video playback is choppy or contains dropped frames**   This typically is not related to the video capture board. For most video capture systems, playback speed and quality is very dependent on machine speed—faster machines with higher-performance equipment will play back video files better than slower, simpler systems. Make sure that your customer's system is equipped with at least the minimum amount of hardware to ensure a proper playback. If playback performance still seems choppy, your customer may have to upgrade the hardware platform. If a platform upgrade is out of the question, try reducing the system load during capture and playback. For example, close all unused Windows and DOS applications, close any unused data files, and select a larger virtual memory size.

This is also a symptom that appears frequently in EISA systems—even on fast EISA systems up to 50 MHz. In many cases, the afflicted EISA system CMOS was not reconfigured properly after adding memory. An EISA configuration disk may have to be run to cache new memory, even though the new memory may be recognized correctly. Try booting the EISA system from its configuration disk and adjusting the system from there.

SYMPTOM 38-57   **You see an initial flash of color when playing back video files**   Chances are that your customer is trying to play video files using an older version of VIDEDIT or VIDCAP utilities in Video for Windows. This is a known problem with these older utilities, and current versions of the software should correct the problem. Until you can download and install updated versions of Video for Windows (**www.microsoft.com**), there is little that you can do other than play back video clips using the Windows Media Player or Media Browser.

SYMPTOM 38-58   **No sound is heard during playback**   Not all video capture products capture sound at the same time video is captured. If no sound was captured (intentionally), no sound will be heard when the video clip is played back through Video for Windows. Most modern capture boards do capture sound and video simultaneously as long as audio is made available on the composite or S-Video signal cables, and the Audio box is checked in the Video Capture options dialog box. Also check the Audio Setup and Audio Level settings in Video for Windows before proceeding.

If all is well with Video for Windows, check to make sure that sound was provided to the capture device. If sound was recorded, you should check the configuration of your sound board. The sound board should contain appropriate hardware settings (such as I/O, IRQ, and DMA). The proper Windows device drivers for the sound board must also be installed, and the driver must be loaded with other Windows drivers. Missing Windows sound drivers will inhibit sound. If the system is configured properly and sound is available but no sound is recorded, the capture board may be defective—try another capture board. If sound is being captured by the sound card, the sound card may be defective.

SYMPTOM 38-59   **When playing video, the system locks up when power management features are enabled**   This typically requires a cold reboot. Unfortunately, video playback is often incompatible with a PC's power management features, such as APM or ACPI (even screen savers can cause this problem). For the immediate future, disable all APM, ACPI, or screen savers when using video playback features. For the long term, check with the capture card maker to see if new drivers or playback software is available that can support power management or screen savers.

SYMPTOM 38-60   **The system locks up when changing resolutions or color depths while using MPEG playback or video capture functions**   This is a common problem that is typically caused by the behavior of the MPEG or capture software. You must close all MPEG and capture functions prior to changing resolutions or color depths.

SYMPTOM 38-61   **There are sound gaps, and the image appears choppy during playback**   This is a symptom associated with capture boards (such as Intel's SVR family) that integrate audio and video into a single AVI capture file. The integrated file prevents audio and video from slipping out of sync. However, playing synchronized capture files requires substantial processing power. If a system is not fast enough, sound can "hiccup" and the video can be choppy. Unfortunately, this kind of playback problem is not a fault or defect—it is a limitation of slower PC systems (usually 486-type systems).

First, remove any Windows or DOS applications running in the background so that Windows can concentrate on Video for Windows or another playback application. If playback does not improve enough, try running the playback in a smaller window. For example, try playing back in a 160×120 window instead of a 320×240 window. Smaller windows require less processing overhead for each frame. Beyond that, the hardware platform may need to be upgraded.

SYMPTOM 38-62   **Blue or green flesh tones appear in the live video and MPEG playback**   This corruption is often caused when an MPEG player application (for example, MPEG Player 4.0) is loaded on a system that already has a video/MPEG player installed. This problem has been reported with the Captivator Pro/TV by Video Logic. You can correct the problem by reinstalling the video/MPEG driver for the particular device:

1.   Close down all MPEG and live windows.

2.   Start a DOS window.

3.   Select the directory where the video/MPEG driver file resides (for the Captivator, the driver is PSTREAM.DRV, normally located in the VLPOWER directory).

4.   Rename this driver file to something else.

5.   Expand the driver file from your original MPEG player installation disk into your current directory, such as: **EXPAND A:\PSTREAM.DR_ PSTREAM.DRV** (assuming that the Microsoft EXPAND utility is on the path).

6.   Exit the DOS window and shut down Windows.

7.   Restart Windows and check the video again.

SYMPTOM 38-63   **You cannot scale an MPEG movie clip to full screen when using 16.7 million colors**   This kind of problem is known to be linked with the Diamond MVP 2000, but it can occur on other video capture/playback platforms. You are usually missing an entry from the video device's INI file. For the MVP 2000, you can add the following line to the [System] section of your STLTHMVP.INI file if you wish to play back MPEG full-screen in 16M color mode:

```
NoVideoSizeLimit=1
```

If you are experiencing lockups when playing MPEG clips full-screen in a 16M color mode, you may be encountering bandwidth limitations on your system. If you encounter this problem, you should change the following line to the [System] section of your STLTHMVP.INI file:

```
NoVideoSizeLimit=0
```

SYMPTOM 38-64   **The video looks grainy (or otherwise has poor quality) when playing back or recording**   This is a symptom that can occur across *all* video capture devices. Image quality is closely related to the color depth of your Windows video driver. Many older Windows 3.1x installations and some low-end Windows 95 platforms use the default 16-color VGA video driver supplied with the Windows operating system. The 16 colors are almost never adequate to define a video image, so the image will look washed out or very grainy. You must install a 256-color (or higher) video driver written for the video board in your system. Contact the video board manufacturer for its latest Windows 9x/Me drivers.

SYMPTOM 38-65   **With Active Movie installed, the MPEG options do not show up as a device under Media Player**   If you install the MPEG video playback drivers while ActiveX (Active Movie) is installed on your system, you will not see the correct menu options in the Media Player. To correct this, uninstall the ActiveX software, and reinstall the MPEG video playback drivers. To remove the Active Movie portion of ActiveX:

1. Click the Start button, select Settings, and choose Control Panel.

2. In Control Panel, double-click the Multimedia icon.

3. Click the Advanced tab.

4. Click the plus (+) symbol next to Video Compression Codecs.

5. When a list of codecs appears, select Intel Indeo(R) Video Interactive 32-bit Driver [IV41], and then click the Properties button.

6. Click the Remove button.

7. Apply or OK the selection.

You are now ready to install the MPEG video player drivers and then reinstall the ActiveX software later.

 ActiveX (Active Movie) is included with most versions of Microsoft Internet Explorer 3.xx and later. If you install the ActiveX software *before* installing the MPEG video playback drivers, you will not have the option to use the MPEG video player for hardware MPEG playback.

Further Study

Aitech   www.aitech.com
Codec Central   www.icanstream.tv/CodecCentral/index.html
Hauppauge   www.hauppauge.com
Intel   www.intel.com
Matrox   www.matrox.com
Pinnacle Systems   www.miro.com
Video Logic   www.videologic.com

39

USB TROUBLESHOOTING

Ever since the earliest PCs, system designers, builders, and users have been searching for ways to ease the time and trouble normally associated with installing or upgrading new PC devices. The adoption of plug-and-play technology was the first major step forward, but it still required you to power down the PC, then add drivers and applets manually—even for devices used "outside the box" such as keyboards, mice, speakers, digital cameras, and so on.

By the early 1990s, designers envisioned the "next generation" of intelligent serial interface. This was dubbed the *Universal Serial Bus* (or simply USB). USB was originally developed by the seven key players in the PC industry: Compaq, DEC, IBM, Intel, Microsoft, NEC, and Northern Telecom and is now receiving broad acceptance in the PC industry. This chapter looks at the general concepts surrounding USB and offers a suite of troubleshooting procedures designed to ease problems with implementation and performance on Windows 9x/Me platforms.

Understanding USB

Traditional device installation continues to present serious problems for system integrators and end-users alike. PC resources (such as IRQs) are scarce, and the time required to install and configure an ever-greater array of devices—then troubleshoot the resulting resource conflicts—can quickly become significant (and expensive).

The USB interface simplifies the integration problems of many external peripheral devices such as printers, scanners, drives, and so on. With USB, there's no need to install cards into dedicated computer slots and reconfigure the system. USB will allow computer peripherals to be automatically configured as soon as they are physically attached—*without* the need to reboot a system or run the CMOS Setup routine. USB will also allow up to 127 USB devices to run simultaneously on a computer.

USB DEVICES

According to the USB SIG (**www.usb.org/**), the potential for USB devices is every bit as diverse as the personal computer itself. Telephones, modems, keyboards, mice, CD-ROM drives, joysticks, tape and floppy drives, scanners, digital cameras, and printers are just a few of the devices which have already been developed for USB. In addition, USB's 12Mbits/s data rate accommodates other unique peripherals, including MPEG-2 video-based products, data gloves, and digitizers. Since computer communication and telephony integration continue to be major growth areas for the PC, USB can also provide an interface for DSL and cable modems.

USB ARCHITECTURE NOTES

The current USB 1.1 architecture has two data rates: a 12Mbits/s rate for devices requiring increased bandwidth and a 1.5Mbits/s rate for lower-speed devices like joysticks and game pads. USB uses a *tiered star topology*, which means that some USB devices—called USB *hubs*—can serve as connection ports for other USB peripherals. Only *one* device needs to be plugged into the port at the PC (though the PC itself may support two or more hubs). Other devices can then be plugged into the hub. USB hubs may be embedded in such key devices as monitors, printers, and keyboards. Stand-alone hubs are also readily available. Hubs feature an *upstream* connection (pointed toward the PC) as well as multiple *downstream* ports (to allow the connection of additional peripheral devices). Up to 127 USB devices can be connected together in this way.

USB host controllers (which are a standard feature of most current PCI and AGP compliant chipsets) manage and control the driver software and data flow required by each peripheral connected to the bus. Users don't need to take any specific configuration action because all the configuration steps happen *automatically*—the USB host controller even allocates electrical power to the USB devices. USB hubs and host controllers can detect attachments and detachments of peripherals occurring downstream and supply appropriate levels of power to downstream devices as needed. Figure 39-1 illustrates a typical USB connector arrangement. The USB connection uses four pins:

Pin 1	Power
Pin 2	Signal (−)
Pin 3	Signal (+)
Pin 4	Ground

IMPLEMENTING USB

Virtually all new motherboards and systems are equipped with one or two USB ports (usually located in the back panel I/O area containing COM and LPT ports). In this case, it is simply a matter of attaching a USB hub (such as a USB keyboard), and then attaching USB devices to the hub. For systems without USB, you'll need a motherboard upgrade that contains a USB-complaint chipset such as Intel's 82801BA I/O Controller Hub (ICH2) used on the D850GB motherboard. Most current ATX and NLX motherboards will sport at least one USB port. Once the new motherboard is in place, USB devices can be attached.

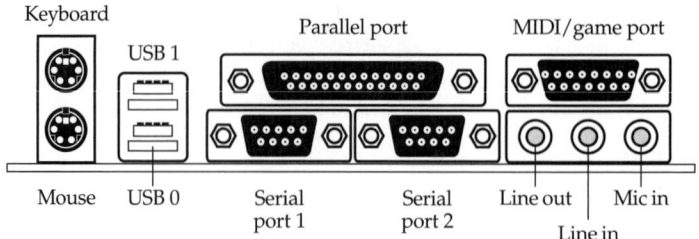

Keyboard

USB 1

Parallel port

MIDI/game port

Mouse   USB 0   Serial
port 1   Serial
port 2   Line out   Mic in
Line in

FIGURE 39-1   A dual-USB port arrangement

If you'd rather *not* upgrade a motherboard to support USB, you may be able to install a PCI-based USB expansion card.

ENABLING USB

USB ports on the motherboard are controlled through the BIOS and are enabled through the system's CMOS Setup utility. Once you've entered the CMOS Setup, locate the USB configuration settings section. These are typically found under the Input/Output Ports configuration menu or the Peripheral Setup menu. If the USB ports are not already enabled by default, you must enable the port(s) before you can use USB. In some cases, you must also assign an IRQ for the USB controller once it's enabled.

USB AND WINDOWS 95

One of the main limiting factors with USB is the operating system itself. The initial release of Windows 95 does *not* support USB (even though the motherboard and BIOS may support USB perfectly). As a minimum, you'll need to be running Windows 95 OSR 2.1 (preferably OSR 2.5) with the USB Supplement in order to implement USB. Many of the bugs and glitches that remain with USB under OSR 2.x can be easily corrected by upgrading the operating system to Windows 98/Me. USB is not supported in the real mode (DOS), though some motherboard designs incorporate a BIOS that will offer real-mode support for USB keyboards (and sometimes mice).

USB HOST CONTROLLER TYPES

There are two types of USB host controllers: the UHCI (*Universal Host Controller Interface*) and the OHCI (*Open Host Controller Interface*). The choice of host controller can have an impact on USB device compatibility. USB devices often work fine with UHCI, but not all USB devices will function properly with OHCI (for example, see Symptom 39-8). This is because many OHCI implementations do not fully comply with industry specifications. Devices used on OHCI platforms may work erratically or may not even be detected. Use the following steps to determine the type of USB host controller in your system:

1.   Click Start | Settings, then choose Control Panel.

2.   Double-click the System icon, then select the Device Manager tab.

3.   Expand the Universal Serial Bus Controller entry by clicking the plus sign (+) in front of it.

4.   You will see the Controller Information dialog. Look for Universal (for UHCI) or Open (for OHCI).

If you cannot get your USB peripheral to work properly (if at all), and you find that you *do* have an OHCI controller, you should contact the motherboard or system manufacturer for updated USB drivers. When you cannot resolve OHCI controller problems, your only real solution to the problem is to exchange the USB version of the peripheral for a PCI bus controller version.

Supported Controllers   Windows 98 and Windows Me support two USB host controller standards: Open Host Controller Interface (OHCI) and Universal Host Controller Interface (UHCI). Windows 98 and Windows Me include drivers that support each of these hardware standards. Windows 98 and Windows Me include drivers for the following OHCI USB host controllers:

- Symbios
- RealTech (based on OPTi hardware)
- CMD Technology (except the REV_04 version)
- Silicon Integrated Systems
- OPTi
- Ali
- National Semiconductor
- NEC

Other OHCI host controllers that comply to the OHCI specification are supported by Windows 98 as a *standard* OHCI USB host controller. Windows 98 and Windows Me include drivers for the following UHCI USB host controllers:

- Intel
- VIA Technologies

Note that other UHCI host controllers that comply to the UHCI specification are supported by Windows 98 as a standard UHCI USB host controller but not all versions of all controllers are supported by the drivers included with Windows 98 and Windows Me.

USB 2.0

The major developers of the original USB specification (that is, Compaq, Hewlett-Packard, Intel, Lucent Microsoft, NEC, Philips, and more) are hard at work creating the "next generation" of USB. This continued development will basically make USB a much *faster* interface. Today, the USB standard (dubbed USB 1.1) will support low-to-mid speed devices at data rates from 1.5Mbps and 12Mbps. The development of USB 2.0 promises to improve this performance by 30 to 40 times—yielding data transfer speeds up to 480Mbps. By supporting faster data rates, USB 2.0 can handle more sophisticated high-bandwidth devices like video cameras. However, since USB 2.0 is intended to be fully backward-compatible with the existing USB 1.1 standard, you'll use the same cables and devices that you have *now*—your current USB devices will *not* be obsolete. The only thing you may need to do is upgrade your USB hubs (if you have lots of USB devices attached) in order to support USB 2.0.

USB 2.0 has been released, but USB 2.0–compliant motherboards may not be appearing until late 2001. If you're interested in learning more about USB, or you want to stay on top of the developments surrounding USB 2.0, check in with the USB Web site at **www.usb.org/developers/usb20/index.html**.

USB Troubleshooting

In spite of its great promise, the early path toward USB has been *anything* but straightforward. Chipset issues, BIOS versions, and operating system bugs (along with a surprisingly slow initial release of USB peripherals by the PC industry) presented serious problems for USB users. This part of the chapter examines many of the more common USB symptoms that you may encounter.

KNOWN USB ISSUES

Before you jump right into the symptoms involved with USB, there are a series of known device-specific issues under Windows 98/Me that you should be familiar with:

- **3Com USB Voice Faxmodem**   Models of this modem that have a firmware revision of 4.9.2 are not USB CDC–compliant devices and will not be supported by Windows Me drivers. You can check the firmware version by querying modem diagnostics in the Modem properties in Control Panel. This modem may still be used in serial mode for dial-up connections.

- **Belkin USB Hubs**   There are two issues with this device. First, the power adapter does not supply enough power for the hub to be able to support four full bus-powered devices. Second, the hub always reports itself as a self-powered device (even when being used as a bus-powered device). If you always use the hub's power adapter, you will avoid having the hub always report itself as a self-powered device. You should note that if you have four devices plugged in to the hub, you may run into intermittent problems.

- **CATC USB Bus-Powered Hubs**   This hub sometimes fails to work with low-speed devices such as keyboards, mice, and joysticks. The solution is to use only self-powered devices with this hub.

- **CMD OHCI USB Controller REV_04**   If you upgrade your computer and have a PCI USB host adapter from CMD, you may see the following string in Device Manager: "Rev 04 CMD USB controller not supported by Microsoft." This device is not supported by Microsoft. You can contact CMD about getting a filter driver that should enable your computer to work.

- **Hitachi Visionbook Plus 4000 Series Laptop**   USB is disabled on these machines due to problems on the laptop with power. The laptop does not properly support high-powered bus-powered devices.

- **Logitech/Storm Pagescan**   This device does not work with the new Windows Image Acquisition architecture available in Windows Me, and therefore it is not supported.

- **NEC Flat Screen Monitor with USB Hub**   This device has problems with low-speed devices (such as keyboards, mouse devices, and joysticks) when plugging in and unplugging. You may have to disconnect and reconnect the device several times to get it to work correctly.

- **NEC NX Series Machines**   These machines come equipped with a legacy-mode USB BIOS that allows the USB keyboard to work in real mode. When you suspend and resume your computer, wake up the machine by using the NEC USB keyboard/mouse, or the device will not work after the computer is resumed. You need to disconnect and reconnect the device.

- **NEC USB OHCI Host Controllers[E5-E11]**   Some older computers ship with a USB OHCI host controller from NEC that has known problems with bulk devices. You may experience problems with this host controller when using bulk USB devices such as scanners, printers, and modems.

- ■ **"Original" Intel USB Camera**   The original USB camera (the square-shaped camera rather than the oval-shaped camera) has problems working on OHCI host controllers. This device should be used on UHCI host controllers.

- ■ **Samsung USB Keyboard with Hub**   The hub on a Samsung USB keyboard does not always identify itself correctly. When it identifies itself as a self-powered device, it confuses the operating system and causes odd behavior with the hub portion of the keyboard. There is no workaround. Use low-powered USB devices (such as a mouse and gaming device) or self-powered devices with this keyboard.

- ■ **Thrustmaster GrandPrix Steering Wheel**   This device has problems working on OHCI host controllers, so this device should be used only on UHCI host controllers.

- ■ **Thrustmaster Top Gun USB Joystick**   This device has problems working on OHCI host controllers, so this device should be used only on UHCI host controllers.

- ■ **Toshiba In-Touch Module**   These devices shipped with Toshiba Infinia computers and allowed multimedia and Internet HID functionality from a USB console. Support for this device has been removed from Windows Me.

- ■ **Unixtar USB Hubs**   This hub always reports itself as a self-powered device—even when being used as a bus-powered device. In order for the hub to work correctly, you must always use the power adapter.

GENERAL USB TROUBLESHOOTING

Most USB problems are not fatal. Since USB devices are PnP devices, there is little that you can do to control or configure them, but most USB problems can be traced to one of the following conditions:

- ■ Hardware failures or configuration problems
- ■ Device driver configuration problems
- ■ Cabling problems
- ■ Firmware/BIOS problems
- ■ Root hub configuration problems

Hardware Failures or Configuration Problems

Many hardware problems (such as high or low power, limited bandwidth, malfunctioning or incorrectly configured firmware, and so on) can cause issues to occur. Check the Device Manager to be certain that the root hub is functioning correctly. If the root hub is displayed with an exclamation point in a yellow circle, verify that the BIOS is assigning an interrupt request (IRQ) line to the root USB controller. This is required for the device driver to be loaded.

If no devices work when you plug the devices into the root hub, verify that the power requirements of the bus are not being exceeded. USB devices can draw a maximum of 500mA for each connection. If a device attempts to draw more power than this, the specification recommends that the computer be able to disable that specific port until the computer power is cycled (this is called "suspending" the port). In contrast, if the device draws less than 50mA, the port never becomes active. Check the Power tab in the USB Root Hub properties to gauge the power usage of the USB bus.

Device Driver Configuration Problems

When you connect a USB device, the computer should load and configure the device without ever requesting a device driver (assuming that the device accepts the standard class drivers). If the computer prompts you for a device driver, check with the manufacturer of the device to determine if a current device-specific driver is available for your particular version of Windows.

Cabling Problems

There are two types of USB cables: high speed and low speed. Low-speed cables differ from high-speed cables primarily in their shielding. If you plug a high-speed device into a low-speed cable, you can cause signal distortion over long distances. Verify the entire USB chain to be certain that a device needing to draw power from the hub is not plugged into the chain on the other side of a non-powered hub—this causes that hub (and all of the devices down the chain) to be suspended. If the hub is a powered hub, verify that the power supply for that hub is configured properly.

Firmware/BIOS Problems

Firmware is the key to all USB devices. The device's firmware contains all of the information about the device. A port is not reset until all of the descriptors in the firmware have been loaded and verified by the root hub—this is critical because it applies to items such as printers and modems. Make certain that you have the most up-to-date firmware that is available for both your computer's BIOS and each individual device.

The symptoms of malfunctioning or incorrectly configured firmware might seem unusual. When you remove and then re-add a USB device, the device simply becomes available again. However, the device may appear as a second instance of that device and load a second copy of itself in Device Manager. If you see duplicates of a device, verify that you have the most up-to-date firmware for that device (this issue is common with USB printers and modems). A similar issue occurs when a device loads a device driver, and then adds a second device for which there appears to be no driver. The second device is displayed with an exclamation point in a yellow circle in Device Manager. The device may work correctly, but you cannot remove the "ghost" device without unplugging the device that seems to have generated the ghost in the first place. You can also generally resolve this issue by updating the firmware or the device driver for that device.

Root Hub Configuration Problems

This problem is normally related to the computer's setup. USB controllers require that an IRQ line be assigned—the IRQ line is assigned in the computer's BIOS, and usually IRQ 9 is assigned. Assign an IRQ through the CMOS Setup.

USB SYMPTOMS

Although the recent releases of Windows have resolved many of the early compatibility problems with USB technology, you can still encounter numerous issues with USB device compatibility and performance. The following symptoms may help you identify corrective action for some of the most common troubles.

SYMPTOM 39-1   Pressing CTRL-ALT-DEL on the USB keyboard has no effect
This problem has been reported when connecting the Microsoft Natural Keyboard Elite (version 1.0) to the Universal Serial Bus (USB) port on a computer running Windows 98. According to Microsoft, this is a problem with Windows 98 itself, and should be corrected in the final release (or Windows 98/SE, as well as Windows Me). To correct the problem in the meantime, revert to a version of OSR 2.x, exchange the keyboard to another model (or use a conventional keyboard), or upgrade Windows to a later version.

SYMPTOM 39-2   You cannot log on to Windows 98 through the USB keyboard
This problem has been reported with the Microsoft Natural Keyboard Elite (version 1.0) under Windows 98. The keyboard does *not* respond the first time you try to log on. This occurs because you must log on to

Windows 98 *before* Windows can detect the keyboard and install the drivers needed to use it. Use the following steps to work around the problem:

1. Shut down and turn off your computer.

2. Connect the keyboard to the USB port on the computer.

3. Connect a PS/2 keyboard to a PS/2 port on the computer.

4. Use the PS/2 keyboard to log on to Windows 98. Windows 98 then detects the keyboard and installs the proper drivers.

5. Shut down and turn off the computer again.

6. Disconnect the PS/2 keyboard.

7. Restart the computer and use the USB keyboard to log on to Windows 98 normally.

SYMPTOM 39-3   **Windows 95 OSR 2.1 hangs while a USB device is "hot inserted"**
Under some conditions, plugging a USB device into the PC can cause an over-current condition. The problem is that Windows 95 OSR 2.1 does not clear the over-current status of the USB hardware, and this causes Windows 95 to service the same over-current error multiple times—hanging up the system. This is a problem with Windows 95 OSR 2.1. OSR 2.5 should fix this problem by updating Windows 95 with the following files:

```
OPENHCI.SYS      2/17/98     31,280     (version 4.03.1217)
USBHUB.SYS       2/17/98     28,448     (version 4.03.1217)
```

This problem is corrected with the release of Windows 98 and Windows Me.

SYMPTOM 39-4   **The computer hangs after attempting to "resume" from a power-saving mode**   This is a known problem that occurs frequently under Windows 95 OSR 2.1 and can manifest itself in two general scenarios. First, the system may hang if you use the PC's sleep button to manually place the PC into a power-saving mode, then use the sleep button again to resume normal operation. Second, the system may hang if it automatically switches to a sleep mode (or other power-saving mode) after some period of inactivity, *then* you use the sleep button to resume normal operation. This is a problem with Windows 95 OSR 2.1. OSR 2.5 should fix this problem by updating Windows 95 with the following file:

```
USBHUB.SYS       8/29/97     28,448     (version 4.03.1215)
```

This problem is corrected with the release of Windows 98 and Windows Me.

SYMPTOM 39-5   **You experience docking and power management trouble with mobile USB-equipped PCs**   There are three general problem modes that can occur when using the USB driver in Windows 95 OSR 2.1 with a USB-equipped mobile PC:

■ The PC's hot docking feature of the mobile PC may function only intermittently (if at all).

■ The automatic power-saving modes (that is, sleep or suspend) may not work properly on some mobile PC models.

■ When entering a power-saving mode, the CPU clock is not properly slowed or stopped by the power management software.

This is a problem with Windows 95 OSR 2.1. OSR 2.5 should fix this problem by updating Windows 95 with the following file:

```
UHCD.SYS          8/13/97    39,872     (version 4.03.1215)
```

This problem is corrected with the release of Windows 98 and Windows Me.

SYMPTOM 39-6   **You find that the PC hangs when working with USB**   This is a known problem under Windows 95 OSR 2.1. The USB-equipped computer may hang in any of several known situations:

- If a mobile PC's PC Card controller is in CardBus mode and the PC is docked to a port replicator, the PC may hang when undocking. This is a known problem with USB-equipped Toshiba portables.

- When suspending and resuming a PC's operation with a USB mouse (such as a Logitech USB mouse), the PC may not complete its resume process successfully.

- When disabling a USB root hub device in the Device Manager while PC Card sockets are enabled, the system may hang, or a "Fatal Exception Error 0E" may appear.

- When rapidly installing and removing a USB game pad (such as an ALPS USB game pad), the PC may hang, or a "Fatal Exception Error 0E" may appear.

This is a problem with Windows 95 OSR 2.1. OSR 2.5 should fix this problem by updating Windows 95 with the following file:

```
OPENHCI.SYS       7/17/97    31,248     (version 4.03.1214)
```

Some Toshiba portable computers also require the following updated file for Windows 95 OSR 2.1:

```
CBSS.VXD          6/13/97    16,249     (version 4.00.1117)
```

This problem is corrected with the release of Windows 98 and Windows Me.

SYMPTOM 39-7   **During the setup of OSR 2.1, you find that the VMM32.VXD file is missing or damaged**   This problem occurs when rebooting the PC after installing OSR 2.1 and may prevent you from restarting Windows 95. This error can occur if the VMM32.VXD file was not rebuilt properly (or was damaged)—resulting in an error message suggesting that "VMM32.VXD is missing or corrupt". The rebuilding of the VMM32.VXD file was unsuccessful, preventing Windows 95 from booting properly and processing the RunOnce section of the Registry. This error can also occur when the addition of USB support causes a conflict with the system, and Windows 95 is unable to boot normally. To correct the problem, you'll need to use either of the following procedures:

- **If the VMM32.VXD file is missing or damaged:**
  You must uninstall OSR2.1 using the OSR 2.1 real-mode uninstall tool (REM.PSS) on the installation disk:
  1. Restart the computer and press F8 when you see "Starting Windows 95".
  2. Choose Safe Mode Command Prompt Only from the Startup menu.

3. Copy the REM.PSS file to the root folder of the boot drive as REMUSB.BAT (do not copy it to REM.BAT because "Rem" is a reserved command and it will not function).

4. Type **REMSUB** to restore the original files that were renamed with an .o20 extension.

5. To complete the uninstall process, restart your computer and use the Add/Remove Programs tool in Control Panel to remove the program WDM/USB Supplement.

6. Delete the REMSUB.BAT file from the root folder of the boot drive.

7. Restart the computer normally, then try reinstalling OSR 2.1 from a known-good source disk.

■ **If Windows 95 cannot boot because of a conflict:**
If there is a conflict between Windows 95 and USB support, follow these steps:

1. Restart the computer and press F8 when you see "Starting Windows 95".

2. Choose Safe Mode from the Startup menu.

3. Rename the DETROIT.BAT file to AUTOEXEC.BAT. The DETROIT.BAT file is actually your original AUTOEXEC.BAT file that was renamed by the OSR 2.1 Setup process.

4. Troubleshoot the conflict while in the Safe Mode, or delete OSR 2.1 as described previously.

SYMPTOM 39-8   **You find that a USB peripheral may not function properly in any USB port**   For example, this is a known problem with the Compaq USB camera. When you attempt to use a Compaq USB camera with an OpenHCI (OHCI) USB host controller, the camera may not be detected and probably will not work properly. This means your particular USB peripheral was probably designed and developed for use on the Intel Universal HCI (UHCI) USB host controller and is *not* supported on an OHCI controller. OHCI host controllers employ optimization which allows multiple transactions to be submitted within a single frame. By comparison, the UHCI host controller sends only a single transaction per frame. This means the peripheral (that is, the Compaq USB camera) cannot respond to a second transaction within a single frame. Such a PC-specific peripheral cannot be used on other PCs. For more information, you'll need to contact the peripheral maker for any patches or workarounds.

SYMPTOM 39-9   **Your USB keyboard does not operate in DOS**   Chances are that this is a fault of the BIOS. Without a USB-aware operating system (such as Windows 98/Me or Windows NT 5.0), USB keyboards rely on the system BIOS for support. If the BIOS does not directly support USB keyboards, your keyboard won't work under DOS. You'll receive a "Keyboard Error" or "Keyboard Not Present" error message when you start the computer. Check with the motherboard or system maker for available BIOS upgrades.

There are generally two ways to work around this issue. First, you can replace the USB keyboard with a PS/2 model outright. Shut down Windows 95 and turn off the computer. Disconnect the USB keyboard and remove the USB adapter. Connect a PS/2 keyboard to a PS/2 port on the computer, and then restart the computer. Second, you can use a dual-keyboard strategy. If you have a PS/2 keyboard available, shut down Windows 95 and turn off the computer. Plug the PS/2 keyboard into a PS/2 port on the computer (leaving the USB keyboard attached), then restart the computer. You can then use the PS/2 keyboard in DOS and use the USB keyboard in Windows.

SYMPTOM 39-10   **You notice that the General tab is missing under your mouse Properties dialog under Windows 98**   The General tab in Windows 95 is intended to provide a location from which you can upgrade the mouse driver. However, the General tab can accommodate only *one* mouse. With the addition of Universal Serial Bus (USB) support in Windows 98, more than one point-ing device may be installed on the computer. You'll need an alternate strategy to upgrade the mouse driver in Windows 98:

1. Click Start | Settings, and then click Control Panel.
2. Double-click the System icon.
3. Click the Device Manager tab, and then double-click the Mouse branch to expand it.
4. Click the desired mouse, then click Properties.
5. Click the Driver tab, and then click Update Driver.
6. Follow the instructions on the screen.

SYMPTOM 39-11   **You notice that USB devices do not seem to work in Safe Mode under Windows 95/98**   After you attempt to start your computer in Safe Mode, your computer may not respond to any keyboard commands, or you may receive the following error message:

```
Windows did not detect a mouse attached to a computer. You can safely attach
a serial mouse now. To attach a mouse to a PS/2 mouse port, you must first
turn the computer off.
```

The fault can occur if you're using a Universal Serial Bus (USB) keyboard or mouse and your system BIOS does *not* support USB devices natively. Windows 98 and Windows 95 do not support the use of a USB keyboard or mouse in Safe Mode (or in real mode) unless the computer's BIOS supports these devices. To circumvent this problem, use a standard (PS/2) keyboard or mouse instead of a USB keyboard or mouse.

SYMPTOM 39-12   **ESD seems to disable USB devices plugged into a hub**   When you employ USB devices connected to an "external" USB hub, one or more devices plugged into that hub may suddenly stop working. This problem is more likely to occur under Windows 98/SE with external USB hubs that are self-powered rather than with USB hubs that are bus-powered. This problem does not seem to occur with devices that are plugged directly into the root hub of the computer itself. This problem is usu-ally caused when the USB hub receives an electrostatic discharge (ESD, or a *static electric shock*). When ESD occurs, Windows may be unable to properly restart an external USB hub to recover from the error. There is a fix that you can download for Windows 98/SE:

```
USBHUB.SYS        08/13/99    36,672 (4.10.2223)
```

To work around this problem in the meantime, simply unplug the external USB hub from the computer (or upstream hub), wait a moment, and then reconnect the external USB hub. The hub should be redetected, and all connected devices should be restored.

SYMPTOM 39-13   **USB device performance is diminished under Windows 98/SE because the USB driver is using the largest report size**   USB devices that support multiple packet sizes send packets using the *largest* supported data field size rather than the *smallest* required data field. Each supported function of the USB device should send packets using the *smallest* required data field size. The overall performance of the USB device suffers since more data is sent over the USB device. This problem occurs because the HID-class driver in Windows 98/SE always uses the *largest* data field the USB device supports to transmit packets. This behavior causes the USB device to transmit unneeded data during an IN or OUT transaction. You can download a fix from Microsoft that should correct the problem:

```
HIDCLASS.SYS              1/10/2000  23,584  (4.10.2223)
```

This fix is generally recommended when you're using multifunction USB devices and will not affect single-purpose (dedicated) USB devices.

SYMPTOM 39-14   **You may hear a high-pitched noise when you enable OHCI USB support under Windows 98/SE**   If you use a USB video capture device, the image may freeze, and Windows may also stop responding to the signal. There is a patch available from Microsoft that should fix this problem:

```
OPENHCI.SYS              01/01/99   24,576 (4.10.2224)
```

To circumvent this problem in the meantime, disable USB support in the Device Manager—disabling USB causes the noise to stop.

SYMPTOM 39-15   **The laptop battery offers less running time when USB devices are attached**   Battery-powered computers that use Windows 9x/Me Advanced Power Management (APM) or the Advanced Configuration and Power Interface (ACPI) may experience additional power consumption (resulting in a faster drain of battery power) when a USB device is attached. The bus activity needed to support communications with the USB device prevents the CPU from switching to the C3 (Clock-Stopped) power state. When a USB device is not connected, the CPU can spend a significant amount of time in the C3 state—this reduces power consumption and extends battery life. Unfortunately, the option to turn off USB devices after a computer is idle is not supported under Windows 9x/Me.

You may need to use other tricks to conserve battery power. One workaround is to disconnect all USB devices if you're not using them. You may also try adjusting the time-out periods for your display and hard drive so that the system will use those standby states sooner.

SYMPTOM 39-16   **You cannot view a USB camera that's in Device Manager under Windows 98**   After you connect your USB digital camera to a USB port, you may not be able to view this device in the Device Manager. This problem can occur if the camera was disabled in Device Manager *before* you removed it—when you reconnect the camera, Device Manager does not refresh the information it's displaying. To avoid this problem, click Refresh in Device Manager.

SYMPTOM 39-17   **Your digital video camera is disabled under Windows 98/SE**
This is a problem with cameras like the Kodak DVC300 or Kodak DVC343. When you view your system devices in Device Manager, you may see a red *X* through the device icon for your USB digital video camera. This issue can occur because Windows 98/SE doesn't include device drivers for the Kodak DVC300 USB or the Kodak DVC323 USB digital video cameras. To correct this issue, download and install the most current driver for the device. If your camera worked before you upgraded your computer, simply re-enable the device drivers:

1.   Click Start | Settings, click Control Panel, double-click the System icon, then click the Device Manager tab.

2. Click Kodak Camera DVC323 or Kodak Camera DVC300, click Properties, click to *select* the Exists in All Hardware Profiles check box, click OK, and then click OK again.

The red *X* may still be displayed on the camera in your Device Manager, but the camera may be working.

SYMPTOM 39-18   **Moving your USB mouse causes a USB printer job to stop under Windows 98**   When a USB printer and a USB mouse are connected to a computer *without* a hub, print jobs in progress may terminate prematurely if the mouse is moved. The USB printer may stop printing in the middle of the job and advance the page instead. This is a known issue with Windows 98/SE, and a patch is available from Microsoft that will fix computers using OHCI controllers:

```
OPENHCI.SYS            5/12/1999   22,816            (4.10.2019)
```

While you may see this issue with printers and mice, any combination of low-speed and high-speed USB devices may also cause this same behavior.

SYMPTOM 39-19   **Scanning stops when using an NEC OHCI controller and HP USB scanner under Windows 98/SE**   When using an HP ScanJet 6200C USB scanner connected to a computer with an NEC OHCI USB controller, you may suddenly be unable to perform a scan after having run a scanning operation (such as a Preview scan). The scanning software may also be listed as Not Responding in the Close Program dialog box. This problem occurs when the NEC controller does not correctly acknowledge a USB packet, which is smaller than the full packet size, and the HP ScanJet 6200C does not properly re-send a packet that has not been acknowledged. A patch for this problem is available from Microsoft:

```
OPENHCI.SYS      11/08/99       24,416 (4.10.0.2226) for WIN98SE
OPENHCI.SYS      11/22/99       22,944 (4.10.0.2021) for WIN98
```

SYMPTOM 39-20   **Your USB keyboard does not work correctly under Windows 98**   When you try to install a new USB keyboard, it may not work after you start your computer. This fault can occur if you install a new USB keyboard while your computer is off and your computer prompts you to log on when you start it. USB keyboards are not enumerated until after you log on to your computer. To resolve this issue, click Cancel when you're prompted to log on, click Start, click Log Off <your user name>, click Yes, and then log on to your computer.

SYMPTOM 39-21   **The PS/2 mouse doesn't work after resuming a docked laptop under Windows 98/SE**   This is a known issue with laptops like the IBM 560Z. If you dock your laptop while the power is on, and you have a USB device connected to it, you may not be able to use your PS/2 mouse when you resume using your computer. This is a driver issue, so contact the laptop manufacturer for updated mouse drivers.

SYMPTOM 39-22   **You cannot use the standby mode with a USB printer**   This is a known issue with the Epson Stylus 740 USB printer under Windows 98/SE. When you try to place your computer in standby mode, you may receive the following error message:

```
Your computer cannot go on standby because a device driver or program won't
allow it. Close all open programs, and then try again.
```

If you click OK, close all running programs, and try to use the standby mode again, you may still receive the same error message. There is a conflict with the third-party Epson printer drivers. To fix this issue, unplug the printer from the USB port *before* placing your computer in standby mode. When you need to print, simply plug the printer back in. You may also check with the printer manufacturer to see if there are updated drivers available.

SYMPTOM 39-23   Your laptop doesn't resume from standby mode when docked
This is a known problem with the Tecra 530CDT laptop under Windows 98/SE. When you attach your Toshiba Tecra 530CDT computer to a DeskStation 5+ docking station, your computer may not resume from the standby mode. This fault can occur if both the docking station's SCSI controller and the laptop's USB controller are enabled. This configuration can cause a USB and SCSI IRQ sharing conflict across the PCI bridge. The docking station's SCSI controller may be allocated the same IRQ as the laptop's USB controller when the computer is docked. This can cause a unique type of resource conflict, resulting in the USB host controller's inability to resume from standby mode.

To work around this issue, either disable the USB controller in Device Manager (if you're not using USB devices), or disable the SCSI controller in Device Manager (if you're not using SCSI devices). If you require the use of both devices simultaneously, configure the System Standby setting in the Power Management icon to Never when docked, and do not manually start the standby mode from the Shut Down Windows dialog box. To disable a device in the Device Manager:

1. Click Start | Settings, click Control Panel, and then click the System icon.
2. Click the Device Manger tab, double-click the branch containing the device you need disabled, and then double-click the exact device to open the Properties dialog.
3. On the General tab, select the Disable in This Hardware Profile check box, click OK, and then click Close.
4. Restart your computer.

SYMPTOM 39-24   The automatic repeat feature for your USB keyboard doesn't work after resuming from the suspend mode   This problem has been addressed by a Windows 98/SE patch that's available from Microsoft:

```
KBDHID.VXD  10/04/99  16,666 (4.10.2223)
```

SYMPTOM 39-25   You encounter performance problems when using a USB camera
When you use a USB camera with certain PCI video cards in Windows 95 OSR2.1, performance may be reduced or your computer may seem to hang up. Video playback may also be affected. This happens because certain PCI video cards may not work well with isochronous transactions (which USB cameras require). The video card may require several attempts to complete an operation. Try reducing your hardware acceleration level:

1. In Control Panel, double-click Display.
2. On the Settings tab, click Advanced Properties.
3. On the Performance tab, move the Hardware Acceleration slider to None.
4. Click OK or Close until you return to Control Panel. Restart the computer when you're prompted to do so.

SYMPTOM 39-26   **You encounter a GPF in the URM.EXE module under Windows 98**
After you install Windows 98 on a Toshiba Infinia computer that uses a USB In Touch module, you may receive the following error message:

```
(file) caused a General Protection Fault in module URM.EXE at 015F:00000055
```

This problem may occur if your version of the In Touch module is not compatible with the revision of the Toshiba Infinia. There are several revisions of the Toshiba Infinia and the USB In Touch module. If you use an In Touch module on a Toshiba Infinia model other than that for which it is designed, this error message can occur—this can occur when you repair or upgrade the In Touch module. To work around this problem temporarily, disconnect the In Touch module. You may also contact Toshiba to inquire about possible driver updates.

SYMPTOM 39-27   **Your computer doesn't recognize a USB device when resuming from standby under Windows 98**   If you connect a USB device to a Windows 98 computer while the computer is in standby mode, the computer does not resume from standby mode to process the USB device connection and immediately recognize the new USB device. The computer remains in standby mode and may not recognize the USB device once resumed. If you disconnect and reconnect the USB device after the computer has resumed, the USB device will be correctly recognized. A fix is available from Microsoft which patches three offending files (though this was fixed in Windows 98/SE):

```
OPENHCI.SYS       07/06/98     21,904 (4.10.2018)
USBD.SYS          07/06/98     17,568 (4.10.2018)
USBHUB.SYS        07/06/98     27,136 (4.10.2018)
```

SYMPTOM 39-28   **Your video capture WDM driver doesn't work under Windows 98**
Programs that use the Microsoft Video for Windows 1.1 (VFW) interface cannot directly communicate with analog video capture devices that use the Windows Driver Model (WDM) video capture interfaces in Windows 98. Such analog capture devices may include PCI adapters with video decoder chips that use WDM drivers. The VFW/WDM mapping files included with Windows 98 do *not* allow WDM-based analog capture devices to be used with the VFW 1.1 interface. Microsoft has a fix that corrects this problem:

```
VFWWDM.DRV        08/10/98     15,344 (4.10.2043)
VFWWDM.DLL        08/10/98     56,832 (4.10.2043)
KSWDMCAP.AX       08/10/98     51,712 (4.10.2043)
```

SYMPTOM 39-29   **The system locks up after clicking the Close button in the Close Program dialog box under Windows 98**   This problem can occur if you're using a USB mouse. The Close Program dialog box is displayed as a fault thread, and the WDM driver message sent by the USB mouse driver cannot be delivered to the window. Microsoft has a patch that should correct this problem (though the problem was corrected under Windows 98/SE):

```
KERNEL32.DLL    02/22/99     452,096 (4.10.2000)
```

To work around this issue, press ESC to close the Close Program dialog box instead of clicking the Close button.

SYMPTOM 39-30 You receive an error when using CTRL-ALT-DEL to shut down using a USB keyboard under Windows 98   If you press CTRL-ALT-DEL twice on a USB keyboard in Windows 98, you may receive the following "blue screen" error message:

```
A fatal exception 06 has occurred at xxxx:xxxxxxxx. The current application
will be terminated.
```

Restarting Windows by pressing CTRL-ALT-DEL twice is *not* recommended—this method causes Windows to suspend most processes and should be used only when the normal shutdown process is not possible. Use the Shut Down command on the Start menu to restart your computer. If you cannot use the Start menu to perform a shutdown, press CTRL-ALT-DEL, then click Shut Down in the Close Program dialog box.

SYMPTOM 39-31 The Creative Labs VideoBlaster WebCam II drivers are not loading properly under Windows 98/Me   After you upgrade to Windows 98/Me, your VideoBlaster WebCam II may not respond, and a yellow exclamation point may appear for that hardware in Device Manager. To correct this issue, unplug and then reconnect the camera to the USB port. The drivers for the camera should then be detected and loaded correctly. The VVLUSB.SYS driver used by the VideoBlaster WebCam II may not be enumerated correctly during the upgrade process. You may also see a Code 10 status for the device in your Device Manager.

SYMPTOM 39-32 You encounter a "File not found" error when installing a 3Com USB modem under Windows 98   When you install a 3Com USB ISDN modem, you're prompted to insert the Windows 98 CD, but you then receive a "File not found" error when Windows attempts to copy the following files:

- Ccport.sys
- Usbser.sys
- Wdmmdmld.vxd

These files are *not* located on the Windows 98 CD *or* the Windows 98 Service Pack 1 (SP1) CD. To resolve the issue, upgrade to Windows 98/Me. The 3Com Web site incorrectly states that the files are available on the Windows 98 SP1 CD. However, the files are only located on the Windows 98/SE CD.

SYMPTOM 39-33 The Windows key may not work on a USB keyboard under Windows 98/SE   This problem can occur if all of the following conditions exist:

- The USB keyboard is the only keyboard attached to your computer.
- The information (.INF) file used for installing the keyboard driver did *not* add the proper setting to the SYSTEM.INI file to correctly identify the keyboard type.
- Your computer contains no legacy devices—having only USB ports for a keyboard and mouse—and has no PS/2-based keyboard and mouse ports.

If a USB keyboard is the only keyboard attached to your computer, the keyboard may not be automatically identified as the correct type of keyboard. The "type=4" setting in the [Keyboard] section of your SYSTEM.INI file overrides this automatic detection so that Windows may correctly interpret the keyboard scan codes. Chances are that the keyboard is being detected as an IBM AT keyboard (type 3 to the

KEYBOARD.DRV file), instead of being detected as an extended keyboard (type 4). Because of this, the keyboard driver is not able to correctly process the extended scan.

To correct this problem, contact the manufacturer of your USB keyboard to download any available fix for this issue. To circumvent this issue, click Start, or press CTRL-ESC, or edit the SYSTEM.INI file. Verify that the following line exists in the [Keyboard] section of your SYSTEM.INI file, and if it does not exist, you can add it:

```
type=4
```

SYMPTOM 39-34   **USB devices may not work under Windows 98/SE**   USB devices that are plugged in to a computer running Windows 98/SE may not work if an AMD processor (running at 350 MHz or faster) and a VIA Technologies USB controller are installed on your system. This problem occurs because there is a timing-specific problem in the Universal Host Controller driver (UHCD.SYS) that may prevent USB devices from enumerating under specific timing conditions. To correct this issue, download and run the appropriate patch file for your version of Windows. For the English version of Windows, try the 240075UP.EXE file from **download.microsoft.com/download/win98SE/Patch/ 4.10.2223/W98/EN-US/240075up.exe**. This patch should have the following file attributes (or later):

```
UHCD.SYS          08/20/99  30,528  (4.10.2223)
```

SYMPTOM 39-35   **Your USB mouse or keyboard is not working with an AMD OHCI USB controller under Windows 98/SE**   When you use AMD's OHCI USB controller, you may experience intermittent instances where Windows does not recognize the USB mouse or USB keyboard. This issue can occur when querying the status of the host controller's registers returns incorrect information. As a result, the mouse and/or keyboard attached to the controller do not initialize properly. To resolve this issue, download the latest version of the OPENHCI.SYS file. The following patch is available for download from Microsoft. For the English version of Windows, try the 241134UP.EXE file from **download.microsoft.com/download/win98SE/amdusb/1/W98/EN-US/241134up.exe**. The patch should have the following attributes (or later):

```
OPENHCI.SYS            10/18/99 24,240   (4.10.2225)
```

SYMPTOM 39-36   **Some camera controls are not available after upgrading NetMeeting 3**   This is a known issue with Kodak DVC323 digital video cameras under Windows 98/SE. After you upgrade to NetMeeting 3.0 or 3.01, the advanced camera controls in NetMeeting may be unavailable. This problem may also occur when you upgrade to Windows 98/SE because it includes NetMeeting 3.0. Click Tools | Options, click the Video tab, click Source, and then click Camera Controls. All of the advanced camera settings may be unavailable (these settings include Zoom, Focus, Exposure, Iris, Tilt, Pan, and Roll). Upgraded drivers for the camera cannot resolve this issue, so you may need to revert to an older version of NetMeeting 3.

SYMPTOM 39-37   **The CAPS LOCK key is on at startup once the USB keyboard is installed under Windows 98/SE**   When you start a non-English version of Windows 98, the CAPS LOCK key is on if both of the following conditions exist:

■   You have a USB keyboard attached to your computer.

■ A language *other* than English is selected on the Language tab of the Keyboard tool in your Control Panel.

This problem occurs if you include the KEYB.COM command in your AUTOEXEC.BAT file which is executed when you start your computer. The KEYB.COM command installs a table that defines the translation of keys to the extended character codes, and then sets the CAPS LOCK state to On. Microsoft has a patch available for Windows 98/SE that should fix the problem:

```
KEYB.COM        01/26/2000  19,927
```

To work around this problem, remove the KEYB.COM command from your AUTOEXEC.BAT file, and then restart your computer. Keep in mind that this workaround is *not* recommended if you use DOS programs that need localized keyboard support (such functionality would not be provided).

SYMPTOM 39-38   **Sound may be disabled when using the PlaySound API with USB HID devices in the system**   On computers running Windows 98/SE, sounds may intermittently be disabled after Windows starts (for example, .WAV files may not play). This problem may occur when the following conditions are true:

■ The program being used to play the sound uses the PlaySound API.

■ The computer has one or more USB HID devices installed (that is, a USB speaker device).

After a sound fails to play, no further attempts to play sounds using the PlaySound API are successful until after you restart Windows (note that the Windows Startup sound may play successfully). This problem can occur if a reference counter is not cleared properly by the WINMM.DLL file when the PlaySound API is processed. This prevents proper initialization during subsequent PlaySound API calls, and this causes the sound to not play.

```
WINMM.DLL   12/29/99  50,688 (4.03.2201)
```

SYMPTOM 39-39   **You have trouble hot-plugging a USB floppy drive under Windows Me**   If you unplug (disconnect) and reconnect a USB floppy drive under Windows Me, or you hot-undock and re-dock a computer running Windows Me while a USB floppy drive is connected to the dock, one of two possible problems may occur:

■ The USB floppy drive may be assigned a drive letter other than drive A:, even if there is no other floppy disk drive present. The drive letter that is assigned to the USB floppy disk drive may be the last drive letter in use. For example, if drive letters C: through F: are used by hard disks and CD-ROM drives, the USB floppy disk drive may appear as drive letter G:.

■ If you hot-undock and re-dock the computer while a USB floppy drive is connected to the dock, the USB floppy disk drive may not be assigned a drive letter.

■ When you disconnect and reconnect the USB floppy drive, it may not have the same drive letter as before you disconnected it. For example, if the USB floppy disk drive appeared as drive G: after startup, it may appear as drive A: after you disconnect and reconnect it.

To restore the original drive letter assignments, simply shut down and restart your computer.

SYMPTOM 39-40   **When connecting USB devices under Windows Me, you get a "USB Power Exceeded" message**   The full error message often appears such as:

```
The hub does not have enough power available to operate the <device>. Would
you like assistance in solving this problem? If you click No, the device may
not function properly.
```

The USB device mentioned in the message probably doesn't work properly. This behavior occurs if there are too many USB devices attached to a passive (unpowered) USB hub. Replace the passive USB hub with an active (powered) hub. To work around this issue, disconnect the affected device from the passive hub and connect it directly to the USB host controller's hub in the back of the computer.

SYMPTOM 39-41   **USB devices perform poorly (if at all) when attached to a Windows Me PC**   This problem can occur if the data bandwidth demands of the combined USB devices exceed the available bandwidth of the USB. To resolve this issue, add an additional USB host controller to the computer and attach some of the USB devices to it to share the bandwidth load. To work around this problem, remove any devices that are using the most bandwidth. You need to determine which devices are using available bandwidth:

1.   When the problem occurs, right-click My Computer, and then click Properties.
2.   Click the Device Manager tab.
3.   Click the plus sign (+) next to Universal Serial Bus Controllers.
4.   Double-click the listed USB universal host controller.
5.   Click the Advanced tab.
6.   Click Bandwidth Usage.
7.   Check to see which devices consume the most bandwidth. The amount of bus bandwidth a device uses appears as a percentage of all available bandwidth.

You can attach any devices that consume the *most* bandwidth to a separate USB host controller's hub or remove a device from the bus so that the remaining devices have more available data transmission bandwidth.

SYMPTOM 39-42   **Windows Me freezes at startup**   This occurs when USB keyboard and USB legacy support are enabled. If you have a USB keyboard installed on a computer with USB legacy support enabled in the BIOS, the computer may occasionally freeze while it is starting up (while the Windows logo screen is displayed)—though this is rather rare. This problem can occur if a System Management Interrupt (SMI) occurs during a very narrow time period during startup while Windows is sizing the base address registers for the USB controller if the controller is already enabled. Microsoft has a fix for this problem:

```
1/18/01   11:18am   4.90.3002   70,539   PCI.VXD
```

SYMPTOM 39-43   The USB device cannot receive data under Windows 98/Me   If your computer is fitted with a non-Intel USB controller, the device may be able to send but not receive any data. For example, a computer equipped with a USB network adapter may not be able to see any other computers on your network. The USB controller driver that Microsoft provides offers advanced buffering to device drivers, but the installed USB controller is not guaranteed to support these features. In most cases, upgrading the USB device's driver will correct the trouble.

SYMPTOM 39-44   Installing Windows Me drivers may cause USB audio device problems   For example, when you install Aureal 8820 drivers on a computer with a USB audio device, the USB device may be removed from the Sounds and Multimedia icon in Control Panel. This trouble can occur if the Preferred device in the Audio tab is not selected. Simply restart the computer to restore the USB functionality.

SYMPTOM 39-45   You encounter noisy playback with a USB amplifier under Windows Me   For example, when you use the Yamaha AP-U70 USB amplifier in six-channel mode under Windows Me, noise may be played when you attempt to play sounds. This occurs because Windows attempts to transfer data to UHCI hardware on nonphysically contiguous memory pages which it cannot properly handle. A supported fix is now available from Microsoft with the following file attributes or later:

```
1/5/2001   8:52:39pm 4.90.0.3001   147,840   Kmixer.sys
1/5/2001   8:52:40pm 4.90.0.3001    24,496   Rt.sys
1/5/2001   8:52:40pm 4.90.3001.0    51,344   Usbaudio.sys
1/5/2001   8:52:40pm 4.90.0.3001   100,208   Wdmaudio.sys
```

SYMPTOM 39-46   You cannot install a USB device under Windows Me   After you add a new USB device, it may appear in Device Manager with a yellow exclamation. The device properties may also indicate "Code 10", and may include an error such as:

```
This device is either not present, not working properly, or does not have
all the drivers installed. (Code 10)
```

This problem may occur during device configuration and initialization. The problem occurs during device configuration and initialization. A USB client driver sends a USB Request Block (URB), and an error is returned. The USBHUB.SYS file incorrectly fails validation. A supported fix is available from Microsoft, and the English version of this fix should have the following file attributes or later:

```
11/13/00   7:06:40pm   4.90.3002.0   41,840   Usbhub.sys
```

Further Study

Intel   developer.intel.com/technology/usb/over.htm
USB   www.usb.org

40

WINDOWS 9X/ME ISSUES

In the early days of computing, hardware was relatively independent of the operating system. With the introduction of Windows, that line between an operating system and hardware began to blur, but it was the shift to Windows 95 (and later to Windows 98/Me) that really began to merge the computer's software and hardware into one inseparable idea. Today, it is almost impossible to troubleshoot a computer without *some* working knowledge of the operating system—even if it's just to navigate between dialogs and update drivers and check the status of each device. Consequently, troubles with the operating system can often manifest themselves as serious system problems, though there may be no problems at all with the hardware. This chapter is intended to offer a series of troubleshooting tips that can help you deal with startup, shutdown, and other miscellaneous problems under Windows 9x/Me.

If you require detailed information regarding Windows 95/98/Me, you should acquire the Resource Kit for your particular Windows version from your local bookstore.

General Techniques

Let's get started with a number of handy support techniques that you can use to deal with common Windows 9x/Me problems. This part of the chapter will show you how to perform basic clean-boot troubleshooting of your Windows platform and handle common Windows troubles such as:

■ Re-creating the SYSTEM.INI file

■ Managing the MSDOS.SYS file

■ Disabling IRQ steering

■ Disabling fast shutdown

■ Troubleshooting stack overflows

CLEAN-BOOT TROUBLESHOOTING

Many of the problems that you encounter with Windows will be due to issues with the computer's environment—such as drivers and TSRs—that are started when the computer boots. The objective of clean-boot troubleshooting is to isolate potential problems related to the computer's environment. By simplifying the environment, you can systematically weed out problem areas. This part of the chapter shows a standard clean boot example for Windows 98/SE. The following environment files are loaded as part of the boot process when Windows 98/SE starts, and these files help to create the environment used by the OS and application programs:

■ **MSDOS.SYS**   The MSDOS.SYS file contains basic information about the location of the Windows folder, startup files, and other options. Many of these options can be edited to adjust the boot performance of the system and Windows. See the "Managing MSDOS.SYS" section later in this chapter for more details.

■ **CONFIG.SYS**   The CONFIG.SYS file is provided for backward-compatibility with DOS-based and older Windows-based programs, and it may not be present on your computer. It loads low-level DOS-based drivers, many with a system (or .SYS) extension.

■ **AUTOEXEC.BAT**   The AUTOEXEC.BAT file is also provided for backward-compatibility with DOS-based and older Windows-based programs, and it may not be present on your computer. It loads DOS-based programs, often with .COM and .EXE extensions.

■ **WINBOOT.INI**   The WINBOOT.INI file is a temporary version of the MSDOS.SYS file that may be present if a program is making changes to your computer that might affect the boot process. Under normal conditions, it is deleted after the program is complete. Until it is deleted, it resides in the root directory and overrides settings in your MSDOS.SYS file.

■ **WINSTART.BAT**   The WINSTART.BAT file is created for programs that need to run a DOS-based program to enable functionality of a Windows-based program. Most users do *not* have this program. The WINSTART.BAT file may not be available as a check box on the General tab in your System Configuration Utility.

■ **SYSTEM.INI**   The SYSTEM.INI file contains critical information about your computer's settings for specific hardware. This file *must* be present in the Windows folder for Windows to start. It is used to load various drivers (including sound and video adapter drivers). It may also contain additional 16-bit drivers for hardware that does not use 32-bit drivers. When you *clear* the Process System.ini File check box in the System Configuration Utility and restart your computer, your display is set to a resolution of 640×480×16 (if you have the display set to a higher resolution, shortcuts on the desktop may overlap and your sound card may no longer operate correctly).

■ **WIN.INI**   The WIN.INI file contains information specific to the overall appearance of Windows. This file *must* be present in the Windows folder (or it is re-created by Windows) and is read at startup for backward-compatibility with Windows 3.x. Many of the settings are duplicated in the Registry. When you *clear* the Process Win.ini File check box in the System Configuration Utility, a generic version of the WIN.INI file is created.

■ **WININIT.INI**   The WININIT.INI file is used to complete the installation of various components for Windows and third-party products. Each time a program needs to copy or remove a file that is in use, instructions are written to the WININIT.INI file. Windows checks for the presence of the WININIT.INI file during the boot process and, if found, performs the instructions. Rename this file to troubleshoot problems.

■ **SYSTEM.DAT**   The SYSTEM.DAT file is one of two Registry files that are required to start Windows. The SYSTEM.DAT file is similar to the SYSTEM.INI file in that it contains computer and software settings. The Load Startup Group option contains the entries that are loaded from the SYSTEM.DAT portion of the Registry.

■ **USER.DAT**   The USER.DAT file is the second of two Registry files that are required to start Windows. The USER.DAT file is similar to the WIN.INI file in that it contains information for running specific programs and information about the overall appearance of Windows.

 You can use the System Configuration Utility to create a backup of the startup files. Click Create Backup on the General tab in the System Configuration Utility. You can choose to save the files to a folder on one of your hard disks or to a floppy disk.

Using MSCONFIG for a Clean Boot

Windows 98 (and later) includes the System Configuration Utility tool (named MSCONFIG.EXE) that can ease the steps needed to perform a clean boot. To start the System Configuration Utility, click Start | Run, type **msconfig.exe**, and then click OK. Once the System Configuration Utility starts (Figure 40-1), select the General tab, click Selective Startup, then click the following check boxes to *clear* them:

■ Process CONFIG.SYS File

■ Process AUTOEXEC.BAT File

■ Process WINSTART.BAT File (if available)

■ Process SYSTEM.INI File

■ Process WIN.INI File

■ Load Startup Group Items

Finally, click OK, then restart your computer when you're prompted to do so. Each check box (except for Load Startup Group Items) represents files that are renamed with a troubleshoot (or .TSH) extension

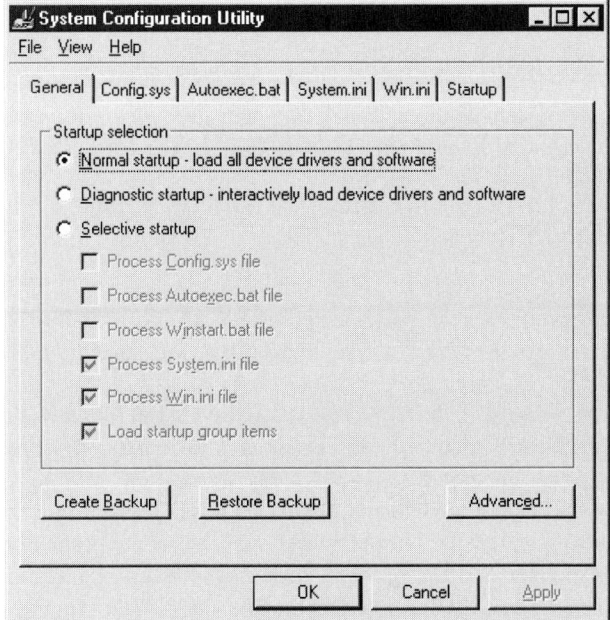

FIGURE 40-1   Using the MSCONFIG utility to control the system boot process

when you clear the check box. By comparison, the Load Startup Group Items entry represents icons in the Startup folder or entries in the following Registry keys:

```
HKEY_LOCAL_MACHINE\SOFTWARE\Microsoft\Windows\CurrentVersion\Run
HKEY_LOCAL_MACHINE\SOFTWARE\Microsoft\Windows\CurrentVersion\RunServices
```

When you click the Load Startup Group Items check box to clear it, the Registry entries are written to the following keys:

```
HKEY_LOCAL_MACHINE\SOFTWARE\Microsoft\Windows\CurrentVersion\Run-
HKEY_LOCAL_MACHINE\SOFTWARE\Microsoft\Windows\CurrentVersion\RunServices-
```

The icons in the Startup folder are moved to the Disabled Startup Items folder in the Windows\Start Menu\Programs folder.

Remember that when you click to clear an entry in a file, a remark statement is placed at the beginning of each line. For the CONFIG.SYS and AUTOEXEC.BAT files, rem tshoot is used (followed by a space). For the SYSTEM.INI and WIN.INI files, ;tshoot is used (followed by a space). These remarks are removed when you click to select an entry that was cleared previously. When you click to select an item in the Startup tab, the corresponding Registry entry is restored to its original location.

You must restart your computer each time you make a change to any of the startup files because they are only read when your computer starts.

Homing in on the Problem

Suppose that your computer no longer displays the problem after you clear all of the entries under the Selective Startup group (that is, after you clean boot the system). You can systematically narrow the focus of the problem by using the System Configuration Utility to restore files or file entries until you determine the specific entry that is causing the problem. Use the General tab and re-select the following entries, restart your computer, and then test the following:

- Process SYSTEM.INI File
- Process WIN.INI File

If the problem occurs again when these files are processed, the problem is related to one of these files. In that case, click to clear one of the files. If the problem still occurs, an entry in the file that is selected is causing the problem.

If the problem does not occur after the SYSTEM.INI and WIN.INI files are selected, click to select the Process Autoexec.bat File check box, restart your computer, and then test. If the problem returns, an entry in the AUTOEXEC.BAT file is responsible.

If the problem does not occur after selecting the AUTOEXEC.BAT file, click to select the Process Config.sys File check box, restart your computer, and then test. If the problem returns, an entry in the CONFIG.SYS file is responsible. If the problem does not reoccur, an item in the Startup group or WINSTART.BAT file is responsible. Click to select the Process Winstart.bat File check box, restart your computer, and then test. If the problem does not return, an item in the Load Startup Items is responsible.

Narrowing Further

Now that you know which file area is causing the problem, you can test the individual files that make up the file area. Click to select the check box for file area causing the problem on the General tab, click the tab representing that file, click to clear the bottom half of the list of check boxes, restart your computer, and then test. For example, if an entry in the Startup group is responsible, click to select the Load Startup Group Items check box on the General tab, click the Startup tab (Figure 40-2), click to clear the bottom half of the entries, click OK, then restart your computer when you're prompted.

If the problem persists, one of the entries that is still selected is causing the problem. If the problem does not occur, one of the entries that you had cleared was causing the problem. In the first case, click to clear half of the remaining entries that are selected, restart your computer, and then test. In the second case, click to select half of the file entries that are cleared, restart your computer, and then test.

Using this systematic process, you can isolate the specific file entry that is causing the problem after restarting your computer several times. Once the specific file entry that is causing the problem is determined, you should edit the appropriate file or Registry entry to remove this entry, and return the System Configuration Utility to its Normal Startup mode:

1. Click Start | Run, type **msconfig** in the Open box, then click OK.
2. On the General tab, click Normal Startup, and then click OK.
3. When you're prompted to restart the computer, click No.

If the problem entry occurred in the CONFIG.SYS, AUTOEXEC.BAT, WIN.INI, or SYSTEM.INI files, use the System Configuration Editor (SYSEDIT.EXE) to edit the file and disable the appropriate line(s):

1. Click Start | Run, type **sysedit** in the Open box, and then click OK.
2. On the Window menu, click the appropriate file name (for example, C:\Windows\System.ini).

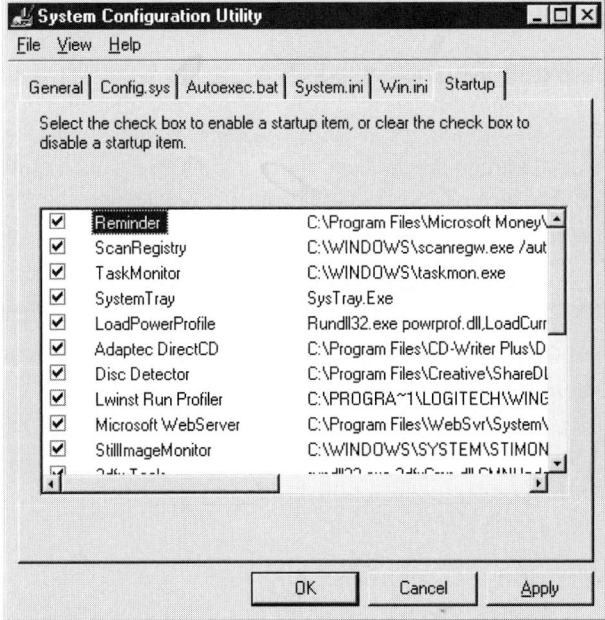

FIGURE 40-2   Using MSCONFIG to isolate problem files or drivers

3. Type **REM** followed by a space at the beginning of the appropriate line that is causing the problem.

4. Click File | Save.

5. Click File | Exit.

6. Restart your computer.

If the problem entry is a program on the Startup tab, remove the program from the Startup folder or delete the program from the Registry:

1. Click Start | Settings | Taskbar and Start Menu.

2. Click the Start Menu Programs tab, then click Remove.

3. Double-click Startup, click the offending entry, then click Remove.

4. Click Close, click OK, and then restart your computer.

If the problem entry is *not* in the Startup folder, the program may be loading in the Registry. Follow these steps to remove the entry from the Registry:

1. Start the Registry Editor and export the appropriate Registry keys (for backup purposes):

```
HKEY_LOCAL_MACHINE\SOFTWARE\Microsoft\Windows\CurrentVersion\Run
HKEY_LOCAL_MACHINE\SOFTWARE\Microsoft\Windows\CurrentVersion\RunServices
```

2. Delete the <filename.exe> value from the appropriate Registry keys:

```
HKEY_LOCAL_MACHINE\SOFTWARE\Microsoft\Windows\CurrentVersion\Run
HKEY_LOCAL_MACHINE\SOFTWARE\Microsoft\Windows\CurrentVersion\RunServices
```

where <filename.exe> is the name of the file that is causing the problem.

3. Quit the Registry Editor and restart the computer.

Advanced Clean-Boot Techniques

If you find that the system problem persists after you have cleared all of the boot entries in the System Configuration Utility, there are three other avenues you can test. Select every check box listed on the Advanced Troubleshooting Settings tab in your System Configuration Utility, change your display adapter to standard Video Graphics Adapter (VGA) mode, or click Diagnostic Startup on the General tab in System Configuration Utility and then do *not* load static VXD files. To check the items on the Advanced Troubleshooting Settings tab:

1. Click Start | Run, type **msconfig.exe**, and then click OK.

2. On the General tab, click Advanced, click to select each check box (Figure 40-3), click OK, then restart your computer when you're prompted to do so.

3. Use the same systematic process that you used previously to isolate the problem. Many of the problems that are isolated through this process are related to hardware- or driver-compatibility issues. When you isolate the problem, contact the hardware or software manufacturer of the affected driver for a possible updated driver or patch.

To change your display adapter driver to standard VGA:

1. Click Start | Settings | Control Panel, then double-click the Display icon.

2. Click the Settings tab, click Advanced, click the Adapter tab, and then click Change.

3. Click Next, click Display a List of All the Drivers in a Specific Location, So You Can Select the Driver You Want, and then click Next.

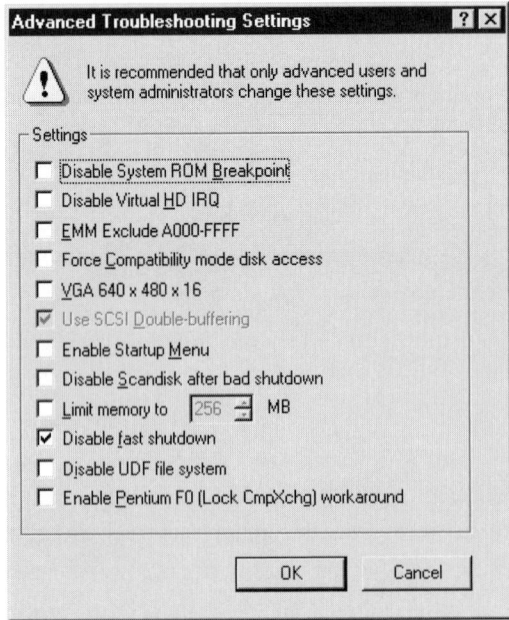

FIGURE 40-3   Advanced troubleshooting with MSCONFIG

4. Click Show All Hardware, click Standard Display Types in the Manufacturer's box, click Standard Display Adapter (VGA) in the Models box, then click Next.

5. Click Yes, click Next, and then click Finish.

6. Click Close, click Close again, and click Yes when you're prompted to restart your computer. If changing your display adapter to the standard VGA driver corrects the problem, contact your video adapter manufacturer for an updated Windows 98/Me video driver.

To select Diagnostic Startup and avoid loading static VXD files:

1. Click Start | Run, type **msconfig.exe**, and then click OK.

2. On the General tab, click Diagnostic Startup—Interactively Load Device Drivers and Software, then click OK.

3. Restart your computer when you're prompted to do so.

4. On the Windows Startup Menu, choose Step-By-Step Confirmation, then press ENTER.

5. Choose the following responses:

   ▓ **Load DoubleSpace Driver?**   Yes

   ▓ **Process the System Registry?**   Yes

   ▓ **Create a Startup Log File (BOOTLOG.TXT)?**   Yes

   ▓ **Process Your Startup Device Drivers (CONFIG.SYS)?**   No

   ▓ **DEVICE=C:\WINDOWS\HIMEM.SYS?**   Yes

   ▓ **DEVICE=C:\WINDOWS\DBLBUFF.SYS?**   Yes

   ▓ **DEVICEHIGH=C:\WINDOWS\IFSHLP.SYS?**   Yes

   ▓ **Process Your Startup Command File (AUTOEXEC.BAT)?**   No

   ▓ **Load the Windows Graphical User Interface?**   Yes

   ▓ **Load All Windows Drivers?**   Yes

6. Note each static VXD file and respond with No to avoid loading each file. Some typical static VXD files that you may encounter are

   ▓ **VNETSUP.VXD**   Microsoft Networking

   ▓ **NDIS.VXD**   Microsoft Networking

   ▓ **NDIS2SUP.VXD**   Microsoft Networking

   ▓ **JAVASUP.VXD**   Microsoft Java

   ▓ **VRTWD.386**   Clock

   ▓ **VFIXD.VXD**   Video Phone helper

   ▓ **VNETBIOS.VXD**   Microsoft Networking

   ▓ **VSERVER.VXD**   Microsoft Networking

   ▓ **VREDIR.VXD**   Microsoft Networking

   ▓ **DFS.VXD**   Microsoft Networking

- ■ **NDISWAN.VXD**   Microsoft Networking
- ■ **MSMOUSE.VXD**   Microsoft Mouse

7. Use this systematic process to isolate and identify the offending VXD file, then delete the incompatible static VxD folder from the following key in the Registry:

    HKEY_LOCAL_MACHINE\System\CurrentControlSet\Services\VxD

REBUILDING THE SYSTEM.INI FILE

Your Windows 9x/Me platform relies heavily on the SYSTEM.INI file to specify the device drivers needed to support various hardware devices on your system. If the SYSTEM.INI file is deleted, damaged, or corrupted (and you don't have a backup available), it may be possible for you to rebuild a basic SYSTEM.INI file that will run without references to third-party drivers. Although some hardware devices may not function, a basic SYSTEM.INI file may allow you to boot Windows. Use the following steps to create your basic SYSTEM.INI file:

> The very best way to protect your system setup is to maintain a current Startup disk which includes all of your key INI files, as well as a complete backup copy of your Registry and REGEDIT utility.

1. Start your computer to the command prompt by booting from a floppy disk or using the Windows Startup Menu.

2. Change to the Windows folder, such as:

    cd \windows

> If you have installed Windows 9x/Me to a drive or folder other than C:\Windows, adjust these instructions accordingly.

3. Rename the current SYSTEM.INI file, such as:

    ren system.ini system.old

4. Create a new SYSTEM.INI file, such as:

    copy system.cb system.ini

5. The following lists the default entries for a SYSTEM.INI file under Windows 98/SE:

```
[386Enh]
device=*vshare
device=*dynapage
device=*vcd
device=*vpd
device=*int13
Keyboard=*vkd
display=*vdd
mouse=*vmouse, msmouse.vxd
Woafont=dosapp.fon
device=*enable

[keyboard]
layout=kbdus.kbd
```

```
subtype=
type=4
keyboard.dll=
oemansi.bin=

[Intl]
ACP=1252
OEMCP=437
SystemLocale=00000409

[boot]
system.drv=system.drv
drivers=mmsystem.dll
user.exe=user.exe
gdi.exe=gdi.exe
sound.drv=mmsound.drv
dibeng.drv=dibeng.dll
comm.drv=comm.drv
shell=Explorer.exe
keyboard.drv=keyboard.drv
fonts.fon=vgasys.fon
fixedfon.fon=vgafix.fon
oemfonts.fon=vgaoem.fon
386Grabber=vgafull.3gr
display.drv=pnpdrvr.drv
mouse.drv=mouse.drv
*DisplayFallback=0

[power.drv]

[drivers]
wavemapper=*.drv

[iccvid.drv]

[mciseq.drv]

[mci]
cdaudio=mcicda.drv
sequencer=mciseq.drv
waveaudio=mciwave.drv
avivideo=mciavi.drv
videodisc=mcipionr.drv
vcr=mcivisca.drv

[NonWindowsApp]

[vcache]

[nwnp32]
```

```
[boot.description]
keyboard.typ=Standard 101/102-Key or Microsoft Natural Keyboard
aspect=100,96,96
display.drv=Standard Display Adapter (VGA)
mouse.drv=Standard mouse
system.drv=Standard PC

[MSNP32]

[display]

[drivers32]
vidc.CVID=iccvid.dll
VIDC.IV31=ir32_32.dll
VIDC.IV32=ir32_32.dll
vidc.MSVC=msvidc32.dll
VIDC.MRLE=msrle32.dll
```

6. Edit the new SYSTEM.INI file, such as:

```
edit system.ini
```

7. Add the following lines at the *top* of the file:

```
[boot]
mouse.drv=mouse.drv
drivers=mmsystem.dll
```

8. Add the following line in the [386Enh] section of the file:

```
mouse=*vmouse
```

9. Save your new SYSTEM.INI file and exit the text editor.

10. Type **win** to start Windows.

If your mouse does not work when Windows starts, it is likely that it is not supported by the standard Windows mouse driver.

11. Click Start | Run, type the path to the Windows Setup program in the Open box, and then click OK. For example, if your Windows CD is in drive D:, type

```
d:\setup
```

12. When the Setup dialog box appears, click Continue, and follow the instructions to set up Windows again. Select the Restore Windows Files That Are Changed or Corrupted option if it's available. If you do not see this option, you'll need to reinstall Windows.

13. After Setup has finished, you may find that some programs, tools, or devices are not working correctly. If this happens, you'll need to reinstall each offending application or device.

MANAGING MSDOS.SYS

The MSDOS.SYS file has been dramatically altered under Windows 9x/Me. Where older stand-alone versions of MS-DOS relied on MSDOS.SYS for disk and file code, all of that functionality has been worked into IO.SYS in Windows 9x/Me. MSDOS.SYS, under Windows 9x/Me, is now little more than a text INI file which is used to configure the boot properties of Windows and list important paths to key Windows files (including the Registry). Normally, there is little need to access the MSDOS.SYS file, but you may be faced with the need to adjust the Windows 9x/Me boot process. This section of the chapter takes you inside the MSDOS.SYS file and illustrates the various options you can use to enhance the Windows platform. A typical example of an MSDOS.SYS file is shown in Figure 40-4.

There are two main sections to the MSDOS.SYS file: the [Paths] section, and the [Options] section. Paths defines the directory paths to major Windows file areas, while Options allow you to configure many of the available attributes used to boot a Windows 95/98 system. The selections for Paths and Options are listed in Table 40-1. The MSDOS.SYS file also contains a section that contains extra *x* characters which may seem like

```
[Paths]
WinDir=c:\windows
WinBootDir=c:\windows
HostWinBootDrv=c
UninstallDir=D:\
[Options]
BootMulti=1
BootGUI=1
;
;The following lines are required for compatibility with other programs.
;Do not remove them (MSDOS.SYS needs to be >1024 bytes).
;xxxxxxxxxxxxxxxxxxxxxxxxxxxxxxxxxxxxxxxxxxxxxxxxxxxxxxxxxxxxxxxxxxxxxxa
;xxxxxxxxxxxxxxxxxxxxxxxxxxxxxxxxxxxxxxxxxxxxxxxxxxxxxxxxxxxxxxxxxxxxxxb
;xxxxxxxxxxxxxxxxxxxxxxxxxxxxxxxxxxxxxxxxxxxxxxxxxxxxxxxxxxxxxxxxxxxxxxc
;xxxxxxxxxxxxxxxxxxxxxxxxxxxxxxxxxxxxxxxxxxxxxxxxxxxxxxxxxxxxxxxxxxxxxxd
;xxxxxxxxxxxxxxxxxxxxxxxxxxxxxxxxxxxxxxxxxxxxxxxxxxxxxxxxxxxxxxxxxxxxxxe
;xxxxxxxxxxxxxxxxxxxxxxxxxxxxxxxxxxxxxxxxxxxxxxxxxxxxxxxxxxxxxxxxxxxxxxf
;xxxxxxxxxxxxxxxxxxxxxxxxxxxxxxxxxxxxxxxxxxxxxxxxxxxxxxxxxxxxxxxxxxxxxxg
;xxxxxxxxxxxxxxxxxxxxxxxxxxxxxxxxxxxxxxxxxxxxxxxxxxxxxxxxxxxxxxxxxxxxxxh
;xxxxxxxxxxxxxxxxxxxxxxxxxxxxxxxxxxxxxxxxxxxxxxxxxxxxxxxxxxxxxxxxxxxxxxi
;xxxxxxxxxxxxxxxxxxxxxxxxxxxxxxxxxxxxxxxxxxxxxxxxxxxxxxxxxxxxxxxxxxxxxxj
;xxxxxxxxxxxxxxxxxxxxxxxxxxxxxxxxxxxxxxxxxxxxxxxxxxxxxxxxxxxxxxxxxxxxxxk
;xxxxxxxxxxxxxxxxxxxxxxxxxxxxxxxxxxxxxxxxxxxxxxxxxxxxxxxxxxxxxxxxxxxxxxl
;xxxxxxxxxxxxxxxxxxxxxxxxxxxxxxxxxxxxxxxxxxxxxxxxxxxxxxxxxxxxxxxxxxxxxxm
;xxxxxxxxxxxxxxxxxxxxxxxxxxxxxxxxxxxxxxxxxxxxxxxxxxxxxxxxxxxxxxxxxxxxxxn
;xxxxxxxxxxxxxxxxxxxxxxxxxxxxxxxxxxxxxxxxxxxxxxxxxxxxxxxxxxxxxxxxxxxxxxo
;xxxxxxxxxxxxxxxxxxxxxxxxxxxxxxxxxxxxxxxxxxxxxxxxxxxxxxxxxxxxxxxxxxxxxxp
;xxxxxxxxxxxxxxxxxxxxxxxxxxxxxxxxxxxxxxxxxxxxxxxxxxxxxxxxxxxxxxxxxxxxxxq
;xxxxxxxxxxxxxxxxxxxxxxxxxxxxxxxxxxxxxxxxxxxxxxxxxxxxxxxxxxxxxxxxxxxxxxr
;xxxxxxxxxxxxxxxxxxxxxxxxxxxxxxxxxxxxxxxxxxxxxxxxxxxxxxxxxxxxxxxxxxxxxxs
DoubleBuffer=1
AutoScan=1
WinVer=4.10.1998
```

FIGURE 40-4 A typical MSDOS.SYS file under Windows 98/SE

TABLE 40-1	TYPICAL OPTIONS FOR THE MSDOS.SYS FILE
[PATHS]	
WinDir=	Indicates the location of the Windows 9x directory specified during Setup.
WinBootDir=	Indicates the location of the necessary startup files. The default is the directory specified during the Setup process (such as C:\WINDOWS).
HostWinBootDrv=c	Indicates the location of the boot drive root directory.
UninstallDir=c	Specifies the location of the W95undo.dat and W95undo.ini files. These files are necessary to uninstall Windows. This setting is present only if you back up your system files when you are prompted to during Windows Setup.
[OPTIONS]	
AutoScan=1	Defines whether or not ScanDisk is run after a bad shutdown. A setting of 0 does not run ScanDisk; 1 prompts before running ScanDisk; 2 does not prompt before running ScanDisk but prompts you before fixing errors if any errors are found. This setting is used only by OSR2 and Windows 98.
BootMulti=	This enables dual-boot capabilities. The default is 0. Setting this value to 1 enables the ability to start MS-DOS by pressing F4 or by pressing F8 to use the Windows Startup menu.
BootGUI=	This enables automatic graphical startup into Windows. The default is 1.
BootMenu=	This enables automatic display of the Windows Startup menu (the user must press F8 in Windows 95 or press and hold the CTRL key in Windows 98 to see the menu). The default is 0. Setting this value to 1 eliminates the need to press F8 to see the menu.
BootKeys=	This enables the startup option keys (such as F5, F6, and F8). The default is 1.
BootWin=	This enables Windows as the default operating system. Setting this value to 0 disables Windows as the default (useful only with MS-DOS version 5 or 6.x on the computer). The default is 1.
BootDelay=n	This sets the initial startup delay to n seconds (default is 2). A BootKeys=0 entry disables the delay. The only purpose of the delay is to give the user sufficient time to press F8 after the Starting Windows message appears. BootDelay is not supported in Windows 98.
BootFailSafe=	This enables safe mode for system startup. The default is 0.
BootMenuDefault=#	This sets the default menu item on the Windows Startup menu; the default is 3 for a computer with no networking components and 4 for a networked computer.
BootMenuDelay=#	This sets the number of seconds to display the Windows Startup menu before running the default menu item. The default is 30 seconds.
Logo=	This enables display of the Windows logo. The default is 1. Setting this value to 0 also avoids hooking a variety of interrupts that can create incompatibilities with certain memory managers from other vendors.
BootWarn=	This enables the safe mode startup warning. The default is 1.
DblSpace=	This enables automatic loading of DBLSPACE.BIN. The default is 1.
DrvSpace=	This enables automatic loading of DRVSPACE.BIN. The default is 1.
DoubleBuffer=	This enables loading of a double-buffering driver for a SCSI controller. The default is 0. Setting this value to 1 enables double-buffering (if required by the SCSI controller).
LoadTop=	This enables the loading of COMMAND.COM or DRVSPACE.BIN at the top of 640KB memory. The default is 1. Set this value to 0 with Novell NetWare or any software that makes assumptions about what is used in specific memory areas.
Network=	This enables Safe Mode with Networking as a menu option. The default is 1 for computers with networking installed. This value should be 0 if network software components are not installed.

useless information. This information is necessary to support programs that expect the MSDOS.SYS file to be at least 1,024 bytes in length. For example, if an antivirus program detects that the MSDOS.SYS file is less than 1,024 bytes, it may assume that the MSDOS.SYS file is infected with a virus. If you delete the MSDOS.SYS file your computer will not start.

Editing MSDOS.SYS

Although it is a relatively simple matter to edit changes in the MSDOS.SYS file, it can be a bit tricky because the file is generally read-only and hidden. Try the following steps to access and edit the file correctly:

1. Click Start | Find, then click Files or Folders.

2. In the Named box, type **msdos.sys**.

3. In the Look In box, click your boot drive (usually drive C:). Click the Find Now button.

4. Right-click the msdos.sys file and then click Properties.

5. Click the Read-Only and Hidden check boxes to *clear* them (removing these attributes from the msdos.sys file), then click OK.

6. Right-click the msdos.sys file, then click Open With.

7. In the Choose the Program You Want to Use box, click WordPad and click OK.

8. Make the changes you need to the msdos.sys file. When you're done, save the file as a text document, and then quit WordPad.

9. Right-click the msdos.sys file, and then click Properties.

10. Click the Read-Only and Hidden check boxes to *select* them (and reset these attributes for the file), then click OK. Close the Find window.

11. Quit and then restart Windows.

MANAGING PCI IRQ BUS STEERING

One of the major complaints about IRQs is that they cannot be "shared"—that is, two devices cannot use the same IRQ. With the introduction of the PCI bus, however, PCI devices can share the interrupts assigned to PCI bus slots. The PCI bus architecture also supports *bus steering* under Windows 98/Me, where Windows can dynamically assign (or "steer") PCI bus IRQs to various PCI devices. PCI IRQ bus steering gives OSR2 and Windows 98/Me the flexibility to reprogram PCI interrupts when it rebalances PnP PCI and ISA resources around non-PnP ISA devices to solve resource conflicts. Windows 95 (the retail release) and OSR1 cannot support this function.

For example, suppose that your computer's BIOS is unaware of non-PnP ISA cards, and the operating system does not have PCI bus IRQ steering. If the BIOS sets a PCI device to IRQ 10, you may have a resource conflict when you add a non-PnP ISA device that is configured for IRQ 10. But with PCI IRQ bus steering, the operating system can resolve this IRQ resource conflict. To handle this, the operating system will:

■ Disable the PCI device.

■ Reprogram a free IRQ to a PCI IRQ (for example, IRQ 11).

■ Assign an IRQ placeholder to IRQ 11.

■ Move the PCI device to IRQ 11.

■ Reprogram IRQ 10 to be an ISA IRQ.

■ Remove the IRQ placeholder for IRQ 10.

The Placeholder

An IRQ Holder for PCI Steering may be displayed when you examine the System Devices branch of your Device Manager. This IRQ Holder for PCI Steering indicates that an IRQ has been programmed to PCI mode and is *unavailable* for ISA devices—even if no PCI devices are currently using the IRQ. To view IRQs that are programmed for PCI mode:

1. Click Start | Settings | Control Panel, then double-click the System icon.
2. Click the Device Manager tab.
3. Double-click the System Devices branch.
4. Double-click the IRQ Holder for PCI Steering you want to view, then click the Resources tab.

Checking for IRQ Steering

You can use the following steps to determine if your computer is using IRQ steering:

1. Click Start | Settings | Control Panel, then double-click the System icon.
2. Click the Device Manager tab.
3. Double-click the System Devices branch.
4. Double-click PCI Bus, then click the IRQ Steering tab (Figure 40-5).
5. You should see *one* of the following settings: IRQ Steering Enabled or IRQ Steering Disabled.

 PCI bus IRQ steering is disabled by default in OSR2. If you're using OSR2 and IRQ steering is disabled, verify that the Use IRQ Steering check box is *selected* on the IRQ Steering tab.

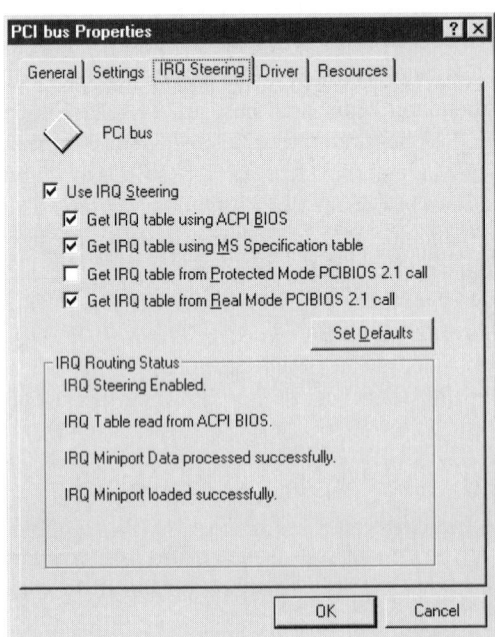

FIGURE 40-5   Checking the status of IRQ steering under Windows 98/SE

The Device Manager may display IRQ Steering as *disabled* for any of the following reasons:

■ The IRQ routing table provided by the BIOS to the operating system may be missing or corrupted (the IRQ routing table provides information on how the motherboard is configured for PCI IRQs).

■ The Use IRQ Steering check box is *not* selected.

■ The Get IRQ Table from Protected Mode PCIBIOS 2.1 Call check box is *not* selected.

■ Your computer's BIOS does not support PCI IRQ bus steering.

Disabling PCI IRQ Bus Steering

When PCI IRQ bus steering is enabled, Windows 98/Me dynamically assigns (or "steers") PCI bus IRQs to the PCI devices. If there are IRQ conflicts between PCI devices, you may need to disable the PCI IRQ bus steering feature to determine where the conflicts occur. You can disable PCI IRQ bus steering with these steps:

1. Click Start | Settings | Control Panel, then double-click the System icon.

2. Click the Device Manager tab.

3. Double-click the System Devices branch.

4. Double-click PCI Bus, then click the IRQ Steering tab.

5. Click the Use IRQ Steering check box to *clear* it, click OK, and then click OK again.

6. Click Yes when you're prompted to restart your computer.

You may also need to disable PCI IRQ bus steering in your computer's BIOS through the CMOS Setup.

The following selections will determine which routing table(s) Windows 98/Me uses when programming IRQ steering:

■ **Get IRQ Table Using ACPI BIOS**   When this box is selected, the ACPI BIOS IRQ routing table is the first table Windows 98/Me tries to use to program IRQ steering. If a PCI device is not working properly, click this check box to *clear* it.

■ **Get IRQ Table Using MS Specification Table**   When this box is selected, the MS Specification routing table is the second table Windows 98/Me tries to use to program IRQ steering.

■ **Get IRQ Table from Protected Mode PCIBIOS 2.1 Call**   When this box is selected, the Protected Mode PCIBIOS 2.1 routing table is the third table Windows 98/Me tries to use to program IRQ steering.

■ **Get IRQ Table from Real Mode PCIBIOS 2.1 Call**   When this box is selected, the Real Mode PCIBIOS 2.1 routing table is the fourth table Windows 98/Me tries to use to program IRQ steering.

By default, the Get IRQ Table from Protected Mode PCIBIOS 2.1 Call check box is *not* selected. You should only select this box if a PCI device is not working properly.

DISABLING FAST SHUTDOWN

When you shut down Windows 98/Me normally, all device drivers are systematically uninitialized. When the fast shutdown feature is enabled in Windows, device drivers are *not* uninitialized. Normally, this results in a faster shutdown, and the fast shutdown feature is enabled by default. Disabling fast shutdown may be necessary if you're troubleshooting shutdown problems in Windows 98/Me. Follow these steps to disable fast shutdown:

1. Click Start | Programs | Accessories, choose System Tools, and then click System Information.

2. Click Tools | System Configuration Utility.

3. On the General tab, click Advanced.

4. Click the Disable Fast Shutdown check box to select it (Figure 40-3, third entry from the end), click OK, and then click OK again.

5. Click Yes when you are prompted to restart your computer.

 Disabling the fast shutdown feature of Windows 98 changes the FastReboot value data from 1 to 0 in the Registry key: HKEY_LOCAL_MACHINE\System\CurrentControlSet\Control\Shutdown.

DEALING WITH STACK OVERFLOW ERRORS

Stacks are reserved memory areas that Windows 9x/Me programs use for processing hardware events—the system state is stored in the stack, the IRQ handler routine is serviced, the system state is "popped" from the stack, and then the system resumes from where it left off. A *stack overflow* occurs when there is not enough space in memory to store the system state before handling the hardware interrupt routines. When Windows displays an error message related to an internal stack overflow, there are several common issues for you to consider:

■ The CONFIG.SYS startup file may not be properly configured for the Windows installation. Try the following values:

```
STACKS=64,512
FILES=60
BUFFERS=40
```

■ If you're using the dual-boot capabilities of Windows, your CONFIG.SYS and AUTOEXEC.BAT files may not contain the correct configuration to run Windows. For example, if you're dual-booting between Windows 3.x and Windows 9x/Me, these files may not have been renamed back to CONFIG.DOS and AUTOEXEC.DOS. Examine the CONFIG.SYS file to determine if files such as HIMEM.SYS or EMM386.EXE are being loaded from a folder *other* than the Windows folder. If so, boot Windows using the Safe Mode Command Prompt Only option. Rename the CONFIG.SYS file to CONFIG.DOS and the AUTOEXEC.BAT file to AUTOEXEC.DOS and then restart the computer.

■ Some TSRs may be interfering with Windows. Disable any nonboot device drivers in the CONFIG.SYS and AUTOEXEC.BAT files. If you're upgrading from Windows 3.x and getting a stack overflow error, check the WIN.INI and SYSTEM.INI files for non-Windows-based programs or drivers loading.

■ There may be an incompatible hardware configuration. Check the port and IRQ settings of your network card, sound card, and modem. Make sure that there are no COM2/COM4 or COM1/COM3 conflicts, and verify that no devices are sharing IRQs. Disable or remove any conflicting devices.

■ Finally, the computer may need a BIOS upgrade. Check the BIOS version and contact the manufacturer of your computer for information about a BIOS upgrade.

RESTORING THE WINDOWS 98 SYSTEM

When a system crash occurs, the most difficult part of the recovery is often restoring the operating system and backup files in the correct order. Windows 98 attempts to resolve this difficulty by providing a System Recovery program that restores your Windows 98 system by using the full backup that you created with

Microsoft Backup. To use System Recovery to restore your system, you must have your Windows 98 CD, a backup device (such as a tape drive) connected to your computer, and a full system backup created with Microsoft Backup. To restore Windows 98 on your computer:

1. Insert your Windows Startup disk into the floppy disk drive, then boot your computer.

2. On the Boot menu, choose Start Your Computer with CD-ROM Support.

3. Switch to your CD-ROM drive by typing its letter and pressing ENTER, such as:

    ```
    d:
    ```

    where D: is the drive letter of your CD-ROM drive.

4. At the DOS command prompt, type the following command and press ENTER:

    ```
    cd tools\sysrec
    ```

    This will switch to the System Recovery directory on the Windows 98 installation CD.

5. At the DOS command prompt, type the following and press ENTER to launch the recovery utility:

    ```
    pcrestor
    ```

6. Follow the instructions that appear on your screen.

This feature will reinstall Windows 98 on your computer. When setup is complete, the System Recovery wizard will start. Use the System Recovery wizard to restore your files:

1. In the System Recovery wizard, click Next.

2. Type your name and company, click Next, and then click Details.

3. In the Help window, read the entire Backup Help topic (this explains the entire recovery process).

4. When you're finished reading the Help topic, click the Close button.

5. In the System Recovery wizard, click Finish.

6. The Microsoft Backup Welcome screen appears.

If you click Cancel, click Yes, and then restart your system, the System Recovery wizard automatically starts.

7. In the Microsoft Backup dialog box, click Restore Backed Up Files. Follow the instructions that appear on your screen. The entire backup of the Registry is restored, along with all selected local drives.

You should restore your hardware settings ONLY if your hardware is the *same* as when you made the backup. This should be true if you maintain consistent backups.

8. If you do *not* click "Restore hardware and system settings to the registry" but continue with the operation, your software settings and configuration will be restored along with all selected local drives.

9. Restore all your new and changed files (ie incremental backups). Begin with the oldest and progress to the most recent incremental backup.

If you cannot access your backup device while running the System Recovery wizard, it's most likely that the driver for the backup device is not installed. Install the driver for your backup device:

1. Click Start | Settings | Control Panel, then double-click the System icon.

2.   Click Device Manager, double-click your backup device, then click Driver.

3.   Click Update Driver, then follow the instructions on your screen.

4.   When you're prompted for a disk, insert the disk that came with your backup device.

RESTORING THE WINDOWS ME SYSTEM

While Windows 98 provides a means for restoring serious system problems, it still requires a fairly comprehensive knowledge of system backup and restore procedures. Windows Me has improved system reliability by providing an integrated System Restore utility designed to automatically monitor and record changes made to the core Windows system files (and to the Registry). System Restore can then allow you to undo (or roll back) a change that caused instability in your system. This is accomplished by periodically recording a Restore Point (or System CheckPoint) at a point in time when your computer was known to function properly.

Keep in mind that System Restore is not intended to be an uninstaller or a backup program and is not intended to take the place of a backup. If Windows does not function properly after installing software or drivers, you should use the Add/Remove Programs wizard in Control Panel (or use the program's uninstaller) to remove the software *before* using System Restore.

Using System Restore

Use the steps here to invoke the System Restore utility:

1.   Click Start | Programs | Accessories | System Tools, and then click System Restore.

2.   The first time you use System Restore, there are two options on the Welcome page: Restore My Computer to an Earlier Time or Create a Restore Point.

3.   Click Restore My Computer to an Earlier Time and click Next.

4.   A calendar appears.

5.   In the calendar, choose which restore point to roll your system back to.

6.   Click Next.

7.   You're prompted to close all applications before completing the Restore process because the computer will restart.

8.   After the restart, a confirmation screen appears. Click OK to continue using your computer.

The next time you start System Restore, you will see a third option called Undo My Last Restoration. This is available in the event that the Restore Point you rolled back to does not correct the original problem that you were having, so you can easily get back to the point in time that you started troubleshooting.

Creating Restore Points

Restore Points are critical for proper operation of the System Restore feature. Restore Points are created under the following conditions:

■ Restore Points are created for every 10 hours of computer time.

■ Restore Points are created by Installer packages that use the new Microsoft Software Installer (MSI) technology.

■ Restore Points are created by Installer packages that use InstallShield 6.1 Pro and later.

■ Restore Points are created when AutoUpdate (AU) installs an update package.

■ Restore Points are created when you use System Restore to roll your system back to a different Restore Point. If this is done in safe mode, however, a Restore Point will not be created.

■ Restore Points are created manually by using the System Restore interface.

The Restore Point files that are created under these conditions are stored in compressed (.CAB) format and are located in the Restore folder (also known as the Data Store) on the Windows Me drive. The Data Store cannot be moved or modified. Each fixed disk on your computer will also contain a Restore folder for indexing and monitoring purposes, and each of these folders will contain a file called SRDISKID.DAT.

Restore Points can be created manually before installing device drivers or software (if you're uncertain how they will affect the overall performance of Windows). If you're then unable to use the program's uninstaller to remove the software, you can roll back to the manual restore point that you created.

Recovering with Restore Points

If your computer becomes nonbootable and System Restore was the last operation performed, you can use the Emergency Boot Disk (EBD) to revert your computer back to the state prior to the Restore operation. When you use the EBD to boot your computer, you will see the following message:

```
System Restore detects that a restore was the last operation completed. It
is recommended you now revert the changes to your system made by System
Restore and restart before you proceed. If you choose not to revert these
changes, this option will no longer be available.
1)Revert the Restore changes made to my system.
2)Do not revert the Restore changes made to my system.
Enter a choice
```

If you select the first option, your computer reverts to the state prior to the restore operation and you are prompted to restart the computer.

Disabling System Restore

Although it is strongly discouraged, you can disable System Restore by following these steps:

1. Open Control Panel and click System.
2. Click the Performance tab.
3. Click the File System button.
4. Click the Troubleshooting tab.
5. Click the Disable System Restore check box.
6. Click OK, and then click Close.
7. Restart your computer when prompted.

Startup Troubleshooting Under Windows 98/Me

Ideally, Windows 98/Me will start flawlessly each time that you boot your computer. In actual practice, however, Windows 98/Me can suffer from numerous hardware and software issues that may prevent a correct startup. In most cases, startup problems are identified when the system hangs up, suffers from fatal exception errors, or encounters invalid VxD errors or other file-related problems at start time. As a technician, you should be comfortable with isolating and correcting typical startup problems.

TRY THE SAFE MODE

If Windows 98/Me refuses to start normally, try booting in safe mode. Starting Windows 98/Me in safe mode bypasses the current real-mode configuration and loads a minimal protected-mode configuration—disabling Windows 98/Me device drivers and using the standard VGA display adapter. To start Windows in safe mode, restart your computer, press and hold down the CTRL key until the Windows Startup menu appears, then choose Safe Mode. If you can't start in safe mode, see the "Won't Start in Safe Mode" section that comes next. If you can start in start mode, pick up the procedure with the "Starts in Safe Mode" section that follows.

WON'T START IN SAFE MODE

If the error(s) persist and the system will *not* start in the safe mode, you should inspect the system carefully for all of the following conditions:

- Your computer may be infected with a virus—probably a boot sector virus. Run a current real-mode antivirus utility from a write-protected boot floppy disk in order to scan the system disks and memory. Remove any viruses (especially boot sector viruses) that you may encounter. It may be necessary to fix the master boot record using the FDISK /MBR command.

- Your computer's CMOS settings may not be correct. Review your computer's CMOS Setup and make sure that every entry is correct for your system's particular hardware configuration. If you're not sure, try selecting the BIOS Default settings for your BIOS. Save any changes and exit in order to reboot the system.

- There may be a hardware conflict. These conflicts can include (but are not limited to) PCI BIOS settings, IRQ conflicts, redundant COM ports (for example, two COM1 ports or an internal modem set to the same COM port as an existing serial port), and defective RAM chips. Simplify (remove) your nonessential system devices and try booting again. If this works, you'll need to reinstall one device at a time until you find the one that's precipitating the trouble, then inspect its condition and setup carefully.

- One or more settings in the MSDOS.SYS file need to be changed (for example, the Logo= setting should be set to 0). See the earlier section "Managing MSDOS.SYS" for details about the MSDOS.SYS file.

- You have a compressed drive that is unable to mount a compressed volume file (CVF). You may need to correct problems with the compression software or remove the compression software outright.

- If you're still unable to start Windows 98/Me in the safe mode, run the Windows Registry Checker (SCANREG.EXE) tool to check for problems with the system Registry. Restart your computer, press and hold CTRL, choose Command Prompt Only, type **scanreg**, then press ENTER. If there is a problem with the Registry, you may be able to correct the problem or select an older working Registry that will allow the system to boot.

- If, after using Registry Checker, you still cannot start Windows 98/Me in the safe mode, try installing Windows 98/Me into a new empty folder. This can help to establish whether the problem is related to a corrupted file or remnant of a previous operating system (such as a configuration setting) or a hardware problem.

STARTS IN SAFE MODE

If Windows 98/Me *does* start in the safe mode, step through the startup process with MSCONFIG to see if any devices do not load properly:

1. Click Start | Run, type **msconfig** in the Open box, then click OK.

2. Click Selective Startup.

3. Try different boot options (such as Boot A, Boot B, Boot C, or Boot D as in Table 40-2).

First, try the Boot A option. If Windows 98/Me does *not* start normally, try the Boot B option. If Windows 98/Me *does* start normally using the Boot A option, there is a problem in the SYSTEM.INI or WIN.INI file. Find which line in the SYSTEM.INI or WIN.INI file is causing the problem:

1. Click Start | Run, type **msconfig** in the Open box, and then click OK.

2. Click the WIN.INI tab.

3. Double-click the \Windows folder.

4. Click the load= and run= check boxes to *remove* the check marks.

5. Click OK.

6. Click Yes when you're prompted to restart your computer.

If this corrects the problem, one or more of the files you unchecked is probably the culprit. Replace each file systematically until you find the one causing the trouble.

If Windows 98/Me starts normally using the Boot B option, there is a problem with a driver or TSR program being loaded from the CONFIG.SYS or AUTOEXEC.BAT file—see "Checking TSR Problems" later in this chapter.

If Windows 98/Me does *not* start normally with the Boot A or Boot B options, try the Boot C option. If Windows 98/Me starts normally using the Boot C option, there is a problem with a program that is run during startup. See the "Checking Startup Problems" section next.

If you're still unable to start Windows 98/Me normally, use the System File Checker tool to check for damaged or replaced system files. To start System File Checker, click Start | Programs | Accessories | System Tools, click System Information, and then click System File Checker on the Tools menu. If problems persist and you're *still* unable to start Windows 98/Me normally, refer to "Checking Protected-Mode Problems" later in this chapter.

TABLE 40-2   BOOT OPTIONS FOR STARTUP TROUBLESHOOTING

	BOOT A	**BOOT B**	**BOOT C**	**BOOT D**
Process SYSTEM.INI file	Yes	No	Yes	Yes
Process WIN.INI file	No	Yes	Yes	Yes
Load Static VxD	Yes	Yes	No	Yes
Load Startup group items	Yes	Yes	Yes	No

CHECKING STARTUP PROBLEMS

If you determine that there's an issue with the Startup folder, the problem may be a result of a program that is run during startup. Determine which program is causing the problem:

1. Click Start | Run, type **msconfig** in the Open box, and then click OK.
2. Click the Startup tab, and then click each check box to *clear* it.
3. Click OK, then restart your computer when you're prompted to do so.

If the problem is resolved, one or more of the programs that you unchecked is probably the culprit. Systematically restore each program until you find the one that's causing the trouble.

There may also be a problem with a TSR being loaded in the WINSTART.BAT file (if the WINSTART.BAT file exists). If the Process Winstart.bat File check box is available on the General tab in System Configuration Utility, click the check box to *clear* it, click OK, and then restart your computer. Keep in mind that the WINSTART.BAT file is usually located in the Windows folder and is used to load TSRs that are required *only* by Windows-based programs.

CHECKING TSR PROBLEMS

It is also possible that the problem may be a driver or TSR being loaded from the CONFIG.SYS or AUTOEXEC.BAT file:

1. Click Start | Run, type **msconfig** in the Open box, and then click OK.
2. Click Selective Startup, then click the Process Autoexec.bat File check box to **clear** it.
3. Click OK, then restart your computer when you're prompted to do so.

If the problem is corrected, the problem driver or TSR is being loaded from the AUTOEXEC.BAT file. If the problem is *not* resolved, the problem driver or TSR is being loaded from the CONFIG.SYS file. To determine which line in the AUTOEXEC.BAT or CONFIG.SYS file is loading the driver or TSR, try these steps:

1. Click Start | Run, type **msconfig** in the Open box, and then click OK.
2. Click the AUTOEXEC.BAT or CONFIG.SYS tab, then click the check boxes for all nonessential drivers and programs to *clear* them.
3. Click OK, then restart your computer when you're prompted to do so.

If the problem is resolved, one or more of the programs that you unchecked is probably the culprit. Systematically restore each program until you find the one that's causing the trouble. If the problem is *not* resolved, run the Windows Registry Checker to examine possible problems with the system Registry. To start the Registry Checker, click Start | Programs | Accessories | System Tools, click System Information, then click Registry Checker on the Tools menu.

CHECKING PROTECTED-MODE PROBLEMS

The startup problem may be in a Windows 98/SE protected-mode driver. Use the following steps to determine if this is the case:

1. Click Start | Run, type **msconfig** in the Open box, and then click OK.
2. On the General tab, click Advanced.
3. Under Settings, click a check box to *select* it.

4. Click OK, click OK again, and then restart your computer.

If the problem persists, repeat these steps to select additional items. When the problem is corrected, the last item to be selected is the culprit. If the problem is *not* resolved, you may try to disable PCI IRQ bus steering in Windows 98/SE. If the problem is *still* not resolved, disable devices in Device Manager:

1. Click Start | Settings, and then click Control Panel.

2. Double-click System.

3. On the Device Manager tab, disable all devices under the following branches:
    Display adapters
    Floppy disk controllers
    Hard disk controllers
    Keyboard
    Mouse
    Network adapters
    Ports
    PCMCIA socket
    SCSI controllers
    Sound, video, and game controllers

4. Double-click the branch containing the device you want to disable, click the device to highlight it, and then click Properties.

5. On the General tab, click the Disable in This Hardware Profile check box to *select* it, and then click OK.

6. Restart your computer.

If the problem *is* resolved, systematically re-enable each of the devices that you disabled (and verify that no devices are conflicting). Click the Resources tab and verify that there are no conflicts listed under the Conflicting Device List.

If the problem is *not* resolved, run the Automatic Skip Driver Agent tool to enable any device that has been disabled. To start Automatic Skip Driver Agent, click Start | Programs | Accessories | System Tools, click System Information, and then click Automatic Skip Driver Agent on the Tools menu. If the problem is not resolved, check for a damaged static virtual device driver (VxD):

1. Restart your computer, press and hold down the CTRL key until the Windows 98 Startup menu appears, then choose Step-By-Step Confirmation.

2. Press Y at each prompt up to (and including) Load All Windows Drivers? and press N to everything else.

3. Note that you should make a list of all the items trying to load after this point. This prevents VxDs from loading, and VxDs in the Windows\System\Vmm32 folder from overriding Windows internal VxDs (that is, VxDs built into the VMM32.VXD file).

Shutdown Troubleshooting Under Windows 98/SE

Windows 98/SE may also suffer from problems during the shutdown phase. When Windows 98/SE shuts down, it performs many functions—it completes all disk write functions, flushes the disk cache, runs the Close Window code to close all currently running programs, and transitions all protected-mode drivers to real mode. Since shutdown problems can result in data loss, it's important that you understand just how to deal with shutdown problems under Windows 98/SE. Shutdown problems in Windows 98/SE can be caused by any of the following issues:

- A video card is not assigned an IRQ in real mode.
- A program or TSR will not close correctly.
- An incompatible, damaged, or conflicting device driver is loaded.
- There is a damaged Exit Windows sound file.
- Hardware is incorrectly configured or damaged.
- There is an incompatible BIOS configuration setting.
- There is an incorrect APM or ACPI setting.
- The Fast Shutdown Registry key is enabled.

To troubleshoot shutdown problems in Windows 98/SE, you must first determine the cause of the problem:

- *Check the programs that are running.* This includes disabling any TSRs, loading in real mode, disabling programs that start from your Startup group, and disabling any nonessential third-party device drivers.
- *Check the hardware configuration.* This includes the BIOS settings and the BIOS version. Disable or remove any hardware that may be responsible.

CHECK THE PROGRAMS

To check the programs that are running, use the System Configuration Utility tool (MSCONFIG.EXE) to clean boot your computer. If a clean boot resolves the issue, you can then use the System Configuration Utility tool to determine the program that is the cause of the shutdown problem.

CHECK THE HARDWARE

To check the hardware configuration on your computer, use Device Manager to troubleshoot the installed hardware:

1. Click Start | Settings | Control Panel, then double-click the System icon.
2. On the Device Manager tab, disable all devices under the following branches:
    Display adapters
    Floppy disk controllers
    Hard disk controllers
    Keyboard
    Mouse
    Network adapters
    PCMCIA socket
    Ports
    SCSI controllers
    Sound, video, and game controllers

When you have a serial mouse and you disable the COM ports, if Windows reports to the BIOS that the COM ports are disabled, you'll have no mouse until you enable the COM ports in the BIOS again.

3. Double-click the branch containing the device you want to disable, click the device to highlight it, then click Properties.

4. On the General tab, click to *select* the Disable in This Hardware Profile check box, then click OK.

5. Restart your computer.

When you disable the mouse and then restart your computer, you may receive an error message such as: "Windows did not detect a mouse attached to the computer. You can safely attach a serial mouse now."

To re-enable your mouse, use the following keyboard commands:

1. Press CTRL-ESC to bring up your Start menu.

2. Press the Up Arrow key until Settings is highlighted, press the Right Arrow key to select Control Panel, and then press ENTER.

3. Press the Down Arrow and Left Arrow keys until System is highlighted, then press ENTER.

4. Press the Left Arrow key to highlight Device Manager, press TAB, press TAB again, and then press the Down Arrow key and highlight the device listed under the expanded Mouse branch.

5. Press TAB once to highlight Properties, press ENTER, press TAB once to select Enable Device, and then press ENTER. The mouse should now work.

6. Click OK and then click Yes to restart your computer.

7. If the mouse still does not work, press TAB and then press ENTER. Press ENTER when you receive the message to restart your computer.

If the problem is resolved, re-enable the devices you disabled previously, then verify that no devices are conflicting. Enable devices in the following order:

■ COM ports

■ Hard disk controllers

■ Floppy disk controllers

■ Other devices

To enable a device and check for possible conflicts, follow these steps:

1. Double-click the branch containing the device that you want to re-enable, click the device, and then click Properties.

2. On the General tab, click to *clear* the Disable in This Hardware Profile check box.

3. On the Resources tab, verify that there are no conflicts in the Conflicting Device List. Note that the Resources tab does *not* appear for each device.

4. Click OK, then restart your computer.

If the problem is *not* corrected, run the Automatic Skip Driver Agent to enable any device that has been disabled:

1. Click Start | Programs | Accessories | System Tools.
2. Click System Information, and then click Automatic Skip Driver Agent on the Tools menu.

If the problem is resolved with these steps, and you determine a specific device to be the cause of your shutdown problem, contact the device manufacturer for an updated version of the driver or firmware for the device.

KNOWN WINDOWS SHUTDOWN ISSUES

In addition to the general troubleshooting guidelines presented above, there are numerous specific issues that may affect a proper Windows shutdown.

IRQ Steering

This powerful feature allows several PCI devices to share the same PCI IRQ. If the BIOS is not fully compliant, this option may result in shutdown problems—even if two or more devices are not sharing an IRQ. To disable PCI IRQ bus steering:

1. Click Start | Settings | Control Panel, then double-click the System icon.
2. On the Device Manager tab, click System Devices.
3. Double-click PCI Bus and click to *clear* the Use IRQ Steering check box on the IRQ Steering tab.
4. Click OK, click OK again, and then restart your computer.
5. After you restart the computer, try to shut down your computer again.

If your computer now shuts down successfully, you may need to change the BIOS configuration, or you may need a BIOS update.

Plug-and-Play BIOS

In some cases, the BIOS and Windows may not be communicating properly with the computer hardware during the shutdown process. It is possible to configure Windows 98/SE to ignore the presence of a PnP BIOS and communicate directly with the hardware. To configure Windows to *not* use the PnP BIOS:

 This should only be done for testing purposes, as leaving the PnP BIOS disabled may cause some hardware to stop working.

1. Reboot your machine and hold the CTRL key until you see the Windows 98 Start menu. Choose Command Prompt Only.
2. Type the following at the command prompt:

    ```
    cd \<Windows>\System
    ```

    where <Windows> is the folder in which Windows is installed.
3. Rename the BIOS.VXD file to BIOS.OLD.
4. Restart your computer.
5. After you restart, attempt to shut down Windows.

If the shutdown is now successful, it's most likely an indication that the system BIOS is contributing to the shutdown problems. You may need to update the system BIOS.

NVRAM/ESCD

There are typically specific settings that dictate how the BIOS and Windows interact during the startup and shutdown processes. To check this, disable the NVRAM/ESCD Updates feature to determine if it resolves the shutdown problem:

1. Click Start | Settings | Control Panel, and then double-click the System icon.

2. On the Device Manager tab, select System Devices.

3. Select Plug and Play BIOS, then click to *select* the Disable NVRAM/ESCD Updates check box on the Settings tab (Figure 40-6).

4. Click OK, click OK again, and then restart your computer.

5. After you restart the computer, try to shut down your computer again.

Fast Shutdown Enabled

The System Configuration Utility includes an option to disable fast shutdown. If this option is unchecked in Windows 98/SE, your system may reboot instead of shutting down. To correct this issue, change the FastReboot value data from 1 to 0 in the following registry key:

`HKEY_LOCAL_MACHINE\System\CurrentControlSet\Control\Shutdown`.

If you apply the Windows 98/SE Shutdown Supplement that addresses shutdown issues, the Disable Fast Shutdown option is no longer listed on the Advanced tab in MSCONFIG.

Antivirus Program

If you have an antivirus program that's configured to scan your floppy disk drive when you shut down your computer, your computer may stop responding. Try disabling or uninstalling the antivirus software on your system.

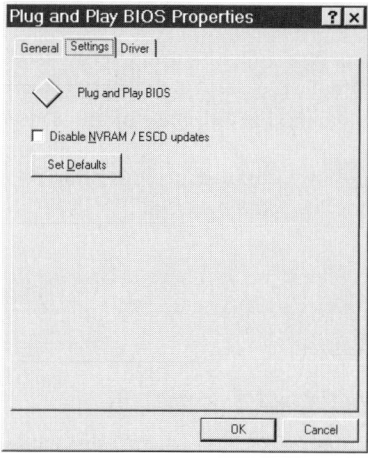

FIGURE 40-6   The PnP BIOS Properties dialog

Shutdown Troubleshooting Under Windows Me

As with older versions of Windows, Windows Me may also suffer from problems during the shutdown process. When Windows Me shuts down, it performs many functions—it completes all disk write functions, flushes the disk cache, runs the Close Window code to close all currently running programs, and transitions all protected-mode drivers to real mode. Since shutdown problems can result in data loss, it's important that you understand just how to deal with shutdown problems under Windows Me. Shutdown problems in Windows Me can be caused by issues such as incompatible, damaged, or conflicting device drivers, a damaged exit sound file, or incorrectly configured or damaged hardware.

The Windows Me Startup and Shutdown Troubleshooting wizard is located in the Help and Support Center in Windows Me, or at the following Microsoft Web site: **support.microsoft.com/support/windows/tshoot/**.

CHECK STARTUP ITEMS

To troubleshoot Windows Me shutdowns, first determine whether a program in the Startup folder conflicts with the startup process:

1. Click Start | Run, type **msconfig** in the Open box, and then click OK.

2. Click Selective Startup, click to clear the Load Startup Group Items check box, click Apply, click OK, and then click Yes to restart your computer.

3. Test to determine if the issue is resolved by restarting your computer. If your computer does not shut down correctly, skip to the next step. If your computer shuts down correctly, one of your startup programs is probably causing this issue.

   To determine which startup program is causing this issue:

1. Click Start | Run, type **msconfig** in the Open box, and then click OK.

2. On the Startup tab, click to select a check box, click OK, and then click Yes to restart your computer.

3. Test to determine if the startup program you disabled caused the issue. If not, repeat the steps, but enable a different program. When your computer does not start correctly, you have determined that the last startup program you enabled is the cause of the issue.

If disabling startup programs does not resolve the problem, re-enable the startup programs by repeating the preceding steps, and then click to select the Load Startup Group Items check box.

CHECK DRIVERS

Now determine if the shutdown problem is caused by a command or driver that is loaded automatically from the WIN.INI or SYSTEM.INI files:

1. Click Start | Run, type **msconfig**, and then click OK.

2. Click Selective Startup, and then click to clear the following check boxes:
   Process Win.ini file
   Process System.ini file

If any of these items is unavailable, that particular file does not contain any items to load. Click OK, and then click Yes to restart the computer.

3. Test to determine if the issue is resolved by restarting your computer. If your computer does not shut down correctly, repeat the steps, but click to select the check boxes, and then continue.

Next, selectively disable device drivers. Some of the most common device drivers that may cause problems are sound card drivers, video adapter drivers, and network adapter drivers. To disable device drivers:

1. Right-click My Computer, click Properties, and then click the Device Manager tab.
2. Double-click a device type, for example, Sound, Video, and Game Controllers, to expand it.
3. Click one of the listed devices, and then click Properties.
4. Click to select the Disable in This Hardware Profile check box.
5. Click OK, click OK again, and then restart your computer.
6. Test to determine if the issue is resolved by restarting your computer. If your computer does not shut down correctly, repeat the steps but disable a different item.
7. To test your video adapter, click Start | Run, type **msconfig**, click OK, click Advanced, click to select the VGA 640×480×16 check box, and then click OK.
8. If you disable your sound card, video adapter, and network adapter, but the issue is still not resolved, re-enable these devices by repeating these steps, but click to clear the Disable in This Hardware Profile check box, and then continue.

CHECK SOUND FILES

At this point, you should determine if a damaged exit sound file causes the shutdown problem:

1. Click Start | Settings | Control Panel, and then double-click the Sounds and Multimedia icon.
2. Record the name and location of the Exit Windows sound, click Exit Windows in the Sound Events box, and then click None in the Name box.
3. Click OK, and then restart your computer.
4. Test to determine if the issue is resolved by restarting your computer. If your computer does not shut down correctly, repeat these steps, but restore your original Exit Windows sound, and then continue.
5. If the issue is resolved, your Exit Windows sound file is damaged and must be replaced. To replace the sound file, restore the file from a backup, or reinstall the program that provided the sound file.

CHECK POWER MANAGEMENT

Not all computers have Advanced Power Management (APM) features. If your computer does not have APM features, skip this step. Otherwise, determine if APM is causing the shutdown problem by disabling it:

1. Click Start | Settings | Control Panel, double-click System, and then click the Device Manager tab.
2. Double-click the System Devices branch to expand it.
3. Double-click Advanced Power Management in the device list, click the Settings tab, and then click to select the Force APM 1.0 Mode and Disable Power Status Polling check boxes.

4. Click OK until you return to Control Panel, and then restart your computer.

5. Test to determine if the issue is resolved by restarting your computer. If your computer does not shut down correctly, repeat these steps, but click to clear the Force APM 1.0 Mode and Disable Power Status Polling check boxes, and then continue.

CHECK VXDS

Buggy or outdated virtual device drivers (or VXD files) can present a serious shutdown problem. Follow the steps here to check for VxD issues:

1. Click Start | Run, type **msconfig**, and then click OK.

2. Click Selective Startup, and then click to clear the Load Static VxDs check box.

3. Click OK, and then click Yes to restart the computer.

4. Test to determine if the issue is resolved by restarting your computer. If your computer does not shut down correctly, repeat these steps, but click to select the check box, and then continue.

5. Check the properties of the VXD file to determine which program it is associated with. Uninstall and then reinstall the program to replace the VXD file with a new copy. To check the properties of a file, click Start | Search, type the name of the file in the For Files or Folders box, and then click Search Now. After the file you are looking for is displayed in the list, right-click the file, and then click Properties.

CHECK THE STARTUP LOG

Determine if the problem is listed in the startup log file. You can look in your startup log file (BOOTLOG.PRV) to find information about problems that occur during shutdown. The BOOTLOG.PRV file is a hidden file in the root folder of drive C. If Windows is configured to hide system files, use these steps to display hidden files:

1. On the Windows desktop, double-click My Computer.

2. On the Tools menu, click Folder Options.

3. Click the View tab.

4. Click to clear the Hide Protected Operating System Files check box, and then click Yes when you are prompted to confirm this action.

5. Click OK, and then look for the BOOTLOG.PRV file again.

If you still cannot find this file on your hard disk, you can create a new one:

1. Click Start | Shut Down, click Shut Down, and then click OK.

2. If your computer does not automatically shut off, press the power button on your computer to turn it off. Leave your computer off for approximately 15 seconds, and then turn your computer back on.

3. While your computer is starting, press and hold the CTRL key. When the Startup menu appears, choose Logged (\BOOTLOG.TXT), and then press ENTER.

4. After Windows starts, click Start | Shut Down, click Restart, and then click OK.

To review your startup log file:

1. Double-click My Computer, double-click drive C, and then look for the BOOTLOG.PRV file.

2. Double-click the BOOTLOG.PRV file. If you are prompted to select a program to use to open the file, click WordPad, Notepad, or any text editor in the list.

3. Look for Terminate= entries. These entries are located at the bottom of the file. If a process that is started by a Terminate= entry is completed successfully, the file contains a matching EndTerminate= entry.

4. Check the last line in the BOOTLOG.PRV file to see if it is one of these items:

-   **Terminate=Query Drivers**   This is a Memory Manager problem. Your computer might have defective memory chips or damaged files. You might need to reinstall Windows.

-   **Terminate=Reset Display**   Try installing an updated video adapter driver.

-   **Terminate=RIT**   There may be timer-related problems with the sound card or an older mouse driver. Try installing updated drivers for these devices.

-   **Terminate=Win32**   A program is not shutting down properly. Try quitting all programs before you shut down Windows.

Print Troubleshooting

Printers are the most common and popular peripheral device for the PC. In the vast majority of cases, using a printer is as simple as connecting it to a parallel port and installing the drivers, but there are situations when the printer may not function properly under Windows 9x/Me. This part of the chapter outlines a series of steps that may help you resolve common printing problems under Windows.

CHECK THE PRINTER'S HARDWARE

Many printing problems can be caused by hardware-related issues. Before you jump into complicated troubleshooting procedures, you should *first* verify that there are no hardware-related printer issues:

-   Verify that your printer is connected to the correct power source and turned on. If the printer has a suspend mode, make sure that the printer is *not* in the suspend mode.

-   Verify that your printer is properly connected to your printer port (such as LPT1). Note that the printer cable must be seated properly in the printer port on your computer and at the printer.

-   Verify that your printer has an adequate supply of paper (or other appropriate printing media), and that the media is *not* jamming the printer.

-   Verify that your printer contains an adequate supply of ink or toner to work properly. Low supplies of ink or toner are usually indicated by an error light or message on the printer itself.

-   If your printer has an online/offline setting or button, verify that your printer is online.

-   Many printing problems are the result of your printer memory being full. Reset your printer and clear its memory by turning it off, waiting 5 to 10 seconds, then turning it back on. Also clear any print buffers in the PC itself.

-   Verify that you've followed all of the installation instructions provided by your printer's manufacturer.

-   Perform a self-test on the printer (according to the manufacturer's instructions). Such self-diagnostic tools can often resolve or diagnose basic issues with your printer hardware. If the printer's self-test doesn't work, your printer may be damaged.

■   If another computer is available, verify that your printer works properly when connected to another computer. If your printer does not work properly when connected to another computer, your printer may be damaged.

CHECK THE PRINTER PROPERTIES

Incorrect printer property settings can cause poor or incomplete output or can cause your printer to not print at all. See that your printer property settings are configured as recommended by the printer's manufacturer:

1.   Click Start | Settings, and then click Printers.

2.   Right-click the printer you want to check, and then click Properties (Figure 40-7).

3.   Verify that all of your printer properties are configured as recommended by your printer manufacturer.

TRY THE PRINT TROUBLESHOOTER

Windows includes a Print Troubleshooter tool that can help to automate the process of testing. Before you perform any of the following troubleshooting steps, try the Print Troubleshooter tool:

1.   For Windows 95, click Start | Help.

2.   On the Contents tab, double-click the Troubleshooting topic.

3.   Double-click the If You Have Trouble Printing topic.

The Windows 95 Resource Kit also includes a Print Troubleshooter tool, and this tool is more detailed than the Print Troubleshooter in Windows. This tool (Epts.exe) is also available on the Windows 95 Upgrade CD-ROM in the Other\Misc\Epts folder.

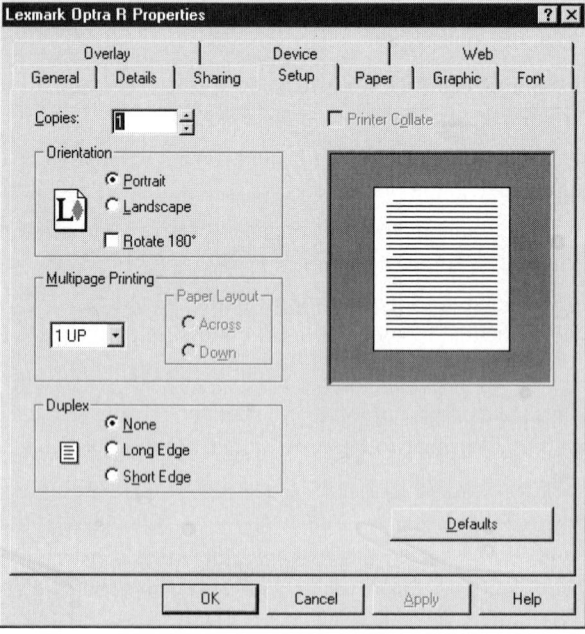

FIGURE 40-7   Checking printer properties under Windows 98/SE

1. For Windows 98, click Start | Help.

2. Click Troubleshooting, click Windows 98 Troubleshooters, and then click Print.

CHECK THE PRINTERS.TXT FILE

Windows 9x/Me includes a file called PRINTERS.TXT located in the Windows folder. This file contains information about known printing issues and may help you identify and resolve many common compatibility and printing problems.

TRY A TEST DOCUMENT

Often, a sophisticated printing application such as Microsoft Word or CorelDraw may not print as expected. Try printing a basic document from WordPad or Notepad. Restart your computer, click Start | Programs | Accessories, and then click Notepad or WordPad. Type some text in the editor, then try to print the text. If you *can* print successfully in Notepad or WordPad, your printing issue may be specific to one application. You should try the steps in the "Printing Problems in Only One Program" section later in this chapter. If you *cannot* print successfully in Notepad or WordPad, try the steps in the "Print from a Command Prompt" section next.

PRINT FROM A COMMAND PROMPT

Try printing from a DOS command prompt to determine if your printer hardware is connected properly and can receive instructions from the computer. Do this by copying a file to your printer:

1. Verify that the printer is turned on and online *without* any printer errors.

2. Check that no printer sharing devices (such as printer switch boxes) or daisy-chained devices (such as parallel port CD-ROMs, Zip drives, and so on) are connected between the computer and printer.

3. Restart your computer to the Safe Mode Command Prompt mode using the Startup menu.

4. At the command prompt, type the appropriate line and then press ENTER:

   ■ For a regular printer, try: **copy c:\windows\mouse.txt lpt1**

   ■ For a laser printer, try: **copy c:\windows\mouse.txt lpt1 /b**

   ■ For a PostScript printer, try: **copy c:\windows\system\testps.txt lpt1**

These commands assume that your printer is connected to LPT1. If your printer is connected to a different printer port, substitute that printer port number in the commands. If you do not have a MOUSE.TXT file in your Windows folder, try substituting the LICENSE.TXT file, the SUPPORT.TXT file, or the CONFIG.TXT file from the Windows folder.

These commands copy the given file to the printer. If the file is *not* printed (or you receive a Write Fault error message), there may be a problem with the printer port, the printer cable, or the printer itself. You may want to try using a different printer cable, or (if possible) test the cable with a different printer. If you determine that you *can* print from a command prompt (but not from Windows 9x/Me), try the steps listed in the "No Windows Support" section next.

When you copy a file to some ink-jet or laser printers, you may need to press the Form Feed or Resume key after the printer has received the print job, or the printer may not eject the paper.

Alternatively, you can try printing from LPT1.DOS. Printing to the LPT1.DOS port is similar to printing to a file and then copying the file to the printer port. Enable the LPT1.DOS port in Windows 9x/Me:

1. Click Start | Settings, and then click Printers.

2. Right-click the printer that you want to use, then click Properties.

3. On the Details tab, click Add Port.

4. In the Add Port dialog box, click Other, click Local Port, and then click OK.

5. Type **lpt1.dos** in the Enter a Port Name box, then click OK.

Remember that printing to the LPT1.DOS port may be slower than printing to the standard LPT1 port. Since printing to LPT1.DOS uses low-level DOS commands to send a print job to the printer, not all of the available signals in the port and printer cable are used. As a result, if printing to LPT1.DOS is successful, this may indicate a problem with the printer port or printer cable. If you *cannot* print to LPT1.DOS in normal mode, try restarting your computer in safe mode and then printing to LPT1.DOS.

NO WINDOWS SUPPORT

If you *can* print from a command prompt but not from *any* Windows-based program, there may be a problem with the system's spool settings, or with bidirectional communication. Determine if either of these issues are the cause of your problem:

1. Click Start | Settings | Printers.

2. Right-click the printer that you're trying to print to, then click Properties.

3. Click the Details tab, click Spool Settings, and then click the Print Directly to the Printer option.

 If the local printer is being shared, the Print Directly to the Printer option is unavailable, so stop sharing the printer.

4. If your printer supports bidirectional communication, click Disable Bidirectional Support for this Printer. Bidirectional printing relies on the IEEE 1284 specification. If your printer cable does not conform to this specification (and is not of reasonable length), bidirectional printing will not work in Windows 9x/Me.

5. Click OK, then click OK again to close Print Properties.

6. Try to print from Notepad or WordPad.

7. If you *can* print from Notepad or WordPad, try different combinations of spool settings and bidirectional support until you find a combination that works. For example, try disabling bidirectional support with RAW and EMF spool data format settings. Also try bidirectional support with the RAW spool data format. Remember that RAW is the only spool data format supported for PostScript printers.

PRINTING PROBLEMS IN ONLY ONE PROGRAM

If your printing problems only occur in one program, this almost always indicates your problem is specific to that one program and is *not* an issue with Windows 9x/Me or your hardware. If you can print from Notepad, WordPad, and other programs, try the following steps to try to narrow the issue within your offending program:

■ As a test, try to print a blank page from the suspect program. If this prints correctly, the program may have problems with memory or fonts. The program may need a patch or update.

■ 32-bit programs use the system Registry to obtain needed information, while 16-bit programs may use INI files. If you're having a printing problem with a 16-bit program, perhaps an INI file needs to be modified to accommodate the program.

■ Uninstall and then reinstall the program.

■ Contact the manufacturer of the program for specific settings or possible known issues with their program that might affect printing.

REMOVE AND REINSTALL THE PRINTER DRIVER

It may be possible that the printer driver that you're using is incorrect or corrupted. Verify that your printer driver is correct, properly installed, and not damaged. To do this, remove and reinstall the printer driver:

1. Click Start | Settings | Printers.

2. Right-click the printer that you want to remove, then click Delete. If you're prompted to remove all the files associated with the printer, click Yes.

3. Click Start | Settings, and then click Printers.

4. Double-click Add Printer, then follow the instructions in the Add Printer wizard to reinstall the appropriate printer driver.

5. Test the printer to determine if your printing issue is resolved.

If your printing issue is not resolved, try using the Generic/Text Only printer driver for your printer. This test can help determine whether or not your printing problem is related to your printer driver. To use the Generic/Text Only printer driver:

1. Click Start | Settings | Printers.

2. Double-click Add Printer, then follow the instructions in the Add Printer wizard to install the Generic/Text Only printer driver as a local printer.

This driver is a very basic driver, and the printed output may be simplified (or appear in a lower resolution).

Test to see if you can print using this driver. If you *can* print successfully using the Generic/Text Only printer driver, your printing issue is most likely specific to the printer driver that you're using. You should contact your printer manufacturer to inquire about the availability of an updated printer driver, a patch (or fix) for your current driver, or information about any known compatibility issues with your driver.

CLEAN UP YOUR HARD DRIVE

Printing issues may sometimes occur if your hard disk contains too many temporary files, the disk is fragmented or damaged, or the disk does not contain more than 3MB of free space. Follow the procedures shown next to clean up the hard disk.

Delete TMP and SPL Files

You should first take some time to locate and delete any temporary (.TMP) or spool (.SPL) files that may be present on the drive:

1. Reboot your computer to a command prompt.

2. At the command prompt, type **set**, then press ENTER.

3. Note the location of the TEMP variable.

4. Change to the TEMP folder. For example, if TEMP is set to c:\windows\temp, type:

    ```
    cd\windows\temp
    ```

    and then press ENTER.

5. Delete any temporary files in this folder. Temporary files typically have a TMP file extension. To delete these files, type:

    ```
    del *.tmp
    ```

    and then press ENTER.

 You should not delete these files from within the Windows 9x/Me GUI because Windows (or a Windows-based program) may be using one of these files.

6. Change to the spool folder. For example, type:

    ```
    cd\windows\spool\printers
    ```

    and then press ENTER.

7. Delete any spool files in this folder. Spool files typically have a SPL file extension. To delete these files, type:

    ```
    del *.spl
    ```

    and then press ENTER.

Perform Basic Drive Maintenance

If your hard disk becomes severely fragmented, the file system is damaged, or the drive has cross-linked files, you may encounter printing problems. Run ScanDisk and Disk Defragmenter to check for these problems:

1. Restart your computer normally.

2. Click Start | Programs | Accessories, select System Tools, and then click ScanDisk.

3. Let ScanDisk run a cycle on each drive in the system. Have ScanDisk fix any errors that it finds.

4. Click Start | Programs | Accessories, select System Tools, and then click Disk Defragmenter.

5. Let Defrag run a cycle on each drive in the system. You may not need to defragment a drive that is less than 5 percent fragmented.

CHECK YOUR PRINTER PORT

If your printer port (LPT port) is not configured and working properly, your printer may not work correctly (or at all). Follow the procedures next to verify the configuration and operation of your printer port.

Check Port Settings with Device Manager

Use Device Manager to verify that your printer port settings are correct and that no resource conflicts exist:

1. Right-click My Computer, click Properties, click the Device Manager tab.

2. Double-click Ports (COM & LPT), then double-click the appropriate port for your printer (for example, Printer Port LPT1).

3. Click the Resources tab, then verify that the settings are correct for your printer port. For example, the I/O range for a standard LPT1 port is 0378h-037Ah (a physical LPT2 port typically uses I/O 278). Also verify that the Conflicting Devices List displays No Conflicts.

4. If you determine that you have one or more devices that are conflicting with your printer port, you'll need to isolate and correct the conflict.

Remove and Reinstall the Printer Port

The printer port itself may have a missing or corrupted driver. You may be able to correct an issue with your printer port by removing and reinstalling it:

1. Right-click My Computer, click Properties, and then click the Device Manager tab.

2. Double-click the Ports (COM & LPT) branch to expand it, then click the appropriate port for your printer (normally Printer Port LPT1).

3. Click Remove, click OK to finish removing your port, and then restart your computer.

When Windows automatically detects your printer port, follow the instructions on the screen to finish reinstalling the port. If your port is *not* automatically detected after you restart your computer:

1. Click Start | Settings | Control Panel, then double-click Add New Hardware.

2. In Windows 95, click Next, click No, and then click Next.

3. In Windows 98/Me, click Next, then click Next again to search for plug-and-play devices. If the port is not found, click No, the Device Isn't in the List, click Next, click No, I Want to Select the Hardware from a List, then click Next.

4. Click Ports (COM & LPT), and then click Next.

5. Click (Standard Port Types) in the Manufacturers box, click Printer Port in the Models box, and then click Next.

6. Follow the directions on the screen, then click Finish.

After you finish reinstalling the printer port, test to see if the issue is resolved. If not, continue with the next section.

Disable ECP Support

If your computer provides an Enhanced Capabilities Port (or ECP), you may need to disable the port in order to remove possible hardware incompatibilities between the ECP and the printer. Determine if your issue is specific to your ECP and disable the ECP by using the following steps for Windows 95:

1. Under Windows 95, click Start | Settings | Control Panel, then double-click the System icon.

2. On the Device Manager tab, double-click the Ports (COM & LPT) branch to expand it.

3. Double-click the ECP port.

4. On the Driver tab, click Change Driver.

5. Click Show All Devices.

6. In the Manufacturers box, click Standard Port Types.

7. In the Models box, click Printer Port, and then click OK until you return to Control Panel.

Disable the ECP by using the following steps for Windows 98/Me:

1.   Under Windows 98, click Start | Settings | Control Panel, then double-click the System icon.

2.   On the Device Manager tab, double-click the Ports (COM & LPT) branch to expand it.

3.   Double-click the ECP port.

4.   On the Driver tab, click Update Driver. When the Update Device Driver wizard appears, click Next.

5.   Click Display a List of All the Device Drivers in a Specific Location, So You Can Select the Driver You Want, and then click Next.

6.   Click Show All Hardware.

7.   In the Manufacturers box, click Standard Port Types.

8.   In the Models box, click Printer Port, and then click Next.

9.   When the Update Driver Warning dialog box appears, click Yes.

10.   Click Finish, then click Yes to restart your computer.

If the ECP port is redetected after you restart your computer, you may also need to disable or reconfigure the LPT port in the CMOS Setup.

UPDATE THE LPT.VXD FILE UNDER WINDOWS 95

If you're using Windows 95, upgrading to Windows 98/Me can often resolve certain printing issues. If you want to continue using Windows 95, you may be able to resolve printing issues by updating to a different LPT.VXD file. The LPT.VXD file is the virtual device driver for your printer port. The standard printer port driver file works correctly with most Windows 95–based computers, but there is an alternate LPT.VXD file that may resolve the following problems:

■   You receive timeout error messages, or you're unable to print if you're printing with a Compaq-based computer and a bidirectional printer.

■   You experience problems printing to any bidirectional printer on a computer with a PS/2-style printer port. Symptoms may include an extra page being printed, PCL commands appearing on the printout, and so on.

■   If you cannot use Device Manager to configure an ECP port to run in standard LPT mode, this may be because your computer has a plug-and-play BIOS that enumerates only ECP parallel ports.

The alternate LPT.VXD file is located in the \Drivers\Printer\Lpt folder on the Windows 95 CD. This file is also available for download from the Microsoft FTP site.

Use these steps to install the alternate LPT.VXD file:

1.   Click Start | Find, then click Files or Folders.

2.   In the Named box, type **lpt.vxd**, then click Find Now.

3.   Right-click the LPT.VXD file in the Windows\System folder, click Rename, type **lpt.old**, and then press ENTER.

4.   Copy the LPT.VXD file from the Drivers\Printer\Lpt folder on the Windows 95 CD to the Windows\System folder on the hard disk.

5.   Restart your computer.

The alternate LPT.VXD file has the same file size and date as the original file. The version number of the alternate LPT.VXD file is 4.00.503 or 4.00.951. To determine the version number, right-click the LPT.VXD file and click Properties.

DISABLE THE CHECK PORT STATE OPTION

The BIOS in some computers incorrectly reports that the printer port is busy or not available. By default, Windows 9x/Me checks for these errors. Clearing the Check Port State check box causes Windows 9x/Me to ignore these messages. If you had to disable the Fast Printing Direct to Port option in Windows 3.1 or WfWG 3.x, you should also disable the Check Port State option in Windows 9x/Me:

1. Click Start | Settings, and then click Printers.
2. Right-click the printer that you want to use, then click Properties.
3. Click the Details tab, click Port Settings, then *clear* the Check Port State Before Printing check box.
4. Restart the computer if necessary.

CHECK FOR A READ-ONLY WIN.INI FILE

Some printing problems can occur if the WIN.INI file has the read-only attribute. Determine if the WIN.INI file has the read-only attribute:

1. Click Start | Find, and then click Files or Folders.
2. In the Named box, type **win.ini**.
3. In the Look In box, click the drive containing the Windows folder, and then click Find Now.
4. Right-click the WIN.INI file, then click Properties.
5. If the Read-Only check box is selected, click to *clear* it.
6. Click OK.
7. Quit the Find tool, then restart your computer.

Further Study

Microsoft   www.microsoft.com

USING THE
COMPANION DISC

The key to a successful PC repair rests in a fast and decisive diagnosis of the problem—determining the source of the problem as quickly and accurately as possible is often the line that separates successful and profitable repair houses from those that are not. *Diagnostics* are the tools that technicians use to "look inside" the behavior of ailing PCs. There are many different kinds of diagnostic tools. Some are hardware-based test instruments (such as digital multimeters, POST reader cards, and high-voltage probes), while others are software-based programs that probe the PC as it runs and report their findings to the display. Your book comes with the DLS Diagnostic CD 4—a CD with over 120 shareware diagnostics and utilities designed to help you identify installed hardware and track down pesky PC problems. This appendix explains how to use the CD and highlights the various software tools you'll find here.

The Shareware Concept

You've probably seen the word "shareware" used before. At this point, we should discuss exactly what shareware is, and how it relates to commercial software. If you already understand the shareware concept, feel free to skip this section. Otherwise, the following section will probably be very helpful to you.

AN ISSUE OF DISTRIBUTION

When we think of diagnostic software, we tend to think of fancy shrink-wrapped boxes lining store shelves. This is *commercial* software sold through distributors. Here's how commercial software works: A bright group of programmers start a small company to write software, but they don't have the marketing or merchandising know-how to get their product into the retail channel. Instead, they will sell (more specifically, "license") their brilliant product to a major software publishing house who will put *their own* name on it, put it in *their own* fancy boxes, and use their clout to get it into the hands of retailers. Retail distributors will buy those products in volume from the publisher (usually at a deep discount) and put them on their store shelves. The publisher then pays the original author(s) a royalty from the volume sales to distributors.

As you might imagine from the scenario above, the people who actually *develop* the software you buy in stores only receive a fraction of the price you actually pay at the store—it's usually the software publishers and retailers that are making the real money. An even more important problem with commercial distribution is that there is only a finite amount of store shelf space to go around, and no distributor is going to stock *everything*. For example, a distributor may choose to carry two or three diagnostics—not 25 or 30. As a result, a lot of very good products never really get the attention they deserve because the people pushing the product just don't have enough clout with the distributor to gain a foothold on their shelves. This means that, as a technician, you're denied a real selection of products.

Another serious problem with commercial distribution is that you rarely (if ever) have an opportunity to try a diagnostic (or any other program) *before* you buy it. The back of the box may look pretty, but it hardly ever reveals the "true" product. How many times have you stood in a store trying to decide between two or three similar products, then gotten home with your choice only to be disappointed? Trying to bring the product back is another challenge entirely. Many software retailers simply will not accept a product return once the box has been opened, and you find yourself out a bundle of money you can barely afford for a product that you can hardly use (if at all). It is a system that is simply not fair to the software buyer.

THE IDEA OF SHAREWARE

The *shareware* concept is a means of product distribution that allows a vast number of software products to be offered on a "try-before-you-buy" basis. Software writers develop a "shareware version" of their product that is then distributed freely through bulletin boards, online services (such as CompuServe or the Internet), or even on diskettes passed between friends. If you like the software and plan to use it, you "register" (a.k.a. "buy") the software with the author. Registration usually involves sending a fee to the author. Some shareware variations, however, only require that you send in your name and mailing address (often referred to as *postcard-ware*), or come complete in its shareware form and no exchange of money is needed (known as *$0 shareware* or *freeware*). When you register a product, you will typically receive benefits such as an updated version of the product, a printed manual, free technical support, or some other combination of benefits. The advantage of shareware is that *anyone* can put their program into distribution—and be assured of a huge distribution network—for virtually no cost.

The important things to remember about shareware are that it is *not* free, it is *not* public domain, and it is *not* a demo version of some shrink-wrapped product. It is fully functional, copyrighted software that commands a purchase price. Once you have a shareware product, you may try the product for a certain period of time (typically 30 days). After that time, you *must* register the product (which means paying the purchase price), or *cease* using it. When you get a shareware product, it will always be marked as such in the startup screen and disk documentation.

THE PROBLEMS WITH SHAREWARE

Shareware is largely regarded as one of the most important developments in the software industry, and many highly respected companies such as Netscape, Id Software, Apogee Games, PKWARE, and McAfee Associates have gone "commercial" from their product's growth as shareware. Vast numbers of other smaller software makers like MVP Software are marketing their products quite successfully where they would never have had a chance through commercial channels. As you venture into the shareware world, however, there *are* some potential pitfalls to beware of.

First, there is a strong potential for "shareware abuse"—people who make productive use of the shareware, but refuse to pay for it. This is the great "gray area" of shareware because there is no real way to regulate distribution. Shareware only works when the authors receive their registration fees. In turn, this allows them to pay the bills and develop even better software. Software authors have several tactics available to encourage registrations. The most common tool is *limited functionality*, where a program may be functional, but limited in its capability. For example, a shareware strategy game I recently found would only allow you to use small and medium-sized play fields with no customized features in the shareware version, but played exactly the same as the registered version that included the added features. In other words, a shareware author will provide you with enough functionality to make the product useful and productive, but not enough functionality where you can do *everything*. Other incentives include the offer of a printed manual—which can be very important for lengthy documentation—and technical support if you need help getting the most from the registered version.

Another issue that some people have with shareware is the inconsistent use of benefits—no two products are alike, and there is no established standard of what you get when you register a product. Some shareware authors provide a wealth of benefits, while others simply send you a registered version on diskette or CD. When you decide to register a product, always look at the shareware documentation to see what the benefits are.

Finally, many people find frustration at the way some shareware authors seem to come and go. Remember that most shareware authors work from home or from a small office where they've hung out their shingle. If the registrations don't come in, they wind up rocketing into oblivion—leaving their shareware product(s) unsupported on BBS libraries and online forums all over the world. It's disappointing to find a handy shareware product, spend time evaluating it, fill out the registration form, send in your money, and get the registration back unopened a few weeks later because the address listed in the documentation has expired or is undeliverable as addressed. As a rule, if you find a shareware product you like, you should look for the most recent shareware version available before registering it.

The DLS Diagnostic CD 4

Now that you understand the idea of shareware, we can finally turn our attention to the CD that accompanies this book. The DLS Diagnostic CD 4 contains over 120 demo, shareware, $0 shareware ("freeware"), and public domain diagnostic programs and PC utilities that have been assembled from some of the finest shareware authors in the world. Whether you are a novice attempting to check your PC's configuration for the first time, or an experienced technician trying to manipulate a partition on your customer's hard drive, you'll find an extensive selection of software for testing, troubleshooting, and mastering the PC.

The CD is arranged as a series of sub-directories where each sub-directory holds an entire product compressed as a single file. Each product resides in its own sub-directory, so once you know the product you are interested in, you can quickly locate the product and install it on your hard drive or floppy disk.

There is *no* Autorun file on the CD, and it will *not* automatically install or launch any product. The CD is intended to serve as an archive (or "library") of shareware products. You can pick and choose the product(s) that you wish to try, then install them individually as required.

THE CD AND FILE COMPRESSION

The DLS Diagnostic CD 4 is intended to serve as an archive rather than a working medium, so each of the programs have been compressed as a .ZIP file or self-extracting .EXE file. To use a program on the CD, you must decompress and install it to your hard drive or a floppy disk. This part of the chapter covers some general guidelines for using the programs on your CD. You might wonder why the programs have been compressed, when they could just have easily been expanded to work (in many cases) directly from the CD itself. Well, there are several important reasons for this decision:

■ *Programs generally run very poorly from slow media such as a CD.* Most of the programs on this CD run much better from a floppy disk, or even better from a hard drive.

■ *Data files can't be written to the CD.* Some of the diagnostic programs on this CD require that data files be written while the program is running. Since you can't write to an ordinary CD, those programs would not be useable from the CD anyway.

■ *Compression conserves space.* Compressed files are smaller and easier to work with than the individual files of an uncompressed product. Using compression allows us to use a minimum amount of space on the CD, and allows the most expansion in future editions of this book.

■ *Many authors prohibit the distribution of their products in an uncompressed form.* Gathering up all of the program files into a single compressed file helps us ensure that the original shareware program package has not been tampered with.

■ *Many products need to be "installed."* Even if the individual program files were uncompressed, some of the products on the CD need to have an installation routine run in order to organize, sort, and initialize the program files properly, so those programs would still not be executable from the CD.

■ *You won't always have a working CD-ROM drive available.* Even if we designed the DLS Diagnostic CD 4 to run each product directly (and successfully) from the CD itself, it means you would need a working CD-ROM drive on the PC you intend to troubleshoot. You understand that this is not always possible.

INSTALLING THE SOFTWARE

Installing software from the CD to your hard disk or floppy drive is not a difficult process, but you need to pay attention to detail. The process typically involves copying, decompressing, virus checking, and installing.

1. Insert the CD into your drive—there is no Autorun or other installer on the disc.
2. Use Windows Explorer to create a folder on your hard drive for the new utility.
3. Use Windows Explorer to locate the directory on the CD containing the utility.
4. Copy the utility file (usually a .ZIP or .EXE file) from the CD to the folder you created.
5. Use WinZip or PKUnzip to decompress the utility copied to your hard drive.
6. Check the decompressed file(s) for viruses.

 Although each of these programs have been tested for viruses, be sure to scan the program files yourself with a current anti-virus tool (such as Symantec's Norton AntiVirus or McAfee VirusScan) before running a given program for the first time. *Do not attempt to execute any file that is flagged with a virus warning.*

7. Review the README file (or any other documentation files) decompressed with the utility.

8.   Now you may run the executable file directly, or start the utility's SETUP routine to install the product (as directed by the product's documentation).

Please do *not* contact Dynamic Learning Systems or McGraw-Hill for information on these programs. We cannot provide support for the installation and use of these programs. For documentation and contact information for each developer, refer to the README file that usually accompanies each program.

REGISTERING SHAREWARE

Most of the shareware products on your CD carry some sort of registration fee. These fees range from $0 (essentially free) to a voluntary contribution of a few dollars to fees of $40 or more. Now there's certainly no reason for you to run right out and register *everything* on the CD. The whole point of shareware is that you can try these products for free to see if they will serve your needs. Chances are that you will try most (if not all) of these programs at one time or another, but you may find only a few programs that you can really use—and these are the ones that you should consider registering. Don't panic, you have plenty of time to try everything!

CARING FOR THE DLS DIAGNOSTIC CD 4

Whether you install several programs of interest and store the CD for a prolonged period, or keep the CD on hand for regular use, you should make it a point to protect the CD. Like any CD, there are few hard and fast rules governing its care, but there are some points to keep in mind. First, keep the CD in a jewel case—one of those clear plastic boxes that audio CDs come in. If you don't have any jewel cases handy, you can buy them at computer stores such as CompUSA or an office store such as Staples.

If you handle the CD carefully and keep it in a jewel case, you should be able to enjoy a long working life from the media. If you should need to clean dust or debris from the CD, use soft, lint-free wipes to gently wipe the disk from hub to edge. Never wipe in a circular motion around the CD's circumference because any scratches can then leave the disk unreadable.

CONTENTS OF THE DLS DIAGNOSTIC CD 4

The DLS Diagnostic CD 4 disc contains over 120 Windows 9*x*/Me compatible utilities that will help you handle tasks ranging from Internet connections to device analysis. This part of the appendix outlines the various shareware products that you'll find on this CD. Table A-1 indexes the products that you'll find on the CD, and you can learn a bit about each product in the descriptions that follow.

Rather than searching for filenames, the following table lists the folder name containing the ZIP or EXE file. This should allow you to locate products of interest more quickly.

BASIC PC MAINTENANCE VIDEO

Whether you're an old hand at PC repair, or just getting started, you can pick up lots of helpful hints and maintenance guidelines from the "Basic PC Maintenance" video located on your DLS Diagnostic CD 4. This real-time, full-motion, 41-minute video clearly explains how to clean your system and peripherals, check the system inside and out, clean your drives, and even optimize your hard drive(s) for peak performance.

To play the "Basic PC Maintenance" video, you'll need Windows 95 or later with a copy of Windows Media Player (or any other .MPG player applet). You can launch Windows Media Player first, then load the VLS001M.MPG file from the /Basic PC Maintenance folder on the CD, or browse the CD in Windows Explorer and simply double-click on the VLS001M.MPG file. The video will play directly from the CD, so just sit back and enjoy the show!

TABLE A-1   DLS DIAGNOSTIC CD 4 SHAREWARE INDEX

PROGRAM	VERSION	DESCRIPTION	PLATFORM	MANUFACTURER	FOLDER NAME
1-Zip	3.00.071	Make self-extracting files	Win95	Boon Docks, Inc.	1ZIP
Access Denied	3.11	Password system	Win95/98	Ivan Mayrakov	Access Denied
AccuSet	5.0b	Time adjusting	Win95	Retsik Software	AccuSet
Adding FreeRAM	1.02	System RAM manager	Win95	Alexandru Dimitriev	Free RAM
AllClear 2000 Pro	2.8f	Year 2000 testing	Win3.x	SIMCOM Software	AllClear 2000
AriTech INI File Editor	1.90a	INI file editor	Win95/NT	AriTech Development	AIN INI Editor
Auto Maintenance	4.06	PC maintenance scheduler	Win95/NT	Comp Time	Auto Maintenance
Backup Registry	3.1	Registry backup utility	Win95/98	Mark A. Sowards	Backup Registry
BCM Diagnostics	1.01.02	PC diagnostics	Win95	BCM Adv. Res. Inc.	BCM Diagnostics
BCWipe	2.34	File shredder	Win95	Jetico, Inc.	BCWipe
Belarc Advisor	4.1	Upgrade advisor	Win95/Inter	Belarc, Inc.	Belarc
BIOS Finder	1.5.3	BIOS upgrade assistant	Win95	Abstract Concepts	BIOS Finder
Boot Locker	7.55	Password system	Win95/98	Steven Eppler	Boot Locker
Boot Log Analyzer	1.2	Checks BOOTLOG.TXT	Win95/98	Vision 4 Ltd.	Boot Log
BootManager	6.10	OS selector	Win95	Nils Hoyer	Boot Manager
Cacheman	3.80	Virtual memory manager	Win95	Ultimatum Productions	Cache Manager
CDCheck	2.0	CD disc checker	Win95/98/NT	Mitja Perko	CD Check
CDLock	1.4	CD drawer lock	Win95/NT	Stefan Luyten	CD Lock
CD-R Diagnostic	1.6.3	CD-ROM/CD-R diagnostic	Win95	CD-ROM Productions	CD-R Diagnostic
CD-ROM Analyzer	2.3	CD-ROM DRIVE TESTER	Win95	Filippof Alex	CD Drive Analyzer
CDSpeed 32	1.01	CD speed tester	Win95/98/NT	---	CD Speed
ChildProof	2.1	Prevent system changes	Win95	George Robertson	Child Proof
Clean Floppy	1.1	Floppy erase/re-label utility	Win95	Jason Hollet	Clean Floppy
CliBench MKII	1.0.0	CPU and HDD benchmark	Win95/98/NT	Marcel Marcus Weber	CliBench
ConfigSafe	3.0	Config. safe and restore	Win95	Artisoft, Inc.	ConfigSafe
Cool Info	2.7i	Win9x system information	Win95	Luke Richey	Cool Info
CPUIdle	5.8	CPU power-down utility	Win95	Andreas Goetz	CPU Idle
CPU Indicator	1.12	CPU usage meter	Win95	PY Software, Inc.	CPU Indicator
Create a DUN	1.0	DUN setup and tutorial	Win95	Julian Maytum	CreateDUN

TABLE A-1   DLS DIAGNOSTIC CD 4 SHAREWARE INDEX *(CONTINUED)*

PROGRAM	VERSION	DESCRIPTION	PLATFORM	MANUFACTURER	FOLDER NAME
Data Advisor	4.10	Drive data diagnostic	---	Ontrack Data Int'l.	Data Advisor
Dialup Constructor	3.75	Setup DUN files	Win95	GRV Consulting	Dialup Constructor
Dial-Up Magic	1.8	Setup DUN files	Win95	TechMagic, LLC	DUN Magic
Disk Editor	3.0	Disk editing utility (FAT 12/16)	DOS 3.0	Jim Webster	Disk Editor
DiskSpeed 32	1.04	Disk speed tester	Win95/98/NT	---	Disk Speed
DiskState	2.1	Drive usage analyzer	Win95	Sveinar Rasmussen	Disk State
DLL Show	4.5	Display DLLs	Win95/98	Software Design	DLL Show
Dr. Hardware	4.00e	PC hardware analyzer	Win95	Gebhard Peter	Dr Hardware
EasyCOM	2.12	Serial device tester	Win95	BT Avance Systems	EasyCOM
Emergency Recover	11.13	Recover system crashes	Win95	Theodore Fattaleh	Emergency Recover
Envite	1.0	Environment variable editor	Win95	McMahon Software	Envite
ErgoTimer	3.2	Ergonomic manager	Win95/98/NT	Silvio Kuczynski	Ergo Timer
Error Scan	2.5	Remove error files	Win95	Lifestyles Technologies	Error Scan
File Rescue	2.0	Undelete from Recycle Bin	Win95/98	Software Shelf	File Rescue
Floppy Eraser	2.2	Floppy disk eraser	Win95	Peter Pearson	Floppy Eraser
FreeMem Pro	4.3	System RAM manager	Win95	Meikel Weber	Free Mem
GodeZIP	7.9	Archiving program	Win95	David Gode	GODE Zip
Graphical Memory	1.1	Memory status indicator	Win95	Jeff Parker	Memory Status
GRD Duplicator	4.0.3	Disk duplicator	Win95	GR Software	GRD Duplicator
Hagi's Boot Editor	1.1	System boot manager	Win95	Hagai Pipko	Boot Editor
HAL	1.01	File browser	Win95/98	Robert J. Dykman	HAL
Hard Info Pro	2.0	System info/ benchmark tool	Win95/98	Ultimate Systems	Hard Info Pro
Header Hunter	1.01	File header reader	Win95	Dan Zentgraf	Header Hunter
Heavy Load	1.0	System load/stress tester	Win95/98/NT	JAM Software	Heavy Load
Hz Tool	1.4	Video refresh rate adjuster	Win95	Stefan Berglind	Hz Tool
Info Pro	2.01	System information utility	Win95	EASTern DiGiTAL	Info Pro
InfoTray	1.08	System information monitor	Win95/98	Markus Schmidt	Info Tray
Internet Firewall 2000	1.0	Internet firewall for PCs	Win95/98	Digital Robotics	Firewall 2000
Internet Support Diags.	1.2	Internet connect testing	Win95	Ken A.	Internet Support

TABLE A-1   DLS DIAGNOSTIC CD 4 SHAREWARE INDEX *(CONTINUED)*

PROGRAM	VERSION	DESCRIPTION	PLATFORM	MANUFACTURER	FOLDER NAME
IRQInfo	3.0	IRQ detection and mapping	DOS	CTS, Inc.	IRQ Info
Keyboard Layout Mgr.	2.66	Keyboard layout control	Win95	Milan Vidakovic	Key Layout Mgr
KeyGO Lite	2.2c	Keyboard management	Win95/98/NT	GDG Systems Inc.	KeyGO Lite
Look RS232	3.0	Serial debugging tool	Win95/98/NT	fCoder Programming	RS 232
Master Booter	3.1	Multi-boot utility	---	Daniel Nagy	Master Booter
MemTurbo	2.0	RAM optimizer	Win95	S P Software	MemTurbo
Modem Doctor	2.0	Modem diagnostic	Win95	Modem Doctor	Modem Doctor
Modem Help Diagnostic	1.0	Modem info tool	Win95	BVRP Software	Modem Help
Modem Status	2.46	Modem status monitor	Win95	TeddyWare	Modem Status
MSDOS Editor	2.0	MSDOS file editor	Win95	Alternative Productions	DOS Editor
NetMon	2.0a	Dialup performance monitor	Win95	Charles Turano	NetMon
OnMark 2000	2.1	Y2K test/fix utility	Win3.1	Viasoft	OnMark
PACT ProfileCopy	21.03b	Save/restore Win profile	Win95	PACT Software	Pact Profile
Partition Manager	Beta 1.91	Analyze/manage partitions	Win95	Mikhail Ranish	Partition Manager
Partition Resizer	1.3.4	Partition management	DOS 5.0	Zofware	Partition Resizer
PC-Config	9.33	System information monitor	DOS 5.0	Holin Datentechnik	PC Config
Performance 95	2.03	Performance monitor	Win95	BonAmi Software	Performance
PortInfo/SPU	5.0	Port management and testing	DOS/Windows	CTS, Inc.	PortInfo
PORTS	2.0	UART identifier	DOS 3.0	MarshallSoft Computing	Ports
PowerTweak	2.02	Hardware optimization	Win95/98/NT	Powertweak	PowerTweak
Print Directory	3.6	Print drive and directory tree	Win95	Brad Prendergast	Print Directory
Procode TrialBlazer	3.0	System protection	Win95	Procode Dev. Pty.	Trial Blazer
ProtectX	4.11	Online protection	Win95/98/NT	JoFBoF Software	ProtectX
Real Uninstall	1.2	Registry cleaner	Win95/NT	D++ Software	Real Uninstall
RegMedic	2.4	Analyze/repair Registry	Win95	Wolf Agency	Registry Medic
RegRepair 2000	3.9	Registry repair	Win95/98	Wolf Agency	Registry Repair
Resplendent Registrar	2.03	Registry editor and manager	Win95	Resplendence Sp	Registrar
Rosenthal Utils.	1.0	Utility suite	Win95/98/NT	Doren Rosenthal	Rosenthal

TABLE A-1   DLS DIAGNOSTIC CD 4 SHAREWARE INDEX *(CONTINUED)*

PROGRAM	VERSION	DESCRIPTION	PLATFORM	MANUFACTURER	FOLDER NAME
SANDRA Std.	2001	PC diagnostic and benchmarking	Win95	3B Software	Sandra
ScanBin	6.0	Binary file scanner	Win95	Jean-Claude Bellamy	ScanBin
Serial	2.0	Serial port reporter	DOS 3.0	Bret Johnson	Serial Reporter
Shortcut Doctor	1.0.2	Remove invalid shortcuts	Win95/98/NT	CronoSoft	Shortcut Dr
Shredder	1.14	File eradicator	Win95	Gale-force	Shredder
Smart Cleaner	3.1	Remove problem files	Win95	PaxWare	SmartClean
SmartFormat	2.1	Format bad floppy disks	DOS 4.0	Tecnolec Software	SmartFormat
SOHO Backup	2.4	Backup to removable media	Win95	Sandy Grant	SOHO Backup
SpeedNet	4.1	Modem speed booster	Win95	Brock Debenham	SpeedNet
Start Editor	3.85	Monitor system boot	Win95	Thomas Reimann	Start Editor
Start Pro	2.0	Control StartUp folder	Win95	Daedalus Software	Start Pro
Stay Alive	2000	Crash prevention/recovery	Win95	TFI Technology, Ltd.	Stay Alive
Super Disk Scanner 98	2.00.4	Test defective disks	Win95	Christian Kassler	Super Scanner
SwapMon	1.6	Swap file analyzer	Win95	FlipTECH	Swap Monitor
System Analyzer	5.2h	PC hardware analyzer	DOS	Hans Niekus	System Analyzer
System Info.	1.8	System information monitor	Win95	Stevens Systems	System Info
Tasks Manager 98	1.12	Manage running applications	Win95	Idyle Software	Tasks Manager
TechFacts 98	2.32	System analyzer utility	Win95	Dean Software Design	TechFacts
Terminal Overdrive	2000	Modem booster	Win95	Digital Robotics	Terminal
Transfer 95	3.0	Create Windows backup	Win95	ITS Systems	Transfer 95
TuneDUN	2.1	DUN manager utility	Win95	Philip Tang & Sons	TuneDUN
TweakDUN	2.23	DUN manager utility	Win95	Patterson Design	TweakDUN
TweakEzy	1.52	Correct drifting PC time	Win95	RealEzy PC Utilities	TweakEzy
TweakI	2.7	Windows optimizing utility	Win95	JerMar Software	TweakI
Uninstall Editor	1.0	Manage uninstall strings	Win95/98	Jacob Degeling	Uninstall Editor
Waterfall Pro	2.01	CPU power-down utility	Win95	Leading WinTech	Waterfall Pro
WinConfig	2.0	Optimize/clean Windows	Win95	TD Software	WinConfig
WinHex	9.7	Hex editor	Win95/98/NT	Stefan Fleischmann	WinHex

TABLE A-1   DLS DIAGNOSTIC CD 4 SHAREWARE INDEX *(CONTINUED)*

PROGRAM	VERSION	DESCRIPTION	PLATFORM	MANUFACTURER	FOLDER NAME
WinImage	5.0	Disk image tool	Win95/98/NT	Gilles Vollant	WinImage
WinRescue 95	10.01	Windows backup/restore	Win95	Super Win Software	Win Rescue
WinSafe 98	3.1.01	System setup protector	Win95	Wolf Agency	WinSafe
WinSystem 98	3.4.7	System information monitor	Win95	NewTech Software	WinSystem
WinTune 98	1.0.43	PC hardware analyzer	Win95	CMP Publications	WinTune
Zip Backup	1.92	Compress/ backup utility	Win95	Gooch Computer Scvs.	Zip Backup
Zip/Jaz Disk Tst.	97-9-9-9	Disk testing utility	Win95/98	Walayat Software	Zip Jaz Tester
Zip Office 98	3.1	Compresses file manager	Win95	Atypie Software	Zip Office

INDEX

DLS Technician's Certificate 4

Information Cover Sheet

Please print clearly

Name: _

Address: _

_ _

City: _ _ _ _ _ _ _ _ _ _ _ _ _ _ _ _ _ _ _

State: _ _   Zip or Postal Code: _ _ _ _ _ _ _ _ _ _

Country (other than USA): _ _ _ _ _ _ _ _ _ _ _ _ _ _ _ _ _

Telephone: _ _ _ _ _ _ _ _ _ _ _ _ _ _

Fax: _ _ _ _ _ _ _ _ _ _ _ _ _ _

♦ the above information is required for proper grading, and to receive proper credit. Tests with incomplete information **cannot** be processed.

Method of Payment

Please Check One

___ Personal or Business *check* for **$50** (US)‡

___ MasterCard *charge* of $50 (US).   Card: _ _ _ _ _ _ _ _ _ _ _ _ _ _ _ _ _

___ VISA *charge* of $50 (US).   Exp: _ / _ / _   Sig: _ _ _ _ _ _ _ _ _ _ _ _

Mail to: **Dynamic Learning Systems, P.O. Box 402, Leicester, MA 01524 USA**

Fax to: **508-892-1482**   (24 hrs/day, 7 days/week)

DLS Technician's Certificate 4

Answer Sheet 1 of 2

*Please Circle Only **One** Letter Corresponding to Each Answer*

1	A B C D	30	A B C D	59	A B C D	88	A B C D
2	A B C D	31	A B C D	60	A B C D	89	A B C D
3	A B C D	32	A B C D	61	A B C D	90	A B C D
4	A B C D	33	A B C D	62	A B C D	91	A B C D
5	A B C D	34	A B C D	63	A B C D	92	A B C D
6	A B C D	35	A B C D	64	A B C D	93	A B C D
7	A B C D	36	A B C D	65	A B C D	94	A B C D
8	A B C D	37	A B C D	66	A B C D	95	A B C D
9	A B C D	38	A B C D	67	A B C D	96	A B C D
10	A B C D	39	A B C D	68	A B C D	97	A B C D
11	A B C D	40	A B C D	69	A B C D	98	A B C D
12	A B C D	41	A B C D	70	A B C D	99	A B C D
13	A B C D	42	A B C D	71	A B C D	100	A B C D
14	A B C D	43	A B C D	72	A B C D	101	A B C D
15	A B C D	44	A B C D	73	A B C D	102	A B C D
16	A B C D	45	A B C D	74	A B C D	103	A B C D
17	A B C D	46	A B C D	75	A B C D	104	A B C D
18	A B C D	47	A B C D	76	A B C D	105	A B C D
19	A B C D	48	A B C D	77	A B C D	106	A B C D
20	A B C D	49	A B C D	78	A B C D	107	A B C D
21	A B C D	50	A B C D	79	A B C D	108	A B C D
22	A B C D	51	A B C D	80	A B C D	109	A B C D
23	A B C D	52	A B C D	81	A B C D	110	A B C D
24	A B C D	53	A B C D	82	A B C D	111	A B C D
25	A B C D	54	A B C D	83	A B C D	112	A B C D
26	A B C D	55	A B C D	84	A B C D	113	A B C D
27	A B C D	56	A B C D	85	A B C D	114	A B C D
28	A B C D	57	A B C D	86	A B C D	115	A B C D
29	A B C D	58	A B C D	87	A B C D	116	A B C D

Answer Sheet 2 of 2

Please Circle Only One Letter Corresponding to Each Answer

117 A B C D	146 A B C D	175 A B C D	204 A B C D
118 A B C D	147 A B C D	176 A B C D	205 A B C D
119 A B C D	148 A B C D	177 A B C D	206 A B C D
120 A B C D	149 A B C D	178 A B C D	207 A B C D
121 A B C D	150 A B C D	179 A B C D	208 A B C D
122 A B C D	151 A B C D	180 A B C D	209 A B C D
123 A B C D	152 A B C D	181 A B C D	210 A B C D
124 A B C D	153 A B C D	182 A B C D	211 A B C D
125 A B C D	154 A B C D	183 A B C D	212 A B C D
126 A B C D	155 A B C D	184 A B C D	213 A B C D
127 A B C D	156 A B C D	185 A B C D	214 A B C D
128 A B C D	157 A B C D	186 A B C D	215 A B C D
129 A B C D	158 A B C D	187 A B C D	216 A B C D
130 A B C D	159 A B C D	188 A B C D	217 A B C D
131 A B C D	160 A B C D	189 A B C D	218 A B C D
132 A B C D	161 A B C D	190 A B C D	219 A B C D
133 A B C D	162 A B C D	191 A B C D	220 A B C D
134 A B C D	163 A B C D	192 A B C D	221 A B C D
135 A B C D	164 A B C D	193 A B C D	222 A B C D
136 A B C D	165 A B C D	194 A B C D	223 A B C D
137 A B C D	166 A B C D	195 A B C D	224 A B C D
138 A B C D	167 A B C D	196 A B C D	225 A B C D
139 A B C D	168 A B C D	197 A B C D	
140 A B C D	169 A B C D	198 A B C D	
141 A B C D	170 A B C D	199 A B C D	<End of Exam>
142 A B C D	171 A B C D	200 A B C D	
143 A B C D	172 A B C D	201 A B C D	
144 A B C D	173 A B C D	202 A B C D	
145 A B C D	174 A B C D	203 A B C D	

INTERNATIONAL CONTACT INFORMATION

AUSTRALIA
McGraw-Hill Book Company Australia Pty. Ltd.
TEL +61-2-9417-9899
FAX +61-2-9417-5687
http://www.mcgraw-hill.com.au
books-it_sydney@mcgraw-hill.com

CANADA
McGraw-Hill Ryerson Ltd.
TEL +905-430-5000
FAX +905-430-5020
http://www.mcgrawhill.ca

GREECE, MIDDLE EAST,
NORTHERN AFRICA
McGraw-Hill Hellas
TEL +30-1-656-0990-3-4
FAX +30-1-654-5525

MEXICO (Also serving Latin America)
McGraw-Hill Interamericana Editores S.A. de C.V.
TEL +525-117-1583
FAX +525-117-1589
http://www.mcgraw-hill.com.mx
fernando_castellanos@mcgraw-hill.com

SINGAPORE (Serving Asia)
McGraw-Hill Book Company
TEL +65-863-1580
FAX +65-862-3354
http://www.mcgraw-hill.com.sg
mghasia@mcgraw-hill.com

SOUTH AFRICA
McGraw-Hill South Africa
TEL +27-11-622-7512
FAX +27-11-622-9045
robyn_swanepoel@mcgraw-hill.com

UNITED KINGDOM & EUROPE
(Excluding Southern Europe)
McGraw-Hill Education Europe
TEL +44-1-628-502500
FAX +44-1-628-770224
http://www.mcgraw-hill.co.uk
computing_neurope@mcgraw-hill.com

ALL OTHER INQUIRIES Contact:
Osborne/McGraw-Hill
TEL +1-510-549-6600
FAX +1-510-883-7600
http://www.osborne.com
omg_international@mcgraw-hill.com